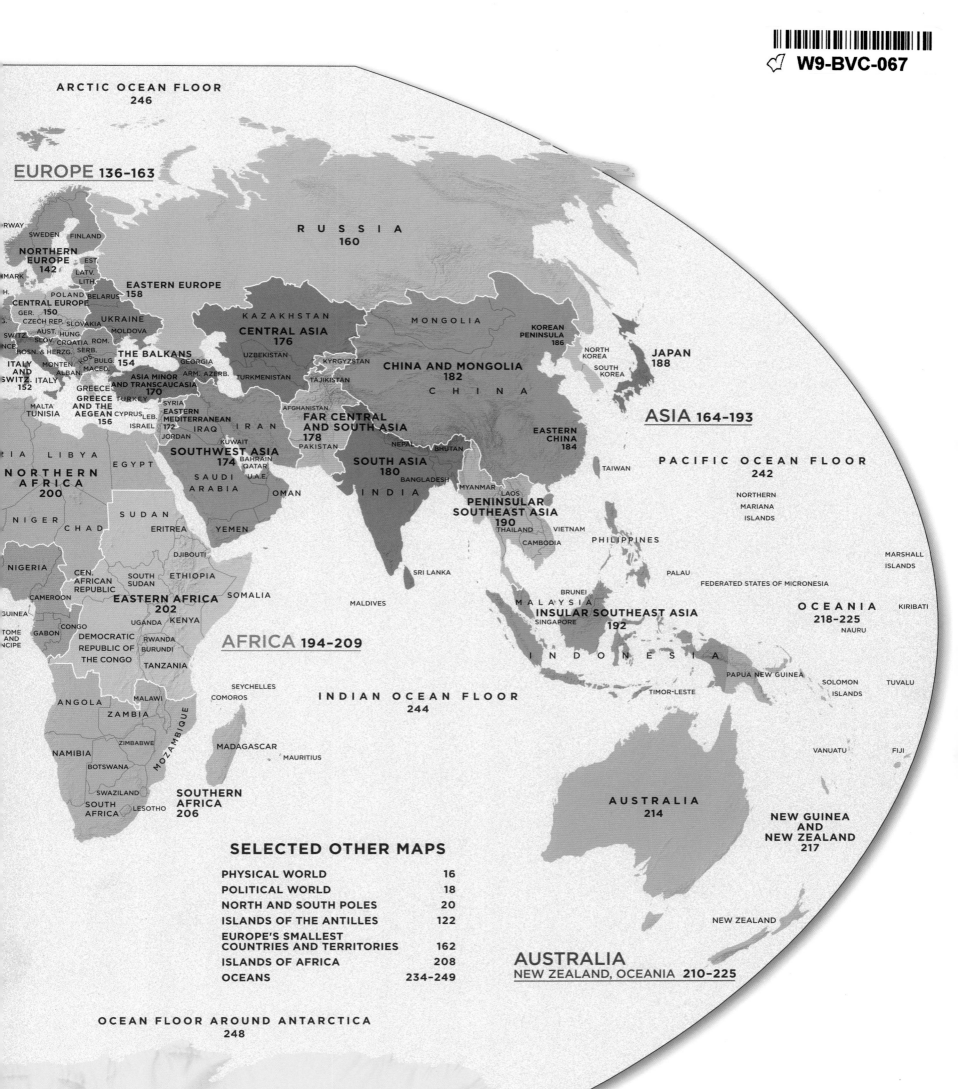

W9-BVC-067

ARCTIC OCEAN FLOOR
246

EUROPE 136-163

RWAY
SWEDEN   FINLAND

NORTHERN
EUROPE
142   EST.
               LATV.
H.   POLAND BELARUS   LITH.
CENTRAL EUROPE   EASTERN EUROPE
GER.   150   158
S.   CZECH REP. SLOVAKIA   UKRAINE
   AUST. HUNG
SWITZ. SLOV.   MOLDOVA
NCE BOSN. & HERZG. CROATIA ROM.
ITALY MONTEN. SERB.
AND   KOS. BULG. MACED.
SWITZ. ITALY   THE BALKANS
152   ALBAN.   154
   GREECE   GEORGIA
MALTA GREECE   ARM. AZERB.
TUNISIA AND THE ASIA MINOR
       AEGEAN AND TRANSCAUCASIA
       156   TURKEY 170
           CYPRUS LEB.
           ISRAEL EASTERN
                MEDITERRANEAN
                172   IRAQ
                JORDAN
RIA   LIBYA   KUWAIT
           EGYPT   SOUTHWEST ASIA
NORTHERN   174 BAHRAIN
AFRICA   QATAR
200   SAUDI   U.A.E.
NIGER CHAD ARABIA
       SUDAN   OMAN
NIGERIA ERITREA YEMEN
   CEN. DJIBOUTI
   AFRICAN SOUTH
   REPUBLIC SUDAN ETHIOPIA
CAMEROON
GUINEA   EASTERN AFRICA SOMALIA
       UGANDA 202
TOME GABON CONGO KENYA
AND   RWANDA
NCIPE DEMOCRATIC BURUNDI
       REPUBLIC OF AFRICA 194-209
       THE CONGO TANZANIA
                   SEYCHELLES
ANGOLA MALAWI   COMOROS
    ZAMBIA
NAMIBIA ZIMBABWE   MADAGASCAR
    BOTSWANA   MAURITIUS
SWAZILAND SOUTHERN
SOUTH LESOTHO AFRICA
AFRICA   206

RUSSIA
160

KAZAKHSTAN

CENTRAL ASIA
176
UZBEKISTAN
        KYRGYZSTAN
TURKMENISTAN
    TAJIKISTAN
AFGHANISTAN FAR CENTRAL
        AND SOUTH ASIA
        178
   PAKISTAN
           SOUTH ASIA
           180
      INDIA   BANGLADESH
                MYANMAR

MONGOLIA   KOREAN
               PENINSULA
               186   NORTH
                     KOREA
               SOUTH
               KOREA
CHINA AND MONGOLIA
182
C H I N A

EASTERN
CHINA
184

JAPAN
188

ASIA 164-193

PACIFIC OCEAN FLOOR
242

TAIWAN   NORTHERN
              MARIANA
              ISLANDS

              PHILIPPINES   MARSHALL
                                   ISLANDS
        PALAU
        FEDERATED STATES OF MICRONESIA

PENINSULAR
SOUTHEAST ASIA
190
THAILAND VIETNAM
    CAMBODIA

BRUNEI
M A L A Y S I A   OCEANIA   KIRIBATI
INSULAR SOUTHEAST ASIA 218-225
SINGAPORE 192   NAURU

I N D O N E S I A

        PAPUA NEW GUINEA
                         SOLOMON   TUVALU
TIMOR-LESTE   ISLANDS

INDIAN OCEAN FLOOR
244

MOZAMBIQUE

VANUATU   FIJI

AUSTRALIA
214   NEW GUINEA
            AND
            NEW ZEALAND
            217

SELECTED OTHER MAPS

PHYSICAL WORLD   16
POLITICAL WORLD   18
NORTH AND SOUTH POLES   20
ISLANDS OF THE ANTILLES   122
EUROPE'S SMALLEST
COUNTRIES AND TERRITORIES   162
ISLANDS OF AFRICA   208
OCEANS   234-249

NEW ZEALAND

AUSTRALIA
NEW ZEALAND, OCEANIA 210-225

OCEAN FLOOR AROUND ANTARCTICA
248

ANTARCTICA 226-233

KEY TO ATLAS MAPS

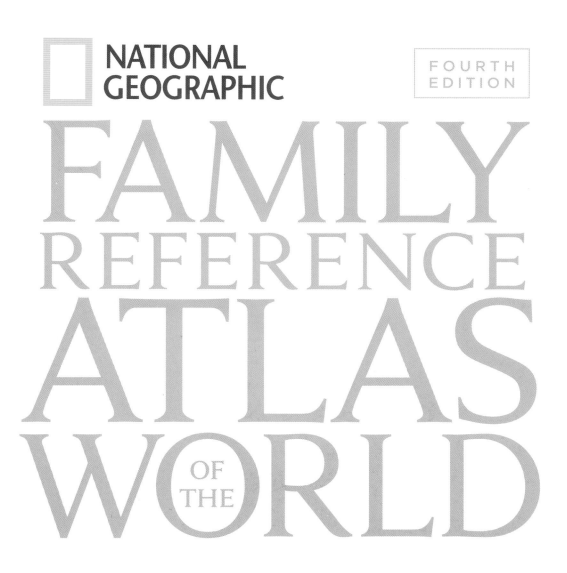

NATIONAL GEOGRAPHIC

FOURTH EDITION

FAMILY REFERENCE ATLAS OF THE WORLD

NATIONAL GEOGRAPHIC

FAMILY REFERENCE ATLAS OF THE WORLD

NATIONAL GEOGRAPHIC
WASHINGTON, D.C.

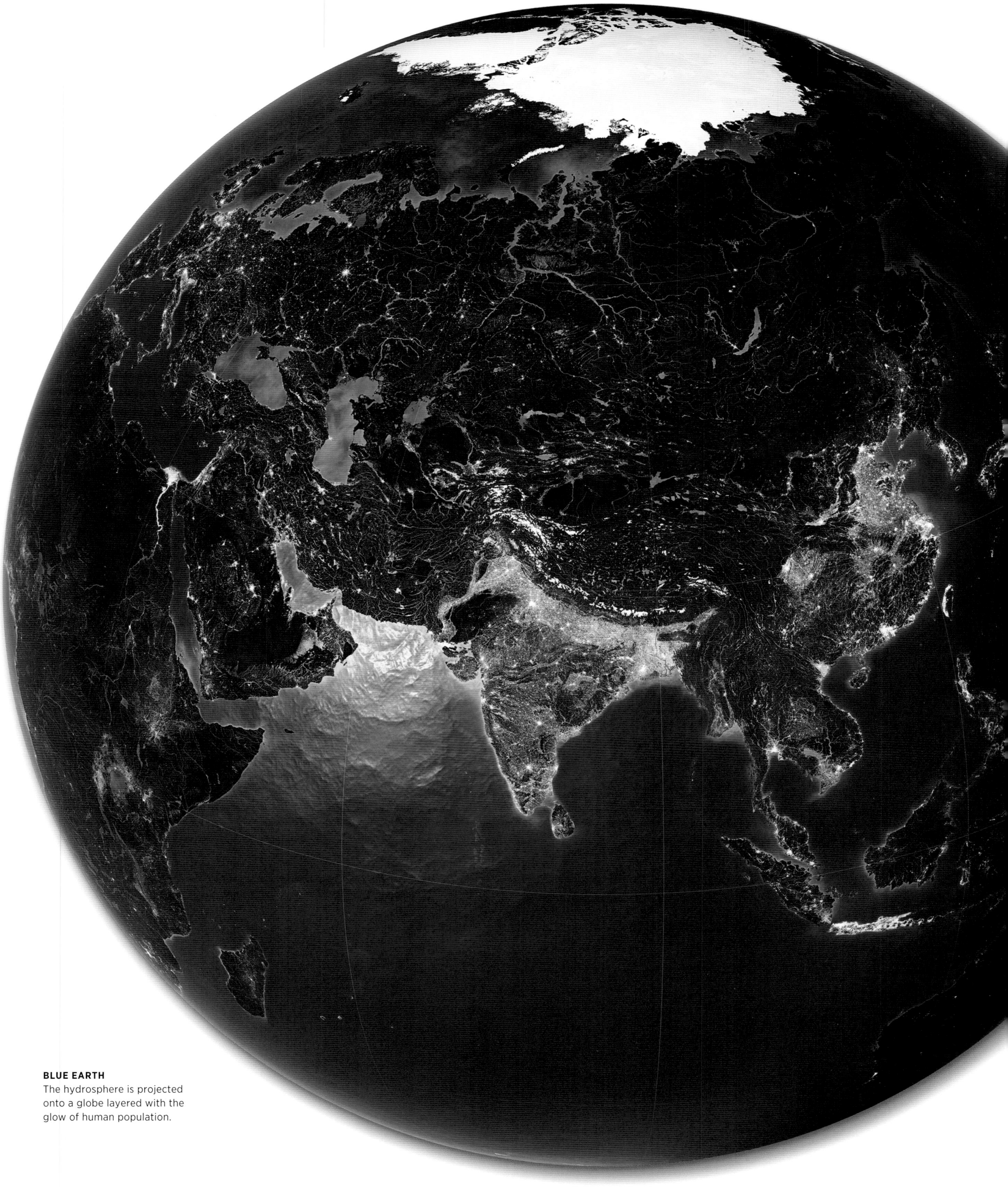

BLUE EARTH
The hydrosphere is projected
onto a globe layered with the
glow of human population.

Foreword

FOR YOUNG MINDS, THE WORLD IS A VAST NEW REALM that encourages their imaginations to soar—to faraway cities where life seems exotically different from their own, to African savannas where lions and giraffes still roam, to the underwater iridescence of tropical coral reefs. As exciting as it is, that limitless world needs a little grounding, and that is what we offer in the *Family Reference Atlas*. It conveys the magnificence of our planet and at the same time makes it more understandable—a home to celebrate, explore, probe, and preserve.

A generation of families—from young children to grandparents—has already grown up with this award-winning atlas, and with our updated fourth edition, we hope to engage the spirit of inquisitiveness and adventure in a new generation. Here at National Geographic, we are committed to motivating lifelong learners and problem solvers who want to see our remarkable planet become an ever more remarkable and hospitable place. We are convinced that the way to create a better world is to foster geographically literate stewards who understand Earth's intricacies and the interconnections that balance it—the give-and-take among different nations and cultures and between the natural and human worlds. In the following pages, we help perpetuate that lifelong learning process with state-of-the-art maps and graphics and compelling words and images that cover the seven continents and the oceanic depths in between and even range to the far reaches of our solar system and the universe beyond. The great rivers and extreme deserts, the monumental cities and memorable landmarks, the nations and peoples that create the current mosaic of life on Earth are all here. And they lead to a deeper understanding of how the realities of life differ from place to place as a result of geography, history, economics, climate, and population pressures—and to a rich awareness of the possibilities and challenges that face us as a global village going forward.

Those challenges can seem daunting, but younger generations have shown themselves to be brave and innovative thinkers in addressing the problems facing global harmony and environmental sustainability. Although a worldwide population explosion has led to new tensions and pressures, the age of technology has gone a long way in knitting together Earth's 7.1 billion people in unprecedented ways, and the young are more inclined to see themselves as global citizens than ever before. We want to encourage them in that pursuit, giving them the curiosity, confidence, and geographic knowledge to engage with this larger, grander world, to take on its problems, and to shepherd it into a promising future.

We're particularly proud to offer this volume on the 100th anniversary of National Geographic mapmaking. For a century our cartographers have pushed the limits of mapmaking to new heights, because an atlas, after all, brings the world to your fingertips. Even in an age of cyber communication, an atlas that can be held in your hands seems to us the best vehicle for exploring the world through maps and engendering a community of engaged, geographically knowledgeable global citizens. We hope this new volume takes you and your fellow citizens on many memorable, fascinating journeys.

MELINA GEROSA BELLOWS
CHIEF EDUCATION OFFICER

Table of Contents

10 Using This Atlas MAP POLICIES • PHYSICAL MAPS • POLITICAL MAPS • WORLD THEMATIC MAPS • REGIONAL MAPS • MAP SYMBOLS

14 THE WORLD

14 Introduction

16 Physical World

18 Political World

20 North and South Poles

22 Structure of the Earth
Continents Adrift in Time • Geologic Time • Geologic Forces Change the Face of the Planet • Plate Tectonics

24 Earth's Rocky Exterior
Rock Classes • The Rock Cycle • Global Distribution of Rock Types • Reading Earth History From Rocks

26 Landforms
Endogenic Landforms • Exogenic Landforms • Other Landforms • Landforms Created by Wind • Landforms Created by Water • Landforms Created by Ice

30 Surface of the Earth
Distribution of Earth's Elevations and Depths (Hypsometry) • Surface by the Numbers • Earth Surface Elevations and Depths • A Slice of Earth

32 Land Cover
Global Land Cover Composition

34 Freshwater
World of Rivers • Water Availability • Mapping Irrigation • Renewable Freshwater Resources • Safe Drinking Water

36 Climate
January and July: Solar Energy, Average Temperature, Cloud Cover, Precipitation • Climate Change • Climate Zones • Climographs

40 Weather
Major Factors That Influence Weather • Cloud Types • Tropical Cyclones • Lightning • El Niño and La Niña

42 Biosphere
The Biosphere From Space • Biosphere Dynamics • Earth System Dynamics • Size of the Biosphere • The Biosphere Over Time

44 Biodiversity
The Natural World • Species Diversity • Biodiversity Hotspots • Threatened Species • Conservation Status of Terrestrial Ecoregions

46 Human Influences
Anthromes • Human Influence Index • Last of the Wild • Human Influences Over Time • Planetary Stewardship

48 Population
Lights of the World • Population Pyramids • Population Growth • Population Density • Regional Population Growth Disparities • Fertility • Urban Population Densities • Urban Population Growth • Life Expectancy • Migration • Most Populous Places • Most Crowded Places • Demographic Extremes

52 Languages
Language Families • Evolution of Languages • How Many Speak What? • Mapping Language Diversity • Vanishing Languages

54 Religions
Dominant Religion • Christianity • Islam • Hinduism • Buddhism • Ethno-Religionism • Judaism • By the Numbers

56 Health and Education
Health Care Availability • Income Levels: Indicators of Health and Literacy • Access to Improved Sanitation • Nutrition • HIV • Global Disease Burden • Under-Five Mortality • Education and Literacy • School Enrollment for Girls • Maternal Mortality • Developing Human Capital

58 Economy
Dominant Economic Sector • Value Added, by Activity • Human Development Index • Top GDP Growth Rates • The World's Richest and Poorest Countries • Gross Domestic Product • Global Innovation Index • Major Exporters

60 Trade
World Economies • Growth of World Trade • Merchandise Exports • Main Trading Nations • World Debt • Trade Blocs • Trade Flow: Fuels • Trade Flow: Agricultural Products • Top Merchandise Exporters and Importers • Top Commercial Services Exporters and Importers

62 Food
Agriculture's Footprint • Where Crop Yields Could Improve • How Our Crops Are Used • Distribution of Major Crops and Livestock • Fishing and Aquaculture • World Food Production • Genetically Modified Crops • Caloric Supply • Food Security

66 Energy
Energy Consumption by Leading Source • Energy Production by Fuel Type • Energy Production by Region • Balancing Consumption and Production • Renewable Resources • Renewable Leaders

68 Minerals
Exports in Nonfuel Mining Products • World Mineral Production by Type • Steel Production by Location • World Mining by Region • World Share of Production

70 Environmental Stresses
Desertification and Land Degradation • Air Pollution: Fine Particulate Matter Levels • Land Degradation and Desertification • Deforestation • Pollution • Deforestation Hot Spots • Water Scarcity • Depletion of the Ozone Layer • Carbon Emissions

72 Protected Areas
World Heritage Sites • Endemism • Growth in Nationally Designated Protected Areas • World Heritage Site Categories

74 Globalization
Globalization Index Scores • Transnational Corporations • Economic Globalization • Social Globalization • International Migration • Political Globalization

76 Digital Connectivity
Booming Mobile-Cellular Subscriptions • Growth in Internet Bandwidth • Interregional Internet Bandwidth • Internet Access

78 NORTH AMERICA

78 Introduction

82 North America: Physical and Political

84 Canada
Canada • Greenland • St.-Pierre and Miquelon

86 United States: Physical

88 United States: Political

90 United States
Temperature and Precipitation • Land Use • Population • Industry and Mining

92 United States: Major Highways

94 United States: National Park Service

96 UNITED STATES REGIONS

NORTHEAST **96**
Connecticut • Maine • Massachusetts • New Hampshire • New Jersey • New York • Pennsylvania • Rhode Island • Vermont

SOUTH ATLANTIC **98**
Delaware • District of Columbia • Florida • Georgia • Maryland • North Carolina • South Carolina • Virginia • West Virginia

GREAT LAKES **100**
Illinois • Indiana • Michigan • Ohio • Wisconsin

MIDDLE SOUTH **102**
Alabama • Arkansas • Kentucky • Louisiana • Mississippi • Tennessee

TEXAS AND OKLAHOMA **104**

NORTHERN PLAINS **106**
Iowa • Kansas • Minnesota • Missouri • Nebraska • North Dakota • South Dakota

ROCKY MOUNTAINS **108**
Arizona • Colorado • Idaho • Montana • New Mexico • Utah • Wyoming

WEST COAST **110**
California • Nevada • Oregon • Washington

ALASKA **112**

HAWAI'I **114**

116 Mexico and Central America
Belize • Costa Rica • El Salvador • Guatemala • Honduras • Mexico • Nicaragua • Panama

118 Bahamas and Greater Antilles
Bahamas • Bermuda • Cayman Islands • Cuba • Dominican Republic • Haiti • Jamaica • Puerto Rico • Turks and Caicos Islands

120 Lesser Antilles
Anguilla • Antigua and Barbuda • Aruba • Barbados • British Virgin Islands • Curaçao • Dominica • Grenada • Guadeloupe • Martinique • Montserrat • Saint-Barthélemy • Saint Kitts and Nevis • Saint Lucia • Saint-Martin • Saint Vincent and the Grenadines • Sint Maarten • Trinidad and Tobago • U.S. Virgin Islands

122 Islands of the Antilles
Abaco Islands • Anguilla • Antigua • Aruba • Barbados • Bermuda Islands • Bimini Islands • Bonaire • Curaçao • Dominica • Eleuthera • Exuma • Grand Bahama Island • Grand Cayman • Grenada • Guadeloupe • Jamaica • Martinique • Montserrat • New Providence • Puerto Rico • San Salvador • Saint Croix • Saint Kitts and Nevis • Saint Lucia • Saint-Martin • Saint Thomas and Saint John • Saint Vincent • Sint Maarten • Tobago • Tortola • Trinidad • Virgin Gorda

124 SOUTH AMERICA

124 Introduction

128 South America: Physical and Political

130 Northern South America
Colombia • Ecuador • French Guiana • Guyana • Suriname • Venezuela

132 Central South America
Bolivia • Brazil • Paraguay • Peru

134 Southern South America
Argentina • Chile • Falkland Islands • Uruguay

136 EUROPE

136 Introduction

140 Europe: Physical and Political

142 Northern Europe
Denmark • Estonia • Finland • Iceland • Latvia • Lithuania • Norway • Sweden • Faroe Islands

144 Britain and Ireland
Ireland • United Kingdom

146 Iberian Peninsula
Portugal • Spain

148 France and the Low Countries
Belgium • France • Luxembourg • Netherlands

150 Central Europe
Austria • Czech Republic • Germany • Hungary • Poland • Slovakia

152 Italy and Switzerland

154 The Balkans
Albania • Bosnia and Herzegovina • Bulgaria • Croatia • Kosovo • Macedonia • Montenegro • Romania • Serbia • Slovenia

156 Greece and the Aegean

158 Eastern Europe
Belarus • Moldova • Ukraine • Western Russia

160 Russia

162 Europe's Smallest Countries and Territories
Andorra • Cyprus • Liechtenstein • Luxembourg • Malta • Monaco • San Marino • Vatican City • Gibraltar

CONTINUES ON NEXT PAGE >

Table of Contents

164 ASIA

- **164** Introduction
- **168** Asia: Physical and Political
- **170** Asia Minor and Transcaucasia
  Armenia • Azerbaijan • Georgia • Turkey
- **172** Eastern Mediterranean
  Israel • Jordan • Lebanon • Syria
- **174** Southwest Asia
  Bahrain • Iran • Iraq • Kuwait • Oman • Qatar • Saudi Arabia • United Arab Emirates • Yemen
- **176** Central Asia
  Kazakhstan • Turkmenistan • Uzbekistan
- **178** Far Central and South Asia
  Afghanistan • Kyrgyzstan • Pakistan • Tajikistan
- **180** South Asia
  Bangladesh • Bhutan • India • Maldives • Nepal • Sri Lanka
- **182** China and Mongolia
- **184** Eastern China
- **186** Korean Peninsula
  North Korea • South Korea
- **188** Japan
- **190** Peninsular Southeast Asia
  Cambodia • Laos • Myanmar • Thailand • Vietnam
- **192** Insular Southeast Asia
  Brunei • Indonesia • Malaysia • Philippines • Singapore • Timor-Leste

194 AFRICA

- **194** Introduction
- **198** Africa: Physical and Political
- **200** Northern Africa
  Algeria • Chad • Egypt • Gambia • Libya • Mali • Mauritania • Morocco • Niger • Senegal • Tunisia • Western Sahara
- **202** Eastern Africa
  Burundi • Central African Republic • Democratic Republic of the Congo • Djibouti • Eritrea • Ethiopia • Kenya • Rwanda • Somalia • South Sudan • Sudan • Tanzania • Uganda
- **204** West Central Africa
  Benin • Burkina Faso • Cameroon • Congo • Côte d'Ivoire • Equatorial Guinea • Gabon • Ghana • Guinea • Guinea-Bissau • Liberia • Nigeria • Sierra Leone • Togo
- **206** Southern Africa
  Angola • Botswana • • Lesotho • Madagascar • Malawi • Mozambique • Namibia • South Africa • Swaziland • Zambia • Zimbabwe
- **208** Islands of Africa
  Bioko • Canary Islands • Cabo Verde • Comoros • Madiera Islands • Mauritius • Mayotte • Réunion • Rodrigues • Sao Tome and Principe • Seychelles

210 AUSTRALIA • NEW ZEALAND • OCEANIA

- **210** Introduction
- **214** Australia: Physical and Political
- **216** Australia
  Temperature and Precipitation • Land Use • Population • Industry and Mining
- **217** New Guinea and New Zealand
  New Zealand • Papua New Guinea
- **218** Islands of Oceania
- **220** Oceania
  Inset Maps • Flags and Facts

226 ANTARCTICA

- **226** Introduction
- **230** Antarctica: Physical
- **232** Exploring Antarctica
  Elevation of the Ice Sheet • Measurements of a Paradox • Ice on the Move • Ultimate Winds • Antarctic Treaty • Antarctic Convergence

234 OCEANS

- **234** World Bathymetry
- **236** Oceanography
  The Ocean Floor • Major Surface Currents • Ocean Conveyor Belt
- **238** Limits of the Oceans and Seas
- **240** Atlantic Ocean Floor
- **242** Pacific Ocean Floor
- **244** Indian Ocean Floor
- **246** Arctic Ocean Floor
- **248** Ocean Floor Around Antarctica

250 SPACE

- **250** Introduction
- **252** Moon: Near Side
- **254** Moon: Far Side
- **256** Inner Solar System
  Sun • Mercury • Venus • Earth • Mars
- **258** Mars: Western Hemisphere
- **260** Mars: Eastern Hemisphere
- **262** Outer Solar System
  Jupiter • Saturn • Uranus • Neptune
- **264** The Universe

266 APPENDIX

266 Abbreviations and Metric Conversions

268 Geographic Comparisons

270 Special Flags
Development of the Stars and Stripes • International Flags •
Religious Flags • Ethnic Flags • Specialized Flags

272 Foreign Terms

274 Time Zones

276 Temperature and Rainfall

280 Major Cities of the World

282 Glossary of Geographic Terms

285 INDEX

285 Place-name Index

392 Moon and Mars Indexes

396 Acknowledgments
Consultants • World Themes • Additional Satellite Imagery • Physical
and Political Maps • Principal Reference Sources • Photographs • Key to
Flags and Facts

A long belt of land and mostly sea—reaching ten degrees
north and ten degrees south of the Equator—wraps
around the globe to form a complete circle of elevation
coverage (top and previous spread).

The round—azimuthal—projection (bottom) represents a
view from atop the world. The geographic North Pole at
90 degrees north latitude is located at the center of the
image. Shown in its entirety, the Northern Hemisphere
radiates from the Pole to the periphery of the map, align-
ing with the Equator at zero degrees latitude.

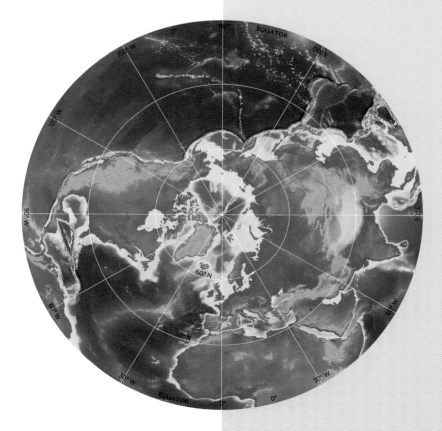

Using This Atlas

MAP POLICIES Maps are a rich, useful, and—to the extent humanly possible—accurate means of depicting the world. Yet maps inevitably make the world seem a little simpler than it really is. A neatly drawn boundary may in reality be a hotly contested war zone. The government-sanctioned, "official" name of a provincial city in an ethnically diverse region may bear little resemblance to the name its citizens routinely use. These cartographic issues often seem obscure and academic. But maps arouse passions. Despite our carefully reasoned map policies, users of National Geographic maps write us strongly worded letters when our maps are at odds with their worldviews.

How do National Geographic cartographers deal with these realities? With constant scrutiny, considerable discussion, and help from many outside experts. Examples:

Nations: Issues of national sovereignty and contested borders often boil down to "de facto versus de jure" discussions. Governments and international agencies frequently make official rulings about contested regions. These de jure decisions, no matter how legitimate, are often at odds with the wishes of individuals and groups, and they often stand in stark contrast to real-world situations. The inevitable conclusion: It is simplest and best to show the world as it is—de facto—rather than as we or others wish it to be.

Africa's Western Sahara, for example, was divided by Morocco and Mauritania after the Spanish government withdrew in 1976. Although Morocco now controls the entire territory, the United Nations does not recognize Morocco's sovereignty over this still disputed area. This atlas shows the de facto Moroccan rule but includes an explanatory note.

Place-names: Ride a barge down the Danube, and you'll hear the river called *Donau, Duna, Dunaj, Dunărea, Dunav, Dunay.* These are local names. This atlas uses the conventional name, "Danube," on physical maps. On political maps, local names are used, with the conventional name in parentheses where space permits. Usage conventions for both foreign and domestic place-names are established by the U.S. Board on Geographic Names, a group with representatives from several federal agencies.

Physical Maps

Physical maps of the world, the continents, and the ocean floor reveal landforms and vegetation in stunning detail. Detailed digital relief is rendered and combined with prevailing land cover based on global satellite data.

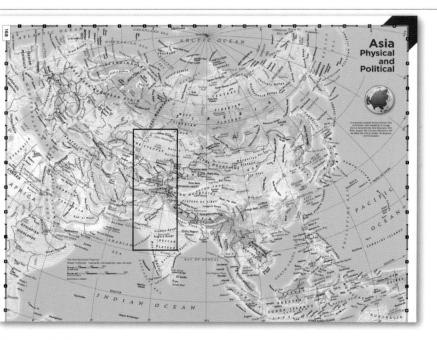

PHYSICAL FEATURES: Colors and shading illustrate variations in elevation, landforms, and vegetation. Patterns indicate specific landscape features, such as sand, glaciers, and swamps.

WATER FEATURES: Blue lines indicate rivers; other water bodies are shown as areas of blue.

BOUNDARIES AND POLITICAL DIVISIONS are shown in red. Dotted lines indicate disputed or uncertain boundaries.

Political Maps

Political maps portray features such as international boundaries, the locations of cities, road networks, and other important elements of the world's human geography. Most index entries are keyed to the political maps, listing the page numbers and then the specific locations on the pages. (See page 285 for details on how to use the index.)

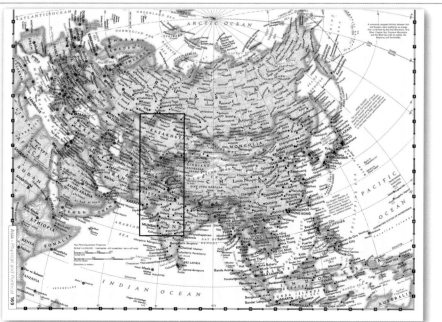

PHYSICAL FEATURES: Gray relief shading depicts surface features such as mountains, hills, and valleys.

WATER FEATURES are shown in blue. Solid lines and filled-in areas indicate perennial water features; dashed lines and patterns indicate intermittent features.

BOUNDARIES AND POLITICAL DIVISIONS are defined with both lines and colored bands; they vary according to whether a boundary is internal or international (for details, see map symbols key at right).

CITIES: The regional political maps that form the bulk of this atlas depict four categories of cities or towns. The largest cities are shown in all capital letters (e.g., LONDON).

World Thematic Maps

Thematic maps reveal the rich patchwork and infinite interrelationships of our changing planet. The thematic section at the beginning of the atlas focuses on physical and biological topics such as geology, landforms, land cover, and biodiversity. It also charts human patterns, with information on population, languages, religions, and the world economy. Two-page spreads on energy and minerals illustrate how people have learned to use Earth's resources, while spreads devoted to environmental stresses and protected lands focus on the far-reaching effects of human activities and the need for resource conservation. Throughout this section of the atlas, maps are coupled with satellite imagery, charts, diagrams, photographs, and tabular information; together, they create a very useful framework for studying geographic patterns.

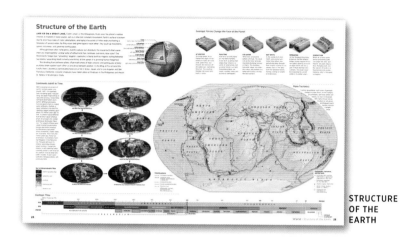

STRUCTURE
OF THE
EARTH

WORLD
POPULATION

Regional Maps

This atlas divides the continents into several subregions, each displayed on a two-page spread. Large-scale maps capture the political divisions and major surface features, whereas accompanying regional thematic maps lend insight into natural and human factors that give character to a region. Fact boxes, which include flag designs and information on populations, languages, religions, and economies, appear alongside the maps as practical reference tools.

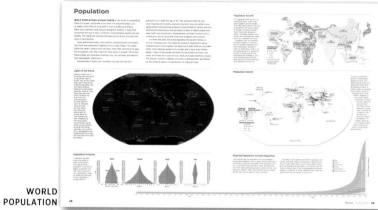

For more details on the regional map spreads, see pages 12–13.

Map Symbols

BOUNDARIES

	Defined
	Undefined or disputed
	Offshore line of separation
	International boundary (Physical Maps)
	Disputed or undefined boundary (Physical Maps)

CITIES

✪ ✪ ⊙ ◎	Capitals
● ● ● •	Towns
○	Farmstead or homestead

TRANSPORTATION

	Superhighway
	Highway
	Road
	Ferry
	Highway tunnel
INTERSTATE 35 STATE 50 FEDERAL 376	Highway numbers

WATER FEATURES

	Drainage
	Intermittent drainage
	Intermittent lake
	Dry salt lake
	Swamp
	Bank or shoal
	Coral reef
51	Water surface elevation in meters
	Falls or rapids
	Aqueduct

PHYSICAL FEATURES

	Relief
◦	Crater
	Lava and volcanic debris
+8,850 (29,035 ft)	Elevation in meters (feet in United States)
-86	Elevation in meters below sea level
⤲	Pass
	Sand
	Salt desert
	Below sea level
	Ice shelf
	Glacier

CULTURAL FEATURES

⚑	Oil field
	Canal
	Dam
	Wall
	U.S. national park
▫	Site
∴	Ruin

Using This Atlas

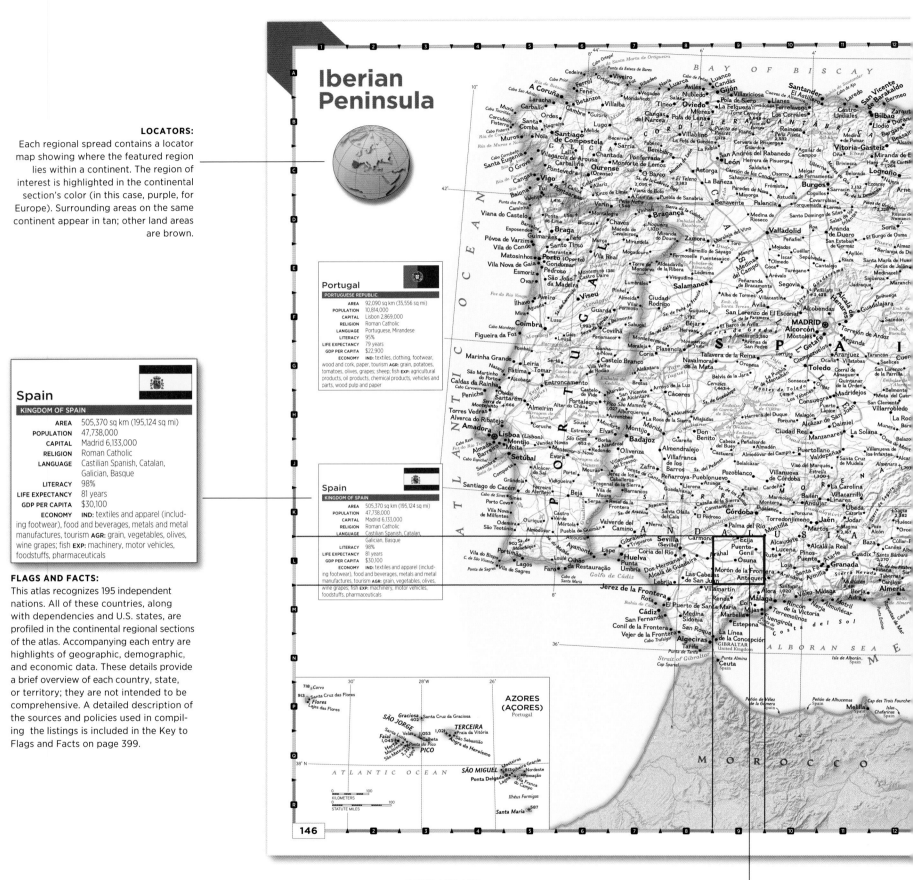

LOCATORS:
Each regional spread contains a locator map showing where the featured region lies within a continent. The region of interest is highlighted in the continental section's color (in this case, purple, for Europe). Surrounding areas on the same continent appear in tan; other land areas are brown.

FLAGS AND FACTS:
This atlas recognizes 195 independent nations. All of these countries, along with dependencies and U.S. states, are profiled in the continental regional sections of the atlas. Accompanying each entry are highlights of geographic, demographic, and economic data. These details provide a brief overview of each country, state, or territory; they are not intended to be comprehensive. A detailed description of the sources and policies used in compiling the listings is included in the Key to Flags and Facts on page 399.

Spain
KINGDOM OF SPAIN
AREA	505,370 sq km (195,124 sq mi)
POPULATION	47,738,000
CAPITAL	Madrid 6,133,000
RELIGION	Roman Catholic
LANGUAGE	Castilian Spanish, Catalan, Galician, Basque
LITERACY	98%
LIFE EXPECTANCY	81 years
GDP PER CAPITA	$30,100
ECONOMY	IND: textiles and apparel (including footwear), food and beverages, metals and metal manufactures, tourism AGR: grain, vegetables, olives, wine grapes; fish EXP: machinery, motor vehicles, foodstuffs, pharmaceuticals

Iberian Peninsula

Portugal
PORTUGUESE REPUBLIC
AREA	92,090 sq km (35,556 sq mi)
POPULATION	10,814,000
CAPITAL	Lisbon 2,869,000
RELIGION	Roman Catholic
LANGUAGE	Portuguese, Mirandese
LITERACY	95%
LIFE EXPECTANCY	79 years
GDP PER CAPITA	$22,900
ECONOMY	IND: textiles, clothing, footwear, wood and cork, paper, tourism AGR: grain, potatoes, tomatoes, olives, grapes; sheep; fish EXP: agricultural products, oil products, chemical products, vehicles and parts, wood pulp and paper

Spain
KINGDOM OF SPAIN
AREA	505,370 sq km (195,124 sq mi)
POPULATION	47,738,000
CAPITAL	Madrid 6,133,000
RELIGION	Roman Catholic
LANGUAGE	Castilian Spanish, Catalan, Galician, Basque
LITERACY	98%
LIFE EXPECTANCY	81 years
GDP PER CAPITA	$30,100
ECONOMY	IND: textiles and apparel (including footwear), food and beverages, metals and metal manufactures, tourism AGR: grain, vegetables, olives, wine grapes; fish EXP: machinery, motor vehicles, foodstuffs, pharmaceuticals

INDEX AND GRID:
Beginning on page 285 is a full index of place-names found in this atlas. The edge of each map is marked with letters (in rows) and numbers (in columns), to which the index entries are referenced. As an example, "Osuna, *Sp.* **146** L9" (see inset section, right) refers to the grid section on page 146 where row L and column 9 meet. More examples and additional details about the index are included on page 285.

Ostrów Wielkopolski, *Pol.* **151** E14
O'Sullivan Dam, *Wash., U.S.* **110** D7
Osŭm, river, *Bulg.* **155** H14
Ōsumi Kaikyō, *Japan* **189** U4
Ōsumi Shotō, *Japan* **189** U4
Osuna, *Sp.* **146** L9
Oswego, *N.Y., U.S.* **96** H8
Oswestry, *Eng., U.K.* **143** T10
Ōta, *Japan* **189** N12
Otaki, *N.Z.* **217** M19
Otar, *Kaz.* **177** H16

MAP PROJECTIONS:
Map projections determine how land shapes are distorted when transferred from a sphere (the Earth) to a flat piece of paper. Many different projections are used in this atlas—each carefully chosen for a map's particular coverage area and purpose.

MAP SCALES:
Scale information indicates the distance on Earth represented by a given length on the map. Here, map scale is expressed in three ways: (1) as a representative fraction where scale is shown as a fraction or ratio as in 1:3,675,000; this means that 1 centimeter or 1 inch on the map represents 3,675,000 centimeters or inches on Earth's surface; (2) as a verbal statement: 1 centimeter equals 37 kilometers or 1 inch equals 58 miles; and (3) as a bar scale, a linear graph symbol subdivided to show map lengths in kilometers and miles in the real world.

THEMATIC MAPS:
In combination, the four thematic maps on each regional spread—Temperature and Precipitation; Population; Land Use; and Industry and Mining—provide a fascinating overview of the area's physical and cultural geography. Temperature and Precipitation maps show which areas receive the most rain, and what the average temperatures are at different times during the year. Population maps allow one to see, at a glance, which areas are the least and most crowded, and where the major urban centers are located. Land Use maps paint a general picture of the ways humans use land resources. And Industry and Mining maps indicate the relative economic well-being of countries (expressed in GDP per capita) and show major centers of mining, mineral processing, and manufacturing. Interesting relationships can be observed: For example, although mines can be located anywhere that mineral deposits occur, processing centers are only feasible in areas with inexpensive electricity and adequate access to transportation.

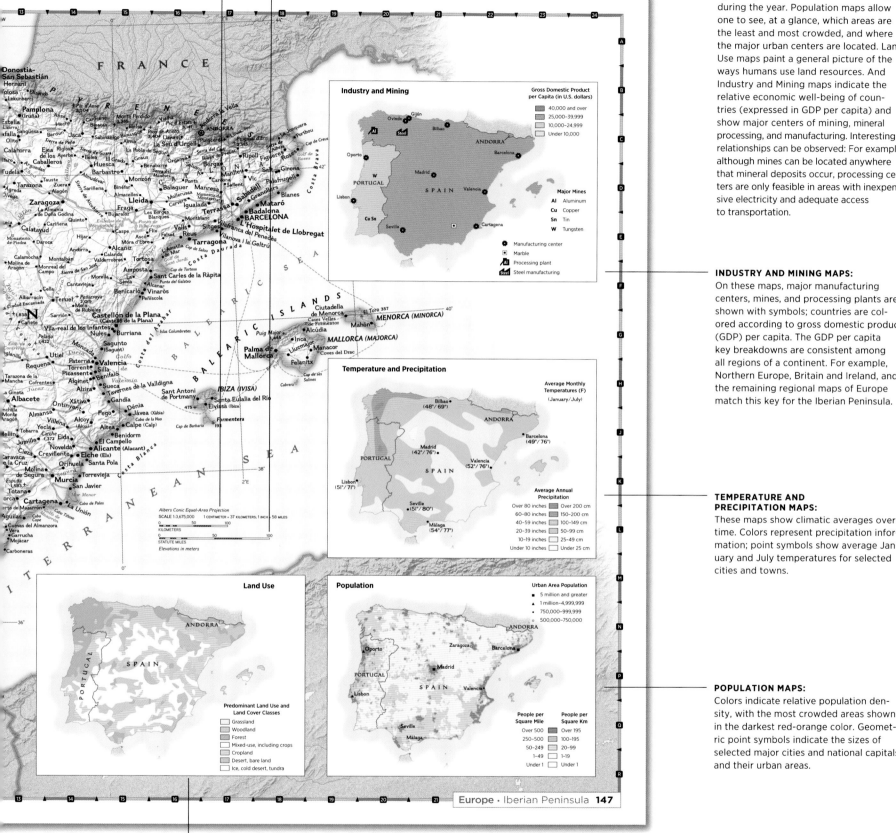

INDUSTRY AND MINING MAPS:
On these maps, major manufacturing centers, mines, and processing plants are shown with symbols; countries are colored according to gross domestic product (GDP) per capita. The GDP per capita key breakdowns are consistent among all regions of a continent. For example, Northern Europe, Britain and Ireland, and the remaining regional maps of Europe match this key for the Iberian Peninsula.

TEMPERATURE AND PRECIPITATION MAPS:
These maps show climatic averages over time. Colors represent precipitation information; point symbols show average January and July temperatures for selected cities and towns.

POPULATION MAPS:
Colors indicate relative population density, with the most crowded areas shown in the darkest red-orange color. Geometric point symbols indicate the sizes of selected major cities and national capitals and their urban areas.

LAND USE MAPS:
The colors on these maps indicate predominant land use and land-cover types—showing, for example, whether an area comprises mainly cropland or forest.

NORTH
AMERICA

EUROPE

AFRICA

SOUTH
AMERICA

The rapid worldwide decline
in the diversity of plant and animal
life ("biodiversity"), an unfortunate
result of human activity, is catching
the growing attention of scientists.
Increasingly, conservationists realize
that to protect the planet's biodiversity
they must look past political boundaries
to work with nature's own organization.
The many hundreds of terrestrial and
coastal marine areas shown on this map
represent eco-regions defined by the World
Wildlife Fund (WWF) and the Nature Conservancy.
Each eco-region has unique species and communities, many found nowhere else on Earth. For detailed
information on each region, see the online maps at:
www.worldwildlife.org/science/
ecoregions/item1267.html.

The World

Some 93 million miles (150 million km) from the sun, Earth whirls in space, its exact origins shrouded in time. According to scientists, our planet and every other object in the solar system originated from a great cloud of interstellar gas and dust that condensed to form the sun and the planets about 4.6 billion years ago. Life is known to have found a foothold on Earth more than 3.5 billion years ago—but in recent years researchers have made intriguing discoveries about potential habitats for life on other planets or their moons.

Scientists continue to study habitats here at home as well. Using the very latest technologies, they are gaining a much better understanding of the natural processes that support life, shape landscapes, and keep the currents of the air and sea always in motion. They are learning, too, how we humans, relative newcomers among life-forms, are affecting our world, for better or worse.

The image at left represents one way to see and understand the diversity of life on Earth. It portrays more than a thousand "eco-regions," charted according to climate, oceanography, plant and animal communities, and other ecological features, rather than political boundaries. Maps such as this can be an invaluable learning tool for scientists and laypeople alike.

The following pages present a wide array of other maps, tables, graphs, images, and text, covering all aspects of physical and cultural geography. Together, they reveal the state of our world, this complex, dynamic realm we call Earth.

ASIA

AUSTRALIA

Physical World

ARCTIC OCEAN

Longitude East of Greenwich (London)

SEA

NORWEGIAN SEA

BARENTS SEA

KARA SEA

LAPTEV SEA

EAST SIBERIAN SEA

ARCTIC CIRCLE

CHUKCHI Range

Wrangel I.

BERING SEA

Spitsbergen 1,712
North East Land
Edge Island
Bear Island
Svalbard

Novaya Zemlya

George Land
Graham Bell Island
Franz Josef Land +606
Vize I.
Komsomolets Island
October Revolution Island
Bol'shevik Island
North Land
Cape Chelyuskin
New Siberian Islands

North Cape
Kolguyev I.
Yamal Pen.
Gyda Peninsula
Taymyr Peninsula
1,146
North Siberian Lowland
Lake Taymyr
1,701
656

Kebnekaise

Saltoppen 2,469

Kola Pen.
White Sea
Lake Onega
Lake Ladoga

Timan Ridge
Narodnaya
1,895

Ob
Yenisey
West Siberian Plain

Central Siberian Plateau

Angara

Verkhoyansk Range
Chersky Range
Lena
1,830
Kolyma
Gora Mus Khaya +2,959

Koryak Range
Kamchatka Peninsula
+4,750
Attu
Aleutian Is.

SEA OF OKHOTSK

NORTH

Northern European Plain
EUROPE
Volga

Ural Mountains

Siberian Plain

SIBERIA

Eastern Sayan Mts.
Lake Baikal
2,412
Stanovoy Range

Sakhalin

Kuril Islands

PACIFIC

Jutland
North Sea
Baltic Sea
Source of the Volga

Central Russian Upland
Highest point in Europe
Caspian Depression
Pinsk Marshes

Kazakh Uplands
Belukha 4,506

Altai Mountains
3,957
Mongolian Plateau

Manchurian Plain
Greater Khingan Range
Amur
Sikhote Alin Range
Tatar Strait
Hokkaido

Corsica
Sardinia
Mt. Olympus +2,917
Balkan Peninsula
ALPS +4,810
Apennines
Crimea
Black Sea
Bosporus
Sea of Azov
Caucasus Mts. +5,642 (18,510 ft)
Elbrus
Aral Sea
Ustyurt Plateau
Turan Lowland
Syr Darya
The Steppes
Dzungarian Basin
Tian Shan
2,584
Turpan Depression
GOBI
North China Plain
Yellow Sea
Korea
Sea of Japan (East Sea)
Honshu
Fuji 3,776
Kyushu
Shikoku
Nampo Islands

Ionian Sea
Crete
Cyprus
ANATOLIA (ASIA MINOR)
Mt. Ararat +5,137
Elburz Mts.
Syrian Desert
Mesopotamia
Zagros Mountains
Amu Darya
Garagum
Kyzyl Kum
Victory Peak 7,495 +7,649
Taklimakan Desert
Altun Shan
Muztag +6,973
Kunlun Mountains
Source of the Yangtze
Plateau of Tibet
Qin Ling
Qinghai Hu
Yangtze

EAST CHINA SEA

Ryukyu Islands

TROPIC OF CANCER

OCEAN

MEDITERRANEAN SEA
Great Eastern Erg
Qattara Depression -133
Western Desert
Libyan Desert
Ahaggar Mts. +Mt. Tahat 3,003
Tibesti Mts.
Nile R. Delta
Sinai
Eastern Desert
An Nafud
Dead Sea -423 (-1,388 ft)
Lowest point in Europe
Kuh-e Taftan
+4,042
HIMALAYA
Mount Everest 8,850 m (29,035 ft)
Highest point in the world
Brahmaputra
Ganges
Taiwan
Hainan
Luzon Strait
Taiwan Str.

PHILIPPINE SEA

Mariana Islands

Wake I.

Taongi Atoll

SAHARA
Emi Koussi 3,415
Air Massif
872
Marra Mts. 3,071
Ras Dejen 4,533
Danakil -155 (-509 ft)
Nubian Desert
ARABIAN PENINSULA
Rub' al Khali
Lowest point in Africa
RED SEA
Socotra
Gulf of Aden
G. of Oman
Persian G.
Syrian Desert
1,893
2,285
Deccan Plateau
Western Ghats
Eastern Ghats
BAY OF BENGAL
Andaman Islands
Andaman Sea
Gulf of Thailand
Indochina Peninsula
Malay Pen.
SOUTH CHINA SEA
Luzon 2,934
Mount Pulog
Mount Pinatubo 1,486
Mindanao
Guam
Chuuk (Ponape) Pohnpei
Caroline Islands
MICRONESIA
Bikini Atoll
Enewetak Atoll
Kwajalein Atoll
Marshall Islands

AFRICA
Lake Chad
Bioko
Gulf of Guinea
São Tomé
Ethiopian Highlands
Somali Peninsula
Nile R.
Maldive Islands
Sri Lanka (Ceylon)
Nicobar Islands
Kinabalu 4,101
Borneo
Sumatra
Kerinci 3,800
INDONESIA
Celebes
Buru
Molucca
Greater Sunda Islands
Java Sea
Banda Sea
New Guinea +4,509
Bismarck Archipelago
New Ireland
New Britain
2,334
Bougainville
Solomon Islands
Solomon Sea
Admiralty Is.
EQUATOR
Nauru
Banaba (Ocean I.)
Nanumea
Tuvalu

Congo Basin
Lower Guinea
Mitumba Mts.
Lake Tanganyika
Lake Victoria
Lake Albert
Lake Turkana (Rudolf)
Mount Kenya +5,199
Kilimanjaro +5,895 m (19,340 ft)
Highest point in Africa
Zanzibar I.
Amirante Isles
Seychelles
Chagos Archipelago
Diego Garcia
Java
Flores
Lesser Sunda Is.
Timor
Arafura Sea
Timor Sea
Cape York Pen.
Gulf of Carpentaria
Guadalcanal
MELANESIA
Vanuatu

Katanga Plateau
Lake Kariba
Namib Desert
1,340
Brandberg 2,606
2,419
Maromokotro 2,876
Madagascar
Mascarene Islands
Mauritius
Rodrigues
Réunion
Comoro Is.
Aldabra Is.
Malawi (L. Nyasa)
Zambezi
INDIAN
Cocos Islands
Christmas I.

Kimberley Plateau
Mount Ord 947
Great Sandy Desert
North West Cape
Macdonnell Ranges
CORAL SEA
New Caledonia +1,628
Fiji Islands

Kalahari Desert
Great Karoo
+2,202
Drakensberg
Cape of Good Hope
Cape Agulhas
OCEAN
Mount Meharry +1,250
Cape Inscription
AUSTRALIA
Western Plateau
Great Artesian Basin
Great Dividing Range
TROPIC OF CAPRICORN
SOUTH PACIFIC

Amsterdam
St. Paul
Cape Naturaliste
Lowest point in Australia
Lake Eyre (-49 ft) -15
Great Victoria Desert
Nullarbor Plain
Great Australian Bight
Murray
Darling
Mt. Kosciuszko +2,228 (7,310 ft)
Highest point in Australia
Lord Howe I.
North Island (Te Ika-a-Maui)
OCEAN

Prince Edward Islands
Crozet Islands
Kerguelen Islands 1,850
Bass Strait
TASMAN SEA
NEW +2,797
Tasmania
(Mt. Cook) Aoraki +3,724
South Island (Te Waipounamu)
ZEALAND
Stewart Island (Rakiura)

Heard Island

Macquarie I.

Auckland Is.

ANTARCTIC CIRCLE
Riiser-Larsen Peninsula
Cosmonaut Sea
Cape Ann
Enderby Land
Prydz Bay
Cape Poinsett
South Magnetic Pole, 2015
Balleny Is.

Queen Maud Land
Wilkes Land
Victoria Land
TRANSANTARCTIC MOUNTAINS
+3,794 +Mt. Erebus
-2,870 (-9,416 ft)
Lowest point in Antarctica
Ross Ice Shelf
Ross Sea

ANTARCTICA

Winkel Tripel Projection

SCALE 1:81,657,000   1 CENTIMETER = 817 KILOMETERS; 1 INCH = 1,289 MILES AT THE EQUATOR

0   500   1000   1500   2000   2500
KILOMETERS

0   500   1000   1500   2000   2500
STATUTE MILES

Political World

Winkel Tripel Projection
SCALE 1:81,657,000   1 CENTIMETER = 817 KILOMETERS; 1 INCH = 1,289 MILES AT THE EQUATOR

Political Poles

North Pole

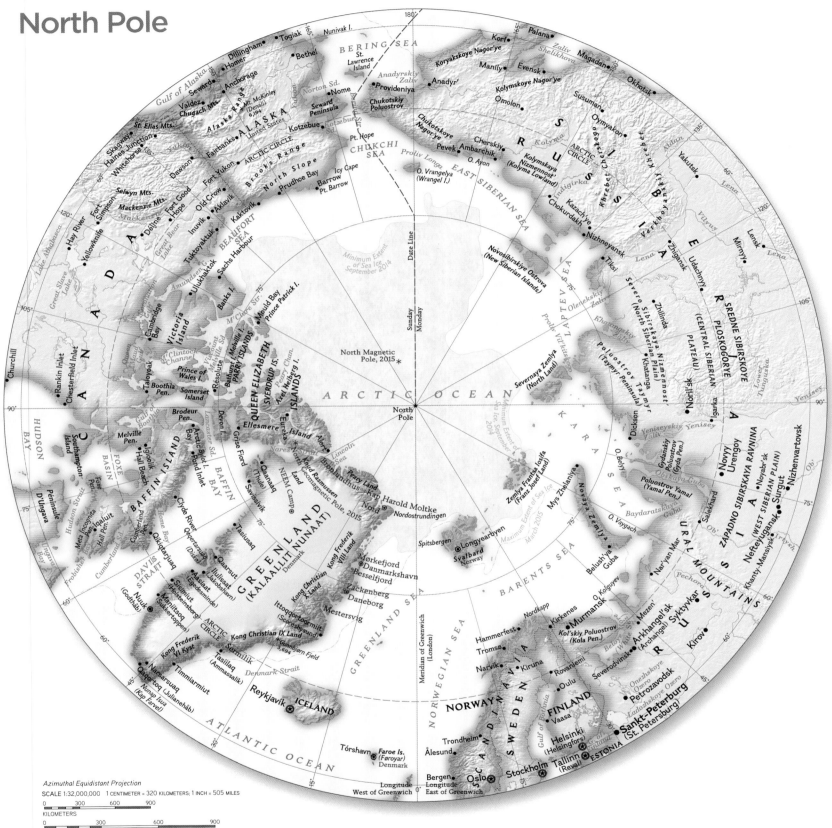

Azimuthal Equidistant Projection
SCALE 1:32,000,000   1 CENTIMETER = 320 KILOMETERS; 1 INCH = 505 MILES

KILOMETERS

STATUTE MILES

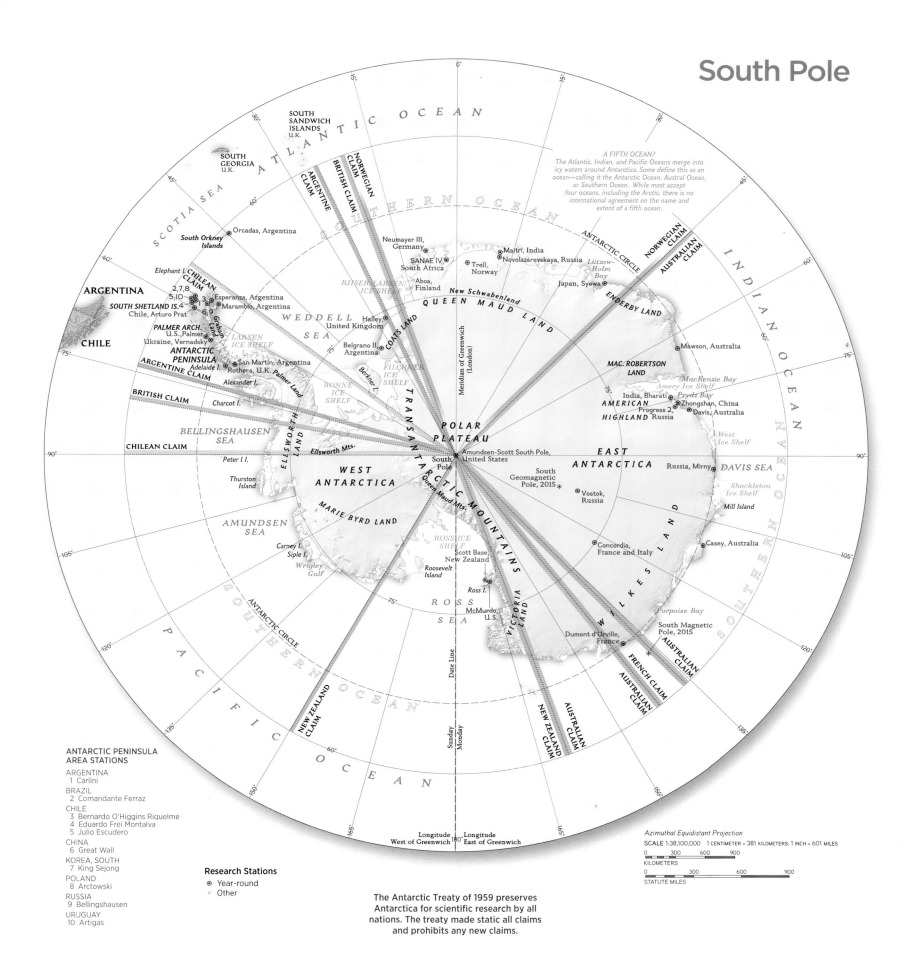

A FIFTH OCEAN?
The Atlantic, Indian, and Pacific Oceans merge into icy waters around Antarctica. Some define this as an ocean—calling it the Antarctic Ocean, Austral Ocean, or Southern Ocean. While most accept four oceans, including the Arctic, there is no international agreement on the name and extent of a fifth ocean.

ATLANTIC OCEAN

SOUTH SANDWICH ISLANDS U.K.

SOUTH GEORGIA U.K.

SCOTIA SEA

SOUTHERN OCEAN

INDIAN OCEAN

ANTARCTIC CIRCLE

South Orkney Islands

Orcadas, Argentina

NORWEGIAN CLAIM

BRITISH CLAIM

ARGENTINE CLAIM

Neumayer III, Germany

Maitri, India
Novolazarevskaya, Russia

SANAE IV, South Africa

Troll, Norway

Japan, Syowa

Lützow-Holm Bay

NORWEGIAN CLAIM

AUSTRALIAN CLAIM

ENDERBY LAND

ARGENTINA

Elephant I.
CHILEAN CLAIM
2,7,8
5,10
3
1
6,9
SOUTH SHETLAND IS.4
Chile, Arturo Prat

CHILE

Esperanza, Argentina
Marambio, Argentina

PALMER ARCH.
U.S., Palmer
Ukraine, Vernadsky

ANTARCTIC PENINSULA

Adelaide I.
Rothera, U.K.

San Martin, Argentina

ARGENTINE CLAIM

BRITISH CLAIM

Alexander I.

Charcot I.

CHILEAN CLAIM

Graham Land

Palmer Land

RIISER-LARSEN ICE SHELF

Aboa, Finland

QUEEN MAUD LAND

New Schwabenland

WEDDELL SEA

Halley, United Kingdom

LARSEN ICE SHELF

Berkner I.

FILCHNER ICE SHELF

COATS LAND

Belgrano II, Argentina

Meridian of Greenwich (London)

Mawson, Australia

MAC. ROBERTSON LAND

MacKenzie Bay
Amery Ice Shelf
Prydz Bay

AMERICAN HIGHLAND

India, Bharati
Progress 2, Russia
Zhongshan, China
Davis, Australia

West Ice Shelf

RONNE ICE SHELF

Ellsworth Mts.

BELLINGSHAUSEN SEA

ELLSWORTH LAND

TRANSANTARCTIC MOUNTAINS

POLAR PLATEAU

South Pole

Amundsen-Scott South Pole, United States

EAST ANTARCTICA

Peter I I.

CHILEAN CLAIM

South Geomagnetic Pole, 2015

Russia, Mirny

DAVIS SEA

Shackleton Ice Shelf

Thurston Island

WEST ANTARCTICA

Queen Maud Mts.

Vostok, Russia

Mill Island

AMUNDSEN SEA

MARIE BYRD LAND

Carney I.
Siple I.

Wrigley Gulf

ROSS ICE SHELF

Scott Base, New Zealand

Roosevelt Island

Concordia, France and Italy

Casey, Australia

WILKES LAND

Porpoise Bay

ANTARCTIC CIRCLE

ROSS SEA

Ross I.

McMurdo, U.S.

VICTORIA LAND

South Magnetic Pole, 2015

Dumont d'Urville, France

AUSTRALIAN CLAIM

FRENCH CLAIM

AUSTRALIAN CLAIM

SOUTHERN OCEAN

PACIFIC OCEAN

NEW ZEALAND CLAIM

Date Line

Sunday Monday

NEW ZEALAND CLAIM

AUSTRALIAN CLAIM

Longitude West of Greenwich
Longitude East of Greenwich

ANTARCTIC PENINSULA AREA STATIONS

ARGENTINA
1 Carlini

BRAZIL
2 Comandante Ferraz

CHILE
3 Bernardo O'Higgins Riquelme
4 Eduardo Frei Montalva
5 Julio Escudero

CHINA
6 Great Wall

KOREA, SOUTH
7 King Sejong

POLAND
8 Arctowski

RUSSIA
9 Bellingshausen

URUGUAY
10 Artigas

Research Stations
◉ Year-round
○ Other

Azimuthal Equidistant Projection

SCALE 1:38,100,000   1 CENTIMETER = 381 KILOMETERS; 1 INCH = 601 MILES

0   300   600   900
KILOMETERS

0   300   600   900
STATUTE MILES

The Antarctic Treaty of 1959 preserves Antarctica for scientific research by all nations. The treaty made static all claims and prohibits any new claims.

Structure of the Earth

LIKE ICE ON A GREAT LAKE, Earth's crust, or the lithosphere, floats over the planet's molten innards, is cracked in many places, and is in slow but constant movement. Earth's surface is broken into 16 enormous slabs of rock, called plates, averaging thousands of miles wide and having a thickness of several miles. As they move and grind against each other, they push up mountains, spawn volcanoes, and generate earthquakes.

Although these often cataclysmic events capture our attention, the movements that cause them are imperceptible—a slow waltz of rafted rock that continues over eons. How slow? The Mid-Atlantic Ridge (see "spreading" diagram, opposite) is being built by magma oozing between two plates, separating North America and Africa at the speed of a growing human fingernail.

The dividing lines between plates often mark areas of high volcanic and earthquake activity as plates strain against each other or one dives beneath another. In the Ring of Fire around the Pacific Basin, disastrous earthquakes have occurred in Kobe, Japan, and in Los Angeles and San Francisco, California. Volcanic eruptions have taken place at Pinatubo in the Philippines and Mount St. Helens in Washington State.

Crust
2 to 45 miles (3 to 72 km) thick
Lithosphere
1 to 120 miles (2 to 193 km) thick
Asthenosphere
60 to 400 miles (97 to 644 km) thick
Upper Mantle
400 miles (644 km) thick
Lower Mantle
1,400 miles (2,253 km) thick
Outer Core
1,400 miles (2,253 km) thick
Inner Core
1,500 miles (2,414 km) in diameter

Continents Adrift in Time

With unceasing movement of Earth's tectonic plates, continents "drift" over geologic time—breaking apart, reassembling, and again fragmenting to repeat the process. Three times during the past billion years, Earth's drifting landmasses have merged to form so-called supercontinents. Rodinia, a supercontinent in the late Precambrian, began breaking apart about 750 million years ago. In time, its pieces reassembled to form another supercontinent, which in turn split into smaller landmasses during the Paleozoic. The largest of these were called Euramerica (ancestral Europe and North America) and Gondwana (ancestral Africa, Antarctica, Arabia, India, and Australia). More than 250 million years ago, these two landmasses recombined, forming Pangaea. In the Mesozoic era, Pangaea split and the Atlantic and Indian Oceans began forming. Though the Atlantic is still widening today, scientists predict it will close as the seafloor recycles back into Earth's mantle. A new supercontinent, Pangaea Ultima, will eventually form.

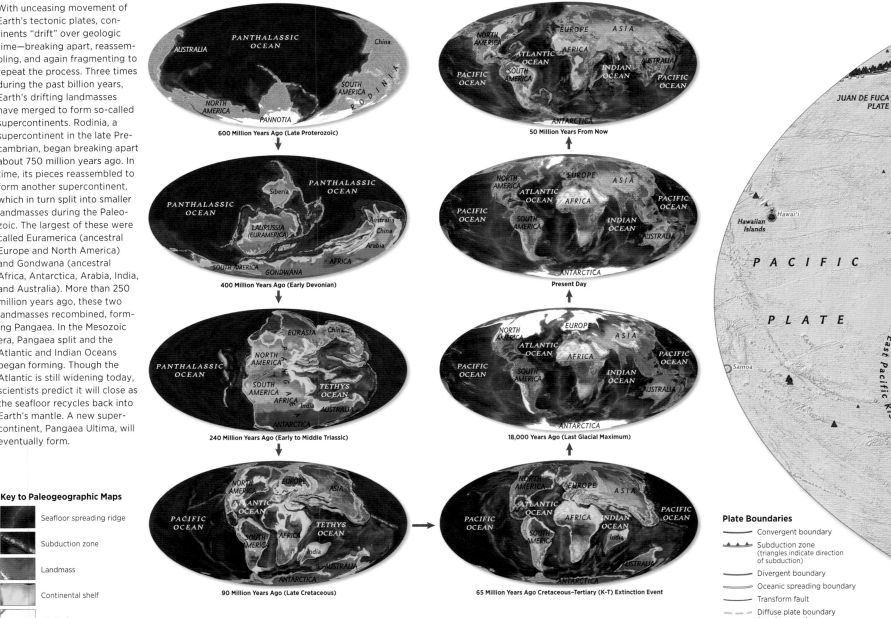

600 Million Years Ago (Late Proterozoic)

400 Million Years Ago (Early Devonian)

240 Million Years Ago (Early to Middle Triassic)

90 Million Years Ago (Late Cretaceous)

50 Million Years From Now

Present Day

18,000 Years Ago (Last Glacial Maximum)

65 Million Years Ago Cretaceous–Tertiary (K-T) Extinction Event

Key to Paleogeographic Maps

Seafloor spreading ridge

Subduction zone

Landmass

Continental shelf

Glacier/ice cap

Plate Boundaries

Convergent boundary

Subduction zone (triangles indicate direction of subduction)

Divergent boundary

Oceanic spreading boundary

Transform fault

Diffuse plate boundary (may be more than 100 mi [161 km] across)

Geologic Time

Millions of years ago (Ma)

	4500			3500		3000		2500		2000		1500		1000

EON	HADEAN		ARCHAEAN				PROTEROZOIC		

ERA		EOARCHAEAN	PALEOARCHAEAN	MESOARCHAEAN	NEOARCHAEAN	PALEOPROTEROZOIC		MESOPROTEROZOIC		NEO- PROTEROZO

PERIOD		*No subdivision into periods*				SIDERIAN	RHYACIAN	OROSIRIAN	STATHERIAN	CALYMMIAN	ECTASIAN	STENIAN	TONIAN

CRYOGENIAN

— PRECAMBRIAN —

JUAN DE FUCA PLATE

Hawaiian Islands

Hawai'i

PACIFIC PLATE

Samoa

East Pacific Ri...

Geologic Forces Change the Face of the Planet

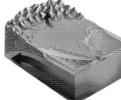

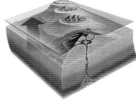

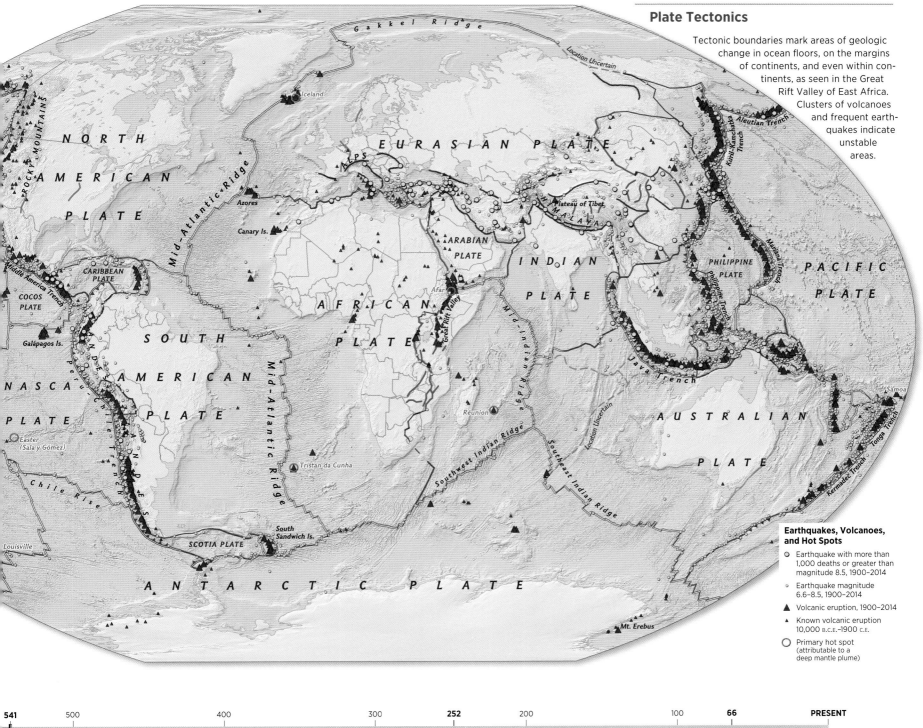

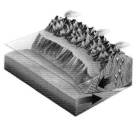

ACCRETION
As ocean plates move toward the edges of continents or island arcs and slide under them, seamounts are skimmed off and piled up in submarine trenches. The resulting buildup can cause continents to grow.

FAULTING
Enormous crustal plates do not slide smoothly. Strain built up along their edges may release in a series of small jumps, felt as minor tremors on land. Extended buildup can cause a sudden jump, producing an earthquake.

COLLISION
When two continental plates converge, the result can be the most dramatic mountain-building process on Earth. The Himalaya mountain range rose when the Indian subcontinent collided with Eurasia, driving the land upward.

HOT SPOTS
In the cauldron of inner Earth, some areas burn hotter than others and periodically blast through their crustal covering as volcanoes. Such a "hot spot" built the Hawaiian Islands, leaving a string of oceanic protuberances.

SPREADING
At the divergent boundary known as the Mid-Atlantic Ridge, oozing magma forces two plates apart by as much as eight inches (20 cm) a year. If that rate had been constant, the ocean could have reached its current width in 30 million years.

SUBDUCTION
When an oceanic plate and a continental plate converge, the older and heavier sea plate takes a dive. Plunging back into the interior of Earth, it is transformed into molten material, only to rise again as magma.

Plate Tectonics

Tectonic boundaries mark areas of geologic change in ocean floors, on the margins of continents, and even within continents, as seen in the Great Rift Valley of East Africa. Clusters of volcanoes and frequent earthquakes indicate unstable areas.

Earthquakes, Volcanoes, and Hot Spots

- ◉ Earthquake with more than 1,000 deaths or greater than magnitude 8.5, 1900–2014
- • Earthquake magnitude 6.6–8.5, 1900–2014
- ▲ Volcanic eruption, 1900–2014
- ▴ Known volcanic eruption 10,000 B.C.E.–1900 C.E.
- ○ Primary hot spot (attributable to a deep mantle plume)

541	500	400	300	252	200	100	66	PRESENT

PHANEROZOIC

PALEOZOIC						MESOZOIC			CENOZOIC
CAMBRIAN	ORDOVICIAN	SILURIAN	DEVONIAN	CARBONIFEROUS	PERMIAN	TRIASSIC	JURASSIC	CRETACEOUS	PALEOGENE

EDIACARAN

NEOGENE
QUATERNARY

Earth's Rocky Exterior

EARTH'S OUTERMOST LAYER, the crust, ranges from 2 to 45 miles (3 to 70 km) thick and comprises a large variety of rocks that are aggregates of one or more types of minerals.

Scientists recognize three main classes of rock. Igneous rock forms when molten material cools and solidifies, either rapidly at Earth's surface—perhaps as a lava flow—or more slowly underground, as an intrusion. Sedimentary rocks form from mineral or rock fragments, or from organic material that is eroded or dissolved and then deposited at Earth's surface. Metamorphic rocks form when rocks of any origin (igneous, sedimentary, or metamorphic) are subjected to very high temperature and pressure; this type also forms as rocks react with fluids deep within the crust. Igneous and metamorphic rocks make up 95 percent of the crust's volume. Sedimentary rocks make up only about 5 percent; even so, they cover a large percentage of Earth's surface.

As a result of plate tectonics, the crust is in constant slow motion; thus, rocks change positions over time. Their compositions also change as they are gradually modified by metamorphism and melting. Rocks form and re-form in a sequence known as the rock cycle (see below). Understanding their nature and origin is important because rocks contain materials that sustain modern civilization. For example, making steel requires the processing of iron, mainly from ancient sedimentary rocks; copper is mined principally from slowly cooled igneous rocks called plutons; and fossil fuels (e.g., coal, oil, natural gas) derive from organic material trapped ages ago in relatively young sedimentary rocks.

Rock Classes

IGNEOUS Igneous rocks form when molten rock (magma) originating from deep within the Earth solidifies. The chemical composition of the magma and its cooling rate determine the final rock type.	**Intrusive (Plutonic)**	**Intrusive** igneous rocks are formed from magma that cools and solidifies deep beneath Earth's surface. The insulating effect of the surrounding rock allows the magma to solidify very slowly. Slow cooling means the individual mineral grains have a long time to grow, so they grow to a relatively large size. Intrusive rocks typically are coarser grained than volcanic rocks.	**Examples:** gabbro, diorite, granite
	Extrusive (Volcanic)	**Extrusive** igneous rocks are formed from magma that cools and solidifies at or near Earth's surface. Exposure to the relatively cool temperature of the atmosphere or water makes the erupted magma solidify very quickly. Rapid cooling means the individual mineral grains have only a short time to grow, so their final size is very tiny, or fine-grained. Sometimes the magma is quenched so rapidly that individual minerals have no time to grow. This is how volcanic glass forms.	**Examples:** basalt, andesite, rhyolite
SEDIMENTARY Sedimentary rocks are formed from preexisting rocks or pieces of once living organisms. They form deposits that accumulate on Earth's surface, generally with distinctive layering or bedding.	**Clastic**	**Clastic** sedimentary rocks are made up of pieces (clasts) of preexisting rocks. Pieces of rock are loosened by weathering and then transported to a basin or depression where sediment is trapped. If the sediment is buried deeply, it becomes compacted and cemented, forming sedimentary rock. Clastic sedimentary rocks may have particles ranging in size from microscopic clay to huge boulders. Their names are based on their grain size.	**Examples:** sandstone, mudstone, conglomerate
	Chemical	**Chemical** sedimentary rocks are formed by chemical precipitation. This process begins when water traveling through rock dissolves some of the minerals, carrying them away from their source. Eventually these minerals are redeposited when the water evaporates.	**Examples:** evaporite, dolomite
	Biologic	**Biologic** sedimentary rocks form from once living organisms. They may comprise accumulated carbon-rich plant material or deposits of animal shells.	**Examples:** coal, chalk, limestone, chert
METAMORPHIC Metamorphic rocks are those rocks that have been substantially changed from their original igneous, sedimentary, or earlier metamorphic form. They form when rocks are subjected to high heat; high pressure; hot, mineral-rich fluids; or, more commonly, some combination of these.	**Foliated**	**Foliated** metamorphic rocks form when pressure deforms tabular minerals within a rock so they become aligned. These rocks develop a platy or sheetlike structure that reflects the directions from which pressure was applied.	**Examples:** schist, gneiss, slate
	Nonfoliated (Massive)	**Nonfoliated** metamorphic rocks do not have a platy or sheetlike structure. There are several ways that nonfoliated rocks can be produced. Some rocks, such as limestone, are made of minerals that are not flat or elongated; no matter how much pressure is applied, the grains will not align despite recrystallization. Contact metamorphism occurs when hot igneous rock intrudes into preexisting rock. The preexisting rock is essentially baked by the heat, which changes mineral composition and texture primarily from heating rather than pressure effects.	**Examples:** marble, quartzite, hornfels

The Rock Cycle

To learn the origin and history of rocks, geologists study their mineralogy, texture, and fabric—characteristics that result from dynamic Earth-shaping processes driven by both internal energy and external forces.

Internal energy is heat contained within the Earth. This intense heat creates convection currents in the mantle, which in turn cause tectonic plate movements and volcanism. External energy comes from the sun, which drives atmospheric processes that produce rain, snow, ice, and wind—powerful agents of weathering and erosion.

As internal energy builds and rebuilds Earth's rocky exterior, the forces of weathering and erosion break down surface materials and wear them away.

Ultimately, soil particles and rock fragments, called sediments, are carried by rivers into the oceans, where they may lithify, or harden into solid rock. In time, these sedimentary rocks may be subjected to heat and pressure at great depth. Mineral and structural changes occur as the rocks break and fold; they are transformed into metamorphic rocks.

Solid rocks subject to high heat and pressure during metamorphism can melt to form magma, which can eventually form igneous rocks, either intrusive or extrusive. The subsurface intrusive rocks (i.e., plutons) can be uplifted later by tectonic forces and/or exposed by erosion. At the surface, the cycle continues as weathering and erosion break it down and wear it away.

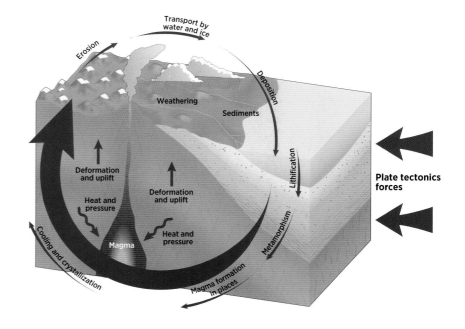

Global Distribution of Rock Types

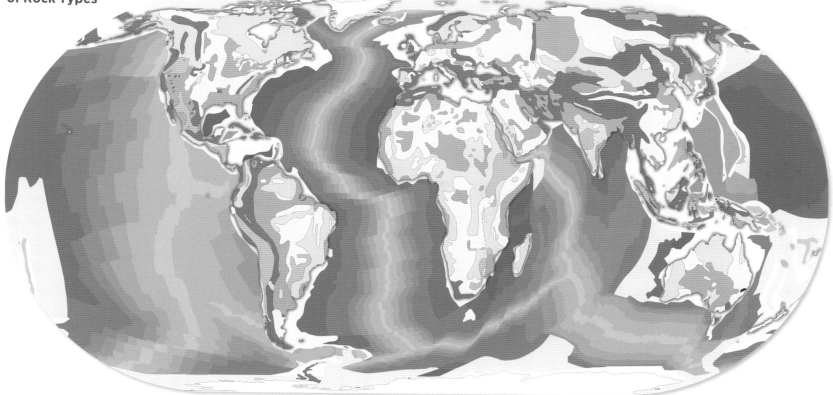

Reading Earth History From Rocks

Earth is 4.6 billion years old, with a long, complex history written in layers of rock.* By reading sequences of sedimentary rock, we can discover information about past environments and processes. The principle of superposition states that, provided rocks are not turned upside down by deformation, the oldest rocks are at the bottom of a sequence and younger rocks are found at the top. Unconformities tell us that uplift and erosion occurred before the deposition of younger sediments resumed. As an example, the rock sequence exposed in the Grand Canyon of Arizona indicates, from oldest to youngest, the following major events:

DURING PRECAMBRIAN TIME

1. Deposition of Vishnu sediment (about 2 billion years ago)
2. Mountain building, metamorphism of Vishnu sediment into Vishnu schist, and intrusion of Zoroaster granite (1.8 to 1.4 billion years ago)
3. Uplift and erosion resulting in an unconformity (1.4 to 1.2 billion years ago)
4. Deposition of Unkar Group sediments (1.2 to 1 billion years ago)
5. Tilting (1 billion years ago)
6. Erosion resulting in angular unconformity (1 billion to 541 million years ago)

DURING THE PHANEROZOIC (CAMBRIAN–RECENT) EON

7. Deposition of Cambrian to Permian (and younger rocks not shown) sediments (541 to 252 million years ago), with disconformities indicating erosion and "missing" time where noted
8. Uplift and erosion of the Grand Canyon (20 million years ago to present)

The ages for these events are broadly defined by the radioisotopic dating of minerals in the metamorphic and igneous rocks, and by fossils and correlation to other rocks for the sedimentary rocks that are younger than the Precambrian-Cambrian boundary (541 million years ago).

Yavapai Point,
Grand Canyon

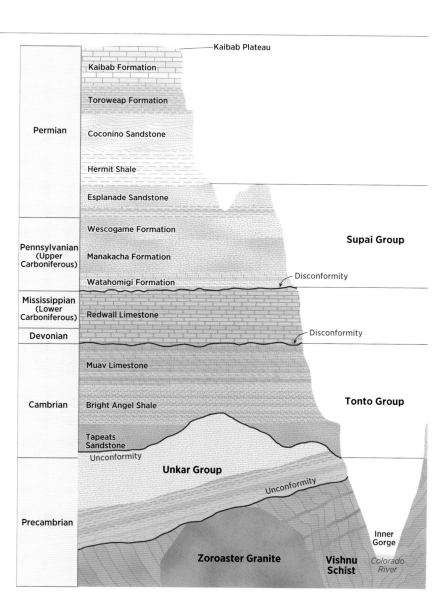

* The oldest-known dated rocks on Earth go back to 4 billion years ago; geologic records of older rocks have been destroyed by more recent geologic events.

Landforms

SEVEN MAJOR LANDFORM TYPES are found on Earth's surface (see map); except for ice caps, all result from tectonic movements and denudational forces.

Mountains, the loftiest landforms, often define the edges of tectonic plates. In places where continental plates converge, Earth's crust crumples into high ranges such as the Himalaya. Where oceanic plates dive beneath continental ones, volcanic mountains can rise. Volcanoes are common along the west coast of South America, which is part of the so-called Ring of Fire, the world's most active mountain-building zone.

Widely spaced mountains are another type, and examples of this landform are seen in the Basin and Range province of the western United States. These features are actually the tops of heavily eroded, faulted mountains. The eroded material filled adjacent valleys, giving these old summits the look of widely spaced mountains.

Extensive, relatively flat lands that are higher than surrounding areas are called plateaus. Formed by uplift, they include the Guiana Highlands of South America. Hills and low plateaus are rounded natural elevations of land with some local relief. The Canadian Shield and Ozarks of North America provide good examples. Depressions are large basins delimited by higher lands, an example of which is the Tarim Basin in western China. Plains are extensive areas of level or rolling treeless country. Examples include the steppes of Eurasia, the Ganges River plains, and the outback of Australia.

Major Landform Types
- Mountains
- Widely spaced mountains
- High plateaus
- Hills and low plateaus
- Depressions
- Plains
- Ice caps

Endogenic Landforms

LANDFORMS THAT RESULT FROM INTERNAL PROCESSES

Forces deep within the Earth give rise to mountains and other endogenic landforms. Some mountains were born when continental plates collided (e.g., the Himalaya). Others rose in the form of volcanoes as sea plates subducted beneath continental plates (e.g., the Cascades of North America, Mount Fuji of Japan) or as plates moved over hot spots in Earth's mantle (e.g., Hawaii). Still others were thrust up by tectonic uplift (parts of the western United States).

Rifting and faulting along plate boundaries and within the plates themselves also generate vertical tectonic landforms; these can be seen in Africa's Great Rift Valley and along the San Andreas Fault of California. Magma released by spreading plates on the Mid-Atlantic seafloor created Iceland.

Clockwise from above: The Wasatch Range in Utah, uplifted by tectonic forces; the San Andreas Fault in California, a fracture in Earth's crust marking a plate boundary; Mount Fuji in Japan, a volcanic peak; Crater Lake in Oregon, a deep lake inside the caldera of Mount Mazama.

Exogenic Landforms

LANDFORMS THAT RESULT FROM EXTERNAL PROCESSES

External agents create exogenic landforms. Weathering by rain, groundwater, and other natural elements slowly breaks down rocks, such as the limestone in karst landscapes or the granite in an exfoliation dome. Erosion removes weathered material and transports it from place to place; collections of such debris at mountain bases are called talus deposits. In the American Southwest, erosion continues to shape the spires of Bryce Canyon and the walls of slot canyons.

Other Landforms

Some landforms are the impact sites (or craters) of asteroids, comets, and meteorites. The most readily observable are Meteor Crater in Arizona and New Quebec Crater in eastern Canada. Other landforms include constructed dams, open-pit and mountaintop removal mines, hillslope terraces, and canals. Coral reefs made by coral polyps and giant termite mounds are known as biogenic features.

Meteor Crater, Arizona

Termite mound, Cape York Peninsula, Australia

Clockwise from above: Tower karst in Thailand, weathered limestone in humid climate; Bryce Canyon in Utah, eroded sedimentary rocks in arid climate; slot canyon in the American Southwest, sedimentary rock eroded by water; Half Dome in Yosemite, California, weathered granite batholith.

Landforms

All of Earth's features are created and continually reshaped by such factors as wind, water, ice, tectonics, and humans. This illustration brings together 41 natural and man-made features to show typical locations and relationships of landforms; it does not depict an actual region. Definitions of most landforms can be found in the glossary.

Mountain range

Mountain peak

Glacier

Iceberg

Dormant volcano

Ocean

Desert

Mesa

Island

Basin

Oasis

Archipelago

Strait

Divide

Plateau

Point

Waterfall

Cape

Sound

Valley

Escarpment

Lake

Canal

Canyon

Plain

River

Fork

Peninsula

Bay

Lagoon

Isthmus

Beach

Delta

Hills

Cliff

Gulf

Spit

Harbor

Tributary

Reef

Breakwater

Landforms Created by Wind

The term "eolian" (from Aeolus, the Greek god of the winds) describes landforms shaped by the wind. The erosive action of wind is characterized by deflation, or the removal of dust and sand from dry soil; sandblasting, the erosion of rock by wind-borne sand; and deposition, the laying down of sediments. The effects of wind erosion are evident in many parts of the world (see map), particularly where there are large deposits of sand or loess (dust and silt dropped by wind). Among desert landforms, sand dunes may be the most spectacular. They come in several types (below): Barchan dunes are crescents with arms pointing downwind; transverse dunes are "waves," with crests perpendicular to the wind; star dunes have curving ridges radiating from their centers; longitudinal dunes lie parallel to the wind; and parabolic dunes are crescents with arms that point upwind.

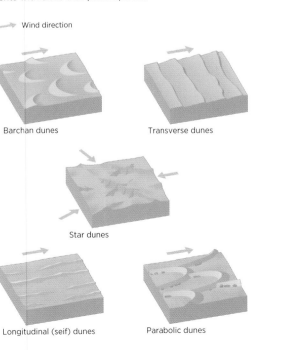

Wind direction

Barchan dunes

Transverse dunes

Star dunes

Longitudinal (seif) dunes

Parabolic dunes

NORTH AMERICA

SOUTH AMERICA

EUROPE

ASIA

AFRICA

AUSTRALIA

ANTARCTICA

Desert

Loess deposit

See Land Cover pp. 32–33

EOLIAN LANDFORMS

Desert dunes, which actually cover only a small portion of desert areas, range in height from just a few feet to more than a thousand feet. Coastal dunes form when wind and waves deposit sediments along the shores of oceans and other large bodies of water. Loess hills are large deposits of wind-borne silt, the most extensive of which are found in North America and Asia.

Desert dunes: Death Valley National Park, California

Coastal dunes: Dune du Nord, Quebec

Loess deposits: Palouse Hills, Washington

Landforms Created by Water

Highlighted on the map at right are Earth's major waters are drainage basins for rivers, which create fluvial (from meaning "river") landforms. Wave action and groundwa produce characteristic landforms.

RIVERS

Some rivers form broad loops (called meanders) as faster currents erode their outer banks and slower currents deposit materials along inner banks. When a river breaks through the narrow neck of a meander, the abandoned curve becomes an oxbow lake.

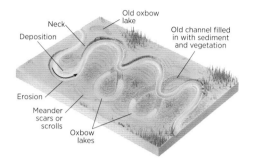

RIVER DELTAS

Sediment deposited at a river's mouth builds a delta, a term first used by the ancient Greeks to describe the Nile Delta; its triangular shape resembles the fourth letter of the Greek alphabet. Not all deltas have that classic shape: The Mississippi River forms a bird's-foot delta.

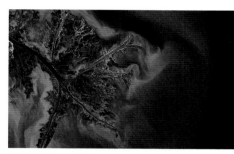

Mississippi River Delta

COASTAL AREAS

Through erosion and deposition, tides and wave action continually reshape the coastlines of the world. Ocean currents transport sand and gravel from one part of a shore to another, sometimes building beach extensions called spits, long ridges that project into open water. Relentless waves undercut coastal cliffs, eroding volumes of material and leaving behind sea stacks and sea arches, remnants made of more resistant rock. As ocean levels rise, narrow arms of the sea (fjords) may reach inland for miles, filling deep valleys once occupied by glaciers flowing to the sea.

Limestone sea stacks at Victoria, Australia. The formation in the foreground collapsed in 2005.

GROUNDWATER

Water in the ground slowly dissolves limestone, a highly soluble rock. Over time, caves form and underground streams flow through the rock; sinkholes develop at the surface as underlying rock gives way. Karst landscapes, named for the rugged Karst region of the former Yugoslavia, are large areas of unusual landforms created by weathered and eroded limestone.

Karst cave: Kickapoo Cave, Texas

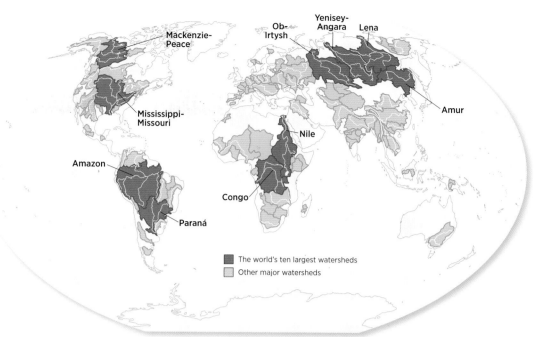

The world's ten largest watersheds

Other major watersheds

Landforms Created by Ice

Among the legacies of Earth's most recent ice age (see map) are landforms shaped by glaciers. There are two kinds of glaciers: valley, or alpine, and continental ice sheets. These large, slow-moving masses of ice can crush or topple anything in their paths; they can even stop rivers in their tracks, creating ice-dammed lakes. Glaciers are also powerful agents of erosion, grinding against the ground and picking up and carrying huge amounts of rock and soil, which they deposit at their margins when they begin to melt; these deposits are called lateral and terminal moraines. The illustrations below show how an ice sheet (upper) leaves a lasting imprint on the land (lower).

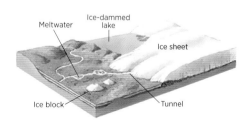

BEFORE AND AFTER

Meltwater deposits material in long, narrow ridges (eskers, left). Ice embedded in the ground melts and forms lakes (kettles). Ice overruns unconsolidated materials and shapes them into hills (drumlins).

Greatest extent of ice during last ice age

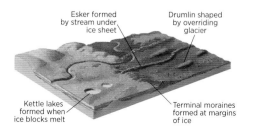

POSTGLACIAL LANDFORMS

As they move, alpine glaciers widen their V-shaped valleys, often leaving behind U-shaped ones when they withdraw. Ice sheets leave an even larger legacy simply because they cover more territory. Among their creations are drumlin fields and lake basins, including the ones now filled by the Great Lakes of North America.

U-shaped glacial valley: Sierra Nevada, California

Drumlins: Kejimkujik Lake, Nova Scotia

Surface of the Earth

EARTH'S LARGEST FEATURES—oceans and continents—can be seen from thousands of miles out in space. So can some of its relatively smaller ones: vast plains and long mountain chains, huge lakes and great ice sheets. The sizes, shapes, locations, and interrelationships of these and innumerable other features, large and small, give Earth its unique appearance.

Mountains, plateaus, and plains give texture to the land. In North and South America, the Rockies and Andes rise above great basins and plains, while in Asia the Himalaya and Plateau of Tibet form the rugged core of Earth's largest continent. All are the result of powerful forces within the planet pushing up the land. Other features, such as valleys and canyons, were created when weathering and erosion wore down parts of the surface.

Landmasses are not the only places with dramatic features: Lying beneath the oceans are enormous mountains and towering volcanoes, high plateaus and seemingly bottomless trenches. Around most continents are shallow seas concealing gently sloping continental shelves. From the margins of these shelves, steeper continental slopes lead ever deeper into the abyss. Although scientists use different terms to describe their studies of the ocean depths (bathymetry) and the lay of the land (topography), Earth's surface is a continuum, with similar features giving texture to lands both above and below the sea level.

Snow Cover

0%   100%

SNOW AND ICE Just over 2 percent of Earth's water is locked in ice, snow, and glaciers. Ice and snow reflect solar energy back into space, thus regulating the temperature. Ocean levels can also be affected, either rising with melt-water from shrinking polar ice sheets or falling as water freezes and becomes ice or snow above sea level.

Earth's Surface Elevations and Depths

Distribution of Earth's Elevations and Depths (Hypsometry)

Hypsometry measures the distribution of elevation and depth as a function of the area covered. At right, the raw percentage curve shows two concentrations of average elevation: about 4,000 meters (13,000 ft) below sea level and about 800 meters (2,600 ft) above sea level. The peaks in the curve reflect the large, nearly flat areas of ocean floor, and vast land areas of Asia, Greenland, and Antarctica. The cumulative percentage curve shows that about 72 percent of Earth's surface is below sea level, based on a worldwide two-minute (latitude-longitude) grid and a 200-meter (650 ft) grouping of vertical data.

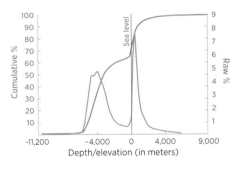

Surface by the Numbers

AREA
TOTAL SURFACE AREA: 196,938,000 square miles (510,066,000 sq km)
LAND AREA: 57,393,000 square miles (148,647,000 sq km), 29.1 percent of total surface area
WATER AREA: 139,545,000 square miles (361,419,000 sq km), 70.9 percent of total surface area

SURFACE FEATURES
HIGHEST LAND: Mount Everest, 29,035 feet (8,850 m) above sea level
LOWEST LAND: Shore of Dead Sea, 1,380 feet (421 m) below sea level

OCEAN DEPTHS
DEEPEST PART OF OCEAN: Challenger Deep, in the Pacific Ocean southwest of Guam, 35,827 feet (10,920 m) below the surface
AVERAGE OCEAN DEPTH: 12,205 feet (3,720 m)

CHEMICAL MAKEUP OF EARTH'S CRUST
AS A PERCENTAGE OF THE CRUST'S WEIGHT:
Oxygen 46.6, silicon 27.7, aluminum 8.1, iron 5.0, calcium 3.6, sodium 2.8, potassium 2.6, magnesium 2.1, and other elements totaling 1.5.

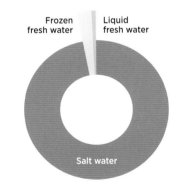

Frozen fresh water   Liquid fresh water

Salt water

Other elements
Magnesium
Potassium
Sodium
Calcium
Iron
Aluminum
Oxygen
Silicon

WORLD IMAGE
Using gradations of color and exaggerated vertical relief, the above image depicts variations in elevation. Mountain ranges and ice caps stand out in shades of orange; lowlands appear in green. Pale blue marks shallow seas along continental margins and over peaks and ridges rising from the ocean floor.

Hawaiian Ridge

PACIFIC OCEAN

Rocky

Middle America Trench

A Slice of Earth

This selection shows some features of the Earth's crust—from the Hawaiian Ridge in the Pacific to the Atlantic's Puerto Rico Trench and Mid-Atlantic Ridge; across Africa's Atlas Mountains, Europe's Alps, and Asia's Himalaya; to the Mariana Trench's Challenger Deep and then back to the Pacific Ocean.

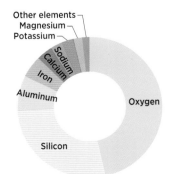

Hawaiian Ridge

Rocky Mountains

PACIFIC OCEAN

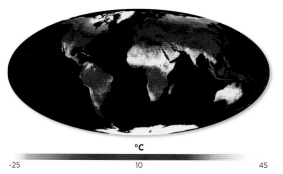

°C

-25   10   45

LAND SURFACE TEMPERATURE Unlike air temperature, surface temperature changes quickly. Land absorbing the sun's heat also warms air above it, a global effect
offset in part by the cooling of air and reflecting of sun's
rays that occur where snow and ice cover is significant.

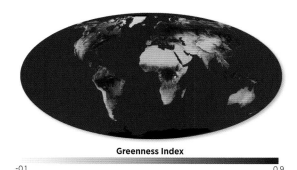

Greenness Index

-0.1   0.9

VEGETATIVE COVER This map depicts the vibrancy of
plant growth and density of vegetative cover during summer in the Northern Hemisphere. By comparing images over
time, scientists can assess environmental health, crop production, human encroachment, and carbon sequestration.

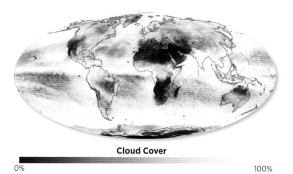

Cloud Cover

0%   100%

CLOUD COVER This composite image shows the regions
with the heaviest cloud cover on a typical June day. The
gradation to blue signifies decreasing cover. Clouds contain moisture, affect temperatures, and on any given day
cover 50 to 70 percent of Earth's surface.

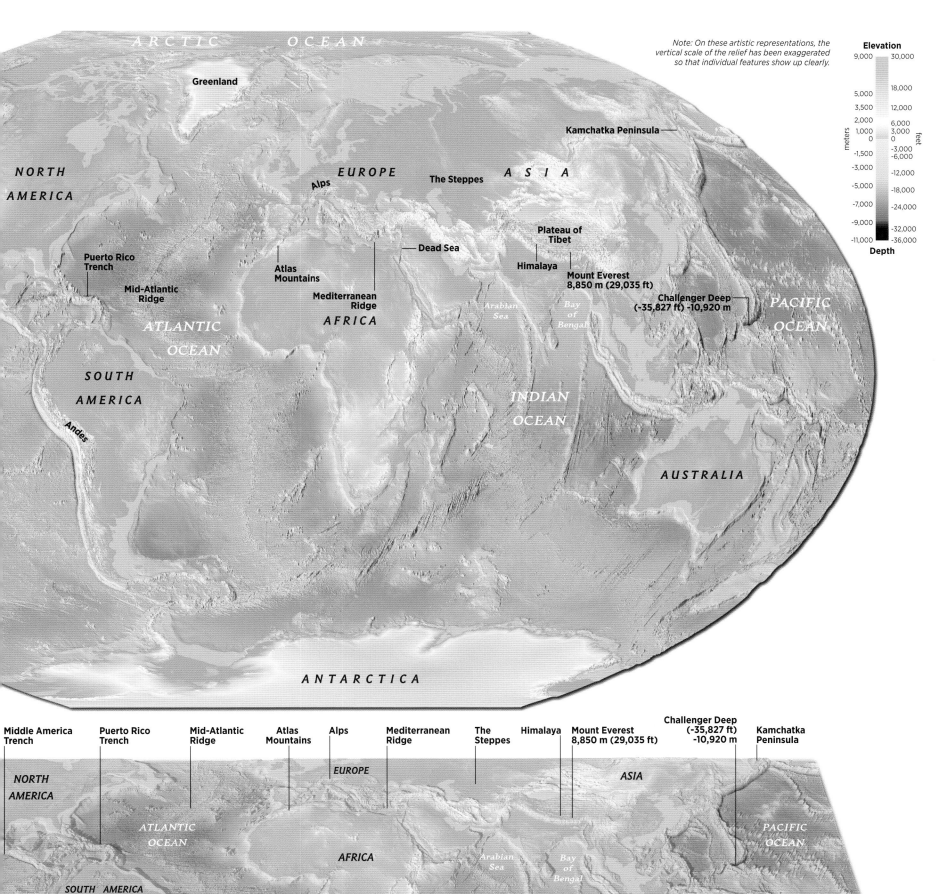

*Note: On these artistic representations, the
vertical scale of the relief has been exaggerated
so that individual features show up clearly.*

Elevation

meters	feet
9,000	30,000
5,000	18,000
3,500	12,000
2,000	6,000
1,000	3,000
0	0
-1,500	-3,000 / -6,000
-3,000	-12,000
-5,000	-18,000
-7,000	-24,000
-9,000	-32,000
-11,000	-36,000

Depth

ARCTIC OCEAN

Greenland

Kamchatka Peninsula

NORTH
AMERICA

EUROPE   The Steppes   ASIA

Alps

Plateau of
Tibet

Dead Sea

Puerto Rico
Trench

Atlas
Mountains

Himalaya

Mount Everest
8,850 m (29,035 ft)

Mid-Atlantic
Ridge

Mediterranean
Ridge

Challenger Deep
(-35,827 ft) -10,920 m

PACIFIC
OCEAN

ATLANTIC
OCEAN

AFRICA

*Arabian
Sea*

*Bay
of
Bengal*

SOUTH
AMERICA

Andes

INDIAN
OCEAN

AUSTRALIA

ANTARCTICA

Middle America
Trench

Puerto Rico
Trench

Mid-Atlantic
Ridge

Atlas
Mountains

Alps

Mediterranean
Ridge

The
Steppes

Himalaya

Mount Everest
8,850 m (29,035 ft)

Challenger Deep
(-35,827 ft)
-10,920 m

Kamchatka
Peninsula

NORTH
AMERICA

EUROPE

ASIA

ATLANTIC
OCEAN

AFRICA

*Arabian
Sea*

*Bay
of
Bengal*

PACIFIC
OCEAN

SOUTH AMERICA

Land Cover

SATELLITE DATA PROVIDE the most reliable picture of global vegetative cover over time. The map at right is based on imagery from the Moderate Resolution Imaging Spectroradiometer (MODIS), at a spatial resolution of 500 meters (1,640 ft). Such maps are used to identify the large-scale effects of many small-scale events (such as brief local weather events) for the global climate models that predict how the Earth system—the physical, chemical, and biological aspects of the planet's terrestrial, oceanic, and atmospheric realms—will change with climate warming. By recording how different wavelengths of the electromagnetic spectrum reflect from the surface, scientists can derive land-cover types through the variation of these reflectances over time. Vast areas of Earth have been altered by humans over millennia, and such changes are captured in the satellite record, contributing to a rich data bank for conservation, biodiversity assessments, and land resource management.

NORTH AMERICA

ATLANTIC OCEAN

PACIFIC OCEAN

SOUTH AMERICA

EVERGREEN NEEDLELEAF FOREST

More than 60 percent of this land is covered by a forest canopy; tree height exceeds 2 m (7 ft). These forests are common in temperate regions of the U.S., Europe, and Asia. In many of them, trees are grown on plantations and are logged for the making of paper and building products.

EVERGREEN BROADLEAF FOREST

More than 60 percent of this land is covered by a forest canopy; tree height exceeds 2 m (7 ft). These include rain forests and dominate in the tropics; they have the greatest concentrations of biodiversity. In many areas, farms, ranches, and tree plantations are replacing this land cover.

Global Land Cover Composition

- Closed Shrubland 0.1%
- Urban and Built-Up 0.5%
- Deciduous Broadleaf Forest 1.0%
- Deciduous Needleleaf Forest 1.1%
- Permanent Wetland 1.1%
- Evergreen Needleleaf Forest 2.0%
- Mixed Forest 5.6%
- Cropland/Natural Vegetation Mosaic 6.2%
- Savanna 6.9%
- Woody Savanna 7.5%
- Cropland 8.4%
- Evergreen Broadleaf Forest 9.0%
- Snow and Ice 10.5%
- Grassland 12.7%
- Barren or Sparsely Vegetated 13.2%
- Open Shrubland 14.2%

DECIDUOUS NEEDLELEAF FOREST

More than 60 percent of this land is covered by a forest canopy; tree height exceeds 2 m (7 ft). Trees respond to cold seasons by shedding their leaves simultaneously. This land cover is present in northeast China but dominant only in Siberia, taking the form of larch forests with a short June-to-August growing season.

DECIDUOUS BROADLEAF FOREST

More than 60 percent of this land is covered by a forest canopy; tree height exceeds 2 m (7 ft). In dry or cold seasons, trees shed their leaves simultaneously. Much of this forest has been converted to cropland in temperate regions; large remnants are increasingly found only on steep and remote slopes.

MIXED FOREST

More than 60 percent of this land is covered by a forest canopy; tree height exceeds 2 m (7 ft). Both evergreen and deciduous types appear, with neither having coverage of less than 25 percent or more than 75 percent. This type is largely found between temperate deciduous and boreal evergreen forests.

WOODY SAVANNA

Land has herbaceous or woody understories and a tree canopy cover of 30 to 60 percent; trees exceed 2 m (7 ft) and may be evergreen or deciduous. This type of land cover is common in the tropics and is most highly degraded in areas with long histories of human habitation, such as West Africa.

SAVANNA

Land has herbaceous or woody understories and a tree canopy cover of 10 to 30 percent; trees exceed 2 m (7 ft) and may be evergreen or deciduous. This type includes classic African savanna as well as open boreal woodlands that demarcate tree lines and the beginning of tundra ecosystems.

CLOSED SHRUBLAND

Bushes or shrubs dominate, with a canopy cover of more than 60 percent. Bushes do not exceed 2 m (7 ft) in height; shrubs or bushes can be evergreen or deciduous. Tree canopy is less than 10 percent. This land cover can be found where prolonged cold or dry seasons limit plant growth.

OPEN SHRUBLAND

Shrubs are dominant, with a canopy cover of between 10 and 60 percent; they do not exceed 2 m (7 ft) in height and can be evergreen or deciduous. The remaining land is either barren or characterized by annual herbaceous cover. This land cover occurs in semiarid or severely cold regions.

ARCTIC OCEAN

EUROPE

ASIA

PACIFIC OCEAN

AFRICA

INDIAN OCEAN

AUSTRALIA

ANTARCTICA

WATER
Surfaces permanently covered with water that never exceed 10 percent vegetated cover during any time of the year. These include salt, fresh, and brackish water bodies. Freshwater is becoming an increasingly scarce resource globally as water is diverted to irrigate agriculture, depleting aquifers.

GRASSLAND
This land has continuous herbaceous cover and less than 10 percent tree or shrub canopy cover. This type occurs in a wide range of habitats. Perennial grasslands in the central United States and Russia, for example, are the most extensive and mark a line of decreased precipitation that limits agriculture.

PERMANENT WETLAND
A permanent mixture of water and herbaceous or woody vegetation. The vegetation can be present in either salt, brackish, or fresh water. The Everglades (pictured) are one of the world's largest permanent wetlands. Other wetlands include the Hudson Bay lowlands and the Sundarbans of India and Bangladesh.

CROPLAND
Crop-producing fields make up more than 60 percent of the landscape. Areas of high-intensity agriculture, including mechanized farming, stretch across temperate regions. Much agriculture in the developing world is fragmented, however, and occurs frequently on small plots of land.

CROPLAND/NATURAL VEGETATION MOSAIC
Lands with a mosaic of croplands, forests, shrubland, and grass-lands in which no one component makes up more than 60 percent of the landscape. This land-cover class can be seen in much of the U.S.; examples include southwestern Wisconsin and the Susquehanna River Valley (pictured).

URBAN AND BUILT-UP
Land cover includes buildings, roads, and other manufactured structures. This class was mapped as an independent layer from MODIS 500-meter-resolution satellite imagery created in 2010. Urban and built-up cover represents the most densely developed areas of human habitation.

BARREN OR SPARSELY VEGETATED
Exposed soil, sand, or rocks are typical; the land never has more than 10 percent vegetated cover during any time of year. This includes true deserts, such as the Sahara (Africa) and Gobi (Asia). Desertification, the expansion of deserts due to land degradation or climate change, is a problem in these areas.

SNOW AND ICE
Land has permanent snow and ice; it never has more than 10 percent vegetated cover at any time of year. The greatest expanses of this class can be seen in Greenland, on other Arctic islands, and in Antarctica. Glaciers at high elevations form significant examples in Alaska, the Himalaya, Chile, and Scandinavia.

Freshwater

ON AVERAGE, HUMAN BEINGS EACH USE TEN GALLONS
(37.8 L) of freshwater a day for drinking, cooking, and cleaning. It seems like so little, and yet more than one billion people around the world lack access to or sufficient supplies of freshwater. In part, that's due to inadequate infrastructure. But freshwater is also naturally distributed unevenly across the globe—in some cases, tragically out of step with the location and need of human populations. In water-rich nations, potable water is sprayed on lawns while rain-water washes down storm drains; in desert regions, every drop is precious.

Agriculture is the main use of freshwater around the world, and some of its applications are shocking. For instance, it takes over 925 gallons (3,500 L) of water to grow and prepare two pounds (900 g) of rice and almost 4,000 gallons (15,140 L) to produce a single pound (450 g) of beef. Awareness of water shortages has spurred interest in foods that have low water inputs and has focused new attention on bringing irrigation to areas where appropriate rivers and lakes already exist.

Worldwide, industry consumes less than a third of agriculture's take. Regional withdrawals vary widely: In South Asia, this sector accounts for 2 percent of the region's consumption; in Western Europe, it claims 77 percent. Freshwater is used not only as a raw material itself, but also for steam, for cleaning and removing waste, and for heating and cooling equipment.

Municipal use currently accounts for 11 percent of global withdrawals, but its share is increasing as urban populations swell. In cities where even present demand is not being met, crises are sure to arise. In a few cases, typically high-consumption, affluent communities are reducing withdrawals as a result of household conservation, improved infrastructure, and consumer awareness. In New York City, for example, consumption in 2010 was 127 gallons (481 L) per capita per day, down from 213 (806 L) in 1980.

Water is usually considered a renewable resource because there is an expectation that what we use will cycle back to us through land, sea, cloud, and rain. For many millennia, the natural recycling of freshwater has been a fair assumption. But climate change is affecting the hydrologic cycle, and weather patterns are shifting in sometimes devastating ways—soaking some formerly dry areas and pushing once wet zones into persistent drought. The warming climate is also melting annual snowpack and ancient glaciers, releasing spring floods for now but threatening downstream areas with chronic water shortages once the frozen reserves are gone.

With 31,700 square miles (82,100 sq km) of surface area, Lake Superior is the largest freshwater lake in the world by area.

NORTH AMERICA

North America

The Amazon River discharges around 4.5 trillion gallons (170.3 trillion L) of water each day— some 15 percent of all the water that rivers send to the sea.

SOUTH AMERICA

South America

World of Rivers
Perennial River
Average discharge, 1961–1990
(gallons per second)
—— More than 130,000
—— 7,500 – 130,000
—— 1,250 – 7,499
—— 250 – 1,249
—— Fewer than 250

Intermittent River
Average discharge, 1961–1990
(gallons per second)
—— More than 7,500
—— 1,250 – 7,500
—— 250 – 1,249
—— Fewer than 250

⬡ Glacier or ice cap

Water Availability

Precious little of Earth's water is suitable for most human use. Of the 2.5 percent of the planet's water that doesn't reside in the salty oceans, most is locked up in the massive ice caps of Antarctica and Greenland, leaving less than one percent that is exploitable for human use. Making seawater safe for human consumption is possible but energy intensive.

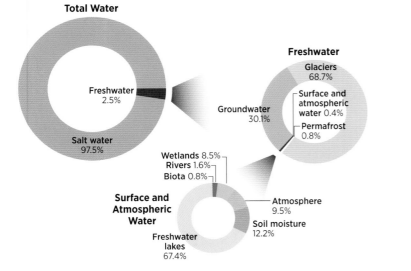

Total Water

Freshwater 2.5%
Salt water 97.5%

Freshwater
Glaciers 68.7%
Surface and atmospheric water 0.4%
Permafrost 0.8%
Groundwater 30.1%

Surface and Atmospheric Water
Wetlands 8.5%
Rivers 1.6%
Biota 0.8%
Freshwater lakes 67.4%
Atmosphere 9.5%
Soil moisture 12.2%

Mapping Irrigation

In many parts of the world, agriculture is impossible without irrigation. While irrigation needs and methods vary regionally, the need for water to grow food is a constant. From California's Central Valley to the coffee farms in Ethiopia's highlands, and from India's Ganges River Valley to the rice paddies of China, irrigation means food for billions of mouths.

Percent Irrigated Area
- 60% – 100%
- 30% – 59%
- 5% – 29%
- Less than 5%
- No data available

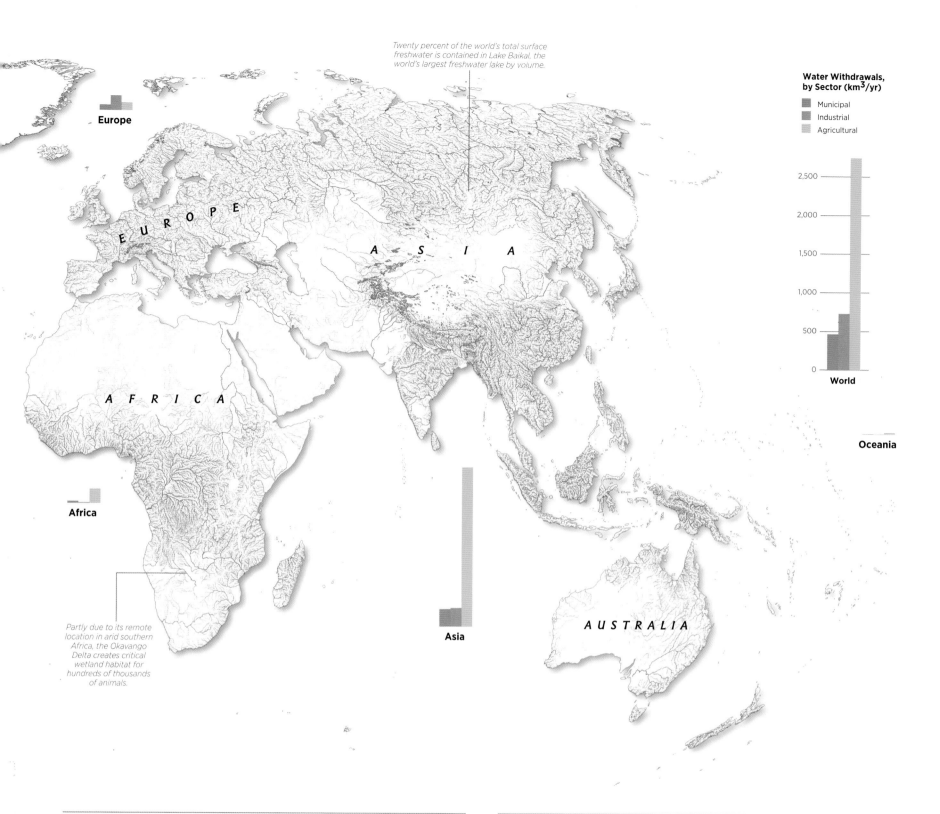

Twenty percent of the world's total surface freshwater is contained in Lake Baikal, the world's largest freshwater lake by volume.

Europe

E U R O P E

A S I A

A F R I C A

Water Withdrawals, by Sector (km³/yr)

- Municipal
- Industrial
- Agricultural

2,500

2,000

1,500

1,000

500

0

World

Oceania

Africa

Partly due to its remote location in arid southern Africa, the Okavango Delta creates critical wetland habitat for hundreds of thousands of animals.

Asia

A U S T R A L I A

Renewable Freshwater Resources

The average annual flow of rivers and recharge of aquifers from precipitation over a 30-year period is referred to as the total actual renewable water resources (TARWR).

A country with more than 1,700 cubic meters annually per inhabitant is said to be water-rich; places where that figure is below 1,000 cubic meters are labeled water-scarce.

Safe Drinking Water

Water quality is as important as quantity. The 1.1 billion people lacking clean drinking water must often resort to using water contaminated with pathogens, disease vectors,

and chemicals. Waterborne diseases—from cholera to dysentery to salmonella-caused illnesses—claim an estimated 2.2 million lives a year; young children are the most vulnerable.

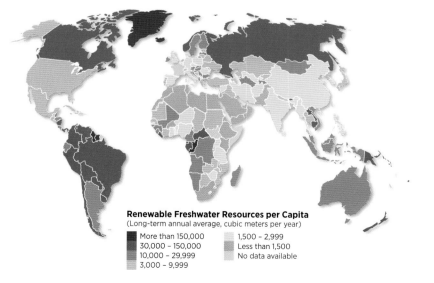

Renewable Freshwater Resources per Capita
(Long-term annual average, cubic meters per year)

- More than 150,000
- 30,000 – 150,000
- 10,000 – 29,999
- 3,000 – 9,999
- 1,500 – 2,999
- Less than 1,500
- No data available

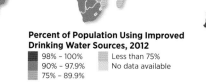

Percent of Population Using Improved Drinking Water Sources, 2012

- 98% – 100%
- 90% – 97.9%
- 75% – 89.9%
- Less than 75%
- No data available

Climate

THE TERM "CLIMATE" describes the average weather conditions, as measured over many years, that prevail at any given point around the world at a given time of the year. Daily weather may differ dramatically from that expected on the basis of climatic statistics.

Energy from the sun drives the global climate system. Much of this incoming energy is absorbed in the tropics. Outgoing heat radiation, much of which exits at high latitudes, balances the absorbed incoming solar energy. To achieve a balance across the globe, huge amounts of heat are moved from the tropics to polar regions by both the atmosphere and the oceans.

The tilt of Earth's axis leads to shifting patterns of incoming solar energy throughout the year. More energy is transported to higher latitudes in winter than in summer, and hence the contrast in temperatures between the tropics and polar regions is greatest at this time of year—especially in the Northern Hemisphere. Scientists present this data in many ways, using climographs (see page 38), which show information about specific places. Alternatively, they produce maps that show regional and worldwide data.

The effects of the climatic contrasts are seen in the distribution of Earth's lifeforms. Temperature, precipitation, and the amount of sunlight all determine both what plants can grow in a region and the animals that live there. People are more adaptable, but climate still exerts powerful constraints on where we live. Climatic conditions affect our planning decisions, such as how much heating oil is needed for the winter and how to irrigate crops given the anticipated summer rainfall. Fluctuations from year to year (e.g., unusually cold winters or summer droughts) make planning more difficult.

In the longer term, continued global warming is changing climatic conditions around the world, which could dramatically alter temperature and precipitation patterns and lead to more frequent heat waves, floods, and droughts. An increase in temperature means more disease-spreading mosquitoes; droughts and floods will lead to more famine. In addition, rising sea levels put much of the world's population at risk, as many of the most densely populated areas are coastal.

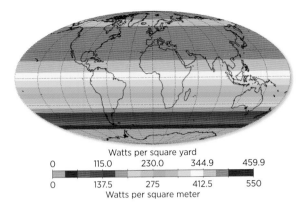

JANUARY SOLAR ENERGY*

Watts per square yard

| 0 | 115.0 | 230.0 | 344.9 | 459.9 |

| 0 | 137.5 | 275 | 412.5 | 550 |

Watts per square meter

JULY SOLAR ENERGY*

Watts per square yard

| 0 | 115.0 | 230.0 | 344.9 | 459.9 |

| 0 | 137.5 | 275 | 412.5 | 550 |

Watts per square meter

Amount of solar energy reaching the upper atmosphere

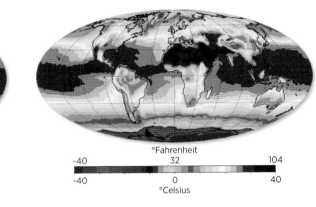

JANUARY AVERAGE TEMPERATURE

°Fahrenheit

| -40 | 32 | 104 |

| -40 | 0 | 40 |

°Celsius

JULY AVERAGE TEMPERATURE

°Fahrenheit

| -40 | 32 | 104 |

| -40 | 0 | 40 |

°Celsius

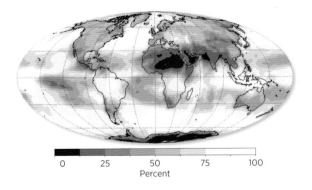

JANUARY CLOUD COVER

| 0 | 25 | 50 | 75 | 100 |

Percent

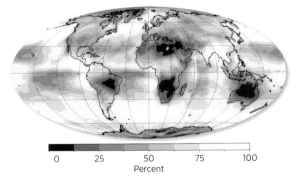

JULY CLOUD COVER

| 0 | 25 | 50 | 75 | 100 |

Percent

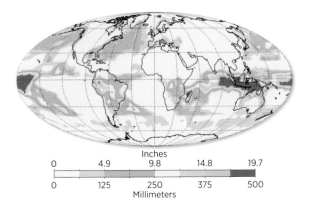

JANUARY PRECIPITATION

Inches

| 0 | 4.9 | 9.8 | 14.8 | 19.7 |

| 0 | 125 | 250 | 375 | 500 |

Millimeters

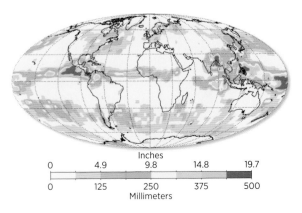

JULY PRECIPITATION

Inches

| 0 | 4.9 | 9.8 | 14.8 | 19.7 |

| 0 | 125 | 250 | 375 | 500 |

Millimeters

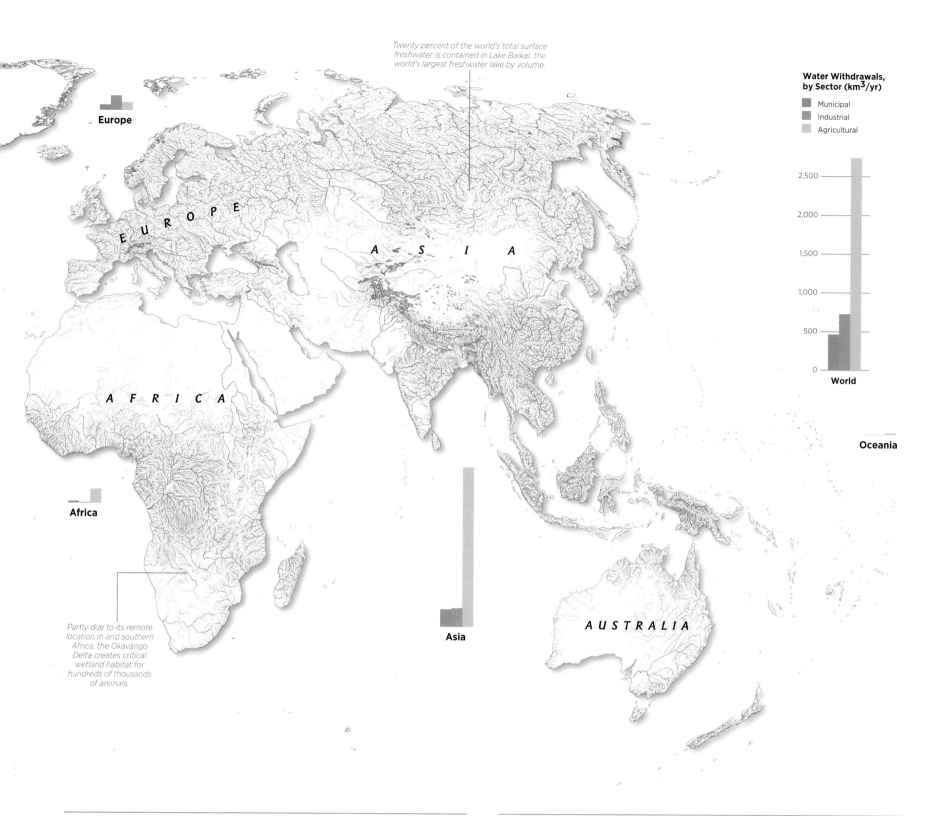

Twenty percent of the world's total surface freshwater is contained in Lake Baikal, the world's largest freshwater lake by volume.

Europe

Africa

Partly due to its remote location in arid southern Africa, the Okavango Delta creates critical wetland habitat for hundreds of thousands of animals.

Asia

Oceania

Renewable Freshwater Resources

The average annual flow of rivers and recharge of aquifers from precipitation over a 30-year period is referred to as the total actual renewable water resources (TARWR).

A country with more than 1,700 cubic meters annually per inhabitant is said to be water-rich; places where that figure is below 1,000 cubic meters are labeled water-scarce.

Safe Drinking Water

Water quality is as important as quantity. The 1.1 billion people lacking clean drinking water must often resort to using water contaminated with pathogens, disease vectors, and chemicals. Waterborne diseases—from cholera to dysentery to salmonella-caused illnesses—claim an estimated 2.2 million lives a year; young children are the most vulnerable.

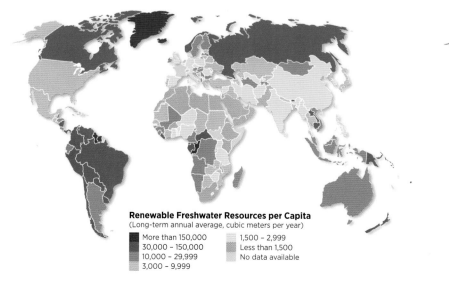

Renewable Freshwater Resources per Capita
(Long-term annual average, cubic meters per year)

- More than 150,000
- 30,000 – 150,000
- 10,000 – 29,999
- 3,000 – 9,999
- 1,500 – 2,999
- Less than 1,500
- No data available

Percent of Population Using Improved Drinking Water Sources, 2012

- 98% – 100%
- 90% – 97.9%
- 75% – 89.9%
- Less than 75%
- No data available

Climate

THE TERM "CLIMATE" describes the average weather conditions, as measured over many years, that prevail at any given point around the world at a given time of the year. Daily weather may differ dramatically from that expected on the basis of climatic statistics.

Energy from the sun drives the global climate system. Much of this incoming energy is absorbed in the tropics. Outgoing heat radiation, much of which exits at high latitudes, balances the absorbed incoming solar energy. To achieve a balance across the globe, huge amounts of heat are moved from the tropics to polar regions by both the atmosphere and the oceans.

The tilt of Earth's axis leads to shifting patterns of incoming solar energy throughout the year. More energy is transported to higher latitudes in winter than in summer, and hence the contrast in temperatures between the tropics and polar regions is greatest at this time of year—especially in the Northern Hemisphere. Scientists present this data in many ways, using climographs (see page 38), which show information about specific places. Alternatively, they produce maps that show regional and worldwide data.

The effects of the climatic contrasts are seen in the distribution of Earth's life-forms. Temperature, precipitation, and the amount of sunlight all determine both what plants can grow in a region and the animals that live there. People are more adaptable, but climate still exerts powerful constraints on where we live. Climatic conditions affect our planning decisions, such as how much heating oil is needed for the winter and how to irrigate crops given the anticipated summer rainfall. Fluctuations from year to year (e.g., unusually cold winters or summer droughts) make planning more difficult.

In the longer term, continued global warming is changing climatic conditions around the world, which could dramatically alter temperature and precipitation patterns and lead to more frequent heat waves, floods, and droughts. An increase in temperature means more disease-spreading mosquitoes; droughts and floods will lead to more famine. In addition, rising sea levels put much of the world's population at risk, as many of the most densely populated areas are coastal.

JANUARY SOLAR ENERGY*

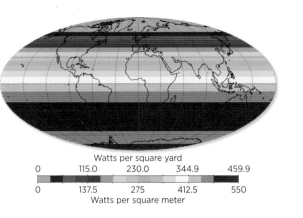

Watts per square yard

0	115.0	230.0	344.9	459.9

0	137.5	275	412.5	550

Watts per square meter

JULY SOLAR ENERGY*

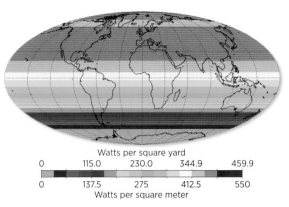

Watts per square yard

0	115.0	230.0	344.9	459.9

0	137.5	275	412.5	550

Watts per square meter

Amount of solar energy reaching the upper atmosphere

JANUARY AVERAGE TEMPERATURE

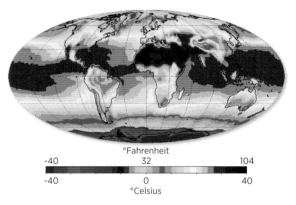

°Fahrenheit

-40	32	104

-40	0	40

°Celsius

JULY AVERAGE TEMPERATURE

°Fahrenheit

-40	32	104

-40	0	40

°Celsius

JANUARY CLOUD COVER

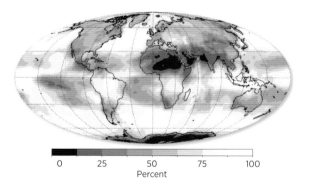

0	25	50	75	100

Percent

JULY CLOUD COVER

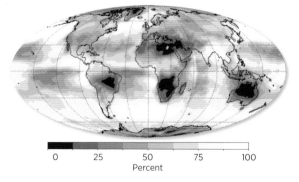

0	25	50	75	100

Percent

JANUARY PRECIPITATION

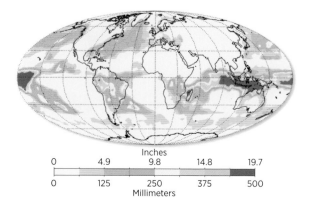

Inches

0	4.9	9.8	14.8	19.7

0	125	250	375	500

Millimeters

JULY PRECIPITATION

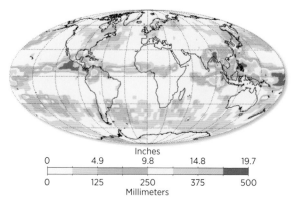

Inches

0	4.9	9.8	14.8	19.7

0	125	250	375	500

Millimeters

Climate Change

The scientific evidence is clear: Earth is warming at a pace that signals an unprecedented shift in the global climate. Such epochal changes have occurred in the past, but they were set in motion by the natural variations in Earth's orbit that affect the amount of sunlight warming the planet. Those cycles of cooling and warming unfolded slowly, over the course of millennia. In fact, only recently did the 10,000-year period of climate stability that helped human civilization flourish come to an end. Now, though, the climate is changing more rapidly than it has for 650,000 years, and humans' burning of fossil fuels—and the attendant rise in greenhouse gases—is the main cause. Scientists believe that unless greenhouse gas emissions are reduced by 50 percent by 2050, the damage to Earth will be irreversible. Already impacts include altered precipitation patterns, melting glaciers and permafrost, more intense weather events, and a rise in sea level. Particularly hard hit will be people in the tropics and poorer countries without the resources to adapt.

Left: As global temperatures rise, drought is becoming more frequent and lasting longer, as evident on the dry bed of Lake Mendocino near Ukiah, California (2014). Right: In some areas where downpours were not common, precipitation, when it does come, arrives in torrents and leads to flooding, as was the case in Vietnam (2011).

TAKING THE PLANET'S RISING TEMPERATURE

The temperature is rising across the planet. The Arctic has seen the greatest change, largely because of its lower albedo rates (how much solar radiation is reflected back into space). Heat waves are becoming more common, often with deadly consequences. Landmasses warm faster than oceans—one reason most heating is observed in the land-dominant Northern Hemisphere—but oceans are also warming. In some areas where oceans are cooling, changing currents are bringing up cold water from the deep.

Surface Temperature Change, 1913–2013
Degrees °C (°F)

- 2.0° – 4.0° (3.6° – 7.2°)
- 1.5° – 1.99° (2.7° – 3.59°)
- 1.0° – 1.49° (1.8° – 2.69°)
- 0.6° – 0.99° (1.1° – 1.79°)
- 0.2° – 0.59° (0.4° – 1.09°)
- -0.19° – 0.19° (-0.39° – 0.39°)
- -0.6° – -0.2° (-1.1° – -0.4°)
- No data available

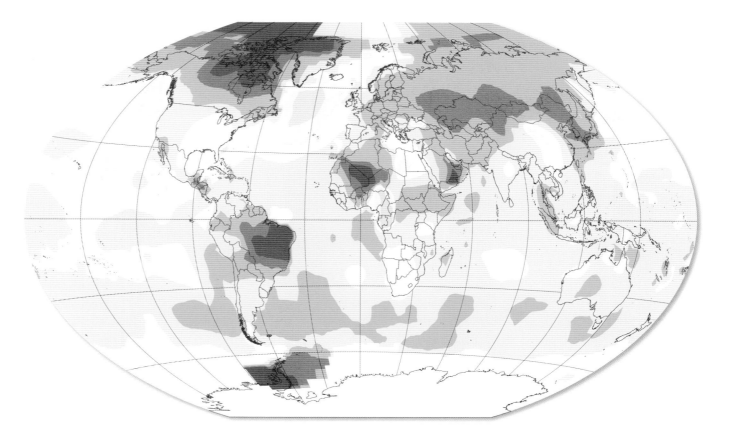

RISING TEMPERATURES AND CO_2

When graphed together, the rise in the global average temperature—an increase of about 1.4°F (0.8°C) since the early 20th century—and the exponential rise in carbon dioxide (CO_2) concentrations track each other closely over the past half century. And the trend is only getting more severe: The ten warmest years on record have all occurred since 1998. This climb is expected to continue, given our unabated appetite for oil, gas, and coal, initiated by the industrial revolution.

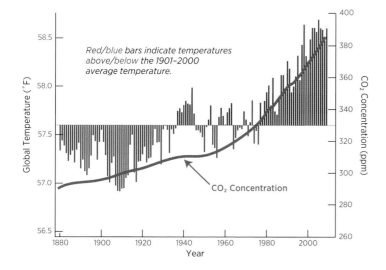

Red/blue bars indicate temperatures above/below the 1901–2000 average temperature.

CO_2 Concentration

SHRINKING POLAR ICE

Often referred to as the "canary in the coal mine" of global climate change, the Arctic is exhibiting change faster than any other part of the world. Sea ice is shrinking at a rapid rate, influencing global climate as it affects ocean circulation. Rapid melting is compounded by a climatic feedback loop: Areas covered by ice, which are light in color, are getting smaller, so less solar radiation is bounced back into the atmosphere; instead, more radiation is being absorbed by the darker ocean waters—which then results in a further reduction of sea ice.

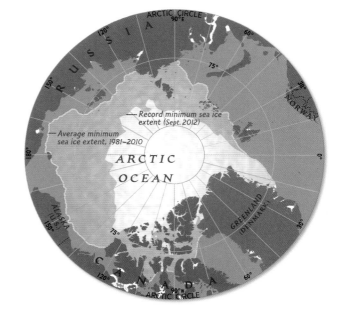

Climate

CLIMATE ZONES ARE PRIMARILY CONTROLLED by latitude—which governs the prevailing winds, the angle of the sun's rays, and the length of day throughout the year—and by geographical location with respect to mountains and oceans. Elevation, surface attributes, and other variables modify the primary controlling factors. Latitudinal banding of climate zones is most pronounced over Africa and Asia, where fewer north-south mountain ranges mean less disruption of prevailing winds. In the Western Hemisphere, the high, almost continuous mountain range that extends from western Canada to southern South America helps create dry regions on its leeward slopes. Over the United States, where westerly winds prevail, areas to the east of the range lie in a "rain shadow" and are therefore drier. In northern parts of South America, where easterly trade winds prevail, the rain shadow lies west of the mountains. Ocean effects dominate much of western Europe and southern parts of Australia.

Climographs

The map at right shows the global distribution of climate zones, while the following 12 climographs (graphs of monthly temperature and precipitation) provide snapshots of the climate at specific places. Each place has a different climate type, which is described in general terms. Rainfall is shown in a bar graph format (scale on right side of the graph); temperature is expressed with a line graph (scale on left side). Places with highland and upland climates were not included because local changes in elevation can produce significant variations in local conditions.

Climate Zones
(based on modified Köppen system)

Tropical
- Tropical wet
- Tropical wet & dry

Dry
- Semiarid
- Arid

Mild
- Marine west coast
- Mediterranean
- Humid subtropical

Continental
- Warm summer
- Cool summer
- Subarctic

Polar
- Tundra
- Ice sheet

High elevations
- Highlands
- Uplands

— Warm ocean current
— Cool ocean current

In 1884, Wladimir Köppen initially developed a system for describing Earth's climate regions that is still widely used today. Based on the idea that natural vegetation regions are best at defining climate boundaries, the system relies on monthly and annual temperature and precipitation data to help delineate climate types.

TROPICAL WET

This climate type has the most predictable conditions. Warm and rainy year-round, regions with a tropical wet climate experience little variation from month to month. This type is mainly found within a zone extending about 10 degrees on either side of the Equator. With as much as 60 inches (152 cm) of rain each year, the tropical wet climate supports lush vegetation.

Singapore climograph

TROPICAL WET AND DRY

Because of seasonal reversals in wind direction (monsoons), this climate type is characterized by a slightly cooler dry season and a warmer, extremely moist wet season. The highest temperatures usually occur just before the wet season. Although average annual conditions may be similar to a tropical wet climate, the rainy season brings much more rain.

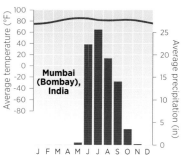

Mumbai (Bombay), India climograph

ARID

Centered between 20 and 30 degrees north and south latitude, this climate type is the result of a persistent high-pressure area and, along the western margins of continents, a cold ocean current. Rainfall amounts in regions with this climate type are negligible, and there is some seasonal variation in temperature. Desert vegetation is typically sparse.

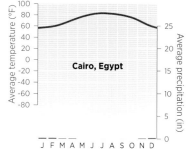

Cairo, Egypt climograph

SEMIARID

Regions with a semiarid climate lie poleward of areas with a desert (arid) climate; they have a much greater range in monthly temperatures and receive significantly more rainfall than deserts. This climate type is often found in inland regions, in the rain shadow of mountain ranges. Annual rainfall amounts support mainly grasses and small shrubs.

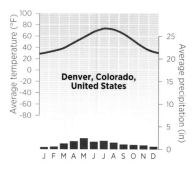

Denver, Colorado, United States climograph

MARINE WEST COAST

This climate type is primarily found between 40 and 60 degrees latitude; it occurs on the west coasts of continents and across much of Europe. Prevailing westerly winds bring milder ocean air ashore, but sunny days are limited and precipitation is frequent. Except in the highest elevations, most precipitation falls as rain. This climate supports extensive forests.

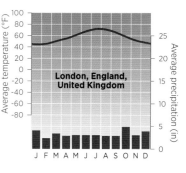

London, England, United Kingdom climograph

The map region includes labels: OCEAN, SIBERIA, BARENTS SEA, EUROPE, Moscow, Lake Baikal, ASIA, GOBI, Aral Sea, BLACK SEA, CASPIAN SEA, MEDITERRANEAN SEA, Athens, Cairo, Nile, RED SEA, ARABIAN SEA, Mumbai (Bombay), HARA, AFRICA, Congo, Lake Victoria, Madagascar, KALAHARI DESERT, INDIAN OCEAN, SOUTH CHINA SEA, Singapore, Borneo, New Guinea, TROPIC OF CANCER, PACIFIC OCEAN, North Equatorial Current, EQUATOR, Equatorial Countercurrent, South Equatorial Current, AUSTRALIA, TROPIC OF CAPRICORN, TASMAN SEA, West Australia Current, West Wind Drift, ANTARCTIC CIRCLE, CTICA

CONTINENTAL WARM SUMMER

Regions with this climate type have warmer year-round temperatures and more rainfall than regions with cool summers. This type is found from about 40 to 50 degrees north (except in Europe, where it extends to about 60 degrees north) and is marked by large variations in average monthly temperature. Summer averages can exceed 70°F (21°C); winter averages can be in the 20s (-7°C).

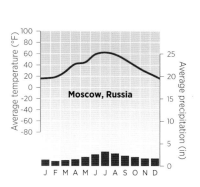

Chicago, Illinois, United States

CONTINENTAL COOL SUMMER

Found only from about 40 to 60 degrees north, this type is marked by temperature extremes. Summers are cool (around 60°F/15°C as a monthly average); winter months may have below-freezing average temperatures. Rainfall is moderate to abundant.

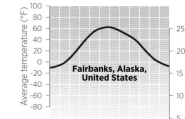

Moscow, Russia

SUBARCTIC

This climate type is found along and just south of the Arctic Circle; it is driven by large seasonal swings in the amount of daylight a region receives. Winter tends to be cold with light snow and little melting. Summer months are quite warm for the latitude, with temperatures 70° or 80°F (39° or 44°C) higher than monthly averages in winter; summer has significant rainfall.

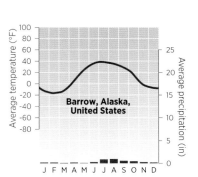

Fairbanks, Alaska, United States

MEDITERRANEAN

This term describes the climate of much of the Mediterranean region. Such a climate is also found in narrow bands along the west coasts of continents that lie around 30 to 35 degrees poleward from the Equator. Summer months are typically warm to hot with dry conditions, while winter months are cool (but not cold) and provide modest precipitation.

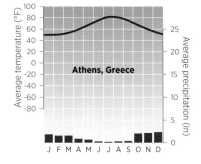

Athens, Greece

TUNDRA

Along the southern boundary of this climatic zone, ground-hugging plants meet the northernmost trees (the tree line). Here, the warmest average monthly temperature is below 50°F (10°C), with only one to four months having an average monthly temperature that is above freezing. Precipitation amounts are low, typically about 10 inches (25 cm) or less annually.

Barrow, Alaska, United States

HUMID SUBTROPICAL

This climate type dominates eastern regions of continents at 30 to 35 degrees latitude. Here, warm ocean waters lead to warm and humid summers. Rainfall is greatest near the coast, supporting forest growth; precipitation is less farther west, supporting grasslands. Winter can bring cold waves and snowy periods, except in areas right on the coast.

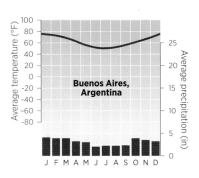

Buenos Aires, Argentina

ICE SHEET

This climate type is found at high latitudes in interior Greenland and across most of Antarctica; average monthly temperatures are around zero degrees Fahrenheit (-18°C) and below. Snow defines the landscape, but precipitation is only about 5 inches (13 cm) or less annually. The combined effects of cold and dryness produce desertlike conditions.

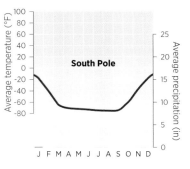

South Pole

Weather

STEP OUTSIDE AND YOU EXPERIENCE many facets of weather. Humidity, air temperature and pressure, wind speed and direction, cloud cover and type, and the amount and form of precipitation are all atmospheric characteristics of the momentary conditions we call weather.

The sun is ultimately responsible for the weather. Its rays are absorbed differently by land and water surfaces (equal amounts of solar radiation heat the ground more quickly than they heat water). Differential warming, in turn, causes variations in the temperature and pressure of overlying air masses.

As an air mass warms, it becomes lighter and rises higher into the atmosphere. As an air mass cools, it becomes heavier and sinks. The pressure differences between masses of air generate winds, which tend to blow from high-pressure areas to areas of low pressure. Fast-moving, upper-atmosphere winds known as jet streams help move weather systems around the world.

Large weather systems called cyclones rotate counterclockwise in the Northern Hemisphere (clockwise in the Southern Hemisphere); they are also called "lows," because their centers are low-pressure areas. Clouds and precipitation are usually associated with these systems. Anticyclones, or "highs," rotate in the opposite direction and are high-pressure areas. They usually bring clearer skies and more settled weather.

The boundary between two air masses is called a front. Here, wind, temperature, and humidity change abruptly, producing atmospheric instability. When things get "out of balance" in the atmosphere, storms may develop, bringing rain or snow and sometimes thunder and lightning as well. Storms are among nature's great equalizers.

The weather you experience is influenced by many factors, including your location's latitude, elevation, and proximity to water bodies. Even the degree of urban development, which creates "heat islands," and the amount of snow cover, which chills an overlying air mass, play important roles. The next time you watch a weather report on television, think about the many factors, some thousands of miles away, that help make the weather what it is.

The swirling cloud pattern and well-formed eye of Hurricane Katrina stand out in this NOAA satellite image from late morning on August 29, 2005. At the time, Katrina was making its third landfall near the border between Louisiana and Mississippi and was by now a weakening Category 2 storm. (The other two landfalls were near Miami, Florida, as a strong tropical storm and just south of New Orleans as a hurricane.) The incredible destruction in the wake of its storm surge, flooding, and high winds led to about 1,200 deaths and caused $108 billion in damages, making Katrina the costliest, and also one of the deadliest, hurricanes ever to strike the United States.

Superstorm Sandy—which had been a hurricane before making landfall in New Jersey on October 29, 2012, as a post-tropical cyclone—generated winds, storm surges, rain, and even snow that affected 24 states, destroyed at least 650,000 houses, and left more than 8 million people without power. It was the deadliest storm in the U.S. since Katrina, causing 159 deaths in 8 states, according to NOAA. The cost of the havoc wreaked by Sandy is in excess of $50 billion, much of that in New York City.

Major Factors That Influence Weather

THE WATER CYCLE

As the sun warms the surface of Earth, water rises in the form of water vapor from lakes, rivers, oceans, plants, the ground, and other sources. This process is called evaporation. Water vapor provides the moisture that forms clouds; it eventually returns to Earth in the form of precipitation, and the cycle continues.

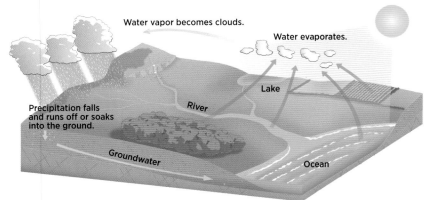

AIR MASSES

When air hovers for a while over a surface area with uniform humidity and temperature, it takes on the characteristics of the area below. For example, an air mass over the tropical Atlantic Ocean would become warm and humid; an air mass over the winter snow and ice of northern Canada would become cold and dry. These massive volumes of air often stretch across thousands of miles and reach to the stratosphere. Over time, midlatitude cyclonic storms and global wind patterns move them to locations far from their source regions.

JET STREAM

A meandering current of high-speed wind, a jet stream is usually found around five to ten miles (8–16 km) above Earth's surface. It generally flows west to east, often in a noncontinuous, wavy fashion, with cold, Equatorward dips (called troughs) and warm, poleward bulges (called ridges). The polar jet separates cold and warm masses of air; the subtropical jet is less likely to be related to temperature differences. Fronts and low-pressure areas are typically located near a jet stream.

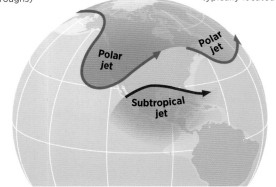

WEATHER FRONTS

The transition zone between two air masses of different humidity and temperature is called a front. Along a cold front, cold air displaces warm air; along a warm front, warm air displaces cold air. When neither air mass displaces the other, a stationary front develops. Towering clouds and intense storms may form along cold fronts, while widespread clouds and rain, snow, sleet, or drizzle may accompany warm fronts.

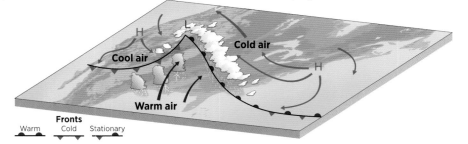

Cloud Types

Clouds are the visible collections of water droplets or ice particles in the atmosphere. Meteorologists classify them according to shape and altitude.

Stratus are low-level clouds that are flat or layered and that may produce drizzle; they are much longer and wider than they are tall. Fog is a stratus cloud that touches the ground. Altostratus (alto means "high") is a stratus cloud about two miles (3.2 km) above Earth. When these clouds rain or snow, they are called nimbostratus. Cirrostratus clouds lie at an altitude of about four miles (6.5 km).

Cumulus clouds have flat bottoms and puffy tops. The flat bottoms mark the altitude at which rising air reaches its condensation level (typically about a mile (1.6 km) above Earth's surface); the puffy tops show how the cloud "bubbles up." Cumulus often develop as sunlight heats the ground and the ground, in turn, heats the air. If cumulus tower, they can transform into cumulonimbus (thunderstorm) clouds, with their tops reaching an

altitude of seven miles (11 km) or more.

Though usually found individually or at some distance from other clouds, cumulus clouds can also develop in layers. Stratocumulus is a layered cumulus cloud about a mile (1.6 km) above the ground. Altocumulus is a similar cloud at an altitude of two miles (3.2 km). Its greater distance from the ground makes the cumulus puffs appear smaller than those of stratocumulus clouds. The cirrocumulus type (with still smaller puffs) is found about four to five miles (6.5–8 km) higher.

Cirrus clouds occur at an altitude of four miles (6.5 km) or more, where the temperature is always below freezing; hence, these clouds are always filled with ice crystals.

As a general forecasting rule, dry weather is most likely when cumulus clouds remain flat or when mid-level (altocumulus) clouds are absent. Precipitation is most likely when two or more clouds occur at the same time or when cumulus clouds tower to great heights or turn into cumulonimbus clouds.

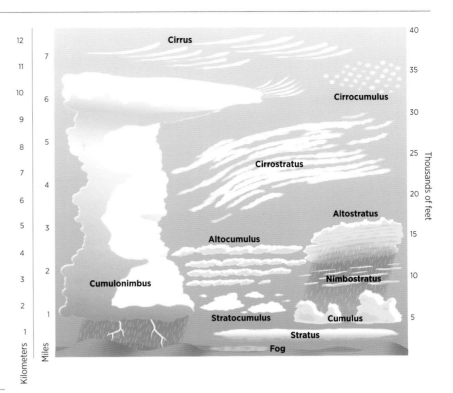

Tropical Cyclones

Hurricanes and their counterparts in other places (typhoons near Japan and cyclones off India and Australia) are moderately large low-pressure systems that form most often during the warmer months of the year. They occur mainly near the Equator, in regions with prevailing easterly winds. These systems develop winds between 75 and 150

miles (120–241 km) an hour and, on some rare occasions, even stronger winds. As the storms move toward the middle latitudes, where the prevailing winds are mainly westerly, they can "recurve" (move toward the east). Some hurricanes have stayed nearly stationary at times, while others have made loops and spirals along their paths.

Lightning

The mean annual distribution of lightning is more than 1.2 billion intracloud and cloud-to-ground flashes. In order to estimate this number, NASA scientists used five years of data taken from a satellite orbiting

460 miles (740 km) above Earth. Unsurprisingly, they observed that lightning distribution is directly linked to climate, with maximal occurrence in areas that see frequent thunderstorms (red areas on the map below).

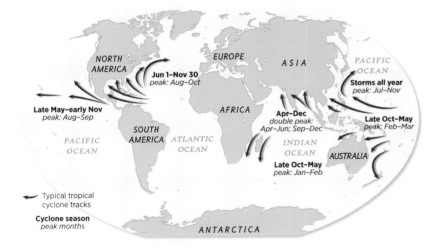

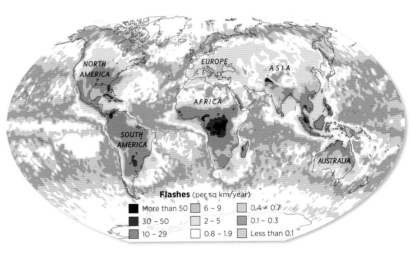

El Niño and La Niña

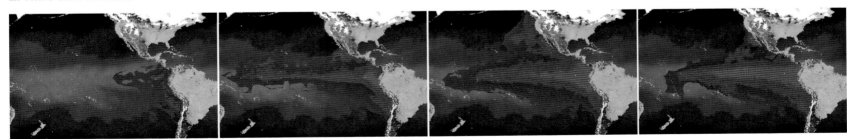

Periodic shifts in wind speed and direction in the tropical eastern Pacific can lead to changes in sea-surface temperatures. In what scientists call El Niño events, prevailing easterly winds weaken or give way to westerly winds, and the normal upwelling process—which brings cool, nutrient-rich waters up from lower levels of the ocean—stops. This stoppage causes sea-surface temperatures to rise, providing an unfavorable habitat for many fish. The warmer ocean conditions can also lead to more rainfall and floods along the west coast of the Americas. A stronger easterly wind flow, on the

other hand, can increase upwelling and make the sea-surface temperatures even colder, producing La Niña.

Both phenomena can have far-reaching weather effects. For example, strong El Niño events often result in a weak Atlantic Ocean hurricane season but produce plentiful precipitation in the normally dry southwestern United States. La Niña events favor more Atlantic hurricanes but can spell drought in the southwestern U.S., even for normally dry southern California.

From left to right, the above image sequence shows how

temperatures in the Pacific Ocean changed as the 1997 to 1998 El Niño event evolved. The first image, from March 10, 1997, shows a mostly cool ocean (blue shades). By mid-June, sea-surface temperatures (red shades) were above average from South America across much of the tropical Pacific. By mid-September, the warmth had extended from California southward to Chile and westward across most of the tropical Pacific. The final image, from late December 1997, shows a major El Niño, with sea-surface temperatures measuring six to eight degrees above average on the Fahrenheit scale.

To learn about weather extremes, see Geographic Comparisons on page 268.

Biosphere

HOME TO ALL LIVING THINGS, the biosphere is an intricate system made up of constantly interacting realms that support life: parts of the atmosphere (air), lithosphere (land), and hydrosphere (water in the ground, at the surface, and in the air).

As a result of the interaction between realms of the biosphere and changes in the distance of Earth's revolution around the sun, Earth's flora and fauna have changed over the eons, sometimes slowly and sometimes rapidly. Some species have continued to evolve; others, like the dinosaurs, have become extinct.

Life, of course, interacts with the land, water, and air, playing a significant role in shaping Earth's face and influencing its natural processes. Billions of years ago one of the smallest life-forms, photosynthetic bacteria

(organisms that produce oxygen as a by-product of their metabolism), helped provide the oxygen in the air we breathe.

Human beings are currently Earth's dominant life-form. Through the ages, we have evolved the means to affect the planet in ways both positive and negative. At present, we are introducing changes to the biosphere at greater rates than natural processes may be able to accommodate, as societies make ever increasing demands on Earth's resources.

It is now clear that human beings are able to greatly influence the fate of the biosphere. It is also clear that developing a better understanding of how the biosphere functions, and how its realms interact, is fundamental to sustaining it. This requires an interdisciplinary perspective that brings together worldviews from the physical, biological, and social sciences.

The Biosphere From Space

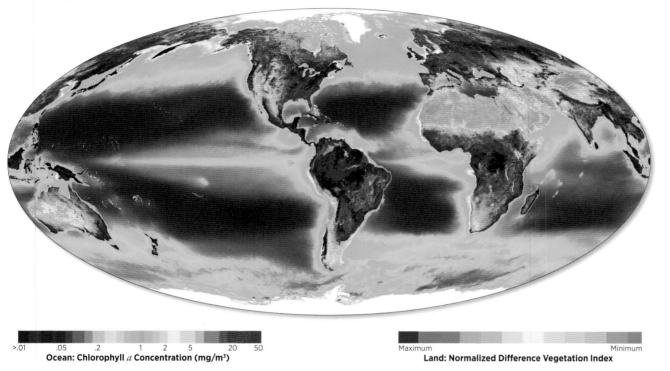

>.01   .05   .2   1   2   5   20   50
Ocean: Chlorophyll *a* Concentration (mg/m³)

Maximum   Minimum
Land: Normalized Difference Vegetation Index

Satellite technology enables us to monitor life on Earth. For example, satellite sensors help us measure the amount of chlorophyll—the green pigment used by plants during photosynthesis—on land and in masses of water. Satellite measurements can also provide an estimate of the distribution and abundance of both terrestrial vegetation and aquatic phytoplankton.

By color-coding data (see the color scales for the world map), we can actually quantify changes in vegetation on land and in the oceans from season to season and from year to year. The map reveals an unequal distribution of life for the June-to-August period. Most of the Northern Hemisphere has become green, except in areas of low rainfall or poor soil. Spectacular phytoplankton blooms are evident in the equatorial Pacific. Vegetation has lightened in the southern winter, as the rays of the sun provide less energy.

Biosphere Dynamics

A fundamental characteristic of the biosphere is the interconnectivity among all of its components. Known as holocoenosis, this interrelationship means that when one part of the biosphere changes, so will others. The biosphere is a dynamic system where interactions are occurring all the time between and within living and non-living components.

The main fuel that keeps the biosphere dynamic is the sun's energy, which is captured by Earth's surface and later harvested by plants and other photosynthetic organisms. The energy flows from these organisms through a living web that includes herbivores (plant feeders), carnivores (flesh feeders), and decomposers (detritus feeders). Energy from the sun also drives the recycling of water and all chemical elements necessary for life. The flow of energy and the continuous recycling of matter are two key processes of the biosphere.

Humans are part of this web of life. We have evolved, we interact with other living organisms, and we may become extinct. We have also developed large-scale organizations (societies, for example) that constitute the "sociosphere." Human interactions within this sphere occur through a diverse array of technologies and cultural frameworks and include activities such as fishing, agriculture, forestry, mining, and urban development. All are resource-utilization processes that can affect the biosphere on a global scale.

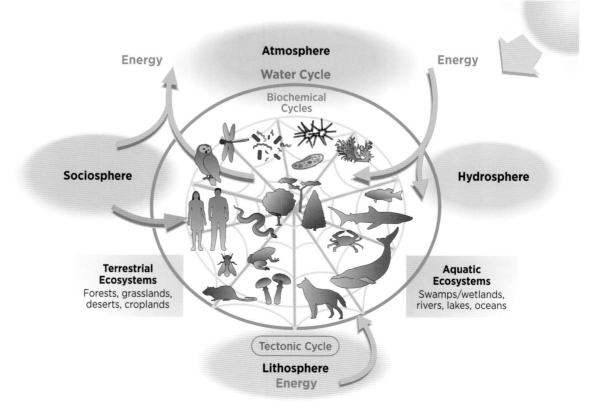

Earth System Dynamics

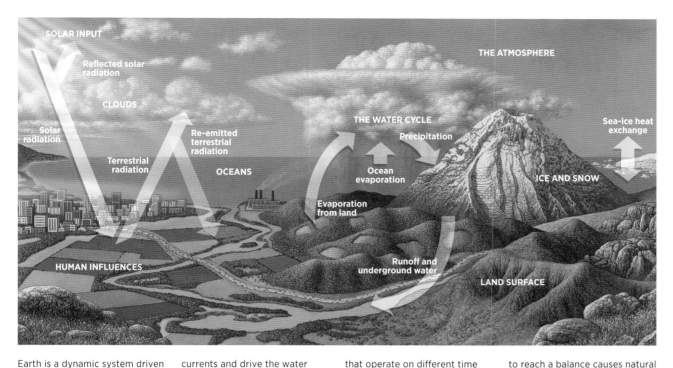

Earth is a dynamic system driven by energy flow from the sun and the planet's interior. Electromagnetic energy from the sun is converted to heat energy in the atmosphere (the greenhouse effect). Energy imbalances cause atmospheric and oceanic currents and drive the water cycle—a result of which is the wearing down of landscapes. Energy flow from Earth's interior drives the tectonic cycle, which builds landscapes.

The cycles vary because they derive from independent forces that operate on different time scales and with changing intensities. Variations in these cycles keep the complex interactions among the biosphere, lithosphere, hydrosphere, and atmosphere from reaching a balance; the tendency of Earth processes to reach a balance causes natural global change.

People can influence these interactions: By modifying the chemical composition of the atmosphere, for example, humans can cause changes in the greenhouse effect.

Size of the Biosphere

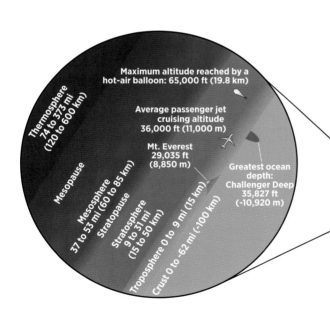

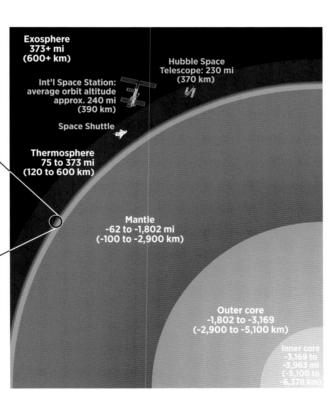

The biosphere reaches from the ocean floor to more than 33,000 feet (10,000 m) above sea level. Most life, however, occurs in a zone extending from about 650 feet (200 m) below the surface of the ocean to 20,000 feet (6,000 m) above sea level. Humans can occupy much of the biosphere and exert influence on all of its regions.

Organisms that make up the biosphere vary greatly in size and number. Small life-forms generally reach very high numbers, whereas large ones may be relatively rare. Mycoplasmas, which are very small parasitic bacteria, can measure 0.2 to 0.3 micrometers. (One micrometer is one-millionth of a meter, or three-millionths of a foot.) Other organisms can be very large: Blue whales, the largest animals on Earth, weigh about 240,000 pounds (110,000 kg) and reach a length of more than 80 feet (25 m). The largest dinosaurs weighed as much as 175,000 pounds (80,000 kg), more than a Boeing 737 at full capacity, and measured up to 108 feet (33 m) long.

The Biosphere Over Time

Ever since life arose on Earth more than three billion years ago, the biosphere has gone through many changes (see time line at right). These have been driven, in part, by drifting continents, ice ages, shifting sea levels, and the consequences of activities within the biosphere itself.

Over millions of years, the addition of oxygen to the atmosphere allowed for the development of terrestrial ecosystems. But in fairly rapid fashion, humans have had a significant effect on the world's ecosystems; our ability to modify species through gene manipulation will further increase our impact.

Thousand Years Ago
- 2 — First transgenic organisms / Industrial metabolism begins
- 4
- 6
- 8
- 10 — First domestication of wild species

Million Years Ago
- 100 — First humans / First grasslands / Dinosaurs become extinct / First flowering plants / First birds
- 200 — First mammals / First dinosaurs
- 300 — First amphibians / First forests
- 400 — Oxygen reaches present level in atmosphere / First land plants
- 500 — First fish
- 600
- 700 — First multicellular animal

Billion Years Ago
- 2.6 — Free oxygen in the atmosphere
- 3.6 — Oldest fossils
- Ocean formation
- 4.6 — Earth formation

Biodiversity

BIODIVERSITY REFERS TO THREE MEASURES of Earth's intricate web of life: the number of different species, the genetic diversity within a species, and the variety of ecosystems in which species live. Greatest in the wet tropics, biodiversity is important for many reasons, including helping to provide food and medicine, breathable air, drinkable water, livable climates, protection from pests and diseases, and ecosystem stability.

Humankind is only one species in a vast array of life-forms. It is, however, an especially influential and increasingly disruptive actor in the huge cast of characters on the stage of planet Earth. Estimates of the total number of plant and animal species range from a few million to a hundred million; of these, only 1.7 million have been described. Yet, a substantial number of those species may be gone before we even have a chance to understand their value.

For most of human history, people have often looked at plants and animals simply as resources for meeting their own basic needs. Scientists today can count over 300,000 plant species, of which just 9 provide three-quarters of all our food; in that respect, biodiversity has been an unimaginable luxury. It is ironic that even as humankind's power to destroy other species grows, so does our ingenuity in finding new and beneficial uses for them.

Sometimes the benefits of preserving a species may have nothing to do with food or medicine. Before a worldwide ban on exports of elephant ivory, the estimated value of such exports was $40 million a year for all of Africa. Now, some wildlife experts estimate that elephants generate more money for ecotourism than their tusks are worth on the black market.

The Natural World
Labeled for their natural vegetation, biomes are defined by their distinctive mix of plants and animals.

1. Tundra
2. Northern coniferous forest (also called boreal forest or taiga)
3. Temperate coniferous forest
4. Temperate broadleaf forest (includes rain forest)
5. Temperate grassland
6. Desert and dry shrub
7. Mediterranean scrub
8. Mountain grassland
9. Flooded grassland and savanna
10. Tropical grassland and savanna
11. Tropical dry forest
12. Tropical coniferous forest
13. Tropical moist broadleaf (includes rain forest)
14. Mangrove
15. Permanent ice cover

Species Diversity

Among fauna and flora, insects make up the largest classification in terms of sheer number of species, with fungi ranked a distant second. At the other extreme, the categories with the smallest numbers—mammals, birds, and mollusks—also happen to be the classes with the greatest percentage of threatened species (see Threatened Species graph, below right). This is not just a matter of proportion: These groups include the most at-risk species in terms of absolute numbers as well.

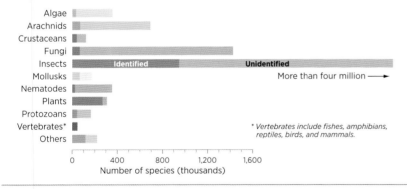

Vertebrates include fishes, amphibians, reptiles, birds, and mammals.

Number of species (thousands)

Biodiversity Hotspots

British ecologist Norman Myers defined the "biodiversity hotspot" concept in 1988 to help address the dilemma of identifying conservation priorities. The biodiversity hotspots hold especially high numbers of endemic species, yet their combined area of remaining habitat covers only 2.3 percent of Earth's land surface. Each hotspot faces extreme threats, and collectively they have lost 85 percent of their original natural vegetation. Of particular concern to scientists is that 69 percent of all threatened terrestrial vertebrates occur only in the hotspots.

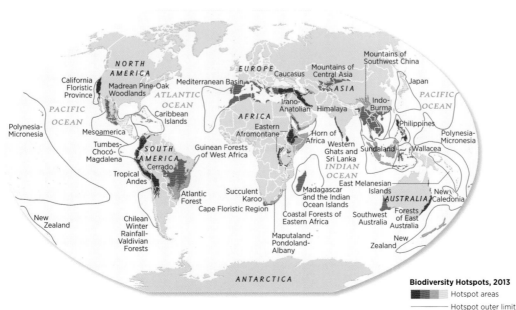

Biodiversity Hotspots, 2013
- Hotspot areas
- Hotspot outer limit

Source: Conservation International

Threatened Species

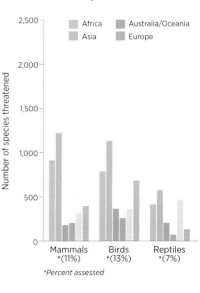

Africa • Australia/Oceania • Asia • Europe

Number of species threatened

Mammals *(11%)* • Birds *(13%)* • Reptiles *(7%)*

Percent assessed

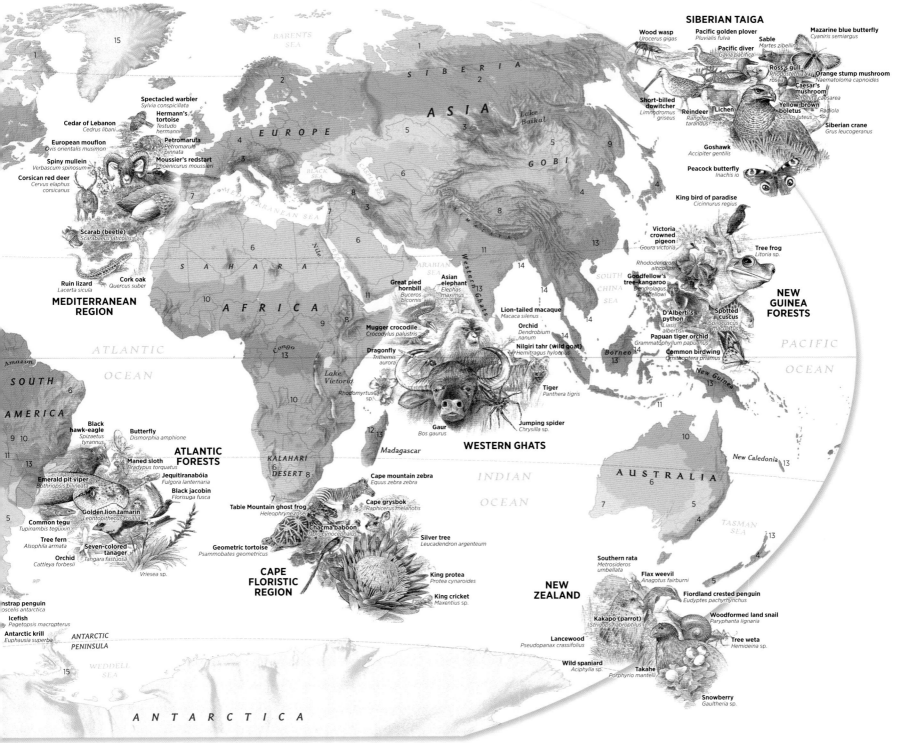

SIBERIAN TAIGA

Wood wasp
Urocerus gigas

Pacific golden plover
Pluvialis fulva

Pacific diver
Gavia pacifica

Mazarine blue butterfly
Cyaniris semiargus

Sable
Martes zibellina

Ross's gull
Rhodostethia rosea

Orange stump mushroom
Naematoloma capnoides

Short-billed dowitcher
Limnodromus griseus

Reindeer
Rangifer tarandus

Lichen

Caesar's mushroom
Amanita caesarea

Yellow-brown boletus
Suillus luteus

Radiola
sp.

Siberian crane
Grus leucogeranus

Goshawk
Accipiter gentilis

Peacock butterfly
Inachis io

King bird of paradise
Cicinnurus regius

Victoria crowned pigeon
Goura victoria

Rhododendron alticolum

Goodfellow's tree-kangaroo
Dendrolagus goodfellowi

Tree frog
Litoria sp.

NEW GUINEA FORESTS

D'Alberti's python
Liasis albertisii

Spotted cuscus
Spilocuscus maculatus

Papuan tiger orchid
Grammatophyllum papuanus

Common birdwing
Ornithoptera priamus

Spectacled warbler
Sylvia conspicillata

Hermann's tortoise
Testudo hermanni

Cedar of Lebanon
Cedrus libani

European mouflon
Ovis orientalis musimon

Petromarula
Petromarula pinnata

Moussier's redstart
Phoenicurus moussieri

Spiny mullein
Verbascum spinosum

Corsican red deer
Cervus elaphus corsicanus

Scarab (beetle)
Scarabaeus laticollis

Ruin lizard
Lacerta sicula

Cork oak
Quercus suber

MEDITERRANEAN REGION

Great pied hornbill
Buceros bicornis

Asian elephant
Elephas maximus

Lion-tailed macaque
Macaca silenus

Mugger crocodile
Crocodylus palustris

Orchid
Dendrobium nanum

Dragonfly
Trithemis aurora

Nilgiri tahr (wild goat)
Hemitragus hylocrius

Rhodomyrtus sp.

Tiger
Panthera tigris

Gaur
Bos gaurus

Jumping spider
Chrysilla sp.

WESTERN GHATS

SOUTH AMERICA

Black hawk-eagle
Spizaetus tyrannus

Butterfly
Dismorphia amphione

Maned sloth
Bradypus torquatus

Jequitiranabóia
Fulgora laternaria

ATLANTIC FORESTS

Emerald pit viper
Bothriopsis bilineata

Black jacobin
Florisuga fusca

Golden lion tamarin
Leontopithecus rosalia

Common tegu
Tupinambis teguixin

Tree fern
Alsophila armata

Seven-colored tanager
Tangara fastuosa

Orchid
Cattleya forbesii

Vriesea sp.

Table Mountain ghost frog
Heleophryne rosei

Cape mountain zebra
Equus zebra zebra

Cape grysbok
Raphicerus melanotis

Chacma baboon
Papio cynocephalus

Silver tree
Leucadendron argenteum

Geometric tortoise
Psammobates geometricus

CAPE FLORISTIC REGION

King protea
Protea cynaroides

King cricket
Maxentius sp.

Southern rata
Metrosideros umbellata

Flax weevil
Anagotus fairburni

Fiordland crested penguin
Eudyptes pachyrhynchus

Woodformed land snail
Paryphanta lignaria

Kakapo (parrot)
Strigops habroptilus

NEW ZEALAND

Lancewood
Pseudopanax crassifolius

Tree weta
Hemideina sp.

Wild spaniard
Aciphylla sp.

Takahe
Porphyrio mantelli

Snowberry
Gaultheria sp.

strap penguin
oscelis antarctica

Icefish
Pagetopsis macropterus

Antarctic krill
Euphausia superba

ANTARCTIC PENINSULA

Conservation Status of Terrestrial Ecoregions

Biodiversity is decreasing at a rapidly increasing rate. According to scientists, current extinction rates are a hundred to a thousand times greater than the normal rate of extinction; furthermore, the number of species threatened with extinction continues to increase (with, for example, one in three amphibians and one in four mammals at risk in the wild). Species are not being killed off directly: The two leading causes of extinction are loss of habitat and the impact of invasive species, although other threats include overexploitation, pollution, disease, and climate change.

North America
South America

Amphibians *(8%)
Fish *(25%)
Mollusks *(8%)
Other invertebrates *(28%)

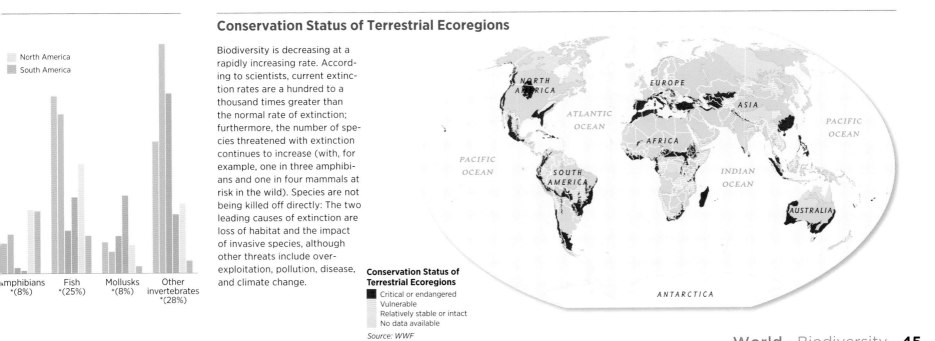

Conservation Status of Terrestrial Ecoregions

Critical or endangered
Vulnerable
Relatively stable or intact
No data available

Source: WWF

Human Influences

EARTH'S 4.5-BILLION-YEAR HISTORY has been characterized by epochs—periods of time that leave a clear record in the planet's rock layers. Each geologic epoch lasts from a few million to tens of millions of years, but the most recent one, the Holocene, which began when the glaciers last receded, may have come to a sudden end after only 11,500 years. Some scientists now believe a new and entirely different phase in Earth's history has begun, and they're calling it the Anthropocene, or "human epoch"—an age in which humans are radically changing the planet.

Humans first began altering Earth's ecology long ago with their use of fire and by hunting large animal species to extinction. Clearing lands for agriculture generated even greater changes in ecology and allowed human populations to grow larger than ever before. Yet, the most rapid and unprecedented changes caused by humans date to the 1800s and the industrial revolution, when humans suddenly acquired an unprecedented ability to exploit energy, especially fossil fuels, and thereby manipulate the environment. These later changes are what are most widely referred to as the origins of the Anthropocene. Now human impacts—habitat conversion for land use, environmental pollution, and plant and animal extinctions—are leaving a record in the rock, the very definition of an epoch.

At the beginning of the industrial revolution, almost half of Earth's land had not yet received the impression of significant human populations or land use; most of the other half, too, was still seminatural, bearing only a light footprint of agriculture or small settlements. But with industrialization, humans' influences on the biosphere began to change dramatically. As urban centers attracted more and more workers, nearby intensive agricultural and forestry techniques altered more and more of the terrestrial biosphere, from its rock layers to its ocean waters to its atmosphere—changing the very nature of planet Earth.

Anthromes

Dense Settlements
- Urban
- Mixed settlements

Villages
- Rice villages
- Irrigated villages
- Rainfed villages
- Pastoral villages

Croplands
- Residential irrigated croplands
- Residential rainfed croplands
- Populated croplands
- Remote croplands

Rangelands
- Residential rangelands
- Populated rangelands
- Remote rangelands

Seminatural
- Residential woodlands
- Populated woodlands
- Remote woodlands
- Inhabited treeless and barren lands

Wildlands
- Wild woodlands
- Wild treeless and barren lands

Human Influence Index

Based on the Human Influence Index created by the Wildlife Conservation Society and Columbia University's Center for International Earth Science Information Network, this map combines data on settlements, transportation infrastructure, landscape transformation, and electric power infrastructure. Such an overview of human influence provides a useful tool for wildlife conservation planning, natural resource management, and research on human-environment interactions.

Last of the Wild

Essentially an inverse of the Human Influence Index map at left (and made by the same researchers), the Last of the Wild map is a tool for finding the best places to preserve wildlife. To help identify priority areas, the scientists looked at the world in terms of biomes. The areas colored in on the map below contain fewer people, less infrastructure, less human land use, and less power—and less human conflict. As such, these places provide the most practical opportunities for conservation efforts.

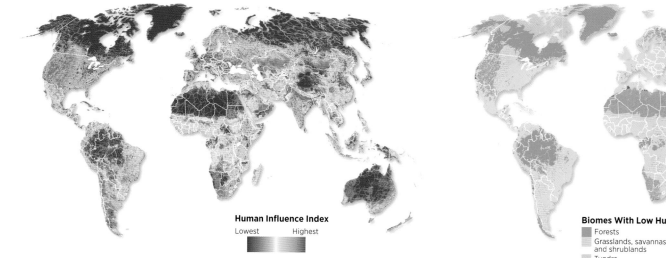

Human Influence Index

Lowest — Highest

Biomes With Low Human Influence
- Forests
- Grasslands, savannas, and shrublands
- Tundra
- Mediterranean
- Desert and xeric shrubland
- Rock and ice

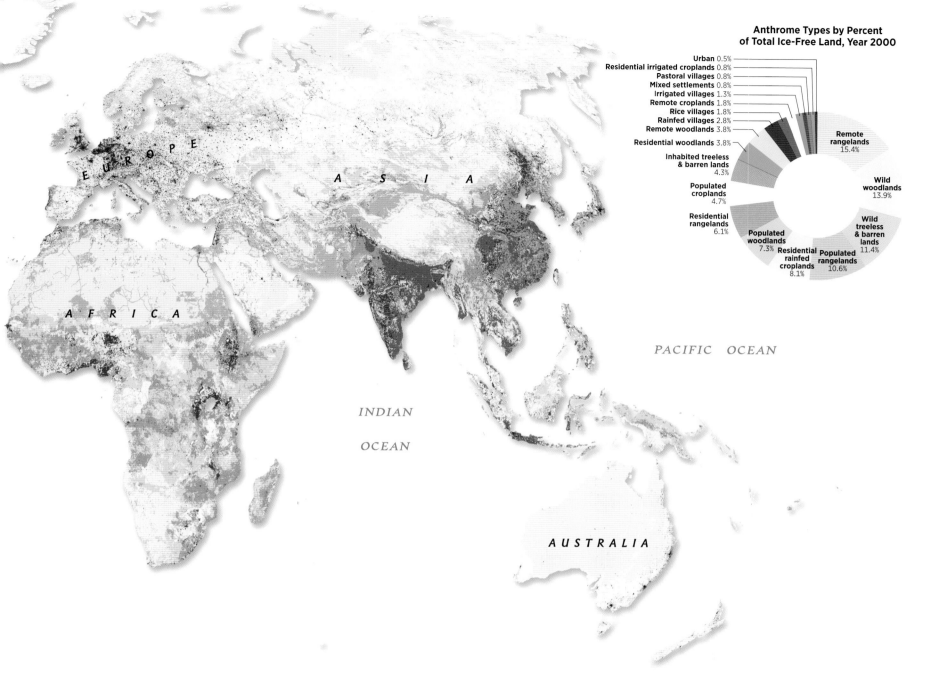

Anthrome Types by Percent of Total Ice-Free Land, Year 2000

Urban 0.5%
Residential irrigated croplands 0.8%
Pastoral villages 0.8%
Mixed settlements 0.8%
Irrigated villages 1.3%
Remote croplands 1.8%
Rice villages 1.8%
Rainfed villages 2.8%
Remote woodlands 3.8%
Residential woodlands 3.8%
Inhabited treeless & barren lands 4.3%
Populated croplands 4.7%
Residential rangelands 6.1%
Populated woodlands 7.3%
Residential rainfed croplands 8.1%
Populated rangelands 10.6%
Wild treeless & barren lands 11.4%
Wild woodlands 13.9%
Remote rangelands 15.4%

Human Influences Over Time

In 1700, 95 percent of the planet's ice-free land was in wildlands and seminatural anthromes, the latter of which supported about half of the human population. The other half of the population at that time lived in croplands and villages. Over the next 300 years, dramatic shifts in land use took place. Humans transformed 55 percent of Earth's ice-free land into rangelands, croplands, villages, and densely settled anthromes. Settlement patterns changed as well: In 2000, seminatural anthromes were home to just 4 percent of Earth's six billion inhabitants; 51 percent were living in villages. Now extensive wildlands mostly remain in the cold or dry biomes where humans prefer not to live.

Planetary Stewardship

We can and should make every effort to preserve areas only lightly touched by humans, but we cannot undo what has been done. People are, as the researchers who coined the term anthrome have said, "in the map." To effect lasting change, conservation efforts need to begin with the mind-set of humans *and* Earth, not humans *versus* Earth. By recognizing that the biosphere is now being reshaped more dramatically by human systems than by biophysical processes alone, we can take on the mantle of stewards instead of invaders or exploiters. In approaching issues such as urbanization and agricultural expansion from this paradigm, we can work toward solutions that address both environmental and human needs.

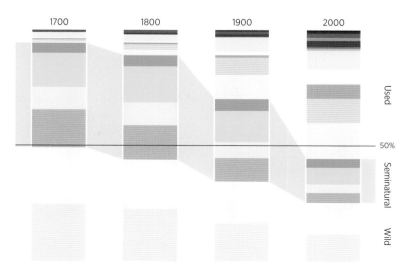

1700   1800   1900   2000

Used
50%
Seminatural
Wild

Dense settlement, China

Mixed settlements, Japan

Barren lands, Bolivia

Rice village, China

Cropland, United Kingdom

Rangeland, United States

Population

WHILE POPULATIONS IN MANY PARTS of the world are expanding, those of Europe—along with some other rich industrial areas such as Japan—show little to no growth or may actually be shrinking. Many such countries must bring in immigrant workers to keep their economies thriving. A clear correlation exists between wealth and low fertility: The higher the incomes and educational levels, the lower the rates of reproduction.

Many governments keep vital statistics, recording births and deaths, and count their populations regularly to try to plan ahead. The United States has taken a census every ten years since 1790, recording the ages, the occupations, and other important facts about its people. The United Nations helps less developed countries carry out censuses and improve their demographic information.

Governments of some poor countries may find that half their

populations are under the age of 20. They are faced with the overwhelming tasks of providing adequate education and jobs while encouraging better family-planning programs. Governments of nations with low birthrates find themselves with growing numbers of elderly people who need health care and pension disbursements but fewer workers able to contribute to the tax base that funds such programs and accounts.

In a mere 150 years, the world population has grown fivefold, at an ever increasing pace. The industrial revolution helped bring about improvements in food supplies and advances in both medicine and public health, which allowed people to live longer and to have more healthy babies. Today, 15,000 people are born into the world every hour, and nearly all of them are in poor African, Asian, and South American nations. This situation concerns planners, who look to demographers (professionals who study all aspects of population) for important data.

Lights of the World

Satellite imagery offers a surprising view of the world at night. Bright lights in Europe, Asia, and the United States give a clear picture of densely populated areas with ample electricity. Reading this map requires great care, however. Some totally dark areas, like most of Australia, do in fact have very small populations, but other light-free areas—in China and Africa, for example—may simply hide dense populations with not enough electricity to be seen by a satellite. Wealthy areas with fewer people, such as Florida, may be visible because residents are using their energy wastefully. Ever since the 1970s, demographers have supplemented census data with information from satellite imagery.

Population Pyramids

A population pyramid shows the number of males and females in every age group of a population. A pyramid for Nigeria reveals that over half—about 55 percent—of the population is under 20, while only 19 percent of Italy's population is younger than 20.

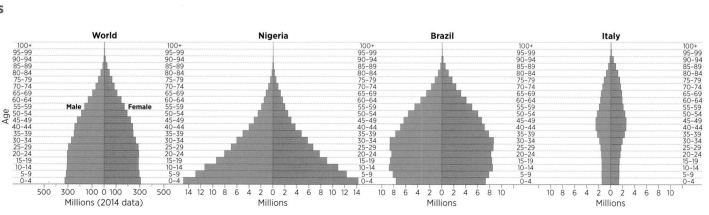

Population Growth

The population of the world is not distributed evenly. In this cartogram, Canada is almost invisible, while India looks enormous because its population is 35 times as large as Canada's. In reality, Canada's area is three times as large as India's. The shape of almost every country looks distorted when populations are compared in this way.

Population sizes are constantly changing, however. In countries that are experiencing many more births than deaths, population totals are ballooning. In others, too few babies are born to replace the number of people who die, and populations are shrinking. A cartogram devoted solely to growth rates around the world would look quite different from this one.

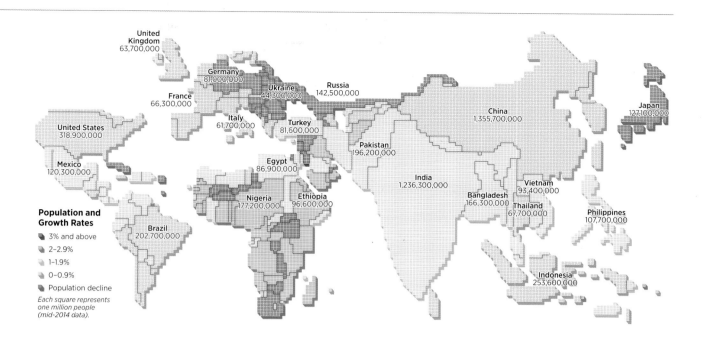

Population and Growth Rates

- 3% and above
- 2–2.9%
- 1–1.9%
- 0–0.9%
- Population decline

Each square represents one million people (mid-2014 data).

United Kingdom 63,700,000
Germany 81,000,000
France 66,300,000
Italy 61,700,000
Ukraine 44,300,000
Russia 142,500,000
China 1,355,700,000
Japan 127,100,000
United States 318,900,000
Turkey 81,600,000
Pakistan 196,200,000
Mexico 120,300,000
Egypt 86,900,000
India 1,236,300,000
Vietnam 93,400,000
Nigeria 177,200,000
Ethiopia 96,600,000
Bangladesh 166,300,000
Thailand 67,700,000
Philippines 107,700,000
Brazil 202,700,000
Indonesia 253,600,000

Population Density

A country's population density is estimated by figuring out how many people would occupy one square mile if they were all spread out evenly. In reality, people live together most closely in cities, on seacoasts, and in river valleys. Singapore, a tiny country largely composed of a single city, has a high population density—more than 20,000 people per square mile. Greenland, by comparison, has less than one person per square mile because it is mostly covered by ice. Its people mainly fish for a living and dwell in small groups near the shore.

People per Square Mile / **People per Square Kilometer**

People per Square Mile	People per Square Kilometer
More than 500	More than 195
150 – 500	60 – 195
25 – 149	10 – 59
1 – 24	1 – 9
Less than 1	Less than 1

Urban Area Population (in millions)
- ■ More than 20
- ▲ 15 – 20
- • 10 – 14.9

Regional Population Growth Disparities

Two centuries ago, the population of the world began a phenomenal expansion. Even so, North America and Australia still have a long way to go before their population numbers equal those of Asia and Africa. China and India now have more than a billion people each, making Asia the most populous continent. Africa, which has the second greatest growth, does not yet approach Asia in numbers.

According to some experts, the world's population, now totaling more than 7 billion, will not start to level off until about the year 2200, when it could reach 11 billion. Nearly all the new growth will take place in Asia, Africa, and Latin America. Africa's share of the world population will almost double, to 24 percent, by 2200, whereas China's share will decline from about 18 percent to 14 percent.

- Asia
- Africa
- Latin America
- Europe
- North America
- Australia & Oceania

Projected growth

Number of People (in billions)

Year: 800 850 900 950 1000 1050 1100 1150 1200 1250 1300 1350 1400 1450 1500 1550 1600 1650 1700 1750 1800 1850 1900 1950 2000 2050

Population

Fertility

Fertility, or birthrate, measures the average number of children born to women in a given population. It can also be expressed as the number of live births per thousand people in a population per year. In low-income countries with limited educational opportunities for girls and women, fertility is often highest.

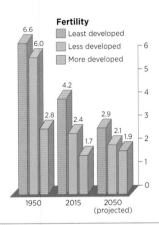

Fertility
- Least developed
- Less developed
- More developed

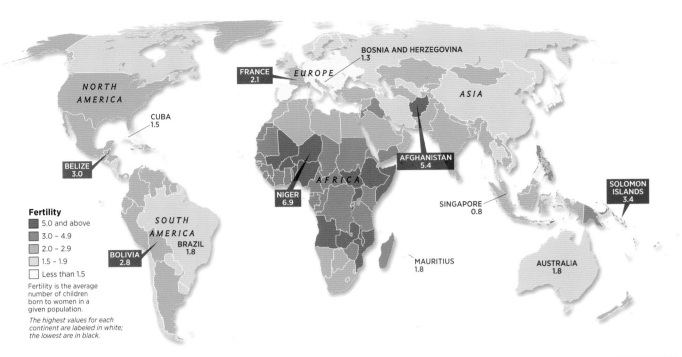

Fertility
- 5.0 and above
- 3.0 – 4.9
- 2.0 – 2.9
- 1.5 – 1.9
- Less than 1.5

Fertility is the average number of children born to women in a given population.

The highest values for each continent are labeled in white; the lowest are in black.

Urban Population Densities

People around the world are leaving farms and moving to cities, where jobs and opportunities are better. By 2008, half the world's people lived in towns or cities. The shift of population from the countryside to urban centers will probably continue in less developed countries for many years to come.

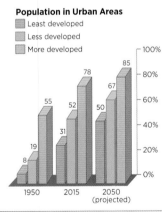

Population in Urban Areas
- Least developed
- Less developed
- More developed

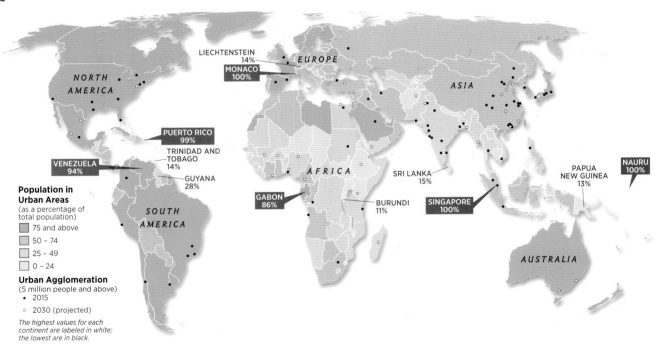

Population in Urban Areas
(as a percentage of total population)
- 75 and above
- 50 – 74
- 25 – 49
- 0 – 24

Urban Agglomeration
(5 million people and above)
- • 2015
- ○ 2030 (projected)

The highest values for each continent are labeled in white; the lowest are in black.

Urban Population Growth

In general, urban populations are growing more than twice as fast as populations as a whole. The world's city dwellers now outnumber its rural inhabitants as towns have become cities and cities have merged into megacities with more than ten million people. Globalization speeds the process. Although cities generate wealth and provide better health care along with benefits such as electricity, clean water, and sewage treatment, they can also cause great ecological damage. Squatter settlements and slums may develop if cities cannot accommodate millions of new arrivals. Smog, congestion, pollution, and crime are other dangers. Good city management is a key to future prosperity.

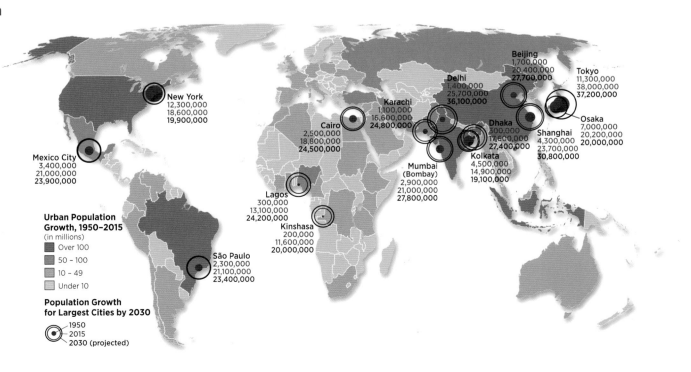

Urban Population Growth, 1950–2015
(in millions)
- Over 100
- 50 – 100
- 10 – 49
- Under 10

Population Growth for Largest Cities by 2030
- 1950
- 2015
- 2030 (projected)

Life Expectancy

Life expectancy for population groups does not mean that all people die by a certain age. It is an average of death statistics. High infant mortality results in low life expectancy: People who live to adulthood will probably reach old age; there are just fewer of them.

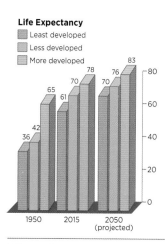

Life Expectancy
- Least developed
- Less developed
- More developed

Life Expectancy
(years)
- 80 and above
- 75 – 79
- 65 – 74
- 55 – 64
- Less than 55

The highest values for each continent are labeled in white; the lowest are in black.

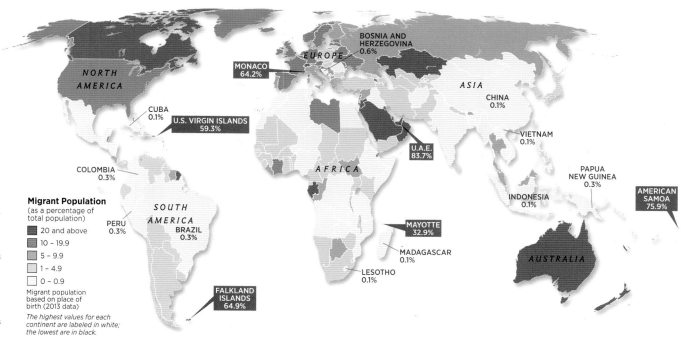

CANADA 82
MOLDOVA 70
EUROPE
MONACO 90
NORTH AMERICA
MOROCCO 77
JAPAN 84
HAITI 63
ASIA
AFGHANISTAN 50
GUYANA 68
AFRICA
CHAD 49
KIRIBATI 65
SOUTH AMERICA
CHILE 78
AUSTRALIA 82

Migration

International migration has reached its highest level, with foreign workers now providing the labor in several Middle Eastern countries and immigrant workers proving essential to rich countries with low birthrates. Refugees continue to escape grim political and environmental conditions, while businesspeople and tourists keep many economies spinning.

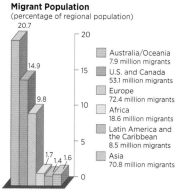

Migrant Population
(percentage of regional population)

- Australia/Oceania — 7.9 million migrants
- U.S. and Canada — 53.1 million migrants
- Europe — 72.4 million migrants
- Africa — 18.6 million migrants
- Latin America and the Caribbean — 8.5 million migrants
- Asia — 70.8 million migrants

Migrant Population
(as a percentage of total population)
- 20 and above
- 10 – 19.9
- 5 – 9.9
- 1 – 4.9
- 0 – 0.9

Migrant population based on place of birth (2013 data)

The highest values for each continent are labeled in white; the lowest are in black.

BOSNIA AND HERZEGOVINA 0.6%
EUROPE
MONACO 64.2%
NORTH AMERICA
ASIA
CHINA 0.1%
CUBA 0.1%
U.S. VIRGIN ISLANDS 59.3%
VIETNAM 0.1%
COLOMBIA 0.3%
U.A.E. 83.7%
AFRICA
PAPUA NEW GUINEA 0.3%
AMERICAN SAMOA 75.9%
SOUTH AMERICA
PERU 0.3%
BRAZIL 0.3%
INDONESIA 0.1%
MAYOTTE 32.9%
MADAGASCAR 0.1%
AUSTRALIA
LESOTHO 0.1%
FALKLAND ISLANDS 64.9%

Most Populous Places

(MID-2014 DATA)

1.	China	1,355,700,000
2.	India	1,236,300,000
3.	United States	318,900,000
4.	Indonesia	253,600,000
5.	Brazil	202,700,000
6.	Pakistan	196,200,000
7.	Nigeria	177,200,000
8.	Bangladesh	166,300,000
9.	Russia	142,500,000
10.	Japan	127,100,000
11.	Mexico	120,300,000
12.	Philippines	107,700,000
13.	Ethiopia	96,600,000
14.	Vietnam	93,400,000
15.	Egypt	86,900,000
16.	Turkey	81,600,000
17.	Germany	81,000,000
18.	Iran	80,800,000
19.	Dem. Rep. of Congo	77,400,000
20.	Thailand	67,700,000

Most Crowded Places

DENSITY (POP/SQ. MI)

1.	Monaco	39,508
2.	Singapore	20,689
3.	Gibraltar (U.K.)	11,629
4.	Vatican City	4,957
5.	Bahrain	4,478
6.	Maldives	3,421
7.	Malta	3,383
8.	Bermuda (U.K.)	3,349
9.	Bangladesh	2,991
10.	Occupied Palestinian Territory	1,893
11.	Barbados	1,746
12.	Mauritius	1,691
13.	Taiwan (China)	1,681
14.	Aruba (Neth.)	1,593
15.	Lebanon	1,466
16.	San Marino	1,391
17.	South Korea	1,274
18.	Rwanda	1,212
19.	Nauru	1,171
20.	Tuvalu	1,075

Demographic Extremes

LIFE EXPECTANCY

LOWEST (FEMALE, IN YEARS)
49	South Africa
50	Swaziland
51	Chad
51	Namibia

HIGHEST (FEMALE, IN YEARS)
94	Monaco
88	Japan
87	Singapore
86	San Marino

LOWEST (MALE, IN YEARS)
48	Chad
48	Guinea-Bissau
49	Afghanistan
50	Somalia

HIGHEST (MALE, IN YEARS)
86	Monaco
82	Singapore
81	Japan
81	San Marino

POPULATION AGE STRUCTURE

HIGHEST % POPULATION UNDER AGE 15
50%	Niger
49%	Uganda
48%	Mali
47%	Malawi

HIGHEST % POPULATION OVER AGE 65
30%	Monaco
26%	Japan
21%	Greece
21%	Italy

Languages

LANGUAGE MAY EASILY BE RANKED as one of humankind's most distinctive and versatile adaptations. Though its exact origins are lost in the recesses of prehistory, spoken language has allowed humans to communicate and develop in ways inconceivable without it. Written language came much later, and even in recent history, many languages were without a written component. Yet today, the written word has a profound impact on daily life, global communications, and human development. It's virtually impossible to imagine a world without it.

As living, organic entities, languages easily morph over time and place to fit cultural and geographical circumstances. In an often cited example of this, Arctic peoples have many different words for snow—words that reflect different qualities, because those qualities can be critical to human survival in a harsh environment. By studying subtle variations in sounds and concepts embedded in languages, linguists have devised systems to classify them into broad families.

Today, Earth's 7 billion people speak some 7,000 languages, but these languages are not equally distributed among the globe's inhabitants. Roughly 78 percent of the world's population, well over 5 billion people, speaks only 85 of the largest languages, while some 3,500 of the smallest languages have only 8.25 million speakers in all. Often speakers of these smaller languages are the elder members of cultural groups that have been marginalized over time by a more dominant culture. As they die out, so too do the languages only they kept alive. Globalization has only exacerbated this trend, but some small cultures, aware of the fragility of their own languages, are working hard to preserve linguistic traditions.

A variety of indigenous languages exist in the Americas, but because their distribution is fairly sparse, many are not shown on this generalized map.

Evolution of Languages

Even as many languages have disappeared, a few dominant linguistic groups have spawned numerous related tongues. Thus, the Germanic language, which derived from Proto-Indo-European and was spoken by tribes that settled in northern and western Europe, has diversified into several major languages today.

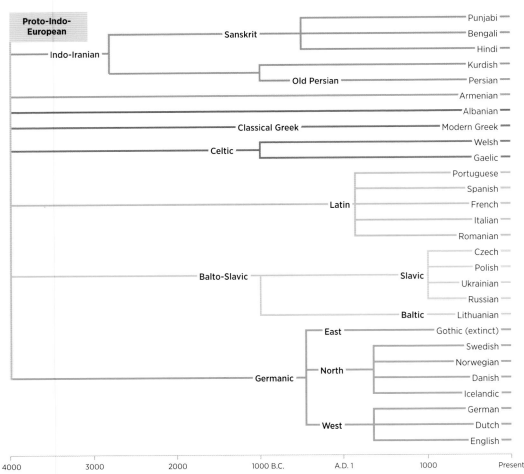

How Many Speak What?

Languages can paint vivid historical pictures of migration and colonization. The languages of a few small European countries are spoken by over a billion people worldwide. In contrast, Australia and Oceania, a constellation of isolated islands in the Pacific, have just 0.5 percent of the world's total population but 19 percent of the world's languages.

World Population and Languages by Region

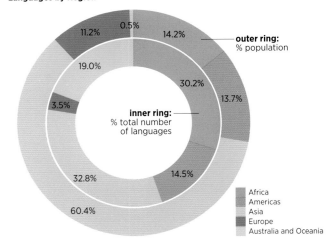

outer ring:
% population

inner ring:
% total number of languages

Africa
Americas
Asia
Europe
Australia and Oceania

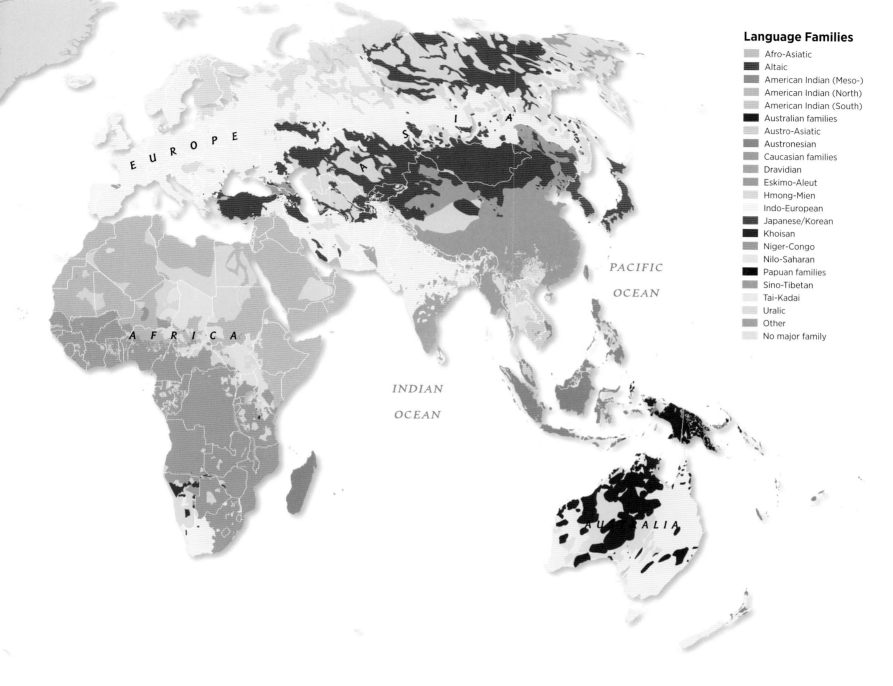

Language Families

- Afro-Asiatic
- Altaic
- American Indian (Meso-)
- American Indian (North)
- American Indian (South)
- Australian families
- Austro-Asiatic
- Austronesian
- Caucasian families
- Dravidian
- Eskimo-Aleut
- Hmong-Mien
- Indo-European
- Japanese/Korean
- Khoisan
- Niger-Congo
- Nilo-Saharan
- Papuan families
- Sino-Tibetan
- Tai-Kadai
- Uralic
- Other
- No major family

Mapping Language Diversity

Measuring language diversity often provides insight into the multicultural nature of countries. Some have high language diversity because of their position in areas of trade or cultural exchange, as seen in Kazakhstan, which was part of the Silk Road. Other countries have high diversity because of multiple surviving ethnic groups, as seen in Bolivia, India, and Chad. Countries with low levels of linguistic diversity, such as Japan and Norway, are often culturally homogeneous.

Vanishing Languages

Every 14 days, another endangered language somewhere in the world dies with its last speaker. These languages tend to be concentrated in hot spots scattered across the world. Linguists fear that by 2100, over half of the 7,000 languages now spoken (many with no recordings for posterity) will be lost forever. Languages become threatened when speakers are past childbearing age and parent-child transmission is unlikely. They are lost when the language is no longer associated with an ethnic identity.

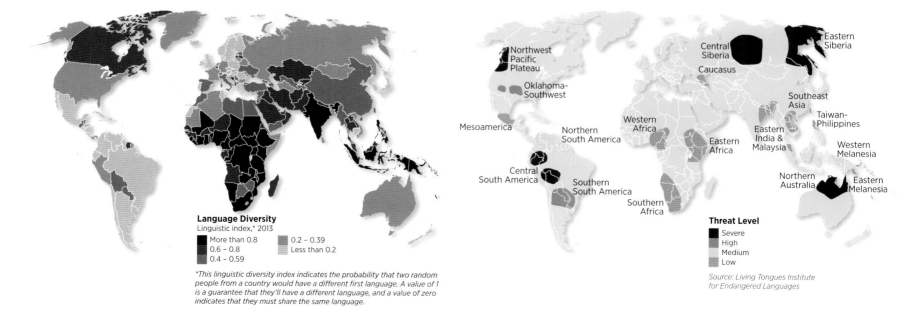

Language Diversity
Linguistic index,* 2013

- More than 0.8
- 0.6 – 0.8
- 0.4 – 0.59
- 0.2 – 0.39
- Less than 0.2

*This linguistic diversity index indicates the probability that two random people from a country would have a different first language. A value of 1 is a guarantee that they'll have a different language, and a value of zero indicates that they must share the same language.

Threat Level
- Severe
- High
- Medium
- Low

Source: Living Tongues Institute for Endangered Languages

Religions

THE GREAT POWER OF RELIGION comes from its ability to speak to the heart and longings of individuals and societies. Since humankind's earliest times, some combination of rituals that acknowledged the mysteries of life and death, practices that honored nature spirits, and beliefs in supreme beings has been part of community life.

In time, an untold number of local religious practices yielded to just a few widespread traditions. Now billions of people are adherents of Hinduism, Buddhism, Judaism, Christianity, and Islam, all of which began in Asia or the Middle East. Universal elements of these faiths include worship, sacred sites, saints and martyrs, ritual clothing, dietary laws and fasting, festivals and holy days, and special ceremonies for life's major moments. Each of these religions gives its followers ways to relate to the spiritual realm as well as moral guidelines that attempt to make life better on Earth. Their tenets and goals are taught not only at the church, synagogue, mosque, or temple, but also through schools, storytelling, and artistic creations.

The world's major religions blossomed from the teachings and revelations of individuals who transmitted the voice of God or discovered a way to salvation that could be understood by others. Abraham and Moses for Jews, the Buddha for Buddhists, Jesus Christ for Christians, and the Prophet Muhammad for Muslims—these individuals fulfilled the roles of divine teachers who experienced essential truths of existence. Leadership was passed to priests, rabbis, ministers, and imams, who have continued to pass down their words, and those found in sacred texts, to faithful followers.

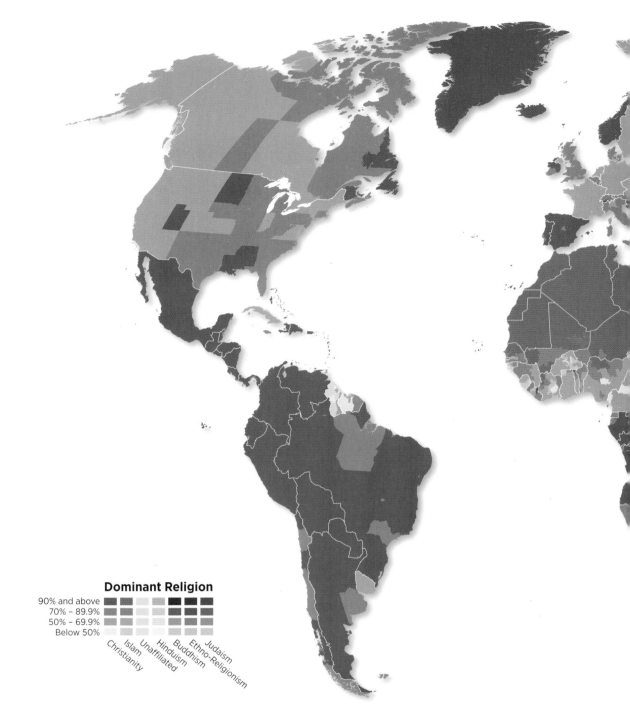

Dominant Religion

90% and above
70% – 89.9%
50% – 69.9%
Below 50%

Christianity
Islam
Unaffiliated
Hinduism
Buddhism
Ethno-Religionism
Judaism

Christianity

Christian belief in eternal life is based on the preaching and example of Jesus Christ, a Jew born some 2,000 years ago. The New Testament tells of his teaching, persecution, Crucifixion and resurrection, and of the early church. Today Christianity is found around the world in three main forms: Roman Catholicism, Eastern Orthodoxy, and Protestantism.

Islam

Muslims believe that the Koran, Islam's sacred book, accurately records the spoken word of God (Allah) as revealed to the Prophet Muhammad, born in Mecca around A.D. 570. Strict adherents pray five times a day, fast during the holy month of Ramadan, and make at least one pilgrimage to Mecca, Islam's holiest city—a trip known as a hajj.

Hinduism

Hinduism began in India more than 4,000 years ago and is still flourishing. Sacred texts known as the Vedas form the basis of Hindu faith and ritual. The main trinity of gods comprises Brahma the creator, Vishnu the preserver, and Shiva the destroyer. Hindus believe in reincarnation and hold that actions in this life affect circumstances of the next (karma).

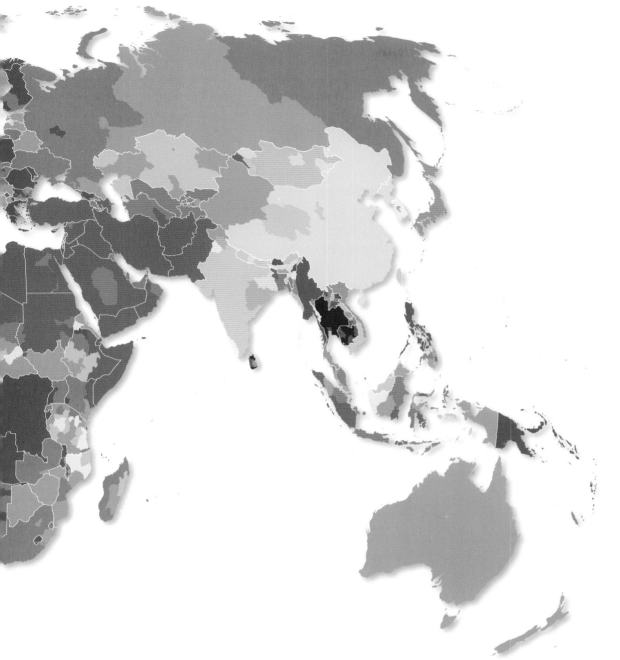

The world's largest religion is Christianity, in its varying forms. The three largest concentrations of Christians are found in the Western Hemisphere, making Christianity the dominant religion of the West because of European colonization. The second largest religion is Islam, which is spreading at a faster rate. All of the leading Islamic nations are in Asia and North Africa, with Indonesia being the most populous Muslim country. Hinduism, the dominant religion of India, also has large concentrations of adherents in other Asian countries, such as Bangladesh and Indonesia. Harder to define as a group are the roughly 1.1 billion people who identify themselves as unaffiliated and are spread throughout the world, with high numbers in Asia and Europe.

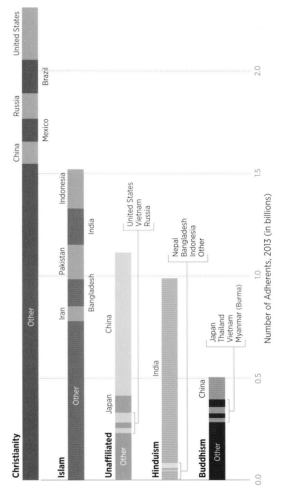

Buddhism

Founded about 2,500 years ago by Shakyamuni Buddha (or Gautama Buddha), Buddhism teaches liberation from suffering through the threefold cultivation of morality, meditation, and wisdom. Buddhists revere the Three Jewels: Buddha (the Awakened One), Dharma (the Truth), and Sangha (the community of monks and nuns).

Ethno-Religionism

As the term implies, ethno-religious traditions combine ethnic and religious identities. Indeed, each of the major faiths are universalized ethno-religions. Some ethno-religions, such as Haitian voodoo, incorporate one of the major faiths; others, such as Sikhism, have branched off. Still more, such as Shinto, are expressions of indigenous and folk religions.

Judaism

The 4,000-year-old religion of the world's 14 million Jews stands as the oldest of the major faiths that believe in a single god (monotheism). Judaism's traditions, customs, laws, and beliefs date back to Abraham, the founder, and to the Torah, the first five books of the Old Testament, believed to have been handed down to Moses on Mount Sinai.

Health and Education

IN THE PAST 50 YEARS, health conditions have improved dramatically. With better economic and living conditions and access to immunization and other basic health services, global life expectancy has risen from 53 to 70 years; the death rate for children under five years old has fallen by half in the past 25 years; and many infectious and parasitic diseases that once killed and disabled millions have been eradicated, eliminated, or greatly reduced in impact.

Despite major strides, however, infant and child mortality from infectious diseases remains relatively high in many of the poorest countries. Each year, more than six million children under five years old die; about four out of every ten of those deaths occur in sub-Saharan Africa and three in South Asia. Undernutrition is a major contributor to half of child deaths, hitting poor families the hardest.

The age-old link between social inequality and ill health is also manifested in the emergence of new health threats. The HIV/AIDS pandemic has erased decades of steady improvements in sub-Saharan Africa, where almost 70 percent of all people living with the disease reside. The death toll in some southern African countries, where adult prevalence exceeds 15 percent, contributed to reversals in life expectancy in the 1990s. Life expectancy is now on the rise again, thanks in part to HIV/AIDS prevention and treatment protocols. At the end of 2013, 36 percent of people living with HIV in low- and middle-income countries were receiving antiretroviral therapy.

Increasingly, lifestyle diseases are also afflicting low-income countries, coming with demographic changes, urbanization, changes in eating habits and physical activity, and environmental degradation. Traffic accidents account for more than a million deaths and upward of 50 million injuries annually; with the rapid increase of automobile use, observers expect that by 2020 the number of traffic deaths will have increased by more than 80 percent in developing countries.

While many international leaders focus on high-profile infectious diseases, the looming challenges of chronic diseases may be even greater. In many high- and middle-income countries, chronic lifestyle-related diseases such as cardiovascular disease and diabetes are becoming the predominant cause of disability and death. In developed countries, smoking is the cause of more than one-third of male deaths in middle age and about one in eight female deaths. Because the focus of policymakers has been on treatment rather than prevention, the costs of dealing with these ailments contributes to high (and increasing) health care spending.

Health Care Availability

Regional differences in health care resources are striking. While countries in Europe and the Americas have relatively large numbers of physicians and nurses, nations with far higher burdens of disease (particularly African countries) are experiencing severe deficits in both health workers and health facilities.

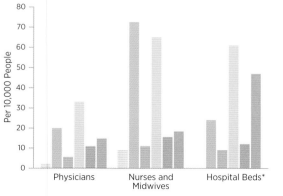

Africa
The Americas
Southeast Asia
Europe
Eastern Mediterranean
Western Pacific

*Hospital beds data unavailable for Africa

Income Levels: Indicators of Health and Literacy

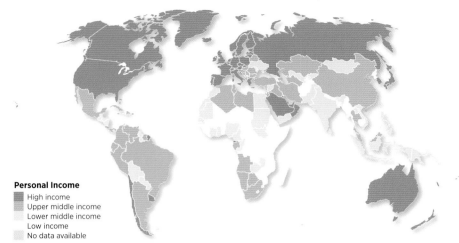

Personal Income
- High income
- Upper middle income
- Lower middle income
- Low income
- No data available

Access to Improved Sanitation

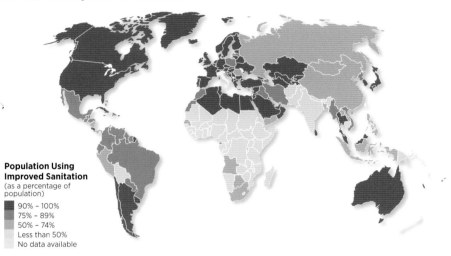

Population Using Improved Sanitation
(as a percentage of population)
- 90% – 100%
- 75% – 89%
- 50% – 74%
- Less than 50%
- No data available

Nutrition

Undernourishment
(as a percentage of population)
- More than 30%
- 15% – 29%
- 10% – 14%
- 5% – 9%
- Less than 5%
- No data available

HIV

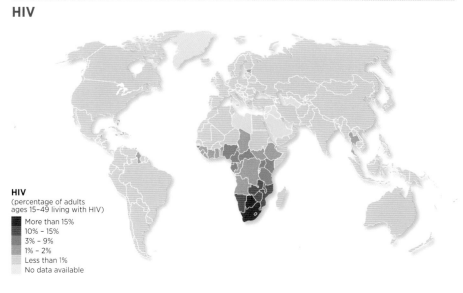

HIV
(percentage of adults ages 15–49 living with HIV)
- More than 15%
- 10% – 15%
- 3% – 9%
- 1% – 2%
- Less than 1%
- No data available

Global Disease Burden

Disease Burden
(percentage of deaths attributable to communicable disease or maternal, perinatal, or nutritional conditions)
- 65% – 100%
- 55% – 64%
- 40% – 54%
- 25% – 39%
- 0% – 24%
- No data available

While infectious and parasitic diseases account for nearly one-quarter of total deaths in developing countries, they result in relatively few deaths in wealthier countries. In contrast, cardiovascular diseases and cancer are more significant causes of death in industrialized countries. Over time, as fertility rates fall, social and living conditions improve, the population ages, and further advances are made against infectious diseases in poorer countries, the differences in causes of death between high-income and low-income countries may converge.

Causes of Death
- Infectious & parasitic diseases
- Cardiovascular diseases
- Respiratory infections
- Perinatal conditions
- Unintentional injuries
- Cancers
- Respiratory diseases
- Digestive diseases
- Intentional injuries
- Maternal conditions
- Neuropsychiatric disorders
- Other

High-Income Countries

Low-Income Countries

Under-Five Mortality

Under-Five Mortality Rate
(per 1,000 live births)
- More than 100
- 60 – 100
- 30 – 59
- 10 – 29
- Less than 10
- No data available

Maternal Mortality

MATERNAL MORTALITY RATIO PER 100,000 LIVE BIRTHS*

COUNTRIES WITH THE HIGHEST MATERNAL MORTALITY RATES		COUNTRIES WITH THE LOWEST MATERNAL MORTALITY RATES	
1. Sierra Leone	1,100	1. Belarus	1
2. Chad	980	2. Israel	2
3. Central African Republic	880	3. Poland	3
4. Somalia	850	4. Austria	4
5. Burundi	740	5. Finland	4
6. Dem. Rep. of the Congo	730	6. Iceland	4
7. South Sudan	730	7. Italy	4
8. Côte d'Ivoire	720	8. Norway	4
9. Guinea	650	9. Spain	4
10. Liberia	640	10. Sweden	4

Adjusted for underreporting and misclassification

Education and Literacy

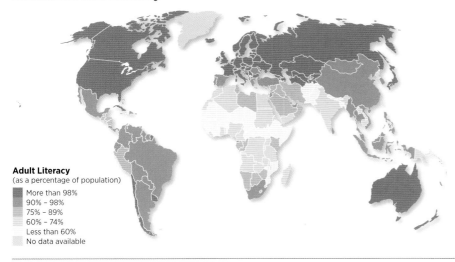

Adult Literacy
(as a percentage of population)
- More than 98%
- 90% – 98%
- 75% – 89%
- 60% – 74%
- Less than 60%
- No data available

Basic education is an investment for the long-term prosperity of a country, generating individual, household, and social benefits. Some countries (e.g., Eastern and Western Europe, the United States) have long traditions of high educational attainment among both genders and now have well-educated populations of all ages. In contrast, many low-income countries have only recently expanded access to primary education; girls still lag behind boys in enrollment and completion of primary school and then in making the transition to secondary school. These countries will have to wait many years before most individuals in the productive ages have even minimal levels of reading, writing, and basic arithmetic skills.

The expansion of secondary schooling tends to lag even further behind, so countries with low educational attainment will likely be at a disadvantage for at least a generation. While no one doubts that the key to long-term economic growth and poverty reduction lies in greater education opportunities for all, many poor countries face the tremendous challenge of paying for schools and teachers today while having to wait 20 years for the economic returns to those investments.

School Enrollment for Girls

Primary Education Enrollment of Girls
(as a percentage of primary school-age girls)
- More than 97%
- 95% – 97%
- 90% – 94%
- 80% – 89%
- Less than 80%
- No data available

Developing Human Capital

In the pyramids below, more orange and blue in the bars indicates a higher level of educational attainment, or "human capital," which contributes greatly to a country's ability for future economic growth. These two countries are similar in population size, but their human capital measures are significantly different.

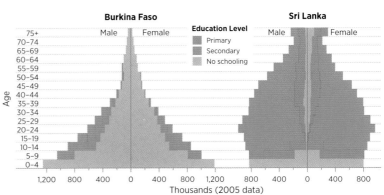

Education Level
- Primary
- Secondary
- No schooling

Thousands (2005 data)

Economy

A GLOBAL ECONOMIC ACTIVITY MAP (right) reveals striking differences between the composition of output in advanced economies and that in less developed economies. The services sector tends to dominate the former, whereas the latter are likely driven by agriculture and industry.

Although countries rich in natural resources can be notable exceptions, economies have generally followed a common trajectory. The majority of an undeveloped economy's employment has been in agriculture. Then, a period of industrialization emerged in which agricultural production became more efficient and less expensive, the market for industrial goods grew in response to demand from customers no longer spending most of their income on food, and those once employed in the shrinking agriculture sector moved on to jobs in the other sectors. As industrial production expanded, both mineral mining and natural resource consumption became more vigorous.

This process now continues to postindustrialization, marked by an evolution in consumer demand—from material goods to services such as health care, education, and entertainment. The number of jobs and proportion of GDP held by the other sectors continue to shrink as efficiency and technological advances increase; however, because in the services sector workers are not easily replaced by machines, employment is relatively stable and costly, raising the sector's share of GDP.

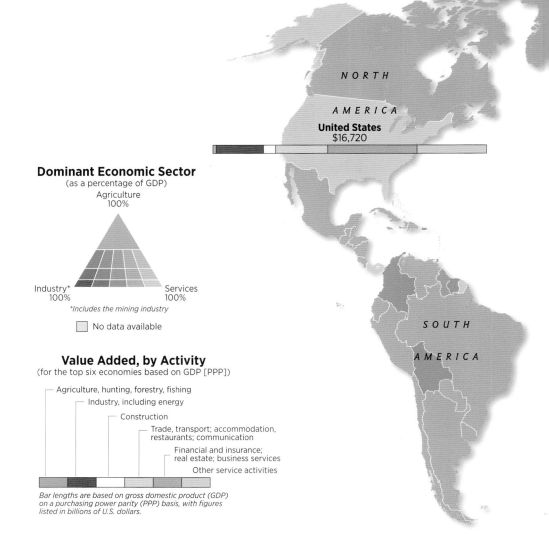

Dominant Economic Sector
(as a percentage of GDP)

Agriculture 100%

Industry* 100%

Services 100%

*Includes the mining industry

No data available

Value Added, by Activity
(for the top six economies based on GDP [PPP])

- Agriculture, hunting, forestry, fishing
- Industry, including energy
- Construction
- Trade, transport; accommodation, restaurants; communication
- Financial and insurance; real estate; business services
- Other service activities

Bar lengths are based on gross domestic product (GDP) on a purchasing power parity (PPP) basis, with figures listed in billions of U.S. dollars.

Human Development Index

Since the UN's first Human Development Index in 1970, quality of life has increased globally. Most gains have been in health, education, and income per capita, which has doubled in the past four decades. But for some countries, especially those in sub-Saharan Africa, the national HDI has been a roller-coaster ride of ups and downs. The current aggregated HDI is influenced by China and India, the most populous nations. In the past 20 years, both have doubled their output per capita, creating an economic maelstrom impacting more humans than did the industrial revolution. Economists predict that by 2050, China, India, and Brazil will control 40 percent of global purchasing power.

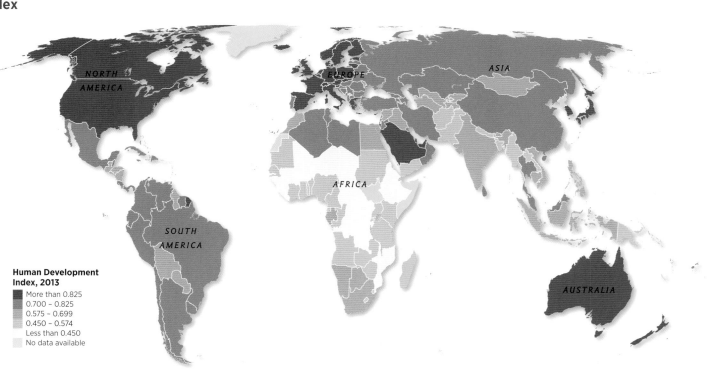

Human Development Index, 2013

- More than 0.825
- 0.700 – 0.825
- 0.575 – 0.699
- 0.450 – 0.574
- Less than 0.450
- No data available

Top GDP Growth Rates
(based on PPP, or purchasing power parity)

2009–2013 AVERAGE

1.	Liberia	11.1%
2.	Afghanistan	10.8%
3.	Ethiopia	10.3%
4.	Qatar	10.3%
5.	Turkmenistan	10.3%
6.	Timor-Leste	10.1%
7.	Sierra Leone	10.0%
8.	Mongolia	9.3%
9.	China	8.9%
10.	Ghana	8.6%

The World's Richest and Poorest Countries (2014 figures, listed in U.S. dollars)

	RICHEST	GDP PER CAPITA (PPP)		POOREST	GDP PER CAPITA (PPP)
1.	Qatar	$108,230	1.	Democratic Republic of the Congo	$415
2.	Luxembourg	$80,660	2.	Zimbabwe	$629
3.	Singapore	$64,880	3.	Burundi	$679
4.	Brunei	$58,700	4.	Liberia	$750
5.	Norway	$58,410	5.	Eritrea	$802
6.	United States	$53,330	6.	Central African Republic	$873
7.	United Arab Emirates	$51,170	7.	Niger	$898
8.	Switzerland	$47,960	8.	Malawi	$940
9.	Australia	$45,860	9.	Madagascar	$1,004
10.	Canada	$45,100	10.	Afghanistan	$1,112

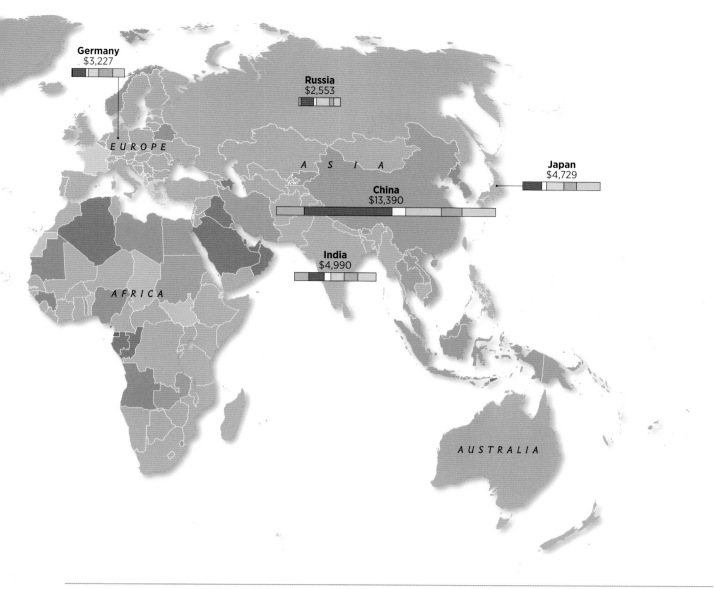

Germany
$3,227

EUROPE

Russia
$2,553

A S I A

Japan
$4,729

China
$13,390

India
$4,990

AFRICA

AUSTRALIA

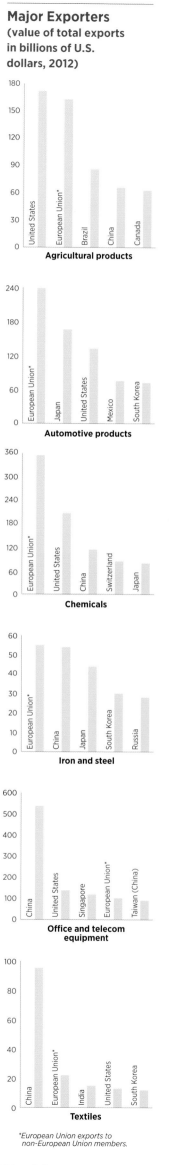

Major Exporters
(value of total exports in billions of U.S. dollars, 2012)

Agricultural products
United States · European Union* · Brazil · China · Canada

Automotive products
European Union* · Japan · United States · Mexico · South Korea

Chemicals
European Union* · United States · China · Switzerland · Japan

Iron and steel
European Union* · China · Japan · South Korea · Russia

Office and telecom equipment
China · United States · Singapore · European Union* · Taiwan (China)

Textiles
China · European Union* · India · United States · South Korea

*European Union exports to non-European Union members.

Gross Domestic Product

The gross domestic product (GDP) is the total market value of goods and services produced by a nation's economy in a given year using global currency exchange rates. It is a convenient way of calculating the level of a nation's international purchasing power and economic strength, but it does not show average wealth of individuals or measure standard of living. For example, a country could have high exports in products but still have a low standard of living.

Gross Domestic Product per Capita
(currency in U.S. dollars)
- More than $25,000
- $10,000 – $25,000
- $5,000 – $9,999
- $1,500 – $4,999
- Less than $1,500
- No data available

NORTH AMERICA · SOUTH AMERICA · EUROPE · AFRICA · ASIA · AUSTRALIA

Global Innovation Index

The Global Innovation Index weighs a country's institutions and infrastructure, human capital and research, and business and market sophistication against its knowledge, technology, and creative outputs to determine world leaders in innovation. While innovation thrives where quality education is available and infrastructure and institutions are strong—as this map shows—creative and critical thinking, openness to risk, and entrepreneurial drive can be found in every country.

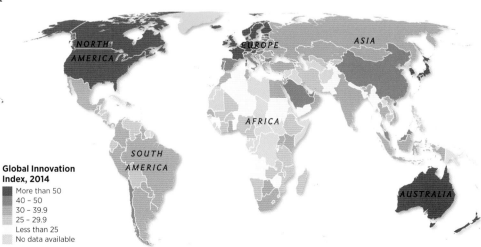

Global Innovation Index, 2014
- More than 50
- 40 – 50
- 30 – 39.9
- 25 – 29.9
- Less than 25
- No data available

NORTH AMERICA · SOUTH AMERICA · EUROPE · AFRICA · ASIA · AUSTRALIA

Trade

WORLD TRADE EXPANDED at a dizzying pace in the half century following World War II. The dollar value of world merchandise exports rose from $61 billion in 1950 to $18.3 trillion in 2013. Adjusted for price changes, world trade grew more than 30 times over the last six decades, much faster than world output. Trade in manufactured goods expanded much faster than that in mining products (including fuels) and agricultural products. In the last decades, many developing countries (e.g., China, South Korea, Mexico) have become important exporters of manufactures. However, there are still many less developed countries—primarily in Africa and the Middle East—that are dependent on a few primary commodities for their export earnings. Commercial services exports have expanded rapidly over the past few decades and amounted to

$4.6 trillion in 2013. While developed countries account for more than two-thirds of world services trade, some developing countries now gain most of their export earnings from services exports. Earnings from tourism in the Caribbean and that from software exports in India are prominent examples of developing countries' dynamic services exports.

Capital flows and worker remittances have gained in importance worldwide and are another important aspect of globalization. The stock of worldwide foreign direct investment was estimated to be $23 trillion at the end of 2012, $13.2 trillion of which was invested in G-20 countries (those with major economies). Capital markets in many developing countries remain small, fragile, and underdeveloped, which hampers household savings and the funding of local enterprises.

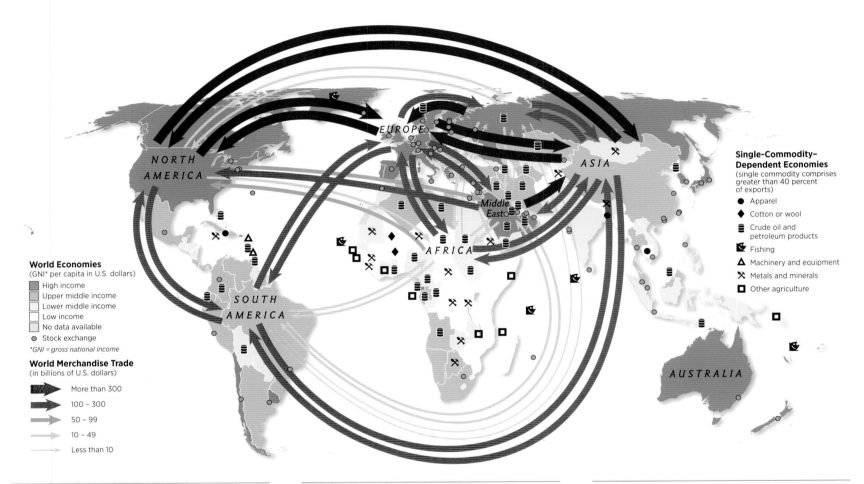

World Economies
(GNI* per capita in U.S. dollars)
- High income
- Upper middle income
- Lower middle income
- Low income
- No data available
- Stock exchange

*GNI = gross national income

World Merchandise Trade
(in billions of U.S. dollars)
- More than 300
- 100 – 300
- 50 – 99
- 10 – 49
- Less than 10

Single-Commodity–Dependent Economies
(single commodity comprises greater than 40 percent of exports)
- Apparel
- Cotton or wool
- Crude oil and petroleum products
- Fishing
- Machinery and equipment
- Metals and minerals
- Other agriculture

Growth of World Trade

After World War II, the export growth of manufactured goods greatly outstripped other exports. This graph shows the volume growth on a semi-log scale (a straight line represents constant growth) rather than a standard scale (a straight line indicates a constant increase in the absolute values in each year).

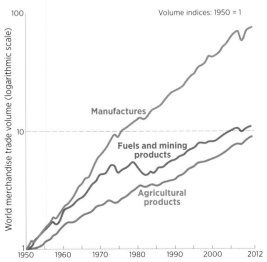

Merchandise Exports

Fuels, because of their heavy concentration in relatively few areas, are the leading category of exports, having increased their share of world exports from 9 percent in 2000 to 19 percent in 2012. Meanwhile, export values for ores and other minerals, raw materials, and iron and steel saw heavy declines from 2011.

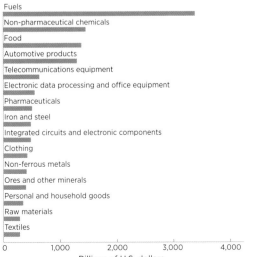

Main Trading Nations

The United States, China, and Germany account for nearly 30 percent of total world merchandise trade. Ongoing negotiations among the 160 member nations of the World Trade Organization are tackling market-access barriers in agriculture, textiles, and clothing—areas where many developing countries hope to compete.

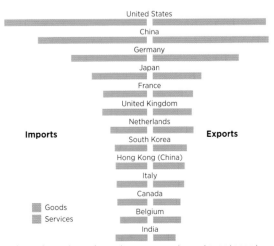

World Debt

Measuring a country's outstanding foreign debt in relation to its GDP indicates the size of future income needed to pay back the debt; it also shows how much a country has relied in the past on foreign savings to finance investment and consumption expenditures. A high external debt ratio can pose a financial risk if debt service payments are not assured.

External Debt
(as a percentage of gross national income [GNI], defined by the World Bank)
- More than 200%
- 100% – 200%
- 50% – 99%
- 25% – 49%
- Less than 25%
- No data available

Trade Blocs

Regional trade is on the rise. Agreements between neighboring countries to offer each other trade benefits can create larger markets and improve the economy of the region as a whole. But they can also lead to discrimination, especially when more efficient suppliers outside the regional agreements are prevented from supplying their goods and services.

Major Regional Trade Agreements
- APEC: Asia-Pacific Economic Cooperation
- ASEAN: Association of Southeast Asian Nations
- APEC & ASEAN
- COMESA: Common Market for Eastern and Southern Africa
- ECOWAS: Economic Community of West African States
- EU: European Union
- MERCOSUR: Southern Common Market
- NAFTA & APEC: North American Free Trade Agreement
- SAFTA: South Asian Free Trade Area

Trade Flow: Fuels

The leading exporters of fuel products are countries in the Middle East, Africa, Russia, and central and western Asia; all export more fuel than they consume. But intra-regional energy trade is growing, with some of the key producers—Canada, Indonesia, Norway, and the United Kingdom, for example—located in regions that are net energy importers.

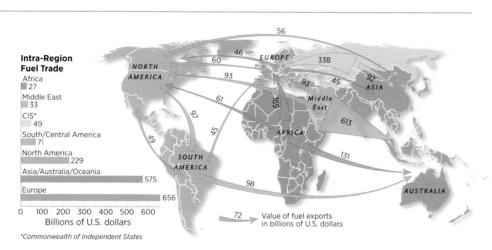

Intra-Region Fuel Trade
- Africa: 27
- Middle East: 33
- CIS*: 49
- South/Central America: 71
- North America: 229
- Asia/Australia/Oceania: 575
- Europe: 656

0 100 200 300 400 500 600
Billions of U.S. dollars

Commonwealth of Independent States

→ 72 Value of fuel exports in billions of U.S. dollars

Trade Flow: Agricultural Products

The world trade in agricultural products is less concentrated than trade in fuels, with processed goods making up the majority. Agricultural products encounter high export barriers, which limit the opportunities for some exporters to expand into foreign markets. Reducing such barriers is a major challenge for governments that are engaged in agricultural trade negotiations.

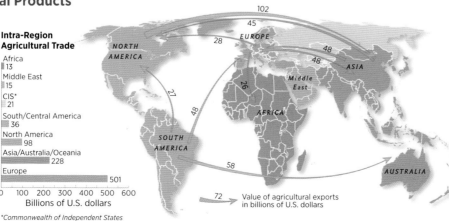

Intra-Region Agricultural Trade
- Africa: 13
- Middle East: 15
- CIS*: 21
- South/Central America: 36
- North America: 98
- Asia/Australia/Oceania: 228
- Europe: 501

0 100 200 300 400 500 600
Billions of U.S. dollars

Commonwealth of Independent States

→ 72 Value of agricultural exports in billions of U.S. dollars

Top Merchandise Exporters and Importers

	PERCENTAGE OF WORLD TOTAL	VALUE (BILLIONS)
TOP EXPORTERS		
China	11.1%	$2,049
United States	8.4%	$1,546
Germany	7.6%	$1,407
Japan	4.3%	$799
Netherlands	3.6%	$656
France	3.1%	$569
South Korea	3.0%	$548
Russia	2.9%	$529
Italy	2.7%	$501
Hong Kong (China)	2.7%	$493
United Kingdom	2.6%	$474
Canada	2.5%	$455
Belgium	2.4%	$447
Singapore	2.2%	$408
Saudi Arabia	2.1%	$388
TOP IMPORTERS		
United States	12.6%	$2,336
China	9.8%	$1,818
Germany	6.3%	$1,167
Japan	4.8%	$886
United Kingdom	3.7%	$690
France	3.6%	$674
Netherlands	3.2%	$591
Hong Kong (China)	3.0%	$553
South Korea	2.8%	$520
India	2.6%	$490
Italy	2.6%	$487
Canada	2.6%	$475
Belgium	2.4%	$437
Mexico	2.0%	$380
Singapore	2.0%	$380

Top Commercial Services Exporters and Importers
(includes transportation, travel, and other services)

	PERCENTAGE OF WORLD TOTAL	VALUE (BILLIONS)
TOP EXPORTERS		
United States	14.3%	$621
United Kingdom	6.4%	$280
Germany	5.9%	$257
France	4.8%	$211
China	4.4%	$190
Japan	3.3%	$142
India	3.2%	$141
Spain	3.1%	$136
Netherlands	3.0%	$131
Hong Kong (China)	2.8%	$123
Ireland	2.7%	$116
Singapore	2.6%	$112
South Korea	2.5%	$110
Italy	2.4%	$103
Belgium	2.2%	$95
TOP IMPORTERS		
United States	9.9%	$411
Germany	7.1%	$293
China	6.7%	$280
Japan	4.2%	$175
United Kingdom	4.2%	$174
France	4.1%	$172
India	3.1%	$127
Netherlands	2.9%	$119
Singapore	2.8%	$118
Ireland	2.7%	$112
South Korea	2.6%	$107
Canada	2.5%	$105
Italy	2.5%	$105
Russia	2.5%	$104
Belgium	2.2%	$92

Food

THE POPULATION OF THE PLANET, which already exceeds seven billion, will grow to nine billion by 2050. To provide everyone with a diet like that available in developed countries by mid-century, food production will need to double.

Yet, food insecurity is already an urgent concern at current population levels. For although the Food and Agriculture Organization of the United Nations reports that 100 million fewer people are chronically undernourished today than a decade ago, over 800 million people (one in nine) still do not have access to the daily recommended minimum of 2,000–2,500 calories per person. The majority of the undernourished live in developing countries; of greatest concern are communities in sub-Saharan Africa and southern Asia. In striking contrast, patterns of consumption in developed countries reveal that changing diets, which incorporate more fat, sugar, and salt, are leading to both undernourishment and widespread obesity.

Feeding an additional two billion people is not only an issue of logistics, however. It is also one of environmental stewardship. The problematic greenhouse gases emitted by agricultural enterprises exceed emissions from automobiles, trains, and airplanes. Water sources are both consumed and polluted by agriculture. Wildlife habitat and biodiversity are lost when undeveloped land is converted for agricultural purposes.

A group of scientists wrestling with the issue of how to make agriculture both more productive and less destructive have created a five-step plan: We must freeze agriculture's footprint, grow more on existing farms, use resources more efficiently, shift our diets, and reduce waste.

Agriculture's Footprint

Almost 40 percent of Earth's ice-free land, and more than 70 percent of land developed by humankind, is used to raise crops or livestock. But even as these practices sustain us, they jeopardize our quality of life and the health of our environment by polluting the ground and waterways, degrading the wildlife habitats around us, and contributing to climate change.

Of the 19.4 million square miles (50.25 million sq km) we already use for agriculture, land with an area about the size of South America supports crops. Even more

land, equal to the size of Africa, is committed to livestock.

So although the obvious approach to increasing food production would be to expand the amount of land under cultivation, this would lead to plowing more grasslands or clearing more forests, the latter likely in tropical areas—far from areas where food security is a pressing concern. This destruction would endanger more species in order to make space for noncritical livestock, soybeans, and palm oil.

Crop Allocation

100% area Pasture	50%	100% Cropland

Where Crop Yields Could Improve

Crop production worldwide has tripled in the last five decades. Gains are largely the result not of expanding the area under cultivation but of increasing yields from existing acreage. Greater yields may indicate that land lay fallow less often, that multiple crops were raised simultaneously, or that planting and growing techniques were improved. They may also be attributable to different inputs—such as more productive crop varieties, better fertilizer, and improved irrigation—or to the introduction of machines. Similar gains were seen in Asia and Latin America in the second half of the 20th century during the so-called green revolution.

Current efforts to apply best practices from both industrial and organic agriculture are focusing on less productive farmland in Africa, Latin America, and Eastern Europe.

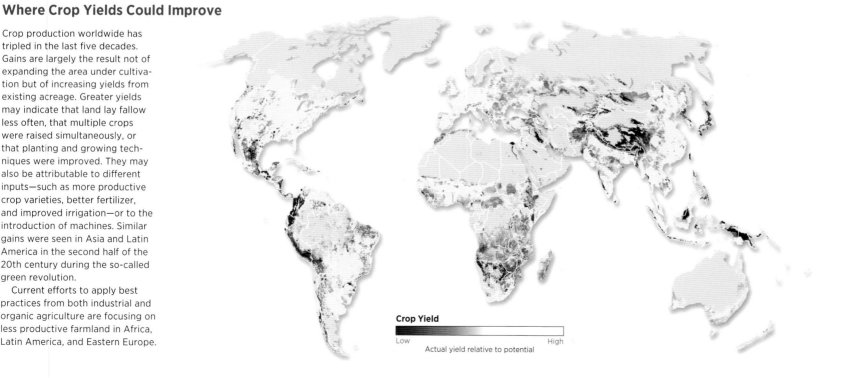

Crop Yield

Low	High

Actual yield relative to potential

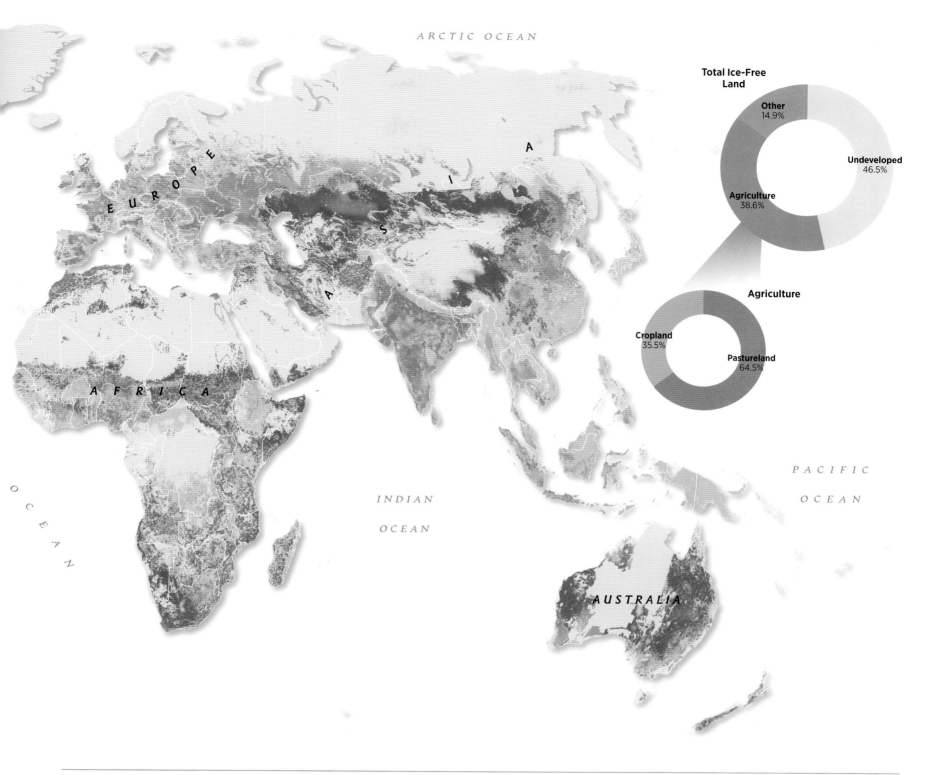

Total Ice-Free Land

Other 14.9%

Undeveloped 46.5%

Agriculture 38.6%

Agriculture

Cropland 35.5%

Pastureland 64.5%

How Our Crops Are Used

Just over half of the calories raised are consumed by humans; the balance are used for biofuels or fed to livestock. However, meat, dairy, and eggs contain only a fraction of the calories that were directed to the animals. For instance, 100 calories of grain fed to cattle produces just 3 calories of beef. Reducing the amount of grain-fed meat in our diet would decrease diverted crops.

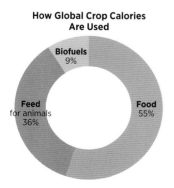

How Global Crop Calories Are Used

Biofuels 9%

Feed for animals 36%

Food 55%

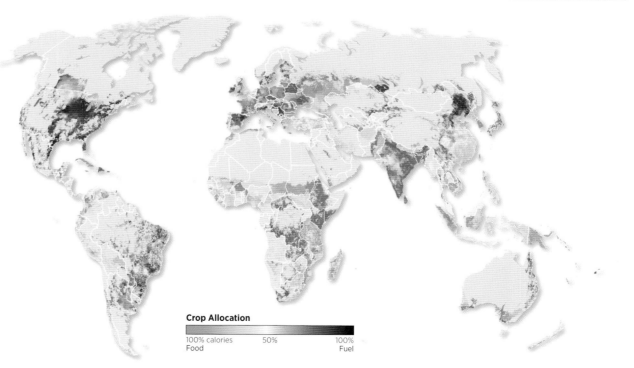

Crop Allocation

100% calories Food — 50% — 100% Fuel

Food

Distribution of Major Crops and Livestock

Humans rely on plant sources for carbohydrates, with grains (the edible parts of cereal plants) providing 80 percent of the food energy (calorie) supply. This means that the major grains—corn, wheat, and rice—are the foods that fuel humanity. Most cereal grains are grown in the Northern Hemisphere, with the United States and France producing enough to be the largest exporters.

In many parts of the world, cereal grains cannot be grown because of the lack of productive farmland or the absence of necessary technology. Again and again throughout history, the actions of countries have been shaped by disparities in the supply and demand of grains as well as by the knowledge that grains equal survival. As food historian Waverley Root once wrote: "Possession of wheat or lack of it sways the destinies of nations; nor is it rare to find wheat being used as a political weapon. . . . It is difficult to foresee any future in which it will not still exert a powerful influence on human history."

Recently, rising standards of living in developing countries have increased the worldwide appetite for meat and other animal products, such as eggs and dairy, further increasing demand for grains that are used in livestock feed. The rapidly expanding livestock sector will soon provide about half of the global agricultural GDP.

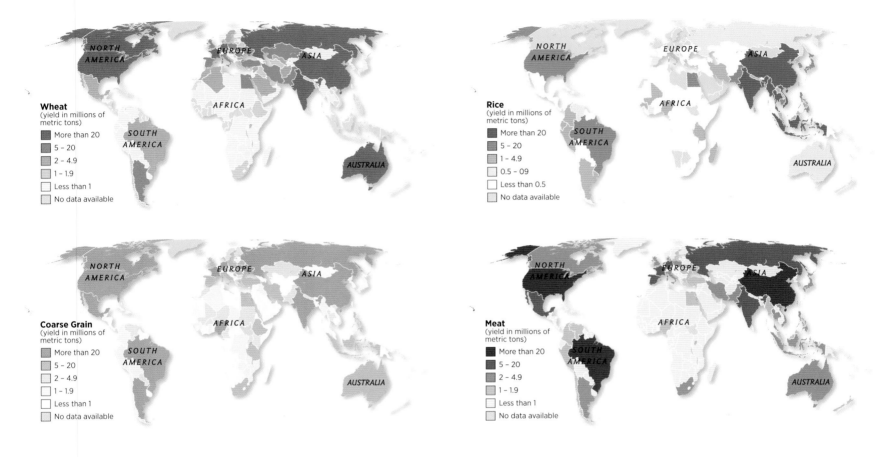

Wheat
(yield in millions of metric tons)
- More than 20
- 5 – 20
- 2 – 4.9
- 1 – 1.9
- Less than 1
- No data available

Rice
(yield in millions of metric tons)
- More than 20
- 5 – 20
- 1 – 4.9
- 0.5 – 09
- Less than 0.5
- No data available

Coarse Grain
(yield in millions of metric tons)
- More than 20
- 5 – 20
- 2 – 4.9
- 1 – 1.9
- Less than 1
- No data available

Meat
(yield in millions of metric tons)
- More than 20
- 5 – 20
- 2 – 4.9
- 1 – 1.9
- Less than 1
- No data available

Fishing and Aquaculture

Marine fisheries are vital for food security in developing countries and are a heavily subsidized industry in developed countries. Today, no parts of the world's oceans are unaffected by our appetite for seafood. Most fish are caught in coastal waters, with the most intense fishing in northern Europe and off China and Southeast Asia. The world's reported catch has more than quadrupled since 1950, but it peaked in the late 1980s and has leveled off since. Fish farming, called aquaculture, is one of the fastest-growing areas of food production. The bulk of marine aquaculture occurs in developing countries, with China accounting for around two-thirds of the total output. Of the 148 million metric tons of fish, crustaceans, and mollusks supplied by marine fisheries and fish farms in 2010, 20 million were used as fishmeal, oil, and animal feed. The other 128 million were for human consumption. On average, fish provides about 17 percent of the animal protein eaten per person per year.

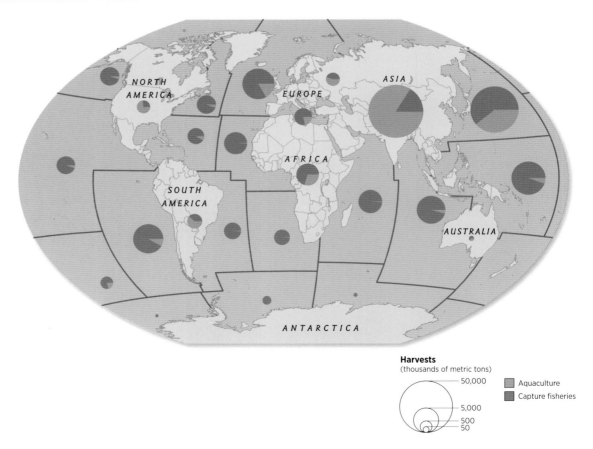

Harvests
(thousands of metric tons)
- 50,000
- 5,000
- 500
- 50
- Aquaculture
- Capture fisheries

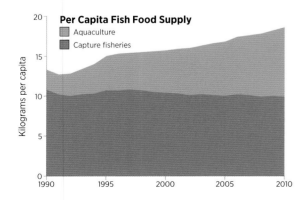

Per Capita Fish Food Supply
- Aquaculture
- Capture fisheries

Kilograms per capita

1990 1995 2000 2005 2010

World Food Production

In the past few decades, world food production has more than kept pace with the burgeoning global population. Meat and cereals account for the most dramatic increases. New high-yield crops, additional irrigated land, and fertilizers have contributed to the rise in production. But there are related problems: Scientists warn that overuse of fertilizers causes nitrogen overload in Earth's waters; on the other hand, the insufficient use of fertilizers, particularly in Africa, has long-term adverse consequences for food security. It is also still the case that farmable land is distributed unequally and is not always available near growing population centers.

Food Security

Food security is a complex and multifaceted issue. While populations facing food shortages can be said to lack food security, the same is true for those who are unable to afford the plentiful food around them or those who are kept from it because of political instability, for example. Even in wealthy countries where food is abundant, like the United States, pockets of the population live in areas where nutritional food is not accessible—places called food deserts. For these reasons, researchers evaluating food security need to consider both causes, such as insufficient supply, poverty, and vulnerability (whether from human or natural causes), and effects, including undernourishment.

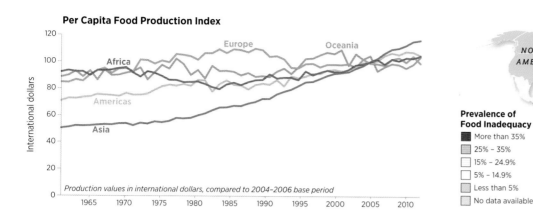

Per Capita Food Production Index

Production values in international dollars, compared to 2004–2006 base period

Prevalence of Food Inadequacy
- More than 35%
- 25% – 35%
- 15% – 24.9%
- 5% – 14.9%
- Less than 5%
- No data available

Genetically Modified Crops

Though it can be said that humans have been manipulating plant and animal species for thousands of years through breeding and hybridization, genetic engineering is a modern practice. In 2013, 12 percent of total crops were genetically modified. Proponents cite benefits such as increased yield, pest resistance without pesticides, improved nutrition, ability to withstand extreme weather, and longer shelf life. Critics emphasize unexpected distribution, unanticipated harmful mutations, unknown effects on wildlife, and farmers' restricted access to patented plant material.

Cropland Planted With Genetically Modified Crops

- Canola 8.2 million hectares
- Other crops 1.2 million hectares
- Cotton 23.9 million hectares
- **Total 175.2 million hectares**
- **Soybeans 84.5 million hectares**
- Maize (corn) 57.4 million hectares

Area of Biotech Crops (millions of hectares)
- More than 40
- 10 – 40
- 1 – 9.9
- 0.1 – 0.9
- Less than 0.1
- No biotech crops planted

Caloric Supply

Changes in diet are largely tied to changes in economic status and urbanization. Low-income and rural populations are often restricted to a diet of roots, tubers, and cereals, which may not provide the minimum daily threshold of 2,000–2,500 calories per person. As communities gain wealth and access to diverse food items, consumption of meat and dairy products as well as of wheat, rice, sugar, and vegetable oils increases. The world now faces a good news–bad news scenario: Many efforts to eradicate undernourishment have been successful; per person daily food availability in recently at-risk countries is nearly 3,000 calories. But in developed countries, where lifestyles are increasingly sedentary and people are eating more saturated fats, salt, and sugar, overnutrition and obesity are more prevalent.

- Cereals
- Fruits
- Meat
- Milk
- Pulses
- Starchy roots
- Sugar and sweeteners
- Vegetable oils
- Vegetables
- Fish and seafood
- Other

Regional Caloric Supply (calories per capita per day)

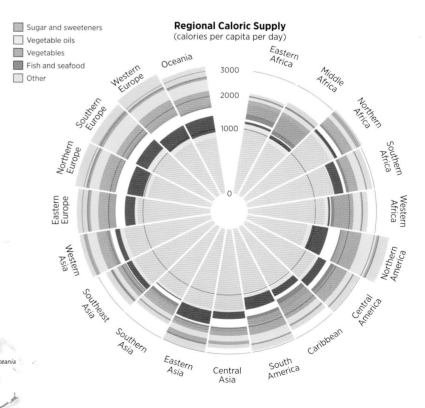

Food Supply (calories per capita per day)
- 3,500 and above
- 3,000 – 3,499
- 2,500 – 2,999
- 2,000 – 2,499
- Less than 2,000
- No data available

Energy

THE WORLD RUNS ON ENERGY, and in the industrialized world that typically means burning oil, natural gas, or coal. Our modern life is built on the idea that energy is cheap and plentiful, powering heavy industry and our homes, our global transportation networks, and even the billions of electronic devices vital to business and communications in the 21st century. Access to fuel is more than a luxury: It can mean the difference between edible food or indigestible grain, and it makes it possible to survive frigid nights and sweltering days. Most energy is consumed in the wealthiest nations or in recently industrialized China and India; in the poorer nations, the fuel likely to be available for everyday life may still be animal dung or gathered firewood. North America, with less than one-tenth of the world's population, consumes about one-quarter of the energy used; Africa, with twice the population, uses five times less than that.

Worldwide, oil accounts for more than 40 percent of energy usage. But as oil supplies dwindle and prices rise, new energy sources are being explored and exploited—from natural gas (obtained by fracking) to renewable energy from the sun, wind, and tides. Not only are these renewable sources inexhaustible, but they are also environmentally neutral, unlike fossil fuels—such as natural gas, petroleum, and coal—whose burning releases greenhouse gases. Those gases, particularly CO_2, are a major cause of the climate change that is now proving so damaging to life and the future of the planet.

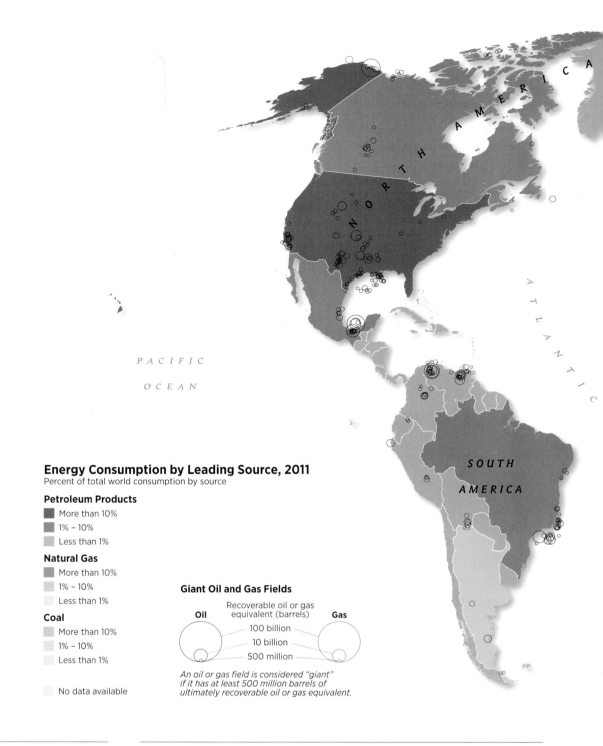

Energy Consumption by Leading Source, 2011
Percent of total world consumption by source

Petroleum Products
- More than 10%
- 1% – 10%
- Less than 1%

Natural Gas
- More than 10%
- 1% – 10%
- Less than 1%

Coal
- More than 10%
- 1% – 10%
- Less than 1%

- No data available

Giant Oil and Gas Fields

Oil   Recoverable oil or gas equivalent (barrels)   Gas
- 100 billion
- 10 billion
- 500 million

An oil or gas field is considered "giant" if it has at least 500 million barrels of ultimately recoverable oil or gas equivalent.

Energy Production by Fuel Type

The production of energy grows yearly to meet the demands of an ever more populous, affluent, and industrialized world. Even the demand for coal, the least clean-burning fuel, has climbed in recent years, but like all fossil fuels, coal's reserves are limited and nonrenewable. Natural gas production is also likely to increase worldwide as previously inaccessible shale gas is recovered via hydraulic fracturing. Geothermal, solar, and wind energies are included in the graph under "other."

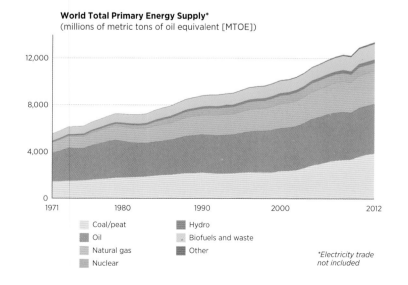

World Total Primary Energy Supply*
(millions of metric tons of oil equivalent [MTOE])

- Coal/peat
- Oil
- Natural gas
- Nuclear
- Hydro
- Biofuels and waste
- Other

Electricity trade not included

Energy Production by Region

The global energy market both influences economic conditions and is influenced by them. For example, the energy crises of the 1970s led to a general downturn in oil consumption in the 1980s, and Asian producers (specifically those in the Middle East) reacted with a drop in production. Yet even with the Great Recession, production between 2000 and 2013 grew in Russia and Saudi Arabia by about 30 percent. China more than doubled its production during that time, from about 1,100 to 2,500 MTOE.

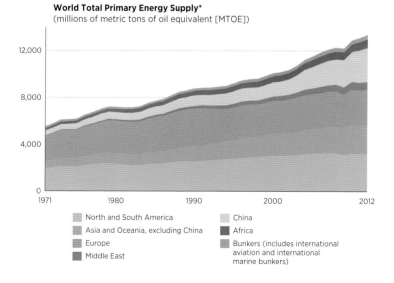

World Total Primary Energy Supply*
(millions of metric tons of oil equivalent [MTOE])

- North and South America
- Asia and Oceania, excluding China
- Europe
- Middle East
- China
- Africa
- Bunkers (includes international aviation and international marine bunkers)

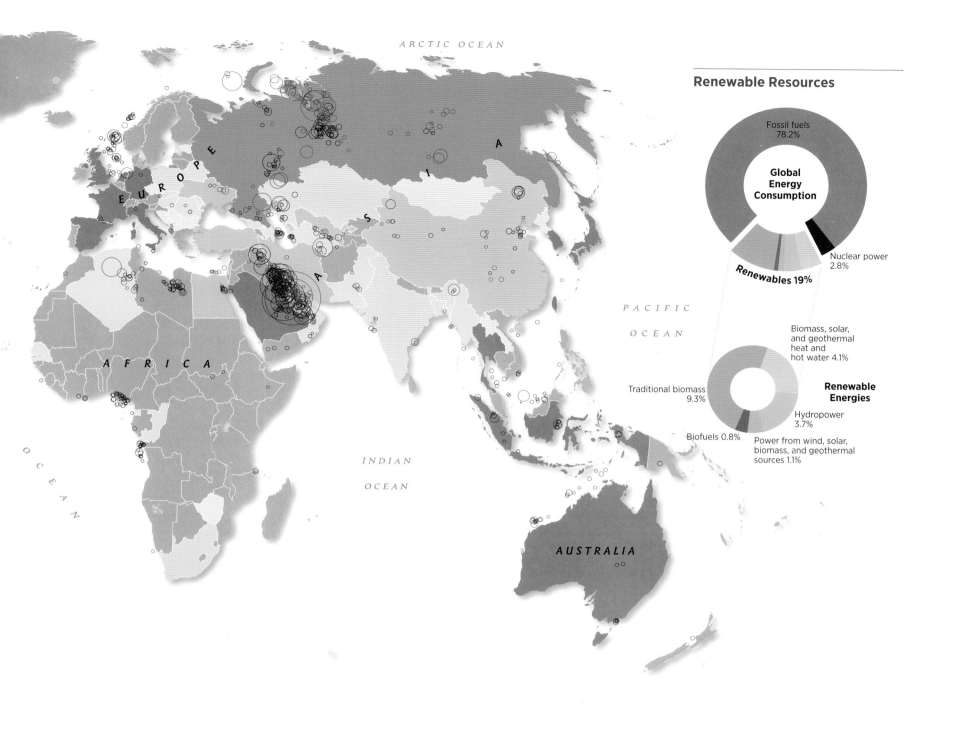

Renewable Resources

Global Energy Consumption

Fossil fuels 78.2%

Nuclear power 2.8%

Renewables 19%

Renewable Energies

Biomass, solar, and geothermal heat and hot water 4.1%

Traditional biomass 9.3%

Hydropower 3.7%

Biofuels 0.8%

Power from wind, solar, biomass, and geothermal sources 1.1%

Balancing Consumption and Production

Few nations have a perfect balance between energy consumption and production. Countries with few energy resources or high consumer populations often have a balance that tips toward net consumption. The United States, followed by Japan and China, has the highest positive consumption balance. Countries rich in energy resources or with small populations often are net energy producers. Russia has the highest production balance, followed by Saudi Arabia.

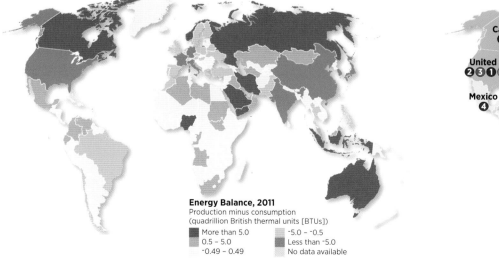

Energy Balance, 2011
Production minus consumption
(quadrillion British thermal units [BTUs])

- More than 5.0
- 0.5 – 5.0
- -0.49 – 0.49
- -5.0 – -0.5
- Less than -5.0
- No data available

Renewable Leaders

Changes in global consumption are visible as much of the world weans itself off fossil fuels. Large economies such as China, the U.S., and Brazil lead in terms of total renewable power capacity. As of 2014, policies in support of renewable energy sources were in place in 144 countries, two-thirds of which are developing or emerging economies.

Renewable Energy, 2012
Countries ranked by capacity

- Total renewable power
- Hydroelectric
- Geothermal
- Wind
- Solar photovoltaics
- Biomass and waste

Countries With Renewable Energy Policies, Early 2013
Number of policy types enacted

- 9 – 13
- 6 – 8
- 3 – 5
- 1 – 2
- No policy or no data available

REN21 Global Status Report, 2013

Minerals

THE MAP AT RIGHT traces more than 90 percent of the total tonnage of mined metallic minerals—generally those with high unit value, measured in dollars to hundreds of dollars per ton—but many other metals are also required to manufacture the products of our modern world. These less glamorous commodities command low unit values but are nonetheless invaluable. Cement, sand and gravel, sulfur, potash, and phosphates all play essential roles, the last two as critical components in the fertilizers the world relies on to feed an ever expanding population.

Geology, climate, economic systems, and social preferences are among the factors that create the global patterns of mineral production. Valuable concentrations of minerals form through the processes of plate movements, volcanism, and sedimentation. The same forces that formed the Andes, for example, are responsible for the porphyry copper deposits along South America's Pacific coast. Other geologic processes concentrate copper in sedimentary basins and in volcanic arcs, while climatic conditions contribute to the formation of bauxite, nickel, and other minerals.

Mineral consumption is generally tied to GDP. Developed countries use larger volumes of materials and, consequently, a wider variety of mineral commodities than are used by less developed countries. Recent economic growth in some parts of the developing world, though, has led to greater demand for many mineral resources. Because extracting and processing minerals both consumes water and energy and generates pollutants, meeting that need without causing harm to the environment will be one of the major challenges of the 21st century.

Major industries that consume processed mineral materials make up 15 percent of the U.S. economy.

Latin America's mineral giant, Brazil is a leading producer of iron and aluminum ores. Chile is the world's leading producer and exporter of copper.

Africa holds a large percentage of the world's untapped mineral reserves. Mineral production is on the rise in Africa and will increase steeply in the coming decade.

Exports in Nonfuel Mining Products, 2013
(in millions of U.S. dollars)

- More than 20,000
- 10,000 – 19,999
- 5,000 – 9,999
- 1,000 – 4,999
- 200 – 999
- Less than 200
- No data available

World Mineral Production by Type

As the chart below indicates, steel vastly outranks all other minerals in production when assessed by value, accounting for more than 83 percent; its closest competitor, precious metals (such as gold, silver, and platinum), accounts for only 4 percent. Steel's economic importance is so pervasive that the health of steelmaking and manufacturing is linked to GDP. Composed of iron, carbon, and various other elements, steel is classified into hundreds of different grades.

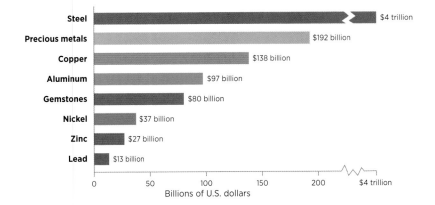

Steel	$4 trillion
Precious metals	$192 billion
Copper	$138 billion
Aluminum	$97 billion
Gemstones	$80 billion
Nickel	$37 billion
Zinc	$27 billion
Lead	$13 billion

Billions of U.S. dollars

Steel Production by Location

In 1950, worldwide crude (raw) steel production was just under 600 million tons annually. In 2012, China alone produced more than 700 million tons, almost half of the world's total output for the year (1,547 million tons). About 35 percent of current production comes from scrap, whose value has doubled in the past decade, instead of from iron ore. Easily separated from the waste stream using magnets, steel is 100 percent recyclable. Its life span is essentially infinite.

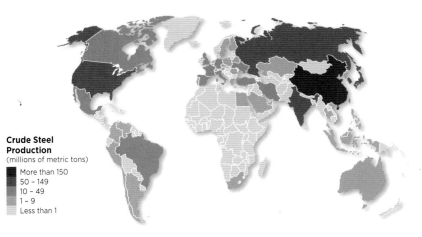

Crude Steel Production
(millions of metric tons)

- More than 150
- 50 – 149
- 10 – 49
- 1 – 9
- Less than 1

China has quickly risen to become the world's dominant producer of many different essential minerals.

PACIFIC OCEAN

INDIAN OCEAN

AUSTRALIA

Australia is the world's largest exporter of nonfuel minerals, exporting more than twice the value of the United States, the second largest exporter.

World Share of Production

Iron Ore
China 45%
Australia 18%
Brazil 13%
Other Countries 24%

Iron ore: Primary iron oxide ores range from 35 to 70 percent iron content. The richer ores, those from Australia, Brazil, and South Africa, can be shipped directly to smelters, whereas the rest require on-site grinding, separation, and concentration. Iron is critical to the production of steel, but the annual 1.5 billion tons of raw steel produced worldwide require large quantities of many other metals as well. In the past few years alone, global steel consumption has increased by about 6 percent annually.

Bauxite
Australia 30%
China 18%
Brazil 13%
Indonesia 12%
Other Countries 27%

Bauxite (aluminum ore): Bauxite, critical to aluminum production, comes from aluminous rocks that have spent millions of years near Earth's surface in tropical or subtropical climates. Deep, prolonged weathering leaches most elements from the parent rock, leaving aluminum and iron oxides. Despite this natural pretreatment, large amounts of energy are still required to convert the ore to aluminum metal. Today, however, a significant percentage of the world's aluminum production comes from recycled products.

Copper
Chile 32%
China 9%
Peru 7%
U.S. 7%
Other Countries 45%

Copper: Humans have used copper for at least 10,000 years, and it ranks third after iron and aluminum in annual consumption. A soft metal, copper was alloyed with zinc to create brass and with tin to create the bronze tools and weapons that ended the Stone Age. Most copper is recovered from sulfide minerals, and historically open-hearth smelting led to severe acid rain. Copper and its alloys are used in building construction (45 percent), electric and electronic products (23 percent), and transportation equipment (12 percent).

Nickel
Indonesia 18%
Philippines 18%
Russia 10%
Australia 10%
Other Countries 44%

Nickel: Globally, stainless steel and non–iron-based alloys and superalloys account for nearly 90 percent of nickel consumption. China's dramatic expansion of its stainless steel industry is certainly the major cause of the nearly threefold price increase in nickel since 2005. Newly discovered sources of nickel in Greenland, Canada, and Russia should help counter what could have been a prolonged global shortage of the mineral, while Indonesia and the Philippines are the new leaders in nickel production.

Zinc
China 37%
Australia 10%
Peru 10%
Other Countries 43%

Zinc: Currently, more than 50 percent of zinc is used in the production of galvanized steel, while nearly 40 percent is consumed as zinc-based alloys, including brass, an alloy of zinc and copper. Zinc sulfide is commonly found in ores with copper sulfide minerals, and thus the original brass was certainly an accidental product. Nearly all the primary cadmium (for nickel-cadmium batteries) and germanium (for fiber-optic cables) come as by-products from zinc mining.

Gold
China 15%
Australia 9%
U.S. 8%
Russia 8%
Other Countries 60%

Precious metals: Gold prices have nearly tripled in the past five years, resulting in the breadth of production seen on the bar graph on page 68. Twenty years ago, South Africa generated nearly 33 percent of the world's annual gold production (falling to 21 percent ten years ago) from the world's deepest mines, but those mines are now nearing exhaustion. Two-thirds of silver production comes from three countries—Mexico, China, and Peru. South Africa accounts for almost 80 percent of platinum.

Lead
China 56%
Australia 13%
U.S. 6%
Other Countries 25%

Lead: Lead-acid automotive batteries continue to be the major end-product for lead sales, accounting for 86 percent of U.S. consumption. Lead is also the recycling king—83 percent of U.S. consumption is recycled (mostly postconsumer) lead. Dramatic expansion of the transportation sector in China in recent years has led to a volatile lead market, with demand and stockpiling causing fluctuations in price. China far outranks all other nations in lead production.

Diamonds
Botswana 28%
Dem. Rep. Congo 21%
Russia 19%
Australia 14%
Other Countries 18%

Gemstones: Diamonds dominate the world gemstone trade, accounting for 95 percent of gem imports. Canadian diamonds from the Northwest Territories have been mined since 1999, and new deposits continue to be found, spurring further exploration across North America. Most diamonds are several billion years old and have been brought to the surface relatively recently as accidental inclusions in unusual volcanic rocks. Other gemstones such as rubies, sapphires, and emeralds occur in different geological settings and thus in different countries.

Note: All figures included in descriptions on pages 68–69 are listed in metric tons.

World Mining by Region

As pioneers of large-scale industrialization, Europe and the United States dominated the mining industry in the 19th and early 20th centuries, respectively. But since World War II, mining has become truly globalized. Partly due to the depletion of easily accessible mineral deposits in Europe and North America, a diverse group of developing countries now provides much of the share of the world's minerals, with China in particular emerging as a critical supplier.

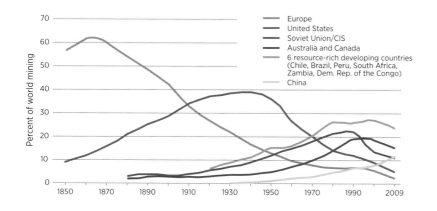

Legend:
- Europe
- United States
- Soviet Union/CIS
- Australia and Canada
- 6 resource-rich developing countries (Chile, Brazil, Peru, South Africa, Zambia, Dem. Rep. of the Congo)
- China

(y-axis: Percent of world mining; x-axis: 1850, 1870, 1890, 1910, 1930, 1950, 1970, 1990, 2009)

Environmental Stresses

LIKE ALL LIFE-FORMS ON EARTH, humans need natural systems—from deserts to forests to riverine biosystems to oceans—to thrive. Yet, through human-caused pollution and exploitation, these systems have been degraded and compromised. The negative consequences of this are already playing out and will continue to do so into the future.

Many types of environmental stresses are interrelated and have far-reaching consequences. For example, the thinning of the protective ozone layer, resulting from the release of chlorofluorocarbons (CFCs) into the atmosphere through aerosol sprays and refrigeration equipment, has already led to more ultraviolet light penetrating the atmosphere, which affects plant growth on land and in the sea and the health of humans. And in the coming decades, global warming caused by the burning of fossil fuels will likely increase water scarcity, desertification, deforestation, and sea-level increase, all of which will create significant problems for humans in both the developed and developing worlds.

Although socioeconomic indicators can reveal a great deal about long-term trends in human impact on the environment, this kind of data is not collected routinely in many countries. But the rapid conversion of countryside to built-up areas is one indicator that change is occurring at a fast pace. While scientists work to develop products and technologies with few or no adverse effects on the environment, their efforts will be nullified if humans' population and consumption of resources continue to increase.

Desertification and Land Degradation

☐ Dryland systems
■ Land degradation in drylands

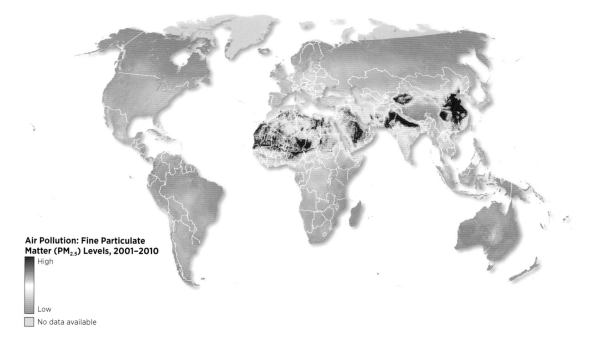

Air Pollution: Fine Particulate Matter (PM$_{2.5}$) Levels, 2001–2010

High

Low

☐ No data available

Land Degradation and Desertification

Deserts exist where rainfall is too little and too erratic to support life except in a few favored localities. Even in these "oases," occasional sandstorms may inhibit agricultural activity. In semiarid zones, lands can easily become degraded or desertlike if they are overused or subject to long or frequent drought. The Sahel of Africa faced this situation in the 1970s and early 1980s, but rainfall subsequently returned to normal, and some of the land recovered.

Often, an extended drought over a wide area can trigger desertification if the land has already been degraded by human actions. Causes of degradation include overgrazing, deforestation, overcultivation, overconsumption of groundwater, and the salinization or waterlogging of irrigated lands.

An emerging issue is the effect of climate change on desertification: Warming will probably lead to more drought in more parts of the world. As glaciers begin to disappear, the meltwater flowing through semiarid downstream areas diminishes as a consequence.

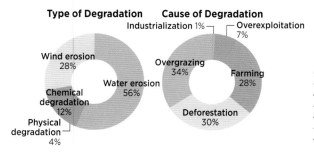

Type of Degradation

- Wind erosion 28%
- Water erosion 56%
- Chemical degradation 12%
- Physical degradation 4%

Cause of Degradation

- Industrialization 1%
- Overexploitation 7%
- Overgrazing 34%
- Farming 28%
- Deforestation 30%

Deforestation

In the latter part of the 20th century, headlines alerted the world to the crisis facing the planet's forests. International agencies and governments responded with efforts to improve the situation through education, restoration, and land protection—efforts that continue today. Yet, while the rate of deforestation is slowing, the decrease is slight: In the 1990s, forests were lost at an annual rate of about 16 million hectares (40 million acres); in the decade that followed, that rate dropped to about 13 million hectares (32 million acres) per year.

Deforestation is closely linked to climate change. Earth's forests sequester about 290 billion metric tons of carbon in their biomass; disrupting or clearing them releases carbon dioxide, a greenhouse gas (see sidebar, page 71), and other gases into the atmosphere. These emissions are significant, comprising up to a fifth of greenhouse gases. Deforestation also results in changes in rainfall patterns, soil erosion, and soil nutrient losses. The main cause of biodiversity loss is the widespread conversion of forest to agricultural use in the wet tropics, home to more than half of the world's species.

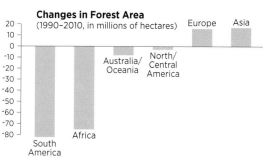

Changes in Forest Area
(1990–2010, in millions of hectares)

- South America
- Africa
- Australia/Oceania
- North/Central America
- Europe
- Asia

Pollution

In the months leading up to the 2008 Summer Olympics in Beijing, horrendous smog threatened not only residents and tourists but also athletes competing in the games. As a temporary solution, the Chinese government halted work at construction sites; closed factories, chemical plants, and mines; and kept more than a million vehicles off the roads. The number of particulates in the air dropped and the games were held, but just a few years later, a 750-mile (1,207 km) band of smog, which reached to Shanghai, was visible from space. This is more than an issue of appearances. Worldwide, 3.7 million deaths are attributed to ambient air pollution annually, and another 4.3 million deaths result from indoor air pollution.

From the contamination of groundwater to the salinization of irrigated lands in semiarid regions and the so-called chemical time bomb issue—where accumulated toxins are suddenly mobilized following a change in external conditions—examples of water and soil pollution are ubiquitous. Oceans and estuaries are also increasingly polluted. A growing problem is the creation of "dead zones" (areas of oxygen depletion), mostly due to agricultural runoff and municipal effluents. Solid and hazardous waste disposal is a universal and ever growing urban strain, and in the world's poorest countries, "garbage pickers" have become symbols of abject poverty. Increasingly, toxic wastes are being transported long distances. This introduces the risk of ocean, highway, and rail accidents, causing serious local contamination.

Addressing these and other problems requires prevention or reduction at the source. Safely disposing of and cleaning up pollution should remain strategies of last resort.

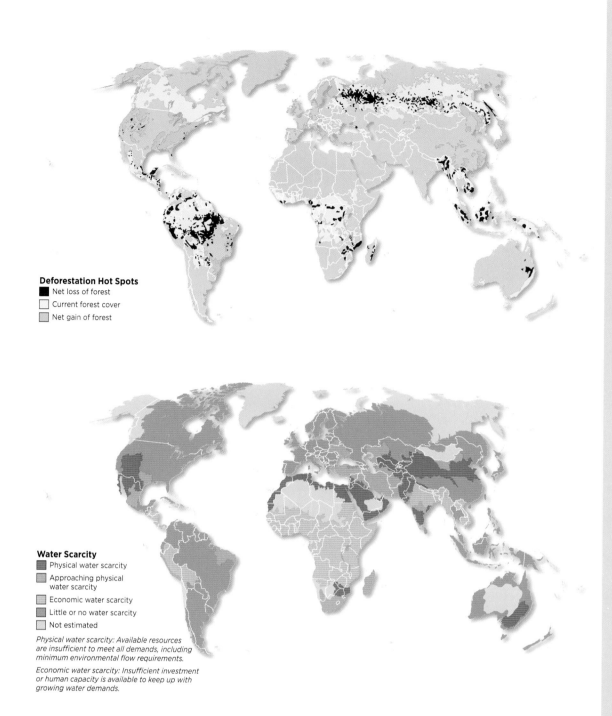

Deforestation Hot Spots
- ■ Net loss of forest
- ☐ Current forest cover
- ▨ Net gain of forest

Water Scarcity
- Physical water scarcity
- Approaching physical water scarcity
- Economic water scarcity
- Little or no water scarcity
- Not estimated

Physical water scarcity: Available resources are insufficient to meet all demands, including minimum environmental flow requirements.

Economic water scarcity: Insufficient investment or human capacity is available to keep up with growing water demands.

Water Scarcity

Shortages of drinking water are increasing in many parts of the world, and the United Nations' Global Environment Outlook (GEO-4) predicts that by 2025, if present trends continue, 1.8 billion people will be living in countries or regions with absolute water scarcity and that two-thirds of the world population could be subject to water stress.

Water is essential for health, hygiene, agriculture, power generation, industry, and transportation, as well as for maintaining healthy freshwater habitats. With increasing pressures from population growth, industrialization, higher standards of living, and climate change, the situation can only worsen. Scarcity of this critical resource will continue to be a major obstacle to economic development in many of the world's poorest regions, from Asia through Central and South America and across most of Africa.

Some countries are pumping groundwater more rapidly than it can be replaced, an activity that will lead to even greater water shortages. In river basins where water is shared among jurisdictions, political tensions are likely to increase. This is particularly so in the Middle East, North Africa, and East Africa, where the availability of freshwater is less than 1,300 cubic yards (1,000 cu m) per person per year; water-rich countries such as Iceland, New Zealand, and Canada enjoy more than a hundred times as much.

Irrigation can be a particularly wasteful use, with up to 70 percent of the water being lost through leaky pipes. In many of the world's cities, aging distribution systems are also a problem, with losses from leakages exceeding 40 percent in cities across North America and Europe.

Depletion of the Ozone Layer

The ozone layer in the stratosphere has long shielded the biosphere from harmful solar ultraviolet radiation. In the 1970s, however, the layer began thinning over Antarctica. This grew into a hole that reached its largest point in September 2006, stretching across nearly the entire area below the 60th parallel south—over 11 million square miles (28.49 million sq km). Fortunately, as a result of the 1987 Montreal Protocol—which called for discontinuing production and consumption of specific chlorine compounds that deplete ozone, including chlorofluorocarbons (CFCs)—progress is being made. From 1986 to 2008, consumption of ozone-depleting substances (ODSs) dropped 98 percent. However, it will take decades to reverse the damage caused by ODSs. The hole grew in size again in 2011 and reached the tip of South America in 2014. And because the area is still saturated in chlorine, experts say it won't really be on the path to total recovery until about 2070.

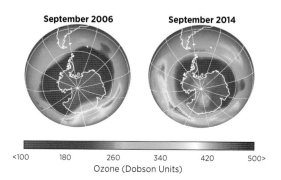

September 2006   September 2014

<100   180   260   340   420   500>
Ozone (Dobson Units)

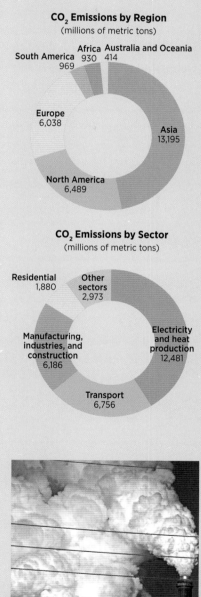

Carbon Emissions

The energy that propels modern industrial society generally comes from burning fossil fuels, which accounts for 80 percent of the extra CO_2 now in the atmosphere. Some 18 percent of the rest comes from land-use changes, primarily the cutting of tropical forests for farmland or timber. As vast tracts of forests have been felled, their vital role in carbon storage has been lost. This has created an imbalance in the carbon cycle: Plants and oceans cannot absorb all of the CO_2 in the atmosphere, and so it lingers, trapping in heat and warming the planet.

Governments need to act to cut emissions before the situation becomes irreversible. While this crisis can seem insurmountable, recent successes in ameliorating other environmental damage—such as the efforts to reduce emissions of chemicals that cause acid rain and deplete ozone—suggest we can work to mitigate climate change.

CO_2 Emissions by Region
(millions of metric tons)

- South America 969
- Africa 930
- Australia and Oceania 414
- Europe 6,038
- Asia 13,195
- North America 6,489

CO_2 Emissions by Sector
(millions of metric tons)

- Residential 1,880
- Other sectors 2,973
- Manufacturing, industries, and construction 6,186
- Electricity and heat production 12,481
- Transport 6,756

Smokestacks of a coal-fired power plant in Kentucky, U.S.A., belch CO_2 into the atmosphere. Such emissions are a major cause of global warming, acid rain, and smog.

Protected Areas

THERE ARE MORE THAN 210,000 protected areas around the globe—on every continent and in every ocean. Some preserve exotic landscapes with rare and imperiled plants and animals; some protect whole ecosystems; some supply natural resources; some offer valuable spiritual, scientific, educational, or recreational opportunities; and some serve as buffer zones for neighboring ecosystems or provide migration corridors for wildlife. Together, these areas are thought to store at least 15 percent of the planet's terrestrial carbon in their soils and plant life.

The International Union for Conservation of Nature (IUCN) evaluates the world's protected areas and places them in seven categories, based on how they are managed and what limits they set on human encroachment. Most restricted are the strict nature reserves, followed by wilderness areas, national parks, national monuments, habitat- and species-management areas, protected landscape/seascapes, and managed resource protection areas.

Local, national, and international governments collaborate with a wide range of environmental agencies to provide protection to these areas. Agencies like WWF (World Wildlife Fund), the Nature Conservancy, and Conservation International work with one another, local shareholders and officials, national agencies, and international organizations like the United Nations to ensure the preservation of environmental and cultural treasures as well as the livelihoods and traditions of local peoples.

PROTECTED AREAS
An array of overlapping conventions designed to preserve everything from wetlands, seas, and wilderness to birds and biogenetic reserves protects approximately 15.4 percent of Earth's land area. In contrast, 3.4 percent of the total ocean area is protected.

Northeast Greenland National Park is the largest terrestrial protected area in the world. At 375,300 square miles (972,000 sq km), it is 77 times larger than Yellowstone. It provides plenty of space for climate change–induced species migration and habitat adaptation.

In 2009, the Canadian government spent $800 million (U.S. $760 million) on parks. Parks in turn contribute $4.6 billion (U.S. $4.4 billion) in revenue.

The U.S. National Park Service reports $14.6 billion in tourism revenue annually—$3.6 million from visits to Yellowstone National Park.

"High seas" (areas falling outside the jurisdiction of any single country) comprise the largest proportion of the global ocean (85 million sq mi/220 million sq km) and the least protected (0.25 percent). Charlie-Gibbs Marine Protected Area is the largest high seas MPA.

Islands represent 5 percent of the world's landmass, but are home to 40 percent of endangered species. Eight Caribbean Small Island Developing States are protecting 20 percent or more of their landmass.

Rain forest plants like those explicitly protected by the Alto Orito Indi-Angue Sanctuary in Colombia contribute to billions of dollars in plant-based pharmaceuticals.

NORTH AMERICA

SOUTH AMERICA

Notes related to climate change
Notes related to health
Notes related to economic impacts
Notes related to marine protected areas

Protected areas larger than 10,000 hectares (24,700 acres)

World Heritage Sites

The World Heritage List was established under the terms of the 1972 UNESCO "Convention Concerning the Protection of the World Cultural and Natural Heritage."

The first 12 World Heritage Sites were named in 1978; among them were L'Anse aux Meadows in Canada, the site of the first Viking settlement in North America; the Galápagos Islands; the cathedral of Aachen, Germany; the historic city center of Kraków, Poland; the island of Gorée, off Senegal; and Mesa Verde and Yellowstone National Parks in the United States.

New sites are added annually. At the time of publication, the list comprised 1,007 sites, with 779 cultural, 197 natural, and 31 mixed sites, located in 161 countries. On average, 30 newly designated sites are added to the list each year, but 2000 must have been considered an auspicious year for listings; 61 sites were added that year, the largest number ever.

World Heritage Sites
- Cultural
- Natural
- Mixed site (site with both cultural and natural value)

The global protected area network stores 15 percent of the world's terrestrial carbon stocks. Europe's Natura 2000 network alone stores 9.6 billion metric tons of carbon.

E U R O P E

A S I A

Protected areas like Ruteng Park, Indonesia, keep air and water clean and reduce the passage of disease vectors. Those living in close proximity to Ruteng experience relatively few instances of tropical disease.

A F R I C A

The transmission of zoonotic diseases, like Ebola, is prevented through environmental education programs operating in and around protected areas that discourage consumption and trade of bush meat.

In Rwanda, tourism revenue from visits to see mountain gorillas in Volcanoes National Park is the country's largest source of foreign exchange, raising $200 million (U.S.) annually.

The Pacific Oceanscape Initiative constitutes the world's largest protected oceanscape (1 million sq mi /2.6 million sq km)— including the Natural Park of the Coral Sea, the world's largest protected area. The initiative aims to conserve 10 percent of the oceans.

A U S T R A L I A

About half of the human population lives in coastal zones. Australia's Marine Reserve network promotes the sustainable use of resources while protecting marine and coastal biodiversity.

A N T A R C T I C A

Endemism

Regional Share of Plant Endemism

- South America 24%
- Africa 10%
- North America 17%
- Europe 2%
- Australia/ Oceania 12%
- Asia 35%

The presence of species found nowhere else—known as endemism—is a key criterion for determining conservation priorities, as areas with high levels of endemism are the most vulnerable to biodiversity loss. The highest levels of endemism occur on oceanic islands and in montane regions.

Growth in Nationally Designated Protected Areas, 1990–2014 (in km²)

- Cumulative total area
- Cumulative terrestrial area
- Cumulative marine area

30 million
20 million
10 million
0

1990   1994   1998   2002   2006   2010   2014

Year

World Heritage Site Categories

NATURAL HERITAGE SITE
Canada's Tatshenshini-Alsek Provincial Wilderness holds a portion of the largest nonpolar ice cap and hundreds of valley glaciers; it is the last major stronghold for North America's grizzly bears. The park designation averted what would have been an enormous open-pit mine.

CULTURAL HERITAGE SITE
Site of some of the most important monuments of ancient Greece, the Acropolis illustrates the civilizations, myths, and religions that flourished there for a period of over a thousand years. Europe claims about half of the world's cultural heritage sites, with more than 300.

MIXED HERITAGE SITE
The town of Ohrid, on the shores of Lake Ohrid in the former Yugoslav Republic of Macedonia, exemplifies a mixed heritage site. The ten-million-year-old lake may be the oldest in Europe, and the town is one of the continent's oldest continuously inhabited sites.

Globalization

ON SOME LEVEL, GLOBALIZATION, like migration, has been a perpetual human trend, historically accomplished through trade. But in the postmodern world, interdependence among humans and cultures over vast distances has accelerated—not just in the economic realm, but also through person-to-person contact, technological connectivity, and political ties. Globalization indices, like the one from the KOF Swiss Economic Institute reflected in the map data here, measure the dimensions of globalization by looking at it country by country and also worldwide through three lenses: political, social, and economic. In the political sphere, the level of cooperation among countries drives the index results; in the economic, real trade and investment volumes are measured, as are trade restrictions; and in the social, the free flow of information and ideas is tracked.

Not surprisingly, the worldwide economic downturn in 2009 slowed the pace of globalization in that sector and somewhat in the social sector. Ireland edges out Belgium, the Netherlands, and Austria at the top of the KOF overall list of most globalized countries, while war-torn Somalia lands at the bottom of the list. Singapore proves to be the most economically and socially globalized country; France heads the list in political globalization. In recent years, Eastern Europe and South and Central Asia have been the regions with the strongest upward trends in globalization. Rankings for countries that experienced some destabilization in the wake of events known collectively as the Arab Spring dropped considerably.

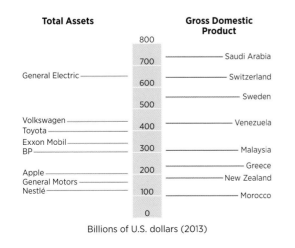

Left: Ibn Battuta Mall, Dubai. One of the United Arab Emirates, Dubai is highly globalized, thanks to long-standing policies that encourage foreign investment. Right: Call center, Philippines. Recently, the Philippines has joined India as a major player in the burgeoning offshore call-center industry.

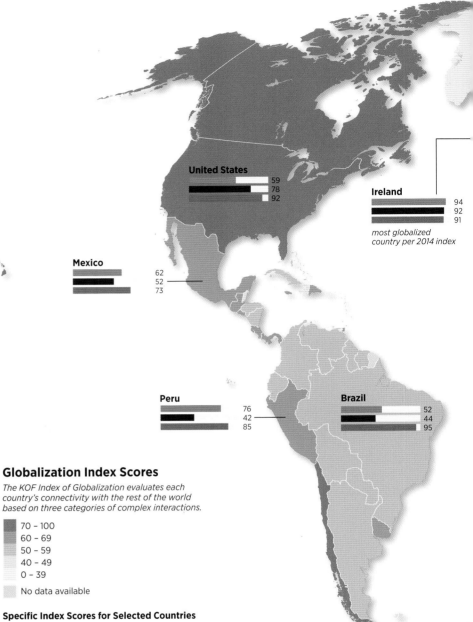

United States
59
78
92

Ireland
94
92
91
most globalized country per 2014 index

Mexico
62
52
73

Peru
76
42
85

Brazil
52
44
95

Globalization Index Scores

The KOF Index of Globalization evaluates each country's connectivity with the rest of the world based on three categories of complex interactions.

- 70 – 100
- 60 – 69
- 50 – 59
- 40 – 49
- 0 – 39
- No data available

Specific Index Scores for Selected Countries

- Economic Globalization
- Social Globalization
- Political Globalization

Transnational Corporations

Transnational corporations have played an important role in global economic integration through sales, investments, and operations in countries around the world. In fact, a number of them have assets equivalent to or larger than the nominal GDPs of some countries. Many of these companies have also made their non-economic influence felt as their products and services shape consumption habits, business practices, and local cultures. These changes, often a type of Westernization, aren't always welcome.

Total Assets		Gross Domestic Product
	800	
	700	Saudi Arabia
General Electric	600	Switzerland
		Sweden
	500	
Volkswagen	400	Venezuela
Toyota		
Exxon Mobil	300	
BP		Malaysia
	200	Greece
Apple		New Zealand
General Motors	100	
Nestlé		Morocco
	0	

Billions of U.S. dollars (2013)

Economic Globalization

Evidence of the global marketplace is ubiquitous, from international food items on grocery store shelves, to clothing tags identifying foreign-made items, to headlines about companies relocating to countries deemed more business friendly. The concept of economic globalization is not new—consider the ancient spice trade, for example—but its reach is unprecedented. The KOF index considers both the actual flow of capital, goods, and services and restrictions such as tariffs, duties, and taxes.

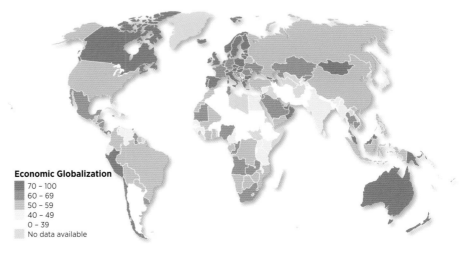

Economic Globalization
- 70 – 100
- 60 – 69
- 50 – 59
- 40 – 49
- 0 – 39
- No data available

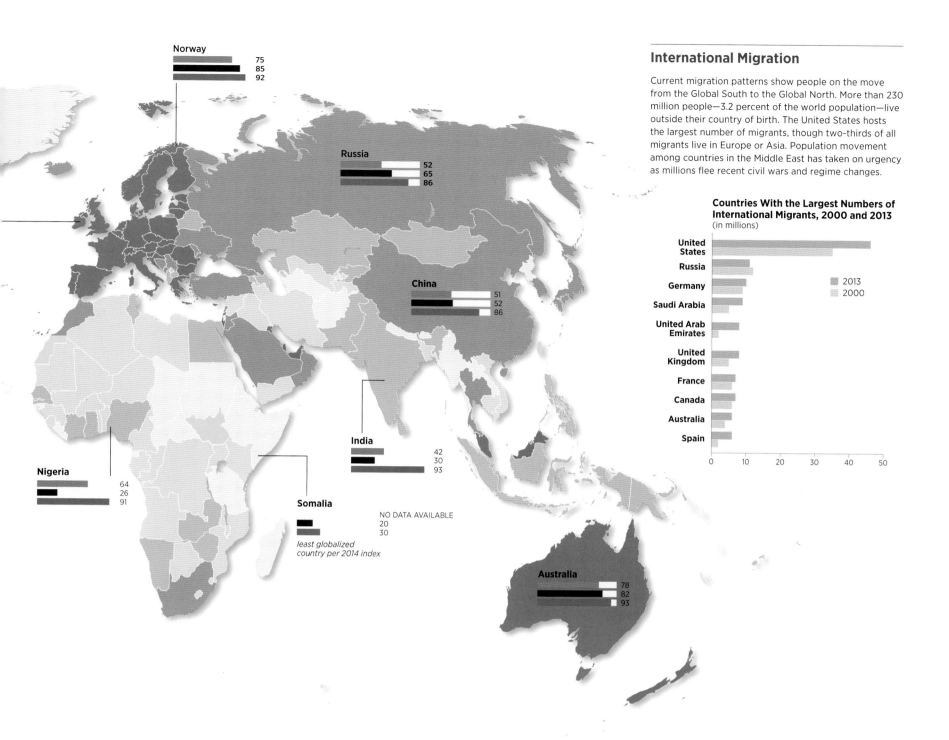

Norway
75
85
92

Russia
52
65
86

China
51
52
86

India
42
30
93

Nigeria
64
26
91

Somalia
NO DATA AVAILABLE
20
30
least globalized country per 2014 index

Australia
78
82
93

International Migration

Current migration patterns show people on the move from the Global South to the Global North. More than 230 million people—3.2 percent of the world population—live outside their country of birth. The United States hosts the largest number of migrants, though two-thirds of all migrants live in Europe or Asia. Population movement among countries in the Middle East has taken on urgency as millions flee recent civil wars and regime changes.

Countries With the Largest Numbers of International Migrants, 2000 and 2013
(in millions)

United States
Russia
Germany
Saudi Arabia
United Arab Emirates
United Kingdom
France
Canada
Australia
Spain

2013
2000

0   10   20   30   40   50

Social Globalization

The seemingly intangible issue of social globalization is evaluated by collecting data on personal contact, information flows, and cultural proximity. The first set of data considers factors such as migration, tourism, and correspondence. Access to television and the Internet and the importing and exporting of newspapers indicate openness to information. When evaluating cultural exchange, foreign book exchange is considered alongside the presence of Ikea stores and McDonald's restaurants.

Social Globalization
70 – 100
60 – 69
50 – 59
40 – 49
0 – 39
No data available

Political Globalization

As countries, cultures, and companies exchange commercial goods and cultural effects, political values are spread as well—regardless of whether such a transmission is intentional or welcome. A government's openness to others' policies is determined by how many foreign embassies it hosts, whether it is a member of international organizations, its participation in United Nations Security Council missions, and the treaties it has signed and ratified. Small island countries are often the most isolated.

Political Globalization
70 – 100
60 – 69
50 – 59
40 – 49
0 – 39
No data available

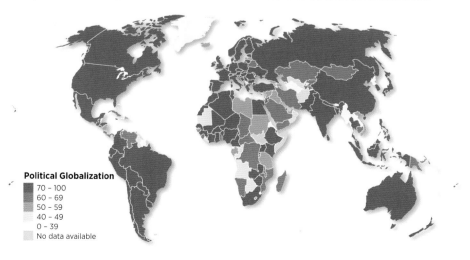

Digital Connectivity

IN THE PAST DECADE, TECHNOLOGICAL ADVANCES have changed the face of communication—and with it everything from geopolitics to finance to health care. For the first time in human history, enormous amounts of data can be shared almost instantaneously across the planet, connecting people and cultures in ways that would have been unimaginable less than a quarter century ago. Voice and Internet communications penetrate virtually every corner of the globe, thanks in large part to the fiber-optic cables, cell-phone towers, and satellites that link humans in ways that copper-wire connectivity never could have. And with increasingly less reliance on infrastructure—poles or cable lines—the latest technologies allow residents in remote areas and developing countries access to global information and the global dialogue in unprecedented ways, fueling business, educational opportunities, and political change.

The speed of these new modes of interacting is at least metaphorically matched by the speed of innovations in the field of global communications and by a new kind of "war"—cyber war. Nations, businesses, and individuals who lead much of their lives online grapple with their vulnerability to hackers, as well as to weather-related interruptions and system breakdowns. Still, from international stock traders to microbusiness owners to citizen journalists broadcasting breaking news from their cell phones, most people will accept these risks in order to be part of the Internet-created global village—a virtual world where distance and time no longer limit human potential.

Left: A specially designed pipe system facilitates the laying of fiber-optic cable in Germany.
Right: A Vietnamese couple reflects the growing reliance on cell phones among young people.

Booming Mobile-Cellular Subscriptions

As the number of traditional telephone lines declines, cell-phone subscriptions are booming. In many developing nations, installing cell-phone towers and selling cell phones with relatively cheap minutes is the most feasible way to bring telecommunications to people. Among developed countries, many nations have more than 100 subscriptions per 100 people. Many people have multiple cell phones and numbers, with some used personally and others for business.

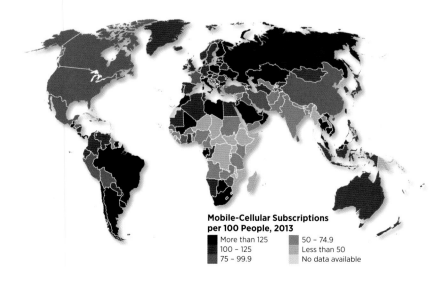

Mobile-Cellular Subscriptions per 100 People, 2013

- More than 125
- 100 – 125
- 75 – 99.9
- 50 – 74.9
- Less than 50
- No data available

U.S. & Canada 3% — Africa 2%
Asia & Pacific 9% — Europe 86%

Africa
571 Gigabits per second

Africa
Europe 26%
U.S. & Canada 44%
Asia & Pacific 30%

Asia & Pacific
9,571 Gigabits per second

Growth in Internet Bandwidth

International Internet bandwidth by region (Gbps)

- Africa
- Latin America & Caribbean
- Asia & Pacific
- U.S. & Canada
- Europe

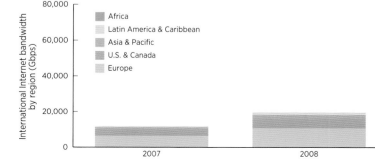

80,000
60,000
40,000
20,000
0

2007   2008

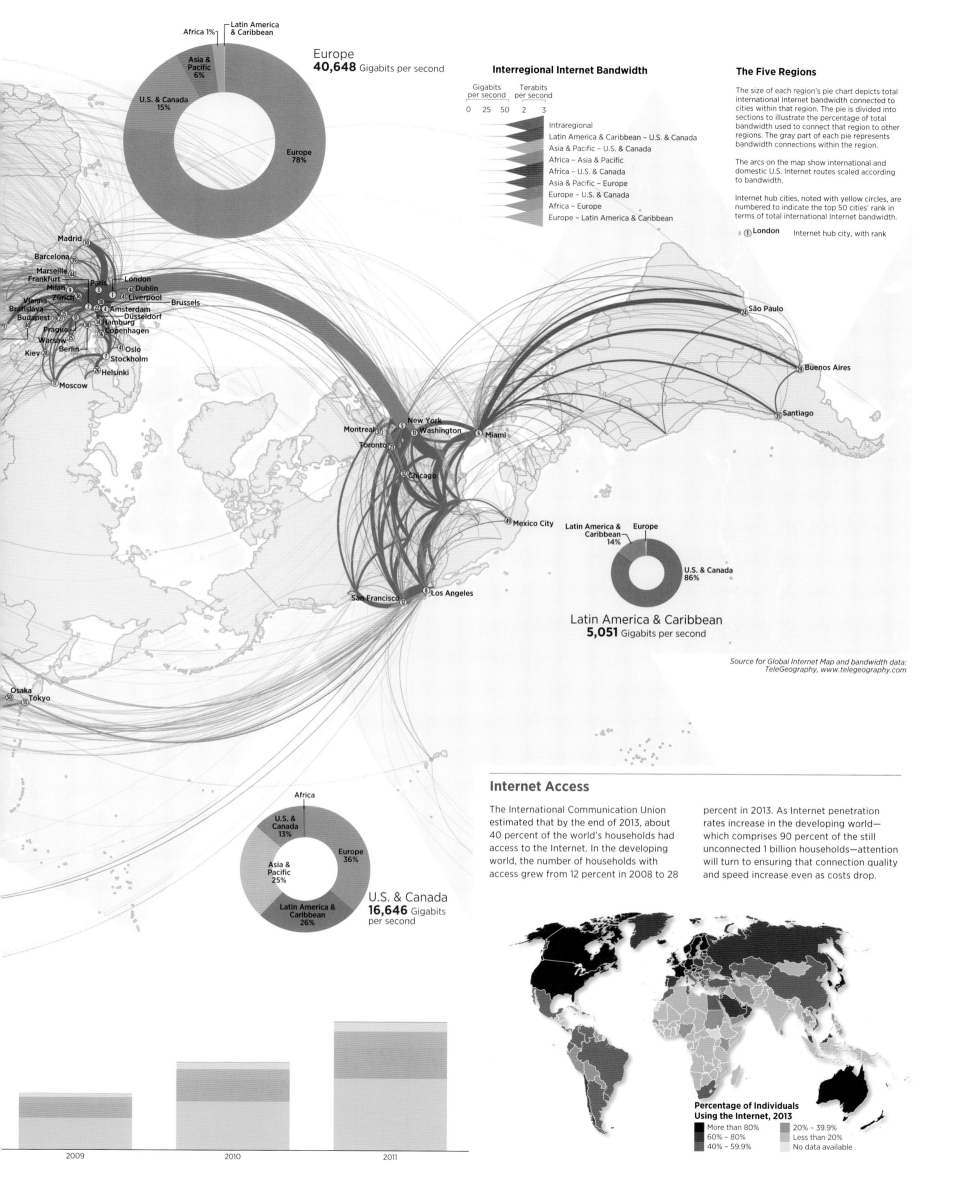

Africa 1%

Latin America & Caribbean

Asia & Pacific 6%

U.S. & Canada 15%

Europe
40,648 Gigabits per second

Europe 78%

Interregional Internet Bandwidth

Gigabits per second   Terabits per second
0   25 50   2   3

Intraregional
Latin America & Caribbean – U.S. & Canada
Asia & Pacific – U.S. & Canada
Africa – Asia & Pacific
Africa – U.S. & Canada
Asia & Pacific – Europe
Europe – U.S. & Canada
Africa – Europe
Europe – Latin America & Caribbean

The Five Regions

The size of each region's pie chart depicts total international Internet bandwidth connected to cities within that region. The pie is divided into sections to illustrate the percentage of total bandwidth used to connect that region to other regions. The gray part of each pie represents bandwidth connections within the region.

The arcs on the map show international and domestic U.S. Internet routes scaled according to bandwidth.

Internet hub cities, noted with yellow circles, are numbered to indicate the top 50 cities' rank in terms of total international Internet bandwidth.

① London   Internet hub city, with rank

Madrid ⑩
Barcelona ㉛
Marseille ㊹
Frankfurt ②
Milan ⑨
Zürich ㊱
Paris ③
London ①
Dublin ㊽
Liverpool ㊸
Brussels
Vienna ㉚
Bratislava
Budapest ⑯ ㊲
Amsterdam ㉒
Düsseldorf ⑭
Hamburg
Copenhagen ⑤
Prague ㉓
Warsaw
Berlin
Oslo ㊶
Stockholm ⑦
Kiev ㉘
Helsinki ㉖
Moscow ⑰
①
㊵

São Paulo ㉔
Buenos Aires ㉙
Santiago

Montreal ㊲
New York ⑤
Toronto ㉕
Washington ⑪
Miami ⑥
Chicago ㉜
Mexico City ㊽
San Francisco ⑫
Los Angeles ⑧

Osaka ㊿
Tokyo ⑮

Latin America & Caribbean 14%

Europe

U.S. & Canada 86%

Latin America & Caribbean
5,051 Gigabits per second

Source for Global Internet Map and bandwidth data:
TeleGeography, www.telegeography.com

Internet Access

The International Communication Union estimated that by the end of 2013, about 40 percent of the world's households had access to the Internet. In the developing world, the number of households with access grew from 12 percent in 2008 to 28 percent in 2013. As Internet penetration rates increase in the developing world—which comprises 90 percent of the still unconnected 1 billion households—attention will turn to ensuring that connection quality and speed increase even as costs drop.

Africa

U.S. & Canada 13%

Asia & Pacific 25%

Europe 36%

Latin America & Caribbean 26%

U.S. & Canada
16,646 Gigabits per second

2009   2010   2011

Percentage of Individuals Using the Internet, 2013
- More than 80%
- 60% – 80%
- 40% – 59.9%
- 20% – 39.9%
- Less than 20%
- No data available

Millions of years of sculpting by wind, rain, snow, heat, cold, and the Colorado River have made the Grand Canyon one of North America's natural icons.

North America

North America is both incredibly old, geologically speaking, and relatively young, when viewed in terms of its human history.

About 200 million years ago, North America separated from Africa and South America when the supercontinent Pangaea began to break apart. For a while, it was attached to Europe, but in time that connection was broken, and the North American landmass began assuming roughly its current shape and size. Meanwhile, the other continents were still separating from one another and jockeying for their new positions across the face of the Earth.

Some of the oldest stones in the world are found in North America. Dating from nearly four billion years ago, they form the stout underbelly of Canada's frozen tundra. In the east, an ancient mountain system—the Appalachians—runs from the southern United States into Canada. But not everything is so deeply ancient: North America's human history is somewhere

North America

between 14,000 and 24,000 years old, while that of Africa, the birthplace of humankind, dates back 200,000 years or more. Just in the past couple of centuries, North America has experienced dramatic changes in its population, landscapes, and environment, an incredible transformation brought about by waves of immigration, booming economies, and relentless development.

PHYSICAL GEOGRAPHY From the world's largest island (Greenland) and greatest concentration of freshwater (the Great Lakes) to such spectacular features as the Grand Canyon and Niagara Falls, North America holds a wealth of superlatives. It is also home to Earth's largest and tallest trees (the sequoias and redwoods of California) and many of its biggest animals (grizzly bears, moose, and bison). The continent is known as well for dramatic extremes of climate—from the sauna-like 134°F (57°C) recorded in California's Death Valley to the brutally cold minus 87°F (-66°C) logged on Greenland's windswept ice cap.

Third largest of the continents, after Asia and Africa, North America encompasses 9.45 million square miles (24.5 million sq km); its northernmost tip is in Greenland (Kaffeklubben Island) and its southernmost point is in Panama (Península de Azuero).

Deeply indented with inlets and bays, North America claims the longest coastline in the western hemisphere. Its land is surrounded by vast oceans and sizable seas: the Atlantic in the east, the Pacific in the west, the Arctic in the north, and the Gulf of Mexico and Caribbean Sea in the south. This geographic circumstance kept the continent isolated for millions of years, greatly influencing the development of its flora and fauna, as well as its human history. Into North America's coastal waters pour a number of mighty rivers, including the Saint Lawrence, Rio Grande, Yukon, Columbia, and Mississippi.

Three significant geologic features dominate the continental landmass: the Canadian (Laurentian) Shield; the great Western Cordillera, which includes the Rocky Mountains, Sierra Nevada, and Sierra Madre; and a colossal flatland that embraces the Great Plains, the Mississippi-Missouri River basin, and most of the Great Lakes region. Other major components include the ancient Appalachian Mountains and the predominantly volcanic islands of the Caribbean Sea. The continent peaks out at 20,320 feet (6,194 m) on the summit of Alaska's Mount McKinley (Denali), and drops to 282 feet (86 m) below sea level in Death Valley.

The climates of North America range from the frigid conditions of the Arctic ice cap to the steamy tropics of Central America (considered part of North America) and the Caribbean; in between are variations of dry, mild, and continental climes.

The continent has an equally diverse biological heritage, ranging from seemingly endless tundra and coniferous forests in the north to vast deserts and dense rain forests in the south. North America once held huge herds of bison, antelope, elk, and other large wildlife, but such populations declined as the human population grew and spread across the continent.

HISTORY Although the exact date will probably never be determined, North America's human history began sometime between 14,000 and 24,000 years ago, when Asiatic nomads crossed the Bering Strait into Alaska. The descendants of these people spread throughout the continent, evolving into distinct tribes with their own lifestyles and more than 400 different languages.

Most of these original Americans were still hunting and gathering

when Europeans arrived in North America; however, several groups had already developed sophisticated cultures. By 1200 B.C., the Olmec of Mexico had created what is generally deemed the first "civilization" in the Western Hemisphere; theirs was a highly advanced society with a calendar, writing system, and stonework architecture. The Maya civilization, which spread through Mexico and Central America, reached an apex around A.D. 700 with the creation of an elaborate religion and sprawling temple cities. In central Mexico, the highly militaristic Toltec and Aztec forged regional empires that drew cultural inspiration from both the Olmec and Maya.

One of the most significant moments for North America—indeed, it was among the most influential events in world history—came in 1492, when a Spanish expedition under Christopher Columbus set foot on an island in the Bahamas. This initial landing ushered in an era of European exploration and settlement that would alter the social fabric of the entire continent. In the next few decades, Hernán Cortés vanquished the Aztec, and Spain claimed virtually the whole Caribbean region and Central America. Other Europeans soon followed—English, French, Germans, Dutch, Russians, and Scandinavians—the leading edge of a migration that would become one of the greatest in human history (more than 70 million people and still counting).

The Native American cultures were unable to compete: They were plagued by European diseases, against which they had little or no resistance; unable to counter the superior firepower of the invaders; and relentlessly driven from their lands. The continent's rich tribal mosaic gradually melted away, replaced by myriad European colonies. By the end of the 19th century, these colonies had been superseded by independent countries such as Canada, Mexico, and the United States. Since 1960, many of the Caribbean isles have gained independence, yet quite a few remain under the British, French, Dutch, and U.S. flags.

During the past century, both the U.S. and Canada have propelled themselves into the ranks of the world's richest nations. But the rest of the continent has failed to keep pace, plagued by poverty, despotic governments, and social unrest. In the decades since World War II, many of the Spanish-speaking nations—Cuba, the Dominican Republic, Nicaragua, El Salvador, and Guatemala—have been racked by bloody conflicts. The U.S., on the other hand, ended the 20th century as the only remaining superpower, with a military presence and political, economic, and cultural influences that extend around the globe.

CULTURE North America's cultural landscape has changed profoundly over the past 500 years. Before the 16th century, the continent was fragmented into hundreds of different cultures developed along tribal lines. From the Inuit people of the Arctic to the Cuña Indians of the Panama jungle, a majority of North America's people had barely risen above Stone Age cultural levels. Noteworthy exceptions included the great civilizations of Mexico and Central America, the Pueblo builders of the southwestern U.S., and the highly organized cultivators of the Great Lakes region and the Mississippi Valley. But for the most part, the

average North American was migratory, had no concept of written language, and used stone or wooden tools.

The arrival of the Europeans brought permanent settlements, metal tools (and weapons), horses, and written languages to the continent. The newcomers founded towns based on Old World models, some of which would evolve into world-class cities—New York, Los Angeles, Toronto, and Mexico City among them. Native tongues gave way to a trio of European languages—English, Spanish, and French—now spoken by most of North America's 561 million people. And ancient beliefs yielded to new religions, like Roman Catholicism and Protestantism, which now dominate the continent's spiritual life. The Europeans also brought ideas—concepts like democracy, capitalism, religious choice, and free speech—that continue to shape political, intellectual, and economic life.

Despite common historical threads, the coat that comprises today's North America is one of many colors. Mexico and Central America are dominated by Hispano-Indian culture and tend to have more in common with South America than with their neighbors north of the Río Bravo del Norte (known in the U.S. as the Rio Grande). Although Anglo-Saxon ways are still clearly evident in the U.S. and Canada, a surge of immigrants from Latin America, Africa, Asia, the Middle East, and the Pacific islands has introduced new cultural traditions. From the Rastafarians of Jamaica to the Creoles of Martinique, the Caribbean islands have fostered myriad microcultures that blend European, African, Native American, and Latin traditions.

ECONOMY When it comes to business and industry, North America—and especially the U.S.—is the envy of much of the world. No other continent produces such an abundance of merchandise or profusion of crops, and no other major region comes close to North America's per capita resource and product consumption. From the high-tech citadels of Silicon Valley to the dream factories of Hollywood, the continent is a world leader in dozens of fields and industries, including computers, entertainment, aerospace, finance, medicine, defense, and agriculture.

The quest for monetary and material success can be traced as far back as the early European immigrants, who saw a land of seemingly limitless resources and unprecedented individual opportunity. Those people, and their cultural descendants, sought to improve their standard of living by exploiting the natural wealth of the land. By the end of the 19th century, North America's forests, minerals, and farmlands had stoked an industrial revolution that had moved the U.S. into the ranks of the richest and most powerful nations. The continent continues to enjoy an abundance of natural resources: expansive agricultural lands; huge coal deposits in the western plains and the Appalachian and Rocky Mountains; with vast petroleum reserves in Alaska, around the Gulf of Mexico, in the Alberta oil sands, and in shale rock, where petroleum—and natural gas—are now accessible through the process of hydraulic fracturing (generally called "fracking").

But North America's most important commodity has always been ideas—the ability of its inhabitants to imagine. Next is the ability to transform those ideas into reality through experimentation and hard work. Many of the innovations that revolutionized modern life—the telephone, electric lighting, motor vehicles, airplanes, computers, shopping malls, television, the Internet, smartphones, and tablets—were either invented or first mass-produced in the U.S.

The ruins of temples, plazas, palaces, and ball courts still stand amid the rain forests of Guatemala's Petén region, marking the site of the once great Maya center of Tikal (top). From its early beginnings as a small village (900–300 B.C.), Tikal grew to house some 50,000 people at its peak (A.D. 600–800). Scholars now believe environmental degradation, overpopulation, and warfare were among the factors that led to the collapse of the mighty Maya. A more sudden form of collapse—from terrorism—changed the skyline of the great modern metropolis of New York on 9/11/2001, when the Twin Towers of the World Trade Center were attacked and destroyed. By 2014, a new monument to endurance—One World Trade Center, tallest building in the Western Hemisphere—had risen in their place (above).

Globalization has spread U.S. goods—and by extension, American ideas and culture—around the planet. This has been facilitated recently by technological innovations in communication and the loosening of trade barriers. The creation of the North American Free Trade Association (NAFTA) in 1994 solidified economic bonds among the continent's three largest countries—the U.S., Canada, and Mexico. But economic successes have brought a host of concerns, not the least of which involves the continued exploitation of natural resources. North America is home to only roughly 8 percent of the planet's people, yet its per capita consumption of energy (most of it by Canada and the U.S.) is more than three times as great as the average for all other continents. Its appetite for timber, metals, and water resources is just as voracious.

Other parts of the continent continue to lag in terms of economic vitality. Most Caribbean nations—along with Costa Rica and Belize—now rely on the tourist industry to generate the bulk of their gross domestic product, while most Central American countries continue to bank on agricultural commodities such as bananas and coffee. Poverty has spurred millions of Mexicans, Central Americans, and Caribbean islanders to migrate northward (legally and illegally) in search of better lives. Finding ways to integrate these disenfranchised people into the continent's economic fabric is one of the greatest challenges facing North America in the 21st century.

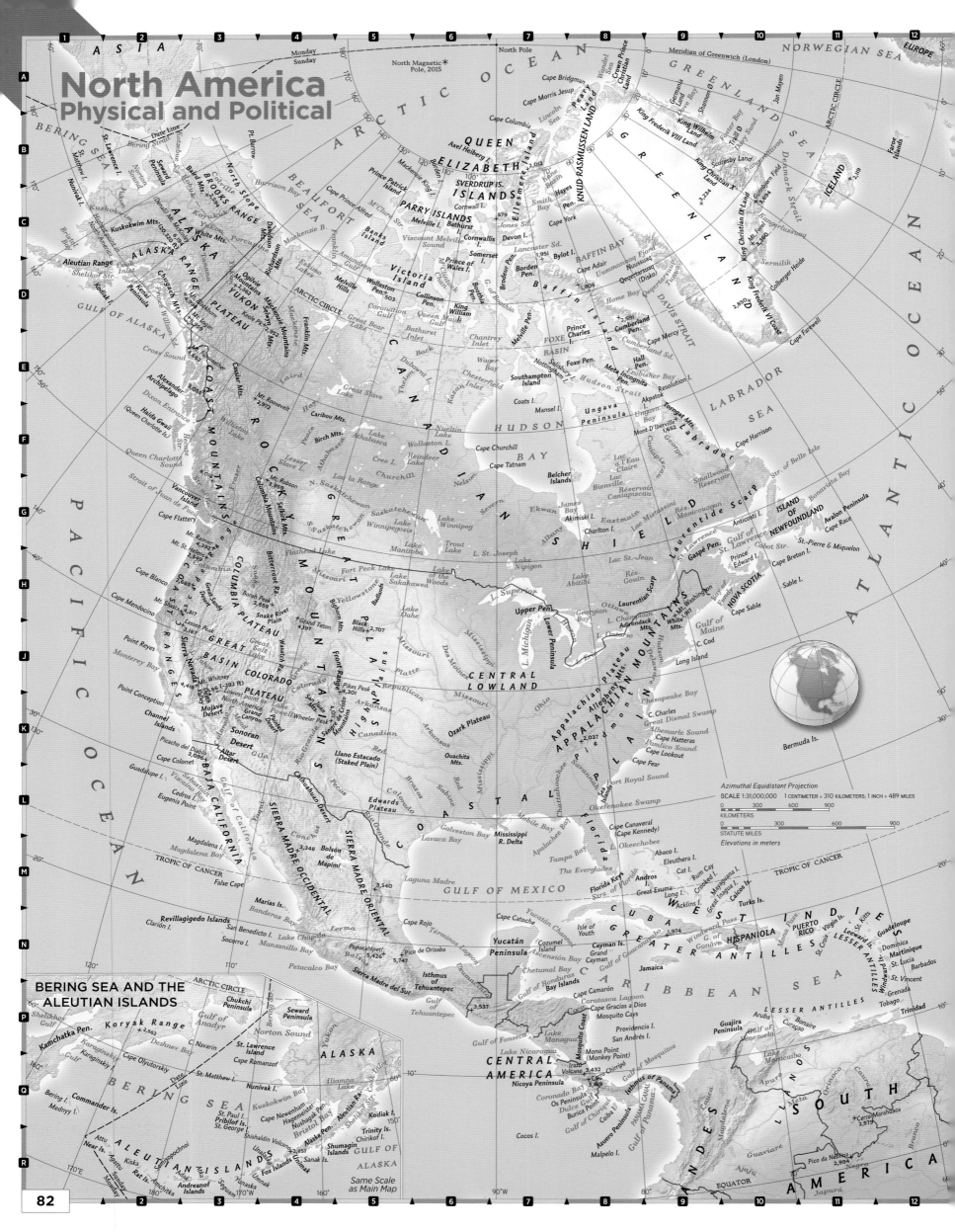

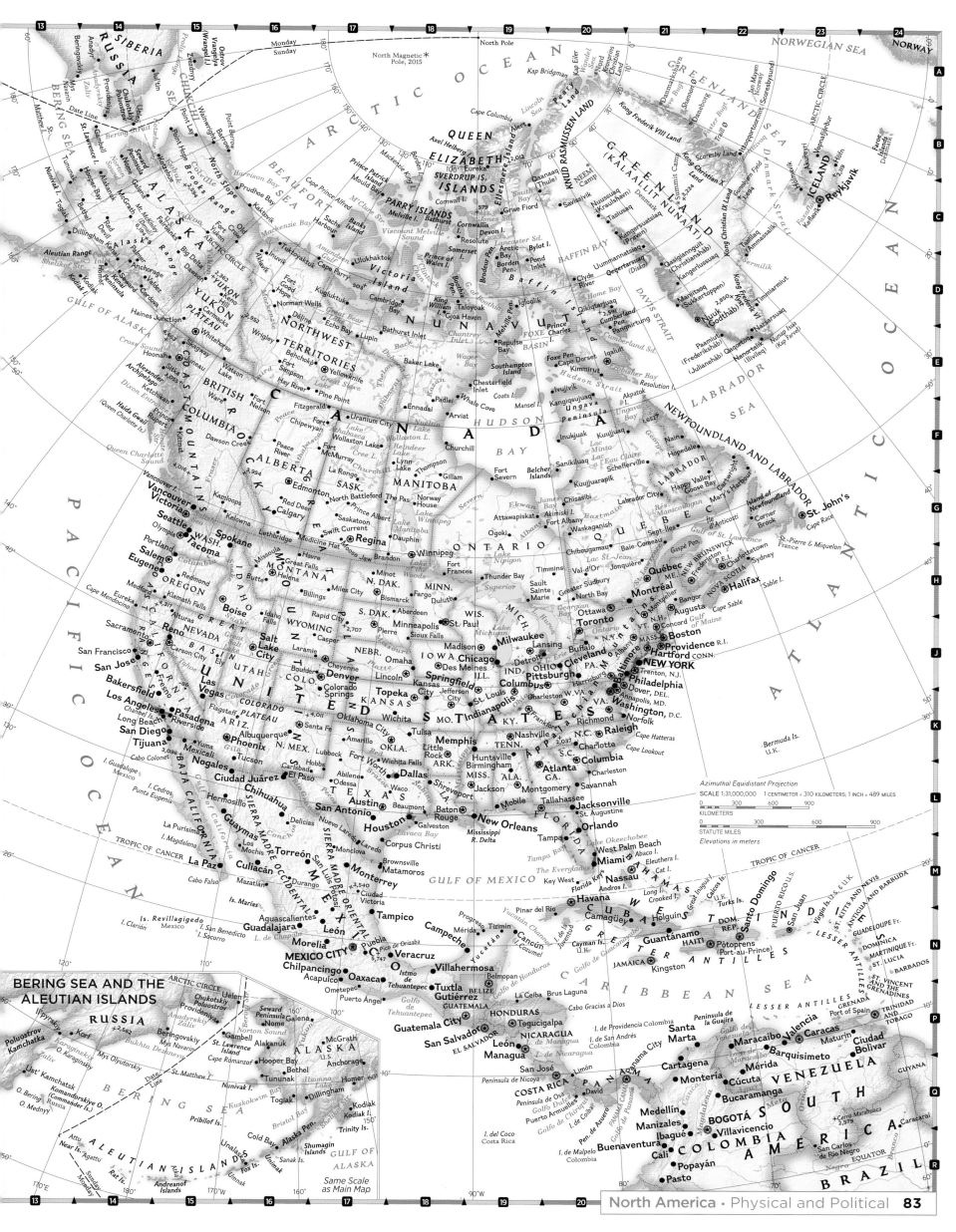

Canada

Temperature and Precipitation

Average Annual Precipitation

Over 80 inches	Over 200 cm
55–80 inches	140–200 cm
40–54 inches	100–139 cm
25–39 inches	60–99 cm
8–24 inches	20–49 cm
Under 8 inches	Under 20 cm

Resolute (-26°/40°)
Inuvik (-20°/57°)
Cambridge Bay (-28°/46°)
Whitehorse (-1°/57°)
Yellowknife (-18°/61°)
Iqaluit (-15°/46°)
C A N A D A
Edmonton (7°/62°)
Churchill (-17°/54°)
Victoria (40°/60°)
Vancouver (37°/63°)
Calgary (14°/62°)
Winnipeg (-2°/67°)
Sept-Îles (6°/59°)
St. John's (24°/59°)
Québec (10°/67°)
Ottawa (12°/69°)
Halifax (22°/65°)
Thunder Bay (5°/64°)
Montréal (15°/70°)
St.-Pierre and Miquelon Fr.
Toronto (23°/70°)

Average Monthly Temperatures (F)

(January/July)

Population

People per Square Mile	People per Square Km
Over 500	Over 195
50–500	20–195
10–49	5–19
1–9	1–4
Under 1	Under 1

C A N A D A

Vancouver
Edmonton
Calgary
Winnipeg
Québec
Ottawa
Montréal
Toronto
Hamilton
St.-Pierre and Miquelon Fr.

Urban Area Population
- ■ 5 million and greater
- ▲ 1 million–4,999,999
- ● 750,000–999,999
- ○ 500,000–749,999

Land Use

Predominant Land Use and Land Cover Classes
- Grassland
- Woodland
- Forest
- Mixed-use, including crops
- Cropland
- Wetland
- Desert, barren land
- Ice, cold desert, tundra
- Urban agglomeration

C A N A D A

St.-Pierre and Miquelon Fr.

Canada
CANADA

AREA	9,984,670 sq km (3,855,103 sq mi)
POPULATION	34,835,000
CAPITAL	Ottawa 1,306,000
RELIGION	Roman Catholic, Protestant
LANGUAGE	English, French
LITERACY	99%
LIFE EXPECTANCY	82 years
GDP PER CAPITA	$43,100
ECONOMY	IND: transportation equipment, chemicals, processed and unprocessed minerals AGR: wheat, barley, oilseed, tobacco, fruits; dairy products; fish EXP: petroleum, natural gas, motor vehicles and parts, industrial machinery, aircraft, gold, lumber

Greenland (Denmark)

SOVEREIGN   LOCAL

GREENLAND

AREA	2,166,086 sq km (836,330 sq mi)
POPULATION	58,000
CAPITAL	Nuuk (Godthåb) 17,000
RELIGION	Evangelical Lutheran, traditional Inuit spiritual beliefs
LANGUAGE	Greenlandic (East Inuit), Danish, English
LITERACY	100%
LIFE EXPECTANCY	72 years
GDP PER CAPITA	$38,400
ECONOMY	IND: fish processing (mainly shrimp and Greenland halibut), mining, hunting, tourism AGR: forage crops, garden and greenhouse vegetables; sheep; fish EXP: fish and fish products, metals

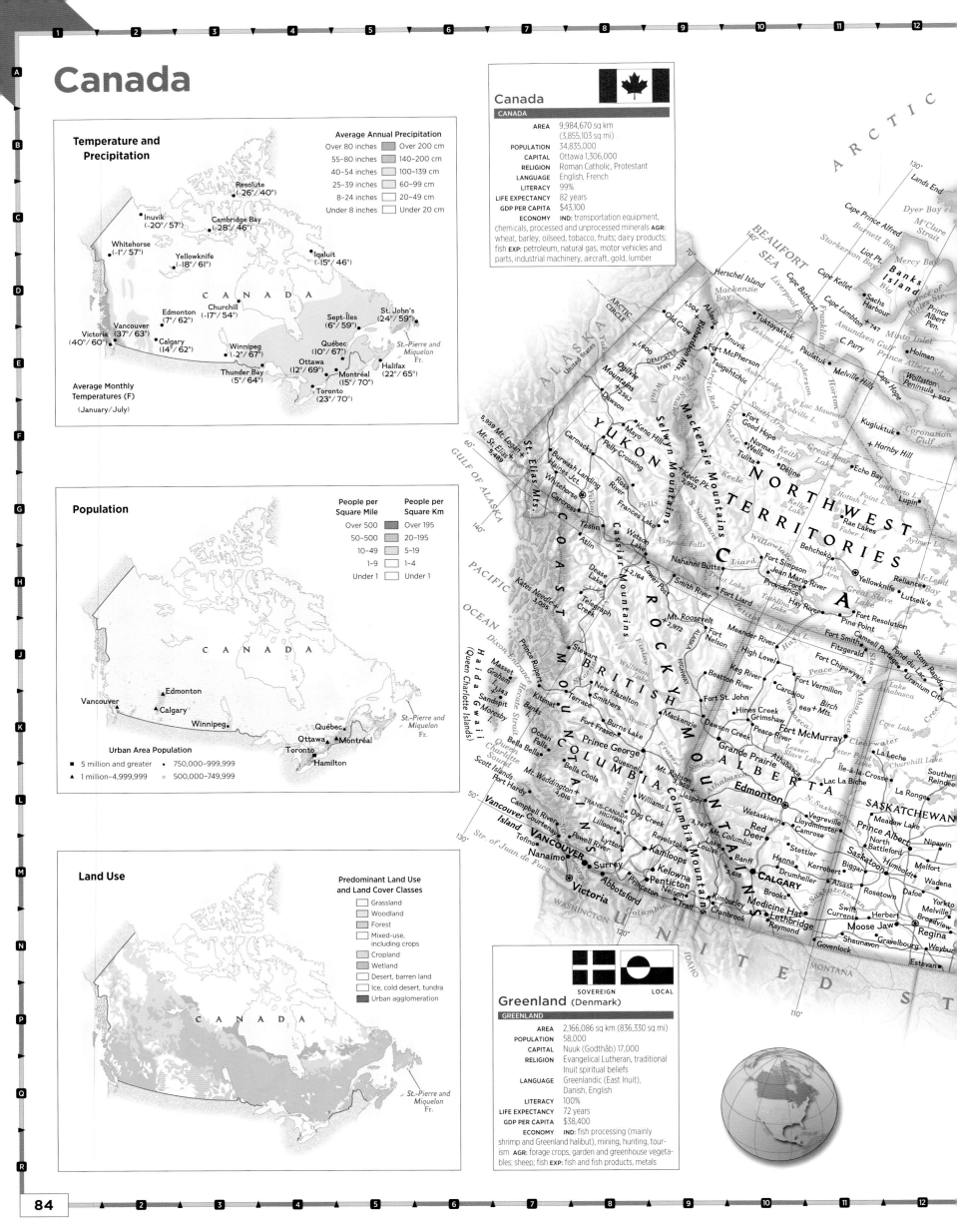

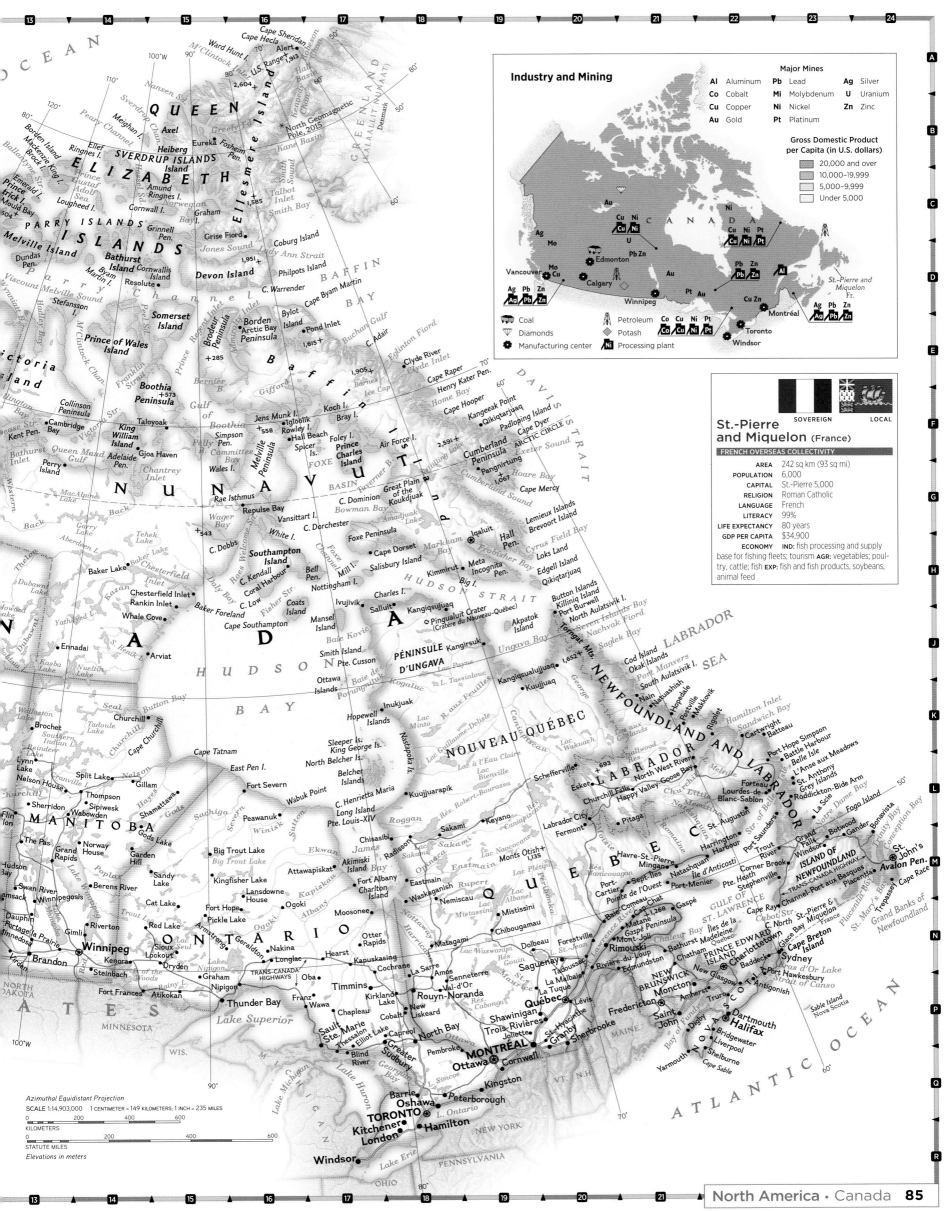

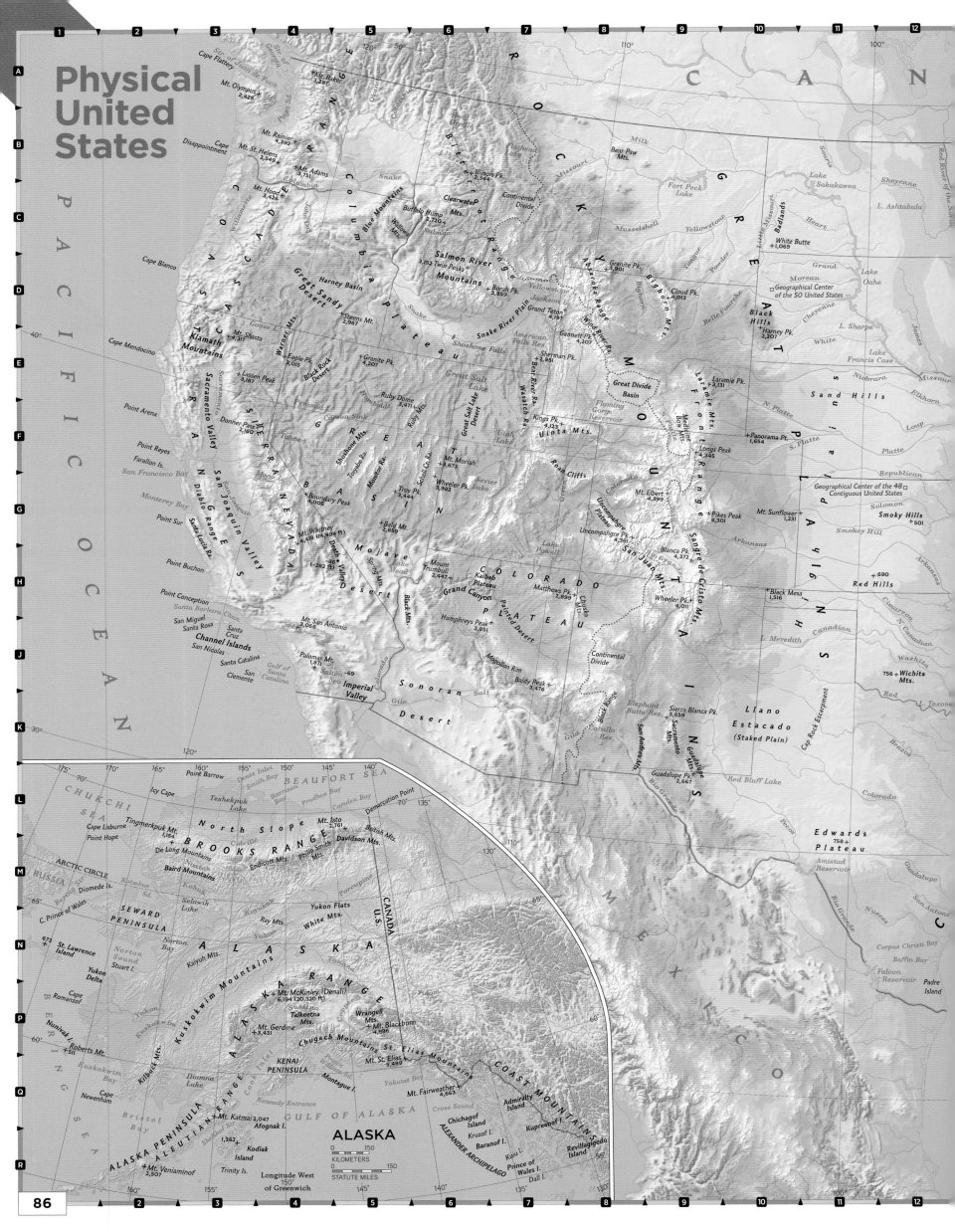

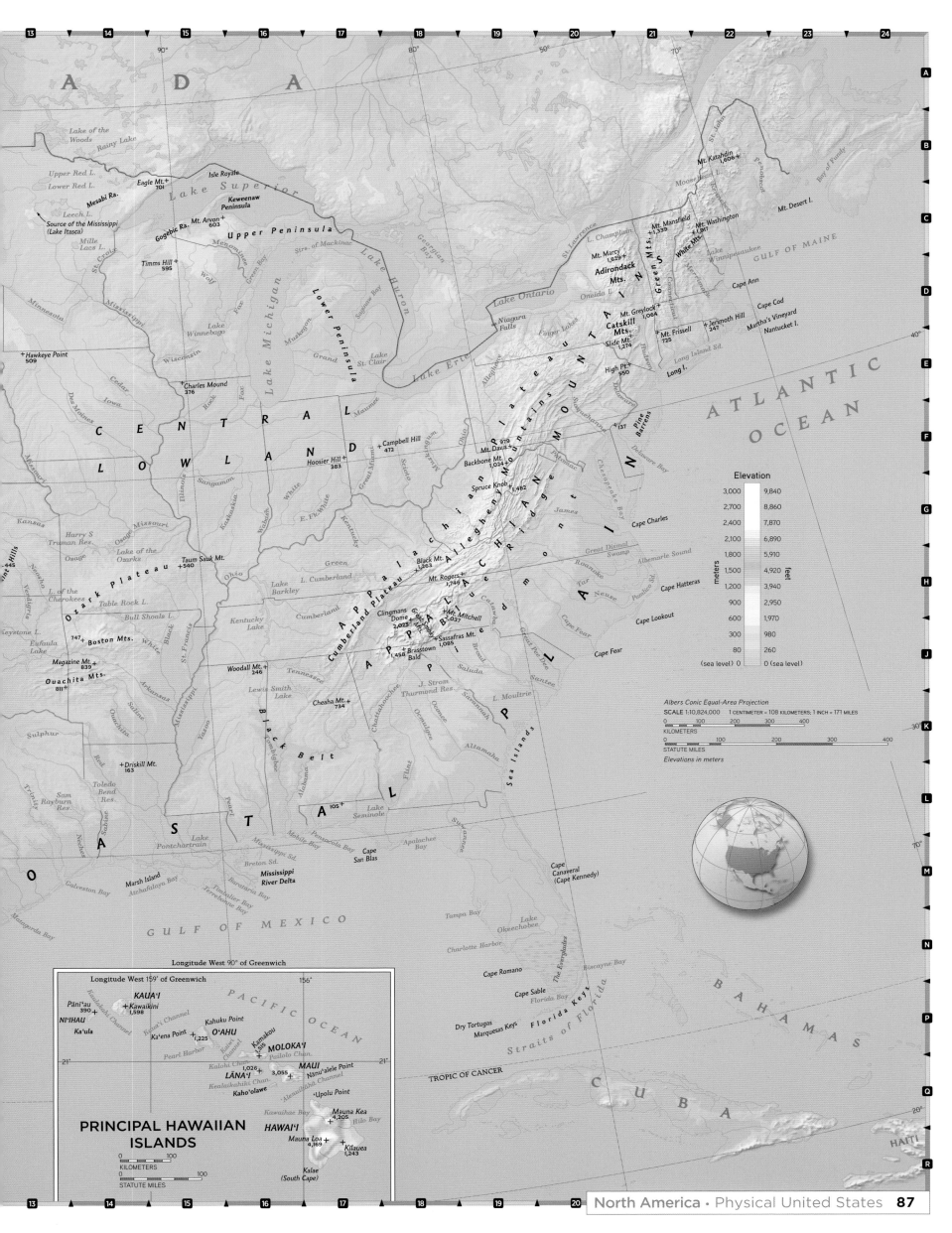

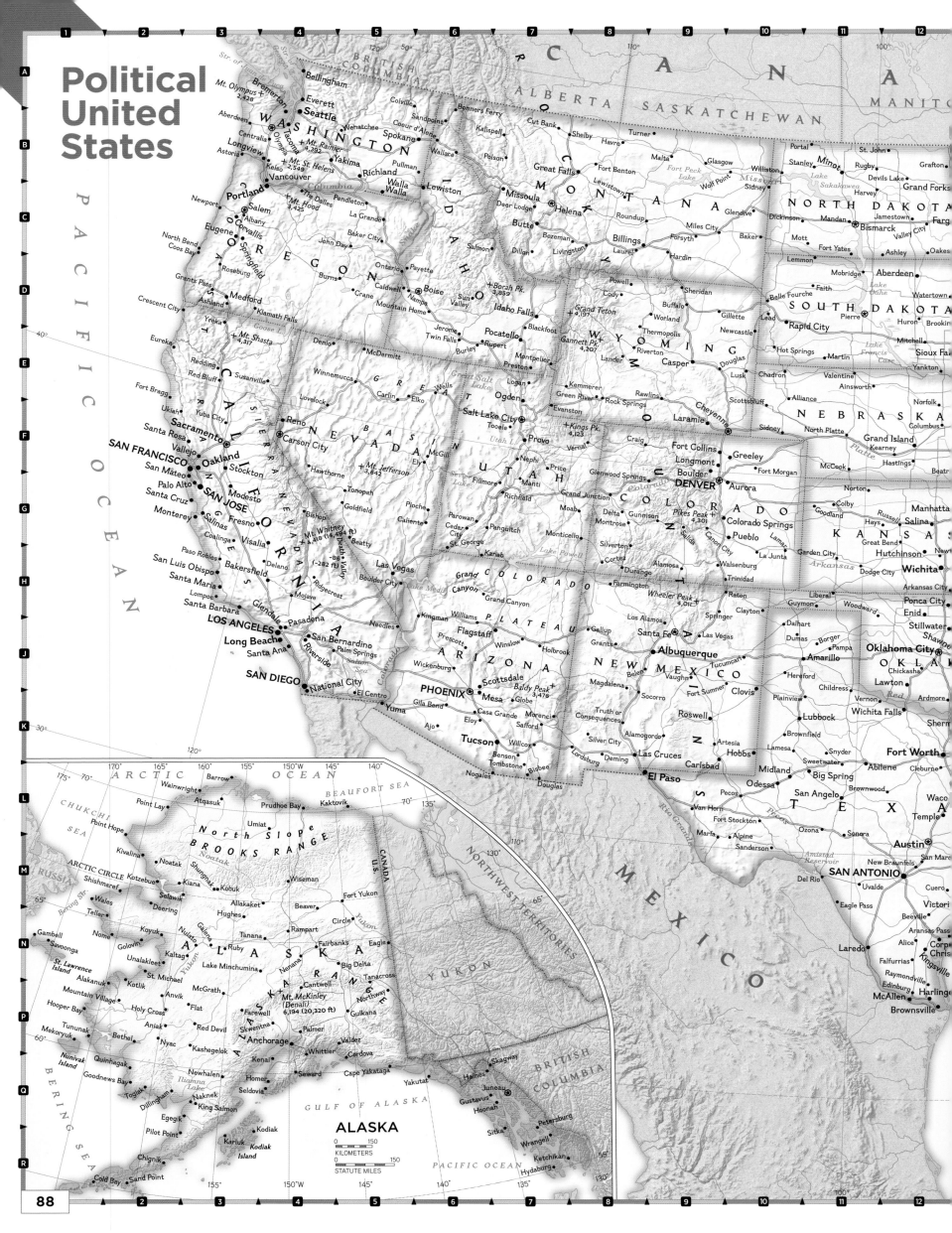

Political United States

ALASKA

KILOMETERS
0   150
STATUTE MILES
0   150

Thematic United States

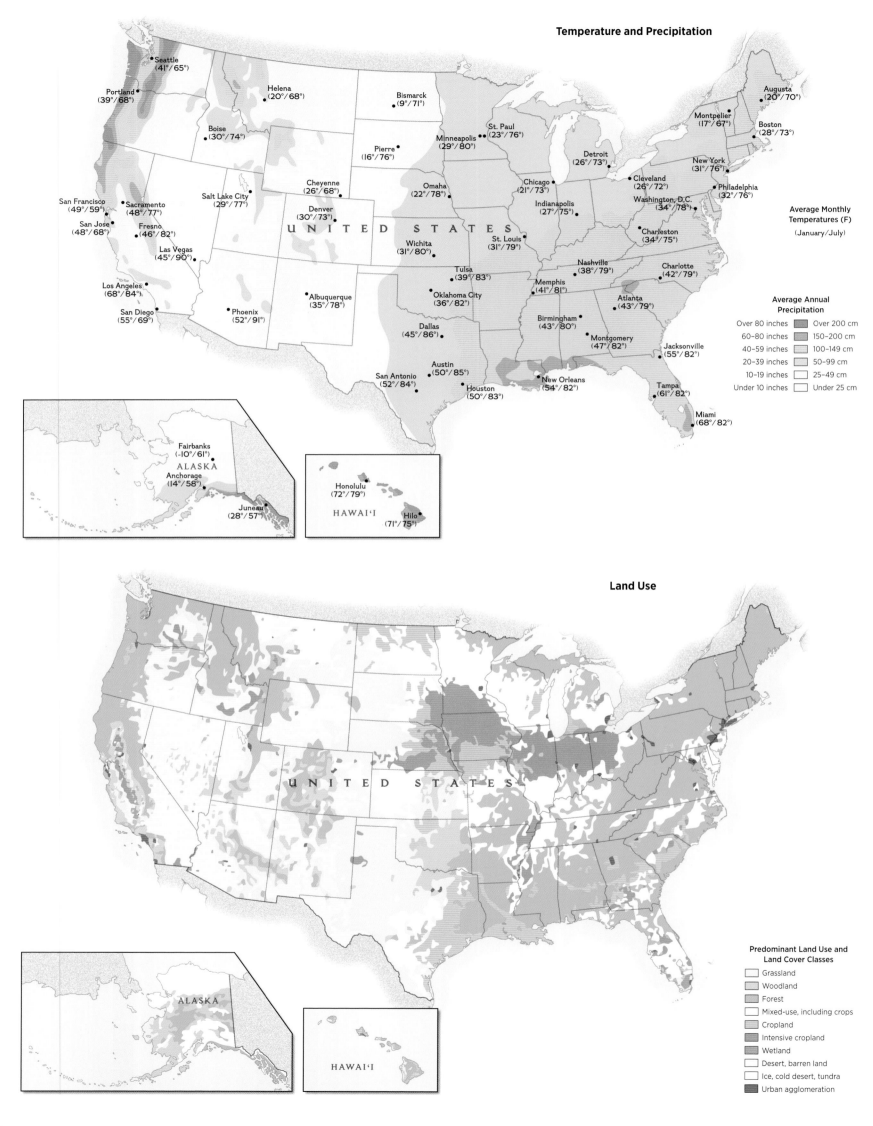

Temperature and Precipitation

Seattle (41°/65°)
Portland (39°/68°)
Helena (20°/68°)
Bismarck (9°/71°)
Boise (30°/74°)
St. Paul (23°/76°)
Minneapolis (29°/80°)
Pierre (16°/76°)
Detroit (26°/73°)
Augusta (20°/70°)
Montpelier (17°/67°)
Boston (28°/73°)
Cheyenne (26°/68°)
Omaha (22°/78°)
Chicago (21°/73°)
Cleveland (26°/72°)
New York (31°/76°)
San Francisco (49°/59°)
Sacramento (48°/77°)
Salt Lake City (29°/77°)
Denver (30°/73°)
Indianapolis (27°/75°)
Washington, D.C. (34°/78°)
Philadelphia (32°/76°)
San Jose (48°/68°)
Fresno (46°/82°)
Wichita (31°/80°)
St. Louis (31°/79°)
Charleston (34°/75°)
Las Vegas (45°/90°)
Tulsa (39°/83°)
Nashville (38°/79°)
Charlotte (42°/79°)
Los Angeles (68°/84°)
Albuquerque (35°/78°)
Oklahoma City (36°/82°)
Memphis (41°/81°)
Atlanta (43°/79°)
San Diego (55°/69°)
Phoenix (52°/91°)
Dallas (45°/86°)
Birmingham (43°/80°)
Montgomery (47°/82°)
Jacksonville (55°/82°)
Austin (50°/85°)
San Antonio (52°/84°)
Houston (50°/83°)
New Orleans (54°/82°)
Tampa (61°/82°)
Miami (68°/82°)

UNITED STATES

Average Monthly Temperatures (F)

(January/July)

Average Annual Precipitation

Over 80 inches	Over 200 cm
60–80 inches	150–200 cm
40–59 inches	100–149 cm
20–39 inches	50–99 cm
10–19 inches	25–49 cm
Under 10 inches	Under 25 cm

Fairbanks (-10°/61°)
ALASKA
Anchorage (14°/58°)
Juneau (28°/57°)

Honolulu (72°/79°)
HAWAI'I
Hilo (71°/75°)

Land Use

UNITED STATES

ALASKA

HAWAI'I

Predominant Land Use and Land Cover Classes

- Grassland
- Woodland
- Forest
- Mixed-use, including crops
- Cropland
- Intensive cropland
- Wetland
- Desert, barren land
- Ice, cold desert, tundra
- Urban agglomeration

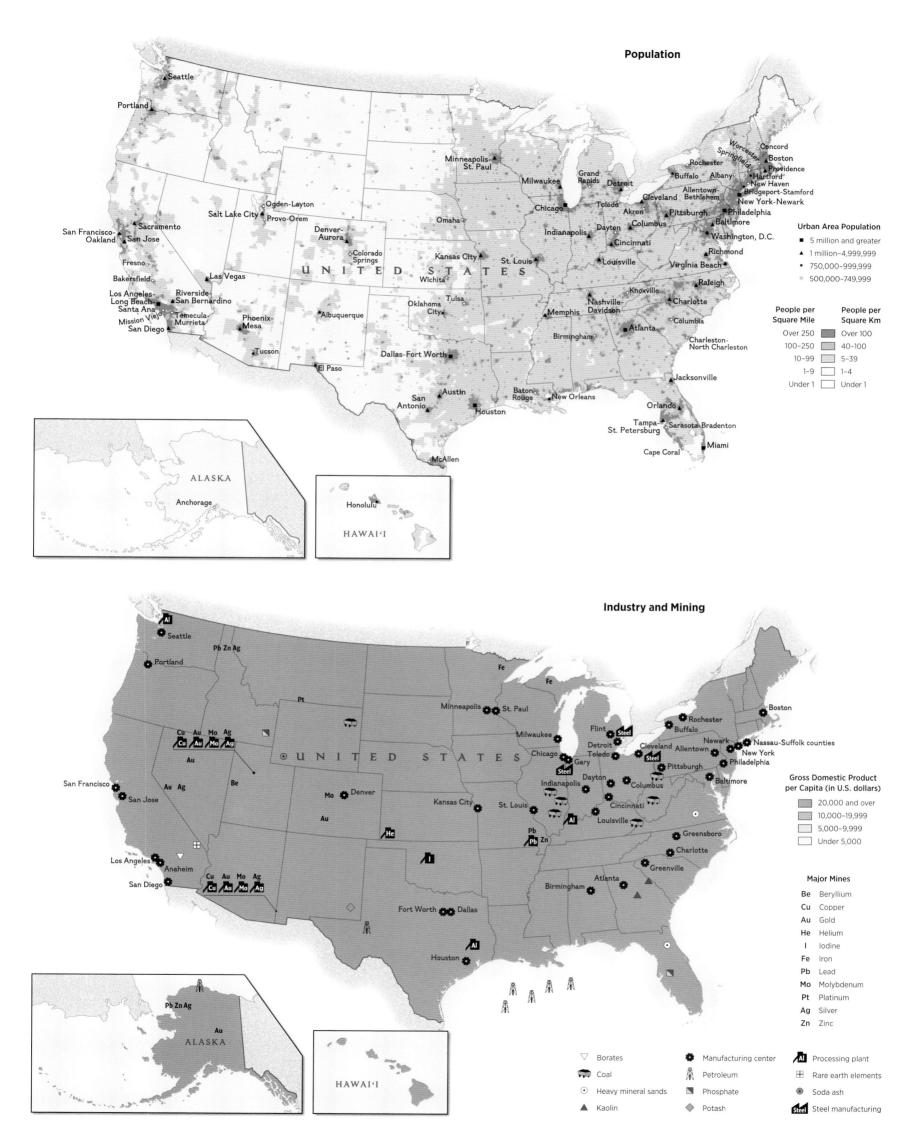

Population

Urban Area Population

- ■ 5 million and greater
- ▲ 1 million–4,999,999
- ● 750,000–999,999
- ○ 500,000–749,999

People per Square Mile		People per Square Km
Over 250		Over 100
100–250		40–100
10–99		5–39
1–9		1–4
Under 1		Under 1

Seattle
Portland
Minneapolis-St. Paul
Grand Rapids
Milwaukee
Detroit
Worcester
Springfield
Concord
Boston
Rochester
Providence
Buffalo
Albany
Hartford
New Haven
Bridgeport-Stamford
Cleveland
Allentown-Bethlehem
Chicago
Toledo
Akron
Pittsburgh
New York-Newark
Philadelphia
Columbus
Baltimore
Ogden-Layton
Salt Lake City
Provo-Orem
Omaha
Denver-Aurora
Indianapolis
Dayton
Cincinnati
Washington, D.C.
Richmond
San Francisco-Oakland
Sacramento
San Jose
Colorado Springs
Kansas City
St. Louis
Louisville
Virginia Beach
Fresno
Wichita
Raleigh
Bakersfield
Las Vegas
Knoxville
Charlotte
UNITED STATES
Los Angeles-Long Beach-Santa Ana
Riverside-San Bernardino
Albuquerque
Oklahoma City
Tulsa
Nashville-Davidson
Columbia
Mission Viejo
Temecula-Murrieta
San Diego
Phoenix-Mesa
Memphis
Atlanta
Charleston-North Charleston
Tucson
Dallas-Fort Worth
Birmingham
El Paso
Jacksonville
Austin
San Antonio
Baton Rouge
New Orleans
Orlando
Houston
Tampa-St. Petersburg
Sarasota-Bradenton
McAllen
Cape Coral
Miami

ALASKA
Anchorage

Honolulu
HAWAI'I

Industry and Mining

Gross Domestic Product per Capita (in U.S. dollars)

- 20,000 and over
- 10,000–19,999
- 5,000–9,999
- Under 5,000

Major Mines

Be	Beryllium
Cu	Copper
Au	Gold
He	Helium
I	Iodine
Fe	Iron
Pb	Lead
Mo	Molybdenum
Pt	Platinum
Ag	Silver
Zn	Zinc

Al Seattle
Portland
Pb Zn Ag
Fe
Fe
Minneapolis
St. Paul
Boston
Rochester
Flint
Steel
Buffalo
Milwaukee
Detroit
Cleveland
Newark
Nassau-Suffolk counties
Cu Au Mo Ag
Chicago
Gary
Toledo
Steel
Allentown
New York
Philadelphia
Au
Pt
Steel
Pittsburgh
Baltimore
San Francisco
Au Ag
Be
Indianapolis
Dayton
Columbus
San Jose
Mo
Denver
Cincinnati
Kansas City
St. Louis
Au
Al
Louisville
Greensboro
He
Los Angeles
Anaheim
Pb
Pb Zn
Greenville
Charlotte
San Diego
Cu Au Mo Ag
I
Birmingham
Atlanta
Greensboro
Fort Worth
Dallas
Al
Houston
UNITED STATES

Pb Zn Ag
Au
ALASKA

HAWAI'I

Legend:

- ▽ Borates
- Coal
- ⊙ Heavy mineral sands
- ▲ Kaolin
- ✿ Manufacturing center
- ⚒ Petroleum
- ◣ Phosphate
- ◇ Potash
- Al Processing plant
- ⊞ Rare earth elements
- ◉ Soda ash
- Steel — Steel manufacturing

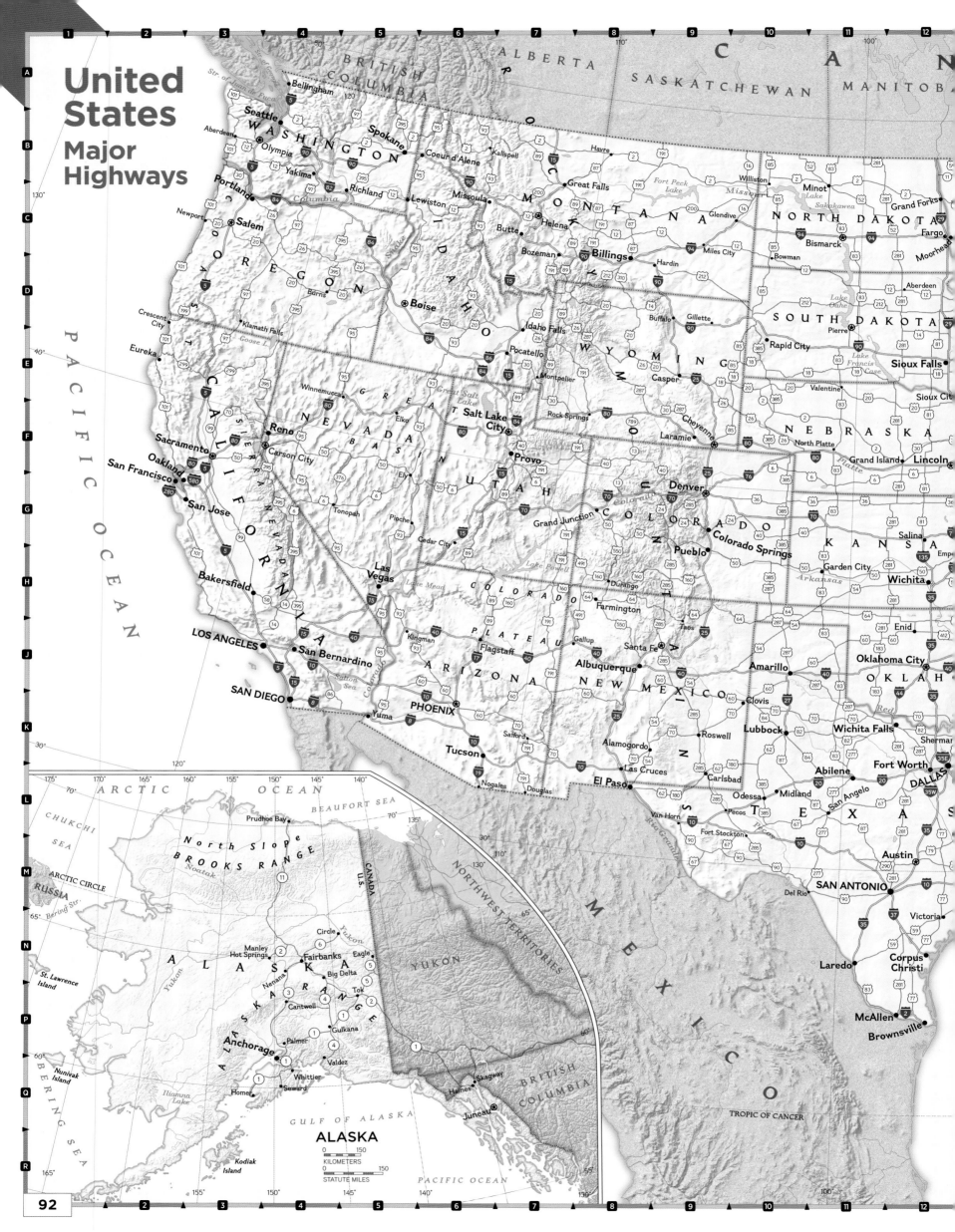

United States
Major Highways

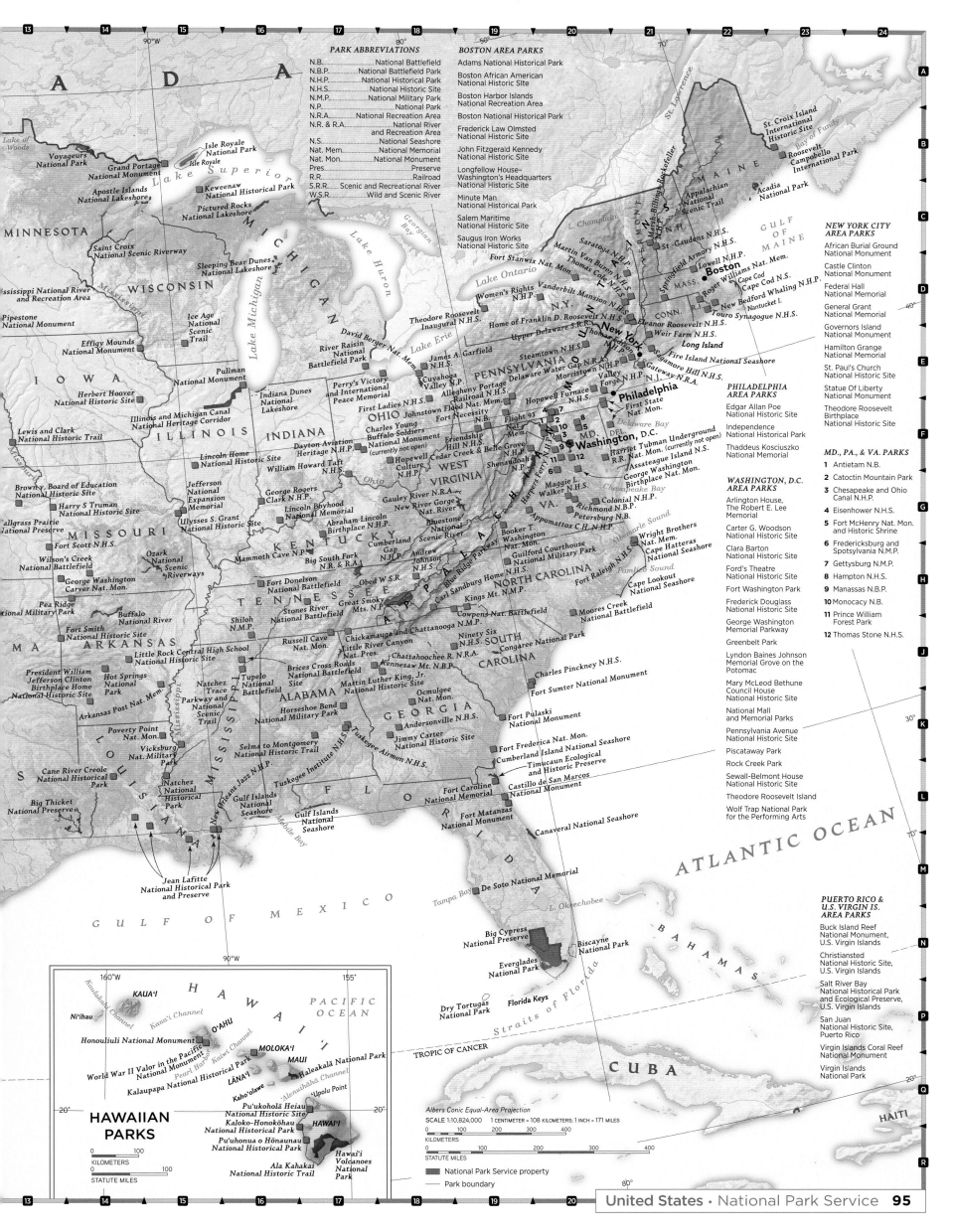

PARK ABBREVIATIONS

N.B.	National Battlefield
N.B.P.	National Battlefield Park
N.H.P.	National Historical Park
N.H.S.	National Historic Site
N.M.P.	National Military Park
N.P.	National Park
N.R.A.	National Recreation Area
N.R. & R.A.	National River and Recreation Area
N.S.	National Seashore
Nat. Mem.	National Memorial
Nat. Mon.	National Monument
Pres.	Preserve
R.R.	Railroad
S.R.R.	Scenic and Recreational River
W.S.R.	Wild and Scenic River

BOSTON AREA PARKS

Adams National Historical Park

Boston African American National Historic Site

Boston Harbor Islands National Recreation Area

Boston National Historical Park

Frederick Law Olmsted National Historic Site

John Fitzgerald Kennedy National Historic Site

Longfellow House–Washington's Headquarters National Historic Site

Minute Man National Historical Park

Salem Maritime National Historic Site

Saugus Iron Works National Historic Site

NEW YORK CITY AREA PARKS

African Burial Ground National Monument

Castle Clinton National Monument

Federal Hall National Memorial

General Grant National Memorial

Governors Island National Monument

Hamilton Grange National Memorial

St. Paul's Church National Historic Site

Statue Of Liberty National Monument

Theodore Roosevelt Birthplace National Historic Site

PHILADELPHIA AREA PARKS

Edgar Allan Poe National Historic Site

Independence National Historical Park

Thaddeus Kosciuszko National Memorial

WASHINGTON, D.C. AREA PARKS

Arlington House, The Robert E. Lee Memorial

Carter G. Woodson National Historic Site

Clara Barton National Historic Site

Ford's Theatre National Historic Site

Fort Washington Park

Frederick Douglass National Historic Site

George Washington Memorial Parkway

Greenbelt Park

Lyndon Baines Johnson Memorial Grove on the Potomac

Mary McLeod Bethune Council House National Historic Site

National Mall and Memorial Parks

Pennsylvania Avenue National Historic Site

Piscataway Park

Rock Creek Park

Sewall-Belmont House National Historic Site

Theodore Roosevelt Island

Wolf Trap National Park for the Performing Arts

MD., PA., & VA. PARKS

1 Antietam N.B.
2 Catoctin Mountain Park
3 Chesapeake and Ohio Canal N.H.P.
4 Eisenhower N.H.S.
5 Fort McHenry Nat. Mon. and Historic Shrine
6 Fredericksburg and Spotsylvania N.M.P.
7 Gettysburg N.M.P.
8 Hampton N.H.S.
9 Manassas N.B.P.
10 Monocacy N.B.
11 Prince William Forest Park
12 Thomas Stone N.H.S.

PUERTO RICO & U.S. VIRGIN IS. AREA PARKS

Buck Island Reef National Monument, U.S. Virgin Islands

Christiansted National Historic Site, U.S. Virgin Islands

Salt River Bay National Historical Park and Ecological Preserve, U.S. Virgin Islands

San Juan National Historic Site, Puerto Rico

Virgin Islands Coral Reef National Monument

Virgin Islands National Park

HAWAIIAN PARKS

National Park Service property
Park boundary

Albers Conic Equal-Area Projection
SCALE 1:10,824,000   1 CENTIMETER = 108 KILOMETERS; 1 INCH = 171 MILES

United States Northeast

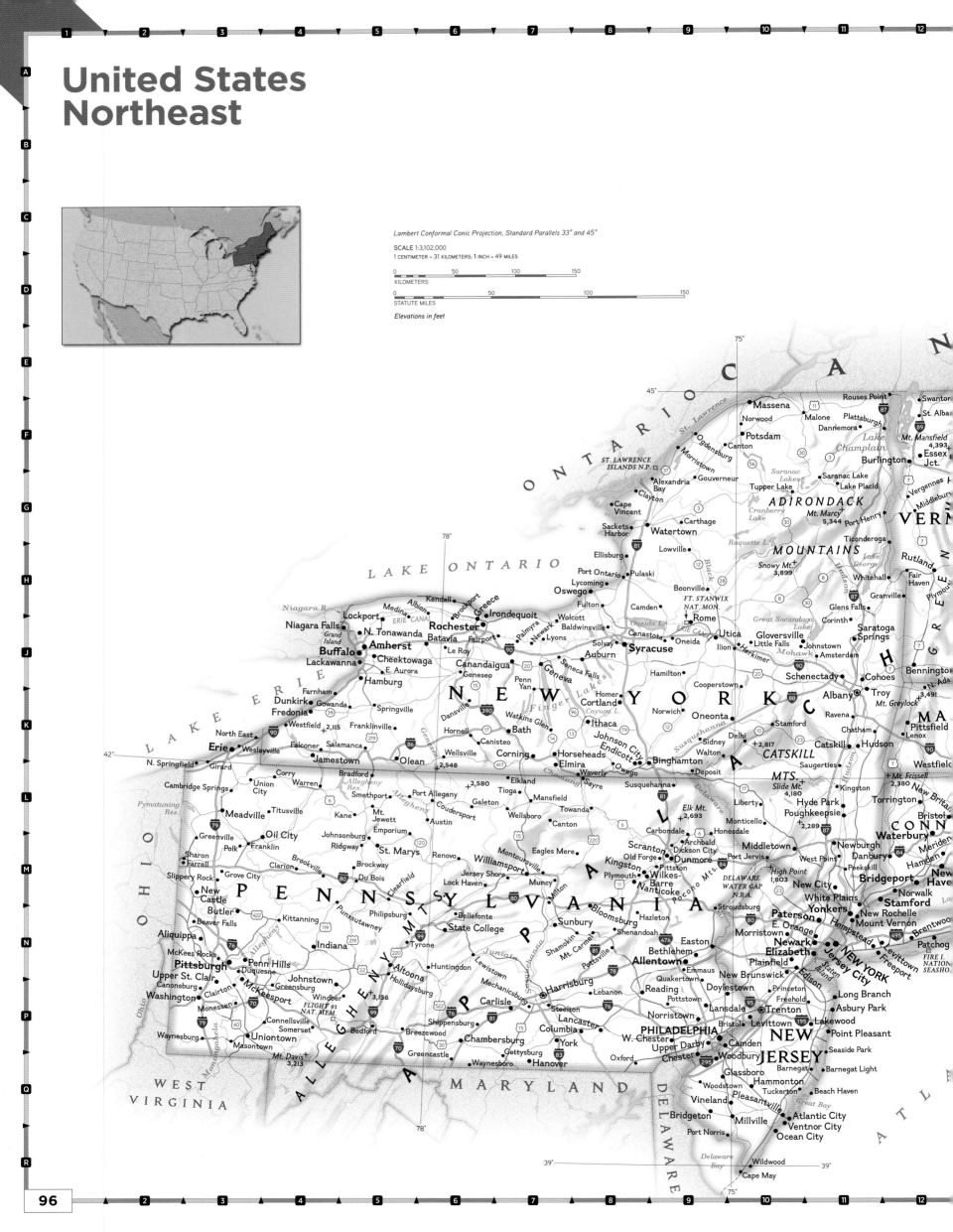

Lambert Conformal Conic Projection, Standard Parallels 33° and 45°

SCALE 1:3,102,000
1 CENTIMETER = 31 KILOMETERS; 1 INCH = 49 MILES

Elevations in feet

Map labels

69°

Madawaska
Fort Kent · Frenchville
St. Francis · Van Buren
Eagle Lake · Limestone
+1,981 · Caribou
Clayton Lake · Washburn · Fort Fairfield
Ashland · Presque Isle
+Peaked Mt. 2,270 · Mars Hill
Churchill L. · Monticello
Pittston Farm
Chesuncook Lake · Houlton
Patten · Island Falls
Chamberlain L. · Sherman Mills
Mt. Katahdin+ 5,268 · Danforth
Rockwood · Millinocket · E. Millinocket · Vanceboro
Jackman · Moosehead L. · Mattawamkeag · Woodland
Greenville · West Grand L. · Calais
+3,196 · Lincoln · St. Croix I.
+3948 · Milo · Howland · Eastport
Guilford · Dover-Foxcroft · ST. CROIX ISLAND I.H.S. · 45°
Stratton · Dexter · Lead Mt. 1,475 · Lubec
Rangeley · Old Town · Machias
Madison · Orono · Bangor · Brewer
Anson · Newport · Graham Lake · Cherryfield
Farmington · Pittsfield · Skowhegan · Milbridge
Andover · Mexico · Waterville · Winslow · Ellsworth · Jonesport
Rumford · Bucksport · Gouldsboro
Winthrop · Belfast · Bar Harbor
Augusta · ACADIA NAT. PARK
Norway · Gardiner · Camden · Mt. Desert I.
Auburn · Lewiston · Richmond · Rockland · Swans I.
Bridgton · Lisbon Falls · Thomaston · Deer Isle
Conway · Fryeburg · Brunswick · Bath · Isle au Haut · Vinalhaven
Freeport · Boothbay Harbor · Matinicus I.
Westbrook · Falmouth · New Harbor · Ragged I.
Portland · S. Portland · To Yarmouth, Nova Scotia (Seasonal)
Saco · Old Orchard Beach · Cape Elizabeth
Biddeford · Kennebunk
Wells

GULF OF MAINE

69°

Maine · MAINE · QUEBEC · NEW BRUNSWICK

State info boxes

New Jersey
GARDEN STATE

AREA	8,271 sq mi (22,588 sq km)
POPULATION	8,938,000
CAPITAL	Trenton
CAPITAL POP.	city proper: 84,000
	metro area: 370,000
LARGEST CITY	Newark
POPULATION	city proper: 278,000
	metro area: part of New York, N.Y.
	metro area (19,950,000)
INCOME	$36,000 per capita
STATEHOOD	December 18, 1787; 3rd state
STATE BIRD	American goldfinch
STATE FLOWER	Violet
HIGHEST POINT	High Point 1,803 ft (550 m)

New York
EMPIRE STATE

AREA	54,556 sq mi (141,299 sq km)
POPULATION	19,746,000
CAPITAL	Albany
CAPITAL POP.	city proper: 98,000
	metro area: 878,000
LARGEST CITY	New York
POPULATION	city proper: 8,406,000
	metro area: 19,950,000
INCOME	$32,400 per capita
STATEHOOD	July 28, 1788; 11th state
STATE BIRD	Eastern bluebird
STATE FLOWER	Rose
HIGHEST POINT	Mount Marcy 5,344 ft (1,629 m)

Maine
PINE TREE STATE

AREA	35,385 sq mi (91,646 sq km)
POPULATION	1,330,000
CAPITAL	Augusta
CAPITAL POP.	city proper: 19,000
	metro area: N/A
LARGEST CITY	Portland
POPULATION	city proper: 66,000
	metro area: 520,000
INCOME	$26,800 per capita
STATEHOOD	March 15, 1820; 23rd state
STATE BIRD	Black-capped chickadee
STATE FLOWER	White pine cone and tassel
HIGHEST POINT	Mt. Katahdin 5,268 ft (1,606 m)

Pennsylvania
KEYSTONE STATE

AREA	46,055 sq mi (119,283 sq km)
POPULATION	12,787,000
CAPITAL	Harrisburg
CAPITAL POP.	city proper: 49,000
	metro area: 558,000
LARGEST CITY	Philadelphia
POPULATION	city proper: 1,553,000
	metro area: 6,035,000
INCOME	$28,500 per capita
STATEHOOD	December 12, 1787; 2nd state
STATE BIRD	Ruffed grouse
STATE FLOWER	Mountain laurel
HIGHEST POINT	Mount Davis 3,213 ft (979 m)

Massachusetts
BAY STATE

AREA	10,555 sq mi (27,336 sq km)
POPULATION	6,745,000
CAPITAL	Boston
CAPITAL POP.	city proper: 646,000
	metro area: 4,684,000
LARGEST CITY	Boston
INCOME	$35,800 per capita
STATEHOOD	February 6, 1788; 6th state
STATE BIRD	Black-capped chickadee
STATE FLOWER	Mayflower
HIGHEST POINT	Mt. Greylock 3,491 ft (1,064 m)

Rhode Island
OCEAN STATE

AREA	1,545 sq mi (4,002 sq km)
POPULATION	1,055,000
CAPITAL	Providence
CAPITAL POP.	city proper: 178,000
	metro area: 1,604,000
LARGEST CITY	Providence
INCOME	$30,500 per capita
STATEHOOD	May 29, 1790; 13th state
STATE BIRD	Rhode Island red
STATE FLOWER	Violet
HIGHEST POINT	Jerimoth Hill 812 ft (247 m)

Connecticut
CONSTITUTION STATE

AREA	5,543 sq mi (14,357 sq km)
POPULATION	3,597,000
CAPITAL	Hartford
CAPITAL POP.	city proper: 125,000
	metro area: 1,215,000
LARGEST CITY	Bridgeport
POPULATION	city proper: 147,000
	metro area: 940,000
INCOME	$37,900 per capita
STATEHOOD	January 9, 1788; 5th state
STATE BIRD	American robin
STATE FLOWER	Mountain laurel
HIGHEST POINT	south slope of Mount Frissell 2,380 ft (725 m)

New Hampshire
GRANITE STATE

AREA	9,350 sq mi (24,216 sq km)
POPULATION	1,327,000
CAPITAL	Concord
CAPITAL POP.	city proper: 42,000
	metro area: N/A
LARGEST CITY	Manchester
POPULATION	city proper: 110,000
	metro area: 404,000
INCOME	$33,100 per capita
STATEHOOD	June 21, 1788; 9th state
STATE BIRD	Purple finch
STATE FLOWER	Purple lilac
HIGHEST POINT	Mt. Washington 6,288 ft (1,917 m)

Vermont
GREEN MOUNTAIN STATE

AREA	9,614 sq mi (24,901 sq km)
POPULATION	627,000
CAPITAL	Montpelier
CAPITAL POP.	city proper: 8,000
	metro area: N/A
LARGEST CITY	Burlington
POPULATION	city proper: 42,000
	metro area: 215,000
INCOME	$29,200 per capita
STATEHOOD	March 4, 1791; 14th state
STATE BIRD	Hermit thrush
STATE FLOWER	Red clover
HIGHEST POINT	Mt. Mansfield 4,393 ft (1,339 m)

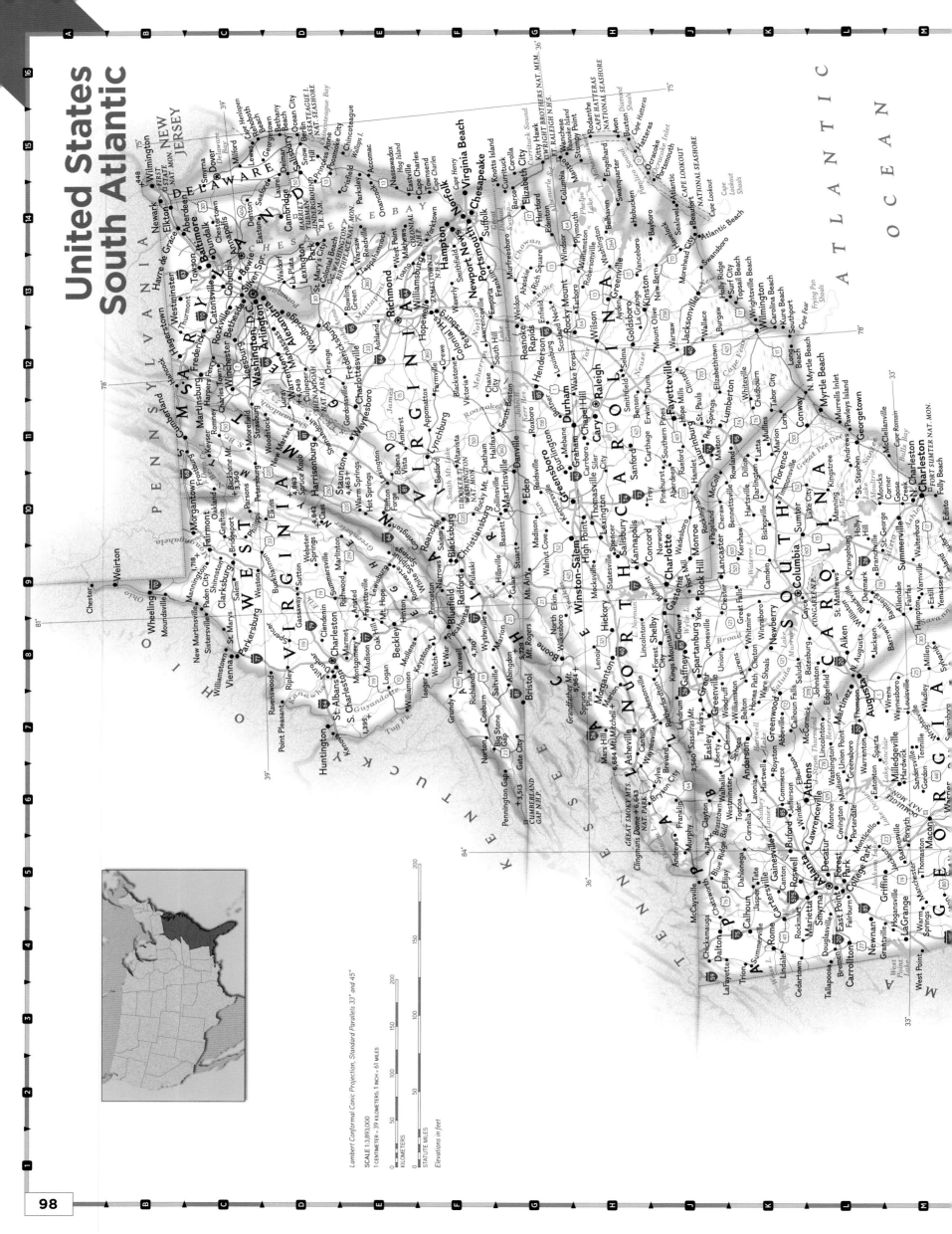

United States
South Atlantic

Lambert Conformal Conic Projection, Standard Parallels 33° and 45°

SCALE 1:3,893,000
1 CENTIMETER = 39 KILOMETERS; 1 INCH = 61 MILES

KILOMETERS
0   50   100   150   200

STATUTE MILES
0   50   100   150   200

Elevations in feet

ATLANTIC OCEAN

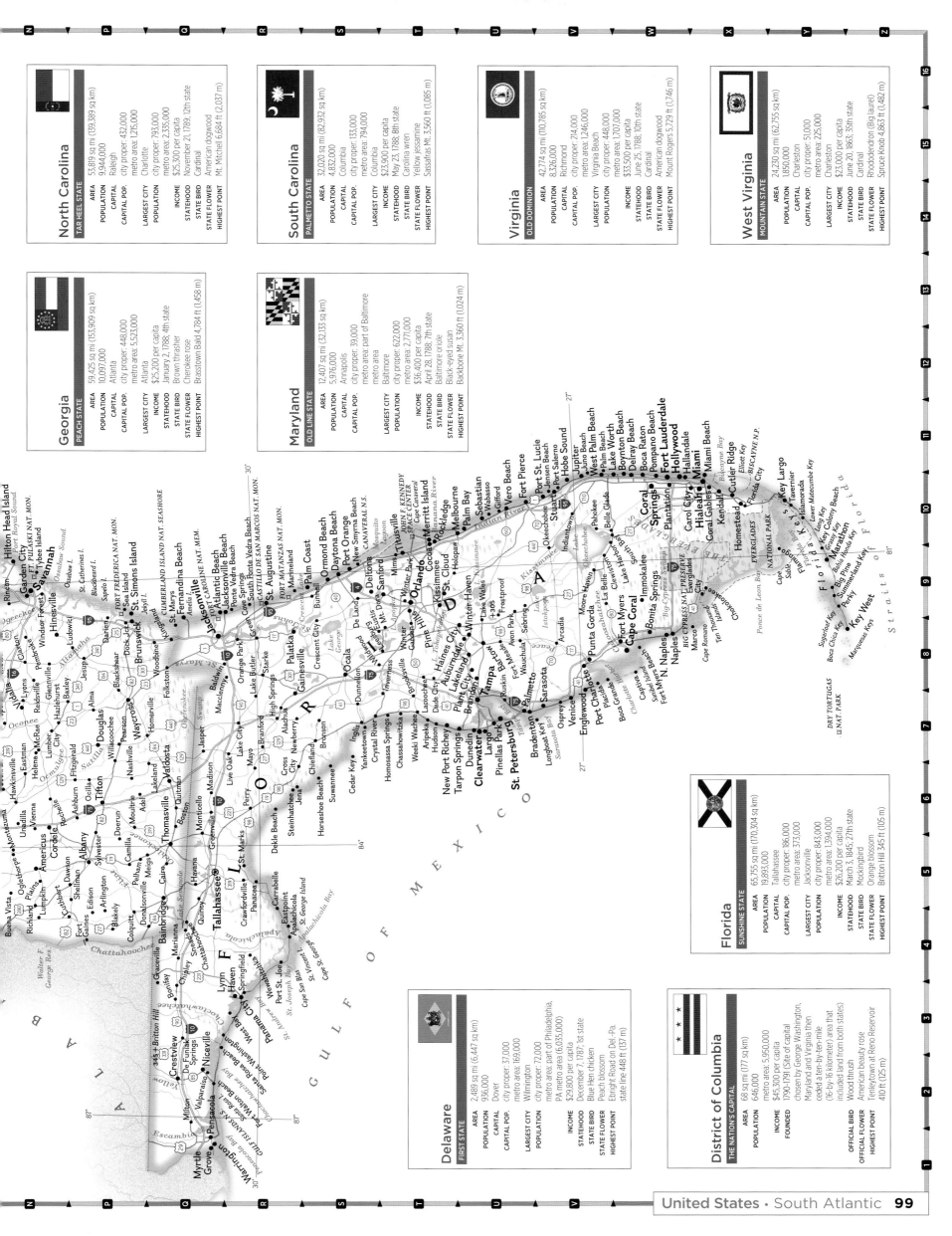

North Carolina
TAR HEEL STATE

AREA	53,819 sq mi (139,389 sq km)
POPULATION	9,944,000
CAPITAL	Raleigh
CAPITAL POP.	city proper: 432,000
	metro area: 1,215,000
LARGEST CITY	Charlotte
POPULATION	city proper: 793,000
	metro area: 2,335,000
INCOME	$25,300 per capita
STATEHOOD	November 21, 1789; 12th state
STATE BIRD	Cardinal
STATE FLOWER	American dogwood
HIGHEST POINT	Mt. Mitchell 6,684 ft (2,037 m)

South Carolina
PALMETTO STATE

AREA	32,020 sq mi (82,932 sq km)
POPULATION	4,832,000
CAPITAL	Columbia
CAPITAL POP.	city proper: 133,000
	metro area: 794,000
LARGEST CITY	Columbia
INCOME	$23,900 per capita
STATEHOOD	May 23, 1788; 8th state
STATE BIRD	Carolina wren
STATE FLOWER	Yellow jessamine
HIGHEST POINT	Sassafras Mt. 3,560 ft (1,085 m)

Virginia
OLD DOMINION

AREA	42,774 sq mi (110,785 sq km)
POPULATION	8,326,000
CAPITAL	Richmond
CAPITAL POP.	city proper: 214,000
	metro area: 1,246,000
LARGEST CITY	Virginia Beach
POPULATION	city proper: 448,000
	metro area: 1,707,000
INCOME	$33,500 per capita
STATEHOOD	June 25, 1788; 10th state
STATE BIRD	Cardinal
STATE FLOWER	American dogwood
HIGHEST POINT	Mount Rogers 5,729 ft (1,746 m)

West Virginia
MOUNTAIN STATE

AREA	24,230 sq mi (62,755 sq km)
POPULATION	1,850,000
CAPITAL	Charleston
CAPITAL POP.	city proper: 51,000
	metro area: 225,000
LARGEST CITY	Charleston
INCOME	$23,000 per capita
STATEHOOD	June 20, 1863; 35th state
STATE BIRD	Cardinal
STATE FLOWER	Rhododendron (Big laurel)
HIGHEST POINT	Spruce Knob 4,863 ft (1,482 m)

Georgia
PEACH STATE

AREA	59,425 sq mi (153,909 sq km)
POPULATION	10,097,000
CAPITAL	Atlanta
CAPITAL POP.	city proper: 448,000
	metro area: 5,523,000
LARGEST CITY	Atlanta
INCOME	$25,200 per capita
STATEHOOD	January 2, 1788; 4th state
STATE BIRD	Brown thrasher
STATE FLOWER	Cherokee rose
HIGHEST POINT	Brasstown Bald 4,784 ft (1,458 m)

Maryland
OLD LINE STATE

AREA	12,407 sq mi (32,133 sq km)
POPULATION	5,976,000
CAPITAL	Annapolis
CAPITAL POP.	city proper: 39,000
	metro area: part of Baltimore
	metro area
LARGEST CITY	Baltimore
POPULATION	city proper: 622,000
	metro area: 2,771,000
INCOME	$36,400 per capita
STATEHOOD	April 28, 1788; 7th state
STATE BIRD	Baltimore oriole
STATE FLOWER	Black-eyed susan
HIGHEST POINT	Backbone Mt. 3,360 ft (1,024 m)

Florida
SUNSHINE STATE

AREA	65,755 sq mi (170,304 sq km)
POPULATION	19,893,000
CAPITAL	Tallahassee
CAPITAL POP.	city proper: 186,000
	metro area: 373,000
LARGEST CITY	Jacksonville
POPULATION	city proper: 843,000
	metro area: 1,394,000
INCOME	$26,200 per capita
STATEHOOD	March 3, 1845; 27th state
STATE BIRD	Mockingbird
STATE FLOWER	Orange blossom
HIGHEST POINT	Britton Hill 345 ft (105 m)

Delaware
FIRST STATE

AREA	2,489 sq mi (6,447 sq km)
POPULATION	936,000
CAPITAL	Dover
CAPITAL POP.	city proper: 37,000
	metro area: 169,000
LARGEST CITY	Wilmington
POPULATION	city proper: 72,000
	metro area: part of Philadelphia,
	PA metro area (6,035,000)
INCOME	$29,800 per capita
STATEHOOD	December 7, 1787; 1st state
STATE BIRD	Blue Hen chicken
STATE FLOWER	Peach blossom
HIGHEST POINT	Ebright Road on Del.-Pa.
	state line 448 ft (137 m)

District of Columbia
THE NATION'S CAPITAL

AREA	68 sq mi (177 sq km)
POPULATION	646,000
	metro area: 5,950,000
INCOME	$45,300 per capita
FOUNDED	1790-1791 (Site of capital
	chosen by George Washington,
	Maryland and Virginia then
	ceded a ten-by-ten-mile
	(16-by-16 kilometer) area that
	included land from both states)
OFFICIAL BIRD	Wood thrush
OFFICIAL FLOWER	American beauty rose
HIGHEST POINT	Tenleytown at Reno Reservoir
	410 ft (125 m)

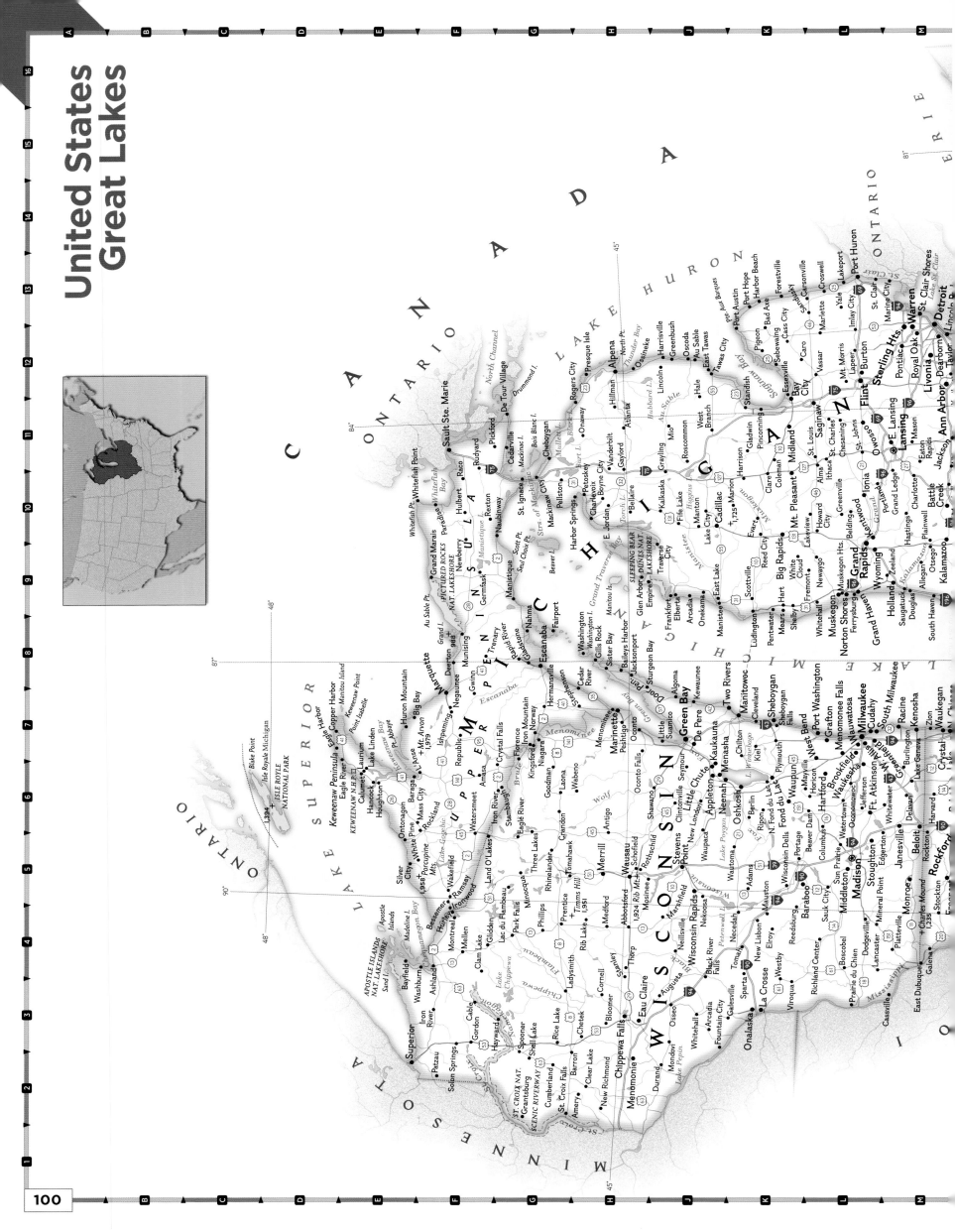

United States
Great Lakes

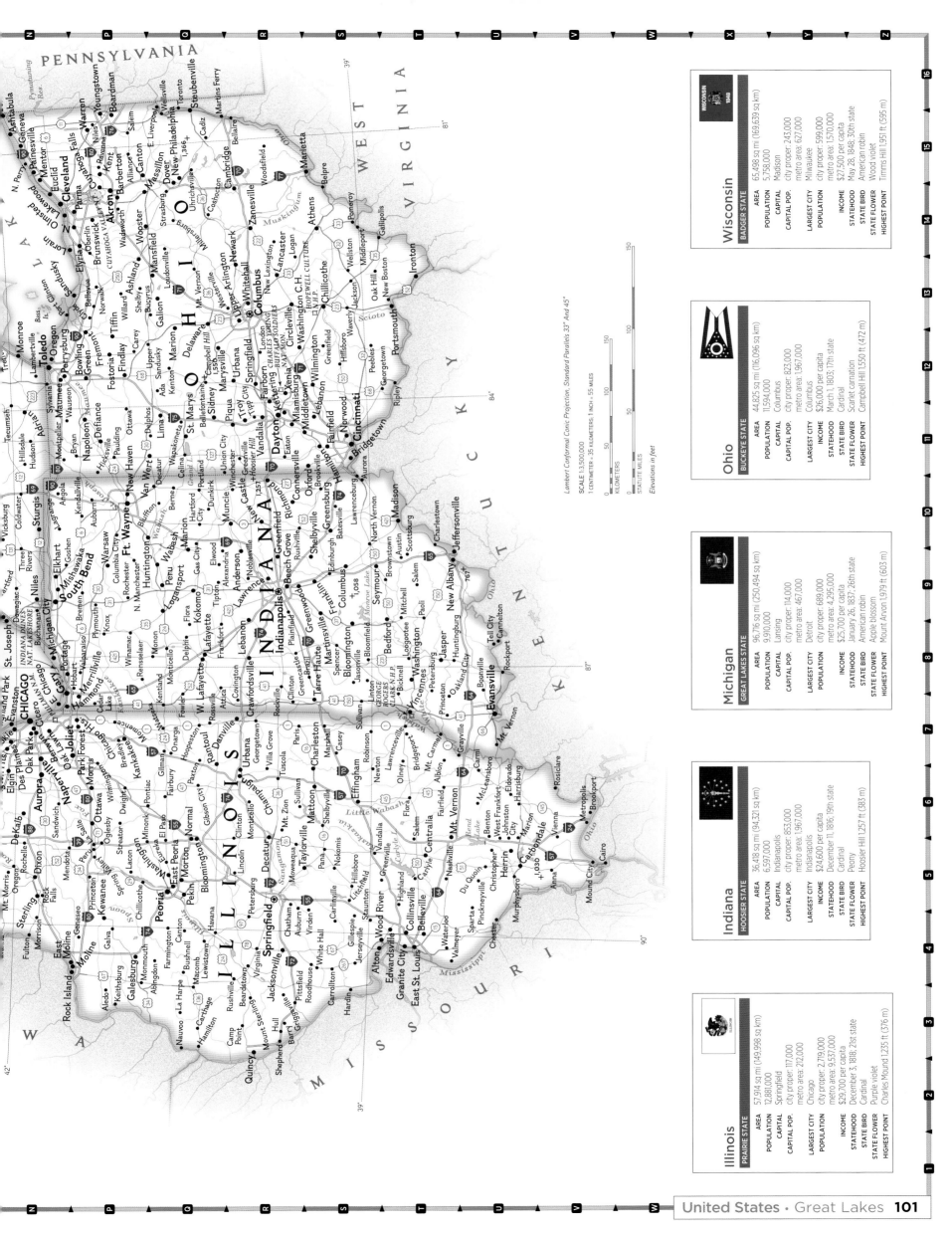

Wisconsin
BADGER STATE
AREA	65,498 sq mi (169,639 sq km)
POPULATION	5,758,000
CAPITAL	Madison
CAPITAL POP.	city proper: 243,000
	metro area: 627,000
LARGEST CITY	Milwaukee
POPULATION	city proper: 599,000
	metro area: 1,570,000
INCOME	$27,500 per capita
STATEHOOD	May 29, 1848; 30th state
STATE BIRD	American robin
STATE FLOWER	Wood violet
HIGHEST POINT	Timms Hill 1,951 ft (595 m)

Ohio
BUCKEYE STATE
AREA	44,825 sq mi (116,096 sq km)
POPULATION	11,594,000
CAPITAL	Columbus
CAPITAL POP.	city proper: 823,000
	metro area: 1,967,000
LARGEST CITY	Columbus
INCOME	$26,000 per capita
STATEHOOD	March 1, 1803; 17th state
STATE BIRD	Cardinal
STATE FLOWER	Scarlet carnation
HIGHEST POINT	Campbell Hill 1,550 ft (472 m)

Michigan
GREAT LAKES STATE
AREA	96,716 sq mi (250,494 sq km)
POPULATION	9,910,000
CAPITAL	Lansing
CAPITAL POP.	city proper: 114,000
	metro area: 467,000
LARGEST CITY	Detroit
POPULATION	city proper: 689,000
	metro area: 4,295,000
INCOME	$25,700 per capita
STATEHOOD	January 26, 1837; 26th state
STATE BIRD	American robin
STATE FLOWER	Apple blossom
HIGHEST POINT	Mount Arvon 1,979 ft (603 m)

Indiana
HOOSIER STATE
AREA	36,418 sq mi (94,321 sq km)
POPULATION	6,597,000
CAPITAL	Indianapolis
CAPITAL POP.	city proper: 853,000
	metro area: 1,967,000
LARGEST CITY	Indianapolis
INCOME	$24,600 per capita
STATEHOOD	December 11, 1816; 19th state
STATE BIRD	Cardinal
STATE FLOWER	Peony
HIGHEST POINT	Hoosier Hill 1,257 ft (383 m)

Illinois
PRAIRIE STATE
AREA	57,914 sq mi (149,998 sq km)
POPULATION	12,881,000
CAPITAL	Springfield
CAPITAL POP.	city proper: 117,000
	metro area: 212,000
LARGEST CITY	Chicago
POPULATION	city proper: 2,719,000
	metro area: 9,537,000
INCOME	$29,700 per capita
STATEHOOD	December 3, 1818; 21st state
STATE BIRD	Cardinal
STATE FLOWER	Purple violet
HIGHEST POINT	Charles Mound 1,235 ft (376 m)

Lambert Conformal Conic Projection, Standard Parallels 33° And 45°

SCALE 1:3,500,000
1 CENTIMETER = 35 KILOMETERS; 1 INCH = 55 MILES

Elevations in feet

United States
Middle South

Lambert Conformal Conic Projection, Standard Parallels 33° And 45°

SCALE 1:3,600,000
1 CENTIMETER = 36 KILOMETERS; 1 INCH = 57 MILES

KILOMETERS

STATUTE MILES

Elevations in feet

Alabama
HEART OF DIXIE

AREA	52,419 sq mi (135,765 sq km)
POPULATION	4,849,000
CAPITAL	Montgomery
CAPITAL POP.	city proper: 201,000
	metro area: 374,000
LARGEST CITY	Birmingham
POPULATION	city proper: 212,000
	metro area: 1,140,000
INCOME	$23,700 per capita
STATEHOOD	December 14, 1819; 22nd state
STATE BIRD	Yellowhammer (Northern flicker)
STATE FLOWER	Camellia
HIGHEST POINT	Cheaha Mt. 2,407 ft (734 m)

Arkansas
NATURAL STATE

AREA	53,179 sq mi (137,732 sq km)
POPULATION	2,966,000
CAPITAL	Little Rock
CAPITAL POP.	city proper: 197,000
	metro area: 724,000
LARGEST CITY	Little Rock
INCOME	$22,200 per capita
STATEHOOD	June 15, 1836; 25th state
STATE BIRD	Mockingbird
STATE FLOWER	Apple blossom
HIGHEST POINT	Magazine Mt. 2,753 ft (839 m)

Kentucky
BLUEGRASS STATE

AREA	40,409 sq mi (104,659 sq km)
POPULATION	4,413,000
CAPITAL	Frankfort
CAPITAL POP.	city proper: 27,000
	metro area: N/A
LARGEST CITY	Louisville
POPULATION	city proper: 757,000
	metro area: 1,262,000
INCOME	$23,500 per capita
STATEHOOD	June 1, 1792; 15th state
STATE BIRD	Cardinal
STATE FLOWER	Goldenrod
HIGHEST POINT	Black Mountain 4,145 ft (1,263 m)

Louisiana
PELICAN STATE

AREA	51,840 sq mi (134,264 sq km)
POPULATION	4,650,000
CAPITAL	Baton Rouge
CAPITAL POP.	city proper: 229,000
	metro area: 820,000
LARGEST CITY	New Orleans
POPULATION	city proper: 379,000
	metro area: 1,241,000
INCOME	$24,400 per capita
STATEHOOD	April 30, 1812; 18th state
STATE BIRD	Brown pelican
STATE FLOWER	Magnolia
HIGHEST POINT	Driskill Mountain 535 ft (163 m)

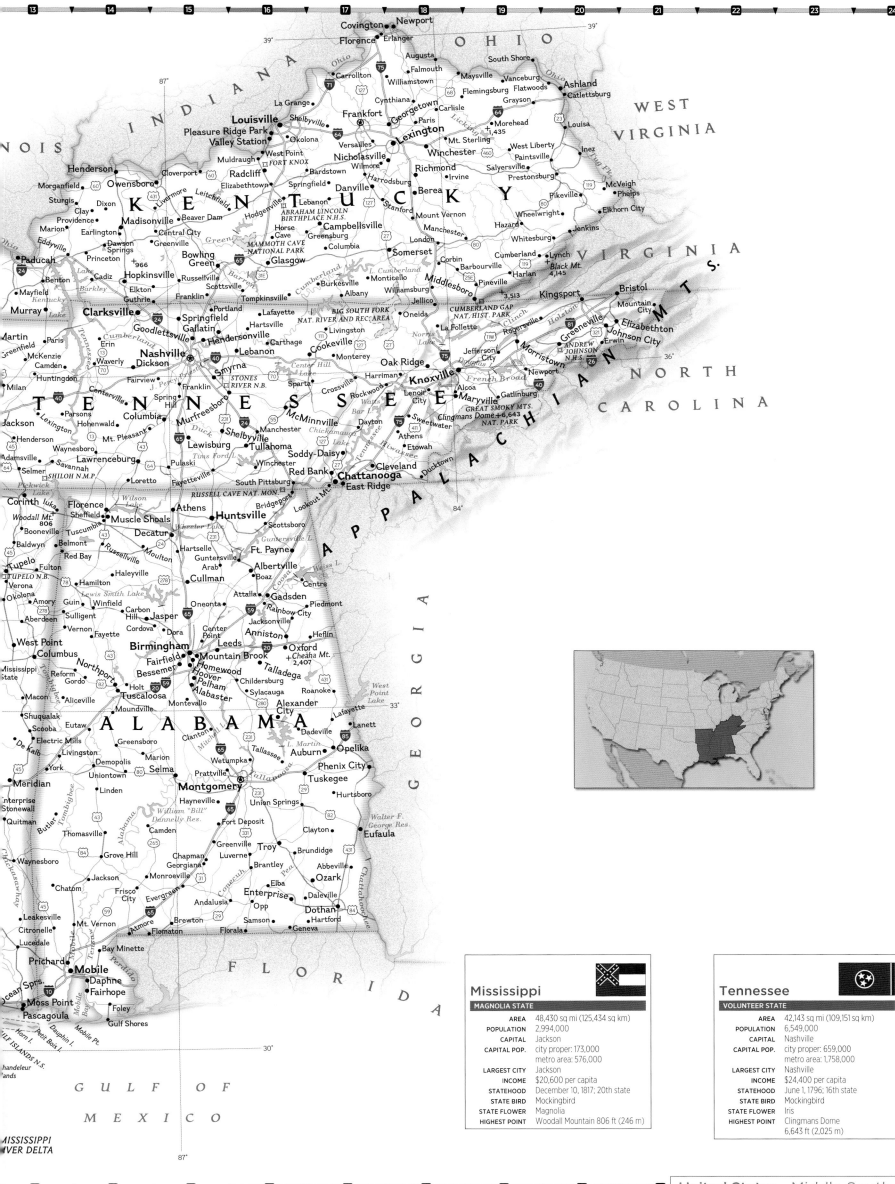

Mississippi
MAGNOLIA STATE

AREA	48,430 sq mi (125,434 sq km)
POPULATION	2,994,000
CAPITAL	Jackson
CAPITAL POP.	city proper: 173,000
	metro area: 576,000
LARGEST CITY	Jackson
INCOME	$20,600 per capita
STATEHOOD	December 10, 1817; 20th state
STATE BIRD	Mockingbird
STATE FLOWER	Magnolia
HIGHEST POINT	Woodall Mountain 806 ft (246 m)

Tennessee
VOLUNTEER STATE

AREA	42,143 sq mi (109,151 sq km)
POPULATION	6,549,000
CAPITAL	Nashville
CAPITAL POP.	city proper: 659,000
	metro area: 1,758,000
LARGEST CITY	Nashville
INCOME	$24,400 per capita
STATEHOOD	June 1, 1796; 16th state
STATE BIRD	Mockingbird
STATE FLOWER	Iris
HIGHEST POINT	Clingmans Dome 6,643 ft (2,025 m)

United States
Texas and Oklahoma

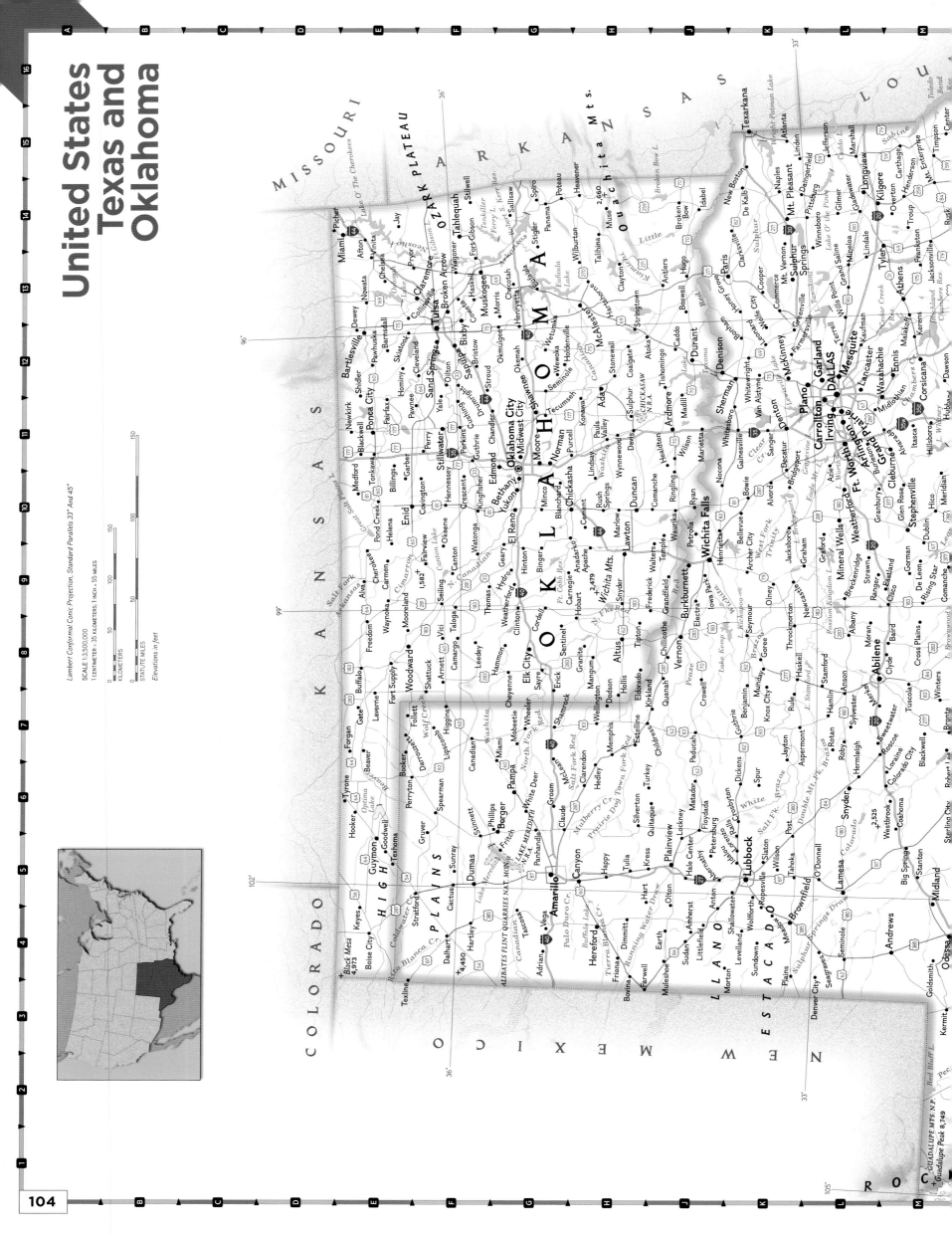

Lambert Conformal Conic Projection, Standard Parallels 33° And 45°

SCALE 1:3,500,000

1 CENTIMETER = 35 KILOMETERS; 1 INCH = 55 MILES

KILOMETERS

STATUTE MILES

Elevations in feet

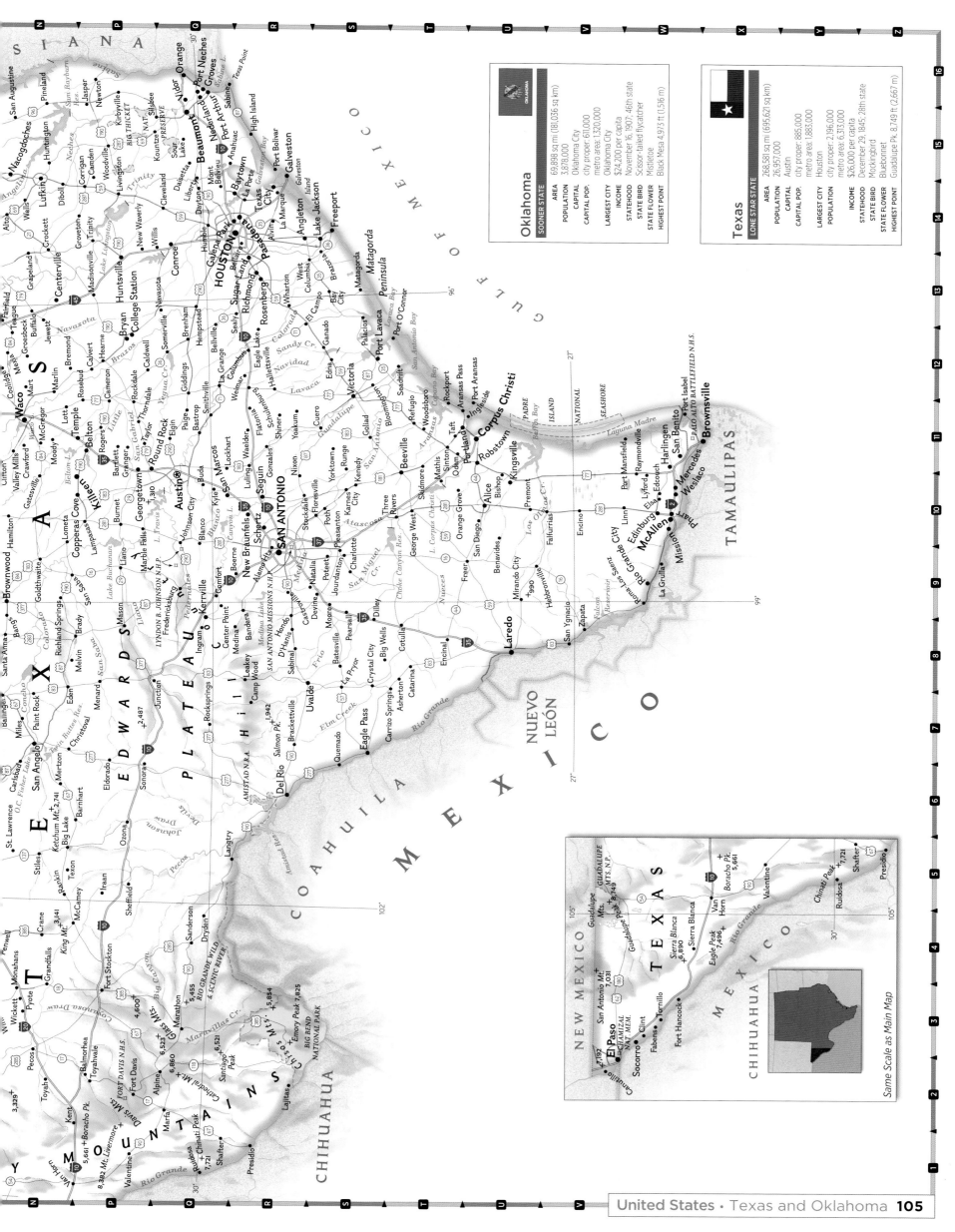

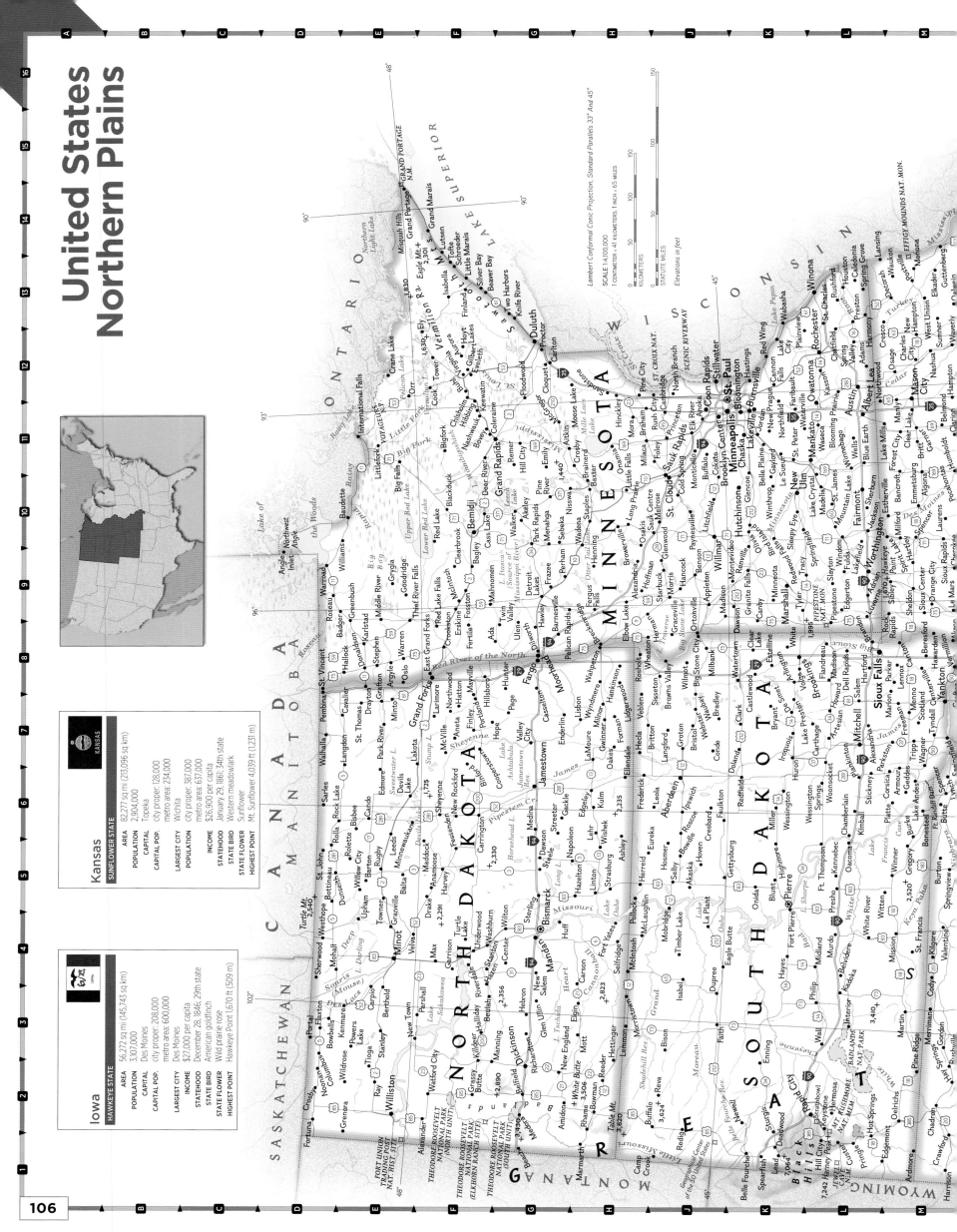

Iowa
HAWKEYE STATE

AREA	56,272 sq mi (145,743 sq km)
POPULATION	3,107,000
CAPITAL	Des Moines
CAPITAL POP.	city proper: 208,000
	metro area: 600,000
LARGEST CITY	Des Moines
INCOME	$27,000 per capita
STATEHOOD	December 28, 1846; 29th state
STATE BIRD	American goldfinch
STATE FLOWER	Wild prairie rose
HIGHEST POINT	Hawkeye Point 1,670 ft (509 m)

Kansas
SUNFLOWER STATE

AREA	82,277 sq mi (213,096 sq km)
POPULATION	2,904,000
CAPITAL	Topeka
CAPITAL POP.	city proper: 128,000
	metro area: 234,000
LARGEST CITY	Wichita
POPULATION	city proper: 387,000
	metro area: 637,000
INCOME	$26,900 per capita
STATEHOOD	January 29, 1861; 34th state
STATE BIRD	Western meadowlark
STATE FLOWER	Sunflower
HIGHEST POINT	Mt. Sunflower 4,039 ft (1,231 m)

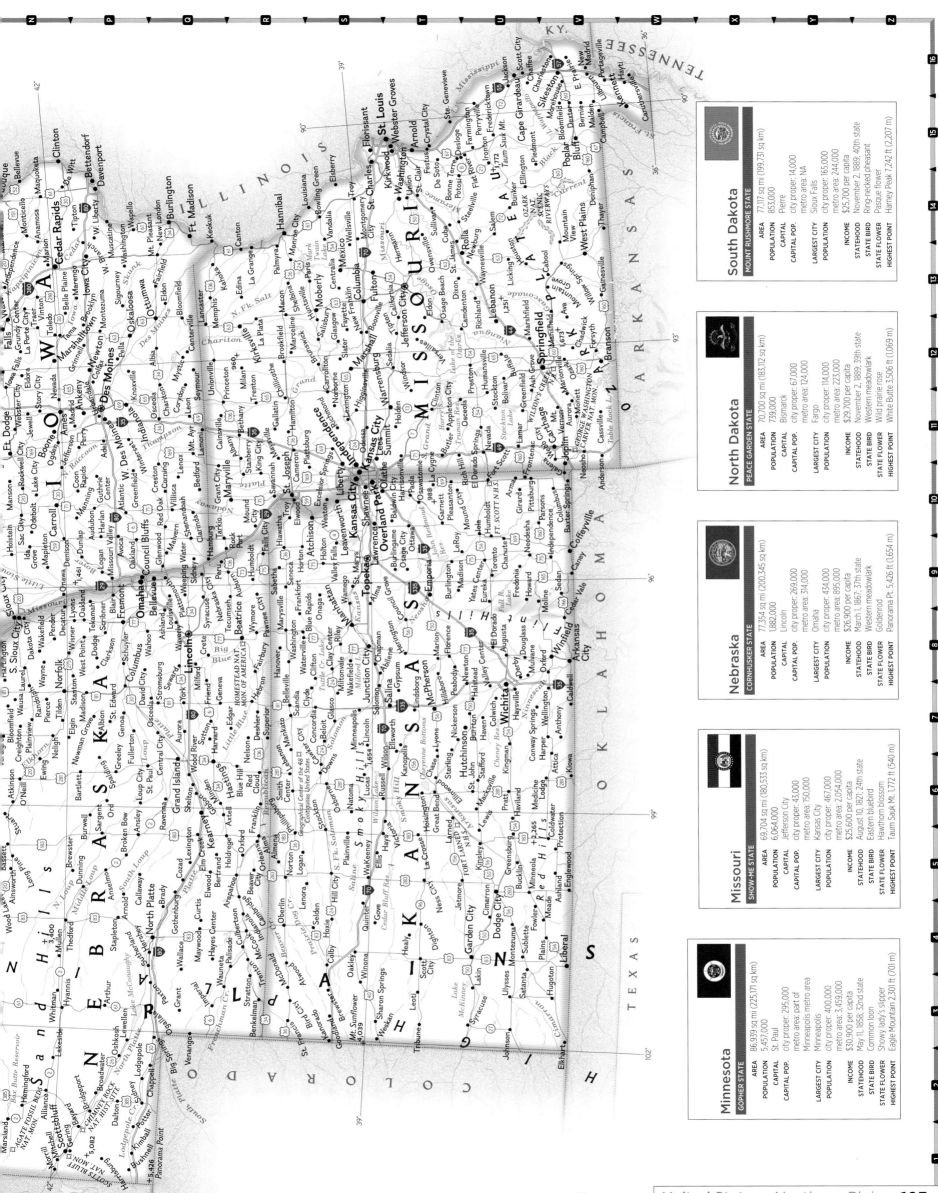

South Dakota
MOUNT RUSHMORE STATE

AREA	77,117 sq mi (199,731 sq km)
POPULATION	853,000
CAPITAL	Pierre
CAPITAL POP.	city proper: 14,000 / metro area: NA
LARGEST CITY	Sioux Falls
POPULATION	city proper: 165,000 / metro area: 244,000
INCOME	$25,700 per capita
STATEHOOD	November 2, 1889; 40th state
STATE BIRD	Ring-necked pheasant
STATE FLOWER	Pasque flower
HIGHEST POINT	Harney Peak 7,242 ft (2,207 m)

North Dakota
PEACE GARDEN STATE

AREA	70,700 sq mi (183,112 sq km)
POPULATION	739,000
CAPITAL	Bismarck
CAPITAL POP.	city proper: 67,000 / metro area: 124,000
LARGEST CITY	Fargo
POPULATION	city proper: 114,000 / metro area: 223,000
INCOME	$29,700 per capita
STATEHOOD	November 2, 1889; 39th state
STATE BIRD	Western meadowlark
STATE FLOWER	Wild prairie rose
HIGHEST POINT	White Butte 3,506 ft (1,069 m)

Nebraska
CORNHUSKER STATE

AREA	77,354 sq mi (200,345 sq km)
POPULATION	1,882,000
CAPITAL	Lincoln
CAPITAL POP.	city proper: 269,000 / metro area: 314,000
LARGEST CITY	Omaha
POPULATION	city proper: 434,000 / metro area: 895,000
INCOME	$26,900 per capita
STATEHOOD	March 1, 1867; 37th state
STATE BIRD	Western meadowlark
STATE FLOWER	Goldenrod
HIGHEST POINT	Panorama Pt. 5,426 ft (1,654 m)

Missouri
SHOW-ME STATE

AREA	69,704 sq mi (180,533 sq km)
POPULATION	6,064,000
CAPITAL	Jefferson City
CAPITAL POP.	city proper: 43,000 / metro area: 150,000
LARGEST CITY	Kansas City
POPULATION	city proper: 467,000 / metro area: 2,054,000
INCOME	$25,600 per capita
STATEHOOD	August 10, 1821; 24th state
STATE BIRD	Eastern bluebird
STATE FLOWER	Hawthorn blossom
HIGHEST POINT	Taum Sauk Mt. 1,772 ft (540 m)

Minnesota
GOPHER STATE

AREA	86,939 sq mi (225,171 sq km)
POPULATION	5,457,000
CAPITAL	St. Paul
CAPITAL POP.	city proper: 295,000 / metro area: part of Minneapolis metro area
LARGEST CITY	Minneapolis
POPULATION	city proper: 400,000 / metro area: 3,459,000
INCOME	$30,900 per capita
STATEHOOD	May 11, 1858; 32nd state
STATE BIRD	Common loon
STATE FLOWER	Showy lady's slipper
HIGHEST POINT	Eagle Mountain 2,301 ft (701 m)

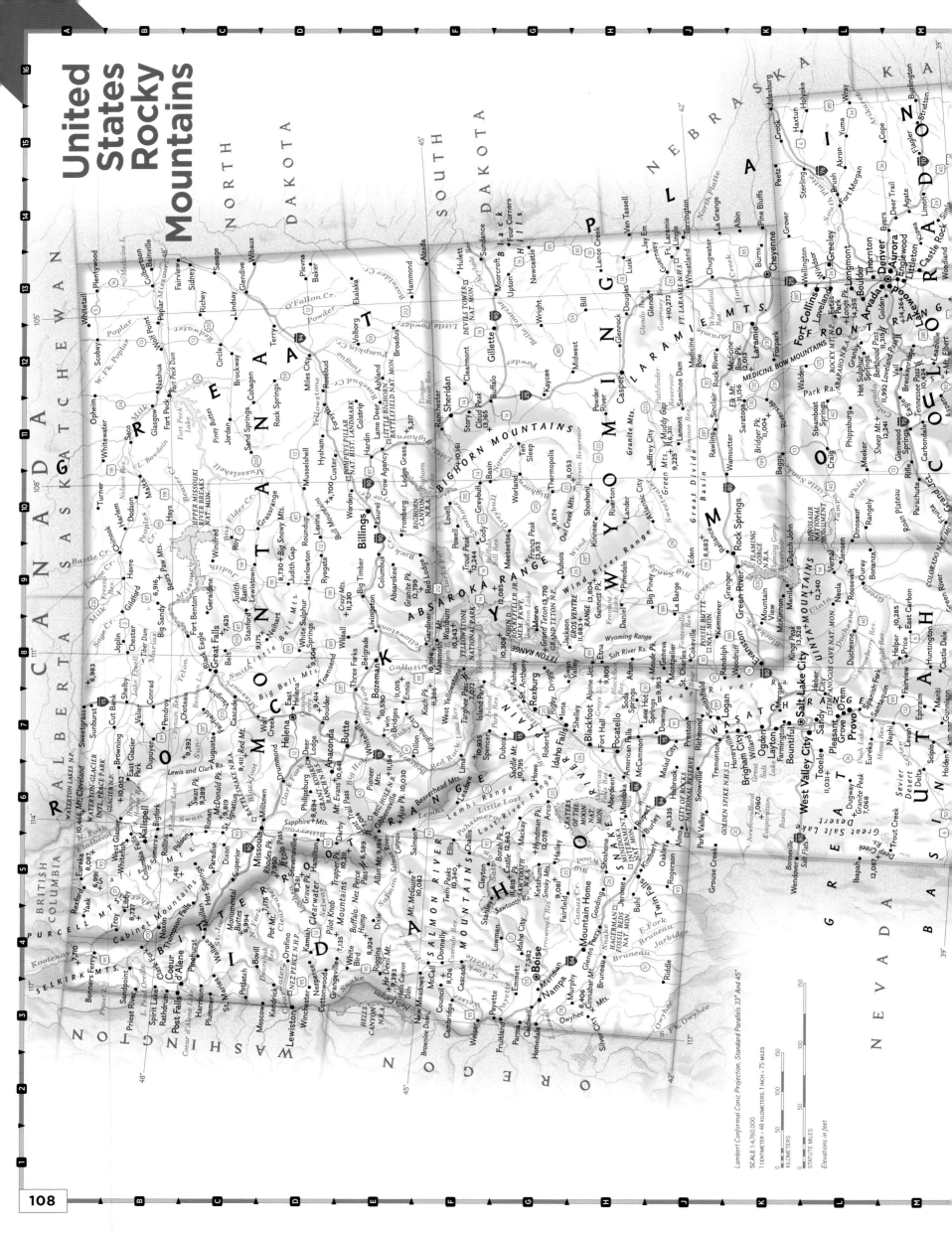

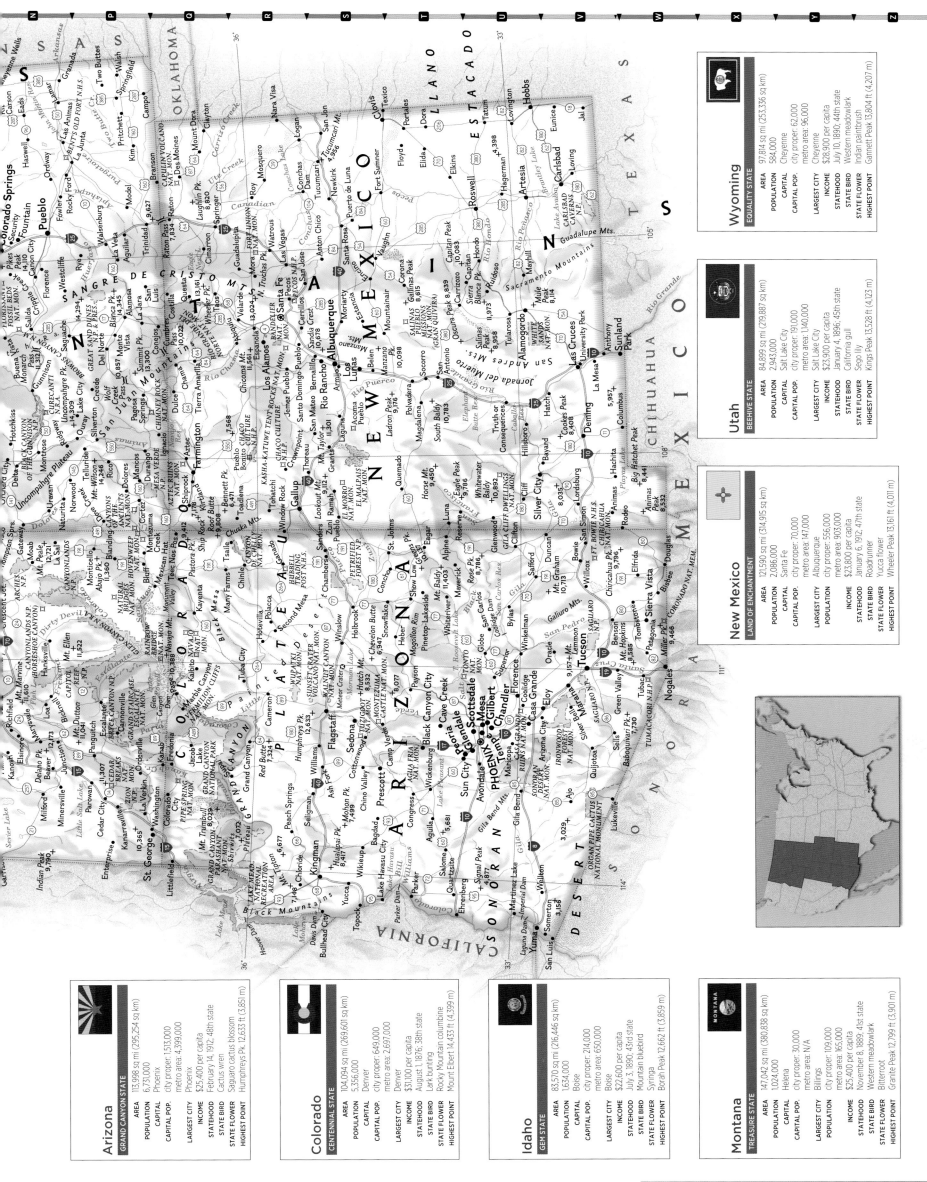

Wyoming
EQUALITY STATE

AREA	97,814 sq mi (253,536 sq km)
POPULATION	584,000
CAPITAL	Cheyenne
CAPITAL POP.	city proper: 62,000 / metro area: 96,000
LARGEST CITY	Cheyenne
INCOME	$28,900 per capita
STATEHOOD	July 10, 1890; 44th state
STATE BIRD	Western meadowlark
STATE FLOWER	Indian paintbrush
HIGHEST POINT	Gannett Peak 13,804 ft (4,207 m)

Utah
BEEHIVE STATE

AREA	84,899 sq mi (219,887 sq km)
POPULATION	2,945,000
CAPITAL	Salt Lake City
CAPITAL POP.	city proper: 191,000 / metro area: 1,140,000
LARGEST CITY	Salt Lake City
INCOME	$27,900 per capita
STATEHOOD	January 4, 1896; 45th state
STATE BIRD	California gull
STATE FLOWER	Sego lily
HIGHEST POINT	Kings Peak 13,528 ft (4,123 m)

New Mexico
LAND OF ENCHANTMENT

AREA	121,590 sq mi (314,915 sq km)
POPULATION	2,086,000
CAPITAL	Santa Fe
CAPITAL POP.	city proper: 70,000 / metro area: 147,000
LARGEST CITY	Albuquerque
POPULATION	city proper: 556,000 / metro area: 903,000
INCOME	$23,800 per capita
STATEHOOD	January 6, 1912; 47th state
STATE BIRD	Roadrunner
STATE FLOWER	Yucca flower
HIGHEST POINT	Wheeler Peak 13,161 ft (4,011 m)

Arizona
GRAND CANYON STATE

AREA	113,998 sq mi (295,254 sq km)
POPULATION	6,731,000
CAPITAL	Phoenix
CAPITAL POP.	city proper: 1,513,000 / metro area: 4,399,000
LARGEST CITY	Phoenix
INCOME	$25,400 per capita
STATEHOOD	February 14, 1912; 48th state
STATE BIRD	Cactus wren
STATE FLOWER	Saguaro cactus blossom
HIGHEST POINT	Humphreys Pk. 12,633 ft (3,851 m)

Colorado
CENTENNIAL STATE

AREA	104,094 sq mi (269,601 sq km)
POPULATION	5,356,000
CAPITAL	Denver
CAPITAL POP.	city proper: 649,000 / metro area: 2,697,000
LARGEST CITY	Denver
INCOME	$31,100 per capita
STATEHOOD	August 1, 1876; 38th state
STATE BIRD	Lark bunting
STATE FLOWER	Rocky Mountain columbine
HIGHEST POINT	Mount Elbert 14,433 ft (4,399 m)

Idaho
GEM STATE

AREA	83,570 sq mi (216,446 sq km)
POPULATION	1,634,000
CAPITAL	Boise
CAPITAL POP.	city proper: 214,000 / metro area: 650,000
LARGEST CITY	Boise
INCOME	$22,600 per capita
STATEHOOD	July 3, 1890; 43rd state
STATE BIRD	Mountain bluebird
STATE FLOWER	Syringa
HIGHEST POINT	Borah Peak 12,662 ft (3,859 m)

Montana
TREASURE STATE

AREA	147,042 sq mi (380,838 sq km)
POPULATION	1,024,000
CAPITAL	Helena
CAPITAL POP.	city proper: 30,000 / metro area: N/A
LARGEST CITY	Billings
POPULATION	city proper: 109,000 / metro area: 165,000
INCOME	$25,400 per capita
STATEHOOD	November 8, 1889; 41st state
STATE BIRD	Western meadowlark
STATE FLOWER	Bitterroot
HIGHEST POINT	Granite Peak 12,799 ft (3,901 m)

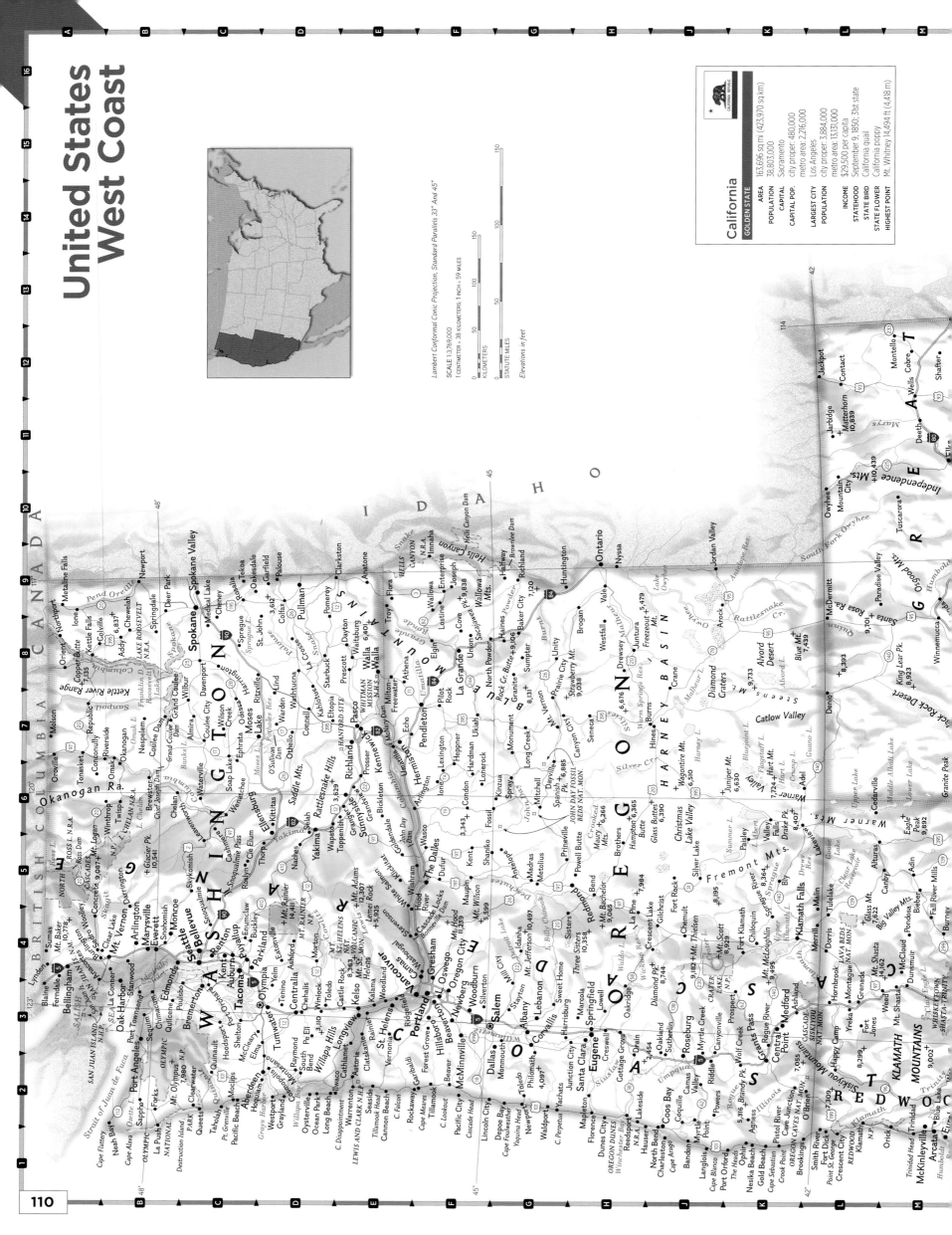

United States West Coast

California
GOLDEN STATE

AREA	163,696 sq mi (423,970 sq km)
POPULATION	38,803,000
CAPITAL	Sacramento
CAPITAL POP.	city proper: 480,000
	metro area: 2,216,000
LARGEST CITY	Los Angeles
POPULATION	city proper: 3,884,000
	metro area 13,131,000
INCOME	$29,500 per capita
STATEHOOD	September 9, 1850; 31st state
STATE BIRD	California quail
STATE FLOWER	California poppy
HIGHEST POINT	Mt. Whitney 14,494 ft (4,418 m)

SCALE 1:3,769,000

1 CENTIMETER = 38 KILOMETERS; 1 INCH = 59 MILES

KILOMETERS

STATUTE MILES

Elevations in feet

Lambert Conformal Conic Projection, Standard Parallels 33° And 45°

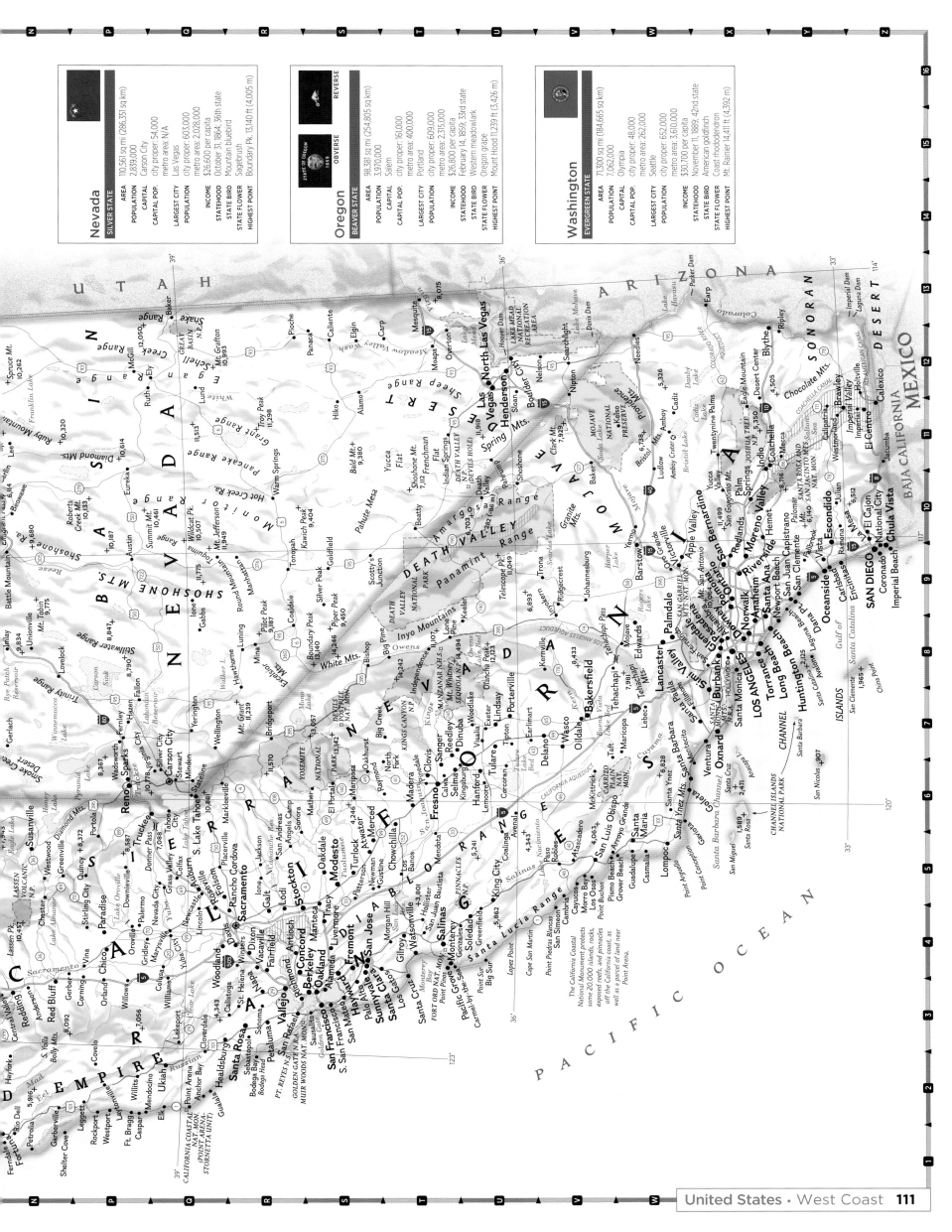

Nevada
SILVER STATE

AREA	110,561 sq mi (286,351 sq km)
POPULATION	2,839,000
CAPITAL	Carson City
CAPITAL POP.	city proper: 54,000
	metro area: N/A
LARGEST CITY	Las Vegas
POPULATION	city proper: 603,000
	metro area: 2,028,000
INCOME	$26,600 per capita
STATEHOOD	October 31, 1864; 36th state
STATE BIRD	Mountain bluebird
STATE FLOWER	Sagebrush
HIGHEST POINT	Boundary Pk. 13,140 ft (4,005 m)

Oregon
BEAVER STATE

AREA	98,381 sq mi (254,805 sq km)
POPULATION	3,970,000
CAPITAL	Salem
CAPITAL POP.	city proper: 161,000
	metro area: 400,000
LARGEST CITY	Portland
POPULATION	city proper: 609,000
	metro area: 2,315,000
INCOME	$26,800 per capita
STATEHOOD	February 14, 1859; 33rd state
STATE BIRD	Western meadowlark
STATE FLOWER	Oregon grape
HIGHEST POINT	Mount Hood 11,239 ft (3,426 m)

Washington
EVERGREEN STATE

AREA	71,300 sq mi (184,665 sq km)
POPULATION	7,062,000
CAPITAL	Olympia
CAPITAL POP.	city proper: 48,000
	metro area: 262,000
LARGEST CITY	Seattle
POPULATION	city proper: 652,000
	metro area: 3,610,000
INCOME	$30,700 per capita
STATEHOOD	November 11, 1889; 42nd state
STATE BIRD	American goldfinch
STATE FLOWER	Coast rhododendron
HIGHEST POINT	Mt. Rainier 14,411 ft (4,392 m)

The California Coastal National Monument protects some 20,000 islands, rocks, exposed reefs, and pinnacles off the California coast, as well as a parcel of land near Point Arena.

Alaska

Area Comparison of Alaska and the Contiguous U.S.

ARCTIC OCEAN

BEAUFORT SEA

Point Barrow
Barrow
IÑUPIAT HERITAGE CENTER
Wainwright
Icy Cape
Point Lay
Peard Bay
Smith Bay
Dease Inlet
Cape Halkett
Harrison Bay
Teshekpuk Lake
Deadhorse
Prudhoe Bay
Kaktovik

matusuk
Kukpowruk Hills
NORTH SLOPE
Meade
Colville
Lookout Ridge +2,344
Mt. Chamberlin +9,020
+ Mt. Isto +9,060

BROOKS RANGE
De Long Mountains
Anaktuvuk Pass
Endicott Mts.
8,025
Philip Smith Mts.
Davidson Mts.
NOATAK NAT. PRESERVE
7,420+
GATES OF THE ARCTIC N.P. AND PRESERVE
Noatak
Baird Mountains
KOBUK VALLEY N.P.
+ Mt. Igikpak 8,510
Arctic Village
Kotzebue
Kiana
Ambler
Kobuk
Shungnak
Noorvik
Selawik
Wiseman
Venetie
Fort Yukon
Chalkyitsik
Deering
Selawik Lake
Evansville
Chandalar
Porcupine

ARCTIC CIRCLE

Koyuk
Hughes
Allakaket
Huslia
Stevens Village
Beaver
ARCTIC CIRCLE
Circle

Koyuk
Nulato
Galena
Ruby
Rampart
Tanana
WHITE MTS. N.R.A.
Central
Shaktoolik
Kaltag
STEESE HWY.
YUKON-CHARLEY RIVERS NATIONAL PRESERVE
Eagle
Unalakleet
Manley Hot Springs
College
Fairbanks
Nenana
Anderson
Delta Junction
TAYLOR HWY.
St. Michael
Koyukuk
Kaiyuh Mts.
Innoko
ALASKA
Yukon
Tanana
ALASKA HWY.
Mt. Hayes +13,832
Tanacross
Tok
Tetlin
Northway Junction
Grayling
Anvik
Shageluk
+4,508
DENALI NATIONAL PARK AND PRESERVE
Healy
Denali Park
RANGE
RICHARDSON HWY.
DENALI HWY.
Mentasta Lake
Holy Cross
Nikolai
(Denali) Mt. McKinley (6,194 m) 20,320
Cantwell
Kuskokwim Mountains
McGrath
Susitna
Talkeetna
Gulkana
Gakona
Kalskag
Aniak
Red Devil
Sleetmute
Kiokluk Mts. 4,093
Talkeetna Mts.
Glennallen
Copper Center
WRANGELL-ST. ELIAS NATIONAL PARK
+ Mt. Blackburn 16,390
Killbuck Mts.
+ Mt. Torbert 11,413
Wasilla
GLENN HWY.
Mt. Marcus Baker 13,176
+ Mt. Bona 16,421
Stony
Birchwood
Palmer
AND PRESERVE
Tyonek
Anchorage
Chugach Mountains
Valdez
Tikchik Lakes
LAKE CLARK N.P. AND PRESERVE
Kenai
Whittier
Mt. Tom White 11,210
St. Elias Mountains
Mt. Foster + 7,127
KLONDIKE GOLD RUSH N.H.P.
Wood River Lakes
Redoubt Volcano + 10,197
Soldotna
Cordova
Mt. St. Elias + 18,008
Bering Glacier
Skagway
Koliganek
Nondalton
Ninilchik
Kenai Peninsula
Seward
Montague Island
Malaspina Glacier
Haines
New Stuyahok
Iliamna Lake
Homer
KENAI FJORDS N.P.
Hinchinbrook Island
Mt. Fairweather + 15,299
GLACIER BAY N.P. AND PRESERVE
Devils Paw + 8,584
Dillingham
Seldovia
Port Graham
Prince William Sound
Yakutat
Juneau
Manokotak
Naknek
KATMAI N.P. AND PRESERVE
Shelikof Strait
Shuyak I.
Hoonah
ADMIRALTY ISLAND N.M.
King Salmon
Mount Katmai + 6,715
Afognak Island
Pelican
Chichagof Island
Angoon
Egegik
Becharof Lake
Port Lions
Kodiak
SITKA N.H.P.
Kake
Bristol Bay
Larsen Bay
Kodiak Island
Kupreanof Island
Petersburg
Pilot Point
ANIAKCHAK N.M. AND PRESERVE
Akhiok
Old Harbor
Sitka
Wrangell
Port Heiden
Sutwik I.
+ Mt. Veniaminof 8,225
Chignik Lagoon
Baranof Island
Thorne Bay
MISTY FIORDS NAT. MON.
Perryville
ALASKA PENINSULA
Trinity Islands
Klawock
Craig
Prince of Wales Island
Ketchikan
Metlakatla
Chirikof Island

NUNAVUT

NORTHWEST TERRITORIES

YUKON

CANADA

BRITISH COLUMBIA

COAST MTS.

ALEXANDER ARCHIPELAGO

Kates Needle + 10,023

Revillagigedo Island

ARCTIC CIRCLE

GULF OF ALASKA

PACIFIC OCEAN

Dixon Entrance

Alaska
LAST FRONTIER

AREA	663,267 sq mi (1,717,854 sq km)
POPULATION	737,000
CAPITAL	Juneau
CAPITAL POP.	city proper: 33,000
	metro area: N/A
LARGEST CITY	Anchorage
POPULATION	city proper: 301,000
	metro area: 396,000
INCOME	$32,700 per capita
STATEHOOD	January 3, 1959; 49th state
STATE BIRD	Willow ptarmigan
STATE FLOWER	Forget-me-not
HIGHEST POINT	Mt. McKinley 20,320 ft (6,194 m)

Azimuthal Equidistant Projection

SCALE 1:7,650,000
1 CENTIMETER = 77 KILOMETERS; 1 INCH = 121 MILES

0   100   200   300
KILOMETERS

0   100   200   300
STATUTE MILES

Elevations in feet

Hawai'i

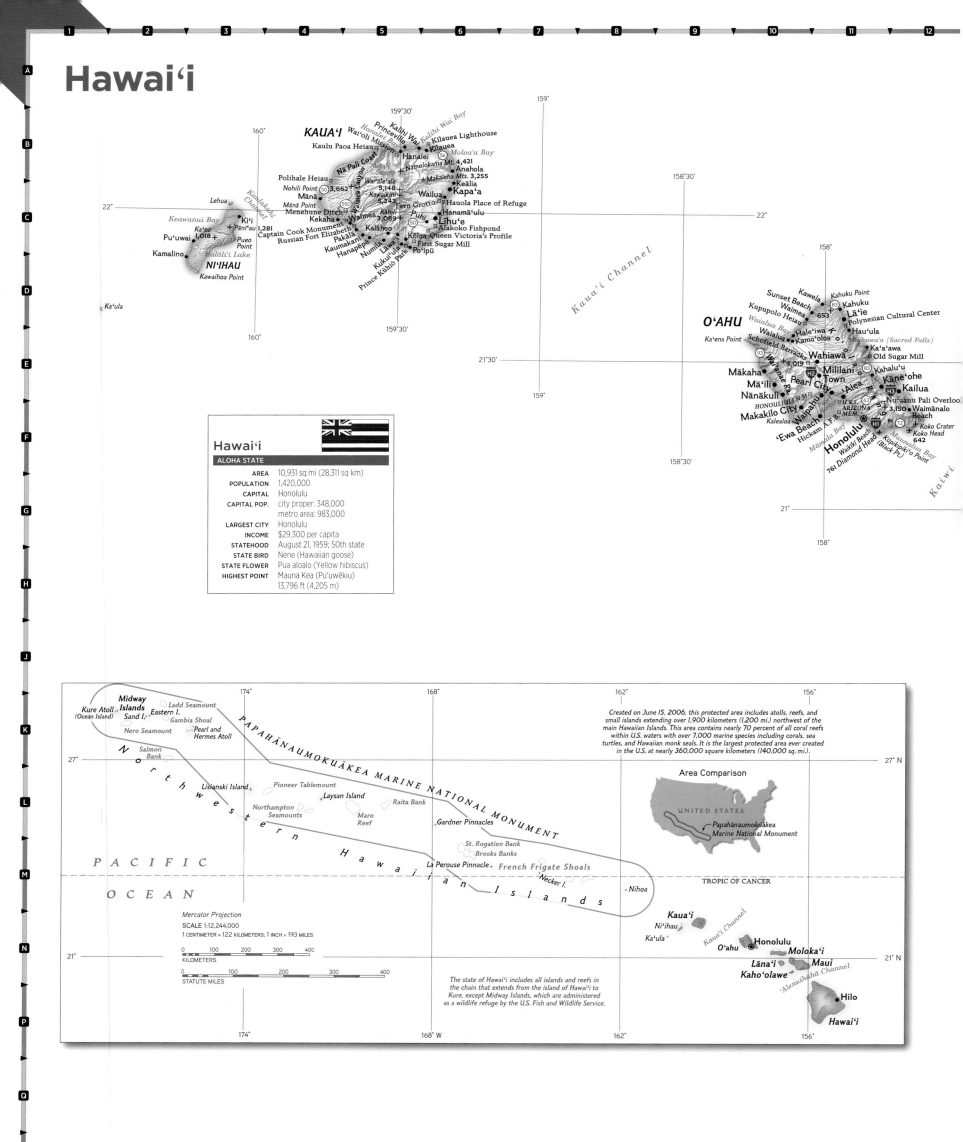

KAUA'I

NI'IHAU

O'AHU

Hawai'i
ALOHA STATE

AREA	10,931 sq mi (28,311 sq km)
POPULATION	1,420,000
CAPITAL	Honolulu
CAPITAL POP.	city proper: 348,000
	metro area: 983,000
LARGEST CITY	Honolulu
INCOME	$29,300 per capita
STATEHOOD	August 21, 1959; 50th state
STATE BIRD	Nene (Hawaiian goose)
STATE FLOWER	Pua aloalo (Yellow hibiscus)
HIGHEST POINT	Mauna Kea (Pu'uwēkiu)
	13,796 ft (4,205 m)

Created on June 15, 2006, this protected area includes atolls, reefs, and small islands extending over 1,900 kilometers (1,200 mi.) northwest of the main Hawaiian Islands. This area contains nearly 70 percent of all coral reefs within U.S. waters with over 7,000 marine species including corals, sea turtles, and Hawaiian monk seals. It is the largest protected area ever created in the U.S. at nearly 360,000 square kilometers (140,000 sq. mi.).

Area Comparison

UNITED STATES

Papahānaumokuākea Marine National Monument

PAPAHĀNAUMOKUĀKEA MARINE NATIONAL MONUMENT

Northwestern Hawaiian Islands

PACIFIC OCEAN

TROPIC OF CANCER

Mercator Projection
SCALE 1:12,244,000
1 CENTIMETER = 122 KILOMETERS; 1 INCH = 193 MILES

KILOMETERS

STATUTE MILES

The state of Hawai'i includes all islands and reefs in the chain that extends from the island of Hawai'i to Kure, except Midway Islands, which are administered as a wildlife refuge by the U.S. Fish and Wildlife Service.

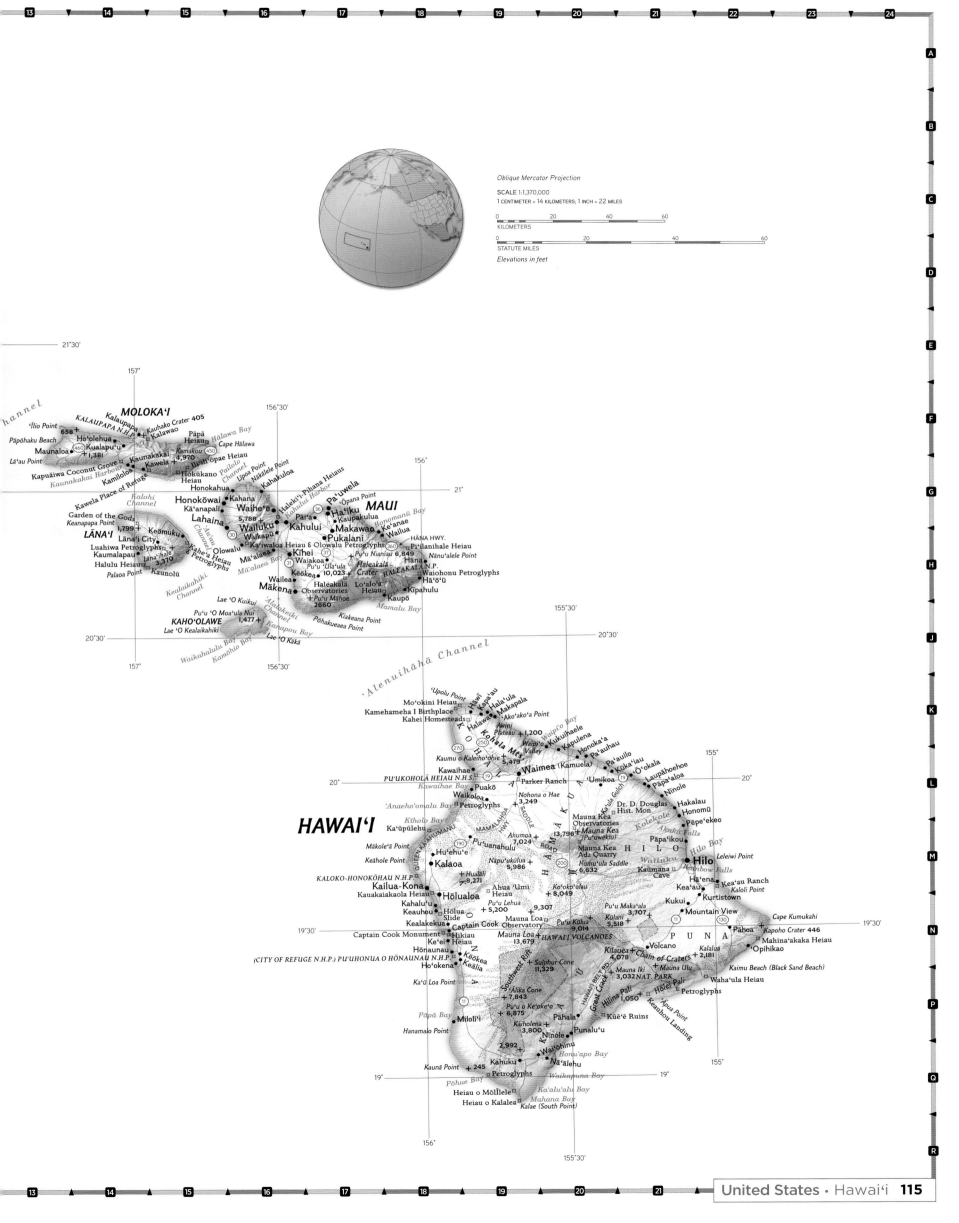

Mexico and Central America

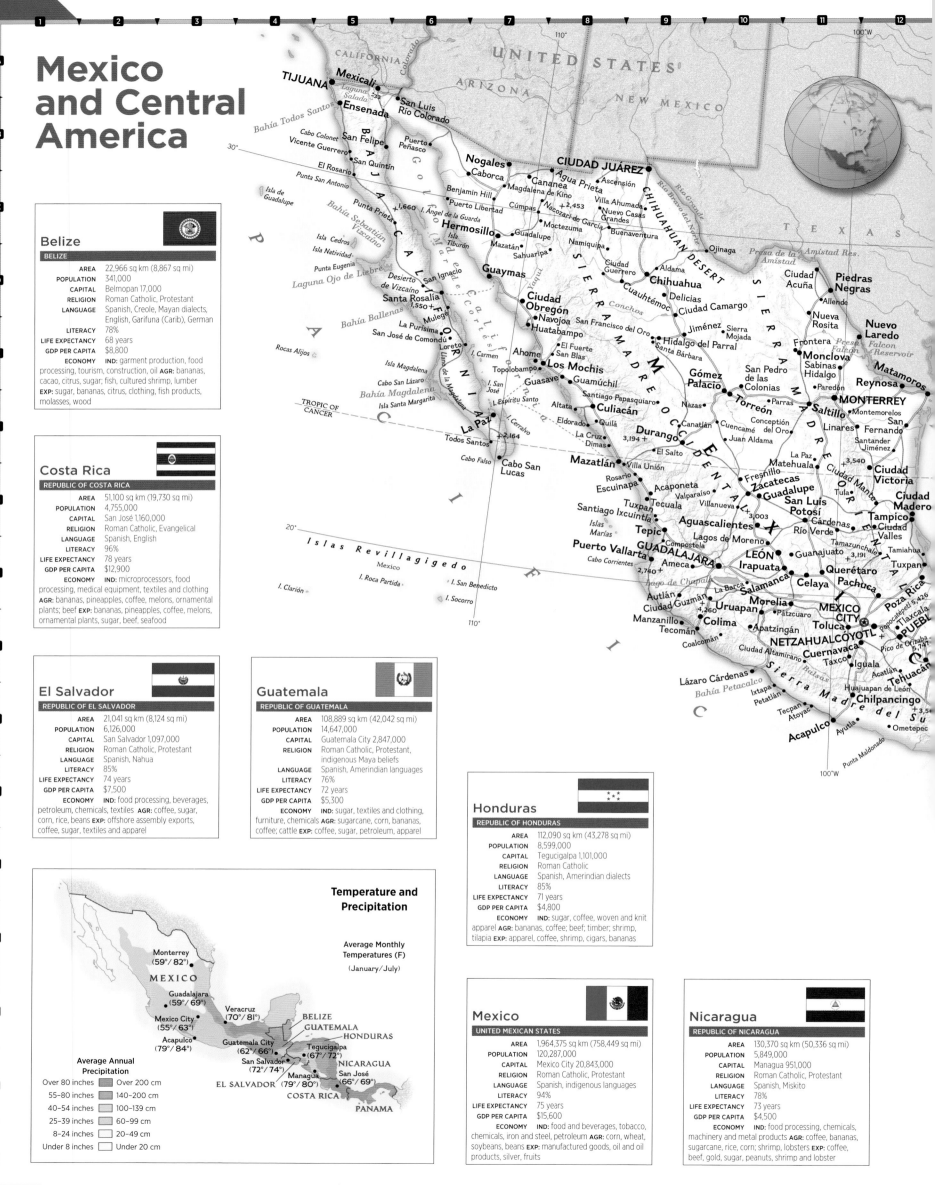

Belize
BELIZE
AREA	22,966 sq km (8,867 sq mi)
POPULATION	341,000
CAPITAL	Belmopan 17,000
RELIGION	Roman Catholic, Protestant
LANGUAGE	Spanish, Creole, Mayan dialects, English, Garifuna (Carib), German
LITERACY	78%
LIFE EXPECTANCY	68 years
GDP PER CAPITA	$8,800

ECONOMY IND: garment production, food processing, tourism, construction, oil AGR: bananas, cacao, citrus, sugar; fish, cultured shrimp, lumber EXP: sugar, bananas, citrus, clothing, fish products, molasses, wood

Costa Rica
REPUBLIC OF COSTA RICA
AREA	51,100 sq km (19,730 sq mi)
POPULATION	4,755,000
CAPITAL	San José 1,160,000
RELIGION	Roman Catholic, Evangelical
LANGUAGE	Spanish, English
LITERACY	96%
LIFE EXPECTANCY	78 years
GDP PER CAPITA	$12,900

ECONOMY IND: microprocessors, food processing, medical equipment, textiles and clothing AGR: bananas, pineapples, coffee, melons, ornamental plants; beef EXP: bananas, pineapples, coffee, melons, ornamental plants, sugar, beef, seafood

El Salvador
REPUBLIC OF EL SALVADOR
AREA	21,041 sq km (8,124 sq mi)
POPULATION	6,126,000
CAPITAL	San Salvador 1,097,000
RELIGION	Roman Catholic, Protestant
LANGUAGE	Spanish, Nahua
LITERACY	85%
LIFE EXPECTANCY	74 years
GDP PER CAPITA	$7,500

ECONOMY IND: food processing, beverages, petroleum, chemicals, textiles AGR: coffee, sugar, corn, rice, beans EXP: offshore assembly exports, coffee, sugar, textiles and apparel

Guatemala
REPUBLIC OF GUATEMALA
AREA	108,889 sq km (42,042 sq mi)
POPULATION	14,647,000
CAPITAL	Guatemala City 2,847,000
RELIGION	Roman Catholic, Protestant, indigenous Maya beliefs
LANGUAGE	Spanish, Amerindian languages
LITERACY	76%
LIFE EXPECTANCY	72 years
GDP PER CAPITA	$5,300

ECONOMY IND: sugar, textiles and clothing, furniture, chemicals AGR: sugarcane, corn, bananas, coffee; cattle EXP: coffee, sugar, petroleum, apparel

Honduras
REPUBLIC OF HONDURAS
AREA	112,090 sq km (43,278 sq mi)
POPULATION	8,599,000
CAPITAL	Tegucigalpa 1,101,000
RELIGION	Roman Catholic
LANGUAGE	Spanish, Amerindian dialects
LITERACY	85%
LIFE EXPECTANCY	71 years
GDP PER CAPITA	$4,800

ECONOMY IND: sugar, coffee, woven and knit apparel AGR: bananas, coffee; beef; timber; shrimp; tilapia EXP: apparel, coffee, shrimp, cigars, bananas

Mexico
UNITED MEXICAN STATES
AREA	1,964,375 sq km (758,449 sq mi)
POPULATION	120,287,000
CAPITAL	Mexico City 20,843,000
RELIGION	Roman Catholic, Protestant
LANGUAGE	Spanish, indigenous languages
LITERACY	94%
LIFE EXPECTANCY	75 years
GDP PER CAPITA	$15,600

ECONOMY IND: food and beverages, tobacco, chemicals, iron and steel, petroleum AGR: corn, wheat, soybeans, beans EXP: manufactured goods, oil and oil products, silver, fruits

Nicaragua
REPUBLIC OF NICARAGUA
AREA	130,370 sq km (50,336 sq mi)
POPULATION	5,849,000
CAPITAL	Managua 951,000
RELIGION	Roman Catholic, Protestant
LANGUAGE	Spanish, Miskito
LITERACY	78%
LIFE EXPECTANCY	73 years
GDP PER CAPITA	$4,500

ECONOMY IND: food processing, chemicals, machinery and metal products AGR: coffee, bananas, sugarcane, rice, corn; shrimp, lobsters EXP: coffee, beef, gold, sugar, peanuts, shrimp and lobster

Temperature and Precipitation

Average Monthly Temperatures (F)

(January/July)

Monterrey (59°/82°)

MEXICO

Guadalajara (59°/69°)

Veracruz (70°/81°)

Mexico City (55°/63°)

Acapulco (79°/84°)

BELIZE
GUATEMALA
HONDURAS

Guatemala City (62°/66°)

Tegucigalpa (67°/72°)

San Salvador (72°/74°)

NICARAGUA

Managua (79°/80°)

San José (66°/69°)

EL SALVADOR

COSTA RICA

PANAMA

Average Annual Precipitation
Over 80 inches	Over 200 cm
55-80 inches	140-200 cm
40-54 inches	100-139 cm
25-39 inches	60-99 cm
8-24 inches	20-49 cm
Under 8 inches	Under 20 cm

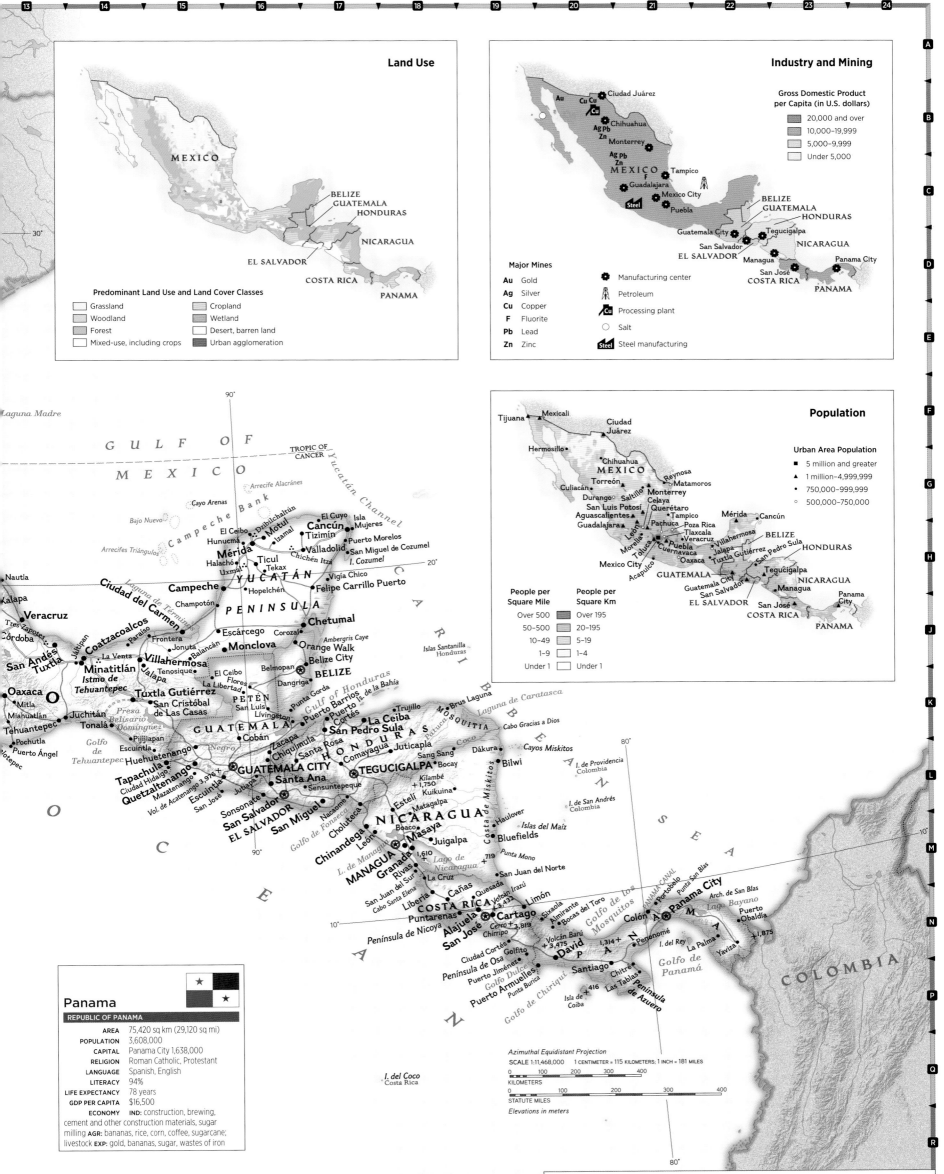

Land Use

Predominant Land Use and Land Cover Classes

- Grassland
- Woodland
- Forest
- Mixed-use, including crops
- Cropland
- Wetland
- Desert, barren land
- Urban agglomeration

Industry and Mining

Gross Domestic Product per Capita (in U.S. dollars)

- 20,000 and over
- 10,000–19,999
- 5,000–9,999
- Under 5,000

Major Mines

- Au Gold
- Ag Silver
- Cu Copper
- F Fluorite
- Pb Lead
- Zn Zinc

- Manufacturing center
- Petroleum
- Cu Processing plant
- Salt
- Steel Steel manufacturing

Population

Urban Area Population

- ■ 5 million and greater
- ▲ 1 million–4,999,999
- ▲ 750,000–999,999
- ○ 500,000–750,000

People per Square Mile	People per Square Km
Over 500	Over 195
50–500	20–195
10–49	5–19
1–9	1–4
Under 1	Under 1

Panama

REPUBLIC OF PANAMA

AREA	75,420 sq km (29,120 sq mi)
POPULATION	3,608,000
CAPITAL	Panama City 1,638,000
RELIGION	Roman Catholic, Protestant
LANGUAGE	Spanish, English
LITERACY	94%
LIFE EXPECTANCY	78 years
GDP PER CAPITA	$16,500
ECONOMY	IND: construction, brewing, cement and other construction materials, sugar milling AGR: bananas, rice, corn, coffee, sugarcane; livestock EXP: gold, bananas, sugar, wastes of iron

Azimuthal Equidistant Projection
SCALE 1:11,468,000   1 CENTIMETER = 115 KILOMETERS; 1 INCH = 181 MILES

KILOMETERS
0   100   200   300   400

STATUTE MILES
0   100   200   300   400

Elevations in meters

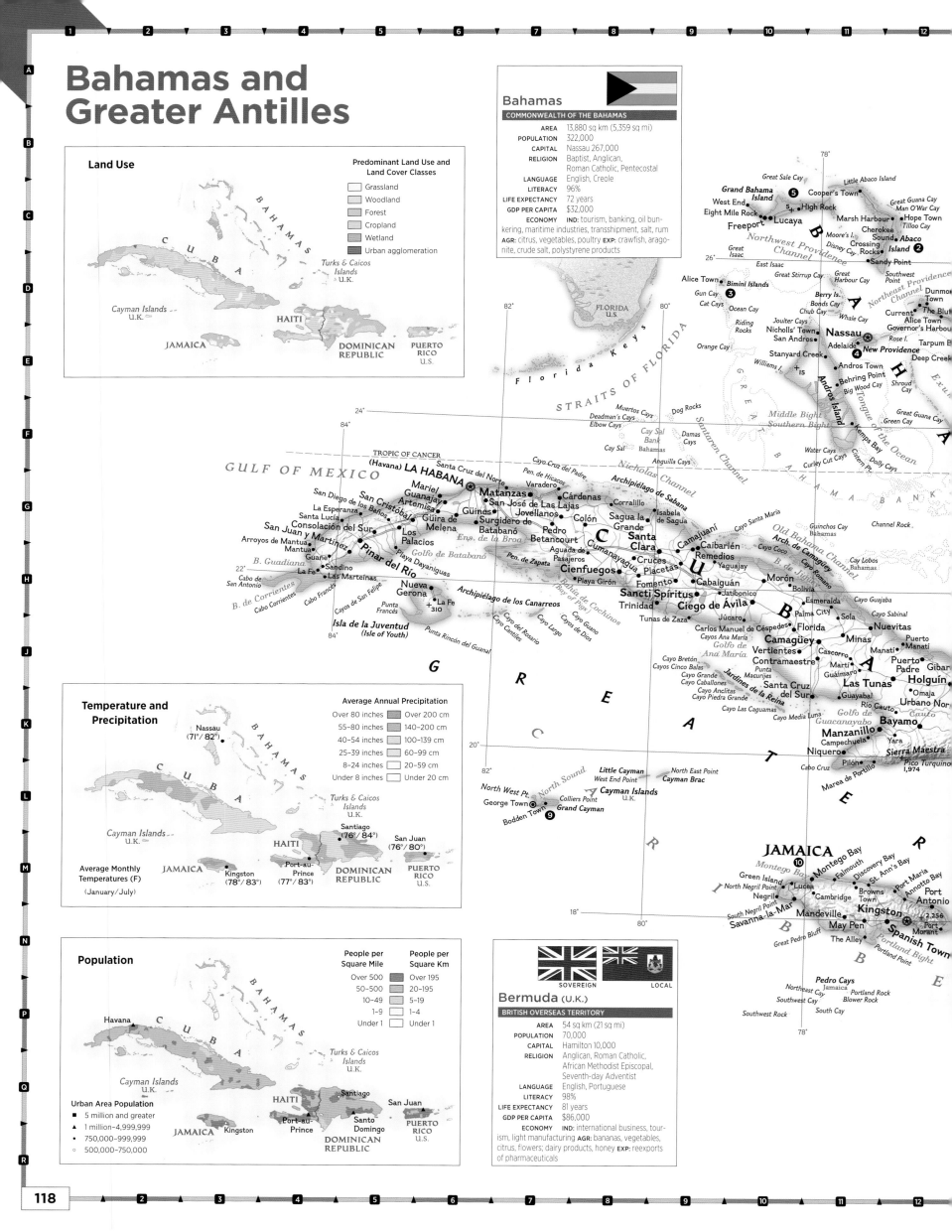

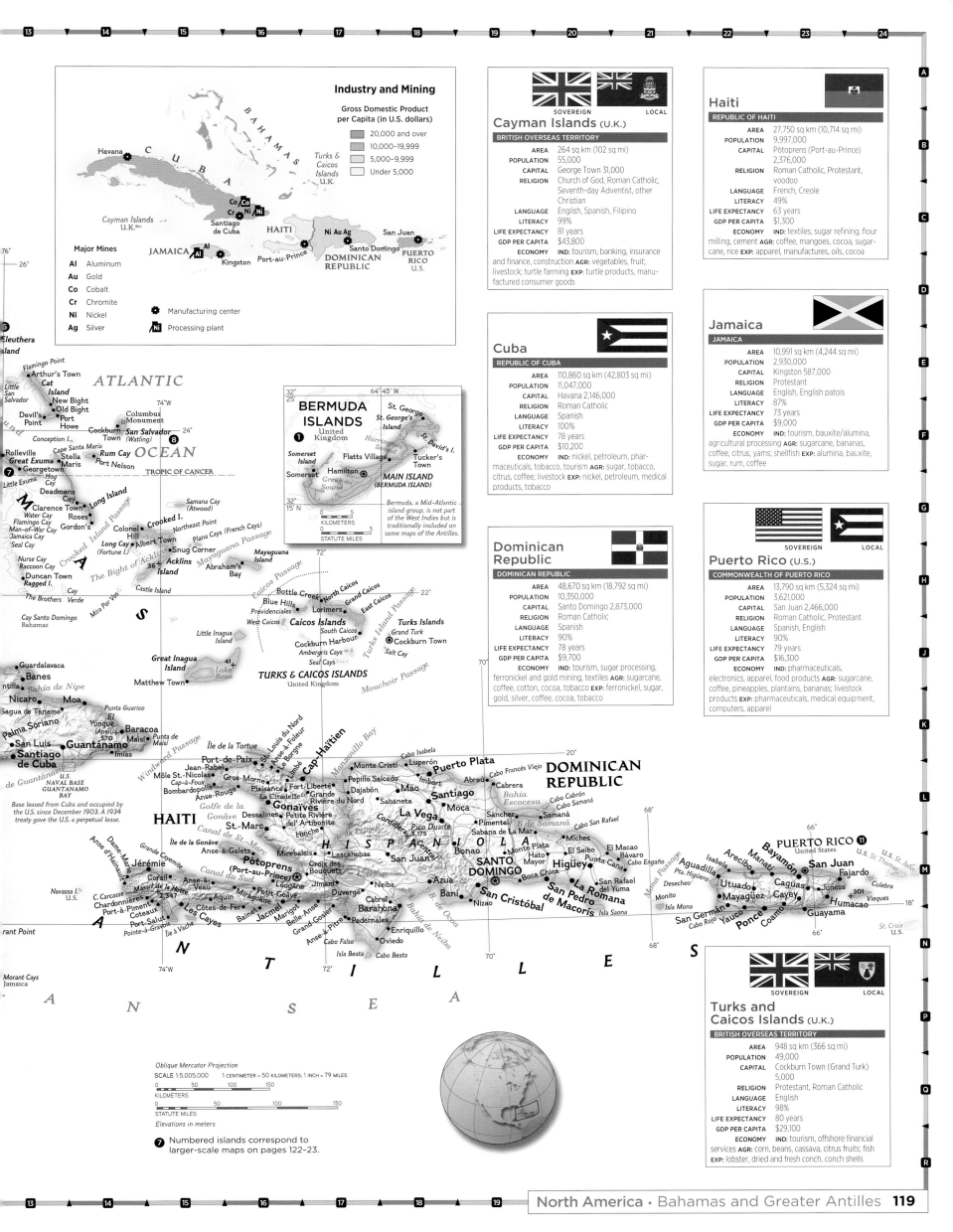

Industry and Mining

Gross Domestic Product per Capita (in U.S. dollars)

- 20,000 and over
- 10,000–19,999
- 5,000–9,999
- Under 5,000

Major Mines

- **Al** Aluminum
- **Au** Gold
- **Co** Cobalt
- **Cr** Chromite
- **Ni** Nickel
- **Ag** Silver

✿ Manufacturing center
[Ni] Processing plant

Cayman Islands (U.K.)

SOVEREIGN | LOCAL

BRITISH OVERSEAS TERRITORY

AREA	264 sq km (102 sq mi)
POPULATION	55,000
CAPITAL	George Town 31,000
RELIGION	Church of God, Roman Catholic, Seventh-day Adventist, other Christian
LANGUAGE	English, Spanish, Filipino
LIFE EXPECTANCY	81 years
GDP PER CAPITA	$43,800
ECONOMY	**IND:** tourism, banking, insurance and finance, construction **AGR:** vegetables, fruit; livestock; turtle farming **EXP:** turtle products, manufactured consumer goods

---

Cuba

REPUBLIC OF CUBA

AREA	110,860 sq km (42,803 sq mi)
POPULATION	11,047,000
CAPITAL	Havana 2,146,000
RELIGION	Roman Catholic
LANGUAGE	Spanish
LITERACY	100%
LIFE EXPECTANCY	78 years
GDP PER CAPITA	$10,200
ECONOMY	**IND:** nickel, petroleum, pharmaceuticals, tobacco, tourism **AGR:** sugar, tobacco, citrus, coffee; livestock **EXP:** nickel, petroleum, medical products, tobacco

---

BERMUDA ISLANDS

United Kingdom

St. George
St. George's Island
St. David's I.
Somerset Island
Somerset
Flatts Village
Tucker's Town
Hamilton ◉
MAIN ISLAND (BERMUDA ISLAND)
Great Sound
Harrington Sound

KILOMETERS
STATUTE MILES

Bermuda, a Mid-Atlantic island group, is not part of the West Indies but is traditionally included on some maps of the Antilles.

Dominican Republic

DOMINICAN REPUBLIC

AREA	48,670 sq km (18,792 sq mi)
POPULATION	10,350,000
CAPITAL	Santo Domingo 2,873,000
RELIGION	Roman Catholic
LANGUAGE	Spanish
LITERACY	90%
LIFE EXPECTANCY	78 years
GDP PER CAPITA	$9,700
ECONOMY	**IND:** tourism, sugar processing, ferronickel and gold mining, textiles **AGR:** sugarcane, coffee, cotton, cocoa, tobacco **EXP:** ferronickel, sugar, gold, silver, coffee, cocoa, tobacco

---

Haiti

REPUBLIC OF HAITI

AREA	27,750 sq km (10,714 sq mi)
POPULATION	9,997,000
CAPITAL	Pòtoprens (Port-au-Prince) 2,376,000
RELIGION	Roman Catholic, Protestant, voodoo
LANGUAGE	French, Creole
LITERACY	49%
LIFE EXPECTANCY	63 years
GDP PER CAPITA	$1,300
ECONOMY	**IND:** textiles, sugar refining, flour milling, cement **AGR:** coffee, mangoes, cocoa, sugarcane, rice **EXP:** apparel, manufactures, oils, cocoa

---

Jamaica

JAMAICA

AREA	10,991 sq km (4,244 sq mi)
POPULATION	2,930,000
CAPITAL	Kingston 587,000
RELIGION	Protestant
LANGUAGE	English, English patois
LITERACY	87%
LIFE EXPECTANCY	73 years
GDP PER CAPITA	$9,000
ECONOMY	**IND:** tourism, bauxite/alumina, agricultural processing **AGR:** sugarcane, bananas, coffee, citrus, yams; shellfish **EXP:** alumina, bauxite, sugar, rum, coffee

---

Puerto Rico (U.S.)

SOVEREIGN | LOCAL

COMMONWEALTH OF PUERTO RICO

AREA	13,790 sq km (5,324 sq mi)
POPULATION	3,621,000
CAPITAL	San Juan 2,466,000
RELIGION	Roman Catholic, Protestant
LANGUAGE	Spanish, English
LITERACY	90%
LIFE EXPECTANCY	79 years
GDP PER CAPITA	$16,300
ECONOMY	**IND:** pharmaceuticals, electronics, apparel, food products **AGR:** sugarcane, coffee, pineapples, plantains, bananas; livestock products **EXP:** pharmaceuticals, medical equipment, computers, apparel

---

Turks and Caicos Islands (U.K.)

SOVEREIGN | LOCAL

BRITISH OVERSEAS TERRITORY

AREA	948 sq km (366 sq mi)
POPULATION	49,000
CAPITAL	Cockburn Town (Grand Turk) 5,000
RELIGION	Protestant, Roman Catholic
LANGUAGE	English
LITERACY	98%
LIFE EXPECTANCY	80 years
GDP PER CAPITA	$29,100
ECONOMY	**IND:** tourism, offshore financial services **AGR:** corn, beans, cassava, citrus fruits; fish **EXP:** lobster, dried and fresh conch, conch shells

---

U.S. NAVAL BASE GUANTANAMO BAY

Base leased from Cuba and occupied by the U.S. since December 1903. A 1934 treaty gave the U.S. a perpetual lease.

Oblique Mercator Projection

SCALE 1:5,005,000   1 CENTIMETER = 50 KILOMETERS; 1 INCH = 79 MILES

KILOMETERS

STATUTE MILES

Elevations in meters

7 Numbered islands correspond to larger-scale maps on pages 122–23.

Lesser Antilles

Anguilla (U.K.)
SOVEREIGN **LOCAL**

BRITISH OVERSEAS TERRITORY
AREA	91 sq km (35 sq mi)
POPULATION	16,000
CAPITAL	The Valley 1,000
RELIGION	Anglican, Methodist, other Protestant, Roman Catholic
LANGUAGE	English
LITERACY	95%
LIFE EXPECTANCY	81 years
GDP PER CAPITA	$12,200

ECONOMY **IND:** tourism, boat building, offshore financial services **AGR:** small quantities of tobacco, vegetables; cattle raising **EXP:** lobster, fish, livestock, salt, concrete blocks, rum

Antigua and Barbuda

ANTIGUA AND BARBUDA
AREA	443 sq km (171 sq mi)
POPULATION	91,000
CAPITAL	St. John's 22,000
RELIGION	Anglican, Seventh-day Adventist, Pentecostal, Moravian, Roman Catholic
LANGUAGE	English, local dialects
LITERACY	99%
LIFE EXPECTANCY	76 years
GDP PER CAPITA	$18,400

ECONOMY **IND:** tourism, construction, light manufacturing (clothing, alcohol, household appliances) **AGR:** cotton, fruits, vegetables, bananas, coconuts, cucumbers, mangoes, sugarcane **EXP:** petroleum products, bedding, handicrafts, electronic components, transport equipment

Aruba (Netherlands)
SOVEREIGN **LOCAL**

AUTONOMOUS COUNTRY
AREA	180 sq km (69 sq mi)
POPULATION	111,000
CAPITAL	Oranjestad 29,000
RELIGION	Roman Catholic
LANGUAGE	Papiamento, Spanish, English, Dutch
LITERACY	97%
LIFE EXPECTANCY	76 years
GDP PER CAPITA	$25,300

ECONOMY **IND:** tourism, transshipment facilities, banking **AGR:** aloes; livestock; fish **EXP:** live animals and animal products, art and collectibles, machinery and electrical equipment, transport equipment

Barbados

BARBADOS
AREA	430 sq km (166 sq mi)
POPULATION	290,000
CAPITAL	Bridgetown 90,000
RELIGION	Anglican, Pentecostal, Adventist
LANGUAGE	English, Bajan
LITERACY	100%
LIFE EXPECTANCY	75 years
GDP PER CAPITA	$25,100

ECONOMY **IND:** tourism, sugar, light manufacturing, component assembly for export **AGR:** sugarcane, vegetables, cotton **EXP:** manufactures, sugar and molasses, rum, other foods and beverages, chemicals

British Virgin Islands (U.K.)
SOVEREIGN **LOCAL**

BRITISH OVERSEAS TERRITORY
AREA	151 sq km (58 sq mi)
POPULATION	33,000
CAPITAL	Road Town 13,000
RELIGION	Methodist, Anglican,
LANGUAGE	English
LITERACY	98%
LIFE EXPECTANCY	78 years
GDP PER CAPITA	$42,300

ECONOMY **IND:** tourism, light industry, construction, rum **AGR:** fruits, vegetables; livestock, poultry **EXP:** rum, fresh fish, fruits, animals; gravel

Curaçao (Neth.)
SOVEREIGN **LOCAL**

AUTONOMOUS COUNTRY
AREA	444 sq km (171 sq mi)
POPULATION	147,000
CAPITAL	Willemstad 145,000
RELIGION	Roman Catholic, Pentecostal
LANGUAGE	Papiamento, Dutch, Spanish
LITERACY	N/A
LIFE EXPECTANCY	N/A
GDP PER CAPITA	$15,000

ECONOMY **IND:** tourism, petroleum refining, petroleum transshipment **AGR:** aloe, sorghum, peanuts, vegetables **EXP:** refined and crude petroleum

Dominica

COMMONWEALTH OF DOMINICA
AREA	751 sq km (290 sq mi)
POPULATION	73,000
CAPITAL	Roseau 15,000
RELIGION	Roman Catholic, Protestant
LANGUAGE	English, French patois
LITERACY	94%
LIFE EXPECTANCY	77 years
GDP PER CAPITA	$14,300

ECONOMY **IND:** soap, coconut oil, tourism, copra, furniture, cement blocks, shoes **AGR:** bananas, citrus, mangos, root crops, coconuts **EXP:** bananas, soap, bay oil, vegetables, grapefruit

Grenada

GRENADA
AREA	344 sq km (133 sq mi)
POPULATION	110,000
CAPITAL	St. George's 38,000
RELIGION	Roman Catholic, Anglican, other Protestant
LANGUAGE	English, French patois
LITERACY	96%
LIFE EXPECTANCY	74 years
GDP PER CAPITA	$13,800

ECONOMY **IND:** food and beverages, textiles, light assembly operations, tourism, construction **AGR:** bananas, cocoa, nutmeg, mace, citrus **EXP:** nutmeg, bananas, cocoa, fruits and vegetables, clothing, mace

Guadeloupe (France)

OVERSEAS DEPARTMENT OF FRANCE
AREA	1,705 sq km (658 sq mi)
POPULATION	406,000
CAPITAL	Basse-Terre 55,000
RELIGION	Roman Catholic, Protestant, Hindu, Muslim, Buddhist, pagan
LANGUAGE	French, Creole patois
LITERACY	N/A
LIFE EXPECTANCY	N/A
GDP PER CAPITA	N/A

ECONOMY **IND:** tourism, sugar and rum production, construction **AGR:** bananas, sugarcane, eggplant, flowers **EXP:** bananas, sugar, rum

Martinique (France)

OVERSEAS DEPARTMENT OF FRANCE
AREA	1,100 sq km (425 sq mi)
POPULATION	386,000
CAPITAL	Fort-de-France 86,000
RELIGION	Roman Catholic, Protestant, Hindu, Muslim, Buddhist
LANGUAGE	French, Creole patois
LITERACY	N/A
LIFE EXPECTANCY	N/A
GDP PER CAPITA	N/A

ECONOMY **IND:** tourism, petroleum refining, rum, sugar **AGR:** pineapples, avocados, bananas, sugarcane **EXP:** fruits, beverages, refined petroleum products

Montserrat (U.K.)
SOVEREIGN **LOCAL**

BRITISH OVERSEAS TERRITORY
AREA	102 sq km (39 sq mi)
POPULATION	5,000
CAPITAL	Brades (administrative) 800; Plymouth (abandoned)
RELIGION	Protestant, Roman Catholic
LANGUAGE	English
LITERACY	97%
LIFE EXPECTANCY	74 years
GDP PER CAPITA	$8,500

ECONOMY **IND:** tourism, rum, textiles, electronic equipment **AGR:** cabbages, carrots, cucumbers, tomatoes; livestock **EXP:** electronic components, plastic bags, apparel, peppers

Saint-Barthélemy (France)

OVERSEAS DEPARTMENT OF FRANCE
AREA	21 sq km (8 sq mi)
POPULATION	7,000
CAPITAL	Gustavia 2,300
RELIGION	Roman Catholic, Protestant, Jehovah's Witnesses
LANGUAGE	French, English
LITERACY	N/A
LIFE EXPECTANCY	N/A
GDP PER CAPITA	N/A

ECONOMY **IND:** tourism, construction, fish products **AGR:** vegetables; fishing **EXP:** art and handicrafts, jewelry, clothing

Saint Kitts and Nevis

FEDERATION OF SAINT KITTS AND NEVIS
AREA	261 sq km (101 sq mi)
POPULATION	52,000
CAPITAL	Basseterre 14,000
RELIGION	Anglican, other Protestant, Roman Catholic
LANGUAGE	English
LITERACY	98%
LIFE EXPECTANCY	75 years
GDP PER CAPITA	$16,300

ECONOMY **IND:** tourism, cotton, salt, copra **AGR:** sugarcane, rice, yams, vegetables; fish **EXP:** machinery, food, electronics, beverages, tobacco

Saint Lucia

SAINT LUCIA
AREA	616 sq km (238 sq mi)
POPULATION	163,000
CAPITAL	Castries 22,000
RELIGION	Roman Catholic, Protestant
LANGUAGE	English, French patois
LITERACY	90%
LIFE EXPECTANCY	77 years
GDP PER CAPITA	$13,100

ECONOMY **IND:** tourism, clothing, assembly of electronic components, beverages, coconut processing **AGR:** bananas, coconuts, vegetables, citrus **EXP:** bananas, clothing, cocoa, avocados

Saint-Martin (France)

FRENCH OVERSEAS COLLECTIVITY
AREA	54 sq km (21 sq mi)
POPULATION	32,000
CAPITAL	Marigot 5,700
RELIGION	Roman Catholic, Jehovah's Witnesses, Protestant, Hindu
LANGUAGE	French, English, Dutch, French Patois, Spanish, Papiamento
LITERACY	N/A
LIFE EXPECTANCY	N/A
GDP PER CAPITA	$19,300

ECONOMY **IND:** tourism, light industry and manufacturing **AGR:** vegetables; fish **EXP:** petroleum products

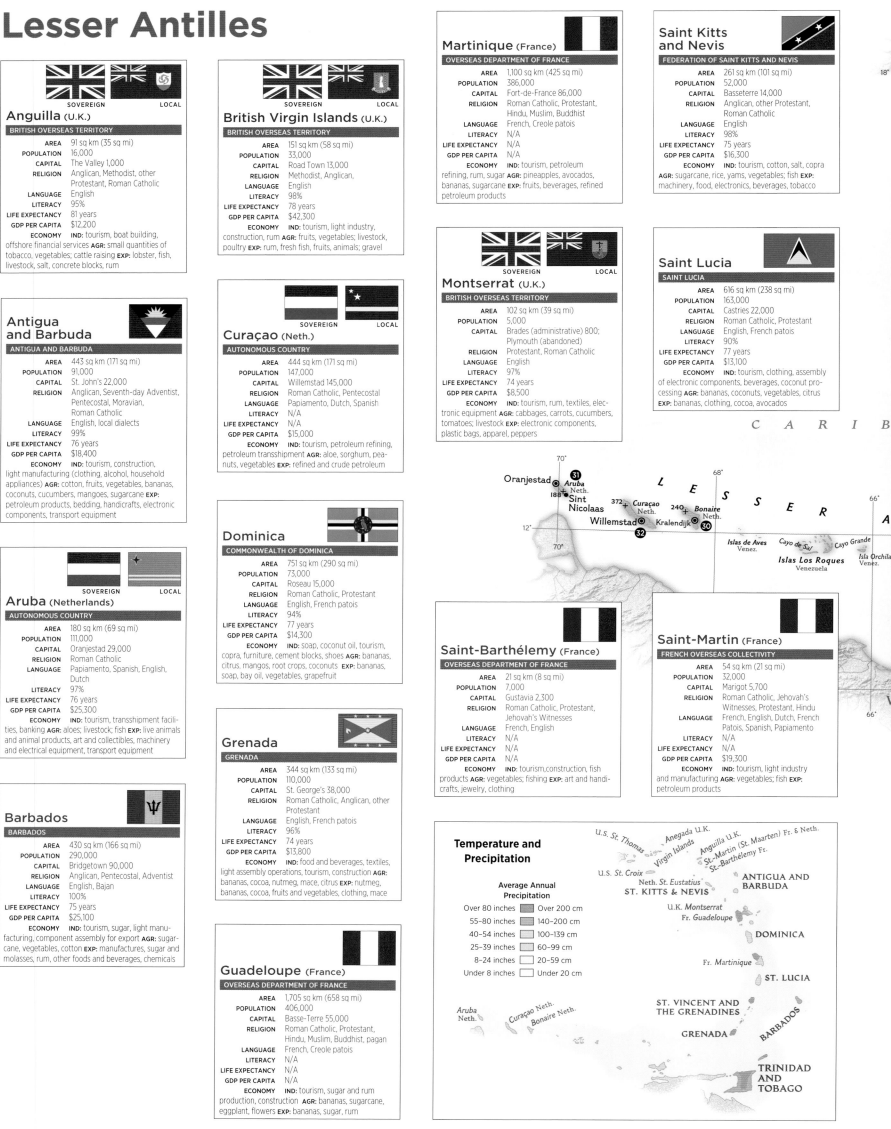

Temperature and Precipitation

Average Annual Precipitation

Over 80 inches	Over 200 cm
55–80 inches	140–200 cm
40–54 inches	100–139 cm
25–39 inches	60–99 cm
8–24 inches	20–59 cm
Under 8 inches	Under 20 cm

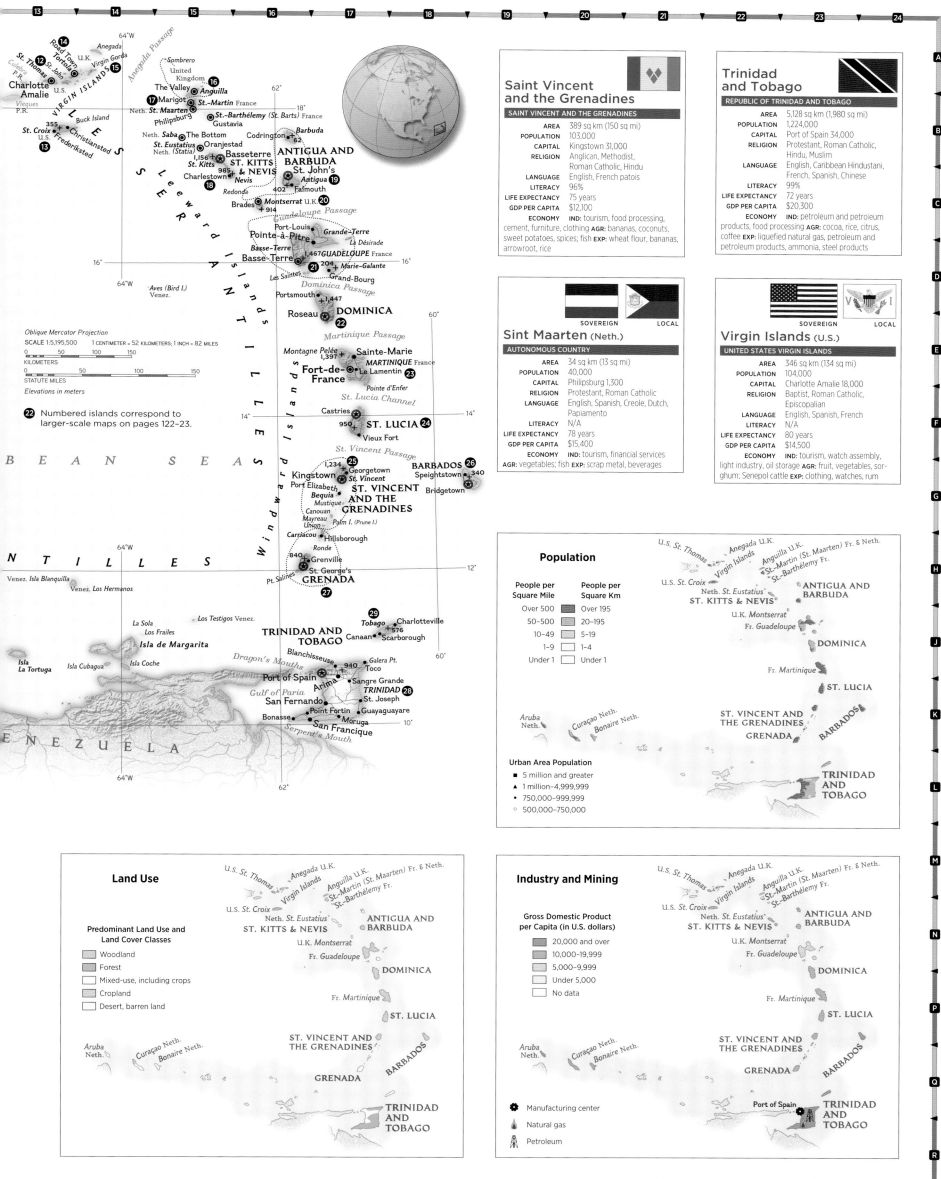

Saint Vincent and the Grenadines

SAINT VINCENT AND THE GRENADINES

AREA	389 sq km (150 sq mi)
POPULATION	103,000
CAPITAL	Kingstown 31,000
RELIGION	Anglican, Methodist, Roman Catholic, Hindu
LANGUAGE	English, French patois
LITERACY	96%
LIFE EXPECTANCY	75 years
GDP PER CAPITA	$12,100
ECONOMY	IND: tourism, food processing, cement, furniture, clothing AGR: bananas, coconuts, sweet potatoes, spices; fish EXP: wheat flour, bananas, arrowroot, rice

Trinidad and Tobago

REPUBLIC OF TRINIDAD AND TOBAGO

AREA	5,128 sq km (1,980 sq mi)
POPULATION	1,224,000
CAPITAL	Port of Spain 34,000
RELIGION	Protestant, Roman Catholic, Hindu, Muslim
LANGUAGE	English, Caribbean Hindustani, French, Spanish, Chinese
LITERACY	99%
LIFE EXPECTANCY	72 years
GDP PER CAPITA	$20,300
ECONOMY	IND: petroleum and petroleum products, food processing AGR: cocoa, rice, citrus, coffee EXP: liquefied natural gas, petroleum and petroleum products, ammonia, steel products

Sint Maarten (Neth.)

SOVEREIGN   LOCAL

AUTONOMOUS COUNTRY

AREA	34 sq km (13 sq mi)
POPULATION	40,000
CAPITAL	Philipsburg 1,300
RELIGION	Protestant, Roman Catholic
LANGUAGE	English, Spanish, Creole, Dutch, Papiamento
LITERACY	N/A
LIFE EXPECTANCY	78 years
GDP PER CAPITA	$15,400
ECONOMY	IND: tourism, financial services AGR: vegetables; fish EXP: scrap metal, beverages

Virgin Islands (U.S.)

SOVEREIGN   LOCAL

UNITED STATES VIRGIN ISLANDS

AREA	346 sq km (134 sq mi)
POPULATION	104,000
CAPITAL	Charlotte Amalie 18,000
RELIGION	Baptist, Roman Catholic, Episcopalian
LANGUAGE	English, Spanish, French
LITERACY	N/A
LIFE EXPECTANCY	80 years
GDP PER CAPITA	$14,500
ECONOMY	IND: tourism, watch assembly, light industry, oil storage AGR: fruit, vegetables, sorghum; Senepol cattle EXP: clothing, watches, rum

Oblique Mercator Projection

SCALE 1:5,195,500
1 CENTIMETER = 52 KILOMETERS; 1 INCH = 82 MILES

KILOMETERS
STATUTE MILES

Elevations in meters

22 Numbered islands correspond to larger-scale maps on pages 122–23.

Population

People per Square Mile	People per Square Km
Over 500	Over 195
50–500	20–195
10–49	5–19
1–9	1–4
Under 1	Under 1

Urban Area Population
- ■ 5 million and greater
- ▲ 1 million–4,999,999
- ● 750,000–999,999
- ○ 500,000–750,000

Land Use

Predominant Land Use and Land Cover Classes
- Woodland
- Forest
- Mixed-use, including crops
- Cropland
- Desert, barren land

Industry and Mining

Gross Domestic Product per Capita (in U.S. dollars)
- 20,000 and over
- 10,000–19,999
- 5,000–9,999
- Under 5,000
- No data

- ☸ Manufacturing center
- Natural gas
- Petroleum

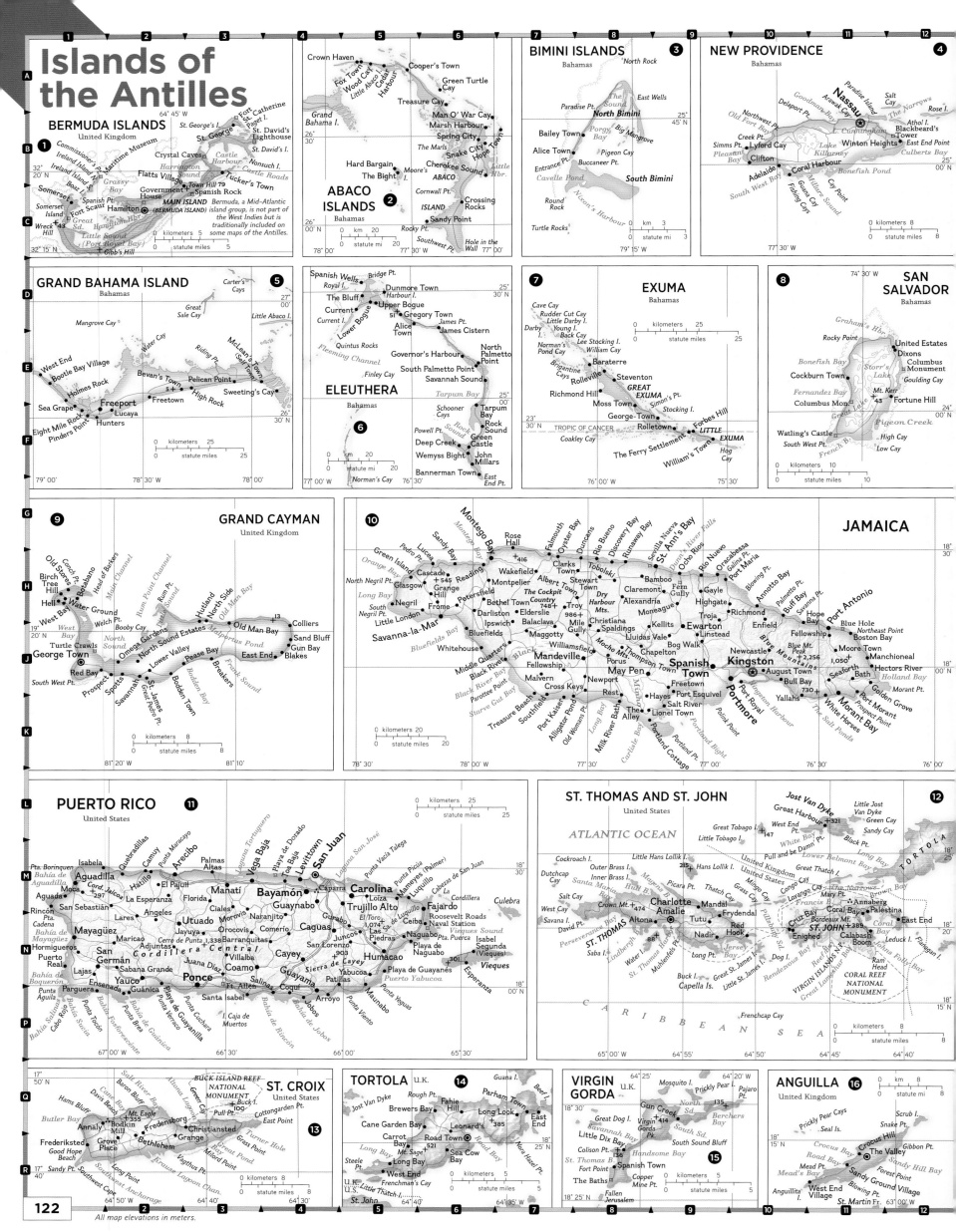

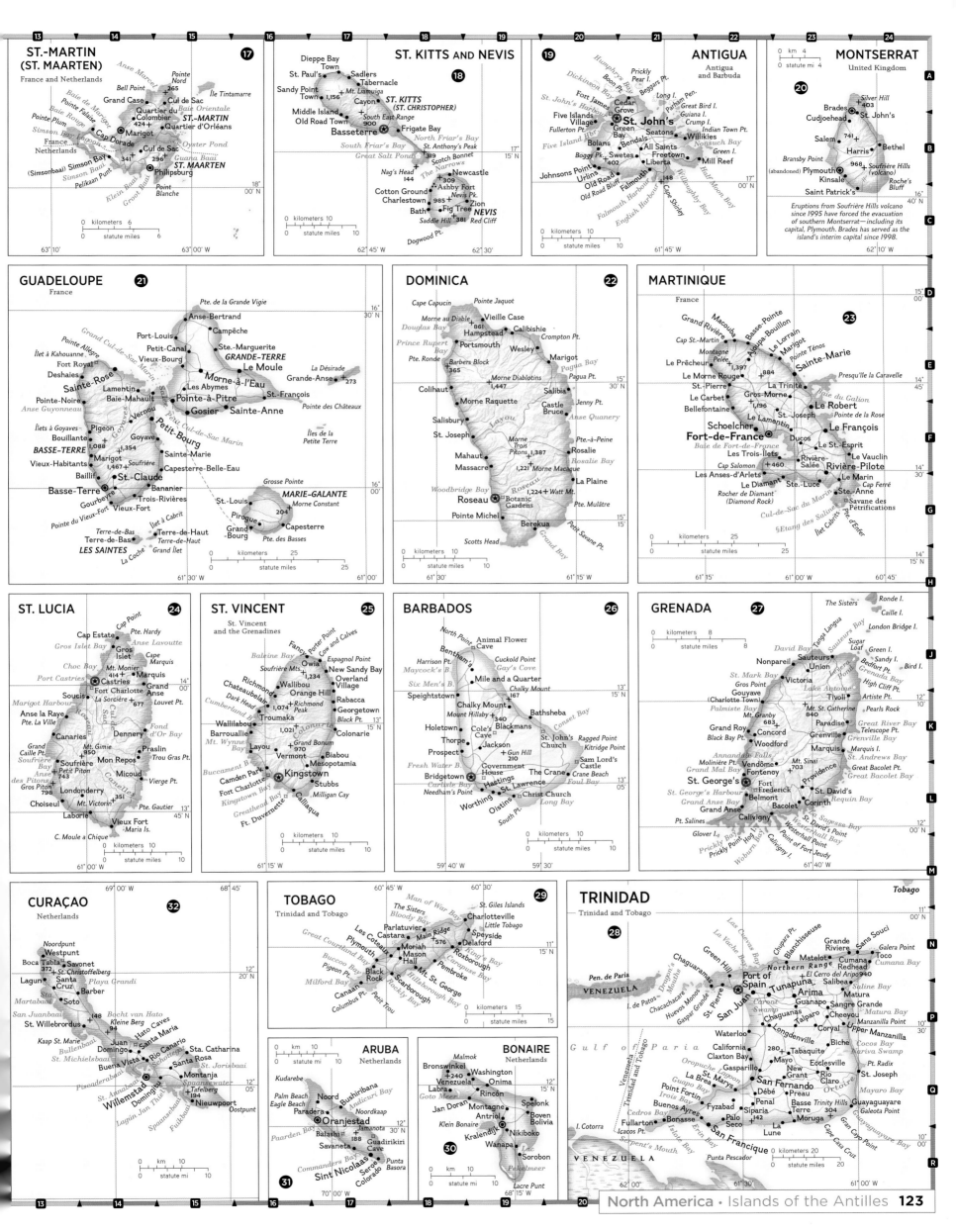

The ice-shrouded Torres del Paine Mountains take pride of place in Chile's windswept Patagonia region. Home to indigenous populations and endemic flora and fauna, Patagonia, which also encompasses a large swath of Argentina, has often been described as "the last place on Earth."

South America

South America is a place of remarkable extremes—sweltering jungle heat and face-numbing cold, endless towering mountains and dense tropical forests that seem to stretch forever, the world's mightiest river (the Amazon), and the planet's driest spot (the Atacama Desert). While the region's coastal areas are highly developed, the heart of the continent remains largely uninhabited, a rugged expanse of mountains, desert, grassland, and forest that constitutes one of the world's last great wilderness treasures.

Although much of the continent remains wild and untamed, South America has its refined side. It provided a cradle for several ancient civilizations and in modern times has given birth to some of the world's largest metropolises. Yet indigenous communities, though only a small percentage of the population, still exist—high in the mountains of Ecuador, deep in the Amazon jungle of Brazil, scattered in the forested

South America

hinterlands of Suriname, and in other pockets. South America has also given us some of the great cultural highlights of the past hundred years—the astonishing discovery of the lost Inca ruins of Machu Picchu in the Peruvian Andes, the building of the modern capital city of Brasília on the Brazilian Highlands, and the writings of Nobel Prize-winning author Gabriel García Márquez of Colombia.

PHYSICAL GEOGRAPHY With a base along the Caribbean coast and an apex at Cape Horn, South America is shaped rather like an elongated triangle. Embracing a total area of nearly 6.9 million square miles (17.8 million sq km), it's the fourth largest continent, bounded by the Atlantic Ocean in the east, the Pacific Ocean in the west, and the Caribbean Sea in the north. Its only connection to another landmass (North America) is the narrow Isthmus of Panama linking Colombia and Panama. In the deep south, just the stormy Drake Passage separates South America from the Antarctic continent.

Despite its hefty size, South America has a relatively short coastline and few islands. However, its offshore elements are distinctive: the untamed grandeur of the Tierra del Fuego archipelago in the far south and the spectacular fjord country of southern Chile; the biological wonderland of the Galápagos; and the river-veined expanses of Marajó Island, the world's largest fluvial island.

Three huge physical features dominate the South American mainland: the Andes mountains, the Amazon Basin, and a wide southern plain that encompasses the Pampas, the Gran Chaco, and much of Patagonia. The Andes cordillera, which runs all the way from northern Venezuela to southern Chile and Argentina, is the world's longest mountain range. It's also one of the highest—more than 50 peaks over 20,000 feet (6,100 m)—and one of the most seismically active.

South America's hydrology is also astounding. Rainwater spilling off the Andes creates the mighty Amazon River and its thousand-plus tributaries, which in turn sustain the world's largest rain forest and greatest diversity of flora and fauna. Although the Amazon itself is not the planet's longest watercourse, it carries more liquid than the next ten biggest rivers combined. Cascading off a tabletop mountain in the northern Amazon is Angel Falls, the world's highest waterfall at 3,212 feet (979 m), and tumbling off an ancient lava cliff between Brazil and Argentina is thunderous Iguazú Falls (spelled Iguaçu in Brazil).

Other notable geographic features are the ferociously arid Atacama Desert, which often goes without rain for hundreds of years; the endless Pampas prairie of Argentina and Uruguay, birthplace of the gaucho culture; and southern Brazil's Pantanal region, one of Earth's great wetlands.

HISTORY Like its continental cousin to the north, South America was first inhabited by nomads whose Asiatic ancestors crossed the Bering Strait during the last great ice age, sometime between 14,000 and 24,000 years ago. Eventually crossing the Isthmus of Panama, they diffused throughout the continent and evolved into hundreds of different tribal groups with their own languages, customs, and traditions.

Starting around 3000 B.C., Amerindians living in the Andes region began to cultivate beans, squash, cotton, and potatoes. By 1000 B.C., villages along Peru's northern coastal plain had evolved into the Chavin culture, the continent's first true civilization. With a religion based on the worship of the jaguar god, the Chavin built great ceremonial centers with mud-brick temples and pyramids. They also developed polychrome pottery, intricate

weaving, and South America's first metallurgy. By the sixth century A.D., the Chavin had been eclipsed by other sophisticated Peruvian cultures such as the Moche, Nasca, and Tiwanaku. The last of the region's great Amerindian cultures was the Inca. Master stonemasons and soldiers, the Inca forged an empire that stretched from present-day southern Colombia to northern Chile and Argentina.

Christopher Columbus "discovered" South America in 1498 on his third voyage to the New World, but the landmass (and adjacent North America) didn't receive its current name until Italian mariner Amerigo Vespucci explored its coast (1499–1502) and first postulated that it was a continent unto itself rather than part of Asia. In their quest for riches, the Spanish conquistadores that followed came into violent contact with local Amerindian groups, climaxing in Francisco Pizarro's invasion of the Andes and bloody triumph over the Inca Empire in the 1530s. While the Spaniards were busy conquering the west coast, the Portuguese were claiming the continent's eastern shore—an area they called Brazil, after a local dyewood tree. Driven off their land, decimated by disease, and pressed into slavery, South America's native population quickly declined in all but the most remote regions. Within half a century of first contact, European hegemony over the entire continent was assured.

By the end of the 16th century, three distinct groups—the military, wealthy families, and the Roman Catholic Church—had come to dominate South America's new Iberian colonies. Using Indian labor and millions of slaves brought from Africa, they developed a society based on sprawling ranches and European-style cities such as Lima and Bogotá. Missions under the direction of the Jesuits and Franciscans were used to convert and control Indians in frontier areas. By the dawn of the 19th century— inspired by popular uprisings in the United States and France—South America's colonies had hatched their own revolutions. Between 1810 and 1824, Simón Bolívar and José de San Martín liberated all of the Spanish-speaking lands on the continent, and in 1822, Brazil declared its independence from Portugal.

Despite impressive economic gains in some countries—most notably Argentina—most of South America's independent states were stagnant by the early 20th century, struggling beneath a twin yoke of brutal military rule and neocolonial economic exploitation. This status quo endured until the late 1980s, when democracy flowered across the continent.

CULTURE A rich blend of Iberian, African, and Amerindian traditions, South America has some of the world's most lively and distinctive cultures. Despite romantic images of the Amazon and Machu Picchu, the vast majority of South Americans live in cities rather than the rain forest or mountains. A massive rural exodus that began in the 1950s has transformed South America into the most urbanized continent after Australia. The region now boasts 3 of the world's 20 largest cities: São Paulo (21 million), Buenos Aires (14 million), and Rio de Janeiro (12 million). Ninety percent of the continent's people live within 200 miles (320 km) of the coast, leaving huge expanses of the interior virtually unpopulated.

Several common threads bind the continent's more than 410 million people. Iberian languages dominate, with about half the population speaking Spanish and the other half Portuguese, though there are linguistic anomalies—French, Dutch, and English in the Guiana region, and Amerindian dialects in the remote Amazon and Andes. Still, most South Americans don't need a translator to talk to one another. And despite recent inroads by Protestant missionaries—especially among remote indigenous groups and the urban poor—about 80 percent of South Americans consider themselves Roman Catholic.

Yet, the continent also flaunts an amazing ethnic diversity. Although the majority of people can still trace their ancestors back to Spain or Portugal, waves of immigration have transformed South America into an ethnic smorgasbord. Amerindians and mixed-blood mestizos make up more than 80 percent of the population in Bolivia, Ecuador, and Peru. More than a third of Argentines have Italian roots. Blond-haired, blue-eyed Germans populate many parts of Chile, Uruguay, and southern Brazil. About half of Brazilians and a high percentage of the residents of coastal Colombia and Venezuela are the descendants of African slaves. Asian Indians comprise the largest ethnic groups in both Suriname and Guyana.

This blend has produced a vibrant modern culture with influence far beyond the bounds of its South American cradle. Argentina's beloved tango—music, lyrics, and dance steps born of the Buenos Aires ghettos—is now an icon of romance around the world. Brazil's port cities hatched steamy Afro-Latino rhythms such as samba and bossa nova, Peruvian pipe music has become synonymous with the Andes, while Colombia has produced a rousing Latino rock. South America's rich literary map includes everything from the imaginative explorations of Jorge Luis Borges to the magical realism of Gabriel García Márquez and Mario Vargas Llosa to the sensual poems of Pablo Neruda. A similar passion flows through soccer, the region's favorite game. Pelé, Maradona, and other legendary players have led Brazil and Argentina to multiple World Cup titles.

ECONOMY Even though South America's colonies gained their independence at a relatively early stage, they were not able to achieve economic autonomy to any large extent. By the early 20th century, nearly all of them were dependent on commodity exports to Europe or the United States: bananas, rubber, sugar, coffee, timber, emeralds, copper, oil, and beef. In the short term, some countries did very well with exports, especially Argentina, which counted itself among the world's richest nations until the 1950s. But failure to make a full transition from resource extraction to modern business and industry spelled economic doom for the entire continent.

By the 1960s, most of South America was mired in negative or neutral economic growth, increasingly dependent on overseas aid, and plagued by unemployment and poverty. Corruption, military rule, and mismanagement worsened an already dire situation. Hyperinflation of several hundred percent per annum battered Brazil and Argentina in the 1980s, nearly crippling the continent's two largest economies. During the same era, narcotics became one of South America's most important money spinners—with cocaine exported in great quantities from Colombia, Bolivia, and Peru. Yet by the 1990s, most countries saw light at the end of

One of the most dramatic ruins in South America, the Inca ceremonial center of Machu Picchu (top) hovers 2,000 feet (610 m) above the Urubamba River in the Peruvian Andes. It was built in the mid- to late 1400s at the behest of Pachacuti, the ruler who greatly enlarged the Inca Empire through conquest and colonization. Soon thereafter, in January 1502, Portuguese explorers sailing along South America's eastern coast entered a bay and named it Rio de Janeiro—"river of January"—now the name of Brazil's second largest city. Today, high-rises arc along that same waterway, renamed Guanabara Bay (above) with the renowned, bulletlike dome of Sugarloaf Mountain looming just beyond, at the entrance to the Atlantic.

their dim economic tunnels. In the early years of the 21st century—though fundamental problems, like huge foreign debt, remained—the region's nouvelle democracies spurred an era of relative prosperity, raising the GDP per capita in many countries.

South America still relies, to a large extent, on commodity exports: oil from Venezuela, coffee from Colombia, and copper from Chile. But recent decades have seen a dramatic shift toward manufacturing and niche agriculture. Brazil now earns more money from making automobiles and aircraft than from shipping rubber overseas, and Chile has earned a worldwide market for its wine, fruit, and salmon.

Despite protests from indigenous and environmental groups, South American governments have tried to spur even more growth by opening the Amazon region to economic exploitation—oil and timber extraction and the transformation of rain forest into cattle ranches. But this practice is already wreaking widespread ecological havoc. The Amazon could very well be the key to the region's economic future—not by the decimation of the world's richest forest but by the sustainable management and commercial development of its largely untapped potential for medical, chemical, and nutritional products. Many researchers believe that treatments for cancer and other ailments may lie undiscovered in South America's rain forest.

South America
Physical and Political

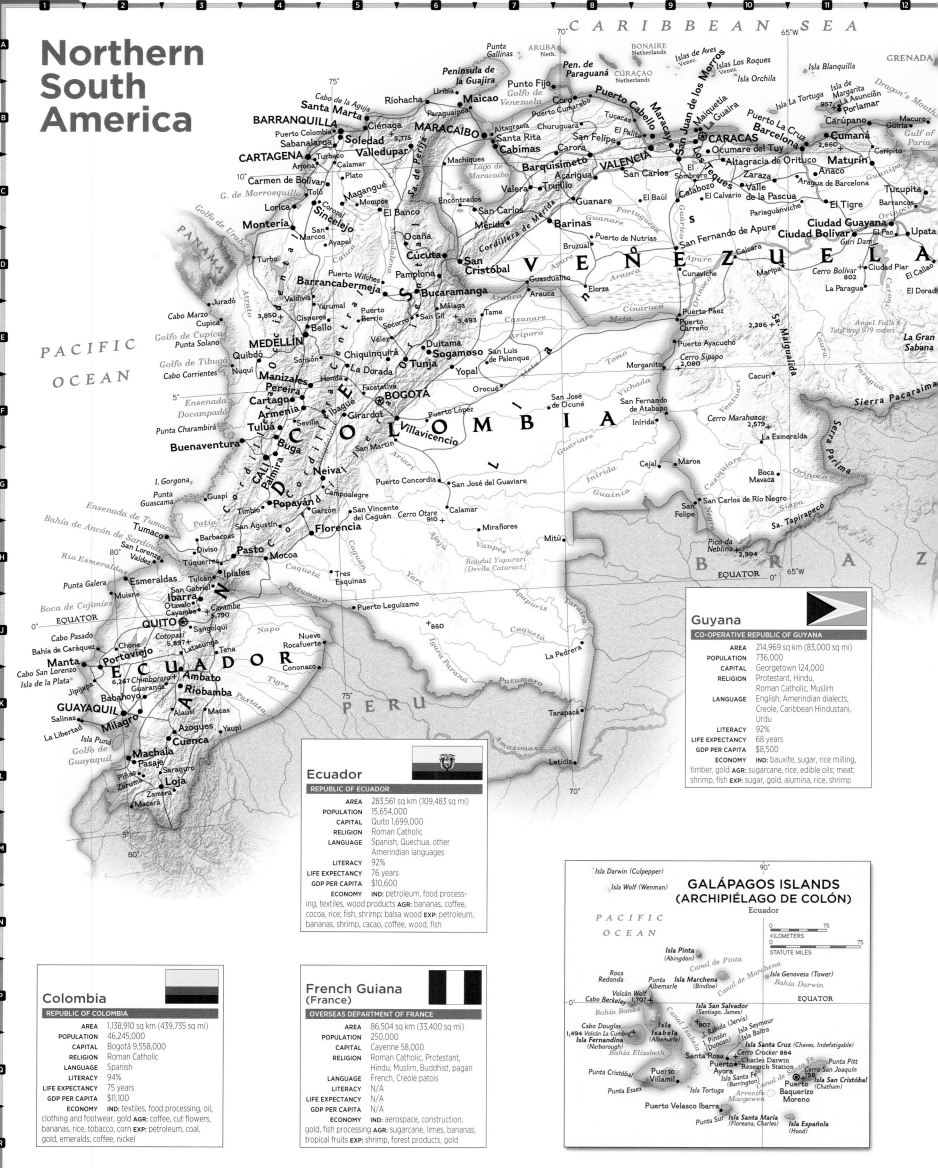

Northern South America

Ecuador
REPUBLIC OF ECUADOR

AREA	283,561 sq km (109,483 sq mi)
POPULATION	15,654,000
CAPITAL	Quito 1,699,000
RELIGION	Roman Catholic
LANGUAGE	Spanish, Quechua, other Amerindian languages
LITERACY	92%
LIFE EXPECTANCY	76 years
GDP PER CAPITA	$10,600
ECONOMY	IND: petroleum, food processing, textiles, wood products AGR: bananas, coffee, cocoa, rice; fish, shrimp; balsa wood EXP: petroleum, bananas, shrimp, cacao, coffee, wood, fish

Guyana
CO-OPERATIVE REPUBLIC OF GUYANA

AREA	214,969 sq km (83,000 sq mi)
POPULATION	736,000
CAPITAL	Georgetown 124,000
RELIGION	Protestant, Hindu, Roman Catholic, Muslim
LANGUAGE	English, Amerindian dialects, Creole, Caribbean Hindustani, Urdu
LITERACY	92%
LIFE EXPECTANCY	68 years
GDP PER CAPITA	$8,500
ECONOMY	IND: bauxite, sugar, rice milling, timber, gold AGR: sugarcane, rice, edible oils; meat; shrimp, fish EXP: sugar, gold, alumina, rice, shrimp

Colombia
REPUBLIC OF COLOMBIA

AREA	1,138,910 sq km (439,735 sq mi)
POPULATION	46,245,000
CAPITAL	Bogotá 9,558,000
RELIGION	Roman Catholic
LANGUAGE	Spanish
LITERACY	94%
LIFE EXPECTANCY	75 years
GDP PER CAPITA	$11,100
ECONOMY	IND: textiles, food processing, oil, clothing and footwear, gold AGR: coffee, cut flowers, bananas, rice, tobacco, corn EXP: petroleum, coal, gold, emeralds, coffee, nickel

French Guiana (France)
OVERSEAS DEPARTMENT OF FRANCE

AREA	86,504 sq km (33,400 sq mi)
POPULATION	250,000
CAPITAL	Cayenne 58,000
RELIGION	Roman Catholic, Protestant, Hindu, Muslim, Buddhist, pagan
LANGUAGE	French, Creole patois
LITERACY	N/A
LIFE EXPECTANCY	N/A
GDP PER CAPITA	N/A
ECONOMY	IND: aerospace, construction, gold, fish processing AGR: sugarcane, limes, bananas, tropical fruits EXP: shrimp, forest products, gold

GALÁPAGOS ISLANDS (ARCHIPIÉLAGO DE COLÓN)
Ecuador

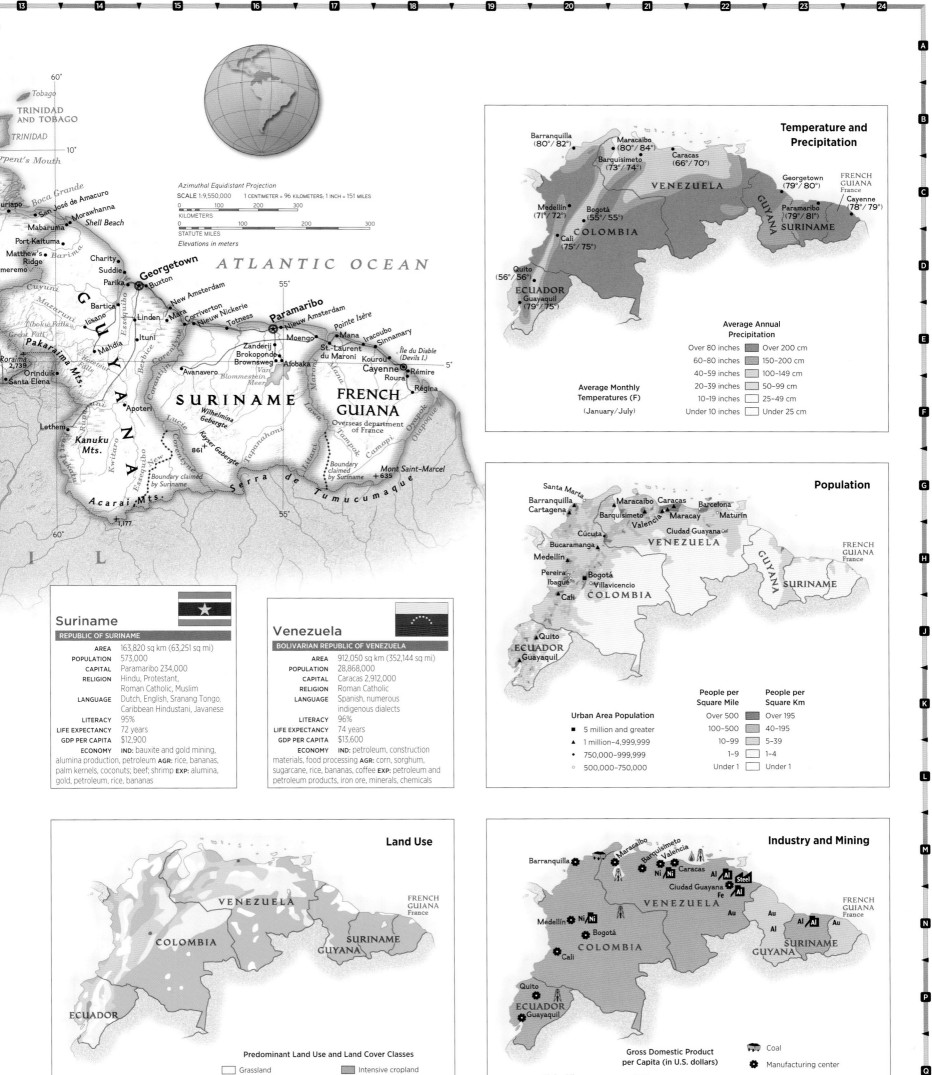

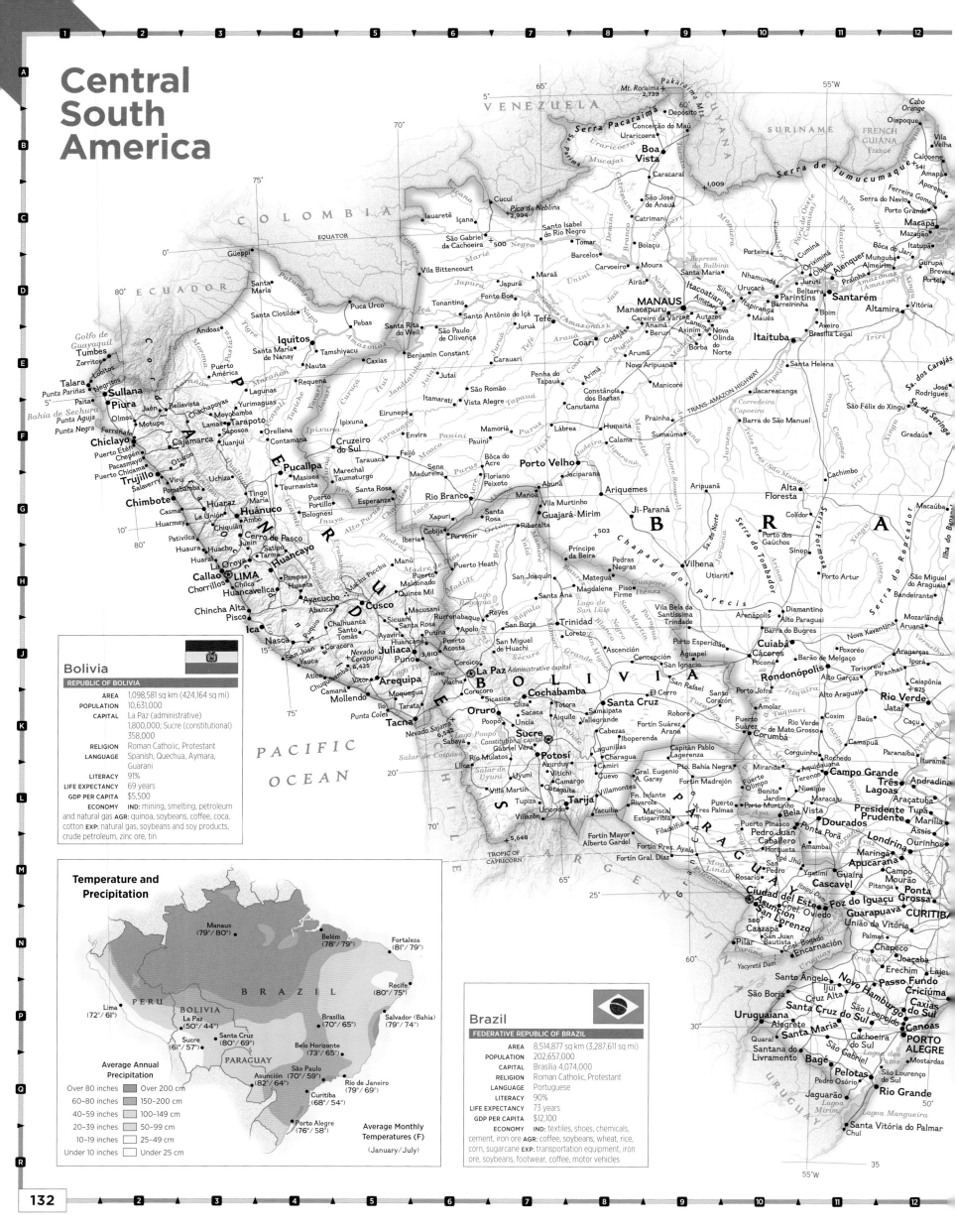

Central South America

Bolivia

REPUBLIC OF BOLIVIA

AREA	1,098,581 sq km (424,164 sq mi)
POPULATION	10,631,000
CAPITAL	La Paz (administrative) 1,800,000; Sucre (constitutional) 358,000
RELIGION	Roman Catholic, Protestant
LANGUAGE	Spanish, Quechua, Aymara, Guarani
LITERACY	91%
LIFE EXPECTANCY	69 years
GDP PER CAPITA	$5,500
ECONOMY	IND: mining, smelting, petroleum and natural gas AGR: quinoa, soybeans, coffee, coca, cotton EXP: natural gas, soybeans and soy products, crude petroleum, zinc ore, tin

Temperature and Precipitation

Manaus (79°/80°)
Belém (78°/79°)
Fortaleza (81°/79°)
Lima (72°/61°)
La Paz (50°/44°)
Santa Cruz (80°/69°)
Sucre (61°/57°)
Recife (80°/75°)
Brasília (70°/65°)
Salvador (Bahia) (79°/74°)
Belo Horizonte (73°/65°)
São Paulo (70°/59°)
Asunción (82°/64°)
Curitiba (68°/54°)
Rio de Janeiro (79°/69°)
Porto Alegre (76°/58°)

Average Annual Precipitation

Over 80 inches	Over 200 cm
60-80 inches	150-200 cm
40-59 inches	100-149 cm
20-39 inches	50-99 cm
10-19 inches	25-49 cm
Under 10 inches	Under 25 cm

Average Monthly Temperatures (F)

(January/July)

Brazil

FEDERATIVE REPUBLIC OF BRAZIL

AREA	8,514,877 sq km (3,287,611 sq mi)
POPULATION	202,657,000
CAPITAL	Brasília 4,074,000
RELIGION	Roman Catholic, Protestant
LANGUAGE	Portuguese
LITERACY	90%
LIFE EXPECTANCY	73 years
GDP PER CAPITA	$12,100
ECONOMY	IND: textiles, shoes, chemicals, cement, iron ore AGR: coffee, soybeans, wheat, rice, corn, sugarcane EXP: transportation equipment, iron ore, soybeans, footwear, coffee, motor vehicles

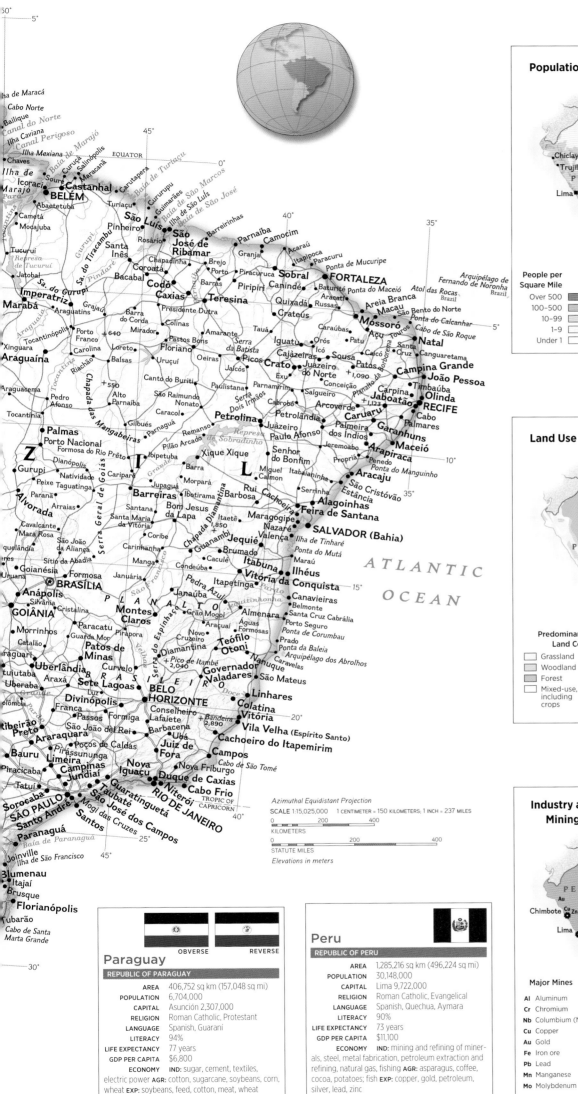

South America • Central

A B C D E F G H J K L M N P Q R

(Main map — partial labels)

Ilha de Maracá
Cabo Norte
Bailique
Ilha Caviana
Ilha Mexiana
Chaves
Ilha de Marajó
Icoaraci
BELÉM
Abaetetuba
Cametá
Mocajuba
Castanhal
Curuçá
Maracanã
Salinópolis
Turiaçu
Carutapera
EQUATOR
Baía de Turiaçu
Baía de São Marcos
Baía de São José
São Luís
Pinheiro
Santa Inês
São José de Ribamar
Rosário
Barreirinhas
Parnaíba
Camocim
Acaraú
Itapipoca
Ponta de Mucuripe
Granja
Caninde
FORTALEZA
Baturité
Ponta do Maceió
Atol das Rocas
Brazil
Arquipélago de Fernando de Noronha
Brazil
Imperatriz
Marabá
Araguaína
Codó
Caxias
Teresina
Sobral
Piripiri
Quixadá
Crateús
Iguatu
Areia Branca
Macau
Mossoró
Açu
Cabo de São Roque
Natal
Campina Grande
João Pessoa
Crato
Juazeiro do Norte
Petrolina
Olinda
RECIFE
Caruaru
Cabo
Garanhuns
Maceió
Arapiraca
Aracaju
Palmas
Porto Nacional
Barreiras
Feira de Santana
SALVADOR (Bahia)
Ilha de Tinharé
Ponta do Mutá
Jequié
Itabuna
Ilhéus
Vitória da Conquista
BRASÍLIA
Anápolis
GOIÂNIA
Uberlândia
Uberaba
Montes Claros
Teófilo Otoni
Governador Valadares
BELO HORIZONTE
Divinópolis
Vitória
Vila Velha (Espírito Santo)
Cachoeiro do Itapemirim
Campos
Cabo de São Tomé
Juiz de Fora
Nova Iguaçu
Duque de Caxias
Niterói
RIO DE JANEIRO
Cabo Frio
SÃO PAULO
Santos
São José dos Campos
Curitiba
Joinville
Florianópolis
Blumenau
Itajaí
Porto Alegre

ATLANTIC OCEAN

TROPIC OF CAPRICORN

Azimuthal Equidistant Projection

SCALE 1:15,025,000 1 CENTIMETER = 150 KILOMETERS; 1 INCH = 237 MILES

KILOMETERS
STATUTE MILES
Elevations in meters

Paraguay
REPUBLIC OF PARAGUAY
OBVERSE   REVERSE

AREA 406,752 sq km (157,048 sq mi)
POPULATION 6,704,000
CAPITAL Asunción 2,307,000
RELIGION Roman Catholic, Protestant
LANGUAGE Spanish, Guaraní
LITERACY 94%
LIFE EXPECTANCY 77 years
GDP PER CAPITA $6,800
ECONOMY IND: sugar, cement, textiles, electric power AGR: cotton, sugarcane, soybeans, corn, wheat EXP: soybeans, feed, cotton, meat, wheat

Peru
REPUBLIC OF PERU

AREA 1,285,216 sq km (496,224 sq mi)
POPULATION 30,148,000
CAPITAL Lima 9,722,000
RELIGION Roman Catholic, Evangelical
LANGUAGE Spanish, Quechua, Aymara
LITERACY 90%
LIFE EXPECTANCY 73 years
GDP PER CAPITA $11,100
ECONOMY IND: mining and refining of minerals, steel, metal fabrication, petroleum extraction and refining, natural gas, fishing AGR: asparagus, coffee, cocoa, potatoes; fish EXP: copper, gold, petroleum, silver, lead, zinc

---

Population

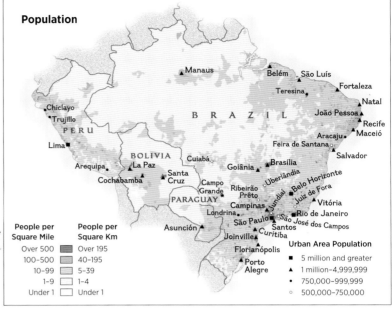

People per Square Mile	People per Square Km
Over 500	Over 195
100–500	40–195
10–99	5–39
1–9	1–4
Under 1	Under 1

Urban Area Population
■ 5 million and greater
▲ 1 million–4,999,999
▴ 750,000–999,999
○ 500,000–750,000

Land Use

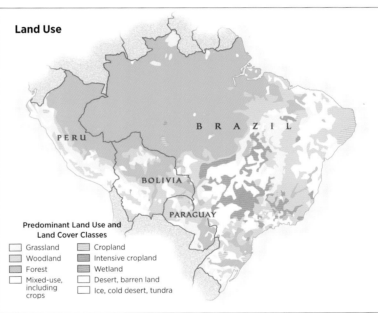

Predominant Land Use and Land Cover Classes
- Grassland
- Woodland
- Forest
- Mixed-use, including crops
- Cropland
- Intensive cropland
- Wetland
- Desert, barren land
- Ice, cold desert, tundra

Industry and Mining

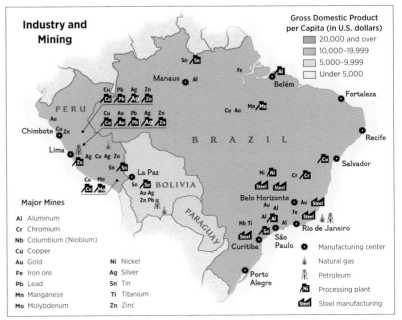

Gross Domestic Product per Capita (in U.S. dollars)
- 20,000 and over
- 10,000–19,999
- 5,000–9,999
- Under 5,000

Major Mines
- Al Aluminum
- Cr Chromium
- Nb Columbium (Niobium)
- Cu Copper
- Au Gold
- Fe Iron ore
- Pb Lead
- Mn Manganese
- Mo Molybdenum
- Ni Nickel
- Ag Silver
- Sn Tin
- Ti Titanium
- Zn Zinc

- ⊕ Manufacturing center
- Natural gas
- Petroleum
- Processing plant
- Steel manufacturing

Southern South America

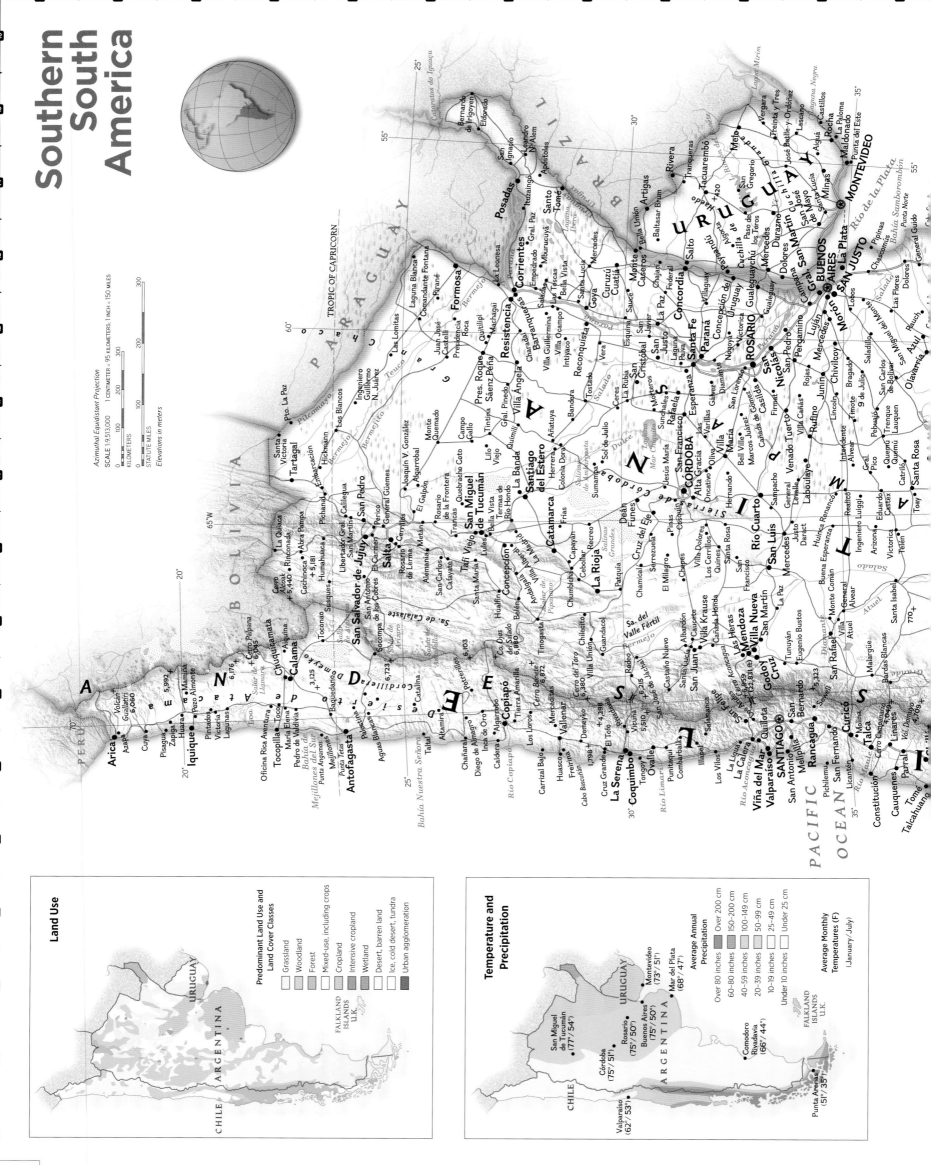

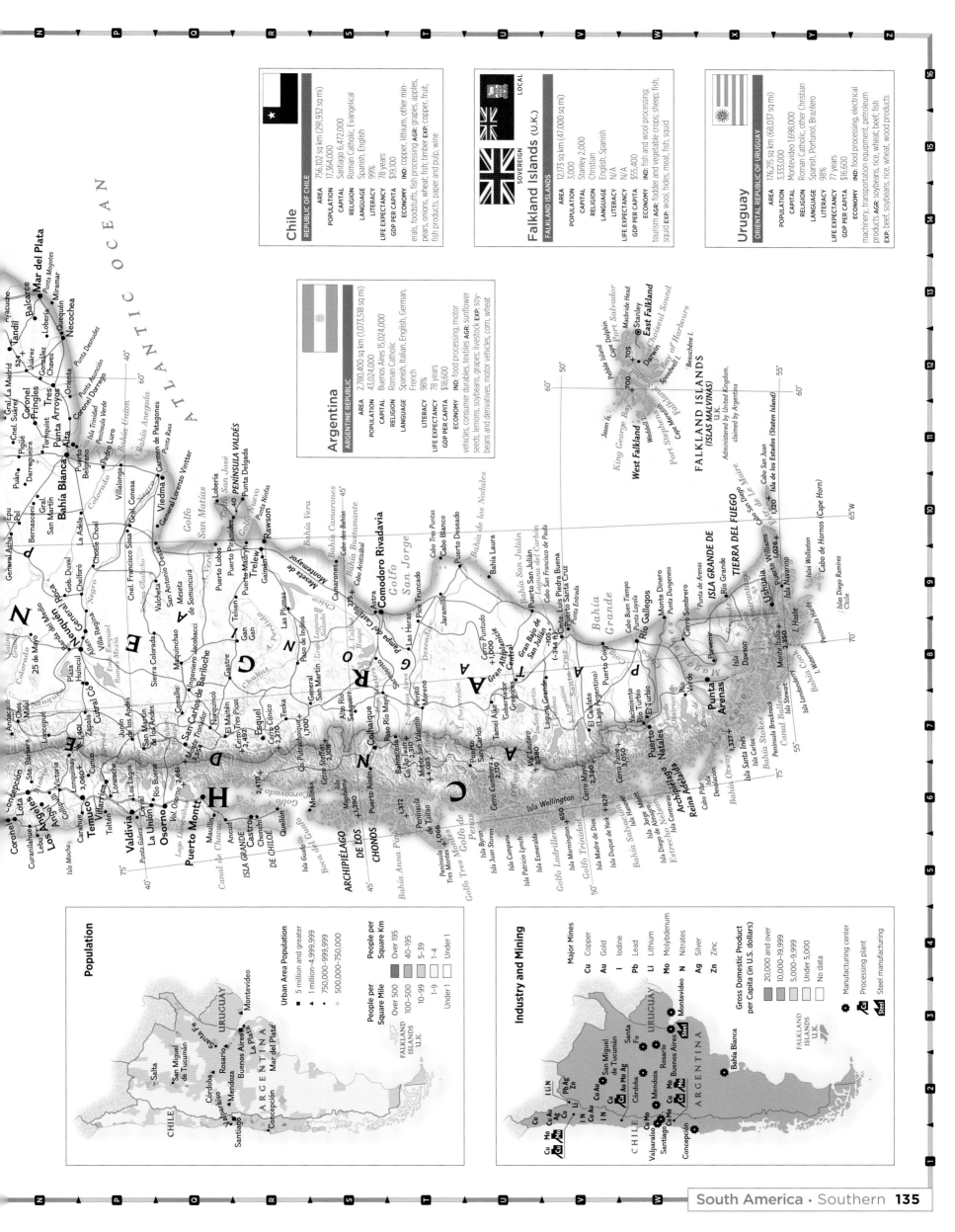

Chile
REPUBLIC OF CHILE

AREA 756,102 sq km (291,932 sq mi)
POPULATION 17,364,000
CAPITAL Santiago 6,472,000
RELIGION Roman Catholic, Evangelical
LANGUAGE Spanish, English
LITERACY 99%
LIFE EXPECTANCY 78 years
GDP PER CAPITA $19,100
ECONOMY IND: copper, lithium, other minerals, foodstuffs, fish processing AGR: grapes, apples, pears, onions, wheat; timber EXP: copper, fruit, fish products, paper and pulp, wine

Falkland Islands (U.K.)
SOVEREIGN / LOCAL

FALKLAND ISLANDS

AREA 12,173 sq km (47,000 sq mi)
POPULATION 3,000
CAPITAL Stanley 2,000
RELIGION Christian
LANGUAGE English, Spanish
LITERACY N/A
LIFE EXPECTANCY N/A
GDP PER CAPITA $55,400
ECONOMY IND: fish and wool processing; tourism AGR: fodder and vegetable crops; sheep; fish, squid EXP: wool, hides, meat, fish, squid

Uruguay
ORIENTAL REPUBLIC OF URUGUAY

AREA 176,215 sq km (68,037 sq mi)
POPULATION 3,333,000
CAPITAL Montevideo 1,698,000
RELIGION Roman Catholic, other Christian
LANGUAGE Spanish, Portunol, Brazilero
LITERACY 98%
LIFE EXPECTANCY 77 years
GDP PER CAPITA $16,600
ECONOMY IND: food processing, electrical machinery, transportation equipment, petroleum products AGR: soybeans, rice, wheat; beef, fish EXP: beef, soybeans, rice, wheat, wood products

Argentina
ARGENTINE REPUBLIC

AREA 2,780,400 sq km (1,073,518 sq mi)
POPULATION 43,024,000
CAPITAL Buenos Aires 15,024,000
RELIGION Roman Catholic
LANGUAGE Spanish, Italian, English, German, French
LITERACY 98%
LIFE EXPECTANCY 78 years
GDP PER CAPITA $18,600
ECONOMY IND: food processing, motor vehicles, consumer durables, textiles AGR: sunflower seeds, lemons, soybeans, grapes; livestock EXP: soybeans and derivatives, motor vehicles, corn, wheat

Population

Urban Area Population
- ■ 5 million and greater
- ▲ 1 million–4,999,999
- ● 750,000–999,999
- ○ 500,000–750,000

People per Square Mile / People per Square Km
- Over 500 / Over 195
- 100–500 / 40–195
- 10–99 / 5–39
- 1–9 / 1–4
- Under 1 / Under 1

Industry and Mining

Major Mines
- Cu Copper
- Au Gold
- I Iodine
- Pb Lead
- Li Lithium
- Mo Molybdenum
- N Nitrates
- Ag Silver
- Zn Zinc

Gross Domestic Product per Capita (in U.S. dollars)
- 20,000 and over
- 10,000–19,999
- 5,000–9,999
- Under 5,000
- No data

- ⚙ Manufacturing center
- Cu Processing plant
- Steel Steel manufacturing

The fantastical Neuschwanstein Castle, built in the late 1800s and later the model for Disneyland's iconic fairy-tale castle, sits high above the Alpsee in the Bavarian Alps. "Mad King Ludwig" intended his creation to be a paean to medieval architecture, but he also incorporated running water, automatic flush toilets, and other revolutionary conveniences of his day.

Europe

Europe is the world's second smallest continent, after Australia. A cluster of peninsulas and islands extending from northwestern Asia to the Atlantic, the continent comprises 46 countries. Despite its northern latitudes, most of its people enjoy a relatively mild climate tempered by warm ocean currents such as the Gulf Stream.

Europe has been inhabited for more than 40,000 years. During the past millennium, Europeans explored the planet and established far-flung empires. Europe led the world in science and invention and launched the industrial revolution. By the end of the 19th century, it dominated world commerce, spreading European ideas, languages, legal systems, and political patterns around the globe.

The 20th century brought unprecedented changes. Germany and its neighbors ignited two world wars. The Russian Revolution introduced communism. And Europe, weakened by war, lost its dominant position in the world along with its empires.

Europe

In 1947, the United States and the Soviet Union entered into the Cold War, pitting capitalism and democracy against communism and state control. Western Europe, backed by the U.S., prospered with market economies, democracy, and free speech; Eastern and Central European countries, their centrally controlled economies closely tied to the Soviet Union's, fell behind and, despite full employment and social benefits, people suffered the lack of personal freedom.

During the same period in the mid to late 20th century, age-old enemies in Western Europe started cooperating with each other and more dynamically with the U.S. and Canda, leading to a still active partnership known as NATO (the North Atlantic Treaty Organization). In 1951, six countries also founded a common market for coal and steel; it soon included more countries and more goods and services until in 1993, the European Community, as it was called, was renamed the European Union (EU). Border controls were eliminated between seven member countries in 1995. In 1999, 11 members introduced a common European currency, the euro. The Cold War ended with the fall of communist governments in Eastern Europe in 1989, Germany's reunification in 1990, and the collapse of the Soviet Union in 1991.

That collapse also created chaos in the Balkans, as Yugoslavia shattered into seven countries and long-simmering ethnic hostilities erupted into violence. Yet, the forces working toward a cohesive, stable Europe prevailed. Today, people move freely throughout the continent; they share the same pop culture, generally urbanized lifestyles, and a heavy reliance on smartphones and the Internet.

Europeans also share environmental hazards. Acid rain from England has killed life in Swedish lakes. A 1986 nuclear accident in Ukraine damaged dozens of countries. The Danube and Rhine Rivers have spread industrial pollution downstream. Wherever possible, regional solutions hold the most promise, such as the ongoing effort to clean up the Baltic Sea being undertaken by nine surrounding countries.

Although the European Union enforces strict environmental laws, Eastern Europe did little to protect the environment until the 1990s, after the fall of communism. Some countries still contain toxic waste dumps, untreated sewage, and other hazards, but they have insufficient funds to meet the high costs of cleanup.

A political United States of Europe will probably never happen, but the economic advantages of the European Union greatly benefited its member countries (currently numbering 28, with 8 more waiting for membership) as they entered a new era of history. In recent years, monetary crises in Greece and other nations have caused some friction among member countries, and inadvertently, the union has contributed to new international unrest in Eastern Europe. In 2014, Ukraine's interest in joining the EU, along with other issues, led Russian president Vladimir Putin to annex Crimea from Ukraine and support separatist rebels hoping to reunite Ukraine with Russia.

PHYSICAL GEOGRAPHY Europe is bounded by the Arctic Ocean in the north, the Atlantic Ocean in the west, the Mediterranean and Black Seas in the south, and the Caspian Sea in the southeast. The traditional land boundary with Asia is a line following Russia's Ural Mountains from the Arctic Ocean south to the Ural River to the Caspian Sea. The line then continues west along the crest of the Caucasus Mountains between the Caspian and Black Seas, making Mount Elbrus (18,510 ft; 5,642 m), on the northern side, the highest peak in Europe. Waterways linking the Black Sea to the Mediterranean place a small part of Turkey in Europe.

Two mountain systems lie between icy tundra and boreal forest in the far north and the warm, dry, hilly Mediterranean coast in the south. Ancient, rugged highlands, worn down by successive Ice Age glaciers, arc southwestward from Scandinavia, through the British Isles to the Iberian Peninsula, while an active Alpine system spreads east to west across southern Europe. Still rising from a collision of tectonic plates, these mountains include the Carpathians, the Alps, the Pyrenees, and their many spurs. The high point is Mont Blanc (15,781 ft; 4,810 m), shared by France and Italy. Three major navigable rivers—the Danube, the Rhine, and the Rhône—rise in the Alps. Europe's longest river, however, is the Volga, flowing southeast across Russia to the Caspian Sea. Movements in Earth's crust cause earthquakes and volcanic eruptions in southern Europe and in Iceland. The best known volcanoes are Vesuvius, Etna, and Stromboli, all three in Italy.

Between Europe's two mountain systems, a rolling, fertile plain stretches across the continent from the Pyrenees to the Urals, well drained by several rivers. Some of the world's greatest cities are located here, including Paris, Berlin, and Moscow. Huge industrial areas on this plain are home to much of Europe's dense population.

HISTORY Named for King Minos, the first civilization in Europe appeared in Crete about 2000 B.C. Minoans traded with Egypt and western Asia, produced impressive art and architecture, and developed a unique form of writing. Around 1450 B.C., their culture disappeared, probably after a major volcanic eruption in the vicinity or an invasion by warlike Mycenaeans. Homer's *Iliad* and *The Odyssey* describe the Mycenaean era that followed.

Classical Greek civilization began in the eighth century B.C. The great achievements of the Greeks in philosophy, mathematics, natural sciences, political thought, and the arts have influenced European civilization ever since. Greece bequeathed its legacy to Rome, known for its builders, engineers, military strategists, and lawmakers. The Roman Empire eventually reached from Britain to Persia and lasted roughly 500 years, until invasions by Germanic tribes from the north destroyed it.

During Roman times, a new religion originating in western Asia, Christianity, gained traction in Europe, eventually spreading to the far western shores of the continent. As the Roman Empire declined, the Christian church became a powerful political, spiritual, and social force, and the common thread binding Europeans together. Throughout the Middle Ages, the church maintained schools and learning in its monasteries. In the 11th century, theological differences created a permanent schism in Christianity. In the east, Orthodoxy became the predominant form of Christianity, led by patriarchs, while in the west, Roman Catholicism continued to hold sway, with authority vested in a pope.

Ottoman Turks introduced Islam to the Balkans through conquest

during the 14th and 15th centuries. A hundred years later, the Protestant Reformation in northern Europe broke the unity of the Roman Catholic Church and provoked a century of wars.

In the 15th and 16th centuries, the Renaissance—a rebirth of arts, science, and culture—spread north from Italy throughout the continent. Political power shifted to Western Europe, where strong nations emerged, notably England, France, Spain, and Portugal. Under powerful kings and queens, worldwide explorations created mercantile empires, even as ideas of democracy and equality started circulating.

In the 18th century, Britain's American colonies became independent and, in the wake of the French Revolution that toppled the monarchy, Napoleon tried but failed to seize all of Europe. In 1815, a balance of power was reestablished among European countries until the forces of imperialism, militarism, defense alliances, and nationalism exploded into two world wars a century later.

Following World War II, the Cold War between the U.S. and the Soviet Union replaced the old balance of power with a deadly balance of nuclear armaments, reducing Europe to lesser status. But by the time the Cold War came to an end in the early 1990s, Western Europe had coalesced into the European Union. A large number of countries were also allied with NATO, and Europe was embarking on a new era of economic and military cooperation.

CULTURE Next to Asia, Europe has the world's densest population. Scores of distinct ethnic groups, speaking some 80 languages, inhabit more than 40 countries, which vary in size from vast European Russia to tiny Vatican City, each with its own history and traditions. Yet, Europe has a more uniform culture than any other continent. Its population is overwhelmingly of one race, Caucasian, despite the recent arrival of immigrants from Africa and Asia. Most of its languages fall into three groups with Indo-European roots: Germanic, Romance, or Slavic. One religion, Christianity, predominates in various forms, and social structures nearly everywhere are based on economic classes.

Great periods of creativity in the arts have occurred at various times all over the continent and shape its collective culture. Classical Greek sculpture and architecture are widely seen as paradigms of beauty. Gothic cathedrals of medieval France still inspire awe. Renaissance works of art, from paintings by Leonardo da Vinci in Italy to plays by Shakespeare in England, are famous worldwide. Music composed by Mozart of Austria, Beethoven of Germany, and Tchaikovsky of Russia has endured, even far beyond Europe. Spanish artist Pablo Picasso transformed the Western world's concept of art. By the 20th century, European culture had penetrated everywhere.

Most Europeans enjoy aspects of American popular culture but are concerned about Americanization. American movies flood the continent; U.S. products and lifestyles are aggressively marketed. English is becoming the preferred second language for students all over Europe. Others see the blending of cultures as an inevitable aspect of globalization and a chance to export their own pop music, plays, architecture, fashions, and gourmet foods to other countries. A more recent shift has come as immigrants arriving as workers, refugees, and asylum seekers have brought their own habits, religions—most notably, Islam—and languages to the continent. European society is becoming multicultural, with political as well as cultural consequences.

Rome's greatest landmark, the Colosseum (top), was completed in A.D. 80; it could hold as many as 50,000 spectators, who would gather for gladiatorial fights and other events. Four stories high, the structure combines Greek aesthetics with the Roman building techniques that have allowed the great stone amphitheater to endure for centuries. The melding of cultures continues to be a hallmark of European success—perhaps most evident today in the cooperative bonds formed among the member nations of the European Union, whose flags proudly fly outside EU headquarters in Brussels, Belgium (above). Created in the aftermath of the Second World War that ravaged the continent, the union has brought stability, economic growth, and cultural cohesion to much of Europe.

ECONOMY Europe is fortunate in having fertile soil, a temperate climate, ample natural resources, and a long, irregular coastline that gives most countries access to the sea and foreign trade. Navigable rivers also often help the 15 landlocked countries.

The progress of many ex-Soviet bloc countries has been slower than anticipated due, in part, to a need for laws preventing corruption and abuses under the new economic system, and for institutions to assure sound financial management. Poland and Slovenia have been among the most successful, and Russia, whose fortunes are dependent on natural resources, has seen its fortunes fluctuate with world energy prices. Belarus, on the other hand, has slipped into worsening poverty, causing some people to clamor for a return to the safety nets of communism.

Despite recent struggles among member nations, the European Union still offers advantages to outside countries that encourage them to practice the tough economic and fiscal policies necessary for membership. Ten countries were admitted in 2004: Estonia, Latvia, Lithuania, Cyprus, Malta, the Czech Republic, Hungary, Poland, Slovakia, and Slovenia. With the addition of Bulgaria and Romania in 2007 and of Croatia in 2013, the European Union now has a population of more than half a billion, firmly cementing it as one of the largest economies in the world. Many Europeans speculate that in time the euro may rival the U.S. dollar as the principal global currency.

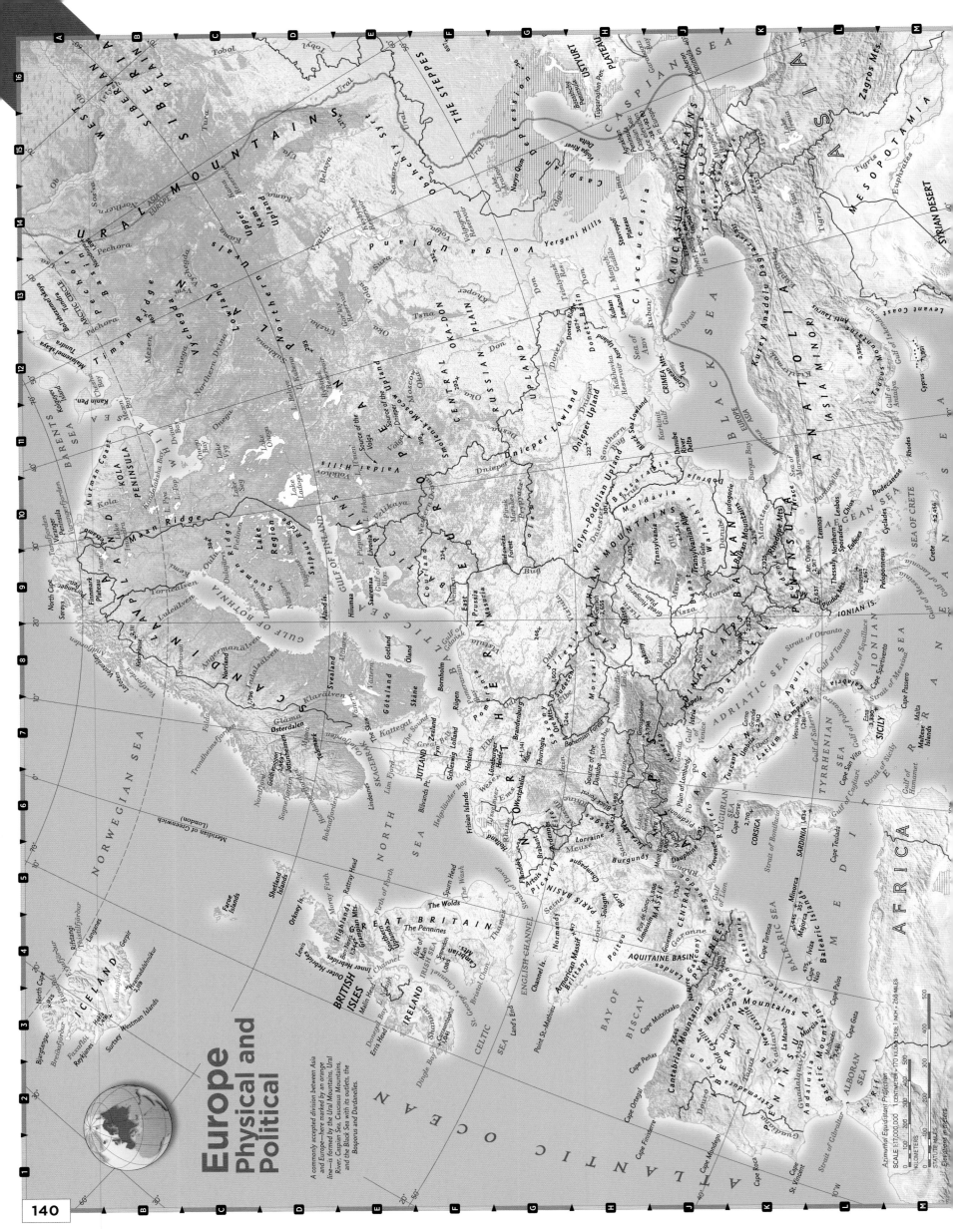

Europe
Physical and Political

A commonly accepted division between Asia and Europe—here marked by an orange line—is formed by the Ural Mountains, Ural River, Caspian Sea, Caucasus Mountains, and the Black Sea with its outlets, the Bosporus and Dardanelles.

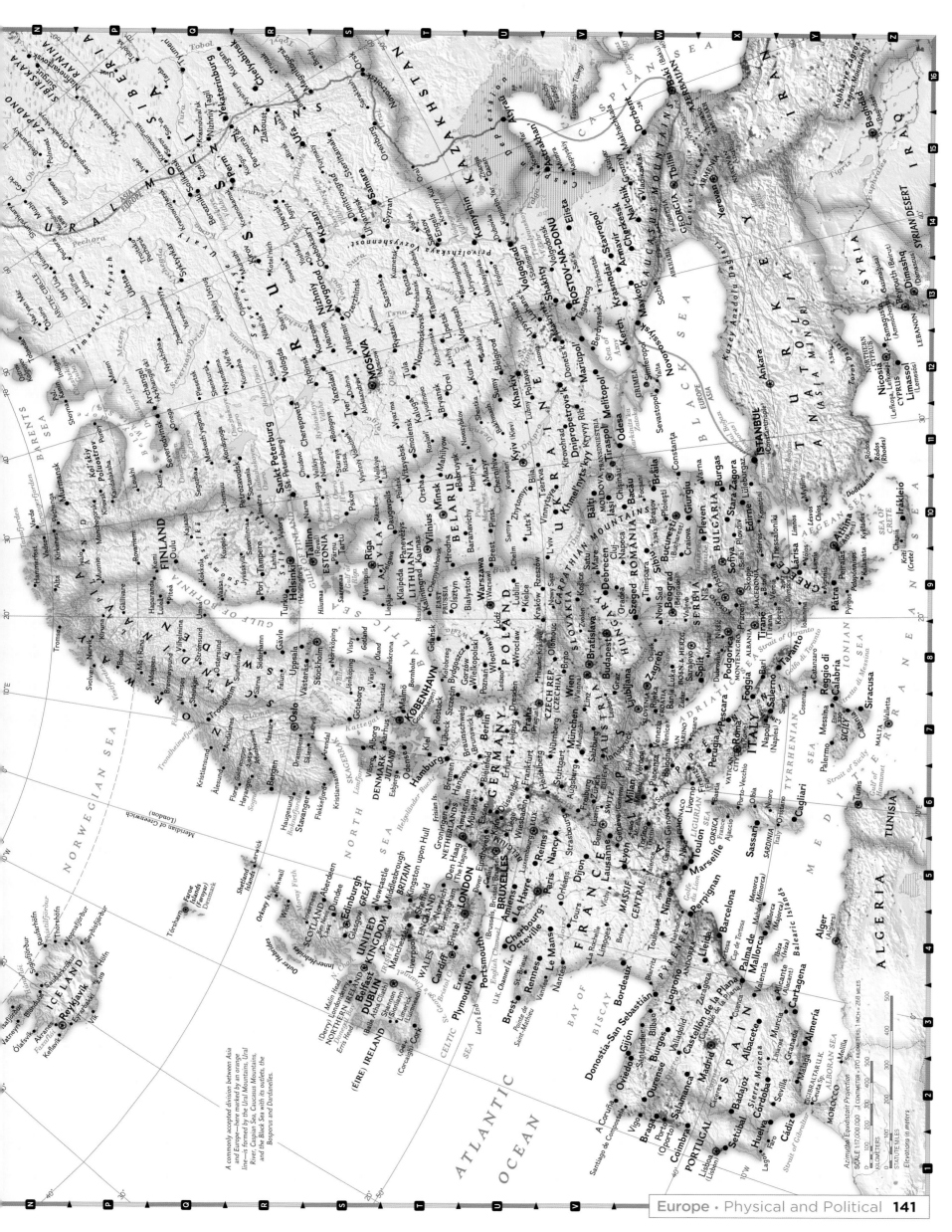

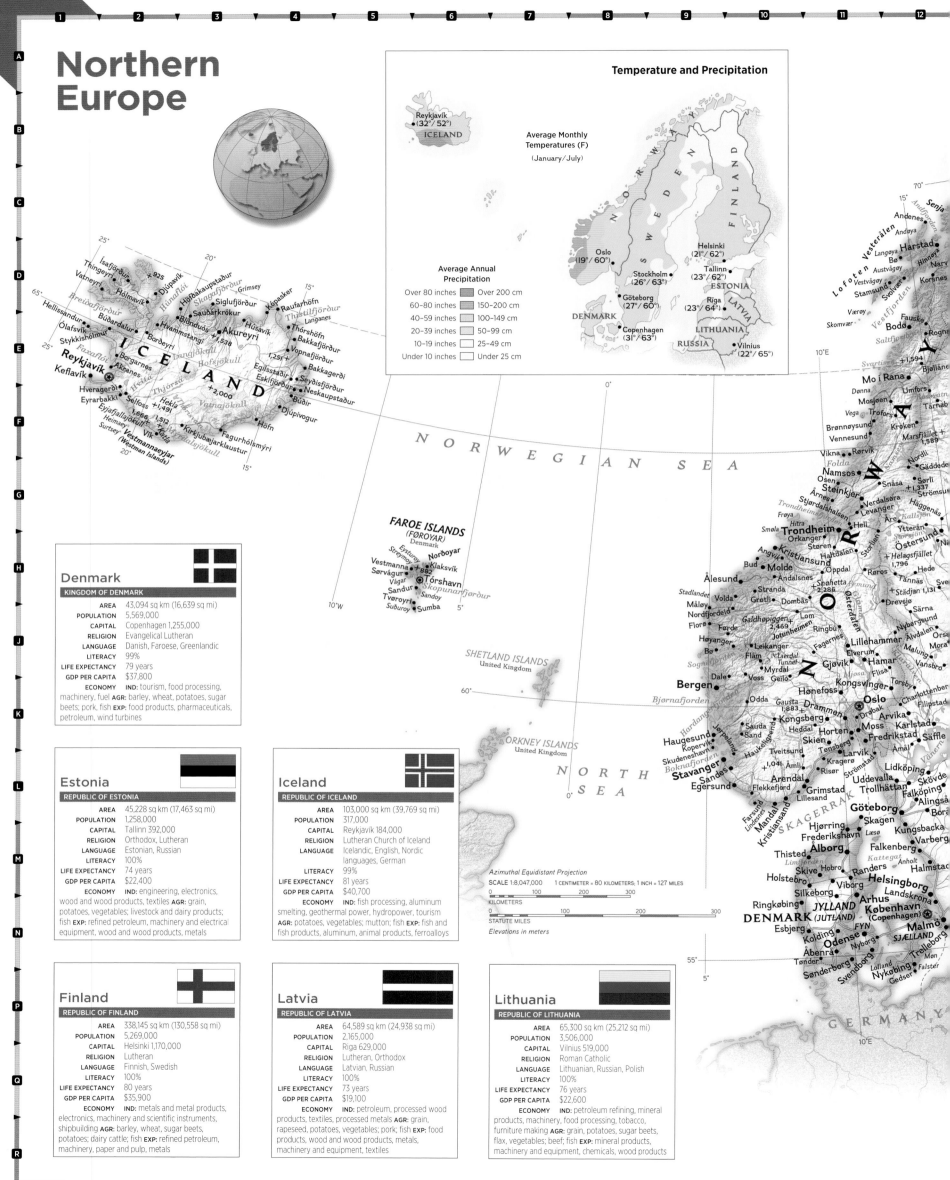

Northern Europe

Temperature and Precipitation

Reykjavík
(32° / 52°)
ICELAND

Average Monthly
Temperatures (F)
(January/July)

Oslo (19° / 60°)
Stockholm (26° / 63°)
Helsinki (21° / 62°)
Tallinn (23° / 62°)
Göteborg (27° / 60°)
Rīga (23° / 64°)
Copenhagen (31° / 63°)
Vilnius (22° / 65°)

Average Annual Precipitation

Over 80 inches	Over 200 cm
60–80 inches	150–200 cm
40–59 inches	100–149 cm
20–39 inches	50–99 cm
10–19 inches	25–49 cm
Under 10 inches	Under 25 cm

NORWEGIAN SEA

FAROE ISLANDS (FØROYAR)
Denmark

SHETLAND ISLANDS
United Kingdom

ORKNEY ISLANDS
United Kingdom

NORTH SEA

Azimuthal Equidistant Projection
SCALE 1:8,047,000   1 CENTIMETER = 80 KILOMETERS; 1 INCH = 127 MILES
KILOMETERS 0 100 200 300
STATUTE MILES 0 100 200 300
Elevations in meters

Denmark
KINGDOM OF DENMARK

AREA	43,094 sq km (16,639 sq mi)
POPULATION	5,569,000
CAPITAL	Copenhagen 1,255,000
RELIGION	Evangelical Lutheran
LANGUAGE	Danish, Faroese, Greenlandic
LITERACY	99%
LIFE EXPECTANCY	79 years
GDP PER CAPITA	$37,800

ECONOMY IND: tourism, food processing, machinery, fuel AGR: barley, wheat, potatoes, sugar beets; pork, fish EXP: food products, pharmaceuticals, petroleum, wind turbines

Estonia
REPUBLIC OF ESTONIA

AREA	45,228 sq km (17,463 sq mi)
POPULATION	1,258,000
CAPITAL	Tallinn 392,000
RELIGION	Orthodox, Lutheran
LANGUAGE	Estonian, Russian
LITERACY	100%
LIFE EXPECTANCY	74 years
GDP PER CAPITA	$22,400

ECONOMY IND: engineering, electronics, wood and wood products, textiles AGR: grain, potatoes, vegetables; livestock and dairy products; fish EXP: refined petroleum, machinery and electrical equipment, wood and wood products, metals

Iceland
REPUBLIC OF ICELAND

AREA	103,000 sq km (39,769 sq mi)
POPULATION	317,000
CAPITAL	Reykjavík 184,000
RELIGION	Lutheran Church of Iceland
LANGUAGE	Icelandic, English, Nordic languages, German
LITERACY	99%
LIFE EXPECTANCY	81 years
GDP PER CAPITA	$40,700

ECONOMY IND: fish processing, aluminum smelting, geothermal power, hydropower, tourism AGR: potatoes, vegetables; mutton; fish EXP: fish and fish products, aluminum, animal products, ferroalloys

Finland
REPUBLIC OF FINLAND

AREA	338,145 sq km (130,558 sq mi)
POPULATION	5,269,000
CAPITAL	Helsinki 1,170,000
RELIGION	Lutheran
LANGUAGE	Finnish, Swedish
LITERACY	100%
LIFE EXPECTANCY	80 years
GDP PER CAPITA	$35,900

ECONOMY IND: metals and metal products, electronics, machinery and scientific instruments, shipbuilding AGR: barley, wheat, sugar beets, potatoes; dairy cattle; fish EXP: refined petroleum, machinery, paper and pulp, metals

Latvia
REPUBLIC OF LATVIA

AREA	64,589 sq km (24,938 sq mi)
POPULATION	2,165,000
CAPITAL	Rīga 629,000
RELIGION	Lutheran, Orthodox
LANGUAGE	Latvian, Russian
LITERACY	100%
LIFE EXPECTANCY	73 years
GDP PER CAPITA	$19,100

ECONOMY IND: petroleum, processed wood products, textiles, processed metals AGR: grain, rapeseed, potatoes, vegetables; pork; fish EXP: food products, wood and wood products, metals, machinery and equipment, textiles

Lithuania
REPUBLIC OF LITHUANIA

AREA	65,300 sq km (25,212 sq mi)
POPULATION	3,506,000
CAPITAL	Vilnius 519,000
RELIGION	Roman Catholic
LANGUAGE	Lithuanian, Russian, Polish
LITERACY	100%
LIFE EXPECTANCY	76 years
GDP PER CAPITA	$22,600

ECONOMY IND: petroleum refining, mineral products, machinery, food processing, tobacco, furniture making AGR: grain, potatoes, sugar beets, flax, vegetables; beef; fish EXP: mineral products, machinery and equipment, chemicals, wood products

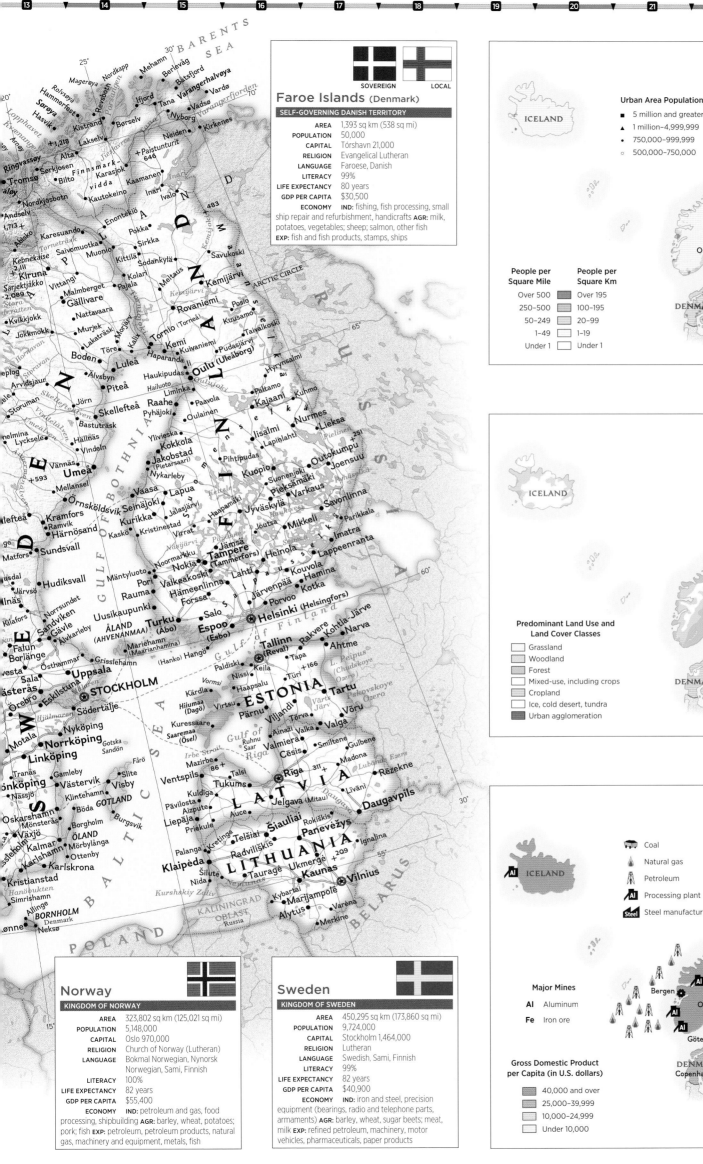

Faroe Islands (Denmark)

SOVEREIGN   LOCAL

SELF-GOVERNING DANISH TERRITORY

AREA	1,393 sq km (538 sq mi)
POPULATION	50,000
CAPITAL	Tórshavn 21,000
RELIGION	Evangelical Lutheran
LANGUAGE	Faroese, Danish
LITERACY	99%
LIFE EXPECTANCY	80 years
GDP PER CAPITA	$30,500

ECONOMY **IND:** fishing, fish processing, small ship repair and refurbishment, handicrafts **AGR:** milk, potatoes, vegetables; sheep; salmon, other fish **EXP:** fish and fish products, stamps, ships

Population

ICELAND

Urban Area Population

- ■ 5 million and greater
- ▲ 1 million–4,999,999
- ● 750,000–999,999
- ○ 500,000–750,000

People per Square Mile	People per Square Km
Over 500	Over 195
250–500	100–195
50–249	20–99
1–49	1–19
Under 1	Under 1

Land Use

ICELAND

Predominant Land Use and Land Cover Classes

- Grassland
- Woodland
- Forest
- Mixed-use, including crops
- Cropland
- Ice, cold desert, tundra
- Urban agglomeration

Industry and Mining

ICELAND

- Coal
- Natural gas
- Petroleum
- **Al** Processing plant
- **Steel** Steel manufacturing

Major Mines

- **Al** Aluminum
- **Fe** Iron ore

Gross Domestic Product per Capita (in U.S. dollars)

- 40,000 and over
- 25,000–39,999
- 10,000–24,999
- Under 10,000

Norway

KINGDOM OF NORWAY

AREA	323,802 sq km (125,021 sq mi)
POPULATION	5,148,000
CAPITAL	Oslo 970,000
RELIGION	Church of Norway (Lutheran)
LANGUAGE	Bokmal Norwegian, Nynorsk Norwegian, Sami, Finnish
LITERACY	100%
LIFE EXPECTANCY	82 years
GDP PER CAPITA	$55,400

ECONOMY **IND:** petroleum and gas, food processing, shipbuilding **AGR:** barley, wheat, potatoes; pork; fish **EXP:** petroleum, petroleum products, natural gas, machinery and equipment, metals, fish

Sweden

KINGDOM OF SWEDEN

AREA	450,295 sq km (173,860 sq mi)
POPULATION	9,724,000
CAPITAL	Stockholm 1,464,000
RELIGION	Lutheran
LANGUAGE	Swedish, Sami, Finnish
LITERACY	99%
LIFE EXPECTANCY	82 years
GDP PER CAPITA	$40,900

ECONOMY **IND:** iron and steel, precision equipment (bearings, radio and telephone parts, armaments) **AGR:** barley, wheat, sugar beets; meat, milk **EXP:** refined petroleum, machinery, motor vehicles, pharmaceuticals, paper products

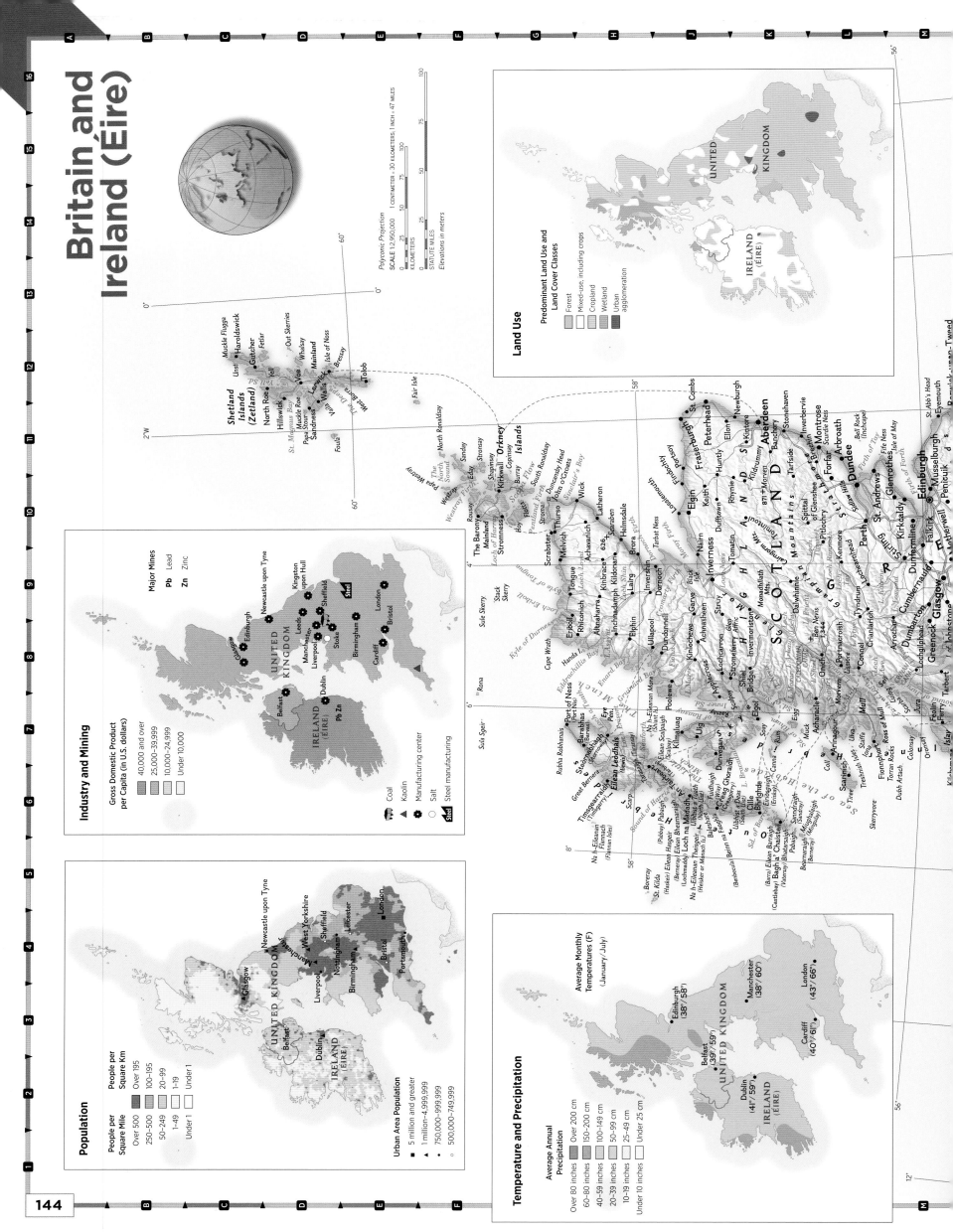

Britain and Ireland (Éire)

Polyconic Projection
SCALE 1:2,950,000 1 CENTIMETER = 30 KILOMETERS; 1 INCH = 47 MILES
KILOMETERS
STATUTE MILES
Elevations in meters

Land Use

Predominant Land Use and Land Cover Classes
- Forest
- Mixed-use, including crops
- Cropland
- Wetland
- Urban agglomeration

Industry and Mining

Gross Domestic Product per Capita (in U.S. dollars)
- 40,000 and over
- 25,000–39,999
- 10,000–24,999
- Under 10,000

Major Mines
- **Pb** Lead
- **Zn** Zinc

- Coal
- Kaolin
- Manufacturing center
- Salt
- Steel manufacturing

Population

People per Square Mile / People per Square Km
- Over 500 / Over 195
- 250–500 / 100–195
- 50–249 / 20–99
- 1–49 / 1–19
- Under 1 / Under 1

Urban Area Population
- 5 million and greater
- 1 million–4,999,999
- 750,000–999,999
- 500,000–749,999

Temperature and Precipitation

Average Monthly Temperatures (F) (January/July)

Average Annual Precipitation
- Over 80 inches / Over 200 cm
- 60–80 inches / 150–200 cm
- 40–59 inches / 100–149 cm
- 20–39 inches / 50–99 cm
- 10–19 inches / 25–49 cm
- Under 10 inches / Under 25 cm

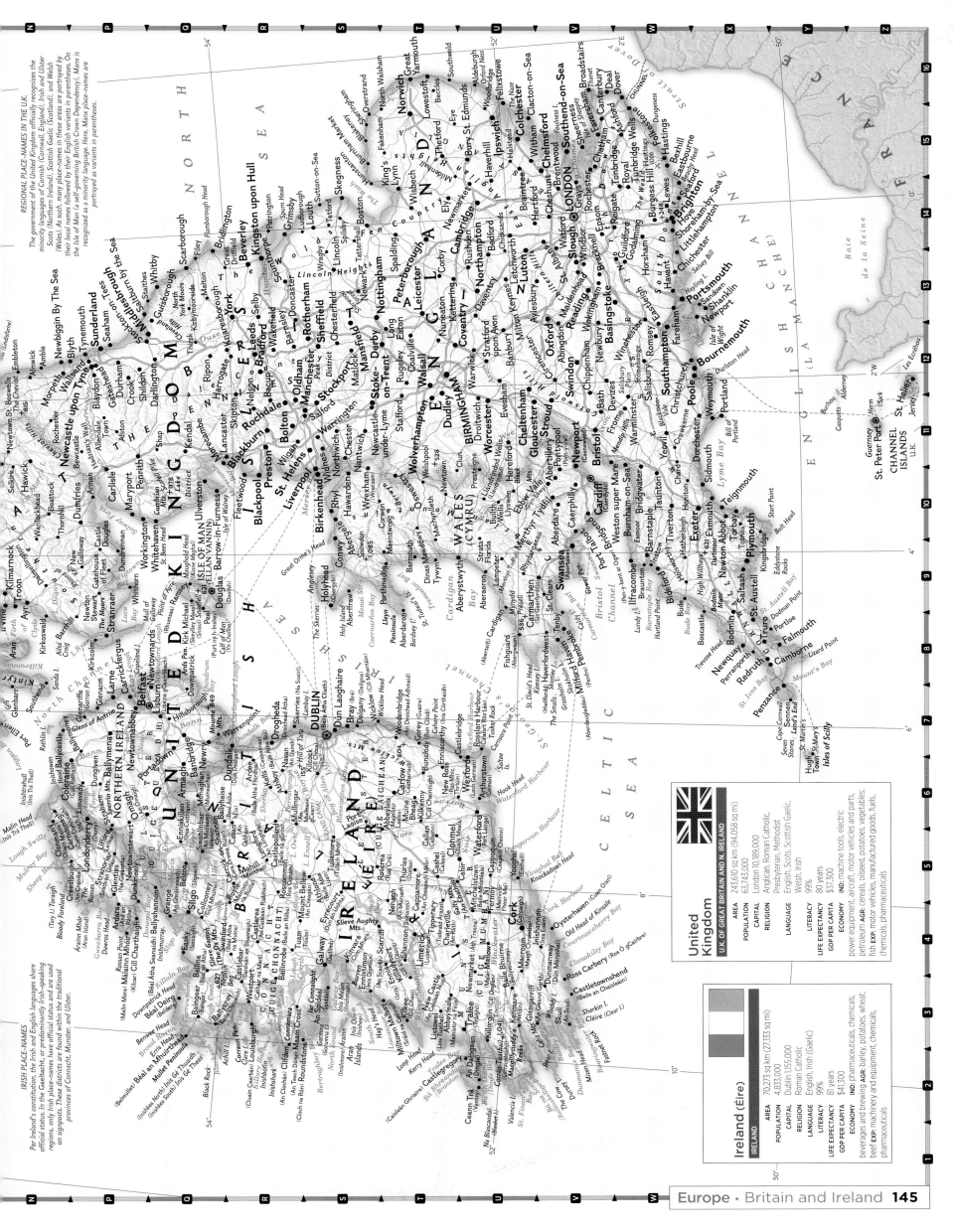

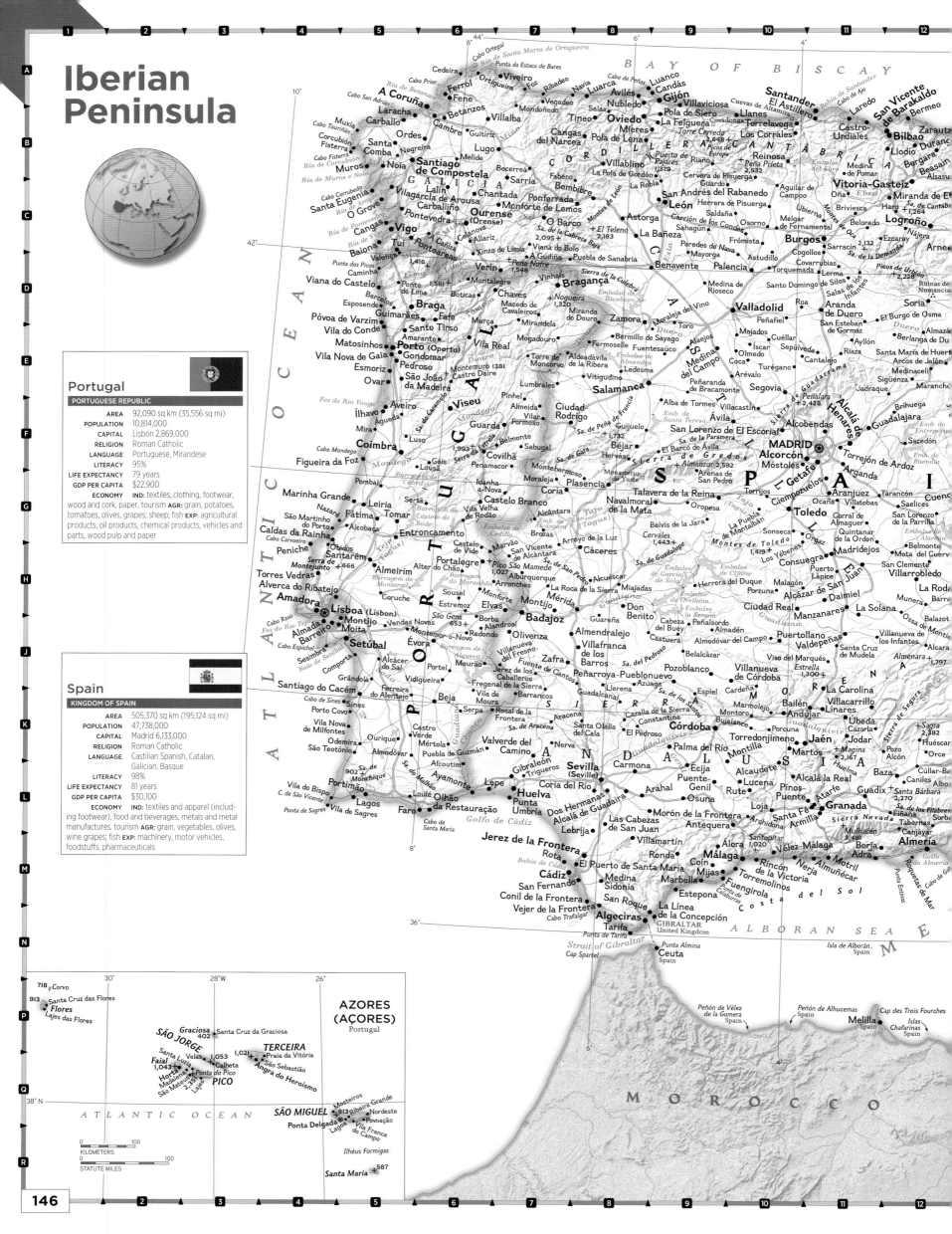

Iberian Peninsula

Portugal

PORTUGUESE REPUBLIC

AREA	92,090 sq km (35,556 sq mi)
POPULATION	10,814,000
CAPITAL	Lisbon 2,869,000
RELIGION	Roman Catholic
LANGUAGE	Portuguese, Mirandese
LITERACY	95%
LIFE EXPECTANCY	79 years
GDP PER CAPITA	$22,900

ECONOMY IND: textiles, clothing, footwear, wood and cork, paper, tourism AGR: grain, potatoes, tomatoes, olives, grapes; sheep; fish EXP: agricultural products, oil products, chemical products, vehicles and parts, wood pulp and paper

Spain

KINGDOM OF SPAIN

AREA	505,370 sq km (195,124 sq mi)
POPULATION	47,738,000
CAPITAL	Madrid 6,133,000
RELIGION	Roman Catholic
LANGUAGE	Castilian Spanish, Catalan, Galician, Basque
LITERACY	98%
LIFE EXPECTANCY	81 years
GDP PER CAPITA	$30,100

ECONOMY IND: textiles and apparel (including footwear), food and beverages, metals and metal manufactures, tourism AGR: grain, vegetables, olives, wine grapes; fish EXP: machinery, motor vehicles, foodstuffs, pharmaceuticals

AZORES (AÇORES)
Portugal

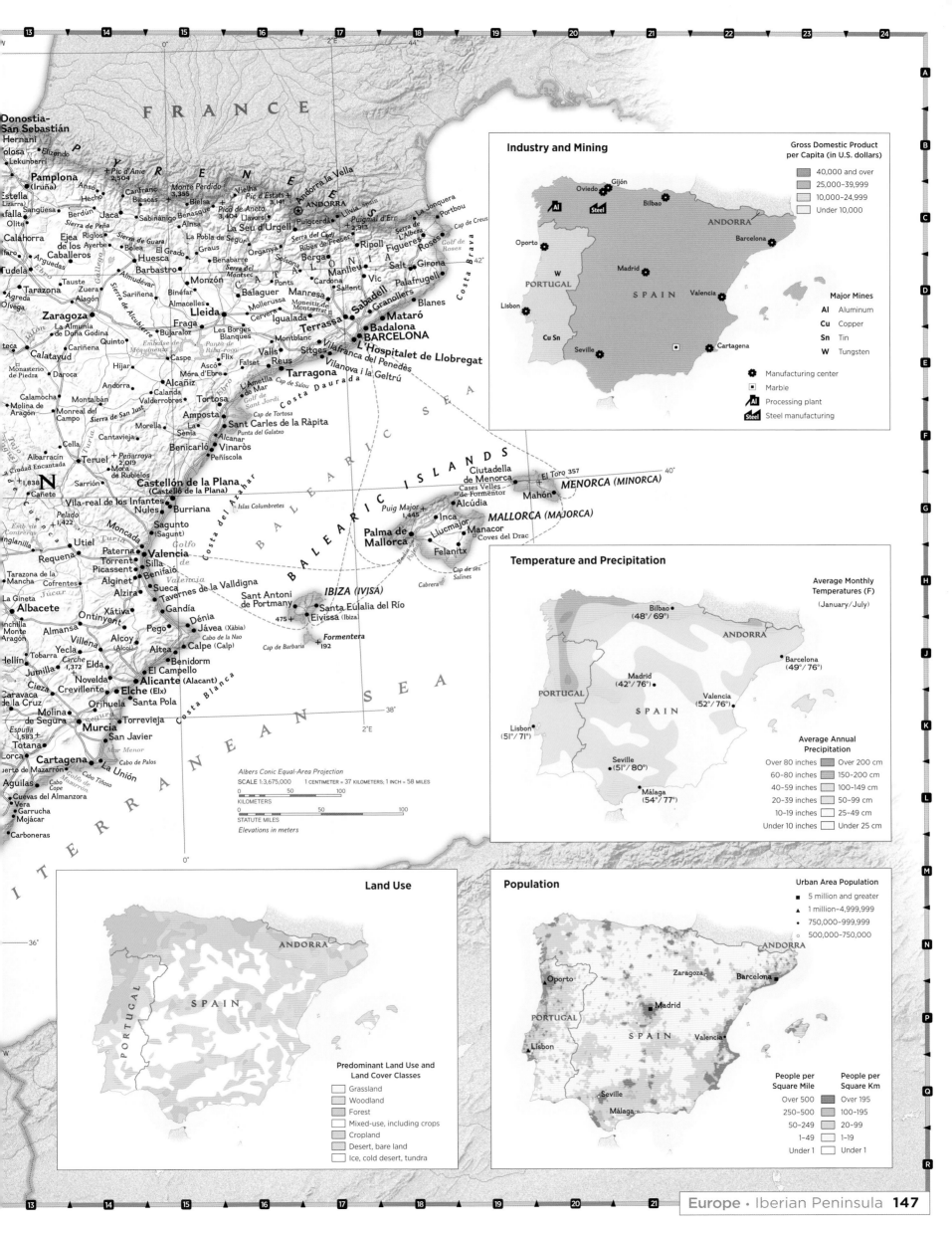

France and the Low Countries

Population

People per Square Mile
- Over 500
- 250-500
- 50-249
- 1-49
- Under 1

People per Square Km
- Over 195
- 100-195
- 20-99
- 1-19
- Under 1

Urban Area Population
- ■ 5 million and greater
- ▲ 1 million-4,999,999
- ○ 750,000-999,999
- ○ 500,000-750,000

Land Use

Predominant Land Use and Land Cover Classes
- Grassland
- Woodland
- Forest
- Mixed-use, including crops
- Cropland
- Ice, cold desert, tundra
- Urban agglomeration

Luxembourg

GRAND DUCHY OF LUXEMBOURG

AREA	2,586 sq km (998 sq mi)
POPULATION	521,000
CAPITAL	Luxembourg 107,000
RELIGION	Roman Catholic
LANGUAGE	Luxembourgish, German, French
LITERACY	100%
LIFE EXPECTANCY	80 years
GDP PER CAPITA	$77,900
ECONOMY	IND: banking and financial services, iron and steel AGR: wine, grapes, barley, oats EXP: machinery, steel products, chemicals

Netherlands

KINGDOM OF THE NETHERLANDS

AREA	41,543 sq km (16,040 sq mi)
POPULATION	16,877,000
CAPITAL	Amsterdam 1,084,000 (seat of government is The Hague)
RELIGION	Roman Catholic, Protestant, Muslim
LANGUAGE	Dutch
LITERACY	99%
LIFE EXPECTANCY	81 years
GDP PER CAPITA	$43,300
ECONOMY	IND: agro-industries, metal and engineering products, electrical machinery and equipment, petroleum AGR: tulips, grains, potatoes, sugar beets, fruits EXP: refined petroleum, machinery and equipment, chemicals, foodstuffs

Industry and Mining

Gross Domestic Product per Capita (in U.S. dollars)
- 40,000 and over
- 25,000-39,999
- 10,000-24,999
- Under 10,000

Major Mines
- S Sulfur

- ✿ Manufacturing center
- Steel Steel manufacturing

Temperature and Precipitation

Average Annual Precipitation
- Over 80 inches — Over 200 cm
- 60-80 inches — 150-200 cm
- 40-59 inches — 100-149 cm
- 20-39 inches — 50-99 cm
- 10-19 inches — 25-49 cm
- Under 10 inches — Under 25 cm

Average Monthly Temperatures (F) (January/July)

Amsterdam (37°/63°)
Brussels (37°/64°)
Paris (34°/66°)
Nantes (41°/65°)
Bordeaux (42°/69°)
Lyon (36°/69°)
Marseille (44°/73°)
Nice (45°/73°)

Albers Conic Equal-Area Projection
SCALE 1:3,869,000   1 CENTIMETER = 39 KILOMETERS; 1 INCH = 61 MILES

Elevations in meters

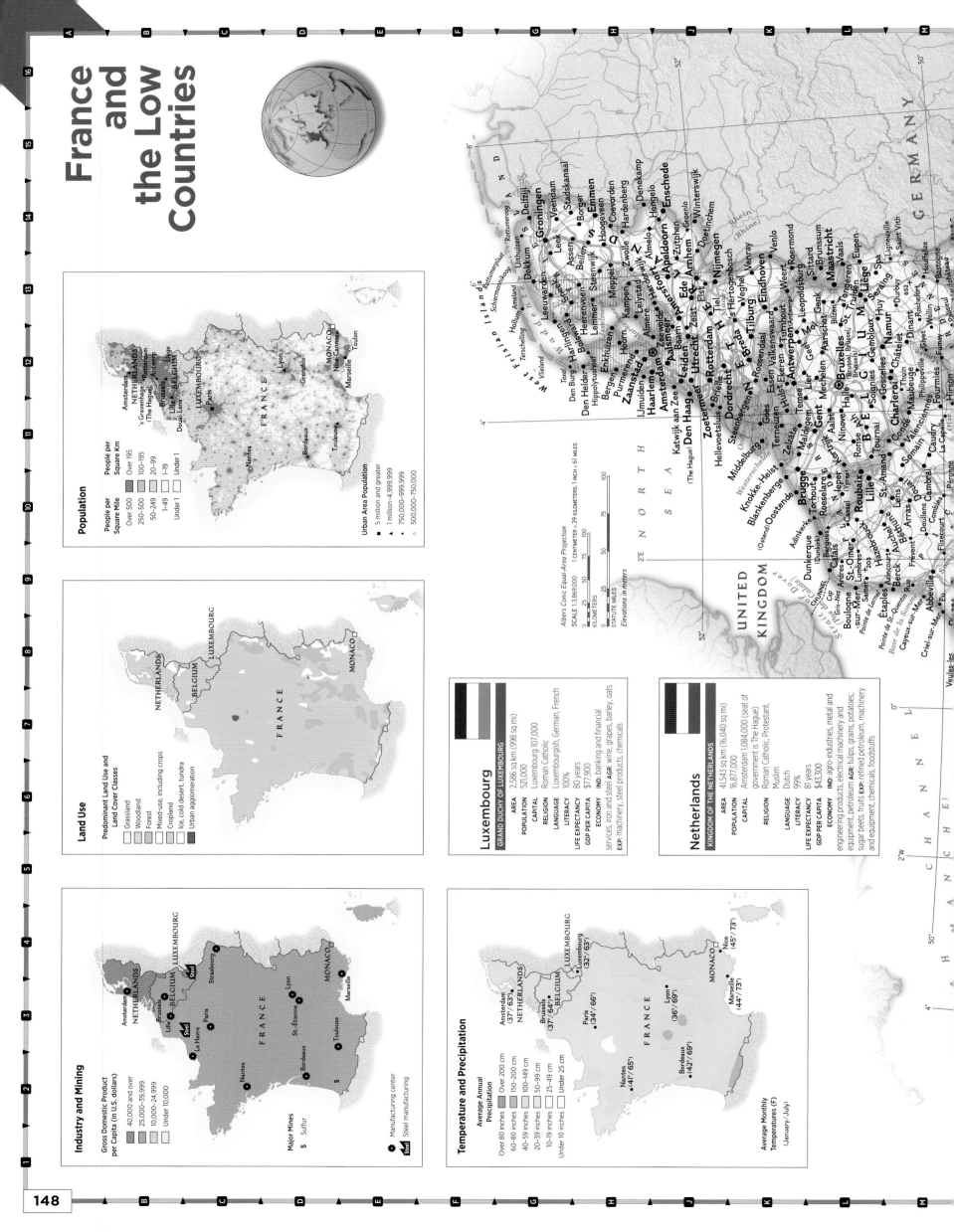

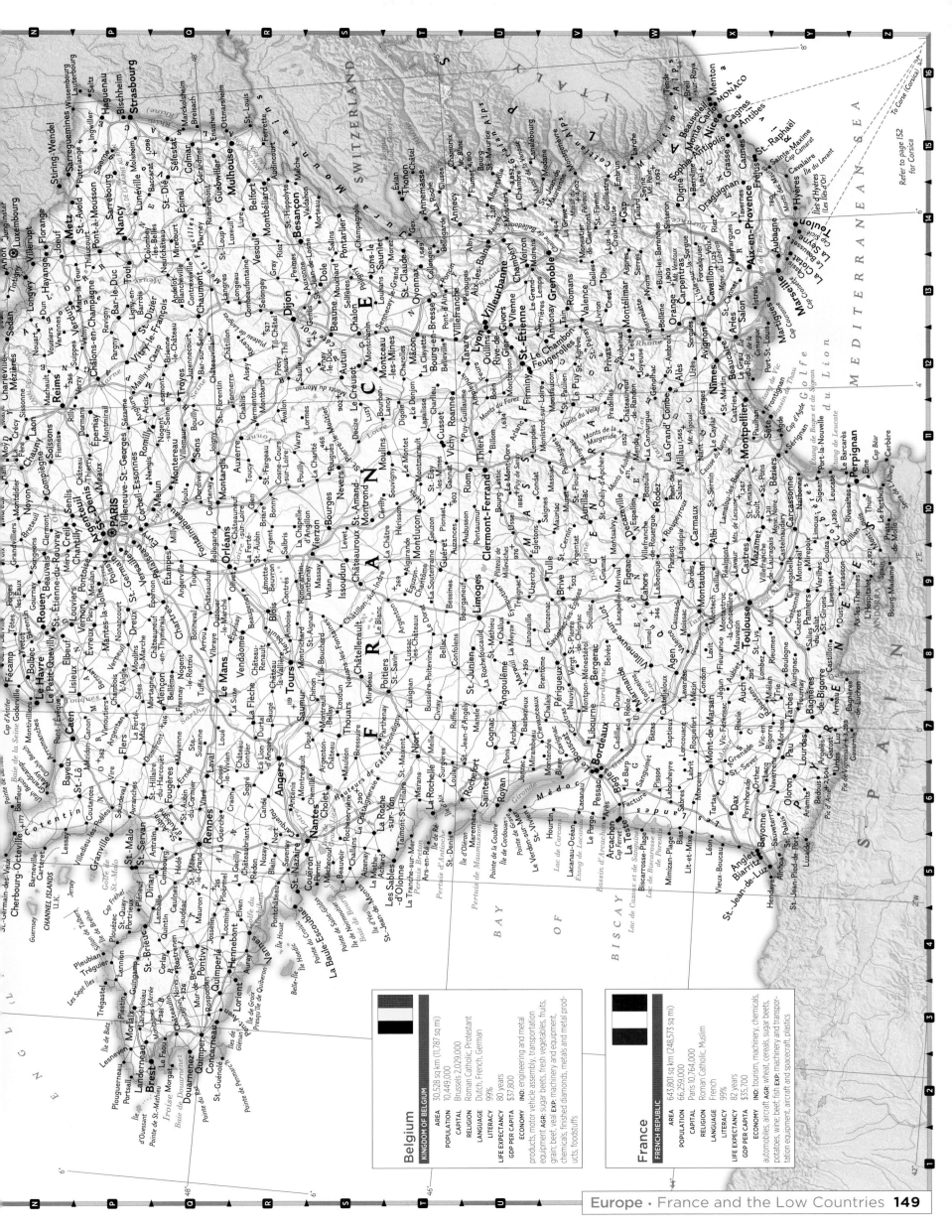

Central Europe

Austria
REPUBLIC OF AUSTRIA
AREA	83,871 sq km (32,383 sq mi)
POPULATION	8,223,000
CAPITAL	Vienna 1,743,000
RELIGION	Roman Catholic, Protestant
LANGUAGE	German, Turkish, Serbian
LITERACY	98%
LIFE EXPECTANCY	80 years
GDP PER CAPITA	$42,600

ECONOMY IND: construction, machinery, vehicles and parts, tourism AGR: grains, potatoes, wine, fruit; dairy products EXP: machinery and equipment, motor vehicles and parts, paper and paperboard, metal goods

Czech Republic (Czechia)
CZECH REPUBLIC
AREA	78,867 sq km (30,451 sq mi)
POPULATION	10,627,000
CAPITAL	Prague 1,303,000
RELIGION	Roman Catholic, Protestant
LANGUAGE	Czech
LITERACY	99%
LIFE EXPECTANCY	78 years
GDP PER CAPITA	$26,300

ECONOMY IND: motor vehicles, metallurgy, machinery and equipment, electronics AGR: wheat, potatoes, sugar beets, hops; pigs EXP: machinery and transport equipment, raw materials and fuel, chemicals

Germany
FEDERAL REPUBLIC OF GERMANY
AREA	357,022 sq km (137,847 sq mi)
POPULATION	80,997,000
CAPITAL	Berlin 3,547,000
RELIGION	Protestant, Roman Catholic
LANGUAGE	German
LITERACY	99%
LIFE EXPECTANCY	80 years
GDP PER CAPITA	$39,500

ECONOMY IND: steel, coal, vehicles, machine tools, electronics AGR: potatoes, wheat, barley, sugar beets; cattle EXP: motor vehicles, machinery, chemicals, computer and electronic products

Land Use

Predominant Land Use and Land Cover Classes
- Grassland
- Woodland
- Forest
- Mixed-use, including crops
- Cropland
- Ice, cold desert, tundra
- Urban agglomeration

Hungary
REPUBLIC OF HUNGARY
AREA	93,028 sq km (35,918 sq mi)
POPULATION	9,919,000
CAPITAL	Budapest 1,717,000
RELIGION	Roman Catholic, Calvinist
LANGUAGE	Hungarian, English, German
LITERACY	99%
LIFE EXPECTANCY	75 years
GDP PER CAPITA	$19,800

ECONOMY IND: metallurgy, construction materials, pharmaceuticals, motor vehicles AGR: wheat, corn, sunflower seeds, potatoes; pigs EXP: machinery and equipment, motor vehicles, electronics, food products

Poland
REPUBLIC OF POLAND
AREA	312,685 sq km (120,728 sq mi)
POPULATION	38,346,000
CAPITAL	Warsaw 1,718,000
RELIGION	Roman Catholic
LANGUAGE	Polish
LITERACY	100%
LIFE EXPECTANCY	77 years
GDP PER CAPITA	$21,100

ECONOMY IND: machine building, iron and steel, coal mining, chemicals AGR: potatoes, fruits, vegetables, wheat; poultry EXP: machinery and transport equipment, refined petroleum, textiles, electronics

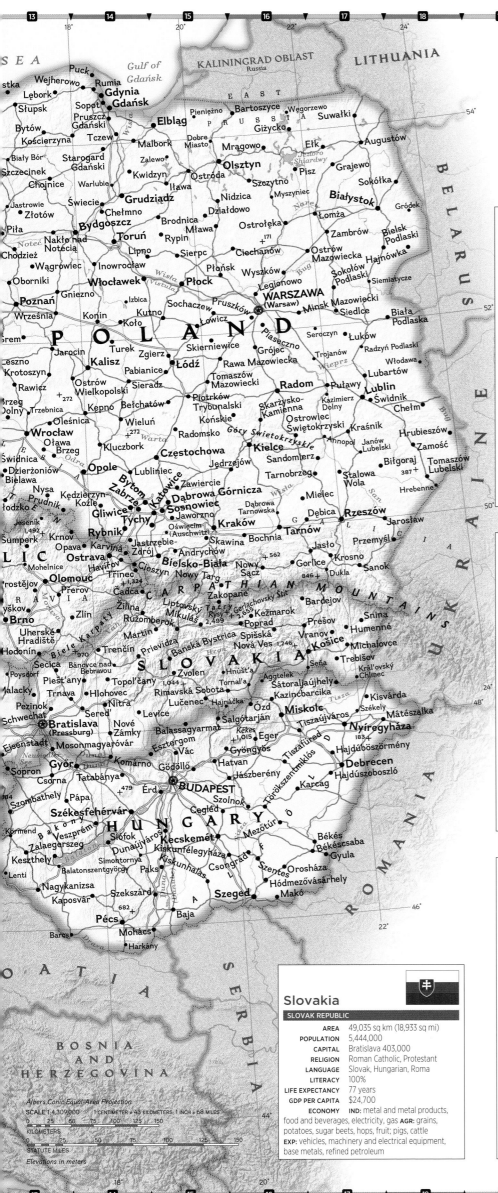

Industry and Mining

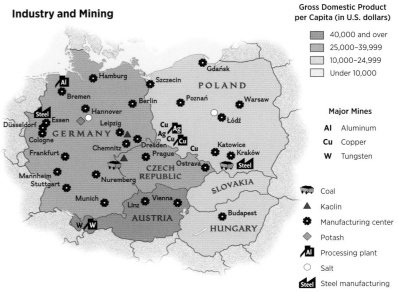

Gross Domestic Product per Capita (in U.S. dollars)

- 40,000 and over
- 25,000–39,999
- 10,000–24,999
- Under 10,000

Major Mines

- Al — Aluminum
- Cu — Copper
- W — Tungsten

- Coal
- Kaolin
- Manufacturing center
- Potash
- Processing plant
- Salt
- Steel manufacturing

Temperature and Precipitation

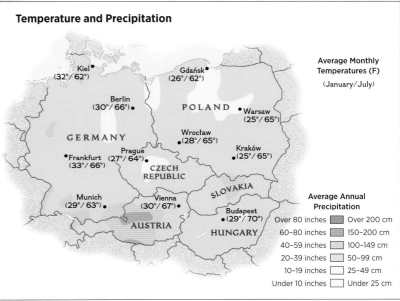

Average Monthly Temperatures (F)

(January/July)

Kiel (32°/ 62°)
Gdańsk (26°/ 62°)
Berlin (30°/ 66°)
Warsaw (25°/ 65°)
Wrocław (28°/ 65°)
Frankfurt (33°/ 66°)
Prague (27°/ 64°)
Kraków (25°/ 65°)
Munich (29°/ 63°)
Vienna (30°/ 67°)
Budapest (29°/ 70°)

Average Annual Precipitation

Over 80 inches	Over 200 cm
60–80 inches	150–200 cm
40–59 inches	100–149 cm
20–39 inches	50–99 cm
10–19 inches	25–49 cm
Under 10 inches	Under 25 cm

Population

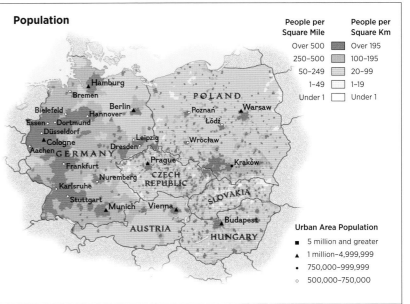

People per Square Mile	People per Square Km
Over 500	Over 195
250–500	100–195
50–249	20–99
1–49	1–19
Under 1	Under 1

Urban Area Population

- 5 million and greater
- 1 million–4,999,999
- 750,000–999,999
- 500,000–750,000

Slovakia

SLOVAK REPUBLIC

- AREA: 49,035 sq km (18,933 sq mi)
- POPULATION: 5,444,000
- CAPITAL: Bratislava 403,000
- RELIGION: Roman Catholic, Protestant
- LANGUAGE: Slovak, Hungarian, Roma
- LITERACY: 100%
- LIFE EXPECTANCY: 77 years
- GDP PER CAPITA: $24,700
- ECONOMY: IND: metal and metal products, food and beverages, electricity, gas AGR: grains, potatoes, sugar beets, hops, fruit; pigs, cattle EXP: vehicles, machinery and electrical equipment, base metals, refined petroleum

Albers Conic Equal-Area Projection
SCALE 1:4,309,000
1 CENTIMETER = 43 KILOMETERS; 1 INCH = 68 MILES
KILOMETERS
STATUTE MILES
Elevations in meters

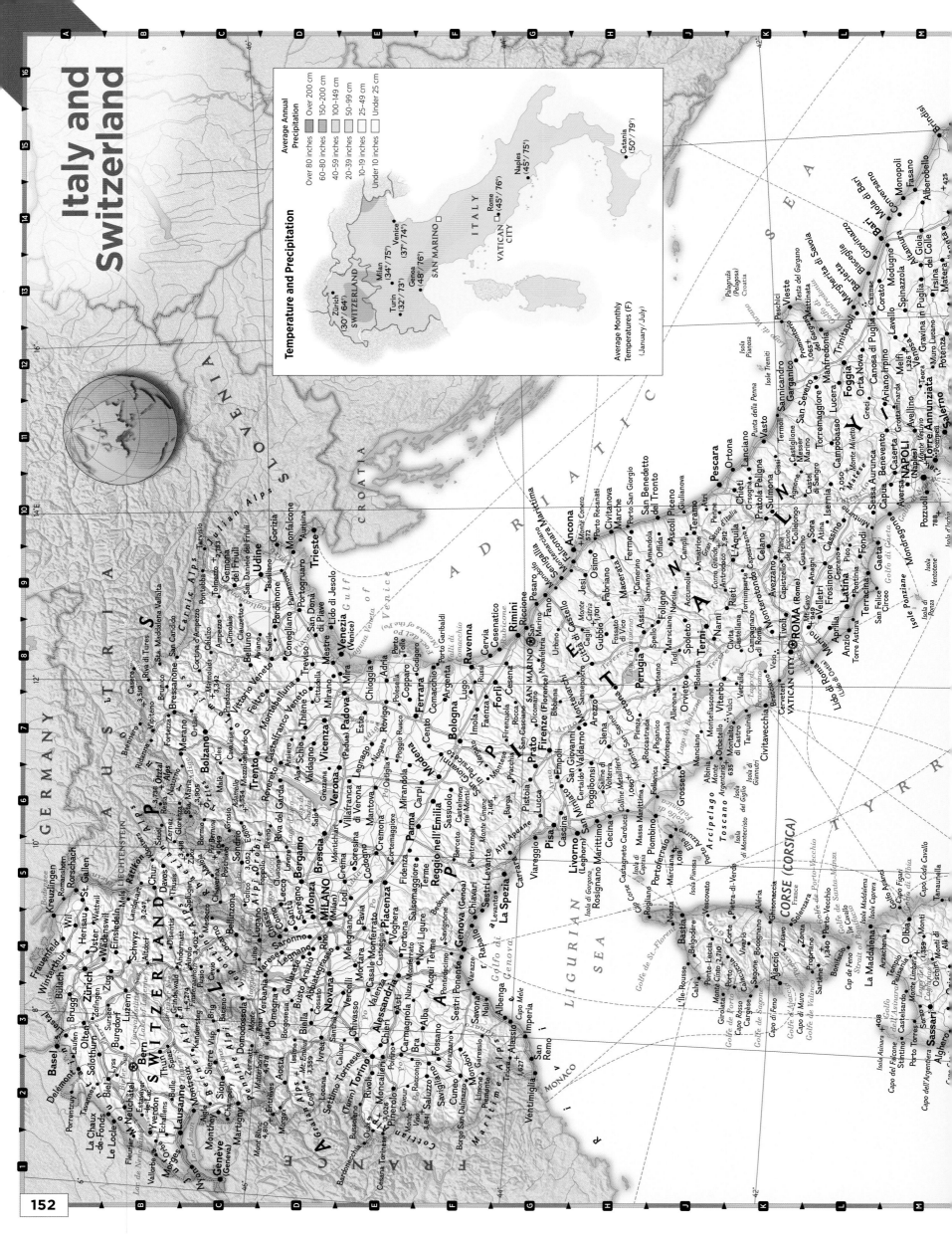

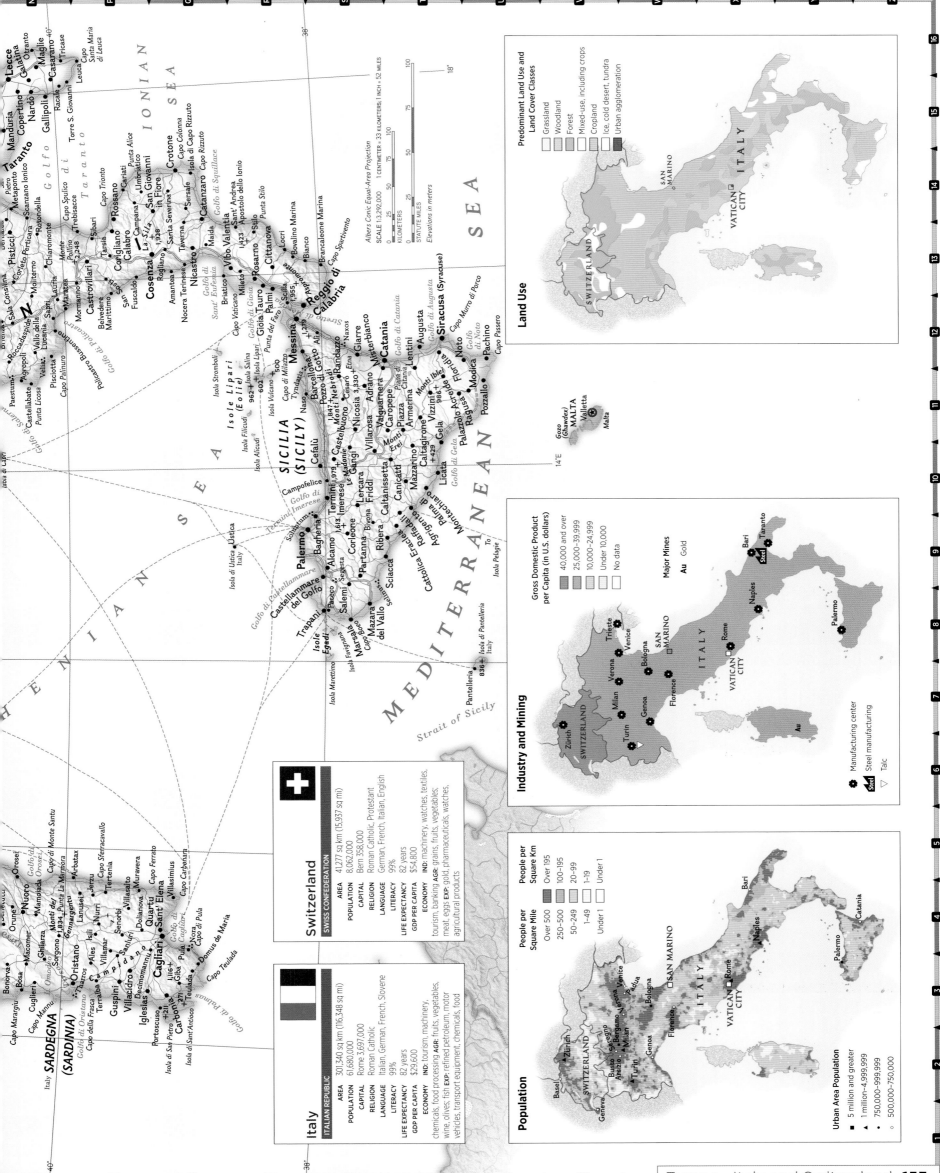

Italy

ITALIAN REPUBLIC

AREA	301,340 sq km (116,348 sq mi)
POPULATION	61,680,000
CAPITAL	Rome 3,697,000
RELIGION	Roman Catholic
LANGUAGE	Italian, German, French, Slovene
LITERACY	99%
LIFE EXPECTANCY	82 years
GDP PER CAPITA	$29,600
ECONOMY	IND: tourism, machinery, chemicals, food processing AGR: fruits, vegetables, wine, olives; fish EXP: refined petroleum, motor vehicles, transport equipment, chemicals, food

Switzerland

SWISS CONFEDERATION

AREA	41,277 sq km (15,937 sq mi)
POPULATION	8,062,000
CAPITAL	Bern 358,000
RELIGION	Roman Catholic, Protestant
LANGUAGE	German, French, Italian, English
LITERACY	99%
LIFE EXPECTANCY	82 years
GDP PER CAPITA	$54,800
ECONOMY	IND: machinery, watches, textiles, tourism, banking AGR: grains, fruits, vegetables; meat, eggs EXP: gold, pharmaceuticals, watches, agricultural products

Albers Conic Equal-Area Projection
SCALE 1:3,292,000 1 CENTIMETER = 33 KILOMETERS; 1 INCH = 52 MILES
Elevations in meters

Land Use

Predominant Land Use and Land Cover Classes
- Grassland
- Woodland
- Forest
- Mixed-use, including crops
- Cropland
- Ice, cold desert, tundra
- Urban agglomeration

Industry and Mining

Gross Domestic Product per Capita (in U.S. dollars)
- 40,000 and over
- 25,000–39,999
- 10,000–24,999
- Under 10,000
- No data

Major Mines
- **Au** Gold

- Manufacturing center
- Steel manufacturing
- ▽ Talc

Population

People per Square Mile / People per Square Km
- Over 500 / Over 195
- 250–500 / 100–195
- 50–249 / 20–99
- 1–49 / 1–19
- Under 1 / Under 1

Urban Area Population
- 5 million and greater
- 1 million–4,999,999
- 750,000–999,999
- 500,000–750,000

The Balkans

THE BALKANS
The Balkan states consist of Albania, Bosnia and Herzegovina, Bulgaria, Croatia, Greece, Kosovo, Macedonia, Montenegro, Romania, Serbia, Slovenia, and the European part of Turkey.

Albania
REPUBLIC OF ALBANIA
AREA	28,748 sq km (11,100 sq mi)
POPULATION	3,020,000
CAPITAL	Tirana 445,000
RELIGION	Muslim, Roman Catholic, Albanian Orthodox
LANGUAGE	Albanian
LITERACY	97%
LIFE EXPECTANCY	78 years
GDP PER CAPITA	$10,700

ECONOMY IND: food and tobacco products, textiles and clothing, lumber, oil AGR: wheat, corn, potatoes, vegetables, fruits EXP: crude oil, textiles and footwear, metals and metallic ores

Bosnia and Herzegovina
BOSNIA AND HERZEGOVINA
AREA	51,197 sq km (19,767 sq mi)
POPULATION	3,872,000
CAPITAL	Sarajevo 322,000
RELIGION	Muslim, Orthodox, Roman Catholic
LANGUAGE	Bosnian, Croatian, Serbian
LITERACY	98%
LIFE EXPECTANCY	76 years
GDP PER CAPITA	$8,300

ECONOMY IND: steel, coal, iron ore, bauxite, aluminum, textiles AGR: wheat, corn, fruits, vegetables; livestock EXP: metals, clothing, wood products

Bulgaria
REPUBLIC OF BULGARIA
AREA	110,879 sq km (42,811 sq mi)
POPULATION	6,925,000
CAPITAL	Sofia 1,222,000
RELIGION	Eastern Orthodox, Muslim
LANGUAGE	Bulgarian, Turkish, Roma
LITERACY	98%
LIFE EXPECTANCY	74 years
GDP PER CAPITA	$14,400

ECONOMY IND: machinery and equipment, base metals, refined petroleum AGR: vegetables, fruits, tobacco, wine, wheat EXP: refined petroleum, metals, machinery and equipment

Croatia
REPUBLIC OF CROATIA
AREA	56,594 sq km (21,851 sq mi)
POPULATION	4,471,000
CAPITAL	Zagreb 687,000
RELIGION	Roman Catholic
LANGUAGE	Croatian
LITERACY	99%
LIFE EXPECTANCY	76 years
GDP PER CAPITA	$17,800

ECONOMY IND: chemicals and plastics, machine tools, fabricated metal, electronics, tourism AGR: wheat, corn, barley, vegetables; livestock EXP: transportation equipment, machinery, textiles, chemicals, fuels

Romania
ROMANIA
AREA	238,391 sq km (92,043 sq mi)
POPULATION	21,730,000
CAPITAL	Bucharest 1,872,000
RELIGION	Eastern Orthodox, Protestant
LANGUAGE	Romanian, Hungarian
LITERACY	98%
LIFE EXPECTANCY	75 years
GDP PER CAPITA	$14,400

ECONOMY IND: electric machinery and equipment, textiles and footwear, vehicle assembly AGR: wheat, corn, barley, sugar beets, grapes EXP: machinery, metals and metal products, textiles

Macedonia
REPUBLIC OF MACEDONIA
AREA	25,713 sq km (9,928 sq mi)
POPULATION	2,092,000
CAPITAL	Skopje 501,000
RELIGION	Macedonian Orthodox, Muslim
LANGUAGE	Macedonian, Albanian, Turkish
LITERACY	97%
LIFE EXPECTANCY	76 years
GDP PER CAPITA	$10,800

ECONOMY IND: food processing, textiles, chemicals, iron, steel AGR: grapes, tobacco, vegetables, fruits EXP: textiles, manufactured goods

KOSOVO
On February 17, 2008, Kosovo declared its independence. Serbia still claims it as a province.

Kosovo
REPUBLIC OF KOSOVO
AREA	10,887 sq km (4,203 sq mi)
POPULATION	1,859,000
CAPITAL	Pristina 600,000
RELIGION	Muslim, Serbian Orthodox, Roman Catholic
LANGUAGE	Albanian, Serbian, Bosnian, Turkish, Roma
LITERACY	92%
LIFE EXPECTANCY	69 years
GDP PER CAPITA	$7,600

ECONOMY IND: mineral mining, construction materials, base metals, leather AGR: wheat, corn, grapes EXP: mining and processed metal products, scrap metals, leather products, machinery

Montenegro
MONTENEGRO
AREA	13,812 sq km (5,333 sq mi)
POPULATION	650,000
CAPITAL	Podgorica 165,000
RELIGION	Orthodox, Muslim
LANGUAGE	Serbian, Montenegrin, Bosnian, Albanian, Serbo-Croat
LITERACY	99%
LIFE EXPECTANCY	N/A
GDP PER CAPITA	$11,900

ECONOMY IND: steelmaking, aluminum, agricultural processing, consumer goods, tourism AGR: tobacco, potatoes, fruits, olives, grapes; sheep EXP: aluminum, ships, wine, metals

Serbia
REPUBLIC OF SERBIA
AREA	77,474 sq km (29,913 sq mi)
POPULATION	7,210,000
CAPITAL	Belgrade 1,181,000
RELIGION	Serbian Orthodox, Catholic
LANGUAGE	Serbian, Hungarian
LITERACY	98%
LIFE EXPECTANCY	75 years
GDP PER CAPITA	$11,100

ECONOMY IND: base metals, food processing, machinery, tires, clothes AGR: wheat, maize, sugar beets, sunflower seeds; beef EXP: corn, metal products, vehicles, rubber tires, fruits and nuts

Slovenia
REPUBLIC OF SLOVENIA
AREA	20,273 sq km (7,827 sq mi)
POPULATION	1,988,000
CAPITAL	Ljubljana 279,000
RELIGION	Catholic
LANGUAGE	Slovene, Serbo-Croatian
LITERACY	100%
LIFE EXPECTANCY	78 years
GDP PER CAPITA	$27,400

ECONOMY IND: ferrous metallurgy and aluminum products, electronics, vehicles and parts AGR: potatoes, hops, wheat, sugar beets; cattle EXP: manufactured goods, machinery and transportation equipment, pharmaceuticals

Industry and Mining

Gross Domestic Product per Capita (in U.S. dollars)

- 40,000 and over
- 25,000–39,999
- 10,000–24,999
- Under 10,000

Major Mines
Cu Copper

☼ Manufacturing center
Cu Processing plant

Temperature and Precipitation

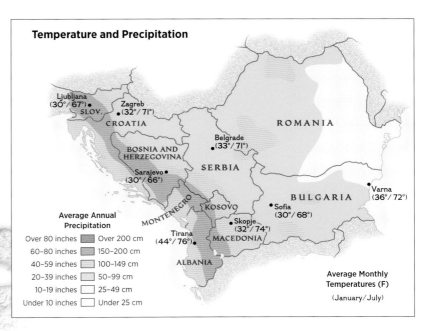

Ljubljana (30°/67°)
Zagreb (32°/71°)
Belgrade (33°/71°)
Sarajevo (30°/66°)
Tirana (44°/76°)
Skopje (32°/74°)
Sofia (30°/68°)
Varna (36°/72°)

Average Annual Precipitation

Over 80 inches	Over 200 cm
60–80 inches	150–200 cm
40–59 inches	100–149 cm
20–39 inches	50–99 cm
10–19 inches	25–49 cm
Under 10 inches	Under 25 cm

Average Monthly Temperatures (F)

(January/July)

Land Use

Predominant Land Use and Land Cover Classes

- Grassland
- Woodland
- Forest
- Mixed-use, including crops
- Cropland
- Ice, cold desert, tundra
- Urban agglomeration

Population

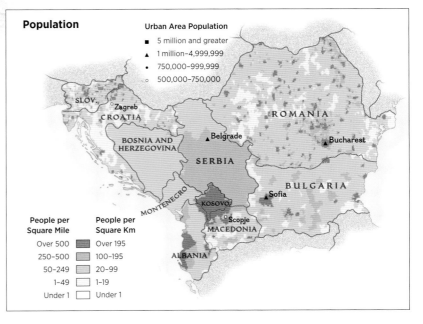

Urban Area Population

- ■ 5 million and greater
- ▲ 1 million–4,999,999
- ● 750,000–999,999
- ○ 500,000–750,000

People per Square Mile	People per Square Km
Over 500	Over 195
250–500	100–195
50–249	20–99
1–49	1–19
Under 1	Under 1

Albers Conic Equal-Area Projection
SCALE 1:4,118,000   1 CENTIMETER = 41 KILOMETERS; 1 INCH = 65 MILES

KILOMETERS
STATUTE MILES
Elevations in meters

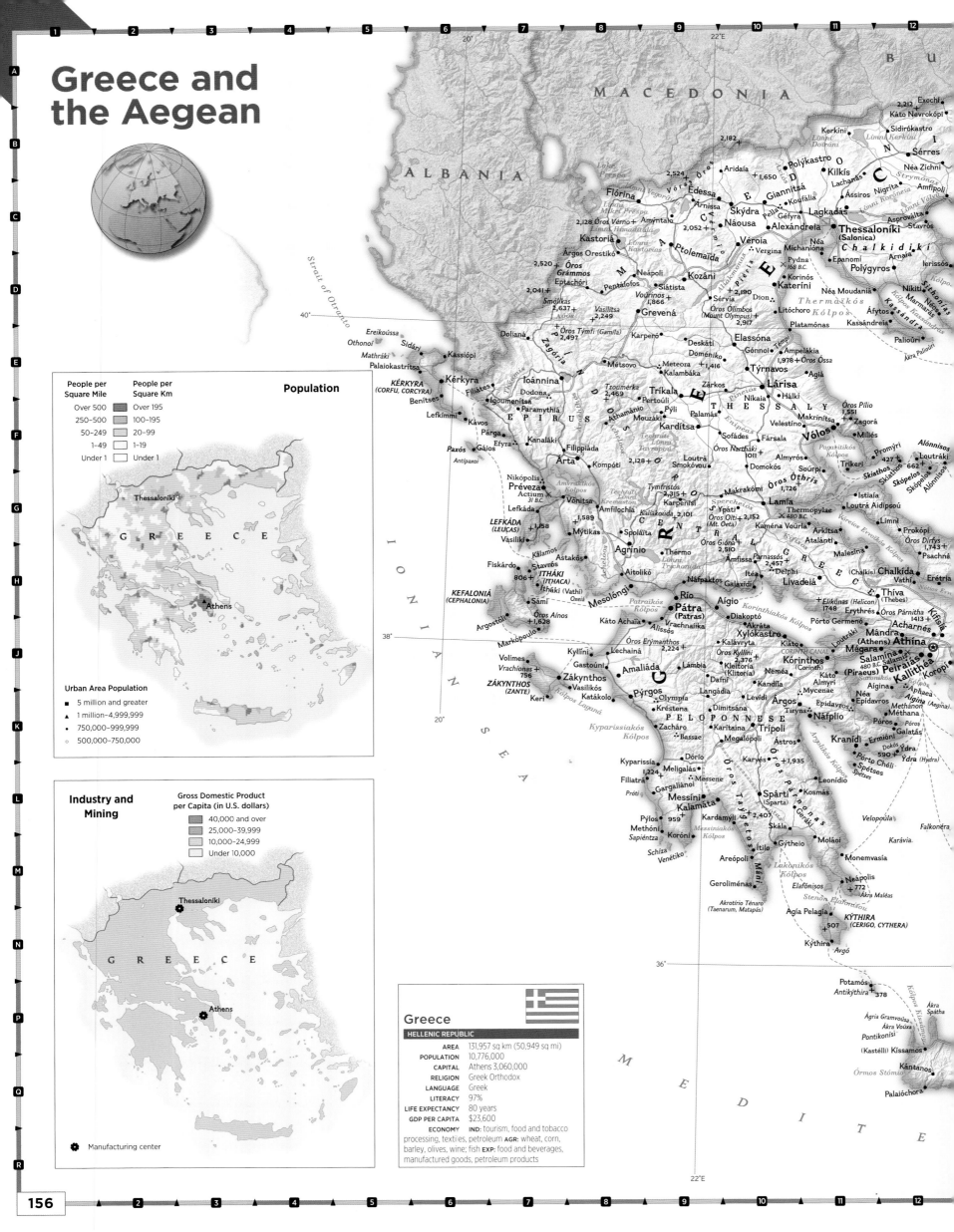

Greece and the Aegean

Population

People per Square Mile	People per Square Km
Over 500	Over 195
250-500	100-195
50-249	20-99
1-49	1-19
Under 1	Under 1

Urban Area Population

- ■ 5 million and greater
- ▲ 1 million-4,999,999
- ● 750,000-999,999
- ○ 500,000-750,000

Industry and Mining

Gross Domestic Product per Capita (in U.S. dollars)

- 40,000 and over
- 25,000-39,999
- 10,000-24,999
- Under 10,000

✿ Manufacturing center

Greece

HELLENIC REPUBLIC

AREA	131,957 sq km (50,949 sq mi)
POPULATION	10,776,000
CAPITAL	Athens 3,060,000
RELIGION	Greek Orthodox
LANGUAGE	Greek
LITERACY	97%
LIFE EXPECTANCY	80 years
GDP PER CAPITA	$23,600
ECONOMY	IND: tourism, food and tobacco processing, textiles, petroleum AGR: wheat, corn, barley, olives, wine; fish EXP: food and beverages, manufactured goods, petroleum products

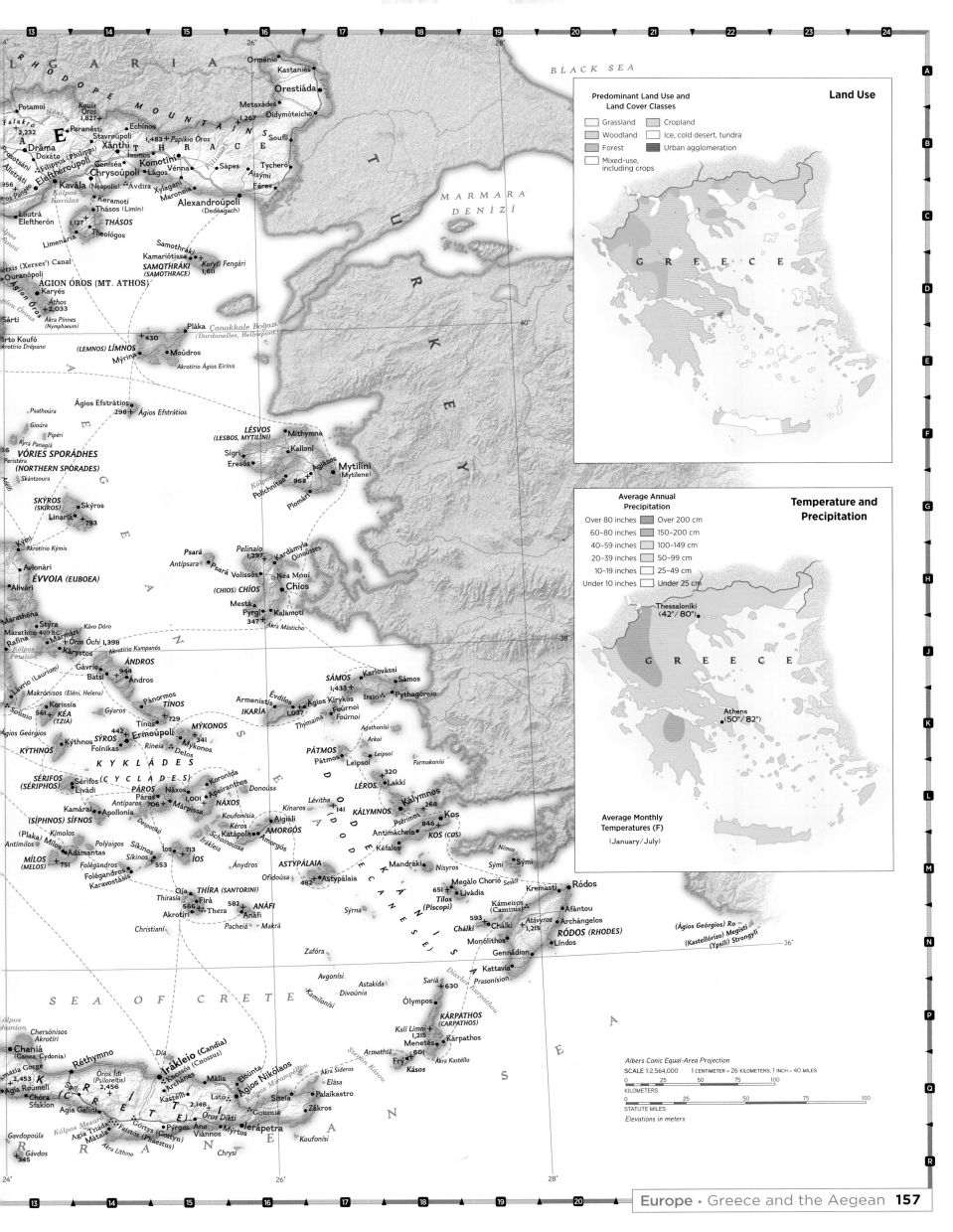

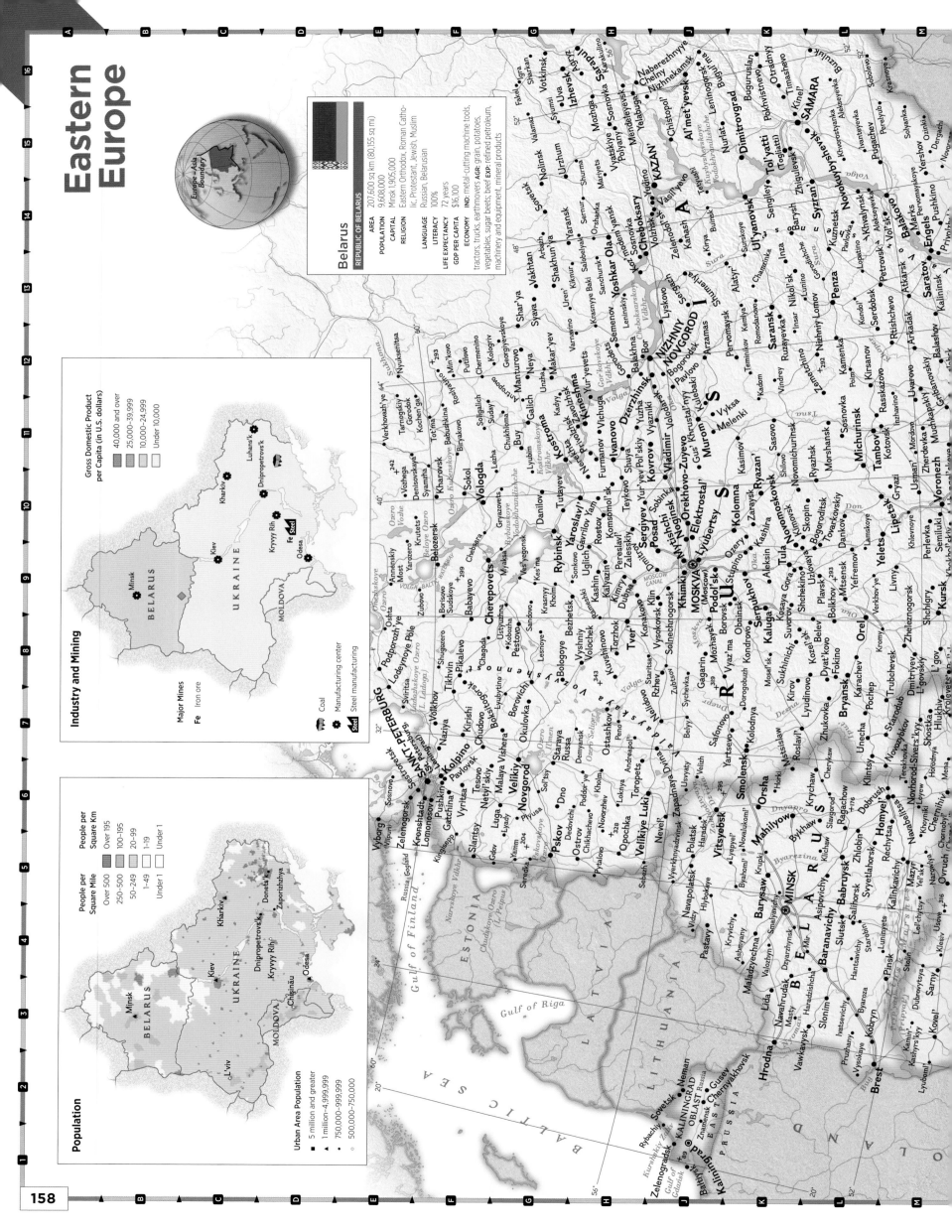

Eastern Europe

Belarus
REPUBLIC OF BELARUS

AREA	207,600 sq km (80,155 sq mi)
POPULATION	9,608,000
CAPITAL	Minsk 1,905,000
RELIGION	Eastern Orthodox, Roman Catholic, Protestant, Jewish, Muslim
LANGUAGE	Russian, Belarusian
LITERACY	100%
LIFE EXPECTANCY	72 years
GDP PER CAPITA	$16,100
ECONOMY	IND: metal-cutting machine tools, tractors, trucks, earthmovers AGR: grain, potatoes, vegetables, sugar beets; beef EXP: refined petroleum, machinery and equipment, mineral products

Industry and Mining

Major Mines
Fe   Iron ore

Coal
Manufacturing center
Steel manufacturing

Population

Urban Area Population
■ 5 million and greater
▲ 1 million–4,999,999
• 750,000–999,999
○ 500,000–750,000

People per Square Mile
Over 500
250–500
50–249
1–49
Under 1

People per Square Km
Over 195
100–195
20–99
1–19
Under 1

Gross Domestic Product per Capita (in U.S. dollars)
40,000 and over
25,000–39,999
10,000–24,999
Under 10,000

Europe–Asia Boundary

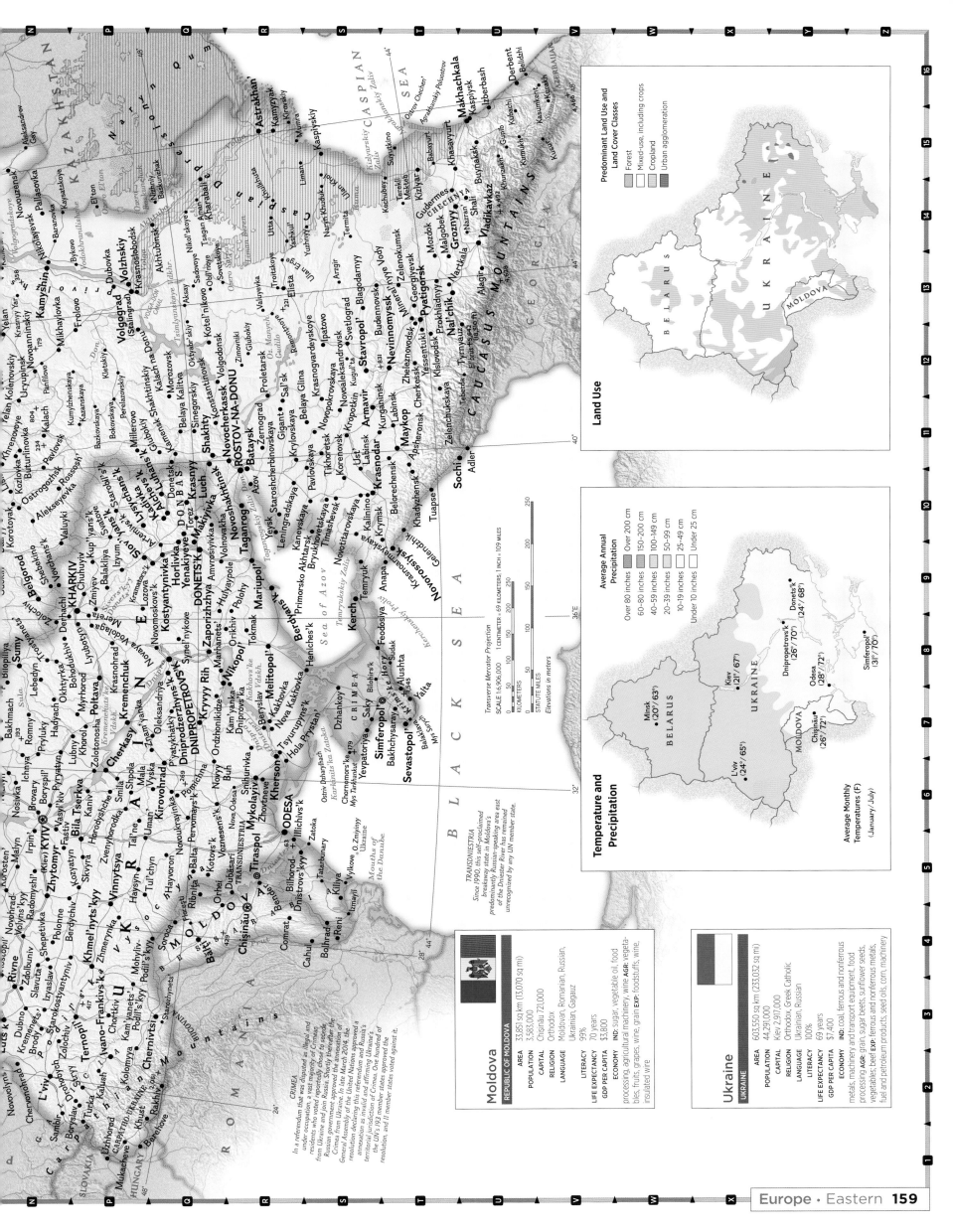

Moldova

REPUBLIC OF MOLDOVA

AREA	33,851 sq km (13,070 sq mi)
POPULATION	3,583,000
CAPITAL	Chișinău 721,000
RELIGION	Orthodox
LANGUAGE	Moldovan, Romanian, Russian, Ukrainian, Gagauz
LITERACY	99%
LIFE EXPECTANCY	70 years
GDP PER CAPITA	$3,800
ECONOMY	IND: sugar, vegetable oil, food processing, agricultural machinery, wine AGR: vegetables, fruits, grapes, wine, grain EXP: foodstuffs, wine, insulated wire

Ukraine

UKRAINE

AREA	603,550 sq km (233,032 sq mi)
POPULATION	44,291,000
CAPITAL	Kiev 2,917,000
RELIGION	Orthodox, Greek Catholic
LANGUAGE	Ukrainian, Russian
LITERACY	100%
LIFE EXPECTANCY	69 years
GDP PER CAPITA	$7,400
ECONOMY	IND: coal, ferrous and nonferrous metals, machinery and transport equipment, food processing AGR: grain, sugar beets, sunflower seeds, vegetables, beef EXP: ferrous and nonferrous metals, fuel and petroleum products, seed oils, corn, machinery

TRANSDNIESTRIA
Since 1990, this self-proclaimed predominantly Russian-speaking area east of the Dniester River has remained unrecognized by any UN member state.

In a referendum that was disputed as illegal and under occupation, a vast majority of Crimea's residents who voted reportedly chose to secede from Ukraine and join Russia. Shortly thereafter the Russian government approved the annexation of Crimea from Ukraine. In late March 2014, the resolution declaring this referendum and Russia's annexation as invalid and affirming Ukraine's territorial jurisdiction of Crimea. One hundred of the UN's 193 member states approved the resolution, and 11 member states voted against it.

Transverse Mercator Projection
SCALE 1:6,906,000
1 CENTIMETER = 69 KILOMETERS; 1 INCH = 109 MILES
KILOMETERS
STATUTE MILES
Elevations in meters

Land Use

Predominant Land Use and Land Cover Classes

- Forest
- Mixed-use, including crops
- Cropland
- Urban agglomeration

Temperature and Precipitation

Average Annual Precipitation

- Over 80 inches — Over 200 cm
- 60–80 inches — 150–200 cm
- 40–59 inches — 100–149 cm
- 20–39 inches — 50–99 cm
- 10–19 inches — 25–49 cm
- Under 10 inches — Under 25 cm

Average Monthly Temperatures (F) (January/July)

Minsk (20°/63°)
L'viv (24°/65°)
Kiev (21°/67°)
Chișinău (26°/72°)
Odesa (28°/72°)
Dnipropetrovs'k (26°/70°)
Donets'k (24°/68°)
Simferopol' (31°/70°)

BELARUS
UKRAINE
MOLDOVA

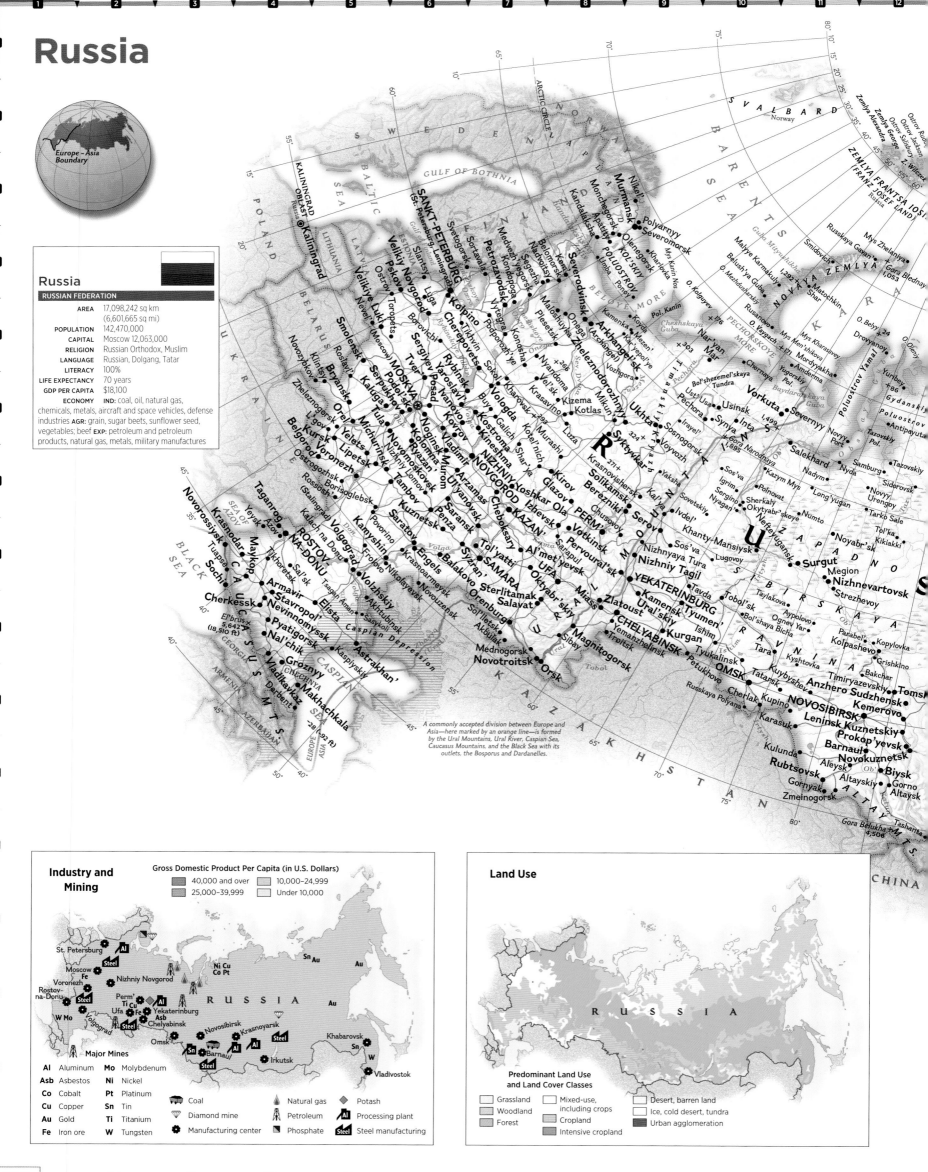

Russia

Russia

RUSSIAN FEDERATION

AREA	17,098,242 sq km (6,601,665 sq mi)
POPULATION	142,470,000
CAPITAL	Moscow 12,063,000
RELIGION	Russian Orthodox, Muslim
LANGUAGE	Russian, Dolgang, Tatar
LITERACY	100%
LIFE EXPECTANCY	70 years
GDP PER CAPITA	$18,100
ECONOMY	IND: coal, oil, natural gas, chemicals, metals, aircraft and space vehicles, defense industries AGR: grain, sugar beets, sunflower seed, vegetables; beef EXP: petroleum and petroleum products, natural gas, metals, military manufactures

Europe – Asia Boundary

A commonly accepted division between Europe and Asia—here marked by an orange line—is formed by the Ural Mountains, Ural River, Caspian Sea, Caucasus Mountains, and the Black Sea with its outlets, the Bosporus and Dardanelles.

Industry and Mining

Gross Domestic Product Per Capita (in U.S. Dollars)
- 40,000 and over
- 25,000–39,999
- 10,000–24,999
- Under 10,000

Major Mines

Al	Aluminum	Mo	Molybdenum
Asb	Asbestos	Ni	Nickel
Co	Cobalt	Pt	Platinum
Cu	Copper	Sn	Tin
Au	Gold	Ti	Titanium
Fe	Iron ore	W	Tungsten

- Coal
- Diamond mine
- Manufacturing center
- Natural gas
- Petroleum
- Phosphate
- Potash
- Al Processing plant
- Steel Steel manufacturing

Land Use

Predominant Land Use and Land Cover Classes
- Grassland
- Woodland
- Forest
- Intensive cropland
- Mixed-use, including crops
- Cropland
- Desert, barren land
- Ice, cold desert, tundra
- Urban agglomeration

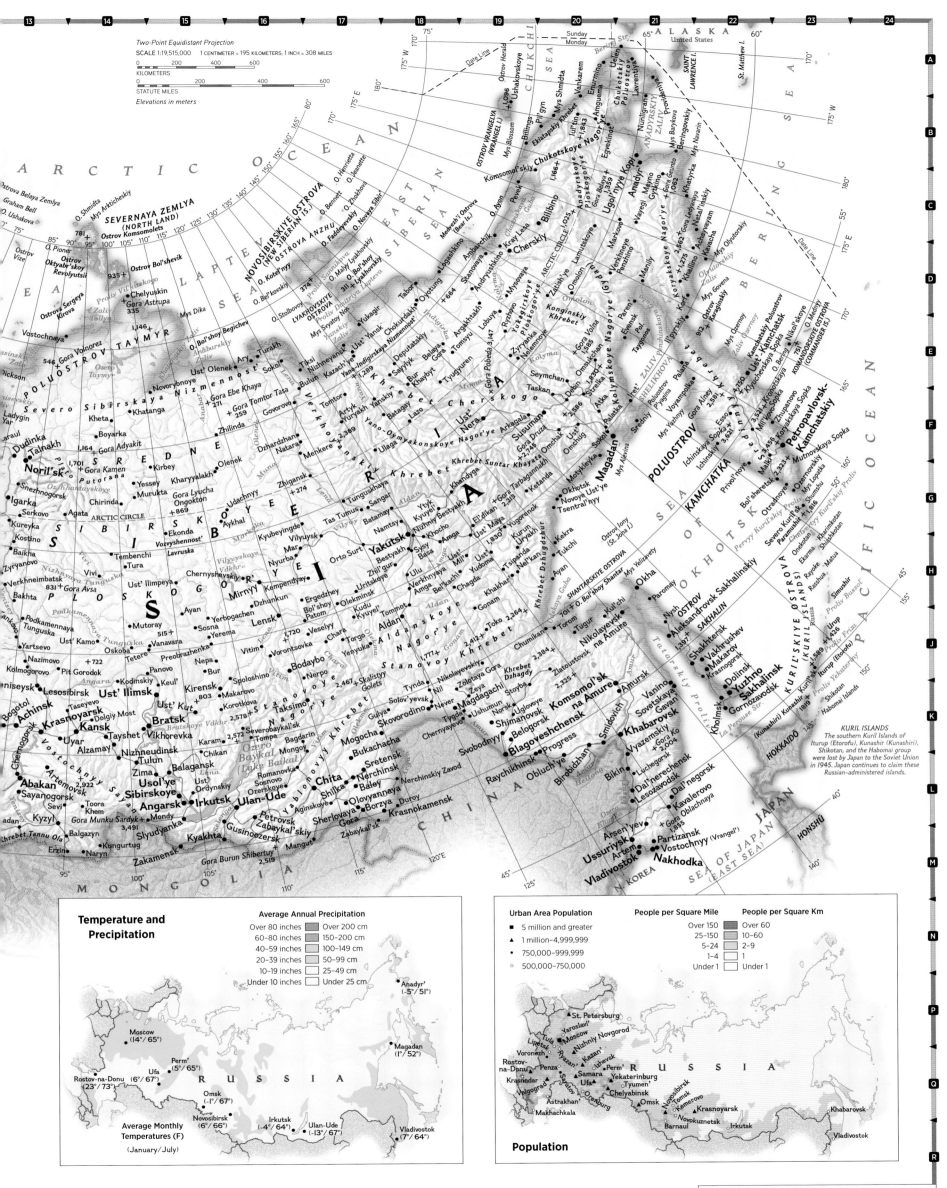

Europe's Smallest Countries and Territories

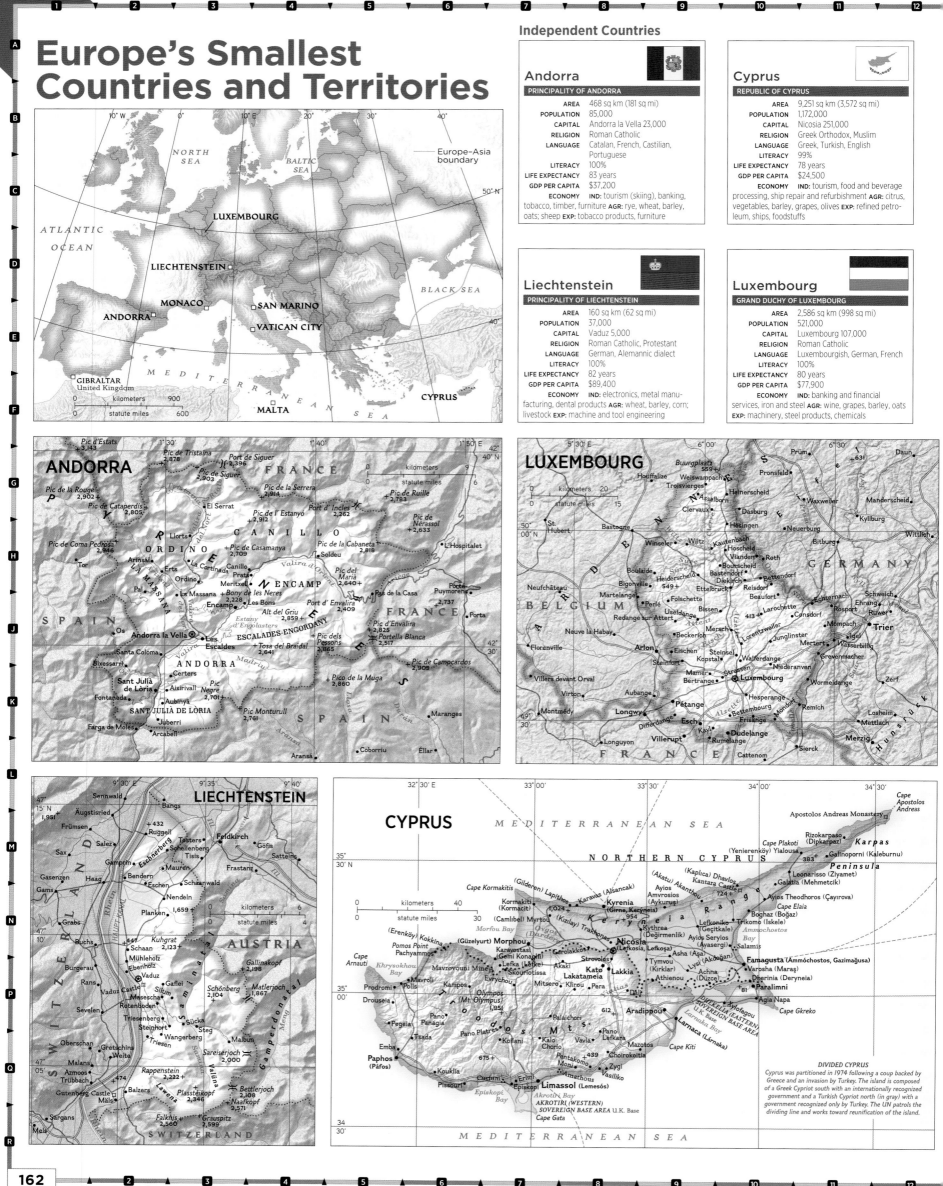

Independent Countries

Andorra
PRINCIPALITY OF ANDORRA

AREA	468 sq km (181 sq mi)
POPULATION	85,000
CAPITAL	Andorra la Vella 23,000
RELIGION	Roman Catholic
LANGUAGE	Catalan, French, Castilian, Portuguese
LITERACY	100%
LIFE EXPECTANCY	83 years
GDP PER CAPITA	$37,200
ECONOMY	IND: tourism (skiing), banking, tobacco, timber, furniture AGR: rye, wheat, barley, oats; sheep EXP: tobacco products, furniture

Cyprus
REPUBLIC OF CYPRUS

AREA	9,251 sq km (3,572 sq mi)
POPULATION	1,172,000
CAPITAL	Nicosia 251,000
RELIGION	Greek Orthodox, Muslim
LANGUAGE	Greek, Turkish, English
LITERACY	99%
LIFE EXPECTANCY	78 years
GDP PER CAPITA	$24,500
ECONOMY	IND: tourism, food and beverage processing, ship repair and refurbishment AGR: citrus, vegetables, barley, grapes, olives EXP: refined petroleum, ships, foodstuffs

Liechtenstein
PRINCIPALITY OF LIECHTENSTEIN

AREA	160 sq km (62 sq mi)
POPULATION	37,000
CAPITAL	Vaduz 5,000
RELIGION	Roman Catholic, Protestant
LANGUAGE	German, Alemannic dialect
LITERACY	100%
LIFE EXPECTANCY	82 years
GDP PER CAPITA	$89,400
ECONOMY	IND: electronics, metal manufacturing, dental products AGR: wheat, barley, corn; livestock EXP: machine and tool engineering

Luxembourg
GRAND DUCHY OF LUXEMBOURG

AREA	2,586 sq km (998 sq mi)
POPULATION	521,000
CAPITAL	Luxembourg 107,000
RELIGION	Roman Catholic
LANGUAGE	Luxembourgish, German, French
LITERACY	100%
LIFE EXPECTANCY	80 years
GDP PER CAPITA	$77,900
ECONOMY	IND: banking and financial services, iron and steel AGR: wine, grapes, barley, oats EXP: machinery, steel products, chemicals

DIVIDED CYPRUS
Cyprus was partitioned in 1974 following a coup backed by Greece and an invasion by Turkey. The island is composed of a Greek Cypriot south with an internationally recognized government and a Turkish Cypriot north (in gray) with a government recognized only by Turkey. The UN patrols the dividing line and works toward reunification of the island.

All map elevations in meters

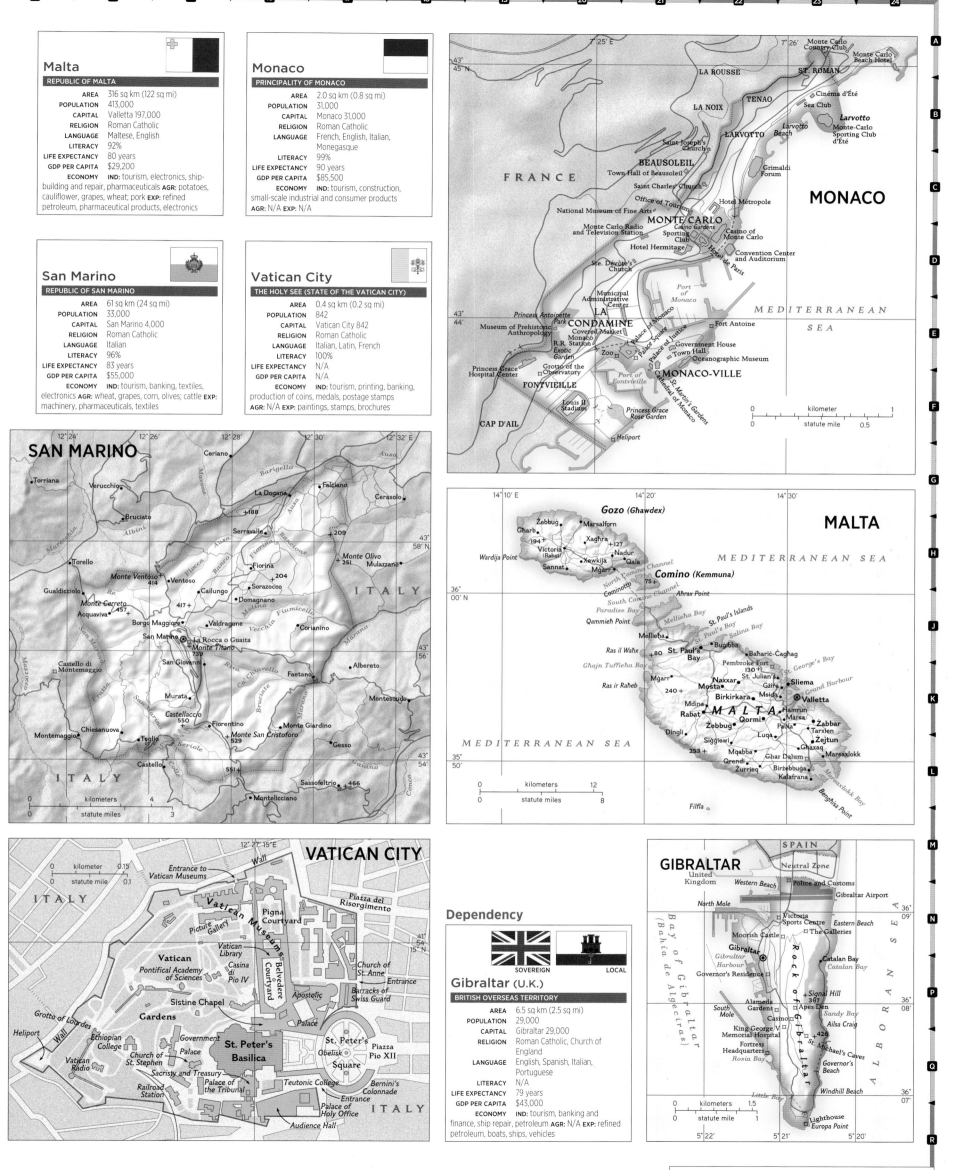

Malta
REPUBLIC OF MALTA

AREA	316 sq km (122 sq mi)
POPULATION	413,000
CAPITAL	Valletta 197,000
RELIGION	Roman Catholic
LANGUAGE	Maltese, English
LITERACY	92%
LIFE EXPECTANCY	80 years
GDP PER CAPITA	$29,200
ECONOMY	IND: tourism, electronics, ship-building and repair, pharmaceuticals AGR: potatoes, cauliflower, grapes, wheat; pork EXP: refined petroleum, pharmaceutical products, electronics

Monaco
PRINCIPALITY OF MONACO

AREA	2.0 sq km (0.8 sq mi)
POPULATION	31,000
CAPITAL	Monaco 31,000
RELIGION	Roman Catholic
LANGUAGE	French, English, Italian, Monegasque
LITERACY	99%
LIFE EXPECTANCY	90 years
GDP PER CAPITA	$85,500
ECONOMY	IND: tourism, construction, small-scale industrial and consumer products AGR: N/A EXP: N/A

San Marino
REPUBLIC OF SAN MARINO

AREA	61 sq km (24 sq mi)
POPULATION	33,000
CAPITAL	San Marino 4,000
RELIGION	Roman Catholic
LANGUAGE	Italian
LITERACY	96%
LIFE EXPECTANCY	83 years
GDP PER CAPITA	$55,000
ECONOMY	IND: tourism, banking, textiles, electronics AGR: wheat, grapes, corn, olives; cattle EXP: machinery, pharmaceuticals, textiles

Vatican City
THE HOLY SEE (STATE OF THE VATICAN CITY)

AREA	0.4 sq km (0.2 sq mi)
POPULATION	842
CAPITAL	Vatican City 842
RELIGION	Roman Catholic
LANGUAGE	Italian, Latin, French
LITERACY	100%
LIFE EXPECTANCY	N/A
GDP PER CAPITA	N/A
ECONOMY	IND: tourism, printing, banking, production of coins, medals, postage stamps AGR: N/A EXP: paintings, stamps, brochures

Dependency

Gibraltar (U.K.)
BRITISH OVERSEAS TERRITORY

SOVEREIGN · LOCAL

AREA	6.5 sq km (2.5 sq mi)
POPULATION	29,000
CAPITAL	Gibraltar 29,000
RELIGION	Roman Catholic, Church of England
LANGUAGE	English, Spanish, Italian, Portuguese
LITERACY	N/A
LIFE EXPECTANCY	79 years
GDP PER CAPITA	$43,000
ECONOMY	IND: tourism, banking and finance, ship repair, petroleum AGR: N/A EXP: refined petroleum, boats, ships, vehicles

Immortalized in art and verse, the beautiful Li River in southern China meanders 105 miles (169 km) through a landscape of towering limestone peaks clad in bamboo forests and ribboned by rushing waterfalls. In riverfront villages, traditional ways of life, like night fishing, still hold sway.

Asia

The continent of Asia, occupying four-fifths of the giant Eurasian landmass, stretches across ten time zones, from the Pacific Ocean in the east to the Ural Mountains and Black Sea in the west. It is the largest of continents, with dazzling geographic diversity and 30 percent of the Earth's land surface. Asia includes numerous island nations, such as Japan, the Philippines, Indonesia, and Sri Lanka, as well as many of the world's major islands: Borneo, Sumatra, Honshu, Celebes, Java, and part of New Guinea.

Siberia, the huge Asian section of Russia, reaches deep inside the Arctic Circle and fills the continent's northern quarter. To its south lie the large countries of Kazakhstan, Mongolia, and China. In all, Asia contains 46 nations, accounting for 60 percent of the Earth's population—more than 4.4 billion people—yet deserts, mountains, jungles, and other inhospitable zones render much of Asia empty or underpopulated.

Asia

For millennia, people have lived near the seas and along great rivers. Early civilizations arose in the Middle East along the Tigris and Euphrates Rivers, in South Asia on the Indus, and in China along the Yellow River. Today, Asia's large populations continue to thrive near inland waterways and coastal regions.

India and China, historically isolated from each other by the high peaks of the Himalaya and by Myanmar's jungles, developed rich, vibrant cultures boasting art, literature, and philosophy of the highest order. China's 1.36 billion people and India's 1.3 billion make up nearly two-thirds of Asia's population. These countries stand as rivals, each trying to modernize and assert itself culturally and economically, while struggling with formidable problems of poverty, pollution, urbanization, and illiteracy.

The breakup of the Soviet Union in 1991 allowed for the creation of eight new Asian countries, five in Central Asia—Kazakhstan, Kyrgyzstan, Uzbekistan, Turkmenistan, and Tajikistan—and three in the Caucasus region—Georgia, Armenia, and Azerbaijan.

Asia's few democracies, including Israel, India, and Japan, contrast with much more numerous and widespread authoritarian governments or military regimes. Monarchies in Bhutan, Jordan, Saudi Arabia, and Brunei (a sultanate) pass rulership through family lines.

Events at the start of the 21st century have put new focus on the Middle East, the role of Islam, and the effects of religious extremism. More than half of Asia's countries are Muslim, yet they possess very different languages, climates, economies, and ethnic groups. But all share emotional links with other Muslims and care deeply about the future of Islam.

PHYSICAL GEOGRAPHY The planet's youngest continent, Asia regularly experiences dramatic geologic activity. Volcanoes form a chain known as the Ring of Fire along the entire Pacific edge, from Siberia's Kamchatka Peninsula to the islands of the Philippines and Indonesia. The Indian subcontinent pushes into the heart of Asia, raising and contorting the towering Karakoram and Himalaya ranges. Earthquakes rattle China, Japan, Indonesia, and West Asia.

Geographic extremes allow Asia to claim many world records. Mount Everest, monarch of the Himalaya, is the planet's highest point at 29,035 feet (8,850 m). The super-salty Dead Sea lies 1,388 feet (423 m) below sea level—Earth's lowest point. A site in Meghalaya, India, receives an astonishing 39 feet (12 m) of rain each year, making it the wettest spot on Earth, and Siberia's ancient Lake Baikal, arcing 395 miles (636 km), plunges down a mile (5,387 ft; 1,642 m), making it the world's deepest lake. It harbors many unique plant and animal species, including tens of thousands of freshwater seals. The Caspian Sea, salty and isolated on the border of Europe and Asia, is Earth's largest lake, measuring more than four times the area of North America's largest lake, Lake Superior.

A 39,000-mile (62,800 km) coastline, longest of any continent, allows all but 12 Asian nations direct access to the sea. These landlocked countries, mostly in Central Asia (excepting Laos), form part of a great band of deserts, mountains, and arid plateaus across the middle latitudes. The vast Tibetan Plateau, home to the yak, snow leopard, wild ass, and migrating antelope, also spawns Asia's vital rivers: the Huang (Yellow), Yangtze, Indus, Ganges, Salween, and Mekong. At the heart of the continent rises a convergence of the world's mighty mountains: the

Himalaya, Karakoram, Hindu Kush, Pamirs, and Kunlun.

Flowing sand dunes of the Arabian Peninsula contrast with steppes that extend for thousands of grassy miles from Europe to Mongolia. To the north, girdling Asia's northern latitudes, grow boreal forests made up of conifers; the taiga, as it's known, comprises the world's largest unbroken woodlands. Farther north, beyond the taiga, stretch frozen expanses of tundra.

Far to the south, monsoon winds bring annual rains to thickly populated regions of South and Southeast Asia. These wet, green domains support some of the world's last rain forests and amazing numbers of plants. Human impact through agriculture, animal grazing, and forestry has altered much of Asia's landscape over time and continues to threaten the natural realm.

HISTORY Asia's great historical breadth encompasses thousands of years, vast distances, and a kaleidoscope of peoples. From China to Lebanon, from Siberia to Sri Lanka, Asia has more ethnic and national groups than any other continent. Their histories have evolved through peaceful growth and migration in part but more often through military conquest.

The Fertile Crescent region of the Middle East saw the emergence of agriculture and early settlements some 10,000 years ago. Later, successful irrigation helped bring forth the first civilization in Sumer, today's southern Iraq; Sumerians invented the first wheeled vehicles, the potter's wheel, the first system of writing—cuneiform—and the first codes of law.

During the second millennium B.C., a pastoral people called the Aryans, or Indo-Iranians, pushed into present-day Afghanistan and eastern Iran, according to one theory. Then they occupied much of the Indian subcontinent and Western and Central Asia.

Central Asia has always been a melting pot of flourishing cultures. More than 2,000 years ago a braid of ancient caravan tracks—the Silk Road—began carrying precious goods between East Asia and the rest of the world: sleek horses, exotic foods, medicines, jewels, birds, and perfume. More practical exports were gunpowder, the magnetic compass, the printing press, mathematical concepts, ceramics, and silk. Trade flourished especially during China's Han dynasty (206 B.C.–A.D. 220), Tang dynasty (A.D. 618–907), and the Yuan, or Mongol, dynasty (13th and 14th centuries). At their height of power, Mongols came closer than any other peoples to conquering all of Asia; they also threatened Europe in the west and twice tried to invade Japan.

Another great expansion was the Russian conquest and settlement of Siberia and Central Asia. The Trans-Siberian Railway, built between 1891 and 1905, opened up Siberia for settlement. During the 19th century, Russian armies and colonizers spread through Central Asia as well, claiming the khanates for an expanding Russian Empire. But even before that expansion, Great Britain, France, and other European countries had begun to lay claim to parts of Asia.

Today, colonial empires have ended and a seemingly stable community of nations with defined borders exists in Asia. Yet, rivalries, threats, and war dominate many regions. Indochina is only now healing after decades of

violence. The Korean Peninsula remains divided. Nuclear-armed India and Pakistan have fought three wars since independence from Britain in 1947. Religious and ethnic hostilities inflame many areas, nowhere more so than in the Middle East. Troubled Afghanistan, victim of almost continuous warfare since 1979, saw a U.S.-led invasion in 2001 to oust the Taliban government and destroy terrorist groups. Civil war broke out in Syria in 2011 and spilled into Iraq in 2014, when Islamic militants invaded northern Iraq. Many claim peace will come to these areas only after economic stability, steps toward more inclusive political systems, and recognition of human rights are achieved.

CULTURE Numerous cultural forces, each linked to broad geographic areas, have formed and influenced Asia's rich civilizations and hundreds of ethnic groups. The two oldest and most dominant are the cultural legacies of the Indian subcontinent and China.

India's culture still reverberates throughout countries as varied as Sri Lanka, Pakistan, Afghanistan, Nepal, Bangladesh, Myanmar (Burma), and across the seas to Thailand, Cambodia, Singapore, and Indonesia. The world religions of Hinduism and Buddhism originated in India and were spread by traders, scholars, and priests seeking distant footholds. The island of Bali in predominantly Muslim Indonesia remains Hindu today. Many regions of Asia first encountered writing in the form of Sanskrit, the holy script of Hinduism.

China's civilization, more than 4,000 years old, has profoundly influenced the development of all of East Asia, much of Southeast Asia, and parts of Central Asia. The Chinese form of government, warfare, architecture, the arts and sciences, and even chopsticks reached to the heart of other lands and peoples. Most important of all were the Chinese written language, a complex script with thousands of characters; and Confucianism, an ethical world view that affected philosophy, politics, and relationships within society. Japan, Korea, and Vietnam especially absorbed these cultural gifts.

Today, most Chinese call themselves "Han," a term that embraces more than 90 percent of the population—a billion-plus people—and thus makes them the world's largest ethnic group. In addition, China's government recognizes 55 other ethnic minorities within its borders.

Islam, a third great cultural influence in Asia, proved formidable in its energy and creative outpouring. From the seventh century on, Arabs, spurred on by their Muslim faith, moved rapidly into Southwest Asia. Their religion and culture, particularly Arabic writing, spread through Iran and Afghanistan to the Indian subcontinent. In time, shipping, commerce, and missionaries carried Islam to the Malay Peninsula and Indonesian archipelago. Indonesia, now the largest Muslim country with more than 200 million believers, and Pakistan and Bangladesh, each with more than 100 million Muslims, attest to Islam's appeal.

Europeans, too, have affected Asia's cultures, from the conquests of Alexander the Great to today's multinational corporations. Colonial powers—especially Britain in India, France in Indochina, the Netherlands in the Indonesian archipelago, and numerous European countries in China—left a lasting mark, even after nationalist movements forced most of them out in the late 1940s and early 1950s.

ECONOMY Blessed with natural resources and teeming with energetic people, Asia still suffers from great disparities between rich and poor. The livelihood of most Asians involves reliance on agriculture and age-old cycles of sowing and harvesting. Many Vietnamese women still turn water-

In 1791, King Bodawpaya of Myanmar commissioned an enormous Buddhist pagoda in Mingun (top). Although construction stopped at the king's death in 1819, the building still measures an astounding 256 feet square (78 m sq) at its base and is 150 feet (45.7 m) tall. Subsequent earthquakes have cracked the structure. Less sedate but just as astonishing is the glittering, captivating sprawl of present-day Shanghai. One the world's most populous cities and China's largest, Shanghai is home to more than 23 million people and growing fast, though a century and a half ago it was no more than a fishing town on the East China Sea. Always a place of paradoxes, Shanghai is a mix of East and West, rich and poor, the future and the past.

wheels by foot, and Iranian farmers plow fields with water buffalo.

Wet-rice cultivation from Japan southward has shaped life for hundreds of millions of Asians. To the west, across north China, Central Asia, and beyond to the Middle East, wheat is the dominant crop. Plantation and cash crops, such as rubber, tea, palm oil, coconuts, sugarcane, and tobacco, continue to sustain regional economies.

In recent decades, country dwellers have flocked in the millions to Asian cities, seeking jobs and a better life. From Jakarta to Baghdad, the growth of megacities represents a dramatic change over the past 50 years. In China, as many as 240 million people form a floating population, moving wherever work can be found.

Economic power in Asia is changing, with China replacing Japan as Asia's largest economy in 2010. Lands in the Persian Gulf region have benefited from the world appetite for petroleum, and many other countries now use light industry as a motor for growth. Tourism also plays its part and has helped of the economies of Thailand, Nepal, and parts of Indonesia and China, including Hong Kong. India's liberalized economy has encouraged a large, growing middle class. Yet, hunger for minerals, water, agricultural land, energy, housing, and animal products poses great challenges for Asia, as nations try to raise the standard of living of their peoples. That ongoing struggle to improve conditions is now exacerbated by climate change.

Asia Minor and Transcaucasia

Conic Projection
SCALE 1:4,604,000   1 CENTIMETER = 46 KILOMETERS; 1 INCH = 73 MILES

KILOMETERS

STATUTE MILES

Elevations in meters

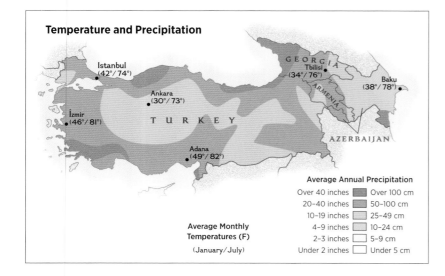

Temperature and Precipitation

Istanbul (42°/74°)
Ankara (30°/73°)
İzmir (46°/81°)
Adana (49°/82°)
Tbilisi (34°/76°)
Baku (38°/78°)

Average Monthly Temperatures (F) (January/July)

Average Annual Precipitation

Over 40 inches	Over 100 cm
20–40 inches	50–100 cm
10–19 inches	25–49 cm
4–9 inches	10–24 cm
2–3 inches	5–9 cm
Under 2 inches	Under 5 cm

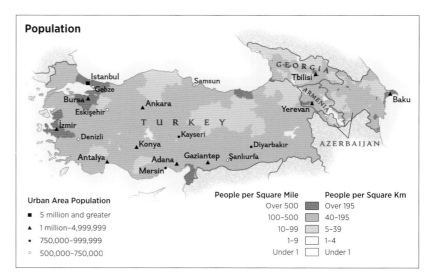

Population

Urban Area Population

- ■ 5 million and greater
- ▲ 1 million–4,999,999
- ● 750,000–999,999
- ● 500,000–750,000

People per Square Mile
- Over 500
- 100–500
- 10–99
- 1–9
- Under 1

People per Square Km
- Over 195
- 40–195
- 5–39
- 1–4
- Under 1

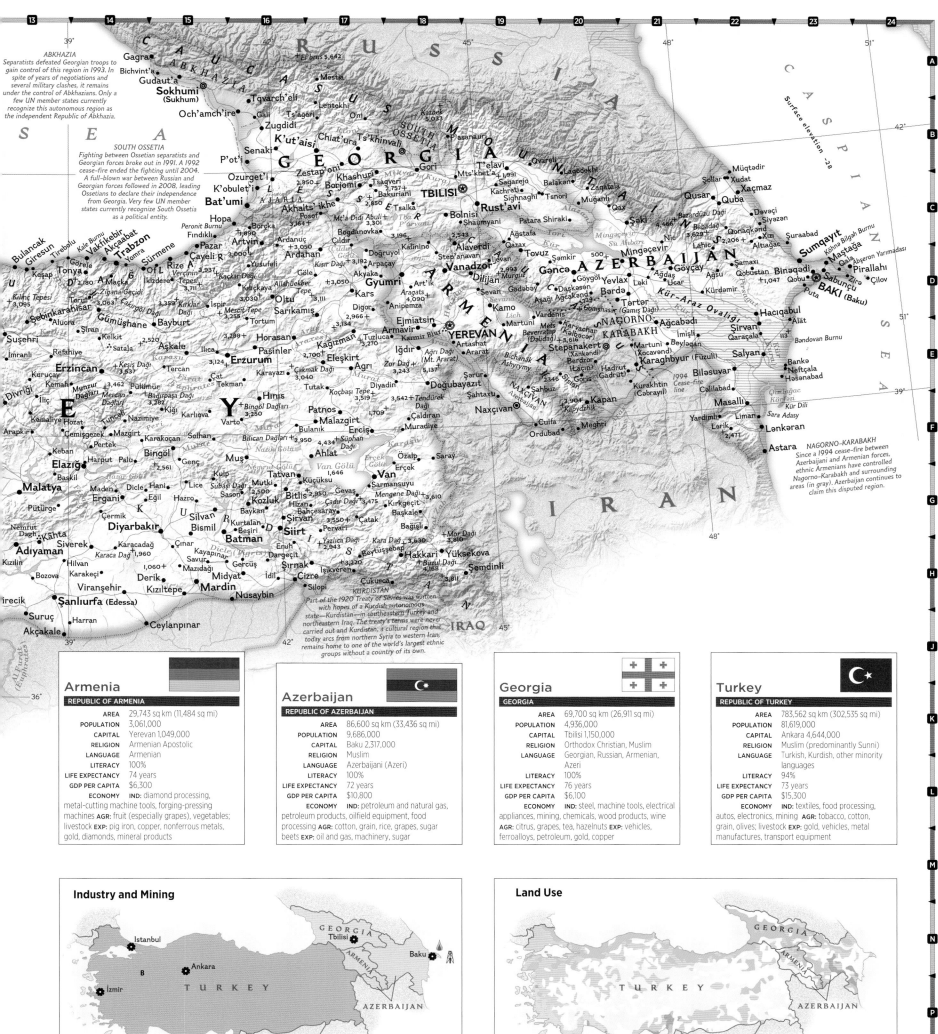

ABKHAZIA
Separatists defeated Georgian troops to gain control of this region in 1993. In spite of years of negotiations and several military clashes, it remains under the control of Abkhazians. Only a few UN member states currently recognize this autonomous region as the independent Republic of Abkhazia.

SOUTH OSSETIA
Fighting between Ossetian separatists and Georgian forces broke out in 1991. A 1992 cease-fire ended the fighting until 2004. A full-blown war between Russian and Georgian forces followed in 2008, leading Ossetians to declare their independence from Georgia. Very few UN member states currently recognize South Ossetia as a political entity.

NAGORNO-KARABAKH
Since a 1994 cease-fire between Azerbaijani and Armenian forces, ethnic Armenians have controlled Nagorno-Karabakh and surrounding areas (in gray). Azerbaijan continues to claim this disputed region.

KURDISTAN
Part of the 1920 Treaty of Sèvres was written with hopes of a Kurdish autonomous state—Kurdistan—in southeastern Turkey and northeastern Iraq. The treaty's terms were never carried out and Kurdistan, a cultural region that today arcs from northern Syria to western Iran, remains home to one of the world's largest ethnic groups without a country of its own.

Armenia
REPUBLIC OF ARMENIA
AREA	29,743 sq km (11,484 sq mi)
POPULATION	3,061,000
CAPITAL	Yerevan 1,049,000
RELIGION	Armenian Apostolic
LANGUAGE	Armenian
LITERACY	100%
LIFE EXPECTANCY	74 years
GDP PER CAPITA	$6,300
ECONOMY	IND: diamond processing, metal-cutting machine tools, forging-pressing machines AGR: fruit (especially grapes), vegetables; livestock EXP: pig iron, copper, nonferrous metals, gold, diamonds, mineral products

Azerbaijan
REPUBLIC OF AZERBAIJAN
AREA	86,600 sq km (33,436 sq mi)
POPULATION	9,686,000
CAPITAL	Baku 2,317,000
RELIGION	Muslim
LANGUAGE	Azerbaijani (Azeri)
LITERACY	100%
LIFE EXPECTANCY	72 years
GDP PER CAPITA	$10,800
ECONOMY	IND: petroleum and natural gas, petroleum products, oilfield equipment, food processing AGR: cotton, grain, rice, grapes, sugar beets EXP: oil and gas, machinery, sugar

Georgia
GEORGIA
AREA	69,700 sq km (26,911 sq mi)
POPULATION	4,936,000
CAPITAL	Tbilisi 1,150,000
RELIGION	Orthodox Christian, Muslim
LANGUAGE	Georgian, Russian, Armenian, Azeri
LITERACY	100%
LIFE EXPECTANCY	76 years
GDP PER CAPITA	$6,100
ECONOMY	IND: steel, machine tools, electrical appliances, mining, chemicals, wood products, wine AGR: citrus, grapes, tea, hazelnuts EXP: vehicles, ferroalloys, petroleum, gold, copper

Turkey
REPUBLIC OF TURKEY
AREA	783,562 sq km (302,535 sq mi)
POPULATION	81,619,000
CAPITAL	Ankara 4,644,000
RELIGION	Muslim (predominantly Sunni)
LANGUAGE	Turkish, Kurdish, other minority languages
LITERACY	94%
LIFE EXPECTANCY	73 years
GDP PER CAPITA	$15,300
ECONOMY	IND: textiles, food processing, autos, electronics, mining AGR: tobacco, cotton, grain, olives; livestock EXP: gold, vehicles, metal manufactures, transport equipment

Industry and Mining

Major Mines
B Boron

✿ Manufacturing center
△ Natural gas
⌖ Petroleum

Gross Domestic Product per Capita (in U.S. dollars)
- 30,000 and over
- 15,000–29,999
- 5,000–14,999
- Under 5,000

Land Use

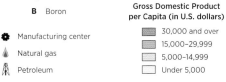

Predominant Land Use and Land Cover Classes
- Grassland
- Woodland
- Forest
- Mixed-use, including crops
- Cropland
- Intensive cropland
- Wetland
- Desert, barren land

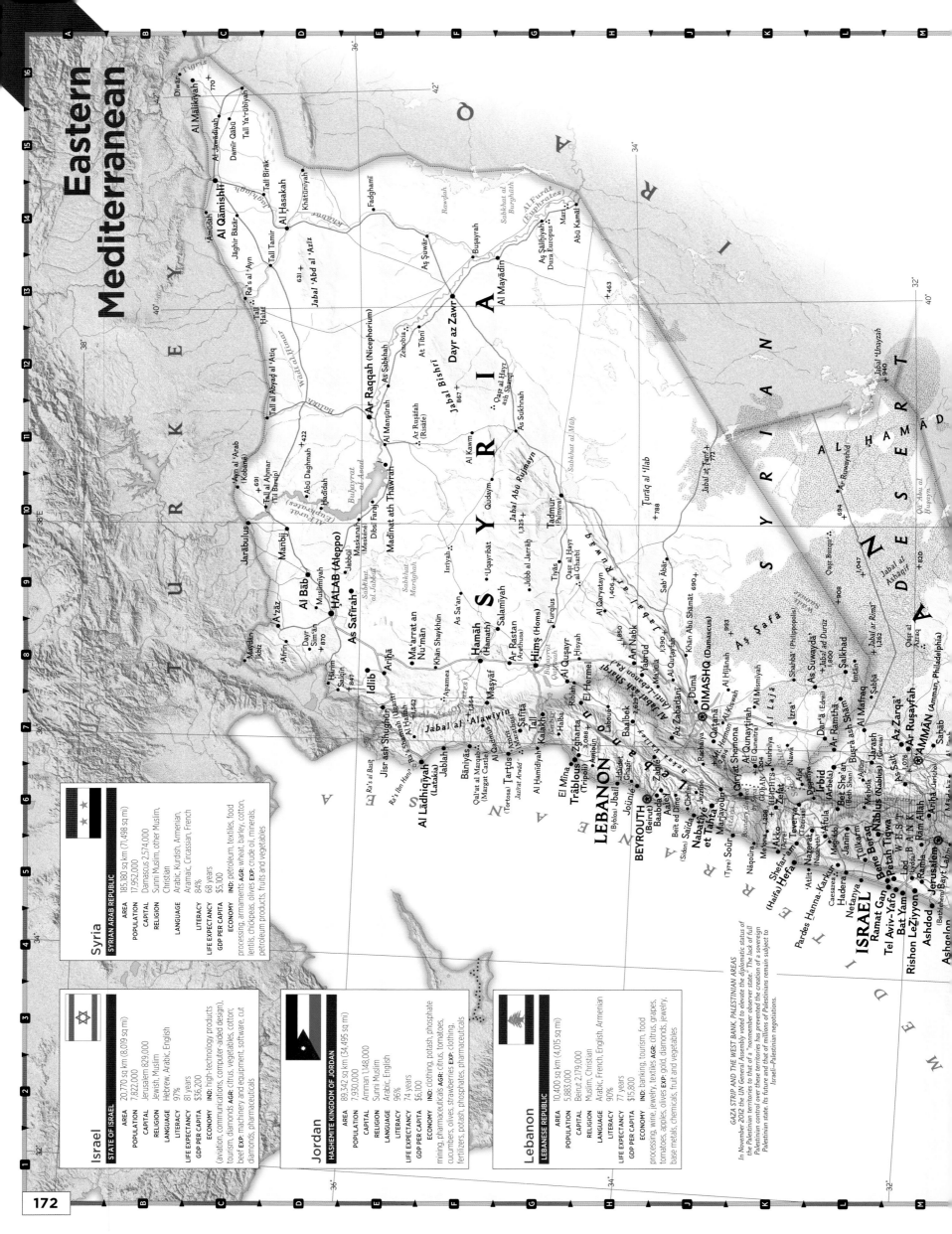

Syria
SYRIAN ARAB REPUBLIC
AREA 185,180 sq km (71,498 sq mi)
POPULATION 17,952,000
CAPITAL Damascus 2,574,000
RELIGION Sunni Muslim, other Muslim, Christian
LANGUAGE Arabic, Kurdish, Armenian, Aramaic, Circassian, French
LITERACY 84%
LIFE EXPECTANCY 68 years
GDP PER CAPITA $5,100
ECONOMY IND: petroleum, textiles, food processing, armaments AGR: wheat, barley, cotton, lentils, chickpeas, olives EXP: crude oil, minerals, petroleum products, fruits and vegetables

Israel
STATE OF ISRAEL
AREA 20,770 sq km (8,019 sq mi)
POPULATION 7,822,000
CAPITAL Jerusalem 829,000
RELIGION Jewish, Muslim
LANGUAGE Hebrew, Arabic, English
LITERACY 97%
LIFE EXPECTANCY 81 years
GDP PER CAPITA $36,200
ECONOMY IND: high-technology products (aviation, communications, computer-aided design), tourism, diamonds AGR: citrus, vegetables, cotton; beef EXP: machinery and equipment, software, cut diamonds, pharmaceuticals

Jordan
HASHEMITE KINGDOM OF JORDAN
AREA 89,342 sq km (34,495 sq mi)
POPULATION 5,883,000
CAPITAL Amman 1,148,000
RELIGION Sunni Muslim
LANGUAGE Arabic, English
LITERACY 96%
LIFE EXPECTANCY 74 years
GDP PER CAPITA $6,100
ECONOMY IND: clothing, potash, phosphate mining, pharmaceuticals AGR: citrus, tomatoes, cucumbers, olives, strawberries EXP: clothing, fertilizers, potash, phosphates, pharmaceuticals

Lebanon
LEBANESE REPUBLIC
AREA 10,400 sq km (4,015 sq mi)
POPULATION 2,179,000
CAPITAL Beirut 2,179,000
RELIGION Muslim, Christian
LANGUAGE Arabic, French, English, Armenian
LITERACY 90%
LIFE EXPECTANCY 77 years
GDP PER CAPITA $15,800
ECONOMY IND: banking, tourism, food processing, wine, jewelry, textiles AGR: citrus, grapes, tomatoes, apples, olives EXP: gold, diamonds, jewelry, base metals, chemicals, fruit and vegetables

GAZA STRIP AND THE WEST BANK, PALESTINIAN AREAS
In November 2012 the UN General Assembly voted to elevate the diplomatic status of the Palestinian territories to that of a "nonmember observer state." The lack of full Palestinian control over these territories has prevented the creation of a sovereign Palestinian state. Its future and that of millions of Palestinians remain subject to Israeli-Palestinian negotiations.

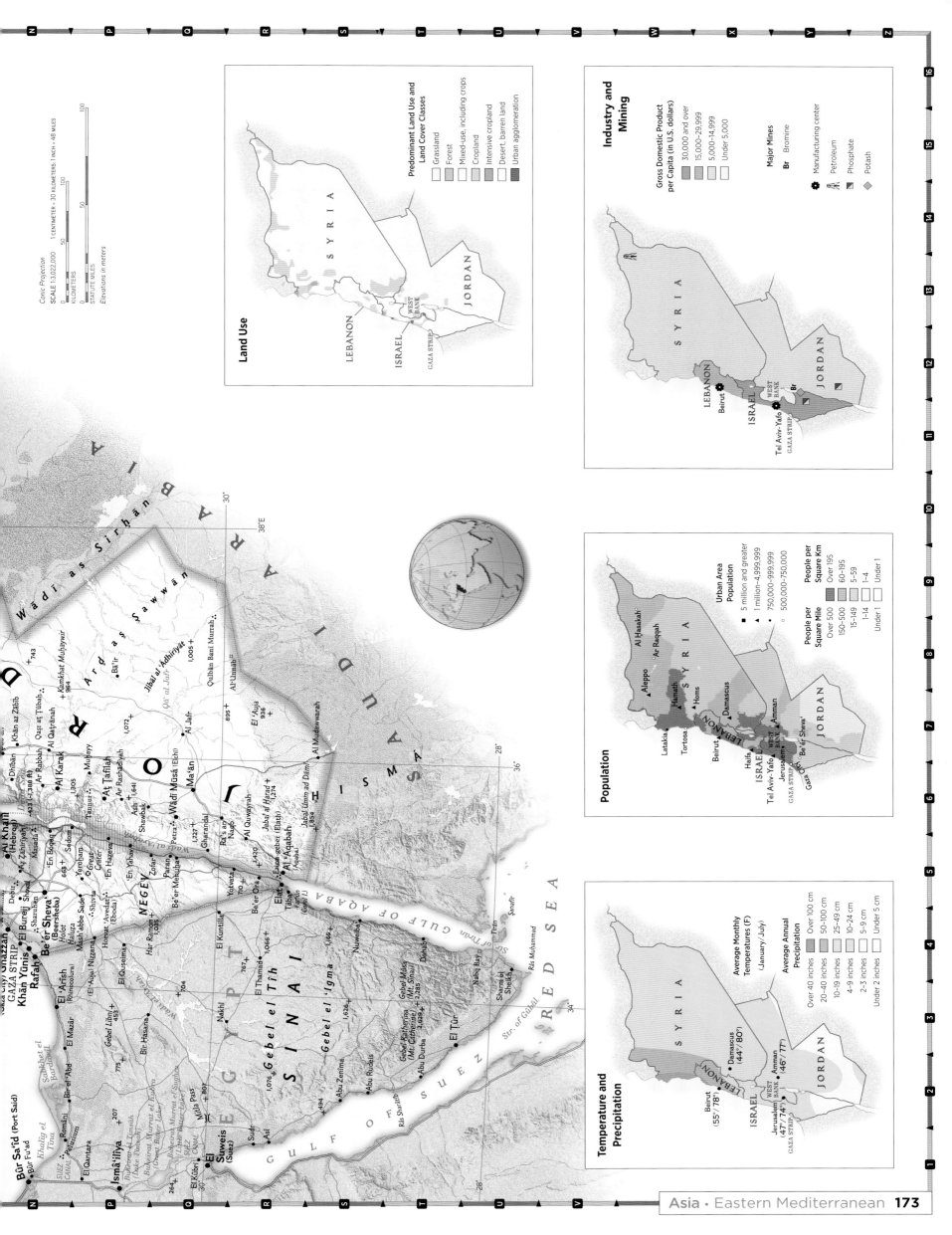

Conic Projection
SCALE 1:3,022,000   1 CENTIMETER = 30 KILOMETERS; 1 INCH = 48 MILES

STATUTE MILES
KILOMETERS

Elevations in meters

Land Use

Predominant Land Use and
Land Cover Classes

- Grassland
- Forest
- Mixed-use, including crops
- Cropland
- Intensive cropland
- Desert, barren land
- Urban agglomeration

LEBANON
SYRIA
ISRAEL
WEST BANK
GAZA STRIP
JORDAN

Industry and Mining

Gross Domestic Product
per Capita (in U.S. dollars)

- 30,000 and over
- 15,000-29,999
- 5,000-14,999
- Under 5,000

Major Mines   Br Bromine

⚙ Manufacturing center
Petroleum
Phosphate
Potash

SYRIA
LEBANON
Beirut
Tel Aviv-Yafo
ISRAEL
WEST BANK
GAZA STRIP
Br
JORDAN

Population

People per
Square Mile
- Over 500
- 150-500
- 15-149
- 1-14
- Under 1

People per
Square Km
- Over 195
- 60-195
- 5-59
- 1-4
- Under 1

Urban Area
Population
■ 5 million and greater
◀ 1 million-4,999,999
● 750,000-999,999
○ 500,000-750,000

Al Ḩasakah
Ar Raqqah
Aleppo
Ḩamath
Homs
SYRIA
Latakia
Tortosa
Damascus
LEBANON
Beirut
Haifa
Tel Aviv-Yafo
ISRAEL
WEST BANK
Jerusalem
GAZA STRIP
Be'ér Sheva'
Amman
JORDAN

Temperature and Precipitation

Average Monthly
Temperatures (F)
(January/July)
- Over 100 inches
- 50-100 cm
- 10-24 inches

Average Annual
Precipitation
- Over 40 inches
- 20-40 inches
- 10-19 inches
- 4-9 inches
- 2-3 inches
- Under 2 inches

Over 40 inches
20-40 inches
10-19 inches
4-9 inches
2-3 inches
Under 2 inches

SYRIA
LEBANON
Beirut (55°/78°)
Damascus (44°/80°)
Amman (46°/77°)
ISRAEL
WEST BANK
Jerusalem (47°/74°)
GAZA STRIP
JORDAN

ARABIA
SAUDI ARABIA
Wādi as Sirḥān
Ard as Sawwān
Jibal al 'Adhiriyāt
Qa' al Jafr
Qubān Bani Murrah
Al 'Umab
HISMA
Jabal Umm ad Dāmi 1,854
Al Mudwwarah
El 'Auja 936

Dhibān
Khān az Zabib
Qaşr aţ Tūbah
Al Qaţranah
Ar Rabbah
Al Karak
Mu'tah
Aţ Ţafilah
Ar Rashadiyah
Wādī Mūsá (Petra)
Ma'ān
Shawbak
Ras an Naqab
Jabal al Harad 1,274
Al Quwayrah
Al 'Aqabah (Aqaba)
Elat
Ṭaba

Al Khalil (Hebron)
Az Zahiriyah
Masada
Sedom
En Boqeq
Great Crater
En Hazeva
En Yahav
Zofar
Paran
Yotvata
Be'ér Ora
Eilat

Be'ér Sheva' (Beersheba)
Holot
Haluza
Mash'abbe Sade
Shivta
'Avedat (Eloda)
Horvat 'Avedat
Har Ramon 1,035
NEGEV
Ḥazeva
Be'ér Mehoqa
El Kuntilla

Gaza City
Gazzah
GAZA STRIP
Khān Yūnis
Rafaḥ
El 'Arish (Rhinocolura)
El Mazār
El Quseima
El 'Auja Nizzana
El Kuntilla

EGYPT
SINAI
Gebel el Tîh
Gebel el 'Igma
Gebel Mûsa (Mt. Sinai) 2,285
Gebel Katherîna (Mt. Catherine) 2,642
El Thamad
Nakhl
El Tûr
Abu Zenima
Abu Rudeis
Ras Sharâtîb

Bûr Sa'îd (Port Said)
Bûr Fu'ad
Khalig el Tina
SUEZ CANAL
Români
El Qantara
Isma'îlîya
El Kûbri
El Suweis (Suez)
Great Bitter Lake
Bir el 'Abd
Bir-el Mazâr
Bir Hasana
Gebel Libni 453
Mitla Pass
Gifgafa
Sudr
Asl

GULF OF SUEZ
RED SEA
GULF OF AQABA
Str. of Jûbâl
Nuweiba
Dahab
Naqb Bay
Sharm el Sheikh
Râs Muḥammad
Ṣanafir
Tiran
Str. of Tiran

Asia · Eastern Mediterranean   173

Southwest Asia

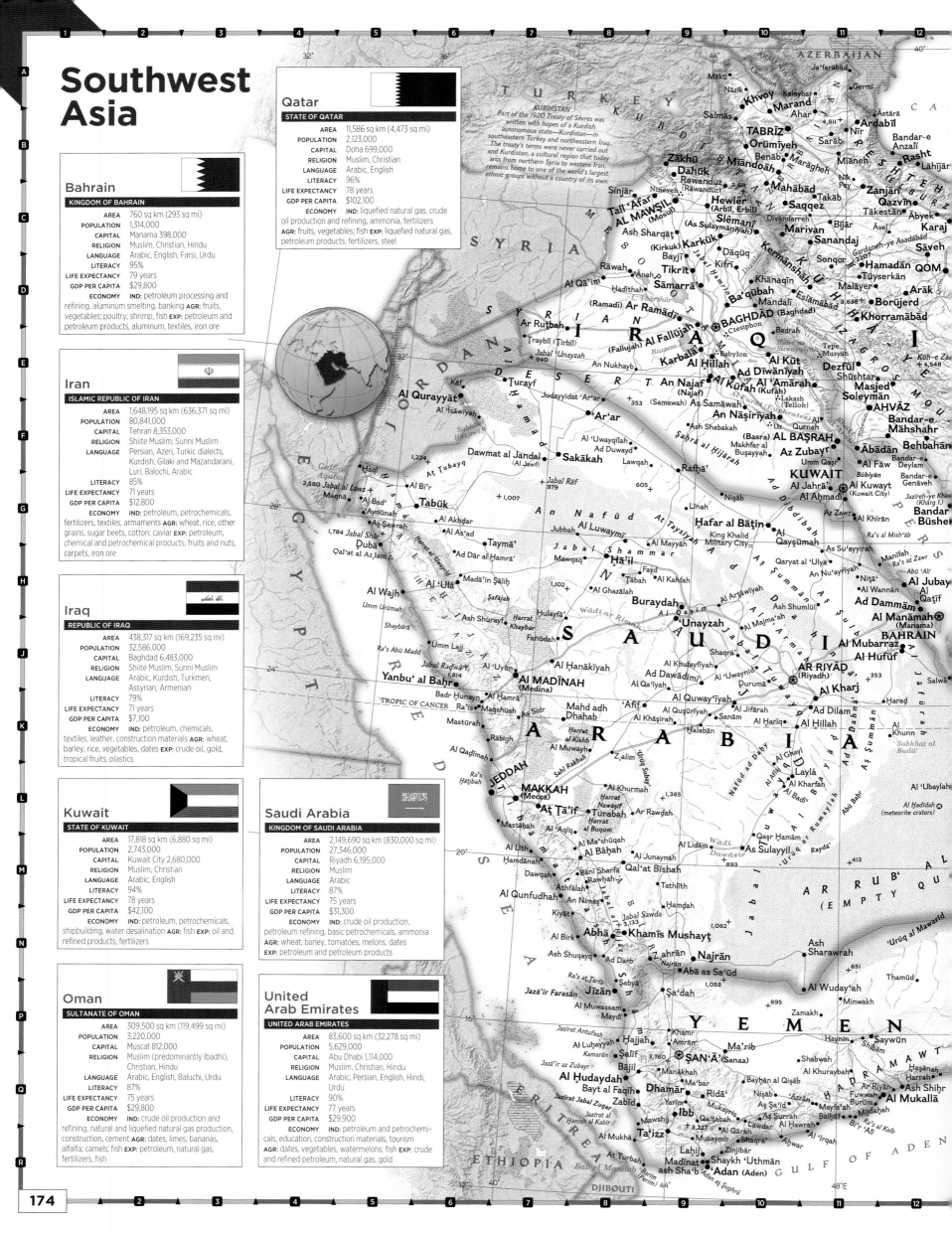

Qatar
STATE OF QATAR

AREA	11,586 sq km (4,473 sq mi)
POPULATION	2,123,000
CAPITAL	Doha 699,000
RELIGION	Muslim, Christian
LANGUAGE	Arabic, English
LITERACY	96%
LIFE EXPECTANCY	78 years
GDP PER CAPITA	$102,100
ECONOMY	IND: liquefied natural gas, crude oil production and refining, ammonia, fertilizers AGR: fruits, vegetables; fish EXP: liquefied natural gas, petroleum products, fertilizers, steel

Bahrain
KINGDOM OF BAHRAIN

AREA	760 sq km (293 sq mi)
POPULATION	1,314,000
CAPITAL	Manama 398,000
RELIGION	Muslim, Christian, Hindu
LANGUAGE	Arabic, English, Farsi, Urdu
LITERACY	95%
LIFE EXPECTANCY	79 years
GDP PER CAPITA	$29,800
ECONOMY	IND: petroleum processing and refining, aluminum smelting, banking AGR: fruits, vegetables; poultry; shrimp, fish EXP: petroleum and petroleum products, aluminum, textiles, iron ore

Iran
ISLAMIC REPUBLIC OF IRAN

AREA	1,648,195 sq km (636,371 sq mi)
POPULATION	80,841,000
CAPITAL	Tehran 8,353,000
RELIGION	Shiite Muslim, Sunni Muslim
LANGUAGE	Persian, Azeri, Turkic dialects, Kurdish, Gilaki and Mazandarani, Luri, Balochi, Arabic
LITERACY	85%
LIFE EXPECTANCY	71 years
GDP PER CAPITA	$12,800
ECONOMY	IND: petroleum, petrochemicals, fertilizers, textiles, armaments AGR: wheat, rice, other grains, sugar beets, cotton; caviar EXP: petroleum, chemical and petrochemical products, fruits and nuts, carpets, iron ore

Iraq
REPUBLIC OF IRAQ

AREA	438,317 sq km (169,235 sq mi)
POPULATION	32,586,000
CAPITAL	Baghdad 6,483,000
RELIGION	Shiite Muslim, Sunni Muslim
LANGUAGE	Arabic, Kurdish, Turkmen, Assyrian, Armenian
LITERACY	79%
LIFE EXPECTANCY	71 years
GDP PER CAPITA	$7,100
ECONOMY	IND: petroleum, chemicals, textiles, leather, construction materials AGR: wheat, barley, rice, vegetables, dates EXP: crude oil, gold, tropical fruits, plastics

Kuwait
STATE OF KUWAIT

AREA	17,818 sq km (6,880 sq mi)
POPULATION	2,743,000
CAPITAL	Kuwait City 2,680,000
RELIGION	Muslim, Christian
LANGUAGE	Arabic, English
LITERACY	94%
LIFE EXPECTANCY	78 years
GDP PER CAPITA	$42,100
ECONOMY	IND: petroleum, petrochemicals, shipbuilding, water desalination AGR: fish EXP: oil and refined products, fertilizers

Saudi Arabia
KINGDOM OF SAUDI ARABIA

AREA	2,149,690 sq km (830,000 sq mi)
POPULATION	27,346,000
CAPITAL	Riyadh 6,195,000
RELIGION	Muslim
LANGUAGE	Arabic
LITERACY	87%
LIFE EXPECTANCY	75 years
GDP PER CAPITA	$31,300
ECONOMY	IND: crude oil production, petroleum refining, basic petrochemicals, ammonia AGR: wheat, barley, tomatoes, melons, dates EXP: petroleum and petroleum products

Oman
SULTANATE OF OMAN

AREA	309,500 sq km (119,499 sq mi)
POPULATION	3,220,000
CAPITAL	Muscat 812,000
RELIGION	Muslim (predominantly Ibadhi), Christian, Hindu
LANGUAGE	Arabic, English, Baluchi, Urdu
LITERACY	87%
LIFE EXPECTANCY	75 years
GDP PER CAPITA	$29,800
ECONOMY	IND: crude oil production and refining, natural gas and liquefied natural gas production, construction, cement AGR: dates, limes, bananas, alfalfa; camels; fish EXP: petroleum, natural gas, fertilizers, fish

United Arab Emirates
UNITED ARAB EMIRATES

AREA	83,600 sq km (32,278 sq mi)
POPULATION	5,629,000
CAPITAL	Abu Dhabi 1,114,000
RELIGION	Muslim, Christian, Hindu
LANGUAGE	Arabic, Persian, English, Hindi, Urdu
LITERACY	90%
LIFE EXPECTANCY	77 years
GDP PER CAPITA	$29,900
ECONOMY	IND: petroleum and petrochemicals, education, construction materials, tourism AGR: dates, vegetables, watermelons; fish EXP: crude and refined petroleum, natural gas, gold

Part of the 1920 Treaty of Sèvres was written with hopes of a Kurdish autonomous state—Kurdistan—in southeastern Turkey and northeastern Iraq. The treaty's terms were never carried out and Kurdistan, a cultural region that today arcs from northern Syria to western Iran, remains home to one of the world's largest ethnic groups without a country of its own.

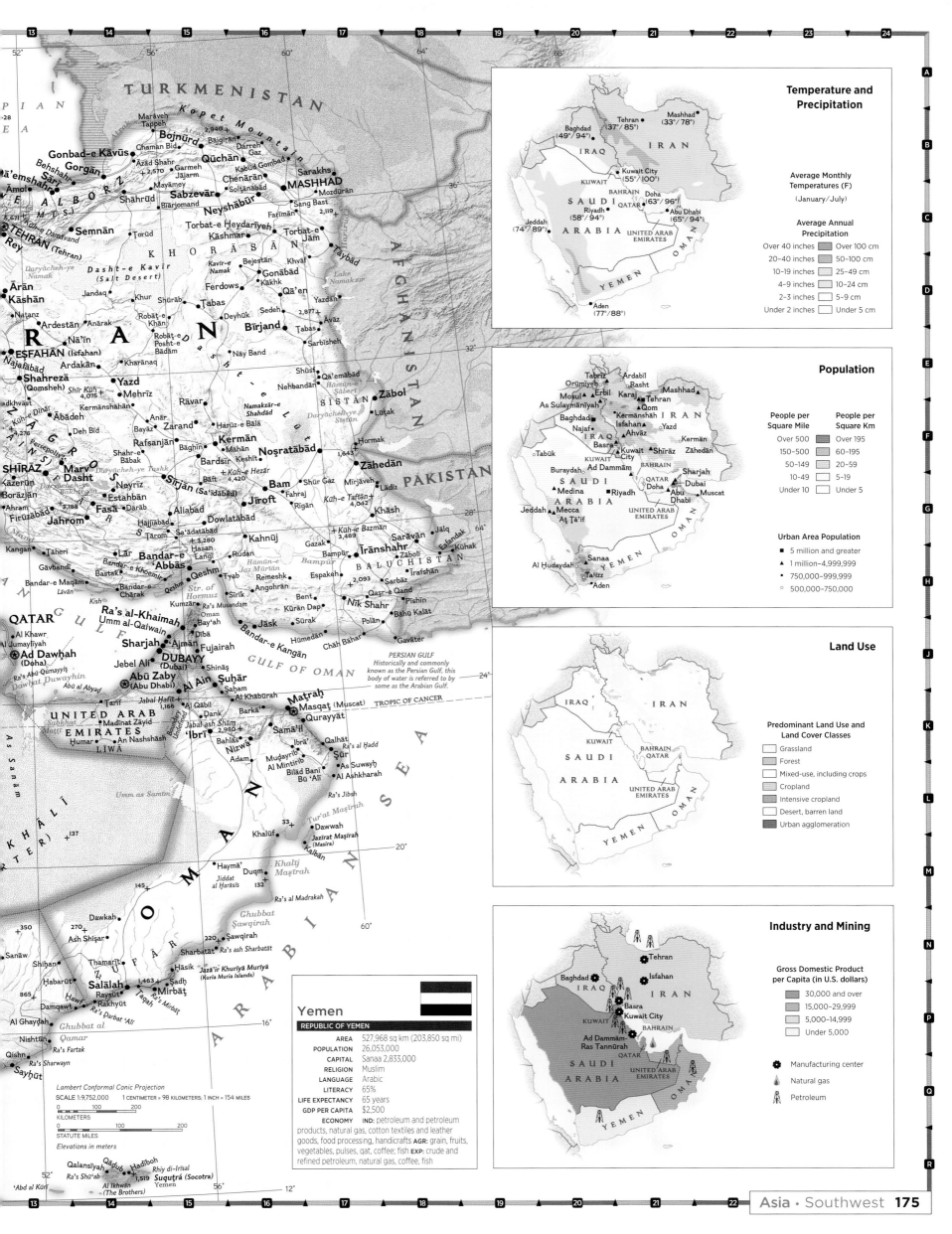

Temperature and Precipitation

Average Monthly Temperatures (F)
(January/July)

Baghdad (49°/94°)
Tehran (37°/85°)
Mashhad (33°/78°)
Kuwait City (55°/100°)
Riyadh (58°/94°)
Doha (63°/96°)
Abu Dhabi (65°/94°)
Jeddah (74°/89°)
Aden (77°/88°)

Average Annual Precipitation

Over 40 inches	Over 100 cm
20–40 inches	50–100 cm
10–19 inches	25–49 cm
4–9 inches	10–24 cm
2–3 inches	5–9 cm
Under 2 inches	Under 5 cm

Population

People per Square Mile	People per Square Km
Over 500	Over 195
150–500	60–195
50–149	20–59
10–49	5–19
Under 10	Under 5

Urban Area Population

- ■ 5 million and greater
- ▲ 1 million–4,999,999
- ● 750,000–999,999
- ○ 500,000–750,000

Land Use

Predominant Land Use and Land Cover Classes

- Grassland
- Forest
- Mixed-use, including crops
- Cropland
- Intensive cropland
- Desert, barren land
- Urban agglomeration

Industry and Mining

Gross Domestic Product per Capita (in U.S. dollars)

- 30,000 and over
- 15,000–29,999
- 5,000–14,999
- Under 5,000

- ✿ Manufacturing center
- 🛢 Natural gas
- ⛏ Petroleum

Yemen

REPUBLIC OF YEMEN

AREA	527,968 sq km (203,850 sq mi)
POPULATION	26,053,000
CAPITAL	Sanaa 2,833,000
RELIGION	Muslim
LANGUAGE	Arabic
LITERACY	65%
LIFE EXPECTANCY	65 years
GDP PER CAPITA	$2,500

ECONOMY **IND:** petroleum and petroleum products, natural gas, cotton textiles and leather goods, food processing, handicrafts **AGR:** grain, fruits, vegetables, pulses, qat, coffee; fish **EXP:** crude and refined petroleum, natural gas, coffee, fish

Lambert Conformal Conic Projection
SCALE 1:9,752,000   1 CENTIMETER = 98 KILOMETERS; 1 INCH = 154 MILES

KILOMETERS
0   100   200

STATUTE MILES
0   100   200

Elevations in meters

PERSIAN GULF
Historically and commonly known as the Persian Gulf, this body of water is referred to by some as the Arabian Gulf.

Central Asia

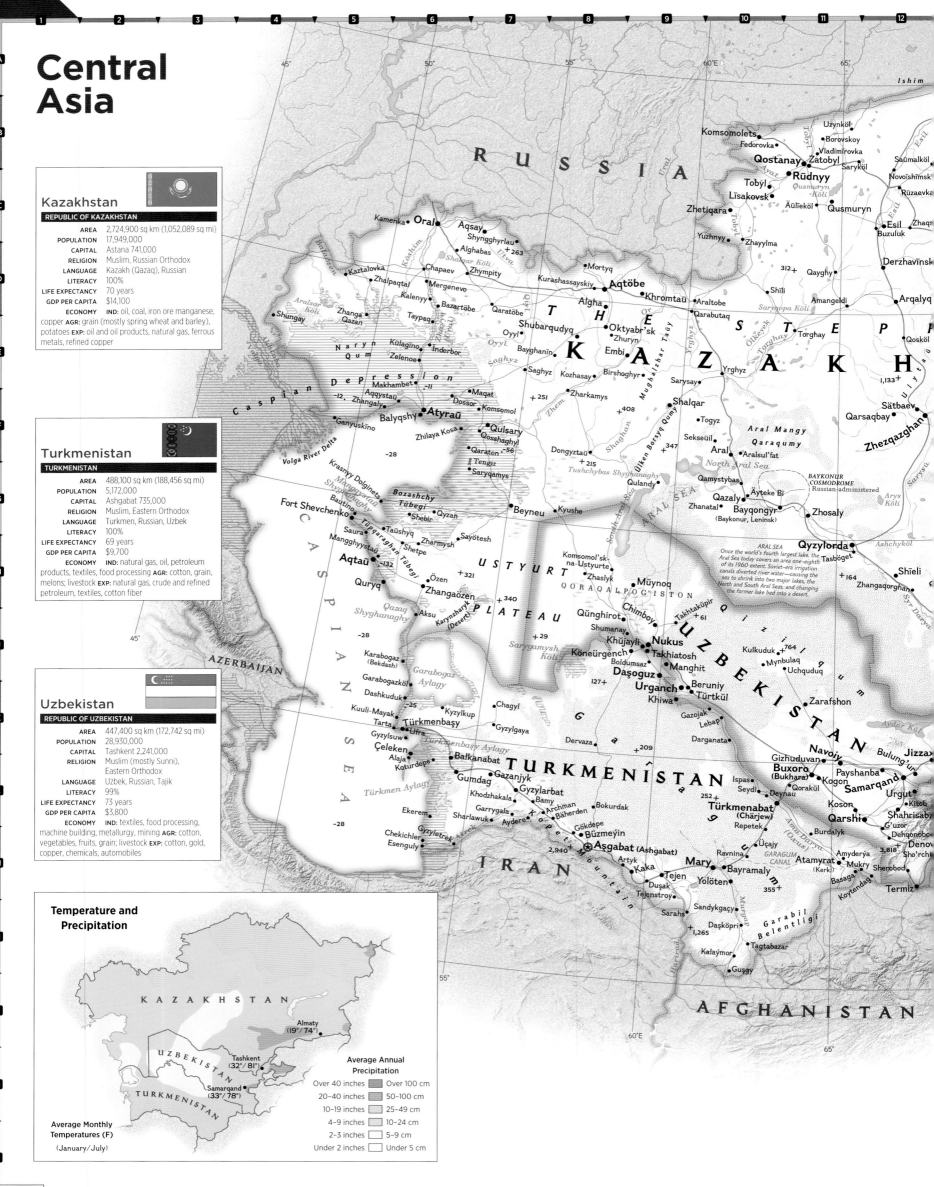

Kazakhstan

REPUBLIC OF KAZAKHSTAN

AREA	2,724,900 sq km (1,052,089 sq mi)
POPULATION	17,949,000
CAPITAL	Astana 741,000
RELIGION	Muslim, Russian Orthodox
LANGUAGE	Kazakh (Qazaq), Russian
LITERACY	100%
LIFE EXPECTANCY	70 years
GDP PER CAPITA	$14,100
ECONOMY	IND: oil, coal, iron ore manganese,

copper AGR: grain (mostly spring wheat and barley), potatoes EXP: oil and oil products, natural gas, ferrous metals, refined copper

Turkmenistan

TURKMENISTAN

AREA	488,100 sq km (188,456 sq mi)
POPULATION	5,172,000
CAPITAL	Ashgabat 735,000
RELIGION	Muslim, Eastern Orthodox
LANGUAGE	Turkmen, Russian, Uzbek
LITERACY	100%
LIFE EXPECTANCY	69 years
GDP PER CAPITA	$9,700
ECONOMY	IND: natural gas, oil, petroleum

products, textiles, food processing AGR: cotton, grain, melons; livestock EXP: natural gas, crude and refined petroleum, textiles, cotton fiber

Uzbekistan

REPUBLIC OF UZBEKISTAN

AREA	447,400 sq km (172,742 sq mi)
POPULATION	28,930,000
CAPITAL	Tashkent 2,241,000
RELIGION	Muslim (mostly Sunni), Eastern Orthodox
LANGUAGE	Uzbek, Russian, Tajik
LITERACY	99%
LIFE EXPECTANCY	73 years
GDP PER CAPITA	$3,800
ECONOMY	IND: textiles, food processing,

machine building, metallurgy, mining AGR: cotton, vegetables, fruits, grain; livestock EXP: cotton, gold, copper, chemicals, automobiles

Temperature and Precipitation

Average Annual Precipitation

Over 40 inches	Over 100 cm
20–40 inches	50–100 cm
10–19 inches	25–49 cm
4–9 inches	10–24 cm
2–3 inches	5–9 cm
Under 2 inches	Under 5 cm

Average Monthly Temperatures (F)

(January/July)

ARAL SEA Once the world's fourth largest lake, the Aral Sea today covers an area one-eighth of its 1960 extent. Soviet-era irrigation canals diverted river water—causing the sea to shrink into two major lakes, the North and South Aral Seas, and changing the former lake bed into a desert.

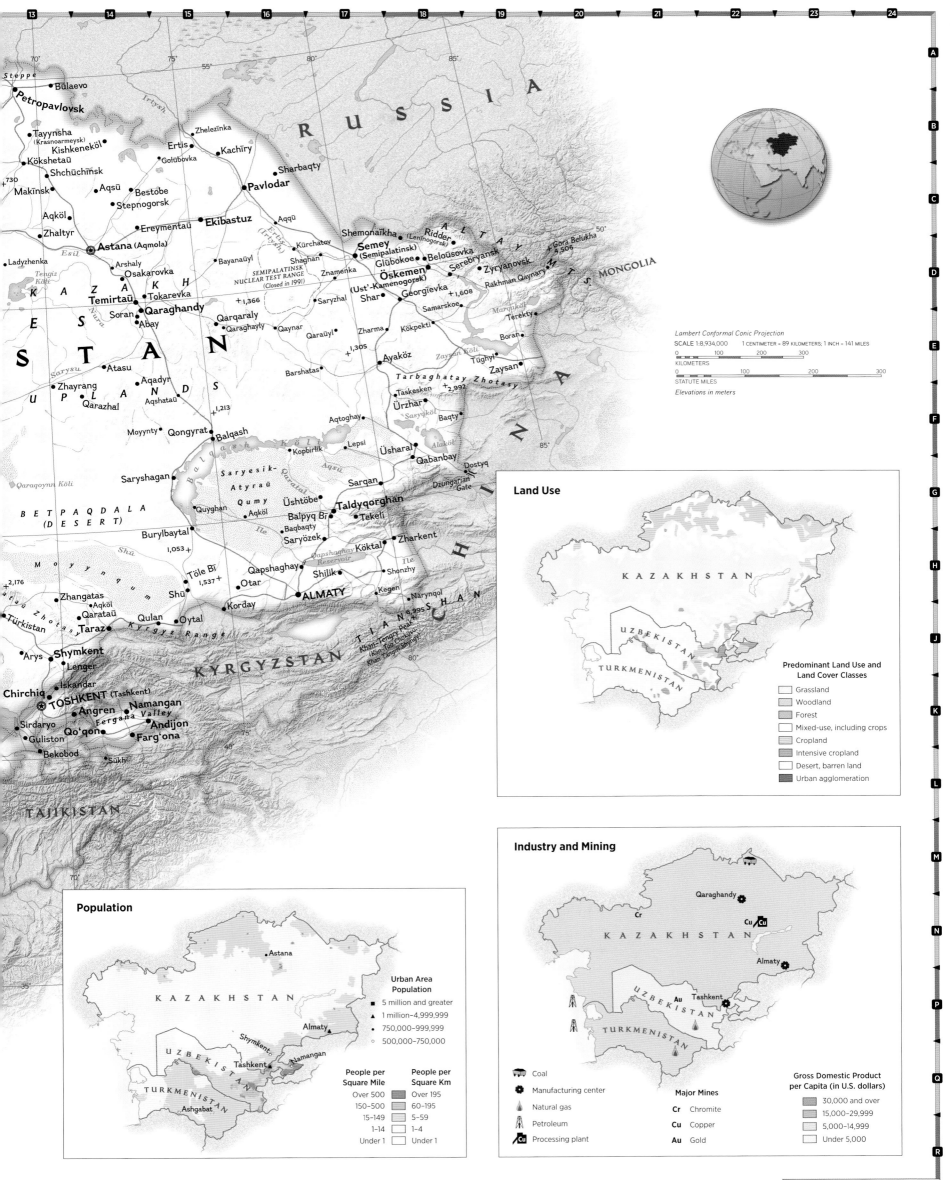

Land Use

Predominant Land Use and Land Cover Classes

- Grassland
- Woodland
- Forest
- Mixed-use, including crops
- Cropland
- Intensive cropland
- Desert, barren land
- Urban agglomeration

Population

Urban Area Population

- ■ 5 million and greater
- ▲ 1 million–4,999,999
- ● 750,000–999,999
- ○ 500,000–750,000

People per Square Mile	People per Square Km
Over 500	Over 195
150–500	60–195
15–149	5–59
1–14	1–4
Under 1	Under 1

Industry and Mining

- Coal
- Manufacturing center
- Natural gas
- Petroleum
- Cu Processing plant

Major Mines

- Cr Chromite
- Cu Copper
- Au Gold

Gross Domestic Product per Capita (in U.S. dollars)

- 30,000 and over
- 15,000–29,999
- 5,000–14,999
- Under 5,000

Lambert Conformal Conic Projection
SCALE 1:8,934,000   1 CENTIMETER = 89 KILOMETERS; 1 INCH = 141 MILES
KILOMETERS
STATUTE MILES
Elevations in meters

Far Central and South Asia

Pakistan

ISLAMIC REPUBLIC OF PAKISTAN

AREA	796,095 sq km (307,374 sq mi)
POPULATION	196,174,000
CAPITAL	Islamabad 1,297,000
RELIGION	Sunni Muslim, Shiite Muslim
LANGUAGE	Punjabi, Sindhi, Saraiki, Pashto, Urdu, Baluchi, Hindko
LITERACY	55%
LIFE EXPECTANCY	67 years
GDP PER CAPITA	$3,100

ECONOMY IND: textiles and apparel, food processing, pharmaceuticals, construction materials **AGR:** cotton, wheat, rice, sugarcane, fruits **EXP:** textiles (garments, bed linen, cotton cloth, yarn), rice, leather goods, carpets and rugs

Kyrgyzstan

KYRGYZ REPUBLIC

AREA	199,951 sq km (77,201 sq mi)
POPULATION	5,604,000
CAPITAL	Bishkek 858,000
RELIGION	Muslim, Russian Orthodox
LANGUAGE	Kyrgyz, Uzbek, Russian
LITERACY	99%
LIFE EXPECTANCY	70 years
GDP PER CAPITA	$2,500

ECONOMY IND: small machinery, textiles, food processing, cement, shoes **AGR:** tobacco, cotton, potatoes, vegetables; sheep **EXP:** gold, cotton, wool, garments, meat, tobacco

Tajikistan

REPUBLIC OF TAJIKISTAN

AREA	143,100 sq km (55,251 sq mi)
POPULATION	8,052,000
CAPITAL	Dushanbe 801,000
RELIGION	Sunni Muslim, Shiite Muslim
LANGUAGE	Tajik, Russian
LITERACY	100%
LIFE EXPECTANCY	67 years
GDP PER CAPITA	$2,300

ECONOMY IND: aluminum, mining, textiles, food processing **AGR:** cotton, grain, fruits, vegetables **EXP:** aluminum, electricity, cotton, lead, fruits

Land Use

Predominant Land Use and Land Cover Classes

- Grassland
- Woodland
- Forest
- Mixed-use, including crops
- Cropland
- Intensive cropland
- Desert, barren land
- Ice, cold desert, tundra
- Urban agglomeration

Temperature and Precipitation

Average Monthly Temperatures (F)
(January / July)

Dushanbe (35° / 81°)
Kabul (29° / 77°)
Lahore (55° / 90°)
Karachi (64° / 86°)

Average Annual Precipitation

- Over 40 inches / Over 100 cm
- 20-40 inches / 50-100 cm
- 10-19 inches / 25-49 cm
- 4-9 inches / 10-24 cm
- 2-3 inches / 5-9 cm
- Under 2 inches / Under 5 cm

Polyconic Projection
SCALE 1:5,829,000   1 CENTIMETER = 58 KILOMETERS; 1 INCH = 92 MILES

Elevations in meters

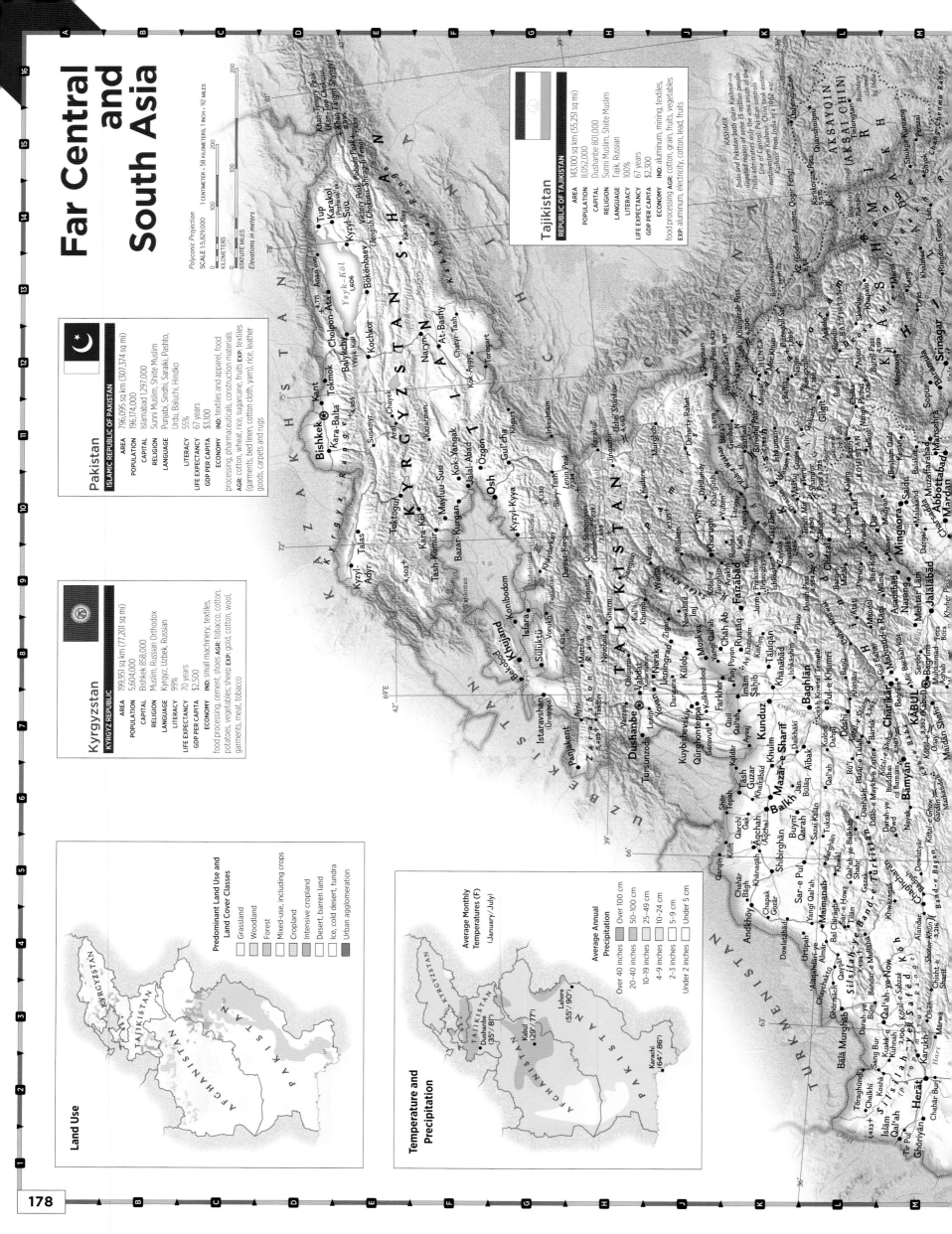

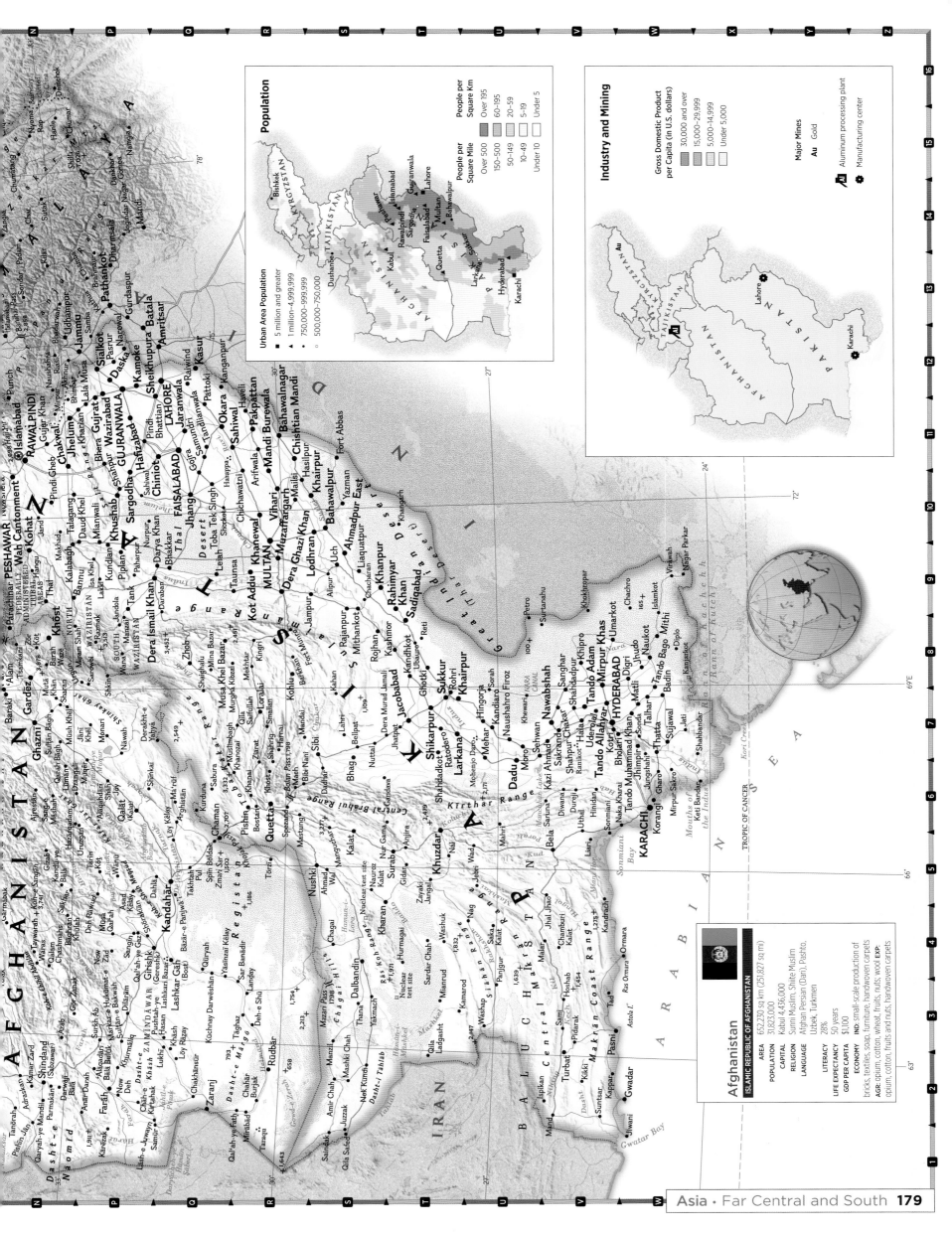

Population

Urban Area Population
- ■ 5 million and greater
- ▲ 1 million–4,999,999
- ▲ 750,000–999,999
- ○ 500,000–750,000

People per Square Mile
- Over 500
- 150–500
- 50–149
- 10–49
- Under 10

People per Square Km
- Over 195
- 60–195
- 20–59
- 5–19
- Under 5

Industry and Mining

Gross Domestic Product per Capita (in U.S. dollars)
- 30,000 and over
- 15,000–29,999
- 5,000–14,999
- Under 5,000

Major Mines
- Au Gold
- Al Aluminum processing plant
- ✾ Manufacturing center

Afghanistan

ISLAMIC REPUBLIC OF AFGHANISTAN

AREA 652,230 sq km (251,827 sq mi)
POPULATION 31,823,000
CAPITAL Kabul 4,436,000
RELIGION Sunni Muslim, Shiite Muslim
LANGUAGE Afghan Persian (Dari), Pashto, Uzbek, Turkmen
LITERACY 28%
LIFE EXPECTANCY 50 years
GDP PER CAPITA $1,100
ECONOMY IND: small-scale production of bricks, textiles, soap, furniture, handwoven carpets AGR: opium, cotton, wheat, fruits, nuts; wool EXP: opium, cotton, fruits and nuts, handwoven carpets

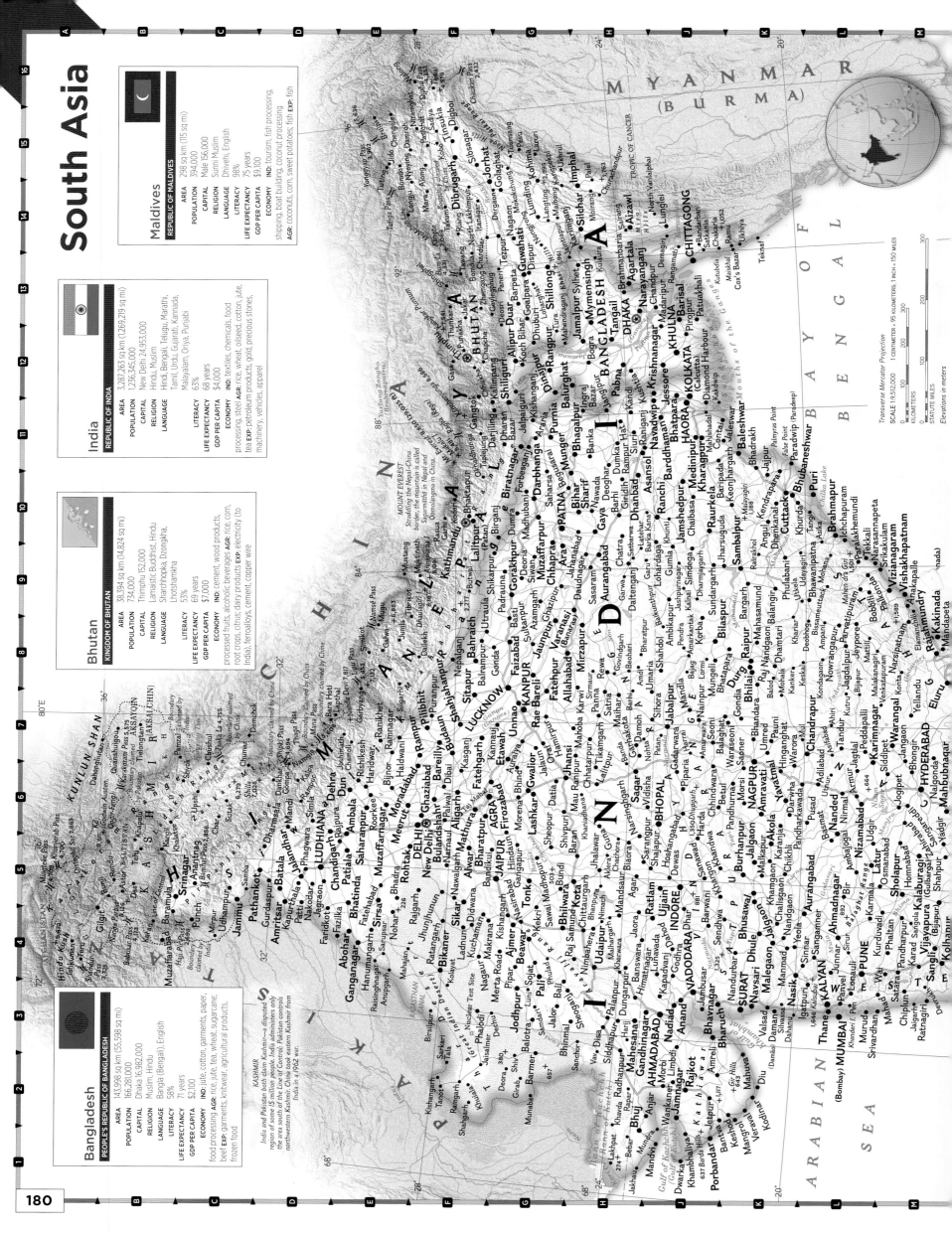

South Asia

Maldives
REPUBLIC OF MALDIVES

AREA	298 sq km (115 sq mi)
POPULATION	394,000
CAPITAL	Male 156,000
RELIGION	Sunni Muslim
LANGUAGE	Divehi, English
LITERACY	98%
LIFE EXPECTANCY	75 years
GDP PER CAPITA	$9,100
ECONOMY	IND: tourism, fish processing, shipping, boat building, coconut processing. AGR: coconuts, corn, sweet potatoes; fish EXP: fish

India
REPUBLIC OF INDIA

AREA	3,287,263 sq km (1,269,219 sq mi)
POPULATION	1,236,345,000
CAPITAL	New Delhi 24,953,000
RELIGION	Hindu, Muslim
LANGUAGE	Hindi, Bengali, Telugu, Marathi, Tamil, Urdu, Gujarati, Kannada, Malayalam, Oriya, Punjabi
LITERACY	63%
LIFE EXPECTANCY	68 years
GDP PER CAPITA	$4,000
ECONOMY	IND: textiles, chemicals, food processing, steel AGR: rice, wheat, oilseed, cotton, jute, tea EXP: petroleum products, gold, precious stones, machinery, vehicles, apparel

Bhutan
KINGDOM OF BHUTAN

AREA	38,394 sq km (14,824 sq mi)
POPULATION	734,000
CAPITAL	Thimphu 152,000
RELIGION	Lamaistic Buddhist, Hindu
LANGUAGE	Sharchhopka, Dzongkha, Lhotshamkha
LITERACY	53%
LIFE EXPECTANCY	69 years
GDP PER CAPITA	$7,000
ECONOMY	IND: cement, wood products, processed fruits, alcoholic beverages AGR: rice, corn, root crops, citrus; dairy products EXP: electricity (to India), ferroalloys, cement, copper wire

Bangladesh
PEOPLE'S REPUBLIC OF BANGLADESH

AREA	143,998 sq km (55,598 sq mi)
POPULATION	166,281,000
CAPITAL	Dhaka 16,982,000
RELIGION	Muslim, Hindu
LANGUAGE	Bangla (Bengali), English
LITERACY	58%
LIFE EXPECTANCY	71 years
GDP PER CAPITA	$2,100
ECONOMY	IND: jute, cotton, garments, paper, food processing AGR: rice, jute, tea, wheat, sugarcane; beef EXP: garments, knitwear, agricultural products, frozen food

KASHMIR
India and Pakistan both claim Kashmir—a disputed region of some 15 million people. India administers only the area south of the Line of Control; Pakistan controls northwestern Kashmir. China took eastern Kashmir from India in a 1962 war.

Transverse Mercator Projection
SCALE 1:9,512,000 1 CENTIMETER = 95 KILOMETERS; 1 INCH = 150 MILES

Elevations in meters

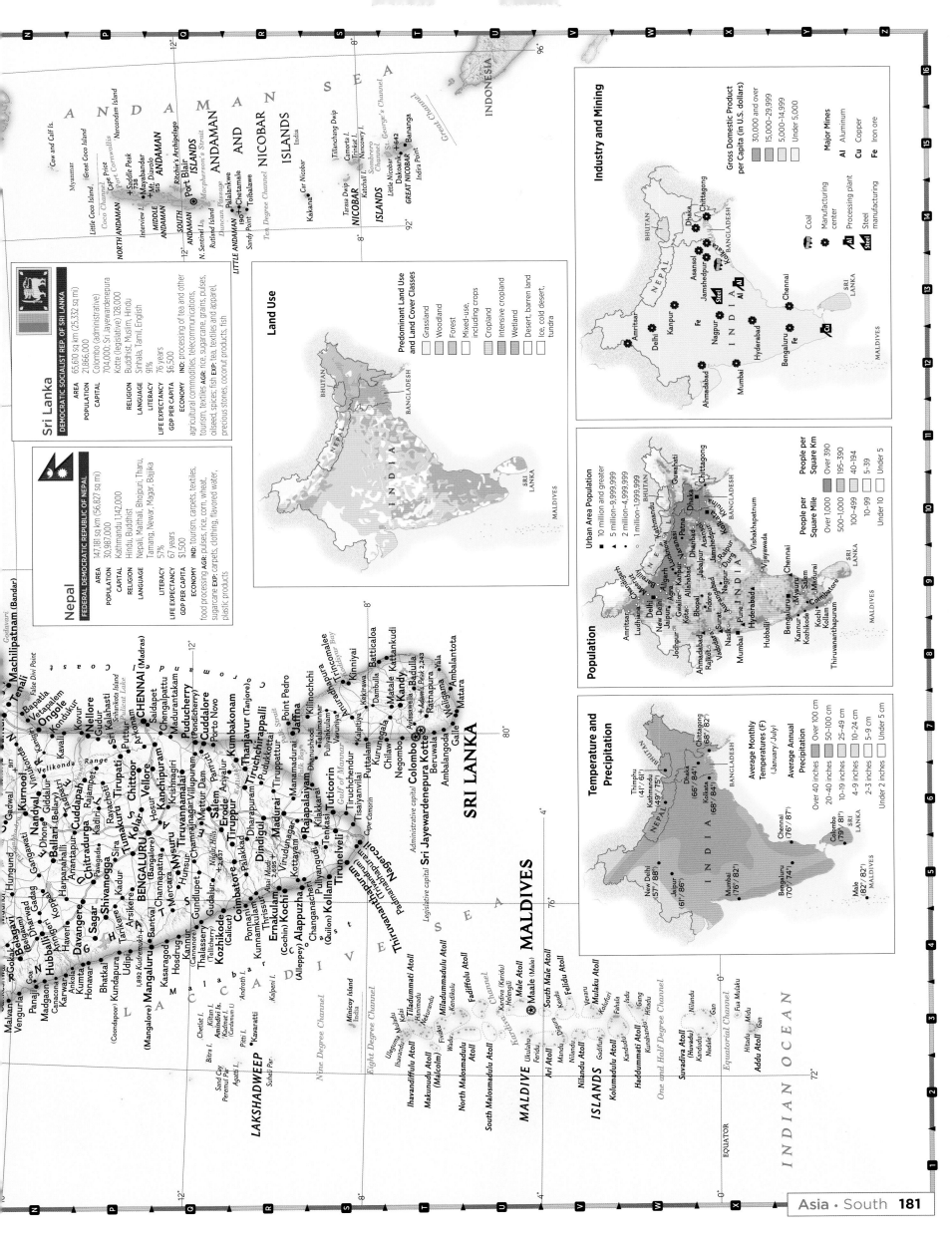

Sri Lanka

DEMOCRATIC SOCIALIST REP. OF SRI LANKA

AREA	65,610 sq km (25,332 sq mi)
POPULATION	21,866,000
CAPITAL	Colombo (administrative) 704,000; Sri Jayewardenepura Kotte (legislative) 128,000
RELIGION	Buddhist, Muslim, Hindu
LANGUAGE	Sinhala, Tamil, English
LITERACY	91%
LIFE EXPECTANCY	76 years
GDP PER CAPITA	$6,500
ECONOMY	IND: processing of tea and other agricultural commodities, telecommunications, tourism, textiles. AGR: rice, sugarcane, grains, pulses, oilseed, spices; fish EXP: tea, textiles and apparel, precious stones, coconut products, fish

Nepal

FEDERAL DEMOCRATIC REPUBLIC OF NEPAL

AREA	147,181 sq km (56,827 sq mi)
POPULATION	30,987,000
CAPITAL	Kathmandu 1,142,000
RELIGION	Hindu, Buddhist
LANGUAGE	Nepali, Maithali, Bhojpuri, Tharu, Tamang, Newar, Magar, Bajjika
LITERACY	57%
LIFE EXPECTANCY	67 years
GDP PER CAPITA	$1,500
ECONOMY	IND: tourism, carpets, textiles, food processing AGR: pulses, rice, corn, wheat, sugarcane EXP: carpets, clothing, flavored water, plastic products

Industry and Mining

Gross Domestic Product per Capita (in U.S. dollars)
- 30,000 and over
- 15,000–29,999
- 5,000–14,999
- Under 5,000

Major Mines
- Al Aluminum
- Cu Copper
- Fe Iron ore

- Coal
- Manufacturing center
- Processing plant
- Steel manufacturing

Land Use

Predominant Land Use and Land Cover Classes
- Grassland
- Woodland
- Forest
- Mixed-use, including crops
- Cropland
- Intensive cropland
- Wetland
- Desert, barren land
- Ice, cold desert, tundra

Population

Urban Area Population
- 10 million and greater
- 5 million–9,999,999
- 2 million–4,999,999
- 1 million–1,999,999

People per Square Mile
- Over 1,000
- 500–1,000
- 100–499
- 10–99
- Under 10

People per Square Km
- Over 390
- 195–390
- 40–194
- 5–39
- Under 5

Temperature and Precipitation

Average Monthly Temperatures (F) (January/July)
- Over 100 cm
- 50–100 cm
- 25–49 cm
- 10–24 cm
- 5–9 cm
- Under 5 cm

Average Annual Precipitation
- Over 40 inches
- 20–40 inches
- 10–19 inches
- 4–9 inches
- 2–3 inches
- Under 2 inches

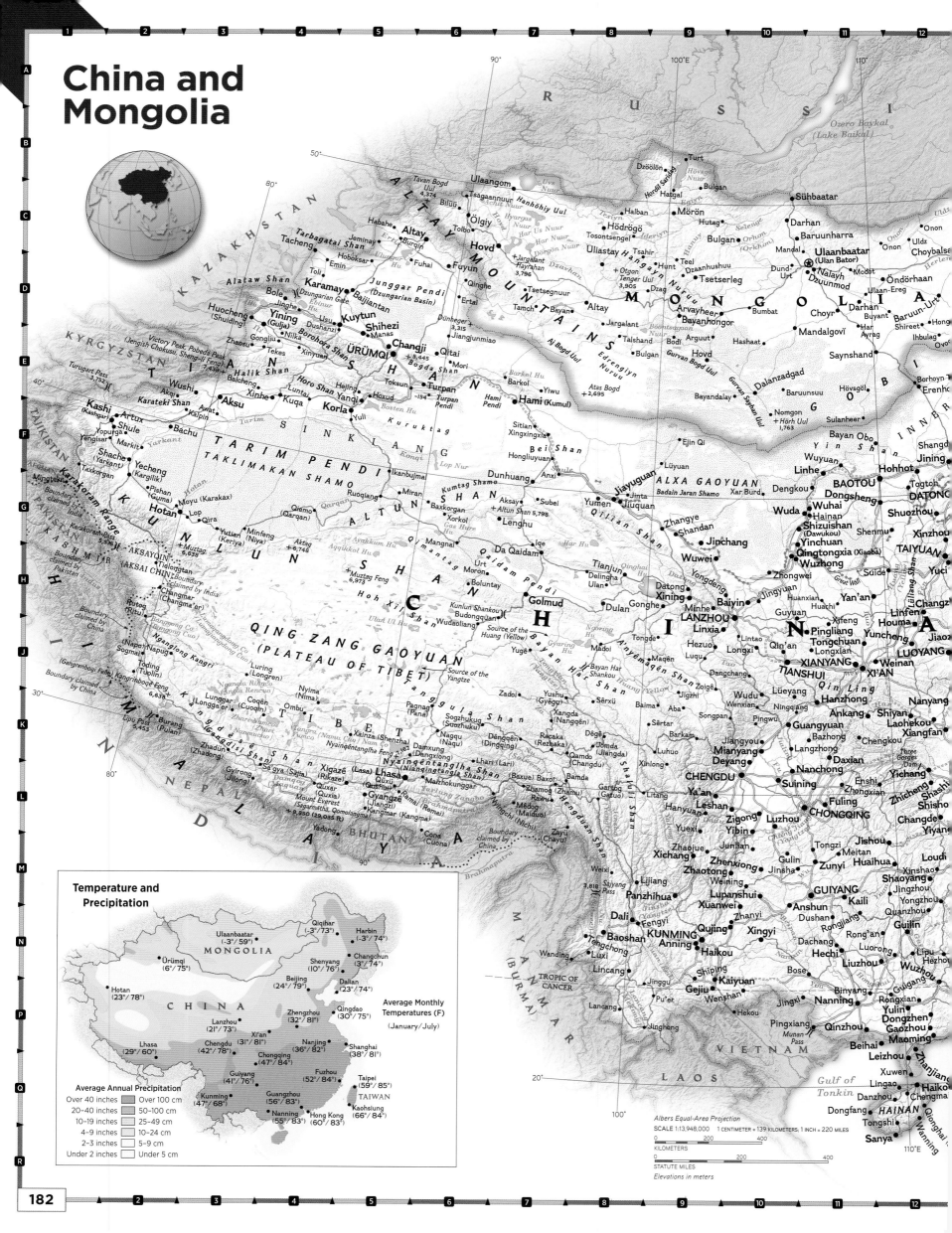

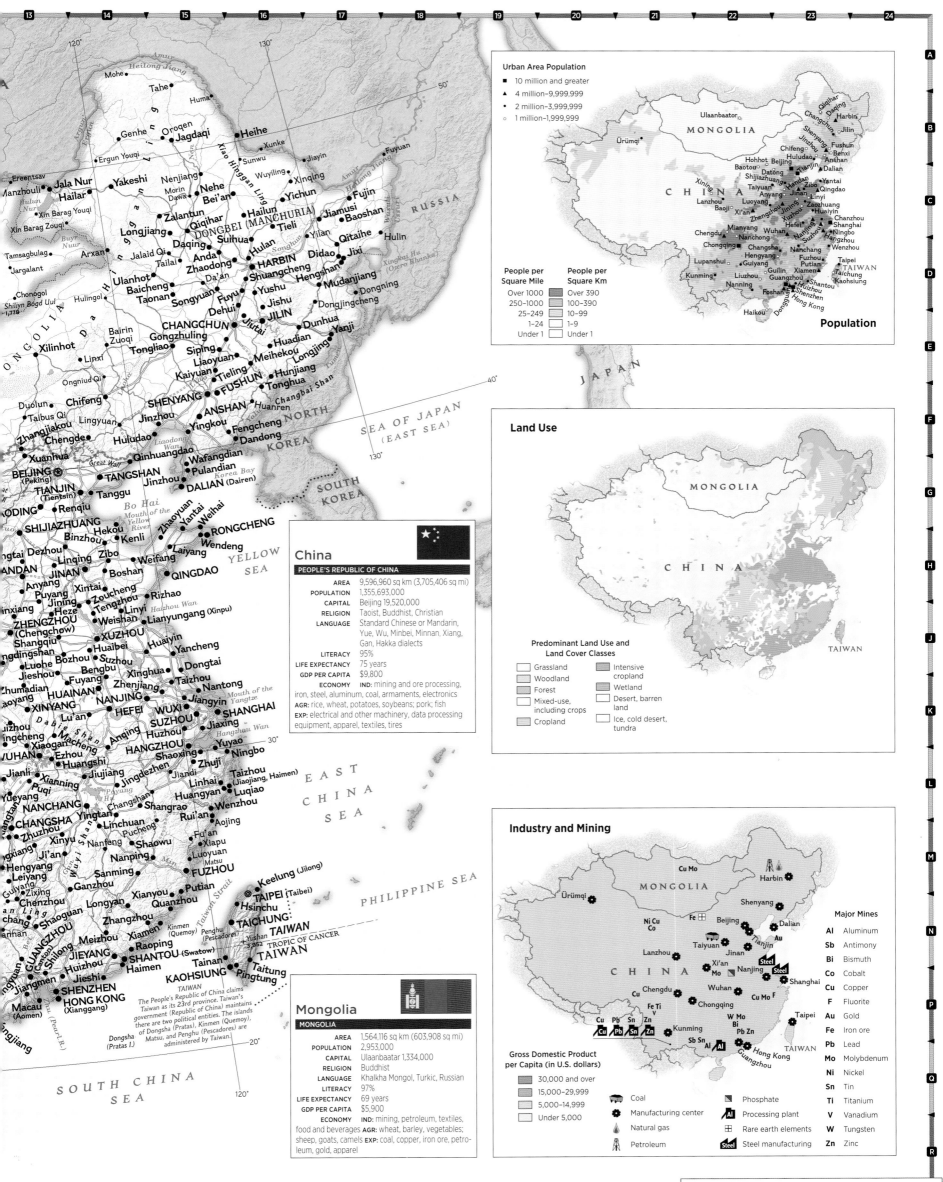

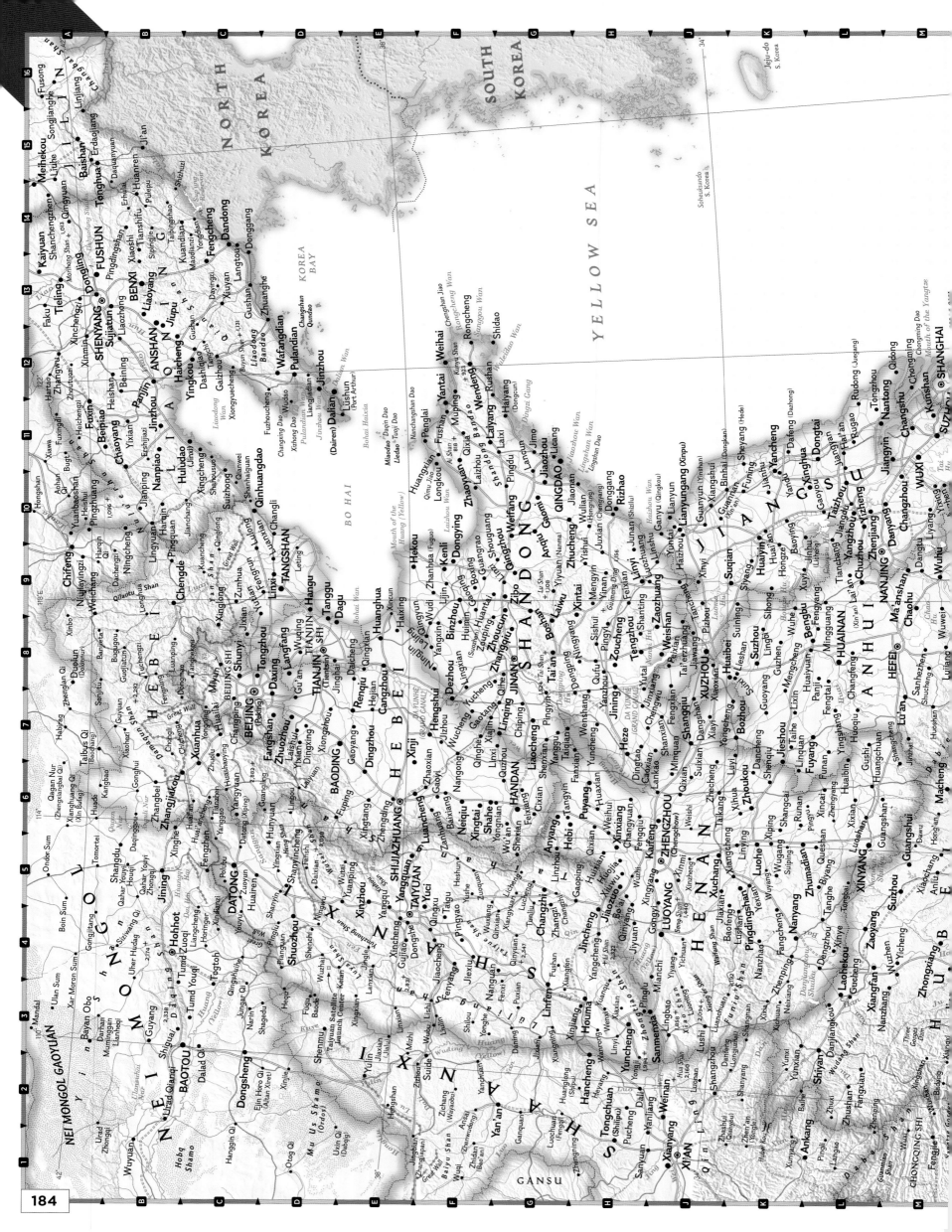

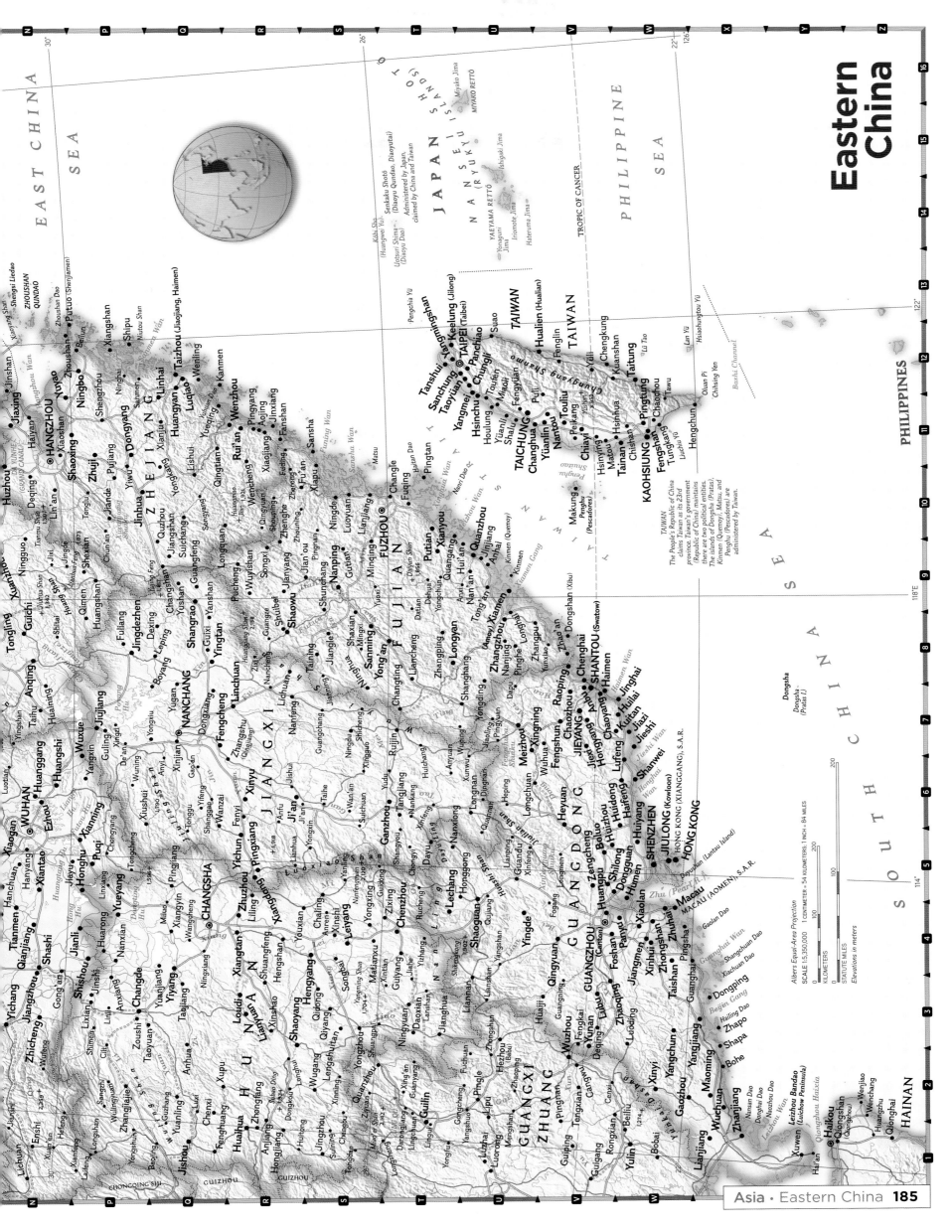

Eastern China

E A S T   C H I N A   S E A

JAPAN

N A N S E I - S H O T O
(R Y U K Y U)
I S L A N D S

Miyako Jima
MIYAKO RETTŌ

Kōbi Sho
(Huangwei Yu)
Uotsuri Shima
(Diaoyu Dao)
Senkaku Shotō
(Diaoyu Qundao, Diaoyutai)
Administered by Japan,
claimed by China and Taiwan.

YAEYAMA RETTŌ
Ishigaki Jima
Yonaguni
Jima
Iriomote Jima
Hateruma Jima

TROPIC OF CANCER

P H I L I P P I N E   S E A

PHILIPPINES

S O U T H   C H I N A   S E A

Pengchia Yü

TAIWAN

Keelung (Jilong)
Tanshui Yangmingshan
Sanchung ⊙ TAIPEI (Taibei)
Taoyüan Panchiao
Yangmei
Chungli
Hsinchu Toufen
Touliu
Miaoli
Puli
Fenglin
Hualien (Hualian)
TAIWAN
Suao

Haitan Dao
Pingtan

TAICHUNG
Changhua
Yüanli
Shalu
Yüanlin
Nantou
Chishan
Yunlin

Nam Dao
Matsu

Matou
Tainan
Hsinhua
Kuanshan
Chengkung
Yüli
Taitung
Pingtung
Fengshan
Tungkang
KAOHSIUNG
Chaochou

Chungyang Shanmo

Lan Yü
Lu Tao
Lüchiu Yü

Olan Pi
Chitsün Yen
Hengchun

Hsiaohungtou Yü

Bashi Channel

TAIWAN
The People's Republic of China
claims Taiwan as its 23rd
province. Taiwan's government
(Republic of China) maintains
there are two political entities.
The islands of Dongsha (Pratas),
Kinmen (Quemoy), Matsu, and
Penghu (Pescadores) are
administered by Taiwan.

Dongsha
Dongsha
(Pratas I.)

ZHEJIANG

Jiaxing
Haiyan
Jinshan
Shengsi Liedao
ZHOUSHAN
QUNDAO
Zhoushan Dao
Putuo (Shenjiamen)
Beilun
Xiangshan
Shipu
Niutou Shan
HANGZHOU ⊙
Shaoxing
Ningbo
Yuyao
Zhuji
Shengzhou
Ninghai
Dongyang
Sanmen
Taizhou (Jiaojiang, Haimen)
Huangyan
Luqiao Wenling
Kanmen
Yueqing
Xianju
Pingyang
Wenzhou
Rui'an
Pingyang
Aojing
Qingtian
Jinxiang
Fanshan
Lishui
Zhenghe
Sansha
Changle

Funing Wan

FUJIAN

FUZHOU ⊙
Fuqing
Lianjiang
Ningde
Luoyuan
Gutian
Minqing
Putian
Xianyou
Quanzhou
Jinjiang
Anhai
Hui'an
Nan'an
Tong'an
Xiamen (Amoy)
Zhangzhou
Longhai

Nanping
Jian'ou
Shaowu
Jianyang
Shunchang
Shaxian
Sanming
Yong'an
Longyan
Zhangping
Yongchun

Dehua
Yongchun
Mingxi
Qingliu
Liancheng
Pinghe
Zhao'an
Dongshan (Xibu)
Dongshan Dao

JIANGXI

NANCHANG ⊙
Fengcheng
Jinxian
Yugan
Dongxiang
Yingtan
Guixi
Yushan
Shangrao
Deqing
Leping
Jingdezhen
Fuliang
Wannian

Ji'an
Fenyi
Xinyu
Zhangshu (Qingjiang)
Fengxin
Xinjian
Gao'an
Wanzai
Yichun
Pingxiang

Ganzhou
Yudu
Xingguo
Ningdu
Guangchang
Nancheng
Nanfeng
Yihuang
Le'an
Fuzhou (Linchuan)

GUANGDONG

SHANTOU (Swatow)
Chenghai
Chaozhou
Raoping
Chaoyang
Puning
JIEYANG
Jiexi
Huilai
Lufeng
Haifeng
Shanwei
Jieshi
Jiazi
Meizhou
Dabu
Fengshun
Wuhua
Xingning
Heyuan

GUANGZHOU ⊙
Foshan
Panyu
Shunde
Dongguan
Humen
SHENZHEN
JIULONG (Kowloon)
HONG KONG
HONG KONG (XIANGGANG), S.A.R.
Bao'an (Lantau Island)
Macau
MACAU (AOMEN), S.A.R.
Zhuhai

Zhaoqing
Qingyuan
Yingde
Lianjiang
Shaoguan
Lechang

GUANGXI ZHUANG

Guilin
Lingchuan
Yangshuo
Gongcheng
Pingle
Lipu

Wuzhou
Cangwu
Fengkai
Yunan
Deqing
Yunfu
Xinxing
Yunan

Yangjiang
Yangchun
Maoming
Gaozhou
Huazhou
Wuchuan
Zhanjiang

HAINAN

Leizhou Bandao
(Luichow Peninsula)
Qiongzhou Haixia
Haikou ⊙
Qiongshan

HUNAN

CHANGSHA ⊙
Zhuzhou
Xiangtan
Liling
Xiangxiang
Liuyang
Shuangfeng
Hengshan
Shaoyang
Hengyang
Leiyang
Youxian
Chaling
Yongxing
Zixing
Chenzhou

JIANGXI

HUBEI

WUHAN ⊙
Huangshi
Ezhou
Huanggang
Xiantao
Xianning
Wuxue
Puqi
Honghu
Chibi

Yichang
Jianli
Shashi
Jingzhou
Jiangling
Tianmen

Yueyang
Yiyang
Changde
Yuanjiang

Loudi
Lianyuan
Shaoyang

PHILIPPINES

Albers Equal-Area Projection
SCALE 1:5,350,000   1 CENTIMETER = 54 KILOMETERS; 1 INCH = 84 MILES

KILOMETERS

STATUTE MILES

Elevations in meters

118°E
122°
126°
30°
26°
22°
114°

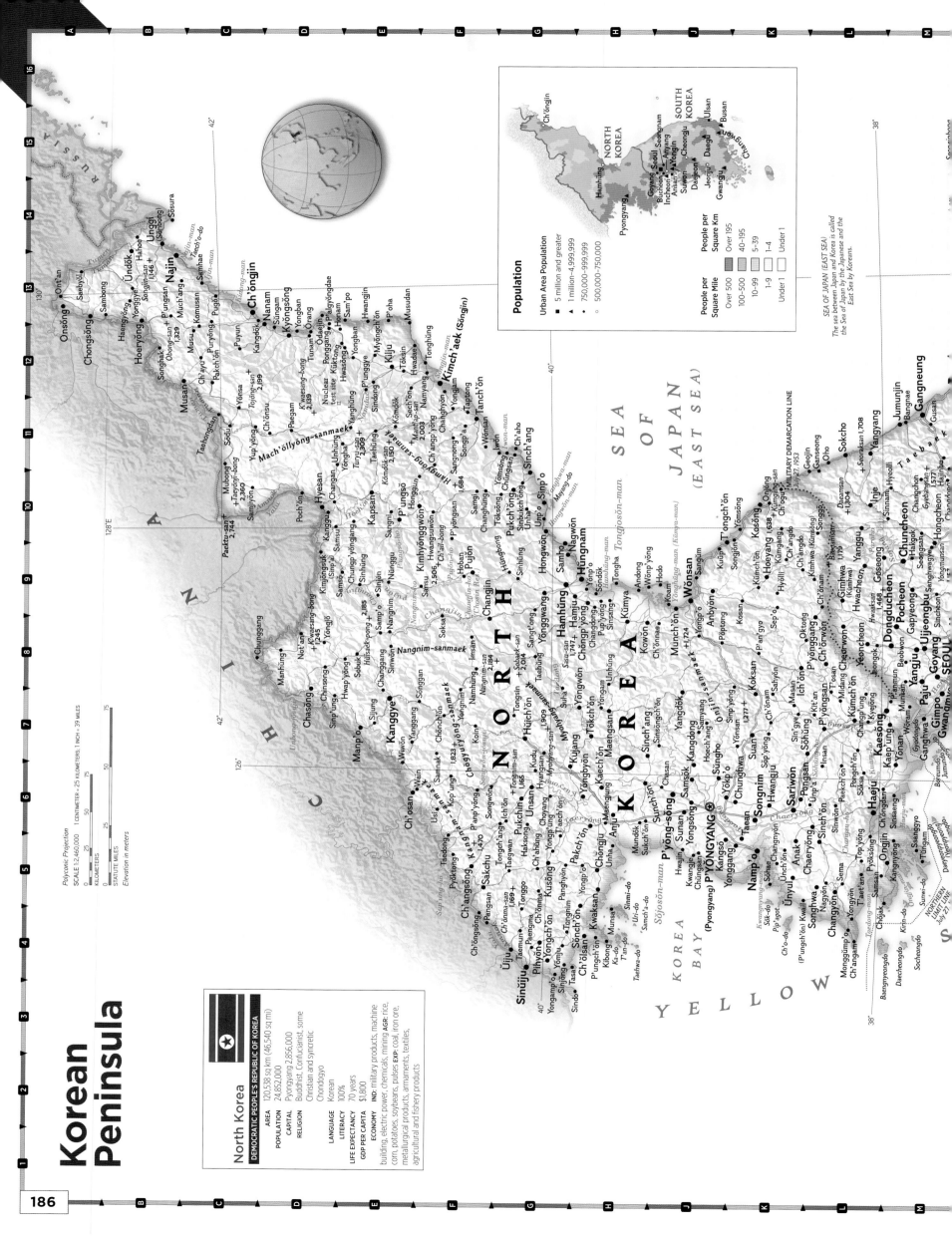

Korean Peninsula

North Korea
DEMOCRATIC PEOPLE'S REPUBLIC OF KOREA

AREA 120,538 sq km (46,540 sq mi)
POPULATION 24,852,000
CAPITAL Pyongyang 2,856,000
RELIGION Buddhist, Confucianist, some Christian and syncretic Chondogyo
LANGUAGE Korean
LITERACY 100%
LIFE EXPECTANCY 70 years
GDP PER CAPITA $1,800
ECONOMY **IND:** military products, machine building, electric power, chemicals, mining **AGR:** rice, corn, potatoes, soybeans, pulses **EXP:** coal, iron ore, metallurgical products, armaments, textiles; agricultural and fishery products

Population

Urban Area Population
- ■ 5 million and greater
- ■ 1 million–4,999,999
- ▲ 750,000–999,999
- • 500,000–750,000

People per Square Mile	People per Square Km
Over 500	Over 195
100–500	40–195
10–99	5–39
1–9	1–4
Under 1	Under 1

SEA OF JAPAN (EAST SEA)
The sea between Japan and Korea is called the Sea of Japan by the Japanese and the East Sea by Koreans.

Polyconic Projection
SCALE 1:2,460,000   1 CENTIMETER = 25 KILOMETERS; 1 INCH = 39 MILES

Elevation in meters

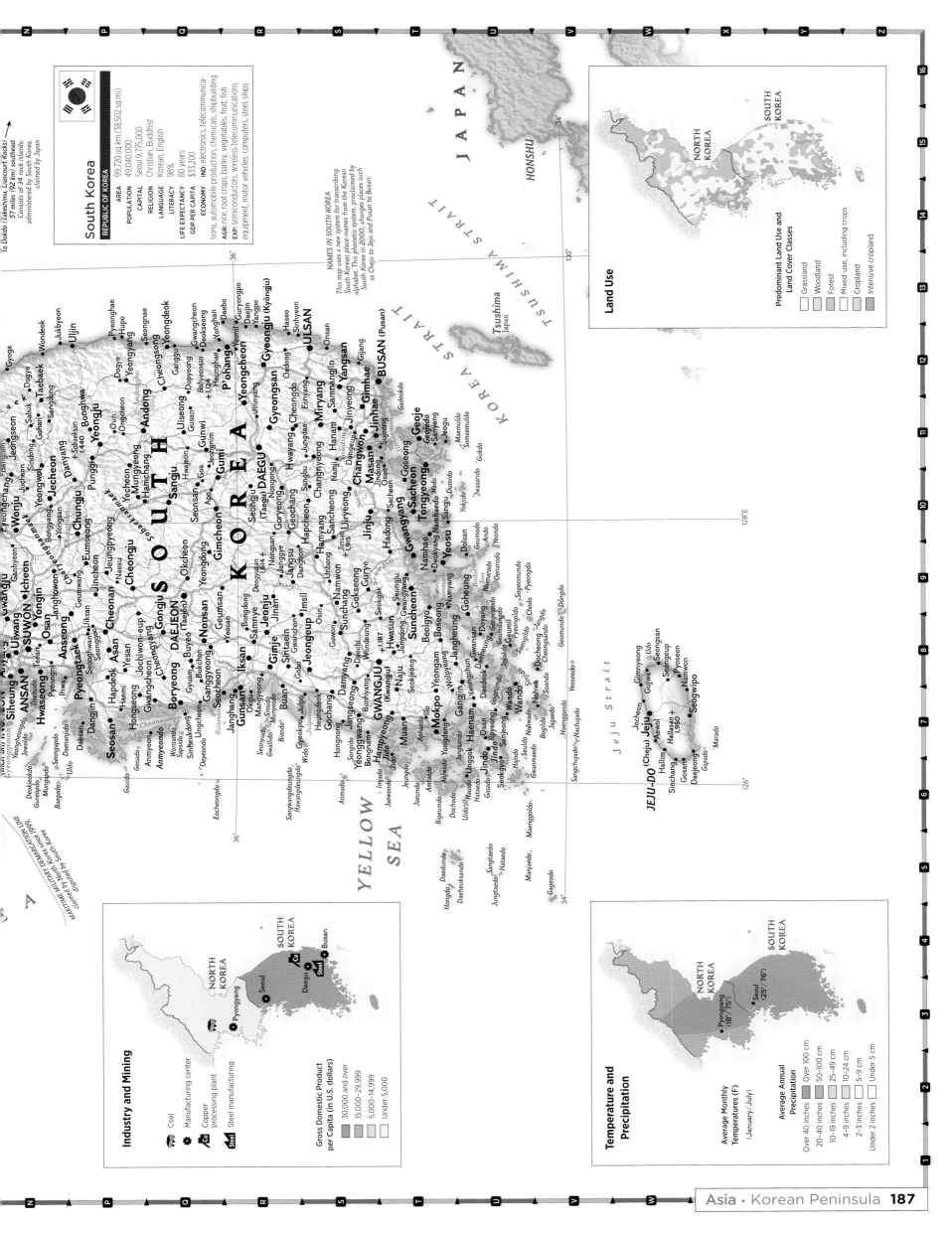

South Korea

REPUBLIC OF KOREA

AREA	99,720 sq km (38,502 sq mi)
POPULATION	49,040,000
CAPITAL	Seoul 9,775,000
RELIGION	Christian, Buddhist
LANGUAGE	Korean, English
LITERACY	98%
LIFE EXPECTANCY	80 years
GDP PER CAPITA	$33,200
ECONOMY	**IND:** electronics, telecommunications, automobile production, chemicals, shipbuilding **AGR:** rice, root crops, barley, vegetables, fruit, fish **EXP:** semiconductors, wireless telecommunications equipment, motor vehicles, computers, steel, ships

To Dokdo (Takeshima, Liancourt Rocks)
57 miles (92 km) southeast
Consists of 34 rock islands;
administered by South Korea,
claimed by Japan

NAMES IN SOUTH KOREA
This map uses a new system for transcribing
South Korean place-names from the Korean
alphabet. This phonetic system, proclaimed by
South Korea in 2000, changes places such
as Cheju to Jeju and Pusan to Busan.

MARITIME MILITARY DEMARCATION LINE
since 1999. Claimed by North Korea
claimed by South Korea

Industry and Mining

- Coal
- Manufacturing center
- Copper processing plant
- Steel manufacturing

Gross Domestic Product per Capita (in U.S. dollars)
- 30,000 and over
- 15,000–29,999
- 5,000–14,999
- Under 5,000

Land Use

Predominant Land Use and Land Cover Classes
- Grassland
- Woodland
- Forest
- Mixed-use, including crops
- Cropland
- Intensive cropland

Temperature and Precipitation

Average Monthly Temperatures (F)
(January / July)

Average Annual Precipitation
- Over 40 inches — Over 100 cm
- 20–40 inches — 50–100 cm
- 10–19 inches — 25–49 cm
- 4–9 inches — 10–24 cm
- 2–3 inches — 5–9 cm
- Under 2 inches — Under 5 cm

YELLOW SEA

KOREA STRAIT

TSUSHIMA STRAIT

JAPAN

HONSHU

Jeju Strait

SOUTH KOREA

NORTH KOREA

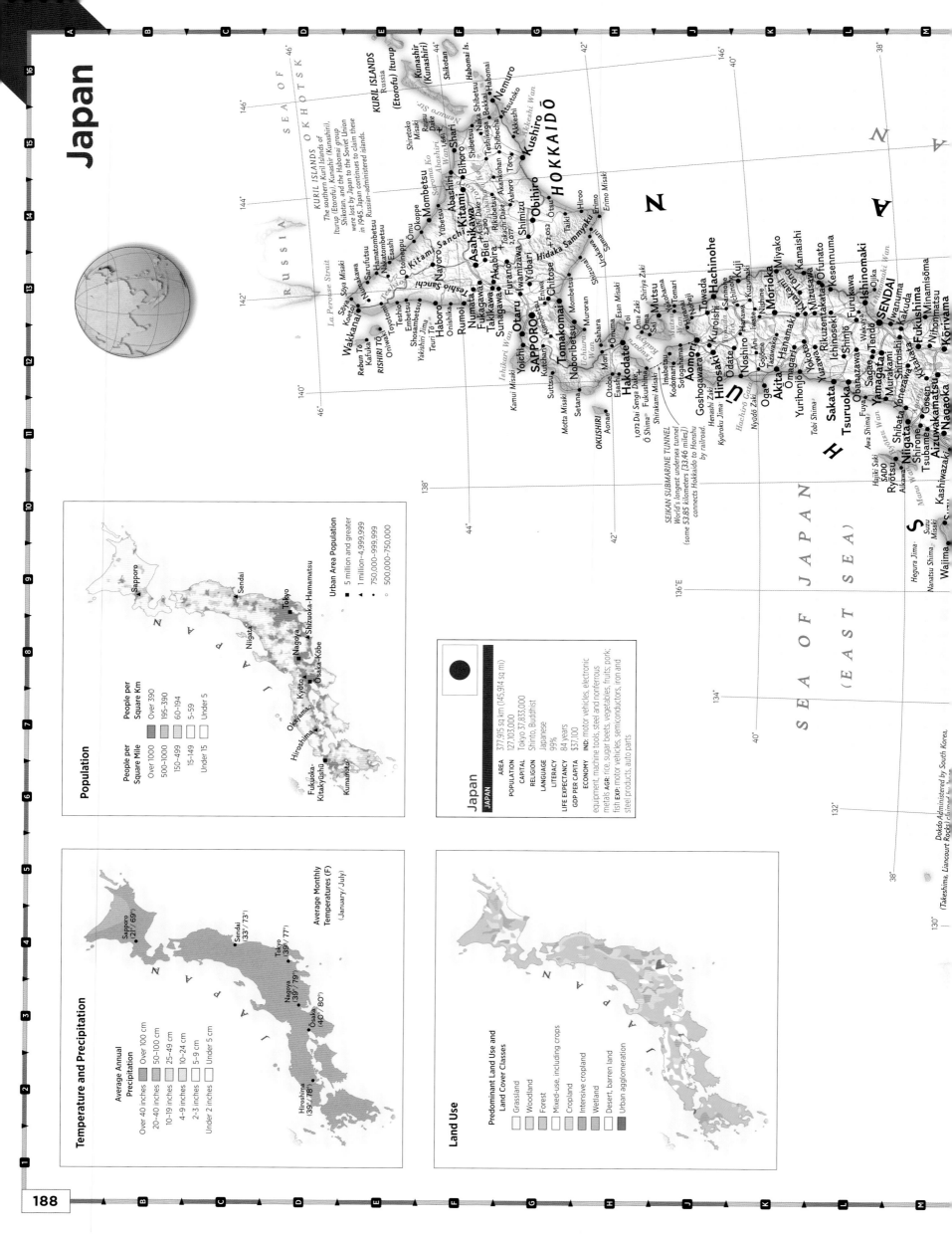

Japan

Temperature and Precipitation

Average Annual Precipitation

- Over 40 inches — Over 100 cm
- 20–40 inches — 50–100 cm
- 10–19 inches — 25–49 cm
- 4–9 inches — 10–24 cm
- 2–3 inches — 5–9 cm
- Under 2 inches — Under 5 cm

Average Monthly Temperatures (F)
(January / July)

- Sapporo (21° / 69°)
- Sendai (33° / 73°)
- Tokyo (39° / 77°)
- Nagoya (39° / 79°)
- Osaka (40° / 80°)
- Hiroshima (39° / 78°)

Land Use

Predominant Land Use and Land Cover Classes

- Grassland
- Woodland
- Forest
- Mixed-use, including crops
- Cropland
- Intensive cropland
- Wetland
- Desert, barren land
- Urban agglomeration

Population

People per Square Mile / **People per Square Km**

- Over 1000 — Over 390
- 500–1000 — 195–390
- 150–499 — 60–194
- 15–149 — 5–59
- Under 15 — Under 5

Urban Area Population

- ■ 5 million and greater
- ▲ 1 million–4,999,999
- ● 750,000–999,999
- ○ 500,000–750,000

Cities: Sapporo, Sendai, Niigata, Tokyo, Nagoya, Shizuoka-Hamamatsu, Kyōto, Osaka-Kōbe, Okayama, Hiroshima, Fukuoka-Kitakyūshū, Kumamoto

Japan

JAPAN	
AREA	377,915 sq km (145,914 sq mi)
POPULATION	127,103,000
CAPITAL	Tokyo 37,833,000
RELIGION	Shinto, Buddhist
LANGUAGE	Japanese
LITERACY	99%
LIFE EXPECTANCY	84 years
GDP PER CAPITA	$37,100
ECONOMY	**IND:** motor vehicles, electronic equipment, machine tools, steel and nonferrous metals **AGR:** rice, sugar beets, vegetables, fruits; pork; fish **EXP:** motor vehicles, semiconductors, iron and steel products, auto parts

SEIKAN SUBMARINE TUNNEL — World's longest undersea tunnel (some 53.85 kilometers [33.46 miles]) connects Hokkaido to Honshu by railroad.

KURIL ISLANDS — The southern Kuril Islands of Iturup (Etorofu), Kunashir (Kunashiri), Shikotan, and the Habomai group were lost by Japan to the Soviet Union in 1945. Japan continues to claim these Russian-administered islands.

Dokdo Administered by South Korea, (Takeshima, Liancourt Rocks) claimed by ...

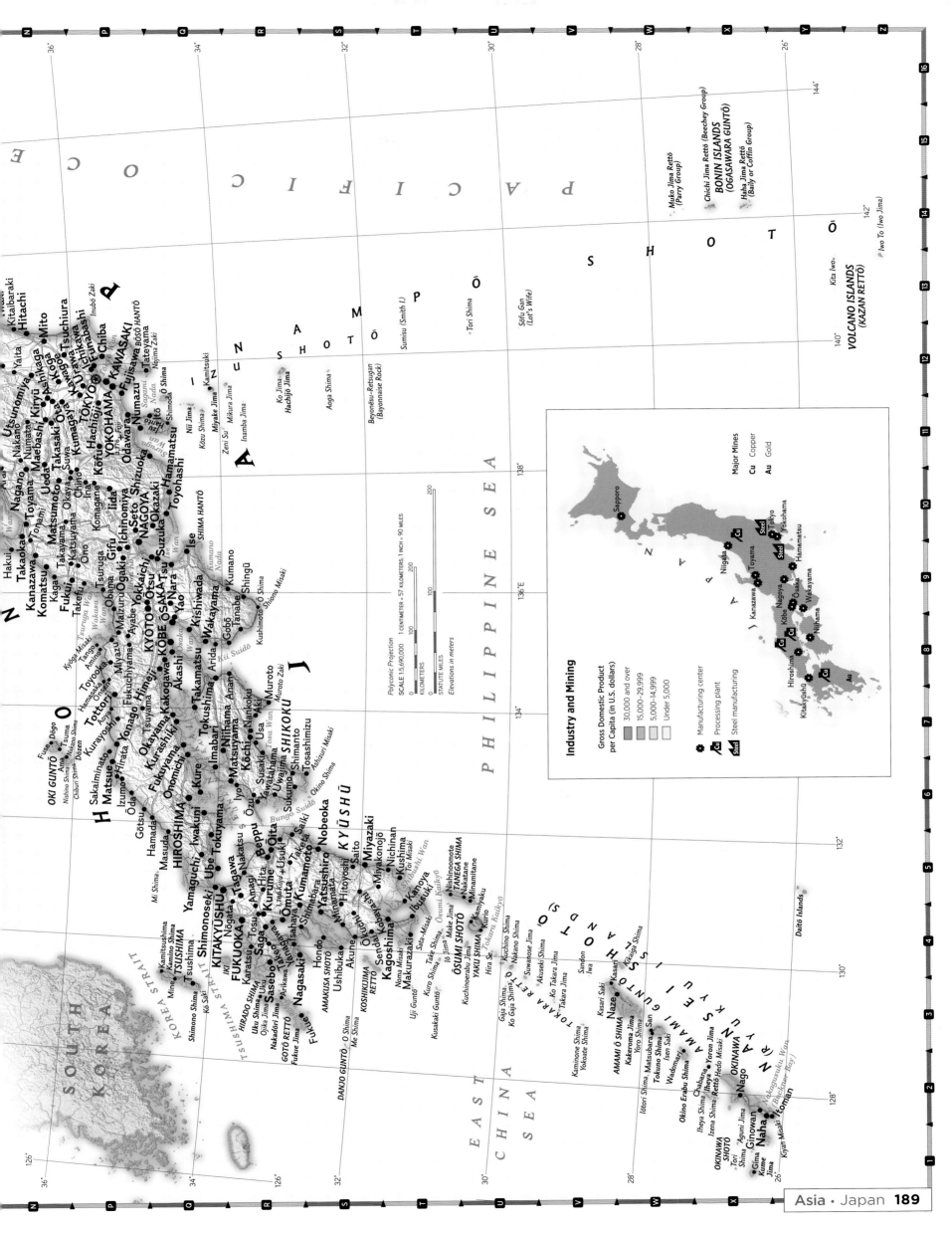

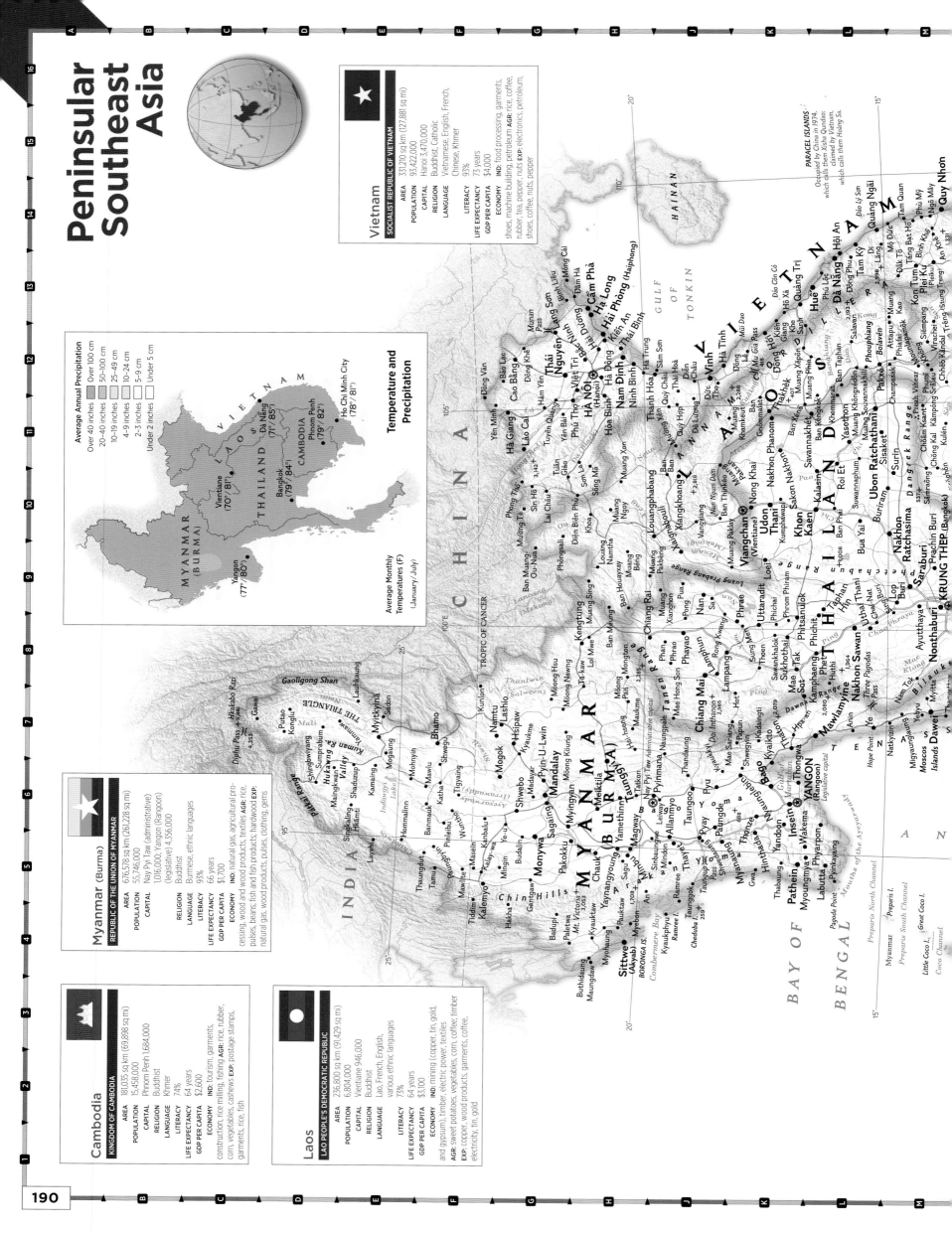

Peninsular Southeast Asia

Vietnam
SOCIALIST REPUBLIC OF VIETNAM
AREA 331,210 sq km (127,881 sq mi)
POPULATION 93,422,000
CAPITAL Hanoi 3,470,000
RELIGION Buddhist, Catholic
LANGUAGE Vietnamese, English, French, Chinese, Khmer
LITERACY 93%
LIFE EXPECTANCY 73 years
GDP PER CAPITA $4,000
ECONOMY **IND:** food processing, garments, shoes, machine building, petroleum **AGR:** rice, coffee, rubber, tea, pepper, nuts **EXP:** electronics, petroleum, shoes, coffee, nuts, pepper

PARACEL ISLANDS
Occupied by China in 1974, which calls them Xisha Qundao; claimed by Vietnam, which calls them Hoàng Sa.

Myanmar (Burma)
REPUBLIC OF THE UNION OF MYANMAR
AREA 676,578 sq km (261,228 sq mi)
POPULATION 55,746,000
CAPITAL Nay Pyi Taw (administrative) 1,016,000; Yangon (Rangoon) (legislative) 4,356,000
RELIGION Buddhist
LANGUAGE Burmese, ethnic languages
LITERACY 93%
LIFE EXPECTANCY 66 years
GDP PER CAPITA $1,700
ECONOMY **IND:** natural gas, agricultural processing, wood and wood products, textiles **AGR:** rice, pulses, beans; fish and fish products; hardwood **EXP:** natural gas, wood products, pulses, clothing, gems

Cambodia
KINGDOM OF CAMBODIA
AREA 181,035 sq km (69,898 sq mi)
POPULATION 15,458,000
CAPITAL Phnom Penh 1,684,000
RELIGION Buddhist
LANGUAGE Khmer
LITERACY 74%
LIFE EXPECTANCY 64 years
GDP PER CAPITA $2,600
ECONOMY **IND:** tourism, garments, construction, rice milling, fishing **AGR:** rice, rubber, corn, vegetables, cashews **EXP:** postage stamps, garments, rice, fish

Laos
LAO PEOPLE'S DEMOCRATIC REPUBLIC
AREA 236,800 sq km (91,429 sq mi)
POPULATION 6,804,000
CAPITAL Vientiane 946,000
RELIGION Buddhist
LANGUAGE Lao, French, English, various ethnic languages
LITERACY 73%
LIFE EXPECTANCY 64 years
GDP PER CAPITA $3,100
ECONOMY **IND:** mining (copper, tin, gold, and gypsum), timber, electric power, textiles **AGR:** sweet potatoes, vegetables, corn, coffee, timber **EXP:** copper, wood products, garments, coffee, electricity, tin, gold

Temperature and Precipitation

Average Annual Precipitation
- Over 40 inches — Over 100 cm
- 20–40 inches — 50–100 cm
- 10–19 inches — 25–49 cm
- 4–9 inches — 10–24 cm
- 2–3 inches — 5–9 cm
- Under 2 inches — Under 5 cm

Average Monthly Temperatures (F) (January/July)

Đà Nẵng (71°/85°)
Phnom Penh (79°/82°)
Ho Chi Minh City (78°/81°)
Vientiane (70°/81°)
Bangkok (79°/84°)
Yangon (77°/80°)

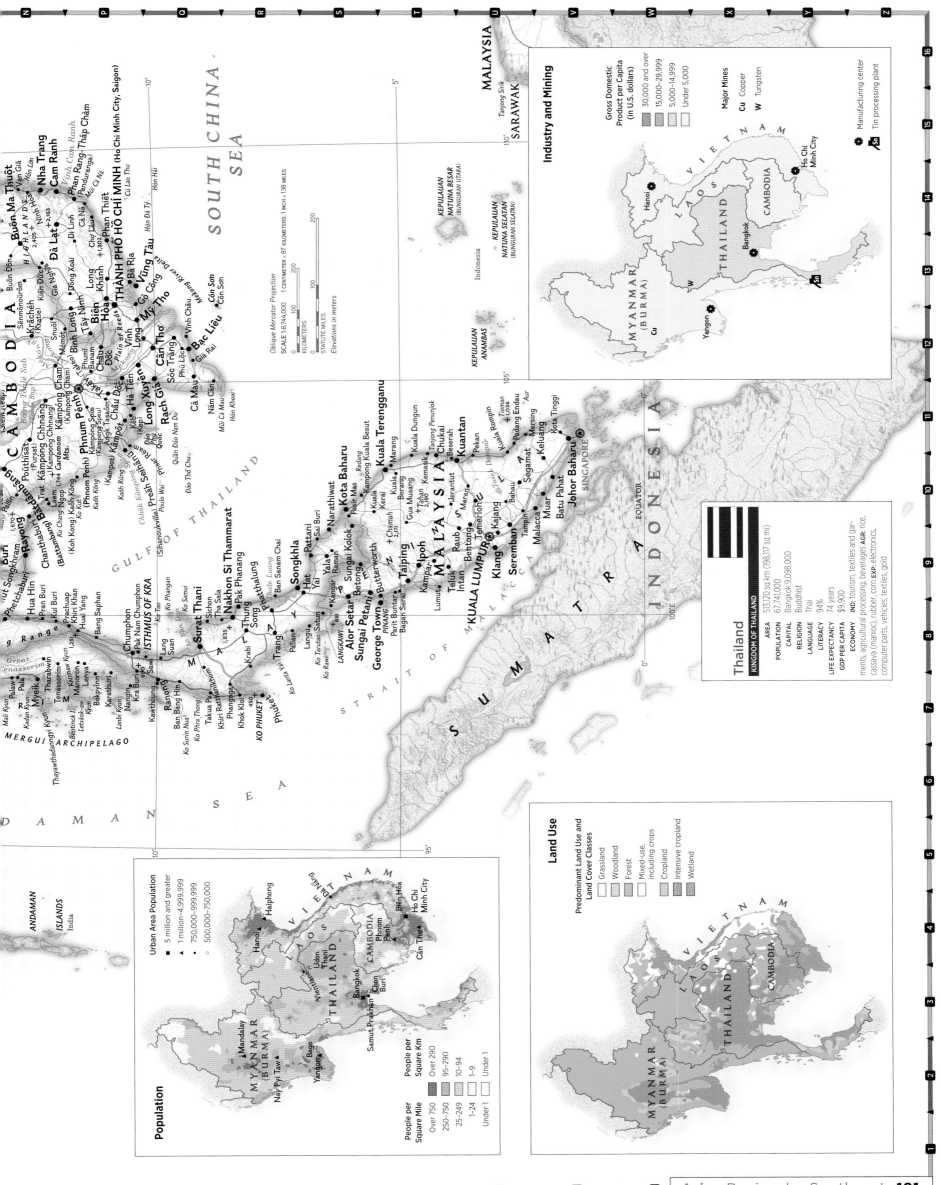

Insular Southeast Asia

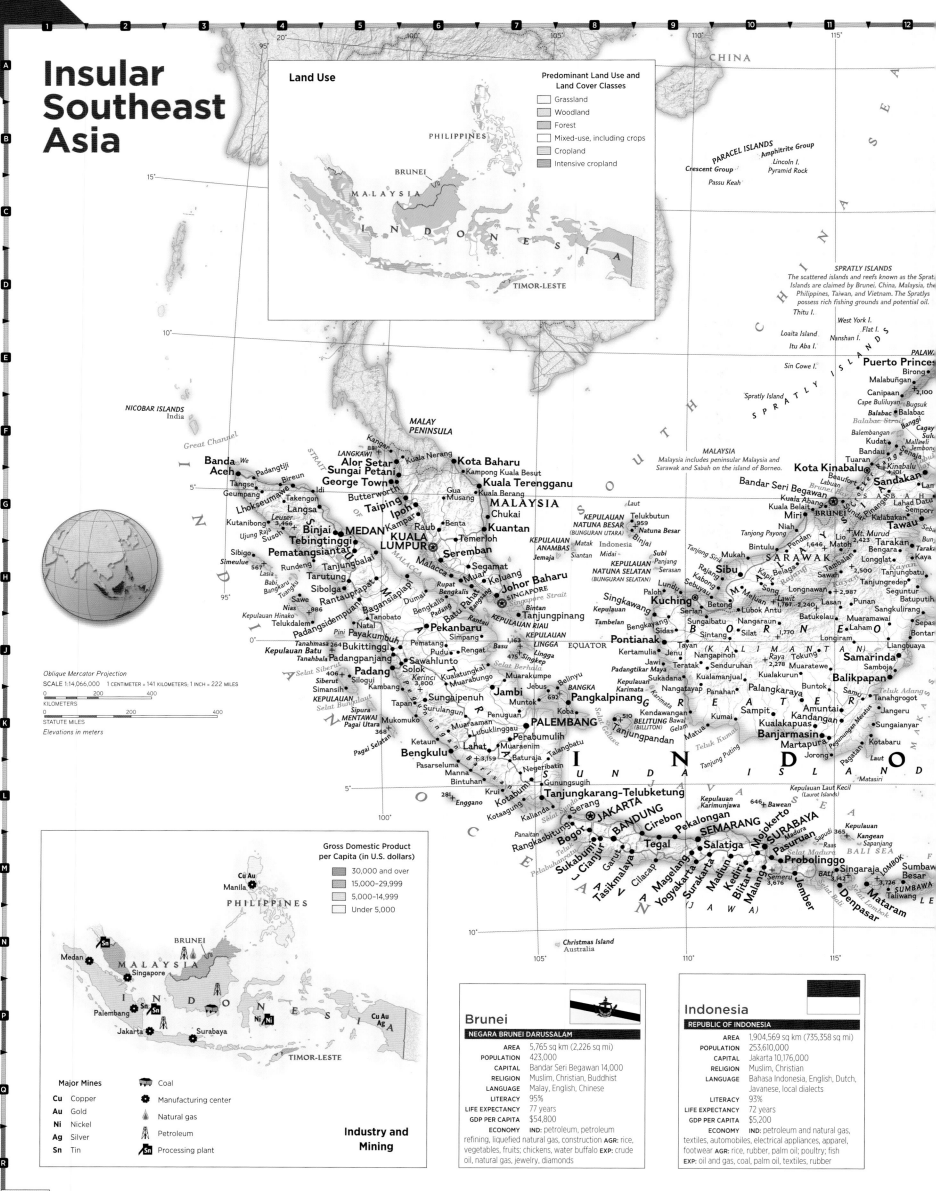

Land Use

Predominant Land Use and Land Cover Classes
- Grassland
- Woodland
- Forest
- Mixed-use, including crops
- Cropland
- Intensive cropland

SPRATLY ISLANDS
The scattered islands and reefs known as the Spratly Islands are claimed by Brunei, China, Malaysia, the Philippines, Taiwan, and Vietnam. The Spratlys possess rich fishing grounds and potential oil.

MALAYSIA
Malaysia includes peninsular Malaysia and Sarawak and Sabah on the island of Borneo.

Oblique Mercator Projection
SCALE 1:14,066,000   1 CENTIMETER = 141 KILOMETERS; 1 INCH = 222 MILES

KILOMETERS
0   200   400

STATUTE MILES
0   200   400

Elevations in meters

Gross Domestic Product per Capita (in U.S. dollars)
- 30,000 and over
- 15,000–29,999
- 5,000–14,999
- Under 5,000

Industry and Mining

Major Mines
- **Cu** Copper
- **Au** Gold
- **Ni** Nickel
- **Ag** Silver
- **Sn** Tin

- 🚃 Coal
- ✳ Manufacturing center
- 💧 Natural gas
- 🛢 Petroleum
- Sn Processing plant

Brunei

NEGARA BRUNEI DARUSSALAM
AREA	5,765 sq km (2,226 sq mi)
POPULATION	423,000
CAPITAL	Bandar Seri Begawan 14,000
RELIGION	Muslim, Christian, Buddhist
LANGUAGE	Malay, English, Chinese
LITERACY	95%
LIFE EXPECTANCY	77 years
GDP PER CAPITA	$54,800
ECONOMY	IND: petroleum, petroleum refining, liquefied natural gas, construction AGR: rice, vegetables, fruits; chickens, water buffalo EXP: crude oil, natural gas, jewelry, diamonds

Indonesia

REPUBLIC OF INDONESIA
AREA	1,904,569 sq km (735,358 sq mi)
POPULATION	253,610,000
CAPITAL	Jakarta 10,176,000
RELIGION	Muslim, Christian
LANGUAGE	Bahasa Indonesia, English, Dutch, Javanese, local dialects
LITERACY	93%
LIFE EXPECTANCY	72 years
GDP PER CAPITA	$5,200
ECONOMY	IND: petroleum and natural gas, textiles, automobiles, electrical appliances, apparel, footwear AGR: rice, rubber, palm oil; poultry; fish EXP: oil and gas, coal, palm oil, textiles, rubber

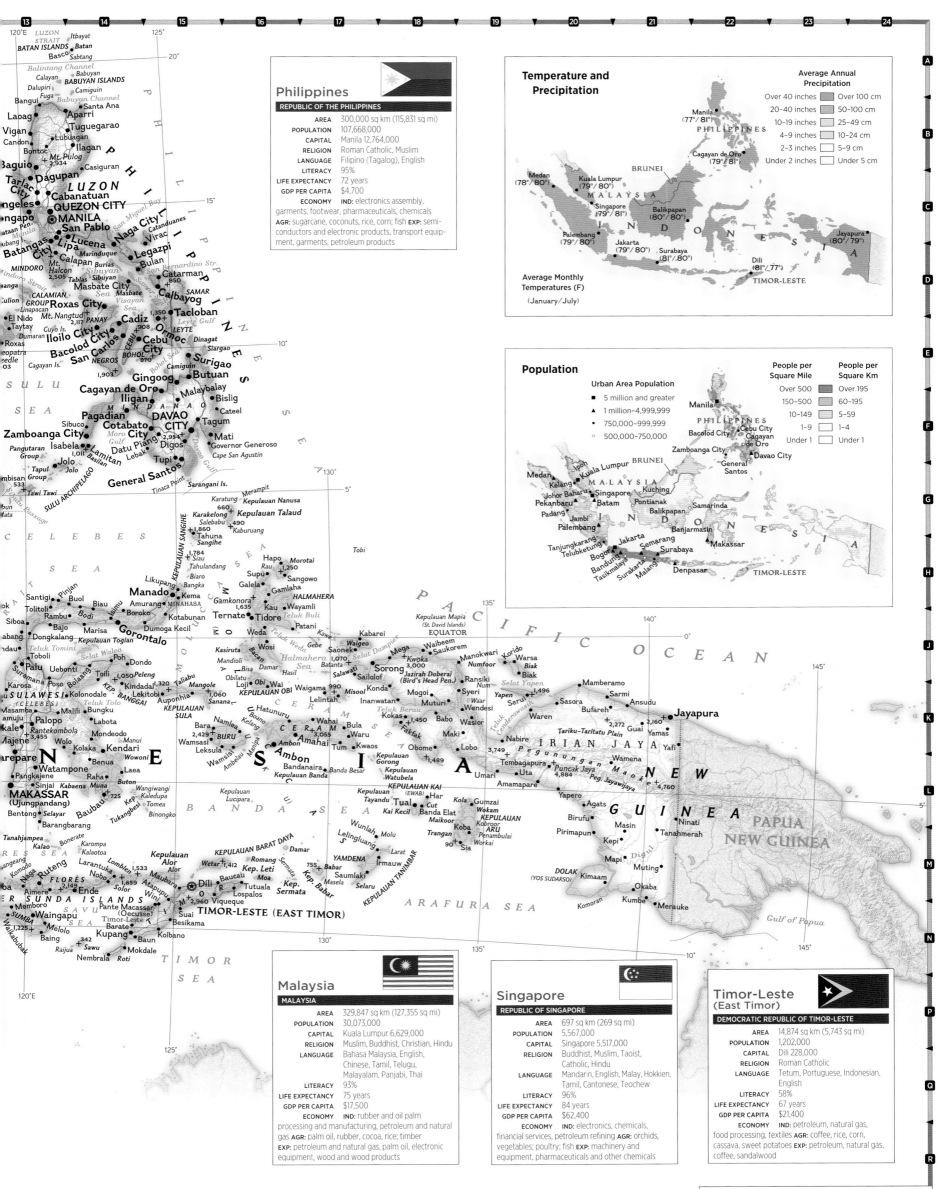

A lone African elephant drinks at a water hole in Chobe National Park, Botswana, where protected enclaves help support some 70,000 of the continent's 470,000 to 690,000 remaining elephants. In the late 1970s, Africa was home to 1.3 million elephants, but poaching and habitat loss have caused a precipitous decline.

Africa

Africa is often called the continent of beginnings. Fossil and bone records of the earliest hominids—humankind's ancestors—go back more than 4 million years here, and perhaps 200,000 years ago the earliest humans departed Africa on the long journey that eventually peopled the Earth. It now seems likely that every person today comes from a lineage that leads back to an ancient African. Innumerable cave paintings and petroglyphs, from the Sahara to South Africa, provide clues to the beliefs and ways of life of these prehistoric hominids.

Second largest continent after Asia, Africa accounts for a fifth of the world's land surface. Its unforgettable form, surrounded by oceans and seas, bulges to the west. Despite its size, Africa can be considered underpopulated, as it is home to only slightly more than 14 percent of the world population, or more than 1.1 billion people; some 60 percent live in the countryside, mostly in coastal regions, near lakes, and along river courses.

Africa

The mighty Sahara, largest hot desert in the world, covers more than a quarter of Africa's surface and divides the continent. Africa's desert zones—the Sahara, Kalahari, and Namib—contrast with immense tropical rain forests. Watered regions of lakes and rivers lie beyond the Sahel, a vast semiarid zone of short grasses that spans the continent south of the Sahara. Most of Africa is made up of savanna—high, rolling, grassy plains.

These savannas have been home since before recorded history to people often called Bantu, a reference to both social groupings and their languages. Other distinct physical types exist around the continent as well: BaMbuti (Pygmies), San (Bushmen), Nilo-Saharans, and Hamito-Semitics (Berbers and Cushites). Africa's astonishing number of spoken languages—2,100—reflects the great diversity of ethnic and social groups. Today, those groups reside in the continent's 54 different countries.

Near the Equator, perpetual ice and snow crown Mount Kilimanjaro, Africa's highest point at 19,340 feet (5,895 m). The Nile, longest river in the world at 4,400 miles (7,081 km), originates in mountains south of the Equator and flows north-northeast, delivering its life-giving waters before reaching the Nile Delta and emptying into the Mediterranean Sea.

Africa, blessed with wondrous deserts, rivers, grasslands, forests, and multihued earth, and possessing huge reserves of mineral wealth and biodiversity, waits expectantly for a prosperous future. Many obstacles, however, complicate the way forward. African countries experience great gaps in wealth between city and country, as is the case with Lagos and the rest of Nigeria or Cairo and most of Egypt.

Nearly 65 African cities have populations numbering more than a million. Lack of clean water and the spread of diseases—malaria, tuberculosis, cholera, Ebola, and AIDS among them—undermine health and with it, the prospects for a better livelihood. In addition, ongoing conflicts and huge concentrations of refugees displaced by fighting, persecution, famine, and drought deter growth and stability. Africa today seems to stand between hope and continued chaos.

PHYSICAL GEOGRAPHY Africa stretches an astounding 5,000 miles (8,047 km) from north to south and 4,600 miles (7,403 km) from east to west. The continent rises from generally narrow coastal strips to form a gigantic plateau, with portions over 2,000 feet (610 m) in height. It has limited harbors and a coastline with few bays and inlets. Though marked by a series of expansive uplands, Africa has few true mountain chains. The main ranges in the north are the Atlas in Morocco and the Ahaggar in Algeria. To the southeast, the Ethiopian Highlands form a broad area of high topography. The massive volcanic peaks of Mount Kilimanjaro and Mount Kenya rise in dramatic isolation from surrounding plains. Between Uganda and the Democratic Republic of the Congo, the Rwenzori Mountains run north to south and fall steeply in the west to the Rift Valley.

The East African Rift System is the continent's most dramatic geologic feature. This great rent actually begins in the Red Sea and then cuts southward to form the stunning landscape of lakes, volcanoes, and deep valleys that finally ends near the mouth of the Zambezi River in Mozambique. The Rift Valley, a region of active plate tectonics, marks the divide where East Africa is being pulled steadily away from the rest of Africa, eventually to become a mini-continent.

The Great Escarpment in southern Africa, a plateau edge that falls off to the coastal strip, is characterized by the stark, highly eroded Drakensberg mountains, which reach altitudes over 11,400 feet (3,482 m).

Madagascar, fourth largest island in the world, lies in the Indian Ocean east of the main continent and is remarkable for its flora and fauna, including medicinal plants and a number of lemur species.

Africa's great rivers include the Niger, Congo, and Zambezi, each regionally important for internal transport and fishing. The Nile drains 6 percent of the continent; its two main branches, the Blue Nile and the White Nile, meet at Khartoum, capital of Sudan.

Wildlife still abounds in eastern and southern Africa and supports ecotourism, but hundreds of plant and animal species live precariously close to extinction.

HISTORY After millions of years of human evolution, one of the first great civilizations, that of ancient Egypt, began to take root along the Nile. With its mastery of agriculture and knowledge of the river's annual flooding cycle, ancient Egypt lasted for some 3,000 years, under a series of dynasties that left an unprecedented legacy of tombs, statuary, pyramids, temples, and hieroglyphic writing.

Long-powerful Carthage, in present-day Tunisia, gripped the western Mediterranean from about 800 B.C. until it was conquered by Rome in 146 B.C. Rome and Byzantium henceforth controlled all of North Africa's coastal strip, until the Arab influx, which began in the seventh century. The Arabs quickly took all of North Africa and spread their language and religion, Islam. Trans-Sahara trade and contact converted many sub-Saharan people, such as the Hausa of Nigeria, to Islam.

Indigenous kingdoms have punctuated Africa's history. Finds from Great Zimbabwe, a massive fortress-city and inland empire that flourished from the 11th to 15th centuries in southern Africa, indicate contact with places as far away as India and China.

Along the Niger River, regional empires rose and fell between A.D. 800 and 1600. Slaves, ivory, gold, and kola nuts (used for flavoring and medicine) formed the basis of trade. In the Niger Delta area, Yoruba, Asante, and Hausa states also had their periods of grandness. Longest lasting of all was Benin, a major African kingdom that survived from the 13th to 19th centuries.

The Swahili (literally, "coastal plain") culture arose from a mix of Arabs, local people, and others. From A.D. 900 onward, it spread to the coastal towns and cities along the Indian Ocean, from Somalia to Zanzibar. The Swahili language remains a major lingua franca in east, central, and southern Africa.

Colonialism's long period of domination, during which Portugal, Great Britain, France, Belgium, Germany, the Netherlands, and Italy held sway over the continent, spans from the mid-1500s to the mid-1900s. The Portuguese arrived first in search of riches and a sea route to India. In time, commerce and Christianity pushed European culture deeper into Africa.

The terrible slave trade lasted centuries and shipped millions of Africans to North and South America and Arab regions. But the European presence also encouraged exploration and led to expeditions that traced the sources of Africa's main rivers and filled blank spots on the map.

In the late 19th century, Europe's powers embarked on a "scramble for Africa," which had led to a partitioning of the entire continent into colonies by 1914. After the two World Wars colonialism weakened. Independence for some countries began in the 1950s and came to most in the 1960s, in power transfers that ranged from peaceful (Ghana, Senegal) to bloody (Kenya, Algeria). Freedom arrived in Rhodesia, with the new name of Zimbabwe in 1980, and in Namibia in 1990. The end of white rule—and a virulent apartheid—in South Africa was marked by the election of Nelson Mandela in 1994.

CULTURE Hunting, fishing, and gathering supported Africa's early humans. In time, agriculture led to permanent settlements and the diversity of skills in societies, first along the Nile River and then in the south.

Village-based communities, resilient and lasting in their institutions, have formed the core of African life for thousands of years. With crop cultivation came domestication of animals—cattle, sheep, and goats. Ironworking reached sub-Saharan Africa from the north by about the fourth century B.C., allowing for new tools and weapons that accelerated change.

Kingdoms grew from the soil of village life. Kings and their courts resembled village elders in their roles as judges, mediators of disputes, and masters of trade. Early kingdoms in Mali, Ghana, and other parts of Africa conducted long-distance trade in gold, ivory, hides, jewels, feathers, and salt.

In some places, religious leaders became kings. Seen as divine, they assumed rights over land and cattle herds and in return took responsibility for the people's well-being.

Settled life allowed time and energy for arts, crafts, and other creative activities. In West Africa, artists, carvers, and bronze casters of the Ife (12th and 13th centuries) and Benin (16th and 17th centuries) kingdoms produced masterpieces in different mediums, culminating in terra-cotta heads and bronze statues and bas-reliefs of exquisite craftsmanship and naturalism. African art, especially sculpture, continues to hold a high place in world culture.

Rich traditions of oral narrative survive to preserve the history and collective memories of different tribes and groups. Bards known as griots tell tales and sing epic songs while playing their instruments.

Traditional religion and ritual still have a powerful place in Africa, ensuring health, wealth, and good harvests, and honoring the forces of nature. The Dogon people retain a complex cosmology and perform a great ceremony every 60 years to mark the appearance of the star Sirius between two mountains.

Most major world religions are represented in Africa: Islam, Christianity, Judaism, and Hinduism. Islam, which predominates in the north, claims 450 million followers, while Christianity, strongest south of the Sahara, has some 500 million African followers. In the region where followers of these two great belief systems come together, tension often leads to conflict.

European languages and schooling, legacies of colonialism, have had lasting effects on modern Africa. Yet far from the cities one can still find blue-turbaned Tuareg wandering the Sahara, slender Maasai on the savannas of East Africa, BaMbuti (Pygmies) in the rain forests, and San (Bushmen) living with the Kalahari Desert's harsh conditions.

ECONOMY Africa ranks among the richest regions in the world in natural resources; it contains vast reserves of fossil fuels, precious metals, ores, and gems, including oil, gold, platinum, chromium, cobalt, copper, coltan, uranium, and diamonds.

The magnificent 13th-century B.C. Temple of Ramses II at Abu Simbel is so revered that when the damming of the Nile at Aswan promised to submerge it, both it and the Temple of Nefertari (not shown in top image) were meticulously dismantled and reassembled (1964–68) on higher ground 600 feet (184 m) to the west. On the far side of the continent, the Nigerian capital of Lagos is a swirl of traffic, humanity, hope, and despair (above). More than 20 million people live within this vast and rapidly growing Atlantic coastal city, the largest in Africa and one of the largest in the world. While roughly two-thirds of them live in slums and dire poverty, better government is gradually improving life here.

Yet Africa ranks as the poorest continent, producing a mere 3.5 percent of the world's economic output. The economies of Nigeria and South Africa equal those of all other sub-Saharan countries combined.

About 65 percent of Africans work in agriculture, accounting for about a third of the continent's economy. Main crops are corn, wheat, rice, yams, potatoes, and cassava. Economic life revolves around farmsteads and village markets. Important cash crops include cacao, coffee, tea, fruit, and palm and vegetable oils. Much of the farmland is community- or state-owned, and many African governments sell or lease agricultural land to foreign corporations or governments. As an example, in 2009 Mozambique signed an agreement with Brazil and Japan to convert 35 million acres (14.16 million ha), including local farms, into large-scale soybean production.

Tourism, while offering hope to numerous countries—most in north, east, and southern Africa—highlights the need for conservation and interdependence among humans and the varied ecosystems that support Africa's plants and wildlife. Stresses today include poaching, overgrazing, and deforestation.

The African Union and numerous regional trading blocs try to encourage the economic cooperation and political stability essential for sustained growth. Economic growth remains promising as investments in education, energy, and health services (which have helped arrest the devastating effects of the HIV-AIDS epidemic) allow Africans to compete in the global economy.

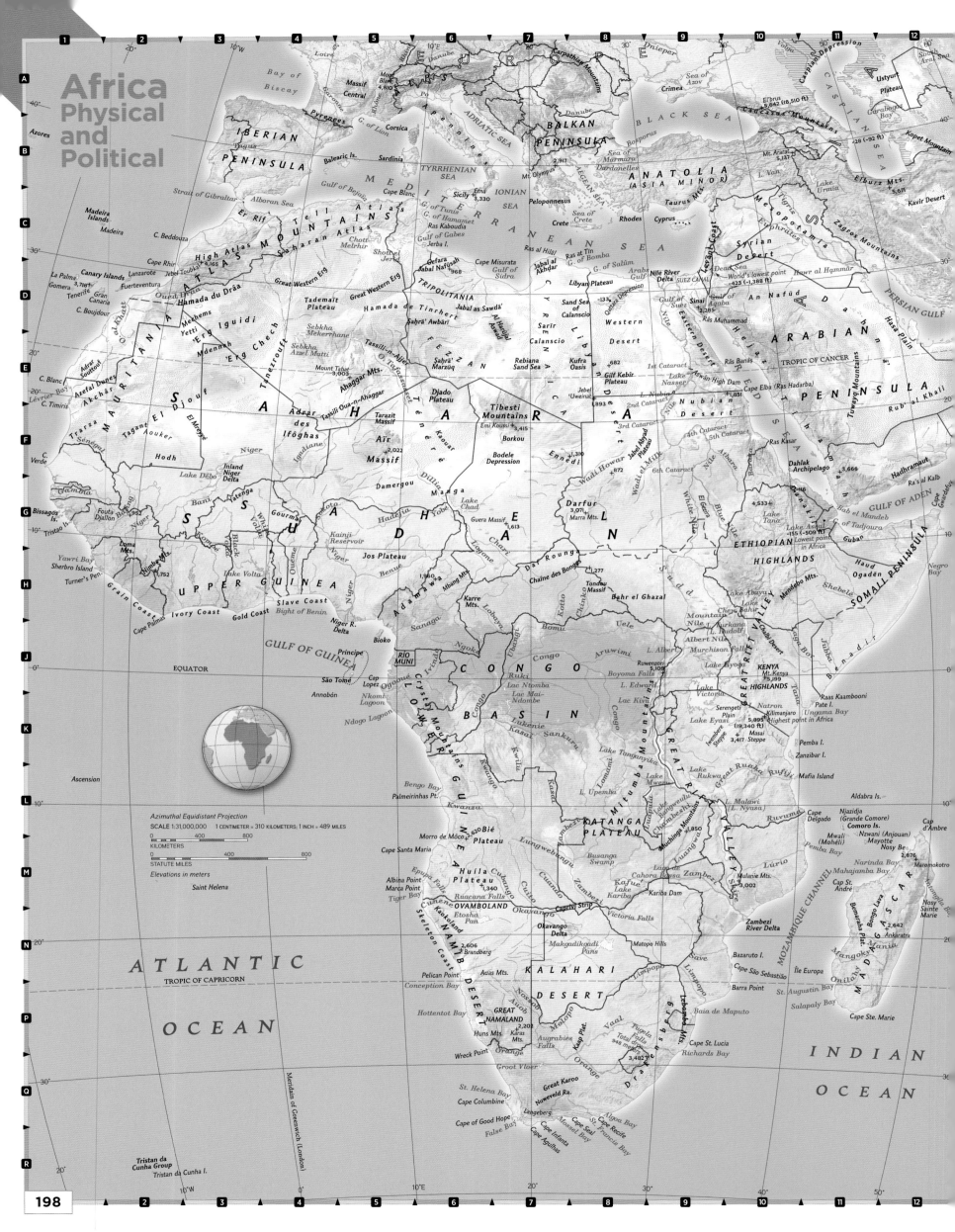

Africa
Physical
and
Political

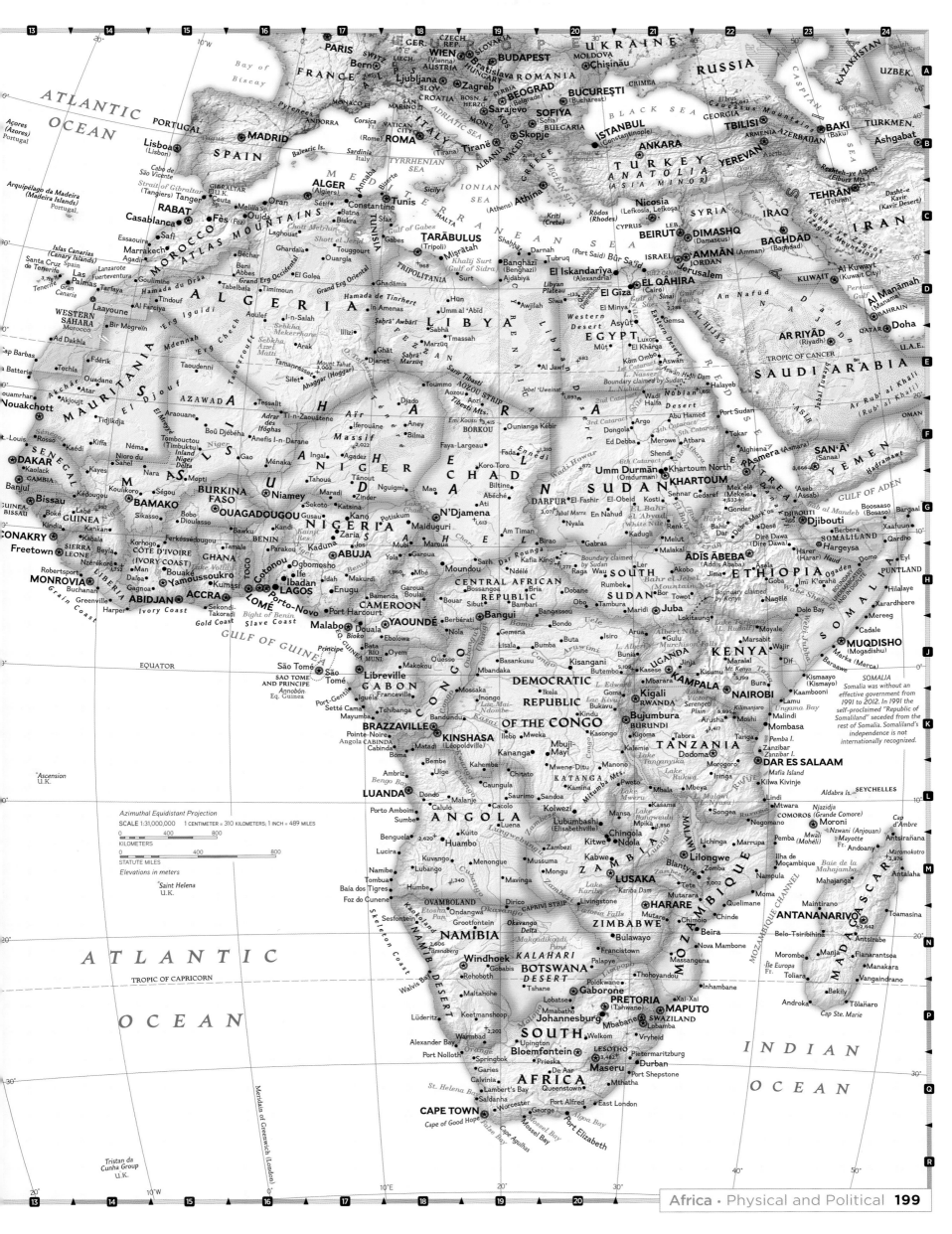

Northern Africa

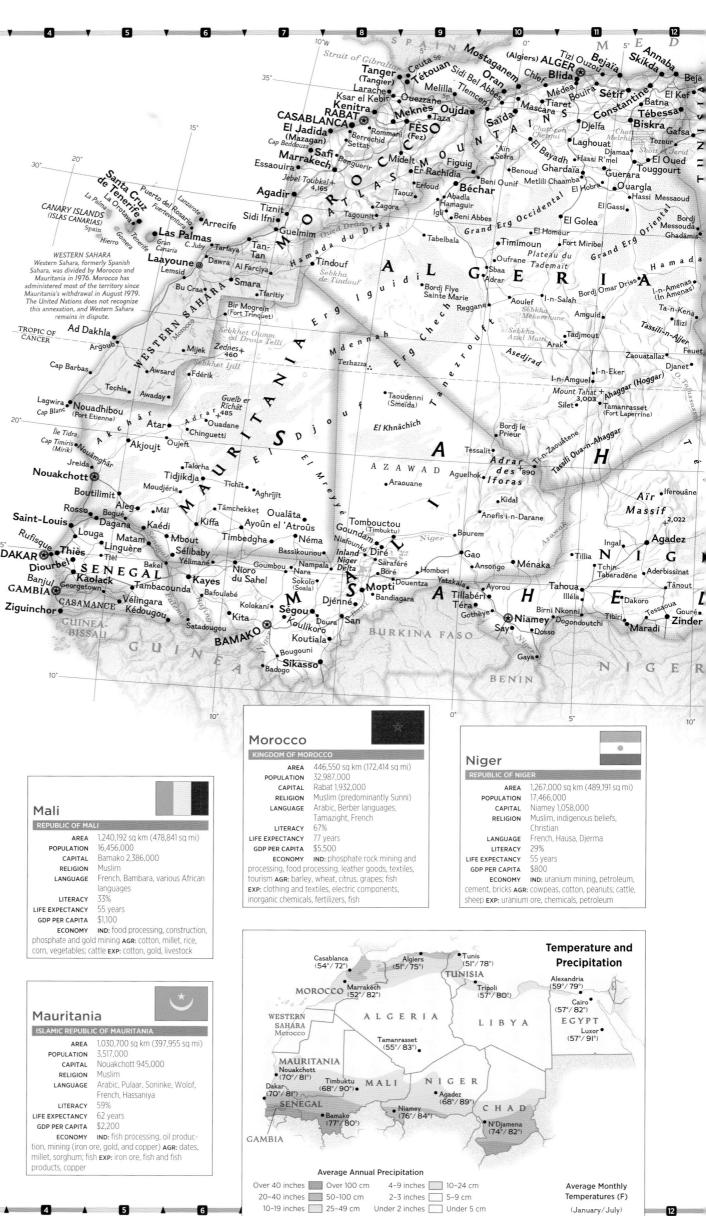

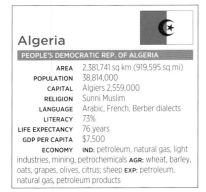

Algeria

PEOPLE'S DEMOCRATIC REP. OF ALGERIA

AREA	2,381,741 sq km (919,595 sq mi)
POPULATION	38,814,000
CAPITAL	Algiers 2,559,000
RELIGION	Sunni Muslim
LANGUAGE	Arabic, French, Berber dialects
LITERACY	73%
LIFE EXPECTANCY	76 years
GDP PER CAPITA	$7,500
ECONOMY	IND: petroleum, natural gas, light industries, mining, petrochemicals AGR: wheat, barley, oats, grapes, olives, citrus; sheep EXP: petroleum, natural gas, petroleum products

Chad

REPUBLIC OF CHAD

AREA	1,284,000 sq km (495,755 sq mi)
POPULATION	11,412,000
CAPITAL	N'Djamena 1,212,000
RELIGION	Muslim, Roman Catholic, Protestant, animist
LANGUAGE	French, Arabic, Sara, more than 120 languages and dialects
LITERACY	35%
LIFE EXPECTANCY	49 years
GDP PER CAPITA	$2,500
ECONOMY	IND: petroleum production and refining, textiles AGR: cotton, sorghum, millet; cattle EXP: crude and refined petroleum

Egypt

ARAB REPUBLIC OF EGYPT

AREA	1,001,450 sq km (386,662 sq mi)
POPULATION	86,895,000
CAPITAL	Cairo 18,419,000
RELIGION	Muslim (mostly Sunni), Coptic Christian
LANGUAGE	Arabic, English, French
LITERACY	74%
LIFE EXPECTANCY	73 years
GDP PER CAPITA	$6,600
ECONOMY	IND: textiles, food processing, tourism, petroleum AGR: cotton, rice, corn, wheat, fruits; cattle EXP: crude oil and petroleum products, cotton, textiles, metal products, chemicals, gold

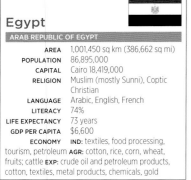

Gambia

REPUBLIC OF THE GAMBIA

AREA	11,295 sq km (4,361 sq mi)
POPULATION	1,926,000
CAPITAL	Banjul 489,000
RELIGION	Muslim, Christian
LANGUAGE	English, Mandinka, Wolof, Fula
LITERACY	51%
LIFE EXPECTANCY	64 years
GDP PER CAPITA	$2,000
ECONOMY	IND: processing peanuts, fish, and hides; tourism, beverages, agricultural machinery assembly AGR: rice, millet, sorghum, peanuts; cattle; fish EXP: peanut products, fish, lumber

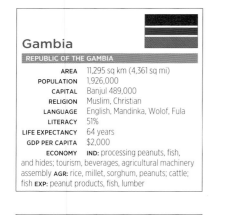

Libya

STATE OF LIBYA (provisional name)

AREA	1,759,540 sq km (679,362 sq mi)
POPULATION	6,244,000
CAPITAL	Tripoli 1,126,000
RELIGION	Sunni Muslim
LANGUAGE	Arabic, Italian, English, Berber
LITERACY	90%
LIFE EXPECTANCY	76 years
GDP PER CAPITA	$11,300
ECONOMY	IND: petroleum, natural gas, petrochemicals, food processing, textiles AGR: wheat, barley, olives, dates, citrus; cattle EXP: petroleum and petroleum products, natural gas, chemicals

Mali

REPUBLIC OF MALI

AREA	1,240,192 sq km (478,841 sq mi)
POPULATION	16,456,000
CAPITAL	Bamako 2,386,000
RELIGION	Muslim
LANGUAGE	French, Bambara, various African languages
LITERACY	33%
LIFE EXPECTANCY	55 years
GDP PER CAPITA	$1,100
ECONOMY	IND: food processing, construction, phosphate and gold mining AGR: cotton, millet, rice, corn, vegetables; cattle EXP: cotton, gold, livestock

Mauritania

ISLAMIC REPUBLIC OF MAURITANIA

AREA	1,030,700 sq km (397,955 sq mi)
POPULATION	3,517,000
CAPITAL	Nouakchott 945,000
RELIGION	Muslim
LANGUAGE	Arabic, Pulaar, Soninke, Wolof, French, Hassaniya
LITERACY	59%
LIFE EXPECTANCY	62 years
GDP PER CAPITA	$2,200
ECONOMY	IND: fish processing, oil production, mining (iron ore, gold, and copper) AGR: dates, millet, sorghum; fish EXP: iron ore, fish and fish products, copper

Morocco

KINGDOM OF MOROCCO

AREA	446,550 sq km (172,414 sq mi)
POPULATION	32,987,000
CAPITAL	Rabat 1,932,000
RELIGION	Muslim (predominantly Sunni)
LANGUAGE	Arabic, Berber languages, Tamazight, French
LITERACY	67%
LIFE EXPECTANCY	77 years
GDP PER CAPITA	$5,500
ECONOMY	IND: phosphate rock mining and processing, food processing, leather goods, textiles, tourism AGR: barley, wheat, citrus, grapes; fish EXP: clothing and textiles, electric components, inorganic chemicals, fertilizers, fish

Niger

REPUBLIC OF NIGER

AREA	1,267,000 sq km (489,191 sq mi)
POPULATION	17,466,000
CAPITAL	Niamey 1,058,000
RELIGION	Muslim, indigenous beliefs, Christian
LANGUAGE	French, Hausa, Djerma
LITERACY	29%
LIFE EXPECTANCY	55 years
GDP PER CAPITA	$800
ECONOMY	IND: uranium mining, petroleum, cement, bricks AGR: cowpeas, cotton, peanuts; cattle, sheep EXP: uranium ore, chemicals, petroleum

Temperature and Precipitation

Average Annual Precipitation

Over 40 inches	Over 100 cm	4-9 inches	10-24 cm		
20-40 inches	50-100 cm	2-3 inches	5-9 cm		
10-19 inches	25-49 cm	Under 2 inches	Under 5 cm		

Average Monthly Temperatures (F)
(January/July)

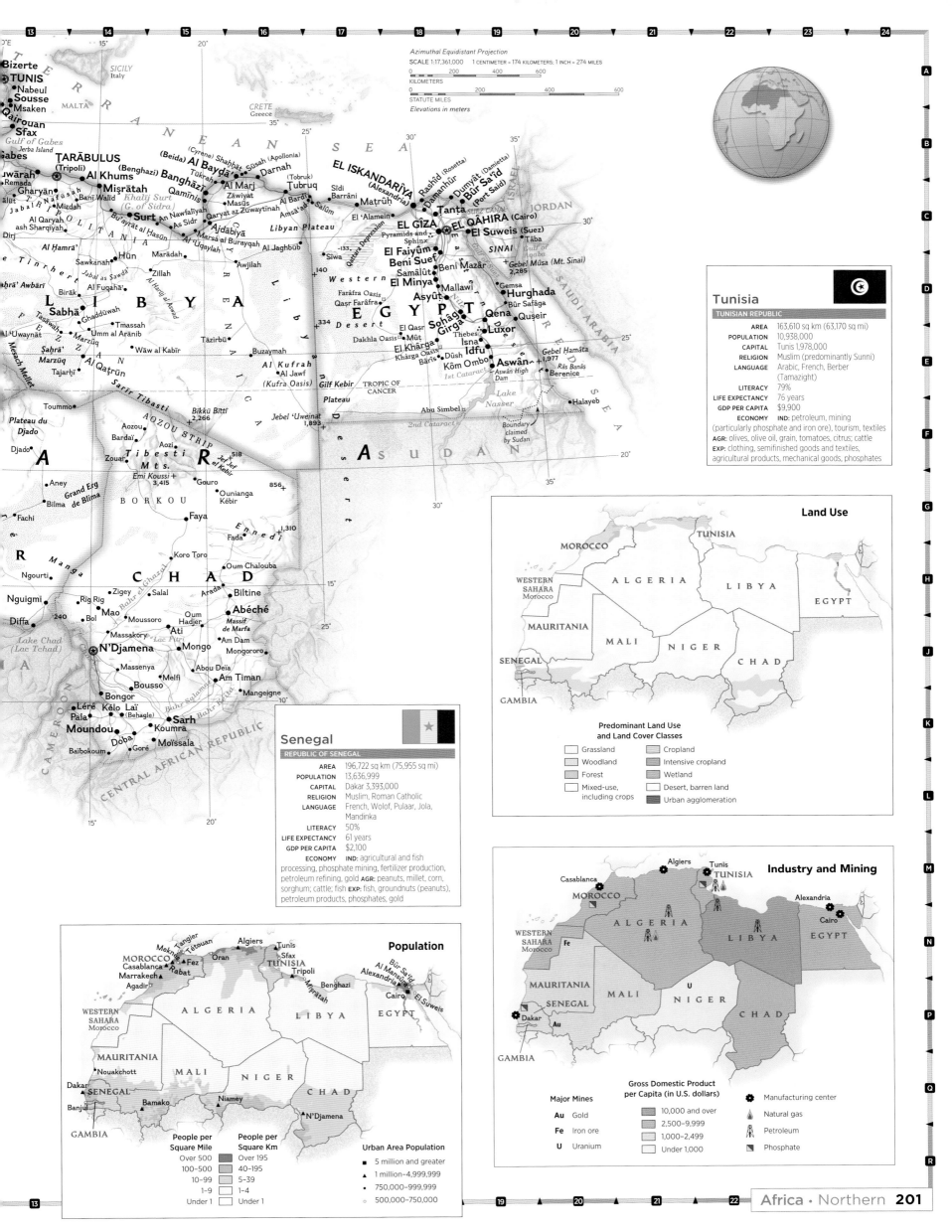

Azimuthal Equidistant Projection

SCALE 1:17,361,000   1 CENTIMETER = 174 KILOMETERS; 1 INCH = 274 MILES

KILOMETERS
0   200   400   600

STATUTE MILES
0   200   400   600

Elevations in meters

Tunisia
TUNISIAN REPUBLIC

AREA 163,610 sq km (63,170 sq mi)
POPULATION 10,938,000
CAPITAL Tunis 1,978,000
RELIGION Muslim (predominantly Sunni)
LANGUAGE Arabic, French, Berber (Tamazight)
LITERACY 79%
LIFE EXPECTANCY 76 years
GDP PER CAPITA $9,900
ECONOMY IND: petroleum, mining (particularly phosphate and iron ore), tourism, textiles AGR: olives, olive oil, grain, tomatoes, citrus; cattle EXP: clothing, semifinished goods and textiles, agricultural products, mechanical goods, phosphates

Senegal
REPUBLIC OF SENEGAL

AREA 196,722 sq km (75,955 sq mi)
POPULATION 13,636,999
CAPITAL Dakar 3,393,000
RELIGION Muslim, Roman Catholic
LANGUAGE French, Wolof, Pulaar, Jola, Mandinka
LITERACY 50%
LIFE EXPECTANCY 61 years
GDP PER CAPITA $2,100
ECONOMY IND: agricultural and fish processing, phosphate mining, fertilizer production, petroleum refining, gold AGR: peanuts, millet, corn, sorghum; cattle; fish EXP: fish, groundnuts (peanuts), petroleum products, phosphates, gold

Land Use

Predominant Land Use and Land Cover Classes

Grassland
Woodland
Forest
Mixed-use, including crops
Cropland
Intensive cropland
Wetland
Desert, barren land
Urban agglomeration

Population

People per Square Mile
Over 500
100–500
10–99
1–9
Under 1

People per Square Km
Over 195
40–195
5–39
1–4
Under 1

Urban Area Population
5 million and greater
1 million–4,999,999
750,000–999,999
500,000–750,000

Industry and Mining

Major Mines
Au Gold
Fe Iron ore
U Uranium

Gross Domestic Product per Capita (in U.S. dollars)
10,000 and over
2,500–9,999
1,000–2,499
Under 1,000

Manufacturing center
Natural gas
Petroleum
Phosphate

Eastern Africa

Burundi
REPUBLIC OF BURUNDI
AREA	27,830 sq km (10,745 sq mi)
POPULATION	10,396,000
CAPITAL	Bujumbura 707,000
RELIGION	Roman Catholic, Protestant
LANGUAGE	Kirundi, French
LITERACY	67%
LIFE EXPECTANCY	60 years
GDP PER CAPITA	$600
ECONOMY	IND: light consumer goods such as blankets, shoes, soap, and beer; assembly of imported components, mining, food processing AGR: coffee, cotton, tea, corn, sorghum, sweet potatoes; beef EXP: gold, coffee, tea, sugar, cotton, hides

Central African Republic
CENTRAL AFRICAN REPUBLIC
AREA	622,984 sq km (240,535 sq mi)
POPULATION	5,278,000
CAPITAL	Bangui 781,000
RELIGION	indigenous beliefs, Protestant, Roman Catholic, Muslim
LANGUAGE	French, Sangho, tribal languages
LITERACY	57%
LIFE EXPECTANCY	51 years
GDP PER CAPITA	$700
ECONOMY	IND: gold and diamond mining, logging, brewing, textiles AGR: cotton, coffee, tobacco, cassava (manioc); timber EXP: timber, cotton, coffee, gold

Congo, Democratic Republic of the
DEMOCRATIC REPUBLIC OF THE CONGO
AREA	2,344,858 sq km (905,354 sq mi)
POPULATION	77,434,000
CAPITAL	Kinshasa 11,116,000
RELIGION	Roman Catholic, Protestant, Kimbanguist, Muslim
LANGUAGE	French, Lingala, Kingwana, Kikongo, Tshiluba
LITERACY	67%
LIFE EXPECTANCY	57 years
GDP PER CAPITA	$400
ECONOMY	IND: mining (copper, cobalt, gold, diamonds, coltan, zinc, tin, tungsten) AGR: coffee, sugar, palm oil; timber EXP: diamonds, copper, cobalt, crude oil

Djibouti
REPUBLIC OF DJIBOUTI
AREA	23,200 sq km (8,958 sq mi)
POPULATION	810,000
CAPITAL	Djibouti 522,000
RELIGION	Muslim, Christian
LANGUAGE	French, Arabic, Somali, Afar
LITERACY	68%
LIFE EXPECTANCY	62 years
GDP PER CAPITA	$2,700
ECONOMY	IND: construction, agricultural processing AGR: fruits, vegetables; goats, sheep, camels, animal hides EXP: reexports, hides and skins, coffee (in transit)

Eritrea
STATE OF ERITREA
AREA	117,600 sq km (45,406 sq mi)
POPULATION	6,381,000
CAPITAL	Asmara 775,000
RELIGION	Muslim, Coptic Christian, Roman Catholic, Protestant
LANGUAGE	Tigrinya, Arabic, English, Tigre, Kunama, Afar
LITERACY	69%
LIFE EXPECTANCY	64 years
GDP PER CAPITA	$1,200
ECONOMY	IND: food processing, beverages, clothing and textiles, light manufacturing, mining AGR: sorghum, lentils, vegetables, corn; livestock EXP: gold, livestock, sorghum, textiles

Ethiopia
FEDERAL DEMOCRATIC REP. OF ETHIOPIA
AREA	1,104,300 sq km (426,372 sq mi)
POPULATION	96,633,000
CAPITAL	Addis Ababa 3,168,000
RELIGION	Ethiopian Orthodox, Muslim, Protestant
LANGUAGE	Oromo, Amharic, Somali, Tigrigna, Sidamo, Wolaytta, Gurage
LITERACY	39%
LIFE EXPECTANCY	61 years
GDP PER CAPITA	$1,300
ECONOMY	IND: food processing, beverages, textiles, leather, chemicals AGR: cereals, pulses, coffee, oilseeds; cattle, sheep EXP: coffee, qat, gold, leather products, live animals, oilseeds

Kenya
REPUBLIC OF KENYA
AREA	580,367 sq km (224,081 sq mi)
POPULATION	45,010,000
CAPITAL	Nairobi 3,768,000
RELIGION	Protestant, Roman Catholic, Muslim
LANGUAGE	English, Kiswahili, indigenous languages
LITERACY	87%
LIFE EXPECTANCY	64 years
GDP PER CAPITA	$1,800
ECONOMY	IND: small-scale consumer goods, agricultural products, horticulture, oil refining, tourism AGR: tea, coffee, corn, wheat, sugarcane, fruit, vegetables EXP: tea, horticultural products, coffee, petroleum products, fish, garments

Rwanda
REPUBLIC OF RWANDA
AREA	26,338 sq km (10,169 sq mi)
POPULATION	12,337,000
CAPITAL	Kigali 1,223,000
RELIGION	Roman Catholic, Protestant
LANGUAGE	Kinyarwanda
LITERACY	71%
LIFE EXPECTANCY	59 years
GDP PER CAPITA	$1,500
ECONOMY	IND: mining, agricultural products, small-scale beverages, soap AGR: coffee, tea, pyrethrum (insecticide made from chrysanthemums), bananas EXP: coffee, tea, hides, tin ore

Temperature and Precipitation

Average Monthly Temperatures (F)
(January/July)

Average Annual Precipitation

Over 40 inches		Over 100 cm	
20–40 inches		50–100 cm	
10–19 inches		25–49 cm	
4–9 inches		10–24 cm	
2–3 inches		5–9 cm	
Under 2 inches		Under 5 cm	

SUDAN
Khartoum (73°/89°)
ERITREA
Asmara (57°/62°) DJIBOUTI
Addis Ababa (61°/60°) Djibouti (77°/95°)
CENTRAL AFRICAN REPUBLIC
Bangui (78°/77°)
SOUTH SUDAN
Juba (83°/78°)
Kisangani (77°/75°)
ETHIOPIA
SOMALIA
UGANDA Kampala (72°/68°)
KENYA
Nairobi (67°/62°)
Mogadishu (80°/79°)
RWANDA
Bujumbura (74°/73°)
DEM. REPUBLIC OF THE CONGO
Kinshasa (77°/71°)
BURUNDI
TANZANIA
Dar es Salaam (81°/74°)
Lubumbashi (69°/64°)

Azimuthal Equidistant Projection
SCALE 1:17,741,000   1 CENTIMETER = 177 KILOMETERS; 1 INCH = 280 MILES
KILOMETERS
STATUTE MILES
Elevations in meters

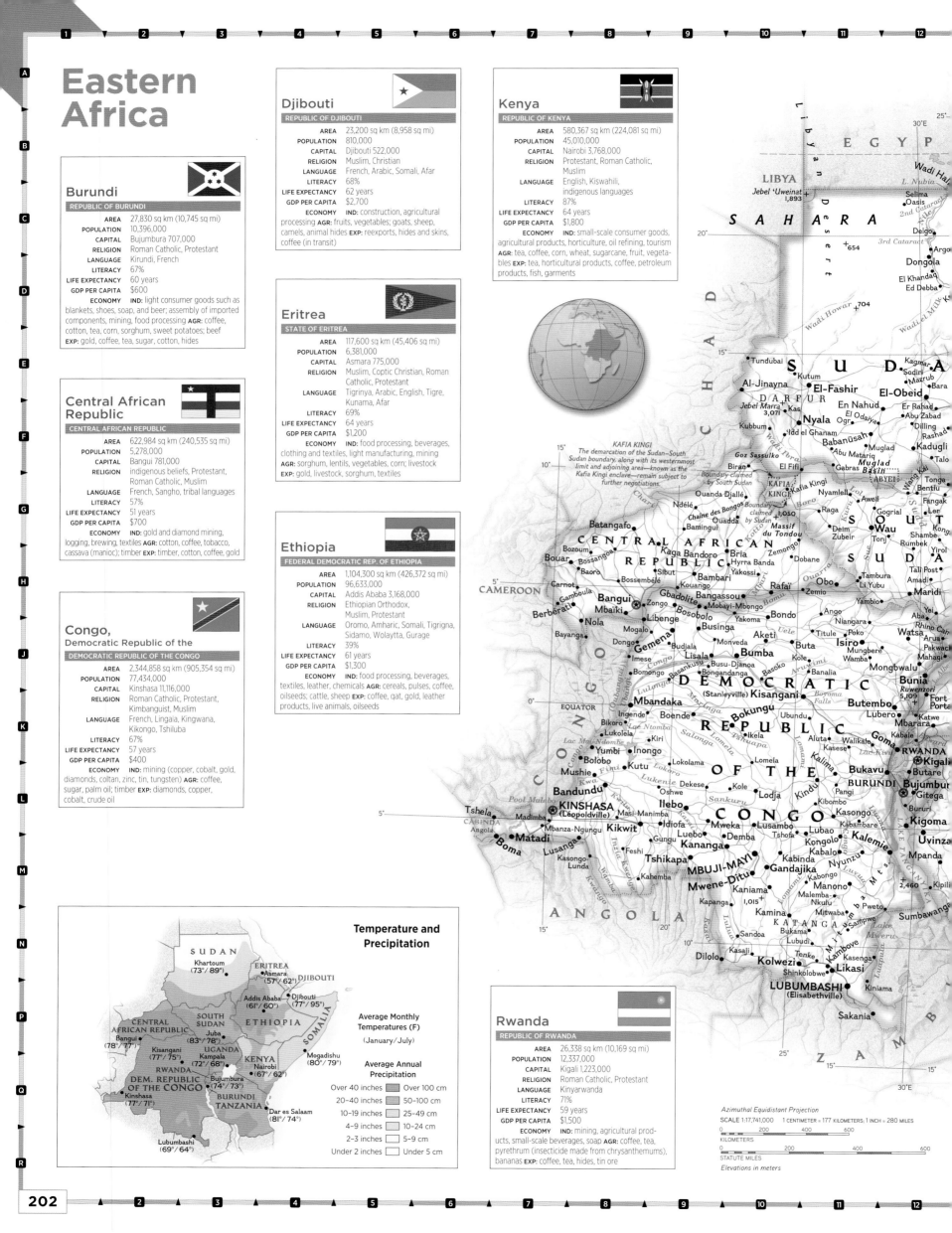

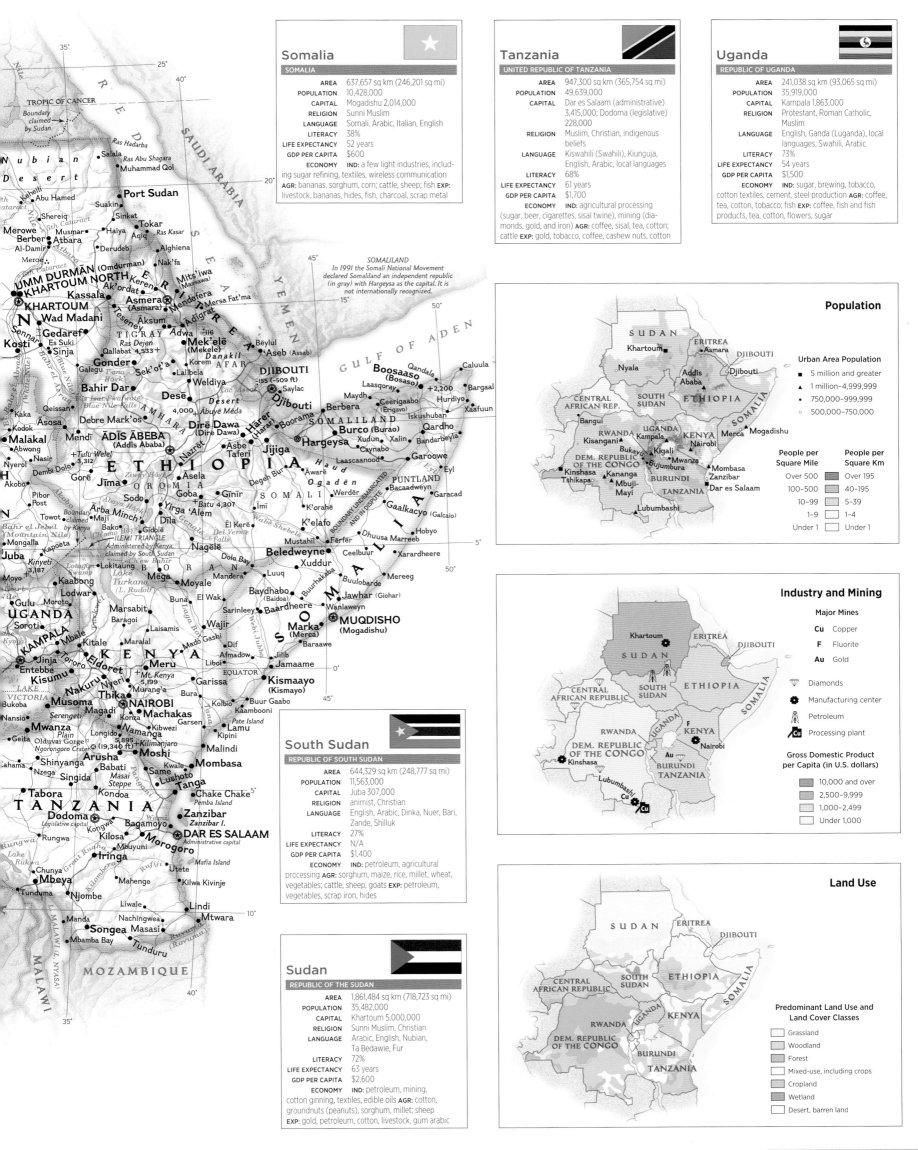

Somalia
SOMALIA

AREA	637,657 sq km (246,201 sq mi)
POPULATION	10,428,000
CAPITAL	Mogadishu 2,014,000
RELIGION	Sunni Muslim
LANGUAGE	Somali, Arabic, Italian, English
LITERACY	38%
LIFE EXPECTANCY	52 years
GDP PER CAPITA	$600
ECONOMY	IND: a few light industries, including sugar refining, textiles, wireless communication AGR: bananas, sorghum, corn; cattle, sheep; fish EXP: livestock, bananas, hides, fish, charcoal, scrap metal

Tanzania
UNITED REPUBLIC OF TANZANIA

AREA	947,300 sq km (365,754 sq mi)
POPULATION	49,639,000
CAPITAL	Dar es Salaam (administrative) 3,415,000; Dodoma (legislative) 228,000
RELIGION	Muslim, Christian, indigenous beliefs
LANGUAGE	Kiswahili (Swahili), Kiunguja, English, Arabic, local languages
LITERACY	68%
LIFE EXPECTANCY	61 years
GDP PER CAPITA	$1,700
ECONOMY	IND: agricultural processing (sugar, beer, cigarettes, sisal twine); mining (diamonds, gold, and iron) AGR: coffee, sisal, tea, cotton; cattle EXP: gold, tobacco, coffee, cashew nuts, cotton

Uganda
REPUBLIC OF UGANDA

AREA	241,038 sq km (93,065 sq mi)
POPULATION	35,919,000
CAPITAL	Kampala 1,863,000
RELIGION	Protestant, Roman Catholic, Muslim
LANGUAGE	English, Ganda (Luganda), local languages, Swahili, Arabic
LITERACY	73%
LIFE EXPECTANCY	54 years
GDP PER CAPITA	$1,500
ECONOMY	IND: sugar, brewing, tobacco, cotton textiles, cement, steel production AGR: coffee, tea, cotton, tobacco; fish EXP: coffee, fish and fish products, tea, cotton, flowers, sugar

South Sudan
REPUBLIC OF SOUTH SUDAN

AREA	644,329 sq km (248,777 sq mi)
POPULATION	11,563,000
CAPITAL	Juba 307,000
RELIGION	animist, Christian
LANGUAGE	English, Arabic, Dinka, Nuer, Bari, Zande, Shilluk
LITERACY	27%
LIFE EXPECTANCY	N/A
GDP PER CAPITA	$1,400
ECONOMY	IND: petroleum, agricultural processing AGR: sorghum, maize, rice, millet, wheat, vegetables; cattle, sheep, goats EXP: petroleum, vegetables, scrap iron, hides

Sudan
REPUBLIC OF THE SUDAN

AREA	1,861,484 sq km (718,723 sq mi)
POPULATION	35,482,000
CAPITAL	Khartoum 5,000,000
RELIGION	Sunni Muslim, Christian
LANGUAGE	Arabic, English, Nubian, Ta Bedawie, Fur
LITERACY	72%
LIFE EXPECTANCY	63 years
GDP PER CAPITA	$2,600
ECONOMY	IND: petroleum, mining, cotton ginning, textiles, edible oils AGR: cotton, groundnuts (peanuts), sorghum, millet; sheep EXP: gold, petroleum, cotton, livestock, gum arabic

SOMALILAND
In 1991 the Somali National Movement declared Somaliland an independent republic (in gray) with Hargeysa as the capital. It is not internationally recognized.

Population

Urban Area Population
- ■ 5 million and greater
- ▲ 1 million–4,999,999
- ● 750,000–999,999
- ○ 500,000–750,000

People per Square Mile	People per Square Km
Over 500	Over 195
100–500	40–195
10–99	5–39
1–9	1–4
Under 1	Under 1

Industry and Mining

Major Mines
- Cu Copper
- F Fluorite
- Au Gold

- ▽ Diamonds
- ✿ Manufacturing center
- ⛏ Petroleum
- Cu Processing plant

Gross Domestic Product per Capita (in U.S. dollars)
- 10,000 and over
- 2,500–9,999
- 1,000–2,499
- Under 1,000

Land Use

Predominant Land Use and Land Cover Classes
- Grassland
- Woodland
- Forest
- Mixed-use, including crops
- Cropland
- Wetland
- Desert, barren land

Map of West Central Africa

Benin
REPUBLIC OF BENIN
AREA	112,622 sq km (43,484 sq mi)
POPULATION	10,161,000
CAPITAL	Porto-Novo (constitutional) 680,000; Cotonou (seat of government) 268,000
RELIGION	Roman Catholic, Muslim, Vodoun, Protestant
LANGUAGE	French, Fon, Yoruba, tribal languages
LITERACY	42%
LIFE EXPECTANCY	61 years
GDP PER CAPITA	$1,600
ECONOMY	IND: textiles, food processing, metals, timber AGR: cotton, corn, cassava (manioc), yams, nuts EXP: gold, cotton, cashews, shea butter, textiles, wood

Burkina Faso
BURKINA FASO
AREA	274,200 sq km (105,869 sq mi)
POPULATION	18,365,000
CAPITAL	Ouagadougou 2,565,000
RELIGION	Muslim, Catholic, animist
LANGUAGE	French, other African languages
LITERACY	29%
LIFE EXPECTANCY	55 years
GDP PER CAPITA	$1,500
ECONOMY	IND: cotton, beverages, agricultural processing, gold AGR: cotton, peanuts, shea nuts, sesame; livestock EXP: gold, cotton, livestock

Cameroon
REPUBLIC OF CAMEROON
AREA	475,440 sq km (183,568 sq mi)
POPULATION	23,131,000
CAPITAL	Yaoundé 2,930,000
RELIGION	indigenous beliefs, Christian, Muslim
LANGUAGE	various African languages, English, French
LITERACY	71%
LIFE EXPECTANCY	57 years
GDP PER CAPITA	$2,400
ECONOMY	IND: petroleum production and refining, aluminum production, food processing, lumber AGR: coffee, cocoa, cotton, rubber, bananas; timber EXP: crude oil and petroleum products, lumber, cocoa beans, bananas

Côte d'Ivoire
(Ivory Coast)
REPUBLIC OF CÔTE D'IVOIRE
AREA	322,463 sq km (124,504 sq mi)
POPULATION	22,849,000
CAPITAL	Abidjan (administrative) 4,708,000; Yamoussoukro (legislative) 259,000
RELIGION	Muslim, Christian, indigenous beliefs
LANGUAGE	French, Dioula, native dialects
LITERACY	57%
LIFE EXPECTANCY	58 years
GDP PER CAPITA	$1,800
ECONOMY	IND: foodstuffs, beverages, wood products, petroleum, gold mining AGR: coffee, cocoa beans, bananas, palm kernels; timber EXP: cocoa, coffee, petroleum, cotton, gold

Equatorial Guinea
REPUBLIC OF EQUATORIAL GUINEA
AREA	28,051 sq km (10,831 sq mi)
POPULATION	722,000
CAPITAL	Malabo 145,000
RELIGION	Roman Catholic, pagan practices
LANGUAGE	Spanish, French, Fang, Bubi
LITERACY	94%
LIFE EXPECTANCY	63 years
GDP PER CAPITA	$25,700
ECONOMY	IND: petroleum, natural gas, sawmilling AGR: coffee, cocoa, rice, yams; livestock; timber EXP: petroleum products, timber

Ghana
REPUBLIC OF GHANA
AREA	238,533 sq km (92,098 sq mi)
POPULATION	25,758,000
CAPITAL	Accra 2,242,000
RELIGION	Christian, Muslim, traditional
LANGUAGE	Asante, Ewe, Fante, Boron (Brong), Dagomba, Dangme, Dagarte (Dagaba), Akyem, Ga, Akuapem, English
LITERACY	72%
LIFE EXPECTANCY	66 years
GDP PER CAPITA	$3,500
ECONOMY	IND: mining, petroleum, lumbering, light manufacturing, food processing AGR: cocoa, rice, coffee, peanuts; timber; fish EXP: gold, cocoa, petroleum, timber, fish

Guinea
REPUBLIC OF GUINEA
AREA	245,857 sq km (94,926 sq mi)
POPULATION	11,474,000
CAPITAL	Conakry 1,886,000
RELIGION	Muslim, Christian, indigenous beliefs
LANGUAGE	French, African languages
LITERACY	41%
LIFE EXPECTANCY	60 years
GDP PER CAPITA	$1,100
ECONOMY	IND: bauxite, gold, diamonds, iron, alumina refining, light manufacturing AGR: rice, coffee, pineapples, palm kernels; fish; timber EXP: bauxite, alumina, gold, diamonds, coffee, fish

Liberia
REPUBLIC OF LIBERIA
AREA	111,369 sq km (43,000 sq mi)
POPULATION	4,092,000
CAPITAL	Monrovia 1,224,000
RELIGION	Christian, Muslim
LANGUAGE	English, ethnic group languages
LITERACY	61%
LIFE EXPECTANCY	58 years
GDP PER CAPITA	$700
ECONOMY	IND: mining (iron ore), rubber processing, timber, diamonds AGR: rubber, coffee, cocoa, rice; sheep, goats; timber EXP: rubber, timber, iron, diamonds, cocoa, petroleum

Congo
REPUBLIC OF THE CONGO
AREA	342,000 sq km (132,047 sq mi)
POPULATION	4,662,000
CAPITAL	Brazzaville 1,827,000
RELIGION	Roman Catholic, Awakening Churches, Protestant
LANGUAGE	French, Lingala, Monokutuba, Kikongo, local languages
LITERACY	84%
LIFE EXPECTANCY	59 years
GDP PER CAPITA	$4,800
ECONOMY	IND: petroleum, natural gas, lumber AGR: cassava (manioc, tapioca), sugar; forest products EXP: petroleum, natural gas, lumber, plywood, sugar, cocoa

Gabon
GABONESE REPUBLIC
AREA	267,667 sq km (103,347 sq mi)
POPULATION	1,673,000
CAPITAL	Libreville 695,000
RELIGION	Christian, animist
LANGUAGE	French, Fang, Myene, Nzebi, Bapounou/Eschira, Bandjabi
LITERACY	89%
LIFE EXPECTANCY	52 years
GDP PER CAPITA	$19,200
ECONOMY	IND: petroleum extraction and refining, manganese, gold, chemicals, ship repair AGR: cocoa, coffee, sugar, palm oil; cattle, okoume (a tropical softwood); fish EXP: petroleum, timber, manganese, rubber

Guinea-Bissau
REPUBLIC OF GUINEA-BISSAU
AREA	36,125 sq km (13,948 sq mi)
POPULATION	1,693,000
CAPITAL	Bissau 473,000
RELIGION	Muslim, indigenous beliefs, Christian
LANGUAGE	Portuguese, Crioulo, African languages
LITERACY	55%
LIFE EXPECTANCY	50 years
GDP PER CAPITA	$1,200
ECONOMY	IND: agricultural products processing, beer, soft drinks AGR: rice, corn, cashew nuts, peanuts; timber; fish EXP: cashew nuts, fish, peanuts, lumber, rubber

Nigeria
FEDERAL REPUBLIC OF NIGERIA
AREA	923,768 sq km (356,669 sq mi)
POPULATION	177,156,000
CAPITAL	Abuja 2,301,000
RELIGION	Muslim, Christian, indigenous beliefs
LANGUAGE	English, Hausa, Yoruba, Igbo (Ibo), Fulani, indigenous languages
LITERACY	61%
LIFE EXPECTANCY	53 years
GDP PER CAPITA	$2,800
ECONOMY	IND: petroleum production and refining, natural gas, rubber products, food products AGR: cocoa, peanuts, cotton, rubber; fish EXP: petroleum and petroleum products, cocoa, rubber

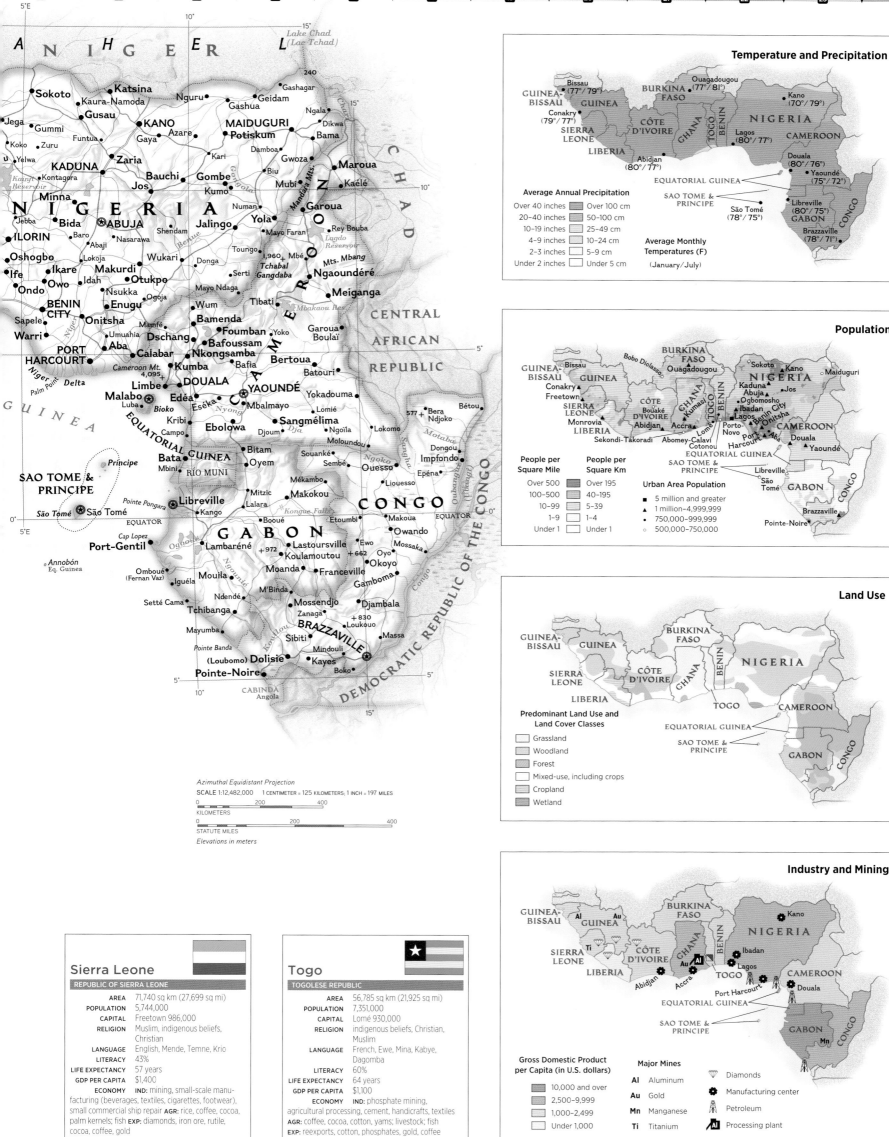

Main Map

NIGER

Lake Chad (Lac Tchad)

Sokoto Katsina Nguru Gashagar Gashua Ngala Dikwa
Kaura-Namoda Gusau Geidam
Jega Gummi Zuru KANO Gaya Azare Potiskum MAIDUGURI Bama
Koko Funtua Kari Damboa Gwoza
Yelwa Kontagora Zaria Bauchi Gombe Kumo Mubi Maroua
KADUNA Jos Biu Kaélé
Minna Numan Garoua
Jebba Bida ABUJA Nasarawa Jalingo Yola Rey Bouba Mandara Mts.
ILORIN Baro Abaji Shendam Mayo Faran 1,960 + Mbé Mts. Mbang
Oshogbo Lokoja Wukari Toungo Tchabal Gangdaba Ngaoundéré
Ife Ikare Makurdi Otukpo Donga Mayo Ndaga Serti Meiganga
Ondo Idah Nsukka Ogoja Wum Tibati
BENIN CITY Enugu Bamenda Foumban Yoko Garoua Boulaï
Sapele Owo Umuahia Dschang Mamfé Mbakaou Res.
Warri Onitsha Bafoussam CENTRAL
Aba Calabar Nkongsamba Bafia Bertoua AFRICAN
PORT HARCOURT Kumba DOUALA Batouri REPUBLIC
Cameroon Mt. 4,095 + Edéa YAOUNDÉ Yokadouma
Malabo Limbe Eséka Nyong Bétou
Luba Bioko Kribi Mbalmayo 577 + Bera Ndjoko
EQUATORIAL GUINEA Campo Ebolowa Sangmélima Lomié Lokomo
GUINEA Djoum Ngoïla Moloundou
SAO TOME & PRINCIPE Bata Bitam Souanké Sembé Ouesso Impfondo
Príncipe Mbini RÍO MUNI Oyem Mékambo Liouesso Epéna Dongou
São Tomé São Tomé Mitzic Makokou
EQUATOR Pointe Pongara Libreville Lalara Kongou Falls CONGO
Cap Lopez Kango Booué Etoumbi Makoua EQUATOR
Port-Gentil Lambaréné + 972 Koulamoutou + 662 Ewo Owando
Annobón Eq. Guinea Omboué (Fernan Vaz) Moanda Oyo Mossaka
Iguéla Mouila Franceville Okoyo Gamboma
Setté Cama Ndendé Lastoursville M'Binda + 830 Djambala
Tchibanga Mossendjo Zanaga Loukouo Massa
Mayumba Sibiti BRAZZAVILLE
Pointe Banda Dolisie Mindouli Kayes Boko
(Loubomo) Pointe-Noire DEMOCRATIC REPUBLIC OF THE CONGO
CABINDA Angola

GABON CAMEROON

Azimuthal Equidistant Projection
SCALE 1:12,482,000   1 CENTIMETER = 125 KILOMETERS; 1 INCH = 197 MILES
0 ... 200 ... 400 KILOMETERS
0 ... 200 ... 400 STATUTE MILES
Elevations in meters

Sierra Leone (flag)

REPUBLIC OF SIERRA LEONE
AREA 71,740 sq km (27,699 sq mi)
POPULATION 5,744,000
CAPITAL Freetown 986,000
RELIGION Muslim, indigenous beliefs, Christian
LANGUAGE English, Mende, Temne, Krio
LITERACY 43%
LIFE EXPECTANCY 57 years
GDP PER CAPITA $1,400
ECONOMY IND: mining, small-scale manufacturing (beverages, textiles, cigarettes, footwear), small commercial ship repair AGR: rice, coffee, cocoa, palm kernels; fish EXP: diamonds, iron ore, rutile, cocoa, coffee, gold

Togo (flag)

TOGOLESE REPUBLIC
AREA 56,785 sq km (21,925 sq mi)
POPULATION 7,351,000
CAPITAL Lomé 930,000
RELIGION indigenous beliefs, Christian, Muslim
LANGUAGE French, Ewe, Mina, Kabye, Dagomba
LITERACY 60%
LIFE EXPECTANCY 64 years
GDP PER CAPITA $1,100
ECONOMY IND: phosphate mining, agricultural processing, cement, handicrafts, textiles AGR: coffee, cocoa, cotton, yams; livestock; fish EXP: reexports, cotton, phosphates, gold, coffee

Temperature and Precipitation

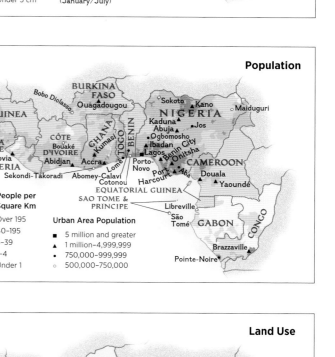

Bissau (77°/79°) Ouagadougou (77°/81°) Kano (70°/79°)
GUINEA-BISSAU BURKINA FASO NIGERIA
Conakry (79°/77°) GUINEA CÔTE D'IVOIRE GHANA TOGO BENIN
SIERRA LEONE LIBERIA Lagos (80°/77°) CAMEROON
Abidjan (80°/77°) EQUATORIAL GUINEA Douala (80°/76°)
SAO TOME & PRINCIPE Yaoundé (75°/72°)
São Tomé (78°/75°) Libreville (80°/75°) GABON CONGO
Brazzaville (78°/71°)

Average Annual Precipitation
Over 40 inches — Over 100 cm
20–40 inches — 50–100 cm
10–19 inches — 25–49 cm
4–9 inches — 10–24 cm
2–3 inches — 5–9 cm
Under 2 inches — Under 5 cm

Average Monthly Temperatures (F) (January/July)

Population

GUINEA-BISSAU Bissau Bobo Dioulasso BURKINA FASO Ouagadougou Sokoto Kano Maiduguri
GUINEA NIGERIA Kaduna
Conakry Freetown Abuja Jos
SIERRA LEONE CÔTE D'IVOIRE GHANA TOGO BENIN Ogbomosho Ibadan Benin City Onitsha
Monrovia Bouaké Kumasi Lagos CAMEROON
LIBERIA Abidjan Accra Lomé Porto-Novo Port Harcourt Douala
Sekondi-Takoradi Abomey-Calavi Cotonou Aba Yaoundé
EQUATORIAL GUINEA
SAO TOME & PRINCIPE Libreville
São Tomé GABON CONGO
Brazzaville Pointe-Noire

People per Square Mile
Over 500
100–500
10–99
1–9
Under 1

People per Square Km
Over 195
40–195
5–39
1–4
Under 1

Urban Area Population
■ 5 million and greater
▲ 1 million–4,999,999
● 750,000–999,999
○ 500,000–750,000

Land Use

GUINEA-BISSAU GUINEA BURKINA FASO NIGERIA
SIERRA LEONE CÔTE D'IVOIRE GHANA BENIN
LIBERIA TOGO CAMEROON
EQUATORIAL GUINEA SAO TOME & PRINCIPE GABON CONGO

Predominant Land Use and Land Cover Classes
Grassland
Woodland
Forest
Mixed-use, including crops
Cropland
Wetland

Industry and Mining

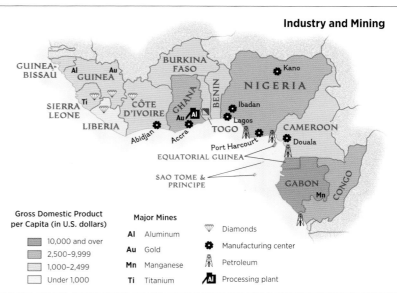

GUINEA-BISSAU GUINEA Al Au BURKINA FASO Kano NIGERIA
SIERRA LEONE Ti CÔTE D'IVOIRE GHANA BENIN Ibadan
LIBERIA Au Al Lagos TOGO CAMEROON
Abidjan Accra Port Harcourt Douala
EQUATORIAL GUINEA
SAO TOME & PRINCIPE GABON Mn CONGO

Gross Domestic Product per Capita (in U.S. dollars)
10,000 and over
2,500–9,999
1,000–2,499
Under 1,000

Major Mines
Al Aluminum
Au Gold
Mn Manganese
Ti Titanium
▽ Diamonds
✿ Manufacturing center
⚑ Petroleum
Al Processing plant

Southern Africa

Azimuthal Equidistant Projection
SCALE 1:14,953,000   1 CENTIMETER = 150 KILOMETERS; 1 INCH = 236 MILES

KILOMETERS
STATUTE MILES
Elevations in meters

Angola
REPUBLIC OF ANGOLA
AREA	1,246,700 sq km (481,353 sq mi)
POPULATION	19,088,000
CAPITAL	Luanda 5,288,000
RELIGION	indigenous beliefs, Roman Catholic, Protestant
LANGUAGE	Portuguese, Bantu, other African languages
LITERACY	70%
LIFE EXPECTANCY	55 years
GDP PER CAPITA	$6,300
ECONOMY	IND: petroleum, natural gas, iron

AGR: bananas, sugarcane, coffee, sisal, corn, cotton; fish EXP: crude and refined petroleum, natural gas

Botswana
REPUBLIC OF BOTSWANA
AREA	581,730 sq km (224,607 sq mi)
POPULATION	2,156,000
CAPITAL	Gaborone 247,000
RELIGION	Christian, Badimo
LANGUAGE	Setswana, Kalanga, Sekgalagadi, English
LITERACY	85%
LIFE EXPECTANCY	54 years
GDP PER CAPITA	$16,400
ECONOMY	IND: diamonds, copper, nickel, salt, soda ash, livestock processing, textiles

AGR: sorghum, maize, millet, beans; livestock
EXP: diamonds, copper, nickel, soda ash, meat, textiles

Lesotho
KINGDOM OF LESOTHO
AREA	30,355 sq km (11,720 sq mi)
POPULATION	1,942,000
CAPITAL	Maseru 267,000
RELIGION	Christian, indigenous beliefs
LANGUAGE	Sesotho, English, Zulu, Xhosa
LITERACY	90%
LIFE EXPECTANCY	53 years
GDP PER CAPITA	$2,200
ECONOMY	IND: food, beverages, textiles, apparel assembly, handicrafts, construction, tourism

AGR: corn, wheat, pulses, sorghum, barley; livestock
EXP: manufactures (clothing, footwear), wool and mohair, food and live animals, water

Madagascar
REPUBLIC OF MADAGASCAR
AREA	587,041 sq km (226,658 sq mi)
POPULATION	23,202,000
CAPITAL	Antananarivo 2,487,000
RELIGION	indigenous beliefs, Christian, Muslim
LANGUAGE	French, Malagasy, English
LITERACY	65%
LIFE EXPECTANCY	65 years
GDP PER CAPITA	$1,000
ECONOMY	IND: meat processing, seafood, soap, breweries, tanneries AGR: coffee, vanilla, sugarcane, cloves; livestock products EXP: coffee, vanilla, cloves, shellfish, sugar, clothing

Malawi
REPUBLIC OF MALAWI
AREA	118,484 sq km (45,747 sq mi)
POPULATION	17,377,000
CAPITAL	Lilongwe 867,000
RELIGION	Christian, Muslim
LANGUAGE	English, Chichewa, other Bantu languages
LITERACY	75%
LIFE EXPECTANCY	60 years
GDP PER CAPITA	$900
ECONOMY	IND: tobacco, tea, sugar, sawmill products AGR: tobacco, sugarcane, cotton, tea; cattle EXP: tobacco, tea, sugar, cotton, coffee

Mozambique
REPUBLIC OF MOZAMBIQUE
AREA	799,380 sq km (308,642 sq mi)
POPULATION	24,962,000
CAPITAL	Maputo 1,174,000
RELIGION	Roman Catholic, Muslim, Zionist Christian, Protestant
LANGUAGE	Emakhuwa, Portuguese, Xichangana, Cisena, Elomwe, Echuwabo, other local languages
LITERACY	56%
LIFE EXPECTANCY	53 years
GDP PER CAPITA	$1,200
ECONOMY	IND: aluminum, petroleum products, chemicals (fertilizer, soap, paints), textiles AGR: cotton, cashew nuts, sugarcane, tea, beef, poultry EXP: aluminum, petroleum, coal, sugar, bulk electricity

Namibia
REPUBLIC OF NAMIBIA
AREA	824,292 sq km (318,261 sq mi)
POPULATION	2,198,000
CAPITAL	Windhoek 356,000
RELIGION	Lutheran, indigenous beliefs
LANGUAGE	Oshiwambo languages, Nama/Damara, Afrikaans, Otjiherero languages, Kavango languages, Caprivi languages, English
LITERACY	89%
LIFE EXPECTANCY	52 years
GDP PER CAPITA	$8,200
ECONOMY	IND: meatpacking, fish processing, mining (diamonds, lead, zinc, tin, silver, tungsten) AGR: millet, sorghum, grapes; fish EXP: diamonds, copper, gold, zinc, lead, uranium, cattle, white fish and mollusks

South Africa
REPUBLIC OF SOUTH AFRICA
AREA	1,219,090 sq km (470,693 sq mi)
POPULATION	48,376,000
CAPITAL	Pretoria (administrative) 1,991,000; Cape Town (legislative) 3,624,000; Bloemfontein (judicial) 496,000
RELIGION	Protestant, Catholic
LANGUAGE	isiZulu, isiXhosa, Afrikaans, English, Sepedi, Setswana, Sesotho, Xitsonga, siSwati, Tshivenda, isiNdebele
LITERACY	93%
LIFE EXPECTANCY	50 years
GDP PER CAPITA	$11,500
ECONOMY	IND: mining (platinum, gold, chromium), automobile assembly, metalworking, machinery, textiles AGR: corn, wheat, sugarcane, fruits; beef, poultry EXP: gold, diamonds, platinum, other metals and minerals, machinery

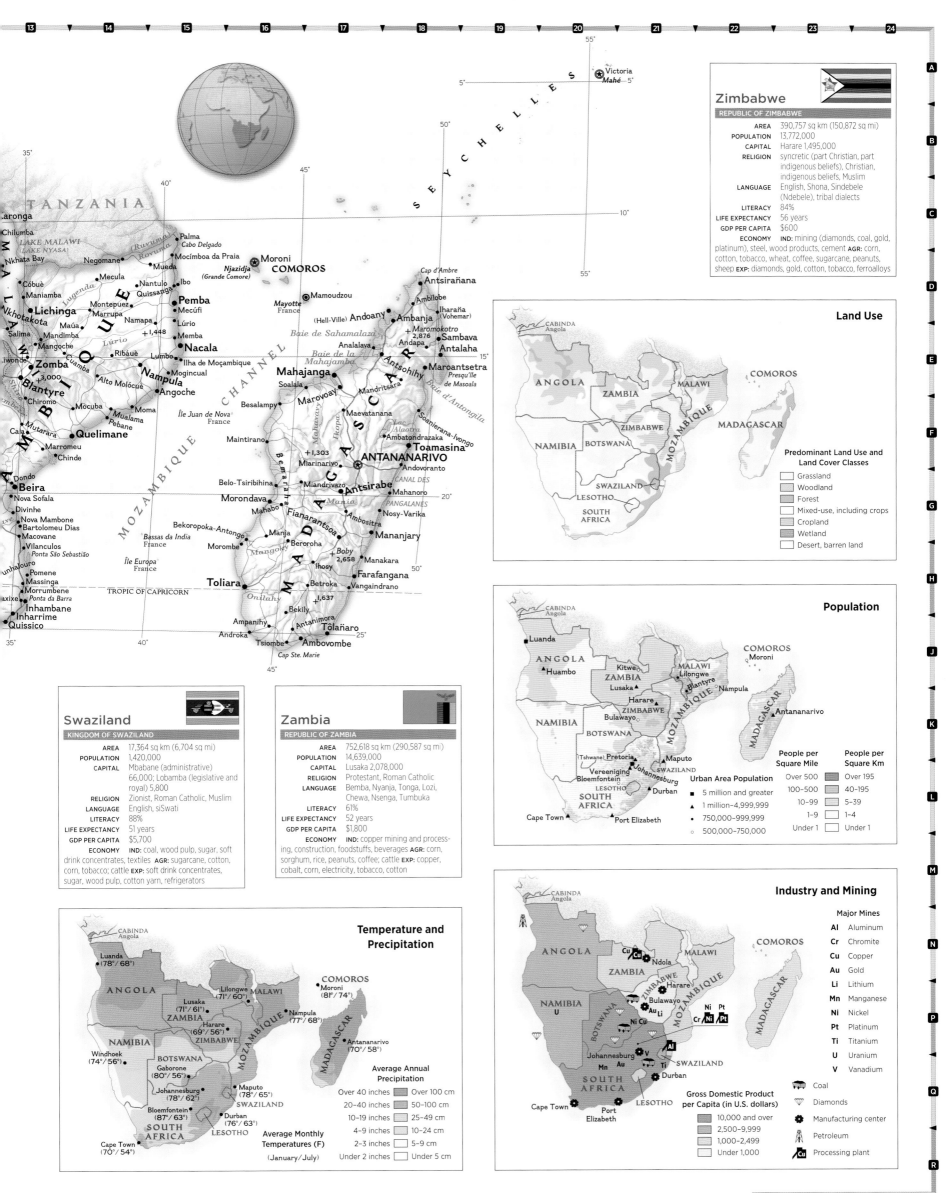

Zimbabwe
REPUBLIC OF ZIMBABWE

AREA	390,757 sq km (150,872 sq mi)
POPULATION	13,772,000
CAPITAL	Harare 1,495,000
RELIGION	syncretic (part Christian, part indigenous beliefs), Christian, indigenous beliefs, Muslim
LANGUAGE	English, Shona, Sindebele (Ndebele), tribal dialects
LITERACY	84%
LIFE EXPECTANCY	56 years
GDP PER CAPITA	$600
ECONOMY	IND: mining (diamonds, coal, gold, platinum), steel, wood products, cement AGR: corn, cotton, tobacco, wheat, coffee, sugarcane, peanuts, sheep EXP: diamonds, gold, cotton, tobacco, ferroalloys

Swaziland
KINGDOM OF SWAZILAND

AREA	17,364 sq km (6,704 sq mi)
POPULATION	1,420,000
CAPITAL	Mbabane (administrative) 66,000; Lobamba (legislative and royal) 5,800
RELIGION	Zionist, Roman Catholic, Muslim
LANGUAGE	English, siSwati
LITERACY	88%
LIFE EXPECTANCY	51 years
GDP PER CAPITA	$5,700
ECONOMY	IND: coal, wood pulp, sugar, soft drink concentrates, textiles AGR: sugarcane, cotton, corn, tobacco; cattle EXP: soft drink concentrates, sugar, wood pulp, cotton yarn, refrigerators

Zambia
REPUBLIC OF ZAMBIA

AREA	752,618 sq km (290,587 sq mi)
POPULATION	14,639,000
CAPITAL	Lusaka 2,078,000
RELIGION	Protestant, Roman Catholic
LANGUAGE	Bemba, Nyanja, Tonga, Lozi, Chewa, Nsenga, Tumbuka
LITERACY	61%
LIFE EXPECTANCY	52 years
GDP PER CAPITA	$1,800
ECONOMY	IND: copper mining and processing, construction, foodstuffs, beverages AGR: corn, sorghum, rice, peanuts, coffee; cattle EXP: copper, cobalt, corn, electricity, tobacco, cotton

Land Use
Predominant Land Use and Land Cover Classes
- Grassland
- Woodland
- Forest
- Mixed-use, including crops
- Cropland
- Wetland
- Desert, barren land

Population
People per Square Mile / People per Square Km
- Over 500 / Over 195
- 100–500 / 40–195
- 10–99 / 5–39
- 1–9 / 1–4
- Under 1 / Under 1

Urban Area Population
- ■ 5 million and greater
- ▲ 1 million–4,999,999
- ▲ 750,000–999,999
- ● 500,000–750,000

Temperature and Precipitation
Average Annual Precipitation
- Over 40 inches / Over 100 cm
- 20–40 inches / 50–100 cm
- 10–19 inches / 25–49 cm
- 4–9 inches / 10–24 cm
- 2–3 inches / 5–9 cm
- Under 2 inches / Under 5 cm

Average Monthly Temperatures (F)
(January/July)

Industry and Mining
Major Mines
- Al Aluminum
- Cr Chromite
- Cu Copper
- Au Gold
- Li Lithium
- Mn Manganese
- Ni Nickel
- Pt Platinum
- Ti Titanium
- U Uranium
- V Vanadium

Gross Domestic Product per Capita (in U.S. dollars)
- 10,000 and over
- 2,500–9,999
- 1,000–2,499
- Under 1,000

- Coal
- Diamonds
- Manufacturing center
- Petroleum
- Processing plant

Islands of Africa

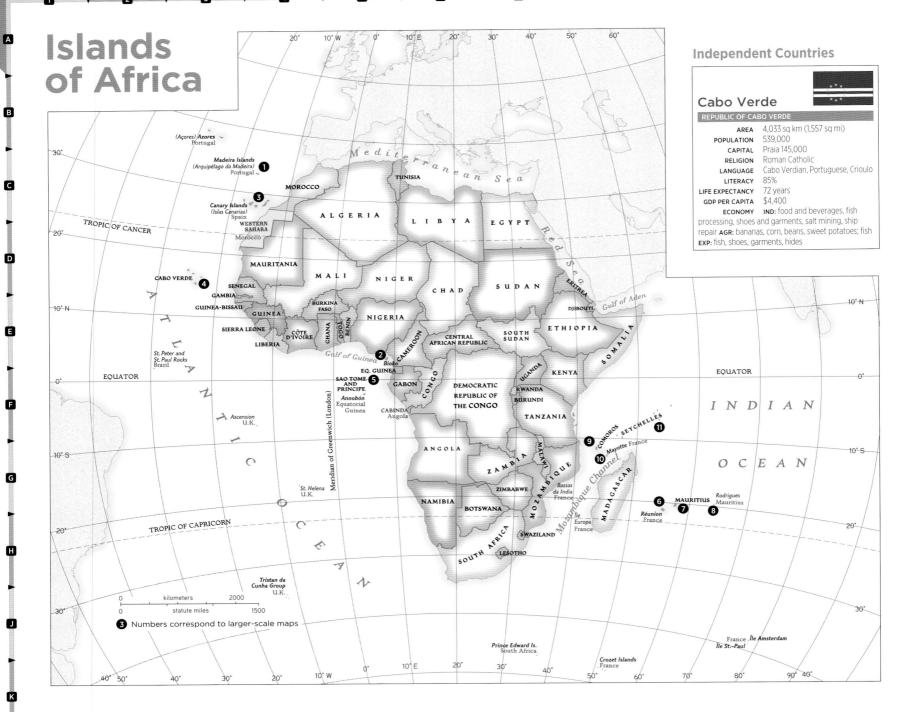

Independent Countries

Cabo Verde

REPUBLIC OF CABO VERDE

AREA	4,033 sq km (1,557 sq mi)
POPULATION	539,000
CAPITAL	Praia 145,000
RELIGION	Roman Catholic
LANGUAGE	Cabo Verdian, Portuguese, Crioulo
LITERACY	85%
LIFE EXPECTANCY	72 years
GDP PER CAPITA	$4,400
ECONOMY	IND: food and beverages, fish processing, shoes and garments, salt mining, ship repair AGR: bananas, corn, beans, sweet potatoes; fish EXP: fish, shoes, garments, hides

(Açores) Azores
Portugal

Madeira Islands
(Arquipélago da Madeira)
Portugal ❶

MOROCCO

TUNISIA

Mediterranean Sea

Canary Islands
(Islas Canarias)
Spain ❸

TROPIC OF CANCER

ALGERIA   LIBYA   EGYPT

WESTERN
SAHARA
Morocco

Red Sea

MAURITANIA

MALI   NIGER   CHAD   SUDAN   ERITREA

Gulf of Aden

CABO VERDE ❹

SENEGAL

GAMBIA

GUINEA-BISSAU

GUINEA

BURKINA
FASO

NIGERIA

DJIBOUTI

10° N

SIERRA LEONE

CÔTE
D'IVOIRE

GHANA

TOGO
BENIN

CENTRAL
AFRICAN REPUBLIC

SOUTH
SUDAN

ETHIOPIA

SOMALIA

LIBERIA

St. Peter and
St. Paul Rocks
Brazil

A T L A N T I C

Gulf of Guinea

Bioko

EQ. GUINEA ❷

CAMEROON

EQUATOR

SAO TOME
AND
PRINCIPE ❺

GABON

CONGO

Annobón
Equatorial
Guinea

UGANDA

KENYA

EQUATOR

0°

RWANDA
BURUNDI

CABINDA
Angola

DEMOCRATIC
REPUBLIC OF
THE CONGO

TANZANIA

INDIAN

O C E A N

Meridian of Greenwich (London)

Ascension
U.K.

10° S

ANGOLA

ZAMBIA

MALAWI

COMOROS ❾

SEYCHELLES ❶❶

10° S

St. Helena
U.K.

O C E A N

Mayotte France ❿

ZIMBABWE

MOZAMBIQUE

Bassas
da India
France

MADAGASCAR

NAMIBIA

BOTSWANA

Mozambique Channel

Europa
France

MAURITIUS ❻

Rodrigues
Mauritius

❼ ❽

TROPIC OF CAPRICORN

20° S

SWAZILAND

Réunion
France

20° S

SOUTH AFRICA

LESOTHO

Tristan da
Cunha Group
U.K.

30° S

| 0 | kilometers | 2000 |
| 0 | statute miles | 1500 |

30° S

France
Île Amsterdam

Île St.-Paul

❸ Numbers correspond to larger-scale maps

Prince Edward Is.
South Africa

Crozet Islands
France

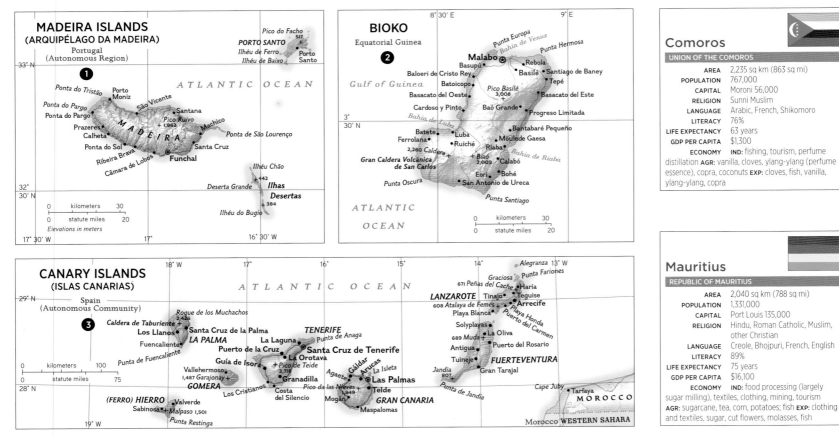

MADEIRA ISLANDS
(ARQUIPÉLAGO DA MADEIRA)

Portugal
(Autonomous Region) ❶

Pico do Facho
517

PORTO SANTO

Ilhéu de Ferro

Ilhéu de Baixo

Porto
Santo

33° N

A T L A N T I C   O C E A N

Ponta do Tristão   Porto
Moniz

São Vicente

Santana

Ponta do Pargo

Ponta do Pargo

Pico Ruivo
1,862

Machico

Prazeres

M A D E I R A

Ponta de São Lourenço

Calheta

Ponta do Sol

Ribeira Brava

Câmara de Lobos

Santa Cruz

Funchal

Ilhéu Chão

Deserta Grande   Ilhas
Desertas
384

32°
30' N

| 0 | kilometers | 30 |
| 0 | statute miles | 20 |

Ilhéu do Bugio

Elevations in meters

17° 30' W   17°   16° 30' W

BIOKO

8° 30' E   9° E

Equatorial Guinea ❷

Punta Europa

Bahía de Venus

Punta Hermosa

Malabo

Basupú

Rebola

Baloeri de Cristo Rey

Basilé   Santiago de Baney

Gulf of Guinea

Batoicopo

Tepé

Basacato del Oeste

Pico Basilé
3,008

Basacato del Este

Cardoso y Pinto

Baó Grande

Progreso Limitada

3°
30' N

Bahía de Luba

Bantabaré Pequeño

Batete

Luba

Môulede Gaesa

Ferrolana

Ruiché

Bahía de Riaba

2,260 Caldera

Biaó
2,009

Riaba

Gran Caldera Volcánica
de San Carlos

Eori

Calabó

Bohé

Punta Oscura

San Antonio de Ureca

A T L A N T I C

Punta Santiago

O C E A N

| 0 | kilometers | 30 |
| 0 | statute miles | 20 |

Comoros

UNION OF THE COMOROS

AREA	2,235 sq km (863 sq mi)
POPULATION	767,000
CAPITAL	Moroni 56,000
RELIGION	Sunni Muslim
LANGUAGE	Arabic, French, Shikomoro
LITERACY	76%
LIFE EXPECTANCY	63 years
GDP PER CAPITA	$1,300
ECONOMY	IND: fishing, tourism, perfume distillation AGR: vanilla, cloves, ylang-ylang (perfume essence), copra, coconuts EXP: cloves, fish, vanilla, ylang-ylang, copra

Mauritius

REPUBLIC OF MAURITIUS

AREA	2,040 sq km (788 sq mi)
POPULATION	1,331,000
CAPITAL	Port Louis 135,000
RELIGION	Hindu, Roman Catholic, Muslim, other Christian
LANGUAGE	Creole, Bhojpuri, French, English
LITERACY	89%
LIFE EXPECTANCY	75 years
GDP PER CAPITA	$16,100
ECONOMY	IND: food processing (largely sugar milling), textiles, clothing, mining, tourism AGR: sugarcane, tea, corn, potatoes; fish EXP: clothing and textiles, sugar, cut flowers, molasses, fish

CANARY ISLANDS
(ISLAS CANARIAS)

18° W   17°   16°   15°   14°   Alegranza 13° W

Spain
(Autonomous Community)

A T L A N T I C   O C E A N

Graciosa   Punta Fariones

29° N

Roque de los Muchachos
2,426

671 Peñas del Cache

LANZAROTE   Tinajo   Teguise

Caldera de Taburiente

608 Atalaya de Femés   Haría

Santa Cruz de la Palma

Playa Blanca   Arrecife

Los Llanos

TENERIFE

Playa Honda

LA PALMA

Puerto del Carmen

Fuencaliente

La Laguna

Punta de Anaga

Solyplayas

Puerto del Rosario

Puerto de la Cruz

689 Muda   La Oliva

Punta de Fuencaliente

Santa Cruz de Tenerife

Antigua

| 0 | kilometers | 100 |
| 0 | statute miles | 75 |

Guía de Isora

Pico de Teide
3,718

La Orotava

Arucas   La Isleta   Tuineje

FUERTEVENTURA

Vallehermoso

Gáldar

Jandia
807

Gran Tarajal

1,487 Garajonay

Granadilla

Las Palmas

GOMERA

Agaete

Pico de las Nieves
1,949

Los Cristianos

Costa
del Silencio

(FERRO) HIERRO

Mogán   Telde

Cape Juby

GRAN CANARIA

Tarfaya

Sabinosa

Malpaso 1,501

MOROCCO

Valverde

28° N

Maspalomas

Punta de Jandia

19° W   Punta Restinga   Morocco WESTERN SAHARA

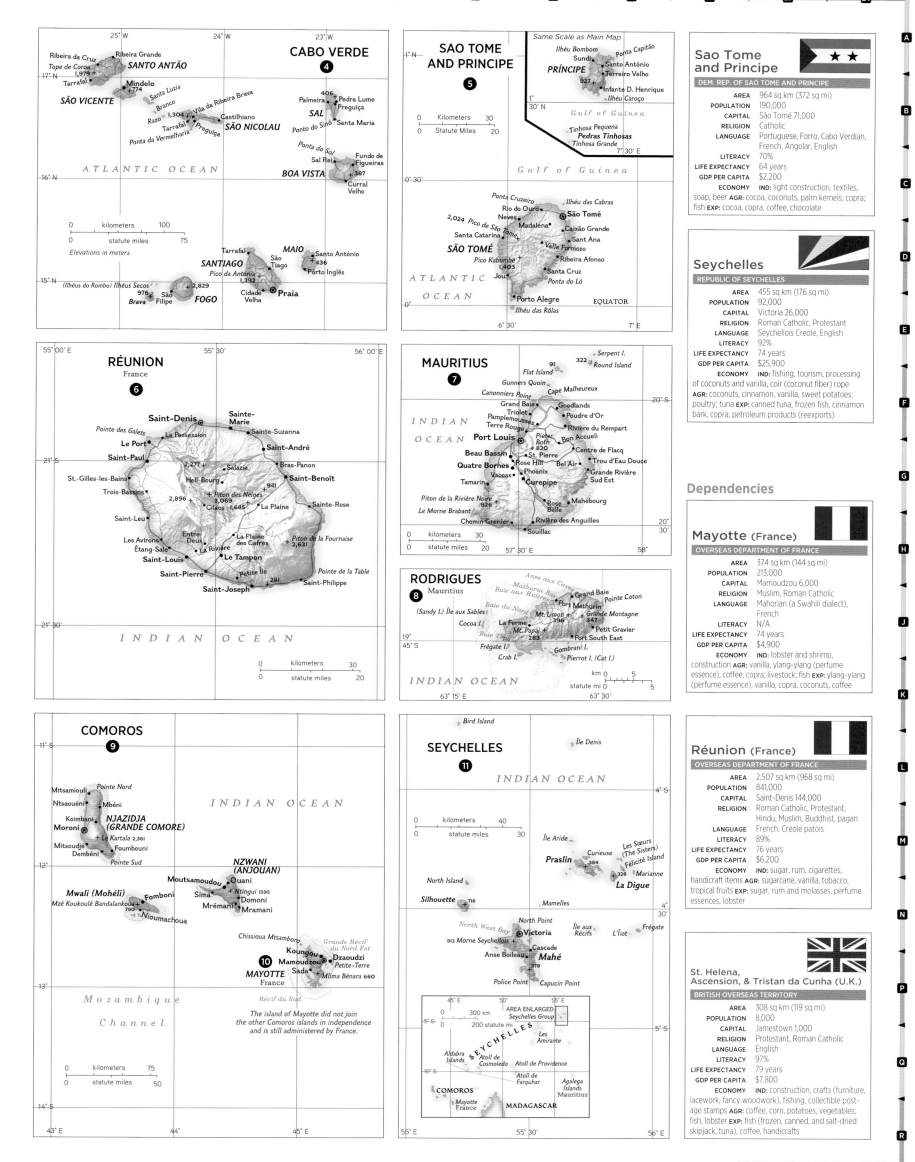

CABO VERDE ④

SAO TOME AND PRINCIPE ⑤

RÉUNION ⑥
France

MAURITIUS ⑦

RODRIGUES ⑧
Mauritius

COMOROS ⑨

SEYCHELLES ⑪

The island of Mayotte did not join the other Comoros islands in independence and is still administered by France.

Sao Tome and Principe
DEM. REP. OF SAO TOME AND PRINCIPE

AREA	964 sq km (372 sq mi)
POPULATION	190,000
CAPITAL	São Tomé 71,000
RELIGION	Catholic
LANGUAGE	Portuguese, Forro, Cabo Verdian, French, Angolar, English
LITERACY	70%
LIFE EXPECTANCY	64 years
GDP PER CAPITA	$2,200
ECONOMY	IND: light construction, textiles, soap, beer AGR: cocoa, coconuts, palm kernels, copra; fish EXP: cocoa, copra, coffee, chocolate

Seychelles
REPUBLIC OF SEYCHELLES

AREA	455 sq km (176 sq mi)
POPULATION	92,000
CAPITAL	Victoria 26,000
RELIGION	Roman Catholic, Protestant
LANGUAGE	Seychellois Creole, English
LITERACY	92%
LIFE EXPECTANCY	74 years
GDP PER CAPITA	$25,900
ECONOMY	IND: fishing, tourism, processing of coconuts and vanilla, coir (coconut fiber) rope AGR: coconuts, cinnamon, vanilla, sweet potatoes; poultry; tuna EXP: canned tuna, frozen fish, cinnamon bark, copra, petroleum products (reexports)

Dependencies

Mayotte (France)
OVERSEAS DEPARTMENT OF FRANCE

AREA	374 sq km (144 sq mi)
POPULATION	213,000
CAPITAL	Mamoudzou 6,000
RELIGION	Muslim, Roman Catholic
LANGUAGE	Mahorian (a Swahili dialect), French
LITERACY	N/A
LIFE EXPECTANCY	74 years
GDP PER CAPITA	$4,900
ECONOMY	IND: lobster and shrimp, construction AGR: vanilla, ylang-ylang (perfume essence), coffee, copra; livestock; fish EXP: ylang-ylang (perfume essence), vanilla, copra, coconuts, coffee

Réunion (France)
OVERSEAS DEPARTMENT OF FRANCE

AREA	2,507 sq km (968 sq mi)
POPULATION	841,000
CAPITAL	Saint-Denis 144,000
RELIGION	Roman Catholic, Protestant, Hindu, Muslim, Buddhist, pagan
LANGUAGE	French, Creole patois
LITERACY	89%
LIFE EXPECTANCY	76 years
GDP PER CAPITA	$6,200
ECONOMY	IND: sugar, rum, cigarettes, handicraft items AGR: sugarcane, vanilla, tobacco, tropical fruits EXP: sugar, rum and molasses, perfume essences, lobster

St. Helena, Ascension, & Tristan da Cunha (U.K.)
BRITISH OVERSEAS TERRITORY

AREA	308 sq km (119 sq mi)
POPULATION	8,000
CAPITAL	Jamestown 1,000
RELIGION	Protestant, Roman Catholic
LANGUAGE	English
LITERACY	97%
LIFE EXPECTANCY	79 years
GDP PER CAPITA	$7,800
ECONOMY	IND: construction, crafts (furniture, lacework, fancy woodwork), fishing, collectible postage stamps AGR: coffee, corn, potatoes, vegetables; fish, lobster EXP: fish (frozen, canned, and salt-dried skipjack, tuna), coffee, handicrafts

The largest structure ever built by living creatures, the Great Barrier Reef dapples the shallow Pacific waters off Australia's northeast coast. Some 600 coral species and 1,625 species of fish inhabit its warm, shallow waters.

Australia,
New Zealand,
and Oceania

Smallest of continents and sixth largest country in the world, Australia is the lowest, flattest, and, apart from Antarctica, driest of Earth's continents.

Though the Australian landmass is generally arid, varied climatic zones give it surprising diversity and a rich ecology. Unlike Europe and North America, where much of the landscape dates back 20,000 years to the time when great ice sheets retreated, Australia's land is many millions of years old; it retains an ancient feeling and distinctive geography and endures extremes of droughts, floods, tropical cyclones, severe storms, and bushfires.

The Great Barrier Reef, the world's largest coral reef, extends about 1,429 miles (2,300 km) along the east coast of Queensland. The reef was formed and expanded over millions of years as tiny marine animals deposited their skeletons. Coral reefs, and the Great Barrier Reef especially, are considered the rain forests of the ocean because of the complexity of their life-forms and their multilayered biodiversity.

Australia, New Zealand, and Oceania

The island of Tasmania lies off Australia's southeast coast. East from there, across the Tasman Sea, is the island nation of New Zealand, composed of South Island and North Island, respectively the 12th and 14th largest islands on Earth. North Island, unlike its southern neighbor, is riddled with geothermal activity.

Thousands of islands—home to 12 independent nations and more than 20 territories—dot the massive Pacific Ocean north and east of Australia and New Zealand. They make up greater Oceania; the term Oceania normally designates islands of the central Pacific and South Pacific, including Australia, New Zealand, and specifically the islands of Melanesia, Micronesia, and Polynesia (including Hawai'i). Eons of isolation have allowed outstanding and bizarre life-forms to evolve, such as the duck-billed platypus—a monotreme, or egg-laying mammal, native to Australia and Tasmania—and New Zealand's kiwi, a timid, nocturnal, flightless bird.

Oceania has many ethnic groups and layers and types of society, from sophisticated cosmopolitan cities to near–Stone Age people in the New Guinea highlands. Owing to a great swell in Christian converts in the 19th century, Christianity is now widespread and dominant in many of the island countries today. Excluding Australia, some 15 million people live in Oceania, three-fourths of whom are found in Papua New Guinea and New Zealand.

Polynesia, which means "many islands," is the most extensive of the ocean realms. It can be seen as a vast triangle of islands in the Pacific, with the points being New Zealand in the southwest, Rapa Nui (Easter Island) in the southeast, and the Hawaiian Islands in the north. Other island groups include Tuvalu, Tokelau, Wallis and Futuna, Samoa, Tonga, the Cook Islands, and French Polynesia.

Micronesia sweeps west of Polynesia and includes the islands and island groups of Nauru, the Marshall Islands, Palau, the Mariana Islands (including Guam), and the Gilbert Islands of Kiribati.

Melanesia, south of Micronesia and west of Polynesia, includes the Solomon Islands, Vanuatu, New Caledonia, the Bismarck Archipelago, and Fiji, and sometimes takes in Papua New Guinea, where some 800 of the giant region's 1,200 languages are spoken.

PHYSICAL GEOGRAPHY The continent of Australia can be divided into three parts: the Western Plateau, Central Lowlands, and Eastern Highlands. The Western Plateau consists of very old rocks, some more than three billion years old. Much of the center of Australia is flat, but some ranges and the famous red sandstone landmark known as Uluru (Ayers Rock) tower above the desert, everything around them having eroded away.

Many of Australia's rivers drain inland; though they erode their valleys near the highland sources, their lower courses fill with alluvium. The rivers often end in salt lakes, dry for much of each year, when they become beds of salt and caked mud. Yet occasional spring rains in the outback can bring spectacular wildflowers.

Nearly all of sparsely populated Australia's 23.5 million people live along the east and southeast coasts, and of these about 40 percent live in the two cities of Sydney and Melbourne. Along the coasts are also some fine harbors, long beaches, and rocky headlands.

The Eastern Highlands rise gently from the Central Lowlands, forming a series of mountains and high plateaus, the highest part around Mount Kosciuszko (7,310 ft; 2,228 m). The Great Escarpment runs from northern Queensland to the Victoria border in the south. Australia's highest waterfalls occur as rivers plunge over the Great Escarpment.

The longest of all Australian river systems—the Murray River and its tributaries, including the long Darling River—drain part of Queensland, the major part of New South Wales, and a large part of Victoria before finally flowing into the Indian Ocean just east of Adelaide. The Great Dividing Range separates rivers flowing to Australia's interior from those draining to the Pacific. The range rises mostly above remarkably flat country dotted with lakes and airstrips. In ancient times, volcanoes erupted in eastern Australia, and lava plains covered large areas.

Australia is blessed with a fascinating mix of native flora and fauna. Its distinctive plants include the ubiquitous eucalyptus, sometimes called a gum tree, and acacia, which Australians call wattle, each with several hundred species. Other common plants include bottlebrushes, paperbarks, and tea trees. Its animals are legendary—the iconic kangaroo, koala, wallaby, wombat, doglike dingo, echidna (a spiny anteater), and numerous beloved birds, such as parrots, cockatoos, kookaburras, and emus, second largest of all birds after the ostrich.

Among the foreign, introduced animals, the rabbit and fox have proven to be particularly noxious pests, overgrazing the land and killing and driving out native species. A fence built in 1907 and still maintained runs 1,139 miles (1,833 km) from the north coast to the south to prevent rabbits from invading Western Australia.

New Zealand is mountainous compared to Australia; it has peaks over 10,000 feet (3,048 m) in the Southern Alps and considerably more rain, resulting in a cooler and more temperate climate. Among New Zealand's oddities is the tuatara, an ancient reptile species that can live up to a hundred years.

Peaks and promontories of the many islands of Polynesia form clouds and capture rain, making these islands very wet. The atolls, mountains, volcanoes, and sandy isles of greater Oceania, with limited land and small or no human populations, have for most of history been isolated from the more settled parts of the world.

HISTORY Australia's first inhabitants, the Aboriginal, migrated there from Asia some 50,000 or more years ago. Until the arrival of Europeans, the Aboriginal remained isolated from outside influences, except for occasional trading in the north with Indonesian islanders.

In 1688, Englishman William Dampier landed on the northwest coast, but his visit aroused little interest in Australia from the outside world. During his 1770 voyage, Capt. James Cook noted the fertile east coast, claimed it for the British Empire, and named it New South Wales.

Australia's formative moment came when Britain began colonizing the east coast in 1788 as a penal colony, to relieve overcrowded English prisons. By 1868, the transplanted convict population numbered 162,000, out of a total colonial population of about 1 million. Most convicts were English, Welsh, or Irish, but other ethnic groups included Chinese and

Maori. Prison transports ended in 1868, and by that time regular emigrants had already begun settling "down under," as Australia was called. By the mid-1800s, systematic, permanent colonization had completely replaced the old penal settlements.

The introduction of sheep in the late 1700s proved vital, and the wool industry flourished. A gold strike in New South Wales in 1851 attracted prospectors from all over the world. Other strikes followed, and with minerals, sheep, and grain forming the base of the economy, Australia developed rapidly, the population expanding across the whole continent.

By 1861, Australians had established the straight-line boundaries between the colonies. The Commonwealth of Australia was born on January 1, 1901, relying on British parliamentary and U.S. federal traditions. Australia and New Zealand share a common British heritage and many similar characteristics; both democracies continue to honor the British monarch.

The great seafaring navigators of Polynesia and Micronesia took part in the last phase of humankind's settlement of the globe, moving into the widely dispersed islands of the Pacific. Their particular genius and contribution was the development of seafaring and navigation skills and canoe technology, which allowed them to travel back and forth among islands across great distances. The more diverse, land-based Melanesians fished along the coasts and practiced horticulture farther inland.

CULTURE Australia's Aboriginal were hunters and gatherers moving with the seasons and taking with them only those possessions necessary for hunting and preparing food. Perhaps 500 or more tribes lived in Australia at the time of Captain Cook's 1770 visit.

Aboriginal society was based on a complex network of intricate kinship relationships. No formal government or authority existed, but social control was maintained by a system of beliefs called the Dreaming, still vital to many Aboriginal today. These beliefs found expression in song, art, and dance. A rich oral tradition exists in which stories of a heroic, sacred time are passed down. Aboriginal rock carvings and paintings date back about 28,000 years.

Australia's Aboriginal have faced two centuries and more of lost land, brutalization, and discrimination. In the 1960s, an Aboriginal movement pressed for full citizenship and improved education. Modern Aboriginal art has undergone a revival as Aboriginal artists have preserved their ancient values while incorporating elements of the contemporary world.

Most Australians are of British and Irish ancestry, and the majority live in urban areas. The population has more than doubled since the end of World War II, spurred by an ambitious postwar immigration program, with many emigrants coming from Greece, Turkey, Italy, and Lebanon. In the 1970s, Australia officially ended some of its discriminatory immigration policies, and substantial Asian immigration followed. Today, Asians make up some 12 percent of the population.

The largest church groups are the Anglican and Roman Catholic, though some say sport is the national religion; Australians are famous for cricket, rugby, and swimming.

The Maori—indigenous Polynesian people of New Zealand—arrived in different migrations starting around 1150, and a "great fleet" arrived in the 14th century. Maori art is characterized by beautiful wood carvings that adorn houses and fish hooks carved out of whale bone. In the 1840

Marking Polynesia's eastern extreme, Rapa Nui—or Easter Island—haunts the imagination with its monumental moai statues (top). The purpose of the carved stone figures, the work of seafaring peoples of vast skill and determination, remains a mystery, as does why those earlier Polynesians chose to settle this particular island sometime between A.D. 800 and 1200. No more than a dot in the endless Pacific, Rapa Nui is 1,100 miles (1,770 km) from its nearest neighbor island. New Zealand's capital city, Wellington (above), has a much more recent and far less mysterious history. Settled by Europeans in 1839–1840, this small city fronting Wellington Harbour has gained a reputation as a sophisticated and livable urban enclave.

Treaty of Waitangi, the Maori gave formal control of their land to the British, though they kept all other rights of livelihood.

ECONOMY Australia dominates all of Oceania economically, its connections to Asia and the rest of the Pacific Rim growing. It supplies raw material to other countries and imports finished manufactured products. China and Japan are Australia's leading trade partners, and thousands of children learn Japanese and Chinese in Australian schools. The standard of living is high, and people have considerable leisure time, a sign for Australians of a good life.

Highly industrialized, Australia counts among its chief industries mining, food processing, the manufacture of industrial and transportation equipment, chemicals, iron and steel, textiles, machinery, and motor vehicles. Service industries, especially travel and professional services, represent about 70 percent of Australia's economy. Tourism is booming, with some 6.5 million visitors coming to see Sydney, the Great Barrier Reef, Kakadu National Park, and many other sites.

Chief export commodities are iron ore, coal, natural gas, gold, oil, wheat, and beef. Air transport and modern communications have shrunk distances, with landing strips on isolated atolls, in the desert outback, and in Papuan jungles.

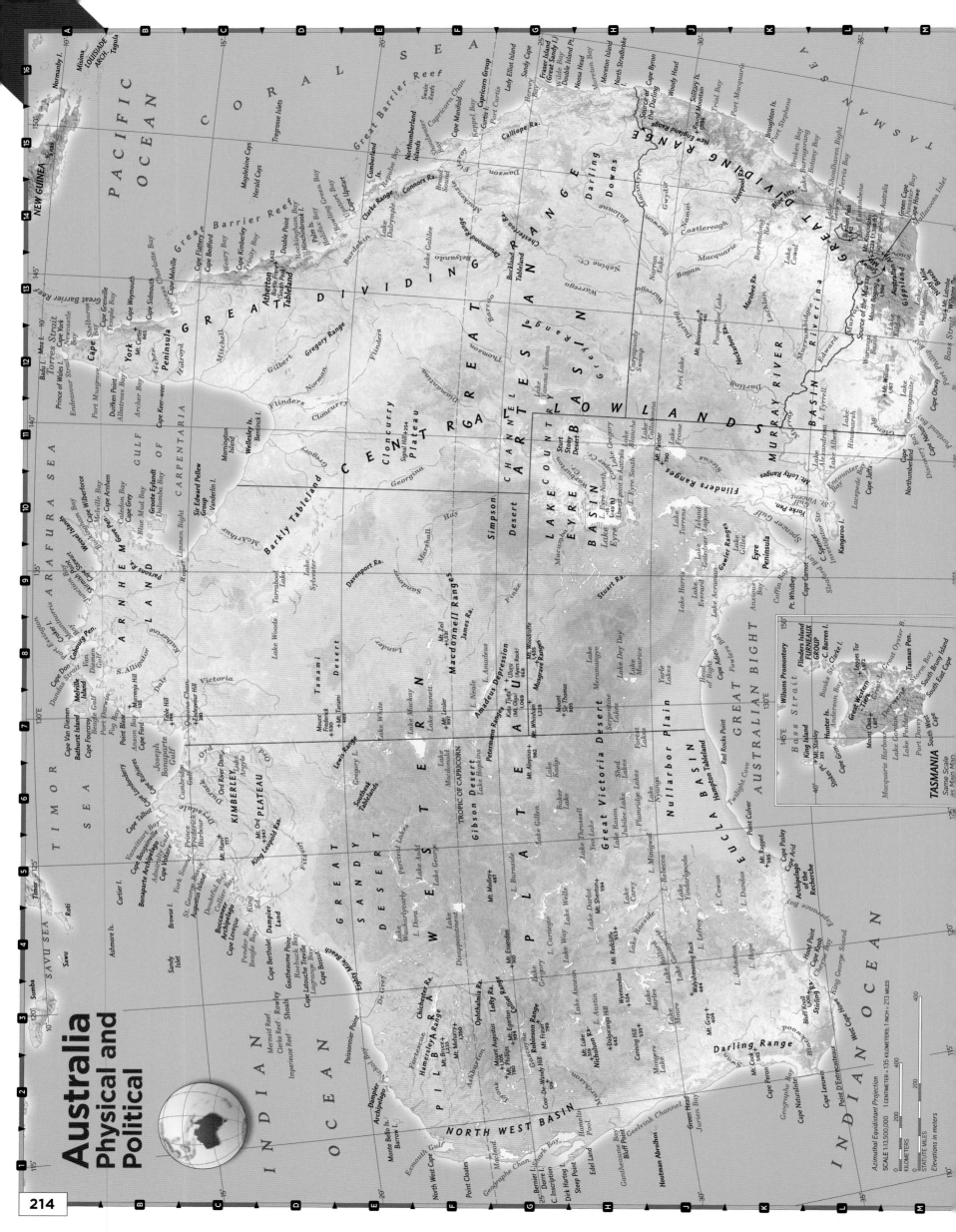

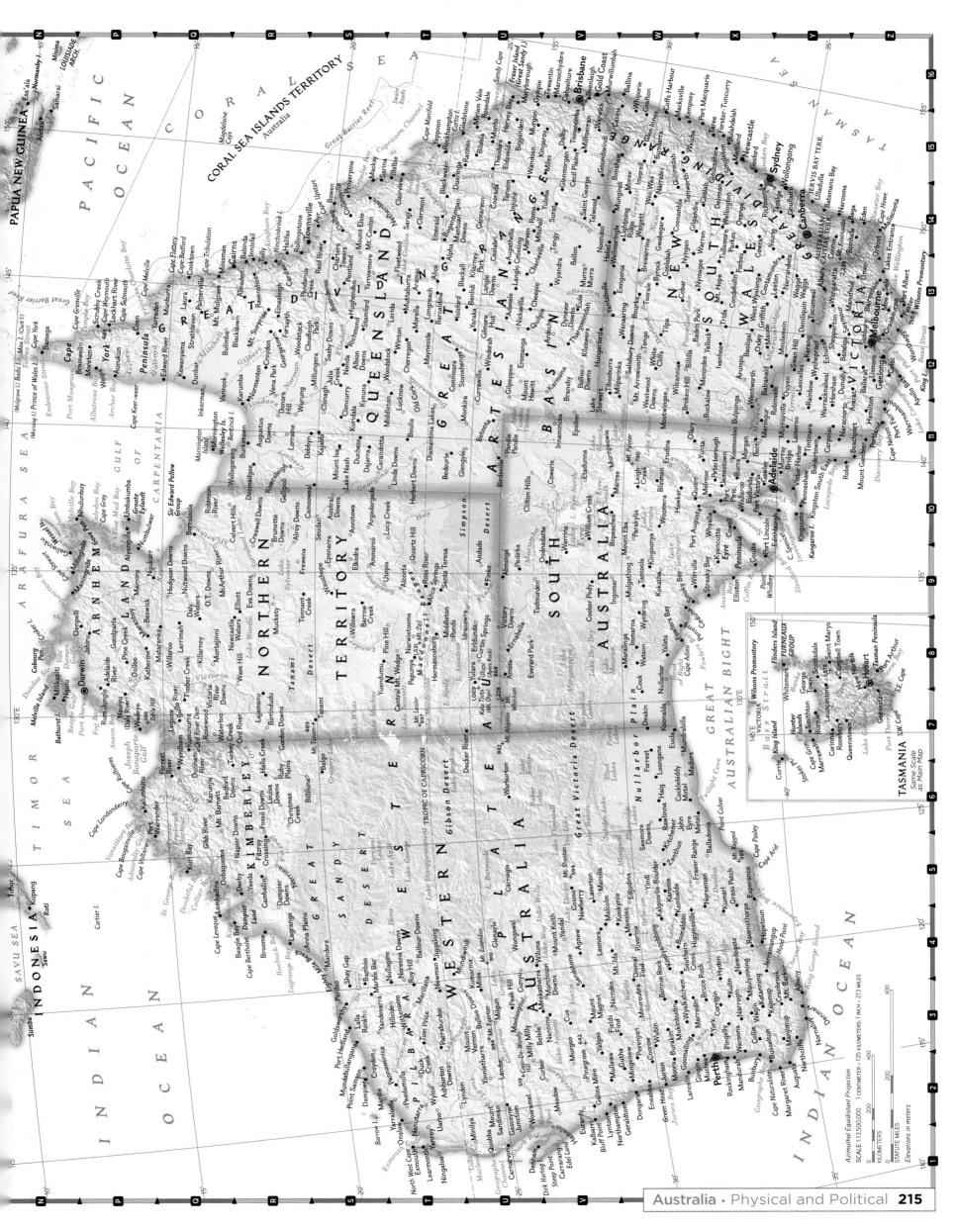

Australia, New Guinea, and New Zealand

Australia
COMMONWEALTH OF AUSTRALIA

AREA	7,741,220 sq km (2,988,901 sq mi)
POPULATION	22,508,000
CAPITAL	Canberra, A.C.T. 415,000
RELIGION	Protestant, Roman Catholic
LANGUAGE	English
LITERACY	99%
LIFE EXPECTANCY	82 years
GDP PER CAPITA	$43,000
ECONOMY	**IND:** mining, industrial and transportation equipment, food processing, chemicals, steel, tourism **AGR:** wheat, barley, sugarcane; cattle **EXP:** coal, iron ore, gold, meat, natural gas

Temperature and Precipitation

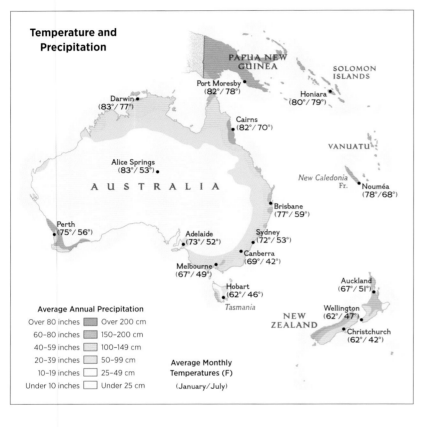

Average Annual Precipitation

Over 80 inches	Over 200 cm
60–80 inches	150–200 cm
40–59 inches	100–149 cm
20–39 inches	50–99 cm
10–19 inches	25–49 cm
Under 10 inches	Under 25 cm

Average Monthly Temperatures (F)
(January/July)

Population

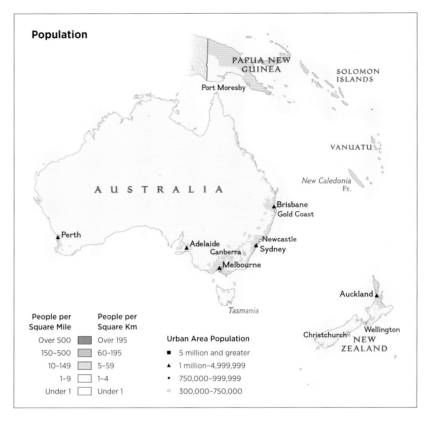

People per Square Mile	People per Square Km
Over 500	Over 195
150–500	60–195
10–149	5–59
1–9	1–4
Under 1	Under 1

Urban Area Population

- ■ 5 million and greater
- ▲ 1 million–4,999,999
- ● 750,000–999,999
- ○ 300,000–750,000

Land Use

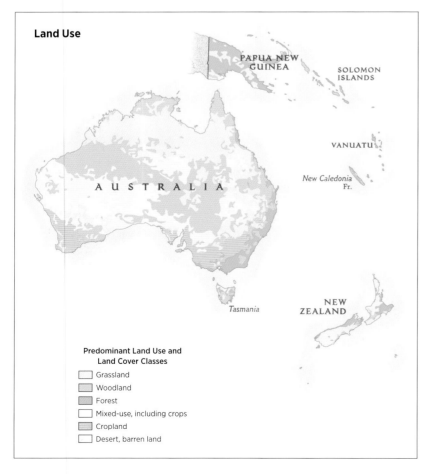

Predominant Land Use and Land Cover Classes

- Grassland
- Woodland
- Forest
- Mixed-use, including crops
- Cropland
- Desert, barren land

Industry and Mining

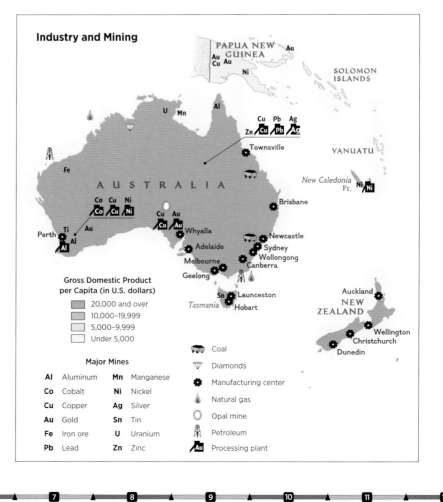

Gross Domestic Product per Capita (in U.S. dollars)

- 20,000 and over
- 10,000–19,999
- 5,000–9,999
- Under 5,000

Major Mines

Al	Aluminum	**Mn**	Manganese
Co	Cobalt	**Ni**	Nickel
Cu	Copper	**Ag**	Silver
Au	Gold	**Sn**	Tin
Fe	Iron ore	**U**	Uranium
Pb	Lead	**Zn**	Zinc

- Coal
- Diamonds
- Manufacturing center
- Natural gas
- Opal mine
- Petroleum
- Processing plant

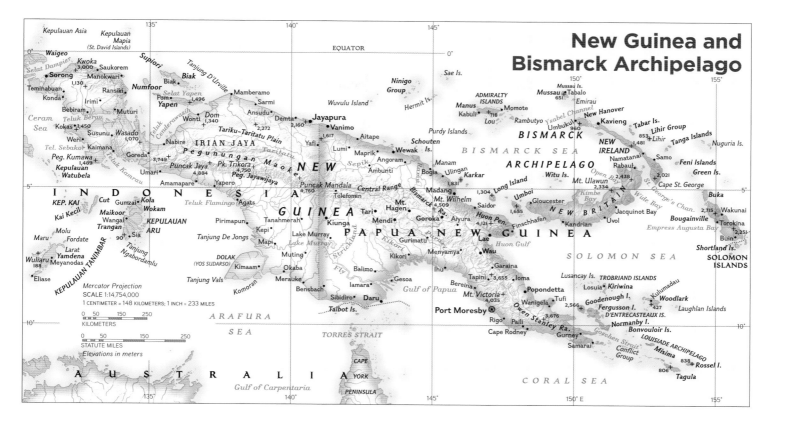

New Guinea and Bismarck Archipelago

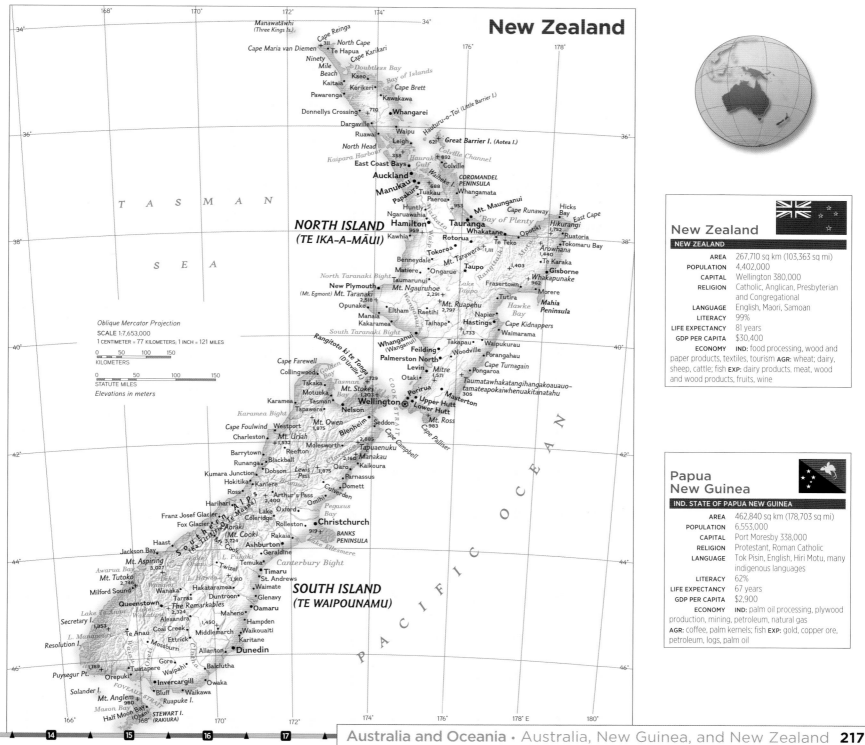

New Zealand

New Zealand

NEW ZEALAND

AREA	267,710 sq km (103,363 sq mi)
POPULATION	4,402,000
CAPITAL	Wellington 380,000
RELIGION	Catholic, Anglican, Presbyterian and Congregational
LANGUAGE	English, Maori, Samoan
LITERACY	99%
LIFE EXPECTANCY	81 years
GDP PER CAPITA	$30,400
ECONOMY	IND: food processing, wood and paper products, textiles, tourism AGR: wheat; dairy, sheep, cattle; fish EXP: dairy products, meat, wood and wood products, fruits, wine

Papua New Guinea

IND. STATE OF PAPUA NEW GUINEA

AREA	462,840 sq km (178,703 sq mi)
POPULATION	6,553,000
CAPITAL	Port Moresby 338,000
RELIGION	Protestant, Roman Catholic
LANGUAGE	Tok Pisin, English, Hiri Motu, many indigenous languages
LITERACY	62%
LIFE EXPECTANCY	67 years
GDP PER CAPITA	$2,900
ECONOMY	IND: palm oil processing, plywood production, mining, petroleum, natural gas AGR: coffee, palm kernels; fish EXP: gold, copper ore, petroleum, logs, palm oil

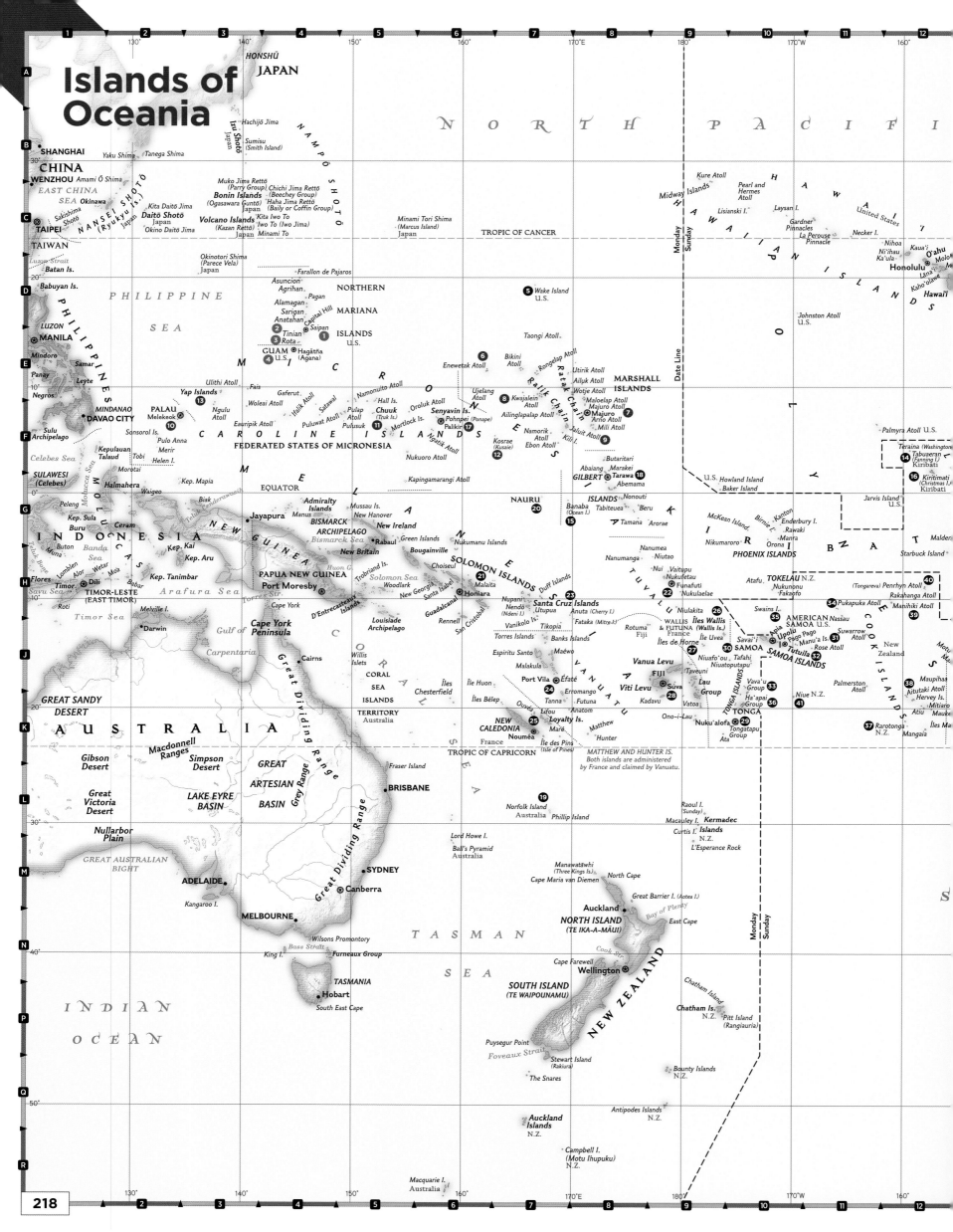

Islands of Oceania

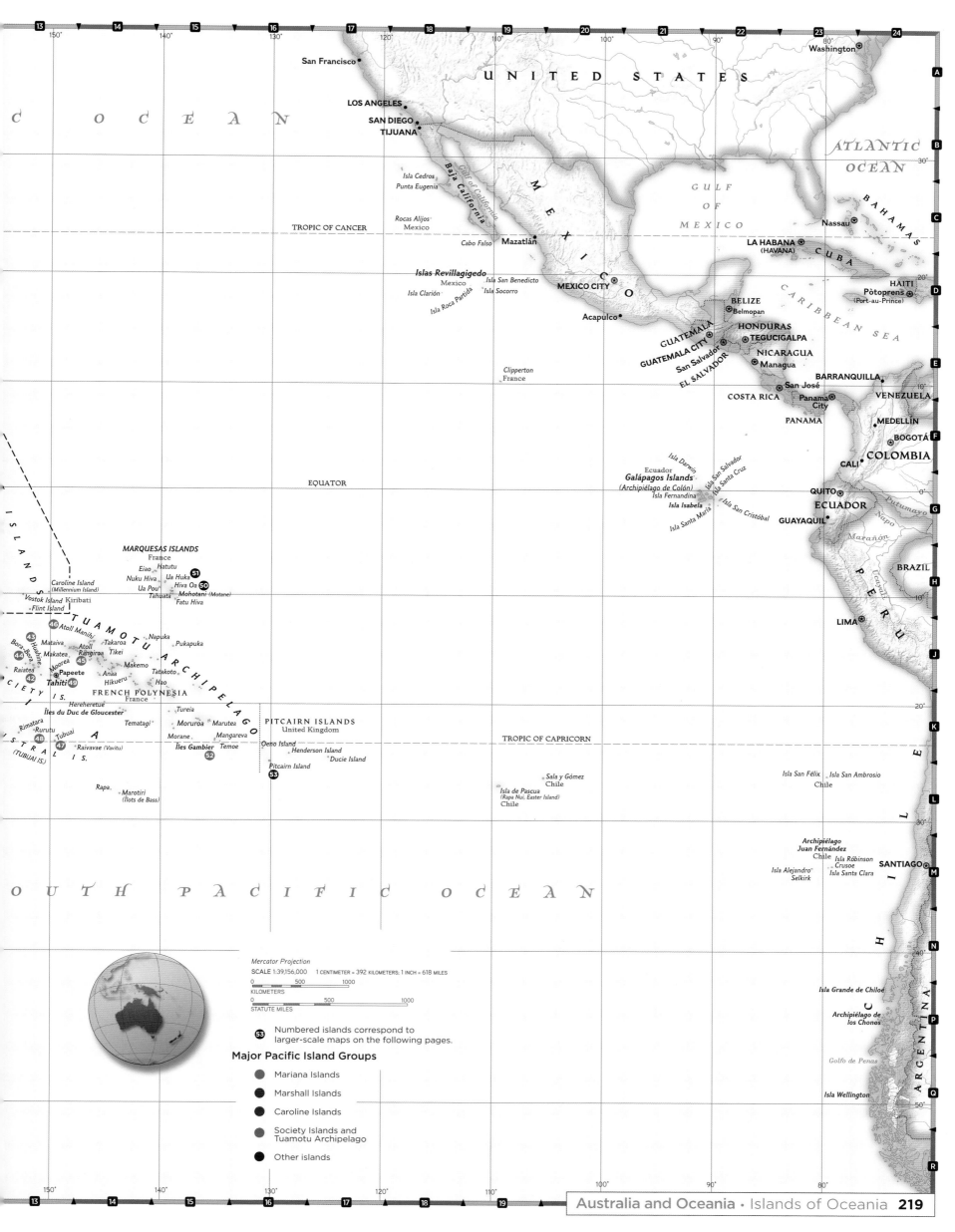

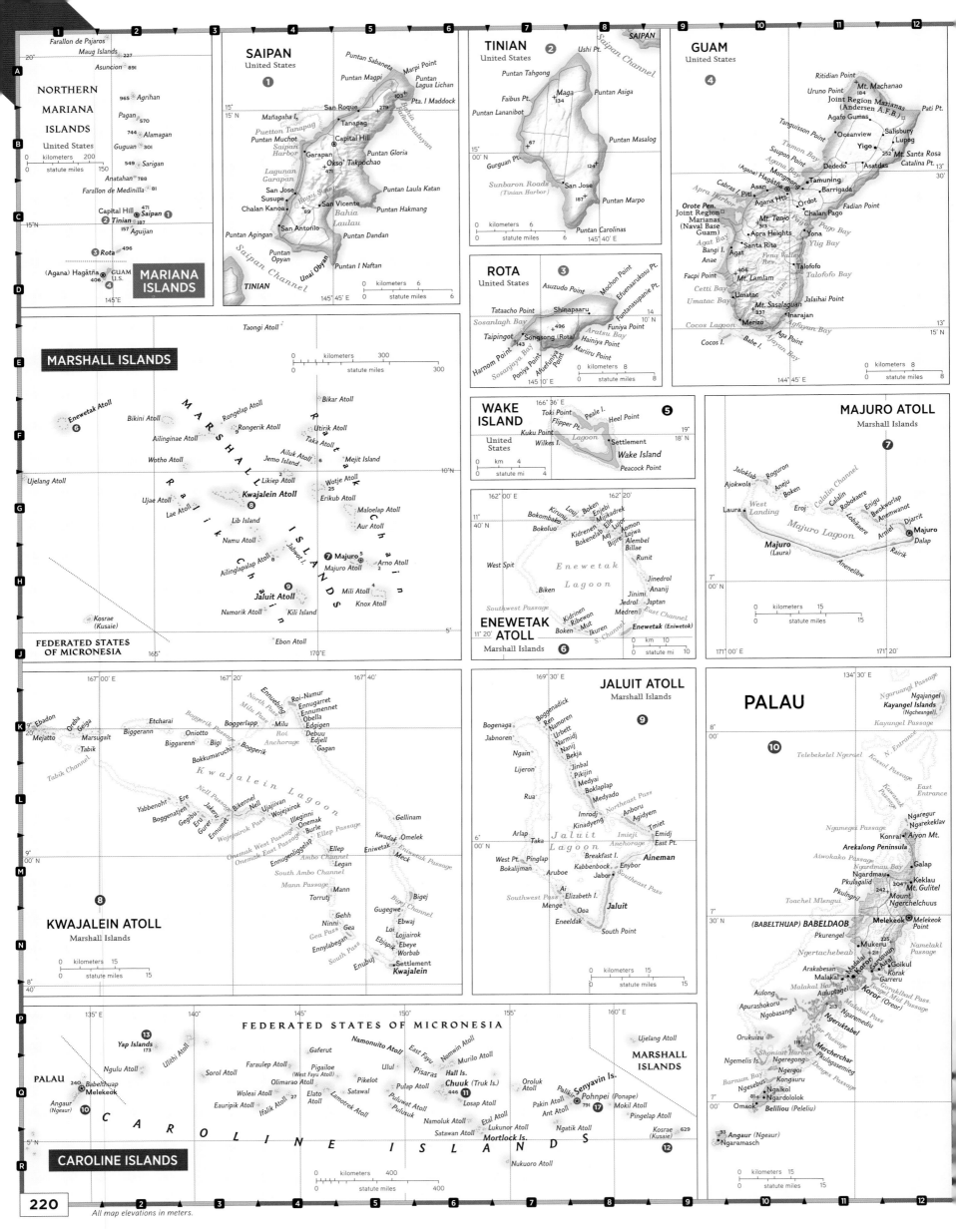

All map elevations in meters.

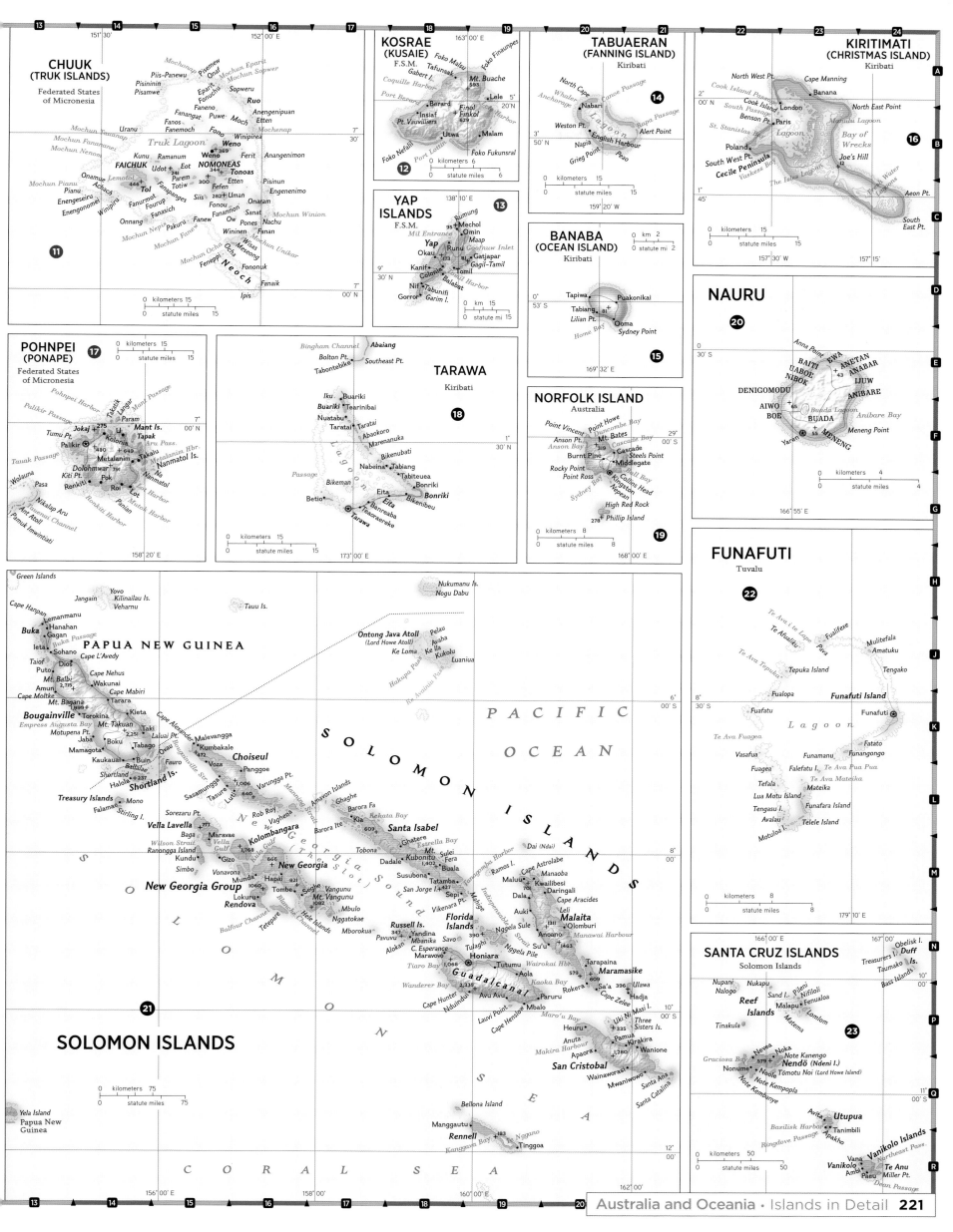

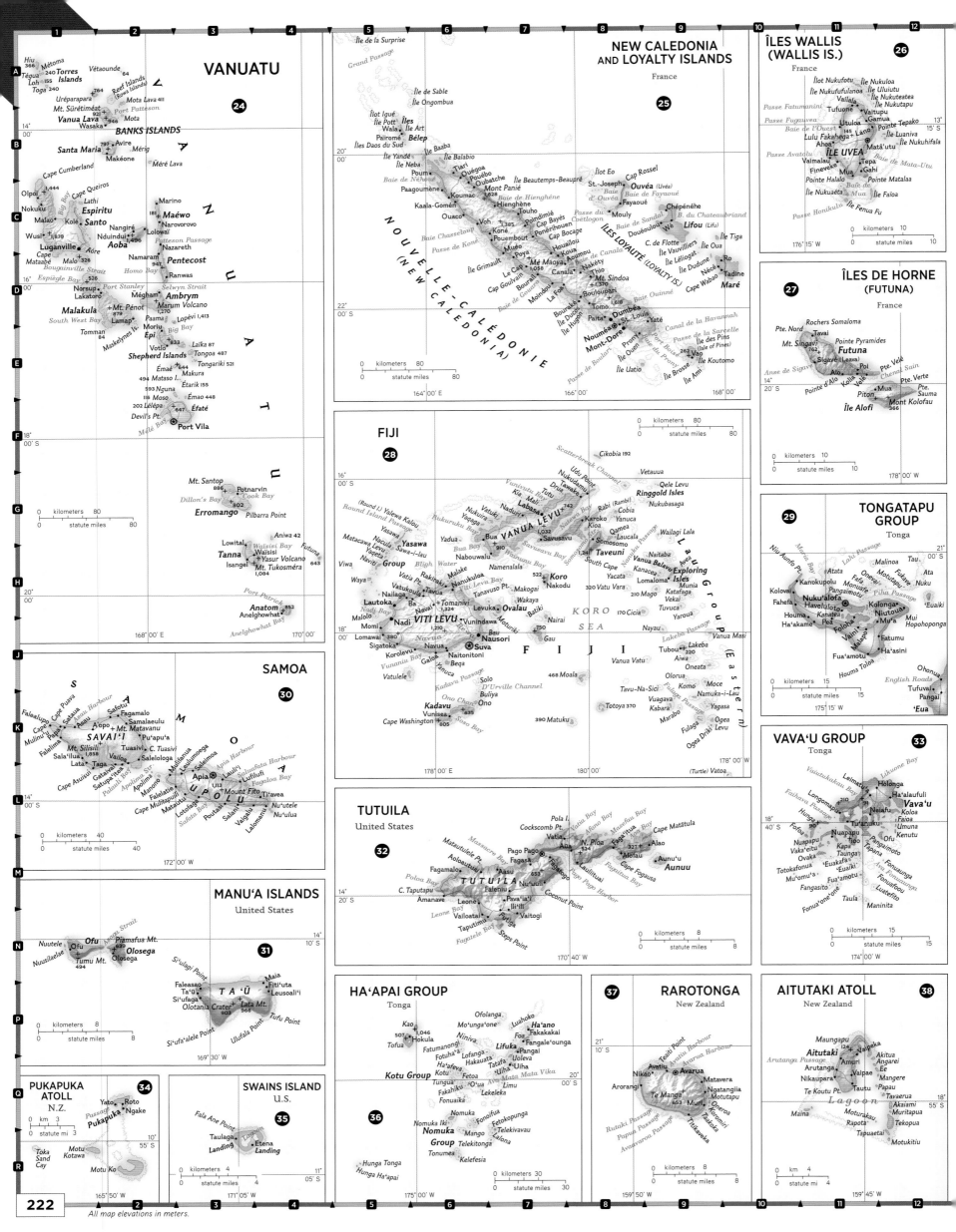

All map elevations in meters.

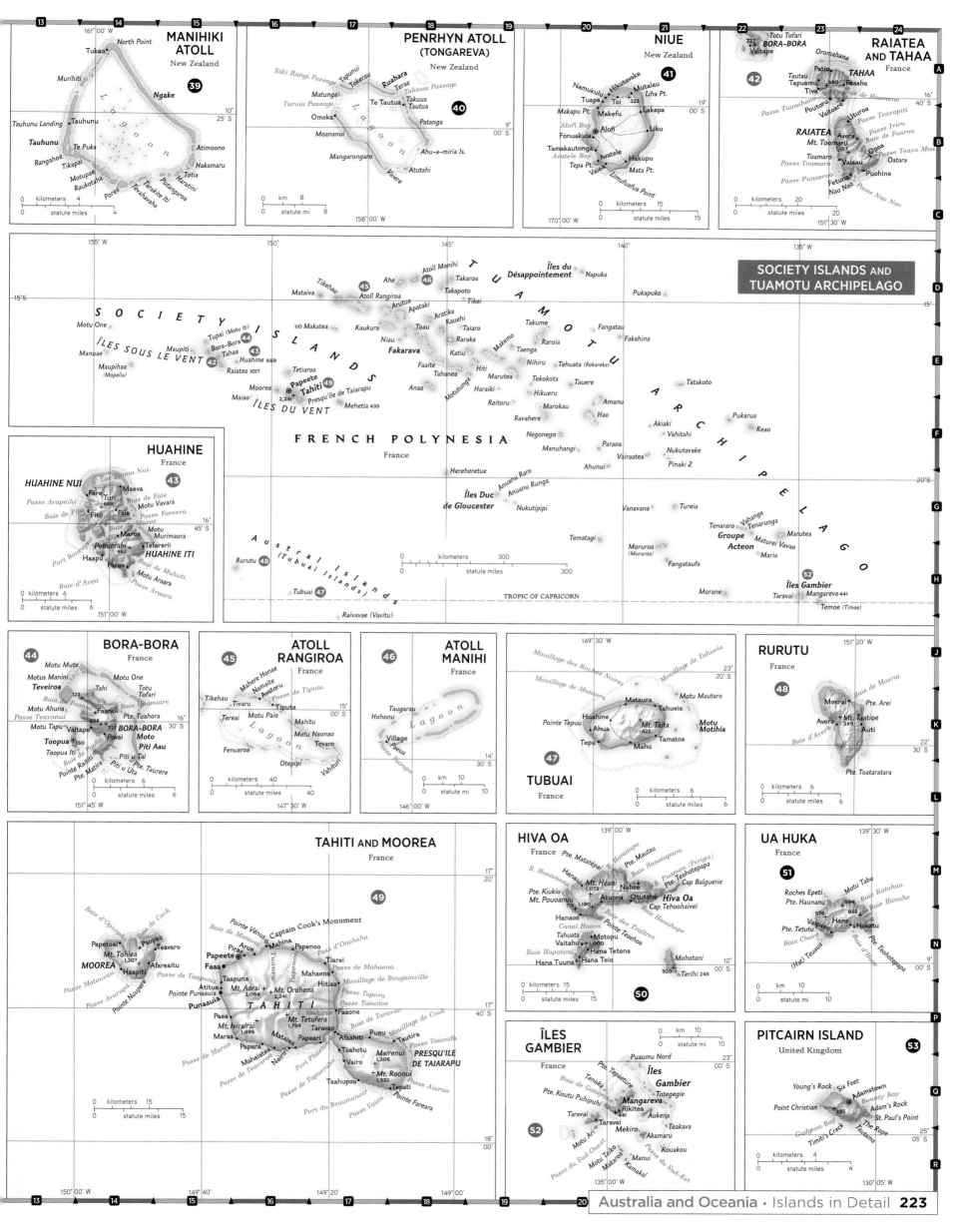

Oceania Flags and Facts

Independent Countries

Federated States of Micronesia
FEDERATED STATES OF MICRONESIA

AREA	702 sq km (271 sq mi)
POPULATION	106,000
CAPITAL	Palikir 7,000
RELIGION	Roman Catholic, Protestant
LANGUAGE	English, Chuukese, Kosrean, Pohnpeian, Yapese, other indigenous languages
LITERACY	89%
LIFE EXPECTANCY	72 years
GDP PER CAPITA	$7,300

ECONOMY **IND:** tourism, construction, fish processing, specialized aquaculture **AGR:** black pepper, tropical fruits and vegetables; pigs; fish **EXP:** fish, garments, bananas, black pepper

Fiji
REPUBLIC OF FIJI

AREA	18,274 sq km (7,056 sq mi)
POPULATION	903,000
CAPITAL	Suva 176,000
RELIGION	Protestant, Hindu, Roman Catholic, Muslim
LANGUAGE	English, Fijian, Hindustani
LITERACY	94%
LIFE EXPECTANCY	72 years
GDP PER CAPITA	$4,900

ECONOMY **IND:** tourism, sugar, clothing, gold **AGR:** sugarcane, coconuts, cassava (manioc); rice; fish **EXP:** sugar, garments, gold, timber, fish

Kiribati
REPUBLIC OF KIRIBATI

AREA	811 sq km (313 sq mi)
POPULATION	104,000
CAPITAL	Tarawa 46,000
RELIGION	Roman Catholic, Kempsville Presbyterian Church
LANGUAGE	I-Kiribati, English
LITERACY	N/A
LIFE EXPECTANCY	65 years
GDP PER CAPITA	$6,400

ECONOMY **IND:** tourism, fishing, handicrafts **AGR:** copra, taro, breadfruit, sweet potatoes, vegetables; fish **EXP:** copra, coconuts, seaweed, fish

Marshall Islands
REPUBLIC OF THE MARSHALL ISLANDS

AREA	181 sq km (70 sq mi)
POPULATION	71,000
CAPITAL	Majuro 31,000
RELIGION	Protestant, Assembly of God, Roman Catholic
LANGUAGE	Marshallese, English
LITERACY	94%
LIFE EXPECTANCY	73 years
GDP PER CAPITA	$8,700

ECONOMY **IND:** copra, tuna processing, tourism, craft items (from seashells, wood, and pearls) **AGR:** coconuts, tomatoes, melons, taro; pigs **EXP:** copra cake, coconut oil, handicrafts, fish

Nauru
REPUBLIC OF NAURU

AREA	21 sq km (8 sq mi)
POPULATION	9,000
CAPITAL	Yaren 9,000
RELIGION	Protestant, Roman Catholic
LANGUAGE	Nauruan, English
LITERACY	N/A
LIFE EXPECTANCY	66 years
GDP PER CAPITA	$5,000

ECONOMY **IND:** phosphate mining, offshore banking, textiles **AGR:** coconuts **EXP:** phosphates, clothing

Palau
REPUBLIC OF PALAU

AREA	459 sq km (177 sq mi)
POPULATION	21,000
CAPITAL	Melekeok 12,000
RELIGION	Roman Catholic, Protestant, Modekngei
LANGUAGE	Palauan, English, Filipino
LITERACY	92%
LIFE EXPECTANCY	73 years
GDP PER CAPITA	$10,500

ECONOMY **IND:** tourism, craft items (from shell, wood, pearls), construction, textiles **AGR:** coconuts, copra, cassava (manioc, tapioca); fish **EXP:** shellfish, tuna, copra, garments

Samoa
INDEPENDENT STATE OF SAMOA

AREA	2,831 sq km (1,093 sq mi)
POPULATION	197,000
CAPITAL	Apia 37,000
RELIGION	Protestant, Roman Catholic, Mormon
LANGUAGE	Samoan (Polynesian), English
LITERACY	99%
LIFE EXPECTANCY	73 years
GDP PER CAPITA	$6,200

ECONOMY **IND:** tourism, food processing, building materials, auto parts **AGR:** coconuts, bananas, taro, yams, coffee; fish **EXP:** fish, coconut oil and cream, copra, taro, automotive parts, tobacco

Solomon Islands
SOLOMON ISLANDS

AREA	28,896 sq km (11,157 sq mi)
POPULATION	610,000
CAPITAL	Honiara 73,000
RELIGION	Protestant, Roman Catholic
LANGUAGE	Melanesian pidgin, English, indigenous languages
LITERACY	84%
LIFE EXPECTANCY	75 years
GDP PER CAPITA	$3,400

ECONOMY **IND:** fish (tuna), mining, timber **AGR:** cocoa, coconuts, palm kernels; fish; timber **EXP:** timber, fish, copra, palm oil, gold

Tonga
KINGDOM OF TONGA

AREA	747 sq km (288 sq mi)
POPULATION	106,000
CAPITAL	Nuku'alofa 25,000
RELIGION	Protestant, Mormon, Roman Catholic
LANGUAGE	Tongan, English
LITERACY	99%
LIFE EXPECTANCY	76 years
GDP PER CAPITA	$8,200

ECONOMY **IND:** tourism, construction, fishing **AGR:** squash, coconuts, copra, bananas; fish **EXP:** squash, fish, vanilla beans, root crops

Tuvalu
TUVALU

AREA	26 sq km (10 sq mi)
POPULATION	11,000
CAPITAL	Funafuti 6,000
RELIGION	Protestant
LANGUAGE	Tuvaluan, English, Samoan, Kiribati
LITERACY	N/A
LIFE EXPECTANCY	66 years
GDP PER CAPITA	$3,500

ECONOMY **IND:** fishing, tourism, copra **AGR:** coconuts; fish **EXP:** copra, fish

Vanuatu
REPUBLIC OF VANUATU

AREA	12,189 sq km (4,706 sq mi)
POPULATION	267,000
CAPITAL	Port Vila 53,000
RELIGION	Protestant, Roman Catholic
LANGUAGE	Bislama, English, French, local languages
LITERACY	83%
LIFE EXPECTANCY	73 years
GDP PER CAPITA	$4,800

ECONOMY **IND:** food and fish freezing, wood processing, meat canning **AGR:** copra, coconuts, cocoa, coffee; beef; fish **EXP:** fish, copra, beef, cocoa, timber, kava, coffee

Dependencies

Australia

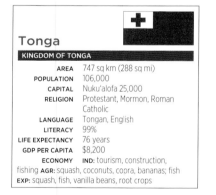

SOVEREIGN | LOCAL

Norfolk Island
AUSTRALIAN EXTERNAL TERRITORY

AREA	36 sq km (14 sq mi)
POPULATION	2,200
CAPITAL	Kingston 900
RELIGION	Protestant, Roman Catholic
LANGUAGE	English, Norfolk Island
LITERACY	N/A
LIFE EXPECTANCY	N/A
GDP PER CAPITA	N/A

ECONOMY **IND:** tourism, light industry, ready-mixed concrete **AGR:** Norfolk Island pine seeds, Kentia palm seeds, cereals, vegetables; cattle **EXP:** postage stamps, pine and palm seeds, avocados

Coral Sea Islands
AUSTRALIAN EXTERNAL TERRITORY

AREA	Less than 3 sq km (1 sq mi)
POPULATION	none

United Kingdom

SOVEREIGN | LOCAL

Pitcairn Islands
BRITISH OVERSEAS TERRITORY

AREA	47 sq km (18 sq mi)
POPULATION	50
CAPITAL	Adamstown 50
RELIGION	Seventh-day Adventist
LANGUAGE	English, Pitkern
LITERACY	N/A
LIFE EXPECTANCY	N/A
GDP PER CAPITA	N/A

ECONOMY **IND:** postage stamps, handicrafts, beekeeping, honey **AGR:** honey, fruits, vegetables; goats; fish **EXP:** fruits, vegetables, curios, stamps

Dependencies

France

French Polynesia

SOVEREIGN · LOCAL

FRENCH OVERSEAS COLLECTIVITY

AREA	4,167 sq km (1,609 sq mi)
POPULATION	280,000
CAPITAL	Papeete 133,000
RELIGION	Protestant, Roman Catholic
LANGUAGE	French, Polynesian
LITERACY	98%
LIFE EXPECTANCY	77 years
GDP PER CAPITA	$22,000

ECONOMY IND: tourism, pearls, agricultural processing, handicrafts, phosphates AGR: coconuts, vanilla, vegetables, fruits, coffee; poultry; fish EXP: cultured pearls, coconut products, vanilla, fish, processed fruits

New Caledonia

FRENCH OVERSEAS COLLECTIVITY

AREA	18,575 sq km (7,172 sq mi)
POPULATION	268,000
CAPITAL	Nouméa 181,000
RELIGION	Roman Catholic, Protestant
LANGUAGE	French, Melanesian-Polynesian dialects
LITERACY	96%
LIFE EXPECTANCY	77 years
GDP PER CAPITA	$37,700

ECONOMY IND: nickel mining and smelting, tourism AGR: vegetables; beef, venison, other livestock products; fish EXP: ferronickels, nickel ore, salt, iron ore, fish

Wallis and Futuna

SOVEREIGN · LOCAL

FRENCH OVERSEAS COLLECTIVITY

AREA	142 sq km (55 sq mi)
POPULATION	16,000
CAPITAL	Matâ'utu 1,000
RELIGION	Roman Catholic
LANGUAGE	Wallisian, Futunian, French
LITERACY	50%
LIFE EXPECTANCY	79 years
GDP PER CAPITA	$3,800

ECONOMY IND: copra, handicrafts, fishing, lumber AGR: coconuts, breadfruit, yams, taro, bananas; pigs; fish EXP: copra, chemicals, fish

Clipperton Island

FRENCH POSSESSION

AREA	7 sq km (3 sq mi)
POPULATION	None

New Zealand

Cook Islands

SOVEREIGN · LOCAL

SELF-GOVERNING NEW ZEALAND TERRITORY

AREA	236 sq km (91 sq mi)
POPULATION	10,000
CAPITAL	Avarua 15,000
RELIGION	Cook Islands Christian Church, Roman Catholic, Seventh-Day Adventist
LANGUAGE	English, Maori
LITERACY	95%
LIFE EXPECTANCY	75 years
GDP PER CAPITA	$9,100

ECONOMY IND: fruit processing, tourism, fishing, clothing, handicrafts AGR: copra, citrus, pineapples, tomatoes; pigs; fish EXP: copra, papayas, fresh and canned citrus fruits, fish, pearls

Niue

SOVEREIGN · LOCAL

SELF-GOVERNING NEW ZEALAND TERRITORY

AREA	260 sq km (100 sq mi)
POPULATION	1,200
CAPITAL	Alofi 1,000
RELIGION	Ekalesia Niue, Mormon, Roman Catholic
LANGUAGE	Niuean, English
LITERACY	95%
LIFE EXPECTANCY	N/A
GDP PER CAPITA	$5,800

ECONOMY IND: handicrafts, food processing, tourism AGR: coconuts, passion fruit, honey, limes; pigs EXP: canned coconut cream, copra, honey, vanilla, passion fruit products

Tokelau

SOVEREIGN · LOCAL

NEW ZEALAND TERRITORY

AREA	12 sq km (5 sq mi)
POPULATION	1,300
CAPITAL	none
RELIGION	Congregational Christian Church, Roman Catholic
LANGUAGE	Tokelauan, English, Samoan, Tuvaluan, Kiribati
LITERACY	N/A
LIFE EXPECTANCY	N/A
GDP PER CAPITA	$1,000

ECONOMY IND: small-scale copra production, woodworking, plaited craft goods, stamps, coins, fishing AGR: coconuts, copra, breadfruit, papayas; fish EXP: stamps, copra, handicrafts

United States

American Samoa

SOVEREIGN · LOCAL

TERRITORY OF AMERICAN SAMOA

AREA	199 sq km (77 sq mi)
POPULATION	55,000
CAPITAL	Pago Pago 48,000
RELIGION	Christian Congregationalist, Roman Catholic, Protestant
LANGUAGE	Samoan, English, Tongan
LITERACY	97%
LIFE EXPECTANCY	75 years
GDP PER CAPITA	$8,000

ECONOMY IND: tuna canneries (largely supplied by foreign fishing vessels), tourism AGR: bananas, coconuts, vegetables, taro, breadfruit, yams, copra; fish EXP: canned tuna

Guam

SOVEREIGN · LOCAL

TERRITORY OF GUAM

AREA	544 sq km (210 sq mi)
POPULATION	161,000
CAPITAL	Hagâtña (Agana) 143,000
RELIGION	Roman Catholic
LANGUAGE	English, Filipino, Chamorro, other Pacific island languages, Asian languages
LITERACY	99%
LIFE EXPECTANCY	79 years
GDP PER CAPITA	$28,700

ECONOMY IND: national defense, tourism, construction, transshipment services, concrete products AGR: fruits, copra, vegetables; pork; fish EXP: transshipments of refined petroleum products, construction materials, fish, food and beverage products

Northern Mariana Islands

SOVEREIGN · LOCAL

COMMONWEALTH OF THE N. MARIANA IS.

AREA	464 sq km (179 sq mi)
POPULATION	51,000
CAPITAL	Saipan (Capital Hill) 49,000
RELIGION	Roman Catholic, traditional beliefs
LANGUAGE	Philippine languages, Chamorro, English, other Pacific island languages, Chinese
LITERACY	97%
LIFE EXPECTANCY	78 years
GDP PER CAPITA	$13,600

ECONOMY IND: tourism, banking, construction, fishing AGR: vegetables, fruits and nuts; livestock; fish EXP: garments

Baker Island

UNINCORPORATED U.S. TERRITORY

AREA	1.4 sq km (0.5 sq mi)
POPULATION	None

Howland Island

UNINCORPORATED U.S. TERRITORY

AREA	1.6 sq km (0.6 sq mi)
POPULATION	None

Jarvis Island

UNINCORPORATED U.S. TERRITORY

AREA	4.5 sq km (1.7 sq mi)
POPULATION	None

Johnston Atoll

UNINCORPORATED U.S. TERRITORY

AREA	2.8 sq km (1.1 sq mi)
POPULATION	None

Kingman Reef

UNINCORPORATED U.S. TERRITORY

AREA	1 sq km (0.4 sq mi)
POPULATION	None

Midway Islands

UNINCORPORATED U.S. TERRITORY

AREA	6.2 sq km (2.4 sq mi)
POPULATION	None

Palmyra Atoll

UNINCORPORATED U.S. TERRITORY

AREA	11.9 sq km (4.6 sq mi)
POPULATION	None

Wake Island

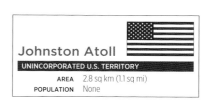

UNORGANIZED, UNINCORPORATED U.S. TERR.

AREA	6.5 sq km (2.5 sq mi)
POPULATION	None

A tabular iceberg drifts in the Bransfield Strait near the tip of the Antarctic Peninsula. These types of icebergs break off of ice shelves and can be very large. B-15, an iceberg that calved from the Ross Ice Shelf in March 2000, measured nearly 4,250 square miles (11,000 sq km), slightly larger than Jamaica, before it broke into relatively smaller bergs.

Antarctica

Often called the last wilderness on Earth, Antarctica's unspoiled expanses of austere frozen beauty remain largely untouched by humans. Antarctica is the driest, coldest, windiest, and least populated of Earth's seven continents, and with an average elevation of 7,200 feet (2,194 m), it is the highest as well. Larger than Europe or Australia, it is 5.1 million square miles (13.2 million sq km) of ice-shrouded land anchoring the bottom of the world.

Antarctica's ice cap, the greatest body of ice in the world, holds some 70 percent of Earth's freshwater. Yet despite all this ice, the Antarctic interior averages only two inches of precipitation per year, making it the largest ice desert in the world; the little snow that does fall, however, almost never melts.

The immensely heavy ice sheet, averaging over a mile (1.6 km) thick and reaching almost three miles (4.8 km) thick in places, compresses much of the continent's surface to below sea level. The weight actually deforms the South Pole, creating a slightly pear-shaped Earth.

Antarctica

Beneath the ice exists a continent of valleys, lakes, islands, and mountains, little dreamed of until the recent compilation of more than 2.5 million ice-thickness measurements revealed the startling topography below. Less than 2 percent of the Antarctic landmass actually breaks through the ice cover to reveal stretches of coastline, islands, and features such as the vast and rugged Transantarctic Mountains, which extend for 2,175 miles (3,500 km) and separate East and West Antarctica.

In spite of perpetual light during the Antarctic summer (also called the austral summer, from December to March), little heat accumulates on the continent because the white, snow-cloaked landscape reflects as much as 90 percent of the sun's incoming rays. During the half year of darkness, terrible cold and storms buffet Antarctica. The winter of 2010 saw the lowest temperature ever recorded on Earth—minus 135.8°F (-93.2°C).

Annual winter temperatures over the elevated central plateau average minus 80°F (-62.2°C), and this cold season causes the ice around Antarctica to grow quickly. Along the continental perimeter, sea ice averaging 6 feet (2 m) deep more than doubles the size of the continent, extending outward to create a belt ranging from 300 miles to more than 1,000 miles (483 to more than 1,610 km) wide.

In the spring, melting ice coincides with the calving of huge white and blue-green icebergs from the Antarctic glaciers. The largest iceberg ever spotted, B-15 in 2000, measured 4,250 square miles (11,000 sq km), making it slightly larger than Jamaica.

Antarctica's circumpolar sea, which some scientists call the Southern Ocean, holds 5.6 percent of the world's seawater and swirls in rhythm with the Antarctic Circumpolar Current; the largest, fastest current in the world, it sweeps clockwise around the globe unimpeded by any land. These high southern latitudes experience extremes of wind and weather. At around 60° south latitude, a remarkable interface of relatively warm waters from the southern Atlantic, Indian, and Pacific Oceans and the cold Southern Ocean creates conditions for an eruption of rich nutrients, phytoplankton, and zooplankton. These plankton form the base for a flourishing marine ecosystem.

Well-known animals of the far south include seals, whales, and distinctive birds such as penguins, albatrosses, terns, and petrels. Though limited in numbers of species—for example, only 322 of the world's 30,000 known species of fish swim here—Antarctica's animal life has adapted extremely well to the harsh climate. Seasonal feeding and energy storage in fats exemplify this specialization. Yet the Antarctic ecosystem is finely tuned, and climatic and other environmental changes can upset its fragile balance.

PHYSICAL GEOGRAPHY Every summer thousands of scientists travel to Antarctica to obtain vital information about Earth's weather and ecology and the state of the southernmost continent. This interest attests to the region's role as a pristine laboratory, where measurements and rates of change in numerous scientific fields can point to larger issues facing the world's environmental health.

Antarctica's oceanic and atmospheric system—indicator of and contributor to climate change—is a main area of focus. Oceanographers attempt to understand more fully the global exchange of heat, sea-ice dynamics, salt and trace elements in those waters, as well as the entire marine biosphere. The critically important research that has emerged from Antarctic studies includes the 1985 discovery of a hole in Earth's protective ozone layer by scientists collecting and analyzing data at the Halley research station operated by the British Antarctic Survey. Their findings brought to prominence a major ecological threat to the planet, and the world community took action to reduce the use of chemical additives affecting the ozone layer, which blocks out harmful ultraviolet rays from the sun.

Ice and sediment cores taken from the southernmost continent also provide insight into the world's ancient climate and allow for comparison with conditions today. Recent studies of Antarctic ice have shown a dramatic contrast in conditions. On the one hand, sea ice has expanded some 7,300 square miles (18,910 sq km), about the size of New Jersey, while Antarctic glaciers, particularly in the west of the continent, have been melting at troubling and unprecedented rates. The addition of this meltwater to the Southern Ocean may account for the increase in sea ice, as freshwater freezes faster than salt water. The glacial melt could also lead to a rise in sea levels worldwide, important news for the three billion people who live in coastal areas. If the Antarctic ice sheet were to melt completely, global seas would rise by an estimated 200 feet (60 m), inundating many oceanic islands and gravely altering the world's coastlines.

Three basic water masses comprise the Southern Ocean: Antarctic Surface Water, Circumpolar Deep Water, and Antarctic Bottom Water. Sharp boundaries separate the water masses, each with its own characteristics. These differences drive circulation around the continent and contribute to the global ocean currents and overall transfer of energy around the world.

Prominent physical features on Antarctica include the Vinson Massif, highest mountain on the continent at 16,067 feet (4,897 m). Rising in the Ellsworth Mountains, the massif was discovered in 1957 by U.S. Navy aircraft and first climbed in 1966 by an American team.

The Antarctic Peninsula, reaching like a long arm 800 miles (1,288 km) into the Southern Ocean toward the tip of South America, is made up of a mountain range and many islands linked together by ice. Seals, penguins, and other seabirds find it a particularly suitable habitat, and the peninsula's relative accessibility makes it the Antarctic area most visited by humans.

The continent's only sizable river, the Onyx, arises from a coastal glacier near McMurdo Sound. Every summer its waters flow inland for some 20 miles (32 km), replenishing and raising the surface level of Lake Vanda, one of several lakes in the Dry Valleys. These valleys, free of snow and ice unlike the rest of Antarctica, were created by ancient glaciers and are among the driest places on Earth. They stretch to the coast from the Transantarctic Mountains, a range high enough here to prevent the great Polar Plateau ice sheet from flowing through the Dry Valleys and down to the sea.

Immense ice shelves, produced as the main plateau disgorges masses of ice, rim much of the continent's coast and extend far into the sea. The largest are the Ross Ice Shelf, which is the size of France, and the Ronne Ice Shelf.

Special names exist for the many different types of ice: frazil ice, an early stage of sea-ice growth in which crystals below the surface form an unstructured slush; nilas, a thin sheen of ice on the sea surface that bends but does not break with wave action; pancake ice, named for its flattened circular shape; pack ice, frozen seawater and floating ice driven together to form a continuous mass; and fast ice, that part of the sea-ice cover attached to land.

Scientists seeking to understand sea ice hover above a surface polka-dotted with pancake ice. This type of ice forms when a thin surface film of crystals breaks up and thickens into irregular disks that can measure from one to ten feet (0.3–3 m) in diameter. Constant battering of the disks against one another causes the turned-up rims.

CULTURE, HISTORY, AND EXPLORATION The search for Antarctica represented the last great adventure of global exploration. British explorer Capt. James Cook crossed three times into Antarctic waters between 1772 and 1775 and was probably the first to cross the Antarctic Circle. Though he never saw the continent, he believed in "a tract of land at the Pole that is the source of all the ice that is spread over this vast southern ocean."

His observations of marine mammals in great numbers lured whalers and sealers into the freezing southern waters in search of skins and oil. First sightings of the continent then followed in 1820.

Those seeking the south magnetic pole included British naval officer James Clark Ross, who between 1839 and 1843 charted unknown territory, including a giant ice shelf later named after him. Ross located the approximate position of the south magnetic pole—the point toward which a compass needle points from any direction throughout surrounding areas.

In 1895, Norwegian whalers landed on the continent beyond the Antarctic Peninsula, and in 1898 a major Belgian scientific expedition overwintered in the Antarctic when their ship became stuck in pack ice for almost 13 months.

Douglas Mawson reached the south magnetic pole as part of Ernest Shackleton's 1907–09 *Nimrod* expedition. Later, Mawson led the Australasian Antarctic Expedition (1911–14), which produced observations in magnetism, geology, biology, and meteorology.

A race to reach the South Pole came to a climax in 1911–12. Norwegian Roald Amundsen's expedition reached the South Pole on December 14, 1911, and returned to base camp on January 25, 1912, after 99 days on the move, relying on Greenland sled dogs to pull their sleds. Simultaneously, the British team of Robert Falcon Scott and four companions set off, unaware of Amundsen's swifter, better-managed effort. Scott's use of Manchurian ponies proved a mistake; his team reached the Pole 34 days later, only to find the Norwegian flag flying. On the bitter return trip, the five men succumbed to cold, hunger, exhaustion, and bad weather just 11 miles (18 km) from supplies. All died.

Another epic adventure involved Ernest Shackleton, whose British expedition aimed to traverse the entire continent. In 1915, Shackleton's main party of 28 men became stranded when sea ice trapped and crushed their ship, *Endurance*. After more than a year on drifting ice, they sailed in lifeboats to Elephant Island at the tip of the Antarctic Peninsula. Shackleton and five others then embarked on an astonishing 800-mile (1,288 km) journey in a small boat to South Georgia. Shackleton eventually returned to Elephant and rescued all of his other men.

In 1935, Caroline Mikkelsen, wife of a Norwegian whaling captain, became the first woman to stand on Antarctica. Almost a dozen years later the U.S. Navy brought 4,700 men, 13 ships, and 23 aircraft to the continent, using icebreakers for the first time. The vast enterprise mapped large areas of the coastline and interior and took 70,000 aerial photographs.

The global scientific community focused its attention on Antarctica in the early 1880s, when 11 countries participated in the first International Polar Year (IPY), which actually ran from 1881 to 1884. This joint research effort inspired in turn the International Geophysical Year (IGY), when for 18 months in 1957–58, many nations participated in advancing knowledge of the continent. There have been subsequent IPYs and IGYs (the last from 2007 to 2009), and they helped lead to the Antarctic Treaty, signed in 1959 by 12 leading IGY participants. The treaty has done much to protect this unique continent.

Today, around 104 research stations and camps stand at many sites around Antarctica, and an ever shifting population, including tourists, can reach as high as 46,000 people in the austral summer. Tourism brings its own troubles. Recently, species of non-native grasses, presumably carried on visitors' clothing, have been found on the continent. Further unintentional aliens, such as algae, crustaceans, and parasites, arrive on floating plastic bottles and other man-made debris.

RESOURCES AT RISK Many believe Antarctica has a wealth of mineral resources, but the harsh climate, short work season, and need to drill through thick ice make the recovery of these resources difficult.

Minerals known to be under the ice include gold, uranium, cobalt, chromium, nickel, copper, iron, and platinum, as well as potentially large deposits of diamonds. Oil probably exists below the ocean floor, and coal deposits have been detected along the coast and throughout the remote and difficult-to-reach Transantarctic Mountains.

A pressing reason to limit mineral exploration and drilling is Antarctica's extreme fragility. Sensitive plants, including rare moss beds on the Antarctic Peninsula, take 300 to 400 years to grow, and a single human boot can cause tremendous damage.

In January 1998, an addition to the Antarctic Treaty, known as the Madrid Protocol, went into force, deeming Antarctica a natural reserve devoted to peace and science. It specifically banned mining and mineral exploitation of any kind until 2048.

Yet pressure builds yearly to find new mineral and petroleum deposits. Despite the Madrid Protocol, Russia and other countries appear to be actively exploring Antarctic oil, gas, and mineral resources. Also significant is the growing commercialization of Southern Ocean fisheries. Particularly vulnerable are the tiny shrimp like krill that form a vital part of Antarctica's food chain. Rising sea temperatures and loss of sea ice is having a devastating impact on their numbers. The collapse of fish and krill species might be analogous to the wholesale slaughter of fur seal populations in the late 1700s and early 1800s and the near destruction of the Southern Ocean's whales in the 20th century.

Antarctica already witnesses vehicle pollution; dumping of plastics, solid wastes, food, and batteries; burning of fossil fuels; and construction of roads and airstrips at the many scientific bases.

The most obvious Antarctic resource of all—ice—may one day serve to relieve thirsty nations. Ships towing icebergs from Antarctica to all parts of the world could deliver this huge potential source of freshwater, but at present such a project is simply too expensive.

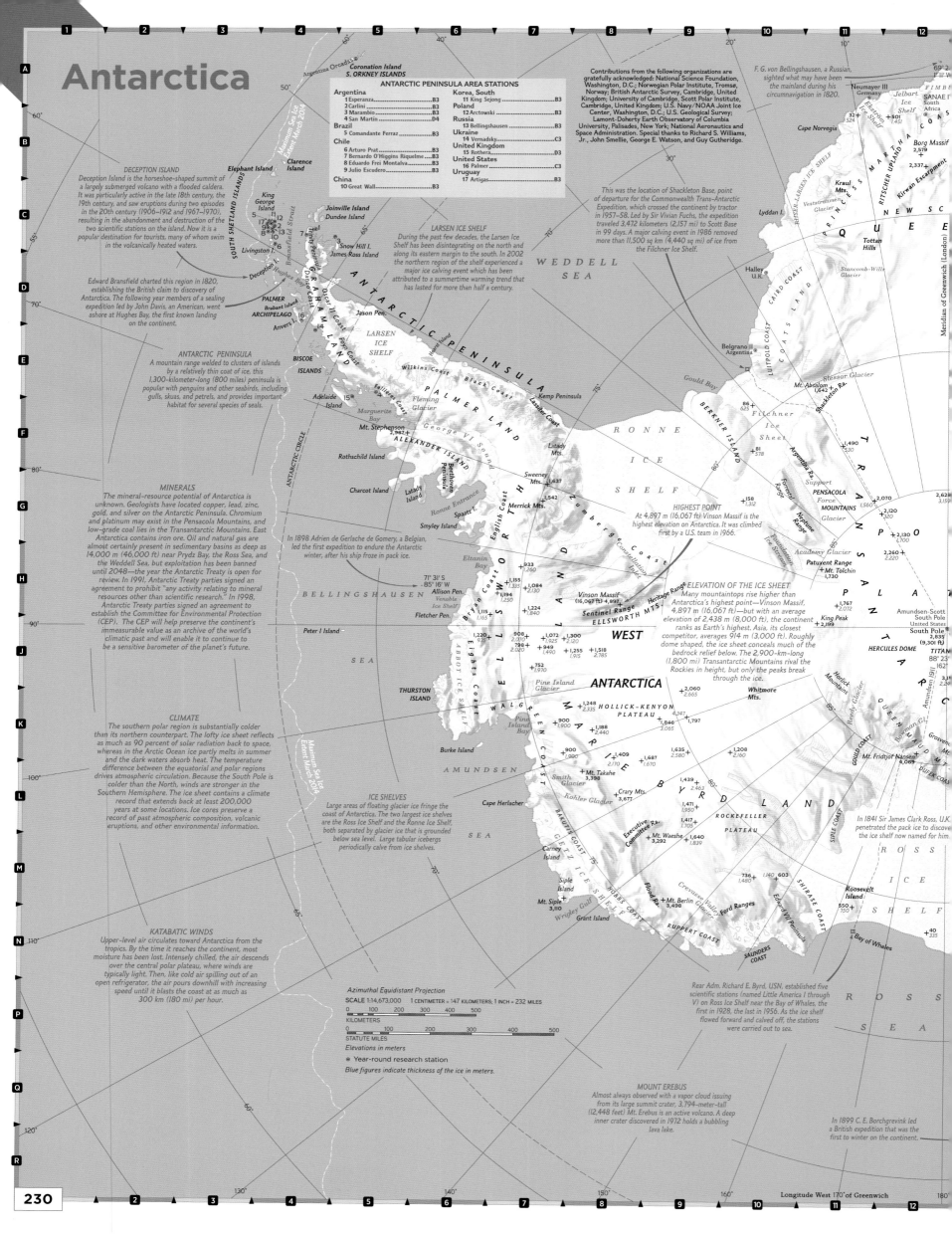

Antarctica

DECEPTION ISLAND
Deception Island is the horseshoe-shaped summit of a largely submerged volcano with a flooded caldera. It was particularly active in the late 18th century, the 19th century, and saw eruptions during two episodes in the 20th century (1906–1912 and 1967–1970), resulting in the abandonment and destruction of the two scientific stations on the island. Now it is a popular destination for tourists, many of whom swim in the volcanically heated waters.

Edward Bransfield charted this region in 1820, establishing the British claim to discovery of Antarctica. The following year members of a sealing expedition led by John Davis, an American, went ashore at Hughes Bay, the first known landing on the continent.

ANTARCTIC PENINSULA
A mountain range welded to clusters of islands by a relatively thin coat of ice, this 1,300-kilometer-long (800 miles) peninsula is popular with penguins and other seabirds, including gulls, skuas, and petrels, and provides important habitat for several species of seals.

MINERALS
The mineral-resource potential of Antarctica is unknown. Geologists have located copper, lead, zinc, gold, and silver on the Antarctic Peninsula. Chromium and platinum may exist in the Pensacola Mountains, and low-grade coal lies in the Transantarctic Mountains. East Antarctica contains iron ore. Oil and natural gas are almost certainly present in sedimentary basins as deep as 14,000 m (46,000 ft) near Prydz Bay, the Ross Sea, and the Weddell Sea, but exploitation has been banned until 2048—the year the Antarctic Treaty is open for review. In 1991, Antarctic Treaty parties signed an agreement to prohibit "any activity relating to mineral resources other than scientific research." In 1998, Antarctic Treaty parties signed an agreement to establish the Committee for Environmental Protection (CEP). The CEP will help preserve the continent's immeasurable value as an archive of the world's climatic past and will enable it to continue to be a sensitive barometer of the planet's future.

CLIMATE
The southern polar region is substantially colder than its northern counterpart. The lofty ice sheet reflects as much as 90 percent of solar radiation back to space, whereas in the Arctic Ocean ice partly melts in summer and the dark waters absorb heat. The temperature difference between the equatorial and polar regions drives atmospheric circulation. Because the South Pole is colder than the North, winds are stronger in the Southern Hemisphere. The ice sheet contains a climate record that extends back at least 200,000 years at some locations. Ice cores preserve a record of past atmospheric composition, volcanic eruptions, and other environmental information.

KATABATIC WINDS
Upper-level air circulates toward Antarctica from the tropics. By the time it reaches the continent, most moisture has been lost. Intensely chilled, the air descends over the central polar plateau, where winds are typically light. Then, like cold air spilling out of an open refrigerator, the air pours downhill with increasing speed until it blasts the coast at as much as 300 km (180 mi) per hour.

ANTARCTIC PENINSULA AREA STATIONS

Argentina		Korea, South	
1 Esperanza	B3	11 King Sejong	B3
2 Carlini	B3	Poland	
3 Marambio	B3	12 Arctowski	B3
4 San Martín	D4	Russia	
Brazil		13 Bellingshausen	B3
5 Comandante Ferraz	B3	Ukraine	
Chile		14 Vernadsky	C3
6 Arturo Prat	B3	United Kingdom	
7 Bernardo O'Higgins Riquelme	B3	15 Rothera	C3
8 Eduardo Frei Montalva	B3	United States	
9 Julio Escudero	B3	16 Palmer	C3
China		Uruguay	
10 Great Wall	B3	17 Artigas	B3

Contributions from the following organizations are gratefully acknowledged: National Science Foundation, Washington, D.C.; Norwegian Polar Institute, Tromsø, Norway; British Antarctic Survey, Cambridge, United Kingdom; University of Cambridge, Scott Polar Institute, Cambridge, United Kingdom; U.S. Navy/NOAA Joint Ice Center, Washington, D.C.; U.S. Geological Survey; Lamont-Doherty Earth Observatory of Columbia University, Palisades, New York; National Aeronautics and Space Administration. Special thanks to Richard S. Williams, Jr., John Smellie, George E. Watson, and Guy Gutheridge.

This was the location of Shackleton Base, point of departure for the Commonwealth Trans-Antarctic Expedition, which crossed the continent by tractor in 1957–58. Led by Sir Vivian Fuchs, the expedition traveled 3,472 kilometers (2,157 mi) to Scott Base in 99 days. A major calving event in 1986 removed more than 11,500 sq km (4,440 sq mi) of ice from the Filchner Ice Shelf.

LARSEN ICE SHELF
During the past few decades, the Larsen Ice Shelf has been disintegrating on the north and along its eastern margin to the south. In 2002 the northern region of the shelf experienced a major ice calving event which has been attributed to a summertime warming trend that has lasted for more than half a century.

HIGHEST POINT
At 4,897 m (16,067 ft) Vinson Massif is the highest elevation on Antarctica. It was climbed first by a U.S. team in 1966.

ELEVATION OF THE ICE SHEET
Many mountaintops rise higher than Antarctica's highest point—Vinson Massif, 4,897 m (16,067 ft)—but with an average elevation of 2,438 m (8,000 ft), the continent ranks as Earth's highest. Asia, its closest competitor, averages 914 m (3,000 ft). Roughly dome shaped, the ice sheet conceals much of the bedrock relief below. The 2,900-km-long (1,800 mi) Transantarctic Mountains rival the Rockies in height, but only the peaks break through the ice.

In 1898 Adrien de Gerlache de Gomery, a Belgian, led the first expedition to endure the Antarctic winter, after his ship froze in pack ice.

ICE SHELVES
Large areas of floating glacier ice fringe the coast of Antarctica. The two largest ice shelves are the Ross Ice Shelf and the Ronne Ice Shelf, both separated by glacier ice that is grounded below sea level. Large tabular icebergs periodically calve from ice shelves.

In 1841 Sir James Clark Ross, U.K., penetrated the pack ice to discover the ice shelf now named for him.

Rear Adm. Richard E. Byrd, USN, established five scientific stations (named Little America I through VI) on Ross Ice Shelf near the Bay of Whales, the first in 1928, the last in 1956. As the ice shelf flowed forward and calved off, the stations were carried out to sea.

MOUNT EREBUS
Almost always observed with a vapor cloud issuing from its large summit crater, 3,794-meter-tall (12,448 feet) Mt. Erebus is an active volcano. A deep inner crater discovered in 1972 holds a bubbling lava lake.

In 1899 C. E. Borchgrevink led a British expedition that was the first to winter on the continent.

Azimuthal Equidistant Projection
SCALE 1:14,673,000 · 1 CENTIMETER = 147 KILOMETERS; 1 INCH = 232 MILES

Elevations in meters
⦿ Year-round research station
Blue figures indicate thickness of the ice in meters.

230

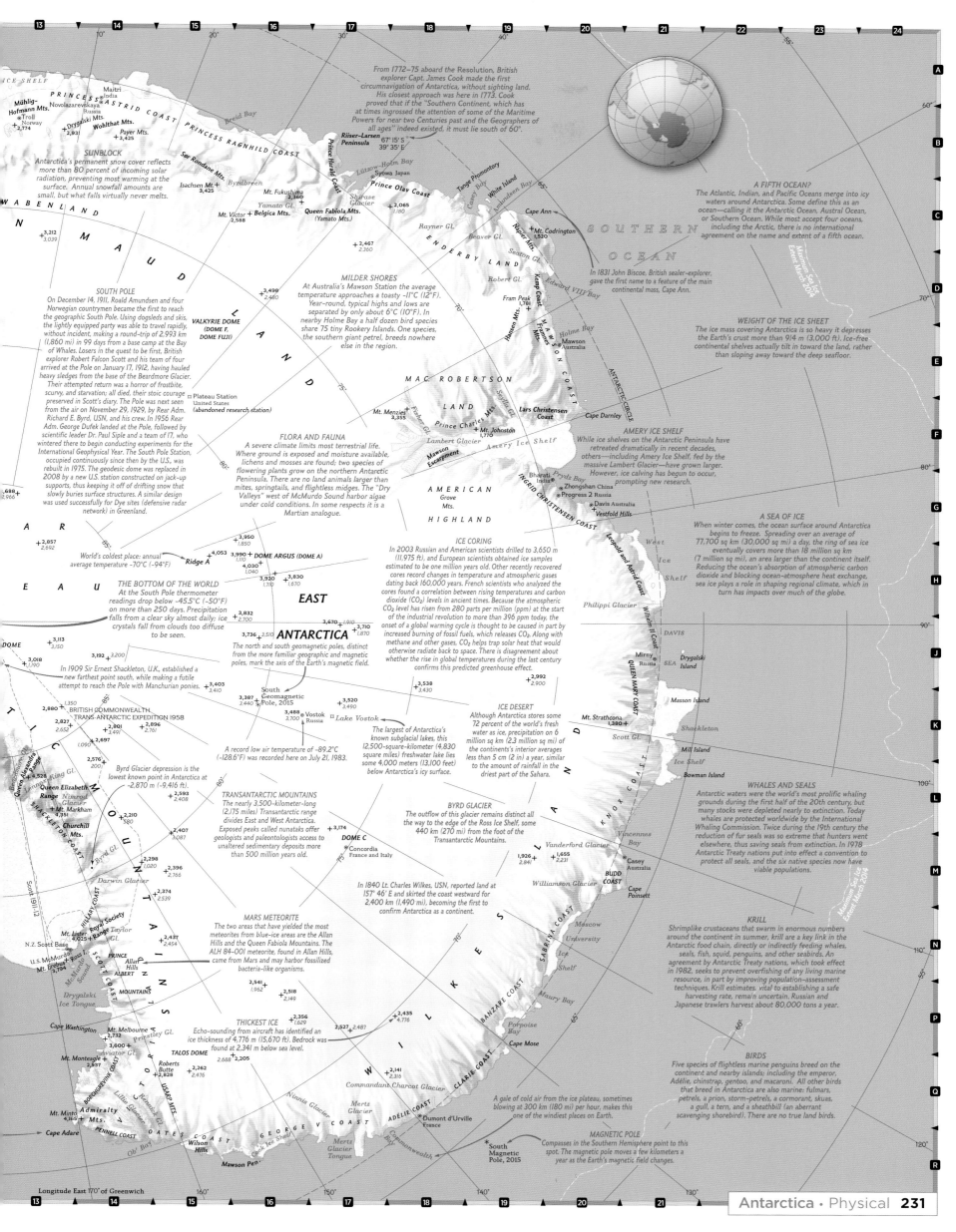

From 1772–75 aboard the Resolution, British explorer Capt. James Cook made the first circumnavigation of Antarctica, without sighting land. His closest approach was here in 1773. Cook proved that if the "Southern Continent, which has at times ingrossed the attention of some of the Maritime Powers for near two Centuries past and the Geographers of all ages" indeed existed, it must lie south of 60°.

SUNBLOCK
Antarctica's permanent snow cover reflects more than 80 percent of incoming solar radiation, preventing most warming at the surface. Annual snowfall amounts are small, but what falls virtually never melts.

A FIFTH OCEAN?
The Atlantic, Indian, and Pacific Oceans merge into icy waters around Antarctica. Some define this as an ocean—calling it the Antarctic Ocean, Austral Ocean, or Southern Ocean. While most accept four oceans, including the Arctic, there is no international agreement on the name and extent of a fifth ocean.

In 1831 John Biscoe, British sealer-explorer, gave the first name to a feature of the main continental mass, Cape Ann.

SOUTH POLE
On December 14, 1911, Roald Amundsen and four Norwegian countrymen became the first to reach the geographic South Pole. Using dogsleds and skis, the lightly equipped party was able to travel rapidly, without incident, making a round-trip of 2,993 km (1,860 mi) in 99 days from a base camp at the Bay of Whales. Losers in the quest to be first, British explorer Robert Falcon Scott and his team of four arrived at the Pole on January 17, 1912, having hauled heavy sledges from the base of the Beardmore Glacier. Their attempted return was a horror of frostbite, scurvy, and starvation; all died, their stoic courage preserved in Scott's diary. The Pole was next seen from the air on November 29, 1929, by Rear Adm. Richard E. Byrd, USN, and his crew. In 1956 Rear Adm. George Dufek landed at the Pole, followed by scientific leader Dr. Paul Siple and a team of 17, who wintered there to begin conducting experiments for the International Geophysical Year. The South Pole Station, occupied continuously since then by the U.S., was rebuilt in 1975. The geodesic dome was replaced in 2008 by a new U.S. station constructed on jack-up supports, thus keeping it off of drifting snow that slowly buries surface structures. A similar design was used successfully for Dye sites (defensive radar network) in Greenland.

WEIGHT OF THE ICE SHEET
The ice mass covering Antarctica is so heavy it depresses the Earth's crust more than half a mile (3,000 ft). Ice-free continental shelves actually tilt in toward the land, rather than sloping away toward the deep seafloor.

MILDER SHORES
At Australia's Mawson Station the average temperature approaches a toasty –11°C (12°F). Year-round, typical highs and lows are separated by only about 6°C (10°F). In nearby Holme Bay a half dozen bird species share 75 tiny Rookery Islands. One species, the southern giant petrel, breeds nowhere else in the region.

FLORA AND FAUNA
A severe climate limits most terrestrial life. Where ground is exposed and moisture available, lichens and mosses are found; two species of flowering plants grow on the northern Antarctic Peninsula. There are no land animals larger than mites, springtails, and flightless midges. The "Dry Valleys" west of McMurdo Sound harbor algae under cold conditions. In some respects it is a Martian analogue.

AMERY ICE SHELF
While ice shelves on the Antarctic Peninsula have retreated dramatically in recent decades, others—including Amery Ice Shelf, fed by the massive Lambert Glacier—have grown larger. However, ice calving has begun to occur, prompting new research.

ICE CORING
In 2003 Russian and American scientists drilled to 3,650 m (11,975 ft), and European scientists obtained ice samples estimated to be one million years old. Other recently recovered cores record changes in temperature and atmospheric gases dating back 160,000 years. French scientists who analyzed the cores found a correlation between rising temperatures and carbon dioxide (CO₂) levels in ancient times. Because the atmospheric CO₂ level has risen from 280 parts per million (ppm) at the start of the industrial revolution to more than 396 ppm today, the onset of a global warming cycle is thought to be caused in part by increased burning of fossil fuels, which releases CO₂. Along with methane and other gases, CO₂ helps trap solar heat that would otherwise radiate back to space. There is disagreement about whether the rise in global temperatures during the last century confirms this predicted greenhouse effect.

A SEA OF ICE
When winter comes, the ocean surface around Antarctica begins to freeze. Spreading over an average of 77,700 sq km (30,000 sq mi) a day, the ring of sea ice eventually covers more than 18 million sq km (7 million sq mi), an area larger than the continent itself. Reducing the ocean's absorption of atmospheric carbon dioxide and blocking ocean-atmosphere heat exchange, sea ice plays a role in shaping regional climate, which in turn has impacts over much of the globe.

THE BOTTOM OF THE WORLD
At the South Pole thermometer readings drop below –45.5°C (–50°F) on more than 250 days. Precipitation falls from a clear sky almost daily; ice crystals fall from clouds too diffuse to be seen.

World's coldest place: annual average temperature –70°C (–94°F)

EAST ANTARCTICA
The north and south geomagnetic poles, distinct from the more familiar geographic and magnetic poles, mark the axis of the Earth's magnetic field.

In 1909 Sir Ernest Shackleton, U.K., established a new farthest point south, while making a futile attempt to reach the Pole with Manchurian ponies.

The largest of Antarctica's known subglacial lakes, this 12,500-square-kilometer (4,830 square miles) freshwater lake lies some 4,000 meters (13,100 feet) below Antarctica's icy surface.

A record low air temperature of –89.2°C (–128.6°F) was recorded here on July 21, 1983.

ICE DESERT
Although Antarctica stores some 72 percent of the world's fresh water as ice, precipitation on 6 million sq km (2.3 million sq mi) of the continent's interior averages less than 5 cm (2 in) a year, similar to the amount of rainfall in the driest part of the Sahara.

BYRD GLACIER
The outflow of this glacier remains distinct all the way to the edge of the Ross Ice Shelf, some 440 km (270 mi) from the foot of the Transantarctic Mountains.

Byrd Glacier depression is the lowest known point in Antarctica at –2,870 m (–9,416 ft).

TRANSANTARCTIC MOUNTAINS
The nearly 3,500-kilometer-long (2,175 miles) Transantarctic range divides East and West Antarctica. Exposed peaks called nunataks offer geologists and paleontologists access to unaltered sedimentary deposits more than 500 million years old.

WHALES AND SEALS
Antarctic waters were the world's most prolific whaling grounds during the first half of the 20th century, but many stocks were depleted nearly to extinction. Today whales are protected worldwide by the International Whaling Commission. Twice during the 19th century the reduction of fur seals was so extreme that hunters went elsewhere, thus saving seals from extinction. In 1978 Antarctic Treaty nations put into effect a convention to protect all seals, and the six native species now have viable populations.

MARS METEORITE
The two areas that have yielded the most meteorites from blue-ice areas are the Allan Hills and the Queen Fabiola Mountains. The ALH 84-001 meteorite, from Allan Hills, came from Mars and may harbor fossilized bacteria-like organisms.

In 1840 Lt. Charles Wilkes, USN, reported land at 157° 46' E and skirted the coast westward for 2,400 km (1,490 mi), becoming the first to confirm Antarctica as a continent.

KRILL
Shrimplike crustaceans that swarm in enormous numbers around the continent in summer, krill are a key link in the Antarctic food chain, directly or indirectly feeding whales, seals, fish, squid, penguins, and other seabirds. An agreement by Antarctic Treaty nations, which took effect in 1982, seeks to prevent overfishing of any living marine resource, in part by improving population-assessment techniques. Krill estimates, vital to establishing a safe harvesting rate, remain uncertain. Russian and Japanese trawlers harvest about 80,000 tons a year.

THICKEST ICE
Echo-sounding from aircraft has identified an ice thickness of 4,776 m (15,670 ft). Bedrock was found at 2,341 m below sea level.

A gale of cold air from the ice plateau, sometimes blowing at 300 km (180 mi) per hour, makes this one of the windiest places on Earth.

BIRDS
Five species of flightless marine penguins breed on the continent and nearby islands, including the emperor, Adélie, chinstrap, gentoo, and macaroni. All other birds that breed in Antarctica are also marine: fulmars, petrels, a prion, storm-petrels, a cormorant, skuas, a gull, a tern, and a sheathbill (an aberrant scavenging shorebird). There are no true land birds.

MAGNETIC POLE
Compasses in the Southern Hemisphere point to this spot. The magnetic pole moves a few kilometers a year as the Earth's magnetic field changes.

Longitude East 170° of Greenwich

Exploring Antarctica

Elevation of the Ice Sheet

Antarctica is Earth's coldest, driest, and on average highest continent (about 7,200 ft; 2,194 m). The continent is covered by a vast ice sheet that blankets over 96 percent of the land mass. The highest point, located in East Antarctica, rises to 13,222 feet (4,030 m). The ice sheet is interrupted only by occasional mountain peaks that pierce the ice. One such peak is the Vinson Massif, Antarctica's highest point, which reaches

an elevation of 16,067 feet (4,897 m) and is located in West Antarctica. Otherwise the icy surface is smooth (surface slopes rarely exceed more than 1 or 2 degrees). The shape of the ice sheet is determined in part by the weight of the ice itself, which causes the ice to flow outward. It is also determined in part by forces acting at the base of the ice sheet that tend to restrain it. The balance of these forces leads to a characteristically

parabola-like shape. Departures from this simple shape occur as the ice from the interior domes spreads slowly over hills and valleys in the rocky base and where coastal mountain ranges channel the flow into outlet glaciers. Ice shelves form where there is sufficient ice to spread over the ocean. Ice shelves are the lowest and flattest parts of the ice sheet and are the source of the huge tabular icebergs that intermittently calve into the coastal ocean.

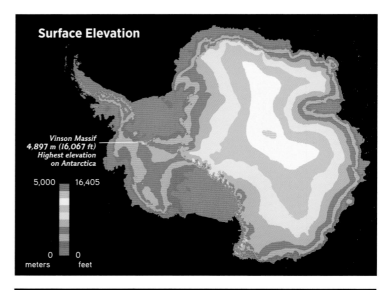

Surface Elevation

Vinson Massif 4,897 m (16,067 ft) Highest elevation on Antarctica

5,000   16,405

0   0
meters   feet

Measurements of a Paradox

Ninety percent of the world's ice and 70 percent of the world's freshwater are found here, yet most of Antarctica is truly a desert. The snow equivalent of less than three inches (76 mm) of rain falls over the high interior of the continent each year. But snow and ice have been slowly accumulating on Antarctica for millions of years. More than 15,600 feet (4,755 m) deep at its thickest, the mean depth of the ice

exceeds 6,600 feet (2,012 m). Ice is generally much thicker on the interior of the ice sheet than at edges. This is because ice flows from the interior to edges, where it eventually returns to the ocean either in the form of icebergs or by melting directly into the ocean. The few areas of thin ice on the interior lie over chains of subglacial mountains. Glaciologists measure ice thickness with either a downward-pointing radar or by

seismic sounding, which records the echo from an explosive shot buried just beneath the surface of the ice sheet. The thickness measurements used for this map were collected by scientists from 15 nations over the last 50 years. Although in theory the amount of ice in the ice sheet is sufficient to raise global sea levels by approximately 200 feet (60 m), it is extremely unlikely that the entire ice sheet could be lost in the foreseeable future.

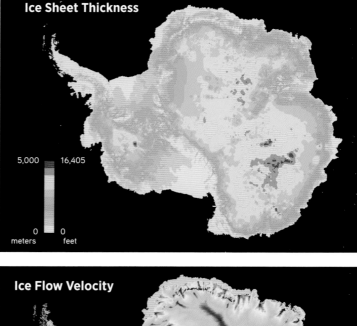

Ice Sheet Thickness

5,000   16,405

0   0
meters   feet

Ice on the Move

Glaciologists once thought that ice motion in Antarctica's interior was slow and relatively uniform, with just a few fast-moving outlet glaciers and some ice streams (in West Antarctica) drawing ice from the interior down to the ice shelves and the sea. A computer model of ice flow, based on new satellite elevation measurements, suggests a more intricate ice-movement pattern. Like rivers, coastal ice flows appear to be fed by

complex systems of tributaries that penetrate hundreds of miles into major drainage basins, and the major streams identified in East Antarctica dwarf those of the West. New satellite-based radar images agree with this more dynamic view. Ice velocities in the streams can be ten times greater than the flow of the adjacent slow-moving ice, and the resulting stream boundaries are often heavily crevassed and detectable from space.

The computer model combines measurements of surface elevation, ice sheet thickness, and snowfall to calculate the pattern of ice flow that would keep Antarctica in balance at its present shape. The resulting continent-wide baseline picture of this "balanced" flow generally resembles the actual situation, and detailed observations can be compared against it to uncover any changes occurring in the size and shape of the ice sheet.

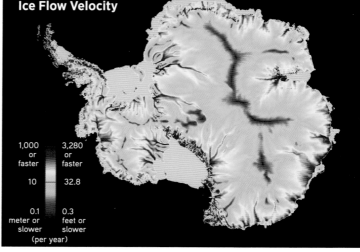

Ice Flow Velocity

1,000 or faster   3,280 or faster

10   32.8

0.1   0.3
meter or   feet or
slower   slower
(per year)

Ultimate Winds

Katabatic winds—cold air pouring down glacial slopes—often blow at 80 miles (129 km) an hour and can exceed 180 miles (290 km) an hour. These winds, which drain cold air masses from central Antarctica under the influence of gravity, are funnelled down valleys outward towards the coast, as indicated by the streamline arrows (right) on the white background of the Antarctic continent. When katabatic winds reach the coastline,

they often turn westward to blow counterclockwise around the continent. Offshore, circumpolar winds and currents push against the sea ice that grows to surround Antarctica each winter, leading to drift distances of up to several miles per day. The resulting near-shore movement of the sea ice is known as the East Wind drift because of the dominant winds from the east. In some locations, such as the Weddell Sea, the drift is forced

northward along the Antarctic Peninsula. In this case, and in the Bellingshausen, Amundsen, and Ross Seas, the combination of winds, currents, bathymetry, and topography leads to clockwise circulations known as gyres. In this image, the average sea-ice drift was determined from meteorological satellites. It illustrates the monthly average drift during the austral midwinter, when sea-ice cover is at its maximum extent.

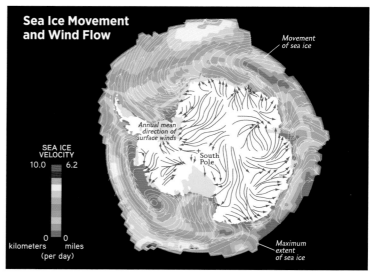

Sea Ice Movement and Wind Flow

Movement of sea ice

Annual mean direction of surface winds

+ South Pole

SEA ICE VELOCITY
10.0   6.2

0   0
kilometers   miles
(per day)

Maximum extent of sea ice

Antarctic Treaty

On December 1, 1959, after a decade of secret meetings, 12 nations—Argentina, Australia, Belgium, Chile, France, Japan, New Zealand, Norway, South Africa, the Soviet Union (Russia), the United Kingdom, and the United States—signed the Antarctic Treaty to preserve the frozen continent for peaceful scientific use only, a major feat during the height of Cold War rivalries. Since then, 32 other nations have joined.

The treaty includes all land, islands, and ice shelves south of 60° south latitude and enshrines the principles of peace, freedom of scientific research and exchange, and total banning of all military activity, nuclear testing, or disposal of radioactive waste. In addition, research stations are fully open to inspection, scientists may travel anywhere on the continent at any time, and countries can carry out aerial observations over any area.

A 1991 meeting prohibited mining in Antarctica. Other gatherings have asserted the importance of protecting wildlife, such as the Ross and fur seals, conserving unique biological habitats, and limiting human impact on sensitive ecological zones. The Antarctic Treaty made static all territorial claims held by 7 of the original 12 countries and prohibits any new claims. The treaty affirms that no country "rules the continent." For more than four decades it has proven to be an unprecedented example of international cooperation.

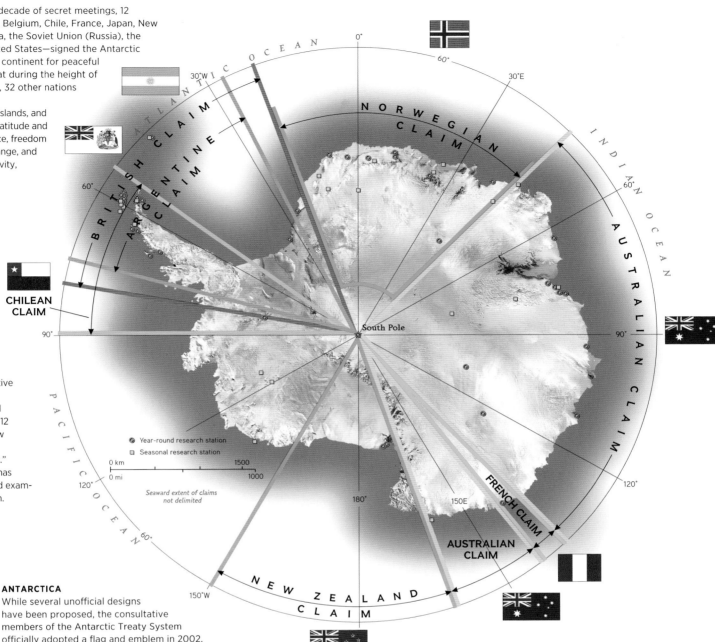

ANTARCTICA
While several unofficial designs have been proposed, the consultative members of the Antarctic Treaty System officially adopted a flag and emblem in 2002, which is now the official symbol of the continent.

Antarctic Convergence

The Antarctic Convergence refers to an undulating boundary in the seas that rings Antarctica roughly 950 miles (1,529 km) off the continental coast, between 50° and 60° south latitude. This narrow zone marks the meeting place of relatively warm waters from the southern Atlantic, Indian, and Pacific Oceans and the cold Antarctic Circumpolar Current. Because cold water sinks, it slips under the more buoyant warmer water and acts to power the great oceanic conveyor belt that affects life and weather around the world. The Antarctic Convergence also generates one of Earth's richest marine ecosystems. Mist and fog often rise at the interface of blended warm and cold waters. Immediately air becomes brisker and marine life alters. Water

temperatures can plummet a dozen degrees (Fahrenheit) or more upon entering the Southern Ocean. The Antarctic Convergence functions as a barrier and forms Antarctica's biological extent. It delimits the Southern Ocean, which holds 5.6 percent of the world's seawater, and thus creates a largely closed ecosystem and isolates the continent from warmer waters. Deep, cold waters permit the proliferation of diatoms—single-celled algae—that in turn support krill, shrimp-like organisms that exist in enormous numbers. Krill form a vital part of the food chain, directly or indirectly providing nutrition for Antarctica's amazing wildlife, particularly fish, seals, whales, and birds, including five species of flightless penguins. Losses of this food source

through over-harvesting by humans would seriously affect marine life. As one travels north into warmer regions beyond the Antarctic Convergence, krill—the basis of Antarctica's life—perish and disappear. The Southern Ocean's rich waters, full of plant and animal life, stand apart from the continent itself, frozen and incredibly harsh, where vegetation is limited to lichens, mosses, and a mere two species of flowering plants. A small insect known as the wingless midge represents the largest land animal. In contrast, large body size and slow growth mark many marine animals, all of which have adapted magnificently to the cold environment.

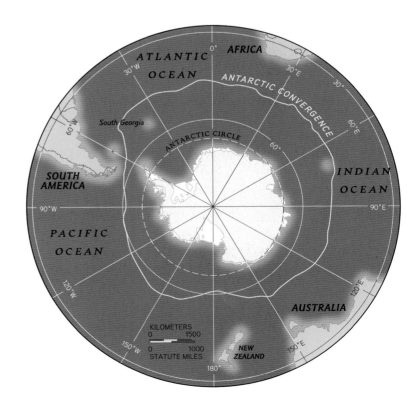

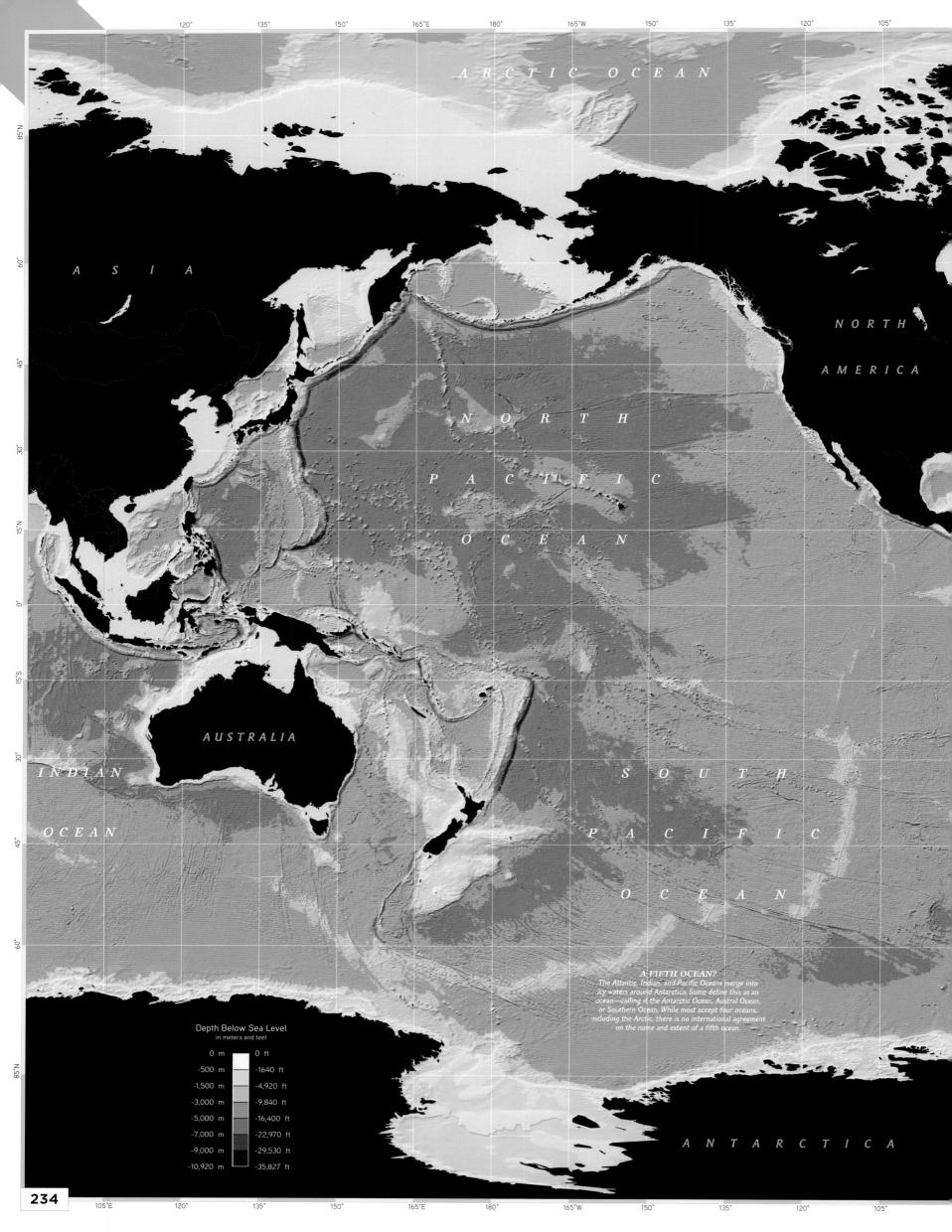

ARCTIC OCEAN

ASIA

NORTH

AMERICA

NORTH

PACIFIC

OCEAN

INDIAN

AUSTRALIA

SOUTH

OCEAN

PACIFIC

OCEAN

A FIFTH OCEAN?
The Atlantic, Indian, and Pacific Oceans merge into
icy waters around Antarctica. Some define this as an
ocean—calling it the Antarctic Ocean, Austral Ocean,
or Southern Ocean. While most accept four oceans,
including the Arctic, there is no international agreement
on the name and extent of a fifth ocean.

Depth Below Sea Level
in meters and feet

0 m	0 ft
-500 m	-1640 ft
-1,500 m	-4,920 ft
-3,000 m	-9,840 ft
-5,000 m	-16,400 ft
-7,000 m	-22,970 ft
-9,000 m	-29,530 ft
-10,920 m	-35,827 ft

ANTARCTICA

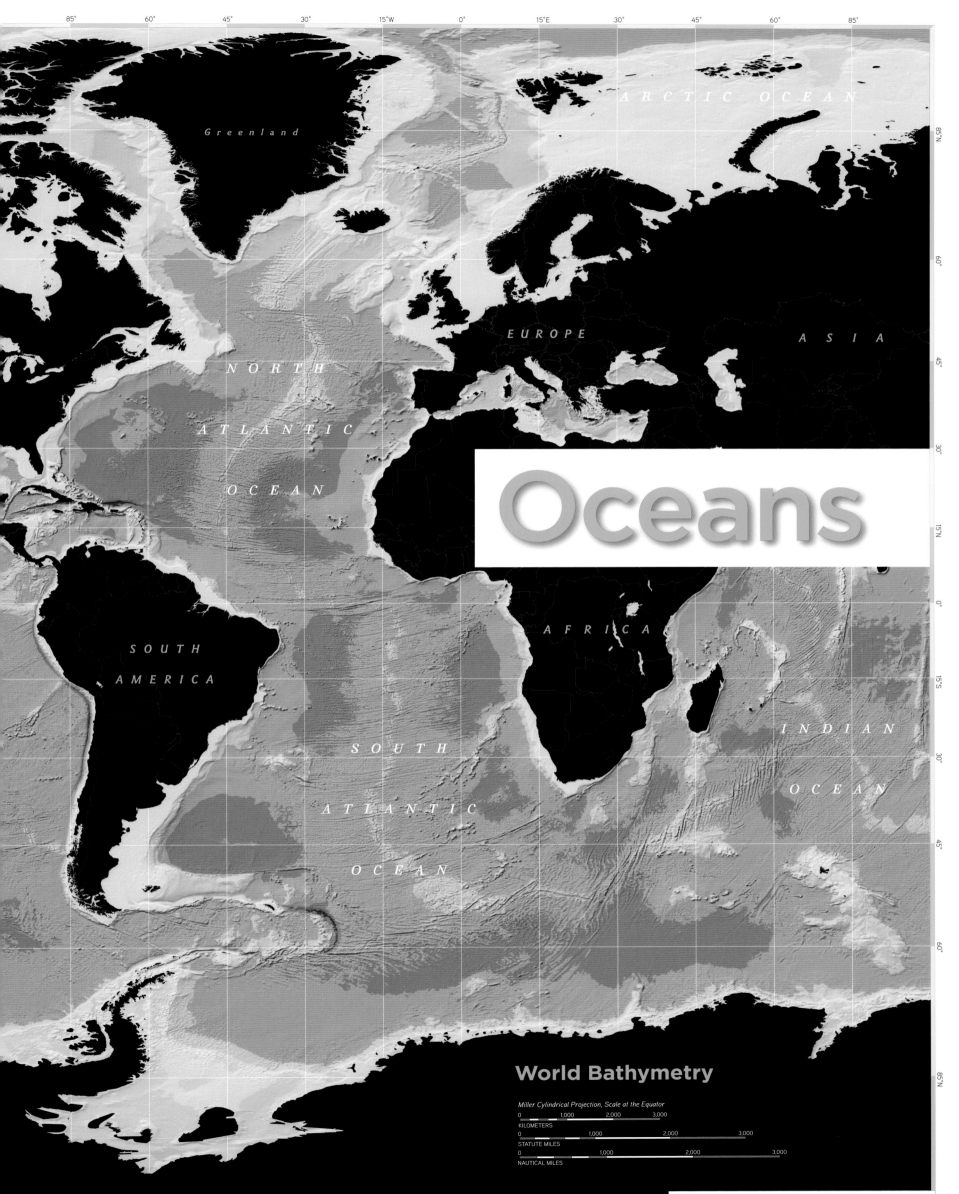

Oceans

World Bathymetry

ARCTIC OCEAN

Greenland

EUROPE

ASIA

NORTH

ATLANTIC

OCEAN

AFRICA

SOUTH
AMERICA

INDIAN

OCEAN

SOUTH

ATLANTIC

OCEAN

Miller Cylindrical Projection, Scale at the Equator

0	1,000	2,000	3,000

KILOMETERS

0	1,000	2,000	3,000

STATUTE MILES

0	1,000	2,000	3,000

NAUTICAL MILES

Oceanography

EARTH IS A WATERY PLANET: More than 70 percent of its surface is covered by interconnected bodies of salt water that together make up a continuous, global ocean. Over the centuries, people have created artificial boundaries that divide this great water body into smaller oceans with numerous seas, gulfs, bays, straits, and channels.

The global ocean is a dynamic participant in Earth's physical, chemical, and biological processes. Millions of years ago, life itself most likely evolved in its waters. These are restless waters, always in motion. Tidal movement—the regular rise and fall of the ocean surface—results from gravitational forces exerted by the sun and the moon. The spin of Earth on its axis, coupled with wind, generates surface currents that redistribute warm and cold water around the planet. Variations in the temperature and salinity of water keep the thermohaline circulation system moving; this enormous system of interconnected currents, at the surface and deep in the ocean, influences climate patterns and circulates vital nutrients.

Where marine and terrestrial realms meet, one may find reefs built by tiny coral polyps or see cliffs and sea stacks shaped by countless waves. Many coastal zones are threatened, however, by overdevelopment, pollution, and overfishing. Farther out, in the deep ocean, lie vast untouched plains, high mountains and ridges, and valleys with floors lying as much as seven miles (11 km) below the sea surface. Teeming with life, the ocean includes "rain forests of the sea" and a host of marine species— even creatures who dwell in superhot waters near hydrothermal vents.

New technology is helping scientists to explore ever deeper and farther and to create more accurate maps of the ocean. Some of this underwater world has been explored with diving vessels and satellite imagery, but so much more remains to be discovered.

The Ocean Floor

The ocean floor is dynamic and varied. From the edge of the continental shelf (the shelf break), the continental slope plunges to the continental rise, which reaches to the abyssal plain. Periodically, terrestrial rocks and sediment flow through submarine canyons and form alluvial fans. The Mid-Ocean Ridge builds new seafloor; erosion and subsidence create atolls and guyots; and subducting tectonic plates form deep trenches in the ocean floor.

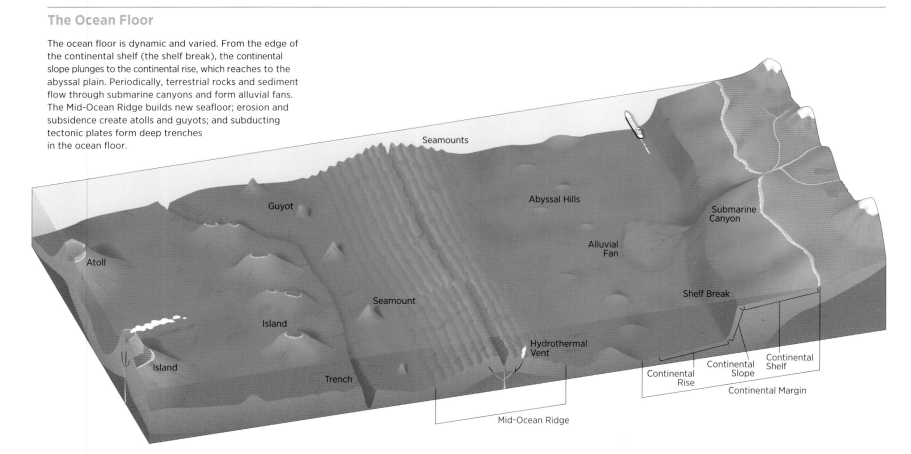

OCEAN WAVES

Waves may be born thousands of miles from shore, a result of large storms churning over the ocean. Wind pushing on the sea surface forms unorganized groups of waves that travel in all directions. In time, they organize into swell—groups of waves that can carry energy over thousands of miles of ocean. As the waves approach a surf zone, they steepen until their crests curl forward and break upon the beach.

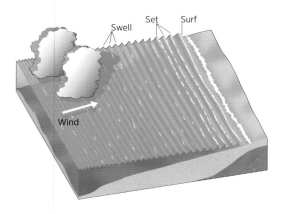

CORAL MORPHOLOGY

Coral reefs—Earth's largest structures with biological origins—form primarily in the tropics, where water is clear and warm. They begin as fringing reefs, colonies built along coastlines by tiny organisms known as coral polyps. As a coastal area subsides, a fringing reef becomes a barrier reef enclosing a protected lagoon. Corals on a reef's seaward side rely on spur and groove formations to withstand powerful waves.

COASTAL MORPHOLOGY

The contours of a coast determine how approaching ocean waves release their energy. In bays, wave energy is dispersed; at headlands, it is concentrated. Waves approaching at an angle produce longshore currents, which flow parallel to shore and transport sediment. Rip currents, generated by wind and the return flow of water, move outward. Over time, waves and currents reshape the coastlines of the world.

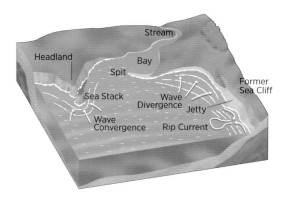

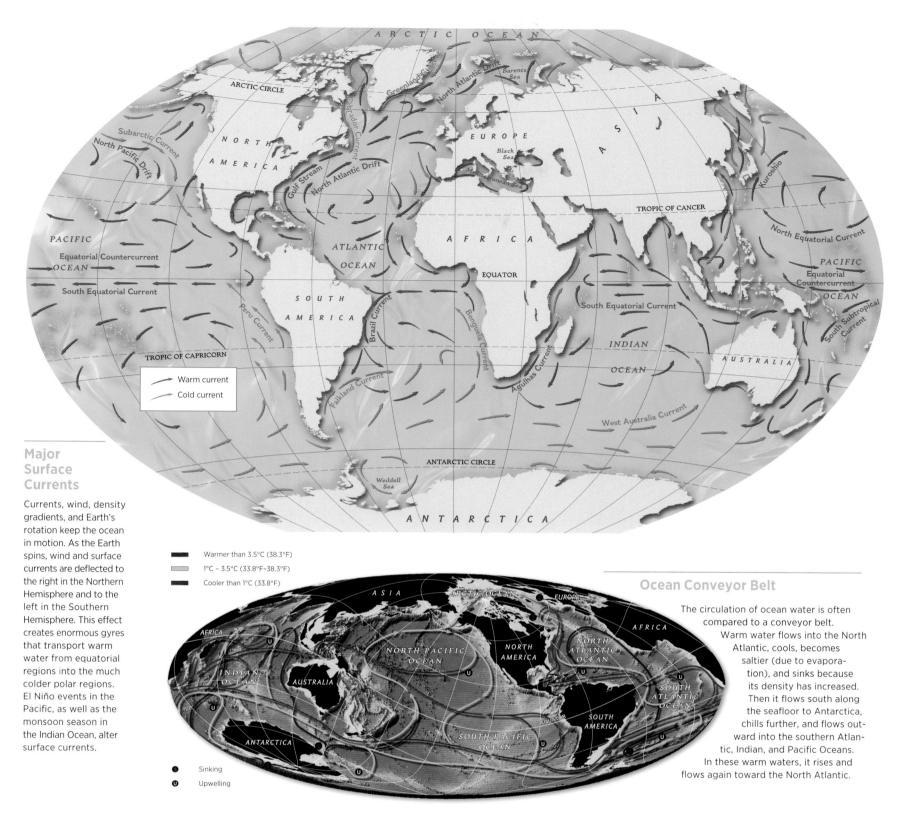

Major Surface Currents

Currents, wind, density gradients, and Earth's rotation keep the ocean in motion. As the Earth spins, wind and surface currents are deflected to the right in the Northern Hemisphere and to the left in the Southern Hemisphere. This effect creates enormous gyres that transport warm water from equatorial regions into the much colder polar regions. El Niño events in the Pacific, as well as the monsoon season in the Indian Ocean, alter surface currents.

Warm current
Cold current

- Warmer than 3.5°C (38.3°F)
- 1°C – 3.5°C (33.8°F–38.3°F)
- Cooler than 1°C (33.8°F)

● Sinking
◎ Upwelling

Ocean Conveyor Belt

The circulation of ocean water is often compared to a conveyor belt. Warm water flows into the North Atlantic, cools, becomes saltier (due to evaporation), and sinks because its density has increased. Then it flows south along the seafloor to Antarctica, chills further, and flows outward into the southern Atlantic, Indian, and Pacific Oceans. In these warm waters, it rises and flows again toward the North Atlantic.

TIDES

Both the sun and moon exert gravitational force on the Earth's ocean, creating tides. But because the moon is closer, its tug is much greater. During spring tides, when the moon is new or full, the combined pull of the sun and moon causes very high and low tides. Neap tides occur during the first and third quarters of the moon; at those times, the difference between tides is much smaller.

MAPPING THE OCEAN

Mapping the ocean requires myriad devices. In space, some satellites carry microwave radars to record data on wind speed and sea height; others use visible and infrared radiometers to collect biological productivity data. Radar altimetry and scatterometry are also used to record wind speed and direction. Out in the ocean, profiling floats collect temperature and salinity data. Ships use acoustics to map the seafloor.

THERMOHALINE CIRCULATION SYSTEM

Differences in the relative densities of volumes of water—determined by temperature (thermo) and salinity (haline)—drive thermohaline circulation. In polar regions, density increases as water cools and as evaporation makes it saltier; the mass of water sinks and flows along the ocean floor. Near the Equator, water warms and rises to the surface. If this system shut down, significant climate effects could occur.

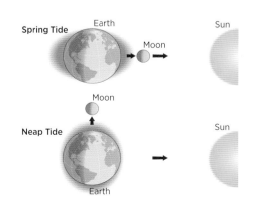

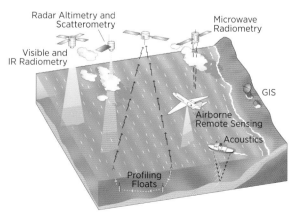

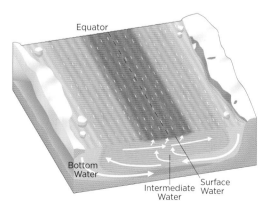

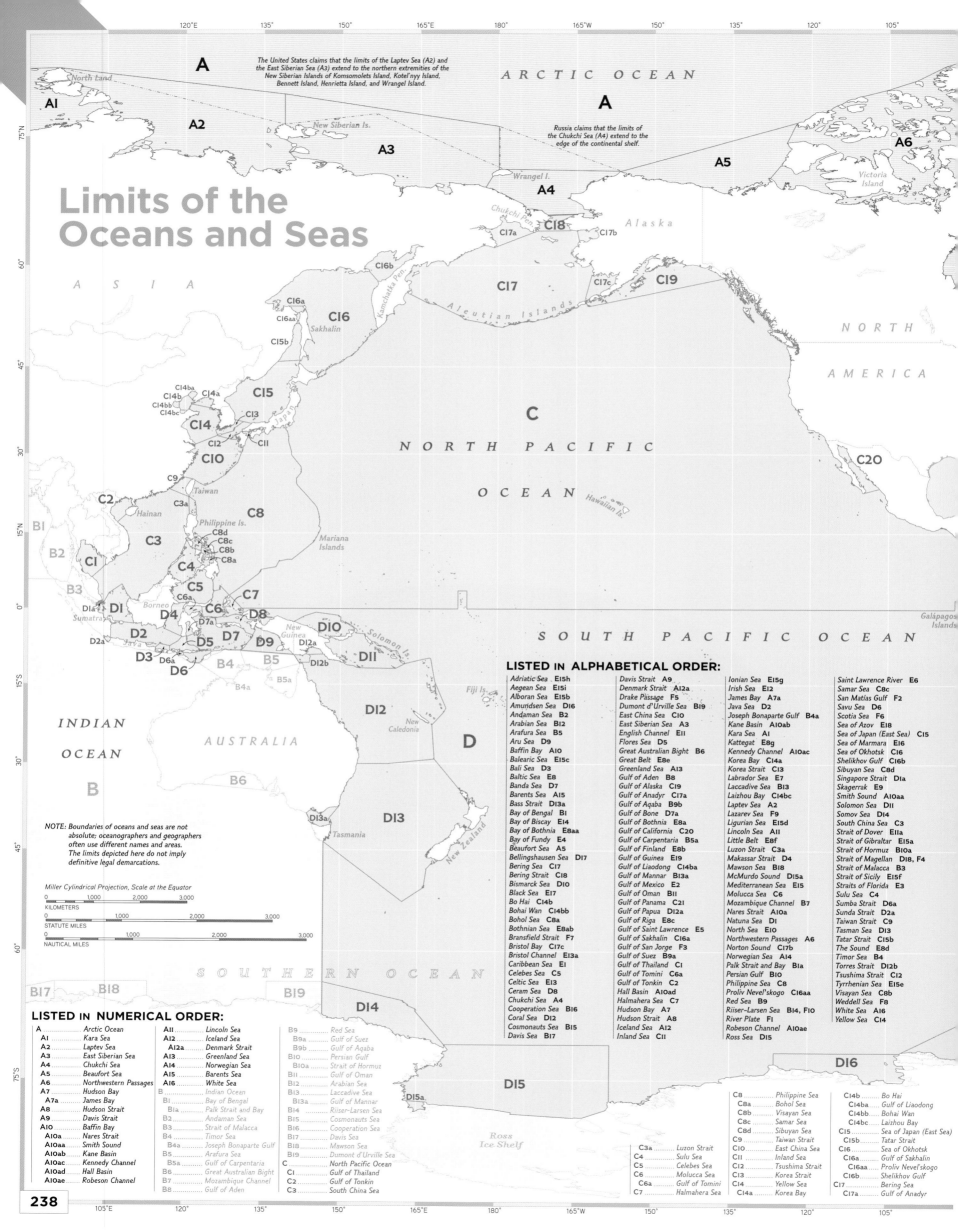

Limits of the Oceans and Seas

The United States claims that the limits of the Laptev Sea (A2) and the East Siberian Sea (A3) extend to the northern extremities of the New Siberian Islands of Komsomolets Island, Kotel'nyy Island, Bennett Island, Henrietta Island, and Wrangel Island.

Russia claims that the limits of the Chukchi Sea (A4) extend to the edge of the continental shelf.

NOTE: Boundaries of oceans and seas are not absolute; oceanographers and geographers often use different names and areas. The limits depicted here do not imply definitive legal demarcations.

Miller Cylindrical Projection, Scale at the Equator

LISTED IN ALPHABETICAL ORDER:

Sea	Code	Sea	Code	Sea	Code	Sea	Code
Adriatic Sea	E15h	Davis Strait	A9	Ionian Sea	E15g	Saint Lawrence River	E6
Aegean Sea	E15i	Denmark Strait	A12a	Irish Sea	E12	Samar Sea	C8c
Alboran Sea	E15b	Drake Passage	F5	James Bay	A7a	San Matías Gulf	F2
Amundsen Sea	D16	Dumont d'Urville Sea	B19	Java Sea	D2	Savu Sea	D6
Andaman Sea	B2	East China Sea	C10	Joseph Bonaparte Gulf	B4a	Scotia Sea	F6
Arabian Sea	B12	East Siberian Sea	A3	Kane Basin	A10ab	Sea of Azov	E18
Arafura Sea	B5	English Channel	E11	Kara Sea	A1	Sea of Japan (East Sea)	C15
Aru Sea	D9	Flores Sea	D5	Kattegat	E8g	Sea of Marmara	E16
Baffin Bay	A10	Great Australian Bight	B6	Kennedy Channel	A10ac	Sea of Okhotsk	C16
Balearic Sea	E15c	Great Belt	E8e	Korea Bay	C14a	Shelikhov Gulf	C16b
Bali Sea	D3	Greenland Sea	A13	Korea Strait	C13	Sibuyan Sea	C8d
Baltic Sea	E8	Gulf of Aden	B8	Laccadive Sea	B13	Singapore Strait	D1a
Banda Sea	D7	Gulf of Alaska	C19	Laizhou Bay	C14bc	Skagerrak	E9
Barents Sea	A15	Gulf of Anadyr	C17a	Laptev Sea	A2	Smith Sound	A10aa
Bass Strait	D13a	Gulf of Aqaba	B9b	Lazarev Sea	F9	Solomon Sea	D11
Bay of Bengal	B1	Gulf of Bone	D7a	Ligurian Sea	E15d	Somov Sea	D14
Bay of Biscay	E14	Gulf of Bothnia	E8a	Lincoln Sea	A11	South China Sea	C3
Bay of Bothnia	E8aa	Gulf of California	C20	Luzon Strait	C3a	Strait of Dover	E11a
Bay of Fundy	E4	Gulf of Carpentaria	B5a	Makassar Strait	D4	Strait of Gibraltar	E15a
Beaufort Sea	A5	Gulf of Finland	E8b	Mawson Sea	B18	Strait of Hormuz	B10a
Bellingshausen Sea	D17	Gulf of Guinea	E19	McMurdo Sound	D15a	Strait of Magellan	D18, F4
Bering Sea	C17	Gulf of Liaodong	C14ba	Mediterranean Sea	E15	Strait of Malacca	B3
Bering Strait	C18	Gulf of Mannar	B13a	Molucca Sea	C6	Strait of Sicily	E15f
Bismarck Sea	D10	Gulf of Mexico	E2	Mozambique Channel	B7	Straits of Florida	E3
Black Sea	E17	Gulf of Oman	B11	Nares Strait	A10a	Sulu Sea	C4
Bo Hai	C14b	Gulf of Panama	C21	Natuna Sea	D1	Sumba Strait	D6a
Bohai Wan	C14bb	Gulf of Papua	D12a	North Sea	E10	Sunda Strait	D2a
Bohol Sea	C8a	Gulf of Riga	E8c	Northwestern Passages	A6	Taiwan Strait	C9
Bothnian Sea	E8ab	Gulf of Saint Lawrence	E5	Norton Sound	C17b	Tasman Sea	D13
Bransfield Strait	F7	Gulf of Sakhalin	C16a	Norwegian Sea	A14	Tatar Strait	C15b
Bristol Bay	C17c	Gulf of San Jorge	F3	Palk Strait and Bay	B1a	The Sound	E8d
Bristol Channel	E13a	Gulf of Suez	B9a	Persian Gulf	B10	Timor Sea	B4
Caribbean Sea	E1	Gulf of Thailand	C1	Philippine Sea	C8	Torres Strait	D12b
Celebes Sea	C5	Gulf of Tomini	C6a	Proliv Nevel'skogo	C16aa	Tsushima Strait	C12
Celtic Sea	E13	Gulf of Tonkin	C2	Red Sea	B9	Tyrrhenian Sea	E15e
Ceram Sea	D8	Hall Basin	A10ad	Riiser-Larsen Sea	B14, F10	Visayan Sea	C8b
Chukchi Sea	A4	Halmahera Sea	C7	River Plate	F1	Weddell Sea	F8
Cooperation Sea	B16	Hudson Bay	A7	Robeson Channel	A10ae	White Sea	A16
Coral Sea	D12	Hudson Strait	A8	Ross Sea	D15	Yellow Sea	C14
Cosmonauts Sea	B15	Iceland Sea	A12				
Davis Sea	B17	Inland Sea	C11				

LISTED IN NUMERICAL ORDER:

A	Arctic Ocean	A11	Lincoln Sea	B9	Red Sea	C8	Philippine Sea
A1	Kara Sea	A12	Iceland Sea	B9a	Gulf of Suez	C8a	Bohol Sea
A2	Laptev Sea	A12a	Denmark Strait	B9b	Gulf of Aqaba	C8b	Visayan Sea
A3	East Siberian Sea	A13	Greenland Sea	B10	Persian Gulf	C8c	Samar Sea
A4	Chukchi Sea	A14	Norwegian Sea	B10a	Strait of Hormuz	C8d	Sibuyan Sea
A5	Beaufort Sea	A15	Barents Sea	B11	Arabian Sea	C9	Taiwan Strait
A6	Northwestern Passages	A16	White Sea	B12	Arabian Sea	C10	East China Sea
A7	Hudson Bay	B	Indian Ocean	B13	Laccadive Sea	C11	Inland Sea
A7a	James Bay	B1	Bay of Bengal	B13a	Gulf of Mannar	C12	Tsushima Strait
A8	Hudson Strait	B1a	Palk Strait and Bay	B14	Riiser-Larsen Sea	C13	Korea Strait
A9	Davis Strait	B2	Andaman Sea	B15	Cosmonauts Sea	C14	Yellow Sea
A10	Baffin Bay	B3	Strait of Malacca	B16	Cooperation Sea	C14a	Korea Bay
A10a	Nares Strait	B4	Timor Sea	B17	Davis Sea	C14b	Bo Hai
A10aa	Smith Sound	B4a	Joseph Bonaparte Gulf	B18	Mawson Sea	C14ba	Gulf of Liaodong
A10ab	Kane Basin	B5	Arafura Sea	B19	Dumont d'Urville Sea	C14bb	Bohai Wan
A10ac	Kennedy Channel	B5a	Gulf of Carpentaria	C	North Pacific Ocean	C14bc	Laizhou Bay
A10ad	Hall Basin	B6	Great Australian Bight	C1	Gulf of Thailand	C15	Sea of Japan (East Sea)
A10ae	Robeson Channel	B7	Mozambique Channel	C2	Gulf of Tonkin	C15b	Tatar Strait
		B8	Gulf of Aden	C3	South China Sea	C16	Sea of Okhotsk
				C3a	Luzon Strait	C16a	Gulf of Sakhalin
				C4	Sulu Sea	C16aa	Proliv Nevel'skogo
				C5	Celebes Sea	C16b	Shelikhov Gulf
				C6	Molucca Sea	C17	Bering Sea
				C6a	Gulf of Tomini	C17a	Gulf of Anadyr
				C7	Halmahera Sea		

A FIFTH OCEAN?
The Atlantic, Indian, and Pacific Oceans merge into icy waters around Antarctica. Some define this as an ocean—calling it the Antarctic Ocean, Austral Ocean, or Southern Ocean. While most accept four oceans, including the Arctic, there is no international agreement on the name and extent of a fifth ocean.

C17b	Norton Sound
C17c	Bristol Bay
C18	Bering Strait
C19	Gulf of Alaska
C20	Gulf of California
C21	Gulf of Panama
D	South Pacific Ocean
D1	Natuna Sea
D1a	Singapore Strait
D2	Java Sea
D2a	Sunda Strait
D3	Bali Sea
D4	Makassar Strait
D5	Flores Sea
D6	Savu Sea
D6a	Sumba Strait
D7	Banda Sea
D7a	Gulf of Bone
D8	Ceram Sea
D9	Aru Sea
D10	Bismarck Sea
D11	Solomon Sea
D12	Coral Sea
D12a	Gulf of Papua
D12b	Torres Strait
D13	Tasman Sea
D13a	Bass Strait
D14	Somov Sea
D15	Ross Sea
D15a	McMurdo Sound
D16	Amundsen Sea
D17	Bellingshausen Sea
D18	Strait of Magellan
E	North Atlantic Ocean
E1	Caribbean Sea
E2	Gulf of Mexico
E3	Straits of Florida
E4	Bay of Fundy
E5	Gulf of St. Lawrence
E6	St. Lawrence River
E7	Labrador Sea
E8	Baltic Sea
E8a	Gulf of Bothnia
E8aa	Bay of Bothnia
E8ab	Bothnian Sea
E8b	Gulf of Finland
E8c	Gulf of Riga
E8d	The Sound
E8e	Great Belt
E8f	Little Belt
E8g	Kattegat
E9	Skagerrak
E10	North Sea
E11	English Channel
E11a	Strait of Dover
E12	Irish Sea
E13	Celtic Sea
E13a	Bristol Channel
E14	Bay of Biscay
E15	Mediterranean Sea
E15a	Strait of Gibraltar
E15b	Alboran Sea
E15c	Balearic Sea
E15d	Ligurian Sea
E15e	Tyrrhenian Sea
E15f	Strait of Sicily
E15g	Ionian Sea
E15h	Adriatic Sea
E15i	Aegean Sea
E16	Sea of Marmara
E17	Black Sea
E18	Sea of Azov
E19	Gulf of Guinea
F	South Atlantic Ocean
F1	River Plate
F2	San Matías Gulf
F3	Gulf of San Jorge
F4	Strait of Magellan
F5	Drake Passage
F6	Scotia Sea
F7	Bransfield Strait
F8	Weddell Sea
F9	Lazarev Sea
F10	Riiser-Larsen Sea

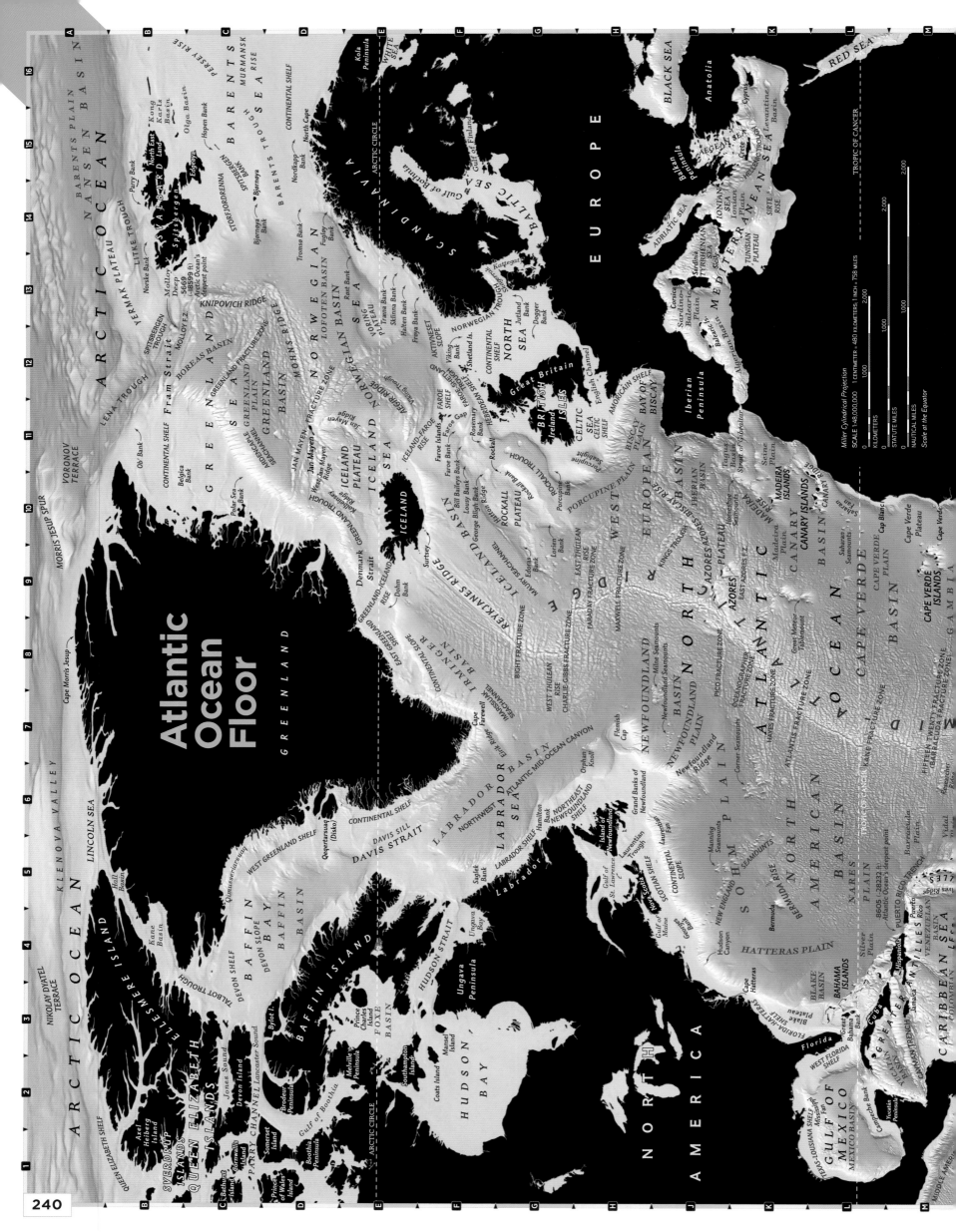

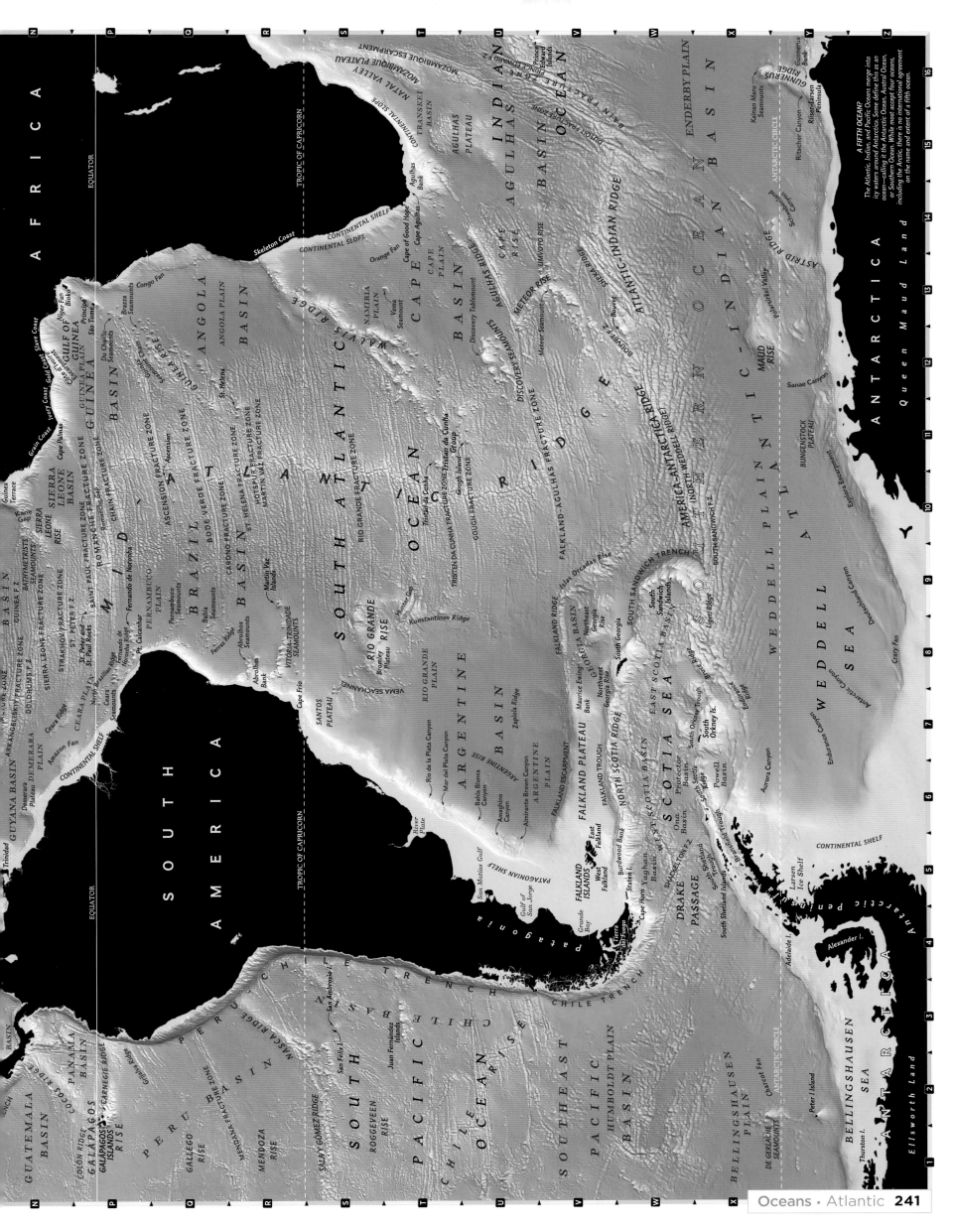

A FIFTH OCEAN?
The Atlantic, Indian, and Pacific Oceans merge into icy waters around Antarctica. Some define this as an ocean—calling it the Antarctic Ocean, Austral Ocean, or Southern Ocean. While most accept four oceans, including the Arctic, there is no international agreement on the name and extent of a fifth ocean.

Pacific
Ocean
Floor

Miller Cylindrical Projection

SCALE 1:51,000,000   1 CENTIMETER = 510 KILOMETERS; 1 INCH = 805 MILES

KILOMETERS
STATUTE MILES
NAUTICAL MILES

Scale at the Equator

CHALLENGER DEEP
The world's deepest point—the Challenger Deep—is located near the southern end of the Mariana Trench and consists of three depressions: an eastern (the deepest), a central, and a western, each of which is six to ten kilometers (4 to 6 mi) long and two kilometers (1 mi) wide. Reports of its maximum depth have varied over the years. To date, UNESCO's Intergovernmental Oceanographic Commission (IOC) and the International Hydrographic Organization (IHO) confirm the recorded depth at 10,920 meters (35,827 ft). This depth reflects the lowest level of vertical uncertainty (±10 meters [±33 ft]) of all current surveys.

On January 23, 1960, Jacques Picard and Lt. Don Walsh, U.S.N., were the first humans to descend 10,912 meters (35,800 ft) into the Challenger Deep in the U.S. Navy bathyscaph Trieste. Over 50 years later, on March 26, 2013, James Cameron piloted the DEEPSEA CHALLENGER to a depth of 10,908 meters (35,787 ft), becoming the first to reach this 11-kilometer-deep (6.8 mi) trough solo.

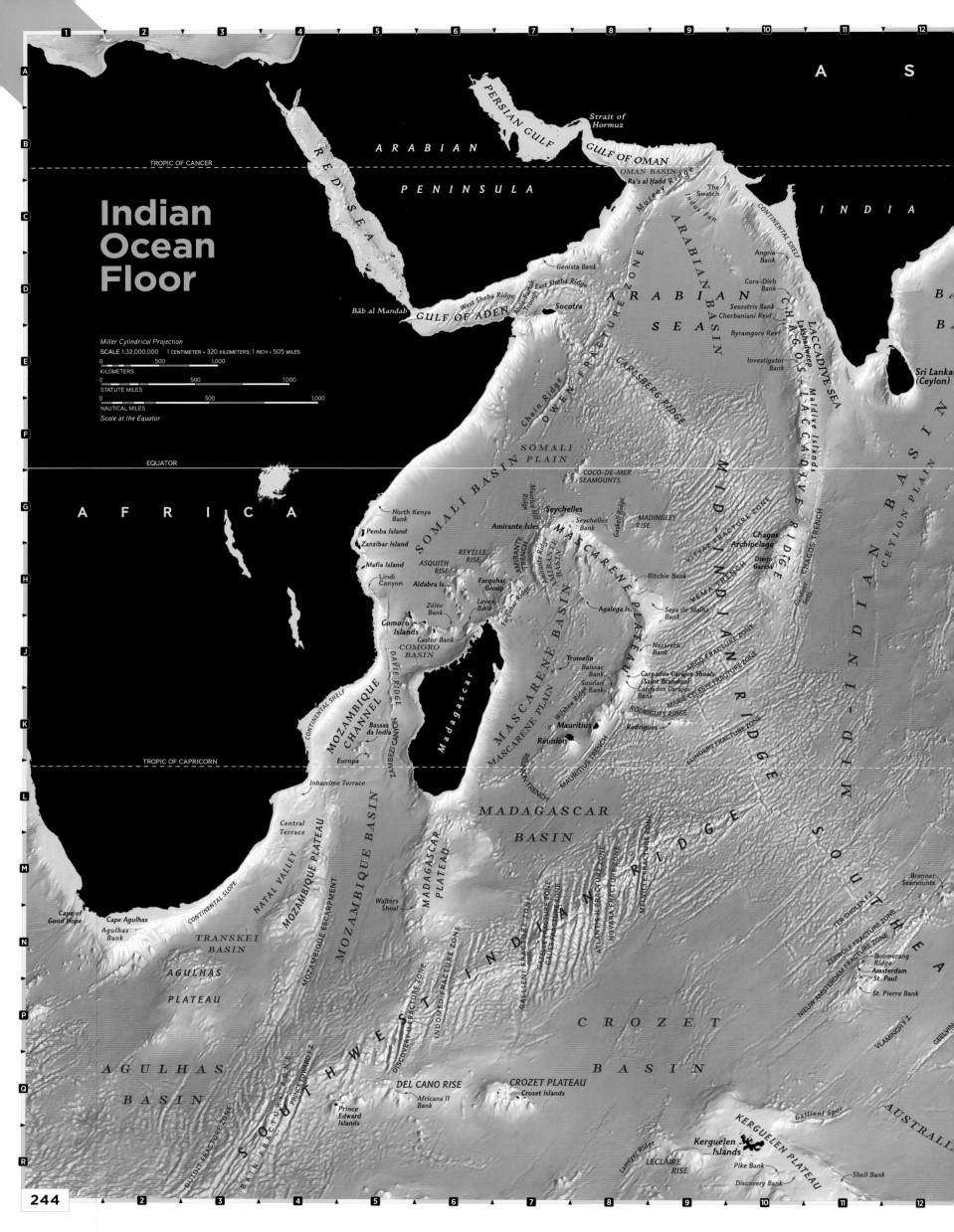

Arctic Ocean Floor

Azimuthal Equidistant Projection

SCALE 1:15,500,000   1 CENTIMETER = 155 KILOMETERS; 1 INCH = 245 MILES

KILOMETERS
0   200   400   600

STATUTE MILES
0   200   400   600

NAUTICAL MILES
0   200   400   600

Scale at the Equator

ARCTIC CIRCLE

A S I A

S I B E R I A

OKHOTSK BASIN

SEA OF OKHOTSK

Sakhalin

Kamchatka Peninsula

Shelikhov Gulf

Commander Islands

COMMANDER BASIN

SHIRSHOV RIDGE

ALEUTIAN BASIN

BERING SEA

Zhemchug Canyon

Pribilof Islands

St. Lawrence Island

CONTINENTAL SHELF

Gulf of Anadyr

Chukchi Peninsula

NORTON PLAIN

Bering Strait
Bering Strait Valley

Nunivak Island

Norton Sound

Seward Peninsula

Kotzebue Sound

ALASKA

Bristol Bay

Kodiak Island

Kenai Peninsula

Alaska Peninsula

PACIFIC OCEAN

GULF OF ALASKA

GULF OF ALASKA SEAMOUNT PROVINCE

ALASKA PLAIN

GILBERT SEAMOUNTS

PATTON SEAMOUNTS

Kolyma Lowland

EAST SIBERIAN SEA

Bear Islands

Ayon Island

Chaun Bay

Kolyma Valley

Wrangel Island

Herald Valley

CHUKCHI SEA

Herald Bank

CHUKCHI SHELF

Hope Valley

Hanna Bank

Point Barrow

Barrow Canyon

LAPTEV SEA

Gulf of Yana

Buor-Khaya Bay

LAPTEV SHELF

Olenëk Valley

Lyakhov Islands

Yana Valley

ANJOU ISLANDS

NEW SIBERIAN ISLANDS

NEW SIBERIAN SHELF

Bennett Island

Zhokhova

Henrietta Island

Jeannette Island

EAST SIBERIAN SHELF

CONTINENTAL SHELF

CONTINENTAL SLOPE

Taymyr Peninsula

NORTH LAND

Bol'shevik Island

October Revolution Island

Komsomolets Island

NANSEN

SADKO VALLEY

EURASIA

GAKKEL

AMUNDSEN

POLE

Rassokho Seamounts

LOMONOSOV

WRANGEL PLAIN

MAKAROV BASIN

KUCHEROV TERRACE

Arlis Spur

SARGO PLATEAU

MENDELEYEV RIDGE

Oden Spur

SHMAKOVES

ARLIS Gap

FLETCHER PLAIN

CHUKCHI PLAIN

Charlie Gap

MENDELEYEV PLAIN

NAUTILUS BASIN

Ryabov Seamounts

CHUKCHI PLATEAU

NAUTILUS SPUR

MARVIN SPUR

ALPHA RIDGE

CHUKCHI BORDERLAND

Skosyrev Ridge

Nautilus Gap

Beal Knoll

Hall Knoll

NORTHWIND PLAIN

NORTHWIND RIDGE

Hanna Canyon

NORTHWIND ESCARPMENT

CANADA PLAIN

CANADA BASIN

STEFANSSON BASIN

Pearya Spur

SEVER SPUR

QUEEN ELIZABETH RISE

CONTINENTAL SLOPE

QUEEN ELIZABETH SHELF

BEAUFORT SHELF

BEAUFORT SLOPE

BEAUFORT RISE

Mackenzie Trough

BEAUFORT TERRACE

BEAUFORT SEA

BANKS RISE

Banks Slope

BANKS SHELF

Banks Island

Amundsen Gulf

MELVILLE TROUGH

ARCTIC CIRCLE

NORTH AMERICA

Borden Island

Prince Patrick Island

Ballantyne Str.

Mackenzie King I.

Prince Gustaf Adolf Sea

Ellef Ringnes Island

Peary Chan.

Axel Heiberg Island

SVERDRUP ISLANDS

QUEEN ELIZABETH IS.

PARRY ISLANDS

Melville Island

M'Clure Strait

Bathurst Island

Cornwallis I.

PARRY CHAN.

Viscount Melville Sound

Victoria Island

M'Clintock Channel

Prince of Wales Island

Somerset Island

Boothia Peninsula

King William Island

Gulf of

Gyda
Peninsula

Yenysey Gulf

Yamal Peninsula

Gulf of Ob

Baydaratta Bay

Pechora Bay

Chesha Bay

WHITE SEA

Kola Peninsula

ARCTIC CIRCLE

EUROPE

KARA SHELF

KARA SEA

BARENTS SHELF

Gulf of Finland

BALTIC SEA

CENTRAL KARA RISE

EAST NOVAYA ZEMLYA TROUGH

Novaya Zemlya

Gusinaya Bank

North Kanin Bank

Kanin Bank

Murman Rise

Gulf of Bothnia

SCANDINAVIA

VORONIN TROUGH

Medvezhy Trough   ADMIRALTEYSTVO TROUGH

Al'banov Bank

WEST NOVAYA ZEMLYA TROUGH

CENTRAL BASIN

Skolpen Bank

SVYATAYA ANNA TROUGH

ADMIRALTEYSTVO RISE

BARENTS

Central Bank

Thor Iversen Bank

Tiddly Bank

CONTINENTAL SHELF

North Cape

Nordkapp Bank

SEA

Graham Bell I.

FRANZ JOSEF LAND

George Land

Ushakov Bank

PERSEY RISE

MURMANSK RISE   BARENTS TROUGH

Real Bank

SVYATAYA ANNA FAN

Alexandra Land

FRANTS VIKTORIYA TROUGH

OLGA BASIN

Stor Bank

Hopen Bank

SPITSBERGEN BANK

Røst Bank

Sklinna Bank

Skagerrak

Kattegat

BARENTS PLAIN

BARENTS BASIN

Kong Karls Basin

North East Land

STOREFJORDRENNA

Edgeøya

Bjørnøya

Bjørnøya Bank

Tromsø Bank

Trøna Bank

Halten Bank

NORTH

Litefjold Ridge

Parry Bank

SVALBARD

Spitsbergen

Sørkapp Bank

Hornsund Valley

Hornsund Bank

Frøya Bank

NORWEGIAN

NORWEGIAN TROUGH

SEA

LITKE TROUGH

Bellsund Valley

Isfjordrenna

LOFOTEN BASIN

VORING PLATEAU

AKTIVNESET SLOPE

SHETLAND ISLANDS

YERMAK PLATEAU

Norske Bank

Isfjord Bank

Molloy Deep -5669 (-18599 ft) Arctic Ocean's deepest point

KNIPOVICH RIDGE

DUMSHAF PLAIN

MOHNS RIDGE

NORWEGIAN BASIN

MERIDIAN OF GREENWICH (LONDON)

FAROE-SHETLAND TROUGH

North Pole

Morozov Ridge

Nansen Ridge

SPITSBERGEN TROUGH

MOLLOY F.Z.

BOREAS BASIN

GREENLAND FRACTURE ZONE

AEGIR RIDGE

VIKING TROUGH

HEBRIDEAN SHELF

Orkney Is.

Great Britain

BRIDGE

BASIN

LENA TROUGH

Fram Strait

GREENLAND

Greenland PLAIN

GREENLAND BASIN

Jan Mayen

JAN MAYEN FRACTURE ZONE

FAROE SHELF

FAROE ISLANDS

BRITISH ISLES

Ob' Bank

CONTINENTAL SHELF

JAN MAYEN RIDGE

Faroe Gap

RIDGE

Morozov Ridge

MORRIS JESUP SPUR

VORONOV TERRACE

Zhilinsky Spur

Belgica Bank

Polar Sea Bank

West Jan Mayen Ridge

ICELAND PLATEAU

ICELAND-FAROE RISE

Faroe Bank

Bill Baileys Bank

Lousy Bank

Rosemary Bank

Hebrides Seamount

NIKOLAY DYBTSEV TERRACE

Cape Morris Jesup

KLENOVA VALLEY

LINCOLN SEA

KOLBEINSEY RIDGE

Seyðisfjarðardjúp

Bakkaflóadjúp

Berufjarðaráll

Lónsdjúp

Hornafjarðardjúp

Anton Dohrn Seamount

George Bligh Bank

ROCKALL TROUGH

GREENLAND TROUGH

Axarfjarðardjúp

Skjálfandadjúp

Breiöamerkurdjúp

Skeiöarárdjúp

Rockall

ROCKALL BANK

GREENLAND

Scoresby Valley

Eyjafjarðardjúp

ICELAND

ROCKALL PLATEAU

Hatton-Rockall Basin

Ellesmere Island

Kane Basin

Denmark Strait

Húnaflóaáll

Reynisdjúp

ICELAND BASIN

HATTON RIDGE

Edoras Bank

Djúpáll

Heimaey

Surtsey

MAURY SEACHANNEL

Garðar Ridge

Ost Bank

GREENLAND-ICELAND RISE

Víkuráll

Kolluáll

Grindavíkurdjúp

Jökuldjúp

Skerjadjúp

TALBOT TROUGH

Kangerlussuaq Valley

EAST GREENLAND SHELF

Dohm Bank

CONTINENTAL SLOPE

Danielsen Canyon

REYKJANES RIDGE

Jones Sound

Qimusseriarsuaq

WEST GREENLAND SHELF

DEVON SLOPE

DEVON SHELF

Sermilik Valley

Skræling Canyon

IRMINGER BASIN

Devon Island

LANCASTER TROUGH

BAFFIN

WEST GREENLAND SLOPE

Bylot I.

BAY

Qeqertarsuaq (Disko)

Skjoldungen Valley

Skjoldungen Bank

BIGHT FRACTURE ZONE

Brodeur Peninsula

BAFFIN BASIN

Disko Bank

Danells Valley

IMARSSUAK SEACHANNEL

Baffin Island

Store Hellefiske Bank

Lindenows Valley

Cape Farewell

CHARLIE-GIBBS FRACTURE ZONE

Boothia

Melville Peninsula

Prince Charles Island

DAVIS STRAIT

DAVIS SILL

Sukkertoppen Bank

Sukkertoppen Valley

Godthåb Valley

Danas Valley

Danish Valley

Frederikshåbs Bank

Nanortalik Bank

Julianehåb Valley

Eirik Ridge

ATLANTIC OCEAN

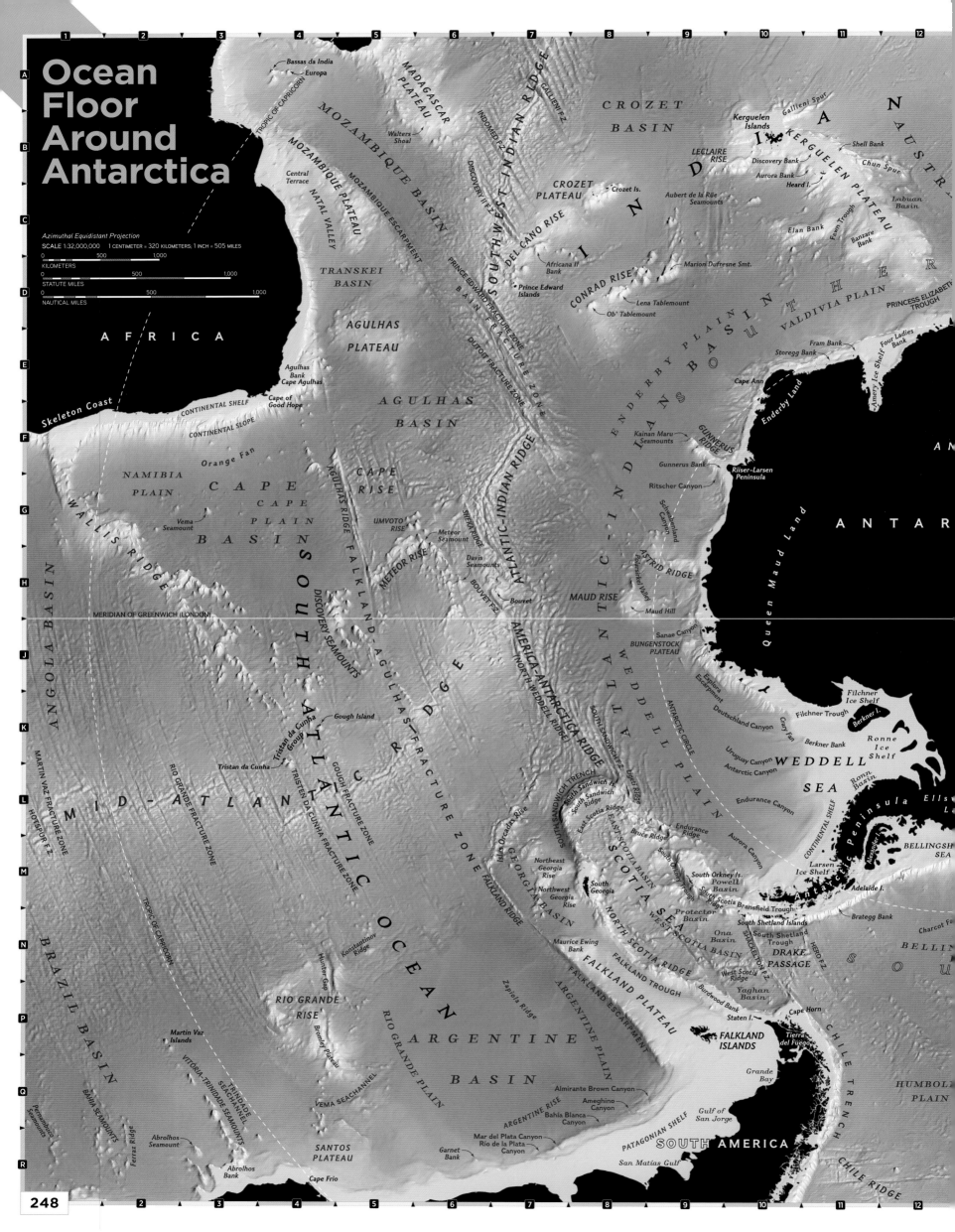

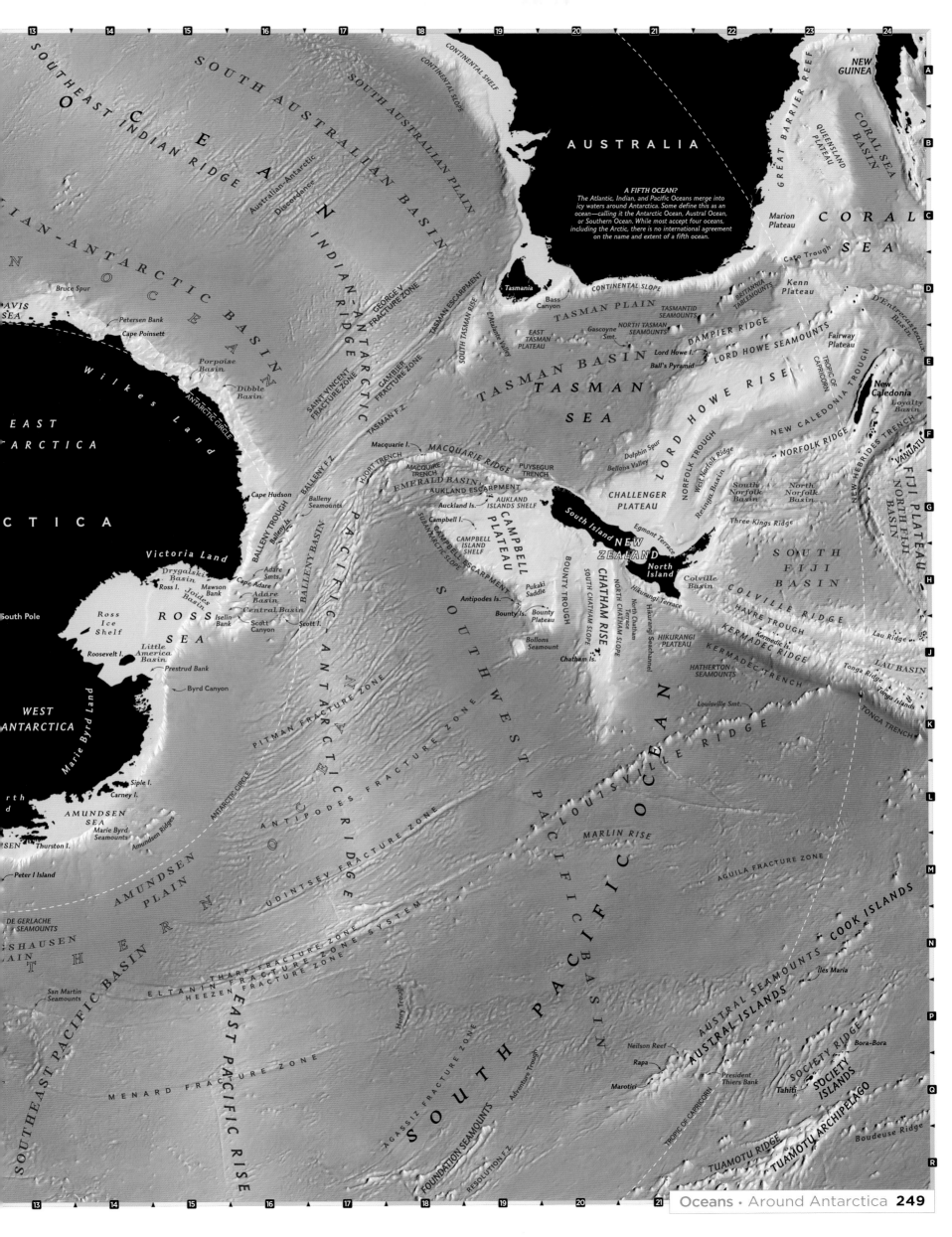

Space

Stellar nurseries are the birthplaces of countless stars in the Milky Way. This dynamic Hubble Space Telescope composite details one small section of the Monkey Head Nebula (NGC 2174). Nearly 6,400 light-years away in the constellation Orion, the whole cloud of gas and dust measures over 475 trillion kilometers (294 trillion mi) across. This false-color image highlights details only seen in the infrared spectrum—billowing rusty-colored dust and bluish gas pockets stirred by energy emitted by many young, hot stars.

In the first decades of the new millennium, astronomers are conducting extensive surveys of new frontiers in space, registering millions of galaxies, each composed of billions of stars. New orbiters and surface rovers are exploring Mars, confirming the presence of liquid water in its distant past and detecting methane in its atmosphere. A probe descended through the atmosphere of Titan, a moon of Saturn, and returned the first pictures from its surface, showing a strange, cold new world complete with flowing hydrocarbon rivers and extensive lakes. A capsule traveling through space returned samples of the sun, and another spacecraft is now studying Pluto and its neighbors. Meanwhile, a copper "cannonball" deployed from a spacecraft created the first man-made impact crater on a comet while another returned comet dust to Earth.

Wherever we look, we see evidence of cataclysmic events, indicating that we live in a 13-billion-year-old universe that is still evolving. Some suns, their atmospheres curiously enriched with telltale elements, may be "death stars" that swallowed whole planets long ago. Our own Milky Way is gradually devouring a small galaxy in the constellation Sagittarius, and elsewhere larger galaxies collide and distort each other. The universe began with a big bang and has been expanding ever since. A mysterious "dark energy" that exceeds all known forms of energy is thought to cause this expansion; space is also pervaded by unseen "dark matter," the dominant component of the universe. In laboratories on Earth and on the drawing boards of aerospace engineers, we are preparing to explore the next frontier of astronomical observation, looking for gravitational waves that may disturb the very fabric of space and time.

Moon
Near Side

YOUNG EARTH HAD NO MOON. At some point in Earth's early history (certainly within the first 100 million years), an object roughly the size of Mars struck Earth a great, glancing blow. Instantly, most of the rogue body and a sizable chunk of Earth were vaporized. The ensuing cloud rose to above 14,000 miles (22,500 km) altitude, where it condensed into innumerable solid particles that orbited Earth as they aggregated into ever larger moonlets, eventually combining to form the moon. This "giant impact" hypothesis of the moon's origin is based on computer simulations and on laboratory analyses of lunar rocks gathered by six teams of Apollo astronauts. It also fits with data on the lunar topography and environment recorded by the United States' Clementine, Lunar Prospector, and Lunar Reconnaisance Orbiter spacecraft.

The airless lunar surface bakes in the sun at up to 243°F (117°C) for two weeks at a time. All the while, it is sprayed with the solar wind of subatomic particles. Then, for an equal period, the same spot is in the dark, cooling to about minus 272°F (-169°C). Day and night, the moon is bombarded by micrometeoroids and larger space rocks. Orbiting at an average distance of 239,000 miles (385,000 km), the moon's rotation is synchronized with its orbital period in such a way that it is gravitationally locked, meaning it always shows the same face, the near side, to Earth. The far side can never be seen from Earth and has been photographed only from spacecraft.

Recently, NASA scientists used Earth-based radio telescopes to produce very detailed radar maps of the southern polar region, revealing that the terrain is much more rugged than had previously been thought. The south pole, specifically the area near the Shackle-ton crater, has been considered as a possible landing site for a future manned mission to the moon. It remains attractive because the bottoms of deep craters in this region may contain water ice, deposited there by previous comet impacts. The ice is a potential source of liquid water for drinking, as well as hydrogen and oxygen for fuel. If future missions to the moon and Mars are able to use local resources, they will not be as reliant on new supplies from Earth. *(Continued on page 254)*

Lambert Azimuthal Equal-Area Projection
SCALE 1:18,825,000
1 CENTIMETER = 188 KILOMETERS; 1 INCH = 297 MILES

STATUTE MILES 0 — 250 — 500
KILOMETERS 0 — 250 — 500

* Spacecraft landing or impact site

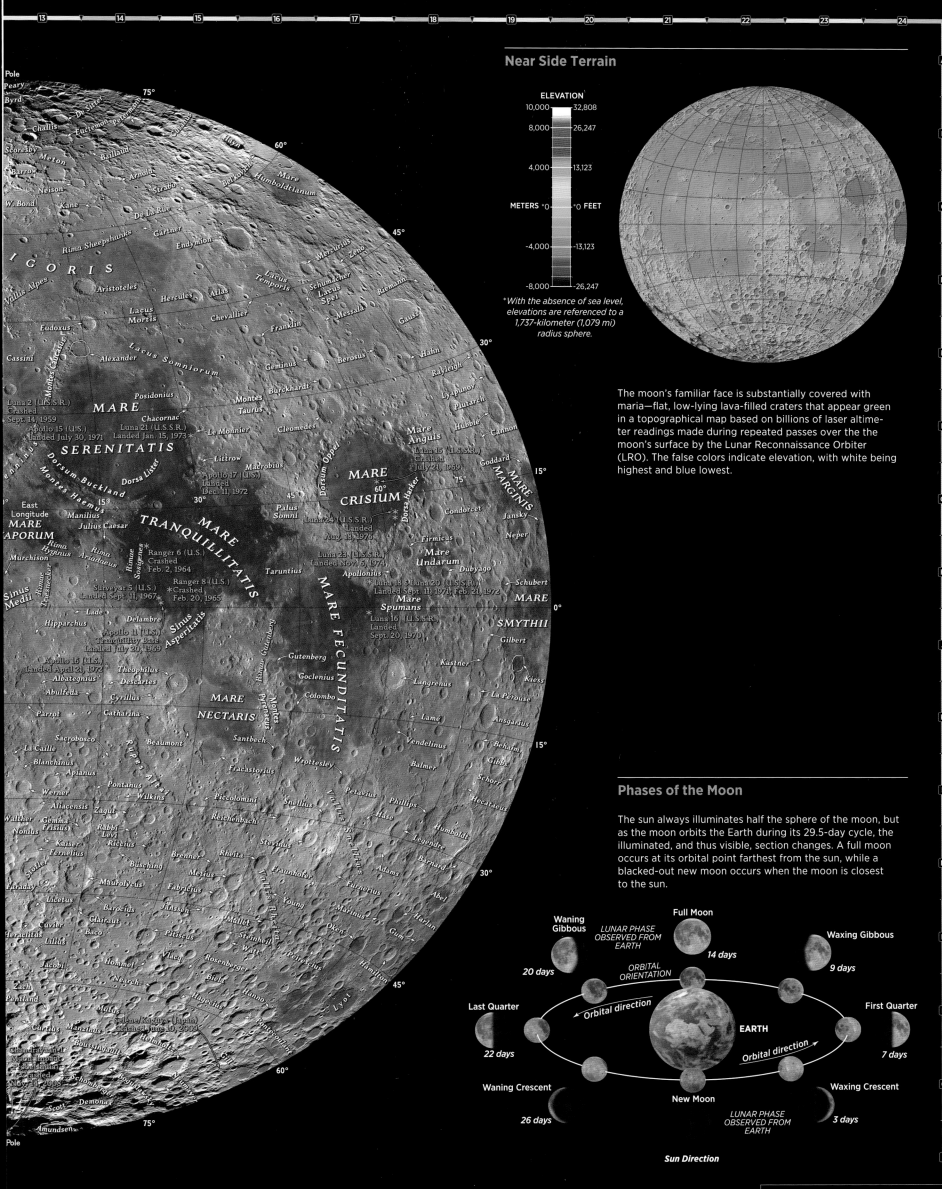

Near Side Terrain

ELEVATION

METERS	FEET
10,000	32,808
8,000	26,247
4,000	13,123
*0	*0
-4,000	-13,123
-8,000	-26,247

*With the absence of sea level, elevations are referenced to a 1,737-kilometer (1,079 mi) radius sphere.

The moon's familiar face is substantially covered with maria—flat, low-lying lava-filled craters that appear green in a topographical map based on billions of laser altimeter readings made during repeated passes over the the moon's surface by the Lunar Reconnaissance Orbiter (LRO). The false colors indicate elevation, with white being highest and blue lowest.

Phases of the Moon

The sun always illuminates half the sphere of the moon, but as the moon orbits the Earth during its 29.5-day cycle, the illuminated, and thus visible, section changes. A full moon occurs at its orbital point farthest from the sun, while a blacked-out new moon occurs when the moon is closest to the sun.

Waning Gibbous — 20 days
Full Moon — 14 days
Waxing Gibbous — 9 days
Last Quarter — 22 days
First Quarter — 7 days
Waning Crescent — 26 days
New Moon
Waxing Crescent — 3 days

LUNAR PHASE OBSERVED FROM EARTH
ORBITAL ORIENTATION
Orbital direction
EARTH
Orbital direction
LUNAR PHASE OBSERVED FROM EARTH
Sun Direction

Moon
Far Side

(Continued from page 252)

The rocks and materials brought back by the Apollo missions are extremely dry; the moon has no indigenous water. However, it is bombarded by water-rich comets and meteoroids. Most of this water is lost to space, but some is trapped and frozen in permanently shadowed areas near the moon's poles.

To the unaided eye, the bright lunar highlands and the dark maria (Latin for "seas") make up the "man in the moon." A telescope shows that they consist of a great variety of round impact features, scars left by objects that struck the moon long ago. In the highlands, craters are closely packed together. In the maria, they are fewer. The largest scars are the impact basins, ranging up to about 1,500 miles (2,400 km) across. The basin floors were flooded with lava some time after the titanic collisions that formed them. The dark lava flows are what the eye discerns as maria. Wrinkled ridges, domed hills, and fissures mark the maria, all familiar aspects of volcanic landscapes. Young craters are centers of radial patterns of bright ejecta, material thrown from the impacts that made them. Because the force of gravity is weaker on the moon (only about one-sixth that on Earth), blocks of rock hurled from impacts travel farther than they would on Earth.

The moon has no mountains like the Himalaya, produced by one tectonic plate bumping into another. There is no continental drift. Everywhere, the lunar surface is sheathed in regolith, a rocky rubble created by the constant bombardment of meteoroids, asteroids, and comets. Lunar mountains consist of volcanic domes, as well as the central peaks and rims of impact craters.

The Lunar Reconnaissance Orbiter, currently studying the rugged surface, is providing exceptionally clear images of the moon's surface, including three-dimensional information and polar illumination observations. It is also performing detailed measurements of the temperature and radiation environment. These data are helping scientists demystify the origins of our neighbor in space, and they provide valuable insight into possible landing sites for future missions of manned exploration.

Lambert Azimuthal Equal-Area Projection
SCALE 1:18,825,000
1 CENTIMETER = 188 KILOMETERS; 1 INCH = 297 MILES

STATUTE MILES 0 250 500
KILOMETERS 0 250 500

∗ Spacecraft landing or impact site

Far Side Terrain

ELEVATION

METERS	FEET
10,000	32,808
8,000	26,247
4,000	13,123
*0	*0
-4,000	-13,123
-8,000	-26,247

*With the absence of sea level, elevations are referenced to a 1,737-kilometer (1,079 mi) radius sphere.

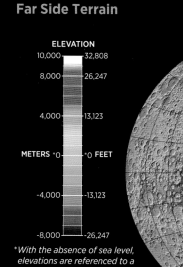

In contrast to the near side, the crater-pocked far side lacks large maria but features much greater heights and deeper depths. Unseen until the age of space travel, major far side features are named after astronauts, scientists, and other recent scholars. The LRO's accurate elevation data could help pave the way for future landings and even moon base construction.

Lunar Influence on Tides

Lunar gravity tugs on Earth's oceans, causing the water to bulge toward the moon. Most coasts experience two low and high tides per day, the magnitude of each affected by local topography, winds, and currents. The sun's gravity also augments or dampens the tidal effect. When the sun, moon, and Earth are aligned—during a new or full moon—a more intense spring tide is produced. A neap tide occurs when the moon's pull is perpendicular to that of the sun.

Full Moon

Orbital direction

Spring Tide

Ocean

Last Quarter

Neap Tide

EARTH

Neap Tide

First Quarter

Ocean

Spring Tide

Orbital direction

New Moon

Sun Direction

Craters labeled in blue commemorate the seven space shuttle Challenger *astronauts. Dashed black lines represent approximate crater perimeters. With the absence of sea level, elevations are referenced to a 1,737-km (1,079 mi) radius sphere.*

Highest point on the moon 10,786 m (35,387 ft)

Okina Selene Orbiter (Japan) Crashed Feb. 12, 2009

Lunar Orbiter 3 (U.S.) Crashed Oct. 9, 1967

Lunar Orbiter 5 (U.S.) Crashed Jan. 31, 1968

Ranger 4 (U.S.) Crashed Apr. 26, 1962

Inner Solar System

OUR SOLAR SYSTEM is mostly the sun. Not in area, perhaps: Measured to its ultimate boundary, the region suffused by solar energy may be 46 billion kilometers (30 billion mi) across, while the diameter of the star itself is just 1.4 million kilometers (865,000 mi). But the sun accounts for about 99.9 percent of the solar system's mass. Everything else—the planets, asteroids, meteoroids, comets, and floating dust and gas— could be considered leftovers from the formation of a medium-size star about 4.6 billion years ago.

The orbits of the inner planets take them from the scorching temperatures of Mercury to the deep winter chill of Mars. Swift Mercury races around the sun, its hemispheres burning and freezing. Torrid Venus bakes under an atmosphere that holds in most of the sun's energy, the greenhouse effect writ large. Uniquely sited, Earth is in the habitable zone, where water can exist as a liquid. Frigid Mars offers tantalizing evidence of a warmer, wetter past. Well studied in the space age, each terrestrial planet has been visited and mapped in detail by spacecraft.

Mercury's speed orbiting the sun—it circles every 88 days on a highly elliptical path—prompted the ancient Romans to name it after the winged messenger of the gods. The planet is densely cratered with a surface like the moon's. Daytime temperatures can reach 465°C (869°F), while readings fall to minus 180°C (−292°F) at night. A nearly vertical axis means relatively little sunlight touches polar regions, where radar reveals hints of water ice at the bottoms of craters.

MERCURY

Average distance from the sun:	57,900,000 km
Perihelion:	46,000,000 km
Aphelion:	69,820,000 km
Revolution period:	88 days
Average orbital speed:	47.9 km/s
Average temperature:	167°C
Rotation period:	58.7 days
Equatorial diameter:	4,879 km
Mass (Earth=1):	0.055
Density:	5.43 g/cm^3
Surface gravity (Earth=1):	0.38
Known satellites:	none

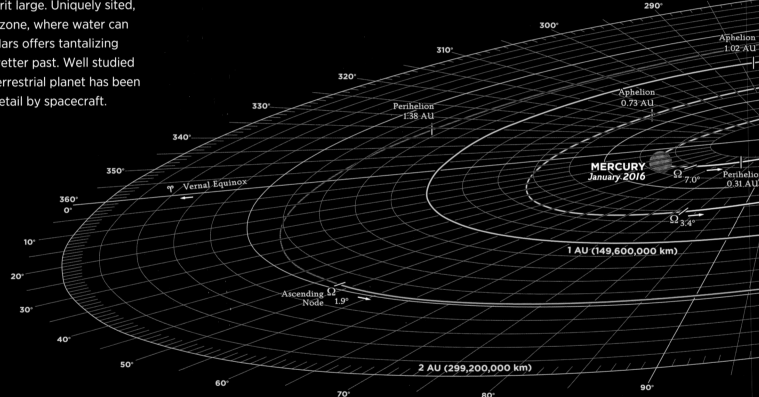

Mapping The Solar System

In this view of the inner reaches of the solar system, the circular grids represent the plane of Earth's orbit around the sun, called the ecliptic. Concentric blue rings show distance from the sun in astronomical units. (One AU is the distance from sun to Earth, about 150 million kilometers or 93 million miles.) Radial lines show degrees of longitude around the sun, and 0° is the vernal equinox. The orbital paths of other planets and dwarf planets are shown in relation to Earth's ecliptic. Above it, they are ascending, with their paths shown as a solid line. Below it, they are descending, with broken lines. Perihelion is the orbital point nearest to the sun; aphelion is the farthest.

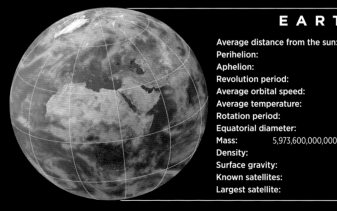

EARTH

Average distance from the sun:	149,600,000 km
Perihelion:	147,090,000 km
Aphelion:	152,100,000 km
Revolution period:	365.26 days
Average orbital speed:	29.8 km/s
Average temperature:	15°C
Rotation period:	23.9 hours
Equatorial diameter:	12,756 km
Mass:	5,973,600,000,000,000,000,000 metric tons
Density:	5.52 g/cm^3
Surface gravity:	9.78 m/s^2
Known satellites:	1
Largest satellite:	Earth's moon

Earth is the only planet known to support life, and perhaps the sole place the primary necessity of life—liquid water—is abundant, covering most of the planet. It's also the most geologically active of the rocky planets, and movements of sections of Earth's crust, called plates, constantly reshape the planet's surface. Its heavy iron core creates a strong magnetic field, providing a shield against the constant bombardment of high-energy particles ejected by the sun.

Venus is almost Earth's twin in size, but its thick atmosphere of mostly carbon dioxide soaks up far more of the sun's energy. This so-called greenhouse effect raises surface temperatures to 475°C (887°F)—making it the hottest planet in the solar system. The surface has rolling plains and mountainous regions, and intense volcanism has buried many impact craters. Above it all, dense sulfuric acid clouds block our direct view of the sweltering surface.

VENUS

Average distance from the sun:	108,200,000 km
Perihelion:	107,480,000 km
Aphelion:	108,940,000 km
Revolution period:	224.7 days
Average orbital speed:	35 km/s
Average temperature:	464°C
Rotation period:	243 days
Equatorial diameter:	12,104 km
Mass (Earth=1):	0.816
Density:	5.24 g/cm³
Surface gravity (Earth=1):	0.91
Known satellites:	none

Sizing Up the Terrestrial Planets

EQUATORIAL DIAMETERS
in kilometers (miles)

Earth	12,756	(7,926)
Venus	12,104	(7,521)
Mars	6,792	(4,220)
Mercury	4,879	(3,032)

Earth

Venus

Mars

Mercury

The inner planets are shown above in proportionate size to one another. Dwarf planets are less than 3,000 kilometers (1,865 mi) in diameter—much smaller than Mercury.

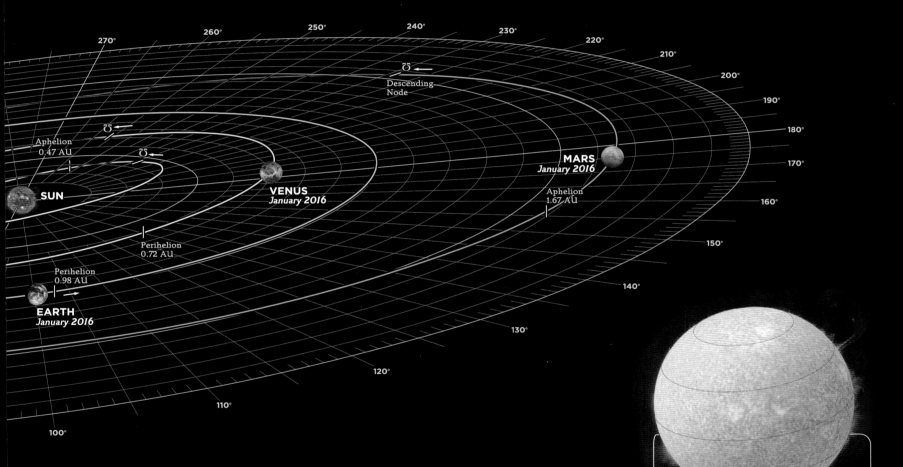

MARS

Average distance from the sun:	227,900,000 km
Perihelion:	206,620,000 km
Aphelion:	249,230,000 km
Revolution period:	687 days
Average orbital speed:	24.1 km/s
Average temperature:	-65°C
Rotation period:	24.6 hours
Equatorial diameter:	6,792 km
Mass (Earth=1):	0.107
Density:	3.93 g/cm³
Surface gravity (Earth=1):	0.38
Known satellites:	2
Largest satellites:	Phobos, Deimos

This outermost of the terrestrial planets bears witness to giant floods, but liquid water vanished three billion years ago. Today, its barren surface is swept by global dust storms that can shroud it in a reddish haze for weeks. Southern latitudes are rugged and heavily cratered, while giant volcanoes rise above plains to the north. Despite a cold climate and thin atmosphere, Mars is more like Earth than any other solar system planet, and it could potentially harbor traces of life.

SUN

Average surface temperature:	5,500°C
Average core temperature:	16,000,000°C
Rotation period:	24.6 days
Equatorial diameter:	1,392,000 km
Mass (Earth=1):	332,950
Density:	1.41 g/cm³
Surface gravity (Earth=1):	28.0

The main actor in our solar system, the sun is scientifically classed as an average star—in the mid-range for temperature, energy output, and size. Its energy is the driving force of weather on every planet and moon with an atmosphere, bringing seasonal variation as orbits progress.

Mars
Western
Hemisphere

SCALE 1:36,718,000

WELL INTO THE 20TH CENTURY, astronomers envisioned a Mars that bore many parallels to Earth. The illusion was shattered by Mariner 4's flyby of the barren planet in 1965. Subsequent exploration has proven it to be a very different place: colder, incomparably drier, and with a thin atmosphere composed mostly of carbon dioxide. Martian topography reveals extremes that far outstrip similar features on Earth. The tallest mountain in the solar system—the mighty volcano Olympus Mons—is more than two and a half times the height of Earth's tallest volcanic peak, Mauna Loa. On the other side of the planet, the bottom of the vast Hellas Planitia crater plunges nearly as deep below the Martian surface as Mount Everest is tall. And Arizona's Grand Canyon would be little more than a gully next to the vast Valles Marineris, a giant crack in Mars's surface that extends nearly 4,000 kilometers (2,500 mi) east to west just south of the Martian equator.

Despite the contrasts, Mars and Earth are unlike the other planets in one key way—liquid water. The surface is rife with features carved by flowing water—in some cases, oceanic volumes of it. In late 2013, scientists announced that instruments aboard NASA's latest rover, Curiosity, had found the seemingly arid surface surprisingly wet, with 2 percent of the soil composed of water. Recent detailed images from the Mars Reconnaissance Orbiter suggest liquid water—essential to the rise of life on Earth—still flows. However, Curiosity surprised researchers by failing to turn up atmospheric methane, a potential sign of biological activity. But there's no sign scientific scrutiny of Mars is slowing. In coming years, several nations' space agencies plan to launch missions that will continue the search for life while delving into the planet's geologic past to increase understanding of how the terrestrial planets formed.

North

75°
60°
45°
30°
15°
0°
15°
30°
45°
60°
75°

South

VASTITAS

Scandia Tholi
Olympia Undae
Scandia Colles
Milankovič
Phoenix (U.S.)
Landed
May 25, 2008

ARCADIA PLANITIA

Erebus Montes
Acheron Fossae

AMAZONIS
PLANITIA

195° 210° 225° 240° 255°

Lycus Sulci
Olympus Mons
Highest point on Mars
69,844 ft
21,287 m

Alba Mons
Alba Patera
Gonnus Mons
Tanaica Montes
Uranius Mons
Uranius Tholus
Ceraunius Tholus
Uranius Patera

Pettit
Eumenides Dorsum
Gordii Dorsum

Jovis Tholus
Ascraeus Mons
Tharsis Tholus

Nicholson
Ulysses Tholus
Biblis Tholus
Pavonis Mons
EQUATOR

Amazonis Mensa
Arsia Mons

THARSIS MONTES

Noctis Labyrinthus
Syria Planum
Oudemans

Marca
Cobres
Burton
Williams
Comas Sola
Bernard

Memnonia Fossae
Medusae Fossae

DAEDALIA
PLANUM

SOLIS

Dejnev
Kovalsky
Pickering

TERRA

SIRENUM

Columbus
Magelhaens
Mariner
Gorgonum Chaos
Newton

Mars 3
(U.S.S.R.)
Landed, contact lost ✱
December 2, 1971

Ptolemaeus
Li Fan
Porter
Brashear
Coblentz

Nordenskjöld
Millman
Clark
Hussey
Ross

Copernicus
Liu Hsin
Dokuchaev
Steno

AONIA
Very
Wright
Chamberlin
Agassiz

TERRA

ARG

Charlier
Stoney
Reynolds
Lau

Parva Planum

Lambert Azimuthal Equal-Area Projection
SCALE 1:36,718,000
1 CENTIMETER = 367 KILOMETERS; 1 INCH = 580 MILES

STATUTE MILES
0   250   500   750   1000

KILOMETERS
0   250   500   750   1000

✱ Spacecraft landing or impact site

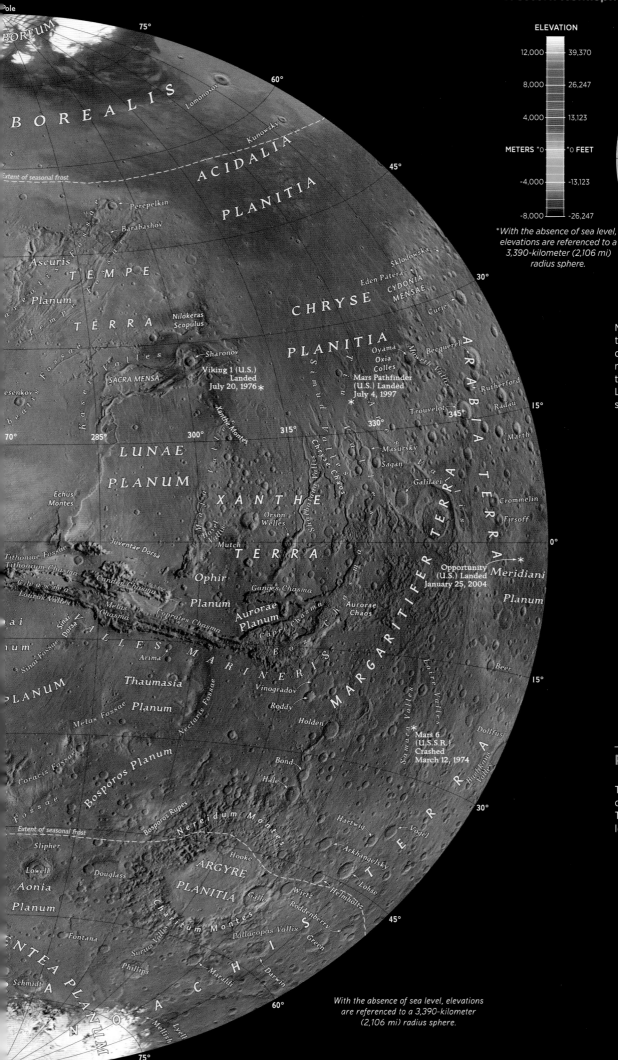

BOREALIS

ACIDALIA

PLANITIA

Extent of seasonal frost

Perepelkin

Barabashov

Ascuris

TEMPE

Planum

TERRA

Nilokeras
Scopulus

Viking 1 (U.S.)
Landed
July 20, 1976 ⚹

SACRA MENSA

LUNAE

PLANUM

Echus
Montes

XANTHE

Orson
Welles

Juventae Dorsa

Tithoniae Fossae
Tithonium Chasma

Ophir

Planum

Aurorae
Planum

Louros Valles

Candor Chasma

Melas
Chasma

Coprates Chasma

Ganges Chasma

Capri Chasma

Aurorae
Chaos

Sinai
Dorsa

VALLES MARINERIS

Arima

Thaumasia

Vinogradov

Roddy

Melas Fossae

Planum

Holden

Nectaris Fossae

Bond

Hale

Coracis Fossae

Bosporos Planum

Fossae

Bosporos Rupes

Nereidum Montes

Slipher

Extent of seasonal frost

Lowell

Douglass

Aonia

Planum

Fontana

Phillips

Charitum Montes

Surius Valles

Pallacopas Vallis

Maraldi

Darwin

Schmidt

Melish

Lyell

CHRYSE
CYDONIA
MENSAE

Eden Patera

PLANITIA

Oyama
Oxia
Colles

Mars Pathfinder
(U.S.) Landed
July 4, 1997 ⚹

Masursky

Sagan

Galilaei

Mutch

Sklodowska

Curie

Becquerel

Rutherford

Trouvelot

Radau

Marth

ARABIA TERRA

Crommelin

Firsoff

Opportunity
(U.S.) Landed
January 25, 2004 ⚹

Meridiani

Planum

MARGARITIFER TERRA

Beer

Mars 6
(U.S.S.R.)
Crashed
March 12, 1974 ⚹

Dollfus

Samara Valles

Loire Valles

Bushlaus Valles

TERRA

Hartwig

Vogel

Arkhangelsky

Lohse

ARGYRE

PLANITIA

Galle

Wirtz

Roddenberry

Green

Hooke

Helmholtz

With the absence of sea level, elevations are referenced to a 3,390-kilometer (2,106 mi) radius sphere.

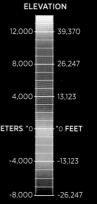

ELEVATION

METERS	FEET
12,000	39,370
8,000	26,247
4,000	13,123
*0	*0
-4,000	-13,123
-8,000	-26,247

With the absence of sea level, elevations are referenced to a 3,390-kilometer (2,106 mi) radius sphere.

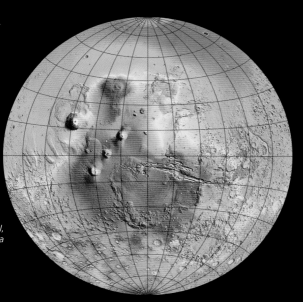

Mars is a planet divided by geology. In the northern latitudes is a low-lying plain, the Vastitas Borealis, a lava-covered expanse that appears blue on this topographic map. Farther south lies jagged, crater-pocked terrain thought to be more ancient than the northern expanse. Lofty mountains, including Olympus Mons, the solar system's highest peak, appear in white.

Phobos

This irregular moon whips around Mars three times a day, orbiting just 6,000 kilometers (3,700 mi) above the surface. The satellite is only 28.6 kilometers (16.7 mi) across on its longest axis.

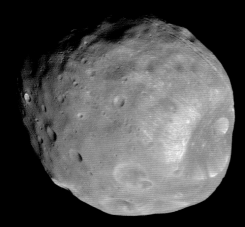

Mars
Eastern
Hemisphere

TWO NOTABLE ASTRONOMERS, Eugène Antoniadi and Giovanni Schiaparelli, crafted maps of the Martian surface based on their observations in the latter half of the 19th century. They used names out of classical mythology, establishing the precedent that the International Astronomical Union (IAU) came to adopt for Mars and most of the other bodies in our solar system. Craters are named in honor of scientists, writers, and mathematicians, both ancient and modern, who have pushed back the boundaries of science.

The Martian landscape is both familiar and alien. All of its features, from rugged riverbeds to shifting sand dunes, are also found on Earth. Yet Mars, with its lower gravity and much thinner atmosphere, imprints its own character on these features: The volcanoes are taller, the canyons wider, the ice caps more ephemeral than on Earth.

Compiled from NASA spacecraft data, the maps on this and the preceding pages depict the remarkable terrain of the arid planet. Mars's polar caps have frozen water, like our Arctic and Antarctic, but during the winters frozen carbon dioxide also coats the poles. Studies of Mars charge on in earnest. NASA's Curiosity rover, now trekking through Gale crater, has found evidence of ancient Martian lakes and flowing water. The search continues for conclusive evidence that life once existed on the red planet.

Lambert Azimuthal Equal-Area Projection
SCALE 1:36,718,000
1 CENTIMETER = 367 KILOMETERS; 1 INCH = 580 MILES

STATUTE MILES
KILOMETERS

0   250   500   750   1000

✳ Spacecraft landing or impact site

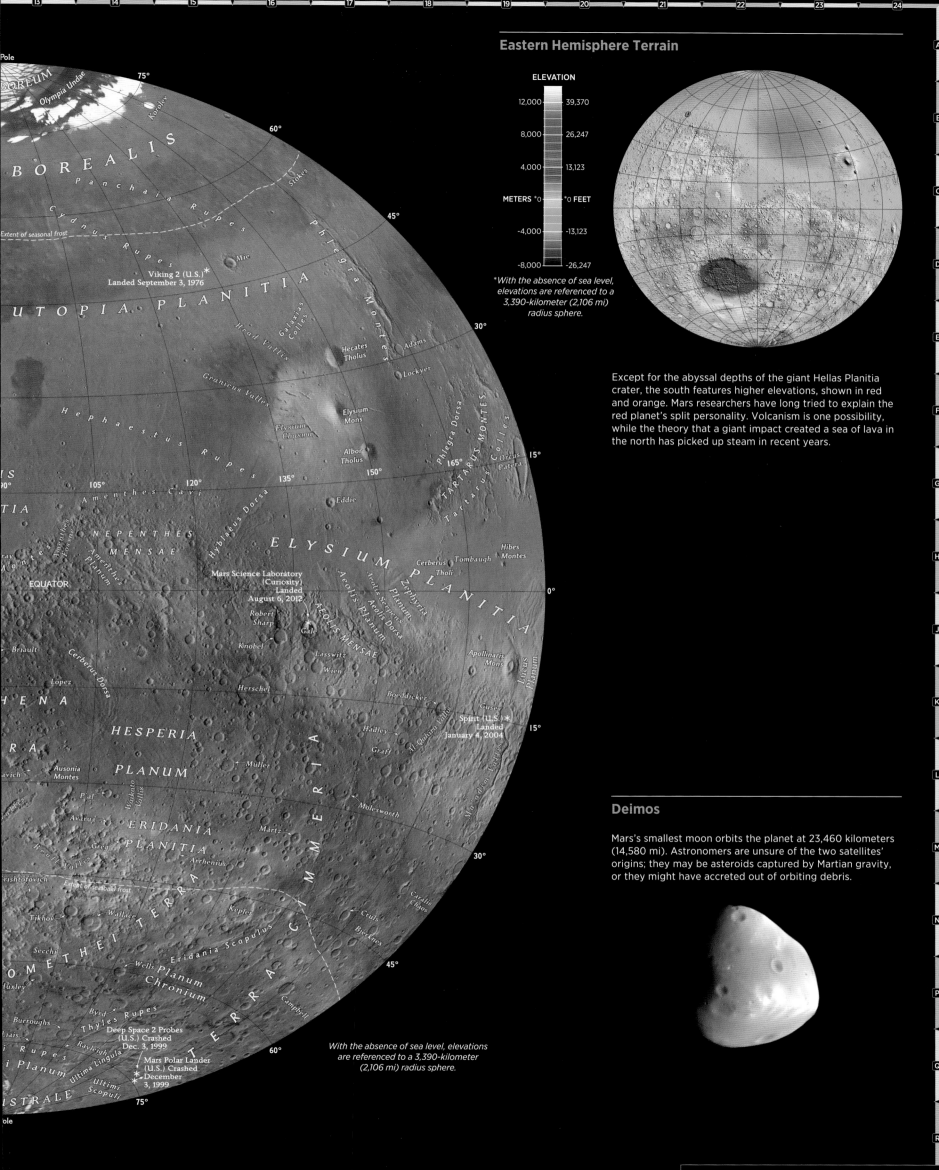

Pole

BOREUM

Olympia Undae

75°

BOREALIS

Panchaia Rupes

60°

Cydnus Rupes

Stokes

Extent of seasonal frost

45°

UTOPIA PLANITIA

Mie

Viking 2 (U.S.)*
Landed September 3, 1976

Phlegra Montes

Hrad Vallis

Galaxias Colles

30°

Granicus Vallis

Hecates
Tholus

Adams

Lockyer

Hephaestus Rupes

Elysium
Mons

Elysium
Chasma

Phlegra Dorsa

TARTARUS MONTES

Albor
Tholus

165°

15°

90°

105°

120°

135°

150°

Orcus
Patera

Tartarus Colles

Amenthes Cavi

Eddie

TIA

NEPENTHES

MENSAE

Hyblaeus Dorsa

ELYSIUM

Hibes
Montes

Amenthes
Fossae

Amenthes
Planum

Cerberus Tombaugh
Tholi

ray

Montes

PLANITIA

EQUATOR

Mars Science Laboratory
(Curiosity)
Landed
August 6, 2012

Zephyria
Planum
Aeolis Serpens

AEOLIS MENSAE

Aeolis Planum

Aeolis Dorsa

0°

Robert
Sharp

Gale

Briault

Knobel

Lasswitz

Wien

Apollinaris
Mons

Lucus
Planum

Cerberus Dorsa

Lopez

Herschel

Boeddicker

Guseu

ENA

Spirit (U.S.)*
Landed
January 4, 2004

15°

avich

HESPERIA

Hadley

Graff

Al Qahira Vallis

Ausonia
Montes

PLANUM

Müller

Molesworth

Ma'adim Vallis

ERIDANIA
PLANITIA

Martz

TERRA CIMMERIA

30°

Catalis
Chaos

Reull Vallis

Greg

Arrhenius

Cruls

Bjerknes

rishtofovich

Extent of seasonal frost

Kepler

Tikhov

Wallace

Eridania Scopulus

45°

Secchi

Wells

Planum

Campbell

Huxley

Chronium

METHEI TERRA

60°

Burroughs

Byrd

Deep Space 2 Probes
(U.S.) Crashed
Dec. 3, 1999

Rupes

Thyles Rupes

Liais

Rayleigh

Mars Polar Lander
(U.S.) Crashed
December
3, 1999

i Planum

Ultima Lingula

Ultimi
Scopuli

75°

ISTRALE

ole

Pole

Eastern Hemisphere Terrain

ELEVATION

METERS	FEET
12,000	39,370
8,000	26,247
4,000	13,123
*0	*0
-4,000	-13,123
-8,000	-26,247

*With the absence of sea level,
elevations are referenced to a
3,390-kilometer (2,106 mi)
radius sphere.

Except for the abyssal depths of the giant Hellas Planitia crater, the south features higher elevations, shown in red and orange. Mars researchers have long tried to explain the red planet's split personality. Volcanism is one possibility, while the theory that a giant impact created a sea of lava in the north has picked up steam in recent years.

With the absence of sea level, elevations
are referenced to a 3,390-kilometer
(2,106 mi) radius sphere.

Deimos

Mars's smallest moon orbits the planet at 23,460 kilometers (14,580 mi). Astronomers are unsure of the two satellites' origins; they may be asteroids captured by Martian gravity, or they might have accreted out of orbiting debris.

Outer Solar System

OUR SOLAR SYSTEM has two classes of planets. Terrestrial planets are small with solid surfaces and mean densities that suggest an iron core surrounded by a rocky, partially molten mantle. The outer Jovian planets are very large, consisting primarily of hydrogen and helium in gas and liquid states with no solid surface. In the past two decades, a large number of rocky, icy bodies have been discovered beyond the orbit of Neptune, in a region known as the Kuiper belt. Some of these objects are comparable to Pluto. One of them, Eris, is slightly larger and has a moon, Dysnomia. The Kuiper belt can thus be considered an icy, distant analog of the asteroid belt between Mars and Jupiter.

In 2006, the International Astronomical Union (IAU), an organization of professional astronomers that provides oversight of the naming and classification of features and bodies in space, decided to redesignate Pluto as a "dwarf planet." Eris and Ceres also share that designation. Large enough to be roughly spherical, they are not of sufficient mass to produce a gravitational field strong enough to clear smaller objects out of their orbital regions.

The discovery of Uranus in 1781 was the first planetary find since classical times. A long-ago collision with an Earth-size object may be the reason Uranus "rolls" on its side around the sun, with its rings more or less perpendicular to those of the other gas giants. Unlike the other outer planets, Uranus absorbs more heat from the sun than it generates. The planet's teal green surface is composed of clouds of methane gas; deeper down could be an ocean of superheated liquid water spiked with ammonia and methane. Like Neptune, it is thought to have a rock and ice core.

URANUS

Average distance from the sun:	2,872,500,000 km
Perihelion:	2,741,300,000 km
Aphelion:	3,003,620,000 km
Revolution period:	83.81 years
Average orbital speed:	6.8 km/s
Average temperature:	-195°C
Rotation period:	17.2 hours
Equatorial diameter:	51,118 km
Mass (Earth=1):	14.5
Density:	1.27 g/cm³
Surface gravity (Earth=1):	0.89
Known satellites:	27
Largest satellites:	Titania, Oberon, Umbriel, Ariel

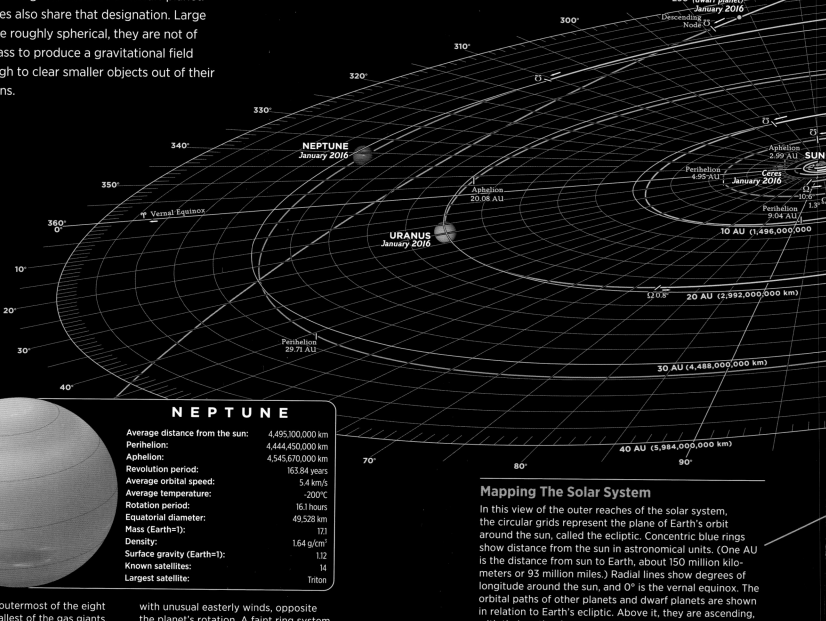

See pages 256–257 for the Inner Solar System

NEPTUNE

Average distance from the sun:	4,495,100,000 km
Perihelion:	4,444,450,000 km
Aphelion:	4,545,670,000 km
Revolution period:	163.84 years
Average orbital speed:	5.4 km/s
Average temperature:	-200°C
Rotation period:	16.1 hours
Equatorial diameter:	49,528 km
Mass (Earth=1):	17.1
Density:	1.64 g/cm³
Surface gravity (Earth=1):	1.12
Known satellites:	14
Largest satellite:	Triton

Neptune is the outermost of the eight planets and smallest of the gas giants, orbiting 30 times farther away from the sun than Earth does. Active weather systems stir a hydrogen-helium atmosphere with unusual easterly winds, opposite the planet's rotation. A faint ring system surrounds Neptune, while the depths of the planet are ammonia, methane, water ice, and rock.

Mapping The Solar System

In this view of the outer reaches of the solar system, the circular grids represent the plane of Earth's orbit around the sun, called the ecliptic. Concentric blue rings show distance from the sun in astronomical units. (One AU is the distance from sun to Earth, about 150 million kilometers or 93 million miles.) Radial lines show degrees of longitude around the sun, and 0° is the vernal equinox. The orbital paths of other planets and dwarf planets are shown in relation to Earth's ecliptic. Above it, they are ascending, with their paths shown as a solid line. Below it, they are descending, with broken lines. Perihelion is the orbital point nearest to the sun; aphelion is the farthest.

The striking cloud bands encircling the solar system's largest planet are caused by alternating east-west winds. Light cloud areas are called zones, while darker regions are belts. The famous Great Red Spot is an intense storm wide enough to swallow several Earths. It has raged for the past 300 years. Jupiter has a hydrogen-helium atmosphere and it is thought to have a rocky center. Its 67 moons are the most of any planet in the solar system; the four largest so-called Galilean moons, Io, Europa, Ganymede, and Callisto, were among Galileo's first telescopic discoveries.

JUPITER

Average distance from the sun:	778,600,000 km
Perihelion:	740,520,000 km
Aphelion:	816,620,000 km
Revolution period:	11.87 years
Average orbital speed:	13.1 km/s
Average temperature:	-110°C
Rotation period:	9.9 hours
Equatorial diameter:	142,984 km
Mass (Earth=1):	317.8
Density:	1.33 g/cm³
Surface gravity (Earth=1):	2.36
Known satellites:	67
Largest satellites:	Ganymede, Callisto, Io, Europa

Planetary Comparison

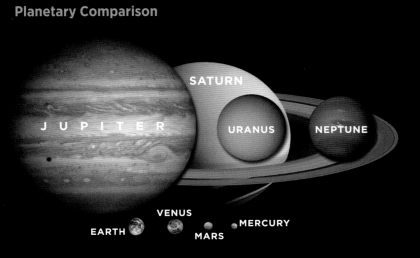

From Jupiter to Mercury, here's how the eight planets of the solar system stack up. The outer gas planets are giants when compared to the inner worlds. Each has a constellation of moons, some even large enough to qualify as planets if they orbited the sun.

Perihelion 29.66 AU

270° 260° 250° 240° 230° 220° 210° 200° 190° 180° 170° 160° 150° 140° 130° 120° 110° 100°

Aphelion 30.39 AU

SATURN January 2016

Aphelion 10.12 AU

ASTEROID BELT
Perihelion 2.55 AU

Aphelion 5.46 AU

JUPITER January 2016

Perihelion 18.32 AU

2.5°

1.8°

17.2° Ascending Node

Comets

Comets are masses of water ice, dust, and rock that mainly orbit far beyond the inner solar system. When they approach the sun, ice begins to vaporize, creating a coma, or atmosphere, around them. The characteristic comet's tail is created when energy from the sun sweeps dust and gas from the coma in a direction opposite our star. Comets travel on widely varying elliptical orbits, usually highly inclined to Earth's ecliptic. They spend most of their time in a comet-filled region outside the Kuiper belt known as the Oort cloud.

Asteroids

Asteroids are rocky remnants left over from the age of planetary formation. They range from gravel-size to gigantic: Ceres, at 950 kilometers (590 mi) in diameter, is classified as a dwarf planet. The greatest concentration is in the asteroid belt between Mars and Jupiter, where Jupiter's gravity prevented them from accreting into a planet. Infrared observation of the belt indicates it could contain well over 1.2 million asteroids with diameters over 1 kilometer (0.62 mi). Concentrations of asteroids known as Trojans also exist in the orbital Lagrange points—islands of gravitational stability—of Earth, Mars, Jupiter, Uranus, and Neptune. A few in orbit near Earth pose a theoretical threat to the planet, though the likelihood of collision is low.

SATURN

Average distance from the sun:	1,433,500,000 km
Perihelion:	1,352,550,000 km
Aphelion:	1,514,500,000 km
Revolution period:	29.44 years
Average orbital speed:	9.7 km/s
Average temperature:	-140°C
Rotation period:	10.7 hours
Equatorial diameter:	120,536 km
Mass (Earth=1):	95.2
Density:	0.69 g/cm³
Surface gravity (Earth=1):	0.92
Known satellites:	62
Largest satellites:	Titan, Rhea, Iapetus, Dione, Tethys

Saturn's ring system is one of the solar system's most majestic sights. Composed of intricately interacting water ice particles, they are vast in diameter but less than 1.6 kilometers (1 mi) thick. In other respects, Saturn is like a slightly smaller Jupiter, with a comparably fast rotational spin of 10.7 hours, and a similar composition. The planet's atmosphere is banded like Jupiter's but not as dramatic in color, Winds can reach 1,800 kilometers an hour (1,100 mph).

The Universe

Looking Back in Time for Origins

Colorful and diverse, an array of galaxies spans a section of sky combining ten years of Hubble data to capture the deepest ever images of the earliest galaxies. They're barely visible in this background image—small bluish blobs of stars one-twentieth the diameter of the Milky Way. Because they are so distant, our current view shows how they existed more than 13 billion years ago, when the universe was perhaps 600 million years old. In the eons following, galaxies combined and grew into larger, more complex structures, with their shapes—whether elliptical like the earliest ones, or spiral like our own—likely determined by the invisible yet massive halos of dark matter surrounding them.

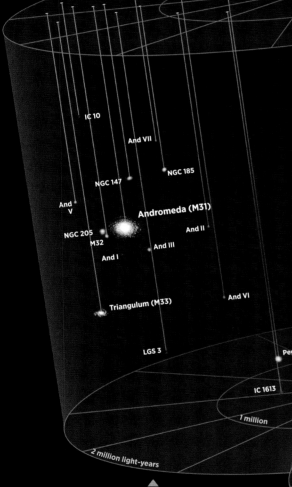

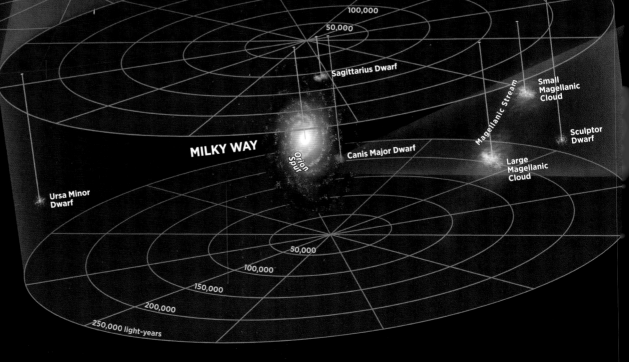

▲
Our Local Galaxy Group

Some of the 30 or so galaxies that make up the Local Group are visible from Earth with the naked eye. The spiral Andromeda galaxy is the largest of the group, and also the most distant object visible without a telescope. Its small companion galaxies, M32 and NGC 205, are easily seen through amateur telescopes. Second in size is the Milky Way, followed by the smaller spiral Triangulum galaxy. Both Andromeda and the Milky Way have many small satellite galaxies arrayed around them, giving the Local Group a binary structure around four million light-years across. The group's center of gravity lies between the two great galaxies, which are being pulled inexorably toward each other. They are expected to collide in four or five billion years, perhaps ending as one massive galaxy.

75 million light-years
50 million
25 million

NGC 5907

NGC 5248

NGC 6946
NGC 5457
NGC 5195
NGC 5236
NGC 5194
NGC 4826
NGC 5055
NGC 4631
NGC 4656
NGC 4565
NGC 4571
M87
M100
Virgo
Virgo III
NGC 4594
NGC 3031

NGC 3628
NGC 3593
NGC 4038

NGC 2903

Local Supercluster

The local supercluster, often called the Virgo supercluster, is a massive group of galaxy clusters 100 million light-years or more across. The Milky Way floats on its periphery. At the center of the supercluster is the smaller Virgo cluster, with a diameter of about 15 million light-years. Among its galaxies, the spiral M100 (as it is known in the Messier Catalogue) is one of the brightest. Meanwhile, M87 may be the dominant galaxy of the cluster—a giant ball of stars larger in diameter than the Milky Way. It is believed to have a black hole at its center 6.4 billion times as massive as the sun. Though the local supercluster has a mass of about a thousand trillion suns, 95 percent of its volume is galaxy-free zones called cosmic voids. This supercluster is still only a tiny speck in relation to the entire universe, which measures many billions of light-years across.

25 million
50 million
75 million light-years

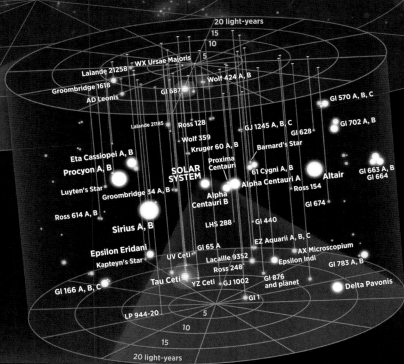

20 light-years
15
10
5

WX Ursae Majoris
Lalande 21258
Groombridge 1618
AD Leonis
Gl 687
Wolf 424 A, B
Gl 570 A, B, C
Lalande 21185
Ross 128
GJ 1245 A, B, C
Gl 702 A, B
Gl 628
Wolf 359
Kruger 60 A, B
Barnard's Star
Eta Cassiopei A, B
Procyon A, B
SOLAR SYSTEM
Proxima Centauri
61 Cygni A, B
Altair
Gl 663 A, B
Gl 664
Luyten's Star
Alpha Centauri A
Ross 154
Groombridge 34 A, B
Alpha Centauri B
Gl 674
Ross 614 A, B
LHS 288
Gl 440
Sirius A, B
EZ Aquarii A, B, C
AX Microscopium
Epsilon Eridani
UV Ceti
Gl 65 A
Lacaille 9352
Epsilon Indi
Gl 783 A, B
Kapteyn's Star
Ross 248
Gl 166 A, B, C
YZ Ceti
Gl 1002
Gl 876 and planet
Delta Pavonis
Tau Ceti
Gl 1
LP 944-20
5
10
15
20 light-years

Our Sun's Neighborhood

The closest stars to the sun make up our solar neighborhood, ranging out to about 20 light-years away. The region is located in the spiral Orion Spur of the Milky Way some 25,000 light-years from the galaxy center. Within the neighborhood confines is Sirius, the brightest star in the night sky, located about 8.6 light-years from Earth. By contrast, the second brightest star from Earth, Canopus, is located far outside the solar neighborhood, some 300 light-years away. In terms of wattage of energy output, Canopus is the far brighter star. Most stars in the solar neighborhood are too dim to see with the naked eye—including tiny Proxima Centauri, the closest star to Earth at 4.2 light-years away.

Galaxy Companions

As galaxies go, the Milky Way ranks as a giant, spanning nearly 100,000 light-years with its spiral disk. In its thrall are several far smaller galaxies that orbit it. The recently discovered Canis Major and Sagittarius dwarf galaxies are the closest, and others include the Ursa Minor and Sculptor dwarf galaxies. The Large and Small Magellanic Clouds, two of the most prominent features of the southern sky, have also long been thought to be satellites of the Milky Way. Recent research, however, indicates they are passersby, and not gravitationally bound.

Our Solar System ▶

On the scale of galaxy clusters and superclusters, our solar system is but a grain of sand in the Sahara at best. In human terms, it is still unmanageably large. One problem that space agencies face as they contemplate human exploration of the nearby planet, Mars, is whether astronauts can safely undertake a round-trip spaceflight of more than a year. A human journey past the most distant point of Pluto's orbit—50 astronomical units (AU) away, or 50 times the distance from the sun to Earth—for now is unthinkable.

KUIPER BELT
Pluto (dwarf planet)
NEPTUNE
SUN
MERCURY
MARS
ASTEROID BELT
URANUS
JUPITER
VENUS
EARTH
SATURN

Appendix

Map and Index Abbreviations

A. Arroio, Arroyo
A.C.T. Australian Capital Territory
A.O. Autonomous Oblast
A. Okr. Autonomous Okrug
Adm. Administrative
Af. Africa
Afghan. Afghanistan
Agr. Agriculture
Ala. Alabama
Alas. Alaska
Alban. Albania
Alg. Algeria
Alta. Alberta
Amer. America-n
Amzns. Amazonas
Anch. Anchorage
And. & Nic. Andaman and Nicobar Islands
Ant. Antilles
Arch. Archipelago, Archipiélago
Arg. Argentina
Ariz. Arizona
Ark. Arkansas
Arkh. Arkhangel'sk
Arm. Armenia
Astrak. Astrakhan'
Atl. Oc. Atlantic Ocean
Aust. Austria
Austral. Australia
Auton. Autonomous
Azerb. Azerbaijan

B. Baai, Baía, Baie, Bahía,Bay, Bugt-en, Buḩayrat
B. Aires Buenos Aires
B.C. British Columbia
B. Qazaq. Batys Qazaqstan
Bashk. Bashkortostan
Belg. Belgium
Bol. Bolivia
Bol. Bol'sh-oy, -aya, -oye
Bosn. & Herzg. Bosnia and Herzegovina
Br. Branch
Braz. Brazil
Bulg. Bulgaria
Burya. Buryatiya

C. Cabo, Cap, Cape, Capo
C.H. Court House
C.P. Conservation Park
C.R. Costa Rica
C.S.I. Terr. Coral Sea Islands Territory
Cach. Cachoeira
Calif. California
Can. Canada
Cap. Capitán
Catam. Catamarca
Cd. Ciudad
Cen. Af. Rep. Central African Republic
Cga. Ciénaga
Chan. Channel
Chap. Chapada
Chech. Chechnya
Chely. Chelyabinsk
Chongq. Chongqing Shi
Chuk. Chukotskiy
Chuv. Chuvashiya
Chyrv. Chyrvony, -aya, -aye
Cmte. Comandante
Cnel. Coronel
Co.-s. Cerro-s
Col. Colombia
Colo. Colorado
Conn. Connecticut

Cord. Cordillera
Corr. Corrientes
Cr. Creek, Crique
Croat. Croatia

D. Danau
D.C. District of Columbia
D.F. Distrito Federal
D.R.C. Democratic Republic of the Congo
Del. Delaware
Dem. Democratic
Den. Denmark
Dist. District, Distrito
Dom. Rep. Dominican Republic
Dr. Doctor
Dz. Dzong

E. East-ern
E. Ríos Entre Ríos
E. Santo Espírito Santo
Ea. Estancia
Ecua. Ecuador
El Salv. El Salvador
Emb. Embalse
Eng. England
Ens. Ensenada
Entr. Entrance
Eq. Equatorial
Esc. Escarpment
Est. Estación
Est. Estonia
Ét. Étang
Eth. Ethiopia
Eur. Europe
Exp. Exports
Ez. Ezers

F. Fiume
F.S.M. Federated States of Micronesia
Falk. Is. Falkland Islands
Fd. Fiord, Fiordo, Fjord
Fed. Federal, Federation
Fin. Finland
Fk. Fork
Fla. Florida
Fn. Fortín
Fr. France, French
ft feet
Ft. Fort
Fy. Ferry
F.Z. Fracture zone

G. Golfe, Golfo, Gulf
G. Altay Gorno-Altay
G.R. Game Reserve
Ga. Georgia
Geb. Gebergte, Gebirge
Gen. General
Ger. Germany
Gez. Gezîra-t, Gezîret
Gezr. Gezâir
Gl. Glacier, Gletscher
Gob. Gobernador
Gr. Greece
Gr. Gross-er
Gral. General
Gt. Great-er
Guang. Guangdong

H.K. Hong Kong
Hbr. Harbor, Harbour
Hdqrs. Headquarters
Heilong. Heilongjiang
Hist. Historic, -al
Hond. Honduras

Hts. Heights
Hung. Hungary
Hwy. Highway

I.H.S. International Historic Site
I.-s. Île-s, Ilha-s, Isla-s, Island-s, Isle, Isol-a, -e
Ice. Iceland
Ig. Igarapé
Igr. Ingeniero
Ill. Illinois
Ind. Indiana
Ind. Industry
Ind. Oc. Indian Ocean
Ingush. Ingushetiya
Intl. International
Ire. Ireland
It. Italy

J. Järvi, Joki
J.A.R. Jewish Autonomous Region
Jab., Jeb. Jabal, Jebel
Jam. Jamaica
Jap. Japan
Jct. Jonction, Junction
Jez. Jezero, Jezioro

K. Kanal
Kalin. Kaliningrad
Kalmy. Kalmykiya
Kamchat. Kamchatka
Kans. Kansas
Karna. Karnataka
Kaz. Kazakhstan
Kemer. Kemerovo
Kep. Kepulauan
Kh. Khor
Khabar. Khabarovsk
Khak. Khakasiya
Khr. Khrebet
Km. Kilómetro
Kól. Kólpos
Kör. Körfez,-i
Kos. Kosovo
Kr. Krasn-yy, -aya, -oye
Krasnod. Krasnodar
Krasnoy. Krasnoyarsk
Ky. Kentucky
Kyrg. Kyrgyzstan

L. Lac, Lago, Lake, Límni, Loch, Lough
La. Louisiana
Lab. Labrador
Lag. Laguna
Lakshad. Lakshadweep
Latv. Latvia
Ldg. Landing
Leb. Lebanon
Lib. Libya
Liech. Liechtenstein
Lith. Lithuania
Lux. Luxembourg

m meters
M.N.M. Marine National Monument
M. Gerais Minas Gerais
M. Grosso Mato Grosso
M. Grosso S. Mato Grosso do Sul
Maced. Macedonia
Madag. Madagascar
Mahar. Maharashtra
Mal. Mal-y-y, -aya, -aye
Man. Manitoba
Maran. Maranhão

Maurit. Mauritius
Mass. Massachusetts
Md. Maryland
Me. Maine
Medit. Sea Mediterranean Sea
Mex. Mexico
Mgne. Montagne
Mich. Michigan
Minn. Minnesota
Miss. Mississippi
Mo. Missouri
Mold. Moldova
Mon. Monument
Mont. Montana
Mont. Montenego
Mor. Morocco
Mt.-s. Mont-s, Mount-ain-s
Mte.-s. Monte-s
Mti., Mtii. Munţi-i
Mun. Municipal
Murm. Murmansk

N. North-ern
NA Not available
Not applicable
N.B. New Brunswick
N.B.P. National Battlefield Park
N.B.S. National Battlefield Site
N.C. North Carolina
N. Dak. North Dakota
N.E. North East
N.H. New Hampshire
N. Ire. Northern Ireland
N.J. New Jersey
N.M. National Monument
N. Mex. New Mexico
N. Mongol Nei Mongol
N.M.P. National Military Park
N.M.S. National Marine Sanctuary
N.P. National Park
N.S. Nova Scotia
N.S.W. New South Wales
N.T. Northern Territory
N.V.M. National Volcanic Monument
N.W.T. Northwest Territories
N.Y. New York
N.Z. New Zealand
Nat. National
Nat. Mem. National Memorial
Nat. Mon. National Monument
Nebr. Nebraska
Neth. Netherlands
Nev. Nevada, Nevado
Nfld. & Lab. Newfoundland and Labrador
Nicar. Nicaragua
Nig. Nigeria
Niz. Nov. Nizhniy Novgorod
Nizh. Nizhn-iy, -yaya, -eye
Nor. Norway
Nov. Nov-yy, -aya, -aye, -oye
Novg. Novgorod
Novo. Novosibirsk
Nr. Nørre

O. Ostrov, Oued
Oc. Ocean
Of. Oficina
Okla. Oklahoma
Ont. Ontario
Ør. Øster
Oreg. Oregon
Orenb. Orenburg
Oz. Ozero

P. Paso, Pass, Passo

P.E.I. Prince Edward Island
P.N.G. Papua New Guinea
P.R. Puerto Rico
Pa. Pennsylvania
Pac. Oc. Pacific Ocean
Pak. Pakistan
Pan. Panama
Pant. Pantano
Para. Paraguay
Pass. Passage
Peg. Pegunungan
Pen. Peninsula, Península, Péninsule
Per. Pereval
Pk. Peak
Pl. Planina
Plat. Plateau
Pol. Poland
Pol. Poluostrov
Port. Portugal
Pres. Presidente
Prov. Province, Provincial
Pt.-e. Point-e
Pta. Ponta, Punta, Puntan
Pto. Puerto
Pul. Pulau

Q. Quebrada
Qnsld. Queensland
Que. Quebec
Qyzyl. Qyzylorda

R. Río, River, Rivière
R.R. Railroad
R. Gr. Norte Rio Grande do Norte
R. Gr. Sul Rio Grande do Sul
R.I. Rhode Island
R. Jan. Rio de Janeiro
R. Negro Río Negro
Ra.-s. Range-s
Rec. Recreation
Reg. Region
Rep. Republic
Res. Reservoir, Reserve, Reservatório
Rk. Rock
Rom. Romania
Russ. Russia

S. South-ern
S.A.R. Special Administrative Region
S. Af. South Africa
S. Aust. South Australia
S.C. South Carolina
S. Dak. South Dakota
S. Estero Santiago del Estero
S. Ossetia South Ossetia
S. Paulo São Paulo
S.W. Southwest
Sa.-s. Serra, Sierra-s
Sal. Salar, Salina
Sask. Saskatchewan
Scot. Scotland
Sd. Sound, Sund
Sel. Selat
Ser. Serranía
Serb. Serbia
Sev. Severn-yy, -aya, -oye
Sgt. Sargento
Shand. Shandong
Sk. Shankou
Slov. Slovenia
Slovak. Slovakia
Smt.-s Seamount-s
Sp. Spain, Spanish
Spr.-s. Spring-s

Sq. Square
Sr. Sønder
St.-e. Saint-e, Sankt, Sint
St. Peter. Saint Petersburg
Sta., Sto. Santa, Station, Santo
Sta. Cata. Santa Catarina
Sta. Cruz. Santa Cruz
Stavr. Stavropol'
Str.-s. Straat, Strait-s
Sv. Svyat-oy, -aya, -oye
Sverd. Sverdlovsk
Sw. Sweden
Switz. Switzerland
Syr. Syria

T. Fuego Tierra del Fuego
Taj. Tajikistan
Tas. Tasmania
Tel. Teluk
Tenn. Tennessee
Terr. Territory
Tex. Texas
Tg. Tanjung
Thai. Thailand
Tmt.-s Tablemount-s
Tocant. Tocantins
Trin. Trinidad
Tun. Tunisia
Turk. Turkey
Turkm. Turkmenistan

U.A.E. United Arab Emirates
U.K. United Kingdom
U.N. United Nations
U.S. United States
Ukr. Ukraine
Ulyan. Ul'yanovsk
Uru. Uruguay
Uzb. Uzbekistan

V.I. Virgin Islands
Va. Virginia
Val. Valley
Vdkhr. Vodokhranil-ishche
Vdskh. Vodoskhovy-shche
Venez. Venezuela
Verkh. Verkhn-iy, -yaya, -eye
Vic. Victoria
Viet. Vietnam
Vol. Volcán, Volcano
Volg. Volgograd
Voz. Vozyera, -yero, -yera
Vozv. Vozvyshennost'
Vr. Vester
Vt. Vermont
Vyal. Vyaliki, -ikaya,-ikaye

W. Wadi, Wâdi, Wādī, Webi
W. West-ern
W. Aust. Western Australia
W.H. Water Hole
W. Va. West Virginia
Wash. Washington
Wis. Wisconsin
Wyo. Wyoming

Yar. Yarımadası
Yaro. Yaroslavl'
Yu. Yuzhn-yy, -aya, -oye

Zakh. Zakhod-ni, -nyaya, -nye
Zal. Zaliv
Zap. Zapadn-yy, -aya, -oye
Zimb. Zimbabwe

QUICK REFERENCE CHART FOR METRIC TO ENGLISH CONVERSION

| 1 METER | 1 METER = 100 CENTIMETERS |
| 1 FOOT | 1 FOOT = 12 INCHES |

| 1 KILOMETER | 1 KILOMETER = 1,000 METERS |
| 1 MILE | 1 MILE = 5,280 FEET |

METERS	1	10	20	50	100	200	500	1,000	2,000	5,000	10,000
FEET	3.28084	32.8084	65.6168	164.042	328.084	656.168	1,640.42	3,280.84	6,561.68	16,404.2	32,808.4
KILOMETERS	1	10	20	50	100	200	500	1,000	2,000	5,000	10,000
MILES	0.621371	6.21371	12.42742	31.06855	62.1371	124.2742	310.6855	621.371	1,242.742	3,106.855	6,213.71

CONVERSION FROM METRIC MEASURES

SYMBOL	WHEN YOU KNOW	MULTIPLY BY	TO FIND	SYMBOL
LENGTH				
cm	centimeters	0.393701	inches	in
m	meters	3.280840	feet	ft
m	meters	1.093613	yards	yd
km	kilometers	0.621371	miles	mi
AREA				
cm^2	square centimeters	0.155000	square inches	in^2
m^2	square meters	10.76391	square feet	ft^2
m^2	square meters	1.195990	square yards	yd^2
km^2	square kilometers	0.386102	square miles	mi^2
ha	hectares	2.471054	acres	--
MASS				
g	grams	0.035274	ounces	oz
kg	kilograms	2.204623	pounds	lb
t	metric tons	1.102311	short tons	--
VOLUME				
mL	milliliters	0.061024	cubic inches	in^3
mL	milliliters	0.033814	liquid ounces	liq oz
L	liters	2.113376	pints	pt
L	liters	1.056688	quarts	qt
L	liters	0.264172	gallons	gal
m^3	cubic meters	35.31467	cubic feet	ft^3
m^3	cubic meters	1.307951	cubic yards	yd^3
TEMPERATURE				
°C	degrees Celsius (centigrade)	9/5 (or 1.8) then add 32	degrees Fahrenheit	°F

CONVERSION TO METRIC MEASURES

SYMBOL	WHEN YOU KNOW	MULTIPLY BY	TO FIND	SYMBOL
LENGTH				
in	inches	2.54	centimeters	cm
ft	feet	0.3048	meters	m
yd	yards	0.9144	meters	m
mi	miles	1.609344	kilometers	km
AREA				
in^2	square inches	6.4516	square centimeters	cm^2
ft^2	square feet	0.092903	square meters	m^2
yd^2	square yards	0.836127	square meters	m^2
mi^2	square miles	2.589988	square kilometers	km^2
--	acres	0.404686	hectares	ha
MASS				
oz	ounces	28.349523	grams	g
lb	pounds	0.453592	kilograms	kg
--	short tons	0.907185	metric tons	t
VOLUME				
in^3	cubic inches	16.387064	milliliters	mL
liq oz	liquid ounces	29.57353	milliliters	mL
pt	pints	0.473176	liters	L
qt	quarts	0.946353	liters	L
gal	gallons	3.785412	liters	L
ft^3	cubic feet	0.028317	cubic meters	m^3
yd^3	cubic yards	0.764555	cubic meters	m^3
TEMPERATURE				
°F	degrees Fahrenheit	5/9 (or 0.55556) after subtracting 32	degrees Celsius (centigrade)	°C

Geographic Comparisons

Planet Facts

Age: Formed 4.54 billion years ago. Life appeared on its surface within a billion years.

Interior: Remains active, with a thick layer of relatively solid mantle, a liquid outer core that generates a magnetic field, and a solid iron inner core.

Mass: 5,973,600,000,000,000,000,000,000—5.9736 sextillion—metric tons (6.5848 sextillion short tons)

Total Area: 510,072,000 sq km (196,940,000 sq mi)

Surface: About 71% of the surface is covered with a saltwater ocean, the remainder consisting of continents and islands.

Land Area: 148,940,000 sq km (57,506,000 sq mi), 29.1% of total

Water Area: 361,132,000 sq km (139,434,000 sq mi), 70.9% of total

Atmosphere Composition: Dry air is 78.08% Nitrogen (N_2), 20.95% Oxygen (O_2), 0.93% Argon (Ar), 0.038% Carbon dioxide (CO_2), and 0.002% other gases. Water vapor is variable and typically about 1%.

Orbit: Earth moves around the sun once for every 366.26 times it rotates about its axis. This time period is a sidereal year, which equals 365.26 solar days.

Equatorial Diameter: 12,756 km (7,926 mi)

Polar Diameter: 12,714 km (7,900 mi)

Planetary Extremes

Hottest Place: Dalol, Danakil Depression, Ethiopia, annual average temperature 34°C (93°F)

Coldest Place: Ridge A, Antarctica, annual average temperature -70°C (-94°F)

Hottest Recorded Air Temperature: Furnace Creek Ranch (Death Valley), California, U.S., 56.7°C (134°F), October 7, 1913

Coldest Recorded Air Temperature: Antarctica, -93.2°C (-135.8°F), August 10, 2010

Wettest Place: Mawsynram, Meghalaya, India, annual average rainfall 1,187 cm (467 in)

Driest Place: Arica, Atacama Desert, Chile, rainfall barely measurable

Largest Hot Desert: Sahara, Africa, 9,000,000 sq km (3,475,000 sq mi)

Largest Ice Desert: Antarctica, 13,209,000 sq km (5,100,000 sq mi)

Largest Canyon: Grand Canyon, Colorado River, Arizona, U.S., 446 km (277 mi) long along river, 180 m (600 ft) to 29 km (18 mi) wide, about 1.6 km (1 mi) deep

Largest Coral Reef Ecosystem: Great Barrier Reef, Australia, 348,300 sq km (134,000 sq mi)

Greatest Tidal Range: Bay of Fundy, Canadian Atlantic Coast, 16 m (53 ft)

Tallest Waterfall: Angel Falls, Venezuela, 979 m (3,212 ft)

Deepest and Oldest Lake: Lake Baikal, Russia, -1,642 m (-5,387 ft), about 25 million years old

Strongest Recorded Wind Gust: Barrow Island, Australia, 408 km/h (254 mph)

Area of Each Continent

	sq km	sq mi	% of land
Asia	44,570,000	17,208,000	30.0
Africa	30,065,000	11,608,000	20.2
North America	24,474,000	9,449,000	16.5
South America	17,819,000	6,880,000	12.0
Antarctica	13,209,000	5,100,000	8.9
Europe	9,947,000	3,841,000	6.7
Australia	7,692,000	2,970,000	5.2

Largest Islands by Area

		sq km	sq mi
1	Greenland	2,166,000	836,000
2	New Guinea	792,500	306,000
3	Borneo	725,500	280,100
4	Madagascar	587,000	226,600
5	Baffin Island	507,500	196,000
6	Sumatra	427,300	165,000
7	Honshu	227,400	87,800
8	Great Britain	218,100	84,200
9	Victoria Island	217,300	83,900
10	Ellesmere Island	196,200	75,800

Lowest Surface Point on Each Continent

	meters	feet
Dead Sea, Asia	-423	-1,388
Lake Assal, Africa	-155	-509
Laguna del Carbón, South America	-105	-344
Death Valley, North America	-86	-282
Caspian Sea, Europe	-28	-92
Lake Eyre, Australia	-15	-49
Byrd Glacier (depression), Antarctica	-2,870	-9,416

Highest Point on Each Continent

	meters	feet
Mount Everest, Asia	8,850	29,035
Cerro Aconcagua, South America	6,959	22,831
Mount McKinley (Denali), N. America	6,194	20,320
Kilimanjaro, Africa	5,895	19,340
El'brus, Europe	5,642	18,510
Vinson Massif, Antarctica	4,897	16,067
Mount Kosciuszko, Australia	2,228	7,310

Mountains and Caves

Tallest Mountain (above and below sea level): Mauna Kea, Hawai'i, U.S., 9,966 m (32,696 ft) above the sea floor and 4,205 m (13,796 ft) above sea level

Highest Mountain (above sea level): Mount Everest, China and Nepal border, 8,850 m (29,035 ft) above sea level

Longest Mountain Range (above sea level): Andes, South America, 7,600 km (4,700 mi)

Longest Mountain Range (above and below sea level): Mid-Ocean Ridge, 60,000 km (37,000 mi), encircles the Earth mostly along the seafloor

Largest Cave Chamber: Sarawak Chamber, Gunung Mulu National Park, Malaysia, 16 hectares and 80 meters high (40.2 acres and 260 feet)

Longest Cave System: Mammoth Cave, Kentucky, U.S., more than 627 km (390 mi) of passageways mapped

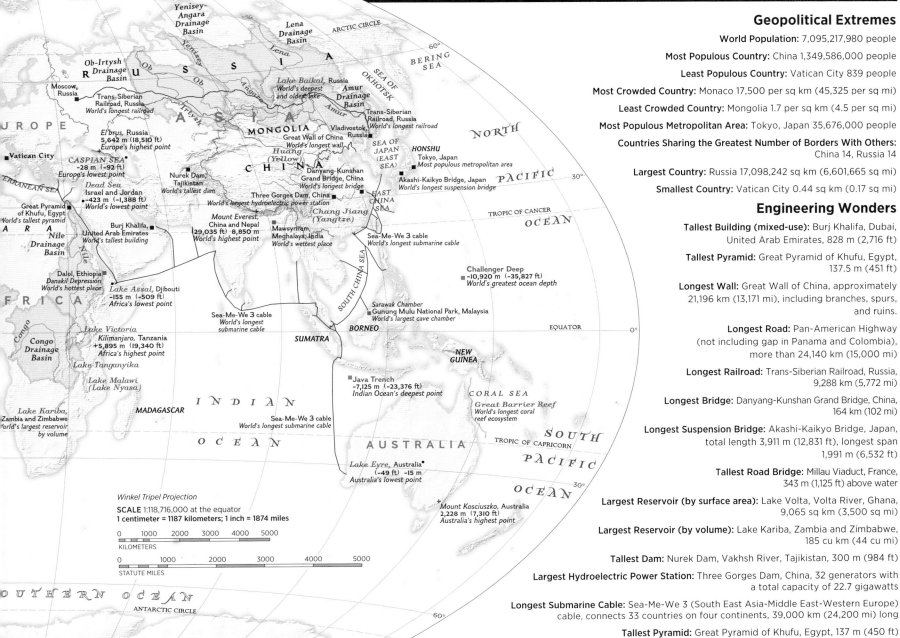

Geopolitical Extremes

World Population: 7,095,217,980 people

Most Populous Country: China 1,349,586,000 people

Least Populous Country: Vatican City 839 people

Most Crowded Country: Monaco 17,500 per sq km (45,325 per sq mi)

Least Crowded Country: Mongolia 1.7 per sq km (4.5 per sq mi)

Most Populous Metropolitan Area: Tokyo, Japan 35,676,000 people

Countries Sharing the Greatest Number of Borders With Others: China 14, Russia 14

Largest Country: Russia 17,098,242 sq km (6,601,665 sq mi)

Smallest Country: Vatican City 0.44 sq km (0.17 sq mi)

Engineering Wonders

Tallest Building (mixed-use): Burj Khalifa, Dubai, United Arab Emirates, 828 m (2,716 ft)

Tallest Pyramid: Great Pyramid of Khufu, Egypt, 137.5 m (451 ft)

Longest Wall: Great Wall of China, approximately 21,196 km (13,171 mi), including branches, spurs, and ruins.

Longest Road: Pan-American Highway (not including gap in Panama and Colombia), more than 24,140 km (15,000 mi)

Longest Railroad: Trans-Siberian Railroad, Russia, 9,288 km (5,772 mi)

Longest Bridge: Danyang-Kunshan Grand Bridge, China, 164 km (102 mi)

Longest Suspension Bridge: Akashi-Kaikyo Bridge, Japan, total length 3,911 m (12,831 ft), longest span 1,991 m (6,532 ft)

Tallest Road Bridge: Millau Viaduct, France, 343 m (1,125 ft) above water

Largest Reservoir (by surface area): Lake Volta, Volta River, Ghana, 9,065 sq km (3,500 sq mi)

Largest Reservoir (by volume): Lake Kariba, Zambia and Zimbabwe, 185 cu km (44 cu mi)

Tallest Dam: Nurek Dam, Vakhsh River, Tajikistan, 300 m (984 ft)

Largest Hydroelectric Power Station: Three Gorges Dam, China, 32 generators with a total capacity of 22.7 gigawatts

Longest Submarine Cable: Sea-Me-We 3 (South East Asia-Middle East-Western Europe) cable, connects 33 countries on four continents, 39,000 km (24,200 mi) long

Tallest Pyramid: Great Pyramid of Khufu, Egypt, 137 m (450 ft)

Deepest Point in Each Ocean

	meters	feet
Challenger Deep, Pacific Ocean	-10,920	-35,827
Puerto Rico Trench, Atlantic Ocean	-8,605	-28,232
Java Trench, Indian Ocean	-7,125	-23,376
Molloy Deep, Arctic Ocean	-5,669	-18,599

Area of Each Ocean

	sq km	sq mi	% ocean area
Pacific	178,800,000	69,000,000	49.5
Atlantic	91,700,000	35,400,000	25.4
Indian	76,200,000	29,400,000	21.0
Arctic	14,700,000	5,600,000	4.1

The Atlantic, Indian, and Pacific Oceans merge into icy waters around Antarctica. Some define this as an ocean— calling it the Antarctic Ocean, Austral Ocean, or Southern Ocean. While most accept four oceans, including the Arctic, there is no international agreement on the name and extent of a fifth ocean. The "Southern Ocean" extends from the Antarctic coast to 60° south latitude and includes portions of the Atlantic, Indian, and Pacific Oceans (estimated area: 20,327,000 sq km, 7,848,000 sq mi).

Largest Seas by Area

		area		avg. depth	
		sq km	sq mi	meters	feet
1	Coral Sea	4,184,000	1,615,500	2,471	8,107
2	South China Sea	3,596,000	1,388,400	1,180	3,871
3	Caribbean Sea	2,834,000	1,094,200	2,596	8,517
4	Bering Sea	2,520,000	973,000	1,832	6,010
5	Mediterranean Sea	2,469,000	953,300	1,572	5,157
6	Sea of Okhotsk	1,625,000	627,400	814	2,671
7	Gulf of Mexico	1,532,000	591,500	1,544	5,066
8	Norwegian Sea	1,425,000	550,200	1,768	5,801
9	Greenland Sea	1,158,000	447,100	1,443	4,734
10	Sea of Japan (East Sea)	1,008,000	389,200	1,647	5,404

Largest Lakes by Area (with maximum depth)

		sq km	sq mi	meters	feet
1	Caspian Sea	371,000	143,200	1,025	3,363
2	Lake Superior	82,100	31,700	406	1,332
3	Lake Victoria	69,500	26,800	82	269
4	Lake Huron	59,600	23,000	229	751
5	Lake Michigan	57,800	22,300	281	922
6	Lake Tanganyika	32,600	12,600	1,470	4,823
7	Lake Baikal	31,500	12,200	1,642	5,387
8	Great Bear Lake	31,300	12,100	446	1,463
9	Lake Malawi (L. Nyasa)	28,900	11,200	695	2,280
10	Great Slave Lake	28,600	11,000	614	2,014

Longest Rivers

		kilometers	miles
1	Nile, Africa	7,081	4,400
2	Amazon, South America	6,679	4,150
3	Chang Jiang (Yangtze), Asia	6,244	3,880
4	Mississippi-Missouri, N. America	6,083	3,780
5	Yenisey-Angara, Asia	5,810	3,610
6	Huang (Yellow), Asia	5,778	3,590
7	Ob-Irtysh, Asia	5,520	3,430
8	Amur, Asia	5,504	3,420
9	Lena, Asia	5,150	3,200
10	Congo, Africa	5,118	3,180

Largest River Drainage Basins by Area

		sq km	sq mi
1	Amazon, South America	6,145,186	2,372,670
2	Congo, Africa	3,730,881	1,440,500
3	Nile, Africa	3,254,853	1,256,706
4	Mississippi-Missouri, N. Amer.	3,202,185	1,236,370
5	Ob-Irtysh, Asia	2,972,493	1,147,686
6	Paraná, South America	2,582,704	997,188
7	Yenisey-Angara, Asia	2,554,388	986,255
8	Lena, Asia	2,306,743	890,638
9	Niger, Africa	2,261,741	873,263
10	Amur, Asia	1,929,955	745,160

Special Flags

IF WE COULD BRING a snapshot back from the future, few images would tell us more about what lies ahead than a flag chart showing the banners of all countries. The independence of new nations, the breakup of empires, even changing political and religious currents—all would be reflected in the symbols and colors of the national flags. This is dramatically evident in the changing flag of the United States (below), but similar visual statements could be made for most countries.

Germany provides another example. In the Middle Ages a gold banner with a black eagle proclaimed its Holy Roman Emperor a successor to the Caesars. A united 19th-century German Empire adopted a black-white-red tricolor for Bismarck's "blood and iron" policies. The liberal Weimar and Federal Republics (1919-1933 and since 1949) hailed a black-red-gold tricolor. The dark years from 1933 to 1945 were under the swastika flag of the Nazi regime. These and similar flags in other countries are more than visual aids to history: Their development and use are a fundamental part of the political and social life of a community.

Like maps, flags are ways to communicate information in condensed form. The study of geography is paralleled by the study of flags, known as vexillology (from the Latin word *vexillum*, for "small sail" or flag). Books, journals, Web sites, and other sources convey information on vexillology; there are also organizations and institutions around the world linked by the International Federation of Vexillological Associations. Even very young students can gain a deeper understanding of countries, populations, political changes, religious movements, and historical events by learning about flags.

All flags embody myths and historical facts, whether they are displayed at the Olympic Games, carried by protesters, placed at a roadside shrine, or arrayed at a ceremony of national significance, such as a presidential inauguration. Flags are powerful symbols, attractive to groups of all kinds; hence their once prominent display by Nazis and Communists to manipulate the masses, their waving by the East Timorese after a successful struggle for independence, and their spontaneous use by people in the United States after September 11, 2001.

Flags of nations may be the most significant flags today, but they are far from the only ones. Sport teams, business enterprises, religious groups, ethnic groups, schools, and international organizations frequently rally, reward, and inspire people through the use of flags. An observant person will also notice advertising banners, nautical signals, warning flags, decorative pennants, the rank flags of important individuals, and many related symbols such as coats of arms and logos.

Examples of flags, as presented on these two pages, only hint at the rich possibilities of design, usage, and symbolism. The vexillophile (flag hobbyist) can easily and inexpensively acquire a substantial collection of flags and flag-related items. The vexillographer (flag designer) can create flags for self or family, club or team, or even for a city or county. The vexillologist (flag scholar) will find endless connections between flags and history, political science, communications theory, social behavior, and other areas. As with geography, the knowledge gained by a study of flags can be a richly rewarding personal experience.

Development of the Stars and Stripes

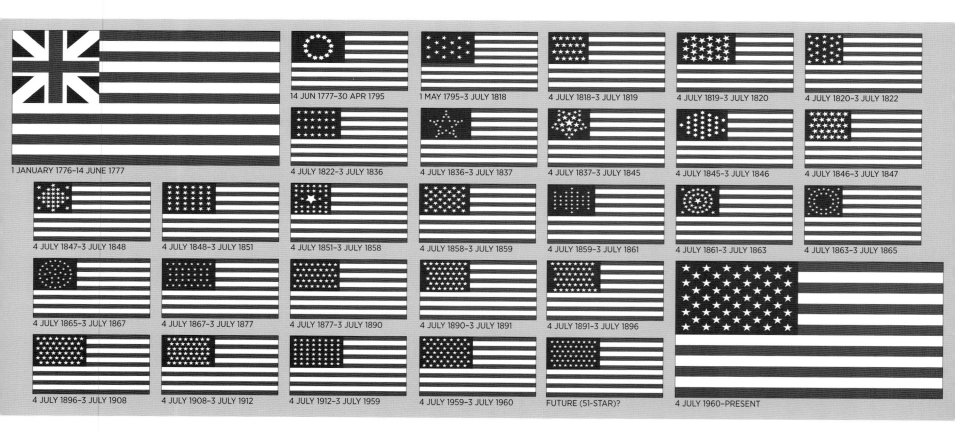

1 JANUARY 1776–14 JUNE 1777 | 14 JUN 1777–30 APR 1795 | 1 MAY 1795–3 JULY 1818 | 4 JULY 1818–3 JULY 1819 | 4 JULY 1819–3 JULY 1820 | 4 JULY 1820–3 JULY 1822

4 JULY 1822–3 JULY 1836 | 4 JULY 1836–3 JULY 1837 | 4 JULY 1837–3 JULY 1845 | 4 JULY 1845–3 JULY 1846 | 4 JULY 1846–3 JULY 1847

4 JULY 1847–3 JULY 1848 | 4 JULY 1848–3 JULY 1851 | 4 JULY 1851–3 JULY 1858 | 4 JULY 1858–3 JULY 1859 | 4 JULY 1859–3 JULY 1861 | 4 JULY 1861–3 JULY 1863 | 4 JULY 1863–3 JULY 1865

4 JULY 1865–3 JULY 1867 | 4 JULY 1867–3 JULY 1877 | 4 JULY 1877–3 JULY 1890 | 4 JULY 1890–3 JULY 1891 | 4 JULY 1891–3 JULY 1896

4 JULY 1896–3 JULY 1908 | 4 JULY 1908–3 JULY 1912 | 4 JULY 1912–3 JULY 1959 | 4 JULY 1959–3 JULY 1960 | FUTURE (51-STAR)? | 4 JULY 1960–PRESENT

No country has changed its flag as frequently as the United States. The Continental Colors (top left) represented the Colonies during the early years of the American Revolution. Its British Union Jack, which signified loyalty to the crown, was replaced on June 14, 1777, by "13 stars . . . representing a new constellation." Congressman Francis Hopkinson was the designer.

The number of stars and stripes was increased to 15 in 1795. In 1817 Congressman Peter Wendover wrote the current flag law. The number of stripes was permanently limited to 13; the stars were to correspond to the number of states, with new stars added to the flag the following Fourth of July.

Star arrangement was not specified, however, and throughout the 19th century a variety of exuberant star designs—"great luminaries," rings, ovals, and diamonds—were actually used. With the increasing number of states, the modern alternating rows of stars became standard. Finally, in 1912, President Taft set forth exact regulations for all flag details.

If a new state joins the Union, a 51-star flag will be needed. There is a logical design for it: alternating rows of nine and eight stars, as shown above.

OLYMPIC GAMES
The colors refer to those in the national flags of participating countries. The Olympic flag was created in 1913.

RED CRESCENT
In Muslim nations, Geneva Convention organizations rejected the red cross in favor of a red crescent, officially recognized in 1906.

RED CROSS
The Geneva Convention chose its symbol and flag in 1864 to identify people, vehicles, and buildings protected during wartime.

TRUCE/PEACE
For a thousand years a white flag has served as a symbol of truce, surrender, noncombatant status, neutrality, and peace.

UNITED NATIONS
Olive branches of peace and a world map form the symbol adopted by the United Nations in 1946. The flag dates from 1947.

AFRICA UNION
Africa stands on a white sun symbolizing hope. The 53 gold stars represent member states. South Sudan became the 54th in July 2011.

ARAB LEAGUE
The color green and the crescent are often symbols in member countries of the League of Arab States, founded in 1945.

ASEAN
A stylized bundle of rice, the principal local crop, appears on the flag of the Association of South East Asian Nations (ASEAN).

COMMONWEALTH
Once the British Empire, the modern Commonwealth under this flag informally links countries with common goals.

EUROPEAN UNION
The number of stars for this flag, adopted in 1955, is permanently set at 12. The ring is a symbol for unity.

OAS
Flags of member nations appear on the flag of the Organization of American States; each new member prompts a flag change.

PACIFIC COMMISSION
The palm tree, surf, and sailboat are found in all of the member nations; each star on the flag represents a country.

BUDDHISM
Designed in 1885 by Henry Olcott of the United States, the Buddhist flag features the auras associated with the Buddha.

CHRISTIANITY
The sacrifice of Christ on the Cross is heralded in this 1897 flag, which features a white field for purity.

ISLAM
"There Is No God but Allah and Muhammad Is the Prophet of Allah" is written on this widely used but unofficial flag.

LA RAZA
Crosses for the ships of Columbus and a golden Inca sun recall the Spanish and Indian heritage of Latin Americans.

PALESTINIANS
Since 1922 Palestinians have used this flag, with traditional Arab dynastic colors, as a symbol of the statehood they desire.

ROMA (GYPSIES)
Against a background of blue sky and green grass, a wheel represents the vehicles (and homes) of the nomadic Roma people.

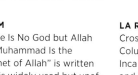

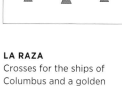

ANARCHISTS
Opposition to all forms of authority is hinted at in the "hand-drawn" rendition of an encircled A in the anarchist flag.

BLUE FLAG
The campaign for the improvement of the environment presents this flag as an award for success.

SCOUTING MOVEMENT
This emblem on a purple background adopted in 1955, with the fleur-de-lis within a rope tied with a reef knot represents scouts worldwide.

CIRCLE CROSS
This ancient religious symbol, related to the swastika, is widely used as a neo-Nazi symbol in Europe and North America.

U.S. DIVERS FLAG
As a warning signal to other boats, this flag flies wherever divers are underwater nearby—and at divers' clubhouses.

ESPERANTO
On the flag promoting Esperanto as a world language, a star signifies unity; green, traditionally, is a symbol of hope.

FRANCOPHONIE
French speakers share their common language and culture in periodic conferences and activities held under this flag.

GAY PRIDE
The Rainbow Flag, in various configurations, has been flown since 1978 by the gay and lesbian community and their families.

GIRL GUIDES/SCOUTS
The trefoil with a compass needle adorns the World Flag of Girl Guides and Girl Scouts, which was adopted in May 1991.

GREEN CROSS
Organizations that display this flag promote public safety in natural disasters, transportation, and the workplace.

MASONS
The unofficial flag of the Masons in the United States displays their traditional logo with symbolic square and compass.

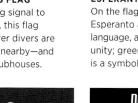

POW-MIA
Aside from Old Glory, no U.S. flag is as popular as the one saluting war prisoners and the missing in action. It recalls those lost but not forgotten.

Foreign Terms

Aaglet — well
Aain — spring
Aauinat — spring
Āb — river, water
Ache — stream
Açude — reservoir
Ada,-sı — island
Adrar — mountain-s, plateau
Ágios — saint
Aguada — dry lake bed
Aguelt — water hole, well
'Ain, Aïn — spring, well
Aïoun-et — spring-s, well
Aivi — mountain
Akra, Akrotírio — cape, promontory
Alb — mountain, ridge
Alföld — plain
Alin' — mountain range
Alpe-n, -s — mountain-s
Altiplanicie — high plain, plateau
Alto — hill-s, mountain-s, ridge
Älv-en — river
Āmba — hill, mountain
Anou — well
Anse — bay, inlet
Ao — bay, cove, estuary
Ap — cape, point
Archipel, Archipiélago — archipelago
Arcipelago, Arkhipelag — archipelago
Arquipélago — archipelago
Arrecife-s — reef-s
Arroio, Arroyo — brook, gully, rivulet, stream
Ås — ridge
Ava — channel
Aylagy — gulf
'Ayn — spring, well

Ba — intermittent stream, river
Baai — bay, cove, lagoon
Bab — gate, strait
Badia — bay
Bælt — strait
Bagh — bay
Bahar — drainage basin
Bahía — bay
Bahr, Baḥr — bay, lake, river, sea, wadi
Baía, Baie — bay
Bajo-s — shoal-s
Ban — village
Bañado-s — flooded area, swamp-s
Banc, Banco-s — bank-s, sandbank-s, shoal-s
Band — dam, lake
Bandao — peninsula
Baño-s — hot spring-s, spa
Baraj-ı — dam, reservoir
Barra — bar, sandbank
Barrage, Barragem — dam, lake, reservoir
Barranca — gorge, ravine
Bazar — marketplace
Belentligi — plateau
Ben, Beinn — mountain
Belt — strait
Bereg — bank, coast, shore
Berg,-e — mountain-s
Bil — lake
Biq'at — plain, valley
Bir, Bîr, Bi'r — spring, well
Birket — lake, pool, swamp
Bjerg-e — mountain-s, range
Boca, Bocca — channel, river, mouth
Bocht — bay
Bodden — bay
Bœng — pond
Boğaz, -ı — strait
Bögeni — reservoir
Boka — gulf, mouth
Bol'sh-oy, -aya, -oye — big
Bolsón — inland basin
Boubairet — lagoon, lake
Bras — arm, branch of a stream
Braţ, -ul — arm, branch of a stream
Bræ-er — glacier
Bre, -en — glacier, ice cap

Bredning — bay, broad water
Bruch — marsh
Bucht — bay
Bugt-en — bay
Buḩayrat, Buheirat — lagoon, lake, marsh
Bukhta, Bukta, Bukt-en — bay
Bulak, Bulaq — spring
Bum — hill, mountain
Burnu, Burun — cape, point
Busen — gulf
Buuraha — hill-s, mountain-s
Büyük — big, large

Cabeza-s — head-s, summit-s
Cabo — cape
Cachoeira — rapids, waterfall
Cal — hill, peak
Caleta — cove, inlet
Campo-s — field-s, flat country
Canal — canal, channel, strait
Caño — channel, stream
Cao Nguyên — plateau
Cap, Capo — cape
Capitán — captain
Càrn — mountain
Castillo — castle, fort
Catarata-s — cataract-s, waterfall-s
Causse — upland
Çay — brook, stream
Cay-s, Cayo-s — island-s, key-s, shoal-s
Cerro-s — hill-s, peak-s
Chaîne, Chaînons — mountain chain, range
Chapada-s — plateau, upland-s
Chedo — archipelago
Chenal — river channel
Chersónisos — peninsula
Chhung — bay
Chi — lake
Chiang — bay
Chiao — cape, point, rock
Ch'ih — lake
Chink — escarpment
Chott — intermittent salt lake, salt marsh
Chou — island
Chroüy — point
Ch'ü — canal
Ch'üntao — archipelago, islands
Chuŏr Phnum — mountains
Chute-s — cataract-s, waterfall-s
Chyrvony, -aya, -aye — red
Ciénaga — marsh
Cima — mountain, peak, summit
Ciudad — city
Co — lake
Col — pass
Collina, Colline — hill, mountains
Con — island
Cordillera — mountain chain
Corno — mountain, peak
Coronel — colonel
Corredeira — cascade, rapids
Costa — coast
Côte — coast, slope
Coxilha, Cuchilla — range of low hills
Crique — creek, stream
Csatorna — canal, channel
Cù Lao — island
Cul de Sac — bay, inlet

Da — great, greater
Daban — pass
Dağ, -ı, Dagh — mountain
Dağlar, -ı — mountains
Dahr — cliff, mesa
Dake — mountain, peak
Dal-en — valley
Dala — steppe
Dan — cape, point
Danau — lake
Dao — island
Đào — island
Dar'ya — lake, river
Daryācheh — lake, marshy lake
Dasht — desert, plain

Dawan — pass
Dawḩat — bay, cove, inlet
Deniz, -i — sea
Dent-s — peak-s
Deo — pass
Deryache — lake
Desēt — hummock, island, land-tied island
Desierto — desert
Détroit — channel, strait
Dhar — hills, ridge, tableland
Ding — mountain
Distrito — district
Djebel — mountain, range
Do — island-s, rock-s
Doi — hill, mountain
Dome — ice dome
Dong — village
Dooxo — floodplain
Dzong — castle, fortress

Eiland-en — island-s
Eilean — island
Ejland — island-s
Elv — river
Embalse — lake, reservoir
Emi — mountain, rock
Enseada, Ensenada — bay, cove
Ér — rivulet, stream
Erg — sand dune region
Est — east
Estación — railroad station
Estany — lagoon, lake
Estero — estuary, inlet, lagoon, marsh
Estrecho — strait
Étang — lake, pond
Eylandt — island
Eżeras — lake
Ezers — lake

Falaise — cliff, escarpment
Farvand-et — channel, sound
Fell — mountain
Feng — mount, peak
Fiord-o — inlet, sound
Firn — snowfield
Fiume — river
Fjäll-et — mountain
Fjällen — mountains
Fjärd-en — fjord
Fjarðar, Fjörður — fjord
Fjeld-e — mountain-s, nunatak-s
Fjell-ene — mountain-s
Fjöll — mountain-s
Fjord-en — inlet, fjord
Fleuve — river
Fljót — large river
Flói — bay, marshland
Foci — river mouths
Főcsatorna — principal canal
Foko — point
Förde — fjord, gulf, inlet
Forsen — rapids, waterfall
Fortaleza — fort, fortress
Fortín — fortified post
Foss-en — waterfall
Foum — pass, passage
Foz — mouth of a river
Fuerte — fort, fortress
Fwafwate — waterfalls

Gacan-ka — hill, peak
Gal — pond, spring, water hole, well
Gang — harbor
Gangri — peak, range
Gaoyuan — plateau
Garaet, Gara'et — lake, lake bed, salt lake
Gardaneh — pass
Garet — hill, mountain
Gat — channel
Gata — bay, inlet, lake
Gattet — channel, strait
Gaud — depression, saline tract
Gave — mountain stream
Gebel — mountain-s, range

Gebergte — mountain range
Gebirge — mountains, range
Geçidi — mountain pass, passage
Geçit — mountain pass, passage
Gezâir — islands
Gezîra-t, Gezîret — island, peninsula
Ghats — mountain range
Ghubb-at, -et — bay, gulf
Giri — mountain
Gjiri — bay
Gletscher — glacier
Gobernador — governor
Gobi — desert
Gol — river, stream
Göl, -ü — lake
Golets — mountain, peak
Golf, -e, -o — gulf
Gor-a, -y, Gór-a, -y — mountain,-s
Got — point
Gowd — depression
Goz — sand ridge
Gran, -de — great, large
Gryada — mountains, ridge
Guan — pass
Guba — bay, gulf
Guelta — well
Guntō — archipelago
Gunung — mountain
Gura — mouth, passage
Guyot — table mount

Hadabat — plateau
Haehyŏp — strait
Haff — lagoon
Hai — lake, sea
Haihsia — strait
Haixia — channel, strait
Hakau — reef, rock
Hakuchi — anchorage
Halvø, Halvøy-a — peninsula
Hama — beach
Hamada, Ḩammādah — rocky desert
Hamn — harbor, port
Hāmūn, Hamun — depression, lake
Hana — cape, point
Hantō — peninsula
Har — hill, mound, mountain
Ḩarrat — lava field
Hasi, Hassi — spring, well
Hauteur — elevation, height
Hav-et — sea
Havn, Havre — harbor, port
Hawr — lake, marsh
Hāyk' — lake, reservoir
He — canal, lake, river
Hegy, -ség — mountain, -s, range
Heiau — temple
Ho — lake, reservoir
Hoek — hook, point
Hög-en — high, hill
Höhe, -n — height, high
Høj — height, hill
Holm, -e, Holmene — island-s, islet -s
Holot — dunes
Hòn — island-s
Hor-a, -y — mountain, -s
Horn — horn, peak
Houma — point
Hoved — headland, peninsula, point
Hraun — lava field
Hsü — island
Hu — lake, reservoir
Huk — cape, point
Hüyük — hill, mound

Idehan — sand dunes
Igarapé — creek, stream
Île-s, Ilha-s, Illa-s, Îlot-s — island-s, islet-s
Îlet, Ilhéu-s — islet, -s
Irhil — mountain-s
'Irq — sand dune-s
Isblink — glacier, ice field
Is-en — glacier
Isebræ — glacier
Isfjord — ice fjord

Iskappe — ice cap
Isla-s, Islote — island-s, islet
Isol-a, -e — island, -s
Isstrøm — glacier, ice field
Istmo — isthmus
Iwa — island, islet, rock

Jabal, Jebel — mountain-s, range
Jahīl — lake
Järv, -i, Jaure, Javrre — lake
Jazā'ir, Jazīrat, Jazīreh — island-s
Jehīl — lake
Jezero, Jezioro — lake
Jiang — river, stream
Jiao — cape
Jibāl — hill, mountain, ridge
Jima — island-s, rock-s
Jøkel, Jökull — glacier, ice cap
Joki, Jokka — river
Jökulsá — river from a glacier
Jõsuji — lake, reservoir
Jūn — bay

Kaap — cape
Kafr — village
Kaikyō — channel, strait
Kaise — mountain
Kaiwan — bay, gulf, sea
Kanal — canal, channel
Kangerlua — fjord
Kangri — mountain-s, peak
Kaôh — island
Kap, Kapp — cape
Kavīr — salt desert
Kefar — village
Kënet' — lagoon, lake
Kep — cape, point
Kepulauan — archipelago, islands
Khalîg, Khalīj — bay, gulf
Khirb-at, -et — ancient site, ruins
Khrebet — mountain range
Kinh — canal
Klint — bluff, cliff
Kō — bay, cove, harbor
Ko — island, lake
Kōh — mountain
Koh — island, mountain, range
Köl-i — lake
Kólpos — gulf
Kong — king, mountain
Körfez, -i — bay, gulf
Kosa — spit of land
Kōtal — pass
Kou — estuary, river mouth
Kowtal-e — pass
Kronprins — crown prince
Krasn-yy, -aya, -oye — red
Kryazh — mountain range, ridge
Kuala — estuary, river mouth
Kuan — mountain pass
Kūh, Kūhhā — mountain-s, range
Kul', Kuli — lake
Kum — sandy desert
Kundo — archipelago
Kuppe — hill-s, mountain-s
Kust — coast, shore
Kyst — coast
Kyun — island

La — pass
Lac, Lac-ul, -us — lake
Lae — cape, point
Lago, -a — lagoon, lake
Lagoen, Lagune — lagoon
Laguna-s — lagoon-s, lake-s
Laht — bay, gulf, harbor
Laje — reef, rock ledge
Laut — sea
Lednik — glacier
Leida — channel
Lhari — mountain
Li — village
Liedao — archipelago, islands
Liehtao — archipelago, islands
Lille — little, small
Liman-ı — bay, estuary

Límni — lake
Ling — mountain-s, range
Linn — pool, waterfall
Lintasan — passage
Liqen — lake
Llano-s — plain-s
Loch, Lough — lake, arm of the sea
Loma-s — hill-s, knoll-s

Mal — mountain, range
Mal-yy, -aya, -oye — little, small
Mamarr — pass, path
Man — bay
Mar, Mare — large lake, sea
Marsa, Marsá — bay, inlet
Masabb — mouth of river
Massif — mountain-s
Mauna — mountain
Mēda — plain
Meer — lake, sea
Melkosopochnik — undulating plain
Mesa, Meseta — plateau, tableland
Mierzeja — sandspit
Minami — south
Mios — island
Misaki — cape, peninsula, point
Mochun — passage
Molsron — harbor
Mong — town, village
Mont-e, -i, -ii, -s — mount, -ain, -s
Montagne, -s — mount, -ain, -s
Montaña, -s — mountain, -s
More — sea
Morne — hill, peak
Morro — bluff, headland, hill
Motu, -s — islands
Mouïet — well
Mouillage — anchorage
Muang — town, village
Mūi — cape, point
Mull — headland, promontory
Munkhafad — depression
Munte — mountain
Munţi-i — mountains
Muong — town, village
Mynydd — mountain
Mys — cape

Nacional — national
Nada — gulf, sea
Næs, Näs — cape, point
Nafūd — area of dunes, desert
Nagor'ye — mountain range, plateau
Nahar, Nahr — river, stream
Nakhon — town
Namakzār — salt waste
Ne — island, reef, rock-s
Neem — cape, point, promontory
Nes, Ness — peninsula, point
Nevado-s — snowcapped mountain-s
Nez — cape, promontory
Ni — village
Nísi, Nísia, Nisís, Nísoi — island-s, islet-s
Nisídhes — islets
Nizhn-iy, -yaya, -eye — lower
Nizmennost' — low country
Noord — north
Nord-re — north-ern
Nørre — north-ern
Nos — cape, nose, point
Nosy — island, reef, rock
Nov-yy, -aya, -aye, -oye — new
Nudo — mountain
Núi — mountains
Numa — lake
Nunaa — area, region
Nunaat — area, island
Nunatak, -s, -ker — peak-s surrounded by ice cap
Nur — lake, salt lake
Nuruu — mountain range, ridge
Nut-en — peak
Nuur — lake

O-n, Ø-er — island-s

Oblast — administrative division, province, region
Oceanus — ocean
Odde-n — cape, point
Øer-ne — islands
Oglat — group of wells
Oguilet — well
Ór-os, -i — mountain, -s
Órmos — bay, port
Ort — place, point
Øst-er — east
Ostrov, -a, Ostrv-o, -a — island, -s
Otoci, Otok — islands, island
Ouadi, Oued — river, watercourse
Ovalığı — plain
Øy-a — island
Øyane — islands
Ozer-o, -a — lake, -s

Pää — mountain, point
Palus — marsh
Pampa-s — grassy plain-s
Pantà — lake, reservoir
Pantanal — marsh, swamp
Pao, P'ao — lake
Parbat — mountain
Parque — park
Pas, -ul — pass
Paso, Passo — pass
Passe — channel, pass
Pasul — pass
Pedra — rock
Pegunungan — mountain range
Pellg — bay, bight
Peña — cliff, rock
Pendi — basin
Penedo-s — rock-s
Péninsule — peninsula
Peñón — point, rock
Pereval — mountain pass
Pertuis — strait
Peski — sands, sandy region
Phnom — hill, mountain, range
Phou — mountain range
Phouphiang — plateau
Phu — mountain
Piana-o — plain
Pic, Pik, Piz — peak
Picacho — mountain, peak
Pico-s — peak-s
Pistyll — waterfall
Piton-s — peak-s
Pivdennyy — southern
Plaja, Playa — beach, inlet, shore
Planalto, Plato — plateau
Planina — mountain, plateau
Plassen — lake
Ploskogor'ye — plateau, upland
Pointe — point
Polder — reclaimed land
Poluostrov — peninsula
Pongo — water gap
Ponta, -l — cape, point
Ponte — bridge
Poolsaar — peninsula
Portezuelo — pass
Porto — port
Poulo — island-s
Praia — beach, seashore
Presa — reservoir
Presidente — president
Presqu'île — peninsula
Prins — prince
Prinsesse — princess
Prokhod — pass
Proliv — strait
Promontorio — promontory
Průsmyk — mountain pass
Przylądek — cape
Puerto — bay, pass, port
Pulao — island-s
Pulau, Pulo — island
Puncak — peak, summit, top
Punt, Punta, -n — point, -s
Pun — peak
Pu'u — hill, mountain
Puy — peak

Qā' — depression, marsh, mud flat
Qal'at — fort
Qal'eh — castle, fort
Qanâ — canal
Qārat — hill-s, mountain-s
Qaşr — castle, fort, hill
Qila — fort
Qiryat — settlement, suburb
Qolleh — peak
Qooriga — anchorage, bay
Qoz — dunes, sand ridge
Qu — canal
Quần Đảo — islands
Quebrada — ravine, stream
Qullai — peak, summit
Qum-y — desert, sand
Qundao — archipelago, islands
Qurayyāt — hills

Raas — cape, point
Rabt — hill
Rada — roadstead
Rade — anchorage, roadstead
Rags — point
Ramat — hill, mountain
Rand — ridge of hills
Rann — swamp
Raqaba — wadi, watercourse
Ras, Râs, Ra's — cape
Ravnina — plain
Récif-s — reef-s
Regreg — marsh
Represa — reservoir
Reservatório — reservoir
Restinga — barrier, sand area
Rettō — chain of islands
Ri — mountain range, village
Ría — estuary
Ribeirão — stream
Río, Rio — river
Rivière — river
Roca-s — cliff, rock-s
Roche-r, -s — rock-s
Rosh — mountain, point
Rt — cape, point
Rubha — headland
Rupes — scarp

Saar — island
Saari, Sari — island
Sabkha-t, Sabkhet — lagoon, marsh, salt lake
Sagar — lake, sea
Sahara, Şaḩrā' — desert
Sahl — plain
Saki — cape, point
Salar — salt flat
Salina — salt pan
Salin-as, -es — salt flat-s, salt marsh-es
Salto — waterfall
Sammyaku — mountain range
San — hill, mountain
San, -ta, -to — saint
Sandur — sandy area
Sankt — saint
Sanmaek — mountain range
São — saint
Sarīr — gravel desert
Sasso — mountain, stone
Savane — savanna
Scoglio — reef, rock
Se — reef, rock-s, shoal-s
Sebjet — salt lake, salt marsh
Sebkha — salt lake, salt marsh
Sebkhet — lagoon, salt lake
See — lake, sea
Selat — strait
Selkä — lake, ridge
Semenanjung — peninsula
Sen — mountain
Seno — bay, gulf
Sermeq — glacier
Sermia — glacier
Serra, Serranía — range of hills or mountains
Severn-ye, -yy, -aya, -oye — northern

Sgùrr — peak
Sha — island, shoal
Sha'ïb — ravine, watercourse
Shamo — desert
Shan — island-s, mountain-s, range
Shankou — mountain pass
Shanmo — mountain range
Sharm — cove, creek, harbor
Shatt, Shaţţ — large river
Shi — administrative division, municipality
Shima — island-s, rock-s
Shō — island, reef, rock
Shotō — archipelago
Shott — intermittent salt lake
Shuiku — reservoir
Shuitao — channel
Shyghanaghy — bay, gulf
Sierra — mountain range
Silsilesi — mountain chain, ridge
Sint — saint
Sinus — bay, sea
Sjö-n — lake
Skarv-et — barren mountain
Skerry — rock
Slieve — mountain
Sø-er — lake-s
Sønder, Søndre — south-ern
Sopka — conical mountain, volcano
Sor — lake, salt lake
Sør, Sör — south-ern
Sory — salt lake, salt marsh
Spitz-e — peak, point, top
Sredn-iy, -yaya, -eye — central, middle
Stagno — lake, pond
Stantsiya — station
Stausee — reservoir
Stenón — channel, strait
Step'-i — steppe-s
Štít — summit, top
Stor-e — big, great
Straat — strait
Straum-en — current-s
Strelka — spit of land
Stretet, Stretto — strait
Su — reef, river, rock, stream
Su Anbarı — reservoir
Sud — south
Sudo — channel, strait
Suidō — channel, strait
Şummān — rocky desert
Sund — sound, strait
Sunden — channel, inlet, sound
Svyat-oy, -aya, -oye — holy, saint
Sziget — island

Tagh — mountain-s
Tai — coast, tide
Tall — hill, mound
T'an — lake
Tanezrouft — desert
Tang — plain, steppe
Tangi — peninsula, point
Tanjong, Tanjung — cape, point
Tao — island-s
Tarso — hill-s, mountain-s
Tassili — plateau, upland
Tau — mountain-s, range
Taūy — hills, mountains
Tchabal — mountain-s
Te Ava — tidal flat
Tel-l — hill, mound
Telok, Teluk — bay
Tepe, -si — hill, peak
Tepuí — mesa, mountain
Terara — hill, mountain, peak
Testa — bluff, head
Thale — lake
Thang — plain, steppe
Tien — lake
Tierra — land, region
Ting — hill, mountain
Tir'at — canal
Tó — lake, pool
To, Tō — island-s, rock-s
Tonle — lake

Tope — hill, mountain, peak
Top-pen — peak-s
Träsk — bog, lake
Tso — lake
Tsui — cape, point
Tübegi — peninsula
Tulu — hill, mountain
Tunturi-t — hill-s, mountain-s

Uad — wadi, watercourse
Udde-m — point
Ujong, Ujung — cape, point
Umi — bay, lagoon, lake
Ura — bay, inlet, lake
'Urūq — dune area
Uul, Uula — mountain, range
'Uyûn — springs

Vaara — mountain
Vaart — canal
Vær — fishing station
Vaïn — channel, strait
Valle, Vallée — valley, wadi
Vallen — waterfall
Valli — lagoon, lake
Vallis — valley
Vanua — land
Varre — mountain
Vatn, Vatten, Vatnet — lake, water
Veld — grassland, plain
Verkhn-iy, -yaya, -eye — higher, upper
Vesi — lake, water
Vest-er — west
Via — road
Vidda — plateau
Vig, Vík, Vik, -en — bay, cove
Vinh — bay
Vodokhranilishche — reservoir
Vodoskhovyshche — reservoir
Volcan, Volcán — volcano
Vostochn-yy, -aya, -oye — eastern
Vötn — stream
Vozvyshennost' — plateau, upland
Vozyera, -yero, -yera — lake-s
Vrchovina — mountains
Vrch-y — mountain-s
Vrh — hill, mountain
Vrůkh — mountain
Vūng — bay
Vyaliki, -ikaya, -ikaye — big, large
Vysočina — highland

Wabē — stream
Wadi, Wâdi, Wādī — valley, watercourse
Wâhât, Wāḩat — oasis
Wald — forest, wood
Wan — bay, gulf
Water — harbor
Webi — stream
Wiek — cove, inlet

Xia — gorge, strait
Xiao — lesser, little

Yanchi — salt lake
Yang — ocean
Yarımadası — peninsula
Yazovir — reservoir
Yŏlto — island group
Yoma — mountain range
Yü — island
Yumco — lake
Yunhe — canal
Yuzhn-yy, -aya, -oye — southern

Zaki — cape, point
Zaliv — bay, gulf
Zan — mountain, ridge
Zangbo — river, stream
Zapadn-yy, -aya, -oye — western
Zatoka — bay, gulf
Zee — bay, sea
Zemlya — land
Zhotasy — mountains

Time Zones

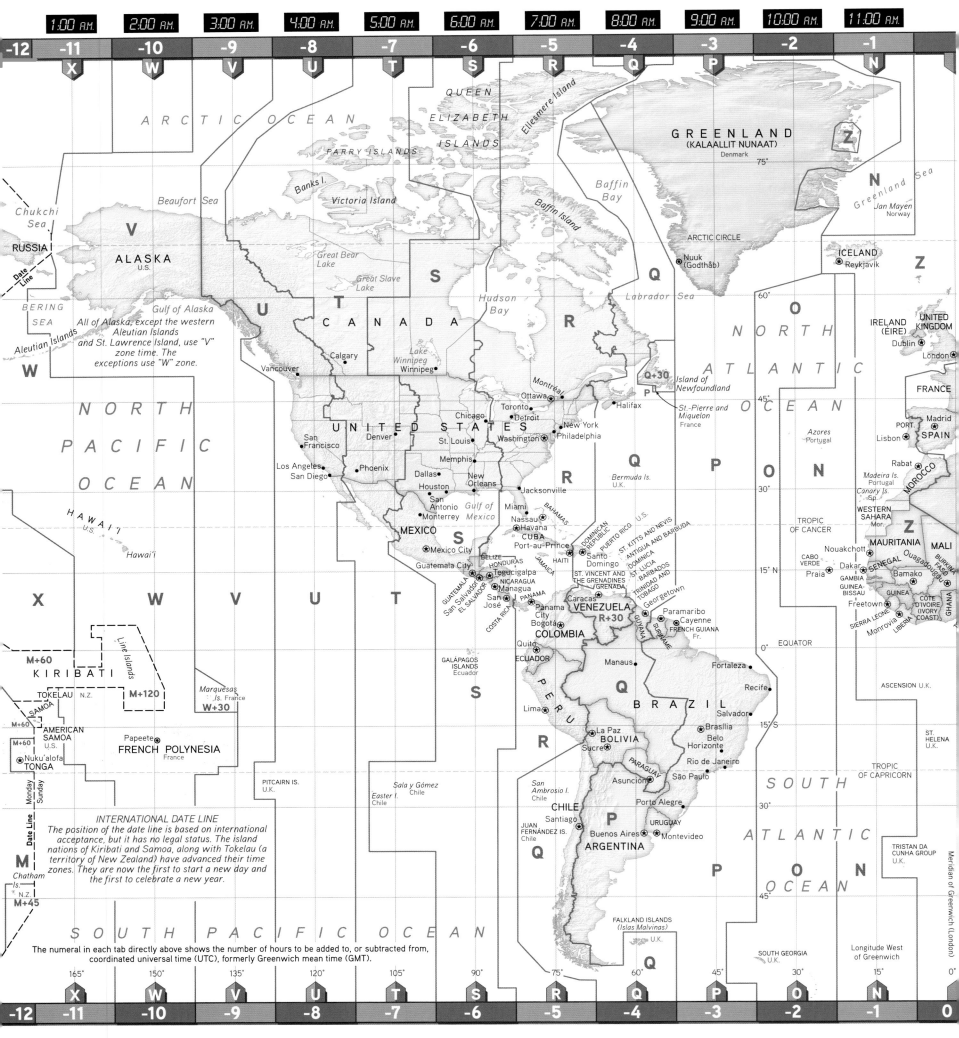

1:00 A.M.	2:00 A.M.	3:00 A.M.	4:00 A.M.	5:00 A.M.	6:00 A.M.	7:00 A.M.	8:00 A.M.	9:00 A.M.	10:00 A.M.	11:00 A.M.
-12	-11	-10	-9	-8	-7	-6	-5	-4	-3	-2	-1
X	W	V	U	T	S	R	Q	P	N

The numeral in each tab directly above shows the number of hours to be added to, or subtracted from, coordinated universal time (UTC), formerly Greenwich mean time (GMT).

165°	150°	135°	120°	105°	90°	75°	60°	45°	30°	15°	0°
X	W	V	U	T	S	R	Q	P	N
-12	-11	-10	-9	-8	-7	-6	-5	-4	-3	-2	-1	0

LEGEND

The map outlines the Earth's 24 time zones with purple lines, with each time zone covering 15° longitude—the distance the Earth rotates in 1 hour in a 24-hour day.

Time zones are measured in reference to the Meridian of Greenwich (0° longitude) in England, sometimes called the prime meridian. Time at Greenwich is known as Greenwich mean time (GMT) or coordinated universal time (UTC) and is the starting point in determining time worldwide. Letters on the map label each time zone,

and the corresponding numbers (with plus or minus signs) indicate the time difference from GMT/UTC. For example, the C time zone is +3. This means that when it is noon in the Greenwich Z zone, it is 3 p.m. standard time in the C zone—the time shown on the clock face (along the top of the map). Daylight savings time, normally one hour ahead of local standard time, is not shown on this map.

Most time zones differ in one-hour increments, but some countries choose to offset time zones by a fraction of an hour. For

example, India (E time zone, +5) shows the label E+30, which means that it is 5 hours and 30 minutes ahead of GMT/UTC time. Nepal is E+45, making it 5 hours and 45 minutes ahead of GMT/UTC.

Many governments choose to have their entire country in one time zone. China is the largest country with only one time zone; normally, it would be divided by five time zones. Other examples of countries in one time zone include India, Iran, and Norway.

274

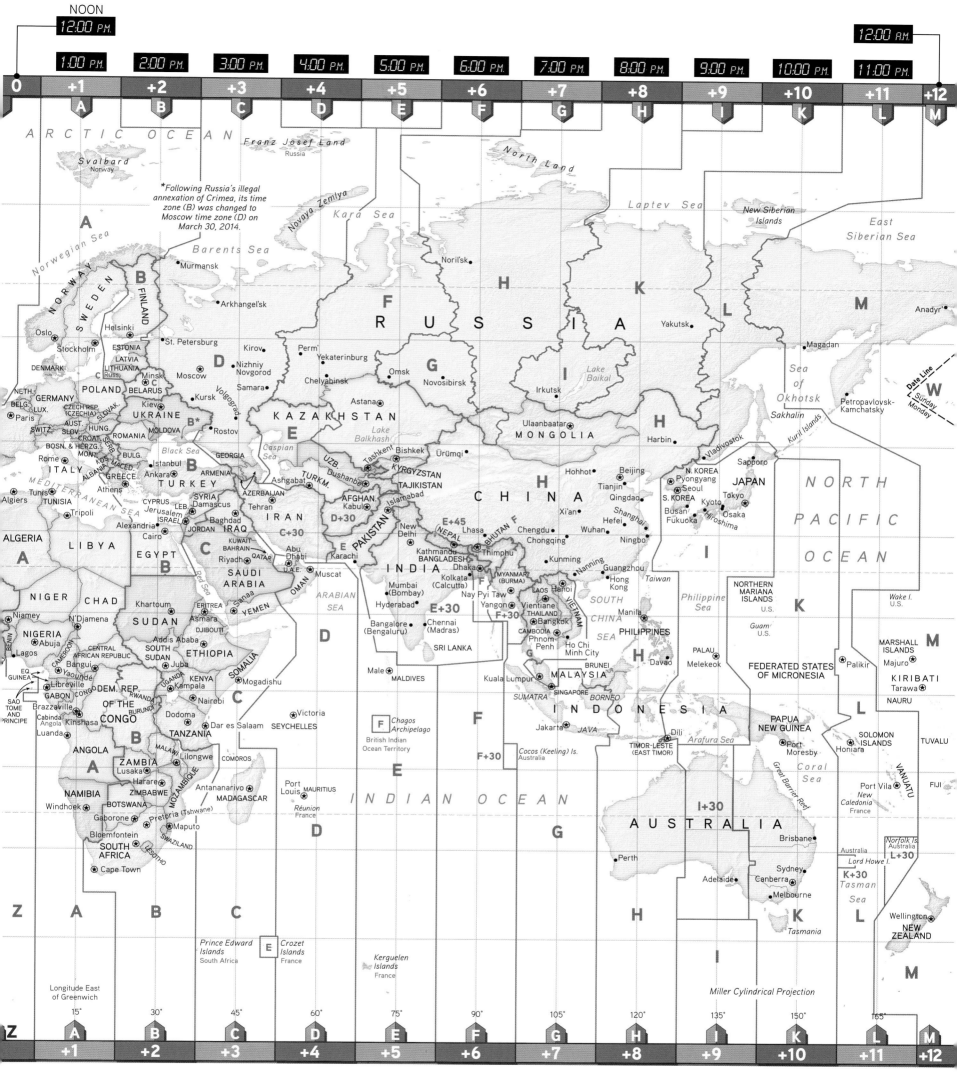

MERIDIAN OF GREENWICH

Britain's Royal Observatory at Greenwich (London) is the home of Greenwich mean time and the "prime meridian of the world" (0° longitude). In 1884, an international conference in Washington, D.C., decided on Greenwich as the location for the prime meridian. At that time, most of the world's commerce depended on sea charts, which already used Greenwich as the prime meridian.

DATE LINE

The international date line, or date line, is an imaginary line located on or near the 180° meridian in the middle of the Pacific Ocean, shown on this map by a dashed black line. The date changes when planes or ships cross it, thus the name date line. A person traveling west across the date line would add a day, but a person traveling east would subtract a day. The position of the date line is based on international acceptance, but it has no legal status. Island countries near the line can choose which date they will observe.

Temperature and Rainfall

Average daily high and low temperatures and monthly rainfall for selected world locations:

	JAN.			FEB.			MARCH			APRIL			MAY			JUNE			JULY			AUG.			SEPT.			OCT.			NOV.			DEC.		
CANADA																																				
CALGARY, *Alberta*	-4	-16	14	-2	-14	15	3	-9	20	11	-3	27	17	3	54	20	7	82	24	9	65	23	8	57	18	3	40	12	-1	18	3	-9	16	-2	-13	14
CHARLOTTETOWN, *P.E.I.*	-3	-11	100	-3	-12	83	1	-7	83	7	-1	77	14	4	79	20	10	75	24	14	78	23	14	86	18	10	91	13	5	106	6	0	106	0	-7	111
CHURCHILL, *Manitoba*	-23	-31	15	-22	-30	12	-15	-25	18	-6	-15	23	2	-5	27	11	1	43	17	7	55	16	7	62	9	2	53	2	-4	44	-9	-16	31	-18	-26	18
EDMONTON, *Alberta*	-9	-18	23	-5	-15	18	0	-9	19	10	-1	24	17	5	45	21	9	79	23	12	87	22	10	64	17	5	36	11	0	20	0	-8	18	-6	-15	22
FORT NELSON, *B.C.*	-18	-27	23	-11	-23	21	-2	-15	21	8	-4	20	16	3	44	21	8	65	23	10	76	21	8	58	15	3	39	6	-4	28	-9	-17	26	-16	-24	23
GOOSE BAY, *Nfld. & Lab.*	-12	-22	1	-10	-21	4	-4	-15	4	3	-7	15	10	0	46	17	5	97	21	10	119	19	9	98	14	4	87	6	-2	58	0	-8	21	-9	-18	7
HALIFAX, *Nova Scotia*	0	-8	139	0	-9	121	3	-5	123	8	0	109	14	5	110	18	9	96	22	13	93	22	14	103	19	10	93	13	5	127	8	1	142	2	-5	141
MONTRÉAL, *Quebec*	-6	-15	71	-4	-13	66	2	-7	71	11	1	74	18	8	69	24	13	84	26	16	87	25	14	91	20	10	84	13	4	76	5	-2	90	-3	-11	85
MOOSONEE, *Ontario*	-14	-27	39	-12	-25	32	-5	-19	37	3	-8	36	11	0	55	18	5	72	22	9	79	20	8	78	15	5	77	8	0	66	-1	-9	53	-11	-21	41
OTTAWA, *Ontario*	-6	-16	67	-5	-15	59	1	-8	67	11	0	60	19	7	72	24	12	82	27	15	86	25	13	80	20	9	77	13	3	69	4	-3	70	-4	-12	74
PRINCE RUPERT, *B.C.*	4	-3	237	6	-1	198	7	0	202	9	2	179	12	5	133	14	8	110	16	10	115	16	10	149	15	8	218	11	5	345	7	1	297	5	-1	275
QUÉBEC, *Quebec*	-7	-17	85	-6	-16	75	0	-9	79	8	-1	76	17	5	93	22	10	108	25	13	112	23	12	109	18	7	113	11	2	89	3	-4	100	-5	-13	104
REGINA, *Saskatchewan*	-12	-23	17	-9	-21	13	-2	-13	18	10	-3	20	18	3	45	23	9	77	26	11	59	25	10	44	19	4	35	11	-2	20	0	-11	16	-8	-19	14
SAINT JOHN, *N.B.*	-3	-14	141	-2	-14	115	3	-7	111	10	-1	111	17	4	116	22	9	103	25	12	100	24	11	100	19	7	108	14	2	118	6	-3	149	-1	-10	157
ST. JOHN'S, *Nfld. & Lab.*	-1	-8	69	-1	-9	69	1	-6	74	5	-2	80	10	1	91	16	6	95	20	11	78	20	11	122	16	8	125	11	3	147	6	0	122	2	-5	91
TORONTO, *Ontario*	-1	-8	68	-1	-9	60	3	-4	66	11	2	65	17	7	71	23	13	68	26	16	77	25	15	70	21	11	73	14	5	62	7	0	70	1	-6	67
VANCOUVER, *B.C.*	5	0	146	8	1	121	10	2	102	13	5	69	17	8	56	19	11	47	22	13	31	22	13	37	19	10	60	14	6	116	9	3	155	6	1	172
WHITEHORSE, *Yukon*	-14	-23	17	-9	-18	13	-2	-13	13	5	-5	9	13	1	14	18	5	30	20	8	37	18	6	39	12	3	31	4	-3	21	-6	-13	20	-12	-20	19
WINNIPEG, *Manitoba*	-13	-23	21	-10	-21	19	-2	-13	26	9	-2	34	18	5	55	23	10	81	26	14	74	25	12	66	19	6	55	12	1	35	-1	-9	26	-9	-18	22
YELLOWKNIFE, *N.W.T.*	-24	-32	14	-20	-30	12	-12	-24	11	-1	-13	10	10	0	16	18	8	20	21	12	35	18	10	39	10	4	29	1	-4	32	-10	-18	23	-20	-28	17
UNITED STATES																																				
ALBANY, *New York*	-1	-12	61	1	-10	59	7	-4	76	14	2	77	21	7	86	26	13	83	29	15	80	27	14	87	23	10	78	17	4	77	9	-1	80	2	-8	74
AMARILLO, *Texas*	9	-6	13	12	-4	14	16	0	23	22	6	28	26	11	71	31	16	88	33	19	70	32	18	74	28	14	50	23	7	35	15	0	15	10	-5	15
ANCHORAGE, *Alaska*	-6	-13	20	-3	-11	21	1	-8	17	6	-2	15	12	4	17	16	8	26	18	11	47	17	10	62	13	5	66	5	-2	47	-3	-9	29	-5	-12	28
ASPEN, *Colorado*	0	-18	32	2	-16	26	5	-11	35	10	-6	28	16	-2	39	22	1	34	26	5	44	25	4	45	21	0	34	15	-5	36	6	-10	31	1	-15	32
ATLANTA, *Georgia*	10	0	117	13	1	117	18	6	139	23	10	103	26	15	100	30	19	92	31	21	134	31	21	93	28	18	91	23	11	77	17	6	95	12	2	105
ATLANTIC CITY, *New Jersey*	5	-6	83	6	-5	78	11	0	98	16	4	86	22	10	82	27	15	63	29	18	103	29	18	103	25	13	78	19	7	72	13	2	84	7	-3	81
AUGUSTA, *Maine*	-2	-11	76	0	-10	71	4	-5	84	11	1	92	19	7	95	23	12	85	26	16	85	25	15	84	20	10	80	14	4	92	7	-1	114	0	-8	93
BIRMINGHAM, *Alabama*	11	0	128	14	1	114	19	6	150	24	10	114	27	14	112	31	18	97	32	21	132	32	20	95	29	17	105	24	10	75	18	5	103	13	2	120
BISMARCK, *North Dakota*	-7	-19	12	-3	-15	11	4	-8	20	13	-1	37	20	6	56	25	11	74	29	14	59	28	12	44	22	6	38	15	0	21	4	-8	14	-4	-16	12
BOISE, *Idaho*	2	-6	38	7	-3	28	12	0	32	16	3	31	22	7	31	27	11	22	32	14	8	31	14	9	25	9	16	18	4	18	9	-1	35	3	-5	35
BOSTON, *Massachusetts*	2	-6	95	3	-5	91	8	0	100	13	5	93	19	10	84	25	15	79	28	18	73	27	18	92	23	14	82	17	8	87	11	4	110	5	-3	105
BROWNSVILLE, *Texas*	21	10	37	22	11	36	26	15	16	29	19	41	31	22	64	33	24	74	34	24	39	34	24	69	32	23	134	30	19	89	26	15	41	22	11	30
BURLINGTON, *Vermont*	-4	-14	46	-3	-13	44	4	-6	55	12	1	71	20	7	78	24	13	85	27	15	90	26	14	101	21	9	85	14	4	77	7	-1	76	-1	-9	59
CHARLESTON, *South Carolina*	14	3	88	16	4	80	20	9	114	24	12	71	28	17	97	31	21	155	32	23	180	32	22	176	29	20	135	25	14	77	21	8	63	16	5	82
CHARLESTON, *West Virginia*	5	-5	87	7	-4	82	14	2	100	19	6	85	24	11	99	28	15	92	30	18	126	29	17	102	26	14	81	20	7	67	14	2	85	8	-2	85
CHEYENNE, *Wyoming*	3	-9	10	5	-8	11	7	-6	26	13	-1	35	18	4	64	24	9	56	28	13	51	27	12	42	22	7	31	16	1	19	8	-5	15	4	-9	10
CHICAGO, *Illinois*	-1	-10	48	1	-7	42	8	-1	72	15	5	97	22	10	83	27	16	103	29	19	103	28	18	89	24	14	79	18	7	70	9	1	73	2	-6	65
CINCINNATI, *Ohio*	3	-6	89	5	-4	67	12	1	97	18	7	94	24	12	101	28	17	99	30	19	102	30	18	86	26	14	75	19	8	62	12	3	81	5	-3	75
CLEVELAND, *Ohio*	1	-7	62	2	-6	58	8	-2	78	15	4	85	21	9	90	26	14	89	28	17	88	27	16	86	23	12	80	17	7	65	10	2	80	3	-4	70
DALLAS, *Texas*	13	1	47	15	4	58	20	8	74	25	13	105	29	18	125	33	22	86	35	24	56	35	24	60	31	20	82	26	14	100	19	8	64	14	3	60
DENVER, *Colorado*	6	-9	14	8	-7	16	11	-3	34	17	1	45	22	6	63	27	11	43	31	15	47	30	14	38	25	9	28	19	2	26	11	-4	23	7	-8	15
DES MOINES, *Iowa*	-2	-12	26	1	-9	30	8	-2	57	17	4	85	23	11	103	28	16	108	30	19	97	29	18	105	24	13	80	18	6	58	9	-1	46	0	-9	31
DETROIT, *Michigan*	-1	-7	42	1	-7	43	7	-2	62	14	4	75	21	10	69	26	15	85	29	18	86	27	18	87	23	14	78	16	7	55	9	2	67	2	-4	67
DULUTH, *Minnesota*	-9	-19	31	-6	-16	21	1	-9	44	9	-2	59	17	4	84	22	9	105	25	13	102	23	12	101	18	7	95	11	2	62	2	-6	48	-6	-15	32
EL PASO, *Texas*	13	-1	11	17	1	11	21	5	8	26	9	7	31	14	9	36	18	17	36	20	38	34	19	39	31	16	34	26	10	20	19	4	11	14	-1	14
FAIRBANKS, *Alaska*	-19	-28	14	-14	-26	11	-5	-19	9	5	-6	7	15	3	15	21	10	35	22	11	45	19	8	46	13	2	28	0	-8	21	-12	-21	18	-17	-26	19
HARTFORD, *Connecticut*	1	-9	83	2	-7	79	8	-2	97	16	3	97	22	9	95	27	14	85	29	17	86	28	16	104	24	11	101	18	5	96	11	0	105	3	-6	99
HELENA, *Montana*	-1	-12	15	3	-9	12	7	-5	18	13	-1	24	19	4	45	24	9	53	29	12	28	28	11	27	21	5	28	15	0	19	6	-6	14	0	-12	16
HONOLULU, *Hawai'i*	27	19	80	27	19	68	28	20	72	28	20	32	29	21	25	30	22	10	31	23	15	32	23	14	31	23	18	31	22	53	29	21	67	27	19	89
HOUSTON, *Texas*	16	4	98	19	6	75	22	10	88	26	15	91	29	18	142	32	21	133	34	22	85	34	22	95	31	20	106	28	14	120	22	10	97	18	6	91
INDIANAPOLIS, *Indiana*	1	-8	69	4	-6	61	11	0	92	17	5	94	23	11	98	28	16	98	30	18	111	29	17	88	25	13	74	19	6	69	11	1	89	4	-5	77
JACKSONVILLE, *Florida*	18	5	83	19	6	89	23	10	100	26	13	77	29	17	92	32	21	140	33	22	164	33	22	186	31	21	199	27	15	99	23	10	52	19	6	65
JUNEAU, *Alaska*	-1	-7	139	1	-5	116	4	-3	113	8	0	105	13	4	109	16	7	88	18	9	120	17	8	160	13	6	217	8	3	255	3	-2	186	0	-5	153
KANSAS CITY, *Missouri*	2	-9	30	5	-6	32	12	0	67	18	7	88	24	12	138	29	17	102	32	20	115	30	19	99	26	14	120	20	8	83	11	1	56	4	-6	43
LAS VEGAS, *Nevada*	14	0	14	17	4	12	20	7	13	25	10	5	31	16	5	38	21	3	41	25	9	40	23	13	35	19	7	28	12	6	20	6	11	14	1	10
LITTLE ROCK, *Arkansas*	9	-1	85	12	1	88	17	6	120	23	11	134	26	15	141	31	20	84	33	22	83	32	21	80	28	18	85	23	11	102	16	6	153	10	1	123
LOS ANGELES, *California*	19	9	70	19	10	61	19	10	51	20	12	20	21	14	3	22	15	1	24	17	1	25	18	2	25	17	5	24	15	7	21	12	38	19	9	43
LOUISVILLE, *Kentucky*	5	-5	85	7	-3	88	14	2	113	20	7	101	24	13	114	29	17	90	31	20	106	30	19	84	27	15	76	21	8	68	14	3	92	7	-2	89
MEMPHIS, *Tennessee*	9	-1	118	12	2	114	17	6	136	23	11	142	27	16	126	32	21	98	34	23	101	33	22	87	29	18	83	24	11	74	17	6	124	11	2	135
MIAMI, *Florida*	24	15	52	25	16	53	26	18	63	28	20	82	30	22	150	31	24	227	32	25	152	32	25	198	31	24	215	29	22	178	27	19	80	25	16	47
MILWAUKEE, *Wisconsin*	-3	-11	32	-1	-8	31	5	-3	54	12	2	87	18	7	73	24	13	87	27	17	85	26	16	94	22	12	95	15	6	66	7	-1	65	0	-7	53
MINNEAPOLIS, *Minnesota*	-6	-16	21	-3	-13	22	4	-5	45	14	2	58	21	9	80	26	14	103	29	17	97	27	16	95	22	10	70	15	4	49	5	-4	37	-4	-12	24
NASHVILLE, *Tennessee*	8	-3	108	10	-1	100	16	4	127	22	9	104	26	14	118	30	18	99	32	21	99	31	20	85	28	16	89	23	9	67	16	4	101	10	-1	112
NEW ORLEANS, *Louisiana*	16	5	136	18	7	147	22	11	124	26	15	119	29	18	135	32	22	147	33	23	167	32	23	157	30	21	138	26	15	76	22	11	101	18	7	132
NEW YORK, *New York*	3	-4	80	4	-3	76	9	1	99	15	7	94	21	12	93	26	17	80	29	21	101	28	20	107	24	16	85	18	10	81	12	5	96	6	-1	90
OKLAHOMA CITY, *Oklahoma*	8	-4	28	11	-1	36	17	4	61	22	9	76	26	14	145	31	19	107	34	21	74	34	21	65	29	17	97	23	10	80	16	4	43	10	-2	37
OMAHA, *Nebraska*	-1	-12	18	2	-9	21	9	-2	61	17	5	73	23	11	118	28	16	105	30	19	96	29	18	95	24	13	90	18	6	60	9	-1	35	1	-9	23
PENSACOLA, *Florida*	15	5	109	17	7	126	21	11	150	25	15	112	28	19	105	32	22	168	32	23	187	32	23	176	30	21	166	26	15	102	21	11	91	17	7	105
PHILADELPHIA, *Pennsylvania*	3	-5	82	5	-4	70	11	1	95	17	6	88	23	12	94	28	17	87	30	20	108	29	19	97	25	15	86	19	8	67	13	3	85	6	-2	86
PHOENIX, *Arizona*	19	3	21	22	5	21	25	7	30	29	9	7	33	13	5	38	18	3	39	23	21	38	22	30	36	18	23	30	12	18	23	7	18	19	3	28
PITTSBURGH, *Pennsylvania*	1	-8	66	3	-7	60	9	-1	85	16	4	80	21	9	92	26	14	91	28	16	98	27	16	83	24	12	74	17	6	61	10	1	69	4	-4	71
PORTLAND, *Oregon*	7	1	133	11	2	105	13	4	92	16	5	61	20	8	53	23	12	38	27	14	15	27	14	23	24	11	41	18	7	76	11	4	135	8	2	149
PROVIDENCE, *Rhode Island*	3	-7	101	4	-6	91	8	-2	111	14	3	102	20	9	89	25	14	77	28	17	77	27	17	102	24	12	88	18	6	93	12	2	117	5	-4	110
RALEIGH, *North Carolina*	9	-2	89	11	0	88	17	4	94	22	8	70	26	13	96	29	18	91	31	20	111	30	20	110	27	16	79	22	9	77	17	4	76	12	0	79
RAPID CITY, *South Dakota*	2	-12	10	4	-10	12	8	-6	26	14	0	52	20	6	84	25	12	89	30	15	63	29	13	43	23	7	32	17	1	26	8	-5	12	3	-11	10
RENO, *Nevada*	7	-6	28	11	-4	24	14	-2	20	18	1	11	23	5	17	28	8	11	33	11	7	32	10	6	26	5	9	20	1	10	12	-3	19	8	-7	27
ST. LOUIS, *Missouri*	3	-6	50	6	-4	54	13	2	84	19	8	97	25	13	100	30	19	103	32	21	92	31	20	76	27	16	73	20	9	70	13	3	78	5	-3	64
SALT LAKE CITY, *Utah*	2	-7	32	6	-4	30	11	0	45	16	3	52	22	8	46	28	13	23	33	18	18	32	17	21	26	11	27	19	5	34	10	-1	34	3	-6	34
SAN DIEGO, *California*	19	9	56	19	10	41	19	12	50	20	13	20	21	15	5	22	17	2	25	19	1	25	20	2	25	19	5	24	16	9	21	12	30	19	9	35
SAN FRANCISCO, *California*	14	8	112	16	9	77	16	9	78	17	10	34	17	10	10	18	11	4	18	12	1	19	13	2	20	13	7	20	13	28	17	11	73	14	8	91

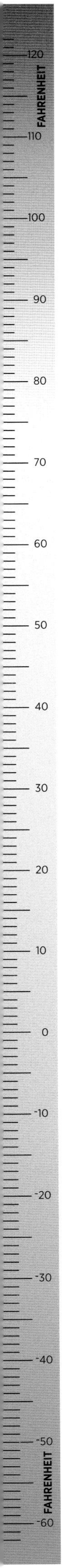

RED FIGURES: Average daily high temperature (°C)

BLUE FIGURES: Average daily low temperature (°C)

BLACK FIGURES: Average monthly rainfall (mm) 1 millimeter = 0.039 inch

	JAN.			FEB.			MARCH			APRIL			MAY			JUNE			JULY			AUG.			SEPT.			OCT.			NOV.			DEC.		
UNITED STATES																																				
SANTA FE, *New Mexico*	6	-10	11	9	-7	9	13	-5	12	18	-1	13	24	4	23	29	9	31	31	12	52	29	11	64	25	7	38	20	1	32	13	-5	14	7	-9	12
SEATTLE, *Washington*	7	2	141	10	3	107	12	4	94	14	5	64	18	8	42	21	11	38	24	13	20	24	13	27	21	11	47	15	8	89	10	5	149	7	2	149
SPOKANE, *Washington*	1	-6	52	5	-3	39	9	-1	37	14	2	28	19	6	35	24	10	33	28	12	15	28	12	16	22	8	20	15	2	31	5	-2	51	1	-6	57
TAMPA, *Florida*	21	10	54	22	11	73	25	14	90	28	16	44	31	20	76	32	23	143	32	24	189	32	24	196	32	23	160	29	18	60	25	14	46	22	11	54
VICKSBURG, *Mississippi*	14	2	155	16	3	131	21	8	160	25	12	147	29	16	130	32	20	88	33	22	106	33	21	80	30	18	85	26	12	106	20	8	126	16	4	168
WASHINGTON, *D.C.*	6	-3	71	8	-2	66	14	3	90	19	8	72	25	14	94	29	19	80	31	22	97	31	21	104	27	17	84	21	10	78	15	5	76	8	0	79
WICHITA, *Kansas*	4	-7	19	8	-5	23	14	1	57	20	7	57	25	12	99	30	18	105	34	21	82	33	20	78	27	15	85	21	8	62	13	1	37	6	-5	29
MIDDLE AMERICA																																				
ACAPULCO, *Mexico*	29	21	8	31	21	1	31	21	0	31	22	1	32	23	36	32	24	325	32	24	231	32	24	236	31	24	353	31	23	170	31	22	30	31	21	10
BALBOA, *Panama*	31	22	34	32	22	16	32	22	14	32	23	73	31	23	198	30	23	203	31	23	176	31	23	200	30	23	197	29	23	271	29	23	260	31	23	133
CHARLOTTE AMALIE, *V.I.*	28	23	50	27	22	41	28	23	49	28	23	63	29	24	105	30	25	67	31	26	71	31	26	112	31	26	132	31	25	139	29	24	131	28	23	69
GUATEMALA CITY, *Guatemala*	23	12	4	25	12	5	27	14	10	28	14	32	29	16	110	27	16	257	26	16	197	26	16	193	26	16	235	24	16	98	23	14	33	22	13	13
GUAYMAS, *Mexico*	23	13	17	24	14	6	26	16	5	29	18	1	31	21	2	34	24	1	34	27	46	35	27	71	35	26	28	32	22	17	28	18	8	23	13	18
HAVANA, *Cuba*	26	18	71	26	18	46	27	19	46	29	21	58	30	22	119	31	23	165	32	24	124	32	24	135	31	24	150	29	23	173	27	21	79	26	19	58
KINGSTON, *Jamaica*	30	19	29	30	19	24	30	20	23	31	21	39	31	22	104	32	23	96	32	23	46	32	23	107	32	23	127	31	23	181	31	22	95	31	21	41
MANAGUA, *Nicaragua*	33	21	2	33	21	3	35	22	4	36	23	3	35	24	136	32	23	237	32	23	132	32	23	121	33	23	213	32	23	315	32	22	42	32	22	10
MÉRIDA, *Mexico*	28	17	30	29	17	23	32	19	18	33	21	20	34	22	81	33	23	142	33	23	132	33	23	142	32	23	173	31	22	97	29	19	33	28	18	33
MEXICO CITY, *Mexico*	19	6	8	21	6	5	24	8	11	25	11	19	26	12	49	24	13	106	23	12	129	23	12	121	23	12	110	21	10	44	20	8	15	19	6	7
MONTERREY, *Mexico*	20	9	18	22	11	23	24	14	16	29	17	29	31	20	40	33	22	68	32	22	62	33	22	76	30	21	151	27	18	78	22	13	26	18	10	20
NASSAU, *Bahamas*	25	18	48	25	18	43	26	19	41	27	21	65	29	22	132	31	23	178	31	24	153	32	24	170	31	24	180	29	23	171	27	21	71	26	19	43
PORT-AU-PRINCE, *Haiti*	31	20	32	31	20	50	32	21	79	32	22	156	32	22	218	33	23	96	34	23	73	34	23	139	33	23	166	32	22	164	31	22	84	31	21	35
PORT OF SPAIN, *Trinidad*	29	19	69	30	19	41	31	19	46	31	21	53	32	21	94	31	22	193	31	21	218	31	22	246	31	22	193	31	22	170	31	21	183	30	21	124
SAN JOSÉ, *Costa Rica*	24	14	11	24	14	5	26	15	14	26	17	46	27	17	224	26	17	276	25	17	215	26	16	243	26	16	326	25	16	323	25	16	148	24	14	42
SAN JUAN, *Puerto Rico*	27	21	75	27	21	56	27	21	59	28	22	95	29	23	156	29	24	112	29	24	115	29	24	133	30	24	136	29	24	140	29	23	148	27	22	118
SAN SALVADOR, *El Salvador*	32	16	7	33	16	7	34	17	13	34	18	53	33	19	179	31	19	315	32	18	312	32	19	307	31	19	317	31	18	230	31	17	40	32	16	12
SANTO DOMINGO, *Dom. Rep.*	29	19	57	29	19	43	29	19	49	29	21	77	30	22	179	31	22	154	31	22	155	31	23	162	31	22	173	31	22	164	30	21	111	29	19	63
TEGUCIGALPA, *Honduras*	25	13	9	27	14	4	29	14	8	30	17	32	29	18	151	28	18	159	28	17	82	28	17	87	28	17	185	27	17	135	26	16	38	25	15	12
SOUTH AMERICA																																				
ANTOFAGASTA, *Chile*	24	17	0	24	17	0	23	16	0	21	14	0	19	13	0	18	11	1	17	11	1	17	11	1	18	12	0	19	13	0	21	14	0	22	16	0
ASUNCIÓN, *Paraguay*	35	22	150	34	22	133	33	21	142	29	18	145	25	14	120	22	12	73	23	12	51	26	14	48	28	16	83	30	17	136	32	18	144	34	21	142
BELÉM, *Brazil*	31	22	351	30	22	412	31	23	441	31	23	370	31	23	282	31	22	164	31	22	154	31	22	122	32	22	129	32	22	105	32	22	101	32	22	202
BOGOTÁ, *Colombia*	19	9	48	20	9	52	19	10	81	19	11	119	19	11	103	18	11	61	18	10	47	18	10	48	19	9	58	19	10	142	19	10	115	19	9	67
BRASÍLIA, *Brazil*	27	18	262	27	18	213	28	18	202	28	17	103	26	13	20	25	11	4	26	11	4	28	13	6	31	16	35	28	18	140	28	19	238	26	18	329
BUENOS AIRES, *Argentina*	29	17	93	28	17	81	26	16	117	22	12	90	18	8	77	14	5	64	14	6	59	16	6	65	18	8	78	21	10	97	24	13	89	28	16	96
CARACAS, *Venezuela*	24	13	41	25	13	27	26	14	22	27	16	20	27	17	36	26	17	52	26	16	53	26	16	53	27	16	48	26	16	47	25	16	50	26	14	58
COM. RIVADAVIA, *Argentina*	26	13	16	25	13	11	22	11	21	18	8	21	13	6	34	11	3	21	11	3	25	12	3	22	14	5	13	19	9	13	22	10	13	24	12	15
CÓRDOBA, *Argentina*	31	16	110	30	16	102	28	14	96	24	11	45	21	7	25	18	3	10	18	3	10	21	4	13	23	7	27	25	11	69	28	13	97	30	16	118
GUAYAQUIL, *Ecuador*	31	21	224	31	22	278	31	22	287	32	22	180	31	20	53	31	20	17	29	19	2	30	18	0	31	19	2	30	20	3	31	20	3	31	21	30
LA PAZ, *Bolivia*	17	6	130	17	6	105	18	6	72	18	4	47	18	3	13	17	1	6	17	1	9	17	2	14	18	3	29	19	4	40	19	6	50	18	6	93
LIMA, *Peru*	28	19	1	28	19	1	28	19	1	27	17	0	23	16	1	20	14	2	19	14	4	19	13	3	20	14	3	22	14	2	23	16	1	26	17	1
MANAUS, *Brazil*	31	24	264	31	24	262	31	24	298	31	24	283	31	24	204	31	24	103	32	24	67	33	24	46	33	24	63	33	24	111	33	24	161	32	24	220
MARACAIBO, *Venezuela*	32	23	5	32	23	5	33	23	6	33	24	39	33	25	65	34	25	55	34	24	25	34	25	53	34	25	76	33	24	119	33	24	134	33	24	22
MONTEVIDEO, *Uruguay*	28	17	95	28	16	100	26	15	111	22	12	83	18	9	76	15	6	74	14	6	86	15	6	84	17	8	90	20	9	98	23	12	78	26	15	84
PARAMARIBO, *Suriname*	29	22	209	29	22	149	29	22	168	30	23	219	30	23	307	30	23	302	31	23	227	32	23	163	33	23	80	33	23	82	32	23	117	30	22	204
PUNTA ARENAS, *Chile*	14	7	35	14	7	28	12	5	39	10	4	41	7	2	42	5	1	32	4	-1	34	6	1	33	8	2	28	11	3	24	12	4	29	14	6	32
QUITO, *Ecuador*	22	8	113	22	8	128	22	8	154	21	8	176	21	8	124	22	7	48	22	7	20	23	7	24	23	7	78	22	8	127	22	7	109	22	8	103
RECIFE, *Brazil*	30	25	62	30	25	102	30	24	197	29	24	252	28	23	301	28	23	302	27	22	254	27	22	156	28	23	78	29	24	36	29	24	29	29	25	40
RIO DE JANEIRO, *Brazil*	29	23	135	29	23	124	28	22	134	27	21	109	25	19	78	24	18	52	24	17	45	24	18	46	24	18	62	25	19	82	26	20	100	28	22	137
SANTIAGO, *Chile*	29	12	3	29	11	3	27	9	5	23	7	13	18	5	64	14	3	84	15	3	76	17	4	56	19	6	30	22	7	15	26	9	8	28	11	5
SÃO PAULO, *Brazil*	27	17	225	28	18	208	27	17	160	26	14	71	23	12	67	22	11	54	22	9	35	23	11	48	23	12	77	24	14	117	26	15	139	27	16	185
VALPARAÍSO, *Chile*	22	13	0	22	13	0	21	12	0	19	11	22	17	10	38	16	9	100	16	8	111	16	8	42	17	9	27	18	10	15	21	11	15	22	12	1
EUROPE																																				
AJACCIO, *Corsica, France*	13	3	76	14	4	58	16	5	66	18	7	56	21	10	41	25	14	23	27	16	71	28	16	18	26	15	43	22	11	97	18	7	112	15	4	79
AMSTERDAM, *Netherlands*	4	1	79	5	1	44	8	3	89	11	6	39	16	10	50	18	13	60	21	15	73	20	15	60	18	13	80	13	9	104	8	5	76	5	2	72
ATHENS, *Greece*	13	6	48	14	7	41	16	8	41	20	11	23	25	16	18	30	20	7	33	23	5	33	23	8	29	19	10	24	15	53	19	12	55	15	8	62
BARCELONA, *Spain*	13	6	38	14	7	38	16	9	47	18	11	47	21	14	44	25	18	38	28	21	28	28	21	44	25	19	76	21	15	96	16	11	51	13	8	44
BELFAST, *N. Ireland, U.K.*	6	2	83	7	2	55	9	3	59	12	4	51	15	6	56	18	9	65	18	11	79	18	11	78	16	9	82	13	7	85	9	4	75	7	3	84
BELGRADE, *Serbia*	3	-3	42	5	-2	39	11	2	43	18	7	57	23	12	73	26	15	84	28	17	63	28	17	53	24	13	47	18	8	50	11	4	55	5	0	52
BERLIN, *Germany*	2	-3	43	3	-3	38	8	0	38	13	4	41	19	8	49	22	12	64	24	14	71	23	13	62	20	10	44	13	6	44	7	2	46	3	-1	48
BIARRITZ, *France*	11	4	106	12	4	93	15	6	92	16	8	95	18	11	97	22	14	93	23	16	64	24	16	74	22	15	102	19	11	129	15	7	135	12	5	134
BORDEAUX, *France*	9	2	76	11	2	65	15	4	66	17	6	65	20	9	71	24	12	65	25	14	52	26	14	59	23	12	70	18	8	87	13	5	88	9	3	86
BRINDISI, *Italy*	12	6	57	13	7	61	15	8	67	18	11	35	22	14	26	26	18	20	29	21	9	29	21	25	26	18	47	22	15	71	18	11	72	14	8	65
BRUSSELS, *Belgium*	4	-1	82	7	0	51	10	2	81	14	5	53	18	8	74	22	11	74	23	12	58	22	12	42	21	11	69	15	7	85	9	3	61	6	0	68
BUCHAREST, *Romania*	1	-7	44	4	-5	37	10	-1	35	18	5	46	23	10	65	27	14	86	30	16	56	30	15	56	25	11	35	18	6	28	10	2	45	4	-3	42
BUDAPEST, *Hungary*	1	-4	41	4	-2	36	10	2	41	17	7	49	22	11	69	26	15	71	28	16	53	27	16	53	23	12	45	16	7	52	8	3	58	4	-1	49
CAGLIARI, *Sardinia, Italy*	14	7	53	15	7	52	17	9	45	19	11	35	23	14	27	27	18	10	30	21	3	30	21	10	27	19	29	23	15	57	19	11	56	16	9	55
CANDIA, *Crete, Greece*	16	9	94	16	9	76	17	10	41	20	12	23	23	15	18	27	19	3	29	21	1	29	22	3	27	19	18	24	17	43	21	14	69	18	11	102
COPENHAGEN, *Denmark*	2	-2	42	2	-3	25	5	-1	35	10	3	40	16	8	42	19	11	52	22	14	67	21	14	75	18	11	51	12	7	53	7	3	52	4	1	51
DUBLIN, *Ireland*	7	2	64	8	2	51	10	3	52	12	5	49	14	7	56	18	9	55	19	11	65	19	11	77	17	10	62	14	7	73	10	4	69	8	3	69
DURAZZO, *Albania*	11	6	76	12	6	84	13	8	99	17	13	56	22	17	41	25	21	48	28	23	13	28	22	48	24	18	43	20	14	180	14	11	216	12	8	185
EDINBURGH, *Scotland, U.K.*	6	1	55	6	1	41	8	2	47	11	4	39	14	6	50	17	9	50	18	11	64	18	11	69	16	9	63	12	7	62	9	4	63	7	2	61
FLORENCE, *Italy*	9	2	64	11	3	62	14	5	69	19	8	71	23	12	73	27	15	56	30	18	34	30	17	47	26	15	83	20	11	99	14	7	103	11	4	79
GENEVA, *Switzerland*	4	-2	55	6	-1	53	10	2	60	15	5	63	19	9	76	23	13	81	25	15	72	24	14	90	21	12	90	14	7	91	8	3	81	4	0	66
HAMBURG, *Germany*	2	-2	61	3	-2	40	7	-1	52	13	3	47	18	7	55	21	11	74	22	13	81	22	12	79	19	10	68	13	6	62	7	3	65	4	0	71
HELSINKI, *Finland*	-3	-9	46	-4	-9	37	0	-7	35	6	-1	37	14	4	42	19	9	46	22	13	62	20	12	75	15	8	67	8	3	69	3	-1	66	-1	-5	55
LISBON, *Portugal*	14	8	95	15	8	87	17	10	85	20	12	60	21	13	44	25	15	18	27	17	4	28	17	5	26	17	33	22	14	75	17	11	100	15	9	97
LIVERPOOL, *England, U.K.*	7	2	69	7	2	48	9	3	38	11	5	41	14	8	56	17	11	51	19	13	71	18	13	79	16	11	66	13	8	76	9	5	76	7	3	64
LONDON, *England, U.K.*	7	2	62	7	2	36	11	8	50	13	4	43	17	7	45	21	11	46	23	13	46	22	12	44	19	11	43	14	7	73	9	4	45	7	2	59
LUXEMBOURG, *Luxembourg*	3	-1	66	4	-1	54	10	1	55	14	4	53	18	8	66	21	11	65	23	13	70	22	12	69	19	10	62	13	6	70	7	3	71	4	0	74
MADRID, *Spain*	9	2	45	11	2	43	15	5	37	18	7	45	21	10	40	27	15	25	31	17	9	30	17	10	25	14	29	19	10	46	13	5	64	9	2	47
MARSEILLE, *France*	10	2	49	12	2	40	15	5	45	18	8	46	22	11	46	26	15	26	29	17	15	28	17	24	25	15	63	20	10	94	15	6	76	11	3	59

Temperature and Rainfall

Average daily high and low temperatures and monthly rainfall for selected world locations:

EUROPE

Location	JAN H	JAN L	JAN R	FEB H	FEB L	FEB R	MARCH H	MARCH L	MARCH R	APRIL H	APRIL L	APRIL R	MAY H	MAY L	MAY R	JUNE H	JUNE L	JUNE R	JULY H	JULY L	JULY R	AUG H	AUG L	AUG R	SEPT H	SEPT L	SEPT R	OCT H	OCT L	OCT R	NOV H	NOV L	NOV R	DEC H	DEC L	DEC R
MILAN, Italy	5	0	61	8	2	58	13	6	72	18	10	85	23	14	98	27	17	81	29	20	68	28	19	81	24	16	82	17	11	116	10	6	106	6	2	75
MOSCOW, Russia	-9	-16	38	-6	-14	36	0	-8	28	10	1	46	19	8	56	21	11	74	23	13	76	22	12	74	16	7	48	9	3	69	2	-3	43	-5	-10	41
MUNICH, Germany	1	-5	49	3	-5	43	9	-1	52	14	3	70	18	7	101	21	11	123	23	13	127	23	12	112	20	9	83	13	4	62	7	0	54	2	-4	51
NANTES, France	8	2	79	9	2	62	13	4	62	15	6	54	19	9	61	22	12	55	24	14	50	24	13	54	21	12	70	16	8	89	11	5	91	8	3	86
NAPLES, Italy	12	4	94	13	5	81	15	6	76	18	9	66	22	12	46	26	16	46	29	18	15	29	18	18	26	16	71	22	12	130	17	9	114	14	6	137
NICE, France	13	4	77	13	5	73	15	7	73	17	9	64	20	13	49	24	16	37	27	18	19	27	18	32	25	16	65	21	12	111	17	8	117	13	5	88
NICOSIA, Cyprus	15	5	70	16	5	50	19	7	35	24	10	21	29	14	26	34	18	9	37	21	1	37	21	2	33	18	6	28	14	23	22	10	41	17	7	74
ODESA, Ukraine	0	-6	25	2	-4	18	5	-1	18	12	6	28	19	12	28	23	16	48	26	18	41	26	18	36	21	14	28	16	9	36	10	4	28	4	-2	28
OSLO, Norway	-2	-7	41	-1	-7	31	4	-4	34	10	1	36	16	6	45	20	10	59	22	13	75	21	12	86	16	8	72	9	3	71	3	-1	57	0	-4	49
PALERMO, Sicily, Italy	16	8	44	16	8	35	17	9	30	20	11	29	24	14	14	27	18	9	30	21	2	30	21	8	28	19	28	25	16	59	21	12	66	18	10	68
PALMA DE MALLORCA, Spain	14	6	39	15	6	35	17	8	37	19	10	35	22	13	34	26	17	20	29	20	8	29	20	18	27	18	52	23	14	77	18	10	54	15	8	54
PARIS, France	6	1	46	7	1	39	12	4	41	16	6	44	20	10	56	23	13	57	25	15	57	24	14	55	21	12	53	16	8	57	10	5	54	7	2	49
PRAGUE, Czech Rep.	1	-4	21	3	-2	19	7	1	26	13	4	36	18	9	59	22	13	68	23	14	67	23	14	62	18	11	41	12	7	30	5	2	27	1	-2	23
RIGA, Latvia	-4	-10	32	-3	-10	24	2	-7	26	10	1	35	16	6	42	21	9	58	22	11	72	21	11	68	17	8	66	11	4	54	4	-1	52	-2	-7	39
ROME, Italy	11	5	80	13	5	71	15	7	69	19	10	67	23	13	52	28	17	34	30	20	16	30	19	24	26	17	69	22	13	113	16	9	111	13	6	97
SAINT PETERSBURG, Russia	-7	-13	25	-5	-12	23	0	-8	23	8	4	25	15	6	41	20	11	51	21	13	64	20	13	71	15	9	53	9	4	46	2	-2	36	-3	-8	30
SEVILLE, Spain	15	6	56	17	7	74	20	9	84	24	11	58	27	13	33	32	17	23	36	20	3	36	20	3	32	18	28	26	14	66	20	10	94	16	7	71
SOFIA, Bulgaria	2	-4	34	4	-3	34	10	1	38	16	5	54	21	10	69	24	14	78	27	16	56	26	15	43	22	11	40	17	8	35	9	3	52	4	-2	44
SPLIT, Croatia	10	5	80	11	5	65	14	7	65	18	11	62	23	16	62	27	19	48	30	22	28	30	22	43	26	19	66	20	14	87	15	10	111	12	7	113
STOCKHOLM, Sweden	-1	-5	31	-1	-5	25	3	-4	26	8	1	29	14	6	34	19	11	44	22	14	64	20	13	66	15	9	49	9	5	51	4	1	44	2	-2	39
VALENCIA, Spain	15	6	23	16	6	38	18	8	23	20	10	30	23	13	28	26	17	33	29	20	10	29	20	13	27	18	56	23	13	41	19	10	64	16	7	33
VALETTA, Malta	14	10	84	15	10	58	16	11	38	18	13	20	22	16	10	26	19	3	29	22	1	29	23	5	27	22	33	24	19	69	20	16	91	16	12	99
VENICE, Italy	6	1	51	8	2	53	12	5	61	17	10	71	21	14	81	25	17	84	27	19	66	27	18	66	24	16	66	19	11	94	12	7	89	8	3	66
VIENNA, Austria	1	-4	38	3	-3	36	8	1	46	15	6	51	19	10	71	23	14	69	25	15	76	24	15	69	20	11	51	14	7	25	7	3	48	3	-1	46
WARSAW, Poland	0	-6	28	0	-6	26	6	-2	31	12	3	37	20	9	50	23	12	66	24	15	77	23	14	72	19	10	47	13	5	41	6	1	38	2	-3	35
ZÜRICH, Switzerland	2	-3	61	5	-2	61	10	1	68	15	4	85	19	8	101	23	12	127	25	14	128	24	13	124	20	11	98	14	6	83	7	2	71	3	-2	72

ASIA

Location	JAN H	JAN L	JAN R	FEB H	FEB L	FEB R	MARCH H	MARCH L	MARCH R	APRIL H	APRIL L	APRIL R	MAY H	MAY L	MAY R	JUNE H	JUNE L	JUNE R	JULY H	JULY L	JULY R	AUG H	AUG L	AUG R	SEPT H	SEPT L	SEPT R	OCT H	OCT L	OCT R	NOV H	NOV L	NOV R	DEC H	DEC L	DEC R
ADEN, Yemen	27	23	8	27	23	7	29	24	8	31	26	4	34	28	3	35	29	1	34	28	2	33	27	3	34	28	4	32	26	2	29	24	2	27	23	4
ALMATY, Kazakhstan	-5	-14	33	-3	-13	23	4	-6	56	13	3	102	20	10	94	24	14	66	27	16	36	27	14	30	22	8	25	13	2	51	4	-5	48	-2	-9	33
ANKARA, Turkey	4	-4	49	6	-3	52	11	-1	45	17	4	44	23	9	56	26	12	37	30	15	13	31	15	8	26	11	28	21	7	21	14	3	28	6	-2	63
ARKHANGEL'SK, Russia	-12	-20	30	-10	-18	28	-4	-13	28	5	-4	18	12	2	33	17	6	48	20	10	66	19	10	69	12	5	56	4	-1	48	-2	-7	41	-8	-15	33
BAGHDAD, Iraq	16	4	27	18	6	28	22	9	27	29	14	19	36	19	7	41	23	0	43	24	0	43	24	0	40	21	0	33	16	3	25	11	20	18	6	26
BALIKPAPAN, Indonesia	29	23	243	30	23	221	30	23	249	29	23	226	29	23	258	29	23	252	28	23	259	29	23	257	29	23	201	29	23	186	29	23	176	29	23	245
BANGKOK, Thailand	32	20	11	33	22	28	34	24	31	35	25	72	34	25	189	33	24	152	32	24	158	32	24	187	32	24	320	31	24	231	31	22	57	31	20	9
BEIJING, China	2	-9	4	5	-7	5	12	-1	8	20	7	18	27	13	33	31	18	78	32	22	224	31	21	170	27	14	58	21	7	18	10	-1	9	3	-7	3
BEIRUT, Lebanon	17	11	187	17	11	151	19	12	96	22	14	51	26	18	19	28	21	2	31	23	0	32	23	0	30	23	6	27	21	48	23	16	119	18	13	176
BRUNEI	30	24	371	30	24	193	31	24	198	32	24	249	32	24	277	31	24	241	31	24	229	31	24	185	31	24	300	31	24	368	31	24	386	30	24	330
CHENNAI (MADRAS), India	29	19	29	31	20	9	33	22	9	35	26	17	38	28	44	38	27	52	36	26	99	35	26	124	34	25	125	32	24	285	29	22	345	29	21	138
CHONGQING, China	9	5	18	13	7	21	18	11	38	23	16	94	27	19	148	29	22	174	34	24	151	35	25	128	29	22	144	22	16	103	16	12	49	13	8	23
COLOMBO, Sri Lanka	30	22	84	31	22	64	31	23	114	31	24	255	31	26	335	29	25	190	29	25	129	29	25	96	29	25	158	29	24	353	29	23	308	29	22	152
DAMASCUS, Syria	12	2	39	14	4	32	18	6	23	24	9	13	29	13	5	33	16	1	36	18	0	37	18	0	33	16	0	27	12	9	19	8	26	13	4	42
DAVAO, Philippines	31	22	117	32	22	110	32	22	109	33	22	149	32	23	223	31	23	205	31	22	171	31	22	161	32	22	177	31	22	184	32	22	139	31	22	139
DHAKA, Bangladesh	26	13	8	28	15	21	32	20	58	33	23	116	33	24	267	32	26	358	31	26	399	31	26	317	32	26	256	31	24	164	29	19	30	26	14	6
HANOI, Vietnam	20	13	20	21	14	30	23	17	64	28	21	91	32	23	104	33	26	284	33	26	302	32	26	386	31	24	254	29	22	89	26	18	66	22	15	71
HO CHI MINH CITY, Vietnam	32	21	14	33	22	4	34	23	9	35	24	51	33	24	213	32	24	309	31	24	295	31	24	271	31	23	342	31	23	261	31	22	119	31	22	47
HONG KONG, China	18	13	27	17	13	44	19	16	75	24	19	140	28	23	298	29	26	399	31	26	371	31	26	377	29	25	297	27	23	119	23	18	38	20	15	25
IRKUTSK, Russia	-16	-26	13	-12	-25	10	-4	-17	8	6	-7	15	13	1	33	20	7	56	21	10	79	20	9	71	14	2	43	5	-6	18	-7	-17	15	-16	-24	15
ISTANBUL, Turkey	8	3	91	9	2	69	11	3	62	16	7	42	21	12	30	25	16	28	28	18	24	28	19	31	24	16	48	20	13	66	15	9	92	11	5	114
JAKARTA, Indonesia	29	23	342	29	23	302	30	23	210	31	24	135	31	24	108	31	23	90	31	23	59	31	23	48	31	23	69	31	23	106	30	23	139	29	23	208
JEDDAH, Saudi Arabia	29	19	5	29	18	1	29	19	1	33	21	1	35	23	1	36	24	0	37	23	1	37	27	1	36	25	1	35	23	1	33	22	25	30	19	30
JERUSALEM, Israel	13	5	140	13	6	111	18	8	116	23	10	17	27	14	6	29	16	0	31	17	0	31	18	0	29	17	0	27	15	11	21	12	68	15	7	129
KABUL, Afghanistan	2	-8	33	4	-6	54	12	1	70	19	6	66	26	11	21	31	13	1	33	16	5	33	15	1	29	11	2	23	6	4	17	1	11	8	-3	21
KARACHI, Pakistan	25	13	7	26	14	10	29	19	10	32	23	3	34	26	0	34	28	10	33	27	90	31	26	58	31	25	27	34	22	3	31	18	3	27	14	5
KATHMANDU, Nepal	18	2	17	19	4	15	25	7	30	28	12	37	30	16	102	29	20	201	29	20	375	28	20	325	28	19	189	27	13	56	23	7	2	19	3	10
KOLKATA (CALCUTTA), India	27	13	12	29	15	25	34	21	32	36	24	53	36	25	129	34	26	291	32	26	329	32	26	338	32	26	266	32	23	131	29	18	21	26	13	7
KUNMING, China	16	3	11	18	4	14	21	7	19	24	11	20	26	14	90	25	17	175	25	17	205	25	17	203	24	15	126	21	12	78	18	7	40	17	3	11
LAHORE, Pakistan	21	4	25	22	7	24	28	12	27	35	17	15	40	22	17	41	26	39	38	27	155	36	26	135	36	23	63	35	15	10	28	8	3	23	4	14
LHASA, China	7	-10	0	9	-7	3	12	-2	4	16	1	6	19	5	24	24	9	72	23	9	132	22	9	128	21	7	58	17	1	9	13	-5	1	9	-9	1
MANAMA, Bahrain	30	14	14	21	15	16	24	17	11	29	21	8	33	26	1	36	28	0	37	29	0	38	29	0	36	27	0	32	24	0	28	21	7	22	16	17
MANDALAY, Myanmar	28	13	2	31	15	13	36	19	7	38	25	35	37	26	142	34	26	124	34	26	83	33	25	113	33	24	155	32	25	125	29	19	45	27	14	10
MANILA, Philippines	30	21	21	31	21	10	33	22	15	34	23	30	34	24	123	33	24	262	31	24	423	31	24	421	31	24	353	31	23	197	31	22	135	30	21	66
MUMBAI (BOMBAY), India	28	19	3	28	19	1	30	22	1	32	24	2	32	27	14	32	26	518	30	25	647	29	24	384	29	24	276	32	24	55	32	23	15	31	21	2
MUSCAT, Oman	25	19	28	25	19	18	28	22	10	32	25	10	37	30	1	38	31	3	36	31	1	33	29	1	34	28	0	34	27	3	30	23	10	26	20	18
NAGASAKI, Japan	9	2	75	10	2	87	14	5	124	19	10	190	23	14	191	26	18	326	29	23	284	31	24	187	27	20	236	22	14	108	17	9	89	12	4	80
NEW DELHI, India	21	7	23	24	9	20	31	14	15	36	20	10	41	26	15	39	28	68	36	27	200	34	26	200	34	24	123	34	18	19	29	11	3	23	8	10
PHNOM PENH, Cambodia	31	21	7	32	22	9	34	23	32	34	24	73	33	24	149	33	24	149	32	24	151	32	24	157	31	24	231	31	24	259	30	23	129	30	22	38
PONTIANAK, Indonesia	31	23	275	32	23	213	32	23	242	33	23	280	33	23	279	32	23	228	32	23	178	32	23	206	32	23	245	32	23	356	31	23	385	31	23	321
RIYADH, Saudi Arabia	21	8	14	23	9	10	28	13	30	28	18	30	38	22	13	42	25	0	42	26	0	42	24	0	39	22	0	34	16	1	29	13	5	21	9	11
SANDAKAN, Malaysia	29	23	454	29	23	271	30	23	200	31	23	118	32	23	153	32	23	196	32	23	185	32	23	205	32	23	240	31	23	263	31	23	356	30	23	470
SAPPORO, Japan	-2	-12	100	-1	-11	79	2	-7	70	11	0	61	16	4	59	21	10	65	24	14	86	26	16	117	22	11	136	16	4	114	8	-2	106	1	-8	102
SEOUL, South Korea	0	-9	21	3	-7	28	8	-2	49	17	5	105	22	11	88	27	16	151	29	21	384	31	21	263	26	15	160	19	7	49	11	0	43	3	-7	24
SHANGHAI, China	8	1	47	8	1	61	13	4	85	19	10	95	25	15	104	28	19	174	32	23	145	32	23	137	28	19	138	23	14	69	17	7	52	12	2	37
SINGAPORE, Singapore	30	23	239	31	23	165	31	24	174	31	24	166	32	24	171	31	24	163	31	24	150	31	24	171	31	24	164	31	23	191	31	23	250	31	23	269
TAIPEI, China	19	12	95	18	12	141	21	14	162	25	17	167	28	21	209	32	23	280	34	24	248	33	24	277	31	23	201	27	19	112	24	17	76	21	14	76
TBILISI, Georgia	6	-2	16	7	-1	21	12	2	30	18	7	52	23	12	83	27	16	73	31	19	49	31	19	40	26	15	44	20	9	37	13	4	30	8	0	21
TEHRAN, Iran	7	-3	42	10	0	37	16	4	37	23	12	33	28	17	14	34	19	3	37	22	2	36	22	2	32	19	2	24	12	9	17	6	21	11	1	32
TEL AVIV-YAFO, Israel	17	9	165	18	9	64	19	10	58	23	12	13	27	16	3	29	19	0	31	22	0	31	23	0	30	20	1	29	17	14	25	15	85	19	11	144
TOKYO, Japan	8	-2	50	9	-1	72	12	2	106	17	8	129	22	12	144	24	17	176	28	21	136	30	22	149	26	19	216	21	13	194	16	6	96	11	1	54
ULAANBAATAR, Mongolia	-19	-32	1	-13	-29	1	-4	-22	3	7	-8	5	13	-2	8	21	7	49	22	11	74	21	9	48	14	2	25	6	-8	5	-6	-20	5	-16	-28	3
VIENTIANE, Laos	28	14	7	30	17	16	33	19	41	34	23	88	32	23	212	32	24	216	31	24	209	31	24	254	31	24	244	31	21	81	29	18	16	28	16	3
VLADIVOSTOK, Russia	-11	-18	8	-6	-14	10	1	-7	18	8	1	30	13	6	53	17	11	74	22	16	84	24	18	119	20	13	109	13	5	48	2	-4	30	-7	-13	15

CELSIUS

50 — 40 — 30 — 20 — 10 — 0 — -10 — -20 — -30 — -40 — -50

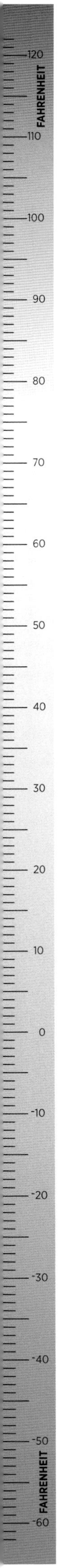

RED FIGURES: Average daily high temperature (°C) **BLUE FIGURES:** Average daily low temperature (°C) **BLACK FIGURES:** Average monthly rainfall (mm) 1 millimeter = 0.039 inch

ASIA	JAN.			FEB.			MARCH			APRIL			MAY			JUNE			JULY			AUG.			SEPT.			OCT.			NOV.			DEC.		
WUHAN, *China*	8	1	41	9	2	57	14	6	92	21	13	136	26	18	165	31	23	212	34	26	165	34	26	114	29	21	73	23	16	74	17	9	49	11	3	30
YAKUTSK, *Russia*	-43	-47	8	-33	-40	5	-18	-29	3	-3	-14	8	9	-1	10	19	9	28	23	12	41	19	9	33	10	1	28	-5	-12	13	-26	-31	10	-39	-43	8
YANGON (RANGOON), *Myanmar*	32	18	4	33	19	4	36	22	17	36	24	47	33	25	307	30	24	478	29	24	535	29	24	511	30	24	368	31	24	183	31	23	62	31	19	11
YEKATERINBURG, *Russia*	-14	-21	8	-10	-17	10	-4	-12	5	6	-3	8	14	4	15	18	9	48	21	12	38	18	10	53	12	5	46	3	-2	23	-7	-12	10	-12	-18	8
AFRICA																																				
ABIDJAN, *Côte d'Ivoire*	31	23	22	32	24	47	32	24	110	32	24	142	31	24	309	29	23	543	28	23	238	28	22	36	28	23	74	29	23	172	31	23	168	31	23	85
ACCRA, *Ghana*	31	23	15	31	24	29	31	24	57	31	24	90	31	24	136	29	23	199	27	23	50	27	22	19	27	23	43	29	23	64	31	24	34	31	24	20
ADDIS ABABA, *Ethiopia*	24	6	17	24	8	38	25	9	68	25	10	86	25	10	86	23	9	132	21	10	268	21	10	281	22	9	186	24	7	28	23	6	11	23	5	10
ALEXANDRIA, *Egypt*	18	11	52	19	11	28	21	13	13	23	15	4	26	18	1	28	21	0	29	23	0	31	23	0	30	23	1	28	20	8	25	17	35	21	13	55
ALGIERS, *Algeria*	15	9	93	16	9	73	17	11	67	20	13	52	23	15	34	26	18	14	28	21	2	29	22	5	27	21	33	23	17	77	19	13	96	16	11	114
ANTANANARIVO, *Madagascar*	26	16	287	26	16	26	26	16	194	24	14	57	23	12	18	21	10	9	20	9	8	21	9	10	23	11	16	27	12	61	27	14	153	27	16	290
ASMARA, *Eritrea*	23	7	0	24	8	20	25	9	1	26	11	7	26	12	23	26	12	48	22	12	114	22	12	123	23	13	49	22	12	4	22	10	3	22	9	0
BAMAKO, *Mali*	33	16	0	36	19	0	39	22	3	39	24	19	39	24	59	34	23	131	32	22	229	31	22	307	32	22	198	34	22	63	34	18	7	33	17	0
BANGUI, *Cen. Af. Rep.*	32	20	20	34	21	39	33	22	107	33	22	133	32	21	163	31	21	143	29	21	181	29	21	225	31	21	190	31	21	202	31	20	93	32	19	29
BEIRA, *Mozambique*	32	24	267	32	24	259	31	23	263	30	22	117	28	18	67	26	16	40	25	16	34	26	17	33	28	18	25	31	22	34	31	22	121	31	23	243
BENGHAZI, *Libya*	17	10	66	18	11	41	21	12	20	23	14	5	26	17	3	28	20	1	29	22	1	29	22	1	28	21	3	27	19	18	23	16	46	19	12	66
BUJUMBURA, *Burundi*	29	20	97	29	20	97	29	20	126	29	20	129	29	20	64	29	19	11	30	19	3	30	19	17	31	20	43	31	20	62	29	20	98	29	20	100
CAIRO, *Egypt*	18	8	5	21	9	4	24	11	4	28	14	2	33	17	1	35	20	0	36	21	0	35	22	0	32	20	0	30	18	1	26	14	3	20	10	6
CAPE TOWN, *South Africa*	26	16	16	26	16	15	25	14	22	22	12	50	19	9	92	18	8	105	17	7	91	18	8	83	18	9	54	21	11	40	23	13	24	24	14	19
CASABLANCA, *Morocco*	17	7	57	18	8	53	19	9	51	21	11	38	22	13	21	24	16	6	26	18	0	27	19	1	26	17	6	24	14	34	21	11	65	18	8	73
CONAKRY, *Guinea*	31	22	1	31	23	1	32	23	6	32	23	21	32	24	141	30	23	503	28	22	1210	28	22	1016	29	23	664	31	23	318	31	24	106	31	23	14
DAKAR, *Senegal*	26	18	1	27	17	1	27	18	0	27	18	0	29	20	1	31	23	15	31	24	75	31	24	215	32	24	146	32	24	42	30	23	3	27	19	4
DAR ES SALAAM, *Tanzania*	31	25	66	31	25	66	31	24	130	30	23	290	29	22	188	29	20	33	28	19	31	28	19	30	28	19	30	29	21	41	30	22	74	31	24	91
DURBAN, *South Africa*	27	21	119	27	21	126	27	20	132	26	18	84	24	14	56	23	12	34	22	11	35	22	13	49	23	15	73	24	17	110	25	18	118	26	19	120
HARARE, *Zimbabwe*	26	16	190	26	16	177	26	14	107	26	13	33	23	9	10	21	7	3	21	7	1	23	8	2	26	12	7	28	14	32	27	16	93	26	16	173
JOHANNESBURG, *South Africa*	26	14	150	25	14	129	24	13	110	22	10	48	19	6	24	17	4	6	17	4	10	20	6	10	23	9	25	25	12	65	25	13	126	26	14	141
KAMPALA, *Uganda*	28	18	58	28	18	68	27	18	128	26	18	185	26	17	134	25	17	71	25	17	55	26	16	87	27	17	100	27	17	119	27	17	142	27	17	95
KHARTOUM, *Sudan*	32	15	0	34	16	0	38	19	0	41	22	0	42	25	4	41	26	7	38	25	49	37	24	69	39	25	21	40	24	5	36	20	0	33	17	0
KINSHASA, *D.R.C.*	31	21	138	31	22	148	32	22	184	32	22	220	31	22	145	29	19	5	27	18	3	29	18	4	31	20	40	31	21	133	31	22	235	30	21	156
KISANGANI, *D.R.C.*	31	21	97	31	21	107	31	21	172	31	21	190	31	21	162	30	21	128	29	19	114	28	20	178	29	20	164	30	20	233	29	20	207	30	20	105
LAGOS, *Nigeria*	31	23	27	32	25	44	32	26	98	32	25	146	31	24	252	29	23	414	28	23	253	28	23	69	28	23	153	29	23	197	31	24	66	31	24	25
LIBREVILLE, *Gabon*	31	23	164	31	22	137	32	23	248	32	23	232	31	22	181	29	21	24	28	20	3	29	21	6	29	22	69	30	22	332	30	22	378	31	22	197
LIVINGSTONE, *Zambia*	29	19	175	29	19	160	29	18	95	30	15	25	28	11	5	25	7	1	25	7	0	28	10	0	32	15	2	34	19	26	33	19	78	31	19	176
LUANDA, *Angola*	28	23	34	29	24	35	30	24	90	29	24	127	28	23	18	25	20	0	23	18	0	23	18	1	24	19	2	26	22	6	28	23	32	28	23	23
LUBUMBASHI, *D.R.C.*	28	16	253	28	17	256	28	16	210	28	14	51	27	10	4	26	7	1	26	6	0	28	8	0	32	11	6	33	14	31	31	16	150	28	17	272
LUSAKA, *Zambia*	26	17	213	26	17	172	26	17	104	26	15	22	25	12	3	23	10	0	23	9	0	25	12	0	29	15	1	31	18	14	29	18	86	27	17	200
LUXOR, *Egypt*	23	6	0	26	7	0	30	10	0	35	15	0	40	21	0	41	21	0	42	23	0	41	23	0	39	22	0	37	18	1	31	12	0	26	7	0
MAPUTO, *Mozambique*	30	22	153	31	22	134	29	21	99	28	19	52	27	16	29	25	13	18	24	13	15	26	14	13	27	16	32	28	18	51	28	19	78	29	21	94
MARRAKECH, *Morocco*	18	4	27	20	6	31	23	9	36	26	11	32	29	14	17	33	17	7	38	19	2	38	20	3	33	17	7	28	14	20	23	9	37	19	6	28
MOGADISHU, *Somalia*	30	23	0	30	23	0	31	24	8	32	26	58	32	25	59	29	23	78	28	23	67	28	23	42	29	23	21	30	24	30	31	24	40	30	24	9
MONROVIA, *Liberia*	30	23	5	29	23	3	31	23	112	31	23	297	30	22	340	27	23	917	27	22	615	27	23	472	27	22	759	28	22	640	29	23	208	30	23	74
NAIROBI, *Kenya*	25	12	45	26	13	43	25	14	73	24	14	160	22	13	119	21	12	30	21	11	13	21	11	13	24	11	26	24	13	42	23	13	121	23	13	77
N'DJAMENA, *Chad*	34	14	0	37	16	0	40	21	0	42	23	8	40	25	31	38	24	62	33	22	150	31	22	215	33	22	91	36	21	22	36	17	0	33	14	0
NIAMEY, *Niger*	34	14	0	37	18	0	41	22	3	42	25	6	41	27	35	38	25	75	34	23	143	32	23	187	34	23	90	38	23	16	38	18	1	34	15	0
NOUAKCHOTT, *Mauritania*	29	14	1	31	15	3	32	17	1	32	18	1	34	21	1	33	23	3	32	23	13	32	24	104	34	24	23	33	22	10	32	18	3	28	13	1
TIMBUKTU, *Mali*	31	13	0	34	14	0	38	19	0	42	22	1	43	26	4	43	27	19	39	25	62	36	24	79	39	24	33	40	23	3	37	18	0	32	13	0
TRIPOLI, *Libya*	16	8	69	17	9	40	19	11	27	22	14	13	24	16	5	27	19	1	29	22	0	30	22	1	29	22	11	27	18	38	23	14	60	18	9	81
TUNIS, *Tunisia*	14	6	62	16	7	52	18	8	46	21	11	38	24	13	22	29	17	10	32	20	3	33	21	7	31	19	32	25	15	55	20	11	54	16	7	63
WADI HALFA, *Sudan*	24	9	0	27	10	0	31	14	0	36	18	0	40	22	1	41	24	0	41	25	1	41	25	0	40	24	0	37	21	0	30	15	0	25	11	0
YAOUNDÉ, *Cameroon*	29	19	26	29	19	55	29	19	140	29	19	193	28	19	216	27	19	163	27	19	62	27	18	80	27	19	216	27	18	292	28	19	120	28	19	28
ZANZIBAR, *Tanzania*	32	24	75	33	24	61	33	25	150	30	25	350	29	24	251	28	23	54	28	22	44	28	22	39	29	22	48	30	23	86	32	24	201	32	24	145
ZOMBA, *Malawi*	27	18	299	27	18	269	26	18	230	26	17	85	24	14	23	22	12	13	22	12	8	24	13	8	27	15	8	29	18	29	29	19	124	27	18	281
ATLANTIC ISLANDS																																				
ASCENSION ISLAND	29	23	4	31	23	8	31	24	23	31	24	27	31	23	10	29	23	14	29	22	12	28	22	10	28	22	8	28	22	7	28	22	4	29	22	3
FALKLAND ISLANDS	13	6	71	13	5	58	12	4	64	9	3	66	7	1	66	5	-1	53	4	-1	51	5	-1	51	7	1	38	9	2	41	11	3	51	12	4	71
FUNCHAL, *Madeira Is.*	19	13	87	18	13	88	19	13	79	19	14	43	21	16	22	22	17	9	24	19	2	24	19	3	24	19	27	23	18	85	22	16	106	19	14	87
HAMILTON, *Bermuda Is.*	20	14	112	20	14	119	20	14	122	22	15	104	24	18	117	27	21	112	29	23	114	30	23	137	29	22	132	26	21	147	23	17	127	21	16	119
LAS PALMAS, *Canary Is.*	21	14	28	22	14	21	22	15	15	22	16	10	23	17	3	24	18	1	25	19	1	26	21	0	26	21	6	26	19	18	24	18	37	22	16	32
NUUK, *Greenland*	-7	-12	36	-7	-13	43	-4	-11	41	-1	-7	30	4	-2	43	8	1	36	11	3	56	11	3	79	6	1	84	2	-3	64	-2	-7	48	-5	-10	38
PONTA DELGADA, *Azores*	17	12	105	17	11	91	17	12	87	18	12	62	20	13	57	22	15	36	25	17	25	26	18	34	25	17	75	22	16	97	20	14	108	18	12	98
PRAIA, *Cape Verde*	25	20	1	25	19	2	26	20	0	26	21	0	27	21	0	28	22	0	28	24	7	29	24	63	29	25	88	29	24	44	28	23	15	26	22	5
REYKJAVÍK, *Iceland*	2	-2	86	3	-2	75	4	-1	76	6	1	56	10	4	42	12	7	45	14	9	51	14	8	62	11	6	71	7	3	88	4	0	83	2	-2	84
THULE, *Greenland*	-17	-27	7	-20	-29	8	-19	-28	4	-13	-23	4	-2	-9	5	5	-1	6	8	2	14	6	1	17	1	-6	13	-5	-13	11	-11	-19	11	-18	-27	5
TRISTAN DA CUNHA	19	15	103	20	16	110	19	14	133	18	14	137	16	12	153	14	11	153	14	10	54	13	9	162	13	9	157	15	11	148	16	12	124	18	14	131
AUSTRALIA and PACIFIC ISLANDS																																				
APIA, *Samoa*	30	24	437	29	24	360	30	23	356	30	24	236	29	23	174	29	23	135	29	23	100	29	24	111	29	23	144	29	24	206	30	23	259	29	23	374
AUCKLAND, *New Zealand*	23	16	70	23	16	86	22	15	77	19	13	96	17	11	115	14	9	126	13	8	131	14	8	112	16	9	94	17	11	93	19	12	82	21	14	78
DARWIN, *Australia*	32	25	396	32	25	331	33	25	282	33	24	97	33	23	18	31	21	3	31	19	1	32	21	4	33	23	15	34	25	60	34	26	130	33	26	239
DUNEDIN, *New Zealand*	19	10	81	19	10	70	17	9	78	15	7	75	12	5	78	9	4	78	9	3	70	11	3	61	13	5	61	15	6	70	17	7	79	18	9	81
GALÁPAGOS IS., *Ecuador*	30	22	20	30	24	36	31	24	28	31	24	18	30	23	1	28	22	1	27	21	1	27	19	1	27	19	1	27	19	1	27	20	1	28	21	1
GUAM, *Mariana Is.*	29	24	138	29	23	116	29	24	121	31	24	108	31	25	164	31	25	150	30	24	274	30	24	368	30	24	374	30	24	334	30	25	231	29	24	160
HOBART, *Tasmania*	22	12	51	22	12	38	20	11	46	17	9	51	14	7	46	12	5	51	11	4	51	13	5	49	15	6	47	17	8	60	19	9	52	21	11	57
MELBOURNE, *Australia*	26	14	48	26	14	47	24	13	52	20	11	57	17	8	58	14	7	49	13	6	49	15	6	50	17	8	59	19	9	67	22	11	60	24	12	59
NAHA, *Okinawa*	19	13	125	19	13	126	21	15	159	24	18	165	27	20	252	29	24	280	32	25	178	31	25	270	31	24	175	27	21	165	24	18	133	21	14	111
NOUMÉA, *New Caledonia*	30	22	111	29	23	130	29	22	155	28	21	121	26	19	106	25	18	107	24	17	91	24	16	73	26	17	56	27	18	53	28	20	55	30	21	77
PAPEETE, *Tahiti*	32	22	335	32	22	292	32	22	165	32	22	173	31	21	124	30	21	81	30	20	66	30	20	48	30	21	58	31	21	86	31	22	165	31	22	302
PERTH, *Australia*	29	17	9	29	17	13	27	16	19	24	14	45	21	12	122	18	10	182	17	9	174	18	9	136	19	10	80	21	12	53	24	14	21	27	16	13
PORT MORESBY, *P.N.G.*	32	24	179	31	24	196	31	24	190	31	24	120	30	24	65	29	23	39	28	23	27	28	23	26	29	23	33	30	24	35	31	24	56	32	24	121
SUVA, *Fiji Islands*	30	23	305	30	23	293	30	23	367	29	23	342	28	22	261	27	21	166	26	20	142	26	20	184	27	21	200	27	21	217	28	22	266	29	23	296
SYDNEY, *Australia*	26	18	103	26	18	111	24	17	131	22	14	130	19	11	123	16	9	129	16	8	103	17	9	80	19	11	69	22	13	83	23	16	81	25	17	78
WELLINGTON, *New Zealand*	21	13	79	21	13	80	19	12	85	17	11	98	14	8	121	13	7	124	12	6	139	12	6	121	14	8	99	16	9	105	17	10	88	19	12	90

Major Cities of the World

NOTES ON MAJOR CITY DATA

The population figures in the following list are from *World Urbanization Prospects: the 2014 Revision,* prepared by the United Nations. All figures are rounded to the nearest hundred. The list shows urban agglomerations with at least 1,000,000 inhabitants in the year 2014. An "urban agglomeration" is a contiguous territory with an urban level of population density; it includes one or more cities or towns and adjacent thickly settled areas. Thus, its geographic extent roughly coincides with the limits of a built-up urban area as seen from on high. Since an urban agglomeration is basically a metropolitan area, the population figure given for each area on the list will naturally be greater than the city-proper population figure cited in many other publications.

It is difficult to compare city populations because definitions of cities and metropolitan areas, as well as the availability of statistics, vary widely among countries. Also, the names given to metropolitan areas and the regions that compose them may vary. As a result, some of the urban agglomeration names and population figures used in this atlas differ from names and figures given for the same general areas included on lists in other publications.

Spellings may vary, too. The UN list sometimes uses spellings that do not agree with ones used on National Geographic maps. In such cases, we have listed the place-names as they appear in the *Family Reference Atlas.* We did not change a United Nations spelling if we included it in the atlas as a parenthetical name or used it as a conventional name on world or physical maps.

Some of the Chinese city names in the following list do not appear on maps in this atlas because of space limitations due to the combination of map scale and the high density of large cities in that country. Populations used to classify the cities as shown on the maps in this atlas are city-proper population figures, which may be much smaller than the urban agglomeration figure.

CITY	COUNTRY	POPULATION
Abidjan	Côte d'Ivoire	4,859,800
Abu Dhabi	U.A.E.	1,145,000
Abuja	Nigeria	2,440,300
Accra	Ghana	2,277,300
Ad-Dammam	Saudi Arabia	1,064,500
Adana	Turkey	1,829,600
Addis Ababa	Ethiopia	3,237,600
Adelaide	Australia	1,255,600
Agra	India	1,966,300
Aguascalientes	Mexico	1,031,500
Ahmadabad	India	7,342,900
Ahvaz	Iran	1,215,800
Alexandria	Egypt	4,777,700
Algiers	Algeria	2,594,200
Aligarh	India	1,037,500
Allahabad	India	1,294,900
Almaty	Kazakhstan	1,522,700
Amman	Jordan	1,154,700
Amritsar	India	1,265,000
Amsterdam	Netherlands	1,090,800
Ankara	Turkey	4,750,000
Anshan	China	1,559,200
Antalya	Turkey	1,072,400
Antananarivo	Madagascar	2,609,800
Anyang	China	1,140,300
Asansol	India	1,313,500
Asunción	Paraguay	2,356,200
Athens	Greece	3,051,900
Atlanta	United States	5,142,200
Auckland	New Zealand	1,344,400
Aurangabad	India	1,344,300
Austin	United States	1,684,500
Baghdad	Iraq	6,642,900
Baixada Santista	Brazil	1,538,600
Baku	Azerbaijan	2,373,700
Baltimore	United States	2,267,000
Bamako	Mali	2,515,000
Bandung	Indonesia	2,543,800
Bangalore	India	10,088,000
Bangkok	Thailand	9,269,900
Baoding	China	1,106,000
Baoji	China	1,000,600
Baotou	China	1,957,100
Barcelona	Spain	5,258,400
Bareilly	India	1,110,800
Barquisimeto	Venezuela	1,038,600
Barranquilla	Colombia	1,991,200
Basra	Iraq	1,019,200
Batam	Indonesia	1,390,600
Beijing	China	20,384,000
Beirut	Lebanon	2,226,500
Belém	Brazil	2,181,700
Belgrade	Serbia	1,181,900
Belo Horizonte	Brazil	5,716,500
Benin City	Nigeria	1,495,800
Benxi	China	1,070,300
Berlin	Germany	3,563,200
Bhopal	India	2,101,700
Birmingham	U.K.	2,514,600
Bogor	Indonesia	1,075,600
Bogotá	Colombia	9,764,800
Boston	United States	4,249,100
Brasília	Brazil	4,155,500
Brazzaville	Congo	1,887,700
Brisbane	Australia	2,202,000
Brussels	Belgium	2,045,000
Bucaramanga	Colombia	1,215,100
Bucharest	Romania	1,867,800
Budapest	Hungary	1,714,000
Buenos Aires	Argentina	15,181,000
Bursa	Turkey	1,922,600
Busan	South Korea	3,216,300
Cairo	Egypt	18,772,000
Calgary	Canada	1,337,200
Cali	Colombia	2,646,000
Campinas	Brazil	3,047,200
Can Tho	Vietnam	1,174,700

CITY	COUNTRY	POPULATION
Cape Town	South Africa	3,660,500
Caracas	Venezuela	2,916,200
Cartagena	Colombia	1,092,400
Casablanca	Morocco	3,515,000
Chandigarh	India	1,134,500
Changchun	China	3,762,400
Changsha	China	3,761,100
Changwon	South Korea	1,038,800
Changzhou, Jiangsu	China	2,584,500
Chaozhou	China	1,333,000
Charlotte	United States	1,615,600
Chelyabinsk	Russia	1,157,400
Chengdu	China	7,555,800
Chennai (Madras)	India	9,890,500
Chicago	United States	8,744,900
Chifeng	China	1,018,300
Chittagong	Bangladesh	4,539,400
Chongqing	China	13,332,000
Cincinnati	United States	1,687,600
Ciudad Juárez	Mexico	1,390,400
Cixi	China	1,303,100
Cleveland	United States	1,772,900
Cochabamba	Bolivia	1,240,400
Coimbatore	India	2,548,600
Cologne	Germany	1,036,800
Columbus, Ohio	United States	1,505,100
Conakry	Guinea	1,936,100
Copenhagen	Denmark	1,268,100
Córdoba	Argentina	1,511,000
Curitiba	Brazil	3,473,700
Daegu	South Korea	2,244,100
Daejon	South Korea	1,563,800
Dakar	Senegal	3,520,300
Dalian	China	4,489,400
Dallas-Fort Worth	United States	5,702,700
Damascus	Syria	2,565,700
Daqing	China	1,621,500
Dar es Salaam	Tanzania	5,115,700
Datong	China	1,531,800
Davao City	Philippines	1,629,600
Delhi	India	25,704,000
Denpasar	Indonesia	1,106,600
Denver-Aurora	United States	2,599,400
Detroit	United States	3,639,100
Dhaka	Bangladesh	17,599,000
Dhanbad	India	1,254,900
Dongguan	China	7,435,000
Douala	Cameroon	2,943,400
Dubai	U.A.E.	2,414,600
Dublin	Ireland	1,169,400
Durban	South Africa	2,901,000
Durg-Bhilainagar	India	1,129,500
Edmonton	Canada	1,272,100
Esfahan	Iran	1,879,900
Faisalabad	Pakistan	3,567,000
Fès	Morocco	1,172,200
Florianópolis	Brazil	1,180,400
Fortaleza	Brazil	3,880,300
Foshan	China	7,036,000
Freetown	Sierra Leone	1,007,200
Fushun, Liaoning	China	1,298,400
Fuzhou, Fujian	China	3,283,000
Gauhati	India	1,042,100
Gaziantep	Turkey	1,528,400
Glasgow	U.K.	1,223,000
Goiânia	Brazil	2,284,900
Grande São Luís	Brazil	1,436,800
Grande Vitória	Brazil	1,636,200
Guadalajara	Mexico	4,843,300
Guangzhou, Guangdong	China	12,459,000
Guatemala City	Guatemala	2,918,400
Guayaquil	Ecuador	2,709,400
Guilin	China	1,039,900
Guiyang	China	2,870,900

CITY	COUNTRY	POPULATION
Gujranwala	Pakistan	2,122,300
Gwalior	India	1,220,800
Gwangju	South Korea	1,536,500
Haifa	Israel	1,096,700
Haikou	China	1,903,100
Haiphòng	Vietnam	1,075,500
Halab (Aleppo)	Syria	3,561,800
Hamah	Syria	1,236,600
Hamburg	Germany	1,830,700
Handan	China	1,634,100
Hangzhou	China	6,390,700
Hànoi	Vietnam	3,629,500
Harare	Zimbabwe	1,501,400
Harbin	China	5,457,500
Havana	Cuba	2,137,100
Hefei	China	3,347,600
Helsinki	Finland	1,180,000
Hengyang	China	1,301,300
Hims (Homs)	Syria	1,641,300
Hiroshima	Japan	2,173,300
Ho Chi Minh City	Vietnam	7,297,800
Hohhot	China	1,784,700
Hong Kong	China	7,313,600
Houston	United States	5,638,100
Huai'an	China	2,000,200
Huainan	China	1,327,500
Huambo	Angola	1,269,300
Hubli-Dharwad	India	1,019,800
Huizhou	China	2,312,400
Hyderabad	India	8,943,600
Hyderabad	Pakistan	1,772,200
Ibadan	Nigeria	3,160,200
Incheon	South Korea	2,685,300
Indianapolis	United States	1,645,700
Indore	India	2,440,800
Irbil (Erbil)	Iraq	1,165,800
Islamabad	Pakistan	1,364,600
Istanbul	Turkey	14,164,000
Izmir	Turkey	3,040,500
Jabalpur	India	1,336,600
Jacksonville, Florida	United States	1,172,000
Jaipur	India	3,460,800
Jakarta	Indonesia	10,324,000
Jamshedpur	India	1,451,300
Ji'nan, Shandong	China	4,032,200
Jiangmen	China	1,572,400
Jiddah	Saudi Arabia	4,075,900
Jilin	China	1,520,500
Jining, Shandong	China	1,385,000
Jinzhou	China	1,035,000
João Pessoa	Brazil	1,093,200
Jodhpur	India	1,284,200
Johannesburg	South Africa	9,398,700
Joinville	Brazil	1,218,800
Kabul	Afghanistan	4,634,900
Kaduna	Nigeria	1,047,900
Kampala	Uganda	1,935,700
Kananga	D.R.C.	1,168,700
Kannur	India	2,152,700
Kano	Nigeria	3,587,100
Kanpur	India	3,020,800
Kansas City	United States	1,604,400
Kaohsiung	China	1,522,800
Karachi	Pakistan	16,618,000
Karaj	Iran	1,807,100
Kathmandu	Nepal	1,182,600
Kazan	Russia	1,162,300
Kharkiv	Ukraine	1,440,900
Khartoum	Sudan	5,129,400
Khulna	Bangladesh	1,022,000
Kiev	Ukraine	2,941,900
Kigali	Rwanda	1,257,000
Kinshasa	D.R.C.	11,587,000
Kisangani	D.R.C.	1,039,700
Kitakyushu	Japan	5,510,500

CITY	COUNTRY	POPULATION
Kochi (Cochin)	India	2,416,100
Kolkata (Calcutta)	India	14,865,000
Kollam	India	1,409,800
Konya	Turkey	1,194,400
Kota	India	1,163,100
Kozhikode (Calicut)	India	2,476,200
Krasnoyarsk	Russia	1,008,400
Kuala Lumpur	Malaysia	6,837,000
Kumasi	Ghana	2,598,800
Kunming	China	3,779,600
Kuwait City	Kuwait	2,778,800

La Paz	Bolivia	1,816,500
Lagos	Nigeria	13,123,000
Lahore	Pakistan	8,741,400
Lanzhou	China	2,723,200
Las Vegas	United States	2,270,200
León	Mexico	1,806,900
Lianyungang	China	1,099,400
Lille	France	1,027,200
Lima	Peru	9,897,100
Linyi, Shandong	China	1,706,000
Lisbon	Portugal	2,884,300
Liuzhou	China	1,619,200
London	U.K.	10,314,000
Los Angeles-Long Beach-Santa Ana		
	United States	12,310,000
Louisville	United States	1,032,000
Luanda	Angola	5,506,000
Lubumbashi	D.R.C.	2,015,100
Lucknow	India	3,221,900
Ludhiana	India	1,716,000
Luoyang	China	2,015,000
Lusaka	Zambia	2,179,500
Lyon	France	1,608,800

Maceió	Brazil	1,266,100
Madrid	Spain	6,199,300
Madurai	India	1,593,200
Makassar (Ujung Pandang)		
	Indonesia	1,488,700
Malappuram	India	2,215,900
Manaus	Brazil	2,025,400
Manchester	U.K.	2,645,600
Mandalay	Myanmar	1,167,000
Manila	Philippines	12,947,000
Maputo	Mozambique	1,187,300
Maracaibo	Venezuela	2,196,500
Maracay	Venezuela	1,166,000
Marrakech	Morocco	1,133,700
Marseille	France	1,605,100
Mashhad	Iran	3,014,500
Mbuji-Mayi	D.R.C.	2,006,700
Mecca	Saudi Arabia	1,770,600
Medan	Indonesia	2,204,100
Medellín	Colombia	3,911,000
Medina	Saudi Arabia	1,280,300
Meerut	India	1,550,400
Melbourne	Australia	4,203,500
Memphis	United States	1,106,100
Mendoza	Argentina	1,009,400
Mérida	Mexico	1,067,800
Mexicali	Mexico	1,034,200
Mexico City	Mexico	20,999,000
Miami	United States	5,817,300
Mianyang	China	1,064,900
Milan	Italy	3,099,000
Milwaukee	United States	1,409,400
Minneapolis-St. Paul	United States	2,791,300
Minsk	Belarus	1,915,400
Mogadishu	Somalia	2,137,900
Mombasa	Kenya	1,103,800
Monrovia	Liberia	1,263,800
Monterrey	Mexico	4,512,600
Montevideo	Uruguay	1,706,900
Montréal	Canada	3,980,800
Moradabad	India	1,023,000
Moscow	Russia	12,166,000
Mosul	Iraq	1,694,300
Multan	Pakistan	1,920,800
Mumbai (Bombay)	India	21,043,000
Munich	Germany	1,437,900
Mysore	India	1,082,400

N'Djaména	Chad	1,260,200
Nagoya	Japan	9,406,300
Nagpur	India	2,675,100
Nairobi	Kenya	3,914,800
Nanchang	China	2,526,900
Nanchong	China	1,049,800
Nanjing, Jiangsu	China	7,369,200
Nanning	China	3,234,400
Nantong	China	1,978,300
Nanyang, Henan	China	1,011,400
Naples	Italy	2,201,800
Nashik	India	1,779,300
Nashville-Davidson	United States	1,105,500
Natal	Brazil	1,166,600

CITY	COUNTRY	POPULATION
Nay Pyi Taw	Myanmar	1,029,800
New York-Newark	United States	18,594,000
Niamey	Niger	1,089,600
Ningbo	China	3,132,000
Nizhniy Novgorod	Russia	1,211,800
Novosibirsk	Russia	1,497,200

Odesa	Ukraine	1,010,500
Omsk	Russia	1,161,900
Onitsha	Nigeria	1,109,300
Orlando	United States	1,730,600
Osaka	Japan	20,238,000
Ottawa-Gatineau	Canada	1,325,900
Ouagadougou	Burkina Faso	2,741,200

P'yongyang	North Korea	2,863,000
Palembang	Indonesia	1,455,300
Panama City	Panama	1,672,900
Paris	France	10,844,000
Patna	India	2,209,600
Pekan Baru	Indonesia	1,120,900
Perth	Australia	1,861,200
Peshawar	Pakistan	1,736,200
Philadelphia	United States	5,585,300
Phnom Penh	Cambodia	1,731,300
Phoenix-Mesa	United States	4,062,700
Pittsburgh	United States	1,719,400
Port Elizabeth	South Africa	1,178,800
Port Harcourt	Nigeria	2,343,400
Port-au-Prince	Haiti	2,439,800
Portland	United States	2,000,900
Porto	Portugal	1,299,500
Pôrto Alegre	Brazil	3,602,600
Prague	Czech Republic	1,313,600
Pretoria	South Africa	2,058,800
Providence	United States	1,196,500
Puebla	Mexico	2,984,100
Pune (Poona)	India	5,727,600
Puning	China	1,004,900
Putian	China	1,437,600

Qingdao	China	4,565,600
Qinhuangdao	China	1,109,300
Qiqihaer	China	1,451,600
Qom	Iran	1,204,200
Quanzhou	China	1,395,400
Querétaro	Mexico	1,267,000
Quetta	Pakistan	1,108,800
Quito	Ecuador	1,726,100

Rabat	Morocco	1,966,900
Raipur	India	1,373,900
Rajkot	India	1,599,300
Raleigh	United States	1,139,800
Ranchi	India	1,262,100
Rawalpindi	Pakistan	2,505,900
Recife	Brazil	3,738,600
Richmond	United States	1,029,600
Rio de Janeiro	Brazil	12,903,000
Riverside-San Bernardino		
	United States	2,194,300
Riyadh	Saudi Arabia	6,369,800
Rizhao	China	1,062,400
Rome	Italy	3,718,000
Rosario	Argentina	1,381,000
Rostov-on-Don	Russia	1,096,600

Sacramento	United States	1,920,400
Saint Louis	United States	2,184,000
Saint Petersburg	Russia	4,993,000
Salem	India	1,002,700
Salt Lake City	United States	1,095,800
Salvador	Brazil	3,583,000
Samara	Russia	1,164,400
Samut Prakan	Thailand	1,814,100
San Antonio	United States	2,029,900
San Diego	United States	3,107,100
San Francisco-Oakland		
	United States	3,300,100
San José	Costa Rica	1,170,200
San Jose	United States	1,729,700
San Juan	Puerto Rico	2,463,300
San Luis Potosí	Mexico	1,147,500
San Salvador	El Salvador	1,098,500
Sana'a'	Yemen	2,962,000
Santa Cruz	Bolivia	2,106,700
Santiago	Chile	6,507,400
Santo Domingo	Dom. Rep.	2,945,400
São Paulo	Brazil	21,067,000
Sapporo	Japan	2,571,500
Seattle	United States	3,248,800
Semarang	Indonesia	1,629,600
Sendai	Japan	2,090,900
Seoul	South Korea	9,773,800
Shanghai	China	23,741,000
Shantou	China	3,948,900
Shaoxing	China	2,075,800
Sharjah	U.A.E.	1,279,400

CITY	COUNTRY	POPULATION
Shenyang	China	6,315,500
Shenzhen	China	10,750,000
Shijiazhuang	China	3,264,500
Shiraz	Iran	1,660,600
Shizuoka	Japan	3,369,000
Singapore	Singapore	5,618,900
Sofia	Bulgaria	1,226,200
Srinagar	India	1,428,600
Stockholm	Sweden	1,485,700
Sulaimaniya	Iraq	1,003,800
Suqian	China	1,049,900
Surabaya	Indonesia	2,853,300
Surat	India	5,650,100
Suweon	South Korea	1,098,900
Suzhou, Jiangsu	China	5,472,100
Sydney	Australia	4,505,400

Tabriz	Iran	1,571,600
Taian, Shandong	China	1,219,600
Taichung	China	1,225,000
Taipei	China	2,665,700
Taiyuan, Shanxi	China	3,481,900
Taizhou, Jiangsu	China	1,184,000
Taizhou, Zhejiang	China	1,648,100
Tampa-St. Petersburg	United States	2,659,200
Tangshan, Hebei	China	2,743,300
Tashkent	Uzbekistan	2,251,200
Tbilisi	Georgia	1,147,500
Tegucigalpa	Honduras	1,122,600
Tehran	Iran	8,432,200
Tel Aviv-Yafo	Israel	3,608,300
Thiruvananthapuram	India	1,964,600
Thrissur	India	2,329,200
Tianjin	China	11,211,000
Tijuana	Mexico	1,986,800
Tiruchirappalli	India	1,106,000
Tiruppur	India	1,230,400
Tokyo	Japan	38,002,000
Toluca de Lerdo	Mexico	2,164,100
Toronto	Canada	5,992,800
Torreón	Mexico	1,332,300
Tripoli	Libya	1,126,200
Tunis	Tunisia	1,993,500
Turin	Italy	1,764,900

Ufa	Russia	1,070,300
Ulaanbaatar	Mongolia	1,377,400
Ürümqi	China	3,498,600

Vadodara	India	1,975,100
Valencia	Venezuela	1,733,700
Vancouver	Canada	2,485,200
Varanasi (Benares)	India	1,541,400
Vereeniging	South Africa	1,155,200
Vienna	Austria	1,752,900
Vijayawada	India	1,759,800
Virginia Beach	United States	1,460,000
Visakhapatnam	India	1,935,300
Volgograd	Russia	1,022,500

Warsaw	Poland	1,722,400
Washington, D.C.	United States	4,955,200
Weifang	China	2,194,600
Wenzhou	China	3,207,900
West Yorkshire	U.K.	1,912,500
Wuhan	China	7,905,600
Wuhu, Anhui	China	1,424,500
Wuxi, Jiangsu	China	3,049,100

Xi'an, Shaanxi	China	6,043,700
Xiamen	China	4,430,100
Xiangtan, Hunan	China	1,009,600
Xiangyang	China	1,533,400
Xining	China	1,323,000
Xuzhou	China	1,917,800

Yancheng, Jiangsu	China	1,435,900
Yangon (Rangoon)	Myanmar	4,802,000
Yangzhou	China	1,765,500
Yantai	China	2,114,500
Yaoundé	Cameroon	3,065,700
Yekaterinburg	Russia	1,379,100
Yerevan	Armenia	1,044,500
Yichang	China	1,263,800
Yinchuan	China	1,596,400
Yingkou	China	1,026,000
Yiwu	China	1,080,500
Yongin	South Korea	1,047,900

Zaozhuang	China	1,028,200
Zhanjiang	China	1,149,100
Zhengzhou	China	4,387,200
Zhenjiang, Jiangsu	China	1,049,900
Zhongshan	China	3,691,400
Zhuhai	China	1,541,900
Zhuzhou	China	1,083,100
Zibo	China	2,430,400
Zürich	Switzerland	1,246,200

Glossary of Geographic Terms

A

abyssal plain a flat, relatively featureless region of the deep ocean floor extending from the mid-ocean ridge to a continental rise or deep-sea trench

acculturation the process of losing the traits of one cultural group while assimilating with another cultural group

alloy a substance that is a mixture of two metals or a metal and a nonmetal

alluvial fan a depositional, fan-shaped feature found where a stream or channel gradient levels out at the base of a mountain

antipode a point that lies diametrically opposite any given point on the surface of the Earth

Archaean (Archean) eon the second eon of Earth's geologic history, ending around 2,500 million years ago

archipelago an associated group of scattered islands in a large body of water

asthenosphere the uppermost zone of Earth's mantle; it consists of rocks in a "plastic" state, immediately below the lithosphere

atmosphere the thin envelope of gases surrounding the solid Earth and comprising mostly nitrogen, oxygen, and various trace gases

atoll a circular coral reef enclosing a lagoon

B

barrier island a low-lying, sandy island parallel to a shoreline but separated from the mainland by a lagoon

basin a low-lying depression in the Earth's surface; some basins are filled with water and sediment, while others are dry most of the time

bathymetry the measurement of depth within bodies of water or the information gathered from such measurements

bay an area of a sea or other body of water bordered on three sides by a curved stretch of coastline but usually smaller than a gulf

biodiversity a broad concept that refers to the variety and range of species (flora and fauna) present in an ecosystem

biogeography the study of the distribution patterns of plants and animals and the processes that produce those patterns

biological weapon a weapon that uses an organism or toxin, such as a bacteria or virus, to harm individuals

biome a very large ecosystem made up of specific plant and animal communities interacting with the physical environment (climate and soil)

biosphere the realm of Earth that includes all plant and animal life-forms

bluff a steep slope or wall of consolidated sediment adjacent to a river or its floodplain

bog soft, spongy, waterlogged ground consisting chiefly of partially decayed plant matter (peat)

breakwater a stone or concrete structure built near a shore to prevent damage to watercraft or construction

butte a tall, steep-sided, flat-topped tower of rock that is a remnant of extensive erosional processes

C

caldera a large, crater-like feature with steep, circular walls and a central depression resulting from the explosion and collapse of a volcano

canal an artificially made channel of water used for navigation or irrigation

canopy the ceiling-like layer of branches and leaves that forms the uppermost layer of a forest

capitalism an economic system characterized by resource allocation primarily through market mechanisms; means of production are privately owned (by either individuals or corporations), and production is organized around profit maximization

capture fishery all of the variables involved in the activities to harvest a given fish (e.g., location, target resource, technology used, social characteristic, purpose, season)

carbon cycle one of the several geochemical cycles by which matter is recirculated through the lithosphere, hydrosphere, atmosphere, and biosphere

carbon neutral process a process resulting in zero net change in the balance between emission and absorption of carbon

carrying capacity the maximum number of animals and/or people a given area can support at a given time under specified levels of consumption

cartogram a map designed to present statistical information in a diagrammatic way, usually not to scale

cartographer a person who interprets, designs, and creates maps and other modes of geographic representation

chemical weapon a weapon that uses toxic properties of chemical substances to harm individuals

chlorofluorocarbon a molecule of industrial origin containing chlorine, fluorine, and carbon atoms; causes severe ozone destruction

civilization a cultural concept suggesting substantial development in the form of agriculture, cities, food and labor surplus, labor specialization, social stratification, and state organization

climate the long-term behavior of the atmosphere; it includes measures of average weather conditions (e.g., temperature, humidity, precipitation, and pressure), as well as trends, cycles, and extremes

colonialism the political, social, or economic domination of a state over another state or people

commodity an economic good or product that can be traded, bought, or sold

composite image a product of combining two or more images

coniferous trees and shrubs with thin leaves and producing cones; also a forest or wood composed of these trees

continental drift a theory that suggests the continents were at one time all part of a prehistoric supercontinent that broke apart; according to the theory, the continents slowly "drifted" across the Earth's surface to their present positions

continental shelf the submerged, offshore extension of a continent

continental slope the steeply graded seafloor connecting the edge of the continental shelf to the deep-ocean floor

convection the transfer of heat within a gas or solid of nonuniform temperature from mass movement or circulatory motion due to gravity and uneven density within the substance

convergent boundary where tectonic plates move toward each other along their common boundary, causing subduction

core the dense, innermost layer of Earth; the outer core is liquid, while the inner core is solid

Coriolis effect the deflection of wind systems and ocean currents (as well as freely moving objects not in contact with the solid Earth) to the right in the Northern Hemisphere and to the left in the Southern Hemisphere as a consequence of the Earth's rotation

crust the rocky, relatively low density, outermost layer of Earth

cultural diffusion the spread of cultural elements from one group to another

culture the "way of life" for a group; it is transmitted from generation to generation and involves a shared system of meanings, beliefs, values, and social relations; it also includes language, religion, clothing, music, laws, and entertainment

D

dead zone oxygen-starved areas in oceans and lakes where marine life cannot be supported, often linked to runoff of excess nutrients

deciduous trees and shrubs that shed their leaves seasonally; also a forest or wood mostly composed of these trees

deformation general term for folding and faulting of rocks due to natural shearing, compression, and extension forces

delta a flat, low-lying, often fan-shaped region at the mouth of a river; it is composed of sediment deposited by a river entering a lake, an ocean, or another large body of water

demography the study of population statistics, changes, and trends based on various measures of fertility, mortality, and migration

denudation the overall effect of weathering, mass wasting, and erosion, which ultimately wears down and lowers the continental surface

desert a region that has little or no vegetation and averages less than ten inches (25 cm) of precipitation a year

desertification the spread of desert conditions in arid and semiarid regions; desertification results from a combination of climatic changes and increasing human pressures in the form of overgrazing, removal of natural vegetation, and cultivation of marginal land

developed country general term for an industrialized country with a diversified and self-sustaining economy, strong infrastructure, and high standard of living

developing country general term for a nonindustrialized country with a weak economy, little modern infrastructure, and low standard of living

dialect a regional variation of one language, with differences in vocabulary, accent, pronunciation, and syntax

diffuse plate boundary a zone of faulting and earthquakes extending to either side of a plate boundary

digital elevation model (DEM) a digital representation of Earth's topography in which data points representing altitude are assigned coordinates and viewed spatially; sometimes called a digital terrain model (DTM)

disconformity a discontinuity in sedimentary rocks in which the rock beds remain parallel

divide a ridge separating watersheds

dormant volcano an active volcano that is temporarily in repose but expected to erupt in the future

E

earthquake vibrations and shock waves caused by volcanic eruptions or the sudden movement of Earth's crustal rocks along fracture zones called faults

easterlies regular winds that blow from the east

ecosystem a group of organisms and the environment with which they interact

elevation the height of a point or place above an established datum, sometimes mean sea level

El Niño a pronounced warming of the surface waters along the coast of Peru and the equatorial region of the east Pacific Ocean; it is caused by weakening (sometimes reversal) of the trade winds, with accompanying changes in ocean circulation (including cessation of upwelling in coastal waters)

emigrant a person migrating away from a country or area; an out-migrant

endangered species a species at immediate risk of extinction

endemic typical of or native to a particular area, people, or environment

endogenous introduced from or originating within a given organism or system

environment the sum of the conditions and stimuli that influence an organism

eon the largest time unit on the geologic time scale; consists of several shorter units called eras

Equator latitude 0°; an imaginary line running east and west around Earth and dividing it into two equal parts known as the Northern and Southern Hemispheres; the Equator always has 12 hours of daylight and 12 hours of darkness

equinox the time of year (usually September 22–23 and March 21–22) when the length of night and day are about equal and the sun is directly overhead at the Equator

era a major subdivision of time on the geologic time scale; consists of several shorter units called periods

erosion the general term for the removal of surface rocks and sediment by the action of water, air, ice, or gravity

escarpment a cliff or steep rock face that separates two comparatively level land surfaces

estuary a broadened seaward end or extension of a river (usually a drowned river mouth), characterized by tidal influences and the mixing of fresh and saline water

ethnic group minority group with a collective self-identity within a larger host population

ethnocentrism a belief in the inherent superiority of one's own ethnic group and culture; a tendency to view all other groups or cultures in terms of one's own

eutrophication the process that occurs when large amounts of nutrients from fertilizers or animal wastes enter a water body and bacteria break down the nutrients; the bacterial action causes depletion of dissolved oxygen

Exclusive Economic Zone (EEZ) an oceanic zone extending up to 200 nautical miles (370 km) from a shoreline, within which a coastal state claims jurisdiction over fishing, mineral exploration, and other economically important activities

exogenous introduced from or originating outside a given organism or system

external debt debt owed to nonresidents; repayable in foreign currency, goods, or services

F

fault a fracture or break in rock where the opposite sides are displaced relative to each other

fjord a coastal inlet that is narrow and deep and reaches far inland; it is usually formed by the sea filling in a glacially scoured valley or trough

flood basalt a huge lava flow that produces thick accumulations of basalt layers over a large area

floodplain a wide, relatively flat area adjacent to a stream or river and subject to flooding and sedimentation; it is the most preferred land area for human settlement and agriculture

food chain the feeding pattern of organisms in an ecosystem, through which energy from food passes from one level to the next in a sequence

fork the place where a river separates into branches; also may refer to one of those branches

fossil fuel fuel in the form of coal, petroleum, or natural gas derived from the remains of ancient plants and animals trapped and preserved in sedimentary rocks

G

galaxy a collection of stars, gas, and dust bound together by gravity; there are billions of galaxies in the universe, and the Earth is in the Milky Way galaxy

genocide the intentional destruction, in whole or in part, of a national, ethnic, racial, or religious group

genome the complete set of genetic material of an organism

geochemistry a branch of geology focusing on the chemical composition of earth materials

geographic information system (GIS) an integrated hardware-software system used to store, organize, analyze, manipulate, model, and display geographic information or data

geography literally means "Earth description"; as a modern academic discipline, geography is concerned with the explanation of the physical and human characteristics and patterns of Earth's surface

geomorphology the study of planetary surface features, especially the processes of landform evolution on Earth

geopolitics the study of how factors such as geography, economics, and demography affect the power and foreign policy of a state

glaciation a period of glacial advancement through the growth of continental ice sheets and/or mountain glaciers

glacier a large, natural accumulation of ice that spreads outward on the land or moves slowly down a slope or valley

global positioning system (GPS) a system of artificial satellites that provides information on three-dimensional position and velocity to users at or near the Earth's surface

global warming the warming of Earth's average global temperature due to a buildup of "greenhouse gases" (e.g., carbon dioxide and methane) released by human activities; increased levels of these gases cause enhanced heat absorption by the atmosphere

globe a scale model of the Earth that correctly represents not only the area, relative size, and shape of physical features but also the distance between points and true compass directions

great circle the largest circle that can be drawn around a sphere such as a globe; a great circle route is the shortest route between two points on the surface of a sphere

greenhouse effect an enhanced near-surface warming that is due to certain atmospheric gases absorbing and re-radiating long-wave radiation that might otherwise have escaped to space had those gases not been present in the atmosphere

gross domestic product (GDP) the total market value of goods and services produced by a nation's economy in a given year using global currency exchange rates

gross national income (GNI) the income derived from the capital and income belonging to nationals employed domestically or abroad

gravitational waves ripples in the fabric of space and time, usually caused by the interaction of two or more large masses

gulf a very large area of an ocean or a sea bordered by coastline on three sides

gyre a large, semicontinuous system of major ocean currents flowing around the outer margins of every major ocean basin

H

habitat the natural environment (including controlling physical factors) in which a plant or animal is usually found or prefers to exist

hemisphere half a sphere; cartographers and geographers, by convention, divide the Earth into the Northern and Southern Hemispheres at the Equator and the Eastern and Western Hemispheres at the prime meridian (longitude 0°) and 180° meridian

herbaceous a type of plant lacking woody tissue, and usually with a life of just one growing season

hot spot a localized and intensely hot region or mantle plume beneath the lithosphere; it tends to stay relatively fixed geographically as a lithospheric plate migrates over it

human geography one of the two major divisions of systematic geography; it is concerned with the spatial analysis of human population, cultures, and social, political, and economic activities

hurricane a large, rotating storm system that forms over tropical waters, with very low atmospheric pressure in the central region and winds in excess of 74 mph (119 km/h); it is called a typhoon over the western Pacific Ocean and a cyclone over the northern Indian Ocean

hydrologic cycle the continuous recirculation of water from the oceans, through the atmosphere, to the continents, through the biosphere and lithosphere, and back to the sea

hydrosphere all of the water found on, under, or over Earth's surface

hypsometry the measurement of contours and elevation of land above sea level

I

ice age a period of pronounced glaciation usually associated with worldwide cooling, a greater proportion of global precipitation falling as snow, and a shorter seasonal snowmelt period

igneous the rock type formed from solidified molten rock (magma) that originates deep within Earth; the chemical composition of the magma and its cooling rate determine the final rock type

immigrant a person migrating into a particular country or area; an in-migrant

impact crater a circular depression on the surface of a planet or moon caused by the collision of another body, such as an asteroid or comet

indigenous native to or occurring naturally in a specific area or environment

industrial metabolism a concept that describes the process of converting raw materials into a final product and waste through energy and labor

infrastructure transportation and communications networks that allow goods, people, and information to flow across space

inorganic not relating to or being derived from living things

interdependence mutual reliance among beings or processes

internally displaced person a person who flees his/her home, to escape danger or persecution, but does not leave the country

International Date Line an imaginary line that roughly follows the 180° meridian in the Pacific Ocean; immediately west of the date line the calendar date is one day ahead of the calendar date east of the line; people crossing the date line in a westward direction lose one calendar day, while those crossing eastward gain one calendar day

intertropical convergence zone (ITCZ) a zone of low atmospheric pressure created by intense solar heating, thereby leading to rising air and horizontal convergence of northeast and southeast trade winds; over the oceans, the ITCZ is usually found between 10° N and 10° S, and over continents the seasonal excursion of the ITCZ is much greater

isthmus a relatively narrow strip of land with water on both sides and connecting two larger land areas

J

jet stream a high-speed west-to-east wind current; jet streams flow in narrow corridors within upper-air westerlies, usually at the interface of polar and tropical air

K

karst a region underlain by limestone and characterized by extensive solution features such as sinkholes, underground streams, and caves

L

lagoon a shallow, narrow water body located between a barrier island and the mainland, with freshwater contributions from streams and saltwater exchange through tidal inlets or breaches throughout the barrier system

La Niña the pronounced cooling of equatorial waters in the eastern Pacific Ocean

latitude the distance north or south of the Equator; lines of latitude, called parallels, are evenly spaced from the Equator to the North and South Poles (from 0° to 90° N and S latitude); latitude and longitude (see below) are measured in terms of the 360 degrees of a circle and are expressed in degrees, minutes, and seconds

leeward the side away from or sheltered by the wind

lingua franca a language used beyond its native speaker population as a common or commercial language

lithosphere the rigid outer layer of the Earth, located above the asthenosphere and comprising the outer crust and the upper, rigid portion of the mantle

longitude the distance measured in degrees east or west of the prime meridian (0° longitude) up to 180°; lines of longitude are called meridians (compare with latitude, above)

M

macroscopic concerned with or considered in large units

magma molten, pressurized rock in the mantle that is occasionally intruded into the lithosphere or extruded to the surface of the Earth by volcanic activity

magnetic poles the points at Earth's surface at which the geomagnetic field is vertical; the location of these points constantly changes

mantle the dense layer of Earth below the crust; the upper mantle is solid, and with the crust forms the lithosphere, the zone containing tectonic plates; the lower mantle is partially molten, making it the pliable base upon which the lithosphere "floats"

map projection the geometric system of transferring information about a round object, such as a globe, to a flat piece of paper or other surface for the purpose of producing a map with known properties and quantifiable distortion

maria volcanic plains on the moon's surface that appear to the naked eye as smooth, dark areas

meridian a north-south line of longitude used to reference distance east or west of the prime meridian (longitude 0°)

mesa a broad, flat-topped hill or mountain with marginal cliffs and/or steep slopes formed by progressive erosion of horizontally bedded sedimentary rocks

metamorphic the rock type formed from preexisting rocks that have been substantially changed from their original igneous, sedimentary, or earlier metamorphic form; catalysts of this change include high heat, high pressure, hot and mineral-rich fluids, or, more commonly, some combination of these

metric ton (tonne) unit of weight equal to 1,000 kilograms or 2,205 pounds

micrometeoroids a tiny particle of rock or dust in space, usually weighing less than a gram

microscopic considered in or concerned with small units

migration the movement of people across a specified boundary for the purpose of establishing a new place of residence

mineral an inorganic solid with a distinctive chemical composition and a specific crystal structure that affect its physical characteristics

moment magnitude scale a measure of the total energy released by an earthquake; preferred to the Richter scale because it more accurately measures strong earthquakes and can be used with data for distant earthquakes

monsoon a seasonal reversal of prevailing wind patterns, often associated with pronounced changes in moisture

N

nation a cultural concept for a group of people bound together by a strong sense of shared values and cultural characteristics, including language, religion, and common history

nebula a cloud of interstellar gas and dust

node a point where distinct lines or objects intersect

Normalized Difference Vegetation Index (NDVI) a measurement of plant growth density over an area of the Earth's surface, measured on a scale of 0.1 to 0.8 (low to high vegetation)

North Pole the most northerly geographic point on the Earth; the northern end of the Earth's axis of rotation; 90° N

nuclear weapon a weapon that utilizes nuclear chain reactions to derive destructive force

O

oasis a fertile area with water and vegetation in a desert

ocean current the regular and persistent flow of water in the oceans, usually driven by atmospheric wind and pressure systems or by regional differences in water density (temperature, salinity)

offshoring relocating business processes to another country, where they are performed by either another branch of the parent company or an external contractor (international outsourcing)

organic relating to or derived from living things

Glossary of Geographic Terms

outsourcing delegating noncore processes from within a business to an external entity such as a subcontractor

oxbow lake a crescent-shaped lake or swamp occupying a channel abandoned by a meandering river

ozone a bluish gas composed of three oxygen atoms and harmful to breathe

ozone layer region of Earth's atmosphere where ozone concentration is relatively high; the ozone layer absorbs harmful ultraviolet rays from the sun

P

paleo-geographic map a map depicting the past positions of the continents, developed from historic magnetic, biological, climatological, and geologic evidence

Pangaea the supercontinent from which today's continents are thought to have originated

peninsula a long piece of land jutting out from a larger piece of land into a body of water

period a basic unit of time on the geologic time scale, generally 35 to 70 million years in duration; a subdivision of an era

Phanerozoic eon an eon of Earth's geologic history that comprises the Paleozoic, Mesozoic, and Cenozoic eras

photosynthesis process by which plants convert carbon dioxide and water to oxygen and carbohydrates

physical geography one of the two major divisions of systematic geography; the spatial analysis of the structure, process, and location of Earth's natural phenomena, such as climate, soil, plants, animals, water, and topography

pilgrimage a typically long and difficult journey to a special place, often of religious importance

plain an extensive flat-lying area characterized generally by the absence of local relief features

planetary nebula an interstellar cloud of gas and dust formed when a star runs out of central nuclear fuel, finally ejecting its outer layers in a gaseous shell

plate tectonics the theory that Earth's lithospheric plates slide or shift slowly over the asthenosphere and that their interactions cause earthquakes, volcanic eruptions, movement of landmasses, and other geologic events

plateau a landform feature characterized by high elevation and gentle upland slopes

point a sharp prominence or headland on the coast that juts out into a body of water

politicide the intentional destruction, in whole or in part, of a group of people based on their political or ideological beliefs

pollution a direct or indirect process resulting from human activity; part of the environment is made potentially or actually unsafe or hazardous to the welfare of the organisms that live in it

porphyry an igneous rock characterized by large crystals within a matrix of much finer crystals

primary energy energy sources as they are found naturally—i.e., before they have been processed or transformed into secondary sources

prime meridian the line of 0° longitude that runs through Greenwich, England, and separates the Eastern and Western Hemispheres

Priscoan eon the earliest eon of Earth's geologic history; also known as the Hadean eon

proliferation the process of growing rapidly and suddenly

Proterozoic eon the eon of geologic time that includes the interval between the Archaean and Phanerozoic eons and is marked by rocks that contain fossils indicating the first appearance of eukaryotic organisms (such as algae)

protogalaxy a cloud of gas, possibly consisting of dark matter, hydrogen, and helium, that is forming into a galaxy

purchasing power parity (PPP) a method of measuring gross domestic product that compares the relative value of currencies based on what each currency will buy in its country of origin; PPP provides a good comparison between national economies and is a decent indicator of living standards

R

rain shadow the dry region on the downwind (leeward) side of a mountain range

raster data spatial data represented as a unified grid of equal-area cells, each with a single numerical value; best suited for contiguous data such as elevation

red dwarf a relatively small, cool, and faint star with a very long estimated life span; the most common type of star

reef a strip of rocks or sand either at or just below the surface of water

refugee a person who flees his/her country of origin to escape danger or persecution for reasons of, for example, race, religion, or political opinion

regolith a layer of disintegrated or partly decomposed rock overlying unweathered parent materials; regolith is usually found in areas of low relief where the physical transport of debris is weak

remote sensing the measurement of some property of an object or terrain by means other than direct contact, usually from aircraft or satellites

renewable resource a resource that can be regenerated or maintained if used at rates that do not exceed natural replenishment

Richter scale a logarithmic scale devised to represent the relative amount of energy released by an earthquake; moment magnitude has superseded the Richter scale as the preferred measurement of earthquake magnitude

rift a long, narrow trough created by plate movement at a divergent boundary

rift valley a long, structural valley formed by the lowering of a block between two parallel faults

Ring of Fire (also Rim of Fire) an arc of volcanoes and tectonic activity along the perimeter of the Pacific Ocean

S

salinization the accumulation of salts in soil

satellite data information collected by a vehicle orbiting a celestial body

savanna a tropical grassland with widely spaced trees; it experiences distinct wet and dry seasons

seamount a submerged volcano rising from the ocean floor

sedimentary the rock type formed from preexisting rocks or pieces of once living organisms; deposits accumulate on Earth's surface, generally with distinctive layering or bedding

solar radiation energy emitted by the sun

solar wind the stream of atoms and ions moving outward from the solar corona at 300 to 500 kilometers per second

solstice a celestial event that occurs twice a year (usually June 20-21 and December 21-22), when the sun appears directly overhead to observers at the Tropic of Cancer or the Tropic of Capricorn

sound a broad channel or passage of water connecting two larger bodies of water or separating an island from the mainland

South Pole the most southerly geographic point on the Earth; the southern end of the Earth's axis of rotation; 90° S

spatial resolution a measure of the smallest distinguishable separation between two objects

spectral resolution a measure of the ability of a sensing system to distinguish electromagnetic radiation of different frequencies

spit beach extension that forms along a shoreline with bays and other indentations

spreading boundary where plates move apart along their common boundary, creating a crack in the Earth's crust (typically at the mid-ocean ridge), which is then filled with upwelling molten rock; also called a divergent boundary

state an area with defined and internationally acknowledged boundaries; a political unit

steppe semiarid, relatively flat, treeless region getting between 10 and 20 inches (25 and 51 cm) of precipitation yearly

strait a narrow passage of water that connects two larger bodies of water

subatomic particle a part of an atom, such as a proton, neutron, or electron

subduction the tectonic process by which the down-bent edge of one lithospheric plate is forced underneath another plate

T

tariff a surcharge on imports levied by a state; a form of protectionism designed to increase imports' market price and thus inhibit their consumption

tectonic plate (also lithospheric or crustal plate) a section of the Earth's rigid outer layer that moves as a distinct unit upon the plastic-like mantle materials in the asthenosphere

temperate mild or moderate

temporal resolution a measure of the frequency with which a sensing system gathers data

terrestrial radiation natural sources of radiation found in earth materials

threatened species species at some, but not immediate, risk of extinction

tide the regular rise and fall of the ocean, caused by the mutual gravitational attraction between the Earth, moon, and sun, as well as the rotation of the Earth-moon system around its center of gravity

ton a unit of weight equal to 2,000 pounds in the U.S. or 2,240 pounds inthe U.K.

tonne (see metric ton)

topography the relief features that are evident on a planetary surface

tornado a violently rotating, funnel-shaped column of air characterized by extremely low atmospheric pressures and exceptional wind speeds generated within intense thunderstorms

tradewind a wind blowing persistently from the same direction; particularly from the subtropical high-pressure centers toward the equatorial low-pressure zone

transgenic an organism artificially or naturally containing one or more genes from a different type of organism

tributary a river or stream flowing into a larger river or stream

tropical warm and moist; occurring in or characteristic of the Tropics

Tropic of Cancer latitude 23.5° N; the farthest northerly excursion of the sun when it is directly overhead

Tropic of Capricorn latitude 23.5° S; the farthest southerly excursion of the sun when it is directly overhead

tsunami a series of ocean waves, often very destructive along coasts, caused by the vertical displacement of the seafloor during an earthquake, submarine landslide, or volcanic eruption

tundra a zone in cold, polar regions (mostly in the Northern Hemisphere) that is transitional between the zone of polar ice and the limit of tree growth; it is usually characterized by low-lying vegetation, with extensive permafrost and waterlogged soils

U

unconformity a discontinuity in sedimentary rocks caused by erosion or nondeposition

uplift the slow, upward movement of Earth's crust

upwelling the process by which water rich in nutrients rises from depth toward the ocean surface; it is usually the result of diverging surface waters

urban agglomeration a group of several cities and/or towns and their suburbs

urbanization a process in which there is an increase in the percentage of people living and working in urban places compared with rural places; a process of change from a rural to urban lifestyle

V

vector data spatial data represented as nodes and connectors identified by geographic coordinates, and related to one another to symbolize geographic features; best suited for geographic features that can be represented as points, lines, or polygons

volcanism the upward movement and expulsion of molten (melted) material and gases from within the Earth's mantle onto the surface, where it cools and hardens, producing characteristic terrain

W

watershed the drainage area of a river and its tributaries

weathering the processes or actions that cause the physical disintegration and chemical decomposition of rock and minerals

westerlies a regular wind that blows from the west

wetland an area of land covered by water or saturated by water sufficiently enough to support vegetation adapted to wet conditions

wilderness a natural environment that has remained essentially undisturbed by human activities and, increasingly, is protected by government or nongovernment organizations

windward the side toward or unsheltered from the wind

X

xerophyte a plant that thrives in a dry environment

Y

yazoo a tributary stream that runs parallel to the main river for some distance

Z

zenith the point in the sky that is immediately overhead; also the highest point above the observer's horizon obtained by a celestial body

zoning the process of subdividing urban areas as a basis for land-use planning and policy

Place-Name Index

Index Marker ———

Bern, *Switz.* **152** B2

Page

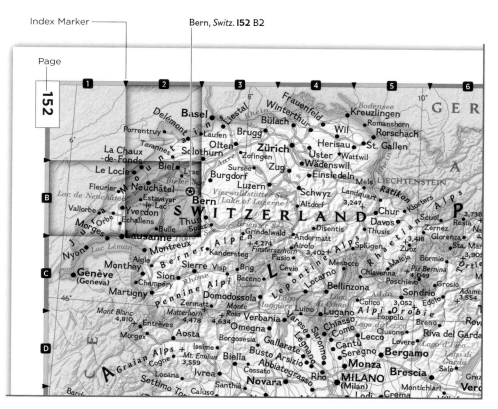

The following system is used to locate a place on a map in the *National Geographic Family Reference Atlas.* The boldface type after an entry refers to the page on which the map is found. The letter-number combination refers to the grid on which the particular place-name is located. The edge of each map is marked horizontally with numbers and vertically with letters. In between, at equally spaced intervals, are index markers (arrows). If these markers were connected with lines, each page would be divided into a grid. Take Bern, Switzerland, for example. The index entry reads "Bern, *Switz.* **152** B2." On page 152, Bern is located within the grid square where row B and column 2 intersect (example at left).

A place-name may appear on several maps, but the index lists only the best presentation. Usually, this means that a feature is indexed to the largest-scale map on which it appears in its entirety. (Note: Rivers are often labeled multiple times even on a single map. In such cases, the rivers are indexed to labels that are closest to their mouths.) The name of the country or continent in which a feature lies is shown in italic type and is usually abbreviated. (A full list of abbreviations appears on page 266.)

The index lists more than proper names. Some entries include a description, as in "Elba, island, *It.* **152** J5" and "Amazon (Solimões), river, *S. Amer.* **128** D5." In languages other than English, the description of a physical feature may be part of the name; e.g., the "Erg" in "Chech, Erg, *Alg., Mali* **200** E9" means "sand dune region." The glossary of Foreign Terms on pages 272–273 translates such terms into English.

When a feature or place can be referred to by more than one name, both may appear in the index with cross-references. For example, the entry for Cairo reads "Cairo *see* El Qâhira, *Egypt* **201** C18." That entry is "El Qâhira (Cairo), *Egypt* **201** C18."

1st Cataract, *Egypt* **201** E19
2nd Cataract, *Sudan* **202** C12
3rd Cataract, *Sudan* **202** C12
4th Cataract, *Sudan* **203** D13
5th Cataract, *Sudan* **203** D13
6th Cataract, *Sudan* **203** D13
9 de Julio, *Arg.* **134** M11
25 de Mayo, *Arg.* **135** N8

A

Aachen, *Ger.* **150** F4
Aalen, *Ger.* **150** J7
Aaley, *Leb.* **172** J6
Aalsmeer, *Neth.* **148** J12
Aalst, *Belg.* **148** L11
Aansluit, *S. Af.* **206** J8
Aare, river, *Switz.* **152** A3
Aarschot, *Belg.* **148** L12
Aasu, *Amer. Samoa, U.S.* **222** M7
Aba, *China* **182** K9
Aba, *Dem. Rep. of the Congo* **202** H12
Aba, *Nigeria* **205** E14
Abā as Saʻūd, *Saudi Arabia* **174** N9
Abaco Island, *Bahamas* **122** B6
Ābādān, *Iran* **174** F11
Ābādeh, *Iran* **175** F13
Abadla, *Alg.* **200** C9
Abaetetuba, *Braz.* **133** D13
Abaiang, island, *Kiribati* **221** E17
Abaji, *Nigeria* **205** D14
Abajo Peak, *Utah, U.S.* **109** P9
Abakan, *Russ.* **161** L13
Abancay, *Peru* **132** H5
Abaokoro, island, *Kiribati* **221** F17
Abashiri, *Japan* **188** F15
Abashiri Wan, *Japan* **188** F15
Abay, *Kaz.* **177** E14
Ābaya Hāyk', *Eth.* **203** H14
Abbaye, Point, *Mich., U.S.* **100** E7
Abbeville, *Ala., U.S.* **103** M17
Abbeville, *Fr.* **148** M9

Abbeville, *La., U.S.* **102** Q8
Abbeville, *S.C., U.S.* **98** K7
Abbeyfeale (Mainistir na Féile), *Ire.* **145** T3
Abbeyleix (Mainistir Laoise), *Ire.* **145** T6
Abbiategrasso, *It.* **152** E4
Abbot Ice Shelf, *Antarctica* **230** J6
Abbotsford, *B.C., Can.* **84** M8
Abbotsford, *Wis., U.S.* **100** H4
Abbottabad, *Pak.* **178** M11
'Abd al Kūrī, island, *Yemen* **175** R13
'Abd al 'Azīz, Jabal, *Syr.* **172** D13
Abéché, *Chad* **201** H16
Abemama, island, *Kiribati* **218** G8
Abengourou, *Côte d'Ivoire* **204** E9
Åbenrå, *Den.* **142** N11
Abeokuta, *Nigeria* **204** D12
Aberaeron, *Wales, U.K.* **145** U9
Aberdare, *Wales, U.K.* **145** V10
Aberdaron, *Wales, U.K.* **145** T9
Aberdaugleddau *see* Milford Haven, *Wales, U.K.* **145** V8
Aberdeen, *Idaho, U.S.* **108** H6
Aberdeen, *Md., U.S.* **98** C14
Aberdeen, *Miss., U.S.* **103** J13
Aberdeen, *N.C., U.S.* **98** J11
Aberdeen, *S. Dak., U.S.* **106** J6
Aberdeen, *Scot., U.K.* **144** K11
Aberdeen, *Wash., U.S.* **110** D2
Aberdeen Lake, *Nunavut, Can.* **85** H14
Aberffraw, *Wales, U.K.* **145** S9
Abergele, *Wales, U.K.* **145** S10
Abergwaun *see* Fishguard, *Wales, U.K.* **145** U8
Abernathy, *Tex., U.S.* **104** J5
Abert, Lake, *Oreg., U.S.* **110** K6
Abertawe *see* Swansea, *Wales, U.K.* **145** V9
Aberteifi *see* Cardigan, *Wales, U.K.* **145** U9
Abertillery, *Wales, U.K.* **145** V10
Aberystwyth, *Wales, U.K.* **145** U9
Abhā, *Saudi Arabia* **174** N8
Abidjan, *Côte d'Ivoire* **204** E9

Abilene, *Kans., U.S.* **107** S8
Abilene, *Tex., U.S.* **104** L8
Abingdon, *Eng., U.K.* **145** V12
Abingdon, *Ill., U.S.* **101** Q4
Abingdon, *Va., U.S.* **98** G8
Abiquiu, *N. Mex., U.S.* **109** R12
Abisko, *Sw.* **143** D13
Abitibi, Lake, *N. Amer.* **82** H8
Abkhazia, republic, *Rep. of Georgia* **171** A15
Abminga, *S. Aust., Austral.* **215** U9
Åbo *see* Turku, *Fin.* **143** J15
Abohar, *India* **180** E4
Abomey, *Benin* **204** E12
Abou Deïa, *Chad* **201** J15
Abraham Lincoln Birthplace National Historic Site, *Ky., U.S.* **103** C16
Abraham's Bay, *Bahamas* **119** H16
Abra Pampa, *Arg.* **134** D9
Abreú, *Dom. Rep.* **119** L19
Abrolhos, Arquipélago dos, *Braz.* **133** K16
Abrolhos Bank, *Atl. Oc.* **241** R8
Abrolhos Seamount, *Atl. Oc.* **248** R2
Abrolhos Seamounts, *Atl. Oc.* **241** R8
Absalom, Mount, *Antarctica* **230** E11
Absaroka Range, *Mont., Wyo., U.S.* **108** F8
Absarokee, *Mont., U.S.* **108** E9
Abşeron Yarımadası, *Azerb.* **171** D23
Abū al Abyaḏ, island, *U.A.E.* **175** K14
Abū 'Alī, island, *Saudi Arabia* **174** H12
Abū Baḥr, plain, *Saudi Arabia* **174** L11
Abū Daghmah, *Syr.* **172** D10
Abu Dhabi *see* Abū Z̧aby, *U.A.E.* **175** J14
Abu Durba, *Egypt* **173** T2
Abu Hamed, *Sudan* **203** C13
Abuja, *Nigeria* **205** D14
Abū Kamāl, *Syr.* **172** H14
Abū Madd, Ra's, *Saudi Arabia* **174** J6
Abu Matariq, *Sudan* **202** F11
Abunã, *Braz.* **132** G7

Abunã, river, *S. Amer.* **132** G7
Abū Qumayyiş, Ra's, *Saudi Arabia* **175** J13
Abu Rudeis, *Egypt* **173** S2
Abū Rujmayn, Jabal, *Syr.* **172** G10
Abu Shagara, Ras, *Sudan* **203** C14
Abu Simbel, site, *Egypt* **201** F19
Ābuyē Mēda, peak, *Eth.* **203** F15
Abu Zabad, *Sudan* **202** F12
Abū Z̧aby (Abu Dhabi), *U.A.E.* **175** J14
Abu Zenîma, *Egypt* **173** S2
Abwong, *S. Sudan* **203** G13
Abyad, El Bahr el (White Nile), river, *Af.* **203** F13
Abyei, region, *Sudan* **202** G12
Ābyek, *Iran* **174** C12
Academy Glacier, *Antarctica* **230** H11
Acadia National Park, *Me., U.S.* **97** F18
A Cañiza, *Sp.* **146** C6
Acaponeta, *Mex.* **116** G9
Acapulco, *Mex.* **116** K11
Acarai Mountains, *S. Amer.* **131** G14
Acaraú, *Braz.* **133** E16
Acarigua, *Venez.* **130** C8
Acatenango, Volcán de, *Guatemala* **117** L15
Acatlán, *Mex.* **116** J12
Accomac, *Va., U.S.* **98** E15
Accra, *Ghana* **204** E10
Accumoli, *It.* **152** J9
Achach, island, *F.S.M.* **221** C14
Acharacle, *Scot., U.K.* **144** L7
Acharnés, *Gr.* **156** J12
Achavanich, *Scot., U.K.* **144** H10
Achayvayam, *Russ.* **161** D22
Acheloós, *Gr.* **156** F8
Acheloós, river, *Gr.* **156** H8
Achill Island, *Ire.* **145** Q3
Achim, *Ger.* **150** C7
Achinsk, *Russ.* **161** K13
Achit Nuur, *Mongolia* **182** C6
Achna (Düzce), *Cyprus* **162** P9
Achnasheen, *Scot., U.K.* **144** J8

Acıgöl, *Turk.* **170** G5
Acıpayam, *Turk.* **170** H5
Ackerman, *Miss., U.S.* **102** K12
Ackley, *Iowa, U.S.* **107** N12
Acklins Island, *Bahamas* **119** H15
Acoma Pueblo, *N. Mex., U.S.* **109** S11
Aconcagua, Cerro, *Arg.* **134** K7
Aconcagua, Río, *Chile* **134** K6
A Coruña, *Sp.* **146** A6
Acquaviva, *San Marino* **163** J14
Acqui Terme, *It.* **152** F3
Acraman, Lake, *Austral.* **214** J9
Acre *see* 'Akko, *Israel* **172** K5
Acre, river, *S. Amer.* **132** G6
Actium, battle, *Gr.* **156** G7
Açu, *Braz.* **133** F17
Ada, *Ghana* **204** E11
Ada, *Minn., U.S.* **106** G8
Ada, *Ohio, U.S.* **101** Q12
Ada, *Okla., U.S.* **104** H12
Ada, *Serb.* **154** D10
Adair, Cape, *Nunavut, Can.* **85** E17
Adak Island, *Alas., U.S.* **112** N5
Adalia *see* Antalya, *Turk.* **170** H6
Adam, *Oman* **175** K10
Adámantas, *Gr.* **157** M13
Adamawa, region, *Af.* **198** H5
Adamello, peak, *It.* **152** C6
Adams, *Minn., U.S.* **106** L12
Adams, *Wis., U.S.* **100** K5
Adams, Mount, *Wash., U.S.* **110** E5
Adam's Bridge, *Asia* **168** K7
Adam's Peak, *Sri Lanka* **181** T7
Adam's Rock, *Pitcairn I., U.K.* **223** Q24
Adamstown, *Pitcairn I., U.K.* **223** Q23
Adamsville, *Tenn., U.S.* **103** G13
'Adan (Aden), *Yemen* **174** R9
Adana, *Turk.* **170** J10
'Adan aş Şughrá, cape, *Yemen* **174** R9
Adang, Teluk, *Indonesia* **192** K12
Adare, Cape, *Antarctica* **231** R13
Adare Basin, *Pac. Oc.* **249** H16
Adare Seamounts, *Pac. Oc.* **249** H16

Adavale, *Qnsld., Austral.* **215** U13
Adda, river, *It.* **152** E5
Ad Dahnā', *Asia* **168** G3
Ad Dakhla, *W. Sahara* **200** E5
Ad Dammām, *Saudi Arabia* **174** H12
Ad Dār al Ḥamrā', *Saudi Arabia* **174** H6
Ad Darb, *Saudi Arabia* **174** N8
Ad Dawādimī, *Saudi Arabia* **174** J9
Ad Dawḥah (Doha), *Qatar* **175** J13
Ad Dibdibah, region, *Iraq, Saudi Arabia* **174** H9
Ad Dilam, *Saudi Arabia* **174** K11
Ad Dīwānīyah, *Iraq* **174** E10
Addu Atoll, *Maldives* **181** X3
Ad Duwayd, *Saudi Arabia* **174** F8
Addy, *Wash., U.S.* **110** B8
Adel, *Ga., U.S.* **99** P6
Adel, *Iowa, U.S.* **107** P11
Adel, *Oreg., U.S.* **110** L6
Adelaide, *Bahamas* **122** B10
Adelaide, *S. Aust., Austral.* **215** X10
Adelaide Island, *Antarctica* **230** F5
Adelaide Peninsula, *Nunavut, Can.* **85** F14
Adelaide River, *N.T., Austral.* **215** P8
Adélfi, island, *Gr.* **157** G13
Adélie Coast, *Antarctica* **231** Q18
Aden, Gulf of, *Ind. Oc.* **168** J3
Aderbissinat, *Niger* **200** H12
'Ādhirīyāt, Jibāl al, *Jordan* **173** Q8
Adieu, Cape, *S. Aust., Austral.* **215** W8
Adige, river, *It.* **152** E7
Ādīgrat, *Eth.* **203** E15
Adilabad, *India* **180** L6
Adin, *Calif., U.S.* **110** M5
Adinkerke, *Belg.* **148** L10
Adirondack Mountains, *N.Y., U.S.* **96** G10
Ādīs Ābeba (Addis Ababa), *Eth.* **203** G15
Adıyaman, *Turk.* **171** H13
Adjud, *Rom.* **155** D16
Adjuntas, *P.R., U.S.* **122** N2
Adler, *Russ.* **159** U11
Admiralteystvo Rise, *Arctic Oc.* **247** E15
Admiralteystvo Trough, *Arctic Oc.* **247** D15
Admiralty Gulf, *Austral.* **214** B5
Admiralty Inlet, *Nunavut, Can.* **85** E16
Admiralty Inlet, *Wash., U.S.* **110** B4
Admiralty Island National Monument, *Alas., U.S.* **113** L22
Admiralty Islands, *P.N.G.* **217** B19
Admiralty Mountains, *Antarctica* **231** Q14
Adour, river, *Fr.* **149** X7
Adra, *Sp.* **146** M11
Adrano, *It.* **153** S11
Adrar, *Alg.* **200** D10
Adrar, region, *Mauritania* **200** F6
Adraskan, *Afghan.* **179** N2
Adria, *It.* **152** E8
Adrian, *Mich., U.S.* **101** N11
Adrian, *Minn., U.S.* **106** L9
Adrian, *Tex., U.S.* **104** G4
Adrianople see Edirne, *Turk.* **170** B3
Adriatic Sea, *Eur.* **140** K7
Adventure Trough, *Pac. Oc.* **249** Q19
Ādwa, *Eth.* **203** E15
Adyakit, Gora, *Russ.* **161** F14
Aegean Sea, *Eur.* **140** L10
Aegina see Aígina, island, *Gr.* **156** K12
Aegir Ridge, *Arctic Oc.* **247** J21
Aej, island, *Marshall Is., U.S.* **220** G8
Aeon Point, *Kiribati* **221** C24
Aewol, *S. Korea* **187** W7
Afaahiti, *Fr. Polynesia, Fr.* **223** P17
Afántou, *Gr.* **157** N20
Afar, region, *Eth.* **203** F15
Afareaitu, *Fr. Polynesia, Fr.* **223** N14
Afghanistan, *Asia* **179** N2
'Afīf, *Saudi Arabia* **174** K8
Afiq, *Israel* **172** K6
Afmadow, *Somalia* **203** K16
Afobaka, *Suriname* **131** E16
Afognak Island, *Alas., U.S.* **113** L15

Afono Bay, *Amer. Samoa, U.S.* **222** L8
Africana II Bank, *Ind. Oc.* **224** Q5
'Afrīn, *Syr.* **172** D8
Afşin, *Turk.* **170** G12
Afton, *Okla., U.S.* **104** E14
Afton, *Wyo., U.S.* **108** H8
Afuefuniya Point, *N. Mariana Is., U.S.* **220** E7
'Afula, *Israel* **172** L6
Afyonkarahisar, *Turk.* **170** F6
Áfytos, *Gr.* **156** D12
Agadez, *Niger* **200** G12
Agadir, *Mor.* **200** C7
Agaete, *Sp.* **208** Q5
Agafo Gumas, *Guam, U.S.* **220** B11
Agana see Hagåtña, *Guam, U.S.* **220** C10
Agana Bay, *Guam, U.S.* **220** C10
Agana Heights, *Guam, U.S.* **220** C10
Agano, river, *Japan* **188** M11
Aga Point, *Guam, U.S.* **220** E10
Agar, *India* **180** H5
Agartala, *India* **180** H13
Agassiz Fracture Zone, *Pac. Oc.* **243** P16
Agat, *Guam, U.S.* **220** D10
Agata, *Russ.* **161** G13
Agat Bay, *Guam, U.S.* **220** C10
Agate, *Colo., U.S.* **108** M14
Agate Fossil Beds National Monument, *Nebr., U.S.* **107** N1
Agathonísi, island, *Gr.* **157** K18
Agats, *Indonesia* **193** L20
Agatti Island, *India* **181** R2
Agattu Island, *Alas., U.S.* **112** L1
Agattu Strait, *Alas., U.S.* **112** L1
Agboville, *Côte d'Ivoire* **204** E9
Ağcabədi, *Azerb.* **171** E21
Ağdaş, *Azerb.* **171** D21
Agde, *Fr.* **149** Y11
Agde, Cap d', *Fr.* **149** Y11
Agen, *Fr.* **149** W8
Agfayan Bay, *Guam, U.S.* **220** E10
Aggtelek, *Hung.* **151** K16
Aghrījīt, *Mauritania* **200** G7
Agiá, *Gr.* **156** E11
Agía Galíni, *Gr.* **157** Q14
Agia Napa, *Cyprus* **162** P10
Agía Pelagía, *Gr.* **156** N11
Agía Roúmeli, *Gr.* **157** Q13
Agiásos, *Gr.* **157** G17
Agía Triáda, ruin, *Gr.* **157** Q14
Agidyem, island, *Marshall Is., U.S.* **220** L8
Agingan, Puntan, *N. Mariana Is., U.S.* **220** C4
Aginskoye, *Russ.* **161** L17
Ágion Óros, *Gr.* **157** D13
Ágion Óros (Athos, Mount), *Gr.* **157** D13
Ágios Efstrátios, *Gr.* **157** F14
Ágios Efstrátios, island, *Gr.* **157** F14
Ágios Eirínis, Akrotírio, *Gr.* **157** E15
Ágios Geórgios see Ro, island, *Gr.* **157** N22
Ágios Geórgios, island, *Gr.* **157** K13
Ágios Kírykos, *Gr.* **157** K17
Ágios Nikólaos, *Gr.* **157** Q16
Agíou Órous, Kólpos, *Gr.* **157** D13
Agness, *Oreg., U.S.* **110** K2
Agnew, *W. Aust., Austral.* **215** V4
Agnita, *Rom.* **155** D14
Agnone, *It.* **152** K11
Agra, *India* **180** G6
Agrakhan Peninsula, *Eur.* **140** H15
Agrakhanskiy Poluostrov, *Russ.* **159** T15
Agrakhanskiy Zaliv, *Russ.* **159** T15
Ágreda, *Sp.* **147** D13
Agrı, *Turk.* **171** E17
Ágria Gramvoúsa, island, *Gr.* **156** P12
Ağrı Dağı (Mount Ararat), *Turk.* **171** E18
Agrigento, *It.* **153** T10
Agrihan, island, *N. Mariana Is., U.S.* **220** A2
Agrínio, *Gr.* **156** H8
Agropoli, *It.* **153** N11
Agryz, *Russ.* **158** H16
Ağstafa, *Azerb.* **171** C19

Ağsu, *Azerb.* **171** D22
Aguada, *P.R., U.S.* **122** M1
Aguada de Pasajeros, *Cuba* **118** H8
Aguadilla, *P.R., U.S.* **122** M1
Aguadilla, Bahía de, *P.R., U.S.* **122** M1
Agua Fria National Monument, *Ariz., U.S.* **109** T7
Aguapeí, *Braz.* **132** J9
Agua Prieta, *Mex.* **116** C8
Aguas Blancas, *Chile* **134** E7
Aguascalientes, *Mex.* **116** G10
Águas Formosas, *Braz.* **133** K16
A Gudiña, *Sp.* **146** D7
Águeda, *Port.* **146** F5
Aguelhok, *Mali* **200** G10
Aguijan, island, *N. Mariana Is., U.S.* **220** C2
Aguila, *Ariz., U.S.* **109** T6
Águila, Punta, *P.R., U.S.* **122** P1
Aguila Fracture Zone, *Pac. Oc.* **243** M13
Aguilar, *Colo., U.S.* **109** P14
Aguilar de Campoo, *Sp.* **146** C10
Aguilas, *Sp.* **147** L13
Aguja, Cabo de la, *Col.* **130** B5
Aguja, Punta, *Peru* **132** F1
Agulhas, Cape, *S. Af.* **206** M8
Agulhas Bank, *Ind. Oc.* **224** M8
Agulhas Basin, *Ind. Oc.* **224** Q2
Agulhas Plateau, *Ind. Oc.* **224** N2
Agulhas Ridge, *Atl. Oc.* **241** U13
Aguni Jima, *Japan* **189** X1
Ahaggar (Hoggar), range, *Alg.* **200** E11
Ahar, *Iran* **174** B11
Ahe, island, *Fr. Polynesia, Fr.* **223** D18
Ahiri, *India* **180** L7
Ahlat, *Turk.* **171** F17
Ahlatlıbel, ruins, *Turk.* **170** E8
Ahmadabad, *India* **180** J3
Ahmadnagar, *India* **180** L4
Ahmadpur East, *Pak.* **179** S9
Ahmad Wal, *Pak.* **179** S5
Ahoa, *Wallis and Futuna, Fr.* **222** B11
Ahome, *Mex.* **116** E7
Ahoskie, *N.C., U.S.* **98** G13
Ahram, *Iran* **175** G13
Aḥrax Point, *Malta* **163** J21
Ahrensburg, *Ger.* **150** C8
Ahtme, *Est.* **143** J17
Ahua, *Fr. Polynesia, Fr.* **223** K20
Ahu-a-miria Islands, *Cook Is., N.Z.* **223** B18
Ahua 'Umi Heiau, *Hawai'i, U.S.* **115** M19
Ahumoa, peak, *Hawai'i, U.S.* **115** M19
Ahuna, Motu, *Fr. Polynesia, Fr.* **223** N13
Ahunui, island, *Fr. Polynesia, Fr.* **223** F20
Ahvāz, *Iran* **174** F11
Ahvenanmaa see Åland, island, *Fin.* **143** J14
Aḩwar, *Yemen* **174** R10
Ai, island, *Marshall Is., U.S.* **220** M7
Aïbak, *Afghan.* **178** L7
'Aiea, *Hawai'i, U.S.* **114** E11
Aigiáli, *Gr.* **157** L16
Aígina, *Gr.* **156** K12
Aígina (Aegina), island, *Gr.* **156** K12
Aígio, *Gr.* **156** H9
Aigle, *Switz.* **152** C2
Aigoual, Mount, *Fr.* **149** W11
Aiguá, *Uru.* **134** L14
Aigurande, *Fr.* **149** T9
Aikawa, *Japan* **188** M11
Aiken, *S.C., U.S.* **98** L8
Ailinginae Atoll, *Marshall Is., U.S.* **220** F3
Ailinglapalap Atoll, *Marshall Is., U.S.* **220** H4
Ailsa Craig, *Gibraltar, U.K.* **163** P23
Ailsa Craig, *Scot., U.K.* **145** N8
Ailuk Atoll, *Marshall Is., U.S.* **220** F4
Aimere, *Indonesia* **193** M13
Ainaži, *Latv.* **143** K16
Aineman, island, *Marshall Is., U.S.* **220** M8
Aînhoa, *Fr.* **149** Y5
Aínos, Óros, *Gr.* **156** J7

Aínsa, *Sp.* **147** C15
'Aïn Sefra, *Alg.* **200** B10
Ainsworth, *Nebr., U.S.* **107** N5
Aiquile, *Bol.* **132** K7
Aiquina, *Chile* **134** D8
Airal, *Palau* **220** N11
Airão, *Braz.* **132** D8
Air Force Island, *Nunavut, Can.* **85** F17
Aïr Massif, *Niger* **200** G12
Airolo, *Switz.* **152** C4
Aisey, *Fr.* **149** R12
Ai Shan, *Shand., China* **184** F11
Aisými, *Gr.* **157** B16
Aitape, *P.N.G.* **217** C18
Aitkin, *Minn., U.S.* **106** G11
Aitoliko, *Gr.* **156** H8
Aitutaki, island, *Cook Is., N.Z.* **222** P11
Aitutaki Atoll, *Cook Is., N.Z.* **218** K12
Aiud, *Rom.* **155** D13
Aiurua, Passe, *Fr. Polynesia, Fr.* **223** Q18
Aix, Île d', *Fr.* **149** T6
Aix-en-Provence, *Fr.* **149** X13
Aixirivall, *Andorra* **162** K2
Aix-les-Bains, *Fr.* **149** U14
Aiyon Mount, *Palau* **220** M12
Aiyura, *P.N.G.* **217** D19
Aizawl, *India* **180** H14
Aizenay, *Fr.* **149** S5
Aizpute, *Latv.* **143** M15
Aizuwakamatsu, *Japan* **188** M12
Ajaccio, *Fr.* **152** K4
Ajaccio, Golfe d', *Fr.* **152** K3
Ajajú, river, *Col.* **130** H6
Ajajú, river, *N. Amer.* **82** R10
Ajaria, republic, *Rep. of Georgia* **171** C16
Ajax Peak, *Idaho, Mont., U.S.* **108** E6
Ajayan Bay, *Guam, U.S.* **220** E10
Aj Bogd Uul, *Mongolia* **182** E7
Ajdābiyā, *Lib.* **201** C15
Ajjer, Tassili-n-, *Alg.* **200** E10
'Ajlūn, *Jordan* **172** L6
'Ajmān, *U.A.E.* **175** J15
Ajmer, *India* **180** G4
Ajo, *Ariz., U.S.* **109** V6
Ajo, Cabo de, *Sp.* **146** B11
Ajokwola, island, *Marshall Is., U.S.* **220** G10
Ajoupa-Bouillon, *Martinique, Fr.* **123** E22
Ajrestān, *Afghan.* **179** N6
Akabira, *Japan* **188** F13
Akademel Nauk Rise, *Pac. Oc.* **242** D8
Akaiami, island, *Cook Is., N.Z.* **222** Q12
Akaki, *Cyprus* **162** P8
Akamaru, island, *Fr. Polynesia, Fr.* **223** R21
Akankohan, *Japan* **188** F15
Akanthou (Akatu), *Cyprus* **162** N9
Akashi, *Japan* **189** Q8
Akaska, *S. Dak., U.S.* **106** J5
Akatu see Akanthou, *Cyprus* **162** N9
Akbulak, *Russ.* **160** J7
Akçaabat, *Turk.* **171** D14
Akçadağ, *Turk.* **170** G12
Akçakale, *Turk.* **171** J13
Akçakışla, *Turk.* **170** E11
Akçakoca, *Turk.* **170** C7
Akçay, *Turk.* **170** E3
Akçay, *Turk.* **170** J5
Akchâr, region, *Mauritania* **200** F5
Akdağ, peak, *Turk.* **170** F2
Akdağ, peak, *Turk.* **170** J7
Ak Dağlar, peak, *Turk.* **170** J5
Akdağmadeni, *Turk.* **170** E11
Akdoğan see Lysi, *Cyprus* **162** P9
Akelay, *Minn., U.S.* **106** G10
Akera, river, *Azerb.* **171** E20
Aketi, *Dem. Rep. of the Congo* **202** J10
Akhalts' ikhe, *Rep. of Georgia* **171** C17

Aínsa, *Sp.* **147** C15
Akḫḏar, Jabal al, *Af.* **198** D7
Akhiok, *Alas., U.S.* **113** M15
Akhisar, *Turk.* **170** F3
Akhnur, *India* **179** N12
Akhtuba, river, *Kaz.* **176** E4
Akhtuba, river, *Russ.* **159** Q14
Akhtubinsk, *Russ.* **159** Q14
Aki, *Japan* **189** R7
Akiachak, *Alas., U.S.* **112** J12
Akiaki, island, *Fr. Polynesia, Fr.* **223** F21
Akimiski Island, *Nunavut, Can.* **85** M17
Akita, *Japan* **188** K12
Akitua, island, *Cook Is., N.Z.* **222** Q11
Akjoujt, *Mauritania* **200** F5
Akkeshi, *Japan* **188** G15
Akkeshi Wan, *Japan* **188** G15
'Akko (Acre), *Israel* **172** K5
Akkuş, *Turk.* **170** D12
Aklavik, *N.W.T., Can.* **84** E9
Aklera, *India* **180** H5
'Ako'ako'a Point, *Hawai'i, U.S.* **115** K19
Akobo, *S. Sudan* **203** G13
Ākobo, river, *Af.* **203** G13
Akola, *India* **180** K5
Ak'ordat, *Eritrea* **203** E14
Akosombo Dam, *Ghana* **204** E11
Akpatok Island, *Nunavut, Can.* **85** J19
Akqi, *China* **182** E2
Akranes, *Ice.* **142** E2
Akráta, *Gr.* **156** J10
Akron, *Colo., U.S.* **108** L15
Akron, *Iowa, U.S.* **106** M8
Akron, *Ohio, U.S.* **101** P14
Akrotíri, *Gr.* **157** N15
Akrotiri Bay, *Cyprus* **162** Q7
Akrotiri (Western) Sovereign Base Area, *U.K.* **162** Q7
Aksai Chin see Aksayqin, region, *China* **180** B7
Akşehir, *Turk.* **170** G7
Akşehir Gölü, *Turk.* **170** G7
Akseki, *Turk.* **170** H7
Aksu, *China* **182** E3
Aksu, *Kaz.* **176** J6
Aksu, river, *Turk.* **170** H6
Āksum, *Eth.* **203** E15
Aktag, peak, *China* **182** H4
Aktivneset Slope, *Atl. Oc.* **240** F12
Akune, *Japan* **189** S4
Akureyri, *Ice.* **142** E3
Akuseki Shima, *Japan* **189** V3
Akutan, *Alas., U.S.* **112** N10
Akyab see Sittwe, *Myanmar* **190** H4
Akyaka, *Turk.* **171** D17
Akyazı, *Turk.* **170** D6
Ala, *It.* **152** D6
Alà, Monti di, *It.* **152** M4
Alabama, *U.S.* **103** K15
Alabama, river, *Ala., U.S.* **103** M14
Alabaster, *Ala., U.S.* **103** K15
Alaca, *Turk.* **170** E10
Alaca Dağ, peak, *Turk.* **170** H7
Alacahöyük, ruins, *Turk.* **170** E10
Alaçam, *Turk.* **170** C10
Alacant see Alicante, *Sp.* **147** J14
Alachua, *Fla., U.S.* **99** R7
Alacránes, Arrecife, *Mex.* **117** G16
Aladağ, peak, *Turk.* **170** G7
Aladağ, peak, *Turk.* **170** H10
Alaejos, *Sp.* **146** E9
Al Aflāj, region, *Saudi Arabia* **174** L10
Alagir, *Russ.* **159** U13
Alagoinhas, *Braz.* **133** H17
Alagón, *Sp.* **147** D14
Al Aḥmadī, *Kuwait* **174** G11
Al Ain, *U.A.E.* **175** K15
Alaja, *Turkm.* **176** L6
Alajuela, *C.R.* **117** N19
Alaka'i Swamp, *Hawai'i, U.S.* **114** B5
Alakanuk, *Alas., U.S.* **112** H12

Al Akhḍar, *Saudi Arabia* **174** G6
Alakoko Fishpond, *Hawai'i, U.S.* **114** C6
Alaköl, lake, *Asia* **168** F8
'Alalakeiki Channel, *Hawai'i, U.S.* **115** J16
Alalakh, ruins, *Turk.* **170** J11
Alamagan, island, *N. Mariana Is., U.S.* **220** B2
Al 'Amārah, *Iraq* **174** E11
Alameda, *Calif., U.S.* **III** S3
Alameda Gardens, *Gibraltar, U.K.* **163** P23
Alamo, *Nev., U.S.* **III** S12
Alamo, *Tenn., U.S.* **102** F12
Alamogordo, *N. Mex., U.S.* **109** U13
Alamo Heights, *Tex., U.S.* **105** R9
Alamosa, *Colo., U.S.* **109** P12
Åland (Ahvenanmaa), island, *Fin.* **143** J14
Alandar, *Afghan.* **178** M4
Åland Islands, *Eur.* **140** D9
Alandroal, *Port.* **146** J6
Alanya, *Turk.* **170** J7
Alao, *Amer. Samoa, U.S.* **222** M9
Alaotra, Lac, *Madagascar* **207** F18
Alappuzha (Alleppey), *India* **181** R5
Al 'Aqabah (Aqaba), *Jordan* **173** R5
'Alāqadārī Bālā Bulūk, *Afghan.* **179** P2
'Alāqahdārī Shāh Jōy, *Afghan.* **179** P6
'Alāqahdārī-ye Almār, *Afghan.* **178** L4
Al 'Aqīq, *Saudi Arabia* **174** L8
Alara, river, *Turk.* **170** J7
Alarcón, Embalse de, *Sp.* **146** G12
Al 'Armah, plateau, *Saudi Arabia* **174** H10
Al Arṭāwīyah, *Saudi Arabia* **174** H9
Al 'Āş (Orontes), river, *Syr.* **172** F7
Al As'ad, *Saudi Arabia* **174** G6
Alaşehir, *Turk.* **170** F4
Al Ashkharah, *Oman* **175** L17
Alaska, *U.S.* **113** G16
Alaska, Gulf of, *Alas., U.S.* **113** L18
Alaska Highway, *Alas., U.S.* **113** G18
Alaska Peninsula, *Alas., U.S.* **113** M13
Alaska Plain, *Pac. Oc.* **243** C15
Alaska Range, *Alas., U.S.* **113** H16
Alassio, *It.* **152** G3
Älät, *Azerb.* **171** E23
Alataw Shan, *China, Kaz.* **182** D3
Alatyr', *Russ.* **158** K13
Alausí, *Ecua.* **130** K3
Alava, Cape, *Wash., U.S.* **110** B1
Alaverdi, *Arm.* **171** D18
'Alawīyīn, Jabal al, *Syr.* **172** F7
Alazani, river, *Rep. of Georgia* **171** C20
Alba, *It.* **152** F3
Al Bāb, *Syr.* **172** D9
Albac, *Rom.* **154** D12
Albacete, *Sp.* **147** H13
Al Bad', *Saudi Arabia* **174** G5
Alba de Tormes, *Sp.* **146** F9
Al Badī', *Saudi Arabia* **174** L10
Al Bāḩah, *Saudi Arabia* **174** M8
Alba Iulia, *Rom.* **155** D13
Albanel, Lac, *Que., Can.* **85** M19
Albania, *Eur.* **154** K10
Al'banov Bank, *Arctic Oc.* **247** D14
Albany, *Ga., U.S.* **99** P5
Albany, *Ky., U.S.* **103** D17
Albany, *Mo., U.S.* **107** R11
Albany, *N.Y., U.S.* **96** K11
Albany, *Oreg., U.S.* **110** G3
Albany, *Tex., U.S.* **104** L8
Albany, *W. Aust., Austral.* **215** Y3
Albany, river, *N. Amer.* **82** G7
Albany, river, *Ont., Can.* **85** N17
Al Bardī, *Lib.* **201** C17
Albardón, *Arg.* **134** J8
Albarracín, *Sp.* **147** F13
Al Başrah (Basra), *Iraq* **174** F11
Albatross Bay, *Austral.* **214** B12
Albatross Plateau, *Pac. Oc.* **243** H19
Al Bayāḍ, plain, *Saudi Arabia* **174** L10
Al Bayḍā' (Beida), *Lib.* **201** B16

Albemarle, Punta, *Ecua.* **130** P9
Albemarle Sound, *N.C., U.S.* **98** G14
Albenga, *It.* **152** G3
Albereto, *It.* **163** K17
Alberobello, *It.* **152** M14
Albert, Lake, *Austral.* **214** L11
Albert, Lake, *Dem. Rep. of the Congo, Uganda* **202** J12
Alberta, *Can.* **84** L10
Albert Lea, *Minn., U.S.* **106** L11
Albert Nile, river, *Af.* **203** J13
Albert Town, *Bahamas* **119** H14
Albert Town, *Jam.* **122** H8
Albertville, *Ala., U.S.* **103** H16
Albertville, *Fr.* **149** U14
Albi, *Fr.* **149** X9
Albia, *Iowa, U.S.* **107** Q12
Albin, *Wyo., U.S.* **108** K14
Albina Point, *Af.* **198** M5
Albini, river, *It.* **163** H14
Albinia, *It.* **152** J7
Albion, *Ill., U.S.* **101** T7
Albion, *Mich., U.S.* **100** M11
Albion, *N.Y., U.S.* **96** H6
Albion, *Nebr., U.S.* **107** P7
Albion Downs, *Qnsld., Austral.* **215** S12
Al Bi'r, *Saudi Arabia* **174** G5
Al Birk, *Saudi Arabia* **174** N8
Alborán, Isla de, *Sp.* **146** N11
Alboran Sea, *Sp.* **146** N10
Ålborg, *Den.* **142** M11
Albox, *Sp.* **146** L12
Albuquerque, *N. Mex., U.S.* **109** S12
Alburquerque, *Sp.* **146** H7
Albury, *N.S.W., Austral.* **215** Y13
Alby, *Fr.* **149** U14
Alcácer do Sal, *Port.* **146** J5
Alcalá de Guadaíra, *Sp.* **146** L8
Alcalá de Henares, *Sp.* **146** F11
Alcalá la Real, *Sp.* **146** L10
Alcamo, *It.* **153** S9
Alcanar, *Sp.* **147** F15
Alcañiz, *Sp.* **147** E15
Alcántara, *Sp.* **146** G7
Alcántara, Embalse de, *Sp.* **146** G7
Alcaraz, *Sp.* **146** J12
Alcaudete, *Sp.* **146** L10
Alcázar de San Juan, *Sp.* **146** H11
Alchevs'k, *Ukr.* **159** Q10
Alcoa, *Tenn., U.S.* **103** F18
Alcoak, Cerro, *Arg.* **134** D8
Alcobaça, *Port.* **146** G5
Alcobendas, *Sp.* **146** F11
Alcock Rise, *Ind. Oc.* **225** E12
Alcoi *see* Alcoy, *Sp.* **147** J14
Alcoota, *N.T., Austral.* **215** T9
Alcorcón, *Sp.* **146** F11
Alcoutim, *Port.* **146** L6
Alcoy, *Sp.* **147** J14
Alcubierre, Sierra de, *Sp.* **147** D14
Alcúdia, *Sp.* **147** G18
Alcuéscar, *Sp.* **146** H8
Aldabra Islands, *Af.* **198** L12
Aldama, *Mex.* **116** D9
Al-Damir, *Sudan* **203** D13
Aldan, *Russ.* **161** J18
Aldan, river, *Asia* **168** D11
Aldan, river, *Russ.* **161** G18
Aldanskoye Nagor'ye, *Russ.* **161** J18
Aldeadávila de la Ribera, *Sp.* **146** E7
Aldeburgh, *Eng., U.K.* **145** U16
Alderney, island, *Channel Is., U.K.* **145** Y12
Aledo, *Ill., U.S.* **101** P3
Aleg, *Mauritania* **200** G5
Alegranza, island, *Sp.* **208** P7
Alegrete, *Braz.* **132** P10
Alejandro Selkirk Island, *S. Amer.* **128** M2
Aleksandrov Gay, *Russ.* **159** N15
Aleksandrovsk Sakhalinskiy, *Russ.* **161** J21
Alekseyevka, *Russ.* **158** L14
Alekseyevka, *Russ.* **158** L16
Alekseyevka, *Russ.* **159** N10
Aleksin, *Russ.* **158** K10
Aleksinac, *Serb.* **154** H11
Alemania, *Arg.* **134** F9
Alembel, island, *Marshall Is., U.S.* **220** H8

Alençon, *Fr.* **149** Q7
Alenquer, *Braz.* **132** D11
'Alenuihāhā Channel, *Hawai'i, U.S.* **115** J18
Aleppo *see* Ḩalab, *Syr.* **172** D9
Aléria, *Fr.* **152** K4
Ales, *It.* **153** P3
Alès, *Fr.* **149** W12
Alessandria, *It.* **152** E4
Ålesund, *Nor.* **142** H10
Aleutian Basin, *Pac. Oc.* **242** B11
Aleutian Islands, *Alas., U.S.* **112** N5
Aleutian Range, *Alas., U.S.* **113** M14
Aleutian Ridge, *Pac. Oc.* **242** C11
Aleutian Trench, *Pac. Oc.* **242** C10
Alevina, Mys, *Russ.* **161** F21
Alexander, *N. Dak., U.S.* **106** F2
Alexander, Cape, *Solomon Is.* **221** K15
Alexander Archipelago, *Alas., U.S.* **113** M22
Alexander Bay, *S. Af.* **206** K6
Alexander City, *Ala., U.S.* **103** K16
Alexander Island, *Antarctica* **230** F6
Alexandra, *N.Z.* **217** Q16
Alexandra, Zemlya, *Russ.* **160** B12
Alexándreia, *Gr.* **156** C10
Alexandria, *Ind., U.S.* **101** Q9
Alexandria, *Jam.* **122** H8
Alexandria, *La., U.S.* **102** N8
Alexandria, *Minn., U.S.* **106** H9
Alexandria, *Rom.* **155** G15
Alexandria, *S. Dak., U.S.* **106** L7
Alexandria, *Va., U.S.* **98** D12
Alexandria *see* El Iskandarîya, *Egypt* **201** C18
Alexandria Bay, *N.Y., U.S.* **96** G9
Alexandrina, Lake, *Austral.* **214** L11
Alexandroúpoli (Dedéagach), *Gr.* **157** C16
Aleysk, *Russ.* **160** L11
Al Fallūjah (Fallujah), *Iraq* **174** E9
Al Farciya, *W. Sahara* **200** D7
Alfaro, *Sp.* **147** D13
Alfatar, *Bulg.* **155** G17
Al Fāw, *Iraq* **174** F11
Alföld, plain, *Hung.* **151** L16
Al Fuqahā', *Lib.* **201** D14
Al Furāt (Euphrates), river, *Iraq* **174** E10
Algarrobal, *Arg.* **134** F10
Algarrobo, *Chile* **134** G6
Algeciras, *Sp.* **146** N8
Algeciras, Bahía de *see* Gibraltar, Bay of, *Gibraltar, U.K.* **163** N21
Alger (Algiers), *Alg.* **200** A11
Algeria, *Af.* **200** D10
Algerian Basin, *Atl. Oc.* **240** J12
Algha, *Kaz.* **176** D8
Alghabas, *Kaz.* **176** D6
Al Ghaydah, *Yemen* **175** P13
Al Ghayl, *Saudi Arabia* **174** K10
Al Ghazālah, *Saudi Arabia* **174** H8
Alghero, *It.* **152** M3
Alghiena, *Eritrea* **203** D15
Algiers *see* Alger, *Alg.* **200** A11
Alginet, *Sp.* **147** H14
Algoa Bay, *Af.* **198** Q8
Algoma, *Wis., U.S.* **100** J7
Algona, *Iowa, U.S.* **106** M11
Algorta, *Uru.* **134** K13
Al Ḩadīdah, crater, *Saudi Arabia* **174** L12
Al Ḩaffah, *Syr.* **172** E7
Al Ḩamād, plain, *Jordan, Saudi Arabia* **174** E7
Alhambra, *Calif., U.S.* **III** X8
Al Ḩamīdīyah, *Syr.* **172** G7
Al Ḩamrā', *Saudi Arabia* **174** K6
Al Ḩamrā', region, *Lib.* **201** C13
Al Ḩanākīyah, *Saudi Arabia* **174** J7
Al Ḩarīq, *Saudi Arabia* **174** K10
Al Harūj al Aswad, range, *Lib.* **201** D15
Al Ḩasakah, *Syr.* **172** D14
Al Ḩawrah, *Yemen* **174** Q11
Al Ḩījānah, *Syr.* **172** K8
Al Ḩijāz (Hejaz), region, *Saudi Arabia* **174** H6

Al Ḩillah, *Iraq* **174** E9
Al Ḩillah, *Saudi Arabia* **174** K10
Alhucemas, Peñón de, *Sp.* **146** P10
Al Ḩudaydah, *Yemen* **174** Q8
Al Hufūf, *Saudi Arabia* **174** J12
Alī, *It.* **153** S12
Aliabad, *Iran* **175** G15
Aliákmonas, river, *Gr.* **156** D10
Alibates Flint Quarries National Monument, *Tex., U.S.* **104** G5
Alicante (Alacant), *Sp.* **147** J14
Alice, *Qnsld., Austral.* **215** T13
Alice, *Tex., U.S.* **105** U10
Alice, Punta, *It.* **153** P14
Alice Springs, *N.T., Austral.* **215** S9
Alice Town, *Bahamas* **122** B7
Alice Town, *Bahamas* **122** D5
Aliceville, *Ala., U.S.* **103** K13
Alicudi, Isola, *It.* **153** R11
Aligarh, *India* **180** F6
'Ālika Cone, *Hawai'i, U.S.* **115** P19
Al Ikhwān (The Brothers), islands, *Yemen* **175** R14
Alindau, *Indonesia* **193** J13
Alingsås, *Sw.* **142** L12
Alipur, *Pak.* **179** S9
Alipur Duar, *India* **180** G12
Aliquippa, *Pa., U.S.* **96** N3
Al 'Irqah, *Yemen* **174** R11
Alişar Hüyük, ruins, *Turk.* **170** E10
Al 'Īsāwīyah, *Saudi Arabia* **174** F6
Alissós, *Gr.* **156** J9
Alistráti, *Gr.* **157** B13
Alivéri, *Gr.* **157** H13
Aliwal North, *S. Af.* **206** L10
Al Jafr, *Jordan* **173** Q7
Al Jāfūrah, desert, *Saudi Arabia* **174** J12
Al Jaghbūb, *Lib.* **201** C16
Al Jahrā', *Kuwait* **174** G10
Al Jawādīyah, *Syr.* **172** C15
Al Jawf, *Lib.* **201** E16
Al Jawf *see* Dawmat al Jandal, *Saudi Arabia* **174** F7
Al Jifārah, *Saudi Arabia* **174** K10
Al-Jinayna, *Sudan* **202** E10
Al Jīzah, *Jordan* **172** M7
Al Jubayl, *Saudi Arabia* **174** H12
Al Jumaylīyah, *Qatar* **175** J13
Al Junaynah, *Saudi Arabia* **174** M8
Al Kahfah, *Saudi Arabia* **174** H9
Al Karak, *Jordan* **173** N6
Al Kawm, *Syr.* **172** F11
Al Khābūrah, *Oman* **175** K16
Al Khalīl (Hebron), *W. Bank* **173** N5
Al Kharfah, *Saudi Arabia* **174** L10
Al Kharj, *Saudi Arabia* **174** K11
Al Khāşirah, *Saudi Arabia* **174** K9
Al Khawr, *Qatar* **175** J13
Al Khīrān, *Kuwait* **174** G11
Al Khufayfīyah, *Saudi Arabia* **174** J9
Al Khums, *Lib.* **201** B14
Al Khunn, *Saudi Arabia* **174** K12
Al Khuraybah, *Yemen* **174** Q11
Al Khurmah, *Saudi Arabia* **174** L8
Al Kiswah, *Syr.* **172** J7
Al Kūfah (Kufah), *Iraq* **174** E9
Al Kufrah (Kufra Oasis), *Lib.* **201** E16
Al Kūt, *Iraq* **174** E10
Al Kuwayt (Kuwait City), *Kuwait* **174** G11
Al Lādhiqīyah (Latakia), *Syr.* **172** F7
Allagash, river, *Me., U.S.* **97** B16
Allahabad, *India* **180** H8
Allahüekber Tepe, peak, *Turk.* **171** D17
Al Lajā, *Syr.* **172** K7
Allakaket, *Alas., U.S.* **113** E16
All American Canal, *Calif., U.S.* **III** Z12
Allan Hills, *Antarctica* **231** N14
Allan Mountain, *Idaho, U.S.* **108** E5
Allanmyo, *Myanmar* **190** J5
Allanton, *N.Z.* **217** Q16
Allaríz, *Sp.* **146** C6
Allegan, *Mich., U.S.* **100** M9
Allegheny, river, *U.S.* **96** L5
Allegheny Mountains, *U.S.* **87** G19
Allegheny Reservoir, *Pa., U.S.* **96** L5

Allègre, Pointe, *Guadeloupe, Fr.* **123** E14
Allen, *Arg.* **135** P8
Allen, Bog of, *Ire.* **145** S6
Allen, Lough, *Ire.* **145** Q5
Allendale, *S.C., U.S.* **98** M9
Allendale Town, *Eng., U.K.* **145** P11
Allende, *Mex.* **116** D11
Allentown, *Pa., U.S.* **96** N9
Alleppey *see* Alappuzha, *India* **181** R5
Aller, river, *Ger.* **150** D8
Allerona, *It.* **152** J8
Alliance, *Nebr., U.S.* **107** N2
Alliance, *Ohio, U.S.* **101** P15
Al Lidām, *Saudi Arabia* **174** M9
Alligator Pond, *Jam.* **122** K7
Allinge, *Den.* **143** N13
Allison Peninsula, *Antarctica* **230** H6
Al Līth, *Saudi Arabia* **174** M7
All Saints, *Antigua and Barbuda* **123** B21
Al Luḩayyah, *Yemen* **174** P8
Al Luwaymī, *Saudi Arabia* **174** G8
Alma, *Ark., U.S.* **102** F6
Alma, *Ga., U.S.* **99** P7
Alma, *Kans., U.S.* **107** S9
Alma, *Mich., U.S.* **100** L11
Alma, *Nebr., U.S.* **107** R5
Almacelles, *Sp.* **147** D15
Almada, *Port.* **146** J4
Almaden, *Qnsld., Austral.* **215** R13
Almadén, *Sp.* **146** J9
Al Madīnah (Medina), *Saudi Arabia* **174** J7
Al Mafraq, *Jordan* **172** L7
Al Majma'ah, *Saudi Arabia* **174** J10
Al Mālikīyah, *Syr.* **172** C16
Al Manāmah (Manama), *Bahrain* **174** J12
Almanor, Lake, *Calif., U.S.* **III** N5
Almansa, *Sp.* **147** J14
Al Manşūrah, *Syr.* **172** E11
Almanzor, peak, *Sp.* **146** F9
Al Marj, *Lib.* **201** C16
Al Ma'shūqah, *Saudi Arabia* **174** M8
Almaty, *Kaz.* **177** H16
Al Mawşil (Mosul), *Iraq* **174** C9
Al Mayādīn, *Syr.* **172** G13
Al Mayyāh, *Saudi Arabia* **174** G9
Almazán, *Sp.* **146** E12
Almeida, *Port.* **146** F7
Almeirim, *Braz.* **132** D12
Almeirim, *Port.* **146** H5
Almelo, *Neth.* **148** H14
Almena, *Kans., U.S.* **107** R5
Almenara, *Braz.* **133** J16
Almenara, peak, *Sp.* **146** J12
Almendra, Embalse de, *Sp.* **146** E8
Almendralejo, *Sp.* **146** J8
Almere, *Neth.* **148** J12
Almería, *Sp.* **146** M12
Almería, Golfo de, *Sp.* **146** M12
Al'met'yevsk, *Russ.* **158** J16
Almina, Punta, *Sp.* **146** N9
Al Mintirib, *Oman* **175** K16
Almira, *Wash., U.S.* **110** C7
Almirantazgo, Seno, *Chile* **135** X8
Almirante, *Pan.* **117** N20
Almirante Brown Canyon, *Atl. Oc.* **241** U6
Al Mismīyah, *Syr.* **172** K7
Almo, *Idaho, U.S.* **108** J6
Almodôvar, *Port.* **146** K5
Almodóvar del Campo, *Sp.* **146** J10
Al Mubarraz, *Saudi Arabia* **174** J12
Al Mudawwarah, *Jordan* **173** S7
Almudévar, *Sp.* **147** D14
Al Mukallā, *Yemen* **174** Q12
Al Mukhā, *Yemen* **174** R8
Almuñécar, *Sp.* **146** M11
Almus, *Turk.* **170** E12
Almus Barajı, *Turk.* **170** D12
Al Muwassam, *Saudi Arabia* **174** P8
Al Muwayh, *Saudi Arabia* **174** K8
Almyrós, *Gr.* **156** F11
Alney, Gora, *Russ.* **161** F22
Alnwick, *Eng., U.K.* **145** N12
Alo, *Wallis and Futuna, Fr.* **222** E11
Alo, Pointe d', *Wallis and Futuna, Fr.* **222** E11
Alofau, *Amer. Samoa, U.S.* **222** M8

Alofi, *Cook Is., N.Z.* **223** B2O
Alofi Bay, *Cook Is., N.Z.* **223** B2O
Alofi, Île, *Wallis and Futuna, Fr.* **222** FII
Alokan, island, *Solomon Is.* **221** NI8
Along, *India* **180** FI5
Alónnisos, *Gr.* **156** FI2
Alónnisos, island, *Gr.* **156** FI2
Alor, island, *Indonesia* **193** MI5
Alor, Kepulauan, *Indonesia* **193** MI5
Álora, *Sp.* **146** M9
Alor Setar, *Malaysia* **191** S9
Alotau, *P.N.G.* **215** NI5
Aloysius, Mount, *Austral.* **214** G7
Alpena, *Mich., U.S.* **100** HI2
Alpha, *Qnsld., Austral.* **215** TI3
Alpha Ridge, *Arctic Oc.* **246** KI2
Alpine, *Ariz., U.S.* **109** T9
Alpine, *Tex., U.S.* **105** Q2
Alpine Junction, *Wyo., U.S.* **108** H8
Alps, *Eur.* **140** J6
Al Qābil, *Oman* **175** KI5
Al Qaḍīmah, *Saudi Arabia* **174** K6
Al Qadmūs, *Syr.* **172** G7
Al Qā'im, *Iraq* **174** D8
Al Qaṭīyah, *Saudi Arabia* **174** J9
Al Qāmishlī, *Syr.* **172** CI4
Al Qārah, *Yemen* **174** R9
Al Qaryah ash Sharqīyah, *Lib.* **201** CI3
Al Qaryatayn, *Syr.* **172** H9
Al Qaşīm, region, *Saudi Arabia* **174** H9
Al Qaţīf, *Saudi Arabia* **174** HI2
Al Qaţrānah, *Jordan* **173** N7
Al Qaţrūn, *Lib.* **201** EI4
Al Qayşūmah, *Saudi Arabia* **174** GIO
Alqueva, Barragem de, *Port.* **146** J6
Al Qunayṭirah (El Quneitra), *Syr.* **172** K6
Al Qunfudhah, *Saudi Arabia* **174** M7
Al Qurayyāt, *Saudi Arabia* **174** E6
Al Qurnah, *Iraq* **174** FII
Al Quşayr, *Syr.* **172** G8
Al Quşūrīyah, *Saudi Arabia* **174** K9
Al Quţayfah, *Syr.* **172** J8
Al Quway'īyah, *Saudi Arabia* **174** KIO
Al Quwayrah, *Jordan* **173** R5
Alroy Downs, *N.T., Austral.* **215** RIO
Alsace, region, *Fr.* **149** QI5
Alsancak see Karavas, *Cyprus* **162** N8
Alsask, *Sask., Can.* **84** MII
Alsasua, *Sp.* **146** BI2
Alston, *Eng., U.K.* **145** PII
Alta, *Iowa, U.S.* **107** N9
Alta, *Nor.* **143** BI4
Alta Floresta, *Braz.* **132** GIO
Alta Gracia, *Arg.* **134** JIO
Altagracia, *Venez.* **130** B7
Altagracia de Orituco, *Venez.* **130** CIO
Altamaha, river, *Ga., U.S.* **99** P8
Altamira, *Braz.* **132** DI2
Altamira, *Chile* **134** F7
Altamura, *It.* **152** MI3
Altan Xiret see Ejin Horo Qi, *N. Mongol, China* **184** D2
Altar Desert, *N. Amer.* **82** K3
Altata, *Mex.* **116** F8
Altavista, *Va., U.S.* **98** FII
Altay, *China* **182** C6
Altay, *Mongolia* **182** D8
Altay Mountains, *Asia* **168** F8
Altayskiy, *Russ.* **160** LI2
Alt del Griu, peak, *Andorra* **162** J4
Altdorf, *Switz.* **152** B4
Altea, *Sp.* **147** JI5
Altenburg, *Ger.* **150** F9
Alter do Chão, *Port.* **146** H6
Altıağac, *Azerb.* **171** C22
Altınekin, *Turk.* **170** G8
Altıntaş, *Turk.* **170** F5
Altınyayla, *Turk.* **170** H5
Altiplano, region, *S. Amer.* **128** G4
Altmühl, river, *Ger.* **150** J8
Altnaharra, *Scot., U.K.* **144** H9
Alto, *Tex., U.S.* **105** NI4
Alto Araguaia, *Braz.* **132** KII
Alto Garças, *Braz.* **132** JII
Alto Molócuè, *Mozambique* **207** EI4

Alton, *Ill., U.S.* **101** S4
Altona, *Virgin Is., U.S.* **122** N9
Altona Lagoon, *Virgin Is., U.S.* **122** Q3
Altoona, *Pa., U.S.* **96** N5
Alto Paraguai, *Braz.* **132** JIO
Alto Parnaíba, *Braz.* **133** GI4
Alto Purús, river, *S. Amer.* **132** G5
Alto Río Senguerr, *Arg.* **135** S7
Altunhisar, *Turk.* **170** G9
Altun Shan, *Asia* **168** G8
Altun Shan, peak, *China* **182** G7
Alturas, *Calif., U.S.* **110** L5
Altus, *Okla., U.S.* **104** H8
Al 'Ubaylah, *Saudi Arabia* **174** LI2
Alucra, *Turk.* **171** EI3
Al 'Ulá, *Saudi Arabia* **174** H6
Alula-Fartak Trough, *Ind. Oc.* **224** D7
Al'Unnāb, site, *Jordan* **173** R8
Al 'Uqaylah, *Lib.* **201** CI5
Alushta, *Ukr.* **159** T8
Aluta, *Dem. Rep. of the Congo* **202** KII
Al 'Uwaynāt, *Lib.* **201** EI3
Al 'Uwaynid, *Saudi Arabia* **174** JIO
Al 'Uwayqīlah, *Saudi Arabia* **174** F8
Al 'Uyūn, *Saudi Arabia* **174** J7
Alva, *Okla., U.S.* **104** E9
Alvarado, *Tex., U.S.* **104** MII
Älvdalen, *Sw.* **142** JI2
Alverca do Ribatejo, *Port.* **146** H4
Alvesta, *Sw.* **143** MI3
Alvin, *Tex., U.S.* **105** RI4
Älvkarleby, *Sw.* **143** JI3
Alvorada, *Braz.* **133** HI3
Alvord, *Tex., U.S.* **104** KIO
Alvord Desert, *Oreg., U.S.* **110** K8
Alvord Lake, *Oreg., U.S.* **110** K8
Älvsbyn, *Sw.* **143** EI4
Al Wajh, *Saudi Arabia* **174** H5
Al Wannān, *Saudi Arabia* **174** HII
Alwar, *India* **180** F5
Al Wuday'ah, *Saudi Arabia* **174** PII
Alxa Gaoyuan, *China* **182** G9
Alyangula, *N.T., Austral.* **215** PIO
Alytus, *Lith.* **143** NI6
Alzada, *Mont., U.S.* **108** FI3
Alzamay, *Russ.* **161** KI4
Alzette, river, *Lux.* **162** JIO
Alzey, *Ger.* **150** H6
Alzira, *Sp.* **147** HI4
Ama, *Japan* **189** N7
Amadeus, Lake, *Austral.* **214** F8
Amadeus Depression, *Austral.* **214** F7
Amadi, *S. Sudan* **202** HI2
Amadjuak Lake, *Nunavut, Can.* **85** GI8
Amadora, *Port.* **146** H4
Amagi, *Japan* **189** R5
Amahai, *Indonesia* **193** KI6
Amakusa Shotō, *Japan* **189** S4
Åmål, *Sw.* **142** KI2
Amalfi, *It.* **152** MII
Amaliáda, *Gr.* **156** G8
Amamapare, *Indonesia* **193** L2O
Amambaí, *Braz.* **132** MII
Amami, island, *Asia* **168** GI3
Amami Guntō, *Japan* **189** W3
Amami Ō Shima, *Japan* **189** W3
Āmanave, *Amer. Samoa, U.S.* **222** M6
Amandola, *It.* **152** J9
Amangeldi, *Kaz.* **176** DII
Amantea, *It.* **153** QI3
Amanu, island, *Fr. Polynesia, Fr.* **223** F2O
Amapá, *Braz.* **132** BI2
Amarante, *Braz.* **133** FI5
Amarante, *Port.* **146** E6
Amargosa Range, *Calif., Nev., U.S.* **III** UIO
Amarillo, *Tex., U.S.* **104** G5
Amarkantak, *India* **180** J8
Amarwara, *India* **180** J7
Amasa, *Mich., U.S.* **100** F6
Amasra, *Turk.* **170** C8
Amasya, *Turk.* **170** DII
Amata, *S. Aust., Austral.* **215** U8
Amatari, *Braz.* **132** D9
Amathous, ruin, *Cyprus* **162** Q8

Amatrice, *It.* **152** J9
Amatuku, island, *Tuvalu* **221** J24
Amatusuk Hills, *Alas., U.S.* **113** CI3
Amavon Islands, *Solomon Is.* **221** LI7
Amazon (Solimões), river, *S. Amer.* **128** D5
Amazon, Mouths of the, *S. Amer.* **128** C8
Amazon Basin, *S. Amer.* **128** E5
Amazon Fan, *Atl. Oc.* **241** N7
Ambajogai, *India* **180** L5
Ambala, *India* **180** E6
Ambalangoda, *Sri Lanka* **181** T7
Ambalantota, *Sri Lanka* **181** T8
Ambanja, *Madagascar* **207** DI8
Ambarchik, *Russ.* **161** CI9
Ambargasta, Salinas de, *Arg.* **134** HIO
Ambato, *Ecua.* **130** K3
Ambatondrazaka, *Madagascar* **207** FI8
Ambelau, island, *Indonesia* **193** KI6
Amberg, *Ger.* **150** H9
Ambergris Caye, island, *Belize* **117** JI7
Ambergris Cays, *Turks & Caicos Is.* **119** JI7
Ambi, *Solomon Is.* **221** R24
Ambikapur, *India* **180** J9
Ambilobe, *Madagascar* **207** DI8
Amble, *Eng., U.K.* **145** NI2
Ambler, *Alas., U.S.* **113** EI4
Ambo, *Peru* **132** G3
Ambo Channel, *Marshall Is., U.S.* **220** M4
Amboise, *Fr.* **149** R8
Ambon, *Indonesia* **193** KI6
Ambon, island, *Indonesia* **193** KI6
Ambositra, *Madagascar* **207** GI7
Ambovombe, *Madagascar* **207** JI7
Amboy, *Calif., U.S.* **III** WII
Amboy Crater, *Calif., U.S.* **III** WII
Ambre, Cap d', *Madagascar* **207** DI8
Ambriz, *Angola* **206** B5
Ambrym, island, *Vanuatu* **222** D2
Ambunti, *P.N.G.* **217** CI8
Amchitka Island, *Alas., U.S.* **112** N3
Amchitka Pass, *Alas., U.S.* **112** N3
Am Dam, *Chad* **201** JI5
Amderma, *Russ.* **160** EII
Amdi, *India* **180** H8
Ameca, *Mex.* **116** H9
Ameghino Canyon, *Atl. Oc.* **241** U6
Ameland, island, *Neth.* **148** GI3
Amelia Island, *Fla., U.S.* **99** Q9
Amerasia Basin, *Arctic Oc.* **246** L9
America-Antarctica Ridge (North Weddell Ridge), *Atl. Oc.* **241** WIO
American Falls, *Idaho, U.S.* **108** H6
American Falls Reservoir, *Idaho, U.S.* **108** H6
American Highland, *Antarctica* **231** GI8
American Samoa, *Pac. Oc.* **218** JIO
Americus, *Ga., U.S.* **99** N5
Amersfoort, *Neth.* **148** JI3
Amery, *Wis., U.S.* **100** H2
Amery Ice Shelf, *Antarctica* **231** FI9
Ames, *Iowa, U.S.* **107** NII
Amfilochía, *Gr.* **156** G8
Amfípoli, *Gr.* **156** CI2
Ámfissa, *Gr.* **156** HIO
Amga, *Russ.* **161** HI8
Amga, river, *Russ.* **161** HI8
Amguema, *Russ.* **161** B2O
Amguid, *Alg.* **200** DII
Amhara, region, *Eth.* **203** FI5
Amherst, *N.S., Can.* **85** P22
Amherst, *N.Y., U.S.* **96** J5
Amherst, *Tex., U.S.* **104** J4
Amherst, *Va., U.S.* **98** EII
Amidon, *N. Dak., U.S.* **106** G2
Amiens, *Fr.* **148** MIO
Ami, Île, *New Caledonia, Fr.* **222** E9
Amindivi Islands, *India* **181** Q3
Amino, *Japan* **189** P8
Aminuis, *Namibia* **206** H7
Amioûn, *Leb.* **172** H6
Amīr, river, *Afghan.* **178** L6
Amirante Basin, *Ind. Oc.* **224** H7
Amirante Ridge, *Ind. Oc.* **224** H7

Amirante Trench, *Ind. Oc.* **224** H7
Amir Chah, *Pak.* **179** S2
Amistad, Presa de la see Amistad Reservoir, *Mex., U.S.* **116** DII
Amistad National Recreation Area, *Tex., U.S.* **105** R6
Amistad Reservoir, *Tex., U.S.* **105** R6
Amite, *La., U.S.* **102** NIO
Amity, *Ark., U.S.* **102** H7
Åmli, *Nor.* **142** LII
Amlia Island, *Alas., U.S.* **112** P6
'Ammān (Amman, Philadelphia), *Jordan* **172** M7
Amman see 'Ammān (Philadelphia), *Jordan* **172** M7**
Ammaroo, *N.T., Austral.* **215** S9
Ammóchostos see Famagusta, *Cyprus* **162** PIO
Ammochostos Bay, *Cyprus* **162** NIO
Amnok, river, *N. Korea* **186** G4
Āmol, *Iran* **175** CI3
Amolar, *Braz.* **132** KIO
Amorgós, *Gr.* **157** MI6
Amorgós, island, *Gr.* **157** LI6
Amoricain Shelf, *Atl. Oc.* **240** HI2
Amory, *Miss., U.S.* **103** JI3
Amos, *Que., Can.* **85** PI8
Amoy see Xiamen, *Fujian, China* **185** U9
Ampani, *India* **180** L8
Ampanihy, *Madagascar* **207** JI6
Ampelákia, *Gr.* **156** EIO
Ampezzo, *It.* **152** C9
Amphitrite Group, *S. China Sea* **192** BIO
Amplepuis, *Fr.* **149** TI2
Amposta, *Sp.* **147** FI5
'Amrān, *Yemen* **174** P9
Amravati, *India* **180** K6
Amreli, *India* **180** J2
'Amrīt (Marathus), ruins, *Syr.* **172** G7
Amritsar, *India* **180** D5
Amsā'ad, *Lib.* **201** CI7
Amsterdam, *N.Y., U.S.* **96** JII
Amsterdam, *Neth.* **148** JI2
Amstetten, *Aust.* **150** KII
Amtaedo, island, *S. Korea* **187** T6
Am Timan, *Chad* **201** JI5
Amu Darya, river, *Asia* **168** F6
Amukta Island, *Alas., U.S.* **112** P7
Amun, *P.N.G.* **221** KI3
Amund Ringnes Island, *Nunavut, Can.* **85** CI5
Amundsen Basin, *Arctic Oc.* **246** GII
Amundsen Bay, *Antarctica* **231** CI9
Amundsen Gulf, *N.W.T., Can.* **84** EII
Amundsen Plain, *Pac. Oc.* **249** MI4
Amundsen Ridges, *Pac. Oc.* **249** MI4
Amundsen-Scott South Pole, station, *Antarctica* **230** JI2
Amundsen Sea, *Antarctica* **230** L6
Amundsen Trough, *Arctic Oc.* **246** P9
Amuntai, *Indonesia* **192** KII
Amur, river, *Asia* **168** EII
Amurang, *Indonesia* **193** HI5
Amuri, *Cook Is., N.Z.* **222** QII
Amursk, *Russ.* **161** K2I
Amvrakikós Kolpos, *Gr.* **156** G8
Amvrosiyivka, *Ukr.* **159** QIO
Amyderýa, *Turkm.* **176** MII
Amýntaio, *Gr.* **156** C9
An, *Myanmar* **190** H5
Anaa, island, *Fr. Polynesia, Fr.* **223** EI8
Anabar, river, *Russ.* **161** FI5
Anabar, region, *Nauru* **221** E23
Anabarskiy Zaliv, *Russ.* **161** EI5
Anacapa Island, *Calif., U.S.* **III** X7
Anaco, *Venez.* **130** CII
Anacoco, *La., U.S.* **102** N7
Anaconda, *Mont., U.S.* **108** D6
Anacortes, *Wash., U.S.* **110** A4
Anadarko, *Okla., U.S.* **104** GIO
Anadyr', river, *Asia* **168** BI2
Anadyr', *Russ.* **161** B2I
Anadyr, Gulf of, *Pac. Oc.* **168** AI2
Anadyrskiy Zaliv, *Russ.* **161** B2I

Anadyrskoye Ploskogor'ye, *Russ.* **161** C2O
Anae, island, *Guam, U.S.* **220** D9
'Anaeho'omalu Bay, *Hawai'i, U.S.* **115** LI8
Anáfi, *Gr.* **157** NI6
Anáfi, island, *Gr.* **157** NI6
Anaga, Punta de, *Sp.* **208** Q5
Anagni, *It.* **152** L9
'Ānah, *Iraq* **174** D8
Anaheim, *Calif., U.S.* **III** X8
Anahola, *Hawai'i, U.S.* **114** B6
Anahuac, *Tex., U.S.* **105** QI5
Anai Mudi, peak, *India* **181** R5
Anak, *N. Korea* **186** K5
Anakapalle, *India* **180** M9
Anaktuvuk Pass, *Alas., U.S.* **113** DI6
Analalava, *Madagascar* **207** EI7
Anamã, *Braz.* **132** E8
Ana María, Cayos, *Cuba* **118** JIO
Ana María, Golfo de, *Cuba* **118** JIO
Anambas, Kepulauan, *Indonesia* **192** H7
Anamoose, *N. Dak., U.S.* **106** F5
Anamosa, *Iowa, U.S.* **107** NI4
Anamur, *Turk.* **170** J8
Anamur Burnu, *Turk.* **170** J8
Anan, *Japan* **189** R8
Anand, *India* **180** J3
Anan'evo, *Kyrg.* **178** DI3
Anangenimon, island, *F.S.M.* **221** BI6
Ananij, island, *Marshall Is., U.S.* **220** H9
Anantapur, *India* **181** P6
Anantnag, *India* **180** C5
Anapa, *Russ.* **159** T9
Anápolis, *Braz.* **133** JI3
Anār, *Iran* **175** FI4
Anārak, *Iran* **175** EI4
Anār Darah, *Afghan.* **179** P2
Anatahan, island, *N. Mariana Is., U.S.* **220** B2
Anatolia (Asia Minor), *Asia* **168** E3
Anatom, island, *Vanuatu* **222** H4
Anatone, *Wash., U.S.* **110** E9
Añatuya, *Arg.* **134** HIO
Anboru, island, *Marshall Is., U.S.* **220** L8
Anbu, *Guang., China* **185** V7
Anbyŏn, *N. Korea* **186** J9
An Cabhán see Cavan, *Ire.* **145** R6
An Caislean Nua see New Castle, *Ire.* **145** T4
An Caisleán Riabhach see Castlerea, *Ire.* **145** R3
Ancenis, *Fr.* **149** R6
An Chathair see Galty Mountains, *Ire.* **145** T4
An Cheapach Mhór see Cappamore, *Ire.* **145** T4
Anchorage, *Alas., U.S.* **113** JI6
Anchor Bay, *Calif., U.S.* **III** Q2
Anclitas, Cayo, *Cuba* **118** KIO
An Clochán see Clifden, *Ire.* **145** R3
Ancona, *It.* **152** H9
Ancón de Sardinas, Bahía de, *Ecua.* **130** H2
An Craoslach see Creeslough, *Ire.* **145** P5
An Creagán see Mount Bellew, *Ire.* **145** R4
Ancud, *Chile* **135** Q6
Ancud, Gulf of, *S. Amer.* **128** N4
Anda, *China* **183** DI5
Andacollo, *Arg.* **135** N7
Andado, *N.T., Austral.* **215** U9
An Daingean (Dingle), *Ire.* **145** U2
Andalgalá, *Arg.* **134** G9
 Åndalsnes, *Nor.* **142** HIO
Andalusia, *Ala., U.S.* **103** NI5
Andalusia, region, *Sp.* **146** K9
Andaman and Nicobar Islands, *India* **181** QI4
Andaman Basin, *Ind. Oc.* **225** EI4
Andaman Islands, *India* **181** QI4
Andaman Sea, *Ind. Oc.* **168** K9
Andapa, *Madagascar* **207** EI8
Andelot-Blancheville, *Fr.* **149** QI3
Andenes, *Nor.* **142** CI2
Andermatt, *Switz.* **152** B4

Andernach, *Ger.* **150** G5
Andersen Air Force Base *see* Joint Region Marianas, *Guam, U.S.* **220** B12
Anderson, *Alas., U.S.* **113** G17
Anderson, *Calif., U.S.* **111** N3
Anderson, *Ind., U.S.* **101** R9
Anderson, *Mo., U.S.* **107** VII
Anderson, *S.C., U.S.* **98** K7
Anderson, river, *N.W.T., Can.* **84** E10
Anderson Bay, *Austral.* **214** L7
Andes, range, *S. Amer.* **128** H4
Andfjorden, bay, *Nor.* **142** C12
Andicuri Bay, *Aruba, Neth.* **123** Q17
Andijon, *Uzb.* **177** K14
Andırın, *Turk.* **170** H11
Andkhōy, *Afghan.* **178** K5
Ando, island, *S. Korea* **187** U9
Andoany (Hell-Ville), *Madagascar* **207** D18
Andoas, *Peru* **132** E3
Andong, *N. Korea* **186** H9
Andong, *S. Korea* **187** Q11
Andongho, lake, *S. Korea* **187** P11
Andorra, *Eur.* **162** E2
Andorra, *Sp.* **147** E14
Andorra la Vella, *Andorra* **162** J3
Andover, *Me., U.S.* **97** F15
Andovoranto, *Madagascar* **207** F18
Andøya, island, *Nor.* **142** C12
Andradina, *Braz.* **132** L12
Andreanof Islands, *Alas., U.S.* **112** N5
Andreapol', *Russ.* **158** H7
Andrew Johnson National Historic Site, *Tenn., U.S.* **103** E20
Andrews, *N.C., U.S.* **98** J5
Andrews, *S.C., U.S.* **98** L11
Andrews, *Tex., U.S.* **104** M4
Andrijevica, *Montenegro* **154** J9
An Droichead Adhmaid *see* Woodenbridge, *Ire.* **145** T7
Androka, *Madagascar* **207** J16
Ándros, *Gr.* **157** J14
Ándros, island, *Gr.* **157** J14
Andros Island, *Bahamas* **118** E11
Andros Town, *Bahamas* **118** E11
Androth Island, *India* **181** R3
Andrychów, *Pol.* **151** H15
Andryushkino, *Russ.* **161** D19
Andselv, *Nor.* **143** C13
Andújar, *Sp.* **146** K10
Anefis i-n-Darane, *Mali* **200** G10
Anegada, island, *British Virgin Is., U.K.* **121** A14
Anegada, Bahía, *Arg.* **135** P11
Anegada Passage, *N. Amer.* **121** A14
Aného, *Togo* **204** E11
Aneju, island, *Marshall Is., U.S.* **220** G10
Anelghowhat, *Vanuatu* **222** H4
Anelghowhat Bay, *Vanuatu* **222** H4
Anemwanot, island, *Marshall Is., U.S.* **220** G11
Anenelibw, island, *Marshall Is., U.S.* **220** H11
Anengenipuan, island, *F.S.M.* **221** B16
Aneta, *N. Dak., U.S.* **106** F7
Anetan, region, *Nauru* **221** E23
Aneto, Pico de, *Sp.* **147** C15
Aney, *Niger* **201** G13
Anfu, *Jiangxi, China* **185** R6
Angamos, Punta, *Chile* **134** E6
Angamos Point, *S. Amer.* **128** J4
Angara, river, *Russ.* **161** J14
Angarei, island, *Cook Is., N.Z.* **222** Q11
Angarsk, *Russ.* **161** L15
Angaur (Ngeaur), island, *Palau* **220** R9
Ånge, *Sw.* **143** H13
Ángel de la Guarda, Isla, *Mex.* **116** C6
Angeles, *P.R., U.S.* **122** N2
Angeles, *Philippines* **193** C13
Angel Falls, *Venez.* **130** E12
Angelina, river, *Tex., U.S.* **105** N14
Angels Camp, *Calif., U.S.* **111** R5
Ångermanälven, river, *Sw.* **143** G13
Angers, *Fr.* **149** R7
Angerville, *Fr.* **149** Q9

An Ghráinseach *see* Grange, *Ire.* **145** Q4
Angkor, ruins, *Cambodia* **190** M11
Ângk Tasaôm, *Cambodia* **191** P11
Angla Rencuo *see* Ngangla Ringco, lake, *China* **182** K3
An Gleann Garbh *see* Glengarriff, *Ire.* **145** V3
Angle Inlet, *Minn., U.S.* **106** D9
Anglem, Mount, *N.Z.* **217** R15
Anglesey, island, *Wales, U.K.* **145** S9
Anglet, *Fr.* **149** X5
Angleton, *Tex., U.S.* **105** R14
Anglure, *Fr.* **149** P11
Ango, *Dem. Rep. of the Congo* **202** H11
Angoche, *Mozambique* **207** E15
Angohrān, *Iran* **175** H16
Angol, *Chile* **135** N6
Angola, *Af.* **206** D7
Angola, *Ind., U.S.* **101** N10
Angola Basin, *Atl. Oc.* **241** Q12
Angola Plain, *Atl. Oc.* **241** Q12
Angoon, *Alas., U.S.* **113** L22
Angora *see* Ankara, *Turk.* **170** E8
Angoram, *P.N.G.* **217** C18
Angoulême, *Fr.* **149** U7
Angra do Heroísmo , *Azores, Port.* **146** Q3
Angren, *Uzb.* **177** K14
Angria Bank, *Ind. Oc.* **224** D10
Anguilla, island, *Lesser Antil.* **121** B15
Anguilla Cays, *Bahamas* **118** F9
Anguillita Island, *British Virgin Is., U.K.* **122** R10
Angul, *India* **180** K10
Anguli Nur, *Hebei, China* **184** B6
Angvik, *Nor.* **142** H10
Anhai, *Fujian, China* **185** U9
Anholt, island, *Den.* **142** M12
Anhua, *Hunan, China* **185** Q3
Anhui, *China* **184** L8
Ani, *Japan* **188** K12
Aniak, *Alas., U.S.* **113** J13
Aniakchak National Monument and Preserve, *Alas., U.S.* **113** M13
Anibare Bay, *Nauru* **221** F24
Anibare, region, *Nauru* **221** E23
Anie, Pic d', *Fr., Sp.* **147** B14
Animal Flower Cave, site, *Barbados* **123** J19
Animas, *N. Mex., U.S.* **109** V10
Animas, river, *Colo., U.S.* **109** P11
Animas Peak, *N. Mex., U.S.* **109** W10
Anin, *Myanmar* **190** L7
Anina, *Rom.* **154** E11
Anipemza, *Arm.* **171** D18
Aniwa, island, *Vanuatu* **222** G4
Anixab, *Namibia* **206** G6
Anjar, *India* **180** J2
Anjiang, *Hunan, China* **185** R1
Anjira, *Pak.* **179** T5
Anjouan *see* Nzwani, *Comoros* **209** N16
Anjou Islands, *Asia* **168** B10
Anju, *N. Korea* **186** H6
Anjwado, island, *S. Korea* **187** T6
Ankang, *Shaanxi, China* **184** L1
Ankara (Angora), *Turk.* **170** E8
Ankara, river, *Turk.* **170** E7
Ankaratra, peak, *Af.* **198** N12
Ankeny, *Iowa, U.S.* **107** P11
An Khê, *Vietnam* **190** M14
Ankola, *India* **181** P4
An Longfort *see* Londford, *Ire.* **145** R5
Anlu, *Hubei, China* **184** M5
Anmado, island, *S. Korea* **187** S6
An Muileann gCearr *see* Mullingar, *Ire.* **145** R6
An Muileann Iarainn *see* Swanlinbar, *Ire.* **145** Q5
Anmyeon, *S. Korea* **187** Q7
Anmyeondo, island, *S. Korea* **187** Q7
Ann, Cape, *Antarctica* **231** C19
Ann, Cape, *Mass., U.S.* **97** K15
Anna, *Ill., U.S.* **101** V5
Anna, Lake, *Va., U.S.* **98** E12
Annaba, *Alg.* **200** A12

Annaberg, ruin, *Virgin Is., U.S.* **122** M11
An Nabk, *Syr.* **172** H8
An Nafūd, desert, *Saudi Arabia* **174** G7
An Najaf (Najaf), *Iraq* **174** E9
Annaly, *Virgin Is., U.S.* **122** Q1
Annam Cordillera, *Asia* **168** J10
Annan, *Scot., U.K.* **145** P10
Annandale Falls, *Grenada* **123** K22
Anna Pink, Bahía, *Chile* **135** T5
Anna Plains, *W. Aust., Austral.* **215** R4
Anna Point, *Nauru* **221** E23
Annapolis, *Md., U.S.* **98** C14
Annapurna I, peak, *Nepal* **180** F9
Ann Arbor, *Mich., U.S.* **100** M12
An Nashshāsh, *U.A.E.* **175** K14
An Nāşirīyah, *Iraq* **174** F10
An Nawfalīyah, *Lib.* **201** C15
Annean, Lake, *Austral.* **214** H3
Annecy, *Fr.* **149** T14
Annecy, Lac d', *Fr.* **149** U14
Annemasse, *Fr.* **149** T14
Annenskiy Most, *Russ.* **158** E9
Annigeri, *India* **181** N4
An Nimāş, *Saudi Arabia* **174** M8
Anning, *China* **182** N9
Anniston, *Ala., U.S.* **103** J16
Annitowa, *N.T., Austral.* **215** S10
Annobón, island, *Eq. Guinea* **205** H13
Annonay, *Fr.* **149** V12
Annopol, *Pol.* **151** F17
Annotto Bay, *Jam.* **122** H10
An Nu'ayrīyah, *Saudi Arabia* **174** H11
An Nukhayb, *Iraq* **174** E8
Anoano, *Solomon Is.* **221** N19
Anoka, *Minn., U.S.* **106** J11
An Ómaigh *see* Omagh, *N. Ire., U.K.* **145** P6
Áno Viánnos, *Gr.* **157** Q15
Anqing, *Anhui, China* **185** N8
Anqiu, *Shand., China* **184** G10
An Ráth *see* Charleville, *Ire.* **145** T4
Anren, *Hunan, China* **185** S4
Ansai (Zhenwudong), *Shaanxi, China* **184** F2
Ansan, *S. Korea* **187** N8
An Scairbh *see* Scarriff, *Ire.* **145** S4
An Scoil *see* Skull, *Ire.* **145** V3
Anse-à-Foleur, *Haiti* **119** L16
Anse-à-Galets, *Haiti* **119** M16
Anse-à-Pitre, *Haiti* **119** N17
Anse-à-Veau, *Haiti* **119** M15
Anse-Bertrand, *Guadeloupe, Fr.* **123** D15
Anse Boileau, *Seychelles* **209** P20
Anse des Pitons, *St. Lucia* **123** L13
Anse d'Hainault, *Haiti* **119** M14
Anse Guyonneau, *Guadeloupe, Fr.* **123** F14
Anse la Raye, *St. Lucia* **123** K13
Anse Lavoutte, *St. Lucia* **123** J14
Anselmo, *Nebr., U.S.* **107** P5
Anse Marcel, *St.-Martin, Fr.* **123** A15
Anseong, *S. Korea* **187** P9
Anse Quanery, *Dominica* **123** F20
Anse-Rouge, *Haiti* **119** L16
Anshan, *Liaoning, China* **184** B13
Anshun, *China* **182** M10
Ansley, *Nebr., U.S.* **107** P5
Ansó, *Sp.* **147** C14
Anson, *Me., U.S.* **97** F16
Anson, *Tex., U.S.* **104** L7
Anson Bay, *Austral.* **214** B7
Anson Bay, *Norfolk I., Austral.* **221** F20
Ansongo, *Mali* **200** H9
Anson Point, *Norfolk I., Austral.* **221** F20
An Spidéal (Spiddal), *Ire.* **145** S3
Ansted, *W. Va., U.S.* **98** E9
Ansudu, *Indonesia* **193** K21
An Tairbeart (Tarbert), *Scot., U.K.* **144** H6
Antakya, *Turk.* **170** J11
Antalaha, *Madagascar* **207** E18
Antalya (Adalia), *Turk.* **170** H6
Antalya Körfezi, *Turk.* **170** J6

Antananarivo, *Madagascar* **207** F17
Antanimora, *Madagascar* **207** J16
An tAonach *see* Nenagh, *Ire.* **145** T5
Antarctic Canyon, *Atl. Oc.* **241** Z7
Antarctic Pacific Ridge, *Pac. Oc.* **243** R14
Antarctic Peninsula, *Antarctica* **230** E5
Ant Atoll, *F.S.M.* **220** Q7
An Teach Dóite *see* Maam Cross, *Ire.* **145** R3
Antelope, *Oreg., U.S.* **110** G5
Antelope Reservoir, *Oreg., U.S.* **110** K9
Antequera, *Sp.* **146** L10
Anthony, *Kans., U.S.* **107** V7
Anthony, *N. Mex., U.S.* **109** V12
Antibes, *Fr.* **149** X15
Anticosti Island, *N. Amer.* **82** G10
Antifer, Cap d', *Fr.* **149** N7
Antigo, *Wis., U.S.* **100** H6
Antigonish, *N.S., Can.* **85** P22
Antigua, *Sp.* **208** Q7
Antigua, island, *Lesser Antil.* **121** C16
Antigua and Barbuda, *N. Amer.* **121** B16
Antikýthira, island, *Gr.* **157** P11
Anti-Lebanon Range *see* Al Jabal ash Sharqī, *Syr.* **172** J7
Antilla, *Cuba* **119** J13
Antimácheia, *Gr.* **157** L18
Antímilos, island, *Gr.* **157** M13
Antioch, *Calif., U.S.* **111** R4
Antioche, Pertuis d', *Fr.* **149** T6
Antíparos, island, *Gr.* **157** L14
Antípaxoi, island, *Gr.* **156** F6
Antipayuta, *Russ.* **160** F12
Antipodes Fracture Zone, *Pac. Oc.* **243** R13
Antipodes Islands, *Pac. Oc.* **218** Q9
Antípsara, island, *Gr.* **157** H15
Antlers, *Okla., U.S.* **104** J13
Antofagasta, *Chile* **134** E6
Antofalla, Salar de, *Arg.* **134** F8
Antoine, Lake, *Grenada* **123** K23
Anton, *Tex., U.S.* **104** J5
Anton Chico, *N. Mex., U.S.* **109** S13
Anton Dohrn Seamount, *Atl. Oc.* **247** L23
Antongila, Baie d', *Madagascar* **207** E18
Antongila Bay, *Af.* **198** M12
Antónia, Pico da, *Cabo Verde* **209** D16
Antrain, *Fr.* **149** Q6
Antrim, Glens of, *N. Ire., U.K.* **145** P7
Antriol, *Bonaire, Neth.* **123** Q19
Antrodoco, *It.* **152** J9
Antropovo, *Russ.* **158** G11
Antsirabe, *Madagascar* **207** G17
Antsiranana, *Madagascar* **207** D18
Antsohihy, *Madagascar* **207** E18
Antufash, Jazīrat, *Yemen* **174** P8
Antwerpen (Antwerp), *Belg.* **148** K12
An Uaimh *see* Navan, *Ire.* **145** R6
Anuanu Raro, island, *Fr. Polynesia, Fr.* **223** G19
Anuanu Runga, island, *Fr. Polynesia, Fr.* **223** G19
Anupgarh, *India* **180** E4
Anuradhapura, *Sri Lanka* **181** S7
Anuta, island, *Solomon Is.* **221** P20
Anvers Island, *Antarctica* **230** D4
Anvik, *Alas., U.S.* **113** H13
Anvil *see* El Yunque, peak, *Cuba* **119** K14
Anxi, *China* **182** G7
Anxi, *Fujian, China* **185** U9
Anxiang, *Hunan, China* **185** P4
Anxious Bay, *Austral.* **214** K9
Anyang, *Henan, China* **184** G6
Anyang, *S. Korea* **187** N8
Ánydros, island, *Gr.* **157** M16
A'nyêmaqên Shan, *China* **182** J8
Anyi, *Jiangxi, China* **185** Q7
Anyuan, *Jiangxi, China* **185** T6
Anzhero Sudzhensk, *Russ.* **160** K12
Anzhu, Ostrova, *Russ.* **161** D16
Anzio, *It.* **152** L8

Aoa Bay, *Amer. Samoa, U.S.* **222** M8
Aoba, island, *Vanuatu* **222** C2
Ao Ban Don, bay, *Thai.* **191** Q8
Aoga Shima, *Japan* **189** S12
Aohan Qi, *N. Mongol, China* **184** A10
Aojing, *Zhejiang, China* **185** R11
Aola, *Solomon Is.* **221** N19
Aoloautuai, *Amer. Samoa, U.S.* **222** M6
Aomen *see* Macau, S.A.R., *China* **185** W4
Aomon, island, *Marshall Is., U.S.* **220** G8
Aomori, *Japan* **188** J12
Aonae, *Japan* **188** H11
Aóös, river, *Gr.* **156** D8
A'opo, *Samoa* **222** K1
Aorai, Mount, *Fr. Polynesia, Fr.* **223** P16
Aoraki (Mount Cook), *N.Z.* **217** P16
Aóre, island, *Vanuatu* **222** C1
Aosta, *It.* **152** D2
Aotea Island *see* Great Barrier Island, *N.Z.* **217** H19
Aouker, island, *Af.* **198** F2
Aoulef, *Alg.* **200** D10
Aoumou, *New Caledonia, Fr.* **222** D8
Aozi, *Chad* **201** F15
Aozou, *Chad* **201** F14
Aozou Strip, region, *Chad* **201** F15
Apa, river, *S. Amer.* **132** L10
Apache, *Okla., U.S.* **104** H9
Apakho, *Solomon Is.* **221** Q23
Apalachee Bay, *U.S.* **87** M18
Apalachicola, *Fla., U.S.* **99** R4
Apalachicola, river, *U.S.* **99** R4
Apalachicola Bay, *Fla., U.S.* **99** R4
Apamea, ruins, *Syr.* **172** F7
Apaora, *Solomon Is.* **221** P20
Apaporis, river, *Col.* **130** H7
Aparri, *Philippines* **193** B14
Apataki, island, *Fr. Polynesia, Fr.* **223** D18
Apatin, *Serb.* **154** E9
Apatity, *Russ.* **160** D8
Apatzingán, *Mex.* **116** J10
Apeíranthos, *Gr.* **157** L15
Apeldoorn, *Neth.* **148** J13
Apennines, *Eur.* **140** K7
Apes Den, *Gibraltar, U.K.* **163** P23
Áphaea, ruin, *Gr.* **156** K12
Aphaedo, island, *S. Korea* **187** T7
Apia, *Samoa* **222** K1
Apia Harbour, *Samoa* **222** L3
Apishapa, river, *Colo., U.S.* **109** P14
Ap Iwan, Cerro, *Arg.* **135** T7
Apo, *S. Korea* **187** Q10
Apolima, island, *Samoa* **222** L2
Apolima Strait, *Samoa* **222** L2
Apollo Bay, *Vic., Austral.* **215** Z12
Apollonia, *Gr.* **157** L14
Apollonia, site, *Alban.* **154** L9
Apolo, *Bol.* **132** J6
Apopka, Lake, *Fla., U.S.* **99** T8
Aporema, *Braz.* **132** C12
Apostle Islands, *Wis., U.S.* **100** E4
Apostle Islands National Lakeshore, *Wis., U.S.* **100** E4
Apóstoles, *Arg.* **134** G14
Apostolic Palace, *Vatican City* **163** P17
Apostolos Andreas, Cape, *Cyprus* **162** L12
Apostolos Andreas Monastery, *Cyprus* **162** M12
Apoteri, *Guyana* **131** F14
Appalachian Mountains, *U.S.* **87** G19
Appalachian Plateau, *U.S.* **87** G19
Appennini, range, *It.* **152** F5
Applecross, *Scot., U.K.* **144** J7
Appleton, *Minn., U.S.* **106** J9
Appleton, *Wis., U.S.* **100** J6
Appleton City, *Mo., U.S.* **107** T11
Apple Valley, *Calif., U.S.* **111** W9
Appomattox, *Va., U.S.* **98** F11
Apra Harbor, *Guam, U.S.* **220** C10
Apra Heights, *Guam, U.S.* **220** C10
Aprilia, *It.* **152** L8
Apsheron Peninsula, *Eur.* **140** J16

Apsheronsk, *Russ.* 159 T11
Apuane, Alpi, *It.* 152 G5
'Āpua Point, *Hawai'i, U.S.* 115 P21
Apucarana, *Braz.* 132 M12
Apulia, *Eur.* 140 K8
Apurashokoru, island, *Palau*
220 P10
Apure, river, *N. Amer.* 82 Q10
Apure, river, *Venez.* 130 D9
Apurímac, river, *Peru* 132 H4
Apuseni Mountains, *Rom.* 154 C12
Aqaba see Al 'Aqabah, *Jordan* 173 R5
Aqaba, Gulf of, *Asia* 168 F2
Aqadyr, *Kaz.* 177 F14
Aqcha see Āqchah, *Afghan.* 178 K5
Āqchah (Aqcha), *Afghan.* 178 K5
Aqiq, *Sudan* 203 D14
Aqköl, *Kaz.* 177 C13
Aqköl, *Kaz.* 177 G16
Aqköl, *Kaz.* 177 I4
Aqmola see Astana, *Kaz.* 177 D14
Aqqikkol Hu, *China* 182 H4
Aqqū, *Kaz.* 177 C16
Aqqystaū, *Kaz.* 176 F6
Aqsay, *Kaz.* 176 C7
Aqshataū, *Kaz.* 177 F15
Aqsū, *Kaz.* 177 C14
Aqsū, river, *Kaz.* 177 G17
Aqtaū, *Kaz.* 176 H5
Aqtöbe, *Kaz.* 176 D8
Aqtoghay, *Kaz.* 177 F17
Aquarius Seachannel, *Pac. Oc.*
243 D14
Aquidauana, *Braz.* 132 L11
Aquin, *Haiti* 119 M15
Aquitaine Basin, *Eur.* 140 J4
Ara, *India* 180 G9
Araara, Passe, *Fr. Polynesia, Fr.*
223 H14
Araara, Motu, *Fr. Polynesia, Fr.*
223 H14
Arab, *Ala., U.S.* 103 H15
'Arab, Shaṭṭ al, *Iraq* 174 F11
'Arabah, Wādī al, *Jordan* 173 Q5
Arabian Basin, *Ind. Oc.* 224 C9
Arabian Peninsula, *Asia* 168 G3
Arabian Sea, *Asia* 168 J5
Arabs Gulf, *Af.* 198 D8
Araç, *Turk.* 170 C8
Araç, river, *Turk.* 170 C9
Aracaju, *Braz.* 133 H17
Aracati, *Braz.* 133 E17
Araçatuba, *Braz.* 132 L12
Aracena, *Sp.* 146 K7
Aracena, Sierra de, *Sp.* 146 K7
Árachthos, river, *Gr.* 156 F8
Aracides, Cape, *Solomon Is.*
221 M20
Araçuaí, *Braz.* 133 K15
Arad, *Rom.* 154 D11
Arada, *Chad* 201 H15
Aradippou, *Cyprus* 162 P9
Arafura Sea, *Asia* 169 M16
Arafura Shelf, *Pac. Oc.* 242 K7
Aragarças, *Braz.* 132 J12
Aragats, peak, *Arm.* 171 D18
Arago, Cape, *Oreg., U.S.* 110 J1
Aragon, *Eur.* 140 K3
Araguacema, *Braz.* 133 F13
Aragua de Barcelona, *Venez.*
130 C11
Araguaia, river, *Braz.* 133 F13
Araguaína, *Braz.* 133 F13
Araguari, *Braz.* 133 K13
Araguari, river, *S. Amer.* 128 C8
Araguatins, *Braz.* 133 E13
Arahal, *Sp.* 146 L8
Arai, *Japan* 189 N11
Árainn (Inishmore), island, *Ire.*
145 S3
Árainn Mhór (Aran Island), *Ire.*
145 P4
Arak, *Alg.* 200 E11
Arāk, *Iran* 174 D12
Arakabesan, island, *Palau* 220 N11
Arakan Yoma, *Myanmar* 190 H5
Arakht, *Afghan.* 178 J9
Aral, *Kaz.* 176 F10
Aral, *Kyrg.* 178 E11
Aral Mangy Qaraqumy, *Kaz.*
176 F10

Aral Sea, *Kaz.* 176 G9
Aralsor, Lake, *Eur.* 140 G14
Aralsköl Köli, *Kaz.* 176 D5
Aralsul'fat, *Kaz.* 176 F10
Araltobe, *Kaz.* 176 D9
Aramac, *Qnsld., Austral.* 215 T13
Aramits, *Fr.* 149 Y6
Ārān, *Iran* 175 D13
Aran, island, *Scot., U.K.* 145 N8
Aranda de Duero, *Sp.* 146 D11
Aranđelovac, *Serb.* 154 G10
Arandu, *Pak.* 178 L9
Aran Island see Árainn Mhór, *Ire.*
145 P4
Aran Islands, *Ire.* 145 S3
Aranjuez, *Sp.* 146 G11
Aransá, *Sp.* 162 L4
Aransá, river, *Sp.* 162 K4
Aransas, river, *Tex., U.S.* 105 T11
Aransas Pass, *Tex., U.S.* 105 T11
Araouane, *Mali* 200 G8
Arapahoe, *Nebr., U.S.* 107 R5
Arapaho National Recreation Area,
Colo., U.S. 108 L12
Arapiraca, *Braz.* 133 G17
Arapkir, *Turk.* 171 F13
'Ar'ar, *Saudi Arabia* 174 F8
Araraquara, *Braz.* 133 L13
Ararat, *Arm.* 171 E19
Ararat, *Vic., Austral.* 215 Z12
Ararat, Mount see Ağrı Dağı, peak,
Turk. 171 E18
Ararat, Mount, *Asia* 168 F4
Araria, *India* 180 G11
Araripe, Chapada do, *S. Amer.*
128 F11
Aras (Araxes), river, *Turk.* 171 E17
Aratika, island, *Fr. Polynesia, Fr.*
223 D18
Aratsu Bay, *N. Mariana Is., U.S.*
220 E8
Arauá, river, *Braz.* 132 E7
Arauca, *Col.* 130 D7
Arauca, river, *S. Amer.* 130 D7
Arauco Gulf, *S. Amer.* 128 M4
Aravalli Range, *India* 180 H4
Arawak Cay, *Bahamas* 122 B11
Araxá, *Braz.* 133 K13
Araxes, river, see Aras, *Turk.* 171 E17
Arayit Dağı, peak, *Turk.* 170 F6
Ārba Minch', *Eth.* 203 H14
Arbatax, *It.* 153 P5
Arbazh, *Russ.* 158 G14
Arbela see Irbid, *Jordan* 172 L6
Arbīl see Hewlêr, *Iraq* 174 C9
Arbroath, *Scot., U.K.* 144 L11
Arcabell, *Sp.* 162 K2
Arcachon, *Fr.* 149 W6
Arcachon, Bassin d', *Fr.* 149 V6
Arcadia, *Fla., U.S.* 99 V8
Arcadia, *La., U.S.* 102 L7
Arcadia, *Mich., U.S.* 100 J9
Arcadia, *Wis., U.S.* 100 J3
Arcata, *Calif., U.S.* 110 M1
Archánes, *Gr.* 157 Q15
Archangel see Arkhangel'sk, *Russ.*
160 E8
Archángelos, *Gr.* 157 N20
Archbald, *Pa., U.S.* 96 M9
Archer, river, *Austral.* 214 B12
Archer Bay, *Austral.* 214 B12
Archer City, *Tex., U.S.* 104 K9
Arches National Park, *Utah, U.S.*
109 N9
Archiac, *Fr.* 149 U7
Archialus see Pomorie, *Bulg.* 155 J17
Archidona, *Sp.* 146 L10
Archipelago, Bonaparte, *Austral.*
214 B5
Archipiélago de Colón see Galápagos
Islands, *Pac. Oc.* 219 G20
Archman, *Turkm.* 176 L7
Arcis, *Fr.* 149 P12
Arco, *Idaho, U.S.* 108 G6
Arcos de Jalón, *Sp.* 146 E12
Arcoverde, *Braz.* 133 G17
Arctic Bay, *Nunavut, Can.* 85 E16
Arctic Ocean, *Arctic Oc.* 240 A13
Arctic Red, river, *N.W.T., Can.* 84 E9
Arctic Village, *Alas., U.S.* 113 D17
Arda, river, *Bulg.* 155 K15

Ardabīl, *Iran* 174 B11
Ardahan, *Turk.* 171 D17
Ardakān, *Iran* 175 E14
Ard an Rátha see Ardara, *Ire.* 145 P5
Ardanuç, *Turk.* 171 D16
Ardara (Ard an Rátha), *Ire.* 145 P5
Ardee (Baile Átha Fhirdhia), *Ire.*
145 R6
Ardencaple Seachannel, *Arctic Oc.*
240 C17
Ardennes, region, *Belg., Fr.* 148 M13
Ardennes, Canal des, *Fr.* 149 N12
Ardestān, *Iran* 175 D13
Ardmore, *India, U.S.* 104 J11
Ardmore, *S. Dak., U.S.* 106 M1
Ardoch, *Qnsld., Austral.* 215 V12
Ardres, *Fr.* 148 L9
Ards Peninsula, *N. Ire., U.K.* 145 Q8
Åre, *Sw.* 142 G12
Arecibo, *P.R., U.S.* 122 M2
Arei, Pointe, *Fr. Polynesia, Fr.*
223 K24
Areia Branca, *Braz.* 133 E17
Arekalong Peninsula, *Palau*
220 M12
Arena, Point, *U.S.* 86 F2
Arenápolis, *Braz.* 132 H10
Arenas, Punta de, *Arg.* 135 X9
Arenas de San Pedro, *Sp.* 146 F9
Arendal, *Nor.* 142 L11
Areópoli, *Gr.* 156 M10
Arequipa, *Peru* 132 J5
Arès, *Fr.* 149 V6
Arethusa see Ar Rastan, *Syr.*
172 G8
Arévalo, *Sp.* 146 E10
Arezzo, *It.* 152 H7
Argadargada, *N.T., Austral.* 215 S10
Argakhtakh, *Russ.* 161 D19
Arganda, *Sp.* 146 F11
Argelès-Gazost, *Fr.* 149 Y7
Argent, *Fr.* 149 R10
Argenta, *It.* 152 F7
Argentan, *Fr.* 149 P7
Argentario, Monte, *It.* 152 J7
Argentat, *Fr.* 149 V9
Argenteuil, *Fr.* 149 P10
Argentiera, Capo dell', *It.* 152 M3
Argentina, *S. Amer.* 134 L10
Argentina Range, *Antarctica*
230 F10
Argentine Basin, *Atl. Oc.* 241 U7
Argentine Plain, *Atl. Oc.* 241 U6
Argentine Rise, *Atl. Oc.* 241 U6
Argentino, Lago, *Arg.* 135 V7
Argenton, *Fr.* 149 T9
Argenton-Château, *Fr.* 149 S7
Argeş, river, *Rom.* 155 F16
Arghandāb, river, *Afghan.* 179 P5
Arghandāb Band, *Afghan.* 179 P5
Arghistān, *Afghan.* 179 Q6
Argo, *Sudan* 202 C12
Argo Fracture Zone, *Ind. Oc.* 224 J9
Argolikós Kólpos, *Gr.* 156 K11
Argonne, range, *Fr.* 149 N13
Árgos, *Gr.* 156 K11
Árgos Orestikó, *Gr.* 156 D8
Argostóli, *Gr.* 156 J7
Argoub, *W. Sahara* 200 E5
Arguedas, *Sp.* 147 D13
Arguello, Point, *Calif., U.S.* 111 W5
Argun', river, *Russ.* 161 L18
Arguut, *Mongolia* 182 E9
Argyle, *Minn., U.S.* 106 E8
Argyle, Lake, *Austral.* 214 C7
Argyrus see Gjirokastër, *Alban.*
154 M10
Arhus, *Den.* 142 M11
Ariano Irpino, *It.* 152 M11
Ariari, river, *Col.* 130 G6
Ari Atoll, *Maldives* 181 V3
Arica, *Chile* 134 B6
Arid, Cape, *Austral.* 214 K5
Arida, *Japan* 189 Q8
Aridaía, *Gr.* 156 B10
Aride, Île, *Seychelles* 209 M20
Ariège, river, *Fr.* 162 H5
Arifwala, *Pak.* 179 R11
Arīḥā, *Syr.* 172 E8
Arīḥā (Jericho), *W. Bank* 172 M6

Arikaree, river, *Colo., Nebr., U.S.*
108 L15
Arikawa, *Japan* 189 R3
Arima, *Trinidad and Tobago* 123 P23
Arimã, *Braz.* 132 E8
Ari, Motu, *Fr. Polynesia, Fr.* 223 R20
Arinagour, *Scot., U.K.* 144 L7
Arinos, river, *Braz.* 132 H10
Aripeka, *Fla., U.S.* 99 T7
Aripo, El Cerro del, *Trinidad and
Tobago* 123 N23
Ariporo, river, *Col.* 130 E7
Aripuanã, *Braz.* 132 G9
Aripuanã, river, *Braz.* 132 F9
Ariquemes, *Braz.* 132 G8
Arîsh, Wâdi el, *Egypt* 173 Q3
Aristizábal, Cabo, *Arg.* 135 S9
Ariyalur, *India* 181 R6
Arizaro, Salar de, *Arg.* 134 F8
Arizona, *Arg.* 134 M9
Arizona, *U.S.* 109 T7
Arizona City, *Ariz., U.S.* 109 V7
Arizoro, Salar de, *S. Amer.* 128 J5
Arjeplog, *Sw.* 143 E13
Arjona, *Col.* 130 C4
Arkadak, *Russ.* 158 M12
Arkadelphia, *Ark., U.S.* 102 H7
Arkagala, *Russ.* 161 F19
Arkaig, Loch, *Scot., U.K.* 144 K8
Arkangeliskiy Fracture Zone, *Atl. Oc.*
241 N7
Arkansas, *U.S.* 102 G8
Arkansas, river, *U.S.* 86 H12
Arkansas City, *Ark., U.S.* 102 J10
Arkansas City, *Kans., U.S.* 107 V8
Arkansas Post National Memorial,
Ark., U.S. 102 H9
Arkhangel'sk (Archangel), *Russ.*
160 E8
Arkhangel'skoye, *Russ.* 158 M11
Arkítsa, *Gr.* 156 G11
Arkoí, island, *Gr.* 157 K17
Arkona, Kap, *Ger.* 150 A10
Arkonam, *India* 181 P7
Arkticheskiy, Mys, *Russ.* 161 C14
Arlanc, *Fr.* 149 U11
Arlap, island, *Marshall Is., U.S.*
220 M7
Arles, *Fr.* 149 X12
Arlington, *Ga., U.S.* 99 P4
Arlington, *Oreg., U.S.* 110 F6
Arlington, *S. Dak., U.S.* 106 K8
Arlington, *Tex., U.S.* 104 L11
Arlington, *Va., U.S.* 98 C13
Arlington, *Wash., U.S.* 110 B4
Arlington Heights, *Ill., U.S.* 101 N6
Arlis Gap, *Arctic Oc.* 246 H11
Arlis Spur, *Arctic Oc.* 246 J8
Arlon, *Belg.* 162 J9
Arma, *Kans., U.S.* 107 U10
Armagh, *N. Ire., U.K.* 145 Q6
Armathiá, island, *Gr.* 157 Q18
Armavir, *Arm.* 171 E18
Armavir, *Russ.* 159 S11
Armenia, *Asia* 171 D17
Armenia, *Col.* 130 F4
Armenistís, *Gr.* 157 K16
Armijo, *N. Mex., U.S.* 109 S12
Armilla, *Sp.* 146 L11
Armorican Massif, *Eur.* 140 G4
Armour, *S. Dak., U.S.* 106 M6
Armstrong, *Ont., Can.* 85 N15
Armur, *India* 180 L6
Arnaía, *Gr.* 156 D12
Arnauti, Cape, *Cyprus* 162 P5
Arnay-le-Duc, *Fr.* 149 S12
Arnedo, *Sp.* 146 C12
Årnes, *Nor.* 142 G11
Arnett, *Okla., U.S.* 104 F8
Arnhem, *Neth.* 148 J13
Arnhem, Cape, *Austral.* 214 B10
Arnhem Land, *Austral.* 214 B9
Arniel, island, *Marshall Is., U.S.*
220 G12
Árnissa, *Gr.* 156 C9
Arno, river, *It.* 152 G6
Arno Atoll, *Marshall Is., U.S.* 220 H5
Arnold, *Mo., U.S.* 107 T15
Arnold, *Nebr., U.S.* 107 P5

Arnøy, island, *Nor.* 143 C13
Arnsberg, *Ger.* 150 F6
Aroab, *Namibia* 206 J8
Arock, *Oreg., U.S.* 110 J9
Arorae, island, *Kiribati* 218 G8
Arorangi, *Cook Is., N.Z.* 222 Q8
Arousa, Ría de, *Sp.* 146 C5
Arowhana, peak, *N.Z.* 217 K20
Arpa, river, *Turk.* 171 D17
Arpaçay, *Turk.* 171 D17
Arqalyq, *Kaz.* 176 D12
Ar Rabbah, *Jordan* 173 N6
Arraias, *Braz.* 133 H14
Ar Ramādī (Ramadi), *Iraq* 174 D9
Ar Ramthā, *Jordan* 172 L7
Ar Raqqah (Nicephorium), *Syr.*
172 E11
Arras, *Fr.* 148 M10
Ar Rashādīyah, *Jordan* 173 P6
Ar Rastan (Arethusa), *Syr.* 172 G8
Ar Rawḍah, *Saudi Arabia* 174 L8
Arreau, *Fr.* 149 Y7
Arrecife, *Sp.* 208 P7
Arrecife Macgowen, *Ecua.*
130 Q10
Arrée, Montagnes d', *Fr.* 149 Q3
Ar Riyāḍ (Riyadh), *Saudi Arabia*
174 J10
Ar Riyān, *Yemen* 174 Q12
Arrochar, *Scot., U.K.* 144 M9
Arromanches, *Fr.* 149 N7
Arronches, *Port.* 146 H6
Arrou, *Fr.* 149 Q8
Arrow, Lough, *Ire.* 145 Q5
Arrowrock Reservoir, *Idaho, U.S.*
108 G4
Arroyo, *P.R., U.S.* 122 P4
Arroyo de la Luz, *Sp.* 146 H7
Arroyo Grande, *Calif., U.S.* 111 W5
Arroyos de Mantua, *Cuba* 118 H4
Ar Rub' Al Khālī (Empty Quarter),
desert, *Saudi Arabia* 174 M11
Ar Ruṣāfah (Risāfe), ruins, *Syr.*
172 F11
Ar Ruṣayfah, *Jordan* 172 M7
Ar Ruṭbah, *Iraq* 174 E7
Ar Ruwayshid, *Jordan* 172 L10
Ars-en-Ré, *Fr.* 149 T5
Arsen'yev, *Russ.* 161 L21
Arshaly, *Kaz.* 177 D14
Arsiero, *It.* 152 D7
Arsikere, *India* 181 P5
Árta, *Gr.* 156 F8
Artamus, island, *Indonesia* 192 K7
Artashat, *Arm.* 171 E18
Artem, *Russ.* 161 M21
Artemisa, *Cuba* 118 G6
Artemivs'k, *Ukr.* 159 Q9
Artemovsk, *Russ.* 161 L13
Artesia, *N. Mex., U.S.* 109 U14
Artesian, *S. Dak., U.S.* 106 L7
Arthur, *Nebr., U.S.* 107 P3
Arthur's Pass, *N.Z.* 217 N17
Arthur's Town, *Bahamas* 119 E13
Arthurstown (Colmán), *Ire.* 145 U6
Artigas, *Uru.* 134 J14
Art, Île, *New Caledonia, Fr.* 222 B5
Artiste Point, *Grenada* 123 K24
Artois, *Eur.* 140 G5
Artova, *Turk.* 170 E11
Artux, *China* 182 F2
Artvin, *Turk.* 171 D16
Artyk, *Uzb.* 176 M8
Artyk Yuryakh, *Russ.* 161 F17
Aru, Kepulauan, *Indonesia* 193 L19
Arua, *Uganda* 202 J12
Aruanã, *Braz.* 132 J12
Aruba, island, *Lesser Antil.* 120 G8
Aruboe, island, *Marshall Is., U.S.*
220 M7
Arucas, *Sp.* 208 Q5
Arue, *Fr. Polynesia, Fr.* 223 N16
Aru Islands, *Asia* 168 L15
Arumã, *Braz.* 132 E8
Arumpo, *N.S.W., Austral.* 215 X12
Aru Passage, *F.S.M.* 221 F14
Arusha, *Tanzania* 203 L14
Arutanga, *Cook Is., N.Z.* 222 Q11
Arutanga Passage, *Cook Is., N.Z.*
222 Q11

Arutua, island, Fr. Polynesia, Fr. 223 D18
Aruwimi, river, Dem. Rep. of the Congo 202 J10
Arvada, Colo., U.S. 108 L13
Arvayheer, Mongolia 182 D9
Arviat, Nunavut, Can. 85 J15
Arvidsjaur, Sw. 143 F13
Arvika, Sw. 142 K12
Arvon, Mount, Mich., U.S. 100 F7
Arxan, China 183 D14
Ary, Russ. 161 E16
Arys, Kaz. 177 J13
Arys Köli, Kaz. 176 G12
Arzachena, It. 152 M4
Arzamas, Russ. 158 J12
Arzgir, Russ. 159 S13
Aşa see Asha, Cyprus 162 N9
Asad, Buḩayrat al, Syr. 172 E10
Asadābād, Afghan. 178 M9
Asadābād, Gardaneh-ye, Iran 174 D11
Asad Kêlay, Afghan. 179 P5
Asaga Strait, Amer. Samoa, U.S. 222 N2
Aşağı Ağcakənd, Arm. 171 D20
Aşağıpınarbaşı, Turk. 170 G8
Asahi Dake, Japan 188 F14
Asahikawa, Japan 188 F13
Asan, Guam, U.S. 220 C10
Asan, S. Korea 187 P8
Asanman, bay, S. Korea 187 P8
Asansol, India 180 H11
Asatdas, Guam, U.S. 220 B11
Asau, Samoa 222 K1
Asau Harbour, Samoa 222 K1
Āsbe Taferī, Eth. 203 G15
Asbury Park, N.J., U.S. 96 P11
Ascención, Bol. 132 L13
Ascensión, Mex. 116 C8
Ascension, island, Af. 198 L1
Ascension Bay, N. Amer. 82 N7
Ascension Fracture Zone, Atl. Oc. 241 Q10
Aschaffenburg, Ger. 150 H7
Ascó, Sp. 147 E15
Ascoli Piceno, It. 152 J10
'Aseb (Assab), Eritrea 203 E16
Asedjrad, range, Alg. 200 E10
Āsela, Eth. 203 G15
Asenovgrad, Bulg. 155 K14
Aşgabat (Ashgabat), Uzb. 176 M8
Asha (Aşa), Cyprus 162 N9
Ashāqif, Jabal al, Jordan 172 M9
Ashburn, Ga., U.S. 99 P6
Ashburton, N.Z. 217 P17
Ashburton, river, Austral. 214 F2
Ashburton Downs, W. Aust., Austral. 215 T2
Ashby Fort, ruin, St. Kitts and Nevis 123 C18
Aschchyköl, lake, Kaz. 176 H12
Ashdod, Israel 172 M5
Ashdown, Ark., U.S. 102 J6
Asherton, Tex., U.S. 105 T8
Asheville, N.C., U.S. 98 H7
Ashford, Eng., U.K. 145 W15
Ashford, Wash., U.S. 110 D4
Ash Fork, Ariz., U.S. 109 S6
Ashgabat see Aşgabat, Uzb. 176 M8
Ash Grove, Mo., U.S. 107 U12
Ashikaga, Japan 189 N12
Ashizuri Misaki, Japan 189 S6
Ashland, Kans., U.S. 107 V5
Ashland, Ky., U.S. 103 B20
Ashland, Me., U.S. 97 B17
Ashland, Mont., U.S. 108 E12
Ashland, Nebr., U.S. 107 Q8
Ashland, Ohio, U.S. 101 P13
Ashland, Oreg., U.S. 110 K3
Ashland, Va., U.S. 98 E13
Ashland, Wis., U.S. 100 F4
Ashley, N. Dak., U.S. 106 H6
Ashley, river, S.C., U.S. 98 M10
Ashmore Islands, Austral. 214 B4
Ashmyany, Belarus 158 K4
Ashoro, Japan 188 G14
Ashqelon, Israel 172 M4
Ash Shabakah, Iraq 174 F9
Ash Sharawrah, Saudi Arabia 174 N11

Ash Sharqāţ, Iraq 174 C9
Ash Shawbak, Jordan 173 P6
Ash Shiḩr, Yemen 174 Q12
Ash Shişar, Oman 175 N14
Ash Shumlūl, Saudi Arabia 174 H11
Ash Shuqayq, Saudi Arabia 174 N8
Ash Shurayf, Saudi Arabia 174 J7
Ashtabula, Ohio, U.S. 101 N15
Ashtabula, Lake, N. Dak., U.S. 106 G7
Ashton, Wyo., U.S. 108 G8
Asia, Kepulauan, Indonesia 217 A14
Asia Minor see Anatolia, Turk. 170 F7
Asifabad, India 180 L7
Asiga, Puntan, N. Mariana Is., U.S. 220 A8
Asika, India 180 L10
Asinara, Golfo dell', It. 152 M3
Asinara, Isola, It. 152 M3
Asipovichy, Belarus 158 L5
'Asīrm, region, Saudi Arabia 174 M8
Aşkale, Turk. 171 E15
Askole, Pak. 178 L13
Asl, Egypt 173 R1
Asmar, Afghan. 178 M9
Asmera (Asmara), Eritrea 203 E15
Āsosa, Sudan 203 F13
Aspen, Colo., U.S. 108 M11
Aspermont, Tex., U.S. 104 K7
Aspiring, Mount, N.Z. 217 P15
Aspres, Fr. 149 W14
Aspromonte, range, It. 153 R13
Asproválta, Gr. 156 C12
Asquith Rise, Ind. Oc. 224 H6
As Sa'an, Syr. 172 F9
As Sabkhah, Syr. 172 E12
Aş Şafā, Syr. 172 K8
As Safīrah, Syr. 172 E9
Aş Şa'īd, Yemen 174 Q10
'Assal, Lac, Djibouti 203 F16
Aş Şāliḩiyah, Syr. 172 G14
As Salţ, Jordan 172 M6
As Samāwah (Samawah), Iraq 174 F10
As Sanām, desert, Saudi Arabia 175 K13
Assateague Island National Seashore, Md., U.S. 98 D15
Aş Şawrah, Saudi Arabia 174 G5
Asselborn, Lux. 162 G9
Assen, Neth. 148 G13
As Sidr, Lib. 201 C15
As Sidr, Saudi Arabia 174 K7
Ássiros, Gr. 156 C11
Assis, Braz. 132 L12
Assisi, It. 152 H8
Assos, ruins, Turk. 170 E2
As Su'ayyirah, Saudi Arabia 174 H11
As Sukhnah, Syr. 172 G11
As Sulaymānīyah see Slêmanî, Iraq 174 C10
As Sulayyil, Saudi Arabia 174 M10
Aş Şulb, region, Saudi Arabia 174 H11
Aş Şummān, plateau, Saudi Arabia 174 H10
Aş Şurrah, Yemen 174 Q10
Aş Şuwār, Syr. 172 F14
As Suwayd', Syr. 172 L8
As Suwayḩ, Oman 175 L17
Assynt, Loch, Scot., U.K. 144 H8
Astakída, island, Gr. 157 P18
Astakós, Gr. 156 H8
Astana (Aqmola), Kaz. 177 D14
Astara, Azerb. 171 F22
Āstārā, Iran 174 B11
Asti, It. 152 E3
Astola Island, Pak. 179 W3
Astor, Pak. 178 L12
Astorga, Sp. 146 C8
Astoria, Oreg., U.S. 110 E2
Astra, Arg. 135 S9
Astrakhan', Russ. 159 R15
Astrid Ridge, Atl. Oc. 241 Y13
Astrolabe, Cape, Solomon Is. 221 M19
Ástros, Gr. 156 K10
Astrupa, Gora, Russ. 161 D14
Astudillo, Sp. 146 D10
Astypálaia, Gr. 157 M17
Astypálaia, island, Gr. 157 M17

Asuisui, Cape, Samoa 222 L1
Asunción, Parag. 132 M10
Asuncion, island, N. Mariana Is., U.S. 220 A2
Asunción, Punta, Arg. 135 N12
Asuzudo Point, N. Mariana Is., U.S. 220 D8
Aswân, Egypt 201 E19
Aswân High Dam, Egypt 201 E19
Asyûţ, Egypt 201 D18
Ata, island, Tonga 222 H12
Atacama, Desierto de, Chile 134 D7
Atacama, Puna de, S. Amer. 128 J5
Atacama, Salar de, Chile 134 E8
Atafu, island, Kiribati 218 H10
Atakapamé, Togo 204 D11
Atalánti, Gr. 156 H11
Atalaya de Femés, peak, Sp. 208 P7
Atamyrat (Kerki), Turkm. 176 M11
Atapupu, Indonesia 193 M15
Atar, Mauritania 200 F6
Atas Bogd, peak, Mongolia 182 E8
Atascadero, Calif., U.S. 111 V5
Atascosa, river, Tex., U.S. 105 S10
Atasu, Kaz. 177 E14
Atbara, Sudan 203 D13
Atbara, river, Sudan 203 D13
At-Bashy, Kyrg. 178 F12
Atchafalaya, river, La., U.S. 102 P9
Atchafalaya Bay, La., U.S. 102 Q9
Atchison, Kans., U.S. 107 S10
Ateca, Sp. 147 E13
Ath, Belg. 148 L11
Athabasca, Alta., Can. 84 L10
Athabasca, river, Sask., Can. 84 K11
Athabasca, Lake, Alta., Sask., Can. 84 J12
Athamánio, Gr. 156 F8
Athboy (Baile Átha Buí), Ire. 145 R6
Athena, Oreg., U.S. 110 E8
Athens, Ala., U.S. 103 G15
Athens, Ga., U.S. 98 L6
Athens, Ohio, U.S. 101 S14
Athens, Tenn., U.S. 103 F18
Athens, Tex., U.S. 104 M13
Athens see Athína, Gr. 156 J12
Atherton Tableland, Austral. 214 D13
Athfālah, Saudi Arabia 174 M8
Athienou, Cyprus 162 P9
Athína (Athens), Gr. 156 J12
Athlone (Baile Átha Luain), Ire. 145 S5
Athol Island, Bahamas 122 B12
Áthos, peak, Gr. 157 D13
Athos, Mount see Ágion Óros, Gr. 157 D13
Áth Trasna see Newmarket, Ire. 145 U4
Ati, Chad 201 J15
Atico, Peru 132 J4
Atikokan, Ont., Can. 85 P15
Atimoono, island, Cook Is., N.Z. 223 B15
Atina, It. 152 L10
Atitue, Fr. Polynesia, Fr. 223 P15
Atiu, island, Cook Is., N.Z. 218 K12
Atka, Alas., U.S. 112 P6
Atka, Russ. 161 F20
Atka Island, Alas., U.S. 112 P6
Atkarsk, Russ. 158 M13
Atkins, Ark., U.S. 102 F8
Atkinson, Nebr., U.S. 107 N6
Atlanta, Ga., U.S. 98 L5
Atlanta, Mich., U.S. 100 H11
Atlanta, Tex., U.S. 104 K15
Atlantic, Iowa, U.S. 107 P10
Atlantic, N.C., U.S. 98 J14
Atlantic Beach, Fla., U.S. 99 Q9
Atlantic Beach, N.C., U.S. 98 J14
Atlantic City, N.J., U.S. 96 Q10
Atlantic City, Wyo., U.S. 108 J10
Atlantic-Indian Basin, Atl. Oc., Ind. Oc. 241 Y10
Atlantic-Indian Ridge, Atl. Oc. 241 W13

Atlantis Fracture Zone, Atl. Oc. 240 K7
Atlantis II Fracture Zone, Ind. Oc. 224 N8
Atlas Mountains, Af. 200 B9
Atlin, B.C., Can. 84 G8
'Atlit, Israel 172 L5
Atmautluak, Alas., U.S. 112 J12
Atmore, Ala., U.S. 103 N14
Atoka, Okla., U.S. 104 H12
Atoyac, Mex. 116 K11
Atrak, river, Iran, Turkm. 175 B14
Atrato, river, Col. 130 D4
Atrek, river, Uzb. 176 M6
Atri, It. 152 J10
Atsutoko, Japan 188 G15
Attalaya, island, Kiribati 218 H10
Aţ Ţafīlah, Jordan 173 P6
Aţ Ţā'if, Saudi Arabia 174 L7
Attalla, Ala., U.S. 103 H16
Attapu, Laos 190 M13
Attawapiskat, Ont., Can. 85 M17
At Taysīyah, plateau, Saudi Arabia 174 G9
Attent, river, Lux. 162 J9
Attica, Ind., U.S. 101 Q8
Attica, Kans., U.S. 107 V6
Attleboro, Mass., U.S. 97 L14
Aţ Ţubayq, region, Saudi Arabia 174 G6
Attu Island, Alas., U.S. 112 K1
At Turbah, Yemen 174 R8
Atuel, river, Arg. 134 M8
Atuona, Fr. Polynesia, Fr. 223 M20
Atutahi, island, Cook Is., N.Z. 223 B18
Atwater, Calif., U.S. 111 S5
Atwood, Kans., U.S. 107 R4
Atwood see Samana Cay, Bahamas 119 G15
Atyraū, Kaz. 176 F6
Aūa, Amer. Samoa, U.S. 222 M8
Auas Mountains, Af. 198 N6
'Au'au Channel, Hawai'i, U.S. 115 H15
Aubagne, Fr. 149 Y13
Aubange, Belg. 162 K8
Aubenas, Fr. 149 W12
Aubert de la Rüe Seamounts, Ind. Oc. 248 C9
Aubiet, Fr. 149 X8
Aubinyà, Andorra 162 K2
Aubrac, Monts d', Fr. 149 W11
Aubry Lake, N.W.T., Can. 84 E10
Auburn, Ala., U.S. 103 L17
Auburn, Calif., U.S. 111 Q5
Auburn, Ill., U.S. 101 R5
Auburn, Ind., U.S. 101 P10
Auburn, Me., U.S. 97 G15
Auburn, N.Y., U.S. 96 J8
Auburn, Nebr., U.S. 107 R9
Auburn, Wash., U.S. 110 C4
Auburndale, Fla., U.S. 99 U8
Aubusson, Fr. 149 U10
Auce, Latv. 143 M16
Auch, Fr. 149 X8
Auchel, Fr. 148 L10
Auckland, N.Z. 217 J19
Auckland Islands, N.Z. 218 Q7
Audience Hall, Vatican City 163 R16
Audincourt, Fr. 149 R15
Audubon, Iowa, U.S. 107 P10
Augathella, Qnsld., Austral. 215 U13
Augrabies Falls, S. Af. 206 K8
Augsburg, Ger. 150 K8
Augusta, Ark., U.S. 102 G9
Augusta, Ga., U.S. 98 L8
Augusta, It. 153 T12
Augusta, Kans., U.S. 107 U8
Augusta, Ky., U.S. 103 A18
Augusta, Me., U.S. 97 G16
Augusta, Mont., U.S. 108 C7
Augusta, W. Aust., Austral. 215 Y2
Augusta, Wis., U.S. 100 J3
Augusta, Golfo di, It. 153 T12
Augustów, Pol. 151 B17
August Town, Jam. 122 J10
Augustus, Mount, Austral. 214 G2
Augustus Downs, Qnsld., Austral. 215 R11

Augustus Island, Austral. 214 C5
Aukena, island, Fr. Polynesia, Fr. 223 Q21
Auki, Solomon Is. 221 N19
Aukland Escarpment, Pac. Oc. 242 R10
Aukland Islands Shelf, Pac. Oc. 249 G19
Auld, Lake, Austral. 214 F5
Auletta, It. 152 M12
Äülieköl, Kaz. 176 C11
Aulong, island, Palau 220 P10
Auluptagel, island, Palau 220 P11
Aunu'u, Amer. Samoa, U.S. 222 M9
Aunuu, island, Amer. Samoa, U.S. 222 M9
Auob, river, Af. 206 J7
Auponhia, Indonesia 193 K15
Aur, island, Malaysia 191 U11
Auraiya, India 180 G7
Aurangabad, India 180 H9
Aurangabad, India 180 L4
Aur Atoll, Marshall Is., U.S. 220 G5
Auray, Fr. 149 R4
Aurich, Ger. 150 C6
Aurignac, Fr. 149 Y8
Aurillac, Fr. 149 V10
Aurisina, It. 152 D10
Aurora, Colo., U.S. 108 M13
Aurora, Ill., U.S. 101 N6
Aurora, Ind., U.S. 101 S10
Aurora, Minn., U.S. 106 F12
Aurora, Mo., U.S. 107 V11
Aurora, Nebr., U.S. 107 Q7
Aurora Bank, Ind. Oc. 248 B11
Aurora Canyon, Atl. Oc. 241 X6
Aurukun, Qnsld., Austral. 215 P12
Aus, Namibia 206 J6
Ausa, river, San Marino 163 G17
Au Sable, Mich., U.S. 100 J12
Au Sable, river, Mich., U.S. 100 J11
Au Sable Point, Mich., U.S. 100 F9
Auschwitz see Oświęcim, Pol. 151 H15
Austin, Ind., U.S. 101 T9
Austin, Minn., U.S. 106 L12
Austin, Nev., U.S. 111 P9
Austin, Pa., U.S. 96 L6
Austin, Tex., U.S. 105 Q10
Austin, Lake, Austral. 214 H3
Austral Downs, N.T., Austral. 215 S10
Austral Fracture Zone, Pac. Oc. 243 M17
Australia, Austral. 217 F15
Australian Alps, Austral. 214 M13
Australian-Antarctic Basin, Ind. Oc. 224 Q12
Australian-Antarctic Discordance, Ind. Oc. 225 R19
Australian Capital Territory, Austral. 215 Y14
Austral Islands (Tubuai Islands), Fr. Polynesia, Fr. 223 H16
Austral Seamounts, Pac. Oc. 243 M14
Austria, Eur. 150 L10
Austriahütte, site, Aust. 150 L10
Austvågøy, island, Nor. 142 D12
Autazes, Braz. 132 D9
Auti, Fr. Polynesia, Fr. 223 K24
Autlán, Mex. 116 H9
Autun, Fr. 149 S12
Auxerre, Fr. 149 R11
Auxonne, Fr. 149 S13
Auzances, Fr. 149 T10
Ava, Mo., U.S. 107 V13
Avaavaroa Passage, Cook Is., N.Z. 222 Q9
Avaha, island, Solomon Is. 221 J18
Avala, peak, Serb. 154 F10
Avalau, island, Tuvalu 221 L23
Avallon, Fr. 149 R11
Avalon, Calif., U.S. 111 Y8
Avalon, Lake, N. Mex., U.S. 109 V14
Avalon Peninsula, Nfld. & Lab., Can. 85 M24
Avanavero, Suriname 131 E15
Avanos, Turk. 170 F10
Avapeihi, Passe, Fr. Polynesia, Fr. 223 G14

Avarapa, Passe, Fr. Polynesia, Fr. 223 P14
Avarua, Cook Is., N.Z. 222 Q9
Avarua Harbour, Cook Is., N.Z. 222 Q9
Avatele, Cook Is., N.Z. 223 B20
Avatele Bay, Cook Is., N.Z. 223 B20
Avatiu, Cook Is., N.Z. 222 Q9
Avatiu Harbour, Cook Is., N.Z. 222 Q9
Avatolu, Passe, Wallis and Futuna, Fr. 222 B11
Avatoru, Fr. Polynesia, Fr. 223 K16
Āvāz, Iran 175 D17
Ávdira, ruin, Gr. 157 C14
Avea, island, Fiji 222 H9
Avea, Baie d', Fr. Polynesia, Fr. 223 H14
Aveiro, Braz. 132 D11
Aveiro, Port. 146 F5
Āvej, Iran 174 C12
Avellino, It. 152 M11
Avenal, Calif., U.S. 111 U6
Avera, Fr. Polynesia, Fr. 223 B23
Avera, Fr. Polynesia, Fr. 223 K23
Avera, Baie d', Fr. Polynesia, Fr. 223 K23
Aversa, It. 152 M10
Aves, island, Lesser Antil. 121 D14
Aves, Islas de, Venez. 130 A9
Aves Ridge, Atl. Oc. 240 M5
Avesta, Sw. 143 K13
Avezzano, It. 152 K9
Avgó, island, Gr. 156 N11
Avgonísi, island, Gr. 157 N17
Aviano, It. 152 D8
Aviator Glacier, Antarctica 231 Q14
Avignon, Fr. 149 X13
Ávila, Sp. 146 F10
Avilés, Sp. 146 A8
Avire, Vanuatu 222 B2
Avissawella, Sri Lanka 181 T7
Avita, Solomon Is. 221 Q23
Avlonári, Gr. 157 H13
Avoca, Iowa, U.S. 107 P9
Avon, N.C., U.S. 98 H15
Avon, river, Eng., U.K. 145 U12
Avon, river, Eng., U.K. 145 V11
Avondale, Ariz., U.S. 109 U6
Avon Park, Fla., U.S. 99 U9
Avranches, Fr. 149 P6
Avsa, Gora, Russ. 161 H13
Avu Avu, Solomon Is. 221 P19
Awaday, W. Sahara 200 E6
Āwarē, Eth. 203 G16
Awarua Bay, N.Z. 217 P15
Awa Shima, Japan 188 L11
Awat, China 182 F3
Awbārī, Ṣaḩrā', desert, Lib. 201 D13
Awe, Loch, Scot., U.K. 144 L8
Aweil, S. Sudan 202 G11
Awini Plateau, Hawai'i, U.S. 115 K19
Awjilah, Lib. 201 D16
Awsard, W. Sahara 200 E5
Axarfjarðardjúp, valley, Arctic Oc. 247 L20
Axel Heiberg Island, Nunavut, Can. 85 B15
Axim, Ghana 204 E10
Axinim, Braz. 132 E9
Axiós, river, Gr. 156 B10
Ax-les-Thermes, Fr. 149 Z9
Axtell, Nebr., U.S. 107 Q6
Ayabe, Japan 189 P8
Ayacucho, Arg. 135 N13
Ayacucho, Peru 132 H4
Ayakkum Hu, China 182 G5
Ayaköz, Kaz. 177 E17
Ayamonte, Sp. 146 L6
Ayan, Russ. 161 H20
Ayan, Russ. 161 J15
Ayancık, Turk. 170 C10
Ayapel, Col. 130 D5
Ayaş, Turk. 170 E8
Ayasergi see Ayios Seryios, Cyprus 162 N10
Ayat, river, Kaz. 176 C10
Ayaviri, Peru 132 J5
Aydar Kŭl, lake, Uzb. 176 K12
Ayden, N.C., U.S. 98 H13
Aydere, Turkm. 176 L7
Aydın, Turk. 170 G3
Aydıncık, Turk. 170 J8
Ayerbe, Sp. 147 C14
Ayers Rock see Uluṟu, peak, N.T., Austral. 215 U8
Ayeyarwady (Irrawaddy), river, Myanmar 190 G6
Ayeyarwady, Mouths of the, Myanmar 190 L5
Ayios Amvrosios (Aykuruş), Cyprus 162 N9
Ayios Seryios (Ayasergi), Cyprus 162 N10
Ayios Theodhoros (Çayırova), Cyprus 162 N10
Aykhal, Russ. 161 G15
Ay Khanom, ruins, Afghan. 178 K8
Aykuruş see Ayios Amvrosios, Cyprus 162 N9
Aylesbury, Eng., U.K. 145 V13
Ayllón, Sp. 146 E11
Aylmer Lake, N.W.T., Can. 84 H12
'Ayn al 'Arab (Kobanê), Syr. 172 C10
Ayní, Taj. 178 H7
'Aynūnah, Saudi Arabia 174 G5
Ayon, Ostrov, Russ. 161 C19
Ayon Island, Asia 168 B11
Ayorou, Niger 200 H10
Ayoûn el 'Atroûs, Mauritania 200 G6
Aypolovo, Russ. 160 J11
Ayr, Qnsld., Austral. 215 S14
Ayr, Scot., U.K. 145 N9
Ayrancı, Turk. 170 H9
Ayre, Point of, Isle of Man, U.K. 145 Q9
Äyteke Bī, Kaz. 176 G10
Aytos, Bulg. 155 J17
Ayutla, Mex. 116 K11
Ayutthaya, Thai. 190 M9
Ayvacık, Turk. 170 E2
Ayvaj, Taj. 178 K7
Ayvalık, Turk. 170 E2
Āzāb, Afghan. 179 N3
Āzād Shahr, Iran 175 B14
Azahar, Costa del, Sp. 147 G16
Azamgarh, India 180 G9
Azapa, Chile 134 B6
Azare, Nigeria 205 B15
Azawad, region, Mali 200 F8
Azawak, river, Mali, Niger 200 G10
A'zāz, Syr. 172 D8
Azdavay, Turk. 170 C8
Azefal Dunes, Af. 198 E1
Azerbaijan, Asia 171 D21
Azerbaijan, region, Iran 174 C10
Azincourt, Fr. 148 M9
Azle, Tex., U.S. 104 L11
Azmoos, Switz. 162 Q1
Azogues, Ecua. 130 K3
Azores-Biscay Rise, Atl. Oc. 240 J10
Azores Plateau, Atl. Oc. 240 J9
Azov, Russ. 159 R10
Azov, Sea of, Russ., Ukr. 159 S9
Azov Upland, Eur. 140 H12
Azraq, El Bahr el (Blue Nile), river, Af. 203 E13
Aztec, N. Mex., U.S. 109 Q11
Aztec Ruins National Monument, N. Mex., U.S. 109 Q10
Azua, Dom. Rep. 119 M18
Azuaga, Sp. 146 J8
Azuero, Península de, Pan. 117 P21
Azuero Peninsula, N. Amer. 82 R8
Azul, Arg. 134 M12
Azurduy, Bol. 132 L8
Az Zabadānī, Syr. 172 J7
Az̧ Z̧āhirīyah, W. Bank 173 N5
'Azzān, Yemen 174 Q11
Az Zarqā', Jordan 172 M7
Az Zawr, Kuwait 174 G11
Azzel Matti, Sebkha, Alg. 200 E10
Az Zubayr, Iraq 174 F11

B

Ba, Fiji 222 H6
Baaba, Île, New Caledonia, Fr. 222 B6
Baabda, Leb. 172 J6
Baalbek, Leb. 172 H7
Baardheere, Somalia 203 J16
Baarn, Neth. 148 J12
Bābā, Kōh-e, Afghan. 178 M6
Baba Burnu, Turk. 170 C7
Baba Burnu, Turk. 170 E2
Baba Dağ, peak, Turk. 170 J4
Babadağ, peak, Azerb. 171 C22
Babaeski, Turk. 170 C3
Babahoyo, Ecua. 130 K2
Babanūsah, Sudan 202 F11
Babar, island, Indonesia 193 M17
Babar, Kepulauan, Indonesia 193 M17
Babar Islands, Asia 168 M15
Babati, Tanzania 203 L14
Babayevo, Russ. 158 F8
Babayurt, Russ. 159 T15
Babe Island, Guam, U.S. 220 E10
Bab el Mandeb, Ind. Oc. 168 J2
Babelthuap see Babledaob, island, Palau 220 N11
Babi, island, Indonesia 192 H4
Babinda, Qnsld., Austral. 215 R13
Babin Nos, peak, Bulg., Serb. 154 G12
Babledaob (Babelthuap), island, Palau 220 N11
Babo, Indonesia 193 K18
Baboquivari Peak, Ariz., U.S. 109 W6
Babruysk, Belarus 158 L5
Babu see Hezhou, Guangxi Zhuang, China 185 U3
Babusar Pass, Pak. 180 B4
Babushkina, Russ. 158 F11
Babuyan, island, Philippines 193 A14
Babuyan Channel, Philippines 193 B13
Babuyan Islands, Philippines 193 A14
Babylon, ruins, Iraq 174 E9
Bacaadweyn, Somalia 203 G18
Bacabal, Braz. 133 E14
Bacan, island, Indonesia 193 J16
Bacău, Rom. 155 C16
Baccarat, Fr. 149 P14
Baceno, It. 152 C3
Bachelor, Mount, Oreg., U.S. 110 H4
Bachu, China 182 F2
Back, river, Nunavut, Can. 85 G13
Bačka, region, Serb. 154 E9
Bačka Palanka, Serb. 154 E9
Bačka Topola, Serb. 154 D9
Backbone Mountain, Md., U.S. 98 C10
Back Cay, Bahamas 122 E7
Bạc Liêu, Vietnam 191 Q12
Bắc Ninh, Vietnam 190 H12
Bacolet, Grenada 123 L23
Bacolod City, Philippines 193 E14
Bacup, Eng., U.K. 145 R11
Bad, river, S. Dak., U.S. 106 L4
Badain Jaran Shamo, China 182 G9
Badajoz, Sp. 146 J7
Badalona, Sp. 147 E17
Bad Axe, Mich., U.S. 100 K12
Baddeck, N.S., Can. 85 N22
Baddo, river, Pak. 179 T4
Baden, Aust. 150 K12
Baden-Baden, Ger. 150 J6
Baden Park, N.S.W., Austral. 215 X12
Baderna, Croatia 154 E4
Bādgah, Afghan. 178 M5
Badger, Minn., U.S. 106 E9
Bad Hersfeld, Ger. 150 F7
Bad Homburg, Ger. 150 G6
Badin, Pak. 179 W7
Bad Ischl, Aust. 150 L10
Bad Kissengen, Ger. 150 G7
Badlands, N. Dak., U.S. 106 G2
Badlands National Park, S. Dak., U.S. 106 L2
Bad Mergentheim, Ger. 150 H7
Badogo, Mali 200 J7
Badong, Chongq., China 184 M2
Badrah, Iraq 174 E10
Bad Reichenhall, Ger. 150 L10
Badr Ḩunayn, Saudi Arabia 174 K6
Bad Säckingen, Ger. 150 L5
Bad Tölz, Ger. 150 L8
Badu Island, Austral. 214 A12
Badulla, Sri Lanka 181 T8
Badupi, Myanmar 190 G4
Baegado, island, S. Korea 187 N6
Baegamsan, peak, S. Korea 186 L9
Baengnyeongdo, island, S. Korea 186 M4
Baetic Mountains, Eur. 140 L2
Bafa Gölü, Turk. 170 G3
Bafatá, Guinea-Bissau 204 B4
Baffin Basin, Arctic Oc. 247 P15
Baffin Bay, Arctic Oc. 247 P14
Baffin Bay, Tex., U.S. 105 U11
Baffin Island, Nunavut, Can. 85 F17
Bafia, Cameroon 205 E15
Bafing, river, Af. 198 G2
Bafoulabé, Mali 200 H6
Bafoussam, Cameroon 205 E15
Bafra, Turk. 170 C11
Bafra Burnu, Turk. 170 C11
Bāft, Iran 175 G15
Baga, island, Solomon Is. 221 M15
Bagamoyo, Tanzania 203 M15
Bagana, Mount, P.N.G. 221 K14
Bagan Serai, Malaysia 191 T9
Bagansiapiapi, Indonesia 192 H6
Bagdad, Ariz., U.S. 109 S6
Bagdarin, Russ. 161 K16
Bagé, Braz. 132 Q11
Bages et de Sigean, Étang de, Fr. 149 Y10
Baggs, Wyo., U.S. 108 K11
Bagh a' Chaisteil (Castlebay), Scot., U.K. 144 K6
Baghdād (Baghdad), Iraq 174 E9
Bagheria, It. 153 S9
Bāghīn, Iran 175 F15
Baghlān, Afghan. 178 L7
Bāghrān Khūlah, Afghan. 179 N4
Bağırpaşa Dağı, peak, Turk. 171 F14
Bağışlı, Turk. 171 G18
Bagley, Minn., U.S. 106 F9
Bagnères-de-Bigorre, Fr. 149 Y7
Bagnères-de-Luchon, Fr. 149 Y8
Bago, Myanmar 190 K6
Bago Yoma, Myanmar 190 H6
Bagrām, Afghan. 178 M8
Bagrimi, Afghan. 178 M8
Baguio, Philippines 193 B13
Bahamas, N. Amer. 118 E12
Baħarić-Ċagħag, Malta 163 J22
Bahau, Malaysia 191 U10
Bahawalnagar, Pak. 179 R11
Bahawalpur, Pak. 179 S10
Bahçe, Turk. 170 H11
Bahçesaray, Turk. 171 G17
Bäherden, Turkm. 176 L8
Bahía, Islas de la, Hond. 117 K17
Bahía Blanca, Arg. 135 N11
Bahía Blanca Canyon, Atl. Oc. 241 U6
Bahía de Caráquez, Ecua. 130 J2
Bahia Honda Key, Fla., U.S. 99 Y9
Bahía Laura, Arg. 135 U9
Bahías, Cabo dos, Arg. 135 S9
Bahia Seamounts, Atl. Oc. 241 Q9
Bahir Dar, Eth. 203 F14
Bahlās, Oman 175 K16
Bahraich, India 180 F8
Bahrain, Asia 174 J12
Bāhū Kalāt, Iran 175 H18
Bai, river, Henan, China 184 L4
Baia de Aramă, Rom. 154 F12
Baia de Maputo, Af. 198 P9
Baía dos Tigres, Angola 206 F5
Baia Mare, Rom. 155 B13
Baia Sprie, Rom. 155 B13
Baïbokoum, Chad 201 K14
Bai Bung, Point, Asia 168 K11
Baicheng, China 182 E3
Baicheng, China 183 D15
Băicoi, Rom. 155 E15
Baie-Mahault, Guadeloupe, Fr. 123 E14
Baihe, Shaanxi, China 184 K2
Baijiantan, China 182 D5
Baikal, Lake see Baykal, Ozero, Russ. 161 L16
Baikha, Russ. 161 H13
Baikunthpur, India 180 J8
Baile an Chaisleáin see Castletownshend, Ire. 145 V3
Baile an Róba see Ballinrobe, Ire. 145 Q3
Baile Átha Buí see Athboy, Ire. 145 R6
Baile Átha Cliath see Dublin, Ire. 145 S7
Baile Átha Fhirdhia see Ardee, Ire. 145 R6
Baile Átha Luain see Athlone, Ire. 145 S5
Baile Bhuirne (Ballyvourney), Ire. 145 U3
Baile Chruaich see Ballycroy, Ire. 145 Q3
Baile Mhistéala see Mitchelstown, Ire. 145 U4
Bailén, Sp. 146 K11
Baile na gCros see Castlepollard, Ire. 145 R6
Băileşti, Rom. 155 G13
Baileys Harbor, Wis., U.S. 100 H8
Bailey Town, Bahamas 122 B8
Bailique, Braz. 133 C13
Baillif, Guadeloupe, Fr. 123 G14
Bailundo, Angola 206 D6
Baily or Coffin Group see Haha Jima Rettō, Japan 218 C4
Baily Group see Haha Jima Rettō, Japan 189 X14
Baima, China 182 K9
Bainbridge, Ga., U.S. 99 Q5
Bainet, Haiti 119 N16
Bain Fracture Zone, Ind. Oc. 224 R3
Baing, Indonesia 193 N13
Baingear (Bangor), Ire. 145 Q3
Bainville, Mont., U.S. 108 B13
Baiona, Sp. 146 C5
Bā'ir, Jordan 173 P8
Baird, Tex., U.S. 104 M8
Baird Inlet, Alas., U.S. 112 J11
Baird Mountains, Alas., U.S. 113 D14
Baird Seamounts, Pac. Oc. 243 H13
Bairin Zuoqi, China 183 E14
Bairnsdale, Vic., Austral. 215 Z13
Baishan, Jilin, China 184 A15
Baissac Bank, Ind. Oc. 224 J8
Baiti, region, Nauru 221 E23
Baixiang, Shanxi, China 184 F6
Baixo, Ilhéu de, Madeira, Port. 208 L4
Baiyin, China 182 H10
Baiyu Shan, Shaanxi, China 184 F1
Baja, Hung. 151 N15
Baja California, Mex. 116 D6
Baja California Seamount Province, Pac. Oc. 243 F17
Bajag, India 180 J8
Bājgīrān, Iran 175 B16
Bājil, Yemen 174 Q8
Bajmok, Serb. 154 D9
Bajo, Indonesia 193 J13
Bakchar, Russ. 160 K12
Bakel, Senegal 200 H5
Baker, Calif., U.S. 111 V11
Baker, Mont., U.S. 108 D13
Baker, Nev., U.S. 111 Q13
Baker, river, Chile 135 U6
Baker, Mount, Wash., U.S. 110 A4
Baker City, Oreg., U.S. 110 G8
Baker Foreland, Nunavut, Can. 85 H15
Baker Island, Pac. Oc. 218 G9
Baker Lake, Austral. 214 G6
Baker Lake, Nunavut, Can. 85 H14
Bakersfield, Calif., U.S. 111 V7
Bakhchysaray, Ukr. 159 T7
Bakhmach, Ukr. 159 N7
Bakhta, Russ. 161 H13
Bakhtegān, Daryācheh-ye, Iran 175 G14
Baki (Baku), Azerb. 171 D23
Bakırdağı, Turk. 170 G11
Bakkafjörður, Ice. 142 E4
Bakkaflóadjúp, valley, Arctic Oc. 247 K21
Bakkagerði, Ice. 142 E4
Bako, Eth. 203 H14
Bakony, range, Hung. 151 M13
Baku see Baki, Azerb. 171 D23
Bakuriani, Rep. of Georgia 171 C17

Bakutis Coast, *Antarctica* **230** L7
Balá, *Turk.* **170** E8
Bala, Cerros de, *S. Amer.* **128** G4
Balabac, *Malaysia* **192** F12
Balabac, island, *Philippines* **192** F12
Balabac Strait, *Philippines* **192** F12
Balabat, *F.S.M.* **221** D18
Balabio, Île, *New Caledonia, Fr.* **222** B6
Balaclava, *Jam.* **122** J7
Balagansk, *Russ.* **161** L15
Balaghat, *India* **180** K7
Balaghat Range, *India* **180** L5
Balaguer, *Sp.* **147** D16
Balakən, *Azerb.* **171** C20
Balakhna, *Russ.* **158** H12
Balaklava, *Ukr.* **159** T7
Balakliya, *Ukr.* **159** P9
Balakot, *Pak.* **178** M11
Balakovo, *Russ.* **158** M14
Bālā Murghāb, *Afghan.* **178** L2
Bălan, *Rom.* **155** C15
Balancán, *Mex.* **117** J15
Balangir, *India* **180** K9
Balaözen, river, *Kaz.* **176** D5
Balashi, site, *Aruba, Neth.* **123** R17
Balashov, *Russ.* **158** M12
Balassagyarmat, *Hung.* **151** K15
Balaton, lake, *Hung.* **151** M14
Balatonszentgyörgy, *Hung.* **151** M13
Balazote, *Sp.* **146** J12
Balbi, Mount, *P.N.G.* **221** J13
Balbina, Represa da, *Braz.* **132** D9
Balcarce, *Arg.* **135** N13
Balchik, *Bulg.* **155** G18
Bal Chirāgh, *Afghan.* **178** L5
Balclutha, *N.Z.* **217** R16
Bald Knob, *Ark., U.S.* **102** F9
Bald Mountain, *Nev., U.S.* **111** S11
Baldwin, *Fla., U.S.* **99** Q8
Baldwin City, *Kans., U.S.* **107** T10
Baldwinsville, *N.Y., U.S.* **96** J8
Baldwyn, *Miss., U.S.* **103** H13
Baldy, Mount, *Ariz., U.S.* **109** T9
Baldy Peak, *U.S.* **86** J7
Balearic Islands, *Sp.* **147** G17
Balearic Sea, *Sp.* **147** G17
Baleia, Ponta da, *Braz.* **133** K16
Baleine Bay, *St. Vincent and the Grenadines* **123** J16
Balembangan, island, *Malaysia* **192** F12
Baleshare, island, *Scot., U.K.* **144** J6
Baleshwar, *India* **180** K11
Baley, *Russ.* **161** L17
Balfour Channel, *Solomon Is.* **221** N16
Balfour Downs, *W. Aust., Austral.* **215** T4
Balgazyn, *Russ.* **161** M13
Balgo, *W. Aust., Austral.* **215** S6
Balguerie, Cap, *Fr. Polynesia, Fr.* **223** M21
Balḩāf, *Yemen* **174** Q11
Bali, *India* **180** G3
Bali, island, *Indonesia* **192** M11
Bali, Selat, *Indonesia* **192** M11
Balıkesir, *Turk.* **170** E4
Balık Gölü, *Turk.* **170** C11
Balīkh, river, *Syr.* **172** D11
Balikpapan, *Indonesia* **192** J12
Balimo, *P.N.G.* **217** D18
Balingen, *Ger.* **150** K6
Balintang Channel, *Philippines* **193** A13
Bali Sea, *Indonesia* **192** M11
Balkanabat, *Turkm.* **176** L6
Balkan Mountains, *Eur.* **154** H12
Balkan Peninsula, *Eur.* **140** K9
Balkh, *Afghan.* **178** K6
Balkhāb, *Afghan.* **178** L6
Balkhash, Lake, *Asia* **168** F7
Balladonia, *W. Aust., Austral.* **215** X5
Ballalae, island, *Solomon Is.* **221** L14
Ballantyne Strait, *N.W.T., Can.* **85** B13
Ballarat, *Vic., Austral.* **215** Z12
Ballard, Lake, *Austral.* **214** J4
Ballenas, Bahía, *Mex.* **116** D6

Ballenero, Canal, *Chile* **135** Y8
Ballenero Bay, *S. Amer.* **128** R5
Balleny Basin, *Pac. Oc.* **249** H17
Balleny Fracture Zone, *Pac. Oc.* **249** G17
Balleny Seamounts, *Pac. Oc.* **249** G16
Balleny Trough, *Pac. Oc.* **249** H16
Ballina, *N.S.W., Austral.* **215** W16
Ballina (Béal an Átha), *Ire.* **145** Q4
Ballinger, *Tex., U.S.* **105** N7
Ballinrobe (Baile an Róba), *Ire.* **145** Q3
Ballinskelligs Bay see Scealg, Bá na, *Ire.* **145** U2
Ball's Pyramid, island, *Coral Sea* **218** M6
Ballycastle, *N. Ire., U.K.* **145** N7
Ballycroy (Baile Chruaich), *Ire.* **145** Q3
Ballyhaise (Beal Átha hÉis), *Ire.* **145** Q6
Ballymena, *N. Ire., U.K.* **145** P7
Ballymoney, *N. Ire., U.K.* **145** Q7
Ballyshannon (Béal Átha Seanaidh), *Ire.* **145** Q5
Ballyvourney see Baile Bhuirne, *Ire.* **145** U3
Balmaceda, *Chile* **135** T7
Balmorhea, *Tex., U.S.* **105** P2
Balod, *India* **180** K8
Baloeri de Cristo Rey, *Eq. Guinea* **208** L7
Balonne, river, *Austral.* **214** H14
Balotra, *India* **180** G3
Balpyq Bī, *Kaz.* **177** G17
Balqash, *Kaz.* **177** F15
Balqash Köli, *Kaz.* **177** G15
Balrampur, *India* **180** F8
Balranald, *N.S.W., Austral.* **215** X12
Balş, *Rom.* **155** F14
Balsas, *Braz.* **133** F14
Balsas, river, *Mex.* **116** J11
Balta, *N. Dak., U.S.* **106** E5
Balta, *Ukr.* **159** Q5
Baltasar Brum, *Uru.* **134** J13
Bălți, *Mold.* **159** Q4
Baltic Plains, *Eur.* **140** E9
Baltic Sea, *Eur.* **140** F8
Baltimore, *Md., U.S.* **98** C13
Baltistan, region, *Pak.* **178** L12
Baltit, *Pak.* **178** K12
Baltiysk, *Russ.* **158** J1
Baltra, Isla, *Ecua.* **130** Q10
Baluchistan, region, *Iran, Pak.* **179** U2
Balurghat, *India* **180** H12
Balya, *Turk.* **170** E3
Balykchy (Ysyk-Köl), *Kyrg.* **178** E12
Balyqshy, *Kaz.* **176** F6
Balzers, *Liech.* **162** Q2
Bam, *Iran* **175** G16
Bama, *Nigeria* **205** B17
Bamaga, *Qnsld., Austral.* **215** N12
Bamako, *Mali* **200** J7
Bambari, *Cen. Af. Rep.* **202** H9
Bamberg, *Ger.* **150** H8
Bamberg, *S.C., U.S.* **98** L9
Bamboo, *Jam.* **122** H8
Bamboo, *W. Aust., Austral.* **215** S3
Bamda, *China* **182** L7
Bamenda, *Cameroon* **205** E15
Bamingui, *Cen. Af. Rep.* **202** G9
Bampūr, *Iran* **175** H17
Bampūr, *Iran* **175** H17
Bamy, *Turkm.* **176** L7
Bāmyān, *Afghan.* **178** M7
Banaba (Ocean Island), *Kiribati* **218** G7
Banalia, *Dem. Rep. of the Congo* **202** J11
Banana, *Kiribati* **221** A23
Bananal, Ilha do, *Braz.* **132** G12
Banana River, *Fla., U.S.* **99** T10
Bananga, *India* **181** T15
Bananier, *Guadeloupe, Fr.* **123** G14
Banaras see Varanasi, *India* **180** H9
Banas, river, *India* **180** G5
Banâs, Râs, *Egypt* **201** E20
Banat, region, *Rom., Serb.* **154** D10
Banaz, *Turk.* **170** F5

Ban Ban, *Laos* **190** J10
Ban Bang Hin, *Thai.* **191** Q7
Banbridge, *N. Ire., U.K.* **145** Q7
Banbury, *Eng., U.K.* **145** U12
Banchory, *Scot., U.K.* **144** K11
Bancroft, *Iowa, U.S.* **106** M11
Banda, *India* **180** H6
Banda, Kepulauan, *Indonesia* **193** L17
Banda, Pointe, *Gabon* **205** J15
Banda Aceh, *Philippines* **192** G3
Banda Besar, island, *Indonesia* **193** L17
Banda Elat, *Indonesia* **193** L18
Bandanaira, *Indonesia* **193** L17
Bandar see Machilipatnam, *India* **181** N11
Bandarban, *Bangladesh* **180** J14
Bandarbeyla, *Somalia* **203** G18
Bandar-e 'Abbās, *Iran* **175** H15
Bandar-e Anzalī, *Iran* **174** B12
Bandar-e Būshehr, *Iran* **174** G12
Bandar-e Chārak, *Iran* **175** H14
Bandar-e Deylam, *Iran* **174** F12
Bandar-e Genāveh, *Iran* **174** G12
Bandar-e Kangān, *Iran* **175** J16
Bandar-e Khoemir, *Iran* **175** H15
Bandar-e Māhshahr, *Iran* **174** F12
Bandar-e Maqām, *Iran* **175** H14
Bandar-e Mullāhā, *Afghan.* **178** L4
Bandar Seri Begawan, *Brunei* **192** G11
Banda Sea, *Indonesia* **193** L15
Bandau, *Malaysia* **192** F12
Bandeira, peak, *Braz.* **133** L15
Bandeirante, *Braz.* **132** H12
Bandelier National Monument, *N. Mex., U.S.* **109** R12
Bandera, *Arg.* **134** H11
Bandera, *Tex., U.S.* **105** R9
Banderas Bay, *N. Amer.* **82** N3
Bandiagara, *Mali* **200** H8
Bandikui, *India* **180** G5
Bandırma, *Turk.* **170** D4
Bandon, *Oreg., U.S.* **110** J1
Bandundu, *Dem. Rep. of the Congo* **202** L8
Bandung, *Indonesia* **192** M8
Banes, *Cuba* **119** J13
Banff, *Alta., Can.* **84** M10
Banfora, *Burkina Faso* **204** C9
Bangalore see Bengaluru, *India* **181** P6
Bangassou, *Cen. Af. Rep.* **202** H10
Banggai, Kepulauan, *Indonesia* **193** K14
Banggi, island, *Malaysia* **192** F12
Banggong Co (Bangong Cuo), *China* **182** H2
Banghāzī (Benghazi), *Lib.* **201** C15
Banghiang, river, *Laos* **190** L12
Bangi Island, *Guam, U.S.* **220** D9
Bangka, island, *Indonesia* **192** K8
Bangka, island, *Indonesia* **193** H15
Bangkaru, island, *Indonesia* **192** H4
Bangkok see Krung Thep, *Thai.* **190** M9
Bangladesh, *Asia* **180** H12
Bangnae, *S. Korea* **186** M11
Bangnim, *S. Korea* **187** N10
Ban Gnômmalat, *Laos* **190** K11
Bangong Cuo see Banggong Co, *China* **182** H2
Bangor, *Me., U.S.* **97** F17
Bangor see Baingear, *Ire.* **145** Q3
Bangs, *Aust.* **162** L2
Bangs, *Tex., U.S.* **105** N8
Bang Saphan, *Thai.* **191** P8
Bangui, *Cen. Af. Rep.* **202** H8
Bangui, *Philippines* **193** B13
Bangweulu, Lake, *Zambia* **206** D11
Ban Houayxay, *Laos* **190** H9
Baní, *Dom. Rep.* **119** M19
Bani, river, *Mali* **200** H8
Banihal Pass, *India* **180** C5
Banī Sharfā, *Saudi Arabia* **174** M8
Banī Walīd, *Lib.* **201** C14
Bāniyās, *Syr.* **172** F7
Banja Luka, *Bosn. & Herzg.* **154** F7
Banjarmasin, *Indonesia* **192** K11
Banjieta, *Hebei, China* **184** A8

Banjul, *Gambia* **200** H4
Banka, *India* **180** H11
Bankə, *Azerb.* **171** E23
Ban Kèngkok, *Laos* **190** L12
Banks, Bahía, *Ecua.* **130** P9
Banks Island, *B.C., Can.* **84** K7
Banks Island, *N.W.T., Can.* **84** D12
Banks Islands, *Vanuatu* **222** B2
Banks Lake, *Wash., U.S.* **110** C7
Banks Peninsula, *N.Z.* **217** P18
Banks Rise, *Arctic Oc.* **246** M9
Banks Shelf, *Arctic Oc.* **246** N9
Banks Slope, *Arctic Oc.* **246** N9
Banks Strait, *Austral.* **214** L8
Banmauk, *Myanmar* **190** F5
Ban Meung, *Laos* **190** H8
Ban Muang- Ou-Nua, *Laos* **190** G9
Bann, river, *N. Ire., U.K.* **145** P7
Bannerman Town, *Bahamas* **122** F6
Bannu, *Pak.* **179** P9
Bánovce nad Bebravou, *Slovakia* **151** J14
Ban Phai, *Thai.* **190** L10
Banreaba, *Kiribati* **221** G17
Ban Sanam Chai, *Thai.* **191** R9
Banská Bystrica, *Slovakia* **151** J15
Banswara, *India* **180** H4
Bantabaré Pequeño, *Eq. Guinea* **208** M7
Ban Taphan, *Laos* **190** L12
Ban Thinkèo, *Laos* **190** J10
Bantry Bay, *Ire.* **145** V3
Bantva, *India* **180** J2
Bantval, *India* **181** Q4
Banū, *Afghan.* **178** L8
Ban Xénô, *Laos* **190** K11
Banzare Bank, *Ind. Oc.* **248** C11
Banzare Coast, *Antarctica* **231** P19
Bao'an see Zhidan, *Shaanxi, China* **184** F1
Baochang see Taibus Qi, *N. Mongol, China* **184** A7
Baode, *Shanxi, China* **184** D3
Baoding, *Hebei, China* **184** E7
Baofeng, *Henan, China* **184** K5
Bao Grande, *Eq. Guinea* **208** M7
Baojing, *Hunan, China* **185** Q1
Bảo Lạc, *Vietnam* **190** G12
Baoro, *Cen. Af. Rep.* **202** H8
Baoshan, *China* **182** N8
Baoshan, *China* **183** C17
Baotou, *N. Mongol, China* **184** C3
Baoying, *Jiangsu, China* **184** K10
Bapatla, *India* **181** N7
Baqbaqty, *Kaz.* **177** H16
Baqty, *Kaz.* **177** F18
Ba'qūbah, *Iraq* **174** D10
Baquedano, *Chile* **134** E7
Bar, *Montenegro* **154** K9
Bara, *Indonesia* **193** K15
Bara, *Sudan* **202** E12
Barkā', *Oman* **175** K16
Baraawe, *Somalia* **203** J16
Barabhas (Barvas), *Scot., U.K.* **144** H7
Baraboo, *Wis., U.S.* **100** K5
Baracoa, *Cuba* **119** K14
Baraga, *Mich., U.S.* **100** E6
Bărăganul, plain, *Rom.* **155** F17
Baragoi, *Kenya* **203** J14
Barahona, *Dom. Rep.* **119** N17
Bara Hoti, *India* **180** D7
Barah Wazē, *Afghan.* **179** N8
Barak, *Turk.* **170** J12
Baraka, river, *Af.* **198** F10
Barakī, *Afghan.* **179** N7
Baramula, *India* **180** B4
Baran, *India* **180** H5
Baranavichy, *Belarus* **158** L4
Barangbarang, *Indonesia* **193** L13
Baranof Island, *Alas., U.S.* **113** L22
Baranovka, *Russ.* **159** N14
Barão de Melgaço, *Braz.* **132** J10
Barataria Bay, *La., U.S.* **102** R11
Barat Daya, Kepulauan, *Indonesia* **193** M16
Barate, *Indonesia* **193** N14
Baraterre, *Bahamas* **122** E8
Barbacena, *Braz.* **133** L14
Barbacoas, *Col.* **130** H3
Barbados, *N. Amer.* **121** G18
Barbaria, Cap de, *Sp.* **147** J17

Barbastro, *Sp.* **147** D15
Barber, *Curaçao, Neth.* **123** P14
Barbers Block, peak, *Dominica* **123** E18
Barberton, *Ohio, U.S.* **101** P14
Barbezieux, *Fr.* **149** U7
Barbourville, *Ky., U.S.* **103** D18
Barbuda, island, *Lesser Antil.* **121** B16
Barcaldine, *Qnsld., Austral.* **215** T13
Barcellona-Pozzo di Gotto, *It.* **153** R12
Barcelona, *Sp.* **147** E17
Barcelona, *Venez.* **130** B11
Barcelos, *Braz.* **132** D8
Barcelos, *Port.* **146** D5
Barco, *N.C., U.S.* **98** G14
Barcoo, river, *Austral.* **214** F13
Barcs, *Hung.* **151** N13
Barda del Medio, *Arg.* **135** N8
Barda Hills, *India* **180** J1
Bardaï, *Chad* **201** F14
Bardas Blancas, *Arg.* **134** M7
Barddhaman, *India* **180** J11
Bardejov, *Slovakia* **151** H16
Bardonecchia, *It.* **152** E1
Bardsey Island, *Wales, U.K.* **145** T8
Bardsīr, *Iran* **175** F15
Bardstown, *Ky., U.S.* **103** C17
Bardwell, *Ky., U.S.* **102** D12
Bareilly, *India* **180** F7
Barentin, *Fr.* **149** N8
Barents Plain, *Arctic Oc.* **247** G14
Barents Sea, *Arctic Oc.* **247** E15
Barents Shelf, *Arctic Oc.* **247** C17
Barents Trough, *Arctic Oc.* **247** F17
Barfak, *Afghan.* **178** L7
Barfleur, *Fr.* **149** N6
Barfleur, Pointe de, *Fr.* **149** N6
Barga, *It.* **152** G6
Bargaal, *Somalia* **203** F19
Bargarh, *India* **180** K9
Barg-e Matāl, *Afghan.* **178** L9
Bar Harbor, *Me., U.S.* **97** F18
Barhi, *India* **180** H10
Barhi, *India* **180** H7
Bari, *It.* **152** L14
Bà Rịa, *Vietnam* **191** P13
Barigello, river, *It.* **163** G16
Barīm (Parim), island, *Yemen* **174** R8
Barima, river, *Guyana* **131** D13
Barinas, *Venez.* **130** C7
Baripada, *India* **180** J11
Bârîs, *Egypt* **201** E18
Barisal, *Bangladesh* **180** J13
Barisan, Pegunungan, *Indonesia* **192** K6
Barisan Mountains, *Asia* **168** M10
Barito, river, *Asia* **168** M12
Barka Kana, *India* **180** J10
Barkam, *China* **182** K9
Barkhan, *Pak.* **179** R8
Barkley, Lake, *Ky., U.S.* **103** D14
Barkly Tableland, *Austral.* **214** D10
Barkol, *China* **182** E7
Barkol Hu, *China* **182** E7
Barla Dağı, peak, *Turk.* **170** G6
Bar-le-Duc, *Fr.* **149** P13
Barlee, Lake, *Austral.* **214** H4
Barletta, *It.* **152** L13
Barlinek, *Pol.* **150** D11
Barmer, *India* **180** G3
Barmouth, *Wales, U.K.* **145** T9
Bärnau, *Ger.* **150** H9
Barnaul, *Russ.* **160** L12
Barnegat, *N.J., U.S.* **96** Q11
Barnegat Light, *N.J., U.S.* **96** Q11
Barnes Ice Cap, *Nunavut, Can.* **85** F17
Barnesville, *Ga., U.S.* **98** M5
Barnesville, *Minn., U.S.* **106** G8
Barneville-Carteret, *Fr.* **149** N5
Barnhart, *Tex., U.S.* **105** P6
Barnsdall, *Okla., U.S.* **104** E12
Barnsley, *Eng., U.K.* **145** R12
Barnstaple, *Eng., U.K.* **145** W9
Barnstaple Bay, *Eng., U.K.* **145** W9
Barnum Bay, *Palau* **220** Q10

Barnwell, *S.C., U.S.* **98** L8
Baro, *Nigeria* **205** D13
Baroghil Pass, *Afghan., Pak.* **178** K11
Baron Bluff, *Virgin Is., U.S.* **122** Q2
Barora Fa, island, *Solomon Is.* **221** L17
Barora Ite,, island, *Solomon Is.* **221** L17
Barpeta, *India* **180** G13
Barques, Pointe Aux, *Mich., U.S.* **100** K13
Barquisimeto, *Venez.* **130** C8
Barra, *Braz.* **133** G15
Barra *see* Eilean Barraigh, island, *Scot., U.K.* **144** K6
Barra, Ponta da, *Mozambique* **207** H13
Barra, Sound of, *Scot., U.K.* **144** K6
Barracks of Swiss Guard, *Vatican City* **163** P17
Barracuda Fracture Zone *see* Fifteen Twenty Fracture Zone, *Atl. Oc.* **240** M7
Barracuda Plain, *Atl. Oc.* **240** M5
Barra do Bugres, *Braz.* **132** J10
Barra do Corda, *Braz.* **133** E14
Barra do São Manuel, *Braz.* **132** F10
Barrancabermeja, *Col.* **130** D5
Barrancas, *Venez.* **130** C12
Barranqueras, *Arg.* **134** G12
Barranquilla, *Col.* **130** B5
Barranquitas, *P.R., U.S.* **122** N3
Barras, *Braz.* **133** E15
Barrax, *Sp.* **146** H12
Barre, *Vt., U.S.* **97** G13
Barreiras, *Braz.* **133** H14
Barreirinha, *Braz.* **132** D10
Barreirinhas, *Braz.* **133** D15
Barreiro, *Port.* **146** J4
Barrême, *Fr.* **149** X14
Barren, river, *Ky., U.S.* **103** D16
Barrhill, *Scot., U.K.* **145** P8
Barrie, *Ont., Can.* **85** Q18
Barrigada, *Guam, U.S.* **220** C11
Barron, *Wis., U.S.* **100** H2
Barroualie, *St. Vincent and the Grenadines* **123** K16
Barrow, *Alas., U.S.* **113** B15
Barrow, river, *Ire.* **145** T6
Barrow, Point, *Alas., U.S.* **113** B15
Barrow Canyon, *Arctic Oc.* **246** L7
Barrow Creek, *N.T., Austral.* **215** S9
Barrow-in-Furness, *Eng., U.K.* **145** Q10
Barrow Island, *Austral.* **214** E2
Barry, *Ill., U.S.* **101** R3
Barrytown, *N.Z.* **217** N16
Barshatas, *Kaz.* **177** E17
Barstow, *Calif., U.S.* **111** W9
Bar-sur-Seine, *Fr.* **149** Q12
Bartica, *Guyana* **131** E14
Bartın, *Turk.* **170** C8
Bartle Frere (South Peak), *Austral.* **214** D13
Bartlesville, *Okla., U.S.* **104** E12
Bartlett, *Nebr., U.S.* **107** P6
Bartlett, *Tex., U.S.* **105** P11
Bartlett Seamounts, *Ind. Oc.* **225** J16
Bartolomeu Dias, *Mozambique* **207** G13
Barton, *N. Dak., U.S.* **106** E5
Barton, *Vt., U.S.* **97** F13
Bartoszyce, *Pol.* **151** B16
Bartow, *Fla., U.S.* **99** U8
Barú, Volcán, *Pan.* **117** N20
Baruunharra, *Mongolia* **182** C10
Baruunsuu, *Mongolia* **182** E10
Baruun-Urt, *Mongolia* **182** D12
Barvas *see* Barabhas, *Scot., U.K.* **144** H7
Barwani, *India* **180** J4
Barwon, river, *Austral.* **214** J14
Barykova, Mys, *Russ.* **161** B21
Barysaw, *Belarus* **158** K5
Barysh, *Russ.* **158** K14
Basacato del Este, *Eq. Guinea* **208** M8
Basacato del Oeste, *Eq. Guinea* **208** M7

Basaga, *Turkm.* **176** M11
Basankusu, *Dem. Rep. of the Congo* **202** J9
Basco, *Philippines* **193** A14
Bascuñán, Cabo, *Chile* **134** H6
Basel, *Switz.* **152** A3
Bashi Channel, *Taiwan, China* **185** X12
Basilan, island, *Philippines* **193** F14
Basile, *La., U.S.* **102** P8
Basilé, *Eq. Guinea* **208** L7
Basilé, Pico, *Eq. Guinea* **208** M7
Basiliano, *It.* **152** D9
Basilisk Harbor, *Solomon Is.* **221** Q23
Basin, *Wyo., U.S.* **108** F10
Basingstoke, *Eng., U.K.* **145** W13
Basīṭ, Ra's al, *Syr.* **172** E7
Başkale, *Turk.* **171** G18
Baskil, *Turk.* **171** G13
Baskunchak, Ozero, *Russ.* **159** Q14
Basmat, *India* **180** L5
Basoko, *Dem. Rep. of the Congo* **202** J10
Basora, Punta, *Aruba, Neth.* **123** R17
Basra *see* Al Başrah, *Iraq* **174** F11
Bassae, ruin, *Gr.* **156** K9
Bass Canyon, *Pac. Oc.* **249** D20
Basse-Pointe, *Martinique, Fr.* **123** E22
Basses, Pointe des, *Guadeloupe, Fr.* **123** G16
Basse Terre, *Trinidad and Tobago* **123** Q23
Basse-Terre, *Guadeloupe, Fr.* **123** G14
Basse-Terre, island, *Guadeloupe, Fr.* **123** F14
Basseterre, *St. Kitts and Nevis* **123** B17
Bassett, *Nebr., U.S.* **107** N5
Bassett, *Va., U.S.* **98** G10
Bassikounou, *Mauritania* **200** H8
Bass Islands, *Ohio, U.S.* **101** N13
Bass Islands, *Solomon Is.* **221** N24
Bass Strait, *Austral.* **214** K7
Bastak, *Iran* **175** H14
Bastendorf, *Lux.* **162** H10
Basti, *India* **180** G8
Bastia, *Fr.* **152** J4
Bastogne, *Belg.* **162** H8
Bastrop, *La., U.S.* **102** K9
Bastrop, *Tex., U.S.* **105** Q11
Bastuträsk, *Sw.* **143** F14
Basu, island, *Indonesia* **192** J7
Basupú, *Eq. Guinea* **208** L7
Bata, *Eq. Guinea* **205** G15
Bataan Peninsula, *Philippines* **193** C13
Batabanó, Golfo de, *Cuba* **118** H6
Batagay, *Russ.* **161** F18
Batala, *India* **180** D5
Batamay, *Russ.* **161** G18
Batan, island, *Philippines* **193** A14
Batangafo, *Cen. Af. Rep.* **202** G8
Batangas City, *Philippines* **193** C13
Batan Islands, *Philippines* **193** A14
Batanta, island, *Indonesia* **193** J17
Batavia, *N.Y., U.S.* **96** J6
Batavia Seasomunt, *Ind. Oc.* **225** L15
Bataysk, *Russ.* **159** R11
Bătdâmbâng (Battambang), *Thai.* **191** N10
Batemans Bay, *N.S.W., Austral.* **215** Y14
Bates, Mount, *Norfolk I., Austral.* **221** F20
Batesburg, *S.C., U.S.* **98** L8
Batesville, *Ark., U.S.* **102** F9
Batesville, *Ind., U.S.* **101** S10
Batesville, *Miss., U.S.* **102** H11
Batesville, *Tex., U.S.* **105** S8
Batete, *Eq. Guinea* **208** M6
Bath, *Eng., U.K.* **145** V11
Bath, *Jam.* **122** J11
Bath, *Me., U.S.* **97** G16
Bath, *N.Y., U.S.* **96** K7
Bath, *St. Kitts and Nevis* **123** C18
Bathsheba, *Barbados* **123** K19

Bathurst, *N.B., Can.* **85** N21
Bathurst, Cape, *N.W.T., Can.* **84** D10
Bathurst Inlet, *Nunavut, Can.* **85** F13
Bathurst Island, *Austral.* **214** A7
Bathurst Island, *Nunavut, Can.* **85** D14
Bathymetrists Seamounts, *Atl. Oc.* **241** N9
Batié, *Burkina Faso* **204** C9
Batiki, island, *Fiji* **222** H7
Batista, Serra da, *Braz.* **133** F16
Batman, *Turk.* **171** G15
Batna, *Alg.* **200** A12
Baton Rouge, *La., U.S.* **102** P9
Batouri, *Cameroon* **205** F17
Båtsfjord, *Nor.* **143** B15
Batsí, *Gr.* **157** J14
Batteau, *Nfld. & Lab., Can.* **85** K22
Batticaloa, *Sri Lanka* **181** S8
Battle Creek, *Can., U.S.* **108** A9
Battle Creek, *Mich., U.S.* **100** M10
Battle Harbour, *Nfld. & Lab., Can.* **85** L23
Battle Mountain, *Nev., U.S.* **111** N9
Batu, peak, *Eth.* **203** H15
Batu, Kepulauan, *Indonesia* **192** J5
Batukelau, *Indonesia* **192** J11
Bat'umi, *Rep. of Georgia* **171** C16
Batu Pahat, *Malaysia* **191** V10
Batuputih, *Indonesia* **192** H12
Baturaja, *Indonesia* **192** K7
Baturité, *Braz.* **133** E17
Bat Yam, *Israel* **172** M5
Batz, Île de, *Fr.* **149** P3
Bau, island, *Fiji* **222** J7
Baubau, *Indonesia* **193** L14
Baucau, *Timor-Leste* **193** M15
Bauchi, *Nigeria* **205** C15
Baudette, *Minn., U.S.* **106** E10
Baudó, Serranía de, *S. Amer.* **128** B2
Bauer Basin, *Pac. Oc.* **243** L20
Bauer Scarp, *Pac. Oc.* **243** L19
Baugé, *Fr.* **149** R7
Bauges, range, *Fr.* **149** U14
Baun, *Indonesia* **193** N14
Baunatal, *Ger.* **150** F6
Baures, river, *Bol.* **132** H8
Bauru, *Braz.* **133** L13
Baús, *Braz.* **132** K11
Bautino, *Kaz.* **176** G5
Bautzen, *Ger.* **150** F11
Bavaria, region, *Ger.* **150** J8
Bávaro, *Dom. Rep.* **119** M21
Bawal, island, *Indonesia* **192** K9
Bawean, island, *Indonesia* **192** L10
Bawku, *Ghana* **204** C11
Baxkorgan, *China* **182** G6
Baxley, *Ga., U.S.* **99** P7
Baxoi (Baxue), *China* **182** L7
Baxter, *Minn., U.S.* **106** H10
Baxter Springs, *Kans., U.S.* **107** V10
Baxue *see* Baxoi, *China* **182** L7
Bay'ah, *Oman* **175** J15
Bayamo, *Cuba* **118** K12
Bayamón, *P.R., U.S.* **122** M4
Bayan, *Mongolia* **182** D7
Bāyan, Band-e, *Afghan.* **178** M5
Bayanaūyl, *Kaz.* **177** D15
Bayandalay, *Mongolia* **182** E10
Bayanga, *Cen. Af. Rep.* **202** J8
Bayan Har Shan, *China* **182** J7
Bayan Har Shankou, *China* **182** J8
Bayanhongor, *Mongolia* **182** D9
Bayan Obo, *N. Mongol, China* **184** A3
Bayard, *N. Mex., U.S.* **109** V10
Bayard, *Nebr., U.S.* **107** P1
Bayat, *Turk.* **170** F6
Bayāz, *Iran* **175** F15
Bayboro, *N.C., U.S.* **98** H14
Bayburt, *Turk.* **171** E16
Bay City, *Mich., U.S.* **100** K11
Bay City, *Tex., U.S.* **105** S13
Baydarata Bay, *Arctic Oc.* **247** B15
Baydaratskaya Guba, *Russ.* **160** F11
Baydhabo (Baidoa), *Somalia* **203** J16
Bayès, Cap, *New Caledonia, Fr.* **222** C7

Bayeux, *Fr.* **149** N6
Bayfield, *Wis., U.S.* **100** E4
Bayghanīn, *Kaz.* **176** E8
Bayḩān al Qiṣāb, *Yemen* **174** Q10
Bayındır, *Turk.* **170** G3
Bay Islands, *N. Amer.* **82** P7
Bayjī, *Iraq* **174** D9
Baykal, Ozero (Lake Baikal), *Russ.* **161** L16
Baykan, *Turk.* **171** G16
Baykonur (Leninsk) *see* Bayqongyr, *Kaz.* **176** G10
Baykonur Cosmodrome, *Kaz.* **176** G11
Bay Minette, *Ala., U.S.* **103** N14
Bay of Whales, site, *Antarctica* **230** N11
Bayonnaise Rock *see* Beyonēsu-Retsugan, *Japan* **189** S12
Bayonne, *Fr.* **149** X5
Bayou Bartholomew, river, *Ark., La., U.S.* **102** K9
Bayqongyr (Baykonur, Leninsk), *Kaz.* **176** G10
Bayramaly, *Turkm.* **176** M10
Bayramiç, *Turk.* **170** E2
Bayreuth, *Ger.* **150** H9
Bay Saint Louis, *Miss., U.S.* **102** P12
Bay Springs, *Miss., U.S.* **102** M12
Bayt al Faqīh, *Yemen* **174** Q8
Bayt Laḩm (Bethlehem), *Israel* **172** M5
Baytown, *Tex., U.S.* **105** R14
Baza, *Sp.* **146** L12
Bāzā'i Gunbad, *Afghan.* **178** K11
Bazardüzü Daği, peak, *Azerb.* **171** C22
Bāzār-e Panjwā'ī, *Afghan.* **179** Q5
Bāzār-e Tālah, *Afghan.* **178** L7
Bazar-Kurgan, *Kyrg.* **178** F10
Bazaruto Island, *Af.* **198** N10
Bazartöbe, *Kaz.* **176** D6
Bazas, *Fr.* **149** W7
Bazhong, *China* **182** K11
Bazkovskaya, *Russ.* **159** P11
Bazmān, Kūh-e, *Iran* **175** G17
Beach, *N. Dak., U.S.* **106** G1
Beach Haven, *N.J., U.S.* **96** Q11
Beachport, *S. Aust., Austral.* **215** Z11
Beachy Head, *Eng., U.K.* **145** W14
Beagle Bay, *Austral.* **214** C4
Beagle Bay, *W. Aust., Austral.* **215** R4
Beagle Gulf, *Austral.* **214** A7
Béal an Átha *see* Ballina, *Ire.* **145** Q4
Béal an Mhuirthead (Belmullet), *Ire.* **145** Q3
Beal Átha hÉis *see* Ballyhaise, *Ire.* **145** Q6
Béal Átha na Muice *see* Swinford, *Ire.* **145** Q4
Béal Átha Seanaidh *see* Ballyshannon, *Ire.* **145** Q5
Béal Deirg (Belderg), *Ire.* **145** Q3
Beal Knoll, *Arctic Oc.* **246** K11
Béar, Cap, *Fr.* **149** Z11
Bearden, *Ark., U.S.* **102** J8
Beardmore Glacier, *Antarctica* **231** L13
Beardstown, *Ill., U.S.* **101** R4
Bear Island, *Ire.* **145** V2
Bear Islands *see* Medvezh'i Ostrova, *Russ.* **161** C19
Bear Lake, *Idaho, Utah, U.S.* **108** J8
Bearnaraigh (Berneray), island, *Scot., U.K.* **144** K6
Bear Paw Mountains, *U.S.* **86** B8
Bear River Range, *Idaho, Utah, U.S.* **108** J7
Bears Paw Mountains, *Mont., U.S.* **108** B9
Beasain, *Sp.* **146** B12
Beata, Cabo, *Dom. Rep.* **119** N17
Beata, Isla, *Dom. Rep.* **119** N17
Beatrice, *Nebr., U.S.* **107** R8
Beattock, *Scot., U.K.* **145** N10
Beatton River, *B.C., Can.* **84** J9
Beatty, *Nev., U.S.* **111** T10
Beau Bassin, *Mauritius* **209** G19
Beaucaire, *Fr.* **149** X12

Beauchêne Island, *Falk. Is., U.K.* **135** W12
Beaufort, *Lux.* **162** H10
Beaufort, *Malaysia* **192** G11
Beaufort, *N.C., U.S.* **98** J14
Beaufort, *S.C., U.S.* **98** M9
Beaufort Rise, *Arctic Oc.* **246** M7
Beaufort Sea, *Arctic Oc.* **246** N8
Beaufort Shelf, *Arctic Oc.* **246** M7
Beaufort Slope, *Arctic Oc.* **246** M7
Beaufort Terrace, *Arctic Oc.* **246** N8
Beaufort West, *S. Af.* **206** L8
Beaugency, *Fr.* **149** R9
Beaumanoir, Port du, *Fr. Polynesia, Fr.* **223** Q17
Beaumont, *Tex., U.S.* **105** Q15
Beaune, *Fr.* **149** S12
Beausoleil, *Fr.* **163** C21
Beautemps-Beaupré, Île, *New Caledonia, Fr.* **222** C8
Beauvais, *Fr.* **149** N9
Beauvoir, *Fr.* **149** S5
Beaver, *Alas., U.S.* **113** E17
Beaver, *Okla., U.S.* **104** E7
Beaver, *Oreg., U.S.* **110** F2
Beaver, *Utah, U.S.* **109** N6
Beaver, river, *Okla., Tex., U.S.* **104** E6
Beaver Bay, *Minn., U.S.* **106** F13
Beaver City, *Nebr., U.S.* **107** R5
Beaver Creek, *Kans., U.S.* **107** R4
Beaver Creek, *Mont., U.S.* **108** B10
Beaver Dam, *Ky., U.S.* **103** C15
Beaver Dam, *Wis., U.S.* **100** L6
Beaver Falls, *Pa., U.S.* **96** N3
Beaver Glacier, *Antarctica* **231** C19
Beaverhead, river, *Mont., U.S.* **108** F6
Beaverhead Mountains, *Mont., U.S.* **108** F6
Beaver Island, *Mich., U.S.* **100** G9
Beaver Lake, *Ark., U.S.* **102** E6
Beaverton, *Oreg., U.S.* **110** F3
Beawar, *India* **180** G4
Bebar, *India* **180** H1
Bebiram, *Indonesia* **217** B14
Beccles, *Eng., U.K.* **145** T16
Bečej, *Serb.* **154** E10
Becerreá, *Sp.* **146** B7
Béchar, *Alg.* **200** C9
Becharof Lake, *Alas., U.S.* **113** L14
Beckerich, *Lux.* **162** J9
Beckley, *W. Va., U.S.* **98** E8
Beddouza, Cap, *Mor.* **200** B7
Bedford, *Eng., U.K.* **145** U13
Bedford, *Ind., U.S.* **101** T9
Bedford, *Iowa, U.S.* **107** Q10
Bedford, *Pa., U.S.* **96** P5
Bedford, *Va., U.S.* **98** F10
Bedford, Cape, *Austral.* **214** C13
Bedford Downs, *W. Aust., Austral.* **215** R6
Bedfort Point, *Grenada* **123** J24
Bedonia, *It.* **152** F5
Bedourie, *Qnsld., Austral.* **215** T11
Bedous, *Fr.* **149** Y6
Beebe, *Ark., U.S.* **102** G9
Beechey Group *see* Chichi Jima Rettō, *Japan* **189** X14
Beech Grove, *Ind., U.S.* **101** R9
Beef Island, *British Virgin Is., U.K.* **122** Q7
Beenleigh, *Qnsld., Austral.* **215** V16
Be'er Menuha, *Israel* **173** Q5
Be'er Ora, *Israel* **173** R5
Beersheba *see* Be'ér Sheva', *Israel* **173** N5
Be'ér Sheva' (Beersheba), *Israel* **173** N5
Beethoven Peninsula, *Antarctica* **230** G6
Beeville, *Tex., U.S.* **105** T10
Bega, *N.S.W., Austral.* **215** Z14
Bega, river, *Rom.* **154** D12
Begejski Kanal, *Rom.* **154** E10
Beggars Point, *Antigua and Barbuda* **123** A21
Bègles, *Fr.* **149** V6
Begusarai, *India* **180** G10
Behbahān, *Iran* **174** F12
Behchokö`, *N.W.T., Can.* **84** H11
Behring Point, *Bahamas* **118** E11
Behshahr, *Iran* **175** C14

Bei, river, *Guang., China* **185** V4
Bei'an, *China* **183** C16
Beida *see* Al Bayḑā', *Lib.* **201** B16
Beihai, *China* **182** P12
Beijing (Peking), *Beijing Shi, China* **184** C7
Beijin Gang, *Guang., China* **185** X3
Beijing Shi, *China* **184** C7
Beilen, *Neth.* **148** H14
Beiliu, *Guangxi Zhuang, China* **185** W1
Beilun, *Zhejiang, China* **185** P12
Beining, *Liaoning, China* **184** B12
Beinn na Faoghla (Benbecula), island, *Scot., U.K.* **144** K6
Beipan, river, *China* **182** N10
Beipiao, *Liaoning, China* **184** A11
Beira, *Mozambique* **207** G13
Beirut *see* Beyrouth, *Leb.* **172** H6
Bei Shan, *China* **182** F7
Beitbridge, *Zimb.* **206** H11
Beït ed Dîne, *Leb.* **172** J6
Beiuş, *Rom.* **154** C12
Beja, *Port.* **146** K6
Beja, *Tun.* **200** A12
Bejaïa, *Alg.* **200** A11
Bejaïa, Gulf of, *Af.* **198** C5
Béjar, *Sp.* **146** F8
Bejestān, *Iran* **175** D16
Bekaa Valley, *Leb.* **172** J7
Bekdash *see* Karabogaz, *Turkm.* **176** J2
Békés, *Hung.* **151** M17
Békéscsaba, *Hung.* **151** M17
Bekily, *Madagascar* **207** H16
Bekja, island, *Marshall Is., U.S.* **220** K7
Bekkai, *Japan* **188** F15
Bekobod, *Taj.* **178** G8
Bekobod, *Uzb.* **177** L13
Bekoropoka-Antongo, *Madagascar* **207** G16
Bekwai, *Ghana* **204** E10
Bela, *Pak.* **179** V5
Belaga, *Malaysia* **192** H11
Belagavi (Belgaum), *India* **181** N4
Bel Air, *Mauritius* **209** G20
Belalcázar, *Sp.* **146** J9
Belarus, *Eur.* **158** L5
Bela Vista, *Braz.* **132** L10
Belaya, river, *Eur.* **140** D15
Belaya, Gora, *Russ.* **161** C20
Belaya Glina, *Russ.* **159** S11
Belaya Gora, *Russ.* **161** E18
Belaya Kalitva, *Russ.* **159** Q11
Belaya Zemlya, Ostrova, *Russ.* **161** C13
Bełchatów, *Pol.* **151** F15
Belcher Islands, *Nunavut, Can.* **85** L17
Belcik, *Turk.* **170** E11
Belcoo, *N. Ire., U.K.* **145** Q5
Belderg *see* Béal Deirg, *Ire.* **145** Q3
Belding, *Mich., U.S.* **100** L10
Beledweyne, *Somalia* **203** H17
Belele, *W. Aust., Austral.* **215** U3
Belém, *Braz.* **133** D13
Belen, *N. Mex., U.S.* **109** S12
Belén, *Arg.* **134** G8
Belentligi, *Uzb.* **176** N10
Bélep, Îles, *New Caledonia, Fr.* **222** B5
Belev, *Russ.* **158** L8
Belfast, *Me., U.S.* **97** F17
Belfast, *N. Ire., U.K.* **145** Q7
Belfast Lough, *N. Ire., U.K.* **145** P7
Belfield, *N. Dak., U.S.* **106** G2
Belfort, *Fr.* **149** R14
Belgaum *see* Belagavi, *India* **181** N4
Belgica Bank, *Arctic Oc.* **247** K16
Belgica Mountains, *Antarctica* **231** C16
Belgium, *Eur.* **148** L12
Belgodère, *Fr.* **152** J4
Belgorod, *Russ.* **159** N9
Belgrade, *Mont., U.S.* **108** E8
Belgrade *see* Beograd, *Serb.* **154** F10
Belgrano II, station, *Antarctica* **230** E10
Belhaven, *N.C., U.S.* **98** H14
Belidzhi, *Russ.* **159** U16

Beliliou (Peleliu), island, *Palau* **220** Q10
Belinyu, *Indonesia* **192** K8
Belisario Domínguez, Presa, *Mex.* **117** K15
Belitung (Billiton), island, *Indonesia* **192** K8
Belize, *N. Amer.* **117** K17
Belize City, *Belize* **117** J17
Bel'kachi, *Russ.* **161** H18
Bel'kovskiy, Ostrov, *Russ.* **161** D16
Bella Bella, *B.C., Can.* **84** K7
Bellac, *Fr.* **149** T8
Bella Coola, *B.C., Can.* **84** K7
Bellaire, *Mich., U.S.* **100** H10
Bellaire, *Ohio, U.S.* **100** R15
Bellaire, *Tex., U.S.* **105** R14
Bellary *see* Ballari, *India* **181** N5
Bella Unión, *Uru.* **134** J13
Bella Vista, *Arg.* **134** G9
Bella Vista, *Arg.* **134** H12
Bellavista, *Peru* **132** F2
Belle-Anse, *Haiti* **119** M17
Belledonne, Chaîne de, *Fr.* **149** U14
Bellefontaine, *Martinique, Fr.* **123** F22
Bellefontaine, *Ohio, U.S.* **101** Q12
Bellefonte, *Pa., U.S.* **96** N6
Belle Fourche, *S. Dak., U.S.* **106** K1
Belle Fourche, river, *S. Dak., Wyo., U.S.* **108** G12
Belle Fourche Reservoir, *S. Dak., U.S.* **106** K1
Bellegarde, *Fr.* **149** Q10
Bellegarde, *Fr.* **149** T14
Belle Glade, *Fla., U.S.* **99** V10
Belle-Île, *Fr.* **149** R4
Belle Isle, *Nfld. & Lab., Can.* **85** L23
Belle Isle, Strait of, *N. Amer.* **85** L22
Bellême, *Fr.* **149** Q8
Belle Plaine, *Iowa, U.S.* **107** N13
Belle Plaine, *Minn., U.S.* **106** K11
Belleville, *Fr.* **149** T12
Belleville, *Ill., U.S.* **101** T4
Belleville, *Kans., U.S.* **107** R7
Bellevue, *Iowa, U.S.* **107** N14
Bellevue, *Nebr., U.S.* **107** Q9
Bellevue, *Ohio, U.S.* **101** P13
Bellevue, *Tex., U.S.* **104** K10
Bellevue, *Wash., U.S.* **110** C4
Bellingham, *Wash., U.S.* **110** A4
Bellingshausen Plain, *Pac. Oc.* **241** X1
Bellingshausen Sea, *Antarctica* **230** H5
Bellinzona, *Switz.* **152** C4
Bello, *Col.* **130** E4
Bellona Island, *Solomon Is.* **221** Q18
Bellona Valley, *Pac. Oc.* **249** F21
Bellows Falls, *Vt., U.S.* **97** J13
Bellpat, *Pak.* **179** S7
Bell Peninsula, *Nunavut, Can.* **85** H17
Bell Point, *St.-Martin, Fr.* **123** A14
Bell Rock (Inchcape), *Scot., U.K.* **144** L11
Bells, *Tenn., U.S.* **102** F12
Bellsund Valley, *Arctic Oc.* **247** G17
Belluno, *It.* **152** C8
Bell Ville, *Arg.* **134** K11
Bellville, *Tex., U.S.* **105** Q12
Belmond, *Iowa, U.S.* **106** M11
Belmont, *Grenada* **123** L22
Belmont, *Miss., U.S.* **103** H13
Belmont, *N.C., U.S.* **98** J9
Belmonte, *Braz.* **133** J16
Belmonte, *Port.* **146** F7
Belmonte, *Sp.* **146** H12
Belmopan, *Belize* **117** K16
Belmullet *see* Béal an Mhuirthead, *Ire.* **145** Q3
Belogorsk, *Russ.* **161** K19
Belo Horizonte, *Braz.* **133** L14
Beloit, *Kans., U.S.* **107** S7
Beloit, *Wis., U.S.* **100** M6
Belomorsk, *Russ.* **160** D8
Belorado, *Sp.* **146** C11
Belorechensk, *Russ.* **159** T11
Belo-Tsiribihina, *Madagascar* **207** G16
Beloŭsovka, *Kaz.* **177** D18
Beloye, Lake, *Eur.* **140** D11

Beloye Ozero, *Russ.* **158** F9
Beloye More, *Russ.* **160** D8
Belozersk, *Russ.* **158** F9
Belpre, *Ohio, U.S.* **101** S15
Belt, *Mont., U.S.* **108** C8
Belterra, *Braz.* **132** D11
Belton, *S.C., U.S.* **98** K7
Belton, *Tex., U.S.* **105** P11
Belton Lake, *Tex., U.S.* **105** N11
Belukha, peak, *Asia* **168** F8
Belukha, Gora, *Russ.* **160** M12
Belush'ya Guba, *Russ.* **160** D10
Belvedere Courtyard, *Vatican City* **163** P16
Belvedere Marittimo, *It.* **153** P13
Belvès, *Fr.* **149** V8
Belvidere, *Ill., U.S.* **100** M6
Belvidere, *S. Dak., U.S.* **106** L4
Belvís de la Jara, *Sp.* **146** G9
Belyando, river, *Austral.* **214** F13
Belyy, *Russ.* **158** J7
Belyy, Ostrov, *Russ.* **160** E12
Belyy Island, *Asia* **168** E8
Belzoni, *Miss., U.S.* **102** K10
Bemaraha, range, *Madagascar* **207** F16
Bemaraha Plateau, *Af.* **198** M11
Bembe, *Angola* **206** B6
Bembibre, *Sp.* **146** C8
Bemidji, *Minn., U.S.* **106** F10
Benāb, *Iran* **174** B10
Benabarre, *Sp.* **147** D15
Benadir, region, *Af.* **198** J11
Benasque, *Sp.* **147** C15
Benavente, *Sp.* **146** D9
Benavides, *Tex., U.S.* **105** U10
Benbecula *see* Beinn na Faoghla, island, *Scot., U.K.* **144** K6
Bend, *Oreg., U.S.* **110** H5
Bendals, *Antigua and Barbuda* **123** B21
Bender, *Mold.* **159** R5
Bendern, *Liech.* **162** M2
Bendigo, *Vic., Austral.* **215** Y12
Bǝndovan Burnu, *Azerb.* **171** E23
Bene Beraq, *Israel* **172** M5
Benetutti, *It.* **153** N4
Benevento, *It.* **152** M11
Bengal, Bay of, *Ind. Oc.* **168** K8
Bengaluru (Bangalore), *India* **181** P6
Bengara, *Indonesia* **192** H12
Bengbu, *Anhui, China* **184** L8
Benghazi *see* Banghāzī, *Lib.* **201** C15
Benghisa Point, *Malta* **163** L23
Bengkalis, *Indonesia* **192** J6
Bengkalis, island, *Indonesia* **192** H6
Bengkayang, *Indonesia* **192** J9
Bengkulu, *Indonesia* **192** K6
Bengo, Baía do, *Angola* **206** C5
Bengo Bay, *Af.* **198** L5
Benguela, *Angola* **206** D5
Benguerir, *Mor.* **200** B8
Beni, river, *Bol.* **132** H7
Beni Abbes, *Alg.* **200** C9
Benicarló, *Sp.* **147** F15
Benidorm, *Sp.* **147** J15
Benifaió, *Sp.* **147** H14
Beni Mazâr, *Egypt* **201** D18
Benin, *Af.* **204** C12
Benin, Bight of, *Af.* **204** F12
Benin City, *Nigeria* **205** E13
Beni Ounif, *Alg.* **200** B10
Beni Suef, *Egypt* **201** D18
Benítses, *Gr.* **156** F6
Benjamin, *Tex., U.S.* **104** K8
Benjamin Constant, *Braz.* **132** E5
Benjamin Hill, *Mex.* **116** C7
Benkelman, *Nebr., U.S.* **107** R3
Benlidi, *Qnsld., Austral.* **215** U13
Bennett, Lake, *Austral.* **214** F8
Bennett, Ostrov, *Russ.* **161** C17
Bennett Peak, *N. Mex., U.S.* **109** Q10
Bennettsville, *S.C., U.S.* **98** J10
Ben Nevis, peak, *Scot., U.K.* **144** L8
Benneydale, *N.Z.* **217** K19
Bennington, *Vt., U.S.* **96** J12
Benoud, *Alg.* **200** B10
Bensbach, *P.N.G.* **217** E17
Bensheim, *Ger.* **150** H6
Benson, *Ariz., U.S.* **109** V8
Benson, *Minn., U.S.* **106** J9

Benson, *N.C., U.S.* **98** H12
Benson Point, *Kiribati* **221** B22
Bent, *Iran* **175** H17
Benta, *Malaysia* **192** G6
Bentham's, *Barbados* **123** J19
Bentinck Island, *Austral.* **214** C11
Bentinck Island, *Myanmar* **191** P7
Bentiu, *S. Sudan* **202** G12
Benton, *Ark., U.S.* **102** H8
Benton, *Ill., U.S.* **101** U6
Benton, *Ky., U.S.* **103** D13
Benton, *La., U.S.* **102** K6
Benton Harbor, *Mich., U.S.* **101** N9
Benton Lake, *Mont., U.S.* **108** C9
Bentonville, *Ark., U.S.* **102** E6
Bent's Old Fort National Historic Site, *Colo., U.S.* **109** N15
Benua, *Indonesia* **193** L14
Benue, river, *Nigeria* **205** D15
Benwee Head, *Ire.* **145** Q3
Benxi, *Liaoning, China* **184** B13
Beobwon, *S. Korea* **186** M8
Beograd (Belgrade), *Serb.* **154** F10
Beohari, *India* **180** H8
Beolgyo, *S. Korea* **187** T9
Beowawe, *Nev., U.S.* **111** N10
Beppu, *Japan* **189** R5
Beqa, island, *Fiji* **222** J6
Bequia, island, *St. Vincent and the Grenadines* **121** G17
Bera Ndjoko, *Congo* **205** F18
Berane, *Montenegro* **154** J9
Berard, *F.S.M.* **221** B18
Berard, Port, *F.S.M.* **221** B18
Berat, *Alban.* **154** L9
Berau, Teluk, *Indonesia* **193** K18
Berber, *Sudan* **203** D13
Berbera, *Somalia* **203** F17
Berbérati, *Cen. Af. Rep.* **202** H8
Berbice, river, *Guyana* **131** E15
Berceto, *It.* **152** F5
Berchers Bay, *British Virgin Is., U.K.* **122** Q9
Berchtesgaden, *Ger.* **150** L10
Berck, *Fr.* **148** M9
Bərdə, *Azerb.* **171** D21
Berdún, *Sp.* **147** C14
Berdyans'k, *Ukr.* **159** R9
Berdychiv, *Ukr.* **159** P5
Berdzor (Laçın), *Azerb.* **171** E20
Berea, *Ky., U.S.* **103** C18
Berehove, *Ukr.* **159** P1
Bereina, *P.N.G.* **217** E19
Berekua, *Dominica* **123** G19
Berenice, *Egypt* **201** E20
Berens River, *Man., Can.* **85** M14
Beresford, *S. Dak., U.S.* **106** M8
Beretău, river, *Rom.* **154** C12
Berezniki, *Russ.* **160** G9
Berga, *Sp.* **147** D17
Bergama, *Turk.* **170** E3
Bergamo, *It.* **152** D5
Bergara, *Sp.* **146** B12
Bergen, *Neth.* **148** H12
Bergen, *Nor.* **142** K9
Bergerac, *Fr.* **149** V8
Bergues, *Fr.* **148** L10
Berhala, Selat, *Indonesia* **192** J7
Bering, Ostrov, *Russ.* **161** E23
Bering Glacier, *Alas., U.S.* **113** K19
Bering Island, *N. Amer.* **82** Q1
Bering Land Bridge National Preserve, *Alas., U.S.* **112** E12
Beringovskiy, *Russ.* **161** B21
Bering Sea, *Pac. Oc.* **246** H2
Bering Strait, *Asia, N. Amer.* **168** A12
Bering Strait Valley, *Arctic Oc.* **246** K4
Berja, *Sp.* **146** M11
Berkeley, *Calif., U.S.* **111** S3
Berkeley, Cabo, *Ecua.* **130** P9
Berkner Bank, *Atl. Oc.* **248** K11
Berkner Island, *Antarctica* **230** F9
Berlanga de Duero, *Sp.* **146** E12
Berlevåg, *Nor.* **143** A15
Berlin, *Ger.* **150** D10
Berlin, *Md., U.S.* **98** D15
Berlin, *N.H., U.S.* **97** F14
Berlin, *Wis., U.S.* **100** K6

Berlin, Mount, *Antarctica* **230** M9
Bermejito, river, *Arg.* **134** E11
Bermejo, river, *Arg.* **134** E10
Bermeo, *Sp.* **146** B12
Bermillo de Sayago, *Sp.* **146** E8
Bermuda Islands, *N. Amer.* **82** K10
Bermuda Rise, *Atl. Oc.* **240** K5
Bern, *Switz.* **152** B2
Bernalda, *It.* **153** N14
Bernalillo, *N. Mex., U.S.* **109** S12
Bernardo de Irigoyen, *Arg.* **134** G15
Bernasconi, *Arg.* **135** N10
Bernau, *Ger.* **150** D10
Bernay, *Fr.* **149** P8
Bernburg, *Ger.* **150** E9
Berne, *Ind., U.S.* **101** Q10
Berner Alpen, *Switz.* **152** C2
Berneray *see* Bearnaraigh, island, *Scot., U.K.* **144** K6
Berneray *see* Eilean Bhearnaraigh, island, *Scot., U.K.* **144** J6
Bernice, *La., U.S.* **102** K8
Bernie, *Mo., U.S.* **107** V15
Bernier Bay, *Nunavut, Can.* **85** E15
Bernier Island, *Austral.* **214** G1
Bernina, Piz, *It., Switz.* **152** C5
Bernina, Piz, *It., Switz.* **152** C5
Bernini's Colonnade, *Vatican City* **163** Q17
Beroroha, *Madagascar* **207** G16
Berre, Étang de, *Fr.* **149** X13
Berrechid, *Mor.* **200** B8
Berri, *S. Aust., Austral.* **215** X11
Berry, *Eur.* **140** H5
Berry Islands, *Bahamas* **118** D11
Berryville, *Ark., U.S.* **102** E7
Berthold, *N. Dak., U.S.* **106** E3
Bertholet, Cape, *Austral.* **214** D4
Berthoud Pass, *Colo., U.S.* **108** L12
Bertoua, *Cameroon* **205** E16
Bertraghboy Bay, *Ire.* **145** S3
Bertrand, *Nebr., U.S.* **107** Q5
Bertrange, *Lux.* **162** K9
Beru, island, *Kiribati* **218** G8
Berufjaröarráll, valley, *Arctic Oc.* **247** L22
Beruniy, *Uzb.* **176** K9
Beruri, *Braz.* **132** E9
Beruwala, *Sri Lanka* **181** T7
Berwick, *La., U.S.* **102** Q9
Berwick-upon-Tweed, *Eng., U.K.* **144** M11
Berwyn, *Ill., U.S.* **101** N7
Berwyn, region, *Wales, U.K.* **145** T10
Beryslav, *Ukr.* **159** R7
Besalampy, *Madagascar* **207** F16
Besançon, *Fr.* **149** R14
Beserah, *Malaysia* **191** T10
Besham Qala, *Pak.* **178** M10
Besikama, *Indonesia* **193** N15
Beşiri, *Turk.* **171** G16
Besni, *Turk.* **170** H12
Beşparmak Dağı, peak, *Turk.* **170** G3
Bessarabia, region, *Mold.* **159** Q4
Bessemer, *Ala., U.S.* **103** J15
Bessemer, *Mich., U.S.* **100** F5
Bessines, *Fr.* **149** T9
Bestobe, *Kaz.* **177** C14
Bestyakh, *Russ.* **161** H18
Beswick, *N.T., Austral.* **215** P8
Betanzos, *Sp.* **146** B6
Betanzos, Ría de, *Sp.* **146** A6
Bethanie, *Namibia* **206** J7
Bethany, *Mo., U.S.* **107** R11
Bethany, *Okla., U.S.* **104** G10
Bethany Beach, *Del., U.S.* **98** D15
Bethel, *Alas., U.S.* **113** J12
Bethel, *Montserrat* **123** B24
Bethel Town, *Jam.* **122** H6
Bethesda, *Md., U.S.* **98** C13
Bethlehem, *Pa., U.S.* **96** N9
Bethlehem, *S. Af.* **206** K10
Bethlehem, *Virgin Is., U.S.* **122** R2
Bethlehem *see* Bayt Laḥm, *Israel* **172** M5
Beth Shan *see* Bet She'an, *Israel* **172** L6
Béthune, *Fr.* **148** L10
Betio, *Kiribati* **221** G17
Betong, *Malaysia* **191** S9
Betoota, *Qnsld., Austral.* **215** U11
Bétou, *Congo* **205** F19

Betpaqdala, desert, *Kaz.* 177 GI3
Betroka, *Madagascar* 207 HI7
Bet She'an (Beth Shan), *Israel* 172 L6
Bettembourg, *Lux.* 162 KIO
Bettendorf, *Iowa, U.S.* 107 PI4
Bettendorf, *Lux.* 162 HIO
Bettlerjoch, peak, *Aust., Liech.* 162 Q3
Betul, *India* 180 J6
Beulah, *N. Dak., U.S.* 106 F3
Bevan's Town, *Bahamas* 122 E2
Beverley, *Eng., U.K.* 145 RI3
Bewcastle, *Eng., U.K.* 145 PII
Bexhill, *Eng., U.K.* 145 WI5
Beycesultan, ruins, *Turk.* 170 G4
Bey Dağı, peak, *Turk.* 170 EI2
Bey Dağı, peak, *Turk.* 170 GII
Beykoz, *Turk.* 170 C5
Beyla, *Guinea* 204 D7
Beyləqan, *Azerb.* 171 E2I
Bēylul, *Eritrea* 203 EI6
Beyneu, *Kaz.* 176 G7
Beyonēsu-Retsugan (Bayonnaise Rock), *Japan* 189 SI2
Beypazarı, *Turk.* 170 E7
Beyrouth (Beirut), *Leb.* 172 H6
Beyşehir, *Turk.* 170 G7
Beyşehir Gölü, *Turk.* 170 G7
Beytüşşebap, *Turk.* 171 HI7
Bezhetsk, *Russ.* 158 H9
Béziers, *Fr.* 149 YII
Bhadarwah, *India* 179 NI3
Bhadra, *India* 180 E5
Bhadrakh, *India* 180 KII
Bhag, *Pak.* 179 S7
Bhagalpur, *India* 180 HII
Bhakkar, *Pak.* 179 Q9
Bhaktapur, *Nepal* 180 FIO
Bhamo, *Myanmar* 190 F7
Bhandara, *India* 180 J7
Bhanpura, *India* 180 H5
Bharati, station, *Antarctica* 231 G2O
Bharatpur, *India* 180 F6
Bharatpur, *India* 180 H8
Bharuch, *India* 180 J3
Bhatapara, *India* 180 K8
Bhatarsaigh (Vatersay), island, *Scot., U.K.* 144 K6
Bhatinda, *India* 180 E5
Bhatkal, *India* 181 P4
Bhatpara, *India* 180 JI2
Bhavnagar, *India* 180 J3
Bhawanipatna, *India* 180 L9
Bhera, *Pak.* 179 PII
Bhilai, *India* 180 K8
Bhilwara, *India* 180 G4
Bhima, river, *India* 180 M5
Bhimbar, *Pak.* 179 NII
Bhind, *India* 180 G6
Bhinmal, *India* 180 H3
Bhisho, *S. Af.* 206 LIO
Bholari, *Pak.* 179 W7
Bhongir, *India* 180 M6
Bhopal, *India* 180 J6
Bhreandáin, Bá (Brandon Bay), *Ire.* 145 U2
Bhubaneshwar, *India* 180 KIO
Bhuj, *India* 180 HI
Bhusawal, *India* 180 K5
Bhutan, *Asia* 180 FI2
Biabou, *St. Vincent and the Grenadines* 123 KI7
Biak, *Indonesia* 193 JI9
Biak, island, *Indonesia* 193 JI9
Biała Podlaska, *Pol.* 151 EI8
Białogard, *Pol.* 150 BI2
Biały Bór, *Pol.* 151 BI3
Białystok, *Pol.* 151 CI7
Bianco, *It.* 153 RI3
Biando, island, *S. Korea* 187 R7
Biaó, peak, *Eq. Guinea* 208 M7
Biaora, *India* 180 H5
Bīārjomand, *Iran* 175 CI5
Biaro, island, *Indonesia* 193 HI5
Biarritz, *Fr.* 149 X5
Bias, *Fr.* 149 W6
Biau, *Indonesia* 193 HI4
Bibala, *Angola* 206 E5
Bibbiena, *It.* 152 G7
Biberach, *Ger.* 150 K7

Bibi Nani, *Pak.* 179 R6
Bicaz, *Rom.* 155 CI5
Bichänäk Ashyrymy, *Arm.* 171 EI9
Biche, *Trinidad and Tobago* 123 P23
Bichvint'a, *Rep. of Georgia* 171 AI5
Bickleton, *Wash., U.S.* 110 E6
Bicknell, *Ind., U.S.* 101 T8
Bicknell, *Utah, U.S.* 109 N7
Bida, *Nigeria* 205 DI3
Biddeford, *Me., U.S.* 97 HI5
Bideford, *Eng., U.K.* 145 W9
Bieber, *Calif., U.S.* 110 M5
Biei, *Japan* 188 FI3
Biel, *Switz.* 152 B2
Bielawa, *Pol.* 151 GI3
Bielefeld, *Ger.* 150 E6
Biele Karpaty, range, *Czech Rep., Slovakia* 151 JI3
Bieler See, *Switz.* 152 B2
Biella, *It.* 152 D3
Bielsa, *Sp.* 147 CI5
Bielsko-Biała, *Pol.* 151 HI5
Bielsk Podlaski, *Pol.* 151 DI7
Biên Hòa, *Vietnam* 191 PI3
Bienville, Lac, *Que., Can.* 85 LI9
Bié Plateau, *Af.* 198 L6
Biescas, *Sp.* 147 CI4
Big, river, *N.W.T., Can.* 84 DI2
Biga, *Turk.* 170 D3
Bigadiç, *Turk.* 170 E4
Big Bay, *Mich., U.S.* 100 E7
Big Bay, *Vanuatu* 222 CI
Big Bay, *Vanuatu* 222 E2
Big Belt Mountains, *Mont., U.S.* 108 D8
Big Bend National Park, *Tex., U.S.* 105 R3
Big Black, river, *Miss., U.S.* 102 LIO
Big Blue, river, *Nebr., U.S.* 107 Q8
Big Bog, swamp, *Minn., U.S.* 106 E9
Big Canyon, river, *Tex., U.S.* 105 Q3
Big Creek, *Calif., U.S.* III T7
Big Cypress National Preserve, *Fla., U.S.* 99 W9
Big Cypress Swamp, *Fla., U.S.* 99 W9
Bigej, island, *Marshall Is., U.S.* 220 M5
Bigej Channel, *Marshall Is., U.S.* 220 M5
Bigeumdo, island, *S. Korea* 187 T6
Big Falls, *Minn., U.S.* 106 EII
Big Fork, river, *Minn., U.S.* 106 EII
Bigfork, *Minn., U.S.* 106 FII
Bigfork, *Mont., U.S.* 108 B6
Biggar, *Sask., Can.* 84 MII
Biggarenn, island, *Marshall Is., U.S.* 220 K3
Biggenden, *Qnsld., Austral.* 215 UI5
Biggerann, island, *Marshall Is., U.S.* 220 K2
Big Hatchet Peak, *N. Mex., U.S.* 109 WIO
Big Hole, river, *Mont., U.S.* 108 E6
Big Hole National Battlefield, *Mont., U.S.* 108 E6
Bighorn, river, *Mont., Wyo., U.S.* 108 GIO
Bighorn Canyon National Recreation Area, *Mont., Wyo., U.S.* 108 FIO
Bighorn Lake, *Mont., Wyo., U.S.* 108 FIO
Bighorn Mountains, *Wyo., U.S.* 108 FIO
Bight Fracture Zone, *Atl. Oc.* 240 G8
Bight of Acklins, The, *Bahamas* 119 HI5
Bigi, island, *Marshall Is., U.S.* 220 K3
Big Island, *Nunavut, Can.* 85 HI8
Big Lake, *Tex., U.S.* 105 NI5
Big Mangrove, *Bahamas* 122 B8
Bigonville, *Lux.* 162 H9
Big Pine, *Calif., U.S.* III T8
Big Pine, *Fla., U.S.* 99 Y9
Big Piney, *Wyo., U.S.* 108 J9
Big Rapids, *Mich., U.S.* 100 KIO
Big Sandy, *Mont., U.S.* 108 B9
Big Sandy, river, *Wyo., U.S.* 108 J9
Big Sioux, river, *S. Dak., U.S.* 106 L8
Big Snowy Mountains, *Mont., U.S.* 108 D9

Big South Fork National River and Recreation Area, *Ky., Tenn., U.S.* 103 EI7
Big Spring, *Tex., U.S.* 104 M5
Big Springs, *Nebr., U.S.* 107 Q3
Big Stone City, *S. Dak., U.S.* 106 J8
Big Stone Gap, *Va., U.S.* 98 G7
Big Stone Lake, *Minn., S. Dak., U.S.* 106 J8
Big Sur, *Calif., U.S.* III U4
Big Thicket National Preserve, *Tex., U.S.* 105 PI5
Big Timber, *Mont., U.S.* 108 E9
Big Trout Lake, *Ont., Can.* 85 MI5
Big Valley Mountains, *Calif., U.S.* 110 M4
Big Wells, *Tex., U.S.* 105 S8
Big Wood, river, *Idaho, U.S.* 108 H5
Big Wood Cay, *Bahamas* 118 EII
Bihać, *Bosn. & Herzg.* 154 F6
Bihar Sharif, *India* 180 HIO
Bihoro, *Japan* 188 FI5
Biinman, bay, *S. Korea* 187 Q7
Bijagós, Arquipélago de, *Guinea-Bissau* 204 B4
Bijapur, *India* 180 L7
Bijapur *see* Vijayapura, *India* 180 M5
Bījār, *Iran* 174 CII
Bijeljina, *Bosn. & Herzg.* 154 F9
Bijire, island, *Marshall Is., U.S.* 220 G8
Bijnor, *India* 180 E6
Bikaner, *India* 180 F4
Bikar Atoll, *Marshall Is., U.S.* 220 F4
Bikeman, island, *Kiribati* 221 GI7
Biken, island, *Marshall Is., U.S.* 220 H7
Bikenibeu, *Kiribati* 221 GI8
Bikennel, island, *Marshall Is., U.S.* 220 L3
Bikenubati, island, *Kiribati* 221 FI7
Bikin, *Russ.* 161 L2I
Bikini Atoll, *Marshall Is., U.S.* 220 F2
Bīkkū Bīttī, peak, *Lib.* 201 FI5
Bikoro, *Dem. Rep. of the Congo* 202 K8
Bilād Banī Bū 'Alī, *Oman* 175 LI7
Bilaspur, *India* 180 J8
Bila Tserkva, *Ukr.* 159 P5
Bilauktaung Range, *Thai.* 190 M8
Bilbao, *Sp.* 146 BI2
Bileća, *Bosn. & Herzg.* 154 H8
Bilecik, *Turk.* 170 D5
Biləsuvar, *Azerb.* 171 E22
Biłgoraj, *Pol.* 151 GI7
Bilhorod-Dnistrovs'kyy, *Ukr.* 159 R5
Bilibino, *Russ.* 161 C2O
Bilican Dağları, peak, *Turk.* 171 FI6
Bill, *Wyo., U.S.* 108 HI3
Billae, island, *Marshall Is., U.S.* 220 H8
Bill Baileys Bank, *Atl. Oc.* 240 FIO
Billila, *N.S.W., Austral.* 215 WI2
Billiluna, *W. Aust., Austral.* 215 R6
Billings, *Mont., U.S.* 108 EIO
Billings, *Okla., U.S.* 104 EII
Billings, *Russ.* 161 BI9
Billiton *see* Belitung, *Indonesia* 192 K8
Bill of Portland, *Eng., U.K.* 145 XII
Billom, *Fr.* 149 UII
Białowieża Forest, *Eur.* 140 G9
Bill Williams, river, *Ariz., U.S.* 109 T5
Billy Chinook, Lake, *Oreg., U.S.* 110 G5
Bilma, *Niger* 201 GI3
Biloela, *Qnsld., Austral.* 215 UI5
Bilo Gora, mountains, *Croatia* 154 D7
Bilohirs'k, *Ukr.* 159 S8
Bilopillya, *Ukr.* 159 N8
Biloxi, *Miss., U.S.* 102 PI2
Biltine, *Chad* 201 HI6
Bilto, *Nor.* 143 CI3
Bilüü, *Mongolia* 182 C6
Bilwi, *Nicar.* 117 LI9
Bilzen, *Belg.* 148 LI3
Bimberi Peak, *Austral.* 214 LI4
Bimini Islands, *Bahamas* 118 D9
Bindura, *Zimb.* 206 FI2
Binéfar, *Sp.* 147 DI5

Binəqədi, *Azerb.* 171 D23
Binford, *N. Dak., U.S.* 106 F7
Bingen, *Ger.* 150 G6
Binger, *Okla., U.S.* 104 G9
Bingham, *Me., U.S.* 97 EI6
Bingham Channel, *Kiribati* 221 EI7
Binghamton, *N.Y., U.S.* 96 L9
Bingöl, *Turk.* 171 FI4
Bingöl Dağları, peak, *Turk.* 171 FI6
Binhai (Dongkan), *Jiangsu, China* 184 JIO
Bình Khê, *Vietnam* 190 MI4
Bình Liêu, *Vietnam* 190 GI3
Bình Long, *Vietnam* 191 PI2
Binjai, *Indonesia* 192 G5
Binjai, *Indonesia* 192 G8
Binongko, island, *Indonesia* 193 LI5
Bintan, island, *Malaysia* 192 H7
Bintuhan, *Indonesia* 192 L7
Bintulu, *Malaysia* 192 HIO
Binyang, *China* 182 PII
Binzhou, *Shand., China* 184 F9
Biobío, river, *Chile* 135 N6
Bioč, peak, *Montenegro* 154 H8
Bioko, island, *Eq. Guinea* 205 FI4
Biokovo, peak, *Croatia* 154 H7
Bir, *India* 180 L5
Birāk, *Lib.* 201 DI4
Bi'r 'Alī, *Yemen* 174 QII
Birao, *Cen. Af. Rep.* 202 FIO
Biratnagar, *Nepal* 180 GII
Birch Mountains, *Alta., Can.* 84 KII
Birch Tree Hill, *Cayman Is.* 122 HI
Birchwood, *Alas., U.S.* 113 JI6
Bird City, *Kans., U.S.* 107 R3
Bird Island, *Grenada* 123 J24
Bird Island, *Minn., U.S.* 106 KIO
Bird Island, *Seychelles* 209 KI9
Bird Island *see* Aves, island, *Lesser Antil.* 121 DI4
Birdsville, *Qnsld., Austral.* 215 UII
Birecik, *Turk.* 171 HI3
Bîr el 'Abd, *Egypt* 173 N2
Bireun, *Indonesia* 192 G4
Birganj, *Nepal* 180 GIO
Bîr Ḥasana, *Egypt* 173 P3
Bīrjand, *Iran* 175 EI6
Birkenhead, *Eng., U.K.* 145 SIO
Birkirkara, *Malta* 163 K22
Bîrlad, river, *Rom.* 155 CI7
Birmingham, *Ala., U.S.* 103 JI5
Birmingham, *Eng., U.K.* 145 TI2
Bir Mogreïn (Fort Trinquet), *Mauritania* 200 D6
Birnie Island, *Kiribati* 218 GIO
Birnin Kebbi, *Nigeria* 204 BI2
Birni Nkonni, *Niger* 200 HII
Birobidzhan, *Russ.* 161 K2O
Birong, *Philippines* 192 EI2
Birrindudu, *N.T., Austral.* 215 R7
Birshoghyr, *Kaz.* 176 E9
Birsilpur, *India* 180 F3
Birtin, *Rom.* 154 CI2
Birufu, *Indonesia* 193 L2O
Biryakovo, *Russ.* 158 FII
Birżebbuġa, *Malta* 163 L23
Bisa, island, *Indonesia* 193 JI6
Bisbee, *Ariz., U.S.* 109 W9
Bisbee, *N. Dak., U.S.* 106 E6
Biscarosse et de Parentis, Lac de, *Fr.* 149 W6
Biscarrosse-Plage, *Fr.* 149 W6
Biscay, Bay of, *Atl. Oc.* 140 H3
Biscayne Bay, *Fla., U.S.* 99 XIO
Biscayne National Park, *Fla., U.S.* 99 XIO
Biscay Plain, *Atl. Oc.* 240 HII
Bisceglie, *It.* 152 LI3
Bischheim, *Fr.* 149 PI5
Biscoe Islands, *Antarctica* 230 E4
Biševo, island, *Croatia* 154 H6
Bishkek, *Kyrg.* 178 DII
Bishop, *Calif., U.S.* III S8
Bishop, *Tex., U.S.* 105 UIO
Bishopville, *S.C., U.S.* 98 KIO
Bishrī, Jabal, *Syr.* 172 FI2
Biskra, *Alg.* 200 BII
Bislig, *Philippines* 193 FI5
Bismarck, *N. Dak., U.S.* 106 G4

Bismarck Archipelago, *P.N.G.* 217 C2O
Bismarck Range, *P.N.G.* 217 CI9
Bismarck Sea, *P.N.G.* 217 C2O
Bismil, *Turk.* 171 GI5
Bison, *S. Dak., U.S.* 106 J3
Bissagos Islands, *Af.* 198 GI
Bissamcuttack, *India* 180 L9
Bissau, *Guinea-Bissau* 204 B4
Bissen, *Lux.* 162 JIO
Bistcho Lake, *Alta., Can.* 84 JIO
Bistineau, Lake, *La., U.S.* 102 L7
Bistreţu, *Rom.* 155 GI3
Bistriţa, *Rom.* 155 CI4
Bistriţa, river, *Rom.* 155 CI5
Bitam, *Gabon* 205 GI6
Bitburg, *Ger.* 162 HII
Bitlis, *Turk.* 171 GI6
Bitola, *Maced.* 154 LII
Bitra Island, *India* 181 Q3
Bitterfontein, *S. Af.* 206 L7
Bitterroot, river, *Mont., U.S.* 108 D6
Bitterroot Range, *Idaho, Mont., U.S.* 108 D5
Biu, *Nigeria* 205 CI6
Bivona, *It.* 153 S9
Biwa Ko, *Japan* 189 P9
Bixby, *Okla., U.S.* 104 FI3
Bixessarri, *Andorra* 162 K2
Biya, river, *Asia* 168 E8
Biyang, *Henan, China* 184 L5
Biysk, *Russ.* 160 LI2
Bizerte, *Tun.* 201 AI3
Bjargtangar, bay, *Atl. Oc.* 140 A3
Bjelolasica, peak, *Croatia* 154 E5
Bjelovar, *Croatia* 154 D7
Bjøllånes, *Nor.* 142 E12
Bjørnafjorden, bay, *Nor.* 142 K9
Bjørnøya Bank, *Arctic Oc.* 247 GI8
Black *see* Dà, river, *Vietnam* 190 HII
Black, river, *Ariz., U.S.* 109 U8
Black, river, *Ark., Mo., U.S.* 102 FIO
Black, river, *Jam.* 122 J7
Black, river, *N.Y., U.S.* 96 H9
Black, river, *Wis., U.S.* 100 J4
Blackall, *Qnsld., Austral.* 215 TI3
Blackball, *N.Z.* 217 NI7
Black Bay Point, *Grenada* 123 K22
Blackbeard Island, *Ga., U.S.* 99 P9
Blackbeard's Tower, site, *Bahamas* 122 BI2
Black Belt, *U.S.* 87 KI6
Blackburn, *Eng., U.K.* 145 RII
Blackburn, Mount, *Alas., U.S.* 113 JI9
Black Canyon City, *Ariz., U.S.* 109 T7
Black Canyon of the Gunnison National Park, *Colo., U.S.* 109 NII
Black Coast, *Antarctica* 230 E6
Blackdown, *Qnsld., Austral.* 215 RI3
Blackduck, *Minn., U.S.* 106 FIO
Black Eagle, *Mont., U.S.* 108 C8
Blackfoot, *Idaho, U.S.* 108 H7
Blackfoot, river, *Mont., U.S.* 108 C6
Blackfoot Reservoir, *Idaho, U.S.* 108 H7
Black Forest, *Ger.* 150 K6
Blackhaw Seamounts, *Pac. Oc.* 243 HI3
Black Hills, *U.S.* 86 DIO
Black Irtysh, river, *Asia* 168 F8
Black Isle, *Scot., U.K.* 144 J9
Black Lake, *Mich., U.S.* 100 GII
Blackmans, *Barbados* 123 KI9
Black Mesa, *Ariz., U.S.* 109 Q8
Black Mesa, peak, *Okla., U.S.* 104 E4
Blackmoor Vale, *Eng., U.K.* 145 WII
Black Mountain, *Ky., U.S.* 103 D2O
Black Mountains, *Ariz., U.S.* 109 R4
BlackMountains, *Wales, U.K.* 145 UIO
Black Point, *British Virgin Is., U.K.* 122 LII
Black Point, *St. Vincent and the Grenadines* 123 KI7
Blackpool, *Eng., U.K.* 145 RIO
Black Range, *U.S.* 86 K8
Black River, *Jam.* 122 J7
Black River Bay, *Jam.* 122 J7
Black River Falls, *Wis., U.S.* 100 J4
Black Rock, *Ire.* 145 Q2

Black Rock, *Trinidad and Tobago*
123 NI7
Black Rock Desert, *Nev., U.S.*
110 M7
Blacksburg, *Va., U.S.* 98 F9
Black Sea, *Eur.* 140 KII
Black Sea Lowland, *Eur.* 140 HII
Blacks Fork, river, *Utah, Wyo., U.S.*
108 K8
Blackshear, *Ga., U.S.* 99 P8
Blacksod Bay, *Ire.* 145 Q3
Blackstone, *Va., U.S.* 98 FI2
Blackville, *S.C., U.S.* 98 L9
Blackwater, *Qnsld., Austral.* 215 TI4
Blackwater, river, *Ire.* 145 U4
Blackwell, *Okla., U.S.* 104 EII
Blackwell, *Tex., U.S.* 104 M7
Blackwood, river, *Austral.* 214 L3
Blagodarnyy, *Russ.* 159 SI3
Blagoevgrad, *Bulg.* 155 KI3
Blagoveshchensk, *Russ.* 161 KI9
Blain, *Fr.* 149 R5
Blaine, *Wash., U.S.* 110 A3
Blair, *Nebr., U.S.* 107 P9
Blaj, *Rom.* 155 DI3
Blake Basin, *Atl. Oc.* 240 L3
Blakely, *Ga., U.S.* 99 P4
Blakeney, *Eng., U.K.* 145 SI5
Blake Plateau, *Atl. Oc.* 240 K3
Blake Point, *Mich., U.S.* 100 C6
Blakes, *Cayman Is.* 122 J4
Blanc, Cap, *Mauritania* 200 F4
Blanc, Mont, *Fr., It.* 152 D2
Blanc, Mount, *Fr., It.* 149 UI5
Blanca, Costa, *Sp.* 147 KI5
Blanca, Portella, *Andorra, Fr.* 162 J5
Blanca Bay, *S. Amer.* 128 M6
Blanca Peak, *Colo., U.S.* 109 PI3
Blanca Peak, *U.S.* 86 H9
Blanchard, *Okla., U.S.* 104 GIO
Blanche, Lake, *Austral.* 214 HII
Blanche Bay, *La., U.S.* 102 R8
Blanche Channel, *Solomon Is.*
221 MI6
Blanchisseuse, *Trinidad and Tobago*
123 N23
Blanco, *Tex., U.S.* 105 Q9
Blanco, river, *Bol.* 132 J8
Blanco, river, *Tex., U.S.* 105 QIO
Blanco, Cape, *Oreg., U.S.* 110 JI
Blanco Fracture Zone, *Pac. Oc.*
243 DI7
Blanding, *Utah, U.S.* 109 P9
Blanes, *Sp.* 147 DI8
Blangy, *Fr.* 148 M9
Blankenberge, *Belg.* 148 KIO
Blanquilla, Isla, *Venez.* 130 AII
Blantyre, *Malawi* 207 EI3
Blasket Island *see* Na Blascaodaí, *Ire.*
145 U2
Blåvands Point, *Eur.* 140 F6
Blaydon, *Eng., U.K.* 145 PI2
Blaye, *Fr.* 149 V6
Blaze, Point, *Austral.* 214 B7
Blednaya, Gora, *Russ.* 160 DI2
Blenheim, *N.Z.* 217 MI8
Blessington Lakes, *Ire.* 145 S6
Blida, *Alg.* 200 AII
Blidinje Jezero, *Bosn. & Herzg.*
154 G7
Bligh Water, *Fiji* 222 H6
Blima, Grand Erg de, *Niger* 201 GI4
Blind River, *Ont., Can.* 85 QI7
Blinman, *S. Aust., Austral.* 215 WIO
Blitar, *Indonesia* 192 MIO
Block Island, *R.I., U.S.* 97 MI4
Bloemfontein, *S. Af.* 206 KIO
Bloemhof, *S. Af.* 206 KIO
Blois, *Fr.* 149 R9
Blönduós, *Ice.* 142 E3
Bloody Bay, *Trinidad and Tobago*
123 NI8
Bloody Foreland, *Ire.* 145 N5
Bloomer, *Wis., U.S.* 100 H3
Bloomfield, *Ind., U.S.* 101 S8
Bloomfield, *Iowa, U.S.* 107 QI3
Bloomfield, *Mo., U.S.* 107 VI5
Bloomfield, *Nebr., U.S.* 107 N7
Blooming Prairie, *Minn., U.S.*
106 LI2
Bloomington, *Ill., U.S.* 101 Q5

Bloomington, *Ind., U.S.* 101 S8
Bloomington, *Minn., U.S.* 106 KII
Bloomington, *Tex., U.S.* 105 SI2
Bloomsburg, *Pa., U.S.* 96 N8
Blossom, Mys, *Russ.* 161 BI9
Blower Rock, *Jam.* 118 PII
Blowing Point, *British Virgin Is., U.K.*
122 RII
Blowing Point, *Jam.* 122 HIO
Bludenz, *Aust.* 150 L7
Blue Earth, *Minn., U.S.* 106 LII
Bluefield, *W. Va., U.S.* 98 F8
Bluefields, *Jam.* 122 J6
Bluefields, *Nicar.* 117 MI9
Bluefields Bay, *Jam.* 122 J6
Blue Hill, *Nebr., U.S.* 107 R6
Blue Hills, *Turks & Caicos Is.* 119 HI6
Blue Hole, site, *Jam.* 122 JII
Bluejoint Lake, *Oreg., U.S.* 110 K6
Blue Lake, *Calif., U.S.* 110 M2
Blue Mountain, *Ark., U.S.* 102 G6
Blue Mountain, *Oreg., U.S.* 110 K8
Blue Mountain Peak, *Jam.* 122 JIO
Blue Mountains, *Austral.* 214 KI4
Blue Mountains, *Jam.* 122 JIO
Blue Mountains, *Oreg., Wash., U.S.*
110 F8
Blue Mud Bay, *Austral.* 214 BIO
Blue Nile *see* Azraq, El Bahr el, river,
Af. 204 EI3
Blue Nile Falls *see* T'is Isat Fwafwatē,
Eth. 204 FI4
Blue Rapids, *Kans., U.S.* 107 R8
Blue Ridge, *Ga., U.S.* 98 J5
Blue Ridge, *U.S.* 98 G9
Bluff, *N.Z.* 217 RI5
Bluff, *Utah, U.S.* 109 P9
Bluff Knoll, *Austral.* 214 L3
Bluff Point, *Austral.* 214 H2
Bluffton, *Ind., U.S.* 101 QIO
Blumenau, *Braz.* 133 NI4
Blunt, *S. Dak., U.S.* 106 K5
Bly, *Oreg., U.S.* 110 K5
Blyth, *Eng., U.K.* 145 PI2
Blythe, *Calif., U.S.* 111 YI2
Blytheville, *Ark., U.S.* 102 FII
Bo, *Sierra Leone* 204 D6
Bø, *Nor.* 142 DI2
Bø, *Nor.* 142 J9
Boaco, *Nicar.* 117 MI8
Bo'ai, *Henan, China* 184 H5
Boano, island, *Indonesia* 193 KI6
Boardman, *Ohio, U.S.* 101 PI5
Boa Vista, *Braz.* 132 B9
Boa Vista, island, *Cabo Verde*
209 CI7
Boaz, *Ala., U.S.* 103 HI6
Boaz Island, *Bermuda* 122 CI
Bobai, *Guangxi Zhuang, China*
185 WI
Bobbili, *India* 180 L9
Bobo Dioulasso, *Burkina Faso*
204 C9
Bobovdol, *Bulg.* 154 JI2
Boby, peak, *Madagascar* 207 HI7
Boca Chica, *Dom. Rep.* 119 MI9
Boca Chica Key, *Fla., U.S.* 99 Y8
Bôca do Acre, *Braz.* 132 F6
Bôca do Jari, *Braz.* 132 DI2
Bocage, Cap, *New Caledonia, Fr.*
222 C7
Boca Grande, *Fla., U.S.* 99 W8
Boca Mavaca, *Venez.* 130 GIO
Boca Raton, *Fla., U.S.* 99 WIO
Bocas del Toro, *Pan.* 117 N2O
Boca Tabla, site, *Curaçao, Neth.*
123 NI3
Bocay, *Nicar.* 117 LI8
Bochnia, *Pol.* 151 HI6
Bocholt, *Ger.* 150 E5
Bochum, *Ger.* 150 E5
Bocognano, *Fr.* 152 K4
Bocşa, *Rom.* 154 EII
Böda, *Sw.* 143 LI4
Bodaybo, *Russ.* 161 JI6
Bodden Bay, *Cayman Is.* 122 J3
Bodden Town, *Cayman Is.* 122 J2
Bodega Bay, *Calif., U.S.* 111 R2
Bodega Head, *Calif., U.S.* 111 R2
Bodele Depression, *Af.* 198 F6
Boden, *Sw.* 143 EI4

Bodensee (Lake Constance), *Aust.,
Ger., Switz.* 150 L6
Bode Verde Fracture Zone, *Atl. Oc.*
241 QIO
Bodi, *Indonesia* 193 JI4
Bodĭ, *Mongolia* 182 E9
Bodkin Mill, site, *Virgin Is., U.S.*
122 Q2
Bodmin, *Eng., U.K.* 145 X8
Bodmin Moor, *Eng., U.K.* 145 X9
Bodø, *Nor.* 142 EI2
Bodŏl Sea, bay, *S. Korea* 187 U9
Bodrum, *Turk.* 170 H3
Boën, *Fr.* 149 UI2
Boende, *Dem. Rep. of the Congo*
202 K9
Bœ̆ng Tônlé Sab (Tonle Sap),
Cambodia 191 NII
Boeo, Capo, *It.* 153 S8
Boe, region, *Nauru* 221 F22
Boerne, *Tex., U.S.* 105 R9
Boeuf, river, *La., U.S.* 102 L9
Boffa, *Guinea* 204 C5
Bogalusa, *La., U.S.* 102 NII
Bogan, river, *Austral.* 214 J13
Bogantungan, *Qnsld., Austral.*
215 TI4
Boğaz *see* Boghaz, *Cyprus* 162 NIO
Boğazkale, *Turk.* 170 EIO
Boğazlıyan, *Turk.* 170 FIO
Bogda Feng, peak, *Asia* 168 F8
Bogdanovka, *Rep. of Georgia*
171 CI7
Bogda Shan, *China* 182 E5
Bogenaga, island, *Marshall Is., U.S.*
220 K7
Boggenadick, island, *Marshall Is., U.S.*
220 K7
Boggenatjen, island, *Marshall Is., U.S.*
220 L3
Boggerik, island, *Marshall Is., U.S.*
220 K3
Boggerik Passage, *Marshall Is., U.S.*
220 K3
Boggerlapp, island, *Marshall Is., U.S.*
220 K4
Boggy Peak, *Antigua and Barbuda*
123 B2O
Boghaz (Boğaz), *Cyprus* 162 NIO
Bogia, *P.N.G.* 217 CI9
Bogildo, island, *S. Korea* 187 V7
Bogong, Mount, *Austral.* 214 LI3
Bogor, *Indonesia* 192 M8
Bogoroditsk, *Russ.* 158 L9
Bogorodsk, *Russ.* 158 JI2
Bogotá, *Col.* 130 F5
Bogotol, *Russ.* 161 KI3
Bogra, *Bangladesh* 180 HI2
Bogué, *Mauritania* 200 G5
Bog Walk, *Jam.* 122 J9
Bo Hai, bay, *Shand., China* 184 EIO
Bohai Haixia, *Shand., China* 184 EII
Bohai Wan, *Tianjin Shi, China* 184 E8
Bohe, *Guang., China* 185 X2
Bohé, *Eq. Guinea* 208 N7
Bohemia, region, *Czech Rep.*
150 HIO
Bohemian Forest, *Ger.* 150 J9
Bohodukhiv, *Ukr.* 159 N8
Bohol, island, *Philippines* 193 EI4
Bohol Sea, *Philippines* 193 EI5
Bohyeonsan, peak, *S. Korea* 187 QI2
Boiaçu, *Braz.* 132 C8
Boim, *Braz.* 132 DII
Boin Sum, *N. Mongol, China* 184 A5
Bois, river, *S. Amer.* 128 G8
Bois Blanc Island, *Mich., U.S.*
100 GII
Boise, *Idaho, U.S.* 108 G4
Boisé, Port, *New Caledonia, Fr.*
222 E9
Boise City, *Okla., U.S.* 104 E4
Bojeador, Cape, *Asia* 168 JI2
Bojnūrd, *Iran* 175 BI5
Bokalijman, island, *Marshall Is., U.S.*
220 M7
Boké, *Guinea* 204 B4
Boken, island, *Marshall Is., U.S.*
220 GIO
Boken, island, *Marshall Is., U.S.*
220 G8

Boken, island, *Marshall Is., U.S.*
220 J8
Bokenelab, island, *Marshall Is., U.S.*
220 G8
Bokkumaruchi, island, *Marshall Is.,
U.S.* 220 K3
Boklaplap, island, *Marshall Is., U.S.*
220 L8
Boknafjorden, bay, *Nor.* 142 K9
Boko, *Congo* 205 KI7
Bokoluo, island, *Marshall Is., U.S.*
220 G7
Bokombako, island, *Marshall Is., U.S.*
220 G7
Bökönbaev, *Kyrg.* 178 EI3
Bokovskaya, *Russ.* 159 PII
Bokpyinn, *Myanmar* 191 P8
Boksitogorsk, *Russ.* 158 F8
Bokungu, *Dem. Rep. of the Congo*
202 K9
Bokurdak, *Turkm.* 176 L8
Bol, *Chad* 201 JI4
Bolaang, *Indonesia* 193 KI4
Bolan Pass, *Pak.* 179 R6
Bolaven, river, *Austral.* 214 J13
Bolbec, *Fr.* 149 N8
Boldumsaz, *Uzb.* 176 J9
Bole, *China* 182 D4
Bole, *Ghana* 204 DIO
Bolea, *Sp.* 147 CI4
Bolesławiec, *Pol.* 150 FI2
Bolgatanga, *Ghana* 204 CIO
Bolhrad, *Ukr.* 159 S4
Bolinao, Cape, *Asia* 168 JI2
Bolivar, *Mo., U.S.* 107 UI2
Bolivar, *Tenn., U.S.* 102 GI2
Bolívar, Cerro, *Venez.* 130 DII
Bolivia, *Cuba* 118 HIO
Bolivia, *S. Amer.* 132 J8
Bolkar Dağları, *Turk.* 170 H9
Bolkhov, *Russ.* 158 L8
Bollène, *Fr.* 149 WI2
Bollnäs, *Sw.* 143 JI3
Bollon, *Qnsld., Austral.* 215 VI4
Bollons Seamount, *Pac. Oc.*
242 QI2
Bolluk Gölü, *Turk.* 170 G8
Bolnisi, *Rep. of Georgia* 171 CI8
Bolobo, *Dem. Rep. of the Congo*
202 K8
Bologna, *It.* 152 F7
Bolognesi, *Peru* 132 G4
Bologoye, *Russ.* 158 G8
Bolsena, *It.* 152 J8
Bolsena, Lago di, *It.* 152 J7
Bol'shaya Bicha, *Russ.* 160 JIO
Bol'sheretsk, *Russ.* 161 G23
Bol'shevik, Ostrov, *Russ.* 161 DI4
Bol'shevik Island, *Asia* 168 B9
Bol'shezemel'skaya Tundra, *Russ.*
160 FIO
Bol'shoy Begichev, Ostrov, *Russ.*
161 EI5
Bol'shoy Lyakhovskiy, Ostrov, *Russ.*
161 DI7
Bol'shoy Patom, *Russ.* 161 JI7
Bol'shoy Shantar, Ostrov, *Russ.*
161 H2O
Bolsón de Mapimí, *N. Amer.* 82 M4
Bolsward, *Neth.* 148 GI3
Bolt Head, *Eng., U.K.* 145 YIO
Bolton, *Eng., U.K.* 145 RII
Bolton Point, *Kiribati* 221 EI7
Bolu, *Turk.* 170 D7
Boluntay, *China* 182 H6
Boluo, *Guang., China* 185 V5
Bolvadin, *Turk.* 170 F6
Bolzano, *It.* 152 C7
Boma, *Dem. Rep. of the Congo*
202 M7
Bomba, Gulf of, *Af.* 198 D8
Bombala, *N.S.W., Austral.* 215 ZI4
Bombardopolis, *Haiti* 119 LI5
Bombay *see* Mumbai, *India* 180 L3
Bombom, Ilhéu, *Sao Tome and Principe*
209 A2O
Bomdila, *India* 180 FI3
Bomdo, *India* 180 EI5
Bom Jesus da Lapa, *Braz.* 133 HI5

Bomongo, *Dem. Rep. of the Congo*
202 J8
Bomu, river, *Af.* 202 HIO
Bona, Mount, *Alas., U.S.* 113 JI9
Bon Accueil, *Mauritius* 209 G2O
Bonaire, island, *Lesser Antil.*
120 HIO
Bonanza, *Utah, U.S.* 108 L9
Bonao, *Dom. Rep.* 119 MI8
Bonaparte Basin, *Ind. Oc.* 225 J2O
Bonasse, *Trinidad and Tobago*
123 Q21
Bonavista, *Nfld. & Lab., Can.* 85 M24
Bonavista Bay, *N. Amer.* 82 GII
Bondo, *Dem. Rep. of the Congo*
202 HIO
Bondoukou, *Côte d'Ivoire* 204 D9
Bonds Cay, *Bahamas* 118 DII
Bone, Gulf of, *Pac. Oc.* 168 MI3
Bone, Teluk, *Indonesia* 218 HI
Bonefish Bay, *Bahamas* 122 EII
Bonefish Pond, *Bahamas* 122 BII
Bonerate, island, *Indonesia* 193 MI3
Bonesteel, *S. Dak., U.S.* 106 M6
Bonete, Cerro, *Arg.* 134 G7
Bongandanga, *Dem. Rep. of the Congo*
202 J9
Bongdong, *S. Korea* 187 R8
Bonghwa, *S. Korea* 187 PII
Bongnam, *S. Korea* 187 S7
Bongo Lava, *Af.* 198 NII
Bongor, *Chad* 201 KI4
Bongos, Chaîne des, *Cen. Af. Rep.*
202 G9
Bongyang, *S. Korea* 187 NIO
Bonham, *Tex., U.S.* 104 KI2
Bonifacio, *Fr.* 152 L4
Bonifacio, Strait of, *Fr.* 152 L4
Bonifay, *Fla., U.S.* 99 Q3
Bonin Islands (Ogasawara Guntō),
Japan 189 XI4
Bonin Trench, *Pac. Oc.* 242 G8
Bonita Springs, *Fla., U.S.* 99 W8
Bonito, *Braz.* 132 LIO
Bonn, *Ger.* 150 F5
Bonners Ferry, *Idaho, U.S.* 108 A4
Bonne Terre, *Mo., U.S.* 107 TI5
Bonneval, *Fr.* 149 Q9
Bonneville Dam, *Oreg., Wash., U.S.*
110 F4
Bonneville Salt Flats, *Utah, U.S.*
108 K5
Bonnie Rock, *W. Aust., Austral.*
215 W3
Bonny, *Fr.* 149 RIO
Bonorva, *It.* 153 N3
Bonriki, *Kiribati* 221 GI8
Bonriki, island, *Kiribati* 221 GI8
Bonshaw, *N.S.W., Austral.* 215 WI5
Bontang, *Indonesia* 192 JI2
Bontoc, *Philippines* 193 BI3
Bonvouloir Islands, *P.N.G.* 217 E21
Bony de les Neres, *Andorra* 162 J3
Booby Cay, *Cayman Is.* 122 J2
Booker, *Tex., U.S.* 104 E7
Booker T. Washington National
Monument, *Va., U.S.* 98 FIO
Booligal, *N.S.W., Austral.* 215 XI2
Boomerang Ridge, *Ind. Oc.* 224 NII
Boonderoo, *Qnsld., Austral.* 215 SI3
Boone, *Iowa, U.S.* 107 NII
Boone, *N.C., U.S.* 98 G8
Booneville, *Ark., U.S.* 102 G6
Booneville, *Miss., U.S.* 103 HI3
Boon Point, *Antigua and Barbuda*
123 A2I
Bööntsagaan Nuur, *Mongolia*
182 E8
Boonville, *Ind., U.S.* 101 U8
Boonville, *Mo., U.S.* 107 SI2
Boonville, *N.Y., U.S.* 96 H9
Boorabbin, *W. Aust., Austral.* 215 W4
Boorama, *Somalia* 203 GI6
Booroondara, Mount, *Austral.*
214 JI3
Boosaaso (Bosaso), *Somalia* 203 FI8
Boothbay Harbor, *Me., U.S.* 97 GI6
Boothia, Gulf of, *Nunavut, Can.*
85 FI5
Boothia Peninsula, *Nunavut, Can.*
85 FI5

Bootle Bay Village, *Bahamas* **122** EI
Boué, *Gabon* **205** HI6
Bopeechee, *S. Aust., Austral.* **215** VIO
Boppard, *Ger.* **150** G5
Boquerón, Bahía de, *P.R., U.S.* **122** NI
Bor, *Russ.* **158** HI2
Bor, *Serb.* **154** GI2
Bor, *Turk.* **170** G9
Bora-Bora, island, *Fr. Polynesia, Fr.* **223** KI4
Boracho Peak, *Tex., U.S.* **105** PI
Borah Peak, *Idaho, U.S.* **108** G6
Boran, *Kaz.* **177** EI9
Boran, region, *Eth.* **203** HI5
Borås, *Sw.* **142** LI2
Borāzjān, *Iran* **175** GI3
Borba, *Braz.* **132** E9
Borba, *Port.* **146** J6
Borborema, Planalto da, *Braz.* **133** FI7
Borchgrevink Coast, *Antarctica* **231** QI4
Borçka, *Rep. of Georgia* **171** CI6
Bordeaux, *Fr.* **149** V6
Bordeaux Mountain, *Virgin Is., U.S.* **122** NII
Borden Island, *N.W.T., Can.* **85** BI3
Borden Peninsula, *Nunavut, Can.* **85** EI6
Bordertown, *S. Aust., Austral.* **215** YII
Borðeyri, *Ice.* **142** E2
Bordj Flye Sainte Marie, *Alg.* **200** D9
Bordj le Prieur, *Alg.* **200** FIO
Bordj Messouda, *Alg.* **200** CI2
Bordj Omar Driss, *Alg.* **200** DI2
Boré, *Mali* **200** H8
Boreas Basin, *Arctic Oc.* **247** JI7
Boreray, island, *Scot., U.K.* **144** H5
Boreumdo, island, *S. Korea* **186** M7
Borgarnes, *Ice.* **142** E2
Borger, *Neth.* **148** HI4
Borger, *Tex., U.S.* **104** G6
Borgholm, *Sw.* **143** MI4
Borg Massif, *Antarctica* **230** BI2
Borgne, Lake, *La., U.S.* **102** QII
Borgo Maggiore, *San Marino* **163** JI5
Borgo San Dalmazzo, *It.* **152** F2
Borgosesia, *It.* **152** D3
Borgou, region, *Benin, Nigeria* **204** CI2
Borhoyn Tal, *Mongolia* **182** EI2
Borinquen, Punta, *P.R., U.S.* **122** MI
Borisoglebsk, *Russ.* **158** MII
BorisovoSudskoye, *Russ.* **158** F9
Borjomi, *Rep. of Georgia* **171** CI7
Borkou, region, *Chad* **201** GI4
Borlänge, *Sw.* **143** JI3
Bormio, *It.* **152** C6
Borneo (Kalimantan), island, *Indonesia* **192** JIO
Bornholm, island, *Den.* **143** NI3
Bornova, *Turk.* **170** F3
Boro, river, *S. Sudan* **202** GII
Borohora Shan, *China* **182** E4
Boroko, *Indonesia* **193** JI4
Boromo, *Burkina Faso* **204** B9
Boronga Islands, *Myanmar* **190** H4
Borotou, *Côte d'Ivoire* **204** D7
Borovichi, *Russ.* **158** G8
Borovo, *Croatia* **154** E9
Borovsk, *Russ.* **158** K9
Borovskoy, *Kaz.* **176** BII
Borroloola, *N.T., Austral.* **215** QIO
Borşa, *Rom.* **155** BI4
Børselv, *Nor.* **143** BI4
Borūjerd, *Iran* **174** DII
Boryeong, *S. Korea* **187** Q7
Boryslav, *Ukr.* **159** P2
Boryspil', *Ukr.* **159** N6
Borzya, *Russ.* **161** LI7
Bosa, *It.* **153** N3
Bosanska Gradiška, *Bosn. & Herzg.* **154** E7
Bosanski Petrovac, *Bosn. & Herzg.* **154** F6
Bosanski Šamac (Šamac), *Bosn. & Herzg.* **154** E8
Boscastle, *Eng., U.K.* **145** X9

Boscobel, *Wis., U.S.* **100** L4
Bose, *China* **182** NII
Boseong, *S. Korea* **187** T8
Boshan, *Shand., China* **184** G9
Bosilegrad, *Serb.* **154** JI2
Bosna, river, *Bosn. & Herzg.* **154** G8
Bosnia and Herzegovina, *Eur.* **154** F7
Bosobolo, *Dem. Rep. of the Congo* **202** H9
Bōsō Hantō, *Japan* **189** PI2
Bosporus see İstanbul Boğazi, strait, *Turk.* **170** C5
Bossangoa, *Cen. Af. Rep.* **202** H8
Bossémbélé, *Cen. Af. Rep.* **202** H8
Bossier City, *La., U.S.* **102** L6
Bossut, Cape, *Austral.* **214** D4
Bost see Lashkar Gāh, *Afghan.* **179** Q4
Bostan, *Pak.* **179** R6
Bosten Hu, *China* **182** F5
Boston, *Eng., U.K.* **145** SI4
Boston, *Ga., U.S.* **99** Q6
Boston, *Mass., U.S.* **97** KI5
Boston Bay, *Jam.* **122** JII
Boston Mountains, *Ark., U.S.* **102** F7
Boswell, *Okla., U.S.* **104** JI3
Botabano, *Cayman Is.* **122** HI
Botanic Gardens, site, *Dominica* **123** GI9
Botany Bay, *Austral.* **214** LI5
Botev, peak, *Bulg.* **155** JI4
Botevgrad, *Bulg.* **155** HI3
Bothnia, Gulf of, *Fin., Sw.* **143** GI4
Boticas, *Port.* **146** D6
Botoşani, *Rom.* **155** BI6
Botswana, *Af.* **206** H9
Bottineau, *N. Dak., U.S.* **106** D5
Bottle Creek, *Turks & Caicos Is.* **119** HI7
Botwood, *Nfld. & Lab., Can.* **85** M23
Bouaflé, *Côte d'Ivoire* **204** D8
Bouaké, *Côte d'Ivoire* **204** D8
Bouar, *Cen. Af. Rep.* **202** H7
Boudeuse Ridge, *Pac. Oc.* **243** KI4
Bougainville, island, *P.N.G.* **221** KI4
Bougainville, Cape, *Austral.* **214** B6
Bougainville, Mouillage de, *Fr. Polynesia, Fr.* **223** PI7
Bougainville Strait, *Solomon Is.* **221** KI5
Bougouni, *Mali* **200** J7
Bouillante, *Guadeloupe, Fr.* **123** FI4
Bouillon, *Belg.* **148** NI2
Bouilly, *Fr.* **149** QII
Bouira, *Alg.* **200** AII
Boujdour, Cap, *Af.* **198** D2
Boulaide, *Lux.* **162** H9
Boulari, Passe de, *New Caledonia, Fr.* **222** E8
Boulder, *Colo., U.S.* **108** LI3
Boulder, *Mont., U.S.* **108** D7
Boulder City, *Nev., U.S.* **111** UI2
Boulia, *Qnsld., Austral.* **215** TII
Boulogne, *Fr.* **149** Y8
Boulogne-sur-Mer, *Fr.* **148** L9
Bouloupari, *New Caledonia, Fr.* **222** D8
Bouna, *Côte d'Ivoire* **204** C9
Boundary Peak, *Nev., U.S.* **111** S8
Boundiali, *Côte d'Ivoire* **204** C8
Bountiful, *Utah, U.S.* **108** K7
Bounty Bay, *Pitcairn I., U.K.* **223** Q24
Bounty Islands, *Pac. Oc.* **218** Q9
Bounty Plateau, *Pac. Oc.* **242** QII
Bounty Trough, *Pac. Oc.* **242** QII
Bourail, *New Caledonia, Fr.* **222** D7
Bouraké, *New Caledonia, Fr.* **222** D8
Bourayne, Port, *Fr. Polynesia, Fr.* **223** GI4
Bourbon-Lancy, *Fr.* **149** TII
Bourem, *Mali* **200** G9
Bourganeuf, *Fr.* **149** U9
Bourg-en-Bresse, *Fr.* **149** TI3
Bourges, *Fr.* **149** SIO
Bourget, Lac du, *Fr.* **149** UI4
Bourg-Lastic, *Fr.* **149** UIO
Bourg-Madame, *Fr.* **149** Z9
Bourgneuf, Baie de, *Fr.* **149** S5
Bourg-Saint-Maurice, *Fr.* **149** UI5
Bourke, *N.S.W., Austral.* **215** WI3

Bournemouth, *Eng., U.K.* **145** XI2
Bourscheid, *Lux.* **162** HIO
Bousso, *Chad* **201** JI4
Boutilimit, *Mauritania* **200** G5
Bouvet Fracture Zone, *Atl. Oc.* **241** WI2
Bovalino Marina, *It.* **153** RI3
Boven Bolivia, *Bonaire, Neth.* **123** QI9
Bovey, *Minn., U.S.* **106** FII
Bovill, *Idaho, U.S.* **108** D4
Bovina, *Tex., U.S.* **104** H4
Bowbells, *N. Dak., U.S.* **106** D3
Bowdle, *S. Dak., U.S.* **106** J5
Bowdoin, Lake, *Mont., U.S.* **108** BII
Bowen, *Qnsld., Austral.* **215** SI4
Bowers Basin, *Pac. Oc.* **242** CII
Bowers Ridge, *Pac. Oc.* **242** CII
Bowie, *Ariz., U.S.* **109** V9
Bowie, *Md., U.S.* **98** CI3
Bowie, *Tex., U.S.* **104** KIO
Bowling Green, *Ky., U.S.* **103** DI5
Bowling Green, *Mo., U.S.* **107** SI4
Bowling Green, *Ohio, U.S.* **101** PI2
Bowling Green, *Va., U.S.* **98** EI3
Bowling Green Bay, *Austral.* **214** DI4
Bowman, *N. Dak., U.S.* **106** H2
Bowman Bay, *Nunavut, Can.* **85** GI8
Bowman Glacier, *Antarctica* **230** KI2
Bowman Island, *Antarctica* **231** L2I
Box Butte Reservoir, *Nebr., U.S.* **107** N2
Box Elder Creek, *Mont., U.S.* **108** CIO
Boxelder Creek, *Mont., U.S.* **108** EI3
Boxing, *Shand., China* **184** F9
Boyabat, *Turk.* **170** CIO
Boyang, *Jiangxi, China* **185** Q8
Boyarka, *Russ.* **161** FI4
Boyce, *La., U.S.* **102** M8
Boyer, river, *Iowa, U.S.* **107** P9
Boyle (Mainistir na Búille), *Ire.* **145** R5
Boyne, river, *Ire.* **145** R6
Boyne City, *Mich., U.S.* **100** HIO
Boynton Beach, *Fla., U.S.* **99** WIO
Boyoma Falls, *Dem. Rep. of the Congo* **202** KII
Boysen Reservoir, *Wyo., U.S.* **108** HIO
Bozashchy Tübegi, *Kaz.* **176** G6
Boz Burun, *Turk.* **170** D4
Bozburun, *Turk.* **170** H3
Bozburun Dağı, peak, *Turk.* **170** H6
Bozcaada, island, *Turk.* **170** E2
Bozdoğan, *Turk.* **170** G4
Bozeman, *Mont., U.S.* **108** E8
Bozhou, *Anhui, China* **184** K7
Bozkir, *Turk.* **170** H7
Bozkurt, *Turk.* **170** C9
Bozouls, *Fr.* **149** WIO
Bozova, *Turk.* **171** HI3
Bozüyük, *Turk.* **170** E5
Bra, *It.* **152** F3
Brabant, *Eur.* **140** G5
Brabant Island, *Antarctica* **230** D4
Brač, island, *Croatia* **154** H6
Bracadale, Loch, *Scot., U.K.* **144** J7
Bracciano, *It.* **152** K8
Bracciano, Lago di, *It.* **152** K8
Brackettville, *Tex., U.S.* **105** R7
Brački Kanal, *Croatia* **154** H6
Bracknell, *Eng., U.K.* **145** VI3
Brad, *Rom.* **154** DI2
Bradenton, *Fla., U.S.* **99** U7
Brades, *Montserrat* **123** A24
Bradford, *Eng., U.K.* **145** RI2
Bradford, *Pa., U.S.* **96** L5
Bradley, *Ill., U.S.* **101** P7
Bradley, *S. Dak., U.S.* **106** J7
Brady, *Nebr., U.S.* **107** Q4
Brady, *Tex., U.S.* **105** P8
Braga, *Port.* **146** D5
Bragado, *Arg.* **134** LI2
Bragança, *Port.* **146** D7
Braham, *Minn., U.S.* **106** HII
Brahmanbaria, *Bangladesh* **180** HI3
Brahmapur, *India* **180** LIO
Brahmaputra, river, *Asia* **168** J9
Brahmaur, *India* **179** PI3

Brăila, *Rom.* **155** EI7
Brainerd, *Minn., U.S.* **106** HIO
Braintree, *Eng., U.K.* **145** UI5
Braintree, *Mass., U.S.* **97** KI5
Bramsche, *Ger.* **150** D6
Bramwell, *Qnsld., Austral.* **215** PI2
Brancaleone Marina, *It.* **153** SI3
Branchville, *S.C., U.S.* **98** L9
Branco, island, *Cabo Verde* **209** BI5
Branco, river, *Braz.* **132** C8
Branco, river, *N. Amer.* **82** RI2
Branco, Cape, *S. Amer.* **128** EI2
Brandberg, peak, *Af.* **198** N6
Brandenburg, *Ger.* **150** D9
Brandenburg, region, *Ger.* **150** EIO
Brandfort, *S. Af.* **206** KIO
Brandon, *Fla., U.S.* **99** U8
Brandon, *Man., Can.* **85** NI3
Brandon, *Miss., U.S.* **102** LII
Brandon, *S. Dak., U.S.* **106** L8
Brandon Bay see Bhreandáin, Bá, *Ire.* **145** U2
Brandvlei, *S. Af.* **206** L8
Brandy Peak, *Oreg., U.S.* **110** K2
Branford, *Fla., U.S.* **99** R7
Bransby, *Qnsld., Austral.* **215** VI2
Bransby Point, *Montserrat* **123** B23
Bransfield Strait, *Antarctica* **230** D4
Bransfield Trough, *Atl. Oc.* **241** X5
Branson, *Colo., U.S.* **109** QI4
Branson, *Mo., U.S.* **107** VI2
Brantley, *Ala., U.S.* **103** MI6
Brantley Lake, *N. Mex., U.S.* **109** VI4
Brantôme, *Fr.* **149** U8
Bras d'Or Lake, *N.S., Can.* **85** N22
Brasília, *Braz.* **133** JI3
Brasília Legal, *Braz.* **132** EII
Braşov, *Rom.* **155** EI5
Bras-Panon, *Réunion, Fr.* **209** GI7
Brasstown Bald, peak, *Ga., U.S.* **98** J6
Brategg Bank, *Pac. Oc.* **248** NII
Brateş, Lacul, *Rom.* **155** EI7
Bratislava (Pressburg), *Slovakia* **151** KI3
Bratsk, *Russ.* **161** KI5
Bratskoye Vodokhranilishche, *Russ.* **161** KI5
Bratsk Reservoir, *Asia* **168** E9
Brattleboro, *Vt., U.S.* **97** JI3
Braunau, *Aust.* **150** KIO
Braunschweig (Brunswick), *Ger.* **150** E8
Braunton, *Eng., U.K.* **145** W9
Brava, island, *Cabo Verde* **209** EI5
Brava, Costa, *Sp.* **147** DI9
Brawley, *Calif., U.S.* **111** YII
Bray (Bré), *Ire.* **145** S7
Bray Island, *Nunavut, Can.* **85** FI7
Brazil, *Ind., U.S.* **101** S8
Brazil, *S. Amer.* **132** GI2
Brazil Basin, *Atl. Oc.* **241** Q9
Brazilian Highlands, *S. Amer.* **128** G3
Brazoria, *Tex., U.S.* **105** SI3
Brazos, river, *U.S.* **86** KI2
Brazza Seamounts, *Atl. Oc.* **241** PI3
Brazzaville, *Congo* **205** JI7
Brčko, *Bosn. & Herzg.* **154** F8
Bré see Bray, *Ire.* **145** S7
Brea, Punta, *P.R., U.S.* **122** P2
Breakers, *Cayman Is.* **122** J3
Breakfast Island, *Marshall Is., U.S.* **220** M8
Breaux Bridge, *La., U.S.* **102** P9
Breaza, *Rom.* **155** EI5
Brechin, *Scot., U.K.* **144** LII
Breckenridge, *Colo., U.S.* **108** MI2
Breckenridge, *Minn., U.S.* **106** H8
Breckenridge, *Tex., U.S.* **104** L9
Brecknock, Península, *Chile* **135** X7
Breda, *Neth.* **148** KI2
Bredasdorp, *S. Af.* **206** M8
Breezewood, *Pa., U.S.* **96** P5
Bregalnica, river, *Maced.* **154** KI2
Bregenz, *Aust.* **150** L7
Bréhat, Île de, *Fr.* **149** P4
Breiðafjörður, bay, *Ice.* **142** D2
Breid Bay, *Antarctica* **231** BI5
Breil-sur-Roya, *Fr.* **149** WI6

Breiöamerkurdjúp, valley, *Arctic Oc.* **247** L22
Breisach, *Fr.* **149** QI5
Brejo, *Braz.* **133** EI5
Bremen, *Ga., U.S.* **98** L4
Bremen, *Ger.* **150** C7
Bremen, *Ind., U.S.* **101** P9
Bremerton, *Wash., U.S.* **110** C3
Bremerhaven, *Ger.* **150** C7
Bremond, *Tex., U.S.* **105** NI2
Brenham, *Tex., U.S.* **105** QI2
Brennero, *It.* **152** B7
Brenner Pass, *Aust.* **150** M8
Brenner Seamounts, *Ind. Oc.* **224** MI2
Breno, *It.* **152** D6
Brentwood, *Eng., U.K.* **145** VI4
Brentwood, *N.Y., U.S.* **96** NI2
Brescia, *It.* **152** D6
Bressanone, *It.* **152** B7
Bressay, island, *Scot., U.K.* **144** DI2
Bressuire, *Fr.* **149** S7
Brest, *Belarus* **158** L2
Brest, *Fr.* **149** P2
Breteuil, *Fr.* **149** NIO
Bretón, Cayo, *Cuba* **118** J9
Breton, Pertuis, *Fr.* **149** T5
Breton Island, Cape, *N. Amer.* **82** HIO
Breton Islands, *La., U.S.* **102** RI2
Breton Sound, *La., U.S.* **102** QI2
Brett, Cape, *N.Z.* **217** HI8
Breu, river, *S. Amer.* **132** G5
Brevard, *N.C., U.S.* **98** J7
Breves, *Braz.* **132** DI2
Brevoort Island, *Nunavut, Can.* **85** GI9
Brewarrina, *N.S.W., Austral.* **215** WI3
Brewer, *Me., U.S.* **97** FI7
Brewers Bay, *British Virgin Is., U.K.* **122** Q6
Brewster, *Kans., U.S.* **107** S3
Brewster, *Nebr., U.S.* **107** N5
Brewster, *Wash., U.S.* **110** B6
Brewton, *Ala., U.S.* **103** NI5
Bria, *Cen. Af. Rep.* **202** HIO
Briare, *Fr.* **149** RIO
Briatico, *It.* **153** QI3
Bridgend (Pen-y-bont ar Ogwr), *Wales, U.K.* **145** VIO
Bridge Point, *Bahamas* **122** D5
Bridgeport, *Ala., U.S.* **103** GI6
Bridgeport, *Calif., U.S.* **111** R7
Bridgeport, *Conn., U.S.* **96** MI2
Bridgeport, *Ill., U.S.* **101** T7
Bridgeport, *Nebr., U.S.* **107** P2
Bridgeport, *Tex., U.S.* **104** KIO
Bridgeport, *W. Va., U.S.* **98** C9
Bridgeport, Lake, *Tex., U.S.* **104** KIO
Bridger Peak, *Wyo., U.S.* **108** KII
Bridgeton, *N.J., U.S.* **96** Q9
Bridgetown, *Barbados* **123** LI9
Bridgetown, *Ohio, U.S.* **101** SII
Bridgewater, *N.S., Can.* **85** P22
Bridgman, Cape, *Greenland, Den.* **82** A8
Bridgton, *Me., U.S.* **97** GI5
Bridgwater, *Eng., U.K.* **145** WII
Bridlington, *Eng., U.K.* **145** QI3
Brielle, *Neth.* **148** JII
Brienne-le-Château, *Fr.* **149** QI2
Brienza, *It.* **153** NI2
Brienzer See, *Switz.* **152** B3
Brig, *Switz.* **152** C3
Brigantine Cays, *Bahamas* **122** E7
Brigham City, *Utah, U.S.* **108** K7
Brighton, *Eng., U.K.* **145** WI4
Brihuega, *Sp.* **146** FI2
Brijuni Otoci, island, *Croatia* **154** E4
Brindisi, *It.* **152** MI5
Brinkley, *Ark., U.S.* **102** GIO
Brisbane, *Qnsld., Austral.* **215** VI6
Bristol, *Conn., U.S.* **96** LI2
Bristol, *Eng., U.K.* **145** VII
Bristol, *Pa., U.S.* **96** P9
Bristol, *S. Dak., U.S.* **106** J7
Bristol, *Tenn., U.S.* **103** D2O
Bristol, *Va., U.S.* **98** G7
Bristol Bay, *Alas., U.S.* **113** LI3
Bristol Bay, *Pac. Oc.* **246** M2

Bristol Channel, *Eng., Wales, U.K.* 145 V9
Bristol Lake, *Calif., U.S.* III WII
Bristol Mountains, *Calif., U.S.* III WII
Bristow, *Okla., U.S.* 104 FI2
Britannia Tablemounts, *Pac. Oc.* 249 D22
British Columbia, *Can.* 84 J8
British Isles, *Eur.* 140 E4
Britstown, *S. Af.* 206 L9
Britt, *Iowa, U.S.* 106 MII
Brittany, region, *Fr.* 149 Q5
Britton, *S. Dak., U.S.* 106 H7
Britton Hill, peak, *Fla., U.S.* 99 Q3
Brive, *Fr.* 149 V9
Briviesca, *Sp.* 146 CII
Brno, *Czech Rep.* 151 JI3
Broa, Ensenada de la, *Cuba* 118 G7
Broad, river, *S.C., U.S.* 98 J8
Broad Haven, *Ire.* 145 Q3
Broad Sound, *Austral.* 214 FI5
Broadstairs, *Eng., U.K.* 145 VI6
Broadus, *Mont., U.S.* 108 EI2
Broadview, *Sask., Can.* 84 NI2
Broadwater, *Nebr., U.S.* 107 P2
Brochet, *Man., Can.* 85 KI3
Brocken, peak, *Ger.* 150 E8
Brock Island, *N.W.T., Can.* 85 BI3
Brockport, *N.Y., U.S.* 96 J6
Brockton, *Mass., U.S.* 97 LI5
Brockway, *Mont., U.S.* 108 CI2
Brockway, *Pa., U.S.* 96 M5
Brodeur Peninsula, *Nunavut, Can.* 85 EI5
Brodnica, *Pol.* 151 CI5
Brody, *Ukr.* 159 N3
Brogan, *Oreg., U.S.* 110 H9
Broken Arrow, *Okla., U.S.* 104 FI3
Broken Bay, *Austral.* 214 KI5
Broken Bow, *Nebr., U.S.* 107 P5
Broken Bow, *Okla., U.S.* 104 JI4
Broken Bow Lake, *Okla., U.S.* 104 JI4
Broken Hill, *N.S.W., Austral.* 215 WII
Broken Ridge, *Ind. Oc.* 225 MI4
Brokopondo, *Suriname* 131 EI6
Bromley Plateau, *Atl. Oc.* 241 S8
Brønnøysund, *Nor.* 142 FII
Bronson, *Fla., U.S.* 99 S7
Bronswinkel, *Bonaire, Neth.* 123 QI8
Bronte, *Tex., U.S.* 104 M7
Brookfield, *Mo., U.S.* 107 RI2
Brookfield, *Wis., U.S.* 100 L7
Brookhaven, *Miss., U.S.* 102 MIO
Brookings, *Oreg., U.S.* 110 LI
Brookings, *S. Dak., U.S.* 106 K8
Brooklyn, *Iowa, U.S.* 107 PI2
Brooklyn Center, *Minn., U.S.* 106 JII
Brookport, *Ill., U.S.* 101 V6
Brooks, *Alta., Can.* 84 MIO
Brooks Banks, *Hawai'i, U.S.* 114 M6
Brooks Range, *Alas., U.S.* 113 DI5
Brooksville, *Fla., U.S.* 99 T7
Brookville, *Ind., U.S.* 101 SIO
Brookville, *Pa., U.S.* 96 M4
Broome, *W. Aust., Austral.* 215 R4
Brora, *Scot., U.K.* 144 H9
Brosse, Île, *New Caledonia, Fr.* 222 E9
Brothers, *Oreg., U.S.* 110 H5
Broughton Islands, *Austral.* 214 KI5
Brouwer Trough, *Ind. Oc.* 225 LI5
Brovary, *Ukr.* 159 N6
Browerville, *Minn., U.S.* 106 HIO
Brown Bay, *Virgin Is., U.S.* 122 MII
Brownfield, *Tex., U.S.* 104 K4
Browning, *Mont., U.S.* 108 B6
Brownlee Dam, *Idaho, Oreg., U.S.* 110 G9
Browns Canyon National Monument, *Colo., U.S.* 109 NI2
Browns Town, *Jam.* 118 MII
Brownstown, *Ind., U.S.* 101 T9
Browns Valley, *Minn., U.S.* 106 J8
Brownsville, *Tenn., U.S.* 102 FI2
Brownsville, *Tex., U.S.* 105 XII
Brownsweg, *Suriname* 131 EI6
Brownwood, *Tex., U.S.* 105 N9
Brownwood, Lake, *Tex., U.S.* 104 M9

Browse Island, *Austral.* 214 B5
Brozas, *Sp.* 146 G7
Bruce, *Miss., U.S.* 102 JI2
Bruce, Mount, *Austral.* 214 F3
Bruce Ridge, *Atl. Oc.* 241 X8
Bruce Rock, *W. Aust., Austral.* 215 X3
Bruce Spur, *Ind. Oc.* 249 DI3
Bruchsal, *Ger.* 150 J6
Bruciate, river, *San Marino* 163 KI6
Bruciato, *It.* 163 HI4
Bruck an der Mur, *Aust.* 150 LI2
Brugg, *Switz.* 152 A3
Brugge, *Belg.* 148 KII
Bruini, *India* 180 EI5
Brule, river, *Wis., U.S.* 100 G6
Brumado, *Braz.* 133 JI5
Brundidge, *Ala., U.S.* 103 MI6
Bruneau, *Idaho, U.S.* 108 H4
Bruneau, river, *Idaho, Nev., U.S.* 108 H4
Brunei, *Asia* 192 GII
Brunei Bay, *Malaysia* 192 GII
Brunette Downs, *N.T., Austral.* 215 RIO
Brunico, *It.* 152 B8
Brunner, Lake, *N.Z.* 217 NI7
Brunssum, *Neth.* 148 LI3
Brunswick, *Ga., U.S.* 99 P8
Brunswick, *Me., U.S.* 97 GI6
Brunswick, *Mo., U.S.* 107 SI2
Brunswick, *Ohio, U.S.* 101 PI4
Brunswick *see* Braunschweig, *Ger.* 150 E8
Brush, *Colo., U.S.* 108 LI4
Brus Laguna, *Hond.* 117 KI8
Brusque, *Braz.* 133 NI3
Brüssel (Brussel) *see* Bruxelles, *Belg.* 148 LI2
Brussels *see* Bruxelles, *Belg.* 148 LI2
Bruxelles (Brüssel, Brussels), *Belg.* 148 LI2
Bruzual, *Venez.* 130 D8
Bryan, *Ohio, U.S.* 101 PII
Bryan, *Tex., U.S.* 105 PI2
Bryan Coast, *Antarctica* 230 H6
Bryansk, *Russ.* 158 L8
Bryant, *Ark., U.S.* 102 H8
Bryant, *S. Dak., U.S.* 106 K7
Bryce Canyon National Park, *Utah, U.S.* 109 P7
Bryson City, *N.C., U.S.* 98 J6
Bryukhovetskaya, *Russ.* 159 SIO
Brzeg, *Pol.* 151 FI3
Brzeg Dolny, *Pol.* 151 FI3
Bua, *Fiji* 222 G6
Bua Bay, *Fiji* 222 H6
Buache, Mount, *F.S.M.* 221 AI9
Buada Lagoon, *Nauru* 221 F23
Buada, region, *Nauru* 221 F23
Buala, *Solomon Is.* 221 MI8
Buan, *S. Korea* 187 R8
Buariki, *Kiribati* 221 FI7
Buariki, island, *Kiribati* 221 FI7
Bua Yai, *Thai.* 190 LIO
Bu'ayrāt al Ḥasūn, *Lib.* 201 CI4
Buba, *Guinea-Bissau* 204 B4
Būbiyān, island, *Kuwait* 174 GII
Bucak, *Turk.* 170 H6
Bucakkışla, *Turk.* 170 H8
Bucaramanga, *Col.* 130 D6
Buccament Bay, *St. Vincent and the Grenadines* 123 LI6
Buccaneer Archipelago, *Austral.* 214 C5
Buccaneer Point, *Bahamas* 122 B8
Buccoo Bay, *Trinidad and Tobago* 123 NI7
Buchanan, *Liberia* 204 E6
Buchanan, *Mich., U.S.* 101 N9
Buchanan, Lake, *Tex., U.S.* 105 P9
Buchan Gulf, *Nunavut, Can.* 85 EI7
Bucharest *see* Bucureşti, *Rom.* 155 FI5
Bucheon, *S. Korea* 186 N8
Buchholz, *Ger.* 150 C8
Buchon, Point, *Calif., U.S.* III V5
Buchs, *Switz.* 162 N3
Buckalow, *N.S.W., Austral.* 215 XII
Buckhannon, *W. Va., U.S.* 98 D9
Buckingham Bay, *Austral.* 214 A9
Buck Island, *Virgin Is., U.S.* 122 N9

Buck Island, *Virgin Is., U.S.* 122 Q3
Buck Island Reef National Monument, *Virgin Is., U.S.* 122 Q3
Buckland Tableland, *Austral.* 214 GI3
Buckley, *Wash., U.S.* 110 C4
Bucklin, *Kans., U.S.* 107 U5
Buckner Bay *see* Nakagusuku Wan, *Japan* 189 X2
Bucksport, *Me., U.S.* 97 FI7
Bucovina, region, *Rom.* 155 AI4
Buco Zau, *Angola* 206 A5
Bu Craa, *W. Sahara* 200 D6
Bucureşti (Bucharest), *Rom.* 155 FI5
Bucyrus, *Ohio, U.S.* 101 QI3
Bud, *Nor.* 142 HIO
Buda, *Tex., U.S.* 105 QIO
Budac, peak, *Rom.* 155 CI5
Budalin, *Myanmar* 190 G5
Budapest, *Hung.* 151 LI5
Būðardalur, *Ice.* 142 E2
Budaun, *India* 180 F7
Budd Coast, *Antarctica* 231 M2O
Buddhas of Bamian, ruins, *Afghan.* 178 M7
Budduso, *It.* 152 M4
Bude, *Eng., U.K.* 145 W9
Bude, *Miss., U.S.* 102 MIO
Bude Bay, *Eng., U.K.* 145 W9
Budennovsk, *Russ.* 159 SI3
Būðir, *Ice.* 142 F4
Budjala, *Dem. Rep. of the Congo* 202 J9
Budongquan, *China* 182 J7
Budū', Sabkhat al, *Saudi Arabia* 174 KI2
Buena Esperanza, *Arg.* 134 L9
Buenaventura, *Col.* 130 F4
Buenaventura, *Mex.* 116 C8
Buenaventura Bay, *S. Amer.* 128 C2
Buena Vista, *Colo., U.S.* 109 NI2
Buena Vista, *Curaçao, Neth.* 123 QI4
Buena Vista, *Ga., U.S.* 99 N5
Buena Vista, *Va., U.S.* 98 EII
Buena Vista Lake Bed, *Calif., U.S.* III V7
Buendía, Embalse de, *Sp.* 146 FI2
Buenos Aires, *Arg.* 134 LI3
Buenos Aires, Lago, *Arg.* 135 T7
Buenos Ayres, *Trinidad and Tobago* 123 Q22
Buen Tiempo, Cabo, *Arg.* 135 W8
Bufareh, *Indonesia* 193 K2O
Buffalo, *Minn., U.S.* 106 JII
Buffalo, *Mo., U.S.* 107 UI2
Buffalo, *N.Y., U.S.* 96 J5
Buffalo, *Okla., U.S.* 104 E8
Buffalo, *S. Dak., U.S.* 106 J2
Buffalo, *Tex., U.S.* 105 NI3
Buffalo, *Wyo., U.S.* 108 FII
Buffalo, river, *Ark., U.S.* 102 E8
Buffalo Bill Reservoir, *Wyo., U.S.* 108 F9
Buffalo Hump, peak, *Idaho, U.S.* 108 E4
Buffalo Lake, *Tex., U.S.* 104 H5
Buffalo National River, *Ark., U.S.* 102 E8
Buff Bay, *Jam.* 122 HIO
Buford, *Ga., U.S.* 98 K5
Buftea, *Rom.* 155 FI5
Bug, river, *Eur.* 140 G9
Buga, *Col.* 130 F4
Buġibba, *Malta* 163 J22
Bugio, Ilhéu do, *Madeira, Port.* 208 N4
Bugsuk, island, *Philippines* 192 FI2
Bugt, *N. Mongol, China* 184 AII
Bugugou, *Hebei, China* 184 B8
Bugul'ma, *Russ.* 158 JI6
Buguruslan, *Russ.* 158 KI6
Buhl, *Idaho, U.S.* 108 H5
Buhl, *Minn., U.S.* 106 FI2
Buhuşi, *Rom.* 155 CI6
Builth Wells, *Wales, U.K.* 145 UIO
Buin, *Solomon Is.* 221 LI4
Buinsk, *Russ.* 158 JI4
Buir Nur, lake, *Asia* 168 FII
Buis-les-Baronnies, *Fr.* 149 WI3

Bujalance, *Sp.* 146 KIO
Bujanovac, *Serb.* 154 JII
Bujaraloz, *Sp.* 147 EI5
Bujumbura, *Burundi* 202 LI2
Buka, island, *P.N.G.* 221 JI3
Bukachacha, *Russ.* 161 LI7
Bukama, *Dem. Rep. of the Congo* 202 NII
Bukanik, Maja, *Alban.* 154 LIO
Buka Passage, *P.N.G.* 221 JI3
Bukavu, *Dem. Rep. of the Congo* 202 LI2
Bukchon, *S. Korea* 187 Q8
Bukhara *see* Buxoro, *Uzb.* 176 LII
Bukittinggi, *Indonesia* 192 J5
Bukoba, *Tanzania* 203 KI3
Bula, *Indonesia* 193 KI7
Bülach, *Switz.* 152 A4
Būlaevo, *Kaz.* 177 AI3
Bulahdelah, *N.S.W., Austral.* 215 XI5
Bulan, *Philippines* 193 DI4
Bulancak, *Turk.* 171 DI3
Bulandshahr, *India* 180 F6
Bulanık, *Turk.* 171 FI6
Buldan, *Turk.* 170 G4
Buldir Island, *Alas., U.S.* 112 M2
Bulgan, *Mongolia* 182 CIO
Bulgan, *Mongolia* 182 C9
Bulgan, *Mongolia* 182 E8
Bulgaria, *Eur.* 155 JI3
Buli, Teluk, *Indonesia* 193 JI6
Buliluyan, Cape, *Philippines* 192 FI2
Bulimba, *Qnsld., Austral.* 215 QI2
Buliya, island, *Fiji* 222 K6
Bull Bay, *Jam.* 122 JIO
Bulle, *Switz.* 152 B2
Bullenbaai, *Curaçao, Neth.* 123 PI4
Bullhead City, *Ariz., U.S.* 109 S4
Bull Mountains, *Mont., U.S.* 108 DIO
Bulloo Downs, *Qnsld., Austral.* 215 VI2
Bullo River, *N.T., Austral.* 215 Q7
Bulls Bay, *S.C., U.S.* 98 MII
Bull Shoals Lake, *Ark., Mo., U.S.* 102 E7
Bulpunga, *N.S.W., Austral.* 215 XII
Bulun, *Russ.* 161 EI6
Bulung'ur, *Uzb.* 176 LI2
Bumba, *Dem. Rep. of the Congo* 202 JIO
Bumbat, *Mongolia* 182 DIO
Bum La, pass, *India* 180 FI3
Buna, *Kenya* 203 JI5
Bunbury, *W. Aust., Austral.* 215 X2
Bunclody (Bun Clóidí), *Ire.* 145 T6
Bun Clóidí *see* Bunclody, *Ire.* 145 T6
Bundarra, *N.S.W., Austral.* 215 WI5
Bundi, *India* 180 G5
Bungalaut, Selat, *Indonesia* 192 K5
Bungenstock Plateau, *Atl. Oc.* 241 YII
Bungku, *Indonesia* 193 KI4
Bungo Strait, *Pac. Oc.* 168 GI3
Bungo Suidō, *Japan* 189 R6
Bunguran Selatan *see* Kepulauan Natuna Selatan, *Indonesia* 192 H9
Bunguran Utara *see* Natuna Besar, Kepulauan, *Indonesia* 192 G8
Bunhyang, *S. Korea* 187 S8
Bunia, *Dem. Rep. of the Congo* 202 JI2
Bunji, *Pak.* 178 LI2
Bunker, *Mo., U.S.* 107 UI4
Bunkie, *La., U.S.* 102 N8
Bunnell, *Fla., U.S.* 99 S9
Buntok, *Indonesia* 192 KII
Bünyan, *Turk.* 170 FII
Bunyu, island, *Indonesia* 192 HI2
Buol, *Indonesia* 193 HI4
Buôn Đôn, *Vietnam* 191 NI3
Buôn Ma Thuột, *Vietnam* 191 NI3
Buor-Khaya Bay, *Arctic Oc.* 246 D8
Buqūm, Ḥarrat al, *Saudi Arabia* 174 L8
Bur, *Russ.* 161 JI5
Bura, *Kenya* 203 KI5
Burakin, *W. Aust., Austral.* 215 W3
Burang (Pulan), *China* 182 K2
Buras, *La., U.S.* 102 RI2

Buraydah, *Saudi Arabia* 174 H9
Burbank, *Calif., U.S.* III X8
Burco (Burao), *Somalia* 203 GI7
Burdalyk, *Turkm.* 176 MII
Burdekin, river, *Austral.* 214 EI3
Burdur, *Turk.* 170 G5
Burdur Gölü, *Turk.* 170 G5
Burdwood Bank, *Atl. Oc.* 241 W5
Bûr Fu'ad, *Egypt* 173 NI
Burg, *Ger.* 150 E9
Burgas, *Bulg.* 155 JI7
Burgas Bay, *Eur.* 140 KIO
Burgaski Zaliv, *Bulg.* 155 JI7
Burgaso Ezero, *Bulg.* 155 JI7
Burgaw, *N.C., U.S.* 98 JI2
Burgdorf, *Switz.* 152 B3
Burgerau, *Switz.* 162 P2
Burgess Hill, *Eng., U.K.* 145 WI4
Burghūth, Sabkhat al, *Syr.* 172 GI4
Burgos, *Sp.* 146 CII
Burgsvik, *Sw.* 143 LI4
Burgundy, region, *Fr.* 149 SI2
Burhaniye, *Turk.* 170 E3
Burhanpur, *India* 180 K5
Burhou, island, *Channel Is., U.K.* 145 YII
Burias, island, *Philippines* 193 DI4
Burica, Punta, *Pan.* 117 PI9
Burica Point, *N. Amer.* 82 Q8
Buriram, *Thai.* 190 LIO
Burkburnett, *Tex., U.S.* 104 J9
Burke, *S. Dak., U.S.* 106 M6
Burke Island, *Antarctica* 230 K6
Burkesville, *Ky., U.S.* 103 DI7
Burketown, *Qnsld., Austral.* 215 RII
Bur Khaybyt, *Russ.* 161 EI8
Burkina Faso, *Af.* 204 BIO
Burle, island, *Marshall Is., U.S.* 220 L4
Burleson, *Tex., U.S.* 104 LII
Burley, *Idaho, U.S.* 108 H5
Burlingame, *Kans., U.S.* 107 T9
Burlington, *Colo., U.S.* 108 MI6
Burlington, *Iowa, U.S.* 107 QI4
Burlington, *Kans., U.S.* 107 T9
Burlington, *N.C., U.S.* 98 GII
Burlington, *Vt., U.S.* 96 FI2
Burlington, *Wash., U.S.* 110 A4
Burlington, *Wis., U.S.* 100 M6
Burma *see* Myanmar, *Asia* 190 H5
Burnet, *Tex., U.S.* 105 PIO
Burnett Bay, *N.W.T., Can.* 84 CII
Burney, *Calif., U.S.* 110 M4
Burnham Market, *Eng., U.K.* 145 SI5
Burnham-on-Sea, *Eng., U.K.* 145 WII
Burnie, *Tas., Austral.* 215 Y7
Burns, *Oreg., U.S.* 110 J7
Burns, *Wyo., U.S.* 108 KI4
Burnside, Lake, *Austral.* 214 G5
Burns Lake, *B.C., Can.* 84 K8
Burnsville, *Minn., U.S.* 106 KII
Burnt, river, *Oreg., U.S.* 110 G8
Burnt Pine, *Norfolk I., Austral.* 221 F2O
Burqin, *China* 182 C5
Burra, *S. Aust., Austral.* 215 XIO
Burragorang, Lake, *Austral.* 214 KI4
Burray, island, *Scot., U.K.* 144 GIO
Burren, region, *Ire.* 145 S4
Burrendong Reservoir, *Austral.* 214 KI4
Burriana, *Sp.* 147 GI5
Burrton, *Kans., U.S.* 107 U7
Burrwood, *La., U.S.* 102 RI2
Bursa, *Turk.* 170 D5
Bûr Safâga, *Egypt* 201 DI9
Bûr Sa'îd (Port Said), *Egypt* 173 NI
Burt Lake, *Mich., U.S.* 100 HII
Burton, *Mich., U.S.* 100 LI2
Burton, *Nebr., U.S.* 106 M5
Buru, island, *Indonesia* 193 KI6
Burūm, *Yemen* 174 QII
Burundi, *Af.* 202 LI2
Burun Shibertuy, Gora, *Russ.* 161 MI6
Bururi, *Burundi* 202 LI2
Burwash Landing, *Yukon, Can.* 84 F7
Burwell, *Nebr., U.S.* 107 P6
Burylbaytal, *Kaz.* 177 GI5

Bury Saint Edmunds, Eng., U.K. 145 U15
Burzil Pass, Pak. 178 M12
Busan (Pusan), S. Korea 187 T12
Busanga Swamp, Zambia 206 E10
Buşayrah, Syr. 172 F13
Bushiribana, Aruba, Neth. 123 Q17
Bushnell, Ill., U.S. 101 Q4
Bushnell, Nebr., U.S. 107 P1
Businga, Dem. Rep. of the Congo 202 J9
Bušk Blato, lake, Bosn. & Herzg. 154 G7
Buşrá ash Shām, Syr. 172 L7
Busselton, W. Aust., Austral. 215 X2
Bussière-Poitevine, Fr. 149 T8
Bussol', Proliv, Russ. 161 J23
Bussoleno, It. 152 E2
Bustamante, Bahía, Arg. 135 S9
Busto Arsizio, It. 152 D4
Busuanga, island, Philippines 193 D13
Busu-Djanoa, Dem. Rep. of the Congo 202 J9
Buta, Dem. Rep. of the Congo 202 J10
Butare, Rwanda 202 L12
Butaritari, island, Kiribati 218 F8
Bute, Island of, Scot., U.K. 144 M8
Butembo, Dem. Rep. of the Congo 202 K12
Buthidaung, Myanmar 190 H4
Butler, Ala., U.S. 103 L13
Butler, Ga., U.S. 98 M5
Butler, Mo., U.S. 107 T11
Butler, Pa., U.S. 96 N3
Butler Bay, Virgin Is., U.S. 122 Q1
Butner, N.C., U.S. 98 G11
Buton, island, Indonesia 193 L14
Butrint, Alban. 154 N9
Butte, Mont., U.S. 108 E7
Butte, Nebr., U.S. 106 M6
Butterworth, Malaysia 191 T9
Butterworth, S. Af. 206 L10
Button Bay, Man., Can. 85 K14
Button Islands, Nfld. & Lab., Can. 85 H20
Butuan, Philippines 193 E15
Buturlinovka, Russ. 159 N11
Butwal, Nepal 180 F9
Buulobarde, Somalia 203 J17
Buur Gaabo, Somalia 203 K16
Buurgplaatz, peak, Fr., Lux. 162 G9
Buurhakaba, Somalia 203 J16
Buxoro (Bukhara), Uzb. 176 L11
Buxtehude, Ger. 150 C7
Buxton, Guyana 131 D15
Buxton, N.C., U.S. 98 H15
Buy, Russ. 158 G11
Buyant, Mongolia 182 D12
Buyeo, S. Korea 187 Q8
Buynaksk, Russ. 159 U15
Buynī Qarah, Afghan. 178 K6
Buyr Nuur, Mongolia 183 D13
Büyük Menderes, river, Turk. 170 G4
Buyun Shan, Liaoning, China 184 C12
Buzău, Rom. 155 E16
Buzău, river, Rom. 155 E16
Buzău, Pasul, Rom. 155 E15
Buzaymah, Lib. 201 E16
Búzi, river, Mozambique 206 G12
Büzmeýin, Uzb. 176 M8
Buzul Dağı, peak, Turk. 171 H18
Buzuluk, Kaz. 176 C12
Buzuluk, Russ. 158 L16
Buzzards Bay, Mass., U.S. 97 M15
Bwokworlap, island, Marshall Is., U.S. 220 G11
Byahoml', Belarus 158 K5
Byala, Bulg. 155 H17
Byala Slatina, Bulg. 155 H13
Byam Martin, Cape, Nunavut, Can. 85 D17
Byam Martin Island, Nunavut, Can. 85 D14
Byarezina, river, Belarus 158 K5
Byaroza, Belarus 158 L3
Byblos see Jbail, Leb. 172 H6
Bydgoszcz, Pol. 151 C14
Byers, Colo., U.S. 108 M14
Bykhaw, Belarus 158 L6
Bykovo, Russ. 159 P13
Bylas, Ariz., U.S. 109 U8
Bylot Island, Nunavut, Can. 85 E16
Bynum Reservoir, Mont., U.S. 108 B7
Byramgore Reef, Ind. Oc. 224 E10
Byrdbreen, glacier, Antarctica 231 C15
Byrd Canyon, Pac. Oc. 249 J15
Byrd Glacier, Antarctica 231 M14
Byrock, N.S.W., Austral. 215 W13
Byron, Cape, Austral. 214 H16
Byron, Isla, Chile 135 U6
Bytom, Pol. 151 G14
Bytów, Pol. 151 B13

C

Caála, Angola 206 D6
Caazapá, Parag. 132 N10
Cabaiguán, Cuba 118 H9
Caballones, Cayo, Cuba 118 J9
Caballo Reservoir, N. Mex., U.S. 109 U11
Cabanatuan, Philippines 193 C13
Cabaneta, Pic de la, Andorra, Fr. 162 H5
Cabeza del Buey, Sp. 146 J9
Cabezas, Bol. 132 K8
Cabimas, Venez. 130 B7
Cabinda, Angola 206 A5
Cabinda, Angola 206 B5
Cabinet Mountains, Idaho, Mont., U.S. 108 B4
Cable, Wis., U.S. 100 F3
Cabo, Braz. 133 G18
Cabo Blanco, Arg. 135 T9
Cabo Carvoeiro, Port. 146 G4
Cabo Frio, Braz. 133 M15
Cabonga, Réservoir, Que., Can. 85 P19
Cabool, Mo., U.S. 107 V13
Caboolture, Qnsld., Austral. 215 V16
Caborca, Mex. 116 C7
Cabo San Lucas, Mex. 116 F7
Cabot, Ark., U.S. 102 G9
Cabot Strait, N. Amer. 82 H10
Cabral, Dom. Rep. 119 M18
Cabras, Ilhéu das, Sao Tome and Principe 209 C20
Cabras Island, Guam, U.S. 220 C10
Cabrera, Dom. Rep. 119 L19
Cabrera, island, Sp. 147 H18
Cabrera Baja, Sierra de la, Sp. 146 C7
Cabril, Barragem do, Port. 146 G6
Cabrit, Îlet à, Guadeloupe, Fr. 123 G14
Cabrits, Îlet, Martinique, Fr. 123 G23
Cabrobó, Braz. 133 G16
Cabrón, Cabo, Dom. Rep. 119 L20
Čačak, Serb. 154 G10
Caccia, Capo, It. 152 M3
Cáceres, Braz. 132 J10
Cáceres, Sp. 146 H8
Cache, river, Ark., U.S. 102 E10
Cache, Peñas del, Sp. 208 P7
Ca' Chiavello, river, San Marino 163 K16
Cachimbo, Braz. 132 G11
Cachoeira, Braz. 133 H16
Cachoeira do Sul, Braz. 132 P11
Cachoeiro do Itapemirim, Braz. 133 L15
Cacine, Guinea-Bissau 204 B4
Cacolo, Angola 206 C7
Cactus, Tex., U.S. 104 F5
Caçu, Braz. 132 K12
Caculé, Braz. 133 J15
Cacuri, Venez. 130 F10
Čadca, Slovakia 151 H14
Caddo, Okla., U.S. 104 J12
Caddo Lake, La., Tex., U.S. 104 L15
Cadena, Punta, P.R., U.S. 122 N1
Cadí, Serra del, Sp. 147 C17
Cadillac, Fr. 149 W7
Cadillac, Mich., U.S. 100 J10
Çadır Dağı, peak, Turk. 171 G17
Cadiz, Calif., U.S. 111 W11
Cadiz, Ky., U.S. 103 D14
Cadiz, Ohio, U.S. 101 Q15
Cadiz, Philippines 193 E14
Cádiz, Sp. 146 M7
Cádiz, Badia de, Sp. 146 M7
Cádiz, Golfo de, Port., Sp. 146 L7
Cadiz Lake, Calif., U.S. 111 X11
Caen, Fr. 149 N7
Caerdydd see Cardiff, Wales, U.K. 145 V10
Caergybi see Holyhead, Wales, U.K. 145 S9
Caernarfon Bay, Wales, U.K. 145 S9
Caerphilly, Wales, U.K. 145 V10
Caesarea, ruins, Israel 172 L5
Cafayate, Arg. 134 F9
Cagayan de Oro, Philippines 193 F15
Cagayan Islands, Philippines 193 E13
Cagayan Sulu Island, Malaysia 192 F12
Cagli, It. 152 H8
Cagliari, It. 153 Q4
Cagliari, Golfo di, It. 153 Q4
Cagnes, Fr. 149 X15
Caguán, river, Col. 130 H5
Caguas, P.R., U.S. 122 N4
Caha Mountains, Ire. 145 V3
Cahir, Ire. 145 T5
Cahora Bassa, Lago de, Mozambique 206 E12
Cahore Point, Ire. 145 T7
Cahors, Fr. 149 W9
Cahul, Mold. 159 S4
Caia, Mozambique 207 F13
Caiapônia, Braz. 132 J12
Caibarién, Cuba 118 H9
Caicara, Venez. 130 D10
Caicó, Braz. 133 F17
Caicos Islands, Turks & Caicos Is. 119 J17
Caicos Passage, N. Amer. 119 H16
Caille Island, Grenada 123 H24
Cailungo, San Marino 163 J15
Cainsville, Mo., U.S. 107 Q11
Caird Coast, Antarctica 230 D10
Cairngorm Mountains, Scot., U.K. 144 K9
Cairns, Qnsld., Austral. 215 R13
Cairo, Ga., U.S. 99 Q5
Cairo, Ill., U.S. 101 V5
Cairo see El Qâhira, Egypt 201 C18
Caiseal see Cashel, Ire. 145 T5
Caisleán an Bharraigh see Castlebar, Ire. 145 R3
Caisleán Ghriaire see Castlegregory, Ire. 145 U2
Caixão Grande, Sao Tome and Principe 209 D20
Cajamarca, Peru 132 F2
Cajàzeiras, Braz. 133 F17
Çakırgöl Dağı, peak, Turk. 171 D14
Cakit, river, Turk. 170 H10
Çakmak, Turk. 170 F7
Çakmak Dağı, peak, Turk. 171 E16
Čakovec, Croatia 154 C6
Çal, Turk. 170 G5
Calabar, Nigeria 205 E14
Calabash Boom, Virgin Is., U.S. 122 N11
Calabó, Eq. Guinea 208 M7
Calabozo, Venez. 130 C9
Calabria, Eur. 140 L8
Calaburras, Punta de, Sp. 146 M9
Calacuccia, Fr. 152 K4
Calafat, Rom. 154 G12
Calafort Ros Láir see Rosslare Harbour, Ire. 145 U7
Calahorra, Sp. 147 C13
Calais, Fr. 148 L9
Calais, Me., U.S. 97 E19
Calais, Pas de see Dover, Strait of, Fr., U.K. 148 L9
Calalaste, Sierra de, Arg. 134 F8
Calalin, island, Marshall Is., U.S. 220 G11
Calalin Channel, Marshall Is., U.S. 220 G11
Calalzo, It. 152 C8
Calama, Braz. 132 F8
Calama, Chile 134 D7
Calamar, Col. 130 C5
Calamar, Col. 130 G6
Calamian Group, Philippines 193 D13
Calamocha, Sp. 147 E13
Călan, Rom. 154 E12
Calanda, Sp. 147 E15
Calanscio, Sand Sea of, Af. 198 D7
Calapan, Philippines 193 D13
Călăraşi, Rom. 155 G17
Calatayud, Sp. 147 E13
Calayan, island, Philippines 193 A13
Calbayog, Philippines 193 D15
Calcanhar, Ponta do, Braz. 133 E18
Calcasieu, river, La., U.S. 102 P7
Calcasieu Lake, La., U.S. 102 Q7
Calçoene, Braz. 132 B12
Calcutta see Kolkata, India 180 J12
Caldas da Rainha, Port. 146 G4
Caldera, Chile 134 G6
Çaldıran, Turk. 171 F18
Caldwell, Idaho, U.S. 108 G3
Caldwell, Kans., U.S. 107 V7
Caldwell, Tex., U.S. 105 P12
Caldy Island, Wales, U.K. 145 V9
Caledon Bay, Austral. 214 B10
Caledonia, Minn., U.S. 106 L13
Caledonian Canal, Scot., U.K. 144 K8
Calexico, Calif., U.S. 111 Z11
Calf of Man (Yn Cholloo), cape, Isle of Man, U.K. 145 R8
Calgary, Alta., Can. 84 M10
Calheta, Azores, Port. 146 Q3
Calheta, Madeira, Port. 208 M2
Calhoun, Ga., U.S. 98 K4
Calhoun City, Miss., U.S. 102 J12
Calhoun Falls, S.C., U.S. 98 K7
Cali, Col. 130 G4
Calibishie, Dominica 123 E19
Calico Rock, Ark., U.S. 102 E9
Calicut see Kozhikode, India 181 Q5
Caliente, Nev., U.S. 111 S12
California, Mo., U.S. 107 T12
California, Trinidad and Tobago 123 P22
California, U.S. 111 S5
California, Golfo de, Mex. 116 D6
California Aqueduct, Calif., U.S. 111 V6
California Coastal National Monument Point Arena-Stornetta Unit, Calif., U.S. 111 Q2
Calilegua, Arg. 134 E9
Calipatria, Calif., U.S. 111 Y11
Calistoga, Calif., U.S. 111 R3
Calivigny, Grenada 123 L22
Calivigny Island, Grenada 123 L22
Callabonna, Lake, Austral. 214 H11
Callainn see Callan, Ire. 145 T5
Callan (Callainn), Ire. 145 T5
Callao, Peru 132 H3
Callaway, Nebr., U.S. 107 P4
Calliaqua, St. Vincent and the Grenadines 123 L16
Calliope Range, Austral. 214 G15
Caloosahatchee, river, Fla., U.S. 99 V8
Calpe, Sp. 147 J15
Caltagirone, It. 153 T11
Caltanissetta, It. 153 T10
Çaltı Burnu, Turk. 170 C12
Calulo, Angola 206 C6
Calumet, Mich., U.S. 100 E6
Caluso, It. 152 E3
Caluula, Somalia 203 F19
Calvert, Tex., U.S. 105 P12
Calvert Hills, N.T., Austral. 215 Q10
Calvi, Fr. 152 J4
Calvinia, S. Af. 206 L8
Calwa, Calif., U.S. 111 T6
Camabatela, Angola 206 C6
Camacupa, Angola 206 D7
Camagüey, Cuba 118 J11
Camagüey, Archipiélago de, Cuba 118 H11
Camajuaní, Cuba 118 H9
Camaná, Peru 132 K4
Camanche Reservoir, Calif., U.S. 111 R5
Camapuã, Braz. 132 K11
Câmara de Lobos, Madeira, Port. 208 M3
Camarat, Cap, Fr. 149 Y15
Çamardı, Turk. 170 G10
Camargo, Bol. 132 L7
Camargo, Okla., U.S. 104 F8
Camargue, Île de la, Fr. 149 X12
Camarón, Cape, N. Amer. 82 P8
Camarones, Arg. 135 S9
Camarones, Bahía, Arg. 135 S9
Camas, Wash., U.S. 110 F4
Camas Creek, Idaho, U.S. 108 H4
Camas Valley, Oreg., U.S. 110 J2
Cà Mau, Vietnam 191 Q12
Camballin, W. Aust., Austral. 215 R5
Cambodia, Asia 191 N11
Camborne, Eng., U.K. 145 Y8
Cambrai, Fr. 148 M11
Cambre, Sp. 146 B6
Cambria, Calif., U.S. 111 V5
Cambrian Mountains, Wales, U.K. 145 U10
Cambridge, Eng., U.K. 145 U14
Cambridge, Idaho, U.S. 108 F3
Cambridge, Jam. 118 M11
Cambridge, Mass., U.S. 97 K15
Cambridge, Md., U.S. 98 D14
Cambridge, Minn., U.S. 106 J11
Cambridge, Nebr., U.S. 107 R5
Cambridge, Ohio, U.S. 101 R14
Cambridge Bay, Nunavut, Can. 85 F13
Cambridge Gulf, Austral. 214 C6
Cambridge Springs, Pa., U.S. 96 L3
Cambundi-Catembo, Angola 206 C7
Çam Burnu, Turk. 170 D12
Camden, Ala., U.S. 103 M15
Camden, Ark., U.S. 102 J8
Camden, Me., U.S. 97 G17
Camden, N.J., U.S. 96 P10
Camden, N.Y., U.S. 96 H9
Camden, S.C., U.S. 98 K9
Camden, Tenn., U.S. 103 E13
Camden, Tex., U.S. 105 P14
Camden Park, St. Vincent and the Grenadines 123 L16
Camdenton, Mo., U.S. 107 U12
Çameli, Turk. 170 H5
Camerino, It. 152 H9
Cameron, Ariz., U.S. 109 R7
Cameron, La., U.S. 102 Q7
Cameron, Mo., U.S. 107 R11
Cameron, Tex., U.S. 105 P11
Cameroon, Af. 205 E16
Cameroon Mountain, Cameroon 205 F15
Cametá, Braz. 133 D13
Camiguin, island, Philippines 193 A14
Camiguin, island, Philippines 193 E15
Camilla, Ga., U.S. 99 P5
Caminha, Port. 146 D5
Camiri, Bol. 132 L8
Camirus see Kámeiros, ruin, Gr. 157 M19
Camissombo, Angola 206 B8
Camlıbel see Myrtou, Cyprus 162 N7
Camocim, Braz. 133 D16
Camooweal, Qnsld., Austral. 215 S10
Camopi, river, Fr. Guiana 131 G17
Camorta Island, India 181 S15
Campagnano di Roma, It. 152 K8
Campana, Arg. 134 L12
Campana, It. 153 P14
Campana, Isla, Chile 135 U6
Campanario, Cerro, Arg. 134 M7
Campania, Eur. 140 K7
Campbell, Mo., U.S. 107 V15
Campbell, Cape, N.Z. 217 M18
Campbell Escarpment, Pac. Oc. 242 R10
Campbell Hill, peak, Ohio, U.S. 101 Q12
Campbell Island (Motu Ihupuku), Pac. Oc. 218 R7
Campbell Island Shelf, Pac. Oc. 249 G19
Campbell Plateau, Pac. Oc. 242 R10

Campbell River, B.C., Can. 84 L7
Campbellsville, Ky., U.S. 103 C17
Campbell Town, Tas., Austral. 215 Y8
Campcardos, Pic de, Fr., Sp. 162 J6
Camp Crook, S. Dak., U.S. 106 J1
Campeche, Mex. 117 H15
Campêche, Guadeloupe, Fr. 123 E15
Campeche Bank, Atl. Oc. 240 L2
Campechuela, Cuba 118 K11
Cẩm Phả, Vietnam 190 H13
Campidano, plain, It. 153 P3
Campina Grande, Braz. 133 F18
Campinas, Braz. 133 M13
Campli, It. 152 J10
Campo, Cameroon 205 F15
Campo, Colo., U.S. 109 P15
Campoalegre, Col. 130 G5
Campobasso, It. 152 L11
Campofelice, It. 153 S10
Campo Gallo, Arg. 134 G10
Campo Grande, Braz. 132 L11
Campo Mourão, Braz. 132 M12
Campos, Braz. 133 L15
Campos, region, S. Amer. 128 J8
Camp Point, Ill., U.S. 101 R3
Campti, La., U.S. 102 M7
Camp Verde, Ariz., U.S. 109 S7
Camp Wood, Tex., U.S. 105 R7
Cam Ranh, Vietnam 191 N14
Camrose, Alta., Can. 84 L10
Camsell Portage, Sask., Can. 84 J12
Camuy, P.R., U.S. 122 M2
Çan, Turk. 170 D3
Cà Ná, Vietnam 191 P14
Canaan, Trinidad and Tobago 123 P17
Canacona, India 181 N4
Canada, N. Amer. 85 J14
Canada Basin, Arctic Oc. 246 M8
Cañada de Gómez, Arg. 134 K11
Cañada Honda, Arg. 134 K8
Canada Plain, Arctic Oc. 246 L8
Canadian, Tex., U.S. 104 F7
Canadian, river, U.S. 86 J11
Canadian Shield, N. Amer. 82 G7
Çanakkale, Turk. 170 D2
Çanakkale Boğazi (Dardanelles), Turk. 170 D2
Canala, New Caledonia, Fr. 222 D8
Canala, Baie de, New Caledonia, Fr. 222 D8
Canalul Bega, Serb. 154 E10
Canandaigua, N.Y., U.S. 96 J7
Cananea, Mex. 116 C7
Canaries, St. Lucia 123 K13
Canarreos, Archipiélago de los, Cuba 118 H7
Canary Basin, Atl. Oc. 240 K9
Canary Islands (Islas Canarias), Sp. 200 C5
Canary Ridge, Atl. Oc. 240 L10
Cañas, C.R. 117 N18
Canastota, N.Y., U.S. 96 J9
Canatlán, Mex. 116 F9
Canaveral, Cape, Fla., U.S. 99 T10
Canaveral National Seashore, Fla., U.S. 99 S9
Canavieiras, Braz. 133 J16
Canberra, A.C.T., Austral. 215 Y14
Canby, Calif., U.S. 110 M5
Canby, Minn., U.S. 106 K9
Cancún, Mex. 117 H17
Çandarlı, Turk. 170 F3
Çandarli Körfezi, Turk. 170 F3
Candás, Sp. 146 A9
Candé, Fr. 149 R6
Candia see Irákleio, Gr. 157 Q15
Cando, N. Dak., U.S. 106 E6
Candon, Philippines 193 B13
Canea see Chaniá, Gr. 157 P13
Cane Bay, Virgin Is., U.S. 122 Q2
Cane Garden Bay, British Virgin Is., U.K. 122 Q6
Canelles, river, St. Lucia 123 L14
Cañete, Sp. 147 G13
Caney, Kans., U.S. 107 V9
Canfranc, Sp. 147 C14
Cangamba, Angola 206 D8
Cangas, Sp. 146 C5
Cangas del Narcea, Sp. 146 B8
Canguaretama, Braz. 133 F18
Cangwu, Guangxi Zhuang, China 185 V2
Cangzhou, Hebei, China 184 E8
Caniapiscau, river, Que., Can. 85 K19
Caniapiscau, Réservoir, Que., Can. 85 L19
Canicattì, It. 153 T10
Caniles, Sp. 146 L12
Canillo, Andorra 162 H3
Canillo, region, Andorra 162 H4
Canindé, Braz. 133 E16
Canipaan, Malaysia 192 F12
Canisteo, N.Y., U.S. 96 K6
Canjáyar, Sp. 146 L12
Çankırı, Turk. 170 D9
Canna, island, Scot., U.K. 144 K7
Cannae, ruin, It. 152 L13
Cannanore see Kannur, India 181 Q4
Cannelton, Ind., U.S. 101 U8
Cannes, Fr. 149 X15
Canning Hill, Austral. 214 H3
Cannonball, river, N. Dak., U.S. 106 H4
Cannon Beach, Oreg., U.S. 110 E2
Cannon Falls, Minn., U.S. 106 K12
Cannonville, Utah, U.S. 109 P7
Canoas, Braz. 132 P12
Canoe Passage, Kiribati 221 A20
Canon City, Colo., U.S. 109 N13
Canonniers Point, Mauritius 209 F20
Canonsburg, Pa., U.S. 96 P3
Canosa di Puglia, It. 152 L13
Canouan, island, St. Vincent and the Grenadines 121 G16
Canso, Strait of, N.S., Can. 85 P22
Cantabria, Sierra, Sp. 146 C12
Cantabrian Mountains, Eur. 140 J2
Cantabrica, Cordillera, Sp. 146 B9
Cantalejo, Sp. 146 E10
Cantavieja, Sp. 147 F14
Canterbury, Eng., U.K. 145 V15
Canterbury Bight, N.Z. 217 P17
Cần Thơ, Vietnam 191 Q12
Cantiles, Cayo, Cuba 118 H6
Canto do Buriti, Braz. 133 F15
Canton, Ga., U.S. 98 K5
Canton, Ill., U.S. 101 Q4
Canton, Miss., U.S. 102 L11
Canton, Mo., U.S. 107 R13
Canton, N.C., U.S. 98 H7
Canton, N.Y., U.S. 96 F9
Canton, Ohio, U.S. 101 P15
Canton, Okla., U.S. 104 F9
Canton, Pa., U.S. 96 L7
Canton, S. Dak., U.S. 106 M8
Canton see Guangzhou, Guang., China 185 V4
Canton Lake, Okla., U.S. 104 F9
Cantù, It. 152 D4
Cantwell, Alas., U.S. 113 H17
Canumã, Braz. 132 E9
Canutama, Braz. 132 F7
Canutillo, Tex., U.S. 105 V2
Cany-Barville, Fr. 149 N8
Canyon, Tex., U.S. 104 H5
Canyon City, Oreg., U.S. 110 G7
Canyon de Chelly National Monument, Ariz., U.S. 109 R9
Canyon Ferry Lake, Mont., U.S. 108 D7
Canyon Grand, N. Amer. 82 K3
Canyon Lake, Tex., U.S. 105 Q10
Canyonlands National Park, Utah, U.S. 109 N9
Canyonlands National Park Horseshoe Canyon, Utah, U.S. 109 N8
Canyons of the Ancients National Monument, Colo., U.S. 109 P10
Canyonville, Oreg., U.S. 110 J3
Cao Bằng, Vietnam 190 G12
Caoxian, Shand., China 184 J7
Caparra, ruin, P.R., U.S. 122 M4
Capayán, Arg. 134 H9
Cap Barbas, W. Sahara 200 E5
Cap d'Ail, Fr. 163 F19
Cap Dorade, St.-Martin, Fr. 123 B14
Cape Barren Island, Austral. 214 L8
Cape Basin, Atl. Oc. 241 T13
Cape Breton Island, N.S., Can. 85 N23
Cape Charles, Va., U.S. 98 F14
Cape Coast, Ghana 204 E10
Cape Cod Bay, Mass., U.S. 97 L16
Cape Cod National Seashore, Mass., U.S. 97 L16
Cape Coral, Fla., U.S. 99 W8
Cape Cornwall, Eng., U.K. 145 Y7
Cape Dorset, Nunavut, Can. 85 H17
Cape Farewell, N.Z. 217 L17
Cape Fear, river, N.C., U.S. 98 K12
Cape Girardeau, Mo., U.S. 107 U16
Cape Hatteras National Seashore, N.C., U.S. 98 H15
Cape Krusenstern National Monument, Alas., U.S. 113 D13
Capella Islands, Virgin Is., U.S. 122 N9
Cape Lookout National Seashore, N.C., U.S. 98 J14
Cape Lookout Shoals, N.C., U.S. 98 J14
Cape May, N.J., U.S. 96 R10
Capenda-Camulembu, Angola 206 C7
Cape Palmas, Liberia 204 F7
Cape Plain, Atl. Oc. 241 T13
Cape Rise, Atl. Oc. 241 U14
Cape Rodney, P.N.G. 217 E20
Cape Shirley, St. Kitts and Nevis 123 C21
Cap Estate, St. Lucia 123 J14
Capesterre, Guadeloupe, Fr. 123 G16
Capesterre-Belle-Eau, Guadeloupe, Fr. 123 F15
Capestrano, It. 152 K10
Cape Town, S. Af. 206 M7
Cape Verde Basin, Atl. Oc. 240 L8
Cape Verde Plain, Atl. Oc. 240 L9
Cape Verde Plateau, Atl. Oc. 240 M10
Cape Vincent, N.Y., U.S. 96 G8
Cape York Peninsula, Austral. 214 B12
Cap-Haïtien, Haiti 119 L17
Capistrello, It. 152 K9
Capital Hill, N. Mariana Is., U.S. 220 B5
Capitan, N. Mex., U.S. 109 U13
Capitán Pablo Lagerenza, Parag. 132 K9
Capitan Peak, N. Mex., U.S. 109 T13
Capitão, Ponta, Sao Tome and Principe 209 A21
Capitol Reef National Park, Utah, U.S. 109 N8
Capodistria see Koper, Slov. 154 D4
Capoeira, falls, Braz. 132 F10
Cappadocia, region, Turk. 170 G10
Cappamore (An Cheapach Mhór), Ire. 145 T4
Cappoquin (Ceapach Choinn), Ire. 145 U5
Capraia, Isola di, It. 152 H5
Capreol, Ont., Can. 85 P18
Caprera, Isola, Fr. 152 L4
Capri, Isola di, It. 153 N10
Capricorn Channel, Austral. 214 F15
Capricorn Group, Austral. 214 F15
Caprivi Strip, region, Namibia 206 F9
Cap Rock Escarpment, U.S. 86 K11
Captain Cook, Hawai'i, U.S. 115 N18
Captain Cook Monument, Hawai'i, U.S. 114 C5
Captain Cook Monument, Hawai'i, U.S. 115 N18
Captain Cook's Monument, Fr. Polynesia, Fr. 223 N16
Captieux, Fr. 149 W7
Captiva, Fla., U.S. 99 W8
Capua, It. 152 M10
Capucin, Cape, Dominica 123 D18
Capucin Point, Seychelles 209 P20
Capulin Volcano National Monument, N. Mex., U.S. 109 Q14
Caquetá, river, Col. 130 J7
Caracal, Rom. 155 G14
Caracaraí, Braz. 132 B9
Caracas, Venez. 130 B9
Caracol, Braz. 133 G15
Carahue, Chile 135 P6
Carajás, Serra dos, Braz. 132 E12
Caramulo, Serra do, Port. 146 F6
Carandotta, Qnsld., Austral. 215 S10
Caransebeş, Rom. 154 E12
Carapuse Bay, Trinidad and Tobago 123 N18
Caratasca, Laguna de, Hond. 117 K19
Caratasca Lagoon, N. Amer. 82 P8
Carauari, Braz. 132 E7
Caraúbas, Braz. 133 F17
Caravaca de la Cruz, Sp. 147 K13
Caravelas, Braz. 133 K16
Caravelle, Presqu'île la, Martinique, Fr. 123 E23
Carballiño, Sp. 146 C6
Carballo, Sp. 146 B5
Carbón, Laguna del, Arg. 135 V8
Carbonara, Capo, It. 153 Q4
Carbondale, Colo., U.S. 108 M11
Carbondale, Ill., U.S. 101 U5
Carbondale, Pa., U.S. 96 M9
Carboneras, Sp. 147 L13
Carbon Hill, Ala., U.S. 103 J14
Carbonia, It. 153 Q3
Carbonne, Fr. 149 Y8
Carcajou, Alta., Can. 84 J10
Carcans, Lac de, Fr. 149 V6
Carcasse, Cap-, Haiti 119 M14
Carcassonne, Fr. 149 Y10
Carche, peak, Sp. 147 J14
Carcross, Yukon, Can. 84 G7
Cardamom Mountains, Cambodia 191 N10
Cardamum Island see Kadmat Island, India 181 Q3
Cardeña, Sp. 146 J10
Cárdenas, Cuba 118 G7
Cárdenas, Mex. 116 G11
Cardiff (Caerdydd), Wales, U.K. 145 V10
Cardigan (Aberteif), Wales, U.K. 145 U9
CardiganBay, Wales, U.K. 145 T9
Cardno Fracture Zone, Atl. Oc. 241 R9
Cardona, Sp. 147 D17
Cardoso y Pinto, Eq. Guinea 208 M7
Cardwell, Qnsld., Austral. 215 R13
Carei, Rom. 154 B12
Careiro da Várzea, Braz. 132 D9
Carey, Ohio, U.S. 101 P12
Carey, Lake, Austral. 214 H5
Cargados Carajos Bank, Ind. Oc. 224 J8
Cargèse, Fr. 152 K3
Carhué, Arg. 134 M11
Cariati, It. 153 P14
Caribbean Sea, Atl. Oc. 240 M3
Caribou, Me., U.S. 97 B18
Caribou Mountains, N. Amer. 82 F4
Cariñena, Sp. 147 E13
Carinhanha, Braz. 133 J15
Cariparé, Braz. 133 H14
Caripito, Venez. 130 B12
Carlin, Nev., U.S. 111 N10
Carlingford Lough, Ire., U.K. 145 R7
Carlinville, Ill., U.S. 101 S4
Carlisle, Ark., U.S. 102 G9
Carlisle, Eng., U.K. 145 P10
Carlisle, Ky., U.S. 103 B18
Carlisle, Pa., U.S. 96 P7
Carlisle Bay, Barbados 123 L19
Carlisle Bay, Jam. 122 K8
Carlos, Isla, Chile 135 X7
Carlos Manuel de Céspedes, Cuba 118 J10
Carlow (Ceatharlach), Ire. 145 T6
Carlsbad, Calif., U.S. 111 Y9
Carlsbad, N. Mex., U.S. 109 V14
Carlsbad, Tex., U.S. 105 N6
Carlsbad Caverns National Park, N. Mex., U.S. 109 V14
Carlsberg Ridge, Ind. Oc. 224 E8
Carlton, Minn., U.S. 106 G12
Carlyle, Ill., U.S. 101 T5
Carlyle Lake, Ill., U.S. 101 T5
Carmacks, Yukon, Can. 84 F8
Carmagnola, It. 152 E3
Carmarthen (Sir Gaerfyrddin), Wales, U.K. 145 V9
Carmarthen Bay, Wales, U.K. 145 V9
Carmaux, Fr. 149 X10
Carmel-by-the-Sea, Calif., U.S. 111 T4
Carmen, Okla., U.S. 104 E9
Carmen, Isla, Mex. 116 E7
Carmen de Bolívar, Col. 130 C5
Carmen de Patagones, Arg. 135 Q10
Carmi, Ill., U.S. 101 U7
Carmona, Sp. 146 L8
Carnarvon, Qnsld., Austral. 215 U14
Carnarvon, S. Af. 206 L8
Carnarvon Terrace, Ind. Oc. 225 L17
Carn Domhnach see Carndonagh, Ire. 145 N6
Carndonagh (Carn Domhnach), Ire. 145 N6
Carnegie, Okla., U.S. 104 G9
Carnegie, W. Aust., Austral. 215 U5
Carnegie, Lake, Austral. 214 G4
Carnegie Ridge, Pac. Oc. 243 K21
Carney Island, Antarctica 230 M7
Carnic Alps, It. 152 C9
Car Nicobar, island, India 181 S14
Carnot, Cen. Af. Rep. 202 H8
Carnot, Cape, Austral. 214 K9
Carnsore Point, Ire. 145 U7
Caro, Mich., U.S. 100 K12
Caroço, Ilhéu, Sao Tome and Principe 209 B21
Carol City, Fla., U.S. 99 X10
Carolina, Braz. 133 F14
Carolina, P.R., U.S. 122 M5
Carolina Beach, N.C., U.S. 98 K13
Carolinas, Puntan, N. Mariana Is., U.S. 220 C8
Caroline Island (Millennium Island), Kiribati 219 H13
Caroline Islands, F.S.M. 221 R4
Caroline Seamounts, Pac. Oc. 242 J8
Caroní, river, Venez. 130 D12
Caroni Swamp, Trinidad and Tobago 123 P22
Carora, Venez. 130 B8
Carp, Nev., U.S. 111 T12
Carpathian Mountains, Eur. 140 H9
Carpathos see Kárpathos, Gr. 157 P18
Carpatho-Ukraine, region, Ukr. 59 P1
Carpentaria, Gulf of, Austral. 214 B11
Carpentras, Fr. 149 W13
Carpi, It. 152 F6
Carpina, Braz. 133 F18
Carpio, N. Dak., U.S. 106 E3
Carpolac, Vic., Austral. 215 Y11
Carquefou, Fr. 149 R6
Carrabelle, Fla., U.S. 99 R5
Carrara, It. 152 G5
Carrarang, W. Aust., Austral. 215 V1
Carrauntoohil see Corrán Tuathail, peak, Ire. 145 U3
Carrboro, N.C., U.S. 98 H11
Carriacou, island, Grenada 121 H16
Carrickfergus, N. Ire., U.K. 145 P7
Carrick-on-Shannon (Cora Droma Rúisc), Ire. 145 R5
Carrington, N. Dak., U.S. 106 F6
Carrión de los Condes, Sp. 146 C10
Carrizal Bajo, Chile 134 G6
Carrizo Creek, N. Mex., Tex., U.S. 109 Q15
Carrizo Plain National Monument, Calif., U.S. 111 V6
Carrizo Springs, Tex., U.S. 105 T7
Carrizozo, N. Mex., U.S. 109 T13
Carroll, Iowa, U.S. 107 N10
Carrollton, Ga., U.S. 98 L4
Carrollton, Ill., U.S. 101 S4
Carrollton, Ky., U.S. 103 A17
Carrollton, Mo., U.S. 107 S11
Carrollton, Tex., U.S. 104 L11
Carrot Bay, British Virgin Is., U.K. 122 R5
Carrowmore Lough, Ire. 145 Q3
Çarşamba, Turk. 170 D11

Çarşamba, river, Turk. 170 H7
Carson, N. Dak., U.S. 106 H4
Carson City, Nev., U.S. III P8
Carson Sink, Nev., U.S. III P8
Carsonville, Mich., U.S. 100 LI3
Cartagena, Col. 130 C4
Cartagena, Sp. 147 KI4
Cartago, C.R. 117 NI9
Cartago, Col. 130 F4
Carter, Mount, Austral. 214 BI2
Carter's Cays, Bahamas 122 D3
Cartersville, Ga., U.S. 98 K4
Carthage, Ark., U.S. 102 H8
Carthage, Ill., U.S. 101 Q3
Carthage, Miss., U.S. 102 KI2
Carthage, Mo., U.S. 107 VII
Carthage, N.C., U.S. 98 HII
Carthage, N.Y., U.S. 96 G9
Carthage, S. Dak., U.S. 106 L7
Carthage, Tenn., U.S. 103 EI6
Carthage, Tex., U.S. 104 MI5
Cartier Island, Austral. 214 B5
Cartwright, Nfld. & Lab., Can. 85 K22
Caruaru, Braz. 133 GI7
Carúpano, Venez. 130 BI2
Carutapera, Braz. 133 DI4
Caruthersville, Mo., U.S. 107 WI6
Carvoeiro, Braz. 132 D8
Cary, N.C., U.S. 98 HII
Caryapundy Swamp, Austral. 214 HI2
Casablanca, Mor. 200 B8
Casa Cruz, Cape, Trinidad and Tobago 123 Q23
Casa Grande, Ariz., U.S. 109 U7
Casa Grande Ruins National Monument, Ariz., U.S. 109 U7
Casale Monferrato, It. 152 E3
Casamance, region, Senegal 200 H4
Casamanya, Pic de, Andorra 162 H3
Casanare, river, Col. 130 E7
Casarano, It. 153 NI5
Cascade, Idaho, U.S. 108 F4
Cascade, Jam. 122 H6
Cascade, Mont., U.S. 108 C7
Cascade, Norfolk I., Austral. 221 F2O
Cascade, Seychelles 209 N2O
Cascade Bay, Norfolk I., Austral. 221 F2O
Cascade Head, Oreg., U.S. 110 F2
Cascade Locks, Oreg., U.S. 110 F4
Cascade Range, N. Amer. 82 J3
Cascade Reservoir, Idaho, U.S. 108 F4
Cascade-Siskiyou National Monument, Oreg., U.S. 110 L3
Cascadia Basin, Pac. Oc. 243 DI7
Cascavel, Braz. 132 MII
Cascina, It. 152 G6
Cascorro, Cuba 118 JII
Casere, It. 152 B8
Caserta, It. 152 MII
Cases Velles de Formentor, Sp. 147 GI9
Casey, Ill., U.S. 101 S7
Casey, station, Antarctica 231 M2I
Casey Bay, Antarctica 231 CI9
Cashel (Caiseal), Ire. 145 T5
Cashmere, Wash., U.S. 110 C6
Casiguran, Philippines 193 BI4
Casilda, Arg. 134 KII
Casina di Pio IV, Vatican City 163 PI6
Casino, N.S.W., Austral. 215 WI6
Casino Gardens, Monaco 163 D2I
Casino of Monte Carlo, Monaco 163 D22
Casiquiare, river, Venez. 130 GIO
Casma, Peru 132 G3
Casmalia, Calif., U.S. III W5
Casnewydd see Newport, Wales, U.K. 145 VII
Caspar, Calif., U.S. III P2
Caspe, Sp. 147 EI5
Casper, Wyo., U.S. 108 HI2
Caspian Depression, Kaz., Russ. 159 RI4
Caspian Sea, Asia 168 F5
Casquets, island, Channel Is., U.K. 145 YII

Cass, W. Va., U.S. 98 DIO
Cass City, Mich., U.S. 100 KI2
Cassel, Fr. 148 LIO
Casselton, N. Dak., U.S. 106 G8
Cassiar Mountains, B.C., Yukon, Can. 84 H8
Cassino, It. 152 LIO
Cassis, Fr. 149 YI3
Cass Lake, Minn., U.S. 106 FIO
Cassville, Mo., U.S. 107 VII
Cassville, Wis., U.S. 100 M3
Castagneto Carducci, It. 152 H6
Castanhal, Braz. 133 DI3
Castaño Nuevo, Arg. 134 J7
Castara, Trinidad and Tobago 123 NI8
Casteggio, It. 152 E4
Castelbuono, It. 153 SIO
Castel di Sangro, It. 152 LIO
Castelfranco Veneto, It. 152 D8
Casteljaloux, Fr. 149 W7
Castellabate, It. 153 NII
Castellaccio, peak, San Marino 163 KI5
Castellammare, Golfo di, It. 153 S9
Castellammare del Golfo, It. 153 S9
Castellaneta, It. 152 MI4
Castello, It. 163 LI5
Castello di Montemaggio, It. 162 KI3
Castellón de la Plana (Castelló de la Plana), Sp. 147 GI5
Castelnaudary, Fr. 149 Y9
Castelnovo ne' Monti, It. 152 F6
Castelo Branco, Port. 146 G6
Castelo de Bode, Barragem de, Port. 146 G5
Castelo de Vide, Port. 146 H6
Castelsardo, It. 152 M3
CastiglioneMesser Marino, It. 152 KII
Castilhiano, Cabo Verde 209 BI6
Castille, region, Sp. 146 FIO
Castillo, Pampa del, Arg. 135 T8
Castillo de San Marcos National Monument, Fla., U.S. 99 R9
Castillon, Fr. 149 Y8
Castillos, Uru. 134 LI5
Castlebar (Caisleán an Bharraigh), Ire. 145 R3
Castlebay see Bagh a' Chaisteil, Scot., U.K. 144 K6
Castlebridge, Ire. 145 U7
Castle Bruce, Dominica 123 F2O
Castle Dale, Utah, U.S. 108 M8
Castle Douglas, Scot., U.K. 145 P9
Castlegregory (Caisleán Ghriaire), Ire. 145 U2
Castle Harbour, Bermuda 122 B3
Castle Island, Bahamas 119 HI4
Castle Peak, Idaho, U.S. 108 G5
Castlepollard (Baile na gCros), Ire. 145 R6
Castlerea (An Caisleán Riabhach), Ire. 145 R3
Castlereagh, river, Austral. 214 JI4
Castle Roads, Bermuda 122 B3
Castle Rock, Colo., U.S. 108 MI3
Castle Rock, Wash., U.S. 110 E3
Castletownshend (Baile an Chaisleáin), Ire. 145 V3
Castlewood, S. Dak., U.S. 106 K8
Castor Bank, Ind. Oc. 224 J6
Castres, Fr. 149 XIO
Castries, Fr. 149 XI2
Castries, St. Lucia 123 JI4
Castro, Chile 135 R6
Castro Daire, Port. 146 E6
Castro-Urdiales, Sp. 146 BII
Castro Verde, Port. 146 K5
Castrovillari, It. 153 PI3
Castroville, Tex., U.S. 105 R9
Castuera, Sp. 146 J8
Çat, Turk. 171 EI5
Catahoula Lake, La., U.S. 102 M8
Çatak, Turk. 171 GI7
Catalan Bay, Gibraltar, U.K. 163 P23
Catalan Bay, Gibraltar, U.K. 163 P23
Catalão, Braz. 133 KI3
Çatalca, Turk. 170 C4
Catalina, Chile 134 F7

Catalina Point, Guam, U.S. 220 BI2
Catalonia, region, Sp. 147 DI7
Catamarca, Arg. 134 H9
Catanduanes, island, Philippines 193 CI5
Catania, It. 153 TI2
Catania, Golfo di, It. 153 TI2
Catania, Piana di, It. 153 TII
Catanzaro, It. 153 QI4
Cataperdís, Pic de, Andorra, Fr. 162 G2
Catarina, Tex., U.S. 105 T8
Catarman, Philippines 193 DI5
Catawba, river, U.S. 87 HI9
Cat Cays, Bahamas 118 D9
Cateel, Philippines 193 FI5
Catete, Angola 206 C5
Cathair na Mart see Westport, Ire. 145 R3
Cathedral Mountain, peak, Tex., U.S. 105 Q2
Cathedral of Monaco, Monaco 163 E2I
Catherine, Mount see Katherîna, Gebel , Egypt 173 T3
Cathlamet, Wash., U.S. 110 E3
Catingas, region, S. Amer. 128 E8
Cat Island, Bahamas 119 EI3
Cat Island, Miss., U.S. 102 PI2
Cat Lake, Ont., Can. 85 NI5
Catlettsburg, Ky., U.S. 103 B2O
Catlow Valley, Oreg., U.S. 110 K7
Catoche, Cape, N. Amer. 82 N7
Catonsville, Md., U.S. 98 CI3
Cato Trough, Pac. Oc. 242 M9
Catria, Monte, It. 152 H8
Catrilló, Arg. 134 MIO
Catrimani, Braz. 132 C8
Catrimani, river, Braz. 132 C8
Catskill, N.Y., U.S. 96 KII
Catskill Mountains, N.Y., U.S. 96 KIO
Cattenom, Fr. 162 LIO
Cattolica Eraclea, It. 153 T9
Cauca, river, Col. 130 D5
Cauca, river, N. Amer. 82 Q9
Caucasus Mountains, Eur., Asia 140 JI4
Caucete, Arg. 134 J8
Caudry, Fr. 148 MII
Caulnes, Fr. 149 Q5
Caungula, Angola 206 C7
Cauquenes, Chile 134 M6
Caura, river, Venez. 130 EII
Caussade, Fr. 149 W9
Causse du Larzac, range, Fr. 149 XII
Cauto, river, Cuba 118 KI2
Cavaillon, Fr. 149 XI3
Cavalaire, Fr. 149 YI5
Cavalcante, Braz. 133 HI3
Cavalese, It. 152 C7
Cavalier, N. Dak., U.S. 106 E7
Cavalla (Cavally), river, Af. 204 E7
Cavallo, Île, Fr. 152 L4
Cavan (An Cabhán), Ire. 145 R6
Cave Cay, Bahamas 122 D7
Cave Creek, Ariz., U.S. 109 T7
Cave Junction, Oreg., U.S. 110 K2
Cavelle Pond, Bahamas 122 B8
Caves, Anse aux, Mauritius 209 J2O
Caviana, Ilha, Braz. 133 CI3
Cavignac, Fr. 149 V7
Cavo, Mount, It. 152 L8
Cavour, It. 152 E2
Çavuş Burnu, Turk. 170 J6
Çavuşçu Gölü, Turk. 170 G7
Cawker City, Kans., U.S. 107 S6
Caxias, Braz. 132 E5
Caxias, Braz. 133 EI5
Caxias do Sul, Braz. 132 PI2
Caxito, Angola 206 C5
Çay, Turk. 170 F6
Cayambe, Ecua. 130 J3
Cayambe, peak, Ecua. 130 J3
Cayce, S.C., U.S. 98 K9
Çaycuma, Turk. 170 C7
Çayeli, Turk. 171 DI5
Cayenne, Fr. Guiana 131 EI8
Cayeux-sur-Mer, Fr. 148 M9
Cayey, P.R., U.S. 122 N4
Cayey, Sierra de, P.R., U.S. 122 N4

Çayıralan, Turk. 170 FIO
Çayırova see Ayios Theodhoros, Cyprus 162 NIO
Cayman Brac, Cayman Is. 118 L9
Cayman Islands, Cayman Is. 118 L8
Cayman Trench, Atl. Oc. 240 M2
Caynabo, Somalia 203 GI7
Cayo Arenas, island, Mex. 117 GI5
Cayon, St. Kitts and Nevis 123 AI7
Cayos Miskitos, islands, Nicar. 117 LI9
Cay Point, Bahamas 122 BII
Cay Sal Bank, Bahamas 118 F8
Cayucos, Calif., U.S. III V5
Cayuga Lake, N.Y., U.S. 96 K8
Cazalla de la Sierra, Sp. 146 K8
Cazaux et de Sanguinet, Lac de, Fr. 149 W6
Cazères, Fr. 149 Y8
Cazombo, Angola 206 D9
Cazorla, Sp. 146 KII
Ceanannas see Kells, Ire. 145 R6
Ceann Trá (Ventry), Ire. 145 U2
Ceapach Choinn see Cappoquin, Ire. 145 U5
Ceara Plain, Atl. Oc. 241 P7
Ceara Ridge, Atl. Oc. 241 N7
Ceara Seamounts, Atl. Oc. 241 P7
Ceatharlach see Carlow, Ire. 145 T6
Cebollar, Arg. 134 H9
Çebrayıl see Kurakhtin, Azerb. 171 E2I
Cebu, island, Philippines 193 EI4
Cebu City, Philippines 193 EI4
Cecile Peninsula, Kiribati 221 B22
Cecil Plains, Qnsld., Austral. 215 VI5
Cecina, It. 152 H6
Cedar, river, Iowa, Minn., U.S. 106 MI2
Cedar Bluff Reservoir, Kans., U.S. 107 T5
Cedar Breaks National Monument, Utah, U.S. 109 P6
Cedar City, Utah, U.S. 109 P6
Cedar Creek Reservoir, Tex., U.S. 104 MI3
Cedar Falls, Iowa, U.S. 107 NI2
Cedar Grove, Antigua and Barbuda 123 A2I
Cedar Harbour, Bahamas 122 A5
Cedar Key, Fla., U.S. 99 S7
Cedar Lake, Ind., U.S. 101 P7
Cedar Rapids, Iowa, U.S. 107 NI3
Cedar River, Wis., U.S. 100 H8
Cedartown, Ga., U.S. 98 K5
Cedar Vale, Kans., U.S. 107 V8
Cedarville, Calif., U.S. 110 L6
Cedarville, Mich., U.S. 100 GII
Cedeira, Sp. 146 A6
Cedillo, Embalse de, Port., Sp. 146 G6
Cedros, Isla, Mex. 116 C5
Cedros Bay, Trinidad and Tobago 123 Q2I
Cedros Island, N. Amer. 82 L3
Cedros Trench, Pac. Oc. 243 FI5
Ceduna, S. Aust., Austral. 215 W9
Ceduna Slope, Ind. Oc. 225 N2O
Ceelbuur, Somalia 203 HI7
Ceerigaabo (Erigavo), Somalia 203 FI7
Cefalù, It. 153 SIO
Cegléd, Hung. 151 LI5
Cehotina, river, Montenegro 154 H9
Ceiba, P.R., U.S. 122 N6
Cejal, Col. 130 G9
Çekerek, Turk. 170 EIO
Çekerek, river, Turk. 170 EIO
Celano, It. 152 K9
Celanova, Sp. 146 C6
Celaya, Mex. 116 HII
Celebes see Sulawesi, island, Indonesia 193 KI3
Celebes Basin, Pac. Oc. 242 J5
Celebes Sea, Indonesia 193 HI3
Çeleken, Turkm. 176 K6
Çelilabad, Azerb. 171 E22
Celje, Slov. 154 D5
Cella, Sp. 147 FI3
Celle, Ger. 150 D8

Celtic Sea, Ire., U.K. 145 V6
Celtic Shelf, Atl. Oc. 240 HII
Cement, Okla., U.S. 104 HIO
Çemişgezek, Turk. 171 FI3
Cenderawasih, Teluk, Indonesia 193 KI9
Cenderawasih Bay, Pac. Oc. 168 LI5
Center, N. Dak., U.S. 106 G4
Center, Tex., U.S. 104 MI5
Center Hill Lake, Tenn., U.S. 103 EI6
Center Point, Ala., U.S. 103 JI5
Center Point, Tex., U.S. 105 Q9
Centerville, Iowa, U.S. 107 QI2
Centerville, S. Dak., U.S. 106 M8
Centerville, Tenn., U.S. 103 FI4
Centerville, Tex., U.S. 105 NI3
Cento, It. 152 F7
Central, Alas., U.S. 113 FI8
Central, Cordillera, Dom. Rep. 119 LI8
Central, Cordillera, P.R., U.S. 122 N2
Central African Republic, Af. 202 G9
Central America, region, N. Amer. 82 Q6
Central Bank, Arctic Oc. 247 EI7
Central Basin, Arctic Oc. 247 DI7
Central Basin, Pac. Oc. 249 HI6
Central Brāhui Range, Pak. 179 T6
Central City, Ky., U.S. 103 DI5
Central City, Nebr., U.S. 107 Q7
Central Greece, region, Gr. 156 HII
Central Highlands, Vietnam 190 MI3
Centralia, Ill., U.S. 101 T5
Centralia, Mo., U.S. 107 SI3
Centralia, Wash., U.S. 110 D3
Central Kara Rise, Arctic Oc. 247 EI3
Central Lowland, U.S. 87 FI6
Central Lowlands, Austral. 214 FII
Central Makrān Range, Pak. 179 V2
Central Mount Wedge, N.T., Austral. 215 T8
Central Pacific Basin, Pac. Oc. 242 HII
Central Point, Oreg., U.S. 110 K3
Central Range, Asia 168 CI3
Central Range, P.N.G. 217 CI8
Central Russian Upland, Eur. 140 FI2
Central Siberian Plateau, Asia 168 D9
Central Terrace, Ind. Oc. 224 L4
Central Valley, Calif., U.S. III N3
Centre, Ala., U.S. 103 HI6
Centre de Flacq, Mauritius 209 G2O
Centreville, Miss., U.S. 102 NIO
Cenxi, Guangxi Zhuang, China 185 V2
Cephalonia see Kefaloniá, island, Gr. 156 H7
Ceprano, It. 152 L9
Ceram, island, Indonesia 193 KI6
Ceram Sea, Indonesia 193 KI7
Ceram Trough, Pac. Oc. 242 K6
Cerasolo, It. 163 GI8
Cerbère, Fr. 149 ZII
Ceres, Arg. 134 HII
Ceres, Braz. 133 JI3
Ceriano, It. 163 GI6
Cerigo see Kýthira, island, Gr. 156 NII
Cérilly, Fr. 149 TIO
Çerkeş, Turk. 170 D8
Çermik, Turk. 171 GI4
Cernavodă, Rom. 155 FI7
Cerralvo, Isla, Mex. 116 F7
Cerredo, Torre, Sp. 146 B9
Cerreto, Monte, San Marino 163 JI4
Cerrillos, Arg. 134 F9
Cerrillos, N. Mex., U.S. 109 RI2
Cerro de Pasco, Peru 132 G3
Cerro de Punta, peak, P.R., U.S. 122 N3
Cerro Sombrero, Chile 135 W8
Certaldo, It. 152 H6
Certers, Andorra 162 K3
Cervales, peak, Sp. 146 G9

Cervera, *Sp.* **147** D16
Cervera de Pisuerga, *Sp.* **146** B10
Cerveteri, *It.* **152** K8
Cervia, *It.* **152** F8
Cesana Torinese, *It.* **152** E1
Cesar, river, *Col.* **130** C5
Cesarò, *It.* **153** S11
Cesena, *It.* **152** G8
Cesenatico, *It.* **152** G8
Cēsis, *Latv.* **143** L17
České Budějovice, *Czech Rep.*
    150 J11
Český Krumlov, *Czech Rep.* **150** J11
Çeşme, *Turk.* **170** F2
Cetinje, *Montenegro* **154** J8
Cetti Bay, *Guam, U.S.* **220** D10
Ceuta, *Sp.* **146** N9
Cévennes, range, *Fr.* **149** W12
Cevio, *Switz.* **152** C4
Ceyhan, *Turk.* **170** H11
Ceyhan, river, *Turk.* **170** H11
Ceylanpınar, *Turk.* **171** J14
Ceylon Plain, *Ind. Oc.* **224** H12
Chabana, *Japan* **189** X2
Chablis, *Fr.* **149** R11
Chacachacare, island, *Trinidad and
    Tobago* **123** P22
Chacao, Canal de, *Chile* **135** Q6
Chacao Channel, *S. Amer.* **128** N4
Chachapoyas, *Peru* **132** F3
Chacharan, *Pak.* **179** S9
Chachora, *India* **180** H5
Chachro, *Pak.* **179** W9
Chaco Austral, region, *S. Amer.*
    128 K6
Chaco Boreal, region, *S. Amer.*
    128 H6
Chaco Central, region, *S. Amer.*
    128 J6
Chaco Culture National Historical
    Park, *N. Mex., U.S.* **109** R10
Chad, *Af.* **201** H15
Chad, Lake (Lac Tchad), *Af.*
    205 A16
Chadan, *Russ.* **161** L13
Chadbourn, *N.C., U.S.* **98** K11
Chadron, *Nebr., U.S.* **106** M2
Chadwick, *Mo., U.S.* **107** V12
Chaeryŏng, *N. Korea* **186** L6
Chaeryŏng, river, *N. Korea* **186** L6
Chafarinas, Islas, *Sp.* **146** P12
Chaffee, *Mo., U.S.* **107** U16
Chagai, *Pak.* **179** S4
Chāgai Hills, *Pak.* **179** S3
Chagda, *Russ.* **161** H8
Chaghcharān, *Afghan.* **178** M5
Chagoda, *Russ.* **158** F8
Chagos Archipelago, *Ind. Oc.*
    168 M5
Chagos-Laccadive Ridge, *Ind. Oc.*
    224 D10
Chagos Trench, *Ind. Oc.* **224** H11
Chaguanas, *Trinidad and Tobago*
    123 P22
Chaguaramas, *Trinidad and Tobago*
    123 P22
Chagyl, *Turkm.* **176** K7
Chāh Āb, *Afghan.* **178** J8
Chahār Bāgh, *Afghan.* **178** K5
Chahār Burj, *Afghan.* **178** M2
Chahār Burjak, *Afghan.* **179** R2
Chāh Bāhar, *Iran* **175** J17
Chāh-e Kirtahak, *Afghan.* **179** P2
Ch'aho, *N. Korea* **186** G11
Ch'ahŭng, *N. Korea* **186** G5
Chaibasa, *India* **180** J10
Ch'ail-bong, peak, *N. Korea*
    186 F9
Chai-Nat, *Thai.* **190** L8
Chain Fracture Zone, *Atl. Oc.*
    241 P10
Chain of Craters, *Hawai'i, U.S.*
    115 N21
Chain Ridge, *Ind. Oc.* **224** F7
Chajarí, *Arg.* **134** J13
Chakar, river, *Pak.* **179** S7
Chakaria, *Bangladesh* **180** J14
Chake Chake, *Tanzania* **203** M15
Chakhānsūr, *Afghan.* **179** Q2
Chakwal, *Pak.* **179** N11
Chalais, *Fr.* **149** V7

Chalan Kanoa, *N. Mariana Is., U.S.*
    220 C4
Chalan Pago, *Guam, U.S.* **220** C11
Chalbi Desert, *Af.* **198** J10
Chaleur Bay, *N.B., Que., Can.* **85** N21
Chalhuanca, *Peru* **132** J4
Chaling, *Hunan, China* **185** S5
Chalisgaon, *India* **180** K4
Chalkhī, *Afghan.* **178** L2
Chálki, bay, *Gr.* **157** N19
Chálki, island, *Gr.* **157** N19
Chalkída (Chalkís), *Gr.* **156** H12
Chalkidikí, Óros, *Gr.* **156** D11
Chalkís see Chalkída, *Gr.* **156** H12
Chalkyitsik, *Alas., U.S.* **113** E18
Chalky Mount, *Barbados* **123** K19
Chalky Mount, *Barbados* **123** K19
Challans, *Fr.* **149** S5
Challenger Deep, *Pac. Oc.* **242** H7
Challenger Fracture Zone, *Pac. Oc.*
    243 N21
Challenger Plateau, *Pac. Oc.*
    242 P10
Challis, *Idaho, U.S.* **108** F5
Chalon, *Fr.* **149** S12
Châlons-en-Champagne, *Fr.*
    149 P12
Châlus, *Fr.* **149** U8
Cham, *Ger.* **150** J9
Chama, *N. Mex., U.S.* **109** Q12
Chamah, peak, *Malaysia* **191** T9
Chaman, *Pak.* **179** Q5
Chaman Bid, *Iran* **175** B15
Chamba, *India* **179** P13
Chambal, river, *India* **180** G5
Chamberlain, *S. Dak., U.S.* **106** L6
Chamberlain Lake, *Me., U.S.* **97** C17
Chamberlin, Mount, *Alas., U.S.*
    113 C18
Chambers, *Ariz., U.S.* **109** S9
Chambersburg, *Pa., U.S.* **96** P6
Chambers Creek, *Tex., U.S.* **104** M11
Chambéry, *Fr.* **149** U14
Chambeshi, river, *Af.* **198** L9
Chambois, *Fr.* **149** P7
Chamburi Kalat, *Pak.* **179** V4
Chamical, *Arg.* **134** J9
Chamizal National Memorial, *Tex.,
    U.S.* **105** V3
Ch'amo Hāyk, *Eth.* **203** H14
Chamoli, *India* **180** E7
Chamonix, *Fr.* **149** T15
Champagne, region, *Fr.* **149** P12
Champagnole, *Fr.* **149** S14
Champaign, *Ill., U.S.* **101** R6
Champasak, *Laos* **190** M12
Champéry, *Switz.* **152** C2
Champlain, Lake, *N.Y., Vt., U.S.*
    96 F12
Champotón, *Mex.* **117** J15
Chamrajnagar, *India* **181** Q5
Chamzinka, *Russ.* **158** K13
Chañaral, *Chile* **134** F6
Chança, river, *Port., Sp.* **146** K6
Chandalar, river, *Alas., U.S.* **113** E17
Chandeleur Islands, *La., U.S.*
    103 Q13
Chandeleur Sound, *La., U.S.*
    102 Q12
Chandigarh, *India* **180** D6
Chandler, *Ariz., U.S.* **109** U7
Chandler, *Okla., U.S.* **104** F11
Chandless, river, *S. Amer.* **132** G5
Chandpur, *Bangladesh* **180** J13
Chandrapur, *India* **180** L7
Ch'angam, *N. Korea* **186** L4
Changan, *N. Korea* **186** D10
Changanacheri, *India* **181** S5
Changane, river, *Mozambique*
    206 H12
Changbai Shan, *Jilin, China* **184** A16
Chang Chenmo Range, *China, India*
    178 M15
Changchon, *S. Korea* **186** M10
Changchun, *China* **183** E16
Changde, *Hunan, China* **185** P3
Ch'angdo, *N. Korea* **186** K9
Changdong, *N. Korea* **186** H9
Changdong, *S. Korea* **186** M10
Changdu see Qamdo, *China* **182** K8
Changfeng, *Anhui, China* **184** L8

Changgang, *N. Korea* **186** E8
Changhua, *Taiwan, China* **185** VII
Changhŭng, *N. Korea* **186** F10
Changhyŏn, *N. Korea* **186** F12
Changji, *China* **182** E5
Chang Jiang (Yangtze), river, *China*
    182 M10
Changjin, *N. Korea* **186** F8
Changjin, river, *N. Korea* **186** E9
Changjin-ho (Chosin Reservoir),
    N. Korea **186** F8
Changle, *Fujian, China* **185** T10
Changli, *Hebei, China* **184** D10
Changma'er see Changmar, *China*
    182 H2
Changmar (Changma'er), *China*
    182 H2
Changnyeong, *S. Korea* **187** S11
Changnyŏn, *N. Korea* **186** K5
Changping, *Beijing Shi, China* **184** C7
Changp'ung, *N. Korea* **186** L7
Ch'angp'yŏng, *N. Korea* **186** F11
Changsha, *Hunan, China* **185** Q4
Changshan, *Jiangxi, China* **185** Q9
Changshan Qundao, islands, *Liaoning,
    China* **184** D12
Changshu, *Jiangsu, China* **184** M11
Ch'angsŏng, *N. Korea* **186** F5
Changsu-ho, lake, *N. Korea* **186** L6
Changting, *Jiangxi, China* **185** T7
Changwon, *S. Korea* **187** S11
Changxing, *Zhejiang, China* **185** N10
Changxing Dao, *Liaoning, China*
    184 D11
Changyŏn, *N. Korea* **186** L5
Changyuan, *Henan, China* **184** H6
Changzhi, *Shanxi, China* **184** G5
Changzhi, *Shanxi, China* **184** G5
Changzhou, *Jiangsu, China* **184** M10
Chaniá (Canea, Cydonia), *Gr.*
    157 P13
Chanión, Kólpos, *Gr.* **157** P13
Channapatna, *India* **181** Q5
Channel Country, *Austral.* **214** G11
Channel Islands, *Calif., U.S.* **111** Y6
Channel Islands, *U.K.* **145** Z11
Channel Islands National Park, *Calif.,
    U.S.* **111** Y5
Channel-Port aux Basques, *Nfld. &
    Lab., Can.* **85** N23
Channel Rock, *Bahamas* **118** G12
Chantada, *Sp.* **146** C6
Chanthaburi, *Thai.* **191** N10
Chantilly, *Fr.* **149** P10
Chantrey Inlet, *Nunavut, Can.*
    85 G14
Chanute, *Kans., U.S.* **107** U9
Chão, Ilhéu, *Madeira, Port.* **208** N4
Chaochou, *Taiwan, China* **185** W11
Chao Hu, *Anhui, China* **184** M8
Chaohu, *Anhui, China* **184** M9
Chao Phraya, river, *Thai.* **190** L8
Chaoyang, *Guang., China* **185** V7
Chaoyang, *Liaoning, China* **184** B11
Chaozhou, *Guang., China* **185** V7
Chapadinha, *Braz.* **133** E15
Chapaev, *Kaz.* **176** D6
Chapak Goz̄ar, *Afghan.* **178** K4
Chapala, Lago de, *Mex.* **116** H10
Chapala, Lake, *N. Amer.* **82** N4
Chapcha, *Bhutan* **180** F12
Chapco, *Braz.* **132** N12
Chapel Hill, *N.C., U.S.* **98** H11
Chapelton, *Jam.* **122** J8
Chapleau, *Ont., Can.* **85** P17
Chapman, *Ala., U.S.* **103** M15
Chapman, *Kans., U.S.* **107** S8
Chappaquiddick Island, *Mass., U.S.*
    97 M15
Chappell, *Nebr., U.S.* **107** P2
Char, *India* **180** C6
Chara, *Russ.* **161** J17
Chara, river, *Russ.* **161** J17
Charadai, *Arg.* **134** G12
Charagua, *Bol.* **132** K8
Charambirá, Punta, *Col.* **130** F3
Charcot Fan, *Pac. Oc.* **241** X2
Charcot Island, *Antarctica* **230** G5
Chard, *Eng., U.K.* **145** W11
Chardonnières, *Haiti* **119** M15
Charduar, *India* **180** F14

Chari, river, *Af.* **198** G6
Chārīkār, *Afghan.* **178** M8
Chariton, *Iowa, U.S.* **107** Q12
Chariton, river, *Iowa, Mo., U.S.*
    107 Q12
Charity, *Guyana* **131** D14
Chärjew see Türkmenabat, *Turkm.*
    176 L10
Charleroi, *Belg.* **148** M12
Charles, Cape, *Va., U.S.* **98** F14
Charles City, *Iowa, U.S.* **106** M12
Charles Darwin Research Station,
    site, *Ecua.* **130** Q10
Charles Island, *Nunavut, Can.*
    85 H18
Charles Mound, peak, *Ill., U.S.*
    100 M4
Charleston, *Ill., U.S.* **101** S6
Charleston, *Miss., U.S.* **102** J11
Charleston, *Mo., U.S.* **107** V16
Charleston, *N.Z.* **217** M17
Charleston, *Oreg., U.S.* **110** J1
Charleston, *S.C., U.S.* **98** M10
Charleston, *W. Va., U.S.* **98** D8
Charles Town, *W. Va., U.S.* **98** C12
Charlestown, *Ind., U.S.* **101** T10
Charlestown, *St. Kitts and Nevis*
    123 C18
Charles Young Buffalo Soldiers
    National Monument, *Ohio, U.S.*
    101 R12
Charleville, *Qnsld., Austral.* **215** U13
Charleville (An Ráth), *Ire.* **145** T4
Charleville-Mézières, *Fr.* **149** N12
Charlevoix, *Mich., U.S.* **100** H10
Charlie Gap, *Arctic Oc.* **246** J8
Charlie-Gibbs Fracture Zone, *Atl. Oc.*
    240 G8
Charlieu, *Fr.* **149** T12
Charlotte, *Mich., U.S.* **100** M10
Charlotte, *N.C., U.S.* **98** J9
Charlotte, *Tex., U.S.* **105** S9
Charlotte Amalie, *Virgin Is., U.S.*
    122 N9
Charlotte Harbor, *Fla., U.S.* **99** W8
Charlottenberg, *Sw.* **142** K12
Charlottesville, *Va., U.S.* **98** E11
Charlotte Town see Gouyave, *Grenada*
    123 K22
Charlottetown, *P.E.I., Can.* **85** N22
Charlotteville, *Trinidad and Tobago*
    123 N19
Charlton Island, *Nunavut, Can.*
    85 M17
Charolles, *Fr.* **149** T12
Charsadda, *Pak.* **178** M10
Charters Towers, *Qnsld., Austral.*
    215 S13
Chartres, *Fr.* **149** Q9
Charyeongsanmaek, range, *S. Korea*
    187 P9
Chasan, *N. Korea* **186** J6
Chascomús, *Arg.* **134** M13
Chase, *Kans., U.S.* **107** T6
Chase City, *Va., U.S.* **98** F12
Chaska, *Minn., U.S.* **106** K11
Chasŏng, *N. Korea* **186** D8
Chassahowitzka, *Fla., U.S.* **99** T7
Chasseloup, Baie, *New Caledonia, Fr.*
    222 C6
Chateaubelair, *St. Vincent and the
    Grenadines* **123** K16
Chateaubriand, Baie du,
    New Caledonia, Fr. **222** C9
Châteaubriant, *Fr.* **149** R6
Châteaudun, *Fr.* **149** Q9
Château-Gontier, *Fr.* **149** R6
Château-la-Vallière, *Fr.* **149** R7
Châteaulin, *Fr.* **149** Q3
Châteauneuf-de-Randon, *Fr.*
    149 W11
Châteauneuf-en-Thymerais, *Fr.*
    149 P8
Châteauneuf-sur-Loire, *Fr.* **149** R10
Château-Renault, *Fr.* **149** R8
Châteauvillain, *Fr.* **149** Q12
Châteaux, Pointe des, *Guadeloupe, Fr.*
    123 E16
Châtel, *Fr.* **149** T15

Châtelet, *Belg.* **148** M12
Châtellerault, *Fr.* **149** S8
Chatfield, *Minn., U.S.* **106** L12
Chatham, *Eng., U.K.* **145** V15
Chatham, *Ill., U.S.* **101** R5
Chatham, *Mass., U.S.* **97** L16
Chatham, *N.B., Can.* **85** N21
Chatham, *N.Y., U.S.* **96** K11
Chatham, *Va., U.S.* **98** F11
Chatham Island, *Pac. Oc.* **218** P9
Chatham Islands, *Pac. Oc.* **218** P9
Chatham Rise, *Pac. Oc.* **242** P11
Chatham Strait, *Alas., U.S.* **113** L22
Châtillon, *Fr.* **149** R12
Châtillon-sur-Indre, *Fr.* **149** S8
Chatom, *Ala., U.S.* **103** M13
Chatra, *India* **180** H10
Chatsworth, *Ga., U.S.* **98** J4
Chattahoochee, *Fla., U.S.* **99** Q4
Chattahoochee, river, *U.S.* **87** K17
Chattanooga, *Tenn., U.S.* **103** G17
Chatyr-Tash, *Kyrg.* **178** F13
Châu Đốc, *Cambodia* **191** P12
Châu Đốc, *Vietnam* **191** P12
Chauk, *Myanmar* **190** H5
Chaukan Pass, *India* **180** F16
Chaumont, *Fr.* **149** Q13
Chaun Bay, *Arctic Oc.* **246** G6
Chaunskaya Guba, *Russ.* **161** C19
Chauny, *Fr.* **149** N11
Chavé, Baie, *Fr. Polynesia, Fr.*
    223 N23
Chaves, *Braz.* **133** C13
Chaves, *Port.* **146** D7
Chaychaktū, *Afghan.* **178** L4
Chayek, *Kyrg.* **178** E11
Ch'ayu, *N. Korea* **186** C12
Chayu see Zayü, *China* **182** L7
Cheaha Mountain, *Ala., U.S.*
    103 J16
Cheb, *Czech Rep.* **150** H9
Cheboksarskoye Vodokhranilishche,
    Russ. **158** H13
Cheboksary, *Russ.* **158** H13
Cheboygan, *Mich., U.S.* **100** G11
Chebsara, *Russ.* **158** F10
Chech, 'Erg, *Af.* **200** E9
Chechen', Ostrov, *Russ.* **159** T15
Chechnya, region, *Russ.* **159** T14
Checotah, *Okla., U.S.* **104** G13
Cheduba Island, *Myanmar* **190** J4
Cheektowaga, *N.Y., U.S.* **96** J5
Cheepie, *Qnsld., Austral.* **215** U13
Cheeyou, *Trinidad and Tobago*
    123 P23
Chehalis, *Wash., U.S.* **110** D3
Cheju see Jeju, *S. Korea* **187** W7
Cheju Island see Jeju Island, *Asia*
    168 G13
Chekichler, *Uzb.* **176** M6
Chelan, *Wash., U.S.* **110** B6
Chelan, Lake, *Wash., U.S.* **110** B6
Chelforó, *Arg.* **135** P9
Chełm, *Pol.* **151** F18
Chełmno, *Pol.* **151** C14
Chelmsford, *Eng., U.K.* **145** V15
Chelsea, *Okla., U.S.* **104** E13
Cheltenham, *Eng., U.K.* **145** U12
Chelyabinsk, *Russ.* **160** J8
Chelyuskin, *Russ.* **161** D14
Chemillé, *Fr.* **149** S6
Chemin Grenier, *Mauritius* **209** H19
Chemnitz, *Ger.* **150** G10
Chemult, *Oreg., U.S.* **110** J4
Chemung, river, *N.Y., Pa., U.S.* **96** L7
Chenab, river, *Pak.* **179** R9
Chenārān, *Iran* **175** B16
Cheney, *Wash., U.S.* **110** C9
Cheney Reservoir, *Kans., U.S.*
    107 U7
Chengalpattu, *India* **181** Q7
Chengbu, *Hunan, China* **185** S2
Chengchow see Zhengzhou, *Henan,
    China* **184** J5
Chengde, *Hebei, China* **184** B9
Chengdu, *China* **182** L10
Chengele, *India* **180** E15
Chenghai, *Guang., China* **185** V7
Chengkou, *China* **182** K11
Chengkung, *Taiwan, China* **185** V12
Chengmai, *China* **182** Q12

Chengshan Jiao, *Shand., China* **184** FI2
Chengwu, *Shand., China* **184** H7
Chengyang *see* Juxian, *Shand., China* **184** H9
Chennai (Madras), *India* **181** P7
Chenxi, *Hunan, China* **185** Q2
Chenzhou, *Hunan, China* **185** T4
Cheonan, *S. Korea* **187** P8
Cheongdo, *S. Korea* **187** RII
Cheongju, *S. Korea* **187** P9
Cheongsando, *island, S. Korea* **187** V8
Cheongsong, *S. Korea* **187** QI2
Cheongyang, *S. Korea* **187** Q8
Cheonsuman, *bay, S. Korea* **187** P7
Cheorwon, *S. Korea* **186** L8
Chepén, *Peru* **132** F2
Chépénéhe, *New Caledonia, Fr.* **222** C9
Chepes, *Arg.* **134** J9
Chequamegon Bay, *Wis., U.S.* **100** F4
Cheraw, *S.C., U.S.* **98** JIO
Cherbaniani Reef, *Ind. Oc.* **224** DIO
Cherbourg-Octeville, *Fr.* **149** N6
Cherepovets, *Russ.* **158** F9
Chergui, Chott ech, *Alg.* **200** BIO
Cherkasy, *Ukr.* **159** P6
Cherkessk, *Russ.* **159** TI2
Cherlak, *Russ.* **160** KIO
Chermenino, *Russ.* **158** FI2
Chernaya, *Russ.* **160** EIO
Chernihiv, *Ukr.* **158** M6
Cherni Vrŭkh, *peak, Bulg.* **155** JI3
Chernivtsi, *Ukr.* **159** Q3
Chernobyl' *see* Chornobyl', *Ukr.* **158** M5
Chernogorsk, *Russ.* **161** LI3
Chernyakhovsk, *Russ.* **158** J2
Chernyayevo, *Russ.* **161** KI9
Chernyshevskiy, *Russ.* **161** HI6
Cherokee, *Iowa, U.S.* **106** M9
Cherokee, *Okla., U.S.* **104** E9
Cherokees, Lake O' the, *Okla., U.S.* **104** EI4
Cherokee Sound, *Bahamas* **122** B6
Cherryfield, *Me., U.S.* **97** FI8
Cherry Island *see* Anuta, *Solomon Is.* **218** H7
Cherskiy, *Russ.* **161** DI9
Cherskiy Range, *Asia* **168** CII
Cherskogo, Khrebet, *Russ.* **161** FI8
Chersónisos Akrotíri, *Gr.* **157** PI3
Cherven Bryag, *Bulg.* **155** HI4
Chervonohrad, *Ukr.* **159** N2
Cherykaw, *Belarus* **158** L6
Chesaning, *Mich., U.S.* **100** LII
Chesapeake, *Va., U.S.* **98** FI4
Chesapeake Bay, *Md., Va., U.S.* **98** DI4
Chesha Bay, *Arctic Oc.* **247** CI8
Cheshskaya Guba, *Russ.* **160** E9
Cheshunt, *Eng., U.K.* **145** VI4
Chester, *Calif., U.S.* **III** N5
Chester, *Eng., U.K.* **145** SII
Chester, *Ill., U.S.* **101** U4
Chester, *Mont., U.S.* **108** B8
Chester, *Pa., U.S.* **96** Q9
Chester, *S.C., U.S.* **98** J9
Chester, *W. Va., U.S.* **98** A9
Chesterfield, *Eng., U.K.* **145** SI2
Chesterfield, Îles, *Coral Sea* **218** K6
Chesterfield Inlet, *Nunavut, Can.* **85** HI5
Chesterfield Inlet, town, *Nunavut, Can.* **85** HI5
Chesterton Range, *Austral.* **214** GI4
Chestertown, *Md., U.S.* **98** CI4
Chesuncook Lake, *Me., U.S.* **97** CI7
Chetamale, *India* **181** SI4
Chetek, *Wis., U.S.* **100** H3
Chetlat Island, *India* **181** Q3
Chetumal, *Mex.* **117** JI7
Chetumal Bay, *N. Amer.* **82** N7
Chetvertyy Kuril'skiy Proliv, *Russ.* **161** G23
Chevak, *Alas., U.S.* **112** HII
Chevanceaux, *Fr.* **149** V7
Chevelon Butte, peak, *Ariz., U.S.* **109** S8
Cheviot Hills, *Scot., U.K.* **145** NII

Ch'ew Bahir, *Eth.* **203** HI4
Chew Bahir, Lake, *Af.* **198** H9
Chewelah, *Wash., U.S.* **110** B8
Cheyenne, *Okla., U.S.* **104** G8
Cheyenne, *Wyo., U.S.* **108** KI3
Cheyenne, river, *U.S.* **106** L3
Cheyenne Bottoms, *Kans., U.S.* **107** T6
Cheyenne Wells, *Colo., U.S.* **109** NI6
Cheyne Bay, *Austral.* **214** L4
Chhâk Kâmpóng Saôm, bay, *Cambodia* **191** PII
Chhapra, *India* **180** GIO
Chhatarpur, *India* **180** H7
Chhêb Kândal, *Cambodia* **190** MI2
Chhim, *Leb.* **172** J6
Chhindwara, *India* **180** J6
Chhukha, *Bhutan* **180** FI2
Chi, river, *Thai.* **190** LIO
Chiang Mai, *Thai.* **190** J8
Chiang Rai, *Thai.* **190** H8
Chiaromonte, *It.* **153** NI3
Chiasso, *Switz.* **152** D4
Chiat'ura, *Rep. of Georgia* **171** BI7
Chiavari, *It.* **152** F4
Chiavenna, *It.* **152** C5
Chiayi, *Taiwan, China* **185** VII
Chiba, *Japan* **189** DI2
Chibemba, *Angola* **206** E6
Chibia, *Angola* **206** E5
Chibougamau, *Que., Can.* **85** NI9
Chiburi Shima, *Japan* **189** P7
Chicago, *Ill., U.S.* **101** N7
Chicago Heights, *Ill., U.S.* **101** P7
Chicapa, river, *Angola* **206** C8
Chichagof Island, *Alas., U.S.* **113** L22
Chichawatni, *Pak.* **179** RIO
Chicheng, *Hebei, China* **184** B7
Chichén Itzá, ruin, *Mex.* **117** HI6
Chichester, *Eng., U.K.* **145** WI3
Chichester Range, *Austral.* **214** F3
Chichi Jima Rettō (Beechey Group), *Japan* **189** XI4
Chickamauga, *Ga., U.S.* **98** J4
Chickamauga Lake, *Tenn., U.S.* **103** FI7
Chickasawhay, river, *Miss., U.S.* **103** MI3
Chickasaw National Recreation Area, *Okla., U.S.* **104** HII
Chickasha, *Okla., U.S.* **104** HIO
Chicksands, *Eng., U.K.* **145** UI3
Chiclayo, *Peru* **132** F2
Chico, *Calif., U.S.* **III** N4
Chico, river, *Arg.* **135** S9
Chicoma Mountain, *N. Mex., U.S.* **109** RI2
Chicomo, *Mozambique* **206** JI2
Chicopee, *Mass., U.S.* **97** KI3
Chief Joseph Dam, *Wash., U.S.* **110** B6
Chiefland, *Fla., U.S.* **99** S7
Chieri, *It.* **152** E3
Chiesanuova, *San Marino* **163** KI4
Chieti, *It.* **152** KIO
Chifeng, *N. Mongol, China* **184** A9
Chignik Lagoon, *Alas., U.S.* **113** MI3
Chihil Abdālān, Kōh-e, *Afghan.* **179** N3
Chihsing Yen, island, *Taiwan, China* **185** XII
Chihuahua, *Mex.* **116** D9
Chihuahuan Desert, *Mex.* **116** C9
Chikan, *Russ.* **161** KI5
Chikhachevo, *Russ.* **158** H6
Chikhli, *India* **180** K5
Chilas, *Pak.* **178** LII
Chilaw, *Sri Lanka* **181** T7
Chilca, *Peru* **132** H3
Childersburg, *Ala., U.S.* **103** KI6
Childress, *Tex., U.S.* **104** J7
Chile, *S. Amer.* **134** M6
Chile Basin, *Pac. Oc.* **243** P22
Chilecito, *Arg.* **134** H8
Chile Fracture Zone, *Pac. Oc.* **243** NI8
Chile Ridge, *Pac. Oc.* **248** RII
Chile Rise, *Pac. Oc.* **243** PI9
Chile Trench, *Pac. Oc.* **243** Q22
Chililabombwe, *Zambia* **206** DIO
Chilka Lake, *India* **180** LIO

Chillán, *Chile* **134** M6
Chillicothe, *Ill., U.S.* **101** P5
Chillicothe, *Mo., U.S.* **107** RII
Chillicothe, *Ohio, U.S.* **101** SI3
Chillicothe, *Tex., U.S.* **104** J8
Chiloé, Isla Grande de, *Chile* **135** R6
Chiloquin, *Oreg., U.S.* **110** K4
Chilpancingo, *Mex.* **116** KII
Chiltern Hills, *Eng., U.K.* **145** VI3
Chilton, *Wis., U.S.* **100** K7
Chilumba, *Malawi* **207** CI3
Chimacum, *Wash., U.S.* **110** B3
Chimbas, *Arg.* **134** K9
Chimborazo, peak, *Ecua.* **130** K3
Chimbote, *Peru* **132** G2
Chimboy, *Uzb.* **176** J9
Chimney Rock National Historic Site, *Nebr., U.S.* **107** PI
Chimney Rock National Monument, *Colo., U.S.* **109** QII
Chimoio, *Mozambique* **206** FI2
Chinandega, *Nicar.* **117** MI7
China, *Asia* **182** H5
China Point, *Calif., U.S.* **III** Z8
Chinati Peak, *Tex., U.S.* **105** QI
Chincha Alta, *Peru* **132** H3
Chinchilla de Monte Aragón, *Sp.* **147** JI3
Chincoteague, *Va., U.S.* **98** EI5
Chincoteague Bay, *Md., U.S.* **98** DI5
Chinde, *Mozambique* **207** FI3
Chindwin, river, *Myanmar* **190** E5
Chingola, *Zambia* **206** DII
Chinhoyi, *Zimb.* **206** FII
Chiniot, *Pak.* **179** QII
Chinko, river, *Af.* **198** H8
Chinle, *Ariz., U.S.* **109** R9
Chino, *Japan* **189** PII
Chinon, *Fr.* **149** S7
Chinook, *Mont., U.S.* **108** B9
Chinook Trough, *Pac. Oc.* **242** EII
Chino Valley, *Ariz., U.S.* **109** S6
Chinsali, *Zambia* **206** CI2
Chinsong, *N. Korea* **186** D8
Chioggia, *It.* **152** E8
Chíos, *Gr.* **157** HI6
Chíos (Chios), island, *Gr.* **157** HI6
Chios *see* Chíos, island, *Gr.* **157** HI6
Chipata, *Zambia* **206** DI2
Chiping, *Shand., China* **184** G7
Chipley, *Fla., U.S.* **99** Q3
Chiplun, *India* **180** M3
Chippenham, *Eng., U.K.* **145** VI2
Chippewa, river, *Wis., U.S.* **100** G3
Chippewa, Lake, *Wis., U.S.* **100** G3
Chippewa Falls, *Wis., U.S.* **100** H3
Chiquián, *Peru* **132** G3
Chiquimula, *Guatemala* **117** LI6
Chiquinata Bay, *S. Amer.* **128** H4
Chiquinquirá, *Col.* **130** E5
Chirchiq, *Uzb.* **177** KI3
Chiredzi, *Zimb.* **206** GI2
Chiricahua National Monument, *Ariz., U.S.* **109** V9
Chiricahua Peak, *Ariz., U.S.* **109** V9
Chirikof Island, *Alas., U.S.* **113** NI4
Chirinda, *Russ.* **161** GI4
Chiriquí, Golfo de, *Pan.* **117** P2O
Chiromo, *Malawi* **207** FI3
Chirpan, *Bulg.* **155** JI5
Chirripó, Cerro, *C.R.* **117** NI9
Chisasibi, *Que., Can.* **85** MI8
Chishan, *Taiwan, China* **185** WII
Chisholm, *Minn., U.S.* **106** FI2
Chisht-e Sharīf, *Afghan.* **178** M3
Chishtian Mandi, *Pak.* **179** RII
Chişinău, *Mold.* **159** R4
Chişineu Criş, *Rom.* **154** CII
Chisos Mountains, *Tex., U.S.* **105** R3
Chissioua Mtsamboro, island, *Mayotte, Fr.* **209** NI7
Chistopol', *Russ.* **158** JI5
Chita, *Russ.* **161** LI7
Chitado, *Angola* **206** F5
Chitato, *Angola* **206** B8
Chitembo, *Angola* **206** D6
Chitipa, *Malawi* **206** CI2
Chitose, *Japan* **188** GI3
Chitradurga, *India* **181** P5
Chitral, *Pak.* **178** LIO

Chitré, *Pan.* **117** P2I
Chittagong, *Bangladesh* **180** JI3
Chittaurgarh, *India* **180** H4
Chittoor, *India* **181** P6
Chitungwiza, *Zimb.* **206** FII
Chiumbe, river, *Angola* **206** C8
Chivasso, *It.* **152** E3
Chivilcoy, *Arg.* **134** LI2
Chlef, *Alg.* **200** AIO
Chloride, *Ariz., U.S.* **109** R5
Chôâm Ksant, *Cambodia* **190** MII
Choc Bay, *St. Lucia* **123** JI4
Chocolate Mountains, *Calif., U.S.* **III** YI2
Choctawhatchee, river, *Fla., U.S.* **99** Q3
Choctawhatchee Bay, *Fla., U.S.* **99** Q2
Ch'o-do, island, *N. Korea* **186** K4
Chodo, island, *S. Korea* **187** U8
Chodzież, *Pol.* **151** DI3
Choele Choel, *Arg.* **135** P9
Chŏgyuryŏng-sanmaek, range, *N. Korea* **186** K6
Choirokoitia, *Cyprus* **162** Q8
Choiseul, *St. Lucia* **123** LI3
Choiseul, island, *Solomon Is.* **221** LI6
Choiseul Sound, *Falk. Is., U.K.* **135** WI2
Chŏjak, *N. Korea* **186** M5
Chojna, *Pol.* **150** DII
Chojnice, *Pol.* **151** CI3
Choke Canyon Reservoir, *Tex., U.S.* **105** T9
Chokoloskee, *Fla., U.S.* **99** X9
Chokurdakh, *Russ.* **161** DI8
Chợ Lâu, *Vietnam* **191** PI3
Cholet, *Fr.* **149** S6
Cholpon-Ata, *Kyrg.* **178** DI3
Choluteca, *Hond.* **117** LI7
Choma, *Zambia* **206** FIO
Chomutov, *Czech Rep.* **150** GIO
Ch'ŏnam, *N. Korea* **186** K7
Ch'ŏnam, *N. Korea* **186** K9
Chon Buri, *Thai.* **191** N9
Chonchi, *Chile* **135** R6
Chŏnch'ŏn, *N. Korea* **186** F7
Chone, *Ecua.* **130** J2
Ch'ŏngdan, *N. Korea* **186** M6
Ch'ŏngjin, *N. Korea* **186** CI3
Chŏngju, *N. Korea* **186** H5
Chŏng Kal, *Cambodia* **190** MII
Chongli, *Hebei, China* **184** B7
Chongming, *Shanghai Shi, China* **184** MI2
Chongming Dao, *Shanghai Shi, China* **184** MI2
Chŏngp'yŏng, *N. Korea* **186** H9
Chongqing, *China* **182** LII
Chongqing Shi, *China* **184** MI
Ch'ŏngsong, *N. Korea* **186** F4
Chongsŏng, *N. Korea* **186** AI3
Chongyang, *Hubei, China* **185** P5
Chongyi, *Jiangxi, China* **185** T5
Ch'ŏnma, *N. Korea* **186** G5
Ch'ŏnma, *N. Korea* **186** G5
Ch'ŏnma-san, peak, *N. Korea* **186** G5
Ch'ŏnnae, *N. Korea* **186** J8
Chonogol, *Mongolia* **183** DI3
Chonos, Archipiélago de los, *Chile* **135** S6
Ch'ŏnsu, *N. Korea* **186** DII
Chóra Sfakíon, *Gr.* **157** QI3
Chornobyl' (Chernobyl'), *Ukr.* **158** M5
Chornomors'ke, *Ukr.* **159** S7
Chorregon, *Qnsld., Austral.* **215** TI2
Chorrillos, *Peru* **132** H3
Chortkiv, *Ukr.* **159** P3
Ch'ŏrwŏn, *N. Korea* **186** L8
Ch'osan, *N. Korea* **186** E6
Chosin Reservoir *see* Changjin-ho, *N. Korea* **186** F8
Chos Malal, *Arg.* **135** N7
Chota Nagpur Plateau, *Asia* **168** J8
Choteau, *Mont., U.S.* **108** C7
Chowan, river, *N.C., U.S.* **98** GI3
Chowchilla, *Calif., U.S.* **III** T6
Choyang, *N. Korea* **186** G6

Choybalsan, *Mongolia* **182** DI2
Choyr, *Mongolia* **182** DII
Christ Church, site, *Barbados* **123** LI9
Christchurch, *Eng., U.K.* **145** XI2
Christchurch, *N.Z.* **217** PI7
Christian, Point, *Pitcairn I., U.K.* **223** Q23
Christiana, *Jam.* **122** J8
Christianí, island, *Gr.* **157** NI5
Christiansburg, *Va., U.S.* **98** F9
Christiansted, *Virgin Is., U.S.* **122** Q3
Christmas Creek, *W. Aust., Austral.* **215** R6
Christmas Island *see* Kiritimati, *Kiribati* **218** GI2
Christmas Lake Valley, *Oreg., U.S.* **110** J6
Christmas Ridge, *Pac. Oc.* **243** JI3
Christmas Rise, *Ind. Oc.* **225** JI5
Christopher, *Ill., U.S.* **101** U5
Christoval, *Tex., U.S.* **105** N7
Chrysí, island, *Gr.* **157** RI6
Chrysoúpoli, *Gr.* **157** BI4
Chub Cay, *Bahamas* **118** DII
Chubut, river, *Arg.* **135** R8
Chudleigh Park, *Qnsld., Austral.* **215** SI3
Chudovo, *Russ.* **158** F7
Chudskoye Ozero (Peipus, Lake), *Russ.* **158** G5
Chugach Mountains, *Alas., U.S.* **113** JI8
Chuginadak Island, *Alas., U.S.* **112** P8
Chugwater, *Wyo., U.S.* **108** JI3
Chuhuyiv, *Ukr.* **159** P9
Chuí, *Braz.* **132** RII
Chukai, *Malaysia* **191** TIO
Chukchi Borderland, *Arctic Oc.* **246** K8
Chukchi Peninsula, *Asia* **168** AI2
Chukchi Plain, *Arctic Oc.* **246** J8
Chukchi Plateau, *Arctic Oc.* **246** K8
Chukchi Range, *Asia* **168** AI2
Chukchi Sea, *Arctic Oc.* **246** J6
Chukchi Shelf, *Arctic Oc.* **246** J6
Chukhloma, *Russ.* **158** GII
Chukotskiy Poluostrov, *Russ.* **161** A2I
Chukotskoye Nagor'ye, *Russ.* **161** B2O
Chula Vista, *Calif., U.S.* **III** Z9
Chumar, *India* **180** C6
Chumatang, *India* **179** NI5
Chumbicha, *Arg.* **134** H9
Chumikan, *Russ.* **161** J2O
Chumphon, *Thai.* **191** P8
Chun'an, *Zhejiang, China* **185** PIO
Chuncheon, *S. Korea* **186** M9
Chunggang, *N. Korea* **186** C8
Chunghwa, *N. Korea* **186** K6
Chungju, *S. Korea* **187** PIO
Chungjuho, lake, *S. Korea* **187** P9
Chungli, *Taiwan, China* **185** UI2
Chungp'yŏngjang, *N. Korea* **186** EIO
Chŭngsan, *N. Korea* **186** GII
Chŭngsan, *N. Korea* **186** J5
Chungyang Shanmo, *Taiwan, China* **185** VI2
Chunnel, *Fr., U.K.* **145** WI6
Chun Spur, *Ind. Oc.* **248** BII
Chunya, *Tanzania* **203** NI3
Chupara Point, *Trinidad and Tobago* **123** N23
Chuquibamba, *Peru* **132** J5
Chuquicamata, *Chile* **134** D7
Chur, *Switz.* **152** B5
Churachandpur, *India* **180** HI4
Churchill, *Man., Can.* **85** KI4
Churchill, river, *N. Amer.* **85** KI4
Churchill, Cape, *Man., Can.* **85** KI5
Churchill Falls, *Nfld. & Lab., Can.* **85** L2I
Churchill Lake, *Me., U.S.* **97** CI6
Churchill Lake, *Sask., Can.* **84** LI2
Churchill Mountains, *Antarctica* **231** LI3
Church of St. Anne, *Vatican City* **163** PI7
Church of St. Stephen, *Vatican City* **163** QI5

Church Point, *La., U.S.* **102** P8
Churuguara, *Venez.* **130** B8
Chushul, *India* **180** C7
Chuska Mountains, *Ariz., N. Mex., U.S.* **109** R9
Chusovoy, *Russ.* **160** H8
Chuuk (Truk Islands), *F.S.M.* **220** Q6
Chuzhou, *Anhui, China* **184** L9
Ciales, *P.R., U.S.* **122** M3
Cianjur, *Indonesia* **192** M8
Çiçekdaği, *Turk.* **170** E9
Cicero, *Ill., U.S.* **101** N7
Cicia, island, *Fiji* **222** H8
Cidade Velha, *Cabo Verde* **209** E16
Cide, *Turk.* **170** C8
Ciechanów, *Pol.* **151** D16
Ciego de Ávila, *Cuba* **118** H10
Ciempozuelos, *Sp.* **146** G11
Ciénaga, *Col.* **130** B5
Cienfuegos, *Cuba* **118** H8
Cieszyn, *Pol.* **151** H14
Cieza, *Sp.* **147** K13
Çiftlik, *Turk.* **170** G9
Cihanbeyli, *Turk.* **170** F8
Cijara, Embalse de, *Sp.* **146** H9
Çikës, Maja e, *Alban.* **154** L10
Cikobia, island, *Fiji* **222** F8
Cilacap, *Indonesia* **192** M9
Cilaos, *Réunion, Fr.* **209** G16
Çıldır, *Turk.* **171** D17
Çıldır Gölü, *Turk.* **171** D17
Cili, *Hunan, China* **185** P2
Cilician Gates, *Turk.* **170** H10
Cill an Dísirt *see* Killadysert, *Ire.* **145** T3
Cill Chainnigh *see* Kilkenny, *Ire.* **145** T6
Cill Chaoi *see* Kilkee, *Ire.* **145** T3
Cill Charthaigh (Kilcar), *Ire.* **145** P4
Cill Choca *see* Kilcock, *Ire.* **145** S6
Cille Bhrìghde, *Scot., U.K.* **144** K6
Cill Mhantáin *see* Wicklow, *Ire.* **145** S7
Cill Orglan *see* Killorglin, *Ire.* **145** U3
Çilov, *Azerb.* **171** D24
Cimarron, *Kans., U.S.* **107** U4
Cimarron, *N. Mex., U.S.* **109** Q13
Cimarron, river, *U.S.* **86** H12
Cimolais, *It.* **152** C8
Cimone, Monte, *It.* **152** G6
Cîmpina, *Rom.* **155** E15
Cîmpulung, *Rom.* **155** E14
Çınar, *Turk.* **171** H15
Cinaruco, river, *Venez.* **130** E9
Cincinnati, *Ohio, U.S.* **101** S11
Cinco Balas, Cayos, *Cuba* **118** J9
Cîndrelu, peak, *Rom.* **155** E13
Çine, *Turk.* **170** G3
Cinéma d'Été, *Monaco* **163** B23
Cinnabar Mountain, *Idaho, U.S.* **108** H3
Cinn Mhara *see* Kinvara, *Ire.* **145** S4
Cintegabelle, *Fr.* **149** Y9
Cinto, Monte, *Fr.* **152** J4
Cioara Doiceşti, *Rom.* **155** F17
Čiovo, island, *Croatia* **154** G6
Cipangu Basin, *Pac. Oc.* **242** E8
Çırçır, *Turk.* **170** E12
Circle, *Alas., U.S.* **113** F18
Circle, *Mont., U.S.* **108** C12
Circleville, *Ohio, U.S.* **101** R13
Cirebon, *Indonesia* **192** L9
Cirencester, *Eng., U.K.* **145** V12
Ciscaucasia, *Eur.* **140** H13
Cisco, *Tex., U.S.* **104** M9
Cisco, *Utah, U.S.* **109** N9
Cisnădie, *Rom.* **155** E14
Cisneros, *Col.* **130** E5
Cistern Point, *Bahamas* **118** F11
Citronelle, *Ala., U.S.* **103** N13
Cittadella, *It.* **152** D7
Città di Castello, *It.* **152** H8
Cittanova, *It.* **153** R13
City of Rocks National Reserve, *Idaho, U.S.* **108** J5
Ciucea, *Rom.* **154** C12
Ciudad Acuña, *Mex.* **116** D11
Ciudad Altamirano, *Mex.* **116** J11
Ciudad Bolívar, *Venez.* **130** D11
Ciudad Camargo, *Mex.* **116** D9
Ciudad Cortés, *C.R.* **117** N19

Ciudad del Carmen, *Mex.* **117** J15
Ciudad del Este, *Parag.* **132** M11
Ciudad Guayana, *Venez.* **130** C12
Ciudad Guerrero, *Mex.* **116** D8
Ciudad Guzmán, *Mex.* **116** H10
Ciudad Hidalgo, *Mex.* **117** L15
Ciudad Juárez, *Mex.* **116** B9
Ciudad Madero, *Mex.* **116** G12
Ciudad Mante, *Mex.* **116** G12
Ciudad Obregón, *Mex.* **116** D7
Ciudad Piar, *Venez.* **130** D12
Ciudad Real, *Sp.* **146** H10
Ciudad-Rodrigo, *Sp.* **146** F7
Ciudad Valles, *Mex.* **116** G12
Ciudad Victoria, *Mex.* **116** G12
Ciutadella de Menorca, *Sp.* **147** G19
Civa Burnu, *Turk.* **170** C11
Civita Castellana, *It.* **152** K8
Civitanova Marche, *It.* **152** H10
Civitavecchia, *It.* **152** K7
Civray, *Fr.* **149** T7
Çivril, *Turk.* **170** G5
Cixian, *Hebei, China* **184** G6
Cizre, *Turk.* **171** H16
Clacton-on-Sea, *Eng., U.K.* **145** U15
Clair Engle Lake, *Calif., U.S.* **110** M3
Clairton, *Pa., U.S.* **96** P3
Clairview, *Qnsld., Austral.* **215** T15
Clam Lake, *Wis., U.S.* **100** F4
Clanton, *Ala., U.S.* **103** K15
Clare, *Mich., U.S.* **100** K10
Clare Island, *Ire.* **145** R3
Claremont, *Jam.* **122** H9
Claremont, *N.H., U.S.* **97** H13
Claremore, *Okla., U.S.* **104** F13
Clarence, river, *N.Z.* **217** N18
Clarence Island, *Antarctica* **230** B4
Clarence Town, *Bahamas* **119** G14
Clarendon, *Ark., U.S.* **102** G10
Clarendon, *Tex., U.S.* **104** H6
Clarie Coast, *Antarctica* **231** Q19
Clarinda, *Iowa, U.S.* **107** Q10
Clarion, *Iowa, U.S.* **106** M11
Clarion, *Pa., U.S.* **96** M4
Clarión, Isla, *Mex.* **116** H4
Clarion Fracture Zone, *Pac. Oc.* **243** H15
Clark, *S. Dak., U.S.* **106** K7
Clark, Lake, *Alas., U.S.* **113** K15
Clark Basin, *Atl. Oc.* **241** N3
Clarke Island, *Austral.* **214** L8
Clarke Range, *Austral.* **214** E14
Clark Fork, *Idaho, U.S.* **108** B4
Clark Fork, river, *Mont., U.S.* **108** D6
Clark Island *see* Moa Island, *Qnsld., Austral.* **215** N12
Clark Mountain, *Calif., U.S.* **111** V11
Clarks, *La., U.S.* **102** L8
Clarksburg, *W. Va., U.S.* **98** C9
Clarksdale, *Miss., U.S.* **102** H10
Clarks Fork, river, *Mont., Wyo., U.S.* **108** F9
Clarkson, *Nebr., U.S.* **107** P8
Clarkston, *Wash., U.S.* **110** D9
Clarks Town, *Jam.* **122** H8
Clarksville, *Ark., U.S.* **102** F7
Clarksville, *Tenn., U.S.* **103** E14
Clarksville, *Tex., U.S.* **104** K14
Clatskanie, *Oreg., U.S.* **110** E2
Claude, *Tex., U.S.* **104** G6
Clauzetto, *It.* **152** C9
Claxton, *Ga., U.S.* **99** N8
Claxton Bay, *Trinidad and Tobago* **123** Q22
Clay, *Ky., U.S.* **103** C14
Clay Center, *Kans., U.S.* **107** S8
Clayton, *Ala., U.S.* **103** M17
Clayton, *Ga., U.S.* **98** J6
Clayton, *Idaho, U.S.* **108** F5
Clayton, *La., U.S.* **102** M9
Clayton, *N. Mex., U.S.* **109** Q15
Clayton, *N.Y., U.S.* **96** G8
Clayton, *Okla., U.S.* **104** H13
Clayton Lake, *Me., U.S.* **97** B16
Clearbrook, *Minn., U.S.* **106** F9
Clear Creek, *Tex., U.S.* **104** K11
Clearfield, *Pa., U.S.* **96** M5
Clear Island *see* Cléire, *Ire.* **145** V3
Clear Lake, *Calif., U.S.* **111** Q3
Clear Lake, *Iowa, U.S.* **106** M11
Clear Lake, *S. Dak., U.S.* **106** K8

Clear Lake, *Wash., U.S.* **110** B4
Clear Lake, *Wis., U.S.* **100** H2
Clear Lake Reservoir, *Calif., U.S.* **110** L5
Clearmont, *Wyo., U.S.* **108** F12
Clearwater, *Fla., U.S.* **99** U7
Clearwater, *Wash., U.S.* **110** C2
Clearwater, river, *Alb. & Sask., Can.* **84** K11
Clearwater, river, *Idaho, Wash., U.S.* **108** D3
Clearwater Mountains, *Idaho, U.S.* **108** D4
Cleburne, *Tex., U.S.* **104** M11
Cle Elum, *Wash., U.S.* **110** C5
Cleethorpes, *Eng., U.K.* **145** S13
Cléire (Clear Island), *Ire.* **145** V3
Clelles, *Fr.* **149** V13
Clemson, *S.C., U.S.* **98** K7
Clendenin, *W. Va., U.S.* **98** D8
Cleopatra Needle, peak, *Philippines* **193** E13
Clermont, *Fr.* **149** N10
Clermont, *Qnsld., Austral.* **215** T14
Clermont-Ferrand, *Fr.* **149** U11
Clervaux, *Lux.* **162** G9
Clervé, river, *Lux.* **162** H9
Cles, *It.* **152** C7
Cleveland, *Miss., U.S.* **102** J10
Cleveland, *Ohio, U.S.* **101** N14
Cleveland, *Okla., U.S.* **104** F12
Cleveland, *Tenn., U.S.* **103** K10
Cleveland, *Tex., U.S.* **105** Q14
Cleveland, *Wis., U.S.* **100** K7
Cleveland, Mount, *Mont., U.S.* **108** A6
Cleveland Hills, *Eng., U.K.* **145** Q12
Clew Bay, *Ire.* **145** R3
Clewiston, *Fla., U.S.* **99** V9
Clifden (An Clochán), *Ire.* **145** R3
Cliff, *N. Mex., U.S.* **109** U10
Clifton, *Ariz., U.S.* **109** U9
Clifton, *Bahamas* **122** B10
Clifton, *Kans., U.S.* **107** S8
Clifton, *Tex., U.S.* **105** N11
Clifton Forge, *Va., U.S.* **98** E10
Clifton Hills, *S. Aust., Austral.* **215** U10
Clinch, river, *Tenn., Va., U.S.* **103** E19
Clingmans Dome, *N.C., Tenn., U.S.* **103** F19
Clint, *Tex., U.S.* **105** W3
Clinton, *Ark., U.S.* **102** F8
Clinton, *Ill., U.S.* **101** R6
Clinton, *Ind., U.S.* **101** R7
Clinton, *Iowa, U.S.* **107** N15
Clinton, *Ky., U.S.* **102** D12
Clinton, *Miss., U.S.* **102** L11
Clinton, *Mo., U.S.* **107** T11
Clinton, *N.C., U.S.* **98** J12
Clinton, *Okla., U.S.* **104** G9
Clinton, *S.C., U.S.* **98** K8
Clintonville, *Wis., U.S.* **100** J6
Clipperton, island, *Pac. Oc.* **219** E19
Clipperton Fracture Zone, *Pac. Oc.* **243** J15
Clipperton Seamounts, *Pac. Oc.* **243** H19
Cliza, *Bol.* **132** K7
Cloates, Point, *Austral.* **214** F1
Cloch na Rón *see* Roundstone, *Ire.* **145** R3
Clonagh, *Qnsld., Austral.* **215** S11
Clonakilty Bay, *Ire.* **145** V4
Cloncurry, river, *Austral.* **214** D11
Cloncurry Plateau, *Austral.* **214** E11
Clonmany (Cluain Maine), *Ire.* **145** N6
Clonmel (Cluain Meala), *Ire.* **145** U5
Cloppenburg, *Ger.* **150** D6
Cloquet, *Minn., U.S.* **106** G12
Cloud Peak, *Wyo., U.S.* **108** F11
Clover, *S.C., U.S.* **98** J8
Cloverdale, *Calif., U.S.* **111** Q3
Cloverport, *Ky., U.S.* **103** C15
Clovis, *Calif., U.S.* **111** T6
Clovis, *N. Mex., U.S.* **109** S15
Cluain Cearbán *see* Louisburgh, *Ire.* **145** R3
Cluain Maine *see* Clonmany, *Ire.* **145** N6

Cluain Meala *see* Clonmel, *Ire.* **145** U5
Cluj-Napoca, *Rom.* **155** C13
Clun, *Eng., U.K.* **145** T10
Cluses, *Fr.* **149** T14
Clusone, *It.* **152** D5
Clutha, river, *N.Z.* **217** Q16
Clyde, *Kans., U.S.* **107** S7
Clyde, *Ohio, U.S.* **101** P13
Clyde, *Tex., U.S.* **104** M8
Clyde, Firth of, *Scot., U.K.* **145** N8
Clyde Inlet, *Nunavut, Can.* **85** E18
Clyde River, *Nunavut, Can.* **85** E18
Cnossus *see* Knossós, ruin, *Gr.* **157** Q15
Coachella, *Calif., U.S.* **111** Y11
Coachella Canal, *Calif., U.S.* **111** Y11
Coahoma, *Tex., U.S.* **104** M6
Coakley Cay, *Bahamas* **122** F8
Coalcomán, *Mex.* **116** J10
Coal Creek, *N.Z.* **217** Q16
Coaldale, *Nev., U.S.* **111** R8
Coalgate, *Okla., U.S.* **104** H12
Coalinga, *Calif., U.S.* **111** U6
Coalville, *Eng., U.K.* **145** T12
Coamo, *P.R., U.S.* **122** N3
Coari, *Braz.* **132** E8
Coari, river, *Braz.* **132** E8
Coari, river, *S. Amer.* **128** E5
Coastal Plain, *U.S.* **87** K19
Coast and Geodetic Survey Seamount Province, *Pac. Oc.* **243** D13
Coast Mountains, *N. Amer.* **82** F3
Coast Range, *S. Amer.* **128** A5
Coast Ranges, *N. Amer.* **82** H3
Coats Island, *Nunavut, Can.* **85** J16
Coats Land, region, *Antarctica* **230** E10
Coatzacoalcos, *Mex.* **117** J14
Cobalt, *Ont., Can.* **85** P18
Cobán, *Guatemala* **117** K16
Cobar, *N.S.W., Austral.* **215** W13
Cobia, island, *Fiji* **222** G8
Cobija, *Bol.* **132** G6
Coborriu, *Sp.* **162** L5
Cobourg Peninsula, *Austral.* **214** A8
Cobre, *Nev., U.S.* **110** M12
Côbuè, *Mozambique* **207** D13
Coburg, *Ger.* **150** G8
Coburg Island, *Nunavut, Can.* **85** D16
Coca, *Sp.* **146** E10
Cocanada *see* Kakinada, *India* **180** M8
Cochabamba, *Bol.* **132** K7
Coche, Isla, *Venez.* **121** J14
Cochin *see* Kochi, *India* **181** R5
Cochinoca, *Arg.* **134** D9
Cochinos, Bahía de, *Cuba* **118** H7
Cochran, *Ga., U.S.* **99** N6
Cochrane, *Ont., Can.* **85** N17
Cockburn Harbour, *Turks & Caicos Is.* **119** J17
Cockburn Town, *Bahamas* **122** E11
Cockburn Town, *Turks & Caicos Is.* **119** J18
Cocklebiddy Motel, *W. Aust., Austral.* **215** W6
Cockroach Island, *Virgin Is., U.S.* **122** M7
Cockscomb Point, *Amer. Samoa, U.S.* **222** L7
Coco, river, *N. Amer.* **117** L19
Coco, Cayo, *Cuba* **118** H10
Coco, Isla del, *C.R.* **117** P22
Cocoa, *Fla., U.S.* **99** T9
Cocoa Island, *Mauritius* **209** J19
Coco Channel, *India* **181** P14
Coco-de-Mer Seamounts, *Ind. Oc.* **224** D2
Coconut Point, *Amer. Samoa, U.S.* **222** M7
Cocos Basin, *Ind. Oc.* **225** H14
Cocos Bay, *Trinidad and Tobago* **123** P24
Cocos Island, *Guam, U.S.* **220** E10
Cocos Island, *N. Amer.* **82** R7
Cocos-Keeling Rise, *Ind. Oc.* **225** J14
Cocos Lagoon, *Guam, U.S.* **220** E10
Cocos Plain, *Ind. Oc.* **225** G14

Cocos Ridge, *Pac. Oc.* **243** J21
Cod, Cape, *Mass., U.S.* **97** L16
Coda Cavallo, Capo, *It.* **152** M5
Codajás, *Braz.* **132** E8
Codigoro, *It.* **152** F8
Cod Island, *Nfld. & Lab., Can.* **85** J21
Codlea, *Rom.* **155** E15
Codó, *Braz.* **133** E15
Codogno, *It.* **152** E5
Codrington, *Antigua and Barbuda* **121** B16
Codrington, Mount, *Antarctica* **231** C19
Cody, *Nebr., U.S.* **106** M4
Cody, *Wyo., U.S.* **108** F10
Coeburn, *Va., U.S.* **98** F7
Coën, *Qnsld., Austral.* **215** P12
Coëtlogon, Passe du, *New Caledonia, Fr.* **222** C8
Coeur d'Alene, *Idaho, U.S.* **108** C3
Coeur d'Alene Lake, *Idaho, U.S.* **108** C3
Coevorden, *Neth.* **148** H14
Coffeyville, *Kans., U.S.* **107** V9
Coffin Bay, *Austral.* **214** K9
Coffin Group *see* Haha Jima Rettō, *Japan* **189** X14
Coffs Harbour, *N.S.W., Austral.* **215** W15
Cofrentes, *Sp.* **147** H14
Coghinas, Lago del, *It.* **152** M4
Cognac, *Fr.* **149** U7
Cogne, *It.* **152** D2
Cogollos, *Sp.* **146** D11
Cohagen, *Mont., U.S.* **108** C11
Cohoes, *N.Y., U.S.* **96** J11
Coiba, Isla de, *Pan.* **117** P20
Coiba Island, *N. Amer.* **82** Q8
Coig, river, *Arg.* **135** W8
Coihaique, *Chile* **135** T7
Coimbatore, *India* **181** R5
Coimbra, *Port.* **146** F5
Coín, *Sp.* **146** M9
Coipasa, Salar de, *Bol.* **132** K6
Cojimíes, Boca de, *Ecua.* **130** J2
Cokato, *Minn., U.S.* **106** J10
Cokeville, *Wyo., U.S.* **108** J8
Colac, *Vic., Austral.* **215** Z12
Colatina, *Braz.* **133** L16
Colberger Heide, *Greenland, Den.* **82** D10
Colby, *Kans., U.S.* **107** S4
Colchester, *Eng., U.K.* **145** U15
Cold Bay, *Alas., U.S.* **112** N11
Cold Spring, *Minn., U.S.* **106** J10
Coldwater, *Kans., U.S.* **107** V5
Coldwater, *Mich., U.S.* **101** N10
Coldwater, river, *Miss., U.S.* **102** H11
Coldwater Creek, *Okla., Tex., U.S.* **104** E4
Colebrook, *N.H., U.S.* **97** F14
Coleman, *Mich., U.S.* **100** K11
Coleman, *Tex., U.S.* **104** M8
Coleraine, *Minn., U.S.* **106** F11
Coleraine (Cúil Rathain), *N. Ire., U.K.* **145** P6
Coles, Punta, *Peru* **132** K5
Colesberg, *S. Af.* **206** L9
Cole's Cave, site, *Barbados* **123** K19
Colfax, *Calif., U.S.* **111** Q5
Colfax, *Iowa, U.S.* **107** P12
Colfax, *La., U.S.* **102** M8
Colfax, *Wash., U.S.* **110** D8
Colhué Huapí, Lago, *Arg.* **135** S9
Colico, *It.* **152** C5
Colídor, *Braz.* **132** G11
Colihaut, *Dominica* **123** E18
Colima, *Mex.* **116** J9
Colinas, *Braz.* **133** F15
Colison Point, *British Virgin Is., U.K.* **122** R8
Coll, island, *Scot., U.K.* **144** L7
Colle, river, *It.* **163** L15
College, *Alas., U.S.* **113** G17
College Park, *Ga., U.S.* **98** L5
College Station, *Tex., U.S.* **105** P12
Collelongo, *It.* **152** K10
Collie, *W. Aust., Austral.* **215** X3
Collier Bay, *Austral.* **214** C5
Collier Range, *Austral.* **214** G3
Colliers, *Cayman Is.* **122** J4

Colliers Point, *Cayman Is.* **118** L7
Collierville, *Tenn., U.S.* **102** G12
Collingwood, *N.Z.* **217** M17
Collins, *Miss., U.S.* **102** M12
Collins Head, *Norfolk I., Austral.* **221** G20
Collinson Peninsula, *Nunavut, Can.* **85** F14
Collinsville, *Ill., U.S.* **101** T4
Collinsville, *Okla., U.S.* **104** E13
Collinsville, *Qnsld., Austral.* **215** S14
Collinsville, *Va., U.S.* **98** G10
Collipulli, *Chile* **135** N6
Collonges, *Fr.* **149** T14
Collooney (Cúil Mhuine), *Ire.* **145** Q4
Colmán *see* Arthurstown, *Ire.* **145** U6
Colmar, *Fr.* **149** Q15
Cologne *see* Köln, *Ger.* **150** F5
Colombey-les-Belles, *Fr.* **149** P13
Colombia, *S. Amer.* **130** F6
Colômbia, *Braz.* **133** L13
Colombian Basin, *Atl. Oc.* **240** M3
Colombian Trench, *Pac. Oc.* **243** J22
Colombo, *Sri Lanka* **181** T7
Colón, *Cuba* **118** G8
Colón, *Pan.* **117** N21
Colonarie, *St. Vincent and the Grenadines* **123** K17
Colonarie, river, *St. Vincent and the Grenadines* **123** K16
Colonel Hill, *Bahamas* **119** G14
Colonet, Cabo, *Mex.* **116** B5
Colonia, *F.S.M.* **221** D18
Colonia Dora, *Arg.* **134** H10
Colonial Beach, *Va., U.S.* **98** D13
Colonial Heights, *Va., U.S.* **98** F13
Colonial National Historical Park, *Va., U.S.* **98** F14
Colonna, Capo, *It.* **153** Q14
Colón Ridge, *Pac. Oc.* **243** J20
Colonsay, island, *Scot., U.K.* **144** M7
Colophon, ruins, *Turk.* **170** G3
Colorado, *U.S.* **108** M13
Colorado, river, *Arg.* **135** N8
Colorado, river, *N. Amer.* **82** K3
Colorado, river, *Tex., U.S.* **104** L5
Colorado City, *Ariz., U.S.* **109** Q6
Colorado City, *Tex., U.S.* **104** M6
Colorado National Monument, *Colo., U.S.* **108** M10
Colorado Plateau, *U.S.* **86** H7
Colorado River Aqueduct, *Calif., U.S.* **111** X12
Colorado Springs, *Colo., U.S.* **109** N13
Colotepec, *Mex.* **117** K13
Colquitt, *Ga., U.S.* **99** P4
Colstrip, *Mont., U.S.* **108** E11
Columbia, *Ky., U.S.* **103** D17
Columbia, *La., U.S.* **102** L8
Columbia, *Md., U.S.* **98** C13
Columbia, *Miss., U.S.* **102** N11
Columbia, *Mo., U.S.* **107** S13
Columbia, *N.C., U.S.* **98** G14
Columbia, *Pa., U.S.* **96** P8
Columbia, *S.C., U.S.* **98** K9
Columbia, *Tenn., U.S.* **103** F15
Columbia, river, *N. Amer.* **82** H3
Columbia, Cape, *N. Amer.* **82** B7
Columbia, Mount, *Alta., B.C., Can.* **84** L9
Columbia City, *Ind., U.S.* **101** P10
Columbia Falls, *Mont., U.S.* **108** B5
Columbia Mountains, *N. Amer.* **82** G3
Columbia Plateau, *U.S.* **86** D5
Columbine, Cape, *S. Af.* **206** L7
Columbretes, Islas, *Sp.* **147** G16
Columbus, *Ga., U.S.* **99** N4
Columbus, *Ind., U.S.* **101** S9
Columbus, *Kans., U.S.* **107** V10
Columbus, *Miss., U.S.* **103** J13
Columbus, *Mont., U.S.* **108** E9
Columbus, *N. Dak., U.S.* **106** D3
Columbus, *N. Mex., U.S.* **109** W11
Columbus, *Nebr., U.S.* **107** P7
Columbus, *Ohio, U.S.* **101** R13
Columbus, *Tex., U.S.* **105** R12
Columbus, *Wis., U.S.* **100** L6
Columbus Monument, site, *Bahamas* **122** E12

Columbus Point, *Trinidad and Tobago* **123** P17
Colusa, *Calif., U.S.* **111** Q4
Colville, *N.Z.* **217** J19
Colville, *Wash., U.S.* **110** A8
Colville, river, *Alas., U.S.* **113** C15
Colville Basin, *Pac. Oc.* **249** H22
Colville Channel, *N.Z.* **217** J19
Colville Lake, *N.W.T., Can.* **84** F10
Colville Ridge, *Pac. Oc.* **242** N11
Colwich, *Kans., U.S.* **107** U7
Comacchio, *It.* **152** F8
Comacchio, Valli di, *It.* **152** F8
Comallo, *Arg.* **135** Q7
Comanche, *Okla., U.S.* **104** J10
Comanche, *Tex., U.S.* **104** M9
Comandante Fontana, *Arg.* **134** F12
Comandante Luis Piedra Buena, *Arg.* **135** V8
Comănești, *Rom.* **155** C16
Coma Pedrosa, Pic de, *Andorra, Sp.* **162** H2
Comarnic, *Rom.* **155** E15
Comayagua, *Hond.* **117** L17
Combarbalá, *Chile* **134** J6
Combeaufontaine, *Fr.* **149** R13
Combermere Bay, *Myanmar* **190** J4
Combles, *Fr.* **148** M10
Combourg, *Fr.* **149** Q5
Comerío, *P.R., U.S.* **122** N4
Comfort, *Tex., U.S.* **105** Q9
Comino (Kemmuna), island, *Malta* **163** H21
Cominotto, island, *Malta* **163** H21
Commandant Charcot Glacier, *Antarctica* **231** Q18
Commander Basin, *Pac. Oc.* **242** B10
Commander Islands *see* Komandorskiye Ostrova, *Russ.* **161** E23
Commanders Bay, *Aruba, Neth.* **123** R17
Commerce, *Ga., U.S.* **98** K6
Commerce, *Tex., U.S.* **104** K13
Commissioner's Point, *Bermuda* **122** B1
Committee Bay, *Nunavut, Can.* **85** F16
Commonwealth Bay, *Antarctica* **231** R18
Communism Peak *see* Qullai Somoniyon, *Asia* **168** G7
Communist Peak *see* Qullai Somoniyon, *Taj.* **178** H10
Como, *It.* **152** D4
Como, Lago di, *It., Switz.* **152** C4
Como, Lake, *Eur.* **140** J6
Comodoro Rivadavia, *Arg.* **135** S9
Comorin, Cape, *India* **181** S6
Comoro Basin, *Ind. Oc.* **224** J6
Comoro Islands, *Af.* **198** L11
Comoros, *Af.* **207** D16
Compiègne, *Fr.* **149** N10
Comporta, *Port.* **146** J5
Compostela, *Mex.* **116** H9
Comrat, *Mold.* **159** N4
Cona (Cuona), *China* **182** L6
Conakry, *Guinea* **204** C5
Conca, river, *It.* **163** L18
Concarneau, *Fr.* **149** Q3
Conceição, *Braz.* **133** F17
Conceição do Maú, *Braz.* **132** B9
Concepción, *Arg.* **134** G9
Concepción, *Bol.* **132** J8
Concepción, *Chile* **135** N6
Concepción del Uruguay, *Arg.* **134** K13
Conception, Point, *Calif., U.S.* **111** W5
Conception Bay, *Af.* **198** P5
Conception Bay, *Nfld. & Lab., Can.* **85** M24
Concepión del Oro, *Mex.* **116** F11
Conception Island, *Bahamas* **119** F14
Conchas, river, *N. Mex., U.S.* **109** R13
Conchas Dam, *N. Mex., U.S.* **109** R14
Conchas Lake, *N. Mex., U.S.* **109** R14
Concho, *Ariz., U.S.* **109** T9
Concho, river, *Tex., U.S.* **105** N7
Conchos, river, *Mex.* **116** D8

Conch Point, *Cayman Is.* **122** H1
Conconully, *Wash., U.S.* **110** A6
Concord, *Calif., U.S.* **111** R4
Concord, *Grenada* **123** K22
Concord, *N.C., U.S.* **98** H9
Concord, *N.H., U.S.* **97** J14
Concordia, *Arg.* **134** J13
Concordia, *Kans., U.S.* **107** S7
Concordia, station, *Antarctica* **231** M17
Concrete, *Wash., U.S.* **110** A4
Condat, *Fr.* **149** U10
Conde, *S. Dak., U.S.* **106** J7
Condé, *Fr.* **148** M11
Condeúba, *Braz.* **133** J15
Condobolin, *N.S.W., Austral.* **215** X13
Condom, *Fr.* **149** X7
Condon, *Oreg., U.S.* **110** F6
Conecuh, river, *Ala., U.S.* **103** N15
Conegliano, *It.* **152** D8
Conejos, *Colo., U.S.* **109** Q12
Conero, Monte, *It.* **152** H10
Conflict Group, *P.N.G.* **217** E21
Confolens, *Fr.* **149** T8
Congaree National Park, *S.C., U.S.* **98** L9
Congo, *Af.* **205** G18
Congo, river, *Af.* **198** J7
Congo, Democratic Republic of the, *Af.* **202** K10
Congo Basin, *Af.* **198** J6
Congo Cay, *Virgin Is., U.S.* **122** M10
Congo Fan, *Atl. Oc.* **241** P13
Congress, *Ariz., U.S.* **109** T6
Cónico, Cerro, *Arg.* **135** R7
Conil de la Frontera, *Sp.* **146** M8
Conn, Lough, *Ire.* **145** Q3
Connacht (Cúige Chonnacht), region, *Ire.* **145** R4
Conneaut, *Ohio, U.S.* **101** N15
Connecticut, *U.S.* **96** L12
Connecticut, river, *U.S.* **97** J13
Connel, *Scot., U.K.* **144** L8
Connell, *Wash., U.S.* **110** D7
Connellsville, *Pa., U.S.* **96** P4
Connemara, region, *Ire.* **145** R3
Connersville, *Ind., U.S.* **101** R10
Connmara, *Qnsld., Austral.* **215** T12
Connors Range, *Austral.* **214** E14
Cononaco, river, *Ecua.* **130** K5
Conrad, *Mont., U.S.* **108** B7
Conrad Rise, *Ind. Oc.* **248** D8
Conroe, *Tex., U.S.* **105** Q14
Consdorf, *Lux.* **162** J10
Conselheiro Lafaiete, *Braz.* **133** L15
Conset Bay, *Barbados* **123** K20
Consolación del Sur, *Cuba* **118** G5
Côn Sơn, *Vietnam* **191** Q13
Côn Sơn, island, *Vietnam* **191** Q13
Constance, Lake *see* Bodensee, *Aust., Ger., Switz.* **150** L6
Constância dos Baetas, *Braz.* **132** E8
Constanța, *Rom.* **155** F18
Constantina, *Sp.* **146** K8
Constantine, *Alg.* **200** A12
Constantinople *see* Istanbul, *Turk.* **170** C5
Constellation Inlet, *Antarctica* **230** H8
Constitución, *Chile* **134** M6
Consuegra, *Sp.* **146** H11
Contact, *Nev., U.S.* **110** L12
Contai, *India* **180** J11
Contamana, *Peru* **132** F4
Contas, river, *S. Amer.* **128** G10
Contramaestre, *Cuba* **118** J11
Contreras, Embalse de, *Sp.* **147** G13
Contreras, Isla, *Chile* **135** W6
Contres, *Fr.* **149** R9
Contrexéville, *Fr.* **149** Q13
Contwoyto Lake, *Nunavut, Can.* **84** G12
Convention Center and Auditorium, *Monaco* **163** D22
Conversano, *It.* **152** M14
Conway, *Ark., U.S.* **102** G8
Conway, *N.H., U.S.* **97** G14
Conway, *S.C., U.S.* **98** K11
Conway Springs, *Kans., U.S.* **107** U7
Conwy, *Wales, U.K.* **145** S10
Coober Pedy, *S. Aust., Austral.* **215** V9

Cook, *Minn., U.S.* **106** F12
Cook, *S. Aust., Austral.* **215** W7
Cook, Bahía, *Chile* **135** Y8
Cook, Mouillage de, *Fr. Polynesia, Fr.* **223** P17
Cook, Mount, *Austral.* **214** K3
Cook, Baie de, *Fr. Polynesia, Fr.* **223** N14
Cook Bay, *S. Amer.* **128** R5
Cook Bay, *Vanuatu* **222** G3
Cookes Peak, *N. Mex., U.S.* **109** V11
Cookeville, *Tenn., U.S.* **103** E17
Cook Ice Shelf, *Antarctica* **231** R16
Cook Inlet, *Alas., U.S.* **113** K16
Cook Island, *Kiribati* **221** B22
Cook Island Passage, *Kiribati* **221** A22
Cook Islands, *Pac. Oc.* **218** J11
Cook, Mount *see* Aoraki, *N.Z.* **217** P16
Cook Strait, *N.Z.* **217** M18
Cooktown, *Qnsld., Austral.* **215** Q13
Coolabah, *N.S.W., Austral.* **215** W13
Coolabri, *Qnsld., Austral.* **215** U13
Coolah, *N.S.W., Austral.* **215** X14
Coolidge, *Ariz., U.S.* **109** U7
Coolidge, *Tex., U.S.* **105** N12
Coolidge Dam, *Ariz., U.S.* **109** U8
Cooma, *N.S.W., Austral.* **215** Y14
Coonamble, *N.S.W., Austral.* **215** W14
Coondapoor *see* Kundapura, *India* **181** P7
Coon Rapids, *Iowa, U.S.* **107** P10
Coon Rapids, *Minn., U.S.* **106** J11
Cooper, *Tex., U.S.* **104** K13
Cooper Creek, *Austral.* **214** H11
Cooper's Town, *Bahamas* **122** A5
Coopertown, *N. Dak., U.S.* **106** F7
Cooperstown, *N.Y., U.S.* **96** J10
Coorada, *Qnsld., Austral.* **215** U14
Coor-De-Wandy Hill, *Austral.* **214** G2
Coorow, *W. Aust., Austral.* **215** W2
Coosa, river, *Ala., Ga., U.S.* **103** H16
Coos Bay, *Oreg., U.S.* **110** J2
Cootamundra, *N.S.W., Austral.* **215** Y13
Copano Bay, *Tex., U.S.* **105** T11
Cope, *Colo., U.S.* **108** M15
Cope, Cabo, *Sp.* **147** L13
Copeland Island, *N. Ire., U.K.* **145** P8
Copenhagen *see* København, *Den.* **142** N12
Copertino, *It.* **153** N15
Copiapó, *Chile* **134** G7
Copiapó, Río, *Chile* **134** G6
Copinsay, island, *Scot., U.K.* **144** G11
Copparo, *It.* **152** E7
Copper, river, *Alas., U.S.* **113** J18
Copperas Cove, *Tex., U.S.* **105** P10
Copper Butte, *Wash., U.S.* **110** A8
Copper Center, *Alas., U.S.* **113** J18
Copper Harbor, *Mich., U.S.* **100** D7
Copper Mine Point, *British Virgin Is., U.K.* **122** R8
Copper Ridge, *Pac. Oc.* **243** H14
Coqên (Cuoqin), *China* **182** K4
Coquí, *P.R., U.S.* **122** P4
Coquille, *Oreg., U.S.* **110** J2
Coquille Harbor, *F.S.M.* **221** A18
Coquimbo, *Chile* **134** J6
Corabia, *Rom.* **155** G14
Coracora, *Peru* **132** J4
Cora-Divh Bank, *Ind. Oc.* **224** D10
Cora Droma Rúisc *see* Carrick-on-Shannon, *Ire.* **145** R5
Corail, *Haiti* **119** M15
Coral Bay, *Virgin Is., U.S.* **122** M11
Coral Bay, *Virgin Is., U.S.* **122** N11
Coral Gables, *Fla., U.S.* **99** X10
Coral Harbour, *Bahamas* **122** B10
Coral Harbour, *Nunavut, Can.* **85** H16
Coral Island *see* Far'ûn, *Israel* **173** R5
Coral Reef National Monument, *Virgin Is., U.S.* **122** N11
Coral Sea, *Pac. Oc.* **218** J5
Coral Sea Basin, *Pac. Oc.* **242** L8
Coral Sea Islands Territory, *Austral.* **215** R15
Coral Springs, *Fla., U.S.* **99** W10

Corangamite, Lake, *Austral.* **214** M12
Corantijn *see* Corentyne, river, *S. Amer.* **131** F15
Corato, *It.* **152** L13
Corbeil-Essonnes, *Fr.* **149** P10
Corbières, range, *Fr.* **149** Y10
Corbin, *Ky., U.S.* **103** D18
Corby, *Eng., U.K.* **145** T13
Corcaigh *see* Cork, *Ire.* **145** U4
Corcoran, *Calif., U.S.* **111** U6
Corcovado, Golfo, *Chile* **135** R6
Corcubión, *Sp.* **146** B5
Corcubión, Ría de, *Sp.* **146** B5
Corcyra *see* Kérkyra, *Gr.* **156** E6
Cordele, *Ga., U.S.* **99** N6
Cordell, *Okla., U.S.* **104** G9
Cordes, *Fr.* **149** X9
Cordillera Central, *Col.* **130** F5
Cordillera de Mérida, *Venez.* **130** D7
Cordillera Occidental, *S. Amer.* **132** H3
Cordillera Oriental, *S. Amer.* **128** H5
Córdoba, *Arg.* **134** J10
Córdoba, *Mex.* **117** J13
Córdoba, *Sp.* **146** K9
Córdoba, Sierras de, *Arg.* **134** J10
Cordouan, Île de, *Fr.* **149** U6
Cordova, *Ala., U.S.* **103** J15
Cordova, *Alas., U.S.* **113** K18
Corentyne, river, *S. Amer.* **131** F15
Corfu *see* Kérkyra, *Gr.* **156** E6
Corguinho, *Braz.* **132** K11
Coria, *Sp.* **146** G7
Coria del Río, *Sp.* **146** L8
Corianino, *San Marino* **163** J16
Coribe, *Braz.* **133** H14
Corigliano Calabro, *It.* **153** P13
Corinna, *Tas., Austral.* **215** Y7
Corinth, *Grenada* **123** L23
Corinth, *Miss., U.S.* **103** G13
Corinth, *N.Y., U.S.* **96** J11
Corinth *see* Kórinthos, *Gr.* **156** J11
Corinth Canal, *Gr.* **156** J11
Cork (Corcaigh), *Ire.* **145** U4
Cork Harbour, *Ire.* **145** U4
Corlay, *Fr.* **149** Q4
Corleone, *It.* **153** S9
Corleto Perticara, *It.* **153** N13
Çorlu, *Turk.* **170** C4
Cornelia, *Ga., U.S.* **98** K6
Cornell, *Wis., U.S.* **100** H3
Corner Brook, *Nfld. & Lab., Can.* **85** M23
Corner Seamounts, *Atl. Oc.* **240** K6
Corning, *Ark., U.S.* **102** E10
Corning, *Calif., U.S.* **111** P4
Corning, *Iowa, U.S.* **107** Q10
Corning, *N.Y., U.S.* **96** K7
Corno Grande, *It.* **152** J9
Cornwall, *Ont., Can.* **85** Q19
Cornwall, region, *Eng., U.K.* **145** X9
Cornwallis, Port, *India* **181** P14
Cornwallis Island, *Nunavut, Can.* **85** D15
Cornwall Island, *Nunavut, Can.* **85** C15
Cornwall Point, *Bahamas* **122** C6
Coro, *Venez.* **130** B8
Coroa, Tope de, *Cabo Verde* **209** B14
Coroatá, *Braz.* **133** E15
Corocoro, *Bol.* **132** K6
Coroico, *Bol.* **132** J6
Corolla, *N.C., U.S.* **98** G15
Coromandel Coast, *India* **181** R8
Coromandel Peninsula, *N.Z.* **217** J19
Corona, *N. Mex., U.S.* **109** T13
Coronado, *Calif., U.S.* **111** Z9
Coronado Bay, *N. Amer.* **82** Q7
Coronado National Memorial, *Ariz., U.S.* **109** W8
Coronation Gulf, *Nunavut, Can.* **84** F12
Coronation Island, *Antarctica* **230** A5
Coronel, *Chile* **135** N6
Coronel Bogado, *Parag.* **132** N10
Coronel Dorrego, *Arg.* **135** N11
Coronel Francisco Sosa, *Arg.* **135** P10
Coronel Oviedo, *Parag.* **132** M10
Coronel Pringles, *Arg.* **135** N11

Coronel Suárez, *Arg.* **135** NII
Coropuna, Nevado, *Peru* **132** J5
Corozal, *Belize* **117** JI6
Corozal, *Col.* **130** C5
Corpus Christi, *Tex., U.S.* **105** UII
Corpus Christi, Lake, *Tex., U.S.*
   105 TIO
Corpus Christi Bay, *U.S.* **86** NI2
Corral, *Chile* **135** P6
Corral de Almaguer, *Sp.* **146** GII
Corralillo, *Cuba* **118** G8
Corrán Tuathail (Carrauntoohil),
   peak, *Ire.* **145** U3
Corraun Peninsula, *Ire.* **145** R3
Corredeir, falls, *Braz.* **132** FIO
Corrib, Lough, *Ire.* **145** R4
Corrientes, *Arg.* **134** GI3
Corrientes, Bahía de, *Cuba* **118** H4
Corrientes, Cabo, *Col.* **130** E3
Corrientes, Cabo, *Cuba* **118** H4
Corrientes, Cabo, *Mex.* **116** H9
Corrigan, *Tex., U.S.* **105** PI4
Corrigin, *W. Aust., Austral.* **215** X3
Corriverton, *Guyana* **131** EI5
Corrubedo, Cabo, *Sp.* **146** C5
Corry, *Pa., U.S.* **96** L4
Corse (Corsica), *island, Fr.* **152** K4
Corse, Cap, *It.* **152** H4
Corse, Cape, *Eur.* **140** K6
Corsica, *S. Dak., U.S.* **106** M6
Corsica *see* Corse, *island, Fr.* **152** K4
Corsicana, *Tex., U.S.* **104** MI2
Corte, *Fr.* **152** K4
Cortemaggiore, *It.* **152** E5
Cortez, *Colo., U.S.* **109** PIO
Cortina d'Ampezzo, *It.* **152** C8
Cortland, *N.Y., U.S.* **96** K8
Cortona, *It.* **152** H8
Coruche, *Port.* **146** H5
Çoruh, *river, Turk.* **171** DI5
Çorum, *Turk.* **170** DIO
Corumbá, *Braz.* **132** KIO
Corumbá, *river, S. Amer.* **128** H9
Corumbau, Ponta de, *Braz.* **133** KI6
Corvallis, *Oreg., U.S.* **110** G3
Corvo, *Azores, Port.* **146** PI
Corwen, *Wales, U.K.* **145** SIO
Coryal, *Trinidad and Tobago* **123** P23
Corydon, *Iowa, U.S.* **107** QI2
Cos *see* Kos, *island, Gr.* **157** MI8
Cosenza, *It.* **153** QI3
Coshocton, *Ohio, U.S.* **101** QI4
Cosmo Newberry, *W. Aust., Austral.*
   215 V5
Cosmopolis, *Wash., U.S.* **110** D2
Cosne-Cours-sur-Loire, *Fr.* **149** RIO
Cosquín, *Arg.* **134** JIO
Cossato, *It.* **152** D3
Cossé-le-Vivien, *Fr.* **149** Q6
Costa del Silencio, *Sp.* **208** R4
Costa Rica, *N. Amer.* **117** NI8
Costeşti, *Rom.* **155** FI4
Costilla, *N. Mex., U.S.* **109** QI3
Cotabato City, *Philippines* **193** FI5
Cotagaita, *Bol.* **132** L7
Coteaux, *Haiti* **119** MI5
Côte d'Ivoire Escarpment, *Atl. Oc.*
   241 NI2
Côte d'Ivoire (Ivory Coast), *Af.*
   204 D8
Côte d'Or, range, *Fr.* **149** SI2
Cotentin, range, *Fr.* **149** N6
Côtes-de-Fer, *Haiti* **119** NI5
Coton, Pointe, *Mauritius* **209** J2I
Cotonou, *Benin* **204** EI2
Cotopaxi, peak, *Ecua.* **130** J3
Cotorra, Isla, *Venez.* **123** R2O
Cotswold Hills, *Eng., U.K.* **145** VII
Cottage Grove, *Oreg., U.S.* **110** H3
Cottbus, *Ger.* **150** EII
Cotter, *Ark., U.S.* **102** E8
Cottian Alps, *Fr., It.* **152** FI
Cottongarden Point, *Virgin Is., U.S.*
   122 Q3
Cotton Ground, *St. Kitts and Nevis*
   123 CI8
Cotton Plant, *Ark., U.S.* **102** GIO
Cotton Valley, *La., U.S.* **102** K7
Cottonwood, *Ariz., U.S.* **109** S7
Cottonwood, *Idaho, U.S.* **108** D3
Cotulla, *Tex., U.S.* **105** T8

Coubre, Pointe de la, *Fr.* **149** U6
Coudersport, *Pa., U.S.* **96** L6
Couëron, *Fr.* **149** S5
Couiza, *Fr.* **149** YIO
Coulee City, *Wash., U.S.* **110** C7
Coulee Dam, *Wash., U.S.* **110** B7
Coulta, *S. Aust., Austral.* **215** X9
Council, *Idaho, U.S.* **108** F3
Council Bluffs, *Iowa, U.S.* **107** P9
Council Grove, *Kans., U.S.* **107** T8
Courland, *Eur.* **140** F9
Couronne, Cap, *Fr.* **149** YI3
Courtenay, *B.C., Can.* **84** M7
Courtenay, *Fr.* **149** QIO
Courtmacsherry Bay, *Ire.* **145** V4
Coutances, *Fr.* **149** P6
Coutras, *Fr.* **149** V7
Covadonga, site, *Sp.* **146** B9
Covarrubias, *Sp.* **146** DII
Cove, *Oreg., U.S.* **110** F8
Covelo, *Calif., U.S.* **111** P2
Coventry, *Eng., U.K.* **145** TI2
Covered Market, *Monaco* **163** E2O
Coves del Drac, site, *Sp.* **147** GI9
Covilhã, *Port.* **146** F6
Covington, *Ga., U.S.* **98** L5
Covington, *Ind., U.S.* **101** R7
Covington, *Ky., U.S.* **103** AI8
Covington, *La., U.S.* **102** PII
Covington, *Okla., U.S.* **104** FIO
Covington, *Tenn., U.S.* **102** FI2
Covington, *Va., U.S.* **98** EIO
Cowal, Lake, *Austral.* **214** KI3
Cowan, Lake, *Austral.* **214** J5
Cow and Calf Islands, *Myanmar*
   181 NI5
Cowarie, *S. Aust., Austral.* **215** VIO
Cowell, *S. Aust., Austral.* **215** XIO
Coweta, *Okla., U.S.* **104** FI3
Cowlitz, *river, Wash., U.S.* **110** D4
Cowra, *N.S.W., Austral.* **215** XI4
Coxim, *Braz.* **132** KII
Coxim, *river, Braz.* **132** KII
Cox's Bazar, *India* **180** KI4
Coyanosa Draw, *river, Tex., U.S.*
   105 P3
Cozad, *Nebr., U.S.* **107** Q5
Cozumel, Isla, *Mex.* **117** HI7
Cozumel Island, *N. Amer.* **82** N7
Crab Island, *Mauritius* **209** J2O
Cradock, *S. Af.* **206** LIO
Craig, *Alas., U.S.* **113** M23
Craig, *Colo., U.S.* **108** LII
Craiova, *Rom.* **155** FI3
Cranberry Lake, *N.Y., U.S.* **96** GIO
Cranbourne, *Vic., Austral.* **215** ZI2
Cranbrook, *B.C., Can.* **84** M9
Cranbrook, *W. Aust., Austral.* **215** Y3
Crandon, *Wis., U.S.* **100** G6
Crane, *Oreg., U.S.* **110** J8
Crane, *Tex., U.S.* **105** N4
Crane Beach, *Barbados* **123** L2O
Crane Lake, *Minn., U.S.* **106** EI2
Craon, *Fr.* **149** R6
Crary Fan, *Atl. Oc.* **241** Z8
Crary Mountains, *Antarctica* **230** L8
Crasna, *Rom.* **155** CI7
Crasna, *river, Rom.* **154** BI2
Crater Lake, *Oreg., U.S.* **110** J4
Crater Lake National Park, *Oreg.,*
   U.S. **110** J4
Craters of the Moon National
   Monument, *Idaho, U.S.* **108** H6
Crateús, *Braz.* **133** EI6
Crato, *Braz.* **133** FI6
Crawford, *Nebr., U.S.* **106** MI
Crawford, *Tex., U.S.* **105** NII
Crawfordsville, *Ind., U.S.* **101** R6
Crawfordville, *Fla., U.S.* **99** R5
Crazy Mountains, *Mont., U.S.*
   108 E9
Creag Ghoraidh (Creagorry), *Scot.,*
   U.K. **144** J6
Creagorry *see* Creag Ghoraidh, *Scot.,*
   U.K. **144** J6
Crécy, *Fr.* **149** NII
Cree, *river, Sask., Can.* **84** KI2
Creede, *Colo., U.S.* **109** PII
Creek Point, *Bahamas* **122** BIO
Cree Lake, *N. Amer.* **82** F5

Cree Lake, *Sask., Can.* **84** KI2
Creeslough (An Craoslach), *Ire.*
   145 P5
Creighton, *Nebr., U.S.* **107** N7
Creil, *Fr.* **149** NIO
Crema, *It.* **152** E5
Cremona, *It.* **152** E5
Cres, island, *Croatia* **154** E4
Cresbard, *S. Dak., U.S.* **106** J6
Crescent, *Okla., U.S.* **104** FIO
Crescent City, *Calif., U.S.* **110** LI
Crescent City, *Fla., U.S.* **99** S8
Crescent Group, *S. China Sea*
   192 BIO
Crescent Junction, *Utah, U.S.*
   109 N9
Crescent Lake, *Fla., U.S.* **99** S8
Crescent Lake, *Oreg., U.S.* **110** J4
Cresco, *Iowa, U.S.* **106** MI3
Crest, *Fr.* **149** VI3
Creston, *Iowa, U.S.* **107** QIO
Crestview, *Fla., U.S.* **99** Q2
Creswell, *Oreg., U.S.* **110** H3
Creswell Downs, *N.T., Austral.*
   215 R9
Crete, *Nebr., U.S.* **107** Q8
Crete *see* Kríti, *island, Gr.* **157** QI4
Crete, Sea of, *Gr.* **157** PI5
Creus, Cap de, *Sp.* **147** CI8
Crevasse Valley Glacier, *Antarctica*
   230 N9
Crevillente, *Sp.* **147** KI4
Crewe, *Va., U.S.* **98** FI2
Crewkerne, *Eng., U.K.* **145** WII
Crianlarich, *Scot., U.K.* **144** L9
Criciúma, *Braz.* **132** PI2
Criel-sur-Mer, *Fr.* **148** M9
Crimea, region, *Ukr.* **159** S7
Crimean Mountains, *Eur.* **140** JI2
Crinian Canal, *Scot., U.K.* **144** M8
Cripple Creek, *Colo., U.S.* **109** NI3
Crisfield, *Md., U.S.* **98** EI4
Cristalina, *Braz.* **133** JI3
Cristóbal, Punta, *Ecua.* **130** Q9
Cristóbal Colón, Pico, *S. Amer.*
   128 A3
Crişul Alb, river, *Rom.* **154** DI2
Crişul Negra, river, *Rom.* **154** CII
Crişul Repede, river, *Rom.* **154** CI2
Crna, river, *Maced.* **154** LII
Croatia, *Eur.* **154** E5
Crocker, Cerro, *Ecua.* **130** QIO
Crocker Range, *Malaysia* **192** GII
Crockett, *Tex., U.S.* **105** NI3
Crocus Bay, *British Virgin Is., U.K.*
   122 RII
Crocus Hill, *British Virgin Is., U.K.*
   122 RII
Crofton, *Nebr., U.S.* **106** M7
Croisette, Cap, *Fr.* **149** YI3
Croisic, Pointe du, *Fr.* **149** R4
Croix des Bouquets, *Haiti* **119** MI7
Croker Island, *Austral.* **214** A8
Cromarty Firth, *Scot., U.K.* **144** J9
Crompton Point, *Dominica* **123** E2O
Crook, *Colo., U.S.* **108** KI5
Crook, *Eng., U.K.* **145** PI2
Crooked, river, *Oreg., U.S.* **110** H6
Crooked Island, *Bahamas* **119** GI5
Crooked Island Passage, *Bahamas*
   119 GI4
Crook Point, *Oreg., U.S.* **110** KI
Crookston, *Minn., U.S.* **106** F8
Crosby, *Minn., U.S.* **106** HII
Crosby, *N. Dak., U.S.* **106** D2
Crosbyton, *Tex., U.S.* **104** K6
Cross City, *Fla., U.S.* **99** R6
Crossett, *Ark., U.S.* **102** K9
Crossing Rocks, *Bahamas* **122** C6
Cross Keys, *Jam.* **122** J8
Cross Plains, *Tex., U.S.* **104** M8
Cross Sound, *Alas., U.S.* **113** K2I
Crossville, *Tenn., U.S.* **103** EI7
Croswell, *Mich., U.S.* **100** LI3
Crotone, *It.* **153** QI4
Crow Agency, *Mont., U.S.* **108** EII
Crowell, *Tex., U.S.* **104** J8
Crowley, *La., U.S.* **102** P8
Crown Haven, *Bahamas* **122** A5
Crown Mountain, *Virgin Is., U.S.*
   122 M8

Crownpoint, *N. Mex., U.S.* **109** RIO
Crown Prince Christian Land,
   Greenland, Den. **82** A8
Croydon, *Qnsld., Austral.* **215** RI2
Crozet Basin, *Ind. Oc.* **224** P8
Crozet Plateau, *Ind. Oc.* **224** Q7
Cruces, *Cuba* **118** H8
Crump Island, *Antigua and Barbuda*
   123 B2I
Crump Lake, *Oreg., U.S.* **110** K6
Cruz, Cabo, *Cuba* **118** LII
Cruz Alta, *Braz.* **132** PII
Cruz Bay, *Virgin Is., U.S.* **122** NIO
Cruz del Eje, *Arg.* **134** J9
Cruz del Padre, Cayo, *Cuba* **118** G8
Cruzeiro, Ponta, *Sao Tome and*
   Principe **209** C2O
Cruzeiro do Sul, *Braz.* **132** F4
Cruz Grande, *Chile* **134** H6
Crystal Caves, site, *Bermuda* **122** B3
Crystal City, *Mo., U.S.* **107** TI5
Crystal City, *Tex., U.S.* **105** S8
Crystal Falls, *Mich., U.S.* **100** G6
Crystal Lake, *Ill., U.S.* **100** M6
Crystal Mountains, *Af.* **198** J6
Crystal River, *Fla., U.S.* **99** S7
Crystal Springs, *Miss., U.S.* **102** MII
Csongrád, *Hung.* **151** MI6
Csorna, *Hung.* **151** LI3
Ctesiphon, ruins, *Iraq* **174** EIO
Cuamba, *Mozambique* **207** EI3
Cuando, river, *Angola* **206** E8
Cuangar, *Angola* **206** F7
Cuanza, river, *Angola* **206** C6
Cuauhtémoc, *Mex.* **116** D8
Cuba, *Mo., U.S.* **107** TI4
Cuba, *N. Amer.* **118** H9
Cubagua, Isla, *Venez.* **121** JI4
Cubal, *Angola* **206** D6
Cubango, river, *Angola* **206** E7
Çubuk, *Turk.* **170** E8
Cuchara, Punta, *P.R., U.S.* **122** P3
Cuckold Point, *Barbados* **123** JI9
Cucuí, *Braz.* **132** C7
Cúcuta, *Col.* **130** D6
Cudahy, *Wis., U.S.* **100** L7
Cuddalore, *India* **181** Q7
Cuddapah, *India* **181** P6
Cudjoehead, *Montserrat* **123** B23
Cue, *W. Aust., Austral.* **215** V3
Cuéllar, *Sp.* **146** EIO
Cuenca, *Ecua.* **130** L3
Cuenca, *Sp.* **146** GI2
Cuenca, Serranía de, *Sp.* **147** GI3
Cuencamé, *Mex.* **116** FIO
Cuernavaca, *Mex.* **116** JI2
Cuero, *Tex., U.S.* **105** SII
Cuevas de Altamira, *Sp.* **146** BIO
Cuevas del Almanzora, *Sp.* **147** LI3
Cuevo, *Bol.* **132** L8
Cugir, *Rom.* **155** DI3
Cuglieri, *It.* **153** N3
Cuiabá, *Braz.* **132** JIO
Cúige Chonnacht *see* Connacht,
   region, *Ire.* **145** R4
Cúige Laighean *see* Leinster, region,
   Ire. **145** S6
Cúige Mumhan *see* Munster, region,
   Ire. **145** U4
Cúige Uladh *see* Ulster, region, *Ire.,*
   U.K. **145** P6
Cúil Mhuine *see* Collooney, *Ire.*
   145 Q4
Cúil Rathain *see* Coleraine, *N. Ire.,*
   U.K. **145** P6
Cuito, river, *Angola* **206** F7
Cuito Cuanavale, *Angola* **206** E7
Çukurca, *Turk.* **171** HI8
Cù Lao Thu, island, *Vietnam*
   191 PI4
Culberts Bay, *Bahamas* **122** BI2
Culbertson, *Mont., U.S.* **108** BI3
Culbertson, *Nebr., U.S.* **107** R4
Cul de Sac, *St. Maarten, Neth.*
   123 BI4
Cul de Sac, *St.-Martin, Fr.* **123** AI5
Cul de Sac, river, *St. Lucia* **123** KI4
Cul-de-Sac du Marin, *Martinique, Fr.*
   123 G23

Culebra, island, *P.R., U.S.* **122** M7
Culebra, Sierra de la, *Sp.* **146** D8
Culfa, *Arm.* **171** FI9
Culiacán, *Mex.* **116** F8
Culion, island, *Philippines* **193** DI3
Cúllar-Baza, *Sp.* **146** LI2
Cullman, *Ala., U.S.* **103** HI5
Culpeper, *Va., U.S.* **98** DI2
Culuene, *river, Braz.* **132** HI2
Culver, Point, *Austral.* **214** K6
Culverden, *N.Z.* **217** NI7
Cumalı, *Turk.* **170** H3
Cumaná, *Venez.* **130** BII
Cumana Bay, *Trinidad and Tobago*
   123 N24
Cumana Redhead, *Trinidad and*
   Tobago **123** N23
Cumanayagua, *Cuba* **118** H8
Cumberland, *Ky., U.S.* **103** DI9
Cumberland, *Md., U.S.* **98** BII
Cumberland, *Wis., U.S.* **100** G2
Cumberland, river, *Ky., Tenn., U.S.*
   103 DI6
Cumberland, river, *U.S.* **87** HI7
Cumberland, Cape, *Vanuatu* **222** BI
Cumberland, Lake, *Ky., U.S.* **103** DI7
Cumberland, Lake, *U.S.* **87** HI7
Cumberland Bay, *St. Vincent and the*
   Grenadines **123** KI6
Cumberland Gap National Historical
   Park, *Ky., Tenn., Va., U.S.* **103** DI9
Cumberland Island National
   Seashore, *Ga., U.S.* **99** Q9
Cumberland Islands, *Austral.*
   214 EI4
Cumberland Peninsula, *Nunavut, Can.*
   85 FI9
Cumberland Plateau, *U.S.* **87** JI7
Cumberland Sound, *Nunavut, Can.*
   85 GI9
Cumbernauld, *Scot., U.K.* **144** M9
Cumbrera, Cerro, *Chile* **135** U7
Cumbres Pass, *Colo., U.S.* **109** QI2
Cumbrian Mountains, *Eng., U.K.*
   145 QIO
Cuminá, *Braz.* **132** DIO
Cúmpas, *Mex.* **116** C7
Çumra, *Turk.* **170** H8
Cunaviche, *Venez.* **130** D9
Cunco, *Chile* **135** P6
Cunene, river, *Af.* **198** M6
Cuneo, *It.* **152** F2
Cùng Sơn, *Vietnam* **191** NI4
Cunningham, Lake, *Bahamas*
   122 BII
Cunyu, *W. Aust., Austral.* **215** U4
Cuona *see* Cona, *China* **182** L6
Cuoqin *see* Coqên, *China* **182** K4
Cupica, *Col.* **130** E3
Cupica, Golfo de, *Col.* **130** E3
Curaçao, *Lesser Antil.* **120** H9
Curanilahue, *Chile* **135** N6
Curbur, *W. Aust., Austral.* **215** V2
Curcubăta, peak, *Rom.* **154** DI2
Curecanti National Recreation Area,
   Colo., U.S. **109** NII
Curepipe, *Mauritius* **209** G2O
Curiapo, *Venez.* **131** CI3
Curicó, *Chile* **134** L6
Curieuse, island, *Seychelles*
   209 M2I
Curitiba, *Braz.* **133** NI3
Curium, ruin, *Cyprus* **162** Q7
Curley Cut Cays, *Bahamas* **118** FII
Curral Velho, *Cabo Verde* **209** CI7
Currawilla, *Qnsld., Austral.* **215** UII
Current, *Bahamas* **122** D5
Current, river, *Ark., Mo., U.S.*
   107 VI4
Current Island, *Bahamas* **122** D5
Currie, *Tas., Austral.* **215** Y7
Curalı *see* Coleraine *see below*
Currituck, *N.C., U.S.* **98** GI4
Currituck Sound, *N.C., U.S.* **98** GI5
Curtea de Argeş, *Rom.* **155** EI4
Curtici, *Rom.* **154** DII
Curtin Springs, *N.T., Austral.* **215** U8
Curtis, *Nebr., U.S.* **107** Q4
Curtis, Port, *Austral.* **214** FI5
Curtis Island, *Austral.* **214** FI5
Curtis Island, *Kermadec Is., N.Z.*
   218 L9

Curuá, river, *Braz.* **132** F11
Curuaés, river, *Braz.* **132** F11
Curuçá, *Braz.* **133** C13
Curuçá, river, *Braz.* **132** E5
Cururupu, *Braz.* **133** D15
Curuzú Cuatiá, *Arg.* **134** H13
Curvelo, *Braz.* **133** K14
Cusco, *Peru* **132** H5
Cushing, *Okla., U.S.* **104** F11
Cusset, *Fr.* **149** T11
Cusson, Pointe, *Que., Can.* **85** J17
Custer, *Mont., U.S.* **108** D11
Custer, *S. Dak., U.S.* **106** L1
Cut, island, *Indonesia* **193** L18
Cut Bank, *Mont., U.S.* **108** B7
Cuthbert, *Ga., U.S.* **99** N4
Cutler Ridge, *Fla., U.S.* **99** X10
Cutral Có, *Arg.* **135** P8
Cuttack, *India* **180** K10
Cuvier Basin, *Ind. Oc.* **225** K17
Cuvier Plateau, *Ind. Oc.* **225** L16
Cuxhaven, *Ger.* **150** B7
Cuya, *Chile* **134** B6
Cuyahoga Falls, *Ohio, U.S.* **101** P14
Cuyahoga Valley National Park, *Ohio, U.S.* **101** P14
Cuyama, river, *Calif., U.S.* **III** W7
Cuyo Islands, *Philippines* **193** E13
Cuyuni, river, *S. Amer.* **131** D13
Cyclades *see* Kykládes, islands, *Gr.* **157** L14
Cydonia *see* Chaniá, *Gr.* **157** P13
Cymru *see* Wales, *Wales, U.K.* **145** U10
Cynthiana, *Ky., U.S.* **103** B18
Cyprus, *Eur.* **162** F6
Cyprus, island, *Asia* **168** E2
Cyrenaica, region, *Lib.* **201** D16
Cyrene *see* Shaḥḥāt, *Lib.* **201** B16
Cyrus Field Bay, *Nunavut, Can.* **85** H19
Cythera *see* Kýthira, island, *Gr.* **156** N11
Czaplinek, *Pol.* **150** C12
Czech Republic (Czechia), *Eur.* **150** H10
Częstochowa, *Pol.* **151** F15
Człopa, *Pol.* **150** D12

D

Dà (Black), river, *Vietnam* **190** H11
Da-an, *China* **183** D15
Ḏabʻah, *Jordan* **173** N7
Dabakala, *Côte d'Ivoire* **204** D9
Daba Shan, *Shaanxi, China* **184** L1
Dabie Shan, *Anhui, China* **184** M7
Dabola, *Guinea* **204** C6
Dabqig *see* Uxin Qi, *N. Mongol, China* **184** E1
Dąbrowa Górnicza, *Pol.* **151** G15
Dąbrowa Tarnowska, *Pol.* **151** G16
Dachang, *China* **182** N11
Dachau, *Ger.* **150** K8
Dachengzi, *N. Mongol, China* **184** B9
Dadale, *Solomon Is.* **221** M18
Daday, *Turk.* **170** C9
Dade City, *Fla., U.S.* **99** T8
Dadeville, *Ala., U.S.* **103** K16
Dadhar, *Pak.* **179** S6
Dadu, *Pak.* **179** U6
Dadu, river, *China* **182** L9
Daeamsan, peak, *S. Korea* **186** L10
Daebo, *S. Korea* **187** R13
Daebudo, island, *S. Korea* **187** N7
Daecheongdo, island, *S. Korea* **186** M4
Daechi, *S. Korea* **187** S8
Daedeok, *S. Korea* **187** U8
Daedundo, island, *S. Korea* **187** T5
Daegu (Taegu), *S. Korea* **187** R11
Daeheuksando, island, *S. Korea* **187** U5
Daeheung, *S. Korea* **187** U8
Daejeon (Taejŏn), *S. Korea* **187** Q9
Daejeong, *S. Korea* **187** X7
Daejin, *S. Korea* **187** R12
Daenanjido, island, *S. Korea* **187** P7

Daesan, *S. Korea* **187** P7
Daeyeonpyeongdo (Yeonpyeong), island, *S. Korea* **186** M6
Dafeng (Dazhong), *Jiangsu, China* **184** K11
Dafní, *Gr.* **156** J9
Dafoe, *Sask., Can.* **84** M12
Dagana, *Senegal* **200** G5
Dagelet *see* Ulleungdo, island, *S. Korea* **186** M15
Dagö *see* Hiiumaa, island, *Est.* **143** K15
Dagu, *Tianjin Shi, China* **184** D8
Dagupan, *Philippines* **193** C13
Dahab, *Egypt* **173** T4
Dahanu, *India* **180** K3
Da Hinggan Ling, *China* **183** E14
Dahlā, *Afghan.* **179** Q5
Dahlak Archipelago, *Af.* **198** F10
Dahlonega, *Ga., U.S.* **98** K5
Dahod, *India* **180** J4
Dahongliutan, *China* **178** K15
Dahūk, *Iraq* **174** B9
Dahuofang Shuiku, *Liaoning, China* **184** A13
Daḫy, Nafūd ad, *Saudi Arabia* **174** L10
Dai (Ndai), island, *Solomon Is.* **221** M19
Daicheng, *Hebei, China* **184** E8
Dai Hai, *N. Mongol, China* **184** C5
Dailekh, *Nepal* **180** F8
Daimiel, *Sp.* **146** H11
Daingerfield, *Tex., U.S.* **104** K14
Daingin, Bá an *see* Dingle Bay, *Ire.* **145** U2
Dairen *see* Dalian, *Liaoning, China* **184** D12
Dai Senga Dake, *Japan* **188** H12
Daisetsu, *Tex., U.S.* **105** Q15
Daitō Islands, *Japan* **189** Y5
Daitō Shotō, *Japan* **218** C2
Daixian, *Shanxi, China* **184** D5
Daiyun Shan, *Fujian, China* **185** T9
Dajabón, *Dom. Rep.* **119** L17
Dajarra, *Qnsld., Austral.* **215** S11
Dajt, Mal, *Alban.* **154** L9
Dakar, *Senegal* **200** H4
Dakhla Oasis, site, *Egypt* **201** E18
Dakoank, *India* **181** T15
Dakoro, *Niger* **200** H11
Dakota City, *Nebr., U.S.* **107** N8
Ðakovica *see* Gjakovë, *Kos.* **154** J10
Ðakovo, *Croatia* **154** E8
Ðâk Tô, *Vietnam* **190** M13
Ðákura, *Nicar.* **117** L19
Dala, *Solomon Is.* **221** M19
Dalad Qi, *N. Mongol, China* **184** C2
Dalaman, river, *Turk.* **170** H4
Dalanzadgad, *Mongolia* **182** E10
Dalap, island, *Marshall Is., U.S.* **220** H12
Ðà Lạt, *Vietnam* **191** N14
Dalbandin, *Pak.* **179** S4
Dalbeg, *Qnsld., Austral.* **215** S14
Dalby, *Qnsld., Austral.* **215** V15
Dale, *Nor.* **142** J10
Dale Country, *Eng., U.K.* **145** R12
Daleville, *Ala., U.S.* **103** N16
Dalgaranga Hill, *Austral.* **214** H3
Dalhart, *Tex., U.S.* **104** F4
Dali, *China* **182** N8
Dali, *Cyprus* **162** P8
Dali, *Shaanxi, China* **184** H2
Dali, river, *Shaanxi, China* **184** F2
Dalian (Dairen), *Liaoning, China* **184** D12
Dalian Wan, *Liaoning, China* **184** D12
Dalkhākī, *Afghan.* **178** K7
Dallas, *Oreg., U.S.* **110** G3
Dallas, *Tex., U.S.* **104** L12
Dalmatia, region, *Croatia* **154** G6
Dalmellington, *Scot., U.K.* **145** N9
Dal'negorsk, *Russ.* **161** L21
Dal'nerechensk, *Russ.* **161** L21
Daloa, *Côte d'Ivoire* **204** D8
Dalrymple, Lake, *Austral.* **214** E14
Daltenganj, *India* **180** H9
Dalton, *Ga., U.S.* **98** J4
Dalton, *Nebr., U.S.* **107** P2

Dalton Highway, *Alas., U.S.* **113** C17
Dalumba Bay, *Austral.* **214** B10
Dalupiri, island, *Philippines* **193** A13
Dalwhinnie, *Scot., U.K.* **144** K9
Daly, river, *Austral.* **214** B8
Daly Bay, *Nunavut, Can.* **85** H15
Daly River *see* Nauiyu, *N.T., Austral.* **215** P7
Daly Waters, *N.T., Austral.* **215** Q8
Daman (Damão), *India* **180** K3
Damanhûr, *Egypt* **201** C18
Damão *see* Daman, *India* **180** K3
Damaqun Shan, *Hebei, China* **184** B7
Damar, island, *Indonesia* **193** J16
Damar, island, *Indonesia* **193** M16
Damas Cays, *Bahamas* **118** F9
Damascus *see* Dimashq, *Syr.* **172** J7
Damāvand, Kūh-e, *Iran* **175** C13
Damboa, *Nigeria* **205** C16
Dambulla, *Sri Lanka* **181** S7
Dame-Marie, *Haiti* **119** M14
Damergou, region, *Af.* **198** G5
Ðâm Hà, *Vietnam* **190** H13
Damietta *see* Dumyât, *Egypt* **201** C18
Damīr Qābū, *Syr.* **172** C15
Damoh, *India* **180** H7
Damongo, *Ghana* **204** D10
Dampier, *W. Aust., Austral.* **215** S2
Dampier, Archipelago, *Austral.* **214** E2
Dampier, Selat, *Indonesia* **193** J17
Dampier Downs, *W. Aust., Austral.* **215** R5
Dampier Land, *Austral.* **214** D4
Dampier Ridge, *Pac. Oc.* **242** M9
Damqawt, *Yemen* **175** P14
Damqog (Maquan), river, *China* **182** L4
Damroh, *India* **180** E15
Damxung (Dangxiong), *China* **182** K6
Damyang, *S. Korea* **187** S8
Dan, river, *N.C., Va., U.S.* **98** G10
Dan, river, *Shaanxi, China* **184** K3
Danakil Desert, *Eth.* **203** F15
Ðà Nẵng, *Vietnam* **190** L13
Dana Point, *Calif., U.S.* **III** Y9
Danas Valley, *Atl. Oc.* **247** R18
Danbury, *Conn., U.S.* **96** M12
Danby Lake, *Calif., U.S.* **III** X12
Dancheng, *Henan, China* **184** K6
Danco Coast, *Antarctica* **230** D4
Dandan, Puntan, *N. Mariana Is., U.S.* **220** C5
Dandong, *Liaoning, China* **184** C14
Danells Valley, *Atl. Oc.* **247** Q20
Danfeng (Longjuzhai), *Shaanxi, China* **184** K2
Danforth, *Me., U.S.* **97** D18
Dangara, *Taj.* **178** J8
Dangbon, *S. Korea* **187** R9
Dangchang, *China* **182** J10
Dangjin, *S. Korea* **187** P7
Dangrek Range, *Thai.* **190** M11
Dangriga, *Belize* **117** K17
Dangshan, *Anhui, China* **184** J7
Dangtu, *Anhui, China* **184** M9
Dangxiong *see* Damxung, *China* **182** K6
Daniel, *Wyo., U.S.* **108** H9
Danielsen Canyon, *Atl. Oc.* **247** N20
Danilov, *Russ.* **158** G10
Daning, *Shanxi, China* **184** G3
Danjiangkou, *Hubei, China* **184** L3
Danjiangkou Shuiku, *Henan, China* **184** L3
Danjo Guntō, *Japan* **189** S3
Ḏank, *Oman* **175** K15
Dankhar Gömpa, *India* **180** D6
Dankov, *Russ.* **158** L10
Dannemora, *N.Y., U.S.* **96** F11
Dansville, *N.Y., U.S.* **96** K6
Danube *see* Donau, Duna, Dunaj, Dunărea, Dunav, Dunay, river, *Eur.* **140** H7
Danube, Mouths of the, *Rom.* **159** S5
Danube, Mouths of the, *Rom.* **155** E19
Danube River Delta, *Eur.* **140** J11
Danville, *Ill., U.S.* **101** R7

Danville, *Ky., U.S.* **103** C17
Danville, *Va., U.S.* **98** G11
Danyang, *Jiangsu, China* **184** M10
Danyang, *S. Korea* **187** P10
Danzhou, *China* **182** Q12
Đào Côn Cỏ, island, *Vietnam* **190** K13
Đào Lý Sơn, island, *Vietnam* **190** L14
Đào Phú Quốc, island, *Vietnam* **191** Q11
Daos du Sud, Îles, *New Caledonia, Fr.* **222** B5
Đào Thổ Chu, island, *Vietnam* **191** Q11
Daoxian, *Hunan, China* **185** T3
Daphne, *Ala., U.S.* **103** P14
Dapu, *Guang., China* **185** U7
Da Qaidam, *China* **182** H7
Daqin Dao, *Shand., China* **184** E11
Daqing, *China* **183** D15
Daqinggou, *Hebei, China* **184** B6
Daqing Shan, *N. Mongol, China* **184** B3
Daquanyuan, *Jilin, China* **184** B14
Dāqūq, *Iraq* **174** D9
Dar'ā (Edrei), *Syr.* **172** L7
Dārāb, *Iran* **175** G14
Daraban, *Pak.* **179** Q9
Darabani, *Rom.* **155** A16
Darah-ye Būm, *Afghan.* **178** L3
Darah-ye Owd, *Afghan.* **178** M6
Ḏarbat ʻAlī, Ra's, *Oman* **175** P14
Darbhanga, *India* **180** G10
Darby, *Mont., U.S.* **108** E5
Darby Island, *Bahamas* **122** E7
Dardanelle, *Ark., U.S.* **102** G7
Dardanelle, Lake, *Ark., U.S.* **102** F7
Dardanelles *see* Çanakkale Boğazı, *Turk.* **170** D2
Dardere *see* Ovgos, river, *Cyprus* **162** N7
Darende, *Turk.* **170** G12
Dar Es Salaam, *Tanzania* **203** M15
Darfur, region, *Sudan* **202** F10
Dargai, *Pak.* **178** M10
Darganata, *Turkm.* **176** K10
Dargaville, *N.Z.* **217** H18
Dargeçit, *Turk.* **171** H16
Dargun, *Ger.* **150** B10
Darhan, *Mongolia* **182** C10
Darhan, *Mongolia* **182** D11
Darhan Mumingaan Lianheqi, *N. Mongol, China* **184** A3
Darien, *Ga., U.S.* **99** P8
Daringali, *Solomon Is.* **221** M20
Darjiling, *India* **180** G11
Dark Head, *St. Vincent and the Grenadines* **123** K16
Darling, river, *Austral.* **214** J12
Darling, Lake, *N. Dak., U.S.* **106** E4
Darling Downs, *Austral.* **214** H14
Darling Range, *Austral.* **214** K3
Darlington, *Eng., U.K.* **145** Q12
Darlington, *S.C., U.S.* **98** K10
Darliston, *Jam.* **122** H6
Darlot, Lake, *Austral.* **214** H4
Darłowo, *Pol.* **150** B12
Darmstadt, *Ger.* **150** H6
Darnah, *Lib.* **201** B16
Darney, *Fr.* **149** Q14
Darnley, Cape, *Antarctica* **231** F20
Daroca, *Sp.* **147** E13
Darongjiang, *Guangxi Zhuang, China* **185** T2
Daroot-Korgon, *Kyrg.* **178** G10
Darregueira, *Arg.* **135** N10
Darreh Gaz, *Iran* **175** B16
Darrington, *Wash., U.S.* **110** B5
Dar Rounga, region, *Af.* **198** H7
Darrouzett, *Tex., U.S.* **104** E7
Darsser Ort, cape, *Ger.* **150** A9
Dartmoor, plateau, *Eng., U.K.* **145** X9
Dartmouth, *N.S., Can.* **85** P22
Daru, *P.N.G.* **217** E18
Darwājī Bālā, *Afghan.* **179** N2
Darwha, *India* **180** K6
Darwin, *Falk., U.K.* **135** W12
Darwin, *N.T., Austral.* **215** P8
Darwin (Culpepper), Isla, *Ecua.* **130** M8

Darwin, Bahía, *Ecua.* **130** P10
Darwin, Port, *Austral.* **214** B7
Darwin Glacier, *Antarctica* **231** M14
Darwin, Isla, *Galápagos Is., Ecua.* **219** G21
Darya Khan, *Pak.* **179** Q9
Das, *Pak.* **180** B5
Dasburg, *Ger.* **162** G10
Dashiqiao, *Liaoning, China* **184** C12
Dashkuduk, *Turkm.* **176** K6
Dasht, river, *Pak.* **179** V2
Dasht-e Kavīr (Salt Desert), *Iran* **175** D14
Dasht-e Lūt, desert, *Iran* **175** E15
Daska, *Pak.* **179** P12
Daşkəsən, *Azerb.* **171** D20
Daşköpri, *Uzb.* **176** N10
Daşoguz, *Turkm.* **176** J9
Datça, *Turk.* **170** H3
Datia, *India* **180** G6
Datian, *Fujian, China* **185** T9
Datong, *China* **182** H9
Datong, *Shanxi, China* **184** C5
Datong (Xiping), *Shanxi, China* **184** C5
Datong, river, *China* **182** H9
Datu, Cape, *Asia* **168** L11
Datu Piang, *Philippines* **193** F15
Daud Khel, *Pak.* **179** P10
Daudnagar, *India* **180** H9
Daugava, river, *Latv.* **143** L17
Daugavpils, *Latv.* **143** L17
Daun, *Ger.* **162** G12
Dauphin, *Man., Can.* **85** N13
Dauphine, *Eur.* **140** J5
Dauphin Island, *Miss., U.S.* **103** P13
Daurada, Costa, *Sp.* **147** E17
Davangere, *India* **181** P5
Davao City, *Philippines* **193** F15
Davao Gulf, *Philippines* **193** F15
Davenport, *Iowa, U.S.* **107** P14
Davenport, *Wash., U.S.* **110** C8
Davenport Range, *Austral.* **214** E9
Daventry, *Eng., U.K.* **145** U13
Davey, Port, *Austral.* **214** M7
David, *Pan.* **117** N20
David Bay, *Grenada* **123** J23
David City, *Nebr., U.S.* **107** P8
David Point, *Virgin Is., U.S.* **122** N8
Davidson Mountains, *Alas., U.S.* **113** D18
Davie Ridge, *Ind. Oc.* **224** J5
Davis, *Calif., U.S.* **III** R4
Davis, *Okla., U.S.* **104** H11
Davis, station, *Antarctica* **231** G20
Davis, Mount, *Pa., U.S.* **96** Q4
Davis Beach, *Virgin Is., U.S.* **122** Q2
Davis Dam, *Ariz., Nev., U.S.* **III** V12
Davis Mountains, *Tex., U.S.* **105** P2
Davis Sea, *Antarctica* **231** J21
Davis Seamounts, *Atl. Oc.* **248** H6
Davis Sill, *Arctic Oc.* **240** E5
Davis Strait, *Arctic Oc.* **240** E5
Davos, *Switz.* **152** B5
Davy Sund, *Greenland, Den.* **82** B10
Dawāsir, Wādī ad, *Saudi Arabia* **174** M9
Dawei, *Myanmar* **190** M7
Dawkah, *Oman* **175** N13
Dawmat al Jandal (Al Jawf), *Saudi Arabia* **174** F7
Dawna Range, *Myanmar* **190** K7
Dawqah, *Saudi Arabia* **174** M7
Dawra, *W. Sahara* **200** D6
Dawros Head, *Ire.* **145** P4
Dawson, *Ga., U.S.* **99** P5
Dawson, *Minn., U.S.* **106** K9
Dawson, *N. Dak., U.S.* **106** G5
Dawson, *Tex., U.S.* **104** M12
Dawson, *Yukon, Can.* **84** E8
Dawson, river, *Austral.* **214** G15
Dawson, Isla, *Chile* **135** X8
Dawson Creek, *B.C., Can.* **84** K9
Dawson Springs, *Ky., U.S.* **103** D14
Dawu, *Hubei, China* **184** M5
Dawukou *see* Shizuishan, *China* **182** G10
Dawwah, *Oman* **175** L17
Dax, *Fr.* **149** X6
Daxian, *China* **182** K11
Daxing, *Beijing Shi, China* **184** D7

Daxue Mountains, *Asia* **168** HIO
Dayingzi, *Liaoning, China* **184** CI3
Dayr az Zawr, *Syr.* **172** FI3
Dayr Sim'ān, *Syr.* **172** D8
Dayton, *Ohio, U.S.* **101** RII
Dayton, *Tenn., U.S.* **103** FI7
Dayton, *Tex., U.S.* **105** QI4
Dayton, *Wash., U.S.* **110** E8
Daytona Beach, *Fla., U.S.* **99** S9
Dayu, *Jiangxi, China* **185** T5
Dayu Ling, *Jiangxi, China* **185** T5
Da Yunhe (Grand Canal), *Zhejiang, China* **185** NII
Dayushan (Lantau Island), *Hong Kong (Xianggang), S.A.R., China* **185** W5
Dayville, *Oreg., U.S.* **110** G7
Dazhong *see* Dafeng, *Jiangsu, China* **184** KII
Dazkırı, *Turk.* **170** G5
De Aar, *S. Af.* **206** L9
Deadhorse, *Alas., U.S.* **113** CI7
Deadmans Cay, *Bahamas* **119** GI4
Deadman's Cays, *Bahamas* **118** F8
Dead Sea, *Israel, Jordan, W. Bank* **173** N6
Deadwood, *S. Dak., U.S.* **106** KI
Deakin, *W. Aust., Austral.* **215** W7
Deal, *Eng., U.K.* **145** VI6
De'an, *Jiangxi, China* **185** P7
Deán Funes, *Arg.* **134** JIO
Dean Passage, *Solomon Is.* **221** R24
Dearborn, *Mich., U.S.* **100** MI2
Dê Arghistān, river, *Afghan.* **179** Q5
Dease Inlet, *Alas., U.S.* **113** BI5
Dease Lake, *B.C., Can.* **84** H8
Dease Strait, *Nunavut, Can.* **85** FI3
Death Valley, *Calif., U.S.* **III** T9
Death Valley, town, *Calif., U.S.* **III** UIO
Death Valley National Park, *Calif., Nev., U.S.* **III** T9
Death Valley National Park Devils Hole, *Nev., U.S.* **III** UIO
Debar, *Maced.* **154** KIO
Débé, *Trinidad and Tobago* **123** Q22
Dębica, *Pol.* **151** GI7
Debin, *Russ.* **161** F2O
Debir, *ruins, Israel* **173** N5
Dębno, *Pol.* **150** DII
Débo, Lake, *Af.* **198** G2
Debrecen, *Hung.* **151** LI7
Debre Mark'os, *Eth.* **203** FI4
Debuu, *island, Marshall Is., U.S.* **220** K4
Decatur, *Ala., U.S.* **103** HI5
Decatur, *Ga., U.S.* **98** L5
Decatur, *Ill., U.S.* **101** R6
Decatur, *Ind., U.S.* **101** QIO
Decatur, *Nebr., U.S.* **107** N8
Decatur, *Tex., U.S.* **104** KII
Decazeville, *Fr.* **149** WIO
Deccan, *plateau, India* **181** N5
Deccan Plateau, *Asia* **168** J7
Deception Island, *Antarctica* **230** D4
Dechu, *India* **180** G3
Decimomannu, *It.* **153** P4
Děčín, *Czech Rep.* **150** GII
Decize, *Fr.* **149** SII
Decorah, *Iowa, U.S.* **106** MI3
Dedéagach *see* Alexandroúpoli, *Gr.* **157** CI6
Dededo, *Guam, U.S.* **220** BII
Dedegöl Dağı, *peak, Turk.* **170** H6
Dédougou, *Burkina Faso* **204** B9
Dedovichi, *Russ.* **158** H6
Deep, *river, N. Dak., U.S.* **106** E4
Deep Creek, *Bahamas* **122** F6
Deep Creek Lake, *Md., U.S.* **98** CIO
Deep Creek Range, *Utah, U.S.* **108** M5
Deering, *Alas., U.S.* **113** EI3
Deer Isle, *Me., U.S.* **97** GI7
Deer Lodge, *Mont., U.S.* **108** D7
Deer Park, *Wash., U.S.* **110** B9
Deerton, *Mich., U.S.* **100** F8
Deer Trail, *Colo., U.S.* **108** MI4
Deeth, *Nev., U.S.* **110** MII
Defiance, *Ohio, U.S.* **101** PII
De Funiak Springs, *Fla., U.S.* **99** Q3

Deganya, *Israel* **172** L6
Dêgê, *China* **182** K8
Degeh Bur, *Eth.* **203** GI6
De Gerlache Seamounts, *Pac. Oc.* **241** XI
Deggendorf, *Ger.* **150** JIO
Değirmenlik *see* Kythrea, *Cyprus* **162** N9
De Grey, *river, Austral.* **214** E3
Deh Bīd, *Iran* **175** FI3
Deh-e Khāwāk, *Afghan.* **178** L8
Deh-e Shū, *Afghan.* **179** R3
Dehqonobod, *Uzb.* **176** MI2
Dehra Dun, *India* **180** E6
Deh Rāwud, *Afghan.* **179** P5
Dehua, *Fujian, China* **185** T9
Dehui, *China* **183** DI6
Deilgne *see* Delgany, *Ire.* **145** S7
Deim Zubeir, *S. Sudan* **202** GII
Dej, *Rom.* **155** CI3
Dejen, Ras, *Eth.* **203** EI5
De Jongs, Tanjung, *Indonesia* **217** DI6
De Kalb, *Miss., U.S.* **103** KI3
De Kalb, *Tex., U.S.* **104** KI4
DeKalb, *Ill., U.S.* **101** N6
Dekese, *Dem. Rep. of the Congo* **202** L9
Dekle Beach, *Fla., U.S.* **99** R6
Delaford, *Trinidad and Tobago* **123** NI8
De Land, *Fla., U.S.* **99** S9
Delano, *Calif., U.S.* **III** V7
Delano Peak, *Utah, U.S.* **109** N6
Delaport Point, *Bahamas* **122** BIO
Delarof Islands, *Alas., U.S.* **112** N4
Delavan, *Wis., U.S.* **100** M6
Delaware, *Ohio, U.S.* **101** QI3
Delaware, *U.S.* **98** CI5
Delaware, *river, U.S.* **96** L9
Delaware Bay, *Del., N.J., U.S.* **96** R9
Delaware Water Gap National Recreation Area, *N.J., Pa., U.S.* **96** MIO
Del Cano Rise, *Ind. Oc.* **224** Q5
Delémont, *Switz.* **152** A2
De Leon, *Tex., U.S.* **104** M9
Delfzijl, *Neth.* **148** GI4
Delgado, Cabo, *Mozambique* **207** CI5
Delgany (Deilgne), *Ire.* **145** S7
Delgo, *Sudan* **202** CI2
Delhi, *India* **180** F6
Delhi, *La., U.S.* **102** L9
Delhi, *N.Y., U.S.* **96** KIO
Delice, *river, Turk.* **170** E9
Delicias, *Mex.* **116** D9
Dalidağ, *peak, see* Mets Beverratap, *Azerb.* **171** E2O
Deliktaş, *Turk.* **170** EIO
Dél̦ne, *N.W.T., Can.* **84** FIO
Delingha, *China* **182** H8
Delitzsch, *Ger.* **150** F9
Dell Rapids, *S. Dak., U.S.* **106** L8
Delmar, *Del., Md., U.S.* **98** DI5
Delmenhorst, *Ger.* **150** C7
Del Norte, *Colo., U.S.* **109** PI3
De Long Mountains, *Alas., U.S.* **113** DI3
Delos, *ruin, Gr.* **157** KI5
Delphi, *Ind., U.S.* **101** Q8
Delphi, *ruin, Gr.* **156** HIO
Delphos, *Ohio, U.S.* **101** QII
Delray Beach, *Fla., U.S.* **99** WIO
Del Rio, *Tex., U.S.* **105** R6
Delta, *Colo., U.S.* **109** NIO
Delta, *Utah, U.S.* **108** M6
Delta Junction, *Alas., U.S.* **113** GI8
Deltona, *Fla., U.S.* **99** S9
Del Verme Falls, *Eth.* **203** HI5
Demagiri, *India* **180** JI4
Demanda, Sierra de la, *Sp.* **146** DII
Demba, *Dem. Rep. of the Congo* **202** MIO
Dembéni, *Comoros* **209** MI4
Dembi Dolo, *Eth.* **203** GI3
Demchok, *India* **180** C7
Demerara Plain, *Atl. Oc.* **241** N6
Demerara Plateau, *Atl. Oc.* **241** N6
Deming, *N. Mex., U.S.* **109** VII
Demini, *river, Braz.* **132** C8

Demirci, *Turk.* **170** F4
Demirköprü Baraji, *Turk.* **170** F4
Demirköy, *Turk.* **170** B4
Demirtaş, *Turk.* **170** J7
Demopolis, *Ala., U.S.* **103** LI4
Demre, *Turk.* **170** J5
Demta, *Indonesia* **217** BI7
Demyansk, *Russ.* **158** H7
Denali *see* McKinley, Mount, *N. Amer.* **82** C2
Denali Highway, *Alas., U.S.* **113** HI7
Denali National Park and Preserve, *Alas., U.S.* **113** GI6
Denali Park, *Alas., U.S.* **113** GI7
Den Burg, *Neth.* **148** GI2
Denekamp, *Neth.* **148** HI4
Denges Passage, *Palau* **220** QII
Dengkou, *China* **182** GII
Dêngqên (Dingqing), *China* **182** K7
Dengzhou, *Henan, China* **184** L4
Den Haag (The Hague), *Neth.* **148** JI2
Denham, *W. Aust., Austral.* **215** UI
Denham Springs, *La., U.S.* **102** PIO
Den Helder, *Neth.* **148** HI2
Dénia, *Sp.* **147** JI5
Denigomodu, *region, Nauru* **221** E23
Deniliquin, *N.S.W., Austral.* **215** YI2
Denio, *Nev., U.S.* **110** L7
Denis, Île, *Seychelles* **209** L2O
Denison, *Iowa, U.S.* **107** N9
Denison, *Tex., U.S.* **104** JI2
Denisovskaya, *Russ.* **158** EII
Denizli, *Turk.* **170** G4
Denman, *N.S.W., Austral.* **215** XI4
Denmark, *Eur.* **142** NII
Denmark, *S.C., U.S.* **98** L9
Denmark, *W. Aust., Austral.* **215** Y3
Denmark Strait, *Arctic Oc.* **247** M2O
Dennery, *St. Lucia* **123** KI4
Denov, *Uzb.* **176** MI2
Denpasar, *Indonesia* **192** MII
Denton, *Md., U.S.* **98** CI4
Denton, *Tex., U.S.* **104** KII
D'Entrecasteaux, Point, *Austral.* **214** L3
D'Entrecasteaux Basin, *Pac. Oc.* **242** L9
D'Entrecasteaux Islands, *P.N.G.* **217** E2I
Denver, *Colo., U.S.* **108** MI3
Denver City, *Tex., U.S.* **104** L4
Deobhog, *India* **180** L8
Deoghar, *India* **180** HII
Deogyusan, *peak, S. Korea* **187** R9
Deokjeokdo, *island, S. Korea* **187** N6
Deokseong, *S. Korea* **187** QI2
Deokyang, *S. Korea* **187** T9
Deora, *India* **180** G2
Deoria, *India* **180** G9
Deosai Mountains, *Pak.* **178** LI2
Deosri, *India* **180** GI3
De Pere, *Wis., U.S.* **100** J7
Depoe Bay, *Oreg., U.S.* **110** G2
Deposit, *N.Y., U.S.* **96** L9
Depósito, *Braz.* **132** B9
Deputatskiy, *Russ.* **161** EI8
Deqing, *Guang., China* **185** V3
Deqing, *Zhejiang, China* **185** NIO
De Queen, *Ark., U.S.* **102** H6
De Quincy, *La., U.S.* **102** P7
Dera Ghazi Khan, *Pak.* **179** R9
Dera Ismail Khan, *Pak.* **179** Q9
Derakht-e Yaḩyá, *Afghan.* **179** Q7
Dera Murad Jamali, *Pak.* **179** T7
Derbent, *Russ.* **159** UI6
Derby, *Eng., U.K.* **145** TI2
Derby, *Kans., U.S.* **107** U8
Derby, *W. Aust., Austral.* **215** R5
Derg, Lough, *Ire.* **145** P5
Derg, Lough, *Ire.* **145** S4
Dergachi, *Russ.* **158** MI5
Dergaon, *India* **180** GI4
Derhachi, *Ukr.* **159** N9
De Ridder, *La., U.S.* **102** N7
Derik, *Turk.* **171** HI5
Dermott, *Ark., U.S.* **102** J9
Dernberg, Cape, *Namibia* **206** K6

Dernieres, Isles, *La., U.S.* **102** RIO
Derravaragh, Lough, *Ire.* **145** R6
Derry *see* Londonderry, *N. Ire., U.K.* **145** P6
Derudeb, *Sudan* **203** DI4
Derventa, *Bosn. & Herzg.* **154** E8
Derwent, *river, Austral.* **214** M7
Deryneia *see* Dherinia, *Cyprus* **162** PIO
Derzhavīnsk, *Kaz.* **176** DI2
Désappointement, Îles du, *Fr. Polynesia, Fr.* **223** D2O
Des Arc, *Ark., U.S.* **102** G9
Deschutes, *river, Oreg., U.S.* **110** G5
Desē, *Eth.* **203** FI5
Deseado, *river, Arg.* **135** T8
Desecheo, *island, P.R., U.S.* **119** M2I
Deserta Grande, *island, Madeira, Port.* **208** N4
Desertas, Ilhas, *Madeira, Port.* **208** N4
Desert Center, *Calif., U.S.* **III** XI2
Deshaies, *Guadeloupe, Fr.* **123** EI4
Deshler, *Nebr., U.S.* **107** R7
Deskáti, *Gr.* **156** E9
Des Lacs, *river, N. Dak., U.S.* **106** D3
Desloge, *Mo., U.S.* **107** TI5
De Smet, *S. Dak., U.S.* **106** K7
Des Moines, *Iowa, U.S.* **107** PII
Des Moines, *N. Mex., U.S.* **109** QI4
Des Moines, *river, Iowa, Mo., U.S.* **107** PI2
Desna, *river, Russ.* **158** K7
Desnuadez, Punta, *Arg.* **135** NI2
Desolación, Isla, *Chile* **135** X6
De Soto, *Mo., U.S.* **107** TI5
Des Plaines, *Ill., U.S.* **101** N7
Despotikó, *island, Gr.* **157** LI4
Dessalines, *Haiti* **119** LI6
Dessau, *Ger.* **150** E9
Destruction Island, *Wash., U.S.* **110** C2
Detmold, *Ger.* **150** E7
De Tour Village, *Mich., U.S.* **100** GII
Detroit, *Mich., U.S.* **100** MI2
Detroit Lake, *Oreg., U.S.* **110** G4
Detroit Lakes, *Minn., U.S.* **106** G9
Deutschland Canyon, *Atl. Oc.* **241** Z9
Deva, *Rom.* **154** DI2
Dəvəçi, *Azerb.* **171** C22
Deveci Dağı, *peak, Turk.* **170** EII
Develi, *Turk.* **170** GIO
Devils, *river, Tex., U.S.* **105** Q6
Devils Lake, *N. Dak., U.S.* **106** F6
Devils Lake, town, *N. Dak., U.S.* **106** E6
Devils Paw, *mountain, Alas., U.S.* **113** K22
Devil's Point, *Bahamas* **119** FI3
Devil's Point, *Vanuatu* **222** F2
Devils Postpile National Monument, *Calif., U.S.* **III** S7
Devils Tower National Monument, *Wyo., U.S.* **108** FI3
Devine, *Tex., U.S.* **105** S9
Devizes, *Eng., U.K.* **145** VI2
Devon Island, *Nunavut, Can.* **85** DI5
Devon Shelf, *Arctic Oc.* **247** PI4
Devon Slope, *Arctic Oc.* **247** PI4
Devrek, *Turk.* **170** C7
Devrekâni, *Turk.* **170** C9
Devrukh, *India* **180** M3
Dewas, *India* **180** J5
Dewey, *Okla., U.S.* **104** EI2
De Witt, *Ark., U.S.* **102** H9
De Witt, *Iowa, U.S.* **107** NI4
Dexing, *Jiangxi, China* **185** Q8
Dexter, *Me., U.S.* **97** EI7
Dexter, *Mo., U.S.* **107** VI5
Deyang, *China* **182** LIO
Dey Dey, Lake, *Austral.* **214** H8
Deyhūk, *Iran* **175** DI5
Deynau, *Turkm.* **176** LIO
Dezfūl, *Iran* **174** EII
Dezhnev Bay, *N. Amer.* **82** P2
Dezhou, *Shand., China* **184** F7
Dhaka, *Bangladesh* **180** HI3
Dhamār, *Yemen* **174** Q9
Dhamtari, *India* **180** K8

Dhanbad, *India* **180** HIO
D'Hanis, *Tex., U.S.* **105** R8
Dhanushkodi, *India* **181** S7
Dhar, *India* **180** J4
Dharan Bazar, *Nepal* **180** GII
Dharapuram, *India* **181** R6
Dharmjaygarh, *India* **180** J9
Dharmsala, *India* **180** D5
Dharwad, *India* **181** N4
Dhaulagiri I, *peak, Nepal* **180** F9
Dhavlos (Kaplıca), *Cyprus* **162** MIO
Dhekelia (Eastern) Sovereign Base Area, *U.K.* **162** P9
Dhenkanal, *India* **180** KIO
Dherinia (Deryneia), *Cyprus* **162** PIO
Dhībān, *Jordan* **173** N6
Dhone, *India* **181** N6
Dhuburi, *India* **180** GI2
Dhule, *India* **180** K4
Dhupgarh, *peak, India* **180** J6
Dhuusa Marreeb, *Somalia* **203** HI7
Día, *island, Gr.* **157** QI5
Diable (Devils Island), Île du, *Fr. Guiana* **131** EI8
Diablo, Picacho del, *N. Amer.* **82** K3
Diablo Range, *Calif., U.S.* **III** T5
Diakoptó, *Gr.* **156** JIO
Diamante, *Arg.* **134** KI2
Diamante, *river, Arg.* **134** L8
Diamantina, *Braz.* **133** KI5
Diamantina, *river, Austral.* **214** FI2
Diamantina, Chapada, *Braz.* **133** HI5
Diamantina Deep, *Ind. Oc.* **225** NI6
Diamantina Escarpment, *Ind. Oc.* **225** MI4
Diamantina Fracture Zone, *Ind. Oc.* **225** MI4
Diamantina Lakes, *Qnsld., Austral.* **215** TII
Diamantina Trench, *Ind. Oc.* **225** NI6
Diamantino, *Braz.* **132** HIO
Diamond Craters, *Oreg., U.S.* **110** J7
Diamond Harbour, *India* **180** JII
Diamond Head, *Hawai'i, U.S.* **114** FII
Diamond Mountains, *Calif., U.S.* **III** N6
Diamond Mountains, *Nev., U.S.* **III** PII
Diamond Peak, *Oreg., U.S.* **110** J4
Diamond Shoals, *N.C., U.S.* **98** HI5
Dianópolis, *Braz.* **133** GI4
Diapaga, *Burkina Faso* **204** BII
Díavlos Karpáthou, *Gr.* **157** NI8
Diavolo, Mount, *India* **181** QI4
Dībā, *U.A.E.* **175** JI5
Dibai, *India* **180** F6
Dibble Basin, *Ind. Oc.* **249** EI5
D'Iberville, Mont, *N. Amer.* **82** F9
Diboll, *Tex., U.S.* **105** NI4
Dibrugarh, *India* **180** FI5
Dibsī Faraj, *Syr.* **172** EIO
Dickens, *Tex., U.S.* **104** K6
Dickinson, *N. Dak., U.S.* **106** G2
Dickinson Bay, *Antigua and Barbuda* **123** A2O
Dickson, *Russ.* **161** EI3
Dickson, *Tenn., U.S.* **103** EI4
Dickson City, *Pa., U.S.* **96** M9
Dicle, *Turk.* **171** GI4
Dicle (Tigris), *river, Turk.* **171** HI6
Dicomano, *It.* **152** G7
Didao, *China* **183** DI7
Didwana, *India* **180** F4
Didymóteicho, *Gr.* **157** BI7
Die, *Fr.* **149** VI3
Diego de Almagro, *Chile* **134** G7
Diego de Almagro, Isla, *Chile* **135** W6
Diego Ramírez, Islas, *Chile* **135** Y9
Diekirch, *Lux.* **162** HIO
Diemal Find, *W. Aust., Austral.* **215** W4
Điện Biên Phủ, *Vietnam* **190** HIO
Diễn Châu, *Vietnam* **190** JI2
Dieppe, *Fr.* **148** M8
Dieppe Bay Town, *St. Kitts and Nevis* **123** AI7
Dierks, *Ark., U.S.* **102** H6

Dif, *Kenya* 203 JI5
Diffa, *Niger* 201 JI3
Differdange, *Lux.* 162 K9
Digboi, *India* 180 FI5
Digby, *N.S., Can.* 85 P21
Dighton, *Kans., U.S.* 107 T4
Digne, *Fr.* 149 WI4
Digoin, *Fr.* 149 TII
Digor, *Turk.* 171 DI7
Digos, *Philippines* 193 FI5
Digri, *Pak.* 179 W8
Digul, river, *Indonesia* 193 M21
Digura, island, *Maldives* 181 V3
Dijlah (Tigris), river, *Iraq* 174 EII
Dijon, *Fr.* 149 RI3
Dika, Mys, *Russ.* 161 EI5
Dikili, *Turk.* 170 E3
Díkti, Óros, *Gr.* 157 QI5
Dikwa, *Nigeria* 205 BI7
Dīla, *Eth.* 203 HI5
Di Lăng, *Vietnam* 190 LI4
Dilārām, *Afghan.* 179 P3
Dildarde Burnu, *Turk.* 170 J7
Díli, *Timor-Leste* 193 MI5
Dilijan, *Arm.* 171 DI9
Di Linh, *Vietnam* 191 PI3
Dillenburg, *Ger.* 150 F6
Dilley, *Tex., U.S.* 105 S8
Dillia, river, *Af.* 198 G6
Dilling, *Sudan* 202 FI2
Dillingham, *Alas., U.S.* 113 LI3
Dillon, *Mont., U.S.* 108 F7
Dillon, *S.C., U.S.* 98 KII
Dillon's Bay, *Vanuatu* 222 G3
Dilolo, *Dem. Rep. of the Congo* 202 N9
Dilworth, *Minn., U.S.* 106 G8
Dimas, *Mex.* 116 F8
Dimashq (Damascus), *Syr.* 172 J7
Dimitrovgrad, *Bulg.* 155 KI5
Dimitrovgrad, *Russ.* 158 KI5
Dimitsána, *Gr.* 156 K9
Dimmitt, *Tex., U.S.* 104 H4
Dinagat, island, *Philippines* 193 EI5
Dinajpur, *Bangladesh* 180 GI2
Dinan, *Fr.* 149 Q5
Dinant, *Belg.* 148 MI2
Dinar, *Turk.* 170 G5
Dīnār, Kūh-e, *Iran* 175 FI3
Dinara, peak, *Bosn. & Herzg., Croatia* 154 G6
Dinara, range, *Bosn. & Herzg., Croatia* 154 F6
Dinaric Alps, *Eur.* 154 D5
Dinas Mawddwy, *Wales, U.K.* 145 TIO
Dindigul, *India* 181 R6
Dingle see *An Daingean, Ire.* 145 U2
Dingle Bay (Daingin, Bá an), *Ire.* 145 U2
Dingli, *Malta* 163 L21
Dingnan, *Jiangxi, China* 185 U6
Dingolfing, *Ger.* 150 J9
Dingqing see *Dêngqên, China* 182 K7
Dingshuzhen, *Jiangsu, China* 184 MIO
Dingtao, *Shand., China* 184 H7
Dinguiraye, *Guinea* 204 B6
Dingxing, *Hebei, China* 184 D7
Dingzhou, *Hebei, China* 184 E6
Dingzi Gang, *Shand., China* 184 GII
Dinosaur, *Colo., U.S.* 108 LIO
Dinosaur National Monument, *Colo., Utah, U.S.* 108 LIO
Dinuba, *Calif., U.S.* III T7
Diomede Islands, *Alas., U.S.* 112 EII
Dion, ruin, *Gr.* 156 DIO
Dios, *P.N.G.* 221 JI3
Dios, Cayos de Cuba 118 H7
Diourbel, *Senegal* 200 H4
Diphu Pass, *India, Myanmar* 190 C7
Dipkarpaz see *Rizokarpaso, Cyprus* 162 MII
Diplo, *Pak.* 179 W8
Dir, *Pak.* 178 LIO
Diré, *Mali* 200 H8
Dirē Dawa (Dire Dawa), *Eth.* 203 GI6
Dírfys, Óros, *Gr.* 156 HI2
Dirico, *Angola* 206 F8
Dirj, *Lib.* 201 CI3

Dirk Hartog Island, *Austral.* 214 GI
Dirty Devil, river, *Utah, U.S.* 109 N8
Disa, *India* 180 H3
Disappointment, Cape, *Wash., U.S.* IIO E2
Disappointment, Lake, *Austral.* 214 F5
Disaster Bay, *Austral.* 214 MI4
Discovery Bank, *Ind. Oc.* 224 RIO
Discovery Bay, *Austral.* 214 MII
Discovery Bay, *Jam.* 122 H8
Discovery II Fracture Zone, *Ind. Oc.* 224 P5
Discovery Seamounts, *Atl. Oc.* 241 UI2
Discovery Tablemount, *Atl. Oc.* 241 UI2
Disentis, *Switz.* 152 B4
Disko, island see *Qeqertarsuaq, island, Greenland, Den.* 82 D9
Disko Bank, *Atl. Oc.* 247 QI6
Disney Cay, *Bahamas* 118 DII
Dispur, *India* 180 GI3
Disteghil Sar, peak, *Pak.* 178 KI2
Diu, *India* 180 K2
Dīvāndarreh, *Iran* 174 CII
Divilacan Bay, *Pac. Oc.* 168 JI3
Divinhe, *Mozambique* 207 GI3
Divinópolis, *Braz.* 133 LI4
Diviso, *Col.* 130 H3
Divo, *Côte d'Ivoire* 204 E8
Divoúnia, island, *Gr.* 157 PI7
Divriği, *Turk.* 171 FI3
Diwana, *Pak.* 179 V6
Dīwār, *Syr.* 172 BI6
Dixie, *Idaho, U.S.* 108 E4
Dixon, *Calif., U.S.* III R4
Dixon, *Ill., U.S.* 101 N5
Dixon, *Ky., U.S.* 103 CI4
Dixon, *Mo., U.S.* 107 TI3
Dixon, *Mont., U.S.* 108 C5
Dixon Entrance, *N. Amer.* 82 F3
Dixons, *Bahamas* 122 EI2
Diyadin, *Turk.* 171 EI8
Diyālá, river, *Iraq* 174 DIO
Diyarbakır, *Turk.* 171 GI5
Dja, river, *Cameroon* 205 FI6
Djado, *Niger* 201 FI3
Djado, Plateau du, *Niger* 201 FI3
Djamaa, *Alg.* 200 BII
Djambala, *Congo* 205 JI7
Djanet, *Alg.* 200 EI2
Djarrit, island, *Marshall Is., U.S.* 220 GI2
Djelfa, *Alg.* 200 BII
Djénné, *Mali* 200 H8
Djibouti, *Af.* 203 FI6
Djibouti, *Djibouti* 203 FI6
Djougou, *Benin* 204 CII
Djoum, *Cameroon* 205 FI6
Djúpáll, valley, *Arctic Oc.* 247 M2O
Djúpavík, *Ice.* 142 D2
Djúpivogur, *Ice.* 142 F4
Dmitriya Lapteva, Proliv, *Russ.* 161 DI7
Dmitriyev L'govskiy, *Russ.* 158 M8
Dmitrov, *Russ.* 158 J9
Dnepr, river, *Russ.* 158 J7
Dnieper see *Dnipro, river, Ukr.* 159 R7
Dnieper Lowland, *Eur.* 140 GII
Dnieper Upland, *Eur.* 140 HII
Dniester, river, *Mold.* 159 R5
Dnipro (Dnieper), river, *Ukr.* 159 R7
Dniprodzerzhyns'k, *Ukr.* 159 Q8
Dnipropetrovs'k, *Ukr.* 159 Q8
Dno, *Russ.* 158 G6
Dnyapro, river, *Belarus* 158 K6
Doba, *Chad* 201 KI4
Dobane, *Cen. Af. Rep.* 202 HIO
Dobbs, Cape, *Nunavut, Can.* 85 HI6
Dobbyn, *Qnsld., Austral.* 215 SII
Doboj, *Bosn. & Herzg.* 154 F8
Dobre Miasto, *Pol.* 151 BI5
Dobrich, *Bulg.* 155 GI7
Dobruja, region, *Bulg., Rom.* 155 GI8
Dobrush, *Belarus* 158 M6
Dobson, *N.Z.* 217 NI7
Docampadó, Ensenada, *Col.* 130 F3
Doce, river, *Braz.* 133 LI5

Docheong, *S. Korea* 187 V8
Dochodo, island, *S. Korea* 187 T6
Docker River, *N.T., Austral.* 215 U7
Dock Junction, *Ga., U.S.* 99 P8
Doctor David Douglas Historical Monument, *Hawai'i, U.S.* II5 L2O
Dodecanese see *Dodekánisa, islands, Gr.* 157 MI8
Dodekánisa (Dodecanese), islands, *Gr.* 157 MI8
Dodge, *Nebr., U.S.* 107 P8
Dodge City, *Kans., U.S.* 107 U5
Dodgeville, *Wis., U.S.* 100 L4
Dodman Point, *Eng., U.K.* 145 Y8
Dodoma, *Tanzania* 203 MI4
Dodona, ruin, *Gr.* 156 E7
Dodson, *Mont., U.S.* 108 BIO
Dodson, *Tex., U.S.* 104 H7
Doerun, *Ga., U.S.* 99 P5
Doetinchem, *Neth.* 148 JI4
Doğanşehir, *Turk.* 170 GI2
Dog Creek, *B.C., Can.* 84 L8
Dogger Bank, *Atl. Oc.* 240 GI3
Dog Island, *Virgin Is., U.S.* 122 NIO
Dōgo, island, *Japan* 189 N7
Dogondoutchi, *Niger* 200 HIO
Dog Rocks, islands, *Bahamas* 118 F9
Doğruyol, *Turk.* 171 DI7
Dogwood Point, *St. Kitts and Nevis* 123 CI8
Dogye, *S. Korea* 187 NI2
Dogye, *S. Korea* 187 PI2
Doha see *Ad Dawḩah, Qatar* 175 JI3
Dohm Bank, *Atl. Oc.* 240 E9
Doi Inthanon, peak, *Thai.* 190 J7
Doïran, Lake see *Dojransko Ezero, Gr., Maced.* 154 LI2
Doïráni, Límni, *Gr.* 156 BII
Dois Irmãos, Serra, *Braz.* 133 GI6
Dojransko Ezero (Doïran, Lake), *Gr., Maced.* 154 LI2
Dokdo (Takeshima, Liancourt Rocks), *S. Korea* 188 M5
Dokkum, *Neth.* 148 GI3
Dokós, island, *Gr.* 156 KI2
Dolak (Yos Sudarso), island, *Indonesia* 193 M2O
Doland, *S. Dak., U.S.* 106 K7
Dolbeau, *Que., Can.* 85 NI9
Doldrums Fracture Zone, *Atl. Oc.* 241 N7
Dole, *Fr.* 149 SI3
Dolgiy Most, *Russ.* 161 KI4
Dolianá, *Gr.* 156 E7
Dolianova, *It.* 153 P4
Dolinsk, *Russ.* 161 K22
Dolisie (Loubomo), *Congo* 205 KI6
Dolly Cays, *Bahamas* 118 FII
Dolo Bay, *Eth.* 203 HI6
Dolohmwar, peak, *F.S.M.* 221 FI4
Dolok (Yos Sudarso), island, *Indonesia* 217 DI6
Dolomites, range, *It.* 152 C7
Dolonnur see *Duolun, N. Mongol, China* 184 A8
Dolores, *Arg.* 134 MI3
Dolores, *Colo., U.S.* 109 PIO
Dolores, *Uru.* 134 LI3
Dolores, river, *Colo., Utah, U.S.* 109 NIO
Dolphin, Cape, *Falk. Is., U.K.* 135 VI2
Dolphin Spur, *Pac. Oc.* 249 F2I
Dolsan, *S. Korea* 187 U9
Đô Lương, *Vietnam* 190 JII
Dom, peak, *Indonesia* 217 BI6
Domagnano, *San Marino* 163 JI6
Domaniç, *Turk.* 170 E5
Domažlice, *Czech Rep.* 150 HIO
Dombás, *Nor.* 142 HII
Dome Argus (Dome A), *Antarctica* 231 HI6
Dome C, *Antarctica* 231 MI7
Doméniko, *Gr.* 156 EIO
Domett, *N.Z.* 217 NI8
Domeyko, *Chile* 134 H6
Domeyko, Cordillera, *Chile* 134 E7
Domfront, *Fr.* 149 P6
Domingitu, *Curaçao* 123 QI5
Dominica, *N. Amer.* 121 EI7

Dominican Republic, *N. Amer.* 119 L2O
Dominica Passage, *N. Amer.* 121 DI6
Dominion, Cape, *Nunavut, Can.* 85 GI7
Domodossola, *It.* 152 C3
Domokós, *Gr.* 156 FIO
Domoni, *Comoros* 209 NI6
Domus de Maria, *It.* 153 Q3
Domuyo, Volcán, *Arg.* 134 M6
Domuyo Volcano, *S. Amer.* 128 M4
Don, river, *Russ.* 159 PI2
Dôn, river, *Laos* 190 LI2
Don, river, *Russ.* 124 A8
Donaldson, *Minn., U.S.* 106 E8
Donaldsonville, *La., U.S.* 102 PIO
Donalsonville, *Ga., U.S.* 99 Q4
Donau (Danube), *Aus.* 150 KII
Donbas, region, *Ukr.* 159 QIO
Don Benito, *Sp.* 146 H8
Doncaster, *Eng., U.K.* 145 RI3
Dondo, *Angola* 206 C6
Dondo, *Indonesia* 193 JI4
Dondo, *Mozambique* 207 GI3
Dondra Head, *Asia* 168 L7
Donegal Bay, *Ire.* 145 Q4
Donets, river, *Eur.* 140 GI2
Donets Basin, *Eur.* 140 HI2
Donets'k, *Ukr.* 159 Q9
Donetsk, *Russ.* 159 QII
Donets Ridge, *Eur.* 140 HI3
Dong, river, *Guang., China* 185 V6
Donga, *Nigeria* 205 DI5
Dongara, *W. Aust., Austral.* 215 W2
Dongbei (Manchuria), region, *China* 183 CI5
Dongcun see *Haiyang, Shand., China* 184 GII
Dongdo, island, *S. Korea* 187 V9
Dongducheon, *S. Korea* 186 M8
Dongeun, *S. Korea* 187 SII
Donghae, *S. Korea* 186 MI2
Donghai Dao, *Guang., China* 185 XI
Đông Hới, *Vietnam* 190 KI2
Dongjingcheng, *China* 183 DI7
Dongkalang, *Indonesia* 193 JI3
Dongkan see *Binhai, Jiangsu, China* 184 JIO
Đông Khê, *Vietnam* 190 GI2
Dongkou, *Hunan, China* 185 R2
Đông Lê, *Vietnam* 190 KI2
Dongling, *Liaoning, China* 184 AI3
Dongmao, *Hebei, China* 184 B7
Dongning, *China* 183 DI7
Dongo, *Dem. Rep. of the Congo* 202 J8
Dongola, *Sudan* 202 DI2
Dongou, *Congo* 205 GI8
Đông Phu, *Vietnam* 190 LI3
Dongping, *Guang., China* 185 X3
Dongping, *Shand., China* 184 H7
Dongping Hu, *Shand., China* 184 G7
Dongsha (Pratas Island), *Other, China* 185 Y7
Dongsha, islands, *Other, China* 185 Y7
Dongshan (Xibu), *Fujian, China* 185 V8
Dongshe, *Shanxi, China* 184 E4
Dongsheng, *N. Mongol, China* 184 C3
Dongtai, *Jiangsu, China* 184 LII
Dongting Hu, *Hunan, China* 185 P4
Đông Văn, *Vietnam* 190 FII
Dongxiang, *Jiangxi, China* 185 Q7
Đồng Xoài, *Vietnam* 191 PI3
Dongyang, *Zhejiang, China* 185 PII
Dongying, *Shand., China* 184 F9
Dongyztaū, *Kaz.* 176 F8
Dongzhen, *China* 182 PI2
Doniphan, *Mo., U.S.* 107 VI4
Dønna, island, *Nor.* 142 FII
Donnelly, *Idaho, U.S.* 108 F4
Donnellys Crossing, *N.Z.* 217 HI8
Donner Pass, *Calif., U.S.* III Q6
Donors Hill, *Qnsld., Austral.* 215 RII

Donostia-San Sebastián, *Sp.* 147 BI3
Donoúsa, island, *Gr.* 157 LI6
Donzenac, *Fr.* 149 V9
Doolish see *Douglas, Isle of Man, U.K.* 145 Q9
Doomadgee, *Qnsld., Austral.* 215 RII
Doon, Loch, *Scot., U.K.* 145 N9
Door Peninsula, *Wis., U.S.* 100 J7
Dopyeong, *S. Korea* 187 QI2
Dora, *Ala., U.S.* 103 JI5
Dora, *N. Mex., U.S.* 109 TI5
Dora, Lake, *Austral.* 214 F5
Dorah Pass, *Afghan., Pak.* 178 L9
Dorchester, *Eng., U.K.* 145 XII
Dorchester, Cape, *Nunavut, Can.* 85 GI7
Dordives, *Fr.* 149 QIO
Dordogne, river, *Fr.* 149 V9
Dordrecht, *Neth.* 148 JI2
Dordrecht Hole, *Ind. Oc.* 225 NI5
Dörgön Nuur, *Mongolia* 182 D7
Dori, *Burkina Faso* 204 AII
Dório, *Gr.* 156 K9
Dormans, *Fr.* 149 PII
Dornbirn, *Aust.* 150 L7
Dornoch, *Scot., U.K.* 144 J9
Dornoch Firth, *Scot., U.K.* 144 J9
Dorogobuzh, *Russ.* 158 K7
Dorohoi, *Rom.* 155 AI5
Dorre Island, *Austral.* 214 GI
Dorris, *Calif., U.S.* IIO L4
Dortmund, *Ger.* 150 E6
Dörtyol, *Turk.* 170 JII
Dos Bahías, Cape, *S. Amer.* 128 P5
Döşemealtı, *Turk.* 170 H6
Dos Hermanas, *Sp.* 146 L8
Dōshī, *Afghan.* 178 L7
Dosso, *Niger* 200 JIO
Dossor, *Kaz.* 176 F6
Dostyq, *Kaz.* 177 GI9
Dothan, *Ala., U.S.* 103 NI7
Douai, *Fr.* 148 MIO
Douala, *Cameroon* 205 FI5
Douarnenez, *Fr.* 149 Q3
Douarnenez, Baie de, *Fr.* 149 Q2
Double Island Point, *Austral.* 214 GI6
Double Mountain Fork Brazos, river, *Tex., U.S.* 104 L6
Double Point, *Austral.* 214 DI3
Doubtful Bay, *Austral.* 214 C5
Doubtless Bay, *N.Z.* 217 GI8
Doué, *Fr.* 149 S7
Douentza, *Mali* 200 H8
Douéoulou, *New Caledonia, Fr.* 222 C9
Douglas, *Ariz., U.S.* 109 W9
Douglas, *Ga., U.S.* 99 P7
Douglas, *Mich., U.S.* 100 M9
Douglas, *Wyo., U.S.* 108 HI3
Douglas (Doolish), *Isle of Man, U.K.* 145 Q9
Douglas, Cabo, *Ecua.* 130 P8
Douglas Bay, *Dominica* 123 DI8
Douglas Lake, *Tenn., U.S.* 103 EI9
Douglass, *Kans., U.S.* 107 U8
Douglasville, *Ga., U.S.* 98 L4
Doullens, *Fr.* 148 MIO
Doura, *Mali* 200 H7
Dourada, Serra, *S. Amer.* 128 G8
Dourados, *Braz.* 132 LII
Douro, river, *Port., Sp.* 146 E8
Dove Bay, *Greenland, Den.* 82 B9
Dove Creek, *Colo., U.S.* 109 PIO
Dover, *Del., U.S.* 98 CI5
Dover, *Eng., U.K.* 145 WI6
Dover, *N.H., U.S.* 97 JI5
Dover, *Ohio, U.S.* 101 QI5
Dover, Strait of (Pas de Calais), *Fr., U.K.* 148 L9
Dover-Foxcroft, *Me., U.S.* 97 EI7
Dowagiac, *Mich., U.S.* 101 N9
Dowlatābād, *Afghan.* 178 K4
Dowlatābād, *Iran* 175 GI5
Dowlatābād, *Afghan.* 178 M5
Dowlatyār, *Afghan.* 178 M5
Downey, *Calif., U.S.* III X8
Downey, *Idaho, U.S.* 108 J7
Downieville, *Calif., U.S.* III P5
Downpatrick, *N. Ire., U.K.* 145 Q7

Downpatrick Head, *Ire.* 145 Q3
Downs, *Kans., U.S.* 107 S6
Doxáto, *Gr.* 157 B13
Doyang, *S. Korea* 187 U8
Doylestown, *Pa., U.S.* 96 P9
Dōzen, island, *Japan* 189 P7
Drâa, Hamada du, *Af.* 200 C8
Drâa, Oued, *Alg., Mor.* 200 C8
Drăgăneşti, *Rom.* 155 G14
Drăgăneşti-Olt, *Rom.* 155 G14
Drăgăşani, *Rom.* 155 F14
Dragon's Mouths, *Trinidad and Tobago, Venez.* 121 J16
Draguignan, *Fr.* 149 X14
Drain, *Oreg., U.S.* 110 H3
Drake, *N. Dak., U.S.* 106 F5
Drakensberg, range, *S. Af.* 206 K11
Drake Passage, *Atl. Oc.* 241 W4
Drake Peak, *Oreg., U.S.* 110 K6
Dráma, *Gr.* 157 B13
Drammen, *Nor.* 142 K11
Dranov, Ostrov, *Rom.* 155 E18
Dras, *India* 178 M13
Drasan, *Pak.* 178 K10
Drau, river, *Aust.* 150 M10
Dráva, river, *Croatia, Hung.* 154 D7
Dravograd, *Slov.* 154 C5
Drayton, *N. Dak., U.S.* 106 E8
Drépano, Akrotírio, *Gr.* 157 E13
Dresden, *Ger.* 150 F10
Dreux, *Fr.* 149 P9
Drevsjø, *Nor.* 142 H12
Drew, *Miss., U.S.* 102 J10
Drewsey, *Oreg., U.S.* 110 H8
Drews Reservoir, *Oreg., U.S.* 110 L5
Driggs, *Idaho, U.S.* 108 G8
Drin, river, *Alban.* 154 J9
Drina, river, *Bosn. & Herzg., Serb.* 154 F9
Drinit, Gjiri i, *Alban.* 154 K9
Driskill Mountain, *La., U.S.* 102 L7
Drøbak, *Nor.* 142 K11
Drobeta-Turnu Severin, *Rom.* 154 F12
Drogheda (Droichead Átha), *Ire.* 145 R7
Drohobych, *Ukr.* 159 P2
Droichead Átha see Drogheda, *Ire.* 145 R7
Droitwich, *Eng., U.K.* 145 U11
Drosh, *Pak.* 178 L10
Drouseia, *Cyprus* 162 P5
Drovyanoy, *Russ.* 160 E12
Drua, island, *Fiji* 222 G7
Drumheller, *Alta., Can.* 84 M10
Drummond, *Mont., U.S.* 108 D6
Drummond Island, *Mich., U.S.* 100 G12
Drummond Range, *Austral.* 214 F14
Drumright, *Okla., U.S.* 104 F12
Druza, Gora, *Russ.* 161 F19
Dryanovo, *Bulg.* 155 H15
Dryden, *Ont., Can.* 85 N15
Dryden, *Tex., U.S.* 105 Q4
Drygalski Basin, *Pac. Oc.* 249 H15
Drygalski Ice Tongue, *Antarctica* 231 P14
Drygalski Island, *Antarctica* 231 J21
Drygalski Mountains, *Antarctica* 231 B13
Dry Harbour Mountains, *Jam.* 122 H8
Drysdale, river, *Austral.* 214 C6
Dry Tortugas, islands, *U.S.* 87 P19
Dry Tortugas National Park, *Fla., U.S.* 99 Y7
Dschang, *Cameroon* 205 E15
Du, river, *Hubei, China* 184 L2
Dūāb-e Maykh-e Zarīn, *Afghan.* 178 L7
Duaringa, *Qnsld., Austral.* 215 T15
Duarte, Pico, *Dom. Rep.* 119 M18
Ḍubā, *Saudi Arabia* 174 H5
Dubai see Dubayy, *U.A.E.* 175 J15
Dubăsari, *Mold.* 159 R5
Dubawnt, river, *N.W.T., Can.* 85 J13
Dubawnt Lake, *Nunavut, Can.* 85 H13
Dubayy (Dubai), *U.A.E.* 175 J15
Dubh Artach, island, *Scot., U.K.* 144 M7
Dublin, *Ga., U.S.* 98 M7

Dublin, *Tex., U.S.* 104 M10
Dublin (Baile Átha Cliath), *Ire.* 145 S7
Dubna, *Russ.* 158 H9
Dubno, *Ukr.* 159 N3
Du Bois, *Pa., U.S.* 96 M5
Dubois, *Idaho, U.S.* 108 G7
Dubois, *Wyo., U.S.* 108 G9
Dubovka, *Russ.* 159 P13
Dubrovnik (Ragusa), *Croatia* 154 J8
Dubrovytsya, *Ukr.* 158 M4
Dubuque, *Iowa, U.S.* 107 N14
Duc de Gloucester, Îles, *Fr. Polynesia, Fr.* 223 G19
Duc de Gloucester, Îles du, *Fr. Polynesia, Fr.* 219 K14
Du Chaillu Seamounts, *Atl. Oc.* 241 P12
Duchesne, *Utah, U.S.* 108 L8
Duchesne, river, *Utah, U.S.* 108 L8
Duchess, *Qnsld., Austral.* 215 S11
Ducie Island, *Pac. Oc.* 219 K17
Duck, river, *Tenn., U.S.* 103 F15
Duck Creek, *W. Aust., Austral.* 215 T2
Duck Hill, *Miss., U.S.* 102 J11
Ducktown, *Tenn., U.S.* 103 G18
Ducos, *Martinique, Fr.* 123 F23
Ducos, Île, *New Caledonia, Fr.* 222 D8
Đức Thọ, *Vietnam* 190 J12
Dudelange, *Lux.* 162 K10
Dudinka, *Russ.* 161 F13
Dudley, *Eng., U.K.* 145 T12
Dudune, Île, *New Caledonia, Fr.* 222 D9
Duero, river, *Sp.* 146 E9
Dufek Coast, *Antarctica* 230 L12
Duff Islands, *Solomon Is.* 221 N24
Dufftown, *Scot., U.K.* 144 J10
Dufur, *Oreg., U.S.* 110 F5
Dugi Otok, island, *Croatia* 154 G5
Dugway, *Utah, U.S.* 108 L6
Duifken Point, *Austral.* 214 B12
Duisburg, *Ger.* 150 E5
Duitama, *Col.* 130 E6
Dukla, *Pol.* 151 H17
Dulan, *China* 182 H8
Dulce, *N. Mex., U.S.* 109 Q11
Dulce, river, *Arg.* 134 H10
Dulce, Golfo, *C.R.* 117 P19
Dulovo, *Bulg.* 155 G16
Duluth, *Minn., U.S.* 106 G12
Dūmā, *Syr.* 172 J7
Dumai, *Indonesia* 192 H6
Dumaran, island, *Philippines* 193 E13
Dumas, *Ark., U.S.* 102 J9
Dumas, *Tex., U.S.* 104 F5
Dumbarton, *Scot., U.K.* 144 M9
Dumbéa, *New Caledonia, Fr.* 222 D8
Dumfries, *Scot., U.K.* 145 P10
Dumido, *S. Korea* 187 T10
Dumka, *India* 180 H11
Dumoga Kecil, *Indonesia* 193 J15
Dumont d'Urville, station, *Antarctica* 231 Q18
Dumra, *India* 180 G10
Dumshaf Plain, *Arctic Oc.* 247 H19
Dumyât (Damietta), *Egypt* 201 C18
Dun, *Fr.* 149 N13
Duna (Danube), river, *Hung.* 151 L14
Dunaj (Danube), river, *Slovakia* 151 L14
Dún an Uchta see Eyrecourt, *Ire.* 145 S5
Dunărea (Danube), river, *Rom., Serb.* 154 F11
Dunaújváros, *Hung.* 151 M15
Dunav, river, *Bulg., Rom.* 155 G16
Dunay (Danube), river, *Rom., Ukr.* 155 E18
Dunbar, *Qnsld., Austral.* 215 Q12
Dunbar, *W. Va., U.S.* 98 D8
Duncan, *Ariz., U.S.* 109 V9
Duncan, *Okla., U.S.* 104 H10
Duncan Passage, *India* 181 R14
Duncans, *Jam.* 122 H8
Duncansby Head, *Scot., U.K.* 144 G10
Duncan Town, *Bahamas* 119 H13
Duncombe Bay, *Norfolk I., Austral.* 221 F20

Dundalk, *Md., U.S.* 98 C13
Dundalk (Dún Dealgan), *Ire.* 145 R7
Dundalk Bay, *Ire.* 145 R7
Dundas, Lake, *Austral.* 214 K5
Dundas Peninsula, *N.W.T., Can.* 85 D13
Dundas Strait, *Austral.* 214 A8
Dún Dealgan see Dundalk, *Ire.* 145 R7
Dundee, *Scot., U.K.* 144 L10
Dundee Island, *Antarctica* 230 C4
Dundonnell, *Scot., U.K.* 144 J8
Dundrennan, *Scot., U.K.* 145 P9
Dundrum Bay, *N. Ire., U.K.* 145 Q7
Dunedin, *Fla., U.S.* 99 U7
Dunedin, *N.Z.* 217 Q16
Dunes City, *Oreg., U.S.* 110 H2
Dunfermline, *Scot., U.K.* 144 M10
Dungarpur, *India* 180 H4
Dungarvan Harbour, *Ire.* 145 U5
Dungeness, cape, *Eng., U.K.* 145 W15
Dungeness, Punta, *Arg.* 135 W9
Dungiven, *N. Ire., U.K.* 145 P6
Dunham River, *W. Aust., Austral.* 215 Q6
Dünheger, peak, *China, Mongolia* 182 D6
Dunhua, *China* 183 E16
Dunhuang, *China* 182 G7
Dunkerque (Dunkirk), *Fr.* 148 L10
Dunkineely, *Ire.* 145 P5
Dunkirk, *Ind., U.S.* 101 Q10
Dunkirk, *N.Y., U.S.* 96 K4
Dunkirk see Dunkerque, *Fr.* 148 L10
Dunkwa, *Ghana* 204 E10
Dún Laoghaire, *Ire.* 145 S7
Dunlap, *Iowa, U.S.* 107 P9
Dún Mánmhaí see Dunmanway, *Ire.* 145 V3
Dunmanus Bay, *Ire.* 145 V3
Dunmanway (Dún Mánmhaí), *Ire.* 145 V3
Dunmore, *Pa., U.S.* 96 M9
Dunmore Town, *Bahamas* 122 D5
Dunn, *N.C., U.S.* 98 H12
Dunnellon, *Fla., U.S.* 99 S7
Dunning, *Nebr., U.S.* 107 P5
Dunn's River Falls, *Jam.* 122 H9
Dunolly, *Vic., Austral.* 215 Y12
Dunseith, *N. Dak., U.S.* 106 D5
Dunsmuir, *Calif., U.S.* 110 M3
Duntroon, *N.Z.* 217 Q16
Dunvegan, *Scot., U.K.* 144 J7
Duolun (Dolonnur), *N. Mongol, China* 184 A8
Dupree, *S. Dak., U.S.* 106 J3
Dupuyer, *Mont., U.S.* 108 B7
Duqm, *Oman* 175 M16
Duque de Caxias, *Braz.* 133 M15
Duque de York, Isla, *Chile* 135 V6
Duquesne, *Pa., U.S.* 96 N3
Du Quoin, *Ill., U.S.* 101 U5
Durack, river, *Austral.* 214 C6
Dura Europus, ruins, *Syr.* 172 G14
Durán, river, *Sp.* 162 K5
Durance, river, *Fr.* 149 W14
Durand, *Wis., U.S.* 100 J2
Durango, *Colo., U.S.* 109 P11
Durango, *Mex.* 116 F9
Durango, *Sp.* 146 B12
Durankulak, *Bulg.* 155 G18
Durant, *Miss., U.S.* 102 K11
Durant, *Okla., U.S.* 104 J12
Duras, *Fr.* 149 W7
Durazno, *Uru.* 134 K14
Durban, *S. Af.* 206 K11
Durbuy, *Belg.* 148 M13
Đurđevac, *Croatia* 154 D7
Dureji, *Pak.* 179 V6
Düren, *Ger.* 150 F5
Durg, *India* 180 K8
Durham, *Eng., U.K.* 145 P12
Durham, *N.C., U.S.* 98 G11
Durham, *N.H., U.S.* 97 J15
Durlas see Thurles, *Ire.* 145 T5
Durlston Head, *Eng., U.K.* 145 X12
Durmitor, peak, *Eur.* 140 K8
Durness, Kyle of, *Scot., U.K.* 144 H8
Duroy, *Russ.* 161 L18

Durrës, *Alban.* 154 L9
Durrësit, Gjiri i, *Alban.* 154 L9
Dursey Island, *Ire.* 145 V2
Dursunbey, *Turk.* 170 E4
Durtal, *Fr.* 149 R7
Duru Gölü, *Turk.* 170 C4
Ḍurumā, *Saudi Arabia* 174 J10
Durūz, Jabal ad, *Syr.* 172 L8
D'Urville, Tanjung, *Indonesia* 217 K5
D'Urville Channel, *Fiji* 222 J6
D'Urville Island see Rangitoto ki te Tonga, *N.Z.* 217 M18
Duşak, *Uzb.* 176 M9
Dûsh, *Egypt* 201 E18
Dūshākh, *Afghan.* 178 L6
Dushan, *China* 182 N11
Dushanbe, *Taj.* 178 H7
Dushanzi, *China* 182 E5
Düsseldorf, *Ger.* 150 F5
Dutchcap Cay, *Virgin Is., U.S.* 122 M7
Dutch John, *Utah, U.S.* 108 K9
Dutoit Fracture Zone, *Ind. Oc.* 224 R3
Dutton, Mount, *Utah, U.S.* 109 P7
Du Vent, Îles, *Fr. Polynesia, Fr.* 223 F16
Duvergé, *Dom. Rep.* 119 M17
Duwayhin, Dawḥat, *Saudi Arabia* 175 J13
Düzce, *Turk.* 170 D7
Düzce see Achna, *Cyprus* 162 P9
Dvina, river, *Asia* 168 D6
Dvina Bay, *Arctic Oc.* 140 B11
Dwarka, *India* 180 J1
Dwight, *Ill., U.S.* 101 P6
Dworshak Reservoir, *Idaho, U.S.* 108 D3
Dyat'kovo, *Russ.* 158 L8
Dyer, Cape, *Nunavut, Can.* 85 F19
Dyer Bay, *N.W.T., Can.* 84 C12
Dyersburg, *Tenn., U.S.* 102 E12
Dyersville, *Iowa, U.S.* 107 N14
Dynevor Downs, *Qnsld., Austral.* 215 V12
Dzaanhushuu, *Mongolia* 182 D9
Dzag, *Mongolia* 182 D9
Dzangalī, *Afghan.* 179 P6
Dzaoudzi, *Mayotte, Fr.* 209 P17
Dzavhan, river, *Mongolia* 182 D7
Dzerzhinsk, *Russ.* 158 J12
Dzhagdy, Khrebet, *Russ.* 161 J19
Dzhagdy Range, *Asia* 168 D11
Dzhankoy, *Ukr.* 159 S7
Dzhardzhan, *Russ.* 161 F16
Dzharty-Rabat, *Taj.* 178 J11
Dzharylhach, Ostriv, *Ukr.* 159 S7
Dzhilandy, *Taj.* 178 J10
Dzhugdzhur, Khrebet, *Russ.* 161 H20
Dzhugdzhur Range, *Asia* 168 D12
Dzhunkun, *Russ.* 161 H16
Działdowo, *Pol.* 151 C15
Dzierżoniów, *Pol.* 151 G13
Dzibilchaltún, ruin, *Mex.* 117 H16
Dzöölön, *Mongolia* 182 B9
Dzungarian Basin see Junggar Pendi, *China* 182 D5
Dzungarian Gate, pass, *China, Kaz.* 177 Q12
Dzuunmod, *Mongolia* 182 D11
Dzvina, river, *Belarus* 158 J6
Dzyarzhynsk, *Belarus* 158 K4

E

Eads, *Colo., U.S.* 109 N15
Eagar, *Ariz., U.S.* 109 T9
Eagle, *Alas., U.S.* 113 F19
Eagle, *Colo., U.S.* 108 M11
Eagle, Mount, *Virgin Is., U.S.* 122 Q2
Eagle Beach, *Aruba, Neth.* 123 Q16
Eagle Butte, *S. Dak., U.S.* 106 J4
Eagle Grove, *Iowa, U.S.* 107 N11
Eagle Harbor, *Mich., U.S.* 100 D7
Eagle Lake, *Calif., U.S.* 111 N5
Eagle Lake, *Me., U.S.* 97 B17
Eagle Lake, *Tex., U.S.* 105 R12

Eagle Mountain, *Calif., U.S.* 111 X12
Eagle Mountain, *Minn., U.S.* 106 F14
Eagle Mountain Lake, *Tex., U.S.* 104 L11
Eagle Nest Lake, *N. Mex., U.S.* 109 Q13
Eagle Pass, *Tex., U.S.* 105 S7
Eagle Peak, *Calif., U.S.* 110 M6
Eagle Peak, *N. Mex., U.S.* 109 T10
Eagle Peak, *Tex., U.S.* 105 X4
Eagle River, *Mich., U.S.* 100 E6
Eagle River, *Wis., U.S.* 100 G5
Eagles Mere, *Pa., U.S.* 96 M8
Earle, *Ark., U.S.* 102 G11
Earlimart, *Calif., U.S.* 111 U7
Earlington, *Ky., U.S.* 103 D14
Earp, *Calif., U.S.* 111 X13
Earth, *Tex., U.S.* 104 J4
Easky (Iascaigh), *Ire.* 145 Q4
Easley, *S.C., U.S.* 98 J7
East Anglia, region, *Eng., U.K.* 145 U15
East Anglian Heights, *Eng., U.K.* 145 U15
East Antarctica, region, *Antarctica* 231 H16
East Aurora, *N.Y., U.S.* 96 J5
East Azores Fracture Zone, *Atl. Oc.* 240 K9
East Bay, *La., U.S.* 102 R12
Eastbourne, *Eng., U.K.* 145 W14
East Caicos, island, *Turks & Caicos Is.* 119 H17
East Cape, *Asia* 168 A12
East Cape, *N.Z.* 217 K21
East Carbon, *Utah, U.S.* 108 M8
East Caroline Basin, *Pac. Oc.* 242 J8
East Channel, *Marshall Is., U.S.* 220 H8
East Chicago, *Ind., U.S.* 101 N7
East China Sea, *Pac. Oc.* 168 H13
East Coast Bays, *N.Z.* 217 J19
East Cote, *La., U.S.* 102 Q9
East Dubuque, *Ill., U.S.* 100 M4
East End, *British Virgin Is., U.K.* 122 Q7
East End, *Cayman Is.* 122 J4
East End, *Virgin Is., U.S.* 122 N12
East End Point, *Bahamas* 122 B12
East End Point, *Bahamas* 122 G6
East Entrance, *Palau* 220 L12
Easter Fracture Zone, *Pac. Oc.* 243 M20
Easter Island see Pascua, Isla de, *Pac. Oc.* 219 L19
Eastern see Lau Group, *Fiji* 222 H9
Eastern Beach, *Gibraltar, U.K.* 163 N23
Eastern Desert, *Egypt* 201 D19
Eastern Ghats, range, *India* 181 Q6
Eastern Island, *Hawai'i, U.S.* 114 K2
Eastern Sayan Mountains, *Asia* 168 E9
East Falkland, island, *Falk. Is., U.K.* 135 W12
East Fayu, island, *F.S.M.* 220 Q6
East Fork Bruneau, river, *Idaho, U.S.* 108 H4
East Fork White, river, *U.S.* 87 G17
East Frisian Islands, *Ger.* 150 B6
East Glacier Park, *Mont., U.S.* 108 B6
East Grand Forks, *Minn., U.S.* 106 F8
East Greenland Shelf, *Atl. Oc.* 240 E8
East Helena, *Mont., U.S.* 108 D7
East Indiaman Ridge, *Ind. Oc.* 225 L14
East Isaac, island, *Bahamas* 118 D10
East Jordan, *Mich., U.S.* 100 H10
East Korea Bay, *Pac. Oc.* 168 F12
East Lake, *Mich., U.S.* 100 J8
Eastland, *Tex., U.S.* 104 M9
East Lansing, *Mich., U.S.* 100 M11
East Liverpool, *Ohio, U.S.* 101 Q15
East London, *S. Af.* 206 M10
Eastmain, *Que., Can.* 85 M18
Eastmain, river, *Que., Can.* 85 M19
Eastman, *Ga., U.S.* 99 N6

East Mariana Basin, *Pac. Oc.* **242** H8
East Millinocket, *Me., U.S.* **97** D17
East Moline, *Ill., U.S.* **101** N4
East Novaya Zemlya Trough, *Arctic Oc.* **247** D15
Easton, *Md., U.S.* **98** C14
Easton, *Pa., U.S.* **96** N9
East Orange, *N.J., U.S.* **96** N11
East Pacific Rise, *Pac. Oc.* **243** Q18
East Pen Island, *Ont., Can.* **85** L16
East Peoria, *Ill., U.S.* **101** Q5
East Point, *Ga., U.S.* **98** L5
East Point, *Marshall Is., U.S.* **220** M9
East Point, *Virgin Is., U.S.* **122** Q4
Eastpoint, *Fla., U.S.* **99** R4
Eastport, *Me., U.S.* **97** E20
East Prairie, *Mo., U.S.* **107** V16
East Prussia, region, *Pol., Russ.* **151** B16
East Ridge, *Tenn., U.S.* **103** G17
East Saint Louis, *Ill., U.S.* **101** T4
East Scotia Basin, *Atl. Oc.* **241** W8
East Scotia Ridge, *Atl. Oc.* **248** L8
East Sea *see* Japan, Sea of, *Pac. Oc.* **168** F13
East Sheba Ridge, *Ind. Oc.* **224** D7
East Siberian Sea, *Arctic Oc.* **246** H6
East Siberian Shelf, *Arctic Oc.* **246** G7
East Takatu *see* Tacutu, river, *S. Amer.* **131** F14
East Tasman Plateau, *Pac. Oc.* **242** P8
East Tasman Saddle, *Ind. Oc.* **225** Q23
East Tawas, *Mich., U.S.* **100** J12
East Thulean Rise, *Atl. Oc.* **240** H9
East Timor *see* Timor-Leste, *Asia* **193** M15
Eastville, *Va., U.S.* **98** E14
East Wells, *Bahamas* **122** A8
Eaton, *Ohio, U.S.* **101** R11
Eaton Rapids, *Mich., U.S.* **100** M11
Eatonton, *Ga., U.S.* **98** L6
Eatonville, *Wash., U.S.* **110** D4
Eau Claire, *Wis., U.S.* **100** H3
Eau Claire, Lac a l', *N. Amer.* **82** F8
Eauripik Atoll, *F.S.M.* **220** Q3
Eauripik Rise, *Pac. Oc.* **242** J7
Ebadon, island, *Marshall Is., U.S.* **220** K1
Ebbw Vale (Glyn Ebwy), *Wales, U.K.* **145** V10
Ebe Khaya, Gora, *Russ.* **161** F15
Ebenholz, *Liech.* **162** P2
Eber Gölü, *Turk.* **170** F7
Eberswalde, *Ger.* **150** D10
Ebeye, island, *Marshall Is., U.S.* **220** N5
Ebinur Hu, *China* **182** D4
Ebjapik, island, *Marshall Is., U.S.* **220** N5
Eboda, ruins *see* Horvat 'Avedat, *Israel* **173** P5
Eboli, *It.* **152** M11
Ebolowa, *Cameroon* **205** F15
Ebon Atoll, *Marshall Is., U.S.* **220** J4
Ebro, river, *Sp.* **147** D13
Ebro, Embalse del, *Sp.* **146** B11
Ebwaj, island, *Marshall Is., U.S.* **220** N5
Ecclesville, *Trinidad and Tobago* **123** Q23
Eceabat, *Turk.* **170** D2
Echallens, *Switz.* **152** B1
Echínos, *Gr.* **157** B14
Echo, *Oreg., U.S.* **110** E7
Echo Bay, *N.W.T., Can.* **84** G11
Echternach, *Lux.* **162** J11
Echuca, *Vic., Austral.* **215** Y12
Écija, *Sp.* **146** L9
Eckenförde, *Ger.* **150** B8
Ecuador, *S. Amer.* **130** K3
Eday, island, *Scot., U.K.* **144** F11
Edcouch, *Tex., U.S.* **105** W10
Ed Debba, *Sudan* **202** D12
Eddrachillis Bay, *Scot., U.K.* **144** H8
Eddystone Rocks, *Eng., U.K.* **145** Y9
Eddyville, *Ky., U.S.* **103** D13

Ede, *Neth.* **148** J13
Edéa, *Cameroon* **205** F15
Edel Land, *Austral.* **214** H1
Eden, *N.C., U.S.* **98** G10
Eden, *N.S.W., Austral.* **215** Z14
Eden, *Tex., U.S.* **105** N7
Eden, *Wyo., U.S.* **108** J9
Edenburg, *S. Af.* **206** K10
Edenton, *N.C., U.S.* **98** G14
Édessa, *Gr.* **156** C9
Edessa *see* Şanlıurfa, *Turk.* **171** H13
Edgar, *Nebr., U.S.* **107** R7
Edgartown, *Mass., U.S.* **97** M15
Edgefield, *S.C., U.S.* **98** L8
Edge Island, *Nor.* **168** A7
Edgeley, *N. Dak., U.S.* **106** H6
Edgell Island, *Nunavut, Can.* **85** H20
Edgemont, *S. Dak., U.S.* **106** M1
Edgerton, *Minn., U.S.* **106** L9
Edgerton, *Wis., U.S.* **100** M5
Edgigen, island, *Marshall Is., U.S.* **220** K4
Edina, *Mo., U.S.* **107** R13
Edinburg, *Tex., U.S.* **105** W10
Edinburgh, *Ind., U.S.* **101** S9
Edinburgh, *Scot., U.K.* **144** M10
Edirne (Adrianople), *Turk.* **170** B3
Edison, *Ga., U.S.* **99** P4
Edison, *N.J., U.S.* **96** N10
Edisto, river, *S.C., U.S.* **98** M9
Edisto Island, *S.C., U.S.* **98** M10
Edithburgh, *S. Aust., Austral.* **215** Y10
Edjell, island, *Marshall Is., U.S.* **220** K4
Edjudina, *W. Aust., Austral.* **215** W5
Edmond, *Okla., U.S.* **104** G11
Edmonds, *Wash., U.S.* **110** B4
Edmonton, *Alta., Can.* **84** L10
Edmore, *N. Dak., U.S.* **106** E6
Edmundston, *N.B., Can.* **85** N21
Edna, *Tex., U.S.* **105** S12
Edolo, *It.* **152** C6
Edoras Bank, *Atl. Oc.* **240** G9
Eduardo Castex, *Arg.* **134** M10
Edward, Lake, *Dem. Rep. of the Congo, Uganda* **202** K12
Edward, river, *Austral.* **214** L12
Edward River, *Qnsld., Austral.* **215** Q12
Edwards, *Calif., U.S.* **III** W8
Edwards Plateau, *Tex., U.S.* **105** P7
Edwardsville, *Ill., U.S.* **101** T4
Edward VIII Bay, *Antarctica* **231** D20
Edward VII Peninsula, *Antarctica* **230** N10
Ee, island, *Cook Is., N.Z.* **222** Q11
Eek, *Alas., U.S.* **112** K12
Eel, river, *Calif., U.S.* **III** N2
Éfaté, island, *Vanuatu* **222** F3
Effigy Mounds National Monument, *Iowa, U.S.* **106** M13
Effingham, *Ill., U.S.* **101** S6
Eflâni, *Turk.* **170** C8
Efuenaarukosu Point, *N. Mariana Is., U.S.* **220** D8
Efyra, ruin, *Gr.* **156** F7
Egadi, Isole, *It.* **153** S8
Egan Range, *Nev., U.S.* **III** Q12
Egegik, *Alas., U.S.* **113** L14
Eger, *Hung.* **151** K16
Egersund, *Nor.* **142** L10
Egerton, Mount, *Austral.* **214** G3
Eğil, *Turk.* **171** G14
Egilsstaðir, *Ice.* **142** E4
Eğirdir, *Turk.* **170** G6
Eğirdir Gölü, *Turk.* **170** G6
Egiyn, river, *Mongolia* **182** C9
Égletons, *Fr.* **149** U9
Eglinton Fiord, *Nunavut, Can.* **85** E18
Egmont Terrace, *Pac. Oc.* **249** G21
Éguzon-Chantôme, *Fr.* **149** T9
Egvekinot, *Russ.* **161** B20
Egypt, *Af.* **201** D18
Ehingen, *Ger.* **150** K7

Ehrang, *Ger.* **162** J11
Ehrenberg, *Ariz., U.S.* **109** T4
Eiao, island, *Fr. Polynesia, Fr.* **219** H14
Eickelberg Ridge, *Pac. Oc.* **243** D16
Eidsvold, *Qnsld., Austral.* **215** U15
Eifel, *Eur.* **140** G6
Eigg, island, *Scot., U.K.* **144** K7
Eight Degree Channel, *Maldives* **181** S3
Eight Mile Rock, *Bahamas* **122** F1
Eights Coast, *Antarctica* **230** J6
Eighty Mile Beach, *Austral.* **214** E4
Eildon, Lake, *Austral.* **214** M13
Eilean Barraigh (Barra), island, *Scot., U.K.* **144** K6
Eilean Bhearnaraigh (Berneray), island, *Scot., U.K.* **144** J6
Eilean Hasgeir (Haskeir), island, *Scot., U.K.* **144** J6
Eilean Leòdhais (Lewis), island, *Scot., U.K.* **144** H7
Eilean Scalpaigh (Scalpay), island, *Scot., U.K.* **144** J6
Einasleigh, *Qnsld., Austral.* **215** R13
Eindhoven, *Neth.* **148** K13
Einsiedeln, *Switz.* **152** B4
Éire *see* Ireland, *Eur.* **145** S5
Eirik Ridge, *Atl. Oc.* **240** E7
Eirunepé, *Braz.* **132** F5
Eiriosgaigh (Eriskay), island, *Scot., U.K.* **144** K6
Eisch, river, *Lux.* **162** J9
Eischen, *Lux.* **162** J9
Eisenach, *Ger.* **150** F8
Eisenerz, *Aust.* **150** L11
Eisenhüttenstad, *Ger.* **150** E11
Eisenstadt, *Aust.* **151** L13
Eita, *Kiribati* **221** G18
Eita, island, *Kiribati* **221** G17
Eivissa (Ibiza), *Sp.* **147** H17
Ejea de los Caballeros, *Sp.* **147** D14
Ejin Horo Qi (Altan Xiret), *N. Mongol, China* **184** D2
Ejin Qi, *China* **182** F9
Ejmiatsin, *Arm.* **171** E18
Ekalaka, *Mont., U.S.* **108** E13
Ekarma, island, *Russ.* **161** H23
Ekerem, *Turkm.* **176** L6
Ekeren, *Belg.* **148** K12
Ekiatapskiy Khrebet, *Russ.* **161** B20
Ekibastuz, *Kaz.* **177** C15
Ekonda, *Russ.* **161** G15
Ekström Ice Shelf, *Antarctica* **230** B11
Ekwan, river, *Ont., Can.* **85** M17
Elafónisos, island, *Gr.* **156** M11
Elafonísou, Stenón, *Gr.* **156** M11
Elaia, Cape, *Cyprus* **162** N10
El 'Alamein, *Egypt* **201** C18
Elamanchili, *India* **180** M9
Elan Bank, *Ind. Oc.* **248** C10
El 'Arîsh (Rhinocolura), *Egypt* **173** N3
Elása, island, *Gr.* **157** Q17
Elassóna, *Gr.* **156** E10
El Astillero, *Sp.* **146** B11
Elat, *Israel* **173** R5
Elato Atoll, *F.S.M.* **220** Q4
El 'Auja *see* Nizzana, *Egypt* **173** P4
El 'Auja, peak, *Jordan* **173** R7
Elazığ, *Turk.* **171** G14
Elba, *Ala., U.S.* **103** M16
Elba, island, *It.* **152** J5
El Banco, *Col.* **130** C5
El Barco de Ávila, *Sp.* **146** F9
Elbasan, *Alban.* **154** L10
El Baúl, *Venez.* **130** C9
El Bayadh, *Alg.* **200** B10
Elbe, river, *Eur.* **140** F7
Elbert, Mount, *Colo., U.S.* **108** M12
Elberta, *Mich., U.S.* **100** J9
Elberton, *Ga., U.S.* **98** K7
Elbeuf, *Fr.* **149** N8
Elbistan, *Turk.* **170** G12
Elbląg, *Pol.* **151** B15
Elbow Cays, *Bahamas* **118** F8
Elbow Lake, *Minn., U.S.* **106** H9
El'brus, peak, *Russ.* **159** U12
El Bureij, *Gaza Strip* **173** N4
El Burgo de Osma, *Sp.* **146** D11

Elburz Mountains *see* Reshteh-Ye Alborz, *Iran* **174** B11
El Cajon, *Calif., U.S.* **III** Z10
El Calafate (Lago Argentino), *Arg.* **135** V7
El Callao, *Venez.* **130** D12
El Calvario, *Venez.* **130** C9
El Campello, *Sp.* **147** J14
El Campo, *Tex., U.S.* **105** R12
El Carmen, *Arg.* **134** E9
El Ceibo, *Guatemala* **117** K15
El Ceibo, *Mex.* **117** H16
El Centro, *Calif., U.S.* **III** Z11
El Cerro, *Bol.* **132** K9
Elche (Elx), *Sp.* **147** K14
Elchi *see* Wādī Mūsā, *Jordan* **173** Q6
El Cuyo, *Mex.* **117** G17
Elda, *Sp.* **147** J14
El'dikan, *Russ.* **161** G19
El Djouf, region, *Mali, Mauritania* **200** F7
Eldon, *Iowa, U.S.* **107** Q13
Eldon, *Mo., U.S.* **107** T12
Eldora, *Iowa, U.S.* **107** N12
El Dorado, *Ark., U.S.* **102** K8
El Dorado, *Kans., U.S.* **107** U8
El Dorado, *Venez.* **130** D12
Eldorado, *Arg.* **134** G15
Eldorado, *Ill., U.S.* **101** U6
Eldorado, *Mex.* **116** F8
Eldorado, *Okla., U.S.* **104** H8
Eldorado, *Tex., U.S.* **105** P6
El Dorado Springs, *Mo., U.S.* **107** U11
Eldoret, *Kenya* **203** K14
Electra, *Tex., U.S.* **104** J9
Electric Mills, *Miss., U.S.* **103** K13
Eleftheroúpoli, *Gr.* **157** C13
Elektrostal', *Russ.* **158** J10
Eléni *see* Makrónisos, island, *Gr.* **157** K13
Elephant Butte Reservoir, *N. Mex., U.S.* **109** U11
Elephant Island, *Antarctica* **230** B4
Eleşkirt, *Turk.* **171** E17
Eleuthera Island, *Bahamas* **119** E13
El Faiyûm, *Egypt* **201** C18
El-Fashir, *Sudan* **202** E11
El Fifi, *Sudan* **202** F10
El Fuerte, *Mex.* **116** E8
El Galpón, *Arg.* **134** F10
El Gassi, *Alg.* **200** C11
El Gezira, region, *Af.* **198** G9
Elgin, *Ill., U.S.* **101** N6
Elgin, *N. Dak., U.S.* **106** H3
Elgin, *Nebr., U.S.* **107** N7
Elgin, *Nev., U.S.* **III** S12
Elgin, *Oreg., U.S.* **110** F8
Elgin, *Scot., U.K.* **144** J10
Elgin, *Tex., U.S.* **105** Q10
El Gîza, *Egypt* **201** C18
Elgol, *Scot., U.K.* **144** K7
El Golea, *Alg.* **200** C11
El Grado, *Sp.* **147** D15
El Hermel, *Leb.* **172** H7
El Hobra, *Alg.* **200** C11
El Homeur, *Alg.* **200** C10
Eliase, *Indonesia* **217** D14
Elida, *N. Mex., U.S.* **109** T15
Elikónas (Helicon), peak, *Gr.* **156** H11
Elim, *Alas., U.S.* **113** F13
El Iskandarîya (Alexandria), *Egypt* **201** C18
Elista, *Russ.* **159** R13
Elizabeth, *La., U.S.* **102** N7
Elizabeth, *N.J., U.S.* **96** N11
Elizabeth, Bahía, *Ecua.* **130** Q9
Elizabeth, Cape, *Asia* **168** D12
Elizabeth, Cape, *Me., U.S.* **97** H16
Elizabeth City, *N.C., U.S.* **98** G14
Elizabeth Island, *Marshall Is., U.S.* **220** M7
Elizabethton, *Tenn., U.S.* **103** E20
Elizabethtown, *Ky., U.S.* **103** C16
Elizabethtown, *N.C., U.S.* **98** J12
Elizondo, *Sp.* **147** B13
El Jadida (Mazagan), *Mor.* **200** B7
Elk, *Calif., U.S.* **III** Q2

Ełk, *Pol.* **151** B17
Elk, river, *W. Va., U.S.* **98** D9
Elkader, *Iowa, U.S.* **106** M13
Elk City, *Okla., U.S.* **104** G8
Elkedra, *N.T., Austral.* **215** S9
El Kef, *Tun.* **200** A12
Ēl Kerē, *Eth.* **203** H16
El Khandaq, *Sudan* **202** D12
El Khârga, *Egypt* **201** E18
Elkhart, *Ind., U.S.* **101** N9
Elkhart, *Kans., U.S.* **107** V3
El Khnâchîch, region, *Mali* **200** F8
Elkhorn, river, *Nebr., U.S.* **107** N6
Elkhorn City, *Ky., U.S.* **103** C20
Elkhovo, *Bulg.* **155** J16
Elkin, *N.C., U.S.* **98** G9
Elkins, *N. Mex., U.S.* **109** T14
Elkins, *W. Va., U.S.* **98** D10
Elkland, *Pa., U.S.* **96** L7
Elk Mountain, *Pa., U.S.* **96** L9
Elk Mountain, *Wyo., U.S.* **108** K12
Elko, *Nev., U.S.* **110** M11
Elk Point, *Nebr., U.S.* **107** N8
Elk River, *Minn., U.S.* **106** J11
Elkton, *Ky., U.S.* **103** D15
Elkton, *Md., U.S.* **98** B14
El Kûbri, *Egypt* **173** Q1
El Kuntilla, *Egypt* **173** Q4
Ellan Vannin *see* Man, Isle of, *U.K.* **145** Q9
Éllar, *Sp.* **162** L6
Elle, island, *Marshall Is., U.S.* **220** G8
Ellef Ringnes Island, *Nunavut, Can.* **85** B14
Ellen, Mount, *Utah, U.S.* **109** N8
Ellendale, *N. Dak., U.S.* **106** H6
Ellensburg, *Wash., U.S.* **110** D6
Ellep, island, *Marshall Is., U.S.* **220** M4
Ellep Passage, *Marshall Is., U.S.* **220** M4
Ellesmere Island, *Nunavut, Can.* **85** B16
Ellesmere, Lake, *N.Z.* **217** P17
Ellice Basin, *Pac. Oc.* **242** K11
Ellice Ridge, *Pac. Oc.* **242** K11
Ellijay, *Ga., U.S.* **98** J5
Ellington, *Mo., U.S.* **107** U14
Ellinwood, *Kans., U.S.* **107** T6
Elliot Lake, *Ont., Can.* **85** P17
Elliott, *N.T., Austral.* **215** R9
Elliott Key, *Fla., U.S.* **99** X10
Ellis, *Idaho, U.S.* **108** F5
Ellis, *Kans., U.S.* **107** S5
Ellisburg, *N.Y., U.S.* **96** H8
Elliston, *S. Aust., Austral.* **215** X9
Ellisville, *Miss., U.S.* **102** M12
Ellon, *Scot., U.K.* **144** J11
Ellsworth, *Kans., U.S.* **107** T7
Ellsworth, *Me., U.S.* **97** F18
Ellsworth Land, *Antarctica* **230** H7
Ellsworth Mountains, *Antarctica* **230** J8
Elma, *Wash., U.S.* **110** D3
El Macao, *Dom. Rep.* **119** M20
Elmadağ, *Turk.* **170** E8
Elma Dağı, *Turk.* **170** E8
El Maitén, *Arg.* **135** Q7
Elmalı, *Turk.* **170** H5
El Malpais National Monument, *N. Mex., U.S.* **109** S10
El Mazâr, *Egypt* **173** N3
Elm Creek, *Nebr., U.S.* **107** Q5
Elm Creek, *Tex., U.S.* **105** S7
El Milagro, *Arg.* **134** J9
El Mîna, *Leb.* **172** G6
El Minya, *Egypt* **201** D18
Elmira, *N.Y., U.S.* **96** L7
El Morro National Monument, *N. Mex., U.S.* **109** S10
El Mreyyé, region, *Af.* **200** F7
Elmshorn, *Ger.* **150** B7
Elne, *Fr.* **149** Z10
El Nido, *Philippines* **193** E13
El-Obeid, *Sudan* **202** E12
Elorza, *Venez.* **130** D8
El Oued, *Alg.* **200** B12
Eloúnta, *Gr.* **157** Q16
Eloy, *Ariz., U.S.* **109** V7
El Pajuil, *P.R., U.S.* **122** M2

El Palito, *Venez.* 130 B9
El Pao, *Venez.* 130 D12
El Paso, *Ill., U.S.* 101 Q6
El Paso, *Tex., U.S.* 105 V2
El Pedroso, *Sp.* 146 G6
Elphin, *Scot., U.K.* 144 H8
El Portal, *Calif., U.S.* III S6
El Puerto de Santa María, *Sp.* 146 M8
El Qâhira (Cairo), *Egypt* 201 C18
El Qanṭara, *Egypt* 173 P1
El Qaṣr, *Egypt* 201 E18
El Quneitra *see* Al Qunayţirah, *Syr.* 172 K6
El Quṣeima, *Egypt* 173 P4
El Reno, *Okla., U.S.* 104 G10
El Rosario, *Mex.* 116 C5
Elroy, *Wis., U.S.* 100 K4
Elsa, *Tex., U.S.* 105 W10
El Salto, *Mex.* 116 F9
El Salvador, *N. Amer.* 117 M16
Elsberry, *Mo., U.S.* 107 S14
El Seibo, *Dom. Rep.* 119 M20
El Serrat, *Andorra* 162 G3
Elsinore, *Utah, U.S.* 109 N7
El Sombrero, *Venez.* 130 C9
Elst, *Neth.* 148 J13
El Suweis (Suez), *Egypt* 173 Q1
El Teleno, peak, *Sp.* 146 C8
Eltham, *N.Z.* 217 L18
El Thamad, *Egypt* 173 R4
El Tigre, *Venez.* 130 C11
El Tofo, *Chile* 134 H6
El'ton, *Russ.* 159 P14
El'ton, Ozero, *Russ.* 159 P14
Eltopia, *Wash., U.S.* 110 D7
El Toro, peak, *P.R., U.S.* 122 N5
El Toro, peak, *Sp.* 147 G20
El Ţûr, *Egypt* 173 T3
El Turbio, *Arg.* 135 W7
Eluru, *India* 180 M8
Elvas, *Port.* 146 H7
Elven, *Fr.* 149 R4
Elverum, *Nor.* 142 J11
El Wak, *Kenya* 203 J15
Elwell, Lake, *Mont., U.S.* 108 B8
Elwood, *Ind., U.S.* 101 Q9
Elwood, *Mo., U.S.* 107 R10
Elwood, *Nebr., U.S.* 107 Q5
Elx *see* Elche, *Sp.* 147 K14
Ely, *Eng., U.K.* 145 T14
Ely, *Minn., U.S.* 106 F12
Ely, *Nev., U.S.* III Q12
Elyria, *Ohio, U.S.* 101 P14
El Yunque, peak, *Cuba* 119 K14
Émaé, island, *Vanuatu* 222 E2
Émao, island, *Vanuatu* 222 E3
Emba, *Cyprus* 162 Q5
Embalse de Ricobayo, *Sp.* 146 D8
Embarcación, *Arg.* 134 E10
Embetsu, *Japan* 188 E13
Embi, *Kaz.* 176 E8
Embleton, *Eng., U.K.* 145 N12
Embrun, *Fr.* 149 W14
Emden, *Ger.* 150 C6
Emerald, *Qnsld., Austral.* 215 T14
Emerald Basin, *Pac. Oc.* 242 R9
Emerald Island, *N.W.T., Can.* 85 C13
Emery, *Utah, U.S.* 109 N8
Emet, *Turk.* 170 E5
Emidj, island, *Marshall Is., U.S.* 220 M9
Emigrant Pass, *Nev., U.S.* III N10
Emi Koussi, peak, *Chad* 201 G15
Emilius, Mount, *It.* 152 D2
Emily, *Minn., U.S.* 106 G11
Emin, *China* 182 D4
Emirau, island, *P.N.G.* 217 B20
Emirdağ, *Turk.* 170 F6
Emir Dağları, peak, *Turk.* 170 F7
Emmaus, *Pa., U.S.* 96 N9
Emmen, *Neth.* 148 H14
Emmetsburg, *Iowa, U.S.* 106 M10
Emmett, *Idaho, U.S.* 108 G3
Emmonak, *Alas., U.S.* 112 G12
Emory Peak, *Tex., U.S.* 105 R3
Empedrado, *Arg.* 134 G13

Emperor Seamounts, *Pac. Oc.* 242 D10
Emperor Trough, *Pac. Oc.* 242 D11
Empire, *Mich., U.S.* 100 J9
Empoli, *It.* 152 G6
Emporia, *Kans., U.S.* 107 T9
Emporia, *Va., U.S.* 98 F13
Emporium, *Pa., U.S.* 96 L5
Empress Augusta Bay, *P.N.G.* 221 K14
Empty Quarter *see* Ar Rub' Al Khālī, desert, *Saudi Arabia* 174 M11
Ems, river, *Ger.* 150 D5
Enard Bay, *Scot., U.K.* 144 H8
'En Boqeq, *Israel* 173 N6
Encamp, *Andorra* 162 H4
Encamp, *Andorra* 162 J3
Encarnación, *Parag.* 132 N10
Encinal, *Tex., U.S.* 105 T8
Encinitas, *Calif., U.S.* III Y9
Encino, *N. Mex., U.S.* 109 S13
Encino, *Tex., U.S.* 105 V10
Encontrados, *Venez.* 130 C6
Encounter Bay, *Austral.* 214 L10
Ende, *Indonesia* 193 M14
Endeavour Hill, *Austral.* 214 C7
Endeavour Strait, *Austral.* 214 A12
Enderbury Island, *Kiribati* 218 G10
Enderby Land, *Antarctica* 231 D19
Enderby Plain, *Ind. Oc.* 248 E9
Enderlin, *N. Dak., U.S.* 106 G7
Endicott, *N.Y., U.S.* 96 L8
Endicott Mountains, *Alas., U.S.* 113 D16
Endurance Canyon, *Atl. Oc.* 241 Y7
Endurance Ridge, *Atl. Oc.* 241 X7
Eneabba, *W. Aust., Austral.* 215 W2
Eneeldak, island, *Marshall Is., U.S.* 220 N8
Enengeseiru, island, *F.S.M.* 221 C14
Enengonomei, island, *F.S.M.* 221 C14
Enewetak (Eniwetok), island, *Marshall Is., U.S.* 220 J8
Enewetak Atoll, *Marshall Is., U.S.* 220 F1
Enewetak Lagoon, *Marshall Is., U.S.* 220 H8
Enez, *Turk.* 170 C2
Enfer, Pointe d', *Martinique, Fr.* 123 G23
Enfield, *Jam.* 122 H10
Enfield, *N.C., U.S.* 98 G13
Engaño, Cabo, *Dom. Rep.* 119 M21
Engelhard, *N.C., U.S.* 98 H15
Engels, *Russ.* 158 M14
Engenenimo, island, *F.S.M.* 221 C16
Enggano, island, *Indonesia* 192 L6
Enggano Basin, *Ind. Oc.* 225 H16
England, *Ark., U.S.* 102 H9
England, *U.K.* 145 T13
Englewood, *Colo., U.S.* 108 M13
Englewood, *Fla., U.S.* 99 V7
Englewood, *Kans., U.S.* 107 V5
English Channel (La Manche), *Fr., U.K.* 145 Y13
English Coast, *Antarctica* 230 G7
English Harbour, *Kiribati* 221 B20
English Harbour, *St. Kitts and Nevis* 123 B21
English Roads, *Tonga* 222 J12
'En Ḥazeva, *Israel* 173 P5
Enid, *Okla., U.S.* 104 E10
Enighed, *Virgin Is., U.S.* 122 N10
Enigu, island, *Marshall Is., U.S.* 220 G11
Eniped, *Marshall Is., U.S.* 220 G11
Eniwa, *Japan* 188 G13
Eniwetak, island, *Marshall Is., U.S.* 220 M5
Eniwetak Passage, *Marshall Is., U.S.* 220 M5
Eniwetok *see* Enewetak, island, *Marshall Is., U.S.* 220 J8
Enjebi, island, *Marshall Is., U.S.* 220 G8
Enkhuizen, *Neth.* 148 H12
Ennadai, *Nunavut, Can.* 85 J13
En Nahud, *Sudan* 202 F11
Ennedi, range, *Chad* 201 G16
Ennell, Lough, *Ire.* 145 S5
Enngonia, *N.S.W., Austral.* 215 V13

Enning, *S. Dak., U.S.* 106 K2
Ennis, *Mont., U.S.* 108 E7
Ennis, *Tex., U.S.* 104 M12
Ennis (Inis), *Ire.* 145 T4
Enniscorthy (Inis Córthaidh), *Ire.* 145 T6
Enniskillen (Inis Ceithlann), *N. Ire., U.K.* 145 Q5
Ennistimon (Inis Díomáin), *Ire.* 145 S3
Ennuebing, island, *Marshall Is., U.S.* 220 K4
Ennugarret, island, *Marshall Is., U.S.* 220 K4
Ennugenliggelap, island, *Marshall Is., U.S.* 220 M4
Ennumennet, island, *Marshall Is., U.S.* 220 K4
Ennumet, island, *Marshall Is., U.S.* 220 M3
Ennylabegan, island, *Marshall Is., U.S.* 220 N5
Enontekiö, *Fin.* 143 C14
Enriquillo, *Dom. Rep.* 119 N18
Enriquillo, Lago, *Dom. Rep.* 119 M17
Enschede, *Neth.* 148 J14
Ensenada, *Mex.* 116 B5
Ensenada, *P.R., U.S.* 122 P2
Enshi, *Hubei, China* 185 N1
Ensisheim, *Fr.* 149 Q15
Entebbe, *Uganda* 203 K13
Enterprise, *Ala., U.S.* 103 N16
Enterprise, *Miss., U.S.* 103 L13
Enterprise, *Utah, U.S.* 109 P5
Enterprise, *Wash., U.S.* 110 F9
Entinas, Punta, *Sp.* 146 M12
Entrada, Punta, *Arg.* 135 V8
Entrance Point, *Bahamas* 122 B7
Entre-Deux, *Réunion, Fr.* 209 H16
Entrepeñas, Embalse de, *Sp.* 146 F12
Entre Ríos, region, *S. Amer.* 128 L6
Entrèves, *It.* 152 D2
Entroncamento, *Port.* 146 G5
Enubuj, island, *Marshall Is., U.S.* 220 N5
Enugu, *Nigeria* 205 E14
Enumclaw, *Wash., U.S.* 110 C4
Enurmino, *Russ.* 161 A20
Envalira, Pic d', *Andorra, Fr.* 162 J5
Envalira, Port d', *Andorra* 162 J5
Envira, *Braz.* 132 F5
'En Yahav, *Israel* 173 P5
Enybor, island, *Marshall Is., U.S.* 220 M8
Eo, Îlot, *New Caledonia, Fr.* 222 B8
Eochaill *see* Youghal, *Ire.* 145 U5
Eocheongdo, island, *S. Korea* 187 Q6
Eolie *see* Lipari, Isole, *It.* 153 R11
Eonyang, *S. Korea* 187 S12
Eori, *Eq. Guinea* 208 N7
Eot, island, *F.S.M.* 221 B15
Epanomí, *Gr.* 156 D11
Eparit, island, *F.S.M.* 221 A15
Eparit, Mochun, *F.S.M.* 221 A15
Epéna, *Congo* 205 G18
Epenarra, *N.T., Austral.* 215 S9
Épernay, *Fr.* 149 P11
Épernon, *Fr.* 149 P9
Ephesus, ruins, *Turk.* 170 G3
Ephraim, *Utah, U.S.* 108 M7
Ephrata, *Wash., U.S.* 110 C7
Epi, island, *Vanuatu* 222 E2
Epidavros, ruin, *Gr.* 156 K11
Épinal, *Fr.* 149 Q14
Epirus, region, *Alban., Gr.* 156 F7
Episkopi, *Cyprus* 162 Q7
Episkopi Bay, *Cyprus* 162 Q7
Epsilon, *Qnsld., Austral.* 215 V11
Epsom, *Eng., U.K.* 145 V14
Eptachóri, *Gr.* 156 D8
Épuisay, *Fr.* 149 R8
Epukiro, *Namibia* 206 H7
Epupa Falls, *Af.* 198 M5
Epu Pel, *Arg.* 135 N10

Erciş, *Turk.* 171 F17
Erciyeş Dağı, peak, *Turk.* 170 G10
Érd, *Hung.* 151 L15
Erdaojiang, *Jilin, China* 184 A15
Erdek, *Turk.* 170 D4
Erdemli, *Turk.* 170 J9
Erding, *Ger.* 150 K9
Ere, island, *Marshall Is., U.S.* 220 L3
Erebus, Mount, *Antarctica* 231 N13
Erechim, *Braz.* 132 N12
Ereentsav, *Mongolia* 183 C13
Ereğli, *Turk.* 170 C7
Ereğli, *Turk.* 170 H9
Erei, Monti, *It.* 153 T11
Ereikoússa, island, *Gr.* 156 E5
Erenhot, *China* 182 E12
Erenköy *see* Kokkina, *Cyprus* 162 N5
Eresós, *Gr.* 157 F16
Erétria, *Gr.* 156 H12
Ereymentaū, *Kaz.* 177 C14
Erfoud, *Mor.* 200 C9
Erfurt, *Ger.* 150 F8
Ergani, *Turk.* 171 G14
Ergedzhey, *Russ.* 161 H16
Ergene, river, *Turk.* 170 C4
Ergun, river, *China* 183 B14
Ergun Youqi, *China* 183 B14
Erhulai, *Liaoning, China* 184 B14
Eriboll, *Scot., U.K.* 144 G9
Eriboll, Loch, *Scot., U.K.* 144 G9
Ericht, Loch, *Scot., U.K.* 144 L9
Erick, *Okla., U.S.* 104 G7
Erie, *Pa., U.S.* 96 K3
Erie, Lake, *N. Amer.* 82 J8
Erie Canal, *N.Y., U.S.* 96 J9
Erikub Atoll, *Marshall Is., U.S.* 220 G4
Erimi, *Cyprus* 162 Q7
Erimo, *Japan* 188 H14
Erimo Misaki, *Japan* 188 H14
Erin, *Tenn., U.S.* 103 D14
Erin Bay, *Trinidad and Tobago* 123 Q21
Eriskay *see* Eiriosgaigh, island, *Scot., U.K.* 144 K6
Erisort, Loch, *Scot., U.K.* 144 H7
Eritrea, *Af.* 203 E15
Erkilet, *Turk.* 170 F10
Erlangen, *Ger.* 150 H8
Erlanger, *Ky., U.S.* 103 A17
Erldunda, *N.T., Austral.* 215 U8
Erling, Lake, *Ark., U.S.* 102 K7
Ermenek, *Turk.* 170 J8
Ermióni, *Gr.* 156 K11
Ermoúpoli, *Gr.* 157 K14
Ernabella, *S. Aust., Austral.* 215 U8
Ernakulam, *India* 181 R5
Ernée, *Fr.* 149 Q6
Erode, *India* 181 Q6
Eroj, island, *Marshall Is., U.S.* 220 G11
Eromanga, *Qnsld., Austral.* 215 U12
Er Rachidia, *Mor.* 200 B9
Er Rahad, *Sudan* 202 F12
Er Rif, range, *Af.* 198 C3
Erris Head, *Ire.* 145 Q3
Erromango, island, *Vanuatu* 222 G3
Ershijiazi, *Liaoning, China* 184 B11
Erskine, *Minn., U.S.* 106 F9
Ertai, *China* 182 D6
Ertis, *Kaz.* 177 B15
Ertis (Irtysh), river, *Kaz.* 177 D16
Ertix, river, *China* 182 C5
Erts, *Andorra* 162 H2
Eru, island, *Marshall Is., U.S.* 220 L3
Erudina, *S. Aust., Austral.* 215 W11
Eruh, *Turk.* 171 H16
Erwin, *N.C., U.S.* 98 H11
Erwin, *Tenn., U.S.* 103 E20
Erýmanthos, Óros, *Gr.* 156 J9
Erythrés, *Gr.* 156 H11
Erzin, *Russ.* 161 M13
Erzincan, *Turk.* 171 E14
Erzurum, *Turk.* 171 E16
Esa'Ala, *P.N.G.* 215 N16
Esan Misaki, *Japan* 188 H13
Esashi, *Japan* 188 E13
Esashi, *Japan* 188 H12
Esbjerg, *Den.* 142 N11
Escalades-Engordany, *Andorra* 162 J4
Escalante, *Utah, U.S.* 109 P7
Erçek, *Turk.* 171 G18
Erçek Gölü, *Turk.* 171 F18

Escalante, river, *Utah, U.S.* 109 P7
Escambia, river, *Ala., Fla., U.S.* 99 Q1
Escanaba, *Mich., U.S.* 100 G8
Escanaba, river, *Mich., U.S.* 100 F7
Escárcego, *Mex.* 117 J16
Esch, *Lux.* 162 K9
Eschen, *Liech.* 162 M2
Eschnerberg, range, *Liech.* 162 M2
Eschwege, *Ger.* 150 F7
Escocesa, Bahia, *Dom. Rep.* 119 L19
Escondido, *Calif., U.S.* III Y10
Escuinapa, *Mex.* 116 G9
Escuintla, *Guatemala* 117 L15
Escuintla, *Mex.* 117 L15
Eséka, *Cameroon* 205 F15
Esenguly, *Uzb.* 176 M6
Eşfahān (Isfahan), *Iran* 175 E13
Esfandak, *Iran* 175 H18
Esil, *Kaz.* 176 C12
Esil, river, *Kaz.* 176 C12
Esker, *Nfld. & Lab., Can.* 85 L20
Eskifjörður, *Ice.* 142 F4
Eskilstuna, *Sw.* 143 K13
Eskimo Lakes, *N.W.T., Can.* 84 E10
Eskipazar, *Turk.* 170 D8
Eskişehir, *Turk.* 170 E6
Esla, river, *Sp.* 146 C9
Eslāmābād, *Iran* 174 D10
Eşler Dağı, peak, *Turk.* 170 G5
Eşme, *Turk.* 170 F4
Esmeralda, *Cuba* 118 H10
Esmeralda, Isla, *Chile* 135 U6
Esmeraldas, *Ecua.* 130 H2
Esmoriz, *Port.* 146 E5
Espagnol Point, *St. Vincent and the Grenadines* 123 J17
Espakeh, *Iran* 175 H17
Espalion, *Fr.* 149 W10
Espanola, *N. Mex., U.S.* 109 R12
Española (Hood), Isla, *Ecua.* 130 R11
Esperance, *W. Aust., Austral.* 215 X5
Esperance, Cape, *Solomon Is.* 221 N18
Esperance Bay, *Austral.* 214 K5
Esperanza, *Arg.* 134 J11
Esperanza, *P.R., U.S.* 122 N6
Esperanza, *Peru* 132 G5
Espichel, Cabo, *Port.* 146 J4
Espiègle Bay, *Vanuatu* 222 D1
Espiel, *Sp.* 146 K9
Espigão Mestre, range, *S. Amer.* 128 F9
Espinhaço, Serra do, *Braz.* 133 K15
Espiritu Santo, island, *Vanuatu* 222 C1
Espíritu Santo, Isla, *Mex.* 116 F7
Espoo (Esbo), *Fin.* 143 J16
Esposende, *Port.* 146 D5
Espuña, peak, *Sp.* 147 K13
Espungabera, *Mozambique* 206 G12
Esquel, *Arg.* 135 R7
Esquina, *Arg.* 134 J12
Essaouira, *Mor.* 200 B7
Essen, *Belg.* 148 K12
Essen, *Ger.* 150 E5
Essendon, Mount, *Austral.* 214 G4
Essequibo, river, *Guyana* 131 G14
Essex, Punta, *Ecua.* 130 Q9
Essex Junction, *Vt., U.S.* 96 F12
Essexville, *Mich., U.S.* 100 K13
Essington, Port, *Austral.* 214 A8
Esslingen, *Ger.* 150 J7
Esso, *Russ.* 161 F22
Es Suki, *Sudan* 203 E13
Estaca de Bares, Punta da, *Sp.* 146 A6
Estados, Isla de los (Staten Island), *Arg.* 135 Y10
Estahbān, *Iran* 175 G14
Estancia, *N. Mex., U.S.* 109 S12
Estância, *Braz.* 133 H17
Estany d'Engolasters, lake, *Andorra* 162 J3
Estanyó, Pic de l', *Andorra* 162 H4
Estats, Pic d', *Fr., Sp.* 162 F1
Estavayer-le-Lac, *Switz.* 152 B2
Este, *It.* 152 E7
Este, Punta del, *S. Amer.* 128 L7
Estelí, *Nicar.* 117 L18
Estella (Lizarra), *Sp.* 147 C13

Estelline, *S. Dak., U.S.* 106 K8
Estelline, *Tex., U.S.* 104 H7
Estepona, *Sp.* 146 M9
Estes Park, *Colo., U.S.* 108 LI3
Estevan, *Sask., Can.* 84 NI2
Estherville, *Iowa, U.S.* 106 MIO
Estill, *S.C., U.S.* 98 M9
Estonia, *Eur.* 143 KI6
Estrela, Serra da, *Port.* 146 F6
Estrella, peak, *Sp.* 146 JII
Estrella Bay, *Solomon Is.* 221 MI8
Estremoz, *Port.* 146 H6
Esztergom, *Hung.* 151 LI5
Etadunna, *S. Aust., Austral.* 215 VIO
Étal Atoll, *F.S.M.* 220 Q6
Étampes, *Fr.* 149 Q9
Étang-Sale, *Réunion, Fr.* 209 HI5
Étaples, *Fr.* 148 L9
Étarik, island, *Vanuatu* 222 E3
Etawah, *India* 180 G7
Etcharai, island, *Marshall Is., U.S.* 220 K2
Etena, *Amer. Samoa, U.S.* 222 R3
Ethiopia, *Af.* 203 GI5
Ethiopian College, *Vatican City* 163 QI4
Ethiopian Highlands, *Af.* 198 H9
Etive, Loch, *Scot., U.K.* 144 L8
Etna, *Wyo., U.S.* 108 H8
Etna, peak, *It.* 153 SII
Etorofu *see* Iturup, island, *Russ.* 161 J23
Etosha Pan, *Namibia* 206 F6
Etoumbi, *Congo* 205 HI7
Etowah, *Tenn., U.S.* 103 FI8
et Tahta, *Leb.* 172 J6
Ettelbruck, *Lux.* 162 HIO
Etten, island, *F.S.M.* 221 BI6
Etten, island, *F.S.M.* 221 CI5
Ettlingen, *Ger.* 150 J6
Ettrick, *N.Z.* 217 QI6
Eu, *Fr.* 148 M9
'Eua, island, *Tonga* 222 KI2
'Euaiki, island, *Tonga* 222 HI2
'Euaiki, island, *Tonga* 222 MII
'Euakafa, island, *Tonga* 222 MII
Euboea *see* Évvoia, island, *Gr.* 157 HI3
Eucla, *W. Aust., Austral.* 215 W7
Eucla Basin, *Austral.* 214 J6
Eucla Canyon, *Ind. Oc.* 225 N2O
Eucla Shelf, *Ind. Oc.* 225 M2O
Euclid, *Ohio, U.S.* 101 NI4
Eucumbene, Lake, *Austral.* 214 LI4
Eudora, *Ark., U.S.* 102 K9
Eudunda, *S. Aust., Austral.* 215 XIO
Eufaula, *Ala., U.S.* 103 MI7
Eufaula, *Okla., U.S.* 104 GI3
Eufaula Lake, *Okla., U.S.* 104 GI3
Eugene, *Oreg., U.S.* 110 H3
Eugenia, Punta, *Mex.* 116 D5
Eugenio Bustos, *Arg.* 134 L7
Eulo, *Qnsld., Austral.* 215 VI3
Eumseong, *S. Korea* 187 P9
Eunice, *La., U.S.* 102 P8
Eunice, *N. Mex., U.S.* 109 VI5
Eupen, *Belg.* 148 LI3
Euphrates, river, *Asia* 168 F3
Eupora, *Miss., U.S.* 102 JI2
Eurardy, *W. Aust., Austral.* 215 V2
Eurasia Basin, *Arctic Oc.* 246 FII
Eureka, *Calif., U.S.* 110 MI
Eureka, *Ill., U.S.* 101 Q5
Eureka, *Kans., U.S.* 107 U9
Eureka, *Mont., U.S.* 108 A5
Eureka, *Nev., U.S.* 111 PII
Eureka, *Nunavut, Can.* 85 BI5
Eureka, *S. Dak., U.S.* 106 J5
Eureka, *Utah, U.S.* 108 L7
Eureka Springs, *Ark., U.S.* 102 E7
Europa, Île, *Af.* 207 HI4
Europa, Picos de, *Sp.* 146 BIO
Europa, Punta, *Eq. Guinea* 208 L7
Europa Point, *Gibraltar, U.K.* 163 R23
Eustis, *Fla., U.S.* 99 T8
Eutaw, *Ala., U.S.* 103 KI4
Eutin, *Ger.* 150 B8
Eva Downs, *N.T., Austral.* 215 R9
Evans, Mount, *Mont., U.S.* 108 E6
Evanston, *Ill., U.S.* 101 N7

Evanston, *Wyo., U.S.* 108 K8
Evansville, *Alas., U.S.* 113 EI6
Evansville, *Ind., U.S.* 101 U7
Evart, *Mich., U.S.* 100 KIO
Évdilos, *Gr.* 157 KI6
Eveleth, *Minn., U.S.* 106 FI2
Evensk, *Russ.* 161 E2I
Everard, Lake, *Austral.* 214 J9
Everard Park, *S. Aust., Austral.* 215 U8
Everest, Mount, *Nepal* 180 FII
Everest, Mount (Sagarmāthā, Qomolangma), *China, Nep.* 182 L4
Everett, *Wash., U.S.* 110 B4
Everglades, The, wetland, *Fla., U.S.* 99 X9
Everglades, The, *U.S.* 87 N2O
Everglades City, *Fla., U.S.* 99 X9
Everglades National Park, *Fla., U.S.* 99 X9
Evergreen, *Ala., U.S.* 103 MI5
Evesham, *Eng., U.K.* 145 UI2
Évian, *Fr.* 149 TI4
Évora, *Port.* 146 J6
Évreux, *Fr.* 149 P8
Évros, river, *Gr.* 157 AI7
Évros, river, *Gr.* 157 CI6
Evrótas, river, *Gr.* 156 LIO
Évry, *Fr.* 149 PIO
Evrychou, *Cyprus* 162 P7
Évvoia (Euboea), island, *Gr.* 157 HI3
Ewab *see* Kai, Kepulauan, *Indonesia* 193 LI8
'Ewa Beach, *Hawai'i, U.S.* 114 FII
Ewa, region, *Nauru* 221 E23
Ewarton, *Jam.* 122 J9
Ewing, *Nebr., U.S.* 107 N6
Ewo, *Congo* 205 HI7
Excelsior Mountains, *Nev., U.S.* 111 R8
Excelsior Springs, *Mo., U.S.* 107 SII
Executive Committee Range, *Antarctica* 230 L8
Exeter, *Calif., U.S.* 111 U7
Exeter, *Eng., U.K.* 145 XIO
Exeter, *N.H., U.S.* 97 JI5
Exeter Sound, *Nunavut, Can.* 85 FI9
Exmoor, plateau, *Eng., U.K.* 145 WIO
Exmouth, *Eng., U.K.* 145 XIO
Exmouth, *W. Aust., Austral.* 215 TI
Exmouth Gulf, *Austral.* 214 FI
Exmouth Plateau, *Ind. Oc.* 225 KI7
Exochí, *Gr.* 156 BI2
Exotic Garden, *Monaco* 163 E2O
Explora Escarpment, *Atl. Oc.* 241 YIO
Exploring Isles, *Fiji* 222 H9
Extremadura, *Eur.* 140 K2
Exu, *Braz.* 133 FI6
Exuma Sound, *Bahamas* 118 EI2
Eyasi, Lake, *Af.* 198 K9
Eye, *Eng., U.K.* 145 TI5
Eyemouth, *Scot., U.K.* 144 MII
Eye Peninsula, *Scot., U.K.* 144 H7
Eyjafjallajökull, peak, *Ice.* 142 F2
Eyjafjaröardjúp, valley, *Arctic Oc.* 247 L2O
Eyjafjörður, bay, *Arctic Oc.* 140 A4
Eyl, *Somalia* 203 GI8
Eyl, river, *Somalia* 203 GI8
Eymoutiers, *Fr.* 149 U9
Eyrarbakki, *Ice.* 142 F2
Eyre, Lake, *Austral.* 214 HIO
Eyre Canyon, *Ind. Oc.* 225 NI9
Eyrecourt (Dún an Uchta), *Ire.* 145 S5
Eyre North, Lake, *Austral.* 214 HIO
Eyre Peninsula, *Austral.* 214 K9
Eyre South, Lake, *Austral.* 214 HIO
Eyre Terrace, *Ind. Oc.* 225 NI9
Eysturoy, island, *Faroe Is., Den.* 142 H6
Ezcaray, *Sp.* 146 CII
Ezequiela Ramos Mexia, Embalse, *Arg.* 135 P8
Ezhou, *Hubei, China* 185 N6
Ezine, *Turk.* 170 E2
Ezion-geber (Elath), ruins, *Jordan* 173 R5

F

Faaa, *Fr. Polynesia, Fr.* 223 NI5
Faaaha, *Fr. Polynesia, Fr.* 223 A23
Faaite, island, *Fr. Polynesia, Fr.* 223 EI8
Faanui, *Fr. Polynesia, Fr.* 223 KI4
Faanui, Baie de, *Fr. Polynesia, Fr.* 223 KI4
Faaone, *Fr. Polynesia, Fr.* 223 PI7
Faaroa, Baie de, *Fr. Polynesia, Fr.* 223 B24
Fabala, *Guinea* 204 C7
Fabens, *Tex., U.S.* 105 W3
Faber Lake, *N.W.T., Can.* 84 GII
Fabero, *Sp.* 146 C8
Fabriano, *It.* 152 H9
Facatativá, *Col.* 130 F5
Fachi, *Niger* 201 GI3
Facho, Pico do, *Madeira, Port.* 208 L5
Facpi Point, *Guam, U.S.* 220 D9
Facture, *Fr.* 149 W6
Fada, *Chad* 201 GI6
Fada N'Gourma, *Burkina Faso* 204 BII
Faddeyevskiy, Ostrov, *Russ.* 161 DI7
Fadghamī, *Syr.* 172 EI4
Fadian Point, *Guam, U.S.* 220 CII
Fadiffolu Atoll, *Maldives* 181 U3
Faenza, *It.* 152 F7
Faetano, *San Marino* 163 KI7
Fafa, island, *Tonga* 222 HII
Fafe, *Port.* 146 D6
Faga'itua, *Amer. Samoa, U.S.* 222 M8
Fagaitua Bay, *Amer. Samoa, U.S.* 222 M8
Fagaloa Bay, *Samoa* 222 L3
Fagamalo, *Amer. Samoa, U.S.* 222 M6
Fagamalo, *Samoa* 222 K2
Fāgăraş, *Rom.* 155 DI4
Fagasā, *Amer. Samoa, U.S.* 222 M7
Fagatele Bay, *Amer. Samoa, U.S.* 222 N7
Fagatogo, *Amer. Samoa, U.S.* 222 M7
Fagernes, *Nor.* 142 JII
Fagnano, Lago, *Arg.* 135 X9
Fagurhólsmýri, *Ice.* 142 F3
Fahala, island, *Maldives* 181 W3
Fahefa, *Tonga* 222 HIO
Fahie Hill, *British Virgin Is., U.K.* 122 Q6
Fahraj, *Iran* 175 GI6
Faial, *Azores, Port.* 146 Q2
Faibus Point, *N. Mariana Is., U.S.* 220 A7
Faichuk, island, *F.S.M.* 221 BI4
Faie, *Fr. Polynesia, Fr.* 223 GI4
Faie, Baie de, *Fr. Polynesia, Fr.* 223 GI4
Faihava Passage, *Tonga* 222 LII
Faioa, island, *Tonga* 222 LI2
Faïoa, Île, *Wallis and Futuna, Fr.* 222 CII
Fairbanks, *Alas., U.S.* 113 GI7
Fairborn, *Ohio, U.S.* 101 RI2
Fairburn, *Ga., U.S.* 98 L5
Fairbury, *Ill., U.S.* 101 Q6
Fairbury, *Nebr., U.S.* 107 R8
Fairfax, *Okla., U.S.* 104 EII
Fairfax, *S.C., U.S.* 98 M9
Fairfield, *Ala., U.S.* 103 JI5
Fairfield, *Calif., U.S.* 111 R4
Fairfield, *Idaho, U.S.* 108 G5
Fairfield, *Ill., U.S.* 101 T6
Fairfield, *Iowa, U.S.* 107 QI3
Fairfield, *Mont., U.S.* 108 C7
Fairfield, *Ohio, U.S.* 101 SII
Fairfield, *Tex., U.S.* 105 NI3
Fair Haven, *Vt., U.S.* 96 HI2
Fairhope, *Ala., U.S.* 103 PI4
Fair Isle, *Scot., U.K.* 144 EI2
Fairmont, *Minn., U.S.* 106 LIO
Fairmont, *W. Va., U.S.* 98 C9
Fairmount, *Ind., U.S.* 101 P8
Fairport, *Mich., U.S.* 100 G8
Fairport, *N.Y., U.S.* 96 J7
Fairview, *Mont., U.S.* 108 BI3
Fairview, *Okla., U.S.* 104 F9
Fairview, *Tenn., U.S.* 103 FI5

Fairview, *Utah, U.S.* 108 M7
Fairway Plateau, *Pac. Oc.* 249 E23
Fairweather, Mount, *Alas., U.S.* 113 K2I
Fais, island, *F.S.M.* 218 E3
Faisalabad, *Pak.* 179 QII
Faizabad, *India* 180 G8
Faīẓābād, *Afghan.* 178 K9
Fajardo, *P.R., U.S.* 122 M6
Fakahiku, island, *Tonga* 222 Q6
Fakahina, island, *Fr. Polynesia, Fr.* 223 E2O
Fakakakai, *Tonga* 222 P7
Fakaofo, island, *Kiribati* 218 HIO
Fakarava, island, *Fr. Polynesia, Fr.* 223 EI8
Fakel, *Russ.* 158 GI6
Fakenham, *Eng., U.K.* 145 TI5
Fakfak, *Indonesia* 193 KI8
Faku, *Liaoning, China* 184 AI3
Fala Ane Point, *Amer. Samoa, U.S.* 222 R3
Falaise, Pointe, *St.-Martin, Fr.* 123 BI4
Falakró, Óros, *Gr.* 157 BI3
Falamae, *Solomon Is.* 221 LI4
Falciano, *San Marino* 163 GI7
Falcon, Cape, *Oreg., U.S.* 110 E2
Falcón, Presa *see* Falcon Reservoir, *Mex., U.S.* 116 EI2
Falconara Marittima, *It.* 152 H9
Falcone, Capo del, *It.* 152 M3
Falconer, *N.Y., U.S.* 96 K4
Falcon Reservoir, *Mex., U.S.* 116 EI2
Falealupo, *Samoa* 222 KI
Faleasao, *Amer. Samoa, U.S.* 222 P3
Falefatu Island, *Tuvalu* 221 L23
Falelatie, *Samoa* 222 L2
Falelima, *Samoa* 222 KI
Falémé, river, *Af.* 200 H6
Faleniu, *Amer. Samoa, U.S.* 222 M7
Falfurrias, *Tex., U.S.* 105 VIO
Falkenberg, *Sw.* 142 MII
Falkensee, *Ger.* 150 DIO
Falkirk, *Scot., U.K.* 144 MIO
Falkland-Agulhas Fracture Zone, *Atl. Oc.* 241 VIO
Falkland Escarpment, *Atl. Oc.* 241 V6
Falkland Islands, *S. Amer.* 135 XII
Falkland Plateau, *Atl. Oc.* 241 V6
Falkland Ridge, *Atl. Oc.* 241 V8
Falkland Sound, *Falk. Is., U.K.* 135 WI2
Falkland Trough, *Atl. Oc.* 241 V6
Falknis, peak, *Liech., Switz.* 162 R3
Falknov *see* Sokolov, *Czech Rep.* 150 G9
Falkonéra, island, *Gr.* 156 LI2
Falköping, *Sw.* 142 LI2
Fallbrook, *Calif., U.S.* 111 Y9
Fallen Jerusalem, island, *British Virgin Is., U.K.* 122 R8
Fallières Coast, *Antarctica* 230 E5
Fallon, *Nev., U.S.* 111 P7
Fall River, *Mass., U.S.* 97 LI5
Fall River Lake, *Kans., U.S.* 107 U9
Fall River Mills, *Calif., U.S.* 110 M4
Falls City, *Nebr., U.S.* 107 R9
Fallujah *see* Al Fallūjah, *Iraq* 174 E9
Falmouth, *Antigua and Barbuda* 121 CI6
Falmouth, *Eng., U.K.* 145 Y8
Falmouth, *Jam.* 122 H7
Falmouth, *Ky., U.S.* 103 AI8
Falmouth, *Me., U.S.* 97 HI6
Falmouth, *St. Kitts and Nevis* 123 B2I
Falmouth Harbour, *St. Kitts and Nevis* 123 B2I
False Bay, *Af.* 198 R6
False Cape, *N. Amer.* 82 M3
False Divi Point, *India* 181 N8
False Pass, *Alas., U.S.* 112 NII
False Point, *India* 180 KII
Falset, *Sp.* 147 EI6
Falso, Cabo, *Dom. Rep.* 119 NI7
Falso, Cabo, *Mex.* 116 F7

Falster, island, *Den.* 142 NI2
Fălticeni, *Rom.* 155 BI5
Falun, *Sw.* 143 JI3
Famagusta (Ammóchostos, Gazimağusa), *Cyprus* 162 PIO
Fanaik, island, *F.S.M.* 221 DI6
Fanan, island, *F.S.M.* 221 CI6
Fanananei, Mochun, *F.S.M.* 221 BI4
Fanangat, island, *F.S.M.* 221 BI5
Fanannon, island, *F.S.M.* 221 CI6
Fanapanges, island, *F.S.M.* 221 CI5
Fanasich, island, *F.S.M.* 221 CI4
Fancy, *St. Vincent and the Grenadines* 123 JI6
Fanemoch, island, *F.S.M.* 221 BI5
Faneno, island, *F.S.M.* 221 BI5
Fanew, island, *F.S.M.* 221 CI5
Fanew, Mochun, *F.S.M.* 221 CI5
Fangak, *S. Sudan* 202 GI2
Fangale'ounga, *Tonga* 222 P7
Fangasito, island, *Tonga* 222 MII
Fangatau, island, *Fr. Polynesia, Fr.* 223 E2O
Fangataufa, island, *Fr. Polynesia, Fr.* 223 H2I
Fangcheng, *Henan, China* 184 K4
Fangshan, *Beijing Shi, China* 184 D7
Fangxian, *Hubei, China* 184 L2
Fanning Island *see* Tabuaeran, *Kiribati* 218 FI2
Fano, *It.* 152 G9
Fanos, island, *F.S.M.* 221 BI5
Fanshan, *Zhejiang, China* 185 RII
Fanshi, *Shanxi, China* 184 D5
Fanūdah, *Saudi Arabia* 174 J7
Fanunchuluyan Bahia, *N. Mariana Is., U.S.* 220 B5
Fanurmot, island, *F.S.M.* 221 CI5
Fanxian, *Shand., China* 184 H7
Faraday Fracture Zone, *Atl. Oc.* 240 H9
Farafangana, *Madagascar* 207 HI7
Farâfra Oasis, site, *Egypt* 201 DI8
Farāh, *Afghan.* 179 P2
Farāh, river, *Afghan.* 179 P2
Farallon de Medinilla, island, *N. Mariana Is., U.S.* 220 C2
Farallon de Pajaros, island, *N. Mariana Is., U.S.* 220 A2
Farallon Islands, *U.S.* 86 F2
Faranah, *Guinea* 204 C6
Farasān, Jazā'ir, *Saudi Arabia* 174 P8
Faraulep Atoll, *F.S.M.* 220 Q4
Fare, *Fr. Polynesia, Fr.* 223 GI4
Fareara, Pointe, *Fr. Polynesia, Fr.* 223 QI8
Fareera, Passe, *Fr. Polynesia, Fr.* 223 GI4
Fareham, *Eng., U.K.* 145 WI3
Farewell, Cape, *Greenland, Den.* 82 EIO
Farewell, Cape, *N.Z.* 218 N8
Farga de Moles, *Andorra* 162 K2
Fargo, *N. Dak., U.S.* 106 G8
Farg'ona, *Uzb.* 177 KI4
Faribault, *Minn., U.S.* 106 KII
Faridkot, *India* 180 D4
Farim, *Guinea-Bissau* 204 B4
Farīmān, *Iran* 175 CI6
Fariones, Punta, *Sp.* 208 P7
Farkhor, *Taj.* 178 J8
Farmakonísi, island, *Gr.* 157 KI8
Farmersville, *Tex., U.S.* 104 KI2
Farmerville, *La., U.S.* 102 K8
Farmington, *Ill., U.S.* 101 Q4
Farmington, *Me., U.S.* 97 FI6
Farmington, *Mo., U.S.* 107 UI5
Farmington, *N. Mex., U.S.* 109 QIO
Farmington, *Utah, U.S.* 108 K7
Farmville, *Va., U.S.* 98 FI2
Farnham, *N.Y., U.S.* 96 K4
Faro, *Port.* 146 L6
Fårö, island, *Sw.* 143 LI4
Faro, Punta del, *It.* 153 RI2
Faroe Bank, *Atl. Oc.* 240 FII
Faroe Gap, *Atl. Oc.* 240 FII
Faroe Islands (Føroyar), *Eur.* 142 H6
Faroe Shelf, *Arctic Oc., Atl. Oc.* 240 FII

Faroe-Shetland Trough, *Arctic Oc., Atl. Oc.* **240** F12
Farquhar Ridge, *Ind. Oc.* **224** J7
Farrell, *Pa., U.S.* **96** M3
Fārs, region, *Iran* **175** G13
Fārsala, *Gr.* **156** F10
Farsund, *Nor.* **142** L10
Fartak, Ra's, *Yemen* **175** P13
Far'ûn (Coral Island), *Israel* **173** R5
Farwell, *Tex., U.S.* **104** H3
Fasā, *Iran* **175** G14
Fasano, *It.* **152** M14
Fastiv, *Ukr.* **159** N5
Fastnet Rock, *Ire.* **145** V3
Fataka (Mitre Island), *Solomon Is.* **218** J8
Fatato, island, *Tuvalu* **221** K24
Fatehabad, *India* **180** E5
Fatehgarh, *India* **180** F7
Fatehpur, *India* **180** G7
Fátima, *Port.* **146** G5
Fatsa, *Turk.* **170** D12
Fatu Hiva, island, *Fr. Polynesia, Fr.* **219** H15
Fatumanini, Passe, *Wallis and Futuna, Fr.* **222** B11
Fatumanongi, island, *Tonga* **222** P6
Fatumu, *Tonga* **222** J12
Faucilles, Monts, *Fr.* **149** Q13
Faulkton, *S. Dak., U.S.* **106** J6
Fauna Nui, Lac, *Fr. Polynesia, Fr.* **223** G14
Fauske, *Nor.* **142** E12
Faversham, *Eng., U.K.* **145** V15
Favignana, Isola, *It.* **153** S8
Fawn Trough, *Ind. Oc.* **248** C11
Faxaflói, bay, *Ice.* **142** E2
Faya, *Chad* **201** G15
Fayaoué, *New Caledonia, Fr.* **222** C8
Fayaoué, Baie de, *New Caledonia, Fr.* **222** C8
Fayd, *Saudi Arabia* **174** H8
Fayette, *Ala., U.S.* **103** J14
Fayette, *Miss., U.S.* **102** M10
Fayette, *Mo., U.S.* **107** S12
Fayetteville, *Ark., U.S.* **102** E6
Fayetteville, *N.C., U.S.* **98** J11
Fayetteville, *Tenn., U.S.* **103** G15
Fayetteville, *W. Va., U.S.* **98** E9
Fazilka, *India* **180** E4
Fdérik, *Mauritania* **200** E6
Fear, Cape, *N.C., U.S.* **98** K12
Fécamp, *Fr.* **149** N8
Federal, *Arg.* **134** J13
Federally Administered Tribal Areas, *Pak.* **179** N8
Federated States of Micronesia, *Pac. Oc.* **220** P5
Fedorovka, *Kaz.* **176** B10
Fefen, island, *F.S.M.* **221** C15
Fehmarn, island, *Ger.* **150** B9
Feijó, *Braz.* **132** F5
Feilding, *N.Z.* **217** L19
Feira de Santana, *Braz.* **133** H16
Feixian, *Shand., China* **184** H9
Feixiang, *Hebei, China* **184** G6
Feke, *Turk.* **170** H10
Felanitx, *Sp.* **147** H19
Feldbach, *Aust.* **150** M12
Feldberg, peak, *Ger.* **150** K6
Feldkirch, *Aust.* **162** M3
Félicité Island, *Seychelles* **209** M21
Felidu Atoll, *Maldives* **181** V3
Felipe Carrillo Puerto, *Mex.* **117** H17
Felixstowe, *Eng., U.K.* **145** U16
Fellowship, *Jam.* **122** J11
Fellowship, *Jam.* **122** J7
Feltre, *It.* **152** C8
Femund, lake, *Nor.* **142** H11
Fen, river, *Shanxi, China* **184** E4
Fena Valley Reservoir, *Guam, U.S.* **220** D10
Fen Country, *Eng., U.K.* **145** T14
Fene, *Sp.* **146** A6
Feneppi, island, *F.S.M.* **221** D15
Fengcheng, *Jiangxi, China* **185** Q7
Fengcheng, *Liaoning, China* **184** C13
Fenghuang, *Hunan, China* **185** Q1
Fengjie, *Chongq., China* **184** M1
Fengkai, *Guang., China* **185** V3

Fenglin, *Taiwan, China* **185** V12
Fengning, *Hebei, China* **184** B8
Fengqi see Luochuan, *Shaanxi, China* **184** G2
Fengqiu, *Henan, China* **184** H6
Fengrun, *Hebei, China* **184** D9
Fengshan, *Taiwan, China* **185** W11
Fengshuba Shuiku, *Guang., China* **185** U6
Fengshun, *Guang., China* **185** V7
Fengtai, *Anhui, China* **184** L8
Fengxian, *Shand., China* **184** J8
Fengyang, *Anhui, China* **184** L8
Fengyi, *China* **182** N8
Fengyüan, *Taiwan, China* **185** U11
Fengzhen, *N. Mongol, China* **184** C5
Feni Islands, *P.N.G.* **217** C22
Feno, Cap de, *Fr.* **152** L4
Feno, Capo di, *Fr.* **152** K3
Fenua Fu, Île, *Wallis and Futuna, Fr.* **222** C11
Fenualoa, island, *Solomon Is.* **221** P23
Fenuaroa, island, *Fr. Polynesia, Fr.* **223** K16
Fenxi, *Shanxi, China* **184** G3
Fenyang, *Shanxi, China* **184** F4
Fenyi, *Jiangxi, China* **185** R6
Feodosiya, *Ukr.* **159** S8
Feolin Ferry, *Scot., U.K.* **144** M7
Fer, Point au, *La., U.S.* **102** R9
Fera, island, *Solomon Is.* **221** M18
Ferdows, *Iran* **175** D15
Féres, *Gr.* **157** C11
Fërfër, *Eth.* **203** H17
Fergana Valley, *Uzb.* **177** K14
Fergus Falls, *Minn., U.S.* **106** H8
Fergusson Island, *P.N.G.* **217** E21
Feridu, island, *Maldives* **181** U3
Ferit, island, *F.S.M.* **221** B16
Ferizaj (Uroševac), *Kos.* **154** J11
Ferkéssédougou, *Côte d'Ivoire* **204** C8
Fermo, *It.* **152** H10
Fermont, *Que., Can.* **85** L20
Fermoselle, *Sp.* **146** E8
Fermoy (Mainistir Fhear Maí), *Ire.* **145** U4
Fernandez Bay, *Bahamas* **122** E11
Fernandina (Narborough), Isla, *Ecua.* **130** Q8
Fernandina Beach, *Fla., U.S.* **99** Q9
Fernandina, Isla, *Galápagos Is., Ecua.* **219** G21
Fernando de Noronha, Arquipélago de, *Braz.* **133** E19
Fernando de Noronha Ridge, *Atl. Oc.* **241** P8
Ferndale, *Calif., U.S.* **111** N1
Ferndale, *Wash., U.S.* **110** A4
Fern Grotto, *Hawai'i, U.S.* **114** C6
Fern Gully, site, *Jam.* **122** H9
Fernley, *Nev., U.S.* **111** P7
Ferrara, *It.* **152** F7
Ferrato, Capo, *It.* **153** Q4
Ferraz Ridge, *Atl. Oc.* **241** Q8
Ferré, Cap, *Martinique, Fr.* **123** G24
Ferreira do Alentejo, *Port.* **146** K5
Ferreira Gomes, *Braz.* **132** C12
Ferreñafe, *Peru* **132** F2
Ferret, Cap, *Fr.* **149** W6
Ferrette, *Fr.* **149** R15
Ferriday, *La., U.S.* **102** M9
Ferro, Ilhéu de, *Madeira, Port.* **208** L4
Ferrol, *Sp.* **146** A6
Ferrolana, *Eq. Guinea* **208** M6
Ferrysburg, *Mich., U.S.* **100** L9
Fertile, *Minn., U.S.* **106** F8
Fès (Fez), *Mor.* **200** B9
Feshi, *Dem. Rep. of the Congo* **202** M8
Fessenden, *N. Dak., U.S.* **106** F5
Festus, *Mo., U.S.* **107** T15
Feteşti, *Rom.* **155** F17
Fethiye, *Turk.* **170** J4
Fethiye Körfezi, *Turk.* **170** J4
Fetlar, island, *Scot., U.K.* **144** C12
Fetoa, island, *Tonga* **222** Q6
Fetokopunga, island, *Tonga* **222** Q7
Fetuna, *Fr. Polynesia, Fr.* **223** B23

Feuet, *Lib.* **200** E12
Feurs, *Fr.* **149** U12
Fevzipaşa, *Turk.* **170** H11
Fezzan, region, *Lib.* **201** E13
Fianarantsoa, *Madagascar* **207** G17
Fidenza, *It.* **152** E5
Fields Find, *W. Aust., Austral.* **215** V3
Fier, *Alban.* **154** L9
Fier-Shegan, *Alban.* **154** L9
Fife Lake, *Mich., U.S.* **100** J10
Fife Ness, *Scot., U.K.* **144** L11
Fifteen Twenty Fracture Zone (Barracuda Fracture Zone), *Atl. Oc.* **240** M7
Figari, Capo, *It.* **152** M5
Figeac, *Fr.* **149** W9
Fig Tree, *St. Kitts and Nevis* **123** C18
Figueira da Foz, *Port.* **146** F5
Figueres, *Sp.* **147** C18
Figuig, *Mor.* **200** B9
Fiji, *Pac. Oc.* **222** J7
Fiji Plateau, *Pac. Oc.* **242** L10
Filabres, Sierra de los, *Sp.* **146** L12
Filadelfia, *Parag.* **132** L9
Filchner Ice Sheet, *Antarctica* **230** F10
Filchner Trough, *Atl. Oc.* **248** K11
Filey, *Eng., U.K.* **145** Q13
Filfla, island, *Malta* **163** M22
Filiaşi, *Rom.* **155** F13
Filiátes, *Gr.* **156** E7
Filiatrá, *Gr.* **156** L9
Filicudi, Isola, *It.* **153** R11
Filiourí, river, *Gr.* **157** B15
Filíppoi (Philippi), ruin, *Gr.* **157** B13
Filipstad, *Sw.* **142** K12
Fillmore, *Calif., U.S.* **111** X7
Fillmore, *Utah, U.S.* **109** N7
Filyos, river, *Turk.* **170** C8
Fimbul Ice Shelf, *Antarctica* **230** A12
Fimi, river, *Dem. Rep. of the Congo* **202** L8
Fiñana, *Sp.* **146** L12
Fındıklı, *Rep. of Georgia* **171** C15
Findlay, *Ohio, U.S.* **101** P12
Findochty, *Scot., U.K.* **144** J10
Fineveke, *Wallis and Futuna, Fr.* **222** B11
Finger Lakes, *N.Y., U.S.* **96** K7
Fíngoè, *Mozambique* **206** E12
Finike, *Turk.* **170** J5
Finisterre, Cape, *Eur.* **140** J2
Finke, *N.T., Austral.* **215** U9
Finke, river, *Austral.* **214** G9
Finland, *Eur.* **143** F15
Finland, *Minn., U.S.* **106** F13
Finland, Gulf of, *Est., Fin.* **143** J15
Finlay, river, *B.C., Can.* **84** J8
Finley, *N. Dak., U.S.* **106** F7
Finley Cay, *Bahamas* **122** E5
Finnmark Plateau, *Eur.* **140** A9
Finnsmarkvidda, island, *Nor.* **143** C14
Finol Finkol, peak, *F.S.M.* **221** B18
Finschhafen, *P.N.G.* **217** D20
Finsteraarhorn, *Switz.* **152** C3
Finsterwalde, *Ger.* **150** E11
Fionn Loch, *Scot., U.K.* **144** J8
Fionnphort, *Scot., U.K.* **144** L7
Fiorentino, *San Marino* **163** K15
Fiorina, *San Marino* **163** H16
Fiorina, river, *San Marino* **163** H16
Firá, *Gr.* **157** M15
Firat, river, *Turk.* **171** G14
Fire Island National Seashore, *N.Y., U.S.* **96** N12
Firenze (Florence), *It.* **152** G7
Firenzuola, *It.* **152** G7
Firmat, *Arg.* **134** K11
Firminy, *Fr.* **149** U12
Firozabad, *India* **180** G6
First State National Monument, *Del., U.S.* **98** B14
First Sugar Mill, *Hawai'i, U.S.* **114** C5
Firth of Forth, *Atl. Oc.* **140** E4
Fīrūzābād, *Iran* **175** G13
Fish, river, *Namibia* **206** H7
Fisher, river, *Can., U.S.* **108** B5
Fisher Glacier, *Antarctica* **231** F18
Fisher Strait, *Nunavut, Can.* **85** J16

Fishguard (Abergwaun), *Wales, U.K.* **145** U8
Fishing Cays, *Bahamas* **122** B10
Fish Lake, *Utah, U.S.* **109** N7
Fiskárdo, *Gr.* **156** H7
Fismes, *Fr.* **149** N11
Fisterra, *Sp.* **146** B5
Fisterra, Cabo, *Sp.* **146** B5
Fitchburg, *Mass., U.S.* **97** K14
Fitii, *Fr. Polynesia, Fr.* **223** G14
Fitii, Baie de, *Fr. Polynesia, Fr.* **223** G14
Fiti'uta, *Amer. Samoa, U.S.* **222** P4
Fito, Mount, *Samoa* **222** L3
Fitri, Lac, *Chad* **201** J15
Fitzgerald, *Alta., Can.* **84** J11
Fitzgerald, *Ga., U.S.* **99** P6
Fitzroy, river, *Austral.* **214** D5
Fitzroy, river, *Austral.* **214** F15
Fitzroy Crossing, *W. Aust., Austral.* **215** R5
Fivaku, island, *Maldives* **181** T3
Five Island Harbour, *Antigua and Barbuda* **123** B20
Five Islands Village, *Antigua and Barbuda* **123** B20
Flagler, *Colo., U.S.* **108** M15
Flagstaff, *Ariz., U.S.* **109** S7
Flagstaff Lake, *Oreg., U.S.* **110** K6
Flåm, *Nor.* **142** J10
Flambeau, river, *Wis., U.S.* **100** G4
Flamborough Head, *Eng., U.K.* **145** Q14
Flaming Gorge National Recreation Area, *Utah, Wyo., U.S.* **108** K9
Flaming Gorge Reservoir, *Utah, Wyo., U.S.* **108** K9
Flamingo, *Fla., U.S.* **99** Y9
Flamingo, Teluk, *Indonesia* **217** C16
Flamingo Cay, *Bahamas* **119** C9
Flamingo Point, *Bahamas* **119** E13
Flanagan Island, *Virgin Is., U.S.* **122** N12
Flanders, region, *Belg., Fr.* **148** L10
Flandreau, *S. Dak., U.S.* **106** L8
Flannach Isles see Na h-Eileanan Flannach, *Scot., U.K.* **144** H6
Flathead Lake, *Mont., U.S.* **108** B6
Flat Island, *Mauritius* **209** F20
Flat Island, *S. China Sea* **192** E11
Flatonia, *Tex., U.S.* **105** R11
Flat River, *Mo., U.S.* **107** U15
Flattery, Cape, *Austral.* **214** C13
Flattery, Cape, *Wash., U.S.* **110** B1
Flatts Village, *Bermuda* **122** C2
Flatwoods, *Ky., U.S.* **103** A20
Flaxton, *N. Dak., U.S.* **106** D3
Fleeming Channel, *Bahamas* **122** E5
Fleetwood, *Eng., U.K.* **145** R10
Fleetwood, *Qnsld., Austral.* **215** T13
Flekkefjord, *Nor.* **142** L10
Fleming Glacier, *Antarctica* **230** F6
Flemingsburg, *Ky., U.S.* **103** B19
Flemish Cap, *Atl. Oc.* **240** H7
Flensburg, *Ger.* **150** A7
Flers, *Fr.* **149** P7
Fletcher Peninsula, *Antarctica* **230** J6
Fletcher Plain, *Arctic Oc.* **246** J11
Fleurance, *Fr.* **149** X8
Fleurier, *Switz.* **152** B1
Flight 93 National Memorial, *Pa., U.S.* **96** P4
Flinders, river, *Austral.* **214** D11
Flinders, river, *Austral.* **214** E12
Flinders Fracture Zone, *Ind. Oc.* **224** K9
Flinders Island, *Austral.* **214** K8
Flinders Ranges, *Austral.* **214** J10
Flin Flon, *Man., Can.* **85** L13
Flint, *Mich., U.S.* **100** L12
Flint, river, *Ga., U.S.* **99** P5
Flint Hills, *Kans., U.S.* **107** U8
Flint Island, *Kiribati* **219** H13
Flipper Point, *Wake I., U.S.* **220** F7
Flisa, *Nor.* **142** J12
Flix, *Sp.* **147** E15
Flixecourt, *Fr.* **148** M9

Flocca, river, *San Marino* **163** H15
Flomaton, *Ala., U.S.* **103** N15
Flood Range, *Antarctica* **230** M9
Floodwood, *Minn., U.S.* **106** G12
Flora, *Ill., U.S.* **101** T6
Flora, *Ind., U.S.* **101** Q8
Flora, *Oreg., U.S.* **110** E9
Florala, *Ala., U.S.* **103** N15
Florange, *Fr.* **149** N14
Florence, *Ala., U.S.* **103** G14
Florence, *Ariz., U.S.* **109** U7
Florence, *Colo., U.S.* **109** N13
Florence, *Kans., U.S.* **107** T8
Florence, *Ky., U.S.* **103** A17
Florence, *Oreg., U.S.* **110** H2
Florence, *S.C., U.S.* **98** K10
Florence, *Wis., U.S.* **100** G7
Florence see Firenze, *It.* **152** G7
Florencia, *Col.* **130** H4
Florenville, *Belg.* **162** J7
Flores, *Azores, Port.* **146** P1
Flores, *Guatemala* **117** K16
Flores, island, *Indonesia* **193** M13
Flores Basin, *Pac. Oc.* **242** K5
Flores Sea, *Indonesia* **192** M13
Floreşti, *Mold.* **159** Q4
Floresville, *Tex., U.S.* **105** S10
Floriano, *Braz.* **133** F15
Floriano Peixoto, *Braz.* **132** G6
Florianópolis, *Braz.* **133** N13
Florida, *Cuba* **118** G6
Florida, *P.R., U.S.* **122** M3
Florida, *U.S.* **99** S7
Florida, peninsula, *N. Amer.* **82** L8
Florida, Straits of, *N. Amer.* **82** M8
Florida Bay, *Fla., U.S.* **99** Y10
Florida City, *Fla., U.S.* **99** X10
Florida-Hatteras Shelf, *Atl. Oc.* **240** K3
Florida Islands, *Solomon Is.* **221** N19
Florida Keys, *Fla., U.S.* **99** Y9
Floridia, *It.* **153** T12
Flórina, *Gr.* **156** C8
Florissant, *Mo., U.S.* **107** S15
Florissant Fossil Beds National Monument, *Colo., U.S.* **109** N13
Florø, *Nor.* **142** J9
Flotta, island, *Scot., U.K.* **144** G10
Flotte, Cap de, *New Caledonia, Fr.* **222** C9
Floyd, *N. Mex., U.S.* **109** T15
Floydada, *Tex., U.S.* **104** J6
Flumet, *Fr.* **149** U14
Fly, river, *P.N.G.* **217** D17
Foa, island, *Tonga* **222** P7
Foča, *Bosn. & Herzg.* **154** H8
Foça, *Turk.* **170** F2
Focşani, *Rom.* **155** D16
Fofoa, island, *Tonga* **222** M11
Fogang, *Guang., China* **185** V4
Fogausa, Cape, *Amer. Samoa, U.S.* **222** M8
Fog Bay, *Austral.* **214** B7
Foggia, *It.* **152** L12
Fogo, island, *Cabo Verde* **209** E15
Fogo Island, *Nfld. & Lab., Can.* **85** L23
Fohnsdorf, *Aust.* **150** L11
Foinikas, *Gr.* **157** K14
Fokino, *Russ.* **158** L8
Foko Finaunpes, cape, *F.S.M.* **221** A19
Foko Fukunsral, cape, *F.S.M.* **221** B19
Foko Malsu, cape, *F.S.M.* **221** A18
Foko Nefalil, cape, *F.S.M.* **221** B18
Folda, bay, *Nor.* **142** G11
Folégandros, *Gr.* **157** M14
Folégandros, island, *Gr.* **157** M14
Foley, *Ala., U.S.* **103** P14
Foley, *Minn., U.S.* **106** J11
Foley Island, *Nunavut, Can.* **85** F17
Foligno, *It.* **152** J8
Folkestone, *Eng., U.K.* **145** W15
Folkston, *Ga., U.S.* **99** Q8
Follett, *Tex., U.S.* **104** E7
Follonica, *It.* **152** J6
Follonica, Golfo di, *It.* **152** J6
Folly Beach, *S.C., U.S.* **98** M10
Foloha, *Tonga* **222** J11
Folschette, *Lux.* **162** J9

Folsom, *Calif., U.S.* III Q5
Folteşti, *Rom.* 155 D17
Fomboni, *Comoros* 209 N15
Fomento, *Cuba* 118 H9
Fond d'Or Bay, *St. Lucia* 123 K14
Fond du Lac, *Wis., U.S.* 100 K6
Fond-du-Lac, *Sask., Can.* 84 J12
Fondi, *It.* 152 L9
Fono, *island, F.S.M.* 221 B15
Fonoifua, *island, Tonga* 222 Q6
Fononuk, *island, F.S.M.* 221 D16
Fonou, *island, F.S.M.* 221 C15
Fonseca, Golfo de, *Hond.* 117 L17
Fontainebleau, *Fr.* 149 Q10
Fontana Lake, *N.C., U.S.* 98 H6
Fontaneda, *Andorra* 162 K2
Fonte Boa, *Braz.* 132 D7
Fontenelle Reservoir, *Wyo., U.S.* 108 J8
Fontenoy, *Grenada* 123 L22
Fontvieille, *Monaco* 163 F19
Fontvieille, Port of, *Monaco* 163 F21
Fonuafoou, *island, Tonga* 222 M12
Fonuaika, *island, Tonga* 222 Q6
Fonua'one'one, *island, Tonga* 222 M11
Fonuaunga, *island, Tonga* 222 M12
Fonuaunga, Ava, *Tonga* 222 M11
Fonuchu, *island, F.S.M.* 221 B15
Foppolo, *It.* 152 D5
Forbes, *N.S.W., Austral.* 215 X14
Forbesganj, *India* 180 G11
Forbes Hill, *Bahamas* 122 F9
Forcalquier, *Fr.* 149 X14
Forchheim, *Ger.* 150 H8
Ford, Cape, *Austral.* 214 B7
Fordate, *island, Indonesia* 217 D14
Førde, *Nor.* 142 J10
Ford Ranges, *Antarctica* 230 N10
Fordyce, *Ark., U.S.* 102 J8
Forécariah, *Guinea* 204 C5
Forel, Mount, *N. Amer.* 82 C10
Foreman, *Ark., U.S.* 102 J6
Forest, *Miss., U.S.* 102 L12
Forest City, *Iowa, U.S.* 106 M11
Forest City, *N.C., U.S.* 98 J8
Forest Grove, *Oreg., U.S.* 110 F3
Forest Lakes, *Austral.* 214 H7
Forest Park, *Ga., U.S.* 98 L5
Forest Point, *British Virgin Is., U.K.* 122 R11
Forestville, *Mich., U.S.* 100 K13
Forestville, *Que., Can.* 85 N20
Forez, Monts du, *Fr.* 149 U11
Forfar, *Scot., U.K.* 144 L10
Forgan, *Okla., U.S.* 104 E7
Forges-les-Eaux, *Fr.* 149 N9
Forks, *Wash., U.S.* 110 B2
Forlì, *It.* 152 G8
Forman, *N. Dak., U.S.* 106 H7
Formentera, *island, Sp.* 147 J17
Formiga, *Braz.* 133 L14
Formigas, Ilhéus, *Azores, Port.* 146 R5
Formosa, *Arg.* 134 F13
Formosa, *Braz.* 133 J13
Formosa, Serra, *Braz.* 132 G11
Formosa do Rio Prêto, *Braz.* 133 G14
Føroyar *see* Faroe Islands, *Eur.* 142 H6
Forrest, *W. Aust., Austral.* 215 W7
Forrestal Range, *Antarctica* 230 G10
Forrest City, *Ark., U.S.* 102 G10
Forrest River, *W. Aust., Austral.* 215 Q6
Forsayth, *Qnsld., Austral.* 215 R12
Forssa, *Fin.* 143 H15
Forst, *Ger.* 150 E11
Forster-Tuncurry, *N.S.W., Austral.* 215 X15
Forsyth, *Ga., U.S.* 98 M5
Forsyth, *Mo., U.S.* 107 V12
Forsyth, *Mont., U.S.* 108 D11
Fort Abbas, *Pak.* 179 S11
Fort Albany, *Ont., Can.* 85 M17
Fort Allen, *site, P.R., U.S.* 122 N3
Fort Antoine, *Monaco* 163 E22

Fort Atkinson, *Wis., U.S.* 100 L6
Fort Benton, *Mont., U.S.* 108 C8
Fort Bowie National Historic Site, *Ariz., U.S.* 109 V9
Fort Bragg, *Calif., U.S.* III P2
Fort Caroline National Memorial, *Fla., U.S.* 99 Q9
Fort Charlotte, *site, St. Lucia* 123 J14
Fort Charlotte, *site, St. Vincent and the Grenadines* 123 L16
Fort Chipewyan, *Alta., Can.* 84 J11
Fort Cobb Reservoir, *Okla., U.S.* 104 G9
Fort Collins, *Colo., U.S.* 108 L13
Fort Davis, *Tex., U.S.* 105 P2
Fort Davis National Historic Site, *Tex., U.S.* 105 P2
Fort-de-France, *Martinique, Fr.* 123 F22
Fort-de-France, Baie de, *Martinique, Fr.* 123 F23
Fort Deposit, *Ala., U.S.* 103 M15
Fort Dick, *Calif., U.S.* 110 L1
Fort Dodge, *Iowa, U.S.* 107 N11
Fort Duvernette, *site, St. Vincent and the Grenadines* 123 L16
Forteau, *Que., Can.* 85 L22
Fortescue, *river, Austral.* 214 F3
Fortezza, *It.* 152 B7
Fort Fairfield, *Me., U.S.* 97 B18
Fort Frances, *Ont., Can.* 85 P14
Fort Fraser, *B.C., Can.* 84 K8
Fort Frederica National Monument, *Ga., U.S.* 99 P9
Fort Frederick, *site, Grenada* 123 L22
Fort Gaines, *Ga., U.S.* 99 P4
Fort Gibson, *Okla., U.S.* 104 F13
Fort Gibson Lake, *Okla., U.S.* 104 F13
Fort Good Hope, *N.W.T., Can.* 84 F10
Forth, Firth of, *Scot., U.K.* 144 M10
Fort Hall, *Idaho, U.S.* 108 H7
Fort Hancock, *Tex., U.S.* 105 W3
Fort Hope, *Ont., Can.* 85 N16
Fortín General Díaz, *Parag.* 132 M9
Fortín Infante Rivarola, *Parag.* 132 L8
Fortín Madrejón, *Parag.* 132 L9
Fortín Mayor Alberto Gardel, *Parag.* 132 M8
Fortín Presidente Ayala, *Parag.* 132 M9
Fortín Suárez Arana, *Bol.* 132 K9
Fort James, *site, Antigua and Barbuda* 123 B20
Fort Jeudy, Point of, *Grenada* 123 L23
Fort Jones, *Calif., U.S.* 110 L3
Fort Kent, *Me., U.S.* 97 A17
Fort Klamath, *Oreg., U.S.* 110 K4
Fort Knox, *site, Ky., U.S.* 103 C16
Fort Laramie, *Wyo., U.S.* 108 J13
Fort Laramie National Historic Site, *Wyo., U.S.* 108 J13
Fort Larned National Historic Site, *Kans., U.S.* 107 T6
Fort Lauderdale, *Fla., U.S.* 99 W10
Fort Liard, *N.W.T., Can.* 84 H9
Fort-Liberté, *Haiti* 119 L17
Fort Madison, *Iowa, U.S.* 107 Q14
Fort Matanzas National Monument, *Fla., U.S.* 99 R9
Fort McMurray, *Alta., Can.* 84 K11
Fort McPherson, *N.W.T., Can.* 84 E9
Fort Meade, *Fla., U.S.* 99 U8
Fort Mill, *S.C., U.S.* 98 J9
Fort Miribel, *Alg.* 200 C11
Fort Morgan, *Colo., U.S.* 108 L14
Fort Munro, *Pak.* 179 R8
Fort Myers, *Fla., U.S.* 99 W8
Fort Myers Beach, *Fla., U.S.* 99 W8
Fort Nelson, *B.C., Can.* 84 J9
Fort Ord National Monument, *Calif., U.S.* III T4
Fort Payne, *Ala., U.S.* 103 H16
Fort Peck, *Mont., U.S.* 108 B12
Fort Peck Dam, *Mont., U.S.* 108 B12
Fort Peck Lake, *Mont., U.S.* 108 C11
Fort Pierce, *Fla., U.S.* 99 U10

Fort Pierre, *S. Dak., U.S.* 106 K5
Fort Point, *British Virgin Is., U.K.* 122 R8
Fort Portal, *Uganda* 202 K12
Fort Providence, *N.W.T., Can.* 84 H10
Fort Pulaski National Monument, *Ga., U.S.* 99 N9
Fort Raleigh National Historic Site, *N.C., U.S.* 98 G15
Fort Randall Dam, *S. Dak., U.S.* 106 M6
Fort Resolution, *N.W.T., Can.* 84 J11
Fortress Headquarters, *Gibraltar, U.K.* 163 Q22
Fort Rock, *Oreg., U.S.* 110 J5
Fort Royal, *site, Guadeloupe, Fr.* 123 E14
Fort Saint Catherine, *site, Bermuda* 122 B3
Fort Saint John, *B.C., Can.* 84 K9
Fort Scaur, *site, Bermuda* 122 C1
Fort Scott, *Kans., U.S.* 107 U10
Fort Scott National Historic Site, *Kans., U.S.* 107 U10
Fort Severn, *Ont., Can.* 85 L16
Fort Shevchenko, *Kaz.* 176 G5
Fort Simpson, *N.W.T., Can.* 84 H10
Fort Smith, *Ark., U.S.* 102 F6
Fort Smith, *N.W.T., Can.* 84 J11
Fort Stanwix National Monument, *N.Y., U.S.* 96 J9
Fort Stockton, *Tex., U.S.* 105 P3
Fort Sumner, *N. Mex., U.S.* 109 S14
Fort Sumter National Monument, *S.C., U.S.* 98 M10
Fort Supply, *Okla., U.S.* 104 E8
Fort Thompson, *S. Dak., U.S.* 106 L5
Fortuna, *Calif., U.S.* III N1
Fortuna, *N. Dak., U.S.* 106 D2
Fortune Hill, *Bahamas* 122 E12
Fortune Island *see* Long Cay, *Bahamas* 119 H14
Fort Union National Monument, *N. Mex., U.S.* 109 R13
Fort Union Trading Post National Historic Site, *N. Dak., U.S.* 106 E1
Fort Valley, *Ga., U.S.* 98 M5
Fort Vermilion, *Alta., Can.* 84 J10
Fort Walton Beach, *Fla., U.S.* 99 Q2
Fort Wayne, *Ind., U.S.* 101 P10
Fort Worth, *Tex., U.S.* 104 L11
Fort Yates, *N. Dak., U.S.* 106 H4
Fort Yukon, *Alas., U.S.* 113 E18
Fosforescénte, Bahía, *P.R., U.S.* 122 P1
Foshan, *Guang., China* 185 V4
Fosheim Peninsula, *Nunavut, Can.* 85 B16
Fossano, *It.* 152 F2
Fossatodi Vico, *It.* 152 H9
Fossil, *Oreg., U.S.* 110 G6
Fossil Butte National Monument, *Wyo., U.S.* 108 J8
Fossil Downs, *W. Aust., Austral.* 215 R6
Fosston, *Minn., U.S.* 106 F9
Foster, *Vic., Austral.* 215 Z13
Foster, Mount, *Can., U.S.* 113 K21
Foster Bay, *Greenland, Den.* 82 B10
Fostoria, *Ohio, U.S.* 101 P12
Fotuha'a, *island, Tonga* 222 P6
Fougères, *Fr.* 149 Q6
Foula, *island, Scot., U.K.* 144 D11
Foul Bay, *Barbados* 123 L20
Foulness Island, *Eng., U.K.* 145 V15
Foulweather, Cape, *Oreg., U.S.* 110 G2
Foulwind, Cape, *N.Z.* 217 M17
Foumban, *Cameroon* 205 E15
Foumbouni, *Comoros* 209 M14
Foundation Ice Stream, *Antarctica* 230 H10
Foundation Seamounts, *Pac. Oc.* 243 N17
Fountain, *Colo., U.S.* 109 N13
Fountain City, *Wis., U.S.* 100 J3
Four Corners, *Wyo., U.S.* 108 G14
Fourcroy, Cape, *Austral.* 214 A7
Four Ladies Bank, *Ind. Oc.* 248 E12
Fourmies, *Fr.* 148 M11

Four Mountains, Islands of, *Alas., U.S.* 112 P8
Fournaise, Piton de la, *Réunion, Fr.* 209 H17
Foúrnoi, *Gr.* 157 K17
Foúrnoi, *island, Gr.* 157 K17
Fourup, *island, F.S.M.* 221 C15
Fouta Djallon, *region, Guinea* 204 B5
Foux, Cap-à-, *Haiti* 119 L15
Foveaux Strait, *N.Z.* 217 R15
Fowler, *Colo., U.S.* 109 N14
Fowler, *Ind., U.S.* 101 Q7
Fowler, *Kans., U.S.* 107 U4
Fowlers Bay, *Austral.* 214 J8
Fowlers Bay, *S. Aust., Austral.* 215 W8
Fox, *river, Ill., U.S.* 100 P6
Fox, *river, Wis., U.S.* 100 K5
Foxe Basin, *Nunavut, Can.* 85 G16
Foxe Channel, *Nunavut, Can.* 85 H17
Foxe Peninsula, *Nunavut, Can.* 85 H17
Fox Glacier, *N.Z.* 217 P16
Fox Islands, *Alas., U.S.* 112 P9
Foxpark, *Wyo., U.S.* 108 K12
Fox Town, *Bahamas* 122 A5
Foyle, Lough, *N. Ire., U.K.* 145 P6
Foyn Coast, *Antarctica* 230 E5
Foz, *Sp.* 146 A7
Foz do Cunene, *Angola* 206 F5
Foz do Iguaçu, *Braz.* 132 N11
Fraga, *Sp.* 147 D15
Fram Bank, *Ind. Oc.* 248 E11
Framnes Mountains, *Antarctica* 231 E19
Fram Peak, *Antarctica* 231 D19
Fram Strait, *Arctic Oc.* 247 J16
Franca, *Braz.* 133 L13
France, *Fr.* 149 S10
Francés, Cabo, *Cuba* 118 H4
Francés, Punta, *Cuba* 118 H5
Frances Lake, *Yukon, Can.* 84 G9
Francés Viejo, Cabo, *Dom. Rep.* 119 L19
Franceville, *Gabon* 205 H17
Francis Bay, *Virgin Is., U.S.* 122 M11
Francis Case, Lake, *S. Dak., U.S.* 106 L5
Francistown, *Botswana* 206 G10
Francs Peak, *Wyo., U.S.* 108 G9
Frankenberg, *Ger.* 150 F6
Frankfort, *Ind., U.S.* 101 Q8
Frankfort, *Kans., U.S.* 107 R8
Frankfort, *Ky., U.S.* 103 B17
Frankfort, *Mich., U.S.* 100 J9
Frankfurt am Main, *Ger.* 150 G6
Frankfurt an der Oder, *Ger.* 150 E11
Franklin, *Ind., U.S.* 101 S9
Franklin, *Ky., U.S.* 103 D15
Franklin, *La., U.S.* 102 Q9
Franklin, *N.C., U.S.* 98 J6
Franklin, *N.H., U.S.* 97 H14
Franklin, *Nebr., U.S.* 107 R6
Franklin, *Pa., U.S.* 96 M3
Franklin, *Pa., U.S.* 96 M3
Franklin, *Tenn., U.S.* 103 F15
Franklin, *Va., U.S.* 98 F13
Franklin Bay, *N.W.T., Can.* 84 D11
Franklin D. Roosevelt Lake, *Wash., U.S.* 110 B8
Franklin Lake, *Nev., U.S.* III N11
Franklin Mountains, *N. Amer.* 82 D4
Franklin Strait, *Nunavut, Can.* 85 E14
Franklinton, *La., U.S.* 102 N11
Franklinville, *N.Y., U.S.* 96 K5
Frank Sound, *Cayman Is.* 122 J3
Frankston, *Tex., U.S.* 105 M13
Frantsa Iosifa, Zemlya (Franz Josef Land), *Russ.* 160 C12
Frants-Viktoriya Trough, *Arctic Oc.* 247 F15
Franz, *Ont., Can.* 85 P17
Franz Josef Glacier, *N.Z.* 217 P16
Franz Josef Land *see* Frantsa Iosifa, Zemlya, *Russ.* 160 C12
Fraserburg, *S. Af.* 206 L8

Fraserburgh, *Scot., U.K.* 144 J11
Fraser Island (Great Sandy Island), *Austral.* 214 G16
Fraser Range, *W. Aust., Austral.* 215 W5
Frasertown, *N.Z.* 217 K20
Frasin, *Rom.* 155 B15
Frastanz, *Aust.* 162 M4
Fratta, *river, San Marino* 163 K14
Frauenfeld, *Switz.* 152 A4
Frazee, *Minn., U.S.* 106 G9
Fredensborg, *Virgin Is., U.S.* 122 Q2
Frederick, *Md., U.S.* 98 C12
Frederick, *Okla., U.S.* 104 J9
Frederick, *S. Dak., U.S.* 106 H6
Frederick, Mount, *Austral.* 214 D7
Fredericksburg, *Tex., U.S.* 105 Q9
Fredericksburg, *Va., U.S.* 98 D13
Fredericktown, *Mo., U.S.* 107 U15
Fredericton, *N.B., Can.* 85 P21
Frederikshåbs Bank, *Atl. Oc.* 247 R18
Frederikshavn, *Den.* 142 M11
Frederiksted, *Virgin Is., U.S.* 121 B13
Frederiksted, *Virgin Is., U.S.* 122 R1
Fredonia, *Ariz., U.S.* 109 Q6
Fredonia, *Kans., U.S.* 107 U9
Fredonia, *N.Y., U.S.* 96 K4
Fredrikstad, *Nor.* 142 K11
Freedom, *Okla., U.S.* 104 E8
Freehold, *N.J., U.S.* 96 P11
Freeman, *S. Dak., U.S.* 106 M7
Freeport, *Bahamas* 118 C10
Freeport, *Bahamas* 122 F1
Freeport, *Ill., U.S.* 100 M5
Freeport, *Me., U.S.* 97 G16
Freeport, *N.Y., U.S.* 96 N11
Freeport, *Tex., U.S.* 105 S14
Freer, *Tex., U.S.* 105 U9
Freetown, *Antigua and Barbuda* 123 B21
Freetown, *Bahamas* 122 E2
Freetown, *Jam.* 122 J9
Freetown, *Sierra Leone* 204 D5
Freezeout Mountain, *Oreg., U.S.* 110 H9
Frégate, *island, Seychelles* 209 N21
Frégate Island, *Mauritius* 209 J19
Fregenal de la Sierra, *Sp.* 146 J7
Fréhel, Cap, *Fr.* 149 P5
Freiberg, *Ger.* 150 F10
Freiburg, *Ger.* 150 K5
Freidberg, *Ger.* 150 K8
Freirina, *Chile* 134 H6
Freisach, *Aust.* 150 M11
Freising, *Ger.* 150 K9
Freistadt, *Aust.* 150 K11
Freital, *Ger.* 150 F10
Fréjus, *Fr.* 149 X15
Fremont, *Calif., U.S.* III S4
Fremont, *Mich., U.S.* 100 L9
Fremont, *Nebr., U.S.* 107 P8
Fremont, *Ohio, U.S.* 101 P12
Fremont, *river, Utah, U.S.* 109 N7
Fremont Lake, *Wyo., U.S.* 108 H9
Fremont Mountains, *Oreg., U.S.* 110 K5
French Bay, *Bahamas* 122 F11
French Broad, *river, Tenn., U.S.* 103 F19
Frenchcap Cay, *Virgin Is., U.S.* 122 P10
French Cays *see* Plana Cays, *Bahamas* 119 G15
French Frigate Shoals, *Hawai'i, U.S.* 114 M7
French Guiana, *S. Amer.* 131 F17
Frenchman Creek, *Colo., Nebr., U.S.* 107 Q3
Frenchman Flat, *Nev., U.S.* III T11
Frenchman's Cay, *British Virgin Is., U.K.* 122 R5
French Polynesia, *Pac. Oc.* 223 F17
Frenchville, *Me., U.S.* 97 A18
Fresh Water Bay, *Barbados* 123 L18
Fresh Water Lagoons, *Kiribati* 221 C24
Fresnay, *Fr.* 149 Q7
Fresnillo, *Mex.* 116 G10
Fresno, *Calif., U.S.* III T6
Fresno Reservoir, *Mont., U.S.* 108 B9

Frévent, Fr. 148 M10
Frewena, N.T., Austral. 215 R9
Freyung, Ger. 150 J10
Fria, Guinea 204 C5
Friars Point, Miss., U.S. 102 H10
Frías, Arg. 134 H9
Fridtjof Nansen, Mount, Antarctica 230 K12
Friedrichshafen, Ger. 150 L7
Friend, Nebr., U.S. 107 Q8
Friesland, region, Neth. 148 G14
Frigate Bay, St. Kitts and Nevis 123 B18
Frio, river, Tex., U.S. 105 S8
Frio, Cabo, S. Amer. 128 J10
Friona, Tex., U.S. 104 H4
Frisange, Lux. 162 K10
Frisco City, Ala., U.S. 103 M14
Frisian Islands, Eur. 140 F6
Frissell, Mount, Conn., U.S. 96 L12
Fritch, Tex., U.S. 104 G5
Friza, Proliv, Russ. 161 J23
Frobisher Bay, Nunavut, Can. 85 H19
Frolovo, Russ. 159 P12
Fromberg, Mont., U.S. 108 E10
Frome, Eng., U.K. 145 W11
Frome, Jam. 122 H6
Frome, Lake, Austral. 214 J11
Frómista, Sp. 146 C10
Frontenac, Kans., U.S. 107 U10
Frontera, Mex. 116 E11
Frontera, Mex. 117 J15
Frontignan, Fr. 149 X11
Front Range, Colo., U.S. 108 L12
Frosinone, It. 152 L9
Frostburg, Md., U.S. 98 C11
Frostproof, Fla., U.S. 99 U9
Frøya, island, Nor. 142 G10
Frøya Bank, Atl. Oc. 240 E13
Fruita, Colo., U.S. 108 M10
Fruitland, Idaho, U.S. 108 G3
Frümsen, Switz. 162 M1
Frý, Gr. 157 Q18
Frydendal, Virgin Is., U.S. 122 N9
Fryeburg, Me., U.S. 97 G15
Frying Pan Shoals, N.C., U.S. 98 L13
Fu, river, China 182 L10
Fu, river, Jiangxi, China 185 R7
Fua'amotu, Tonga 222 J11
Fua'amotu, island, Tonga 222 M11
Fuafatu, island, Tuvalu 221 K22
Fuagea, island, Tuvalu 221 L22
Fualifexe, island, Tuvalu 221 J23
Fualopa, island, Tuvalu 221 K22
Fua Mulaku, island, Maldives 181 X3
Fu'an, Fujian, China 185 S10
Fuchuan, Guangxi Zhuang, China 185 U2
Fucino, Piana del, It. 152 K9
Fuding, Fujian, China 185 R11
Fuencaliente, Sp. 208 Q3
Fuencaliente, Punta de, Sp. 208 Q3
Fuengirola, Sp. 146 M9
Fuente de Cantos, Sp. 146 J8
Fuentesaúco, Sp. 146 E9
Fuerte Olimpo, Parag. 132 L10
Fuerteventura, island, Sp. 208 Q7
Fuga, island, Philippines 193 B13
Fugauvea, Passe, Wallis and Futuna, Fr. 222 B11
Fugløy Bank, Atl. Oc. 240 D14
Fugu, Shaanxi, China 184 D3
Fuguo see Zhanhua, Shand., China 184 F9
Fuhai, China 182 D5
Fuidhaigh (Wiay), island, Scot., U.K. 144 J6
Fuikbaai, Curaçao, Neth. 123 Q15
Fujairah, U.A.E. 175 J15
Fuji, peak, Japan 189 P11
Fujian, China 185 T8
Fujin, China 183 C17
Fujisawa, Japan 189 P12
Fukagawa, Japan 188 F13
Fukave, island, Tonga 222 H12
Fukuchiyama, Japan 189 P8
Fukue, Japan 189 R3
Fukue Jima, Japan 189 R3
Fukui, Japan 189 P9
Fukuoka, Japan 189 R4
Fukushima, Japan 188 H12
Fukushima, Japan 188 M12
Fukushima, Mount, Antarctica 231 C16
Fukuyama, Japan 189 Q7
Fulaga, island, Fiji 222 K9
Fulaga Passage, Fiji 222 J9
Fulda, Ger. 150 G7
Fulda, Minn., U.S. 106 L9
Fuliang, Jiangxi, China 185 P8
Fuling, China 182 L11
Fullarton, Trinidad and Tobago 123 Q21
Fullerton, Nebr., U.S. 107 P7
Fullerton Point, Antigua and Barbuda 123 B20
Fulton, Ill., U.S. 101 N4
Fulton, Ky., U.S. 102 E12
Fulton, Miss., U.S. 103 H13
Fulton, Mo., U.S. 107 S13
Fulton, N.Y., U.S. 96 H8
Fumay, Fr. 148 M12
Fumel, Fr. 149 W8
Funabashi, Japan 189 P12
Funafara Island, Tuvalu 221 L23
Funafuti, Tuvalu 221 K24
Funafuti Island, Tuvalu 221 K24
Funamanu, island, Tuvalu 221 K23
Funan, Anhui, China 184 L7
Funangongo, island, Tuvalu 221 K23
Funchal, Madeira, Port. 208 M3
Fundo de Figueiras, Cabo Verde 209 C18
Fundy, Bay of, N. Amer. 82 H9
Funhalouro, Mozambique 207 H13
Funing, Jiangsu, China 184 K10
Funing Wan, Fujian, China 185 S11
Funiu Shan, Henan, China 184 K3
Funiya Point, N. Mariana Is., U.S. 220 E8
Funtanasupanie Point, N. Mariana Is., U.S. 220 D8
Funtua, Nigeria 205 B14
Fuping, Hebei, China 184 D6
Fuqing, Fujian, China 185 T10
Furano, Japan 188 G13
Furmanov, Russ. 158 H11
Furnas Reservoir, S. Amer. 128 H9
Furneaux Group, Austral. 214 L8
Furqlus, Syr. 172 G8
Fürstenfeldbruck, Ger. 150 K8
Fürstenwalde, Ger. 150 D11
Fürth, Ger. 150 H8
Furth im Wald, Ger. 150 J10
Furukawa, Japan 188 L13
Fuscaldo, It. 153 P13
Fuse, Japan 189 N7
Fushan, Shand., China 184 F11
Fushan, Shanxi, China 184 G4
Fushun, Liaoning, China 184 A13
Fusio, Switz. 152 C4
Fusong, Jilin, China 184 A16
Füssen, Ger. 150 L8
Futiga, Amer. Samoa, U.S. 222 N7
Futou Hu, Hubei, China 185 P5
Futun, river, Fujian, China 185 S8
Futuna, island, Vanuatu 222 H4
Futuna, island, Wallis and Futuna, Fr. 222 E11
Fuwwah, Yemen 174 Q12
Fuxin, Liaoning, China 184 A11
Fuxingdi, Liaoning, China 184 A11
Fuya, Japan 188 L12
Fuyang, Anhui, China 184 L7
Fuyu, China 183 D16
Fuyuan, China 183 B18
Fuyun, China 182 D6
Fuzhou, Fujian, China 185 T10
Fuzhoucheng, Liaoning, China 184 D12
Füzuli see Karaghbyur, Azerb. 171 E21
Fyn, island, Den. 142 N11
Fyne, Loch, Scot., U.K. 144 M8
Fyzabad, Trinidad and Tobago 123 Q22

G

Gaalkacyo (Galcaio), Somalia 203 H18
Gabbs, Nev., U.S. 111 Q8
Gabela, Angola 206 D6
Gabert Island, F.S.M. 221 A18
Gabes, Tun. 201 B13
Gabes, Gulf of, Tun. 201 B13
Gabon, Af. 205 H16
Gaborone, S. Af. 206 J10
Gabras, Sudan 202 F11
Gabriel Vera, Bol. 132 K7
Gabrovo, Bulg. 155 H15
Gackle, N. Dak., U.S. 106 G6
Gadag, India 181 N5
Gadarwara, India 180 J6
Gäddede, Sw. 142 G12
Gadeokdo, island, S. Korea 187 T11
Gadifuri, island, Maldives 181 V3
Gadrut see Hadrut, Azerb. 171 E21
Gadsden, Ala., U.S. 103 H16
Gadwal, India 181 N6
Găeşti, Rom. 155 F15
Gaeta, It. 152 L10
Gaeta, Golfo di, It. 152 M10
Gaferut, island, F.S.M. 220 P4
Gaffney, S.C., U.S. 98 J8
Gaflei, Liech. 162 P2
Gafsa, Tun. 200 B12
Gagan, P.N.G. 221 J13
Gagan, island, Marshall Is., U.S. 220 K4
Gagarin, Russ. 158 J8
Gageodo, island, S. Korea 187 V5
Gagil-Tamil, island, F.S.M. 221 D19
Gagnoa, Côte d'Ivoire 204 E8
Gagra, Rep. of Georgia 171 A15
Gahi, Wallis and Futuna, Fr. 222 B11
Gaiano, river, It. 163 L17
Gaillac, Fr. 149 X9
Gaillimh see Galway, Ire. 145 S4
Gaimán, Arg. 135 R9
Gainesville, Fla., U.S. 99 R7
Gainesville, Ga., U.S. 98 K5
Gainesville, Mo., U.S. 107 V13
Gainesville, Tex., U.S. 104 K11
Gáios, Gr. 156 F6
Gairdner, Lake, Austral. 214 J9
Gaizhou, Liaoning, China 184 C12
Gaja Shima, Japan 189 U3
Gakkel Ridge, Arctic Oc. 246 F11
Gakona, Alas., U.S. 113 H18
Gakuch, Pak. 178 L11
Galap, Palau 220 M12
Galápagos Fracture Zone, Pac. Oc. 243 K15
Galápagos Islands (Archipiélago de Colón), Ecua. 130 N10
Galápagos Rise, Pac. Oc. 243 J20
Galashiels, Scot., U.K. 145 N11
Galatás, Gr. 156 K12
Galaţi, Rom. 155 E17
Galatia (Mehmetcik), Cyprus 162 M10
Galatina, It. 153 N15
Galatxo, Punta del, Sp. 147 F16
Galax, Va., U.S. 98 G9
Galaxidi, Gr. 156 H10
Gáldar, Sp. 208 Q5
Galdhøpiggen, peak, Nor. 142 J10
Galegu, Sudan 203 F14
Galela, Indonesia 193 H16
Galena, Alas., U.S. 113 F14
Galena, Ill., U.S. 100 M4
Galena, Kans., U.S. 107 V10
Galena Park, Tex., U.S. 105 R14
Galeota Point, Trinidad and Tobago 123 Q24
Galera, Punta, Chile 135 P6
Galera, Punta, Ecua. 130 H2
Galera Point, S. Amer. 128 D2
Galera Point, S. Amer. 128 N4
Galera Point, Trinidad and Tobago 123 N24
Galesburg, Ill., U.S. 101 P4
Galesville, Wis., U.S. 100 K3
Galeton, Pa., U.S. 96 L6
Galets, Pointe des, Réunion, Fr. 209 F15
Gali, Rep. of Georgia 171 B16
Galich, Russ. 158 G11
Galicia, region, Pol., Ukr. 151 G17
Galicia, region, Sp. 146 C6
Galilee, Lake, Austral. 214 F13
Galilee, Sea of, Israel 172 K6
Galina Mine, W. Aust., Austral. 215 V2
Galina Point, Jam. 122 H9
Galinoporni (Kaleburnu), Cyprus 162 M11
Galion, Ohio, U.S. 101 Q13
Galion, Baie du, Martinique, Fr. 123 E23
Galiuro Mountains, Ariz., U.S. 109 V8
Galiwinku, N.T., Austral. 215 N9
Gallarate, It. 152 D4
Gallatin, Mo., U.S. 107 R11
Gallatin, Tenn., U.S. 103 E15
Gallatin, river, Mont., U.S. 108 E8
Galle, Sri Lanka 181 T7
Gállego, river, Sp. 147 D14
Gallego Rise, Pac. Oc. 243 K20
Gallegos, river, S. Amer. 128 Q5
Gallieni Fracture Zone, Ind. Oc. 224 N7
Gallieni Spur, Ind. Oc. 224 Q11
Gallinakopf, peak, Aust., Liech. 162 P4
Gallinas, Punta, Col. 130 A7
Gallinas Peak, N. Mex., U.S. 109 T13
Gallipoli, It. 153 N15
Gallipoli, N.T., Austral. 215 R10
Gallipoli see Gelibolu, Turk. 170 D3
Gallipolis, Ohio, U.S. 101 S14
Gällivare, Sw. 143 E13
Gallup, N. Mex., U.S. 109 R10
Galoa, Fiji 222 J6
Galt, Calif., U.S. 111 R4
Galty Mountains (An Chathair), Ire. 145 T4
Galva, Ill., U.S. 101 P4
Galveston, Tex., U.S. 105 R15
Galveston Bay, Tex., U.S. 105 R14
Galveston Island, Tex., U.S. 105 R14
Gálvez, Arg. 134 K11
Galwa, Nepal 180 E8
Galway (Gaillimh), Ire. 145 S4
Galway Bay, Ire. 145 S3
Gambaga, Ghana 204 C10
Gambell, Alas., U.S. 112 F10
Gambia, Af. 200 H4
Gambia, river, Af. 198 G1
Gambia Basin, Atl. Oc. 240 M9
Gambia Plain, Atl. Oc. 240 M9
Gambia Shoal, Hawai'i, U.S. 114 K2
Gambier, Îles, Fr. Polynesia, Fr. 223 Q21
Gambier Fracture Zone, Pac. Oc. 249 E18
Gamboma, Congo 205 H17
Gamboula, Cen. Af. Rep. 202 H7
Gamíla see Týmfi, Óros, Gr. 156 E7
Gamış Dağı see Gomshasar, peak, Azerb. 171 D20
Gamkonora, peak, Indonesia 193 H16
Gamlaha, Indonesia 193 H16
Gamleby, Sw. 143 L13
Gamperdonatal, valley, Aust. 162 P4
Gamprin, Liech. 162 M2
Gams, Switz. 162 N1
Gamua, Wallis and Futuna, Fr. 222 B11
Gan, island, Maldives 181 X3
Gan, river, Jiangxi, China 185 S6
Ganado, Ariz., U.S. 109 R9
Ganado, Tex., U.S. 105 S12
Gandajika, Dem. Rep. of the Congo 202 M10
Gandava, Pak. 179 T6
Gander, Nfld. & Lab., Can. 85 M23
Gandhinagar, India 180 J3
Gandía, Sp. 147 H15
Gang, island, Maldives 181 W3
Ganga (Ganges), river, India 180 G7
Gan Gan, Arg. 135 R8
Ganganagar, India 180 E4
Gangapur, India 180 G5
Gangawati, India 181 N5
Gangdisi Shan see Kangdêsê Shan, China 182 K3
Ganges, Fr. 149 X11
Ganges, river, Bangladesh, India 180 G7
Ganges, Mouths of the, Bangladesh, India 180 K12
Ganges Fan, Ind. Oc. 225 D13
Ganges Plain, Asia 168 H8
Ganges River Delta, Asia 168 J8
Ganggu, S. Korea 187 Q12
Ganggyeong, S. Korea 187 Q8
Ganghwa, S. Korea 186 M7
Gangi, It. 153 S10
Gangjin, S. Korea 187 U8
Gangneung, S. Korea 186 M11
Gangrenboqi Feng see Kangrinboqê Feng, China 182 J2
Gangtok, Bhutan 180 F12
Ganhyeon, S. Korea 187 N9
Gannat, Fr. 149 T11
Gannett Peak, Wyo., U.S. 108 H10
Ganquan, Shaanxi, China 184 G2
Ganseong, S. Korea 186 L11
Gansu, China 184 G1
Ganta, Guinea 204 D7
Gantgaw, Myanmar 190 G5
Gantheaume Bay, Austral. 214 H2
Ganyu (Qingkou), Jiangsu, China 184 J10
Ganyuskīno, Kaz. 176 F5
Ganzhou, Jiangxi, China 185 T6
Gao, Mali 200 H9
Gao'an, Jiangxi, China 185 Q6
Gaolan Dao, Guang., China 185 X4
Gaoligong Shan, Myanmar 190 D8
Gaomi, Shand., China 184 G10
Gaoping, Shanxi, China 184 H5
Gaoqing, Shand., China 184 F9
Gaotang, Shand., China 184 G7
Gaoua, Burkina Faso 204 C9
Gaoual, Guinea 204 B5
Gaoyang, Hebei, China 184 E7
Gaoyi, Hebei, China 184 F6
Gaoyou, Jiangsu, China 184 L10
Gaoyou Hu, Jiangsu, China 184 L10
Gaozhou, Guang., China 185 W2
Gap, Fr. 149 W14
Gapado, island, S. Korea 187 X7
Gapyeong, S. Korea 186 M9
Garabil, Uzb. 176 N10
Garabogaz Aylagy, bay, Turkm. 176 J6
Garabogaz Bay, Asia 168 F5
Garabogazköl, Turkm. 176 K6
Garacad, Somalia 203 G18
Garagum, Turkm. 176 K8
Garagum Canal, Turkm. 176 M10
Garaina, P.N.G. 217 D19
Garajonay, peak, Sp. 208 Q4
Garanhuns, Braz. 133 G17
Garapan, N. Mariana Is., U.S. 220 B4
Garapan, Lagunan, N. Mariana Is., U.S. 220 B4
Garavuti, Taj. 178 J7
Garber, Okla., U.S. 104 E10
Garberville, Calif., U.S. 111 N2
Garbyang, India 180 E8
García de Sola, Embalse de, Sp. 146 H9
Garda, Lago di, It. 152 D6
Garda, Lake, Eur. 140 J6
Gardar Ridge, Atl. Oc. 247 N22
Garden City, Ga., U.S. 99 N9
Garden City, Kans., U.S. 107 U4
Garden Hill, Man., Can. 85 M14
Garden Island Bay, La., U.S. 102 R12
Garden of the Gods, Hawai'i, U.S. 115 G14
Gardēz, Afghan. 179 N8
Gardiner, Me., U.S. 97 G16
Gardiner, Mont., U.S. 108 F8
Gardiner Seamounts, Ind. Oc. 224 H11
Gardner Pinnacles, Hawai'i, U.S. 114 L6
Garessio, It. 152 F3
Garfield, Wash., U.S. 110 D9
Gargaliánoi, Gr. 156 L9
Gargano, Promontorio del, It. 152 L12
Gargano, Testa del, It. 152 K13
Garhakota, India 180 H7
Garibaldi, Oreg., U.S. 110 F2
Garies, S. Af. 206 L7
Garim Island, F.S.M. 221 D18
Garissa, Kenya 203 K15
Garland, Tex., U.S. 104 L12
Garmābak, Afghan. 179 N4
Garmeh Jājarm, Iran 175 B15

Garmisch-Partenkirchen, *Ger.* **150** L8
Garmna (Gorumna Island), *Ire.* **145** S3
Garner, *Iowa, U.S.* **106** M11
Garnet Bank, *Atl. Oc.* **248** R6
Garnett, *Kans., U.S.* **107** T10
Garonne, river, *Fr.* **149** X8
Garoowe, *Somalia* **203** G18
Garoua, *Cameroon* **205** C16
Garoua Boulaï, *Cameroon* **205** E17
Garreru, island, *Palau* **220** P11
Garrett Fracture Zone, *Pac. Oc.* **243** L18
Garrison, *N. Dak., U.S.* **106** F4
Garrison, *Utah, U.S.* **109** N5
Garron Point, *N. Ire., U.K.* **145** P7
Garrucha, *Sp.* **147** L13
Garrygala, *Turkm.* **176** L7
Garry Lake, *Nunavut, Can.* **85** G14
Garsen, *Kenya* **203** L15
Gartog (Gatuo) *China* **182** L8
Garu, *India* **180** J9
Garub, *Namibia* **206** J6
Garusuun, *Palau* **220** N11
Garut, *Indonesia* **192** M8
Garve, *Scot., U.K.* **144** J9
Garwa, *India* **180** H9
Gary, *Ind., U.S.* **101** N8
Garzón, *Col.* **130** G4
Gasa, *Bhutan* **180** F12
Gasado, island, *S. Korea* **187** U6
Gas City, *Ind., U.S.* **101** Q10
Gasconade, river, *Mo., U.S.* **107** V13
Gascony, region, *Fr.* **149** X7
Gascoyne, river, *Austral.* **214** G2
Gascoyne Junction, *W. Aust., Austral.* **215** U2
Gascoyne Plain, *Ind. Oc.* **225** J17
Gascoyne Seamount, *Pac. Oc.* **249** E21
Gasenzen, *Switz.* **162** M1
Gashagar, *Nigeria* **205** B16
Gashua, *Nigeria* **205** B15
Gas Hure Hu, *China* **182** G6
Gaskell Ridge, *Ind. Oc.* **224** G8
Gaspar Grande, *Trinidad and Tobago* **123** P21
Gasparillo, *Trinidad and Tobago* **123** Q22
Gaspé, *Que., Can.* **85** N21
Gaspé Peninsula, *Que., Can.* **85** N21
Gassaway, *W. Va., U.S.* **98** D9
Gaston, Lake, *N.C., Va., U.S.* **98** G12
Gastonia, *N.C., U.S.* **98** J9
Gastoúni, *Gr.* **156** J8
Gastre, *Arg.* **135** Q8
Gata, Cabo de, *Sp.* **146** M12
Gata, Cape, *Cyprus* **162** R7
Gata, Sierra de, *Sp.* **146** F8
Gataivai, *Samoa* **222** L2
Gatayake, Baie de, *Fr. Polynesia, Fr.* **223** Q20
Gatchina, *Russ.* **158** F6
Gate, *Okla., U.S.* **104** E7
Gate City, *Va., U.S.* **98** G7
Gatehouse of Fleet, *Scot., U.K.* **145** P9
Gateshead, *Eng., U.K.* **145** P12
Gates of the Arctic National Park and Preserve, *Alas., U.S.* **113** D16
Gatesville, *Tex., U.S.* **105** N10
Gateway, *Colo., U.S.* **109** N10
Gatjapar, *F.S.M.* **221** D19
Gatlinburg, *Tenn., U.S.* **103** F19
Gatuo *see* Gartog, *China* **182** L8
Gau, island, *Fiji* **222** J7
Gauido, island, *S. Korea* **187** P6
Gauss Fracture Zone, *Ind. Oc.* **224** N7
Gausta, peak, *Nor.* **142** K10
Gautheaume Point, *Austral.* **214** D4
Gautier, Pointe, *St. Lucia* **123** L14
Gavarnie, *Fr.* **149** Z7
Gavāter, *Iran* **175** J18
Gāvbandī, *Iran* **175** H14
Gavdopoúla, island, *Gr.* **157** R13
Gávdos, island, *Gr.* **157** R13
Gaviota, *Calif., U.S.* **111** W6
Gävle, *Sw.* **143** J13
Gavrilov Yam, *Russ.* **158** H10

Gávrio, *Gr.* **157** J14
Gawachab, *Namibia* **206** J7
Gawai, *Myanmar* **190** C7
Gawler, *S. Aust., Austral.* **215** X10
Gawler Ranges, *Austral.* **214** J9
Gaya, *India* **180** H10
Gaya, *Niger* **200** J10
Gaya, *Nigeria* **205** B14
Gayle, *Jam.* **122** H9
Gaylord, *Mich., U.S.* **100** H11
Gaylord, *Minn., U.S.* **106** K10
Gay's Cove, *Barbados* **123** J19
Gaza City *see* Ghazzah, *Gaza Strip* **173** N4
Gazak, *Afghan.* **178** L5
Gazak, *Iran* **175** G17
Gazanjyk, *Turkm.* **176** L7
Gaza Strip, *Asia* **173** N4
Gazelle Fracture Zone, *Ind. Oc.* **224** N7
Gaziantep, *Turk.* **170** H12
Gazimağusa *see* Famagusta, *Cyprus* **162** P10
Gazipaşa, *Turk.* **170** J7
Gazojak, *Turkm.* **176** K10
Gbadolite, *Dem. Rep. of the Congo* **202** H9
Gdańsk, *Pol.* **151** B14
Gdańsk, Gulf of, *Pol., Russ.* **151** A14
Gdov, *Russ.* **158** G5
Gdynia, *Pol.* **151** B14
Gea, island, *Marshall Is., U.S.* **220** N4
Gea Pass, *Marshall Is., U.S.* **220** N5
Geary, *Okla., U.S.* **104** G9
Gebe, island, *Indonesia* **193** J17
Gebiz, *Turk.* **170** H6
Gebze, *Turk.* **170** D5
Geçitkale *see* Lefkoniko, *Cyprus* **162** N9
Gedaref, *Sudan* **203** E14
Geddes, *S. Dak., U.S.* **106** M6
Gədəbəy, *Azerb.* **171** D19
Gediz, *Turk.* **170** F5
Gediz, river, *Turk.* **170** F3
Gedser, *Den.* **142** N12
Geel, *Belg.* **148** K12
Geelong, *Vic., Austral.* **215** Z12
Geelvinck Fracture Zone, *Ind. Oc.* **224** P12
Geelvink Channel, *Austral.* **214** J2
Geesthacht, *Ger.* **150** C8
Geeveston, *Tas., Austral.* **215** Z7
Gefara, region, *Af.* **198** D6
Géfyra, *Gr.* **156** C11
Gegibu, island, *Marshall Is., U.S.* **220** L3
Gehh, island, *Marshall Is., U.S.* **220** N5
Geidam, *Nigeria* **205** B16
Geiga, island, *Marshall Is., U.S.* **220** K1
Geilo, *Nor.* **142** J10
Geita, *Tanzania* **203** L13
Gejiu, *China* **182** P9
Gela, *It.* **153** T11
Gela, Golfo di, *It.* **153** T10
Gelam, island, *Indonesia* **192** K9
Gelasa, Selat, *Indonesia* **192** K8
Gelendzhik, *Russ.* **159** T10
Gelibolu (Gallipoli), *Turk.* **170** D3
Gellinam, island, *Marshall Is., U.S.* **220** L5
Gelsenkirchen, *Ger.* **150** E5
Gembloux, *Belg.* **148** L12
Gemena, *Dem. Rep. of the Congo* **202** J9
Gemerek, *Turk.* **170** F11
Gemi Konaghi *see* Karavostasi, *Cyprus* **162** N7
Gemlik, *Turk.* **170** D5
Gemlik Körfezi, *Turk.* **170** D4
Gemona del Friuli, *It.* **152** C9
Gemsa, *Egypt* **201** D9
Genalē, river, *Eth.* **203** H15
Genç, *Turk.* **171** F15
Gəncə, *Azerb.* **171** D20
General Acha, *Arg.* **135** N10
General Alvear, *Arg.* **134** L8
General Carrera, Lago, *Chile* **135** T7
General Conesa, *Arg.* **135** P10

General Eugenio A. Garay, *Parag.* **132** L8
General Güemes, *Arg.* **134** E9
General Guido, *Arg.* **134** M13
General Juan Madariaga, *Arg.* **134** M13
General La Madrid, *Arg.* **135** N11
General Levalle, *Arg.* **134** L10
General Lorenzo Vintter, *Arg.* **135** Q10
General Paz, *Arg.* **134** G13
General Pico, *Arg.* **134** M10
General Pinedo, *Arg.* **134** G11
General Roca, *Arg.* **135** P8
General San Martín, *Arg.* **134** L13
General San Martín, *Arg.* **135** N10
General San Martín, *Arg.* **135** S7
General Santos, *Philippines* **193** F15
Genesee, river, *N.Y., U.S.* **96** K6
Geneseo, *Ill., U.S.* **101** P4
Geneseo, *N.Y., U.S.* **96** J6
Geneva, *Ala., U.S.* **103** N16
Geneva, *Idaho, U.S.* **108** J8
Geneva, *N.Y., U.S.* **96** J7
Geneva, *Nebr., U.S.* **107** Q7
Geneva, *Ohio, U.S.* **101** N15
Geneva *see* Genève, *Switz.* **152** C1
Geneva, Lake *see* Léman, Lac, *Fr.* **149** T15
Genève (Geneva), *Switz.* **152** C1
Genhe, *China* **183** B14
Genil, river, *Sp.* **146** L9
Geniséa, *Gr.* **157** B14
Genista Bank, *Ind. Oc.* **224** D7
Genk, *Belg.* **148** L13
Genlis, *Fr.* **149** R13
Gennádion, *Gr.* **157** N19
Gennargentu, Monti del, *It.* **153** N4
Genoa, *Nebr., U.S.* **107** P7
Genoa *see* Genova, *It.* **152** F4
Génolhac, *Fr.* **149** W12
Genova (Genoa), *It.* **152** F4
Genova, Golfo di, *It.* **152** G4
Genovesa (Tower), Isla, *Ecua.* **130** P10
Gent, *Belg.* **148** L11
Geoado, island, *S. Korea* **187** P7
Geochang, *S. Korea* **187** R10
Geogeumdo, island, *S. Korea* **187** U8
Geographe Bay, *Austral.* **214** K2
Geographe Channel, *Austral.* **214** G1
Geoje, *S. Korea* **187** T11
Geojedo, island, *S. Korea* **187** T11
Geojin, *S. Korea* **186** L11
Geomundo, island, *S. Korea* **187** V8
George, *S. Af.* **206** M8
George, river, *N. Amer.* **82** F9
George, river, *Que., Can.* **85** K20
George, Lake, *Austral.* **214** F5
George, Lake, *Austral.* **214** L14
George, Lake, *Fla., U.S.* **99** S8
George, Lake, *N.Y., U.S.* **96** H11
George, Zemlya, *Russ.* **160** B12
George Bligh Bank, *Atl. Oc.* **240** F10
George Land, *Asia* **168** B8
George Rogers Clark National Historical Park, *Ind., U.S.* **101** T7
Georges Bank, *Atl. Oc.* **240** J4
George Town, *Cayman Is.* **122** J1
George Town, *Malaysia* **191** T8
George Town, *Tas., Austral.* **215** Y7
George-Town, *Bahamas* **122** F9
Georgetown, *Bahamas* **119** F13
Georgetown, *Del., U.S.* **98** D15
Georgetown, *Gambia* **200** H4
Georgetown, *Guyana* **131** D15
Georgetown, *Ill., U.S.* **101** R7
Georgetown, *Ky., U.S.* **103** B18
Georgetown, *Ohio, U.S.* **101** T12
Georgetown, *Qnsld., Austral.* **215** R12
Georgetown, *S.C., U.S.* **98** L11
Georgetown, *St. Vincent and the Grenadines* **123** K17
Georgetown, *Tex., U.S.* **105** P10
George V Coast, *Antarctica* **231** R16
George V Fracture Zone, *Ind. Oc.* **249** D18
George VI Sound, *Antarctica* **230** F6
George Washington Birthplace National Monument, *Va., U.S.* **98** D13

George Washington Carver National Monument, *Mo., U.S.* **107** VII
George West, *Tex., U.S.* **105** T10
Georgia, *Asia* **171** B17
Georgia, *U.S.* **98** M6
Georgia, Strait of, *N. Amer.* **82** G3
Georgia Basin, *Atl. Oc.* **241** V8
Georgiana, *Ala., U.S.* **103** M15
Georgian Bay, *Ont., Can.* **85** Q18
Georgīevka, *Kaz.* **177** D18
Georgina, river, *Austral.* **214** E10
Georgiyevsk, *Russ.* **159** T13
Georgiyevskoye, *Russ.* **158** G12
Gera, *Ger.* **150** F9
Geráki, *Gr.* **156** L10
Geral, Serra, *S. Amer.* **128** J8
Geral de Goiás, Serra, *Braz.* **133** H14
Geraldine, *Mont., U.S.* **108** C9
Geraldine, *N.Z.* **217** P17
Geraldton, *Ont., Can.* **85** N16
Geraldton, *W. Aust., Austral.* **215** W2
Gérardmer, *Fr.* **149** Q14
Gerasa *see* Jarash, *Jordan* **172** L7
Gerber, *Calif., U.S.* **111** N4
Gercüş, *Turk.* **171** H16
Gerede, *Turk.* **170** D7
Gereshk *see* Girishk, *Afghan.* **179** Q4
Geretsried, *Ger.* **150** K8
Gering, *Nebr., U.S.* **107** N1
Gerlach, *Nev., U.S.* **111** N7
Gerlach, peak, *Eur.* **140** H9
Gerlachovský Štít, peak, *Slovakia* **151** J16
Germania Land, *Greenland, Den.* **82** A9
Germantown, *Tenn., U.S.* **102** G11
Germany, *Eur.* **150** F8
Germering, *Ger.* **150** K8
Germfask, *Mich., U.S.* **100** F9
Germī, *Iran* **174** A11
Gerolakkos, *Cyprus* **162** N8
Geroliménas, *Gr.* **156** M10
Gerpir, *Eur.* **140** B4
Gersthofen, *Ger.* **150** K8
Gerze, *Turk.* **170** C10
Gesoa, *P.N.G.* **217** D18
Gesso, *It.* **163** L17
Getafe, *Sp.* **146** F11
Gettysburg, *Pa., U.S.* **96** Q7
Gettysburg, *S. Dak., U.S.* **106** J5
Getz Ice Shelf, *Antarctica* **230** M8
Geum, river, *S. Korea* **187** R8
Geumdangdo, island, *S. Korea* **187** U8
Geumil, *S. Korea* **187** U8
Geumodo, island, *S. Korea* **187** U8
Geumpang, *Indonesia* **192** G4
Geumsan, *S. Korea* **187** R9
Geumwang, *S. Korea* **187** P9
Geunto, Gora, *Russ.* **161** C21
Gevaş, *Turk.* **171** G17
Gex, *Fr.* **149** T14
Geylegphug, *Bhutan* **180** G13
Geyve, *Turk.* **170** D6
Gezhouba Dam, *Hubei, China* **185** N3
Ghadāmis, *Lib.* **200** C12
Ghaddūwah, *Lib.* **201** D14
Ghaghe, island, *Solomon Is.* **221** L17
Għajn Tuffieħa Bay, *Malta* **163** K21
Ghana, *Af.* **204** D10
Ghanzi, *Botswana* **206** G8
Gharandal, *Jordan* **173** Q5
Għarb, *Malta* **163** H19
Ghardaïa, *Alg.* **200** B11
Ghar Dalum, site, *Malta* **163** L23
Gharm, *Taj.* **178** H8
Gharo, *Pak.* **179** W6
Gharyān, *Lib.* **201** C13
Ghatere, *Solomon Is.* **221** M18
Għawdex *see* Gozo, island, *Malta* **163** H20
Għaxaq, *Malta* **163** L23
Ghazal, Bahr el, *Chad* **201** H14
Ghaziabad, *India* **180** F6
Ghazipur, *India* **180** G9
Ghaznī, *Afghan.* **179** N7
Ghazzah (Gaza City), *Gaza Strip* **173** N4
Gheorghieni, *Rom.* **155** C15
Gherla, *Rom.* **155** C13
Ghilarza, *It.* **153** N3
Ghisonaccia, *Fr.* **152** K4

Ghōriyān, *Afghan.* **178** M2
Ghōrmāch, *Afghan.* **178** L3
Ghotki, *Pak.* **179** T8
Ghubbat al Qamar, *Ind. Oc.* **168** J4
Gia Nghĩa, *Vietnam* **191** N13
Giannitsá, *Gr.* **156** C10
Giannutri, Isola di, *It.* **152** K6
Giá Rai, *Vietnam* **191** Q12
Giarre, *It.* **153** S12
Giba, *It.* **153** Q3
Gibara, *Cuba* **118** J12
Gibbon, *Nebr., U.S.* **107** Q6
Gibbon Point, *British Virgin Is., U.K.* **122** R12
Gibbonsville, *Idaho, U.S.* **108** E6
Gibb River, *W. Aust., Austral.* **215** Q6
Gibb's Hill, peak, *Bermuda* **122** C1
Gibeon, *Namibia* **206** J7
Gibraleón, *Sp.* **146** L7
Gibraltar, *Gibraltar, U.K.* **163** F1
Gibraltar, Bay of (Bahía de Algeciras), *Gibraltar, U.K.* **163** N21
Gibraltar, Rock of, *Gibraltar, U.K.* **163** P23
Gibraltar, Strait of, *Af. Eur.* **146** N8
Gibraltar Airport, *Gibraltar, U.K.* **163** N23
Gibraltar Harbour, *Gibraltar, U.K.* **163** P22
Gibsland, *La., U.S.* **102** L7
Gibson City, *Ill., U.S.* **101** Q6
Gibson Desert, *Austral.* **214** F6
Gidar, *Pak.* **179** T5
Giddalur, *India* **181** N6
Giddings, *Tex., U.S.* **105** Q12
Gīdolē, *Eth.* **203** H14
Gien, *Fr.* **149** R10
Giessen, *Ger.* **150** G6
Gifford, *Fla., U.S.* **99** U10
Gifford, river, *Nunavut, Can.* **85** F16
Gifhorn, *Ger.* **150** D8
Gifu, *Japan* **189** P9
Gigant, *Russ.* **159** R11
Gigha Island, *Scot., U.K.* **145** N7
Giglio, Isola del, *It.* **152** K6
Gijang, *S. Korea* **187** S12
Gijón, *Sp.* **146** A9
Gila, river, *Ariz., N. Mex., U.S.* **109** U5
Gila Bend, *Ariz., U.S.* **109** U6
Gila Bend Mountains, *Ariz., U.S.* **109** U6
Gila Cliff Dwellings National Monument, *N. Mex., U.S.* **109** U10
Gilbert, *Ariz., U.S.* **109** U7
Gilbert, *Minn., U.S.* **106** F12
Gilbert, river, *Austral.* **214** D12
Gilbert Islands, *Kiribati* **218** G8
Gilbert Ridge, *Pac. Oc.* **242** J10
Gilbert Seamounts, *Pac. Oc.* **243** C14
Gilbués, *Braz.* **133** G14
Gilchrist, *Oreg., U.S.* **110** J4
Gilderen *see* Lapithos, *Cyprus* **162** N8
Gildford, *Mont., U.S.* **108** B9
Gilf Kebir Plateau, *Egypt* **201** E17
Gilgandra, *N.S.W., Austral.* **215** W14
Gilgit, *Pak.* **178** L12
Gilgit, region, *Pak.* **178** L11
Gilgit, river, *Pak.* **178** L12
Gill, Lough, *Ire.* **145** Q4
Gillam, *Man., Can.* **85** L14
Gillen, Lake, *Austral.* **214** G5
Gilles, Lake, *Austral.* **214** K10
Gillespie, *Ill., U.S.* **101** S4
Gillett, *Ark., U.S.* **102** H9
Gillette, *Wyo., U.S.* **108** G12
Gills Rock, *Wis., U.S.* **100** H8
Gilman, *Ill., U.S.* **101** Q7
Gilmer, *Tex., U.S.* **105** N15
Gilmore Hut, *Qnsld., Austral.* **215** U13
Gilpeppee, *Qnsld., Austral.* **215** U12
Gilroy, *Calif., U.S.* **111** T4
Gima, *Japan* **189** X1
Gimcheon, *S. Korea* **187** Q10
Gimhae, *S. Korea* **187** S11
Gimhwa (Kŭmhwa), *S. Korea* **186** L9
Gimie, Mount, *St. Lucia* **123** K14
Gimje, *S. Korea* **187** R8
Gimli, *Man., Can.* **85** N14
Gimnyeong, *S. Korea* **187** W8

Gimpo, *S. Korea* **186** M7
Gingin, *W. Aust., Austral.* **215** X2
Gingoog, *Philippines* **193** E15
Gīnīr, *Eth.* **203** G15
Ginowan, *Japan* **189** X2
Gioia, Golfo di, *It.* **153** R13
Gioiadel Colle, *It.* **152** M14
Gioia Tauro, *It.* **153** R13
Gióna, Óros, *Gr.* **156** H10
Gioúra, island, *Gr.* **157** F13
Giovinazzo, *It.* **152** L13
Gippsland, region, *Austral.* **214** M13
Girab, *India* **180** G2
Girard, *Kans., U.S.* **107** U10
Girard, *Pa., U.S.* **96** L3
Girardot, *Col.* **130** F5
Giresun, *Turk.* **171** D13
Girga, *Egypt* **201** D19
Gir Hills, *India* **180** K2
Giridih, *India* **180** H10
Girishk (Gereshk), *Afghan.* **179** Q4
Girne see Kyrenia, *Cyprus* **162** N8
Girolata, *Fr.* **152** J3
Girona, *Sp.* **147** D18
Gironde, bay, *Fr.* **149** U6
Gisborne, *N.Z.* **217** K20
Gissi, *It.* **152** K11
Gitega, *Burundi* **202** L12
Giulianova, *It.* **152** J10
Giurgiu, *Rom.* **155** G15
Givet, *Fr.* **148** M12
Givors, *Fr.* **149** U12
Gizab, *Afghan.* **179** N5
Gizhuduvan, *Uzb.* **176** L11
Gizo, *Solomon Is.* **221** M15
Giżycko, *Pol.* **151** B16
Gjakovë (Dakovica), *Kos.* **154** J10
Gjeravica, peak, *Kos.* **154** J10
Gjilan (Gnjilane), *Kos.* **154** J11
Gjirokastër (Argyrus), *Alban.* **154** M10
Gjoa Haven, *Nunavut, Can.* **85** F14
Gjøvik, *Nor.* **142** J11
Gkreko, Cape , *Cyprus* **162** P10
Glachau, *Ger.* **150** G9
Glacier Bay, *Alas., U.S.* **113** K21
Glacier Bay National Park and Preserve, *Alas., U.S.* **113** L21
Glacier National Park, *Mont., U.S.* **108** B6
Glacier Peak, *Wash., U.S.* **110** B5
Gladewater, *Tex., U.S.* **104** L14
Gladstone, *Mich., U.S.* **100** G8
Gladstone, *Qnsld., Austral.* **215** T15
Gladwin, *Mich., U.S.* **100** K11
Glåma, river, *Nor.* **142** J11
Glasco, *Kans., U.S.* **107** S7
Glasgow, *Jam.* **122** H6
Glasgow, *Ky., U.S.* **103** D16
Glasgow, *Mo., U.S.* **107** S12
Glasgow, *Mont., U.S.* **108** B11
Glasgow, *Scot., U.K.* **144** M9
Glassboro, *N.J., U.S.* **96** Q9
Glass Buttes, *Oreg., U.S.* **110** J6
Glass Mountain, *Calif., U.S.* **110** L4
Glass Mountains, *Tex., U.S.* **105** Q3
Glen Affric, *Scot., U.K.* **144** K8
Glénan, Îles de, *Fr.* **149** R3
Glen Arbor, *Mich., U.S.* **100** H9
Glenariffe, *N. Ire., U.K.* **145** P7
Glenarm, *N. Ire., U.K.* **145** P7
Glenavy, *N.Z.* **217** Q17
Glenayle, *W. Aust., Austral.* **215** U4
Glenbarr, *Scot., U.K.* **145** N7
Glen Canyon Dam, *Ariz., U.S.* **109** Q7
Glen Canyon National Recreation Area, *Utah, U.S.* **109** P8
Glencoe, *Minn., U.S.* **106** K11
Glendale, *Ariz., U.S.* **109** U7
Glendale, *Calif., U.S.* **III** X8
Glendive, *Mont., U.S.* **108** C13
Glendo, *Wyo., U.S.* **108** J13
Glendo Reservoir, *Wyo., U.S.* **108** H13
Glenelg, river, *Austral.* **214** M11
Glengarriff (An Gleann Garbh), *Ire.* **145** V3
Glengyle, *Qnsld., Austral.* **215** T11
Glen Innes, *N.S.W., Austral.* **215** W15
Glen Mor, *Scot., U.K.* **144** K9
Glenmora, *La., U.S.* **102** N8
Glenmorgan, *Qnsld., Austral.* **215** V14

Glennallen, *Alas., U.S.* **113** H18
Glenn Highway, *Alas., U.S.* **113** J17
Glenns Ferry, *Idaho, U.S.* **108** H4
Glennville, *Ga., U.S.* **99** N8
Glenrock, *Wyo., U.S.* **108** H12
Glen Rose, *Tex., U.S.* **104** M10
Glenrothes, *Scot., U.K.* **144** M10
Glens Falls, *N.Y., U.S.* **96** H11
Glenties (Na Gleannta), *Ire.* **145** P5
Glen Ullin, *N. Dak., U.S.* **106** G3
Glenwood, *Ark., U.S.* **102** H7
Glenwood, *Iowa, U.S.* **107** Q9
Glenwood, *Minn., U.S.* **106** J9
Glenwood, *N. Mex., U.S.* **109** U10
Glenwood Springs, *Colo., U.S.* **108** M11
Glidden, *Wis., U.S.* **100** F4
Glina, *Croatia* **154** E6
Gliwice, *Pol.* **151** G14
Globe, *Ariz., U.S.* **109** U8
Głogów, *Pol.* **150** E12
Glorenza, *It.* **152** C6
Gloria, Puntan, *N. Mariana Is., U.S.* **220** B5
Glossglockner, peak, *Aust.* **150** M9
Gloster, *Miss., U.S.* **102** N10
Gloucester, *Eng., U.K.* **145** U11
Gloucester, *Mass., U.S.* **97** K15
Gloucester, *N.S.W., Austral.* **215** X15
Gloucester, *P.N.G.* **217** C20
Glover Island, *Grenada* **123** M22
Gloversville, *N.Y., U.S.* **96** J10
Glubokiy, *Russ.* **159** Q11
Glubokiy, *Russ.* **159** R12
Glūbokoe, *Kaz.* **177** D18
Glyn Ebwy see Ebbw Vale, *Wales, U.K.* **145** V10
Gmunden, *Aust.* **150** K10
Gniezno, *Pol.* **151** D13
Gnjilane see Gjilan, *Kos.* **154** J11
Goa, *India* **181** N4
Goa, *S. Korea* **187** Q10
Goalpara, *India* **180** G13
Goba, *Eth.* **203** G15
Gobabis, *Namibia* **206** H7
Gobernador Duval, *Arg.* **135** N9
Gobernador Gregores, *Chile* **135** U8
Gobi, desert, *China, Mongolia* **182** F11
Gobō, *Japan* **189** R8
Gobu, *S. Korea* **187** S8
Gochang, *S. Korea* **187** S7
Gò Công, *Vietnam* **191** Q13
Godalming, *Eng., U.K.* **145** W13
Godavari, river, *India* **180** L5
Godavari, Mouths of the, *India* **181** N8
Goderville, *Fr.* **149** N8
Godhra, *India* **180** J4
Gödöllő, *Hung.* **151** L15
Godoy Cruz, *Arg.* **134** K7
Gods, river, *Man., Can.* **85** L15
Gods Lake, *Man., Can.* **85** L14
Godthåb Valley, *Atl. Oc.* **247** R17
Godwin Austen see K2, peak, *China, Pak.* **178** L13
Goélands, Lac aux, *Que., Can.* **85** K20
Goes, *Neth.* **148** K11
Gofar Fracture Zone, *Pac. Oc.* **243** K19
Göfis, *Aust.* **162** M4
Gogebic, Lake, *Mich., U.S.* **100** F5
Gogebic Range, *U.S.* **87** C15
Gogeumdo, island, *S. Korea* **187** U8
Gogland, *Russ.* **158** E5
Gogrial, *S. Sudan* **202** G11
Gohan, *S. Korea* **187** N11
Goheung, *S. Korea* **187** U9
Goianésia, *Braz.* **133** J13
Goiânia, *Braz.* **133** J13
Goikul, *Palau* **220** N12
Góis, *Port.* **146** F6
Gojōme, *Japan* **188** K12
Gojra, *Pak.* **179** Q10
Gök, river, *Turk.* **170** C10
Gokak, *India* **181** N4
Gökçeada (Imbros), island, *Turk.* **170** D2
Gökdepe, *Uzb.* **176** M8
Gökova Körfezi, *Turk.* **170** H3
Gokseong, *S. Korea* **187** S9

Göksu, river, *Turk.* **170** G11
Göksu, river, *Turk.* **170** H8
Göksun, *Turk.* **170** G11
Golaghat, *India* **180** G14
Golan Heights, *Israel* **172** K6
Gölbaşı, *Turk.* **170** E8
Gölbaşı, *Turk.* **170** H12
Golconda, *Nev., U.S.* **110** M9
Gölcük, *Turk.* **170** D5
Gold Beach, *Oreg., U.S.* **110** K1
Gold Coast, *Af.* **204** F10
Gold Coast, *Qnsld., Austral.* **215** V16
Golden, *Colo., U.S.* **108** M13
Golden Bay, *N.Z.* **217** M17
Golden Bo'sunbird Seamounts, *Ind. Oc.* **225** J16
Goldendale, *Wash., U.S.* **110** E5
Golden Gate, *Calif., U.S.* **III** S3
Golden Gate National Recreation Area, *Calif., U.S.* **III** R3
Golden Grove, *Jam.* **122** J11
Golden Meadow, *La., U.S.* **102** R11
Golden Spike National Historic Site, *Utah, U.S.* **108** K6
Goldfield, *Nev., U.S.* **III** S9
Goldsboro, *N.C., U.S.* **98** H12
Goldsborough Seamounts, *Pac. Oc.* **242** H12
Goldsmith, *Tex., U.S.* **104** M4
Goldsworthy, *W. Aust., Austral.* **215** S3
Goldthwaite, *Tex., U.S.* **105** N9
Göle, *Turk.* **171** D17
Goleniów, *Pol.* **150** C11
Goleta, *Calif., U.S.* **III** W7
Golfito, *C.R.* **117** N6
Golfo Aranci, *It.* **152** M5
Goliad, *Tex., U.S.* **105** S11
Gölköy, *Turk.* **170** D12
Golmud, *China* **182** H7
Golo, river, *Fr.* **152** J4
Gölören, *Turk.* **170** G9
Golovin, *Alas., U.S.* **112** F12
Gölpazarı, *Turk.* **170** D6
Golūbovka, *Kaz.* **177** D10
Golyama Kamchiya, river, *Bulg.* **155** H16
Golyam Perelik, peak, *Bulg.* **155** K14
Goma, *Dem. Rep. of the Congo* **202** K12
Gombe, *Nigeria* **205** C15
Gombrani Island, *Mauritius* **209** J20
Gomera, island, *Sp.* **208** Q4
Gómez Palacio, *Mex.* **116** F10
Gomshasar, peak, (Gamış Dağı), *Azerb.* **171** D20
Gonābād, *Iran* **175** D16
Gonaïves, *Haiti* **119** L16
Gonam, *Russ.* **161** H19
Gonam, river, *Russ.* **161** J18
Gonâve, Golfe de la, *Haiti* **119** L16
Gonâve, Île de la, *Haiti* **119** M15
Gonbad-e Kāvūs, *Iran* **175** B14
Gonda, *India* **180** G8
Gonder, *Eth.* **203** F14
Gondia, *India* **180** K7
Gondomar, *Port.* **146** E5
Gönen, *Turk.* **170** D3
Gong'an, *Hubei, China* **185** N3
Gongcheng, *Guangxi Zhuang, China* **185** U2
Gonghe, *China* **182** H9
Gonghui, *Hebei, China* **184** B6
Gongjitang, *N. Mongol, China* **184** A4
Gongju, *S. Korea* **187** Q8
Gonglee, *Liberia* **204** E7
Gongliu, *China* **182** E4
Gongola, river, *Nigeria* **205** C16
Gongyi, *Henan, China* **184** J5
Gongzhuling, *China* **183** E16
Gónnoi, *Gr.* **156** E10
Gonzales, *Calif., U.S.* **III** U4
Gonzales, *Tex., U.S.* **105** R10
González Chaves, *Arg.* **135** N12
Goodenough Island, *P.N.G.* **217** E21
Good Hope, Cape of, *S. Af.* **206** M7
Good Hope Beach, *Virgin Is., U.S.* **122** R1
Goodhouse, *S. Af.* **206** K7
Gooding, *Idaho, U.S.* **108** H5
Goodland, *Kans., U.S.* **107** S3
Goodlands, *Mauritius* **209** F20

Goodlettsville, *Tenn., U.S.* **103** E15
Goodman, *Miss., U.S.* **102** K11
Goodman, *Wis., U.S.* **100** G6
Goodman Bay, *Bahamas* **122** B11
Goodnews Bay, *Alas., U.S.* **112** K12
Goodparla, *N.T., Austral.* **215** P8
Goodridge, *Minn., U.S.* **106** E9
Goodwell, *Okla., U.S.* **104** E5
Goodwin Inlet, *F.S.M.* **221** C19
Goomalling, *W. Aust., Austral.* **215** W3
Goondiwindi, *Qnsld., Austral.* **215** V15
Goongarrie, Lake, *Austral.* **214** J4
Goose Creek, *S.C., U.S.* **98** M10
Goose Lake, *Calif., Oreg., U.S.* **110** L6
Gora Belukha, peak, *Kaz.* **177** D20
Gorakhpur, *India* **180** G9
Goraklbad Passage, *Palau* **220** P11
Gora Mus Khaya, peak, *Asia* **168** C11
Gorda Ridges, *Pac. Oc.* **243** E17
Gördes, *Turk.* **170** F4
Gordion, ruins, *Turk.* **170** E7
Gordo, *Ala., U.S.* **103** K14
Gordon, *Ga., U.S.* **98** M6
Gordon, *Nebr., U.S.* **106** M3
Gordon, *Wis., U.S.* **100** F3
Gordon, Lake, *Austral.* **214** M7
Gordon Downs, *W. Aust., Austral.* **215** R7
Gordon's, *Bahamas* **119** G14
Gordonsville, *Va., U.S.* **98** E12
Gore, *N.Z.* **217** R16
Goré, *Chad* **201** K14
Gorē, *Eth.* **203** G14
Goreda, *Indonesia* **217** C15
Goree, *Tex., U.S.* **104** K8
Görele, *Turk.* **171** D14
Gorey (Guaire), *Ire.* **145** T7
Gorgān, *Iran* **175** B14
Gorgona, Isla, *Col.* **130** G3
Gorgona, Isola di, *It.* **152** H5
Gorham, *N.H., U.S.* **97** G14
Gori, *Rep. of Georgia* **171** C18
Goris, *Arm.* **171** E20
Gorizia, *It.* **152** D10
Gor'kiy Reservoir, *Eur.* **140** E13
Gor'kovskoye Vodokhranilishche, *Russ.* **158** H12
Gorlice, *Pol.* **151** H16
Görlitz, *Ger.* **150** F11
Gorman, *Tex., U.S.* **104** M9
Gorna Oryakhovitsa, *Bulg.* **155** H15
Gornja Radgona, *Slov.* **154** C6
Gornji Milanovac, *Serb.* **154** G10
Gorno Altaysk, *Russ.* **160** L12
Gornozavodsk, *Russ.* **161** K22
Gornyak, *Russ.* **160** L11
Gorodets, *Russ.* **158** H12
Gorodishche, *Russ.* **158** L13
Goroka, *P.N.G.* **217** D19
Gorong, Kepulauan, *Indonesia* **193** L17
Gorontalo, *Indonesia* **193** J14
Gorror, *F.S.M.* **221** D18
Gortyn see Górtys, ruin, *Gr.* **157** Q14
Górtys (Gortyn), ruin, *Gr.* **157** Q14
Gorumna Island see Garmna, *Ire.* **145** S3
Goryeong, *S. Korea* **187** R10
Góry Swietokrzyskie, range, *Pol.* **151** F16
Gör Zanak, *Afghan.* **179** P3
Gorzów Wielkopolski, *Pol.* **150** D12
Gosan, *S. Korea* **187** W6
Goschen Strait, *P.N.G.* **217** E21
Gosen, *Japan* **188** M11
Goseong, *S. Korea* **186** L9
Goseong, *S. Korea* **187** T10
Gosford, *N.S.W., Austral.* **215** X15
Goshen, *Ind., U.S.* **101** N9
Goshogawara, *Japan* **188** J12
Gosier, *Guadeloupe, Fr.* **123** F15
Goslar, *Ger.* **150** E8
Gosnel, *Ark., U.S.* **102** F11
Gospić, *Croatia* **154** F5
Gosselies, *Belg.* **148** L11
Gostivar, *Maced.* **154** K10
Götaland, *Eur.* **140** E7
Göteborg, *Sw.* **142** L12
Gotha, *Ger.* **150** F8
Gothenburg, *Nebr., U.S.* **107** Q5
Gothèye, *Niger* **200** H10

Gotland, island, *Sw.* **143** L14
Goto Meer, *Bonaire, Neth.* **123** Q18
Gotse Delchev, *Bulg.* **155** K13
Gotska Sandön, island, *Sw.* **143** L14
Gōtsu, *Japan* **189** P6
Göttingen, *Ger.* **150** E7
Gouaro, Baie de, *New Caledonia, Fr.* **222** D7
Gough Fracture Zone, *Atl. Oc.* **241** U10
Gouin, Réservoir, *Que., Can.* **85** N19
Goulburn, *N.S.W., Austral.* **215** Y14
Gould, *Ark., U.S.* **102** H9
Gould Bay, *Antarctica* **230** E9
Gould Coast, *Antarctica* **230** K11
Goulding Cay, *Bahamas* **122** E12
Gouldsboro, *Me., U.S.* **97** F18
Goulvain, Cap, *New Caledonia, Fr.* **222** D7
Goumbou, *Mali* **200** H7
Goundam, *Mali* **200** G8
Gourbeyre, *Guadeloupe, Fr.* **123** G14
Gouré, *Niger* **200** H12
Gourma, region, *Af.* **198** G4
Gournay, *Fr.* **149** N9
Gourniá, ruin, *Gr.* **157** Q16
Gouro, *Chad* **201** G15
Gouverneur, *N.Y., U.S.* **96** G9
Gouyave, *Grenada* **123** K22
Gouzon, *Fr.* **149** T10
Gove, *Kans., U.S.* **107** S4
Govena, Mys, *Russ.* **161** D22
Govenlock, *Sask., Can.* **84** N11
Gove Peninsula, *Austral.* **214** B10
Governador Valadares, *Braz.* **133** K15
Government House, *Monaco* **163** E21
Government House, site, *Barbados* **123** L19
Government House, site, *Bermuda* **122** C2
Government Palace, *Vatican City* **163** Q15
Governor Generoso, *Philippines* **193** F15
Governor's Beach, *Gibraltar, U.K.* **163** Q23
Governor's Harbour, *Bahamas* **122** E6
Governor's Residence, *Gibraltar, U.K.* **163** P22
Govindgarh, *India* **180** H8
Govorovo, *Russ.* **161** F16
Gowanda, *N.Y., U.S.* **96** K5
Gower Peninsula, *Wales, U.K.* **145** V9
Gowon, *S. Korea* **187** S8
Goya, *Arg.* **134** H12
Goyang, *S. Korea* **186** M8
Goyave, *Guadeloupe, Fr.* **123** F15
Goyaves, river, *Guadeloupe, Fr.* **123** F14
Goyaves, Îlets à, *Guadeloupe, Fr.* **123** F14
Göyçay, *Azerb.* **171** D21
Göygöl, *Azerb.* **171** D20
Göynük, *Turk.* **170** D6
Gozo (Għawdex), island, *Malta* **163** H20
Graaff-Reinet, *S. Af.* **206** L9
Grabs, *Switz.* **162** N1
Gračac, *Croatia* **154** F6
Gračanica, *Bosn. & Herzg.* **154** F8
Graceville, *Fla., U.S.* **99** Q3
Graceville, *Minn., U.S.* **106** J8
Gracias a Dios, Cabo, *Nicar.* **117** K19
Graciosa, island, *Sp.* **208** P7
Graciosa Bay, *Solomon Is.* **221** Q22
Gradaús, *Braz.* **132** F12
Graford, *Tex., U.S.* **104** L10
Grafton, *N. Dak., U.S.* **106** E7
Grafton, *N.S.W., Austral.* **215** W15
Grafton, *W. Va., U.S.* **98** C10
Grafton, *Wis., U.S.* **100** L7
Grafton, Mount, *Nev., U.S.* **III** Q12
Graham, *N.C., U.S.* **98** G11
Graham, *Ont., Can.* **85** P15
Graham, *Tex., U.S.* **104** L9
Graham, Mount, *Ariz., U.S.* **109** V9
Graham Bell, Ostrov, *Russ.* **161** C13
Graham Bell Island, *Asia* **168** B8
Graham Island, *B.C., Can.* **84** J6
Graham Island, *Nunavut, Can.* **85** C15

Graham Lake, *Me., U.S.* **97** F18
Graham Land, region, *Antarctica* **230** D4
Graham's Harbour, *Bahamas* **122** E11
Grahamstown, *S. Af.* **206** M10
Graian Alps, *Fr., It.* **152** D2
Grain Coast, *Af.* **204** E6
Grajaú, *Braz.* **133** E14
Grajaú, river, *S. Amer.* **128** E9
Grajewo, *Pol.* **151** B17
Gramat, *Fr.* **149** V9
Grámmos, Óros, *Gr.* **156** D8
Grampian Mountains, *Scot., U.K.* **144** K9
Granada, *Colo., U.S.* **109** N16
Granada, *Nicar.* **117** M18
Granada, *Sp.* **146** L12
Granadilla, *Sp.* **208** Q4
Gran Altiplanicie Central, *Arg.* **135** U8
Granbury, *Tex., U.S.* **104** L10
Granby, *Colo., U.S.* **108** L12
Granby, *Que., Can.* **85** P20
Granby, Mount, *Grenada* **123** K22
Gran Canaria, island, *Sp.* **208** R5
Gran Cayo Point, *Trinidad and Tobago* **123** Q23
Gran Chaco, region, *S. Amer.* **128** J6
Grand, river, *Mich., U.S.* **100** L10
Grand, river, *Mo., U.S.* **107** R12
Grand, river, *S. Dak., U.S.* **106** J3
Grand Anse, *Grenada* **123** L22
Grand Anse, *St. Lucia* **123** J14
Grand Anse Bay, *Grenada* **123** L22
Grand Bahama Island, *Bahamas* **122** A4
Grand Baie, *Mauritius* **209** F20
Grand Baie, *Mauritius* **209** J20
Grand Banks of Newfoundland, *N. Amer.* **85** N24
Grand-Bassam, *Côte d'Ivoire* **204** E9
Grand Bay, *Dominica* **123** G19
Grand Bonum, peak, *St. Vincent and the Grenadines* **123** K16
Grand-Bourg, *Guadeloupe, Fr.* **123** G16
Grand Caicos, island, *Turks & Caicos Is.* **119** H17
Grand Caille Point, *St. Lucia* **123** K13
Grandcamp-Maisy, *Fr.* **149** N6
Grand Canal, *Ire.* **145** S6
Grand Canyon, *Ariz., U.S.* **109** R6
Grand Canyon, town, *Ariz., U.S.* **109** R7
Grand Canyon National Park, *Ariz., U.S.* **109** Q6
Grand Canyon-Parashant National Monument, *Ariz., U.S.* **109** Q5
Grand Case, *St.-Martin, Fr.* **123** A14
Grand Cayman, island, *Cayman Is.* **118** L7
Grand Cess, *Liberia* **204** F7
Grand Coulee, *Wash., U.S.* **110** B8
Grand Coulee Dam, *Wash., U.S.* **110** B7
Grand Cul-de-Sac Marin, *Guadeloupe, Fr.* **123** E14
Grande, river, *Arg.* **134** M7
Grande, river, *Bol.* **132** J8
Grande, river, *Braz.* **133** H15
Grande, river, *Braz.* **133** L13
Grande, Bahía, *Arg.* **135** V8
Grande, Boca, *Venez.* **131** C13
Grande, Cayo, *Cuba* **118** J9
Grande, Cuchilla, *Uru.* **134** K14
Grande, Salina, *Arg.* **135** N8
Grande-Anse, *Guadeloupe, Fr.* **123** E17
Grande Bay, *Atl. Oc.* **241** V4
Grande Cayemite, island, *Haiti* **119** M15
Grande Comore see Njazidja, *Comoros* **209** M14
Grande Montagne, peak, *Mauritius* **209** J20
Grande Prairie, *Alta., Can.* **84** K9
Grande Riviere, *Trinidad and Tobago* **123** N23
Grande Rivière du Nord, *Haiti* **119** L17

Grande Rivière Sud Est, *Mauritius* **209** G21
Grande Ronde, river, *Oreg., U.S.* **110** F8
Grandes, Salinas, *Arg.* **134** H9
Grande-Terre, island, *Guadeloupe, Fr.* **123** E15
Grande Vigie, Pointe de la, *Guadeloupe, Fr.* **123** D15
Grandfalls, *Tex., U.S.* **105** N3
Grand Falls-Windsor, *Nfld. & Lab., Can.* **85** M23
Grandfather Mountain, *N.C., U.S.* **98** G8
Grandfield, *Okla., U.S.* **104** J9
Grand Forks, *N. Dak., U.S.* **106** F8
Grand-Gosier, *Haiti* **119** M17
Grand Harbour, *Malta* **163** K23
Grand Haven, *Mich., U.S.* **100** L9
Grandi, Playa, *Curaçao, Neth.* **123** P14
Grand Îlet, *Guadeloupe, Fr.* **123** H14
Grand Island, *Mich., U.S.* **100** F8
Grand Island, *N.Y., U.S.* **96** J5
Grand Island, *Nebr., U.S.* **107** Q6
Grand Island Bay, *S. Amer.* **128** J9
Grand Isle, *La., U.S.* **102** R11
Grand Junction, *Colo., U.S.* **108** M10
Grand Lake, *La., U.S.* **102** Q7
Grand Lake, *Ohio, U.S.* **101** Q11
Grand Ledge, *Mich., U.S.* **100** M10
Grand Lieu, Lac de, *Fr.* **149** S5
Grand Mal Bay, *Grenada* **123** L22
Grand Marais, *Mich., U.S.* **100** F9
Grand Marais, *Minn., U.S.* **106** F14
Grândola, *Port.* **146** J5
Grand Passage, *New Caledonia, Fr.* **222** A5
Grand Portage, *Minn., U.S.* **106** E14
Grand Portage National Monument, *Minn., U.S.* **106** E14
Grand Prairie, *Tex., U.S.* **104** L11
Grand Rapids, *Man., Can.* **85** M13
Grand Rapids, *Mich., U.S.* **100** L9
Grand Rapids, *Minn., U.S.* **106** G11
Grand Rivière, *Martinique, Fr.* **123** E22
Grand Roy, *Grenada* **123** K22
Grand Saline, *Tex., U.S.* **104** L13
Grand Staircase-Escalante National Monument, *Utah, U.S.* **109** P7
Grand Teton, peak, *Wyo., U.S.* **108** G8
Grand Teton National Park, *Wyo., U.S.* **108** G8
Grand Traverse Bay, *Mich., U.S.* **100** H10
Grand Turk, island, *Turks & Caicos Is.* **119** J18
Grandview, *Wash., U.S.* **110** E6
Grandvilliers, *Fr.* **149** N9
Grange, *Virgin Is., U.S.* **122** R2
Grange (An Ghráinseach), *Ire.* **145** S4
Grange Hill, *Jam.* **122** H6
Granger, *Tex., U.S.* **105** P11
Granger, *Wash., U.S.* **110** E6
Granger, *Wyo., U.S.* **108** K9
Grangeville, *Idaho, U.S.* **108** E4
Granite, *Okla., U.S.* **104** H8
Granite, *Oreg., U.S.* **110** G8
Granite City, *Ill., U.S.* **101** T4
Granite Falls, *Minn., U.S.* **106** K9
Granite Mountains, *Calif., U.S.* **111** V10
Granite Mountains, *Wyo., U.S.* **108** H11
Granite Peak, *Mont., U.S.* **108** F9
Granite Peak, *Nev., U.S.* **110** M7
Granite Peak, *Utah, U.S.* **108** L6
Granja, *Braz.* **133** D14
Gran Laguna Salada, *Arg.* **135** S8
Granollers, *Sp.* **147** D17
Gran Sasso d'Italia, *It.* **152** J10
Grant, *Nebr., U.S.* **107** Q3
Grant, Mount, *Nev., U.S.* **111** R7
Gran Tarajal, *Sp.* **208** Q7
Grant City, *Mo., U.S.* **107** Q10
Grant Island, *Antarctica* **230** N8
Grant-Kohrs Ranch National Historic Site, *Mont., U.S.* **108** D6
Grant Range, *Nev., U.S.* **111** R11

Grants, *N. Mex., U.S.* **109** S11
Grantsburg, *Wis., U.S.* **100** G2
Grants Pass, *Oreg., U.S.* **110** K2
Grantville, *Ga., U.S.* **98** M4
Granville, *Fr.* **149** P6
Granville, *N. Dak., U.S.* **106** E4
Granville, *N.Y., U.S.* **96** H12
Granville Lake, *Man., Can.* **85** L13
Grão Mogol, *Braz.* **133** J15
Grapeland, *Tex., U.S.* **105** N13
Grapevine Lake, *Tex., U.S.* **104** L11
Grass Cay, *Virgin Is., U.S.* **122** M10
Grasse, *Fr.* **149** X15
Grassholm Island, *Wales, U.K.* **145** V8
Grass Patch, *W. Aust., Austral.* **215** X5
Grass Point, *Virgin Is., U.S.* **122** R3
Grassrange, *Mont., U.S.* **108** D10
Grass Valley, *Calif., U.S.* **111** Q5
Grassy Bay, *Bermuda* **122** B2
Grassy Butte, *N. Dak., U.S.* **106** F2
Grassy Key, *Fla., U.S.* **99** Y9
Graus, *Sp.* **147** C15
Grauspitz, peak, *Liech., Switz.* **162** R3
Grave, Pointe de, *Fr.* **149** U6
Gravelbourg, *Sask., Can.* **84** N11
Grave Peak, *Idaho, U.S.* **108** D5
Gravette, *Ark., U.S.* **102** E6
Gravina in Puglia, *It.* **152** M13
Gray, *Fr.* **149** R13
Grayland, *Wash., U.S.* **110** D2
Grayling, *Alas., U.S.* **113** H13
Grayling, *Mich., U.S.* **100** J10
Grays, *Eng., U.K.* **145** V14
Grays Harbor, *Wash., U.S.* **110** D2
Grays Lake, *Idaho, U.S.* **108** H7
Grayson, *Ky., U.S.* **103** B19
Grayville, *Ill., U.S.* **101** U7
Graz, *Aust.* **150** M12
Great Artesian Basin, *Austral.* **214** G12
Great Australian Bight, *Austral.* **214** K7
Great Bacolet Bay, *Grenada* **123** L23
Great Bacolet Point, *Grenada* **123** L23
Great Bahama Bank, *Atl. Oc.* **240** L3
Great Barrier Island (Aotea Island), *N.Z.* **217** H19
Great Barrier Reef, *Qnsld., Austral.* **214** D14
Great Basin, *U.S.* **86** F5
Great Basin National Park, *Nev., U.S.* **111** Q12
Great Bay, *N.J., U.S.* **96** Q10
Great Bear Lake, *N.W.T., Can.* **84** F11
Great Belt, *Atl. Oc.* **140** F7
Great Bend, *Kans., U.S.* **107** T5
Great Bernera, island, *Scot., U.K.* **144** H6
Great Bird Island, *Antigua and Barbuda* **123** A21
Great Bitter Lake see Murrat el Kubra, Buheirat, *Egypt* **173** Q1
Great Britain, *U.K.* **145** Q12
Great Channel, *India, Indonesia* **181** T15
Great Channel, *Philippines* **192** F3
Great Coco Island, *Myanmar* **190** M4
Great Courtland Bay, *Trinidad and Tobago* **123** N17
Great Crack, *Hawai'i, U.S.* **115** P20
Great Crater, *Israel* **173** P5
Great Dismal Swamp, *N.C., Va., U.S.* **98** G14
Great Divide Basin, *Wyo., U.S.* **108** J10
Great Dividing Range, *Austral.* **214** G14
Great Dog Island, *British Virgin Is., U.K.* **122** L8
Great Driffield, *Eng., U.K.* **145** R13
Great Eastern Erg see Oriental, Grand Erg, *Af.* **198** D5
Greater Antilles, islands, *N. Amer.* **119** M13
Greater Khingan Range, *Asia* **168** F11
Greater Sudbury, *Ont., Can.* **85** P17
Greater Sunda Islands, *Indonesia* **192** K7
Great Exuma, island, *Bahamas* **122** E8

Great Fall, *Guyana* **131** E13
Great Falls, *Mont., U.S.* **108** C8
Great Falls, *S.C., U.S.* **98** K9
Great Guana Cay, *Bahamas* **118** C12
Great Guana Cay, *Bahamas* **118** F12
Great Harbour, *British Virgin Is., U.K.* **122** L11
Great Harbour Cay, *Bahamas* **118** D11
Greathead Bay, *St. Vincent and the Grenadines* **123** L16
Great Hungarian Plain, *Eur.* **140** J9
Great Inagua Island, *Bahamas* **119** J15
Great Indian Desert (Thar Desert), *India, Pak.* **179** U8
Great Isaac, island, *Bahamas* **118** D10
Great Karoo, region, *Af.* **198** Q7
Great Lake, *Austral.* **214** L7
Great Lake, *Bahamas* **122** F11
Great Lameshur Bay, *Virgin Is., U.S.* **122** P10
Great Meteor Tablemount, *Atl. Oc.* **240** K8
Great Miami, river, *U.S.* **87** G17
Great Namaland, region, *Namibia* **206** J7
Great Nicobar, island, *India* **181** T15
Great Orme's Head, *Eng., U.K.* **145** S9
Great Oyster Bay, *Austral.* **214** L8
Great Pedro Bluff, *Jam.* **119** N11
Great Pedro Point, *Cayman Is.* **122** J2
Great Pee Dee, river, *S.C., U.S.* **98** L12
Great Plains, *N. Amer.* **82** H5
Great Pond Bay, *Virgin Is., U.S.* **122** R3
Great Rift Valley, *Af.* **198** K10
Great River Bay, *Grenada* **123** K24
Great Ruaha, river, *Tanzania* **203** M14
Great Sacandaga Lake, *N.Y., U.S.* **96** J11
Great Saint James Island, *Virgin Is., U.S.* **122** N10
Great Sale Cay, *Bahamas* **123** D3
Great Salt Lake, *Utah, U.S.* **108** K6
Great Salt Lake Desert, *Utah, U.S.* **108** L6
Great Salt Plains Lake, *Okla., U.S.* **104** E10
Great Salt Pond, *St. Kitts and Nevis* **123** B18
Great Sand Dunes National Park & Preserve, *Colo., U.S.* **109** P13
Great Sandy Desert, *Austral.* **214** E5
Great Sandy Desert, *U.S.* **86** D4
Great Sandy Island see Fraser Island, *Austral.* **214** G16
Great Sitkin Island, *Alas., U.S.* **112** N5
Great Slave Lake, *N.W.T., Can.* **84** H11
Great Smoky Mountains, *U.S.* **87** J18
Great Smoky Mountains National Park, *N.C., Tenn., U.S.* **103** F19
Great Sound, *Bermuda* **122** C1
Great Stirrup Cay, *Bahamas* **118** D11
Great Tenasserim, river, *Myanmar* **191** N8
Great Thatch Island, *British Virgin Is., U.K.* **122** M11
Great Tobago Island, *British Virgin Is., U.K.* **122** L10
Great Victoria Desert, *Austral.* **214** H6
Great Wall, *Hebei, China* **184** C9
Great Western Erg see Occidental, Grand Erg, *Af.* **198** D4
Great Western Tiers, *Austral.* **214** L7
Great Yarmouth, *Eng., U.K.* **145** T16
Great Zab, river, *Turk.* **171** H18
Great Zimbabwe, ruin, *Zimb.* **206** G11
Greci, *It.* **152** L12
Gredos, Sierra de, *Sp.* **146** F9
Greece, *Eur.* **156** F9
Greece, *N.Y., U.S.* **96** J6
Greeley, *Colo., U.S.* **108** L13
Greeley, *Nebr., U.S.* **107** P6
Greely Fjord, *Nunavut, Can.* **85** B15
Green, river, *Ky., U.S.* **103** D15
Green, river, *U.S.* **86** G7

Green, river, *U.S.* **87** H17
Green, river, *U.S.* **108** M9
Green Bay, *Antigua and Barbuda* **123** B20
Green Bay, *U.S.* **87** D16
Green Bay, *Wis., U.S.* **100** H7
Green Bay, town, *Wis., U.S.* **100** J7
Greenbrier, river, *W. Va., U.S.* **98** E10
Greenbush, *Mich., U.S.* **100** J12
Greenbush, *Minn., U.S.* **106** E9
Green Cape, *Austral.* **214** M14
Green Castle, *Bahamas* **122** F6
Greencastle, *Ind., U.S.* **101** R8
Greencastle, *Pa., U.S.* **96** Q6
Green Cay, *Bahamas* **118** F12
Green Cay, *British Virgin Is., U.K.* **122** L11
Green Cay, *Virgin Is., U.S.* **122** Q3
Green Cove Springs, *Fla., U.S.* **99** R8
Greeneville, *Tenn., U.S.* **103** E20
Greenfield, *Calif., U.S.* **111** U4
Greenfield, *Ind., U.S.* **101** R9
Greenfield, *Iowa, U.S.* **107** P10
Greenfield, *Mass., U.S.* **97** K13
Greenfield, *Mo., U.S.* **107** U11
Greenfield, *Ohio, U.S.* **101** S12
Greenfield, *Tenn., U.S.* **103** E13
Greenfield, *Wis., U.S.* **100** L7
Green Head, *Austral.* **214** J2
Green Hill, *Trinidad and Tobago* **123** N22
Green Island, *Antigua and Barbuda* **123** B22
Green Island, *Grenada* **123** J24
Green Island, *Jam.* **122** H5
Green Islands, *P.N.G.* **217** C22
Greenland, *N. Amer.* **82** C9
Greenland Basin, *Arctic Oc.* **247** J18
Greenland Fracture Zone, *Arctic Oc.* **247** J17
Greenland-Iceland Rise, *Arctic Oc., Atl. Oc.* **247** M20
Greenland Plain, *Arctic Oc.* **247** J18
Greenland Sea, *Arctic Oc.* **247** J17
Greenland Trough, *Arctic Oc.* **247** L19
Green Mountains, *Vt., U.S.* **96** H12
Green Mountains, *Wyo., U.S.* **108** J11
Greenock, *Scot., U.K.* **144** M8
Greenport, *N.Y., U.S.* **97** L13
Green River, *Utah, U.S.* **108** M9
Green River, *Wyo., U.S.* **108** K9
Greensboro, *Ala., U.S.* **103** K14
Greensboro, *Ga., U.S.* **98** L6
Greensboro, *N.C., U.S.* **98** G10
Greensburg, *Ind., U.S.* **101** S10
Greensburg, *Kans., U.S.* **107** U5
Greensburg, *Ky., U.S.* **103** D17
Greensburg, *Pa., U.S.* **96** P4
Greens Peak, *Ariz., U.S.* **109** T9
Green Turtle Cay, *Bahamas* **122** A6
Green Valley, *Ariz., U.S.* **109** V7
Greenville, *Ala., U.S.* **103** M15
Greenville, *Calif., U.S.* **111** N5
Greenville, *Ga., U.S.* **99** Q6
Greenville, *Ill., U.S.* **101** T5
Greenville, *Ky., U.S.* **103** D15
Greenville, *Liberia* **204** E7
Greenville, *Me., U.S.* **97** D16
Greenville, *Mich., U.S.* **100** L10
Greenville, *Miss., U.S.* **102** J10
Greenville, *N.C., U.S.* **98** H13
Greenville, *Ohio, U.S.* **100** R11
Greenville, *Pa., U.S.* **96** M3
Greenville, *S.C., U.S.* **98** J7
Greenville, *Tex., U.S.* **104** K12
Greenwood, *Ark., U.S.* **102** F6
Greenwood, *Ind., U.S.* **101** R9
Greenwood, *Miss., U.S.* **102** J11
Greenwood, *S.C., U.S.* **98** K7
Greer, *S.C., U.S.* **98** J7
Greers Ferry Lake, *Ark., U.S.* **102** F8
Gregory, *S. Dak., U.S.* **106** M5
Gregory, river, *Austral.* **214** D11
Gregory, Lake, *Austral.* **214** G4
Gregory, Lake, *Austral.* **214** H11
Gregory Lake, *Austral.* **214** E6
Gregory Range, *Austral.* **214** D12
Gregory Town, *Bahamas* **122** D5
Greifswald, *Ger.* **150** B10
Greiz, *Ger.* **150** G9

Grenada, *Calif., U.S.* 110 L3
Grenada, *Miss., U.S.* 102 J11
Grenada, island, *N. Amer.* 121 H16
Grenada Bay, *Grenada* 123 J24
Grenade, *Fr.* 149 X7
Grenoble, *Fr.* 149 V14
Grenora, *N. Dak., U.S.* 106 E2
Grenville, *Grenada* 121 H17
Grenville, *Grenada* 123 K23
Grenville, Cape, *Austral.* 214 A12
Grenville, Point, *Wash., U.S.* 110 C2
Grenville Bay, *Grenada* 123 K23
Gresham, *Oreg., U.S.* 110 F4
Gretna, *La., U.S.* 102 Q11
Gretschins, *Switz.* 162 Q2
Grevená, *Gr.* 156 D8
Grevenmacher, *Lux.* 162 J11
Grey, Cape, *Austral.* 214 B10
Grey, Mount, *Austral.* 214 J3
Greybull, *Wyo., U.S.* 108 F10
Greybull, river, *Wyo., U.S.* 108 G10
Grey Islands, *Nfld. & Lab., Can.*
  85 L23
Greylock, Mount, *Mass., U.S.* 96 K12
Grey Range, *Austral.* 214 H12
Grezzana, *It.* 152 D6
Gribanovskiy, *Russ.* 158 M11
Gridley, *Calif., U.S.* 111 P4
Grieg Point, *Kiribati* 221 B20
Griekwastad (Griquatown), *S. Af.*
  206 K9
Griffin, *Ga., U.S.* 98 M5
Griffith, *N.S.W., Austral.* 215 X13
Griggsville, *Ill., U.S.* 101 R3
Grijalva Ridge, *Pac. Oc.* 243 K21
Grim, Cape, *Austral.* 214 L7
Grimaldi Forum, *Monaco* 163 C22
Grimault, Île, *New Caledonia, Fr.*
  222 D7
Grimsby, *Eng., U.K.* 145 R14
Grímsey, island, *Ice.* 142 D3
Grimshaw, *Alta., Can.* 84 K10
Grimstad, *Nor.* 142 L11
Grindavíkurdjúp, valley, *Atl. Oc.*
  247 M21
Grindelwald, *Switz.* 152 B3
Grinnell, *Iowa, U.S.* 107 P12
Grinnell Peninsula, *Nunavut, Can.*
  85 C15
Grintavec, peak, *Slov.* 154 C5
Grise Fiord, *Nunavut, Can.* 85 C16
Grishkino, *Russ.* 160 J12
Gris-Nez, Cap, *Fr.* 148 L9
Grisslehamn, *Sw.* 143 J14
Gródek, *Pol.* 151 C18
Groenlo, *Neth.* 148 J14
Groesbeck, *Tex., U.S.* 105 N12
Groix, Île de, *Fr.* 149 R3
Grójec, *Pol.* 151 E16
Gronau, *Ger.* 150 D5
Groningen, *Neth.* 148 G14
Groom, *Tex., U.S.* 104 G6
Groot Baai, *St. Maarten, Neth.*
  123 B14
Groote Eylandt, *Austral.* 214 B10
Grootfontein, *Namibia* 206 G7
Groot Vloer, *Af.* 198 Q7
Grosio, *It.* 152 C6
Gros Islet, *St. Lucia* 123 J14
Gros Islet Bay, *St. Lucia* 123 J14
Gros-Morne, *Haiti* 119 L16
Gros-Morne, *Martinique, Fr.*
  123 E23
Gros Piton, peak, *St. Lucia* 123 L13
Gros Point, *Grenada* 123 J22
Grosse Pointe, *Guadeloupe, Fr.*
  123 G16
Grosseto, *It.* 152 J6
Grossglockner, peak, *Eur.* 140 H7
Grossvenediger, peak, *Aust.* 150 L8
Grosvenor Mountains, *Antarctica*
  230 K12
Gros Ventre Range, *Wyo., U.S.*
  108 H8
Grotli, *Nor.* 142 H10
Groton, *S. Dak., U.S.* 106 J7
Grottaminarda, *It.* 152 M11
Grotto of Lourdes, *Vatican City*
  163 Q14
Grotto of the Observatory, *Monaco*
  163 F19

Groupe Acteon, island, *Fr. Polynesia,
  Fr.* 223 G22
Grouse Creek, *Utah, U.S.* 108 J5
Grove City, *Pa., U.S.* 96 M3
Grove Hill, *Ala., U.S.* 103 M14
Grove Mountains, *Antarctica*
  231 G18
Grove Place, *Virgin Is., U.S.* 122 R2
Grover, *Colo., U.S.* 108 K14
Grover Beach, *Calif., U.S.* 111 W5
Groves, *Tex., U.S.* 105 Q16
Groveton, *N.H., U.S.* 97 F14
Groveton, *Tex., U.S.* 105 P14
Groznyy, *Russ.* 159 T14
Grudovo, *Bulg.* 155 J17
Grudziądz, *Pol.* 151 C14
Gruinard Bay, *Scot., U.K.* 144 J8
Grundy, *Va., U.S.* 98 F7
Grundy Center, *Iowa, U.S.* 107 N12
Gruver, *Tex., U.S.* 104 F5
Gryazi, *Russ.* 158 M10
Gryazovets, *Russ.* 158 G10
Gryfino, *Pol.* 150 C11
Grygla, *Minn., U.S.* 106 E9
Guacanayabo, Golfo de, *Cuba* 118 K11
Guadalajara, *Mex.* 116 H10
Guadalajara, *Sp.* 146 F11
Guadalcanal, *Sp.* 146 K8
Guadalcanal, island, *Solomon Is.*
  221 N19
Guadalquivir, river, *Sp.* 146 K9
Guadalupe, *Calif., U.S.* 111 W5
Guadalupe, *Mex.* 116 C7
Guadalupe, *Mex.* 116 G10
Guadalupe, river, *Tex., U.S.* 105 S11
Guadalupe, Isla de, *Mex.* 116 C4
Guadalupe, Sierra de, *Sp.* 146 H9
Guadalupe Island, *N. Amer.* 82 L2
Guadalupe Mountains, *N. Mex., Tex.,
  U.S.* 105 V5
Guadalupe Mountains National Park,
  Tex., U.S. 104 M1
Guadalupe Peak, *Tex., U.S.* 104 M1
Guadalupita, *N. Mex., U.S.* 109 R13
Guadarrama, Sierra de, *Sp.* 146 E10
Guadeloupe, island, *Lesser Antil.*
  121 D17
Guadeloupe Passage, *N. Amer.*
  121 C16
Guadiana, river, *Sp.* 146 H8
Guadiana, Bahía, *Cuba* 118 H4
Guadirikiri Cave, site, *Aruba, Neth.*
  123 R17
Guadix, *Sp.* 146 L11
Guafo, Boca del, *Chile* 135 R6
Guafo, Isla, *Chile* 135 R5
Guafo Fracture Zone, *Pac. Oc.*
  243 Q21
Guai, *Indonesia* 193 K21
Guáimaro, *Cuba* 118 J11
Guainía, river, *Col.* 130 G8
Guaíra, *Braz.* 132 M11
Guaire *see* Gorey, *Ire.* 145 T7
Guajaba, Cayo, *Cuba* 118 H11
Guajará-Mirim, *Braz.* 132 G7
Guajira, Península de la, *Col.* 130 A7
Guajira Peninsula, *N. Amer.* 82 P9
Gualala, *Calif., U.S.* 111 Q2
Gualdicciolo, *San Marino* 162 J13
Gualeguay, *Arg.* 134 K12
Gualeguaychú, *Arg.* 134 K12
Gualicho, Salina, *Arg.* 135 P9
Guallatiri, Volcán, *Chile* 134 B7
Guam, island, *Guam, U.S.* 220 D2
Guamúchil, *Mex.* 116 E8
Gua Musang, *Malaysia* 191 T10
Gu'an, *Hebei, China* 184 D7
Guana Baai, *St. Maarten, Neth.*
  123 B15
Guanabara Bay, *S. Amer.* 128 J10
Guana Cay, *Bahamas* 122 B10
Guana Island, *British Virgin Is., U.K.*
  122 Q7
Guanajay, *Cuba* 118 G6
Guanajuato, *Mex.* 116 H11
Guanambi, *Braz.* 133 J15
Guanapo, *Trinidad and Tobago*
  123 P23
Guanare, *Venez.* 130 C8
Guanare, river, *Venez.* 130 C8
Guandacol, *Arg.* 134 H8

Guandu, *Guang., China* 185 U5
Guane, *Cuba* 118 H4
Guangchang, *Jiangxi, China* 185 S7
Guangdong, *China* 185 V4
Guangfeng, *Jiangxi, China* 185 Q9
Guanghai, *Guang., China* 185 X4
Guanghai Wan, *Guang., China*
  185 X4
Guangling, *Shanxi, China* 184 D6
Guangning, *Guang., China* 185 V3
Guangrao, *Shand., China* 184 F9
Guangshan, *Henan, China* 184 M6
Guangshui, *Hubei, China* 184 M5
Guangyuan, *China* 182 K10
Guangze, *Fujian, China* 185 R8
Guangzhou (Canton), *Guang., China*
  185 V4
Guánica, *P.R., U.S.* 122 P2
Guánica, Bahía de, *P.R., U.S.* 122 P2
Guanipa, river, *Venez.* 130 C12
Guanmian Shan, *Chongq., China*
  184 M1
Guannan (Xin'an), *Jiangsu, China*
  184 J10
Guano, Cayo, *Cuba* 118 H7
Guano Lake, *Oreg., U.S.* 110 L7
Guantánamo, *Cuba* 119 K13
Guantánamo, Bahía de, *Cuba, U.S.*
  119 L13
Guanyang, *Guangxi Zhuang, China*
  185 T2
Guanyun (Yinshan), *Jiangsu, China*
  184 J10
Guapí, *Col.* 130 G3
Guapo Bay, *Trinidad and Tobago*
  123 Q22
Guaporé *see* Iténez, river, *S. Amer.*
  132 H8
Guara, Sierra de, *Sp.* 147 C14
Guaranda, *Ecua.* 130 K3
Guarapuava, *Braz.* 132 N12
Guaratinguetá, *Braz.* 133 M14
Guarcino, *It.* 152 L9
Guarda, *Port.* 146 F7
Guardalavaca, *Cuba* 119 J13
Guarda Mor, *Braz.* 133 K13
Guardo, *Sp.* 146 C9
Guareña, *Sp.* 146 H8
Guárico, river, *Venez.* 130 C9
Guarico, Punta, *Cuba* 119 K14
Guasave, *Mex.* 116 E8
Guascama, Punta, *Col.* 130 G3
Guasdualito, *Venez.* 130 D7
Guatemala, *N. Amer.* 117 K16
Guatemala Basin, *Pac. Oc.* 243 J20
Guatemala City, *Guatemala* 117 L16
Guaviare, river, *Col.* 130 G8
Guaviare, river, *N. Amer.* 82 R10
Guayabal, *Cuba* 118 K11
Guayaguayare, *Trinidad and Tobago*
  123 Q24
Guayaguayare Bay, *Trinidad and
  Tobago* 123 Q24
Guayama, *P.R., U.S.* 122 P4
Guayaquil, *Ecua.* 130 K2
Guayaquil, Golfo de, *Ecua.* 130 L2
Guaymas, *Mex.* 116 D7
Guaynabo, *P.R., U.S.* 122 M4
Gûbâl, Strait of, *Egypt* 173 U3
Guban, region, *Af.* 198 G11
Gubbio, *It.* 152 H8
Gubin, *Pol.* 150 E11
Gubkin, *Russ.* 159 N9
Gucheng, *Hubei, China* 184 L3
Gudalur, *India* 181 Q5
Gudaut'a, *Rep. of Georgia* 171 A15
Gudermes, *Russ.* 159 T14
Gudgeon Bay, *Pitcairn I., U.K.*
  223 Q23
Gudur, *India* 181 P7
Guebwiller, *Fr.* 149 Q15
Guelb er Rîchât, peak, *Mauritania*
  200 F6
Guelma *see* ... *Uganda* 203 J13
Guelmim, *Mor.* 200 C7
Güeppí, *Peru* 132 C3
Guera Massif, peak, *Af.* 198 G6
Guerara, *Alg.* 200 B11
Guéret, *Fr.* 149 T9
Guernsey, *Wyo., U.S.* 108 J13
Guernsey, island, *Channel Is., U.K.*
  145 Z11

Guernsey Reservoir, *Wyo., U.S.*
  108 J13
Gueydan, *La., U.S.* 102 P8
Gugegwe, island, *Marshall Is., U.S.*
  220 N5
Guguan, island, *N. Mariana Is., U.S.*
  220 B2
Gui, river, *Guangxi Zhuang, China*
  185 U2
Guía de Isora, *Sp.* 208 Q4
Guiana Highlands, *S. Amer.* 128 C6
Guiana Island, *Antigua and Barbuda*
  123 B21
Guichi, *Anhui, China* 185 N8
Guidong, *Hunan, China* 185 S5
Guienne, region, *Fr.* 149 W8
Guigang, *Guangxi Zhuang, China*
  185 V1
Guiglo, *Côte d'Ivoire* 204 E7
Guijá, *Mozambique* 206 H12
Guijuelo, *Sp.* 146 F8
Guilden Draak Seamount, *Ind. Oc.*
  225 M15
Guildford, *Eng., U.K.* 145 W13
Guilford, *Me., U.S.* 97 E16
Guilin, *Guangxi Zhuang, China* 185 T2
Guillaume-Delisle, Lac, *Que., Can.*
  85 L18
Guillestre, *Fr.* 149 V15
Guimarães, *Braz.* 133 D15
Guimarães, *Port.* 146 D6
Guimeng Ding, *Shand., China* 184 H9
Guin, *Ala., U.S.* 103 J14
Guinchos Cay, *Bahamas* 118 G11
Guinea, *Af.* 204 C6
Guinea, Gulf of, *Af.* 204 F12
Guinea Basin, *Atl. Oc.* 241 P11
Guinea-Bissau, *Af.* 204 B4
Guinea Fracture Zone, *Atl. Oc.*
  241 N9
Guinea Plain, *Atl. Oc.* 241 P12
Guinea Rise, *Atl. Oc.* 241 Q12
Guinea Seamount Chain, *Atl. Oc.*
  241 P12
Guinea Terrace, *Atl. Oc.* 241 N10
Güines, *Cuba* 118 G6
Güiria, *Venez.* 130 B12
Guingamp, *Fr.* 149 P4
Guiping, *Guangxi Zhuang, China*
  185 V1
Güira de Melena, *Cuba* 118 G6
Guisborough, *Eng., U.K.* 145 Q13
Guitiriz, *Sp.* 146 B6
Guixi, *Jiangxi, China* 185 Q8
Guiyang, *Hunan, China* 185 T4
Guizhou, *China* 185 Q1
Gujar Khan, *Pak.* 179 N11
Gujiao, *Shanxi, China* 184 E4
Gujranwala, *Pak.* 179 P12
Gujrat, *Pak.* 179 P11
Gujwa, *S. Korea* 187 W8
Gukdo, island, *S. Korea* 187 U11
Gul Bahâr, *Afghan.* 178 M8
Gulbarga *see* Kalaburagi, *India*
  180 M5
Gulbene, *Latv.* 143 L17
Gul'cha, *Kyrg.* 178 G11
Gulf Islands National Seashore, *Miss.,
  U.S.* 103 P13
Gulfport, *Miss., U.S.* 102 P12
Gulf Shores, *Ala., U.S.* 103 P14
Gulin, *China* 182 M10
Guling, *Jiangxi, China* 185 P7
Guliston, *Uzb.* 177 K13
Gulitel, Mount, *Palau* 220 M12
Gulja *see* Yining, *China* 182 D4
Gulkana, *Alas., U.S.* 113 H17
Güllük, *Turk.* 170 H3
Gülnar, *Turk.* 170 J8
Gülşehir, *Turk.* 170 F9
Gulu, *Uganda* 203 J13
Gülübovo, *Bulg.* 155 J15
Gulya, *Russ.* 161 K18
Gulyantsi, *Bulg.* 155 G14
Guma *see* Pishan, *China* 182 G2
Gumdag, *Turkm.* 176 L6
Gumi, *S. Korea* 187 Q10
Gumla, *India* 180 J9
Gummi, *Nigeria* 205 B13

Gümüşhacıköy, *Turk.* 170 D10
Gümüşhane, *Turk.* 171 D14
Gümüşören, *Turk.* 170 G10
Gumzai, *Indonesia* 193 L19
Guna, *India* 180 H6
Gun Bay, *Cayman Is.* 122 J4
Gun Cay, *Bahamas* 118 D9
Gun Creek, *British Virgin Is., U.K.*
  122 Q9
Gundlupet, *India* 181 Q5
Gündoğmuş, *Turk.* 170 J7
Güney, *Turk.* 170 G4
Gungu, *Dem. Rep. of the Congo*
  202 M9
Gun Hill, peak, *Barbados* 123 K19
Gunib, *Russ.* 159 U15
Gunnbjørn Fjeld, peak, *N. Amer.*
  82 C10
Gunnedah, *N.S.W., Austral.* 215 W14
Gunners Quoin, island, *Mauritius*
  209 F20
Gunnerus Bank, *Ind. Oc.* 241 Y16
Gunnerus Ridge, *Ind. Oc.* 241 Y16
Gunnison, *Colo., U.S.* 109 N11
Gunnison, *Utah, U.S.* 108 M7
Gunsan, *S. Korea* 187 R8
Gunt, river, *Taj.* 178 J10
Guntersville, *Ala., U.S.* 103 H16
Guntersville Lake, *Ala., U.S.* 103 H16
Guntur, *India* 181 N7
Gunungsugih, *Indonesia* 192 L7
Gunwi, *S. Korea* 187 Q11
Guojiatun, *Hebei, China* 184 B8
Guoyang, *Anhui, China* 184 K7
Gupis, *Pak.* 178 K11
Gurabo, *P.R., U.S.* 122 N5
Gura Humorului, *Rom.* 155 B15
Gurdaspur, *India* 179 P13
Gurdon, *Ark., U.S.* 102 J7
Güre, *Turk.* 170 F5
Gureopdo, island, *S. Korea* 187 N6
Gurer, island, *Marshall Is., U.S.*
  220 L3
Gurguan Point, *N. Mariana Is., U.S.*
  220 B7
Guri Dam, *Venez.* 130 D11
Guri i Topit, peak, *Alban.* 154 L9
Gurimatu, *P.N.G.* 217 D19
Gurkovo, *Bulg.* 155 J15
Gurney, *P.N.G.* 217 E21
Gürün, *Turk.* 170 F12
Gurupá, *Braz.* 132 D12
Gurupá Island, *S. Amer.* 128 D8
Gurupi, *Braz.* 133 H13
Gurupi, river, *Braz.* 133 E14
Gurupi, Cape, *S. Amer.* 128 D9
Gurupi, Serra do, *Braz.* 133 E13
Gurvan Bogd Uul, *Mongolia* 182 E9
Gurvan Sayhan Uul, *Mongolia*
  182 E10
Gurye, *S. Korea* 187 S9
Guryongpo, *S. Korea* 187 R13
Gusan, *S. Korea* 186 M11
Gusan, *S. Korea* 187 Q11
Gusau, *Nigeria* 205 B14
Gusev, *Russ.* 158 J2
Gushgy, *Uzb.* 176 N10
Gushan, *Liaoning, China* 184 C12
Gushan, *Liaoning, China* 184 C13
Gushi, *Henan, China* 184 L7
Gusinaya Bank, *Arctic Oc.* 247 D17
Gusinoozersk, *Russ.* 161 L15
Gus' Khrustal'nyy, *Russ.* 158 J11
Guspini, *It.* 153 P3
Güssing, *Aust.* 150 M12
Gustavia, *St.-Barthélemy, Fr.* 121 B15
Gustine, *Calif., U.S.* 111 S5
Güstrow, *Ger.* 150 C9
Gutâiu, peak, *Rom.* 155 B13
Gutcher, *Scot., U.K.* 144 C12
Gutenberg Castle, ruin, *Liech.*
  162 Q1
Gütersloh, *Ger.* 150 E6
Gutha, *W. Aust., Austral.* 215 W2
Guthrie, *Ky., U.S.* 103 D15
Guthrie, *Okla., U.S.* 104 F11
Guthrie, *Tex., U.S.* 104 K7
Guthrie Center, *Iowa, U.S.* 107 P10
Gutian, *Fujian, China* 185 S9
Guttenberg, *Iowa, U.S.* 106 M14
Güvem, *Turk.* 170 D8

Guwahati, *India* 180 G13
Guyana, *S. Amer.* 131 F14
Guyana Basin, *Atl. Oc.* 241 N6
Guyandotte, river, *W. Va., U.S.* 98 E7
Guyang, *N. Mongol, China* 184 B3
Guymon, *Okla., U.S.* 104 E5
Guyuan, *China* 182 H10
Guyuan, *Hebei, China* 184 B7
Güzeloluk, *Turk.* 170 J9
Güzelyurt, *Turk.* 170 G9
Güzelyurt *see* Morphou, *Cyprus* 162 N7
Guzhang, *Hunan, China* 185 Q2
Guzhen, *Anhui, China* 184 K8
G'uzor, *Uzb.* 176 M12
Gwa, *Myanmar* 190 K5
Gwabegar, *N.S.W., Austral.* 215 W14
Gwadar, *Pak.* 179 W2
Gwai, *Zimb.* 206 G10
Gwalior, *India* 180 G6
Gwallido, island, *S. Korea* 187 R7
Gwanchon, *S. Korea* 187 R8
Gwanda, *Zimb.* 206 G11
Gwangcheon, *S. Korea* 187 Q12
Gwangcheon, *S. Korea* 187 Q7
Gwangju, *S. Korea* 187 N8
Gwangju (Kwangju), *S. Korea* 187 T8
Gwangmyeong, *S. Korea* 186 N8
Gwangyang, *S. Korea* 187 T9
Gwangyang, *S. Korea* 187 T9
Gwanmaedo, island, *S. Korea* 187 U6
Gwansan, *S. Korea* 187 U8
Gwardafuy, Cape, *Af.* 198 G12
Gwardafuy, Cape, *Asia* 168 J3
Gwatar Bay, *Iran, Pak.* 179 W1
Gweebarra Bay, *Ire.* 145 P4
Gweru, *Zimb.* 206 G11
Gwinn, *Mich., U.S.* 100 F7
Gwinner, *N. Dak., U.S.* 106 H7
Gwoza, *Nigeria* 205 C16
Gwydir, river, *Austral.* 214 J14
Gyangzê (Jiangzi), *China* 182 L5
Gyaring Hu, *China* 182 J8
Gýaros, island, *Gr.* 157 K14
Gydan *see* Kolymskoye Nagor'ye, range, *Russ.* 161 E20
Gydanskiy Poluostrov, *Russ.* 160 F12
Gyda Peninsula, *Asia* 168 C8
Gyebangsan, peak, *S. Korea* 186 M11
Gyêgu *see* Yushu, *China* 182 K7
Gyeokpo, *S. Korea* 187 S7
Gyeonggiman, bay, *S. Korea* 187 N7
Gyeongju (Kyŏngju), *S. Korea* 187 R12
Gyeongsan, *S. Korea* 187 R11
Gyirong (Jilong), *China* 182 L3
Gympie, *Qnsld., Austral.* 215 U16
Gyodongdo, island, *S. Korea* 186 M7
Gyoga, *S. Korea* 187 N12
Gyöngyös, *Hung.* 151 K15
Győr, *Hung.* 151 L14
Gypsum, *Kans., U.S.* 107 T7
Gýtheio, *Gr.* 156 M10
Gyuam, *S. Korea* 187 Q8
Gyula, *Hung.* 151 M17
Gyumri, *Arm.* 171 D18
Gyzylarbat, *Turkm.* 176 L7
Gyzyletrek, *Uzb.* 176 M6
Gyzylgaya, *Turkm.* 176 K7
Gyzylsuw, *Turkm.* 176 K6
Gżira, *Malta* 163 K23

Ha'afeva, island, *Tonga* 222 Q6
Haag, *Switz.* 162 M2
Ha'akame, *Tonga* 222 J11
Ha'alaufuli, *Tonga* 222 L12
Haamaire, Baie, *Fr. Polynesia, Fr.* 223 K14
Haamene, Baie de, *Fr. Polynesia, Fr.* 223 A23
Ha'ano, island, *Tonga* 222 P7
Ha'apai Group, *Tonga* 218 K10
Haapamäki, *Fin.* 143 G15
Haapiti, *Fr. Polynesia, Fr.* 223 N14
Haapsalu, *Est.* 143 K16
Haapu, *Fr. Polynesia, Fr.* 223 H14

Haarlem, *Neth.* 148 J12
Ha'asini, *Tonga* 222 J12
Haast, *N.Z.* 217 P16
Haava, Canal, *Fr. Polynesia, Fr.* 223 N20
Hab, river, *Pak.* 179 V6
Habahe, *China* 182 C5
Ḩabarūt, *Yemen* 175 N14
Habirag, *N. Mongol, China* 184 A7
Habomai, *Japan* 188 F16
Habomai Islands, *Russ.* 161 K23
Haboro, *Japan* 188 F13
Hachijō Jima, *Japan* 189 R12
Hachinohe, *Japan* 188 J13
Hachiōji, *Japan* 189 P11
Hachirō Gata, *Japan* 188 K12
Hachita, *N. Mex., U.S.* 109 V10
Hachujado, island, *S. Korea* 187 V7
Hacıbektaş, *Turk.* 170 F9
Hacıqabul, *Azerb.* 171 D22
Hadarba, Ras, *Sudan* 203 C14
Ḩadd, Ra's al, *Oman* 175 K17
Haddummati Atoll, *Maldives* 181 W3
Hadejia, river, *Af.* 198 G5
Ḩadera, *Israel* 172 L5
Hadhramaut, *Asia* 168 J3
Hadīboh, *Yemen* 175 R14
Ḩadīdah, *Syr.* 172 D10
Hadim, *Turk.* 170 H7
Ḩadīthah, *Iraq* 174 D8
Hadja, *Solomon Is.* 221 P21
Hadley Bay, *Nunavut, Can.* 85 E13
Hado, island, *S. Korea* 187 T10
Hà Đông, *Vietnam* 190 H12
Hadong, *S. Korea* 187 T9
Ḩaḑramawt, region, *Yemen* 174 Q11
Hadrian's Wall, *Eng., U.K.* 145 P11
Hadrut (Gadrut), *Azerb.* 171 E21
Hadyach, *Ukr.* 159 N7
Haedo, Cuchilla de, *Uru.* 134 K13
Haeju, *N. Korea* 186 L6
Haeju-man, bay, *N. Korea* 186 M6
Haemi, *S. Korea* 187 P7
Hā'ena, *Hawai'i, U.S.* 115 M22
Haenam, *S. Korea* 187 U9
Haengyŏng, *N. Korea* 186 B13
Ḩafar al Bāţin, *Saudi Arabia* 174 G10
Hafik, *Turk.* 170 E12
Ḩafīt, Jabal, *Oman, U.A.E.* 175 K15
Hafizabad, *Pak.* 179 P11
Hag's Head, *Ire.* 145 S3
Hagåtna (Agana), *Guam, U.S.* 220 C10
Hagemeister Island, *Alas., U.S.* 112 L12
Hagen, *Ger.* 150 F5
Hagerman, *N. Mex., U.S.* 109 U14
Hagerman Fossil Beds National Monument, *Idaho, U.S.* 108 H4
Hagerstown, *Md., U.S.* 98 B12
Häggenås, *Sw.* 142 G12
Hà Giang, *Vietnam* 190 G11
Hagoi Susupe, lake, *N. Mariana Is., U.S.* 220 C4
Hague, Cap de la, *Fr.* 149 N5
Hague, The *see* Den Haag, *Neth.* 148 J12
Haguenau, *Fr.* 149 P15
Haha Jima Rettō (Baily or Coffin Group), *Japan* 189 X14
Hahoe, *N. Korea* 186 B14
Hai'an, *Guang., China* 185 Y1
Hai'an, *Jiangsu, China* 184 L11
Haicheng, *Liaoning, China* 184 B12
Haida Gwaii (Queen Charlotte Islands), *B.C., Can.* 84 J6
Hài Dương, *Vietnam* 190 H12
Haifa *see* Ḩefa, *Israel* 172 K5
Haifeng, *Guang., China* 185 W6
Haig, *W. Aust., Austral.* 215 W6
Haiger, *Ger.* 150 F6
Haikou, *China* 182 N9
Haikou, *China* 182 Q12
Haikou, *Hainan, China* 185 Y1
Ha'iku, *Hawai'i, U.S.* 115 G17
Ḩā'il, *Saudi Arabia* 174 H8
Hailar, *China* 183 C14
Hailey, *Idaho, U.S.* 108 G5
Hailing Dao, *Guang., China* 185 X3
Hailun, *China* 183 C16
Hailuoto, island, *Fin.* 143 F15

Haimen, *Guang., China* 185 V7
Haimen *see* Taizhou, *Zhejiang, China* 185 Q12
Haimen Wan, *Guang., China* 185 W7
Hainan, *China* 182 G11
Hainan, *China* 185 Z1
Hainan, island, *China* 182 Q12
Haines, *Alas., U.S.* 113 K21
Haines, *Oreg., U.S.* 110 G8
Haines City, *Fla., U.S.* 99 U8
Haines Junction, *Yukon, Can.* 84 G7
Hainiya Point, *N. Mariana Is., U.S.* 220 E8
Hải Phòng (Haiphong), *Vietnam* 190 H12
Haiphong *see* Hải Phòng, *Vietnam* 190 H12
Haitan Dao, *Fujian, China* 185 T10
Haiti, *N. Amer.* 119 L15
Haixing, *Hebei, China* 184 E8
Haiya, *Sudan* 203 D14
Haiyan, *Zhejiang, China* 185 N11
Haiyang (Dongcun), *Shand., China* 184 G11
Haizhou, *Jiangsu, China* 184 J10
Haizhou Wan, *Jiangsu, China* 184 J10
Hajdúböszörmény, *Hung.* 151 L17
Hajdúdorog, *Hung.* 151 L17
Hajdúszoboszló, *Hung.* 151 L17
Hajiki Saki, *Japan* 188 L11
Hajinbu, *S. Korea* 186 M11
Haji Pir Pass, *India, Pak.* 179 N11
Ḩajjah, *Yemen* 174 P9
Ḩajjīābād, *Iran* 175 G15
Hajnáčka, *Slovakia* 151 K15
Hajnówka, *Pol.* 151 D18
Hajodo, island, *S. Korea* 187 U6
Hakalau, *Hawai'i, U.S.* 115 L21
Hakamaru, island, *Cook Is., N.Z.* 223 B15
Hakataramea, *N.Z.* 217 Q16
Hakauata, island, *Tonga* 222 Q7
Hakdam, *S. Korea* 186 M10
Hakgok, *S. Korea* 186 M9
Hakha, *Myanmar* 190 G4
Hakkari, *Turk.* 171 H18
Hakmang, Puntan, *N. Mariana Is., U.S.* 220 C5
Hakodate, *Japan* 188 H12
Haksong, *N. Korea* 186 G6
Hakui, *Japan* 189 N9
Hakupa Pass, *Solomon Is.* 221 J18
Hakupu, *Cook Is., N.Z.* 223 B21
Hala, *Pak.* 179 V7
Halab (Aleppo), *Syr.* 172 D9
Ḩalabān, *Saudi Arabia* 174 K9
Halachó, *Mex.* 117 H16
Halāli'i Lake, *Hawai'i, U.S.* 114 D3
Halalo, Pointe, *Wallis and Futuna, Fr.* 222 C11
Hala'ula, *Hawai'i, U.S.* 115 K19
Halawa, *Hawai'i, U.S.* 115 K19
Hālawa, Cape, *Hawai'i, U.S.* 115 F15
Hālawa Bay, *Hawai'i, U.S.* 115 F15
Halayeb, *Egypt* 201 F20
Halba, *Leb.* 172 G7
Halban, *Mongolia* 182 C8
Halberstadt, *Ger.* 150 E8
Halcon, Mount, *Philippines* 193 D13
Haldwani, *India* 180 E7
Hale, *Mich., U.S.* 100 J12
Haleakalā Crater, *Hawai'i, U.S.* 115 H17
Haleakalā National Park, *Hawai'i, U.S.* 115 H18
Haleakalā Observatories, *Hawai'i, U.S.* 115 H17
Hale Center, *Tex., U.S.* 104 J5
Hale'iwa, *Hawai'i, U.S.* 114 E10
Haleki'i-Pihana Heiaus, *Hawai'i, U.S.* 115 G16
Haleyville, *Ala., U.S.* 103 H14
Halfeti, *Turk.* 170 H12
Half Moon Bay, *Antigua and Barbuda* 123 B22
Half Moon Bay (Oban), *N.Z.* 217 R15
Halfway, *Oreg., U.S.* 110 G9
Halfweg, *Turk.* 171 G15

Halkett, Cape, *Alas., U.S.* 113 B16
Hálki, *Gr.* 156 F10
Hall, *Aust.* 150 L8
Hallandale, *Fla., U.S.* 99 W10
Hallasan, peak, *S. Korea* 187 W7
Hall Basin, *Nunavut, Can.* 85 F16
Hall Beach, *Nunavut, Can.* 85 F16
Halle, *Belg.* 148 L13
Halle, *Ger.* 150 F9
Hallein, *Aust.* 150 L10
Hallettsville, *Tex., U.S.* 105 R12
Halley, station, *Antarctica* 230 D10
Halliday, *N. Dak., U.S.* 106 F3
Hallim, *S. Korea* 187 W7
Hall Islands, *F.S.M.* 220 Q6
Hall Knoll, *Arctic Oc.* 246 K11
Hällnäs, *Sw.* 143 F14
Hallock, *Minn., U.S.* 106 E8
Hall Peninsula, *Nunavut, Can.* 85 H19
Halls, *Tenn., U.S.* 102 F12
Halls Creek, *W. Aust., Austral.* 215 R6
Hallstadt, *Nor.* 142 H11
Hallstatt, *Aust.* 150 L10
Halmeu, *Rom.* 154 A12
Halmstad, *Sw.* 142 M12
Halmahera, island, *Indonesia* 193 H16
Halmahera Sea, *Indonesia* 193 J16
Halstead, *Eng., U.K.* 145 U15
Halstead, *Kans., U.S.* 107 U7
Haltdalen, *Nor.* 142 H11
Halten Bank, *Atl. Oc.* 240 E13
Halulu Heiau, *Hawai'i, U.S.* 115 H14
Ham, *Fr.* 149 N10
Hamada, *Japan* 189 Q6
Hamadān, *Iran* 174 D11
Hamaguir, *Alg.* 200 C9
Ḩamāh (Hamath), *Syr.* 172 F8
Hāmākua, region, *Hawai'i, U.S.* 115 M20
Hamamatsu, *Japan* 189 Q10
Hamamet, Gulf of, *Af.* 198 C6
Hamar, *Nor.* 142 H11
Hamasaka, *Japan* 189 P8
Ḩamâta, Gebel, *Egypt* 201 E20
Hamath *see* Ḩamāh, *Syr.* 172 F8
Hamatombetsu, *Japan* 188 E13
Hamburg, *Ark., U.S.* 102 K9
Hamburg, *Ger.* 150 C8
Hamburg, *Iowa, U.S.* 107 Q9
Hamburg, *N.Y., U.S.* 96 J5
Hamchang, *S. Korea* 187 Q10
Ḩamdah, *Saudi Arabia* 174 M9
Ḩamdānah, *Saudi Arabia* 174 M7
Hamden, *Conn., U.S.* 96 M12
Hämeenlinna, *Fin.* 143 H16
Hamelin, *W. Aust., Austral.* 215 V1
Hamelin Pool, *Austral.* 214 H1
Hameln, *Ger.* 150 E7
Hamersley Range, *Austral.* 214 F3
Hamgyŏng-sanmaek, range, *N. Korea* 186 F10
Hamhŭng, *N. Korea* 186 G9
Hamhŭng-man, bay, *N. Korea* 186 H9
Hami (Kumul), *China* 182 F7
Hamilton, *Ala., U.S.* 103 H14
Hamilton, *Bermuda* 122 C2
Hamilton, *Ill., U.S.* 101 Q3
Hamilton, *Mo., U.S.* 107 R11
Hamilton, *Mont., U.S.* 108 D5
Hamilton, *N.Y., U.S.* 96 J9
Hamilton, *N.Z.* 217 K19
Hamilton, *Ohio, U.S.* 101 S11
Hamilton, *Ont., Can.* 85 R18
Hamilton, *Scot., U.K.* 144 M9
Hamilton, *Tex., U.S.* 105 N10
Hamilton, *Vic., Austral.* 215 Z11
Hamilton, Lake, *Ark., U.S.* 102 H7
Hamilton Bank, *Atl. Oc.* 240 G6
Hamilton Harbour, *Bermuda* 122 C2
Hamilton Inlet, *Nfld. & Lab., Can.* 85 K22
Hamina, *Fin.* 143 H17
Hami Pendi, *China* 182 F6
Hamirpur, *India* 180 G7
Hamju, *N. Korea* 186 H9
Hamlet, *N.C., U.S.* 98 J10
Hamlin, *Tex., U.S.* 104 L7
Hamm, *Ger.* 150 E6
Hammerfest, *Nor.* 143 B14

Hammon, *Okla., U.S.* 104 G8
Hammond, *Ind., U.S.* 101 N7
Hammond, *La., U.S.* 102 P10
Hammond, *Mont., U.S.* 108 E13
Hammonton, *N.J., U.S.* 96 Q10
Hampden, *N.Z.* 217 Q16
Hampstead, *Dominica* 123 E19
Hampton, *Ark., U.S.* 102 J8
Hampton, *Iowa, U.S.* 106 M12
Hampton, *S.C., U.S.* 98 M9
Hampton, *Va., U.S.* 98 F14
Hampton Bays, *N.Y., U.S.* 97 N13
Hampton Butte, *Oreg., U.S.* 110 H6
Hampton Tableland, *Austral.* 214 J6
Hampyeong, *S. Korea* 187 T7
Ḩamrīn, Jabal, *Iraq* 174 D9
Hamrun, *Malta* 163 K23
Hams Bluff, *Virgin Is., U.S.* 122 Q1
Hāmūn Şāberī, Daryācheh-ye, *Afghan., Iran* 179 Q1
Hamyang, *S. Korea* 187 S9
Hàm Yên, *Vietnam* 190 G11
Han, river, *Guang., China* 185 V7
Han, river, *S. Korea* 186 M8
Han, river, *Shaanxi, China* 184 K2
Hāna, *Hawai'i, U.S.* 115 H18
Hanahan, *P.N.G.* 221 J13
Hanahe, Baie, *Fr. Polynesia, Fr.* 223 N24
Hāna Highway, *Hawai'i, U.S.* 115 H18
Hanahupe, Baie, *Fr. Polynesia, Fr.* 223 N21
Hanaiapa, Baie, *Fr. Polynesia, Fr.* 223 M20
Hanaiapaoa, Baie, *Fr. Polynesia, Fr.* 223 M21
Hanalei, *Hawai'i, U.S.* 114 B5
Hanalei Bay, *Hawai'i, U.S.* 114 B5
Hanam, *S. Korea* 186 M8
Hanam, *S. Korea* 187 S11
Hanamaki, *Japan* 188 K13
Hanamalo Point, *Hawai'i, U.S.* 115 P18
Hanamā'ulu, *Hawai'i, U.S.* 114 C6
Hanamenu, Baie, *Fr. Polynesia, Fr.* 223 M20
Hanaoo, *Fr. Polynesia, Fr.* 223 N20
Hanapēpē, *Hawai'i, U.S.* 114 C5
Hana Teio, *Fr. Polynesia, Fr.* 223 N20
Hana Tetena, *Fr. Polynesia, Fr.* 223 N20
Hana Tuuna, *Fr. Polynesia, Fr.* 223 N20
Hanau, *Ger.* 150 G6
Hanaui, *Fr. Polynesia, Fr.* 223 M20
Hanawa, *Japan* 188 K12
Hancheng, *Shaanxi, China* 184 H2
Hanchuan, *Hubei, China* 185 N5
Hancock, *Md., U.S.* 98 B12
Hancock, *Mich., U.S.* 100 E6
Hancock, *Minn., U.S.* 106 J9
Handa Island, *Scot., U.K.* 144 H9
Handan, *Hebei, China* 184 G6
Handsome Bay, *British Virgin Is., U.K.* 122 R8
Hane, *Fr. Polynesia, Fr.* 223 N23
Hane, Baie d', *Fr. Polynesia, Fr.* 223 N23
Hanford, *Calif., U.S.* 111 U6
Hanford Site, *Wash., U.S.* 110 E7
Hangayn Nuruu, *Mongolia* 182 D8
Hanggin Qi, *N. Mongol, China* 184 C2
Hangö (Hanko), *Fin.* 143 J15
Hangu, *Pak.* 179 N9
Hangu, *Tianjin Shi, China* 184 D9
Hangzhou, *Zhejiang, China* 185 N11
Hangzhou Bay, *Pac. Oc.* 168 G12
Hangzhou Wan, *Zhejiang, China* 185 N11
Hanhöhiy Uul, *Mongolia* 182 C7
Hani, *Turk.* 171 G15
Hanimadu, island, *Maldives* 181 T3
Ḩanīsh al Kabīr, Jazīrat al, *Yemen* 174 Q8
Hankinson, *N. Dak., U.S.* 106 H8
Hanko *see* Hangö, *Fin.* 143 J15
Hanksville, *Utah, U.S.* 109 N8
Hanle, *India* 179 N15
Hann, Mount, *Austral.* 214 C5
Hanna, *Alta., Can.* 84 M10
Hanna Bank, *Arctic Oc.* 246 K7
Hanna Canyon, *Arctic Oc.* 246 L7

Hannibal, *Mo., U.S.* **107** R14
Hannover (Hanover), *Ger.* **150** D7
Hanöbukten, *bay, Sw.* **143** N13
Hà Nội (Hanoi), *Vietnam* **190** H12
Hanoi *see* Hà Nội, *Vietnam* **190** H12
Hanover, *Kans., U.S.* **107** R8
Hanover, *N.H., U.S.* **97** H13
Hanover, *Pa., U.S.* **96** Q7
Hanover, *Isla, Chile* **135** W6
Hanpan, Cape, *P.N.G.* **221** j13
Hansen Mountains, *Antarctica* **231** E19
Hans Lollik Island, *Virgin Is., U.S.* **122** M9
Hantsavichy, *Belarus* **158** L4
Hanumangarh, *India* **180** E4
Hanuy, *river, Mongolia* **182** C9
Hanyang, *Hubei, China* **185** N5
Hanyuan, *China* **182** L9
Hanzhong, *China* **182** K11
Hao, *island, Fr. Polynesia, Fr.* **223** F20
Haora, *India* **181** J12
Hāʻōʻū, *Hawaiʻi, U.S.* **115** H18
Hapai, *Solomon Is.* **221** M16
Haparanda, *Sw.* **143** E15
Hapatoni, Baie, *Fr. Polynesia, Fr.* **223** N20
Hapcheon, *S. Korea* **187** S10
Hapdeok, *S. Korea* **187** P8
Hapo, *Indonesia* **193** H16
Happy, *Tex., U.S.* **104** H5
Happy Camp, *Calif., U.S.* **110** L2
Happy Valley-Goose Bay, *Nfld. & Lab., Can.* **85** L21
Ḩaql, *Saudi Arabia* **174** F5
Har, *Indonesia* **193** L18
Ḩaraḑ, *Saudi Arabia* **174** K12
Ḩarad, Jabal al, *Jordan* **173** R6
Haradok, *Belarus* **158** J6
Haradzishcha, *Belarus* **158** L4
Haraiki, *island, Fr. Polynesia, Fr.* **223** E19
Harappa, *ruins, Pak.* **179** R11
Harare, *Zimb.* **206** F11
Ḩarāsīs, Jiddat al, *Oman* **175** M15
Haratini, *island, Cook Is., N.Z.* **223** C15
Har Ayrag, *Mongolia* **182** E11
Harbin, *China* **183** D16
Harbor Beach, *Mich., U.S.* **100** K13
Harbor Pearl, *Hawaiʻi, U.S.* **114** F11
Harbor Springs, *Mich., U.S.* **100** H10
Harbour Island, *Bahamas* **122** D5
Harbours, Bay of, *Falk. Is., U.K.* **135** W12
Harda, *India* **180** J5
Hardangerfjorden, *bay, Nor.* **142** K10
Hard Bargain, *Bahamas* **122** B5
Hardenberg, *Neth.* **148** H14
Harderwijk, *Neth.* **148** J13
Hardin, *Ill., U.S.* **101** S3
Hardin, *Mont., U.S.* **108** E11
Harding, *S. Af.* **206** L11
Hardman, *Oreg., U.S.* **110** F6
Hardwick, *Ga., U.S.* **98** M6
Hardy, *Ark., U.S.* **102** E9
Hardy, Península, *Chile* **135** Y9
Hardy, Pointe, *St. Lucia* **123** J14
Hārer (Harar), *Eth.* **203** G16
Hargeysa, *Somalia* **203** G16
Har Hu, *China* **182** H7
Harī, *river, Afghan., Iran* **178** L1
Haría, *Sp.* **208** P7
Haridwar, *India* **180** E6
Harihari, *N.Z.* **217** N16
Harij, *India* **180** H3
Ḩārim, *Syr.* **172** D8
Haripur, *Pak.* **179** N11
Harirud, *river, Asia* **175** C17
Harkány, *Hung.* **151** N14
Harlan, *Iowa, U.S.* **107** P10
Harlan, *Ky., U.S.* **103** D19
Harlem, *Mont., U.S.* **108** B10
Harlingen, *Neth.* **148** G13
Harlingen, *Tex., U.S.* **105** W11
Harlowton, *Mont., U.S.* **108** D9
Harmancık, *Turk.* **170** E5
Harmony, *Minn., U.S.* **106** L13
Harnai, *Pak.* **179** R7
Harney Basin, *Oreg., U.S.* **110** J7
Harney Lake, *Oreg., U.S.* **110** J7

Harney Peak, *S. Dak., U.S.* **106** L1
Harnom Point, *N. Mariana Is., U.S.* **220** E7
Härnösand, *Sw.* **143** H13
Har Nuur, *Mongolia* **182** C7
Haro, *Sp.* **146** C12
Haroldswick, *Scot., U.K.* **144** C12
Harpanahalli, *India* **181** N5
Harper, *Kans., U.S.* **107** V7
Harper, *Liberia* **204** F7
Harper Lake, *Calif., U.S.* **111** W9
Harpers Ferry, *W. Va., U.S.* **98** C12
Harput, *Turk.* **171** G14
Harqin, *Liaoning, China* **184** B10
Harqin Qi, *N. Mongol, China* **184** A9
Ḩarrah, *Yemen* **174** Q12
Harrai, *India* **180** J7
Harran, *Turk.* **171** J13
Harray, Loch of, *Scot., U.K.* **144** F10
Harricana, *river, Ont., Que., Can.* **85** N18
Harriet Tubman Underground Railroad National Monument, *Md., U.S.* **98** D15
Harriman, *Tenn., U.S.* **103** E18
Harrington, *Wash., U.S.* **110** C8
Harrington Harbour, *Que., Can.* **85** M22
Harrington Sound, *Bermuda* **122** B3
Harris, *Montserrat* **123** B24
Harris, Lake, *Austral.* **214** J9
Harris, Sound of, *Scot., U.K.* **144** J6
Harrisburg, *Ark., U.S.* **102** F10
Harrisburg, *Ill., U.S.* **101** U6
Harrisburg, *Nebr., U.S.* **107** P1
Harrisburg, *Oreg., U.S.* **110** G3
Harrisburg, *Pa., U.S.* **96** P7
Harrison, *Ark., U.S.* **102** E7
Harrison, *Idaho, U.S.* **108** C3
Harrison, *Mich., U.S.* **100** K10
Harrison, *Nebr., U.S.* **106** M1
Harrison, Cape, *N. Amer.* **82** F10
Harrison Bay, *Alas., U.S.* **113** B16
Harrisonburg, *La., U.S.* **102** M9
Harrisonburg, *Va., U.S.* **98** D11
Harrison Point, *Barbados* **123** J18
Harrisonville, *Mo., U.S.* **107** T10
Harrisville, *Mich., U.S.* **100** J12
Harrodsburg, *Ky., U.S.* **103** C17
Harrogate, *Eng., U.K.* **145** R12
Harry S. Truman Reservoir, *Mo., U.S.* **107** T11
Harşit, *river, Turk.* **171** D13
Harstad, *Nor.* **142** D12
Hart, *Mich., U.S.* **100** K9
Hart, *Tex., U.S.* **104** H5
Hartao, *Liaoning, China* **184** A12
Hartford, *Ala., U.S.* **103** N17
Hartford, *Ark., U.S.* **102** G6
Hartford, *Conn., U.S.* **97** L13
Hartford, *Mich., U.S.* **101** N9
Hartford, *S. Dak., U.S.* **106** L8
Hartford, *Vt., U.S.* **97** H13
Hartford, *Wis., U.S.* **100** L6
Hartford City, *Ind., U.S.* **101** Q10
Hartington, *Nebr., U.S.* **107** N8
Hart Lake, *Oreg., U.S.* **110** K6
Hartland Point, *Eng., U.K.* **145** W9
Hartley, *Iowa, U.S.* **106** M9
Hartley, *Tex., U.S.* **104** F4
Hart Mountain, *Oreg., U.S.* **110** K6
Hartog Ridge, *Ind. Oc.* **225** M16
Hartselle, *Ala., U.S.* **103** H15
Hartshorne, *Okla., U.S.* **104** H13
Hartsville, *S.C., U.S.* **98** K10
Hartsville, *Tenn., U.S.* **103** E16
Hartwell, *Ga., U.S.* **98** K7
Hartwell Lake, *Ga., S.C., U.S.* **98** K7
Har Us Nuur, *Mongolia* **182** C7
Hārūt, *river, Afghan.* **179** P1
Harūz-e Bālā, *Iran* **175** F15
Harvard, *Ill., U.S.* **100** M6
Harvard, *Nebr., U.S.* **107** Q7
Harvey, *N. Dak., U.S.* **106** F5
Harz, *range, Ger.* **150** E8
Ḩaşānah, *Yemen* **174** Q12
Hasan Dağı, *peak, Turk.* **170** G9
Ḩasan Langī, *Iran* **175** H15
Hasa Plain, *Asia* **168** H4
Haseo, *S. Korea* **187** R12
Hashaat, *Mongolia* **182** E10

Ḩāsik, *Oman* **175** N15
Hasil, *island, Indonesia* **193** J16
Hasilpur, *Pak.* **179** R10
Haskeir *see* Eilean Hasgeir, *island, Scot., U.K.* **144** J6
Haskell, *Okla., U.S.* **104** F13
Haskell, *Tex., U.S.* **104** K8
Hassel Sound, *Nunavut, Can.* **85** B14
Hassi Messaoud, *Alg.* **200** C11
Hassi R'mel, *Alg.* **200** B11
Hässleholm, *Sw.* **143** M13
Hastings, *Barbados* **123** L19
Hastings, *Eng., U.K.* **145** W15
Hastings, *Mich., U.S.* **100** M10
Hastings, *Minn., U.S.* **106** K12
Hastings, *N.Z.* **217** L20
Hastings, *Nebr., U.S.* **107** Q6
Hastings, battlefied, *Eng., U.K.* **145** W15
Hasvik, *Nor.* **143** B13
Haswell, *Colo., U.S.* **109** N15
Hat *see* Teuaua, *point, Fr. Polynesia, Fr.* **223** N23
Hataedo, *island, S. Korea* **187** U5
Hataedo, *island, S. Korea* **187** U6
Hatch, *N. Mex., U.S.* **109** V11
Hatchie, *river, Tenn., U.S.* **102** F12
Haţeg, *Rom.* **154** E12
Hatgal, *Mongolia* **182** C9
Hatherleigh, *Eng., U.K.* **145** W9
Hatherton Seamounts, *Pac. Oc.* **249** J22
Ḩāţibah, Ra's, *Saudi Arabia* **174** L6
Hà Tiên, *Cambodia* **191** P11
Hatillo, *P.R., U.S.* **122** M2
Hà Tĩnh, *Vietnam* **190** J12
Hato, Bocht van, *Curaçao, Neth.* **123** P14
Hato Caves, *site, Curaçao, Neth.* **123** P14
Hato Mayor, *Dom. Rep.* **119** M20
Hà Trung, *Vietnam* **190** H12
Hatteras, *N.C., U.S.* **98** H15
Hatteras, Cape, *N.C., U.S.* **98** H15
Hatteras Plain, *Atl. Oc.* **240** K4
Hattiesburg, *Miss., U.S.* **102** N12
Hatton, *N. Dak., U.S.* **106** F7
Hatton Ridge, *Atl. Oc.* **240** F10
Hatton-Rockall Basin, *Atl. Oc.* **247** M23
Hatunuru, *Indonesia* **193** K16
Hatutu, *island, Fr. Polynesia, Fr.* **219** H15
Hatvan, *Hung.* **151** L15
Hat Yai, *Thai.* **191** S9
Haud, *region, Eth.* **203** G17
Haugesund, *Nor.* **142** K9
Haugsdorf, *Aust.* **150** J12
Hauido, *island, S. Korea* **187** U6
Haukeligrend, *Nor.* **142** K10
Haukipudas, *Fin.* **143** F15
Haukivesi, *lake, Fin.* **143** G17
Haulover, *Nicar.* **117** M19
Haunanu, Pointe, *Fr. Polynesia, Fr.* **223** M23
Hauola Place of Refuge, *Hawaiʻi, U.S.* **114** C6
Haupt Kanal, *Liech.* **162** N2
Hauraki Gulf, *N.Z.* **217** J19
Hauser, *Oreg., U.S.* **110** H2
Haut, Isle au, *Me., U.S.* **97** G18
Hauteurs de Gâtine, *Fr.* **149** S6
Hauturu-o-Toi (Little Barrier Island), *N.Z.* **217** H19
Hauʻula, *Hawaiʻi, U.S.* **114** E11
Havana, *Fla., U.S.* **99** Q5
Havana, *Ill., U.S.* **101** Q4
Havana *see* La Habana, *Cuba* **118** G6
Havannah, Canal de la, *New Caledonia, Fr.* **222** E9
Havant, *Eng., U.K.* **145** W13
Havasu, Lake, *Ariz., Calif., U.S.* **111** W13
Havel, *river, Ger.* **150** C10
Havelberg, *Ger.* **150** D9
Haveli, *Pak.* **179** R11
Havelock, *N.C., U.S.* **98** J14
Haveluloto, *Tonga* **222** H11
Haven, *Kans., U.S.* **107** U7
Haverfordwest (Hwlffordd), *Wales, U.K.* **145** V8

Haverhill, *Eng., U.K.* **145** U14
Haverhill, *Mass., U.S.* **97** J15
Haveri, *India* **181** N4
Haviland, *Kans., U.S.* **107** U6
Havíŕov, *Czech Rep.* **151** H14
Havlíčkův Brod, *Czech Rep.* **150** H12
Havre, *Mont., U.S.* **108** B9
Havre de Grace, *Md., U.S.* **98** B14
Havre-Saint-Pierre, *Que., Can.* **85** M21
Havre Trough, *Pac. Oc.* **249** H22
Havza, *Turk.* **170** D11
Hawaiʻi, *island, Hawaiʻi, U.S.* **115** M17
Hawaiian Islands, *Pac. Oc.* **218** C10
Hawaiian Ridge, *Pac. Oc.* **242** F11
Hawaiʻi Belt Road, *Hawaiʻi, U.S.* **115** P20
Hawaiʻi Volcanoes National Park, *Hawaiʻi, U.S.* **115** N20
Hawangdeungdo, *island, S. Korea* **187** R6
Hawarden, *Iowa, U.S.* **106** M8
Hawarden, *Wales, U.K.* **145** S10
Hāwea, Lake, *N.Z.* **217** P16
Ḩawf, *Yemen* **175** P14
Hāwī, *Hawaiʻi, U.S.* **115** K19
Hawick, *Scot., U.K.* **145** N11
Hawke Bay, *N.Z.* **217** L20
Hawker, *S. Aust., Austral.* **215** W10
Hawkeye Point, *peak, Iowa, U.S.* **106** M9
Hawkinsville, *Ga., U.S.* **99** N6
Hawley, *Minn., U.S.* **106** G8
Hawr al Hammār, *lake, Asia* **168** G3
Hawthorne, *Nev., U.S.* **111** R8
Haxtun, *Colo., U.S.* **108** K15
Hay, *river, Alta., Can.* **84** J10
Hay, *river, Austral.* **214** F10
Hayange, *Fr.* **149** N13
Hayes, *Jam.* **122** K8
Hayes, *S. Dak., U.S.* **106** K4
Hayes, *river, Man., Can.* **85** L14
Hayes, Mount, *Alas., U.S.* **113** G17
Hayes Center, *Nebr., U.S.* **107** Q4
Hayes Fracture Zone, *Atl. Oc.* **240** K7
Hayes Peninsula, *Greenland, Den.* **82** C7
Hayfork, *Calif., U.S.* **111** N2
Hayling Island, *Eng., U.K.* **145** W13
Haymā', *Oman* **175** M15
Haymana, *Turk.* **170** E8
Haynesville, *La., U.S.* **102** K7
Hayneville, *Ala., U.S.* **103** L15
Haynin, *Yemen* **174** P11
Hayrabolu, *Turk.* **170** C3
Hay River, *N.W.T., Can.* **84** H11
Hays, *Kans., U.S.* **107** S5
Hays, *Mont., U.S.* **108** B10
Hay Springs, *Nebr., U.S.* **106** M2
Haysville, *Kans., U.S.* **107** U7
Haysyn, *Ukr.* **159** P5
Hayti, *Mo., U.S.* **107** W16
Hayvoron, *Ukr.* **159** Q5
Hayward, *Calif., U.S.* **111** S4
Hayward, *Wis., U.S.* **100** G3
Hazārah Jāt, *region, Afghan.* **179** N5
Hazard, *Ky., U.S.* **103** C19
Hazar Gölü, *Turk.* **171** G14
Hazārqadam, *Afghan.* **179** P6
Ḩaz̧ awz̧ ā', Sabkhat, *Saudi Arabia* **174** F6
Hazebrouck, *Fr.* **148** L10
Hazelton, *N. Dak., U.S.* **106** H5
Hazen, *Ark., U.S.* **102** G9
Hazen, *N. Dak., U.S.* **106** F4
Hazen, *Nev., U.S.* **111** P7
Hazlehurst, *Ga., U.S.* **99** N7
Hazlehurst, *Miss., U.S.* **102** M11
Hazleton, *Pa., U.S.* **96** N8
Hazro, *Turk.* **171** G15
Head of Barkers, *Cayman Is.* **122** H1
Head of Bight, *Austral.* **214** J8
Healdsburg, *Calif., U.S.* **111** Q3
Healdton, *Okla., U.S.* **104** J11
Healy, *Alas., U.S.* **113** G17
Healy, *Kans., U.S.* **107** T4
Héani, Mount, *Fr. Polynesia, Fr.* **223** M20
Hearne, *Tex., U.S.* **105** P12
Hearst, *Ont., Can.* **85** N17

Hearst Island, *Antarctica* **230** E6
Heart, *river, N. Dak., U.S.* **106** G3
Heath, Pointe, *Que., Can.* **85** M22
Heavener, *Okla., U.S.* **104** H14
Hebbronville, *Tex., U.S.* **105** U9
Hebei, *China* **184** E6
Hebel, *Qnsld., Austral.* **215** V14
Heber, *Ariz., U.S.* **109** T8
Heber City, *Utah, U.S.* **108** L7
Heber Springs, *Ark., U.S.* **102** F9
Hebgen Lake, *Mont., U.S.* **108** F8
Hebi, *Henan, China* **184** G6
Hefeng, *Hubei, China* **185** N2
Heflin, *Ala., U.S.* **103** J17
Hegura Jima, *Japan* **188** M10
Heiau o Kalalea, *Hawaiʻi, U.S.* **115** Q19
Heiau o Mōʻīlele, *Hawaiʻi, U.S.* **115** Q19
Heichengzi, *Liaoning, China* **184** A11
Heide, *Ger.* **150** B7
Heidelberg, *Ger.* **150** H6
Heidelberg, *Miss., U.S.* **102** M12
Heidenheim, *Ger.* **150** J7
Heiderscheid, *Lux.* **162** H9
Heihe, *China* **183** B16
Heilbronn, *Ger.* **150** J7
Heilong Jiang, *river, China* **183** A14
Heimaey, *island, Ice.* **142** F2
Heinerscheid, *Lux.* **162** G10
Heinola, *Fin.* **143** H16
Heishan, *Liaoning, China* **184** B12
Heishui, *Liaoning, China* **184** A10
Heisker Islands *see* Na h-Eileanan Theisgeir, *Scot., U.K.* **144** J6
Hejaz *see* Al Ḩijāz, *region, Saudi Arabia* **174** H6
Hejian, *Hebei, China* **184** E7
Hejing, *China* **182** E5
Hekimhan, *Turk.* **170** F12
Hekla, *peak, Ice.* **142** F2
Hekou, *China* **182** P10
Hekou, *Shand., China* **184** E9
Helagsfjället, *peak, Sw.* **142** H12
Hele Islands, *Solomon Is.* **221** N16
Helena, *Ark., U.S.* **102** H10
Helena, *Ga., U.S.* **99** N7
Helena, *Mont., U.S.* **108** D7
Helena, *Okla., U.S.* **104** E10
Helena *see* Makrónisos, *island, Gr.* **157** K13
Helengili, *island, Maldives* **181** U3
Helen Islands, *Palau* **218** F2
Helgoländer Bay, *Atl. Oc.* **140** F6
Helgoländer Bucht, *Ger.* **150** B6
Helicon *see* Elikónas, *peak, Gr.* **156** H12
Hell, *Cayman Is.* **122** H1
Hell, *Nor.* **142** G11
Hell-Bourg, *Réunion, Fr.* **209** G15
Hellenic Trough, *Atl. Oc.* **240** K15

Hellevoetsluis, *Neth.* **148** J11
Hellín, *Sp.* **147** J13
Hellissandur, *Ice.* **142** E1
Hells Canyon, *Idaho, Oreg., U.S.* **110** F9
Hells Canyon Dam, *Idaho, Oreg., U.S.* **110** F9
Hells Canyon National Recreation Area, *Idaho, Oreg., U.S.* **110** E9
Helmand, river, *Afghan.* **179** P5
Helmsdale, *Scot., U.K.* **144** H10
Helper, *Utah, U.S.* **108** M8
Helsingborg, *Sw.* **142** M11
Helsinki (Helsingfors), *Fin.* **143** J16
Hemet, *Calif., U.S.* **111** W10
Hemingford, *Nebr., U.S.* **107** N2
Hempstead, *N.Y., U.S.* **96** N11
Hempstead, *Tex., U.S.* **105** Q13
Henan, *China* **184** J4
Henashi Zaki, *Japan* **188** J12
Hendaye, *Fr.* **149** X5
Hendek, *Turk.* **170** D6
Henderson, *Ky., U.S.* **103** C14
Henderson, *N.C., U.S.* **98** G12
Henderson, *Nev., U.S.* **111** U12
Henderson, *Tenn., U.S.* **103** F13
Henderson, *Tex., U.S.* **104** M14
Henderson Island, *Pac. Oc.* **219** K16
Hendersonville, *N.C., U.S.* **98** J7
Hendersonville, *Tenn., U.S.* **103** E15
Hengchun, *Taiwan, China* **185** X12
Hengduan Shan, *China* **182** L7
Hengelo, *Neth.* **148** J14
Heng Shan, *Shanxi, China* **184** D5
Hengshan, *China* **183** D17
Hengshan, *Hunan, China* **185** R4
Hengshan, *Shaanxi, China* **184** E2
Hengshui, *Hebei, China* **184** F7
Hengyang, *Hunan, China* **185** S4
Heniches'k, *Ukr.* **159** S8
Henlopen, Cape, *Del., U.S.* **98** C15
Hennebont, *Fr.* **149** R4
Hennessey, *Okla., U.S.* **104** F10
Hennigsdorf, *Ger.* **150** D10
Henning, *Minn., U.S.* **106** H9
Henrietta, *Tex., U.S.* **104** J10
Henrietta, Ostrov, *Russ.* **161** C17
Henrietta Maria, Cape, *Ont., Can.* **85** L17
Henry, Cape, *Va., U.S.* **98** F14
Henryetta, *Okla., U.S.* **104** G12
Henry Kater Peninsula, *Nunavut, Can.* **85** F18
Henrys Fork, river, *Idaho, U.S.* **108** G7
Henry Trough, *Pac. Oc.* **243** Q16
Henslow, Cape, *Solomon Is.* **221** P19
Heping, *Guang., China* **185** U6
Heppner, *Oreg., U.S.* **110** F6
Hequ, *Shanxi, China* **184** D3
Herald, Ostrov, *Russ.* **161** A19
Herald Bank, *Arctic Oc.* **246** K6
Herald Cays, *Austral.* **214** C14
Herald Valley, *Arctic Oc.* **246** J6
Herāt, *Afghan.* **178** M2
Herbault, *Fr.* **149** R8
Herbert, *Sask., Can.* **84** N11
Herbert Downs, *Qnsld., Austral.* **215** T11
Hercules Dome, *Antarctica* **230** J12
Hereford, *Eng., U.K.* **145** U11
Hereford, *Tex., U.S.* **104** H4
Hereheretue, island, *Fr. Polynesia, Fr.* **223** G18
Herford, *Ger.* **150** E6
Herington, *Kans., U.S.* **107** T8
Herisau, *Switz.* **152** A4
Hérisson, *Fr.* **149** T10
Heritage Range, *Antarctica* **230** H9
Herkimer, *N.Y., U.S.* **96** J10
Herlacher, Cape, *Antarctica* **230** L7
Herlen, river, *Mongolia* **183** D12
Herm, island, *Channel Is., U.K.* **145** Z11
Herman, *Minn., U.S.* **106** H8
Hermann, *Mo., U.S.* **107** T14
Hermannsburg, *N.T., Austral.* **215** T8
Hermansville, *Mich., U.S.* **100** G7
Hermanus, *S. Af.* **206** M7
Hermiston, *Oreg., U.S.* **110** E7
Hermit Islands, *P.N.G.* **217** B19

Hermleigh, *Tex., U.S.* **104** L6
Hermon, Mount, *Leb.* **172** J7
Hermosa, *S. Dak., U.S.* **106** L2
Hermosa, Punta, *Eq. Guinea* **208** L8
Hermosillo, *Mex.* **116** C7
Hernando, *Arg.* **134** K10
Hernando, *Miss., U.S.* **102** G11
Hernani, *Sp.* **147** B13
Herne, *Ger.* **150** E5
Hero Fracture Zone, *Pac. Oc.* **248** N11
Herreid, *S. Dak., U.S.* **106** H5
Herrera, *Arg.* **134** H10
Herrera del Duque, *Sp.* **146** H9
Herrera de Pisuerga, *Sp.* **146** C10
Herrin, *Ill., U.S.* **101** U5
Herschel Island, *Yukon, Can.* **84** D9
Hershey, *Nebr., U.S.* **107** P4
Hertford, *Eng., U.K.* **145** V14
Hertford, *N.C., U.S.* **98** G14
Hervás, *Sp.* **146** F8
Hervey Bay, *Austral.* **214** G16
Hervey Bay, *Qnsld., Austral.* **215** U16
Hervey Islands, *Cook Is., N.Z.* **218** K12
Herzberg, *Ger.* **150** E10
Həsənabad, *Azerb.* **171** E23
Heshun, *Shanxi, China* **184** F5
Hesperange, *Lux.* **162** K10
Hess Rise, *Pac. Oc.* **242** E11
Hettinger, *N. Dak., U.S.* **106** H3
Heungdeok, *S. Korea* **187** S7
Heunghae, *S. Korea* **187** Q12
Heuru, *Solomon Is.* **221** P20
Hewlêr (Arbîl, Erbil), *Iraq* **174** C9
Heyang, *Shaanxi, China* **184** H2
Heyuan, *Guang., China* **185** V6
Hezār, Kūh-e, *Iran* **175** G15
Heze, *Shand., China* **184** H7
Hezhou (Babu), *Guangxi Zhuang, China* **185** U3
Hezuo, *China* **182** J9
Hialeah, *Fla., U.S.* **99** X10
Hiawatha, *Kans., U.S.* **107** R9
Hibbing, *Minn., U.S.* **106** F11
Hicacos, Península de, *Cuba* **118** G7
Hickam Air Force Base, *Hawai'i, U.S.* **114** F11
Hickman, *Ky., U.S.* **102** E12
Hickmann, *Arg.* **134** E10
Hickory, *N.C., U.S.* **98** H8
Hicks Bay, *N.Z.* **217** J20
Hicksville, *Ohio, U.S.* **101** P11
Hico, *Tex., U.S.* **104** M10
Hidaka Sammyaku, *Japan* **188** G14
Hidalgo del Parral, *Mex.* **116** E9
Hienghène, *New Caledonia, Fr.* **222** C7
Hienghéne, Baie de, *New Caledonia, Fr.* **222** C7
Hierro (Ferro), island, *Sp.* **208** R3
Higgins, *Tex., U.S.* **104** F7
Higgins Lake, *Mich., U.S.* **100** J10
Higginsville, *Mo., U.S.* **107** S11
Higginsville, *W. Aust., Austral.* **215** W4
High Atlas, range, *Af.* **198** C3
High Cay, *Bahamas* **122** F11
High Cliff Point, *Grenada* **123** J24
Highgate, *Jam.* **122** H9
High Island, *Tex., U.S.* **105** R15
Highland, *Ill., U.S.* **101** T5
Highland Park, *Ill., U.S.* **101** N7
Highlands, *Scot., U.K.* **144** K9
High Level, *Alta., Can.* **84** J10
Highmore, *S. Dak., U.S.* **106** K5
High Plains, *N. Amer.* **82** K5
High Point, *N.C., U.S.* **98** H10
High Point, peak, *N.J., U.S.* **96** M10
High Red Rock, *Norfolk I., Austral.* **221** G20
High Rock, *Bahamas* **122** E3
High Springs, *Fla., U.S.* **99** R7
High Willhays, peak, *Eng., U.K.* **145** X9
Higüero, Punta, *P.R., U.S.* **119** M22
Higüey, *Dom. Rep.* **119** M20
Hiiumaa (Dagö), island, *Est.* **143** K15
Híjar, *Sp.* **147** E14
Ḩijārah, Şaḩrā al, *Iraq* **174** F9
Ḩijāz, Jabal al, *Saudi Arabia* **174** M8
Hikiau Heiau, *Hawai'i, U.S.* **115** N18
Hiko, *Nev., U.S.* **111** S11

Hikueru, island, *Fr. Polynesia, Fr.* **223** E19
Hikurangi, peak, *N.Z.* **217** K20
Hikurangi Plateau, *Pac. Oc.* **242** P12
Hikurangi Seachannel, *Pac. Oc.* **249** I21
Hikurangi Terrace, *Pac. Oc.* **242** P11
Hikutavake, *Niue, N.Z.* **223** A20
Hilāl, Ras al, *Af.* **198** C7
Hildesheim, *Ger.* **150** E7
Hilina Pali, *Hawai'i, U.S.* **115** P20
Hillaby, Mount, *Barbados* **123** K19
Hillary Coast, *Antarctica* **231** N14
Hill City, *Kans., U.S.* **107** S5
Hill City, *Minn., U.S.* **106** G11
Hill City, *S. Dak., U.S.* **106** L1
Hill Country, *Tex., U.S.* **105** Q8
Hillman, *Mich., U.S.* **100** H11
Hillsboro, *Ill., U.S.* **101** S5
Hillsboro, *Kans., U.S.* **107** T8
Hillsboro, *N. Dak., U.S.* **106** F8
Hillsboro, *N. Mex., U.S.* **109** U11
Hillsboro, *Ohio, U.S.* **101** S12
Hillsboro, *Oreg., U.S.* **110** F3
Hillsboro, *Tex., U.S.* **104** M11
Hillsborough, *Grenada* **121** H17
Hillsborough, *N. Ire., U.K.* **145** Q7
Hillsborough Bay, *Trinidad and Tobago* **123** N18
Hillsdale, *Mich., U.S.* **101** N11
Hillside, *W. Aust., Austral.* **215** T3
Hillsville, *Va., U.S.* **98** G9
Hillswick, *Scot., U.K.* **144** D12
Hilo, *Hawai'i, U.S.* **115** M21
Hilo, region, *Hawai'i, U.S.* **115** M21
Hilo Bay, *Hawai'i, U.S.* **115** M21
Hilton Head Island, *S.C., U.S.* **99** N9
Hilvan, *Turk.* **171** H13
Himadítida, Límni, *Gr.* **156** C9
Himalaya, range, *Asia* **168** H7
Himatnagar, *India* **180** H3
Himeji, *Japan* **189** Q8
Ḩimş (Homs), *Syr.* **172** G8
Hinako, Kepulauan, *Indonesia* **192** J4
Hinche, *Haiti* **119** L17
Hinchinbrook Island, *Alas., U.S.* **113** K18
Hinchinbrook Island, *Austral.* **214** D13
Hinckley, *Minn., U.S.* **106** H12
Hindaun, *India* **180** G6
Hindmarsh, Lake, *Austral.* **214** L11
Hindu Kush, *Afghan., Pak.* **178** L8
Hines, *Oreg., U.S.* **110** J7
Hines Creek, *Alta., Can.* **84** K10
Hinesville, *Ga., U.S.* **99** N8
Hinganghat, *India* **180** K6
Hingol, river, *Pak.* **179** V4
Hingorja, *Pak.* **179** U7
Hinidan, *Pak.* **179** V6
Ḩinis, *Turk.* **171** F16
Hinnøya, island, *Nor.* **142** D12
Hinthada, *Myanmar* **190** K5
Hinton, *Okla., U.S.* **104** G9
Hinton, *W. Va., U.S.* **98** E8
Hippolytushoef, *Neth.* **148** H12
Hirado Shima, *Japan* **189** R4
Hiranai, *Japan* **188** J12
Hira Se, island, *Japan* **189** U4
Hirata, *Japan* **189** P6
Hirfanlı Barajı, *Turk.* **170** F9
Hiroo, *Japan* **188** H14
Hirosaki, *Japan* **188** J12
Hiroshima, *Japan* **189** Q6
Hirson, *Fr.* **148** M11
Hîrşova, *Rom.* **155** F17
Hisarönü, *Turk.* **170** C7
Ḩismá, plain, *Saudi Arabia* **174** G5
Hispaniola, island, *N. Amer.* **119** M18
Ḩisyah, *Syr.* **172** H8
Hita, *Japan* **189** R5
Hitachi, *Japan* **189** P8
Hitadu, island, *Maldives* **181** W3
Hitadu, island, *Maldives* **181** X3
Hiti, island, *Fr. Polynesia, Fr.* **223** E19
Hitiaa, *Fr. Polynesia, Fr.* **223** P17
Hitoyoshi, *Japan* **189** S5
Hitra, island, *Nor.* **142** G10
Hiu, island, *Vanuatu* **222** A1
Hiva Oa, island, *Fr. Polynesia, Fr.* **223** M21

Hiwassee, river, *N.C., Tenn., U.S.* **103** F17
Hizan, *Turk.* **171** G17
Hjälmaren, lake, *Sw.* **143** K13
Hjørring, *Den.* **142** M11
Hjort Trench, *Pac. Oc.* **249** G17
Hkakabo Razi, peak, *Myanmar* **190** C7
Hlohovec, *Slovakia* **151** K14
Hlukhiv, *Ukr.* **158** M7
Hlybokaye, *Belarus* **158** J5
Hněvkovice, *Czech Rep.* **150** H11
Hnúšťa, *Slovakia* **151** J15
Ho, *Ghana* **204** E11
Hòa Bình, *Vietnam* **190** H12
Hoanib, river, *Namibia* **206** G5
Hoare Bay, *Nunavut, Can.* **85** G19
Hoban, *N. Korea* **186** F9
Hobart, *Ind., U.S.* **101** P8
Hobart, *Okla., U.S.* **104** H8
Hobart, *Tas., Austral.* **215** Z8
Hobbs, *N. Mex., U.S.* **109** U15
Hobbs Coast, *Antarctica* **230** M8
Hobe Sound, *Fla., U.S.* **99** V10
Hoboksar, *China* **182** D5
Hobq Shamo, *N. Mongol, China* **184** B1
Hobro, *Den.* **142** M11
Hobucken, *N.C., U.S.* **98** H14
Hobyo, *Somalia* **203** H18
Ho Chi Minh City *see* Thành Phố Hồ Chí Minh (Saigon), *Vietnam* **191** P13
Hŏch'ŏn, river, *N. Korea* **186** E10
Hodge, *La., U.S.* **102** L8
Hodgenville, *Ky., U.S.* **103** C16
Hodgson Downs, *N.T., Austral.* **215** Q9
Hodh, region, *Af.* **198** F2
Hódmezővásárhely, *Hung.* **151** M16
Hodo, *N. Korea* **186** J9
Hodonín, *Czech Rep.* **151** J13
Hödrögö, *Mongolia* **182** C8
Hoech'ang, *N. Korea* **186** J7
Hoedic, Île, *Fr.* **149** R4
Hoedspruit, *S. Af.* **206** H11
Hoenggando, island, *S. Korea* **187** V7
Hoengseong, *S. Korea* **187** N10
Hoeryŏng, *N. Korea* **186** B12
Hoeyang, *N. Korea* **186** K9
Hof, *Ger.* **150** G9
Höfðakaupstaður, *Ice.* **142** D3
Hoffman, *N.C., U.S.* **98** H9
Höfn, *Ice.* **142** F4
Hofsjökull, glacier, *Ice.* **142** E3
Hogansville, *Ga., U.S.* **98** M4
Hog Cay, *Bahamas* **122** F9
Hog Island, *Grenada* **123** L22
Hog Island, *Va., U.S.* **98** E15
Hohenems, *Aust.* **150** L7
Hohenwald, *Tenn., U.S.* **103** F14
Hohe Tauern, range, *Aust.* **150** M9
Hohhot, *N. Mongol, China* **184** B4
Hohonu, island, *Fr. Polynesia, Fr.* **223** K18
Hoh Xil Shan, *China* **182** H5
Hội An, *Vietnam* **190** L13
Hoisington, *Kans., U.S.* **107** T6
Hokatu, *Fr. Polynesia, Fr.* **223** N24
Hokitika, *N.Z.* **217** N17
Hokkaidō, island, *Japan* **188** G14
Hokkaido Rise *see* Zenkevich Rise, *Pac. Oc.* **242** E8
Hōkūkano Heiau, *Hawai'i, U.S.* **115** G15
Hokula, *Tonga* **222** P6
Hola Prystan', *Ukr.* **159** R7
Holbrook, *Ariz., U.S.* **109** S8
Holbrook, *Idaho, U.S.* **108** J6
Holden, *Mo., U.S.* **107** T11
Holden, *Utah, U.S.* **108** M7
Holdenville, *Okla., U.S.* **104** G12
Holdrege, *Nebr., U.S.* **107** Q5
Hole in the Wall, *Bahamas* **122** C6
Hōlei Pali, *Hawai'i, U.S.* **115** P21
Holetown, *Barbados* **123** K18
Holguín, *Cuba* **118** J12
Holland, *Eur.* **140** G5
Holland, *Mich., U.S.* **100** M9
Hollandale, *Miss., U.S.* **102** K10
Holland Bay, *Jam.* **122** J11

Hollick-Kenyon Plateau, *Antarctica* **230** K8
Hollidaysburg, *Pa., U.S.* **96** N5
Hollis, *Okla., U.S.* **104** H7
Hollister, *Calif., U.S.* **111** T4
Hollum, *Neth.* **148** G13
Holly Hill, *S.C., U.S.* **98** L10
Holly Ridge, *N.C., U.S.* **98** J13
Holly Springs, *Miss., U.S.* **102** G12
Hollywood, *Calif., U.S.* **111** X8
Hollywood, *Fla., U.S.* **99** W10
Holman, *N.W.T., Can.* **84** E12
Hólmavík, *Ice.* **142** D2
Holme Bay, *Antarctica* **231** E20
Holmes Rock, *Bahamas* **122** E1
Holonga, *Tonga* **222** L11
Holopaw, *Fla., U.S.* **99** T9
H_olot _Haluẓa, *Israel* **173** N4
Holroyd, river, *Austral.* **214** B12
Holstebro, *Den.* **142** M10
Holstein, *Eur.* **140** F7
Holstein, *Iowa, U.S.* **107** N9
Holston, river, *Tenn., Va., U.S.* **103** E20
Holsworthy, *Eng., U.K.* **145** W9
Holt, *Ala., U.S.* **103** K14
Holton, *Kans., U.S.* **107** S9
Holtville, *Calif., U.S.* **111** Z12
Hōlualoa, *Hawai'i, U.S.* **115** N18
Hōlua Slide, *Hawai'i, U.S.* **115** N18
Holy Cross, *Alas., U.S.* **113** H13
Holyhead (Caergybi), *Wales, U.K.* **145** S9
Holy Island, *Wales, U.K.* **145** S9
Holy Island (Lindisfarne), *Eng., U.K.* **145** N12
Holyoke, *Colo., U.S.* **108** L16
Holyoke, *Mass., U.S.* **97** K13
Hombori, *Mali* **200** H9
Homburg, *Ger.* **150** H5
Home Bay, *Kiribati* **221** E20
Home Bay, *Nunavut, Can.* **85** F18
Homedale, *Idaho, U.S.* **108** G3
Homer, *Alas., U.S.* **113** K16
Homer, *La., U.S.* **102** K7
Homer, *Mich., U.S.* **101** N10
Homer, *N.Y., U.S.* **96** K8
Homerville, *Ga., U.S.* **99** Q7
Homestead, *Fla., U.S.* **99** X10
Homestead National Monument of America, *Nebr., U.S.* **107** R8
Homewood, *Ala., U.S.* **103** J15
Hominy, *Okla., U.S.* **104** E12
Hommalinn, *Myanmar* **190** E5
Homnabad, *India* **180** M5
Homo Bay, *Vanuatu* **222** D2
Homosassa Springs, *Fla., U.S.* **99** T7
Homs *see* Ḩimş, *Syr.* **172** G8
Homuz, Strait of, *Ind. Oc.* **168** H5
Homyel', *Belarus* **158** M6
Honam, *N. Korea* **186** D12
Hōnaunau, *Hawai'i, U.S.* **115** N18
Honavar, *India* **181** P4
Honaz, *Turk.* **170** G5
Honda, *Col.* **130** F5
Hòn Đá Tý, island, *Vietnam* **191** Q14
Hondo, *Japan* **189** S4
Hondo, *N. Mex., U.S.* **109** U13
Hondo, *Tex., U.S.* **105** R8
Honduras, *N. Amer.* **117** L17
Honduras, Gulf of, *N. Amer.* **117** K17
Honea Path, *S.C., U.S.* **98** K7
Hønefoss, *Nor.* **142** K11
Honesdale, *Pa., U.S.* **96** M9
Honey Grove, *Tex., U.S.* **104** K13
Honey Lake, *Calif., U.S.* **111** N6
Honeyville, *Utah, U.S.* **108** K7
Hồng (Red), river, *Vietnam* **190** G11
Hong'an, *Hubei, China* **184** M6
Hongcheon, *S. Korea* **186** M10
Hongdo, island, *S. Korea* **187** T5
Honggong, *Guang., China* **185** U5
Honggun, *N. Korea* **186** E10
Honghai, *Guang., China* **185** W6
Hong Hu, *Hubei, China* **185** P5
Honghu, *Hubei, China* **185** P5
Hongjiang, *Hunan, China* **185** R1
Hong Kong, *Hong Kong (Xianggang), S.A.R., China* **185** W5
Hong Kong (Xianggang), S.A.R., *China* **185** W5

Hongliu, river, *N. Mongol, China*
184 E1
Hongliuyuan, *China* **182** F7
Hongning *see* Wulian, *Shand., China*
184 H10
Hongnong, *S. Korea* **187** S7
Hongor, *Mongolia* **182** D12
Hongseong, *S. Korea* **187** P7
Hongshan, *N. Mongol, China* **184** A10
Hongshui, river, *China* **182** N11
Hongwŏn, *N. Korea* **186** G10
Hongwŏn-man, bay, *N. Korea*
186 G10
Hongyang, *Guang., China* **185** V7
Hongze, *Jiangsu, China* **184** K10
Hongze Hu, *Jiangsu, China* **184** K9
Hòn Hải, island, *Vietnam* **191** Q14
Honiara, *Solomon Is.* **221** N19
Honikulu, Passe, *Wallis and Futuna, Fr.*
222 C11
Honiton, *Eng., U.K.* **145** W10
Hòn Khoai, island, *Vietnam* **191** R11
Hòn Lớn, island, *Vietnam* **191** N14
Honoka'a, *Hawai'i, U.S.* **115** L20
Honokahua, *Hawai'i, U.S.* **115** G16
Honokōwai, *Hawai'i, U.S.* **115** G15
Honolulu, *Hawai'i, U.S.* **114** F11
Honomanū Bay, *Hawai'i, U.S.* **115** G17
Honomū, *Hawai'i, U.S.* **115** L21
Honouliuli National Monument,
Hawai'i, U.S. **114** E10
Honshū, island, *Japan* **189** P6
Honu'apo Bay, *Hawai'i, U.S.* **115** Q20
Hood, Mount, *Oreg., U.S.* **110** F4
Hood Point, *Austral.* **214** L4
Hood River, *Oreg., U.S.* **110** E4
Hoodsport, *Wash., U.S.* **110** C3
Hoogeveen, *Neth.* **148** H14
Ho'okena, *Hawai'i, U.S.* **115** N18
Hooker, *Okla., U.S.* **104** E6
Hook Head, *Ire.* **145** U6
Ho'olehua, *Hawai'i, U.S.* **115** F14
Hoonah, *Alas., U.S.* **113** L22
Hooper, Cape, *Nunavut, Can.* **85** F18
Hooper Bay, *Alas., U.S.* **112** H11
Hoopeston, *Ill., U.S.* **101** Q7
Hoorn, *Neth.* **148** H12
Hoosier Hill, *Ind., U.S.* **101** R10
Hoover, *Ala., U.S.* **103** J15
Hoover Dam, *Ariz., Nev., U.S.* **111** U12
Hopa, *Rep. of Georgia* **171** C16
Hope, *Ark., U.S.* **102** J7
Hope, *N. Dak., U.S.* **106** G7
Hope, Cape, *Nunavut, Can.* **84** F12
Hope, Lake, *Austral.* **214** K4
Hope Bay, *Jam.* **122** H10
Hopedale, *Nfld. & Lab., Can.* **85** K21
Hopelchén, *Mex.* **117** H16
Hope Mills, *N.C., U.S.* **98** J11
Hopen Bank, *Arctic Oc.* **247** F16
Hope Point, *Myanmar* **190** L7
Hopetoun, *W. Aust., Austral.* **215** X4
Hope Town, *Bahamas* **122** B7
Hopetown, *S. Af.* **206** K9
Hope Valley, *Arctic Oc.* **246** K5
Hopewell, *Va., U.S.* **98** F13
Hopewell Culture National Historical
Park, *Ohio, U.S.* **101** S13
Hopewell Islands, *Nunavut, Can.*
85 K17
Hopkins, Lake, *Austral.* **214** F7
Hopkins, Mount, *Ariz., U.S.* **109** W8
Hopkinsville, *Ky., U.S.* **103** D14
Hopohoponga, Mui, *Tonga* **222** J12
Hoquiam, *Wash., U.S.* **110** D2
Horasan, *Turk.* **171** E16
Hordil Saridag, range, *Mongolia*
182 C8
Horgos, *Serb.* **154** D10
Hörh Uul, *Mongolia* **182** F10
Horicon, *Wis., U.S.* **100** L6
Horinger, *N. Mongol, China* **184** C4
Horizon Ridge, *Ind. Oc.* **225** J16
Horki, *Belarus* **158** K6
Horlick Mountains, *Antarctica*
230 J11
Horlivka, *Ukr.* **159** Q9
Ḩormak, *Iran* **175** F17
Hormigueros, *P.R., U.S.* **122** N1
Hormuz, Strait of, *Iran, Oman*
175 H15

Horn, Cape *see* Hornos, Cabo de,
S. Amer. **128** R5
Hornafjarðardjúp, valley, *Atl. Oc.*
247 L22
Hornavan, lake, *Sw.* **143** E13
Hornbeck, *La., U.S.* **102** M6
Hornbrook, *Calif., U.S.* **110** L3
Hornby Hill, peak, *Nunavut, Can.*
84 F11
Horne, Îles de, *Pac. Oc.* **218** J9
Hornell, *N.Y., U.S.* **96** K6
Horn Island, *Miss., U.S.* **103** P13
Hornos, Cabo de (Cape Horn), *Chile*
135 Y9
Hornsund Bank, *Arctic Oc.* **247** G17
Hornsund Valley, *Arctic Oc.* **247** G17
Horodnya, *Ukr.* **158** M6
Horodyshche, *Ukr.* **159** P6
Horo Shan, *China* **182** E4
Horqueta, *Parag.* **132** M10
Horse Cave, *Ky., U.S.* **103** D16
Horse Creek, *Wyo., U.S.* **108** K13
Horsehead Lake, *N. Dak., U.S.*
106 G5
Horseheads, *N.Y., U.S.* **96** K7
Horse Mountain, *N. Mex., U.S.*
109 T10
Horseshoe Beach, *Fla., U.S.* **99** S6
Horseshoe Bend, *Ark., U.S.* **102** E9
Horseshoe Seamounts, *Atl. Oc.*
240 J10
Horsham, *Eng., U.K.* **145** W14
Horsham, *Vic., Austral.* **215** Y11
Horta , *Azores, Port.* **146** Q2
Horten, *Nor.* **142** K11
Horton, *Kans., U.S.* **107** R9
Horton, river, *N.W.T., Can.* **84** E11
Horvat 'Avedat (Eboda), ruins, *Israel*
173 P5
Hoscheid, *Lux.* **162** H10
Hosdrug, *India* **181** Q4
Hoshab, *Pak.* **179** V3
Hoshangabad, *India* **180** J6
Hosingen, *Lux.* **162** H10
Hosmer, *S. Dak., U.S.* **106** J5
Hoste, Isla, *Chile* **135** Y8
Hosur, *India* **181** Q6
Hot, *Thai.* **190** K7
Hotan, *China* **182** G2
Hotan, river, *China* **182** G3
Hotchkiss, *Colo., U.S.* **109** N11
Hot Creek Range, *Nev., U.S.* **111** R10
Hotel de Paris, *Monaco* **163** D22
Hotel Hermitage, *Monaco* **163** D21
Hotel Métropole, *Monaco* **163** C22
Hotevilla, *Ariz., U.S.* **109** R8
Hot Springs, *Ark., U.S.* **102** H7
Hot Springs, *Mont., U.S.* **108** C5
Hot Springs, *S. Dak., U.S.* **106** L1
Hot Springs, *Va., U.S.* **98** E10
Hot Springs National Park, *Ark., U.S.*
102 H7
Hotspur Fracture Zone, *Atl. Oc.*
241 R10
Hot Sulphur Springs, *Colo., U.S.*
108 L12
Hottah Lake, *N.W.T., Can.* **84** G11
Hotte, Massif de la, *Haiti* **119** M15
Hottentot Bay, *Namibia* **206** J6
Houaïlou, *New Caledonia, Fr.* **222** C7
Houat, Île, *Fr.* **149** R4
Houffalize, *Belg.* **162** G9
Houghton, *Mich., U.S.* **100** E6
Houlton, *Me., U.S.* **97** C18
Houlung, *Taiwan, China* **185** U11
Houma, *La., U.S.* **102** Q10
Houma, *Shanxi, China* **184** H3
Houma, *Tonga* **222** J11
Houma Toloa, *Tonga* **222** J11
Hourtin, *Fr.* **149** V6
Houston, *Minn., U.S.* **106** L13
Houston, *Miss., U.S.* **102** J12
Houston, *Mo., U.S.* **107** U13
Houston, *Tex., U.S.* **105** R14
Houtman Abrolhos, islands, *Austral.*
214 J1
Hovd, *Mongolia* **182** C7
Hovd, *Mongolia* **182** E9
Hovd, river, *Mongolia* **182** C7
Hove, *Eng., U.K.* **145** W14
Hoven, *S. Dak., U.S.* **106** J5

Hovenweep National Monument,
Utah, U.S. **109** P9
Hövsgöl, *Mongolia* **182** E11
Hövsgöl Nuur, *Mongolia* **182** B9
Howar, Wadi, *Sudan* **202** D11
Howard, *Kans., U.S.* **107** U9
Howard, *S. Dak., U.S.* **106** L7
Howard City, *Mich., U.S.* **100** L10
Howard Lake, *N.W.T., Can.* **85** H13
Howe, *Idaho, U.S.* **108** G6
Howe, Cape, *Austral.* **214** M14
Howe, Point, *Norfolk I., Austral.*
221 F20
Howland, *Me., U.S.* **97** E17
Howland Island, *Pac. Oc.* **218** G9
Hồ Xá, *Vietnam* **190** K13
Hoxie, *Ark., U.S.* **102** E10
Hoxie, *Kans., U.S.* **107** S4
Hoxud, *China* **182** E5
Hoy, island, *Scot., U.K.* **144** G10
Høyanger, *Nor.* **142** J10
Hoyerswerda, *Ger.* **150** F11
Hoyt Lakes, *Minn., U.S.* **106** F12
Hozat, *Turk.* **171** F14
Hpa-an, *Myanmar* **190** K7
Hradec Králové, *Czech Rep.* **150** G12
Hrazdan, river, *Arm.* **171** D18
Hrebenne, *Pol.* **151** G18
Hrodna, *Belarus* **158** K3
Hron, river, *Slovakia* **151** J15
Hrubieszów, *Pol.* **151** F18
Hsiaohungtou Yü, *Taiwan, China*
185 X12
Hsi-hseng, *Myanmar* **190** H7
Hsinchu, *Taiwan, China* **185** U11
Hsinhua, *Taiwan, China* **185** W11
Hsinying, *Taiwan, China* **185** V11
Hsipaw, *Myanmar* **190** G7
Huachi, *China* **182** H11
Huacho, *Peru* **132** H3
Huade, *N. Mongol, China* **184** A6
Huadian, *China* **183** E16
Hua Hin, *Thai.* **191** N8
Huahine, *Fr. Polynesia, Fr.* **223** K20
Huahine, island, *Fr. Polynesia, Fr.*
223 E16
Huahine Iti, island, *Fr. Polynesia, Fr.*
223 H14
Huahine Nui, island, *Fr. Polynesia, Fr.*
223 G14
Huai, river, *Anhui, China* **184** L7
Huai'an, *Hebei, China* **184** C6
Huai'an, *Jiangsu, China* **184** K10
Huai'ancheng, *Shanxi, China* **184** C6
Huaibei, *Anhui, China* **184** K8
Huaibin, *Henan, China* **184** L7
Huaihua, *Hunan, China* **185** R1
Huaiji, *Guang., China* **185** V3
Huailai, *Hebei, China* **184** C7
Huainan, *Anhui, China* **184** L8
Huaining, *Anhui, China* **185** N8
Huairen, *Shanxi, China* **184** C5
Huai Yang, *Thai.* **191** P8
Huaiyin, *Jiangsu, China* **184** K10
Huaiyuan, *Anhui, China* **184** L8
Huajuapan de León, *Mex.* **116** K12
Huālālī, peak, *Hawai'i, U.S.* **115** M20
Hualapai Peak, *Ariz., U.S.* **109** S5
Hualfín, *Arg.* **134** G8
Hualian *see* Hualien, *Taiwan, China*
185 V12
Hualien (Hualian), *Taiwan, China*
185 V12
Huallaga, river, *Peru* **132** F3
Huambo, *Angola* **206** D6
Huancané, *Peru* **132** J6
Huancavelica, *Peru* **132** H4
Huancayo, *Peru* **132** H4
Huang (Yellow), river, *N. Mongol,
China* **184** C3
Huangchuan, *Henan, China* **184** L6
Huanggang, *Hubei, China* **185** N6
Huanggang Shan, *Fujian, China*
185 R9
Huanghua, *Hebei, China* **184** E8
Huanglong (Shipu), *Shaanxi, China*
184 H2
Huangmao Jian, peak, *Zhejiang, China*
185 R10
Huang, Mouth of the (Yellow), *Shand.,
China* **184** E9

Huangpu, *Guang., China* **185** V4
Huangqi Hai, *N. Mongol, China*
184 B5
Huang Shan, *Anhui, China* **185** N9
Huangshan, *Anhui, China* **185** P9
Huangshi, *Hubei, China* **185** N6
Huangtang Hu, *Hubei, China* **185** N5
Huangxian, *Shand., China* **184** F11
Huangyan, *Zhejiang, China* **185** Q12
Huangzhu, *Hainan, China* **185** Z1
Huanren, *Liaoning, China* **184** B14
Huanta, *Peru* **132** H4
Huantai (Suozhen), *Shand., China*
184 F9
Huánuco, *Peru* **132** G3
Huanxian, *China* **182** H11
Huara, *Chile* **134** C7
Huaral, *Peru* **132** H3
Huaraz, *Peru* **132** G3
Huarmey, *Peru* **132** G3
Huarong, *Hunan, China* **185** P4
Huascarán, Nevado, *S. Amer.* **128** F2
Huasco, *Chile* **134** H6
Hua Shan, *Shaanxi, China* **184** J2
Huashaoying, *Hebei, China* **184** C6
Huashi Shan, *Guang., China* **185** U5
Huatabampo, *Mex.* **116** E7
Huaura, *Peru* **132** H3
Huaxian, *Henan, China* **184** H6
Hubballi, *India* **181** N4
Hubbard, *Tex., U.S.* **104** M12
Hubbard Lake, *Mich., U.S.* **100** H12
Hubbell Trading Post National
Historic Site, *Ariz., U.S.* **109** R9
Hubei, *China* **184** M3
Hubei Kou, pass, *Shaanxi, China*
184 K1
Hudiksvall, *Sw.* **143** H13
Hudson, *Fla., U.S.* **99** T7
Hudson, *Mich., U.S.* **101** N11
Hudson, *N.Y., U.S.* **96** K11
Hudson, river, *N.Y., U.S.* **96** H11
Hudson Bay, *N. Amer.* **82** F7
Hudson Bay, *Sask., Can.* **85** M13
Hudson Canyon, *Atl. Oc.* **240** J4
Hudson Strait, *N. Amer.* **85** H18
Hudson Strait, *Nunavut, Can.* **240** F4
Huề, *Vietnam* **190** L13
Hu'ehu'e, *Hawai'i, U.S.* **115** M18
Huehuetenango, *Guatemala* **117** L15
Huelma, *Sp.* **146** K11
Huelva, *Sp.* **146** L7
Huerfano, river, *Colo., U.S.* **109** P13
Huesca, *Sp.* **147** D14
Huéscar, *Sp.* **146** K12
Huevos Monos, *Trinidad and Tobago*
123 P21
Huff, *N. Dak., U.S.* **106** G4
Hughenden, *Qnsld., Austral.* **215** S13
Hughes, *Alas., U.S.* **113** F15
Hughes, *Ark., U.S.* **102** G11
Hughes Bay, *Antarctica* **230** D4
Hugh Town, *Eng., U.K.* **145** Y7
Hugli, estuary, *India* **180** J11
Hugo, *Okla., U.S.* **104** J13
Hugon, Île, *New Caledonia, Fr.* **222** E8
Hugoton, *Kans., U.S.* **107** V3
Hui'an, *Fujian, China* **185** U9
Huichang, *Jiangxi, China* **185** T7
Huidong, *Guang., China* **185** W6
Huilai, *Guang., China* **185** W7
Huíla Plateau, *Af.* **198** M6
Huimin, *Shand., China* **184** F8
Huinca Renancó, *Arg.* **134** L10
Hŭisaek-pong, peak, *N. Korea* **186** E8
Huitong, *Hunan, China* **185** R1
Huîtres, Baie aux, *Mauritius*
209 J20
Huixian, *Henan, China* **184** H5
Huiyang, *Guang., China* **185** W5
Huizhou, *Guang., China* **185** V5
Hukawng Valley, *Myanmar* **190** D6
Hulan, *China* **183** D16
Hulbert, *Mich., U.S.* **100** F10
Hulett, *Wyo., U.S.* **108** F13
Hulin, *China* **183** C18
Hulingol, *China* **183** D14
Hull, *Ill., U.S.* **101** R3
Hull Bay, *Virgin Is., U.S.* **122** M8

Hulst, *Neth.* **148** K11
Huludao (Jinxi), *Liaoning, China*
184 C11
Hulun Nur, *China* **183** C13
Hulyaypole, *Ukr.* **159** Q9
Huma, *China* **183** B15
Humacao, *P.R., U.S.* **122** N5
Humahuaca, *Arg.* **134** E9
Humaitá, *Braz.* **132** F8
Humansdorp, *S. Af.* **206** M9
Humansville, *Mo., U.S.* **107** U11
Ḩumar, *U.A.E.* **175** K14
Humbe, *Angola* **206** F6
Humber, river, *Eng., U.K.* **145** R13
Humble, *Tex., U.S.* **105** Q14
Humboldt, *Iowa, U.S.* **106** M11
Humboldt, *Kans., U.S.* **107** U10
Humboldt, *Nebr., U.S.* **107** R9
Humboldt, *Sask., Can.* **84** M12
Humboldt, *Tenn., U.S.* **103** F13
Humboldt, river, *Nev., U.S.* **110** M9
Humboldt Bay, *Calif., U.S.* **110** M1
Humboldt Plain, *Pac. Oc.* **243** R21
Hūmedān, *Iran* **175** J17
Humen, *Guang., China* **185** W5
Humenné, *Slovakia* **151** J17
Humphreys Peak, *Ariz., U.S.* **109** R7
Humphrys Bay, *Antigua and Barbuda*
123 A21
Humu'ula Saddle, *Hawai'i, U.S.*
115 M20
Ḩūn, *Lib.* **201** D14
Hun, river, *Liaoning, China* **184** B12
Húnaflóaáll, valley, *Arctic Oc.*
247 L20
Húnaflói, bay, *Ice.* **142** D2
Hunan, *China* **184** M3
Hunedoara, *Rom.* **154** E12
Hunga, island, *Tonga* **222** L11
Hunga Ha'apai, island, *Tonga* **222** R5
Hungary, *Eur.* **151** M15
Hunga Tonga, island, *Tonga* **222** R5
Hŭngbong, *N. Korea* **186** G9
Hungerford, *Qnsld., Austral.* **215** V12
Hŭngnam, *N. Korea* **186** H9
Hungry Horse Reservoir, *Mont., U.S.*
108 B6
Hungund, *India* **181** N5
Hunjiang, *China* **183** E16
Huns Mountains, *Af.* **198** P6
Hunsrück, range, *Ger.* **162** K12
Hunstanton, *Eng., U.K.* **145** S14
Hunsur, *India* **181** Q5
Hunt, *Mongolia* **182** D9
Hunter, *N. Dak., U.S.* **106** G8
Hunter, island, *Vanuatu* **218** K8
Hunter, Cape, *Solomon Is.* **221** P18
Hunter Gap, *Atl. Oc.* **241** T9
Hunter Islands, *Austral.* **214** L7
Hunters, *Bahamas* **122** F1
Huntingburg, *Ind., U.S.* **101** T8
Huntingdon, *Pa., U.S.* **96** N6
Huntingdon, *Tenn., U.S.* **103** E13
Huntington, *Ind., U.S.* **101** Q10
Huntington, *Oreg., U.S.* **110** G9
Huntington, *Tex., U.S.* **105** N15
Huntington, *Utah, U.S.* **108** M8
Huntington, *W. Va., U.S.* **98** D7
Huntington Beach, *Calif., U.S.* **111** Y8
Huntly, *N.Z.* **217** J19
Huntly, *Scot., U.K.* **144** J11
Huntsville, *Ala., U.S.* **103** G15
Huntsville, *Ark., U.S.* **102** E7
Huntsville, *Mo., U.S.* **107** S12
Huntsville, *Tex., U.S.* **105** P13
Hunucmá, *Mex.* **117** H16
Hunyuan, *Shanxi, China* **184** D5
Hunza, region, *Pak.* **178** K12
Huocheng (Shuiding), *China* **182** D3
Huojia, *Henan, China* **184** H5
Huon Gulf, *P.N.G.* **217** D20
Huon, Île, *Coral Sea* **218** J7
Huon Peninsula, *P.N.G.* **217** D19
Huoqiu, *Anhui, China* **184** L7
Huoshan, *Anhui, China* **184** M7
Hupo, *S. Korea* **187** P12
Hurdiyo, *Somalia* **203** F19
Hurghada, *Egypt* **201** D19
Hurley, *Wis., U.S.* **100** F4
Hurmagai, *Pak.* **179** T4
Huron, *S. Dak., U.S.* **106** K7

Huron, Lake, *N. Amer.* **82** J7
Huron Mountain, *Mich., U.S.* **100** E7
Hurtsboro, *Ala., U.S.* **103** LI7
Húsavík, *Ice.* **142** E3
Huşi, *Rom.* **155** CI7
Huslia, *Alas., U.S.* **113** FI4
Husum, *Ger.* **150** A7
Hutag, *Mongolia* **182** C9
Hutchinson, *Kans., U.S.* **107** U7
Hutchinson, *Minn., U.S.* **106** KIO
Hutch Mountain, *Ariz., U.S.* **109** S7
Huthi, *Thai.* **190** L8
Hutland, *Cayman Is.* **122** H3
Huttig, *Ark., U.S.* **102** K8
Hutuo, river, *Shanxi, China* **184** E5
Huvadu *see* Suvadiva Atoll, *Maldives* **181** W3
Huy, *Belg.* **148** LI3
Hüyük, *Turk.* **170** G7
Huzhou, *Zhejiang, China* **185** NIO
Hvammstangi, *Ice.* **142** E2
Hvannadalshnúkur, peak, *Eur.* **140** B4
Hvar (Pharus), island, *Croatia* **154** H6
Hvarski Kanal, *Croatia* **154** H6
Hveragerði, *Ice.* **142** F2
Hvítá, river, *Ice.* **142** F2
Hwaaksan, peak, *S. Korea* **186** L9
Hwacheon, *S. Korea* **186** L9
Hwadae, *N. Korea* **186** EI2
Hwajeon, *S. Korea* **187** QII
Hwajin, *N. Korea* **186** J5
Hwange, *Zimb.* **206** FIO
Hwangjin, *N. Korea* **186** EI3
Hwangju, *N. Korea* **186** K6
Hwangsuwŏn, *N. Korea* **186** FIO
Hwap'yŏng, *N. Korea* **186** E8
Hwaseong, *S. Korea* **187** N8
Hwasŏng, *N. Korea* **186** EI2
Hwasun, *S. Korea* **187** T8
Hwayang, *S. Korea* **187** RII
Hwlffordd *see* Haverfordwest, *Wales, U.K.* **145** V8
Hyangsan, *N. Korea* **186** G7
Hyannis, *Mass., U.S.* **97** LI6
Hyannis, *Nebr., U.S.* **107** N3
Hyargas Nuur, *Mongolia* **182** C7
Hyden, *W. Aust., Austral.* **215** X4
Hyde Park, *N.Y., U.S.* **96** LII
Hyderabad, *India* **180** M6
Hyderabad, *Pak.* **179** V7
Hydra *see* Ýdra, island, *Gr.* **156** KI2
Hydro, *Okla., U.S.* **104** G9
Hyeolli, *S. Korea* **186** MIO
Hyères, *Fr.* **149** YI4
Hyères, Îles d' (Les Îles d'Or), *Fr.* **149** YI4
Hyesan, *N. Korea* **186** DIO
Hyndman Peak, *Idaho, U.S.* **108** G5
Hyŏlli, *N. Korea* **186** K9
Hyrra Banda, *Cen. Af. Rep.* **202** HIO
Hyrynsalmi, *Fin.* **143** FI6
Hysham, *Mont., U.S.* **108** DII

I

Iaco, river, *Braz.* **132** G6
Iaeger, *W. Va., U.S.* **98** F8
Ialomiţa, river, *Rom.* **155** FI6
Iamara, *P.N.G.* **217** EI8
Iar Connaught, region, *Ire.* **145** S3
Iascaigh *see* Easky, *Ire.* **145** Q4
Iaşi, *Rom.* **155** BI7
Íasmos, *Gr.* **157** BI5
Iauaretê, *Braz.* **132** C6
Ibadan, *Nigeria* **204** DI2
Ibagué, *Col.* **130** F5
Ibapah, *Utah, U.S.* **108** L5
Ibarra, *Ecua.* **130** J3
Ibb, *Yemen* **174** Q9
Iberá, Laguna, *Arg.* **134** HI3
Iberia, *Peru* **132** G6
Iberian Basin, *Atl. Oc.* **240** JIO
Iberian Mountains, *Eur.* **140** K3
Iberian Peninsula, *Eur.* **140** K3
Ibiapaba, Serra da, *S. Amer.* **128** EIO
Ibipetuba, *Braz.* **133** GI4
Ibiza (Ivisa), island, *Sp.* **147** HI7

Ibiza *see* Eivissa, *Sp.* **147** HI7
Iblei, Monti, *It.* **153** TII
Ibn Hani', Ras, *Syr.* **172** E6
Ibo, *Mozambique* **207** DI5
Iboperenda, *Bol.* **132** K8
Ibotirama, *Braz.* **133** HI5
Ibrā', *Oman* **175** KI6
Ibra, Wadi, *Sudan* **202** FIO
'Ibrī, *Oman* **175** KI5
Ibusuki, *Japan* **189** T4
Ica, *Peru* **132** J4
Ica, river, *Peru* **132** J4
Icacos Point, *Trinidad and Tobago* **123** R2O
Içana, *Braz.* **132** C6
Içana, river, *S. Amer.* **132** C6
Iceland, *Eur.* **142** E3
Iceland Basin, *Atl. Oc.* **240** F9
Iceland-Faroe Rise, *Arctic Oc., Atl. Oc.* **247** K22
Iceland Plateau, *Arctic Oc.* **247** KI9
Iceland Sea, *Arctic Oc.* **247** L2O
Ichchapuram, *India* **180** LIO
Icheon, *S. Korea* **187** N9
Ichikawa, *Japan* **189** PI2
Ichinohe, *Japan* **188** KI3
Ichinomiya, *Japan* **189** P9
Ichinoseki, *Japan* **188** LI2
Ichinskaya Sopka, *Russ.* **161** F22
Ichinskiy, *Russ.* **161** F22
Ichnya, *Ukr.* **159** N7
Ich'ŏn, *N. Korea* **186** G6
Ich'ŏn, *N. Korea* **186** K8
Icó, *Braz.* **133** FI7
Iconium *see* Konya, *Turk.* **170** G8
Icoraci, *Braz.* **133** DI3
Icy Cape, *Alas., U.S.* **113** BI3
Idabel, *Okla., U.S.* **104** JI4
Ida Grove, *Iowa, U.S.* **107** N9
Idah, *Nigeria* **205** DI4
Idaho, *U.S.* **108** G5
Idaho City, *Idaho, U.S.* **108** G4
Idaho Falls, *Idaho, U.S.* **108** G7
Idalou, *Tex., U.S.* **104** K5
Idanha, *Oreg., U.S.* **110** G4
Idanha-a-Nova, *Port.* **146** G7
'Idd el Ghanam, *Sudan* **202** FIO
Ideriyn, river, *Mongolia* **182** C8
Idfu, *Egypt* **201** EI9
Idi, *Indonesia* **192** G4
Ídi, Óros (Psiloreítis), *Gr.* **157** QI4
İdil, *Turk.* **171** HI6
Idiofa, *Dem. Rep. of the Congo* **202** L9
Idlib, *Syr.* **172** E8
Idracowra, *N.T., Austral.* **215** U9
Ieper (Ypres), *Belg.* **148** LIO
Ierápetra, *Gr.* **157** QI6
Ierissós, *Gr.* **156** DI2
Ieta, *P.N.G.* **221** JI3
Ifalik Atoll, *F.S.M.* **220** Q4
Ife, *Nigeria* **205** DI3
Iferouâne, *Niger* **200** GI2
Ifjord, *Nor.* **143** BI4
Iforas, Adrar des, *Af.* **200** FIO
Igadiane, river, *Af.* **198** F4
Igara Paraná, river, *Col.* **130** J6
Igarka, *Russ.* **161** GI3
Igatpuri, *India* **180** L3
Iğdır, *Turk.* **171** EI8
Igel, *Ger.* **162** JII
Iglesias, *It.* **153** P3
Igli, *Alg.* **200** C9
Igloolik, *Nunavut, Can.* **85** FI6
'Igma, Gebel el, *Egypt* **173** S3
Ignacio, *Colo., U.S.* **109** QII
Ignalina, *Lith.* **143** MI7
İğneada, *Turk.* **170** B4
İğneada Burnu, *Turk.* **170** B4
Igoumenítsa, *Gr.* **156** F7
Igra, *Russ.* **158** GI6
Igrim, *Russ.* **160** GIO
Iguaçu, Cataratas do, *Arg., Braz.* **134** FI5
Iguala, *Mex.* **116** JII
Igualada, *Sp.* **147** DI7
Iguatu, *Braz.* **133** FI6
Iguazú Falls, *S. Amer.* **128** J7
Igué, Îlot, *New Caledonia, Fr.* **222** B5
Iguéla, *Gabon* **205** HI5
Iguidi, 'Erg, *Af.* **200** D8

Iharana (Vohemar), *Madagascar* **207** DI8
Ihavandiffulu Atoll, *Maldives* **181** T3
Ihavandu, island, *Maldives* **181** T3
Ih Bogd Uul, peak, *Asia* **168** FIO
Ihbulag, *Mongolia* **182** EI2
Iheya Rettō, *Japan* **189** X2
Iheya Shima, *Japan* **189** X2
Ihosy, *Madagascar* **207** HI7
Ihu, *P.N.G.* **217** DI9
Ihwa, *S. Korea* **187** N8
Ii, *Fin.* **143** EI5
Iida, *Japan* **189** PIO
Iisalmi, *Fin.* **143** FI6
Ijevan, *Arm.* **171** DI9
Ijill, Sebkhet, *Mauritania* **200** E6
IJmuiden, *Neth.* **148** HI2
IJsselmeer, bay, *Neth.* **148** HI3
Ijuí, *Braz.* **132** PII
Ijuw, region, *Nauru* **221** E24
Ikanbujmal, *China* **182** G5
Ikare, *Nigeria* **205** DI3
Ikaría, island, *Gr.* **157** KI6
Ikela, *Dem. Rep. of the Congo* **202** KIO
Ikhtiman, *Bulg.* **155** JI3
Iki, island, *Japan* **189** R4
İkizdere, *Turk.* **171** DI5
Ikopa, river, *Madagascar* **207** FI7
Ikorodu, *Nigeria* **204** EI2
Iksan, *S. Korea* **187** R8
Ikuren, island, *Marshall Is., U.S.* **220** J8
Ilagan, *Philippines* **193** BI4
Ilave, *Peru* **132** J6
Iława, *Pol.* **151** CI5
Ilbilbie, *Qnsld., Austral.* **215** TI5
Ile, river, *Kaz.* **177** HI8
Île-à-la-Crosse, *Sask., Can.* **84** LI2
Ilebo, *Dem. Rep. of the Congo* **202** L9
Île d'Anticosti, *Que., Can.* **85** M2I
Ilemi Triangle, region, *Kenya, S. Sudan* **203** HI4
Îles de la Madeleine, *Que., Can.* **85** N22
Ilfracombe, *Eng., U.K.* **145** W9
Ilgaz, *Turk.* **170** D9
Ilgaz Dağları, *Turk.* **170** D9
Ilgın, *Turk.* **170** G7
Ilha de Moçambique, *Mozambique* **207** EI5
Ílhavo, *Port.* **146** F5
Ilhéus, *Braz.* **133** JI6
Ili, river, *China* **182** E3
Iliamna Lake, *Alas., U.S.* **113** KI4
Iliç, *Turk.* **170** FI2
Ilıca, *Turk.* **171** EI5
Iligan, *Philippines* **193** FI5
Ili'ili, *Amer. Samoa, U.S.* **222** N7
Ili'ili'ōpae Heiau, *Hawai'i, U.S.* **115** GI5
Ilinden, *Bulg.* **155** KI3
Ilion, *N.Y., U.S.* **96** JIO
'Īlio Point, *Hawai'i, U.S.* **115** FI3
Ill, river, *Aust.* **162** M3
Illapel, *Chile* **134** J4
Illeginni, island, *Marshall Is., U.S.* **220** L4
Illéla, *Niger* **200** HII
Illichivs'k, *Ukr.* **159** R5
Illinois, *U.S.* **101** R5
Illinois, river, *Ill., U.S.* **101** Q4
Illinois, river, *Oreg., U.S.* **110** K2
Illinois Peak, *U.S.* **86** B6
Illizi, *Alg.* **200** DI2
Illo, *S. Korea* **187** T7
Il'men', Lake, *Eur.* **140** EIO
Ilmen, Ozero, *Russ.* **158** G7
Ilmenau, *Ger.* **150** G8
Ilo, *Peru* **132** K5
Iloilo City, *Philippines* **193** EI4
Ilorin, *Nigeria* **205** DI3
Îlots de Bass *see* Marotiri, *Fr. Polynesia, Fr.* **219** LI4
Ilovik, island, *Croatia* **154** F4
Ilpyeong, *S. Korea* **187** U7
Il'pyrskiy, *Russ.* **161** E2I
Ilwaco, *Wash., U.S.* **110** E2
Imabari, *Japan* **189** Q6
Imabetsu, *Japan* **188** JI2

I Maddock, Puntan, *N. Mariana Is., U.S.* **220** A6
İmam Şāḩib, *Afghan.* **178** K7
Imandra, Lake, *Eur.* **140** BIO
Imarssuak Seachannel, *Atl. Oc.* **240** FI2
Imataca, Sierra de, *S. Amer.* **128** B6
Imatra, *Fin.* **143** HI7
Imbert, *Dom. Rep.* **119** LI8
Imbros, island, *see* Gökçeada, *Turk.* **170** D2
Imese, *Dem. Rep. of the Congo* **202** J8
Īmī, *Eth.* **203** HI6
Imías, *Cuba* **119** KI4
Imieji Anchorage, *Marshall Is., U.S.* **220** M8
İmişli, *Azerb.* **171** E22
Imjado, island, *S. Korea* **187** T6
Imjin-man, bay, *N. Korea* **186** CI3
Imlay, *Nev., U.S.* **111** N8
Imlay City, *Mich., U.S.* **100** LI2
Immarna, *S. Aust., Austral.* **215** W8
Immokalee, *Fla., U.S.* **99** W9
Imnaha, *Wash., U.S.* **110** F9
Imola, *It.* **152** F7
Imotski, *Croatia* **154** H7
Imperatriz, *Braz.* **133** EI3
Imperia, *It.* **152** G3
Imperial, *Calif., U.S.* **III** ZII
Imperial, *Nebr., U.S.* **107** Q3
Imperial Beach, *Calif., U.S.* **III** Z9
Imperial Dam, *Ariz., Calif., U.S.* **III** ZI3
Imperial Valley, *Calif., U.S.* **105** ZII
Impfondo, *Congo* **205** GI8
Imphal, *India* **180** HI4
İmralı, island, *Turk.* **170** D4
İmranlı, *Turk.* **171** EI3
Imrodj, island, *Marshall Is., U.S.* **220** L8
Imsan, *N. Korea* **186** F8
Imsil, *S. Korea* **187** S9
Imtān, *Syr.* **172** L8
Ina, *Japan* **189** PIO
Inamba Jima, *Japan* **189** RII
I-n-Amenas (In Amenas), *Alg.* **200** DI2
I-n-Amguel, *Alg.* **200** EII
Inanwatan, *Indonesia* **193** KI8
Inarajan, *Guam, U.S.* **220** DIO
Inari, *Fin.* **143** CI5
Inari, lake, *Fin.* **143** CI5
Inca, *Sp.* **147** GI8
Inca de Oro, *Chile* **134** G7
İncekum Burnu, *Turk.* **170** J9
İncesu, *Turk.* **170** GIO
Inchcape *see* Bell Rock, *Scot., U.K.* **144** LII
Incheon (Inch'ŏn), *S. Korea* **187** N8
Inch Island, *Ire.* **145** P6
Inchnadamph, *Scot., U.K.* **144** H8
Inch'ŏn *see* Incheon, *S. Korea* **187** N8
Incles, Port d', *Andorra, Fr.* **162** G5
Indalsälven, river, *Eur.* **140** C8
Indawgyi Lake, *Myanmar* **190** E6
Independence, *Calif., U.S.* **III** T8
Independence, *Iowa, U.S.* **107** NI3
Independence, *Kans., U.S.* **107** V9
Independence, *Mo., U.S.* **107** SIO
Independence Mountains, *Nev., U.S.* **110** MIO
İnderbor, *Kaz.* **176** E6
India, *Asia* **180** H6
India, Bassas da, *Af.* **207** GI4
Indiana, *Pa., U.S.* **96** N4
Indiana, *U.S.* **101** R9
Indiana Dunes National Lakeshore, *Ind., U.S.* **101** N8
Indian-Antarctic Ridge, *Ind. Oc.* **249** DI7
Indianapolis, *Ind., U.S.* **101** R9
Indian Ocean, *Ind. Oc.* **241** UI5
Indianola, *Iowa, U.S.* **107** PII
Indianola, *Miss., U.S.* **102** JIO
Indianola, *Nebr., U.S.* **107** R4
Indian Peak, *Utah, U.S.* **109** N5
Indian River, *Fla., U.S.* **99** UIO
Indian Springs, *Nev., U.S.* **III** TII
Indiantown, *Fla., U.S.* **99** VIO
Indian Town Point, *Antigua and Barbuda* **123** B22

Indigirka, river, *Asia* **168** BII
Indija, *Serb.* **154** EIO
Indio, *Calif., U.S.* **III** XII
Indira Point, *India* **181** TI5
Indispensable Strait, *Solomon Is.* **221** NI9
Indochina Peninsula, *Asia* **168** KIO
Indomed Fracture Zone, *Ind. Oc.* **224** P6
Indonesia, *Indonesia* **192** L8
Indore, *India* **180** J5
Indravati, river, *India* **180** L8
Indus, river, *India, Pak.* **179** Q9
Indus, Mouths of the, *Pak.* **179** W6
Indus Fan, *Ind. Oc.* **224** C9
İnebolu, *Turk.* **170** C9
İnegöl, *Turk.* **170** E5
I-n-Eker, *Alg.* **200** EII
Ineu, *Rom.* **154** DII
Inez, *Ky., U.S.* **103** B2O
Infanta, Cape, *Af.* **198** Q7
Infante D. Henrique, *Sao Tome and Principe* **209** B2I
Ingal, *Niger* **200** GII
Ingende, *Dem. Rep. of the Congo* **202** K8
Ingeniero Guillermo N. Juárez, *Arg.* **134** EII
Ingeniero Jacobacci, *Arg.* **135** Q8
Ingeniero Luiggi, *Arg.* **134** MIO
Inglesa Bay, *S. Amer.* **128** K4
Ingleside, *Tex., U.S.* **105** UII
Inglis, *Fla., U.S.* **99** S7
Ingolstadt, *Ger.* **150** J8
Ingomar, *S. Aust., Austral.* **215** V9
Ingraj Bazar, *India* **180** HII
Ingram, *Tex., U.S.* **105** Q8
Ingrid Christensen Coast, *Antarctica* **231** G2O
Ingwiller, *Fr.* **149** PI5
Inhambane, *Mozambique* **207** HI3
Inharrime, *Mozambique* **207** HI3
Inharrime Terrace, *Ind. Oc.* **224** L4
Inírida, *Col.* **130** F9
Inírida, river, *Col.* **130** G8
Inis *see* Ennis, *Ire.* **145** T4
Inis Ceithlann *see* Enniskillen, *N. Ire., U.K.* **145** Q5
Inis Córthaidh *see* Enniscorthy, *Ire.* **145** T6
Inis Díomáin *see* Ennistimon, *Ire.* **145** S3
Inis Eoáin *see* Inishannon, *Ire.* **145** V4
Inis Gé Theas (Inishkea South), island, *Ire.* **145** Q2
Inis Gé Thuaidh (Inishkea North), island, *Ire.* **145** Q2
Inishannon (Inis Eoáin), *Ire.* **145** V4
Inishbofin, island, *Ire.* **145** R2
Inisheer *see* Inis Oírr, *Ire.* **145** S3
Inishkea North *see* Inis Gé Thuaidh, island, *Ire.* **145** Q2
Inishkea South *see* Inis Gé Theas, island, *Ire.* **145** Q2
Inishmaan *see* Inis Meáin, island, *Ire.* **145** S3
Inishmore *see* Árainn, island, *Ire.* **145** S3
Inishmurray, island, *Ire.* **145** Q4
Inishowen Head, *Ire.* **145** N6
Inishshark, island, *Ire.* **145** R2
Inishtrahull (Inis Trá Tholl), island, *Ire.* **145** N6
Inis Meáin (Inishmaan), island, *Ire.* **145** S3
Inis Oírr (Inisheer), island, *Ire.* **145** S3
Inis Trá Tholl *see* Inishtrahull, island, *Ire.* **145** N6
Inis Trá Tholl *see* Malin Head, *Ire.* **145** N5
Inje, *S. Korea* **186** LIO
Injune, *Qnsld., Austral.* **215** UI4
Inkerman, *Qnsld., Austral.* **215** QI2
Inland Niger Delta, *Mali* **200** H8
Inland Sea *see* Seto Naikai, *Japan* **189** Q6
Inn, river, *Aust., Ger.* **150** KIO
Innamincka, *S. Aust., Austral.* **215** VII
Inner Brass Island, *Virgin Is., U.S.* **122** M8

Inner Hebrides, islands, Scot., U.K. 144 L7
Inner Sound, Scot., U.K. 144 J7
Innisfail, Qnsld., Austral. 215 R13
Innoko, river, Alas., U.S. 113 G14
Innsbruck, Aust. 150 L8
Inongo, Dem. Rep. of the Congo 202 K8
Ïnönü, Turk. 170 E6
Inowrocław, Pol. 151 D14
I-n-Salah, Alg. 200 D10
Insan, N. Korea 186 L7
Insar, Russ. 158 K12
Inscription, Cape, Austral. 214 G1
Insein, Myanmar 190 K6
Insiaf, F.S.M. 221 B18
Instow, Eng., U.K. 145 W9
Inta, Russ. 160 F10
Intendente Alvear, Arg. 134 L10
Interior, S. Dak., U.S. 106 L3
International Falls, Minn., U.S. 106 E11
Interview Island, India 181 P14
Intiyaco, Arg. 134 H12
Inubō Zaki, Japan 189 P13
Inukjuak, Que., Can. 85 K17
Iñupiat Heritage Center, Alas., U.S. 113 B15
Inuvik, N.W.T., Can. 84 E10
Inuya, river, Peru 132 G4
Inverbervie, Scot., U.K. 144 K11
Invercargill, N.Z. 217 R15
Inverell, N.S.W., Austral. 215 W15
Invermoriston, Scot., U.K. 144 K9
Inverness, Fla., U.S. 99 T7
Inverness, Scot., U.K. 144 J9
Invershin, Scot., U.K. 144 H9
Investigator Bank, Ind. Oc. 224 E10
Investigator Ridge, Ind. Oc. 225 H14
Investigator Strait, Austral. 214 L10
Inyokern, Calif., U.S. III V9
Inyo Mountains, Calif., U.S. III T8
Inza, Russ. 158 K13
Inzhavino, Russ. 158 M12
Inzia, river, Dem. Rep. of the Congo 202 M7
Ioánnina, Gr. 156 E7
Iō Jima, Japan 189 T4
Iola, Kans., U.S. 107 U10
Ioma, P.N.G. 217 D20
Iona, Idaho, U.S. 108 G7
Iona, island, Scot., U.K. 144 L7
Ione, Calif., U.S. III R5
Ione, Nev., U.S. III Q9
Ione, Oreg., U.S. 110 F6
Ione, Wash., U.S. 110 A9
Ionia, Mich., U.S. 100 L10
Ionian Islands, Eur. 140 L9
Ionian Plain, Atl. Oc. 240 K14
Ionian Sea, Eur. 140 L8
Iony, Ostrov (Saint Jona Island), Russ. 161 H20
Iori, river, Azerb., Rep. of Georgia 171 B19
Íos, Gr. 157 M15
Íos, island, Gr. 157 M15
Iōtori Shima, Japan 189 W2
Iowa, U.S. 107 N12
Iowa, river, Iowa, U.S. 107 P12
Iowa City, Iowa, U.S. 107 P13
Iowa Falls, Iowa, U.S. 107 N12
Iowa Park, Tex., U.S. 104 J9
Ipatovo, Russ. 159 S12
Ipiales, Col. 130 H3
Ipis, island, F.S.M. 221 D16
Ipixuna, Braz. 132 F5
Ipixuna, river, Braz. 132 F4
Ipoh, Malaysia 191 T9
Iporá, Braz. 132 J12
Ïpsala, Turk. 170 C2
Ipswich, Eng., U.K. 145 U15
Ipswich, Jam. 122 H7
Ipswich, S. Dak., U.S. 106 J6
Iput', river, Russ. 158 L7
Iqaluit, Nunavut, Can. 85 H19
Iqe, China 182 H7
Iquique, Chile 134 C7
Iquitos, Peru 132 E4
Iraan, Tex., U.S. 105 P5
Iracoubo, Fr. Guiana 131 E17
Ïrafshān, Iran 175 H18

Iraio, ruin, Gr. 157 K17
Irákleia, island, Gr. 157 M15
Irákleio (Candia), Gr. 157 Q15
Iran, Asia 174 E12
Ïrānshahr, Iran 175 H17
Irapuata, Mex. 116 H11
Iraq, Asia 174 E8
Irayel', Russ. 160 F9
Irazú, Volcán, C.R. 117 N19
Irbe Strait, Est., Latv. 143 L15
Irbid (Arbela), Jordan 172 L6
Ireland (Éire), Eur. 145 S5
Ireland, island, Ireland, U.K. 145 S5
Ireland Island North, Bermuda 122 B1
Ireland Island South, Bermuda 122 C1
Iret', Russ. 161 F21
Irian Jaya, Indonesia 193 K20
Irimi, Indonesia 217 B14
Iringa, Tanzania 203 M14
Iriri, river, Braz. 132 E11
Iriru, Passe, Fr. Polynesia, Fr. 223 B24
Irish Sea, Atl. Oc. 140 F4
Irkeshtam, Kyrg. 178 G11
Irkutsk, Russ. 161 L15
Irmauw, Indonesia 193 M17
Irminger Basin, Atl. Oc. 240 F8
Irois Bay, Trinidad and Tobago 123 Q21
Iroise, bay, Fr. 149 Q2
Irondequoit, N.Y., U.S. 96 J6
Iron Gate, Eur. 140 J9
Iron Gate Dam, Rom., Serb. 154 F12
Iron Mountain, Mich., U.S. 100 G7
Iron River, Mich., U.S. 100 G6
Iron River, Wis., U.S. 100 F3
Ironton, Mo., U.S. 107 U15
Ironton, Ohio, U.S. 101 T13
Ironwood, Mich., U.S. 100 F4
Ironwood Forest National Monument, Ariz., U.S. 109 V7
Iroquois, S. Dak., U.S. 106 K7
Irpin', Ukr. 159 N6
Irrawaddy see Ayeyarwady, river, Myanmar 190 G6
Irsina, It. 152 M13
Irtysh, river, Russ. 160 H10
Iruña see Pamplona, Sp. 147 C13
Irvine, Ky., U.S. 103 C18
Irvine, Scot., U.K. 145 N9
Irving, Tex., U.S. 104 L11
Isabel, S. Dak., U.S. 106 J4
Isabela, P.R., U.S. 122 M1
Isabela, Philippines 193 F14
Isabela, Cabo, Dom. Rep. 119 K18
Isabela, Canal, Ecua. 130 P9
Isabela (Albemarle), Isla, Ecua. 130 P9
Isabela de Sagua, Cuba 118 G9
Isabela, Isla, Galápagos Is., Ecua. 219 G22
Isabella, Minn., U.S. 106 F13
Isabelle, Point, Mich., U.S. 100 E7
Isabel Segunda, P.R., U.S. 122 N6
Isachsen Mountain, Antarctica 231 C15
Ísafjörður, Ice. 142 D2
Isahaya, Japan 189 R4
Isa Khel, Pak. 179 P9
Isangel, Vanuatu 222 H3
Isar, river, Ger. 150 K9
Íscar, Sp. 146 E10
Ischia, Isola d', It. 152 M10
Isdu, island, Maldives 181 W3
Ise, Japan 189 Q9
Iselin Bank, Pac. Oc. 249 J15
Isen Saki, Japan 189 W3
Iseo, Lago d', It. 152 D5
Isère, Pointe, Fr. Guiana 131 E17
Isernia, It. 152 L10
Ise Wan, Japan 189 Q9
Isfahan see Eşfahān, Iran 175 E13
Isfara, Taj. 178 G9
Isfjord Bank, Arctic Oc. 247 H17
Isfjordrenna, valley, Arctic Oc. 247 H17
Ishikari Wan, Japan 188 G12
Ishim, Russ. 160 J10
Ishim, river, Russ. 160 J10
Ishim Steppe, Kaz. 176 A13
Ishinomaki, Japan 188 L13
Ishinomaki Wan, Japan 188 L13

Ishkāshem, Afghan. 178 K9
Ishkāshim, Afghan. 178 K8
Ishkuman, Pak. 178 K11
Ishpeming, Mich., U.S. 100 F7
Işık Dağı, peak, Turk. 170 D8
Ishkveren, Turk. 171 H17
Isili, It. 153 P4
Isimu, Indonesia 193 J14
Isiro, Dem. Rep. of the Congo 202 J11
Isisford, Qnsld., Austral. 215 T13
Iskandar, Uzb. 177 K13
Iskele see Trikomo, Cyprus 162 N10
İskenderun, Turk. 170 J11
İskenderun Körfezi, Turk. 170 J10
İskilip, Turk. 170 D9
Iskŭr, river, Bulg. 155 H14
Iskushuban, Somalia 203 F18
Ïslâhiye, Turk. 170 H11
Islamabad, Pak. 179 N11
Islamkot, Pak. 179 W9
Islamorada, Fla., U.S. 99 Y10
Islām Qal'ah, Afghan. 178 M1
Isla Mujeres, Mex. 117 H17
Island Falls, Me., U.S. 97 C18
Island Lagoon, Austral. 214 J10
Island Park, Idaho, U.S. 108 F8
Island Park Reservoir, Idaho, U.S. 108 F7
Island Pond, Vt., U.S. 97 F14
Islands, Bay of, N.Z. 217 H18
Islas Canarias see Canary Islands, Sp. 200 C5
Islas Malvinas see Falkland Islands, S. Amer. 135 XII
Islas Orcadas Rise, Atl. Oc. 241 V9
Islay, island, Scot., U.K. 144 M7
Isle Royle National Park, Mich., U.S. 100 D6
Islote Bay, Trinidad and Tobago 123 Q21
Ismâ'îlîya, Egypt 173 P1
Isna, Egypt 201 E19
Isoka, Zambia 206 C12
Isola di Capo Rizzuto, It. 153 Q14
Isonzo, river, It. 152 D9
Isparta, Turk. 170 G6
Ispas, Turkm. 176 L10
Ispikan, Pak. 179 V2
İspir, Turk. 171 D15
Israel, Asia 172 L5
Isrïyah, ruins, Syr. 172 F9
Issano, Guyana 131 E14
Issime, It. 152 D3
Issoudun, Fr. 149 S9
Ist, island, Croatia 154 F5
Istādāh-ye Muqur, Āb-e, Afghan. 179 P7
Istanbul (Constantinople), Turk. 170 C5
İstanbul Boğazı (Bosporus), Turk. 170 C5
Istaravshan (Ŭroteppa), Taj. 178 G7
Istiaía, Gr. 156 G11
Isto, Mount, Alas., U.S. 113 C18
Istokpoga, Lake, Fla., U.S. 99 V9
Istres, Fr. 149 X13
Istria, peninsula, Croatia 154 E4
Itabaianinha, Braz. 133 H17
Itabuna, Braz. 133 J16
Itacoatiara, Braz. 132 D9
Itaetê, Braz. 133 H16
Itaipú Dam, Braz., Parag. 132 M10
Itaituba, Braz. 132 E10
Itajaí, Braz. 133 N13
Itamarati, Braz. 132 F6
Itambé, Pico de, Braz. 133 K15
Itanagar, India 180 F14
Itapetinga, Braz. 133 J16
Itapipoca, Braz. 133 E16
Itapiranga, Braz. 132 D10
Itatupã, Braz. 132 C12
Itbayat, island, Philippines 193 A14
Itéa, Gr. 156 H10
Iténez see Guaporé, river, S. Amer. 132 H8
Itezhi-Tezhi, Lake, Zambia 206 E10
Ithaca, Mich., U.S. 100 L11

Ithaca, N.Y., U.S. 96 K8
Ithaca see Ithāki, island, Gr. 156 H7
Ithāki (Ithaca), island, Gr. 156 H7
Ithāki (Vathí), Gr. 156 H7
Ítilo, Gr. 156 M10
Iti, Motu see Tupai, Fr. Polynesia, Fr. 223 E15
Itiquira, river, Braz. 132 K10
Itō, Japan 189 Q11
Itoman, Japan 189 Y2
Itta Bena, Miss., U.S. 102 J11
Ittiri, It. 152 M3
Itu Aba Island, S. China Sea 192 E11
Ituí, river, Braz. 132 E5
Ituiutaba, Braz. 133 K13
Ituni, Guyana 131 E14
Iturama, Braz. 132 K12
Iturup (Etorofu), island, Russ. 161 J23
Ituxi, river, Braz. 132 F7
Ituzaingó, Arg. 134 G14
Itzehoe, Ger. 150 B8
Iuka, Miss., U.S. 103 G13
Iva, island, Scot., U.K. 144 M7
Ivaí, river, Braz. 132 M11
Ivalo, Fin. 143 C15
Ivanhoe, N.S.W., Austral. 215 X12
Ivanić Grad, Croatia 154 D6
Ivanjica, Serb. 154 H10
Ivano-Frankivs'k, Ukr. 159 P2
Ivanovo, Russ. 158 H11
Ivanteyevka, Russ. 158 L15
Ivatsevichy, Belarus 158 L3
Ivaylovgrad, Bulg. 155 K16
Ivdel', Russ. 160 G9
Ivindo, river, Af. 198 J6
Ivirairai, Mount, Fr. Polynesia, Fr. 223 P16
Ivisa see Ibiza, island, Sp. 147 H17
Iviza, island, Eur. 140 L4
Ivory Coast, Af. 204 F8
Ivrea, It. 152 D3
Ivujivik, Que., Can. 85 H17
Iwaki, Japan 189 N13
Iwakuni, Japan 189 Q6
Iwamizawa, Japan 188 G13
Iwanuma, Japan 188 M13
Iwate, Japan 188 K13
Iwembere Steppe, Af. 198 K9
Iwo, Nigeria 204 D12
Iwo Jima see Iwo To, island, Japan 189 Z13
Iwo Jima Ridge, Pac. Oc. 242 F7
Iwŏn, N. Korea 186 G11
Iwon-man, bay, N. Korea 186 G11
Iwo To (Iwo Jima), island, Japan 189 Z13
Ixtapa, Mex. 116 K10
Iyo, Japan 189 R6
Iž, island, Croatia 154 G5
Ïzadkhvāst, Iran 175 F13
Izamal, Mex. 117 H16
Izberbash, Russ. 159 U15
Izbica, Pol. 151 D14
Izena Shima, Japan 189 X2
Izhevsk, Russ. 158 G16
Izmayil, Ukr. 159 S4
Izmir (Smyrna), Turk. 170 F3
Ïzmit see Kocaeli, Turk. 170 D5
İznik (Nicaea), Turk. 170 D5
İznik Gölü, Turk. 170 D5
Izozog, Bañados del, S. Amer. 128 H6
Izra', Syr. 172 K7
Izu Hantō, Japan 189 Q11
Izu Islands, Asia 168 F14
Izumo, Japan 189 P6
Izu-Ogasawara Rise, Pac. Oc. 242 F7
Izu-Ogasawara Trench, Pac. Oc. 242 F8
Izu Shotō, Japan 189 Q12
Izyaslav, Ukr. 159 N4
Izyum, Ukr. 159 P9

Jabbūl, Syr. 172 E9
Jabbūl, Sabkhat a, Syr. 172 E9
Jabal Abyad Plateau, Af. 198 F8
Jabiru, N.T., Austral. 215 P8
Jablah, Syr. 172 F7
Jablaničko Jezero, Bosn. & Herzg. 154 G8
Jablonec, Czech Rep. 150 G11
Jabnoren, island, Marshall Is., U.S. 220 K7
Jaboatão, Braz. 133 G18
Jabor, Marshall Is., U.S. 220 M8
Jabuka, island, Croatia 154 H5
Jabwot Island, Marshall Is., U.S. 220 H4
Jaca, Sp. 147 C14
Jacareacanga, Braz. 132 E10
Jaciparaná, Braz. 132 G7
Jackman, Me., U.S. 97 D15
Jackpot, Nev., U.S. 110 L12
Jacksboro, Tex., U.S. 104 K10
Jackson, Ala., U.S. 103 M14
Jackson, Barbados 123 K19
Jackson, Calif., U.S. III R5
Jackson, Ga., U.S. 98 L5
Jackson, La., U.S. 102 N9
Jackson, Mich., U.S. 100 M11
Jackson, Minn., U.S. 106 L10
Jackson, Miss., U.S. 102 L11
Jackson, Mo., U.S. 107 U16
Jackson, Ohio, U.S. 101 S13
Jackson, S.C., U.S. 98 L8
Jackson, Tenn., U.S. 103 F13
Jackson, Wyo., U.S. 108 G8
Jackson, Ostrov, Russ. 160 C12
Jackson Bay, N.Z. 217 P15
Jackson Lake, Ga., U.S. 98 L5
Jackson Lake, Wyo., U.S. 108 G8
Jacksonport, Wis., U.S. 100 H8
Jacksonville, Ala., U.S. 103 J16
Jacksonville, Ark., U.S. 102 G8
Jacksonville, Fla., U.S. 99 Q8
Jacksonville, Ill., U.S. 101 R4
Jacksonville, N.C., U.S. 98 J13
Jacksonville, Tex., U.S. 104 M14
Jacksonville Beach, Fla., U.S. 99 R9
Jacmel, Haiti 119 M16
Jacobabad, Pak. 179 T7
Jacob Lake, Ariz., U.S. 109 Q7
Jacquinot Bay, P.N.G. 217 C21
Jacumba, Calif., U.S. III Z11
Jadraque, Sp. 146 E12
Jaén, Peru 132 F2
Jaén, Sp. 146 K11
Jaeundo, island, S. Korea 187 T6
Jaewondo, island, S. Korea 187 T6
Ja'farābād, Iran 174 A11
Jaffa, Cape, Austral. 214 L11
Jaffna, Sri Lanka 181 R7
Jagaedo, island, S. Korea 187 V7
Jagdalpur, India 180 L8
Jagdaqi, China 183 B15
Jāghir Bāzār, Syr. 172 C14
Jaghjagh, river, Syr. 172 C14
Jagodina, Serb. 154 G11
Jagraon, India 180 D5
Jagtial, India 180 L6
Jaguarão, Braz. 132 Q11
Jahanabad, India 180 H10
Jahorina, peak, Bosn. & Herzg. 154 G8
Jahrom, Iran 175 G14
Jaicoa, Cordillera, P.R., U.S. 122 M1
Jaicós, Braz. 133 F16
Jaigarh, India 180 M3
Jaintiapur, India 180 H13
Jaipur, India 180 G5
Jaisalmer, India 180 G2
Jajpur, India 180 K10
Jakar, Bhutan 180 F13
Jakarta, Indonesia 192 L8
Jakeru, island, Marshall Is., U.S. 220 L3
Jakhau, India 180 H1
Jakobstad (Pietarsaari), Fin. 143 G15
Jal, N. Mex., U.S. 109 V15
Jalaid Qi, China 183 D15
Jalaihai Point, Guam, U.S. 220 D11
Jalal-Abad, Kyrg. 178 F10
Jalālābād, Afghan. 178 M9

Jalandhar, *India* **180** D5
Jala Nur, *China* **183** C13
Jalapa, *Mex.* **117** J14
Jalasjärvi, *Fin.* **143** G15
Jalaun, *India* **180** G7
Jaleswar, *India* **180** K11
Jalgaon, *India* **180** K5
Jalgaon, *India* **180** K5
Jalingo, *Nigeria* **205** D15
Jalkot, *Pak.* **178** L11
Jaloklab, island, *Marshall Is., U.S.* **220** G10
Jalón, river, *Sp.* **147** E13
Jalor, *India* **180** G3
Jalpaiguri, *India* **180** G12
Jālq, *Iran* **175** G18
Jáltipan, *Mex.* **117** J14
Jaluit, island, *Marshall Is., U.S.* **220** N8
Jaluit Atoll, *Marshall Is., U.S.* **220** H4
Jaluit Lagoon, *Marshall Is., U.S.* **220** M7
Jamaame, *Somalia* **203** K16
Jamaica, *N. Amer.* **118** N10
Jamaica, island, *N. Amer.* **82** N8
Jamaica Cay, *Bahamas* **119** G13
Jamalpur, *Bangladesh* **180** H12
Jamanota, peak, *Aruba, Neth.* **123** R17
Jaman Pass, *Afghan., Taj.* **178** J12
Jambi, *Indonesia* **192** K7
Jambusar, *India* **180** J3
James, river, *N. Dak., U.S.* **106** G6
James, river, *Va., U.S.* **98** E11
James Bay, *N. Amer.* **85** M17
James Cistern, *Bahamas* **122** D6
James Point, *Bahamas* **122** D6
James Range, *Austral.* **214** F8
James Ross Island, *Antarctica* **230** D4
Jamestown, *N. Dak., U.S.* **106** G6
Jamestown, *N.Y., U.S.* **96** K4
Jamestown, *S. Aust., Austral.* **215** X10
Jamestown National Historic Site, *Va., U.S.* **98** F13
Jamestown Reservoir, *N. Dak., U.S.* **106** G6
Jammu, *India* **180** C5
Jamnagar, *India* **180** J2
Jampur, *Pak.* **179** S9
Jämsä, *Fin.* **143** H15
Jamshedpur, *India* **180** J10
Jamuna, river, *Bangladesh* **180** H12
Janaúba, *Braz.* **133** J15
Jān Būlāq, *Afghan.* **178** K6
Jand, *Pak.* **179** N10
Jandaq, *Iran* **175** D14
Jandia, peak, *Sp.* **208** Q7
Jandia, Punta de, *Sp.* **208** Q6
Jandiatuba, river, *Braz.* **132** E5
Jandola, *Pak.* **179** P8
Jan Doran, *Bonaire, Neth.* **123** Q19
Janesville, *Wis., U.S.* **100** M6
Jangain, island, *P.N.G.* **221** H14
Jangaon, *India* **180** M7
Jangdo, island, *S. Korea* **187** V8
Jangdong, *S. Korea* **187** T8
Jangeru, *Indonesia* **192** K12
Janggye, *S. Korea* **187** R9
Janghang, *S. Korea* **187** R7
Jangheung, *S. Korea* **187** U8
Janghowon, *S. Korea* **187** N9
Jangipur, *India* **180** H11
Jangpyeong, *S. Korea* **186** M11
Jangsando, island, *S. Korea* **187** U7
Jangseong, *S. Korea* **187** S8
Jangsu, *S. Korea* **187** R9
Jānī Khēl, *Afghan.* **179** P7
Janīn, *W. Bank* **172** L6
Jan Mayen Fracture Zone, *Arctic Oc.* **247** K19
Jan Mayen Ridge, *Arctic Oc.* **247** K19
Janów Lubelski, *Pol.* **151** F17
Jansenville, *S. Af.* **206** M9
Jan Thiel, Lagún, *Curaçao, Neth.* **123** Q15
Januária, *Braz.* **133** J14
Jaora, *India* **180** H4
Japan, *Asia* **189** R8

Japan, Sea of (East Sea), *Pac. Oc.* **168** F13
Japan Basin, *Pac. Oc.* **242** E6
Japanese Guyots, *Pac. Oc.* **242** F8
Japan Rise, *Pac. Oc.* **242** E8
Japan Trench, *Pac. Oc.* **242** E8
Japtan, island, *Marshall Is., U.S.* **220** H8
Japurá, *Braz.* **132** D7
Japurá, river, *N. Amer.* **82** R11
Japurá, river, *S. Amer.* **132** D6
Jaquot, Pointe, *Dominica* **123** D19
Jarābulus, *Syr.* **172** C10
Jaramillo, *Arg.* **135** T9
Jaranwala, *Pak.* **179** Q11
Jarash (Gerasa), *Jordan* **172** L7
Jarbidge, *Nev., U.S.* **110** L11
Jarbidge, river, *Idaho, Nev., U.S.* **108** J4
Jardim, *Braz.* **132** L10
Jardines de la Reina, *Cuba* **118** K10
Jargalant, *Mongolia* **182** D8
Jargalant, *Mongolia* **183** D13
Jargalant Hayrahan, peak, *Mongolia* **182** D7
Jarghān, *Afghan.* **178** L5
Jari, river, *Braz.* **132** C12
Jarocin, *Pol.* **151** E13
Jarosław, *Pol.* **151** G18
Järvenpää, *Fin.* **143** J16
Jarvis Island, *Pac. Oc.* **218** G12
Järvsö, *Sw.* **143** H13
Jashpurnagar, *India* **180** J9
Jāsk, *Iran* **175** J16
Jasło, *Pol.* **151** H17
Jason Islands, *Falk. Is., U.K.* **135** V11
Jason Peninsula, *Antarctica* **230** D5
Jasonville, *Ind., U.S.* **101** S8
Jasper, *Ala., U.S.* **103** J14
Jasper, *Alta., Can.* **84** L9
Jasper, *Ark., U.S.* **102** E7
Jasper, *Fla., U.S.* **98** Q7
Jasper, *Ga., U.S.* **98** K5
Jasper, *Ind., U.S.* **101** T8
Jasper, *Tex., U.S.* **105** P15
Jastrowie, *Pol.* **151** C13
Jastrzębie-Zdrój, *Pol.* **151** H14
Jászberény, *Hung.* **151** L16
Jataí, *Braz.* **132** K12
Jati, *Pak.* **179** W7
Jatibonico, *Cuba* **118** H9
Jatobal, *Braz.* **133** E13
Jaú, river, *Braz.* **132** D8
Jauaperi, river, *Braz.* **132** C9
Jaunpur, *India* **180** G8
Java (Jawa), island, *Indonesia* **192** M8
Javari see Yavarí, river, *S. Amer.* **132** F4
Java Ridge, *Ind. Oc.* **225** H16
Java Sea, *Indonesia* **192** L9
Java Trench (Sunda Trench), *Ind. Oc.* **225** G15
Jávea (Xàbia), *Sp.* **147** J15
Jawa see Java, island, *Indonesia* **192** M8
Jawhar (Giohar), *Somalia* **203** J17
Jawi, *Indonesia* **192** J9
Jawoldo, island, *S. Korea* **187** N7
Jaworzno, *Pol.* **151** G15
Jay, *Okla., U.S.* **104** E14
Jaya, Puncak, *Indonesia* **217** C16
Jayapura, *Indonesia* **193** K21
Jayawijaya, Pegunungan, *Indonesia* **193** L20
Jay Em, *Wyo., U.S.* **108** H13
Jayton, *Tex., U.S.* **104** K7
Jayuya, *P.R., U.S.* **122** N3
Jazirah Doberai (Bird's Head Peninsula), *Indonesia* **193** J18
Jazīrat Arwād, island, *Syr.* **172** G7
Jazīrat Maşīrah, *Asia* **168** J4
Jaz Mūrīān, Hāmūn-e, *Iran* **175** H16
Jbail (Byblos), *Leb.* **172** H6
Jdaïdet Ghazīr, *Leb.* **172** H6
Jeanerette, *La., U.S.* **102** Q9
Jeanette, Ostrov, *Russ.* **161** C17
Jean Marie River, *N.W.T., Can.* **84** H10
Jean-Rabel, *Haiti* **119** L16
Jebba, *Nigeria* **205** D13

Jebel, Bahr el (Mountain Nile), river, *Af.* **203** H13
Jebel Alī, *U.A.E.* **175** J15
Jebri, *Pak.* **179** U5
Jebus, *Indonesia* **192** K7
Jecheon, *S. Korea* **187** N10
Jeddah, *Saudi Arabia* **174** L7
Jedrol, island, *Marshall Is., U.S.* **220** H8
Jędrzejów, *Pol.* **151** G16
Jefferson, *Ga., U.S.* **98** K6
Jefferson, *Iowa, U.S.* **107** N10
Jefferson, *Tex., U.S.* **104** L15
Jefferson, *Wis., U.S.* **100** L6
Jefferson, river, *Mont., U.S.* **108** E7
Jefferson, Mount, *Nev., U.S.* **111** Q9
Jefferson, Mount, *Oreg., U.S.* **110** G4
Jefferson City, *Mo., U.S.* **107** T13
Jefferson City, *Tenn., U.S.* **103** E19
Jeffersonville, *Ind., U.S.* **101** T9
Jeffrey City, *Wyo., U.S.* **108** J11
Jef Jef el Kebir, desert, *Chad* **201** F15
Jega, *Nigeria* **205** B13
Jeju (Cheju), *S. Korea* **187** W7
Jeju-do, island, *S. Korea* **187** W6
Jeju Island (Cheju Island), *Asia* **168** G13
Jeju Strait, *S. Korea* **187** W7
Jekyll Island, *Ga., U.S.* **99** P9
Jelbart Ice Shelf, *Antarctica* **230** A12
Jelenia Góra, *Pol.* **150** F12
Jelgava (Mitau), *Latv.* **143** L16
Jellico, *Tenn., U.S.* **103** D18
Jemaja, island, *Indonesia* **192** H8
Jember, *Indonesia* **192** M11
Jembongan, island, *Malaysia* **192** F12
Jemez Pueblo, *N. Mex., U.S.* **109** R12
Jeminay, *China* **182** C5
Jemo Island, *Marshall Is., U.S.* **220** F4
Jena, *Fla., U.S.* **99** R6
Jena, *Ger.* **150** F9
Jena, *La., U.S.* **102** M8
Jengish Chokusu see Pobeda Peak, *China, Kyrg.* **178** E15
Jenkins, *Ky., U.S.* **103** C20
Jennings, *La., U.S.* **102** P7
Jenny Point, *Dominica* **123** F20
Jensen, *Utah, U.S.* **108** L9
Jensen Beach, *Fla., U.S.* **99** V10
Jens Munk Island, *Nunavut, Can.* **85** F16
Jenu, *Indonesia* **192** J9
Jeogu, *S. Korea* **187** T11
Jeongeup, *S. Korea* **187** S8
Jeongnim, *S. Korea* **187** Q11
Jeongok, *S. Korea* **186** L8
Jeongseon, *S. Korea* **187** N11
Jeonju, *S. Korea* **187** R8
Jequié, *Braz.* **133** J16
Jequitinhonha, river, *Braz.* **133** J16
Jerantut, *Malaysia* **191** T10
Jerba Island, *Tun.* **201** B13
Jérémie, *Haiti* **119** M15
Jeremoabo, *Braz.* **133** G17
Jerez de la Frontera, *Sp.* **146** M4
Jerez de los Caballeros, *Sp.* **146** J7
Jericho see Arīḩā, *W. Bank* **172** M6
Jericoacoara, Point, *S. Amer.* **128** E11
Jerid, Shott el, *Tun.* **200** D12
Jerimoth Hill, *R.I., U.S.* **97** L14
Jerome, *Idaho, U.S.* **108** H5
Jerramungup, *W. Aust., Austral.* **215** X4
Jersey, island, *Channel Is., U.K.* **145** Z12
Jersey Bay, *Virgin Is., U.S.* **122** N9
Jersey City, *N.J., U.S.* **96** N11
Jersey Shore, *Pa., U.S.* **96** M7
Jerseyville, *Ill., U.S.* **101** S4
Jerusalem, *Israel* **172** M5
Jervis Bay, *Austral.* **214** L14
Jervis Bay Territory, *Austral.* **215** Y14
Jerzu, *It.* **153** P4
Jesenice, *Slov.* **154** C4
Jeseník, *Czech Rep.* **151** G13
Jesi, *It.* **152** H9
Jessore, *Bangladesh* **180** J12
Jesup, *Ga., U.S.* **99** P8
Jesús María, *Arg.* **134** J10

Jetmore, *Kans., U.S.* **107** T5
Jetpur, *India* **180** J2
Jeungdo, island, *S. Korea* **187** T6
Jeungpyeong, *S. Korea* **187** P9
Jewel Cave National Monument, *S. Dak., U.S.* **106** L1
Jewell, *Iowa, U.S.* **107** N11
Jewett, *Tex., U.S.* **105** N12
Jeypore, *India* **180** L8
Jezercë, Maja, *Alban.* **154** J9
Jezioro Shiardwy, lake, *Pol.* **151** B16
Jezzîne, *Leb.* **172** J6
Jhalawar, *India* **180** H5
Jhal Jhao, *Pak.* **179** V5
Jhang, *Pak.* **179** Q10
Jhansi, *India* **180** H6
Jharsuguda, *India* **180** K9
Jhatpat, *Pak.* **179** T7
Jhelum, *Pak.* **179** N11
Jhelum, river, *Pak.* **179** Q10
Jhimpir, *Pak.* **179** W7
Jhudo, *Pak.* **179** W8
Jhunjhunun, *India* **180** F5
Jiahe, *Hunan, China* **185** T4
Jiaji see Qionghai, *China* **182** Q12
Jialing, river, *China* **182** K10
Jialu see Jiaxian, *Shaanxi, China* **184** E3
Jiamusi, *China* **183** C17
Ji'an, *Jiangxi, China* **185** R6
Ji'an, *Jiangxi, China* **185** R6
Ji'an, *Jilin, China* **184** B15
Jian, river, *Fujian, China* **185** S9
Jianchang, *Liaoning, China* **184** C10
Jiande, *Zhejiang, China* **185** P10
Jiangda see Jomda, *China* **182** K8
Jiangdu, *Jiangsu, China* **184** L10
Jianghua, *Hunan, China* **185** T3
Jiangjunmiao, *China* **182** E6
Jiangle, *Fujian, China* **185** S8
Jiangmen, *Guang., China* **185** W3
Jiangshan, *Jiangxi, China* **185** Q9
Jiangsu, *China* **184** J10
Jiangxi, *China* **185** R6
Jiangyan, *Jiangsu, China* **184** L11
Jiangyin, *Jiangsu, China* **184** M11
Jiangyou, *China* **182** K10
Jiangzhou, *Hubei, China* **185** N4
Jiangzi see Gyangzê, *China* **182** L5
Jianhu, *Jiangsu, China* **184** K10
Jianli, *Hubei, China* **185** P4
Jianning, *Fujian, China* **185** S8
Jian'ou, *Fujian, China* **185** S9
Jianping, *Liaoning, China* **184** B10
Jianshi, *Hubei, China* **185** N2
Jianyang, *Fujian, China* **185** R9
Jiaocheng, *Shanxi, China* **184** F4
Jiaojiang see Taizhou, *Zhejiang, China* **185** Q12
Jiaoling, *Guang., China* **185** U7
Jiaonan, *Shand., China* **184** H10
Jiaozhou, *Shand., China* **184** G10
Jiaozhou Wan, *Shand., China* **184** G11
Jiaozuo, *Henan, China* **184** H5
Jiawang, *Jiangsu, China* **184** J8
Jiaxian, *Henan, China* **184** J5
Jiaxian (Jialu), *Shaanxi, China* **184** E3
Jiaxing, *Zhejiang, China* **185** N11
Jiayin, *China* **183** B17
Jiayu, *Hubei, China* **185** P5
Jiayuguan, *China* **182** G8
Jiazi, *Guang., China* **185** W7
Jibsh, Ra's, *Oman* **175** L17
Jido, *India* **180** E15
Jido, *S. Korea* **187** T7
Jido, island, *S. Korea* **187** T7
Jieshi, *Guang., China* **185** W7
Jieshi Wan, *Guang., China* **185** W6
Jieshou, *Anhui, China* **184** K7
Jiesjavrre, lake, *Nor.* **143** C14
Jiexi, *Guang., China* **185** V7
Jiexiu, *Shanxi, China* **184** F4
Jieyang, *Guang., China* **185** V7
Jiggalong, *W. Aust., Austral.* **215** T4
Jigüey, Bahía de, *Cuba* **118** H10
Jigzhi, *China* **182** K9
Jihlava, *Czech Rep.* **150** H12
Jijia, river, *Rom.* **155** B16
Jijiga, *Eth.* **203** G16
Jiksan, *S. Korea* **187** P8
Jilib, *Somalia* **203** K16

Jilin, *China* **183** E16
Jilin, *China* **184** A15
Jilong see Gyirong, *China* **182** L3
Jilong see Keelung, *Taiwan, China* **185** T12
Jīma, *Eth.* **203** G14
Jimaní, *Dom. Rep.* **119** M17
Jimbolia, *Rom.* **154** D10
Jiménez, *Mex.* **116** E9
Jimo, *Shand., China* **184** G11
Jin, river, *Fujian, China* **185** S8
Jin, river, *Jiangxi, China* **185** Q6
Jinan, *S. Korea* **187** R9
Jinan, *Shand., China* **184** G8
Jinbal, island, *Marshall Is., U.S.* **220** L8
Jinchang, *China* **182** G9
Jincheng, *Shanxi, China* **184** H4
Jincheon, *S. Korea* **187** P9
Jindo, *S. Korea* **187** U7
Jindo, island, *S. Korea* **187** U7
Jindong, *S. Korea* **187** T11
Jindřichův Hradec, *Czech Rep.* **150** J11
Jinedrol, island, *Marshall Is., U.S.* **220** H8
Jing, river, *Shaanxi, China* **184** J1
Jingazhir, *Taj.* **178** H11
Jingbian (Zhangjiapan), *Shaanxi, China* **184** F1
Jingde, *Anhui, China* **185** N9
Jingdezhen, *Jiangxi, China* **185** P8
Jinggu, *China* **182** P9
Jinghai, *Guang., China* **185** W7
Jinghai, *Tianjin Shi, China* **184** D8
Jinghe, *China* **182** D4
Jinghong, *China* **182** P9
Jingle, *Shanxi, China* **184** E4
Jingmen, *Hubei, China* **184** M3
Jingxi, *China* **182** P11
Jingyuan, *China* **182** H10
Jingzhou, *Hunan, China* **185** S1
Jinhae, *S. Korea* **187** S11
Jinhaemen, bay, *S. Korea* **187** T11
Jinhu (Licheng), *Jiangsu, China* **184** L10
Jinhua, *Zhejiang, China* **185** P10
Jinimi, island, *Marshall Is., U.S.* **220** H8
Jining, *N. Mongol, China* **184** B5
Jining, *Shand., China* **184** H8
Jinja, *Uganda* **203** K13
Jinjiang, *Fujian, China* **185** U9
Jinju, *S. Korea* **187** S10
Jinnyang, *S. Korea* **187** R11
Jinsha, *China* **182** M10
Jinsha (Yangtze), river, *China* **182** L8
Jinshan, *Shanghai Shi, China* **185** N12
Jinshi, *Hunan, China* **185** P3
Jinta, *China* **182** G8
Jinxi see Huludao, *Liaoning, China* **184** C11
Jinxiang, *Fujian, China* **185** R11
Jinxiang, *Shand., China* **184** H7
Jinyeong, *S. Korea* **187** S11
Jinzhai, *Anhui, China* **184** M7
Jinzhou, *Liaoning, China* **184** B11
Jinzhou, *Liaoning, China* **184** D12
Jinzhou Wan, *Liaoning, China* **184** D12
Ji-Paraná, *Braz.* **132** G8
Jiparaná, river, *Braz.* **132** F8
Jipijapa, *Ecua.* **130** K2
Jirgatol, *Taj.* **178** H9
Jirisan, peak, *S. Korea* **187** S9
Jīroft, *Iran* **175** G16
Jishou, *Hunan, China* **185** Q1
Jishu, *China* **183** D16
Jishui, *Jiangxi, China* **185** R6
Jisr ash Shughūr, *Syr.* **172** E7
Jiu, river, *Rom.* **155** G13
Jiuhua Shan, *Anhui, China* **185** N9
Jiujiang, *Jiangxi, China* **185** P7
Jiulian Shan, *Guang., China* **185** U5
Jiuling Shan, *Jiangxi, China* **185** Q6
Jiulong (Kowloon), *Hong Kong (Xianggang), S.A.R., China* **185** W5
Jiupu, *Liaoning, China* **184** B13
Jiuquan, *China* **182** G8
Jiutai, *China* **183** E16
Jiwani, *Pak.* **179** W1

Jixi, *Anhui, China* 185 N9
Jixi, *China* 183 D17
Jixian, *Beijing Shi, China* 184 C8
Jixian, *Shanxi, China* 184 G3
Jiyuan, *Henan, China* 184 H4
Jīzān, *Saudi Arabia* 174 P8
Jizhou, *Hebei, China* 184 F7
Jizzax, *Uzb.* 176 L12
Joaçaba, *Braz.* 132 N12
João Pessoa, *Braz.* 133 F18
Joaquín V. González, *Arg.* 134 F10
Jobos, *P.R., U.S.* 122 P4
Jobos, Bahía de, *P.R., U.S.* 122 P4
Jocheon, *S. Korea* 187 W7
Jochiwon-eup, *S. Korea* 187 P9
Jodar, *Sp.* 146 K11
Jodhpur, *India* 180 G3
Joensuu, *Fin.* 143 G17
Joe's Hill, *Kiribati* 221 B23
Jōetsu, *Japan* 188 M11
Joeuf, *Fr.* 149 N14
Joey Rise, *Ind. Oc.* 225 J17
Jogindar Nagar, *India* 179 P14
Jogipet, *India* 180 M6
Johannesburg, *Calif., U.S.* 111 V9
Johannesburg, *S. Af.* 206 J10
John Day, river, *Oreg., U.S.* 110 G6
John Day Dam, *Oreg., Wash., U.S.* 110 E5
John Day Fossil Beds National Monument, *Oreg., U.S.* 110 G6
John D. Rockefeller Jr. Memorial Parkway, *Wyo., U.S.* 108 G8
John Eyre Motel, *W. Aust., Austral.* 215 X6
John F. Kennedy Space Center, *Fla., U.S.* 99 T10
John H. Kerr Reservoir, *N.C., Va., U.S.* 98 G12
John Martin Reservoir, *Colo., U.S.* 109 N15
John Millars, *Bahamas* 122 F6
John o'Groats, site, *Scot., U.K.* 144 G10
John Redmond Reservoir, *Kans., U.S.* 107 T9
Johns Folly Bay, *Virgin Is., U.S.* 122 N11
Johnson, *Kans., U.S.* 107 U3
Johnsonburg, *Pa., U.S.* 96 M5
Johnson City, *N.Y., U.S.* 96 L8
Johnson City, *Tenn., U.S.* 103 E20
Johnson City, *Tex., U.S.* 105 Q9
Johnson Draw, river, *Tex., U.S.* 105 Q6
Johnsons Point, *Antigua and Barbuda* 123 B20
Johnston, *S.C., U.S.* 98 L7
Johnston, Lake, *Austral.* 214 K4
Johnston, Mount, *Antarctica* 231 F19
Johnston Atoll, *Pac. Oc.* 218 D10
Johnston City, *Ill., U.S.* 101 U6
Johnstone, *Scot., U.K.* 144 M9
Johnston Seamounts, *Pac. Oc.* 242 H12
Johnstown, *N.Y., U.S.* 96 J11
Johnstown, *Pa., U.S.* 96 P4
Johor Baharu, *Malaysia* 191 V11
Joides Basin, *Pac. Oc.* 249 H15
Joigny, *Fr.* 149 Q11
Joint Region Marianas (Andersen Air Force Base), *Guam, U.S.* 220 B12
Joint Region Marianas (Naval Base Guam), *Guam, U.S.* 220 C10
Joinville, *Braz.* 133 N13
Joinville Island, *Antarctica* 230 C4
Jokaj, island, *F.S.M.* 221 F14
Jokkmokk, *Sw.* 143 E13
Jökuldjúp, valley, *Atl. Oc.* 247 M21
Joliet, *Ill., U.S.* 101 P7
Joliette, *Que., Can.* 85 P19
Jolo, *Philippines* 193 G13
Jolo, island, *Philippines* 193 G13
Jomda (Jiangda), *China* 182 K8
Jonesboro, *Ark., U.S.* 102 F10
Jonesboro, *La., U.S.* 102 L8
Jonesport, *Me., U.S.* 97 F19
Jones Sound, *Arctic Oc.* 247 N13
Jones Sound, *Nunavut, Can.* 85 D15
Jonesville, *La., U.S.* 102 M9

Jonesville, *S.C., U.S.* 98 J8
Jönköping, *Sw.* 143 L13
Jonuta, *Mex.* 117 J15
Jonzac, *Fr.* 149 U7
Joplin, *Mo., U.S.* 107 VII
Joplin, *Mont., U.S.* 108 B8
Jordan, *Asia* 173 P7
Jordan, *Minn., U.S.* 106 K11
Jordan, *Mont., U.S.* 108 C11
Jordan, river, *Jordan* 172 M6
Jordan Valley, *Oreg., U.S.* 110 J9
Jorhat, *India* 180 F14
Jorge Montt, Isla, *Chile* 135 W6
Jörn, *Sw.* 143 F14
Jornada del Muerto, *N. Mex., U.S.* 109 U12
Jorong, *Indonesia* 192 K11
Jørpeland, *Nor.* 142 L10
Jos, *Nigeria* 205 C14
José Batlle-y-Ordóñez, *Uru.* 134 L14
Joseph, *Wash., U.S.* 110 F9
Joseph Bonaparte Gulf, *Austral.* 214 B7
José Rodrigues, *Braz.* 132 E12
Joshimath, *India* 180 E7
Joshua Tree National Park, *Calif., U.S.* 111 X11
Josipdol, *Croatia* 154 E5
Jos Plateau, *Af.* 198 H5
Josselin, *Fr.* 149 Q4
Jost Van Dyke, island, *British Virgin Is., U.K.* 122 L11
Jotunheimen, range, *Nor.* 142 J10
Jou, *Sao Tome and Principe* 209 D19
Joulter Cays, *Bahamas* 118 D11
Joûnié, *Leb.* 172 H6
Jourdanton, *Tex., U.S.* 105 S9
Joutsa, *Fin.* 143 H16
Jovellanos, *Cuba* 118 G7
Joyakdo, island, *S. Korea* 187 U8
Joyeuse, *Fr.* 149 W12
J. Percy Priest Lake, *Tenn., U.S.* 103 E15
Jreida, *Mauritania* 200 F5
J. Strom Thurmond Reservoir, *Ga., S.C., U.S.* 98 L6
Ju, river, *Hubei, China* 184 M3
Juana Díaz, *P.R., U.S.* 122 N3
Juan Aldama, *Mex.* 116 F10
Juan de Fuca, Strait of, *N. Amer.* 82 G2
Juan de Fuca Ridge, *Pac. Oc.* 243 D17
Juan de Nova, Île, *Fr.* 207 F16
Juan Domingo, *Curaçao, Neth.* 123 P14
Juan Fernández Islands, *S. Amer.* 128 M2
Juan José Castelli, *Arg.* 134 F12
Juanjuí, *Peru* 132 F3
Juan Stuven, Isla, *Chile* 135 U6
Juárez, *Arg.* 135 N12
Juàzeiro, *Braz.* 133 G16
Juazeiro do Norte, *Braz.* 133 F16
Juba, *S. Sudan* 203 H13
Jubba, river, *Af.* 198 J11
Jubba, Webi, *Somalia* 203 J16
Jubbah, *Saudi Arabia* 174 G8
Jubb al Jarrāḥ, *Syr.* 172 G9
Juberri, *Andorra* 162 K2
Jubilee Lake, *Austral.* 214 H6
Juby, Cap, *Mor.* 200 C6
Júcar, river, *Sp.* 147 H13
Júcaro, *Cuba* 118 J10
Jucheon, *S. Korea* 187 N10
Juchitán, *Mex.* 117 K14
Judayyidat 'Ar'ar, *Saudi Arabia* 174 E8
Judenberg, *Aust.* 150 L11
Judith, river, *Mont., U.S.* 108 C9
Judith Basin, *Mont., U.S.* 108 C9
Judith Gap, *Mont., U.S.* 108 D9
Judsonia, *Ark., U.S.* 102 F9
Juegang see Rudong, *Jiangsu, China* 184 L11
Juigalpa, *Nicar.* 117 M18
Juiz de Fora, *Braz.* 133 L18
Jukbyeon, *S. Korea* 187 N12
Julesburg, *Colo., U.S.* 108 K16
Juliaca, *Peru* 132 J6
Julia Creek, *Qnsld., Austral.* 215 S12

Julian, *Calif., U.S.* 111 Y10
Julian Alps, *Slov.* 152 C10
Julianehåb Valley, *Atl. Oc.* 247 R20
Julpo, *S. Korea* 187 S7
Julpoman, bay, *S. Korea* 187 S7
Jumilla, *Sp.* 147 J13
Jumla, *Nepal* 180 E8
Jumundo, island, *S. Korea* 186 M7
Jumunjin, *S. Korea* 186 M11
Junan (Shizilu), *Shand., China* 184 H9
Juncos, *P.R., U.S.* 122 N5
Junction, *Tex., U.S.* 105 Q8
Junction, *Utah, U.S.* 109 N7
Junction Bay, *Austral.* 214 A9
Junction City, *Ark., U.S.* 102 K8
Junction City, *Kans., U.S.* 107 S8
Junction City, *Oreg., U.S.* 110 H3
Jundiaí, *Braz.* 133 M13
Juneau, *Alas., U.S.* 113 K22
Jungar Qi, *N. Mongol, China* 184 C3
Jungdae, *S. Korea* 187 S11
Junggar Pendi (Dzungarian Basin), *China* 182 D5
Junglinster, *Lux.* 162 J10
Jungshahi, *Pak.* 179 W7
Jungtaedo, island, *S. Korea* 187 U5
Juniper Mountain, *Oreg., U.S.* 110 J6
Junian, *China* 182 M10
Junín, *Arg.* 134 L11
Junín, *Peru* 132 H3
Junín de los Andes, *Arg.* 135 P7
Junnar, *India* 180 L4
Juno Beach, *Fla., U.S.* 99 V10
Juntura, *Oreg., U.S.* 110 H8
Jupaguá, *Braz.* 133 H15
Jupiter, *Fla., U.S.* 99 V10
Jura, island, *Scot., U.K.* 144 M7
Jura, Sound of, *Scot., U.K.* 144 M7
Juradó, *Col.* 130 E3
Jura Mountains, *Fr., Switz.* 152 B1
Jurien, *W. Aust., Austral.* 215 W2
Jurien Bay, *Austral.* 214 J2
Jurm, *Afghan.* 178 K9
Juruá, *Braz.* 132 E7
Juruá, river, *Braz.* 132 G4
Juruena, river, *Braz.* 132 F10
Juruti, *Braz.* 132 D10
Justo Daract, *Arg.* 134 L9
Jutaí, *Braz.* 132 E6
Jutaí, river, *Braz.* 132 E6
Jutiapa, *Guatemala* 117 L16
Juticalpa, *Hond.* 117 L18
Jutland, *Eur.* 140 F6
Jutland Bank, *Atl. Oc.* 240 G13
Juventud, Isla de la, *Cuba* 118 J4
Juxian (Chengyang), *Shand., China* 184 H9
Juzennecourt, *Fr.* 149 Q12
Južna Morava, river, *Serb.* 154 H11
Juzzak, *Pak.* 179 S1
Jwasarido, island, *S. Korea* 187 U10
Jylland (Jutland), region, *Den.* 142 N11
Jyväskylä, *Fin.* 143 G16

K

K2 (Godwin Austen, Qogir Feng), peak, *China, Pak.* 178 L13
Ka'a'awa, *Hawai'i, U.S.* 114 E11
Kaabong, *Uganda* 203 J13
Kaala-Gomén, *New Caledonia, Fr.* 222 C6
Ka'alu'alu Bay, *Hawai'i, U.S.* 115 Q19
Kaamanen, *Fin.* 143 C15
Kaambooni, *Somalia* 203 K16
Kaambooni, Raas, *Af.* 198 K11
Kā'anapali, *Hawai'i, U.S.* 115 G15
Kaap Plateau, *Af.* 198 P8
Kabaena, island, *Indonesia* 193 L14
Kabala, *Sierra Leone* 204 C6
Kabale, *Uganda* 202 K12
Kabalo, *Dem. Rep. of the Congo* 202 M11
Kabambare, *Dem. Rep. of the Congo* 202 L11

Kabara, island, *Fiji* 222 K9
Kabarei, *Indonesia* 193 J17
Kabbenbock, island, *Marshall Is., U.S.* 220 M8
Kabena, island, *Asia* 168 M13
Kabinda, *Dem. Rep. of the Congo* 202 M10
Kabīr, river, *Leb.* 172 G7
Kabong, *Malaysia* 192 H10
Kabongo, *Dem. Rep. of the Congo* 202 M11
Kaboudia, Ras, *Af.* 198 C6
Kabūd Gombad, *Iran* 175 B16
Kābul (Kabul), *Afghan.* 178 M8
Kābul, river, *Afghan.* 178 M8
Kabuli, *P.N.G.* 217 B19
Kabumbé, Pico, *Sao Tome and Principe* 209 D20
Kaburuang, island, *Indonesia* 193 G16
Kabwe, *Zambia* 206 E11
Kachchh, Gulf of (Gulf of Kutch), *India* 180 J1
Kachchh, Rann of (Kutch, Rann of), *India, Pak.* 179 X7
Kachīry, *Kaz.* 177 B15
Kachreti, *Rep. of Georgia* 171 C19
Kaçkar Dağı, peak, *Turk.* 171 D15
Kadaingti, *Myanmar* 190 K7
Kadan Kyun, island, *Myanmar* 191 N7
Kadavu, island, *Fiji* 222 K6
Kadavu Passage, *Fiji* 222 K6
Kadé, *Guinea* 204 B5
Kadgo, Lake, *Austral.* 214 G6
Kadıköy, *Turk.* 170 D2
Kading, river, *Thai.* 190 K12
Kadınhanı, *Turk.* 170 G7
Kadiri, *India* 181 P6
Kadirli, *Turk.* 170 H11
Kadivka, *Ukr.* 159 Q10
Kadmat Island (Cardamum Island), *India* 181 Q3
Ka-do, island, *N. Korea* 186 H4
Kadoka, *S. Dak., U.S.* 106 L3
Kadom, *Russ.* 158 K12
Kadoma, *Zimb.* 206 F11
Kadugli, *Sudan* 202 F12
Kaduna, *Nigeria* 205 C14
Kadur, *India* 181 P5
Kadyy, *Russ.* 158 G12
Kaech'ŏn, *N. Korea* 186 H6
Kaédi, *Mauritania* 200 G5
Kaélé, *Cameroon* 205 C17
Ka'ena Point, *Hawai'i, U.S.* 114 E10
Ka'eo, peak, *Hawai'i, U.S.* 114 C3
Kaeo, *N.Z.* 217 H18
Kaep'ung, *N. Korea* 186 M7
Kaesŏng, *N. Korea* 186 M7
Kāf, *Saudi Arabia* 174 E6
Kāfar Jar Ghar, range, *Afghan.* 179 P5
Kafia Kingi, *S. Sudan* 202 G10
Kafia Kingi, region, *S. Sudan* 202 G10
Kafue, *Zambia* 206 E10
Kafue, river, *Zambia* 206 E10
Kafuka, *Japan* 188 E12
Kaga, *Japan* 189 N9
Kaga Bandoro, *Cen. Af. Rep.* 202 H9
Kagan, *Pak.* 178 M10
Kağızman, *Turk.* 171 E17
Kagmar, *Sudan* 202 E12
Kagoshima, *Japan* 189 T4
Kahakuloa, *Hawai'i, U.S.* 115 G16
Kahalu'u, *Hawai'i, U.S.* 114 E11
Kahalu'u, *Hawai'i, U.S.* 115 N18
Kahama, *Tanzania* 203 L13
Kahan, *Pak.* 179 S7
Kahana, *Hawai'i, U.S.* 115 G16
Kahe'a Heiau & Petroglyphs, *Hawai'i, U.S.* 115 H15
Kahei Homesteads, *Hawai'i, U.S.* 115 K19
Kahemba, *Dem. Rep. of the Congo* 202 M8
Kāhili, peak, *Hawai'i, U.S.* 114 C5
Kahlotus, *Wash., U.S.* 110 D8
Kahnūj, *Iran* 175 G16
Kahoka, *Mo., U.S.* 107 Q13
Kaho'olawe, Island, *Hawai'i, U.S.* 115 J15

Kahouanne, Îlet à, *Guadeloupe, Fr.* 123 E14
Kahramanmaraş, *Turk.* 170 H12
Kâhta, *Turk.* 171 H13
Kahuku, *Hawai'i, U.S.* 114 D11
Kahuku, *Hawai'i, U.S.* 115 Q19
Kahuku Point, *Hawai'i, U.S.* 114 D11
Kahului, *Hawai'i, U.S.* 115 G16
Kahului Harbor, *Hawai'i, U.S.* 115 G16
Kahuwa'a (Sacred Falls), *Hawai'i, U.S.* 114 E11
Kai, Kepulauan (Ewab), *Indonesia* 193 L18
Kaiama, *Nigeria* 204 C12
Kaibab Plateau, *U.S.* 86 H6
Kaibito, *Ariz., U.S.* 109 Q8
Kaieteur Falls, *Guyana* 131 E14
Kaifeng, *Henan, China* 184 J6
Kaiholena, peak, *Hawai'i, U.S.* 115 P20
Kai Kecil, island, *Indonesia* 193 L18
Kai, Kepulauan, *Indonesia* 217 C14
Kaikoura, *N.Z.* 217 N18
Kailas Range, *Asia* 168 H7
Kaili, *China* 182 M11
Kailua, *Hawai'i, U.S.* 114 E12
Kailua-Kona, *Hawai'i, U.S.* 115 M18
Kaimana, *Indonesia* 217 C15
Kaimu Beach (Black Sand Beach), *Hawai'i, U.S.* 115 P22
Kainan Maru Seamounts, *Ind. Oc.* 248 F9
Kainji Reservoir, *Nigeria* 205 C13
Kaipara Harbour, *N.Z.* 217 J18
Kaiserslautern, *Ger.* 150 H6
Kaitaia, *N.Z.* 217 H18
Ka'iwaloa Heiau & Olowalu Petroglyphs, *Hawai'i, U.S.* 115 H16
Kaiwi Channel, *Hawai'i, U.S.* 114 G12
Kaiyuan, *China* 182 N9
Kaiyuan, *Liaoning, China* 184 A13
Kaiyuh Mountains, *Alas., U.S.* 113 G14
Kajaani, *Fin.* 143 F16
Kajabbi, *Qnsld., Austral.* 215 S11
Kajakī, Band-e, *Afghan.* 179 P5
Kajang, *Malaysia* 191 U10
Kaka, *S. Sudan* 203 F13
Kaka, *Uzb.* 176 M9
Kakamas, *S. Af.* 206 K8
Kakana, *India* 181 S14
Kakaramea, *N.Z.* 217 L18
Kakdwip, *India* 180 J11
Kake, *Alas., U.S.* 113 L22
Kakeroma Jima, *Japan* 189 W3
Kākhk, *Iran* 175 D16
Kakhovka, *Ukr.* 159 R7
Kakhovka Reservoir, *Eur.* 140 H12
Kakhovs'ke Vodoskhovyshche, *Ukr.* 159 R7
Kakinada (Cocanada), *India* 180 M8
Kakogawa, *Japan* 189 Q8
Kakshaal Range, *China, Kyrg.* 178 F13
Kaktovik, *Alas., U.S.* 113 C18
Kakuda, *Japan* 188 M12
Kalabagh, *Pak.* 179 N9
Kalabakan, *Malaysia* 192 G12
Kalabo, *Zambia* 206 E8
Kalaburagi (Gulbarga), *India* 180 M5
Kalach, *Russ.* 159 N11
Kalach na Donu, *Russ.* 159 P12
Kalae (South Point), *Hawai'i, U.S.* 115 Q19
Kalafrana, *Malta* 163 L23
Kalahari Desert, *Af.* 206 H8
Kalāheo, *Hawai'i, U.S.* 114 C5
Kal'ai Khumb, *Taj.* 178 H9
Kalalua, peak, *Hawai'i, U.S.* 115 N22
Kalam, *Pak.* 178 L10
Kalama, *Wash., U.S.* 110 E3
Kalamáta, *Gr.* 156 L9
Kalamazoo, *Mich., U.S.* 100 M10
Kalamazoo, river, *Mich., U.S.* 100 M9
Kalambáka, *Gr.* 156 E9
Kálamos, island, *Gr.* 156 H7
Kalamotí, *Gr.* 157 H16
Kalaniopuu Basin, *Pac. Oc.* 242 G10
Kalao, island, *Indonesia* 193 M13
Kalaoa, *Hawai'i, U.S.* 115 M18
Kalaotoa, island, *Indonesia* 193 M14
Kalasin, *Thai.* 190 L10
Kalat, *Pak.* 179 S6
Kalat see Qalāt, *Afghan.* 179 P6

Kalaupapa, *Hawai'i, U.S.* 115 F14
Kalaupapa National Historical Park, *Hawai'i, U.S.* 115 F14
Kalávryta, *Gr.* 156 J9
Kalawao, *Hawai'i, U.S.* 115 F15
Kalaýmor, *Uzb.* 176 N1O
Kalay-wa, *Myanmar* 190 F5
Kalb, Ra's al, *Yemen* 174 Q11
Kalbān, *Oman* 175 M17
Kalbarri, *W. Aust., Austral.* 215 V2
Kaldār, *Afghan.* 178 K6
Kalealoa, *Hawai'i, U.S.* 114 F1O
Kale Burnu, *Turk.* 171 D14
Kaleburnu see Galinoporni, *Cyprus* 162 M11
Kalecik, *Turk.* 170 E9
Kaledupa, island, *Indonesia* 193 L14
Kalemie, *Dem. Rep. of the Congo* 202 M12
Kalemyo, *Myanmar* 190 F5
Kalenyy, *Kaz.* 176 D6
Kaleybar, *Iran* 174 A1O
Kalgoorlie-Boulder, *W. Aust., Austral.* 215 W4
Kaliakoúda, peak, *Gr.* 156 G9
Kaliakra, Nos, *Bulg.* 155 H18
Kalianda, *Indonesia* 192 L7
Kalihi Wai, *Hawai'i, U.S.* 114 B5
Kalihi Wai Bay, *Hawai'i, U.S.* 114 B6
Kalí Límni, peak, *Gr.* 157 P18
Kalima, *Dem. Rep. of the Congo* 202 L11
Kalimantan see Borneo, island, *Indonesia* 192 J1O
Kalimpang, *India* 180 G11
Kaliningrad, *Russ.* 158 J1
Kaliningrad Oblast, *Russ.* 158 J2
Kalinino, *Arm.* 171 C18
Kalinino, *Russ.* 159 S1O
Kalininsk, *Russ.* 158 M13
Kalinkavichy, *Belarus* 158 M5
Kalispell, *Mont., U.S.* 108 B5
Kalisz, *Pol.* 151 E14
Kalix, *Sw.* 143 E14
Kalkan, *Turk.* 170 J5
Kalkaska, *Mich., U.S.* 100 J1O
Kallithéa, *Gr.* 156 J12
Kalloní, *Gr.* 157 F16
Kallonís, Kólpos, *Gr.* 157 F16
Kallsjön, lake, *Sw.* 142 G12
Kalmar, *Sw.* 143 M13
Kalnai, *India* 180 J9
Kalnik, peak, *Croatia* 154 D6
Kalo Chorio, *Cyprus* 162 Q7
Kalohi Channel, *Hawai'i, U.S.* 115 G14
Kaloko-Honokōhau National Historical Park, *Hawai'i, U.S.* 115 M18
Kaloli Point, *Hawai'i, U.S.* 115 M22
Kalpa, *India* 180 D6
Kalpeni Island, *India* 181 R3
Kalpin, *China* 182 F3
Kalpitiya, *Sri Lanka* 181 S7
Kalskag, *Alas., U.S.* 113 J13
Kalsubai, peak, *India* 180 L4
Kaltag, *Alas., U.S.* 113 G14
Kaluga, *Russ.* 158 K9
Kalumburu, *W. Aust., Austral.* 215 P5
Kalush, *Ukr.* 159 P2
Kal'ya, *Russ.* 160 G9
Kalyan, *India* 180 L3
Kalyazin, *Russ.* 158 H9
Kálymnos, *Gr.* 157 L18
Kálymnos, island, *Gr.* 157 L18
Kama, river, *Russ.* 160 H7
Kamaing, *Myanmar* 190 E6
Kamaishi, *Japan* 188 K13
Kamakal, island, *Fr. Polynesia, Fr.* 223 R21
Kamakou, peak, *Hawai'i, U.S.* 115 G15
Kamalino, *Hawai'i, U.S.* 114 D2
Kaman, *Turk.* 170 F9
Kamárai, *Gr.* 157 L14
Kamarān, island, *Yemen* 174 Q8
Kama Reservoir, *Eur.* 140 C14
Kamariótissa, *Gr.* 157 D15
Kamarod, *Pak.* 179 T3
Kamar Zard, *Afghan.* 179 N2
Kambalda, *W. Aust., Austral.* 215 W4
Kambang, *Indonesia* 192 K6

Kambove, *Dem. Rep. of the Congo* 202 N11
Kamchatka, Gulf of, *Pac. Oc.* 168 C13
Kamchatka Peninsula, *Asia* 168 B13
Kamchatka Poluostrov, *Russ.* 161 F22
Kamchatskiy Poluostrov, *Russ.* 161 E22
Kamchiya, river, *Bulg.* 155 H17
Kamehameha Basin, *Pac. Oc.* 243 N11
Kamehameha I Birthplace, *Hawai'i, U.S.* 115 K18
Kámeiros (Camirus), ruin, *Gr.* 157 M19
Kamen, Gora, *Russ.* 161 G14
Kaména Voúrla, *Gr.* 156 G11
Kamenjak, Rt, *Croatia* 154 E3
Kamenka, *Kaz.* 176 C6
Kamenka, *Russ.* 158 L12
Kamenka, *Russ.* 160 E9
Kamenskiy, *Russ.* 159 N13
Kamensk Shakhtinskiy, *Russ.* 159 Q11
Kamensk Ural'skiy, *Russ.* 160 J9
Kamiah, *Idaho, U.S.* 108 D4
Kaminone Shima, *Japan* 189 V3
Kamino Shima, *Japan* 189 Q4
Kamitsuki, *Japan* 189 Q12
Kamitsushima, *Japan* 189 Q4
Kamiyaku, *Japan* 189 U4
Kamkhat Muḥaywir, peak, *Jordan* 173 N7
Kamloops, *B.C., Can.* 84 M8
Kamo, *Arm.* 171 D19
Kamōhio Bay, *Hawai'i, U.S.* 115 J16
Kamoke, *Pak.* 179 P12
Kamo'oloa, *Hawai'i, U.S.* 114 E1O
Kampala, *Uganda* 203 K13
Kampanós, Akrotírio, *Gr.* 157 J14
Kampar, *Malaysia* 191 T9
Kampen, *Neth.* 148 H13
Kamphaeng Phet, *Thai.* 190 L8
Kâmpóng Cham (Kompong Cham), *Cambodia* 191 N12
Kampong Cham see Kâmpóng Cham, *Cambodia* 191 N12
Kâmpóng Chhnăng (Kompong Chhnang), *Cambodia* 191 N11
Kampong Chhnang see Kâmpóng Chhnăng, *Cambodia* 191 N11
Kampong Kuala Besut, *Malaysia* 191 S1O
Kampong Speu see Kâmpóng Spœ, *Cambodia* 191 P11
Kâmpóng Spœ (Kampong Speu), *Cambodia* 191 P11
Kampos, *Cyprus* 162 P6
Kâmpôt (Kampot), *Cambodia* 191 P11
Kampot see Kâmpôt, *Cambodia* 191 P11
Kamrau, Teluk, *Indonesia* 217 C15
Kamsack, *Sask., Can.* 85 M13
Kamsar, *Guinea* 204 C4
Kamui Misaki, *Japan* 188 G12
Kam'yanets-Podil's'kyy, *Ukr.* 159 P3
Kam'yanka-Dniprovs'ka, *Ukr.* 159 R8
Kamyshin, *Russ.* 159 N13
Kamyzyak, *Russ.* 159 R15
Kanab, *Utah, U.S.* 109 Q6
Kanab Creek, *Ariz., Utah, U.S.* 109 Q6
Kanacea, island, *Fiji* 222 G13
Kanaga Island, *Alas., U.S.* 112 N5
Kanak, river, *Turk.* 170 E1O
Kanaláki, *Gr.* 156 F7
Kananga, *Dem. Rep. of the Congo* 202 M9
Kanapou Bay, *Hawai'i, U.S.* 115 J16
Kanarraville, *Utah, U.S.* 109 P6
Kanash, *Russ.* 158 J14
Kanatea, island, *Tonga* 222 J11
Kanawha, river, *W. Va., U.S.* 98 D7
Kanazawa, *Japan* 189 N9
Kanbalu, *Myanmar* 190 F6
Kānchenjunga, peak, *Nepal* 180 F11
Kanchipuram, *India* 181 Q7

Kandahār, *Afghan.* 179 Q5
Kandalaksha, *Russ.* 160 D8
Kandalaksha Bay, *Eur.* 140 B1O
Kandalakshskiy Zaliv, *Russ.* 160 D8
Kandangan, *Indonesia* 192 K11
Kandersteg, *Switz.* 152 C3
Kandhkot, *Pak.* 179 T8
Kandi, *Benin* 204 C12
Kandi, *India* 180 H11
Kandiaro, *Pak.* 179 U7
Kandíla, *Gr.* 156 J1O
Kandıra, *Turk.* 170 C6
Kandrach, *Pak.* 179 V5
Kandrian, *P.N.G.* 217 D2O
Kandudu, island, *Maldives* 181 W3
Kandudu, island, *Maldives* 181 X3
Kandū-ye Bālā, *Afghan.* 179 N5
Kandy, *Sri Lanka* 181 T7
Kane, *Pa., U.S.* 96 L5
Kane Basin, *Arctic Oc.* 247 M14
Kane Basin, *Nunavut, Can.* 85 B16
Kane Fracture Zone, *Atl. Oc.* 240 L7
Kane Gap, *Atl. Oc.* 241 N1O
Kāne'ohe, *Hawai'i, U.S.* 114 E11
Kanevskaya, *Russ.* 159 S1O
Kangal, *Turk.* 170 F12
Kangan, *Iran* 175 H13
Kanganpur, *Pak.* 179 Q12
Kangar, *Malaysia* 191 S8
Kangaroo Island, *Austral.* 214 L1O
Kangbao, *Hebei, China* 184 A6
Kangdêsê Shan (Gangdisi Shan), *China* 182 K3
Kangdŏk, *N. Korea* 186 C13
Kangdong, *N. Korea* 186 J7
Kangean, Kepulauan, *Indonesia* 192 L11
Kangeeak Point, *Nunavut, Can.* 85 F19
Kangerlussuaq, *Greenland, Den.* 82 C1O
Kangerlussuaq Valley, *Atl. Oc.* 247 N19
Kangertittivaq, *Greenland, Den.* 82 B1O
Kanggava Bay, *Solomon Is.* 221 R19
Kanggu, *N. Korea* 186 D1O
Kanggye, *N. Korea* 186 E7
Kangiqsualujjuaq, *Que., Can.* 85 J2O
Kangiqsujuaq, *Que., Can.* 85 J18
Kangirsuk, *Que., Can.* 85 J19
Kangkar Punsum, peak, *Bhutan* 180 F13
Kangma see Kangmar, *China* 182 L5
Kangmar (Kangma), *China* 182 L5
Kangnam-sanmaek, range, *N. Korea* 186 F5
Kangnyŏng, *N. Korea* 186 M5
Kango, *Gabon* 205 H15
Kangpokpi, *India* 180 G14
Kangrinboqê Feng (Gangrenboqi Feng), *China* 182 J2
Kangsŏ, *N. Korea* 186 J5
Kangto, peak, *India* 180 F14
Kaniama, *Dem. Rep. of the Congo* 202 M1O
Kaniere, *N.Z.* 217 N17
Kanif, *F.S.M.* 221 D18
Kanigiri, *India* 181 N7
Kanin, Poluostrov, *Russ.* 160 E9
Kanin Bank, *Arctic Oc.* 247 D18
Kanin Nos, Mys, *Russ.* 160 D9
Kanin Peninsula, *Eur.* 140 A12
Kanish, ruins, *Turk.* 170 F1O
Kaniv, *Ukr.* 159 P6
Kanjarkot, site, *Pak.* 179 W8
Kanjiža, *Serb.* 154 D1O
Kankakee, *Ill., U.S.* 101 P7
Kankakee, river, *Ill., Ind., U.S.* 101 P7
Kankan, *Guinea* 204 C7
Kanker, *India* 180 K8
Kanmaw Kyun, island, *Myanmar* 191 P7
Kanmen, *Zhejiang, China* 185 Q12
Kannapolis, *N.C., U.S.* 98 H9
Kannauj, *India* 180 G7
Kannur (Cannanore), *India* 181 Q4
Kano, *Nigeria* 205 B14
Kanokopolu, *Tonga* 222 H11
Kanopolis, *Kans., U.S.* 107 T7
Kanorado, *Kans., U.S.* 107 S3

Kanosh, *Utah, U.S.* 109 N6
Kanoya, *Japan* 189 T5
Kanpur, *India* 180 G7
Kansas, *U.S.* 107 T6
Kansas, river, *U.S.* 107 S8
Kansas City, *Kans., U.S.* 107 S1O
Kansas City, *Mo., U.S.* 107 S1O
Kansk, *Russ.* 161 K14
Kant, *Kyrg.* 178 D11
Kántanos, *Gr.* 156 Q12
Kantara Castle, ruin, *Cyprus* 162 N1O
Kanton, island, *Kiribati* 218 G1O
Kan-Too Chokusu see Khan-Tengry Peak, *Kaz., Kyrg.* 178 E15
Kanuku Mountains, *Guyana* 131 F14
Kanye, *Botswana* 206 J9
Kao, island, *Tonga* 222 P6
Kaôh Kŏng (Koh Kong), *Thai.* 191 P1O
Kaôh Kŏng, island, *Cambodia* 191 P1O
Kaôh Nhêk, *Cambodia* 191 N13
Kaôh Rŭng, island, *Cambodia* 191 P1O
Kaohsiung, *Taiwan, China* 185 W11
Kaoka Bay, *Solomon Is.* 221 P19
Kaokoland, region, *Namibia* 206 F5
Kaolack, *Senegal* 200 H4
Kaoma, *Zambia* 206 E9
Kaouar, oasis, *Af.* 198 F6
Kapa, island, *Tonga* 222 M11
Kapa'a, *Hawai'i, U.S.* 114 C6
Kapa'au, *Hawai'i, U.S.* 115 K19
Kapadvanj, *India* 180 J3
Kapan, *Arm.* 171 F2O
Kapanga, *Dem. Rep. of the Congo* 202 M1O
Kapela, mountains, *Croatia* 154 E5
Kapfenberg, *Aust.* 150 L12
Kapıdağı, peak, *Turk.* 170 D4
Kapingamarangi Atoll, *F.S.M.* 218 G5
Kapiri Mposhi, *Zambia* 206 E11
Kapiskau, *Ont., Can.* 85 M17
Kapit, *Malaysia* 192 H1O
Kaplan, *La., U.S.* 102 P8
Kaplıca see Dhavlos, *Cyprus* 162 M1O
Kapoeta, *S. Sudan* 203 H13
Kapoho Crater, *Hawai'i, U.S.* 115 N22
Kaposvár, *Hung.* 151 M14
Kappar, *Pak.* 179 V2
Kapsan, *N. Korea* 186 E1O
Kapuāiwa Coconut Grove, *Hawai'i, U.S.* 115 G14
Kapulena, *Hawai'i, U.S.* 115 L2O
Kapurthala, *India* 180 D5
Kapuskasing, *Ont., Can.* 85 N17
Kapydzhik, peak, *Arm.* 171 F2O
Kara-Balta, *Kyrg.* 178 D11
Karabiga, *Turk.* 170 D3
Karabogaz (Bekdash), *Turkm.* 176 J6
Karabük, *Turk.* 170 C8
Kara Burun, *Turk.* 170 J7
Karaburun, *Turk.* 170 F2
Karaburun, cape, *Alban.* 154 M9
Karacabey, *Turk.* 170 D4
Karaca Dağ, peak, *Turk.* 171 H14
Karacadağ, *Turk.* 171 H14
Karacaköy, *Turk.* 170 C4
Karachev, *Russ.* 158 L8
Karachi, *Pak.* 179 W6
Karad, *India* 180 M4
Kara Dağ, peak, *Turk.* 170 H8
Kara Dağ, peak, *Turk.* 171 H18
Karaghbyur (Füzuli), *Azerb.* 171 E21
Karaginskiy, Ostrov, *Russ.* 161 E22
Karaginskiy Gulf, *Pac. Oc.* 168 B13
Karahallı, *Turk.* 170 G5
Karahüyük, *Turk.* 170 G7
Karaisalı, *Turk.* 170 H1O
Karaj, *Iran* 174 C12
Karakax see Moyu, *China* 182 G2
Karakeçi, *Turk.* 171 H14
Karakelong, island, *Indonesia* 193 G16
Karakoçan, *Turk.* 171 F14
Kara-Köl, *Kyrg.* 178 F1O
Karakol (Przheval'sk), *Kyrg.* 178 D14
Karakoram Pass, *China, India* 178 L14
Karakoram Range, *India, Pak.* 178 K12
Karakul', *Taj.* 178 H11
Karakulino, *Russ.* 158 H16
Karakuwisa, *Namibia* 206 F8

Karam, *Russ.* 161 K15
Karaman, *Turk.* 170 H8
Karamay, *China* 182 D5
Karamea, *N.Z.* 217 M17
Karamea Bight, *N.Z.* 217 M17
Karamürsel, *Turk.* 170 D5
Karanja, *India* 180 K6
Karapınar, *Turk.* 170 H8
Kara-Say, *Kyrg.* 178 E14
Karasburg, *Namibia* 206 K7
Kara Sea, *Arctic Oc.* 247 D14
Kara Shelf, *Arctic Oc.* 247 C14
Karasjok, *Nor.* 143 C14
Karas Mountains, *Af.* 198 P7
Karasu, *Turk.* 170 D6
Karasu, river, *Turk.* 171 E15
Karasuk, *Russ.* 160 K11
Karataş, *Turk.* 170 J1O
Karateki Shan, *China* 182 F2
Karatepe, *Turk.* 170 H11
Karathuri, *Myanmar* 191 P7
Karatsu, *Japan* 189 R4
Karatung, island, *Indonesia* 193 G16
Karaul, *Russ.* 161 F13
Karavas (Alsancak), *Cyprus* 162 N8
Karávia, island, *Gr.* 156 M12
Karavostasi (Gemi Konaghi), *Cyprus* 162 N7
Karavostásis, *Gr.* 157 M14
Karawanken, mountains, *Aust., Slov.* 154 C4
Karayazı, *Turk.* 171 E16
Karayün, *Turk.* 170 E12
Karbalā', *Iraq* 174 E9
Karcag, *Hung.* 151 L16
Kardámyla, *Gr.* 157 H16
Kardamýli, *Gr.* 156 L1O
Kardítsa, *Gr.* 156 F9
Kardiva (Karidu), island, *Maldives* 181 U3
Kardiva Channel, *Maldives* 181 U3
Kärdla, *Est.* 143 K15
Karesuando, *Sw.* 143 D14
Kārēzak, *Afghan.* 179 P1
Kargı, *Turk.* 170 D1O
Kargil, *India* 180 B5
Kargilik see Yecheng, *China* 182 F2
Kari, *Nigeria* 205 C15
Kariba, *Zimb.* 206 E11
Kariba, Lake, *Zambia, Zimb.* 206 F1O
Karidu see Kardiva, island, *Maldives* 181 U3
Karikari, Cape, *N.Z.* 217 G18
Karimata, island, *Indonesia* 192 K1O
Karimata, Kepulauan, *Indonesia* 192 J8
Karimganj, *India* 180 H14
Karimnagar, *India* 180 L7
Karimunjawa, Kepulauan, *Indonesia* 192 L9
Karítaina, *Gr.* 156 K9
Karitane, *N.Z.* 217 Q16
Karkar, island, *P.N.G.* 217 C19
Karkinit Gulf, *Eur.* 140 J11
Karkinits'ka Zatoka, *Ukr.* 159 S7
Karkük (Kirkuk), *Iraq* 174 C9
Karlıova, *Turk.* 171 F15
Karlovac, *Croatia* 154 E5
Karlovássi, *Gr.* 157 J17
Karlovy Vary, *Czech Rep.* 150 G1O
Karlshamn, *Sw.* 143 M13
Karlskrona, *Sw.* 143 M13
Karlsruhe, *Ger.* 150 J6
Karlstad, *Minn., U.S.* 106 E8
Karlstad, *Sw.* 142 K12
Karmala, *India* 180 L4
Karmir Blur, ruins, *Arm.* 171 E18
Karmona, *Qnsld., Austral.* 215 V12
Karnali, river, *Nepal* 180 E8
Karnaphuli Reservoir, *Bangladesh* 180 J14
Karnes City, *Tex., U.S.* 105 S1O
Karnobat (Polyanovgrad), *Bulg.* 155 J16
Karoi, *Zimb.* 206 F11
Karoko, *Fiji* 222 G8
Karompa, island, *Indonesia* 193 M14
Karonga, *Malawi* 207 C13
Karonie, *W. Aust., Austral.* 215 W5
Karosa, *Indonesia* 193 K13

Karpas Peninsula, *Cyprus* **162** MII
Kárpathos, *Gr.* **157** P18
Kárpathos (Carpathos), *Gr.* **157** P18
Karpenísi, *Gr.* **156** G9
Karperó, *Gr.* **156** E9
Karre Mountains, *Af.* **198** H6
Kars, *Turk.* **171** D17
Kartal, *Turk.* **170** C5
Karukh, *Afghan.* **178** M3
Karumba, *Qnsld., Austral.* **215** RII
Kārūn, *Iran* **174** FII
Karunjie, *W. Aust., Austral.* **215** Q6
Karvachar (Kǝlbǝcǝr), *Azerb.* **171** E2O
Karviná, *Czech Rep.* **151** HI4
Karwar, *India* **181** N4
Karwi, *India* **180** H8
Kar'yepol'ye, *Russ.* **160** E9
Karyés, *Gr.* **156** LIO
Karyés, *Gr.* **157** DI3
Karynzharyk, desert, *Kaz.* **176** J6
Kárystos, *Gr.* **157** JI3
Kas, *Sudan* **202** FIO
Kaş, *Turk.* **170** J5
Kasai, river, *Af.* **198** K7
Kasaji, *Dem. Rep. of the Congo* **202** NIO
Kasama, *Zambia* **206** CI2
Kasane, *Botswana* **206** F9
Kasar, Ras, *Eritrea* **203** DI5
Kasaragod, *India* **181** Q4
Kasari, *Japan* **189** V3
Kasari Saki, *Japan* **189** V3
Kasba Lake, *N.W.T., Can.* **85** JI3
Kasempa, *Zambia* **206** DIO
Kasenga, *Dem. Rep. of the Congo* **202** NII
Kasese, *Dem. Rep. of the Congo* **202** KII
Kasganj, *India* **180** F6
Kasha-Katuwe Tent Rocks National Monument, *N. Mex., U.S.* **109** RI2
Kāshān, *Iran* **175** DI3
Kashgar see Kashi, *China* **182** F2
Kashi (Kashgar), *China* **182** F2
Kashin, *Russ.* **158** H9
Kashira, *Russ.* **158** K9
Kashiwazaki, *Japan* **188** MII
Kashkandyow, *Afghan.* **178** KIO
Kāshmar, *Iran* **175** CI6
Kashmir, region, *China, India, Pak.* **178** MI2
Kashmir, Vale of, *India* **178** MI2
Kashmor, *Pak.* **179** T8
Kasimov, *Russ.* **158** KII
Kasiruta, island, *Indonesia* **193** JI6
Kaskaskia, river, *Ill., U.S.* **101** S5
Kaskö, *Fin.* **143** HI4
Kasongo, *Dem. Rep. of the Congo* **202** LII
Kasongo-Lunda, *Dem. Rep. of the Congo* **202** M8
Kásos, island, *Gr.* **157** QI8
Kaspiysk, *Russ.* **159** UI5
Kaspiyskiy, *Russ.* **159** SI5
Kassala, *Sudan* **203** EI4
Kassándra, peninsula, *Gr.* **156** DI2
Kassándras, Kólpos, *Gr.* **156** DI2
Kassándreia, *Gr.* **156** EI2
Kassel, *Ger.* **150** F7
Kassiópi, *Gr.* **156** E6
Kasson, *Minn., U.S.* **106** LI2
Kastamonu, *Turk.* **170** C9
Kastaniés, *Gr.* **157** AI7
Kastélli, *Gr.* **157** QI5
Kastélli see Kíssamos, *Gr.* **156** PI2
Kastéllo, Ákra, *Gr.* **157** QI8
Kastellórizo see Megísti, island, *Gr.* **157** N22
Kastoriá, *Gr.* **156** C8
Kastorías, Límni, *Gr.* **156** C8
Kasumkent, *Russ.* **159** VI6
Kasur, *Pak.* **179** QI2
Katafaga, island, *Fiji* **222** H9
Katahdin, Mount, *Me., U.S.* **97** DI7
Katákolo, *Gr.* **156** K8
Katanga, region, *Dem. Rep. of the Congo* **202** NIO
Katanning, *W. Aust., Austral.* **215** X3
Katápola, *Gr.* **157** MI6
Kata Tjuṭa (Olga, Mount), *Austral.* **214** G8

Katchall Island, *India* **181** SI5
Kateríni, *Gr.* **156** DIO
Kates Needle, peak, *Alas., U.S.* **113** L23
Katha, *Myanmar* **190** F6
Katherîna, Gebel (Mount Catherine), *Egypt* **173** T3
Katherine, river, *Austral.* **214** B8
Kathiawar, peninsula, *India* **180** J2
Kathmandu, *Nepal* **180** FIO
Kathua, *India* **179** PI3
Ka Tiritiri O Te Moana see Southern Alps, *N.Z.* **217** PI6
Katiu, island, *Fr. Polynesia, Fr.* **223** EI8
Katla, peak, *Ice.* **142** F2
Katlanovo, *Maced.* **154** KII
Katmai, Mount, *Alas., U.S.* **113** LI5
Katmai National Park and Preserve, *Alas., U.S.* **113** LI5
Káto Achaḯa, *Gr.* **156** J8
Káto Almyrí, *Gr.* **156** JII
Katohau, Baie, *Fr. Polynesia, Fr.* **223** M24
Kato Lakatameia, *Cyprus* **162** P8
Káto Nevrokópi, *Gr.* **156** BI2
Katowice, *Pol.* **151** GI6
Katrancık Dağı, peak, *Turk.* **170** H5
Katrine, Loch, *Scot., U.K.* **144** L9
Katsina, *Nigeria* **205** BI4
Katsuyama, *Japan* **189** P9
Kattankudi, *Sri Lanka* **181** T8
Kattavía, *Gr.* **157** NI9
Kattegat, strait, *Den., Sw.* **142** MI2
Katun', river, *Russ.* **160** LI2
Katwe, *Uganda* **202** KI2
Katwijk aan Zee, *Neth.* **148** JI2
Ka'ū, peak, *Hawai'i, U.S.* **115** P2O
Kau, *Indonesia* **193** HI6
Kaua'i, island, *Hawai'i, U.S.* **114** B4
Kaua'i Channel, *Hawai'i, U.S.* **114** D8
Kauakaiakaola Heiau, *Hawai'i, U.S.* **115** NI8
Kauehi, island, *Fr. Polynesia, Fr.* **223** EI8
Kaufbeuren, *Ger.* **150** K8
Kaufman, *Tex., U.S.* **104** LI2
Kauhako Crater, *Hawai'i, U.S.* **115** FI4
Kaukauai, *Solomon Is.* **221** LI4
Kaukauna, *Wis., U.S.* **100** J6
Kaukura, island, *Fr. Polynesia, Fr.* **223** EI7
Ka'ula, island, *Hawai'i, U.S.* **114** DI
Ka'ula Gulch, *Hawai'i, U.S.* **115** L2O
Kaulakahi Channel, *Hawai'i, U.S.* **114** C3
Ka'ū Loa Point, *Hawai'i, U.S.* **115** PI8
Kaulu Paoa Heiau, *Hawai'i, U.S.* **114** B5
Kaumakani, *Hawai'i, U.S.* **114** C5
Kaumalapau, *Hawai'i, U.S.* **115** HI4
Kaūmana Cave, *Hawai'i, U.S.* **115** M2I
Kaumu o Kaleihoʻohie, peak, *Hawai'i, U.S.* **115** LI9
Kaunakakai, *Hawai'i, U.S.* **115** GI4
Kaunakakai Harbour, *Hawai'i, U.S.* **115** GI4
Kaunā Point, *Hawai'i, U.S.* **115** QI8
Kaunas, *Lith.* **143** MI7
Kaunolū, *Hawai'i, U.S.* **115** HI5
Kaupakulua, *Hawai'i, U.S.* **115** GI7
Kaupō, *Hawai'i, U.S.* **115** HI8
Ka'ūpūlehu, *Hawai'i, U.S.* **115** MI8
Kaura-Namoda, *Nigeria* **205** BI4
Kautenbach, *Lux.* **162** H9
Kautokeino, *Nor.* **143** CI4
Kavacha, *Russ.* **161** D22
Kavadarci, *Maced.* **154** KI2
Kavajë, *Alban.* **154** L9
Kavak, *Turk.* **170** DII
Kavála (Neapolis), *Gr.* **157** CI3
Kaválas, Kólpos, *Gr.* **157** CI3
Kavalerovo, *Russ.* **161** L2I
Kavali, *India* **181** N7
Kavaratti, *India* **181** R3
Kavieng, *P.N.G.* **217** B2I
Kavir Desert, *Asia* **168** G5
Kavīr-e Namak, salt desert, *Iran* **175** DI5
Kávo Dóro, *Gr.* **157** JI4
Kávos, *Gr.* **156** F6

Kawagoe, *Japan* **189** PI2
Kawaihae, *Hawai'i, U.S.* **115** LI9
Kawaihae Bay, *Hawai'i, U.S.* **115** LI8
Kawaihoa Point, *Hawai'i, U.S.* **114** D3
Kawaikini, peak, *Hawai'i, U.S.* **114** C5
Kawakawa, *N.Z.* **217** HI8
Kawambwa, *Zambia* **206** CII
Kawasaki, *Japan* **189** PI2
Kawasak Passage, *Palau* **220** LI2
Kawe, island, *Indonesia* **193** JI7
Kawela, *Hawai'i, U.S.* **114** DII
Kawela, *Hawai'i, U.S.* **115** GI4
Kawela Place of Refuge, *Hawai'i, U.S.* **115** GI4
Kawhia, *N.Z.* **217** KI9
Kawich Peak, *Nev., U.S.* **III** RIO
Kawthoung, *Myanmar* **191** Q7
Kaya, *Burkina Faso* **204** BIO
Kaya, *Indonesia* **192** HI2
Kayanl, river, *Indonesia* **192** HII
Kayangel Islands (Ngcheangel), *Palau* **220** KI2
Kayangel Passage, *Palau* **220** KI2
Kayapınar, *Turk.* **171** HI5
Kaycee, *Wyo., U.S.* **108** GI2
Kayenta, *Ariz., U.S.* **109** Q8
Kayes, *Congo* **205** KI6
Kayes, *Mali* **200** H6
Kayl, *Lux.* **162** K9
Kaymaz, *Turk.* **170** E6
Kaynar, *Turk.* **170** FII
Kaysatskoye, *Russ.* **159** NI4
Kayseri, *Turk.* **170** FIO
Kazach'ye, *Russ.* **161** EI7
Kazakh, *Kaz.* **177** DI4
Kazakhstan, *Asia* **176** E8
Kazakh Uplands, *Asia* **168** E7
Kazan, river, *Nunavut, Can.* **85** HI4
Kazan', *Russ.* **158** JI4
Kazan Rettō see Volcano Islands, *Japan* **189** ZI3
Kazanskaya, *Russ.* **159** PII
Kazarman, *Kyrg.* **178** FII
Kazbek, peak, *Rep. of Georgia* **171** BI8
Kaz Dağı, peak, *Turk.* **170** E3
Kāzerūn, *Iran* **175** GI3
Kazi Ahmad, *Pak.* **179** V7
Kazimierz Dolny, *Pol.* **151** FI7
Kazincbarcika, *Hung.* **151** KI6
Kaztalovka, *Kaz.* **176** D5
Kazym Mys, *Russ.* **160** GIO
Kea (Tzia), island, *Gr.* **157** KI3
Kea'au, *Hawai'i, U.S.* **115** M22
Kea'au Ranch, *Hawai'i, U.S.* **115** M22
Keadu, island, *Maldives* **181** V3
Keāhole Point, *Hawai'i, U.S.* **115** MI8
Kealaikahiki Channel, *Hawai'i, U.S.* **115** HI5
Kealakekua, *Hawai'i, U.S.* **115** NI8
Keālia, *Hawai'i, U.S.* **114** C6
Keālia, *Hawai'i, U.S.* **115** NI8
Ke'anae, *Hawai'i, U.S.* **115** HI7
Keanapapa Point, *Hawai'i, U.S.* **115** GI4
Kearney, *Nebr., U.S.* **107** Q6
Keauhou, *Hawai'i, U.S.* **115** NI8
Keauhou Landing, *Hawai'i, U.S.* **115** P2I
Ke Avainiu Pass, *Solomon Is.* **221** JI8
Keawanui Bay, *Hawai'i, U.S.* **114** C3
Kêb (Kep), *Cambodia* **191** PII
Keban, *Turk.* **171** FI3
Kebnekaise, peak, *Sw.* **143** HI3
Kech, river, *Pak.* **179** V3
Keçiborlu, *Turk.* **170** G6
Kecil, Kai, *Indonesia* **217** DI4
Kecskemét, *Hung.* **151** MI5
Kediri, *Indonesia* **192** MIO
Kédougou, *Senegal* **200** H5
Kędzierzyn-Koźle, *Pol.* **151** GI4
Ke'ei, *Hawai'i, U.S.* **115** NI8
Keele, river, *N.W.T., Can.* **84** G9
Keele Peak, *Yukon, Can.* **84** G9
Keeler, *Calif., U.S.* **III** U8
Keeling (Jilong), *Taiwan, China* **185** TI2
Keene, *N.H., U.S.* **97** JI3
Keer-Weer, Cape, *Austral.* **214** BI2
Keeler, *Calif., U.S.* **III** U8
Keetmanshoop, *Namibia* **206** J7

Keewatin, *Minn., U.S.* **106** FII
Kefaloniá (Cephalonia), island, *Gr.* **156** H7
Kéfalos, *Gr.* **157** MI8
Kefaluka, *Turk.* **170** H3
Keflavík, *Ice.* **142** EI
Kegen, *Kaz.* **177** HI7
Keg River, *Alta., Can.* **84** JIO
Keheili, *Sudan* **203** CI3
Kehl, *Ger.* **150** J5
Keila, *Est.* **143** JI6
Kéita, Bahr, *Chad* **201** KI5
Keitele, lake, *Fin.* **143** GI6
Keith, *Scot., U.K.* **144** JIO
Keith Arm, *N.W.T., Can.* **84** FIO
Keithsburg, *Ill., U.S.* **101** P3
Kekaha, *Hawai'i, U.S.* **114** C4
Kékes, peak, *Hung.* **151** KI6
Kekirawa, *Sri Lanka* **181** S7
Keklau, *Palau* **220** MI2
Kekra, *Russ.* **161** H2O
Kekri, *India* **180** G4
K'elafo, *Eth.* **203** HI6
Kelai, island, *Maldives* **181** T3
Kelan, *Shanxi, China* **184** E4
Kelang, island, *Indonesia* **193** KI6
Kǝlbǝcǝr see Karvachar, *Azerb.* **171** E2O
Kélcyrë, *Alban.* **154** MIO
Kelefesia, island, *Tonga* **222** R6
Kelheim, *Ger.* **150** J9
Kelibia, *Tun.* **199** TI7
Kelkit, *Turk.* **171** EI4
Kelkit, river, *Turk.* **170** DI2
Ke Ila, island, *Solomon Is.* **221** JI8
Keller Lake, *N.W.T., Can.* **84** GIO
Kellet, Cape, *N.W.T., Can.* **84** DII
Kellits, *Jam.* **122** J8
Kells (Ceanannas), *Ire.* **145** R6
Ke Loma, island, *Solomon Is.* **221** JI8
Kelowna, *B.C., Can.* **84** M9
Kelso, *Calif., U.S.* **III** WII
Kelso, *Wash., U.S.* **110** E3
Keluang, *Malaysia* **191** VIO
Kem', *Russ.* **160** D8
Kema, *Indonesia* **193** HI5
Kemah, *Turk.* **171** EI3
Kemaliye, *Turk.* **171** FI3
Kemasik, *Malaysia* **191** TIO
Kemer, *Turk.* **170** D3
Kemer, *Turk.* **170** G4
Kemer, *Turk.* **170** J5
Kemer, *Turk.* **170** J6
Kemerovo, *Russ.* **160** KI2
Kemi, *Fin.* **143** EI5
Kemi, river, *Eur.* **140** C9
Kemijärvi, *Fin.* **143** DI5
Kemijärvi, lake, *Fin.* **143** DI5
Kemijoki, river, *Fin.* **143** DI5
Kemlya, *Russ.* **158** KI3
Kemmerer, *Wyo., U.S.* **108** J8
Kemmuna see Comino, island, *Malta* **163** H2I
Kemp, Lake, *Tex., U.S.* **104** J8
Kemp Coast, *Antarctica* **231** DI9
Kempendyay, *Russ.* **161** HI7
Kemp Peninsula, *Antarctica* **230** F7
Kemps Bay, *Bahamas* **118** FII
Kempsey, *N.S.W., Austral.* **215** WI5
Kempten, *Ger.* **150** L7
Kenai, *Alas., U.S.* **113** KI6
Kenai Fjords National Park, *Alas., U.S.* **113** KI6
Kenai Peninsula, *Alas., U.S.* **113** KI6
Kendal, *Eng., U.K.* **145** QII
Kendall, *Fla., U.S.* **99** XIO
Kendall, *N.Y., U.S.* **96** H6
Kendall, Cape, *Nunavut, Can.* **85** HI6
Kendallville, *Ind., U.S.* **101** PIO
Kendari, *Indonesia* **193** KI4
Kendawangan, *Indonesia* **192** K9
Kendikolu, island, *Maldives* **181** T3
Kendrapara, *India* **180** KIO
Kendrick, *Idaho, U.S.* **108** D3
Kenedy, *Tex., U.S.* **105** SIO
Kenema, *Sierra Leone* **204** D6
Kengtung, *Myanmar* **190** H8
Kenhardt, *S. Af.* **206** K8
Kenitra, *Mor.* **200** B8
Kenli, *Shand., China* **184** F9

Kenmare, *N. Dak., U.S.* **106** E3
Kenmare (Neidín), *Ire.* **145** U3
Kenmore, *Scot., U.K.* **144** L9
Kennebec, *S. Dak., U.S.* **106** L5
Kennebec, river, *Me., U.S.* **97** EI6
Kennebunk, *Me., U.S.* **97** HI5
Kennedy, Cape see Canaveral, Cape, *N. Amer.* **82** L8
Kennedy Channel, *Nunavut, Can.* **85** BI6
Kenner, *La., U.S.* **102** QII
Kennett, *Mo., U.S.* **107** WI5
Kennewick, *Wash., U.S.* **110** E7
Kenn Plateau, *Pac. Oc.* **242** M9
Keno Hill, *Yukon, Can.* **84** F8
Kenora, *Ont., Can.* **85** NI4
Kenosha, *Wis., U.S.* **100** M7
Kenova, *W. Va., U.S.* **98** D7
Kent, *Ohio, U.S.* **101** PI5
Kent, *Oreg., U.S.* **110** F5
Kent, *Tex., U.S.* **105** N2
Kent, *Wash., U.S.* **110** C4
Kentland, *Ind., U.S.* **101** Q7
Kenton, *Ohio, U.S.* **101** QI2
Kent Peninsula, *Nunavut, Can.* **85** FI3
Kentucky, *U.S.* **103** CI7
Kentucky, river, *U.S.* **87** GI7
Kentucky Lake, *Ky., Tenn., U.S.* **103** DI3
Kentwood, *La., U.S.* **102** NIO
Kentwood, *Mich., U.S.* **100** LIO
Kenutu, island, *Tonga* **222** MI2
Kenya, *Af.* **203** KI4
Kenya, Mount, *Kenya* **203** KI4
Kenya Highlands, *Af.* **198** JIO
Kēōkea, *Hawai'i, U.S.* **115** HI7
Kēōkea, *Hawai'i, U.S.* **115** NI8
Keokuk, *Iowa, U.S.* **107** QI4
Keōmuku, *Hawai'i, U.S.* **115** HI5
Keonjhargarh, *India* **180** KIO
Kep see Kêb, *Cambodia* **191** PII
Kepi, *Indonesia* **193** M2I
Kępno, *Pol.* **151** FI4
Keppel Bay, *Austral.* **214** FI5
Kepsut, *Turk.* **170** E4
Keramotí, *Gr.* **157** CI4
Keran, *Pak.* **180** B4
Kerang, *Vic., Austral.* **215** YI2
Kerch, *Ukr.* **159** S9
Kerchenskiy Proliv, *Ukr.* **159** S9
Kerch Strait, *Eur.* **140** JI2
Kerempe Burnu, *Turk.* **170** B9
Keren, *Eritrea* **203** EI5
Kerens, *Tex., U.S.* **104** MI2
Kerguelen Plateau, *Ind. Oc.* **224** QIO
Keri, *Gr.* **156** K7
Kerikeri, *N.Z.* **217** HI8
Kerinci, peak, *Indonesia* **192** K6
Keriya see Yutian, *China* **182** G3
Kerki see Atamyrat, *Turkm.* **176** MII
Kerkíni, *Gr.* **156** BII
Kerkíni, Límni, *Gr.* **156** BII
Kérkyra, *Gr.* **156** E6
Kérkyra (Corfu, Corcyra), *Gr.* **156** E6
Kermadec Islands, *Pac. Oc.* **218** L9
Kermadec Ridge, *Pac. Oc.* **242** NII
Kermadec Trench, *Pac. Oc.* **242** NI2
Kermān, *Iran* **175** FI5
Kermānshāh, *Iran* **174** DII
Kermānshāhān, *Iran* **175** FI4
Kermit, *Tex., U.S.* **104** M3
Kern, river, *Calif., U.S.* **III** V7
Kernersville, *N.C., U.S.* **98** GIO
Kernville, *Calif., U.S.* **III** V8
Kéros, island, *Gr.* **157** LI6
Kerr, Mount, *Bahamas* **122** EII
Kerrobert, *Sask., Can.* **84** MII
Kerrville, *Tex., U.S.* **105** Q8
Kerry Head, *Ire.* **145** T2
Kershaw, *S.C., U.S.* **98** K9
Kertamulia, *Indonesia* **192** J8
Keryíneia see Kyrenia, *Cyprus* **162** N8
Keryneia Range, *Cyprus* **162** N9
Keşan, *Turk.* **170** C3
Keşap, *Turk.* **171** DI3
Kesennuma, *Japan* **188** LI3
Keshīt, *Iran* **175** FI6
Keshod, *India* **180** K2
Keskal, *India* **180** L8

Keskin, *Turk.* **170** E9
Kes'ma, *Russ.* **158** G9
Keszthely, *Hung.* **151** M13
Ketanda, *Russ.* **161** G19
Ketaun, *Indonesia* **192** K6
Ketchikan, *Alas., U.S.* **113** M24
Ketchum, *Idaho, U.S.* **108** G5
Ketchum Mountain, *Tex., U.S.*
    105 N6
Kete Krachi, *Ghana* **204** D11
Keti Bandar, *Pak.* **179** X6
Kettering, *Eng., U.K.* **145** T13
Kettering, *Ohio, U.S.* **101** R11
Kettle Falls, *Wash., U.S.* **110** A8
Kettle River Range, *Wash., U.S.*
    110 B7
Keul', *Russ.* **161** K15
Kewanee, *Ill., U.S.* **101** P4
Kewaunee, *Wis., U.S.* **100** J7
Keweenaw Bay, *Mich., U.S.* **100** E6
Keweenaw National Historical Park,
    Mich., U.S. **100** E6
Keweenaw Peninsula, *Mich., U.S.*
    100 D7
Keweenaw Point, *Mich., U.S.* **100** E7
Key, Lough, *Ire.* **145** Q5
Keyano, *Que., Can.* **85** L19
Keya Paha, river, *Nebr., S. Dak., U.S.*
    106 M4
Key Colony Beach, *Fla., U.S.* **99** Y9
Keyes, *Okla., U.S.* **104** E4
Keyhole Reservoir, *Wyo., U.S.*
    108 F13
Key Largo, *Fla., U.S.* **99** Y10
Keyser, *W. Va., U.S.* **98** C11
Keystone, *S. Dak., U.S.* **106** L2
Keystone, *W. Va., U.S.* **98** F8
Keystone Lake, *U.S.* **87** J13
Key West, *Fla., U.S.* **99** Z8
Kežmarok, *Slovakia* **151** J16
Khabarovsk, *Russ.* **161** K21
Khābūr, river, *Syr.* **172** D14
Khadyzhensk, *Russ.* **159** T10
Khailino, *Russ.* **161** D21
Khaīrābād, *Afghan.* **178** K6
Khairpur, *Pak.* **179** S10
Khairpur, *Pak.* **179** T7
Khakhar', *Russ.* **161** H19
Khalatse, *India* **180** B6
Khalīg el Tîna, *Egypt* **173** N1
Khalīj Surt *see* Gulf of Sidra, *Lib.*
    201 C14
Khalūf, *Oman* **175** M16
Khambhaliya, *India* **180** J1
Khambhat, Gulf of, *India* **180** K3
Khamgaon, *India* **180** K5
Khamīs Mushayṭ, *Saudi Arabia*
    174 N8
Khamr, *Yemen* **174** P9
Khānābād, *Afghan.* **178** K8
Khān Abū Shāmāt, *Syr.* **172** J8
Khanai, *Pak.* **179** R6
Khānaqāh, *Afghan.* **178** K5
Khānaqīn, *Iraq* **174** D10
Khān az Zabīb, *Jordan* **173** N7
Khanderi Island, *India* **180** L3
Khandwa, *India* **180** J5
Khandyga, *Russ.* **161** G18
Khanewal, *Pak.* **179** R10
Khangarh, *Pak.* **179** T10
Khaniadhana, *India* **180** H6
Khanka, Lake, *Asia* **168** E12
Khanka, Ozero, *Russ.* **161** L21
Khanka, Ozero *see* Xingkai Hu, *China,*
    Russ. **183** D17
Khanozai, *Pak.* **179** R6
Khanpur, *Pak.* **179** S9
Khān Shaykhūn, *Syr.* **172** F8
Khan Tängiri Shyngy *see*
    Khan-Tengry Peak, *Kaz., Kyrg.*
    178 E15
Khantayskoye, Ozero, *Russ.* **161** G13
Khan-Tengry Peak (Kan-Too
    Chokusu, Khan Tängiri Shyngy),
    Kaz., Kyrg. **178** E15
Khanty-Mansiysk, *Russ.* **160** H10
Khān Yūnis, *Gaza Strip* **173** N4
Khapalu, *Pak.* **178** L13
Kharabali, *Russ.* **159** Q14
Kharagpur, *India* **180** J11
Kharan, *Pak.* **179** S5

Kharānaq, *Iran* **175** E14
Kharasavey, Mys, *Russ.* **160** E11
Khārga Oasis, site, *Egypt* **201** E18
Khārg Island *see* Khārk, Jazīreh-ye,
    Iran **174** G12
Khargon, *India* **180** J5
Khargüsh, *Taj.* **178** J10
Kharian, *Pak.* **179** P11
Khariar, *India* **180** K8
Kharimkotan, island, *Russ.* **161** H23
Khārk, Jazīreh-ye (Khārg Island),
    Iran **174** G12
Kharkiv, *Ukr.* **159** P9
Kharlovka, *Russ.* **160** D9
Kharmanli, *Bulg.* **155** K15
Kharovsk, *Russ.* **158** F10
Khartoum, *Sudan* **203** E13
Khartoum North, *Sudan* **203** E13
Kharyyalakh, *Russ.* **161** G15
Khasavyurt, *Russ.* **159** T15
Khāsh, *Afghan.* **179** Q3
Khāsh, *Iran* **175** G17
Khāsh, river, *Afghan.* **179** P4
Khāsh, Dasht-e, *Afghan.* **179** P2
Khashuri, *Rep. of Georgia* **171** C17
Khasi Hills, *India* **180** G13
Khaskovo, *Bulg.* **155** K15
Khatanga, *Russ.* **161** F14
Khatanga Gulf, *Arctic Oc.* **168** C9
Khatangskiy Zaliv, *Russ.* **161** E15
Khatt, Oued al, *Af.* **198** E2
Khātūnīyah, *Syr.* **172** D15
Khatyrka, *Russ.* **161** C21
Khavda, *India* **180** H2
Khaybar, Ḥarrat, *Saudi Arabia* **174** J7
Khaydarkan, *Kyrg.* **178** G9
Khemmarat, *Thai.* **190** L12
Kherson, *Ukr.* **159** R7
Kherwara, *India* **180** H4
Khe Sanh, *Vietnam* **190** K12
Kheta, *Russ.* **161** F14
Kheta, river, *Asia* **168** C9
Khewari, *Pak.* **179** U7
Khimki, *Russ.* **158** J9
Khinjān, *Afghan.* **178** L7
Khipro, *Pak.* **179** V8
Khiri Ratthanikhom, *Thai.* **191** Q8
Khiwa, *Uzb.* **176** K9
Khlevnoye, *Russ.* **158** M10
Khmel'nyts'kyy, *Ukr.* **159** P4
Khoa, *Laos* **190** H10
Khocho, *Russ.* **161** H18
Khodzhakala, *Turkm.* **176** L7
Khojak Pass, *Pak.* **179** Q6
Khokhol'skiy, *Russ.* **158** M10
Khokhropar, *Pak.* **179** V9
Khok Kloi, *Thai.* **191** R7
Kholm, *Russ.* **158** H6
Kholmsk, *Russ.* **161** K22
Khŏng, *Laos* **190** M12
Khon Kaen, *Thai.* **190** L10
Khoper, river, *Russ.* **158** M12
Khorāsān, region, *Iran* **175** D15
Khorol, *Ukr.* **159** P7
Khorramābād, *Iran* **174** D11
Khorugh, *Taj.* **178** J9
Khost, *Pak.* **179** R6
Khōst, *Afghan.* **179** N8
Khoyniki, *Belarus* **158** M5
Khrenovoye, *Russ.* **159** N11
Khromtaü, *Kaz.* **176** D9
Khrysokhou Bay, *Cyprus* **162** P5
Khudabad, *Pak.* **178** K12
Khuiala, *India* **180** F2
Khujand, *Taj.* **178** G8
Khūjayli, *Uzb.* **176** J9
Khulkhuta, *Russ.* **159** R14
Khulm, *Afghan.* **178** K6
Khulna, *Bangladesh* **180** J12
Khunjerab Pass, *China, Pak.* **178** K12
Khunti, *India* **180** J10
Khunzakh, *Russ.* **159** U15
Khur, *Iran* **175** D14
Khurda, *India* **180** K10
Khurīyā Murīyā, Jazā'ir (Kuria
    Muria Islands), *Oman* **175** N15
Khurmāliq, *Afghan.* **179** P2
Khushab, *Pak.* **179** P10
Khust, *Ukr.* **159** P2
Khuzdar, *Pak.* **179** T5
Khvāf, *Iran* **175** D17

Khvalynsk, *Russ.* **158** L14
Khvorostyanka, *Russ.* **158** L15
Khvoy, *Iran* **174** A10
Khwāl, *Afghan.* **178** L5
Khwāzagak, *Afghan.* **178** M5
Khyber Pass, *Afghan., Pak.* **178** M9
Kia, *Solomon Is.* **221** L17
Kia, island, *Fiji* **222** G7
Kiakeana Point, *Hawai'i, U.S.* **115** J17
Kiamichi, river, *Okla., U.S.* **104** H13
Kiana, *Alas., U.S.* **113** E13
Kiáto, *Gr.* **156** J11
Kibombo, *Dem. Rep. of the Congo*
    202 L11
Kibong, *N. Korea* **186** H4
Kibwezi, *Kenya* **203** L15
Kičevo, *Maced.* **154** K10
Kickapoo, Lake, *Tex., U.S.* **104** K8
Kidal, *Mali* **200** G10
Kidnappers, Cape, *N.Z.* **217** L20
Kidong-man, bay, *N. Korea* **186** C13
Kidrenen, island, *Marshall Is., U.S.*
    220 G8
Kidrinen, island, *Marshall Is., U.S.*
    220 J7
Kiel, *Ger.* **150** B8
Kiel, *Wis., U.S.* **100** K7
Kielce, *Pol.* **151** F16
Kieler Bucht, *Den., Ger.* **150** A8
Kiến An, *Vietnam* **190** H12
Kiến Đức, *Vietnam* **191** N13
Kiến Giang, *Vietnam* **190** K13
Kieta, *P.N.G.* **221** K14
Kiev *see* Kyiv, *Ukr.* **159** N6
Kiffa, *Mauritania* **200** G6
Kifisiá, *Gr.* **156** J12
Kifisós, river, *Gr.* **156** G10
Kifrī, *Iraq* **174** D10
Kigali, *Rwanda* **202** K12
Kiği, *Turk.* **171** F15
Kigoma, *Tanzania* **202** L12
Kīhei, *Hawai'i, U.S.* **115** H16
Kīholo Bay, *Hawai'i, U.S.* **115** M18
Ki'i, *Hawai'i, U.S.* **114** C3
Kii Channel, *Pac. Oc.* **168** F13
Kii Suidō, *Japan* **189** Q8
Kikaiga Shima, *Japan* **189** W4
Kikiakki, *Russ.* **160** H12
Kikinda, *Serb.* **154** D10
Kikki, *Pak.* **179** V2
Kiknur, *Russ.* **158** H13
Kikori, *P.N.G.* **217** D18
Kikori, river, *P.N.G.* **217** D18
Kikwit, *Dem. Rep. of the Congo*
    202 L8
Kil, river, *Pak.* **179** V3
Kilafors, *Sw.* **143** J13
Kilakkarai, *India* **181** S6
Kilambé, peak, *Nicar.* **117** L18
Kilar, *India* **179** N13
Kilarney Park, *Qnsld., Austral.*
    215 U13
Kīlauea, *Hawai'i, U.S.* **114** B6
Kīlauea, peak, *Hawai'i, U.S.* **115** N21
Kīlauea Lighthouse, *Hawai'i, U.S.*
    114 B6
Kilbrannan Sound, *Scot., U.K.* **145** N8
Kilbuck Mountains, *Alas., U.S.* **113** J13
Kilcar *see* Cill Charthaigh, *Ire.* **145** P4
Kilchoman, *Scot., U.K.* **144** M7
Kilcock (Cill Choca), *Ire.* **145** S6
Kilcowera, *Qnsld., Austral.* **215** V12
Kildonan, *Scot., U.K.* **144** H9
Kildrummy, *Scot., U.K.* **144** K10
Kilgore, *Nebr., U.S.* **106** M4
Kilgore, *Tex., U.S.* **104** L14
Kılıçkaya, *Turk.* **171** D16
Kılınç Tepesi, peak, *Turk.* **171** D13
Kilinochchi, *Sri Lanka* **181** S7
Kilis, *Turk.* **170** J12
Kiliya, *Ukr.* **159** S5
Kilju, *N. Korea* **186** E12
Kilkee (Cill Chaoi), *Ire.* **145** T3
Kilkenny (Cill Chainnigh), *Ire.* **145** T6
Kilkís, *Gr.* **156** B11
Killadysert (Cill an Dísirt), *Ire.*
    145 T3

Killala Bay, *Ire.* **145** Q4
Killarney, *N.T., Austral.* **215** Q8
Killarney, Lake, *Bahamas* **122** B11
Killary Harbour, *Ire.* **145** R3
Killdeer, *N. Dak., U.S.* **106** F3
Killeen, *Tex., U.S.* **105** P10
Killiniq Island, *Nfld. & Lab., Can.*
    85 J20
Killorglin (Cill Orglan), *Ire.* **145** U3
Kilmaluag, *Scot., U.K.* **144** J7
Kilmarnock, *Scot., U.K.* **145** N9
Kilnovec, peak, *Czech Rep.* **150** G10
Kilombero, river, *Tanzania* **203** N14
Kilosa, *Tanzania* **203** M14
Kiltan Island, *India* **181** Q3
Kilwa Kivinje, *Tanzania* **203** N15
Kim, *Colo., U.S.* **109** P15
Kimaam, *Indonesia* **193** M20
Kimball, *Nebr., U.S.* **107** P1
Kimball, *S. Dak., U.S.* **106** L6
Kimbe Bay, *P.N.G.* **217** C21
Kimberley, *B.C., Can.* **84** M9
Kimberley, *S. Af.* **206** K9
Kimberley, Cape, *Austral.* **214** C13
Kimberley, region, *W. Aust., Austral.*
    215 R6
Kimberley Plateau, *Austral.* **214** C6
Kimberly, *Idaho, U.S.* **108** H5
Kimch'aek (Sŏngjin), *N. Korea*
    186 F12
Kimhwa (Kŭmsŏng), *N. Korea* **186** L9
Kimhyŏnggwŏn, *N. Korea* **186** F10
Kimjŏngsuk (Sinp'a), *N. Korea* **186** D9
Kimmirut, *Nunavut, Can.* **85** H18
Kimobetsu, *Japan* **188** G12
Kímolos, island, *Gr.* **157** M14
Kimovsk, *Russ.* **158** K10
Kimry, *Russ.* **158** H9
Kinabalu, peak, *Malaysia* **192** G12
Kinadyeng, island, *Marshall Is., U.S.*
    220 L8
Kínaros, island, *Gr.* **157** L17
Kinbrace, *Scot., U.K.* **144** H9
Kindadal, *Indonesia* **193** K14
Kinder, *La., U.S.* **102** P7
Kindia, *Guinea* **204** C5
Kindu, *Dem. Rep. of the Congo*
    202 L11
Kinel', *Russ.* **158** K15
Kineshma, *Russ.* **158** H11
Kingaroy, *Qnsld., Austral.* **215** V15
King Christian IX Land, *Greenland,*
    Den. **82** C10
King Christian X Land, *Greenland,*
    Den. **82** B9
King City, *Calif., U.S.* **III** U5
King City, *Mo., U.S.* **107** R10
King Cove, *Alas., U.S.* **112** N11
Kingfisher, *Okla., U.S.* **104** F10
Kingfisher Lake, *Ont., Can.* **85** M15
King Frederik VI Coast, *Greenland,*
    Den. **82** D10
King Frederik VIII Land, *Greenland,*
    Den. **82** B9
King George Bay, *Falk. Is., U.K.*
    135 W11
King George Island, *Antarctica*
    230 C4
King George Islands, *Nunavut, Can.*
    85 K17
King George Sound, *Austral.* **214** L3
King George V Memorial Hospital,
    Gibraltar, U.K. **163** P23
Kingisepp, *Russ.* **158** F5
King Island, *Alas., U.S.* **112** F11
King Island, *Austral.* **214** L7
King Khalid Military City, site,
    Saudi Arabia **174** H10
King Lear Peak, *Nev., U.S.* **110** M8
King Leopold Ranges, *Austral.*
    214 D5
Kingman, *Ariz., U.S.* **109** S5
Kingman, *Kans., U.S.* **107** U7
Kingman Basin, *Pac. Oc.* **242** J12
Kingman Reef, *Pac. Oc.* **243** J13
King Mountain, *Tex., U.S.* **105** N4
Kingoonya, *S. Aust., Austral.* **215** W9
King Peak, *Antarctica* **230** J11
Kingri, *Pak.* **179** R8
Kings, river, *Calif., U.S.* **III** T7
King Salmon, *Alas., U.S.* **113** L14

King's Bay, *Trinidad and Tobago*
    123 N18
Kingsbridge, *Eng., U.K.* **145** X10
Kingsburg, *Calif., U.S.* **III** U6
Kings Canyon National Park, *Calif.,*
    U.S. **III** T7
Kingscote, *S. Aust., Austral.* **215** Y10
Kingsford, *Mich., U.S.* **100** G7
Kingsland, *Ga., U.S.* **99** Q8
King's Lynn, *Eng., U.K.* **145** T14
Kings Mountain, *N.C., U.S.* **98** J8
King Sound, *Austral.* **214** C5
Kings Peak, *Utah, U.S.* **108** L8
Kingsport, *Tenn., U.S.* **103** D20
Kingston, *Jam.* **122** J10
Kingston, *N.Y., U.S.* **96** L11
Kingston, *Norfolk I., Austral.* **221** G20
Kingston, *Ont., Can.* **85** Q19
Kingston, *Pa., U.S.* **96** M8
Kingston Harbour, *Jam.* **122** J10
Kingston South East, *S. Aust., Austral.*
    215 Y11
Kingston upon Hull, *Eng., U.K.* **145**
    R13
Kingstown, *St. Vincent and the*
    Grenadines **123** L16
Kingstown Bay, *St. Vincent and the*
    Grenadines **123** L16
Kingstree, *S.C., U.S.* **98** L10
Kings Trough, *Atl. Oc.* **240** J9
Kingsville, *Tex., U.S.* **105** U10
King Wilhelm Land, *Greenland, Den.*
    82 B9
King William Island, *Nunavut, Can.*
    85 F14
Kiniama, *Dem. Rep. of the Congo*
    202 P11
Kinlochewe, *Scot., U.K.* **144** J8
Kinmen, *Fujian, China* **185** U9
Kinmen (Quemoy), *Fujian, China*
    185 U9
Kinnear, *Wyo., U.S.* **108** H10
Kinniyai, *Sri Lanka* **181** S8
Kinsale, *Montserrat* **123** B23
Kinshasa (Léopoldville), *Dem. Rep. of*
    the Congo **202** L7
Kinsley, *Kans., U.S.* **107** U5
Kinston, *N.C., U.S.* **98** H13
Kintore, *Scot., U.K.* **144** K11
Kintyre, peninsula, *Scot., U.K.*
    145 N8
Kinvara (Cinn Mhara), *Ire.* **145** S4
Kinyeti, peak, *S. Sudan* **203** H13
Kinzua, *Oreg., U.S.* **110** G6
Kioa, island, *Fiji* **222** G8
Kiokluk Mountains, *Alas., U.S.*
    113 J14
Kione Maghal *see* Maughold Head,
    Isle of Man, U.K. **145** Q9
Kiowa, *Colo., U.S.* **108** M14
Kiowa, *Kans., U.S.* **107** V6
Kīpahulu, *Hawai'i, U.S.* **115** H18
Kipili, *Tanzania* **202** M12
Kipini, *Kenya* **203** L15
Kipnuk, *Alas., U.S.* **112** K11
Kirakira, *Solomon Is.* **221** P21
Kiraz, *Turk.* **170** G4
Kirbey, *Russ.* **161** G15
Kirbymoorside, *Eng., U.K.* **145** Q13
Kirbyville, *Tex., U.S.* **105** P16
Kirensk, *Russ.* **161** K15
Kiri, *Dem. Rep. of the Congo* **202** K9
Kiribati, *Pac. Oc.* **218** G10
Kırıkhan, *Turk.* **170** J11
Kırıkkale, *Turk.* **170** E9
Kirin-do, island, *S. Korea* **186** M5
Kirishi, *Russ.* **158** F7
Kiritimati (Christmas Island), *Kiribati*
    218 G12
Kiriwina, island, *P.N.G.* **217** E21
Kırka, *Turk.* **170** F6
Kırkağaç, *Turk.* **170** E3
Kirkcaldy, *Scot., U.K.* **144** M10
Kirkcolm, *Scot., U.K.* **145** P8
Kirkenes, *Nor.* **143** B15
Kırkgeçit, *Turk.* **171** G18
Kirkjubæjarklaustur, *Ice.* **142** F3
Kirkland, *Tex., U.S.* **104** J7
Kirkland Lake, *Ont., Can.* **85** P18
Kırklar *see* Tymvou, *Cyprus* **162** N9
Kırklar Dağı, peak, *Turk.* **171** D15

Kırklareli, *Turk.* **170** B3
Kirk Michael (Skeylley Maayl),
   Isle of Man, U.K. **145** Q9
Kirkoswald, *Scot., U.K.* **145** N8
Kirksville, *Mo., U.S.* **107** R12
Kirkuk see Karkūk, *Iraq* **174** C9
Kirkwall, *Scot., U.K.* **144** G10
Kirkwood, *Mo., U.S.* **107** T15
Kirn, *Ger.* **150** H5
Kirov, *Russ.* **158** K8
Kirov, *Russ.* **160** G8
Kirovohrad, *Ukr.* **159** Q6
Kirovskiy, *Russ.* **159** R15
Kirsanov, *Russ.* **158** L12
Kırşehir, *Turk.* **170** F9
Kīrthar Range, *Pak.* **179** T6
Kirtland, *N. Mex., U.S.* **109** Q10
Kiruna, *Sw.* **143** D13
Kirunu, island, *Marshall Is., U.S.*
   220 G7
Kirwan Escarpment, *Antarctica*
   230 C12
Kirya, *Russ.* **158** J13
Kiryū, *Japan* **189** N11
Kisangani (Stanleyville), *Dem. Rep. of*
   the Congo **202** K11
Kish, island, *Iran* **175** H14
Kishanganj, *India* **180** G11
Kishangarh, *India* **180** F2
Kishangarh, *India* **180** G4
Kishb, Ḥarrat al, *Saudi Arabia* **174** K8
Kishim, *Afghan.* **178** K8
Kishiwada, *Japan* **189** Q8
Kishkeneköl, *Kaz.* **177** B14
Kısır Dağı, peak, *Turk.* **171** D17
Kiska Island, *Alas., U.S.* **112** M2
Kiskunfélegyháza, *Hung.* **151** M15
Kiskunhalas, *Hung.* **151** M15
Kislovodsk, *Russ.* **159** T12
Kismaayo (Kismayo), *Somalia*
   203 K16
Kiso, river, *Japan* **189** P10
Kíssamos (Kastélli), *Gr.* **156** P12
Kissámou, Kólpos, *Gr.* **156** P12
Kissidougou, *Guinea* **204** C6
Kissimmee, *Fla., U.S.* **99** T9
Kissimmee, river, *Fla., U.S.* **99** U9
Kissimmee, Lake, *Fla., U.S.* **99** U9
Kistrand, *Nor.* **143** B14
Kisumu, *Kenya* **203** K13
Kisvárda, *Hung.* **151** K17
Kita, *Mali* **200** H6
Kita Daitō Jima, *Japan* **218** C2
Kitaibaraki, *Japan* **189** N12
Kita Iwo, island, *Japan* **189** Y13
Kita Iwo To, *Japan* **218** C3
Kitakami, *Japan* **188** K13
Kitakata, *Japan* **188** M12
Kitakyūshū, *Japan* **189** Q5
Kitale, *Kenya* **203** J14
Kitami, *Japan* **188** F14
Kitami Sanchi, *Japan* **188** F14
Kit'an, *N. Korea* **186** L7
Kit Carson, *Colo., U.S.* **109** N15
Kitchener, *Ont., Can.* **85** R18
Kitchener, *W. Aust., Austral.* **215** W5
Kiti, Cape, *Cyprus* **162** Q9
Kitimat, *B.C., Can.* **84** K7
Kiti Point, *F.S.M.* **221** G14
Kitob, *Uzb.* **176** L12
Kitridge Point, *Barbados* **123** K20
Kittanning, *Pa., U.S.* **96** N4
Kittery, *Me., U.S.* **97** J15
Kittilä, *Fin.* **143** D14
Kittitas, *Wash., U.S.* **110** D6
Kitty Hawk, *N.C., U.S.* **98** G15
Kitwe, *Zambia* **206** D10
Kitzingen, *Ger.* **150** H7
Kiukiu, Pointe, *Fr. Polynesia, Fr.*
   223 M20
Kiunga, *P.N.G.* **217** D17
Kivalina, *Alas., U.S.* **112** D12
Kivu, Lac, *Dem. Rep. of the Congo,*
   Rwanda **202** K11
Kiyan Misaki, *Japan* **189** Y2
Kiyāt, *Saudi Arabia* **174** N8
Kıyıköy, *Turk.* **170** C4
Kizema, *Russ.* **160** F8
Kızılay see Trakhonas, *Cyprus* **162** N8
Kızılcahamam, *Turk.* **170** D7
Kızılin, *Turk.* **171** H13

Kızılırmak, *Turk.* **170** D9
Kızılırmak, river, *Turk.* **170** F11
Kızılliman Burnu, *Turk.* **170** J8
Kızıltepe, *Turk.* **171** H15
Kizlyar, *Russ.* **159** T15
Kizlyarskiy Zaliv, *Russ.* **159** S15
Kladno, *Czech Rep.* **150** G11
Klagenfurt, *Aust.* **150** M11
Klaipėda, *Lith.* **143** M15
Klaksvík, *Faroe Is., Den.* **142** H6
Klamath, *Calif., U.S.* **110** L2
Klamath, river, *Calif., Oreg., U.S.*
   110 L2
Klamath Falls, *Oreg., U.S.* **110** K4
Klamath Mountains, *Calif., U.S.*
   110 M2
Klang, *Malaysia* **191** U9
Klarälven, river, *Sw.* **142** J12
Klatovy, *Czech Rep.* **150** H10
Klawer, *S. Af.* **206** L7
Klawock, *Alas., U.S.* **113** M23
Kle, *Liberia* **204** D6
Klein Baai, *St. Maarten, Neth.* **123** B14
Klein Bonaire, island, *Bonaire, Neth.*
   123 Q19
Kleine Berg, peak, *Curaçao, Neth.*
   123 P14
Kleitoría (Klitoría), *Gr.* **156** J10
Klekovača, peak, *Bosn. & Herzg.*
   154 F6
Klenova Valley, *Arctic Oc.* **247** K13
Klerksdorp, *S. Af.* **206** J10
Klesiv, *Ukr.* **158** M4
Kletskiy, *Russ.* **159** P12
Klichaw, *Belarus* **158** L5
Klickitat, *Wash., U.S.* **110** E5
Klin, *Russ.* **158** J9
Klintehamn, *Sw.* **143** L14
Klintsy, *Belarus* **158** L7
Klirou, *Cyprus* **162** P8
Klitoría see Kleitoría, *Gr.* **156** J10
Kłodzko, *Pol.* **151** G13
Klondike Gold Rush National
   Historical Park, *Alas., U.S.* **113** K22
Klosterneuburg, *Aust.* **150** K12
Klosters, *Switz.* **152** B5
Kluczbork, *Pol.* **151** F14
Klyuchevskaya Sopka, *Russ.* **161** F22
Knaresborough, *Eng., U.K.* **145** R12
Knezha, *Bulg.* **155** H14
Knife River, *Minn., U.S.* **106** G13
Knin, *Croatia* **154** G6
Knipovich Ridge, *Arctic Oc.* **247** H17
Knittlefeld, *Aust.* **150** L11
Knjaževac, *Serb.* **154** H12
Knob, Cape, *Austral.* **214** L4
Knockadoon Head, *Ire.* **145** U5
Knokke-Heist, *Belg.* **148** K11
Knossós (Cnossus), ruin, *Gr.* **157** Q15
Knotts Island, *N.C., U.S.* **98** G14
Knox, *Ind., U.S.* **101** P8
Knox Atoll, *Marshall Is., U.S.* **220** H5
Knox City, *Tex., U.S.* **104** K8
Knox Coast, *Antarctica* **231** L20
Knoxville, *Iowa, U.S.* **107** P12
Knoxville, *Tenn., U.S.* **103** E18
Knud Rasmussen Land, *Greenland,*
   Den. **82** B8
Knysna, *S. Af.* **206** M9
Ko, Gora, *Russ.* **161** K21
Koam, *N. Korea* **186** J9
Koba, *Indonesia* **192** K8
Koba, *Indonesia* **193** M18
Kobanê see 'Ayn al 'Arab, *Syr.*
   172 C10
Kobarid, *Slov.* **154** C4
Kobayashi, *Japan* **189** S5
Kōbe, *Japan* **189** Q8
København (Copenhagen), *Den.*
   142 N12
Koblenz, *Ger.* **150** G5
Kobo, *India* **180** F15
Kobozha, *Russ.* **158** G8
Kobroor, island, *Indonesia* **193** L19
Kobryn, *Belarus* **158** L3
Kobuk, *Alas., U.S.* **113** E14
Kobuk, river, *Alas., U.S.* **113** E14
Kobuk Valley National Park, *Alas., U.S.*
   113 E14
K'obulet'i, *Rep. of Georgia* **171** C16
Kocaeli (İzmit), *Turk.* **170** D5

Kočani, *Maced.* **154** K12
Koçarlı, *Turk.* **170** G3
Koçbaşı Tepe, peak, *Turk.* **171** F17
Ko Chang, island, *Thai.* **191** N10
Koch Bihar, *India* **180** G12
Kochen'ga, *Russ.* **158** F12
Kōchi, *Japan* **189** R7
Kochi (Cochin), *India* **181** R5
Koch Island, *Nunavut, Can.* **85** F17
Kochkor, *Kyrg.* **178** E12
Kochubey, *Russ.* **159** T15
Kodari, *Nepal* **180** F10
Koddiyar Bay, *Sri Lanka* **181** S8
Kodiak, *Alas., U.S.* **113** M15
Kodiak Island, *Alas., U.S.* **113** M15
Kodinar, *India* **180** K2
Kodinskiy, *Russ.* **161** J14
Kodok, *S. Sudan* **203** G13
Kodomari, *Japan* **188** J12
Köes, *Namibia* **206** J7
Koetoi, *Japan* **188** E13
Kofarnihon see Vahdat, *Taj.* **178** H7
Köflach, *Aust.* **150** M11
Koforidua, *Ghana* **204** E11
Kōfu, *Japan* **189** P11
Koga, *Japan* **189** N12
Ko Gaja Shima, *Japan* **189** U3
Kogalnik, river, *Que., Can.* **85** K18
Kögart, *Kyrg.* **178** G11
Kogon, *Uzb.* **176** L11
Kohala, region, *Hawai'i, U.S.* **115** K19
Kohala Mountains, *Hawai'i, U.S.*
   115 K19
Kohat, *Pak.* **179** N9
Kohima, *India* **180** G15
Kohistan, region, *Pak.* **178** L10
Koh Kong see Kaôh Kŏng, *Thai.*
   191 P10
Kohler Glacier, *Antarctica* **230** L7
Kohlu, *Pak.* **179** R8
Köhnə Bilgəh Burnu, *Azerb.* **171** D23
Kohtla-Järve, *Est.* **143** J17
Koilani, *Cyprus* **162** Q7
Koimbani, *Comoros* **209** M14
Koin, *N. Korea* **186** F7
Ko Jima, *Japan* **189** R12
Kojonup, *W. Aust., Austral.* **215** X3
Kokas, *Indonesia* **193** K18
Kokatha, *S. Aust., Austral.* **215** W9
Kök-Aygyr, *Kyrg.* **178** F12
Kokkina (Erenköy), *Cyprus* **162** N5
Kokkola, *Fin.* **143** F15
Koko, *Nigeria* **205** C13
Koko Crater, *Hawai'i, U.S.* **114** F12
Koko Head, peak, *Hawai'i, U.S.*
   114 F12
Kokomo, *Ind., U.S.* **101** Q9
Kökpekti, *Kaz.* **177** E18
Koksan, *N. Korea* **186** K7
Kökshetaū, *Kaz.* **177** C13
Köktal, *Kaz.* **177** H17
Ko Kut, island, *Cambodia* **191** P10
Kok-Yangak, *Kyrg.* **178** F10
Kola, island, *Indonesia* **193** L19
Kola, river, *Eur.* **140** A10
Kolachi, river, *Pak.* **179** T6
Kolaka, *Indonesia* **193** K14
Kola Peninsula, *Eur.* **140** B10
Kolar, *India* **181** P6
Kolari, *Fin.* **143** D14
Kolarovgrad see Shumen, *Bulg.*
   155 H16
Kolayat, *India* **180** F3
Kolbano, *Indonesia* **193** N15
Kolbeinsey Ridge, *Arctic Oc.* **247** K19
Kolbio, *Kenya* **203** K15
Kolding, *Den.* **142** N11
Kole, *Dem. Rep. of the Congo* **202** J11
Kole, *Dem. Rep. of the Congo* **202** L10
Kolé, *Vanuatu* **222** C1
Kolekole, river, *Hawai'i, U.S.* **115** M21
Kolguyev, Ostrov, *Russ.* **160** E10
Kolguyev Island, *Asia* **168** C7
Kolhapur, *India* **180** M4
Kolia, *Wallis and Futuna, Fr.* **222** E11
Koliganek, *Alas., U.S.* **113** K14
Kolín, *Czech Rep.* **150** H12
Kolkata (Calcutta), *India* **180** J12
Kolkhozobod, *Taj.* **178** J7
Kollam (Quilon), *India* **181** S5

Kollidam, river, *India* **181** R6
Kolluáll, valley, *Atl. Oc.* **247** M21
Kolmogorovo, *Russ.* **161** J13
Koło, *Pol.* **151** E14
Köln (Cologne), *Ger.* **150** F5
Kōloa, *Hawai'i, U.S.* **114** C5
Koloa, island, *Tonga* **222** L12
Kolodnya, *Russ.* **158** K7
Kologriv, *Russ.* **158** F12
Kolokani, *Mali* **200** H7
Kolomna, *Russ.* **158** K10
Kolomyya, *Ukr.* **159** P3
Kolonga, *Tonga* **222** H12
Kolonia, *F.S.M.* **221** F14
Kolonodale, *Indonesia* **193** K14
Kolovai, *Tonga* **222** H10
Kolpashevo, *Russ.* **160** J12
Kolpino, *Russ.* **158** F6
Kol'skiy Poluostrov, *Russ.* **160** D8
Kolufuri, island, *Maldives* **181** V3
Kolumadulu Atoll, *Maldives* **181** V3
Kolwezi, *Dem. Rep. of the Congo*
   202 N10
Kolyma, river, *Asia* **168** C12
Kolyma Lowland, *Asia* **168** B11
Kolyma Range, *Asia* **168** B12
Kolyma Valley, *Arctic Oc.* **246** G6
Kolymskoye Nagor'ye (Gydan), *Russ.*
   161 E20
Kom, peak, *Bulg.* **155** H13
Komagane, *Japan* **189** P10
Komandorskiye Ostrova (Commander
   Islands), *Russ.* **161** E23
Komárno, *Slovakia* **151** L14
Komatsu, *Japan* **189** N9
Kŏmdŏk, *N. Korea* **186** E11
Kŏmdŏk-san, peak, *N. Korea* **186** E11
Komo, *Fiji* **222** J9
Komodo, island, *Indonesia* **193** M13
Komoé, river, *Côte d'Ivoire* **204** D9
Komoran, island, *Indonesia* **193** M20
Komotiní, *Gr.* **157** B15
Ko, Motu, *Cook Is., N.Z.* **222** R2
Komovi, peak, *Montenegro* **154** J9
Kompóti, *Gr.* **156** F8
Komsomol, *Kaz.* **176** F7
Komsomolets, *Kaz.* **176** B10
Komsomolets, Ostrov, *Russ.* **161** C14
Komsomol'sk, *Russ.* **158** H10
Komsomol'skiy, *Russ.* **161** C19
Komsomol'sk na Amure, *Russ.*
   161 K20
Komsomol'sk-na-Ustyurte, *Uzb.*
   176 H8
Komusan, *N. Korea* **186** C12
Kona, region, *Hawai'i, U.S.* **115** N19
Konakovo, *Russ.* **158** H9
Konakpınar, *Turk.* **170** F12
Konawa, *Okla., U.S.* **104** H11
Konda, *Indonesia* **193** K18
Kondagaon, *India* **180** L8
Kondoa, *Tanzania* **203** L14
Kondol', *Russ.* **158** L13
Kondopoga, *Russ.* **160** E7
Kondrovo, *Russ.* **158** K8
Kondukur, *India* **181** N7
Koné, *New Caledonia, Fr.* **222** C7
Koné, Passe de, *New Caledonia, Fr.*
   222 C6
Köneürgench, *Uzb.* **176** J9
Kong, river, *Laos* **190** L13
Kongauru, island, *Palau* **220** Q10
Kongiganak, *Alas., U.S.* **112** K12
Konginskiy Khrebet, *Russ.* **161** D20
Kong Karls Basin, *Arctic Oc.* **247** G16
Konglu, *Myanmar* **190** F7
Kongolo, *Dem. Rep. of the Congo*
   202 M11
Kongor, *S. Sudan* **202** G12
Kongsberg, *Nor.* **142** K11
Kongsvinger, *Nor.* **142** K12
Kongue Falls, *Gabon* **205** G16
Kongur Shan, peak, *Asia* **168** G7
Kongwa, *Tanzania* **203** M14
Konibodom, *Taj.* **178** G8
Königswinter, *Ger.* **150** F5
Konin, *Pol.* **151** E14

Konispol, *Alban.* **154** N10
Konjuh, peak, *Bosn. & Herzg.* **154** F8
Konosha, *Russ.* **160** E7
Konotop, *Ukr.* **159** N7
Konqi, river, *China* **182** F5
Konrai, *Palau* **220** M12
Końskie, *Pol.* **151** F16
Konstantinov Ridge, *Atl. Oc.* **241** T8
Konstantinovsk, *Russ.* **159** Q11
Konstanz, *Ger.* **150** L6
Konta, *India* **180** M8
Kontagora, *Nigeria* **205** C13
Kon Tum, *Vietnam* **190** M13
Konya (Iconium), *Turk.* **170** G8
Konza, *Kenya* **203** K14
Ko'oko'olau, peak, *Hawai'i, U.S.*
   115 M20
Kookooligit Mountains, *Alas., U.S.*
   112 F10
Kookynie, *W. Aust., Austral.* **215** V4
Ko'olau Range, *Hawai'i, U.S.* **114** E11
Koolyanobbing, *W. Aust., Austral.*
   215 W4
Koomooloo, *S. Aust., Austral.* **215** XII
Koonalda, *S. Aust., Austral.* **215** W7
Kootenay, river, *Can., U.S.* **108** A4
Kopaonik, mountains, *Kos., Serb.*
   154 H10
Kópasker, *Ice.* **142** E4
Kopbirlik, *Kaz.* **177** F16
Köpekkayası Burnu, *Turk.* **170** C8
Koper (Capodistria), *Slov.* **154** D4
Kopervik, *Nor.* **142** K9
Kopet Mountain, *Asia* **168** F5
Kopište, island, *Croatia* **154** J6
Koppal, *India* **181** N5
Koprivnica, *Croatia* **154** D7
Köprü, river, *Turk.* **170** H6
Kopstal, *Lux.* **162** J10
Kop'ung, *N. Korea* **186** F6
Kopylovka, *Russ.* **160** J12
Korab, Mal, *Alban., Maced.* **154** K10
K'orahē, *Eth.* **203** H16
Korak, island, *Palau* **220** N12
Korangi, *Pak.* **179** W6
Ko Rawi, island, *Thai.* **191** S8
Korba, *India* **180** J8
Korçë, *Alban.* **154** M10
Korčula, island, *Croatia* **154** H6
Korčulanski Kanal, *Croatia* **154** H6
Korday, *Kaz.* **177** J15
Korea, *Asia* **168** F12
Korea Bay, *China, N. Korea* **184** D13
Korea Strait, *Japan, S. Korea* **187** U11
Korem, *Eth.* **203** F15
Korenovsk, *Russ.* **159** S10
Korf, *Russ.* **161** D21
Korhogo, *Côte d'Ivoire* **204** C8
Kori Creek, *India* **180** H1
Korido, *Indonesia* **193** J19
Korinós, *Gr.* **156** D10
Korinthiakós Kólpos, *Gr.* **156** H10
Kórinthos (Corinth), *Gr.* **156** J11
Korissía, *Gr.* **157** K13
Kōriyama, *Japan* **188** M12
Korkuteli, *Turk.* **170** H5
Korla, *China* **182** F5
Kormacit see Kormakiti, *Cyprus*
   162 N7
Kormakiti (Kormacit), *Cyprus* **162** N7
Kormakitis, Cape, *Cyprus* **162** N7
Körmend, *Hung.* **151** M13
Kornat, island, *Croatia* **154** G5
Koro, island, *Fiji* **222** H7
Korolevu, *Fiji* **222** J6
Koromiri, island, *Cook Is., N.Z.*
   222 Q9
Koróneia, Límni, *Gr.* **156** C11
Koróni, *Gr.* **156** M9
Koronída, *Gr.* **157** L15
Koropí, *Gr.* **156** J12
Koror, *Palau* **220** N11
Koror (Oreor), island, *Palau* **220** P11
Koro Sea, *Fiji* **222** H8
Korosten', *Ukr.* **159** N5
Korotkova, *Russ.* **161** K15
Korotoyak, *Russ.* **159** N10
Korsnes, *Nor.* **142** D12
Korti, *Sudan* **202** D12
Kortrijk, *Belg.* **148** L11

Koryak Range, *Asia* **168** BI2
Koryak Range, *N. Amer.* **82** P2
Koryakskaya Sopka, *Russ.* **161** F23
Koryakskoye Nagor'ye, *Russ.* **161** D2I
Koryfí Fengári, peak, *Gr.* **157** DI5
Kos, *Gr.* **157** LI8
Kos (Cos), island, *Gr.* **157** MI8
Kō Saki, *Japan* **189** Q3
Kosan, *N. Korea* **186** K9
Kosaya Gora, *Russ.* **158** K9
Kościerzyna, *Pol.* **151** BI4
Kosciusko, *Miss., U.S.* **102** KI2
Kosciuszko, Mount, *Austral.* **214** LI3
Koshikijima Rettō, *Japan* **189** S4
Köshim, river, *Kaz.* **176** D6
Koshk, *Afghan.* **178** M2
Košice, *Slovakia* **151** JI7
Kosmás, *Gr.* **156** LII
Kosomolets Island, *Asia* **168** B9
Koson, *Uzb.* **176** LII
Kosŏng, *N. Korea* **186** KIO
Kosovo, *Eur.* **154** JIO
Kosovska Mitrovica see Mitrovicë, *Kos.* **154** HIO
Kosrae (Kusaie), island, *F.S.M.* **220** JI
Kossol Passage, *Palau* **220** LI2
Kossou, Lac de, *Côte d'Ivoire* **204** D8
Kosti, *Sudan* **203** EI3
Kostino, *Russ.* **161** HI3
Kostopil', *Ukr.* **159** N4
Kostroma, *Russ.* **158** GII
Kostromskoye Vodokhranilishche, *Russ.* **158** GII
Kostyantynivka, *Ukr.* **159** Q9
Koszalin, *Pol.* **150** BI2
Kota, *India* **180** H5
Kotaagung, *Indonesia* **192** L7
Kotabaru, *Indonesia* **192** KI2
Kotabumi, *Indonesia* **192** L7
Kotabunan, *Indonesia* **193** JI5
Kot Addu, *Pak.* **179** R9
Ko Takara Jima, *Japan* **189** V3
Kota Kinabalu, *Malaysia* **192** GII
Ko Tarutao, island, *Thai.* **191** S8
Kota Tinggi, *Malaysia* **191** VII
Kotawa, Motu, *Cook Is., N.Z.* **222** RI
Kotel'nich, *Russ.* **160** G7
Kotel'nikovo, *Russ.* **159** QI2
Kotel'nyy, Ostrov, *Russ.* **161** DI6
Köthen, *Ger.* **150** E9
Kotka, *Fin.* **143** HI6
Kotlas, *Russ.* **160** F8
Kotlik, *Alas., U.S.* **112** GI2
Kotorska, Boka, *Montenegro* **154** J8
Kotovs'k, *Russ.* **158** MII
Kotovsk, *Ukr.* **159** Q5
Kotri, *Pak.* **179** V7
Kottayam, *India* **181** R5
Kotto, river, *Cen. Af. Rep.* **202** GIO
Kotu, island, *Tonga* **222** Q6
Kotu Group, *Tonga* **222** Q6
Koturdepe, *Turkm.* **176** L6
Kotzebue, *Alas., U.S.* **113** EI3
Kotzebue Sound, *Alas., U.S.* **113** EI3
Koua, *New Caledonia, Fr.* **222** D7
Kouakou, island, *Fr. Polynesia, Fr.* **223** R2I
Kouango, *Cen. Af. Rep.* **202** H9
Koudougou, *Burkina Faso* **204** BIO
Koufália, *Gr.* **156** CIO
Koufonísi, island, *Gr.* **157** RI6
Koufonísia, island, *Gr.* **157** LI5
Kouilou, river, *Congo* **205** JI6
Koukdjuak, Great Plain of the, *Nunavut, Can.* **85** GI8
Kouklia, *Cyprus* **162** Q6
Koúla Óros, *Gr.* **157** BI4
Koulamoutou, *Gabon* **205** HI6
Koulikoro, *Mali* **200** H7
Koumac, *New Caledonia, Fr.* **222** C6
Koumra, *Chad* **201** KI5
Koungou, *Mayotte, Fr.* **209** PI7
Kountze, *Tex., U.S.* **105** QI5
Kourou, *Fr. Guiana* **131** EI8
Kouroussa, *Guinea* **204** C6
Koutiala, *Mali* **200** J8
Koutomo, Île, *New Caledonia, Fr.* **222** E9

Koutu Puhipuhi, Pointe, *Fr. Polynesia, Fr.* **223** Q20
Kouvola, *Fin.* **143** HI6
Kovel', *Ukr.* **158** M3
Kovic, Baie, *Que., Can.* **85** JI7
Kovin, *Serb.* **154** FII
Kovrov, *Russ.* **158** JII
Kovur, *India* **181** P7
Kowanyama, *Qnsld., Austral.* **215** PI2
Kowloon see Jiulong, Hong Kong (Xianggang), S.A.R., China **185** W5
Kowŏn, *N. Korea* **186** H8
Köyceğiz, *Turk.* **170** H4
Koyda, *Russ.* **160** E9
Koytendag, *Turkm.* **176** MI2
Koyuk, *Alas., U.S.* **113** FI3
Koyukuk, *Alas., U.S.* **113** FI4
Koyukuk, river, *Alas., U.S.* **113** EI5
Koyulhisar, *Turk.* **170** EI2
Kozan, *Turk.* **170** HII
Kozáni, *Gr.* **156** D9
Kozel'sk, *Russ.* **158** K8
Kozhasay, *Kaz.* **176** E8
Kozhikode (Calicut), *India* **181** Q5
Kozjak, peak, *Maced.* **154** LII
Kozlovka, *Russ.* **159** NII
Kozlu, *Turk.* **170** C7
Kozluk, *Turk.* **171** GI6
Koz'modem'yansk, *Russ.* **158** HI3
Kōzu Shima, *Japan* **189** QII
Kozyatyn, *Ukr.* **159** P5
Kpalimé, *Togo* **204** DII
Kra, Isthmus of, *Thai.* **191** Q8
Krabi, *Thai.* **191** R8
Kra Buri, *Thai.* **191** P8
Krâchéh (Kratie), *Cambodia* **191** NI2
Kragerø, *Nor.* **142** LI4
Kragujevac, *Serb.* **154** GIO
Kraków, *Pol.* **151** GI5
Kralendijk, *Bonaire, Neth.* **123** QI9
Kraljevo, *Serb.* **154** GIO
Kráľovský Chlmec, *Slovakia* **151** JI7
Kramators'k, *Ukr.* **159** Q9
Kramfors, *Sw.* **143** HI3
Kraníd, *Gr.* **156** KII
Kranj, *Slov.* **154** D4
Krasavino, *Russ.* **160** F8
Kraśnik, *Pol.* **151** FI7
Krasnoarmeysk see Tayynsha, *Kaz.* **177** BI3
Krasnoarmeyskaya, *Russ.* **159** SIO
Krasnodar, *Russ.* **159** SIO
Krasnogorsk, *Russ.* **161** J22
Krasnogvardeyskoye, *Russ.* **159** SII
Krasnohrad, *Ukr.* **159** P8
Krasnokamensk, *Russ.* **161** LI8
Krasnoslobodsk, *Russ.* **159** PI3
Krasnovishersk, *Russ.* **160** G9
Krasnoyarsk, *Russ.* **161** KI3
Krasnoye, *Russ.* **158** MI6
Krasnyy Dolginets, *Kaz.* **176** G5
Krasnyye Baki, *Russ.* **158** HI3
Krasnyy Kholm, *Russ.* **158** G9
Krasnyy Luch, *Ukr.* **159** QIO
Krasnyy Yar, *Russ.* **159** NI3
Kratie see Krâchéh, *Cambodia* **191** NI2
Kraul Mountains, *Antarctica* **230** CII
Krause Lagoon Channel, *Virgin Is., U.S.* **122** R2
Kray Lesa, *Russ.* **161** DI9
Krefeld, *Ger.* **150** F5
Kremastí, *Gr.* **157** M2O
Kremen, peak, *Croatia* **154** F6
Kremenchuk, *Ukr.* **159** P7
Kremenchuts'ke Vodoskovyshche, *Ukr.* **159** P7
Kremenets', *Ukr.* **159** N3
Krems, *Aust.* **150** KI2
Kress, *Tex., U.S.* **104** J5
Kréstena, *Gr.* **156** K9
Kretinga, *Lith.* **143** MI5
Kreuzlingen, *Switz.* **152** A4
Kribi, *Cameroon* **205** FI5
Krim, peak, *Slov.* **154** D4
Krims'ke Hory, *Ukr.* **159** T7
Krishna, river, *India* **181** N5
Krishnagiri, *India* **181** Q6
Krishnanagar, *India* **180** JI2
Kristiansand, *Nor.* **142** MIO

Kristianstad, *Sw.* **143** MI3
Kristiansund, *Nor.* **142** HIO
Kristinestad, *Fin.* **143** HI4
Kríti (Crete), island, *Gr.* **157** QI4
Krk, island, *Croatia* **154** E4
Krnov, *Czech Rep.* **151** HI3
Kroken, *Nor.* **142** FI2
Krolevets', *Ukr.* **158** M7
Kromy, *Russ.* **158** M8
Kronotskaya Sopka, *Russ.* **161** F22
Kronotskiy Gulf, *Pac. Oc.* **168** CI3
Kronshtadt, *Russ.* **158** F6
Kroonstad, *S. Af.* **206** KIO
Kropotkin, *Russ.* **159** SII
Krosno, *Pol.* **151** HI7
Krosno Odrzańskie, *Pol.* **150** EII
Krotoszyn, *Pol.* **151** EI3
Krstača, peak, *Montenegro, Serb.* **154** HIO
Krui, *Indonesia* **192** L7
Krumovgrad, *Bulg.* **155** KI5
Krung Thep (Bangkok), *Thai.* **190** M9
Krupá, *Czech Rep.* **150** GIO
Krupište, *Maced.* **154** KI2
Krupki, *Belarus* **158** K5
Krusenstern Trough, *Pac. Oc.* **242** CIO
Kruševac, *Serb.* **154** GII
Krutets, *Russ.* **158** FIO
Krychaw, *Belarus* **158** L6
Krylovskaya, *Russ.* **159** RII
Krymsk, *Russ.* **159** TIO
Kryvichy, *Belarus* **158** K4
Kryvyy Rih, *Ukr.* **159** Q7
Ksar el Kebir, *Mor.* **200** A8
Ksenen Rise, *Ind. Oc.* **225** GI4
Kufah see Al Kūfah, *Iraq* **174** E9
Kufra Oasis, *Af.* **198** E8
Kufstein, *Aust.* **150** L9
Kugluktuk, *Nunavut, Can.* **84** FI2
Kugul'ta, *Russ.* **159** SI2
Kūhak, *Iran* **175** HI8
Kūh-e Taftān, peak, *Asia* **168** H5
Kuhgrat, peak, *Liech.* **162** N3

Kūhhā-Ye Zāgros (Zagros Mountains), *Iran* **174** DII
Kuhmo, *Fin.* **143** FI6
Kui Buri, *Thai.* **191** N8
Kuikuina, *Nicar.* **117** LI8
Kuiseb, river, *Namibia* **206** H6
Kuitan, *Guang., China* **185** W7
Kuito, *Angola* **206** D7
Kuivaniemi, *Fin.* **143** EI5
Kujang, *N. Korea* **186** G6
Kuji, *Japan* **188** KI3
Kuju, peak, *Japan* **189** R5
Kūka'iau, *Hawai'i, U.S.* **115** L2O
Kukës, *Alban.* **154** KIO
Kukolu, island, *Solomon Is.* **221** JI8
Kukpowruk, river, *Alas., U.S.* **113** CI3
Kukui, *Hawai'i, U.S.* **115** N2I
Kukuihaele, *Hawai'i, U.S.* **115** K2O
Kukui'ula, *Hawai'i, U.S.* **114** C5
Kuku Point, *Wake I., U.S.* **220** F7
Kula, *Serb.* **154** E9
Kula, *Turk.* **170** F4
Kūlagīno, *Kaz.* **176** E6
Kula Gulf, *Solomon Is.* **221** MI6
Kūlani, peak, *Hawai'i, U.S.* **115** N2I
Kulaura, *Bangladesh* **180** HI3
Kul'chi, *Russ.* **161** J2O
Kuldīga, *Latv.* **143** LI5
Kule, *Botswana* **206** H8
Kulebaki, *Russ.* **158** JII
Kulén, *Cambodia* **190** MII
Kulin, *W. Aust., Austral.* **215** X3
Kulkuduk, *Uzb.* **176** JIO
Kulm, *N. Dak., U.S.* **106** H6
Kulmbach, *Ger.* **150** G8
Kūlob, *Taj.* **178** J8
Kulōrō Dahşil, *Afghan.* **178** L7
Kulp, *Turk.* **171** GI5
Kulu, *Turk.* **170** F8
Kulumadau, *P.N.G.* **217** E2I
Kulunda, *Russ.* **160** LII
Kuma, river, *Russ.* **159** SI4
Kumagaya, *Japan* **189** NII
Kumai, *Indonesia* **192** KIO
Kumai, Teluk, *Indonesia* **192** KIO
Kumamoto, *Japan* **189** R5
Kumano, *Japan* **189** R9
Kumano Nada, *Japan* **189** Q9
Kumanovo, *Maced.* **154** KII
Kuman Range, *Myanmar* **190** E7
Kumara Junction, *N.Z.* **217** NI7
Kumarina Mine, *W. Aust., Austral.* **215** U3
Kumarl, *W. Aust., Austral.* **215** X4
Kumasi, *Ghana* **204** EIO
Kumawa, Pegunungan, *Indonesia* **217** CI4
Kumba, *Cameroon* **205** FI5
Kumbakale, *Solomon Is.* **221** KI5
Kumbakonam, *India* **181** R7
Kumbe, *Indonesia* **193** M2I
Kümch'ŏn, *N. Korea* **186** K9
Kümch'ŏn, *N. Korea* **186** L7
Kume Jima, *Japan* **189** XI
Kumejima, *Japan* **189** XI
Kümgang, *N. Korea* **186** KIO
Kümgang-san, peak, *N. Korea* **186** KIO
Kümhwa see Gimhwa, *S. Korea* **186** L9
Kumo, *Nigeria* **205** CI5
Kumphawapi, *Thai.* **190** KIO
Kümsŏng see Kimhwa, *N. Korea* **186** L9
Kumta, *India* **181** P4
Kumtag Shamo, *China* **182** G6
Kumukahi, Cape, *Hawai'i, U.S.* **115** N22
Kumukh, *Russ.* **159** UI5
Kumul see Hami, *China* **182** F7
Kümya, *N. Korea* **186** H8
Kümya-man see Yŏnghüng-man, bay, *N. Korea* **186** J9
Kumylzhenskaya, *Russ.* **159** PI2
Kumzār, *Oman* **175** HI5
Kunahandu, island, *Maldives* **181** W3
Kunashir (Kunashiri), island, *Russ.* **188** EI6
Kunashiri see Kunashir, island, *Russ.* **161** K23

Kundapura (Coondapoor), *India* **181** P4
Kundar, river, *Afghan., Pak.* **179** Q7
Kundian, *Pak.* **179** P9
Kundu, *Solomon Is.* **221** MI5
Kunduz, *Afghan.* **178** K7
Kunduz, river, *Afghan.* **178** L7
Kunene (Cunene), river, *Af.* **206** F5
Kungsbacka, *Sw.* **142** MI2
Kungurtug, *Russ.* **161** MI4
Kunlon, *Myanmar* **190** F8
Kunlun Mountains, *Asia* **168** G7
Kunlun Shan, *China* **180** A6
Kunlun Shankou, *China* **182** H7
Kunming, *China* **182** N9
Kunnamkulam, *India* **181** R5
Kunshan, *Jiangsu, China* **184** MII
Kunu, island, *F.S.M.* **221** BI4
Kununurra, *W. Aust., Austral.* **215** Q7
Kunyu Shan, *Shand., China* **184** FI2
Kuopio, *Fin.* **143** GI6
Kupa, river, *Croatia* **154** E5
Kupang, *Indonesia* **193** NI4
Küpikipiki'o Point (Black Point), *Hawai'i, U.S.* **114** FII
Kupino, *Russ.* **160** KII
Kupreanof Island, *Alas., U.S.* **113** M23
Kupuas, river, *Asia* **168** LI2
Kupupolo Heiau, *Hawai'i, U.S.* **114** DIO
Kup''yans'k, *Ukr.* **159** P9
Kuqa, *China* **182** E4
Kür (Kura), river, *Azerb.* **171** E22
Kura, river see Mtkvari, *Rep. of Georgia* **171** CI8
Kura, river, see Kür, *Azerb.* **171** E22
Kurakh, *Russ.* **159** VI6
Kurakhtin (Cəbrayıl), *Azerb.* **171** E2I
Kūrān Dap, *Iran* **175** HI7
Kür-Araz Ovalığı, *Azerb.* **171** D2I
Kurashassayskiy, *Kaz.* **176** D8
Kurashiki, *Japan* **189** Q7
Kurayoshi, *Japan* **189** P7
Kurbağa Gölü, *Turk.* **170** GIO
Kürchatov, *Kaz.* **177** DI6
Kürdəmir, *Azerb.* **171** D22
Kür Dili, *Azerb.* **171** F23
Kurdistan, region, *Iran, Iraq., Turk.* **174** B9
Kurduna, *Pak.* **179** Q6
Kurduvadi, *India* **180** M4
Kürdzhali, *Bulg.* **155** KI5
Kure, *Japan* **189** Q7
Küre, *Turk.* **170** C9
Kure Atoll, *Hawai'i, U.S.* **114** K2
Kure Beach, *N.C., U.S.* **98** KI3
Kuressaare, *Est.* **143** KI5
Kureyka, *Russ.* **161** GI3
Kurgan, *Russ.* **160** J9
Kurganinsk, *Russ.* **159** TII
Kuria Muria Islands see Khurīyā Murīyā, Jazā'ir, *Oman* **175** NI5
Kuri Bay, *W. Aust., Austral.* **215** Q5
Kuridala, *Qnsld., Austral.* **215** SII
Kurikka, *Fin.* **143** GI5
Kuril Basin, *Pac. Oc.* **242** D8
Kuril Islands see Kuril'skiye Ostrova, *Russ.* **161** J23
Kuril-Kamchatka Trench, *Pac. Oc.* **242** D8
Kuril'sk, *Russ.* **161** J23
Kuril'skiye Ostrova (Kuril Islands), *Russ.* **161** J23
Kurio, *Japan* **189** U4
Kurnool, *India* **181** N6
Kuroishi, *Japan* **188** JI2
Kuroiso, *Japan* **189** NI2
Kuro Shima, *Japan* **189** T4
Kurshskiy Zaliv, *Lith., Russ.* **158** JI
Kursk, *Russ.* **158** M9
Kurşunlu, *Turk.* **170** D8
Kurtalan, *Turk.* **171** GI6
Kurtistown, *Hawai'i, U.S.* **115** N22
Kurtoğlu Burnu, *Turk.* **170** J4
Kuruçay, *Turk.* **171** EI3
Kuru, river, *S. Sudan* **202** GII
Kuruktag, range, *China* **182** F5
Kuruman, *S. Af.* **206** K9
Kurume, *Japan* **189** R4
Kurunegala, *Sri Lanka* **181** S7
Kurun Uryakh, *Russ.* **161** HI9

Kuryong, river, N. Korea **186** G6
Kuşadası, Turk. **170** G3
Kuşadası Körfezi, Turk. **170** G3
Kusaie see Kosrae, island, F.S.M. **220** J1
Kusakaki Guntō, Japan **189** T3
Kuş Gölü, Turk. **170** D4
Kushima, Japan **189** T5
Kushimoto, Japan **189** R9
Kushiro, Japan **188** G15
Kushk-e Kuhnah, Afghan. **178** M3
Kushnïya, Israel **172** K6
Kushtia, Bangladesh **180** H12
Kuskokwim, river, Alas., U.S. **113** H14
Kuskokwim Bay, Alas., U.S. **112** K12
Kuskokwim Mountains, Alas., U.S. **113** H14
Kusŏng, N. Korea **186** G5
Kussharo Ko, Japan **188** F15
Kusur, Russ. **159** V15
Kütahya, Turk. **170** E5
K'ut'aisi, Rep. of Georgia **171** B17
Kutanibong, Indonesia **192** G4
Kutch, Gulf of see Kachchh, Gulf of, India **180** J1
Kutch, Rann of see Rann of Kachchh, Rann of, India, Pak. **179** X7
Kutchan, Japan **188** G12
Kutina, Croatia **154** E7
Kutno, Pol. **151** E15
Kutru, India **180** L7
Kutu, Dem. Rep. of the Congo **202** L8
Kutubdia, island, Bangladesh **180** J13
Kutum, Sudan **202** E10
Kuujjuaq, Que., Can. **85** K19
Kuujjuarapik, Que., Can. **85** L18
Kuuli-Mayak, Turkm. **176** K6
Kuŭp, N. Korea **186** J9
Kuusamo, Fin. **143** E16
Kuvango, Angola **206** E6
Kuvshinovo, Russ. **158** H8
Kuwait, Asia **174** G10
Kuwait City see Al Kuwayt, Kuwait **174** G11
Kuybishevskiy, Taj. **178** J7
Kuybyshev, Russ. **160** K11
Kuybyshev Reservoir, Eur. **140** E14
Kuybyshevskoye Vodokhranilishche, Russ. **158** J14
Kuye, river, Shaanxi, China **184** D3
Kuytun, China **182** D5
Kuzey Anadolu Dağlari, Turk. **170** C9
Kuznetsk, Russ. **158** L14
Kuzumaki, Japan **188** K13
Kvænangen, bay, Nor. **143** B13
Kvaløy, island, Nor. **143** C13
Kvarner, gulf, Croatia **154** F4
Kvarnerić, bay, Croatia **154** E4
Kvikkjokk, Sw. **143** E13
Kwa, river, Dem. Rep. of the Congo **202** L8
Kwadak, island, Marshall Is., U.S. **220** M5
K'waesang-bong, peak, N. Korea **186** D11
K'waesang-bong, peak, N. Korea **186** D8
Kwail (P'ungch'ŏn), N. Korea **186** K5
Kwailibesi, Solomon Is. **221** M19
Kwajalein, island, Marshall Is., U.S. **220** N5
Kwajalein Atoll, Marshall Is., U.S. **220** G3
Kwajalein Lagoon, Marshall Is., U.S. **220** L3
Kwaksan, N. Korea **186** H5
Kwale, Kenya **203** L15
Kwangje, N. Korea **186** J5
Kwangju see Gwangju, S. Korea **187** T8
Kwangnyang-man, bay, N. Korea **186** K5
Kwango, river, Af. **198** K6
Kwanza, river, Af. **198** L6
Kwaos, Indonesia **193** K17
Kwekwe, Zimb. **206** G11
Kwenge, river, Dem. Rep. of the Congo **202** M8
Kwethluk, Alas., U.S. **112** J12
Kwidzyn, Pol. **151** C14
Kwigillingok, Alas., U.S. **112** K12

Kwilu, river, Dem. Rep. of the Congo **202** L8
Kwitaro, river, Guyana **131** G14
Kwoka, peak, Indonesia **193** J18
Kyaikto, Myanmar **190** K7
Kyakhta, Russ. **161** M15
Kyancutta, S. Aust., Austral. **215** X9
Kyaukkyi, Myanmar **190** J6
Kyaukme, Myanmar **190** G7
Kyaukphyu, Myanmar **190** J4
Kyauktaw, Myanmar **190** H4
Kybartai, Lith. **143** N16
Kyejŏng, N. Korea **186** L7
Kyiv (Kiev), Ukr. **159** N6
Kykládes (Cyclades), islands, Gr. **157** L14
Kyle, Tex., U.S. **105** Q10
Kyll, river, Ger. **162** H11
Kyllburg, Ger. **162** G11
Kyllíni, Gr. **156** J8
Kyllíni, Óros, Gr. **156** J10
Kými, Gr. **157** H13
Kýmis, Akrotírio, Gr. **157** H13
Kynuna, Qnsld., Austral. **215** S12
Kyoga, Lake, Uganda **203** J13
Kyōga Misaki, Japan **189** P8
Kyŏngju see Gyeongju, S. Korea **187** R12
Kyŏngsŏng, N. Korea **186** D12
Kyōto, Japan **189** Q9
Kyparissía, Gr. **156** L9
Kyparissiakós Kólpos, Gr. **156** K8
Kyrá Panagiá, island, Gr. **157** F13
Kyrenia (Girne, Kerýneia), Cyprus **162** N8
Kyrgyz Range, Kaz., Kyrg. **178** D9
Kyrgyzstan, Asia **178** E10
Kyshtovka, Russ. **160** J11
Kýthira, Gr. **156** N11
Kýthira (Cerigo, Cythera), island, Gr. **156** N11
Kýthnos, Gr. **157** K13
Kýthnos, island, Gr. **157** K13
Kythrea (Değirmenlik), Cyprus **162** N9
Kyubeyingde, Russ. **161** G16
Kyūroku Jima, Japan **188** J11
Kyushe, Kaz. **176** G8
Kyūshū, island, Japan **189** S5
Kyushu-Palau Ridge, Pac. Oc. **242** F6
Kyustendil, Bulg. **154** J12
Kyzyl, Russ. **161** L13
Kyzyl-Adyr, Kyrg. **178** E9
Kyzylkup, Turkm. **176** K6
Kyzyl-Kyya, Kyrg. **178** G10
Kyzyl-Suu, Kyrg. **178** E14

L

La Adela, Arg. **135** P10
La Almunia de Doña Godina, Sp. **147** E13
Laascaanood, Somalia **203** G17
Laasqoray, Somalia **203** F18
La Asunción, Venez. **130** B11
Laatzen, Ger. **150** D7
Lā'au Point, Hawai'i, U.S. **115** G13
Laayoune, W. Sahara **200** D6
La Banda, Arg. **134** G10
La Bañeza, Sp. **146** C8
La Barca, Mex. **116** H10
La Barge, Wyo., U.S. **108** J9
Labasa, Fiji **222** G7
La Baule-Escoublac, Fr. **149** R5
Labé, Guinea **204** B5
Labe, river, Czech Rep. **150** H12
La Belle, Fla., U.S. **99** V9
Labinsk, Russ. **159** T11
Laborie, St. Lucia **123** L14
Labota, Indonesia **193** K14
Labouheyre, Fr. **149** W6
Laboulaye, Arg. **134** L10
Labra, Bonaire, Neth. **123** Q18
Labrador, region, Nfld. & Lab., Can. **85** L21
Labrador Basin, Atl. Oc. **240** F6

Labrador City, Nfld. & Lab., Can. **85** M20
Labrador Sea, Atl. Oc. **240** G6
Labrador Shelf, Atl. Oc. **240** G5
La Brea, Trinidad and Tobago **123** Q22
Lábrea, Braz. **132** F7
Labuan, island, Malaysia **192** G11
Labuan Basin, Ind. Oc. **248** C12
Labuk Bay, Malaysia **192** F12
Labutta, Myanmar **190** L5
La Calera, Chile **134** K6
Lacanau, Fr. **149** W6
Lacanau, Étang de, Fr. **149** V6
Lacanau-Océan, Fr. **149** V6
La Canourgue, Fr. **149** W11
La Capelle, Fr. **148** M11
Lacapelle-Marival, Fr. **149** V9
La Carolina, Sp. **146** J11
Lacaune, Monts de, Fr. **149** X10
Laccadive Sea, India **181** P4
Lac du Flambeau, Wis., U.S. **100** G5
La Ceiba, Hond. **117** K17
Lacepede Bay, Austral. **214** L11
La Chambre, Fr. **149** U14
Lachanás, Gr. **156** C11
La Chapelle-d'Angillon, Fr. **149** R9
La Charité, Fr. **149** S10
La Châtaigneraie, Fr. **149** S6
La Châtre, Fr. **149** T9
La Chaux-de-Fonds, Switz. **152** B2
Lachlan, river, Austral. **214** K13
Laçın see Berdzor, Azerb. **171** E20
La Ciotat, Fr. **149** Y14
La Citadelle, site, Haiti **119** L17
La Ciudad Encantada, Sp. **147** G13
Lackawanna, N.Y., U.S. **96** J5
Lac La Biche, Alta., Can. **84** L11
La Clayette, Fr. **149** T12
La Coche, Guadeloupe, Fr. **123** H14
Lacon, Ill., U.S. **101** P5
La Condamine, Monaco **163** E20
Laconia, N.H., U.S. **97** H14
Laconia, Gulf of, Gr. **140** M9
La Conner, Wash., U.S. **110** B4
Lacoochee, Fla., U.S. **99** T8
La Cordillera, islands, P.R., U.S. **122** M6
La Cortinada, Andorra **162** H3
Lacq, Fr. **149** X6
Lacre Punt, Bonaire, Neth. **123** R19
La Crosse, Kans., U.S. **107** T5
La Crosse, Wash., U.S. **110** D8
La Crosse, Wis., U.S. **100** K3
La Cruz, C.R. **117** M18
La Cruz, Mex. **116** F7
La Cumbre, Volcán, Ecua. **130** P9
La Cygne, Kans., U.S. **107** T10
Ladakh, region, India **180** B6
Ladakh Range, India **180** B6
Ladd Seamount, Hawai'i, U.S. **114** K2
La Désirade, island, Guadeloupe, Fr. **123** E17
La Digue, island, Seychelles **209** N21
Ladik, Turk. **170** D11
Lādīz, Iran **175** G17
Ladnun, India **180** F4
Ladoga, Lake see Ladozhskoye Ozero, Russ. **158** F7
La Dogana, San Marino **163** G16
La Dorada, Col. **130** E5
Ladozhskoye Ozero (Ladoga, Lake), Russ. **158** F7
Ladrillero, Golfo, Chile **135** V6
Ladron Peak, N. Mex., U.S. **109** T11
Lady Ann Strait, Nunavut, Can. **85** D16
Lady Elliot Island, Austral. **214** G16
Ladygin Yar, Russ. **161** F13
Ladysmith, S. Af. **206** K11
Ladysmith, Wis., U.S. **100** G3
Ladyzhenka, Kaz. **177** D13
Lae, P.N.G. **217** D19
Laea, Indonesia **193** L14
Lae Atoll, Marshall Is., U.S. **220** G3
Laem Ngop, Cambodia **191** N10
Lae 'O Kākā, Hawai'i, U.S. **115** J16
Lae 'O Kealaikahiki, Hawai'i, U.S. **115** J15
Lae 'O Kuikui, Hawai'i, U.S. **115** J16

Laerdal Tunnel, Nor. **142** J10
La Esmeralda, Venez. **130** F10
Læsø, island, Den. **142** M11
La Esperanza, Cuba **118** G5
La Esperanza, P.R., U.S. **122** M2
Lafayette, Ala., U.S. **103** K17
LaFayette, Ga., U.S. **98** J4
Lafayette, Ind., U.S. **101** Q8
Lafayette, La., U.S. **102** P8
Lafayette, Tenn., U.S. **103** E16
La Fe, Cuba **118** H4
La Fe, Cuba **118** H6
La Felguera, Sp. **146** B9
La Fère, Fr. **149** N11
La Ferme, Mauritius **209** J20
La Ferté-Macé, Fr. **149** P7
La Ferté-Saint-Aubin, Fr. **149** R9
La Flèche, Fr. **149** R7
La Foa, New Caledonia, Fr. **222** D7
La Follette, Tenn., U.S. **103** E18
Laga Bor, river, Kenya **203** J15
La Gacilly, Fr. **149** R5
Laghouat, Alg. **200** B11
La Gineta, Sp. **147** H13
Lagkadás, Gr. **156** C11
Lagkadía, Gr. **156** K9
Lagdo Reservoir, Cameroon **205** D17
Laggan Bay, Scot., U.K. **145** N7
Laghouat, Alg. **200** B11
La Gineta, Sp. **147** H13
Lagoa, Azores, Port. **146** Q5
Lagodekhi, Rep. of Georgia **171** C20
Lagos, Nigeria **204** E12
Lagos, Port. **146** L5
Lágos, Gr. **157** B14
Lagos de Moreno, Mex. **116** H10
Lagosta see Lastovo, island, Croatia **154** J6
La Grand' Combe, Fr. **149** W12
La Grande, Oreg., U.S. **110** F8
La Grange, Ky., U.S. **103** B17
La Grange, Mo., U.S. **107** R13
La Grange, N.C., U.S. **98** H13
La Grange, Tex., U.S. **105** Q12
La Grange, Wyo., U.S. **108** J14
LaGrange, Ga., U.S. **98** M4
Lagrange, Ind., U.S. **101** N10
Lagrange, W. Aust., Austral. **215** R4
Lagrange Bay, Austral. **214** D4
La Gran Sabana, region, Venez. **130** E12
La Grave, Fr. **149** V14
La Grulla, Tex., U.S. **105** W9
La Guaira, Venez. **130** B9
Lagua Lichan, Puntan, N. Mariana Is., U.S. **220** A6
Laguépie, Fr. **149** W9
La Guerche, Fr. **149** Q6
Lagun, Curaçao, Neth. **123** N13
Laguna, N. Mex., U.S. **109** S11
Laguna Beach, Calif., U.S. **111** Y9
Laguna Blanca, Arg. **134** F13
Laguna Dam, Ariz., Calif., U.S. **111** Z13
Laguna Grande, Arg. **135** V8
Laguna Madre, Tex., U.S. **105** V11
Laguna Ojo de Liebre, Mex. **116** D5
Laguna Paiva, Arg. **134** J13
Lagunas, Chile **134** C7
Lagunas, Peru **132** E3
Lagunillas, Bol. **132** K8
Lagwira, Mauritania **200** F4
La Habana, Cuba **118** G6
Lahad Datu, Malaysia **192** G12
Lahaina, Hawai'i, U.S. **115** G16
Laham, Indonesia **192** J11
La Harpe, Ill., U.S. **101** Q3
Lahat, Indonesia **192** K7
Lahıc, Azerb. **171** D22
Lāhījān, Iran **174** B12
Lahi Passage, Tonga **222** H11
Lahn, river, Ger. **150** G6
Lahnstein, Ger. **150** G5
Lahontan Reservoir, Nev., U.S. **111** P7
Lahore, Pak. **179** Q12
Lahr, Ger. **150** K5
Lahri, Pak. **179** S7
Lahti, Fin. **143** H16
Laï (Behagle), Chad **201** K14
Lai'an (Xin'an), Anhui, China **184** L9
Lai Châu, Vietnam **190** G10
Lā'ie, Hawai'i, U.S. **114** D11

Laifeng, Hubei, China **185** P1
L'Aigle, Fr. **149** P8
Laïka, island, Vanuatu **222** E3
Laingsburg, S. Af. **206** M8
Laird, river, N. Amer. **82** E4
Lairg, Scot., U.K. **144** H9
Laisamis, Kenya **203** J14
Laishui, Hebei, China **184** D7
La Isleta, island, Sp. **208** Q6
Laiwu, Shand., China **184** G8
Laixi, Shand., China **184** G11
Laiyang, Shand., China **184** F11
Laiyuan, Hebei, China **184** D6
Laizhou, Shand., China **184** F10
Laizhou Wan, Shand., China **184** F10
Lajamanu, N.T., Austral. **215** R7
La Jara, Colo., U.S. **109** P12
Lajes, Braz. **132** N12
Lajes, Azores, Port. **146** Q3
Lajes, Azores, Port. **146** P1
Lajes das Flores, Azores, Port. **146** P1
Lajitas, Tex., U.S. **105** R2
La Jonquera, Sp. **147** C18
La Junta, Colo., U.S. **109** P15
Lakash (Telloh), ruins, Iraq **174** F10
Lakatoro, Vanuatu **222** D2
Lakaträsk, Sw. **143** E14
Lake, Poopelloe, N.S.W., Austral. **215** W12
Lake Andes, S. Dak., U.S. **106** M6
Lake Arthur, La., U.S. **102** P7
Lakeba, island, Fiji **222** J9
Lakeba Passage, Fiji **222** J9
Lake Butler, Fla., U.S. **99** R7
Lake Charles, La., U.S. **102** P7
Lake Chelan National Recreation Area, Wash., U.S. **110** B5
Lake City, Colo., U.S. **109** P11
Lake City, Iowa, U.S. **107** N10
Lake City, Mich., U.S. **100** J10
Lake City, Minn., U.S. **106** K12
Lake City, S.C., U.S. **98** L10;R7
Lake Clark National Park and Preserve, Alas., U.S. **113** J15
Lake Coleridge, N.Z. **217** P16
Lake Crystal, Minn., U.S. **106** L10
Lake District, Eng., U.K. **145** Q10
Lake Eyre Basin, Austral. **214** G10
Lakefield, Minn., U.S. **106** L10
Lake Geneva, Wis., U.S. **100** M6
Lake Harbor, Fla., U.S. **99** V10
Lake Havasu City, Ariz., U.S. **109** S4
Lake Jackson, Tex., U.S. **105** S14
Lakeland, Fla., U.S. **99** U8
Lakeland, Ga., U.S. **99** Q6
Lake Linden, Mich., U.S. **100** E6
Lake Louise, Alta., Can. **84** M9
Lake Mead National Recreation Area, Ariz., Nev., U.S. **111** U12
Lake Meredith National Recreation Area, Tex., U.S. **104** G5
Lake Mills, Iowa, U.S. **106** M11
Lake Murray, P.N.G. **217** D17
Lake Nash, N.T., Austral. **215** S10
Lake Oswego, Oreg., U.S. **110** F3
Lakepa, Cook Is., N.Z. **223** B21
Lake Placid, N.Y., U.S. **96** G11
Lakeport, Calif., U.S. **111** Q3
Lakeport, Mich., U.S. **100** L13
Lake Preston, S. Dak., U.S. **106** K7
Lake Providence, La., U.S. **102** K10
Lake Region, Eur. **140** D9
Lake Roosevelt National Recreation Area, Wash., U.S. **110** B8
Lakes Entrance, Vic., Austral. **215** Z13
Lakeside, Nebr., U.S. **107** N2
Lakeside, Oreg., U.S. **110** H2
Lake Stewart, N.S.W., Austral. **215** V11
Lakeview, Mich., U.S. **100** L10
Lakeview, Oreg., U.S. **110** L6
Lake Village, Ark., U.S. **102** K9
Lakeville, Minn., U.S. **106** K11
Lake Vostok, site, Antarctica **231** K17
Lake Wales, Fla., U.S. **99** U8
Lakewood, Colo., U.S. **108** M13
Lakewood, N.J., U.S. **96** P11
Lakewood, Ohio, U.S. **101** N14
Lake Worth, Fla., U.S. **99** W10
Lakhpat, India **180** H1
Lakin, Kans., U.S. **107** U3

Lakki, Pak. 179 P9
Lakkí, Gr. 157 L18
Lakkia, Cyprus 162 P8
Lakonikós Kólpos, Gr. 156 M10
Lakota, N. Dak., U.S. 106 F7
Lakselv, Nor. 143 B14
Lakshadweep, islands, India 181 R2
La Laguna, Sp. 208 Q5
Lala Musa, Pak. 179 P11
Lalara, Gabon 205 G16
Lalbenque, Fr. 149 W9
L'Albera, Serra de, Sp. 147 C18
La Leonesa, Arg. 134 G13
Lalëzit, Gjiri i, Alban. 154 K9
Lalībela, Eth. 203 F15
La Libertad, Ecua. 130 K1
La Libertad, Guatemala 117 K15
La Ligua, Chile 134 K6
Lalín, Sp. 146 C6
La Línea de la Concepción, Sp. 146 N9
Lalitpur, India 180 H6
Lalitpur (Patan), Nepal 180 F10
Lalla Rookh, W. Aust., Austral. 215 S3
La Loche, Sask., Can. 84 K11
Lalomanu, Samoa 222 L4
Lalona, island, Tonga 222 R7
Laluai Point, P.N.G. 221 K14
La Lune, Trinidad and Tobago 123 Q23
La Maddalena, Fr. 152 L4
La Madrid, Arg. 134 G9
Lamag, Malaysia 192 G12
La Malbaie, Que., Can. 85 N20
Lamalou-les-Bains, Fr. 149 X11
La Mancha, Eur. 140 K3
La Manche see English Channel, Fr., U.K. 145 Y13
Lamap, Vanuatu 222 D2
Lamar, Colo., U.S. 109 N15
Lamar, Mo., U.S. 107 U11
Lamar Hayes Ridge, Ind. Oc. 225 N16
La Marmora, Punta, It. 153 N4
La Marque, Tex., U.S. 105 R14
Lamas, Peru 132 F3
Lamas, Turk. 170 J9
La Massana, Andorra 162 H2
La Massana, Andorra 162 J3
Lamballe, Fr. 149 Q5
Lambaréné, Gabon 205 H15
Lambay Island, Ire. 145 S7
Lambert Glacier, Antarctica 231 F18
Lambert's Bay, S. Af. 206 L7
Lambertville, Mich., U.S. 101 N12
Lámbia, Gr. 156 J9
Lambton, Cape, N.W.T., Can. 84 D11
Lame Deer, Mont., U.S. 108 E11
Lamentin, Guadeloupe, Fr. 123 E14
Lameroo, S. Aust., Austral. 215 Y11
La Mesa, Calif., U.S. 111 Z10
La Mesa, N. Mex., U.S. 109 V12
Lamesa, Tex., U.S. 104 L5
L'Ametlla, de Mar, Sp. 147 E16
Lameyer Ridge, Ind. Oc. 224 R8
La Meyze, Fr. 149 U8
Lamía, Gr. 156 G10
Lamitan, Philippines 193 F14
Lamlam, Mount, Guam, U.S. 220 D10
Lamoille, Nev., U.S. 110 M11
Lamoni, Iowa, U.S. 107 Q11
Lamont, Wyo., U.S. 108 J11
La Montaña, region, S. Amer. 128 E3
La Mothe-Achard, Fr. 149 S5
Lamotrek Atoll, F.S.M. 220 Q4
Lamotte-Beuvron, Fr. 149 R9
LaMoure, N. Dak., U.S. 106 H7
Lampang, Thai. 190 J8
Lampasas, Tex., U.S. 105 P10
Lampertheim, Ger. 150 H6
Lampeter, Wales, U.K. 145 U9
Lamphun, Thai. 190 J8
Lamskoye, Russ. 158 L9
Lamu, Kenya 203 L15
Lamutskoye, Russ. 161 C20
Lānaʻi, island, Hawaiʻi, U.S. 115 H14
Lānaʻi City, Hawaiʻi, U.S. 115 H15
Lānaʻihale, peak, Hawaiʻi, U.S. 115 H15
Lananibot, Puntan, N. Mariana Is., U.S. 220 B7
Lanbi Kyun, island, Myanmar 191 P7
Lancang, China 182 P8
Lancang (Mekong), river, China 182 P8
Lancaster, Calif., U.S. 111 W8
Lancaster, Eng., U.K. 145 R11
Lancaster, Mo., U.S. 107 Q12
Lancaster, N.H., U.S. 97 F14
Lancaster, Ohio, U.S. 101 R13
Lancaster, Pa., U.S. 96 P8
Lancaster, S.C., U.S. 98 J9
Lancaster, Tex., U.S. 104 L12
Lancaster, Wis., U.S. 100 L4
Lancaster Sound, N. Amer. 82 C7
Lancaster Trough, Arctic Oc. 247 P13
Lance Creek, Wyo., U.S. 108 H13
Lancelin, W. Aust., Austral. 215 W2
Lanciano, It. 152 K11
Lancun, Shand., China 184 G11
Landau, Ger. 150 H6
Landay, Afghan. 179 R3
Landeck, Aust. 150 L8
Lander, Wyo., U.S. 108 H10
Lander, river, Austral. 214 E8
Landerneau, Fr. 149 P3
Landes, Eur. 140 J4
Landivisiau, Fr. 149 P3
Land O'Lakes, Wis., U.S. 100 F5
Landor, W. Aust., Austral. 215 U2
Landquart, Switz. 152 B5
Landrum, S.C., U.S. 98 J7
Landsberg, Ger. 150 K8
Land's End, cape, Eng., U.K. 145 Y7
Lands End, cape, N.W.T., Can. 84 C12
Landshut, Ger. 150 K9
Landskrona, Sw. 142 N12
Lanett, Ala., U.S. 103 K17
Langádia, Gr. 156 K9
Langanes, island, Ice. 142 E4
Langao, Shaanxi, China 184 L1
Langar, Taj. 178 K10
Langar, island, F.S.M. 221 F14
Langdon, N. Dak., U.S. 106 E7
Langeac, Fr. 149 V11
Langeberg, range, Af. 198 Q7
Langenhangen, Ger. 150 D7
Langfang, Hebei, China 184 D8
Langford, S. Dak., U.S. 106 J7
Langjökull, glacier, Ice. 142 E3
Langkawi, island, Malaysia 191 S8
Langlo Crossing, Qnsld., Austral. 215 U13
Langlo Downs, Qnsld., Austral. 215 U13
Langlois, Oreg., U.S. 110 J1
Langøya, island, Nor. 142 D12
Langres, Fr. 149 R13
Langres, Plateau de, Fr. 149 R12
Langsa, Indonesia 192 G4
Langseth Ridge, Arctic Oc. 247 H13
Lạng Sơn, Vietnam 190 G12
Lang Suan, Thai. 191 Q8
Langting, India 180 G14
Langtou, Liaoning, China 184 C14
Langtry, Tex., U.S. 105 R5
Langu, Thai. 191 S8
Languedoc, region, Fr. 149 W11
Langzhong, China 182 K10
Lankao, Henan, China 184 J6
Lannion, Fr. 149 P4
Lano, Wallis and Futuna, Fr. 222 B11
La Noix, Fr. 163 B22
Lanouaille, Fr. 149 U8
Lansdale, Pa., U.S. 96 P9
Lansdowne House, Ont., Can. 85 M16
L'Anse, Mich., U.S. 100 F6
L'Anse aux Meadows, Nfld. & Lab., Can. 85 L23
Lanshan, Hunan, China 185 T3
Lansing, Iowa, U.S. 106 L13
Lansing, Mich., U.S. 100 M11
Lanslebourg, Fr. 149 U15
Lanta Yai, Ko, Thai. 191 R8
Lanusei, It. 153 P4
Lanxian, Shanxi, China 184 E4
Lan Yü, Taiwan, China 185 W12
Lanzarote, island, Sp. 208 P7
Lanzhou, China 182 J10
Laoag, Philippines 193 B13
Lào Cai, Vietnam 190 G11
Laoha, river, Liaoning, China 184 A10
Laohekou, Hubei, China 184 L3
La Oliva, Sp. 208 Q7
Laon, Fr. 149 N11
Laona, Wis., U.S. 100 G6
La Orotava, Sp. 208 Q4
La Oroya, Peru 132 H3
Laos, Asia 190 J11
Lapalisse, Fr. 149 T11
La Palma, Pan. 117 N22
La Palma, island, Sp. 208 Q3
La Paloma, Uru. 134 L15
La Paragua, Venez. 130 D11
La Paz, Arg. 134 J12
La Paz, Arg. 134 K8
La Paz, Bol. 132 J6
La Paz, Mex. 116 F11
La Paz, Mex. 116 F7
La Pedrera, Col. 130 J8
Lapeer, Mich., U.S. 100 L12
La Perouse Pinnacle, Hawaiʻi, U.S. 114 M6
La Perouse Strait, Japan, Russ. 188 D13
La Perouse Strait, Russ. 161 K22
La Pine, Oreg., U.S. 110 H4
Lapinlahti, Fin. 143 F16
Lapithos (Gilderen), Cyprus 162 N8
La Place, La., U.S. 102 P10
La Plaine, Dominica 123 G20
La Plaine, Réunion, Fr. 209 G16
La Plaine des Cafres, Réunion, Fr. 209 H16
Lapland, region, Fin., Russ., Sw. 143 D14
La Plant, S. Dak., U.S. 106 J4
La Plata, Arg. 134 L13
La Plata, Md., U.S. 98 D13
La Plata, Mo., U.S. 107 R12
La Pobla de Segur, Sp. 147 C16
La Pola de Gordón, Sp. 146 B9
La Porte, Tex., U.S. 105 R14
La Porte City, Iowa, U.S. 107 N13
La Possession, Réunion, Fr. 209 G15
Lappajärvi, lake, Eur. 140 D9
Lappeenranta, Fin. 143 H17
La Pryor, Tex., U.S. 105 S8
Lapseki, Turk. 170 D3
Laptev Sea, Arctic Oc. 246 D9
Laptev Shelf, Arctic Oc. 246 D9
Lapthal, India 180 E7
Lapua, Fin. 143 G15
La Puebla de Montalbán, Sp. 146 G9
La Purísima, Mex. 116 E6
La Push, Wash., U.S. 110 B2
La Quiaca, Arg. 134 D9
L'Aquila, It. 152 K9
Lār, Iran 175 H14
Laracha, Sp. 146 B5
Larache, Mor. 200 A8
Laramie, Wyo., U.S. 108 K13
Laramie, river, Colo., Wyo., U.S. 108 J12
Laramie Mountains, Wyo., U.S. 108 J12
Laramie Peak, U.S. 86 E9
Larantuka, Indonesia 193 M14
Larat, island, Indonesia 193 M18
Larche, Fr. 149 W15
Laredo, Sp. 146 B11
Laredo, Tex., U.S. 105 U8
La Réole, Fr. 149 W7
Lares, P.R., U.S. 122 N2
Largo, Fla., U.S. 99 U7
Largo, Cayo, Cuba 118 H7
Lari see Lhari, China 182 L6
Larimore, N. Dak., U.S. 106 F7
La Rioja, Arg. 134 H8
Lárisa, Gr. 156 E10
La Rivière, Réunion, Fr. 209 H15
Larkana, Pak. 179 T7
Larnaca (Lárnaka), Cyprus 162 P9
Lárnaka see Larnaca, Cyprus 162 P9
Larnaka Bay, Cyprus 162 P9
Larne, N. Ire., U.K. 145 P7
Larned, Kans., U.S. 107 T6
La Robla, Sp. 146 C9
La Roca de la Sierra, Sp. 146 H7
La Rocca o Guaita, San Marino 163 J15
La Roche, Fr. 149 T14
La Rochefoucauld, Fr. 149 U8
La Rochelle, Fr. 149 T6
La Roche-sur-Yon, Fr. 149 S6
Larochette, Lux. 162 J10
La Roda, Sp. 146 H12
La Romana, Dom. Rep. 119 M20
La Ronge, Sask., Can. 84 L12
Larose, La., U.S. 102 Q10
La Rousse, Fr. 163 A22
Larrimah, N.T., Austral. 215 Q8
Lars Christensen Coast, Antarctica 231 F19
Larsen Bay, Alas., U.S. 113 M15
Larsen Ice Shelf, Antarctica 230 E5
La Rubia, Arg. 134 J11
Laruri, India 180 G15
Larvik, Nor. 142 L11
Larvotto, Monaco 163 B22
Larvotto, peninsula, Monaco 163 B23
Larvotto Beach, Monaco 163 B23
Lasa see Lhasa, China 182 L5
La Sagesse Bay, Grenada 123 L23
La Sal, Utah, U.S. 109 N9
La Salle, Ill., U.S. 101 P5
Lasan, Indonesia 192 H11
Las Animas, Colo., U.S. 109 N15
La Sarre, Que., Can. 85 P18
Las Cabezas de San Juan, Sp. 146 L8
Las Caguamas, Cayo, Cuba 118 K10
Lascahobas, Haiti 119 M17
Lascano, Uru. 134 L15
Lascelles, Vic., Austral. 215 Y12
La Scie, Nfld. & Lab., Can. 85 L23
Las Cruces, N. Mex., U.S. 109 V12
Las Cuevas Bay, Trinidad and Tobago 123 N22
La Sènia, Sp. 147 F15
La Serena, Chile 134 J7
La Seu d'Urgell, Sp. 147 C16
La Seyne, Fr. 149 Y14
Las Flores, Arg. 134 M12
Lāsh-e Juwayn, Afghan. 179 Q2
Las Heras, Arg. 134 K8
Las Heras, Arg. 135 T8
Lashio, Myanmar 190 G7
Lashkar, India 180 G6
Lashkar Gāh (Bost), Afghan. 179 Q4
Lashkari Bazar, ruins, Afghan. 179 Q4
Lasia, island, Indonesia 192 H4
La Sila, range, It. 153 P13
Las Lomitas, Arg. 134 F12
Las Marteínas, Cuba 118 H4
La Sola, island, Venez. 121 J14
La Solana, Sp. 146 H11
La Sorcière, peak, St. Lucia 123 K14
La Souterraine, Fr. 149 T9
Las Palmas, Sp. 208 Q5
La Spezia, It. 152 G5
Las Piedras, P.R., U.S. 122 N5
Las Plumas, Arg. 135 R9
Lassen Peak, Calif., U.S. 111 N4
Lassen Volcanic National Park, Calif., U.S. 111 N5
Lassiter Coast, Antarctica 230 F7
Las Tablas, Pan. 117 P21
Las Toscas, Arg. 134 H12
Lastoursville, Gabon 205 H16
Lastovo (Lagosta), island, Croatia 154 J6
Lastovski Kanal, Croatia 154 H6
Las Tunas, Cuba 118 J12
La Suze, Fr. 149 R7
Las Varillas, Arg. 134 K11
Las Vegas, N. Mex., U.S. 109 R13
Las Vegas, Nev., U.S. 111 U12
Lata, Samoa 222 K1
Latacunga, Ecua. 130 J3
Latady Island, Antarctica 230 G6
Latady Mountains, Antarctica 230 F7
Latakia see Al Lādhiqīyah, Syr. 172 F7
L'Atalante Valley, Pac. Oc. 242 Q8
Lata Mountain, Amer. Samoa, U.S. 222 P3
Latehar, India 180 H9
La Teste, Fr. 149 W6
Latheron, Scot., U.K. 144 H10
Lathi, island, Vanuatu 222 C1
Latiano, It. 152 M15
Latina, It. 152 L9
Latium, Eur. 140 K7
Lató, ruin, Gr. 157 Q15
La Tortuga, Isla, Venez. 130 B10
Latouche Treville, Cape, Austral. 214 D4
La Tranche-sur-Mer, Fr. 149 T5
La Trinité, Martinique, Fr. 123 E23
Latrobe, Mount, Austral. 214 M13
Latta, S.C., U.S. 98 K11
La Tuque, Que., Can. 85 P19
Latur, India 180 L5
Latvia, Eur. 143 L16
Lau Basin, Pac. Oc. 242 L12
Laucala, island, Fiji 222 G8
Laufen, Switz. 152 A3
Laughlan Islands, P.N.G. 217 E22
Laughlin Peak, N. Mex., U.S. 109 Q14
Lau Group (Eastern), Fiji 222 H9
Lauhkaung, Myanmar 190 E7
Laula Katan, Puntan, N. Mariana Is., U.S. 220 C5
Laulau, Bahia, N. Mariana Is., U.S. 220 C5
Lauliʻi, Samoa 222 L3
Lauliituai, Amer. Samoa, U.S. 222 M8
Launceston, Tas., Austral. 215 Y8
La Unión, Chile 135 P6
La Unión, Peru 132 G3
La Unión, Sp. 147 K14
Laupāhoehoe, Hawaiʻi, U.S. 115 L21
Laura, Marshall Is., U.S. 220 G10
Laura, Qnsld., Austral. 215 Q13
Laura see Majuro, island, Marshall Is., U.S. 220 H10
Laurel, Del., U.S. 98 D14
Laurel, Miss., U.S. 102 M12
Laurel, Mont., U.S. 108 E10
Laurel, Nebr., U.S. 107 N8
Laurens, Iowa, U.S. 106 M10
Laurens, S.C., U.S. 98 K8
Laurentian Fan, Atl. Oc. 240 J6
Laurentian Scarp, N. Amer. 82 H8
Laurentian Trough, Atl. Oc. 240 H5
Laurentide Scarp, N. Amer. 82 H9
Lauria, It. 153 N12
Lau Ridge, Pac. Oc. 242 M11
Laurinburg, N.C., U.S. 98 J11
Laurium, Mich., U.S. 100 E6
Laurium see Lávrio, Gr. 157 K13
Laurot Islands see Laut Kecil, Kepulauan, Indonesia 192 L11
Lausanne, Switz. 152 C1
Laut, island, Indonesia 192 G8
Laut, island, Indonesia 192 K12
Lautaro, Volcán, Chile 135 U6
Lauterbourg, Fr. 149 P16
Laut Kecil, Kepulauan (Laurot Islands), Indonesia 192 L11
Lautoka, Fiji 222 H5
Lauvi Point, Solomon Is. 221 P19
Lava Beds National Monument, Calif., U.S. 110 L4
Lavaca, river, Tex., U.S. 105 R12
Lavaca Bay, Tex., U.S. 105 S12
La Vache Bay, Trinidad and Tobago 123 N22
Lava Hot Springs, Idaho, U.S. 108 H7
Laval, Fr. 149 Q6
Lava, Mota, Vanuatu 222 A2
Lāvān, island, Iran 175 H14
Lavardac, Fr. 149 W7
Lavaur, Fr. 149 X9
L'Avedy, Cape, P.N.G. 221 J14
La Vega, Dom. Rep. 119 L18
Lavelanet, Fr. 149 Y9
Lavello, It. 152 M12
La Venta, ruin, Mex. 117 J14
La Verkin, Utah, U.S. 109 P6
Laverne, Okla., U.S. 104 E7
Laverton, W. Aust., Austral. 215 V5
La Veta, Colo., U.S. 109 P13
La Ville, Pointe, St. Lucia 123 K13
Lavina, Mont., U.S. 108 D10
Lavit, Fr. 149 X8
Lavonia, Ga., U.S. 98 K6
Lavrentiya, Russ. 161 A21
Lávrio (Laurium), Gr. 157 K13
Lawa, river, S. Amer. 131 F17

Lāwa'i, *Hawai'i, U.S.* 114 C5
Lawdar, *Yemen* 174 Q10
Lawena, valley, *Liech.* 162 Q2
Lawit, peak, *Indonesia* 192 H10
Lawqah, *Saudi Arabia* 174 F9
Lawra, *Ghana* 204 C10
Lawrence, *Ind., U.S.* 101 R9
Lawrence, *Kans., U.S.* 107 S10
Lawrence, *Mass., U.S.* 97 J14
Lawrenceburg, *Ind., U.S.* 101 S10
Lawrenceburg, *Tenn., U.S.* 103 G14
Lawrenceville, *Ga., U.S.* 98 L5
Lawrenceville, *Ill., U.S.* 101 T7
Lawrenceville, *Va., U.S.* 98 F12
Lawton, *Okla., U.S.* 104 H9
Lawz, Jabal al, *Saudi Arabia* 174 G4
Laylá, *Saudi Arabia* 174 L10
Layou, *St. Vincent and the Grenadines* 123 K16
Layou, river, *Dominica* 123 F19
Laysan Island, *Hawai'i, U.S.* 114 L4
Layshi, *Myanmar* 190 E5
Layton, *Utah, U.S.* 108 K7
Laytonville, *Calif., U.S.* 111 P2
Lázaro Cárdenas, *Mex.* 116 J9
Lazo, *Russ.* 161 F18
Leachville, *Ark., U.S.* 102 F11
Lead, *S. Dak., U.S.* 106 K1
Lead Mountain, *Me., U.S.* 97 E18
Leadore, *Idaho, U.S.* 108 F6
Leadville, *Colo., U.S.* 108 M12
Leaf, river, *Miss., U.S.* 102 M12
Leakesville, *Miss., U.S.* 103 N13
Leakey, *Tex., U.S.* 105 R8
Leandro N. Alem, *Arg.* 134 G14
Leane, Lough, *Ire.* 145 U3
Learmonth, *W. Aust., Austral.* 215 T1
l'Eau Claire, Lac à, *Que., Can.* 85 L18
Leava *see* Sigavé, *Wallis and Futuna, Fr.* 222 E11
Leavenworth, *Kans., U.S.* 107 S10
Leavenworth, *Wash., U.S.* 110 C5
Lebak, *Philippines* 193 F15
Lebanon, *Asia* 172 H6
Lebanon, *Ind., U.S.* 101 R8
Lebanon, *Kans., U.S.* 107 R6
Lebanon, *Ky., U.S.* 103 C17
Lebanon, *Leb.* 172 J6
Lebanon, *Mo., U.S.* 107 U12
Lebanon, *N.H., U.S.* 97 H13
Lebanon, *Ohio, U.S.* 101 S11
Lebanon, *Oreg., U.S.* 110 G3
Lebanon, *Pa., U.S.* 96 P8
Lebanon, *Tenn., U.S.* 103 E16
Lebap, *Turkm.* 176 K10
Le Barcarès, *Fr.* 149 Y10
Le Barp, *Fr.* 149 W6
Le Beausset, *Fr.* 149 Y14
Lebec, *Calif., U.S.* 111 W7
Lebedyn, *Ukr.* 159 N8
Le Blanc, *Fr.* 149 S8
Lebombo Mountains, *Af.* 198 P9
Le Borgne, *Haiti* 119 L16
Lębork, *Pol.* 151 B13
Le Bouscat, *Fr.* 149 V6
Lebrija, *Sp.* 146 L8
Lebu, *Chile* 135 N5
Le Cap, *New Caledonia, Fr.* 222 D7
Le Carbet, *Martinique, Fr.* 123 E22
Le Caylar, *Fr.* 149 X11
Lecce, *It.* 153 N15
Lecco, *It.* 152 D5
Lecco, Lago di, *It.* 152 D5
Lechainá, *Gr.* 156 J8
Le Chambon-Feugerolles, *Fr.* 149 U12
Lechang, *Guang., China* 185 T4
Leclaire Rise, *Ind. Oc.* 224 R9
Lecompte, *La., U.S.* 102 N8
Le Creusot, *Fr.* 149 S12
Ledesma, *Sp.* 146 E8
Le Diamant, *Martinique, Fr.* 123 G23
Le Donjon, *Fr.* 149 T11
Le Dorat, *Fr.* 149 T8
Leduck Island, *Virgin Is., U.S.* 122 N12
Ledyanaya, Gora, *Russ.* 161 C21
Lee, *Nev., U.S.* 111 N11
Leech Lake, *Minn., U.S.* 106 G10
Leedey, *Okla., U.S.* 104 F8
Leeds, *Ala., U.S.* 103 J15
Leeds, *Eng., U.K.* 145 R12

Leeds, *N. Dak., U.S.* 106 E6
Leek, *Neth.* 148 G13
Leer, *Ger.* 150 C6
Leesburg, *Fla., U.S.* 99 T8
Leesburg, *Va., U.S.* 98 C12
Lees Summit, *Mo., U.S.* 107 S11
Lee Stocking Island, *Bahamas* 122 E8
Leesville, *La., U.S.* 102 N7
Leeton, *N.S.W., Austral.* 215 Y13
Leeuwarden, *Neth.* 148 G13
Leeuwin, Cape, *Austral.* 214 L2
Leeward Islands, *Lesser Antil.* 121 C15
Le Faou, *Fr.* 149 Q3
Lefka (Lefke), *Cyprus* 162 P7
Lefkáda (Leucas), island, *Gr.* 156 G7
Lefkada (Leucas), island, *Gr.* 156 G7
Lefkímmi, *Gr.* 156 F6
Lefkoniko (Geçitkale), *Cyprus* 162 N9
Lefkoşa *see* Nicosia, *Cyprus* 162 N8
Lefkosía *see* Nicosia, *Cyprus* 162 N8
Le François, *Martinique, Fr.* 123 F23
Lefroy, Lake, *Austral.* 214 J4
Legan, river, *Marshall Is., U.S.* 220 M4
Legazpi, *Philippines* 193 D14
Legges Tor, peak, *Austral.* 214 L8
Leggett, *Calif., U.S.* 111 P2
Leghorn *see* Livorno, *It.* 152 H6
Legionowo, *Pol.* 151 D16
Legnago, *It.* 152 E7
Legnano, *It.* 152 D4
Legnica, *Pol.* 150 F12
Le Grand-Lemps, *Fr.* 149 U13
Le Grau-du-Roi, *Fr.* 149 X12
Legune, *N.T., Austral.* 215 Q7
Leh, *India* 178 M14
Le Havre, *Fr.* 149 N7
Lehr, *N. Dak., U.S.* 106 H6
Lehrte, *Ger.* 150 D8
Lehua, island, *Hawai'i, U.S.* 114 C3
Lehututu, *Botswana* 206 H8
Lei, river, *Hunan, China* 185 S4
Leiah, *Pak.* 179 Q9
Leicester, *Eng., U.K.* 145 T13
Leiden, *Neth.* 148 J12
Leifear *see* Lifford, *Ire.* 145 P6
Leigh, *N.Z.* 217 H19
Leigh Creek, *S. Aust., Austral.* 215 W10
Leikanger, *Nor.* 142 J10
Leimatu'a, *Tonga* 222 L11
Leine, river, *Ger.* 150 E7
Leinster (Cúige Laighean), region, *Ire.* 145 S6
Leipsoí, *Gr.* 157 K17
Leipsoí, island, *Gr.* 157 K17
Leipzig, *Ger.* 150 F9
Leiria, *Port.* 146 G5
Leisler, Mount, *Austral.* 214 F7
Leitchfield, *Ky., U.S.* 103 C15
Leiway, *Myanmar* 190 J6
Leiyang, *Hunan, China* 185 S4
Leizhou, *China* 182 Q12
Leizhou Bandao (Luichow Peninsula), *Guang., China* 185 Y1
Leizhou Peninsula, *Asia* 168 J11
Leizhou Wan, *Guang., China* 185 X1
Le Kartala, peak, *Comoros* 209 M14
Lekeleka, island, *Tonga* 222 Q6
Leki, *Azerb.* 171 D21
Lekitobi, *Indonesia* 193 K15
Leksula, *Indonesia* 193 K15
Lekunberri, *Sp.* 147 B13
Le Lamentin, *Martinique, Fr.* 123 F23
Leland, *Miss., U.S.* 102 J10
Lel'chytsy, *Belarus* 158 M5
Lele, *F.S.M.* 221 A19
Lele Harbor, *F.S.M.* 221 B19
Lélépa, island, *Vanuatu* 222 F2
Leli, island, *Solomon Is.* 221 N20
Leling, *Shand., China* 184 F8
Lelingluang, *Indonesia* 193 M17
Lelintah, *Indonesia* 193 K17
Lêliogat, Île, *New Caledonia, Fr.* 222 D9
Le Lion-d'Angers, *Fr.* 149 R6
Le Locle, *Switz.* 152 B2
Le Lorrain, *Martinique, Fr.* 123 E22
Lelystad, *Neth.* 148 H13
Le Madonie, range, *It.* 153 S10

Le Maire, Estrecho de, *Arg.* 135 Y10
Léman, Lac (Lake Geneva), *Fr.* 149 T15
Lemanmanu, *P.N.G.* 221 J13
Le Mans, *Fr.* 149 Q7
Le Marin, *Martinique, Fr.* 123 G23
Le Mars, *Iowa, U.S.* 106 M9
Lemei Rock, peak, *Wash., U.S.* 110 E4
Lemesós *see* Limassol, *Cyprus* 162 Q7
Lemgo, *Ger.* 150 E7
Lemhi, river, *Idaho, U.S.* 108 F6
Lemhi Range, *Idaho, U.S.* 108 F6
Lemieux Islands, *Nunavut, Can.* 85 G19
Lemmer, *Neth.* 148 H13
Lemmon, *S. Dak., U.S.* 106 H3
Lemmon, Mount, *Ariz., U.S.* 109 V8
Lemnos *see* Límnos, island, *Gr.* 157 E14
Le Mont-Dore, *Fr.* 149 U10
Le Montet, *Fr.* 149 T10
Lemoore, *Calif., U.S.* 111 U6
Le Morne Brabant, cape, *Mauritius* 209 H18
Le Morne Rouge, *Martinique, Fr.* 123 E22
Le Moule, *Guadeloupe, Fr.* 123 E16
Lempdes, *Fr.* 149 U11
Lemsid, *W. Sahara* 200 D6
Lena, river, *Asia* 168 C10
Lena, river, *Russ.* 161 G17
Lena River Delta, *Asia* 168 C10
Lena Tablemount, *Ind. Oc.* 248 D8
Lena Trough, *Arctic Oc.* 247 J15
Lencouacq, *Fr.* 149 W7
Lenger, *Kaz.* 177 J13
Lenghu, *China* 182 G7
Lengshuitan, *Hunan, China* 185 S3
Lengua de Vaca Point, *S. Amer.* 128 L4
Lenin, *Taj.* 178 J7
Leningrad, *Taj.* 178 J8
Leningrad *see* Sankt-Peterburg, *Russ.* 158 F6
Leningradskaya, *Russ.* 159 R10
Leninogorsk, *Russ.* 158 J16
Leninogorsk *see* Ridder, *Kaz.* 177 D18
Lenin Peak, *Kyrg., Taj.* 178 H10
Leninsk *see* Bayqongyr (Baykonur), *Kaz.* 176 G10
Leninskiy, *Russ.* 158 H13
Leninsk Kuznetskiy, *Russ.* 160 K12
Leninskiy, *Russ.* 158 G8
Lennox, *S. Dak., U.S.* 106 M8
Lennox-King Glacier, *Antarctica* 231 L13
Lenoir, *N.C., U.S.* 98 H8
Lenoir City, *Tenn., U.S.* 103 F18
Lenora, *Kans., U.S.* 107 R5
Lenox, *Iowa, U.S.* 107 Q10
Lenox, *Mass., U.S.* 97 K12
Lens, *Fr.* 148 M10
Lensk, *Russ.* 161 J16
Lentekhi, *Rep. of Georgia* 171 B17
Lenti, *Hung.* 151 M13
Lentini, *It.* 153 T12
Lenya, *Myanmar* 191 P8
Léo, *Burkina Faso* 204 C10
Leoben, *Aust.* 150 L11
Léogâne, *Haiti* 119 M16
Leola, *S. Dak., U.S.* 106 J6
Leominster, *Mass., U.S.* 97 K14
Leon, *Eur.* 140 J2
Leon, *Iowa, U.S.* 107 Q11
León, *Mex.* 116 H10
León, *Nicar.* 117 M17
León, *Sp.* 146 C9
Léon, *Fr.* 149 X5
Leon, river, *Tex., U.S.* 104 M9
León, Montes de, *Sp.* 146 C8
Leonard, *Tex., U.S.* 104 K12
Leonard's, *British Virgin Is., U.K.* 122 Q6
Leonarisso (Ziyamet), *Cyprus* 162 M10
Leonberg, *Ger.* 150 J6
Leonding, *Aust.* 150 K11
Leone, *Amer. Samoa, U.S.* 222 M6
Leone Bay, *Amer. Samoa, U.S.* 222 M6
Leonídio, *Gr.* 156 L11

Leonora, *W. Aust., Austral.* 215 V4
Leopold and Astrid Coast, *Antarctica* 231 H21
Leopoldsburg, *Belg.* 148 K13
Leoti, *Kans., U.S.* 107 T3
Lepanto, *Ark., U.S.* 102 F11
Lepe, *Sp.* 146 L6
Le Perthus, *Fr.* 149 Z10
Le Petit-Quevilly, *Fr.* 149 N8
Leping, *Jiangxi, China* 185 Q8
Lepontine Alps, *Switz.* 152 C4
Le Porge, *Fr.* 149 V6
Le Port, *Réunion, Fr.* 209 G15
Le Prêcheur, *Martinique, Fr.* 123 E22
Lepsi, *Kaz.* 177 F17
Le Puy, *Fr.* 149 V11
Ler, *S. Sudan* 202 G12
LercaraFriddi, *It.* 153 S10
Léré, *Chad* 201 K14
Lerida, *Qnsld., Austral.* 215 T13
Lerik, *Azerb.* 171 F22
Lerma, *Sp.* 146 D11
Lerma, river, *N. Amer.* 82 N4
Le Robert, *Martinique, Fr.* 123 F23
Léros, island, *Gr.* 157 L17
Le Roy, *N.Y., U.S.* 96 J6
LeRoy, *Kans., U.S.* 107 T9
Lerwick, *Scot., U.K.* 144 D12
Les Abymes, *Guadeloupe, Fr.* 123 E15
Le Saint-Esprit, *Martinique, Fr.* 123 F23
Les Anses-d'Arlets, *Martinique, Fr.* 123 G22
Les Avirons, *Réunion, Fr.* 209 H15
Les Bons, *Andorra* 162 J3
Les Borges Blanques, *Sp.* 147 D16
Les Cayes, *Haiti* 119 M15
Les Coteaux, *Trinidad and Tobago* 123 N18
Les Ecréhou, island, *Channel Is., U.K.* 145 Z12
Les Escaldes, *Andorra* 162 J3
Leskovac, *Serb.* 154 H11
Les Landes, *Fr.* 149 W6
Leslie, *Ark., U.S.* 102 F8
Lesmont, *Fr.* 149 Q12
Lesneven, *Fr.* 149 P3
Lesnoye, *Russ.* 158 G8
Lesosibirsk, *Russ.* 161 K13
Lesotho, *Af.* 206 K10
Lesozavodsk, *Russ.* 161 L21
L'Esperance Rock, *Kermadec Is., N.Z.* 218 M9
Les Sables-d'Olonne, *Fr.* 149 T5
Les Saintes, islands, *Guadeloupe, Fr.* 123 H14
Lessay, *Fr.* 149 N6
Les Sept Îles, *Fr.* 149 P4
Lesser Antilles, *N. Amer.* 121 B14
Lesser Caucasus, range, *Rep. of Georgia* 171 C17
Lesser Khingan Range, *Asia* 168 E11
Lesser Slave Lake, *Alta., Can.* 84 K10
Lesser Sunda Islands, *Indonesia* 192 M13
Les Soeurs, islands (The Sisters), *Seychelles* 209 M21
Les Trois-Îlets, *Martinique, Fr.* 123 F23
Le Sueur, *Minn., U.S.* 106 K10
Lésvos (Lesbos, Mytilíni), island, *Gr.* 157 F16
Leszno, *Pol.* 151 E13
Le Tampon, *Réunion, Fr.* 209 H16
Letchworth, *Eng., U.K.* 145 U14
Letea, Ostrov, *Rom.* 155 E18
Le Teil, *Fr.* 149 W12
Lethbridge, *Alta., Can.* 84 N10
Lethem, *Guyana* 131 F14
Leti, Kepulauan, *Indonesia* 193 M16
Leticia, *Col.* 130 L8
Leti Islands, *Asia* 168 M14
Leting, *Hebei, China* 184 D9
Letsâok-aw Kyun, island, *Myanmar* 191 P7
Leuca, *It.* 153 P16
Leucas *see* Lefkada, island, *Gr.* 156 G7

Leucate, *Fr.* 149 Y10
Leucate, Étang de, *Fr.* 149 Y10
Leulumoega, *Samoa* 222 L3
Leuser, peak, *Indonesia* 192 G4
Leusoali'i, *Amer. Samoa, U.S.* 222 P4
Levan, *Utah, U.S.* 108 M7
Levanger, *Nor.* 142 G11
Levant, Île du, *Fr.* 149 Y15
Levant Coast, *Asia* 168 F3
Levantine Basin, *Atl. Oc.* 240 K15
Levanto, *It.* 152 G5
Le Vauclin, *Martinique, Fr.* 123 F23
Levelland, *Tex., U.S.* 104 K4
Leven Bank, *Ind. Oc.* 224 J6
Leveque, Cape, *Austral.* 214 C4
Levera Pond, *Grenada* 123 J24
Le Verdon-sur-Mer, *Fr.* 149 U6
Leverkusen, *Ger.* 150 F5
Levet, *Fr.* 149 S10
Levice, *Slovakia* 151 K14
Lévis, *Que., Can.* 85 P20
Lévitha, island, *Gr.* 157 L17
Levin, *N.Z.* 217 M19
Levittown, *N.Y., U.S.* 96 N12
Levittown, *P.R., U.S.* 122 M4
Levittown, *Pa., U.S.* 96 P10
Levski, *Bulg.* 155 H15
Levu, Vanua, *Fiji* 218 J9
Levuka, *Fiji* 222 H7
Lewellen, *Nebr., U.S.* 107 P3
Lewes, *Del., U.S.* 98 C15
Lewes, *Eng., U.K.* 145 W14
Lewis, *Kans., U.S.* 107 U5
Lewis *see* Eilean Leòdhais, island, *Scot., U.K.* 144 H7
Lewis, river, *Wash., U.S.* 110 E4
Lewis and Clark National Historical Park, *Oreg., U.S.* 110 E2
Lewis and Clark Range, *Mont., U.S.* 108 C6
Lewisburg, *Tenn., U.S.* 103 F15
Lewisburg, *W. Va., U.S.* 98 E9
Lewis Pass, *N.Z.* 217 N17
Lewis Range, *Austral.* 214 E7
Lewis Smith Lake, *Ala., U.S.* 103 H14
Lewiston, *Idaho, U.S.* 108 D3
Lewiston, *Me., U.S.* 97 G16
Lewistown, *Ill., U.S.* 101 Q4
Lewistown, *Mont., U.S.* 108 C9
Lewistown, *Pa., U.S.* 96 N6
Lewisville, *Ark., U.S.* 102 J7
Lewisville Lake, *Tex., U.S.* 104 K11
Lexington, *Ky., U.S.* 103 B18
Lexington, *Miss., U.S.* 102 K11
Lexington, *Mo., U.S.* 107 S11
Lexington, *N.C., U.S.* 98 H10
Lexington, *Nebr., U.S.* 107 Q5
Lexington, *Oreg., U.S.* 110 F6
Lexington, *Tenn., U.S.* 103 F13
Lexington, *Va., U.S.* 98 E10
Lexington Park, *Md., U.S.* 98 D14
Leydsdorp, *S. Af.* 206 H11
Leyte, island, *Philippines* 193 E15
Leyte Gulf, *Philippines* 193 E15
Lezha, *Russ.* 158 G10
Lezhë, *Alban.* 154 K9
L'gov, *Russ.* 158 M8
Lhari (Lari), *China* 182 L6
Lhasa (Lasa), *China* 182 L5
Lhokseumawe, *Indonesia* 192 G4
L'Hospitalet, *Fr.* 162 H6
L'Hospitalet de Llobregat, *Sp.* 147 E17
Li, river, *Hunan, China* 185 P2
Liamuiga, Mount, *St. Kitts and Nevis* 123 A17
Lian, river, *Guang., China* 185 U4
Liancheng, *Fujian, China* 185 T8
Liancourt Rocks *see* Dokdo, *S. Korea* 188 M5
Liangbuaya, *Indonesia* 192 J12
Liangcheng, *N. Mongol, China* 184 C4
Liangjiadian, *Liaoning, China* 184 D12
Liangzi Hu, *Hubei, China* 185 N6
Lianhua, *Jiangxi, China* 185 R5
Lianhua Feng, *Anhui, China* 185 P9
Lianjiang, *Fujian, China* 185 S10
Lianjiang, *Guang., China* 185 X1
Liannan, *Guang., China* 185 U3

Lianping, *Guang., China* **185** U5
Lianshan, *Guang., China* **185** U3
Lianyuan, *Hunan, China* **185** R3
Lianyun, *Jiangsu, China* **184** JIO
Lianyungang (Xinpu), *Jiangsu, China* **184** JIO
Liao, river, *Liaoning, China* **184** BI2
Liaocheng, *Shand., China* **184** G7
Liaodong Bandao, *Liaoning, China* **184** CI2
Liaodong Wan, *Liaoning, China* **184** CII
Liaoning, *China* **184** BII
Liaoyang, *Liaoning, China* **184** BI3
Liaoyuan, *China* **183** EI6
Liaozhong, *Liaoning, China* **184** BI2
Liaquatpur, *Pak.* **179** S9
Liard, river, *N.W.T., Can.* **84** HIO
Liari, *Pak.* **179** V5
Libby, *Mont., U.S.* **108** B4
Libenge, *Dem. Rep. of the Congo* **202** J8
Liberal, *Kans., U.S.* **107** V4
Liberec, *Czech Rep.* **150** GII
Liberia, *Af.* **204** E6
Liberia, *C.R.* **117** NI8
Liberta, *Antigua and Barbuda* **123** B2I
Libertador General San Martín, *Arg.* **134** E9
Liberty, *Mo., U.S.* **107** SIO
Liberty, *N.Y., U.S.* **96** LIO
Liberty, *S.C., U.S.* **98** J7
Liberty, *Tex., U.S.* **105** QI4
Lib Island, *Marshall Is., U.S.* **220** G3
Libni, Gebel, *Egypt* **173** P3
Liboi, *Kenya* **203** KI5
Libourne, *Fr.* **149** V7
Libreville, *Gabon* **205** GI5
Libya, *Af.* **201** DI4
Libyan Desert, *Af.* **198** E8
Libyan Plateau, *Egypt, Lib.* **201** CI6
Licang, *Shand., China* **184** GII
Licantén, *Chile* **134** L6
Licata, *It.* **153** TIO
Lice, *Turk.* **171** GI5
Licheng, *Shanxi, China* **184** G5
Licheng *see* Jinhu, *Jiangsu, China* **184** LIO
Lichinga, *Mozambique* **207** DI3
Lichtenfels, *Ger.* **150** G8
Lichuan, *Hubei, China* **185** NI
Lichuan, *Jiangxi, China* **185** R8
Licking, *Mo., U.S.* **107** UI3
Licking, river, *Ky., U.S.* **103** BI8
Ličko Lešće, *Croatia* **154** F5
Licosa, Punta, *It.* **153** NII
Lida, *Belarus* **158** K3
Lidgerwood, *N. Dak., U.S.* **106** H8
Lidköping, *Sw.* **142** LI2
Lido di Jesolo, *It.* **152** D8
Lido di Ostia *see* Lido di Roma, *It.* **152** L8
Lido di Roma (Lido di Ostia), *It.* **152** L8
Liechtenstein, *Eur.* **162** C3
Liège, *Belg.* **148** LI3
Lieksa, *Fin.* **143** FI7
Lienz, *Aust.* **150** M9
Liepāja, *Latv.* **143** MI5
Lier, *Belg.* **148** KI2
Lieshan, *Anhui, China* **184** K8
Liestal, *Switz.* **152** A3
Liffey, river, *Ire.* **145** S6
Lifford (Leifear), *Ire.* **145** P6
Lifou (Lifu), island, *New Caledonia, Fr.* **222** C9
Lifu *see* Lifou, island, *New Caledonia, Fr.* **222** C9
Lifuka, island, *Tonga* **222** P7
Ligeti Ridge, *Atl. Oc.* **241** X8
Lightning Ridge, *N.S.W., Austral.* **215** WI4
Ligneuville, *Belg.* **148** MI3
Ligny-en-Barrois, *Fr.* **149** PI3
Ligurian Sea, *It.* **152** H4
Liha Point, *Niue, N.Z.* **223** A2I
Lihir, island, *P.N.G.* **217** C2I
Lihir Group, *P.N.G.* **217** B2I
Līhu'e, *Hawai'i, U.S.* **114** C6
L'Îiot, island, *Seychelles* **209** N2I

Lijeron, island, *Marshall Is., U.S.* **220** L7
Lijiang, *China* **182** M8
Lijin, *Shand., China* **184** F9
Likasi, *Dem. Rep. of the Congo* **202** NII
Likiep Atoll, *Marshall Is., U.S.* **220** G4
Liku, *Cook Is., N.Z.* **223** B2I
Likuone Bay, *Tonga* **222** LI2
Likupang, *Indonesia* **193** HI5
Lilbourn, *Mo., U.S.* **107** VI6
L'Île-Bouchard, *Fr.* **149** S8
L'Île-Rousse, *Fr.* **152** J4
Lilian Point, *Kiribati* **221** D2O
Liling, *Hunan, China* **185** R5
Liliuokalani Ridge, *Pac. Oc.* **242** FI2
Lille, *Fr.* **148** LIO
Lillehammer, *Nor.* **142** JII
Lillesand, *Nor.* **142** LIO
Lillie Glacier, *Antarctica* **231** QI4
Lillooet, *B.C., Can.* **84** L8
Lilongwe, *Malawi* **206** EI2
Lilo Viejo, *Arg.* **134** GIO
Lim, river, *Serb.* **154** H9
Lima, *Mont., U.S.* **108** F7
Lima, *Ohio, U.S.* **101** QII
Lima, *Peru* **132** H3
Lima, river, *Port.* **146** D5
Liman, *Azerb.* **171** F22
Liman, *Russ.* **159** RI5
Liman Beren, lake, *Russ.* **159** RI3
Lima Reservoir, *Mont., U.S.* **108** F7
Limarí, Río, *Chile* **134** J6
Limassol (Lemesós), *Cyprus* **162** Q7
Limavady, *N. Ire., U.K.* **145** P6
Limay, river, *S. Amer.* **128** N4
Limbara, Monte, *It.* **152** M4
Limbdi, *India* **180** J3
Limbe, *Cameroon* **205** FI4
Limbé, *Haiti* **119** LI6
Limburg, *Ger.* **150** G6
Limeira, *Braz.* **133** L8
Limenária, *Gr.* **157** CI4
Limerick (Luimneach), *Ire.* **145** T4
Limestone, *Me., U.S.* **97** BI8
Lim Fjord, *Atl. Oc.* **140** E7
Limfjorden, lake, *Den.* **142** MII
Limia, river, *Sp.* **146** D6
Limín *see* Thásos, *Gr.* **157** CI4
Liminka, *Fin.* **143** FI5
Límni, *Gr.* **156** GI2
Límnos (Lemnos), island, *Gr.* **157** EI4
Limoges, *Fr.* **149** U8
Limon, *Colo., U.S.* **108** MI4
Limón, *C.R.* **117** NI9
Limon, Mount, *Mauritius* **209** J2O
Limone Piemonte, *It.* **152** F2
Limousin, *Eur.* **140** H4
Limoux, *Fr.* **149** YIO
Limpopo, river, *Af.* **198** N8
Limu, island, *Tonga* **222** Q7
Limufuafua Point, *Niue, N.Z.* **223** B2O
Līnah, *Saudi Arabia* **174** G9
Lin'an, *Zhejiang, China* **185** NIO
Linapacan, island, *Philippines* **193** DI3
Linares, *Chile* **134** M6
Linares, *Mex.* **116** FII
Linares, *Sp.* **146** KII
Linariá, *Gr.* **157** GI4
Lincang, *China* **182** N8
Linchuan, *Jiangxi, China* **185** R7
Lincoln, *Arg.* **134** LII
Lincoln, *Calif., U.S.* **III** Q4
Lincoln, *Eng., U.K.* **145** SI3
Lincoln, *Ill., U.S.* **100** R5
Lincoln, *Kans., U.S.* **107** S7
Lincoln, *Me., U.S.* **97** EI8
Lincoln, *Mich., U.S.* **100** JI2
Lincoln, *N.H., U.S.* **97** GI4
Lincoln, *Nebr., U.S.* **107** Q8
Lincoln City, *Oreg., U.S.* **110** F2
Lincoln Heights, *Eng., U.K.* **145** SI3
Lincoln Island, island, *S. China Sea* **192** BIO
Lincoln Park, *Mich., U.S.* **100** MI2
Lincoln Sea, *N. Amer.* **82** B7
Lincolnton, *Ga., U.S.* **98** L7
Lincolnton, *N.C., U.S.* **98** H8

Lind, *Wash., U.S.* **IIO** D7
Linda Downs, *Qnsld., Austral.* **215** TIO
Lindale, *Ga., U.S.* **98** K4
Lindale, *Tex., U.S.* **104** LI3
Lindau, *Ger.* **150** L7
Lindberg Bay, *Virgin Is., U.S.* **122** N8
Linden, *Ala., U.S.* **103** LI4
Linden, *Guyana* **131** EI4
Linden, *Tex., U.S.* **104** KI5
Lindenows Valley, *Atl. Oc.* **247** R2O
Lindesnes, cape, *Nor.* **142** MIO
Lindi, *Tanzania* **203** NI5
Lindi Canyon, *Ind. Oc.* **224** H5
Lindisfarne *see* Holy Island, *Eng., U.K.* **145** NI2
Líndos, *Gr.* **157** N2O
Lindsay, *Calif., U.S.* **III** U7
Lindsay, *Mont., U.S.* **108** CI3
Lindsay, *Okla., U.S.* **104** HIO
Lindsborg, *Kans., U.S.* **107** T7
Line Islands, *Pac. Oc.* **218** FI2
Linfen, *Shanxi, China* **184** G3
Lingao, *China* **182** QI2
Lingbao, *Henan, China* **184** J3
Lingbi, *Anhui, China* **184** K8
Lingchuan, *Guangxi Zhuang, China* **185** T2
Lingen, *Ger.* **150** D6
Lingga, island, *Indonesia* **192** J7
Lingga, Kepulauan, *Indonesia* **192** J7
Lingle, *Wyo., U.S.* **108** JI4
Lingou, *Shanxi, China* **184** D6
Ling Qu, *Guangxi Zhuang, China* **185** T2
Lingshan Dao, *Shand., China* **184** HII
Lingshan Wan, *Shand., China* **184** HII
Linguère, *Senegal* **200** G5
Lingui, *Guangxi Zhuang, China* **185** TI
Lingxian, *Shand., China* **184** F8
Lingyuan, *Liaoning, China* **184** BIO
Linhai, *Zhejiang, China* **185** QII
Linhares, *Braz.* **133** LI6
Linhe, *China* **182** GII
Linjiang, *Jilin, China* **184** AI5
Linköping, *Sw.* **143** LI3
Linli, *Hunan, China* **185** P3
Linn, *Tex., U.S.* **105** WIO
Linnhe, Loch, *Scot., U.K.* **144** L8
Linqing, *Shand., China* **184** G7
Linquan, *Anhui, China* **184** K6
Linshu, *Shand., China* **184** J9
Linstead, *Jam.* **122** J9
Lintao, *China* **182** JIO
Linton, *Ind., U.S.* **101** S8
Linton, *N. Dak., U.S.* **106** H5
Linxi, *China* **183** EI4
Linxi, *Hebei, China* **184** D9
Linxi, *Shand., China* **184** G7
Linxia, *China* **182** J9
Linxian, *Shanxi, China* **184** E3
Linxiang, *Hunan, China* **185** P5
Linyi, *Shand., China* **184** H9
Linyi, *Shanxi, China* **184** H3
Linying, *Henan, China* **184** K5
Linz, *Aust.* **150** KII
Linzhou, *Henan, China* **184** G5
Linzi, *Shand., China* **184** G9
Lio Matoh, *Malaysia* **192** HII
Lion, Golfe du, *Fr.* **149** YI2
Lionel Town, *Jam.* **122** K8
Lions Den, *Zimb.* **206** FII
Lios na gCearrbhach *see* Lisburn, *N. Ire., U.K.* **145** Q7
Lios Tuathail *see* Listowel, *Ire.* **145** T3
Liot Point, *N.W.T., Can.* **84** DII
Liouesso, *Congo* **205** GI7
Lipa, *Philippines* **193** DI3
Lipari, Isola, *It.* **153** RII
Lipari, Isole(Eolie), *It.* **153** RII
Lipetsk, *Russ.* **158** MIO
Lipno, *Pol.* **151** DI4
Līpoa Point, *Hawai'i, U.S.* **115** GI6
Lipova, *Rom.* **154** DII
Lipscomb, *Tex., U.S.* **104** F7
Liptovský Mikuláš, *Slovakia* **151** JI5
Lipu, *Guangxi Zhuang, China* **185** U2
Lipu Pass, *China, India, Nepal* **180** E8
Liri, river, *It.* **152** LIO
Līsakovsk, *Kaz.* **176** CIO

Lisala, *Dem. Rep. of the Congo* **202** J9
Lisboa (Lisbon), *Port.* **146** H4
Lisbon, *N. Dak., U.S.* **106** H7
Lisbon *see* Lisboa, *Port.* **146** H4
Lisbon Falls, *Me., U.S.* **97** GI6
Lisburn (Lios na gCearrbhach), *N. Ire., U.K.* **145** Q7
Lisburne, Cape, *Alas., U.S.* **112** CI2
Liscannor Bay, *Ire.* **145** S3
Li Shan, *Shanxi, China* **184** H4
Lishi, *Shanxi, China* **184** F3
Lishui, *Zhejiang, China* **185** QIO
Lisianski Island, *Hawai'i, U.S.* **114** L3
Lisieux, *Fr.* **149** P7
Liski, *Russ.* **159** NIO
L'Isle-sur-la-Sorgue, *Fr.* **149** XI3
Lismore, *Vic., Austral.* **215** ZI2
Lismore, island, *Scot., U.K.* **144** L8
Lissa *see* Vis, island, *Croatia* **154** H6
Lister, Mount, *Antarctica* **231** NI4
Listowel (Lios Tuathail), *Ire.* **145** T3
Litang, *China* **182** L8
Litani, river, *S. Amer.* **131** GI7
Lîtâni, river, *Leb.* **172** K6
Litchfield, *Ill., U.S.* **101** S5
Litchfield, *Minn., U.S.* **106** JIO
Lit-et-Mixe, *Fr.* **149** W6
Líthino, Ákra, *Gr.* **157** RI4
Lithuania, *Eur.* **143** MI6
Litke Trough, *Arctic Oc.* **247** HI5
Litóchoro, *Gr.* **156** DIO
Little, river, *La., U.S.* **102** M8
Little, river, *Nfld. & Lab., Que., Can.* **85** L2I
Little, river, *Okla., U.S.* **104** HI4
Little, river, *Tex., U.S.* **105** PII
Little Abaco Island, *Bahamas* **122** A5
Little America Basin, *Pac. Oc.* **249** JI4
Little Andaman, island, *India* **181** RI4
Little Barrier Island *see* Hauturu-o-Toi, *N.Z.* **217** HI9
Little Bay, *Gibraltar, U.K.* **163** Q23
Little Belt Mountains, *Mont., U.S.* **108** D9
Little Bighorn, river, *Mont., Wyo., U.S.* **108** FII
Little Bighorn Battlefield National Monument, *Mont., U.S.* **108** EII
Little Bitter Lake *see* Murrat el Sughra, Buheirat, *Egypt* **173** QI
Little Blue, river, *Nebr., U.S.* **107** R7
Little Cayman, island, *Cayman Is.* **118** L8
Little Chute, *Wis., U.S.* **100** J6
Little Coco Island, *Myanmar* **190** M4
Little Colorado, river, *Ariz., U.S.* **109** R7
Little Darby Island, *Bahamas* **122** D7
Little Dix Bay, *British Virgin Is., U.K.* **122** R8
Little Exuma, island, *Bahamas* **122** F9
Little Falls, *Minn., U.S.* **106** HIO
Little Falls, *N.Y., U.S.* **96** JIO
Littlefield, *Ariz., U.S.* **109** Q5
Littlefield, *Tex., U.S.* **104** J4
Little Fork, river, *Minn., U.S.* **106** EII
Littlefork, *Minn., U.S.* **106** EII
Littlehampton, *Eng., U.K.* **145** WI3
Little Hans Lollik Island, *Virgin Is., U.S.* **122** M9
Little Harbour, *Bahamas* **122** B6
Little Inagua Island, *Bahamas* **119** JI6
Little Jost Van Dyke, island, *British Virgin Is., U.K.* **122** LII
Little London, *Jam.* **122** H6
Little Lost, river, *Idaho, U.S.* **108** F6
Little Marais, *Minn., U.S.* **106** FI3
Little Missouri, river, *U.S.* **86** CIO
Little Nicobar, island, *India* **181** TI5
Little Powder, river, *Mont., Wyo., U.S.* **108** FI3
Little Red, river, *Ark., U.S.* **102** F8
Little Rock, *Ark., U.S.* **102** G8
Little Saint James Island, *Virgin Is., U.S.* **122** NIO
Little Salt Lake, *Utah, U.S.* **109** P6
Little San Salvador, island, *Bahamas* **119** EI3

Little Snake, river, *Colo., Wyo., U.S.* **108** LIO
Little Sound, *Bermuda* **122** CI
Little Sound, *Cayman Is.* **122** J2
Little Suamico, *Wis., U.S.* **100** J7
Little Thatch Island, *British Virgin Is., U.K.* **122** R5
Little Tobago, island, *Trinidad and Tobago* **123** NI9
Little Tobago Island, *British Virgin Is., U.K.* **122** M9
Littleton, *Colo., U.S.* **108** MI3
Littleton, *N.H., U.S.* **97** GI4
Little Wabash, river, *Ill., U.S.* **101** S6
Liuchiu Yü, *Taiwan, China* **185** WII
Liuhe, *Jilin, China* **184** AI5
Liulin, *Shanxi, China* **184** F3
Liuwa Plain, *Zambia* **206** E9
Liuzhou, *China* **182** NI2
Livadeiá, *Gr.* **156** HII
Livádi, *Gr.* **157** LI4
Livádia, *Gr.* **157** MI8
Līvāni, *Latv.* **143** LI7
Live Oak, *Fla., U.S.* **99** R7
Livermore, *Calif., U.S.* **III** S4
Livermore, *Ky., U.S.* **103** CI5
Livermore, Mount, *Tex., U.S.* **105** P2
Liverpool, *Eng., U.K.* **145** SIO
Liverpool, *N.S., Can.* **85** P22
Liverpool Bay, *N.W.T., Can.* **84** DIO
Liverpool Range, *Austral.* **214** KI4
Livingston, *Ala., U.S.* **103** LI3
Livingston, *Mont., U.S.* **108** E8
Livingston, *Tenn., U.S.* **103** EI7
Livingston, *Tex., U.S.* **105** PI4
Lívingston, *Guatemala* **117** KI6
Livingston, Lake, *Tex., U.S.* **105** PI4
Livingstone, *Zambia* **206** FIO
Livingston Island, *Antarctica* **230** D4
Livny, *Russ.* **158** M9
Livonia, *Eur.* **140** E9
Livonia, *Mich., U.S.* **100** MI2
Livorno (Leghorn), *It.* **152** H6
Livron, *Fr.* **149** VI3
Līwā, region, *U.A.E.* **175** KI4
Liwale, *Tanzania* **203** NI4
Liwonde, *Malawi* **207** EI3
Lixian, *Hunan, China* **185** P3
Lixin, *Anhui, China* **184** K7
Liyang, *Jiangsu, China* **184** MIO
Li Yubu, *S. Sudan* **202** HII
Lizard Point, *Eng., U.K.* **145** Y8
Lizarra *see* Estella, *Sp.* **147** CI3
Ljubljana, *Slov.* **154** D5
Ljusdal, *Sw.* **143** HI3
Llamara, Salar de, *Chile* **134** D7
Llandrindod *see* Llandrindod Wells, *Wales, U.K.* **145** UIO
Llandrindod Wells (Llandrindod), *Wales, U.K.* **145** UIO
Llanes, *Sp.* **146** BIO
Llano, *Tex., U.S.* **105** P9
Llano, river, *Tex., U.S.* **105** P8
Llano Estacado (Staked Plain), *U.S.* **86** KIO
Llanos, plain, *S. Amer.* **128** B4
Llanquihue, Lago, *Chile* **135** Q6
Llavorsí, *Sp.* **147** CI6
Lleida, *Sp.* **147** DI6
Llerena, *Sp.* **146** J8
LleynPeninsula, *Wales, U.K.* **145** T9
Llica, *Bol.* **132** L6
Llívia, *Sp.* **147** CI7
Llodio, *Sp.* **146** BI2
Llorts, *Andorra* **162** H3
Llosa, river, *Sp.* **162** K5
Lloydminster, *Alta., Can.* **84** LII
Llucmajor, *Sp.* **147** GI8
Lluidas Vale, *Jam.* **122** J9
Llyswen, *Wales, U.K.* **145** UIO
Lô, river, *Vietnam* **190** GII
Ló, Ponta do, *Sao Tome and Principe* **209** D2O
Loa, *Utah, U.S.* **109** N7
Loa, river, *Chile* **134** D7
Loaita Island, *S. China Sea* **192** EII
Lo'alo'a Heiau, *Hawai'i, U.S.* **115** HI8
Lobamba, *Swaziland* **206** JII
Lobatse, *Botswana* **206** JIO
Lobaya, river, *Af.* **198** H6
Lobería, *Arg.* **135** NI2

Lobería, *Arg.* 135 Q10
Lobikaere, island, *Marshall Is., U.S.* 220 G11
Lobito, *Angola* 206 D5
Lobitos, *Peru* 132 E1
Lobo, *Indonesia* 193 K19
Lobos, *Arg.* 134 L12
Lobos, Cay, *Bahamas* 118 H11
Lobuya, *Russ.* 161 E19
Locana, *It.* 152 D2
Locarno, *Switz.* 152 C4
Lochcarron, *Scot., U.K.* 144 J8
Lochearnhead, *Scot., U.K.* 144 L9
Loch Garman see Wexford, *Ire.* 145 U7
Lochgilphead, *Scot., U.K.* 144 M8
Lochmaddy see Loch na Madadh, *Scot., U.K.* 144 J6
Loch na Madadh (Lochmaddy), *Scot., U.K.* 144 J6
Lochsa, river, *Idaho, U.S.* 108 D4
Lochy, Loch, *Scot., U.K.* 144 K8
Lockesburg, *Ark., U.S.* 102 H6
Lockhart, *Tex., U.S.* 105 Q11
Lockhart River, *Qnsld., Austral.* 215 P13
Lock Haven, *Pa., U.S.* 96 M6
Lockney, *Tex., U.S.* 104 J5
Lockport, *N.Y., U.S.* 96 J5
Locminé, *Fr.* 149 Q4
Locri, *It.* 153 R13
Lod (Lydda), *Israel* 172 M5
Lodeynoye Pole, *Russ.* 158 E8
Lodge Creek, *Can., U.S.* 108 A9
Lodge Grass, *Mont., U.S.* 108 E11
Lodgepole, *Nebr., U.S.* 107 N2
Lodgepole Creek, *Nebr., U.S.* 107 P1
Lodhran, *Pak.* 179 S9
Lodi, *Calif., U.S.* III R4
Lodi, *It.* 152 E5
Lodja, *Dem. Rep. of the Congo* 202 L10
Lodwar, *Kenya* 203 J13
Łódź, *Pol.* 151 E15
Loei, *Thai.* 190 K9
Lofanga, island, *Tonga* 222 P6
Lofoten, archipelago, *Nor.* 142 D12
Lofoten Basin, *Arctic Oc.* 247 H19
Lofty Range, *Austral.* 214 G3
Lofty Ranges, Mount, *Austral.* 214 K10
Logan, *Iowa, U.S.* 107 P9
Logan, *Kans., U.S.* 107 R5
Logan, *N. Mex., U.S.* 109 R15
Logan, *Ohio, U.S.* 101 R14
Logan, *Utah, U.S.* 108 J7
Logan, *W. Va., U.S.* 98 E8
Logan, Mount, *Wash., U.S.* 110 A5
Logan, Mount, *Yukon, Can.* 84 F7
Logansport, *Ind., U.S.* 101 Q9
Logansport, *La., U.S.* 102 L6
Logashkino, *Russ.* 161 D18
Logone, river, *Af.* 198 G6
Logoniégué, *Burkina Faso* 204 C9
Logroño, *Sp.* 146 C12
Loh, island, *Vanuatu* 222 A1
Lōʻīhi Seamount, *Pac. Oc.* 243 G14
Loi Mwe, *Myanmar* 190 H8
Loire, river, *Fr.* 149 Q10
Loíza, *P.R., U.S.* 122 M5
Loja, *Ecua.* 130 L3
Loja, *Sp.* 146 L10
Loji, *Indonesia* 193 K16
Lojjairok, island, *Marshall Is., U.S.* 220 N5
Lojwa, island, *Marshall Is., U.S.* 220 G8
Lokhwabe, *Botswana* 206 H8
Lokitaung, *Kenya* 203 H14
Loknya, *Russ.* 158 H6
Lokoja, *Nigeria* 205 D14
Lokolama, *Dem. Rep. of the Congo* 202 L9
Lokomo, *Cameroon* 205 F17
Lokoro, river, *Dem. Rep. of the Congo* 202 L9

Lokuru, *Solomon Is.* 221 M16
Lol, river, *S. Sudan* 202 G11
Lolland, island, *Den.* 142 N12
Lolo Pass, *Idaho, Mont., U.S.* 108 D5
Lolowaï, *Vanuatu* 222 C2
Lom, *Bulg.* 155 G13
Lom, *Nor.* 142 J10
Lomaloma, *Fiji* 222 H9
Lomami, river, *Dem. Rep. of the Congo* 202 M10
Loma Mountains, *Guinea, Sierra Leone* 204 C6
Lomawai, *Fiji* 222 J5
Lombadina, *W. Aust., Austral.* 215 Q4
Lombak Basin, *Ind. Oc.* 225 H17
Lombardy, Plain of, *Eur.* 140 J6
Lombez, *Fr.* 149 X8
Lombien, island, *Asia* 168 M14
Lomblen, island, *Indonesia* 193 M14
Lombok, island, *Indonesia* 192 M12
Lombok, Selat, *Indonesia* 192 M11
Lomé, *Togo* 204 E11
Lomela, *Dem. Rep. of the Congo* 202 K10
Lomela, river, *Dem. Rep. of the Congo* 202 K9
Lometa, *Tex., U.S.* 105 N9
Lomié, *Cameroon* 205 F17
Lomlom, island, *Solomon Is.* 221 P23
Lomond, Loch, *Scot., U.K.* 144 M9
Lomonosov, *Russ.* 158 F6
Lomonosov Ridge, *Arctic Oc.* 246 G11
Lompoc, *Calif., U.S.* III W5
Łomża, *Pol.* 151 C17
Lonauli, *India* 180 L3
Loncoche, *Chile* 135 P6
Loncopué, *Arg.* 135 N7
London, *Eng., U.K.* 145 V14
London, *Kiribati* 221 A23
London, *Ky., U.S.* 103 D18
London, *Ohio, U.S.* 101 R12
London, *Ont., Can.* 85 R18
London Bridge Island, *Grenada* 123 J24
Londonderry, *St. Lucia* 123 L14
Londonderry (Derry), *N. Ire., U.K.* 145 P6
Londonderry, Cape, *Austral.* 214 B6
Londonderry, Isla, *Chile* 135 Y8
Londrina, *Braz.* 132 M12
Lone Pine, *Calif., U.S.* III T8
Lonerock, *Oreg., U.S.* 110 F6
Longa, river, *Angola* 206 C6
Long Bay, *Barbados* 123 L20
Long Bay, *British Virgin Is., U.K.* 122 R5
Long Bay, *British Virgin Is., U.K.* 122 R5
Long Bay, *Jam.* 122 H5
Long Bay, *Jam.* 122 K8
Long Beach, *Calif., U.S.* III X8
Long Beach, *Miss., U.S.* 102 P12
Long Beach, *N.C., U.S.* 98 K12
Long Beach, *Wash., U.S.* 110 D2
Longboat Key, *Fla., U.S.* 99 V7
Long Branch, *N.J., U.S.* 96 P11
Long Cay, *Bahamas* 119 H14
Longchuan, *Guang., China* 185 U6
Long Creek, *Oreg., U.S.* 110 G7
Longdenville, *Trinidad and Tobago* 123 P22
Long Eaton, *Eng., U.K.* 145 T12
Longeau, *Fr.* 149 R13
Longford (An Longfort), *Ire.* 145 R5
Longgaʼer see Lunggar, *China* 182 K3
Longglat, *Indonesia* 192 H12
Longhai, *Fujian, China* 185 U9
Longhua, *N. Mongol, China* 184 B9
Longhui, *Hunan, China* 185 R2
Longido, *Tanzania* 203 L14
Longiram, *Indonesia* 192 J11
Long Island, *Antigua and Barbuda* 123 A21
Long Island, *Bahamas* 119 G14
Long Island, *N.Y., U.S.* 97 N13
Long Island, *Nunavut, Can.* 85 L17
Long Island, *P.N.G.* 217 C19
Long Island Sound, *U.S.* 97 M13
Longjiang, *China* 183 C15
Longjing, *China* 183 E17

Longju, *India* 180 E14
Longjuzhai see Danfeng, *Shaanxi, China* 184 K2
Long Key, *Fla., U.S.* 99 Y10
Long Khánh, *Vietnam* 191 P13
Longkou, *Shand., China* 184 F11
Longlac, *Ont., Can.* 85 N16
Long Lake, *N. Dak., U.S.* 106 G5
Long Look, *British Virgin Is., U.K.* 122 Q7
Longmen, *Guang., China* 185 V5
Longmont, *Colo., U.S.* 108 L13
Longnan, *Jiangxi, China* 185 U6
Longnawan, *Indonesia* 192 H11
Longomapu, *Tonga* 222 L11
Long Pine, *Nebr., U.S.* 107 N5
Long Point, *Virgin Is., U.S.* 122 N9
Long Prairie, *Minn., U.S.* 106 H10
Longquan, *Zhejiang, China* 185 R10
Longreach, *Qnsld., Austral.* 215 T13
Longren see Luring, *China* 182 J3
Longshan, *Hunan, China* 185 P1
Longsheng, *Guangxi Zhuang, China* 185 T1
Longs Peak, *Colo., U.S.* 108 L13
Long Strait, *Arctic Oc.* 168 A11
Longuyon, *Fr.* 162 L8
Longview, *Tex., U.S.* 104 L14
Longview, *Wash., U.S.* 110 E3
Longville, *La., U.S.* 102 P7
Longwy, *Fr.* 162 K8
Longxi, *China* 182 J10
Longxian, *China* 182 J11
Long Xuyên, *Vietnam* 191 P12
Longyan, *Fujian, China* 185 T8
Longʼyugan, *Russ.* 160 G11
Lonoke, *Ark., U.S.* 102 G9
Lonquimay, *Chile* 135 N7
Lónsdjúp, valley, *Atl. Oc.* 247 L22
Lons-le-Saunier, *Fr.* 149 S13
Loogootee, *Ind., U.S.* 101 T8
Loon, river, *Can.* 84 W11
Lookout, Cape, *N.C., U.S.* 98 J14
Lookout, Cape, *Oreg., U.S.* 110 F2
Lookout Mountain, *N. Mex., U.S.* 109 S10
Lookout Mountain, *Tenn., U.S.* 103 G16
Lookout Ridge, *Alas., U.S.* 113 C14
Loongana, *W. Aust., Austral.* 215 W6
Loop Head, *Ire.* 145 T3
Lop, *China* 182 G3
Lopatino, *Russ.* 158 L13
Lopatka, Cape, *Asia* 168 C13
Lopatka, Mys, *Russ.* 161 G23
Lop Buri, *Thai.* 190 M9
Lopévi, island, *Vanuatu* 222 D2
Lopez, Cap, *Gabon* 205 H14
Lopez Point, *Calif., U.S.* III U4
Lop Nur, lake, *China* 182 F6
Lopphavet, bay, *Nor.* 143 B13
Lora, Hamun-i-, *Pak.* 179 S4
Lorain, *Ohio, U.S.* 101 P14
Loraine, *Tex., U.S.* 104 M6
Loralai, *Pak.* 179 R7
Lorca, *Sp.* 147 K13
Lord Howe Atoll see Ontong Java Atoll, *Solomon Is.* 221 J18
Lord Howe Island see Tōmotu Noi, *Solomon Is.* 221 Q23
Lord Howe Rise, *Pac. Oc.* 242 M9
Lord Howe Seamounts, *Pac. Oc.* 242 M9
Lordsburg, *N. Mex., U.S.* 109 V10
Lorentzweiler, *Lux.* 162 J10
Lorenzo, *Tex., U.S.* 104 K5
Loreto, *Bol.* 132 J7
Loreto, *Braz.* 133 F14
Loreto, *Mex.* 116 E6
Loretto, *Tenn., U.S.* 103 G14
Lorica, *Col.* 130 C4
Lorien Bank, *Atl. Oc.* 240 G10
Lorient, *Fr.* 149 R4
Lorimers, *Turks & Caicos Is.* 119 H17
Loris, *S.C., U.S.* 98 K11
Lormes, *Fr.* 149 R11
Lormi, *India* 180 J8
Lorn, Firth of, *Scot., U.K.* 144 L7
Lornel, Pointe de, *Fr.* 148 L9
Lörrach, *Ger.* 150 K5
Lorraine, *Qnsld., Austral.* 215 R11
Lorraine, region, *Fr.* 149 P13

Los Alamos, *N. Mex., U.S.* 109 R12
Los Andes, *Chile* 134 K7
Los Angeles, *Calif., U.S.* III X8
Los Ángeles, *Chile* 135 N6
Los Angeles Aqueduct, *Calif., U.S.* III V8
Los Banos, *Calif., U.S.* III T5
Los Blancos, *Arg.* 134 E11
Los Cerrillos, *Arg.* 134 K9
Los Corrales, *Sp.* 146 B10
Los Cristianos, *Sp.* 208 Q4
Los Frailes, islands, *Venez.* 121 J14
Los Gatos, *Calif., U.S.* III T4
Los Hermanos, island, *Venez.* 121 H13
Los Lagos, *Chile* 135 P6
Los Llanos, *Sp.* 208 Q3
Los Loros, *Chile* 134 G7
Los Lunas, *N. Mex., U.S.* 109 S12
Los Mochis, *Mex.* 116 E7
Los Olmos Creek, *Tex., U.S.* 105 U10
Los Osos, *Calif., U.S.* III V5
Los Palacios, *Cuba* 118 G5
Lospalos, *Timor-Leste* 193 M16
Los Roques, Islas, *Venez.* 130 A10
Los Teques, *Venez.* 130 B9
Los Testigos, islands, *Venez.* 121 J15
Lostine, *Oreg., U.S.* 110 F9
Lost River Range, *Idaho, U.S.* 108 G6
Lost Trail Pass, *Idaho, Mont., U.S.* 108 E6
Losuia, *P.N.G.* 217 E21
Los Vilos, *Chile* 134 K6
Los Yébenes, *Sp.* 146 G10
Lot, *F.S.M.* 221 G14
Lot, river, *Fr.* 149 W11
Lot's Wife see Sōfu Gan, island, *Japan* 189 U12
Lota, *Chile* 135 N6
Lotagipi Swamp, *Kenya* 203 H14
Lot Harbor, *F.S.M.* 221 G14
Lotofaga, *Samoa* 222 L3
Lott, *Tex., U.S.* 105 N11
Lottin, Port, *F.S.M.* 221 B18
Lou, island, *P.N.G.* 217 B19
Louang Namtha, *Laos* 190 H9
Louangphabang, *Laos* 190 J10
Loudéac, *Fr.* 149 Q4
Loudi, *Hunan, China* 185 R3
Loudonville, *Ohio, U.S.* 101 Q14
Loudun, *Fr.* 149 S7
Loué, *Fr.* 149 Q7
Louga, *Senegal* 200 G4
Lougheed Island, *Nunavut, Can.* 85 C13
Louhans, *Fr.* 149 S13
Louisa, *Ky., U.S.* 103 B20
Louisa Downs, *W. Aust., Austral.* 215 R6
Louisburg, *N.C., U.S.* 98 G12
Louisburgh (Cluain Cearbán), *Ire.* 145 R3
Louisiade Archipelago, *P.N.G.* 217 E22
Louisiade Plateau, *Pac. Oc.* 242 L9
Louisiana, *Mo., U.S.* 107 S14
Louisiana, *U.S.* 102 N8
Louisiana Point, *La., U.S.* 102 Q6
Louis II Stadium, *Monaco* 163 F20
Louisville, *Ga., U.S.* 98 M7
Louisville, *Ky., U.S.* 103 B16
Louisville, *Miss., U.S.* 102 K12
Louisville, *Nebr., U.S.* 107 Q9
Louisville Ridge, *Pac. Oc.* 242 N12
Louisville Seamount, *Pac. Oc.* 249 K22
Louis-XIV, Pointe, *Que., Can.* 85 L17
Louj, island, *Marshall Is., U.S.* 220 G8
Loukouo, *Congo* 205 J17
Loulay, *Fr.* 149 T6
Loulé, *Port.* 146 L5
Loup, river, *Nebr., U.S.* 107 P6
Loup City, *Nebr., U.S.* 107 P6
Lourdes, *Fr.* 149 Y7
Lourdes-de-Blanc-Sablon, *Que., Can.* 85 L22

Lousã, *Port.* 146 F6
Lousy Bank, *Atl. Oc.* 240 F10
Louth, *Eng., U.K.* 145 S14
Loutrá Aidipsoú, *Gr.* 156 G11
Loutrá Elefthéron, *Gr.* 157 C13
Loutráki, *Gr.* 156 F12
Loutráki, *Gr.* 156 J11
Loutrá Smokóvou, *Gr.* 156 F9
Louvet Point, *St. Lucia* 123 K14
Louviers, *Fr.* 149 N8
Lovango Cay, *Virgin Is., U.S.* 122 M10
Lovech, *Bulg.* 155 H14
Loveland, *Colo., U.S.* 108 L13
Loveland Pass, *Colo., U.S.* 108 M12
Lovell, *Wyo., U.S.* 108 F10
Lovelock, *Nev., U.S.* III N8
Lovere, *It.* 152 D5
Loving, *N. Mex., U.S.* 109 V14
Lovington, *N. Mex., U.S.* 109 U15
Low, Cape, *Nunavut, Can.* 85 H16
Low Cay, *Bahamas* 122 F11
Lowell, *Mass., U.S.* 97 K14
Lowell, *Oreg., U.S.* 110 H3
Lowell, Lake, *Idaho, U.S.* 108 G3
Lower Belmont Bay, *British Virgin Is., U.K.* 122 M11
Lower Bogue, *Bahamas* 122 D5
Lower Guinea, *Af.* 198 K6
Lower Hutt, *N.Z.* 217 M19
Lower Lake, *Calif., U.S.* 110 M6
Lower Lough Erne, *N. Ire., U.K.* 145 Q5
Lower Matecumbe Key, *Fla., U.S.* 99 Y10
Lower Peninsula, *U.S.* 87 D17
Lower Post, *B.C., Can.* 84 H8
Lower Red Lake, *Minn., U.S.* 106 F9
Lower Valley, *Cayman Is.* 122 J2
Lowestoft, *Eng., U.K.* 145 T16
Łowicz, *Pol.* 151 E15
Lowitai, *Vanuatu* 222 H3
Lowman, *Idaho, U.S.* 108 G4
Lowreenne Seamounts, *Ind. Oc.* 225 Q22
Lowville, *N.Y., U.S.* 96 H9
Loyal, Loch, *Scot., U.K.* 144 H9
Loyalty Basin, *Pac. Oc.* 242 L10
Loyalty Islands see Loyauté, Îles, *New Caledonia, Fr.* 222 C9
Loyauté, Îles (Loyalty Islands), *New Caledonia, Fr.* 222 C9
Loyew, *Belarus* 158 M6
Lōy Kêlay, *Afghan.* 179 Q5
Loyola, Punta, *Arg.* 135 W8
Lōy Rāzay, *Afghan.* 179 Q2
Loznica, *Serb.* 154 F9
Lozova, *Ukr.* 159 P9
Lu, river, *Shaanxi, China* 184 E2
Luahiwa Petroglyphs, *Hawaiʻi, U.S.* 115 H15
Luahoko, island, *Tonga* 222 P7
Luama, river, *Dem. Rep. of the Congo* 202 L11
Lua Motu Island, *Tuvalu* 221 L23
Luʻan, *Anhui, China* 184 M7
Luan, river, *Hebei, China* 184 C9
Luancheng, *Hebei, China* 184 F6
Luanchuan, *Shaanxi, China* 184 K3
Luanco, *Sp.* 146 A8
Luanda, *Angola* 206 C5
Luang Prabang Range, *Laos* 190 J9
Luangwa, *Zambia* 206 E11
Luangwa, river, *Zambia* 206 E11
Luaniua, island, *Solomon Is.* 221 J18
Luaniva, Île, *Wallis and Futuna, Fr.* 222 B12
Luanping, *Hebei, China* 184 B8
Luanshya, *Zambia* 206 D11
Luanxian, *Hebei, China* 184 D9
Luapula, river, *Af.* 198 L9
Luarca, *Sp.* 146 A8
Luatefito, island, *Tonga* 222 M11
Luau, *Angola* 206 C8
Luba, *Eq. Guinea* 208 M7
Luba, Bahia de, *Eq. Guinea* 208 M7
Lubāns Ezers, lake, *Latv.* 143 L17
Lubang Island, *Philippines* 193 D13
Lubango, *Angola* 206 E5
Lubao, *Dem. Rep. of the Congo* 202 L11
Lubartów, *Pol.* 151 E17

Lübbenau, *Ger.* **150** E11
Lubbock, *Tex., U.S.* **104** K5
Lubec, *Me., U.S.* **97** E19
Lübeck, *Ger.* **150** B8
Lubero, *Dem. Rep. of the Congo* **202** K12
Lubéron, Montagne du, *Fr.* **149** X13
Lubin, *Pol.* **150** F12
Lublin, *Pol.* **151** F17
Lubliniec, *Pol.* **151** G14
Lubny, *Ukr.* **159** P7
Lubok Antu, *Indonesia* **192** H10
Luboten, peak, *Kos.* **154** J11
Lubu, *Guang., China* **185** V3
Lubuagan, *Philippines* **193** B13
Lubudi, *Dem. Rep. of the Congo* **202** N11
Lubuklinggau, *Indonesia* **192** K6
Lubumbashi (Elisabethville), *Dem. Rep. of the Congo* **202** P11
Lucas, *Kans., U.S.* **107** S6
Lucaya, *Bahamas* **122** F2
Lucca, *It.* **152** G6
Lucea, *Jam.* **122** H6
LuceBay, *Scot., U.K.* **145** P8
Lucedale, *Miss., U.S.* **103** N13
Lucena, *Philippines* **193** C14
Lucena, *Sp.* **146** L10
Lučenec, *Slovakia* **151** K15
Lucera, *It.* **152** L12
Lucerne, Lake of *see* Vierwaldstätter See, *Switz.* **152** B3
Luchegorsk, *Russ.* **161** L21
Lucheng, *Shanxi, China* **184** G5
Lucie, river, *Suriname* **131** F15
Lucipara, Kepulauan, *Indonesia* **193** L16
Lucira, *Angola* **206** E5
Lucknow, *India* **180** G8
Lucknow, *Qnsld., Austral.* **215** T11
Lücongpo, *Hubei, China* **185** N2
Lucy Creek, *N.T., Austral.* **215** T10
Luda Kamchiya, river, *Bulg.* **155** H16
Ludborough, *Eng., U.K.* **145** S14
Lüdenscheid, *Ger.* **150** F6
Lüderitz, *Namibia* **206** J6
Ludhiana, *India* **180** D5
Ludington, *Mich., U.S.* **100** K9
Ludlow, *Calif., U.S.* **111** W11
Ludlow, *Vt., U.S.* **97** H13
Ludogorie, *Eur.* **140** K10
Ludogorsko Plato, mountains, *Bulg.* **155** G16
Ludowici, *Ga., U.S.* **99** P8
Ludus, *Rom.* **155** C13
Ludwigsburg, *Ger.* **150** J7
Ludwigshafen, *Ger.* **150** H6
Luebo, *Dem. Rep. of the Congo* **202** M9
Luena, *Angola* **206** D8
Lüeyang, *China* **182** K10
Lufeng, *Guang., China* **185** W6
Lufilufi, *Samoa* **222** L3
Lufkin, *Tex., U.S.* **105** N14
Luga, *Russ.* **158** G6
Lugano, *Switz.* **152** D4
Luganville, *Vanuatu* **222** C1
Lugenda, river, *Mozambique* **207** D14
Lugo, *It.* **152** F7
Lugo, *Sp.* **146** B7
Lugoj, *Rom.* **154** E11
Lugovoy, *Russ.* **160** H10
Luhans'k, *Ukr.* **159** Q10
Luhuo, *China* **182** K9
Luiana, river, *Angola* **206** F8
Luichow Peninsula *see* Leizhou Bandao, *Guang., China* **185** Y1
Luimneach *see* Limerick, *Ire.* **145** T4
Luing, island, *Scot., U.K.* **144** M8
Luino, *It.* **152** D4
Luitpold Coast, *Antarctica* **230** E10
Luján, *Arg.* **134** L12
Lujiang, *Anhui, China* **184** M8
Lujor, island, *Marshall Is., U.S.* **220** G8
Luke, Mount, *Austral.* **214** H3
Lukenie, river, *Dem. Rep. of the Congo* **202** L8
Lukeville, *Ariz., U.S.* **109** V6
Lukhī, *Afghan.* **179** Q3
Lukolela, *Dem. Rep. of the Congo* **202** K8

Lukovit, *Bulg.* **155** H14
Łuków, *Pol.* **151** E17
Lukulu, *Zambia* **206** E9
Lukunor Atoll, *F.S.M.* **220** R6
Luleå, *Sw.* **143** E14
Luleälven, river, *Eur.* **140** B9
Lüleburgaz, *Turk.* **170** C3
Lules, *Arg.* **134** G9
Lüliang Shan, *Shanxi, China* **184** G3
Luling, *Tex., U.S.* **105** R10
Lulong, *Hebei, China* **184** C9
Lulonga, river, *Dem. Rep. of the Congo* **202** K8
Lulua, river, *Dem. Rep. of the Congo* **202** N10
Lulu Fakahega, peak, *Wallis and Futuna, Fr.* **222** B11
Lumajiangdong Cuo *see* Lumaqangdong Co, *China* **182** H3
Lüman, *Afghan.* **179** N4
Lumaqangdong Co (Lumajiangdong Cuo), *China* **182** H3
Lumbala N'guimbo, *Angola* **206** E8
Lumber City, *Ga., U.S.* **99** N7
Lumberton, *Miss., U.S.* **102** M4
Lumberton, *N.C., U.S.* **98** J11
Lumbo, *Mozambique* **207** E15
Lumbrales, *Sp.* **146** E9
Lumbres, *Fr.* **148** L9
Lumding, *India* **180** G14
Lumi, *Indonesia* **217** C18
Lumphät, *Cambodia* **190** M13
Lumpkin, *Ga., U.S.* **99** N4
Lumu, *Indonesia* **193** K13
Lumut, *Malaysia* **191** T9
Luna, *N. Mex., U.S.* **109** T10
Lunavada, *India* **180** J4
Lund, *Nev., U.S.* **111** Q12
Lundazi, *Zambia* **206** D12
Lundu, *Malaysia* **192** H9
Lundy Island, *Eng., U.K.* **145** W9
Lüneburg, *Ger.* **150** C8
Lüneburger Heide, region, *Ger.* **150** C8
Lunéville, *Fr.* **149** P14
Lunggar (Longga'er), *China* **182** K3
Lunglei, *India* **180** J14
Lungwebungu, river, *Angola* **206** D8
Luni, *India* **180** G3
Luni, river, *India* **180** G3
Luning, *Nev., U.S.* **111** R8
Lunino, *Russ.* **158** L13
Luninyets, *Belarus* **158** M4
Luntai, *China* **182** E4
Luo, river, *Shaanxi, China* **184** H2
Luochuan (Fengqi), *Shaanxi, China* **184** G2
Luoding, *Guang., China* **185** W3
Luohe, *Henan, China* **184** K5
Luoma Hu, *Jiangsu, China* **184** J9
Luonan, *Shaanxi, China* **184** J2
Luoning, *Henan, China* **184** J3
Luorong, *Guangxi Zhuang, China* **185** U1
Luoshan, *Henan, China* **184** L6
Luotian, *Hubei, China* **185** N6
Luoxiao Shan, *Jiangxi, China* **185** R5
Luoyang, *Henan, China* **184** J4
Luoyuan, *Fujian, China* **185** S10
Luozhuang, *Shand., China* **184** H9
Lupanshui, *China* **182** M10
Luperón, *Dom. Rep.* **119** L18
Lupin, *Nunavut, Can.* **84** G12
Lupog, *Guam, U.S.* **220** B12
Luqa, *Malta* **L22**
Luqiao, *Zhejiang, China* **185** Q12
Luqu, *China* **182** J9
Luquillo, *P.R., U.S.* **122** M5
Luquillo, Sierra de, *P.R., U.S.* **122** N5
Luray, *Va., U.S.* **98** D11
Lure, *Fr.* **149** R14
Luring (Longren), *China* **182** J3
Lúrio, *Mozambique* **207** D15
Lúrio, river, *Mozambique* **207** E14
Lusaka, *Zambia* **206** E11
Lusambo, *Dem. Rep. of the Congo* **202** L10
Lusancay Islands, *P.N.G.* **217** D21
Lusanga, *Dem. Rep. of the Congo* **202** M8
Lu Shan, *Shand., China* **184** G9

Lushan, *Henan, China* **184** K4
Lushi, *Shaanxi, China* **184** J3
Lushnjë, *Alban.* **154** L9
Lushoto, *Tanzania* **203** L15
Lüshun (Port Arthur), *Liaoning, China* **184** E11
Lusignan, *Fr.* **149** T7
Lusk, *Wyo., U.S.* **108** H13
Lus-la-Croix-Haute, *Fr.* **149** V14
Luso, *Port.* **146** F5
Lussac-les-Châteaux, *Fr.* **149** T8
Lustenau, *Ger.* **150** L7
Lūţak, *Iran* **175** F17
Lü Tao, *Taiwan, China* **185** W12
Lutcher, *La., U.S.* **102** P10
Lut Desert, *Asia* **168** G5
Luti, *Solomon Is.* **221** L16
Luton, *Eng., U.K.* **145** U13
Łutselk'e, *N.W.T., Can.* **84** H12
Lutsen, *Minn., U.S.* **106** F14
Luts'k, *Ukr.* **159** N3
Lützow-Holm Bay, *Antarctica* **231** C17
Luuq, *Somalia* **203** J16
Luverne, *Ala., U.S.* **103** M16
Luverne, *Minn., U.S.* **106** L9
Luvua, river, *Dem. Rep. of the Congo* **202** M11
Luxembourg, *Eur.* **162** C3
Luxembourg, *Lux.* **162** K10
Luxeuil, *Fr.* **149** R14
Luxi, *China* **182** N8
Luxi, *Hunan, China* **185** Q2
Luxor, *Egypt* **201** E19
Luxora, *Ark., U.S.* **102** F11
Luya Shan, *Shanxi, China* **184** E4
Luyi, *Henan, China* **184** K7
Lüyuan, *China* **182** F9
Luz, *Braz.* **133** L14
Luz, *Fr.* **149** Y7
Luza, *Russ.* **160** F8
Luzaide, *Fr.* **149** Y5
Luzern, *Switz.* **152** B3
Luzhai, *Guangxi Zhuang, China* **185** U1
Luzhou, *China* **182** L10
Luzon, island, *Philippines* **193** C13
Luzon Ridge, *Pac. Oc.* **242** G5
Luzon Strait, *Philippines* **193** A13
Luzy, *Fr.* **149** S11
L'viv, *Ukr.* **159** N2
Lwarah, river, *Afghan.* **179** P6
Lyady, *Russ.* **158** G5
Lyakhov Islands, *Asia* **168** B10
Lyakhovskiye, Ostrova, *Russ.* **161** D17
Lycksele, *Sw.* **143** F13
Lycoming, *N.Y., U.S.* **96** H8
Lydda *see* Lod, *Israel* **172** M5
Lyddan Island, *Antarctica* **230** C10
Lyepyel', *Belarus* **158** K5
Lyford, *Tex., U.S.* **105** W10
Lyford Cay, *Bahamas* **122** B10
Lyme Bay, *Eng., U.K.* **145** X11
Lynch, *Ky., U.S.* **103** D20
Lynch, *Nebr., U.S.* **106** M6
Lynchburg, *Va., U.S.* **98** F11
Lynden, *Wash., U.S.* **110** A4
Lyndon, *W. Aust., Austral.* **215** T2
Lyndon B. Johnson National Historical Park, *Tex., U.S.* **105** Q9
Lyndonville, *Vt., U.S.* **97** F13
Lynn, *Mass., U.S.* **97** K15
Lynn Haven, *Fla., U.S.* **99** R3
Lynn Lake, *Man., Can.* **85** L13
Lynton, *W. Aust., Austral.* **215** V2
Lyon, *Fr.* **149** U12
Lyons, *Ga., U.S.* **99** N7
Lyons, *Kans., U.S.* **107** T7
Lyons, *N.Y., U.S.* **96** J7
Lyons, *Nebr., U.S.* **107** P8
Lyons, river, *Austral.* **214** G2
Lyra Basin, *Pac. Oc.* **242** J8
Lysi (Akdoğan), *Cyprus* **162** P9
Lyskovo, *Russ.* **158** J13
Lyss, *Switz.* **152** B2
Lysychans'k, *Ukr.* **159** P10
Lytton, *B.C., Can.* **84** M8
Lyubertsy, *Russ.* **158** J9
Lyubim, *Russ.* **158** G10
Lyubimets, *Bulg.* **155** K16
Lyuboml', *Ukr.* **158** M2
Lyubotyn, *Ukr.* **159** P8

Lyubytino, *Russ.* **158** G7
Lyucha Ongokton, Gora, *Russ.* **161** G15
Lyudinovo, *Russ.* **158** L8

M

Māʻalaea, *Hawaiʻi, U.S.* **115** H16
Māʻalaea Bay, *Hawaiʻi, U.S.* **115** H16
Maale (Male), *Maldives* **181** U3
Maam Cross (An Teach Dóite), *Ire.* **145** R3
Maʻān, *Jordan* **173** Q6
Maan Ridge, *Eur.* **140** B10
Maanselkä, region, *Fin.* **143** E16
Maʻanshan, *Anhui, China* **184** M9
Maap, island, *F.S.M.* **221** C19
Maarianhamina *see* Mariehamn, *Fin.* **143** J14
Maʻarrat an Nuʻmān, *Syr.* **172** E8
Maas, river, *Neth.* **148** J13
Maastricht, *Neth.* **148** L13
Maʻbar, *Yemen* **174** Q9
Mabaruma, *Guyana* **131** C14
Mabiri, Cape, *P.N.G.* **221** K14
MacAlpine Lake, *Nunavut, Can.* **85** G13
Macapá, *Braz.* **132** C12
Macará, *Ecua.* **130** L2
Macas, *Ecua.* **130** K3
Macau, *Braz.* **133** E17
Macau, *Guang., China* **185** W4
Macaúba, *Braz.* **132** G12
Macauley Island, *Kermadec Is., N.Z.* **218** L9
Macau (Aomen), S.A.R., *China* **185** W4
Macbride Head, *Falk. Is., U.K.* **135** W12
Macclenny, *Fla., U.S.* **99** R8
Macdonald, Lake, *Austral.* **214** F7
Macdonnell Ranges, *Austral.* **214** F8
Macedo de Cavaleiros, *Port.* **146** D7
Macedonia, *Eur.* **154** K10
Macedonia, region, *Gr.* **156** C10
Maceió, *Braz.* **133** G18
Maceió, Ponta do, *Braz.* **133** E17
Macenta, *Guinea* **204** D7
Macerata, *It.* **152** H9
Macgillycuddy'sReeks, *Ire.* **145** U2
Mach, *Pak.* **179** R6
Machagai, *Arg.* **134** G12
Machakos, *Kenya* **203** K14
Machala, *Ecua.* **130** L2
Machanao, Mount, *Guam, U.S.* **220** A11
Machault, *Fr.* **149** N12
Machecoul, *Fr.* **149** S5
Macheng, *Hubei, China* **184** M6
Macherla, *India* **181** N7
Machias, *Me., U.S.* **97** F19
Machico, *Madeira, Port.* **208** M3
Machilipatnam (Bandar), *India* **181** N8
Machiques, *Venez.* **130** C6
Mach'ŏllyŏng-sanmaek, range, *N. Korea* **186** D11
Machu Picchu, ruin, *Peru* **132** H5
Machynlleth, *Wales, U.K.* **145** T10
Măcin, *Rom.* **155** E17
Macintyre, river, *Austral.* **214** H14
Maçka, *Turk.* **171** D14
Mackay, *Idaho, U.S.* **108** G6
Mackay, *Qnsld., Austral.* **215** S15
Mackay, Lake, *Austral.* **214** E7
Mackenzie, *B.C., Can.* **84** K9
Mackenzie, river, *Austral.* **214** F14
Mackenzie, river, *N.W.T., Can.* **84** F10
Mackenzie Bay, *N.W.T., Can.* **84** D9
Mackenzie King Island, *N.W.T., Can.* **85** B13
Mackenzie Mountains, *N.W.T., Can.* **84** F9
Mackenzie Trough, *Arctic Oc.* **246** N7
Mackinac, Straits of, *Mich., U.S.* **100** G10
Mackinac Island, *Mich., U.S.* **100** G11

Mackinaw City, *Mich., U.S.* **100** G10
Mačkovci, *Slov.* **154** C6
Macksville, *Kans., U.S.* **107** U6
Macksville, *N.S.W., Austral.* **215** W15
Maclear, *S. Af.* **206** L10
Macleod, Lake, *Austral.* **214** G1
Macomb, *Ill., U.S.* **101** Q4
Macomer, *It.* **153** N3
Macon, *Ga., U.S.* **98** M6
Macon, *Miss., U.S.* **103** K13
Macon, *Mo., U.S.* **107** R13
Mâcon, *Fr.* **149** T12
Macondo, *Angola* **206** D9
Macouba, *Martinique, Fr.* **123** E22
Macovane, *Mozambique* **207** G13
Macpherson's Strait, *India* **181** Q14
Macquarie, river, *Austral.* **214** J13
Macquarie, Port, *Austral.* **214** K15
Macquarie Harbour, *Austral.* **214** M7
Macquarie Island, *Pac. Oc.* **218** R6
Macquarie Ridge, *Pac. Oc.* **242** R9
MacquireTrench, *Pac. Oc.* **249** F18
Mac. Robertson Land, region, *Antarctica* **231** F18
Macroom (Maigh Chromtha), *Ire.* **145** U4
Macumba, river, *Austral.* **214** G9
Macurijes, Punta, *Cuba* **118** J10
Macuro, *Venez.* **130** B12
Macusani, *Peru* **132** H5
Mad, river, *Calif., U.S.* **111** N2
Mādabā, *Jordan* **172** M6
Madagascar, *Af.* **207** G17
Madagascar Basin, *Ind. Oc.* **224** L7
Madagascar Plateau, *Ind. Oc.* **224** M6
Madāʻin Şāliḥ, *Saudi Arabia* **174** H6
Madalai, *Palau* **220** N11
Madalena, *Sao Tome and Principe* **209** D20
Madalena, *Azores, Port.* **146** Q3
Madan, *Bulg.* **155** K14
Madang, *P.N.G.* **217** C19
Madaripur, *Bangladesh* **180** J13
Madawaska, *Me., U.S.* **97** A18
Madayar, *Myanmar* **190** G6
Maddalena, Isola, *It.* **152** L4
Maddock, *N. Dak., U.S.* **106** F5
Madeira, island, *Madeira, Port.* **208** M2
Madeira, river, *S. Amer.* **132** F8
Madeira Plain, *Atl. Oc.* **240** K9
Madeira Rise, *Atl. Oc.* **240** K10
Madelia, *Minn., U.S.* **106** L10
Madeline Island, *Wis., U.S.* **100** E4
Maden, *Turk.* **171** G14
Madera, *Calif., U.S.* **111** T6
Madera, *Mex.* **116** D9
Madgaon, *India* **181** N4
Madhubani, *India* **180** G10
Madidi, river, *Bol.* **132** H6
Madill, *Okla., U.S.* **104** J12
Madimba, *Dem. Rep. of the Congo* **202** L7
Madīnat ash Shaʻb, *Yemen* **174** R9
Madīnat ath Thawrah, *Syr.* **172** E11
Madīnat Zāyid, *U.A.E.* **175** K14
Madingley Rise, *Ind. Oc.* **224** G8
Madison, *Fla., U.S.* **98** Q6
Madison, *Ga., U.S.* **98** L6
Madison, *Ind., U.S.* **101** T10
Madison, *Kans., U.S.* **107** T9
Madison, *Me., U.S.* **97** F16
Madison, *Minn., U.S.* **106** J9
Madison, *N.C., U.S.* **98** G10
Madison, *Nebr., U.S.* **107** P7
Madison, *S. Dak., U.S.* **106** L8
Madison, *W. Va., U.S.* **98** E8
Madison, *Wis., U.S.* **100** L5
Madisonville, *Ky., U.S.* **103** C14
Madisonville, *Tex., U.S.* **105** P13
Madiun, *Indonesia* **192** M10
Madley, Mount, *Austral.* **214** F5
Mado Gashi, *Kenya* **203** K15
Madoi, *China* **182** J8
Madona, *Latv.* **143** L17
Madrakah, Raʻs al, *Oman* **175** M16
Madras, *Oreg., U.S.* **110** G5
Madras *see* Chennai, *India* **181** P7
Madre, Laguna, *Mex.* **116** F12
Madre de Dios, river, *S. Amer.* **132** H6
Madre de Dios, Isla, *Chile* **135** V6

Madrid, *Iowa, U.S.* **107** P11
Madrid, *Sp.* **146** F11
Madridejos, *Sp.* **146** H11
Madrid Point, *S. Amer.* **128** H4
Madriu, *river, Andorra* **162** J3
Madura, *W. Aust., Austral.* **215** W6
Madura, *island, Indonesia* **192** M11
Madura, Selat, *Indonesia* **192** M11
Madurai, *India* **181** R6
Madurantakam, *India* **181** Q7
Madyan, *Pak.* **178** M10
Maebashi, *Japan* **189** N11
Mae Hong Son, *Thai.* **190** J7
Mae Klong, *river, Thai.* **190** M8
Maemuldo, *island, S. Korea* **187** U11
Maenggoldo, *island, S. Korea* **187** U6
Maengjung, *N. Korea* **186** H6
Maengsan, *N. Korea* **186** H7
Maentwrog, *Wales, U.K.* **145** T9
Mae Sariang, *Thai.* **190** K7
Mae Sot, *Thai.* **190** K8
Maeva, *Fr. Polynesia, Fr.* **223** G14
Maevatanana, *Madagascar* **207** F17
Maéwo, *island, Vanuatu* **222** C2
Mafia Island, *Tanzania* **203** M15
Magadan, *Russ.* **161** F20
Magadi, *Kenya* **203** K14
Magallanes, Estrecho de *see* Strait of
  Magellan, *S. Amer.* **135** X8
Magangué, *Col.* **130** C5
Maga, *peak, N. Mariana Is., U.S.*
  220 A7
Magazine Mountain, *Ark., U.S.*
  102 G7
Magdagachi, *Russ.* **161** K18
Magdalena, *Bol.* **132** H8
Magdalena, *N. Mex., U.S.* **109** T11
Magdalena, *river, N. Amer.* **82** R10
Magdalena, *river, S. Amer.* **130** G5
Magdalena, Bahía, *Mex.* **116** F6
Magdalena, Isla, *Chile* **135** S6
Magdalena, Isla, *Mex.* **116** E6
Magdalena, Llano de la, *Mex.* **116** E6
Magdalena Bay, *N. Amer.* **82** M3
Magdalena de Kino, *Mex.* **116** C7
Magdeburg, *Ger.* **150** E9
Magdelaine Cays, *Austral.* **214** C15
Magee, *Miss., U.S.* **102** M11
Magelang, *Indonesia* **192** M9
Magellan, Strait of, *S. Amer.* **128** R5
Magellan Rise, *Pac. Oc.* **242** J11
Magellan Seamounts, *Pac. Oc.*
  242 H9
Magens Bay, *Virgin Is., U.S.* **122** M9
Magerøya, *island, Nor.* **143** B14
Maggiore, Lago, *It.* **152** C4
Maggotty, *Jam.* **122** J7
Magina, *peak, Sp.* **146** K11
Maglić, *peak, Bosn. & Herzg.,*
  Montenegro **154** H8
Maglie, *It.* **153** N16
Magnitogorsk, *Russ.* **160** J8
Magnolia, *Ark., U.S.* **102** J7
Magnolia, *Miss., U.S.* **102** N10
Mago, *island, Fiji* **222** H9
Magpi, Puntan, *N. Mariana Is., U.S.*
  220 A5
Magude, *Mozambique* **206** J12
Magway, *Myanmar* **190** H5
Mahābād, *Iran* **174** C10
Mahabharat Range, *Nepal* **180** F8
Mahabo, *Madagascar* **207** G16
Mahad, *India* **180** M3
Mahaena, *Fr. Polynesia, Fr.* **223** N16
Mahaena, Passe de, *Fr. Polynesia, Fr.*
  223 N17
Mahagi, *Dem. Rep. of the Congo*
  202 D12
Mahaiatea, *Fr. Polynesia, Fr.* **223** P16
Mahajamba, Baie de la, *Madagascar*
  207 E17
Mahajamba Bay, *Af.* **198** M11
Mahajan, *India* **180** E4
Mahajanga, *Madagascar* **207** E17
Mahalapye, *Botswana* **206** H10
Māhān, *Iran* **175** F15
Mahana Bay, *Hawai'i, U.S.* **115** Q19
Mahanadi, *river, India* **180** K9
Mahanoro, *Madagascar* **207** G18
Mahasamund, *India* **180** K8
Mahaut, *Dominica* **123** F19

Mahavavy, *river, Madagascar*
  207 F17
Mahbubnagar, *India* **180** M6
Mahd adh Dhahab, *Saudi Arabia*
  174 K7
Mahdia, *Guyana* **131** E14
Mahé, *island, Seychelles* **209** P20
Mahébourg, *Mauritius* **209** G20
Mahendraganj, *India* **180** G12
Mahen dra Giri, *peak, India* **180** L9
Mahenge, *Tanzania* **203** N14
Maheno, *N.Z.* **217** Q16
Mahere Honae, *island, Fr. Polynesia,*
  Fr. **223** K16
Mahesana, *India* **180** H3
Mahia Peninsula, *N.Z.* **217** L20
Mahige, *island, Solomon Is.* **221** M19
Mahilyow, *Belarus* **158** K6
Mahina, *Fr. Polynesia, Fr.* **223** N17
Mahina'akaka Heiau, *Hawai'i, U.S.*
  115 N22
Mahishadal, *India* **180** J11
Mahitu, *island, Fr. Polynesia, Fr.*
  223 K16
Maḥmūd-e Rāqī, *Afghan.* **178** M8
Mahmudiye, *Turk.* **170** E6
Mahoba, *India* **180** H7
Mahón, *Sp.* **147** G20
Mahri, *Pak.* **179** U6
Mahu, *Fr. Polynesia, Fr.* **223** K21
Mahuti, Baie de, *Fr. Polynesia, Fr.*
  223 H14
Mahuva, *India* **180** K2
Maia, *Amer. Samoa, U.S.* **222** P4
Maiao, *island, Fr. Polynesia, Fr.*
  223 F16
Maibong, *India* **180** G14
Maicao, *Col.* **130** B6
Maîche, *Fr.* **149** R14
Maicuru, *river, Braz.* **132** C11
Maida, *It.* **153** Q13
Maïdān Shahr, *Afghan.* **178** M7
Maidenhead, *Eng., U.K.* **145** V13
Maiduguri, *Nigeria* **205** B16
Maiduo *see* Mêdog, *China* **182** L7
Maigh Chromtha *see* Macroom, *Ire.*
  145 U4
Maigualida, Sierra, *Venez.* **130** E10
Maihar, *India* **180** H7
Maikoor, *island, Indonesia* **193** L18
Mā'ili, *Hawai'i, U.S.* **114** E10
Mailly-le-Camp, *Fr.* **149** P12
Mailsi, *Pak.* **179** R10
Maïmanah, *Afghan.* **178** L4
Main, *river, Ger.* **150** H8
Maina, *island, Cook Is., N.Z.* **222** Q11
Main Channel, *Cayman Is.* **122** H2
Mai-Ndombe, Lac, *Dem. Rep. of the*
  Congo **202** K7
Maine, *It.* **153** N16
Maine, Gulf of, *N. Amer.* **82** J9
Maingkwan, *Myanmar* **190** D6
Main Island (Bermuda Island),
  Bermuda **122** C2
Mainistir Fhear Maí *see* Fermoy, *Ire.*
  145 U4
Mainistir Laoise *see* Abbeyleix, *Ire.*
  145 T6
Mainistir na Búille *see* Boyle, *Ire.*
  145 R5
Mainistir na Féile *see* Abbeyfeale, *Ire.*
  145 T3
Mainland, *island, Scot., U.K.* **144** D12
Mainland, *island, Scot., U.K.* **144** F10
Mainoru, *N.T., Austral.* **215** P9
Main Ridge, *Trinidad and Tobago*
  123 N18
Maintirano, *Madagascar* **207** F16
Mainz, *Ger.* **150** G6
Maio, *island, Cabo Verde* **209** D17
Maiquetía, *Venez.* **130** B9
Mairenui, *peak, Fr. Polynesia, Fr.*
  223 Q17
Maisí, *Cuba* **119** K15
Maisí, Punta de, *Cuba* **119** K15
Maiskhal, *island, India* **180** K13
Maitland, *N.S.W., Austral.* **215** X15
Maitri, *station, Antarctica* **231** A14
Maíz, Islas del, *Nicar.* **117** M19
Maizhokunggar, *China* **182** L6

Maizuru, *Japan* **189** P8
Majene, *Indonesia* **193** K13
Majī, *Eth.* **203** H14
Majorca *see* Mallorca, *island, Sp.*
  147 G18
Majuro, *Marshall Is., U.S.* **220** G12
Majuro (Laura), *island, Marshall Is.,*
  U.S. **220** H10
Majuro Atoll, *Marshall Is., U.S.*
  220 H5
Majuro Lagoon, *Marshall Is., U.S.*
  220 G10
Mākaha, *Hawai'i, U.S.* **114** E10
Makakilo City, *Hawai'i, U.S.* **114** F10
Makale, *Indonesia* **193** K13
Makaleha Mountains, *Hawai'i, U.S.*
  114 C6
Makalu I, *peak, Nepal* **180** F11
Makapala, *Hawai'i, U.S.* **115** K19
Makapu Point, *Cook Is., N.Z.*
  223 B20
Makaroa, *island, Fr. Polynesia, Fr.*
  223 R21
Makarov, *Russ.* **161** J22
Makarov Basin, *Arctic Oc.* **246** H10
Makarov, *Russ.* **161** K15
Makar'yev, *Russ.* **158** G12
Makassar (Ujungpandang), *Indonesia*
  193 L13
Makassar Strait, *Indonesia* **192** K12
Makatea, *island, Fr. Polynesia, Fr.*
  223 E17
Makawao, *peak, Hawai'i, U.S.* **115** H17
Makefu, *Cook Is., N.Z.* **223** B20
Make Jima, *Japan* **189** T5
Makemo, *island, Fr. Polynesia, Fr.*
  223 E19
Mākena, *Hawai'i, U.S.* **115** H16
Makeni, *Sierra Leone* **204** D6
Makéone, *Vanuatu* **222** B2
Makgadikgadi Pans, *Botswana*
  206 G9
Makhachkala, *Russ.* **159** U15
Makhad, *Pak.* **179** N10
Makhado (Louis Trichardt), *S. Af.*
  206 H11
Makhambet, *Kaz.* **176** E6
Makhfar al Buşayyah, *Iraq* **174** F10
Maki, *Indonesia* **193** K19
Makīnsk, *Kaz.* **177** C13
Makira Harbour, *Solomon Is.* **221** P20
Makiyivka, *Ukr.* **159** Q10
Makkah (Mecca), *Saudi Arabia* **174** L7
Makkovik, *Nfld. & Lab., Can.* **85** K21
Makó, *Hung.* **151** M16
Makogai, *island, Fiji* **222** H7
Makokou, *Gabon* **205** D16
Mākole'ā Point, *Hawai'i, U.S.* **115** M18
Makoua, *Congo* **205** H18
Makrá, *island, Gr.* **157** N16
Makrakómi, *Gr.* **156** G10
Makrana, *India* **180** G4
Makrān Coast Range, *Pak.* **179** V2
Makrinítsa, *Gr.* **156** F11
Makrónisos (Eléni, Helena), *island,*
  Gr. **157** K13
Mākū, *Iran* **174** A10
Makukung, *Taiwan, China* **185** V10
Makura, *island, Vanuatu* **222** E3
Makurazaki, *Japan* **189** T4
Makurdi, *Nigeria* **205** D14
Māl, *Mauritania* **200** G5
Mala *see* Mallow, *Ire.* **145** U4
Malabar Coast, *India* **181** Q4
Malabo, *Eq. Guinea* **208** L7
Malabuñgan, *Philippines* **192** E12
Malacca, *Malaysia* **191** V10
Malacca, Strait of, *Asia* **191** U8
Malacky, *Slovakia* **151** K13
Malad City, *Idaho, U.S.* **108** J7
Maladzyechna, *Belarus* **158** K4
Málaga, *Col.* **130** E6
Málaga, *Sp.* **146** M10
Malagón, *Sp.* **146** H10
Málainn Mhóir (Malin More), *Ire.*
  145 Q3
Malaita, *island, Solomon Is.* **221** N20
Malakal, *Palau* **220** P11
Malakal, *S. Sudan* **203** G13

Malakal Harbor, *Palau* **220** P11
Malakal Pass, *Palau* **220** P11
Malakanagiri, *India* **180** L8
Malakand, *Pak.* **178** M10
Malake, *island, Fiji* **222** H6
Malakoff, *Tex., U.S.* **104** M13
Malakula, *island, Vanuatu* **222** D2
Malam, *F.S.M.* **221** B19
Malang, *Indonesia* **192** M10
Malanje, *Angola* **206** C6
Malans, *Switz.* **162** Q1
Malanville, *Benin* **204** B12
Malao, *Vanuatu* **222** C1
Malapo, *Tonga* **222** J11
Malapu, *Solomon Is.* **221** P23
Malar, *Pak.* **179** V4
Malargüe, *Arg.* **134** M7
Malaspina Glacier, *Alas., U.S.* **113** K20
Malatya, *Turk.* **171** G13
Mala Vyska, *Ukr.* **159** Q6
Malawi, *Af.* **207** D13
Malawi, Lake (Lake Nyasa), *Af.*
  198 L10
Malayagiri, *peak, India* **180** K10
Malaya Vishera, *Russ.* **158** G7
Malaybalay, *Philippines* **193** F15
Malāyer, *Iran* **174** D11
Malay Peninsula, *Thai.* **191** R8
Malaysia, *Asia* **192** G7
Malazgirt, *Turk.* **171** F17
Malbork, *Pol.* **151** B14
Malbun, *Liech.* **162** Q3
Malcolm, *W. Aust., Austral.* **215** V4
Malcolm *see* Makunudu Atoll,
  Maldives **181** T3
Maldegem, *Belg.* **148** K11
Malden, *Mo., U.S.* **107** V15
Malden Island, *Kiribati* **218** G12
Maldive Islands, *Maldives* **181** U3
Maldives, *Asia* **181** U3
Maldonado, *Uru.* **134** L14
Maldonado, Punta, *Mex.* **116** K12
Malè, *It.* **152** C6
Male *see* Maale, *Maldives* **181** U3
Male Atoll, *Maldives* **181** U3
Maléas, Ákra, *Gr.* **156** M11
Malegaon, *India* **180** K4
Malemba-Nkulu, *Dem. Rep. of the*
  Congo **202** M11
Malesína, *Gr.* **156** H11
Malevangga, *Solomon Is.* **221** K15
Malgobek, *Russ.* **159** T13
Malhão, Serra do, *Port.* **146** L6
Malhargarh, *India* **180** H4
Malheur, *river, Oreg., U.S.* **110** H8
Malheureux, Cape, *Mauritius*
  209 F20
Malheur Lake, *Oreg., U.S.* **110** J7
Mali, *Af.* **200** H8
Mali, *island, Fiji* **222** G7
Mali, *river, Myanmar* **190** D7
Mália, *Gr.* **157** Q15
Mali Drvenik, *island, Croatia* **154** G6
Mali Kyun, *island, Myanmar* **191** N7
Malili, *Indonesia* **193** K13
Malin, *Oreg., U.S.* **110** L5
Malin Head (Inis Trá Tholl), *Ire.*
  145 N5
Malin More *see* Málainn Mhóir, *Ire.*
  145 Q3
Malinoa, *island, Tonga* **222** H11
Malkapur, *India* **180** K5
Malkara, *Turk.* **170** C3
Malki, *Russ.* **161** F22
Malko Tŭrnovo, *Bulg.* **155** J17
Mallacoota, *Vic., Austral.* **215** Z14
Mallacoota Inlet, *Austral.* **214** M14
Mallawi, *Egypt* **201** D18
Mallwli, *island, Malaysia* **192** F12
Mallorca (Majorca), *island, Sp.*
  147 G18
Mallow (Mala), *Ire.* **145** U4
Malmberget, *Sw.* **143** D13
Malmesbury, *S. Af.* **206** M7
Malmö, *Sw.* **142** N12
Malmok, *Bonaire, Neth.* **123** Q18
Malo, *island, Vanuatu* **222** D1
Maloelap Atoll, *Marshall Is., U.S.*
  220 G5

Maloja, *Switz.* **152** C5
Malolo, *island, Fiji* **222** H5
Malone, *N.Y., U.S.* **96** F11
Maloshuyka, *Russ.* **160** E8
Måløy, *Nor.* **142** J9
Malozemel'skaya Tundra, *Eur.*
  140 A12
Malpaso, *peak, Sp.* **208** R3
Malpelo Island, *S. Amer.* **128** C1
Malportas Pond, *Cayman Is.* **122** J3
Mäls, *Liech.* **162** Q2
Malta, *Eur.* **162** F4
Malta, *Mont., U.S.* **108** B10
Malta, *island, Malta* **162** K22
Maltahöhe, *Namibia* **206** J7
Maltese Islands, *Eur.* **140** M7
Malton, *Eng., U.K.* **145** Q13
Maluku *see* Moluccas, *island,*
  Indonesia **193** H16
Ma'lūlā, *Syr.* **172** J8
Malung, *Sw.* **142** J12
Maluu, *Solomon Is.* **221** M19
Malvan, *India* **181** N3
Malvern, *Ark., U.S.* **102** H8
Malvern, *Iowa, U.S.* **107** Q9
Malvern, *Jam.* **122** J7
Malyn, *Ukr.* **159** N5
Malyye Karmakuly, *Russ.* **160** D10
Malyy Lyakhovskiy, Ostrov, *Russ.*
  161 D17
Mamagota, *P.N.G.* **221** K14
Māmala Bay, *Hawai'i, U.S.* **114** F11
Mamalahoa Highway, *Hawai'i, U.S.*
  115 M19
Mamalu Bay, *Hawai'i, U.S.* **115** J17
Mamberamo, *Indonesia* **193** K20
Mamelles, *island, Seychelles*
  209 N20
Mamer, *Lux.* **162** K9
Mameyes, *P.R., U.S.* **122** M5
Mamfé, *Cameroon* **205** E14
Mamiña, *Chile* **134** C7
Mammoth, *Wyo., U.S.* **108** F8
Mammoth Cave National Park, *Ky.,*
  U.S. **103** D16
Mammoth Spring, *Ark., U.S.* **102** E9
Mamoiada, *It.* **153** N4
Mamoré, *river, S. Amer.* **132** G7
Mamoriá, *Braz.* **132** F7
Mamou, *Guinea* **204** C5
Mamou, *La., U.S.* **102** P8
Mamoudzou, *Mayotte, Fr.* **209** P17
Mampong, *Ghana* **204** D10
Mamuju, *Indonesia* **193** K13
Man, *Côte d'Ivoire* **204** D7
Man, Isle of (Ellan Vanninn), *U.K.*
  145 Q9
Mana, *Fr. Guiana* **131** E17
Mānā, *Hawai'i, U.S.* **114** C4
Mana, *river, Fr. Guiana* **131** E17
Manacapuru, *Braz.* **132** D9
Manacor, *Sp.* **147** G19
Manado, *Indonesia* **193** H15
Mañagaha Island, *N. Mariana Is., U.S.*
  220 B4
Managua, *Nicar.* **117** M18
Managua, Lago de, *Nicar.* **117** M18
Manaia, *N.Z.* **217** L18
Manakara, *Madagascar* **207** H17
Manakau, *peak, N.Z.* **217** N18
Manākhah, *Yemen* **174** Q9
Manam, *island, P.N.G.* **217** C19
Manama *see* Al Manāmah, *Bahrain*
  174 J12
Manamadurai, *India* **181** R6
Mananjary, *Madagascar* **207** G17
Manaoba, *island, Solomon Is.*
  221 M19
Mana Pass, *India* **180** D7
Mānā Point, *Hawai'i, U.S.* **114** C4
Manapouri, Lake, *N.Z.* **217** Q15
Manas, *China* **182** E5
Manassas, *Va., U.S.* **98** D12
Manatí, *Cuba* **118** J12
Manatí, *P.R., U.S.* **122** M3
Manaus, *Braz.* **132** D9
Manavgat, *Turk.* **170** J6
Manawai Harbour, *Solomon Is.*
  221 N20
Manawatāwhi (Three Kings Islands),
  N.Z. **217** G17

Manbij, *Syr.* 172 DIO
Manchester, *Conn., U.S.* 97 LI3
Manchester, *Eng., U.K.* 145 SII
Manchester, *Ga., U.S.* 98 M5
Manchester, *Iowa, U.S.* 107 NI3
Manchester, *Ky., U.S.* 103 DI9
Manchester, *N.H., U.S.* 97 JI4
Manchester, *Tenn., U.S.* 103 FI6
Manchhar Lake, *Pak.* 179 U6
Manchioneal, *Jam.* 122 JII
Manchuria see Dongbei, region, *China* 183 CI5
Manchurian Plain, *Asia* 168 FI2
Manciano, *It.* 152 J7
Mancos, *Colo., U.S.* 109 PIO
Mand, *Iran* 175 GI3
Mand, *Pak.* 179 V2
Manda, *Tanzania* 203 NI3
Mandai, *Pak.* 179 R7
Mandal, *Mongolia* 182 CIO
Mandal, *N. Mongol, China* 184 A3
Mandal, *Nor.* 142 MIO
Mandal, *Virgin Is., U.S.* 122 M9
Mandala, Puncak, *Indonesia* 217 CI7
Mandalay, *Myanmar* 190 G6
Mandalgovĭ, *Mongolia* 182 EIO
Mandalī, *Iraq* 174 DIO
Mandan, *N. Dak., U.S.* 106 G4
Mandapeta, *India* 180 M8
Mandara Mountains, *Cameroon, Nigeria* 205 CI6
Mandeb, Bab el, *Djibouti, Yemen* 174 R8
Mandera, *Kenya* 203 JI6
Manderscheid, *Ger.* 162 GI2
Mandeville, *Jam.* 122 J8
Mandi, *India* 180 D6
Mandi Burewala, *Pak.* 179 RII
Mandimba, *Mozambique* 207 EI3
Mandioli, island, *Indonesia* 193 JI6
Mandla, *India* 180 J7
Mandōl, *Afghan.* 178 L8
Mandora, *W. Aust., Austral.* 215 S4
Mándra, *Gr.* 156 JI2
Mandráki, *Gr.* 157 MI8
Mandritsa, *Bulg.* 155 KI6
Mandritsara, *Madagascar* 207 EI8
Mandsaur, *India* 180 H4
Mandu, island, *Maldives* 181 V3
Mandurah, *W. Aust., Austral.* 215 X2
Manduria, *It.* 153 NI5
Mandvi, *India* 180 JI
Manfredonia, *It.* 152 LI2
Manfredonia, Golfo di, *It.* 152 LI3
Manga, *Braz.* 133 JI5
Manga, region, *Chad, Niger* 201 HI3
Mangabeiras, Chapada das, *Braz.* 133 GI4
Mangaia, island, *Cook Is., N.Z.* 218 KI2
Mangalia, *Rom.* 155 GI8
Mangalore see Mangaluru, *India* 181 Q4
Mangaluru (Mangalore), *India* 181 Q4
Mangareva, island, *Fr. Polynesia, Fr.* 223 Q2I
Mangarongaro, island, *Cook Is., N.Z.* 223 BI7
Mangeigne, *Chad* 201 KI6
Mangere, island, *Cook Is., N.Z.* 222 QI2
Manggautu, *Solomon Is.* 221 QI9
Mangghyystaū, *Kaz.* 176 H5
Manghit, *Uzb.* 176 J9
Mangkalihat, Cape, *Asia* 168 LI3
Mangnai, *China* 182 G6
Mango, island, *Tonga* 222 R6
Mangoche, *Malawi* 207 EI3
Mangoky, river, *Madagascar* 207 HI6
Mangole, island, *Indonesia* 193 KI5
Mangqystaū Shyghanaghy, bay, *Kaz.* 176 G5
Mangrol, *India* 180 K2
Mangrove Cay, *Bahamas* 122 D2
Manguchar, *Pak.* 179 S6
Mangueira, Lagoa, *Braz.* 132 QII
Manguinho, Ponta do, *Braz.* 133 GI7
Mangum, *Okla., U.S.* 104 H8
Mangut, *Russ.* 161 MI7
Mangyeong, *S. Korea* 187 R8

Manhattan, *Kans., U.S.* 107 S8
Manhattan, *Nev., U.S.* III R9
Manhŭng, *N. Korea* 186 D8
Máni, peninsula, *Gr.* 156 MIO
Mania, river, *Madagascar* 207 GI7
Maniamba, *Mozambique* 207 DI3
Manica, *Mozambique* 206 FI2
Manicoré, *Braz.* 132 E9
Manicouagan, Réservoir, *Que., Can.* 85 M2O
Manīfah, *Saudi Arabia* 174 HI2
Manifold, Cape, *Austral.* 214 FI5
Manihi, Atoll, *Fr. Polynesia, Fr.* 223 DI8
Manihiki Atoll, *Cook Is., N.Z.* 218 HI2
Manihiki Plateau, *Pac. Oc.* 243 KI3
Manila, *Ark., U.S.* 102 FII
Manila, *Philippines* 193 CI3
Manila, *Utah, U.S.* 108 K9
Manila Bay, *Philippines* 193 CI3
Manily, *Russ.* 161 D2I
Maningrida, *N.T., Austral.* 215 N9
Maninita, island, *Tonga* 222 MII
Manipa, island, *Indonesia* 193 KI6
Manisa, *Turk.* 170 F3
Manistee, *Mich., U.S.* 100 J9
Manistee, river, *Mich., U.S.* 100 J9
Manistique, *Mich., U.S.* 100 G9
Manistique Lake, *Mich., U.S.* 100 F9
Manitoba, *Can.* 85 LI3
Manitoba, Lake, *Man., Can.* 85 NI3
Manitou Island, *Mich., U.S.* 100 E7
Manitou Islands, *Wis., U.S.* 100 H9
Manitowoc, *Wis., U.S.* 100 K7
Manizales, *Col.* 130 F4
Manja, *Madagascar* 207 GI6
Manjaedo, island, *S. Korea* 187 U5
Manjimup, *W. Aust., Austral.* 215 Y3
Manjra, river, *India* 180 M6
Mankato, *Kans., U.S.* 107 R7
Mankato, *Minn., U.S.* 106 LII
Manley Hot Springs, *Alas., U.S.* 113 FI6
Manlleu, *Sp.* 147 DI7
Manly, *Iowa, U.S.* 106 MII
Manmad, *India* 180 K4
Mann, island, *Marshall Is., U.S.* 220 M4
Manna, *Indonesia* 192 L6
Mannar, Gulf of, *India* 181 S6
Mannheim, *Ger.* 150 H6
Manning, *Iowa, U.S.* 107 PIO
Manning, *N. Dak., U.S.* 106 G3
Manning, *S.C., U.S.* 98 LIO
Manning, Cape, *Kiribati* 221 A23
Manning Seamounts, *Atl. Oc.* 240 J5
Manning Strait, *Solomon Is.* 221 LI6
Mannington, *W. Va., U.S.* 98 C9
Mann Passage, *Marshall Is., U.S.* 220 M4
Mannu, Capo, *It.* 153 N3
Manoa, *Bol.* 132 G7
Man of War Bay, *Trinidad and Tobago* 123 NI8
Man-of-War Cay, *Bahamas* 119 GI3
Manokotak, *Alas., U.S.* 113 LI3
Manokwari, *Indonesia* 193 JI9
Manono, *Dem. Rep. of the Congo* 202 MII
Manono, island, *Samoa* 222 L2
Manoron, *Myanmar* 191 P8
Mano Wan, *Japan* 188 MII
Man O' War Cays, *Bahamas* 122 B6
Manp'o, *N. Korea* 186 E7
Manra, island, *Kiribati* 218 GIO
Manresa, *Sp.* 147 DI7
Mansa, *Zambia* 206 DII
Mansehra, *Pak.* 178 MII
Mansel Island, *Nunavut, Can.* 85 JI7
Manseriche, Pongo de, *S. Amer.* 128 E2
Mansfield, *Ark., U.S.* 102 G6
Mansfield, *Eng., U.K.* 145 SI2
Mansfield, *La., U.S.* 102 L6
Mansfield, *Mo., U.S.* 107 VI3
Mansfield, *Ohio, U.S.* 101 QI3
Mansfield, *Pa., U.S.* 96 L7
Mansfield, *Vic., Austral.* 215 YI3
Mansfield, Mount, *Vt., U.S.* 96 FI2
Mansle, *Fr.* 149 U7

Manson, *Iowa, U.S.* 107 NIO
Manta, *Ecua.* 130 J2
Manta Bay, *S. Amer.* 128 DI
Mant'ap-san, peak, *N. Korea* 186 EII
Manteca, *Calif., U.S.* III S5
Manteo, *N.C., U.S.* 98 GI5
Mantes-la-Jolie, *Fr.* 149 P9
Manti, *Utah, U.S.* 108 M7
Mantiqueira, Serra da, *S. Amer.* 128 J9
Mant Islands, *F.S.M.* 221 FI4
Manton, *Mich., U.S.* 100 JIO
Mantova, *It.* 152 E6
Mant Passage, *F.S.M.* 221 FI4
Mantua, *Cuba* 118 H4
Mantuan Downs, *Qnsld., Austral.* 215 UI4
Manturovo, *Russ.* 158 GI2
Mäntyluoto, *Fin.* 143 HI5
Manú, *Peru* 132 H5
Manuae, island, *Fr. Polynesia, Fr.* 223 EI4
Manu'a Islands, *Amer. Samoa, U.S.* 218 JIO
Manuhangi, island, *Fr. Polynesia, Fr.* 223 F2O
Manui, island, *Fr. Polynesia, Fr.* 223 R2I
Manui, island, *Indonesia* 193 KI4
Manukau, *N.Z.* 217 JI9
Manulu Lagoon, *Kiribati* 221 B23
Manus, island, *P.N.G.* 217 BI9
Many, *La., U.S.* 102 M7
Manych Gudilo, Ozero, *Russ.* 159 RI2
Manych Guidilo, Lake, *Eur.* 140 HI3
Many Farms, *Ariz., U.S.* 109 Q8
Manzai, *Pak.* 179 P8
Manzanares, *Sp.* 146 HII
Manzanar National Historic Site, *Calif., U.S.* III T8
Manzanilla Point, *Trinidad and Tobago* 123 P24
Manzanillo, *Cuba* 118 KII
Manzanillo, *Mex.* 116 J9
Manzanillo Bay, *Haiti* 119 LI7
Manzano Mountains, *N. Mex., U.S.* 109 SI2
Manzano Peak, *N. Mex., U.S.* 109 SI2
Manzhouli, *China* 183 CI3
Manzil, *Pak.* 179 S3
Mao, *Chad* 201 HI4
Mao, *Dom. Rep.* 119 LI8
Maodianzi, *Liaoning, China* 184 CI4
Maoming, *Guang., China* 185 X2
Maothail see Mohill, *Ire.* 145 R5
Mapai, *Mozambique* 206 HI2
Mapi, *Indonesia* 193 M2I
Mapia, Kepulauan (Saint David Islands), *Indonesia* 193 JI9
Mapleton, *Iowa, U.S.* 107 N9
Mapleton, *Oreg., U.S.* 110 H2
Mapmaker Seamounts, *Pac. Oc.* 242 FIO
Maprik, *P.N.G.* 217 CI8
Mapuera, river, *Braz.* 132 CIO
Maputo, *Mozambique* 206 JI2
Maputo, Baía de, *Mozambique* 206 JI2
Maqat, *Kaz.* 176 F6
Maqellarë, *Alban.* 154 KIO
Maqên, *China* 182 J9
Maqnā, *Saudi Arabia* 174 G4
Maqshūsh, *Saudi Arabia* 174 K6
Maquan see Damqog, river, *China* 182 L4
Maquela do Zombo, *Angola* 206 B6
Maquinchao, *Arg.* 135 Q8
Maquoketa, *Iowa, U.S.* 107 NI4
Mar, *Russ.* 161 HI6
Mar, Serra do, *S. Amer.* 128 K8
Mara, *Guyana* 131 EI5
Mara, *India* 180 FI4
Maraa, *Fr. Polynesia, Fr.* 223 PI6
Maraã, *Braz.* 132 D7
Maraa, Passe de, *Fr. Polynesia, Fr.* 223 PI6
Marabá, *Braz.* 133 EI3
Marabo, island, *Fiji* 222 K9

Maracá, Ilha de, *Braz.* 133 BI3
Maracaibo, *Venez.* 130 B7
Maracaibo, Lago de, *Venez.* 130 C7
Maracaibo Basin, *S. Amer.* 128 A3
Maracá Island, *S. Amer.* 128 C8
Maracaju, *Braz.* 132 LII
Maracaju, Serra de, *S. Amer.* 128 H7
Maracanã, *Braz.* 133 DI4
Maracay, *Venez.* 130 B9
Maracayo, Punta, *P.R., U.S.* 122 M2
Marādah, *Lib.* 201 DI5
Maradi, *Niger* 200 JI2
Marado, island, *S. Korea* 187 X7
Marāghah, Sabkhat, *Syr.* 172 E9
Marāgheh, *Iran* 174 BIO
Maragogipe, *Braz.* 133 HI6
Marahuaca, Cerro, *N. Amer.* 82 QII
Marahuaca, Cerro, *Venez.* 130 FIO
Marajó, Baía de, *Braz.* 133 CI3
Marajó, Ilha de, *Braz.* 133 CI3
Marakei, island, *Kiribati* 218 F8
Maralal, *Kenya* 203 JI4
Maralinga, *S. Aust., Austral.* 215 W8
Maramasike, island, *Solomon Is.* 221 N2O
Maran, *Malaysia* 191 UIO
Marana, *Ariz., U.S.* 109 V7
Maranboy, *N.T., Austral.* 215 P8
Maranchón, *Sp.* 146 EI2
Marand, *Iran* 174 BIO
Marang, *Malaysia* 191 TIO
Maranges, *Sp.* 162 K6
Maranhão, Barragem do, *Port.* 146 H6
Marano, river, *It., San Marino* 163 JI7
Marañón, river, *Peru* 132 E3
Marans, *Fr.* 149 T6
Marargiu, Capo, *It.* 153 N3
Mara Rosa, *Braz.* 133 HI3
Maraş see Varosha, *Cyprus* 162 PIO
Mărăşeşti, *Rom.* 155 DI6
Maratea, *It.* 153 NI2
Marathon, *Fla., U.S.* 99 Y9
Marathon, *Tex., U.S.* 105 Q3
Marathon, battle, *Gr.* 157 JI3
Marathóna, *Gr.* 157 JI3
Marathus, ruins see 'Amrīt, *Syr.* 172 G7
Maraú, *Braz.* 133 JI6
Maravae, *Solomon Is.* 221 MI5
Marāveh Tappeh, *Iran* 175 BI5
Maravillas Creek, *Tex., U.S.* 105 Q3
Maravovo, *Solomon Is.* 221 NI8
Marbella, *Sp.* 146 M9
Marble Bar, *W. Aust., Austral.* 215 S3
Marble Canyon, *Ariz., U.S.* 109 Q7
Marble Falls, *Tex., U.S.* 105 PIO
Marburg, *Ger.* 150 F6
Marca Point, *Af.* 198 M5
Marceline, *Mo., U.S.* 107 RI2
Marchena, Canal de, *Ecua.* 130 PIO
Marchena (Bindloe), Isla, *Ecua.* 130 PIO
Mar Chiquita, Laguna, *Arg.* 134 JIO
Marciana, *It.* 152 J5
Marckolsheim, *Fr.* 149 QI5
Marco, *Fla., U.S.* 99 X8
Marcola, *Oreg., U.S.* 110 H3
Marcos Juárez, *Arg.* 134 KII
Marcus Baker, Mount, *Alas., U.S.* 113 JI7
Marcus Island see Minami Tori Shima, *Pac. Oc.* 218 C5
Marcus-Wake Seamounts, *Pac. Oc.* 242 G8
Marcy, Mount, *N.Y., U.S.* 96 GII
Mardan, *Pak.* 178 MIO
Mar del Plata, *Arg.* 135 NI3
Mar del Plata Canyon, *Atl. Oc.* 241 T6
Mardie, *W. Aust., Austral.* 215 S2
Mardin, *Turk.* 171 HI5
Maré, island, *New Caledonia, Fr.* 222 DIO
Marea de Portillo, *Cuba* 118 LII
Marecchia, river, *It.* 162 HI3
Marechal Taumaturgo, *Braz.* 132 G4
Maree, Loch, *Scot., U.K.* 144 J8
Marenanuka, island, *Kiribati* 221 FI7
Marengo, *Iowa, U.S.* 107 PI3
Marennes, *Fr.* 149 U6

Marettimo, Isola, *It.* 153 S8
Mareuil, *Fr.* 149 U8
Marfa, *Tex., U.S.* 105 Q2
Marfa, Massif de, *Chad* 201 JI6
Margaret River, *W. Aust., Austral.* 215 Y2
Margarita, Isla de, *Venez.* 130 BII
Margat Castle, ruins see Qal'at al Marqab, *Syr.* 172 F7
Margeride, Monts de la, *Fr.* 149 VII
Margherita di Savoia, *It.* 152 LI3
Marghita, *Rom.* 154 BI2
Mārgō, Dasht-e, *Afghan.* 179 R2
Marguerite Bay, *Antarctica* 230 F5
Marhanets', *Ukr.* 159 Q8
Mari, ruins, *Syr.* 172 GI4
Maria, island, *Fr. Polynesia, Fr.* 223 H22
Mariá, Pic del, *Andorra* 162 H5
Maria Bay, *Tonga* 222 HII
María Elena, *Chile* 134 D7
Maria, Îles, *Fr. Polynesia, Fr.* 218 KI2
Maria Islands, *St. Lucia* 123 LI4
Mariana Islands, *Asia* 168 HI6
Mariana Trench, *Pac. Oc.* 242 H8
Mariana Trough, *Pac. Oc.* 242 G8
Marianna, *Ark., U.S.* 102 GIO
Marianna, *Fla., U.S.* 99 Q4
Marianne, *Seychelles* 209 M2I
Mariánské Lázně, *Czech Rep.* 150 H9
Marias, river, *Mont., U.S.* 108 B8
Marías, Islas, *Mex.* 116 G8
Marías Islands, *N. Amer.* 82 M3
Maria van Diemen, Cape, *N.Z.* 217 GI7
Ma'rib, *Yemen* 174 PIO
Maribor, *Slov.* 154 C6
Maricao, *P.R., U.S.* 122 N2
Maricopa, *Ariz., U.S.* 109 U7
Maricopa, *Calif., U.S.* III W7
Maridi, *S. Sudan* 202 HII
Marié, river, *Braz.* 132 D6
Marie Byrd Land, region, *Antarctica* 230 L9
Marie Byrd Seamounts, *Pac. Oc.* 249 LI4
Marie Celeste Fracture Zone, *Ind. Oc.* 224 K9
Marie-Galante, island, *Guadeloupe, Fr.* 123 GI6
Mariehamn (Maarianhamina), *Fin.* 143 JI4
Mariel, *Cuba* 118 G6
Mariental, *Namibia* 206 J7
Marietta, *Ga., U.S.* 98 L5
Marietta, *Ohio, U.S.* 101 SI5
Marietta, *Okla., U.S.* 104 JII
Marigot, *Dominica* 123 E2O
Marigot, *Guadeloupe, Fr.* 123 FI4
Marigot, *Haiti* 119 MI6
Marigot, *Martinique, Fr.* 123 E23
Marigot, *St.-Martin, Fr.* 123 BI4
Marigot, Baie de, *St.-Martin, Fr.* 123 BI4
Marigot Harbour, *St. Lucia* 123 KI3
Mariiru Point, *N. Mariana Is., U.S.* 220 E8
Marijampolė, *Lith.* 143 NI6
Marília, *Braz.* 132 LI2
Marillana, *W. Aust., Austral.* 215 T3
Marinduque, island, *Philippines* 193 DI4
Marine City, *Mich., U.S.* 100 MI3
Marineland, *Fla., U.S.* 99 R9
Marinette, *Wis., U.S.* 100 H7
Maringá, *Braz.* 132 MI2
Maringa, river, *Dem. Rep. of the Congo* 202 K9
Marinha Grande, *Port.* 146 G5
Marino, *It.* 152 L8
Marino, *Vanuatu* 222 C2
Marion, *Ala., U.S.* 103 LI4
Marion, *Ark., U.S.* 102 GII
Marion, *Ill., U.S.* 101 U6
Marion, *Ind., U.S.* 101 Q9
Marion, *Iowa, U.S.* 107 NI3
Marion, *Kans., U.S.* 107 T8
Marion, *Ky., U.S.* 103 C9
Marion, *Mich., U.S.* 100 KIO
Marion, *N.C., U.S.* 98 H8
Marion, *Ohio, U.S.* 101 QI2

Marion, *S. Dak., U.S.* **106** M8
Marion, *S.C., U.S.* **98** K11
Marion, *Va., U.S.* **98** G8
Marion, Lake, *S.C., U.S.* **98** L10
Marion Dufresne Seamount, *Ind. Oc.* **248** D9
Marion Plateau, *Pac. Oc.* **242** M8
Marionville, *Mo., U.S.* **107** VII
Maripa, *Venez.* **130** D10
Mariposa, *Calif., U.S.* **III** S6
Marisa, *Indonesia* **193** J14
Mariscal Estigarribia, *Parag.* **132** L9
Maritime Alps, *Fr., It.* **152** G2
Maritime Museum, site, *Bermuda* **122** B1
Maritsa, river, *Bulg.* **155** K15
Mariupol', *Ukr.* **159** R9
Marivan, *Iran* **174** C10
Mariyets, *Russ.* **158** H15
Marjayoûn, *Leb.* **172** J6
Marka (Merca), *Somalia* **203** J17
Markandeh, ruins, *Afghan.* **178** M6
Markaz-e Ḥukūmat-e Sulṭān-e Bakwāh, *Afghan.* **179** P3
Marked Tree, *Ark., U.S.* **102** F11
Markermeer, bay, *Neth.* **148** H12
Markham, Mount, *Antarctica* **231** L13
Markham Bay, *Nunavut, Can.* **85** H18
Markit, *China* **182** F2
Markleeville, *Calif., U.S.* **III** Q6
Markópoulo, *Gr.* **156** J7
Markovo, *Russ.* **161** C21
Marks, *Miss., U.S.* **102** H11
Marks, *Russ.* **158** M14
Marksville, *La., U.S.* **102** N8
Mark Twain Lake, *Mo., U.S.* **107** S13
Marle, *Fr.* **149** N11
Marlette, *Mich., U.S.* **100** L12
Marlin, *Tex., U.S.* **105** N12
Marlin Rise, *Pac. Oc.* **243** P14
Marlinton, *W. Va., U.S.* **98** D10
Marlow, *Okla., U.S.* **104** H10
Marmande, *Fr.* **149** W7
Marmara, island, *Turk.* **170** D4
Marmara Denizi, *Turk.* **170** D4
Marmara Ereğlisi (Perinthus), *Turk.* **170** C4
Marmara Gölü, *Turk.* **170** F4
Marmarás, *Gr.* **156** D12
Marmári, *Gr.* **157** J13
Marmaris, *Turk.* **170** H4
Marmarth, *N. Dak., U.S.* **106** H1
Marmelos, river, *Braz.* **132** F8
Marmet, *W. Va., U.S.* **98** E8
Marmolada, peak, *It.* **152** C7
Marmolejo, *Sp.* **146** K10
Marne, river, *Fr.* **149** P12
Marne au Rhin, Canal de la, *Fr.* **149** P14
Maroa, *Venez.* **130** G9
Maroantsetra, *Madagascar* **207** E18
Marobee Range, *Austral.* **214** K13
Maroe, *Fr. Polynesia, Fr.* **223** G14
Maroe, Baie de, *Fr. Polynesia, Fr.* **223** G14
Marokau, island, *Fr. Polynesia, Fr.* **223** F19
Marol, *Pak.* **178** M13
Maromokotro, peak, *Madagascar* **207** E18
Maroneía, *Gr.* **157** C15
Maroni, river, *S. Amer.* **128** B7
Maroochydore, *Qnsld., Austral.* **215** V16
Maro Reef, *Hawai'i, U.S.* **114** L5
Marotiri (Îlots de Bass), *Fr. Polynesia, Fr.* **219** L14
Maroua, *Cameroon* **205** C17
Maro'u Bay, *Solomon Is.* **221** P20
Marovoay, *Madagascar* **207** E17
Marpi Point, *N. Mariana Is., U.S.* **220** A5
Márpissa, *Gr.* **157** L15
Marpo, Puntan, *N. Mariana Is., U.S.* **220** C8
Marqaköl, *Kaz.* **177** D19
Marquesas Fracture Zone, *Pac. Oc.* **243** L16
Marquesas Islands, *Fr. Polynesia, Fr.* **219** H14

Marquesas Keys, *Fla., U.S.* **99** Z8
Marquette, *Mich., U.S.* **100** F7
Marquis, *Grenada* **123** K23
Marquis, *St. Lucia* **123** J14
Marquis, Cape, *St. Lucia* **123** J14
Marquis Island, *Grenada* **123** K24
Marra, *Jebel, Sudan* **202** F10
Marrakech, *Mor.* **200** B8
Marrawah, *Tas., Austral.* **215** Y7
Marree, *S. Aust., Austral.* **215** V10
Marrero, *La., U.S.* **102** Q11
Marromeu, *Mozambique* **207** F13
Marrupa, *Mozambique* **207** D14
Marsa, *Malta* **163** K23
Marsá al Burayqah, *Lib.* **201** C15
Marsabit, *Kenya* **203** J14
Marsala, *It.* **153** S8
Marsalforn, *Malta* **163** H20
Marsaxlokk, *Malta* **163** L23
Marsaxlokk Bay, *Malta* **163** L23
Marsciano, *It.* **152** J8
Marseille, *Fr.* **149** Y13
Marsfjället, peak, *Sw.* **142** F12
Marshall, *Alas., U.S.* **111** F13
Marshall, *Ark., U.S.* **102** E8
Marshall, *Ill., U.S.* **100** S7
Marshall, *Mich., U.S.* **100** M10
Marshall, *Minn., U.S.* **106** K9
Marshall, *Mo., U.S.* **107** S12
Marshall, *Tex., U.S.* **104** L15
Marshall, river, *Austral.* **214** F9
Marshall Islands, *Pac. Oc.* **220** F3
Marshall Seamounts, *Pac. Oc.* **242** H10
Marshalltown, *Iowa, U.S.* **107** N12
Marshfield, *Mo., U.S.* **107** U12
Marshfield, *Wis., U.S.* **100** J7
Marsh Harbour, *Bahamas* **122** B6
Mars Hill, *Me., U.S.* **97** C18
Mars Hill, *N.C., U.S.* **98** H7
Marsh Island, *La., U.S.* **102** Q8
Marsh Island, *U.S.* **87** M15
Marsland, *Nebr., U.S.* **107** N2
Mars-la-Tour, *Fr.* **149** P13
Marsugalt, island, *Marshall Is., U.S.* **220** K1
Mart, *Tex., U.S.* **105** N12
Martaban, Gulf of, *Myanmar* **190** K6
Martapura, *Indonesia* **192** K11
Martelange, *Lux.* **162** J8
Martha's Vineyard, *Mass., U.S.* **97** M15
Martí, *Cuba* **118** J11
Martigny, *Switz.* **152** C2
Martigues, *Fr.* **149** X13
Martin, *S. Dak., U.S.* **106** M3
Martin, *Slovakia* **151** J15
Martin, *Tenn., U.S.* **103** E13
Martin, Lake, *Ala., U.S.* **103** L16
Martinez, *Ga., U.S.* **98** L8
Martinez Lake, *Ariz., U.S.* **109** U4
Martinique, island, *Lesser Antil.* **121** E17
Martinique Passage, *N. Amer.* **121** E17
Martinsburg, *W. Va., U.S.* **98** C12
Martins Ferry, *Ohio, U.S.* **101** Q15
Martinsville, *Ind., U.S.* **101** S9
Martinsville, *Va., U.S.* **98** G10
Martin Vaz Fracture Zone, *Atl. Oc.* **241** R10
Martos, *Sp.* **146** K10
Martuni, *Arm.* **171** E19
Martuni (Xocavənd), *Azerb.* **171** E21
Maru, island, *Indonesia* **217** D14
Ma'rūf, *Afghan.* **179** Q6
Marum Volcano, *Vanuatu* **222** D2
Marutea, island, *Fr. Polynesia, Fr.* **223** E19
Marutea, island, *Fr. Polynesia, Fr.* **223** G23
Marvão, *Port.* **146** H7
Marv Dasht, *Iran* **175** F13
Marvine, Mount, *Utah, U.S.* **109** N7
Marvin Spur, *Arctic Oc.* **246** K12
Mārwā, *Afghan.* **178** M3
Mary, *Uzb.* **176** M10
Maryborough, *Qnsld., Austral.* **215** U16
Maryland, *U.S.* **98** C13
Mary Point, *Virgin Is., U.S.* **122** M11
Maryport, *Eng., U.K.* **145** P10

Marys, river, *Nev., U.S.* **110** M11
Marysvale, *Utah, U.S.* **109** N7
Marysville, *Calif., U.S.* **III** Q4
Marysville, *Kans., U.S.* **107** R8
Marysville, *Ohio, U.S.* **101** Q12
Marysville, *Wash., U.S.* **110** B4
Maryville, *Mo., U.S.* **107** R10
Maryville, *Tenn., U.S.* **103** F18
Marzo, Cabo, *Col.* **130** E3
Marzûq, *Lib.* **201** E14
Marzūq, Şaḩrā'', desert, *Lib.* **201** E13
Masada, ruins, *Israel* **173** N6
Masai Steppe, *Tanzania* **203** L14
Masallı, *Azerb.* **171** F22
Masalog, Puntan, *N. Mariana Is., U.S.* **220** B8
Masamba, *Indonesia* **193** K13
Masan, *N. Korea* **186** K7
Masan, *S. Korea* **187** S11
Masasi, *Tanzania* **203** N15
Masaya, *Nicar.* **117** M18
Masbate, island, *Philippines* **193** D14
Masbate City, *Philippines* **193** D14
Mascara, *Alg.* **200** A10
Mascarene Basin, *Ind. Oc.* **224** K7
Mascarene Plain, *Ind. Oc.* **224** K7
Mascarene Plateau, *Ind. Oc.* **224** G7
Masefau Bay, *Amer. Samoa, U.S.* **222** L8
Masein, *Myanmar* **190** F5
Masela, island, *Indonesia* **193** M17
Maseru, *Lesotho* **206** K10
Masescha, *Liech.* **162** P2
Mash'abbe Sade, *Israel* **173** P5
Mashhad, *Iran* **175** C16
Mashkai, river, *Pak.* **179** U5
Mashkel, river, *Pak.* **179** T3
Māshkel, Hāmūn-i-, *Pak.* **179** T2
Mashki Chah, *Pak.* **179** S2
Masi-Manimba, *Dem. Rep. of the Congo* **202** L8
Masin, *Indonesia* **193** M21
Masira *see* Maşīrah, Jazīrat, *Oman* **175** M17
Masira, Gulf of, *Ind. Oc.* **168** J4
Maşīrah, Jazīrat (Masira), *Oman* **175** M17
Maşīrah, Khalīj, *Oman* **175** M16
Masisea, *Peru* **132** G4
Masjed Soleymān, *Iran* **174** E12
Mask, Lough, *Ire.* **145** R3
Maskanah (Meskéné), *Syr.* **172** E10
Maskelynes Islands, *Vanuatu* **222** D2
Maslenica, *Croatia* **154** F5
Maslen Nos, *Bulg.* **155** J17
Masoala, Presqu'île de, *Madagascar* **207** E18
Mason, *Mich., U.S.* **100** M11
Mason, *Tex., U.S.* **105** P8
Mason Bay, *N.Z.* **217** R15
Mason City, *Iowa, U.S.* **106** M12
Mason Hall, *Trinidad and Tobago* **123** N23
Masontown, *Pa., U.S.* **96** P3
Maspalomas, *Sp.* **208** R5
Masqaţ (Muscat), *Oman* **175** K16
Massa, *Congo* **205** J17
Massachusetts, *U.S.* **97** K14
Massachusetts Bay, *Mass., U.S.* **97** K16
Massacre, *Dominica* **123** F19
Massacre Bay, *Amer. Samoa, U.S.* **222** M7
Massafra, *It.* **152** M14
Massakory, *Chad* **201** J14
Massa Marittima, *It.* **152** H6
Massangena, *Mozambique* **206** G12
Massay, *Fr.* **149** S9
Mass City, *Mich., U.S.* **100** F6
Massena, *N.Y., U.S.* **96** F10
Massenya, *Chad* **201** J14
Masset, *B.C., Can.* **84** J7
Massiac, *Fr.* **149** V11
Massif Central, *Fr.* **149** U10
Massif du Tondou, *Cen. Af. Rep.* **202** G10
Massillon, *Ohio, U.S.* **101** P14
Massinga, *Mozambique* **207** H13
Masson Island, *Antarctica* **231** K21
Mastābah, *Saudi Arabia* **174** L7
Maştağa, *Azerb.* **171** D23

Masterton, *N.Z.* **217** M19
Másticho, Ákra, *Gr.* **157** J16
Mastuj, *Pak.* **178** K10
Mastung, *Pak.* **179** R6
Mastūrah, *Saudi Arabia* **174** K6
Masty, *Belarus* **158** K3
Masuda, *Japan* **189** Q6
Masuria, *Eur.* **140** F9
Masvingo, *Zimb.* **206** G11
Maşyāf, *Syr.* **172** F7
Mat, river, *Alban.* **154** K9
Mataabé, Cape, *Vanuatu* **222** D1
Matacawa Levu, island, *Fiji* **222** H5
Matadi, *Dem. Rep. of the Congo* **202** M7
Matador, *Tex., U.S.* **104** J6
Matagalpa, *Nicar.* **117** L18
Matagami, *Que., Can.* **85** N18
Matagorda, *Tex., U.S.* **105** S13
Matagorda Bay, *U.S.* **87** N13
Matagorda Peninsula, *Tex., U.S.* **105** S13
Mataiea, *Fr. Polynesia, Fr.* **223** P16
Mataiva, island, *Fr. Polynesia, Fr.* **223** D17
Matak, island, *Indonesia* **192** H8
Mátala, *Gr.* **157** R14
Matalaa, Pointe, *Wallis and Futuna, Fr.* **222** C11
Matale, *Sri Lanka* **181** T7
Matam, *Senegal* **200** G5
Mata Mata Vika, Ava, *Tonga* **222** Q7
Matamoros, *Mex.* **116** E12
Matane, *Que., Can.* **85** N21
Matanzas, *Cuba* **118** G7
Matapás *see* Ténaro, Akrotírio, *Gr.* **156** M10
Mata Point, *Cook Is., N.Z.* **223** B21
Matara, *Sri Lanka* **181** T7
Mataram, *Indonesia* **192** M12
Mataranka, *N.T., Austral.* **215** Q8
Mataró, *Sp.* **147** D18
Matasiri, island, *Indonesia* **192** L11
Mataso Island, *Vanuatu* **222** E2
Matatépai, Pointe, *Fr. Polynesia, Fr.* **223** M20
Matatiele, *S. Af.* **206** L11
Matātula, Cape, *Amer. Samoa, U.S.* **222** L9
Mataura, *Fr. Polynesia, Fr.* **223** K21
Mataura, Mouillage de, *Fr. Polynesia, Fr.* **223** K20
Matā'utu, *Wallis and Futuna, Fr.* **222** B11
Matautu, *Samoa* **222** L3
Mata-Utu, Baie de, *Wallis and Futuna, Fr.* **222** B11
Matautulele Point, *Amer. Samoa, U.S.* **222** M6
Matauvau, Passe, *Fr. Polynesia, Fr.* **223** N14
Matavai, Baie de, *Fr. Polynesia, Fr.* **223** N16
Matavanu, Mount, *Samoa* **222** K2
Matavera, *Cook Is., N.Z.* **222** Q9
Matcha, *Taj.* **178** H8
Mateguá, *Bol.* **132** H8
Matehuala, *Mex.* **116** G11
Mateika, island, *Tuvalu* **221** L23
Matelot, *Trinidad and Tobago* **123** N23
Matema, island, *Solomon Is.* **221** P23
Matera, *It.* **152** M13
Matese, range, *It.* **152** L10
Matészalka, *Hung.* **151** K17
Matfors, *Sw.* **143** H13
Mathematician Seamounts, *Pac. Oc.* **243** H19
Mather, *Calif., U.S.* **III** S6
Mathews, *Va., U.S.* **98** E14
Mathis, *Tex., U.S.* **105** T10
Mathráki, island, *Gr.* **156** E5
Mathura, *India* **180** F6
Mathurin Bay, *Mauritius* **209** J20
Mati, *Philippines* **193** F15
Matianxu, *Hunan, China* **185** S4
Matiere, *N.Z.* **217** K19
Matinicus Island, *Me., U.S.* **97** G17
Matira, Pointe, *Fr. Polynesia, Fr.* **223** L14
Matlerjoch, peak, *Aust., Liech.* **162** P4

Matli, *Pak.* **179** W7
Matlock, *Eng., U.K.* **145** S12
Matochkin Shar, *Russ.* **160** D11
Matopo Hills, *Af.* **198** N8
Matosinhos, *Port.* **146** E5
Matou, *Taiwan, China* **185** VII
Mátra, *Eur.* **140** H9
Maţraḥ, *Oman* **175** K16
Maţrûḥ, *Egypt* **201** C17
Matsu, island, *Fujian, China* **185** S11
Matsubara, *Japan* **189** W3
Matsue, *Japan* **189** P7
Matsumoto, *Japan* **189** N10
Matsuyama, *Japan* **189** R6
Mattamuskeet, Lake, *N.C., U.S.* **98** H14
Mattaponi, river, *Va., U.S.* **98** E13
Mattawamkeag, *Me., U.S.* **97** D18
Matterhorn, peak, *It., Switz.* **152** C3
Matterhorn, peak, *Nev., U.S.* **110** L11
Matthew, island, *Vanuatu* **218** K8
Matthews Peak, *U.S.* **86** H8
Matthew's Ridge, *Guyana* **131** D13
Matthew Town, *Bahamas* **119** J14
Maţţī, Sabkhat, *Saudi Arabia, U.A.E.* **175** K13
Mattili, *India* **180** L8
Mattinata, *It.* **152** L13
Mattoon, *Ill., U.S.* **101** S6
Matua, *Indonesia* **192** K9
Matua, island, *Russ.* **161** H23
Matuku, island, *Fiji* **222** K8
Matunga, island, *Cook Is., N.Z.* **223** A17
Matunuck, *R.I., U.S.* **97** M14
Matura, *Trinidad and Tobago* **123** P23
Matura Bay, *Trinidad and Tobago* **123** P24
Maturei Vavao, island, *Fr. Polynesia, Fr.* **223** G22
Maturín, *Venez.* **130** C12
Matxitxako, Cape, *Eur.* **140** J3
Maúa, *Mozambique* **207** E14
Maubara, *Timor-Leste* **193** M15
Maubeuge, *Fr.* **148** M11
Maude, *N.S.W., Austral.* **215** X12
Maud Hill, *Atl. Oc.* **248** H8
Maud Rise, *Atl. Oc.* **241** X12
Maués, *Braz.* **132** D10
Maughold Head (Kione Maghal), *Isle of Man, U.K.* **145** Q9
Maug Islands, *N. Mariana Is., U.S.* **220** A2
Maui, island, *Hawai'i, U.S.* **115** G17
Mauke, island, *Cook Is., N.Z.* **218** K12
Maukme, *Myanmar* **190** H7
Maule, river, *Chile* **134** M6
Mauléon, *Fr.* **149** S6
Maullín, *Chile* **135** Q6
Maumee, *Ohio, U.S.* **101** N12
Maumee, river, *Ohio, U.S.* **101** P11
Maumusson, Pertuis de, *Fr.* **149** U6
Maun, *Botswana* **206** G9
Maunabo, *P.R., U.S.* **122** N5
Mauna Iki, peak, *Hawai'i, U.S.* **115** P20
Mauna Kea (Pu'uwēkiu), peak, *Hawai'i, U.S.* **115** M20
Mauna Kea Adz Quarry, *Hawai'i, U.S.* **115** M20
Mauna Kea Observatories, *Hawai'i, U.S.* **115** M20
Mauna Loa, peak, *Hawai'i, U.S.* **115** N19
Maunaloa, *Hawai'i, U.S.* **115** F14
Mauna Loa Observatory, *Hawai'i, U.S.* **115** N20
Maunalua Bay, *Hawai'i, U.S.* **114** F12
Mauna Ulu, peak, *Hawai'i, U.S.* **115** N21
Maungapu, peak, *Cook Is., N.Z.* **222** P11
Maungdaw, *Myanmar* **190** H4
Maunoir, Lac, *N.W.T., Can.* **84** F10
Maupihaa (Mopelia), island, *Fr. Polynesia, Fr.* **223** E14
Maupin, *Oreg., U.S.* **110** F5
Maupiti, island, *Fr. Polynesia, Fr.* **223** E15
Mau Ranipur, *India* **180** H7
Mauren, *Liech.* **162** M2
Maurepas, Lake, *La., U.S.* **102** P10

Maures, Monts des, *Fr.* **149** Y14
Mauriac, *Fr.* **149** V10
Maurice, Lake, *Austral.* **214** H8
Maurice Ewing Bank, *Atl. Oc.* **241** V7
Maurice Hill Ridge, *Ind. Oc.* **224** G7
Mauritania, *Af.* **200** F6
Mauritania, region, *Af.* **198** F2
Mauritius Trench, *Ind. Oc.* **224** L7
Mauron, *Fr.* **149** Q5
Maury Bay, *Antarctica* **231** P19
Maury Mountains, *Oreg., U.S.* **110** H6
Maury Seachannel, *Atl. Oc.* **240** G9
Mauston, *Wis., U.S.* **100** K4
Mautaro, Motu, *Fr. Polynesia, Fr.* **223** K21
Mautau, Pointe, *Fr. Polynesia, Fr.* **223** M21
Mauvezin, *Fr.* **149** X8
Maverick, *Ariz., U.S.* **109** T9
Mavinga, *Angola* **206** E8
Mavone, river, *It.* **163** G15
Mavroli, *Cyprus* **162** P6
Mavrovouni Mine, *Cyprus* **162** P7
Mawarīd, 'Urūq al, *Yemen* **174** N12
Mawlamyine, *Myanmar* **190** L7
Mawlite, *Myanmar* **190** F5
Mawlu, *Myanmar* **190** F6
Mawqaq, *Saudi Arabia* **174** H8
Mawshij, *Yemen* **174** Q8
Mawson, station, *Antarctica* **231** E20
Mawson Bank, *Pac. Oc.* **249** H15
Mawson Coast, *Antarctica* **231** E20
Mawson Escarpment, *Antarctica* **231** F18
Mawson Peninsula, *Antarctica* **231** R16
Max, *N. Dak., U.S.* **106** F4
Maxixe, *Mozambique* **207** H13
Maxton, *N.C., U.S.* **98** J11
Maxwell Fracture Zone, *Atl. Oc.* **240** H9
May, Isle of, *Scot., U.K.* **144** M11
Mayabandar, *India* **181** P14
Mayaguana Island, *Bahamas* **119** H16
Mayaguana Passage, *Bahamas* **119** H15
Mayagüez, *P.R., U.S.* **122** N1
Mayagüez, Bahía de, *P.R., U.S.* **122** N1
Mayāmey, *Iran* **175** C15
Mayang-do, island, *N. Korea* **186** G10
Mayaro Bay, *Trinidad and Tobago* **123** Q24
Maycock's Bay, *Barbados* **123** J18
Maydān Ikbiz, *Syr.* **172** C8
Maydh, *Somalia* **203** F17
Maydī, *Yemen* **174** P8
Mayenne, *Fr.* **149** Q6
Mayfa'ah, *Yemen* **174** Q11
Mayfield, *Ky., U.S.* **103** D13
Mayhill, *N. Mex., U.S.* **109** U13
Maykop, *Russ.* **159** T11
Mayluu-Suu, *Kyrg.* **178** F10
Mayneside, *Qnsld., Austral.* **215** T12
Mayno Gytkino, *Russ.* **161** C21
Mayo, *Fla., U.S.* **99** R6
Mayo, *Trinidad and Tobago* **123** Q22
Mayo, *Yukon, Can.* **84** F8
Mayo, Cerro, *Chile* **135** V6
Mayo Faran, *Nigeria* **205** D16
Mayo Ndaga, *Nigeria* **205** E16
Mayorga, *Sp.* **146** D9
Mayotte, island, *Mayotte, Fr.* **209** P17
May Pen, *Jam.* **122** J8
Mayreau, island, *St. Vincent and the Grenadines* **121** G16
Maysville, *Ky., U.S.* **103** A18
Maysville, *Mo., U.S.* **107** R11
Mayumba, *Gabon* **205** J15
Mayville, *N. Dak., U.S.* **106** F8
Mayville, *Wis., U.S.* **100** L6
Maywood, *Nebr., U.S.* **107** Q4
Mazabuka, *Zambia* **206** E10
Mazagão, *Braz.* **132** C12
Mazamet, *Fr.* **149** X10
Mazaradel Vallo, *It.* **153** S8
Mazār-e Sharīf, *Afghan.* **178** K6
Mazari Pass, *Pak.* **179** S3
Mazarrón, Golfo de, *Sp.* **147** L13
Mazaruni, river, *Guyana* **131** E13
Mazatán, *Mex.* **116** D7
Mazatenango, *Guatemala* **117** L15
Mazatlán, *Mex.* **116** F8
Mazgirt, *Turk.* **171** F14
Mazıdağı, *Turk.* **171** H15
Mazirbe, *Latv.* **143** L15
Mazotos, *Cyprus* **162** Q9
Mazrub, *Sudan* **202** E12
Mazyr, *Belarus* **158** M5
Mazzarino, *It.* **153** T10
Mazzocco, river, *It.* **162** K13
Mbabane, *Swaziland* **206** J11
Mbaïki, *Cen. Af. Rep.* **202** H8
Mbakaou Reservoir, *Cameroon* **205** E16
Mbala, *Zambia* **206** C12
Mbale, *Uganda* **203** J13
Mbalmayo, *Cameroon* **205** F16
Mbalo, *Solomon Is.* **221** P19
Mbamba Bay, *Tanzania* **203** P13
Mbandaka, *Dem. Rep. of the Congo* **202** K8
Mbang, Monts, *Cameroon* **205** D17
Mbanika, island, *Solomon Is.* **221** N18
M'banza Congo, *Angola* **206** B6
Mbanza-Ngungu, *Dem. Rep. of the Congo* **202** L7
Mbarara, *Uganda* **202** K12
Mbari, river, *Cen. Af. Rep.* **202** H10
Mbé, *Cameroon* **205** D16
Mbéni, *Comoros* **209** M14
Mbeya, *Tanzania* **203** N13
M'Binda, *Congo* **205** J16
Mbini, *Eq. Guinea* **205** G15
Mborokua, island, *Solomon Is.* **221** N17
Mbout, *Mauritania* **200** G6
Mbuji-Mayi, *Dem. Rep. of the Congo* **202** M10
Mbulo, island, *Solomon Is.* **221** N17
Mburucuyá, *Arg.* **134** G13
Mbuyuni, *Tanzania* **203** M14
McAlester, *Okla., U.S.* **104** H13
McAllen, *Tex., U.S.* **105** W10
McArthur, river, *Austral.* **214** C10
McArthur River, *N.T., Austral.* **215** Q9
McCall, *Idaho, U.S.* **108** F4
McCamey, *Tex., U.S.* **105** P4
McCammon, *Idaho, U.S.* **108** H7
McCaysville, *Ga., U.S.* **98** J5
McCleary, *Wash., U.S.* **110** C3
McClellanville, *S.C., U.S.* **98** M11
McCloud, *Calif., U.S.* **110** M4
McColl, *S.C., U.S.* **98** J10
McComb, *Miss., U.S.* **102** N10
McConaughy, Lake, *Nebr., U.S.* **107** P3
McCook, *Nebr., U.S.* **107** R4
McCormick, *S.C., U.S.* **98** L7
McCrory, *Ark., U.S.* **102** G10
McDermitt, *Nev., U.S.* **110** L9
McDonald, *Kans., U.S.* **107** R3
McDonald Peak, *Mont., U.S.* **108** C6
McGehee, *Ark., U.S.* **102** J9
McGill, *Nev., U.S.* **111** P12
McGrath, *Alas., U.S.* **113** H15
McGregor, *Minn., U.S.* **106** G11
McGregor, *Tex., U.S.* **105** N11
McGuire, Mount, *Idaho, U.S.* **108** E5
Mchinji, *Malawi* **206** E12
McIntosh, *Minn., U.S.* **106** F9
McIntosh, *S. Dak., U.S.* **106** H4
McKean Island, *Kiribati* **218** G10
McKeesport, *Pa., U.S.* **96** P3
McKees Rocks, *Pa., U.S.* **96** N3
McKenzie, *Tenn., U.S.* **103** E13
McKinley, Mount (Denali), *Alas., U.S.* **113** H16
McKinleyville, *Calif., U.S.* **110** M2
McKinney, *Tex., U.S.* **104** K12
McKinney, Lake, *Kans., U.S.* **107** U3
McKinnon, *Wyo., U.S.* **108** K9
McKittrick, *Calif., U.S.* **111** V6
McLaughlin, *S. Dak., U.S.* **106** H4
McLean, *Tex., U.S.* **104** G7
McLeansboro, *Ill., U.S.* **101** U6
McLean's Town (Self Town), *Bahamas* **122** E3
McLeod Bay, *N.W.T., Can.* **84** H12
M'Clintock Channel, *Nunavut, Can.* **85** E14
M'Clintock Inlet, *Nunavut, Can.* **85** A15
McLoughlin, Mount, *Oreg., U.S.* **110** K4
M'Clure Strait, *N.W.T., Can.* **84** C12
McMahon Line, *India* **180** F14
McMinnville, *Oreg., U.S.* **110** F3
McMinnville, *Tenn., U.S.* **103** F16
McMurdo, station, *Antarctica* **231** N13
McMurdo Sound, *Antarctica* **231** N14
McNary Dam, *Oreg., Wash., U.S.* **110** E7
McPherson, *Kans., U.S.* **107** T7
McRae, *Ga., U.S.* **99** N7
McVeigh, *Ky., U.S.* **103** C20
McVille, *N. Dak., U.S.* **106** F7
Mdennah, region, *Af.* **200** E8
Mdina, *Malta* **163** K22
Mead, Lake, *Ariz., Nev., U.S.* **111** U12
Meade, *Kans., U.S.* **107** V4
Meade, river, *Alas., U.S.* **113** C15
Meade Peak, *Idaho, U.S.* **108** J8
Meadow, *Tex., U.S.* **104** K4
Meadow, *W. Aust., Austral.* **215** V2
Meadow Lake, *Sask., Can.* **84** L11
Meadow Valley Wash, river, *Nev., U.S.* **111** T12
Mead Point, *British Virgin Is., U.K.* **122** R11
Mead's Bay, *British Virgin Is., U.K.* **122** R11
Meadville, *Pa., U.S.* **96** L3
Meander River, *Alta., Can.* **84** J10
Meares, Cape, *Oreg., U.S.* **110** F2
Mears, *Mich., U.S.* **100** K9
Meaux, *Fr.* **149** P10
Mebane, *N.C., U.S.* **98** G11
Mecatina, river, *Nfld. & Lab., Que., Can.* **85** L22
Mecca, *Calif., U.S.* **111** Y11
Mecca *see* Makkah, *Saudi Arabia* **174** L7
Mechanicsburg, *Pa., U.S.* **96** P7
Mechelen, *Belg.* **148** L12
Mechems, region, *Af.* **198** D3
Mechol, *F.S.M.* **221** C18
Mecitözü, *Turk.* **170** D10
Meck, island, *Marshall Is., U.S.* **220** M5
Mecklenburger Bucht, *Ger.* **150** B9
Mecúfi, *Mozambique* **207** D15
Mecula, *Mozambique* **207** D14
Medan, *Indonesia* **192** G5
Medanosa Point, *S. Amer.* **128** Q5
Médéa, *Alg.* **200** A11
Medellín, *Col.* **130** E4
Medford, *Okla., U.S.* **104** E10
Medford, *Oreg., U.S.* **110** K3
Medford, *Wis., U.S.* **100** H4
Medgidia, *Rom.* **155** F18
Media Luna, Cayo, *Cuba* **118** K11
Medical Lake, *Wash., U.S.* **110** C8
Medicine Bow, *Wyo., U.S.* **108** J12
Medicine Bow Mountains, *Colo., Wyo., U.S.* **108** K12
Medicine Bow Peak, *Wyo., U.S.* **108** K12
Medicine Hat, *Alta., Can.* **84** N11
Medicine Lake, *Mont., U.S.* **108** B13
Medicine Lodge, *Kans., U.S.* **107** V6
Medina, *N. Dak., U.S.* **106** G6
Medina, *N.Y., U.S.* **96** H5
Medina, *Tex., U.S.* **105** R8
Medina *see* Al Madīnah, *Saudi Arabia* **174** J7
Medina, river, *Tex., U.S.* **105** R9
Medinaceli, *Sp.* **146** E12
Medina del Campo, *Sp.* **146** E9
Medina de Pomar, *Sp.* **146** B11
Medina de Rioseco, *Sp.* **146** D9
Medina Lake, *Tex., U.S.* **105** R9
Medina Sidonia, *Sp.* **146** M8
Medinipur, *India* **180** J11
Mediterranean Sea, *Eur.* **240** J13
Mednogorsk, *Russ.* **160** J7
Mednyy, Ostrov, *Russ.* **161** E23
Mednyy Island, *N. Amer.* **82** Q1
Médoc, region, *Fr.* **149** V6
Mêdog (Maiduo), *China* **182** L7
Medora, *N. Dak., U.S.* **106** G2
Medren, island, *Marshall Is., U.S.* **220** H8
Medvezh'i Ostrova (Bear Islands), *Russ.* **161** C19
Medvezh'yegorsk, *Russ.* **160** D7
Medvezhy Trough, *Arctic Oc.* **247** D14
Medyado, island, *Marshall Is., U.S.* **220** L8
Medyai, island, *Marshall Is., U.S.* **220** L8
Meekatharra, *W. Aust., Austral.* **215** U3
Meeker, *Colo., U.S.* **108** L11
Meerut, *India* **180** E6
Meeteetse, *Wyo., U.S.* **108** G10
Mega, *Indonesia* **193** J18
Mēga, *Eth.* **203** H15
Megálo Chorió, *Gr.* **157** M18
Megalópoli, *Gr.* **156** K10
Mégara, *Gr.* **156** J12
Mégham, *Vanuatu* **222** D2
Meghri, *Arm.* **171** F20
Megiddo, *Israel* **172** L5
Megion, *Russ.* **160** H11
Megísti (Kastellórizo), island, *Gr.* **157** N22
Mehadia, *Rom.* **154** F12
Mehamn, *Nor.* **143** A14
Mehar, *Pak.* **179** U7
Meharry, Mount, *Austral.* **214** F3
Meherrin, river, *Va., U.S.* **98** F12
Mehetia, island, *Fr. Polynesia, Fr.* **223** F17
Mehmetcik *see* Galatia, *Cyprus* **162** M10
Me_h_ola, *W. Bank* **172** L6
Mehrīz, *Iran* **175** E14
Mehtar Lām, *Afghan.* **178** M8
Mei, river, *Guang., China* **185** U7
Meiganga, *Cameroon* **205** E17
Meighan Island, *Nunavut, Can.* **85** B14
Meigs, *Ga., U.S.* **99** Q5
Meihekou, *Jilin, China* **186** A14
Meiktila, *Myanmar* **190** H6
Meiningen, *Ger.* **150** G8
Meissen, *Ger.* **150** F10
Meitan, *China* **182** M11
Meizhou, *Guang., China* **185** U7
Meizhou Wan, *Fujian, China* **185** U10
Mejatto, island, *Marshall Is., U.S.* **220** K1
Mejillones, *Chile* **134** E6
Mejillones del Sur, Bahía de, *Chile* **134** E5
Mejit Island, *Marshall Is., U.S.* **220** F5
Mékambo, *Gabon* **205** G17
Mek'elē (Mekele), *Eth.* **203** E15
Mekerrhane, Sebkha, *Alg.* **200** D10
Mekhtar, *Pak.* **179** R8
Mekiro, island, *Fr. Polynesia, Fr.* **223** R21
Meknès, *Mor.* **200** B8
Mekong (Lancang, Mékôngk, Mènam) river, *Asia* **168** H9
Mékôngk (Mekong), river, *Cambodia* **191** N12
Mekong River Delta, *Vietnam* **191** P13
Mekoryuk, *Alas., U.S.* **112** J11
Melanesia, island, *Pac. Oc.* **218** G4
Melanesian Basin, *Pac. Oc.* **242** J9
Melbourne, *Fla., U.S.* **99** U10
Melbourne, *Vic., Austral.* **215** Z12
Melbourne, Mount, *Antarctica* **231** P14
Mele, Capo, *It.* **152** G3
Mélé Bay, *Vanuatu* **222** F2
Melegnano, *It.* **152** E4
Melekeok, *Palau* **220** N12
Melekeok Point, *Palau* **220** N12
Melenki, *Russ.* **158** J11
Melfi, *Chad* **201** J15
Melfi, *It.* **152** M12
Melfort, *Sask., Can.* **84** M12
Melgar de Fernamental, *Sp.* **146** C10
Melide, *Sp.* **146** B6
Meligalás, *Gr.* **156** L9
Melilla, *Sp.* **146** P11
Melinka, *Chile* **135** S6
Melipilla, *Chile* **134** L6
Melita *see* Mljet, island, *Croatia* **154** J7
Melitopol', *Ukr.* **159** R8
Mellansel, *Sw.* **143** G13
Melle, *Fr.* **149** T7
Melle, *Ger.* **150** D6
Mellen, *Wis., U.S.* **100** F4
Mellieħa, *Malta* **163** J21
Mellieħa Bay, *Malta* **163** J21
Mellish Rise, *Pac. Oc.* **242** L9
Mělník, *Czech Rep.* **150** G11
Melo, *Uru.* **134** K15
Melolo, *Indonesia* **193** N13
Melos *see* Mílos, island, *Gr.* **157** M13
Melrhir, Chott, *Alg.* **200** B12
Melrose, *Minn., U.S.* **106** J10
Melrose, *S. Aust., Austral.* **215** X10
Mels, *Switz.* **162** R1
Meltaus, *Fin.* **143** D15
Meluan, *Malaysia* **192** H10
Melun, *Fr.* **149** Q10
Melvich, *Scot., U.K.* **144** G9
Melville, *Sask., Can.* **84** N12
Melville, Cape, *Austral.* **214** B13
Melville, Lake, *Nfld. & Lab., Can.* **85** L22
Melville Bay, *Austral.* **214** A10
Melville Fracture Zone, *Ind. Oc.* **224** M8
Melville Hills, *Nunavut, N.W.T., Can.* **84** E11
Melville Island, *Austral.* **214** A7
Melville Island, *Nunavut, N.W.T., Can.* **85** C13
Melville Peninsula, *Nunavut, Can.* **85** G16
Melville Trough, *Arctic Oc.* **246** P10
Melvin, *Tex., U.S.* **105** N8
Melvin, Lough, *N. Ire., U.K.* **145** Q5
Mé Maoya, peak, *New Caledonia, Fr.* **222** D7
Memba, *Mozambique* **207** E15
Memboro, *Indonesia* **193** N13
Memmingen, *Ger.* **150** K7
Mémót, *Cambodia* **191** N12
Memphis, *Mo., U.S.* **107** Q13
Memphis, *Tenn., U.S.* **102** G11
Memphis, *Tex., U.S.* **104** H7
Mena, *Ark., U.S.* **102** G6
Mena, *Ukr.* **158** M7
Menahga, *Minn., U.S.* **106** G10
Menai Strait, *Wales, U.K.* **145** S9
Ménaka, *Mali* **200** H10
Mènam (Mekong), river, *Laos* **190** J9
Menard, *Tex., U.S.* **105** P8
Menard Fracture Zone, *Pac. Oc.* **243** Q17
Menasha, *Wis., U.S.* **100** J6
Mendana Fracture Zone, *Pac. Oc.* **243** L20
Mende, *Fr.* **149** W11
Mendebo Mountains, *Af.* **198** H10
Mendefera, *Eritrea* **203** E15
Mendeleyev Plain, *Arctic Oc.* **246** J9
Mendeleyev Ridge, *Arctic Oc.* **246** H9
Mendeleyevsk, *Russ.* **158** H16
Mendenhall, *Miss., U.S.* **102** M11
Mendi, *P.N.G.* **217** D18
Mendī, *Eth.* **203** G14
Mendip Hills, *Eng., U.K.* **145** W11
Mendocino, *Calif., U.S.* **111** P2
Mendocino, Cape, *U.S.* **86** E2
Mendocino Escarpment, *Pac. Oc.* **243** E15
Mendocino Fracture Zone, *Pac. Oc.* **243** E13
Mendocino Ridge, *Pac. Oc.* **243** E17
Mendota, *Calif., U.S.* **111** T5
Mendota, *Ill., U.S.* **101** N5
Mendoza, *Arg.* **134** K8
Mendoza Rise, *Pac. Oc.* **243** M20
Menehune Ditch, *Hawai'i, U.S.* **114** C5
Meneng Point, *Nauru* **221** F23
Meneng, region, *Nauru* **221** F23
Menetés, *Gr.* **157** P18
Meng, river, *Aust.* **162** P4
Mengcheng, *Anhui, China* **184** K7
Menge, island, *Marshall Is., U.S.* **220** N7
Mengen, *Turk.* **170** D7

Mengene Dağı, peak, *Turk.* 171 G18
Mengshan, *Guangxi Zhuang, China* 185 U2
Mengyin, *Shand., China* 184 H9
Menindee, *N.S.W., Austral.* 215 X12
Menkere, *Russ.* 161 F16
Menno, *S. Dak., U.S.* 106 M7
Menominee, *Wis., U.S.* 100 H7
Menominee, river, *Mich., Wis., U.S.* 100 G7
Menomonee Falls, *Wis., U.S.* 100 L7
Menomonie, *Wis., U.S.* 100 H2
Menongue, *Angola* 206 E7
Menor, Mar, *Sp.* 147 K14
Menorca (Minorca), island, *Sp.* 147 G20
Men'shikova, Mys, *Russ.* 160 E10
Mentasta Lake, *Alas., U.S.* 113 H18
Mentawai, Kepulauan, *Indonesia* 192 K5
Mentawai Islands, *Asia* 168 M10
Mentawei Basin, *Ind. Oc.* 225 G15
Mentawei Ridge, *Ind. Oc.* 225 G15
Mentawei Trough, *Ind. Oc.* 225 G15
Menton, *Fr.* 149 X16
Mentor, *Ohio, U.S.* 101 N15
Menyamya, *P.N.G.* 217 D19
Menzies, *W. Aust., Austral.* 215 W4
Menzies, Mount, *Antarctica* 231 F18
Me'ona, *Israel* 172 K6
Meppel, *Neth.* 148 H13
Meppen, *Ger.* 150 D6
Mequinenza, Embalse de, *Sp.* 147 E15
Meramangye, Lake, *Austral.* 214 H8
Meramec, river, *Mo., U.S.* 107 T14
Merampit, island, *Indonesia* 193 G16
Merano, *It.* 152 C7
Meratus, Pegunungan, *Indonesia* 192 K11
Merauke, *Indonesia* 193 N21
Mercan Dağları, peak, *Turk.* 171 F14
Mercara, *India* 181 Q5
Mercator Basin, *Pac. Oc.* 242 F10
Merced, *Calif., U.S.* 111 S5
Mercedes, *Arg.* 134 H13
Mercedes, *Arg.* 134 L12
Mercedes, *Arg.* 134 L9
Mercedes, *Tex., U.S.* 105 W10
Mercedes, *Uru.* 134 K13
Merceditas, *Chile* 134 H7
Mercherchar, island, *Palau* 220 P11
Mercy, Cape, *Nunavut, Can.* 85 G19
Mercy Bay, *N.W.T., Can.* 84 D12
Meredith, Cape, *Falk. Is., U.K.* 135 W11
Meredith, Lake, *Tex., U.S.* 104 G5
Mereeg, *Somalia* 203 J17
Merefa, *Ukr.* 159 P8
Méré Lava, *Vanuatu* 222 B2
Mergenevo, *Kaz.* 176 D6
Mergui Archipelago, *Myanmar* 191 N7
Mergui Terrace, *Ind. Oc.* 225 E15
Meriç, *Turk.* 170 C2
Meriç, river, *Turk.* 170 C2
Mérida, *Mex.* 117 H16
Mérida, *Sp.* 146 H8
Mérida, *Venez.* 130 C7
Meriden, *Conn., U.S.* 96 M12
Meridian, *Idaho, U.S.* 108 G3
Meridian, *Miss., U.S.* 103 L13
Meridian, *Tex., U.S.* 104 M10
Mérig, island, *Vanuatu* 222 B2
Meringur, *Vic., Austral.* 215 X11
Merir, island, *Palau* 218 F2
Meritxell, *Andorra* 162 H4
Merizo, *Guam, U.S.* 220 E10
Merkel, *Tex., U.S.* 104 L7
Merkine, *Lith.* 143 N17
Meroe, ruin, *Sudan* 203 D13
Merolia, *W. Aust., Austral.* 215 V5
Merowe, *Sudan* 203 D13
Merredin, *W. Aust., Austral.* 215 W3
Merrick Mountains, *Antarctica* 230 G7
Merrill, *Oreg., U.S.* 110 L4
Merrill, *Wis., U.S.* 100 H5
Merrillville, *Ind., U.S.* 101 P8
Merrimack, river, *N.H., U.S.* 97 H14
Merriman, *Nebr., U.S.* 106 M3
Merritt Island, *Fla., U.S.* 99 T10
Mer Rouge, *La., U.S.* 102 K9
Merryville, *La., U.S.* 102 N6
Mersa Fat'ma, *Eritrea* 203 E15
Mersch, *Lux.* 162 J10
Merseburg, *Ger.* 150 F9
Mersey River, *Eng., U.K.* 145 S10
Mersin, *Turk.* 170 J9
Mersing, *Malaysia* 191 U11
Merta Road, *India* 180 G4
Mertert, *Lux.* 162 J11
Merthyr Tudful *see* Merthyr Tydfil, *Wales, U.K.* 145 V10
Merthyr Tydfil (Merthyr Tudfu), *Wales, U.K.* 145 V10
Mértola, *Port.* 146 K6
Mertz Glacier, *Antarctica* 231 Q17
Mertz Glacier Tongue, *Antarctica* 231 R17
Mertzon, *Tex., U.S.* 105 N6
Meru, *Kenya* 203 K14
Méru, *Fr.* 149 N9
Merzifon, *Turk.* 170 D10
Merzig, *Ger.* 162 K11
Mesa, *Ariz., U.S.* 109 U7
Mesabi Range, *U.S.* 87 C14
Mesach Mellet, region, *Lib.* 201 E13
Mesará, Kólpos, *Gr.* 157 Q14
Mesa Verde National Park, *Colo., U.S.* 109 Q10
Mescit Tepe, peak, *Turk.* 171 D15
Meseong, island, *F.S.M.* 221 C16
Meseta, *Eur.* 140 K2
Me Shima, *Japan* 189 S3
Meskéné *see* Maskanah, *Syr.* 172 E10
Mesocco, *Switz.* 152 C4
Mesolóngi, *Gr.* 156 H8
Mesopotamia, *St. Vincent and the Grenadines* 123 L16
Mesopotamia, region, *Iraq* 174 C8
Mesquite, *Nev., U.S.* 111 T13
Mesquite, *Tex., U.S.* 104 L12
Messene, *Gr.* 156 L9
Messina, *It.* 153 R12
Messina, *S. Af.* 206 H11
Messina, Stretto di, *It.* 153 R12
Messíni, *Gr.* 156 L9
Messinia, Gulf of, *Eur.* 140 M9
Messiniakós Kólpos, *Gr.* 156 L9
Mestá, *Gr.* 157 H16
Mestia, *Rep. of Georgia* 171 A17
Mestre, *It.* 152 D8
Mesudiye, *Turk.* 170 D12
Meta, river, *N. Amer.* 82 Q10
Meta, river, *S. Amer.* 130 E8
Meta Incognita Peninsula, *Nunavut, Can.* 85 H19
Metairie, *La., U.S.* 102 Q11
Metalanim, *F.S.M.* 221 F14
Metalanim Harbor, *F.S.M.* 221 F14
Metaline Falls, *Wash., U.S.* 110 A9
Metallifere, Colline, *It.* 152 H6
Metán, *Arg.* 134 F9
Metaponto, *It.* 153 N14
Metaxádes, *Gr.* 157 A16
Meteora, ruin, *Gr.* 156 E9
Meteor Crater, *Ariz., U.S.* 109 S8
Meteor Rise, *Atl. Oc.* 241 U13
Meteor Seamount, *Atl. Oc.* 241 V13
Méthana, *Gr.* 156 K12
Methánon, island, *Gr.* 156 K12
Methóni, *Gr.* 156 L9
Metković, *Croatia* 154 H7
Metlakatla, *Alas., U.S.* 113 M24
Metlili Chaamba, *Alg.* 200 B11
Metolius, *Oreg., U.S.* 110 G5
Métoma, island, *Vanuatu* 222 A1
Metropolis, *Ill., U.S.* 101 V6
Mets Beverratap (Dəlidağ), peak, *Azerb.* 171 E20
Métsovo, *Gr.* 156 E8
Metter, *Ga., U.S.* 99 N8
Mettlach, *Ger.* 162 K11
Mettur Dam, *India* 181 Q6
Metz, *Fr.* 149 P14
Meulan, *Fr.* 149 P9
Meuse, river, *Belg., Fr.* 148 M12
Mexia, *Tex., U.S.* 105 N12
Mexiana, Ilha, *Braz.* 133 C13
Mexicali, *Mex.* 116 A5
Mexican Hat, *Utah, U.S.* 109 Q9
Mexico, *Me., U.S.* 97 F15
Mexico, *Mo., U.S.* 107 S13
Mexico, *N. Amer.* 116 H11
Mexico, Gulf of, *N. Amer.* 82 M6
Mexico Basin, *Atl. Oc.* 240 L1
Mexico City, *Mex.* 116 J12
Meyanodas, *Indonesia* 217 D14
Meyrargues, *Fr.* 149 X13
Mezdra, *Bulg.* 155 H13
Mezen', *Russ.* 160 E9
Mezen', river, *Russ.* 160 F9
Mezen' Bay, *Arctic Oc.* 140 B12
Mezhdusharskiy, Ostrov, *Russ.* 160 E10
Mézidon-Canon, *Fr.* 149 P7
Mézin, *Fr.* 149 W7
Mezőtúr, *Hung.* 151 L16
Mezzolombardo, *It.* 152 C7
Mġarr, *Malta* 163 H20
Mġarr, *Malta* 163 K21
Mi, river, *Hunan, China* 185 S5
Miahuatlán, *Mex.* 117 K13
Miajadas, *Sp.* 146 H8
Miami, *Fla., U.S.* 99 X10
Miami, *Okla., U.S.* 104 E14
Miami, *Tex., U.S.* 104 G7
Miami Beach, *Fla., U.S.* 99 X10
Miamisburg, *Ohio, U.S.* 101 R11
Mianchi, *Henan, China* 184 J4
Mīāndoāh, *Iran* 174 B10
Miandrivazo, *Madagascar* 207 G16
Mīāneh, *Iran* 174 B11
Miani Hor, lake, *Pak.* 179 V5
Mianrud, *Pak.* 179 T3
Mianwali, *Pak.* 179 P10
Mianyang, *China* 182 K10
Miaodao Liedao, islands, *Shand., China* 184 E11
Miao'er Shan, *Guangxi Zhuang, China* 185 T2
Miaoli, *Taiwan, China* 185 U11
Miarinarivo, *Madagascar* 207 F17
Miass, *Russ.* 160 J8
Michalovce, *Slovakia* 151 J17
Miches, *Dom. Rep.* 119 M20
Michigan, *U.S.* 100 H10
Michigan, Lake, *N. Amer.* 82 J7
Michigan City, *Ind., U.S.* 101 N8
Michurinsk, *Russ.* 158 L11
Micoud, *St. Lucia* 123 L14
Micronesia, islands, *Pac. Oc.* 218 E3
Midai, island, *Indonesia* 192 H8
Midang, *N. Korea* 186 L7
Mid-Atlantic Ridge, *Atl. Oc.* 240 M7
Middelburg, *Neth.* 148 K11
Middelburg, *S. Af.* 206 L9
Middle Alkali Lake, *Calif., U.S.* 110 M6
Middle America Trench, *Pac. Oc.* 243 G19
Middle Andaman, island, *India* 181 Q14
Middle Bight, *Bahamas* 118 F11
Middlebury, *Vt., U.S.* 96 G12
Middlegate, *Norfolk I., Austral.* 221 F20
Middle Island, *St. Kitts and Nevis* 123 B17
Middle Loup, river, *Nebr., U.S.* 107 P5
Middlemarch, *N.Z.* 217 Q16
Middleport, *Ohio, U.S.* 101 S14
Middle Quarters, *Jam.* 122 J7
Middle River, *Minn., U.S.* 106 E9
Middlesboro, *Ky., U.S.* 103 D19
Middlesbrough, *Eng., U.K.* 145 Q12
Middleton, *Qnsld., Austral.* 215 T12
Middleton, *Wis., U.S.* 100 L5
Middleton Ponds, *N.T., Austral.* 215 T8
Middletown, *Conn., U.S.* 97 M13
Middletown, *N.Y., U.S.* 96 M10
Middletown, *Ohio, U.S.* 101 S11
Midelt, *Mor.* 200 B8
Midi, Canal du, *Fr.* 149 Y9
Mid-Indian Basin, *Ind. Oc.* 224 L11
Mid-Indian Ridge, *Ind. Oc.* 224 G9
Midland, *Mich., U.S.* 100 K11
Midland, *S. Dak., U.S.* 106 L4
Midland, *Tex., U.S.* 104 M5
Midlothian, *Tex., U.S.* 104 L11
Mid-Pacific Mountains, *Pac. Oc.* 242 G11
Midu, island, *Maldives* 181 X3
Midway Islands, *Hawai'i, U.S.* 114 K2
Midwest, *Wyo., U.S.* 108 H12
Midwest City, *Okla., U.S.* 104 G11
Midyat, *Turk.* 171 H16
Midžor, peak, *Bulg., Serb.* 154 H12
Międzyrzecz, *Pol.* 150 D12
Miélan, *Fr.* 149 X7
Mielec, *Pol.* 151 G16
Miercurea-Ciuc, *Rom.* 155 D15
Mieres, *Sp.* 146 B9
Miguel Calmon, *Braz.* 133 H16
Migyaunglaung, *Myanmar* 190 M7
Mihalıççık, *Turk.* 170 E7
Mijas, *Sp.* 146 M9
Mijdaḩah, *Yemen* 174 Q11
Mijek, *W. Sahara* 200 E6
Mijikadrek, island, *Marshall Is., U.S.* 220 G8
Mikhaylovka, *Russ.* 159 N12
Mikkeli, *Fin.* 143 H16
Mikrí Préspa, Límni, *Gr.* 156 C8
Mikun', *Russ.* 160 F8
Mikura Jima, *Japan* 189 R12
Milaca, *Minn., U.S.* 106 H11
Miladummadulu Atoll, *Maldives* 181 T3
Milagro, *Ecua.* 130 K2
Milan, *Mo., U.S.* 107 R12
Milan, *Tenn., U.S.* 103 F13
Milan *see* Milano, *It.* 152 D4
Milano (Milan), *It.* 152 D4
Milas, *Turk.* 170 H3
Milazzo, Capo di, *It.* 153 R12
Milbank, *S. Dak., U.S.* 106 J8
Milbridge, *Me., U.S.* 97 F18
Mildenhall, *Eng., U.K.* 145 T14
Mile and a Quarter, *Barbados* 123 J19
Mile Gully, *Jam.* 122 J8
Mil Entrance, *F.S.M.* 221 C18
Miles, *Qnsld., Austral.* 215 V15
Miles, *Tex., U.S.* 105 N7
Miles City, *Mont., U.S.* 108 D12
Mileto, *It.* 153 R13
Miletto, Monte, *It.* 152 L11
Miletus, ruins, *Turk.* 170 G3
Milford, *Del., U.S.* 98 C15
Milford, *Iowa, U.S.* 106 M10
Milford, *Mass., U.S.* 97 K14
Milford, *Nebr., U.S.* 107 Q8
Milford, *Utah, U.S.* 109 N6
Milford Bay, *Trinidad and Tobago* 123 P17
Milford Haven (Aberdaugleddau), *Wales, U.K.* 145 V8
Milford Lake, *Kans., U.S.* 107 S8
Milford Sound, *N.Z.* 217 Q15
Milgun, *W. Aust., Austral.* 215 U3
Mili Atoll, *Marshall Is., U.S.* 220 H5
Miliés, *Gr.* 156 F11
Milikapiti, *N.T., Austral.* 215 N7
Mililani Town, *Hawai'i, U.S.* 114 E11
Milingimbi, *N.T., Austral.* 215 N9
Milk, river, *Can., U.S.* 86 B8
Milk, Wadi el, *Sudan* 202 D12
Mil'kovo, *Russ.* 161 F22
Milk River Bath, *Jam.* 122 K8
Millars Sound, *Bahamas* 122 B10
Millau, *Fr.* 149 W11
Mill City, *Oreg., U.S.* 110 G3
Milledgeville, *Ga., U.S.* 98 M6
Mille Lacs Lake, *Minn., U.S.* 106 H11
Millen, *Ga., U.S.* 98 M8
Millennium Island *see* Caroline Island, *Kiribati* 219 H13
Miller, *S. Dak., U.S.* 106 K6
Millerovo, *Russ.* 159 P11
Miller Peak, *Ariz., U.S.* 109 W8
Miller Point, *Solomon Is.* 221 R24
Millersburg, *Ohio, U.S.* 101 Q14
Millevaches, Plateau de, *Fr.* 149 U9
Milligan Cay, *St. Vincent and the Grenadines* 123 L17
Millington, *Tenn., U.S.* 102 F11
Millinocket, *Me., U.S.* 97 D17
Mill Island, *Antarctica* 231 K21
Mill Island, *Nunavut, Can.* 85 H17
Millmerran, *Qnsld., Austral.* 215 V15
Mill Reef, *Antigua and Barbuda* 123 B22
Milltown, *Mont., U.S.* 108 D6
Milltown Malbay (Sráid na Cathrach), *Ire.* 145 T3
Millungera, *Qnsld., Austral.* 215 S12
Millville, *N.J., U.S.* 96 Q10
Milly, *Fr.* 149 Q10
Milly Milly, *W. Aust., Austral.* 215 U2
Milne Seamounts, *Atl. Oc.* 240 J8
Milnor, *N. Dak., U.S.* 106 H7
Milo, *Me., U.S.* 97 E17
Milo, river, *Guinea* 204 C7
Miloli'i, *Hawai'i, U.S.* 115 P18
Milord Point, *Virgin Is., U.S.* 122 R3
Mílos (Melos), island, *Gr.* 157 M13
Mílos (Plaka), *Gr.* 157 M13
Milparinka, *N.S.W., Austral.* 215 V12
Milton, *Fla., U.S.* 99 Q2
Milton, *Pa., U.S.* 96 M7
Milton-Freewater, *Oreg., U.S.* 110 E8
Milton Keynes, *Eng., U.K.* 145 U13
Miltonvale, *Kans., U.S.* 107 S7
Milu, island, *Marshall Is., U.S.* 220 K4
Miluo, *Hunan, China* 185 Q5
Milu Pass, *Marshall Is., U.S.* 220 K4
Milwaukee, *Wis., U.S.* 100 L7
Mimizan-Plage, *Fr.* 149 W6
Mims, *Fla., U.S.* 99 T9
Min, river, *China* 182 K10
Min, river, *Fujian, China* 185 S9
Mina, *Nev., U.S.* 111 R8
Mina Bazar, *Pak.* 179 Q8
Minahasa, *Indonesia* 193 H15
Minamata, *Japan* 189 S4
Minamisōma, *Japan* 188 M13
Minamitane, *Japan* 189 U5
Minami To, *Japan* 218 C3
Minami Tori Shima (Marcus Island), *Pac. Oc.* 218 C5
Minas, *Cuba* 118 J11
Minas, *Uru.* 134 L14
Minatitlán, *Mex.* 117 J14
Minbu, *Myanmar* 190 H5
Minco, *Okla., U.S.* 104 G10
Mindanao, island, *Philippines* 193 F15
Mindelo, *Cabo Verde* 209 B15
Minden, *Ger.* 150 D7
Minden, *La., U.S.* 102 K7
Minden, *Nebr., U.S.* 107 Q6
Minden, *Nev., U.S.* 111 Q6
Mindon, *Myanmar* 190 J5
Mindoro, island, *Philippines* 193 D13
Mindoro Strait, *Philippines* 193 D13
Mindouli, *Congo* 205 J17
Mine, *Japan* 189 Q4
Mineloa, *Tex., U.S.* 104 L13
Mineral'nyye Vody, *Russ.* 159 T13
Mineral Point, *Wis., U.S.* 100 L4
Mineral Wells, *Tex., U.S.* 104 L10
Minersville, *Utah, U.S.* 109 N6
Minfeng (Niya), *China* 182 G3
Mingan, *Que., Can.* 85 M21
Mingaora, *Pak.* 178 M10
Mingəçevir, *Azerb.* 171 D21
Mingəçevir Su Anbarı, *Azerb.* 171 C20
Mingenew, *W. Aust., Austral.* 215 W2
Mingguang, *Anhui, China* 184 L9
Mingin, *Myanmar* 190 G5
Minglanilla, *Sp.* 147 H13
Mingo Cay, *Virgin Is., U.S.* 122 M10
Mingteke, *China* 182 G1
Mingteke Pass, *Pak.* 180 A5
Mingulay Miughalaigh, island, *Scot., U.K.* 144 K6
Mingxi, *Fujian, China* 185 S8
Minhe, *China* 182 H9
Minho, river, *Jam.* 122 J8
Minho, river, *Port., Sp.* 146 D5
Minicoy Island, *India* 181 S3
Minidoka, *Idaho, U.S.* 108 H6
Minidoka Internment National Monument, *Idaho, U.S.* 108 H5
Minigwal, Lake, *Austral.* 214 J5
Minilya, *W. Aust., Austral.* 215 U1
Minimarg, *Pak.* 178 M12
Min'kovo, *Russ.* 158 F12
Minna, *Nigeria* 205 C13
Minneapolis, *Kans., U.S.* 107 S7
Minneapolis, *Minn., U.S.* 106 K11
Minnedosa, *Man., Can.* 85 N13
Minneola, *Kans., U.S.* 107 U5
Minneota, *Minn., U.S.* 106 K9
Minnesota, *U.S.* 106 H10

Minnesota, river, *Minn., U.S.* 106 K10
Minnewaukan, *N. Dak., U.S.* 106 E6
Miño, river, *Sp.* 146 B7
Minocqua, *Wis., U.S.* 100 G5
Minonk, *Ill., U.S.* 101 Q5
Minorca see Menorca, island, *Sp.* 147 G20
Minot, *N. Dak., U.S.* 106 E4
Minqing, *Fujian, China* 185 S10
Minquan, *Henan, China* 184 J6
Minsk, *Belarus* 158 K4
Minsk Mazowiecki, *Pol.* 151 E16
Minto, *N. Dak., U.S.* 106 E7
Minto, Lac, *Que., Can.* 85 K18
Minto, Mount, *Antarctica* 231 Q14
Minto Inlet, *N.W.T., Can.* 84 E12
Minturno, *It.* 152 L10
Minwakh, *Yemen* 174 P11
Mio, *Mich., U.S.* 100 J11
Mir, *Belarus* 158 L4
Mira, *It.* 152 E8
Mira, *Port.* 146 F5
Mīrābād, *Afghan.* 179 R2
Mirador, *Braz.* 133 F15
Miraflores, *Col.* 130 H7
Miragoâne, *Haiti* 119 M16
Miramar, *Arg.* 135 N13
Mirambeau, *Fr.* 149 U6
Mirampéllou, Kólpos, *Gr.* 157 Q16
Miram Shah, *Pak.* 179 P8
Miran, *China* 182 G5
Miranda, *Braz.* 132 L10
Miranda, river, *Braz.* 132 K10
Miranda de Ebro, *Sp.* 146 C12
Miranda do Douro, *Port.* 146 D8
Mirandela, *Port.* 146 D7
Mirando City, *Tex., U.S.* 105 U9
Mirandola, *It.* 152 E6
Mirano, *It.* 152 D8
Mira Por Vos, island, *Bahamas* 119 H14
Mīr Bachah Kōṭ, *Afghan.* 178 M8
Mirbāṭ, *Oman* 175 P15
Mirbāṭ, Ra's, *Oman* 175 P15
Mirebalais, *Haiti* 119 M17
Mirebeau, *Fr.* 149 S7
Mirecourt, *Fr.* 149 P13
Mirepoix, *Fr.* 149 Y9
Miri, *Malaysia* 192 G11
Miriam Vale, *Qnsld., Austral.* 215 U15
Mirim, Lagoa, *Uru.* 134 K15
Mirim Lagoon, *S. Amer.* 128 L8
Mīrjāveh, *Iran* 175 G17
Mirny, station, *Antarctica* 231 J21
Mirnyy, *Russ.* 161 H16
Mirpur, *Pak.* 179 N11
Mirpur Khas, *Pak.* 179 V8
Mirpur Sakro, *Pak.* 179 W6
Miryang, *S. Korea* 187 S11
Mirzapur, *India* 180 H8
Misgar, *Pak.* 178 K12
Mish'āb, Ra's al, *Saudi Arabia* 174 G11
Mishawaka, *Ind., U.S.* 101 N9
Mi Shima, *Japan* 189 Q5
Misima, island, *P.N.G.* 217 E22
Miskitos, Costa de, *Nicar.* 117 M19
Miskolc, *Hung.* 151 K16
Misool, island, *Indonesia* 193 K17
Misquah Hills, *Minn., U.S.* 106 E14
Miṣrātah, *Lib.* 201 C14
Mission, *S. Dak., U.S.* 106 M4
Mission, *Tex., U.S.* 105 W10
Mississippi, *U.S.* 102 L11
Mississippi, river, *N. Amer.* 82 J6
Mississippi Fan, *Atl. Oc.* 240 L2
Mississippi River Delta, *La., U.S.* 103 R13
Mississippi Sound, *Miss., U.S.* 102 P12
Mississippi State, *Miss., U.S.* 103 J13
Missoula, *Mont., U.S.* 108 D6
Missouri, *U.S.* 107 T13
Missouri, river, *N. Amer.* 82 H4
Missouri Valley, *Iowa, U.S.* 107 P9
Mistassini, Lac, *Que., Can.* 85 N19
Misterbianco, *It.* 153 S12
Mistissini, *Que., Can.* 85 N19
Misty Fiords National Monument, *Alas., U.S.* 113 M24

Misurata, Cape, *Af.* 198 D6
Mitau see Jelgava, *Latv.* 143 L16
Mitchell, *Ind., U.S.* 101 T9
Mitchell, *Nebr., U.S.* 107 N1
Mitchell, *Oreg., U.S.* 110 G6
Mitchell, *Qnsld., Austral.* 215 U14
Mitchell, *S. Dak., U.S.* 106 L7
Mitchell, river, *Austral.* 214 C12
Mitchell, Mount, *N.C., U.S.* 98 H7
Mitchell Lake, *Ala., U.S.* 103 K15
Mitchelstown (Baile Mhistéala), *Ire.* 145 U4
Mithankot, *Pak.* 179 S9
Mithi, *Pak.* 179 W8
Míthymna, *Gr.* 157 F16
Mitiaro, island, *Cook Is., N.Z.* 218 K12
Mitla, *Mex.* 117 K13
Mitla Pass, *Egypt* 173 Q2
Mito, *Japan* 189 N12
Mitre, peak, *N.Z.* 217 M19
Mitre Island see Fataka, *Solomon Is.* 218 J8
Mitrovica see Mitrovicë, *Kos.* 154 H10
Mitrovicë (Kosovska Mitrovica, Mitrovica), *Kos.* 154 H10
Mitsamiouli, *Comoros* 209 L14
Mitsero, *Cyprus* 162 P8
Mits'iwa (Massawa), *Eritrea* 203 E15
Mitsoudjé, *Comoros* 209 M14
Mitú, *Col.* 130 H8
Mitumba Mountains, *Dem. Rep. of the Congo* 202 N11
Mitwaba, *Dem. Rep. of the Congo* 202 N11
Mityushikha, Guba, *Russ.* 160 D11
Mitzic, *Gabon* 205 G16
Miughalaigh, island, *Scot., U.K.* 144 K6
Miyake Jima, *Japan* 189 Q12
Miyako, *Japan* 188 K13
Miyakonojō, *Japan* 189 S5
Miyazaki, *Japan* 189 S5
Miyazu, *Japan* 189 P8
Miyun, *Beijing Shi, China* 184 C8
Miyun Shuiku, *Beijing Shi, China* 184 C8
Mizdah, *Lib.* 201 C13
Mizen Head, *Ire.* 145 V3
Mizhi, *Shaanxi, China* 184 E3
Mizil, *Rom.* 155 E16
Mizo Hills, *India* 180 H14
Mizusawa, *Japan* 188 L13
Mjøsa, lake, *Nor.* 142 J11
Mladá Boleslav, *Czech Rep.* 150 G11
Mladenovac, *Serb.* 154 F10
Mława, *Pol.* 151 C15
Mlima Bénara, peak, *Mayotte, Fr.* 209 P17
Mljet (Melita), island, *Croatia* 154 J7
Mljetski Kanal, *Croatia* 154 H7
Mmabatho, *S. Af.* 206 J10
Moa, *Cuba* 119 K14
Moa, island, *Indonesia* 193 M16
Moa, river, *Af.* 204 D6
Moab, *Utah, U.S.* 109 N9
Moaco, river, *Braz.* 132 F6
Moa Island, *Austral.* 214 A12
Moala, island, *Fiji* 222 J7
Moananui, island, *Cook Is., N.Z.* 223 B17
Moanda, *Gabon* 205 H16
Moapa, *Nev., U.S.* 111 T12
Mobayi-Mbongo, *Dem. Rep. of the Congo* 202 H9
Mobeetie, *Tex., U.S.* 104 G7
Moberly, *Mo., U.S.* 107 S13
Mobile, *Ala., U.S.* 103 N14
Mobile, river, *Ala., U.S.* 103 N14
Mobile Bay, *Ala., U.S.* 103 P14
Mobile Point, *Ala., U.S.* 103 P14
Mobridge, *S. Dak., U.S.* 106 J5
Moca, *Dom. Rep.* 119 L18
Moca, *P.R., U.S.* 122 M1
Mocajuba, *Braz.* 133 D13
Moce, island, *Fiji* 222 J9
Moch, island, *F.S.M.* 221 B16
Mocha, Isla, *Chile* 135 N5
Mochenap, bay, *F.S.M.* 221 B16
Mocho Mountains, *Jam.* 122 J8

Mochonap, bay, *F.S.M.* 221 A15
Mochon Point, *N. Mariana Is., U.S.* 220 D8
Mochudi, *Botswana* 206 H10
Mocímboa da Praia, *Mozambique* 207 D15
Mocksville, *N.C., U.S.* 98 H9
Moclips, *Wash., U.S.* 110 C2
Môco, Morro de, *Af.* 198 M6
Mocoa, *Col.* 130 H4
Moctezuma, *Mex.* 116 C7
Moctezuma Trough, *Pac. Oc.* 243 H19
Mocuba, *Mozambique* 207 F14
Modane, *Fr.* 149 V15
Model, *Colo., U.S.* 109 P14
Modena, *It.* 152 F6
Modesto, *Calif., U.S.* 111 S5
Modica, *It.* 153 U11
Modot, *Mongolia* 182 D11
Mộ Đức, *Vietnam* 190 M14
Modugno, *It.* 152 M14
Moe, *Vic., Austral.* 215 Z13
Moengo, *Suriname* 131 E17
Moerai, *Fr. Polynesia, Fr.* 223 K23
Moerai, Baie de, *Fr. Polynesia, Fr.* 223 K23
Mogadishu see Muqdisho, *Somalia* 203 J17
Mogadouro, *Port.* 146 E7
Mogalo, *Dem. Rep. of the Congo* 202 J9
Mogán, *Sp.* 208 R5
Mogaung, *Myanmar* 190 E7
Mogi das Cruzes, *Braz.* 133 M14
Mogincual, *Mozambique* 207 E15
Mogocha, *Russ.* 161 K17
Mogoi, *Indonesia* 193 K18
Mogok, *Myanmar* 190 G6
Mogollon Rim, *Ariz., U.S.* 109 T8
Mogotes, Punta, *Arg.* 135 N13
Mohács, *Hung.* 151 N15
Mohala, *India* 180 K7
Mohall, *N. Dak., U.S.* 106 D4
Mohana, *India* 180 L9
Mohave, Lake, *Ariz., Nev., U.S.* 111 V12
Mohawk, river, *N.Y., U.S.* 96 J10
Mohe, *China* 183 A14
Mohéli see Mwali, *Comoros* 209 N15
Mohelnice, *Czech Rep.* 151 H13
Mohenjo Daro, ruins, *Pak.* 179 U7
Mohill (Maothail), *Ire.* 145 R5
Mohns Ridge, *Arctic Oc.* 247 H18
Mohnyin, *Myanmar* 190 E6
Mohon Peak, *Ariz., U.S.* 109 S5
Mohotani, island, *Fr. Polynesia, Fr.* 223 N21
Mohyliv-Podil's'kyy, *Ukr.* 159 Q4
Moindou, *New Caledonia, Fr.* 222 D7
Moineşti, *Rom.* 155 C16
Mo i Rana, *Nor.* 142 E12
Moirang, *India* 180 H14
Moirans, *Fr.* 149 U13
Moisie, river, *Que., Can.* 85 M20
Moissac, *Fr.* 149 W8
Moïssala, *Chad* 201 K15
Moita, *Port.* 146 J5
Mojácar, *Sp.* 147 L13
Mojados, *Sp.* 146 E10
Mojave, *Calif., U.S.* 111 W8
Mojave, river, *Calif., U.S.* 111 W10
Mojave Desert, *U.S.* 86 H5
Mojave National Preserve, *Calif., U.S.* 111 V11
Mojokerto, *Indonesia* 192 M10
Mokdale, *Indonesia* 193 N14
Mokil Atoll, *F.S.M.* 220 Q8
Mokokchung, *India* 180 G15
Mokpo, *S. Korea* 187 T7
Mol, *Belg.* 148 K12
Mola di Bari, *It.* 152 M14
Moláoi, *Gr.* 156 M11
Molat, island, *Croatia* 154 F5
Moldavia, region, *Rom.* 155 B16
Molde, *Nor.* 142 H10
Moldova, *Eur.* 159 Q4
Moldova, river, *Rom.* 155 B16
Moldova Nouă, *Rom.* 154 F11
Moldovearu, peak, *Rom.* 155 E14
Molepolole, *Botswana* 206 H10
Môle Saint-Nicolas, *Haiti* 119 L15

Molesworth, *N.Z.* 217 N18
Molina, *Chile* 134 L7
Molina de Aragón, *Sp.* 147 F13
Molina de Segura, *Sp.* 147 K14
Moline, *Ill., U.S.* 101 P4
Moline, *Kans., U.S.* 107 U9
Molinière Point, *Grenada* 123 L22
Molino, river, *San Marino* 163 J16
Moliterno, *It.* 153 N13
Mollendo, *Peru* 132 K5
Mollerussa, *Sp.* 147 D16
Molloy Deep, *Arctic Oc.* 247 H17
Molloy Fracture Zone, *Arctic Oc.* 247 H16
Molopo, river, *Af.* 206 J9
Moloundou, *Cameroon* 205 G17
Molsheim, *Fr.* 149 P15
Molson, *Wash., U.S.* 110 A7
Moltke, Cape, *P.N.G.* 221 K13
Molu, island, *Indonesia* 193 M17
Moluccas (Maluku), islands, *Indonesia* 193 K16
Molucca Sea, *Indonesia* 193 J15
Moma, *Mozambique* 207 F14
Moma, river, *Russ.* 161 E19
Mombasa, *Kenya* 203 L15
Mombetsu, *Japan* 188 F14
Mombetsu, *Japan* 188 G13
Momence, *Ill., U.S.* 101 P7
Momi, *Fiji* 222 J5
Momote, *P.N.G.* 217 B20
Mompach, *Lux.* 162 J11
Mompós, *Col.* 130 C5
Møn, island, *Den.* 142 N12
Mona, Isla, *P.R., U.S.* 119 N21
Monach Islands see Na h-Eileanan Theisgeir, *Scot., U.K.* 144 J6
Monaco, *Eur.* 162 E3
Monaco, Port of, *Monaco* 163 D21
Monaco R.R. Station, *Monaco* 163 E20
Monaco-Ville, *Monaco* 163 E21
Monadhliath Mountains, *Scot., U.K.* 144 K9
Monaghan (Muineachán), *Ire.* 145 Q6
Monahans, *Tex., U.S.* 105 N3
Mona Passage, *N. Amer.* 119 M21
Monarch Pass, *Colo., U.S.* 109 N12
Mona Reservoir, *Utah, U.S.* 108 M7
Monari, *Afghan.* 179 P7
Moncada, *Sp.* 147 H14
Moncalieri, *It.* 152 E2
Monchegorsk, *Russ.* 160 D8
Mönchengladbach, *Ger.* 150 F4
Monchique, Serra de, *Port.* 146 L5
Moncks Corner, *S.C., U.S.* 98 L10
Monclova, *Mex.* 116 E11
Monclova, *Mex.* 117 J16
Moncton, *N.B., Can.* 85 P21
Mondego, river, *Port.* 146 F6
Mondego, Cabo, *Port.* 146 F5
Mondego, Cape, *Eur.* 140 J1
Mondeodo, *Indonesia* 193 K14
Mondolfo, *It.* 152 G9
Mondoñedo, *Sp.* 146 B7
Mondorf, *Lux.* 162 K10
Mondovi, *Wis., U.S.* 100 J3
Mondovì, *It.* 152 F3
Mondragone, *It.* 152 M10
Mondy, *Russ.* 161 L15
Moneague, *Jam.* 122 H9
Monemvasía, *Gr.* 156 M11
Monessen, *Pa., U.S.* 96 P3
Monestier-de-Clermont, *Fr.* 149 V13
Monett, *Mo., U.S.* 107 V11
Monfalcone, *It.* 152 D9
Monforte, *Port.* 146 H6
Monforte de Lemos, *Sp.* 146 C7
Mongalla, *S. Sudan* 203 H13
Mongbwalu, *Dem. Rep. of the Congo* 202 J12
Móng Cái, *Vietnam* 190 G13
Mongers Lake, *Austral.* 214 J3
Monggümp'o, *N. Korea* 186 L4
Mongmong, *Guam, U.S.* 220 C11
Mongo, *Chad* 201 J15

Mongolia, *Asia* 182 D8
Mongolian Plateau, *Asia* 168 F10
Mongororo, *Chad* 201 J16
Mongoy, *Russ.* 161 K17
Mongton, *Myanmar* 190 H8
Mongu, *Zambia* 206 E9
Moni, *Cyprus* 162 Q8
Monier, Mount, *St. Lucia* 123 J14
Monistrol-sur-Loire, *Fr.* 149 V12
Monito, island, *P.R., U.S.* 119 M21
Monitor Range, *Nev., U.S.* 111 R10
Monkey Point see Mono Point, *N. Amer.* 82 Q8
Monkira, *Qnsld., Austral.* 215 U11
Monmouth, *Ill., U.S.* 101 P4
Monmouth, *Oreg., U.S.* 110 G3
Mono, island, *Solomon Is.* 221 L14
Mono, Punta, *Nicar.* 117 M19
Mono Lake, *Calif., U.S.* 111 R7
Monólithos, *Gr.* 157 N19
Monomoy Island, *Mass., U.S.* 97 L16
Monon, *Ind., U.S.* 101 Q8
Monona, *Iowa, U.S.* 106 M13
Monongahela, river, *Pa., W. Va., U.S.* 96 Q3
Mono Point, *N. Amer.* 82 Q8
Monopoli, *It.* 152 M14
Monreal del Campo, *Sp.* 147 F13
Mon Repos, *St. Lucia* 123 K14
Monroe, *Ga., U.S.* 98 L6
Monroe, *La., U.S.* 102 L9
Monroe, *Mich., U.S.* 100 N12
Monroe, *N.C., U.S.* 98 J9
Monroe, *Wash., U.S.* 110 B4
Monroe, *Wis., U.S.* 100 M5
Monroe City, *Mo., U.S.* 107 R13
Monroe Lake, *Ind., U.S.* 101 S9
Monroeville, *Ala., U.S.* 103 M14
Monrovia, *Liberia* 204 E6
Monschau, *Ger.* 150 G4
Monsoon Rise, *Ind. Oc.* 225 J15
Mönsterås, *Sw.* 143 M13
Montagne, *Bonaire, Neth.* 123 Q19
Montagne Pelée, peak, *Martinique, Fr.* 123 E22
Montague, *Calif., U.S.* 110 L3
Montague Island, *Alas., U.S.* 113 K17
Montalbán, *Sp.* 147 F14
Montalegre, *Port.* 146 D6
Montalto di Castro, *It.* 152 K7
Montana, *Bulg.* 155 H13
Montana, *U.S.* 108 D9
Montanja, *Curaçao, Neth.* 123 Q15
Montargil, Barragem de, *Port.* 146 H5
Montargis, *Fr.* 149 Q10
Montastruc-la-Conseillère, *Fr.* 149 X9
Montauban, *Fr.* 149 X9
Montauk Point, *N.Y., U.S.* 97 M14
Montbard, *Fr.* 149 R12
Montbéliard, *Fr.* 149 R14
Mont Belvieu, *Tex., U.S.* 105 Q14
Mont Blanc, *Eur.* 140 J5
Montblanc, *Sp.* 147 E16
Montbrison, *Fr.* 149 U12
Montceau-les-Mines, *Fr.* 149 S12
Montchanin, *Fr.* 149 S12
Mont-de-Marsan, *Fr.* 149 X6
Montdidier, *Fr.* 149 N10
Mont-Dore, *New Caledonia, Fr.* 222 E8
Monteagle, Mount, *Antarctica* 231 Q14
Monte Bello Islands, *Austral.* 214 E2
Montebelluna, *It.* 152 D8
Monte Carlo, *Monaco* 163 C21
Monte Carlo Beach Hotel, *Fr.* 163 A24
Monte Carlo Country Club, *Fr.* 163 A23
Monte-Carlo Radio and Television Station, *Monaco* 163 D21
Monte-Carlo Sporting Club d'Été, *Monaco* 163 B23
Monte Caseros, *Arg.* 134 J13
Montech, *Fr.* 149 X8
Montecito, *Calif., U.S.* 111 X6
Monte Comán, *Arg.* 134 L8
Monte Cristi, *Dom. Rep.* 119 L17
Montecristo, Isola di, *It.* 152 K5

Monte Dinero, *Arg.* **135** W9
Montefiascone, *It.* **152** J8
Monte Giardino, *San Marino* **163** K16
Montego Bay, *Jam.* **122** H6
Montego Bay, town, *Jam.* **122** H6
Montehermoso, *Sp.* **146** G8
Montejinni, *N.T., Austral.* **215** Q8
Montejunto, Serra de, *Port.* **146** H4
Montelicciano, *It.* **163** L16
Montélimar, *Fr.* **149** W12
Monte Lindo, river, *Parag.* **132** M9
Montello, *Nev., U.S.* **110** M12
Montemaggio, *It.* **163** L14
Montemarciano, *It.* **152** G9
Montemayor, Meseta de, *Arg.* **135** S9
Montemorelos, *Mex.* **116** F11
Montemor-o-Novo, *Port.* **146** J5
Montemuro, peak, *Port.* **146** E6
Montendre, *Fr.* **149** V7
Montenegro, *Eur.* **154** H8
Montepescali, *It.* **152** J6
Monte Plata, *Dom. Rep.* **119** M19
Montepuez, *Mozambique* **207** D14
Monte Quemado, *Arg.* **134** F10
Montereau, *Fr.* **149** Q10
Monterey, *Calif., U.S.* **111** T4
Monterey, *Tenn., U.S.* **103** E17
Monterey Bay, *Calif., U.S.* **111** T4
Monterey Canyon, *Pac. Oc.* **243** E17
Montería, *Col.* **130** D4
Monterotondo, *It.* **152** K8
Monterrey, *Mex.* **116** F11
Montesano, *Wash., U.S.* **110** D2
Monte San Savino, *It.* **152** H7
Monte Santu, Capo di, *It.* **153** N5
Montes Claros, *Braz.* **133** J15
Montescudo, *It.* **163** K18
Montese, *It.* **152** F6
Montevallo, *Ala., U.S.* **103** K15
Montevarchi, *It.* **152** H7
Montevideo, *Minn., U.S.* **106** K9
Montevideo, *Uru.* **134** L14
Monte Vista, *Colo., U.S.* **109** P12
Montezuma, *Ga., U.S.* **99** N5
Montezuma, *Iowa, U.S.* **107** P12
Montezuma, *Kans., U.S.* **107** U4
Montezuma Castle National
  Monument, *Ariz., U.S.* **109** S7
Montezuma Creek, *Utah, U.S.* **109** P9
Montfaucon, *Fr.* **149** V12
Montgenèvre, *Fr.* **149** V15
Montgomery, *Ala., U.S.* **103** L16
Montgomery, *W. Va., U.S.* **98** E8
Montgomery City, *Mo., U.S.* **107** S14
Monthey, *Switz.* **152** C2
Monti, *It.* **152** M4
Monticello, *Ark., U.S.* **102** J9
Monticello, *Fla., U.S.* **99** Q6
Monticello, *Ga., U.S.* **98** L6
Monticello, *Ill., U.S.* **101** R6
Monticello, *Ind., U.S.* **101** Q8
Monticello, *Iowa, U.S.* **107** N14
Monticello, *Ky., U.S.* **103** D17
Monticello, *Me., U.S.* **97** C18
Monticello, *Minn., U.S.* **106** J11
Monticello, *Miss., U.S.* **102** M11
Monticello, *N.Y., U.S.* **96** L10
Monticello, *Utah, U.S.* **109** P9
Montichiari, *It.* **152** E6
Montijo, *Port.* **146** J5
Montijo, *Sp.* **146** H7
Montilla, *Sp.* **146** K10
Montivilliers, *Fr.* **149** N7
Mont-Joli, *Que., Can.* **85** N20
Mont Kolofau, *Wallis and Futuna, Fr.*
  222 F12
Mont-Louis, *Fr.* **149** Z9
Montluçon, *Fr.* **149** T10
Montmarault, *Fr.* **149** T10
Montmédy, *Fr.* **162** K7
Montmirail, *Fr.* **149** P11
Monto, *Qnsld., Austral.* **215** U15
Montoro, *Sp.* **146** K10
Montoursville, *Pa., U.S.* **96** M7
Montpelier, *Idaho, U.S.* **108** J8
Montpelier, *Jam.* **122** H6
Montpelier, *Ohio, U.S.* **101** N11
Montpelier, *Vt., U.S.* **97** G13
Montpellier, *Fr.* **149** X11
Montpon-Ménestérol, *Fr.* **149** V7
Montreal, *Wis., U.S.* **100** F4

Montréal, *Fr.* **149** Y9
Montréal, *Que., Can.* **85** P19
Montreuil-Bellay, *Fr.* **149** S7
Montreux, *Switz.* **152** C2
Montrevault, *Fr.* **149** R6
Montrichard, *Fr.* **149** R8
Montrose, *Colo., U.S.* **109** N11
Montrose, *Scot., U.K.* **144** L11
Montsalvy, *Fr.* **149** V10
Montsec, Serra del, *Sp.* **147** D16
Montserrat, island, *Lesser Antil.*
  121 C16
Montserrat, Monestir de, *Sp.*
  147 D17
Monturull, Pic, *Andorra, Sp.* **162** K3
Monuafe, island, *Tonga* **222** H11
Monument, *Oreg., U.S.* **110** G7
Monumental Buttes, peak, *Idaho, U.S.*
  108 C4
Monument Valley, *Ariz., Utah, U.S.*
  109 Q8
Monveda, *Dem. Rep. of the Congo*
  202 J9
Monywa, *Myanmar* **190** G5
Monza, *It.* **152** D4
Monze, *Zambia* **206** F10
Monzón, *Sp.* **147** D15
Moody, *Tex., U.S.* **105** N11
Moʻokini Heiau, *Hawaiʻi, U.S.* **115** K18
Mooloogool, *W. Aust., Austral.* **215** U3
Möong Hsu, *Myanmar* **190** G7
Möong Köung, *Myanmar* **190** G7
Möong Nawng, *Myanmar* **190** G7
Möong Pan, *Myanmar* **190** H7
Moonless Mountains, *Pac. Oc.*
  243 F15
Moora, *W. Aust., Austral.* **215** W2
Moorcroft, *Wyo., U.S.* **108** G13
Moore, *Okla., U.S.* **104** G11
Moore, *Tex., U.S.* **105** S9
Moore, Lake, *Austral.* **214** J3
Moorea, island, *Fr. Polynesia, Fr.*
  223 N14
Moorefield, *W. Va., U.S.* **98** C11
Moore Haven, *Fla., U.S.* **99** V9
Mooreland, *Okla., U.S.* **104** E8
Moore's Island, *Bahamas* **122** B5
Moore Town, *Jam.* **122** J11
Moorhead, *Minn., U.S.* **106** G8
Moorhead, *Miss., U.S.* **102** J10
Moorish Castle, *Gibraltar, U.K.*
  163 N23
Moosehead Lake, *Me., U.S.* **97** D16
Moose Jaw, *Sask., Can.* **84** N12
Moose Lake, *Minn., U.S.* **106** H12
Mooselook-meguntic Lake, *Me., U.S.*
  97 F15
Moosonee, *Ont., Can.* **85** N17
Mootwingee, *N.S.W., Austral.*
  215 W12
Mopelia *see* Maupihaa, island,
  Fr. Polynesia, Fr. **223** E14
Mopti, *Mali* **200** H8
Moquegua, *Peru* **132** K5
Mora, *Minn., U.S.* **106** H11
Mora, *N. Mex., U.S.* **109** R13
Mora, *Sw.* **142** J12
Morača, river, *Montenegro* **154** J9
Moradabad, *India* **180** F6
Móra d'Ebre, *Sp.* **147** E16
Mora de Rubielos, *Sp.* **147** F14
Moraleda, Channel, *S. Amer.* **128** P4
Moraleja, *Sp.* **146** G7
Moraleja del Vino, *Sp.* **146** E9
Moran, *Tex., U.S.* **104** L8
Moran, *Wyo., U.S.* **108** G8
Morane, island, *Fr. Polynesia, Fr.*
  223 H22
Morant Bay, *Jam.* **122** J11
Morant Cays, *Jam.* **119** N13
Morant Point, *Jam.* **122** J12
Morar, Loch, *Scot., U.K.* **144** K7
Morava, river, *Czech Rep.* **151** J13
Moravia, region, *Czech Rep.* **151** H13
Morawhanna, *Guyana* **131** C14
Moray Firth, *Scot., U.K.* **144** J10
Morbi, *India* **180** J2
Morbihan, Golfe du, *Fr.* **149** R4
Mörbylånga, *Sw.* **143** M13
Morcenx, *Fr.* **149** X6
Mor Dağı, peak, *Turk.* **171** H18

Mordovo, *Russ.* **158** M11
Mordyyakha, *Russ.* **160** F11
Moreau, river, *S. Dak., U.S.* **106** J2
Morecambe, *Eng., U.K.* **145** Q11
Morecambe Bay, *Eng., U.K.* **145** R10
Moree, *N.S.W., Austral.* **215** W14
Morehead, *Ky., U.S.* **103** B19
Morehead City, *N.C., U.S.* **98** J14
Morehouse, *Mo., U.S.* **107** V16
Morelia, *Mex.* **116** H11
Morella, *Qnsld., Austral.* **215** T12
Morella, *Sp.* **147** F15
Morena, *India* **180** G6
Morena, Sierra, *Sp.* **146** K10
Moreni, *Rom.* **155** F15
Moreno Bay, *S. Amer.* **128** J4
Moreno Valley, *Calif., U.S.* **111** X9
Morere, *N.Z.* **217** K20
Moresby Island, *B.C., Can.* **84** K6
Moresby Seachannel, *Pac. Oc.*
  243 D16
Moreton, *Qnsld., Austral.* **215** P12
Moreton Bay, *Austral.* **214** H16
Moreton Island, *Austral.* **214** H16
Moreuil, *Fr.* **149** N10
Morez, *Fr.* **149** T14
Morfou Bay, *Cyprus* **162** N7
Morgan, *S. Aust., Austral.* **215** X11
Morgan, *Utah, U.S.* **108** K7
Morgan City, *La., U.S.* **102** Q9
Morganfield, *Ky., U.S.* **103** C14
Morgan Hill, *Calif., U.S.* **111** T4
Morganito, *Venez.* **130** E9
Morgantown, *N.C., U.S.* **98** H8
Morgantown, *W. Va., U.S.* **98** C10
Morgat, *Fr.* **149** Q2
Morges, *Switz.* **152** C1
Morgex, *It.* **152** D2
Mori, *China* **182** E6
Mori, *Japan* **188** H12
Moriah, *Trinidad and Tobago* **123** N18
Moriah, Mount, *U.S.* **86** F6
Moriarty, *N. Mex., U.S.* **109** S12
Morihong Shan, *Liaoning, China*
  184 A14
Morin Dawa, *China* **183** C15
Morioka, *Japan* **188** K13
Moriu, *Vanuatu* **222** E2
Morjärv, *Sw.* **143** E14
Mor Khun, *Pak.* **178** K12
Morkoka, river, *Russ.* **161** G16
Morlaas, *Fr.* **149** Y7
Morlaix, *Fr.* **149** P3
Mormanno, *It.* **153** P13
Mormon Lake, *Ariz., U.S.* **109** S7
Morne-à-l'Eau, *Guadeloupe, Fr.*
  123 E15
Morne au Diable, peak, *Dominica*
  123 D19
Morne Constant, peak, *Guadeloupe,*
  Fr. **123** G16
Morne Diablotins, peak, *Dominica*
  123 E19
Morne Macaque, peak, *Dominica*
  123 F19
Morne Raquette, *Dominica* **123** F18
Morne Seychellois, peak, *Seychelles*
  209 N20
Morne Trois Pitons, peak, *Dominica*
  123 F19
Mornington, *Qnsld., Austral.* **215** Q11
Mornington, Isla, *Chile* **135** V6
Mornington Island, *Austral.* **214** C11
Moro, *Pak.* **179** U7
Morocco, *Af.* **200** B8
Morogoro, *Tanzania* **203** M14
Moro Gulf, *Philippines* **193** F14
Morombe, *Madagascar* **207** H16
Morón, *Arg.* **134** L12
Morón, *Cuba* **118** H10
Mörön, *Mongolia* **182** C9
Morona, river, *Peru* **132** E3
Morondava, *Madagascar* **207** G16
Morón de la Frontera, *Sp.* **146** L10
Moroni, *Comoros* **209** M14
Morotai, island, *Indonesia* **193** H16
Moroto, *Uganda* **203** J13
Morovis, *P.R., U.S.* **122** M3
Morozov Ridge, *Arctic Oc.* **247** J13
Morozovsk, *Russ.* **159** Q12
Morpará, *Braz.* **133** H15

Morpeth, *Eng., U.K.* **145** N12
Morphou (Güzelyurt), *Cyprus* **162** N7
Morrill, *Nebr., U.S.* **107** N1
Morrilton, *Ark., U.S.* **102** G8
Morrinhos, *Braz.* **133** K13
Morris, *Ill., U.S.* **101** P6
Morris, *Minn., U.S.* **106** J9
Morris, *Okla., U.S.* **104** G13
Morris Jesup, Cape, *Greenland, Den.*
  82 A8
Morris Jesup Spur, *Arctic Oc.*
  247 J14
Morrison, *Ill., U.S.* **101** N4
Morristown, *N.J., U.S.* **96** N10
Morristown, *N.Y., U.S.* **96** F9
Morristown, *S. Dak., U.S.* **106** H3
Morristown, *Tenn., U.S.* **103** E19
Morrisville, *Vt., U.S.* **97** F13
Morro Bay, *Calif., U.S.* **111** V5
Morro Point, *S. Amer.* **128** K4
Morrosquillo, Golfo de, *Col.* **130** C4
Morrumbene, *Mozambique* **207** H13
Morshansk, *Russ.* **158** L11
Morsi, *India* **180** K6
Mortagne, *Fr.* **149** Q8
Mortara, *It.* **152** E4
Morteau, *Fr.* **149** S14
Morteros, *Arg.* **134** J11
Mortes, Rio das, *S. Amer.* **128** G8
Mortlock Islands, *F.S.M.* **220** R6
Morton, *Ill., U.S.* **101** Q5
Morton, *Miss., U.S.* **102** L11
Morton, *Tex., U.S.* **104** K4
Morton, *Wash., U.S.* **110** D4
Mortyq, *Kaz.* **176** D8
Moruga, *Trinidad and Tobago*
  123 Q23
Moruroa (Mururoa), island,
  Fr. Polynesia, Fr. **223** H21
Morvan, Monts du, *Fr.* **149** S12
Morven, *Qnsld., Austral.* **215** U14
Morven, peak, *Scot., U.K.* **144** K10
Morvern, peninsula, *Scot., U.K.*
  144 L7
Mosal'sk, *Russ.* **158** K8
Moscos Islands, *Myanmar* **190** M7
Moscow, *Idaho, U.S.* **108** D3
Moscow *see* Moskva, *Russ.* **158** J9
Moscow Canal, *Russ.* **158** J9
Moscow University Ice Shelf,
  Antarctica **231** N20
Mose, Cape, *Antarctica* **231** P19
Mosel, river, *Ger.* **150** G5
Moselle, river, *Eur.* **140** G6
Moses Lake, *Wash., U.S.* **110** C7
Moses Lake, town, *Wash., U.S.* **110** C7
Moshi, *Tanzania* **203** L14
Mosinee, *Wis., U.S.* **100** H5
Mosjøen, *Nor.* **142** F12
Moskva, *Taj.* **178** J8
Moskva, river, *Russ.* **158** J8
Moskva(Moscow), *Russ.* **158** J9
Moso, island, *Vanuatu* **222** E2
Mosonmagyaróvár, *Hung.* **151** K13
Mosquero, *N. Mex., U.S.* **109** R14
Mosquitia, region, *Hond.* **117** K18
Mosquito Cays, *N. Amer.* **82** P8
Mosquito Coast, *N. Amer.* **82** Q8
Mosquito Island, *British Virgin Is., U.K.*
  122 Q9
Mosquito Lagoon, *Fla., U.S.* **99** T9
Mosquitos, Golfo de los, *Pan.* **117** N20
Moss, *Nor.* **142** K11
Mossaka, *Congo* **205** H18
Mossburn, *N.Z.* **217** Q15
Mossel Bay, *S. Af.* **206** M8
Mossendjo, *Congo* **205** J16
Mossman, *Qnsld., Austral.* **215** Q13
Mossoró, *Braz.* **133** E17
Moss Point, *Miss., U.S.* **103** P13
Moss Town, *Bahamas* **122** F8
Most, *Czech Rep.* **150** G10
Mosta, *Malta* **163** K22
Mostaganem, *Alg.* **200** A10
Mostar, *Bosn. & Herzg.* **154** H7
Mostardas, *Braz.* **132** Q12
Mosteiros , *Azores, Port.* **146** Q4
Móstoles, *Sp.* **146** F10
Mosul *see* Al Mawşil, *Iraq* **174** C9
Mota, island, *Vanuatu* **222** B2
Motaba, river, *Congo* **205** F18

Mota del Cuervo, *Sp.* **146** H12
Motala, *Sw.* **143** L13
Motane *see* Mohotani, island, *Fr.*
  Polynesia, Fr. **219** H15
Motherwell, *Scot., U.K.* **144** M9
Motihia, Motu, *Fr. Polynesia, Fr.*
  223 K21
Motopu, *Fr. Polynesia, Fr.* **223** N20
Motril, *Sp.* **146** M11
Motru, *Rom.* **154** F12
Motru, river, *Rom.* **154** F12
Mott, *N. Dak., U.S.* **106** H3
Motta Misaki, *Japan* **188** G12
Motu, river, *N.Z.* **217** K20
Motueka, *N.Z.* **217** M18
Motu Ihupuku *see* Campbell Island,
  Pac. Oc. **218** R7
Motukitiu, island, *Cook Is., N.Z.*
  222 R12
Motul, *Mex.* **117** H16
Motuloa Island, *Tuvalu* **221** L23
Motupae, island, *Cook Is., N.Z.*
  223 B14
Motupe, *Peru* **132** F2
Motupupu Point, *P.N.G.* **221** K14
Moturakau, island, *Cook Is., N.Z.*
  222 Q11
Moturiki, island, *Fiji* **222** H7
Motus Manini, island, *Fr. Polynesia, Fr.*
  223 J13
Mututapu, island, *Cook Is., N.Z.*
  222 Q9
Mututapu, island, *Tonga* **222** H12
Motutunga, island, *Fr. Polynesia, Fr.*
  223 E19
Motykleyka, *Russ.* **161** F20
Mouchard, *Fr.* **149** S13
Mouchoir Passage, *N. Amer.* **119** J18
Moudjéria, *Mauritania* **200** G5
Moúdros, *Gr.* **157** E15
Mouila, *Gabon* **205** H15
Moulamein, *N.S.W., Austral.* **215** Y12
Mould Bay, *N.W.T., Can.* **85** C13
Moule a Chique, Cap, *St. Lucia*
  123 M14
Mòulede Gaesa, *Eq. Guinea* **208** M7
Moulins, *Fr.* **149** T11
Moulins-la-Marche, *Fr.* **149** P8
Moulton, *Ala., U.S.* **103** H14
Moultrie, *Ga., U.S.* **99** P6
Moultrie, Lake, *S.C., U.S.* **98** L10
Mouly, *New Caledonia, Fr.* **222** C8
Moulyinning, *W. Aust., Austral.*
  215 X3
Mound Bayou, *Miss., U.S.* **102** J10
Mound City, *Ill., U.S.* **101** V5
Mound City, *Kans., U.S.* **107** R10
Mound City, *Mo., U.S.* **107** R10
Moundou, *Chad* **201** K14
Moundsville, *W. Va., U.S.* **98** B9
Moundville, *Ala., U.S.* **103** K14
Mountainair, *N. Mex., U.S.* **109** T12
Mountain Brook, *Ala., U.S.* **103** J15
Mountain City, *Nev., U.S.* **110** L10
Mountain City, *Tenn., U.S.* **103** D21
Mountain Grove, *Mo., U.S.* **107** V13
Mountain Home, *Ark., U.S.* **102** E8
Mountain Home, *Idaho, U.S.* **108** H4
Mountain Lake, *Minn., U.S.* **106** L10
Mountain Nile *see* Jebel, Bahr el, *Af.*
  204 H13
Mountain View, *Ark., U.S.* **102** F9
Mountain View, *Hawaiʻi, U.S.* **115** N21
Mountain View, *Mo., U.S.* **107** V14
Mountain View, *Wyo., U.S.* **108** K8
Mountain Village, *Alas., U.S.* **112** H12
Mount Airy, *N.C., U.S.* **98** G9
Mount Arrowsmith, *N.S.W., Austral.*
  215 W11
Mount Ayr, *Iowa, U.S.* **107** Q11
Mount Barker, *W. Aust., Austral.*
  215 Y3
Mount Barnett, *W. Aust., Austral.*
  215 Q6
Mount Bellew (An Creagán), *Ire.*
  145 R4
Mount Carmel, *Ill., U.S.* **101** T6
Mount Carmel, *Pa., U.S.* **96** N8
Mount Cook, *N.Z.* **217** P16

Mount Coolon, *Qnsld., Austral.* 215 SI4
Mount Desert Island, *Me., U.S.* 97 GI8
Mount Dora, *Fla., U.S.* 99 T8
Mount Dora, *N. Mex., U.S.* 109 QI5
Mount Eba, *S. Aust., Austral.* 215 W9
Mount Egmont *see* Mount Taranaki, peak, *N.Z.* 217 LI8
Mount Elsie, *Qnsld., Austral.* 215 SI4
Mount Enterprise, *Tex., U.S.* 104 MI4
Mount Gambier, *S. Aust., Austral.* 215 ZII
Mount Hagen, *P.N.G.* 217 DI8
Mount Hope, *N.S.W., Austral.* 215 XI3
Mount Hope, *W. Va., U.S.* 98 E8
Mount Howitt, *Qnsld., Austral.* 215 UI2
Mount Ida, *W. Aust., Austral.* 215 V4
Mount Isa, *Qnsld., Austral.* 215 SII
Mount Jewett, *Pa., U.S.* 96 L5
Mount Keith, *W. Aust., Austral.* 215 V4
Mount Magnet, *W. Aust., Austral.* 215 V3
Mount Maunganui, *N.Z.* 217 JI9
Mount Morris, *Ill., U.S.* 100 N5
Mount Morris, *Mich., U.S.* 100 LI2
Mount Mulgrave, *Qnsld., Austral.* 215 QI3
Mountnorris Bay, *Austral.* 214 A8
Mount Olive, *Miss., U.S.* 102 MII
Mount Olive, *N.C., U.S.* 98 JI2
Mount Pleasant, *Iowa, U.S.* 107 QI3
Mount Pleasant, *Mich., U.S.* 100 KIO
Mount Pleasant, *Tenn., U.S.* 103 FI4
Mount Pleasant, *Tex., U.S.* 104 KI4
Mount Rainier National Park, *Wash., U.S.* 110 D4
Mount Rushmore National Memorial, *S. Dak., U.S.* 106 L2
Mount Saint George, *Trinidad and Tobago* 123 NI8
Mount Saint Helens National Volcanic Monument, *Wash., U.S.* 110 E4
Mount Sandiman, *W. Aust., Austral.* 215 U2
Mount's Bay, *Eng., U.K.* 145 Y8
Mount Shasta, *Calif., U.S.* 110 M3
Mount Sterling, *Ill., U.S.* 101 R3
Mount Sterling, *Ky., U.S.* 103 BI8
Mount Surprise, *Qnsld., Austral.* 215 RI3
Mount Taranaki (Mount Egmont), peak, *N.Z.* 217 LI8
Mount Vernon, *Ala., U.S.* 103 NI4
Mount Vernon, *Ill., U.S.* 101 T6
Mount Vernon, *Ind., U.S.* 101 U7
Mount Vernon, *Ky., U.S.* 103 CI8
Mount Vernon, *Mo., U.S.* 107 VII
Mount Vernon, *N.Y., U.S.* 96 NII
Mount Vernon, *Ohio, U.S.* 101 QI3
Mount Vernon, *Oreg., U.S.* 110 G7
Mount Vernon, *Tex., U.S.* 104 KI4
Mount Vernon, *W. Aust., Austral.* 215 U3
Mount Vernon, *Wash., U.S.* 110 B4
Mount Wynne Bay, *St. Vincent and the Grenadines* 123 KI6
Mount Zion, *Ill., U.S.* 101 R6
Moura, *Braz.* 132 D8
Mourão, *Port.* 146 J6
MourneMountains, *N. Ire., U.K.* 145 Q7
Mouroubra, *W. Aust., Austral.* 215 W3
Moussoro, *Chad* 201 JI4
Moutiers, *Fr.* 149 UI4
Moutsamoudou, *Comoros* 209 NI6
Mouzáki, *Gr.* 156 F9
Moweaqua, *Ill., U.S.* 101 R5
Moÿ, *Fr.* 149 NII
Moyale, *Kenya* 203 JI5
Moyo, *Uganda* 203 JI3
Moyobamba, *Peru* 132 F3
Moyu (Karakax), *China* 182 G2
Moyynqum, *Kaz.* 177 HI3
Moyynty, *Kaz.* 177 FI5
Mozambique, *Af.* 207 FI3
Mozambique Basin, *Ind. Oc.* 224 N5
Mozambique Channel, *Af.* 207 FI5

Mozambique Escarpment, *Ind. Oc.* 224 N4
Mozambique Plateau, *Ind. Oc.* 224 N4
Mozarlândia, *Braz.* 132 JI2
Mozdok, *Russ.* 159 TI3
Mozdūrān, *Iran* 175 CI7
Mozhaysk, *Russ.* 158 J8
Mozhga, *Russ.* 158 HI6
Mpanda, *Tanzania* 202 MI2
Mpandamatenga, *Botswana* 206 FIO
Mpika, *Zambia* 206 DI2
Mqabba, *Malta* 163 L23
Mrągowo, *Pol.* 151 BI6
Mrémani, *Comoros* 209 NI6
Mrkojević, Zaliv, *Montenegro* 154 K9
Msaken, *Tun.* 201 BI3
Msida, *Malta* 163 K23
Mstsislaw, *Belarus* 158 K6
Mt'a Didi Abuli, peak, *Rep. of Georgia* 171 CI8
Mthatha, *S. Af.* 206 LII
Mtkvari (Kura), river, *Rep. of Georgia* 171 CI8
Mtsensk, *Russ.* 158 L9
Mts'khet'a, *Rep. of Georgia* 171 CI8
Mtwara, *Tanzania* 203 NI5
Mu'a, *Tonga* 222 JI2
Mua, *Wallis and Futuna, Fr.* 222 BII
Mua, *Wallis and Futuna, Fr.* 222 EII
Mua, Baie de, *Wallis and Futuna, Fr.* 222 CII
Mualama, *Mozambique* 207 FI4
Muan, *S. Korea* 187 T7
Muang Béng, *Laos* 190 H9
Muang Kao, *Laos* 190 MI3
Muang Khamkeut, *Laos* 190 KII
Muang Khôngxédôn, *Laos* 190 LI2
Muang Ngoy, *Laos* 190 HIO
Muang Pakbèng, *Laos* 190 J9
Muang Paklay, *Laos* 190 K9
Muang Paksan, *Laos* 190 JII
Muang Phin, *Laos* 190 LI2
Muang Sing, *Myanmar* 190 H9
Muang Souvannakhili, *Laos* 190 LI2
Muang Xépôn, *Laos* 190 KI2
Muang Xianghon, *Laos* 190 J9
Muang Xon, *Laos* 190 HIO
Muar, *Malaysia* 191 VIO
Muaraaman, *Indonesia* 192 K6
Muarabungo, *Indonesia* 192 J6
Muaraenim, *Indonesia* 192 K7
Muarakumpe, *Indonesia* 192 J7
Muaramawai, *Indonesia* 192 JI2
Muaratewe, *Indonesia* 192 JII
Mubi, *Nigeria* 205 CI6
Mubong, *N. Korea* 186 CII
Mucajaí, river, *Braz.* 132 B8
Muchachos, Roque de los, *Sp.* 208 Q3
Much'ang, *N. Korea* 186 BI3
Muchea, *W. Aust., Austral.* 215 X2
Muchinga Mountains, *Zambia* 206 DI2
Muchkapskiy, *Russ.* 158 MI2
Muchot, Puntan, *N. Mariana Is., U.S.* 220 B4
Muck, island, *Scot., U.K.* 144 K7
Muckety, *N.T., Austral.* 215 R9
Muckle Flugga, island, *Scot., U.K.* 144 CI2
Muckle Roe, island, *Scot., U.K.* 144 DI2
Muconda, *Angola* 206 C8
Mucur, *Turk.* 170 F9
Mucuripe, Ponta de, *Braz.* 133 EI7
Mucusso, *Angola* 206 F8
Muda, peak, *Sp.* 208 Q7
Mudanjiang, *China* 183 DI7
Mudanya, *Turk.* 170 D4
Muḍayrib, *Oman* 175 KI6
Muddy Gap, *Wyo., U.S.* 108 JII
Mudhol, *India* 181 N4
Mud Lake, *Idaho, U.S.* 108 G7
Mudurnu, *Turk.* 170 D7
Mueda, *Mozambique* 207 DI5
Muéo, *New Caledonia, Fr.* 222 D7
Muertos, Isla Caja de, *P.R., U.S.* 122 P3
Muertos Cays, *Bahamas* 118 F9
Mufulira, *Zambia* 206 DII

Muga, Pico de la, *Sp.* 162 K5
Muğanlı, *Azerb.* 171 C2O
Mughalzhar Taüy, *Kaz.* 176 E9
Mu Gia Pass, *Vietnam* 190 KI2
Muğla, *Turk.* 170 H4
Muglad, *Sudan* 202 FII
Muglad Basin, *Sudan* 202 FII
Mugu, *Nepal* 180 E8
Mūḩ, Sabkhat al, *Syr.* 172 GIO
Muhammad Āghah Wuluswālī, *Afghan.* 178 M8
Muhammad Qol, *Sudan* 203 CI4
Muḩayy, *Jordan* 173 P6
Muhembo, *Botswana* 206 F8
Mühleholz, *Liech.* 162 P2
Muhlenfels Point, *Virgin Is., U.S.* 122 N9
Mühlhausen, *Ger.* 150 F8
Mühlig-Hofmann Mountains, *Antarctica* 231 BI3
Mūi Cà Mau, *Vietnam* 191 RII
Mūi Cà Ná, *Vietnam* 191 PI4
Mūi Dao, *Vietnam* 190 KI2
Muineachán *see* Monaghan, *Ire.* 145 Q6
Muine Bheag, *Ire.* 145 T6
Muir Woods National Monument, *Calif., U.S.* 111 R3
Muisne, *Ecua.* 130 J2
Mukacheve, *Ukr.* 159 PI
Mukah, *Malaysia* 192 HIO
Mukayris, *Yemen* 174 QIO
Mukeru, *Palau* 220 NII
Muko Jima Rettō (Parry Group), *Japan* 189 WI4
Mukomuko, *Indonesia* 192 K6
Mukry, *Turkm.* 176 MII
Muktinath, *Nepal* 180 F9
Mul, *India* 180 L7
Mula, river, *India* 180 L4
Muladu, island, *Maldives* 181 T3
Mulaku Atoll, *Maldives* 181 V3
Mulanie Mountains, *Af.* 198 MIO
Mulâtre, Pointe, *Dominica* 123 G2O
Mulazzano, *It.* 163 HI8
Mulberry, *Ark., U.S.* 102 F6
Mulberry Creek, *Tex., U.S.* 104 H6
Mulchatna, river, *Alas., U.S.* 113 KI4
Muldraugh, *Ky., U.S.* 103 CI6
Mulegé, *Mex.* 116 D6
Mule Peak, *N. Mex., U.S.* 109 UI3
Muleshoe, *Tex., U.S.* 104 J4
Mulgathing, *S. Aust., Austral.* 215 W9
Mulgrave Island *see* Badu Island, *Qnsld., Austral.* 215 NI2
Mulhacén, peak, *Sp.* 146 LII
Mülheim, *Ger.* 150 E5
Mulhouse, *Fr.* 149 RI5
Mulifanua, *Samoa* 222 L2
Mulinu'u, Cape, *Samoa* 222 KI
Mulitapuili, Cape, *Samoa* 222 L3
Mulitefala, island, *Tuvalu* 221 J24
Mull, island, *Scot., U.K.* 144 L7
Mull, Sound of, *Scot., U.K.* 144 L7
Mullan, *Idaho, U.S.* 108 C4
Mullen, *Nebr., U.S.* 107 N4
Mullens, *W. Va., U.S.* 98 E8
Mullet Peninsula, *Ire.* 145 Q3
Mullett Lake, *Mich., U.S.* 100 GII
Mullewa, *W. Aust., Austral.* 215 V2
Mullingar (An Muileann gCearr), *Ire.* 145 R6
Mullins, *S.C., U.S.* 98 KII
Mull of Galloway, cape, *Scot., U.K.* 145 P8
Mulobezi, *Zambia* 206 F9
Mulroy Bay, *Ire.* 145 N5
Multan, *Pak.* 179 RIO
Mulvane, *Kans., U.S.* 107 U8
Mumbai (Bombay), *India* 180 L3
Mumbwa, *Zambia* 206 EIO
Mumra, *Russ.* 159 RI5
Muna, island, *Indonesia* 193 LI4
Muna, river, *Russ.* 161 GI6
Munaba, *India* 180 G2
Munan Pass, *China, Vietnam* 190 GI2

Muncie, *Ind., U.S.* 101 RIO
Muncy, *Pa., U.S.* 96 M7
Munda, *Solomon Is.* 221 MI6
Mundabullangana, *W. Aust., Austral.* 215 S3
Munday, *Tex., U.S.* 104 K8
Münden, *Ger.* 150 F7
Mundiwindi, *W. Aust., Austral.* 215 T4
Mundōk, *N. Korea* 186 H6
Mundra, *India* 180 JI
Mundrabilla, *W. Aust., Austral.* 215 W7
Munera, *Sp.* 146 HI2
Mungapdo, island, *S. Korea* 187 N6
Mungbere, *Dem. Rep. of the Congo* 202 JI2
Mungeli, *India* 180 J8
Munger, *India* 180 HIO
Mungindi, *N.S.W., Austral.* 215 VI4
Munguba, *Braz.* 132 DI2
Mungyeong, *S. Korea* 187 PIO
Munia, island, *Fiji* 222 H9
Munich *see* München, *Ger.* 150 K9
Municipal Administrative Center, *Monaco* 163 E2O
Munising, *Mich., U.S.* 100 F8
Munku Sardyk, Gora, *Russ.* 161 LI4
Munsa, *N. Korea* 186 H5
Munsan, *S. Korea* 186 M8
Münster, *Ger.* 150 E6
Munster (Cúige Mumhan), region, *Ire.* 145 U4
Muntok, *Indonesia* 192 K7
Munyeodo, island, *S. Korea* 187 R7
Munzur Dağları, *Turk.* 171 FI4
Mu'omu'a, island, *Tonga* 222 MII
Mường Tè, *Laos* 190 GIO
Mường Xén, *Vietnam* 190 JII
Muonio, *Fin.* 143 DI4
Muping, *Shand., China* 184 FI2
Muqdisho (Mogadishu), *Somalia* 203 JI7
Muqêr, *Afghan.* 179 P7
Müqtǝdir, *Azerb.* 171 C22
Mur, river, *Aust.* 150 MIO
Muradiye, *Turk.* 171 FI8
Murakami, *Japan* 188 MI2
Muralag Island *see* Prince of Wales Island, *Qnsld., Austral.* 215 NI2
Murang'a, *Kenya* 203 KI4
Murashi, *Russ.* 160 G8
Murat, *Fr.* 149 VIO
Murat, river, *Turk.* 171 FI6
Murata, San Marino 163 KI5
Murat Dağı, peak, *Turk.* 170 F5
Muratlı, *Turk.* 170 C3
Muravera, *It.* 153 P4
Murazzano, *It.* 152 F2
Murça, *Port.* 146 E7
Murchison, river, *Austral.* 214 H2
Murchison Downs, *W. Aust., Austral.* 215 V3
Murchison Falls, *Af.* 198 J9
Murcia, *Sp.* 147 KI4
Murcuripe Point, *S. Amer.* 128 EII
Mur-de-Bretagne, *Fr.* 149 Q4
Murdo, *S. Dak., U.S.* 106 L4
Mureş, river, *Rom.* 154 DII
Muret, *Fr.* 149 X9
Murfreesboro, *Ark., U.S.* 102 H7
Murfreesboro, *N.C., U.S.* 98 GI3
Murgap, river, *Uzb.* 176 NIO
Murgha Kibzai, *Pak.* 179 R8
Murghob, *Taj.* 178 JII
Murghob, river, *Taj.* 178 JII
Murgon, *Qnsld., Austral.* 215 UI5
Murgoo, *W. Aust., Austral.* 215 V2
Murguz, peak, *Arm.* 171 DI9
Muri, *Cook Is., N.Z.* 222 Q9
Murihiti, island, *Wallis and Futuna, Fr.* 223 AI4
Murilo Atoll, *F.S.M.* 220 Q6
Murimaora, Motu, *Fr. Polynesia, Fr.* 223 GI4
Muritapua, island, *Cook Is., N.Z.* 222 QI2
Müritz, lake, *Ger.* 150 CIO
Murjek, *Sw.* 143 EI4
Murman Coast, *Eur.* 140 AIO
Murman Rise, *Arctic Oc.* 247 DI8
Murmansk, *Russ.* 160 D9

Murmansk Rise, *Arctic Oc.* 247 EI6
Murnpeowie, *S. Aust., Austral.* 215 VII
Muro, Capo di, *Fr.* 152 K3
Muro Lucano, *It.* 152 MI2
Murom, *Russ.* 158 JII
Muroran, *Japan* 188 HI2
Muros, *Sp.* 146 B5
Muros e Noia, Ría de, *Sp.* 146 B5
Muroto, *Japan* 189 R7
Muroto Zaki, *Japan* 189 R7
Murphy, *Idaho, U.S.* 108 H3
Murphy, *N.C., U.S.* 98 J5
Murphysboro, *Ill., U.S.* 101 U5
Murra Murra, *Qnsld., Austral.* 215 VI3
Murrat el Sughra, Buheirat (Little Bitter Lake), *Egypt* 173 QI
Murray, *Ky., U.S.* 103 EI3
Murray, river, *Austral.* 214 LI3
Murray, Lake, *P.N.G.* 217 DI7
Murray, Lake, *S.C., U.S.* 98 K8
Murray Bridge, *S. Aust., Austral.* 215 YII
Murray Fracture Zone, *Pac. Oc.* 243 FI4
Murray River Basin, *Austral.* 214 KII
Murrayville, *Vic., Austral.* 215 YII
Murrells Inlet, *S.C., U.S.* 98 LII
Murrenja Hill, *Austral.* 214 B7
Murrey Ridge, *Ind. Oc.* 224 C8
Murro di Porco, Capo, *It.* 153 TI2
Murrumbidgee, river, *Austral.* 214 KI2
Murska Sobota, *Slov.* 154 C6
Mursko Središće, *Croatia* 154 C6
Murter, island, *Croatia* 154 G5
Murud, *India* 180 L3
Murud, Mount, *Malaysia* 192 GII
Murukta, *Russ.* 161 GI4
Mururoa *see* Moruroa, island, *Fr. Polynesia, Fr.* 223 H2I
Murwillumbah, *N.S.W., Austral.* 215 VI6
Mürzzuschlag, *Aust.* 150 LI2
Muş, *Turk.* 171 FI6
Mûsa, Gebel (Mount Sinai), *Egypt* 173 T3
Musa Dağ, peak, *Turk.* 170 JII
Musa Khel Bazar, *Pak.* 179 Q8
Musala, peak, *Bulg.* 155 JI3
Musan, *N. Korea* 186 BI2
Musandam, Ra's, *Oman* 175 HI5
Mūsá Qal'ah, *Afghan.* 179 P4
Musaymīr, *Yemen* 174 R9
Muscat *see* Masqaṭ, *Oman* 175 KI6
Muscatine, *Iowa, U.S.* 107 PI4
Muscle Shoals, *Ala., U.S.* 103 GI4
Muse, *Okla., U.S.* 104 HI4
Museum of Prehistoric Anthropology, *Monaco* 163 E2O
Musgrave, Port, *Austral.* 214 AI2
Musgrave Ranges, *Austral.* 214 G8
Mushie, *Dem. Rep. of the Congo* 202 L8
Mūsh Khēl, *Afghan.* 179 N7
Musicians Seamounts, *Pac. Oc.* 243 FI3
Muskegon, *Mich., U.S.* 100 L9
Muskegon, river, *Mich., U.S.* 100 KIO
Muskegon Heights, *Mich., U.S.* 100 L9
Muskingum, river, *Ohio, U.S.* 101 RI4
Muskogee, *Okla., U.S.* 104 FI3
Muslimbagh, *Pak.* 179 R6
Muslimīyah, *Syr.* 172 D9
Musmar, *Sudan* 203 DI4
Musoma, *Tanzania* 203 KI3
Mussau, island, *P.N.G.* 217 B2O
Mussau Islands, *P.N.G.* 217 B2O
Musselburgh, *Scot., U.K.* 144 MIO
Musselshell, *Mont., U.S.* 108 DIO
Musselshell, river, *Mont., U.S.* 108 CII
Mussuma, *Angola* 206 E8
Mustafakemalpaşa, *Turk.* 170 D4
Mustaḩīl, *Eth.* 203 HI7
Mustang, *Nepal* 180 E9
Musters, Lago, *Arg.* 135 S8
Mustique, island, *St. Vincent and the Grenadines* 121 GI7

Musu, *N. Korea* 186 CI2
Musudan, *N. Korea* 186 EI3
Mut, *Turk.* 170 J8
Mût, *Egypt* 201 EI8
Mut, *island, Marshall Is., U.S.* 220 J8
Mutá, Ponta do, *Braz.* 133 JI6
Mutā Khān, *Afghan.* 179 N7
Mutalau, *Niue, N.Z.* 223 A2I
Mutarara, *Mozambique* 207 FI3
Mutare, *Mozambique* 206 FI2
Mute, Motu, *Fr. Polynesia, Fr.* 223 JI4
Muting, *Indonesia* 193 M2I
Mutki, *Turk.* 171 GI6
Mutnovskaya Sopka, *Russ.* 161 F23
Mutok Harbor, *F.S.M.* 221 GI4
Mutoray, *Russ.* 161 JI4
Mutsu, *Japan* 188 JI3
Mutsu Wan, *Japan* 188 JI3
Muttaburra, *Qnsld., Austral.* 215 TI3
Muturi, *Indonesia* 193 KI8
Mu Us Shamo (Ordos), *N. Mongol, China* 184 DI
Muxía, *Sp.* 146 B5
Mŭynoq, *Uzb.* 176 H9
Muzaffarabad, *Pak.* 178 MII
Muzaffargarh, *Pak.* 179 R9
Muzaffarnagar, *India* 180 E6
Muzaffarpur, *India* 180 GIO
Muztag, peak, *China* 182 H3
Muztag Feng, *China* 182 H5
Mwali, *island (Mohéli), Comoros* 209 NI5
Mwaniwowo, *Solomon Is.* 221 Q2I
Mwanza, *Tanzania* 203 LI3
Mweka, *Dem. Rep. of the Congo* 202 L9
Mwene-Ditu, *Dem. Rep. of the Congo* 202 M9
Mwenezi, *Zimb.* 206 GII
Mweru, Lake, *Dem. Rep. of the Congo, Zambia* 206 CII
Mwinilunga, *Zambia* 206 D9
Myaksa, *Russ.* 158 G9
Myanaung, *Myanmar* 190 J5
Myanmar (Burma), *Asia* 190 H5
Mycenae, ruin, *Gr.* 156 KII
Myebon, *Myanmar* 190 H4
Myeik, *Myanmar* 191 N7
Myingyan, *Myanmar* 190 G6
Myitkyinā, *Myanmar* 190 E7
Myitta, *Myanmar* 190 M7
Mykolayiv, *Ukr.* 159 R6
Mýkonos, *Gr.* 157 KI5
Mýkonos, *island, Gr.* 157 KI5
Mymensingh, *Bangladesh* 180 HI3
Mynbulaq, *Uzb.* 176 JIO
Mynydd Preseli, peak, *Wales, U.K.* 145 U9
Myohaung, *Myanmar* 190 H4
Myohyang-san, peak, *N. Korea* 186 G7
Myohyang-sanmaek, range, *N. Korea* 186 G7
Myŏngch'ŏn, *N. Korea* 186 EI2
Myoungmya, *Myanmar* 190 L5
Myrdal, *Nor.* 142 JIO
Mýrdalsjökull, glacier, *Ice.* 142 F2
Myrhorod, *Ukr.* 159 P7
Myrina, *Gr.* 157 EI4
Myrtle Beach, *S.C., U.S.* 98 LII
Myrtle Creek, *Oreg., U.S.* 110 J3
Myrtle Grove, *Fla., U.S.* 99 QI
Myrtle Point, *Oreg., U.S.* 110 J2
Mýrtos, *Gr.* 157 QI5
Myrtou (Camlibel), *Cyprus* 162 N7
Mysovaya, *Russ.* 161 DI9
Mys Shmidta, *Russ.* 161 B2O
Mystic, *Conn., U.S.* 97 MI4
Mystic, *Iowa, U.S.* 107 QI2
Mysuru, *India* 181 Q5
Mys Zhelaniya, *Russ.* 160 DI2
Myszyniec, *Pol.* 151 CI6
Mỹ Tho, *Vietnam* 191 PI2
Mýtikas, *Gr.* 156 G8
Mytilene see Mytilíni, *Gr.* 157 GI7
Mytilíni (Mytilene), *Gr.* 157 GI7
Mytilíni see Lésvos, *island, Gr.* 157 FI6
Mytishchi, *Russ.* 158 J9

Mzé Koukoulé Bandalankoua, peak, *Comoros* 209 NI5
Mzuzu, *Malawi* 206 DI2

N

Na, *island, F.S.M.* 221 GI4
Naafkopf, peak, *Aust., Liech, Switz.* 162 Q3
Nāʻālehu, *Hawaiʻi, U.S.* 115 Q2O
Nabari, *Kiribati* 221 B2O
Nabatîyé, *Leb.* 172 J6
Nabeina, *Kiribati* 221 FI7
Naberezhnyye Chelny, *Russ.* 158 HI6
Nabeul, *Tun.* 201 AI3
Nabire, *Indonesia* 193 KI9
Na Blascaodaí (Blasket Island), *Ire.* 145 U2
Nāblus (Nablus), *W. Bank* 172 L6
Nabouwalu, *Fiji* 222 H7
Nabq Bay, site, *Egypt* 173 U4
Nacala, *Mozambique* 207 EI5
Nacaome, *Hond.* 117 LI7
Naches, *Wash., U.S.* 110 D5
Nachingwea, *Tanzania* 203 NI5
Náchod, *Czech Rep.* 150 GI2
Nachu, *island, F.S.M.* 221 CI6
Nachvak Fiord, *Nfld. & Lab., Can.* 85 J2O
Nacimiento, Lake, *Calif., U.S.* III V5
Nacogdoches, *Tex., U.S.* 105 NI4
Nacozari de García, *Mex.* 116 C7
Nacula, *island, Fiji* 222 H5
Nadale, *island, Maldives* 181 X3
Nadezhda Basin, *Pac. Oc.* 242 F8
Nadi, *Fiji* 222 J5
Nadiad, *India* 180 J3
Nadi Bay, *Fiji* 222 H5
Nadir, *Virgin Is., U.S.* 122 N9
Nădlac, *Rom.* 154 DIO
Nadur, *Malta* 163 H2O
Naduri, *Fiji* 222 G7
Nadvoitsy, *Russ.* 160 D8
Nadym, *Russ.* 160 GII
Naenarodo, *island, S. Korea* 187 U9
Naesu, *S. Korea* 187 P9
Náfpaktos, *Gr.* 156 H9
Náfplio, *Gr.* 156 KII
Nafūsah, Jabal, *Lib.* 201 CI3
Nag, *Pak.* 179 U4
Naga, *Indonesia* 193 MI3
Naga City, *Philippines* 193 CI4
Naga Hills, *India* 180 GI5
Nagano, *Japan* 189 NII
Nagaoka, *Japan* 188 MII
Nagaon, *India* 180 GI4
Nagar Parkar, *Pak.* 179 W9
Nagasaki, *Japan* 189 R4
Nagaur, *India* 180 G3
Nagēlē, *Eth.* 203 HI5
Nagercoil, *India* 181 S5
Nagir, *Pak.* 178 KI2
Na Gleannta see Glenties, *Ire.* 145 P5
Nago, *Japan* 189 X2
Nagorno-Karabakh, region, *Azerb.* 171 E2O
Nagoya, *Japan* 189 PIO
Nagpur, *India* 180 K7
Nagqu (Naqu), *China* 182 K6
Nag's Head, *St. Kitts and Nevis* 123 BI8
Naguabo, *P.R., U.S.* 122 N5
Nagwŏn, *N. Korea* 186 G9
Nagykanizsa, *Hung.* 151 MI3
Nagyŏn, *N. Korea* 186 L5
Naha, *Japan* 189 X2
Nahanni Butte, *N.W.T., Can.* 84 H9
Na h-Eileanan Flannach (Flannach Isles), *Scot., U.K.* 144 H6
Na h-Eileanan Mora (Shiant Islands), *Scot., U.K.* 144 H7
Na h-Eileanan Theisgeir (Heisker Islands), *Scot., U.K.* 144 J6
Nahma, *Mich., U.S.* 100 G8
Nahoe, *Fr. Polynesia, Fr.* 223 M2I
Nahuei Huapí, Lago, *Arg.* 135 Q7
Nailaga, *Fiji* 222 H5
Naʻīn, *Iran* 175 EI3

Nain, *Nfld. & Lab., Can.* 85 K2I
Nainpur, *India* 180 J7
Nairai, *island, Fiji* 222 J7
Nairiri, *Fr. Polynesia, Fr.* 223 PI6
Nairn, *Scot., U.K.* 144 J9
Nairobi, *Kenya* 203 KI4
Naitaba, *island, Fiji* 222 H9
Naitonitoni, *Fiji* 222 J6
Najaf see An Najaf, *Iraq* 174 E9
Najafābād, *Iran* 175 EI3
Najd, region, *Saudi Arabia* 174 H8
Nájera, *Sp.* 146 CI2
Najin, *N. Korea* 186 BI3
Najin-man, bay, *N. Korea* 186 BI3
Najran, *Saudi Arabia* 174 N9
Najrān, oasis, *Saudi Arabia* 174 N9
Naju, *S. Korea* 187 T8
Nakadōri Jima, *Japan* 189 R3
Nakagusuku Wan (Buckner Bay), *Japan* 189 X2
Naka Kharai, *Pak.* 179 W6
Nakālele Point, *Hawaiʻi, U.S.* 115 GI6
Nakano, *Japan* 189 NII
Nakano Shima, *Japan* 189 N7
Nakano Shima, *Japan* 189 U4
Naka Shibetsu, *Japan* 188 FI5
Nakatane, *Japan* 189 U5
Nakatombetsu, *Japan* 188 EI3
Nakatsu, *Japan* 189 R5
Nakdong river, *S. Korea* 187 SII
Nakéty, *New Caledonia, Fr.* 222 D8
Nak'fa, *Eritrea* 203 DI5
Nakhl, *Egypt* 173 Q3
Nakhodka, *Russ.* 161 M2I
Nakhon Phanom, *Thai.* 190 KII
Nakhon Ratchasima, *Thai.* 190 MIO
Nakhon Sawan, *Thai.* 190 L8
Nakhon Si Thammarat, *Thai.* 191 R8
Nakina, *Ont., Can.* 85 NI6
Naknek, *Alas., U.S.* 113 LI4
Nakodar, *India* 180 D5
Nakodu, *Fiji* 222 H7
Nakuru, *Kenya* 203 KI4
Nal, *Pak.* 179 T5
Nalayh, *Mongolia* 182 DII
Nal'chik, *Russ.* 159 TI3
Nalgonda, *India* 180 M7
Nallıhan, *Turk.* 170 D7
Nalogo, *island, Solomon Is.* 221 P22
Nālūt, *Lib.* 201 CI3
Nam, river, *S. Korea* 187 SIO
Namaite, *island, Fr. Polynesia, Fr.* 223 KI6
Namak, Daryācheh-ye, *Iran* 175 DI3
Namaksār, lake, *Afghan.* 179 NI
Namakzar, Lake, *Afghan., Iran* 175 DI7
Namakzār-e Shahdād, salt desert, *Iran* 175 FI6
Namanga, *Kenya* 203 LI4
Namangan, *Uzb.* 177 KI4
Namapa, *Mozambique* 207 DI5
Namaram, *Vanuatu* 222 D2
Namatanai, *P.N.G.* 217 C2I
Năm Căn, *Vietnam* 191 QI2
Nam Co (Namu Cuo), *China* 182 K5
Namdae, river, *N. Korea* 186 EII
Nam Định, *Vietnam* 190 HI2
Namekagon, river, *Wis., U.S.* 100 G3
Namelakl Passage, *Palau* 220 NI2
Namenalala, *island, Fiji* 222 H7
Namgia, *India* 180 D6
Namhae, *S. Korea* 187 TIO
Namhaedo, *island, S. Korea* 187 TIO
Namhŭng, *N. Korea* 186 F8
Namib Desert, *Namibia* 206 H6
Namibe, *Angola* 206 E5
Namibia, *Af.* 206 G7
Namibia Plain, *Atl. Oc.* 241 SI3
Namiquipa, *Mex.* 116 D8
Namji, *S. Korea* 187 SII
Namlea, *Indonesia* 193 KI6
Nam Ngum Dam, *Laos* 190 JIO
Namoi, river, *Austral.* 214 JI4
Nāmolokama Mountain, *Hawaiʻi, U.S.* 114 B5
Namoluk Atoll, *F.S.M.* 220 Q6
Namonuito Atoll, *F.S.M.* 220 Q5

Namoren, *island, Marshall Is., U.S.* 220 K7
Namorik Atoll, *Marshall Is., U.S.* 220 H4
Nampa, *Idaho, U.S.* 108 G3
Nampala, *Mali* 200 H8
Namp'o, *N. Korea* 186 K5
Nampo Islands, *Asia* 168 FI4
Nampō Shotō, *Japan* 189 RI2
Nampula, *Mozambique* 207 EI4
Namsen, river, *Nor.* 142 FI2
Namsê Pass, *Nepal* 180 E8
Namsos, *Nor.* 142 GII
Nam Tok, *Thai.* 190 M8
Namtsy, *Russ.* 161 GI8
Namtu, *Myanmar* 190 G7
Namu Atoll, *Marshall Is., U.S.* 220 G4
Namu Cuo see Nam Co, *China* 182 K5
Namuka-i-Lau, *island, Fiji* 222 K9
Namukulu, *Niue, N.Z.* 223 A2O
Namur, *Belg.* 148 LI2
Namutoni, *Namibia* 206 F7
Namwon, *S. Korea* 187 S9
Namwon, *S. Korea* 187 W7
Namyang, *N. Korea* 186 FI2
Namyang, *S. Korea* 187 T9
Nan, river, *Hubei, China* 184 L3
Nan, river, *Thai.* 190 K9
Nanaimo, *B.C., Can.* 84 M7
Nānākuli, *Hawaiʻi, U.S.* 114 EIO
Nanam, *N. Korea* 186 DI3
Nanao, *Japan* 189 NIO
Nanatsu Shima, *Japan* 188 M9
Nanchang, *Jiangxi, China* 185 Q7
Nanchangshan Dao, *Shand., China* 184 EII
Nancheng, *Jiangxi, China* 185 R8
Nanchong, *China* 182 LIO
Nancowry Island, *India* 181 SI5
Nancy, *Fr.* 149 PI4
Nanda Devi, pass, *India* 180 E7
Nanded, *India* 180 L6
Nandgaon, *India* 180 K4
Nandurbar, *India* 180 K4
Nandyal, *India* 181 N6
Nanfeng, *Jiangxi, China* 185 R7
Nanfengmian, peak, *Hunan, China* 185 S5
Nanga Parbat, peak, *Pak.* 178 LI2
Nangapinoh, *Indonesia* 192 JIO
Nangaraun, *Indonesia* 192 JIO
Nangatayap, *Indonesia* 192 K9
Nangin, *Myanmar* 191 P7
Nangiré, *Vanuatu* 222 C2
Nangis, *Fr.* 149 QIO
Nangnim, *N. Korea* 186 E8
Nangnim-ho, *lake, N. Korea* 186 E8
Nangnim-san, peak, *N. Korea* 186 F8
Nangnim-sanmaek, range, *N. Korea* 186 E8
Nangong, *Hebei, China* 184 F7
Nangqên see Xangda, *China* 182 K7
Nangtud, Mount, *Philippines* 193 DI4
Nanguan, *Shanxi, China* 184 G4
Nanij, *island, Marshall Is., U.S.* 220 K7
Nanjing, *Fujian, China* 185 U8
Nanjing, *Jiangsu, China* 184 L9
Nankang, *Jiangxi, China* 185 T6
Nankoku, *Japan* 189 R7
Nan Ling, *Hunan, China* 185 T4
Nanma see Yiyuan, *Shand., China* 184 G9
Nanmatol, *island, F.S.M.* 221 GI4
Nanmatol Islands, *F.S.M.* 221 FI5
Nannine, *W. Aust., Austral.* 215 V3
Nanning, *China* 182 PII
Nanortalik Bank, *Atl. Oc.* 247 R2O
Nanpan, river, *China* 182 NIO
Nanpiao, *Liaoning, China* 184 BII
Nanping, *Fujian, China* 185 S9
Nanri Dao, *Fujian, China* 185 TIO
Nansan Dao, *Guang., China* 185 X2
Nansei Shotō (Ryukyu Islands), *Japan* 189 X2
Nansen Basin, *Arctic Oc.* 246 FI2
Nansen Sound, *Nunavut, Can.* 85 AI4
Nanshan Island, *S. China Sea* 192 EII

Nansi Hu, *Shand., China* 184 J8
Nansio, *Tanzania* 203 KI3
Nant, *Fr.* 149 XII
Nantes, *Fr.* 149 S5
Nanticoke, *Pa., U.S.* 96 M8
Nantong, *Jiangsu, China* 184 LII
Nantou, *Taiwan, China* 185 VII
Nantucket, *Mass., U.S.* 97 MI6
Nantucket Island, *Mass., U.S.* 97 MI6
Nantucket Sound, *Mass., U.S.* 97 MI6
Nantulo, *Mozambique* 207 DI4
Nantwich, *Eng., U.K.* 145 SII
Nānuʻalele Point, *Hawaiʻi, U.S.* 115 HI8
Nanukuloa, *Fiji* 222 H6
Nanuku Passage, *Fiji* 222 H8
Nanumanga, *island, Tuvalu* 218 H8
Nanumea, *island, Tuvalu* 218 H8
Nanuque, *Braz.* 133 KI6
Nanusa, Kepulauan, *Indonesia* 193 GI6
Nanutarra, *W. Aust., Austral.* 215 T2
Nanwan Shuiku, *Henan, China* 184 L5
Nanxian, *Hunan, China* 185 P4
Nanxiong, *Guang., China* 185 T5
Nanyang, *Henan, China* 184 K4
Nanzhang, *Hubei, China* 184 M3
Nanzhao, *Henan, China* 184 K4
Nao, Cabo de la, *Sp.* 147 JI5
Nao, Cape, *Eur.* 140 G4
Naococane, Lac, *Que., Can.* 85 MI9
Nāomīd, Dasht-e, *Afghan., Iran* 179 NI
Nao Nao, *island, Fr. Polynesia, Fr.* 223 C23
Naonao, Motu, *Fr. Polynesia, Fr.* 223 KI6
Nao Nao, Passe, *Fr. Polynesia, Fr.* 223 C23
Náousa, *Gr.* 156 CIO
Naozhou Dao, *Guang., China* 185 X2
Napa, *Calif., U.S.* III R3
Nā Pali Coast, *Hawaiʻi, U.S.* 114 B5
Naperville, *Ill., U.S.* 101 N6
Napia, *island, Kiribati* 221 B2O
Napier, *N.Z.* 217 L2O
Napier Downs, *W. Aust., Austral.* 215 R5
Napier Mountains, *Antarctica* 231 CI9
Naples, *Fla., U.S.* 99 W8
Naples, *Tex., U.S.* 104 KI4
Naples see Napoli, *It.* 152 MIO
Napo see Napug, *China* 182 J2
Napo, river, *S. Amer.* 130 J4
Napoleon, *N. Dak., U.S.* 106 H5
Napoleon, *Ohio, U.S.* 101 PII
Napoleonville, *La., U.S.* 102 QIO
Napoli (Naples), *It.* 152 MIO
Napoli, Golfo di, *It.* 152 MIO
Napug (Napo), *China* 182 J2
Napuka, *island, Fr. Polynesia, Fr.* 223 D2O
Nāpuʻukūlua, peak, *Hawaiʻi, U.S.* 115 MI9
Nâqoûra, *Leb.* 172 K5
Naqu see Nagqu, *China* 182 K6
Nara, *Japan* 189 Q9
Nara, *Mali* 200 H7
Nara, river, *Pak.* 179 V8
Naracoorte, *S. Aust., Austral.* 215 YII
Narang, *Afghan.* 178 M9
Naranjito, *P.R., U.S.* 122 N4
Narasannapeta, *India* 180 L9
Narathiwat, *Thai.* 191 S9
Nara Visa, *N. Mex., U.S.* 109 RI5
Narbonne, *Fr.* 149 YIO
Narcondam Island, *India* 181 PI5
Nardò, *It.* 153 NI5
Nares Plain, *Atl. Oc.* 240 L5
Narew, river, *Pol.* 151 CI6
Narib, *Namibia* 206 H7
Narin, *N. Mongol, China* 184 C3
Narinda Bay, *Af.* 198 MII
Nariva Swamp, *Trinidad and Tobago* 123 P23
Narli, *Turk.* 170 HI2
Narmada, river, *India* 180 J4

Narmidj, island, *Marshall Is., U.S.* 220 K7
Narnaul, *India* 180 F5
Narndee, *W. Aust., Austral.* 215 V3
Narni, *It.* 152 J8
Narodnaya, peak, *Asia* 168 D7
Narodnaya, Gora, *Russ.* 160 FIO
Narooma, *N.S.W., Austral.* 215 Y14
Narovorovo, *Vanuatu* 222 C2
Narowal, *Pak.* 179 PI2
Narowlya, *Belarus* 158 M5
Narrabri, *N.S.W., Austral.* 215 W14
Narragansett Pier, *R.I., U.S.* 97 MI4
Narrandera, *N.S.W., Austral.* 215 YI3
Narran Lake, *Austral.* 214 JI3
Narrogin, *W. Aust., Austral.* 215 X3
Narrows, *Va., U.S.* 98 F9
Narsinghgarh, *India* 180 H5
Narsipatnam, *India* 180 M8
Nartës, Laguna e, *Alban.* 154 M9
Narthákí, Óros, *Gr.* 156 FIO
Nartkala, *Russ.* 159 TI3
Narva, *Est.* 143 JI7
Narvik, *Nor.* 142 DI2
Narvskoye Vodokhranilishche, *Russ.* 158 F5
Narwietooma, *N.T., Austral.* 215 T8
Nar'yan Mar, *Russ.* 160 EIO
Naryn, *Kyrg.* 178 FI2
Naryn, *Russ.* 161 MI4
Naryn, river, *Kyrg.* 178 FIO
Naryn Khuduk, *Russ.* 159 SI4
Narynqol, *Kaz.* 177 HI8
Naryn Qum, desert, *Kaz.* 176 E5
Näs, *Sw.* 142 HI2
Nasarawa, *Nigeria* 205 DI4
Nasca, *Peru* 132 J4
Nasca Ridge, *Pac. Oc.* 243 M22
Na Sceirí see Skerries, *Ire.* 145 R7
Nashua, *Iowa, U.S.* 106 MI2
Nashua, *Mont., U.S.* 108 BI2
Nashua, *N.H., U.S.* 97 JI4
Nashville, *Ark., U.S.* 102 H6
Nashville, *Ga., U.S.* 99 P6
Nashville, *Ill., U.S.* 101 T5
Nashville, *Tenn., U.S.* 103 EI5
Nashwauk, *Minn., U.S.* 106 FII
Našice, *Croatia* 154 E8
Näsijärvi, lake, *Fin.* 143 HI5
Nasik, *India* 180 K4
Nasir, *S. Sudan* 203 GI3
Nasirabad, *India* 180 G4
Naso, *It.* 153 RII
Nassau, *Bahamas* 122 BII
Nassau, island, *Cook Is., N.Z.* 218 HII
Nassau Bay, *S. Amer.* 128 R5
Nassawadox, *Va., U.S.* 98 EI4
Nasser, Lake, *Egypt* 201 EI9
Nässjö, *Sw.* 143 LI3
Nastapoka Islands, *Nunavut, Can.* 85 KI8
Nata, *Botswana* 206 GIO
Natal, *Braz.* 133 FI8
Natal, *Indonesia* 192 J5
Natalia, *Tex., U.S.* 105 S9
Natal'inskiy, *Russ.* 161 C22
Natal Valley, *Ind. Oc.* 224 M4
Naţanz, *Iran* 175 DI3
Natara, *Russ.* 161 FI6
Natashquan, *Que., Can.* 85 M22
Natashquan, river, *Nfld. & Lab., Que., Can.* 85 L2I
Natchez, *Miss., U.S.* 102 M9
Natchitoches, *La., U.S.* 102 M7
Natewa Bay, *Fiji* 222 H6
National City, *Calif., U.S.* III Z9
National Museum of Fine Arts, *Monaco* 163 C2I
Natitingou, *Benin* 204 CII
Natividad, Isla, *Mex.* 116 D5
Natividade, *Braz.* 133 HI3
Natkyizin, *Myanmar* 190 M7
Natoma, *Kans., U.S.* 107 S6
Natron, Lake, *Af.* 198 KIO
Nattavaara, *Sw.* 143 EI4
Natuashish, *Nfld. & Lab., Can.* 85 K2I
Natuna Besar, island, *Indonesia* 192 G9
Natuna Besar, Kepulauan (Bunguran Utara), *Indonesia* 192 G8
Natuna Islands, *Asia* 168 LII

Natuna Selatan, Kepulauan (Bunguran Selatan), *Indonesia* 192 H9
Natural Bridges National Monument, *Utah, U.S.* 109 P9
Naturaliste, Cape, *Austral.* 214 K2
Naturaliste Fracture Zone, *Ind. Oc.* 225 MI6
Naturaliste Plateau, *Ind. Oc.* 225 NI7
Naturaliste Trough, *Ind. Oc.* 225 NI7
Naturita, *Colo., U.S.* 109 NIO
Naturno, *It.* 152 C6
Naubinway, *Mich., U.S.* 100 GIO
Nauiyu (Daly River), *N.T., Austral.* 215 P7
Naukot, *Pak.* 179 W8
Naungpale, *Myanmar* 190 J7
Nauroz Kalat, *Pak.* 179 S5
Nauru, *Pac. Oc.* 218 G7
Naushahra, *India* 179 NI2
Naushahro Firoz, *Pak.* 179 U7
Nausori, *Fiji* 222 J6
Nauta, *Peru* 132 E4
Nautilus Basin, *Arctic Oc.* 246 J9
Nautilus Gap, *Arctic Oc.* 246 K9
Nautilus Spur, *Arctic Oc.* 246 KII
Nautla, *Mex.* 117 HI3
Nauvoo, *Ill., U.S.* 101 Q3
Navabelitsa, *Belarus* 158 M6
Navadwip, *India* 180 JII
Navahrudak, *Belarus* 158 K4
Navai, *Fiji* 222 H6
Navajo Mountain, *Utah, U.S.* 109 Q8
Navajo National Monument, *Ariz., U.S.* 109 Q8
Navajo Reservoir, *Colo., N. Mex., U.S.* 109 QII
Naval Base Guam see Joint Region Marianas, *Guam, U.S.* 220 CIO
Navalmoral de la Mata, *Sp.* 146 G9
Navan (An Uaimh), *Ire.* 145 R6
Navapolatsk, *Belarus* 158 J5
Navarin, Cape, *Asia* 168 AI2
Navarin, Cape, *N. Amer.* 82 P3
Navarin, Mys, *Russ.* 161 B2I
Navarino, Isla, *Chile* 135 Y9
Navarre, *Eur.* 140 J3
Navarrenx, *Fr.* 149 Y6
Navasota, *Tex., U.S.* 105 QI3
Navasota, river, *Tex., U.S.* 105 NI2
Navassa Island, *U.S.* 119 MI4
Navia, *Sp.* 146 A7
Navidad, river, *Tex., U.S.* 105 RI2
Naviti, island, *Fiji* 222 H5
Năvodari, *Rom.* 155 FI8
Navoiy, *Uzb.* 176 LII
Navojoa, *Mex.* 116 E7
Navrongo, *Ghana* 204 CIO
Navsari, *India* 180 K3
Navua, *Fiji* 222 J6
Navua, river, *Fiji* 222 J6
Nawá, *Syr.* 172 K7
Nawabshah, *Pak.* 179 V7
Nawada, *India* 180 JII
Nāwah, *Afghan.* 179 P7
Nawalgarh, *India* 180 F5
Nawāşīf, Ḥarrat, *Saudi Arabia* 174 L8
Naxçivan, region, *Arm.* 171 FI9
Naxçivan, *Arm.* 171 FI9
Náxos, *Gr.* 157 LI5
Náxos, island, *Gr.* 157 LI5
Naxos, ruin, *It.* 153 SI2
Naxxar, *Malta* 163 K22
Nay, Cape, *Asia* 168 KII
Nayak, *Afghan.* 178 M6
Nayau, island, *Fiji* 222 J9
Nāy Band, *Iran* 175 EI6
Nayoro, *Japan* 188 FI3
Nay Pyi Taw, *Myanmar* 190 J6
Nazaré, *Braz.* 133 HI6
Nazaré, *Port.* 146 G4
Nazareth, *Vanuatu* 222 C2
Nazareth see Naẕerat, *Israel* 172 L6
Nazareth Bank, *Ind. Oc.* 224 J9
Nazas, *Mex.* 116 F9
Naze, *Japan* 189 W3
Naẕerat (Nazareth), *Israel* 172 L6
Nāzīk, *Iran* 174 AIO
Nazik Gölü, *Turk.* 171 FI6

Nazilli, *Turk.* 170 G4
Nazimiye, *Turk.* 171 FI4
Nazimovo, *Russ.* 161 JI3
Naziya, *Russ.* 158 F7
Nazran', *Russ.* 159 UI4
Nazrēt, *Eth.* 203 GI5
Ndai see Dai, island, *Solomon Is.* 221 MI9
N'dalatando, *Angola* 206 C6
Ndélé, *Cen. Af. Rep.* 202 G9
Ndendé, *Gabon* 205 JI6
N'Djamena, *Chad* 201 JI4
Ndogo Lagoon, *Af.* 198 K5
Ndola, *Zambia* 206 DII
Nduindui, *Solomon Is.* 221 PI9
Nduindui, *Vanuatu* 222 C2
Néa Epídavros, *Gr.* 156 KII
Neagh, Lake, *Eur.* 140 E4
Neagh, Lough, *N. Ire., U.K.* 145 P7
Neah Bay, *Wash., U.S.* 110 B2
Neale, Lake, *Austral.* 214 F7
Néa Michanióna, *Gr.* 156 DII
Néa Moní, *Gr.* 157 HI6
Néa Moudaniá, *Gr.* 156 DII
Neápoli, *Gr.* 156 D8
Neápolis, *Gr.* 156 MII
Neapolis see Kavála, *Gr.* 157 CI3
Near Islands, *Alas., U.S.* 112 LI
Néa Zíchni, *Gr.* 156 BI2
Neba, Île, *New Caledonia, Fr.* 222 B6
Nebine Creek, *Austral.* 214 HI3
Neblina, Pico da, *S. Amer.* 130 HIO
Nebraska, *U.S.* 107 P5
Nebraska City, *Nebr., U.S.* 107 Q8
Nebrodi, Monti, *It.* 153 RII
Nécé, *New Caledonia, Fr.* 222 D9
Necedah, *Wis., U.S.* 100 K4
Neches, river, *Tex., U.S.* 105 NI5
Neckar, river, *Ger.* 150 J6
Neckarboo Range, *Austral.* 214 KI2
Necker Island, *Hawai'i, U.S.* 114 M7
Necker Ridge, *Pac. Oc.* 243 GI3
Necochea, *Arg.* 135 NI2
Nederland, *Tex., U.S.* 105 QI6
Needham's Point, *Barbados* 123 LI9
Needles, *Calif., U.S.* III WI2
Neenah, *Wis., U.S.* 100 J6
Neftçala, *Azerb.* 171 E23
Nefteyugansk, *Russ.* 160 HII
Negaunee, *Mich., U.S.* 100 F7
Negeribatin, *Indonesia* 192 L7
Negev, region, *Israel* 173 P5
Negoiul, peak, *Rom.* 155 EI4
Negomane, *Mozambique* 207 DI4
Negombo, *Sri Lanka* 181 T7
Negonego, island, *Fr. Polynesia, Fr.* 223 F2O
Negotin, *Serb.* 154 GI2
Negra, Laguna, *Uru.* 134 LI5
Negra, Punta, *Peru* 132 FI
Negre, Pic, *Andorra, Sp.* 162 K3
Negreira, *Sp.* 146 B5
Negreşti-Oaş, *Rom.* 155 BI3
Negril, *Jam.* 122 H5
Negritos, *Peru* 132 EI
Negro, river, *Guatemala* 117 LI5
Negro, river, *S. Amer.* 130 G9
Negro Bay, *Af.* 198 HI2
Negros, island, *Philippines* 193 EI4
Negru Vodă, *Rom.* 155 GI8
Nehbandān, *Iran* 175 EI7
Nehe, *China* 183 CI5
Néhoué, Baie de, *New Caledonia, Fr.* 222 C6
Nehus, Cape, *P.N.G.* 221 JI4
Neiafu, *Tonga* 222 LII
Neiba, *Dom. Rep.* 119 MI7
Neiba, Bahía de, *Dom. Rep.* 119 MI8
Neiden, *Nor.* 143 BI5
Neidín see Kenmare, *Ire.* 145 U3
Neiges, Piton des, *Réunion, Fr.* 209 GI6
Neihart, *Mont., U.S.* 108 D8
Neillsville, *Wis., U.S.* 100 J4
Neilson Reef, *Pac. Oc.* 249 P2I
Nei Mongol, *China* 184 BI
Nei Mongol Gaoyuan, *N. Mongol, China* 184 AI
Neiqiu, *Hebei, China* 184 F6

Neiva, *Col.* 130 G5
Neixiang, *Henan, China* 184 K3
Nekoosa, *Wis., U.S.* 100 J5
Neksø, *Den.* 143 NI3
Nekurandu, island, *Maldives* 181 T3
Nelemnoye, *Russ.* 161 EI9
Nelidovo, *Russ.* 158 J7
Neligh, *Nebr., U.S.* 107 N7
Nel'kan, *Russ.* 161 HI9
Nellore, *India* 181 P7
Nell, island, *Marshall Is., U.S.* 220 L3
Nell Passage, *Marshall Is., U.S.* 220 L3
Nelson, *B.C., Can.* 84 M9
Nelson, *Eng., U.K.* 145 RII
Nelson, *N.Z.* 217 MI8
Nelson, *Nebr., U.S.* 107 R7
Nelson, *Nev., U.S.* III VI2
Nelson, river, *Man., Can.* 85 LI4
Nelson, Cape, *Austral.* 214 MII
Nelson, Estrecho, *Chile* 135 W6
Nelson House, *Man., Can.* 85 LI3
Nelson Island, *Alas., U.S.* 112 JII
Nelson Lagoon, *Alas., U.S.* 112 NI2
Nelson Reservoir, *Mont., U.S.* 108 BII
Néma, *Mauritania* 200 G7
Neman, *Russ.* 158 J2
Neman, river, *Eur.* 140 F9
Nembrala, *Indonesia* 193 NI4
Neméa, *Gr.* 156 JIO
Nemiscau, *Que., Can.* 85 MI8
Nemrut Dagh, ruins, *Turk.* 171 HI3
Nemrut Gölü, *Turk.* 171 GI6
Nemunas, river, *Lith.* 143 MI6
Nemuro, *Japan* 188 FI6
Nemuro Strait, *Japan* 188 FI5
Nen, river, *China* 183 BI5
Nenagh (An tAonach), *Ire.* 145 T5
Nenana, *Alas., U.S.* 113 GI7
Nendeln, *Liech.* 162 N2
Nendö (Ndeni Island), *Solomon Is.* 221 Q23
Nenjiang, *China* 183 CI5
Nenom, Mochun, *F.S.M.* 221 BI4
Neoch, islands, *F.S.M.* 221 DI5
Neodesha, *Kans., U.S.* 107 U9
Neola, *Utah, U.S.* 108 L9
Néos, *Gr.* 156 DI2
Neosho, *Mo., U.S.* 107 VII
Neosho, river, *U.S.* 87 HI3
Nepa, *Russ.* 161 JI5
Nepal, *Asia* 180 F8
Nepalganj, *India* 180 F8
Nepean, island, *Norfolk I., Austral.* 221 G2O
Nephi, *Utah, U.S.* 108 M7
Nephin Beg, peak, *Ire.* 145 Q3
Nepis, Mochun, *F.S.M.* 221 CI5
Neptune Range, *Antarctica* 230 GIO
Nèrassol, Pic de, *Fr.* 162 H6
Nerchinsk, *Russ.* 161 LI7
Nerchinskiy Zavod, *Russ.* 161 LI8
Nerekhta, *Russ.* 158 HIO
Neretva, river, *Bosn. & Herzg.* 154 H7
Neretvanski Kanal, *Croatia* 154 H7
Neriquinha, *Angola* 206 E8
Néris, *Fr.* 149 TIO
Nerja, *Sp.* 146 MIO
Nero Seamount, *Hawai'i, U.S.* 114 K2
Nerpo, *Russ.* 161 JI7
Nerrima, *W. Aust., Austral.* 215 R5
Nerva, *Sp.* 146 K7
Nesika Beach, *Oreg., U.S.* 110 KI
Neskaupstaður, *Ice.* 142 F4
Nespelem, *Wash., U.S.* 110 B7
Ness, Loch, *Scot., U.K.* 144 K9
Ness City, *Kans., U.S.* 107 T5
Néstos, river, *Gr.* 157 BI3
Netanya, *Israel* 172 L5
Netherdale, *Qnsld., Austral.* 215 SI4
Netherlands, *Eur.* 148 JI3
Nettilling Lake, *Nunavut, Can.* 85 GI8
Netzahualcóyotl, *Mex.* 116 JI2
Neuberg, *Ger.* 150 J8
Neubrandenburg, *Ger.* 150 CIO
Neuchâtel, *Switz.* 152 B2
Neuchâtel, Lac de, *Switz.* 152 B2
Neuerburg, *Ger.* 162 HIO
Neufchâteau, *Belg.* 162 H7

Neufchâteau, *Fr.* 149 QI3
Neumagen, *Ger.* 150 G5
Neumayer III, station, *Antarctica* 230 AII
Neumünster, *Ger.* 150 B8
Neun, river, *Vietnam* 190 HII
Neunkirchen, *Aust.* 150 LI2
Neunkirchen, *Ger.* 150 H5
Neuquén, *Arg.* 135 P8
Neuquén, river, *Arg.* 135 N7
Neuruppin, *Ger.* 150 DIO
Neuschwanstein, site, *Ger.* 150 L8
Neuse, river, *N.C., U.S.* 98 HI2
Neusiedler Lake, *Eur.* 140 H8
Neusiedler See, *Aust.* 151 LI3
Neuss, *Ger.* 150 F5
Neustadt, *Ger.* 150 H6
Neustrelitz, *Ger.* 150 CIO
Neu-Ulm, *Ger.* 150 K7
Neuve la Habay, *Belg.* 162 J8
Neuvic, *Fr.* 149 V8
Neuwied, *Ger.* 150 G5
Nevada, *Iowa, U.S.* 107 NII
Nevada, *Mo., U.S.* 107 UII
Nevada, *U.S.* III QIO
Nevada, Sierra de, *Sp.* 146 LII
Nevada City, *Calif., U.S.* III Q5
Nevea, *Solomon Is.* 221 Q22
Nevel', *Russ.* 158 J6
Never, *Russ.* 161 KI8
Nevers, *Fr.* 149 SII
Neves, *Sao Tome and Principe* 209 D2O
Nevinnomyssk, *Russ.* 159 TI2
Nevis, island, *St. Kitts and Nevis* 123 CI9
Nevis, Loch, *Scot., U.K.* 144 K8
Nevis Peak, *St. Kitts and Nevis* 123 CI8
Nevşehir, *Turk.* 170 GIO
New, river, *Guyana* 131 GI5
New, river, *N.C., U.S.* 98 JI3
New, river, *Va., W. Va., U.S.* 98 F9; JI3
New Albany, *Ind., U.S.* 101 T9
New Albany, *Miss., U.S.* 102 HI2
New Amsterdam, *Guyana* 131 EI5
Newark, *Ark., U.S.* 102 F9
Newark, *Del., U.S.* 98 BI4
Newark, *Eng., U.K.* 145 SI3
Newark, *N.J., U.S.* 96 NII
Newark, *N.Y., U.S.* 96 J7
Newark, *Ohio, U.S.* 101 RI3
Newaygo, *Mich., U.S.* 100 L9
New Bedford, *Mass., U.S.* 97 LI5
Newberg, *Oreg., U.S.* 110 F3
New Bern, *N.C., U.S.* 98 JI3
Newbern, *Tenn., U.S.* 102 EI2
Newberry, *Fla., U.S.* 99 R7
Newberry, *Mich., U.S.* 100 FIO
Newberry, *S.C., U.S.* 98 K8
Newbiggin By The Sea, *Eng., U.K.* 145 NI2
New Bight, *Bahamas* 119 FI3
New Boston, *Ohio, U.S.* 101 TI3
New Boston, *Tex., U.S.* 104 KI5
New Braunfels, *Tex., U.S.* 105 RIO
New Britain, *Conn., U.S.* 96 LI2
New Britain, island, *P.N.G.* 217 C2I
New Brunswick, *Can.* 85 P2I
New Brunswick, *N.J., U.S.* 96 NIO
Newburg, *Mo., U.S.* 107 UI3
Newburgh, *N.Y., U.S.* 96 MII
Newburgh, *Scot., U.K.* 144 KII
Newbury, *Eng., U.K.* 145 VI2
New Caledonia see Nouvelle-Calédonie, island, *New Caledonia, Fr.* 222 C6
New Caledonia Trough, *Pac. Oc.* 242 MIO
New Castile, *Eur.* 140 K3
New Castle, *Ind., U.S.* 101 RIO
New Castle, *Pa., U.S.* 96 M3
New Castle (An Caisleán Nua), *Ire.* 145 T4
Newcastle, *Calif., U.S.* III Q5
Newcastle, *Jam.* 122 JIO
Newcastle, *N.S.W., Austral.* 215 XI5
Newcastle, *St. Kitts and Nevis* 123 BI8
Newcastle, *Tex., U.S.* 104 K9

Newcastle, *Wyo., U.S.* **108** G14
Newcastle Bay, *Austral.* **214** A12
Newcastle-under-Lyme, *Eng., U.K.* **145** S11
Newcastle upon Tyne, *Eng., U.K.* **145** P12
Newcastle Waters, *N.T., Austral.* **215** R8
New City, *N.Y., U.S.* **96** M11
Newdegate, *W. Aust., Austral.* **215** X4
New Delhi, *India* **180** F6
Newell, *S. Dak., U.S.* **106** K2
New England, *N. Dak., U.S.* **106** G2
New England Range, *Austral.* **214** J15
New England Seamounts, *Atl. Oc.* **240** J5
Newenham, Cape, *Alas., U.S.* **112** L12
Newfoundland, Island of, *Nfld. & Lab., Can.* **85** M23
Newfoundland and Labrador, *Can.* **85** K21
Newfoundland Basin, *Atl. Oc.* **240** H7
Newfoundland Evaporation Basin, *Utah, U.S.* **108** K6
Newfoundland Plain, *Atl. Oc.* **240** J7
Newfoundland Ridge, *Atl. Oc.* **240** J6
Newfoundland Seamounts, *Atl. Oc.* **240** J7
New Franklin, *Mo., U.S.* **107** S12
New Galloway, *Scot., U.K.* **145** P9
New Georgia, island, *Solomon Is.* **221** M16
New Georgia Group, islands, *Solomon Is.* **221** M15
New Georgia Sound (The Slot), *Solomon Is.* **221** M17
New Glasgow, *N.S., Can.* **85** P22
New Grant, *Trinidad and Tobago* **123** Q23
New Guinea, *Indonesia* **217** C17
New Guinea Trench, *Pac. Oc.* **242** J7
New Hampshire, *U.S.* **97** H14
New Hampton, *Iowa, U.S.* **106** M12
New Hanover, island, *P.N.G.* **217** B21
New Harbor, *Me., U.S.* **97** G17
New Haven, *Conn., U.S.* **96** M12
New Haven, *Ind., U.S.* **101** P10
New Hazelton, *B.C., Can.* **84** J8
New Hebrides Trench, *Pac. Oc.* **242** L10
New Iberia, *La., U.S.* **102** Q9
New Ipswich, *N.H., U.S.* **97** J14
New Ireland, *P.N.G.* **217** C21
New Jersey, *U.S.* **96** P10
Newkirk, *N. Mex., U.S.* **109** S14
Newkirk, *Okla., U.S.* **104** E11
New Lexington, *Ohio, U.S.* **101** R14
New Lisbon, *Wis., U.S.* **100** K4
New Liskeard, *Ont., Can.* **85** P18
New London, *Conn., U.S.* **97** M13
New London, *Iowa, U.S.* **107** Q13
New London, *Wis., U.S.* **100** J6
New Madrid, *Mo., U.S.* **107** V16
Newman, *Calif., U.S.* **111** S5
Newman, *W. Aust., Austral.* **215** T3
Newman Grove, *Nebr., U.S.* **107** P7
New Market, *Va., U.S.* **98** D11
Newmarket, *Eng., U.K.* **145** U14
Newmarket (Áth Trasna), *Ire.* **145** U4
New Martinsville, *W. Va., U.S.* **98** C9
New Meadows, *Idaho, U.S.* **108** F4
New Mexico, *U.S.* **109** S12
Newnan, *Ga., U.S.* **98** L4
New Norfolk, *Tas., Austral.* **215** Z8
New Orleans, *La., U.S.* **102** Q11
New Philadelphia, *Ohio, U.S.* **101** Q15
New Plymouth, *N.Z.* **217** K18
Newport, *Ark., U.S.* **102** F10
Newport, *Eng., U.K.* **145** X13
Newport, *Jam.* **122** J8
Newport, *Ky., U.S.* **103** A18
Newport, *Me., U.S.* **97** F17
Newport, *Oreg., U.S.* **110** G2
Newport, *R.I., U.S.* **97** M14
Newport, *Tenn., U.S.* **103** E19
Newport, *Vt., U.S.* **97** F13
Newport, *Wash., U.S.* **110** B9

Newport (Casnewydd), *Wales, U.K.* **145** V11
Newport Beach, *Calif., U.S.* **111** Y8
Newport News, *Va., U.S.* **98** F14
New Port Richey, *Fla., U.S.* **99** T7
New Prague, *Minn., U.S.* **106** K11
New Providence, island, *Bahamas* **118** E11
Newquay, *Eng., U.K.* **145** X8
New Richmond, *Wis., U.S.* **100** H2
New Roads, *La., U.S.* **102** N9
New Rochelle, *N.Y., U.S.* **96** N11
New Rockford, *N. Dak., U.S.* **106** F6
New Ross (Ros Mhic Thriúin), *Ire.* **145** T6
New Salem, *N. Dak., U.S.* **106** G4
New Sandy Bay, *St. Vincent and the Grenadines* **123** J17
New Schwabenland, region, *Antarctica* **231** C13
New Siberian Islands see Novosibirskiye Ostrova, *Russ.* **161** D16
New Siberian Shelf, *Arctic Oc.* **246** F9
New Smyrna Beach, *Fla., U.S.* **99** S9
New South Wales, *Austral.* **215** X13
New Stuyahok, *Alas., U.S.* **113** K14
Newton, *Ill., U.S.* **101** S6
Newton, *Iowa, U.S.* **107** P12
Newton, *Kans., U.S.* **107** U7
Newton, *Mass., U.S.* **97** K14
Newton, *Miss., U.S.* **102** L12
Newton, *Tex., U.S.* **105** P16
Newton Abbot, *Eng., U.K.* **145** X10
Newton Stewart, *Scot., U.K.* **145** P9
New Town, *N. Dak., U.S.* **106** E3
Newtown, *Wales, U.K.* **145** T10
Newtownabbey, *N. Ire., U.K.* **145** P7
Newtownards, *N. Ire., U.K.* **145** Q8
Newtown Saint Boswells, *Scot., U.K.* **145** N11
Newtownstewart, *N. Ire., U.K.* **145** P6
New Ulm, *Minn., U.S.* **106** K10
New Waverly, *Tex., U.S.* **105** P13
New York, *N.Y., U.S.* **96** N11
New York, *U.S.* **96** K8
Neya, *Russ.* **158** G12
Neyrīz, *Iran* **175** G14
Neyshābūr, *Iran* **175** C16
Nezperce, *Idaho, U.S.* **108** D4
Nez Perce National Historical Park, *Idaho, U.S.* **108** D3
Nez Perce Pass, *Idaho, Mont., U.S.* **108** E5
Ngabordamlu, Tanjung, *Indonesia* **217** D15
Ngain, island, *Marshall Is., U.S.* **220** K7
Ngajangel, island, *Palau* **220** K12
Ngake, *Cook Is., N.Z.* **222** Q2
Ngake, island, *Cook Is., N.Z.* **223** A14
Ngala, *Nigeria* **205** B17
Ngalkol, *Palau* **220** Q10
Ngamegei Passage, *Palau* **220** L12
Ngami, Lake, *Botswana* **206** G8
Ngangla Ringco (Angla Rencuo), lake, *China* **182** K3
Nganglong Kangri, *China* **182** J2
Ngaoundéré, *Cameroon* **205** D16
Ngaramasch, *Palau* **220** R9
Ngardmau, *Palau* **220** M12
Ngardmau Bay, *Palau* **220** M12
Ngardololok, *Palau* **220** Q10
Ngaregur, island, *Palau* **220** L12
Ngaremediu, island, *Palau* **220** P11
Ngaruangl Passage, *Palau* **220** K12
Ngaruawahia, *N.Z.* **217** J19
Ngatangiia, *Cook Is., N.Z.* **222** Q9
Ngatik Atoll, *F.S.M.* **220** D18
Ngauruhoe, Mount, *N.Z.* **217** L19
Ngcheangel see Kayangel Islands, *Palau* **220** K12
Ngeaur see Angaur, island, *Palau* **220** R9
Ngemelis Islands, *Palau* **220** Q10
Ngerchelchuus, Mount, *Palau* **220** M12
Ngeregong, island, *Palau* **220** Q11

Ngergoi, island, *Palau* **220** Q10
Ngertachebeab, bay, *Palau* **220** N11
Ngeruktabel, island, *Palau* **220** P11
Ngesebus, island, *Palau* **220** Q10
Nggatokae, island, *Solomon Is.* **221** N17
Nggela Pile, island, *Solomon Is.* **221** N19
Nggela Sule, island, *Solomon Is.* **221** N19
Ngobasangel, island, *Palau* **220** P10
Ngoïla, *Cameroon* **205** F17
Ngoko, river, *Cameroon, Congo* **205** G17
Ngô Mây, *Vietnam* **190** M14
Ngoring Hu, *China* **182** J8
Ngorongoro Crater, *Tanzania* **203** L14
Ngounié, river, *Gabon* **205** H15
Ngourti, *Niger* **201** H13
Nguigmi, *Niger* **201** H13
Nguiu, *N.T., Austral.* **215** N7
Ngukurr, *N.T., Austral.* **215** P9
Ngulu Atoll, *F.S.M.* **221** Q2
Nguna, island, *Vanuatu* **222** E2
Nguru, *Nigeria* **205** B15
Nhamundá, *Braz.* **132** D10
Nha Trang, *Vietnam* **191** N14
Nhulunbuy, *N.T., Austral.* **215** P10
Niafounké, *Mali* **200** H8
Niagara, *Wis., U.S.* **100** G7
Niagara, river, *N.Y., U.S.* **96** H4
Niagara Falls, *N.Y., U.S.* **96** J5
Niah, *Malaysia* **192** G11
Niamey, *Niger* **200** H10
Niangara, *Dem. Rep. of the Congo* **202** J11
Niangua, river, *Mo., U.S.* **107** U12
Nianqingtangla Shan see Nyainqêntanglha Shan, *China* **182** L5
Nias, island, *Indonesia* **192** H4
Niau, island, *Fr. Polynesia, Fr.* **223** E18
Nibok, region, *Nauru* **221** E23
Nic, *Azerb.* **171** C21
Nicaea see İznik, *Turk.* **170** D5
Nicaragua, *N. Amer.* **117** M18
Nicaragua, Lago de, *Nicar.* **117** M18
Nicaro, *Cuba* **119** K13
Nicastro, *It.* **153** Q13
Nice, *Fr.* **149** X15
Nicephorium see Ar Raqqah, *Syr.* **172** E11
Niceville, *Fla., U.S.* **99** Q2
Nichi see Nyingchi, *China* **182** L7
Nichinan, *Japan* **189** T5
Nicholas Channel, *N. Amer.* **118** F8
Nicholasville, *Ky., U.S.* **103** C18
Nicholls' Town, *Bahamas* **118** E11
Nicholson Range, *Austral.* **214** H3
Nickavilla, *Qnsld., Austral.* **215** U12
Nickerson, *Kans., U.S.* **107** T7
Nickol Bay, *Austral.* **214** E2
Nicobar Fan, *Ind. Oc.* **225** F14
Nicobar Islands, *India* **181** S15
Nicosia, *It.* **153** S11
Nicosia (Lefkosía, Lefkoşa), *Cyprus* **162** N8
Nicoya, Península de, *C.R.* **117** N18
Nida, *Lith.* **143** M15
Nidzica, *Pol.* **151** C15
Niederanven, *Lux.* **162** J10
Niedere Tauern, range, *Aust.* **150** L10
Nienburg, *Ger.* **150** D7
Nienhawn Amsterdam, *Suriname* **131** E16
Nieuw Amsterdam Fracture Zone, *Ind. Oc.* **224** N11
Nieuw Nickerie, *Suriname* **131** E15
Nieuwpoort, *Curaçao, Neth.* **123** Q15
Nieves, Pico da las, *Sp.* **208** R5
Nif, *F.S.M.* **220** Q7
Nifiloli, island, *Solomon Is.* **221** P23
Niğde, *Turk.* **170** G10
Niger, *Af.* **200** H12
Niger, river, *Af.* **198** G2
Niger Delta, *Nigeria* **205** F13
Niger Fan, *Atl. Oc.* **241** N13
Nigeria, *Af.* **205** C14
Nigríta, *Gr.* **156** C12
Nihing, river, *Pak.* **179** V2

Nihiru, island, *Fr. Polynesia, Fr.* **223** E19
Nihoa, *Hawai'i, U.S.* **114** M8
Nihonmatsu, *Japan* **188** M12
Niigata, *Japan* **188** M11
Niihama, *Japan* **189** Q7
Ni'ihau, Island, *Hawai'i, U.S.* **114** D3
Nii Jima, *Japan* **189** Q11
Nijmegen, *Neth.* **148** J13
Níkaia, *Gr.* **156** F10
Nişāb, *Saudi Arabia* **174** G9
Nişāb, *Yemen* **174** Q10
Nišava, river, *Serb.* **154** H12
Nishine, *Japan* **188** K13
Nishinoomote, *Japan* **189** T5
Nishino Shima, *Japan* **189** N6
Nishtūn, *Yemen* **175** P13
Nissi, *Est.* **143** K16
Nisswa, *Minn., U.S.* **106** G10
Nísyros, island, *Gr.* **157** M18
Niţă', *Saudi Arabia* **174** H11
Niterói, *Braz.* **133** M15
Nitra, *Slovakia* **151** K14
Nitro, *W. Va., U.S.* **98** D8
Niuafo'ou, island, *Tonga* **218** J10
Niuatoputapu, island, *Tonga* **218** J10
Niue, island, *Pac. Oc.* **218** K10
Niujiayingzi, *N. Mongol, China* **184** A9
Niulakita, island, *Tuvalu* **218** H9
Niutao, island, *Tuvalu* **218** H9
Niutoua, *Tonga* **222** J12
Niutou Shan, island, *Zhejiang, China* **185** P12
Nixon, *Tex., U.S.* **105** R10
Nixon's Harbour, *Bahamas* **122** C8
Niya see Minfeng, *China* **182** G3
Nizamabad, *India* **180** L6
Nizamghat, *India* **180** F15
Nizam Sagar, lake, *India* **180** M6
Nizao, *Dom. Rep.* **119** M19
Nizhnekamsk, *Russ.* **158** H16
Nizhneudinsk, *Russ.* **161** L14
Nizhnevartovsk, *Russ.* **160** H11
Nizhneyansk, *Russ.* **161** E17
Nizhniy Baskunchak, *Russ.* **159** Q14
Nizhniy Bestyakh, *Russ.* **161** G18
Nizhniy Lomov, *Russ.* **158** L12
Nizhniy Novgorod, *Russ.* **158** J12
Nizhniy Tagil, *Russ.* **160** H9
Nizhnyaya Tunguska, river, *Russ.* **161** H13
Nizhnyaya Tura, *Russ.* **160** H9
Nizhyn, *Ukr.* **159** N6
Nizip, *Turk.* **170** J12
Nizip, river, *Turk.* **170** H12
Nizwá, *Oman* **175** K16
Nizza Monferrato, *It.* **152** E3
Nizzana (El 'Auja), *Egypt* **173** P4
Njazidja, island (Grande Comore), *Comoros* **209** M14
Njegoš, peak, *Montenegro* **154** H8
Njombe, *Tanzania* **203** N13
Nkhata Bay, *Malawi* **207** D13
Nkhotakota, *Malawi* **207** D13
Nkomi Lagoon, *Af.* **198** K5
Nkongsamba, *Cameroon* **205** E15
Nmai, river, *Myanmar* **190** D7
Noatak, *Alas., U.S.* **113** D13
Noatak National Preserve, *Alas., U.S.* **113** D14
Nobeoka, *Japan* **189** S5
Noblesville, *Ind., U.S.* **101** R9
Nobo, *Indonesia* **193** M14
Noboribetsu, *Japan* **188** G13
Nocera Terinese, *It.* **153** Q13
Nocona, *Tex., U.S.* **104** J10
Nodales, Bahía de los, *Arg.* **135** U9
Nodaway, river, *Iowa, Mo., U.S.* **107** R10
Nofre, Peña, *Sp.* **146** D7
Nogales, *Ariz., U.S.* **109** W8
Nogales, *Mex.* **116** B7
Nogara, *It.* **152** E7
Nōgata, *Japan* **189** R5
Nogent-le-Rotrou, *Fr.* **149** Q8
Nogent-sur-Seine, *Fr.* **149** Q11
Noginsk, *Russ.* **158** J10
Nogoyá, *Arg.* **134** K12
Nogu Dabu, island, *P.N.G.* **221** H18
Nogueira, peak, *Port.* **146** D7
Nohar, *India* **180** E4

Noheji, *Japan* 188 JI3
Nohili Point, *Hawai'i, U.S.* 114 C4
Nohona o Hae, peak, *Hawai'i, U.S.* 115 LI9
Nohta, *India* 180 J7
Nohwa, *S. Korea* 187 V7
Nohwado, island, *S. Korea* 187 U7
Noia, *Sp.* 146 B5
Noire, Montagne, *Fr.* 149 XI0
Noires, Montagnes, *Fr.* 149 Q3
Noirmoutier, Île de, *Fr.* 149 S5
Nojima Zaki, *Japan* 189 QI2
Noka, *Solomon Is.* 221 Q22
Nokaneng, *Botswana* 206 G8
Nokia, *Fin.* 143 HI5
Nok Kundi, *Pak.* 179 S2
Nokomis, *Ill., U.S.* 101 S5
Nokuku, *Vanuatu* 222 CI
Nola, *Cen. Af. Rep.* 202 J8
Noli, *It.* 152 F3
Nolinsk, *Russ.* 158 GI4
Noma Misaki, *Japan* 189 T4
Nomans Land, *Mass., U.S.* 97 MI5
Nome, *Alas., U.S.* 112 FI2
Nomgon, *Mongolia* 182 FI0
Nomoneas, island, *F.S.M.* 221 BI5
Nomuka, island, *Tonga* 222 Q6
Nomuka Group, *Tonga* 222 R6
Nomuka Iki, island, *Tonga* 222 Q6
Nomwin Atoll, *F.S.M.* 220 Q6
Nonancourt, *Fr.* 149 P8
Nonda, *Qnsld., Austral.* 215 SI2
Nondalton, *Alas., U.S.* 113 KI5
Nongjrong, *India* 180 GI4
Nong Khai, *Thai.* 190 KI0
Nongong, *S. Korea* 187 RII
Nongsan, *S. Korea* 187 RI0
Nonouti, island, *Kiribati* 218 G8
Nonpareil, *Grenada* 123 J23
Nonsan, *S. Korea* 187 Q8
Nonsuch Bay, *Antigua and Barbuda* 123 B22
Nonsuch Island, *Bermuda* 122 B3
Nonthaburi, *Thai.* 190 M9
Nonume, *Solomon Is.* 221 Q22
Nonza, *Fr.* 152 J4
Noole, *Solomon Is.* 221 Q22
Noonan, *N. Dak., U.S.* 106 D2
Noondoo, *Qnsld., Austral.* 215 VI4
Noord, *Aruba, Neth.* 123 QI7
Noordkaap, *Aruba, Neth.* 123 QI7
Noordpunt, *Curaçao, Neth.* 123 NI3
Noormarkku, *Fin.* 143 HI5
Noorvik, *Alas., U.S.* 113 EI3
Noosa Head, *Austral.* 214 HI6
Nóqui, *Angola* 206 B5
Nora, ruin, *It.* 153 T4
Nora Hazel Point, *British Virgin Is., U.K.* 122 R7
Norak, *Taj.* 178 J8
Norborne, *Mo., U.S.* 107 SII
Norcia, *It.* 152 X9
Nord, Baie du, *Mauritius* 209 J20
Nord, Pointe, *Comoros* 209 LI4
Nord, Pointe, *St.-Martin, Fr.* 123 AI5
Nord, Pointe, *Wallis and Futuna, Fr.* 222 EII
Norden, *Ger.* 150 C6
Norderstedt, *Ger.* 150 C8
Nord Est, Grande Récif du, *Mayotte, Fr.* 209 NI7
Nordeste, *Azores, Port.* 146 Q5
Nordfjord, *Atl. Oc.* 140 D6
Nordfjordeid, *Nor.* 142 JI0
Nordhausen, *Ger.* 150 F8
Nordhorn, *Ger.* 150 D5
Nordkapp, cape, *Nor.* 143 BI4
Nordkapp Bank, *Arctic Oc.* 247 FI8
Nordkjosbotn, *Nor.* 143 CI3
Nordli, *Nor.* 142 GI2
Norðoyar, island, *Faroe Is., Den.* 142 H6
Nore, river, *Ire.* 145 T6
Noreena Downs, *W. Aust., Austral.* 215 T4
Norfolk, *Nebr., U.S.* 107 N7
Norfolk, *Va., U.S.* 98 FI4
Norfolk Island, *Norfolk Is., Austral.* 218 L7
Norfolk Ridge, *Pac. Oc.* 242 MI0
Norfolk Trough, *Pac. Oc.* 242 NI0

Norfork Lake, *Ark., U.S.* 102 E9
Noril'sk, *Russ.* 161 FI3
Normal, *Ill., U.S.* 101 Q6
Norman, *Ark., U.S.* 102 H7
Norman, *Okla., U.S.* 104 GII
Norman, river, *Austral.* 214 DI2
Norman, Lake, *N.C., U.S.* 98 H9
Normanby Island, *P.N.G.* 217 E2I
Normandy, region, *Fr.* 149 P8
Norman's Cay, *Bahamas* 122 G5
Norman's Pond Cay, *Bahamas* 122 E7
Normanton, *Qnsld., Austral.* 215 RI2
Norman Wells, *N.W.T., Can.* 84 FI0
Nornalup, *W. Aust., Austral.* 215 Y3
Ñorquincó, *Arg.* 135 Q7
Norris Lake, *Tenn., U.S.* 103 EI8
Norristown, *Pa., U.S.* 96 P9
Norrköping, *Sw.* 143 LI3
Norrland, *Eur.* 140 C8
Norrsundet, *Sw.* 143 JI3
Norseman, *W. Aust., Austral.* 215 X5
Norsk, *Russ.* 161 KI9
Norske Bank, *Arctic Oc.* 247 HI6
Nort, *Fr.* 149 R6
Norte, Cabo, *Braz.* 133 CI3
Norte, Canal do, *Braz.* 133 CI3
Norte, Punta, *Arg.* 134 MI3
Norte, Serra do, *Braz.* 132 G9
North, Cape, *N.S., Can.* 85 N22
North Adams, *Mass., U.S.* 97 KI2
North Albanian Alps, *Alban.* 154 J9
North Aleutian Slope, *Pac. Oc.* 242 CI2
North American Basin, *Atl. Oc.* 240 K5
Northampton, *Eng., U.K.* 145 UI3
Northampton, *Mass., U.S.* 97 KI3
Northampton, *W. Aust., Austral.* 215 V2
Northampton Seamounts, *Hawai'i, U.S.* 114 L4
North Andaman, island, *India* 181 PI4
North Aral Sea, *Kaz.* 176 GI0
North Arm, *N.W.T., Can.* 84 HII
North Atlantic Ocean, *Atl. Oc.* 240 J8
North Augusta, *S.C., U.S.* 98 L8
North Aulatsivik Island, *Nfld. & Lab., Can.* 85 J20
North Australian Basin, *Ind. Oc.* 225 JI8
North Banda Basin, *Pac. Oc.* 242 K5
North Battleford, *Sask., Can.* 84 MII
North Bay, *Ont., Can.* 85 PI8
North Belcher Islands, *Nunavut, Can.* 85 LI7
North Bend, *Oreg., U.S.* 110 J2
North Bimini, *Bahamas* 122 B8
North Branch, *Minn., U.S.* 106 JI2
North Branch Potomac, river, *Md., W. Va., U.S.* 98 CI0
North Brazilian Ridge, *Atl. Oc.* 241 P8
North Caicos, island, *Turks & Caicos Is.* 119 HI7
North Canadian, river, *U.S.* 86 JI2
North Cape, *Eur.* 140 A3
North Cape, *Eur.* 140 A9
North Cape, *Kiribati* 221 A20
North Cape, *N.Z.* 217 GI8
North Carolina, *U.S.* 98 HI0
North Cascades National Park, *Wash., U.S.* 110 A5
North Channel, *Can., U.S.* 100 FI2
North Channel, *Ire., U.K.* 145 P8
North Charleston, *S.C., U.S.* 98 MI0
North Chatham Slope, *Pac. Oc.* 249 H2I
North Chatham Terrace, *Pac. Oc.* 249 H2I
North Chicago, *Ill., U.S.* 100 M7
North China Plain, *Asia* 168 GII
Northcliffe, *W. Aust., Austral.* 215 Y3
North Comino Channel, *Malta* 163 H2I
North Dakota, *U.S.* 106 F4
North Downs, *Eng., U.K.* 145 VI4
North East, *Pa., U.S.* 96 K3
Northeast Cay, *Jam.* 118 PII

Northeast Georgia Rise, *Atl. Oc.* 241 V8
North East Land, *Nor.* 168 A7
Northeast Newfoundland Shelf, *Atl. Oc.* 240 G6
Northeast Pacific Basin, *Pac. Oc.* 243 EI3
Northeast Pass, *Marshall Is., U.S.* 220 L8
Northeast Passage, *Solomon Is.* 221 R24
North East Point, *Cayman Is.* 118 L9
North East Point, *Kiribati* 221 B23
Northeast Point, *Bahamas* 119 GI5
Northeast Point, *Jam.* 122 JII
Northeast Providence Channel, *Bahamas* 118 DI2
Northeim, *Ger.* 150 E7
North Entrance, *Palau* 220 KI2
Northern Cyprus, *Cyprus* 162 N9
Northern Dvina, river, *Eur.* 140 CI2
Northern European Plain, *Eur.* 140 G7
Northern Ireland, *N. Ire., U.K.* 145 P6
Northern Light Lake, *Can., U.S.* 106 EI4
Northern Mariana Islands, *Pac. Oc.* 220 AI
Northern Range, *Trinidad and Tobago* 123 N23
Northern Sporades see Vóries Sporádhes, islands, *Gr.* 157 FI3
Northern Territory, *Austral.* 215 R8
Northern Urals, *Asia* 168 D6
Northern Uvals, *Eur.* 140 DI3
Northfield, *Minn., U.S.* 106 KII
Northfield, *Vt., U.S.* 97 GI3
North Fiji Basin, *Pac. Oc.* 242 LI0
North Fond du Lac, *Wis., U.S.* 100 K6
North Fork, *Calif., U.S.* 111 T6
North Fork Clearwater, river, *Idaho, U.S.* 108 C4
North Fork Flathead, river, *Can., U.S.* 108 A5
North Fork Payette, river, *Idaho, U.S.* 108 G4
North Fork Red, river, *Okla., Tex., U.S.* 104 G6
North Fork Salt, river, *Mo., U.S.* 107 RI3
North Friar's Bay, *St. Kitts and Nevis* 123 BI8
North Frisian Islands, *Den., Ger.* 150 A6
North Head, *N.Z.* 217 JI8
North Island, *Seychelles* 209 NI9
North Island (Te Ika-A-Māui), *N.Z.* 217 HI9
North Kanin Bank, *Arctic Oc.* 247 DI7
North Kenya Bank, *Ind. Oc.* 224 G5
North Korea, *Asia* 186 G7
North Kosovo, region, *Kos.* 154 HI0
North Lakhimpur, *India* 180 FI4
North Land see Severnaya Zemlya, *Russ.* 161 CI2
North Las Vegas, *Nev., U.S.* 111 UI2
North Little Rock, *Ark., U.S.* 102 G8
North Loup, river, *Nebr., U.S.* 107 N5
North Magellan Rise, *Pac. Oc.* 242 HI2
North Malosmadulu Atoll, *Maldives* 181 U3
North Manchester, *Ind., U.S.* 101 P9
North Mole, *Gibraltar, U.K.* 163 N22
North Myrtle Beach, *S.C., U.S.* 98 LI2
North Naples, *Fla., U.S.* 99 W8
North Negril Point, *Jam.* 122 H5
North Norfolk Basin, *Pac. Oc.* 242 MI0
North Olmsted, *Ohio, U.S.* 101 PI4
North Pacific Ocean, *Pac. Oc.* 218 BII
North Palmetto Point, *Bahamas* 122 E6
North Pass, *Marshall Is., U.S.* 220 K4
North Perry, *Ohio, U.S.* 101 NI5
North Pioa, peak, *Amer. Samoa, U.S.* 222 M8
North Platte, *Nebr., U.S.* 107 Q4

North Platte, river, *U.S.* 86 F9
North Point, *Barbados* 123 JI9
North Point, *Cook Is., N.Z.* 223 AI4
North Point, *Mich., U.S.* 100 HI2
North Point, *S. Amer.* 128 M7
North Point, *Seychelles* 209 N20
Northport, *Ala., U.S.* 103 KI4
Northport, *Wash., U.S.* 110 A8
North Powder, *Oreg., U.S.* 110 F8
North Raccoon, river, *Iowa, U.S.* 107 PII
North Rock, *Bahamas* 122 A8
North Roe, *Scot., U.K.* 144 DI2
North Ronaldsay, island, *Scot., U.K.* 144 FI0
North Saskatchewan, river, *Alb. & Sask., Can.* 84 LI2
North Scotia Ridge, *Atl. Oc.* 241 W6
North Sea, *Eur.* 140 E5
North Sentinel Island, *India* 181 QI4
North Siberian Lowland, *Asia* 168 C9
North Side, *Cayman Is.* 122 H3
North Slope, *Alas., U.S.* 113 CI6
North Solomon Trough, *Pac. Oc.* 242 K9
North Sound, *British Virgin Is., U.K.* 122 Q9
North Sound, *Cayman Is.* 122 J2
North Sound, *Ire.* 145 S3
North Sound, The, *Scot., U.K.* 144 FI0
North Sound Estates, *Cayman Is.* 122 J2
North Springfield, *Pa., U.S.* 96 L3
North Stradbroke Island, *Austral.* 214 HI6
North Taranaki Bight, *N.Z.* 217 KI7
North Tasman Seamounts, *Pac. Oc.* 249 E2I
North Tonawanda, *N.Y., U.S.* 96 J5
North Truchas Peak, *N. Mex., U.S.* 109 RI3
North Uist see Uibhist a Tuath, island, *Scot., U.K.* 144 J6
Northumberland, Cape, *Austral.* 214 MII
Northumberland Islands, *Austral.* 214 EI5
North Vanlaiphai, *India* 180 JI4
North Vernon, *Ind., U.S.* 101 SI0
North Walsham, *Eng., U.K.* 145 TI5
Northway Junction, *Alas., U.S.* 113 HI9
North Wazīristān, region, *Pak.* 179 N8
North Weddell Ridge see America-Antarctica Ridge, *Atl. Oc.* 241 WI0
Northwest Angle, *Minn., U.S.* 106 DI0
Northwest Atlantic Mid-Ocean Canyon, *Atl. Oc.* 240 F6
North West Basin, *Austral.* 214 G2
North West Bay, *Seychelles* 209 NI9
North West Cape, *Austral.* 214 FI
Northwestern Hawaiian Islands, *Hawai'i, U.S.* 114 M5
Northwest Georgia Rise, *Atl. Oc.* 241 V8
Northwest Pacific Basin, *Pac. Oc.* 242 E8
North West Point, *Cayman Is.* 118 L7
North West Point, *Kiribati* 221 A22
Northwest Point, *Bahamas* 122 BI0
Northwest Providence Channel, *Bahamas* 118 CI0
North West River, *Nfld. & Lab., Can.* 85 L2I
Northwest Territories, *Can.* 84 GI0
Northwich, *Eng., U.K.* 145 SII
North Wilkesboro, *N.C., U.S.* 98 G9
Northwind Escarpment, *Arctic Oc.* 246 K8
Northwind Plain, *Arctic Oc.* 246 K8
Northwind Ridge, *Arctic Oc.* 246 L8
Northwood, *Iowa, U.S.* 106 LI2
Northwood, *N. Dak., U.S.* 106 F7
Northwood, *Ohio, U.S.* 101 PI4
NorthYork Moors, *Eng., U.K.* 145 QI3
Norton, *Kans., U.S.* 107 R5
Norton, *Va., U.S.* 98 F7
Norton Bay, *Alas., U.S.* 113 FI3

Norton Plain, *Pac. Oc.* 246 L3
Norton Shores, *Mich., U.S.* 100 L9
Norton Sound, *Alas., U.S.* 112 GI2
Norvegia, Cape, *Antarctica* 230 BII
Norwalk, *Calif., U.S.* III X8
Norwalk, *Conn., U.S.* 96 MI2
Norwalk, *Ohio, U.S.* 101 PI3
Norway, *Eur.* 142 GII
Norway, *Me., U.S.* 97 GI5
Norway, *Mich., U.S.* 100 G7
Norway House, *Man., Can.* 85 MI4
Norwegian Basin, *Arctic Oc.* 240 EI2
Norwegian Bay, *Nunavut, Can.* 85 CI5
Norwegian Sea, *Arctic Oc.* 140 B6
Norwegian Trough, *Atl. Oc.* 240 FI3
Norwich, *Conn., U.S.* 97 MI3
Norwich, *Eng., U.K.* 145 TI5
Norwich, *N.Y., U.S.* 96 K9
Norwood, *Colo., U.S.* 109 NI0
Norwood, *N.C., U.S.* 98 JI0
Norwood, *N.Y., U.S.* 96 FI0
Norwood, *Ohio, U.S.* 101 SII
Noshiro, *Japan* 188 KI2
Nosivka, *Ukr.* 159 N6
Noşratābād, *Iran* 175 FI7
Noss, Isle of, *Scot., U.K.* 144 DI2
Nossob, river, *Af.* 206 J8
Nosy Be, island, *Af.* 198 MI2
Nosy Sainte Marie, island, *Af.* 198 MI2
Nosy-Varika, *Madagascar* 207 GI8
Not'an, *N. Korea* 186 D8
Noteć, river, *Pol.* 151 CI3
Note Kanengo, cape, *Solomon Is.* 221 Q23
Note Kembanye, cape, *Solomon Is.* 221 Q22
Note Kempopla, cape, *Solomon Is.* 221 Q22
Nótios Evvoïkós Kólpos, *Gr.* 156 HI2
Noto, *It.* 153 TI2
Noto, *Japan* 188 MI0
Noto, Golfo di, *It.* 153 UI2
Noto Hantō, *Japan* 188 M9
Noto Peninsula, *Asia* 168 FI3
Notre Dame Bay, *Nfld. & Lab., Can.* 85 M23
Nottaway, river, *Que., Can.* 85 NI8
Nottingham, *Eng., U.K.* 145 SI3
Nottingham Island, *Nunavut, Can.* 85 HI7
Nottoway, river, *Va., U.S.* 98 FI2
Nouadhibou (Port Etienne), *Mauritania* 200 F4
Nouakchott, *Mauritania* 200 G5
Nouâmghâr, *Mauritania* 200 F4
Nouans-les-Fontaines, *Fr.* 149 S9
Nouart, *Fr.* 149 NI2
Nouméa, *New Caledonia, Fr.* 222 E8
Nouna, *Burkina Faso* 204 B9
Nouveau Québec, *Que., Can.* 85 LI8
Nouvelle-Calédonie (New Caledonia), island, *New Caledonia, Fr.* 222 C6
Novafeltria, *It.* 152 G8
Nova Friburgo, *Braz.* 133 MI5
Nova Gorica, *Slov.* 154 D4
Nova Gradiška, *Croatia* 154 E7
Nova Iguaçu, *Braz.* 133 MI4
Nova Kakhovka, *Ukr.* 159 R7
Novalukoml', *Belarus* 158 K5
Nova Mambone, *Mozambique* 207 GI3
Nova Odesa, *Ukr.* 159 R6
Nova Olinda do Norte, *Braz.* 132 E9
Novara, *It.* 152 D4
Novara Fracture Zone, *Ind. Oc.* 224 N8
Nova Scotia, *Can.* 85 P22
Nova Sofala, *Mozambique* 207 GI3
Nova Xavantina, *Braz.* 132 JI2
Novaya Sibir', Ostrov, *Russ.* 161 CI7
Novaya Vodolaga, *Ukr.* 159 P8
Novaya Zemlya, *Russ.* 160 DII
Nova Zagora, *Bulg.* 155 JI6
Novelda, *Sp.* 147 JI4
Nové Zámky, *Slovakia* 151 KI4
Novhorod-Sivers'kyy, *Ukr.* 158 M7
Novi Bečej, *Serb.* 154 EI0
Novi Ligure, *It.* 152 F4

Nov–Oka

Novi Pazar, Bulg. 155 H17
Novi Pazar, Serb. 154 H10
Novi Sad, Serb. 154 E9
Novoaleksandrovsk, Russ. 159 S11
Novoanninskiy, Russ. 159 N12
Novo Aripuanã, Braz. 132 E9
Novobod, Taj. 178 H8
Novocherkassk, Russ. 159 R11
Novo Cruzeiro, Braz. 133 K15
Novo Hamburgo, Braz. 132 P12
Novohrad-Volyns'kyy, Ukr. 159 N4
Novoīshīmskīy, Kaz. 176 C12
Novokuybyshevsk, Russ. 158 L15
Novokuznetsk, Russ. 160 L12
Novolazarevskaya, station, Antarctica 231 B14
Novo Mesto, Slov. 154 D5
Novomichurinsk, Russ. 158 K10
Novomoskovs'k, Ukr. 159 Q8
Novomoskovsk, Russ. 158 K9
Novopokrovskaya, Russ. 159 S11
Novorepnoye, Russ. 158 M15
Novorossiysk, Russ. 159 T9
Novorybnoye, Russ. 161 F15
Novorzhev, Russ. 158 H6
Novoshakhtinsk, Russ. 159 Q11
Novosibirsk, Russ. 160 K12
Novosibirskiye Ostrova (New Siberian Islands), Russ. 161 D16
Novotitarovskaya, Russ. 159 S10
Novotroitsk, Russ. 160 J7
Novoukrayinka, Ukr. 159 Q6
Novouzensk, Russ. 159 N15
Novovolyns'k, Ukr. 159 N2
Novoye Ust'ye, Russ. 161 G20
Novozybkov, Russ. 158 M6
Novyy Buh, Ukr. 159 Q6
Novyy Port, Russ. 160 F11
Novyy Urengoy, Russ. 160 G12
Nowābād Īmj, Afghan. 178 J9
Nowa Sól, Pol. 150 E12
Nowata, Okla., U.S. 104 E13
Now Deh, Afghan. 179 P2
Nowood, river, Wyo., U.S. 108 G11
Nowrangapur, India 180 L8
Nowshāk, peak, Afghan., Pak. 178 K10
Nowshera, Pak. 179 N10
Nowy Sącz, Pol. 151 H16
Nowy Targ, Pol. 151 H15
Now Zād, Afghan. 179 P4
Noxon, Mont., U.S. 108 B4
Noyabr'sk, Russ. 160 H11
Noyon, Fr. 149 N10
Nozay, Fr. 149 R5
Nsukka, Nigeria 205 E14
Ntingui, peak, Comoros 209 N16
Ntomba, Lac, Dem. Rep. of the Congo 202 K8
Ntsaouéni, Comoros 209 M14
Nu (Salween), river, Asia 168 H9
Nuapapu, Tonga 222 M11
Nuapapu, island, Tonga 222 M11
Nuatabu, Kiribati 221 F17
Nubia, Lake, Sudan 202 C12
Nubian Desert, Sudan 203 C13
Nubledo, Sp. 146 A8
Nuclear test site, N. Korea 186 D11
Nuclear test site, Pak. 179 S4
Nuclear test site, Pak. 179 T3
Nueces, river, Tex., U.S. 105 T9
Nueltin Lake, Nunavut, Can. 85 J14
Nuestra Señora, Bahía, Chile 134 F6
Nueva Gerona, Cuba 118 H6
Nueva Rosita, Mex. 116 D11
Nuevitas, Cuba 118 J11
Nuevo, Bajo, Mex. 117 G15
Nuevo, Golfo, Arg. 135 R10
Nuevo Casas Grandes, Mex. 116 C8
Nuevo Laredo, Mex. 116 F12
Nuevo Rocafuerte, Ecua. 130 J5
Nuguria Islands, P.N.G. 217 C22
Nui, island, Tuvalu 218 H9
Nukapu, island, Solomon Is. 221 P22
Nuku, island, Tonga 222 H12
Nukuaéta, Île, Wallis and Futuna, Fr. 222 C11
Nuku'alofa, Tonga 222 H11
Nukubasaga, island, Fiji 222 G9
Nukudamu, Fiji 222 G8
Nukufetau, island, Tuvalu 218 H9
Nukufotu, Îlot, Wallis and Futuna, Fr. 222 A11
Nukufufulanoa, Île, Wallis and Futuna, Fr. 222 A11
Nukuhifala, Île, Wallis and Futuna, Fr. 222 B12
Nuku Hiva, island, Fr. Polynesia, Fr. 219 H15
Nukuira, island, Fiji 222 G7
Nukulaelae, island, Tuvalu 218 H9
Nukuloa, Île, Wallis and Futuna, Fr. 222 A11
Nukumanu Islands, P.N.G. 221 H18
Nukunonu, island, Kiribati 218 H10
Nukuoro Atoll, F.S.M. 220 R7
Nukus, Uzb. 176 J9
Nukutapu, Île, Wallis and Futuna, Fr. 222 B11
Nukutavake, island, Fr. Polynesia, Fr. 223 F21
Nukuteatea, Île, Wallis and Futuna, Fr. 222 A11
Nukutipipi, island, Fr. Polynesia, Fr. 223 G19
Nulato, Alas., U.S. 113 F14
Nules, Sp. 147 G15
Nullagine, W. Aust., Austral. 215 T3
Nullarbor, S. Aust., Austral. 215 W8
Nullarbor Plain, Austral. 214 J6
Nulu'erhu Shan, Liaoning, China 184 B10
Num, island, Indonesia 193 K19
Numakawa, Japan 188 E13
Numan, Nigeria 205 C16
Numata, Japan 188 F13
Numata, Japan 189 N11
Numazu, Japan 189 P11
Numbulwar, N.T., Austral. 215 P9
Numfoor, island, Indonesia 193 J19
Numila, Hawai'i, U.S. 114 C5
Numto, Russ. 160 G11
Nunavut, Can. 85 G14
Nuneaton, Eng., U.K. 145 T12
Nünggu, N. Korea 186 E9
Nunivak Island, Alas., U.S. 112 J10
Nunligran, Russ. 161 A21
Nuoro, It. 153 N4
Nupani, island, Solomon Is. 221 P22
Nuquí, Col. 130 E3
Nura, river, Kaz. 177 E14
Nuremberg see Nürnberg, Ger. 150 H8
Nur Gama, Pak. 179 T6
Nurlat, Russ. 158 J15
Nurmes, Fin. 143 F16
Nürnberg (Nuremberg), Ger. 150 H8
Nurpur, Pak. 179 P10
Nurri, It. 153 P4
Nurse Cay, Bahamas 119 H13
Nusaybin, Turk. 171 H16
Nushagak Peninsula, N. Amer. 82 R4
Nushki, Pak. 179 S5
Nuttal, Pak. 179 S7
Nutwood Downs, N.T., Austral. 215 Q9
Nu'uanu Pali Overlook, Hawai'i, U.S. 114 F11
Nu'ulua, island, Samoa 222 L4
Nuupere, Pointe, Fr. Polynesia, Fr. 223 N14
Nuusilaelae, island, Amer. Samoa, U.S. 222 N1
Nuussuaq, island, Greenland, Den. 82 D9
Nu'utele, island, Samoa 222 L4
Nuutele, island, Amer. Samoa, U.S. 222 N1
Nu'uuli, Amer. Samoa, U.S. 222 M7
Nuweiba', Egypt 173 S4
Nuweveld Range, Af. 198 Q7
Nyagan', Russ. 160 G10
Nyainqêntanglha Feng, China 182 K5
Nyainqêntanglha Shan (Nianqingtangla Shan), China 182 L5
Nyala, Sudan 202 F10
Nyamlell, S. Sudan 202 G11
Nyandoma, Russ. 160 E7
Nyanga, Lake, Austral. 214 J6
Nyaunglebin, Myanmar 190 K6
Nybergsund, Nor. 142 J12
Nyborg, Den. 142 N11
Nyborg, Nor. 143 B15
Nyda, Russ. 160 G11
Nyeri, Kenya 203 K14
Nyerol, S. Sudan 203 G13
Nyeying, India 180 E14
Nyima (Nima), China 182 K4
Nyingchi (Nichi), China 182 L7
Nyíregyháza, Hung. 151 K17
Nykarleby, Fin. 143 G15
Nykøbing, Den. 142 N12
Nyköping, Sw. 143 K13
Nymagee, N.S.W., Austral. 215 X13
Nymphaeum see Pínnes, Ákra, Gr. 157 D13
Nyngan, N.S.W., Austral. 215 W13
Nyoman, river, Belarus 158 K3
Nyoma Rap, India 179 N15
Nyon, Switz. 152 C1
Nyong, river, Cameroon 205 F15
Nyons, Fr. 149 W13
Nysa, Pol. 151 G13
Nysh, Russ. 161 J21
Nyssa, Oreg., U.S. 110 H9
Nyūdō Zaki, Japan 188 K12
Nyuksenitsa, Russ. 158 E12
Nyunzu, Dem. Rep. of the Congo 202 M11
Nyurba, Russ. 161 H16
Nzega, Tanzania 203 L13
Nzérékoré, Guinea 204 D7
N'zeto, Angola 206 B5
Nzwani, island (Anjouan), Comoros 209 N16

O

Oacoma, S. Dak., U.S. 106 L5
Oahe, Lake, N. Dak., S. Dak., U.S. 106 H4
O'ahu, Island, Hawai'i, U.S. 114 D9
Oak Bluffs, Mass., U.S. 97 M15
Oakdale, Calif., U.S. 111 S5
Oakdale, La., U.S. 102 N8
Oakes, N. Dak., U.S. 106 H7
Oakesdale, Wash., U.S. 110 C9
Oak Grove, La., U.S. 102 K9
Oak Harbor, Wash., U.S. 110 B3
Oak Hill, Ohio, U.S. 101 S13
Oak Hill, W. Va., U.S. 98 E8
Oakhurst, Calif., U.S. 111 S6
Oakland, Calif., U.S. 111 S3
Oakland, Iowa, U.S. 107 P9
Oakland, Md., U.S. 98 C10
Oakland, Nebr., U.S. 107 P8
Oakland, Oreg., U.S. 110 J3
Oakland City, Ind., U.S. 101 T7
Oak Lawn, Ill., U.S. 101 N7
Oakley, Idaho, U.S. 108 J5
Oakley, Kans., U.S. 107 S4
Oak Park, Ill., U.S. 101 N7
Oak Ridge, Tenn., U.S. 103 E18
Oakridge, Oreg., U.S. 110 H3
Oamaru, N.Z. 217 Q17
Oaro, N.Z. 217 N18
Oatara, island, Fr. Polynesia, Fr. 223 B24
Oates Coast, Antarctica 231 R15
Oaxaca, Mex. 117 K13
Ob', river, Russ. 160 G10
Ob, Gulf of, Arctic Oc. 168 C8
Oba, Ont., Can. 85 P17
Obama, Japan 189 P9
Oban see Half Moon Bay, N.Z. 217 R15
Obanazawa, Japan 188 L12
O Barco, Sp. 146 C7
Ob' Bank, Arctic Oc. 247 J16
Ob' Bay, Antarctica 231 R14
Ōbêh, Afghan. 178 M3
Obelisk, site, Vatican City 163 Q17
Obelisk Island, Solomon Is. 221 N24
Obella, island, Marshall Is., U.S. 220 K4
Oberdrauburg, Aust. 150 M10
Oberhausen, Ger. 150 E5
Oberlin, Kans., U.S. 107 R4
Oberlin, La., U.S. 102 P7
Oberlin, Ohio, U.S. 101 P14
Oberschan, Switz. 162 Q1
Oberursel, Ger. 150 G6
Obervellach, Aust. 150 M10
Oberwart, Aust. 150 L12
Obi, island, Indonesia 193 K16
Obi, Kepulauan, Indonesia 193 K16
Óbidos, Braz. 132 D11
Óbidos, Port. 146 H4
Obigarm, Taj. 178 H8
Obihiro, Japan 188 G14
Obilatu, island, Indonesia 193 J16
Obil'noye, Russ. 159 Q13
Obion, Tenn., U.S. 102 E12
Oblachnaya, Gora, Russ. 161 L21
Obluch'ye, Russ. 161 L20
Obninsk, Russ. 158 K9
Obo, Cen. Af. Rep. 202 H11
Obome, Indonesia 193 K18
Obong-san, peak, N. Korea 186 B13
Oborniki, Pol. 151 D13
Obrenovac, Serb. 154 F10
O'Brien, Oreg., U.S. 110 L2
Obrovac, Croatia 154 F5
Obruk, Turk. 170 G8
Obshchiy Syrt, Eur. 140 E15
Obskaya Guba, Russ. 160 F12
Obstrucción, Fiordo, Chile 135 W7
Ob' Tablemount, Ind. Oc. 248 D8
Ob' Trench, Ind. Oc. 225 M15
Oca, Montes de, Sp. 146 C11
Ocala, Fla., U.S. 99 S8
Ocaña, Col. 130 D6
Ocaña, Sp. 146 G11
Occidental, Grand Erg, Alg. 200 C10
Ocean Cay, Bahamas 118 D10
Ocean City, Md., U.S. 98 D15
Ocean City, N.J., U.S. 96 R10
Ocean Falls, B.C., Can. 84 K7
Ocean Island see Banaba, Kiribati 218 G7
Ocean Island see Kure Atoll, Hawai'i, U.S. 114 K2
Oceanographer Fracture Zone, Atl. Oc. 240 K7
Oceanographic Museum, Monaco 163 E21
Ocean Park, Wash., U.S. 110 D2
Oceanside, Calif., U.S. 111 Y9
Ocean Springs, Miss., U.S. 103 P13
Oceanview, Guam, U.S. 220 B11
O.C. Fisher Lake, Tex., U.S. 105 N7
Óch, Óros, Gr. 157 J13
Ocha, island, F.S.M. 221 C15
Och'amch'ire, Rep. of Georgia 171 B16
Ocha, Mochun, F.S.M. 221 C15
Ochlockonee, river, Fla., Ga., U.S. 99 Q5
Ocho Rios, Jam. 122 H9
Ocilla, Ga., U.S. 99 P6
Ocmulgee, river, Ga., U.S. 99 N6
Ocmulgee National Monument, Ga., U.S. 98 M6
Ocna Mureş, Rom. 155 D13
Ocoa, Bahía de, Dom. Rep. 119 M18
Oconee, river, Ga., U.S. 99 N7
Oconee, Lake, Ga., U.S. 98 L6
Oconomowoc, Wis., U.S. 100 L6
Oconto, Wis., U.S. 100 H7
Oconto Falls, Wis., U.S. 100 H7
Ocracoke, N.C., U.S. 98 H15
Ocracoke Inlet, N.C., U.S. 98 J15
October Revolution Island, Asia 168 B9
Ocumare del Tuy, Venez. 130 B9
Ōda, Japan 189 P6
Ŏdaejin, N. Korea 186 D13
Ōdate, Japan 188 K12
Odawara, Japan 189 P11
Odda, Nor. 142 K10
Odebolt, Iowa, U.S. 107 N10
Odem, Tex., U.S. 105 T11
Odemira, Port. 146 K5
Ödemiş, Turk. 170 G3
Odense, Den. 142 N11
Oden Spur, Arctic Oc. 246 H11
Oder, river, Ger. 150 D11
Odesa, Ukr. 159 R6
Odessa, Mo., U.S. 107 S11
Odessa, Tex., U.S. 104 M4
Odessa, Wash., U.S. 110 C7
Odienné, Côte d'Ivoire 204 C7
O'Donnell, Tex., U.S. 104 L5
Odra, river, Pol. 150 D11
Odžaci, Serb. 154 E9
Oecusse see Pante Macassar, Timor-Leste 193 N15
Oedong, S. Korea 187 R12
Oeiras, Braz. 133 F15
Oelrichs, S. Dak., U.S. 106 M2
Oelwein, Iowa, U.S. 106 M13
Oenarodo, island, S. Korea 187 U9
Oeno Island, Pac. Oc. 219 K16
Oenpelli, N.T., Austral. 215 P8
Oeta, Mount see Oíti Óros, Gr. 156 G10
Oeyeondo, island, S. Korea 187 Q6
Of, Turk. 171 D15
O'Fallon Creek, Mont., U.S. 108 D13
Offenbach, Ger. 150 G6
Offenburg, Ger. 150 J6
Office of Tourism, Monaco 163 C21
Offida, It. 152 J10
Oficina Rica Aventura, Chile 134 D7
Ofidoúsa, island, Gr. 157 M16
Ofolanga, island, Tonga 222 P7
Ofu, Amer. Samoa, U.S. 222 N1
Ofu, island, Amer. Samoa, U.S. 222 N1
Ofu, island, Tonga 222 M12
Ōfunato, Japan 188 L13
Oga, Japan 188 K12
Ogadēn, region, Eth. 203 G17
Ōgaki, Japan 189 P9
Ogallala, Nebr., U.S. 107 Q3
Ogasawara Guntō see Bonin Islands, Japan 189 X14
Ogbomosho, Nigeria 204 D12
Ogden, Iowa, U.S. 107 N11
Ogden, Utah, U.S. 108 K7
Ogdensburg, N.Y., U.S. 96 F9
Ogea Driki, island, Fiji 222 K9
Ogea Levu, island, Fiji 222 K9
Ogeechee, river, Ga., U.S. 99 N8
Ogilvie Mountains, Yukon, Can. 84 E8
Oglesby, Ill., U.S. 101 P5
Oglethorpe, Ga., U.S. 99 N5
Ognev Yar, Russ. 160 J11
Ogoja, Nigeria 205 E14
Ogoki, Ont., Can. 85 N16
Ogoki, river, Ont., Can. 85 N16
Ogooué, river, Gabon 205 H15
Ogr, Sudan 202 F11
O Grove, Sp. 146 C5
Ogulin, Croatia 154 E5
Ohau, Lake, N.Z. 217 P17
O'Higgins, Lago, Arg., Chile 135 U7
Ohio, U.S. 101 Q13
Ohio, river, N. Amer. 82 K7
Oho, S. Korea 186 L11
Ohonua, Tonga 222 J12
Ohrid, Maced. 154 L10
Ohrid, Lake see Ohridsko Jezero, Alban., Maced. 154 L10
Ohridsko Jezero (Ohrid, Lake), Alban., Maced. 154 L10
Oía, Gr. 157 M15
Oiapoque, Braz. 132 B12
Oiapoque see Oyapok, river, S. Amer. 131 F18
Oil City, Pa., U.S. 96 M4
Oildale, Calif., U.S. 111 V7
Oilton, Okla., U.S. 104 F12
Oinoússes, island, Gr. 157 H16
Oise, river, Fr. 149 N10
Oistins, Barbados 123 L19
Ōita, Japan 189 R5
Oíti, Óros (Oeta, Mount), Gr. 156 G10
Ojika, Japan 188 L13
Ojika Jima, Japan 189 R3
Ojinaga, Mex. 116 D10
Ōjin Rise, Pac. Oc. 242 E10
Ojiya, Japan 188 M11
Ojos del Salado, Cerro, Arg. 134 G8
Oka, river, Russ. 158 K9
Oka-Don Plain, Eur. 140 F12
Okaba, Indonesia 193 M21
Okahandja, Namibia 206 H7
Okak Islands, Nfld. & Lab., Can. 85 J21
Okanogan, Wash., U.S. 110 B7

Okanogan, river, Can., U.S. 86 A5
Okanogan Range, Can., U.S. 110 A6
Okara, Pak. 179 Q11
Okau, F.S.M. 221 D18
Okaukuejo, Namibia 206 G6
Okavango, river, Af. 206 F7
Okavango Delta, Botswana 206 G9
Okaya, Japan 189 P10
Okayama, Japan 189 Q7
Okazaki, Japan 189 Q10
Okcheon, S. Korea 187 Q9
Okeechobee, Fla., U.S. 99 V9
Okeechobee, Lake, Fla., U.S. 99 V9
Okeene, Okla., U.S. 104 F9
Okefenokee Swamp, Fla., Ga., U.S. 99 Q7
Okemah, Okla., U.S. 104 G12
Okgu, S. Korea 187 R7
Okha, Russ. 161 H21
Okhaldhunga, Nepal 180 F10
Okhotsk, Russ. 161 G20
Okhotsk, Sea of, Russ. 161 H22
Okhotsk Basin, Pac. Oc. 242 C8
Okhtyrka, Ukr. 159 N8
Okiep, S. Af. 206 K7
Oki Guntō, Japan 189 N7
Okinawa, island, Japan 189 X2
Okinawa Shotō, Japan 189 X1
Okinawa Trough, Pac. Oc. 242 F6
Okino Daitō Jima, Japan 218 C2
Okino Erabu Shima, Japan 189 W2
Okino Shima, Japan 189 S6
Okinotori Shima (Parece Vela), Japan 218 D3
Oklahoma, U.S. 104 G11
Oklahoma City, Okla., U.S. 104 G11
Okmulgee, Okla., U.S. 104 G12
Okolona, Ky., U.S. 103 B16
Okolona, Miss., U.S. 103 J13
Okoppe, Japan 188 F14
Okoyo, Congo 205 H17
Okso Takpochao, peak, N. Mariana Is., U.S. 220 B4
Oktong, N. Korea 186 K8
Oktyabr'sk, Kaz. 176 E8
Oktyabr'skiy, Russ. 159 Q13
Oktyabr'skiy, Russ. 160 H7
Ōkuchi, Japan 189 S4
Okulovka, Russ. 158 G7
Okushiri, island, Japan 188 H11
Okwa, river, Botswana 206 H8
Okytyabr'skoye, Russ. 160 G10
Ola, Ark., U.S. 102 G7
Ólafsvík, Ice. 142 E1
Olancha Peak, Calif., U.S. 111 U8
Öland, island, Sw. 143 M14
Olary, S. Aust., Austral. 215 W11
Olathe, Kans., U.S. 107 S10
Olavarría, Arg. 134 M12
Oława, Pol. 151 F13
Olbia, It. 152 M4
Olbia, Golfo di, It. 152 M5
Old Bahama Channel, N. Amer. 118 G10
Old Bight, Bahamas 119 F13
Old Castile, Eur. 140 J3
Old Cork, Qnsld., Austral. 215 T12
Old Crow, Yukon, Can. 84 D9
Oldenburg, Ger. 150 C6
Old Forge, Pa., U.S. 96 M9
Old Fort Bay, Bahamas 122 B10
Oldham, Eng., U.K. 145 R11
Old Harbor, Alas., U.S. 113 M15
Old Head of Kinsale, Ire. 145 V4
Old Man Bay, Cayman Is. 122 H3
Old Man Bay, town, Cayman Is. 122 J3
Old Orchard Beach, Me., U.S. 97 H15
Old Road, St. Kitts and Nevis 123 B20
Old Road Bluff, St. Kitts and Nevis 123 C20
Old Road Town, St. Kitts and Nevis 123 B17
Old Stores, Cayman Is. 122 H1
Old Sugar Mill, Hawai'i, U.S. 114 E11
Old Town, Me., U.S. 97 E17
Olduvai Gorge, site, Tanzania 203 L14
Old Womans Point, Jam. 122 K8
Olean, N.Y., U.S. 96 K5
Olekma, river, Russ. 161 K17

Olekminsk, Russ. 161 H17
Oleksandriya, Ukr. 159 Q7
Olenegorsk, Russ. 160 D8
Olenek, Russ. 161 G15
Olenek, river, Asia 168 C10
Olenek, river, Russ. 161 F16
Olenëk Valley, Arctic Oc. 246 D10
Oleniy, Ostrov, Russ. 160 E12
Oléron, Île d', Fr. 149 T6
Oleśnica, Pol. 151 F13
Olga, Mount see Kata Tjuṯa, Austral. 214 G8
Olga Basin, Arctic Oc. 247 F16
Ölgiy, Mongolia 182 C6
Olhão da Restauração, Port. 146 L6
Olib, island, Croatia 154 F5
Olifantshoek, S. Af. 206 K8
Olimarao Atoll, F.S.M. 220 Q4
Ólimbos, Óros (Olympus, Mount), Gr. 156 D10
Olinda, Braz. 133 G18
Olite, Sp. 147 C13
Oliva, Arg. 134 K10
Olivenza, Sp. 146 J7
Olivet, Fr. 149 R9
Olivia, Minn., U.S. 106 K10
Olivo, Monte, It. 163 H17
Ölkeyek, river, Kaz. 176 E10
Olla, La., U.S. 102 M8
Olmedo, Sp. 146 E10
Olmos, Peru 132 F2
Olney, Ill., U.S. 101 T7
Olney, Tex., U.S. 104 K9
'Olomburi, Solomon Is. 221 N20
Olomouc, Czech Rep. 151 H13
Olongapo, Philippines 193 C13
Oloron, Fr. 149 Y6
Olorua, island, Fiji 222 J9
Olosega, Amer. Samoa, U.S. 222 N2
Olosega, island, Amer. Samoa, U.S. 222 N2
Olotania Crater, Amer. Samoa, U.S. 222 P3
Olovyannaya, Russ. 161 L17
Olowalu, Hawai'i, U.S. 115 H16
Olpoï, Vanuatu 222 C1
Olsztyn, Pol. 151 B15
Olt, river, Rom. 155 G14
Olten, Switz. 152 A3
Olteniţa, Rom. 155 G16
Olton, Tex., U.S. 104 J5
Oltu, Turk. 171 D16
Oltu, river, Turk. 171 D16
Oluan Pi, point, Taiwan, China 185 X11
Ólvega, Sp. 147 D13
Olympia, Wash., U.S. 110 D3
Olympia, ruin, Gr. 156 K9
Olympic National Park, Wash., U.S. 110 B3
Ólympos, Gr. 157 P18
Olympos (Mount Olympus), Cyprus 162 P7
Olympus, Mount see Ulu Dağ, Turk. 170 E5
Olympus, Mount, Wash., U.S. 110 B2
Olympus, Mount see Ólimbos, Óros, Gr. 156 D10
Olyutorskiy, Cape, Asia 168 B13
Olyutorskiy, Mys, Russ. 161 D22
Olyutorskiy Zaliv, Russ. 161 D22
Ōma, Japan 188 H12
Ōmagari, Japan 188 K12
Omagh (An Ómaigh), N. Ire., U.K. 145 P6
Omaha, Nebr., U.S. 107 P9
Omaha Beach, Fr. 149 N6
Omaja, Cuba 118 K12
Omak, Wash., U.S. 110 B7
Omak Lake, Wash., U.S. 110 B7
Oman, Asia 175 N14
Oman, Gulf of, Iran, Oman 175 J16
Oman Basin, Ind. Oc. 224 B8
Omaok, Palau 220 Q10
Ōma Zaki, Japan 188 H12
Omboué (Fernan Vaz), Gabon 205 H15
Ombu, China 182 K4
Omchak, Russ. 161 F20
Omega Gardens, Cayman Is. 122 J2
Omegna, It. 152 D3

Omelek, island, Marshall Is., U.S. 220 M5
Omeo, Vic., Austral. 215 Z13
Ometepec, Mex. 116 K12
Omihi, N.Z. 217 N17
Omin, F.S.M. 221 C18
Omodeo, Lago, It. 153 N4
Omoka, Cook Is., N.Z. 223 B17
Omolon, Russ. 161 D20
Omolon, river, Russ. 161 D20
Omsk, Russ. 160 K10
Omsukchan, Russ. 161 E20
Ōmu, Japan 188 E14
Omul, peak, Rom. 155 E15
Ōmuta, Japan 189 R4
Oña, Sp. 146 C11
Ona Basin, Atl. Oc. 241 W6
Onaf, island, F.S.M. 221 A15
Onaga, Kans., U.S. 107 S9
Onalaska, Wis., U.S. 100 K3
Onamia, Minn., U.S. 106 H11
Onamue, island, F.S.M. 221 C14
Onancock, Va., U.S. 98 E14
Onaram, island, F.S.M. 221 C16
Onarga, Ill., U.S. 101 Q7
Onawa, Iowa, U.S. 107 N9
Onaway, Mich., U.S. 100 H11
Ōnay, Kōtal-e, Afghan. 178 M7
Oncativo, Arg. 134 K10
Ondangwa, Namibia 206 F6
Ondjiva, Angola 206 F6
Ondo, Nigeria 205 D13
Öndörhaan, Mongolia 182 D12
Ondor Sum, N. Mongol, China 184 A5
One, Motu, Fr. Polynesia, Fr. 223 E14
One, Motu, Fr. Polynesia, Fr. 223 J14
One and Half Degree Channel, Maldives 181 W3
Oneata, island, Fiji 222 J9
Onega, Russ. 160 E8
Onega, river, Russ. 160 E7
Onega, Lake, Eur. 140 D11
Onega Bay, Arctic Oc. 140 C11
Oneida, N.Y., U.S. 96 J9
Oneida, Tenn., U.S. 103 E18
Oneida Lake, N.Y., U.S. 96 J8
O'Neill, Nebr., U.S. 107 N6
Onekama, Mich., U.S. 100 J9
Onekotan, island, Russ. 161 H23
Onemak, island, Marshall Is., U.S. 220 L4
Onemak East Passage, Marshall Is., U.S. 220 L4
Onemak West Passage, Marshall Is., U.S. 220 L4
Oneonta, Ala., U.S. 103 J15
Oneonta, N.Y., U.S. 96 K10
Oneroa, island, Cook Is., N.Z. 222 Q9
Oneşti, Rom. 155 D16
Onevai, island, Tonga 222 H12
Ongarue, N.Z. 217 K19
Ongcheon, S. Korea 187 P11
Ongjin, N. Korea 186 M5
Ongjin-man, bay, N. Korea 186 M5
Ongole, India 181 N7
Ongombua, Île, New Caledonia, Fr. 222 A6
Oni, Rep. of Georgia 171 B17
Onich, Scot., U.K. 144 L8
Onida, S. Dak., U.S. 106 K5
Onilahy, river, Madagascar 207 H16
Onima, Bonaire, Neth. 123 Q19
Oniotto, island, Marshall Is., U.S. 220 K3
Onishika, Japan 188 F13
Onitsha, Nigeria 205 E14
Oniwaki, Japan 188 E12
Önjin-sanmaek, range, N. Korea 186 J7
Onjŏng, N. Korea 186 K10
Onnang, island, F.S.M. 221 C14
Ōno, Japan 189 P9
Ono, island, Fiji 222 K6
Ono Channel, Fiji 222 K6
Onoheha, Pass d', Fr. Polynesia, Fr. 223 N17
Ono-i-Lau, island, Fiji 218 K9
Onomichi, Japan 189 Q6
Onon, Mongolia 182 C11
Onon, river, Mongolia 182 C12

Onsan, S. Korea 187 S12
Onsen, Japan 189 P8
Onslow, W. Aust., Austral. 215 T2
Onsŏng, N. Korea 186 A13
Ont'an, N. Korea 186 A13
Ontario, Calif., U.S. 111 X9
Ontario, Can. 85 N16
Ontario, Oreg., U.S. 110 H9
Ontario, Lake, N. Amer. 82 J8
Ontinyent, Sp. 147 J14
Ontonagon, Mich., U.S. 100 E5
Ontong Java Atoll (Lord Howe Atoll), Solomon Is. 221 J18
Ontong-Java Rise, Pac. Oc. 242 J9
Ōnuma, Japan 188 H12
Ooa, island, Marshall Is., U.S. 220 N8
Oobagooma, W. Aust., Austral. 215 Q5
Oodnadatta, S. Aust., Austral. 215 V9
'Ō'okala, Hawai'i, U.S. 115 L21
Oolloo, N.T., Austral. 215 P8
Oologah Lake, Okla., U.S. 104 E13
Ooma, Kiribati 221 D20
Oostende (Ostend), Belg. 148 K10
Oosterschelde, bay, Neth. 148 K11
Oostpunt, Curaçao, Neth. 123 Q15
Opava, Czech Rep. 151 H14
Opelika, Ala., U.S. 103 L17
Opelousas, La., U.S. 102 P8
Open Bay, P.N.G. 217 C21
Opheim, Mont., U.S. 108 A12
Ophir, Oreg., U.S. 110 K1
Ophthalmia Range, Austral. 214 F3
'Opihikao, Hawai'i, U.S. 115 N22
Opinaca, river, Que., Can. 85 M18
Opoa, Fr. Polynesia, Fr. 223 B24
Opochka, Russ. 158 H5
Opole, Pol. 151 G14
Oporto see Porto, Port. 146 E5
Opotiki, N.Z. 217 K20
Opp, Ala., U.S. 103 N16
Oppdal, Nor. 142 H11
Optima Lake, Okla., U.S. 104 E6
Opunake, N.Z. 217 L18
Opunohu, Baie d', Fr. Polynesia, Fr. 223 N14
Opuwo, Namibia 206 F5
Opyan, Puntan, N. Mariana Is., U.S. 220 C4
Or, river, Kaz. 176 D9
Or, Les Îles d' see Hyères, Îles d', Fr. 149 Y14
Oracabessa, Jam. 122 H9
Oracle, Ariz., U.S. 109 V8
Oradea, Rom. 154 C11
Orai, India 180 G7
Oral, Kaz. 176 C6
Oran, Alg. 200 A10
Orange, Fr. 149 W13
Orange, N.S.W., Austral. 215 X14
Orange, Tex., U.S. 105 Q16
Orange, Va., U.S. 98 D12
Orange, river, Af. 206 K7
Orange, Cabo, Braz. 132 B12
Orange Bay, Jam. 122 H5
Orangeburg, S.C., U.S. 98 L9
Orange Cay, Bahamas 118 E9
Orange City, Iowa, U.S. 106 M9
Orange Fan, Atl. Oc. 241 S13
Orange Grove, Tex., U.S. 105 T10
Orange Hill, St. Vincent and the Grenadines 123 K17
Orange Park, Fla., U.S. 99 R8
Orange Walk, Belize 117 J16
Oranienburg, Ger. 150 D10
Oranjemund, Namibia 206 K6
Oranjestad, Aruba, Neth. 123 Q17
Oranjestad, St. Eustatius, Neth. 121 B15
Oraviţa, Rom. 154 F11
Orbe, Switz. 152 B1
Orbetello, It. 152 J7
Orbost, Vic., Austral. 215 Z13
Orcadas, station, Antarctica 230 A5
Orce, Sp. 146 K12
Orchard City, Colo., U.S. 109 N10
Orchila, Isla, Venez. 130 A10
Ord, Nebr., U.S. 107 P6
Ord, river, Austral. 214 C7
Ord, Mount, Austral. 214 D5

Orderville, Utah, U.S. 109 P6
Ordes, Sp. 146 B6
Ordino, Andorra 162 H3
Ordino, Andorra 162 H3
Ordos see Mu Us Shamo, N. Mongol, China 184 D1
Ordot, Guam, U.S. 220 C10
Ord River, W. Aust., Austral. 215 R7
Ord River Dam, Austral. 214 C7
Ordu, Turk. 170 D12
Ordubad, Arm. 171 F20
Ordway, Colo., U.S. 109 N14
Ordzhonikidze, Ukr. 159 Q7
Oreba, island, Marshall Is., U.S. 220 K1
Örebro, Sw. 143 K13
Oregon, Ill., U.S. 101 N5
Oregon, Ohio, U.S. 101 N12
Oregon, U.S. 110 H5
Oregon Caves National Monument, Oreg., U.S. 110 K2
Oregon City, Oreg., U.S. 110 F3
Oregon Dunes National Recreation Area, Oreg., U.S. 110 H2
Orekhovo-Zuyevo, Russ. 158 J10
Orel, Russ. 158 L8
Orellana, Peru 132 F4
Orellana, Embalse de, Sp. 146 H9
Orem, Utah, U.S. 108 L7
Ore Mountains, Czech Rep., Ger. 150 G9
Ören, Turk. 170 H3
Orenburg, Russ. 160 J7
Orense see Ourense, Sp. 146 C6
Orenşehir, Turk. 170 F11
Oreor see Koror, island, Palau 220 P11
Orepuki, N.Z. 217 R15
Orestiáda, Gr. 157 A17
Oreti, river, N.Z. 217 R15
Orfanoú, Kólpos, Gr. 156 C12
Orford Ness, cape, Eng., U.K. 145 U16
Organ Pipe Cactus National Monument, Ariz., U.S. 109 V6
Organyà, Sp. 147 C16
Orgaz, Sp. 146 G10
Orhangazi, Turk. 170 D5
Orhei, Mold. 159 Q5
Orhon (Orkhon), river, Mongolia 182 C10
Orick, Calif., U.S. 110 M2
Oricum see Orikon, site, Alban. 154 M9
Orient, Wash., U.S. 110 A8
Oriental, Grand Erg, Alg. 200 C12
Orientale, Baie, St.-Martin, Fr. 123 A15
Oriente, Arg. 135 N12
Orihuela, Sp. 147 K14
Orikhiv, Ukr. 159 R8
Orikon (Oricum), site, Alban. I 54 M9
Orinduik, Guyana 131 F13
Orinoco, river, S. Amer. 128 B5
Orinoco River Delta, S. Amer. 128 A6
Oristano, It. 153 N3
Oristano, Golfo di, It. 153 P3
Oriximiná, Braz. 132 D11
Orizaba, Pico de, Mex. 116 J12
Orjen, peak, Montenegro 154 J8
Orkanger, Nor. 142 H11
Orkhon see Orhon, river, Mongolia 182 C10
Orkney Islands, Scot., U.K. 144 F10
Orland, Calif., U.S. 111 P3
Orlando, Fla., U.S. 99 T9
Orleans, Nebr., U.S. 107 R5
Orleans, Vt., U.S. 97 F13
Orléans, Fr. 149 R9
Ormara, Pak. 179 W4
Ormara, Ras, Pak. 179 W4
Orménio, Gr. 157 A16
Ormoc, Philippines 193 E15
Ormond Beach, Fla., U.S. 99 S9
Örnsköldsvik, Sw. 143 G13
Orobie, Alpi, It. 152 C5
Orocovis, P.R., U.S. 122 N3
Orocué, Col. 130 F7
Orofino, Idaho, U.S. 108 D4
Oro Grande, Calif., U.S. 111 W9

Orohena, Mount, Fr. Polynesia, Fr. 223 P16
Oroluk Atoll, F.S.M. 220 Q7
Oromahana, island, Fr. Polynesia, Fr. 223 A23
Oromia, region, Eth. 203 G15
Orona, island, Kiribati 218 G10
Orono, Me., U.S. 97 E17
Oronsay, island, Scot., U.K. 144 M7
Orontes, river see Al ʿĀş, Syr. 172 F7
Oropesa, Sp. 146 G9
Oropuche Lagoon, Trinidad and Tobago 123 Q22
Oroqen, China 183 B15
Orós, Braz. 133 F17
Orosei, It. 153 N5
Orosei, Golfo di, It. 153 N5
Orosháza, Hung. 151 M16
Orote Peninsula, Guam, U.S. 220 C9
Oroville, Calif., U.S. 111 P4
Oroville, Wash., U.S. 110 A7
Oroville, Lake, Calif., U.S. 111 P4
Orphan Knoll, Atl. Oc. 240 H7
Orr, Minn., U.S. 106 E12
Orsa, Sw. 142 J12
Orsha, Belarus 158 K6
Orshanka, Russ. 158 H14
Orsk, Russ. 160 J7
Orsogna, It. 152 K10
Orşova, Rom. 154 F12
Orta, Turk. 170 D8
Ortaca, Turk. 170 H4
Orta Nova, It. 152 L12
Ortegal, Cabo, Sp. 146 A6
Ortegal, Cape, Eur. 140 H2
Orthez, Fr. 149 X6
Ortigueira, Sp. 146 A6
Ortisei, It. 152 C7
Ortles, range, It. 152 C6
Ortoire, river, Trinidad and Tobago 123 Q23
Ortón, river, Bol. 132 G7
Ortona, It. 152 K11
Ortonville, Minn., U.S. 106 J8
Orto Surt, Russ. 161 H17
Orukuizu, island, Palau 220 P10
Orūmīyeh, Iran 174 B10
Orūmīyeh, Daryācheh-ye (Urmia, Lake), Iran 174 B10
Orune, It. 153 N4
Oruro, Bol. 132 K7
Orvieto, It. 152 J8
Oryakhovo, Bulg. 155 G13
Os, Fr. 162 J2
Os, river, Andorra 162 K2
Osa, Península de, Pan. 117 P19
Osage, Iowa, U.S. 106 M12
Osage, river, Mo., U.S. 107 T13
Osage Beach, Mo., U.S. 107 T12
Osage City, Kans., U.S. 107 T9
Ōsaka, Japan 189 Q8
Osakarovka, Kaz. 177 D14
Ōsaka Wan, Japan 189 Q8
Osakis, Minn., U.S. 106 H10
Osan, S. Korea 187 N8
Osan, S. Korea 187 U7
Osawatomie, Kans., U.S. 107 T10
Osborne, Kans., U.S. 107 S6
Osborn Plateau, Ind. Oc. 225 J13
Oscar II Coast, Antarctica 230 D4
Osceola, Ark., U.S. 102 F11
Osceola, Iowa, U.S. 107 Q11
Osceola, Mo., U.S. 107 U11
Osceola, Nebr., U.S. 107 Q7
Oschiri, It. 152 M4
Oscoda, Mich., U.S. 100 J12
Oscura, Punta, Eq. Guinea 208 N6
Oscura Peak, N. Mex., U.S. 109 T12
Ösel see Saaremaa, island, Est. 143 K15
Osen, Nor. 142 G11
Oseo, S. Korea 187 T11
Osgood Mountains, Nev., U.S. 110 M9
Osh, Kyrg. 178 G10
Oshawa, Ont., Can. 85 Q18
O Shima, Japan 189 S3
Ō Shima, Japan 188 H11
Ō Shima, Japan 189 Q12
Ō Shima, Japan 189 R9
Oshkosh, Nebr., U.S. 107 P2
Oshkosh, Wis., U.S. 100 K6
Oshogbo, Nigeria 205 D13
Oshta, Russ. 158 E8
Oshwe, Dem. Rep. of the Congo 202 L9
Osijek, Croatia 154 E8
Osimo, It. 152 H9
Osin, S. Korea 187 S9
Oskaloosa, Iowa, U.S. 107 P12
Oskarshamn, Sw. 143 L13
Öskemen (Ust'-Kamenogorsk), Kaz. 177 D18
Oskoba, Russ. 161 J14
Oslo, Minn., U.S. 106 E8
Oslo, Nor. 142 K11
Oslofjorden, Atl. Oc. 140 D7
Osmanabad, India 180 M5
Osmancık, Turk. 170 D10
Osmaniye, Turk. 170 H11
Osnabrück, Ger. 150 D6
Osorno, Chile 135 Q6
Osorno, Sp. 146 C10
Osorno, Volcán, Chile 135 Q6
Os Peninsula, N. Amer. 82 Q7
Osprey, Fla., U.S. 99 V7
Ossa, Mount, Austral. 214 L7
Óssa, Óros, Gr. 156 E11
Ossabaw Island, Ga., U.S. 99 N9
Ossabaw Sound, Ga., U.S. 99 N9
Ossa de Montiel, Sp. 146 H12
Osseo, Wis., U.S. 100 J3
Ossetia, republic, Rep. of Georgia 171 B18
Ossineke, Mich., U.S. 100 H12
Ostashkov, Russ. 158 H7
Ost Bank, Atl. Oc. 247 N20
Ostend see Oostende, Belg. 148 K10
Østerdalen, valley, Nor. 142 J11
Osterholz-Scharmbeck, Ger. 150 C7
Östersund, Sw. 142 G12
Östhammar, Sw. 143 J14
Ostiglia, It. 152 E7
Ostrava, Czech Rep. 151 H14
Ostróda, Pol. 151 C15
Ostrogozhsk, Russ. 159 N10
Ostrołęka, Pol. 151 C16
Ostrov, Russ. 158 H5
Ostrowiec Świętokrzyski, Pol. 151 F16
Ostrów Mazowiecka, Pol. 151 D17
Ostrów Wielkopolski, Pol. 151 E14
O'Sullivan Dam, Wash., U.S. 110 D7
Osŭm, river, Bulg. 155 H14
Ōsumi Kaikyō, Japan 189 T4
Ōsumi Shotō, Japan 189 U4
Osuna, Sp. 146 L9
Oswego, N.Y., U.S. 96 H8
Oswestry, Eng., U.K. 145 T10
Oświęcim (Auschwitz), Pol. 151 H15
Ōta, Japan 189 N11
Otaki, N.Z. 217 M19
Otar, Kaz. 177 H16
Otare, Cerro, Col. 130 G6
Otaru, Japan 188 G12
Otavalo, Ecua. 130 J3
Otavi, Namibia 206 G7
O.T. Downs, N.T., Austral. 215 Q9
Oţelu Roşu, Rom. 154 E12
Otepipi, island, Fr. Polynesia, Fr. 223 L16
Otgon Tenger Uul, Mongolia 182 D8
Othello, Wash., U.S. 110 D7
Othonoí, island, Gr. 156 E5
Óthris, Óros, Gr. 156 G10
Otish, Monts, Que., Can. 85 M20
Otjiwarongo, Namibia 206 G7
Otobe, Japan 188 H12
Otog Qi, N. Mongol, China 184 D1
Otoineppu, Japan 188 E13
Otradnoye, Russ. 161 G23
Otradnyy, Russ. 158 K16
Otranto, It. 153 N16
Otranto, Strait of, Eur. 140 L8
Otsego, Mich., U.S. 100 M9
Ōtsu, Japan 188 G14
Ōtsu, Japan 189 Q9
Ottawa, Ill., U.S. 101 P6
Ottawa, Kans., U.S. 107 T10
Ottawa, Ohio, U.S. 101 P11
Ottawa, Ont., Can. 85 Q19
Ottawa, river, Ont., Que., Can. 85 P18
Ottawa Islands, Nunavut, Can. 85 K17
Ottenby, Sw. 143 M14
Otter Rapids, Ont., Can. 85 N17
Otter Tail Lake, Minn., U.S. 106 H9
Ottmarsheim, Fr. 149 Q15
Ottumwa, Iowa, U.S. 107 Q12
Otukpo, Nigeria 205 D14
Otutéhé, Fr. Polynesia, Fr. 223 M21
Otuzco, Peru 132 F2
Otway, Bahía, Chile 135 X7
Otway, Cape, Austral. 214 M12
Otway, Seno de, Chile 135 X8
Ötztal Alps, It. 152 B6
Ou, river, Hunan, China 185 T5
Ou, river, Laos 190 G10
Ou, river, Zhejiang, China 185 Q11
ʻOʻua, island, Tonga 222 Q6
Oua, Île, New Caledonia, Fr. 222 C9
Ouachita, river, U.S. 87 K14
Ouachita, Lake, Ark., U.S. 102 G7
Ouachita Mountains, U.S. 87 J13
Ouaco, New Caledonia, Fr. 222 C6
Ouadane, Mauritania 200 F6
Ouadda, Cen. Af. Rep. 202 G10
Ouagadougou, Burkina Faso 204 B10
Ouahigouya, Burkina Faso 204 B10
Oualâta, Mauritania 200 G7
Oua-n-Ahaggar, Tassili, Alg. 200 F11
Ouanda Djallé, Cen. Af. Rep. 202 G10
Ouani, Comoros 209 N16
Ouargla, Alg. 200 C11
Ouarra, river, Cen. Af. Rep. 202 H11
Oubangui (Ubangi), river, Af. 205 G18
Oubatche, New Caledonia, Fr. 222 C6
Oudtshoorn, S. Af. 206 M8
Ouégoa, New Caledonia, Fr. 222 B6
Ouéme, river, Af. 198 H4
Ouen, Île, New Caledonia, Fr. 222 E8
Ouessa, Burkina Faso 204 C9
Ouessant, Île d', Fr. 149 P2
Ouesso, Congo 205 G18
Ouest, Baie de l', Wallis and Futuna, Fr. 222 B11
Ouest, Pointe de l', Que., Can. 85 M21
Ouezzane, Mor. 200 A9
Oufrane, Alg. 200 D10
Ouinné, Baie, New Caledonia, Fr. 222 D8
Oujda, Mor. 200 B9
Oujeft, Mauritania 200 F6
Oulainen, Fin. 143 F15
Oullins, Fr. 149 U12
Oulu (Uleåborg), Fin. 143 F15
Oulu, river, Eur. 140 C9
Oulujärvi, lake, Eur. 140 C9
Oulujoki, river, Fin. 143 F15
Oulx, It. 152 E1
Oum Chalouba, Chad 201 H16
Oum Hadjer, Chad 201 J15
Oumm ed Drous Telli, Sebkhet, Mauritania 200 E6
Oun, S. Korea 187 P11
Ounianga Kébir, Chad 201 G15
Our, river, Ger., Lux. 162 G10
Ouranópoli, Gr. 157 D13
Ouray, Colo., U.S. 109 P11
Ouray, Utah, U.S. 108 L9
Ourense (Orense), Sp. 146 C6
Ourinhos, Braz. 132 M12
Ourique, Port. 146 K5
Ouse, river, Eng., U.K. 145 Q12
Oust, Fr. 149 Y8
Outer Brass Island, Virgin Is., U.S. 122 M8
Outer Hebrides, islands, Scot., U.K. 144 J6
Outjo, Namibia 206 G6
Outokumpu, Fin. 143 G17
Out Skerries, Scot., U.K. 144 D12
Ouvéa (Uvéa), island, New Caledonia, Fr. 222 C8
Ouvéa, Baie d', New Caledonia, Fr. 222 C8
Ouyen, Vic., Austral. 215 Y12
Ouzouer-le-Marché, Fr. 149 R9
Ovacık, Turk. 170 J8
Ovaka, island, Tonga 222 M11
Ovalau, island, Fiji 222 H7
Ovalle, Chile 134 J6
Ovamboland, region, Namibia 206 F6
Ovar, Port. 146 E5
Ovau, island, Solomon Is. 221 K15
Overland Park, Kans., U.S. 107 S10
Overland Village, St. Vincent and the Grenadines 123 J17
Overstrand, Eng., U.K. 145 S15
Overton, Nev., U.S. 111 T12
Overton, Tex., U.S. 104 M14
Ovgos (Dardere), river, Cyprus 162 N7
Oviedo, Dom. Rep. 119 N18
Oviedo, Sp. 146 B8
Ovoot, Mongolia 182 E12
Ovruch, Ukr. 158 M5
Ow, island, F.S.M. 221 C16
Owaka, N.Z. 217 R16
Owando, Congo 205 H18
Owatonna, Minn., U.S. 106 L11
Owego, N.Y., U.S. 96 L8
Owel, Lough, Ire. 145 R6
Owen Fracture Zone, Ind. Oc. 224 F7
Owen, Mount, N.Z. 217 M17
Owens, river, Calif., U.S. 111 T8
Owensboro, Ky., U.S. 103 C15
Owens Lake Bed, Calif., U.S. 111 U8
Owen Stanley Range, P.N.G. 217 E20
Owensville, Mo., U.S. 107 T14
Owia, St. Vincent and the Grenadines 123 J17
Owl Creek Mountains, Wyo., U.S. 108 G10
Owo, Nigeria 205 D13
Owosso, Mich., U.S. 100 L11
Owyhee, Nev., U.S. 110 L10
Owyhee, river, Oreg., U.S. 110 J8
Owyhee, Lake, Oreg., U.S. 110 J9
Owyhee Mountains, Idaho, U.S. 108 H3
Oxeiá, island, Gr. 156 H8
Oxford, Ala., U.S. 103 J16
Oxford, Eng., U.K. 145 V13
Oxford, Kans., U.S. 107 V8
Oxford, Miss., U.S. 102 H12
Oxford, N.Z. 217 N17
Oxford, Nebr., U.S. 107 R5
Oxford, Ohio, U.S. 101 S11
Oxford, Pa., U.S. 96 Q8
Oxley, N.S.W., Austral. 215 X12
Oxnard, Calif., U.S. 111 X7
Oyapok see Oiapoque, river, S. Amer. 131 F18
Oyem, Gabon 205 G16
Oyo, Congo 205 H18
Oyo, Nigeria 204 D12
Oyonnax, Fr. 149 T13
Oyotung, Russ. 161 D18
Oyster Bay, Jam. 122 H7
Oysterhaven (Cuan Oisrí), Ire. 145 V4
Oyster Pond, St.-Martin, Fr. 123 B15
Oysterville, Wash., U.S. 110 D2
Oytal, Kaz. 177 J15
Oyyl, Kaz. 176 E7
Oyyl, river, Kaz. 176 E7
Özalp, Turk. 171 F18
Ozark, Ala., U.S. 103 M17
Ozark, Ark., U.S. 102 F6
Ozark, Mo., U.S. 107 V12
Ozark National Scenic Riverways, Mo., U.S. 107 U14
Ozark Plateau, U.S. 87 H14
Ozarks, Lake of the, Mo., U.S. 107 T12
Ózd, Hung. 151 K16
Özen, Kaz. 176 H6
Ozernovskiy, Russ. 161 G23
Ozernoy, Mys, Russ. 161 E22
Ozernoy, Zaliv, Russ. 161 E22
Ozery, Russ. 158 K10
Ozette Lake, Wash., U.S. 110 B2
Özgön, Kyrg. 178 F11
Ozieri, It. 152 M4
Ozinki, Russ. 158 M15
Ozona, Tex., U.S. 105 P6
Ōzu, Japan 189 R6
Ozurget'i, Rep. of Georgia 171 C16

P

Paagoumène, New Caledonia, Fr. 222 C6
Paama, island, Vanuatu 222 D2
Paarden Bay, Aruba, Neth. 123 Q17
Paarl, S. Af. 206 M7
Paʻauhau, Hawaiʻi, U.S. 115 L20
Paʻauilo, Hawaiʻi, U.S. 115 L20
Paavola, Fin. 143 F15
Pabaigh (Pabbay), island, Scot., U.K. 144 J6
Pabaigh, island, Scot., U.K. 144 K6
Pabbay see Pabaigh, island, Scot., U.K. 144 J6
Pabianice, Pol. 151 E15
Pabna, Bangladesh 180 H12
Pacaraimã, Serra see Pacaraima, Sierra, S. Amer. 132 B8
Pacaraima, Sierra, S. Amer. 130 F11
Pacasmayo, Peru 132 F2
Paceco, It. 153 S8
Pacheiá, island, Gr. 157 N16
Pachino, It. 153 U12
Pachuca, Mex. 116 H12
Pachyammos, Cyprus 162 N6
Pacific-Antarctic Ridge, Pac. Oc. 249 H17
Pacific Beach, Wash., U.S. 110 C2
Pacific City, Oreg., U.S. 110 F2
Pacific Grove, Calif., U.S. 111 T4
Pacy, Fr. 149 P9
Padam, India 179 N14
Padang, Indonesia 192 J5
Padang, island, Indonesia 192 J6
Padang Endau, Malaysia 191 U11
Padangpanjang, Indonesia 192 J5
Padangsidempuan, Indonesia 192 H5
Padangtiji, Indonesia 192 G4
Padangtikar Maya, island, Indonesia 192 J8
Paden City, W. Va., U.S. 98 C9
Paderborn, Ger. 150 E7
Padeş, peak, Rom. 154 E12
Padloping Island, Nunavut, Can. 85 F19
Padma (Ganges), river, Bangladesh 180 H12
Padmanabhapuram, India 181 S5
Padova (Padua), It. 152 E7
Padrauna, India 180 G9
Padre Island, U.S. 87 P12
Padre Island National Seashore, Tex., U.S. 105 U11
Padua see Padova, It. 152 E7
Paducah, Ky., U.S. 103 D13
Paducah, Tex., U.S. 104 J7
Paea, Fr. Polynesia, Fr. 223 P15
Paegam, N. Korea 186 D11
Paekch'ŏn, N. Korea 186 L6
Paektu-san, peak, N. Korea 186 C10
Paengma, N. Korea 186 G4
Paeroa, N.Z. 217 J19
Paestum, ruin, It. 153 N11
Paeu, Solomon Is. 221 R24
Paeua, island, Fr. Polynesia, Fr. 223 K18
Páfos see Paphos, Cyprus 162 Q5
Pafúri, Mozambique 206 H12
Pag, island, Croatia 154 F5
Pagadian, Philippines 193 F14
Pagai Selatan, island, Indonesia 192 K5
Pagai Utara, island, Indonesia 192 K5
Pagan, island, N. Mariana Is., U.S. 220 B2
Paganico, It. 152 J7
Pagasitikós Kólpos, Gr. 156 F11
Pagatan, Indonesia 192 K11
Page, Ariz., U.S. 109 Q7
Page, N. Dak., U.S. 106 G7
Pageland, S.C., U.S. 98 J10
Paget Island, Bermuda 122 B3
Pagnag (Pana), China 182 K6
Pago Bay, Guam, U.S. 220 C11
Pagoda Point, Myanmar 190 L5
Pago Pago, Amer. Samoa, U.S. 222 M7
Pago Pago Harbor, Amer. Samoa, U.S. 222 M8

Pago, river, *Guam, U.S.* **220** C1O
Pagosa Springs, *Colo., U.S.* **109** P11
Pagua Bay, *Dominica* **123** E2O
Pagua Point, *Dominica* **123** E2O
Pāhala, *Hawai'i, U.S.* **115** P2O
Paharpur, *Pak.* **179** P9
Pāhoa, *Hawai'i, U.S.* **115** N22
Pahokee, *Fla., U.S.* **99** V1O
Pahrump, *Nev., U.S.* **111** U11
Pahsimeroi, river, *Idaho, U.S.* **108** F6
Pahute Mesa, *Nev., U.S.* **111** S1O
Pāi'a, *Hawai'i, U.S.* **115** G17
Paige, *Tex., U.S.* **105** Q11
Päijänne, lake, *Fin.* **143** H16
Paili, *P.N.G.* **217** E2O
Pailĭn (Pailin), *Thai.* **191** N1O
Pailolo Channel, *Hawai'i, U.S.* **115** G15
Paine, Cerro, *Chile* **135** W7
Painesville, *Ohio, U.S.* **101** N15
Painted Desert, *Ariz., U.S.* **109** R8
Painter, Mount, *Austral.* **214** J11
Paint Rock, *Tex., U.S.* **105** N7
Paintsville, *Ky., U.S.* **103** C2O
Paio, Motu, *Fr. Polynesia, Fr.* **223** K16
Païrömé, *New Caledonia, Fr.* **222** B5
Paisley, *Oreg., U.S.* **110** K5
Paistunturit, peak, *Fin.* **143** B14
Paita, *New Caledonia, Fr.* **222** D8
Paita, *Peru* **132** F1
Pajala, *Sw.* **143** D14
Pajares, Puerto de, *Sp.* **146** B9
Pajaro Point, *British Virgin Is., U.K.* **122** Q1O
Paju, *S. Korea* **186** M8
Pakālā, *Hawai'i, U.S.* **114** C5
Pakaraima Mountains, *S. Amer.* **131** E13
Pakch'ŏn, *N. Korea* **186** C12
Pakch'ŏn, *N. Korea* **186** H6
Pakin Atoll, *F.S.M.* **220** Q7
Pakistan, *Asia* **179** U5
Pakleni Otoci, island, *Croatia* **154** H6
Pak Nam Chumphon, *Thai.* **191** P8
Pakokku, *Myanmar* **190** G5
Pakpattan, *Pak.* **179** R11
Pak Phanang, *Thai.* **191** R8
Paks, *Hung.* **151** M15
Pakuru, island, *F.S.M.* **221** C15
Pakwach, *Uganda* **202** J12
Pakxé, *Laos* **190** L12
Pal, *Andorra* **162** H2
Pala, *Chad* **201** K14
Pala, *Myanmar* **191** N7
Palace of Holy Office, *Vatican City* **163** R17
Palace of Justice, *Monaco* **163** E21
Palace of Monaco, *Monaco* **163** E21
Palace of the Tribunal, *Vatican City* **163** Q15
Palace Square, *Monaco* **163** E21
Palacios, *Tex., U.S.* **105** S13
Palafrugell, *Sp.* **147** D16
Palagruža (Pelagosa), island, *Croatia* **154** J6
Palaichori, *Cyprus* **162** P7
Palaíkastro, *Gr.* **157** Q17
Palaióchora, *Gr.* **156** Q12
Palaiokastrítsa, *Gr.* **156** E6
Palaiseau, *Fr.* **149** P1O
Palakkad, *India* **181** R5
Palalankwe, *India* **181** R14
Palamás, *Gr.* **156** F9
Palana, *Russ.* **161** E21
Palanga, *Lith.* **143** M15
Palangkaraya, *Indonesia* **192** K11
Palanpur, *India* **180** H3
Palaoa Point, *Hawai'i, U.S.* **115** H14
Palapye, *Botswana* **206** H1O
Palatka, *Fla., U.S.* **99** R8
Palatka, *Russ.* **161** F2O
Palau, *Pac. Oc.* **220** Q1
Palauk, *Myanmar* **191** N7
Palauli Bay, *Samoa* **222** L2
Palau Trench, *Pac. Oc.* **242** J6
Palaw, *Myanmar* **191** N7
Palawan, island, *Philippines* **192** E12
Palawan Trough, *Pac. Oc.* **242** J4
Palazzolo Acreide, *It.* **153** T11
Paldiski, *Est.* **143** J16
Palel, *India* **180** H15
Palembang, *Indonesia* **192** K7

Palencia, *Sp.* **146** D1O
Palermo, *Calif., U.S.* **111** P4
Palermo, *It.* **153** R9
Palestina, *Chile* **134** E7
Palestina, *Virgin Is., U.S.* **122** M11
Palestine, *Tex., U.S.* **104** M13
Paletwa, *Myanmar* **190** G4
P'algyŏngdae, *N. Korea* **186** D13
Pali, *India* **180** G3
Palian, *Thai.* **191** R8
Palikir, *F.S.M.* **221** F14
Palikir Passage, *F.S.M.* **221** F13
Palinuro, Capo, *It.* **153** N12
Palioúri, *Gr.* **156** E12
Palioúri, Ákra, *Gr.* **156** E12
Palisade, *Nebr., U.S.* **107** R4
Paliseul, *Belg.* **148** M12
Palk Bay, *India* **181** R6
Palkonda, *India* **180** L9
Palk Strait, *India* **181** R7
Pallasovka, *Russ.* **159** N14
Palliser, Cape, *N.Z.* **217** M19
Palma, *Mozambique* **207** C15
Palma, Badia de, *Sp.* **147** G18
Palma City, *Cuba* **118** H11
Palma del Río, *Sp.* **146** K9
Palma de Mallorca, *Sp.* **147** G18
Palma di Montechiaro, *It.* **153** T1O
Palmanova, *It.* **152** D9
Palmares, *Braz.* **133** G18
Palmas, *Braz.* **132** N12
Palmas, *Braz.* **133** G18
Palmas, Cape, *Af.* **198** J2
Palmas, Golfo di, *It.* **153** Q3
Palmas Altas, *P.R., U.S.* **122** M3
Palma Soriano, *Cuba* **118** K13
Palm Bay, *Fla., U.S.* **99** U1O
Palm Beach, *Aruba, Neth.* **123** Q16
Palm Beach, *Fla., U.S.* **99** V11
Palm Coast, *Fla., U.S.* **99** S9
Palmdale, *Calif., U.S.* **111** W8
Palmeira, *Cabo Verde* **209** B17
Palmeira dos Índios, *Braz.* **133** G17
Palmeirinhas, Ponta das, *Angola* **206** C5
Palmer, *Alas., U.S.* **113** J17
Palmer Archipelago, *Antarctica* **230** D4
Palmer Land, region, *Antarctica* **230** F6
Palmer see Mameyes, *P.R., U.S.* **122** M5
Palmerston Atoll, *Cook Is., N.Z.* **218** J11
Palmerston North, *N.Z.* **217** L19
Palmerville, *Qnsld., Austral.* **215** Q13
Palmetto, *Fla., U.S.* **99** U7
Palmetto Point, *Jam.* **122** H1O
Palmi, *It.* **153** R13
Palmira, *Col.* **130** G4
Palm Island, *St. Vincent and the Grenadines* **121** G17
Palm Islands, *Austral.* **214** D14
Palmiste Bay, *Grenada* **123** K22
Palm Point, *Nigeria* **205** F13
Palm Springs, *Calif., U.S.* **111** X1O
Palmyra, *Mo., U.S.* **107** R13
Palmyra, *N.Y., U.S.* **96** J7
Palmyra see Tadmur, *Syr.* **172** G1O
Palmyra Atoll, *Pac. Oc.* **218** F11
Palmyras Point, *India* **180** K11
Palo Alto, *Calif., U.S.* **111** S3
Palo Alto Battlefield National Historic Site, *Tex., U.S.* **105** W11
Palo Duro Creek, *Tex., U.S.* **104** H4
Paloh, *Indonesia* **192** H9
Palomar Mountain, *Calif., U.S.* **111** Y1O
Palopo, *Indonesia* **193** K13
Palos, Cabo de, *Sp.* **147** K14
Palos, Cape, *Eur.* **140** L3
Palo Seco, *Trinidad and Tobago* **123** Q22
Palouse, *Wash., U.S.* **110** D9
Palouse, river, *Wash., U.S.* **110** D8
Palpana, Cerro, *Chile* **134** D7
Paltamo, *Fin.* **143** F16
Palu, *Indonesia* **193** J13
Palu, *Turk.* **171** F14
Palwal, *India* **180** F6
Pamiers, *Fr.* **149** Y9

Pamir see Pomir, river, *Afghan., Taj.* **178** K1O
Pamirs, range, *Taj.* **178** J1O
Pamlico Sound, *N.C., U.S.* **98** H14
Pampa, *Tex., U.S.* **104** G6
Pampas, *Peru* **132** H4
Pampas, region, *S. Amer.* **128** M6
Pamplemousses, *Mauritius* **209** F2O
Pamplona, *Col.* **130** D6
Pamplona (Iruña), *Sp.* **147** C13
Pamua, *Solomon Is.* **221** P2O
Pamuk Imwintiati, island, *F.S.M.* **221** G13
Pamzal, *India* **180** C7
Pana, *Ill., U.S.* **101** S5
Pana see Pagnag, *China* **182** K6
Panaca, *Nev., U.S.* **111** S12
Panacea, *Fla., U.S.* **99** R5
Panagyurishte, *Bulg.* **155** J14
Panahan, *Indonesia* **192** K1O
Panaitan, island, *Indonesia* **192** M7
Panaji, *India* **181** N4
Panama, *N. Amer.* **117** N21
Panama, *Okla., U.S.* **104** G14
Panamá, Golfo de, *Pan.* **117** P21
Panama, Isthmus of, *N. Amer.* **82** Q8
Panama Basin, *Pac. Oc.* **243** J21
Panama Canal, *Pan.* **117** N21
Panama City, *Fla., U.S.* **99** R3
Panama City, *Pan.* **117** N21
Panamint Range, *Calif., U.S.* **111** U9
Panay, island, *Philippines* **193** E14
Pancake Range, *Nev., U.S.* **111** R11
Pančevo, *Serb.* **154** F1O
Panchiao, *Taiwan, China* **185** U12
Pančiév Vrh, peak, *Kos., Serb.* **154** F1O
Pandanus Creek, *Qnsld., Austral.* **215** R13
Panduranga see Phan Rang-Tháp Chàm, *Vietnam* **191** P14
Paneri, *India* **180** G13
Panevėžys, *Lith.* **143** M16
Panfilovo, *Russ.* **159** N12
Pangai, *Tonga* **222** K12
Pangai, *Tonga* **222** P7
Pangaimoto, island, *Tonga* **222** M11
Pangaimotu, island, *Tonga* **222** H11
Pangalanes, Canal des, *Madagascar* **207** G18
Pangani, river, *Tanzania* **203** L14
Pangéo, Óros, *Gr.* **157** C13
Panggoe, *Solomon Is.* **221** L16
Panghyŏn, *N. Korea* **186** G5
Pangi, *Dem. Rep. of the Congo* **202** L11
Pangkajene, *Indonesia* **193** L13
Pangkalpinang, *Indonesia* **192** K8
Pangnirtung, *Nunavut, Can.* **85** G19
Pangong Tso, lake, *India* **180** C7
Pangsan, *N. Korea* **186** F4
Panguitch, *Utah, U.S.* **109** P6
Pangutaran Group, *Philippines* **193** F13
P'an'gyo, *N. Korea* **186** K8
Panhandle, *Tex., U.S.* **104** G6
Panian, island, *F.S.M.* **221** G14
Pānī'au, peak, *Hawai'i, U.S.* **114** C3
Panié, Mont, *New Caledonia, Fr.* **222** C6
Panj, river, *Afghan., Taj.* **178** J9
Panjakent, *Taj.* **178** H6
Panjang, island, *Indonesia* **192** H1O
Panjgur, *Pak.* **179** U3
Panji, *Anhui, China* **184** L8
Panjin, *Liaoning, China* **184** B12
Panj Poyon, *Taj.* **178** K8
Panjshayr, river, *Afghan.* **178** L8
P'anmun, *N. Korea* **186** M7
Panna, *India* **180** H7
Pannawonica, *W. Aust., Austral.* **215** T2
Pano Lefkara, *Cyprus* **162** P8
Pano Panagia, *Cyprus* **162** P6
Pano Platres, *Cyprus* **162** P7

Panorama Point, peak, *Nebr., U.S.* **107** P1
Pánormos, *Gr.* **157** K14
Panovo, *Russ.* **161** J15
P'anp'yŏng, *N. Korea* **186** F6
Panruti, *India* **181** Q7
Pantà de Riba-roga, *Sp.* **147** E15
Pantanal, marsh, *S. Amer.* **128** H7
Pantelleria, *It.* **153** U7
Pantelleria, Isola di, *It.* **153** U8
Pante Macassar (Oecusse), *Timor-Leste* **193** N15
Panvel, *India* **180** L3
Panyu, *Guang., China* **185** W4
Panzhihua, *China* **182** L9
Pao, river, *Thai.* **190** K1O
Paola, *Kans., U.S.* **107** T1O
Paola, *Malta* **163** K23
Paoli, *Ind., U.S.* **101** T9
Paopao, *Fr. Polynesia, Fr.* **223** N14
Papa, *Samoa* **222** K1
Pápa, *Hung.* **151** L13
Pāpa'aloa, *Hawai'i, U.S.* **115** L21
Pāpā Bay, *Hawai'i, U.S.* **115** P18
Papahānaumokuākea Marine National Monument, *Hawai'i, U.S.* **114** L5
Pāpā Heiau, *Hawai'i, U.S.* **115** F15
Papai, Mount, *Mauritius* **209** J2O
Pāpa'ikou, *Hawai'i, U.S.* **115** M21
Papakura, *N.Z.* **217** J19
Papara, *Fr. Polynesia, Fr.* **223** P16
Papa Stour, island, *Scot., U.K.* **144** D12
Papau, island, *Cook Is., N.Z.* **222** Q11
Papa Westray, island, *Scot., U.K.* **144** F1O
Papeari, *Fr. Polynesia, Fr.* **223** P17
Papeete, *Fr. Polynesia, Fr.* **223** N16
Papenoo, *Fr. Polynesia, Fr.* **223** N16
Papenoo, river, *Fr. Polynesia, Fr.* **223** N16
Papenburg, *Ger.* **150** C6
Papetoai, *Fr. Polynesia, Fr.* **223** N14
Paphos (Páfos), *Cyprus* **162** Q5
Papíkio Óros, *Gr.* **157** B15
Pāpōhaku Beach, *Hawai'i, U.S.* **115** F13
Papua, Gulf of, *P.N.G.* **217** E19
Papua New Guinea, *P.N.G.* **217** D19
Papua Passage, *Cook Is., N.Z.* **222** Q9
Papun, *Myanmar* **190** K7
Papunya, *N.T., Austral.* **215** T8
Pará, river, *Braz.* **133** D13
Parabel, *Russ.* **160** J12
Paracas Peninsula, *S. Amer.* **128** G3
Paracatu, *Braz.* **133** K14
Paracel Islands, *S. China Sea* **192** B1O
Parachinar, *Pak.* **179** N8
Parachute, *Colo., U.S.* **108** M1O
Paraćin, *Serb.* **154** G11
Paracuru, *Braz.* **133** E17
Parada Point, *S. Amer.* **128** G3
Paradeep see Paradwip, *India* **180** K11
Paradera, *Aruba, Neth.* **123** Q17
Paradise, *Calif., U.S.* **111** P4
Paradise, *Grenada* **123** K23
Paradise, *Mich., U.S.* **100** F1O
Paradise, *Mont., U.S.* **108** C5
Paradise Bay, *Malta* **163** J21
Paradise Island, *Bahamas* **122** B11
Paradise Point, *Bahamas* **122** A8
Paradise Valley, *Nev., U.S.* **110** L9
Paradwip (Paradeep), *India* **180** K11
Paragould, *Ark., U.S.* **102** E11
Paragua, river, *Venez.* **130** E11
Paraguá, river, *Bol.* **132** H8
Paraguaipoa, *Venez.* **130** B6
Paraguaná, Península de, *Venez.* **130** A8
Paraguay, *S. Amer.* **132** M9
Paraguay, river, *S. Amer.* **128** H7
Paraíso, *Mex.* **117** N15
Parakou, *Benin* **204** C12
Parakylia, *S. Aust., Austral.* **215** W1O
Paralakhemundi, *India* **180** L9
Paralimni, *Cyprus* **162** P1O
Param, island, *F.S.M.* **221** F14
Paramaribo, *Suriname* **131** E16
Paramera, Sierra de la, *Sp.* **146** F9

Paramushir, island, *Russ.* **161** G23
Paramythiá, *Gr.* **156** F7
Paran, *Israel* **173** Q5
Paraná, *Arg.* **134** J12
Paranã, *Braz.* **133** H13
Paraná, river, *S. Amer.* **128** K7
Paranaguá, *Braz.* **133** N13
Paranaguá, Baía de, *Braz.* **133** N13
Paranaíba, *Braz.* **132** K12
Paranaíba, river, *Braz.* **132** K12
Paranapanema, river, *S. Amer.* **128** J8
Paranésti, *Gr.* **157** B13
Paraoa, island, *Fr. Polynesia, Fr.* **223** F2O
Parchim, *Ger.* **150** C9
Pardes_H_anna-Karkur, *Israel* **172** L5
Pardo, river, *Braz.* **132** L11
Pardo, river, *Braz.* **133** J16
Pardoo, *W. Aust., Austral.* **215** S3
Pardubice, *Czech Rep.* **150** H12
Parea, *Fr. Polynesia, Fr.* **223** H14
Parece Vela see Okinotori Shima, *Japan* **218** D3
Parecis, Chapada dos, *Braz.* **132** H9
Paredes de Nava, *Sp.* **146** D1O
Paredón, *Mex.* **116** E11
Parem, island, *F.S.M.* **221** C15
Paren', *Russ.* **161** D21
Parepare, *Indonesia* **193** L13
Párga, *Gr.* **156** F7
Pargny, *Fr.* **149** P12
Pargo, Ponta do, *Madeira, Port.* **208** M2
Parguera, *P.R., U.S.* **122** P1
Parham Peninsula, *Antigua and Barbuda* **123** B21
Parham Town, *British Virgin Is., U.K.* **122** Q7
Paria, river, *Ariz., Utah, U.S.* **109** P7
Paria, Gulf of, *Trinidad and Tobago, Venez.* **121** K16
Pariaguánviche, *Venez.* **130** C11
Paria Peninsula, *S. Amer.* **128** A6
Parika, *Guyana* **131** D14
Parikkala, *Fin.* **143** G17
Parim see Barīm, island, *Yemen* **174** R8
Parima, Serra, *S. Amer.* **130** F11
Pariñas, Punta, *Peru* **132** E1
Parintins, *Braz.* **132** D1O
Paris, *Ark., U.S.* **102** F7
Paris, *Fr.* **149** P1O
Paris, *Ill., U.S.* **101** R7
Paris, *Ky., U.S.* **103** B18
Paris, *Mo., U.S.* **107** S13
Paris, *Tenn., U.S.* **103** E13
Paris, *Tex., U.S.* **104** K13
Paris Basin, *Eur.* **140** H5
Parisot, *Fr.* **149** W9
Parit Buntar, *Malaysia* **191** T9
Parker, *Ariz., U.S.* **109** T5
Parker, *S. Dak., U.S.* **106** M8
Parker Dam, *Ariz., Calif., U.S.* **111** X13
Parker Dam, *Ariz., U.S.* **109** T5
Parker Ranch, *Hawai'i, U.S.* **115** L19
Parkersburg, *W. Va., U.S.* **98** C5
Parkes, *N.S.W., Austral.* **215** X14
Park Falls, *Wis., U.S.* **100** G4
Park Forest, *Ill., U.S.* **101** P7
Parkin, *Ark., U.S.* **102** G1O
Parkland, *Wash., U.S.* **110** C4
Park Range, *Colo., U.S.* **108** L12
Park Rapids, *Minn., U.S.* **106** G1O
Park River, *N. Dak., U.S.* **106** E7
Parksley, *Va., U.S.* **98** E15
Parkston, *S. Dak., U.S.* **106** M7
Park Valley, *Utah, U.S.* **108** J6
Parlatuvier, *Trinidad and Tobago* **123** N18
Parma, *Idaho, U.S.* **108** G3
Parma, *It.* **152** F6
Parma, *Ohio, U.S.* **101** P14
Parmakān, *Afghan.* **179** N2
Parnaguá, *Braz.* **133** G14
Parnaíba, *Braz.* **133** D16
Parnaíba, river, *Braz.* **133** E15
Parnamirim, *Braz.* **133** F16
Parnassós, peak, *Gr.* **156** H1O
Parnassus, *N.Z.* **217** N18
Parnassus, peak, *Eur.* **140** L9

Párnitha, Óros, *Gr.* **156** J12
Párnonas, Óros, *Gr.* **156** L10
Pärnu, *Est.* **143** K16
Paroho, lake, *S. Korea* **186** L9
Paromay, *Russ.* **161** H21
Paropamisus Range *see* Silsilah-ye Safēd Kōh, *Afghan.* **178** M2
Páros, *Gr.* **157** L15
Páros, island, *Gr.* **157** L15
Parottee Point, *Jam.* **122** J7
Parowan, *Utah, U.S.* **109** P6
Parraburdoo, *W. Aust., Austral.* **215** T3
Parral, *Chile* **134** M6
Parras, *Mex.* **116** F10
Parry, Cape, *N.W.T., Can.* **84** E11
Parry Bank, *Arctic Oc.* **247** G15
Parry Channel, *Nunavut, N.W.T., Can.* **85** D14
Parry Group *see* Muko Jima Rettō, *Japan* **189** W14
Parry Islands, *Nunavut, N.W.T., Can.* **85** C13
Parshall, *N. Dak., U.S.* **106** F3
Parsons, *Kans., U.S.* **107** V10
Parsons, *Tenn., U.S.* **103** F13
Parsons, *W. Va., U.S.* **98** C10
Parsons Range, *Austral.* **214** B9
Partanna, *It.* **153** S9
Parthenay, *Fr.* **149** S7
Partizansk, *Russ.* **161** M21
Paru, river, *Braz.* **132** C11
Paru de Oeste (Cumina), river, *Braz.* **132** C11
Pārūn, *Afghan.* **178** L9
Paruru, *Solomon Is.* **221** P19
Parvatipuram, *India* **180** L9
Pasa, island, *F.S.M.* **221** G13
Pasadena, *Calif., U.S.* **111** X8
Pasadena, *Tex., U.S.* **105** R14
Pasado, Cabo, *Ecua.* **130** J2
Pasaje, *Ecua.* **130** L2
P'asanauri, *Rep. of Georgia* **171** B18
Pasarseluma, *Indonesia* **192** L6
Pascagoula, *Miss., U.S.* **103** P13
Paşcani, *Rom.* **155** B16
Pasco, *Wash., U.S.* **110** E7
Pascua, Isla de (Rapa Nui, Easter Island), *Pac. Oc.* **219** L19
Pas de la Casa, *Andorra* **162** J5
Pasewalk, *Ger.* **150** C11
Pasighat, *India* **180** F15
Pasinler, *Turk.* **171** E16
Pasir Mas, *Malaysia* **191** S10
Pasley, Cape, *Austral.* **214** K5
Pašman, island, *Croatia* **154** G5
Pasni, *Pak.* **179** V3
Paso de Indios, *Arg.* **135** R8
Paso de los Toros, *Uru.* **134** K14
Paso Río Mayo, *Arg.* **135** S7
Paso Robles, *Calif., U.S.* **111** V5
Pasrur, *Pak.* **179** P12
Passage, *Cook Is., N.Z.* **222** Q2
Passau, *Ger.* **150** K10
Pass Christian, *Miss., U.S.* **102** P12
Passero, Capo, *It.* **153** U12
Passo Fundo, *Braz.* **132** P11
Passos, *Braz.* **133** L14
Passu Keah, island, *S. China Sea* **192** C10
Pastavy, *Belarus* **158** J4
Pastaza, river, *S. Amer.* **128** D2
Pasto, *Col.* **130** H3
Pastora Peak, *Ariz., U.S.* **109** Q9
Pastos Bons, *Braz.* **133** F15
Pasuruan, *Indonesia* **192** M10
Patagonia, *Ariz., U.S.* **109** W8
Patagonia, region, *S. Amer.* **128** Q5
Patagonian Shelf, *Atl. Oc.* **241** U5
Patan, *India* **180** J7
Patan *see* Lalitpur, *Nepal* **180** F10
Patanga, island, *Cook Is., N.Z.* **223** B18
Patani, *Indonesia* **193** J16
Patara Shiraki, *Rep. of Georgia* **171** C20
Patchogue, *N.Y., U.S.* **96** N12
Pate Island, *Kenya* **203** L15
Paterna, *Sp.* **147** H14
Paterson, *N.J., U.S.* **96** N11
Pathankot, *India* **180** D5
Pathein, *Myanmar* **190** K5

Pathfinder Reservoir, *Wyo., U.S.* **108** J11
Patía, river, *Col.* **130** H3
Patiala, *India* **180** E5
Patience, Cape, *Asia* **168** D13
Patillas, *P.R., U.S.* **122** N4
Patio, *Fr. Polynesia, Fr.* **223** A23
Pati Point, *Guam, U.S.* **220** B12
Pativilca, *Peru* **132** G3
Pātkai Range, *Myanmar* **190** D6
Pátmos, *Gr.* **157** K17
Pátmos, island, *Gr.* **157** K17
Patna, *India* **180** G10
Patnos, *Turk.* **171** F17
Patos, *Braz.* **133** F17
Patos, Isla de, *Venez.* **123** P21
Patos, Lagoa dos, *Braz.* **132** Q12
Patos de Minas, *Braz.* **133** K14
Patquía, *Arg.* **134** H8
Pátra (Patras), *Gr.* **156** H9
Patraïkós Kólpos, *Gr.* **156** H9
Patras *see* Pátra, *Gr.* **156** H9
Patricio Lynch, Isla, *Chile* **135** U6
Patrick, Port, *Vanuatu* **222** H4
Patrington, *Eng., U.K.* **145** R14
Pattani, *Thai.* **191** S9
Patten, *Me., U.S.* **97** C18
Patterson, *Calif., U.S.* **111** S5
Patterson, *La., U.S.* **102** Q9
Patteson, Port, *Vanuatu* **222** B2
Patteson Passage, *Vanuatu* **222** C2
Patti, *India* **180** D5
Pattoki, *Pak.* **179** Q11
Patton Escarpment, *Pac. Oc.* **243** E17
Patton Seamounts, *Pac. Oc.* **243** C15
Patu, *Braz.* **133** F17
Patuakhali, *Bangladesh* **180** J13
Patuca, river, *Hond.* **117** K18
Patuxent Range, *Antarctica* **230** H11
Patzau, *Wis., U.S.* **100** F2
Pátzcuaro, *Mex.* **116** J10
Pau, *Fr.* **149** Y7
Pauini, *Braz.* **132** F6
Pauini, river, *Braz.* **132** F6
Pauktaw, *Myanmar* **190** H4
Paulatuk, *N.W.T., Can.* **84** E10
Paulding, *Ohio, U.S.* **101** P11
Paulhaguet, *Fr.* **149** V11
Paulhan, *Fr.* **149** X11
Paulistana, *Braz.* **133** F16
Paulo Afonso, *Braz.* **133** G17
Pauls Valley, *Okla., U.S.* **104** H11
Paungbyin, *Myanmar* **190** F5
Paungde, *Myanmar* **190** J6
Pauni, *India* **180** K7
Pa'uwela, *Hawai'i, U.S.* **115** G17
Pava, island, *Tuvalu* **221** J23
Pava'ia'i, *Amer. Samoa, U.S.* **222** M7
Pavia, *It.* **152** E4
Pāvilosta, *Latv.* **143** L15
Pavlikeni, *Bulg.* **155** H15
Pavlodar, *Kaz.* **177** C16
Pavlof Volcano, *Alas., U.S.* **112** N12
Pavlovka, *Russ.* **158** L14
Pavlovo, *Russ.* **158** J12
Pavlovsk, *Russ.* **158** F6
Pavlovsk, *Russ.* **159** N11
Pavlovskaya, *Russ.* **159** S11
Pavuvu, island, *Solomon Is.* **221** N18
Pawarenga, *N.Z.* **217** H18
Pawhuska, *Okla., U.S.* **104** E12
Pawleys Island, *S.C., U.S.* **98** L11
Pawnee, *Okla., U.S.* **104** E11
Pawnee City, *Nebr., U.S.* **107** R9
Paw Paw, *Mich., U.S.* **100** M9
Pawtucket, *R.I., U.S.* **97** L14
Paxós, island, *Gr.* **156** F6
Paxton, *Ill., U.S.* **101** Q7
Paxton, *Nebr., U.S.* **107** Q3
Payakumbuh, *Indonesia* **192** J6
Payer Mountains, *Antarctica* **231** B14
Payette, *Idaho, U.S.* **108** G3
Payette, river, *Idaho, U.S.* **108** G3
Payette Lake, *Idaho, U.S.* **108** F4
Payne, Lac, *Que., Can.* **85** J18
Paynesville, *Minn., U.S.* **106** J10
Paysandú, *Uru.* **134** K13
Payshanba, *Uzb.* **176** L12
Payson, *Ariz., U.S.* **109** T7

Pazar, *Turk.* **170** D8
Pazar, *Turk.* **170** E11
Pazar, *Turk.* **171** D15
Pazarcık, *Turk.* **170** H12
Pazardzhik, *Bulg.* **155** J14
Pazin, *Croatia* **154** E4
Pčinja, river, *Maced.* **154** K11
Pea, *Tonga* **222** J11
Pea, river, *Ala., Fla., U.S.* **103** M16
Peabody, *Kans., U.S.* **107** T8
Peace, river, *N. Amer.* **84** J11
Peace River, *Alta., Can.* **84** K10
Peach Springs, *Ariz., U.S.* **109** R5
Peacock Point, *Wake I., U.S.* **220** G8
Peak District, *Eng., U.K.* **145** S12
Peaked Mountain, *Me., U.S.* **97** C17
Peak Hill, *W. Aust., Austral.* **215** U3
Peale, Mount, *Utah, U.S.* **109** N9
Peale Island, *Wake I., U.S.* **220** F8
Peao, island, *Kiribati* **221** B20
Peard Bay, *Alas., U.S.* **113** B14
Pea Ridge National Military Park, *Ark., U.S.* **102** E6
Pearl, *Miss., U.S.* **102** L11
Pearl *see* Zhu, river, *Guang., China* **185** W5
Pearl, river, *La., Miss., U.S.* **102** L11
Pearl and Hermes Atoll, *Hawai'i, U.S.* **114** K3
Pearl City, *Hawai'i, U.S.* **114** E11
Pearl River, *Asia* **168** J12
Pearls Rock, island, *Grenada* **123** K24
Pearsall, *Tex., U.S.* **105** S9
Pearson, *Ga., U.S.* **99** P7
Pearya Spur, *Arctic Oc.* **246** L11
Peary Channel, *Nunavut, Can.* **85** B14
Peary Land, *Greenland, Den.* **82** A8
Pease, river, *Tex., U.S.* **104** J8
Pease Bay, *Cayman Is.* **122** J2
Peawanuk, *Ont., Can.* **85** L16
Pebane, *Mozambique* **207** F14
Pebas, *Peru* **132** D5
Pebble Island, *Falk. Is., U.K.* **135** V12
Peć *see* Pejë, *Kos.* **154** J10
Pecan Island, *La., U.S.* **102** Q8
Pechora, *Russ.* **160** F9
Pechora, river, *Russ.* **160** F9
Pechora Basin, *Eur.* **140** A13
Pechora Bay, *Arctic Oc.* **247** B16
Pechorskoye More, *Russ.* **160** E10
Pecos, *N. Mex., U.S.* **109** R13
Pecos, *Tex., U.S.* **105** N3
Pecos, river, *N. Mex., Tex., U.S.* **104** M2
Pecos National Historical Park, *N. Mex., U.S.* **109** R13
Pécs, *Hung.* **151** N14
Peddapalli, *India* **180** L7
Pedder, Lake, *Austral.* **214** M7
Pedernales, *Dom. Rep.* **119** N17
Pedernales, river, *Tex., U.S.* **105** Q8
Pedirka, *S. Aust., Austral.* **215** U9
Pedra Azul, *Braz.* **133** J15
Pedra Lume, *Cabo Verde* **209** B17
Pedras Negras, *Braz.* **132** H8
Pedro Afonso, *Braz.* **133** G13
Pedro Betancourt, *Cuba* **118** G7
Pedro Cays, *Jam.* **118** P11
Pedro de Valdivia, *Chile* **134** D7
Pedro Juan Caballero, *Parag.* **132** L10
Pedro Luro, *Arg.* **135** P11
Pedro Osório, *Braz.* **132** Q11
Pedro Point, *Jam.* **122** H6
Pedroso, *Port.* **146** E5
Pedroso, Sierra del, *Sp.* **146** J8
Peebles, *Ohio, U.S.* **101** S12
Peedamulla, *W. Aust., Austral.* **215** T2
Peekskill, *N.Y., U.S.* **96** M11
Peel (Purt ny h-Inshey), *Isle of Man, U.K.* **145** Q9
Peel, river, *Yukon, Can.* **84** E9
Pe Ell, *Wash., U.S.* **110** D3
Peel Sound, *Nunavut, Can.* **85** D14
Peetz, *Colo., U.S.* **108** K15
Pegasus Bay, *N.Z.* **217** N18
Pegeia, *Cyprus* **162** P5
Pego, *Sp.* **147** J15
Pehuajó, *Arg.* **134** M11
Peikang, *Taiwan, China* **185** V11
Peine, *Ger.* **150** D8
Peine, Pointe-à-, *Dominica* **123** F20

Peipus, Lake *see* Chudskoye Ozero, *Russ.* **158** G5
Peiraiás (Piraeus), *Gr.* **156** J12
Peixe, *Braz.* **133** H13
Peixian, *Jiangsu, China* **184** J8
Pejē (Peć), *Kos.* **154** J10
Pekalongan, *Indonesia* **192** M9
Pekan, *Malaysia* **191** U10
Pekanbaru, *Indonesia* **192** J6
Pekelmeer, *Bonaire, Neth.* **123** R19
Pekin, *Ill., U.S.* **101** Q5
Peking *see* Beijing, *Beijing Shi, China* **184** C7
Pelabuhanratu, Teluk, *Indonesia* **192** M8
Pelado, peak, *Sp.* **147** G13
Pelagosa *see* Palagruža, island, *Croatia* **154** J6
Pelahatchie, *Miss., U.S.* **102** L11
Pelat, Mount, *Fr.* **149** W15
Pelau, island, *Solomon Is.* **221** J18
Peleaga, peak, *Rom.* **154** E12
Peleliu *see* Beliliou, island, *Palau* **220** Q10
Peleng, island, *Indonesia* **193** J14
Pelham, *Ala., U.S.* **103** K15
Pelham, *Ga., U.S.* **99** P5
Pelican, *Alas., U.S.* **113** L21
Pelican Lake, *Minn., U.S.* **106** E12
Pelican Point, *Af.* **198** N6
Pelican Point, *Bahamas* **122** E3
Pelican Rapids, *Minn., U.S.* **106** G9
Péligre, Lac de, *Haiti* **119** M17
Pelikaan Punt, *St. Maarten, Neth.* **123** B14
Pelinaío, peak, *Gr.* **157** H16
Pelister, peak, *Maced.* **154** L11
Peljēšac, island, *Croatia* **154** H7
Pella, *Iowa, U.S.* **107** P12
Pella, ruin, *Gr.* **156** C10
Pellston, *Mich., U.S.* **100** G10
Pelly, river, *Yukon, Can.* **84** G8
Pelly Bay, *Nunavut, Can.* **85** F15
Pelly Crossing, *Yukon, Can.* **84** F8
Peloponnese, region, *Gr.* **156** K9
Peloponnesus, *Eur.* **140** M9
Pelotas, *Braz.* **132** Q11
Pelvoux, Massif du, *Fr.* **149** V14
Pematang, *Indonesia* **192** J6
Pematangsiantar, *Indonesia* **192** H5
Pemba, *Mozambique* **207** D15
Pemba Bay, *Af.* **198** M11
Pemba Island, *Tanzania* **203** M15
Pembina, *N. Dak., U.S.* **106** D8
Pembroke, *Ga., U.S.* **99** N8
Pembroke, *Ont., Can.* **85** Q18
Pembroke, *Trinidad and Tobago* **123** N18
Pembroke (Penfro), *Wales, U.K.* **145** V8
Pembroke Fort, *Malta* **163** K22
Pen, *India* **180** L3
Peña, Sierra de, *Sp.* **147** C14
Peña de Francia, Sierra de, *Sp.* **146** F8
Peñafiel, *Sp.* **146** D10
Penal, *Trinidad and Tobago* **123** Q22
Peñalara, peak, *Sp.* **146** F10
Peñalsordo, *Sp.* **146** J9
Penamacor, *Port.* **146** F7
Penambulai, island, *Indonesia* **193** M19
Peñaranda de Bracamonte, *Sp.* **146** E9
Peñarroya, peak, *Sp.* **147** F14
Peñarroya-Pueblonuevo, *Sp.* **146** J9
Peñas, Cabo de, *Sp.* **146** A8
Penas, Cape, *Eur.* **140** J3
Penas, Golfo de, *Chile* **135** T6
Pendan, *Indonesia* **192** H11
Pendembu, *Sierra Leone* **204** D6
Pender, *Nebr., U.S.* **107** N8
Pender Bay, *Austral.* **214** C4
Pendleton, *Oreg., U.S.* **110** F7
Pend Oreille, river, *Idaho, Wash., U.S.* **110** A9
Pend Oreille, Lake, *Idaho, U.S.* **108** B4
Pendra, *India* **180** J8
Pendroy, *Mont., U.S.* **108** B7

Penedo, *Braz.* **133** G17
Penfro *see* Pembroke, *Wales, U.K.* **145** V8
Pengchia Yü, *Taiwan, China* **185** T13
Penghu (Pescadores), isalnds, *Taiwan, China* **185** V10
Penghu, Shuitao, *Taiwan, China* **185** V10
Penglai, *Shand., China* **184** F11
Penha do Tapauá, *Braz.* **132** E7
Peniche, *Port.* **146** H4
Penicuik, *Scot., U.K.* **144** M10
Péninsule D'Ungava, *Que., Can.* **85** J18
Peñíscola, *Sp.* **147** F15
Penmarc'h, Pointe de, *Fr.* **149** Q2
Penna, Punta della, *It.* **152** K11
Penne, *It.* **152** J10
Pennell Coast, *Antarctica* **231** R14
Penner, river, *India* **181** P6
Penneshaw, *S. Aust., Austral.* **215** Y10
Penn Hills, *Pa., U.S.* **96** N3
Pennine Alpi, *Switz.* **152** C2
Pennington Gap, *Va., U.S.* **98** G6
Pennsylvania, *U.S.* **96** M6
Penn Yan, *N.Y., U.S.* **96** J7
Peno, *Russ.* **158** H7
Penobscot, river, *U.S.* **87** B22
Penobscot Bay, *Me., U.S.* **97** F17
Penong, *S. Aust., Austral.* **215** W8
Penonomé, *Pan.* **117** N21
Pénot, Mount, *Vanuatu* **222** D2
Penrhyn Atoll (Tongareva), *Cook Is., N.Z.* **218** H12
Penrhyn Basin, *Pac. Oc.* **243** L14
Penrith, *Eng., U.K.* **145** P11
Pensacola, *Fla., U.S.* **99** Q1
Pensacola Bay, *Fla., U.S.* **99** Q1
Pensacola Mountains, *Antarctica* **230** G11
Pentakomo, *Cyprus* **162** Q8
Pentálofos, *Gr.* **156** D8
Pentecost, island, *Vanuatu* **222** D2
Penticton, *B.C., Can.* **84** M8
Pentland, *Qnsld., Austral.* **215** S13
Pentland Firth, *Scot., U.K.* **144** G10
Pentwater, *Mich., U.S.* **100** K9
Pen-y-bont ar Ogwr *see* Bridgend, *Wales, U.K.* **145** V10
Penza, *Russ.* **158** L13
Penzance, *Eng., U.K.* **145** Y7
Penzhinskaya Guba, *Russ.* **161** E21
Peoples Creek, *Mont., U.S.* **108** B10
Peoria, *Ariz., U.S.* **109** U6
Peoria, *Ill., U.S.* **101** Q5
Pēpe'ekeo, *Hawai'i, U.S.* **115** M21
Pepillo Salcedo, *Dom. Rep.* **119** L17
Pepin, Lake, *Minn., Wis., U.S.* **100** J2
Pera, *Cyprus* **162** P8
Perabumilih, *Indonesia* **192** K7
Percival Lakes, *Austral.* **214** E5
Perdido, river, *Ala., Fla., U.S.* **103** N14
Perdido, Arroyo, *Arg.* **135** R8
Perdido, Monte, *Sp.* **147** C15
Pereira, *Col.* **130** F4
Perelazovskiy, *Russ.* **159** P12
Perelyub, *Russ.* **158** M16
Peremul Par, island, *India* **181** Q2
Perenjori, *W. Aust., Austral.* **215** W2
Pereslavl' Zalesskiy, *Russ.* **158** H10
Perga, ruins, *Turk.* **170** H6
Pergamino, *Arg.* **134** L12
Perham, *Minn., U.S.* **106** G9
Peri, river, *Turk.* **171** F15
Péribonka, river, *Que., Can.* **85** M20
Perico, *Arg.* **134** E9
Perigoso, Canal, *Braz.* **133** C13
Perigot *see* Puamau, Bay, *Fr. Polynesia, Fr.* **223** M21
Périgueux, *Fr.* **149** V8
Perijá, Sierra de, *S. Amer.* **130** C6
Peri Lake, *Austral.* **214** J12
Perinthus *see* Marmara Ereğlisi, *Turk.* **170** C4
Peristéra, island, *Gr.* **157** F13
Perito Moreno, *Arg.* **135** T7
Perkins, *Okla., U.S.* **104** F11
Perky, *Fla., U.S.* **99** Y9
Perlé, *Lux.* **162** J9

Perlevka, *Russ.* **158** M10
Perm', *Russ.* **160** H8
Pernambuco Plain, *Atl. Oc.* **241** Q9
Pernambuco Seamounts, *Atl. Oc.*
 241 Q9
Pernik, *Bulg.* **154** J12
Peron, Cape, *Austral.* **214** K2
Peronit Burnu, *Rep. of Georgia*
 171 C15
Péronne, *Fr.* **148** M10
Pérouges, *Fr.* **149** U13
Perpetua, Cape, *Oreg., U.S.* **110** G2
Perpignan, *Fr.* **149** Z10
Perranporth, *Eng., U.K.* **145** X8
Perry, *Fla., U.S.* **99** R6
Perry, *Ga., U.S.* **99** N6
Perry, *Iowa, U.S.* **107** P11
Perry, *Okla., U.S.* **104** F11
Perry Island, *Nunavut, Can.* **85** G13
Perrysburg, *Ohio, U.S.* **101** N12
Perryton, *Tex., U.S.* **104** E6
Perryville, *Alas., U.S.* **113** N13
Perryville, *Mo., U.S.* **107** U15
Persephone, ruins, *Iran* **175** F13
Perseverance Bay, *Virgin Is., U.S.*
 122 N8
Persey Rise, *Arctic Oc.* **247** F16
Persian Gulf, *Ind. Oc.* **168** G4
Pertek, *Turk.* **171** F14
Perth, *Scot., U.K.* **144** L10
Perth, *W. Aust., Austral.* **215** X2
Perth Basin, *Ind. Oc.* **225** L15
Pertóuli, *Gr.* **156** F9
Peru, *Ill., U.S.* **101** P5
Peru, *Ind., U.S.* **101** Q9
Peru, *Nebr., U.S.* **107** Q9
Peru, *S. Amer.* **132** G4
Peru Basin, *Pac. Oc.* **243** K21
Peru-Chile Trench, *Pac. Oc.* **243** L22
Perugia, *It.* **152** H8
Pervari, *Turk.* **171** G17
Pervomays'k, *Ukr.* **159** Q6
Pervomaysk, *Russ.* **158** K12
Pervomayskoye, *Russ.* **158** M14
Pervoural'sk, *Russ.* **160** H8
Pervyy Kuril'skiy Proliv, *Russ.*
 161 G23
Pesaro, *It.* **152** G9
Pescador, Punta, *Venez.* **123** R22
Pescadores *see* Penghu, islands,
 Taiwan, China **185** V10
Pescara, *It.* **152** J10
Peschici, *It.* **152** K13
Peshawar, *Pak.* **179** N9
Peshkopi, *Alban.* **154** K10
Peshtera, *Bulg.* **155** K14
Peshtigo, *Wis., U.S.* **100** H7
Pesmes, *Fr.* **149** R13
Pessac, *Fr.* **149** V6
Pessons, Pic dels, *Andorra* **162** J4
Pestovo, *Russ.* **158** G8
Pesu, *India* **180** G15
Petacalco, Bahía, *Mex.* **116** J9
Petacalco Bay, *N. Amer.* **82** N4
Petah Tiqwa, *Israel* **172** M5
Petal, *Miss., U.S.* **102** N12
Petalión, Kólpos, *Gr.* **157** J13
Petaluma, *Calif., U.S.* **111** R3
Pétange, *Lux.* **162** K9
Petatlán, *Mex.* **116** K11
Petén, region, *Guatemala* **117** K16
Petenwell Lake, *Wis., U.S.* **100** J5
Peterborough, *Eng., U.K.* **145** T14
Peterborough, *N.H., U.S.* **97** J13
Peterborough, *Ont., Can.* **85** Q18
Peterborough, *S. Aust., Austral.*
 215 X10
Peterhead, *Scot., U.K.* **144** J11
Peter I Island, *Antarctica* **230** J5
Petermann Ranges, *Austral.* **214** F7
Peter Pond Lake, *Sask., Can.* **84** L12
Petersburg, *Alas., U.S.* **113** L23
Petersburg, *Ill., U.S.* **101** R4
Petersburg, *Ind., U.S.* **101** T8
Petersburg, *Tex., U.S.* **104** J5
Petersburg, *Va., U.S.* **98** F13
Petersburg, *W. Va., U.S.* **98** C11
Petersen Bank, *Ind. Oc.* **249** D14
Petersfield, *Jam.* **122** H6
Peter the Great Gulf, *Pac. Oc.*
 168 F12

Petit Bois Island, *Miss., U.S.* **103** P13
Petit-Bourg, *Guadeloupe, Fr.* **123** F14
Petit-Canal, *Guadeloupe, Fr.* **123** E15
Petit Cul-de-Sac Marin, *Guadeloupe,*
 Fr. **123** F15
Petite Île, *Réunion, Fr.* **209** H16
Petite Rivière del' Artibonite, *Haiti*
 119 L16
Petite-Terre, island, *Mayotte, Fr.*
 209 P17
Petite-Terre, Îles de la, *Guadeloupe,*
 Fr. **123** F17
Petit-Goâve, *Haiti* **119** M16
Petit Gravier, *Mauritius* **209** J21
Petitot, river, *N. Amer.* **84** H10
Petit Piton, peak, *St. Lucia* **123** L13
Petit Savane Point, *Dominica*
 123 G20
Petit Trou, *Trinidad and Tobago*
 123 P17
Petoskey, *Mich., U.S.* **100** H10
Petra, ruins, *Jordan* **173** Q6
Petrich, *Bulg.* **155** K13
Petrified Forest National Park, *Ariz.,*
 U.S. **109** S9
Petrila, *Rom.* **155** E13
Petrinja, *Croatia* **154** E6
Petro, *Pak.* **179** U8
Petrolândia, *Braz.* **133** G17
Petrolia, *Calif., U.S.* **111** N1
Petrolia, *Tex., U.S.* **104** J10
Petrolina, *Braz.* **133** G16
Petropavlovsk, *Kaz.* **177** B13
Petropavlovsk-Kamchatskiy, *Russ.*
 161 F23
Petrovac, *Montenegro* **154** J8
Petrovaradin, *Serb.* **154** E9
Petrovgrad *see* Zrenjanin, *Serb.*
 154 E10
Petrovsk, *Russ.* **158** L13
Petrovsk Zabaykal'skiy, *Russ.*
 161 L16
Petrozavodsk, *Russ.* **160** E7
Petsamo, *Eur.* **140** A10
Petukhovo, *Russ.* **160** J9
Pevek, *Russ.* **161** C19
Peyrehorade, *Fr.* **149** X6
Pezinok, *Slovakia* **151** K13
Pfaffenhofen, *Ger.* **150** K8
Pforzheim, *Ger.* **150** J6
Phaestus *see* Faistós, ruin, *Gr.*
 157 Q14
Phaeton, Port, *Fr. Polynesia, Fr.*
 223 P17
Phagwara, *India* **180** D5
Phalodi, *India* **180** F3
Phaltan, *India* **180** M4
Phan, *Thai.* **190** J8
Phangan, Ko, *Thai.* **191** Q8
Phangnga, *Thai.* **191** R7
Phan Rang-Tháp Chàm
 (Panduranga), *Vietnam* **191** P14
Phan Thiêt, *Vietnam* **191** P13
Pharr, *Tex., U.S.* **105** W10
Pharus *see* Hvar, island, *Croatia*
 154 H6
Phatthalung, *Thai.* **191** R8
Phayao, *Thai.* **190** J8
Phelps, *Ky., U.S.* **103** C21
Phelps Lake, *N.C., U.S.* **98** H14
Phenix City, *Ala., U.S.* **103** L17
Phetchabun Range, *Thai.* **190** L9
Phetchaburi, *Thai.* **191** N8
Phiafai, *Laos* **190** M12
Phichai, *Thai.* **190** K8
Phichit, *Thai.* **190** L9
Philadelphia, *Miss., U.S.* **102** K12
Philadelphia, *Pa., U.S.* **96** P9
Philadelphia *see* 'Ammān (Ammān),
 Jordan **172** M7
Philip, *S. Dak., U.S.* **106** L3
Philippeville, *Belg.* **148** M12
Philippi, *W. Va., U.S.* **98** C10
Philippi *see* Fílippoi, ruin, *Gr.* **157** B13
Philippi Glacier, *Antarctica* **231** H21
Philippine Basin, *Pac. Oc.* **242** G6
Philippine Islands, *Asia* **168** J13
Philippines, *Asia* **193** C13
Philippine Sea, *Pac. Oc.* **168** J14
Philippine Trench, *Pac. Oc.* **242** H5
Philippolis, *S. Af.* **206** L9

Philippopolis *see* Plovdiv, *Bulg.*
 155 J14
Philippopolis *see* Shahbā', *Syr.* **172** K8
Philipsburg, *Mont., U.S.* **108** D6
Philipsburg, *Pa., U.S.* **96** N5
Philipsburg, *St. Maarten, Neth.*
 123 B14
Philip Smith Mountains, *Alas., U.S.*
 113 D17
Phillip Island, *Norfolk I., Austral.*
 221 G20
Phillips, *Tex., U.S.* **104** G6
Phillips, *Wis., U.S.* **100** G4
Phillips, Mount, *Austral.* **214** G2
Phillipsburg, *Kans., U.S.* **107** R5
Philomath, *Oreg., U.S.* **110** G3
Philpots Island, *Nunavut, Can.*
 85 D16
Phippsburg, *Colo., U.S.* **108** L11
Phitsanulok, *Thai.* **190** K8
Phnom Penh *see* Phnum Pénh,
 Cambodia **191** P11
Phnum Pénh (Phnom Penh),
 Cambodia **191** P11
Phoenix, *Ariz., U.S.* **109** U7
Phoenix, *Mauritius* **209** G20
Phoenix Islands, *Kiribati* **218** H10
Phoenix Seamounts, *Pac. Oc.*
 242 K12
Phôngsali, *Laos* **190** G10
Phong Thô, *Vietnam* **190** G10
Phouphiang Bolavén, *Laos* **190** L12
Phrae, *Thai.* **190** K8
Phrao, *Thai.* **190** J8
Phra Thong, Ko, *Thai.* **191** Q7
Phrom Phiram, *Thai.* **190** K8
Phsar Réam, *Cambodia* **191** P11
Phuket, *Thai.* **191** R7
Phuket, Ko, *Thai.* **191** R7
Phulabani, *India* **180** K9
Phulad, *India* **180** G4
Phú Lôc, *Vietnam* **190** L13
Phú Lôc, *Vietnam* **191** Q12
Phumi Banam, *Cambodia* **191** P12
Phumi Kâmpóng Srâlau, *Cambodia*
 190 M12
Phumi Lvéa Kraôm, *Cambodia*
 191 N10
Phumi Thalabârivât, *Cambodia*
 190 M12
Phù Mỹ, *Vietnam* **190** M14
Phú Tho, *Vietnam* **190** G11
Phyarpon, *Myanmar* **190** L6
Pi', *Burkina Faso* **204** C10
Piacenza, *It.* **152** E5
Piamafua Mountain, *Amer. Samoa,*
 U.S. **222** N2
Piangan, *Shanxi, China* **184** D4
Pianosa, Isola, *It.* **152** J5
Pianosa, Isola, *It.* **152** K12
Pianu, island, *F.S.M.* **221** C14
Pianu, Mochun, *F.S.M.* **221** C14
Piasecznto, *Pol.* **151** E16
Piatra Neamt, *Rom.* **155** C16
Piaui, river, *S. Amer.* **128** E10
Piave, river, *It.* **152** C8
Piazza Armerina, *It.* **153** T11
Piazza del Risorgimento, *It.* **163** N17
Piazza Pio XII, *Vatican City* **163** Q17
Pibor Post, *S. Sudan* **203** H13
Picara Point, *Virgin Is., U.S.* **122** M10
Picardy, region, *Fr.* **148** M10
Picassent, *Sp.* **147** H14
Picayune, *Miss., U.S.* **102** P11
Pichanal, *Arg.* **134** E10
Picher, *Okla., U.S.* **104** D14
Pichilemu, *Chile* **134** L6
Pickens, *Miss., U.S.* **102** K11
Pickford, *Mich., U.S.* **100** F11
Pickle Lake, *Ont., Can.* **85** N15
Pickwick Lake, *Ala., Miss., Tenn., U.S.*
 103 G13
Pico, *Azores, Port.* **146** Q3
Pico, *It.* **152** L10
Pico, Ponta do, *Azores, Port.* **146** Q3
Pico Fracture Zone, *Atl. Oc.* **240** J8
Picos, *Braz.* **133** F16
Picos, Punta dos, *Sp.* **146** D5
Pico Truncado, *Arg.* **135** T8
Pictured Rocks National Lakeshore,
 Mich., U.S. **100** F9

Picture Gallery, *Vatican City* **163** N15
Picúa, Punta, *P.R., U.S.* **122** M5
Pidarak, *Pak.* **179** V3
Piedmont, *Ala., U.S.* **103** J17
Piedmont, *Eur.* **140** J6
Piedmont, *Mo., U.S.* **107** U15
Piedmont, range, *U.S.* **87** H19
Piedra, Monasterio de, *Sp.* **147** E13
Piedra Grande, Cayo, *Cuba* **118** K10
Piedras, river, *Peru* **132** G5
Piedras Blancas, Point, *Calif., U.S.*
 111 V4
Piedras Negras, *Mex.* **116** D11
Pieksämäki, *Fin.* **143** G16
Pielinen, lake, *Fin.* **143** F17
Pieniężno, *Pol.* **151** B15
Pienza, *It.* **152** H7
Piepus, Lake, *Eur.* **140** E10
Pierce, *Nebr., U.S.* **107** N7
Piéria, Óros, *Gr.* **156** D10
Pierre, *S. Dak., U.S.* **106** K5
Pierrelatte, *Fr.* **149** W12
Pierrot Island (Cat Island), *Mauritius*
 209 K20
Piešt'any, *Slovakia* **151** K14
Pietarsaari *see* Jakobstad, *Fin.*
 143 G15
Pietermaritzburg, *S. Af.* **206** K11
Pietra-di-Verde, *Fr.* **152** K4
Pietrosu, peak, *Rom.* **155** C14
Pietrosul, peak, *Rom.* **155** B14
Pigafetta Basin, *Pac. Oc.* **242** G8
Pigailoe (West Fayu Atoll), *F.S.M.*
 220 Q4
Pigeon, *Guadeloupe, Fr.* **123** F14
Pigeon, *Mich., U.S.* **100** K12
Pigeon Cay, *Bahamas* **122** B8
Pigeon Creek, *Bahamas* **122** F11
Pigeon Point, *Trinidad and Tobago*
 123 N17
Piggott, *Ark., U.S.* **102** E11
Pigna Courtyard, *Vatican City*
 163 N16
Pigs, Bay of *see* Cochinos, Bahía de,
 Cuba **118** H7
Pigüé, *Arg.* **135** N11
Piha Passage, *Tonga* **222** H12
Pihtipudas, *Fin.* **143** G15
Pihyön, *N. Korea* **186** G4
Pi'ilanihale Heiau, *Hawai'i, U.S.*
 115 H18
Piis-Panewu, island, *F.S.M.* **221** A15
Pijijiapan, *Mex.* **117** K14
Pikalevo, *Russ.* **158** F8
Pike Bank, *Ind. Oc.* **224** R10
Pikelot, island, *F.S.M.* **220** Q5
Pikes Peak, *Colo., U.S.* **109** N13
Pikeville, *Ky., U.S.* **103** C20
Pikijin, island, *Marshall Is., U.S.*
 220 L8
Piła, *Pol.* **151** C13
Pilão Arcado, *Braz.* **133** G15
Pilar, *Parag.* **132** N10
Pilar, Cabo, *Chile* **135** X6
Pilbara, region, *Austral.* **214** F2
Pilbarra Point, *Vanuatu* **222** G3
Pilcomayo, river, *S. Amer.* **128** J6
Pileni, island, *Solomon Is.* **221** P23
Pil'gyn, *Russ.* **161** B20
Pilibhit, *India* **180** F7
Pílio, Óros, *Gr.* **156** F11
Pillsbury Sound, *Virgin Is., U.S.*
 122 N10
Pilón, *Cuba* **118** L11
Pilot Knob, peak, *Idaho, U.S.* **108** E4
Pilot Peak, *Nev., U.S.* **111** R8
Pilot Point, *Alas., U.S.* **113** M13
Pilot Rock, *Oreg., U.S.* **110** F7
Pilot Station, *Alas., U.S.* **112** H12
Pilottown, *La., U.S.* **102** R12
Pilsen *see* Plzeň, *Czech Rep.* **150** H10
Pimentel, *Dom. Rep.* **119** L19
Pinaki 2, island, *Fr. Polynesia, Fr.*
 223 F21
Pinang, island, *Malaysia* **191** T9
Pinangah, *Malaysia* **192** G12
Pınarbaşı, *Turk.* **170** G11
Pinar del Río, *Cuba* **118** G5
Pinas, *Arg.* **134** J9

Piñas, *Ecua.* **130** L2
Pinatubo, Mount, *Asia* **168** J13
Pinckneyville, *Ill., U.S.* **101** U5
Pinconning, *Mich., U.S.* **100** K11
Pindaré, river, *Braz.* **133** E14
Pinders Point, *Bahamas* **122** F1
Pindi Bhattian, *Pak.* **179** P11
Pindi Gheb, *Pak.* **179** N10
Píndos Óros, *Gr.* **156** F8
Pindus Mountains, *Alban., Gr.*
 154 M10
Pine Barrens, *U.S.* **87** F21
Pine Bluff, *Ark., U.S.* **102** H9
Pine Bluffs, *Wyo., U.S.* **108** K14
Pine City, *Minn., U.S.* **106** H12
Pine Creek, *N.T., Austral.* **215** P8
Pinedale, *Calif., U.S.* **111** T6
Pinedale, *Wyo., U.S.* **108** H9
Pinega, river, *Eur.* **140** C12
Pinegrove, *W. Aust., Austral.* **215** V2
Pine Hill, *N.T., Austral.* **215** T8
Pine Hills, *Fla., U.S.* **99** T9
Pinehurst, *Idaho, U.S.* **108** C4
Pinehurst, *N.C., U.S.* **98** J11
Pineiós, river, *Gr.* **156** E10
Pine Island Bay, *Antarctica* **230** K7
Pine Island Glacier, *Antarctica*
 230 J7
Pineland, *Tex., U.S.* **105** N15
Pinellas Park, *Fla., U.S.* **99** U7
Pine Point, *N.W.T., Can.* **84** J11
Pine Ridge, S. *Dak., U.S.* **106** M2
Pine River, *Minn., U.S.* **106** G10
Pinerolo, *It.* **152** E2
Pines, Isle of *see* Pins, Île,
 New Caledonia, Fr. **222** E9
Pines, Lake O' the, *Tex., U.S.*
 104 L14
Pinetop-Lakeside, *Ariz., U.S.* **109** T9
Pineville, *Ky., U.S.* **103** D19
Pineville, *La., U.S.* **102** N8
Piney Buttes, *Mont., U.S.* **108** C11
Ping, river, *Thai.* **190** L8
Pingdingshan, *Henan, China* **184** K5
Pingdingshan, *Liaoning, China*
 184 B14
Pingdu, *Shand., China* **184** G10
Pingelap Atoll, *F.S.M.* **220** Q8
Pingelly, *W. Aust., Austral.* **215** X3
Pinghe, *Fujian, China* **185** U8
Pingjiang, *Hunan, China* **185** Q5
Pinglap, island, *Marshall Is., U.S.*
 220 M7
Pingle, *Guangxi Zhuang, China*
 185 U2
Pingli, *Shaanxi, China* **184** L1
Pingliang, *China* **182** J11
Pinglu, *Shanxi, China* **184** D4
Pinglu, *Shanxi, China* **184** H3
Pingnan, *Fujian, China* **185** S10
Pingnan, *Guangxi Zhuang, China*
 185 V2
Pingquan, *Hebei, China* **184** B9
Pingsha, *Guang., China* **185** W4
Pingtan, *Fujian, China* **185** T10
Pingtung, *Taiwan, China* **185** W11
Pingualuit Crater (Cratère du
 Nouveau-Québec), *Que., Can.*
 85 J18
Pingwu, *China* **182** K10
Pingxiang, *China* **182** P11
Pingxiang, *Jiangxi, China* **185** R5
Pingyang, *Zhejiang, China* **185** R11
Pingyao, *Shanxi, China* **184** F4
Pingyi, *Shand., China* **184** H8
Pingyin, *Shand., China* **184** G7
Pingyu, *Henan, China* **184** L6
Pingyuan, *Guang., China* **185** U7
Pingzhuang, *N. Mongol, China*
 184 A10
Pinheiro, *Braz.* **133** D14
Pinhel, *Port* **146** F7
Pini, island, *Indonesia* **192** J5
Pinjan, *Indonesia* **193** H13
Pinleibu, *Myanmar* **190** F6
Pinnacles National Park, *Calif., U.S.*
 111 U5
Pinneberg, *Ger.* **150** C7
Pínnes, Ákra (Nymphaeum), *Gr.*
 157 D13
Pinos, Point, *Calif., U.S.* **111** T4

Pinos-Puente, *Sp.* **146** LII
Pins, Île (Pines, Isle of), *New Caledonia, Fr.* **222** E9
Pins, Île des (Isle of Pines), *New Caledonia, Fr.* **218** K7
Pinsk, *Belarus* **158** M4
Pinsk Marshes, *Belarus* **158** M4
Pinta, Canal de, *Ecua.* **130** P9
Pinta (Abingdon), Isla, *Ecua.* **130** N9
Pintados, *Chile* **134** C7
Pinzón (Duncan), Isla, *Ecua.* **130** Q9
Pioche, *Nev., U.S.* **III** R12
Piombino, *It.* **152** J6
Pioneer Fracture Zone, *Pac. Oc.* **243** E15
Pioneer Mountains, *Mont., U.S.* **108** E6
Pioneer Tablemount, *Hawai'i, U.S.* **114** L4
Pioner, Ostrov, *Russ.* **161** D14
Pionsat, *Fr.* **149** T10
Piotrków Trybunalski, *Pol.* **151** F15
Pip'agol, point, *N. Korea* **186** K5
Pipanaco, Salar de, *Arg.* **134** H9
Pipar, *India* **180** G4
Piparia, *India* **180** J6
Pipéri, island, *Gr.* **157** F13
Piper Peak, *Nev., U.S.* **III** S8
Pipe Spring National Monument, *Ariz., U.S.* **109** Q6
Pipestem Creek, river, *N. Dak., U.S.* **106** G6
Pipestone, *Minn., U.S.* **106** L8
Pipestone National Monument, *Minn., U.S.* **106** L8
Pipinas, *Arg.* **134** MI3
Piplan, *Pak.* **179** P9
Piqua, *Ohio, U.S.* **101** RII
Piracicaba, *Braz.* **133** MI3
Piracuruca, *Braz.* **133** E16
Pirae, *Fr. Polynesia, Fr.* **223** NI6
Piraeus *see* Peiraiás, *Gr.* **156** JI2
Pirallahı, *Azerb.* **171** D23
Pirané, *Arg.* **134** FI2
Piranhas, *Braz.* **132** JI2
Pirapora, *Braz.* **133** KI4
Pirássununga, *Braz.* **133** LI3
Pirimapun, *Indonesia* **193** M2O
Pirin, mountains, *Bulg.* **155** KI3
Piripiri, *Braz.* **133** E16
Pirmasens, *Ger.* **150** H5
Pirna, *Ger.* **150** FII
Pirogue, *Guadeloupe, Fr.* **123** GI6
Pirojpur, *Bangladesh* **180** JI2
Pirot, *Serb.* **154** HI2
Pir Panjal Range, *India* **179** NI2
Pirsagat, river, *Azerb.* **171** D22
Pisa, *It.* **152** G6
Pisagua, *Chile* **134** C6
Pisamwe, island, *F.S.M.* **221** AI5
Pisaras, island, *F.S.M.* **220** Q5
Piscaderabaai, *Curaçao, Neth.* **123** QI4
Pisciotta, *It.* **153** NI2
Pisco, *Peru* **132** J3
Piscopi *see* Tílos, island, *Gr.* **157** MI8
Písek, *Czech Rep.* **150** JII
Pisemew, island, *F.S.M.* **221** AI5
Pishan (Guma), *China* **182** G2
Pishin, *Pak.* **179** R6
Pīshīn, *Iran* **175** HI8
Pishīn Jān, *Afghan.* **179** N2
Pisininin, island, *F.S.M.* **221** AI5
Pisinun, island, *F.S.M.* **221** CI6
Pismo Beach, *Calif., U.S.* **III** V5
Piso Firme, *Bol.* **132** H8
Pissos, *Fr.* **149** W6
Pissouri, *Cyprus* **162** Q6
Pisticci, *It.* **153** NI3
Pistoia, *It.* **152** G6
Pistol River, *Oreg., U.S.* **110** KI
Pisz, *Pol.* **151** CI6
Pitaga, *Nfld. & Lab., Can.* **85** L2O
Pitanga, *Braz.* **132** MI2
Pitav, *Afghan.* **178** K8
Pitcairn Island, *Pac. Oc.* **219** LI6
Pitcairn Islands, *Pac. Oc.* **219** KI6
Piteå, *Sw.* **143** FI4
Piteşti, *Rom.* **155** FI4
Pit Gorodok, *Russ.* **161** JI3
Piti, *Guam, U.S.* **220** CIO

Piti Aau, Moto, *Fr. Polynesia, Fr.* **223** KI4
Piti u Tai, island, *Fr. Polynesia, Fr.* **223** LI4
Piti u Uta, island, *Fr. Polynesia, Fr.* **223** LI4
Pitlochry, *Scot., U.K.* **144** LIO
Pitman Fracture Zone, *Pac. Oc.* **249** KI6
Piton, peak, *Wallis and Futuna, Fr.* **222** FII
Pitt, Punta, *Ecua.* **130** QII
Pitti Island, *India* **181** R3
Pitt Island (Rangiauria), *Pac. Oc.* **218** P9
Pittsburg, *Kans., U.S.* **107** UIO
Pittsburg, *Tex., U.S.* **104** LI4
Pittsburgh, *Pa., U.S.* **96** N2
Pittsfield, *Ill., U.S.* **101** R3
Pittsfield, *Mass., U.S.* **97** KI2
Pittsfield, *Me., U.S.* **97** FI7
Pittston, *Pa., U.S.* **96** M9
Pittston Farm, *Me., U.S.* **97** DI6
Piua Petrii, *Rom.* **155** FI7
Piura, *Peru* **132** F2
Piva, river, *Montenegro* **154** H8
Pīwār Kandow, pass, *Afghan., Pak.* **179** N8
Pizhou, *Jiangsu, China* **184** J9
Pkulagalid, cape, *Palau* **220** MII
Pkulagasemieg, island, *Palau* **220** QII
Pkulngril, cape, *Palau* **220** MII
Pkurengel, cape, *Palau* **220** NII
Placentia, *Nfld. & Lab., Can.* **85** M24
Placentia Bay, *Nfld. & Lab., Can.* **85** M24
Placerville, *Calif., U.S.* **III** Q5
Placetas, *Cuba* **118** H9
Placida, *Fla., U.S.* **99** V8
Plain Dealing, *La., U.S.* **102** K6
Plainfield, *Ind., U.S.* **101** R9
Plainfield, *N.J., U.S.* **96** NIO
Plain of Reeds, *Vietnam* **191** PI2
Plains, *Ga., U.S.* **99** N5
Plains, *Kans., U.S.* **107** V4
Plains, *Tex., U.S.* **104** K4
Plainview, *Minn., U.S.* **106** KI2
Plainview, *Nebr., U.S.* **107** N7
Plainview, *Tex., U.S.* **104** J5
Plainville, *Kans., U.S.* **107** S5
Plainwell, *Mich., U.S.* **100** MIO
Plaisance, *Haiti* **119** LI6
Pláka, *Gr.* **157** EI5
Plaka *see* Mílos, *Gr.* **157** MI3
Plakoti, Cape , *Cyprus* **162** MII
Plana Cays, *Bahamas* **119** GI5
Planalto Brasileiro, *Braz.* **133** KI5
Planken, *Liech.* **162** N2
Plankinton, *S. Dak., U.S.* **106** L6
Plano, *Tex., U.S.* **104** LI2
Plantation, *Fla., U.S.* **99** WIO
Plant City, *Fla., U.S.* **99** U8
Plaquemine, *La., U.S.* **102** P9
Plasencia, *Sp.* **146** G8
Plasstéikopf, peak, *Liech.* **162** Q3
Plata, Isla de la, *Ecua.* **130** KI
Plata, Río de la, *Arg.* **134** LI3
Platamónas, *Gr.* **156** HIO
Plateau Fairway, *Pac. Oc.* **242** M9
Plateau Station, site, *Antarctica* **231** FI5
Plato, *Col.* **130** C5
Plato Putorana, *Russ.* **161** GI4
Platte, *S. Dak., U.S.* **106** M6
Platte, river, *U.S.* **86** FI2
Platteville, *Wis., U.S.* **100** M4
Plattsburg, *Mo., U.S.* **107** SIO
Plattsburgh, *N.Y., U.S.* **96** FII
Plattsmouth, *Nebr., U.S.* **107** Q8
Platypus Spur, *Ind. Oc.* **225** JI7
Plauen, *Ger.* **150** G9
Plavsk, *Russ.* **158** L9
Playa Blanca, *Sp.* **208** Q7
Playa Dayaniguas, *Cuba* **118** H5
Playa de Dorado, site, *P.R., U.S.* **122** M4
Playa de Guayanés, *P.R., U.S.* **122** N5
Playa de Guayanilla, *P.R., U.S.* **122** P2
Playa de Naguabo, *P.R., U.S.* **122** N5
Playa Girón, *Cuba* **118** H8

Playa Honda, *Sp.* **208** P7
Playas Lake, *N. Mex., U.S.* **109** WIO
Plaza Huincul, *Arg.* **135** P8
Pleasant, Lake, *Ariz., U.S.* **109** T6
Pleasant Bay, *Bahamas* **122** BIO
Pleasant Grove, *Utah, U.S.* **108** L7
Pleasanton, *Kans., U.S.* **107** TIO
Pleasanton, *Tex., U.S.* **105** S9
Pleasantville, *N.J., U.S.* **96** QIO
Pleasure Ridge Park, *Ky., U.S.* **103** BI6
Plei Ku (Pleiku), *Vietnam* **190** MI3
Pleiku *see* Plei Ku, *Vietnam* **190** MI3
Pléneuf, *Fr.* **149** P4
Plenty, Bay of, *N.Z.* **217** K2O
Plentywood, *Mont., U.S.* **108** AI3
Plesetsk, *Russ.* **160** E8
Plestin, *Fr.* **149** P3
Plétipi, Lac, *Que., Can.* **85** M2O
Pleubian, *Fr.* **149** P4
Pleven, *Bulg.* **155** HI4
Plevna, *Mont., U.S.* **108** DI3
Pljevlja, *Montenegro* **154** H9
Ploče, *Croatia* **154** H7
Płock, *Pol.* **151** DI5
Ploërmel, *Fr.* **149** Q5
Ploieşti, *Rom.* **155** FI5
Plomári, *Gr.* **157** GI7
Płońsk, *Pol.* **151** DI5
Plouézec, *Fr.* **149** P4
Plouguerneau, *Fr.* **149** P2
Plovdiv (Philippopolis), *Bulg.* **155** JI4
Plum, Pointe, *St.-Martin, Fr.* **123** BI3
Plummer, *Idaho, U.S.* **108** C3
Plumridge Lakes, *Austral.* **214** H6
Plumtree, *Zimb.* **206** GIO
Plymouth, *Eng., U.K.* **145** X9
Plymouth, *Ind., U.S.* **100** P9
Plymouth, *Mass., U.S.* **97** LI5
Plymouth, *Montserrat* **123** B23
Plymouth, *N.C., U.S.* **98** HI4
Plymouth, *N.H., U.S.* **97** HI4
Plymouth, *Pa., U.S.* **96** M8
Plymouth, *Trinidad and Tobago* **123** NI7
Plymouth, *Vt., U.S.* **96** HI2
Plymouth, *Wis., U.S.* **100** K7
Plyusa, *Russ.* **158** G6
Plzeň (Pilsen), *Czech Rep.* **150** HIO
Pniewy, *Pol.* **150** DI2
Po, river, *It.* **152** E6
Po, Foci del (Po, Mouths of the), *It.* **152** F8
Po, Mouths of the *see* Po, Foci del, *It.* **152** F8
Pobeda, Gora, *Russ.* **161** FI9
Pobeda Peak (Victory Peak, Jengish Chokusu, Sheng-li Feng), *China, Kyrg.* **178** EI5
Pocahontas, *Ark., U.S.* **102** EIO
Pocahontas, *Iowa, U.S.* **106** MIO
Pocahontas, *W. Va., U.S.* **98** F8
Pocatello, *Idaho, U.S.* **108** H7
Pocheon, *S. Korea* **186** M8
Pochep, *Russ.* **158** L7
Poch'ŏn, *N. Korea* **186** DIO
Pochutla, *Mex.* **117** KI3
Pocomoke City, *Md., U.S.* **98** DI5
Poconé, *Braz.* **132** JIO
Pocono Mountains, *Pa., U.S.* **96** M9
Poços de Caldas, *Braz.* **133** LI3
Poddor'ye, *Russ.* **158** H6
Poděbrady, *Czech Rep.* **150** GII
Podgorica, *Montenegro* **154** J8
Podil's'ka Vysochyna, *Ukr.* **159** P4
Podkamennaya Tunguska, river, *Russ.* **161** JI4
Podol'sk, *Russ.* **158** J9
Podporozh'ye, *Russ.* **158** E8
Podravska Slatina, *Croatia* **154** D7
Poggibonsi, *It.* **152** H7
Poggio Rusco, *It.* **152** E7
Poh, *Indonesia* **193** JI4
P'oha, *N. Korea* **186** EI3
Pōhakueaea Point, *Hawai'i, U.S.* **115** JI7
P'ohang, *S. Korea* **187** RI2
Pohnpei (Ponape), island, *F.S.M.* **220** Q8
Pohnpei Harbor, *F.S.M.* **221** FI4
Pohorje, mountains, *Slov.* **154** C5

Pōhue Bay, *Hawai'i, U.S.* **115** QI9
Pohuerahi, peak, *Fr. Polynesia, Fr.* **223** HI4
Poi, *Wallis and Futuna, Fr.* **222** EII
Poim, *Russ.* **158** LI2
Poindimié, *New Caledonia, Fr.* **222** C7
Poinsett, Cape, *Antarctica* **231** M2I
Point, Cap, *St. Lucia* **123** JI4
Point Arena, *Calif., U.S.* **III** Q2
Point Blanche, *St. Maarten, Neth.* **123** BI5
Pointe-à-Gravois, *Haiti* **119** NI5
Pointe a la Hache, *La., U.S.* **102** QII
Pointe-à-Pitre, *Guadeloupe, Fr.* **123** EI5
Pointe Michel, *Dominica* **123** GI9
Pointe-Noire, *Congo* **205** KI6
Pointe-Noire, *Guadeloupe, Fr.* **123** FI4
Point Fortin, *Trinidad and Tobago* **123** Q22
Point Hope, *Alas., U.S.* **112** CI2
Point Lake, *N.W.T., Can.* **84** GI2
Point Lay, *Alas., U.S.* **113** CI3
Point Pedro, *Sri Lanka* **181** R7
Point Pleasant, *N.J., U.S.* **96** PII
Point Pleasant, *W. Va., U.S.* **98** D7
Point Reyes National Seashore, *Calif., U.S.* **III** R2
Point Ross, *Norfolk I., Austral.* **221** G2O
Point Samson, *W. Aust., Austral.* **215** S2
Point Sur, *Calif., U.S.* **III** U4
Point Washington, *Fla., U.S.* **99** Q3
Po'ipū, *Hawai'i, U.S.* **114** C5
Poirino, *It.* **152** E3
Poissonnier Point, *Austral.* **214** E3
Poissy, *Fr.* **149** P9
Poitiers, *Fr.* **149** T7
Poitou, *Eur.* **140** H4
Poix, *Fr.* **149** N9
Pok, *F.S.M.* **221** GI4
Pokhvistnevo, *Russ.* **158** KI6
Pokka, *Fin.* **143** CI5
Poko, *Dem. Rep. of the Congo* **202** JII
Pola *see* Pula, *Croatia* **154** E4
Polacca, *Ariz., U.S.* **109** R8
Pola de Lena, *Sp.* **146** B8
Pola de Siero, *Sp.* **146** B9
Pola Island, *Amer. Samoa, U.S.* **222** L7
Polān, *Iran* **175** JI8
Poland, *Eur.* **151** EI3
Poland, *Kiribati* **221** B22
Polar Plateau, *Antarctica* **230** HI2
Polar Sea Bank, *Arctic Oc.* **247** KI7
Polarsirkel Valley, *Atl. Oc.* **241** YI3
Polatlı, *Turk.* **170** E7
Polatsk, *Belarus* **158** J5
Pole Plain, *Arctic Oc.* **246** GII
Poles', *Eur.* **140** GIO
Polesella, *It.* **152** E7
Policastro, Golfo di, *It.* **153** NI2
Policastro Bussentino, *It.* **153** NI2
Police, *Pol.* **150** CII
Police Point, *Seychelles* **209** P2O
Polichnítos, *Gr.* **157** GI6
Poligny, *Fr.* **149** SI3
Polihale Heiau, *Hawai'i, U.S.* **114** B4
Polink Point, *Jam.* **122** K9
Polis, *Cyprus* **162** P5
Polisella, *It.*
Politica *Russ.*
Polkowice, *Russ.*
Polk, *Pa., U.S.* **96** M3
Pollino, Monte, *It.* **153** PI3
Pollock, *S. Dak., U.S.* **106** H5
Polnovat, *Russ.* **160** GIO
Poloa Bay, *Amer. Samoa, U.S.* **222** M6
Polohy, *Ukr.* **159** R9
Polokwane (Pietersburg), *S. Af.* **206** HII
Polonne, *Ukr.* **159** N4
Polson, *Mont., U.S.* **108** C5
Poltava, *Ukr.* **159** P8
Polubu, *Shanxi, China* **184** C5
Polvadera, *N. Mex., U.S.* **109** TI2
Polýaigos, island, *Gr.* **157** MI4
Polyanovgrad *see* Karnobat, *Bulg.* **155** HI6
Polyarnyy, *Russ.* **160** C9
Polýgyros, *Gr.* **156** DI2
Polýkastro, *Gr.* **156** BIO
Polynesia, islands, *Pac. Oc.* **218** DIO

Polynesian Cultural Center, *Hawai'i, U.S.* **114** DII
Pom, *Indonesia* **217** BI5
Pomabamba, *Peru* **132** G3
Pombal, *Port.* **146** G5
Pomene, *Mozambique* **207** HI3
Pomerania, region, *Ger., Pol.* **150** CII
Pomeranian Bay, *Atl. Oc.* **140** F7
Pomeroy, *Ohio, U.S.* **101** SI4
Pomeroy, *Wash., U.S.* **110** D9
Pomichna, *Ukr.* **159** Q6
Pomir (Pamir), river, *Afghan., Taj.* **178** KIO
Pomîrla, *Rom.* **155** AI5
Pomona, *Calif., U.S.* **III** X9
Pomorie (Archialus), *Bulg.* **155** JI7
Pomos Point, *Cyprus* **162** N6
Pompano Beach, *Fla., U.S.* **99** WIO
Pompeii, ruin, *It.* **152** MII
Pompeiopolis, ruins, *Turk.* **170** J9
Pompeys Pillar National Historic Landmark, *Mont., U.S.* **108** EIO
Ponape *see* Pohnpei, island, *F.S.M.* **220** Q8
Ponca City, *Okla., U.S.* **104** EII
Ponce, *P.R., U.S.* **122** N3
Ponce de Leon Bay, *Fla., U.S.* **99** X9
Ponchatoula, *La., U.S.* **102** PIO
Poncin, *Fr.* **149** TI3
Pond Creek, *Okla., U.S.* **104** EIO
Pondicherry *see* Puducherry, *India* **181** Q7
Pond Inlet, *Nunavut, Can.* **85** EI7
Pondosa, *Calif., U.S.* **110** M4
Ponérihouen, *New Caledonia, Fr.* **222** C7
Pones, island, *F.S.M.* **221** CI6
Ponferrada, *Sp.* **146** C8
Pong, *Thai.* **190** J8
Pongara, Pointe, *Gabon* **205** GI5
Pongaroa, *N.Z.* **217** MI9
Pongch'ŏn, *N. Korea* **186** L7
Ponggang, *N. Korea* **186** DI2
Pongsan, *N. Korea* **186** K6
Poniya Point, *N. Mariana Is., U.S.* **220** E7
Ponnani, *India* **181** R5
Ponoy, *Russ.* **160** D9
Pons, *Fr.* **149** U6
Ponta Delgada , *Azores, Port.* **146** Q5
Ponta do Pargo, *Madeira, Port.* **208** M2
Ponta do Sol, *Madeira, Port.* **208** M2
Ponta Grossa, *Braz.* **132** MI2
Pont-à-Mousson, *Fr.* **149** PI4
Ponta Porã, *Braz.* **132** LIO
Pontarlier, *Fr.* **149** s
Pontaumur, *Fr.* **149** UIO
Pont-Aven, *Fr.* **149** Q3
Pontchartrain, Lake, *La., U.S.* **102** PII
Pontchâteau, *Fr.* **149** R5
Pont-d'Ain, *Fr.* **149** TI3
Pont-de-Salars, *Fr.* **149** WIO
Ponteareas, *Sp.* **146** C5
Pontebba, *It.* **152** C9
Pontedecimo, *It.* **152** F4
Ponte de Lima, *Port.* **146** D5
Ponte-Leccia, *Fr.* **152** J4
Pontevedra, *Sp.* **146** C5
Pontevedra, Ría de, *Sp.* **146** C5
Ponte Vedra Beach, *Fla., U.S.* **99** R9
Pontiac, *Ill., U.S.* **101** Q6
Pontiac, *Mich., U.S.* **100** MI2
Pontianak, *Indonesia* **192** J8
Pontifical Academy of Sciences, *Vatican City* **163** PI5
Pontikonísi, island, *Gr.* **156** PI2
Pontinia, *It.* **152** L9
Pontivy, *Fr.* **149** Q4
Pont-l'Évêque, *Fr.* **149** N7
Pontoise, *Fr.* **149** P9
Pontotoc, *Miss., U.S.* **102** HI2
Pontremoli, *It.* **152** F5
Ponts, *Sp.* **147** DI6
Pontypool (Pont-y-pwl), *Wales, U.K.* **145** VIO
Pont-y-pwl *see* Pontypool, *Wales, U.K.* **145** VIO
Ponza, Isola di, *It.* **152** M9
Ponziane, Isole, *It.* **152** M9

Poofai, Baie de, Fr. Polynesia, Fr. 223 K14
Poole, Eng., U.K. 145 X12
Poolewe, Scot., U.K. 144 J8
Pool Malebo, Dem. Rep. of the Congo 202 L7
Poopelloe Lake, Austral. 214 J12
Poopó, Bol. 132 K7
Poopó, Lago, Bol. 132 K7
Popayán, Col. 130 G4
Poplar, Mont., U.S. 108 B13
Poplar, river, Can., U.S. 108 B12
Poplar, river, Man., Can. 85 M14
Poplar Bluff, Mo., U.S. 107 V15
Poplarville, Miss., U.S. 102 N12
Popocatépetl, peak, Mex. 116 J12
Popondetta, P.N.G. 217 E20
Popovo, Bulg. 155 H16
Poprad, Slovakia 151 J16
Pŏptong, N. Korea 186 J8
Porali, river, Pak. 179 U5
Porangahau, N.Z. 217 L20
Porbandar, India 180 J1
Porcuna, Sp. 146 K10
Porcupine, river, Can., U.S. 113 E18
Porcupine Bank, Atl. Oc. 240 G10
Porcupine Mountains, Mich., U.S. 100 F5
Porcupine Plain, Atl. Oc. 240 H10
Porcupine Seabight, Atl. Oc. 240 H11
Pordenone, It. 152 D8
Porea, island, Cook Is., N.Z. 223 C14
Poreč, Croatia 154 E3
Porga, Benin 204 C11
Porgy Bay, Bahamas 122 B8
Pori, Fin. 143 H15
Porirua, N.Z. 217 M19
Porlamar, Venez. 130 B11
Pornic, Fr. 149 S5
Póros, Gr. 156 K12
Póros, island, Gr. 156 K12
Porpoise Basin, Ind. Oc. 249 E15
Porpoise Bay, Antarctica 231 P19
Porrentruy, Switz. 152 A2
Porsangen, bay, Nor. 143 B14
Porsanger Peninsula, Eur. 140 A9
Porsuk, river, Turk. 170 E6
Porta, Fr. 162 J6
Portadown, N. Ire., U.K. 145 Q7
Portage, Ind., U.S. 101 N8
Portage, Mich., U.S. 101 N10
Portage, Wis., U.S. 100 K5
Portage la Prairie, Man., Can. 85 N13
Portageville, Mo., U.S. 107 V16
Portal, N. Dak., U.S. 106 D3
Port Albert, Vic., Austral. 215 Z13
Portalegre, Port. 146 H6
Portales, N. Mex., U.S. 109 T15
Port Alfred, S. Af. 206 M10
Port Allegany, Pa., U.S. 96 L5
Port Allen, La., U.S. 102 P9
Port Angeles, Wash., U.S. 110 B3
Port Antonio, Jam. 122 J11
Port-à-Piment, Haiti 119 M15
Port Aransas, Tex., U.S. 105 U11
Port Arthur, Tas., Austral. 215 Z8
Port Arthur, Tex., U.S. 105 Q16
Port Arthur see Lüshun, Liaoning, China 184 E11
Port Augusta, S. Aust., Austral. 215 X10
Port-au-Prince see Pòtoprens, Haiti 119 M16
Port Austin, Mich., U.S. 100 K12
Port Blair, India 181 Q14
Port Bolivar, Tex., U.S. 105 R15
Portbou, Sp. 147 C18
Port Burwell, Nfld. & Lab., Can. 85 J20
Port-Cartier, Que., Can. 85 M21
Port Castries, St. Lucia 123 J14
Port Charlotte, Fla., U.S. 99 V8
Port Clinton, Ohio, U.S. 101 N13
Port-de-Paix, Haiti 119 L16
Port Eads, La., U.S. 102 R12
Port Edward, S. Af. 206 L11
Porteira, Braz. 132 D10
Portel, Braz. 132 D12
Portel, Port. 146 J6
Port Elizabeth, S. Af. 206 M10
Port Elizabeth, St. Vincent and the Grenadines 121 G17
Port Ellen, Scot., U.K. 145 N7
Porté-Puymorens, Fr. 162 H6
Porterdale, Ga., U.S. 98 L5
Porter Point, St. Vincent and the Grenadines 123 J17
Porterville, Calif., U.S. 111 U7
Porterville, S. Af. 206 M7
Port Esquivel, Jam. 122 J9
Port Fairy, Vic., Austral. 215 Z11
Port-Gentil, Gabon 205 H14
Port Gibson, Miss., U.S. 102 M10
Port Graham, Alas., U.S. 113 L16
Port Harcourt, Nigeria 205 E14
Port Hardy, B.C., Can. 84 L7
Port Hawkesbury, N.S., Can. 85 P22
Port Hedland, W. Aust., Austral. 215 S3
Port Heiden, Alas., U.S. 113 M13
Port Henry, N.Y., U.S. 96 G11
Porthmadog, Wales, U.K. 145 T9
Port Hope, Mich., U.S. 100 K13
Port Hope Simpson, Nfld. & Lab., Can. 85 L22
Port Howe, Bahamas 119 F13
Port Huron, Mich., U.S. 100 L13
Portimão, Port. 146 L5
Port Isabel, Tex., U.S. 105 W11
Portiţei, Gura, Rom. 155 F18
Port Jervis, N.Y., U.S. 96 M10
Port Kaiser, Jam. 122 K7
Port Kaituma, Guyana 131 D13
Port Láirge see Waterford, Ire. 145 U6
Portland, Eng., U.K. 145 X11
Portland, Ind., U.S. 101 Q10
Portland, Me., U.S. 97 H15
Portland, Mich., U.S. 100 L10
Portland, N. Dak., U.S. 106 F7
Portland, Oreg., U.S. 110 F3
Portland, Tenn., U.S. 103 E15
Portland, Tex., U.S. 105 T11
Portland, Vic., Austral. 215 Z11
Portland Bay, Austral. 214 M11
Portland Bight, Jam. 122 K9
Portland Cottage, Jam. 122 K8
Portland Point, Jam. 122 K9
Portland Rock, island, Jam. 118 P11
Port-la-Nouvelle, Fr. 149 Y11
Port Laoise, Ire. 145 S6
Port Lavaca, Tex., U.S. 105 S12
Port Lincoln, S. Aust., Austral. 215 X9
Port Lions, Alas., U.S. 113 M15
Portloe, Eng., U.K. 145 Y8
Port Loko, Sierra Leone 204 D5
Port Louis, Mauritius 209 G20
Port-Louis, Guadeloupe, Fr. 123 E15
Port Macquarie, N.S.W., Austral. 215 X15
Port Mansfield, Tex., U.S. 105 W11
Port Manvers, Nfld. & Lab., Can. 85 J21
Port Maria, Jam. 122 H9
Port Mathurin, Mauritius 209 J20
Port-Menier, Que., Can. 85 M21
Port Morant, Jam. 122 J11
Portmore, Jam. 122 J9
Port Moresby, P.N.G. 217 E19
Portnacroish, Scot., U.K. 144 L8
Portnahaven, Scot., U.K. 145 N7
Port Neches, Tex., U.S. 105 Q16
Port Nelson, Bahamas 119 F14
Port Nis see Port of Ness, Scot., U.K. 144 G7
Port Nolloth, S. Af. 206 K7
Port Norris, N.J., U.S. 96 R9
Porto, Braz. 133 E15
Porto, Fr. 152 K3
Porto (Oporto), Port. 146 E5
Porto, Golfe de, Fr. 152 K3
Porto Alegre, Braz. 132 P12
Porto Alegre, Sao Tome and Principe 209 E20
Porto Amboim, Angola 206 C5
Porto Artur, Braz. 132 H11
Porto Azzurro, It. 152 J6
Portobelo, Pan. 117 N21
Pórto Chéli, Gr. 156 K11
Port O'Connor, Tex., U.S. 105 T12
Porto Covo, Port. 146 K5
Porto dos Gaúchos, Braz. 132 G10
Porto Esperidião, Braz. 132 J10
Portoferraio, It. 152 J6
Port of Ness (Port Nis), Scot., U.K. 144 G7
Porto Franco, Braz. 133 F14
Port of Spain, Trinidad and Tobago 123 P22
Porto Garibaldi, It. 152 F8
Pórto Germenó, Gr. 156 J11
Porto Grande, Braz. 132 C12
Portogruaro, It. 152 D9
Pôrto Inglês, Cabo Verde 209 D17
Porto Jofre, Braz. 132 K10
Pórto Koufó, Gr. 157 E13
Portola, Calif., U.S. 111 P5
Porto Moniz, Madeira, Port. 208 M2
Porto Murtinho, Braz. 132 L10
Porto Nacional, Braz. 133 G13
Porto Novo, India 181 Q7
Porto-Novo, Benin 204 E12
Port Ontario, N.Y., U.S. 96 H8
Port Orange, Fla., U.S. 99 S9
Port Orchard, Wash., U.S. 110 C3
Porto Recanati, It. 152 H10
Port Orford, Oreg., U.S. 110 K1
Porto San Giorgio, It. 152 H10
Porto Santo, Madeira, Port. 208 L5
Porto Santo, island, Madeira, Port. 208 L4
Portoscuso, It. 153 Q3
Porto Seguro, Braz. 133 K16
Porto Tolle, It. 152 E8
Porto Torres, It. 152 M3
Porto-Vecchio, Fr. 152 L4
Porto-Vecchio, Golfe de, Fr. 152 L4
Porto Velho, Braz. 132 F8
Portoviejo, Ecua. 130 J2
Port Phillip Bay, Austral. 214 M12
Port Pirie, S. Aust., Austral. 215 X10
Port Royal, Jam. 122 J10
Port Royal, S.C., U.S. 99 N9
Port Royal Bay see Little Sound, Bermuda 122 C1
Port Royal Sound, S.C., U.S. 99 N9
Port Said see Bûr Sa'îd, Egypt 173 N1
Port Saint Joe, Fla., U.S. 99 R4
Port Saint Johns, S. Af. 206 L11
Port-Saint-Louis, Fr. 149 X13
Port Saint Lucie, Fla., U.S. 99 V10
Port Salerno, Fla., U.S. 99 V10
Portsall, Fr. 149 P2
Port-Salut, Haiti 119 N15
Port Salvador, Falk. Is., U.K. 135 W12
Port Saunders, Nfld. & Lab., Can. 85 L23
Port Shepstone, S. Af. 206 L11
Portsmouth, Dominica 121 D16
Portsmouth, Dominica 123 E18
Portsmouth, Eng., U.K. 145 W13
Portsmouth, N.C., U.S. 98 J15
Portsmouth, N.H., U.S. 97 J15
Portsmouth, Ohio, U.S. 101 T13
Portsmouth, Va., U.S. 98 F14
Port South East, Mauritius 209 J20
Portsoy, Scot., U.K. 144 J11
Port Stephens, Falk. Is., U.K. 135 W11
Port Sudan, Sudan 203 C14
Port Sulphur, La., U.S. 102 Q11
Port Talbot, Wales, U.K. 145 V10
Port Townsend, Wash., U.S. 110 B3
Portugal, Eur. 146 K6
Portuguesa, river, Venez. 130 C8
Port Victoria, S. Aust., Austral. 215 X10
Port Vila, Vanuatu 222 F2
Port Warrender, W. Aust., Austral. 215 P6
Port Washington, Wis., U.S. 100 L7
Porus, Jam. 122 J8
Porvenir, Bol. 132 G6
Porvenir, Chile 135 X8
Porvoo, Fin. 143 J16
Porzuna, Sp. 146 H10
Posadas, Arg. 134 G14
Poschiavo, Switz. 152 C5
Posio, Fin. 143 E16
Poso, Indonesia 193 J13
Posof, Rep. of Georgia 171 C17
Possum Kingdom Lake, Tex., U.S. 104 L9
Post, Tex., U.S. 104 K6
Post Falls, Idaho, U.S. 108 B3
Postville, Iowa, U.S. 106 M13
Postville, Nfld. & Lab., Can. 85 K21
Posušje, Bosn. & Herzg. 154 H7
Potamoí, Gr. 157 B13
Potamós, Gr. 156 P11
Poteau, Okla., U.S. 104 G14
Poteet, Tex., U.S. 105 S9
Potenza, It. 152 M12
Poth, Tex., U.S. 105 S10
Potholes Reservoir, Wash., U.S. 110 D7
P'ot'i, Rep. of Georgia 171 B16
Potiskum, Nigeria 205 B15
Potlatch, Idaho, U.S. 108 C3
Pot Mountain, Idaho, U.S. 108 D4
Potnarvin, Vanuatu 222 G3
Potomac, river, Md., Va., U.S. 98 D13
Pòtoprens, Haiti 119 M16
Potosi, Mo., U.S. 107 T14
Potosí, Bol. 132 K7
Potrerillos, Chile 134 G7
Potsdam, Ger. 150 D10
Potsdam, N.Y., U.S. 96 F10
Pott, Île, New Caledonia, Fr. 222 B5
Potter, Nebr., U.S. 107 P1
Pottstown, Pa., U.S. 96 P9
Pottsville, Pa., U.S. 96 N8
Poudre d'Or, Mauritius 209 F20
Pouébo, New Caledonia, Fr. 222 C6
Pouembout, New Caledonia, Fr. 222 C7
Poughkeepsie, N.Y., U.S. 96 L11
Pougues, Fr. 149 S10
Pouilly, Fr. 149 R10
Poulo Wai, island, Cambodia 191 Q10
Poulsbo, Wash., U.S. 110 C3
Poum, New Caledonia, Fr. 222 B6
Pouoanuu, Mount, Fr. Polynesia, Fr. 223 M20
Poutasi, Samoa 222 L3
Poŭthĭsăt (Pursat), Cambodia 191 N11
Poutoru, Fr. Polynesia, Fr. 223 A23
Povai, Fr. Polynesia, Fr. 223 K14
Poverty Point National Monument, La., U.S. 102 L9
Povoação, Azores, Port. 146 Q5
Póvoa de Varzim, Port. 146 D5
Povorino, Russ. 159 N12
Povungnituk, Baie de, Que., Can. 85 J17
Powder, river, Oreg., U.S. 110 G9
Powder River, Wyo., U.S. 108 H11
Powell, Wyo., U.S. 108 F10
Powell, Lake, Ariz., Utah, U.S. 109 Q7
Powell Basin, Atl. Oc. 241 X6
Powell Butte, Oreg., U.S. 110 H5
Powell Point, Bahamas 122 F5
Powell River, B.C., Can. 84 M8
Powers, Oreg., U.S. 110 J2
Powers Lake, N. Dak., U.S. 106 E3
Poxoréo, Braz. 132 J11
Poya, New Caledonia, Fr. 222 D7
Poyang Hu, Jiangxi, China 185 P7
Poygan, Lake, Wis., U.S. 100 J6
Poysdorf, Aust. 151 J13
Pōzak, Jahīl-e, Afghan. 179 Q2
Pozantı, Turk. 170 H10
Požarevac, Serb. 154 F11
Poza Rica, Mex. 116 H12
Požega, Croatia 154 E7
Poznań, Pol. 151 D13
Pozo Alcón, Sp. 146 K12
Pozo Almonte, Chile 134 C7
Pozoblanco, Sp. 146 J9
Pozzallo, It. 153 U11
Pozzuoli, It. 152 M10
Pracchia, It. 152 G6
Prachin Buri, Thai. 190 M9
Prachuap Khiri Khan, Thai. 191 P8
Pradelles, Fr. 149 V11
Prado, Braz. 133 K16
Prague see Praha, Czech Rep. 150 H11
Praha (Prague), Czech Rep. 150 H11
Praia, Cabo Verde 209 E16
Praia da Vitória, Azores, Port. 146 Q4
Prainha, Braz. 132 D11
Prainha, Braz. 132 F9
Prairie City, Oreg., U.S. 110 G7
Prairie Dog Creek, Kans., U.S. 107 S4
Prairie Dog Town Fork Red, river, Tex., U.S. 104 H6
Prairie du Chien, Wis., U.S. 100 L3
Prairie Grove, Ark., U.S. 102 E6
Pran Buri, Thai. 191 N8
Praslin, St. Lucia 123 K14
Praslin, island, Seychelles 209 M20
Prasonísion, island, Gr. 157 N19
Prato, It. 152 G7
Pratola Peligna, It. 152 K10
Prats, Andorra 162 H4
Prats-de-Mollo, Fr. 149 Z10
Pratt, Kans., U.S. 107 U6
Prattville, Ala., U.S. 103 L15
Prazeres, Madeira, Port. 208 M2
Preăh Seihânŭ (Sihanoukville), Cambodia 191 P11
Preah Vihear, ruins, Cambodia 190 M11
Preau, Trinidad and Tobago 123 Q23
Précy-sous-Thil, Fr. 149 R12
Predazzo, It. 152 C7
Preguiça, Cabo Verde 209 B15
Preguiça, Cabo Verde 209 B17
Prehistoric Petroglyphs, ruins, Afghan. 178 K9
Premont, Tex., U.S. 105 U10
Premuda, island, Croatia 154 F4
Prentice, Wis., U.S. 100 G4
Prentiss, Miss., U.S. 102 M11
Prenzlau, Ger. 150 C10
Preobrazhenka, Russ. 161 J15
Preparis Island, Myanmar 190 M4
Preparis North Channel, Myanmar 190 L4
Preparis South Channel, Myanmar 190 M4
Přerov, Czech Rep. 151 H13
Prescott, Ariz., U.S. 109 S6
Prescott, Ark., U.S. 102 J7
Prescott, Wash., U.S. 110 E8
Presho, S. Dak., U.S. 106 L5
Presidencia Roca, Arg. 134 F12
Presidente Dutra, Braz. 133 E15
Presidente Prudente, Braz. 132 L12
Presidente Roque Sáenz Peña, Arg. 134 G12
President Thiers Bank, Pac. Oc. 249 Q22
Presidio, Tex., U.S. 105 R1
Prešov, Slovakia 151 J16
Prespa, peak, Bulg. 155 K14
Prespa, Lake see Prespansko Jezero, Alban., Maced. 154 L10
Prespansko Jezero (Prespa, Lake), Alban., Maced. 154 L10
Presque Isle, Me., U.S. 97 B18
Presque Isle, Mich., U.S. 100 H12
Presqu'île de Taiarapu, island, Fr. Polynesia, Fr. 223 F16
Pressburg see Bratislava, Slovakia 151 K13
Presteigne, Wales, U.K. 145 U10
Preston, Eng., U.K. 145 R11
Preston, Idaho, U.S. 108 J7
Preston, Minn., U.S. 106 L13
Preston, Mo., U.S. 107 U12
Prestonsburg, Ky., U.S. 103 C20
Prestrud Bank, Pac. Oc. 249 J15
Pretoria (Tshwane), S. Af. 206 J10
Préveza, Gr. 156 G7
Pribilof Islands, Alas., U.S. 112 L9
Priboj, Serb. 154 G9
Priboj, Serb. 154 J12
Příbram, Czech Rep. 150 H11
Price, Utah, U.S. 108 M8
Price, river, Utah, U.S. 108 M8
Price, Cape, India 181 P14
Prichard, Ala., U.S. 103 N13
Prickly Bay, Grenada 123 L22
Prickly Pear Cays, Anguilla 122 Q10
Prickly Pear Island, Antigua and Barbuda 123 A21
Prickly Pear Island, British Virgin Is., U.K. 122 Q9
Prickly Point, Grenada 123 M22
Priekule, Latv. 143 M15
Prieska, S. Af. 206 K9
Priest Lake, Idaho, U.S. 108 B3
Priestley Glacier, Antarctica 231 P14

Priest River, *Idaho, U.S.* **108** B3
Prieta, Peña, *Sp.* **146** B1O
Prievidza, *Slovakia* **151** J14
Prijedor, *Bosn. & Herzg.* **154** E6
Prijepolje, *Serb.* **154** H9
Prilep, *Maced.* **154** L11
Primorsko Akhtarsk, *Russ.* **159** S1O
Prince Albert, *S. Af.* **206** M8
Prince Albert, *Sask., Can.* **84** M12
Prince Albert Mountains, *Antarctica* **231** N14
Prince Albert Peninsula, *N.W.T., Can.* **84** D12
Prince Albert Sound, *N.W.T., Can.* **84** E11
Prince Alfred, Cape, *N.W.T., Can.* **84** C12
Prince Charles Island, *Nunavut, Can.* **85** F17
Prince Charles Mountains, *Antarctica* **231** F18
Prince Edward Fracture Zone, *Ind. Oc.* **224** Q4
Prince Edward Island, *Can.* **85** N22
Prince Frederick Harbour, *Austral.* **214** C5
Prince George, *B.C., Can.* **84** K8
Prince Gustaf Adolf Sea, *Nunavut, Can.* **85** C14
Prince Harald Coast, *Antarctica* **231** B17
Prince Kūhiō Park, *Hawai'i, U.S.* **114** C5
Prince of Wales, Cape, *Alas., U.S.* **112** E11
Prince of Wales Island, *Alas., U.S.* **113** M23
Prince of Wales Island, *Austral.* **214** A12
Prince of Wales Island, *Nunavut, Can.* **85** E14
Prince of Wales Strait, *N.W.T., Can.* **84** D12
Prince Olav Coast, *Antarctica* **231** C18
Prince Patrick Island, *N.W.T., Can.* **85** C13
Prince Regent Inlet, *Nunavut, Can.* **85** E15
Prince Rupert, *B.C., Can.* **84** J7
Prince Rupert Bay, *Dominica* **123** E18
Princess Anne, *Md., U.S.* **98** D15
Princess Antoinette Park, *Monaco* **163** E2O
Princess Astrid Coast, *Antarctica* **231** A14
Princess Charlotte Bay, *Austral.* **214** B13
Princess Elizabeth Trough, *Ind. Oc.* **248** D12
Princess Grace Hospital Center, *Monaco* **163** E19
Princess Grace Rose Garden, *Monaco* **163** F21
Princess Martha Coast, *Antarctica* **230** B11
Princess Ragnhild Coast, *Antarctica* **231** B15
Princeton, *B.C., Can.* **84** M8
Princeton, *Ill., U.S.* **101** P5
Princeton, *Ind., U.S.* **101** T7
Princeton, *Ky., U.S.* **103** D14
Princeton, *Minn., U.S.* **106** J11
Princeton, *Mo., U.S.* **107** Q11
Princeton, *N.J., U.S.* **96** P1O
Princeton, *W. Va., U.S.* **98** F9
Princeville, *Hawai'i, U.S.* **114** B5
Prince William Sound, *Alas., U.S.* **113** K17
Príncipe, island, *Sao Tome and Principe* **209** B2O
Príncipe da Beira, *Braz.* **132** H8
Prineville, *Oreg., U.S.* **110** G5
Pringle, *S. Dak., U.S.* **106** L1
Prior, Cabo, *Sp.* **146** A6
Pripyat' *see* Pryp'yat', river, *Ukr.* **158** M3
Prishtinë *see* Pristina, *Kos.* **154** J11
Prislop, Pasul, *Rom.* **155** B14
Pristina (Prishtinë, Priština), *Kos.* **154** J11

Pritchett, *Colo., U.S.* **109** P15
Pritzwalk, *Ger.* **150** C9
Privas, *Fr.* **149** V12
Privol'noye, *Russ.* **161** G22
Privolzhsk, *Russ.* **158** H11
Privolzhskaya Vozvyshennost', *Russ.* **159** N13
Privolzhskiy, *Russ.* **158** M14
Prizren, *Kos.* **154** J1O
Probolinggo, *Indonesia* **192** M1O
Proctor, *Minn., U.S.* **106** G12
Prodromi, *Cyprus* **162** P5
Progreso Limitada, *Eq. Guinea* **208** M8
Progress, *Russ.* **161** K2O
Progress 2, station, *Antarctica* **231** G2O
Prokhladnyy, *Russ.* **159** T13
Prokhod Sveti Nikola, peak, *Bulg., Serb.* **154** H12
Prokópi, *Gr.* **156** G12
Prokop'yevsk, *Russ.* **160** L12
Prokuplje, *Serb.* **154** H11
Proletarsk, *Russ.* **159** R12
Promýri, *Gr.* **156** F11
Pronsfeld, *Ger.* **162** G1O
Prony, *New Caledonia, Fr.* **222** E8
Prony, Baie du, *New Caledonia, Fr.* **222** E8
Propriá, *Braz.* **133** G17
Propriano, *Fr.* **152** L4
Proserpine, *Qnsld., Austral.* **215** S14
Prosotsáni, *Gr.* **157** B13
Prospect, *Barbados* **123** K18
Prospect, *Cayman Is.* **122** J2
Prospect, *Oreg., U.S.* **110** K3
Prospect Point, *Jam.* **122** K11
Prosser, *Wash., U.S.* **110** E6
Prostějov, *Czech Rep.* **151** H13
Protection, *Kans., U.S.* **107** V5
Protector Basin, *Atl. Oc.* **241** W6
Próti, island, *Gr.* **156** L8
Provadiya, *Bulg.* **155** H17
Provence, region, *Fr.* **149** X14
Providence, *Grenada* **123** L23
Providence, *Ky., U.S.* **103** C14
Providence, *R.I., U.S.* **97** L14
Providence Mountains, *Calif., U.S.* **111** W11
Providencia, Isla de, *Col.* **117** L2O
Providenciales, island, *Bahamas* **119** H16
Providenciya, *Russ.* **161** A21
Provincetown, *Mass., U.S.* **97** L16
Provo, *Utah, U.S.* **108** L7
Prudhoe Bay, *Alas., U.S.* **113** C17
Prudnik, *Pol.* **151** G13
Prüm, *Ger.* **162** G11
Prüm, river, *Ger.* **162** G11
Prune Island *see* Palm Island, *St. Vincent and the Grenadines* **121** G17
Pruszcz Gdański, *Pol.* **151** B14
Pruszków, *Pol.* **151** E16
Prut, river, *Mold., Rom.* **155** D17
Pruzhany, *Belarus* **158** L3
Prvić, island, *Croatia* **154** E5
Prydz Bay, *Antarctica* **231** G2O
Pryluky, *Ukr.* **159** N7
Pryor, *Okla., U.S.* **104** E13
Pryor Creek, *Mont., U.S.* **108** E1O
Pryp'yat' (Pripyat'), river, *Ukr.* **158** M3
Prypyats', river, *Eur.* **140** G1O
Przemyśl, *Pol.* **151** H18
Przheval'sk *see* Karakol, *Kyrg.* **178** D14
Psachná, *Gr.* **156** H12
Psará, *Gr.* **157** H15
Psará, island, *Gr.* **157** H15
Psathoúra, island, *Gr.* **157** F13
Psérimos, island, *Gr.* **157** L18
Psiloreítis *see* Ídi, Óros, *Gr.* **157** Q14
Pskov, *Russ.* **158** G5
Pskov, Lake, *Eur.* **140** E1O
PskovskoyeOzero, *Russ.* **158** G5
Ptolemaḯda, *Gr.* **156** C9
Ptolemy Basin, *Pac. Oc.* **242** F9
Ptuj, *Slov.* **154** C6
Pua, *Thai.* **190** J9
Puakō, *Hawai'i, U.S.* **115** L19

Puakonikai, *Kiribati* **221** D2O
Puamau, Bay (Perigot), *Fr. Polynesia, Fr.* **223** M21
Puán, *Arg.* **135** N11
Pu'apu'a, *Samoa* **222** K2
Puaumu Nord, island, *Fr. Polynesia, Fr.* **223** Q21
Puava, Cape, *Samoa* **222** K1
Pucallpa, *Peru* **132** F4
Puca Urco, *Peru* **132** D5
Pucheng, *Fujian, China* **185** R9
Pucheng, *Shaanxi, China* **184** H2
Pucioasa, *Rom.* **155** E15
Puck, *Pol.* **151** A14
Pudasjärvi, *Fin.* **143** E15
Pudimoe, *S. Af.* **206** K9
Pudu, *Indonesia* **192** J6
Puducherry (Pondicherry), *India* **181** Q7
Pudukkottai, *India* **181** R6
Puebla, *Mex.* **116** J12
Puebla de Guzmán, *Sp.* **146** K6
Puebla de Sanabria, *Sp.* **146** D7
Pueblo, *Colo., U.S.* **109** N14
Pueblo Bonito, *N. Mex., U.S.* **109** R11
Puente-Genil, *Sp.* **146** L9
Pueo Point, *Hawai'i, U.S.* **114** C3
Puerca, Punta, *P.R., U.S.* **122** N6
Puerco, river, *Ariz., N. Mex., U.S.* **109** S9
Puerto Acosta, *Bol.* **132** J6
Puerto Aisén, *Chile* **135** S6
Puerto América, *Peru* **132** E3
Puerto Ángel, *Mex.* **117** K13
Puerto Armuelles, *Pan.* **117** P19
Puerto Ayacucho, *Venez.* **130** E9
Puerto Ayora, *Ecua.* **130** Q1O
Puerto Bahía Negra, *Parag.* **132** L1O
Puerto Baquerizo Moreno, *Ecua.* **130** Q11
Puerto Barrios, *Guatemala* **117** K17
Puerto Belgrano, *Arg.* **135** P11
Puerto Berrío, *Col.* **130** E5
Puerto Cabello, *Venez.* **130** B9
Puerto Carreño, *Venez.* **130** E9
Puerto Chicama, *Peru* **132** F2
Puerto Coig, *Arg.* **135** V8
Puerto Colombia, *Col.* **130** B5
Puerto Concordia, *Col.* **130** G6
Puerto Cortés, *Hond.* **117** K17
Puerto Cumarebo, *Venez.* **130** B8
Puerto de la Cruz, *Sp.* **208** Q4
Puerto del Carmen, *Sp.* **208** P7
Puerto del Rosario, *Sp.* **208** Q7
Puerto de Luna, *N. Mex., U.S.* **109** S14
Puerto de Mazarrón, *Sp.* **147** L13
Puerto de Nutrias, *Venez.* **130** D8
Puerto Deseado, *Arg.* **135** T9
Puerto Etén, *Peru* **132** F2
Puerto Heath, *Bol.* **132** H6
Puerto Jiménez, *C.R.* **117** P19
Puerto La Cruz, *Venez.* **130** B11
Puerto La Paz, *Arg.* **134** D11
Puerto Lápice, *Sp.* **146** H11
Puerto Leguízamo, *Col.* **130** J5
Puerto Libertad, *Mex.* **116** C6
Puertollano, *Sp.* **146** J1O
Puerto Lobos, *Arg.* **135** Q9
Puerto López, *Col.* **130** F6
Puerto Madryn, *Arg.* **135** R1O
Puerto Maldonado, *Peru* **132** H6
Puerto Manatí, *Cuba* **118** J11
Puerto Montt, *Chile* **135** Q6
Puerto Morelos, *Mex.* **117** H17
Puerto Natales, *Chile* **135** W7
Puerto Obaldía, *Pan.* **117** N22
Puerto Páez, *Venez.* **130** E9
Puerto Padre, *Cuba* **118** J12
Puerto Peñasco, *Mex.* **116** B6
Puerto Pinasco, *Parag.* **132** L1O
Puerto Pirámides, *Arg.* **135** R1O
Puerto Plata, *Dom. Rep.* **119** L18
Puerto Portillo, *Peru* **132** G4
Puerto Princesa, *Philippines* **192** E12
Puerto Real, *P.R., U.S.* **122** N1
Puerto Rico, island, *N. Amer.* **119** M23
Puerto Rico Trench, *Atl. Oc.* **240** M4
Puerto San Carlos, *Chile* **135** U6
Puerto San Julián, *Arg.* **135** U9

Puerto Santa Cruz, *Arg.* **135** V8
Puerto Suárez, *Bol.* **132** K1O
Puerto Tres Palmas, *Parag.* **132** L1O
Puerto Vallarta, *Mex.* **116** H9
Puerto Velasco Ibarra, *Ecua.* **130** R1O
Puerto Villamil, *Ecua.* **130** Q9
Puerto Wilches, *Col.* **130** D5
Puerto Williams, *Chile* **135** Y9
Puerto Yabucoa, *P.R., U.S.* **122** N5
Puetton Tanapag, bay, *N. Mariana Is., U.S.* **220** B4
Pueu, *Fr. Polynesia, Fr.* **223** P17
Pugachev, *Russ.* **158** L15
Pugŏ, *N. Korea* **186** C13
Puget Sound, *U.S.* **86** B4
Pugu, *N. Korea* **186** E12
Pudimoe, *S. Af.* **206** K9
Puhi, *Hawai'i, U.S.* **114** C6
Puigcerdà, *Sp.* **147** C17
Puig Major, peak, *Sp.* **147** G18
Puigmal d'Err, peak, *Sp.* **147** C17
Pujehun, *Sierra Leone* **204** D6
Pujiang, *Zhejiang, China* **185** P1O
Pujŏn, *N. Korea* **186** F9
Pujŏn, river, *N. Korea* **186** E9
Pujŏn-ho, lake, *N. Korea* **186** F9
Pukaki, Lake, *N.Z.* **217** P16
Pukalani, *Hawai'i, U.S.* **115** H17
Pukapuka, island, *Cook Is., N.Z.* **222** Q2
Pukapuka, island, *Fr. Polynesia, Fr.* **223** D21
Pukapuka Atoll, *Cook Is., N.Z.* **218** H11
Pukapukae Ridge, *Pac. Oc.* **243** L16
Pukarua, island, *Fr. Polynesia, Fr.* **223** F22
Pukchin, *N. Korea* **186** G6
Pukch'ŏng, *N. Korea* **186** G1O
Pula, *It.* **153** Q4
Pula (Pola), *Croatia* **154** E4
Pula, Capo di, *It.* **153** Q4
Pulan *see* Burang, *China* **182** K2
Pulandian, *Liaoning, China* **184** D12
Pulandian Wan, *Liaoning, China* **184** D12
Pulap Atoll, *F.S.M.* **220** Q5
Pulaski, *N.Y., U.S.* **96** H8
Pulaski, *Tenn., U.S.* **103** G15
Pulaski, *Va., U.S.* **98** F9
Puławy, *Pol.* **151** F17
Pul-e 'Alam, *Afghan.* **179** N8
Pul-e Khumrī, *Afghan.* **178** L7
Pulepu, *Liaoning, China* **184** B14
Puli, *Taiwan, China* **185** V12
Pulicat Lake, *India* **181** P7
Puliyangudi, *India* **181** S5
Puliyankulam, *Sri Lanka* **181** S7
Pull and be Damn' Point, *British Virgin Is., U.K.* **122** L11
Pullman, *Wash., U.S.* **110** D9
Pullman National Monument, *Ill., U.S.* **101** N7
Pull Point, *Virgin Is., U.S.* **122** Q3
Pulo Anna, island, *Palau* **218** F2
Pulog, Mount, *Philippines* **193** B13
Pülümür, *Turk.* **171** F14
Pulusuk, island, *F.S.M.* **220** Q5
Puluwat Atoll, *F.S.M.* **220** Q5
Pumpkin Creek, *Mont., U.S.* **108** E12
Puná, Isla, *Ecua.* **130** L2
Puna, region, *Hawai'i, U.S.* **115** N21
Punaauia, *Fr. Polynesia, Fr.* **223** P15
Punaauia, Pointe, *Fr. Polynesia, Fr.* **223** P15
Punaeroa, Passe, *Fr. Polynesia, Fr.* **223** B23
Punakha, *Bhutan* **180** F12
Punalu'u, *Hawai'i, U.S.* **115** P2O
Punan, *Indonesia* **192** H11
Puncak Jaya, peak, *Indonesia* **193** L2O
Punch, *India* **180** C4
Pune, *India* **180** L4
P'ungch'ŏn, *N. Korea* **186** H4
P'ungch'ŏn *see* Kwail, *N. Korea* **186** K5
Punggi, *S. Korea* **187** P11
P'unggye, *N. Korea* **186** E12
P'ungsan, *N. Korea* **186** B13

P'ungsŏ, *N. Korea* **186** E1O
P'ungsŏ-ho, lake, *N. Korea* **186** E1O
Punitaqui, *Chile* **134** J6
Puno, *Peru* **132** J6
Punta Alta, *Arg.* **135** N11
Punta Arenas, *Chile* **135** X8
Punta Cana, *Dom. Rep.* **119** M21
Punta del Este, *Uru.* **134** L14
Punta Delgada, *Arg.* **135** R1O
Punta Gorda, *Belize* **117** K16
Punta Gorda, *Fla., U.S.* **99** V8
Punta Prieta, *Mex.* **116** C6
Puntarenas, *C.R.* **117** N18
Punta Umbría, *Sp.* **146** L7
Puntland, region, *Somalia* **203** G18
Punto Fijo, *Venez.* **130** B7
Puntudo, Cerro, *Arg.* **135** U8
Punxsutawney, *Pa., U.S.* **96** N4
Puohine, *Fr. Polynesia, Fr.* **223** B24
Pup'yŏng, *N. Korea* **186** H9
Puqi, *Hubei, China* **185** P5
Puquio, *Peru* **132** J4
Puranpur, *India* **180** F7
Purari, river, *P.N.G.* **217** D19
Purcell, *Okla., U.S.* **104** H11
Purcell Mountains, *Can., U.S.* **108** A4
Purdy Islands, *P.N.G.* **217** B19
Purgatoire, river, *Colo., U.S.* **109** P14
Puri, *India* **180** L1O
Purmerend, *Neth.* **148** H12
Purna, river, *India* **180** K5
Purnia, *India* **180** G11
Pursat *see* Poŭthĭsăt, *Cambodia* **191** N11
Purt ny h-Inshey *see* Peel, *Isle of Man, U.K.* **145** Q9
Purus, river, *Braz.* **132** F7
Purvis, *Miss., U.S.* **102** N12
Puryŏng, *N. Korea* **186** C13
Pusad, *India* **180** L6
Pusan *see* Busan, *S. Korea* **187** T12
Pushkin, *Russ.* **158** F6
Pushkino, *Russ.* **158** M14
Pushtah-ye Ḩasan, *Afghan.* **179** Q3
Puta, *Azerb.* **171** D23
Putangaroa, island, *Cook Is., N.Z.* **223** C15
Putao, *Myanmar* **190** D7
Putian, *Fujian, China* **185** T1O
Putilovo, *Russ.* **158** F12
Putina, *Peru* **132** J6
Puto, *P.N.G.* **221** J13
Putorana Plateau, *Asia* **168** C9
Putrachoique, Cerro, *Arg.* **135** R7
Puttalam, *Sri Lanka* **181** S7
Puttelange, *Fr.* **149** P14
Puttur, *India* **181** P7
Putumayo, river, *S. Amer.* **130** H4
Putuo (Shenjiamen), *Zhejiang, China* **185** P13
Pütürge, *Turk.* **171** G13
Pu'uanahulu, *Hawai'i, U.S.* **115** M19
Pu'uhonua O Hōnaunau National Historical Park (City of Refuge National Historical Park), *Hawai'i, U.S.* **115** N18
Pu'ukoholā Heiau National Historic Site, *Hawai'i, U.S.* **115** L19
Pu'u Kūlua, peak, *Hawai'i, U.S.* **115** N2O
Pu'u Lehua, peak, *Hawai'i, U.S.* **115** N19
Pu'u Māhoe, peak, *Hawai'i, U.S.* **115** H17
Pu'u Maka'ala, peak, *Hawai'i, U.S.* **115** N21
Pu'u Nianiau, peak, *Hawai'i, U.S.* **115** H17
Pu'u o Ke'oke'o, peak, *Hawai'i, U.S.* **115** P19
Pu'u 'O Moa'ula Nui, peak, *Hawai'i, U.S.* **115** J16
Pu'u 'Ula'ula, peak, *Hawai'i, U.S.* **115** H17
Pu'uwai, *Hawai'i, U.S.* **114** C3
Puwe, island, *F.S.M.* **221** B15
Puxian, *Shanxi, China* **184** G3
Puyallup, *Wash., U.S.* **110** C4
Puyang, *Henan, China* **184** H6
Puy de Sancy, peak, *Fr.* **149** U1O
Puy-Guillaume, *Fr.* **149** U11

Puysegur Point, *N.Z.* 217 R14
Puysegur Trench, *Pac. Oc.* 249 GI9
Puyun, *N. Korea* 186 C12
Pweto, *Dem. Rep. of the Congo* 202 M12
Pya, Lake, *Eur.* 140 B10
P'yagina, Poluostrov, *Russ.* 161 F21
Pyasinskiy Zaliv, *Russ.* 161 E13
Pyatigorsk, *Russ.* 159 T13
P'yatykhatky, *Ukr.* 159 Q7
Pyay, *Myanmar* 190 J5
Pydna, battle, *Gr.* 156 D10
Pyeongchang, *S. Korea* 187 N10
Pyeonghae, island, *S. Korea* 187 U9
Pyeonghae, *S. Korea* 187 P12
Pyeongildo, island, *S. Korea* 187 U8
Pyeongni, *S. Korea* 187 N8
Pyeongtaek, *S. Korea* 187 P8
Pyhäjoki, *Fin.* 143 F15
Pyhäselkä, lake, *Fin.* 143 G17
Pyinkayaing, *Myanmar* 190 L5
Pyinmana, *Myanmar* 190 J6
Pyin-U-Lwin, *Myanmar* 190 G6
Pýli, *Gr.* 156 F9
Pýlos, *Gr.* 156 L9
Pymatuning Reservoir, *Ohio, Pa., U.S.* 96 L3
Pyŏksŏng, *N. Korea* 186 L6
Pyŏktong, *N. Korea* 186 F5
P'yŏnggang, *N. Korea* 186 L9
P'yŏngsan, *N. Korea* 186 F10
P'yŏngsan, *N. Korea* 186 L7
P'yŏng-sŏng, *N. Korea* 186 J6
P'yŏngyang (Pyongyang), *N. Korea* 186 J6
Pyongyang see P'yŏngyang, *N. Korea* 186 J6
Pyoseon, *S. Korea* 187 W8
Pyote, *Tex., U.S.* 105 N3
Pyramides, Pointe, *Wallis and Futuna, Fr.* 222 E11
Pyramid Lake, *Nev., U.S.* 111 P6
Pyramid Rock, island, *S. China Sea* 192 B10
Pyramids and Sphinx, ruin, *Egypt* 201 C18
Pyrenees, range, *Eur.* 140 J4
Pyrgí, *Gr.* 157 H16
Pýrgos, *Gr.* 156 K8
Pýrgos, *Gr.* 157 R15
Pyryatyn, *Ukr.* 159 N7
Pytalovo, *Russ.* 158 H5
Pythagóreio, *Gr.* 157 K18
Pyu, *Myanmar* 190 J6

Q

Qā' Abu al Ḥuṣayn, *Jordan* 172 M10
Qā' al Jafr, *Jordan* 173 Q7
Qabanbay, *Kaz.* 177 G18
Qāḍub, *Yemen* 175 R14
Qā'emābād, *Iran* 175 E17
Qā'emshahr, *Iran* 175 C13
Qā'en, *Iran* 175 D16
Qagan Nur, *N. Mongol, China* 184 B6
Qagan Nur (Zhengxiangbai Qi), *N. Mongol, China* 184 A6
Qahar Youyi Houqi, *N. Mongol, China* 184 B5
Qahar Youyi Zhongqi, *N. Mongol, China* 184 B5
Qaidam Basin, *Asia* 168 G9
Qaidam Pendi, *China* 182 H6
Qairouan, *Tun.* 201 B13
Qala, *Azerb.* 171 D23
Qala, *Malta* 163 H21
Qal'ah, *Afghan.* 178 L6
Qal'ah-ye Fath, *Afghan.* 179 R2
Qal'ah-ye Gaz, *Afghan.* 179 P4
Qal'ah-ye Now, *Afghan.* 178 M3
Qal'ah-ye Shahr, *Afghan.* 178 L5
Qalam Chashmahs, *Afghan.* 179 N4
Qalansīyah, *Yemen* 175 R14
Qalāt (Kalat), *Afghan.* 179 P6
Qal'at al Az Jam, ruins, *Saudi Arabia* 174 H4
Qal'at al Marqab (Margat Castle), ruins, *Syr.* 172 F7

Qal'at Bīshah, *Saudi Arabia* 174 M8
Qalhāt, *Oman* 175 K17
Qallabat, *Eth.* 203 E14
Qamar, Ghubbat al, *Yemen* 175 P13
Qamdo (Changdu), *China* 182 K8
Qamea, island, *Fiji* 222 G8
Qamīnis, *Lib.* 201 C15
Qammieh Point, *Malta* 163 J21
Qamystybas, *Kaz.* 176 G10
Qandala, *Somalia* 203 F18
Qapshaghay, *Kaz.* 177 H16
Qapshaghay Reservoir, *Kaz.* 177 H17
Qarabutaq, *Kaz.* 176 D9
Qaraçala, *Azerb.* 171 E22
Qaraghandy, *Kaz.* 177 E14
Qaraghayly, *Kaz.* 177 E15
Qarah Bāgh, *Afghan.* 179 N7
Qaratal, river, *Kaz.* 177 G16
Qarataū, *Kaz.* 177 J14
Qarataū Zhotasy, *Kaz.* 176 J13
Qaratöbe, *Kaz.* 176 D7
Qaraton, *Kaz.* 176 F7
Qaraūyl, *Kaz.* 177 E17
Qarazhal, *Kaz.* 177 F14
Qarchī Gak, *Afghan.* 178 K6
Qardho, *Somalia* 203 G18
Qarokŭl, lake, *Taj.* 178 H10
Qarqan see Qiemo, *China* 182 G4
Qarqan, river, *China* 182 G4
Qarqaraly, *Kaz.* 177 E15
Qarqīn, *Afghan.* 178 J5
Qarsaqbay, *Kaz.* 176 F12
Qarshi, *Uzb.* 176 L12
Qaryah-ye Mandil, *Afghan.* 179 N2
Qaryat al 'Ulyā, *Saudi Arabia* 174 H11
Qaryat az Zuwaytīnah, *Lib.* 201 C15
Qaşr al Azraq, ruins, *Jordan* 172 M8
Qaşr al Ḥayr al Gharbī, ruins, *Syr.* 172 H9
Qaşr al Ḥayr ash Sharqī, ruins, *Syr.* 172 G11
Qaşr aţ Ṭūbah, ruins, *Jordan* 173 N7
Qaşr Burqu', ruins, *Jordan* 172 L10
Qaşr-e Qand, *Iran* 175 H17
Qaşr Farāfra, *Egypt* 201 D17
Qaşr Ḥamām, *Saudi Arabia* 174 M10
Qa'ţabah, *Yemen* 174 Q9
Qaţanā, *Syr.* 172 J7
Qatar, *Asia* 175 J13
Qattara Depression, *Egypt* 201 C17
Qaţţīnah, Buḥayrat, *Syr.* 172 G8
Qax, *Azerb.* 171 C20
Qayghy, *Kaz.* 176 D11
Qaynar, *Kaz.* 177 E16
Qayşār, *Afghan.* 178 L4
Qazaly, *Kaz.* 176 G10
Qazaq Shyghanaghy, bay, *Kaz.* 176 J6
Qazax, *Azerb.* 171 C19
Qāzī Deh, *Afghan.* 178 K10
Qazvīn, *Iran* 174 C12
Qeissan, *Sudan* 203 F13
Qele Levu, island, *Fiji* 222 G9
Qena, *Egypt* 201 D19
Qeqertarsuaq, island, *Greenland, Den.* 82 D9
Qeqertarsuup Tunua, *Greenland, Den.* 82 D9
Qeshm, *Iran* 175 H15
Qeshm, island, *Iran* 175 H15
Qianjiang, *Hubei, China* 185 N4
Qian Shan, *Liaoning, China* 184 C12
Qianwei, *Liaoning, China* 184 C10
Qianyou see Zhashui, *Shaanxi, China* 184 K1
Qidong, *Hunan, China* 185 S3
Qidong, *Jiangsu, China* 184 M12
Qiemo (Qarqan), *China* 182 G4
Qihe, *Shand., China* 184 G8
Qikiqtarjuaq, *Nunavut, Can.* 85 F19
Qikiqtarjuaq, island, *Nunavut, Can.* 85 H20
Qila Ladgasht, *Pak.* 179 T2
Qila Safed, *Pak.* 179 S1
Qila Saifullah, *Pak.* 179 R7
Qilaotu Shan, *Hebei, China* 184 B9
Qilian Shan, *China* 182 G8
Qimantag, range, *China* 182 G5
Qimen, *Anhui, China* 185 P8
Qimu Jiao, *Shand., China* 184 F11

Qimusseriarsuaq, bay, *Greenland, Den.* 247 N15
Qin, river, *Shanxi, China* 184 G4
Qin'an, *China* 182 J10
Qing, river, *Hubei, China* 185 N2
Qingdao, *Shand., China* 184 G11
Qinghai Hu, *China* 182 H8
Qinghe, *China* 182 D6
Qinghe, *Hebei, China* 184 F7
Qingjiang see Zhangshu, *Jiangxi, China* 185 R7
Qingkou see Ganyu, *Jiangsu, China* 184 J10
Qinglong, *Hebei, China* 184 C9
Qingshuihe, *N. Mongol, China* 184 C4
Qingtian, *Zhejiang, China* 185 Q11
Qingtongxia (Xiaoba), *China* 182 H10
Qingxian, *Hebei, China* 184 E8
Qingxu, *Shanxi, China* 184 F4
Qingyuan, *Guang., China* 185 V4
Qingyuan, *Liaoning, China* 184 A14
Qingyuan, *Zhejiang, China* 185 R10
Qingyun, *Shand., China* 184 F8
Qing Zang Gaoyuan (Tibet, Plateau of), *China* 182 J3
Qingzhou, *Shand., China* 184 G9
Qinhuangdao, *Hebei, China* 184 C10
Qin Lin, *Asia* 168 G10
Qin Ling, range, *China* 182 J11
Qinxian, *Shanxi, China* 184 G4
Qinyang, *Henan, China* 184 H5
Qinyuan, *Shanxi, China* 184 G4
Qinzhou, *China* 182 P11
Qionghai, *Hainan, China* 185 Z1
Qiongshan (Qiongzhou), *Hainan, China* 185 Y1
Qiongzhou see Qiongshan, *Hainan, China* 185 Y1
Qiongzhou Haixia, *Guang., China* 185 Y1
Qiongzhou Strait, *Pac. Oc.* 168 J11
Qiqihar, *China* 183 C15
Qira, *China* 182 G3
Qiryat Shemona, *Israel* 172 K6
Qishn, *Yemen* 175 Q13
Qitai, *China* 182 E6
Qitaihe, *China* 183 D17
Qixia, *Shand., China* 184 F11
Qixian, *Henan, China* 184 H6
Qixian, *Henan, China* 184 J6
Qiyang, *Hunan, China* 185 S3
Qiyl, river, *Kaz.* 176 D7
Qizilağac Körfəzi, *Azerb.* 171 F22
Qizil Qal'ah, *Afghan.* 178 K7
Qizilqum, *Uzb.* 176 J10
Qobu, *Azerb.* 171 D23
Qobustan, *Azerb.* 171 D22
Qogir Feng see K2, *China, Pak.* 178 L13
Qom, *Iran* 174 D12
Qom, river, *Iran* 174 D12
Qomolangma see Everest, Mount, *China, Nep.* 182 L4
Qomsheh see Shahrezā, *Iran* 175 E13
Qonaqkend, *Azerb.* 171 C22
Qongyrat, *Kaz.* 177 F15
Qo'qon, *Uzb.* 177 K14
Qorakŭl, *Uzb.* 176 L11
Qoraqalpog'iston, region, *Uzb.* 176 H9
Qormi, *Malta* 163 K22
Qoskӧl, *Kaz.* 176 E12
Qosshaghyl, *Kaz.* 176 F7
Qostanay, *Kaz.* 176 N1
Qrendi, *Malta* 163 L22
Quakertown, *Pa., U.S.* 96 P9
Quanah, *Tex., U.S.* 104 J8
Quân Đảo Nam Du, island, *Vietnam* 191 Q11
Quangang, *Fujian, China* 185 T10
Quảng Ngãi, *Vietnam* 190 L14
Quảng Trị, *Vietnam* 190 K13
Quannan, *Jiangxi, China* 185 U6
Quanshuigou, *China* 178 L16
Quanzhou, *Fujian, China* 185 U9
Quanzhou, *Guangxi Zhuang, China* 185 S2
Quaraí, *Braz.* 132 P10
Quartier d'Orléans, *St.-Martin, Fr.* 123 B15

Quartier du Colombier, *St.-Martin, Fr.* 123 B14
QuartuSant' Elena, *It.* 153 Q4
Quartz Hill, *N.T., Austral.* 215 T9
Quartzsite, *Ariz., U.S.* 109 T5
Quatre Bornes, *Mauritius* 209 G20
Quba, *Azerb.* 171 C22
Qūchān, *Iran* 175 B16
Qudaym, *Syr.* 172 F10
Quebec, *Can.* 85 M19
Québec, *Que., Can.* 85 P20
Quebracho Coto, *Arg.* 134 F10
Quebrada Fracture Zone, *Pac. Oc.* 243 K19
Quebradillas, *P.R., U.S.* 122 M2
Queen Adelaida Archipelago, *S. Amer.* 128 R4
Queen Alexandra Range, *Antarctica* 231 L13
Queen Charlotte Islands see Haida Gwaii, *Can.* 84 J6
Queen Charlotte Sound, *B.C., Can.* 84 K7
Queen Elizabeth Islands, *Nunavut, N.W.T., Can.* 85 B14
Queen Elizabeth Range, *Antarctica* 231 L13
Queen Elizabeth Rise, *Arctic Oc.* 246 L11
Queen Elizabeth Shelf, *Arctic Oc.* 246 M12
Queen Fabiola Mountains (Yamato Mountains), *Antarctica* 231 C17
Queen Ka'ahumanu Highway, *Hawai'i, U.S.* 115 M18
Queen Mary Coast, *Antarctica* 231 J21
Queen Maud Gulf, *Nunavut, Can.* 85 F14
Queen Maud Land, region, *Antarctica* 231 D14
Queen Maud Mountains, *Antarctica* 230 K12
Queens Channel, *Austral.* 214 C7
Queensland, *Austral.* 215 S12
Queensland Plateau, *Pac. Oc.* 242 L8
Queenstown, *N.Z.* 217 Q15
Queenstown, *S. Af.* 206 L10
Queenstown, *Tas., Austral.* 215 Y7
Queen Victoria's Profile, *Hawai'i, U.S.* 114 C6
Queets, *Wash., U.S.* 110 C2
Queiros, Cape, *Vanuatu* 222 C1
Quelimane, *Mozambique* 207 F14
Quellón, *Chile* 135 R6
Quemado, *N. Mex., U.S.* 109 T10
Quemado, *Tex., U.S.* 105 S6
Quemoy see Kinmen, *Fujian, China* 185 U9
Quemú Quemú, *Arg.* 134 M10
Quequén, *Arg.* 135 N12
Quercy, region, *Fr.* 149 W9
Querétaro, *Mex.* 116 H11
Quesada, *C.R.* 117 N19
Queshan, *Henan, China* 184 L5
Quesnel, *B.C., Can.* 84 L8
Questa, *N. Mex., U.S.* 109 Q13
Quetta, *Pak.* 179 R6
Quetzaltenango, *Guatemala* 117 L15
Quezon City, *Philippines* 193 C13
Qufu, *Shand., China* 184 H8
Quibala, *Angola* 206 C6
Quibdó, *Col.* 130 E4
Quiberon, Presqu'île de, *Fr.* 149 R4
Quijotoa, *Ariz., U.S.* 109 V7
Quilá, *Mex.* 116 F8
Quilcene, *Wash., U.S.* 110 B3
Quillan, *Fr.* 149 Y10
Quillota, *Chile* 134 K6
Quilon see Kollam, *India* 181 S5
Quilpie, *Qnsld., Austral.* 215 U12
Quimilí, *Arg.* 134 G11
Quimper, *Fr.* 149 Q3
Quimperlé, *Fr.* 149 Q3
Quinault, *Wash., U.S.* 110 C2
Quinault, river, *Wash., U.S.* 110 C2
Quince Mil, *Peru* 132 H5
Quincy, *Calif., U.S.* 111 P5
Quincy, *Fla., U.S.* 99 Q5
Quincy, *Ill., U.S.* 101 R3
Quincy, *Mass., U.S.* 97 K15

Quines, *Arg.* 134 K9
Quinhagak, *Alas., U.S.* 112 K12
Quinn, river, *Nev., Oreg., U.S.* 110 L8
Quintanar de la Orden, *Sp.* 146 G11
Quinter, *Kans., U.S.* 107 S4
Quintin, *Fr.* 149 Q4
Quinto, *Sp.* 147 E14
Quintus Rocks, island, *Bahamas* 122 E4
Quipungo, *Angola* 206 E6
Quiros Fracture Zone, *Pac. Oc.* 243 M20
Quissanga, *Mozambique* 207 D15
Quissico, *Mozambique* 207 J13
Quitaque, *Tex., U.S.* 104 J6
Quitilipi, *Arg.* 134 G12
Quitman, *Ga., U.S.* 99 Q6
Quitman, *Miss., U.S.* 103 M13
Quito, *Ecua.* 130 J3
Quixadá, *Braz.* 133 E17
Qujiang, *Guang., China* 185 U5
Qujing, *China* 182 N10
Qulan, *Kaz.* 177 J15
Qulandy, *Kaz.* 176 G9
Qulbān Banī Murrah, ruins, *Jordan* 173 Q8
Qullai Somoniyon (Communist Peak), *Taj.* 178 H10
Qulsary, *Kaz.* 176 F7
Qŭnghirot, *Uzb.* 176 J9
Quobba, *W. Aust., Austral.* 215 U1
Quogue, *N.Y., U.S.* 97 N13
Quokka Rise, *Ind. Oc.* 225 K16
Quorn, *S. Aust., Austral.* 215 W10
Qurayyāt, *Oman* 175 K16
Qŭrghonteppa, *Taj.* 178 J7
Qŭryah, *Afghan.* 179 Q4
Quryq, *Kaz.* 176 H5
Qusar, *Azerb.* 171 C22
Quṣeir, *Egypt* 201 D19
Qushui see Qüxü, *China* 182 L5
Qusmuryn, *Kaz.* 176 C11
Qusmuryn Köli, *Kaz.* 176 C11
Quxar (Quxia), *China* 182 L4
Quxia see Quxar, *China* 182 L4
Qüxü (Qushui), *China* 182 L5
Quỳ Châu, *Vietnam* 190 J11
Quyghan, *Kaz.* 177 G15
Quỳ Hợp, *Vietnam* 190 J11
Quy Nhơn, *Vietnam* 190 M14
Quzhou, *Hebei, China* 184 G6
Quzhou, *Zhejiang, China* 185 Q10
Qvareli, *Rep. of Georgia* 171 B19
Qyzan, *Kaz.* 176 G6
Qyzylorda, *Kaz.* 176 H11

R

Raahe, *Fin.* 143 F15
Raas, island, *Indonesia* 192 M11
Raasay, island, *Scot., U.K.* 144 J7
Raasay, Sound of, *Scot., U.K.* 144 J7
Rab, island, *Croatia* 154 F5
Raba, *Indonesia* 193 M13
Rabacca, *St. Vincent and the Grenadines* 123 K17
Rabastens, *Fr.* 149 Y7
Rabat, *Malta* 163 K22
Rabat, *Mor.* 200 B8
Rabat see Victoria, *Malta* 163 H20
Rabaul, *P.N.G.* 217 C21
Rabi (Rambi), island, *Fiji* 222 G8
Rábida (Jervis), Isla, *Ecua.* 130 Q9
Rābigh, *Saudi Arabia* 174 K6
Racaka (Rezhaka), *China* 182 K7
Racale, *It.* 153 N15
Răcari, *Rom.* 155 F15
Racconigi, *It.* 152 F2
Raccoon Cay, *Bahamas* 119 H13
Raccoon Point, *La., U.S.* 102 R10
Race, Cape, *Nfld. & Lab., Can.* 85 M24
Raceland, *La., U.S.* 102 Q10
Rachaïya, *Leb.* 172 J6
Rạch Giá, *Vietnam* 191 Q12
Racine, *Wis., U.S.* 100 M7
Raco, *Mich., U.S.* 100 F10
Rădăuți, *Rom.* 155 B15

Radcliff, *Ky., U.S.* **103** C16
Radford, *Va., U.S.* **98** F9
Radhanpur, *India* **180** H3
Radisson, *Que., Can.* **85** M18
Radix, Point, *Trinidad and Tobago* **123** Q24
Radnevo, *Bulg.* **155** J15
Radom, *Pol.* **151** F16
Radomsko, *Pol.* **151** F15
Radomyshl', *Ukr.* **159** N5
Radviliškis, *Lith.* **143** M16
Radwá, Jabal, *Saudi Arabia* **174** J6
Radzyń Podlaski, *Pol.* **151** E17
Rae Bareli, *India* **180** G8
Raeford, *N.C., U.S.* **98** J11
Rae Isthmus, *Nunavut, Can.* **85** G16
Rae Lakes, *N.W.T., Can.* **84** G11
Raeside, Lake, *Austral.* **214** H4
Raetihi, *N.Z.* **217** L19
Rāf, Jabal, *Saudi Arabia* **174** G7
Rafaela, *Arg.* **134** J11
Rafaḥ, *Gaza Strip* **173** N4
Rafaï, *Cen. Af. Rep.* **202** H10
Raffadali, *It.* **153** T10
Rafḥā', *Saudi Arabia* **174** F9
Rafína, *Gr.* **157** J13
Rafsanjān, *Iran* **175** F15
Raga, *S. Sudan* **202** G11
Ragachow, *Belarus* **158** L6
Ragba (Rega), pass, *Nepal* **180** F11
Ragged, Mount, *Austral.* **214** K5
Ragged Island, *Bahamas* **119** H13
Ragged Island, *Me., U.S.* **97** G17
Ragged Point, *Barbados* **123** K20
Ragusa, *It.* **153** T11
Ragusa *see* Dubrovnik, *Croatia* **154** J8
Raha, *Indonesia* **193** L14
Raḥeb, Ras ir, *Malta* **163** K21
Rahimyar Khan, *Pak.* **179** T9
Raiatea, island, *Fr. Polynesia, Fr.* **223** B23
Raijua, island, *Indonesia* **193** N14
Railk Ridge, *Pac. Oc.* **242** H10
Rainbow, *Vic., Austral.* **215** Y11
Rainbow Bridge National Monument, *Utah, U.S.* **109** P8
Rainbow City, *Ala., U.S.* **103** J16
Rainbow Falls, *Hawai‘i, U.S.* **115** M21
Rainier, *Oreg., U.S.* **110** E3
Rainier, Mount, *Wash., U.S.* **110** D4
Rainy, river, *Can., U.S.* **106** E10
Rainy Lake, *Can., U.S.* **106** E11
Raipur, *India* **180** K8
Rairakhol, *India* **180** K9
Rairik, island, *Marshall Is., U.S.* **220** H12
Ra'īs, *Saudi Arabia* **174** K6
Raisinghnagar, *India* **180** E4
Raita Bank, *Hawai‘i, U.S.* **114** L5
Raititi, Pointe, *Fr. Polynesia, Fr.* **223** K14
Raitt Rise, *Ind. Oc.* **225** J14
Raivavae (Vavitu), island, *Fr. Polynesia, Fr.* **223** J17
Raiwind, *Pak.* **179** Q12
Rajahmundry, *India* **180** M8
Rajampet, *India* **181** P6
Rajang, *Malaysia* **192** H9
Rajangl, river, *Malaysia* **192** H11
Rajanpur, *Pak.* **179** S9
Rajapalaiyam, *India* **181** S6
Rajasthan Canal, *India* **180** F3
Rajgarh, *India* **180** F5
Rajkot, *India* **180** J2
Raj Nandgaon, *India* **180** K8
Rajpura, *India* **180** E5
Raj Samund, *India* **180** H4
Rakahanga Atoll, *Cook Is., N.Z.* **218** H12
Rakaia, *N.Z.* **217** P17
Rakaposhi, peak, *Pak.* **178** L12
Rakbah, Sahl, *Saudi Arabia* **174** L7
Rakhiv, *Ukr.* **159** Q2
Rakhman Qaynary, *Kaz.* **177** D20
Rakhshan, river, *Pak.* **179** U4
Rakhyūt, *Oman* **175** P14
Rakiraki, *Fiji* **222** H6
Rakiura *see* Stewart Island, *N.Z.* **217** R15
Rakops, *Botswana* **206** G9

Rakvere, *Est.* **143** J17
Raleigh, *Miss., U.S.* **102** L12
Raleigh, *N.C., U.S.* **98** H11
Ralik Chain, islands, *Marshall Is., U.S.* **220** G3
Ralls, *Tex., U.S.* **104** K5
Ramadi *see* Ar Ramādī, *Iraq* **174** D9
Ramah, *N. Mex., U.S.* **109** S10
Ramai (Remai), *China* **182** L5
Rām Allāh, *W. Bank* **172** M5
Raman, *Thai.* **191** S9
Ramanum, island, *F.S.M.* **221** B15
Ramat Gan, *Israel* **172** M5
Rambi *see* Rabi, island, *Fiji* **222** G8
Rambu, *Indonesia* **193** J14
Rambutyo, island, *P.N.G.* **217** B20
Rameshki, *Russ.* **158** H8
Ramgarh, *India* **180** F2
Ram Head, *Virgin Is., U.S.* **122** N11
Ramla, *Israel* **172** M5
Ramnagar, *India* **180** E7
Râmnicu Vâlcea, *Rom.* **155** E14
Ramon, Har, *Israel* **173** Q4
Ramona, *Calif., U.S.* **111** Y10
Ramos Island, *Solomon Is.* **221** M19
Rampart, *Alas., U.S.* **113** F16
Rampur, *India* **180** D6
Rampur, *India* **180** F7
Rampur Hat, *India* **180** H11
Ramree, *Myanmar* **190** J5
Ramree Island, *Myanmar* **190** J4
Ramsay, *Mich., U.S.* **100** F5
Ramsey (Rhumsaa), *Isle of Man, U.K.* **145** Q9
Ramsey Island, *Wales, U.K.* **145** V8
Ramu, *India* **180** K14
Ramu, river, *P.N.G.* **217** C19
Ramvik, *Sw.* **143** H13
Rancagua, *Chile* **134** L7
Ranchester, *Wyo., U.S.* **108** F11
Ranchi, *India* **180** J10
Rancho Cordova, *Calif., U.S.* **111** R4
Rancione, river, *San Marino* **163** H16
Ranco, river, *San Marino* **163** H15
Ranco, Lago, *Chile* **135** P6
Randazzo, *It.* **153** S11
Randers, *Den.* **142** M11
Randolph, *Nebr., U.S.* **107** N7
Randolph, *Utah, U.S.* **108** K8
Randolph, *Vt., U.S.* **97** G13
Rangahoe, island, *Cook Is., N.Z.* **223** B13
Rangamati, *Bangladesh* **180** J14
Rangeley, *Me., U.S.* **97** E15
Rangely, *Colo., U.S.* **108** L10
Ranger, *Tex., U.S.* **104** L9
Rangiauria *see* Pitt Island, *Pac. Oc.* **218** P9
Rangiroa, Atoll, *Fr. Polynesia, Fr.* **223** D17
Rangitaiki, river, *N.Z.* **217** K20
Rangitoto ki te Tonga (D'Urville Island), *N.Z.* **217** M18
Rangkasbitung, *Indonesia* **192** L8
Rangoon *see* Yangon, *Myanmar* **190** K6
Rangpur, *Bangladesh* **180** G12
Rangsang, island, *Indonesia* **192** H6
Raniganj, *India* **180** J11
Ranikhet, *India* **180** E7
Ranikot, ruins, *Pak.* **179** V7
Rankin, *Tex., U.S.* **105** N5
Rankin Inlet, *Nunavut, Can.* **85** H15
Rannes, *Qnsld., Austral.* **215** U15
Rannoch, Loch, *Scot., U.K.* **144** L9
Rann of Kachchh (Rann of Kutch), lake, *India* **180** H2
Rann of Kutch *see* Rann of Kachchh, lake, *India* **180** H2
Ranong, *Thai.* **191** Q7
Ranongga Island, *Solomon Is.* **221** M15
Rano Rahi Seamounts, *Pac. Oc.* **243** L18
Rans, *Switz.* **162** P2
Ransiki, *Indonesia* **193** J19
Rantau, island, *Indonesia* **192** J6
Rantauprapat, *Indonesia* **192** H5
Rantekombola, peak, *Indonesia* **193** K13
Rantoul, *Ill., U.S.* **101** Q7

Ranwas, *Vanuatu* **222** D2
Raoping, *Guang., China* **185** V8
Raoul Island (Sunday), *Kermadec Is., N.Z.* **218** L9
Rapa, island, *Fr. Polynesia, Fr.* **219** L14
Rapallo, *It.* **152** F4
Rapa Nui *see* Pascua, Isla de, *Pac. Oc.* **219** L19
Rapa Passage, *Kiribati* **221** B21
Rapar, *India* **180** H2
Raper, Cape, *Nunavut, Can.* **85** E18
Rapid, river, *Minn., U.S.* **106** E10
Rapid City, *S. Dak., U.S.* **106** L2
Rapid River, *Mich., U.S.* **100** G8
Rapota, island, *Cook Is., N.Z.* **222** Q11
Rappenstein, peak, *Liech.* **162** Q3
Rápulo, river, *Bol.* **132** J7
Raquette Lake, *N.Y., U.S.* **96** H10
Raraka, island, *Fr. Polynesia, Fr.* **223** E18
Raroia, island, *Fr. Polynesia, Fr.* **223** E19
Rarotonga, island, *Cook Is., N.Z.* **218** K12
Rasa, Punta, *Arg.* **135** Q11
Ra's al 'Ayn, *Syr.* **172** C13
Ra's al Ḥadd, *Asia* **168** H5
Ra's al Kalb, *Asia* **168** J3
Ra's al-Khaimah, *Oman* **175** J15
Ra's an Naqb, *Jordan* **173** Q6
Ra's ash Sharbatāt, *Asia* **168** J4
Ra's Fartak, *Asia* **168** J3
Rashad, *Sudan* **202** F12
Rashîd (Rosetta), *Egypt* **201** C18
Rasht, *Iran* **175** B12
Ra's Koh Range, *Pak.* **179** S4
Rās Muḥammad, island, *Egypt* **173** U4
Raso, Cabo, *Port.* **146** H4
Rason, Lake, *Austral.* **214** H5
Ra's Shamrah (Ugarit), ruins, *Syr.* **172** E6
Rasshua, island, *Russ.* **161** H23
Rasskazovo, *Russ.* **158** L11
Rassokho Seamounts, *Arctic Oc.* **246** F12
Rasua Garhi, *Nepal* **180** F10
Ratak Chain, islands, *Marshall Is., U.S.* **220** G5
Ratak Ridge, *Pac. Oc.* **242** H10
Ratangarh, *India* **180** F4
Rathdrum, *Idaho, U.S.* **108** B3
Rathenow, *Ger.* **150** D9
Rathlin Island, *Scot., U.K.* **145** N7
Rätikon, range, *Switz.* **152** B5
Ratingen, *Ger.* **150** F5
Ratisbon *see* Regensburg, *Ger.* **150** J9
Rat Island, *Alas., U.S.* **112** M3
Rat Islands, *Alas., U.S.* **112** M2
Ratlam, *India* **180** J4
Ratnagiri, *India* **180** M3
Ratnapura, *Sri Lanka* **181** T7
Ratodero, *Pak.* **179** T7
Raton, *N. Mex., U.S.* **109** Q14
Raton Pass, *N. Mex., U.S.* **109** Q14
Rattlesnake Creek, *Oreg., U.S.* **110** K8
Rattlesnake Hills, *Wash., U.S.* **110** D6
Rattlesnake National Recreation Area, *Mont., U.S.* **108** C6
Rattray Head, *Eur.* **140** E5
Rau, island, *Indonesia* **193** H16
Raub, *Malaysia* **191** U9
Rauch, *Arg.* **134** M12
Raudal Yupurari (Devils Cataract), *Col.* **130** H7
Raufarhöfn, *Ice.* **142** D4
Raukotaha, island, *Cook Is., N.Z.* **223** C14
Rauma, *Fin.* **143** H15
Raurkela, *India* **180** J10
Rausu Dake, *Japan* **188** F15
Ravahere, island, *Fr. Polynesia, Fr.* **223** F19
Rāvar, *Iran* **175** F15
Ravena, *N.Y., U.S.* **96** K11
Ravenna, *It.* **152** F8
Ravenna, *Nebr., U.S.* **107** Q6
Ravenna, *Ohio, U.S.* **101** P15

Ravensburg, *Ger.* **150** K7
Ravenshoe, *Qnsld., Austral.* **215** R13
Ravensthorpe, *W. Aust., Austral.* **215** X4
Ravenswood, *W. Va., U.S.* **98** D8
Ravi, river, *Pak.* **179** Q11
Ravnina, *Turkm.* **176** M10
Rāwah, *Iraq* **174** D8
Rawaki, island, *Kiribati* **218** G10
Rawalpindi, *Pak.* **179** N11
Rawa Mazowiecka, *Pol.* **151** E15
Rāwandūz *see* Rewanduz, *Iraq* **174** C9
Rawḍah, lake, *Syr.* **172** F14
Rawḥah, *Saudi Arabia* **174** M8
Rawicz, *Pol.* **151** E13
Rawlinna, *W. Aust., Austral.* **215** W6
Rawlins, *Wyo., U.S.* **108** J11
Rawson, *Arg.* **135** R10
Rawu, *China* **182** L7
Ray, *N. Dak., U.S.* **106** E2
Ray, Cape, *Nfld. & Lab., Can.* **85** N22
Raya, peak, *Indonesia* **192** J10
Rayachoti, *India* **181** P6
Raychikhinsk, *Russ.* **161** L19
Raydā', plain, *Saudi Arabia* **174** M11
Raymond, *Alta., Can.* **84** N10
Raymond, *Calif., U.S.* **111** T6
Raymond, *Wash., U.S.* **110** D2
Raymondville, *Tex., U.S.* **105** W10
Rayne, *La., U.S.* **102** P8
Rayner Glacier, *Antarctica* **231** C18
Rayoke, island, *Russ.* **161** H23
Rayong, *Thai.* **191** N9
Raysūt, *Oman* **175** P14
Rayville, *La., U.S.* **102** L9
Raz, Pointe du, *Fr.* **149** Q2
Razelm, Lacul, *Rom.* **155** F18
Razgrad, *Bulg.* **155** G16
Razlog, *Bulg.* **155** K13
Razmak, *Pak.* **179** P8
Razo, island, *Cabo Verde* **209** B15
Razzaza Lake, *Iraq* **174** E9
Re, river, *San Marino* **163** J14
Ré, Île de, *Fr.* **149** T5
Reading, *Eng., U.K.* **145** V13
Reading, *Jam.* **122** H6
Reading, *Pa., U.S.* **96** P8
Real Bank, *Arctic Oc.* **247** F18
Realicó, *Arg.* **134** L10
Réalmont, *Fr.* **149** X10
Reao, island, *Fr. Polynesia, Fr.* **223** F22
Rebecca, Lake, *Austral.* **214** J5
Rebiana Sand Sea, *Af.* **198** E7
Rebola, *Eq. Guinea* **208** L7
Rebun Tō, *Japan* **188** E12
Recey, *Fr.* **149** R12
Recherche, Archipelago of the, *Austral.* **214** K5
Rechytsa, *Belarus* **158** M6
Recife, *Braz.* **133** G18
Recife, Cape, *S. Af.* **206** M10
Récifs, Île aux, *Seychelles* **209** N21
Recklinghausen, *Ger.* **150** E5
Reconquista, *Arg.* **134** H12
Recreo, *Arg.* **134** H9
Rector, *Ark., U.S.* **102** E11
Red *see* Hồng, river, *Vietnam* **190** G11
Red *see* Yuan, river, *China* **182** N9
Red, river, *U.S.* **86** K12
Redang, island, *Malaysia* **191** S10
Redange sur Attert, *Lux.* **162** J9
Red Bank, *Tenn., U.S.* **103** G17
Red Bay, *Ala., U.S.* **103** H13
Red Bay, *Cayman Is.* **122** J1
Red Bluff, *Calif., U.S.* **111** N3
Red Bluff Lake, *Tex., U.S.* **104** M2
Red Butte, *Ariz., U.S.* **109** R7
Red Cliff, *St. Kitts and Nevis* **123** C19
Redcliffe, Mount, *Austral.* **214** H4
Red Cloud, *Nebr., U.S.* **107** R6
Red Deer, *Alta., Can.* **84** M10
Red Devil, *Alas., U.S.* **113** J14
Redding, *Calif., U.S.* **111** N3
Redfield, *S. Dak., U.S.* **106** K6
Red Hills, *Kans., U.S.* **107** V5
Red Hook, *Virgin Is., U.S.* **122** N11
Redig, *S. Dak., U.S.* **106** J2
Red Lake, *Minn., U.S.* **106** F10
Red Lake, *Ont., Can.* **85** N14

Red Lake Falls, *Minn., U.S.* **106** F8
Redlands, *Calif., U.S.* **111** X9
Red Lodge, *Mont., U.S.* **108** F9
Redmond, *Oreg., U.S.* **110** H5
Red Mountain, *Mont., U.S.* **108** C7
Red Oak, *Iowa, U.S.* **107** Q10
Redon, *Fr.* **149** R5
Redonda, island, *Lesser Antil.* **121** C15
Redondo, *Port.* **146** J6
Redoubt Volcano, *Alas., U.S.* **113** K15
Red River of the North, river, *Can., U.S.* **86** B12
Red Rock, river, *Mont., U.S.* **108** F6
Red Rocks Point, *Austral.* **214** J7
Redruth, *Eng., U.K.* **145** X8
Red Sea, *Af., Asia* **268** h2
Red Springs, *N.C., U.S.* **98** J11
Redwater, river, *Mont., U.S.* **108** C12
Red Wing, *Minn., U.S.* **106** K12
Redwood Empire, region, *Calif., U.S.* **111** N2
Redwood Falls, *Minn., U.S.* **106** K10
Redwood National Park, *Calif., U.S.* **110** L2
Ree, Lough, *Ire.* **145** R5
Reed City, *Mich., U.S.* **100** K10
Reeder, *N. Dak., U.S.* **106** H2
Reedley, *Calif., U.S.* **111** T7
Reedsburg, *Wis., U.S.* **100** K4
Reedsport, *Oreg., U.S.* **110** H2
Reedville, *Va., U.S.* **98** E14
Reedy Glacier, *Antarctica* **230** K11
Reef Bay, *Virgin Is., U.S.* **122** N11
Reef Islands, *Solomon Is.* **221** P22
Reef Islands (Rowa Islands), *Vanuatu* **222** A2
Reefton, *N.Z.* **217** N17
Reese, river, *Nev., U.S.* **111** N9
Refahiye, *Turk.* **171** E13
Reform, *Ala., U.S.* **103** J14
Refugio, *Tex., U.S.* **105** T11
Regência Point, *S. Amer.* **128** H10
Regensburg (Ratisbon), *Ger.* **150** J9
Reggane, *Alg.* **200** D10
Reggio di Calabria, *It.* **153** R12
Reggio nell'Emilia, *It.* **152** F6
Reghin, *Rom.* **155** C14
Regina, *Sask., Can.* **84** N12
Régina, *Fr. Guiana* **131** F18
Registan, range, *Afghan.* **179** R4
Rehoboth, *Namibia* **206** H7
Rehoboth Beach, *Del., U.S.* **98** C15
Reid River, *Qnsld., Austral.* **215** S14
Reidsville, *Ga., U.S.* **98** N11
Reidsville, *N.C., U.S.* **98** G10
Reigate, *Eng., U.K.* **145** W14
Reims, *Fr.* **149** N11
Reina Adelaida, Archipiélago, *Chile* **135** W6
Reindeer Lake, *Sask., Man., Can.* **85** K13
Reinga, Cape, *N.Z.* **217** G17
Reinga Basin, *Pac. Oc.* **242** N10
Reinosa, *Sp.* **146** B10
Reisdorf, *Lux.* **162** H10
Reitoru, island, *Fr. Polynesia, Fr.* **223** F19
Rekareka *see* Tehuata, island, *Fr. Polynesia, Fr.* **223** E20
Rekata Bay, *Solomon Is.* **221** L17
Reliance, *N.W.T., Can.* **84** H12
Reliance, *Wyo., U.S.* **108** K9
Remada, *Tun.* **201** C13
Remai *see* Ramai, *China* **182** L5
Remanso, *Braz.* **133** G15
Remedios, *Cuba* **118** H9
Remer, *Minn., U.S.* **106** G11
Remeshk, *Iran* **175** H16
Remich, *Lux.* **162** K11
Rémire, *Fr. Guiana* **131** E18
Remiremont, *Fr.* **149** Q14
Remontnoye, *Russ.* **159** R13
Ren, island, *Marshall Is., U.S.* **220** K7
Rendezvous Bay, *Virgin Is., U.S.* **122** N11
Rend Lake, *Ill., U.S.* **101** U5
Rendova, island, *Solomon Is.* **221** M16
Rendsburg, *Ger.* **150** B7
Rengat, *Indonesia* **192** J6
Reni, *Ukr.* **159** S4
Rennell, island, *Solomon Is.* **221** R19

Rennes, *Fr.* **149** Q5
Rennick Glacier, *Antarctica* **231** Q15
Reno, *Nev., U.S.* **III** P6
Renovo, *Pa., U.S.* **96** M6
Renqiu, *Hebei, China* **184** E7
Rensselaer, *Ind., U.S.* **101** P8
Renton, *Wash., U.S.* **110** C4
Renville, *Minn., U.S.* **106** K10
Repetek, *Turkm.* **176** M10
Republic, *Mich., U.S.* **100** F7
Republic, *Wash., U.S.* **110** A7
Republican, river, *U.S.* **86** G12
Repulse Bay, *Austral.* **214** E14
Repulse Bay, *Nunavut, Can.* **85** G16
Requena, *Peru* **132** E4
Requena, *Sp.* **147** H14
Requin Bay, *Grenada* **123** L23
Reşadiye, *Turk.* **170** E12
Researcher Ridge, *Atl. Oc.* **240** M6
Reserve, *La., U.S.* **102** P10
Reserve, *N. Mex., U.S.* **109** T10
Reshteh-Ye Alborz (Elburz Mountains), *Iran* **174** B11
Resia, *It.* **152** B6
Resistencia, *Arg.* **134** G12
Reşiţa, *Rom.* **154** E11
Resolute, *Nunavut, Can.* **85** D15
Resolution Fracture Zone, *Pac. Oc.* **243** N16
Resolution Island, *N. Amer.* **82** E9
Resolution Island, *N.Z.* **217** Q14
Rest, *Jam.* **122** J8
Restinga, Punta, *Sp.* **208** R3
Réthymno, *Gr.* **157** Q13
Reti, *Pak.* **179** T8
Réunion Trench, *Ind. Oc.* **224** L7
Reus, *Sp.* **147** E16
Reutlingen, *Ger.* **150** J7
Reva, *S. Dak., U.S.* **106** J2
Reval *see* Tallinn, *Est.* **143** J16
Revelle Rise, *Ind. Oc.* **224** H6
Revelstoke, *B.C., Can.* **84** M9
Revigny, *Fr.* **149** P12
Revillagigedo, Islas, *Mex.* **116** H5
Revillagigedo Island, *Alas., U.S.* **113** M24
Revolyutsii Oktyabr'skoy, Ostrov, *Russ.* **161** D14
Revsbotn, *Nor.* **143** B14
Rewa, *India* **180** H8
Rewa, river, *Fiji* **222** J6
Rewanduz (Rāwandūz), *Iraq* **174** C9
Rexburg, *Idaho, U.S.* **108** G7
Rexford, *Mont., U.S.* **108** A5
Rexton, *Mich., U.S.* **100** F10
Rey, *Iran* **175** C13
Rey, Isla del, *Pan.* **117** N21
Rey Bouba, *Cameroon* **205** D17
Reyes, *Bol.* **132** H6
Reyes, Point, *U.S.* **86** F2
Reyhanlı, *Turk.* **170** J11
Reykjanes, *Eur.* **140** A3
Reykjanes Ridge, *Atl. Oc.* **247** N21
Reykjavík, *Ice.* **142** E2
Reynisdjúp, valley, *Atl. Oc.* **247** M21
Reynosa, *Mex.* **116** E12
Rēzekne, *Latv.* **143** L17
Rezhaka *see* Racaka, *China* **182** K7
Rgotina, *Serb.* **154** G12
Rhaetian Alps, *Switz.* **152** C5
Rhame, *N. Dak., U.S.* **106** H2
Rhein (Rhine), river, *Switz.* **152** A3
Rheine, *Ger.* **150** D6
Rhiconich, *Scot., U.K.* **144** H8
Rhin (Rhine), *Eur.* **149** Q15
Rhine *see* Rhein, Rhin, river, *Eur.* **140** G6
Rhinelander, *Wis., U.S.* **100** G5
Rhinns of Kells, region, *Scot., U.K.* **145** P9
Rhino Camp, *Uganda* **202** J12
Rhinocolura *see* El 'Arîsh, *Egypt* **173** N3
Rhir, Cape, *Af.* **198** D2
Rhiy di-Irīsal, cape, *Yemen* **175** R14
Rho, *It.* **152** D4
Rhode Island, *U.S.* **97** L14
Rhodes *see* Ródos, island, *Gr.* **157** N20
Rhodes Peak, *Idaho, U.S.* **108** D5

Rhodope Mountains, *Bulg., Gr.* **155** K13
Rhône, river, *Fr., Switz.* **149** W12
Rhône au Rhin, Canal du, *Fr.* **149** R15
Rhum, Sound of, *Scot., U.K.* **144** K7
Rhumsaa *see* Ramsey, *Isle of Man, U.K.* **145** Q9
Rhydargaeau, *Wales, U.K.* **145** U9
Rhyl, *Eng., U.K.* **145** S10
Rhynie, *Scot., U.K.* **144** K10
Riaba, *Eq. Guinea* **208** M7
Riaba, Bahia de, *Eq. Guinea* **208** M7
Riachão, *Braz.* **133** F14
Rialb, river, *Andorra* **162** G3
Riang, *India* **180** K12
Riaño, *Sp.* **146** B9
Riasi, *India* **179** N12
Riau, Kepulauan, *Indonesia* **192** J7
Riaza, *Sp.* **146** E11
Ribadeo, *Sp.* **146** A7
Ribáuè, *Mozambique* **207** E14
Ribeira Afonso, *Sao Tome and Principe* **209** D20
Ribeira Brava, *Madeira, Port.* **208** M2
Ribeira da Cruz, *Cabo Verde* **209** A14
Ribeira Grande, *Cabo Verde* **209** A14
Ribeira Grande , *Azores, Port.* **146** Q5
Ribeirão Preto, *Braz.* **133** L13
Ribera, *It.* **153** T9
Riberalta, *Bol.* **132** G7
Ribes de Freser, *Sp.* **147** C17
Ribewon, island, *Marshall Is., U.S.* **220** J8
Riblah, *Leb.* **172** H8
Rib Lake, *Wis., U.S.* **100** H4
Rib Mountain, *Wis., U.S.* **100** H5
Ribniţa, *Mold.* **159** Q5
Ribnitz-Damgarten, *Ger.* **150** B9
Riccione, *It.* **152** G8
Rice Lake, *Wis., U.S.* **100** G3
Richards Bay, *S. Af.* **206** K12
Richardson Highway, *Alas., U.S.* **113** H18
Richardson Mountains, *N.W.T., Yukon, Can.* **84** D9
Richardton, *N. Dak., U.S.* **106** G3
Richey, *Mont., U.S.* **108** C13
Richfield, *Utah, U.S.* **109** N7
Richford, *Vt., U.S.* **97** F13
Rich Hill, *Mo., U.S.* **107** R11
Richland, *Ga., U.S.* **99** N5
Richland, *Mo., U.S.* **107** U13
Richland, *Oreg., U.S.* **110** G9
Richland, *Wash., U.S.* **110** E7
Richland Center, *Wis., U.S.* **100** L4
Richland Chambers Reservoir, *Tex., U.S.* **104** M13
Richlands, *Va., U.S.* **98** F8
Richland Springs, *Tex., U.S.* **105** N9
Richmond, *Calif., U.S.* **III** R3
Richmond, *Ind., U.S.* **101** R10
Richmond, *Jam.* **122** H9
Richmond, *Ky., U.S.* **103** C18
Richmond, *Me., U.S.* **97** G16
Richmond, *Mo., U.S.* **107** S11
Richmond, *N.S.W., Austral.* **215** X14
Richmond, *Qnsld., Austral.* **215** S12
Richmond, *S. Af.* **206** L9
Richmond, *St. Vincent and the Grenadines* **123** K16
Richmond, *Tex., U.S.* **105** R13
Richmond, *Utah, U.S.* **108** J7
Richmond, *Va., U.S.* **98** E13
Richmond Hill, *Bahamas* **122** E8
Richmond Peak, *St. Vincent and the Grenadines* **123** K16
Rich Square, *N.C., U.S.* **98** G13
Richton, *Miss., U.S.* **102** M12
Richwood, *W. Va., U.S.* **98** E9
Rico, *Colo., U.S.* **109** P10
Ridā', *Yemen* **174** Q9
Ridanna, *It.* **152** B7
Ridder (Leninogorsk), *Kaz.* **177** D18
Riddle, *Idaho, U.S.* **108** J3
Riddle, *Oreg., U.S.* **110** J2
Ridge A, *Antarctica* **231** H15
Ridgecrest, *Calif., U.S.* **III** V9
Ridgefield, *Wash., U.S.* **110** E3
Ridgeland, *S.C., U.S.* **98** M9
Ridgway, *Colo., U.S.* **109** N11

Ridgway, *Pa., U.S.* **96** M5
Riding Point, *Bahamas* **122** E3
Riding Rocks, islands, *Bahamas* **118** E10
Riesa, *Ger.* **150** F10
Rieti, *It.* **152** K9
Rieumes, *Fr.* **149** X8
Rieupeyroux, *Fr.* **149** W10
Riez, *Fr.* **149** X14
Rifle, *Colo., U.S.* **108** M11
Rifstangi, *Eur.* **140** A4
Rīga, *Latv.* **143** L16
Riga, Gulf of, *Est., Latv.* **143** L16
Rīgān, *Iran* **175** G16
Rigby, *Idaho, U.S.* **108** G7
Riggins, *Idaho, U.S.* **108** E4
Riglos, *Sp.* **147** C14
Rigo, *P.N.G.* **217** E20
Rigolet, *Nfld. & Lab., Can.* **85** K22
Rig Rig, *Chad* **201** H14
Riiser-Larsen Ice Shelf, *Antarctica* **230** C10
Riiser-Larsen Peninsula, *Antarctica* **231** B17
Rijeka (Fiume), *Croatia* **154** E4
Rijeka Crnojevića, *Montenegro* **154** J9
Rikaze *see* Xigazê, *China* **182** L5
Rikitea, *Fr. Polynesia, Fr.* **223** Q20
Rikubetsu, *Japan* **188** F14
Rikuzentakata, *Japan* **188** L13
Rila, mountains, *Bulg.* **155** K13
Riley, *Kans., U.S.* **107** S8
Rilly, *Fr.* **149** P11
Rimā', Jabal ar, *Jordan* **172** L8
Rimah, Wādī ar, *Saudi Arabia* **174** H8
Rimatara, island, *Fr. Polynesia, Fr.* **219** K13
Rimavská Sobota, *Slovakia* **151** K15
Rimini, *It.* **152** G8
Rîmnicu Sărat, *Rom.* **155** E16
Rimouski, *Que., Can.* **85** N20
Rincon, *Ga., U.S.* **99** N9
Rincón, *Bonaire, Neth.* **123** Q19
Rincón, *P.R., U.S.* **122** M1
Rincón, Bahía de, *P.R., U.S.* **122** P4
Rinconada, *Arg.* **134** D9
Rincón de la Victoria, *Sp.* **146** M10
Rincón del Bonete, Lago, *Uru.* **134** K14
Rincón del Guanal, Punta, *Cuba* **118** J6
Ríneia, island, *Gr.* **157** K15
Ringbu, *Nor.* **142** J11
Ringdom Gompa, *India* **178** M13
Ringdove Passage, *Solomon Is.* **221** R23
Ringgold, *La., U.S.* **102** L7
Ringgold Isles, *Fiji* **222** G9
Ringkøbing, *Den.* **142** N10
Ringling, *Okla., U.S.* **104** J10
Ringvassøy, island, *Nor.* **143** C13
Río, *Gr.* **156** H9
Riobamba, *Ecua.* **130** K3
Rio Branco, *Braz.* **132** G6
Río Bravo del Norte, river *see* Rio Grande, *N. Amer.* **116** C9
Rio Bueno, *Jam.* **122** H8
Río Bueno, *Chile* **135** P6
Rio Canario, *Curaçao, Neth.* **123** Q14
Río Cauto, *Cuba* **118** K12
Rio Chama, river, *N. Mex., U.S.* **109** Q12
Rio Claro, *Trinidad and Tobago* **123** Q23
Río Cuarto, *Arg.* **134** K10
Rio de Janeiro, *Braz.* **133** M15
Río de la Plata Canyon, *Atl. Oc.* **241** T6
Rio Dell, *Calif., U.S.* **III** N1
Rio do Ouro, *Sao Tome and Principe* **209** C20
Río Esmeraldas, river, *Ecua.* **130** H2
Río Gallegos, *Arg.* **135** W8
Río Grande, *Braz.* **132** Q12
Río Grande, *Arg.* **135** X9
Rio Grande, river, *N. Amer.* **82** K4
Rio Grande City, *Tex., U.S.* **105** W9
Río Grande del Norte National Monument, *N. Mex., U.S.* **109** Q12

Rio Grande Fracture Zone, *Atl. Oc.* **241** S10
Rio Grande Plain, *Atl. Oc.* **241** T8
Rio Grande Rise, *Atl. Oc.* **241** S8
Rio Grande Wild & Scenic River, *Tex., U.S.* **105** Q4
Ríohacha, *Col.* **130** B6
Rio Hondo, river, *N. Mex., U.S.* **109** U13
Riom, *Fr.* **149** U11
Río Mulatos, *Bol.* **132** K7
Río Muni, region, *Eq. Guinea* **205** G15
Rio Nuevo, *Jam.* **122** H9
Río Peñasco, river, *N. Mex., U.S.* **109** U13
Rio Puerco, river, *N. Mex., U.S.* **109** S11
Rio Rancho, *N. Mex., U.S.* **109** S12
Rio Tejo, Foz do, *Port.* **146** J4
Rio Verde, *Braz.* **132** K12
Río Verde, *Chile* **135** W7
Río Verde, *Mex.* **116** G11
Rio Verde de Mato Grosso, *Braz.* **132** K11
Rio Vouga, Foz do, *Port.* **146** F5
Rioz, *Fr.* **149** R14
Ripley, *Calif., U.S.* **III** Y12
Ripley, *Miss., U.S.* **102** G12
Ripley, *Ohio, U.S.* **101** T12
Ripley, *Tenn., U.S.* **102** F12
Ripley, *W. Va., U.S.* **98** D8
Ripoll, *Sp.* **147** C17
Ripon, *Eng., U.K.* **145** Q12
Ripon, *Wis., U.S.* **100** K6
Risāfe, ruins *see* Ar Ruşāfah, *Syr.* **172** F11
Riscle, *Fr.* **149** X7
Rishikesh, *India* **180** E6
Rishiri Tō, *Japan* **188** E12
Rishon LeZiyyon, *Israel* **172** M5
Rising Star, *Tex., U.S.* **104** M9
Rison, *Ark., U.S.* **102** H8
Risør, *Nor.* **142** L11
Rita Blanca Creek, *N. Mex., Tex., U.S.* **104** E4
Ritchie Bank, *Ind. Oc.* **224** H8
Ritchie's Archipelago, *India* **181** Q14
Ritidian Point, *Guam, U.S.* **220** A11
Ritscher Canyon, *Ind. Oc.* **241** Y15
Ritscher Upland, *Antarctica* **230** C12
Ritu *see* Rutog, *China* **182** H2
Ritzville, *Wash., U.S.* **110** C8
Riva, river, *San Marino* **163** K16
Rivadavia, *Chile* **134** H7
Riva del Garda, *It.* **152** D6
Riva di Tures, *It.* **152** B8
Rivas, *Nicar.* **117** M18
Rive-de-Gier, *Fr.* **149** U12
Riveire aux Feuilles, river, *Que., Can.* **85** K18
Rivera, *Uru.* **134** J14
River Cess, *Liberia* **204** E6
Riverdale, *N. Dak., U.S.* **106** F4
Riverhead, *N.Y., U.S.* **97** N13
Riverina, *W. Aust., Austral.* **215** W4
Riverina, region, *Austral.* **214** L13
River Plate, *Atl. Oc.* **241** T6
Riverside, *Calif., U.S.* **III** X9
Riverside, *Wash., U.S.* **110** B7
Riverside, *Wyo., U.S.* **108** K11
Riversleigh, *Qnsld., Austral.* **215** R11
Riverton, *Man., Can.* **85** N14
Riverton, *Wyo., U.S.* **108** H10
Rivesaltes, *Fr.* **149** Z10
Riviera, *Fr., It.* **140** J6
Rivière des Anguilles, *Mauritius* **209** H20
Rivière-du-Loup, *Que., Can.* **85** N20
Rivière du Rempart, *Mauritius* **209** F20
Rivière Noire, Piton de la, *Mauritius* **209** G19
Rivière-Pilote, *Martinique, Fr.* **123** F23
Rivière-Salée, *Martinique, Fr.* **123** F23
Rivne, *Ukr.* **159** N3
Rivoli, *It.* **152** E2

Riyadh *see* Ar Riyāḍ, *Saudi Arabia* **174** J10
Rize, *Turk.* **171** D15
Rizhao, *Shand., China* **184** H10
Rizokarpaso (Dipkarpaz), *Cyprus* **162** M11
Rizzuto, Capo, *It.* **153** Q14
Ro, *New Caledonia, Fr.* **222** D10
Ro (Ágios Geórgios), island, *Gr.* **157** N22
Roa, *Sp.* **146** D10
Road Bay, *British Virgin Is., U.K.* **122** R11
Road Bay, *British Virgin Is., U.K.* **122** R6
Road Town, *British Virgin Is., U.K.* **122** R6
Roan Cliffs, *U.S.* **86** F7
Roanne, *Fr.* **149** T12
Roanoke, *Ala., U.S.* **103** K17
Roanoke, *Va., U.S.* **98** F10
Roanoke, river, *N.C., Va., U.S.* **98** F11
Roanoke Island, *N.C., U.S.* **98** G15
Roanoke Rapids, *N.C., U.S.* **98** G12
Roan Plateau, *Colo., U.S.* **108** M10
Roaringwater Bay, *Ire.* **145** V3
Robāṭ-e Khān, *Iran* **175** D15
Robāṭ-e Posht-e Bādām, *Iran* **175** E15
Robbie Ridge, *Pac. Oc.* **242** L12
Robe, *S. Aust., Austral.* **215** Y11
Robersonville, *N.C., U.S.* **98** H13
Robert-Bourassa, Réservoir, *Que., Can.* **85** L18
Robert Glacier, *Antarctica* **231** D19
Robert Lee, *Tex., U.S.* **104** M7
Roberts, *Idaho, U.S.* **108** G7
Roberts Butte, *Antarctica* **231** Q15
Roberts Creek Mountain, *Nev., U.S.* **III** P10
Robert S. Kerr Reservoir, *Okla., U.S.* **104** G14
Robertsport, *Liberia* **204** E6
Robeson Channel, *Nunavut, Can.* **85** A17
Robinson, *Ill., U.S.* **101** S7
Róbinson Crusoe, Isla, *S. Amer.* **128** L3
Robinson Range, *Austral.* **214** G3
Robinson River, *N.T., Austral.* **215** Q10
Robinvale, *N.S.W., Austral.* **215** X12
Robokaere, island, *Marshall Is., U.S.* **220** G11
Roboré, *Bol.* **132** K9
Rob Roy, island, *Solomon Is.* **221** Li6
Robson, Mount, *B.C., Can.* **84** L9
Robstown, *Tex., U.S.* **105** U11
Roby, *Tex., U.S.* **104** L7
Roca, Cape, *Eur.* **140** K1
Roca Partida, Isla, *Mex.* **116** H6
Roca Redonda, *Ecua.* **130** P8
Rocas, Atol das, *Braz.* **133** E18
Rocas Alijos, islands, *Mex.* **116** E5
Roccadaspide, *It.* **153** N12
Rocca San Casciano, *It.* **152** G7
Roccastrada, *It.* **152** H7
Rocha, *Uru.* **134** L15
Rochdale, *Eng., U.K.* **145** R11
Rochedo, *Braz.* **132** K11
Rochefort, *Belg.* **148** M13
Rochefort, *Fr.* **149** U6
Rochelle, *Ga., U.S.* **99** N6
Rochelle, *Ill., U.S.* **101** N5
Rocher de Diamant (Diamond Rock), island, *Martinique, Fr.* **123** G22
Rochers Somaloma, island, *Wallis and Futuna, Fr.* **222** E11
Roche's Bluff, *Montserrat* **123** B24
Roches Epeti, island, *Fr. Polynesia, Fr.* **223** M23
Roches Noires, Mouillage des, *Fr. Polynesia, Fr.* **223** J20
Rocheservière, *Fr.* **149** S5
Rochester, *Eng., U.K.* **145** N11
Rochester, *Ind., U.S.* **145** V15
Rochester, *Ind., U.S.* **101** P9
Rochester, *Minn., U.S.* **106** L12
Rochester, *N.H., U.S.* **97** H15
Rochester, *N.Y., U.S.* **96** J6
Rock, river, *Ill., Wis., U.S.* **101** N5
Rockall Bank, *Atl. Oc.* **240** G10

Rockall Plateau, *Atl. Oc.* **240** GIO
Rockall Trough, *Atl. Oc.* **240** GIO
Rockaway, *Oreg., U.S.* **110** F2
Rock Creek, *Mont., U.S.* **108** E9
Rock Creek Butte, *Oreg., U.S.* **110** G8
Rockdale, *Tex., U.S.* **105** PII
Rockefeller Plateau, *Antarctica* **230** LIO
Rock Falls, *Ill., U.S.* **101** N5
Rockford, *Ill., U.S.* **100** M5
Rockhampton, *Qnsld., Austral.* **215** TI5
Rock Hill, *S.C., U.S.* **98** J9
Rockingham, *N.C., U.S.* **98** JIO
Rockingham, *W. Aust., Austral.* **215** X2
Rockingham Bay, *Austral.* **214** DI3
Rock Island, *Ill., U.S.* **101** P4
Rock Lake, *N. Dak., U.S.* **106** E6
Rockland, *Me., U.S.* **97** GI7
Rockland, *Mich., U.S.* **100** F6
Rockledge, *Fla., U.S.* **99** TIO
Rockly Bay, *Trinidad and Tobago* **123** NI8
Rockmart, *Ga., U.S.* **98** K4
Rock Port, *Mo., U.S.* **107** Q9
Rockport, *Calif., U.S.* **III** P2
Rockport, *Ind., U.S.* **101** U8
Rockport, *Tex., U.S.* **105** TII
Rock Rapids, *Iowa, U.S.* **106** M9
Rock River, *Wyo., U.S.* **108** JI2
Rock Sound, *Bahamas* **122** F6
Rock Sound, *Bahamas* **122** F6
Rock Springs, *Mont., U.S.* **108** DI2
Rock Springs, *Wyo., U.S.* **108** K9
Rocksprings, *Tex., U.S.* **105** Q7
Rockton, *Ill., U.S.* **100** M5
Rockville, *Ind., U.S.* **101** R8
Rockville, *Md., U.S.* **98** CI3
Rockwell City, *Iowa, U.S.* **107** NIO
Rockwood, *Me., U.S.* **97** DI6
Rockwood, *Tenn., U.S.* **103** FI8
Rocky Ford, *Colo., U.S.* **109** NI4
Rocky Mount, *N.C., U.S.* **98** GI2
Rocky Mount, *Va., U.S.* **98** FIO
Rocky Mountain National Park, *Colo., U.S.* **108** LI2
Rocky Mountains, *N. Amer.* **82** H4
Rocky Point, *Bahamas* **122** C6
Rocky Point, *Bahamas* **122** EII
Rocky Point, *Norfolk I., Austral.* **221** G20
Rodanthe, *N.C., U.S.* **98** HI5
Roddickton-Bide Arm, *Nfld. & Lab., Can.* **85** L23
Rodeo, *Arg.* **134** J7
Rodeo, *N. Mex., U.S.* **109** WIO
Rodez, *Fr.* **149** WIO
Rodonit, Kepi i, *Alban.* **154** K9
Ródos, *Gr.* **157** M2O
Ródos (Rhodes), island, *Gr.* **157** N2O
Rodrigues Ridge, *Ind. Oc.* **224** K8
Roebuck Bay, *Austral.* **214** D4
Roermond, *Neth.* **148** KI3
Roeselare, *Belg.* **148** LIO
Roes Welcome Sound, *Nunavut, Can.* **85** HI6
Rogagua, Lago, *Bol.* **132** H7
Rogers, *Ark., U.S.* **102** E6
Rogers, *Tex., U.S.* **105** PII
Rogers, Mount, *Va., U.S.* **98** G8
Rogers City, *Mich., U.S.* **100** HII
Rogers Lake, *Calif., U.S.* **III** W9
Rogerson, *Idaho, U.S.* **108** J5
Rogersville, *Tenn., U.S.* **103** EI9
Roggan, river, *Que., Can.* **85** LI8
Roggeveen Basin, *Pac. Oc.* **243** NI9
Roggeveen Rise, *Pac. Oc.* **243** N2I
Rogliano, *Fr.* **152** J4
Rogliano, *It.* **153** QI3
Rognan, *Nor.* **142** EI2
Rogue, river, *Oreg., U.S.* **110** K2
Rogue River, *Oreg., U.S.* **110** K3
Roguron, island, *Marshall Is., U.S.* **220** GIO
Rohrbach, *Aust.* **150** KIO
Rohri, *Pak.* **179** T7
Rohtak, *India* **180** E5
Roi, *Fr.* **152** K8
Roi, *Marshall Is., U.S.* **221** GI4
Roi Anchorage, *Marshall Is., U.S.* **220** K4
Roi Et, *Thai.* **190** LII

Roi-Namur, island, *Marshall Is., U.S.* **220** K4
Rojas, *Arg.* **134** LII
Rojhan, *Pak.* **179** S8
Rojo, Cabo, *P.R., U.S.* **122** PI
Rokera, *Solomon Is.* **221** P2O
Rokiškis, *Lith.* **143** LI7
Rôlas, Ilhéu das, *Sao Tome and Principe* **209** E2O
Rolette, *N. Dak., U.S.* **106** E5
Rolla, *Mo., U.S.* **107** UI3
Rolla, *N. Dak., U.S.* **106** D5
Rolleston, *N.Z.* **217** PI7
Rolletown, *Bahamas* **122** F9
Rolleville, *Bahamas* **122** E8
Rolling Fork, *Miss., U.S.* **102** KIO
Rollingstone, *Qnsld., Austral.* **215** RI4
Rollins, *Mont., U.S.* **108** B5
Rolvsøya, island, *Nor.* **143** BI4
Roma, *Qnsld., Austral.* **215** UI4
Roma (Rome), *It.* **152** K8
Romain, Cape, *S.C., U.S.* **98** MII
Romaine, river, *Que., Can.* **85** M2I
Roma-Los Saenz, *Tex., U.S.* **105** W9
Roman, *Rom.* **155** CI6
Romanche Fracture Zone, *Atl. Oc.* **241** P9
Romanche Gap, *Atl. Oc.* **241** PIO
Romang, island, *Indonesia* **193** MI6
Români, *Egypt* **173** NI
Romania, *Eur.* **154** DII
Romanija, peak, *Bosn. & Herzg.* **154** G8
Romano, Cape, *Fla., U.S.* **99** X8
Romano, Cayo, *Cuba* **118** HII
Romans, *Fr.* **149** VI3
Romanshorn, *Switz.* **152** A5
Romanzof, Cape, *N. Amer.* **82** Q3
Rome, *Ga., U.S.* **98** K4
Rome, *N.Y., U.S.* **96** J9
Rome see Roma, *It.* **152** K8
Romilly, *Fr.* **149** QII
Romorantin-Lanthenay, *Fr.* **149** R9
Romsey, *Eng., U.K.* **145** WI2
Rona, island, *Scot., U.K.* **144** F8
Ronan, *Mont., U.S.* **108** C6
Roncador, Serra do, *Braz.* **132** HI2
Ronceverte, *W. Va., U.S.* **98** E9
Ronda, *Sp.* **146** M9
Ronde, Pointe, *Dominica* **123** EI8
Ronde Island, *Grenada* **123** H24
Rondonópolis, *Braz.* **132** JII
Rondu, *Pak.* **178** LI2
Rong'an, *China* **182** NI2
Rongcheng, *Shand., China* **184** FI2
Rongcheng Wan, *Shand., China* **184** FI2
Ronge, Lac la, *N. Amer.* **82** G5
Rongelap Atoll, *Marshall Is., U.S.* **220** F3
Rongerik Atoll, *Marshall Is., U.S.* **220** F3
Rongjiang, *China* **182** NII
Rong Kwang, *Thai.* **190** J9
Rongxian, *Guangxi Zhuang, China* **185** V2
Ronkiti, *F.S.M.* **221** GI4
Ronkiti Harbor, *F.S.M.* **221** GI4
Ronn Basin, *Atl. Oc.* **248** LII
Rønne, *Den.* **143** NI3
Ronne Entrance, *Antarctica* **230** G6
Ronne Ice Shelf, *Antarctica* **230** F8
Ronse, *Belg.* **148** LII
Roodhouse, *Ill., U.S.* **101** S4
Rosport, *Lux.* **162** JII
Roof Butte, *Ariz., U.S.* **109** Q9
Roonui, Mount, *Fr. Polynesia, Fr.* **223** QI7
Roo Rise, *Ind. Oc.* **225** JI7
Roorkee, *India* **180** E6
Roosendaal, *Neth.* **148** KI2
Roosevelt, *Utah, U.S.* **108** L9
Roosevelt, Mount, *B.C., Can.* **84** J9
Roosevelt Island, *Antarctica* **230** MII
Roosevelt Roads Naval Station, site, *P.R., U.S.* **122** N6

Root, river, *Minn., U.S.* **106** LI3
Rope, The, *Pitcairn I., U.K.* **223** Q24
Roper, river, *Austral.* **214** B9
Ropesville, *Tex., U.S.* **104** K5
Roquefort, *Fr.* **149** X7
Roquetas de Mar, *Sp.* **146** MI2
Roraima, Monte, *S. Amer.* **131** EI3
Røros, *Nor.* **142** HII
Rorschach, *Switz.* **152** A5
Rørvik, *Nor.* **142** FII
Rosa, Lake, *Bahamas* **119** JI5
Rosa, Monte, *It., Switz.* **152** D3
Rosal de la Frontera, *Sp.* **146** K7
Rosalia, *Wash., U.S.* **110** C9
Rosalie, *Dominica* **123** F2O
Rosalie Bay, *Dominica* **123** F2O
Rosario, *Arg.* **134** KI2
Rosario, *Mex.* **116** G9
Rosario, *Parag.* **132** MIO
Rosário, *Braz.* **133** DI5
Rosario, Cayo del, *Cuba* **118** H7
Rosario de la Frontera, *Arg.* **134** F9
Rosario de Lerma, *Arg.* **134** F9
Rosarno, *It.* **153** RI3
Roscoe, *S. Dak., U.S.* **106** J6
Roscoe, *Tex., U.S.* **104** M7
Ros Comáin see Roscommon, *Ire.* **145** R5
Roscommon, *Mich., U.S.* **100** JII
Roscommon (Ros Comáin), *Ire.* **145** R5
Ros Cré see Roscrea, *Ire.* **145** S5
Roscrea (Ros Cré), *Ire.* **145** S5
Rose, Pointe de la, *Martinique, Fr.* **123** F23
Rose Atoll, *Amer. Samoa, U.S.* **218** JII
Roseau, *Dominica* **123** GI9
Roseau, *Minn., U.S.* **106** D9
Roseau, river, *Can., U.S.* **106** D8
Roseau, river, *Dominica* **123** GI9
Roseau, river, *St. Lucia* **123** KI4
Rose Belle, *Mauritius* **209** G2O
Rosebery, *Tas., Austral.* **215** Y7
Rosebud, *Mont., U.S.* **108** DI2
Rosebud, *Tex., U.S.* **105** PII
Rosebud Creek, *Mont., U.S.* **108** EI2
Roseburg, *Oreg., U.S.* **110** J3
Rosedale, *Miss., U.S.* **102** JIO
Rosedale, *Qnsld., Austral.* **215** UI5
Rose Hall, *Jam.* **122** G7
Rose Hill, *Mauritius* **209** G2O
Rose Island, *Bahamas* **122** BI2
Rosemary Bank, *Atl. Oc.* **240** FII
Rosenbach, *Aust.* **150** MIO
Rosenberg, *Tex., U.S.* **105** RI3
Rosenheim, *Ger.* **150** K9
Rose Peak, *Ariz., U.S.* **109** U9
Rosepine, *La., U.S.* **102** N7
Roses, *Bahamas* **119** GI4
Roses, *Sp.* **147** CI8
Roses, Golf de, *Sp.* **147** CI8
Rosetown, *Sask., Can.* **84** MII
Roseville, *Calif., U.S.* **III** Q4
Rosewood, *N.T., Austral.* **215** Q7
Rosholt, *S. Dak., U.S.* **106** H8
Rosht-Kala, *Taj.* **178** KIO
Rosia Bay, *Gibraltar, U.K.* **163** Q22
Rosiclare, *Ill., U.S.* **101** V6
Rosignano Marittimo, *It.* **152** H6
Roşiori de Vede, *Rom.* **155** GI4
Roslavl', *Russ.* **158** K7
Roslyatino, *Russ.* **158** FI2
Roslyn, *Wash., U.S.* **110** C5
Ros Mhic Thriúin see New Ross, *Ire.* **145** T6
Ros Ó gCairbre see Ross Carbery, *Ire.* **145** V3
Rosporden, *Fr.* **149** Q3
Ross, *N.Z.* **217** NI6
Rossano, *It.* **153** PI4
Rossan Point, *Ire.* **145** P4
Ross Barnett Reservoir, *Miss., U.S.* **102** LII
Ross Carbery (Ros Ó gCairbre), *Ire.* **145** V3
Ross Dam, *Wash., U.S.* **110** A5
Rosse Island, *P.N.G.* **217** F22
Ross Ice Shelf, *Antarctica* **230** MI2
Ross Island, *Antarctica* **231** NI3
Ross Lake, *Wash., U.S.* **110** A5

Ross Lake National Recreation Area, *Wash., U.S.* **110** A5
Rosslare Harbour (Calafort Ros Láir), *Ire.* **145** U7
Ross, Mount, *N.Z.* **217** MI9
Rosso, *Mauritania* **200** G4
Rosso, Capo, *Fr.* **152** K3
Ross of Mull, peninsula, *Scot., U.K.* **144** L7
Rossosh', *Russ.* **159** NIO
Ross River, *N.T., Austral.* **215** T9
Ross River, *Yukon, Can.* **84** G8
Ross Sea, *Antarctica* **230** PI2
Røssvatnet, lake, *Nor.* **142** FI2
Rossville, *Ill., U.S.* **101** Q7
Røst Bank, *Arctic Oc.* **247** G2O
Rostock, *Ger.* **150** B9
Rostov, *Russ.* **158** HIO
Rostov-na-Donu, *Russ.* **159** RII
Rostrenen, *Fr.* **149** Q4
Roswell, *Ga., U.S.* **98** K5
Roswell, *N. Mex., U.S.* **109** UI4
Rota, *Sp.* **146** M7
Rota see Songsong, *N. Mariana Is., U.S.* **220** E7
Rota, island, *Asia* **168** HI6
Rota, island, *N. Mariana Is., U.S.* **220** D2
Rotan, *Tex., U.S.* **104** L7
Rotenboden, *Liech.* **162** P2
Roth, *Ger.* **150** J8
Roth, *Ger.* **162** HIO
Rotherham, *Eng., U.K.* **145** SI2
Rothschild, *Wis., U.S.* **100** H5
Rothschild Island, *Antarctica* **230** F5
Roti, island, *Indonesia* **193** NI4
Roto, *Cook Is., N.Z.* **222** Q2
Rotondella, *It.* **153** NI3
Rotorua, *N.Z.* **217** KI9
Rotterdam, *Neth.* **148** JI2
Rottumeroog, island, *Neth.* **148** GI4
Rottumerplaat, island, *Neth.* **148** GI4
Rotuma, island, *Fiji* **218** J8
Roubaix, *Fr.* **148** LIO
Rouen, *Fr.* **149** N8
Rouge, Baie, *St.-Martin, Fr.* **123** BI4
Rouge, Pic de la, *Fr., Sp.* **162** G2
Rough Point, *British Virgin Is., U.K.* **122** Q6
Round Island, *Mauritius* **209** E2I
Round Island see Yalewa Kalou, *Fiji* **222** G6
Round Island Passage, *Fiji* **222** G5
Round Mountain, *Austral.* **214** JI5
Round Mountain, *Nev., U.S.* **III** Q9
Round Rock, *Bahamas* **122** C7
Round Rock, *Tex., U.S.* **105** PIO
Roundstone (Cloch na Rón), *Ire.* **145** R3
Roundup, *Mont., U.S.* **108** DIO
Roura, *Fr. Guiana* **131** FI8
Rousay, island, *Scot., U.K.* **144** FIO
Rouses Point, *N.Y., U.S.* **96** FI2
Rouyn-Noranda, *Que., Can.* **85** PI8
Rovaniemi, *Fin.* **143** EI5
Rovereto, *It.* **152** D7
Rôviĕng, *Cambodia* **191** NI2
Rovigo, *It.* **152** E7
Rovinj, *Croatia* **154** E4
Rovuma (Ruvuma), river, *Af.* **207** DI5
Rowa Islands see Reef Islands, *Vanuatu* **222** A2
Rowland, *N.C., U.S.* **98** KII
Rowley Island, *Nunavut, Can.* **85** FI7
Rowley Reefs, *Ind. Oc.* **225** JI8
Rowley Shelf, *Ind. Oc.* **225** KI8
Roxas, *Philippines* **193** EI3
Roxas City, *Philippines* **193** DI4
Roxboro, *N.C., U.S.* **98** GII
Roxborough, *Trinidad and Tobago* **123** NI8
Roy, *Mont., U.S.* **108** CIO
Roy, *N. Mex., U.S.* **109** RI4
Royale, Isle, *Mich., U.S.* **100** D6
Royal Island, *Bahamas* **122** D4
Royal Oak, *Mich., U.S.* **100** MI2
Royal Society Range, *Antarctica* **231** NI4
Royal Tunbridge Wells, *Eng., U.K.* **145** WI4

Royan, *Fr.* **149** U6
Roy Hill, *W. Aust., Austral.* **215** T3
Royston, *Ga., U.S.* **98** K6
Roznov, *Rom.* **155** CI6
Rrogozhinë, *Alban.* **154** L9
Rtishchevo, *Russ.* **158** MI2
Rua, island, *Marshall Is., U.S.* **220** L7
Ruacaná Falls, *Angola, Namibia* **206** F5
Ruahara, island, *Cook Is., N.Z.* **223** AI7
Ruapehu, Mount, *N.Z.* **217** LI9
Ruapuke Island, *N.Z.* **217** RI5
Ruatoria, *N.Z.* **217** K2I
Ruawai, *N.Z.* **217** HI8
Rub' al Khali, *Asia* **168** H3
Rubha Robhanais, cape, *Scot., U.K.* **144** G7
Rubicone, river, *It.* **152** G8
Rubtsovsk, *Russ.* **160** LI
Ruby, *Alas., U.S.* **113** GI5
Ruby, river, *Mont., U.S.* **108** E7
Ruby Dome, peak, *U.S.* **86** F6
Ruby Mountains, *Nev., U.S.* **III** NII
Ruby Plains, *W. Aust., Austral.* **215** R6
Rucheng, *Hunan, China* **185** T5
Rudan, *Iran* **175** HI6
Rūdbār, *Afghan.* **179** R2
Rudder Cut Cay, *Bahamas* **122** D7
Rūdnyy, *Kaz.* **176** CII
Rudong (Juegang), *Jiangsu, China* **184** LII
Rudyard, *Mich., U.S.* **100** FII
Rue, *Fr.* **148** M9
Ruffec, *Fr.* **149** T7
Rufiji, river, *Tanzania* **203** MI4
Rufino, *Arg.* **134** LII
Rufisque, *Senegal* **200** H4
Rugao, *Jiangsu, China* **184** LII
Rugby, *N. Dak., U.S.* **106** E5
Rugeley, *Eng., U.K.* **145** TI2
Rügen, island, *Ger.* **150** BIO
Ruggell, *Liech.* **162** M2
Ruhnu Saar, island, *Est.* **143** LI6
Ruhr, river, *Ger.* **150** F6
Rui'an, *Zhejiang, China* **185** RII
Rui Barbosa, *Braz.* **133** HI6
Ruiché, *Eq. Guinea* **208** M7
Ruidosa, *Tex., U.S.* **105** QI
Ruidoso, *N. Mex., U.S.* **109** UI3
Ruijin, *Jiangxi, China* **185** T7
Ruille, Pic de, *Fr.* **162** G5
Ruinas de Numancia, *Sp.* **146** DI2
Ruivo, Pico, *Madeira, Port.* **208** M3
Ruj, peak, *Bulg. Serb.* **154** HI2
Rujen, peak, *Bulg.* **154** JI2
Ruki, river, *Af.* **198** J7
Rukuruku Bay, *Fiji* **222** G6
Rukwa, Lake, *Tanzania* **203** MI4
Rule, *Tex., U.S.* **104** K7
Ruleville, *Miss., U.S.* **102** JIO
Rulhieres, Cape, *Austral.* **214** B6
Rum, island, *Scot., U.K.* **144** K7
Ruma, *Serb.* **154** F9
Rumaylah, 'Urūq ar, *Saudi Arabia* **174** MIO
Rumbek, *S. Sudan* **202** HI2
Rum Cay, *Bahamas* **119** FI4
Rumelange, *Lux.* **162** K9
Rumford, *Me., U.S.* **97** FI5
Rumia, *Pol.* **151** AI4
Rum Jungle, *N.T., Austral.* **215** P8
Rumoi, *Japan* **188** FI3
Rum Point, *Cayman Is.* **122** H2
Rum Point Channel, *Cayman Is.* **122** H2
Rumung, island, *F.S.M.* **221** CI8
Runan, *Henan, China* **184** K6
Runanga, *N.Z.* **217** NI7
Runaway, Cape, *N.Z.* **217** J2O
Runaway Bay, *Jam.* **122** H8
Runde, river, *Zimb.* **206** GII
Rundeng, *Indonesia* **192** H4
Rundu, *Namibia* **206** F8
Runge, *Tex., U.S.* **105** SII
Rungwa, *Tanzania* **203** MI3
Rungwa, river, *Tanzania* **203** MI3

Runit, island, *Marshall Is., U.S.* 220 H8
Running Water Draw, river, *Tex., U.S.* 104 H4
Runu, *F.S.M.* 221 CI8
Ruo, island, *F.S.M.* 221 AI6
Ruoqiang, *China* 182 G5
Rupat, island, *Indonesia* 192 H6
Rupert, *Idaho, U.S.* 108 H6
Rupert, river, *Que., Can.* 85 MI9
Ruppert Coast, *Antarctica* 230 N9
Rupununi, river, *Guyana* 131 FI4
Rurrenabaque, *Bol.* 132 J6
Rurutu, island, *Fr. Polynesia, Fr.* 223 HI6
Rusanovo, *Russ.* 160 EIO
Ruse, *Bulg.* 155 GI5
Rushan, *Shand., China* 184 FI2
Rushan, *Taj.* 178 J9
Rush City, *Minn., U.S.* 106 JI2
Rushden, *Eng., U.K.* 145 UI3
Rushford, *Minn., U.S.* 106 LI3
Rush Springs, *Okla., U.S.* 104 HIO
Rushville, *Ill., U.S.* 101 R4
Rushville, *Ind., U.S.* 101 RIO
Rushville, *Nebr., U.S.* 106 M2
Rusk, *Tex., U.S.* 104 MI4
Ruskin, *Fla., U.S.* 99 U7
Russas, *Braz.* 133 EI7
Russell, *Kans., U.S.* 107 S6
Russell Cave National Monument, *Ala., U.S.* 103 GI6
Russell Islands, *Solomon Is.* 221 NI8
Russellville, *Ala., U.S.* 103 HI4
Russellville, *Ark., U.S.* 102 F7
Russellville, *Ky., U.S.* 103 DI5
Rüsselsheim, *Ger.* 150 G6
Russi, *It.* 152 F8
Russia, *Eur. Asia* 160 HI2
Russian, river, *Calif., U.S.* 111 Q2
Russian Fort Elizabeth, *Hawai'i, U.S.* 114 C5
Russian Mission, *Alas., U.S.* 112 HI2
Russkaya Gavan', *Russ.* 160 DI2
Russkaya Polyana, *Russ.* 160 KIO
Rustāq, *Afghan.* 178 K8
Rust'avi, *Rep. of Georgia* 171 CI9
Ruston, *La., U.S.* 102 L8
Rutaki Passage, *Cook Is., N.Z.* 222 Q9
Rute, *Sp.* 146 LIO
Ruteng, *Indonesia* 193 MI3
Ruth, *Nev., U.S.* 111 QI2
Rutherfordton, *N.C., U.S.* 98 J8
Rutland, *Vt., U.S.* 96 HI2
Rutland Island, *India* 181 QI4
Rutog (Ritu), *China* 182 H2
Ruvuma (Rovuma), river, *Af.* 203 NI5
Ruwāq, Jabal ar, *Syr.* 172 J9
Ruwenzori, range, *Dem. Rep. of the Congo, Uganda* 202 KI2
Ruwer, *Ger.* 162 JI2
Rūzaevka, *Kaz.* 176 CI2
Ruzayevka, *Russ.* 158 KI3
Ružomberok, *Slovakia* 151 JI5
Rwanda, *Af.* 202 KI2
Ryabov Seamounts, *Arctic Oc.* 246 JII
Ryan, *Okla., U.S.* 104 JIO
Ryan, Loch, *Scot., U.K.* 145 P8
Ryazan', *Russ.* 158 KIO
Ryazhsk, *Russ.* 158 LIO
Rybachiy, *Russ.* 158 J2
Rybinsk, *Russ.* 158 GIO
Rybinskoye Vodokhranilishche, *Russ.* 158 GIO
Rybinsk Reservoir, *Eur.* 140 DI2
Rybnik, *Pol.* 151 GI4
Rye, *Colo., U.S.* 109 PI3
Ryegate, *Mont., U.S.* 108 D9
Rye Patch Reservoir, *Nev., U.S.* 111 N8
Ryl'sk, *Russ.* 158 M8
Ryōtsu, *Japan* 188 MII
Ryōtsu Wan, *Japan* 188 MII
Rypin, *Pol.* 151 CI5
Rysy, peak, *Pol., Slovakia* 151 JI5
Ryukyu Islands *see* Nansei Shotō, *Japan* 218 C2
Ryukyu Ridge, *Pac. Oc.* 242 G6
Ryukyu Trench, *Pac. Oc.* 242 G6

Ryżhovo, *Russ.* 161 EI9
Rzeszów, *Pol.* 151 GI7
Rzhev, *Russ.* 158 J8

Sa, *Thai.* 190 J9
Sa'a, *Solomon Is.* 221 P2O
Sa'ādatābād, *Iran* 175 GI5
Saale, river, *Ger.* 150 G9
Saalfeld, *Ger.* 150 G8
Saar, river, *Ger.* 162 KII
Saarbrücken, *Ger.* 150 H5
Saaremaa (Ösel), island, *Est.* 143 KI5
Saba, island, *Neth.* 121 BI5
Sab' Ābār, *Syr.* 172 J9
Šabac, *Serb.* 154 F9
Sabadell, *Sp.* 147 DI7
Sabah, *Malaysia* 192 GI2
Saba Island, *Virgin Is., U.S.* 122 N8
Sabana, Archipiélago de, *Cuba* 118 G8
Sabana de La Mar, *Dom. Rep.* 119 L2O
Sabana Grande, *P.R., U.S.* 122 N2
Sabanalarga, *Col.* 130 B5
Sabaneta, *Dom. Rep.* 119 LI8
Sabaneta, Puntan, *N. Mariana Is., U.S.* 220 A5
Sabang, *Indonesia* 193 JI3
Şabanözü, *Turk.* 170 D8
Sabaya, *Bol.* 132 K6
Şāberī, Hāmūn-e, *Iran* 175 EI7
Sabetha, *Kans., U.S.* 107 R9
Sabhā, *Lib.* 201 DI4
Şabḩā, *Jordan* 172 L7
Sabinal, *Tex., U.S.* 105 R8
Sabinal, Cayo, *Cuba* 118 JII
Sabiñánigo, *Sp.* 147 CI4
Sabinas Hidalgo, *Mex.* 116 EII
Sabine, *Tex., U.S.* 105 QI6
Sabine, river, *U.S.* 87 LI4
Sabine Lake, *La., Tex., U.S.* 105 QI6
Sabinosa, *Sp.* 208 R3
Sabkhet el Bardawîl, *Egypt* 173 N2
Sable, Cape, *Fla., U.S.* 99 Y9
Sable, Cape, *N.S., Can.* 85 Q22
Sable, Île de, *New Caledonia, Fr.* 222 A6
Sable Island, *N.S., Can.* 85 P23
Sables, Île aux (Sandy Island), *Mauritius* 209 JI9
Sabres, *Fr.* 149 W6
Sabrina Coast, *Antarctica* 231 N2O
Sabtang, island, *Philippines* 193 AI4
Sabugal, *Port.* 146 F7
Sabuk, *S. Korea* 187 NII
Sabunçu, *Azerb.* 171 D23
Sabura, *Pak.* 179 Q6
Şabyā, *Saudi Arabia* 174 P8
Sabzak, Kōtal-e, *Afghan.* 178 M3
Sabzawar *see* Shīndand, *Afghan.* 179 N2
Sabzevār, *Iran* 175 CI5
Sacaca, *Bol.* 132 K7
Sacajawea Peak, *Oreg., U.S.* 110 F9
Sac City, *Iowa, U.S.* 107 NIO
Sacedón, *Sp.* 146 FI2
Săcel, *Rom.* 155 BI4
Săcele, *Rom.* 155 EI5
Sacheon, *S. Korea* 187 TIO
Sacheon, *S. Korea* 187 TIO
Sachigo, river, *Ont., Can.* 85 LI5
Sachs Harbour, *N.W.T., Can.* 84 DII
Sacile, *It.* 152 D8
Sackets Harbor, *N.Y., U.S.* 96 G8
Saco, *Me., U.S.* 97 HI5
Saco, *Mont., U.S.* 108 BII
Sacramento, *Calif., U.S.* 111 R4
Sacramento, river, *Calif., U.S.* 111 N4
Sacramento Mountains, *N. Mex., U.S.* 109 UI3
Sacramento Valley, *U.S.* 86 F3
Sacristy and Treasury, *Vatican City* 163 QI6
Sada, *Mayotte, Fr.* 209 PI7
Şa'dah, *Yemen* 174 P9
Saddle Hill, peak, *St. Kitts and Nevis* 123 CI4
Saddle Mountain, *Idaho, U.S.* 108 G6

Saddle Mountains, *Wash., U.S.* 110 D6
Saddle Peak, *India* 181 PI4
Saddle Road, *Hawai'i, U.S.* 115 LI9
Şadḥ, *Oman* 175 PI5
Sadiqabad, *Pak.* 179 T8
Sadiya, *India* 180 FI5
Sadko Valley, *Arctic Oc.* 246 EIO
Sadlers, *St. Kitts and Nevis* 123 AI7
Sado, island, *Japan* 188 MII
Sado, river, *Port.* 146 J5
Sadon, *Myanmar* 190 E7
Sadovoye, *Russ.* 159 QI3
Saebyŏl, *N. Korea* 186 AI3
Sae Islands, *P.N.G.* 217 BI9
Saelices, *Sp.* 146 GI2
Saengildo, island, *S. Korea* 187 U8
Şafājah, region, *Saudi Arabia* 174 H6
Safata Bay, *Samoa* 222 L3
Safed Khirs, range, *Afghan.* 178 J9
Säffle, *Sw.* 142 KI2
Safford, *Ariz., U.S.* 109 U9
Safi, *Mor.* 200 B7
Şāfītā, *Syr.* 172 G7
Safonovo, *Russ.* 158 K7
Safotu, *Samoa* 222 K2
Safranbolu, *Turk.* 170 C8
Saga, *Japan* 189 R4
Sagae, *Japan* 188 LI2
Sagaing, *Myanmar* 190 G6
Sagami Nada, *Japan* 189 QII
Sagar, *India* 180 H6
Sagar, *India* 181 P4
Sagarejo, *Rep. of Georgia* 171 CI9
Sagarmāthā *see* Everest, Mount, *China, Nep.* 182 L4
Sage, Mount, *British Virgin Is., U.K.* 122 R6
Sage Creek, *Mont., U.S.* 108 A8
Sag Harbor, *N.Y., U.S.* 97 NI3
Saghyz, *Kaz.* 176 E7
Saghyz, river, *Kaz.* 176 E7
Saginaw, *Mich., U.S.* 100 LII
Saginaw Bay, *Mich., U.S.* 100 KI2
Sagittarius Seachannel, *Pac. Oc.* 243 DI4
Sagone, *Fr.* 152 K3
Sagone, Golfe de, *Fr.* 152 K3
Sagra, peak, *Sp.* 146 KI2
Sagres, Ponta de, *Port.* 146 L4
Sagu, *Myanmar* 190 H5
Saguache, *Colo., U.S.* 109 NI2
Sagua de Tánamo, *Cuba* 119 KI3
Sagua la Grande, *Cuba* 118 G8
Saguaro National Park, *Ariz., U.S.* 109 V8
Saguenay, *Que., Can.* 85 N2O
Sa'gya (Sajia), *China* 182 L4
Şaḥāb, *Jordan* 172 M7
Sahagún, *Sp.* 146 C9
Şaḩam, *Oman* 175 KI5
Sahamalaza, Baie de, *Madagascar* 207 EI7
Sahara, *Japan* 188 HI2
Sahara, desert, *Af.* 198 F3
Saharan Atlas, range, *Af.* 198 C4
Saharan Fan, *Atl. Oc.* 240 LIO
Saharanpur, *India* 180 E6
Saharan Seamounts, *Atl. Oc.* 240 L9
Saharsa, *India* 180 GIO
Şahbuz, *Arm.* 171 FI9
Sahel, plain, *Af.* 198 G6
Sahiwal, *Pak.* 179 PIO
Sahiwal, *Pak.* 179 RII
Şahtaxtı, *Arm.* 171 FI9
Sahuaripa, *Mex.* 116 D8
Sahul Banks, *Ind. Oc.* 225 JI9
Sahul Shelf, *Ind. Oc.* 225 JI9
Sahyŏn, *N. Korea* 186 K7
Sai, *Japan* 188 HI2
Sai Buri, *Thai.* 191 S9
Saïda, *Alg.* 200 BIO
Saïda (Sidon), *Leb.* 172 J6
Sa'īdābād *see* Sīrjān, *Iran* 175 GI5
Saidapet, *India* 181 Q7
Saidor, *P.N.G.* 217 CI9
Saidu, *Pak.* 178 MIO
Saignes, *Fr.* 149 VIO

Saigon *see* Thành Phô'Hô Chí Minh (Ho Chi Minh City), *Vietnam* 191 PI3
Saiki, *Japan* 189 R6
Sailolof, *Indonesia* 193 JI7
Saimaa, lake, *Fin.* 143 HI7
Saimbeyli, *Turk.* 170 GII
Sain, Chenal, *Wallis and Futuna, Fr.* 222 EI2
Saindak, *Pak.* 179 SI
Saint-Mathieu, Point, *Eur.* 140 G3
Saint-Agrève, *Fr.* 149 VI2
Saint-Aignan, *Fr.* 149 S9
Saint Albans, *Eng., U.K.* 145 VI4
Saint Albans, *Vt., U.S.* 96 FI2
Saint Albans, *W. Va., U.S.* 98 D8
Saint-Amand, *Fr.* 148 MII
Saint-Amand-Montrond, *Fr.* 149 SIO
Saint-Amans-Soult, *Fr.* 149 XIO
Saint-Ambroix, *Fr.* 149 WI2
Saint-André, *Réunion, Fr.* 209 GI6
Saint André, Cap, *Af.* 198 MII
Saint Andrew Bay, *Fla., U.S.* 99 R3
Saint Andrews, *N.Z.* 217 PI7
Saint Andrews, *Scot., U.K.* 144 LII
Saint Andrews Bay, *Grenada* 123 K23
Saint Annabaai, *Curaçao, Neth.* 123 QI4
Saint Ann's Bay, *Jam.* 122 H9
Saint Anthony, *Idaho, U.S.* 108 G7
Saint Anthony, *Nfld. & Lab., Can.* 85 L23
Saint Anthony's Peak, *St. Kitts and Nevis* 123 BI8
Saint-Aubin-d'Aubigné, *Fr.* 149 Q5
Saint-Aubin-du-Cormier, *Fr.* 149 Q6
Saint-Augustin, *Que., Can.* 85 L22
Saint Augustin Bay, *Af.* 198 PIO
Saint Augustine, *Fla., U.S.* 99 R9
Saint Austell, *Eng., U.K.* 145 X8
Saint Austell Bay, *Eng., U.K.* 145 X8
Saint-Avold, *Fr.* 149 PI4
Saint-Barthélemy, island, *Lesser Antil.* 121 BI5
Saint Barts *see* Saint-Barthélemy, island, *Lesser Antil.* 121 BI5
Saint Bees Head, *Eng., U.K.* 145 QIO
Saint-Benoît, *Réunion, Fr.* 209 GI7
Saint-Brieuc, *Fr.* 149 P4
Saint-Cannat, *Fr.* 149 XI3
Saint Catherine, Mount, *Grenada* 123 K23
Saint Catherines Island, *Ga., U.S.* 99 P9
Saint-Cernin, *Fr.* 149 VIO
Saint Charles, *Idaho, U.S.* 108 J8
Saint Charles, *Mich., U.S.* 100 LII
Saint Charles, *Minn., U.S.* 106 LI3
Saint Charles, *Mo., U.S.* 107 SI5
Saint Charles' Church, *Monaco* 163 C22
Saint-Chély-d'Apcher, *Fr.* 149 VII
Saint Christoffelberg, peak, *Curaçao, Neth.* 123 NI3
Saint Christopher *see* Saint Kitts, island, *St. Kitts and Nevis* 123 AI7
Saint Clair, *Mich., U.S.* 100 LI3
Saint Clair, *Mo., U.S.* 107 TI4
Saint Clair, river, *Can., U.S.* 100 MI3
Saint Clair, Lake, *Mich., U.S.* 100 MI3
Saint Clair Shores, *Mich., U.S.* 100 MI3
Saint-Claude, *Fr.* 149 TI4
Saint-Claude, *Guadeloupe, Fr.* 123 GI4
Saint Clears, *Wales, U.K.* 145 V9
Saint Cloud, *Fla., U.S.* 99 T9
Saint Cloud, *Minn., U.S.* 106 JIO
Saint Combs, *Scot., U.K.* 144 JII
Saint Croix, island, *Virgin Is., U.S.* 121 BI3
Saint Croix, river, *Can., U.S.* 97 DI9
Saint Croix, river, *Minn., Wis., U.S.* 100 HI
Saint Croix Falls, *Wis., U.S.* 100 G2
Saint Croix Island International Historic Site, *Can., U.S.* 97 EI9

Saint Croix National Scenic Riverway, *Wis., U.S.* 100 GI
Saint David Islands *see* Mapia, Kepulauan, *Indonesia* 193 JI9
Saint David's, *Grenada* 123 L23
Saint David's Head, *Wales, U.K.* 145 U8
Saint David's Island, *Bermuda* 122 B3
Saint David's Lighthouse, site, *Bermuda* 122 B3
Saint David's Point, *Grenada* 123 L23
Saint-Denis, *Fr.* 149 PIO
Saint-Denis, *Fr.* 149 T6
Saint-Denis, *Réunion, Fr.* 209 FI6
Saint-Dié, *Fr.* 149 QI5
Saint-Dizier, *Fr.* 149 PI2
Sainte-Anne, *Guadeloupe, Fr.* 123 FI5
Sainte-Anne, *Martinique, Fr.* 123 G23
Ste. Dévôte's Church, *Monaco* 163 D2I
Saint Edward, *Nebr., U.S.* 107 P7
Sainte Genevieve, *Mo., U.S.* 107 TI5
Saint Elias, Mount, *Can., U.S.* 113 KI9
Saint-Éloy-les-Mines, *Fr.* 149 TIO
Sainte-Luce, *Martinique, Fr.* 123 G23
Sainte-Marguerite, *Guadeloupe, Fr.* 123 EI5
Sainte-Marie, *Guadeloupe, Fr.* 123 FI5
Sainte-Marie, *Martinique, Fr.* 123 E23
Sainte-Marie, *Réunion, Fr.* 209 FI6
Sainte Marie, Cap, *Madagascar* 207 JI6
Sainte-Maxime, *Fr.* 149 XI5
Sainte-Rose, *Guadeloupe, Fr.* 123 EI4
Sainte-Rose, *Réunion, Fr.* 209 GI7
Saintes, *Fr.* 149 U6
Sainte-Suzanna, *Réunion, Fr.* 209 FI6
Sainte-Suzanne, *Fr.* 149 Q7
Saint-Étienne, *Fr.* 149 UI2
Saint-Étienne-du-Rouvray, *Fr.* 149 N8
Saint Eustatius, island, *Lesser Antil.* 121 BI5
Saint-Fargeau, *Fr.* 149 RIO
Saint Finan's Bay, *Ire.* 145 U2
Saint-Firmin, *Fr.* 149 VI4
Saint-Florent, Golfe de, *It.* 152 J4
Saint-Florentin, *Fr.* 149 QII
Saint-Flour, *Fr.* 149 VII
Saint Francis, *Kans., U.S.* 107 R3
Saint Francis, *Me., U.S.* 97 LI4
Saint Francis, *S. Dak., U.S.* 106 M4
Saint Francis, river, *Ark., Mo., U.S.* 102 EII
Saint Francis Bay, *Af.* 198 Q8
Saint-François, *Guadeloupe, Fr.* 123 EI6
Saint Gallen, *Switz.* 152 A5
Saint George, *Bermuda* 122 B3
Saint George, *Qnsld., Austral.* 215 VI4
Saint George, *S.C., U.S.* 98 L9
Saint George, *Utah, U.S.* 109 Q5
Saint George, Cape, *Fla., U.S.* 99 R4
Saint George, Cape, *P.N.G.* 217 C22
Saint George, Point, *Calif., U.S.* 110 LI
Saint George Basin, *Austral.* 214 C5
Saint George Island, *Alas., U.S.* 112 L9
Saint George Island, *Fla., U.S.* 99 S4
Saint George's, *Grenada* 123 L22
St. George's Bay, *Malta* 163 K23
Saint George's Channel, *India* 181 TI5
Saint George's Channel, *Ire., U.K.* 145 U7
Saint George's Channel, *P.N.G.* 217 C2I
Saint George's Harbour, *Grenada* 123 L22
Saint George's Island, *Bermuda* 122 B3
Saint-Germain, *Fr.* 149 P9
Saint-Germain-des-Vaux, *Fr.* 149 N5
Saint-Gildas, Pointe de, *Fr.* 149 S5
Saint Giles Islands, *Trinidad and Tobago* 123 MI9
Saint-Gilles-les-Bains, *Réunion, Fr.* 209 GI5

Saint-Girons, *Fr.* **149** Y8
Saint-Guénolé, *Fr.* **149** Q2
Saint Helena, *Calif., U.S.* **III** R3
Saint Helena, island, *Af.* **198** M3
Saint Helena Bay, *S. Af.* **206** L7
Saint Helena Fracture Zone, *Atl. Oc.* **241** RIO
Saint Helena Sound, *S.C., U.S.* **99** NIO
Saint Helens, *Eng., U.K.* **145** SII
Saint Helens, *Oreg., U.S.* **110** E3
Saint Helens, Mount, *Wash., U.S.* **110** E4
Saint Helier, *Channel Is., U.K.* **145** ZI2
Saint-Hillaire-du-Harcouët, *Fr.* **149** P6
Saint-Hippolyte, *Fr.* **149** RI4
St. Hubert, *Belg.* **162** H7
Saint Ignace, *Mich., U.S.* **100** GIO
Saint Ignatius, *Mont., U.S.* **108** C6
Saint Ives Bay, *Eng., U.K.* **145** Y8
Saint James, *Cayman Is.* **122** J2
Saint James, *Minn., U.S.* **106** LIO
Saint James, *Mo., U.S.* **107** TI3
Saint-Jean, Lac, *Que., Can.* **85** N2O
Saint-Jean-d'Angély, *Fr.* **149** U6
Saint-Jean-de-Losne, *Fr.* **149** SI3
Saint-Jean-de-Luz, *Fr.* **149** X5
Saint-Jean-de-Monts, *Fr.* **149** S5
Saint-Jean-Pied-de-Port, *Fr.* **149** Y6
Saint Joe, river, *Idaho, U.S.* **108** C4
Saint John, *Kans., U.S.* **107** U6
Saint John, *N. Dak., U.S.* **106** D5
Saint John, *N.B., Can.* **85** P2I
Saint John, *Wash., U.S.* **110** D9
Saint John, island, *Virgin Is., U.S.* **122** NII
Saint John, river, *Can., U.S.* **97** BI6
Saint John's, *Antigua and Barbuda* **123** B2I
Saint John's, *Montserrat* **123** B24
Saint John's, *Nfld. & Lab., Can.* **85** M24
Saint Johns, *Ariz., U.S.* **109** T9
Saint Johns, *Mich., U.S.* **100** LII
Saint Johns, river, *Fla., U.S.* **99** S8
Saint Johnsbury, *Vt., U.S.* **97** FI3
Saint John's Church, site, *Barbados* **123** K2O
Saint John's Harbour, *Antigua and Barbuda* **123** B2O
Saint Jona Island *see* Iony, Ostrov, *Russ.* **161** H2O
Saint Jorisbaai, *Curaçao, Neth.* **123** QI5
Saint Joseph, *Dominica* **123** FI9
Saint Joseph, *La., U.S.* **102** M9
Saint Joseph, *Mich., U.S.* **101** N8
Saint Joseph, *Mo., U.S.* **107** RIO
Saint Joseph, *Trinidad and Tobago* **123** Q24
Saint Joseph, river, *Ind., Ohio, U.S.* **101** PIO
Saint-Joseph, *Martinique, Fr.* **123** F23
Saint-Joseph, *New Caledonia, Fr.* **222** C8
Saint-Joseph, *Réunion, Fr.* **209** JI6
Saint Joseph Bay, *Fla., U.S.* **99** R4
Saint Joseph's Church, *Fr.* **163** B22
St. Julian's, *Malta* **163** K23
Saint-Junien, *Fr.* **149** U8
Saint Kilda, island, *Scot., U.K.* **144** J5
Saint Kitts, island, *St. Kitts and Nevis* **123** AI8
Saint Kitts and Nevis, *N. Amer.* **121** CI6
Saint-Laurent du Maroni, *Fr. Guiana* **131** EI7
Saint Lawrence, *Barbados* **123** LI9
Saint Lawrence, *Tex., U.S.* **105** N5
Saint Lawrence, river, *N. Amer.* **82** H9
Saint Lawrence, Gulf of, *Que., Can.* **85** N24
Saint Lawrence Island, *Alas., U.S.* **112** FIO
Saint Lawrence Islands National Park, *N.Y., U.S.* **96** F9
Saint Lawrence River, *N. Amer.* **85** N2O

Saint-Leu, *Réunion, Fr.* **209** HI5
Saint-Lô, *Fr.* **149** P6
Saint Louis, *Mich., U.S.* **100** LII
Saint Louis, *Mo., U.S.* **107** TI5
Saint Louis, river, *Minn., U.S.* **106** GI2
Saint-Louis, *Fr.* **149** RI5
Saint-Louis, *Guadeloupe, Fr.* **123** GI6
Saint-Louis, *New Caledonia, Fr.* **222** D8
Saint-Louis, *Réunion, Fr.* **209** HI5
Saint-Louis, *Senegal* **200** G4
Saint-Louis du Nord, *Haiti* **119** LI6
Saint-Loup, *Fr.* **149** QI4
Saint Lucia, *N. Amer.* **121** FI7
Saint Lucia, Cape, *Af.* **198** P9
Saint Lucia, Lake, *S. Af.* **206** KI2
Saint Lucia Channel, *N. Amer.* **121** FI7
Saint-Lys, *Fr.* **149** X8
Saint Maarten, island, *Lesser Antil.* **123** BI5
Saint Magnus Bay, *Scot., U.K.* **144** DII
Saint-Maixent, *Fr.* **149** T7
Saint-Malo, *Fr.* **149** P5
Saint-Malo, Golfe de, *Fr.* **149** P5
Saint-Marc, *Haiti* **119** LI6
Saint-Marc, Canal de, *Haiti* **119** MI6
Saint-Marcel, Mont, *Fr. Guiana* **131** GI8
Saint Marie, Kaap, *Curaçao, Neth.* **123** PI4
Saint Maries, *Idaho, U.S.* **108** C4
Saint Mark Bay, *Grenada* **123** J23
Saint Marks, *Fla., U.S.* **99** R5
Saint-Martin, *Fr.* **149** XII
Saint-Martin, island, *Lesser Antil.* **123** BI5
Saint-Martin, Cap, *Martinique, Fr.* **123** E22
Saint Martin's, island, *Eng., U.K.* **145** Y7
St. Martin's Gardens, *Monaco* **163** F2I
Saint Martinville, *La., U.S.* **102** P9
Saint Mary's, island, *Eng., U.K.* **145** Y7
Saint Marys, *Ga., U.S.* **98** Q8
Saint Marys, *Kans., U.S.* **107** S9
Saint Marys, *Ohio, U.S.* **101** QII
Saint Marys, *Pa., U.S.* **96** M5
Saint Marys, *Tas., Austral.* **215** Y8
Saint Marys, *Trinidad and Tobago* **123** Q22
Saint Marys, *W. Va., U.S.* **98** C8
Saint Marys, river, *Fla., Ga., U.S.* **99** Q8
Saint Mary's Bay, *Nfld. & Lab., Can.* **85** M24
Saint Mary's City, *Md., U.S.* **98** DI4
Saint Mary's Loch, *Scot., U.K.* **145** NIO
Saint-Mathieu, *Fr.* **149** U8
Saint-Mathieu, Pointe de, *Fr.* **149** Q2
Saint Matthew Island, *Alas., U.S.* **112** H9
Saint Matthews, *S.C., U.S.* **98** L9
Saint-Maurice, river, *Que., Can.* **85** PI9
Saint-Méen-le-Grand, *Fr.* **149** Q5
Saint Michael, *Alas., U.S.* **113** GI3
St. Michael's Caves, *Gibraltar, U.K.* **163** Q23
Saint Michielsbaai, *Curaçao, Neth.* **123** QI4
Saint-Nazaire, *Fr.* **149** R5
Saint-Omer, *Fr.* **148** LIO
Saint-Palais, *Fr.* **149** Y6
Saint Patrick's, *Montserrat* **123** C24
Saint Paul, *Minn., U.S.* **106** JI2
Saint Paul, *Nebr., U.S.* **107** P6
Saint-Paul, *Réunion, Fr.* **209** GI5
Saint Paul Fracture Zone, *Atl. Oc.* **241** P9
Saint-Paulien, *Fr.* **149** VII
Saint Paul Island, *Alas., U.S.* **112** L9
Saint Paul's, *St. Kitts and Nevis* **123** AI7
Saint Pauls, *N.C., U.S.* **98** JII
St. Paul's Bay, *Malta* **163** J2I
St. Paul's Bay, *Malta* **163** J22

St. Paul's Islands, *Malta* **163** J22
Saint Paul's Point, *Pitcairn I., U.K.* **223** Q24
Saint-Péray, *Fr.* **149** VI2
Saint Peter, *Minn., U.S.* **106** KII
Saint Peter Fracture Zone, *Atl. Oc.* **241** P8
Saint Peter Port, *Channel Is., U.K.* **145** ZII
St. Peter's Basilica, *Vatican City* **163** QI6
Saint Petersburg, *Fla., U.S.* **99** U7
Saint Petersburg *see* Sankt-Peterburg, *Russ.* **158** F6
St. Peter's Square, *Vatican City* **163** QI7
Saint-Philippe, *Réunion, Fr.* **209** HI7
Saint Pierre, *Mauritius* **209** G2O
Saint Pierre, *Trinidad and Tobago* **123** P22
Saint-Pierre, *Martinique, Fr.* **123** E22
Saint-Pierre, *Réunion, Fr.* **209** HI6
Saint-Pierre & Miquelon, *N. Amer.* **85** N23
Saint Pierre Bank, *Ind. Oc.* **224** PII
Saint-Pierre-de-Chignac, *Fr.* **149** V8
Saint-Pierre-le-Moûtier, *Fr.* **149** SII
St. Pölten, *Aust.* **150** KI2
Saint-Pons, *Fr.* **149** XIO
Saint-Quay-Portrieux, *Fr.* **149** P4
Saint-Quentin, *Fr.* **148** MII
Saint-QuentinPointe de, *Fr.* **148** M9
Saint-Raphaël, *Fr.* **149** XI5
Saint Rogatien Bank, *Hawai'i, U.S.* **114** M6
St. Roman, *Monaco* **163** A23
Saint-Savin, *Fr.* **149** T8
Saint-Sernin, *Fr.* **149** XIO
Saint-Servan, *Fr.* **149** P5
Saint-Sever, *Fr.* **149** X6
Saint Simons Island, *Ga., U.S.* **99** P9
Saint Stanislas Bay, *Kiribati* **221** B22
Saint Stephen, *S.C., U.S.* **98** LIO
Saint Elias Mountains, *Can., U.S.* **113** K2O
Saint Thomas, *N. Dak., U.S.* **106** E7
Saint Thomas, island, *Virgin Is., U.S.* **122** N8
Saint Thomas Bay, *British Virgin Is., U.K.* **122** R8
Saint Thomas Harbor, *Virgin Is., U.S.* **122** N9
Saint Truiden, *Belg.* **148** LI2
Saint Tudwal's Islands, *Wales, U.K.* **145** T9
St. Veit, *Aust.* **150** MII
Saint Vincent, *Minn., U.S.* **106** D8
Saint Vincent, island, *St. Vincent and the Grenadines* **121** GI7
Saint Vincent, Cape, *Eur.* **140** KI
Saint Vincent, Gulf, *Austral.* **214** KIO
Saint Vincent and the Grenadines, *N. Amer.* **121** GI7
Saint Vincent Fracture Zone, *Ind. Oc.* **249** EI7
Saint Vincent Island, *Fla., U.S.* **99** R4
Saint Vincent Passage, *N. Amer.* **121** FI7
Saint Vith, *Belg.* **148** MI3
Saint-Vivien, *Fr.* **149** U6
St. Wendel, *Ger.* **150** H5
Saint Willebrordus, *Curaçao, Neth.* **123** PI4
Saipan, island, *Asia* **168** HI6
Saipan, island, *N. Mariana Is., U.S.* **220** C2
Saipan Channel, *N. Mariana Is., U.S.* **220** C4
Saipan Harbor, *N. Mariana Is., U.S.* **220** B4
Sairang, *India* **180** HI4
Saito, *Japan* **189** S5
Saivomuotka, *Sw.* **143** DI4
Sajama, Nevado, *Bol.* **132** K6
Sajia *see* Sa'gya, *China* **182** L4
Sajyang Pass, *China, Myanmar* **182** M8
Sakaiminato, *Japan* **189** P7
Sakākah, *Saudi Arabia* **174** F7
Saka Kalat, *Pak.* **179** U4

Sakakawea, Lake, *N. Dak., U.S.* **106** F3
Sakami, *Que., Can.* **85** MI8
Sakami, river, *Que., Can.* **85** MI8
Sakami, Lac, *Que., Can.* **85** MI8
Sakania, *Dem. Rep. of the Congo* **202** PII
Sakarya, *Turk.* **170** D6
Sakarya, river, *Turk.* **170** E6
Sakata, *Japan* **188** LI2
Sakçagöze, *Turk.* **170** HI2
Sakchu, *N. Korea* **186** F5
Sakhalin, island, *Asia* **168** DI3
Sakhalin, Ostrov, *Russ.* **161** J2I
Sākhar, *Afghan.* **179** N5
Sakishima Shotō, *Japan* **218** CI
Sakon Nakhon, *Thai.* **190** KII
Sakrand, *Pak.* **179** V7
Saky, *Ukr.* **159** S7
Sal, island, *Cabo Verde* **209** BI7
Sal, Cay, *Bahamas* **118** F8
Sal, Cayo de, *Venez.* **120** HII
Sala, *Sw.* **143** KI3
Sala Consilina, *It.* **153** NI2
Saladas, *Arg.* **134** GI3
Saladillo, *Arg.* **134** HII
Salado, river, *Arg.* **134** HII
Salado, river, *Arg.* **134** MI2
Salado, river, *Arg.* **134** M9
Salaga, *Ghana* **204** DIO
Sala'ilua, *Samoa* **222** KI
Salal, *Chad* **201** HI5
Salala, *Sudan* **203** CI4
Salālah, *Oman* **175** PI4
Salamanca, *Chile* **134** K6
Salamanca, *Mex.* **116** HII
Salamanca, *N.Y., U.S.* **96** K5
Salamanca, *Sp.* **146** E8
Salamat, Bahr, *Chad* **201** KI5
Salamína, *Gr.* **156** JI2
Salamis, battle, *Gr.* **156** JI2
Salamis, ruin, *Cyprus* **162** NIO
Salamīyah, *Syr.* **172** G8
Sālang, Kōtal-e, *Afghan.* **178** L7
Salani, *Samoa* **222** L3
Salapaly Bay, *Af.* **198** PIO
Salas, *Sp.* **146** B8
Salas de los Infantes, *Sp.* **146** DII
Salatiga, *Indonesia* **192** M9
Salavan, *Laos* **190** LI2
Salavat, *Russ.* **160** J7
Salaverry, *Peru* **132** G2
Salawati, island, *Indonesia* **193** JI7
Sala y Gómez, Isla, *Pac. Oc.* **219** L2O
Sala y Gómez Ridge, *Pac. Oc.* **243** M2O
Salazie, *Réunion, Fr.* **209** GI6
Salbris, *Fr.* **149** R9
Salda Gölü, *Turk.* **170** H5
Saldaña, *Sp.* **146** CIO
Saldanha, *S. Af.* **206** M7
Sale, *Vic., Austral.* **215** ZI3
Salebabu, island, *Indonesia* **193** GI6
Salée, strait, *Guadeloupe, Fr.* **123** EI5
Saleimoa, *Samoa* **222** L3
Salekhard, *Russ.* **160** FII
Salelologa, *Samoa* **222** K2
Salem, *Ark., U.S.* **102** E9
Salem, *Ill., U.S.* **101** T6
Salem, *Ind., U.S.* **101** T9
Salem, *India* **181** Q6
Salem, *Mass., U.S.* **97** KI5
Salem, *Mo., U.S.* **107** UI4
Salem, *Montserrat* **123** B23
Salem, *N.H., U.S.* **97** JI4
Salem, *Ohio, U.S.* **101** PI5
Salem, *Oreg., U.S.* **110** G3
Salem, *S. Dak., U.S.* **106** L7
Salem, *Va., U.S.* **98** FIO
Salem, *W. Va., U.S.* **98** C9
Salemi, *It.* **153** S9
Salerno, *It.* **152** MII
Salerno, Golfo di, *It.* **153** NII
Salez, *Switz.* **162** M2
Salford, *Eng., U.K.* **145** SII
Salgótarján, *Hung.* **151** KI5
Salgueiro, *Braz.* **133** FI6
Salibea, *Trinidad and Tobago* **123** P23
Salibia, *Dominica* **123** E2O
Salida, *Colo., U.S.* **109** NI2

Salies-du-Salat, *Fr.* **149** Y8
Şalīf, *Yemen* **174** Q8
Salihli, *Turk.* **170** F4
Salihorsk, *Belarus* **158** L4
Salima, *Malawi* **207** EI3
Salina, *Kans., U.S.* **107** T7
Salina, *Utah, U.S.* **109** N7
Salina, Isola, *It.* **153** RII
Salinas, *Calif., U.S.* **III** T4
Salinas, *Ecua.* **130** KI
Salinas, *P.R., U.S.* **122** P4
Salinas, river, *Calif., U.S.* **III** U5
Salinas, Bahía, *P.R., U.S.* **122** PI
Salinas Bay, *S. Amer.* **128** F2
Salinas Peak, *N. Mex., U.S.* **109** UI2
Salinas Pueblo Missions National Monument Gran Quivira, *N. Mex., U.S.* **109** TI2
Saline, river, *U.S.* **87** KI4
Saline Bay, *Trinidad and Tobago* **123** P24
Saline di Volterra, *It.* **152** H6
Salines, Cap de ses, *Sp.* **147** HI8
Salines, Étang des, *Martinique, Fr.* **123** G23
Salines, Point, *Grenada* **123** L22
Salinópolis, *Braz.* **133** CI4
Salins, *Fr.* **149** SI4
Salisbury, *Dominica* **123** FI9
Salisbury, *Eng., U.K.* **145** WI2
Salisbury, *Guam, U.S.* **220** BI2
Salisbury, *Md., U.S.* **98** DI5
Salisbury, *Mo., U.S.* **107** SI2
Salisbury, *N.C., U.S.* **98** H9
Salisbury, Ostrov, *Russ.* **160** CI2
Salisbury Downs, *N.S.W., Austral.* **215** WI2
Salisbury Island, *Nunavut, Can.* **85** HI7
Salisbury Plain, *Eng., U.K.* **145** WI2
Salish Mountains, *Mont., U.S.* **108** B5
Salish Sea, *Can., U.S.* **110** A3
Şalkhad, *Syr.* **172** L8
Sallent, *Sp.* **147** DI7
Sallfelden, *Aust.* **150** LIO
Sallisaw, *Okla., U.S.* **104** GI4
Salluit, *Que., Can.* **85** HI8
Salmās, *Iran* **174** BIO
Salmon, *Idaho, U.S.* **108** F6
Salmon, river, *Idaho, U.S.* **108** E5
Salmon Bank, *Hawai'i, U.S.* **114** K2
Salmon Peak, *Tex., U.S.* **105** R7
Salmon River Canyon, *Idaho, U.S.* **108** E5
Salmon River Mountains, *Idaho, U.S.* **108** F4
Salo, *Fin.* **143** JI5
Salò, *It.* **152** D6
Salobelyak, *Russ.* **158** HI4
Salome, *Ariz., U.S.* **109** T5
Salomon, Cap, *Martinique, Fr.* **123** F22
Salon, *Fr.* **149** XI3
Salonga, river, *Dem. Rep. of the Congo* **202** K9
Salonica *see* Thessaloníki, *Gr.* **156** CII
Salonta, *Rom.* **154** CII
Salou, Cap de, *Sp.* **147** EI6
Salpaus Ridge, *Eur.* **140** D9
Salpausselkä, range, *Fin.* **143** HI6
Salqīn, *Syr.* **172** E8
Sal Rei, *Cabo Verde* **209** CI7
Sal'sk, *Russ.* **159** RII
Salsomaggiore Terme, *It.* **152** F5
Salt, *Sp.* **147** DI8
Salt, river, *Ariz., U.S.* **109** U7
Salta, *Arg.* **134** F9
Saltash, *Eng., U.K.* **145** X9
Saltburn by the Sea, *Eng., U.K.* **145** PI3
Salt Cay, *Bahamas* **122** AI2
Salt Cay, *Turks & Caicos Is.* **119** JI8
Salt Cay, *Virgin Is., U.S.* **122** M7
Saltee Islands, *Ire.* **145** U6
Saltfjorden, bay, *Nor.* **142** EI2
Salt Fork Arkansas, river, *Kans., Okla., U.S.* **104** E9
Salt Fork Brazos, river, *Tex., U.S.* **104** K6

Salt Fork Red, river, Okla., Tex., U.S. 104 H6
Saltillo, Mex. 116 F11
Salt Lake City, Utah, U.S. 108 L7
Salto, Uru. 134 J13
Salton Sea, Calif., U.S. 111 Y11
Salt Range, Pak. 179 P10
Salt River, Jam. 122 K9
Salt River Bay, Virgin Is., U.S. 122 Q2
Salt River Range, Wyo., U.S. 108 H8
Saltville, Va., U.S. 98 F8
Saluafata Harbour, Samoa 222 L3
Saluda, S.C., U.S. 98 K8
Saluda, river, S.C., U.S. 98 K8
Salûm, Egypt 201 C17
Salûm, Gulf of, Af. 198 D8
Saluzzo, It. 152 F2
Salvación, Bahía, Chile 135 W6
Salvador (Bahia), Braz. 133 H17
Salvador, Lake, La., U.S. 102 Q11
Salwá, Saudi Arabia 174 J12
Salween (Nu, Thanlwin), river, Asia 168 H9
Salyan, Azerb. 171 E22
Salyersville, Ky., U.S. 103 C19
Salzbrunn, Namibia 206 H7
Salzburg, Aust. 150 L10
Salzgitter, Ger. 150 E8
Salzwedal, Ger. 150 D8
Šamac see Bosanski Šamac, Bosn. & Herzg. 154 E8
Samā'il, Oman 175 K16
Samaipata, Bol. 132 K8
Samalaeulu, Samoa 222 K2
Samâlût, Egypt 201 D18
Samaná, Dom. Rep. 119 L20
Samaná, Bahía de, Dom. Rep. 119 L19
Samaná, Cabo, Dom. Rep. 119 L20
Samana Cay, Bahamas 119 G15
Samandağ, Turk. 170 K11
Samani, Japan 188 H14
Samar, island, Philippines 193 D15
Samara, Russ. 158 K15
Samara, river, Eur. 140 E14
Samarai, P.N.G. 217 E21
Samaria Gorge, Gr. 157 Q13
Samarinda, Indonesia 192 J12
Samarqand, Uzb. 176 L12
Sāmarrā', Iraq 174 D9
Samar Sea, Philippines 193 D15
Samarskoe, Kaz. 177 D18
Samawah As Samāwah, Iraq 174 F10
Şamaxı, Azerb. 171 D22
Samba, India 180 C5
Sambalpur, India 180 K9
Sambava, Madagascar 207 E18
Sambir, Ukr. 159 N2
Samboja, Indonesia 192 J12
Sambong, N. Korea 186 A13
Samborombón, Bahía, Arg. 134 M13
Samburg, Russ. 160 G12
Samch'a-do, island, N. Korea 186 H4
Samcheok, S. Korea 187 N12
Samdari, India 180 G3
Same, Tanzania 203 L14
Samer, Fr. 148 L9
Samgi, N. Korea 186 F10
Samhae, N. Korea 186 C13
Samho, N. Korea 186 G10
Sami, Pak. 179 V3
Sámi, Gr. 156 H7
Samīm, Umm as, Oman, Saudi Arabia 175 L15
Samina, river, Aust., Liech. 162 N3
Saminatal, valley, Liech. 162 P3
Samjiyŏn, N. Korea 186 C10
Sam Lord's Castle, site, Barbados 123 K20
Samnak, N. Korea 186 F7
Samnangjin, S. Korea 187 S11
Samnye, S. Korea 187 R8
Samo, P.N.G. 217 C22
Samoa, Pac. Oc. 222 K1
Samoa Basin, Pac. Oc. 242 L12
Samoa Islands, Pac. Oc. 218 J10
Samokov, Bulg. 155 J13
Sámos, Gr. 157 J18
Sámos, island, Gr. 157 J17
Samothrace see Samothráki, Gr. 157 D15
Samothráki, Gr. 157 D15
Samothráki (Samothrace), Gr. 157 D15
Sampacho, Arg. 134 K10
Sampit, Indonesia 192 K10
Sam'po, N. Korea 186 E13
Samp'o, N. Korea 186 E8
Sampwe, Dem. Rep. of the Congo 202 N11
Sâmraông, Cambodia 190 M10
Sam Rayburn Reservoir, Tex., U.S. 105 N15
Samsan, N. Korea 186 L5
Samsŏ, N. Korea 186 E9
Samsŏk, N. Korea 186 J6
Sầm Sơn, Vietnam 190 J12
Samson, Ala., U.S. 103 N16
Samsu, N. Korea 186 D10
Samsun, Turk. 170 C11
Samu, Indonesia 192 K11
Samui, island, Asia 168 L10
Samui, Ko, Thai. 191 Q8
Samundri, Pak. 179 Q11
Samūr, Afghan. 179 Q2
Samur, river, Russ. 159 V15
Samut Prakhan, Thai. 190 M9
Samut Songkhram, Thai. 191 N8
Samyang, N. Korea 186 J7
San, Japan 189 W3
San, Mali 200 H8
San, river, Pol. 151 G17
San, river, Vietnam 190 M13
Şan'ā'(Sanaa), Yemen 174 Q9
Sana, river, Bosn. & Herzg. 154 E6
Sanaa see Şan'ā', Yemen 174 Q9
San Adrián, Cabo, Sp. 146 B5
SANAE IV, station, Antarctica 230 B12
Sanae Canyon, Atl. Oc. 241 Y12
Şanafīr, island, Egypt 173 U4
Sanaga, river, Af. 198 J5
San Agustín, Col. 130 H4
San Agustin, Cape, Philippines 193 F15
Sanak Islands, Alas., U.S. 112 P11
Sanām, Saudi Arabia 174 K9
San Ambrosio Island, S. Amer. 128 K2
Sanana, island, Indonesia 193 K15
Sanandaj, Iran 174 C11
San Andés Tuxtla, Mex. 117 J13
San Andreas, Calif., U.S. 111 R5
San Andrés, Isla de, Col. 117 L20
San Andrés del Rabanedo, Sp. 146 C9
San Andres Mountains, N. Mex., U.S. 109 U12
San Andros, Bahamas 118 E11
San Angelo, Tex., U.S. 105 N7
San Antonio, Chile 134 L6
San Antonio, N. Mariana Is., U.S. 220 C4
San Antonio, N. Mex., U.S. 109 T12
San Antonio, Tex., U.S. 105 R9
San Antonio, river, Tex., U.S. 105 S11
San Antonio, Cabo, Arg. 134 M13
San Antonio, Cabo de, Cuba 118 H3
San Antonio, Mount, Calif., U.S. 111 X9
San Antonio, Punta, Mex. 116 C5
San Antonio Bay, Tex., U.S. 105 T12
San Antonio de los Cobres, Arg. 134 E9
San Antonio de Ureca, Eq. Guinea 208 N7
San Antonio Missions National Historical Park, Tex., U.S. 105 R9
San Antonio Mountain, peak, Tex., U.S. 105 V4
San Antonio Oeste, Arg. 135 Q9
Sanat, island, F.S.M. 221 C16
San Augustine, Tex., U.S. 105 N15
Sanāw, Yemen 175 N13
Sanawad, India 180 J5
San Benedetto del Tronto, It. 152 J10
San Benedicto, Isla, Mex. 116 H6
San Benito, Tex., U.S. 105 W11
San Bernardino, Calif., U.S. 111 X9
San Bernardino Strait, Philippines 193 D15
San Bernardo, Chile 134 L7
San Blas, Mex. 116 E8
San Blas, Archipiélago de, Pan. 117 N22
San Blas, Cape, Fla., U.S. 99 R4
San Blas, Punta, Pan. 117 N21
San Borja, Bol. 132 J7
San Candido, It. 152 B8
San Carlos, Arg. 134 F9
San Carlos, Ariz., U.S. 109 U8
San Carlos, Philippines 193 E14
San Carlos, Venez. 130 C7
San Carlos, Gran Caldera Volcánica de, Eq. Guinea 208 M6
San Carlos de Bariloche, Arg. 135 Q7
San Carlos de Bolívar, Arg. 134 M11
San Carlos de Río Negro, Venez. 130 G9
San Carlos Reservoir, Ariz., U.S. 109 U8
Sancheong, S. Korea 187 S10
Sánchez, Dom. Rep. 119 L19
Sanchor, India 180 H3
Sanchung, Taiwan, China 185 U12
Sanchursk, Russ. 158 H13
San Clemente, Calif., U.S. 111 Y9
San Clemente, Sp. 146 H12
San Clemente, island, Calif., U.S. 111 Z8
San Cristóbal, Isla, Galápagos Is., Ecua. 219 G22
San Cristóbal, Arg. 134 J11
San Cristóbal, Cuba 118 G5
San Cristóbal, Dom. Rep. 119 M19
San Cristóbal, Venez. 130 D6
San Cristobal, island, Solomon Is. 221 Q20
San Cristóbal (Chatham), Isla, Ecua. 130 Q11
San Cristóbal de Las Casas, Mex. 117 K15
San Cristoforo, Monte, San Marino 163 L16
Sancti Spíritus, Cuba 118 H9
Sand, Nor. 142 K10
Sanda Island, Scot., U.K. 145 N8
Sandakan, Malaysia 192 G12
Sandal, Baie de, New Caledonia, Fr. 222 C9
San Daniele del Friuli, It. 152 C9
Sanday, island, Scot., U.K. 144 F11
Sand Bluff, Cayman Is. 122 J4
Sand Cay, India 181 Q2
Sanders, Ariz., U.S. 109 S9
Sanderson, Tex., U.S. 105 Q4
Sandersville, Ga., U.S. 98 M7
Sandes, Nor. 142 L10
Sand Hills, Nebr., U.S. 107 N3
Sandia Crest, N. Mex., U.S. 109 S12
San Diego, Calif., U.S. 111 Z9
San Diego, Tex., U.S. 105 U10
San Diego, Cabo, Arg. 135 X10
San Diego de los Baños, Cuba 118 G5
Sandıklı, Turk. 170 F6
Sandino, Cuba 118 H4
Sand Island, Hawai'i, U.S. 114 K2
Sand Island, Solomon Is. 221 P23
Sand Island, Wis., U.S. 100 E4
Sandness, Scot., U.K. 144 D12
Sandoa, Dem. Rep. of the Congo 202 N10
Sandomierz, Pol. 151 F17
San Donà di Piave, It. 152 D8
Sandon Iwa, Japan 189 V4
Sandover, river, Austral. 214 E9
Sandovo, Russ. 158 G9
Sandown, Eng., U.K. 145 X13
Sandoy, island, Faroe Is., Den. 142 H6
Sand Point, Alas., U.S. 112 N12
Sandpoint, Idaho, U.S. 108 B4
Sandray Sanndraigh, island, Scot., U.K. 144 K6
Sandspit, B.C., Can. 84 K7
Sand Springs, Mont., U.S. 108 C11
Sand Springs, Okla., U.S. 104 F12
Sandstone, Minn., U.S. 106 H12
Sandstone, W. Aust., Austral. 215 V3
Sandur, Faroe Is., Den. 142 H6
Sandusky, Mich., U.S. 100 L13
Sandusky, Ohio, U.S. 101 P13
Sandviken, Sw. 143 J13
Sandwich, Ill., U.S. 101 N6
Sandwich Bay, Nfld. & Lab., Can. 85 K22
Sandy, Utah, U.S. 108 L7
Sandy Bay, Gibraltar, U.K. 163 P23
Sandy Bay, Jam. 122 H6
Sandy Cape, Austral. 214 G16
Sandy Cay, British Virgin Is., U.K. 122 L11
Sandy Creek, Tex., U.S. 105 R12
Sandy Ground Village, British Virgin Is., U.K. 122 R11
Sandy Hill Bay, British Virgin Is., U.K. 122 R12
Sandy Island, Grenada 123 J24
Sandy Islet, Austral. 214 B4
Sandykgaçy, Uzb. 176 N10
Sandy Lake, Ont., Can. 85 M15
Sandy Point, Bahamas 122 C6
Sandy Point, India 181 R14
Sandy Point, Virgin Is., U.S. 122 R1
Sandy Point Town, St. Kitts and Nevis 123 A17
San Esteban de Gormaz, Sp. 146 D11
San FeliceCirceo, It. 152 L9
San Felipe, Chile 134 K7
San Felipe, Col. 130 G9
San Felipe, Mex. 116 B5
San Felipe, Venez. 130 B8
San Felipe, Cayos de, Cuba 118 H5
San Félix Island, S. Amer. 128 K2
San Fernando, Calif., U.S. 111 X8
San Fernando, Chile 134 L7
San Fernando, Mex. 116 F12
San Fernando, Sp. 146 M8
San Fernando, Trinidad and Tobago 123 Q22
San Fernando de Apure, Venez. 130 D9
San Fernando de Atabapo, Venez. 130 F9
Sanford, Fla., U.S. 98 T9
Sanford, Me., U.S. 97 H15
Sanford, N.C., U.S. 98 H11
San Francique, Trinidad and Tobago 123 Q22
San Francisco, Arg. 134 J11
San Francisco, Arg. 134 K9
San Francisco, Calif., U.S. 111 S3
San Francisco, river, N. Mex., U.S. 109 U10
San Francisco Bay, U.S. 86 G3
San Francisco del Oro, Mex. 116 E9
San Francisco de Paula, Cabo, Arg. 135 V9
San Gabriel, Ecua. 130 H3
San Gabriel, river, Tex., U.S. 105 P11
San Gabriel Mountains National Monument, Calif., U.S. 111 X8
Sangamner, India 180 L4
Sangamon, river, Ill., U.S. 101 R5
Sangān, Kōh-e, Afghan. 179 N4
Sangar, Russ. 161 G17
Sangareddi, India 180 M6
Sang Bast, Iran 175 C16
Sangbu, S. Korea 187 S10
Sang Bur, Afghan. 178 M2
Sangchujado, island, S. Korea 187 V7
Sangdong, S. Korea 187 N11
Sangeang, island, Indonesia 193 M13
Sang-e Māshah, Afghan. 179 N6
Sanger, Calif., U.S. 111 T6
Sanger, Tex., U.S. 104 K11
San Germán, P.R., U.S. 122 N1
Sanggan, river, Shanxi, China 184 C5
Sanggou Wan, Shand., China 184 F12
Sangha, river, Cameroon, Congo 205 G18
Sanghar, Pak. 179 V7
Sanghwagye, S. Korea 186 M9
Sangihe, island, Indonesia 193 H15
Sangihe, Kepulauan, Indonesia 193 H15
San Gil, Col. 130 E6
Sangīn, Afghan. 179 P4
San Giovanni, San Marino 163 K15
San Giovanniin Fiore, It. 153 Q14
San Giovanni in Persiceto, It. 152 F7
San Giovanni Valdarno, It. 152 H7
Sangju, S. Korea 187 Q10
Sangju, S. Korea 187 T10
Sangkulirang, Indonesia 192 H12
Sangli, India 180 M4
Sangmélima, Cameroon 205 F16
Sangni, N. Korea 186 E10
Sangnong, N. Korea 186 F11
Sangola, India 180 M4
Sangolquí, Ecua. 130 J3
San Gorgonio Mountain, Calif., U.S. 111 X10
Sangowo, Indonesia 193 H16
Sangre de Cristo Mountains, Colo., N. Mex., U.S. 109 Q13
San Gregorio, Uru. 134 K14
Sangre Grande, Trinidad and Tobago 123 P23
Sang Sang, Nicar. 117 L18
Sangtaedo, island, S. Korea 187 U5
Sangt'ong, N. Korea 186 G9
Sangüesa, Sp. 147 C13
Sanguinet, Fr. 149 W6
Sangŭm, N. Korea 186 J9
Sangvor, Taj. 178 H9
Sangwangdeungdo, island, S. Korea 187 R6
Sangzhi, Hunan, China 185 P2
Sanhezhen, Anhui, China 184 M8
Sanibel Island, Fla., U.S. 99 W8
San Ignacio, Arg. 134 G14
San Ignacio, Bol. 132 J9
San Ignacio, Mex. 116 D6
Saniquellie, Liberia 204 D7
San Javier, Arg. 134 J12
San Javier, Sp. 147 K14
Sanjeong, S. Korea 187 U7
San Joaquín, Bol. 132 H7
San Joaquin, river, Calif., U.S. 111 T6
San Joaquín, Cerro, Ecua. 130 Q11
San Joaquin Valley, U.S. 86 G3
San Jon, N. Mex., U.S. 109 S15
San Jorge, Golfo, Arg. 135 T9
San Jorge Island, Solomon Is. 221 M18
San Jose, Calif., U.S. 111 S4
San Jose, N. Mariana Is., U.S. 220 C4
San Jose, N. Mex., U.S. 109 R13
San José, C.R. 117 N19
San José, Guatemala 117 L15
San José, Golfo, Arg. 135 Q10
San José, Isla, Mex. 116 E7
San José, Laguna, P.R., U.S. 122 M5
San José de Amacuro, Venez. 131 C13
San José de Comondú, Mex. 116 E6
San José de Jáchal, Arg. 134 J7
San José de Las Lajas, Cuba 118 G6
San José del Guaviare, Col. 130 G6
San José de Mayo, Uru. 134 L13
San José de Ocuné, Col. 130 F7
San Juan, Arg. 134 J8
San Juan, Dom. Rep. 119 M18
San Juan, P.R., U.S. 122 M4
San Juan, Peru 132 J4
San Juan, Trinidad and Tobago 123 P22
San Juan, river, Utah, U.S. 109 P8
San Juan, Cabezas de, P.R., U.S. 122 M6
San Juan, Cabo, Arg. 135 X10
San Juanbaai, Curaçao, Neth. 123 P13
San Juan Bautista, Calif., U.S. 111 T4
San Juan Bautista, Parag. 132 N10
San Juan Capistrano, Calif., U.S. 111 Y9
San Juan del Norte, Nicar. 117 M19
San Juan de los Morros, Venez. 130 C9
San Juan del Sur, Nicar. 117 M18
San Juan Island National Historical Park, Wash., U.S. 110 A3
San Juan Islands, Wash., U.S. 110 A3
San Juan Islands National Monument, Wash., U.S. 110 A3
San Juan Mountains, Colo., N. Mex., U.S. 109 P11
San Juan y Martinez, Cuba 118 H5
San Julián, Bahía, Arg. 135 U9
San Julián, Gran Bajo de, Arg. 135 U8
San Just, Sierra de, Sp. 147 F14
San Justo, Arg. 134 J12
San Justo, Arg. 134 L12
Sankeshwar, India 181 N4

Sankt-Peterburg (Saint Petersburg, Leningrad), *Russ.* **158** F6
Sankuru, river, *Dem. Rep. of the Congo* **202** L9
San Lázaro, Cabo, *Mex.* **116** E6
Şanlıurfa (Edessa), *Turk.* **171** HI3
San Lorenzo, *Arg.* **134** KII
San Lorenzo, *Ecua.* **130** H2
San Lorenzo, *P.R., U.S.* **122** N5
San Lorenzo, *Parag.* **132** MIO
San Lorenzo, Cabo, *Ecua.* **130** KI
San Lorenzo de El Escorial, *Sp.* **146** FIO
San Lorenzo de la Parrilla, *Sp.* **146** GI2
San Luis, *Arg.* **134** K9
San Luis, *Ariz., U.S.* **109** V4
San Luis, *Colo., U.S.* **109** PI3
San Luis, *Cuba* **119** KI3
San Luis, *Guatemala* **117** KI6
San Luis, Lago de, *Bol.* **132** H8
San Luis de Palenque, *Col.* **130** E7
San Luis Obispo, *Calif., U.S.* **III** V5
San Luis Potosí, *Mex.* **116** GII
San Luis Reservoir, *Calif., U.S.* **III** T5
San Luis Río Colorado, *Mex.* **116** B6
Sanluri, *It.* **153** P4
San Marcos, *Col.* **130** D5
San Marcos, *Tex., U.S.* **105** QIO
San Marino, *San Marino* **163** E4
San Marino, *San Marino* **163** JI5
San Marino, river, *It., San Marino* **163** JI4
San Martín, *Arg.* **134** K8
San Martín, *Col.* **130** F5
San Martín, river, *Bol.* **132** H8
San Martin, Cape, *Calif., U.S.* **III** U4
San Martín, Lago, *Chile* **135** U7
San Martín de los Andes, *Arg.* **135** P7
San Martin Seamounts, *Pac. Oc.* **249** PI3
San Mateo, *Calif., U.S.* **III** S3
San Mateo, *N. Mex., U.S.* **109** SII
San Matías, Golfo, *Arg.* **135** QIO
Sanmen, *Zhejiang, China* **185** PI2
Sanmen Wan, *Zhejiang, China* **185** PI2
Sanmenxia, *Henan, China* **184** J3
San Miguel, *El Salv.* **117** LI7
San Miguel, island, *Calif., U.S.* **III** X5
San Miguel, river, *Bol.* **132** J8
San Miguel Bay, *Philippines* **193** CI4
San Miguel Creek, *Tex., U.S.* **105** S9
San Miguel de Cozumel, *Mex.* **117** HI7
San Miguel de Huachi, *Bol.* **132** J7
San Miguel del Monte, *Arg.* **134** MI2
San Miguel de Tucumán, *Arg.* **134** G9
Sanming, *Fujian, China* **185** S8
San Miniato, *It.* **152** G6
Sannat, *Malta* **163** H2O
Sanndraigh, island, *Scot., U.K.* **144** K6
SannicandroGarganico, *It.* **152** KI2
San Nicolás, *Arg.* **134** KI2
San Nicolas, island, *Calif., U.S.* **III** Y6
Sannikova, Proliv, *Russ.* **161** DI7
Sannohe, *Japan* **188** JI3
Sanok, *Pol.* **151** HI7
San Pablo, *Philippines* **193** CI4
San Pedro, *Arg.* **134** E9
San Pedro, *Arg.* **134** LI2
San Pedro, *Parag.* **132** MIO
San Pedro, river, *Ariz., U.S.* **109** V8
San Pedro, Sierra de, *Sp.* **146** H7
San Pedro de las Colonias, *Mex.* **116** EIO
San Pedro de Macorís, *Dom. Rep.* **119** M2O
San Pedro Sula, *Hond.* **117** KI7
San Pietro, island, *It.* **153** NI4
San Pietro, Isola di, *It.* **153** Q3
Sanpoil, river, *Wash., U.S.* **110** B7
San Quintín, *Mex.* **116** B5
San Rafael, *Arg.* **134** L8
San Rafael, *Bol.* **132** J9
San Rafael, *Calif., U.S.* **III** R3
San Rafael, Cabo, *Dom. Rep.* **119** L2O
San Rafael del Yuma, *Dom. Rep.* **119** M2O
San Remo, *It.* **152** G2
San Roque, *N. Mariana Is., U.S.* **220** B5

San Roque, *Sp.* **146** N9
San Saba, *Tex., U.S.* **105** N9
San Saba, river, *Tex., U.S.* **105** P8
San Salvador, *El Salv.* **117** LI6
San Salvador, island, *Bahamas* **119** FI4
San Salvador (Santiago, James), Isla, *Ecua.* **130** P9
San Salvador, Isla, *Galápagos Is., Ecua.* **219** G22
San Salvador de Jujuy, *Arg.* **134** E9
Sansanné-Mango, *Togo* **204** CII
San Sebastián, *Sp.* **122** M2
Sansepolcro, *It.* **152** H8
San Severo, *It.* **152** LI2
Sansha, *Fujian, China* **185** SII
Sansha Wan, *Fujian, China* **185** SIO
San Simeon, *Calif., U.S.* **III** V4
San Simon, *Ariz., U.S.* **109** V9
Sanski Most, *Bosn. & Herzg.* **154** F6
San Sosti, *It.* **153** PI3
Sans Souci, *Trinidad and Tobago* **123** N24
Sansu, *N. Korea* **186** F9
Santa Ana, *Bol.* **132** H7
Santa Ana, *Calif., U.S.* **III** X8
Santa Ana, *El Salv.* **117** LI6
Santa Ana, *Philippines* **193** BI4
Santa Ana, island, *Solomon Is.* **221** Q2I
Santa Anna, *Tex., U.S.* **105** N8
Santa Barbara, *Calif., U.S.* **III** W6
Santa Bárbara, *Chile* **135** N6
Santa Bárbara, *Mex.* **116** E9
Santa Barbara, island, *Calif., U.S.* **III** Y7
Santa Bárbara, peak, *Sp.* **146** LI2
Santa Barbara Channel, *Calif., U.S.* **III** X6
Santa Catalina, island, *Calif., U.S.* **III** Y8
Santa Catalina, island, *Solomon Is.* **221** Q2I
Santa Catalina, Gulf of, *Calif., U.S.* **III** Y8
Santa Catarina, *Sao Tome and Principe* **209** DI9
Santa Catarina Island, *S. Amer.* **128** K8
Santa Catharina, *Curaçao, Neth.* **123** PI5
Santa Clara, *Calif., U.S.* **III** S4
Santa Clara, *Cuba* **118** H9
Santa Clara, *Oreg., U.S.* **110** H3
Santa Clara, Isla, *Pac. Oc.* **219** M23
Santa Clotilde, *Peru* **132** D4
Santa Coloma, *Andorra* **162** J2
Santa Comba, *Sp.* **146** B5
Santa Cruz, *Bol.* **132** K8
Santa Cruz, *Braz.* **133** FI8
Santa Cruz, *Calif., U.S.* **III** T4
Santa Cruz, *Curaçao, Neth.* **123** PI3
Santa Cruz, *Madeira, Port.* **208** M3
Santa Cruz, *Sao Tome and Principe* **209** D2O
Santa Cruz, island, *Calif., U.S.* **III** X6
Santa Cruz, river, *Arg.* **135** V8
Santa Cruz, river, *Ariz., U.S.* **109** W8
Santa Cruz (Chaves, Indefatigable), Isla, *Ecua.* **130** QIO
Santa Cruz, Isla, *Galápagos Is., Ecua.* **219** G22
Santa Cruz Cabrália, *Braz.* **133** JI6
Santa Cruz da Graciosa, *Azores, Port.* **146** P3
Santa Cruz das Flores , *Azores, Port.* **146** PI
Santa Cruz de la Palma, *Sp.* **208** Q3
Santa Cruz del Norte, *Cuba* **118** G7
Santa Cruz del Sur, *Cuba* **118** KII
Santa Cruz de Mudela, *Sp.* **146** JII
Santa Cruz de Tenerife, *Sp.* **208** Q5
Santa Cruz do Sul, *Braz.* **132** PII
Santa Cruz Islands, *Solomon Is.* **218** H7
Santa Elena, *Venez.* **131** FI3
Santa Elena, Cabo, *C.R.* **117** NI8
Santa Elena Peninsula, *S. Amer.* **128** DI
Santa Eugenia, *Sp.* **146** C5
Santa Eulalia del Río, *Sp.* **147** HI7

Santa Fe, *Arg.* **134** JI2
Santa Fe, *N. Mex., U.S.* **109** RI2
Santa Fé, *Sp.* **146** LII
Santa Fe, Canal de, *Ecua.* **130** QIO
Santa Fe (Barrington), Isla, *Ecua.* **130** QIO
Santa Helena, *Braz.* **132** EIO
Santa Inês, *Braz.* **133** EI4
Santa Inés, Isla, *Chile* **135** X7
Santa Isabel, *Arg.* **134** M9
Santa Isabel, *P.R., U.S.* **122** P3
Santa Isabel, island, *Solomon Is.* **221** LI7
Santa Lucía, *Arg.* **134** HI2
Santa Lucía, *Arg.* **134** J8
Santa Lucía, *Cuba* **118** G5
Santa Lucía, *Uru.* **134** LI4
Santa Lucia Range, *Calif., U.S.* **III** U4
Santa Luzia , *Azores, Port.* **146** Q3
Santa Luzia, island, *Cabo Verde* **209** BI5
Santa Maddalena Vallalta, *It.* **152** B8
Santa-Manza, Golfe de, *Fr.* **152** L4
Santa Margarita, Isla, *Mex.* **116** F6
Santa Maria, *Azores, Port.* **146** R5
Santa Maria, *Braz.* **132** D9
Santa Maria, *Braz.* **132** PII
Santa Maria, *Cabo Verde* **209** BI7
Santa Maria, *Calif., U.S.* **III** W5
Santa Maria, *Curaçao, Neth.* **123** PI4
Santa María, *Arg.* **134** G9
Santa María, *Peru* **132** D4
Santa Maria, island, *Vanuatu* **222** B2
Santa Maria, Cabo de, *Angola* **206** D5
Santa Maria, Cabo de, *Port.* **146** L6
Santa María, Cape, *Bahamas* **119** FI3
Santa María, Cayo, *Cuba* **118** GIO
Santa María (Floreana, Charles), Isla, *Ecua.* **130** RIO
Santa María, Isla, *Galápagos Is., Ecua.* **219** G22
Santa Maria Bay, *Virgin Is., U.S.* **122** M8
Santa Maria da Vitória, *Braz.* **133** HI5
Santa María de Huerta, *Sp.* **146** EI2
Santa María de Nanay, *Peru* **132** E4
Santa Maria di Leuca, Capo, *It.* **153** PI6
Santa Marta, *Col.* **130** B5
Santa Martabaai, *Curaçao, Neth.* **123** PI3
Santa Marta de Ortigueira, Ría de, *Sp.* **146** A6
Santa Marta Grande, Cabo de, *Braz.* **133** PI3
Santa Monica, *Calif., U.S.* **III** X8
Santa Monica Mountains National Recreation Area, *Calif., U.S.* **III** X7
Sant Ana, *Sao Tome and Principe* **209** D2O
Santana, *Braz.* **133** HI5
Santana, *Madeira, Port.* **208** M3
Santana do Livramento, *Braz.* **132** PII
Santander, *Sp.* **146** BII
Santander, Bahía de, *Sp.* **146** BII
Santander Jiménez, *Mex.* **116** FI2
Sant' Andrea Apostolo dello Ionio, *It.* **153** RI3
Santanilla Honduras, Islas, *Hond.* **117** JI9
Sant'Antioco, Isola di, *It.* **153** Q3
Sant Antoni de Portmany, *Sp.* **147** HI6
Santa Olalla del Cala, *Sp.* **146** K8
Santa Paula, *Calif., U.S.* **III** X7
Santa Pola, *Sp.* **147** KI4
Santaquin, *Utah, U.S.* **108** L7
Santarém, *Braz.* **132** DII
Santarém, *Port.* **146** H5
Santaren Channel, *Bahamas* **118** F9
Santa Rita, *Guam, U.S.* **220** CIO
Santa Rita, *Venez.* **130** B7
Santa Rita do Weil, *Braz.* **132** E5
Santa Rosa, *Arg.* **134** K9
Santa Rosa, *Arg.* **134** MIO
Santa Rosa, *Bol.* **132** G6
Santa Rosa, *Calif., U.S.* **III** R3

Santa Rosa, *Curaçao, Neth.* **123** QI5
Santa Rosa, *Ecua.* **130** QIO
Santa Rosa, *Hond.* **117** LI6
Santa Rosa, *N. Mex., U.S.* **109** SI4
Santa Rosa, *Peru* **132** G5
Santa Rosa, *Peru* **132** J5
Santa Rosa, island, *Calif., U.S.* **III** X6
Santa Rosa, Mount, *Guam, U.S.* **220** BI2
Santa Rosa and San Jacinto Mountains National Monument, *Calif., U.S.* **III** YIO
Santa Rosa Beach, *Fla., U.S.* **99** Q3
Santa Rosa Island, *Fla., U.S.* **99** Q2
Santa Rosalía, *Mex.* **116** D6
Santa Rosa Range, *Nev., U.S.* **110** L9
Santa Severina, *It.* **153** QI4
Santa Teresa, *N.T., Austral.* **215** T9
Santa Teresa, Embalse de, *Sp.* **146** F9
Santa Victoria, *Arg.* **134** DII
Santa Vitória do Palmar, *Braz.* **132** QII
Santa Ynez, *Calif., U.S.* **III** W6
Santa Ynez Mountains, *Calif., U.S.* **III** W6
Sant Carles de la Ràpita, *Sp.* **147** FI6
Santee, river, *S.C., U.S.* **98** LII
Sant' Eufemia, Golfo di, *It.* **153** QI3
Santhià, *It.* **152** E3
Santiago, *Chile* **134** L7
Santiago, *Dom. Rep.* **119** LI8
Santiago, *Pan.* **117** P2O
Santiago, island, *Cabo Verde* **209** DI6
Santiago, Punta, *Eq. Guinea* **208** N7
Santiago de Baney, *Eq. Guinea* **208** L8
Santiago de Compostela, *Sp.* **146** B5
Santiago de Cuba, *Cuba* **119** KI3
Santiago del Estero, *Arg.* **134** GIO
Santiago do Cacém, *Port.* **146** K5
Santiago Ixcuintla, *Mex.* **116** G9
Santiago Papasquiaro, *Mex.* **116** F9
Santiago Peak, *Tex., U.S.* **105** Q3
Santigi, *Indonesia* **193** HI3
Sant Jordi, Golf de, *Sp.* **147** FI6
Sant Julià de Lòria, *Andorra* **162** K2
Sant Julià de Lòria, *Andorra* **162** K2
Santo André, *Braz.* **133** MI3
Santo Ângelo, *Braz.* **132** PII
Santo Antão, island, *Cabo Verde* **209** AI5
Santo António, *Cabo Verde* **209** DI7
Santo António, *Sao Tome and Principe* **209** A2I
Santo Antônio do Içá, *Braz.* **132** D6
Santo Corazón, *Bol.* **132** K9
Santo Domingo, *Dom. Rep.* **119** MI9
Santo Domingo, Cay, *Bahamas* **119** JI3
Santo Domingo de Silos, *Sp.* **146** DII
Santo Domingo Pueblo, *N. Mex., U.S.* **109** RI2
Santo Isabel do Rio Negro, *Braz.* **132** C7
Santop, Mount, *Vanuatu* **222** G3
Santopitar, peak, *Sp.* **146** MIO
Santorini see Thíra, island, *Gr.* **157** MI5
Santos, *Braz.* **133** MI4
Santos, Sierra de los, *Sp.* **146** K9
Santos Plateau, *Atl. Oc.* **241** S7
Santo Tirso, *Port.* **146** E5
Santo Tomás, *Peru* **132** J5
Santo Tomé, *Arg.* **134** HI4
San Valentín, Cerro, *Chile* **135** T6
San Vicente, *N. Mariana Is., U.S.* **220** C4
San Vicente de Alcántara, *Sp.* **146** H7
San Vicente de Barakaldo, *Sp.* **146** BI2
San Vincente del Caguán, *Col.* **130** G5
San Vito, Cape, *Eur.* **140** L7
Sanya, *China* **182** RI2
Sanyang, *S. Korea* **187** TII
San Ygnacio, *Tex., U.S.* **105** V8
Sanyuan, *Shaanxi, China* **184** JI
São Bento do Norte, *Braz.* **133** EI8
São Borja, *Braz.* **132** PIO

São Cristóvão, *Braz.* **133** HI7
São Félix do Xingu, *Braz.* **132** FI2
São Filipe, *Cabo Verde* **209** EI5
São Francisco, river, *Braz.* **133** JI4
São Francisco, Ilha de, *Braz.* **133** NI3
São Gabriel, *Braz.* **132** PII
São Gabriel da Cachoeira, *Braz.* **132** C6
São Gens, peak, *Port.* **146** J6
São João da Aliança, *Braz.* **133** JI3
São João da Madeira, *Port.* **146** E5
São João del Rei, *Braz.* **133** LI4
São Jorge, *Azores, Port.* **146** Q3
São José, Baía de, *Braz.* **133** DI5
São José de Anauá, *Braz.* **132** C8
São José de Ribamar, *Braz.* **133** DI5
São José dos Campos, *Braz.* **133** MI4
São Leopoldo, *Braz.* **132** PII
São Lourenço, Ponta de, *Madeira, Port.* **208** M4
São Lourenço do Sul, *Braz.* **132** QI2
São Luís, *Braz.* **133** DI5
São LuÍs, Ilha de, *Braz.* **133** DI5
São Mamede, Pico, *Port.* **146** H6
São Marcos, Baía de, *Braz.* **133** DI5
São Martinho do Porto, *Port.* **146** G4
São Mateus, *Braz.* **133** KI6
São Mateus , *Azores, Port.* **146** Q3
São Miguel, *Azores, Port.* **146** Q5
São Miguel do Araguaia, *Braz.* **132** HI2
Saona, Isla, *Dom. Rep.* **119** N2O
Saône, river, *Eur.* **140** H5
Saonek, *Indonesia* **193** JI7
Saoner, *India* **180** K6
São Nicolau, island, *Cabo Verde* **209** BI6
São Paulo, *Braz.* **133** MI3
São Paulo de Olivença, *Braz.* **132** E6
São Raimundo Nonato, *Braz.* **133** GI5
São Romão, *Braz.* **132** E6
São Roque, Cabo de, *Braz.* **133** FI8
São Sebastião , *Azores, Port.* **146** Q4
São Sebastião, Ponta de, *Mozambique* **207** HI3
São Sebastião Island, *S. Amer.* **128** J9
São Teotónio, *Port.* **146** K5
São Tiago, *Cabo Verde* **209** DI6
São Tomé, *Sao Tome and Principe* **209** C2O
São Tomé, island, *Sao Tome and Principe* **209** DI9
São Tomé, *Sao Tome and Principe* **205** HI4
São Tomé, Cabo de, *Braz.* **133** MI5
São Tomé, Pico de, *Sao Tome and Principe* **209** D2O
Sao Tome & Principe, *Af.* **205** GI4
São Vicente, island, *Madeira, Port.* **208** M3
São Vicente, *Cabo Verde* **209** BI4
São Vicente, Cabo de, *Port.* **146** L4
Sapanca, *Turk.* **170** D6
Sapanjang, island, *Indonesia* **192** MII
Sapele, *Nigeria* **205** EI3
Sapelo Island, *Ga., U.S.* **99** P9
Sápes, *Gr.* **157** BI5
Sapiéntza, island, *Gr.* **156** M9
Saphire Mountains, *Mont., U.S.* **108** D6
Sappho, *Wash., U.S.* **110** B2
Sapporo, *Japan* **188** GI3
Sapri, *It.* **153** NI2
Sapsido, island, *S. Korea* **187** Q7
Sapudi, island, *Indonesia* **192** MII
Sapulpa, *Okla., U.S.* **104** FI2
Saqqez, *Iran* **174** CIO
Sara Adasy, island, *Azerb.* **171** F22
Sarāb, *Iran* **174** BII
Saraburi, *Thai.* **190** M9
Saraféré, *Mali* **200** H8
Saraguro, *Ecua.* **130** L3
Sarahs, *Uzb.* **176** N9
Sarajevo, *Bosn. & Herzg.* **154** G8
Saraji, *Qnsld., Austral.* **215** TI4
Sarakhs, *Iran* **175** BI7
Saranac Lake, *N.Y., U.S.* **96** GII
Saranac Lakes, *N.Y., U.S.* **96** GIO

Sarandë, *Alban.* 154 N9
Sarangani Islands, *Philippines* 193 G15
Sarangpur, *India* 180 J5
Saransk, *Russ.* 158 K13
Sarapul, *Russ.* 158 H16
Sarasota, *Fla., U.S.* 99 V7
Sarasota Bay, *Fla., U.S.* 99 V7
Saratoga, *Wyo., U.S.* 108 K11
Saratoga Springs, *N.Y., U.S.* 96 J11
Saratov, *Russ.* 158 M13
Sarāvān, *Iran* 175 G18
Sarawak, *Malaysia* 192 H10
Saray, *Turk.* 170 C4
Saray, *Turk.* 171 F18
Sarayköy, *Turk.* 170 G4
Sar Banādir, *Afghan.* 179 R4
Sarbāz, *Iran* 175 H18
Sarbīsheh, *Iran* 175 E17
Sarcelle, Passe de la, *New Caledonia, Fr.* 222 E9
Sardar Chah, *Pak.* 179 T4
Sardegna (Sardinia), island, *It.* 153 N3
Sardinia see Sardegna, island, *It.* 153 N3
Sardino-Balearic Plain, *Atl. Oc.* 240 J13
Sardis, *Miss., U.S.* 102 H11
Sardis, ruins, *Turk.* 170 F4
Sardis Lake, *Miss., U.S.* 102 H11
Sar-e Howz, *Afghan.* 178 L4
Sareiserjoch, peak, *Liech.* 162 Q3
Sar-e Pul, *Afghan.* 178 L5
Sargans, *Switz.* 162 R1
Sargent, *Nebr., U.S.* 107 P5
Sargodha, *Pak.* 179 P10
Sargo Plateau, *Arctic Oc.* 246 J8
Sarh, *Chad* 201 K15
Sarḩad, *Afghan.* 178 K12
Sārī, *Iran* 175 C13
Sariá, island, *Gr.* 157 P18
Sarigan, island, *N. Mariana Is., U.S.* 220 B2
Sarıgöl, *Turk.* 170 G4
Sarıkamış, *Turk.* 171 D17
Sarina, *Qnsld., Austral.* 215 S15
Sariñena, *Sp.* 147 D15
Sarinleey, *Somalia* 203 J16
Sarīr Calanscio, *Af.* 198 D7
Sarīr Tibasti, region, *Lib.* 201 E14
Sariwŏn, *N. Korea* 186 K6
Sarıyar Baraji, *Turk.* 170 E7
Sarıyer, *Turk.* 170 C5
Sarız, *Turk.* 170 G11
Sarjektjåkko, peak, *Sw.* 143 D13
Sark, island, *Channel Is., U.K.* 145 Z11
Sarkari Tala, *India* 180 F2
Şarkîkaraağaç, *Turk.* 170 G7
Şarkışla, *Turk.* 170 F11
Şarköy, *Turk.* 170 D3
Sarles, *N. Dak., U.S.* 106 D6
Sarmansuyu, *Turk.* 171 G17
Sarmi, *Indonesia* 193 K20
Sarmiento, *Arg.* 135 S8
Särna, *Sw.* 142 J12
Sarny, *Ukr.* 158 M4
Sarōbī, *Afghan.* 178 M8
Saroma Ko, *Japan* 188 F14
Saronikós Kólpos, *Gr.* 156 J12
Saronno, *It.* 152 D4
Saros Körfezi, *Turk.* 170 D3
Sarowbi, *Afghan.* 179 P8
Sarpa, Ozero, *Russ.* 159 Q14
Sar Passage, *Palau* 220 P11
Sarqan, *Kaz.* 177 G17
Sarracín, *Sp.* 146 C11
Sarrebourg, *Fr.* 149 P15
Sarreguemines, *Fr.* 149 N15
Sarria, *Sp.* 146 B7
Sarrión, *Sp.* 147 G14
Sarteano, *It.* 152 J7
Sartène, *Fr.* 152 L4
Sarthe, river, *Fr.* 149 Q7
Sárti, *Gr.* 157 D13
Sarufutsu, *Japan* 188 E13
Saruna, *Pak.* 179 V6
Sarupsar, *India* 180 E4
Sarych, Mys, *Ukr.* 159 T7

Saryesik-Atryrau Desert, *Asia* 168 F7
Saryesik-Atyraū Qumy, *Kaz.* 177 G16
Sarygamysh Köli, lake, *Turkm.* 176 J8
Saryköl, *Kaz.* 176 B11
Saryözek, *Kaz.* 177 H17
Saryqamys, *Kaz.* 176 G6
Saryqopa Köli, *Kaz.* 176 D11
Sarysay, *Kaz.* 176 E9
Saryshagan, *Kaz.* 177 G15
Sarysu, river, *Kaz.* 177 E13
Sary-Tash, *Kyrg.* 178 G10
Saryzhal, *Kaz.* 177 D17
Sasalaguan, Mount, *Guam, U.S.* 220 D10
Sasamungga, *Solomon Is.* 221 L15
Sasaram, *India* 180 H9
Sasebo, *Japan* 189 R4
Saseno see Sazan, island, *Alban.* 154 M9
Saskatchewan, *Can.* 84 L11
Saskatchewan, river, *N. Amer.* 82 G5
Saskatoon, *Sask., Can.* 84 M12
Sason, *Turk.* 171 G16
Sasora, *Indonesia* 193 K20
Sasovo, *Russ.* 158 K11
Sassafras Mountain, *S.C., U.S.* 98 J7
Sassandra, *Côte d'Ivoire* 204 E8
Sassari, *It.* 152 M3
Sassnitz, *Ger.* 150 B10
Sassofeltrio, *It.* 163 L17
Sasstown, *Liberia* 204 E7
Sassulko, Goz, *Cen. Af. Rep., Sudan* 202 F10
Sassuolo, *It.* 152 F5
Sasu-san, peak, *N. Korea* 186 G8
Sasyqköl, *Kaz.* 177 F18
Satadougou, *Mali* 200 J6
Satala, ruins, *Turk.* 171 E14
Sata-Misaki, *Japan* 189 T4
Satanta, *Kans., U.S.* 107 U4
Satara, *India* 180 M4
Sataua, *Samoa* 222 K1
Satawal, island, *F.S.M.* 218 F4
Satawan Atoll, *F.S.M.* 220 R6
Sätbaev, *Kaz.* 176 F12
Satbarwa, *India* 180 H9
Satilla, river, *Ga., U.S.* 99 P6
Satipo, *Peru* 132 N4
Satkania, *Bangladesh* 180 J14
Satna, *India* 180 H7
Šator, peak, *Bosn. & Herzg.* 154 G6
Sátoraljaújhely, *Hung.* 151 K17
Satpura Range, *India* 180 K4
Satteins, *Aust.* 162 M4
Satulung, *Rom.* 155 B13
Satu Mare, *Rom.* 154 B12
Satun, *Thai.* 191 S8
Satupa'itea, *Samoa* 222 L2
Sauce, *Arg.* 134 J13
Sauda, *Nor.* 142 K10
Sauðárkrókur, *Ice.* 142 E3
Saudi Arabia, *Asia* 174 J8
Saugatuck, *Mich., U.S.* 100 M9
Saugerties, *N.Y., U.S.* 96 L11
Sauk Centre, *Minn., U.S.* 106 J10
Sauk City, *Wis., U.S.* 100 L5
Saukorem, *Indonesia* 193 J18
Sauk Rapids, *Minn., U.S.* 106 J11
Saulieu, *Fr.* 149 R12
Sault Sainte Marie, *Mich., U.S.* 100 F11
Sault Sainte Marie, *Ont., Can.* 85 P17
Sauma, Pointe, *Wallis and Futuna, Fr.* 222 E12
Saūmalköl, *Kaz.* 176 B12
Saumlaki, *Indonesia* 193 M17
Saumur, *Fr.* 149 S7
Saunders Coast, *Antarctica* 230 N10
Saupon Point, *Guam, U.S.* 220 B11
Saura, *Kaz.* 176 G5
Saurimo, *Angola* 206 C8
Sausalito, *Calif., U.S.* III S3
Sauteurs, *Grenada* 123 J23
Sauteurs Bay, *Grenada* 123 J23
Sauveterre, *Fr.* 149 X6
Sava, river, *Bosn. & Herzg., Croatia* 154 E7
Savage, *Mont., U.S.* 108 C13
Savai'i, island, *Samoa* 222 K2

Savalou, *Benin* 204 D12
Savana Island, *Virgin Is., U.S.* 122 N7
Savane des Pétrifications, site, *Martinique, Fr.* 123 G23
Savaneta, *Aruba, Neth.* 123 R17
Savanna, *Ill., U.S.* 101 N4
Savannah, *Cayman Is.* 122 J2
Savannah, *Ga., U.S.* 99 N9
Savannah, *Mo., U.S.* 107 R10
Savannah, *Tenn., U.S.* 103 G13
Savannah, river, *Ga., S.C., U.S.* 98 M8
Savannah, river, *N. Amer.* 82 L8
Savannah, river, *U.S.* 87 K19
Savannah Bay, *British Virgin Is., U.K.* 122 R8
Savannah Sound, *Bahamas* 122 E6
Savannakhét, *Laos* 190 L11
Savanna-la-Mar, *Jam.* 122 H6
Savanna Point, *Jam.* 122 H10
Savaştepe, *Turk.* 170 E3
Save, river, *Mozambique* 207 G13
Sāveh, *Iran* 174 C12
Savenay, *Fr.* 149 R5
Saverne, *Fr.* 149 P15
Savigliano, *It.* 152 F2
Savignac-les-Églises, *Fr.* 149 V8
Savignone, *It.* 152 F3
Savo, island, *Solomon Is.* 221 N18
Savona, *It.* 152 F3
Savonet, *Curaçao, Neth.* 123 N13
Savonlinna, *Fin.* 143 G17
Savoonga, *Alas., U.S.* 112 F10
Savu Basin, *Pac. Oc.* 242 L5
Savukoski, *Fin.* 143 D15
Savur, *Turk.* 171 H15
Savusavu, *Fiji* 222 G7
Savusavu Bay, *Fiji* 222 G7
Savu Sea, *Indonesia* 193 N14
Sawah, *Indonesia* 192 H11
Sawahlunto, *Indonesia* 192 J6
Sawa-i-lau, island, *Fiji* 222 H5
Sawai Madhopur, *India* 180 G5
Sawankhalok, *Thai.* 190 K8
Sawatch Range, *Colo., U.S.* 108 M12
Sawda, Jabal, *Saudi Arabia* 174 N8
Sawdā', Jabal as, *Lib.* 201 D14
Sawe, *Indonesia* 192 H4
Sawi, *Thai.* 191 Q8
Sawkanah, *Lib.* 201 D14
Şawqirah, *Oman* 175 N15
Şawqirah, Ghubbat, *Oman* 175 N16
Sawtooth Mountains, *Minn., U.S.* 106 F13
Sawtooth National Recreation Area, *Idaho, U.S.* 108 G5
Sawtooth Range, *Idaho, U.S.* 108 G5
Sawu, island, *Indonesia* 193 N14
Sax, *Switz.* 162 M1
Saxby Downs, *Qnsld., Austral.* 215 S12
Saxony, region, *Ger.* 150 F10
Say, *Niger* 200 J10
Saya de Malha Bank, *Ind. Oc.* 224 H9
Sayanogorsk, *Russ.* 161 L13
Sayḩūt, *Yemen* 175 Q13
Saylac, *Somalia* 203 F16
Saynshand, *Mongolia* 182 E11
Sayötesh, *Kaz.* 176 H6
Sayram Hu, *China* 182 D4
Sayre, *Okla., U.S.* 104 G8
Sayre, *Pa., U.S.* 96 L8
Saywūn, *Yemen* 174 P11
Sayylyk, *Russ.* 161 E18
Sazaī Kalān, *Afghan.* 178 L5
Sazan (Saseno), island, *Alban.* 154 M9
Sazin, *Pak.* 178 L11

Scarinish, *Scot., U.K.* 144 L6
Scarp, island, *Scot., U.K.* 144 H6
Scarriff (An Scairbh), *Ire.* 145 S4
Scatterbreak Channel, *Fiji* 222 G8
Scealg, Bá na (Ballinskelligs Bay), *Ire.* 145 U2
Šćedro, island, *Croatia* 154 H6
Schaan, *Liech.* 162 N2
Schaanwald, *Liech.* 162 N3
Schefferville, *Que., Can.* 85 L20
Schell Creek Range, *Nev., U.S.* III Q12
Schellenberg, *Liech.* 162 M3
Schenectady, *N.Y., U.S.* 96 J11
Schertz, *Tex., U.S.* 105 R10
Schiermonnikoog, island, *Neth.* 148 G13
Schio, *It.* 152 D7
Schíza, island, *Gr.* 156 M9
Schleswig, *Ger.* 150 A7
Schoelcher, *Martinique, Fr.* 123 F22
Schofield, *Wis., U.S.* 100 H5
Schofield Barracks, *Hawai'i, U.S.* 114 E10
Schoinoússa, island, *Gr.* 157 L15
Schönberg, peak, *Liech.* 162 P3
Schönebeck, *Ger.* 150 E9
Schooner Cays, *Bahamas* 122 F6
Schottegat, *Curaçao, Neth.* 123 Q14
Schouten Islands, *P.N.G.* 217 C19
Schrems, *Aust.* 150 J11
Schroeder, *Minn., U.S.* 106 F13
Schuckmannsburg, *Namibia* 206 F9
Schulenburg, *Tex., U.S.* 105 R12
Schuyler, *Nebr., U.S.* 107 P8
Schwabach, *Ger.* 150 H8
Schwabenland Canyon, *Atl. Oc., Ind. Oc.* 241 Y14
Schwäbische Alb, range, *Ger.* 150 K6
Schwäbisch Hall, *Ger.* 150 J7
Schwaz, *Aust.* 150 L9
Schwechat, *Aust.* 151 K13
Schwedt, *Ger.* 150 D11
Schweich, *Ger.* 162 J12
Schweinfurt, *Ger.* 150 G8
Schwerin, *Ger.* 150 C9
Schwyz, *Switz.* 152 B4
Sciacca, *It.* 153 T9
Scilla, *It.* 153 R12
Scilly, Isles of, *Eng., U.K.* 145 Y7
Scioto, river, *Ohio, U.S.* 101 S13
Scipio, *Utah, U.S.* 108 M7
Scobey, *Mont., U.S.* 108 A12
Scofield Reservoir, *Utah, U.S.* 108 M8
Scooba, *Miss., U.S.* 103 K13
Scoresby Land, *Greenland, Den.* 82 B10
Scoresby Valley, *Arctic Oc.* 247 L19
Scotch Bonnet, *St. Kitts and Nevis* 123 B18
Scotian Shelf, *Atl. Oc.* 240 J5
Scotia Sea, *Atl. Oc.* 241 W6
Scotland, *S. Dak., U.S.* 106 M7
Scotland, *Scot., U.K.* 144 K9
Scotland Neck, *N.C., U.S.* 98 G13
Scott, Mount, *Oreg., U.S.* 110 J4
Scott Base, station, *Antarctica* 231 N13
Scott Canyon, *Pac. Oc.* 249 H16
Scott City, *Kans., U.S.* 107 T4
Scott City, *Mo., U.S.* 107 U16
Scott Coast, *Antarctica* 231 N14
Scott Glacier, *Antarctica* 231 K21
Scott Islands, *B.C., Can.* 84 L7
Scott Plateau, *Ind. Oc.* 225 J18
Scott Point, *Mich., U.S.* 100 G10
Scottsbluff, *Nebr., U.S.* 107 N1
Scotts Bluff National Monument, *Nebr., U.S.* 107 N1
Scottsboro, *Ala., U.S.* 103 G16
Scottsburg, *Ind., U.S.* 101 T9
Scottsdale, *Ariz., U.S.* 109 U7
Scottsdale, *Tas., Austral.* 215 Y8
Scotts Head, *Dominica* 123 G19
Scottsville, *Ky., U.S.* 103 D16
Scottville, *Mich., U.S.* 100 K9
Scotty's Junction, *Nev., U.S.* III S9
Scrabster, *Scot., U.K.* 144 G10
Scranton, *Pa., U.S.* 96 M9
Scribner, *Nebr., U.S.* 107 P8
Scrubby Creek, *Qnsld., Austral.* 215 P13

Scrub Island, *Anguilla* 122 Q12
Sculpin Ridge, *Pac. Oc.* 243 H13
Scunthorpe, *Eng., U.K.* 145 R13
Scuol, *Switz.* 152 B6
Scurdie Ness, cape, *Scot., U.K.* 144 L11
Scutari see Shkodër, *Alban.* 154 K9
Scutari, Lake see Skadarsko Jezero, *Alban., Montenegro* 154 J9
Sea Club, *Monaco* 163 B23
Sea Cow Bay, *British Virgin Is., U.K.* 122 R6
Seadrift, *Tex., U.S.* 105 T12
Seaford, *Del., U.S.* 98 D14
Seaford, *Eng., U.K.* 145 W14
Seaforth, *Jam.* 122 J11
Seaforth, Loch, *Scot., U.K.* 144 J7
Sea Grape, *Bahamas* 122 F1
Seagraves, *Tex., U.S.* 104 L4
Seaham, *Eng., U.K.* 145 P12
Sea Island, *Ga., U.S.* 99 P9
Sea Islands, *U.S.* 87 K19
Seal, river, *Man., Can.* 85 K14
Seal, Cape, *S. Af.* 206 M9
Seal Cay, *Bahamas* 119 H13
Seal Cays, *Turks & Caicos Is.* 119 J17
Sealevel, *N.C., U.S.* 98 J14
Seal Islands, *Anguilla* 122 Q11
Sealy, *Tex., U.S.* 105 R13
Searchlight, *Nev., U.S.* III V12
Searcy, *Ark., U.S.* 102 G9
Searles Lake, *Calif., U.S.* III V9
Seaside, *Oreg., U.S.* 110 E2
Seaside Park, *N.J., U.S.* 96 Q11
Seaton Glacier, *Antarctica* 231 D19
Seatons, *Antigua and Barbuda* 123 B21
Seattle, *Wash., U.S.* 110 C4
Sebago Lake, *Me., U.S.* 97 G15
Sebakor, Teluk, *Indonesia* 217 C14
Sebastian, *Fla., U.S.* 99 U10
Sebastian, Cape, *Oreg., U.S.* 110 K1
Sebastián Vizcaíno, Bahía, *Mex.* 116 C5
Sebastopol, *Calif., U.S.* III R3
Sebatik, island, *Indonesia* 192 G12
Sebeka, *Minn., U.S.* 106 G10
Seben, *Turk.* 170 D7
Sebeş, *Rom.* 155 D13
Sebewaing, *Mich., U.S.* 100 K12
Sebezh, *Russ.* 158 H5
Şebinkarahisar, *Turk.* 171 E13
Sebring, *Fla., U.S.* 99 U9
Sebuyau, *Malaysia* 192 H9
Sech'ŏn, *N. Korea* 186 E12
Sechura, Bahía de, *Peru* 132 F1
Sechura Desert, *S. Amer.* 128 E2
Secica, *Slovakia* 151 J12
Secondigny, *Fr.* 149 S7
Second Mesa, *Ariz., U.S.* 109 R8
Secos, Ilhéus (Ilhéus do Rombo), *Cabo Verde* 209 D15
Secretary Island, *N.Z.* 217 Q15
Sécure, river, *Bol.* 132 J7
Security, *Colo., U.S.* 109 N13
Sedalia, *Mo., U.S.* 107 T12
Sedan, *Fr.* 149 N12
Sedan, *Kans., U.S.* 107 V9
Seddon, *N.Z.* 217 M18
Sedeh, *Iran* 175 D16
Sedom, *Israel* 173 P6
Sedona, *Ariz., U.S.* 109 S7
Sedro Woolley, *Wash., U.S.* 110 A4
Seeheim, *Namibia* 206 J7
Seemore Downs, *W. Aust., Austral.* 215 W6
Sées, *Fr.* 149 P7
Seevetal, *Ger.* 150 C8
Seferihisar, *Turk.* 170 F2
Seg, Lake, *Eur.* 140 C10
Segamat, *Malaysia* 191 U10
Segbana, *Benin* 204 C12
Segesta, ruin, *It.* 153 S9
Segezha, *Russ.* 160 D7
Seghe, *Solomon Is.* 221 M16
Ségou, *Mali* 200 H7
Segovia, *Sp.* 146 E10
Segré, *Fr.* 149 R6
Seguam Island, *Alas., U.S.* 112 P7
Séguéla, *Côte d'Ivoire* 204 D8
Seguin, *Tex., U.S.* 105 R10

Seguntur, *Indonesia* **192** HI2
Segura, river, *Sp.* **147** KI4
Segura, Sierra de, *Sp.* **146** KI2
Sehwan, *Pak.* **179** U7
Seikan Submarine Tunnel, *Japan* **188** JI2
Seil, island, *Scot., U.K.* **144** L8
Seiling, *Okla., U.S.* **104** F9
Seinäjoki, *Sw.* **143** GI4
Seine, river, *Fr.* **149** P9
Seine, Baie de la, *Fr.* **149** N7
Seine Plain, *Atl. Oc.* **240** KII
Şäki, *Azerb.* **171** C2I
Sekondi-Takoradi, *Ghana* **204** EIO
Sek'ot'a, *Eth.* **203** FI5
Sekseüil, *Kaz.* **176** FIO
Selah, *Wash., U.S.* **110** D6
Selaru, island, *Indonesia* **193** MI7
Selawik, *Alas., U.S.* **113** EI4
Selawik Lake, *Alas., U.S.* **113** EI3
Selayar, island, *Indonesia* **193** LI3
Selby, *Eng., U.K.* **145** RI3
Selby, *S. Dak., U.S.* **106** J5
Selden, *Kans., U.S.* **107** S4
Seldovia, *Alas., U.S.* **113** KI6
Selendi, *Turk.* **170** F4
Selenga, river, *Russ.* **161** LI5
Selenge, river, *Mongolia* **182** CIO
Sélestat, *Fr.* **149** QI5
Selfoss, *Ice.* **142** F2
Selfridge, *N. Dak., U.S.* **106** H4
Sélibaby, *Mauritania* **200** H6
Seliger, Ozero, *Russ.* **158** H7
Seligman, *Ariz., U.S.* **109** S6
Selima Oasis, *Sudan* **202** CI2
Selinus, ruin, *It.* **153** S9
Selkirk, *Scot., U.K.* **145** NII
Selkirk Mountains, *Can., U.S.* **108** A3
Selkirk Rise, *Pac. Oc.* **243** P2I
Sellières, *Fr.* **149** SI3
Sells, *Ariz., U.S.* **109** V7
Selma, *Ala., U.S.* **103** LI5
Selma, *Calif., U.S.* **111** T6
Selma, *N.C., U.S.* **98** HI2
Selmer, *Tenn., U.S.* **103** GI3
Selongey, *Fr.* **149** RI3
Selsey Bill, cape, *Eng., U.K.* **145** XI3
Seltz, *Fr.* **149** PI6
Selvas, region, *S. Amer.* **128** E5
Selway, river, *Idaho, U.S.* **108** D4
Selwyn Mountains, *Yukon, Can.* **84** F9
Selwyn Strait, *Vanuatu* **222** D2
Sema, *N. Korea* **186** L5
Semarang, *Indonesia* **192** M9
Sembé, *Congo* **205** GI7
Şemdinli, *Turk.* **171** HI9
Semenov, *Russ.* **158** HI2
Semeru, peak, *Indonesia* **192** MIO
Semey (Semipalatinsk), *Kaz.* **177** DI7
Semichi Islands, *Alas., U.S.* **112** L2
Semiluki, *Russ.* **158** MIO
Seminoe Dam, *Wyo., U.S.* **108** JII
Seminoe Reservoir, *Wyo., U.S.* **108** JII
Seminole, *Okla., U.S.* **104** GI2
Seminole, *Tex., U.S.* **104** L4
Seminole, Lake, *Fla., Ga., U.S.* **99** Q4
Semipalatinsk see Semey, *Kaz.* **177** DI7
Semipalatinsk Nuclear Test Range, *Kaz.* **177** DI6
Semisopochnoi Island, *Alas., U.S.* **112** N3
Şämkir, *Azerb.* **171** D2O
Semnān, *Iran* **175** CI4
Semporna, *Malaysia* **192** GI2
Sên, river, *Cambodia* **190** MII
Seňa, *Slovakia* **151** JI7
Senaja, *Malaysia* **192** FI2
Senaki, *Rep. of Georgia* **171** BI6
Sena Madureira, *Braz.* **132** G6
Senanga, *Zambia* **206** E9
Senatobia, *Miss., U.S.* **102** HII
Sendai, *Japan* **188** LI3
Sendai, *Japan* **189** S4
Sendhwa, *India* **180** K4
Senduruhan, *Indonesia* **192** J9
Seneca, *Kans., U.S.* **107** R9
Seneca, *Oreg., U.S.* **110** H7
Seneca, *S.C., U.S.* **98** K7

Seneca Falls, *N.Y., U.S.* **96** J7
Senegal, *Af.* **200** H5
Sénégal, river, *Af.* **200** G5
Senftenberg, *Ger.* **150** FII
Sengiley, *Russ.* **158** KI4
Senhor do Bonfim, *Braz.* **133** GI6
Senigallia, *It.* **152** G9
Senj, *Croatia* **154** E5
Senja, island, *Nor.* **142** CI2
Senjitu, *Hebei, China* **184** A8
Sen'ko Valley, *Arctic Oc.* **246** JI2
Senlis, *Fr.* **149** NIO
Sênmônoŭrôm, *Cambodia* **191** NI3
Sennar, *Sudan* **203** EI3
Sennecey-le-Grand, *Fr.* **149** SI2
Sennen, *Eng., U.K.* **145** Y7
Senneterre, *Que., Can.* **85** PI8
Sennwald, *Switz.* **162** L2
Senorbi, *It.* **153** P4
Sens, *Fr.* **149** QII
Sensuntepeque, *El Salv.* **117** LI7
Senta, *Serb.* **154** DII
Šentilj, *Slov.* **154** C6
Sentinel, *Okla., U.S.* **104** G8
Sentinel Range, *Antarctica* **230** H8
Senyavin Islands, *F.S.M.* **220** Q8
Seocheon, *S. Korea* **187** R7
Seogwipo, *S. Korea* **187** X7
Seogkok, *S. Korea* **187** T8
Seokgyo, *S. Korea* **187** U7
Seokjeong, *S. Korea* **187** T8
Seomjin, river, *S. Korea* **187** S9
Seongapdo, island, *S. Korea* **187** N6
Seongeup, *S. Korea* **187** W8
Seonggeo, *S. Korea* **187** P8
Seonghwan, *S. Korea* **187** P8
Seonginbong, peak, *S. Korea* **186** MI5
Seongju, *S. Korea* **187** RIO
Seongmodo, island, *S. Korea* **186** M7
Seongnae, *S. Korea* **187** QI2
Seongnam, *S. Korea* **187** N8
Seongsan, *S. Korea* **186** MIO
Seongsan, *S. Korea* **187** W8
Seoni, *India* **180** J7
Seonsan, *S. Korea* **187** QIO
Seonyudo, island, *S. Korea* **187** R7
Seoraksan, peak, *S. Korea* **186** LII
Seosan, *S. Korea* **187** P7
Seoul, *S. Korea* **186** M8
Sepasu, *Indonesia* **192** JI2
Sepi, *Solomon Is.* **221** MI8
Sepik, river, *P.N.G.* **217** CI8
Sep'o, *N. Korea* **186** K9
Sept-Îles, *Que., Can.* **85** M2I
Sepúlveda, *Sp.* **146** EII
Sepupa, *Botswana* **206** F8
Sequim, *Wash., U.S.* **110** B3
Sequoia National Park, *Calif., U.S.* **111** U7
Seraing, *Belg.* **148** LI3
Serang, *Indonesia* **192** L8
Serasan, island, *Indonesia* **192** H9
Serbia, *Eur.* **154** GIO
Serdobsk, *Russ.* **158** LI2
Serebryansk, *Kaz.* **177** DI8
Sered', *Slovakia* **151** KI4
Seredka, *Russ.* **158** G5
Şereflikoçhisar, *Turk.* **170** F9
Seregno, *It.* **152** D4
Seremban, *Malaysia* **191** UIO
Serena, Embalse la, *Sp.* **146** H9
Serengeti Plain, *Tanzania* **203** KI3
Sergach, *Russ.* **158** JI3
Sergeya Kirova, Ostrova, *Russ.* **161** DI3
Sergino, *Russ.* **160** GIO
Sergiyev Posad, *Russ.* **158** J9
Serian, *Malaysia* **192** H9
Sérifos, *Gr.* **157** LI4
Sérifos (Sériphos), island, *Gr.* **157** LI3
Sérignan, *Fr.* **149** YII
Serik, *Turk.* **170** H6
Seringa, Serra da, *Braz.* **132** FI2
Seriole, river, *San Marino* **163** LI5
Sériphos see Sérifos, island, *Gr.* **157** LI3
Serkovo, *Russ.* **161** GI3
Sermata, island, *Indonesia* **193** MI6
Sermata, Kepulauan, *Indonesia* **193** MI6
Sermilik, *Greenland, Den.* **82** DIO

Sermilik Valley, *Atl. Oc.* **247** PI9
Sernur, *Russ.* **158** HI4
Seroczyn, *Pol.* **151** EI7
Seroe Colorado, *Aruba, Neth.* **123** RI7
Serov, *Russ.* **160** H9
Serowe, *Botswana* **206** HIO
Serpa, *Port.* **146** K6
Serpentine Lakes, *Austral.* **214** H7
Serpent Island, *Mauritius* **209** E2I
Serpent's Mouth, *Trinidad and Tobago, Venez.* **121** KI6
Serpukhov, *Russ.* **158** K9
Serra de L'Albera, range, *Fr., Sp.* **149** ZIO
Serra do Navio, *Braz.* **132** CI2
Serravalle, *San Marino* **163** JI6
Serre-Ponçon, Lac de, *Fr.* **149** WI4
Serrera, Pic de la, *Andorra, Fr.* **162** G4
Serres, *Fr.* **149** WI4
Sérres, *Gr.* **156** BI2
Serrezuela, *Arg.* **134** J9
Serrières, *Fr.* **149** VI2
Serrinha, *Braz.* **133** HI6
Sersale, *It.* **153** QI4
Sertã, *Port.* **146** G6
Sertão, region, *S. Amer.* **128** FIO
Sêrtar, *China* **182** K9
Serti, *Nigeria* **205** DI5
Serui, *Indonesia* **193** KI9
Şәrur, *Arm.* **171** EI9
Sérvia, *Gr.* **156** D9
Sêrxü, *China* **182** K8
Sesfontein, *Namibia* **206** G5
Sesheke, *Zambia* **206** F9
Sesimbra, *Port.* **146** J4
Sesklí, island, *Gr.* **157** MI9
Sessa Aurunca, *It.* **152** LIO
Sestri Levante, *It.* **152** F5
Sestri Ponente, *It.* **152** F4
Sestroretsk, *Russ.* **158** F6
Setana, *Japan* **188** HI2
Sète, *Fr.* **149** XII
Sete Lagoas, *Braz.* **133** KI4
Sete Quedas Falls, *S. Amer.* **128** J7
Sétif, *Alg.* **200** AII
Seto, *Japan* **189** PIO
Seto Naikai (Inland Sea), *Japan* **189** Q6
Settat, *Mor.* **200** B8
Setté Cama, *Gabon* **205** JI5
Settimo Torinese, *It.* **152** E3
Settlement, *Marshall Is., U.S.* **220** N5
Settlement, *Wake I., U.S.* **220** F8
Setúbal, *Port.* **146** J5
Setúbal, Baía de, *Port.* **146** J5
Seul, Lac, *Ont., Can.* **85** NI5
Seul Choix Point, *Mich., U.S.* **100** G9
Seuldo, island, *S. Korea* **187** U7
Seungju, *S. Korea* **187** T9
Sevan, *Arm.* **171** DI9
Sevana Lich, *Arm.* **171** DI9
Sevastopol', *Ukr.* **159** T7
Sevelen, *Switz.* **162** P2
Seven Islands Bay, *Nfld. & Lab., Can.* **85** J2O
Seven Stones, island, *Eng., U.K.* **145** Y7
Severn, *Ont., Can.* **85** LI6
Severn, *S. Af.* **206** J9
Severn, river, *N. Amer.* **82** G6
Severnaya Dvina, river, *Russ.* **160** F8
Severnaya Zemlya (North Land), *Russ.* **161** CI4
Severnyy, *Russ.* **160** FII
Severobaykal'sk, *Russ.* **161** KI6
Severodvinsk, *Russ.* **160** E8
Severo Kuril'sk, *Russ.* **161** G23
Severomorsk, *Russ.* **160** D9
Severo Sibirskaya Nizmennost', *Russ.* **161** FI4
Sever Spur, *Atl. Oc.* **246** LII
Sevi, river, *Russ.* **161** LI3
Sevier, river, *Utah, U.S.* **108** M6
Sevier Desert, *Utah, U.S.* **108** M6
Sevier Lake, *Utah, U.S.* **109** N6
Sevilla, *Col.* **130** F4
Sevilla (Seville), *Sp.* **146** L8
Sevilla Nueva, site, *Jam.* **122** H8
Sevlievo, *Bulg.* **155** HI5
Seward, *Alas., U.S.* **113** KI6

Seward, *Nebr., U.S.* **107** Q8
Seward Peninsula, *Alas., U.S.* **112** EI2
Sewell, *Chile* **134** L7
Sewell Rise, *Ind. Oc.* **225** EI2
Seychelles, *Af.* **207** BI9
Seychelles Bank, *Ind. Oc.* **224** G8
Seydi, *Turkm.* **176** LIO
Seydişehir, *Turk.* **170** H7
Seyðisfjörður, *Ice.* **142** E4
Seyfe Gölü, *Turk.* **170** F9
Seyhan, river, *Turk.* **170** HIO
Seyhan Barajı, *Turk.* **170** HIO
Seyitgazi, *Turk.* **170** E6
Seylla Glacier, *Antarctica* **231** FI9
Seymchan, *Russ.* **161** E2O
Seymour, *Ind., U.S.* **101** S9
Seymour, *Iowa, U.S.* **107** QI2
Seymour, *Tex., U.S.* **104** K8
Seymour, *Vic., Austral.* **215** YI2
Seymour, *Wis., U.S.* **100** J6
Seymour, Isla, *Ecua.* **130** RIO
Seyne, *Fr.* **149** WI4
Seyöisfjarðardjúp, valley, *Arctic Oc.* **247** K2O
Sézanne, *Fr.* **149** PII
Sfântu Gheorghe, *Rom.* **155** DI5
Sfântu-Gheorghe, Ostrov, *Rom.* **155** EI9
Sfântu-Gheorghe Braţul, river, *Rom.* **155** EI9
Sfax, *Tun.* **201** BI3
Sha, river, *Fujian, China* **185** S8
Shaanxi, *China* **184** HI
Shabla, Nos, *Bulg.* **155** GI8
Shabwah, *Yemen* **174** QIO
Shache (Yarkant), *China* **182** F2
Shackleton Fracture Zone, *Atl. Oc.* **241** W5
Shackleton Coast, *Antarctica* **231** LI3
Shackleton Ice Shelf, *Antarctica* **231** K2I
Shackleton Range, *Antarctica* **230** FII
Shadehill Reservoir, *S. Dak., U.S.* **106** H3
Shaduzup, *Myanmar* **190** E6
Shafter, *Nev., U.S.* **110** MI2
Shafter, *Tex., U.S.* **105** QI
Shagedu, *N. Mongol, China* **184** D3
Shageluk, *Alas., U.S.* **113** HI3
Shaghan, *Kaz.* **177** DI7
Shaghan, river, *Kaz.* **176** F8
Shahbā' (Philippopolis), *Syr.* **172** K8
Shahbandar, *Pak.* **179** X7
Shahdadkot, *Pak.* **179** T7
Shahdadpur, *Pak.* **179** V7
Shahdol, *India* **180** J8
Shahe, *Hebei, China* **184** F6
Shahgarh, *India* **180** F2
Shahhāt (Cyrene), *Lib.* **201** BI6
Shahjahanpur, *India* **180** F7
Shāh Maqşūd, Kōh-e, *Afghan.* **179** Q4
Shahousuo, *Liaoning, China* **184** CII
Shahpur, *India* **180** M5
Shahpur, *Pak.* **179** PIO
Shahpur Chakar, *Pak.* **179** V7
Shahr-e Bābak, *Iran* **175** FI4
Shahrezā (Qomsheh), *Iran* **175** EI3
Shahrig, *Pak.* **179** R7
Shahrisabz, *Uzb.* **176** LI2
Shāhrūd, *Iran* **175** CI4
Shaighalu, *Pak.* **179** Q7
Shajapur, *India* **180** J5
Shakhtersk, *Russ.* **161** J2I
Shakhty, *Russ.* **159** QII
Shakhun'ya, *Russ.* **158** GI3
Shaktoolik, *Alas., U.S.* **113** GI3
Shali, *Russ.* **159** UI4
Shallowater, *Tex., U.S.* **104** K5
Shalqar, *Kaz.* **176** F9
Shalqar Köli, *Kaz.* **176** D6
Shalu, *Taiwan, China* **185** UII
Shaluli Shan, *China* **182** L8
Shām, Jabal ash, *Oman* **175** KI6
Shamattawa, river, *Man., Can.* **85** LI5
Shambe, *S. Sudan* **202** GI2
Shammar, Jabal, *Saudi Arabia* **174** H7
Shamokin, *Pa., U.S.* **96** N8
Shamrock, *Tex., U.S.* **104** G7

Shamva, *Zimb.* **206** FI2
Shanchengzhen, *Jilin, China* **184** AI4
Shandan, *China* **182** G9
Shandong, *China* **184** G8
Shandong Bandao, *Shand., China* **184** GIO
Shandur Pass, *Pak.* **178** LIO
Shangcai, *Henan, China* **184** K6
Shangcheng, *Henan, China* **184** M7
Shangchuan Dao, *Guang., China* **185** X4
Shangdu, *N. Mongol, China* **184** B5
Shanggao, *Jiangxi, China* **185** Q6
Shanghai, *Shanghai Shi, China* **184** MI2
Shanghai Shi, *China* **184** MI2
Shanghang, *Fujian, China* **185** U7
Shangnan, *Shaanxi, China* **184** K3
Shangombo, *Zambia* **206** E8
Shangqiu, *Henan, China* **184** J7
Shangrao, *Jiangxi, China* **185** Q9
Shangyou, *Jiangxi, China* **185** T5
Shangzhou, *Shaanxi, China* **184** J2
Shanhaiguan, *Liaoning, China* **184** CIO
Shaniko, *Oreg., U.S.* **110** F5
Shanklin, *Eng., U.K.* **145** XI3
Shannon (Sionainn), *Ire.* **145** T4
Shannon, River, *Ire.* **145** T3
Shannon Ø, island, *Greenland, Den.* **82** B9
Shantar Islands, *Asia* **168** DI2
Shantarskiye Ostrova, *Russ.* **161** H2O
Shanting, *Shand., China* **184** H8
Shantou (Swatow), *Guang., China* **185** V8
Shanwei, *Guang., China* **185** W6
Shanxi, *China* **184** G4
Shanxian, *Shand., China* **184** J7
Shanyang, *Shaanxi, China* **184** K2
Shanyin, *Shanxi, China* **184** D5
Shanyincheng, *Shanxi, China* **184** D5
Shaoguan, *Guang., China* **185** U5
Shaowu, *Fujian, China* **185** R8
Shaoxing, *Zhejiang, China* **185** PII
Shaoyang, *Hunan, China* **185** R3
Shap, *Eng., U.K.* **145** QII
Shapa, *Guang., China* **185** X3
Shapinsay, island, *Scot., U.K.* **144** FIO
Shaqrā', *Saudi Arabia* **174** JIO
Shaqrā', *Yemen* **174** RIO
Shar, *Kaz.* **177** DI7
Shār, Jabal, *Saudi Arabia* **174** G5
Sharan, *Afghan.* **179** N7
Sharbaqty, *Kaz.* **177** CI6
Sharbatāt, *Oman* **175** NI5
Sharbatāt, Ra's ash, *Oman* **175** NI5
Shari, *Japan* **188** FI5
Sharjah, *U.A.E.* **175** JI5
Sharkan, *Russ.* **158** GI6
Shark Bay, *Austral.* **214** GI
Sharlawuk, *Turkm.* **176** L7
Sharm el Sheikh, *Egypt* **173** U4
Sharon, *Pa., U.S.* **96** M3
Sharon Springs, *Kans., U.S.* **107** S3
Sharpe, Lake, *S. Dak., U.S.* **106** L5
Sharqī, Al Jabal ash (Anti-Lebanon Range), *Syr.* **172** J7
Sharuhen, ruins, *Israel* **173** N4
Sharwayn, Ra's, *Yemen* **175** QI3
Shar'ya, *Russ.* **158** GI3
Shashe, river, *Af.* **206** GIO
Shashi, *Hubei, China* **185** N4
Shasta, Mount, *Calif., U.S.* **110** M4
Shasta Lake, *Calif., U.S.* **110** M4
Shatskiy Rise, *Pac. Oc.* **242** F9
Shattuck, *Okla., U.S.* **104** F7
Shaumyani, *Rep. of Georgia* **171** CI8
Shaunavon, *Sask., Can.* **84** NII
Shaw, *Miss., U.S.* **102** JIO
Shawano, *Wis., U.S.* **100** J6
Shawinigan, *Que., Can.* **85** PI9
Shawnee, *Kans., U.S.* **107** SIO
Shawnee, *Okla., U.S.* **104** GII
Shaxian, *Fujian, China* **185** S9
Shaybārā, island, *Saudi Arabia* **174** J5
Shay Gap, *W. Aust., Austral.* **215** S3
Shaykh 'Uthmān, *Yemen* **174** R9
Shayman, *Taj.* **178** JI2
Shchekino, *Russ.* **158** K9
Shchigry, *Russ.* **158** M9

Shchŭchīnsk, *Kaz.* **177** CI3
Shebekino, *Russ.* **159** N9
Shebelē, river, *Af.* **198** HII
Shebelē, Wabē, *Af.* **203** HI6
Shebir, *Kaz.* **176** G6
Sheboygan, *Wis., U.S.* **100** K7
Sheboygan Falls, *Wis., U.S.* **100** K7
Shed Lakes, *Austral.* **214** H6
Sheelin, Lough, *Ire.* **145** R6
Sheep Haven, *Ire.* **145** N5
Sheep Mountain, *Colo., U.S.* **108** LII
Sheep Range, *Nev., U.S.* **III** TI2
Sheerness, *Eng., U.K.* **145** VI5
Shefar'am, *Israel* **172** K5
Sheffield, *Ala., U.S.* **103** GI4
Sheffield, *Eng., U.K.* **145** SI2
Sheffield, *Tex., U.S.* **105** P5
Sheikhupura, *Pak.* **179** QI2
Sheka Ridge, *Atl. Oc.* **241** VI3
Shelbina, *Mo., U.S.* **107** RI3
Shelburne, *N.S., Can.* **85** Q22
Shelburne Bay, *Austral.* **214** AI2
Shelby, *Mich., U.S.* **100** K9
Shelby, *Miss., U.S.* **102** JIO
Shelby, *Mont., U.S.* **108** B7
Shelby, *N.C., U.S.* **98** J8
Shelby, *Ohio, U.S.* **100** PI3
Shelbyville, *Ill., U.S.* **101** S6
Shelbyville, *Ind., U.S.* **101** S9
Shelbyville, *Ky., U.S.* **103** BI7
Shelbyville, *Tenn., U.S.* **103** FI5
Sheldon, *Iowa, U.S.* **106** M9
Sheldon Point, *Alas., U.S.* **112** HII
Shelikhova, Zaliv, *Russ.* **161** E2I
Shelikhov Gulf, *Pac. Oc.* **168** CI2
Shelikof Strait, *Alas., U.S.* **113** LI5
Shell Bank, *Ind. Oc.* **224** RII
Shell Beach, *Guyana* **131** CI4
Shelley, *Idaho, U.S.* **108** H7
Shell Lake, *Wis., U.S.* **100** G2
Shellman, *Ga., U.S.* **99** P5
Shelter Cove, *Calif., U.S.* **III** NI
Shelton, *Nebr., U.S.* **107** Q6
Shelton, *Wash., U.S.* **110** C3
Shemonaïkha, *Kaz.* **177** DI8
Shemya Island, *Alas., U.S.* **112** L2
Shenandoah, *Iowa, U.S.* **107** Q9
Shenandoah, *Pa., U.S.* **96** N8
Shenandoah, *Va., U.S.* **98** DII
Shenandoah, river, *Va., U.S.* **98** DII
Shenandoah National Park, *Va., U.S.* **98** DII
Shenchi, *Shanxi, China* **184** D4
Shendam, *Nigeria* **205** DI5
Sheng-li Feng see Pobeda Peak, *China, Kyrg.* **178** EI5
Shengsi Liedao, islands, *Zhejiang, China* **185** NI3
Shengzhou, *Zhejiang, China* **185** PII
Shenjiamen see Putuo, *Zhejiang, China* **185** PI3
Shenmu, *Shaanxi, China* **184** D3
Shenqiu, *Henan, China* **184** K6
Shenton, Mount, *Austral.* **214** H5
Shenxian, *Shand., China* **184** G7
Shenyang, *Liaoning, China* **184** AI3
Shenzha see Xainza, *China* **182** K5
Shenzhen, *Hong Kong (Xianggang), S.A.R., China* **185** W5
Sheoganj, *India* **180** H3
Sheopur, *India* **180** G5
Shepetivka, *Ukr.* **159** N4
Shepherd, *Ill., U.S.* **101** R3
Shepherd Islands, *Vanuatu* **222** E2
Shepparton, *Vic., Austral.* **215** YI3
Sheppey, Isle of, *Eng., U.K.* **145** VI5
Sherbo Island, *Sierra Leone* **204** D5
Sherbrooke, *Que., Can.* **85** P2O
Sherburn, *Minn., U.S.* **106** LIO
Shereiq, *Sudan* **203** DI3
Sheridan, *Ark., U.S.* **102** H8
Sheridan, *Wyo., U.S.* **108** FII
Sheridan, Cape, *Nunavut, Can.* **85** AI6
Sheringham, *Eng., U.K.* **145** SI5
Sherkaly, *Russ.* **160** GIO
Sherkin Island, *Ire.* **145** V3
Sherlovaya Gora, *Russ.* **161** LI7
Sherman, *Tex., U.S.* **104** KI2
Sherman Mills, *Me., U.S.* **97** DI8
Sherman Peak, *U.S.* **86** E7

Sherobod, *Uzb.* **176** MI2
Sherridon, *Man., Can.* **85** LI3
's Hertogenbosch, *Neth.* **148** KI3
Sherwood, *N. Dak., U.S.* **106** D4
Sherwood Forest, *Eng., U.K.* **145** SI3
Shetland Islands (Zetland), *Scot., U.K.* **144** CI2
Shetpe, *Kaz.* **176** H6
Shexian, *Anhui, China* **185** P9
Shexian, *Shanxi, China* **184** G5
Sheyang (Hede), *Jiangsu, China* **184** KII
Sheyenne, *N. Dak., U.S.* **106** F6
Sheyenne, river, *N. Dak., U.S.* **106** F7
Shiant Islands see Na h-Eileanan Mora, islands, *Scot., U.K.* **144** H7
Shiashkotan, island, *Russ.* **161** H23
Shibām, *Yemen* **174** PII
Shibar, Kōtal-e, *Afghan.* **178** M6
Shibata, *Japan* **188** MII
Shibecha, *Japan* **188** GI5
Shibetsu, *Japan* **188** FI5
Shibirghān, *Afghan.* **178** K5
Shibushi Wan, *Japan* **189** T5
Shicheng, *Jiangxi, China* **185** S7
Shidao, *Shand., China* **184** FI2
Shidler, *Okla., U.S.* **104** EI2
Shiel, Loch, *Scot., U.K.* **144** L8
Shiel Bridge, *Scot., U.K.* **144** K8
Shīeli, *Kaz.* **176** HI2
Shiguai, *N. Mongol, China* **184** B3
Shiḥan, *Yemen* **175** NI3
Shihezi, *China* **182** E5
Shijiazhuang, *Hebei, China* **184** E6
Shikarpur, *India* **180** G9
Shikarpur, *Pak.* **179** T7
Shikengkong, peak, *Guang., China* **185** U4
Shikoku, island, *Japan* **189** R7
Shikoku Basin, *Pac. Oc.* **242** F7
Shikotan, island, *Russ.* **188** FI6
Shildon, *Eng., U.K.* **145** PI2
Shīli, *Kaz.* **176** DIO
Shiliguri, *India* **180** GII
Shilik, *Kaz.* **177** HI7
Shilipu see Tongchuan, *Shaanxi, China* **184** HI
Shiliyn Bogd Uul, *China, Mongolia* **183** EI3
Shilka, *Russ.* **161** LI7
Shilla, peak, *India* **180** D6
Shillong, *India* **180** GI3
Shiloh National Military Park, *Tenn., U.S.* **103** GI3
Shilong, *Guang., China* **185** V5
Shilou, *Shanxi, China* **184** F3
Shilovo, *Russ.* **158** KII
Shimabara, *Japan* **189** R4
Shima Hantō, *Japan* **189** QIO
Shimanovsk, *Russ.* **161** KI9
Shimanto, *Japan* **189** R6
Shimen, *Hunan, China* **185** P3
Shimizu, *Japan* **188** GI4
Shimoda, *Japan* **189** QII
Shimonoseki, *Japan* **189** Q5
Shimono Shima, *Japan* **189** Q3
Shin, Loch, *Scot., U.K.* **144** H9
Shinapaaru, *N. Mariana Is., U.S.* **220** D8
Shinās, *Oman* **175** JI5
Shīndand (Sabzawar), *Afghan.* **179** N2
Shiner, *Tex., U.S.* **105** RII
Shingbwiyang, *Myanmar* **190** D6
Shingphel, *Bhutan* **180** FI3
Shingū, *Japan* **189** R9
Shinjō, *Japan* **188** LI2
Shīnkaī, *Afghan.* **179** P6
Shīnkay Ghar, range, *Afghan.* **179** P7
Shinkolobwe, *Dem. Rep. of the Congo* **202** NII
Shinnston, *W. Va., U.S.* **98** C9
Shinyanga, *Tanzania* **203** LI3
Shiono Misaki, *Japan* **189** R9
Shiping, *China* **182** N9
Ship Island, *Miss., U.S.* **102** PI2
Shipki Pass, *India* **180** D7
Shippensburg, *Pa., U.S.* **96** P6
Ship Rock, peak, *N. Mex., U.S.* **109** QIO
Shiprock, *N. Mex., U.S.* **109** QIO

Shipu, *Zhejiang, China* **185** PI2
Shipu see Huanglong, *Shaanxi, China* **184** H2
Shirakami Misaki, *Japan* **188** HI2
Shirase Coast, *Antarctica* **230** MII
Shirase Glacier, *Antarctica* **231** CI7
Shīrāz, *Iran* **175** GI3
Shire, river, *Malawi* **207** EI3
Shireet, *Mongolia* **182** DI2
Shiretoko Misaki, *Japan* **188** EI5
Shiriya Zaki, *Japan* **188** HI3
Shīr Kūh, peak, *Iran* **175** EI4
Shiroishi, *Japan* **188** MI2
Shirone, *Japan* **188** MII
Shirshov Ridge, *Pac. Oc.* **246** GI
Shishaldin Volcano, *Alas., U.S.* **112** NII
Shishmaref, *Alas., U.S.* **112** EI2
Shishou, *Hubei, China* **185** P4
Shitai, *Anhui, China* **185** N8
Shiv, *India* **180** G2
Shivamogga, *India* **181** P5
Shivpuri, *India* **180** G6
Shivta, ruins, *Israel* **173** P4
Shivwits Plateau, *Ariz., U.S.* **109** R5
Shiyan, *Hubei, China* **184** L3
Shizhuzi, *Liaoning, China* **184** BI4
Shizilu see Junan, *Shand., China* **184** H9
Shizuishan (Dawukou), *China* **182** GIO
Shizunai, *Japan* **188** HI3
Shizuoka, *Japan* **189** QII
Shkīn, *Afghan.* **179** P8
Shkodër (Scutari), *Alban.* **154** K9
Shkumbin, river, *Alban.* **154** L9
Shmakov Escarpment, *Arctic Oc.* **246** HI2
Shmidta, Ostrov, *Russ.* **161** CI4
Shoalhaven Bight, *Austral.* **214** LI4
Shoals, Isles of, *N.H., U.S.* **97** JI5
Shoalwater Bay, *Austral.* **214** FI5
Shoghot, *Pak.* **178** LIO
Sholapur, *India* **180** M5
Shonian Harbor, *Palau* **220** QIO
Shonzhy, *Kaz.* **177** HI7
Shōrakīan, *Afghan.* **179** P4
Sho'rchi, *Uzb.* **176** MI2
Shoreham-by-Sea, *Eng., U.K.* **145** WI4
Shorkot, *Pak.* **179** QIO
Shorobe, *Botswana* **206** G9
Shōr Tepah, *Afghan.* **178** K6
Shortland, island, *Solomon Is.* **221** LI4
Shortland Islands, *Solomon Is.* **221** LI4
Shosambetsu, *Japan* **188** EI3
Shoshone, *Calif., U.S.* **III** UIO
Shoshone, *Idaho, U.S.* **108** H5
Shoshone, river, *Wyo., U.S.* **108** FIO
Shoshone Falls, *U.S.* **86** E6
Shoshone Lake, *Wyo., U.S.* **108** G8
Shoshone Mountain, *Nev., U.S.* **III** TIO
Shoshone Mountains, *Nev., U.S.* **III** Q9
Shoshone Range, *Nev., U.S.* **III** N9
Shoshoni, *Wyo., U.S.* **108** HIO
Shostka, *Ukr.* **158** M7
Shotor Khūn, pass, *Afghan.* **178** M4
Shouguang, *Shand., China* **184** G9
Shouning, *Fujian, China* **185** RIO
Shoval, *Israel* **173** N5
Show Low, *Ariz., U.S.* **109** T9
Shpola, *Ukr.* **159** P6
Shreveport, *La., U.S.* **102** L6
Shroud Cay, *Bahamas* **118** EI2
Shū, *Kaz.* **177** HI5
Shū, river, *Kaz.* **177** HI4
Shū'ab, Ra's, *Yemen* **175** RI4
Shuangcheng, *China* **183** DI6
Shuangfeng, *Hunan, China* **185** R4
Shuangpai, *Hunan, China* **185** S3
Shubarqudyq, *Kaz.* **176** E8
Shucheng, *Anhui, China* **184** M8
Shugozero, *Russ.* **158** F8
Shuibei, *Jiangxi, China* **185** R8
Shuiding see Huocheng, *China* **182** D3
Shukpa Kunzang, *India* **178** MI5
Shule, *China* **182** F2

Shule, river, *China* **182** G7
Shumagin Islands, *Alas., U.S.* **112** NI2
Shumanay, *Uzb.* **176** J9
Shumen (Kolarovgrad), *Bulg.* **155** HI6
Shumerlya, *Russ.* **158** JI3
Shumshu, island, *Russ.* **161** G23
Shunchang, *Fujian, China* **185** S9
Shungay, *Kaz.* **176** E4
Shungnak, *Alas., U.S.* **113** EI4
Shunyi, *Beijing Shi, China* **184** C8
Shuozhou, *Shanxi, China* **184** D4
Shupenzë, *Alban.* **154** KIO
Shuqualak, *Miss., U.S.* **103** KI3
Shūrāb, *Iran* **175** DI5
Shūr Gaz, *Iran* **175** GI6
Shurma, *Russ.* **158** HI5
Shurugwi, *Zimb.* **206** GII
Shūsf, *Iran* **175** EI7
Shūshtar, *Iran* **174** EII
Shuya, *Russ.* **158** HII
Shuyak Island, *Alas., U.S.* **113** LI5
Shwebo, *Myanmar* **190** G6
Shwedaung, *Myanmar* **190** J5
Shwegu, *Myanmar* **190** F6
Shwegyin, *Myanmar* **190** K6
Shweli, river, *Myanmar* **190** F7
Shymkent, *Kaz.* **177** JI3
Shyngghyrlau, *Kaz.* **176** C7
Shyok, *India* **180** C6
Shyok, river, *Pak.* **178** LI3
Sia, *Indonesia* **193** MI9
Siāhān Range, *Pak.* **179** U3
Sialkot, *Pak.* **179** PI2
Siantan, island, *Indonesia* **192** H8
Siapa, river, *Venez.* **130** GIO
Siargao, island, *Philippines* **193** EI5
Siátista, *Gr.* **156** D9
Siau, island, *Indonesia* **193** HI5
Šiauliai, *Lith.* **143** MI6
Sibari, *It.* **153** PI3
Sibay, *Russ.* **160** J8
Siberia, region, *Asia* **168** D8
Siberut, island, *Indonesia* **192** J5
Siberut, Selat, *Indonesia* **192** J5
Sibi, *Pak.* **179** S7
Sibidiro, *P.N.G.* **217** EI8
Sibigo, *Indonesia* **192** H4
Sibiti, *Congo* **205** JI6
Sibiu, *Rom.* **155** DI4
Sibley, *Iowa, U.S.* **106** M9
Siboa, *Indonesia* **193** JI3
Sibolga, *Indonesia* **192** H5
Sibsagar, *India* **180** FI5
Sibu, *Malaysia* **192** HIO
Sibuco, *Philippines* **193** FI4
Sibut, *Cen. Af. Rep.* **202** H9
Sibutu Passage, *Philippines* **193** GI3
Sibuyan, island, *Philippines* **193** DI4
Sibuyan Sea, *Philippines* **193** DI4
Sicasica, *Bol.* **132** K6
Siccus, river, *Austral.* **214** JII
Sichon, *Thai.* **191** Q8
Sichuan Basin, *Asia* **168** HIO
Sicié, Cap, *Fr.* **149** YI4
Sicilia (Sicily), island, *It.* **153** SII
Sicily see Sicilia, island, *It.* **153** SII
Sicily, Strait of, *It.* **153** T7
Sicuani, *Peru* **132** J5
Sidári, *Gr.* **156** E6
Sidas, *Indonesia* **192** J9
Siddhapur, *India* **180** H3
Siddipet, *India* **180** M6
Side, ruins, *Turk.* **170** C5
Síderos, Ákra, *Gr.* **157** QI7
Sīdi Barrâni, *Egypt* **201** CI7
Sidi Bel Abbès, *Alg.* **200** AIO
Sidi Ifni, *Mor.* **200** C7
Sidirókastro, *Gr.* **156** BI2
Sidlaw Hills, *Scot., U.K.* **144** LIO
Sidmouth, *Eng., U.K.* **145** XIO
Sidmouth, Cape, *Austral.* **214** BI3
Sidney, *Iowa, U.S.* **107** Q9
Sidney, *Mont., U.S.* **108** CI3
Sidney, *N.Y., U.S.* **96** K9
Sidney, *Nebr., U.S.* **107** P2
Sidney, *Ohio, U.S.* **101** QII
Sidney Lanier, Lake, *Ga., U.S.* **98** K7
Sidon see Saïda, *Leb.* **172** J6
Sidorovsk, *Russ.* **160** GI2

Sidra, Gulf of see Khalīj Surt, *Lib.* **201** CI4
Siedlce, *Pol.* **151** DI7
Siegen, *Ger.* **150** F6
Siemiatycze, *Pol.* **151** DI7
Siĕmpang, *Cambodia* **190** MI2
Siĕmréab (Siem Reap), *Cambodia* **191** NII
Siem Reap see Siĕmréab, *Cambodia* **191** NII
Siena, *It.* **152** H7
Sieradz, *Pol.* **151** EI4
Sierck, *Fr.* **162** LII
Sierpc, *Pol.* **151** DI5
Sierra Blanca, peak, *Tex., U.S.* **105** W4
Sierra Blanca Peak, *N. Mex., U.S.* **109** UI3
Sierra Colorada, *Arg.* **135** P8
Sierra Leone, *Af.* **204** C6
Sierra Leone Basin, *Atl. Oc.* **241** NIO
Sierra Leone Fracture Zone, *Atl. Oc.* **241** N8
Sierra Leone Rise, *Atl. Oc.* **241** NIO
Sierra Madre del Sur, *Mex.* **116** KII
Sierra Madre Occidental, *Mex.* **116** E9
Sierra Madre Oriental, *Mex.* **116** FII
Sierra Maestra, *Cuba* **118** KI2
Sierra Mojada, *Mex.* **116** EIO
Sierra Nevada, *Calif., U.S.* **III** S7
Sierra Vista, *Ariz., U.S.* **109** W8
Sierre, *Switz.* **152** C2
Sífnos (Síphnos), island, *Gr.* **157** LI4
Sigatoka, *Fiji* **222** J5
Sigavé (Leava), *Wallis and Futuna, Fr.* **222** EII
Sigave, Anse de, *Wallis and Futuna, Fr.* **222** EII
Sigean, *Fr.* **149** YIO
Siġġiewi, *Malta* **163** L22
Sighetul Marmatiei, *Rom.* **155** AI3
Sighişoara, *Rom.* **155** DI4
Sighnaghi, *Rep. of Georgia* **171** CI9
Siglufjörður, *Ice.* **142** D3
Signal Hill, *Austral.* **214** EII
Signal Hill, *Gibraltar, U.K.* **163** P23
Signal Peak, *Ariz., U.S.* **109** U5
Sigourney, *Iowa, U.S.* **107** PI3
Sígri, *Gr.* **157** FI6
Sigüenza, *Sp.* **146** EI2
Siguer, Port de, *Andorra, Fr.* **162** G3
Siguiri, *Guinea* **204** B7
Sihanoukville see Preăh Seihânŭ, *Cambodia* **191** PII
Siheung, *S. Korea* **187** N8
Sihong, *Jiangsu, China* **184** K9
Sihora, *India* **180** J7
Siirt, *Turk.* **171** GI6
Siis, island, *F.S.M.* **221** CI5
Sijung, *N. Korea* **186** E7
Sikar, *India* **180** F5
Sikasso, *Mali* **200** J7
Sikeston, *Mo., U.S.* **107** VI6
Sikhote Alin' Range, *Asia* **168** EI3
Síkinos, *Gr.* **157** MI5
Síkinos, island, *Gr.* **157** MI5
Siki Rangi Passage, *Cook Is., N.Z.* **223** AI7
Sil, river, *Sp.* **146** C7
Sila Fracture Zone, *Pac. Oc.* **243** CI4
Silat, *Indonesia* **192** JIO
Silba, island, *Croatia* **154** F4
Silchar, *India* **180** HI4
Şile, *Turk.* **170** C5
Siler City, *N.C., U.S.* **98** HII
Silesia, region, *Pol.* **151** FI3
Silet, *Alg.* **200** FII
Siletitengi, Lake, *Asia* **168** E7
Silgarhi, *Nepal* **180** F5
Silhouette, island, *Seychelles* **209** NI9
Silifke, *Turk.* **170** J9
Silisili, Mount, *Samoa* **222** K2
Silistra, *Bulg.* **155** GI7
Silivri, *Turk.* **170** C4
Siljan, lake, *Sw.* **142** JI2
Silkeborg, *Den.* **142** MIO
Silla, *Sp.* **147** HI4
Siloam Springs, *Ark., U.S.* **102** E6
Silogui, *Indonesia* **192** J5

Silopi, *Turk.* 171 HI7
Silsbee, *Tex., U.S.* 105 PI5
Silsilah-ye Band-e Turkistān, range, *Afghan.* 178 L3
Silsilah-ye Safēd Kōh (Paropamisus Range), *Afghan.* 178 M2
Silum, *Liech.* 162 P3
Šilutė, *Lith.* 143 MI5
Silvan, *Turk.* 171 GI5
Silvânia, *Braz.* 133 JI3
Silvassa, *India* 180 K3
Silver Bay, *Minn., U.S.* 106 FI3
Silver Bell, *Ariz., U.S.* 109 V7
Silver City, *Idaho, U.S.* 108 H3
Silver City, *Mich., U.S.* 100 E5
Silver City, *N. Mex., U.S.* 109 UIO
Silver City, *Nev., U.S.* III Q6
Silver Creek, *Oreg., U.S.* 110 H6
Silver Hill, peak, *Montserrat* 123 A24
Silver Lake, *Oreg., U.S.* 110 J5
Silver Peak, *Nev., U.S.* III S9
Silver Plain, *Atl. Oc.* 240 L4
Silver Spring, *Md., U.S.* 98 CI3
Silverton, *Colo., U.S.* 109 PII
Silverton, *Oreg., U.S.* 110 F3
Silverton, *Tex., U.S.* 104 H6
Silves, *Braz.* 132 DIO
Silvies, river, *Oreg., U.S.* 110 H7
Sima, *Comoros* 209 NI6
Simansih, *Indonesia* 192 K5
Şīmareh, river, *Iran* 174 DIO
Simav, *Turk.* 170 F4
Simav, river, *Turk.* 170 E4
Simbo, island, *Solomon Is.* 221 MI5
Simcoe, Lake, *Ont., Can.* 85 QI8
Simdega, *India* 180 J9
Simeria, *Rom.* 154 DI2
Simeulue, island, *Indonesia* 192 H4
Simferopol', *Ukr.* 159 T7
Simikot, *Nepal* 180 E8
Simi Valley, *Calif., U.S.* III X7
Simla, *Colo., U.S.* 108 MI4
Simla, *India* 180 D6
Şimleu Silvaniei, *Rom.* 154 BI2
Simms Point, *Bahamas* 122 BIO
Simon's Point, *Bahamas* 122 F9
Simontornya, *Hung.* 151 MI4
Simpang, *Indonesia* 192 J7
Simpson Desert, *Austral.* 214 GIO
Simpson Peninsula, *Nunavut, Can.* 85 FI5
Simrishamn, *Sw.* 143 NI3
Simson Baai, *St. Maarten, Neth.* 123 BI4
Simsonbaai see Simson Bay, *St. Maarten, Neth.* 123 BI4
Simson Bay, *St. Maarten, Neth.* 123 BI4
Simson Bay Lagoon, *St. Maarten, St.–Martin* 123 BI3
Simushir, island, *Russ.* 161 H23
Sinai, peninsula, *Egypt* 173 R3
Sinai, region, *Egypt* 201 CI9
Sinai, Mount, *Grenada* 123 L23
Sinai, Mount see Mûsa, Gebel, *Egypt* 201 DI9
Sinbaungwe, *Myanmar* 190 J5
Sinbukch'ŏng, *N. Korea* 186 GIO
Sincelejo, *Col.* 130 C4
Sinch'ang, *N. Korea* 186 GII
Sinch'ang, *N. Korea* 186 H7
Sinchang, *S. Korea* 187 W6
Sincheon, *S. Korea* 186 M9
Sinch'ŏn, *N. Korea* 186 L5
Sinclair, *Wyo., U.S.* 108 JII
Sinclair, Lake, *Ga., U.S.* 98 M6
Sinclair's Bay, *Scot., U.K.* 144 GIO
Sin Cowe Island, *S. China Sea* 192 EII
Sındırgı, *Turk.* 170 E4
Sindo, *N. Korea* 186 H3
Sindoa, Mount, *New Caledonia, Fr.* 222 D8
Sindong, *N. Korea* 186 EI2
Sindong, *S. Korea* 187 NII
Sinegorskiy, *Russ.* 159 QII
Sines, *Port.* 146 K5
Sines, Cabo de, *Port.* 146 K5
Singapore, *Asia* 191 VII
Singapore Strait, *Asia* 192 H7
Singaraja, *Indonesia* 192 MII

Singavi, Mount, *Wallis and Futuna, Fr.* 222 EII
Sing Buri, *Thai.* 190 M9
Singen, *Ger.* 150 K6
Singida, *Tanzania* 203 LI3
Singkaling Hkämti, *Myanmar* 190 E6
Singkawang, *Indonesia* 192 H9
Singkep, island, *Indonesia* 192 J7
Singleton, *N.S.W., Austral.* 215 XI5
Sin'gye, *N. Korea* 186 K7
Sinheukdong, *S. Korea* 187 Q7
Sìn Hô, *Vietnam* 190 GIO
Sinhŭng, *N. Korea* 186 G9
Sinhŭng, *N. Korea* 186 G9
Sinhyeon, *S. Korea* 187 RI2
Siniscola, *It.* 152 M5
Sini Vrükh, peak, *Bulg.* 155 KI5
Sinj, *Croatia* 154 G6
Sinja, *Sudan* 203 FI3
Sinjai, *Indonesia* 193 LI3
Sinjār, *Iraq* 174 C8
Sinjido, island, *S. Korea* 187 U8
Sinjŏn, *N. Korea* 186 E9
Sinjŏng, *N. Korea* 186 G4
Sinkat, *Sudan* 203 DI4
Sinkiang, region, *China* 182 F4
Sinmi-do, island, *N. Korea* 186 H5
Sinnam, *S. Korea* 186 MIO
Sinnamary, *Fr. Guiana* 131 EI8
Sinnar, *India* 180 L4
Sînnicolau Mare, *Rom.* 154 DIO
Sinó, Ponto do, *Cabo Verde* 209 BI7
Sinoe, Lacul, *Rom.* 155 FI8
Sinop, *Braz.* 132 HII
Sinop (Sinope), *Turk.* 170 CIO
Sinop Burnu, *Turk.* 170 BIO
Sinope see Sinop, *Turk.* 170 CIO
Sinp'a see Kimjŏngsuk, *N. Korea* 186 D9
Sinp'o, *N. Korea* 186 GIO
Sinp'ung, *N. Korea* 186 D7
Sinp'yŏng, *N. Korea* 186 K8
Sinsaeng, *N. Korea* 186 M6
Sinsang, *N. Korea* 186 H9
Sinsheim, *Ger.* 150 H6
Sinsido, island, *S. Korea* 187 R7
Sinsŏngch'ŏn, *N. Korea* 186 J7
Sintaein, *S. Korea* 187 R8
Sintang, *Indonesia* 192 JIO
Sint Maarten, island, *Lesser Antil.* 121 BI4
Sint Nicolaas, *Aruba, Neth.* 123 RI7
Sinton, *Tex., U.S.* 105 TII
Sinŭiju, *N. Korea* 186 G4
Sinwŏn, *N. Korea* 186 E8
Sinwŏn, *N. Korea* 186 L6
Sinzig, *Ger.* 150 G5
Siófok, *Hung.* 151 MI4
Sion, *Switz.* 152 C2
Sionainn see Shannon, *Ire.* 145 T4
Sioux Center, *Iowa, U.S.* 106 M9
Sioux City, *Iowa, U.S.* 107 N8
Sioux Falls, *S. Dak., U.S.* 106 L8
Sioux Lookout, *Ont., Can.* 85 NI5
Sioux Rapids, *Iowa, U.S.* 106 MIO
Sipapo, Cerro, *Venez.* 130 E9
Siparia, *Trinidad and Tobago* 123 Q22
Síphnos see Sífnos, island, *Gr.* 157 LI4
Siping, *China* 183 EI5
Sipingjie, *Liaoning, China* 184 BI4
Sipiwesk, *Man., Can.* 85 LI4
Siple, Mount, *Antarctica* 230 M7
Siple Coast, *Antarctica* 230 MII
Siple Island, *Antarctica* 230 M7
Sipura, island, *Indonesia* 192 K5
Siqueires Fracture Zone, *Pac. Oc.* 243 JI9
Sira, *India* 181 P5
Siracusa (Syracuse), *It.* 153 TI2
Şiran, *Turk.* 171 EI4
Sirdaryo, *Uzb.* 177 KI3
Sir Edward Pellew Group, *Austral.* 214 CIO
Siret, river, *Rom.* 155 EI7
Sir Gaerfyrddin see Carmarthen, *Wales, U.K.* 145 V9
Sirḥān, Wādī as, *Jordan* 173 N9
Sīrīk, *Iran* 175 HI6
Sīrjān (Sa'īdābād), *Iran* 175 GI5
Sirkka, *Fin.* 143 DI4

Sirmaur, *India* 180 H8
Şırnak, *Turk.* 171 HI7
Sirsa, *India* 180 E5
Sirte Rise, *Atl. Oc.* 240 KI4
Sir Thomas, Mount, *Austral.* 214 G7
Sirur, *India* 180 L4
Şirvan, *Azerb.* 171 E22
Şirvan, *Turk.* 171 GI6
Sisak, *Croatia* 154 E6
Sisaket, *Thai.* 190 MII
Sishui, *Shand., China* 184 H8
Sisian, *Arm.* 171 E2O
Sisimiut see Holsteinsborg, ... [no]
Siskiyou Mountains, *Calif., Oreg., U.S.* 110 L2
Sisŏphŏn, *Cambodia* 190 MIO
Sisseton, *S. Dak., U.S.* 106 J8
Sissonne, *Fr.* 149 NII
Sīstān, region, *Iran* 175 FI7
Sīstān, Daryācheh-ye, *Iran* 175 FI7
Sister Bay, *Wis., U.S.* 100 H8
Sisteron, *Fr.* 149 WI4
Sisters, *Oreg., U.S.* 110 H4
Sistersville, *W. Va., U.S.* 98 C9
Sistine Chapel, *Vatican City* 163 PI6
Sitapur, *India* 180 F7
Siteía, *Gr.* 157 QI6
Sithonías, peninsula, *Gr.* 156 DI2
Sitian, *China* 182 F7
Sítio da Abadia, *Braz.* 133 JI4
Sitka, *Alas., U.S.* 113 M22
Sitka National Historical Park, *Alas., U.S.* 113 L22
Sittard, *Neth.* 148 LI3
Sittwe (Akyab), *Myanmar* 190 H4
Si'ufa'alele Point, *Amer. Samoa, U.S.* 222 P3
Si'ufaga, *Amer. Samoa, U.S.* 222 P3
Si'ulagi Point, *Amer. Samoa, U.S.* 222 P3
Siuri, *India* 180 HII
Siuslaw, river, *Oreg., U.S.* 110 H2
Sivac, *Serb.* 154 E9
Sivas, *Turk.* 170 EI2
Siverek, *Turk.* 171 HI4
Sivers'kyy Donets', river, *Ukr.* 159 P9
Sivrihisar, *Turk.* 170 E7
Sîwa, *Egypt* 201 DI7
Siwalik Range, *India* 180 C5
Siwan, *India* 180 G9
Sixaola, *Pan.* 117 N2O
Six Feet, point, *Pitcairn I., U.K.* 223 Q23
Six Men's Bay, *Barbados* 123 JI8
Siyang, *Jiangsu, China* 184 K9
Siyəzən, *Azerb.* 171 C22
Siziwang Qi, *N. Mongol, China* 184 B4
Sjælland, island, *Den.* 142 NI2
Sjenica, *Serb.* 154 HIO
Skadarsko Jezero (Scutari, Lake), *Alban., Montenegro* 154 J9
Skagafjörður, bay, *Ice.* 142 E3
Skagen, *Den.* 142 LII
Skagerrak, strait, *Den., Nor.* 142 MIO
Skagit, river, *Wash., U.S.* 110 B4
Skagway, *Alas., U.S.* 113 K22
Skála, *Gr.* 156 LIO
Skalistyy Golets, peak, *Russ.* 161 KI7
Skåne, *Eur.* 140 F7
Skántzoura, island, *Gr.* 157 GI3
Škarda, island, *Croatia* 154 F4
Skardu, *Pak.* 178 LI3
Skarżysko-Kamienna, *Pol.* 151 FI6
Skawina, *Pol.* 151 HI5
Skeena, river, *B.C., Can.* 84 J8
Skegness, *Eng., U.K.* 145 SI4
Skeiðarárdjúp, valley, *Atl. Oc.* 247 L22
Skeleton Coast, *Af.* 206 G5
Skellefteå, *Sw.* 143 FI4
Skellefteälven, river, *Sw.* 143 FI4
Skerjadjúp, valley, *Arctic Oc.* 247 M2I
Skerries (Na Sceirí), *Ire.* 145 R7
Skerryvore, island, *Scot., U.K.* 144 L6
Skeylley Maayl see Kirk Michael, *Isle of Man, U.K.* 145 Q9
Skíathos, *Gr.* 156 FI2
Skíathos, island, *Gr.* 156 FI2
Skiatook, *Okla., U.S.* 104 EI2
Skidmore, *Tex., U.S.* 105 TII

Skien, *Nor.* 142 KII
Skierniewice, *Pol.* 151 EI5
Skikda, *Alg.* 200 AI2
Skipton, *Eng., U.K.* 145 RII
Skirmish Point, *Austral.* 214 A9
Skíros see Skýros, island, *Gr.* 157 GI3
Skive, *Den.* 142 MII
Skjálfandadjúp, valley, *Arctic Oc.* 247 L2O
Skjoldungen Bank, *Atl. Oc.* 247 Q2O
Skjoldungen Valley, *Atl. Oc.* 247 Q2O
Sklinna Bank, *Atl. Oc.* 240 EI3
Skokholm Island, *Wales, U.K.* 145 V8
Skokie, *Ill., U.S.* 101 N7
Skolpen Bank, *Arctic Oc.* 247 DI8
Skomer Island, *Wales, U.K.* 145 V8
Skomvær, island, *Nor.* 142 EI2
Skópelos, *Gr.* 156 GI2
Skópelos, island, *Gr.* 156 GI2
Skopin, *Russ.* 158 LIO
Skopje, *Maced.* 154 KII
Skopunarfjørður, bay, *Faroe Is., Den.* 142 H4
Skosyrev Ridge, *Arctic Oc.* 246 K8
Skouriotissa, *Cyprus* 162 P7
Skövde, *Sw.* 142 LI2
Skovorodino, *Russ.* 161 KI8
Skowhegan, *Me., U.S.* 97 FI6
Skrælling Canyon, *Atl. Oc.* 247 P2O
Skudeneshavn, *Nor.* 142 K9
Skull (An Scoil), *Ire.* 145 V3
Skunk, river, *Iowa, U.S.* 107 PI3
Skvyra, *Ukr.* 159 P5
Skýdra, *Gr.* 156 CIO
Skye, island, *Scot., U.K.* 144 K7
Skykomish, *Wash., U.S.* 110 C5
Skýros, *Gr.* 157 GI4
Skýros (Skíros), island, *Gr.* 157 GI3
Slantsy, *Russ.* 158 F5
Slater, *Mo., U.S.* 107 SI2
Slatina, *Rom.* 155 FI4
Slaton, *Tex., U.S.* 104 K5
Slave, river, *N. Amer.* 84 JII
Slave Coast, *Af.* 204 FII
Slavgorod, *Belarus* 158 L6
Slavonia, region, *Croatia* 154 E7
Slavonski Brod, *Croatia* 154 E8
Slavuta, *Ukr.* 159 N4
Sławno, *Pol.* 150 BI2
Slayton, *Minn., U.S.* 106 L9
Sleaford Bay, *Austral.* 214 L9
Sleat, Sound of, *Scot., U.K.* 144 K7
Sleeper Islands, *Nunavut, Can.* 85 KI7
Sleeping Bear Dunes National Lakeshore, *Mich., U.S.* 100 H9
Sleepy Eye, *Minn., U.S.* 106 KIO
Sleetmute, *Alas., U.S.* 113 JI4
Slêmanî (As Sulaymānīyah), *Iraq* 174 CIO
Slessor Glacier, *Antarctica* 230 EII
Slidell, *La., U.S.* 102 PII
Slide Mountain, *N.Y., U.S.* 96 LIO
Sliema, *Malta* 163 K23
Slieve Aughty Mountains, *Ire.* 145 S4
Slieve Gamph (The Ox Mountains), *Ire.* 145 Q4
Sligeach see Sligo, *Ire.* 145 Q4
Sligo (Sligeach), *Ire.* 145 Q4
Sligo Bay, *Ire.* 145 Q4
Slippery Rock, *Pa., U.S.* 96 M3
Slite, *Sw.* 143 LI4
Sliven, *Bulg.* 155 JI6
Sloan, *Nev., U.S.* III UI2
Slobozia, *Rom.* 155 FI7
Slonim, *Belarus* 158 L3
Slough, *Eng., U.K.* 145 VI3
Slovakia, *Eur.* 151 JI5
Slovenia, *Eur.* 154 D4
Slov''yans'k, *Ukr.* 159 P9
Słupsk, *Pol.* 151 BI3
Slutsk, *Belarus* 158 L4
Slyudyanka, *Russ.* 161 LI5
Smackover, *Ark., U.S.* 102 J8
Smallan, *Pak.* 179 R7
Smallwood Reservoir, *Nfld. & Lab., Can.* 85 L2I
Smalyavichy, *Belarus* 158 K5
Smara, *W. Sahara* 200 D6
Smederevo, *Serb.* 154 FIO

Smethport, *Pa., U.S.* 96 L5
Smidovich, *Russ.* 160 DII
Smidovich, *Russ.* 161 K2O
Smila, *Ukr.* 159 P6
Smiltene, *Latv.* 143 LI7
Smith, river, *Mont., U.S.* 108 C8
Smith Arm, *N.W.T., Can.* 84 FIO
Smith Bay, *Alas., U.S.* 113 BI5
Smith Bay, *Nunavut, Can.* 85 CI6
Smith Center, *Kans., U.S.* 107 R6
Smithers, *B.C., Can.* 84 K8
Smithfield, *N.C., U.S.* 98 HI2
Smithfield, *Utah, U.S.* 108 J7
Smithfield, *Va., U.S.* 98 FI4
Smith Glacier, *Antarctica* 230 L7
Smith Island, *Nunavut, Can.* 85 JI7
Smith Island see Sumisu, *Japan* 189 TI2
Smith Mountain Lake, *Va., U.S.* 98 FIO
Smith River, *B.C., Can.* 84 H9
Smith River, *Calif., U.S.* 110 LI
Smith Sound, *Nunavut, Can.* 85 CI6
Smithton, *Tas., Austral.* 215 Y7
Smithville, *Tex., U.S.* 105 QII
Smoke Creek Desert, *Nev., U.S.* III N6
Smokey Hill, river, *Kans., U.S.* 86 GII
Smoky, river, *Alta., Can.* 84 L9
Smoky Bay, *S. Aust., Austral.* 215 W9
Smoky Hill, river, *Kans., U.S.* 107 T6
Smoky Hills, *Kans., U.S.* 107 S6
Smoky Mountains, *Idaho, U.S.* 108 G5
Smøla, island, *Nor.* 142 HIO
Smolensk, *Russ.* 158 K7
Smolensk-Moscow Upland, *Eur.* 140 FII
Smólikas, peak, *Gr.* 156 D8
Smolyan, *Bulg.* 155 KI4
Smyley Island, *Antarctica* 230 G6
Smyrna, *Del., U.S.* 98 CI4
Smyrna, *Ga., U.S.* 98 L5
Smyrna, *Tenn., U.S.* 103 EI5
Smyrna see Izmir, *Turk.* 170 F3
Snaefell (Sniaul), peak, *Isle of Man, U.K.* 145 Q9
Snake, river, *U.S.* 86 B5
Snake, river, *Yukon, Can.* 84 E9
Snake City, *Bahamas* 122 B6
Snake Point, *Anguilla* 122 QI2
Snake Range, *Nev., U.S.* III QI3
Snake River Plain, *Idaho, U.S.* 108 H6
Snåsa, *Nor.* 142 GII
Sneads, *Fla., U.S.* 99 Q4
Sneek, *Neth.* 148 GI3
Snezhnogorsk, *Russ.* 161 GI3
Sněžka, peak, *Czech Rep., Pol.* 150 GI2
Sniaul see Snaefell, peak, *Isle of Man, U.K.* 145 Q9
Snihurivka, *Ukr.* 159 R7
Snina, *Slovakia* 151 JI7
Snøhetta, peak, *Nor.* 142 HII
Snohomish, *Wash., U.S.* 110 B4
Snoqualmie, *Wash., U.S.* 110 C4
Snoqualmie Pass, *Wash., U.S.* 110 C5
Snowden Seamounts, *Pac. Oc.* 243 HI4
Snowdon, peak, *Wales, U.K.* 145 S9
Snowflake, *Ariz., U.S.* 109 T9
Snow Hill, *Md., U.S.* 98 DI5
Snow Hill Island, *Antarctica* 230 C5
Snowville, *Utah, U.S.* 108 J6
Snowy, river, *Austral.* 214 MI3
Snowy Mountain, *N.Y., U.S.* 96 HIO
Snowy Mountains, *Austral.* 214 LI3
Snug Corner, *Bahamas* 119 HI5
Snuŏl, *Cambodia* 191 NI2
Snyder, *Okla., U.S.* 104 H9
Snyder, *Tex., U.S.* 104 L6
Soalala, *Madagascar* 207 EI7
Soando, island, *S. Korea* 187 V7
Soanierana-Ivongo, *Madagascar* 207 FI8
Soap Lake, *Wash., U.S.* 110 C7
Soay, island, *Scot., U.K.* 144 K7
Sobaek-san, peak, *N. Korea* 186 G8
Sobaeksan, peak, *S. Korea* 187 PII
Sobaeksanmaek, range, *S. Korea* 187 QIO
Sobinka, *Russ.* 158 JIO

Sobolevo, *Russ.* 158 L16
Sobradinho, Represa de, *Braz.* 133 G15
Sobral, *Braz.* 133 E16
Sobuk, *N. Korea* 186 E8
Soča, river, *Slov.* 154 C4
Sochaczew, *Pol.* 151 E15
Socheongdo, island, *S. Korea* 186 M4
Sochi, *Russ.* 159 U11
Society Islands, *Fr. Polynesia, Fr.* 223 E16
Societyridge, *Pac. Oc.* 243 L14
Socompa, *Chile* 134 E8
Socorro, *Col.* 130 E6
Socorro, *N. Mex., U.S.* 109 T12
Socorro, *Tex., U.S.* 105 W3
Socorro, Isla, *Mex.* 116 H6
Socotra *see* Suquţrá, island, *Yemen* 175 R14
Sóc Trăng, *Vietnam* 191 Q12
Soda Lake, *Calif., U.S.* 111 V11
Sodankylä, *Fin.* 143 D15
Soda Springs, *Idaho, U.S.* 108 H7
Soddy-Daisy, *Tenn., U.S.* 103 G16
Södertälje, *Sw.* 143 K14
Sodiri, *Sudan* 202 E12
Sodo, *Eth.* 203 H14
Sŏdu, *N. Korea* 186 C11
Soekmekaar (Morebeng), *S. Af.* 206 H11
Sofádes, *Gr.* 156 F10
Sofia *see* Sofiya, *Bulg.* 155 J13
Sofiya (Sofia), *Bulg.* 155 J13
Sōfu Gan (Lot's Wife), island, *Japan* 189 U12
Sogamoso, *Col.* 130 E6
Soğanlı, river, *Turk.* 170 C8
Sogeomundo, island, *S. Korea* 187 U9
Sogmai, *China* 182 J2
Sognefjorden, bay, *Nor.* 142 J10
Sŏgŭt, *Turk.* 170 E6
Sŏgŭt Gölü, *Turk.* 170 H5
Sogzhukug (Suozhuku), *China* 182 K6
Sŏhae, *N. Korea* 186 K5
Sohâg, *Egypt* 201 D19
Sohano, *P.N.G.* 221 J13
Sohm Plain, *Atl. Oc.* 240 K5
Sŏhŭng, *N. Korea* 186 L7
Sŏhŭng-ho, lake, *N. Korea* 186 L6
Soignies, *Belg.* 148 L11
Soissons, *Fr.* 149 N11
Sojat, *India* 180 G4
Sŏjosŏn-man, bay, *N. Korea* 186 J5
Sokcho, *S. Korea* 186 L11
Sŏk-do, island, *N. Korea* 186 K5
Söke, *Turk.* 170 G3
Sokhumi (Sukhum), *Rep. of Georgia* 171 A15
Sokodé, *Togo* 204 C11
Sokol, *Russ.* 158 F10
Sokol, *Russ.* 161 E16
Sokol, *Russ.* 161 F20
Sokółka, *Pol.* 151 C18
Sokolo (Soala), *Mali* 200 H7
Sokolov (Falknov), *Czech Rep.* 150 G9
Sokołów Podlaski, *Pol.* 151 D17
Sokoto, *Nigeria* 205 B13
Sokoto, river, *Nigeria* 204 B12
Soksa, *N. Korea* 186 F9
Sŏksa, *N. Korea* 186 L6
Sol, Costa del, *Sp.* 146 N10
Sol, Ponta do, *Cabo Verde* 209 C17
Sola, *Cuba* 118 J11
Solander Island, *N.Z.* 217 R15
Solano, Punta, *Col.* 130 E3
Sol de Julio, *Arg.* 134 H10
Soldeu, *Andorra* 162 H4
Soldotna, *Alas., U.S.* 113 K16
Soledad, *Calif., U.S.* 111 U4
Soledad, *Col.* 130 B5
Solenzara, *Fr.* 152 K4
Solhan, *Turk.* 171 F15
Soligalich, *Russ.* 158 F11
Solikamsk, *Russ.* 160 G9
Solimões *see* Amazon, river, *S. Amer.* 128 D5
Solingen, *Ger.* 150 F5
Solitary Islands, *Austral.* 214 J16
Şollar, *Azerb.* 171 C22
Sollefteå, *Sw.* 143 G13
Sol'Iletsk, *Russ.* 160 J7

Solnechnogorsk, *Russ.* 158 J9
Solo, island, *Fiji* 222 J6
Sologne, *Eur.* 140 H5
Solok, *Indonesia* 192 J6
Solomon, *Kans., U.S.* 107 S7
Solomon, river, *Kans., U.S.* 107 S7
Solomon Basin, *Pac. Oc.* 242 K8
Solomon Islands, *Pac. Oc.* 221 L18
Solomon Sea, *P.N.G.* 217 D21
Solon Springs, *Wis., U.S.* 100 F3
Solor, island, *Indonesia* 193 M14
Solothurn, *Switz.* 152 A3
Solov'yevsk, *Russ.* 161 K18
Solsona, *Sp.* 147 D15
Šolta, island, *Croatia* 154 H6
Solţānābād, *Iran* 175 C16
Sol'tsy, *Russ.* 158 G6
Soluntum, ruin, *It.* 153 S10
Solvay, *N.Y., U.S.* 96 J13
Solway Firth, *Eng., Scot., U.K.* 145 P10
Solwezi, *Zambia* 206 D10
Solyanka, *Russ.* 158 M15
Solyplayas, *Sp.* 208 Q7
Soma, *Turk.* 170 E3
Somaemuldo, island, *S. Korea* 187 U11
Somain, *Fr.* 148 M11
Somali, region, *Eth.* 203 G16
Somalia, *Af.* 203 H17
Somali Basin, *Ind. Oc.* 224 G6
Somaliland, region, *Somalia* 203 F17
Somali Peninsula, *Af.* 198 H11
Somali Plain, *Ind. Oc.* 224 F7
Sombor, *Croatia* 154 D9
Sombrero, island, *U.K.* 121 A15
Sombrero Channel, *India* 181 S15
Somers, *Mont., U.S.* 108 B5
Somerset, *Bermuda* 122 C1
Somerset, *Colo., U.S.* 109 N11
Somerset, *Ky., U.S.* 103 D18
Somerset, *Pa., U.S.* 96 P4
Somerset Island, *Bermuda* 122 C1
Somerset Island, *Nunavut, Can.* 85 E15
Somersworth, *N.H., U.S.* 97 H15
Somerton, *Ariz., U.S.* 109 V4
Somerville, *Tenn., U.S.* 102 G12
Somerville, *Tex., U.S.* 105 Q12
Someş, river, *Rom.* 155 B13
Somme, river, *Fr.* 148 M9
Somme, Baie de la, *Fr.* 148 M9
Somosomo, *Fiji* 222 G8
Somosomo Strait, *Fiji* 222 H8
Somuncurá, Meseta de, *Arg.* 135 Q9
Son, river, *India* 180 H8
Sŏnbong *see* Unggi, *N. Korea* 186 B14
Sŏnch'ŏn, *N. Korea* 186 H5
Sonda, *Pak.* 179 W7
Sondar, *India* 179 N13
Sønderborg, *Den.* 142 N11
Sondershausen, *Ger.* 150 F8
Sŏndŏk, *N. Korea* 186 H9
Sondrio, *It.* 152 C5
Song, *Malaysia* 192 H10
Songbai, *Hunan, China* 185 S4
Sông Câu, *Vietnam* 190 M14
Songea, *Tanzania* 203 N14
Songeons, *Fr.* 149 N9
Sŏnggan, *N. Korea* 186 F7
Sŏnggŏ, *N. Korea* 186 L10
Songhak, *N. Korea* 186 B12
Songhua, river, *China* 183 D16
Sŏnghwa, *N. Korea* 186 L5
Songido, island, *S. Korea* 187 S7
Songjiang, *Shanghai Shi, China* 185 N12
Songjianghe, *Jilin, China* 184 A16
Sŏngjin *see* Kimch'aek, *N. Korea* 186 F12
Sŏngjin-man, bay, *N. Korea* 186 F12
Songjin-san, peak, *N. Korea* 186 B13
Sŏngjŏn, *N. Korea* 186 K9
Songkhla, *Thai.* 191 R9
Sông Mã, *Vietnam* 190 H11
Songnim, *N. Korea* 186 K6
Songp'a, *N. Korea* 186 F11
Songpan, *China* 182 K10
Song Shan, *Henan, China* 184 J5
Songsong (Rota), *N. Mariana Is., U.S.* 220 E7
Songwŏn, *N. Korea* 186 F6

Songwŏn-jōsuji, lake, *N. Korea* 186 F6
Songxi, *Fujian, China* 185 R9
Songyang, *Zhejiang, China* 185 Q10
Songyuan, *China* 183 D15
Sonja Ridge, *Ind. Oc.* 225 K16
Sonkovo, *Russ.* 158 H9
Sơn La, *Vietnam* 190 H11
Sonmiani, *Pak.* 179 V6
Sonmiani Bay, *Pak.* 179 W5
Sonneberg, *Ger.* 150 G8
Sonoma, *Braz.* 133 F17
Sonoma, *Calif., U.S.* 111 R3
Sonora, *Calif., U.S.* 111 R6
Sonora, *Tex., U.S.* 105 P6
Sonoran Desert, *N. Amer.* 82 K3
Sonoran Desert National Monument, *Ariz., U.S.* 109 U6
Sonqor, *Iran* 174 D11
Sonseca, *Sp.* 146 G10
Sonsón, *Col.* 130 E5
Sonsonate, *El Salv.* 117 L16
Sonsorol Islands, *Palau* 218 F2
Soperton, *Ga., U.S.* 99 N7
Sophia-Antipolis, *Fr.* 149 X15
Sopot, *Pol.* 151 B14
Sopron, *Hung.* 151 L13
Sopur, *India* 178 M12
Sopwer, Mochun, *F.S.M.* 221 A15
Sopweru, island, *F.S.M.* 221 A15
Sŏp'yŏng, *N. Korea* 186 K7
Sora, *It.* 152 L10
Sorah, *Pak.* 179 U7
Soran, *Kaz.* 177 E14
Sorazocco, *San Marino* 163 J16
Sorbas, *Sp.* 146 L12
Soresina, *It.* 152 E5
Sorezaru Point, *Solomon Is.* 221 L15
Sorgono, *It.* 153 N4
Sorgues, *Fr.* 149 X13
Sorgun, *Turk.* 170 E10
Soria, *Sp.* 146 D12
Sorkapp Bank, *Arctic Oc.* 247 G17
Sorkh Kowtal Temple, ruins, *Afghan.* 178 L7
Sørkjosen, *Nor.* 143 C13
Sørli, *Nor.* 142 G12
Sorobon, *Bonaire, Neth.* 123 R19
Soroca, *Mold.* 159 Q4
Sorocaba, *Braz.* 133 M13
Sorong, *Indonesia* 193 J17
Soroti, *Uganda* 203 J13
Sørøya, island, *Nor.* 143 B13
Sør Rondane Mountains, *Antarctica* 231 B15
Sorsele, *Sw.* 143 F13
Sorso, *It.* 152 M3
Sørvágur, *Faroe Is., Den.* 142 H5
Sosanjaya Bay, *N. Mariana Is., U.S.* 220 E7
Sosanlagh Bay, *N. Mariana Is., U.S.* 220 E7
Sosna, *Russ.* 161 J15
Sosnogorsk, *Russ.* 160 F9
Sosnovka, *Russ.* 158 H13
Sosnovka, *Russ.* 158 H15
Sosnovka, *Russ.* 158 L11
Sosnovo, *Russ.* 158 E6
Sosnovo Ozerskoye, *Russ.* 161 L16
Sosnowiec, *Pol.* 151 G15
Soso Bay, *Fiji* 222 K6
Sōsura, *N. Korea* 186 B14
Sos'va, *Russ.* 160 G10
Sos'va, *Russ.* 160 H9
Soto, *Curaçao, Neth.* 123 P13
Sotogahama, *Japan* 188 J12
Souanké, *Congo* 205 G17
Soubré, *Côte d'Ivoire* 204 E8
Soucis, *St. Lucia* 123 K14
Soudan, *N.T., Austral.* 215 S10
Soudan Bank, *Ind. Oc.* 224 K8
Soufli, *Gr.* 157 B16
Soufrière, *St. Lucia* 123 K13
Soufrière, peak, *Guadeloupe, Fr.* 123 F14
Soufrière Bay, *St. Lucia* 123 K13
Soufrière Hills, volcano, *Montserrat* 123 B24
Soufrière Mountains, *St. Vincent and the Grenadines* 123 J16
Souillac, *Fr.* 149 V9
Souillac, *Mauritius* 209 H20

Soúnio, ruin, *Gr.* 157 K13
Soûr (Tyre), *Leb.* 172 K6
Sourdeval, *Fr.* 149 P6
Soure, *Braz.* 133 C13
Souris (Mouse), river, *Can., U.S.* 106 D3
Souris, river, *Can., U.S.* 86 B11
Sour Lake, *Tex., U.S.* 105 Q15
Soúrpi, *Gr.* 156 G11
Sousa, *Braz.* 133 F17
Sousel, *Port.* 146 H6
Sous Le Vent, Îles, *Fr. Polynesia, Fr.* 223 E14
Sousse, *Tun.* 201 A13
South Africa, *Af.* 206 L9
South Aleutian Slope, *Pac. Oc.* 242 C12
South Alligator, river, *Austral.* 214 B8
South Ambo Channel, *Marshall Is., U.S.* 220 M4
Southampton, *Eng., U.K.* 145 W12
Southampton, *N.Y., U.S.* 97 N13
Southampton, Cape, *Nunavut, Can.* 85 J16
Southampton Island, *Nunavut, Can.* 85 H16
South Andaman, island, *India* 181 Q14
South Aral Sea, *Uzb.* 176 G9
South Atlantic Ocean, *Atl. Oc.* 241 S9
South Aulatsivik Island, *Nfld. & Lab., Can.* 85 K21
South Australia, *Austral.* 215 V9
South Australian Basin, *Ind. Oc.* 225 P16
South Australian Plain, *Ind. Oc.* 225 N19
Southaven, *Miss., U.S.* 102 G11
South Baldy, peak, *N. Mex., U.S.* 109 T11
South Banda Basin, *Pac. Oc.* 242 K6
South Bay, *Fla., U.S.* 99 V10
South Bend, *Ind., U.S.* 101 N9
South Bend, *Wash., U.S.* 110 D2
South Bimini, *Bahamas* 122 B8
South Boston, *Va., U.S.* 98 G11
South Branch Potomac, river, *Md., W. Va., U.S.* 98 C11
South Bruny Island, *Austral.* 214 M8
South Caicos, island, *Turks & Caicos Is.* 119 J17
South Cape, *Fiji* 222 H8
South Carolina, *U.S.* 98 K9
South Cay, *Jam.* 118 P11
South Channel, *Marshall Is., U.S.* 220 J8
South Charleston, *W. Va., U.S.* 98 E8
South Chatham Slope, *Pac. Oc.* 249 H20
South China Basin, *Pac. Oc.* 242 H4
South China Sea, *Pac. Oc.* 168 K12
South Comino Channel, *Malta* 163 J21
South Dakota, *U.S.* 106 K5
South Downs, *Eng., U.K.* 145 W14
South East Cape, *Austral.* 214 M7
Southeast Indian Ridge, *Ind. Oc.* 224 M11
Southeast Pacific Basin, *Pac. Oc.* 243 Q19
Southeast Pass, *Marshall Is., U.S.* 220 M8
South East Point, *Kiribati* 221 C24
Southeast Point, *Kiribati* 221 E17
South East Range, *St. Kitts and Nevis* 123 B17
Southend, *Scot., U.K.* 145 N8
Southend-on-Sea, *Eng., U.K.* 145 V15
Southend Reindeer, *Sask., Can.* 85 L13
Southern Alps (Ka Tiritiri O Te Moana), *N.Z.* 217 P16
Southern Bight, *Bahamas* 118 F11
Southern Bug, river, *Eur.* 140 H11
Southern Cross, *W. Aust., Austral.* 215 W4
Southern Indian Lake, *Man., Can.* 85 K14
Southern Ocean, 241 X9
Southern Pines, *N.C., U.S.* 98 J11
Southern Uplands, *Eur.* 140 E4

Southern Uplands, *Scot., U.K.* 145 N10
Southesk Tablelands, *Austral.* 214 E6
Southfield, *Jam.* 122 K7
South Fiji Basin, *Pac. Oc.* 242 M11
South Fork Owyhee, river, *Idaho, Nev., U.S.* 108 J3
South Fork Shenandoah, *Va., U.S.* 98 D11
South Fork Solomon, river, *Kans., U.S.* 107 S5
South Friar's Bay, *St. Kitts and Nevis* 123 B18
South Fulton, *Tenn., U.S.* 102 E12
South Georgia Island, *S. Amer.* 128 R10
South Grand, river, *Mo., U.S.* 107 T11
South Haven, *Mich., U.S.* 100 M9
South Henik Lake, *Nunavut, Can.* 85 J14
South Hill, *Va., U.S.* 98 F12
South Island (Te Waipounamu), *N.Z.* 217 P17
South Korea, *Asia* 187 Q9
South Lake Tahoe, *Calif., U.S.* 111 Q6
South Loup, river, *Nebr., U.S.* 107 P5
South Male Atoll, *Maldives* 181 V3
South Malosmadulu Atoll, *Maldives* 181 U3
South Milwaukee, *Wis., U.S.* 100 L7
South Mole, *Gibraltar, U.K.* 163 P22
South Nahanni, river, *N.W.T., Can.* 84 G9
South Negril Point, *Jam.* 122 H5
South Norfolk Basin, *Pac. Oc.* 242 N10
South Orkney Islands, *Antarctica* 230 A5
South Orkney Trough, *Atl. Oc.* 241 X7
South Ossetia, republic, *Rep. of Georgia* 171 B18
South Pacific Ocean, *Pac. Oc.* 219 M16
South Palmetto Point, *Bahamas* 122 E6
South Pass, *Marshall Is., U.S.* 220 N5
South Passage, *Kiribati* 221 B22
South Peak *see* Bartle Frere, *Austral.* 214 D13
South Pittsburg, *Tenn., U.S.* 103 G16
South Platte, river, *U.S.* 86 F11
South Point, *Barbados* 123 L19
South Point, *Marshall Is., U.S.* 220 N8
South Ponte Vedra Beach, *Fla., U.S.* 99 R9
Southport, *N.C., U.S.* 98 K12
South Portland, *Me., U.S.* 97 H16
South Ronaldsay, island, *Scot., U.K.* 144 G10
South Sandwich Fracture Zone, *Atl. Oc.* 241 X10
South Sandwich Ridge, *Atl. Oc.* 248 L8
South Sandwich Trench, *Atl. Oc.* 241 W9
South San Francisco, *Calif., U.S.* 111 S3
South Saskatchewan, river, *Alta., Sask., Can.* 84 N11
South Scotia Ridge, *Atl. Oc.* 241 X6
South Shetland Islands, *Antarctica* 230 C3
South Shetland Trough, *Atl. Oc., Pac. Oc.* 248 N10
South Shore, *Ky., U.S.* 103 A19
South Sioux City, *Nebr., U.S.* 107 N8
South Solomon Trough, *Pac. Oc.* 242 L9
South Sound, *British Virgin Is., U.K.* 122 Q9
South Sound, *Ire.* 145 S3
South Sound Bluff, *British Virgin Is., U.K.* 122 R9
South Sudan, *Af.* 202 G12
South Taranaki Bight, *N.Z.* 217 L18
South Tasman Rise, *Ind. Oc., Pac. Oc.* 249 E19
South Tasman Saddle, *Ind. Oc.* 225 Q22

Tehuantepec Ridge, *Pac. Oc.* **243** H2O
Tehuata (Rekareka), island, *Fr. Polynesia, Fr.* **223** E2O
Teide, Pico de, *Sp.* **208** Q4
Teignmouth, *Eng., U.K.* **145** X1O
Te Ika-A-Māui *see* North Island, *N.Z.* **217** K19
Teiko, Motu, *Fr. Polynesia, Fr.* **223** R2O
Tejen, *Uzb.* **176** M9
Tejenstroy, *Uzb.* **176** M9
Tejo (Tagus), river, *Port.* **146** H5
Tekamah, *Nebr., U.S.* **107** P9
Te Karaka, *N.Z.* **217** K2O
Tekax, *Mex.* **117** H16
Tekeli, *Kaz.* **177** G17
Tekes, *China* **182** E4
Tekirdağ, *Turk.* **170** C3
Tekirova, *Turk.* **170** J6
Tekkali, *India* **180** L9
Tekman, *Turk.* **171** E16
Teknaf, *India* **180** K14
Tekoa, *Wash., U.S.* **110** C9
Tekokota, island, *Fr. Polynesia, Fr.* **223** E19
Tekopua, island, *Cook Is., N.Z.* **222** Q12
Te Koutu Point, *Cook Is., N.Z.* **222** Q11
T'elavi, *Rep. of Georgia* **171** B19
Tel Aviv-Yafo, *Israel* **172** M5
Telde, *Sp.* **208** R5
Telebekelel Ngerael, *Palau* **220** K11
Telefomin, *P.N.G.* **217** C17
Telegraph Creek, *B.C., Can.* **84** H8
Telekitonga, island, *Tonga* **222** R7
Telekivavau, island, *Tonga* **222** R7
Telele Island, *Tuvalu* **221** L23
Telemark, *Eur.* **140** D7
Telén, *Arg.* **134** M9
Telescope Peak, *Calif., U.S.* **III** U9
Telescope Point, *Grenada* **123** K24
Teles Pires (São Manuel), river, *Braz.* **132** F1O
Tel Lakhish, ruins, *Israel* **173** N5
Tell Atlas, range, *Af.* **198** C4
Tell City, *Ind., U.S.* **101** U8
Teller, *Alas., U.S.* **112** F12
(Tellicherry *see* Thalassery, *India* **181** Q4
Telloh *see* Lakash, ruins, *Iraq* **174** F1O
Tell Tayinat, ruins, *Turk.* **170** J11
Telluride, *Colo., U.S.* **109** P11
Telsen, *Arg.* **135** R9
Telšiai, *Lith.* **143** M16
Telukbutun, *Indonesia* **192** G8
Telukdalem, *Indonesia* **192** J4
Teluk Intan, *Malaysia* **191** T9
Tema, *Ghana* **204** E11
Te Manga, peak, *Cook Is., N.Z.* **222** Q9
Tematagi, island, *Fr. Polynesia, Fr.* **223** G2O
Tembagapura, *Indonesia* **193** L2O
Tembenchi, *Russ.* **161** H14
Temerin, *Serb.* **154** E1O
Temerloh, *Malaysia* **191** U1O
Teminabuan, *Indonesia* **217** B14
Teminikov, *Russ.* **158** K12
Temirtaū, *Kaz.* **177** D14
Temoe (Timoe), island, *Fr. Polynesia, Fr.* **223** H23
Tempe, *Ariz., U.S.* **109** U7
Témpi, valley, *Gr.* **156** E1O
Tempio Pausania, *It.* **152** M4
Temple, *Tex., U.S.* **104** J1O
Temple, *Tex., U.S.* **105** P11
Temple Bay, *Austral.* **214** B12
Temryuk, *Russ.* **159** S9
Temryukskiy Zaliv, *Russ.* **159** S8
Temse, *Belg.* **148** K11
Temuco, *Chile* **135** P6
Temuka, *N.Z.* **217** P17
Tena, *Ecua.* **130** J3
Tenali, *India* **181** N7
Tenao, *Monaco* **163** B22
Tenararo, island, *Fr. Polynesia, Fr.* **223** G22
Ténaro, Akrotírio (Taenarum, Matapás), *Gr.* **156** M1O

Tenarunga, island, *Fr. Polynesia, Fr.* **223** G22
Tenasserim, *Myanmar* **190** L7
Tenasserim, *Myanmar* **191** N8
Tenby, *Wales, U.K.* **145** V8
Tende, *Fr.* **149** W16
Ten Degree Channel, *India* **181** R14
Tendō, *Japan* **188** L12
Tendürek Dağı, peak, *Turk.* **171** F18
Ténéré, region, *Niger* **201** G13
Tenerife, island, *Sp.* **208** Q5
Tengako, island, *Tuvalu* **221** J24
Tengasu Island, *Tuvalu* **221** L23
Tengchong, *China* **182** N8
Te Nggano, *Solomon Is.* **221** R19
Tengiz, oil well, *Kaz.* **176** G6
Tengiz, Lake, *Asia* **168** E7
Tengiz Köli, *Kaz.* **177** D14
Tengxian, *Guangxi Zhuang, China* **185** V2
Tengzhou, *Shand., China* **184** H8
Tenino, *Wash., U.S.* **110** D3
Tenjo, Mount, *Guam, U.S.* **220** C1O
Tenkasi, *India* **181** S5
Tenke, *Dem. Rep. of the Congo* **202** N11
Tenkiller Ferry Lake, *Okla., U.S.* **104** F14
Tenkodogo, *Burkina Faso* **204** B11
Tennant Creek, *N.T., Austral.* **215** R9
Tennessee, *U.S.* **103** F15
Tennessee, river, *U.S.* **103** E14
Tennessee Pass, *Colo., U.S.* **108** M12
Tennille, *Ga., U.S.* **98** M7
Tenoka, island, *Fr. Polynesia, Fr.* **223** Q2O
Ténos, Pointe, *Martinique, Fr.* **123** E23
Tenosique, *Mex.* **117** K15
Tensaw, river, *Ala., U.S.* **103** N14
Ten Sleep, *Wyo., U.S.* **108** G11
Ten Thousand Islands, *Fla., U.S.* **99** X9
Teófilo Otoni, *Braz.* **133** K15
Teohotepapa, Pointe, *Fr. Polynesia, Fr.* **223** M21
Teora, *It.* **152** M12
Tepa, *Wallis and Futuna, Fr.* **222** B11
Tepaeture, Pointe, *Fr. Polynesia, Fr.* **223** Q21
Tepako, Pointe, *Wallis and Futuna, Fr.* **222** B11
Tepa Point, *Cook Is., N.Z.* **223** B2O
Tepati, *Fr. Polynesia, Fr.* **223** Q18
Tepé, *Eq. Guinea* **208** L8
Tepe, peak, *Kos., Serb.* **154** J11
Tepe Musyan, ruins, *Iran* **174** E11
Tepic, *Mex.* **116** G9
Tepu, *Fr. Polynesia, Fr.* **223** K2O
Te Puka, island, *Cook Is., N.Z.* **223** B13
Tepuka Island, *Tuvalu* **221** J23
Tepuu, Pointe, *Fr. Polynesia, Fr.* **223** K2O
Téra, *Niger* **200** H9
Terae, island, *Cook Is., N.Z.* **223** A18
Teraina (Washington Island), *Kiribati* **218** F12
Teramo, *It.* **152** J1O
Teratak, *Indonesia* **192** J9
Tercan, *Turk.* **171** E15
Terceira, *Azores, Port.* **146** Q3
Tereai, island, *Fr. Polynesia, Fr.* **223** K15
Terekhovka, *Belarus* **158** M6
Terekli Mekteb, *Russ.* **159** T14
Terekty, *Kaz.* **177** E19
Terenos, *Braz.* **132** L11
Teresina, *Braz.* **133** E15
Terhazza, ruin, *Mali* **200** E8
Terihi, island, *Fr. Polynesia, Fr.* **223** N21
Termas de Río Hondo, *Arg.* **134** G9
Terme, *Turk.* **170** D12
Termini Imerese, *It.* **153** S1O
Termini Imerese, Golfo di, *It.* **153** S1O
Términos, Laguna de, *Mex.* **117** J15
Termita, *Russ.* **159** S14
Termiz, *Uzb.* **176** M12
Termoli, *It.* **152** K11
Ternate, *Indonesia* **193** J16

Terneuzen, *Neth.* **148** K11
Terni, *It.* **152** J8
Ternitz, *Aust.* **150** L12
Ternopil', *Ukr.* **159** P3
Terrace, *B.C., Can.* **84** K7
Terrace Beachport, *Ind. Oc.* **225** N22
Terrace Ceduna, *Ind. Oc.* **225** N2O
Terracina, *It.* **152** L9
Terralba, *It.* **153** P3
Terrassa, *Sp.* **147** D17
Terre-de-Bas, *Guadeloupe, Fr.* **123** G14
Terre-de-Bas, island, *Guadeloupe, Fr.* **123** G14
Terre-de-Haut, *Guadeloupe, Fr.* **123** G15
Terre-de-Haut, island, *Guadeloupe, Fr.* **123** G15
Terre Haute, *Ind., U.S.* **101** S7
Terreiro Velho, *Sao Tome and Principe* **209** B21
Terrell, *Tex., U.S.* **104** L12
Terre Rouge, *Mauritius* **209** F2O
Terry, *Mont., U.S.* **108** D12
Tersakan Gölü, *Turk.* **170** G8
Terschelling, island, *Neth.* **148** G12
Tertenia, *It.* **153** P4
Tartar, *Azerb.* **171** D21
Ter Tholen Fracture Zone, *Ind. Oc.* **224** N11
Teru, *Pak.* **178** L1O
Teruel, *Sp.* **147** F14
Teseney, *Eritrea* **203** E14
Teshekpuk Lake, *Alas., U.S.* **113** B15
Teshikaga, *Japan* **188** F15
Teshio, *Japan* **188** E13
Teshio, river, *Japan* **188** E13
Teshio Sanchi, *Japan* **188** F13
Tesiyn, river, *Mongolia* **182** C8
Teslić, *Bosn. & Herzg.* **154** F8
Teslin, *Yukon, Can.* **84** G8
Tesovo Netyl'skiy, *Russ.* **158** F6
Tessalit, *Mali* **200** F1O
Tessaoua, *Niger* **200** H12
Tetas, Punta, *Chile* **134** E6
Te Tautua, *Cook Is., N.Z.* **223** B18
Tete, *Mozambique* **206** E12
Te Teko, *N.Z.* **217** K2O
Tetepare, island, *Solomon Is.* **221** N16
Tetere, *Russ.* **161** J14
Teteven, *Bulg.* **155** H14
Tetford, *Eng., U.K.* **145** S14
Tetiaroa, island, *Fr. Polynesia, Fr.* **223** E16
Tetlin, *Alas., U.S.* **113** H19
Teton, river, *Mont., U.S.* **108** C8
Tétouan, *Mor.* **200** A9
Tetovo-Skopje, *Maced.* **154** K1O
Tetufera, Mount, *Fr. Polynesia, Fr.* **223** P16
Tetutu, Pointe, *Fr. Polynesia, Fr.* **223** N23
Tetyushi, *Russ.* **158** J14
Teuauua (Hat), point, *Fr. Polynesia, Fr.* **223** N23
Teuco, river, *Arg.* **134** F11
Teulada, *It.* **153** Q3
Teulada, Capo, *It.* **153** Q3
Teuri Tō, *Japan* **188** F13
Teutonic College, *Vatican City* **163** Q16
Tevahavaha, island, *Cook Is., N.Z.* **223** C14
Tevaro, island, *Fr. Polynesia, Fr.* **223** K17
Teveiroa, island, *Fr. Polynesia, Fr.* **223** K13
Tevere (Tiber), river, *It.* **152** J8
Teverya (Tiberias), *Israel* **172** K6
Te Waipounamu *see* South Island, *N.Z.* **217** P17
Tewantin, *Qnsld., Austral.* **215** V16
Texarkana, *Tex., U.S.* **104** K15
Texas, *U.S.* **105** N9
Texas City, *Tex., U.S.* **105** R14
Texas-Lousiana Shelf, *Atl. Oc.* **240** L1
Texas Point, *Tex., U.S.* **105** R16
Texel, island, *Neth.* **148** G12

Texhoma, *Okla., U.S.* **104** E5
Texico, *N. Mex., U.S.* **109** S15
Texline, *Tex., U.S.* **104** E3
Texoma, Lake, *Okla., Tex., U.S.* **104** J12
Texon, *Tex., U.S.* **105** N5
Teykovo, *Russ.* **158** H1O
Tezpur, *India* **180** G14
Tfaritiy, *W. Sahara* **200** D7
Thabana Ntlenyana, peak, *S. Af.* **206** K11
Thabaung, *Myanmar* **190** K5
Thaga Pass, *India* **180** D7
Thagyettaw, *Myanmar* **190** M7
Thái Hoà, *Vietnam* **190** J12
Thái Bình, *Vietnam* **190** H12
Thailand, *Asia* **190** L8
Thailand, Gulf of, *Pac. Oc.* **168** K1O
Thái Nguyên, *Vietnam* **190** G12
Thakhèk, *Laos* **190** K11
Thal, *Pak.* **179** N9
Thalassery (Tellicherry), *India* **181** Q4
Thal Desert, *Pak.* **179** Q9
Thale Luang, lake, *Thai.* **191** R8
Thamarīt, *Oman* **175** N14
Thames, River, *Eng., U.K.* **145** V15
Thamūd, *Yemen* **174** N12
Thana, *Pak.* **179** S3
Thandaung, *Myanmar* **190** J6
Thane, *India* **180** L3
Thanet, island, *Eng., U.K.* **145** V16
Thanh Hóa, *Vietnam* **190** J12
Thành Phố Hồ Chí Minh (Ho Chi Minh City, Saigon), *Vietnam* **191** P13
Thanjavur (Tanjore), *India* **181** R6
Thanlwin *see* Salween, river, *Asia* **168** H9
Tharabwin, *Myanmar* **191** N8
Thar Desert *see* Great Indian Desert, *India, Pak.* **179** U8
Thargomindah, *Qnsld., Austral.* **215** V12
Tharp Fracture Zone, *Pac. Oc.* **243** R16
Tharthār, Lake, *Iraq* **174** D9
Tha Sala, *Thai.* **191** Q8
Thásos (Limín), *Gr.* **157** C14
Thasos, island, *Gr.* **157** C14
Thatch Cay, *Virgin Is., U.S.* **122** M9
Thaton, *Myanmar* **190** K7
Thatta, *Pak.* **179** W7
Thau, Bassin de, *Fr.* **149** X11
Thaungdut, *Myanmar* **190** F5
Thayawthadanngyi Kyun, island, *Myanmar* **191** N7
Thayer, *Mo., U.S.* **107** V14
Thayet, *Myanmar* **190** J5
The Alley, *Jam.* **122** K8
The Barony, *Scot., U.K.* **144** F1O
The Baths, site, *British Virgin Is., U.K.* **122** R8
Thebes *see* Thíva, *Gr.* **156** H12
Thebes, ruin, *Egypt* **201** E19
The Bight, *Bahamas* **122** B5
The Bluff, *Bahamas* **122** D5
The Bottom, *Saba, Neth.* **121** B15
The Brothers *see* Al Ikhwān, islands, *Yemen* **175** R14
The Brothers, islands, *Bahamas* **119** H13
The Cheviot, peak, *Eng., U.K.* **145** N11
The Cockpit Country, *Jam.* **122** H7
The Cow, island, *Ire.* **145** V2
The Crane, *Barbados* **123** L2O
The Dalles, *Oreg., U.S.* **110** F5
The Deeps, bay, *Scot., U.K.* **144** D12
Thedford, *Nebr., U.S.* **107** N4
The Ferry Settlement, *Bahamas* **122** F9
The Galleries, *Gibraltar, U.K.* **163** N23
The Heads, *Oreg., U.S.* **110** K1
The Isles Lagoon, *Kiribati* **221** B23
The Little Minch, bay, *Scot., U.K.* **144** J6
Thelon, river, *N. Amer.* **85** H13
The Marls, *Bahamas* **122** B6
The Minch, bay, *Scot., U.K.* **144** H7
The Moors, *Scot., U.K.* **145** P9

The Narrows, *Bahamas* **122** B12
The Narrows, *St. Kitts and Nevis* **123** B18
The Narrows, *V.I.* **122** M11
The Naze, cape, *Eng., U.K.* **145** U15
Theodore, *Qnsld., Austral.* **215** U15
Theodore Roosevelt, river, *Braz.* **132** F9
Theodore Roosevelt National Park Elkhorn Ranch Site, *N. Dak., U.S.* **106** F2
Theodore Roosevelt National Park North Unit, *N. Dak., U.S.* **106** F2
Theodore Roosevelt National Park South Unit, *N. Dak., U.S.* **106** G2
Theológos, *Gr.* **157** C14
The Ox Mountains *see* Slieve Gamph, *Ire.* **145** Q4
The Pas, *Man., Can.* **85** M13
The Pennines, region, *Eng., U.K.* **145** Q11
Thera, ruin, *Gr.* **157** N15
The Remarkables, peak, *N.Z.* **217** Q16
Thermaïkós Kólpos, *Gr.* **156** D11
Thérmo, *Gr.* **156** H9
Thermopolis, *Wyo., U.S.* **108** G1O
Thermopylae, battle, *Gr.* **156** G1O
The Rosses, region, *Ire.* **145** P5
The Salt Ponds, *Jam.* **122** K11
The Sisters, *Trinidad and Tobago* **123** N18
The Sisters, islands, *Grenada* **123** H23
The Skaw, *Eur.* **140** E7
The Skerries, islands, *Wales, U.K.* **145** S9
The Slot *see* New Georgia Sound, *Solomon Is.* **221** M17
The Smalls, *Wales, U.K.* **145** V7
The Snares, islands, *N.Z.* **218** Q7
The Solent, bay, *Eng., U.K.* **145** X12
The Sound, *Atl. Oc.* **140** F7
The Sound, *Bahamas* **122** A8
Thessalon, *Ont., Can.* **85** G17
Thessaloníki (Salonica), *Gr.* **156** C11
Thessaly, region, *Gr.* **156** F1O
The Steppes, *Kaz.* **176** E11
The Swatch, trough, *Ind. Oc.* **224** C9
Thetford, *Eng., U.K.* **145** T15
The Valley, *Anguilla* **121** B15
The Valley, *British Virgin Is., U.K.* **122** R11
The Wash, bay, *Eng., U.K.* **145** S14
The Weald, region, *Eng., U.K.* **145** W14
The Wolds, region, *Eng., U.K.* **145** R13
Thiaucourt, *Fr.* **149** P13
Thibodaux, *La., U.S.* **102** Q1O
Thief River Falls, *Minn., U.S.* **106** E9
Thielsen, Mount, *Oreg., U.S.* **110** J4
Thiene, *It.* **152** D7
Thiers, *Fr.* **149** U11
Thiès, *Senegal* **200** H4
Thika, *Kenya* **203** K14
Thimphu, *Bhutan* **180** F12
Thingeyri, *Ice.* **142** D2
Thio, *New Caledonia, Fr.* **222** D8
Thíra (Santorini), island, *Gr.* **157** M15
Thirasía, island, *Gr.* **157** M15
Thirsk, *Eng., U.K.* **145** Q12
Thiruvananthapuram (Trivandrum), *India* **181** S5
Thisted, *Den.* **142** M11
Thistilfjörður, bay, *Ice.* **142** E4
Thitu Island, *S. China Sea* **192** D11
Thíva (Thebes), *Gr.* **156** H12
Thjórsá, river, *Ice.* **142** F2
Thoen, *Thai.* **190** K8
Thohoyandou, *S. Af.* **206** H11
Thomas, *Okla., U.S.* **104** F9
Thomaston, *Ga., U.S.* **98** M5
Thomaston, *Me., U.S.* **97** G17
Thomasville, *Ala., U.S.* **103** M14
Thomasville, *Ga., U.S.* **98** Q5
Thomasville, *N.C., U.S.* **98** H1O
Thompson, *Man., Can.* **85** L14
Thompson, river, *Iowa, Mo., U.S.* **107** P11
Thompson Falls, *Mont., U.S.* **108** C5

Thompson Springs, *Utah, U.S.* 109 N9
Thompson Town, *Jam.* 122 J8
Thomson, *Ga., U.S.* 98 L7
Thomson, *river, Austral.* 214 FI2
Thongwa, *Myanmar* 190 K6
Thonon, *Fr.* 149 TI4
Thonze, *Myanmar* 190 K6
Thoreau, *N. Mex., U.S.* 109 SIO
Thórisvatn, *lake, Ice.* 142 F2
Thor Iversen Bank, *Arctic Oc.* 247 EI7
Thorndale, *Tex., U.S.* 105 PII
Thorne Bay, *Alas., U.S.* 113 M23
Thornhill, *Scot., U.K.* 145 NIO
Thornton, *Colo., U.S.* 108 LI3
Thorp, *Wash., U.S.* 110 D5
Thorp, *Wis., U.S.* 100 H4
Thorpe, *Barbados* 123 KI9
Thórshöfn, *Ice.* 142 E4
Thouars, *Fr.* 149 S7
Thrace, *region, Gr.* 157 BI5
Three Forks, *Mont., U.S.* 108 E8
Three Gorges Dam, *Hubei, China* 185 N3
Three Kings Islands *see* Manawatāwhi, *N.Z.* 217 GI7
Three Kings Ridge, *Pac. Oc.* 242 NII
Three Lakes, *Wis., U.S.* 100 G5
Three Pagodas Pass, *Myanmar* 190 L7
Three Points, Cape, *Ghana* 204 EIO
Three Rivers, *Mich., U.S.* 101 N9
Three Rivers, *Tex., U.S.* 105 TIO
Three Sisters, *peak, Oreg., U.S.* 110 H4
Three Sisters Islands, *Solomon Is.* 221 P2I
Thrissur, *India* 181 R5
Throckmorton, *Tex., U.S.* 104 K8
Throssell, Lake, *Austral.* 214 H5
Thuin, *Belg.* 148 MI2
Thuir, *Fr.* 149 ZIO
Thun, *Switz.* 152 B3
Thunder Bay, *Mich., U.S.* 100 HI2
Thunder Bay, *Ont., Can.* 85 PI5
Thuner See, *Switz.* 152 B3
Thung Song, *Thai.* 191 R8
Thunkar, *Bhutan* 180 FI3
Thuringia, *Eur.* 140 G7
Thurles (Durlas), *Ire.* 145 T5
Thurmont, *Md., U.S.* 98 BI2
Thurso, *Scot., U.K.* 144 GIO
Thurston Island, *Antarctica* 230 K6
Thusis, *Switz.* 152 B5
Thýamis, *river, Gr.* 156 E7
Thýmaina, *island, Gr.* 157 KI7
Tiamahana, Passe, *Fr. Polynesia, Fr.* 223 A23
Tianchang, *Anhui, China* 184 LIO
Tianjin (Tientsin), *Tianjin Shi, China* 184 D8
Tianjin Shi, *China* 184 D8
Tianjun, *China* 182 H8
Tianmen, *Hubei, China* 185 N4
Tianmu Shan, *Zhejiang, China* 185 NIO
Tian Shan, *Asia* 168 G7
Tianshifu, *Liaoning, China* 184 BI4
Tianshui, *China* 182 JIO
Tiantangzhai, *peak, Hubei, China* 184 M7
Tianzhen, *Shanxi, China* 184 C6
Tiarei, *Fr. Polynesia, Fr.* 223 NI7
Tiaret, *Alg.* 200 AIO
Tiari, *New Caledonia, Fr.* 222 B6
Tiaro Bay, *Solomon Is.* 221 NI8
Ti'avea, *Samoa* 222 L4
Tibagi, *river, Braz.* 132 MI2
Tibati, *Cameroon* 205 EI6
Tibé, Pic de, *Guinea* 204 D7
Tiber *see* Tevere, *river, It.* 152 J8
Tiber Dam, *Mont., U.S.* 108 B8
Tiberias *see* Teverya, *Israel* 172 K6
Tibesti Mountains, *Chad* 201 FI5
Tibet, *region, China* 182 K4
Tibet, Plateau of, *Asia* 168 H8
Tibet, Plateau of *see* Qing Zang Gaoyuan, *China* 182 J3
Tibiri, *Niger* 200 HII
Tiboku Falls, *Guyana* 131 EI4

Tibooburra, *N.S.W., Austral.* 215 VI2
Tibrikot, *Nepal* 180 E9
Tibugá, Golfo de, *Col.* 130 E3
Tiburón, Isla, *Mex.* 116 C6
Tîchît, *Mauritania* 200 G7
Ticonderoga, *N.Y., U.S.* 96 GII
Ticul, *Mex.* 117 HI6
Tiddim, *Myanmar* 190 F5
Tiddly Bank, *Arctic Oc.* 247 EI8
Tidjikdja, *Mauritania* 200 G6
Tidore, *Indonesia* 193 JI6
Tidra, Île, *Mauritania* 200 F4
Tiel, *Neth.* 148 JI3
Tièl, *Senegal* 200 H5
Tieli, *China* 183 CI6
Tieling, *Liaoning, China* 184 AI3
Tielongtan, *China* 182 H2
Tientsin *see* Tianjin, *Tianjin Shi, China* 184 D8
Tierra Amarilla, *Chile* 134 G7
Tierra Amarilla, *N. Mex., U.S.* 109 QI2
Tierra Blanca Creek, *Tex., U.S.* 104 H4
Tierra del Fuego, Isla Grande de, *S. Amer.* 135 X9
Tietê, *river, S. Amer.* 128 J9
Tiffin, *Ohio, U.S.* 101 PI2
Tifton, *Ga., U.S.* 99 P6
Tiga, Île, *New Caledonia, Fr.* 222 C9
Tiger Bay, *Af.* 198 M5
Tigray, *region, Eth.* 203 EI4
Tigre, *river, S. Amer.* 132 D3
Tigris, *river, Asia* 168 F4
Tigyaing, *Myanmar* 190 F6
Tîh, Gebel el, *Egypt* 173 R3
Tihāmah, *Asia* 168 H2
Tihāmat ash Shām, *region, Saudi Arabia, Yemen* 174 L7
Tijuana, *Mex.* 116 A5
Tikamgarh, *India* 180 H6
Tikapai, *island, Cook Is., N.Z.* 223 BI4
Tikchik Lakes, *Alas., U.S.* 113 KI3
Tikehau, *island, Fr. Polynesia, Fr.* 223 DI7
Tikei, *island, Fr. Polynesia, Fr.* 223 DI8
Tikhoretsk, *Russ.* 159 SII
Tikhvin, *Russ.* 158 F7
Tiki Basin, *Pac. Oc.* 243 LI6
Tikopia, *island, Solomon Is.* 218 J7
Tikrīt, *Iraq* 174 D9
Tiksi, *Russ.* 161 GI6
Tiladummati Atoll, *Maldives* 181 T3
Tilân, *Afghan.* 178 L4
Til Barsip *see* Tall al Aḥmar, *Syr.* 172 DIO
Tilburg, *Neth.* 148 KI2
Til-Châtel, *Fr.* 149 RI3
Tilden, *Nebr., U.S.* 107 N7
Tillabéri, *Niger* 200 HIO
Tillamook, *Oreg., U.S.* 110 F2
Tillamook Head, *Oreg., U.S.* 110 E2
Tillanchang Dwip, *island, India* 181 SI5
Tillia, *Niger* 200 HII
Tilloo Cay, *Bahamas* 118 CI2
Tílos (Piscopi), *island, Gr.* 157 MI8
Tilpa, *N.S.W., Austral.* 215 WI2
Timan Ridge, *Eur.* 140 BI2
Timanskiy Kryazh, *Russ.* 160 CI2
Timaru, *N.Z.* 217 PI7
Timashevo, *Russ.* 158 KI6
Timashevsk, *Russ.* 159 SIO
Timbalier Bay, *La., U.S.* 102 RIO
Timbalier Island, *La., U.S.* 102 RIO
Timbaúba, *Braz.* 133 FI8
Timbedgha, *Mauritania* 200 G7
Timber Creek, *N.T., Austral.* 215 Q7
Timber Lake, *S. Dak., U.S.* 106 J4
Timbío, *Col.* 130 G4
Timbuktu *see* Tombouctou, *Mali* 200 G8
Timbun Mata, *island, Malaysia* 193 GI3
Timimoun, *Alg.* 200 CIO
Timiris, Cap (Mirik), *Mauritania* 200 F4
Timiryazevskiy, *Russ.* 160 KI2
Timiš, *river, Rom.* 154 EII
Timişoara, *Rom.* 154 DII

Timiti's Crack, *point, Pitcairn I., U.K.* 223 Q23
Timmins, *Ont., Can.* 85 PI7
Timmonsville, *S.C., U.S.* 98 KIO
Timms Hill, *Wis., U.S.* 100 H4
Timoe *see* Temoe, *island, Fr. Polynesia, Fr.* 223 H23
Timor, *island, Asia* 193 NI5
Timor-Leste (East Timor), *Asia* 193 MI5
Timor Sea, *Ind. Oc.* 168 MI4
Timor Trough, *Ind. Oc.* 225 HI9
Timote, *Arg.* 134 LII
Timpanogos Cave National Monument, *Utah, U.S.* 108 L7
Timpson, *Tex., U.S.* 104 MI5
Timsâh, Buheirat el (Lake Timsah), *Egypt* 173 PI
Timsah, Lake *see* Buheirat el Timsâh, *Egypt* 173 PI
Tims Ford Lake, *Tenn., U.S.* 103 GI6
Timsgarry *see* Timsgearraidh, *Scot., U.K.* 144 H6
Timsgearraidh (Timsgarry), *Scot., U.K.* 144 H6
Tîn, Ras at, *Af.* 198 D8
Tinaca Point, *Philippines* 193 GI5
Tinajo, *Sp.* 208 P7
Tinakula, *island, Solomon Is.* 221 P22
Tindouf, *Alg.* 200 D7
Tindouf, Sebkha de, *Alg.* 200 D8
Tineo, *Sp.* 146 B8
Ting, *river, Fujian, China* 185 T7
Tinggoa, *Solomon Is.* 221 RI9
Tingo María, *Peru* 132 G3
Tinharé, Ilha de, *Braz.* 133 HI6
Tinhosa Grande, *Sao Tome and Principe* 209 B20
Tinhosa Pequena, *island, Sao Tome and Principe* 209 B20
Tinhosas, Pedras, *Sao Tome and Principe* 209 B20
Tinian, *island, N. Mariana Is., U.S.* 220 C2
Tinian Harbor *see* Sunbaron Roads, *N. Mariana Is., U.S.* 220 C7
Tinogasta, *Arg.* 134 G8
Tínos, *Gr.* 157 KI5
Tínos, *island, Gr.* 157 KI5
Tiñoso, Cabo, *Sp.* 147 LI4
Tinrhert, Hamada de, *Alg., Lib.* 200 DI2
Tinsukia, *India* 180 FI5
Tintamarre, Île, *St.-Martin, Fr.* 123 AI5
Tintigny, *Belg.* 149 NI3
Tintina, *Arg.* 134 GII
Tintinara, *S. Aust., Austral.* 215 YII
Ti-n-Zaouâtene, *Alg.* 200 FIO
Tiobraid Árann *see* Tipperary, *Ire.* 145 T5
Tioga, *N. Dak., U.S.* 106 E2
Tioga, *Pa., U.S.* 96 L7
Tioman, *peak, Malaysia* 191 UII
Tipp City, *Ohio, U.S.* 101 RII
Tipperary (Tiobraid Árann), *Ire.* 145 T5
Tipton, *Calif., U.S.* 111 U7
Tipton, *Ind., U.S.* 101 Q9
Tipton, *Iowa, U.S.* 107 PI4
Tipton, *Mo., U.S.* 107 TI2
Tipton, *Okla., U.S.* 104 H8
Tipton, Mount, *Ariz., U.S.* 109 R5
Tiptonville, *Tenn., U.S.* 102 EI2
Tiputa, *Fr. Polynesia, Fr.* 223 KI6
Tiputa, Passe de, *Fr. Polynesia, Fr.* 223 KI6
Tiracambu, Serra do, *Braz.* 133 EI4
Tīrān, *island, Egypt* 173 U4
Tīrān, Strait of, *Egypt* 173 U4
Tirana *see* Tiranë, *Alban.* 154 L9
Tiranë (Tirana), *Alban.* 154 L9
Tiraspol, *Mold.* 159 R5
Ţirbīl *see* Ţraybīl, *Iraq* 174 E7
Tire, *Turk.* 170 G3
Tirebolu, *Turk.* 171 DI3
Tiree, *island, Scot., U.K.* 144 L6
Tîrgu Frumos, *Rom.* 155 BI6
Tîrgu Lăpuş, *Rom.* 155 BI3
Tîrgu Neamţ, *Rom.* 155 BI5
Tîrgu Ocna, *Rom.* 155 DI6

Tîrgu Secuiesc, *Rom.* 155 DI5
Tirich Mir, *peak, Pak.* 178 LIO
Tîrna Mare, *Rom.* 155 AI3
Tîrnăveni, *Rom.* 155 DI4
Tir Pul, *Afghan.* 178 MI
Tirso, *river, It.* 153 N4
Tiruchchendur, *India* 181 S6
Tiruchchirappalli, *India* 181 R6
Tirunelveli, *India* 181 S5
Tirupati, *India* 181 P7
Tiruppattur, *India* 181 R6
Tiruppur, *India* 181 R5
Tiruvannamalai, *India* 181 Q6
Tiryns, *ruin, Gr.* 156 KII
Tisa, *river, Rom.* 154 DIO
Tisaiyanvilai, *India* 181 S6
Tishomingo, *Okla., U.S.* 104 JI2
Tisis, *Aust.* 162 M3
T'is Isat Fwafwatē (Blue Nile Falls), *Eth.* 203 FI4
Tista, *river, India* 180 GI2
Tisza, *river, Hung.* 151 KI7
Tiszafüred, *Hung.* 151 LI6
Tiszaújváros, *Hung.* 151 KI6
Titan Dome, *Antarctica* 230 JI2
Titano, Monte, *San Marino* 163 JI5
Titicaca, Lago, *Peru* 132 K6
Titikaveka, *Cook Is., N.Z.* 222 Q9
Titule, *Dem. Rep. of the Congo* 202 JII
Titusville, *Fla., U.S.* 99 T9
Titusville, *Pa., U.S.* 96 L4
Tiva, *Fr. Polynesia, Fr.* 223 A23
Tivaru, *island, Fr. Polynesia, Fr.* 223 KI5
Tiverton, *Eng., U.K.* 145 WIO
Tiverton, *R.I., U.S.* 97 LI5
Tivoli, *Grenada* 123 K23
Tivoli, *It.* 152 K9
Tiyās, *Syr.* 172 G9
Tizimín, *Mex.* 117 HI7
Tizi Ouzou, *Alg.* 200 AII
Tiznit, *Mor.* 200 C7
Tlaxcala, *Mex.* 116 JI2
Tlemcen, *Alg.* 200 A9
Tmassah, *Lib.* 201 EI4
Tmiet, *island, Marshall Is., U.S.* 220 L9
Toa Baja, *P.R., U.S.* 122 M4
Toachel Mlengui, *Palau* 220 MII
Toadlena, *N. Mex., U.S.* 109 RIO
Toagel Mid Passage, *Palau* 220 PII
Toahotu, *Fr. Polynesia, Fr.* 223 PI7
Toamaro, *island, Fr. Polynesia, Fr.* 223 B23
Toamaro, Passe, *Fr. Polynesia, Fr.* 223 B23
Toamasina, *Madagascar* 207 FI8
Toano, *Va., U.S.* 98 EI3
Toataratara, Pointe, *Fr. Polynesia, Fr.* 223 L23
Toau, *island, Fr. Polynesia, Fr.* 223 EI8
Toay, *Arg.* 134 MIO
Tobago, *Trinidad and Tobago* 123 NI8
Toba Kākar Range, *Pak.* 179 R6
Tobarra, *Sp.* 147 JI3
Toba Tek Singh, *Pak.* 179 QIO
Tobi, *island, Palau* 218 F2
Tobi Shima, *Japan* 188 LII
Tobin, Mount, *Nev., U.S.* 111 N9
Tobol, *river, Asia* 168 E7
Toboli, *Indonesia* 193 JI3
Tobol'sk, *Russ.* 160 JIO
Tobolski, *Jam.* 122 H8
Tobona, *island, Solomon Is.* 221 MI7
Tobruk *see* Ţubruq, *Lib.* 201 CI6
Tobyl, *Kaz.* 176 CIO
Tobyl, *river, Kaz.* 176 BII
Tocantínia, *Braz.* 133 GI3
Tocantinópolis, *Braz.* 133 FI3
Tocantins, *river, Braz.* 133 FI3
Toccoa, *Ga., U.S.* 98 K6
Toco, *Chile* 134 D7
Toco, *Trinidad and Tobago* 123 N24
Tocón, Punta, *P.R., U.S.* 122 PI
Toconao, *Chile* 134 E8
Tocopilla, *Chile* 134 D6
Tocumwal, *N.S.W., Austral.* 215 YI3
Todi, *It.* 152 J8
Toding (Tuolin), *China* 182 J2
Todmorden, *S. Aust., Austral.* 215 U9

Todos os Santos Bay, *S. Amer.* 128 GII
Todos Santos, *Mex.* 116 F7
Todos Santos, Bahía, *Mex.* 116 B5
Tofino, *B.C., Can.* 84 M7
Tofte, *Minn., U.S.* 106 FI3
Tofua, *island, Tonga* 222 P5
Toga, *island, Vanuatu* 222 AI
Togiak, *Alas., U.S.* 113 KI3
Togian, Kepulauan, *Indonesia* 193 JI4
Togliatti *see* Tol'yatti, *Russ.* 158 KI5
Togo, *Af.* 204 DII
Togtoh, *N. Mongol, China* 184 C3
Togyz, *Kaz.* 176 F9
Tohatchi, *N. Mex., U.S.* 109 RIO
Tohiea, Mount, *Fr. Polynesia, Fr.* 223 NI4
Tohma, *river, Turk.* 170 FI2
Tohopekaliga, Lake, *Fla., U.S.* 99 T9
Toi, *Cook Is., N.Z.* 223 A2O
Toi, *Japan* 188 HI2
Toibalawe, *India* 181 RI4
Toili, *Indonesia* 193 JI4
Toi Misaki, *Japan* 189 T5
Toiyabe Range, *U.S.* 86 F5
Tojŏng-san, *peak, N. Korea* 186 CI2
Tok, *Alas., U.S.* 113 GI9
Tokachi Dake, *Japan* 188 GI4
Tōkamachi, *Japan* 189 NII
Tokar, *Sudan* 203 DI4
Tokara Kaikyō, *Japan* 189 U4
Tokara Rettō, *Japan* 189 V3
Tokarevka, *Kaz.* 177 DI4
Toka Sand Cay, *Cook Is., N.Z.* 222 RI
Tokat, *Turk.* 170 EI2
Tōkch'ŏn, *N. Korea* 186 H7
Tokelau, *island, Kiribati* 218 HIO
Tokelau Basin, *Pac. Oc.* 242 KI2
Tokerau, *island, Cook Is., N.Z.* 223 AI7
Toki Point, *Wake I., U.S.* 220 F8
Tokmak, *Ukr.* 159 R8
Tokmok, *Kyrg.* 178 DI2
Toko, *Russ.* 161 JI9
Tokomaru Bay, *N.Z.* 217 K2O
Tokoro, *river, Japan* 188 FI4
Tokoroa, *N.Z.* 217 KI9
Tŏksin, *N. Korea* 186 EI2
Tŏksŏng, *N. Korea* 186 GIO
Toksook Bay, *Alas., U.S.* 112 JII
Toksun, *China* 182 E5
Toktogul, *Kyrg.* 178 EIO
Tokung, *Indonesia* 192 JII
Tokuno Shima, *Japan* 189 W3
Tokushima, *Japan* 189 Q8
Tokuyama, *Japan* 189 Q6
Tōkyō, *Japan* 189 PI2
Tōkyō Wan, *Japan* 189 PI2
Tol, *island, F.S.M.* 221 CI4
Tôlanaro, *Madagascar* 207 JI7
Tolbo, *Mongolia* 182 C6
Tolchin, Mount, *Antarctica* 230 HII
Tôle Bī, *Kaz.* 177 HI5
Toledo, *Iowa, U.S.* 107 NI2
Toledo, *Ohio, U.S.* 101 NI2
Toledo, *Oreg., U.S.* 110 G2
Toledo, *Sp.* 146 GIO
Toledo, *Wash., U.S.* 110 D3
Toledo, Montes de, *Sp.* 146 HIO
Toledo Bend Reservoir, *La., Tex., U.S.* 104 MI6
Toli, *China* 182 D4
Toliara, *Madagascar* 207 HI6
Tolitoli, *Indonesia* 193 HI3
Tol'ka, *Russ.* 160 HI2
Tollya, Zaliv, *Russ.* 161 DI4
Tolmezzo, *It.* 152 C9
Tolo, Teluk, *Indonesia* 193 KI4
Tolob, *Scot., U.K.* 144 EI2
Tolosa, *Sp.* 147 BI3
Toltén, *Chile* 135 P6
Tolti, *Pak.* 180 B5
Tolú, *Col.* 130 C4
Toluca, *Mex.* 116 JII
Tol'yatti (Togliatti), *Russ.* 158 KI5
Tomah, *Wis., U.S.* 100 K4
Tomahawk, *Wis., U.S.* 100 G5
Tomakomai, *Japan* 188 GI3
Tomanivi, *peak, Fiji* 222 H6
Tomar, *Braz.* 132 C8

Tomar, Port. 146 G5
Tomari, Japan 188 J13
Tomaszów Lubelski, Pol. 151 G18
Tomaszów Mazowiecki, Pol. 151 E15
Tomatin, Scot., U.K. 144 K9
Tombador, Serra do, Braz. 132 H10
Tombe, Solomon Is. 221 M16
Tombigbee, river, Ala., Miss., U.S. 103 J13
Tombouctou (Timbuktu), Mali 200 G8
Tombstone, Ariz., U.S. 109 W9
Tombua, Angola 206 E5
Tomé, Chile 134 M5
Tomea, island, Indonesia 193 L15
Tomil, F.S.M. 221 D18
Tomil Harbor, F.S.M. 221 D18
Tomini, Gulf of, Pac. Oc. 168 L13
Tomini, Teluk, Indonesia 193 J13
Tomintoul, Scot., U.K. 144 K10
Tomman, island, Vanuatu 222 E2
Tommot, Russ. 161 H18
Tomo, New Caledonia, Fr. 222 D8
Tomo, river, Col. 130 E8
Tomorit, Maja e, Alban. 154 M10
Tomortei, N. Mongol, China 184 A5
Tömotu Noi (Lord Howe Island), Solomon Is. 221 Q23
Tompa, Russ. 161 K16
Tompkinsville, Ky., U.S. 103 D16
Tom Price, W. Aust., Austral. 215 T3
Tomsk, Russ. 160 K12
Tomsyu, Russ. 161 E18
Tomtor, Russ. 161 F17
Tomtor Tasa, Gora, Russ. 161 F16
Tom White, Mount, Alas., U.S. 113 J18
Tonalá, Mex. 117 K14
Tonami, Japan 189 N10
Tonantins, Braz. 132 D6
Tonasket, Wash., U.S. 110 A7
Tonbridge, Eng., U.K. 145 W14
Tønder, Den. 142 N11
Tondou Massif, Af. 198 H8
Tonga, Pac. Oc. 218 K10
Tonga, S. Sudan 202 G12
Tonga Islands, Pac. Oc. 218 K10
Tong'an, Fujian, China 185 U9
Tongareva see Penrhyn Atoll, Cook Is., N.Z. 218 H12
Tonga Ridge, Pac. Oc. 242 M12
Tongariki, island, Vanuatu 222 E3
Tongatapu Group, Tonga 218 K10
Tonga Trench, Pac. Oc. 242 M12
Tongbai, Henan, China 184 L5
Tongch'ang, N. Korea 186 G6
Tongcheng, Hubei, China 185 P5
T'ongch'ŏn, N. Korea 186 J10
Tongchuan (Shilipu), Shaanxi, China 184 H1
Tongdao, Hunan, China 185 S1
Tongde, China 182 J9
Tongeren, Belg. 148 L13
Tonggo, N. Korea 186 G5
Tonggu, Jiangxi, China 185 Q6
Tongha, N. Korea 186 H9
Tonghua, Jilin, China 184 A15
Tonghŭng, N. Korea 186 F12
Tongjosŏn-man, bay, N. Korea 186 H9
Tongliao, China 183 E15
Tongling, Anhui, China 185 N9
Tonglu, Zhejiang, China 185 P10
Tongnim, N. Korea 186 G4
Tongnim-san, peak, N. Korea 186 G6
Tongo, N.S.W., Austral. 215 W12
Tongoa, island, Vanuatu 222 E3
Tongoy, Chile 134 J6
Tongshi, China 182 Q12
Tongsin, N. Korea 186 G7
Tongtian (Yangtze), river, China 182 J7
Tongue, Scot., U.K. 144 G9
Tongue, river, Mont., Wyo., U.S. 108 E12
Tongue, Kyle of, Scot., U.K. 144 G9
Tongue of the Ocean, Bahamas 118 F11
Tongue River Reservoir, Mont., U.S. 108 F11
Tongy, Qnsld., Austral. 215 V14
Tongyeong, S. Korea 187 T11
Tongzhou, Beijing Shi, China 184 C8
Tongzhou, Jiangsu, China 184 L11
Tongzi, China 182 M11
Tonj, S. Sudan 202 G12
Tonk, India 180 G5
Tonkawa, Okla., U.S. 104 E11
Tonkin, Gulf of, Asia 190 J13
Tonle Sap see Bœ̆ng Tônlé Sab, Cambodia 191 N11
Tonneins, Fr. 149 W7
Tonnerre, Fr. 149 R11
Tōno, Japan 188 K13
Tonoas, island, F.S.M. 221 B15
Tonopah, Nev., U.S. 111 R9
Tønsberg, Nor. 142 K11
Tonto National Monument, Ariz., U.S. 109 U8
Tonumea, island, Tonga 222 R6
Tonya, Turk. 171 D14
Tooele, Utah, U.S. 108 L7
Toomaru, Mount, Fr. Polynesia, Fr. 223 B23
Toopua, island, Fr. Polynesia, Fr. 223 K13
Toopua Iti, island, Fr. Polynesia, Fr. 223 K13
Toora Khem, Russ. 161 L14
Toorale, N.S.W., Austral. 215 W13
Toowoomba, Qnsld., Austral. 215 V15
Top, Lake, Eur. 140 B10
Topaze, Baie, Mauritius 209 J20
Topeka, Kans., U.S. 107 S9
Toplița, Rom. 155 C15
Topock, Ariz., U.S. 109 S4
Topol'čany, Slovakia 151 K14
Topolobampo, Mex. 116 E7
Toppenish, Wash., U.S. 110 E6
Topsail Beach, N.C., U.S. 98 K13
Top'yŏng, N. Korea 186 L5
Toquima Range, Nev., U.S. 111 Q9
Tor, Sp. 162 H1
Tora Bora, site, Afghan. 178 M8
Tōraghūndī, Afghan. 178 L2
Toraigh (Tory Island), Ire. 145 N5
Torbalı, Turk. 170 G3
Torbat-e Ḩeydarīyeh, Iran 175 C16
Torbat-e Jām, Iran 175 C17
Torbay, Eng., U.K. 145 X10
Torbert, Mount, Alas., U.S. 113 J16
Torch Lake, Mich., U.S. 100 H10
Töre, Sw. 143 E14
Torello, It. 162 H13
Torez, Ukr. 159 Q10
Torghay, Kaz. 176 E11
Torghay, river, Kaz. 176 E10
Torgo, Russ. 161 J17
Torhout, Belg. 148 L10
Torino (Turin), It. 152 E2
Tori Shima, Japan 189 U12
Tori Shima, Japan 189 X1
Torixoreu, Braz. 132 J12
Tornal'a, Slovakia 151 K16
Torneå see Tornio, Fin. 143 E15
Torneälven, river, Eur. 140 B9
Torneträsk, lake, Sw. 143 D13
Torngat Mountains, Nfld. & Lab., Can. 85 J20
Tornillo, Tex., U.S. 105 W3
Tornimparte, It. 152 K9
Tornio (Torneå), Fin. 143 E15
Torniojoki, river, Fin., Sw. 143 D14
Tornquist, Arg. 135 N11
Toro, Sp. 146 D9
Tōro, Japan 188 G15
Toro, Cerro del, S. Amer. 134 H7
Torokina, P.N.G. 221 K14
Törökszentmiklós, Hung. 151 L16
Torom, Russ. 161 J20
Toronto, Kans., U.S. 107 U9
Toronto, Ohio, U.S. 101 Q16
Toronto, Ont., Can. 85 Q18
Toropets, Russ. 158 H6
Tororo, Uganda 203 K13
Toros Dağı, Turk. 170 H9
Toros Dağlari (Taurus), Turk. 170 J8
Torquemada, Sp. 146 D10
Torrance, Calif., U.S. 111 X8
Torran Rocks, Scot., U.K. 144 M7
Torre Annunziata, It. 152 M11
Torre Astura, It. 152 L8
Torre de Moncorvo, Port. 146 E7
Torredonjimeno, Sp. 146 K10
Torrejón de Ardoz, Sp. 146 F11
Torrelavega, Sp. 146 B10
Torremaggiore, It. 152 L12
Torremolinos, Sp. 146 M10
Torrens, Lake, Austral. 214 J10
Torrent, Sp. 147 H14
Torreón, Mex. 116 F10
Torre San Giovanni, It. 153 N15
Torres Islands, Vanuatu 222 A1
Torres Strait, Austral. 214 A12
Torres Vedras, Port. 146 H4
Torrevieja, Sp. 147 K14
Torriana, It. 162 G13
Torrijos, Sp. 146 G10
Torrington, Conn., U.S. 96 L12
Torrington, Wyo., U.S. 108 J14
Torrutj, island, Marshall Is., U.S. 220 M4
Torsby, Sw. 142 K12
Tórshavn, Faroe Is., Den. 142 H6
Tortola, British Virgin Is., U.K. 122 Q6
Tortona, It. 152 E4
Tortosa, Sp. 147 F15
Tortosa see Ţarţūs, Syr. 172 G7
Tortosa, Cap de, Sp. 147 F16
Tortosa, Cape, Eur. 140 K4
Tortue, Île de la, Haiti 119 K15
Tortuga, Isla, Ecua. 130 Q9
Tortuguero, Laguna, P.R., U.S. 122 M3
Tortum, Turk. 171 E16
Ţorūd, Iran 175 C14
Torugart, Kyrg. 178 F12
Torul, Turk. 171 D14
Toruń, Pol. 151 D14
Tõrva, Est. 143 K17
Tory Island see Toraigh, Ire. 145 N5
Torzhok, Russ. 158 H8
Tōrzī, Afghan. 179 R5
Tosa del Braidal, peak, Andorra 162 J4
T'osan, N. Korea 186 L8
Tosashimizu, Japan 189 S6
Tosa Wan, Japan 189 R7
Tosca, S. Af. 206 J9
Toscano, Arcipelago, It. 152 J6
Toshkent (Tashkent), Uzb. 177 K13
Tosontsengel, Mongolia 182 C8
Tostado, Arg. 134 H11
Tosters, Aust. 162 M3
Tosu, Japan 189 R4
Tosya, Turk. 170 D9
Totana, Sp. 147 K13
Totegegie, island, Fr. Polynesia, Fr. 223 Q21
Toteng, Botswana 206 G9
Tôtes, Fr. 149 N8
Totia, island, Cook Is., N.Z. 223 C15
Totiw, island, F.S.M. 221 C15
Tot'ma, Russ. 158 F11
Totnes, Eng., U.K. 145 X10
Totness, Suriname 131 E16
Toto, Angola 206 B6
Totokafonua, island, Tonga 222 M11
Totora, Bol. 132 K7
Totoya, island, Fiji 222 K8
Tottan Hills, Antarctica 230 C11
Tottori, Japan 189 P7
Totu Tofari, island, Fr. Polynesia, Fr. 223 A22
Toubkal, Jebel, Mor. 200 C8
Toucy, Fr. 149 R11
Toufen, Taiwan, China 185 U11
Tougan, Burkina Faso 204 B9
Touggourt, Alg. 200 B12
Touho, New Caledonia, Fr. 222 C7
Toul, Fr. 149 P13
Touliu, Taiwan, China 185 V11
Toulon, Fr. 149 Y14
Toulouse, Fr. 149 X9
Toummo, Lib. 201 F13
Toungo, Nigeria 205 D16
Touques, river, Fr. 149 P7
Touriñán, Cabo, Sp. 146 B5
Tournai, Belg. 148 L11
Tournavista, Peru 132 G4
Tournay, Fr. 149 Y7
Touros, Braz. 133 F18
Tours, Fr. 149 R8
Toury, Fr. 149 Q9
Touwsrivier, S. Af. 206 M8
Tovarkovskiy, Russ. 158 L9
Tovuz, Azerb. 171 D19
Towada, Japan 188 J13
Towada Ko, Japan 188 J12
Towanda, Pa., U.S. 96 L8
Tower, Minn., U.S. 106 F12
Towner, N. Dak., U.S. 106 E5
Town Hall, Monaco 163 E21
Town Hall of Beausoleil, Fr. 163 C21
Town Hill, peak, Bermuda 122 C3
Townsend, Mont., U.S. 108 D8
Townsend, Va., U.S. 98 F14
Townsville, Qnsld., Austral. 215 R14
Towot, S. Sudan 203 H13
Towson, Md., U.S. 98 C13
Toyah, Tex., U.S. 105 N2
Toyahvale, Tex., U.S. 105 P2
Toyama, Japan 189 N10
Toyama Wan, Japan 189 N10
Toyohashi, Japan 189 Q10
Toyooka, Japan 189 P8
Toyotomi, Japan 188 E13
Tozeur, Tun. 200 B12
Tqvarch'eli, Rep. of Georgia 171 B16
Trâblous (Tripoli), Leb. 172 H7
Trabzon, Turk. 171 D14
Tracy, Calif., U.S. 111 S4
Tracy, Minn., U.S. 106 K9
Træna Bank, Atl. Oc. 240 E13
Traer, Iowa, U.S. 107 N12
Trafalgar, Cabo, Sp. 146 N8
Tráighlí see Tralee, Ire. 145 U3
Trail, B.C., Can. 84 M9
Traill Ø, island, Greenland, Den. 82 B10
Traíra see Taraira, river, S. Amer. 132 C5
Traîtres, Baie des, Fr. Polynesia, Fr. 223 N20
Trakhonas (Kızılay), Cyprus 162 N8
Tralee (Tráighlí), Ire. 145 U3
Tralee Bay, Ire. 145 U3
Tranås, Sw. 143 L13
Trancas, Arg. 134 F9
Trang, Thai. 191 R8
Trangan, island, Indonesia 193 M18
Tranqueras, Uru. 134 J14
Trans-Amazon Highway, Braz. 132 F9
Transantarctic Mountains, Antarctica 231 K13
Trans-Canada Highway, Can. 84 L8
Transdniestria, region, Mold., Ukr. 159 R5
Transkei Basin, Ind. Oc. 224 N3
Transylvania, region, Rom. 155 C13
Transylvanian Alps, Rom. 154 F12
Trapani, It. 153 S8
Trapper Peak, Mont., U.S. 108 E5
Trarza, regions, Af. 198 F1
Trasimeno, Lago, It. 152 H8
Trat, Cambodia 191 N10
Traun, Aust. 150 K11
Traunreut, Ger. 150 K9
Traverse, Lake, Minn., S. Dak., U.S. 106 J8
Traverse City, Mich., U.S. 100 J9
Travis, Lake, Tex., U.S. 105 Q10
Travnik, Bosn. & Herzg. 154 G7
Ţraybīl (Ţirbīl), Iraq 174 E7
Trbovlje, Slov. 154 D5
Treasure Beach, Jam. 122 J7
Treasure Cay, Bahamas 122 A6
Treasurers Island, Solomon Is. 221 N24
Treasury Islands, Solomon Is. 221 L14
Třebíč, Czech Rep. 150 J12
Trebinje, Bosn. & Herzg. 154 J8
Trebisacce, It. 153 P13
Trebišov, Slovakia 151 J17
Třeboň, Czech Rep. 150 J11
Trégastel, Fr. 149 P3
Tregrosse Islets, Austral. 214 D15
Tréguier, Fr. 149 P4
Treignac, Fr. 149 U9
Treinta y Tres, Uru. 134 K15
Trelew, Arg. 135 R9
Trelleborg, Sw. 142 N12
Tremadoc Bay, Wales, U.K. 145 T9
Tremiti, Isole, It. 152 K12
Tremonton, Utah, U.S. 108 J7
Trenary, Mich., U.S. 100 F8
Trenčín, Slovakia 151 J14
Trenque Lauquen, Arg. 134 M11
Trento, It. 152 C7
Trenton, Mich., U.S. 101 N12
Trenton, Mo., U.S. 107 R11
Trenton, N.J., U.S. 96 P10
Trenton, Nebr., U.S. 107 R4
Trenton, Tenn., U.S. 102 F12
Trepassey, Nfld. & Lab., Can. 85 M24
Tres Arroyos, Arg. 135 N12
Tres Esquinas, Col. 130 H5
Treshnish Isles, Scot., U.K. 144 L7
Três Lagoas, Braz. 132 L12
Três Marias Reservoir, S. Amer. 128 H9
Tres Montes, Golfo, Chile 135 T6
Tres Montes, Península, Chile 135 T5
Tres Picos, Cerro, Arg. 135 R7
Tres Puntas, Cabo, Arg. 135 T9
Tres Zapotes, ruin, Mex. 117 J13
Treviso, It. 152 D8
Trevose Head, Eng., U.K. 145 X8
Trgovı̌ste, Serb. 154 J12
Trial Bay, Austral. 214 J15
Triangle, The, Myanmar 190 E7
Triángulos, Arrecifes, Mex. 117 H15
Tribulation, Cape, Qnsld., Austral. 215 Q13
Tribune, Kans., U.S. 107 T3
Tricarico, It. 152 M13
Tricase, It. 153 N16
Trichonida, Límni, Gr. 156 H9
Trida, N.S.W., Austral. 215 X13
Trie, Fr. 149 Y7
Trier, Ger. 162 J12
Triesen, Liech. 162 Q2
Triesenberg, Liech. 162 P2
Trieste, It. 152 D10
Triglav, peak, Slov. 154 C4
Trigueros, Sp. 146 L7
Tríkala, Gr. 156 E9
Tríkeri, Gr. 156 G11
Trikomo (Iskele), Cyprus 162 N10
Trikora, peak, Indonesia 217 C16
Trincomalee, Sri Lanka 181 S8
Trindade Seachannel, Atl. Oc. 248 Q3
Třinec, Czech Rep. 151 H14
Trinidad, Bol. 132 J7
Trinidad, Calif., U.S. 110 M1
Trinidad, Colo., U.S. 109 P14
Trinidad, Cuba 118 H9
Trinidad, island, Trinidad and Tobago 121 K17
Trinidad, Golfo, Chile 135 V6
Trinidad, Isla, Arg. 135 P11
Trinidad and Tobago, N. Amer. 121 J17
Trinidad Head, Calif., U.S. 110 M1
Trinitapoli, It. 152 L13
Trinity, Tex., U.S. 105 P14
Trinity, river, Calif., U.S. 110 M2
Trinity, river, Tex., U.S. 105 P14
Trinity Bay, Austral. 214 C13
Trinity Bay, Nfld. & Lab., Can. 85 M24
Trinity Hills, peaks, Trinidad and Tobago 123 Q23
Trinity Islands, Alas., U.S. 113 N15
Trinity Peninsula, Antarctica 230 C4
Trinity Range, Nev., U.S. 111 N7
Trinkat Island, India 181 S15
Triolet, Mauritius 209 F20
Trion, Ga., U.S. 98 K4
Trionto, Capo, It. 153 P14
Triora, It. 152 G2
Trípoli, Gr. 156 K10
Tripoli see Ţarābulus, Lib. 201 B13
Tripoli see Trâblous, Leb. 172 H7
Tripolitania, region, Lib. 201 C13
Tripp, S. Dak., U.S. 106 M7
Tristaina, river, Andorra 162 G3
Tristaina, Pic de, Andorra, Fr. 162 G2
Tristan da Cunha Group, islands, Af. 198 R2
Tristan da Cunha Island, Af. 198 R2
Tristao, Îles, Guinea 204 C4
Tristão, Ponta do, Madeira, Port. 208 M2
Tristen da Cunha Fracture Zone, Atl. Oc. 241 T9

Trivandrum see Thiruvananthapuram, India 181 S5
Trnava, Slovakia 151 K13
Trobriand Islands, P.N.G. 217 D21
Trofors, Nor. 142 F12
Trois-Bassins, Réunion, Fr. 209 G16
Troisdorf, Ger. 150 F5
Trois Fourches, Cap des, Mor. 146 P11
Trois-Rivières, Guadeloupe, Fr. 123 G14
Trois-Rivières, Que., Can. 85 P20
Troisvierges, Lux. 162 G9
Troitsk, Russ. 160 J8
Troitskoye, Russ. 159 R13
Troja, Jam. 122 H9
Trojanów, Pol. 151 E17
Troll, station, Antarctica 231 B13
Trollhättan, Sw. 142 L12
Trombetas, river, Braz. 132 C10
Tromsø, Nor. 143 C13
Tromsø Bank, Arctic Oc. 247 F18
Trona, Calif., U.S. 111 V9
Tronador, Monte, Arg. 135 Q7
Trondheim, Nor. 142 G12
Trondheimsfjorden, bay, Nor. 142 G11
Troodos Mountains, Cyprus 162 P7
Troon, Scot., U.K. 145 N9
T. Roosevelt Lake, Ariz., U.S. 109 T8
Trostyanets', Ukr. 159 N8
Trou d'Eau Douce, Mauritius 209 G21
Trou Gras Point, St. Lucia 123 K14
Troumaka, St. Vincent and the Grenadines 123 K16
Troup, Tex., U.S. 104 M14
Trout Creek, Utah, U.S. 108 M5
Trout Lake, N.W.T., Can. 84 H10
Trout Lake, Ont., Can. 85 N14
Trout Peak, Wyo., U.S. 108 F9
Trout River, Nfld. & Lab., Can. 85 M23
Troy, Ala., U.S. 103 M16
Troy, Jam. 122 H7
Troy, Kans., U.S. 107 R10
Troy, Mo., U.S. 107 S14
Troy, Mont., U.S. 108 B4
Troy, N.C., U.S. 98 H10
Troy, N.Y., U.S. 96 K11
Troy, Ohio, U.S. 101 R11
Troy, Oreg., U.S. 110 E9
Troy, ruins, Turk. 170 D2
Troyes, Fr. 149 Q14
Troy Peak, Nev., U.S. 111 R11
Trübbach, Switz. 162 Q1
Trubchevsk, Russ. 158 M7
Truckee, Calif., U.S. 111 Q6
Truckee, river, Calif., Nev., U.S. 111 P6
Trujillo, Hond. 117 K18
Trujillo, Peru 132 G2
Trujillo, Venez. 130 C7
Trujillo Alto, P.R., U.S. 122 M5
Truk Islands see Chuuk, F.S.M. 220 Q6
Truk Lagoon, F.S.M. 221 B15
Trumann, Ark., U.S. 102 F10
Trumbull, Mount, Ariz., U.S. 109 Q6
Truro, Eng., U.K. 145 X8
Truro, N.S., Can. 85 P22
Truth or Consequences, N. Mex., U.S. 109 U11
Trutnov, Czech Rep. 150 G12
Tryavna, Bulg. 155 H15
Trzebnica, Pol. 151 F13
Tsada, Cyprus 162 Q6
Tsagaannuur, Mongolia 182 C6
Tsagan Aman, Russ. 159 Q14
Ts'ageri, Rep. of Georgia 171 B17
Tsagveri, Rep. of Georgia 171 C17
Tsahir, Mongolia 182 D8
Tsaile, Ariz., U.S. 109 R9
Tsaka La, peak, India 180 C7
Tsalka, Rep. of Georgia 171 C18
Tsamkanī, Afghan. 179 N8
Tsarevo, Bulg. 155 J17
Tsau (Tsao), Botswana 206 G8
Tschida, Lake, N. Dak., U.S. 106 G3
Tsentral'nyy, Russ. 161 G20
Tses, Namibia 206 J7
Tsetsegnuur, Mongolia 182 D7
Tsetserleg, Mongolia 182 D9

Tshabong, Botswana 206 J8
Tshane, Botswana 206 H8
Tshela, Dem. Rep. of the Congo 202 L6
Tshikapa, Dem. Rep. of the Congo 202 M9
Tshofa, Dem. Rep. of the Congo 202 L10
Tshootsha, Botswana 206 H8
Tshuapa, river, Dem. Rep. of the Congo 202 K10
Tshwane see Pretoria, S. Af. 206 J10
Tsiigehtchic, N.W.T., Can. 84 E9
Tsimlyanskoye Vodokhranilishche, Russ. 159 Q12
Tsimlyansk Reservoir, Eur. 140 G13
Tsiombe, Madagascar 207 J16
Tsipanda, Russ. 161 H19
Ts'khinvali, Rep. of Georgia 171 B18
Tsna, river, Russ. 158 L11
Tsnori, Rep. of Georgia 171 C20
Tsu, Japan 189 Q9
Tsubame, Japan 188 M11
Tsuchiura, Japan 189 N12
Tsugaru Kaikyō, Japan 188 J12
Tsuma, Japan 189 N7
Tsumeb, Namibia 206 G7
Tsuruga, Japan 189 P9
Tsuruga Wan, Japan 189 P9
Tsuruoka, Japan 188 L12
Tsushima, Japan 189 Q4
Tsushima, island, Japan 189 Q4
Tsushima Strait, Japan, S. Korea 187 V13
Tsuyama, Japan 189 P7
Tsyurupyns'k, Ukr. 159 R7
Tuahora, Pointe, Fr. Polynesia, Fr. 223 K14
Tuaim see Taum, Ire. 145 R4
Tuakau, N.Z. 217 J19
Tual, Indonesia 193 L18
Tuam (Tuaim), Ire. 145 R4
Tuamotu Archipelago, Fr. Polynesia, Fr. 223 E19
Tuamotu Ridge, Pac. Oc. 243 L15
Tuân Giáo, Vietnam 190 G10
Tuangku, island, Indonesia 192 H4
Tu'anuku, Tonga 222 L11
Tuapa, Niue, N.Z. 223 A20
Tuapse, Russ. 159 T10
Tuaran, Malaysia 192 F12
Tuasivi, Samoa 222 K2
Tuasivi, Cape, Samoa 222 K2
Tuatapere, N.Z. 217 R15
Tuath, Loch a, Scot., U.K. 144 H7
Tuauru, river, Fr. Polynesia, Fr. 223 N16
Tubac, Ariz., U.S. 109 W8
Tuba City, Ariz., U.S. 109 R7
Tubarão, Braz. 133 P13
Tubarão, Point, S. Amer. 128 E11
Tübingen, Ger. 150 J6
Tubmanburg, Liberia 204 D6
Tubou, Fiji 222 J9
Ţubruq (Tobruk), Lib. 201 C16
Tubuai, island, Fr. Polynesia, Fr. 223 H16
Tubuai Islands see Austral Islands, Fr. Polynesia, Fr. 223 H16
Tucacas, Venez. 130 B9
Tucavaca, river, Bol. 132 K9
Tuchengzi, Hebei, China 184 B8
Tuckerman, Ark., U.S. 102 F10
Tucker's Town, Bermuda 122 B3
Tuckerton, N.J., U.S. 96 Q10
Tucson, Ariz., U.S. 109 V8
Tucumcari, N. Mex., U.S. 109 S15
Tucumcari, N. Mex., U.S. 109 S15
Tucupita, Venez. 130 C12
Tucuruí, Braz. 133 E13
Tucuruí, Represa de, Braz. 133 E13
Tudela, Sp. 147 D13
Tuensang, India 180 G15
Tuffé, Fr. 149 Q8
Tufi, P.N.G. 217 E20
Tufts Plain, Pac. Oc. 243 D15
Tufuone, Wallis and Futuna, Fr. 222 B11
Tufu Point, Amer. Samoa, U.S. 222 P4
Tufuvai, Tonga 222 K12
Tugela Falls, Af. 198 P8

Tug Fork, river, Ky., W. Va., U.S. 103 B20
Tūghyl, Kaz. 177 E19
Tuguegarao, Philippines 193 B14
Tugur, Russ. 161 J20
Tui, Sp. 146 C5
Tuineje, Sp. 208 Q7
Tukangbesi Kepulauan, Indonesia 193 L14
Tukao, Cook Is., N.Z. 223 A14
Tukchi, Russ. 161 H20
Tukosméra, Mount, Vanuatu 222 H4
Tūkrah, Lib. 201 C15
Tuktoyaktuk, N.W.T., Can. 84 D10
Tukums, Latv. 143 L16
Tukzār, Afghan. 178 L6
Tula, Mex. 116 G11
Tula, Russ. 158 K9
Tulach Mhór see Tullamore, Ire. 145 S5
Tulaghi, island, Solomon Is. 221 N19
Tūlak, Afghan. 179 N3
Tulare, Calif., U.S. 111 U7
· Tulare Lake Bed, Calif., U.S. III U6
Tularosa, N. Mex., U.S. 109 U12
Tulcán, Ecua. 130 H3
Tulcea, Rom. 155 E18
Tul'chyn, Ukr. 159 P5
Tulelake, Calif., U.S. 110 L4
Tuli, Zimb. 206 H11
Tulia, Tex., U.S. 104 H5
Tulita, N.W.T., Can. 84 F10
Ţūlkarm, W. Bank 172 L5
Tullahoma, Tenn., U.S. 103 F16
Tullamore, N.S.W., Austral. 215 X13
Tullamore (Tulach Mhór), Ire. 145 S5
Tulle, Fr. 149 V9
Tully, Qnsld., Austral. 215 R13
Tulsa, Okla., U.S. 104 F12
Tuluá, Col. 130 F4
Tulun, Russ. 161 L14
Tulu Welel, peak, Eth. 203 G14
Tum, Indonesia 193 K17
Tumacacori National Historical Park, Ariz., U.S. 109 W7
Tumaco, Col. 130 H3
Tumaco, Ensenada de, Col. 130 H3
Tumakuru, India 181 P5
Tuman, river, China 186 A13
Tumbes, Peru 132 E2
Tumd Youqi, N. Mongol, China 184 C3
Tumd Zuoqi, N. Mongol, China 184 B3
Tumen, river, N. Korea 186 A13
Tumeremo, Venez. 131 D13
Tummel, Loch, Scot., U.K. 144 L9
Tumon Bay, Guam, U.S. 220 B11
Tumucumaque, Serra de, S. Amer. 131 G17
Tumu Mountain, Amer. Samoa, U.S. 222 N1
Tumu Point, F.S.M. 221 F13
Tumwater, Wash., U.S. 110 D3
Tunam, N. Korea 186 D12
Tunapuna, Trinidad and Tobago 123 P22
Tunas de Zaza, Cuba 118 J9
Tunceli, Turk. 171 F14
Tundubai, Sudan 202 E10
Tunduma, Tanzania 203 N13
Tunduru, Tanzania 203 N14
Tundzha, river, Bulg. 155 J15
Tungabhadra, river, India 181 N5
Tŭngam, N. Korea 186 M5
Tunga Pass, India 180 E14
Tungkang, Taiwan, China 185 W11
Tungua, island, Tonga 222 Q6
Tunguska Nizhnaya, river, Asia 168 D9
Tunguska Podkamennaya, Russ. 161 J13
Tunguskhaya, Russ. 161 G17
Tunica, Miss., U.S. 102 G11
Tunis, Tun. 201 A13
Tunis, Gulf of, Af. 198 C6
Tunisia, Af. 200 B12
Tunisian Plateau, Atl. Oc. 240 K13
Tunja, Col. 130 E6
Tunliu, Shanxi, China 184 G5
Tununak, Alas., U.S. 112 J11
Tunuyán, Arg. 134 L7
Tuoji Dao, Shand., China 184 E11

Tuolin see Toding, China 182 J2
Tuolumne, river, Calif., U.S. 111 S5
Tup, Kyrg. 178 D14
Tupã, Braz. 132 L12
Tupai (Iti, Motu), island, Fr. Polynesia, Fr. 223 E15
Tupelo, Miss., U.S. 103 H13
Tupelo National Battlefield, Miss., U.S. 103 H13
Tupi, Philippines 193 F15
Tupiza, Bol. 132 L7
Tupper Lake, N.Y., U.S. 96 G10
Túpqaraghan Tübegi, Kaz. 176 G5
Túquerres, Col. 130 H3
Tura, India 180 G12
Tura, Russ. 161 H14
Turabah, Saudi Arabia 174 L8
Turakh, Russ. 161 E16
Turan Lowland, Asia 168 F5
Tur'at Maşīrah, Oman 175 L17
Ţurayf, Saudi Arabia 174 E7
Turbaco, Col. 130 C5
Turbat, Pak. 179 V2
Turbo, Col. 130 D4
Turda, Rom. 155 C13
Turégano, Sp. 146 E10
Tureia, island, Fr. Polynesia, Fr. 223 G21
Turek, Pol. 151 E14
Türghān, Kōtal-e, Afghan. 178 J9
Türgovishte, Bulg. 155 H16
Turgut, Turk. 170 F7
Turgutlu, Turk. 170 F3
Turhal, Turk. 170 D11
Türi, Est. 143 K16
Turi, peak, Fr. Polynesia, Fr. 223 G14
Turia, river, Sp. 147 F14
Turiaçu, Braz. 133 D14
Turiaçu, Baía de, Braz. 133 D14
Turin see Torino, It. 152 E2
Turka, Ukr. 159 P2
Turkana, Lake (Lake Rudolf), Kenya 203 J14
Türkeli, island, Turk. 170 D3
Turkey, Asia 170 F6
Turkey, Tex., U.S. 104 J6
Turkey, river, Iowa, U.S. 106 M13
Turkey Creek, W. Aust., Austral. 215 Q6
Türkistan, Kaz. 177 J13
Turkmenabat (Chärjew), Turkm. 176 L10
Türkmen Aylagy, Turkm. 176 L6
Türkmenbaşy, Turkm. 176 K6
Türkmenbaşy Aylagy, Turkm. 176 K6
Türkmen Dağı, Turk. 170 E6
Turkmenistan, Asia 176 L8
Turks & Caicos Islands, N. Amer. 119 J17
Turks Island Passage, Turks & Caicos Is. 119 J17
Turks Islands, Turks & Caicos Is. 119 J18
Turku (Åbo), Fin. 143 J15
Turkwel, river, Kenya 203 J14
Turlock, Calif., U.S. 111 S5
Turnagain, Cape, N.Z. 217 L20
Turner, Mont., U.S. 108 A10
Turner's Peninsula, Af. 198 H1
Turner Hole, Virgin Is., U.S. 122 Q3
Turnhout, Belg. 148 K12
Turnu Măgurele, Rom. 155 G14
Turnu Roşu, Pasul, Rom. 155 E14
Turpan, China 182 E6
Turpan Depression, Asia 168 G8
Turpan Pendi, China 182 E6
Turquino, Pico, Cuba 118 K12
Tursunzoda, Taj. 178 H7
Turt, Mongolia 182 B9
Türtkül, Uzb. 176 K9
Turtle see Vatoa, island, Fiji 222 L9
Turtle Crawls, site, Cayman Is. 122 J1
Turtle Lake, N. Dak., U.S. 106 F4
Turtle Mountain, N. Dak., U.S. 106 D5
Turtle Rocks, Bahamas 122 C7
Turugart Pass, China, Kyrg. 182 E2
Turyu-san, peak, N. Korea 186 E11
Tuscaloosa, Ala., U.S. 103 K14
Tuscany, Eur. 140 K6

Tuscarora, Nev., U.S. 110 M10
Tuscola, Ill., U.S. 101 R6
Tuscola, Tex., U.S. 104 M8
Tuscumbia, Ala., U.S. 103 G14
Tushchybas Shyghanaghy, bay, Kaz. 176 G9
Tuskar Rock, Ire. 145 U7
Tuskegee, Ala., U.S. 103 L16
Tutak, Turk. 171 E17
Tutayev, Russ. 158 G10
Tuticorin, India 181 S6
Tuting, India 180 E15
Tutira, N.Z. 217 L20
Tutoko, Mount, N.Z. 217 P15
Tutrakan, Bulg. 155 G16
Tuttle Creek Lake, Kans., U.S. 107 S8
Tuttlingen, Ger. 150 K6
Tutu, Virgin Is., U.S. 122 N9
Tutu, island, Fiji 222 G7
Tutuala, Timor-Leste 193 M16
Tutuila, island, Amer. Samoa, U.S. 222 M6
Tutumu, Solomon Is. 221 N19
Tuvalu, Pac. Oc. 218 H8
Tuvuca, island, Fiji 222 H9
Ţuwayq, Jabal, Saudi Arabia 174 L10
Tuwayq Mountains, Asia 168 H3
Tuxpan, Mex. 116 G9
Tuxpan, Mex. 116 H12
Tuxtla Gutiérrez, Mex. 117 K14
Tuy Hòa, Vietnam 191 N14
Tūyserkān, Iran 174 D11
Tuz Gölü, Turk. 170 F8
Tuzigoot National Monument, Ariz., U.S. 109 S7
Tuzla, Bosn. & Herzg. 154 F8
Tuzla Gölü, Turk. 170 F11
Tuzluca, Turk. 171 E18
Tveitsund, Nor. 142 L11
Tver', Russ. 158 H8
Tvøroyri, Faroe Is., Den. 142 H6
Twentynine Palms, Calif., U.S. III XII
Twilight Cove, Austral. 214 K6
Twin Bridges, Mont., U.S. 108 E7
Twin Buttes Reservoir, Tex., U.S. 105 N7
Twin City, Ga., U.S. 98 M8
Twin Falls, Idaho, U.S. 108 H5
Twin Peaks, Idaho, U.S. 108 F5
Twin Valley, Minn., U.S. 106 G8
Twisp, Wash., U.S. 110 B6
Twizel, N.Z. 217 P16
Two Butte Creek, Colo., U.S. 109 P15
Two Buttes, Colo., U.S. 109 P16
Two Harbors, Minn., U.S. 106 G13
Two Rivers, Wis., U.S. 100 K7
Tyab, Iran 175 H15
Tybee Island, Ga., U.S. 99 N9
Tycheró, Gr. 157 B16
Tychy, Pol. 151 G15
Tygda, Russ. 161 K19
Tyler, Minn., U.S. 106 K9
Tyler, Tex., U.S. 104 M14
Tylertown, Miss., U.S. 102 N11
Týmfi, Óros (Gamíla), Gr. 156 E7
Tymfristós, peak, Gr. 156 G9
Tymvou (Kırklar), Cyprus 162 N9
Tynda, Russ. 161 K18
Tyndall, S. Dak., U.S. 106 M7
Tyndaris, ruin, It. 153 R11
Tyndrum, Scot., U.K. 144 L9
Tynemouth, Eng., U.K. 145 P12
Tyonek, Alas., U.S. 113 J16
Tyre see Soûr, Leb. 172 K6
Týrnavos, Gr. 156 E10
Tyrnyauz, Russ. 159 U12
Tyrol, region, Aust., It. 152 C6
Tyrone, Okla., U.S. 104 E6
Tyrone, Pa., U.S. 96 N5
Tyrrell, Lake, Austral. 214 L12
Turtle Lake, N. Dak., U.S. 106 F4
Tyrrhenian Sea, It. 152 N7
Tyugyuren, Russ. 161 E18
Tyukalinsk, Russ. 160 J10
Tyumen', Russ. 160 J9
Tywyn, Wales, U.K. 145 T9
Tzaneen, S. Af. 206 H11
Tzia see Kea, island, Gr. 157 K13
Tzoumérka, peak, Gr. 156 E8

U

U, F.S.M. 221 F14
Uaboe, region, Nauru 221 E23
Ua Huka, island, Fr. Polynesia, Fr. 219 H15
Ua Pou, island, Fr. Polynesia, Fr. 219 H15
Uaroo, W. Aust., Austral. 215 T2
Uatio, Île, New Caledonia, Fr. 222 E8
Ubá, Braz. 133 L15
Ubangi (Oubangui), river, Af. 202 K8
Ubauro, Pak. 179 T8
Ube, Japan 189 Q5
Úbeda, Sp. 146 K11
Uberaba, Braz. 133 K13
Uberlândia, Braz. 133 K13
Ubierna, Sp. 146 C11
Ubon Ratchathani, Thai. 190 L11
Ubundu, Dem. Rep. of the Congo 202 K11
Üçajy, Turkm. 176 M10
Ucar, Azerb. 171 D21
Ucayali, river, Peru 132 F4
Uch, Pak. 179 S9
Uchiura Wan, Japan 188 H12
Uchiza, Peru 132 G3
Uchquduq, Uzb. 176 J11
Udachnyy, Russ. 161 G16
Udaipur, India 180 H4
Uda Spur, Pac. Oc. 242 G8
Udayagiri, India 180 L9
Uddevalla, Sw. 142 L12
Uderolal, Pak. 179 V7
Udgir, India 180 L5
Udhampur, India 180 C5
Udine, It. 152 D9
Udintsev Fracture Zone, Pac. Oc. 243 R14
Udipi, India 181 P4
Udo, island, S. Korea 187 W8
Udon Thani, Thai. 190 K10
Udot, island, F.S.M. 221 B15
Udskaya Guba, Russ. 161 J20
Udu Point, Fiji 222 G8
Uebonti, Indonesia 193 J14
Ueda, Japan 189 N11
Uele, river, Dem. Rep. of the Congo 202 J10
Uelen, Russ. 161 A21
Uelzen, Ger. 150 D8
Ufa, Russ. 160 H8
Ufa, river, Eur. 140 D15
Ufra, Turkm. 176 K6
Ugab, river, Namibia 206 G6
Uganda, Af. 203 J13
Ugarit, ruins see Ra's Shamrah, Syr. 172 E6
Uglich, Russ. 158 H9
Ugljan, island, Croatia 154 F5
Ugljane, Croatia 154 G6
Uglovoye, Russ. 161 K19
Ugol'nyye Kopi, Russ. 161 B21
Ugum, river, Guam, U.S. 220 D10
Uher Hudag, N. Mongol, China 184 B4
Uherské Hradiště, Czech Rep. 151 J13
Uhrichsville, Ohio, U.S. 101 Q15
Uibhist a Deas (South Uist), island, Scot., U.K. 144 K6
Uibhist a Tuath (North Uist), island, Scot., U.K. 144 J6
Uido, island, S. Korea 187 U6
Uig, Scot., U.K. 144 J7
Uíge, Angola 206 B6
'Uiha, Tonga 222 Q7
'Uiha, island, Tonga 222 Q7
Uijeongbu, S. Korea 186 M8
Ŭiju, N. Korea 186 G4
Uinta, river, Utah, U.S. 108 L9
Uinta Mountains, Utah, U.S. 108 L8
Uiryeong, S. Korea 187 S10
Uiseong, S. Korea 187 Q11
Uitenhage, S. Af. 206 M9
Uithuizen, Neth. 148 G14
Uiwang, S. Korea 187 N8
Ujae Atoll, Marshall Is., U.S. 220 G2
Ujajiivan, island, Marshall Is., U.S. 220 L4
Ujelang Atoll, Marshall Is., U.S. 220 P8
Uji Guntō, Japan 189 T3
Ujjain, India 180 J5
Ujungpandang see Makassar, Indonesia 193 L13
Ujung Raja, Indonesia 192 G4
Ukhiya, India 180 K14
Ukhrul, India 180 G15
Ukhta, Russ. 160 F9
Ukiah, Calif., U.S. 111 Q2
Ukiah, Oreg., U.S. 110 F7
Uki Ni Masi Island, Solomon Is. 221 P20
Ukmergė, Lith. 143 M17
Ukraine, Eur. 159 P6
Uku, Japan 189 R3
Ukulahu, island, Maldives 181 U3
Uku Shima, Japan 189 R3
Ula, Turk. 170 H4
Ulaanbaatar (Ulan Bator), Mongolia 182 D11
Ulaan-Ereg, Mongolia 182 D11
Ulaangom, Mongolia 182 C7
Ulaga, Russ. 161 F17
Ulan, China 182 H8
Ulan Bator see Ulaanbaatar, Mongolia 182 D11
Ulan Erge, Russ. 159 R13
Ulanhot, China 183 D15
Ulan Khol, Russ. 159 S15
Ulansuhai Nur, N. Mongol, China 184 B2
Ulan Sum, N. Mongol, China 184 A3
Ulan-Ude, Russ. 161 L16
Ulan Ul Hu, China 182 J5
Ulaş, Turk. 170 F12
Ulawa, island, Solomon Is. 221 P21
Ulawun, Mount, P.N.G. 217 C21
Ulcinj, Montenegro 154 K9
Uldo, island, S. Korea 187 P6
Uldz, Mongolia 182 C12
Uldz, river, Mongolia 182 C12
Uleåborg see Oulu, Fin. 143 F15
Uleguma, island, Maldives 181 T3
Ulen, Minn., U.S. 106 G8
Uliastay, Mongolia 182 D8
Ulingan, P.N.G. 217 C19
Ulithi Atoll, F.S.M. 221 P3
Uljin, S. Korea 187 P12
Uljma, Serb. 154 F11
Ülken Borsyq Qumy, Kaz. 176 G10
Ulladulla, N.S.W., Austral. 215 Y14
Ullapool, Scot., U.K. 144 J8
Ulleung, S. Korea 187 N15
Ulleungdo (Dagelet), island, S. Korea 186 M15
Ulm, Ger. 150 K7
Ulsan, S. Korea 187 S12
Ulster (Cúige Uladh), region, Ire., U.K. 145 P6
Ulu, Russ. 161 H18
UlubatGölü, Turk. 170 D4
Uluborlu, Turk. 170 G6
Ulu Dağ (Mount Olympus), Turk. 170 E5
Ulufala Point, Amer. Samoa, U.S. 222 P4
Uluiutu, Île, Wallis and Futuna, Fr. 222 A11
Ulukışla, Turk. 170 H9
Ulul, island, F.S.M. 220 Q5
uLundi, S. Af. 206 K11
Ulungur Hu, China 182 D5
Uluru (Ayers Rock), peak, Austral. 214 G8
Ulus, Turk. 170 C8
Ulva, island, Scot., U.K. 144 L7
Ulverston, Eng., U.K. 145 Q10
Ul'yanovsk, Russ. 158 K14
Ulysses, Kans., U.S. 107 U3
Ulytaū, Kaz. 176 E12
Uman, island, F.S.M. 221 C15
Uman', Ukr. 159 P5
Umari, Indonesia 193 L19
Umaria, India 180 J7
Umarkot, Pak. 179 V8
Umatac, Guam, U.S. 220 D10
Umatac Bay, Guam, U.S. 220 D10
Umatilla, Oreg., U.S. 110 E7
Umatilla, river, Oreg., U.S. 110 F7
Umba, Russ. 160 D8
Umbakumba, N.T., Austral. 215 P10
Umboi, island, P.N.G. 217 C20
Umbria, Eur. 140 K7
Umbriatico, It. 153 P14
Umbukul, P.N.G. 217 B20
Umeå, Sw. 143 G14
Umeälven, river, Sw. 143 F13
Umfors, Sw. 142 F12
'Umikoa, Hawai'i, U.S. 115 L20
Umm ad Dāmī, Jabal, Jordan 173 S6
Umm al Arānib, Lib. 201 E14
Umm al-Qaiwain, U.A.E. 175 J15
Umm Durmān (Omdurman), Sudan 203 E13
Umm Lajj, Saudi Arabia 174 J6
Umm Qaşr, Iraq 174 F11
Umm Urūmah, island, Saudi Arabia 174 H5
Umnak Island, Alas., U.S. 112 P9
Umpqua, river, Oreg., U.S. 110 J2
Umred, India 180 K7
Umuahia, Nigeria 205 E14
Umuna, island, Tonga 222 L12
Umvoto Rise, Atl. Oc. 241 V14
Una, river, Bosn. & Herzg., Croatia 154 E6
Unadilla, Ga., U.S. 99 N6
Unai Obyan, peninsula, N. Mariana Is., U.S. 220 D4
Unalakleet, Alas., U.S. 113 G13
Unalaska, Alas., U.S. 112 P10
Unalaska Island, Alas., U.S. 112 P9
'Unayzah, Saudi Arabia 174 J9
'Unayzah, Jabal, Iraq 174 E7
'Unayzah, Jabal, Jordan 172 M12
Unbong, S. Korea 187 S9
Unbong-jŏsuji, lake, N. Korea 186 D7
Ŭnch'ŏn, N. Korea 186 K5
Uncía, Bol. 132 K7
Uncompahgre Peak, Colo., U.S. 109 N11
Uncompahgre Plateau, Colo., U.S. 109 N10
Underwood, N. Dak., U.S. 106 F4
Ŭndŏk, N. Korea 186 B13
Unecha, Russ. 158 L7
Ungama Bay, Af. 198 K11
Ungava Bay, N. Amer. 85 J19
Ungava Bay, Que., Can. 240 F4
Ungava Peninsula, N. Amer. 82 F8
Ungcheon, S. Korea 187 Q7
Unggi (Sŏnbong), N. Korea 186 B14
Unggok, S. Korea 187 U6
Unha, N. Korea 186 G10
Unha, N. Korea 186 H5
Unhŭng, N. Korea 186 D11
Unhŭng, N. Korea 186 H8
União da Vitória, Braz. 132 N12
Unije, island, Croatia 154 F4
Unikar, Mochun, F.S.M. 221 C16
Unimak Island, Alas., U.S. 112 N11
Unimak Pass, Alas., U.S. 112 N10
Unini, river, Braz. 132 D8
Union, Grenada 123 J23
Union, Miss., U.S. 102 L12
Union, Mo., U.S. 107 T14
Union, Oreg., U.S. 110 F8
Union, S.C., U.S. 98 J8
Union, island, St. Vincent and the Grenadines 121 G16
Uníon, Bahía, Arg. 135 P11
Union City, Ohio, U.S. 101 R11
Union City, Pa., U.S. 96 L3
Union City, Tenn., U.S. 102 E12
Union Point, Ga., U.S. 98 L6
Union Springs, Ala., U.S. 103 L16
Uniontown, Ala., U.S. 103 L14
Uniontown, Pa., U.S. 96 P3
Unionville, Mo., U.S. 107 Q12
Unionville, Nev., U.S. 111 N8
United Arab Emirates, Asia 175 K13
United Estates, Bahamas 122 E12
United Kingdom, Eur. 145 Q6
United States, N. Amer. 88 J12
Unity, Oreg., U.S. 110 G8
University Park, N. Mex., U.S. 109 V12
Unnao, India 180 G7
Ŭnp'a, N. Korea 186 L6
Unp'o, N. Korea 186 G10
Unsan, N. Korea 186 G6
Unst, island, Scot., U.K. 144 C12
Ünye, Turk. 170 D12
Ŭnyul, N. Korea 186 K5
Unzha, Russ. 158 G12
Unzha, river, Eur. 140 D13
Uoleva, island, Tonga 222 Q7
Upata, Venez. 130 D12
Upemba, Lake, Af. 198 L8
Upham, N. Dak., U.S. 106 E4
Upington, S. Af. 206 K8
Uplands, Kaz. 177 F14
Upolu, island, Samoa 222 L3
'Upolu Point, Hawai'i, U.S. 115 K19
Upper Arlington, Ohio, U.S. 101 R13
Upper Bogue, Bahamas 122 D5
Upper Darby, Pa., U.S. 96 P9
Upper Guinea, region, Af. 198 H3
Upper Hutt, N.Z. 217 M19
Upper Kama Upland, Eur. 140 C14
Upper Klamath Lake, Oreg., U.S. 110 K4
Upper Lake, Calif., U.S. 110 L6
Upper Lough Erne, N. Ire., U.K. 145 Q5
Upper Manzanilla, Trinidad and Tobago 123 P23
Upper Missouri River Breaks National Monument, Mont., U.S. 108 C10
Upper Peninsula, Mich., U.S. 100 F9
Upper Red Lake, Minn., U.S. 106 E10
Upper Saint Clair, Pa., U.S. 96 P3
Upper Sandusky, Ohio, U.S. 101 Q12
Uppsala, Sw. 143 K14
Upshi, India 180 C6
Upstart, Cape, Austral. 214 E14
Upstart Bay, Austral. 214 E14
Upton, Wyo., U.S. 108 G13
'Uqayribāt, Syr. 172 F9
Ur, ruins, Iraq 174 F10
Urabá, Golfo de, Col. 130 D4
Urad Qianqi, N. Mongol, China 184 B2
Urad Zhongqi, N. Mongol, China 184 A2
Urakawa, Japan 188 H14
Ural, river, Asia 168 E6
Ural Mountains, Asia 168 D6
Urania, La., U.S. 102 M8
Uranium City, Sask., Can. 84 J12
Uranu, island, F.S.M. 221 B14
Uraricoera, Braz. 132 B9
Uraricoera, river, Braz. 132 B8
Uravan, Colo., U.S. 109 N10
Urawa, Japan 189 P12
Urbana, Ill., U.S. 101 R7
Urbana, Ohio, U.S. 101 R12
Urbandale, Iowa, U.S. 107 P11
Urbano Noris, Cuba 118 K12
Urbett, island, Marshall Is., U.S. 220 K7
Urbino, It. 152 G8
Urbión, Picos de, Sp. 146 D12
Urdos, Fr. 149 Y6
Uren', Russ. 158 G13
Uréparapara, island, Vanuatu 222 A1
Urganch, Uzb. 176 K9
Urgūn, Afghan. 179 P8
Urgut, Uzb. 176 L12
Uriah, Mount, N.Z. 217 N17
Uribia, Col. 130 B6
Uri-do, island, N. Korea 186 H4
Uriondo, Bol. 132 L7
Uritskoye, Russ. 161 H17
Urla, Turk. 170 F2
Urlaţi, Rom. 155 E16
Urlins, Antigua and Barbuda 123 B20
Urmia, Lake see Orūmīyeh, Daryācheh-ye, Iran 174 B10
Uroševac see Ferizaj, Kos. 154 J11
Ŭroteppa see Istaravshan, Taj. 178 G7
Urtipah, Afghan. 178 L4
Urt Moron, China 182 H6
Uruana, Braz. 133 J13
Uruapan, Mex. 116 J10
Urubamba, river, Peru 132 H5
Urucará, Braz. 132 D10
Uruçuí, Braz. 133 F15
Uruçuí, Serra do, S. Amer. 128 F10
Uruguai see Uruguay, river, Arg. 134 H14
Uruguaiana, Braz. 132 P10
Uruguay, S. Amer. 134 K14
Uruguay, river, S. Amer. 128 K7
Uruguay Canyon, Atl. Oc. 248 K10
Ürümqi, China 182 E5
Uruno Point, Guam, U.S. 220 A11
Urup, Russ. 161 J23
Urup, island, Asia 168 D14
Uruzgān, Afghan. 179 P6
Uryupinsk, Russ. 159 N11
Ürzhar, Kaz. 177 F18
Urzhum, Russ. 158 G15
Urziceni, Rom. 155 F16
Usa, Japan 189 R7
Usa, river, Eur. 140 A13
Uşak, Turk. 170 F5
Usakos, Namibia 206 H6
Usarp Mountains, Antarctica 231 Q15
Usedom, island, Ger. 150 B10
Useldange, Lux. 162 J9
Ushakova, Ostrov, Russ. 161 C13
Ushakov Bank, Arctic Oc. 247 F15
Ushakovskoye, Russ. 161 B19
Üsharal, Kaz. 177 F18
Ushibuka, Japan 189 S4
Ushi Point, N. Mariana Is., U.S. 220 A8
Üshtöbe, Kaz. 177 G17
Ushuaia, Arg. 135 X9
Ushumun, Russ. 161 K19
Usi, N. Korea 186 F6
Usinsk, Russ. 160 F10
Usman', Russ. 158 M10
U.S. Naval Base Guantanamo Bay, U.S. 119 L14
Usol'ye Sibirskoye, Russ. 161 L15
Usove, Ukr. 158 M4
U.S. Range, Nunavut, Can. 85 A16
U.S.S. Arizona Memorial, Hawai'i, U.S. 114 F11
Ussel, Fr. 149 U10
Ussuri, river, Russ. 161 L21
Ussuriysk, Russ. 161 M21
Uster, Switz. 152 A4
Ustica, It. 153 R9
Ustica, Isola di, It. 153 R9
Ust' Ilimpeya, Russ. 161 H15
Ust' Ilimsk, Russ. 161 K15
Ustí nad Labem, Czech Rep. 150 G11
Ustka, Pol. 151 A13
Ust'-Kamchatsk, Russ. 161 E22
Ust'-Kamenogorsk see Öskemen, Kaz. 177 D18
Ust' Kamo, Russ. 161 J14
Ust' Kut, Russ. 161 K15
Ust' Labinsk, Russ. 159 S11
Ust' Maya, Russ. 161 G19
Ust' Mil', Russ. 161 H19
Ust' Nera, Russ. 161 F19
Ust' Olenek, Russ. 161 E16
Ust' Omchug, Russ. 161 F20
Ust' Ordynskiy, Russ. 161 L15
Ust' Usa, Russ. 160 F10
Ust' Yansk, Russ. 161 E17
Ust' Yudoma, Russ. 161 H19
Ustyurt Plateau, Kaz. 176 H7
Ustyuzhna, Russ. 158 G9
Usu, China 182 D4
Usuki, Japan 189 R5
Usumacinta, river, N. Amer. 82 N6
Usvyaty, Russ. 158 J6
Uta, Indonesia 193 L19
Utah, U.S. 108 M7
Utah Beach, Fr. 149 N6
Utah Lake, Utah, U.S. 108 L7
Ute Creek, N. Mex., U.S. 109 Q14
Utete, Tanzania 203 M15
Uthai Thani, Thai. 190 L8
Uthal, Pak. 179 V6
Utiariti, Braz. 132 H10
Utica, N.Y., U.S. 96 J9
Utiel, Sp. 147 H14
Utirik Atoll, Marshall Is., U.S. 220 F4
Utkela, India 180 L9
Utnur, India 180 L6
Utopia, N.T., Austral. 215 S9

Utraula, *India* 180 F8
Utrecht, *Neth.* 148 J12
Utsunomiya, *Japan* 189 N12
Utta, *Russ.* 159 R14
Uttaradit, *Thai.* 190 K8
Utuado, *P.R., U.S.* 122 N2
Utuloa, *Wallis and Futuna, Fr.* 222 B11
Utupua, island, *Solomon Is.* 221 Q23
Uturoa, *Fr. Polynesia, Fr.* 223 B23
Utva, river, *Kaz.* 176 D7
Utwa, *F.S.M.* 221 B18
Uummannaq Fjord, *Greenland, Den.* 82 D8
Uusikaupunki, *Fin.* 143 J15
Uva, *Russ.* 158 G16
Uvalde, *Tex., U.S.* 105 R8
Uvarovo, *Russ.* 158 M11
Uvéa see Ouvéa, island, *New Caledonia, Fr.* 222 C8
Uvea, Île, *Wallis and Futuna, Fr.* 222 B11
Uvinza, *Tanzania* 202 L12
Uvol, *P.N.G.* 217 D21
Uvs Nuur, *Mongolia* 182 C7
Uwajima, *Japan* 189 R6
'Uwayriḍ, Ḥarrat al, *Saudi Arabia* 174 G6
'Uweinat, Jebel, *Sudan* 202 C11
Uxin Qi (Dabqig), *N. Mongol, China* 184 E1
Uxmal, ruin, *Mex.* 117 H16
Uyar, *Russ.* 161 K13
Uys Nuur, lake, *Asia* 168 F9
Uyuni, *Bol.* 132 L7
Uyuni, Salar de, *Bol.* 132 L6
Uzbekistan, *Asia* 176 J10
Uzbel Shankou, pass, *China, Taj.* 178 H11
Uzerche, *Fr.* 149 U9
Uzès, *Fr.* 149 X12
Uzhhorod, *Ukr.* 159 P1
Užice, *Serb.* 154 G9
Uzlovaya, *Russ.* 158 K9
Üzümlü, *Turk.* 170 H4
Uzunköprü, *Turk.* 170 C3
Uzynköl, *Kaz.* 176 B11

V

Vaal, river, *S. Af.* 206 K10
Vaals, *Neth.* 148 L13
Vaasa, *Fin.* 143 G14
Vác, *Hung.* 151 L15
Vacaville, *Calif., U.S.* 111 R4
Vache, Île à, *Haiti* 119 N15
Vacía Talega, Punta, *P.R., U.S.* 122 M5
Vacoas, *Mauritius* 209 G20
Vadodara, *India* 180 J3
Vadsø, *Nor.* 143 B15
Vaduz, *Liech.* 162 P2
Vaduz Castle, ruin, *Liech.* 162 P2
Værøy, island, *Nor.* 142 E11
Vágar, island, *Faroe Is., Den.* 142 H5
Vaghena, island, *Solomon Is.* 221 L16
Vagthus Point, *Virgin Is., U.S.* 122 R2
Váh, river, *Slovakia* 151 J14
Vahanga, island, *Fr. Polynesia, Fr.* 223 G22
Vahdat (Kofarnihon), *Taj.* 178 H7
Vahitahi, island, *Fr. Polynesia, Fr.* 223 F21
Vahituri, island, *Fr. Polynesia, Fr.* 223 L17
Vaiaau, *Fr. Polynesia, Fr.* 223 B23
Vaiau, Passe, *Fr. Polynesia, Fr.* 223 Q17
Vaiden, *Miss., U.S.* 102 K11
Vaiea, *Cook Is., N.Z.* 223 B20
Vaiere, island, *Cook Is., N.Z.* 223 B17
Vaigalu, *Samoa* 222 L3
Vaihiria, Lake, *Fr. Polynesia, Fr.* 223 P16
Vail, *Colo., U.S.* 108 M12
Vaila, island, *Scot., U.K.* 144 D12
Vailala, *Wallis and Futuna, Fr.* 222 B11
Vailoa, *Samoa* 222 K2
Vailoatai, *Amer. Samoa, U.S.* 222 N6

Vaimalau, *Wallis and Futuna, Fr.* 222 B11
Vaini, *Tonga* 222 J11
Vaionifa, Passe, *Fr. Polynesia, Fr.* 223 P18
Vaipae, *Cook Is., N.Z.* 222 Q11
Vaipaee, *Fr. Polynesia, Fr.* 223 N23
Vaipeka, *Cook Is., N.Z.* 222 P11
Vairaatea, island, *Fr. Polynesia, Fr.* 223 F21
Vairo, *Fr. Polynesia, Fr.* 223 Q17
Vaitahu, *Fr. Polynesia, Fr.* 223 N20
Vaitape, *Fr. Polynesia, Fr.* 223 K14
Vaitoare, *Fr. Polynesia, Fr.* 223 A23
Vaitogi, *Amer. Samoa, U.S.* 222 N7
Vaitupu, *Wallis and Futuna, Fr.* 222 B11
Vaiutukakau Bay, *Tonga* 222 L11
Vaka'eitu, island, *Tonga* 222 M11
Vakfıkebir, *Turk.* 171 D14
Vakhrushev, *Russ.* 161 J22
Vakhsh, river, *Taj.* 178 H8
Vakhtan, *Russ.* 158 G13
Valamaz, *Russ.* 158 G15
Valcheta, *Arg.* 135 Q9
Valdagno, *It.* 152 D7
Valdahon, *Fr.* 149 S14
Valdai Hills, *Eur.* 140 E11
Valdayskaya Vozvyshennost', *Russ.* 158 H7
Valdepeñas, *Sp.* 146 J11
Valderrobres, *Sp.* 147 F15
Valdés, Península, *Arg.* 135 R10
Valdez, *Alas., U.S.* 113 J18
Valdez, *Ecua.* 130 H2
Valdivia, *Chile* 135 P6
Valdivia, *Col.* 130 D4
Valdivia Fracture Zone, *Pac. Oc.* 243 P20
Valdivia Plain, *Ind. Oc.* 248 D11
Val-d'Or, *Que., Can.* 85 P18
Valdosta, *Ga., U.S.* 99 Q6
Valdragone, *San Marino* 163 J15
Vale, *Oreg., U.S.* 110 H9
Valea lui Mihai, *Rom.* 154 B12
Valença, *Braz.* 133 H16
Valença, *Port.* 146 D5
Valence, *Fr.* 149 V13
Valence, *Fr.* 149 W8
Valencia, *Sp.* 147 H14
Valencia, *Venez.* 130 B9
Valencia, Golfo de, *Sp.* 147 H15
Valencia, Lake, *S. Amer.* 128 A4
Valencia Island, *Ire.* 145 U2
Valenciennes, *Fr.* 148 M11
Valentine, *Nebr., U.S.* 106 M4
Valentine, *Tex., U.S.* 105 P1
Valenza, *It.* 152 E4
Valera, *Venez.* 130 C7
Valga, *Est.* 143 K17
Valguarnera Caropepe, *It.* 153 T11
Valier, *Mont., U.S.* 108 B7
Valinco, Golfe de, *Fr.* 152 L4
Valira del Nort, river, *Andorra* 162 J3
Valira d'Orient, river, *Andorra* 162 H4
Valjevo, *Serb.* 154 G9
Valka, *Latv.* 143 K16
Valkeakoski, *Fin.* 143 H15
Valkenswaard, *Neth.* 148 K12
Valkyrie Dome (Dome F, Dome Fuji), *Antarctica* 231 E15
Valladolid, *Mex.* 117 H17
Valladolid, *Sp.* 146 D10
Valle de la Pascua, *Venez.* 130 C10
Valledupar, *Col.* 130 B6
Valle Fértil, Sierra del, *Arg.* 134 J8
Valle Formozo, *Sao Tome and Principe* 209 D20
Vallegrande, *Bol.* 132 K8
Vallehermoso, *Sp.* 208 Q4
Vallejo, *Calif., U.S.* 111 R3
Vallenar, *Chile* 134 H6
Valletta, *Malta* 163 K23
Valley Center, *Kans., U.S.* 107 U7
Valley City, *N. Dak., U.S.* 106 G7
Valley Falls, *Kans., U.S.* 107 S9
Valley Falls, *Oreg., U.S.* 110 K6
Valley Mills, *Tex., U.S.* 105 N11
Valley Station, *Ky., U.S.* 103 B16
Vallo della Lucania, *It.* 153 N12

Vallorbe, *Switz.* 152 B1
Valls, *Sp.* 147 E16
Valmeyer, *Ill., U.S.* 101 T4
Valmiera, *Latv.* 143 K17
Valmy, *Fr.* 149 P12
Valona see Vlorë, *Alban.* 154 M9
Valozhyn, *Belarus* 158 K4
Valparaíso, *Fla., U.S.* 99 Q2
Valparaiso, *Ind., U.S.* 101 P8
Valparaíso, *Chile* 134 K6
Valparaíso, *Mex.* 116 G10
Vals, Cape, *Asia* 168 L16
Vals, Tanjung, *Indonesia* 217 D16
Valsad, *India* 180 K3
Valüna, valley, *Liech.* 162 Q3
Valuyevka, *Russ.* 159 R13
Valuyki, *Russ.* 159 N10
Valverde, *Sp.* 208 R3
Valverde del Camino, *Sp.* 146 K7
Van, *Turk.* 171 G17
Van, Lake, *Asia* 168 F4
Vana, *Solomon Is.* 221 R24
Vanadzor, *Arm.* 171 D18
Van Alstyne, *Tex., U.S.* 104 K12
Vanavana, island, *Fr. Polynesia, Fr.* 223 G21
Vanavara, *Russ.* 161 J15
Van Blommestein Meer, *Suriname* 131 E16
Van Buren, *Ark., U.S.* 102 F6
Van Buren, *Me., U.S.* 97 A18
Vanceboro, *Me., U.S.* 97 D19
Vanceboro, *N.C., U.S.* 98 H13
Vanceburg, *Ky., U.S.* 103 A19
Vancouver, *B.C., Can.* 84 M8
Vancouver, *Wash., U.S.* 110 F3
Vancouver Island, *B.C., Can.* 84 L7
Vandalia, *Ill., U.S.* 101 S5
Vandalia, *Mo., U.S.* 107 S14
Vandalia, *Ohio, U.S.* 101 R11
Vanderbilt, *Mich., U.S.* 100 H11
Vanderford Glacier, *Antarctica* 231 M20
Vanderlin Island, *Austral.* 214 C10
Van Diemen, Cape, *Austral.* 214 A7
Van Diemen Gulf, *Austral.* 214 A8
Vänern, lake, *Sw.* 142 L12
Vangaindrano, *Madagascar* 207 H17
Vạn Giã, *Vietnam* 191 N14
Van Gölü, *Turk.* 171 G17
Vangunu, island, *Solomon Is.* 221 M17
Vangunu, Mount, *Solomon Is.* 221 M17
Vangviang, *Laos* 190 J10
Van Horn, *Tex., U.S.* 105 N1
Vanikolo, island, *Solomon Is.* 221 R24
Vanikolo Islands, *Solomon Is.* 221 R24
Vanimo, *P.N.G.* 217 B17
Vanino, *Russ.* 161 K21
Vanj, *Taj.* 178 J9
Vankarem, *Russ.* 161 A20
Vännäs, *Sw.* 143 G14
Vannes, *Fr.* 149 R4
Vannøy, island, *Nor.* 143 C13
Vanoise, Massif de la, *Fr.* 149 U15
Vanrhynsdorp, *S. Af.* 206 L7
Vanrook, *Qnsld., Austral.* 215 Q12
Vansbro, *Sw.* 142 J12
Vansittart Bay, *Austral.* 214 B6
Vansittart Island, *Nunavut, Can.* 85 G16
Van Tassell, *Wyo., U.S.* 108 H14
Vanua Balavuc, island, *Fiji* 222 H9
Vanua Lava, island, *Vanuatu* 222 B2
Vanua Levu, island, *Fiji* 222 G7
Vanua Masi, island, *Fiji* 222 J9
Vanua Vatu, island, *Fiji* 222 J9
Van Wert, *Ohio, U.S.* 101 Q11
Vao, *New Caledonia, Fr.* 222 E9
Varadero, *Cuba* 118 G7
Varangerfjorden, bay, *Nor.* 143 B15
Varangerhalvøya, peninsula, *Nor.* 143 B15
Varanger Peninsula, *Eur.* 140 A10
Varano, Lago di, *It.* 152 K12
Varaždin, *Croatia* 154 D6
Varazze, *It.* 152 F4
Varberg, *Sw.* 142 M12
Vardar, river, *Maced.* 154 K11

Vardenis, *Arm.* 171 E19
Vardø, *Nor.* 143 B15
Varéna, *Lith.* 143 N17
Varennes, *Fr.* 149 N12
Varese, *It.* 152 D4
Varilhes, *Fr.* 149 Y9
Varkaus, *Fin.* 143 G16
Varna, *Bulg.* 155 H17
Varnavino, *Russ.* 158 H12
Varnenski Zaliv, *Bulg.* 155 H17
Varnensko Ezero, *Bulg.* 155 H17
Varnville, *S.C., U.S.* 98 M9
Varosha (Maraş), *Cyprus* 162 P10
Varto, *Turk.* 171 F16
Värts Järv, lake, *Est.* 143 K17
Varungga Point, *Solomon Is.* 221 L16
Varzob, *Taj.* 178 H7
Varzy, *Fr.* 149 R11
Vasafua, island, *Tuvalu* 221 K22
Vasilikí, *Gr.* 156 G7
Vasiliko, *Cyprus* 162 Q8
Vasilikós, *Gr.* 156 K8
Vasilítsa, peak, *Gr.* 156 D8
Vasil'yevo, *Russ.* 158 J14
Vaskess Bay, *Kiribati* 221 B22
Vaslui, *Rom.* 155 C17
Vassar, *Mich., U.S.* 100 L12
Västerås, *Sw.* 143 K13
Västervik, *Sw.* 143 L13
Vasto, *It.* 152 K11
Vatan, *Fr.* 149 S9
Vatersay see Bhatarsaigh, island, *Scot., U.K.* 144 K6
Vathí, *Gr.* 156 H12
Vathí see Itháki, *Gr.* 156 H7
Vatia, *Amer. Samoa, U.S.* 222 M7
Vatia Bay, *Amer. Samoa, U.S.* 222 M8
Vatia Point, *Fiji* 222 H6
Vatican City, *Eur.* 162 E4
Vatican Gardens, *Vatican City* 163 P15
Vatican Library, *Vatican City* 163 N16
Vatican Museums, *Vatican City* 163 N16
Vaticano, Capo, *It.* 153 R13
Vatican Radio, *Vatican City* 163 Q14
Vatnajökull, glacier, *Ice.* 142 F3
Vatneyri, *Ice.* 142 D2
Vatoa (Turtle), island, *Fiji* 222 L9
Vatra Dornei, *Rom.* 155 B15
Vättern, lake, *Sw.* 143 L13
Vatuki, island, *Fiji* 222 G6
Vatukoula, *Fiji* 222 H6
Vatulele, island, *Fiji* 222 J5
Vatu Vara, island, *Fiji* 222 H8
Vaughn, *Mont., U.S.* 108 C7
Vaughn, *N. Mex., U.S.* 109 S13
Vaupés, river, *Col.* 130 H7
Vauvilliers, Île, *New Caledonia, Fr.* 222 D9
Vauvilliers, Point, *F.S.M.* 221 B18
Vav, *India* 180 H3
Vava'u, island, *Tonga* 222 L12
Vava'u Group, *Tonga* 218 J10
Vavitu see Raivavae, island, *Fr. Polynesia, Fr.* 223 J17
Vavla, *Cyprus* 162 Q8
Vavuniya, *Sri Lanka* 181 S7
Vawkavysk, *Belarus* 158 L3
Växjö, *Sw.* 143 M13
Vayegi, *Russ.* 161 C21
Vaygach, Ostrov, *Russ.* 160 E10
Vaygach Island, *Asia* 168 C7
Veblen, *S. Dak., U.S.* 106 H7
Vecchia, river, *San Marino* 163 J16
Vedea, river, *Rom.* 155 G15
Veendam, *Neth.* 148 G14
Vega, *Tex., U.S.* 104 G4
Vega, island, *Nor.* 142 F11
Vega Baja, *P.R., U.S.* 122 M3
Vegadeo, *Sp.* 146 A7
Veghel, *Neth.* 148 K13
Vegorítida, Límni, *Gr.* 156 C9
Vegreville, *Alta., Can.* 84 L11
Veharnu, island, *P.N.G.* 221 H14
Veio, ruin, *It.* 152 K8
Vejer de la Frontera, *Sp.* 146 M8

Vekai, island, *Fiji* 222 H9
Velarde, *N. Mex., U.S.* 109 R12
Velas, *Azores, Port.* 146 Q3
Velay,, Monts du, *Fr.* 149 V11
Velbert, *Ger.* 150 F5
Velden, *Aust.* 150 M10
Velé, *Wallis and Futuna, Fr.* 222 E11
Velé, Pointe, *Wallis and Futuna, Fr.* 222 E12
Velebit, mountains, *Croatia* 154 F5
Velenje, *Slov.* 154 C5
Veles, *Maced.* 154 K11
Velestíno, *Gr.* 156 F11
Vélez, *Col.* 130 E5
Velež, peak, *Bosn. & Herzg.* 154 H8
Vélez de la Gomera, Peñón de , *Sp.* 146 P9
Vélez-Málaga, *Sp.* 146 M10
Velhas, river, *Braz.* 133 K14
Velia, ruin, *It.* 153 N12
Velika Ljubuša, peak, *Bosn. & Herzg.* 154 G7
Velika Morava, river, *Serb.* 154 F11
Velika Plana, *Serb.* 154 F11
Velikaya, river, *Eur.* 140 E10
Veliki Drvenik, island, *Croatia* 154 G6
Veliki Snežnik, peak, *Slov.* 154 D4
Veliki Troglav, peak, *Bosn. & Herzg.* 154 G6
Velikiye Luki, *Russ.* 158 J6
Velikiy Novgorod, *Russ.* 158 G6
Velikonda Range, *India* 181 N6
Veliko Türnovo, *Bulg.* 155 H15
Vélingara, *Senegal* 200 H5
Velingrad, *Bulg.* 155 K14
Velizh, *Russ.* 158 J6
Vella Gulf, *Solomon Is.* 221 M15
Vella Lavella, island, *Solomon Is.* 221 L15
Velletri, *It.* 152 L9
Vellore, *India* 181 Q6
Velopoúla, island, *Gr.* 156 L12
Vel'sk, *Russ.* 160 F7
Velva, *N. Dak., U.S.* 106 E4
Vema Fracture Zone, *Atl. Oc.* 241 N7
Vema Seachannel, *Atl. Oc.* 241 T7
Vema Seamount, *Atl. Oc.* 241 T13
Vema Trench, *Ind. Oc.* 224 H9
Venable Ice Shelf, *Antarctica* 230 H6
Venado Tuerto, *Arg.* 134 L11
Venango, *Nebr., U.S.* 107 Q3
Vena Park, *Qnsld., Austral.* 215 R12
Vendâome, *Fr.* 149 R8
Vendas Novas, *Port.* 146 J5
Vendôme, *Grenada* 123 L23
Venetie, *Alas., U.S.* 113 E17
Venétiko, island, *Gr.* 156 M9
Veneto, *Eur.* 140 J7
Veneta, Laguna, *It.* 152 E8
Venezia (Venice), *It.* 152 E8
Venezuela, Bonaire, Neth. 123 Q19
Venezuela, *S. Amer.* 130 D10
Venezuela, Golfo de, *S. Amer.* 130 B7
Venezuelan Basin, *Atl. Oc.* 240 M4
Vengurla, *India* 181 N3
Veniaminof, Mount, *Alas., U.S.* 113 N13
Venice, *Fla., U.S.* 99 V7
Venice, *La., U.S.* 102 R12
Venice see Venezia, *It.* 152 E8
Venice, Gulf of, *It.* 152 E9
Vening Melnesz Rise, *Ind. Oc.* 225 H15
Vening Melnesz Seamounts, *Ind. Oc.* 225 H15
Venkatapuram, *India* 180 M7
Venlo, *Neth.* 148 K13
Vénna, *Gr.* 157 B15
Vennesund, *Nor.* 142 F11
Venosa, *It.* 152 M12
Venray, *Neth.* 148 K13
Ventana, Sierra de la, *S. Amer.* 128 M6
Ventimiglia, *It.* 152 G2
Ventnor City, *N.J., U.S.* 96 Q10
Ventoso, *San Marino* 163 H15
Ventoso, Monte, *San Marino* 163 H15
Ventotene, Isola, *It.* 152 M9
Ventoux, Mount, *Fr.* 149 W13
Ventry see Ceann Trá, *Ire.* 145 U2
Ventspils, *Latv.* 143 L15

Ventuari, river, *Venez.* 130 F10
Ventura, *Calif., U.S.* III X7
Venus, Bahia de, *Eq. Guinea* 208 L7
Vénus, Pointe, *Fr. Polynesia, Fr.* 223 N16
Vera, *Arg.* 134 H12
Vera, *Sp.* 147 L13
Vera, Bahía, *Arg.* 135 R9
Veracruz, *Mex.* 117 J13
Veraval, *India* 180 K2
Verbania, *It.* 152 D4
Vercelli, *It.* 152 E3
Verçinin Tepesi, peak, *Turk.* 171 D15
Verdalsøra, *Nor.* 142 G11
Verde, river, *Ariz., U.S.* 109 T7
Verde, river, *S. Amer.* 128 H8
Verde, Arroyo, *Arg.* 135 Q9
Verde, Cabo, *Af.* 198 FI
Verde, Cay, *Bahamas* 119 H14
Verde, Península, *Arg.* 135 P11
Verdigre, *Nebr., U.S.* 107 N7
Verdigris, river, *U.S.* 87 H13
Verdun, *Fr.* 149 N13
Vereeniging, *S. Af.* 206 J10
Verga, Cap, *Guinea* 204 C4
Vergara, *Uru.* 134 K15
Vergato, *It.* 152 F6
Vergennes, *Vt., U.S.* 96 G12
Vergina, ruin, *Gr.* 156 D10
Vergt, *Fr.* 149 V8
Verín, *Sp.* 146 D6
Verkhneimbatsk, *Russ.* 161 H13
Verkhneye Penzhino, *Russ.* 161 D20
Verkhnyaya Amga, *Russ.* 161 H18
Verkhovazh'ye, *Russ.* 158 E11
Verkhov'ye, *Russ.* 158 L9
Verkhoyanskiy Khrebet, *Russ.* 161 F17
Verkhoyansk Range, *Asia* 168 C10
Vermelharia, Ponta da, *Cabo Verde* 209 B15
Vermelho, river, *Braz.* 132 J12
Vermenton, *Fr.* 149 R11
Vermilion Bay, *La., U.S.* 102 Q8
Vermilion Cliffs National Monument, *Ariz., U.S.* 109 Q7
Vermilion Lake, *Minn., U.S.* 106 F12
Vermilion Range, *Minn., U.S.* 106 F13
Vermillion, *S. Dak., U.S.* 106 M8
Vérmio, Óros, *Gr.* 156 C9
Vermont, *St. Vincent and the Grenadines* 123 K16
Vermont, *U.S.* 96 G12
Vernal, *Utah, U.S.* 108 L9
Verneuil, *Fr.* 149 P8
Vérno, Óros, *Gr.* 156 C8
Vernon, *Ala., U.S.* 103 J13
Vernon, *Fr.* 149 P9
Vernon, *Tex., U.S.* 104 J8
Vernonia, *Oreg., U.S.* 110 E3
Vernou, *Guadeloupe, Fr.* 123 F14
Vero Beach, *Fla., U.S.* 99 U10
Véroia, *Gr.* 156 C10
Verona, *It.* 152 E6
Verona, *Miss., U.S.* 103 H13
Verraco, Punta, *P.R., U.S.* 122 P2
Versailles, *Fr.* 149 P9
Versailles, *Ky., U.S.* 103 B17
Versailles, *Mo., U.S.* 107 T12
Verte, Pointe, *Wallis and Futuna, Fr.* 222 E12
Vertientes, *Cuba* 118 J10
Verucchio, *It.* 163 G14
Verzy, *Fr.* 149 P12
Vescovato, *Fr.* 152 J4
Veselyy, *Russ.* 161 J17
Vesoul, *Fr.* 149 R14
Vesterålen, archipelago, *Nor.* 142 D12
Vestfjorden, bay, *Nor.* 142 E11
Vestfold Hills, *Antarctica* 231 G20
Vestmanna, *Faroe Is., Den.* 142 H5
Vestmannaeyjar (Westman Islands), *Ice.* 142 F2
Veststraumen Glacier, *Antarctica* 230 C11
Vestvågøy, island, *Nor.* 142 D12
Vesuvio, Monte, *It.* 152 M11
Vesuvius, peak, *Eur.* 140 K7
Ves'yegonsk, *Russ.* 158 G9
Veszprém, *Hung.* 151 L14

Vétaounde, island, *Vanuatu* 222 A2
Vetapalem, *India* 181 N7
Vetauua, island, *Fiji* 222 G8
Vetralla, *It.* 152 K8
Veules-les-Roses, *Fr.* 148 M8
Vevaru, island, *Maldives* 181 V3
Vezhen, peak, *Bulg.* 155 J14
Vezirköprü, *Turk.* 170 D10
Viacha, *Bol.* 132 J6
Viana do Bolo, *Sp.* 146 C7
Viana do Castelo, *Port.* 146 D5
Vianden, *Lux.* 162 H10
Viangchan (Vientiane), *Laos* 190 K10
Viareggio, *It.* 152 G5
Viborg, *Den.* 142 M11
Vibo Valentia, *It.* 153 R13
Vibraye, *Fr.* 149 Q8
Vic, *Sp.* 147 D17
Vic, Étang de, *Fr.* 149 X11
Vic-en-Bigorre, *Fr.* 149 Y7
Vicente Guerrero, *Mex.* 116 B5
Vicenza, *It.* 152 D7
Vic-Fézensac, *Fr.* 149 X7
Vichada, river, *Col.* 130 F8
Vichuga, *Russ.* 158 H11
Vichy, *Fr.* 149 T11
Vici, *Okla., U.S.* 104 F8
Vicksburg, *Mich., U.S.* 101 N10
Vicksburg, *Miss., U.S.* 102 L10
Vicksburg National Military Park, *Miss., U.S.* 102 L10
Vicovu de Sus, *Rom.* 155 A15
Victor, Mount, *Antarctica* 231 C16
Victor Harbor, *S. Aust., Austral.* 215 Y10
Victoria, *Austral.* 215 Z12
Victoria, *B.C., Can.* 84 M8
Victoria, *Chile* 134 C7
Victoria, *Chile* 135 N6
Victoria, *Grenada* 123 J23
Victoria, *Kans., U.S.* 107 T6
Victoria, *Seychelles* 209 N20
Victoria, *Tex., U.S.* 105 S12
Victoria, *Va., U.S.* 98 F12
Victoria (Rabat), *Malta* 163 H20
Victoria, river, *Austral.* 214 C8
Victoria, Lake, *Af.* 198 J9
Victoria, Mount, *Myanmar* 190 H5
Victoria, Mount, *P.N.G.* 217 E20
Victoria Falls, *Zambia, Zimb.* 206 F10
Victoria Falls, *Zambia, Zimb.* 206 F10
Victoria Island, *Nunavut, N.W.T., Can.* 85 E13
Victoria Land, region, *Antarctica* 231 P14
Victoria River Downs, *N.T., Austral.* 215 Q8
Victoria Sports Centre, *Gibraltar, U.K.* 163 N23
Victoria Strait, *Nunavut, Can.* 85 F14
Victorica, *Arg.* 134 K12
Victorica, *Arg.* 134 M9
Victorin, Mount, *St. Lucia* 123 L14
Victorville, *Calif., U.S.* III W9
Victory Downs, *N.T., Austral.* 215 U8
Victory Peak *see* Pobeda Peak, *China, Kyrg.* 178 E15
Vicuña, *Chile* 134 J7
Vidalia, *Ga., U.S.* 99 N7
Vidalia, *La., U.S.* 102 M9
Vidal Plain, *Atl. Oc.* 240 M6
Videle, *Rom.* 155 F15
Vidigueira, *Port.* 146 J6
Vidin, *Bulg.* 154 G12
Vidisha, *India* 180 J6
Vidor, *Tex., U.S.* 105 Q16
Vidzy, *Belarus* 158 J4
Viedma, *Arg.* 135 Q10
Viedma, Lago, *Arg.* 135 V7
Vieille Case, *Dominica* 123 D19
Vielha, *Sp.* 147 C16
Vienna, *Ga., U.S.* 99 N6
Vienna, *Ill., U.S.* 101 V6
Vienna, *W. Va., U.S.* 98 C8
Vienna *see* Wien, *Aust.* 150 K11
Vienne, *Fr.* 149 U13
Vientiane *see* Viangchan, *Laos* 190 K10
Viento, Punta, *P.R., U.S.* 122 P5

Vieques *see* Isabel Segunda, *P.R., U.S.* 122 N6
Vieques, island, *P.R., U.S.* 122 N6
Vieques Sound, *P.R., U.S.* 122 N6
Vierge Point, *St. Lucia* 123 L14
Vierwaldstätter See (Lake of Lucerne), *Switz.* 152 B3
Vierzon, *Fr.* 149 S9
Vieste, *It.* 152 K13
Vietnam, *Asia* 190 J12
Việt Trì, *Vietnam* 190 H12
Vieux-Boucau, *Fr.* 149 X5
Vieux-Bourg, *Guadeloupe, Fr.* 123 E15
Vieux Fort, *St. Lucia* 123 L14
Vieux-Fort, *Guadeloupe, Fr.* 123 G14
Vieux-Fort, Pointe du, *Guadeloupe, Fr.* 123 G14
Vieux-Habitants, *Guadeloupe, Fr.* 123 F14
Vigan, *Philippines* 193 B13
Vigía Chico, *Mex.* 117 H17
Vignemale, Pic de, *Fr.* 149 Y6
Vigo, *Sp.* 146 C5
Vigo, Ría de, *Sp.* 146 C5
Vihari, *Pak.* 179 R10
Viipuri *see* Vyborg, *Russ.* 158 E6
Vijayapura (Bijapur), *India* 180 M5
Vijayawada, *India* 181 N7
Vík, *Ice.* 142 F2
Vikenara Point, *Solomon Is.* 221 M19
Vikhorevka, *Russ.* 161 K14
Vikhren, peak, *Bulg.* 155 K13
Vikna, *Nor.* 142 F11
Viking Bank, *Atl. Oc.* 240 F12
Viking Trough, *Arctic Oc.* 247 J21
Víkuáall, *Atl. Oc.* 247 M20
Vila Bela da Santíssima Trindade, *Braz.* 132 J9
Vila Bittencourt, *Braz.* 132 D6
Vila da Ribeira Brava, *Cabo Verde* 209 B15
Vila de Moura, *Port.* 146 K6
Vila de Sagres, *Port.* 146 L4
Vila do Bispo, *Port.* 146 L4
Vila do Conde, *Port.* 146 E5
Vilafranca del Penedès, *Sp.* 147 E17
Vila Franca do Campo, *Azores, Port.* 146 Q5
Vilagarcĺa de Arousa, *Sp.* 146 C5
Vila Murtinho, *Braz.* 132 G7
Vilanculos, *Mozambique* 207 H13
Vila Nova de Gaia, *Port.* 146 E5
Vila Nova de Milfontes, *Port.* 146 K5
Vilanova i la Geltrú, *Sp.* 147 E17
Vila Real, *Port.* 146 E6
Vila-real de los Infantes, *Sp.* 147 G14
Vilar Formoso, *Port.* 146 F7
Vila Velha, *Braz.* 132 B12
Vila Velha (Espírito Santo), *Braz.* 133 L16
Vila Velha de Rodão, *Port.* 146 G6
Vilhelmina, *Sw.* 143 F13
Vilhena, *Braz.* 132 H9
Viljandi, *Est.* 143 K16
Vil'kitskogo, Proliv, *Russ.* 161 D14
Villa Ahumada, *Mex.* 116 C9
Villa Alberdi, *Arg.* 134 G9
Villa Ángela, *Arg.* 134 G12
Villa Atuel, *Arg.* 134 L8
Villablino, *Sp.* 146 B8
Villa Cañás, *Arg.* 134 L11
Villacarrillo, *Sp.* 146 K11
Villacastín, *Sp.* 146 F10
Villach, *Aust.* 150 M10
Villacidro, *It.* 153 P3
Villa Dolores, *Arg.* 134 K9
Villafranca de los Barros, *Sp.* 146 J8
Villafrancadi Verona, *It.* 152 E6
Village, *Fr. Polynesia, Fr.* 223 K17
Villa Grove, *Ill., U.S.* 101 R7
Villaguay, *Arg.* 134 K12
Villa Guillermina, *Arg.* 134 H12
Villahermosa, *Mex.* 117 J14
Villa Krause, *Arg.* 134 K8
Villalba, *P.R., U.S.* 122 N3
Villalonga, *Arg.* 135 P11
Villamar, *It.* 153 P4
Villa María, *Arg.* 134 K10
Villa Martín, *Bol.* 132 L6
Villamartín, *Sp.* 146 M8

Villamontes, *Bol.* 132 L8
Villa Nueva, *Arg.* 134 K8
Villanueva, *Mex.* 116 G10
Villanueva de Córdoba, *Sp.* 146 J10
Villanueva del Fresno, *Sp.* 146 J7
Villanueva de los Infantes, *Sp.* 146 J11
Villa Ocampo, *Arg.* 134 H12
Villa Regina, *Arg.* 135 P9
Villarosa, *It.* 153 S10
Villarrica, *Chile* 135 P6
Villarrica, Lago, *Chile* 135 P6
Villarrobledo, *Sp.* 146 H12
Villasalto, *It.* 153 P4
Villasimius, *It.* 153 Q4
Villatobas, *Sp.* 146 G11
Villa Unión, *Arg.* 134 H7
Villa Unión, *Mex.* 116 G8
Villavicencio, *Col.* 130 F6
Villaviciosa, *Sp.* 146 A9
Villazón, *Bol.* 132 L7
Villedieu-les-Poêles, *Fr.* 149 P6
Villefranche, *Fr.* 149 T12
Villefranche-de-Lauragais, *Fr.* 149 Y9
Villefranche-de-Rouergue, *Fr.* 149 W9
Villemaur, *Fr.* 149 Q11
Villena, *Sp.* 147 J14
Villeneuve-Saint-Georges, *Fr.* 149 P10
Villeneuve-sur-Lot, *Fr.* 149 W8
Ville Platte, *La., U.S.* 102 N8
Villers devant Orval, *Belg.* 162 K7
Villerupt, *Fr.* 162 L9
Villeurbanne, *Fr.* 149 U13
Villingen-Schwenningen, *Ger.* 150 K6
Villisca, *Iowa, U.S.* 107 Q10
Villupuram, *India* 181 Q7
Vilnius, *Lith.* 143 M17
Vilyuy, river, *Asia* 168 D10
Vilyuysk, *Russ.* 161 H17
Vilyuyskoye Vodokhranilishche, *Russ.* 161 H13
Vimoutiers, *Fr.* 149 P7
Vina, *Calif., U.S.* III P4
Viña del Mar, *Chile* 134 K6
Vinalhaven, *Me., U.S.* 97 G17
Vinaròs, *Sp.* 147 F15
Vincennes, *Ind., U.S.* 101 T7
Vincennes Bay, *Antarctica* 231 M20
Vincent, Point, *Norfolk I., Austral.* 221 F20
Vindelälven, river, *Sw.* 143 F13
Vindeln, *Sw.* 143 G14
Vindhya Range, *India* 180 J5
Vindrey, *Russ.* 158 K12
Vineland, *N.J., U.S.* 96 Q10
Vinh, *Vietnam* 190 J12
Vinhais, *Port.* 146 D7
Vịnh Cam Ranh, bay, *Vietnam* 191 N14
Vĩnh Châu, *Vietnam* 191 Q12
Vĩnh Long, *Vietnam* 191 P12
Vinita, *Okla., U.S.* 104 E13
Vinkovci, *Croatia* 154 E8
Vinnytsya, *Ukr.* 159 P5
Vinson Massif, *Antarctica* 230 H8
Vinton, *Iowa, U.S.* 107 N13
Vinton, *La., U.S.* 102 P6
Vinukonda, *India* 181 N7
Vipiteno, *It.* 152 B7
Viqueque, *Timor-Leste* 193 M15
Vir, *Taj.* 178 J10
Vir, island, *Croatia* 154 F5
Virac, *Philippines* 193 C15
Virachei, *Cambodia* 190 M13
Viranşehir, *Turk.* 171 H14
Virawah, *Pak.* 179 W9
Virden, *Ill., U.S.* 101 S5
Virden, *Man., Can.* 85 N13
Vire, *Fr.* 149 P6
Vîrfurile, *Rom.* 154 D12
Vírgenes, Cape, *S. Amer.* 128 Q5
Virgin, river, *Ariz., Nev., U.S.* III T13
Virgin Gorda, island, *British Virgin Is., U.K.* 121 A14
Virgin Gorda Peak, *British Virgin Is., U.K.* 122 Q9
Virginia, *Ill., U.S.* 101 R4
Virginia, *Minn., U.S.* 106 F12

Virginia, *U.S.* 98 E11
Virginia Beach, *Va., U.S.* 98 F14
Virginia City, *Mont., U.S.* 108 E7
Virginia City, *Nev., U.S.* III Q6
Virginia Falls, *N.W.T., Can.* 84 H9
Virgin Islands, *U.K., U.S.* 121 B13
Virgin Islands National Park, *Virgin Is., U.S.* 122 N11
Viroqua, *Wis., U.S.* 100 K3
Virovitica, *Croatia* 154 D7
Virrat, *Fin.* 143 H15
Virton, *Belg.* 162 K8
Virtsu, *Est.* 143 K16
Virú, *Peru* 132 G2
Virudunagar, *India* 181 R6
Vis (Lissa), island, *Croatia* 154 H6
Visalia, *Calif., U.S.* III U7
Visayan Sea, *Philippines* 193 D14
Visby, *Sw.* 143 L14
Viscount Melville Sound, *Nunavut, N.W.T., Can.* 85 D13
Višegrad, *Bosn. & Herzg.* 154 G9
Viseu, *Port.* 146 F6
Vişeu de Sus, *Rom.* 155 B14
Vishakhapatnam, *India* 180 M9
Viški Kanal, *Croatia* 154 H6
Viso, Monte, *It.* 152 F2
Viso del Marqués, *Sp.* 146 J11
Visp, *Switz.* 152 C3
Vista, *Calif., U.S.* III Y9
Vista Alegre, *Braz.* 132 F6
Vistula, river, *Eur.* 140 F8
Vit, river, *Bulg.* 155 H14
Viterbo, *It.* 152 J8
Vitichi, *Bol.* 132 L7
Vitigudino, *Sp.* 146 E8
Viti Levu, island, *Fiji* 222 J6
Viti Levu Bay, *Fiji* 222 H6
Vitim, *Russ.* 161 J16
Vitim, river, *Russ.* 161 J16
Vítor, *Peru* 132 J5
Vitória, *Braz.* 132 D12
Vitória, *Braz.* 133 L16
Vitória da Conquista, *Braz.* 133 J16
Vitoria-Gasteiz, *Sp.* 146 C12
Vitória-Trinidade Seamounts, *Atl. Oc.* 241 R8
Vitré, *Fr.* 149 Q6
Vitry-le-François, *Fr.* 149 P12
Vitsyebsk, *Belarus* 158 J6
Vittangi, *Sw.* 143 D13
Vittorio Veneto, *It.* 152 D8
Vityaz Fracture Zone, *Ind. Oc.* 224 H9
Vityaz Trench, *Pac. Oc.* 242 K10
Vivario, *Fr.* 152 K4
Viveiro, *Sp.* 146 A7
Vivi, *Russ.* 161 H14
Vivi, river, *Russ.* 161 H14
Vivian, *La., U.S.* 102 K6
Viwa, island, *Fiji* 222 H5
Vizcaíno, Desierto de, *Mex.* 116 D6
Vize, *Turk.* 170 C4
Vize, Ostrov, *Russ.* 161 D13
Vizianagaram, *India* 180 M9
Vizzini, *It.* 153 T11
Vjosë, river, *Alban.* 154 M9
Vlădeasa, peak, *Rom.* 154 C12
Vladikavkaz, *Russ.* 159 U14
Vladimir, *Russ.* 158 J10
Vladīmīrovka, *Kaz.* 176 B11
Vladivostok, *Russ.* 161 M21
Vlamingh Fracture Zone, *Ind. Oc.* 224 P12
Vlasenica, *Bosn. & Herzg.* 154 G9
Vlasinje, *Bosn. & Herzg.* 154 F7
Vlorë (Valona), *Alban.* 154 M9
Vlorës, Gjiri i, *Alban.* 154 M9
Vltava, river, *Czech Rep.* 150 J11
Vöcklabruck, *Aust.* 150 K10
Voe, *Scot., U.K.* 144 D12
Vogelsberg, range, *Ger.* 150 G7
Voghera, *It.* 152 E4
Voh, *New Caledonia, Fr.* 222 C6
Voiron, *Fr.* 149 U13
Voitsberg, *Aust.* 150 M11
Vojvodina, region, *Serb.* 154 E9
Volborg, *Mont., U.S.* 108 E12
Volcano, *Hawai'i, U.S.* 115 N21

Volcano Islands (Kazan Rettō), *Japan* **189** Z13
Volda, *Nor.* **142** H10
Volga, *S. Dak., U.S.* **106** K8
Volga, river, *Russ.* **158** L15
Volga-Baltic Waterway, *Russ.* **158** F9
Volga-Don Canal, *Russ.* **159** Q13
Volga River Delta, *Eur.* **140** H15
Volga Upland, *Eur.* **140** F14
Volgodonsk, *Russ.* **159** Q12
Volgograd (Stalingrad), *Russ.* **159** P13
Volgograd Reservoir, *Eur.* **140** F14
Volgogradskoye Vodokhranilishche, *Russ.* **159** N13
Volímes, *Gr.* **156** J7
Volissós, *Gr.* **157** H16
Volkhov, *Russ.* **158** F7
Volkhov, river, *Eur.* **140** E10
Völklingen, *Ger.* **150** H5
Volksrust, *S. Af.* **206** K11
Volna, Gora, *Russ.* **161** E20
Volnorez, Gora, *Russ.* **161** E13
Volnovakha, *Ukr.* **159** Q9
Volodarsk, *Russ.* **158** J12
Vologda, *Russ.* **158** F10
Vólos, *Gr.* **156** F11
Vol'sk, *Russ.* **158** M14
Volta, Lake, *Ghana* **204** D10
Voltaire, Cape, *Austral.* **214** B5
Volturno, river, *It.* **152** L10
Vólvi, Límni, *Gr.* **156** C12
Volx, *Fr.* **149** X14
Volyn-Podolian Upland, *Eur.* **140** H10
Volzhsk, *Russ.* **158** J14
Volzhskiy, *Russ.* **159** P13
Vonavona, island, *Solomon Is.* **221** M16
Vónitsa, *Gr.* **156** G8
Vopnafjörður, *Ice.* **142** E4
Vóras Óros, *Gr.* **156** C9
Vóreios Evvoïkós Kólpos, *Gr.* **156** G11
Vóries Sporádhes (Northern Sporades), islands, *Gr.* **157** F13
Voring Plateau, *Arctic Oc.* **247** H21
Vorkuta, *Russ.* **160** F10
Vormsi, island, *Est.* **143** K16
Voronezh, *Russ.* **158** M10
Voronin Trough, *Arctic Oc.* **247** E13
Voronov Terrace, *Arctic Oc.* **247** J15
Vorontsovka, *Russ.* **161** J16
Võru, *Est.* **143** K17
Vorukh, *Kyrg.* **178** G9
Vosges, range, *Fr.* **149** P15
Voss, *Nor.* **142** J10
Vostochnaya, *Russ.* **161** E13
Vostochnyy (Vrangel'), *Russ.* **161** M21
Vostochnyy Sayan, *Russ.* **161** L14
Vostok, station, *Antarctica* **231** K16
Vostok Island, *Kiribati* **219** H13
Votice, *Czech Rep.* **150** H11
Votkinsk, *Russ.* **158** G16
Votlo, *Vanuatu* **222** E2
Voulx, *Fr.* **149** Q10
Voúrinos, peak, *Gr.* **156** D9
Voúxa, Ákra, *Gr.* **156** P12
Vouziers, *Fr.* **149** N12
Vovchans'k, *Ukr.* **159** N9
Voyager Seamounts, *Pac. Oc.* **242** G12
Voyageurs National Park, *Minn., U.S.* **106** E12
Voyampolka, *Russ.* **161** E21
Voyvozh, *Russ.* **160** F9
Voza, *Solomon Is.* **221** L15
Vozhe, Ozero, *Russ.* **158** E10
Vozhega, *Russ.* **158** E10
Vozhgora, *Russ.* **160** F9
Voznesens'k, *Ukr.* **159** Q6
Vozvyshennost' Lavruska, *Russ.* **161** H15
Vrachíonas, peak, *Gr.* **156** J7
Vrachnaíika, *Gr.* **156** J9
Vrang, *Taj.* **178** K10
Vrangel' *see* Vostochnyy, *Russ.* **161** M21
Vrangelya, Ostrov (Wrangel Island), *Russ.* **161** B19
Vranica, peak, *Bosn. & Herzg.* **154** G7

Vranje, *Serb.* **154** J11
Vranov, *Slovakia* **151** J17
Vransko Jezero, *Croatia* **154** G5
Vratsa, *Bulg.* **155** H13
Vrbas, river, *Bosn. & Herzg.* **154** F7
Vrchovina Českomoravská, range, *Czech Rep.* **150** J12
Vršac, *Serb.* **154** E11
Vryburg, *S. Af.* **206** J9
Vryheid, *S. Af.* **206** K11
Vuagava, island, *Fiji* **222** K9
Vučitrn *see* Vushtrri, *Kos.* **154** J10
Vulcano, Isola, *It.* **153** R11
Vulci, ruin, *It.* **152** K7
Vunaniu Bay, *Fiji* **222** J6
Vũng Tàu, *Vietnam* **191** P13
Vunindawa, *Fiji* **222** J6
Vunisea, *Fiji* **222** K6
Vunivutu Bay, *Fiji* **222** G7
Vushtrri (Vučitrn), *Kos.* **154** J10
Vyatka, river, *Eur.* **140** D14
Vyatskiye Polyany, *Russ.* **158** H15
Vyazemskiy, *Russ.* **161** K21
Vyaz'ma, *Russ.* **158** K8
Vyazniki, *Russ.* **158** J11
Vyborg (Viipuri), *Russ.* **158** E6
Vychegda, river, *Eur.* **140** C13
Vychegda Lowland, *Eur.* **140** C12
Vyerkhnyadzvinsk, *Belarus* **158** J5
Vyg, Lake, *Eur.* **140** C11
Vyksa, *Russ.* **158** J11
Vylkove, *Ukr.* **159** S5
Vym', river, *Eur.* **140** C13
Vyritsa, *Russ.* **158** F6
VyshniyVolochek, *Russ.* **158** H8
Vyškov, *Czech Rep.* **151** J13
Vysokaye, *Belarus* **158** L2
Vysokovsk, *Russ.* **158** J9
Vytegra, *Russ.* **160** E7

W

Wa, *Ghana* **204** C10
Waar, island, *Indonesia* **193** K19
Wabao, Cape, *New Caledonia, Fr.* **222** D9
Wabasca, river, *Alta., Can.* **84** K10
Wabash, *Ind., U.S.* **101** Q9
Wabash, river, *Ill., Ind., U.S.* **101** T7
Wabasha, *Minn., U.S.* **106** K13
Wabasso, *Fla., U.S.* **99** U10
Wabeno, *Wis., U.S.* **100** H6
Wabowden, *Man., Can.* **85** L13
Wabuk Point, *Ont., Can.* **85** L16
Waco, *Tex., U.S.* **105** N11
Waco Lake, *Tex., U.S.* **105** N11
Wad, *Pak.* **179** U5
Waddenzee, bay, *Neth.* **148** G13
Waddington, Mount, *B.C., Can.* **84** L8
Wadena, *Minn., U.S.* **106** H10
Wadena, *Sask., Can.* **84** M12
Wädenswil, *Switz.* **152** B4
Wadesboro, *N.C., U.S.* **98** J10
Wadeye, *N.T., Austral.* **215** P7
Wadi Halfa, *Sudan* **202** C12
Wādī Mūsá (Elchi), *Jordan* **173** Q6
Wadley, *Ga., U.S.* **98** M7
Wad Madani, *Sudan* **203** E13
Wadomari, *Japan* **189** W3
Wadsworth, *Nev., U.S.* **111** P7
Wadsworth, *Ohio, U.S.* **101** P14
Wadu, island, *Maldives* **181** T3
Waelder, *Tex., U.S.* **105** R11
Waeshe, Mount, *Antarctica* **230** M9
Wafangdian, *Liaoning, China* **184** D12
Wager Bay, *N. Amer.* **82** E6
Wager Bay, *Nunavut, Can.* **85** G15
Wagga Wagga, *N.S.W., Austral.* **215** Y13
Wagin, *W. Aust., Austral.* **215** X3
Wagner, *S. Dak., U.S.* **106** M7
Wagoner, *Okla., U.S.* **104** F13
Wagontire Mountain, *Oreg., U.S.* **110** J6
Wągrowiec, *Pol.* **151** D13
Wahai, *Indonesia* **193** K17
Waha'ula Heiau, *Hawai'i, U.S.* **115** P22
Wah Cantonment, *Pak.* **179** N10

Wahiawā, *Hawai'i, U.S.* **114** E11
Wahoo, *Nebr., U.S.* **107** P8
Wahpeton, *N. Dak., U.S.* **106** H8
Waħx, Ras il, *Malta* **163** J21
Wai, *India* **180** M4
Wai, *Indonesia* **193** K16
Waiakoa, *Hawai'i, U.S.* **115** H17
Wai'ale'ale, peak, *Hawai'i, U.S.* **114** C5
Waialua, *Hawai'i, U.S.* **114** E10
Waialua Bay, *Hawai'i, U.S.* **114** E10
Wai'anae Range, *Hawai'i, U.S.* **114** E10
Waiau, river, *N.Z.* **217** Q15
Waibeem, *Indonesia* **193** J18
Waifang Shan, *Henan, China* **184** J4
Waigama, *Indonesia* **193** K17
Waigeo, island, *Indonesia* **193** J17
Waihe'e, *Hawai'i, U.S.* **115** G16
Waiheke Island, *N.Z.* **217** J19
Waikabubak, *Indonesia* **193** N13
Waikahalulu Bay, *Hawai'i, U.S.* **115** J16
Waikapū, *Hawai'i, U.S.* **115** H16
Waikapuna Bay, *Hawai'i, U.S.* **115** Q20
Waikato, river, *N.Z.* **217** J19
Waikawa, *N.Z.* **217** R16
Waikīkī Beach, *Hawai'i, U.S.* **114** F11
Waikoloa, *Hawai'i, U.S.* **115** L19
Waikouaiti, *N.Z.* **217** Q16
Wailagi Lala, island, *Fiji* **222** G9
Wailea, *Hawai'i, U.S.* **115** H16
Wailua, *Hawai'i, U.S.* **114** C6
Wailua, *Hawai'i, U.S.* **115** H18
Wailuku, *Hawai'i, U.S.* **115** G16
Wailuku, river, *Hawai'i, U.S.* **115** M21
Waimānalo Beach, *Hawai'i, U.S.* **114** F12
Waimarama, *N.Z.* **217** L20
Waimate, *N.Z.* **217** Q17
Waimea, *Hawai'i, U.S.* **114** C6
Waimea, *Hawai'i, U.S.* **114** D10
Waimea (Kamuela), *Hawai'i, U.S.* **115** L19
Waimea Canyon, *Hawai'i, U.S.* **114** C5
Wain, *N. Korea* **186** F6
Wainaworasi, *Solomon Is.* **221** Q21
Waingapu, *Indonesia* **193** N13
Wainunu Bay, *Fiji* **222** H7
Wainwright, *Alas., U.S.* **113** B14
Wai'ōhinu, *Hawai'i, U.S.* **115** Q19
Waiohonu Petroglyphs, *Hawai'i, U.S.* **115** H18
Wai'oli Mission, *Hawai'i, U.S.* **114** B5
Waipa, river, *N.Z.* **217** K19
Waipahi, *N.Z.* **217** R16
Waipahu, *Hawai'i, U.S.* **114** E11
Waipi'o Bay, *Hawai'i, U.S.* **115** K20
Waipi'o Valley, *Hawai'i, U.S.* **115** K19
Waipu, *N.Z.* **217** H18
Waipukurau, *N.Z.* **217** L20
Wairokai Harbor, *Solomon Is.* **221** N20
Waïsisi, *Vanuatu* **222** H4
Waïsisi Bay, *Vanuatu* **222** H4
Waitsburg, *Wash., U.S.* **110** E8
Wajima, *Japan* **188** M9
Wajir, *Kenya* **203** D15
Wakasa Wan, *Japan* **189** P9
Wakatipu, Lake, *N.Z.* **217** Q15
Wakaya, island, *Fiji* **222** H7
Wakayama, *Japan* **189** Q8
WaKeeney, *Kans., U.S.* **107** S5
Wakefield, *Eng., U.K.* **145** R12
Wakefield, *Jam.* **122** H7
Wakefield, *Kans., U.S.* **107** S8
Wakefield, *Mich., U.S.* **100** F5
Wakefield, *Nebr., U.S.* **107** N8
Wake Forest, *N.C., U.S.* **98** H12
Wake Island, *Wake I., U.S.* **220** F8
Wakema, *Myanmar* **190** L5
Wakenaam Island, *S. Amer.* **128** B7
Wākhān, region, *Afghan.* **178** K10
Wākhān, Kōh-e, *Afghan.* **178** K10
Wakhjir Pass, *Afghan., China* **178** K12
Wakkanai, *Japan* **188** N3
Wakuach, Lac, *Que., Can.* **85** K20
Wakunai, *P.N.G.* **221** J14
Wakuya, *Japan* **188** L13
Wala, *New Caledonia, Fr.* **222** B5
Walachia, region, *Rom.* **155** F14
Wałbrzych, *Pol.* **150** G12

Walcha, *N.S.W., Austral.* **215** W15
Walcott, Lake, *Idaho, U.S.* **108** H6
Wałcz, *Pol.* **150** C12
Walden, *Colo., U.S.* **108** L12
Waldkraiburg, *Ger.* **150** K9
Waldo, *Ark., U.S.* **102** J7
Waldo Lake, *Oreg., U.S.* **110** H4
Waldorf, *Md., U.S.* **98** D13
Waldport, *Oreg., U.S.* **110** G2
Waldron, *Ark., U.S.* **102** G6
Walea, Selat, *Indonesia* **193** J14
Wales, *Alas., U.S.* **112** E11
Wales, *Wales, U.K.* **145** U10
Wales Island, *Nunavut, Can.* **85** G16
Walferdange, *Lux.* **162** J10
Walgett, *N.S.W., Austral.* **215** W14
Walgreen Coast, *Antarctica* **230** K7
Walhalla, *N. Dak., U.S.* **106** D7
Walhalla, *S.C., U.S.* **98** J6
Walikale, *Dem. Rep. of the Congo* **202** K11
Walker, *Minn., U.S.* **106** G10
Walker Lake, *Nev., U.S.* **111** Q7
Wall, *S. Dak., U.S.* **106** L3
Wallaby Saddle, *Ind. Oc.* **225** L17
Wallace, *Idaho, U.S.* **108** C4
Wallace, *N.C., U.S.* **98** J12
Wallace, *Nebr., U.S.* **107** Q4
Wallaroo, *S. Aust., Austral.* **215** X10
Walla Walla, *Wash., U.S.* **110** E8
Wallibou, *St. Vincent and the Grenadines* **123** J16
Wallilabou, *St. Vincent and the Grenadines* **123** K16
Wallis, Îles (Wallis Islands), *Pac. Oc.* **218** J9
Wallis & Futuna, *Pac. Oc.* **218** J9
Wallis Islands *see* Wallis, Îles, *Pac. Oc.* **218** J9
Wallis Ridge, *Atl. Oc.* **248** G1
Wallops Island, *Va., U.S.* **98** E15
Wallowa, *Wash., U.S.* **110** F9
Wallowa Mountains, *Oreg., U.S.* **110** F9
Walls, *Scot., U.K.* **144** D12
Wallsend, *Eng., U.K.* **145** P12
Walney, Isle of, *Eng., U.K.* **145** Q10
Walnut Canyon National Monument, *Ariz., U.S.* **109** S7
Walnut Cove, *N.C., U.S.* **98** G10
Walnut Ridge, *Ark., U.S.* **102** E10
Walong, *India* **180** E16
Walsall, *Eng., U.K.* **145** T12
Walsenburg, *Colo., U.S.* **109** P13
Walsh, *Colo., U.S.* **109** P16
Walsrode, *Ger.* **150** D7
Walterboro, *S.C., U.S.* **98** M9
Walter F. George Reservoir, *Ala., Ga., U.S.* **103** M17
Walters, *Okla., U.S.* **104** J9
Walters Shoal, *Ind. Oc.* **224** N5
Walton, *N.Y., U.S.* **96** K9
Walvis Bay, *Namibia* **206** H6
Walvis Ridge, *Atl. Oc.* **241** S12
Walyahmoning Rock, *Austral.* **214** J3
Wāmā, *Afghan.* **178** M9
Wamba, *Dem. Rep. of the Congo* **202** J11
Wamba, river, *Dem. Rep. of the Congo* **202** M8
Wamego, *Kans., U.S.* **107** S9
Wamena, *Indonesia* **193** L20
Wami, river, *Tanzania* **203** M15
Wamsasi, *Indonesia* **193** K15
Wamsisi, *Indonesia* **193** K16
Wamsutter, *Wyo., U.S.* **108** K10
Wana, *Pak.* **179** P8
Wanaaring, *N.S.W., Austral.* **215** W12
Wanaka, *N.Z.* **217** Q16
Wanaka, Lake, *N.Z.* **217** P16
Wan'an, *Jiangxi, China* **185** S6
Wanapa, *Bonaire, Neth.* **123** R19
Wanchese, *N.C., U.S.* **98** G15
Wanderer Bay, *Solomon Is.* **221** P18
Wandoan, *Qnsld., Austral.* **215** U15
Wangal, *Indonesia* **217** D15
Wanganui *see* Whanganui, *N.Z.* **217** L19

Wanganui, river, *N.Z.* **217** L19
Wangaratta, *Vic., Austral.* **215** Y13
Wangcheng, *Hunan, China* **185** Q4
Wangerberg, *Liech.* **162** Q2
Wangiwangi, island, *Indonesia* **193** L14
Wang Kai, *S. Sudan* **202** G12
Wanigela, *P.N.G.* **217** E20
Wanione, *Solomon Is.* **221** P21
Wankaner, *India* **180** J2
Wanlaweyn, *Somalia* **203** J17
Wanlockhead, *Scot., U.K.* **145** N10
Wanning, *China* **182** Q12
Wanrong, *Shanxi, China* **184** H3
Wānū, *Afghan.* **179** P5
Wanzai, *Jiangxi, China* **185** Q6
Wapakoneta, *Ohio, U.S.* **101** Q11
Wapato, *Wash., U.S.* **110** D6
Wapello, *Iowa, U.S.* **107** P14
Wappapello, Lake, *Mo., U.S.* **107** V15
Wapsipinicon, river, *Iowa, U.S.* **107** N13
War, *W. Va., U.S.* **98** F8
Waranga Basin, *Austral.* **214** L12
Warangal, *India* **180** M7
Waras, *Afghan.* **179** N4
Waraseoni, *India* **180** K7
Warburg, *Ger.* **150** E7
Warburton, *W. Aust., Austral.* **215** U6
Warburton Creek, *Austral.* **214** H10
Warden, *Wash., U.S.* **110** D7
Ward Hunt Island, *Nunavut, Can.* **85** A15
Wardija Point, *Malta* **163** H19
Waren, *Ger.* **150** C10
Waren, *Indonesia* **193** K19
Ware Shoals, *S.C., U.S.* **98** K7
Warlubie, *Pol.* **151** C14
Warmbad, *Namibia* **206** K7
Warminster, *Eng., U.K.* **145** W11
Warm Springs, *Ga., U.S.* **98** M5
Warm Springs, *Nev., U.S.* **111** R10
Warm Springs, *Oreg., U.S.* **98** E10
Warm Springs Reservoir, *Oreg., U.S.* **110** H8
Warner Mountains, *Calif., Oreg., U.S.* **110** L6
Warner Robins, *Ga., U.S.* **98** M6
Warner Valley, *Oreg., U.S.* **110** K6
Waroona, *W. Aust., Austral.* **215** X3
Warora, *India* **180** K6
Warracknabeal, *Vic., Austral.* **215** Y12
Warrego, river, *Austral.* **214** H13
Warren, *Ark., U.S.* **102** J8
Warren, *Mich., U.S.* **100** M12
Warren, *Minn., U.S.* **106** E8
Warren, *N.S.W., Austral.* **215** W14
Warren, *Ohio, U.S.* **101** P15
Warren, *Pa., U.S.* **96** L4
Warrender, Cape, *Nunavut, Can.* **85** D16
Warrenpoint, *N. Ire., U.K.* **145** Q7
Warrensburg, *Mo., U.S.* **107** T11
Warrenton, *Ga., U.S.* **98** L7
Warrenton, *Oreg., U.S.* **110** E2
Warrenton, *S. Af.* **206** K9
Warrenton, *Va., U.S.* **98** D12
Warri, *Nigeria* **205** E13
Warrina, *S. Aust., Austral.* **215** V9
Warrington, *Eng., U.K.* **145** S11
Warrington, *Fla., U.S.* **99** Q1
Warrnambool, *Vic., Austral.* **215** Z11
Warroad, *Minn., U.S.* **106** D9
Warsa, *Indonesia* **193** J19
Warsaw, *Ind., U.S.* **101** P9
Warsaw, *N.C., U.S.* **98** J12
Warsaw, *Va., U.S.* **98** E13
Warszawa (Warsaw), *Pol.* **151** D16
Warta, river, *Pol.* **151** F14
Waru, *Indonesia* **193** K17
Warwick, *Eng., U.K.* **145** U12
Warwick, *Qnsld., Austral.* **215** V15
Warwick, *R.I., U.S.* **97** L14
Wasado, peak, *Indonesia* **217** C15
Wasaka, *Vanuatu* **222** B2
Wasam, *Pak.* **178** K11
Wasatch Range, *Utah, U.S.* **108** K7
Wasco, *Calif., U.S.* **111** V7
Wasco, *Oreg., U.S.* **110** F5
Waseca, *Minn., U.S.* **106** L11
Washap, *Pak.* **179** U3

Washburn, *Me., U.S.* **97** B18
Washburn, *N. Dak., U.S.* **106** F4
Washburn, *Wis., U.S.* **100** F4
Washburn, Mount, *Wyo., U.S.* **108** F8
Washington, *Bonaire, Neth.* **123** Q19
Washington, *D.C., U.S.* **98** C13
Washington, *Ga., U.S.* **98** L7
Washington, *Ill., U.S.* **101** Q5
Washington, *Ind., U.S.* **101** T8
Washington, *Iowa, U.S.* **107** P13
Washington, *Kans., U.S.* **107** R8
Washington, *Mo., U.S.* **107** T14
Washington, *N.C., U.S.* **98** H13
Washington, *Pa., U.S.* **96** P3
Washington, *U.S.* **110** C5
Washington, *Utah, U.S.* **109** Q5
Washington, *Wis., U.S.* **100** H8
Washington, Cape, *Antarctica* **231** P14
Washington, Cape, *Fiji* **222** K6
Washington, Mount, *N.H., U.S.* **97** G14
Washington Court House, *Ohio, U.S.* **101** R12
Washington Island, *Wis., U.S.* **100** H8
Washington Island see Teraina, *Kiribati* **218** F12
Washita, river, *Okla., Tex., U.S.* **104** F7
Washougal, *Wash., U.S.* **110** F4
Washtucna, *Wash., U.S.* **110** D8
Washuk, *Pak.* **179** T4
Wasilla, *Alas., U.S.* **113** J16
Wasior, *Indonesia* **193** K19
Waskaganish, *Que., Can.* **85** N18
Wasserbillig, *Lux.* **162** J11
Waswanipi, Lac, *Que., Can.* **85** N18
Watampone, *Indonesia* **193** L13
Waterbury, *Conn., U.S.* **96** M12
Water Cays, *Bahamas* **122** E2
Water Cays, *Bahamas* **118** F11
Wateree Lake, *S.C., U.S.* **98** K9
Waterford (Port Láirge), *Ire.* **145** U6
Waterford Harbour, *Ire.* **145** U6
Water Ground, *Cayman Is.* **122** H1
Water Island, *Virgin Is., U.S.* **122** N8
Waterloo, *Ill., U.S.* **101** T4
Waterloo, *Iowa, U.S.* **107** N12
Waterloo, *N.T., Austral.* **215** Q7
Waterloo, *Trinidad and Tobago* **123** P22
Waterman, Isla, *Chile* **135** Y8
Watersmeet, *Mich., U.S.* **100** F6
Waterton-Glacier International Peace Park, *Mont., U.S.* **108** A6
Waterton Lakes National Park, *Alberta, Can.* **108** A6
Watertown, *N.Y., U.S.* **96** G9
Watertown, *S. Dak., U.S.* **106** K8
Watertown, *Wis., U.S.* **100** L6
Water Valley, *Miss., U.S.* **102** H12
Waterville, *Kans., U.S.* **107** R8
Waterville, *Me., U.S.* **97** F16
Waterville, *Minn., U.S.* **106** K11
Waterville, *Wash., U.S.* **110** C6
Watford, *Eng., U.K.* **145** V14
Watford City, *N. Dak., U.S.* **106** F2
Watkins Glen, *N.Y., U.S.* **96** K7
Watling see San Salvador, island, *Bahamas* **119** F14
Watling's Castle, site, *Bahamas* **122** F11
Watonga, *Okla., U.S.* **104** F9
Watrous, *N. Mex., U.S.* **109** R13
Watsa, *Dem. Rep. of the Congo* **202** J12
Watseka, *Ill., U.S.* **101** Q7
Watson, *S. Aust., Austral.* **215** W8
Watson Lake, *Yukon, Can.* **84** H8
Watsonville, *Calif., U.S.* **111** T4
Watt Mount, *Dominica* **123** G20
Watts Bar Lake, *Tenn., U.S.* **103** F17
Wattwil, *Switz.* **152** A4
Watubela, Kepulauan, *Indonesia* **193** L18
Wau, *P.N.G.* **217** D19
Wau, *S. Sudan* **202** G11
Waubay, *S. Dak., U.S.* **106** J7
Wauchope, *N.T., Austral.* **215** S9
Wauchula, *Fla., U.S.* **99** U8
Waukarlycarly, Lake, *Austral.* **214** E4

Waukegan, *Ill., U.S.* **100** M7
Waukesha, *Wis., U.S.* **100** L6
Waukon, *Iowa, U.S.* **106** M13
Wauneta, *Nebr., U.S.* **107** Q3
Waupaca, *Wis., U.S.* **100** J6
Waupun, *Wis., U.S.* **100** K6
Waurika, *Okla., U.S.* **104** J10
Wausa, *Nebr., U.S.* **107** N7
Wausau, *Wis., U.S.* **100** H5
Wauseon, *Ohio, U.S.* **101** N11
Wautoma, *Wis., U.S.* **100** K5
Wauwatosa, *Wis., U.S.* **100** L7
Wave Hill, *N.T., Austral.* **215** R8
Waverly, *Iowa, U.S.* **106** M12
Waverly, *N.Y., U.S.* **96** L8
Waverly, *Nebr., U.S.* **107** Q8
Waverly, *Ohio, U.S.* **101** S13
Waverly, *Tenn., U.S.* **103** E14
Waverly, *Va., U.S.* **98** F13
Wawa, *Ont. Can.* **85** P17
Wāw al Kabīr, *Lib.* **201** E14
Waxahachie, *Tex., U.S.* **104** M12
Waxweiler, *Ger.* **162** G11
Way, Lake, *Austral.* **214** G4
Waya, island, *Fiji* **222** H5
Wayamli, *Indonesia* **193** H16
Wayaobu see Zichang, *Shaanxi, China* **184** F2
Waycross, *Ga., U.S.* **99** P7
Wayne, *Nebr., U.S.* **107** N8
Waynesboro, *Ga., U.S.* **98** M8
Waynesboro, *Miss., U.S.* **103** M13
Waynesboro, *Pa., U.S.* **96** Q6
Waynesboro, *Tenn., U.S.* **103** F14
Waynesboro, *Va., U.S.* **98** E11
Waynesburg, *Pa., U.S.* **96** P3
Waynesville, *Mo., U.S.* **107** U13
Waynesville, *N.C., U.S.* **98** H6
Waynoka, *Okla., U.S.* **104** E9
Wazirabad, *Pak.* **179** P12
Wé, *New Caledonia, Fr.* **222** C9
We, island, *Philippines* **192** F3
Weary Bay, *Austral.* **214** C13
Weatherford, *Okla., U.S.* **104** G9
Weatherford, *Tex., U.S.* **104** L10
Weaverville, *Calif., U.S.* **110** M3
Webb City, *Mo., U.S.* **107** V11
Weber Basin, *Pac. Oc.* **242** K6
Webster, *Mass., U.S.* **97** L14
Webster, *S. Dak., U.S.* **106** J7
Webster City, *Iowa, U.S.* **107** N11
Webster Groves, *Mo., U.S.* **107** T15
Webster Springs, *W. Va., U.S.* **98** D9
Weda, *Indonesia* **193** J16
Weda, Teluk, *Indonesia* **193** J16
Weddell Island, *Falk. Is., U.K.* **135** W11
Weddell Plain, *Atl. Oc.* **241** Y8
Weddell Sea, *Antarctica* **230** D8
Wedemark, *Ger.* **150** D7
Weed, *Calif., U.S.* **110** M3
Weeki Wachee, *Fla., U.S.* **99** T7
Weeping Water, *Nebr., U.S.* **107** Q9
Weert, *Neth.* **148** K13
Wee Waa, *N.S.W., Austral.* **215** W14
Węgorzewo, *Pol.* **151** B16
Wei, river, *Shaanxi, China* **184** J2
Wei, river, *Shand., China* **184** G7
Weichang, *Hebei, China* **184** A9
Weiden, *Ger.* **150** H9
Weifang, *Shand., China* **184** G10
Weihai, *Shand., China* **184** F12
Weihui, *Henan, China* **184** H6
Weilheim, *Ger.* **150** K8
Weilmoringle, *N.S.W., Austral.* **215** V13
Weimar, *Ger.* **150** F8
Weimar, *Tex., U.S.* **105** R12
Weinan, *Shaanxi, China* **184** J2
Weining, *China* **182** M10
Weinsberger Wald, *Aust.* **150** K11
Weipa, *Qnsld., Austral.* **215** P12
Weirton, *W. Va., U.S.* **98** B9
Weiser, *Idaho, U.S.* **108** F3
Weiser, river, *Idaho, U.S.* **108** F3
Weishan, *Shand., China* **184** J8
Weishi, *Henan, China* **184** J6
Weissenburg, *Ger.* **150** J8
Weissenfels, *Ger.* **150** F9
Weiss Lake, *Ala., Ga., U.S.* **98** K4
Weiswampach, *Lux.* **162** G10
Weite, *Switz.* **162** Q2
Weixi, *China* **182** M8

Wejherowo, *Pol.* **151** A14
Welch, *W. Va., U.S.* **98** F8
Welch Point, *Cayman Is.* **122** J1
Weldiya, *Eth.* **203** F15
Weldon, *N.C., U.S.* **98** G13
Weligama, *Sri Lanka* **181** T7
Welkom, *S. Af.* **206** K10
Wellesley Islands, *Austral.* **214** C11
Wellin, *Belg.* **148** M12
Wellington, *Colo., U.S.* **108** L13
Wellington, *Kans., U.S.* **107** V7
Wellington, *N.S.W., Austral.* **215** X14
Wellington, *N.Z.* **217** M18
Wellington, *Nev., U.S.* **111** Q7
Wellington, *Tex., U.S.* **104** H7
Wellington, Isla, *Chile* **135** V6
Wellington, Lake, *Austral.* **214** M13
Wellington Bay, *Nunavut, Can.* **85** F13
Wells, *Me., U.S.* **97** H15
Wells, *Minn., U.S.* **106** L11
Wells, *Nev., U.S.* **110** M12
Wells, *Tex., U.S.* **105** N14
Wells, Lake, *Austral.* **214** G5
Wellsboro, *Pa., U.S.* **96** L7
Wellston, *Ohio, U.S.* **101** S13
Wellsville, *Mo., U.S.* **107** S13
Wellsville, *N.Y., U.S.* **96** K6
Wellsville, *Ohio, U.S.* **101** Q15
Wellton, *Ariz., U.S.* **109** V5
Wels, *Aust.* **150** K11
Welsh, *La., U.S.* **102** P7
Welshpool, *Wales, U.K.* **145** T10
Wemyss Bight, *Bahamas* **122** F6
Wenatchee, *Wash., U.S.* **110** C6
Wenchang, *Hainan, China* **185** Z2
Wencheng, *Zhejiang, China* **185** R11
Wenchi, *Ghana* **204** D10
Wendeng, *Shand., China* **184** F12
Wendesi, *Indonesia* **193** K19
Wendover, *Nev., U.S.* **110** M12
Wendover, *Utah, U.S.* **108** K5
Wenjiao, *Hainan, China* **185** Z2
Wenling, *Zhejiang, China* **185** Q12
Weno, *F.S.M.* **221** B15
Weno, island, *F.S.M.* **221** B15
Wenshan, *China* **182** P10
Wenshang, *Shand., China* **184** H7
Wentworth, *N.S.W., Austral.* **215** X11
Wenxi, *Shanxi, China* **184** H3
Wenxian, *China* **182** K10
Wenzhou, *Zhejiang, China* **185** R11
Werdau, *Ger.* **150** F9
Werder, *Ger.* **150** D10
Werdēr, *Eth.* **203** G17
Weri, *Indonesia* **217** C14
Weser, river, *Ger.* **150** E7
Weskan, *Kans., U.S.* **107** S3
Weslaco, *Tex., U.S.* **105** W10
Wesley, *Dominica* **123** E19
Wesleyville, *Pa., U.S.* **96** K3
Wessel Islands, *Austral.* **214** A10
Wessington, *S. Dak., U.S.* **106** K6
Wessington Springs, *S. Dak., U.S.* **106** L6
Wesson, *Miss., U.S.* **102** M11
West, *Tex., U.S.* **104** M11
West Allis, *Wis., U.S.* **100** L7
West Antarctica, region, *Antarctica* **230** J8
West Bank, *Asia* **172** M5
West Bay, *Cayman Is.* **122** J1
West Bay, *Fla., U.S.* **99** R3
West Bay, *La., U.S.* **102** R12
West Bay, town, *Cayman Is.* **122** H1
West Bend, *Wis., U.S.* **100** L7
West Branch, *Iowa, U.S.* **107** P13
West Branch, *Mich., U.S.* **100** J11
Westbrook, *Me., U.S.* **97** H15
Westbrook, *Tex., U.S.* **104** M6
West Burra, island, *Scot., U.K.* **144** E11
Westby, *Wis., U.S.* **100** K4
West Caicos, island, *Turks & Caicos Is.* **119** J16
West Cape Howe, *Austral.* **214** L3
West Caroline Basin, *Pac. Oc.* **242** J7
West Cay, *Virgin Is., U.S.* **122** M7
West Chester, *Pa., U.S.* **96** P9
Westcliffe, *Colo., U.S.* **109** N13

West Columbia, *Tex., U.S.* **105** R13
West Des Moines, *Iowa, U.S.* **107** P11
West End, *Bahamas* **122** E1
West End, *British Virgin Is., U.K.* **122** R5
West End Point, *British Virgin Is., U.K.* **122** L10
West End Point, *Cayman Is.* **118** L8
West End Village, *British Virgin Is., U.K.* **122** R11
Westerhall Bay, *Grenada* **123** L23
Westerhall Point, *Grenada* **123** L23
Westerland, *Ger.* **150** A7
Westerly, *R.I., U.S.* **97** M14
Western, river, *Nunavut, Can.* **85** G13
Western Australia, *Austral.* **215** T4
Western Beach, *Gibraltar, U.K.* **163** N23
Western Desert, *Egypt* **201** D17
Western Dvina, river, *Eur.* **140** F10
Western Ghats, range, *India* **180** L3
Western Plateau, *Austral.* **214** F6
Western Sahara, *Af.* **200** D6
Western Sayan Mountains, *Asia* **168** E9
Westerschelde, bay, *Neth.* **148** K11
Westerville, *Ohio, U.S.* **101** R13
West European Basin, *Atl. Oc.* **240** H10
West Falkland, island, *Falk. Is., U.K.* **135** W11
Westfall, *Oreg., U.S.* **110** H8
West Fayu Atoll see Pigailoe, *F.S.M.* **220** Q4
Westfield, *Mass., U.S.* **96** L12
Westfield, *N.Y., U.S.* **96** K4
West Florida Shelf, *Atl. Oc.* **240** L2
West Fork Poplar, river, *Mont., U.S.* **108** A12
West Fork Trinity, river, *Tex., U.S.* **104** K9
West Frankfort, *Ill., U.S.* **101** U6
West Frisian Islands, *Neth.* **148** G12
West Glacier, *Mont., U.S.* **108** B6
West Grand Lake, *Me., U.S.* **97** E18
West Greenland Shelf, *Arctic Oc.* **247** N15
West Helena, *Ark., U.S.* **102** H10
Westhope, *N. Dak., U.S.* **106** D4
West Ice Shelf, *Antarctica* **231** H21
West Indies, *N. Amer.* **82** N9
West Jan Mayen Ridge, *Arctic Oc.* **247** K19
West Lafayette, *Ind., U.S.* **101** Q8
West Landing, *Marshall Is., U.S.* **220** G10
West Liberty, *Iowa, U.S.* **107** P14
West Liberty, *Ky., U.S.* **103** B19
Westman Islands see Vestmannaeyjar, *Ice.* **142** F2
West Mariana Basin, *Pac. Oc.* **242** H7
West Melanesian Trench, *Pac. Oc.* **242** J8
West Memphis, *Ark., U.S.* **102** G10
Westminster, *Md., U.S.* **98** B13
Westminster, *S.C., U.S.* **98** K6
West Monroe, *La., U.S.* **102** L8
Westmorland, *Calif., U.S.* **111** Y11
West Nicholson, *Zimb.* **206** G11
West Norfolk Ridge, *Pac. Oc.* **242** N10
West Novaya Zemlya Trough, *Arctic Oc.* **247** D17
Weston, *Mo., U.S.* **107** S10
Weston, *W. Va., U.S.* **98** C9
Weston Point, *Kiribati* **221** B20
Weston super Mare, *Eng., U.K.* **145** V11
West Palm Beach, *Fla., U.S.* **99** V10
Westphalia, *Eur.* **140** G6
West Plains, *Mo., U.S.* **107** V13
West Point, *Ga., U.S.* **98** M4
West Point, *Ky., U.S.* **103** B16
West Point, *Marshall Is., U.S.* **220** M7
West Point, *Miss., U.S.* **103** J13
West Point, *N.Y., U.S.* **96** M11
West Point, *Nebr., U.S.* **107** P8
West Point, *Va., U.S.* **98** E13
West Point Lake, *Ala., Ga., U.S.* **103** K17

Westport, *Calif., U.S.* **111** P2
Westport, *N.Z.* **217** M17
Westport, *Wash., U.S.* **110** D2
Westport (Cathair na Mart), *Ire.* **145** R3
Westpunt, *Curaçao, Neth.* **123** N13
Westray, island, *Scot., U.K.* **144** F10
Westray Firth, *Scot., U.K.* **144** F10
West Scotia Basin, *Atl. Oc.* **241** W6
West Scotia Ridge, *Atl. Oc.* **248** N10
West Sheba Ridge, *Ind. Oc.* **224** D6
West Siberian Plain, *Asia* **168** D8
West Spit, *Marshall Is., U.S.* **220** H7
West Thulean Rise, *Atl. Oc.* **240** G8
West Union, *Iowa, U.S.* **106** M13
West Valley City, *Utah, U.S.* **108** L7
West Virginia, *U.S.* **98** D9
Westwego, *La., U.S.* **102** Q11
Westwood, *Calif., U.S.* **111** N5
Westwood Downs, *N.S.W., Austral.* **215** W11
West Wyalong, *N.S.W., Austral.* **215** X13
West Yellowstone, *Mont., U.S.* **108** F8
West York Island, *S. China Sea* **192** E11
Wetar, island, *Indonesia* **193** M15
Wetaskiwin, *Alta., Can.* **84** L10
Wetumka, *Okla., U.S.* **104** G12
Wetumpka, *Ala., U.S.* **103** L16
Wetzlar, *Ger.* **150** G6
Wewahitchka, *Fla., U.S.* **99** R4
Wewak, *P.N.G.* **217** C18
Wewoka, *Okla., U.S.* **104** G12
Wexford (Loch Garman), *Ire.* **145** U7
Wexford Harbour, *Ire.* **145** U7
Weyburn, *Sask., Can.* **84** N12
Weyer, *Aust.* **150** L11
Weymouth, *Eng., U.K.* **145** X11
Weymouth, Cape, *Austral.* **214** B13
Whakapunake, peak, *N.Z.* **217** K20
Whakatane, *N.Z.* **217** K20
Whale Cay, *Bahamas* **118** D10
Whale Cove, *Nunavut, Can.* **85** J15
Whaler Anchorage, *F.S.M.* **221** A20
Whalsay, island, *Scot., U.K.* **144** D12
Whangamata, *N.Z.* **217** J19
Whanganui (Wanganui), *N.Z.* **217** L19
Whangarei, *N.Z.* **217** H18
Wharton, *Tex., U.S.* **105** R13
Wharton Basin, *Ind. Oc.* **225** K14
Wheatland, *Wyo., U.S.* **108** J13
Wheatland Reservoir, *Wyo., U.S.* **108** J13
Wheaton, *Minn., U.S.* **106** H8
Wheeler, *Tex., U.S.* **104** G7
Wheeler Lake, *Ala., U.S.* **103** H15
Wheeler Peak, *N. Mex., U.S.* **109** Q13
Wheeling, *W. Va., U.S.* **98** B9
Wheelwright, *Ky., U.S.* **103** C20
Whidbey, Point, *Austral.* **214** K9
Whiddy Island, *Ire.* **145** V3
Whinham, Mount, *Austral.* **214** G7
Whiporie, *N.S.W., Austral.* **215** W16
Whiskeytown Shasta-Trinity National Recreation Area, *Calif., U.S.* **110** M3
Whitby, *Eng., U.K.* **145** Q13
White, *S. Dak., U.S.* **106** K8
White, river, *Ark., U.S.* **102** E8
White, river, *Colo., Utah, U.S.* **108** L10
White, river, *Ind., U.S.* **101** T7
White, river, *Nev., U.S.* **111** R12
White, river, *S. Dak., U.S.* **106** L4
White, river, *Tex., U.S.* **104** K6
White, Lake, *Austral.* **214** E7
White Bay, *British Virgin Is., U.K.* **122** L11
White Bird, *Idaho, U.S.* **108** E4
White Butte, peak, *N. Dak., U.S.* **106** H2
White Cliffs, *N.S.W., Austral.* **215** W12
White Cloud, *Mich., U.S.* **100** K9
White Deer, *Tex., U.S.* **104** G6
Whitefish, *Mont., U.S.* **108** B5
Whitefish Bay, *Mich., U.S.* **100** F10
Whitefish Point, *Mich., U.S.* **100** F10
Whitefish Point, town, *Mich., U.S.* **100** F10

White Hall, *Ark., U.S.* 102 H9
White Hall, *Ill., U.S.* 101 S4
Whitehall, *Mich., U.S.* 100 L9
Whitehall, *Mont., U.S.* 108 E7
Whitehall, *N.Y., U.S.* 96 H12
Whitehall, *Ohio, U.S.* 101 R13
Whitehall, *Wis., U.S.* 100 J3
Whitehaven, *Eng., U.K.* 145 Q10
Whitehorse, *Yukon, Can.* 84 G8
White Horses, *Jam.* 122 K11
Whitehouse, *Jam.* 122 J6
White Island, *Antarctica* 231 C19
White Island, *Nunavut, Can.* 85 G16
White Lake, *La., U.S.* 102 Q8
Whitemark, *Tas., Austral.* 215 Y8
White Mountain, *Alas., U.S.* 112 F12
White Mountains, *Calif., U.S.* 111 S8
White Mountains, *Me., N.H., U.S.* 97 F14
White Mountains National Recreation Area, *Alas., U.S.* 113 F17
White Nile, river, *Af.* 198 G9
White Pine, *Mich., U.S.* 100 F5
White Plains, *N.Y., U.S.* 96 M11
White River, *S. Dak., U.S.* 106 L4
Whiteriver, *Ariz., U.S.* 109 T9
White River Junction, *Vt., U.S.* 97 H13
White Salmon, *Wash., U.S.* 110 E5
White Sands National Monument, *N. Mex., U.S.* 109 U12
Whitesboro, *Tex., U.S.* 104 K11
Whitesburg, *Ky., U.S.* 103 D20
White Sea, *Arctic Oc.* 247 C19
White Sulphur Springs, *Mont., U.S.* 108 D8
White Sulphur Springs, *W. Va., U.S.* 98 E9
Whitetail, *Mont., U.S.* 108 A13
Whiteville, *N.C., U.S.* 98 K12
Whiteville, *Tenn., U.S.* 102 F12
Whitewater, *Mont., U.S.* 108 B11
Whitewater, *Wis., U.S.* 100 M6
Whitewater Baldy, peak, *N. Mex., U.S.* 109 U10
Whitewright, *Tex., U.S.* 104 K12
Whithorn, *Scot., U.K.* 145 P9
Whitman, *Nebr., U.S.* 107 N3
Whitman Mission National Historic Site, *Wash., U.S.* 110 E8
Whitmire, *S.C., U.S.* 98 K8
Whitmore Mountains, *Antarctica* 230 K10
Whitney, Lake, *Tex., U.S.* 104 M11
Whitney, Mount, *Calif., U.S.* 111 T8
Whittier, *Alas., U.S.* 113 J17
Wholdaia Lake, *N.W.T., Can.* 85 J13
Whyalla, *S. Aust., Austral.* 215 X10
Wiay see Fuidhaigh, island, *Scot., U.K.* 144 J6
Wibaux, *Mont., U.S.* 108 C13
Wichita, *Kans., U.S.* 107 U7
Wichita, river, *Tex., U.S.* 104 K9
Wichita Falls, *Tex., U.S.* 104 J9
Wichita Mountains, *Okla., U.S.* 104 H9
Wick, *Scot., U.K.* 144 H10
Wickenburg, *Ariz., U.S.* 109 T6
Wickett, *Tex., U.S.* 105 N3
Wickiup Reservoir, *Oreg., U.S.* 110 H4
Wickliffe, *Ky., U.S.* 102 D12
Wicklow (Cill Mhantáin), *Ire.* 145 S7
Wicklow Head, *Ire.* 145 S7
Wicklow Mountains, *Ire.* 145 S7
Wide Bay, *P.N.G.* 217 C21
Widnes, *Eng., U.K.* 145 S11
Wido, island, *S. Korea* 187 S7
Wieleń, *Pol.* 150 D12
Wieluń, *Pol.* 151 F14
Wien (Vienna), *Aust.* 150 K11
Wiener Neustadt, *Aust.* 150 L12
Wieprz, river, *Pol.* 151 E17
Wiesbaden, *Ger.* 150 G6
Wigan, *Eng., U.K.* 145 R11
Wiggins, *Miss., U.S.* 102 N12
Wight, Isle of, *Eng., U.K.* 145 X13
Wigtown Bay, *Scot., U.K.* 145 P9
Wikieup, *Ariz., U.S.* 109 S5
Wil, *Switz.* 152 A4
Wilberforce, Cape, *Austral.* 214 A10
Wilbur, *Wash., U.S.* 110 C7

Wilburton, *Okla., U.S.* 104 H13
Wilcannia, *N.S.W., Austral.* 215 W12
Wilczek, Zemlya, *Russ.* 160 C12
Wildcat Peak, *Nev., U.S.* 111 Q10
Wilde Bay, *Austral.* 214 G16
Wildespitze, peak, *Aust.* 150 M8
Wildrose, *N. Dak., U.S.* 106 E2
Wildwood, *Fla., U.S.* 99 S8
Wildwood, *N.J., U.S.* 96 R10
Wilhelm, Mount, *P.N.G.* 217 C19
Wilhelm II Coast, *Antarctica* 231 J21
Wilhelmina Gebergte, peak, *Suriname* 131 F15
Wilhelmshaven, *Ger.* 150 C6
Wilkes-Barre, *Pa., U.S.* 96 M8
Wilkes Fracture Zone, *Pac. Oc.* 243 K19
Wilkes Island, *Wake I., U.S.* 220 F7
Wilkes Land, region, *Antarctica* 231 N19
Wilkins Coast, *Antarctica* 230 E6
Willacoochee, *Ga., U.S.* 99 P7
Willamette, river, *Oreg., U.S.* 110 G3
Willapa Bay, *Wash., U.S.* 110 D2
Willapa Hills, *Wash., U.S.* 110 D2
Willard, *Ohio, U.S.* 101 P13
Willard, *Utah, U.S.* 108 K7
Willcox, *Ariz., U.S.* 109 V9
Willemstad, *Curaçao, Neth.* 123 Q14
Willeroo, *N.T., Austral.* 215 Q8
William, Mount, *Austral.* 214 L12
William "Bill" Dannelly Reservoir, *Ala., U.S.* 103 L15
William Cay, *Bahamas* 122 E8
William Creek, *S. Aust., Austral.* 215 V10
Williams, *Ariz., U.S.* 109 S7
Williams, *Calif., U.S.* 111 Q4
Williams, *Minn., U.S.* 106 E10
Williamsburg, *Ky., U.S.* 103 D18
Williamsburg, *Va., U.S.* 98 F13
Williamsfield, *Jam.* 122 J8
Williams Island, *Bahamas* 118 E10
Williams Lake, *B.C., Can.* 84 L8
Williamson, *W. Va., U.S.* 98 D7
Williamson Glacier, *Antarctica* 231 M20
Williamsport, *Pa., U.S.* 96 M7
Williamston, *N.C., U.S.* 98 H13
Williamston, *S.C., U.S.* 98 K7
William's Town, *Bahamas* 122 F9
Williamstown, *Ky., U.S.* 103 A18
Williamstown, *W. Va., U.S.* 98 C8
Willikies, *Antigua and Barbuda* 123 B21
Willis, *Tex., U.S.* 105 Q14
Willis Islets, *Austral.* 218 J5
Williston, *N. Dak., U.S.* 106 E2
Williston, *S.C., U.S.* 98 L8
Williston Lake, *B.C., Can.* 84 J9
Willits, *Calif., U.S.* 111 P2
Willmar, *Minn., U.S.* 106 J10
Willoughby Bay, *Antigua and Barbuda* 123 B21
Willow City, *N. Dak., U.S.* 106 E5
Willowlake, river, *N.W.T., Can.* 84 H10
Willowra, *N.T., Austral.* 215 S8
Willows, *Calif., U.S.* 111 P3
Willow Springs, *Mo., U.S.* 107 V13
Wills Point, *Tex., U.S.* 104 L13
Wilmington, *Del., U.S.* 98 B14
Wilmington, *Ill., U.S.* 101 P7
Wilmington, *N.C., U.S.* 98 K12
Wilmington, *Ohio, U.S.* 101 S12
Wilmore, *Ky., U.S.* 103 C17
Wilmot, *Ark., U.S.* 102 K9
Wilmot, *S. Dak., U.S.* 106 J8
Wilshaw Ridge, *Ind. Oc.* 224 K7
Wilson, *Ark., U.S.* 102 F11
Wilson, *Kans., U.S.* 107 T6
Wilson, *N.C., U.S.* 98 H12
Wilson, *Okla., U.S.* 104 J11
Wilson, *Tex., U.S.* 104 K5
Wilson, Mount, *Colo., U.S.* 109 P10
Wilson, Mount, *Oreg., U.S.* 110 F4
Wilson Creek, *Wash., U.S.* 110 C7
Wilson Hills, *Antarctica* 231 R15
Wilson Lake, *Ala., U.S.* 103 G14
Wilson Lake, *Kans., U.S.* 107 S6
Wilson's Creek National Battlefield, *Mo., U.S.* 107 V12

Wilsons Promontory, *Austral.* 214 M13
Wilson Strait, *Solomon Is.* 221 M15
Wilton, *N. Dak., U.S.* 106 G4
Wiltz, *Lux.* 162 H9
Wiltz, river, *Lux.* 162 H9
Wiluna, *W. Aust., Austral.* 215 U4
Winamac, *Ind., U.S.* 101 P8
Winchester, *Eng., U.K.* 145 W13
Winchester, *Idaho, U.S.* 108 D3
Winchester, *Ind., U.S.* 101 R10
Winchester, *Ky., U.S.* 103 B18
Winchester, *Tenn., U.S.* 103 G16
Winchester, *Va., U.S.* 98 C12
Winchester Bay, *Oreg., U.S.* 110 H2
Wind, river, *Wyo., U.S.* 108 H9
Wind, river, *Yukon, Can.* 84 E9
Windber, *Pa., U.S.* 96 P5
Winder, *Ga., U.S.* 98 K6
Windhill Beach, *Gibraltar, U.K.* 163 Q23
Windhoek, *Namibia* 206 H7
Windom, *Minn., U.S.* 106 L10
Windorah, *Qnsld., Austral.* 215 U12
Window Rock, *Ariz., U.S.* 109 R10
Wind River Range, *Wyo., U.S.* 108 H9
Windsor, *Colo., U.S.* 108 L13
Windsor, *Conn., U.S.* 97 L13
Windsor, *Eng., U.K.* 145 V13
Windsor, *N.C., U.S.* 98 G13
Windsor, *Ont., Can.* 85 R17
Windsor, *Vt., U.S.* 97 H13
Windsor Forest, *Ga., U.S.* 99 N9
Windsor Lake, *Mo., U.S.* 107 T11
Windward Islands, *Lesser Antil.* 121 H16
Windward Passage, *N. Amer.* 119 K15
Winfield, *Ala., U.S.* 103 J14
Winfield, *Kans., U.S.* 107 V8
Wini, *Indonesia* 193 M15
Winifred, *Mont., U.S.* 108 C9
Wininen, island, *F.S.M.* 221 C16
Winion, Mochun, *F.S.M.* 221 C16
Winipirea, island, *F.S.M.* 221 B16
Winipiru, island, *F.S.M.* 221 C14
Winisk, river, *Ont., Can.* 85 M16
Wink, *Tex., U.S.* 105 N3
Winkelman, *Ariz., U.S.* 109 U8
Winlock, *Wash., U.S.* 110 D3
Winneba, *Ghana* 204 E10
Winnebago, *Minn., U.S.* 106 L11
Winnebago, Lake, *Wis., U.S.* 100 K6
Winnemucca, *Nev., U.S.* 110 M8
Winnemucca Lake, *Nev., U.S.* 111 N7
Winner, *S. Dak., U.S.* 106 M5
Winnfield, *La., U.S.* 102 M8
Winnibigoshish, Lake, *Minn., U.S.* 106 F10
Winnipeg, *Man., Can.* 85 N14
Winnipeg, Lake, *Man., Can.* 85 M14
Winnipegosis, *Man., Can.* 85 M13
Winnipegosis, Lake, *N. Amer.* 82 G5
Winnipesaukee, Lake, *N.H., U.S.* 97 H14
Winnsboro, *La., U.S.* 102 L9
Winnsboro, *S.C., U.S.* 98 K9
Winnsboro, *Tex., U.S.* 104 L14
Winona, *Kans., U.S.* 107 S3
Winona, *Minn., U.S.* 106 L11
Winona, *Miss., U.S.* 102 J11
Winseler, *Lux.* 162 H9
Winsen, *Ger.* 150 C8
Winslow, *Ariz., U.S.* 109 S8
Winslow, *Me., U.S.* 97 F16
Winston-Salem, *N.C., U.S.* 98 G10
Winter Garden, *Fla., U.S.* 99 T8
Winter Haven, *Fla., U.S.* 99 U8
Winter Park, *Fla., U.S.* 99 T9
Winters, *Calif., U.S.* 111 R4
Winters, *Tex., U.S.* 104 M7
Winterset, *Iowa, U.S.* 107 P11
Winterswijk, *Neth.* 148 J14
Winterthur, *Switz.* 152 A4
Winthrop, *Me., U.S.* 97 G16
Winthrop, *Minn., U.S.* 106 K10
Winthrop, *Wash., U.S.* 110 B6
Winton, *Qnsld., Austral.* 215 T12
Winton Heights, *Bahamas* 122 B12
Wippra, *Ger.* 150 E8
Wirrulla, *S. Aust., Austral.* 215 W9
Wisas, island, *F.S.M.* 221 C16

Wisbech, *Eng., U.K.* 145 T14
Wiscasset, *Me., U.S.* 97 G16
Wisconsin, *U.S.* 100 J5
Wisconsin, river, *Wis., U.S.* 100 J5
Wisconsin Dells, *Wis., U.S.* 100 K5
Wisconsin Rapids, *Wis., U.S.* 100 J5
Wiseman, *Alas., U.S.* 113 E16
Wishek, *N. Dak., U.S.* 106 H5
Wishram, *Wash., U.S.* 110 F5
Wismar, *Ger.* 150 B9
Wisner, *La., U.S.* 102 M9
Wisner, *Nebr., U.S.* 107 N8
Wissembourg, *Fr.* 149 P15
Witham, *Eng., U.K.* 145 U15
Witsand, *S. Af.* 206 M8
Witten, *S. Dak., U.S.* 106 M4
Wittenberg, *Ger.* 150 E10
Wittenberge, *Ger.* 150 D9
Wittenoom, *W. Aust., Austral.* 215 T3
Wittlich, *Ger.* 162 H12
Wittstock, *Ger.* 150 C9
Witu Islands, *P.N.G.* 217 C20
Wiwǒn, *N. Korea* 186 E7
Włocławek, *Pol.* 151 D14
Włodawa, *Pol.* 151 E18
Wöbbelin, *Ger.* 150 C9
Woburn Bay, *Grenada* 123 L22
Wohlthat Mountains, *Antarctica* 231 B14
Wojejairok, island, *Marshall Is., U.S.* 220 L4
Wojejairok Pass, *Marshall Is., U.S.* 220 L4
Wokam, island, *Indonesia* 193 L19
Wokingham, *Eng., U.K.* 145 V13
Wolauna, island, *F.S.M.* 221 C16
Wolcott, *N.Y., U.S.* 96 J7
Woleai Atoll, *F.S.M.* 220 Q4
Wolf, river, *Wis., U.S.* 100 H6
Wolf (Wenman), Isla, *Ecua.* 130 N8
Wolf, Volcán, *Ecua.* 130 P9
Wolf Creek, *Mont., U.S.* 108 D7
Wolf Creek, *Okla., Tex., U.S.* 104 F7
Wolf Creek, *Oreg., U.S.* 110 K2
Wolf Creek Pass, *Colo., U.S.* 109 P12
Wolfeboro, *N.H., U.S.* 97 H14
Wolfe City, *Tex., U.S.* 104 K12
Wolfen, *Ger.* 150 E9
Wolfenbüttel, *Ger.* 150 E8
Wolfforth, *Tex., U.S.* 104 K5
Wolf Point, *Mont., U.S.* 108 B12
Wolfsberg, *Aust.* 150 M11
Wolfsburg, *Ger.* 150 D8
Wollaston, Islas, *Chile* 135 Y9
Wollaston Lake, *Sask., Can.* 85 K13
Wollaston Peninsula, *Nunavut, N.W.T., Can.* 84 E12
Wollogorang, *N.T., Austral.* 215 R10
Wollongong, *N.S.W., Austral.* 215 Y14
Wolo, *Indonesia* 193 K13
Wolpyeong, *S. Korea* 187 T7
Wolverhampton, *Eng., U.K.* 145 T11
Wombat Plateau, *Ind. Oc.* 225 J17
Wondeok, *S. Korea* 187 N12
Wondeung, *S. Korea* 187 S8
Wongawal, *W. Aust., Austral.* 215 U4
Wonju, *S. Korea* 187 N10
Wǒnp'yǒng, *N. Korea* 186 H9
Wǒnsan, *N. Korea* 186 F11
Wǒnsan, *N. Korea* 186 J9
Wonsando, island, *S. Korea* 187 Q7
Wonthaggi, *Vic., Austral.* 215 Z12
Wonti, *Indonesia* 217 B16
Woodall Mountain, *Miss., U.S.* 103 G13
Woodbine, *Ga., U.S.* 99 Q8
Woodbridge, *Eng., U.K.* 145 U15
Woodbridge, *Va., U.S.* 98 D13
Woodbridge Bay, *Dominica* 123 G19
Woodburn, *Oreg., U.S.* 110 F3
Woodbury, *N.J., U.S.* 96 Q9
Wood Cay, *Bahamas* 122 A5
Woodenbridge (An Droichead Adhmaid), *Ire.* 145 T7
Woodford, *Grenada* 123 K22
Wood Lake, *Nebr., U.S.* 107 N5
Woodlake, *Calif., U.S.* 111 U7
Woodland, *Calif., U.S.* 111 Q4
Woodland, *Me., U.S.* 97 E19
Woodland, *Wash., U.S.* 110 E3
Woodland Park, *Colo., U.S.* 108 M13

Woodlark, island, *P.N.G.* 217 E22
Wood River, *Ill., U.S.* 101 T4
Wood River, *Nebr., U.S.* 107 Q6
Wood River Lakes, *Alas., U.S.* 113 K13
Woodroffe, Mount, *Austral.* 214 G8
Woodruff, *S.C., U.S.* 98 J8
Woodruff, *Utah, U.S.* 108 K8
Woods, Lake, *Austral.* 214 D9
Woods, Lake of the, *N. Amer.* 82 H6
Woodsboro, *Tex., U.S.* 105 T11
Woodsfield, *Ohio, U.S.* 101 R15
Woods Hole, *Mass., U.S.* 97 M15
Woodstock, *Qnsld., Austral.* 215 R12
Woodstock, *Qnsld., Austral.* 215 T12
Woodstock, *Va., U.S.* 98 D11
Woodstown, *N.J., U.S.* 96 Q9
Woodsville, *N.H., U.S.* 97 G13
Woodville, *Miss., U.S.* 102 N9
Woodville, *N.Z.* 217 L19
Woodville, *Tex., U.S.* 105 P15
Woodward, *Okla., U.S.* 104 E8
Woody Head, *Austral.* 214 J16
Woomera, *S. Aust., Austral.* 215 W10
Woonsocket, *R.I., U.S.* 97 L14
Woonsocket, *S. Dak., U.S.* 106 L7
Wooramel, *W. Aust., Austral.* 215 U1
Wooster, *Ohio, U.S.* 101 P14
Wǒram, *N. Korea* 186 M7
Worbab, island, *Marshall Is., U.S.* 220 N5
Worcester, *Eng., U.K.* 145 U11
Worcester, *Mass., U.S.* 97 K14
Worcester, *S. Af.* 206 M8
Worden, *Mont., U.S.* 108 E10
Workai, island, *Indonesia* 193 M19
Workington, *Eng., U.K.* 145 P10
Worland, *Wyo., U.S.* 108 G10
Wormeldange, *Lux.* 162 K11
Worms, *Ger.* 150 H6
Worth, Lake, *Tex., U.S.* 104 L11
Wortham, *Tex., U.S.* 104 M12
Worthing, *Barbados* 123 L19
Worthington, *Minn., U.S.* 106 L9
Wosi, *Indonesia* 193 J16
Wotho Atoll, *Marshall Is., U.S.* 220 F3
Wotje Atoll, *Marshall Is., U.S.* 220 G4
Wowoni, island, *Indonesia* 193 L14
Wragby, *Eng., U.K.* 145 S13
Wrangel Island, *Asia* 168 A11
Wrangell, *Alas., U.S.* 113 M23
Wrangell, Cape, *Alas., U.S.* 112 K1
Wrangell-Saint Elias National Park and Preserve, *Alas., U.S.* 113 J18
Wrangel Plain, *Arctic Oc.* 246 H10
Wrath, Cape, *Scot., U.K.* 144 G8
Wray, *Colo., U.S.* 108 L8
Wreck Hill, peak, *Bermuda* 122 C1
Wreck Point, *Af.* 198 Q6
Wrecks, Bay of, *Kiribati* 221 B23
Wrecsam see Wrexham, *Wales, U.K.* 145 S10
Wrens, *Ga., U.S.* 98 M7
Wrexham (Wrecsam), *Wales, U.K.* 145 S10
Wright, *Wyo., U.S.* 108 G13
Wright Brothers National Memorial, *N.C., U.S.* 98 G15
Wright Patman Lake, *Tex., U.S.* 104 K15
Wrightsville, *Ga., U.S.* 98 M7
Wrightsville Beach, *N.C., U.S.* 98 K13
Wrigley Gulf, *Antarctica* 230 M8
Wrocław, *Pol.* 151 F13
Września, *Pol.* 151 E13
Wu, river, *China* 182 M11
Wu'an, *Hebei, China* 184 G6
Wubin, *W. Aust., Austral.* 215 W3
Wubu, *Shaanxi, China* 184 F3
Wucheng, *Shand., China* 184 F7
Wuchuan, *Guang., China* 185 X2
Wuda, *China* 182 G11
Wudāb, *Afghan.* 178 J9
Wudang Shan, *Hubei, China* 184 L2
Wudao, *Liaoning, China* 184 D11
Wudaoliang, *China* 182 J6
Wudi, *Shand., China* 184 F8
Wuding, river, *Shaanxi, China* 184 F3
Wudu, *China* 182 K10
Wufeng, *Hubei, China* 185 N2

Wugang, *Henan, China* 184 K5
Wugang, *Hunan, China* 185 S2
Wuhai, *China* 182 G11
Wuhan, *Hubei, China* 185 N6
Wuhe, *Jiangsu, China* 184 K9
Wuhu, *Anhui, China* 184 M9
Wuhua, *Guang., China* 185 V7
Wukari, *Nigeria* 205 D15
Wular Lake, *India* 178 M12
Wuleidao Wan, *Shand., China* 184 F12
Wulian (Hongning), *Shand., China* 184 H10
Wuliaru, island, *Indonesia* 217 D14
Wuling Shan, *Hunan, China* 185 Q1
Wulingyuan, *Hunan, China* 185 P2
Wum, *Cameroon* 205 E15
Wuning, *Jiangxi, China* 185 P6
Wunlah, *Indonesia* 193 M17
Wuntho, *Myanmar* 190 F6
Wupatki National Monument, *Ariz., U.S.* 109 R7
Wuping, *Fujian, China* 185 U7
Wuppertal, *Ger.* 150 F5
Wuqi, *Shaanxi, China* 184 F1
Wuqing, *Tianjin Shi, China* 184 D8
Wurung, *Qnsld., Austral.* 215 R11
Würzburg, *Ger.* 150 H7
Wushan, *Chongq., China* 184 M2
Wushi, *China* 182 E3
Wusi, *Vanuatu* 222 C1
Wusuli, river, *China* 183 C18
Wutai, *Shanxi, China* 184 E5
Wutai Shan, *Shanxi, China* 184 D5
Wuvulu Island, *P.N.G.* 217 B18
Wuwei, *Anhui, China* 184 M9
Wuwei, *China* 182 H9
Wuxi, *Chongq., China* 184 M1
Wuxi, *Jiangsu, China* 184 M11
Wuxiang, *Shanxi, China* 184 F5
Wuxue, *Hubei, China* 185 P7
Wuyang, *Henan, China* 184 K5
Wuyiling, *China* 183 C16
Wuyi Shan, *Jiangxi, China* 185 T7
Wuyishan, *Fujian, China* 185 R9
Wuyuan, *N. Mongol, China* 184 B1
Wuzhai, *Shanxi, China* 184 D4
Wuzhen, *Hubei, China* 184 M4
Wuzhi, *Henan, China* 184 H5
Wuzhong, *China* 182 H10
Wuzhou, *Guangxi Zhuang, China* 185 V2
Wyalkatchem, *W. Aust., Austral.* 215 W3
Wyandra, *Qnsld., Austral.* 215 V13
Wycheproof, *Vic., Austral.* 215 Y12
Wye, river, *Eng., Wales, U.K.* 145 U11
Wyemandoo, peak, *Austral.* 214 H3
Wyk, *Ger.* 150 A7
Wylie Lake, *N.C., S.C., U.S.* 98 J9
Wyloo, *W. Aust., Austral.* 215 T2
Wymore, *Nebr., U.S.* 107 R8
Wynbring, *S. Aust., Austral.* 215 W9
Wyndham, *W. Aust., Austral.* 215 Q6
Wyndmere, *N. Dak., U.S.* 106 H7
Wynne, *Ark., U.S.* 102 G10
Wynnewood, *Okla., U.S.* 104 H11
Wynniatt Bay, *N.W.T., Can.* 85 E13
Wyoming, *Mich., U.S.* 100 L9
Wyoming, *U.S.* 108 H11
Wyoming Range, *Wyo., U.S.* 108 H8
Wyszków, *Pol.* 151 D16
Wytheville, *Va., U.S.* 98 F9

X

Xaafuun, *Somalia* 203 F19
Xàbia see Jávea, *Sp.* 147 J15
Xaçmaz, *Azerb.* 171 C22
Xagħra, *Malta* 163 H20
Xaignabouli, *Laos* 190 J9
Xainza (Shenzha), *China* 182 K5
Xai-Xai, *Mozambique* 206 J12
Xalapa, *Mex.* 117 J13
Xalin, *Somalia* 203 G18
Xangda (Nangqên), *China* 182 K7
Xangongo, *Angola* 206 F6

Xankəndi see Stepanakert, *Azerb.* 171 E20
Xánthi, *Gr.* 157 B14
Xanthus, ruins, *Turk.* 170 J4
Xapuri, *Braz.* 132 G6
Xarardheere, *Somalia* 203 H18
Xar Burd, *China* 182 G10
Xar Moron Sum, *N. Mongol, China* 184 A4
Xátiva, *Sp.* 147 H14
Xau, Lake, *Botswana* 206 G9
X`éng, river, *Laos* 190 H10
Xenia, *Ohio, U.S.* 101 R12
Xerxes' see Xérxis Canal, *Gr.* 157 D13
Xérxis (Xerxes') Canal, *Gr.* 157 D13
Xewkija, *Malta* 163 H20
Xi, river, *Guang., China* 185 V3
Xiachuan Dao, *Guang., China* 185 X4
Xiajin, *Shand., China* 184 F7
Xiamen (Amoy), *Fujian, China* 185 U9
Xiamen Gang, *Fujian, China* 185 U9
Xi'an, *Shaanxi, China* 184 J1
Xianfeng, *Hubei, China* 185 P1
Xiang, river, *Hunan, China* 185 S3
Xiangcheng, *Henan, China* 184 K5
Xiangdong, *Jiangxi, China* 185 R5
Xiangfan, *Hubei, China* 184 L4
Xiangfen, *Shanxi, China* 184 G3
Xianggang see Hong Kong S.A.R., *China* 185 W5
Xianghuang Qi (Xin Bulag), *N. Mongol, China* 184 A6
Xiangkhoang, *Laos* 190 J10
Xiangning, *Shanxi, China* 184 G3
Xiangshan, *Zhejiang, China* 185 P12
Xiangshui, *Jiangsu, China* 184 J10
Xiangtan, *Hunan, China* 185 R4
Xiangxi, *Hubei, China* 184 M2
Xiangyin, *Hunan, China* 185 Q4
Xiangyuan, *Shanxi, China* 184 G5
Xianju, *Zhejiang, China* 185 Q11
Xianning, *Hunan, China* 185 P5
Xiantao, *Hubei, China* 185 N5
Xianyang, *Shaanxi, China* 184 J1
Xianyou, *Fujian, China* 185 T9
Xiao, river, *Hunan, China* 185 S3
Xiaoba see Qingtongxia, *China* 182 H10
Xiaochang, *Hubei, China* 184 M5
Xiaogan, *Hubei, China* 185 N5
Xiaohezi, *N. Mongol, China* 184 B7
Xiao Hinggan Ling, *China* 183 B15
Xiaojiang, *Zhejiang, China* 185 R11
Xiaolan, *Guang., China* 185 W4
Xiao Shan, *Henan, China* 184 J3
Xiaoshan, *Zhejiang, China* 185 N11
Xiaoshi, *Liaoning, China* 184 B13
Xiaoxian, *Anhui, China* 184 J8
Xiaoyang Shan, island, *Zhejiang, China* 185 N12
Xiapu, *Fujian, China* 185 S11
Xiawa, *N. Mongol, China* 184 A11
Xiaxian, *Shanxi, China* 184 H3
Xiayi, *Henan, China* 184 J7
Xichang, *China* 182 M9
Xichuan, *Henan, China* 184 K3
Xifeng, *China* 182 J11
Xigazê (Rikaze), *China* 182 L5
Xihua, *Henan, China* 184 K6
Xilinhot, *China* 183 E13
Xin, river, *Jiangxi, China* 185 Q8
Xin'an see Guannan, *Jiangsu, China* 184 J10
Xin'an see Lai'an, *Anhui, China* 184 L9
Xin'anjiang Shuiku, *Zhejiang, China* 185 P10
Xin Barag Youqi, *China* 183 C13
Xin Barag Zouqi, *China* 183 C13
Xinbo, *Hebei, China* 184 A9
Xin Bulag see Xianghuang Qi, *N. Mongol, China* 184 A6
Xincai, *Henan, China* 184 L6
Xincheng, *Shanxi, China* 184 E4
Xinchengzi, *Liaoning, China* 184 A13
Xincun, *Hebei, China* 184 E9
Xindianzi, *Shanxi, China* 184 C4
Xinfeng, *Guang., China* 185 U5
Xinfeng, *Jiangxi, China* 185 T6

Xinfengjiang Shuiku, *Guang., China* 185 V5
Xing'an, *Guangxi Zhuang, China* 185 T2
Xingcheng, *Liaoning, China* 184 C11
Xingguo, *Jiangxi, China* 185 S6
Xinghe, *N. Mongol, China* 184 B6
Xinghua, *Jiangsu, China* 184 L10
Xinghua Wan, *Fujian, China* 185 T10
Xingkai Hu (Khanka, Ozero), *China, Russ.* 183 D17
Xinglong, *Beijing Shi, China* 184 C8
Xingning, *Guang., China* 185 U7
Xingshan, *Hubei, China* 184 M2
Xingtai, *Hebei, China* 184 F6
Xingtang, *Hebei, China* 184 E6
Xingu, river, *Braz.* 132 F12
Xinguara, *Braz.* 133 F13
Xingxian, *Shanxi, China* 184 E3
Xingxingxia, *China* 182 F7
Xingyang, *Henan, China* 184 J5
Xingyi, *China* 182 N10
Xingzi, *Jiangxi, China* 185 P7
Xinhe, *China* 182 E4
Xinhui, *Guang., China* 185 W4
Xining, *China* 182 H9
Xinji, *Hebei, China* 184 E7
Xinjian, *Jiangxi, China* 185 Q7
Xinjiang, *Shanxi, China* 184 H3
Xinjie, *N. Mongol, China* 184 D2
Xinlong, *Henan, China* 182 L9
Xinmi, *Henan, China* 184 J5
Xinmin, *Liaoning, China* 184 A12
Xinning, *Hunan, China* 185 S2
Xinpu see Lianyungang, *Jiangsu, China* 184 J10
Xinqing, *China* 183 C16
Xinshao, *Hunan, China* 185 R3
Xinshi, *Hunan, China* 185 S4
Xintai, *Shand., China* 184 H9
Xintian, *Hunan, China* 185 T3
Xinxiang, *Henan, China* 184 H5
Xinyang, *Henan, China* 184 L5
Xinye, *Henan, China* 184 L4
Xinyi, *Guang., China* 185 W2
Xinyi, *Jiangsu, China* 184 J9
Xinyu, *Jiangxi, China* 185 R6
Xinyuan, *China* 182 E4
Xinzheng, *Henan, China* 184 J5
Xinzhou, *Shanxi, China* 184 E4
Xinzo de Limia, *Sp.* 146 D6
Xiong'er Shan, *Henan, China* 184 J3
Xiongyuecheng, *Liaoning, China* 184 C12
Xiongzhou, *Hebei, China* 184 D7
Xiping, *Henan, China* 184 K5
Xiping see Datong, *Shanxi, China* 184 C5
Xique Xique, *Braz.* 133 G15
Xiushui, *Jiangxi, China* 185 P6
Xiuwu, *Henan, China* 184 H5
Xiuyan, *Liaoning, China* 184 C13
Xixia, *Henan, China* 184 K3
Xixian, *Henan, China* 184 L6
Xizhong Dao, *Liaoning, China* 184 D11
Xizhou, *Shan., Shanxi, China* 184 E5
Xızı, *Azerb.* 171 C22
Xocavənd see Martuni, *Azerb.* 171 E21
Xorkol, *China* 182 G6
Xuan'en, *Hubei, China* 185 N1
Xuanhua, *Hebei, China* 184 C6
Xuanwei, *China* 182 M10
Xuanzhou, *Anhui, China* 185 N9
Xuchang, *Henan, China* 184 J5
Xudat, *Azerb.* 171 C22
Xuddur, *Somalia* 203 H16
Xudun, *Somalia* 203 G17
Xun, river, *Guangxi Zhuang, China* 185 V2
Xun, river, *Shaanxi, China* 184 K1
Xunke, *China* 183 B16
Xunwu, *Jiangxi, China* 185 U7
Xunyang, *Shaanxi, China* 184 K1
Xupu, *Hunan, China* 185 Q2
Xuwen, *Guang., China* 185 Y1
Xuyi, *Jiangsu, China* 184 K9
Xuzhou, *Jiangsu, China* 184 J8
Xylaganí, *Gr.* 157 B15
Xylofagou, *Cyprus* 162 P10
Xylókastro, *Gr.* 156 J10

Y

Yaak, *Mont., U.S.* 108 A4
Ya'an, *China* 182 L9
Yabbenohr, island, *Marshall Is., U.S.* 220 L2
Yablonovyy Khrebet, *Russ.* 161 L17
Yablonovyy Range, *Asia* 168 E10
Yabrūd, *Syr.* 172 H8
Yabucoa, *P.R., U.S.* 122 N5
Yacata, island, *Fiji* 222 H8
Yachats, *Oreg., U.S.* 110 G2
Yacimiento Río Turbio, *Arg.* 135 W7
Yacuiba, *Bol.* 132 L8
Yacyretá Dam, *Arg., Parag.* 132 N10
Yadgir, *India* 180 M5
Yadkin, river, *N.C., U.S.* 98 G9
Yadong, *China* 182 M5
Yadua, island, *Fiji* 222 G6
Yafi, *Indonesia* 193 K21
Yagasa, island, *Fiji* 222 K9
Yağca, *Turk.* 170 H5
Yaghan Basin, *Atl. Oc.* 241 W5
Yaguajay, *Cuba* 118 H9
Yahyalı, *Turk.* 170 G10
Yaita, *Japan* 189 N12
Yakacık, *Turk.* 170 J11
Yakapınar, *Turk.* 170 J10
Yakeshi, *China* 183 C14
Yakima, *Wash., U.S.* 110 D6
Yakima, river, *Wash., U.S.* 110 D5
Yakishiri Jima, *Japan* 188 F13
Yakmach, *Pak.* 179 S3
Yakoma, *Dem. Rep. of the Congo* 202 H10
Yakossi, *Cen. Af. Rep.* 202 H10
Yaksha, *Russ.* 160 G9
Yaku, island, *Asia* 168 G13
Yaku Shima, *Japan* 189 U4
Yakutat, *Alas., U.S.* 113 K20
Yakutat Bay, *Alas., U.S.* 113 K20
Yakutsk, *Russ.* 161 G18
Yala, *Sri Lanka* 181 T8
Yala, *Thai.* 191 S9
Yalata, *S. Aust., Austral.* 215 W8
Yale, *Mich., U.S.* 100 L13
Yale, *Okla., U.S.* 104 F12
Yalewa Kalou (Round Island), *Fiji* 222 G6
Yalgoo, *W. Aust., Austral.* 215 V3
Yallahs, *Jam.* 122 K10
Yallock, *N.S.W., Austral.* 215 X12
Yalobusha, river, *Miss., U.S.* 102 J11
Yalong, river, *China* 182 L9
Yalova, *Turk.* 170 D5
Yalta, *Ukr.* 159 T7
Yalu, river, *China, N. Korea* 186 G4
Yalvaç, *Turk.* 170 G6
Yamagata, *Japan* 188 L12
Yamaguchi, *Japan* 189 Q5
Yamal, Poluostrov, *Russ.* 160 F11
Yamal Peninsula, *Asia* 168 C8
Yamas, *Indonesia* 193 K21
Yamato Glacier, *Antarctica* 231 C16
Yamato Mountains see Queen Fabiola Mountains, *Antarctica* 231 C17
Yambio, *S. Sudan* 202 H11
Yambol, *Bulg.* 155 J16
Yamdena, island, *Indonesia* 193 M17
Yamethinn, *Myanmar* 190 H6
Yamm, *Russ.* 158 G5
Yammaw, *Myanmar* 190 E7
Yamma Yamma, Lake, *Austral.* 214 G11
Yamoussoukro, *Côte d'Ivoire* 204 D8
Yampa, river, *Colo., U.S.* 108 L10
Yan, river, *Shaanxi, China* 184 G2
Yana, river, *Russ.* 161 F17
Yana, Gulf of, *Arctic Oc.* 246 D8
Yanagawa, *Japan* 189 R4
Yan'an, *Shaanxi, China* 184 G2
Yana Valley, *Arctic Oc.* 246 E9
Yanbu' al Baḥr, *Saudi Arabia* 174 J6
Yancheng, *Jiangsu, China* 184 K11
Yanchuan, *Shaanxi, China* 184 F2
Yandal, *W. Aust., Austral.* 215 V4
Yandé, Île, *New Caledonia, Fr.* 222 B6
Yandeearra, *W. Aust., Austral.* 215 S3
Yandina, *Solomon Is.* 221 N18

Yandoon, *Myanmar* 190 K6
Yandu, *Jiangsu, China* 184 K10
Yangcheng, *Shanxi, China* 184 H4
Yangchun, *Guang., China* 185 W3
Yangdŏk, *N. Korea* 186 J7
Yanggang, *N. Korea* 186 E7
Yanggao, *Shanxi, China* 184 C5
Yanggu, *S. Korea* 186 L10
Yanggu, *Shand., China* 184 G7
Yanghŭng, *N. Korea* 186 E11
Yanghwa-man, bay, *N. Korea* 186 G10
Yangī Qal'ah, *Afghan.* 178 J8
Yangī Qal'ah, *Afghan.* 178 L4
Yangjiang, *Guang., China* 185 X3
Yangju, *S. Korea* 186 M8
Yangmei, *Taiwan, China* 185 U12
Yangming Shan, *Hunan, China* 185 S3
Yangmingshan, *Taiwan, China* 185 T12
Yangon (Rangoon), *Myanmar* 190 K6
Yangpo, *S. Korea* 187 R12
Yangquan, *Shanxi, China* 184 E4
Yangquan, *Shanxi, China* 184 E5
Yangsan, *S. Korea* 187 S12
Yangshan, *Guang., China* 185 U4
Yangshuo, *Guangxi Zhuang, China* 185 U2
Yangtze see Chang Jiang, Jinsha, river, *China* 182 M10
Yangtze Gorges, *Chongq., China* 184 M1
Yangtze, Mouth of the, *Shanghai Shi, China* 184 M12
Yangxin, *Hubei, China* 185 P6
Yangxin, *Shand., China* 184 F8
Yangyang, *S. Korea* 186 L11
Yangyuan, *Hebei, China* 184 C6
Yangzhou, *Jiangsu, China* 184 L10
Yanji, *China* 183 E17
Yankeetown, *Fla., U.S.* 99 S7
Yankton, *S. Dak., U.S.* 106 M7
Yanliang, *Shaanxi, China* 184 J1
Yanling, *Hunan, China* 185 S5
Yano-Indigirskaya Nizmennost', *Russ.* 161 E17
Yano-Oymyakonskoye Nagor'ye, *Russ.* 161 F18
Yanqi, *China* 182 F5
Yanrey, *W. Aust., Austral.* 215 T1
Yan Shan, *Hebei, China* 184 C9
Yanshan, *Jiangxi, China* 185 Q8
Yanskiy, *Russ.* 161 F17
Yanskiy Zaliv, *Russ.* 161 E17
Yantabulla, *N.S.W., Austral.* 215 V13
Yantai, *Shand., China* 184 F11
Yantra, river, *Bulg.* 155 H15
Yanuca, island, *Fiji* 222 G8
Yanuca, island, *Fiji* 222 J6
Yanzhou, *Shand., China* 184 H8
Yao, *Japan* 189 Q9
Yaoundé, *Cameroon* 205 F16
Yap, island, *F.S.M.* 221 C18
Yapen, island, *Indonesia* 193 K19
Yapen, Selat, *Indonesia* 193 K19
Yapero, *Indonesia* 193 L20
Yap Islands, *F.S.M.* 220 P2
Yap Trench, *Pac. Oc.* 242 J7
Yaqaga, island, *Fiji* 222 G6
Yaqeta, island, *Fiji* 222 H5
Yaqui, river, *Mex.* 116 D7
Yaquina Head, *Oreg., U.S.* 110 G2
Yara, *Cuba* 118 K12
Yaraka, *Qnsld., Austral.* 215 U12
Yaralıgöz, peak, *Turk.* 170 C9
Yaransk, *Russ.* 158 G14
Yardımcı Burnu, *Turk.* 170 J5
Yardımlı, *Azerb.* 171 F22
Yaren, *Nauru* 221 F23
Yarí, river, *Col.* 130 H6
Yarīm, *Yemen* 174 Q9
Yarkant see Shache, *China* 182 F2
Yarkant, river, *China* 182 F2
Yarle Lakes, *Austral.* 214 J8
Yarlung Zangbo (Brahmaputra), river, *China* 182 L6
Yarma, *Turk.* 170 G8
Yarmouth, *N.S., Can.* 85 Q21
Yaroslavl', *Russ.* 158 H10
Yaroua, island, *Fiji* 222 H9
Yarozero, *Russ.* 158 E10
Yarraden, *Qnsld., Austral.* 215 Q12

Yarraloola, *W. Aust., Austral.* **215** T2
Yarrowmere, *Qnsld., Austral.* **215** S13
Yartsevo, *Russ.* **158** K7
Yartsevo, *Russ.* **161** JI3
Yarumal, *Col.* **130** E4
Yasawa, island, *Fiji* **222** G5
Yasawa Group, *Fiji* **222** H5
Yashkul', *Russ.* **159** R14
Yasin, *Pak.* **178** KII
Yāsīnzaī Kêlay, *Afghan.* **179** Q4
Yasothon, *Thai.* **190** LII
Yasun Burnu, *Turk.* **170** DI2
Yasur Volcano, *Vanuatu* **222** H4
Yata, river, *Bol.* **132** G7
Yatağan, *Turk.* **170** H3
Yatakala, *Niger* **200** H9
Yaté, *New Caledonia, Fr.* **222** D9
Yatenga, region, *Af.* **198** G3
Yates Center, *Kans., U.S.* **107** U9
Yathkyed Lake, *Nunavut, Can.* **85** JI4
Yato, *Cook Is., N.Z.* **222** Q2
Yatsushiro, *Japan* **189** S4
Yauca, *Peru* **132** J4
Yauco, *P.R., U.S.* **122** N2
Yaupi, *Ecua.* **130** K3
Yavarí *see* Javari, river, *S. Amer.* **132** F4
Yavatmal, *India* **180** K6
Yaviza, *Pan.* **117** N22
Yawatahama, *Japan* **189** R6
Yawri Bay, *Sierra Leone* **204** D5
Yaylâdağı, *Turk.* **170** KII
Yaynangyoung, *Myanmar* **190** H5
Yazd, *Iran* **175** EI4
Yazdān, *Iran* **175** DI7
Yazılıkaya, *Turk.* **170** F6
Yazlıca Dağı, peak, *Turk.* **171** HI7
Yazman, *Pak.* **179** SIO
Yazoo, river, *Miss., U.S.* **102** KIO
Yazoo City, *Miss., U.S.* **102** KII
Ýdra, *Gr.* **156** KI2
Ýdra (Hydra), island, *Gr.* **156** KI2
Ye, *Myanmar* **190** L7
Yebyu, *Myanmar* **190** M7
Yecheng (Kargilik), *China* **182** F2
Yecheon, *S. Korea* **187** PII
Yecla, *Sp.* **147** JI4
Yeeda, *W. Aust., Austral.* **215** R5
Yefremov, *Russ.* **158** L9
Yegua Creek, *Tex., U.S.* **105** QII
Yeguas, Punta, *P.R., U.S.* **122** N5
Yei, *S. Sudan* **202** HI2
Yekaterinburg, *Russ.* **160** H9
Yekateriny, Proliv, *Russ.* **161** K23
Yelabuga, *Russ.* **158** HI6
Yela Island, *P.N.G.* **221** QI3
Yelan', *Russ.* **159** NI2
Yelan Kolenovskiy, *Russ.* **159** NII
Yelets, *Russ.* **158** MIO
Yélimané, *Mali* **200** H6
Yelizavety, Mys, *Russ.* **161** H2I
Yell, island, *Scot., U.K.* **144** DI2
Yellandu, *India* **180** M7
Yellow *see* Huang, river, *N. Mongol, China* **184** C3
Yellow, river, *Ala., Fla., U.S.* **99** Q2
Yellow, Mouth of the *see* Huang, Mouth of the (Yellow), *Shand., China* **184** E9
Yellowknife, *N.W.T., Can.* **84** HII
Yellow Sea, *Pac. Oc.* **168** GI2
Yellowstone, river, *Mont., Wyo., U.S.* **108** DII
Yellowstone Lake, *Wyo., U.S.* **108** F8
Yellowstone National Park, *Idaho, Mont., Wyo., U.S.* **108** F8
Yell Sound, *Scot., U.K.* **144** DI2
Yellville, *Ark., U.S.* **102** E8
Yelm, *Wash., U.S.* **110** D3
Yel'sk, *Belarus* **158** M5
Yelwa, *Nigeria* **205** CI3
Yemanzhelinsk, *Russ.* **160** J8
Yemassee, *S.C., U.S.* **98** M9
Yemen, *Asia* **174** P9
Yenakiyeve, *Ukr.* **159** QIO
Yên Bái, *Vietnam* **190** GII
Yendi, *Ghana* **204** CII
Yengisar, *China* **182** F2
Yeniçağa, *Turk.* **170** D7
Yenice, *Turk.* **170** F8
Yenice, river, *Turk.* **170** GII

Yeniceoba, *Turk.* **170** F8
Yenierenköy *see* Yialousa, *Cyprus* **162** MII
Yenişehir, *Turk.* **170** D5
Yenisey, river, *Asia* **168** D8
Yenisey Gulf, *Arctic Oc.* **168** C8
Yeniseysk, *Russ.* **161** KI3
Yeniseyskiy Zaliv, *Russ.* **161** FI3
Yên Minh, *Vietnam* **190** FII
Yenyuka, *Russ.* **161** JI7
Yeola, *India* **180** K4
Yeoncheon, *S. Korea* **186** L8
Yeondo, island, *S. Korea* **187** U9
Yeongam, *S. Korea* **187** T7
Yeongcheon, *S. Korea* **187** RII
Yeongchun, *S. Korea* **187** U7
Yeongdeok, *S. Korea* **187** QI2
Yeongdong, *S. Korea* **187** Q9
Yeonggwang, *S. Korea* **187** S7
Yeongheungdo, island, *S. Korea* **187** N7
Yeongjongdo, island, *S. Korea* **187** N7
Yeongju, *S. Korea* **187** PII
Yeongwol, *S. Korea* **187** NII
Yeongyang, *S. Korea* **187** PI2
Yeonil, *S. Korea* **187** RI2
Yeonpyeong *see* Daeyeonpyeongdo, island, *S. Korea* **186** M6
Yeoryang, *S. Korea* **187** NII
Yeosan, *S. Korea* **187** R8
Yeoseodo, island, *S. Korea* **187** V8
Yeosu, *S. Korea* **187** T9
Yeovil, *Eng., U.K.* **145** WII
Yeppoon, *Qnsld., Austral.* **215** TI5
Yerbogachen, *Russ.* **161** JI5
Yerema, *Russ.* **161** JI5
Yerevan, *Arm.* **171** EI8
Yergeni Hills, *Eur.* **140** GI4
Yerington, *Nev., U.S.* **111** Q7
Yerköy, *Turk.* **170** E9
Yermak Plateau, *Arctic Oc.* **247** HI5
Yermo, *Calif., U.S.* **111** WIO
Yeroḥam, *Israel* **173** P5
Yershov, *Russ.* **158** MI5
Yeşilhisar, *Turk.* **170** GIO
Yeşilırmak, river, *Turk.* **170** DII
Yeşilkent, *Turk.* **170** JII
Yeşilova, *Turk.* **170** H5
Yesŏng, river, *N. Korea* **186** L7
Yessentuki, *Russ.* **159** TI2
Yessey, *Russ.* **161** GI4
Yetti, region, *Af.* **198** E3
Ye-u, *Myanmar* **190** G6
Yeu, Île d', *Fr.* **149** S5
Yevlax, *Azerb.* **171** D2I
Yevpatoriya, *Ukr.* **159** S7
Yexian, *Henan, China* **184** K5
Yeysk, *Russ.* **159** RIO
Ygatimí, *Parag.* **132** MII
Yí, river, *Uru.* **134** KI4
Yialias, river, *Cyprus* **162** P8
Yialousa (Yenierenköy), *Cyprus* **162** MII
Yibin, *China* **182** LIO
Yichang, *Hubei, China* **185** N3
Yicheng, *Hubei, China* **184** M4
Yichuan, *Henan, China* **184** J4
Yichun, *China* **183** CI6
Yichun, *Jiangxi, China* **185** R5
Yifeng, *Jiangxi, China* **185** Q6
Yigo, *Guam, U.S.* **220** BII
Yilan, *China* **183** CI7
Yıldız Dağları, peak, *Turk.* **170** B4
Yıldızeli, *Turk.* **170** EII
Yinan, *Shand., China* **184** H9
Yinchuan, *China* **182** HIO
Yindarlgooda, Lake, *Austral.* **214** J5
Yindi, *W. Aust., Austral.* **215** W5
Yingcheng, *Hubei, China* **185** N5
Yingde, *Guang., China* **185** U4
Yingkou, *Liaoning, China* **184** CI2
Yingshan, *Hubei, China* **185** N7
Yingshang, *Anhui, China* **184** L7
Yingtan, *Jiangxi, China* **185** Q8
Yingxian, *Shanxi, China* **184** D5
Yining (Gulja), *China* **182** D4
Yinnietharra, *W. Aust., Austral.* **215** U2
Yin Shan, *China* **182** FII

Yinshan *see* Guanyun, *Jiangsu, China* **184** JIO
Yirga 'Alem, *Eth.* **203** HI5
Yirol, *S. Sudan* **202** HI2
Yishui, *Shand., China* **184** H9
Yiwu, *China* **182** E7
Yiwu, *Zhejiang, China* **185** PII
Yixian, *Hebei, China* **184** D7
Yixian, *Liaoning, China* **184** BII
Yixing, *Jiangsu, China* **184** MIO
Yiyang, *Henan, China* **184** J4
Yiyang, *Hunan, China* **185** Q4
Yiyuan (Nanma), *Shand., China* **184** G9
Yizhang, *Hunan, China* **185** T4
Yizheng, *Jiangsu, China* **184** LIO
Ylig Bay, *Guam, U.S.* **220** CII
Ylivieska, *Fin.* **143** FI5
Yn Cholloo *see* Calf of Man, cape, *Isle of Man, U.K.* **145** R8
Yoakum, *Tex., U.S.* **105** RII
Yobe, river, *Af.* **198** G6
Yocona, river, *Miss., U.S.* **102** HII
Yogyakarta, *Indonesia* **192** M9
Yoichi, *Japan* **188** GI2
Yokadouma, *Cameroon* **205** FI7
Yokjido, island, *S. Korea* **187** UIO
Yokkaichi, *Japan* **189** Q9
Yoko, *Cameroon* **205** EI6
Yokoate Shima, *Japan* **189** V3
Yokohama, *Japan* **188** JI3
Yokohama, *Japan* **189** PI2
Yokote, *Japan* **188** KI2
Yŏkp'o, *N. Korea* **186** J6
Yola, *Nigeria* **205** DI6
Yolöten, *Uzb.* **176** MIO
Yom, river, *Thai.* **190** K8
Yŏmju, *N. Korea* **186** G4
Yomra, *Turk.* **171** DI4
Yŏmsŏng, *N. Korea* **186** GII
Yŏmsŏng, *N. Korea* **186** KIO
Yona, *Guam, U.S.* **220** CII
Yonago, *Japan* **189** P7
Yŏnan, *N. Korea* **186** M7
Yonezawa, *Japan* **188** MI2
Yongam, *N. Korea* **186** H7
Yongamp'o, *N. Korea* **186** G4
Yong'an, *Fujian, China* **185** T8
Yongban, *N. Korea* **186** DI2
Yongban, *N. Korea* **186** EI2
Yŏngbyŏn, *N. Korea* **186** H6
Yongcheng, *Henan, China* **184** K7
Yongch'ŏn, *N. Korea* **186** G4
Yongchun, *Fujian, China* **185** T9
Yongdang, *S. Korea* **187** T7
Yongdeng, *China* **182** HIO
Yongdian, *Liaoning, China* **184** CI4
Yongding, *Fujian, China* **185** U8
Yongdu, *S. Korea* **186** M9
Yongfu, *Guangxi Zhuang, China* **185** TI
Yonggang, *N. Korea* **186** K5
Yŏnggwang, *N. Korea* **186** G9
Yonggyap Pass, *India* **180** EI5
Yŏngha, *N. Korea* **186** EII
Yonghan, *S. Korea* **187** QI2
Yonghe, *Shanxi, China* **184** F3
Yŏnghŭng-man (Kŭmya-man), bay, *N. Korea* **186** J9
Yongin, *S. Korea* **187** N8
Yongjam, *N. Korea* **186** FII
Yongji, *Shanxi, China* **184** H2
Yŏngjŏ, *N. Korea* **186** D8
Yongkang, *Zhejiang, China* **185** QII
Yongle *see* Zhen'an, *Shaanxi, China* **184** KI
Yongmunsan, peak, *S. Korea* **186** M9
Yongnian, *Hebei, China* **184** G6
Yongnim, *N. Korea* **186** F8
Yongning, *Beijing Shi, China* **184** C7
Yongp'o, *N. Korea* **186** H5
Yongp'o, *N. Korea* **186** J8
Yongp'ung, *N. Korea* **186** G5
Yongsan, *S. Korea* **187** NIO
Yongshun, *Hunan, China* **185** PI
Yongsŏng, *N. Korea* **186** J5
Yŏngwŏn, *N. Korea* **186** H7
Yongxin, *Jiangxi, China* **185** S5
Yongxing, *Hunan, China* **185** S4
Yongxiu, *Jiangxi, China* **185** Q7

Yongyŏn, *N. Korea* **186** L4
Yongzhou, *Hunan, China* **185** S3
Yonkers, *N.Y., U.S.* **96** NII
Yonne, river, *Fr.* **149** RII
Yŏnp'o, *N. Korea* **186** H9
Yŏnsa, *N. Korea* **186** CII
Yŏnsan, *N. Korea* **186** K7
Yopal, *Col.* **130** E6
Yopurga, *China* **182** F2
York, *Ala., U.S.* **103** LI3
York, *Eng., U.K.* **145** RI3
York, *Nebr., U.S.* **107** Q7
York, *Pa., U.S.* **96** P7
York, *S.C., U.S.* **98** J9
York, *W. Aust., Austral.* **215** X3
York, Cape, *Austral.* **214** AI2
York, Cape, *Greenland, Den.* **82** C7
Yorke Peninsula, *Austral.* **214** KIO
York Sound, *Austral.* **214** C5
Yorkton, *Sask., Can.* **84** NI2
Yorktown, *Tex., U.S.* **105** SII
Yorktown, *Va., U.S.* **98** FI4
Yoron Jima, *Japan* **189** X2
Yoro Shima, *Japan* **189** W3
Yortan Tepe, ruins, *Turk.* **170** F3
Yosemite National Park, *Calif., U.S.* **111** S6
Yoshkar Ola, *Russ.* **158** HI4
Yos Sudarso *see* Dolak, island, *Indonesia* **193** M2O
Yotvata, *Israel* **173** R5
You, river, *China* **182** PII
Youghal (Eochaill), *Ire.* **145** U5
Youghal Bay, *Ire.* **145** U5
Young, *N.S.W., Austral.* **215** XI4
Young Island, *Bahamas* **122** E7
Young's Rock, *Pitcairn I., U.K.* **223** Q23
Youngstown, *Ohio, U.S.* **101** PI5
Youth, Isle of *see* Juventud, Isla de la, *Cuba* **118** J4
Youxian, *Hunan, China* **185** S4
Youyu, *Shanxi, China* **184** C4
Yovan, *Taj.* **178** J8
Yovkovo, *Bulg.* **155** GI7
Yovo, island, *P.N.G.* **221** HI4
Yozgat, *Turk.* **170** EIO
Ypáti, *Gr.* **156** GIO
Ypé Jhú, *Parag.* **132** MII
Ypres *see* Ieper, *Belg.* **148** LIO
Ypsilanti, *Mich., U.S.* **100** MI2
Ypsilí *see* Strongylí, island, *Gr.* **157** N22
Yreka, *Calif., U.S.* **110** L3
Yrghyz, *Kaz.* **176** EIO
Yrghyz, river, *Kaz.* **176** E9
Ysabel Channel, *P.N.G.* **217** B2O
Ysyk, Lake, *Asia* **168** G8
Ysyk-Köl, *Kyrg.* **178** EI2
Ysyk-Köl *see* Balykchy, *Kyrg.* **178** EI2
Ytterån, *Sw.* **142** GI2
Ytyk Kyuyel', *Russ.* **161** GI8
Yu, river, *Guangxi Zhuang, China* **185** VI
Yuan (Red), river, *China* **182** N9
Yuan, river, *Hunan, China* **185** Q2
Yuan, river, *Jiangxi, China* **185** R6
Yuanbaoshan, *N. Mongol, China* **184** AIO
Yuanjiang, *Hunan, China* **185** Q4
Yuanli, *Taiwan, China* **185** UII
Yüanlin, *Taiwan, China* **185** VII
Yuanling, *Hunan, China* **185** Q2
Yuanping, *Shanxi, China* **184** E5
Yuanqu, *Shanxi, China* **184** H4
Yuba, river, *Calif., U.S.* **111** Q4
Yuba City, *Calif., U.S.* **111** Q4
Yūbari, *Japan* **188** GI3
Yuben', *Taj.* **178** KIO
Yūbetsu, *Japan* **188** FI4
Yucatán Basin, *Atl. Oc.* **240** M2
Yucatán Channel, *N. Amer.* **82** N7
Yucatán Peninsula, *N. Amer.* **117** HI6
Yucca, *Ariz., U.S.* **109** S5
Yucca Flat, *Nev., U.S.* **111** TII
Yucca Valley, *Calif., U.S.* **111** XIO
Yucheng, *Shand., China* **184** G8
Yuci, *Shanxi, China* **184** F5
Yudino, *Russ.* **158** JI4
Yudu, *Jiangxi, China* **185** T6
Yuendumu, *N.T., Austral.* **215** S8

Yueqing, *Zhejiang, China* **185** QII
Yuexi, *China* **182** L9
Yueyang, *Hunan, China* **185** P4
Yugan, *Jiangxi, China* **185** Q8
Yugê, *China* **182** J7
Yugorenok, *Russ.* **161** GI9
Yugorskiy Poluostrov, *Russ.* **160** FII
Yuhuan Dao, *Zhejiang, China* **185** QI2
Yujing Feng, *Jiangxi, China* **185** Q9
Yukagir, *Russ.* **161** EI7
Yukagirskoye Ploskogor'ye, *Russ.* **161** DI9
Yukon, *Can.* **84** F8
Yukon, *Okla., U.S.* **104** GIO
Yukon, river, *N. Amer.* **82** C3
Yukon-Charley Rivers National Preserve, *Alas., U.S.* **113** FI8
Yukon Delta, *Alas., U.S.* **112** GI2
Yukon Plateau, *N. Amer.* **82** D3
Yüksekova, *Turk.* **171** HI8
Yulara, *N.T., Austral.* **215** U8
Yuleba, *Qnsld., Austral.* **215** VI4
Yuli, *China* **182** F5
Yüli, *Taiwan, China* **185** VI2
Yulin, *Guangxi Zhuang, China* **185** WI
Yulin, *Shaanxi, China* **184** E2
Yulin, river, *Shaanxi, China* **184** E2
Yuma, *Ariz., U.S.* **109** U4
Yuma, *Colo., U.S.* **108** LI5
Yumbi, *Dem. Rep. of the Congo* **202** K8
Yumen, *China* **182** G8
Yumrukaya Burnu, *Turk.* **170** BIO
Yumurtalık, *Turk.* **170** JIO
Yunan, *Guang., China* **185** V3
Yunaska Island, *Alas., U.S.* **112** P8
Yuncheng, *Shand., China* **184** H7
Yuncheng, *Shanxi, China* **184** H3
Yungas, region, *S. Amer.* **128** G5
Yunkai Dashan, *Guangxi Zhuang, China* **185** WI
Yunta, *S. Aust., Austral.* **215** XII
Yuntai, *Jiangsu, China* **184** JIO
Yunxi, *Hubei, China* **184** K2
Yunxian, *Hubei, China* **184** K3
Yunxiao, *Fujian, China* **185** V8
Yunzhong Shan, *Shanxi, China* **184** E4
Yuoxi, *Fujian, China* **185** S9
Yupanqui Basin, *Pac. Oc.* **243** MI9
Yup'yŏng, *N. Korea* **186** CII
Yuribey, *Russ.* **160** FI2
Yurihonjō, *Japan* **188** KI2
Yurimaguas, *Peru* **132** F3
Yur'yevets, *Russ.* **158** HI2
Yur'yev Pol'skiy, *Russ.* **158** HIO
Yushan, *Jiangxi, China* **185** Q9
Yushan, peak, *Taiwan, China* **185** VI2
Yushe, *Shanxi, China* **184** F5
Yushu, *China* **183** DI6
Yushu (Gyêgu), *China* **182** K7
Yuste, Monasterio de, *Sp.* **146** G8
Yusufeli, *Turk.* **171** DI6
Yutai, *Shand., China* **184** H8
Yutian, *Hebei, China* **184** D9
Yutian (Keriya), *China* **182** G3
Yuyao, *Zhejiang, China* **185** NI2
Yuzawa, *Japan* **188** LI2
Yuzha, *Russ.* **158** HII
Yuzhno Sakhalinsk, *Russ.* **161** K22
Yuzhnyy, *Kaz.* **176** CIO
Yuzhnyy, *Russ.* **159** SI4
Yuzhnyy, Mys, *Russ.* **161** F2I
Yverdon, *Switz.* **152** BI
Yvetot, *Fr.* **149** N8

Z

Za, river, *China* **182** K7
Zaanstad, *Neth.* **148** HI2
Zabaykal'sk, *Russ.* **161** LI7
Żabbar, *Malta* **163** K23
Zabīd, *Yemen* **174** Q8
Zābol, *Iran* **175** EI7
Zābolī, *Iran* **175** HI8
Zabrze, *Pol.* **151** GI4
Zacapa, *Guatemala* **117** LI6
Zacatecas, *Mex.* **116** GIO
Zácharo, *Gr.* **156** K9

Zadar (Zara), *Croatia* **154** G5
Zadoi, *China* **182** K7
Zafóra, island, *Gr.* **157** N17
Zafra, *Sp.* **146** J7
Żagań, *Pol.* **150** F12
Zagora, *Mor.* **200** C8
Zagorá, *Gr.* **156** F11
Zagória, range, *Gr.* **156** E7
Zagreb, *Croatia* **154** D6
Zagros Mountains *see* Kūhhā-Ye
 Zāgros, *Iran* **174** D11
Zāhedān, *Iran* **175** F17
Zahirabad, *India* **180** M6
Zaḥlé, *Leb.* **172** J7
Z̧ahrān, *Saudi Arabia* **174** N9
Zaječar, *Serb.* **154** G12
Zakamensk, *Russ.* **161** M15
Zakhodnyaya, river, *Belarus* **158** J6
Zākhū, *Iraq* **174** B9
Zakopane, *Pol.* **151** H15
Zákros, *Gr.* **157** Q17
Zákynthos, *Gr.* **156** J7
Zákynthos (Zante), island, *Gr.* **156** J7
Zalaegerszeg, *Hung.* **151** M13
Zalantun, *China* **183** C15
Zalău, *Rom.* **155** C13
Zalewo, *Pol.* **151** B15
Zalew Szczeciński *see* Stettiner Haff,
 Ger., Pol. **150** C11
Z̧alim, *Saudi Arabia* **174** K8
Zamakh, *Yemen* **174** P11
Zambeze *see* Zambezi, river, *Af.*
 207 F13
Zambezi, *Zambia* **206** D9
Zambezi, river, *Af.* **198** M7
Zambezi Canyon, *Ind. Oc.* **224** K5
Zambezi River Delta, *Af.* **198** N10
Zambia, *Af.* **206** E11
Zamboanga City, *Philippines* **193** F14
Zambrów, *Pol.* **151** C17
Zamīndāwar, region, *Afghan.* **179** P3
Zamora, *Ecua.* **130** L3
Zamora, *Sp.* **146** D8
Zamość, *Pol.* **151** F18
Zanaga, *Congo* **205** M4
Zanderij, *Suriname* **131** E16
Zanesville, *Ohio, U.S.* **101** R14
Zangla, *India* **179** N14
Zanguinasso, *Côte d'Ivoire* **204** C8
Zanhuang, *Hebei, China* **184** F6
Zanjān, *Iran* **174** C11
Zante *see* Zákynthos, island, *Gr.*
 156 J7
Zanthus, *W. Aust., Austral.* **215** W5
Zanzibar, *Tanzania* **203** M15
Zanzibar Island, *Tanzania* **203** M15
Zaouatallaz, *Alg.* **200** E12
Zaoyang, *Hubei, China* **184** L4
Zaozhuang, *Shand., China* **184** J8
Zapadna Morava, river, *Serb.*
 154 G10
Zapadnaya Dvina, *Russ.* **158** J7
Zapadno Sibirskaya Ravnina, *Russ.*
 160 H11
Zapala, *Arg.* **135** P7
Zapata, *Tex., U.S.* **105** V8
Zapata, Península de, *Cuba* **118** H7
Zapiga, *Chile* **134** C7
Zapiola Ridge, *Atl. Oc.* **241** U7
Zaporizhzhya, *Ukr.* **159** Q8
Zaqatala, *Azerb.* **171** C20
Zara, *Turk.* **170** E12
Zara *see* Zadar, *Croatia* **154** G5
Zarafshon, *Uzb.* **176** K11
Zarafshon Range, *Taj.* **178** H7
Zaragoza, *Sp.* **147** D14
Zarand, *Iran* **175** F15
Zaranj, *Afghan.* **179** Q2
Zarautz, *Sp.* **146** B12
Zaraysk, *Russ.* **158** K10
Zaraza, *Venez.* **130** C10
Zard, Kūh-e, *Iran* **174** E12
Zaria, *Nigeria* **205** C14
Zárkos, *Gr.* **156** E10
Zărneşti, *Rom.* **155** E15
Zaruma, *Ecua.* **130** L2
Żary, *Pol.* **150** E11
Zaskar Mountains, *India* **180** C6
Zatish'ye, *Russ.* **161** D20
Zatobyl, *Kaz.* **176** B11
Zatoka, *Ukr.* **159** S5

Zavolzhsk, *Russ.* **158** H11
Zawiercie, *Pol.* **151** G15
Zāwiyat Masūs, *Lib.* **201** C16
Zawr, Ra's az, *Saudi Arabia* **174** H12
Zayaki Jangal, *Pak.* **179** T5
Zaybāk, *Afghan.* **178** K9
Zaysan, *Kaz.* **177** E19
Zaysan, Lake, *Asia* **168** F8
Zaysan Köli, *Kaz.* **177** E19
Zayü (Chayu), *China* **182** L7
Zdolbuniv, *Ukr.* **159** N3
Zealand, island, *Eur.* **140** F7
Żebbuġ, *Malta* **163** H20
Żebbuġ, *Malta* **163** K22
Zeča, island, *Croatia* **154** E4
Zednes, peak, *Mauritania* **200** E6
Zeehaen Fracture Zone, *Ind. Oc.*
 225 R17
Zeeland, *Mich., U.S.* **100** M9
Zeewolde, *Neth.* **148** J13
Zeewolf Fracture Zone, *Ind. Oc.*
 224 N11
Zeewyk Ridge, *Ind. Oc.* **225** L15
Zefat, *Israel* **172** K6
Zeil, Mount, *Austral.* **214** F8
Zeist, *Neth.* **148** J12
Żejtun, *Malta* **163** L23
Zelee, Cape, *Solomon Is.* **221** P20
Zélée Bank, *Ind. Oc.* **224** J6
Zelenchukskaya, *Russ.* **159** T12
Zelenodol'sk, *Russ.* **158** J14
Zelenoe, *Kaz.* **176** E6
Zelenogorsk, *Russ.* **158** E6
Zelenogradsk, *Russ.* **158** J1
Zelenokumsk, *Russ.* **159** T13
Železná Ruda, *Czech Rep.* **150** J10
Železnik, *Serb.* **154** F10
Zelzate, *Belg.* **148** K11
Zemetchino, *Russ.* **158** L12
Zemio, *Cen. Af. Rep.* **202** H11
Zemongo, *Cen. Af. Rep.* **202** G10
Zencirli, site, *Turk.* **170** H11
Zengcheng, *Guang., China* **185** V5
Zenica, *Bosn. & Herzg.* **154** G8
Zeni Su, island, *Japan* **189** R11
Zenith Plateau, *Ind. Oc.* **225** K16
Zenkevich Rise (Hokkaido Rise),
 Pac. Oc. **242** E8
Zenobia, ruins, *Syr.* **172** E12
Žepče, *Bosn. & Herzg.* **154** F8
Zerah, Gowd-e, *Afghan.* **179** R2
Zerf, *Ger.* **162** K12
Zermatt, *Switz.* **152** C3
Zernez, *Switz.* **152** B5
Zernograd, *Russ.* **159** R11
Zestap'oni, *Rep. of Georgia* **171** B17
Zetland *see* Shetland Islands, *Scot.,*
 U.K. **144** C12
Zeya, *Russ.* **161** K19
Zgharta, *Leb.* **172** H7
Zgierz, *Pol.* **151** E15
Zgorzelec, *Pol.* **150** F11
Zhadong *see* Zhadün, *China* **182** K3
Zhadün (Zhadong), *China* **182** K3
Zhalpaqtal, *Kaz.* **176** D5
Zhaltyr, *Kaz.* **177** C13
Zhamog (Zhamu), *China* **182** L7
Zhamu *see* Zhamog, *China* **182** L7
Zhanatal, *Kaz.* **176** G10
Zhang, river, *Henan, China* **184** G5
Zhangaly, *Kaz.* **176** F5
Zhangaözen, *Kaz.* **176** H6
Zhanga Qazan, *Kaz.* **176** D5
Zhangaqorghan, *Kaz.* **176** H12
Zhangatas, *Kaz.* **177** H13
Zhangbei, *Hebei, China* **184** B6
Zhangjiajie, *Hunan, China* **185** P2
Zhangjiakou, *Hebei, China* **184** B6
Zhangjiapan *see* Jingbian, *Shaanxi,*
 China **184** F1
Zhangping, *Fujian, China* **185** T8
Zhangpu, *Fujian, China* **185** V8
Zhangqiu, *Shand., China* **184** G8
Zhangshu (Qingjiang), *Jiangxi, China*
 185 R7
Zhangwu, *Liaoning, China* **184** A12
Zhangye, *China* **182** G9
Zhangzhou, *Fujian, China* **185** U8
Zhangzi, *Shanxi, China* **184** G5
Zhanhua (Fuguo), *Shand., China*
 184 F9

Zhanjiang, *Guang., China* **185** X1
Zhanyi, *China* **182** N10
Zhao'an, *Fujian, China* **185** V8
Zhaodong, *China* **183** D16
Zhaojue, *China* **182** M9
Zhaoping, *Guangxi Zhuang, China*
 185 U2
Zhaoqing, *Guang., China* **185** V3
Zhaosu, *China* **182** E3
Zhaotong, *China* **182** M10
Zhaoxian, *Hebei, China* **184** F6
Zhaoyuan, *Shand., China* **184** F11
Zhapo, *Guang., China* **185** X3
Zhaqsy, *Kaz.* **176** C12
Zhari Namco (Zhari Nanmucuo),
 lake, *China* **182** K4
Zhari Nanmucuo *see* Zhari Namco,
 lake, *China* **182** K4
Zharkamys, *Kaz.* **176** F8
Zharkent, *Kaz.* **177** E19
Zharma, *Kaz.* **177** E17
Zharmysh, *Kaz.* **176** H6
Zhashui (Qianyou), *Shaanxi, China*
 184 K1
Zhaslyk, *Uzb.* **176** H8
Zhayrang, *Kaz.* **177** F13
Zhayylma, *Kaz.* **176** C10
Zhayyq (Ural), river, *Kaz.* **176** E6
Zhecheng, *Henan, China* **184** J6
Zhejiang, *China* **185** Q10
Zhelezīnka, *Kaz.* **177** B15
Zheleznodorozhnyy, *Russ.* **160** F9
Zheleznogorsk, *Russ.* **158** M8
Zheleznovodsk, *Russ.* **159** T12
Zhem, river, *Kaz.* **176** F8
Zhemchug Canyon, *Pac. Oc.* **242** B12
Zhemgang, *Bhutan* **180** F13
Zhen'an (Yongle), *Shaanxi, China*
 184 K1
Zhengding, *Hebei, China* **184** E6
Zhenghe, *Fujian, China* **185** R10
Zhenglan Qi, *N. Mongol, China*
 184 A7
Zhengning, *Gansu, China* **184** H1
Zhengxiangbai Qi *see* Qagan Nur,
 N. Mongol, China **184** A6
Zhengyang, *Henan, China* **184** L6
Zhengzhou (Chengchow), *Henan,*
 China **184** J4
Zhenjiang, *Jiangsu, China* **184** L10
Zhenping, *Henan, China* **184** K4
Zhenping, *Shaanxi, China* **184** L1
Zhenwudong *see* Ansai, *Shaanxi, China*
 184 F2
Zhenxiong, *China* **182** M10
Zherdevka, *Russ.* **158** M11
Zherong, *Fujian, China* **185** R10
Zhetiqara, *Kaz.* **176** C10
Zhezqazghan, *Kaz.* **176** F12
Zhicheng, *Hubei, China* **185** N2
Zhidan (Bao'an), *Shaanxi, China*
 184 F1
Zhigansk, *Russ.* **161** G17
Zhigulevsk, *Russ.* **158** K15
Zhilaya Kosa, *Kaz.* **176** F6
Zhil'gur, *Russ.* **161** H18
Zhilinda, *Russ.* **161** F15
Zhilinsky Spur, *Arctic Oc.* **247** J15
Zhlobin, *Belarus* **158** L6
Zhmerynka, *Ukr.* **159** P4
Zhob, *Pak.* **179** Q8
Zhob, river, *Pak.* **179** Q8
Zhokhova, Ostrov, *Russ.* **161** C17
Zhongfang, *Hunan, China* **185** R1
Zhongshan, *Guang., China* **185** W4
Zhongshan, *Guangxi Zhuang, China*
 185 U2
Zhongshan, station, *Antarctica*
 231 G20
Zhongtiao Shan, *Shanxi, China*
 184 H3
Zhongwei, *China* **182** H10
Zhongxian, *China* **182** L11
Zhongxiang, *Hubei, China* **184** M4
Zhosaly, *Kaz.* **176** G11
Zhoucun, *Shand., China* **184** G9
Zhoukou, *Henan, China* **184** K6
Zhouning, *Fujian, China* **185** R10
Zhoushan, *Zhejiang, China* **185** N12
Zhoushan Dao, *Zhejiang, China*
 185 N12

Zhoushan Qundao, islands, *Zhejiang,*
 China **185** N13
Zhoutuozi, *Liaoning, China* **184** A12
Zhovtneve, *Ukr.* **159** R6
Zhu (Pearl), river, *Guang., China*
 185 W5
Zhuanghe, *Liaoning, China* **184** D13
Zhucheng, *Shand., China* **184** G10
Zhuhai, *Guang., China* **185** W4
Zhuji, *Zhejiang, China* **185** P11
Zhukovka, *Russ.* **158** L7
Zhumadian, *Henan, China* **184** K5
Zhuolu, *Hebei, China* **184** C7
Zhuozhou, *Beijing Shi, China* **184** D7
Zhupanovo, *Russ.* **161** F23
Zhuryn, *Kaz.* **176** E8
Zhushan, *Hubei, China* **184** L2
Zhuxi, *Hubei, China* **184** L2
Zhuzhou, *Hunan, China* **185** R4
Zhympity, *Kaz.* **176** D6
Zhytomyr, *Ukr.* **159** N5
Zi, river, *Hunan, China* **185** Q3
Ziarat, *Pak.* **179** R7
Zibo, *Shand., China* **184** G9
Zicavo, *Fr.* **152** K4
Zichang (Wayaobu), *Shaanxi, China*
 184 F2
Zielona Góra, *Pol.* **150** E12
Zigana Geçidi, *Turk.* **171** D14
Zigar, *Taj.* **178** J8
Zigey, *Chad* **201** H14
Zigong, *China* **182** L10
Ziguinchor, *Senegal* **200** H4
Zile, *Turk.* **170** E11
Žilina, *Slovakia* **151** J14
Zillah, *Lib.* **201** D15
Zima, *Russ.* **161** L15
Zimbabwe, *Af.* **206** F11
Zimnicea, *Rom.* **155** G15
Zimovniki, *Russ.* **159** R12
Zinder, *Niger* **200** H12
Zinjibār, *Yemen* **174** R10
Zion, *Ill., U.S.* **100** M7
Zion, *St. Kitts and Nevis* **123** C19
Zion National Park, *Utah, U.S.*
 109 P6
Zirə, *Azerb.* **171** D23
Žirje, island, *Croatia* **154** G5
Zirndorf, *Ger.* **150** H8
Zittau, *Ger.* **150** F11
Živinice, *Bosn. & Herzg.* **154** F8
Ziway Hāyk', *Eth.* **203** G15
Zixi, *Jiangxi, China* **185** R8
Zixing, *Hunan, China* **185** T4
Ziyamet *see* Leonarisso, *Cyprus*
 162 M10
Ziyuan, *Guangxi Zhuang, China*
 185 S2
Zizhou, *Shaanxi, China* **184** F2
Zlarin, island, *Croatia* **154** G6
Zlatoust, *Russ.* **160** J8
Zlatoustovsk, *Russ.* **161** J20
Zlín, *Czech Rep.* **151** J14
Złotów, *Pol.* **151** C13
Zmari Sar, peak, *Afghan.* **179** Q5
Zmeica, Lacul, *Rom.* **155** F17
Zmeinogorsk, *Russ.* **160** L11
Zmiyev, *Ukr.* **159** P9
Zmiyinyy, Ostriv, *Ukr.* **159** S5
Znamenka, *Kaz.* **177** D17
Znamensk, *Russ.* **158** J2
Znam'yanka, *Ukr.* **159** Q7
Znojmo, *Czech Rep.* **150** J12
Zoetermeer, *Neth.* **148** J12
Z̧ofar, *Israel* **173** Q5
Zofingen, *Switz.* **152** A4
Zoigê, *China* **182** J9
Zolochiv, *Ukr.* **159** N3
Zolochiv, *Ukr.* **159** N8
Zolotaya Gora, *Russ.* **161** K18
Zolotonosha, *Ukr.* **159** P6
Zomba, *Malawi* **207** E13
Zongo, *Dem. Rep. of the Congo*
 202 H9
Zonguldak, *Turk.* **170** C7
Zonza, *Fr.* **152** L4
Zoo, *Monaco* **163** E20
Zor Dağ, peak, *Turk.* **171** E18
Zorkol Lake, *Taj.* **178** J11
Z̧ōr Kōt̨, *Afghan.* **179** N8

Zorritos, *Peru* **132** E2
Zouar, *Chad* **201** F14
Zoucheng, *Shand., China* **184** H8
Zouping, *Shand., China* **184** F8
Zoushi, *Hunan, China* **185** P3
Zrenjanin (Petrovgrad), *Serb.*
 154 E10
Zubayr, Jazā'ir az, *Yemen* **174** Q8
Zubovo, *Russ.* **158** F9
Zubtsov, *Russ.* **158** J8
Zuera, *Sp.* **147** D14
Z̧ufār, region, *Oman* **175** N14
Zug, *Switz.* **152** B4
Zugdidi, *Rep. of Georgia* **171** B16
Zugspitze, peak, *Aust., Ger.* **150** L8
Zululand, region, *S. Af.* **206** K12
Žumberačka Gora, *Croatia, Slov.*
 154 D5
Zumberge Coast, *Antarctica* **230** G8
Zumbo, *Mozambique* **206** E11
Zunhua, *Hebei, China* **184** C9
Zuni, river, *Ariz., N. Mex., U.S.*
 109 S9
Zuni Pueblo, *N. Mex., U.S.* **109** S10
Zunyi, *China* **182** M11
Zuoquan, *Shanxi, China* **184** F5
Zuoyun, *Shanxi, China* **184** C5
Zuoz, *Switz.* **152** C5
Zürich, *Switz.* **152** A3
Żurrieq, *Malta* **163** L22
Zuru, *Nigeria* **205** C13
Žut, island, *Croatia* **154** G5
Zutphen, *Neth.* **148** J13
Zuwārah, *Lib.* **201** B13
Zvenyhorodka, *Ukr.* **159** P6
Zvishavane, *Zimb.* **206** G11
Zvolen, *Slovakia* **151** J15
Zvornik, *Bosn. & Herzg.* **154** F9
Zwettl, *Aust.* **150** K12
Zwickau, *Ger.* **150** G9
Zwolle, *La., U.S.* **102** M6
Zwolle, *Neth.* **148** H13
Zygi, *Cyprus* **162** Q8
Zyryanka, *Russ.* **161** E19
Zyryanovo, *Russ.* **161** H13
Zyryanovsk, *Kaz.* **177** D19

Moon and Mars Indexes

Latin Equivalents

Catena, catenae _____ chain of craters
Cavus, cavi _____ hollows, irregular steep-sided depressions, usually in arrays or clusters
Chaos, chaoses _____ distinctive area of broken terrain
Chasma, chasmata _____ deep elongated steep-sided depression
Collis, colles _____ small hills or knobs
Crater, craters _____ circular depression
Dorsum, dorsa _____ ridge
Fossa, fossae _____ long, narrow depression
Labyrinthus, labyrinthi _____ area of intersecting valleys or ridges

Lacus _____ lake; small plain; small, dark area with discrete, sharp edges
Mare, maria _____ sea; large, circular plain
Mensa, mensae _____ flat prominence with cliff-like edges
Mons, montes _____ mountain
Oceanus, oceani _____ very large, dark area
Palus, paludes _____ swamp; small plain
Patera, paterae _____ irregular crater, often with scalloped edges
Planitia, planitiae _____ low plain
Planum, plana _____ plateau or high plain
Promontorium, promontoria _____ cape; headland promontoria

Rima, rimae _____ fissure
Rupes, Rupii _____ scarp
Scopulus, scopuli _____ lobate or irregular scarp
Sinus _____ bay; small plain
Sulcus, sulci _____ subparallel furrows and ridges
Terra, terrae _____ extensive area
Tholus, tholi _____ small, dome-shaped mountain or hill
Unda, undae _____ dunes
Vallis, valles _____ valley
Vastitas, vastitates _____ extensive plain

Moon Index

Note: Entries without a generic descriptor are craters.

Abbe, *Far Side,* **254** NI2
Abel, *Near Side,* **253** MI8
Abulfeda, *Near Side,* **253** KI3
Abul Wáfa, *Far Side,* **254** H7
Adams, *Near Side,* **253** MI7
Aestuum, Sinus, *Near Side,* **252** GI2
Agricola, Montes, *Near Side,* **252** F8
Aitken, *Far Side,* **254** KI2
Albategnius, *Near Side,* **253** KI3
Al-Biruni, *Far Side,* **254** F6
Alden, *Far Side,* **254** L7
Alder, *Far Side,* **255** NI3
Alekhin, *Far Side,* **255** QI4
Alexander, *Near Side,* **253** EI4
Aliacensis, *Near Side,* **253** LI3
Al-Khwarizmi, *Far Side,* **254** H7
Alpes, Montes, *Near Side,* **252** DI2
Alpes, Vallis, *Near Side,* **253** DI3
Alphonsus, *Near Side,* **252** KI2
Altai, Rupes, *Near Side,* **253** LI4
Alter, *Far Side,* **255** GI8
Amici, *Far Side,* **255** JI3
Amundsen, *Near Side,* **253** RI3
Anaximander, *Near Side,* **252** CII
Anaximenes, *Near Side,* **252** BII
Anderson, *Far Side,* **254** GI2
Anguis, Mare, *Near Side,* **253** FI8
Ansgarius, *Near Side,* **253** KI9
Antoniadi, *Far Side,* **255** PI3
Anuchin, *Far Side,* **254** P8
Apenninus, Montes, *Near Side,* **252** GI2
Apianus, *Near Side,* **253** LI3
Apollo, *Far Side,* **255** MI4
Apollonius, *Near Side,* **253** HI7
Appleton, *Far Side,* **254** EII
Archimedes, *Near Side,* **252** FI2
Ariadaeus, Rima, *Near Side,* **253** HI4
Aristarchus, *Near Side,* **252** F9
Aristillus, *Near Side,* **253** FI3
Aristoteles, *Near Side,* **253** DI4
Arnold, *Near Side,* **253** CI4
Arrhenius, *Far Side,* **255** PI6
Artamonov, *Far Side,* **254** F7
Artem'ev, *Far Side,* **255** HI5
Arzachel, *Near Side,* **252** KI2
Ashbrook, *Far Side,* **255** QI3
Asperitatis, Sinus, *Near Side,* **253** JI5
Atlas, *Near Side,* **253** DI5
Australe, Mare, *Far Side,* **254** N7
Autumni, Lacus, *Near Side,* **252** K6
Avicenna, *Far Side,* **255** DI8
Avogadro, *Far Side,* **254** CI2

Baade, *Near Side,* **252** N8
Baade, Vallis, *Near Side,* **252** N8

Babbage, *Near Side,* **252** CIO
Babcock, *Far Side,* **254** H6
Backlund, *Far Side,* **254** K7
Baco, *Near Side,* **253** NI4
Baillaud, *Near Side,* **253** BI4
Bailly, *Near Side,* **252** QIO
Balboa, *Near Side,* **252** F6
Baldet, *Far Side,* **255** NI4
Balmer, *Near Side,* **253** LI8
Barbier, *Far Side,* **254** LII
Barnard, *Near Side,* **253** MI8
Barocius, *Near Side,* **253** MI4
Barringer, *Far Side,* **255** LI5
Barrow, *Near Side,* **253** CI3
Beaumont, *Near Side,* **253** KI5
Bečvář, *Far Side,* **254** J8
Behaim, *Near Side,* **253** KI9
Beijerinck, *Far Side,* **254** KIO
Bel'kovich, *Far Side,* **254** B9
Bel'kovich, *Near Side,* **253** BI6
Bell, *Far Side,* **255** FI9
Bellinsgauzen, *Far Side,* **255** PI3
Belopol'skiy, *Far Side,* **255** KI7
Belyaev, *Far Side,* **254** F9
Berkner, *Far Side,* **255** FI8
Berlage, *Far Side,* **255** PI3
Berosus, *Near Side,* **253** EI7
Bettinus, *Near Side,* **252** PII
Bhabha, *Far Side,* **255** NI3
Biela, *Near Side,* **253** PI5
Birkeland, *Far Side,* **254** LI2
Birkhoff, *Far Side,* **255** CI4
Birmingham, *Near Side,* **252** CI2
Blackett, *Far Side,* **255** MI7
Blancanus, *Near Side,* **252** PII
Blanchinus, *Near Side,* **253** LI3
Blazhko, *Far Side,* **255** FI5
Boguslawsky, *Near Side,* **253** QI4
Bohr, *Near Side,* **252** G6
Bolyai, *Far Side,* **254** M9
Bonpland, *Near Side,* **252** JII
Boole, *Near Side,* **252** BIO
Bose, *Far Side,* **255** NI3
Boussingault, *Near Side,* **253** QI4
Bouvard, Vallis, *Near Side,* **252** N7
Boyle, *Far Side,* **254** NI2
Bragg, *Far Side,* **255** DI7
Brashear, *Far Side,* **255** QI3
Bredikhin, *Far Side,* **255** GI4
Brenner, *Near Side,* **253** MI5
Brianchon, *Near Side,* **252** BII
Bridgman, *Far Side,* **254** DIO
Bronk, *Far Side,* **255** FI6
Brouwer, *Far Side,* **255** MI6
Buckland, Dorsum, *Near Side,* **253** GI3
Buffon, *Far Side,* **255** MI6
Buisson, *Far Side,* **254** J7
Bullialdus, *Near Side,* **252** KII

Bunsen, *Near Side,* **252** D7
Burckhardt, *Near Side,* **253** EI7
Büsching, *Near Side,* **253** MI4
Buys-Ballot, *Far Side,* **254** GI2
Byrd, *Near Side,* **253** BI3
Byrgius, *Near Side,* **252** L7

Cabannes, *Far Side,* **255** PI3
Cajori, *Far Side,* **254** NI2
Campbell, *Far Side,* **254** DII
Cannon, *Near Side,* **253** FI9
Cantor, *Far Side,* **254** D8
Capuanus, *Near Side,* **252** MII
Cardanus, Rima, *Near Side,* **252** G7
Carnot, *Far Side,* **255** DI5
Carpatus, Montes, *Near Side,* **252** GII
Carpenter, *Near Side,* **252** BII
Carver, *Far Side,* **254** N9
Cassegrain, *Far Side,* **254** P9
Cassini, *Near Side,* **253** EI3
Catharina, *Near Side,* **253** KI4
Caucasus, Montes, *Near Side,* **253** EI3
Cavalerius, *Near Side,* **252** H7
Cavendish, *Near Side,* **252** L8
Chacornac, *Near Side,* **253** FI5
Challis, *Near Side,* **253** BI3
Chamberlin, *Far Side,* **254** P9
Champollion, *Far Side,* **254** EI2
Chandler, *Far Side,* **254** EI2
Chaplygin, *Far Side,* **254** JIO
Chapman, *Far Side,* **255** CI7
Chappell, *Far Side,* **255** DI3
Charlier, *Far Side,* **255** EI6
Chauvenet, *Far Side,* **254** K9
Chebyshev, *Far Side,* **255** MI6
Chernyshev, *Far Side,* **254** DI2
Chevallier, *Near Side,* **253** DI6
Chrétien, *Far Side,* **254** NII
Clairaut, *Near Side,* **253** NI3
Clavius, *Near Side,* **252** PI2
Cleomedes, *Near Side,* **253** FI7
Cleostratus, *Near Side,* **252** C9
Cockcroft, *Far Side,* **255** FI4
Cognitum, Mare, *Near Side,* **252** JIO
Colombo, *Near Side,* **253** KI6
Compton, *Far Side,* **254** C9
Comrie, *Far Side,* **255** FI8
Comstock, *Far Side,* **255** FI7
Condorcet, *Near Side,* **253** GI8
Congreve, *Far Side,* **255** JI3
Copernicus, *Near Side,* **252** HII
Cordillera, Montes, **252; 255** L7; KI8
Cori, *Far Side,* **255** NI4
Coriolis, *Far Side,* **254** HI2
Coulomb, *Far Side,* **255** CI6

Cremona, **252; 255** BIO; BI5
Crisium, Mare, *Near Side,* **253** GI7
Crocco, *Far Side,* **254** NII
Crommelin, *Far Side,* **255** QI4
Crüger, *Near Side,* **252** K7
Curie, *Far Side,* **254** L6
Curtius, *Near Side,* **253** PI3
Cusanus, *Near Side,* **253** BI5
Cuvier, *Near Side,* **253** NI3
Cyrano, *Far Side,* **254** KII
Cyrillus, *Near Side,* **253** KI4

D'Alembert, *Far Side,* **254** DII
Daedalus, *Far Side,* **254** JI2
Dalton, *Near Side,* **252** G6
Danjon, *Far Side,* **254** K8
Dante, *Far Side,* **254** FI2
Darwin, *Near Side,* **252** L7
Davisson, *Far Side,* **255** MI3
Debye, *Far Side,* **255** DI3
De Forest, *Far Side,* **255** QI3
Delambre, *Near Side,* **253** JI4
De La Rue, *Near Side,* **253** CI5
Dellinger, *Far Side,* **254** J9
Demonax, *Near Side,* **253** QI4
De Moraes, *Far Side,* **254** DIO
Desargues, *Near Side,* **252** BIO
Descartes, *Near Side,* **253** KI4
De Sitter, *Near Side,* **253** BI3
Deslandres, *Near Side,* **252** LI2
Deutsch, *Far Side,* **254** F7
De Vries, *Far Side,* **255** KI3
Doerfel, *Far Side,* **255** QI5
Donner, *Far Side,* **254** M7
Doppelmayer, *Near Side,* **252** L9
Doppler, *Far Side,* **255** KI4
Dreyer, *Far Side,* **254** G6
Dryden, *Far Side,* **255** LI4
Drygalski, *Near Side,* **252** RII
Dubyago, *Near Side,* **253** HI8
Dunér, *Far Side,* **255** EI3
Dyson, *Far Side,* **255** CI5
Dziewulski, *Far Side,* **254** F6

Eddington, *Near Side,* **252** F7
Edison, *Far Side,* **254** F7
Eijkman, *Far Side,* **255** PI4
Einstein, *Near Side,* **252** G6
Einthoven, *Far Side,* **254** J7
Elvey, *Far Side,* **255** GI9
Emden, *Far Side,* **255** CI3
Endymion, *Near Side,* **253** DI5
Eötvös, *Far Side,* **254** M9
Epidemiarum, Palus, *Near Side,* **252** LIO
Epigenes, *Near Side,* **252** CI2
Eratosthenes, *Near Side,* **252** GII
Erro, *Far Side,* **254** H6
Esnault-Pelterie, *Far Side,* **255** DI5

Espin, *Far Side,* **254** F7
Euctemon, *Near Side,* **253** BI3
Eudoxus, *Near Side,* **253** EI4
Euler, *Near Side,* **252** FIO
Evans, *Far Side,* **255** JI6
Evershed, *Far Side,* **255** EI4
Excellentiae, Lacus, *Near Side,* **252** M9

Fabricius, *Near Side,* **253** MI5
Fabry, *Far Side,* **254** D8
Faraday, *Near Side,* **253** MI3
Fecunditatis, Mare, *Near Side,* **253** JI7
Fermi, *Far Side,* **254** K8
Fernelius, *Near Side,* **253** MI3
Fersman, *Far Side,* **255** GI7
Finsen, *Far Side,* **255** MI3
Firmicus, *Near Side,* **253** HI8
Firsov, *Far Side,* **254** H7
Fitzgerald, *Far Side,* **255** FI3
Fizeau, *Far Side,* **255** PI5
Flammarion, *Near Side,* **252** JI2
Flamsteed, *Near Side,* **252** J9
Fleming, *Far Side,* **254** G7
Florensky, *Far Side,* **254** F9
Florey, *Near Side,* **252** AI2
Fourier, *Near Side,* **252** M9
Fowler, *Far Side,* **255** EI5
Fracastorius, *Near Side,* **253** LI5
Fra Mauro, *Near Side,* **252** JII
Franklin, *Near Side,* **253** EI6
Fraunhofer, *Near Side,* **253** MI6
Freundlich, *Far Side,* **254** FI2
Fridman, *Far Side,* **255** KI7
Frigoris, Mare, *Near Side,* **252** CI2
Froelich, *Far Side,* **255** BI4
Frost, *Far Side,* **255** EI7
Furnerius, *Near Side,* **253** MI7

Gadomski, *Far Side,* **255** EI5
Gagarin, *Far Side,* **254** KIO
Galois, *Far Side,* **255** KI5
Galvani, *Near Side,* **252** C8
Gamow, *Far Side,* **254** CII
Ganswindt, *Far Side,* **254** QI2
Garavito, *Far Side,* **254** NII
Gärtner, *Near Side,* **253** CI4
Gassendi, *Near Side,* **252** K9
Gauricus, *Near Side,* **252** MI2
Gauss, *Near Side,* **253** EI8
Gavrilov, *Far Side,* **254** G9
Geminus, *Near Side,* **253** EI6
Gemma Frisius, *Near Side,* **253** LI3
Gerard, *Near Side,* **252** D8
Gerasimovich, *Far Side,* **255** LI6
Gibbs, *Near Side,* **253** LI9
Gilbert, *Near Side,* **253** JI9
Gill, *Near Side,* **253** QI5

Ginzel, *Far Side*, **254** G6
Goclenius, *Near Side*, **253** JI6
Goddard, *Near Side*, **253** GI9
Goldschmidt, *Near Side*, **252** BI2
Green, *Far Side*, **254** H9
Gregory, *Far Side*, **254** H8
Grimaldi, *Near Side*, **252** J7
Grissom, *Far Side*, **255** NI5
Gruemberger, *Near Side*, **252** PI2
Gruithuisen, *Near Side*, **252** FIO
Guericke, *Near Side*, **252** KII
Guillaume, *Far Side*, **255** EI3
Gum, *Near Side*, **253** NI8
Gutenberg, *Near Side*, **253** JI6
Gutenberg, Rimae, *Near Side*, **253** JI6
Guthnick, *Far Side*, **255** PI7
Guyot, *Far Side*, **254** G7

H. G. Wells, *Far Side*, **254** D9
Haber, *Far Side*, **255** AI3
Haemus, Montes, *Near Side*, **253** GI3
Hagecius, *Near Side*, **253** PI5
Hahn, *Near Side*, **253** EI8
Hainzel, *Near Side*, **252** MIO
Hale, *Far Side*, **254** QII
Hamilton, *Near Side*, **253** NI7
Hanno, *Near Side*, **253** PI6
Harbinger, Montes, *Near Side*, **252** F9
Harker, Dorsa, *Near Side*, **253** GI8
Harkhebi, *Far Side*, **254** D7
Harlan, *Near Side*, **253** NI8
Harriot, *Far Side*, **254** E8
Hartmann, *Far Side*, **254** H9
Hartwig, *Near Side*, **252** J6
Harvey, *Far Side*, **255** GI5
Hase, *Near Side*, **253** LI7
Haskin, *Far Side*, **254** BII
Hausen, *Far Side*, **255** QI5
Hausen, *Near Side*, **252** QIO
Hayn, *Near Side*, **253** BI5
Heaviside, *Far Side*, **254** JII
Hecataeus, *Near Side*, **253** LI8
Helberg, *Far Side*, **255** FI8
Helmholtz, *Near Side*, **253** QI5
Henyey, *Far Side*, **255** GI5
Heraclitus, *Near Side*, **253** NI3
Hercules, *Near Side*, **253** DI5
Hermite, *Near Side*, **252** AI2
Herodotus, *Near Side*, **252** F9
Hertz, *Far Side*, **254** G7
Hertzsprung, *Far Side*, **255** HI7
Hesiodus, Rima, *Near Side*, **252** LII
Hess, *Far Side*, **254** NI2
Hevelius, *Near Side*, **252** H7
Hilbert, *Far Side*, **254** L7
Hippalus, *Near Side*, **252** LIO
Hipparchus, *Near Side*, **253** JI3
Hippocrates, *Far Side*, **255** BI4
Hirayama, *Near Side*, **254** J6
Hommel, *Near Side*, **253** NI4
Hopmann, *Far Side*, **254** NII
Houzeau, *Far Side*, **255** KI7
Hubble, *Near Side*, **253** FI9
Humboldt, *Near Side*, **253** MI8
Humboldtianum, Mare, *Near Side*, **253** CI6
Humorum, Mare, *Near Side*, **252** L9
Hyginus, Rima, *Near Side*, **253** HI3

Ibn Firnas, *Far Side*, **254** H8
Ibn Yunus, *Far Side*, **254** G6
Icarus, *Far Side*, **255** JI3
Imbrium, Mare, *Near Side*, **252** FII
Ingenii, Mare, *Far Side*, **254** LII
Inghirami, *Near Side*, **252** N9
Inghirami, Vallis, *Near Side*, **252** N8
Insularum, Mare, *Near Side*, **252** HIO
Ioffe, *Far Side*, **255** KI7
Iridum, Sinus, *Near Side*, **252** DIO
Isaev, *Far Side*, **254** KIO

J. Herschel, *Near Side*, **252** CII

Jackson, *Far Side*, **255** GI4
Jacobi, *Near Side*, **253** NI3
Jansky, *Near Side*, **253** GI9
Janssen, *Near Side*, **253** NI5
Jarvis, *Far Side*, **255** MI5
Jeans, *Far Side*, **254** P9
Jenner, *Far Side*, **254** N8
Joliot, *Far Side*, **254** E6
Joule, *Far Side*, **255** FI5
Jules Verne, *Far Side*, **254** MIO
Julius Caesar, *Near Side*, **253** HI4

Kaiser, *Near Side*, **253** MI3
Kamerlingh Onnes, *Far Side*, **255** GI8
Kane, *Near Side*, **253** CI4
Karpinskiy, *Far Side*, **254** BI2
Karrer, *Far Side*, **255** NI5
Kästner, *Near Side*, **253** JI9
Keeler, *Far Side*, **254** JII
Kekulé, *Far Side*, **255** GI6
Kepler, *Near Side*, **252** H9
Khvol'son, *Far Side*, **254** K7
Kibal'chich, *Far Side*, **255** HI5
Kidinnu, *Far Side*, **254** E9
Kiess, *Near Side*, **253** JI9
King, *Far Side*, **254** H8
Kircher, *Near Side*, **252** PII
Kirkwood, *Far Side*, **255** CI3
Klaproth, *Near Side*, **252** PI2
Kleymenov, *Far Side*, **255** LI6
Klute, *Far Side*, **255** EI5
Koch, *Far Side*, **254** MIO
Kohlschütter, *Far Side*, **254** GIO
Kolhörster, *Far Side*, **255** GI8
Komarov, *Far Side*, **254** FIO
Kondratyuk, *Far Side*, **254** K7
Konstantinov, *Far Side*, **254** GII
Korolev, *Far Side*, **255** JI4
Kostinskiy, *Far Side*, **254** G7
Kovalevskaya, *Far Side*, **255** EI6
Kozyrev, *Far Side*, **254** N9
Krafft, *Near Side*, **252** G7
Kramers, *Far Side*, **255** DI5
Krasovskiy, *Far Side*, **255** HI3
Kugler, *Far Side*, **254** P9
Kulik, *Far Side*, **255** EI4
Kurchatov, *Far Side*, **254** EIO
Kurchatov, Catena, *Far Side*, **254** E9

La Caille, *Near Side*, **253** LI3
Lacchini, *Far Side*, **255** DI7
Lade, *Near Side*, **253** JI3
Lagrange, *Near Side*, **252** M7
Lamarck, *Near Side*, **252** L7
Lamb, *Far Side*, **254** N8
Lambert, *Near Side*, **252** FII
Lamé, *Near Side*, **253** KI8
Lampland, *Far Side*, **254** L9
Landau, *Far Side*, **255** DI6
Lane, *Far Side*, **254** J9
Langemak, *Far Side*, **254** J8
Langevin, *Far Side*, **254** EII
Langmuir, *Far Side*, **255** MI6
Langrenus, *Near Side*, **253** KI8
La Pérouse, *Near Side*, **253** KI9
Larmor, *Far Side*, **255** FI3
Laue, *Far Side*, **255** EI8
Lavoisier, *Near Side*, **252** D7
Leavitt, *Far Side*, **255** MI5
Lebedev, *Far Side*, **254** N8
Lebedinskiy, *Far Side*, **255** HI4
Leeuwenhoek, *Far Side*, **255** LI3
Legendre, *Near Side*, **253** MI8
Le Gentil, *Near Side*, **252** QII
Lehmann, *Near Side*, **252** M9
Leibnitz, *Far Side*, **254** MI2
Lemaître, *Far Side*, **255** PI4
Le Monnier, *Near Side*, **253** FI5
Leucippus, *Far Side*, **255** FI7
Leuschner, Catena, *Far Side*, **255** HI8
Levi-Civita, *Far Side*, **254** L9
Ley, *Far Side*, **254** EII
Licetus, *Near Side*, **253** NI3
Lilius, *Near Side*, **253** NI3

Lindblad, *Far Side*, **255** BI5
Lippmann, *Far Side*, **255** PI6
Lipskiy, *Far Side*, **254** JI2
Lister, Dorsa, *Near Side*, **253** GI4
Littrow, *Near Side*, **253** GI5
Lobachevskiy, *Far Side*, **254** G7
Lodygin, *Far Side*, **255** KI5
Lomonosov, *Far Side*, **254** E7
Longomontanus, *Near Side*, **252** NII
Lorentz, *Far Side*, **255** EI8
Love, *Far Side*, **254** J8
Lovelace, *Far Side*, **255** BI3
Lowell, *Far Side*, **255** KI9
Lucretius, *Far Side*, **255** JI7
Lucretius, Catena, *Far Side*, **255** JI7
Lundmark, *Far Side*, **254** MII
Lyapunov, *Near Side*, **253** EI9
Lyman, *Far Side*, **254** PI2
Lyot, *Near Side*, **253** PI7

Mach, *Far Side*, **255** GI5
Macrobius, *Near Side*, **253** GI6
Maginus, *Near Side*, **252** NI2
Mairan, *Near Side*, **252** EIO
Maksutov, *Far Side*, **255** MI3
Malapert, *Near Side*, **253** QI3
Mallet, *Near Side*, **253** NI6
Mandel'shtam, *Far Side*, **254** HII
Manilius, *Near Side*, **253** GI3
Manzinus, *Near Side*, **253** PI3
Marconi, *Far Side*, **254** JIO
Marginis, Mare, *Near Side*, **253** GI9
Marinus, *Near Side*, **253** NI7
Mariotte, *Far Side*, **255** LI6
Maunder, *Far Side*, **255** KI9
Maurolycus, *Near Side*, **253** MI4
Maxwell, *Far Side*, **254** E7
McAuliffe, *Far Side*, **255** LI5
McKellar, *Far Side*, **255** KI3
McLaughlin, *Far Side*, **255** CI7
McMath, *Far Side*, **255** GI4
McNair, *Far Side*, **255** MI5
Mechnikov, *Far Side*, **255** KI5
Medii, Sinus, *Near Side*, **253** HI3
Mee, *Near Side*, **252** MIO
Meggers, *Far Side*, **254** F8
Meitner, *Far Side*, **254** K7
Mendel, *Far Side*, **255** NI6
Mendeleev, *Far Side*, **254** H9
Mercurius, *Near Side*, **253** DI6
Merrill, *Far Side*, **255** BI4
Mersenius, *Near Side*, **252** L8
Meshcherskiy, *Far Side*, **254** G8
Messala, *Near Side*, **253** EI7
Metius, *Near Side*, **253** MI5
Meton, *Near Side*, **253** BI3
Mezentsev, *Far Side*, **255** BI4
Michelson, *Far Side*, **255** HI7
Michelson, Catena, *Far Side*, **255** JI8
Milankovič, *Far Side*, **254** BI2
Miller, *Near Side*, **253** MI3
Millikan, *Far Side*, **254** D9
Milne, *Far Side*, **254** M8
Mineur, *Far Side*, **255** FI4
Minkowski, *Far Side*, **255** NI4
Minnaert, *Far Side*, **254** PI2
Mitra, *Far Side*, **255** GI5
Mohorovičić, *Far Side*, **255** KI4
Moiseev, *Far Side*, **254** G6
Montes Jura, *Near Side*, **252** DIO
Montgolfier, *Far Side*, **255** DI4
Moore, *Far Side*, **255** EI3
Moretus, *Near Side*, **252** PI2
Morse, *Far Side*, **255** GI3
Mortis, Lacus, *Near Side*, **253** EI4
Moscoviense, Mare, *Far Side*, **254** FIO
Mouchez, *Near Side*, **252** BI2
Murchison, *Near Side*, **253** HI3
Mutus, *Near Side*, **253** PI4

Nansen, *Far Side*, **254** AII
Nasmyth, *Near Side*, **252** N9

Nassau, *Far Side*, **254** LI2
Nearch, *Near Side*, **253** PI4
Nectaris, Mare, *Near Side*, **253** KI5
Neison, *Near Side*, **253** CI3
Neper, *Near Side*, **253** HI9
Nernst, *Far Side*, **255** EI8
Neujmin, *Far Side*, **254** L8
Neumayer, *Near Side*, **253** QI5
Newton, *Near Side*, **252** QI2
Niepce, *Far Side*, **255** BI4
Nishina, *Far Side*, **255** NI3
Nonius, *Near Side*, **253** MI3
Nöther, *Far Side*, **255** BI5
Nubium, Mare, *Near Side*, **252** KII
Numerov, *Far Side*, **255** PI3
Nušl, *Far Side*, **254** FII

O'Day, *Far Side*, **254** LII
Oberth, *Far Side*, **254** CII
Obruchev, *Far Side*, **254** MII
Oenopides, *Near Side*, **252** C9
Ohm, *Far Side*, **255** GI8
Oken, *Near Side*, **253** NI7
Olbers, *Near Side*, **252** H6
Olcott, *Far Side*, **254** F8
Olivier, *Far Side*, **254** CIO
Omar Khayyam, *Far Side*, **255** CI6
Onizuka, *Far Side*, **255** MI5
Oppel, Dorsum, *Near Side*, **253** GI7
Oppenheimer, *Far Side*, **255** MI3
Oresme, *Far Side*, **254** MI2
Orientale, Mare, *Far Side*, **255** LI9
Orlov, *Far Side*, **255** LI3
Orontius, *Near Side*, **252** MI2
Ostwald, *Far Side*, **254** H8

Paneth, *Far Side*, **255** BI6
Pannekoek, *Far Side*, **254** J9
Papaleksi, *Far Side*, **254** HII
Paracelsus, *Far Side*, **254** LII
Paraskevopoulos, *Far Side*, **255** DI4
Parenago, *Far Side*, **255** FI8
Parkhurst, *Far Side*, **254** M7
Parrot, *Near Side*, **253** KI3
Pascal, *Near Side*, **252** BII
Paschen, *Far Side*, **255** KI6
Pasteur, *Far Side*, **254** K6
Pauli, *Far Side*, **254** NIO
Pavlov, *Far Side*, **254** LIO
Pawsey, *Far Side*, **254** DIO
Peary, *Near Side*, **253** AI3
Peirescius, *Near Side*, **253** NI6
Pentland, *Near Side*, **253** PI3
Perepelkin, *Far Side*, **254** J8
Perkin, *Far Side*, **255** DI3
Perrine, *Far Side*, **255** DI6
Petavius, *Near Side*, **253** LI7
Petermann, *Near Side*, **253** BI4
Petropavlovskiy, *Far Side*, **255** EI7
Pettit, Rimae, *Far Side*, **255** MI9
Petzval, *Far Side*, **255** PI5
Phillips, *Near Side*, **253** LI8
Philolaus, *Near Side*, **252** BI2
Phocylides, *Near Side*, **252** P9
Piazzi, *Near Side*, **252** M8
Piccolomini, *Near Side*, **253** LI5
Pingré, *Near Side*, **252** P9
Pirquet, *Far Side*, **254** K9
Pitatus, *Near Side*, **252** LII
Pitiscus, *Near Side*, **253** NI4
Planck, *Far Side*, **254** PIO
Planck, Vallis, *Far Side*, **254** PIO
Plaskett, *Far Side*, **254** BI2
Plato, *Near Side*, **252** DI2
Plummer, *Far Side*, **255** LI4
Plutarch, *Near Side*, **253** FI8
Poczobutt, *Far Side*, **255** CI6
Poincaré, *Far Side*, **254** NII
Poinsot, *Far Side*, **255** BI3
Polzunov, *Far Side*, **254** F8
Poncelet, *Near Side*, **252** BII
Pontanus, *Near Side*, **253** LI4
Pontécoulant, *Near Side*, **253** PI6
Popov, *Far Side*, **254** G6
Porter, *Near Side*, **252** NI2

Posidonius, *Near Side*, **253** FI5
Poynting, *Far Side*, **255** GI6
Prager, *Far Side*, **254** J8
Prandtl, *Far Side*, **254** PII
Procellarum, Oceanus, *Near Side*, **252** H8
Proctor, *Near Side*, **252** NI2
Ptolemaeus, *Near Side*, **252** JI2
Purbach, *Near Side*, **252** LI2
Putredinis, Palus, *Near Side*, **253** FI3
Pyrenaeus, Montes, *Near Side*, **253** KI6
Pythagoras, *Near Side*, **252** CIO

Quételet, *Far Side*, **255** EI6

Rabbi Levi, *Near Side*, **253** MI4
Racah, *Far Side*, **255** KI3
Raimond, *Far Side*, **255** GI4
Ramsay, *Far Side*, **254** MIO
Rayleigh, *Near Side*, **253** EI9
Razumov, *Far Side*, **255** EI7
Réaumur, *Near Side*, **252** JI2
Regiomontanus, *Near Side*, **252** LI2
Reichenbach, *Near Side*, **253** LI6
Reiner, *Near Side*, **252** H8
Reinhold, *Near Side*, **252** HIO
Repsold, *Near Side*, **252** C9
Resnik, *Far Side*, **255** MI5
Rheita, *Near Side*, **253** MI6
Rheita, Vallis, *Near Side*, **253** MI6
Riccioli, *Near Side*, **252** J6
Riccius, *Near Side*, **253** MI4
Ricco, *Far Side*, **254** BI2
Richardson, *Far Side*, **254** E7
Riemann, *Near Side*, **253** DI8
Riphaeus, Montes, *Near Side*, **252** JIO
Roberts, *Far Side*, **255** CI3
Robertson, *Far Side*, **255** FI8
Rocca, *Near Side*, **252** K7
Roche, *Far Side*, **254** MIO
Röntgen, *Far Side*, **255** EI8
Rook, Montes, **252**; **255** K6; LI8
Roris, Sinus, *Near Side*, **252** DIO
Rosenberger, *Near Side*, **253** NI5
Rosseland, *Far Side*, **254** M9
Rowland, *Far Side*, **255** DI3
Rozhdestvenskiy, *Far Side*, **255** BI3
Rumford, *Far Side*, **255** LI3
Russell, *Near Side*, **252** F7
Rydberg, *Far Side*, **255** NI7
Rynin, *Far Side*, **255** DI7

Sacrobosco, *Near Side*, **253** KI3
Saenger, *Far Side*, **254** H6
Saha, *Far Side*, **254** J6
Sanford, *Far Side*, **255** EI5
Santbech, *Near Side*, **253** KI6
Sarton, *Far Side*, **255** DI6
Sasserides, *Near Side*, **252** MI2
Saussure, *Near Side*, **252** MI2
Scaliger, *Far Side*, **254** L7
Schaeberle, *Far Side*, **254** L8
Scheiner, *Near Side*, **252** PII
Schickard, *Near Side*, **252** N9
Schiller, *Near Side*, **252** NIO
Schjellerup, *Far Side*, **254** CI2
Schlesinger, *Far Side*, **255** DI5
Schliemann, *Far Side*, **254** JIO
Schlüter, *Near Side*, **252** J6
Schneller, *Far Side*, **255** EI4
Schomberger, *Near Side*, **253** QI3
Schorr, *Near Side*, **253** LI9
Schrödinger, *Far Side*, **254** QII
Schrödinger, Vallis, *Far Side*, **254** QIO
Schröteri, Vallis, *Near Side*, **252** F9
Schubert, *Near Side*, **253** HI9
Schumacher, *Near Side*, **253** DI6
Schuster, *Far Side*, **254** HIO
Schwarzschild, *Far Side*, **254** BII
Scobee, *Far Side*, **255** LI5
Scoresby, *Near Side*, **253** BI3
Scott, *Near Side*, **253** QI3

Seares, *Far Side,* **254** B11
Sechenov, *Far Side,* **255** J16
Segner, *Near Side,* **252** P10
Seidel, *Far Side,* **254** L10
Serenitatis, Mare, *Near Side,* **253** F14
Seyfert, *Far Side,* **254** F8
Sharonov, *Far Side,* **254** G12
Shayn, *Far Side,* **254** F12
Sheepshanks, Rima, *Near Side,* **253** F14
Shirakatsi, *Far Side,* **254** K8
Shternberg , *Far Side,* **255** F18
Siedentopf, *Far Side,* **254** F9
Sierpinski, *Far Side,* **254** L11
Sikorsky, *Far Side,* **254** Q10
Sirsalis, *Near Side,* **252** K8
Sirsalis, Rimae, *Near Side,* **252** K8
Sklodowska, *Far Side,* **254** L6
Slipher, *Far Side,* **254** D11
Smith, *Far Side,* **255** L15
Smoluchowski, *Far Side,* **255** B16
Smythii, Mare, *Near Side,* **253** H19
Snellius, *Near Side,* **253** L17
Snellius, Vallis, *Near Side,* **253** L17
Solitudinis, Lacus, *Far Side,* **254** M7
Sommerfeld, *Far Side,* **255** C13
Somni, Palus, *Near Side,* **253** G16
Somniorum, Lacus, *Near Side,* **253** E15

Sosigenes, Rimae, *Near Side,* **253** H14
South, *Near Side,* **252** C10
Spei, Lacus, *Near Side,* **253** D17
Spencer Jones, *Far Side,* **254** G11
Spumans, Mare, *Near Side,* **253** H18
St. John, *Far Side,* **254** G10
Stadius, *Near Side,* **252** H11
Stebbins, *Far Side,* **255** C14
Stefan, *Far Side,* **255** D17
Steinheil, *Near Side,* **253** N15
Sternfeld, *Far Side,* **255** K15
Stetson, *Far Side,* **255** N17
Stevinus, *Near Side,* **253** M16
Stöfler, *Near Side,* **253** M13
Störmer, *Far Side,* **254** C11
Strabo, *Near Side,* **253** C15
Stratton, *Far Side,* **254** J11
Strömgren, *Far Side,* **255** L16
Struve, *Near Side,* **252** F7
Subbotin, *Far Side,* **254** L9
Suess, Rima, *Near Side,* **252** H8
Sumner, Catena, *Far Side,* **254** D8
Sylvester, *Near Side,* **252** A12
Szilard, *Far Side,* **254** E7

Taruntius, *Near Side,* **253** H16
Taurus, Montes, *Near Side,* **253** F16
Teisserenc, *Far Side,* **255** E16

Temporis, Lacus, *Near Side,* **253** D16
Thebit, *Near Side,* **252** K12
Theophilus, *Near Side,* **253** J15
Thiessen, *Far Side,* **255** B13
Thomson, *Far Side,* **254** L11
Tikhov, *Far Side,* **254** C12
Timiryazev, *Far Side,* **255** J15
Timocharis, *Near Side,* **252** F12
Tiselius, *Far Side,* **254** H12
Titius, *Far Side,* **254** M7
Tranquillitatis, Mare, *Near Side,* **253** H15
Triesnecker, Rimae, *Near Side,* **253** H13
Trumpler, *Far Side,* **254** F12
Tsander, *Far Side,* **255** H15
Tseraskiy, *Far Side,* **254** N10
Tsiolkovskiy, *Far Side,* **254** K9
Tycho, *Near Side,* **252** M12

Ulugh Beigh, *Near Side,* **252** E7
Undarum, Mare, *Near Side,* **253** H18

Valier, *Far Side,* **254** H12
Van't Hoff, *Far Side,* **255** C15
Van de Graaff, *Far Side,* **254** L12
Van der Waals, *Far Side,* **254** N9
Van Maanen, *Far Side,* **254** E9
Vaporum, Mare, *Near Side,* **253** G13

Vasco da Gama, *Near Side,* **252** G6
Vavilov, *Far Side,* **255** J16
Vendelinus, *Near Side,* **253** K18
Vening Meinesz, *Far Side,* **254** J11
Ventris, *Far Side,* **254** J11
Veris, Lacus, *Near Side,* **252** K6
Vernadskiy, *Far Side,* **254** F9
Vertregt, *Far Side,* **254** K12
Vesalius, *Far Side,* **254** J7
Vestine, *Far Side,* **254** E7
Vetchinkin, *Far Side,* **254** H8
Vieta, *Near Side,* **252** L8
Vlacq, *Near Side,* **253** N15
Volta, *Near Side,* **252** C9
Volterra, *Far Side,* **254** C10
Von Békésy, *Far Side,* **254** D9
Von Braun, *Near Side,* **252** D8
Von der Pahlen, *Far Side,* **255** L16
Von Kármán, *Far Side,* **254** M12
Von Neumann, *Far Side,* **254** E11
Von Zeipel, *Far Side,* **255** E15

W. Bond, *Near Side,* **253** C13
Walther, *Near Side,* **253** L13
Wan-Hoo, *Far Side,* **255** J16
Wargentin, *Near Side,* **252** N9
Waterman, *Far Side,* **254** L8
Watson, *Far Side,* **255** P15
Watt, *Near Side,* **253** N15
Wegener, *Far Side,* **255** D17
Werner, *Near Side,* **253** L13

Weyl, *Far Side,* **255** G17
Wiener, *Far Side,* **254** E10
Wilhelm, *Near Side,* **252** M11
Wilkins, *Near Side,* **253** L14
Wilsing, *Far Side,* **255** K14
Wilson, *Near Side,* **252** Q11
Winlock, *Far Side,* **255** E17
Wood, *Far Side,* **255** D16
Wrottesley, *Near Side,* **253** L17
Wurzelbauer, *Near Side,* **252** M11
Wyld, *Far Side,* **254** J6

Xenophanes, *Near Side,* **252** C9

Yablochkov, *Far Side,* **254** C10
Yamamoto, *Far Side,* **254** D12
Young, *Near Side,* **253** M16

Zach, *Near Side,* **253** P13
Zagut, *Near Side,* **253** L14
Zeeman, *Far Side,* **255** Q14
Zelinskiy, *Far Side,* **254** L11
Zeno, *Near Side,* **253** D17
Zhukovskiy, *Far Side,* **255** H14
Zsigmondy, *Far Side,* **255** C16
Zucchius, *Near Side,* **252** P10
Zwicky, *Far Side,* **254** K11

Moon Landing Sites

NEAR SIDE

Apollo 11 (U.S.)—Tranquillity Base Landed July 20, 1969 **H15**
Apollo 12 (U.S.)—Landed Nov. 19, 1969 **J10**
Apollo 14 (U.S.)—Landed Feb. 5, 1971 **J11**
Apollo 15 (U.S.)—Landed July 30, 1971 **F13**
Apollo 16 (U.S.)—Landed April 21, 1972 **J14**
Apollo 17 (U.S.)—Landed Dec. 11, 1972 **G15**
Chandrayaan-1 Moon Impact Probe(India)—Crashed Nov. 14, 2008 **R13**
Chang'e 3 (China)—Landed Dec. 14, 2013 **E11**
GRAIL A (Ebb) (U.S.)—Crashed Dec. 17, 2012 **B12**
GRAIL B (Flow) (U.S.)—Crashed Dec. 17, 2012 **B12**
Hiten (Japan)—Crashed April 10, 1993 **D11**
LCROSS, Centaur Impactor (U.S.)—Crashed Oct. 9, 2009 **Q12**
Luna 13 (U.S.S.R.)—Landed Dec. 24, 1966 **G8**
Luna 15 (U.S.S.R.)—Crashed July 21, 1969 **G17**

Luna 16 (U.S.S.R.)—Landed Sept. 20, 1970 **J17**
Luna 17 (U.S.S.R.)—Landed Nov. 17, 1970 **E10**
Luna 2 (U.S.S.R.)—Crashed Sept. 14, 1959 **F13**
Luna 5 (U.S.S.R.)—Crashed May 10, 1965 **H11**
Luna 7 (U.S.S.R.)—Crashed Oct. 7, 1965 **H8**
Luna 8 (U.S.S.R.)—Crashed Dec. 6, 1965 **H7**
Luna 9 (U.S.S.R.)—Crashed Feb. 3, 1966 **H7**
Luna 18 (U.S.S.R.)—Landed Sept. 11, 1971 **H17**
Luna 20 (U.S.S.R.)—Landed Feb. 21, 1972 **H17**
Luna 21 (U.S.S.R.)—Landed Jan. 15, 1973 **F15**
Luna 23 (U.S.S.R.)—Landed Nov. 6, 1974 **G18**
Luna 24 (U.S.S.R.)—Landed Aug. 18, 1976 **G18**
Lunar Prospector (U.S.)—Crashed July 31, 1999 **R12**
Ranger 6 (U.S.)—Crashed Feb. 2, 1964 **H14**
Ranger 7 (U.S.)—Crashed July 31, 1964 **J11**
Ranger 8 (U.S.)—Crashed Feb. 20, 1965 **H15**
Ranger 9 (U.S.)—Crashed Mar. 24, 1965 **K12**

Selene/Kaguya (Japan)—Crashed June 10, 2009 **Q15**
SMART-1 (ESA)—Crashed Sept. 3, 2006 **M9**
Surveyor 1 (U.S.)—Landed June 2, 1966 **J9**
Surveyor 2 (U.S.)—Crashed Sept. 22, 1966 **J12**
Surveyor 3 (U.S.)—Landed Apr. 20, 1967 **J10**
Surveyor 4 (U.S.)—Crashed July 17, 1967 **H12**
Surveyor 5 (U.S.)—Landed Sept. 11, 1967 **H14**
Surveyor 6 (U.S.)—Landed Nov. 10, 1967 **H12**
Surveyor 7 (U.S.)—Landed Jan. 10, 1968 **M12**

FAR SIDE

Lunar Orbiter 1 (U.S.)—Crashed Oct. 29, 1966 **H11**
Lunar Orbiter 2 (U.S.)—Crashed Oct. 11, 1967 **H7**
Lunar Orbiter 3 (U.S.)—Crashed Oct. 9, 1967 **G19**
Lunar Orbiter 5 (U.S.)—Crashed Jan. 31, 1968 **J16**
Okina, Selene Orbiter (Japan)—Crashed Feb. 12, 2009 **F14**
Ranger 4 (U.S.)—Crashed Apr. 26, 1962 **K16**

Mars Index

Note: Entries without a generic descriptor are craters.

Acheron Fossae, *W. Hemis.,* **258** E9
Acidalia Planitia, *W. Hemis.,* **259** D16
Adams, *E. Hemis.,* **261** E18
Aeolis Dorsa, *E. Hemis.,* **261** J17
Aeolis Mensae, *E. Hemis.,* **261** J17
Aeolis Planum, *E. Hemis.,* **261** J17
Aeolis Serpens, *E. Hemis.,* **261** J17
Aganippe Fossa, *W. Hemis.,* **258** J9
Agassiz, *W. Hemis.,* **258** P12
Al-Qahira Vallis, *E. Hemis.,* **261** L18
Alba Fossae, *W. Hemis.,* **258** E11
Alba Mons, *W. Hemis.,* **258** E11
Alba Patera, *W. Hemis.,* **258** E11
Albor Tholus, *E. Hemis.,* **261** G17
Alpheus Colles, *E. Hemis.,* **260** M10
Amazonis Mensae, *W. Hemis.,* **258** J8
Amazonis Planitia, *W. Hemis.,* **258** F7
Amenthes Cavi, *E. Hemis.,* **261** G14
Amenthes Fossae, *E. Hemis.,* **261** H13
Amenthes Planum, *E. Hemis.,* **261** H14

Amphitrites Patera, *E. Hemis.,* **260** P11
Antoniadi, *E. Hemis.,* **260** G10
Aonia Planum, *W. Hemis.,* **259** N13
Aonia Terra, *W. Hemis.,* **258** P10
Apollinaris Mons, *E. Hemis.,* **261** J19
Arabia Terra, 259; **260** G19; E8
Arago, *E. Hemis.,* **260** H7
Arcadia Planitia, *W. Hemis.,* **258** C8
Arena Colles, *E. Hemis.,* **260** F12
Ares Vallis, *W. Hemis.,* **259** G18
Argentea Planum, *W. Hemis.,* **259** P13
Argyre Planitia, *W. Hemis.,* **259** N15
Arima, *W. Hemis.,* **259** K15
Arkhangelsky, *W. Hemis.,* **259** N17
Arrhenius, *E. Hemis.,* **261** M15
Arsia Mons, *W. Hemis.,* **258** J10
Ascraeus Mons, *W. Hemis.,* **258** G11
Ascuris Planum, *W. Hemis.,* **259** E13
Astapus Colles, *E. Hemis.,* **260** E12
Aurorae Chaos, *W. Hemis.,* **259** J17
Aurorae Planum, *W. Hemis.,* **259** K16

Ausonia Montes, *E. Hemis.,* **261** L13
Australe, Planum, *E. Hemis.,* **260** R12
Avarua, *E. Hemis.,* **261** M14

Bakhuysen, *E. Hemis.,* **260** L6
Baldet, *E. Hemis.,* **260** F10
Barabashov, *W. Hemis.,* **259** D14
Barnard, *E. Hemis.,* **260** P11
Bashkaus Valles, *W. Hemis.,* **259** M19
Becquerel, *W. Hemis.,* **259** F19
Beer, *W. Hemis.,* **259** K19
Bernard, *W. Hemis.,* **258** L8
Biblis Tholus, *W. Hemis.,* **258** H10
Bjerknes, *E. Hemis.,* **261** N17
Boeddicker, *E. Hemis.,* **261** K18
Bond, *W. Hemis.,* **259** M16
Boreum, Planum, 258; **260** A12; B12
Bosporos Planum, *W. Hemis.,* **259** M14
Bosporos Rupes, *W. Hemis.,* **259** M15
Bouguer, *E. Hemis.,* **260** L7
Brashear, *W. Hemis.,* **258** N11
Brevia, Dorsa, *E. Hemis.,* **260** P11

Briault, *E. Hemis.,* **261** J13
Burroughs, *E. Hemis.,* **261** Q13
Burton, *W. Hemis.,* **258** K7
Byrd, *E. Hemis.,* **261** P14

Campbell, *E. Hemis.,* **261** P16
Candor Chasma, *W. Hemis.,* **259** J14
Cankuzo, *E. Hemis.,* **260** K9
Capen, *E. Hemis.,* **260** H6
Capri Chasma, *W. Hemis.,* **259** K16
Caralis Chaos, *E. Hemis.,* **261** N18
Cassini, *E. Hemis.,* **260** F8
Ceraunius Fossae, *W. Hemis.,* **258** F11
Ceraunius Tholus, *W. Hemis.,* **258** F12
Cerberus Dorsa, *E. Hemis.,* **261** K14
Cerberus Tholi, *E. Hemis.,* **261** H18
Cerulli, *E. Hemis.,* **260** E8
Chamberlin, *W. Hemis.,* **258** P11
Charitum Montes, *W. Hemis.,* **259** P15
Charlier, *W. Hemis.,* **258** Q10
Chronium, Planum, *E. Hemis.,* **261** P15
Chryse Chaos, *W. Hemis.,* **259** G17
Chryse Planitia, *W. Hemis.,* **259** E17

Cimmeria, Terra, *E. Hemis.,* **261** N16
Claritas Fossae, *W. Hemis.,* **258** L11
Claritas Rupes, *W. Hemis.,* **258** L11
Clark, *W. Hemis.,* **258** N10
Coblentz, *W. Hemis.,* **258** N12
Cobres, *W. Hemis.,* **258** K7
Coloe Fossae, *E. Hemis.,* **260** E10
Columbus, *W. Hemis.,* **258** M7
Comas Sola, *W. Hemis.,* **258** L7
Copernicus, *W. Hemis.,* **258** P8
Coprates Chasma, *W. Hemis.,* **259** K15
Coracis Fossae, *W. Hemis.,* **259** M13
Crommelin, *W. Hemis.,* **259** H19
Cruls, *E. Hemis.,* **261** N17
Curie, *W. Hemis.,* **259** E18
Cyane Fossae, *W. Hemis.,* **258** E10
Cydnus Rupes, *E. Hemis.,* **261** D14
Cydonia Mensae, *W. Hemis.,* **259** E18

Daedalia Planum, *W. Hemis.,* **258** K9
Dao Vallis, *E. Hemis.,* **260** M12
Darwin, *W. Hemis.,* **259** P16
Dawes, *E. Hemis.,* **260** J8

Dejnev, *W. Hemis.,* **258** L7
Denning, *E. Hemis.,* **260** K8
Deuteronilus Mensae, *E. Hemis.,* **260** D8
Dokuchaev, *W. Hemis.,* **258** PII
Dollfus, *W. Hemis.,* **259** LI9
Douglass, *W. Hemis.,* **259** NI4
Du Martheray, *E. Hemis.,* **261** HI3

Echus Montes, *W. Hemis.,* **259** HI3
Eddie, *E. Hemis.,* **261** GI7
Eden Patera, *W. Hemis.,* **259** EI8
Elysium Chasma, *E. Hemis.,* **261** FI6
Elysium Mons, *E. Hemis.,* **261** FI7
Elysium Planitia, *E. Hemis.,* **261** HI7
Eos Chasma, *W. Hemis.,* **259** KI6
Erebus Montes, *W. Hemis.,* **258** E7
Eridania Planitia, *E. Hemis.,* **261** MI5
Eridania Scopulus, *E. Hemis.,* **261** NI6
Eumenides Dorsum, *W. Hemis.,* **258** H7

Fesenkov, *W. Hemis.,* **259** GI3
Firsoff, *W. Hemis.,* **259** HI9
Flammarion, *E. Hemis.,* **260** F9
Flaugergues, *E. Hemis.,* **260** K7
Fontana, *W. Hemis.,* **259** PI3
Fournier, *E. Hemis.,* **260** JII

Galaxias Colles, *E. Hemis.,* **261** EI6
Gale, *E. Hemis.,* **261** JI6
Galilaei, *W. Hemis.,* **259** HI8
Galle, *W. Hemis.,* **259** NI6
Ganges Chasma, *W. Hemis.,* **259** JI6
Gilbert, *E. Hemis.,* **260** PI2
Gill, *E. Hemis.,* **260** G6
Gonnus Mons, *W. Hemis.,* **258** EI2
Gordii Dorsum, *W. Hemis.,* **258** H8
Gorgonum Chaos, *W. Hemis.,* **258** N7
Graff, *E. Hemis.,* **261** LI7
Granicus Valles, *E. Hemis.,* **261** FI5
Green, *W. Hemis.,* **259** PI7
Greg, *E. Hemis.,* **261** MI4
Gusev, *E. Hemis.,* **261** KI9

Hadley, *E. Hemis.,* **261** KI8
Hadriacus Palus, *E. Hemis.,* **260** LI2
Hale, *W. Hemis.,* **259** MI6
Harris, *E. Hemis.,* **260** LII
Hartwig, *W. Hemis.,* **259** NI7
Havel Vallis, *W. Hemis.,* **259** HI5
Hecates Tholus, *E. Hemis.,* **261** EI7
Hellas Chaos, *E. Hemis.,* **260** NII
Hellas Planitia, *E. Hemis.,* **260** MII
Hellespontus Montes, *E. Hemis.,* **260** M9
Helmholtz, *W. Hemis.,* **259** NI7
Henry, *E. Hemis.,* **260** G7
Hephaestus Rupes, *E. Hemis.,* **261** FI4
Herschel, *E. Hemis.,* **261** KI6
Hesperia Planum, *E. Hemis.,* **261** LI4
Hibes Montes, *E. Hemis.,* **261** HI9

Holden, *W. Hemis.,* **259** LI7
Holmes, *E. Hemis.,* **260** QI2
Hooke, *W. Hemis.,* **259** NI5
Hrad Vallis, *E. Hemis.,* **261** EI6
Hussey, *W. Hemis.,* **258** NIO
Huxley, *E. Hemis.,* **261** PI3
Huygens, *E. Hemis.,* **260** KIO
Hyblaeus Dorsa, *E. Hemis.,* **261** HI5

Icaria Planum, *W. Hemis.,* **258** MII
Isidis Planitia, *E. Hemis.,* **260** GI2
Ismenia Patera, *E. Hemis.,* **260** D7
Ius Chasma, *W. Hemis.,* **259** JI3

Janssen, *E. Hemis.,* **260** H8
Jarry-Desloges, *E. Hemis.,* **260** JI2
Jovis Tholus, *W. Hemis.,* **258** GIO
Juventae Dorsa, *W. Hemis.,* **259** JI4

Kaiser, *E. Hemis.,* **260** N8
Kasei Valles, *W. Hemis.,* **259** FI4
Kepler, *E. Hemis.,* **261** NI6
Knobel, *E. Hemis.,* **261** JI6
Korolev, *E. Hemis.,* **261** BI4
Koval'sky, *W. Hemis.,* **258** L9
Krishtofovich, *E. Hemis.,* **261** MI3
Kunowsky, *W. Hemis.,* **259** CI6

Labeatis Fossae, *W. Hemis.,* **259** GI3
Lasswitz, *E. Hemis.,* **261** JI7
Lau, *W. Hemis.,* **258** QI2
Le Verrier, *E. Hemis.,* **260** M8
Liais, *E. Hemis.,* **261** QI3
Libya Montes, *E. Hemis.,* **260** HI2
Li Fan, *E. Hemis.,* **258** N9
Liu Hsin, *W. Hemis.,* **258** P9
Lockyer, *E. Hemis.,* **261** FI8
Lohse, *W. Hemis.,* **259** NI7
Loire Valles, *W. Hemis.,* **259** KI8
Lomonosov, *W. Hemis.,* **259** BI5
López, *E. Hemis.,* **261** KI3
Louros Valles, *W. Hemis.,* **259** JI3
Lowell, *W. Hemis.,* **259** NI3
Lucus Planum, *E. Hemis.,* **261** KI9
Lunae Planum, *W. Hemis.,* **259** GI4
Luzin, *E. Hemis.,* **260** F8
Lycus Sulci, *W. Hemis.,* **258** F8
Lyell, *W. Hemis.,* **259** QI5
Lyot, *E. Hemis.,* **260** D9

Ma'Adim Vallis, *E. Hemis.,* **261** LI9
Mädler, *E. Hemis.,* **260** K6
Mad Vallis, *E. Hemis.,* **260** PI2
Magelhaens, *W. Hemis.,* **258** M7
Maggini, *E. Hemis.,* **260** E7
Maja Valles, *W. Hemis.,* **259** HI5
Malea Planum, *E. Hemis.,* **260** PII
Mamers Valles, *E. Hemis.,* **260** D8
Mangala Fossa, *W. Hemis.,* **258** K8
Mangala Valles, *W. Hemis.,* **258** J7
Maraldi, *W. Hemis.,* **259** PI5
Marca, *W. Hemis.,* **258** K7
Mareotis Fossae, *W. Hemis.,* **259** EI3
Margaritifer Terra, *W. Hemis.,* **259** JI8
Marikh Vallis, *E. Hemis.,* **260** L6
Mariner, *W. Hemis.,* **258** M7

Marineris, Valles, *W. Hemis.,* **259** KI5
Marth, *W. Hemis.,* **259** GI9
Martz, *E. Hemis.,* **261** MI6
Masursky, *W. Hemis.,* **259** GI7
Maunder, *E. Hemis.,* **260** P8
Mawrth Vallis, *W. Hemis.,* **259** FI8
Melas Chasma, *W. Hemis.,* **259** JI4
Melas Fossae, *W. Hemis.,* **259** LI4
Mellish, *W. Hemis.,* **259** QI4
Memnonia Fossae, *W. Hemis.,* **258** L7
Meridiani Planum, **259; 260** JI9; J6
Micoud, *E. Hemis.,* **260** C9
Mie, *E. Hemis.,* **261** DI5
Milanković, *W. Hemis.,* **258** CIO
Millman, *W. Hemis.,* **258** P9
Millochau, *E. Hemis.,* **260** KI2
Mitchel, *E. Hemis.,* **260** PI2
Molesworth, *E. Hemis.,* **261** LI7
Moreux, *E. Hemis.,* **260** E9
Müller, *E. Hemis.,* **261** LI5
Mutch, *W. Hemis.,* **259** JI5

Nectaris Fossae, *W. Hemis.,* **259** LI5
Nepenthes Mensae, *E. Hemis.,* **261** HI4
Nereidum Montes, *W. Hemis.,* **259** MI5
Newcomb, *E. Hemis.,* **260** L6
Newton, *W. Hemis.,* **258** N8
Nicholson, *W. Hemis.,* **258** H6
Niesten, *E. Hemis.,* **260** LIO
Nili, Colles, *E. Hemis.,* **260** EII
Nili Fossae, *E. Hemis.,* **260** GII
Nilokeras Scopulus, *W. Hemis.,* **259** EI5
Nilosyrtis Mensae, *E. Hemis.,* **260** FII
Noachis Terra, **259; 260** NI7; N8
Noctis Fossae, *W. Hemis.,* **258** JI2
Noctis Labyrinthus, *W. Hemis.,* **258** JII
Nordenskiöld, *W. Hemis.,* **258** P9

Oenotria Plana, *E. Hemis.,* **260** JII
Oenotria Scopulus, *E. Hemis.,* **260** JII
Okavango Valles, *E. Hemis.,* **260** E7
Olympia Undae, **258; 261** BII; BI3
Olympica Fossae, *W. Hemis.,* **258** FII
Olympus Mons, *W. Hemis.,* **258** G9
Ophir Planum, *W. Hemis.,* **259** JI5
Orcus Patera, *E. Hemis.,* **261** GI9
Orson Welles, *W. Hemis.,* **259** HI6
Oudemans, *W. Hemis.,* **258** KI2
Oxia Colles, *W. Hemis.,* **259** FI7
Oyama, *W. Hemis.,* **259** FI7

P'Al, *E. Hemis.,* **261** LI4
Pallacopas Vallis, *W. Hemis.,* **259** PI6
Panchaia Rupes, *E. Hemis.,* **261** CI4
Parva Planum, *W. Hemis.,* **258** QI2
Pasteur, *E. Hemis.,* **260** G8
Pavonis Mons, *W. Hemis.,* **258** HIO
Perepelkin, *W. Hemis.,* **259** DI4
Peridier, *E. Hemis.,* **260** FI2

Pettit, *W. Hemis.,* **258** G6
Phillips, *W. Hemis.,* **259** PI4
Phlegra Dorsa, *E. Hemis.,* **261** FI8
Phlegra Montes, *E. Hemis.,* **261** DI7
Pickering, *W. Hemis.,* **258** M9
Pityusa Patera, *E. Hemis.,* **260** QIO
Pollack, *E. Hemis.,* **260** J7
Porter, *W. Hemis.,* **258** NII
Proctor, *E. Hemis.,* **260** N9
Promethei Planum, *E. Hemis.,* **260** QI2
Promethei Rupes, *E. Hemis.,* **260** QI2
Promethei Terra, *E. Hemis.,* **261** NI4
Protonilus Mensae, *E. Hemis.,* **260** DIO
Ptolemaeus, *W. Hemis.,* **258** N9

Quenisset, *E. Hemis.,* **260** E9

Rabe, *E. Hemis.,* **260** N9
Radau, *W. Hemis.,* **259** GI9
Rayleigh, *E. Hemis.,* **261** QI3
Renaudot, *E. Hemis.,* **260** EII
Reull Vallis, *E. Hemis.,* **261** MI3
Reynolds, *W. Hemis.,* **258** QII
Robert Sharp, *E. Hemis.,* **261** JI6
Roddenberry, *W. Hemis.,* **259** PI7
Roddy, *W. Hemis.,* **259** LI6
Ross, *W. Hemis.,* **258** NI2
Rudaux, *E. Hemis.,* **260** EIO
Russell, *E. Hemis.,* **260** P9
Rutherford, *W. Hemis.,* **259** FI9

Sabaea, Terra *E. Hemis.,* **260** J8
Sacra Mensa, *W. Hemis.,* **259** FI4
Sagan, *W. Hemis.,* **259** GI7
Saheki, *E. Hemis.,* **260** KII
Samara Valles, *W. Hemis.,* **259** LI8
Savich, *E. Hemis.,* **261** LI3
Scandia Colles, *W. Hemis.,* **258** CIO
Scandia Tholi, *W. Hemis.,* **258** BII
Schaeberle, *E. Hemis.,* **260** L9
Schiaparelli, *E. Hemis.,* **260** J6
Schmidt, *W. Hemis.,* **259** QI3
Schöner, *E. Hemis.,* **260** G9
Schroeter, *E. Hemis.,* **260** J9
Secchi, *E. Hemis.,* **261** NI3
Shalbatana Vallis, *W. Hemis.,* **259** HI7
Sharonov, *W. Hemis.,* **259** FI5
Simud Valles, *W. Hemis.,* **259** GI7
Sinai Dorsa, *W. Hemis.,* **259** KI3
Sinai Fossae, *W. Hemis.,* **259** KI3
Sinai Planum, *W. Hemis.,* **258** KI2
Sirenum, Terra, *W. Hemis.,* **258** M8
Sisyphi Planum, *E. Hemis.,* **260** QIO
Sklodowska, *W. Hemis.,* **259** EI8
Slipher, *W. Hemis.,* **259** NI3
Solis Planum, *W. Hemis.,* **258** LI2
South, *E. Hemis.,* **260** QII
Steno, *W. Hemis.,* **258** PI2
Stokes, *E. Hemis.,* **261** CI6
Stoney, *W. Hemis.,* **258** QII
Surius Vallis, *W. Hemis.,* **259** PI4
Syria Planum, *W. Hemis.,* **258** KII
Syrtis Major Planum, *E. Hemis.,* **260** HII

Tanaica Montes, *W. Hemis.,* **258** EI2
Tantalus Fossae, *W. Hemis.,* **258** EI2
Tartarus Colles, *E. Hemis.,* **261** GI9
Tartarus Montes, *E. Hemis.,* **261** FI9
Teisserenc de Bort, *E. Hemis.,* **260** H9
Tempe Fossae, *W. Hemis.,* **259** EI4
Tempe Terra, *W. Hemis.,* **259** EI4
Terby, *E. Hemis.,* **260** LII
Tharsis Montes, *W. Hemis.,* **258** JIO
Tharsis Tholus, *W. Hemis.,* **258** GI2
Thaumasia Fossae, *W. Hemis.,* **258** NI2
Thaumasia Planum, *W. Hemis.,* **259** KI4
Thyles Rupes, *E. Hemis.,* **261** QI4
Tikhonravov, *E. Hemis.,* **260** G8
Tikhov, *E. Hemis.,* **261** NI3
Tithoniae Fossae, *W. Hemis.,* **259** JI3
Tithonium Chasma, *W. Hemis.,* **259** JI3
Tiu Valles, *W. Hemis.,* **259** GI7
Tombaugh, *E. Hemis.,* **261** HI8
Tractus Catena, *W. Hemis.,* **258** FII
Trouvelot, *W. Hemis.,* **259** GI8
Tyrrhena Terra, *E. Hemis.,* **260** KI2

Ultima Lingula, *E. Hemis.,* **261** QI4
Ultimi Scopuli, *E. Hemis.,* **261** QI4
Ulysses Fossae, *W. Hemis.,* **258** HIO
Ulysses Tholus, *W. Hemis.,* **258** HIO
Uranius Mons, *W. Hemis.,* **258** FI2
Uranius Patera, *W. Hemis.,* **258** FI2
Uranius Tholus, *W. Hemis.,* **258** FI2
Utopia Planitia, *E. Hemis.,* **261** EI5

Vastitas Borealis, **258; 260** CI2; CI2
Very, *W. Hemis.,* **258** P8
Vinogradov, *W. Hemis.,* **259** KI7
Vogel, *W. Hemis.,* **259** MI8

Waikato Vallis, *E. Hemis.,* **261** LI4
Wallace, *E. Hemis.,* **261** NI4
Wells, *E. Hemis.,* **261** PI4
Wien, *E. Hemis.,* **261** KI7
Williams, *W. Hemis.,* **258** K7
Wirtz, *W. Hemis.,* **259** NI6
Wislicenus, *E. Hemis.,* **260** L6
Wright, *W. Hemis.,* **258** PIO

Xanthe Montes, *W. Hemis.,* **259** GI5
Xanthe Terra, *W. Hemis.,* **259** HI6

Zarqa Valles, *E. Hemis.,* **260** JI2
Zephyria Planum, *E. Hemis.,* **261** JI8

Mars Landing Sites

WESTERN HEMISPHERE

Mars 3 (U.S.S.R.)—Landed, contact lost December 2, 1971 **N8**
Mars 6 (U.S.S.R.)—Crashed March 12, 1974 **L18**
Mars Pathfinder (U.S.)—Landed July 4, 1997 **G17**
Opportunity (U.S.)—Landed January 25, 2004 **J19**
Phoenix (U.S.)—Landed May 25, 2008 **C11**
Viking I (U.S.)—Landed July 20, 1976 **F16**

EASTERN HEMISPHERE

Beagle 2 (U.K.)—
  Landed, contact lost December 25, 2003 **H12**
Deep Space 2 Probes (U.S.)—Crashed Dec. 3, 1999 **Q14**
Mars 2 (U.S.S.R.)—Crashed November 27, 1971 **N10**
Mars Polar Lander (U.S.)—Crashed December 3, 1999 **Q14**
Mars Science Laboratory (Curiosity) (U.S.)—
  Landed August 6, 2012 **J16**
Spirit (U.S.)—Landed January 4, 2004 **K19**
Viking 2 (U.S.)—Landed September 3, 1976 **D15**

Acknowledgments

COVER AND FULL TITLE GLOBES

IMAGE: Félix Pharand-Deschênes / Globaïa. globaia.org

DATA SOURCES: *Lakes and wetlands:* Global Lakes and Wetlands Database (GLWD) from WWF, the Center for Environmental Systems Research, and University of Kassel; *Rivers:* HydroSHEDS, hydrosheds.org; *Ice:* Randolph Glacier Inventory (RGI 3.2); *Sea ice:* National Snow and Ice Data Center, nsidc.org; *Ocean color:* Earth Observatory Group in coordination with Gene Feldman and Norman Kuring, NASA Goddard Ocean Color Group.

FOREWORD

IMAGE AND DATA SOURCES: Same as Cover and Full Title as listed above, plus (for population) LandScan Global Population Database. Developed by Oak Ridge National Laboratory (ORNL), distributed by East View Geospatial: geospatial.com and East View Information Services: eastview.com/online/landscan

WORLD THEMES

Introduction   pp. 14–15

CONSULTANT

John Morrison
World Wildlife Fund (WWF)

GRAPHICS

ECOREGIONS: Terrestrial Ecoregions of the World were developed by D.M. Olson, E. Dinerstein, E.D. Wikramanayake, N.D. Burgess, G.V.N. Powell, E.C. Underwood, J.A. D'Amico, I. Itoua, H.E. Strand, J.C. Morrison, C.J. Loucks, T.F. Allnutt, T.H. Ricketts, Y. Kura, J.F. Lamoreux, W.W. Wettengel, P. Hedao, K.R. Kassem, World Wildlife Fund. Marine Ecoregions of the World (MEOW) were developed by the MEOW Working Group, co-chaired by The Nature Conservancy and the World Wildlife Fund (Mark Spalding, Helen Fox, Gerald Allen, Nick Davidson, Zach Ferdana, Max Finlayson, Ben Halpern, Miguel Jorge, Al Lombana, Sara Lourie, Kirsten Martin, Edmund McManus, Jennifer Molnar, Kate Newman, Cheri Recchia, James Robertson).

Structure of the Earth   pp. 22–23

CONSULTANTS

Ron Blakey
Colorado Plateau Geosystems, Inc.

Robert I. Tilling
U.S. Geological Survey (USGS)

GRAPHICS

CONTINENTS ADRIFT IN TIME: Ron Blakey, © Colorado Geosystems, Inc. cpgeosystems.com

CUTAWAY OF THE EARTH: Tibor G. Tóth

TECTONIC BLOCK DIAGRAMS: Susan Sanford

PLATE TECTONICS: *Earthquake data:* USGS Earthquake Hazards Program and USGS National Earthquake Information Center (NEIC). earthquake.usgs.gov. *Volcanism data:* Smithsonian Institution, Global Volcanism Program. volcano.si.edu; USGS and the International Association of Volcanology and Chemistry of the Earth's Interior. vulcan.wr.usgs.gov

GEOLOGIC TIME: International Commission on Stratigraphy. *International Chronostratigraphic Chart,* v2014/10. stratigraphy.org

Earth's Rocky Exterior   pp. 24–25

CONSULTANTS

Jon Spencer
Arizona Geological Survey

Robert I. Tilling
U.S. Geological Survey (USGS)

GRAPHICS

ROCK CYCLE AND READING EARTH HISTORY: Chapel Design & Marketing and XNR Productions

GLOBAL DISTRIBUTION OF ROCK TYPES: Global distribution of surface rock from *The National Geographic Desk Reference.* Washington, D.C.: The National Geographic Society, 1999. Age of oceanic crust from Simkin et al., *This Dynamic Planet: World Map of Volcanoes, Earthquakes, Impact Craters, and Plate Tectonics,* 3rd ed. Washington, D.C.: USGS, 2006.

Landforms   pp. 26–29

CONSULTANTS

Sharon Johnson
University of California, Berkeley

Mike Slattery
Texas Christian University

GRAPHICS

FICTIONAL LANDFORMS: *National Geographic World Atlas for Young Explorers.* Washington, D.C.: The National Geographic Society, 2003.

DUNES: Chapel Design & Marketing

RIVERS: Steven Fick/Canadian Geographic

GLACIAL LANDFORMS: Steven Fick

SATELLITE IMAGERY

MISSISSIPPI RIVER DELTA: Centre National d'Etudes Spatiales (CNES)

Surface of the Earth   pp. 30–31

SATELLITE IMAGERY

EARTH'S SURFACE ELEVATIONS AND DEPTHS, A SLICE OF EARTH: Natural Earth CleanTOPO2. naturalearthdata.com

SNOW AND ICE, LAND SURFACE TEMPERATURE, VEGETATIVE COVER, CLOUD COVER: NASA Earth Observatory. earthobservatory.nasa.gov

Land Cover   pp. 32–33

CONSULTANTS

Mark Friedl and Damien Sulla-Menashe
Global Land Cover Project, Boston University

SATELLITE IMAGERY

GLOBAL LAND COVER: Boston University Department of Geography and Environment Global Land Cover Project. Source data provided by NASA's Moderate Resolution Imaging Spectraradiometer.

Freshwater   pp. 34–35

GRAPHICS

MAP: *National Geographic,* 2010. Water: A Special Issue. Sources: World Wildlife Fund; Igor A. Shiklomanov, State Hydrological Institute, Russia; USGS; University of Kassel Center for Environmental Systems Research, Germany; National Snow and Ice Data Center, University of Colorado.

WATER WITHDRAWALS, BY SECTOR: UNESCO. *Managing Water under Uncertainty and Risk, The United Nations World Water Development Report 4.* 2012, p. 443.

MAPPING IRRIGATION: Food and Agricultural Organization of the United Nations (FAO), 2008.

RENEWABLE WATER RESOURCES: United Nations Statistics Division. *Renewable Freshwater Resources per Capita: Long Term Annual Average.* unstats.un.org (accessed Oct. 2014).

SAFE DRINKING WATER: WHO / UNICEF Joint Monitoring Programme (JMP) for Water Supply and Sanitation. wssinfo.org (accessed Oct. 2014).

Climate   pp. 36–39

CONSULTANT

Vladimir Ryabinin
World Climate Research Programme

GRAPHICS

TAKING THE PLANET'S RISING TEMPERATURE: Source map created by Makiko Sato. Original data source: NASA GISS.

RISING TEMPERATURES AND CO2: NCDC/NOAA: "The Global Surface Temperature is Rising." ncdc.noaa.gov/indicators/

SHRINKING POLAR ICE: National Snow and Ice Data Center. nsidc.org/data/seaice_index

SATELLITE IMAGERY

Images originally created for the GLOBE program by NOAA's National Geophysical Data Center, Boulder, Colorado, U.S.A.

CLOUD COVER: International Satellite Cloud Climatology Project (ISCCP); National Aeronautics and Space Administration (NASA); Goddard Institute for Space Studies (GISS)

PRECIPITATION: Global Precipitation Climatology Project (GPCP); International Satellite Land Surface Climatology Project (ISLSCP)

SOLAR ENERGY: Earth Radiation Budget Experiment (ERBE); Greenhouse Effect Detection Experiment (GEDEX)

TEMPERATURE: National Center for Environmental Prediction (NCEP); National Center for Atmospheric Research (NCAR); National Weather Service (NWS)

Weather   pp. 40–41

CONSULTANTS

Gerry Bell
National Oceanic and Atmospheric Administration (NOAA)

H. Michael Mogil
Certified Consulting Meteorologist (CCM)

GRAPHICS

WATER CYCLE, AIR MASSES, JET STREAM, WEATHER FRONTS, CLOUD TYPES: Chapel Design & Marketing

SATELLITE IMAGERY

HURRICANE IMAGE: NASA Goddard Space Flight Center (GSFC), data from NOAA

EL NIÑO IMAGE SEQUENCE: Courtesy Robert M. Carey, NOAA

LIGHTNING IMAGE: NASA Marshall Space Flight Center Lightning Imaging Sensor (LIS) Instrument Team, Huntsville, Alabama, U.S.

Biosphere   pp. 42–43

CONSULTANTS

Manuel Colunga-Garcia (Entomology), **Patrick J. Webber** (Plant Biology), **David T. Long** (Geological Sciences), **Stuart H. Gage** (Entomology), **Craig K. Harris** (Sociology)
Earth Systems Science Ed. Program, Michigan State University

Jane Robertson Vernhes
World Network of Biosphere Reserves, UNESCO

GRAPHICS

BIOSPHERE DYNAMICS: Earth Systems Science Education Program, Michigan State University, and Chapel Design & Marketing

EARTH SYSTEM DYNAMICS: Edward Gazsi

SIZE OF THE BIOSPHERE: The COMET Program and Chapel Design & Marketing

BIOSPHERE OVER TIME: Earth Systems Science Education Program, Michigan State University

SATELLITE IMAGERY

BIOSPHERE FROM SPACE: SeaWiFS, NASA/Goddard Space Flight Center, Gene Carl Feldman and ORBIMAGE

Biodiversity   pp. 44–45

CONSULTANTS

Craig Hilton-Taylor
International Union for Conservation of Nature and Natural Resources (IUCN)

Kellee Koenig
Conservation International

John Morrison
World Wildlife Fund (WWF)

GENERAL REFERENCE

Catalogue of Life: catalogueoflife.org

GRAPHICS

THE NATURAL WORLD AND SPECIES DIVERSITY: *Biodiversity.* NG Maps for *National Geographic* magazine, February 1999.

BIODIVERSITY HOTSPOTS: Conservation International. conservation.org

THREATENED SPECIES: International Union for Conservation of Nature and Natural Resources (IUCN): iucnredlist.org

CONSERVATION STATUS OF TERRESTRIAL ECOREGIONS: World Wildlife Fund. wwf.panda.org

Human Influences   pp. 46–47

CONSULTANT

Erle Ellis
University of Maryland, Baltimore County

GRAPHICS

ANTHROMES (MAIN MAP) AND HUMAN INFLUENCES OVER TIME: Ellis, E. C., K. Klein Goldewijk, S. Siebert, D. Lightman, and N. Ramankutty. 2010. "Anthropogenic transformation of the biomes, 1700 to 2000." *Global Ecology and Biogeography* 19(5):589–606.

HUMAN INFLUENCE INDEX, LAST OF THE WILD: Wildlife Conservation Society - WCS, and Center for International Earth Science Information Network - CIESIN - Columbia University. 2005. Last of the Wild Project, Version 2, 2005 (LWP-2): Global Human Influence Index (HII) Dataset (IGHP). Palisades, NY: NASA Socioeconomic Data and Applications Center (SEDAC). sedac.ciesin.columbia.edu/data/set/wildareas-v2-human-influence-index-ighp

Population   pp. 48–51

CONSULTANT

Carl Haub
Population Reference Bureau

GENERAL REFERENCES

CIA. *The World Factbook.* cia.gov (accessed 2014); United Nations Department of Economic and Social Affairs Population Division. *World Urbanization Prospects: The 2014 Revision; World Population Prospects: The 2012 Revision;* and *Trends in International Migrant Stock: The 2013 Revision.*

GRAPHICS

POPULATION PYRAMIDS: U.S. Census Bureau

POPULATION DENSITY: LandScan 2012 Global Population Database. Developed by Oak Ridge National Laboratory (ORNL), July 2013. Distributed by East View Geospatial: geospatial.com and East View Information Services: eastview.com/online/landscan

SATELLITE IMAGERY

LIGHTS OF THE WORLD: NASA. NASA Visible Earth 2012. visibleearth.nasa.gov

Languages   pp. 52–53

GRAPHICS

LANGUAGE FAMILIES (MAIN MAP): Global Mapping International (GMI) and SIL International. World Language Mapping System, version 3.2.1.

EVOLUTION OF LANGUAGES: *National Geographic Almanac of Geography.* Washington, D.C.: The National Geographic Society, 2005.

HOW MANY SPEAK WHAT: Loh, Jonathan and Dave Harmon. 2013. Data from Gordon, R.G. (ed.), 2005. *Ethnologue: Languages of the World,* Fifteenth edition. Dallas, Tex.: SIL International.

MAPPING LANGUAGE DIVERSITY: Ethnologue (2013 data). ethnologue.com

VANISHING LANGUAGES: Living Tongues Institute for Endangered Languages/National Geographic. *Language Hotspots map.* travel.nationalgeographic.com/travel/enduring-voices

Religions
pp. 54–55

CONSULTANT

Todd Johnson
Center for the Study of Global Christianity,
Gordon-Conwell Theological Seminary

GRAPHICS

DOMINANT RELIGION (MAIN MAP): World Religion Database, research version, 2014. worldreligiondatabase.org

BY THE NUMBERS: World Religion Database; Pew Research Center, pewforum.org (accessed 2013)

Health and Education
pp. 56–57

CONSULTANTS

Carlos Castillo-Salgado
Pan American Health Organization (PAHO)/
World Health Organization (WHO)

George Ingram and Annababette Wils
Education Policy and Data Center

Margaret Kruk
United Nations Millennium Project and
University of Michigan School of Public Health

Ruth Levine
Center for Global Development

GRAPHICS

INCOME LEVELS: World Bank. data.worldbank.org

ACCESS TO IMPROVED SANITATION: UNICEF. 2014 Update: Progress on Drinking Water and Sanitation. unicef.org

NUTRITION: Food and Agriculture Organization. The State of Food Insecurity in the World, 2014. fao.org

HIV: UNAIDS. unaids.org

HEALTH CARE AVAILABILITY: World Health Organization. World Health Statistics 2012. who.org

GLOBAL DISEASE BURDEN: World Health Organization. WHO Mortality Database; Mortality and Global Burden of Disease (GBD), 2012.

UNDER-FIVE MORTALITY: United Nations Statistics Division. Millennium Development Goals Indicators. mdgs.un.org

EDUCATION AND LITERACY: CIA. The World Factbook. cia.gov (accessed Oct. 2014).

SCHOOL ENROLLMENT FOR GIRLS: UNICEF. The State of the World's Children 2015. unicef.org

MATERNAL MORTALITY: World Bank, with WHO, UNICEF, UNFPA, and UN Population Division. who.int

DEVELOPING HUMAN CAPITAL: Adapted from Human Capital Projections developed by Education Policy and Data Center. epdc.org

Economy
pp. 58–59

GRAPHICS

DOMINANT ECONOMIC SECTOR (MAIN MAP): CIA. The World Factbook. cia.gov (accessed Sept. 2014); "Value added, by activity" data from OECD Factbook 2013: Economic, Environmental and Social Statistics. oecd.org

HUMAN DEVELOPMENT INDEX: United Nations Development Programme. UNDP 2014 Human Development Report. undp.org

TOP GDP GROWTH RATES: World Bank. data.worldbank.org (accessed Oct. 2014)

THE WORLD'S RICHEST AND POOREST COUNTRIES, GROSS DOMESTIC PRODUCT: International Monetary Fund. imf.org (accessed Oct. 2014).

GLOBAL INNOVATION INDEX: The Global Innovation Index 2014. globalinnovationindex.org

MAJOR EXPORTERS: World Trade Organization. International Trade Statistics 2013. wto.org

Trade
pp. 60–61

CONSULTANTS

Peter Werner and Michael Finger
World Trade Organization (WTO)

GRAPHICS

WORLD ECONOMIES: World Bank. data.worldbank.org (accessed Oct. 2014)

SINGLE-COMMODITY DEPENDENT ECONOMIES: International Trade Centre. intracen.org (accessed Oct. 2014)

STOCK EXCHANGES: World Federation of Exchanges. world-exchanges.org (accessed Oct. 2014)

WORLD MERCHANDISE TRADE, GROWTH OF WORLD TRADE, MERCHANDISE EXPORTS, MAIN TRADING NATIONS, TRADE FLOW: FUELS, TRADE FLOW: AGRICULTURAL PRODUCTS, TOP MERCHANDISE EXPORTERS AND IMPORTERS, TOP COMMERCIAL SERVICES EXPORTERS AND IMPORTERS: World Trade Organization. International Trade Statistics 2013.

WORLD DEBT: CIA. The World Factbook. cia.gov (accessed Oct. 2014)

TRADE BLOCS: APEC (apec.org), ASEAN (asean.org), COMESA (about.comesa.int), ECOWAS (comm.ecowas.int), EU (europa.eu), MERCOSUR (mercosur.int), NAFTA (ustr.gov), SAFTA (saarc-sec.org)

Food
pp. 62–65

GENERAL REFERENCES

Foley, Jonathan. "A Five-Step Plan to Feed the World." National Geographic, May 2014. Available online at nationalgeographic.com/foodfeatures/feeding-9-billion/

Food and Agriculture Organization of the United Nations (FAO). FAO Statistical Yearbook 2013. Available online at fao.org/docrep/018/i3107e/i3107e.PDF

GRAPHICS

AGRICULTURE'S FOOTPRINT (MAIN MAP), WHERE CROP YIELDS COULD IMPROVE, HOW OUR CROPS ARE USED: Global Landscapes Initiative, Institute on the Environment, University of Minnesota.

AGRICULTURE'S FOOTPRINT (CHART): "Land Transformation by Humans: A Review." Roger LeB. Hooke, José F. Martín-Duque. GSA Today, Volume 22, Issue 12.

DISTRIBUTION OF MAJOR CROPS AND LIVESTOCK, FISHING AND AQUACULTURE, FOOD SECURITY: Food and Agriculture Organization of the United Nations Statistics Division (FAOSTAT). FAO Statistical Yearbook 2013.

WORLD FOOD PRODUCTION: FAOSTAT. faostat.fao.org (accessed Oct. 2014)

GENETICALLY MODIFIED CROPS: International Service for the Acquisition of Agri-Biotech Applications. isaaa.org (accessed Oct. 2014)

CALORIC SUPPLY: FAOSTAT Food Balance Sheets. faostat.fao.org (accessed Oct. 2014)

Energy
pp. 66–67

GRAPHICS

ENERGY CONSUMPTION BY LEADING SOURCE (MAIN MAP): Energy Information Administration, U.S. Department of Energy. eia.gov (accessed Oct. 2013); Horn, M.K. Giant Oil and Gas Fields of the World. Available online via the American Association of Petroleum Geologists/AAPG Datapages. datapages.com

ENERGY PRODUCTION BY FUEL TYPE, ENERGY PRODUCTION BY REGION: International Energy Agency. 2014 Key World Energy Statistics.

BALANCING CONSUMPTION AND PRODUCTION: Energy Information Administration, U.S. Department of Energy. eia.gov

RENEWABLE RESOURCES (GRAPH) AND RENEWABLE LEADERS (MAP): Renewable Energy Policy Network for the 21st Century (REN21). Renewables 2013 Global Status Report. Paris: REN21, 2014. ren21.net

Minerals
pp. 68–69

CONSULTANT

Philip Brown
University of Wisconsin—Madison

GENERAL REFERENCES

EXPORTS IN NON-FUEL MINING PRODUCTS (MAIN MAP): World Trade Organization. International Trade and Market Access Data. wto.org (accessed Nov. 2014)

WORLD MINERAL PRODUCTION BY TYPE: Philip Brown, University of Wisconsin—Madison.

STEEL PRODUCTION BY LOCATION: World Steel Association. World Steel in Figures 2014. worldsteel.org

WORLD MINING BY REGION: International Council on Mining and Metals. Trends in the Mining and Metals Industry, October 2012. Available online at icmm.com/document/4441

WORLD SHARE OF PRODUCTION: USGS Mineral Commodity Summaries, 2014. minerals.usgs.gov

Environmental Stresses
pp. 70–71

GRAPHICS

DESERTIFICATION AND LAND DEGRADATION, DEFORESTATION: Millennium Ecosystem Assessment. Ecosystems and Human Well-Being, Synthesis.

CHANGES IN FOREST AREA: Earth Policy Institute. FAO Forest Resources Assessment 2010.

AIR POLLUTION: van Donkelaar, A., R.V. Martin, M. Brauer, R. Kahn, R. Levy, C. Verduzco, and P.J. Villeneuve. "Global estimates of exposure to fine particulate matter concentrations from satellite-based aerosol optical depth." Environ. Health Perspec., doi:10.1289/ehp.0901623, 118(6), 2010.

CARBON EMISSIONS: International Energy Agency. CO_2 Emissions From Fuel Combustion Highlights 2013. iea.org/publications

SATELLITE IMAGERY

DEPLETION OF THE OZONE LAYER: NASA. Ozone Hole Watch. ozonewatch.gsfc.nasa.gov/monthly/ (accessed Nov. 2014)

Protected Areas
pp. 72–73

CONSULTANTS

Amy Milam
EcoLogic, LLC

UNEP-WCMC

UNESCO World Heritage Centre

GRAPHICS

PROTECTED AREAS (MAIN MAP AND GROWTH GRAPH): IUCN and UNEP-WCMC 2014, The World Database on Protected Areas (WDPA), November 2014 Release. Cambridge, UK: UNEP-WCMC. protectedplanet.net

WORLD HERITAGE SITES: UNESCO. whc.unesco.org/en/list (Nov. 2014)

Globalization
pp. 74–75

GRAPHICS

GLOBALIZATION INDEX (ALL MAPS): Swiss Federal Institute of Technology Zurich. ETH: KOF Index of Globalization, 2014 Rankings. globalization.kof.ethz.ch

INTERNATIONAL MIGRATION: UN Department of Economic and Social Affairs. International Migration 2013, Graphs and Maps from the 2013 Wallchart. un.org/en/development/desa

TRANSNATIONAL CORPORATIONS: The World Bank. World Development Indicators. data.worldbank.org (accessed Nov. 2014); UN Conference on Trade and Development. World Investment Report 2014. unctad.org

Digital Connectivity
pp. 76–77

GRAPHICS

INTERREGIONAL INTERNET BANDWIDTH (MAIN MAP) AND GROWTH IN INTERNET BANDWIDTH (GRAPH): Telegeography. 2012 Global Internet Map. telegeography.com

BOOMING MOBILE-CELLULAR SUBSCRIPTIONS, INTERNET ACCESS: International Telecommunication Union (ITU). ITU World Telecommunication/ICT Indicators Database 2013. itu.int

ADDITIONAL SATELLITE IMAGERY

Antarctica
pp. 232–233

PAGE 232, SURFACE ELEVATION: Byrd Polar Research Center, Ohio State University. Ice Sheet Thickness: Bedmap Project. Ice Flow Velocity: Roland Warner, Antarctic Cooperative Research Centre and Australian Antarctic Division. Sea Ice Movement and Wind Flow: Sea ice velocity data: Mark R. Drinkwater and Xiang Liu, Jet Propulsion Laboratory/California Institute of Technology. Surface winds: based on data from David H. Bromwich, Ohio State University, and Thomas R. Parish, University of Wyoming.

SPACE

Space Introduction
pp. 250–251

IMAGE

PAGES 250–251, MONKEY HEAD NEBULA, SHARPLESS SH2-252: NASA, ESA, and the Hubble Heritage Team (STScI/AURA)

Moon
pp. 252–255

DATA SOURCES

PHYSICAL FEATURE NAMES: Gazetteer of Planetary Nomenclature. Planetary Geomatics Group of the USGS (United States Geological Survey) Astrogeology Science Center. planetarynames.wr.usgs.gov (accessed Aug. 2014).

TERRAIN, MAIN MAP GLOBAL MOSAICS: Lunar Reconnaissance Orbiter (LRO); NASA; Arizona State University

PHASES OF THE MOON, LUNAR INFLUENCE ON TIDES: National Geographic Society, Lunar Reconnaissance Orbiter (LRO); NASA

Inner Solar System
pp. 256–257

IMAGES

NASA/JPL-Caltech, Johns Hopkins University Applied Physics Laboratory, Carnegie Institution of Washington.

Mars
pp. 258–261

DATA SOURCES

PHYSICAL FEATURE NAMES: Gazetteer of Planetary Nomenclature. Planetary Geomatics Group of the USGS (United States Geological Survey) Astrogeology Science Center. planetarynames.wr.usgs.gov (accessed Aug. 2014).

GLOBAL MOSAICS: NASA Mars Global Surveyor (MGS); National Geographic Society

TERRAIN: NASA Mars Global Surveyor (MGS); Mars Orbital Laser Altimeter (MOLA)

IMAGES

Phobos: NASA/JPL-Caltech/University of Arizona

Outer Solar System
pp. 262–263

IMAGES

NASA/JPL-Caltech, Johns Hopkins University Applied Physics Laboratory, Carnegie Institution of Washington

Universe
pp. 264–265

ARTWORK

Ken Eward, National Geographic Society

IMAGES

LOOKING BACK IN TIME FOR ORIGINS (BACKGROUND): Hubble Ultra Deep Field 2012; NASA, ESA, R. Ellis (Caltech), and the UDF 2012 Team

Acknowledgments

ADDITIONAL CONSULTANTS

Regional Thematic Maps

Carl Haub
Population Reference Bureau

W. David Menzie and J. Michael Eros
USGS Minerals Information Team

Freddy Nachtergaele
Food and Agriculture Organization of the United Nations (FAO)

Gregory Yetman
Center for International Earth Science Information Network (CIESIN), Columbia University

Flags and Facts

Graham Bartram
Chief Vexillologist, The Flag Institute, London, United Kingdom

Carl Haub
Population Reference Bureau

Whitney Smith
Flag Research Center

Antarctica pp. 226–233

Graham Bartram
The Flag Institute

Scott Borg
National Science Foundation (NSF)—Antarctic Division

Mark R. Drinkwater
European Space Agency

Kenneth Jezek
Byrd Polar Research Center, Ohio State University

Tony K. Meunier
USGS Polar Program

David G. Vaughan
Bedmap Consortium, British Antarctic Survey

Roland Warner
Antarctic Cooperative Research Centre and Australian Antarctic Division

Oceans pp. 234–249

Eric J. Lindstrom
National Aeronautics and Space Administration (NASA)

Keelin Kuipers
National Oceanic and Atmospheric Administration (NOAA)

Bob Molinari
NOAA

Bruce Parker
NOAA/National Ocean Service (NOS)

Richard A. Schmalz, Jr.
NOAA

Limits of the Oceans and Seas pp. 238–239

Adam J. Kerr
International Hydrographic Management Consulting

Space pp. 250–265

Alexei V. Filippenko
Department of Astronomy, University of California, Berkeley

Sanjay S. Limaye and Rosalyn A. Pertzborn
Space Science and Engineering Center, University of Wisconsin—Madison

Stephen P. Maran
Robert E. Pratt
National Geographic Maps

The Moon pp. 252–255

Paul D. Spudis
Lunar and Planetary Institute, Houston, Texas

Inner Solar System pp. 256–257

Lucy McFadden
University of Maryland, College Park

Mars pp. 258–261

Damond Benningfield
StarDate radio series

Outer Solar System pp. 262–263

Henry Kline
NASA Jet Propulsion Laboratory (JPL)

The Universe pp. 264–265

Todd J. Henry
Harvard-Smithsonian Center for Astrophysics

Edmund Bertschinger
Massachusetts Institute of Technology

Donald P. Schneider
Pennsylvania State University

Marc Postman
Space Telescope Science Institute (STScI)

Christopher D. Impey
University of Arizona

R. Brent Tully
University of Hawai'i

August E. Evrard
University of Michigan

Geographic Comparisons pp. 268–269

John Kammerer
National Geospatial-Intelligence Agency (NGA)

George Sharman
NOAA/NESDIS/NGDC

Peter H. Gleick
Pacific Institute for Studies in Development, Environment, and Security

R. L. Fisher
Scripps Institution of Oceanography

Philip Micklin
Western Michigan University

Special Flags pp. 270–271

Graham Bartram
The Flag Institute

Glossary pp. 282–284

Rex Honey
University of Iowa

Bernard O. Bauer
University of Southern California

PHYSICAL AND POLITICAL MAPS

Bureau of the Census, U.S. Department of Commerce

Bureau of Land Management, U.S. Department of the Interior

Central Intelligence Agency (CIA)

National Geographic Maps

National Geospatial-Intelligence Agency (NGA)

National Park Service, U.S. Department of the Interior

Office of the Geographer and Global Issues, U.S. Department of State

U.S. Board on Geographic Names (BGN)

U.S. Geological Survey, U.S. Department of the Interior

PRINCIPAL REFERENCE SOURCES

Columbia Gazetteer of the World. Cohen, Saul B., ed. New York: Columbia University Press

Encarta World English Dictionary. New York: St. Martin's Press and Microsoft Encarta

Human Development Reports. New York: United Nations Development Programme (UNDP)

International Trade Statistics. Geneva, Switzerland: World Trade Organization

McKnight, Tom L. *Physical Geography: A Landscape Appreciation.* 5th ed. Upper Saddle River, New Jersey: Prentice Hall, 1996

National Geographic Atlas of the World. 10th ed. Washington, D.C.: The National Geographic Society, 2014

Strahler, Alan, and Arthur Strahler. *Physical Geography: Science and Systems of the Human Environment.* 2nd ed. Hoboken, New Jersey: John Wiley & Sons, Inc., 2002

Tarbuck, Edward J. and Frederick K. Lutgens. *Earth: An Introduction to Physical Geology.* 7th ed. Upper Saddle River, New Jersey: Prentice Hall, 2002

World Development Indicators, Washington, D.C.: World Bank

The World Factbook. Washington, D.C.: Central Intelligence Agency

The World Health Report. Geneva: World Health Organization

World Investment Report. New York and Geneva: United Nations Conference on Trade and Development

Cambridge Dictionaries Online
dictionary.cambridge.org

Central Intelligence Agency
cia.gov

CIESIN
ciesin.org

Conservation International
conservation.org

Energy Information Agency
eia.doe.gov

Food and Agriculture Organization of the UN
fao.org

International Monetary Fund
imf.org

Merriam-Webster OnLine
m-w.com

National Aeronautics and Space Administration
nasa.gov

National Climatic Data Center
ncdc.noaa.gov

National Geophysical Data Center
ngdc.noaa.gov

National Oceanic and Atmospheric Administration
noaa.gov

National Park Service
nps.gov

National Renewable Energy Laboratory
nrel.gov

Population Reference Bureau
prb.org

United Nations
un.org

UN Conference on Trade and Development
unctad.org

UN Development Programme
undp.org

UN Educational, Cultural, and Scientific Organization
unesco.org

UNESCO Institute for Statistics
uis.unesco.org

UNEP-WCMC
unep-wcmc.org

UN Millennium Development Goals
un.org/millenniumgoals

UN Population Division
unpopulation.org

UN Refugee Agency
unhcr.org

UN Statistics Division
unstats.un.org

U.S. Board on Geographic Names
geonames.usgs.gov

U.S. Bureau of Economic Analysis
bea.gov

U.S. Census Bureau
census.gov

U.S. Geological Survey
usgs.gov

World Bank
worldbank.org

World Health Organization
who.int

World Trade Organization
wto.org

WWF
worldwildlife.org

PHOTOGRAPHS

FRONT JACKET

(LE) Kerrick James/Corbis
(CT LE) David McGlynn/Getty Images
(CT) NASA Visible Earth: Image created by Reto Stöckli with the help of Alan Nelson, under the leadership of Fritz Hasler
(CT RT) Multi-bits/Getty Images
(RT) Bob Smith/National Geographic Creative

INTERIOR

PAGE 24, (UP) R. D. Griggs, USGS
PAGE 24, (CT) Sharon Johnson Edell
PAGE 24, (LO) Muench Photography Inc.
PAGE 25, (UP) Raymond Gehman/National Geographic Creative
PAGE 26, (LE) Joel Sartore/National Geographic Creative
PAGE 26, (CT) David Parker/Science Source
PAGE 26, (UP RT) George F. Mobley/National Geographic Creative
PAGE 26, (LO RT) James D. Balog/National Geographic Creative
PAGE 27, (UP LE) Wolfgang Kaehler/Corbis
PAGE 27, (UP CT) Lyle Rosbotham
PAGE 27, (UP RT) Adriel Heisey
PAGE 27, (LO LE) Marc Moritsch/National Geographic Creative
PAGE 27, (LO CT) Peter Essick
PAGE 27, (LO RT) Sam Abell/National Geographic Creative
PAGE 28, (LE) Peter Essick
PAGE 28, (CT) Douglas R. Grant
PAGE 28, (RT) Tom and Pat Leeson
PAGE 29, (UP CT) Rob Brander
PAGE 29, (UP RT) George Veni & James Jasek
PAGE 29, (LO LE) Sharon Johnson Edell
PAGE 29, (LO RT) Douglas R. Grant/Parks Canada
PAGE 32, (UP LE) Tom and Pat Leeson/Science Source
PAGE 32, (UP RT) Michael Nichols/National Geographic Creative
PAGE 32, (LO-A) Stephen J. Krasemann/Science Source
PAGE 32, (LO-B) Rod Planck/Science Source
PAGE 32, (LO-C) James Steinberg/Science Source
PAGE 32, (LO-D) Matthew C. Hansen
PAGE 32, (LO-E) Gregory G. Dimijian/Science Source
PAGE 32, (LO-F) Sharon Johnson Edell
PAGE 32, (LO-G) Adam Burton/Robert Harding World Imagery/Corbis
PAGE 33, (A) Rod Planck/Science Source
PAGE 33, (B) James Randklev/Getty Images
PAGE 33, (C) George Steinmetz/Corbis
PAGE 33, (D) Jim Richardson/National Geographic Creative
PAGE 33, (E) Steve McCurry/National Geographic Creative
PAGE 33, (F) George Steinmetz/National Geographic Creative
PAGE 33, (G) B. & C. Alexander/Science Source

PAGE 37, (LE) Rob Whitworth/Corbis
PAGE 37, (RT) AP Photo/Rich Pedroncelli
PAGE 47, (UP LE) QILAI SHEN/epa/Corbis
PAGE 47, (UP CT) Frank Chen/Getty Images
PAGE 47, (UP RT) Sara Winter/Getty Images
PAGE 47, (LO LE) David Santiago Garcia/Getty Images
PAGE 47, (LO CT) Andrew Holt/Getty Images
PAGE 47, (LO RT) Galen Rowell/Corbis
PAGE 54, (LE) James L. Stanfield/National Geographic Creative
PAGE 54, (CT) Thomas J. Abercrombie/National Geographic Creative
PAGE 54, (RT) Tony Heiderer/National Geographic Creative
PAGE 55, (LE) Jodi Cobb/National Geographic Creative
PAGE 55, (CT) MORANDI Bruno/Hemis/Corbis
PAGE 55, (RT) Annie Griffiths/National Geographic Creative
PAGE 71, Andre Kudyusov/Getty Images
PAGE 73, (LE) Art Wolfe/artwolfe.com
PAGE 73, (CT) Richard Nowitz/National Geographic Creative
PAGE 73, (RT) Sarah Leen/National Geographic Creative
PAGE 74, (LE) Nico Tondini/Robert Harding World Imagery/Corbis
PAGE 74, (RT) Julian Abram Wainwright/Bloomberg via Getty Images
PAGE 76, (LE) JENS BUETTNER/epa/Corbis
PAGE 76, (RT) xPACIFICA/Corbis
PAGE 78-79, Ron Watts/Corbis
PAGE 81, (UP) Kenneth Garrett/National Geographic Creative
PAGE 81, (LO) Danny Lehman/Corbis
PAGE 124-5, Skip Brown/National Geographic Creative
PAGE 127, (UP) L. Scott Shelton
PAGE 127, (LO) Danny Lehman/Corbis
PAGE 136-7, George F. Mobley/National Geographic Creative
PAGE 139, (UP) Winfield Parks/National Geographic Creative
PAGE 139, (LO) FREDERICK FLORIN/AFP/Getty Images
PAGE 164-5, J Yip//Panoramic Images
PAGE 167, (UP) Steve McCurry/National Geographic Creative
PAGE 167, (LO) Xu Xiaolin/Corbis
PAGE 194-5, Beverly Joubert/National Geographic Creative
PAGE 197, (UP) David S. Boyer/National Geographic Creative
PAGE 197, (LO) Kelechi Amadi-Obi
PAGE 210-1, Theo Allofs/Corbis
PAGE 213, (UP) Diane Cook and Len Jenshel/Getty Images
PAGE 213, (LO) Doug Pearson/Getty Images
PAGE 226-7, Paul A. Souders/Corbis
PAGE 229, Maria Stenzel/National Geographic Creative

KEY TO FLAGS AND FACTS

The National Geographic Society, whose cartographic policy is to recognize de facto countries, counted 195 independent nations in the spring of 2015. Within this atlas, fact boxes for independent nations, most dependencies, and U.S. states are placed on or next to regional maps that show the areas they represent. Each box includes the flag of the political entity, as well as important statistical data. Boxes for some dependencies show two flags—a local flag and the flag of the administering country. Since Paraguay and the state of Oregon have different designs on the obverse and reverse sides of their flags, their fact boxes show both sides of their flags.

The statistical data provide highlights of geography, demography, and economy. These details offer a brief overview of each entity; they present general characteristics and are not intended to be comprehensive studies. The structured nature of the text results in some generic collective or umbrella terms. The industry category, for instance, includes services in addition to traditional manufacturing sectors. Space limitations dictate the amount of information included. For example, the only languages listed for the U.S. are English and Spanish, although many others are spoken.

Fact boxes are arranged alphabetically by the conventional short forms of the country or dependency names (except for the Oceania, Islands of Africa, and Europe's Smallest Countries fact boxes, where country and dependency boxes are grouped separately). The short-form names for dependencies are followed by the name of the administering country in parentheses. The short-form names for Côte d'Ivoire, Myanmar, and Timor-Leste are followed by alternate, commonly referred to names in parentheses. The conventional long-form names of the country or dependency appear within colored stripes below the short-form names; if there are no long forms, the short forms are repeated. This policy has two exceptions: For U.S. states, nicknames are shown inside the colored stripes, and for French overseas departments, the words "Overseas Department of France" appear inside the colored stripes. These departments of France are the equivalent of states in the United States, and thus not considered dependencies. NA indicates that data are not available or not applicable.

AREA accounts for the total area of a country, U.S. state, or dependency, including all land and inland water features as delimited by coastlines and international boundaries. Figures do not include territorial waters. Area information comes from the CIA *World Factbook* and the U.S. State Department. Figures for the U.S. states and the District of Columbia come from the U.S. Census Bureau.

In the POPULATION category, the figures for U.S. state populations are from the U.S. Census Bureau's 2014 midyear estimates. Two population figures are listed for the CAPITAL and LARGEST CITY of each state. The city-proper figure, from data provided by the U.S. Census Bureau, shows the estimated number of people who lived within the incorporated city limits on July 1, 2013. The larger metro-area figure represents the number of people who live within a U.S. Office of Management and Budget-defined metropolitan statistical area—a broader designation that includes both a city proper and the surrounding urbanized region. These July 1, 2013, estimates are from the U.S. Census Bureau's table of Annual Estimates of the Population of Metropolitan and Micropolitan Statistical Areas. Metropolitan statistical areas and their geographic boundaries can cross state borders and are defined on the basis of population as well as other factors. Some state capitals with small populations are not defined as part of a metropolitan statistical area and thus do not have a metro-area figure.

POPULATION figures for independent nations and dependencies are mid-2014 figures from the 2014 CIA *World Factbook*. Next to CAPITAL is the name of the seat of government, followed by the city's population. Capital city populations for both independent nations and dependencies are estimates from the United Nations' 2014 *World Urbanization Prospects* and represent the population of the city's urban agglomeration, which usually includes both city proper and adjacent suburbs. Both POPULATION and CAPITAL population figures for countries, dependencies, and U.S. states are rounded to the nearest thousand.

Under RELIGION, the most widely practiced faith appears first. "Traditional" or "indigenous" connotes beliefs of important local sects, such as Maya in Middle America. Under LANGUAGE, the most widely spoken language is listed first. Both RELIGION and LANGUAGE are in rank ordering, taken from the 2014 CIA *World Factbook*.

LITERACY generally indicates the percentage of the population above the age of 15 who can read and write. There are no universal standards of literacy, so these estimates (from the 2014 CIA *World Factbook*) are based on the most common definition available for a nation. LIFE EXPECTANCY (from the 2014 CIA *World Factbook*) represents the average number of years a group of infants born in the same year can be expected to live if the mortality rate at each age remains constant in the future.

GDP PER CAPITA is gross domestic product (GDP) based on purchasing-power parity (PPP) in current international dollars divided by midyear population estimates. GDP per capita estimates, rounded to the nearest hundred, are from the 2014 CIA *World Factbook*. Gross domestic product is the value of all final goods and services produced within a region in a given year. These estimates are calculated using the PPP conversion factor designed to equalize the purchasing powers of different countries. For U.S. states, equivalent measurements to GDP on the intranational level have been used. 2013 per capita INCOME figures from the U.S. Census Bureau's 2009–2013 5-year *American Community Survey* are presented.

Individual income estimates such as GDP PER CAPITA and per capita INCOME are among the many indicators used to assess a nation's well-being. As statistical averages, they hide extremes of poverty and wealth. Furthermore, they take no account of factors that affect quality of life, such as environmental degradation, educational opportunities, and health care.

ECONOMY information for the independent nations and dependencies is divided into three general categories: industry, agriculture, and exports. Because of structural limitations, only the primary industries (IND), agricultural commodities (AGR), and exports (EXP) as listed in the 2014 CIA *World Factbook* are reported. Agriculture serves as an umbrella term not only for crops but also for livestock, products, and fish. In the interest of conciseness, agriculture for the independent nations presents, when applicable but not limited to, four major crops, followed by leading entries for livestock, products, and fish. For the other two categories, the leading industries and export products are listed as data and space limitations allow. The information provided for each category is listed in rank order, starting with the largest by value or importance.

In certain cases, the 2014 CIA World Factbook *did not include some data for specific nations or dependencies. Various official government figures and other reputable sources were then used to complete the fact boxes.*

FAMILY REFERENCE ATLAS OF THE WORLD

FOURTH EDITION

Published by the National Geographic Society

Gary E. Knell	President and Chief Executive Officer
John M. Fahey	Chairman of the Board
Declan Moore	Chief Media Officer
Chris Johns	Chief Content Officer

Prepared by the Book Division

Hector Sierra	Senior Vice President and General Manager
Lisa Thomas	Senior Vice President and Editorial Director
Jonathan Halling	Creative Director
Marianne R. Koszorus	Design Director
R. Gary Colbert	Production Director
Jennifer A. Thornton	Director of Managing Editorial
Susan S. Blair	Director of Photography
Meredith C. Wilcox	Director, Administration and Rights Clearance

Staff for This Atlas

Carl Mehler	Project Editor and Director of Maps
Juan José Valdés	The Geographer NGS
Matthew W. Chwastyk	Map Production Manager
Maureen J. Flynn, Julie A. Ibinson	Map Editors
Michael McNey, Gregory Ugiansky, and XNR Productions	Map Research and Production
Jennifer Conrad Seidel	Contibuting Writer and Editor

Elisabeth B. Booz, Patrick Booz, Philip Brown, William Burroughs, Carlos Castillo-Salgado, Manuel Colunga-Garcia, Byron Crape, Ellen Ficklen, Michael Finger, Richard Fix, Stuart H. Gage, Matthew C. Hansen, Craig K. Harris, Mike Hoffmann, Tim Kelly, K. M. Kostyal, Ruth Levine, Eric Lindstrom, David T. Long, Enrique Loyola-Elizondo, Stephen P. Maran, Carl Mehler, W. David Menzie, David B. Miller, H. Michael Mogil, John Morrison, Rhea Muchow, Ted Munn, Margaret Murray, Sarah Parks, Janet Pau, Josh Polterock, Antony Shugaar, Brad Singer, Peter W. Sloss, Whitney Smith, Paul D. Spudis, Robert Tilling, Simon Walker, Patrick J. Webber, Joe Yogerst   Contributing Writers

Marshall Kiker	Associate Managing Editor
Judith Klein	Senior Production Editor
George Bounelis	Manager, Production Services

The National Geographic Society is one of the world's largest nonprofit scientific and educational organizations. Founded in 1888 to "increase and diffuse geographic knowledge," the member-supported Society works to inspire people to care about the planet. Through its online community, members can get closer to explorers and photographers, connect with other members around the world, and help make a difference. National Geographic reflects the world through its magazines, television programs, films, music and radio, books, DVDs, maps, exhibitions, live events, school publishing programs, interactive media, and merchandise. *National Geographic* magazine, the Society's official journal, published in English and 38 local-language editions, is read by more than 60 million people each month. The National Geographic Channel reaches 440 million households in 171 countries in 38 languages. National Geographic Digital Media receives more than 25 million visitors a month. National Geographic has funded more than 10,000 scientific research, conservation, and exploration projects and supports an education program promoting geography literacy. For more information, visit www.nationalgeographic.com.

For more information, please call 1-800-NGS LINE (647-5463) or write to the following address:

National Geographic Society
1145 17th Street NW
Washington, D.C. 20036-4688 U.S.A.

For information about special discounts for bulk purchases, please contact National Geographic Books Special Sales: ngspecsales@ngs.org

For rights or permissions inquiries, please contact National Geographic Books Subsidiary Rights: ngbookrights@ngs.org

Library of Congress Cataloging-in-Publication Data

National Geographic Society (U.S.), author, issuing body.
 National Geographic Family reference atlas of the world / National Geographic, Washington, D.C. -- Fourth edition.
    pages cm
 "Copyright © 2016"
 Includes bibliographical references and indexes.
 ISBN 978-1-4262-1543-8 (hardcover : alk. paper)
 1. Geography--Maps. 2. Physical geography--Maps.
    3. Political geography--Maps. I. Title. II. Title: Family reference atlas of the world.
 G1021.N393 2016
 912--dc23

                                                   2015006195

Printed in Hong Kong
15/THK/1

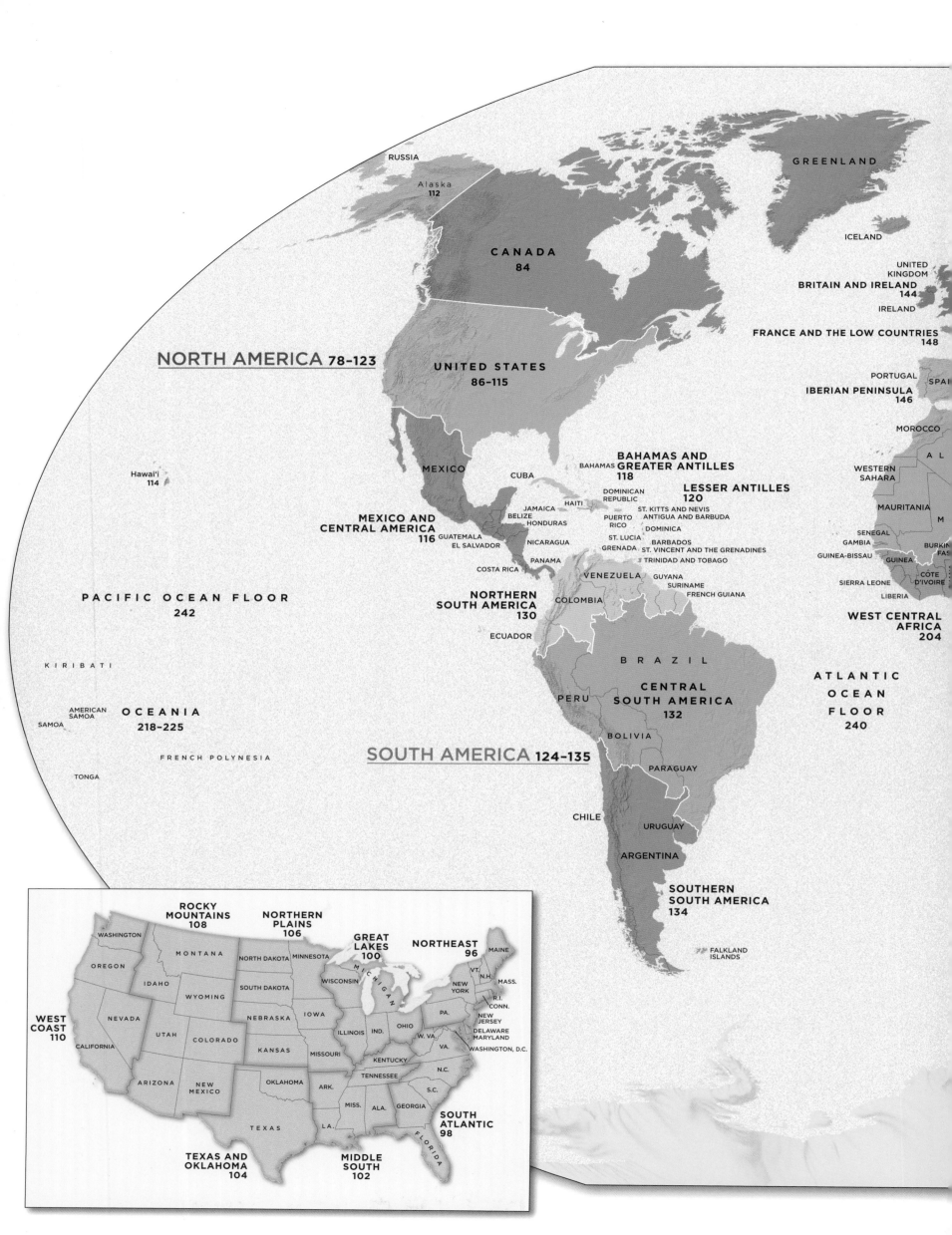

RUSSIA

GREENLAND

Alaska
112

ICELAND

CANADA
84

UNITED
KINGDOM

BRITAIN AND IRELAND
144

IRELAND

FRANCE AND THE LOW COUNTRIES
148

NORTH AMERICA 78-123

UNITED STATES
86-115

PORTUGAL

SPAI

IBERIAN PENINSULA
146

Hawai'i
114

MEXICO

CUBA

BAHAMAS AND
BAHAMAS GREATER ANTILLES
118

LESSER ANTILLES
120

MOROCCO

A L

WESTERN
SAHARA

DOMINICAN
REPUBLIC

MEXICO AND
CENTRAL AMERICA
116

JAMAICA
BELIZE

HAITI

GUATEMALA
EL SALVADOR

HONDURAS

NICARAGUA

PUERTO
RICO

ST. LUCIA

ST. KITTS AND NEVIS
ANTIGUA AND BARBUDA

DOMINICA

MAURITANIA

M

SENEGAL

GAMBIA

COSTA RICA

PANAMA

GRENADA

BARBADOS
ST. VINCENT AND THE GRENADINES

TRINIDAD AND TOBAGO

GUINEA-BISSAU

BURKIN
FAS

GUINEA

VENEZUELA

GUYANA
SURINAME

SIERRA LEONE

CÔTE
D'IVOIRE

PACIFIC OCEAN FLOOR
242

NORTHERN
SOUTH AMERICA
130

COLOMBIA

FRENCH GUIANA

LIBERIA

WEST CENTRAL
AFRICA
204

ECUADOR

KIRIBATI

B R A Z I L

ATLANTIC

OCEAN

FLOOR

240

AMERICAN
SAMOA

OCEANIA
218-225

PERU

CENTRAL
SOUTH AMERICA
132

SAMOA

FRENCH POLYNESIA

BOLIVIA

SOUTH AMERICA 124-135

TONGA

PARAGUAY

CHILE

URUGUAY

ARGENTINA

SOUTHERN
SOUTH AMERICA
134

FALKLAND
ISLANDS

ROCKY
MOUNTAINS
108

NORTHERN
PLAINS
106

GREAT
LAKES
100

NORTHEAST
96

MAINE

WASHINGTON

MONTANA

NORTH DAKOTA

MINNESOTA

VT.
N.H.

MASS.

OREGON

IDAHO

SOUTH DAKOTA

WISCONSIN

M
I
C
H
I
G
A
N

NEW
YORK

PA.

R.I.
CONN.

WEST
COAST
110

NEVADA

WYOMING

NEBRASKA

IOWA

ILLINOIS

IND.

OHIO

W. VA.

NEW
JERSEY

DELAWARE
MARYLAND

WASHINGTON, D.C.

CALIFORNIA

UTAH

COLORADO

KANSAS

MISSOURI

KENTUCKY

VA.

ARIZONA

NEW
MEXICO

OKLAHOMA

ARK.

TENNESSEE

N.C.

S.C.

MISS.

ALA.

GEORGIA

TEXAS

LA.

F
L
O
R
I
D
A

SOUTH
ATLANTIC
98

TEXAS AND
OKLAHOMA
104

MIDDLE
SOUTH
102